Features

ISBN 0-16-038080-4

9 780160 380808

90000

For sale by the U.S. Government Printing Office
Superintendent of Documents, Mail Stop: SSOP, Washington, DC 20402-9328
ISBN 0-16-038080-4

112th Edition

Statistical Abstract of the United States 1992

U.S. Department of Commerce
Barbara Hackman Franklin, Secretary
Rockwell A. Schnabel, Deputy Secretary

Economics and Statistics Administration
J. Antonio Villamil, Under Secretary
for Economic Affairs

BUREAU OF THE CENSUS
Barbara Everitt Bryant, Director

Economics and Statistics Administration
J. Antonio Villamil, Under Secretary for Economic Affairs

BUREAU OF THE CENSUS
Barbara Everitt Bryant, Director
C. L. Kincannon, Deputy Director
John J. Connolly, Assistant Director for Communications

DATA USER SERVICES DIVISION
Marshall L. Turner, Jr., Chief

Acknowledgments

Glenn W. King, Chief, Statistical Compendia Staff, was responsible for general supervision and compilation of this volume under the direction of **Marie Argana**. **Lars B. Johanson** was responsible for technical supervision and coordination. Assisting in the research and analytical phases of assigned sections and in the developmental aspects of new tables were **Rosemary E. Clark**, **Edward C. Jagers** and **Rachael LaPorte**. The latter two were also responsible for content and preparation of graphics. **Geraldine W. Blackburn** provided primary editorial assistance. Other editorial assistance was rendered by **Kelvin Elmore, Patricia S. Lancaster, Joyce Mori, Dolores M. Roberson**, and **Marjorie M. Sproesser**.

The staff of the Administrative and Publications Services Division, **Walter C. Odom**, Chief, performed publication planning, editorial review, design, composition, and printing planning and procurement. **Patricia Heiston** provided publication coordination and editing. **Janet Sweeney** provided design and graphics services.

The cooperation of many contributors to this volume is gratefully acknowledged. The source note below each table credits the various government and private agencies which have collaborated in furnishing information for the **Statistical Abstract**. In a few instances, contributors have requested that their data be designated as subject to copyright restrictions, as indicated in the source notes to the tables affected. Permission to use copyright material should be obtained directly from the copyright owner.

Library of Congress Card No. 4–18089

SUGGESTED CITATION

U.S. Bureau of the Census, *Statistical Abstract of the United States: 1992*
(112th edition.) Washington, DC, 1992

For sale by Superintendent of Documents, U.S. Government Printing Office, Washington, DC 20402, Tel. 202–783–3238.

Preface

The *Statistical Abstract of the United States,* published since 1878, is the standard summary of statistics on the social, political, and economic organization of the United States. It is designed to serve as a convenient volume for statistical reference and as a guide to other statistical publications and sources. The latter function is served by the introductory text to each section, the source note appearing below each table, and Appendix I, which comprises the Guide to Sources of Statistics, the Guide to State Statistical Abstracts, and the Guide to Foreign Statistical Abstracts.

This volume includes a selection of data from many statistical publications, both government and private. Publications cited as sources usually contain additional statistical detail and more comprehensive discussions of definitions and concepts than can be presented here. Data not available in publications issued by the contributing agency but obtained from unpublished records are identified in the source notes as "unpublished data." More information on the subjects covered in the tables so noted may generally be obtained from the source.

Except as indicated, figures are for the United States as presently constituted. Although emphasis in the *Statistical Abstract* is primarily given to national data, many tables present data for regions and individual States and a smaller number for metropolitan areas and cities. Appendix II, Metropolitan Area Concepts and Components, presents explanatory text, a complete current listing and population data for metropolitan statistical areas (MSA's), the primary metropolitan statistical areas (PMSA's), and the consolidated metropolitan statistical areas (CMSA's). Table 34 in section 1 presents selected population characteristics for MSA's with population of 250,000 or more. Statistics for the Commonwealth of Puerto Rico and for outlying areas of the United States are included in many State tables and are supplemented by information in section 30. Additional information for States, cities, counties, metropolitan areas, and other small units, as well as more historical data, are available in

various supplements to the *Abstract* (see inside back cover).

Changes in this edition.—We have restructured our text material into a two column format with a larger type size and have included summary statistical highlights to give an overview of the scope of data in each section. The revised format and "In Brief" items should provide a more user-friendly text presentation.

Subject matter content changes include expanded coverage of 1990 census data in the Population and the Construction and Housing sections. A special presentation of 1990 census sample data begins on page xii with six pages of national and State data. Among other areas in which we have introduced new material are data on consumer finances in the Banking section and data on the communications industry in the Communications section. Other selected new topics include family planning services, outpatient surgery, crimes involving handguns, high-tech employment, household net worth, and minority-owned businesses. (See Appendix VI, pp. 927-929 for a complete list of new tables introduced in this edition.)

As mentioned in last year's preface, we have spent considerable time and effort in converting much of the *Abstract* into electronic form. We are now working toward the goal of providing the book on a CD-ROM. For price and availability, see inside back cover.

Statistics in this edition are generally for the most recent year or period available by late 1991. Special effort was made to include economic series which became available in early 1992 including series covering the labor force, the consumer price index, and wholesale trade. Each year almost 1,500 tables and charts are reviewed and evaluated, new tables and charts of current interest are added, continuing series are updated, and less timely data are condensed or eliminated. Text notes and appendices are revised as appropriate.

USA Statistics in Brief, 1992, a pocket-size pamphlet highlighting many statistical series in the *Abstract,* is available sepa-rately. Price and ordering information can be obtained from U.S. Bureau of the Census, Customer Services, Washington, DC 20233 (telephone 301- 763-4100). A 25 percent discount will be available on orders of 100 copies or more sent to the same address.

Historical statistics.—Specific head-note references in this *Abstract* link many tables to earlier data shown in *Historical Statistics of the United States, Colonial Times to 1970.* (See Appendix IV, pp. 920 and 921).

Statistics for States and metropolitan areas.—Data for States and metro areas may also be found in the *State and Metropolitan Area Data Book, 1991* and its 1992 update, due out in the fall 1992.

Statistical reliability and responsibility.—The contents of this volume were taken from many sources. All data from either censuses and surveys or from administrative records are subject to error arising from a number of factors: Sampling variability (for statistics based on samples), reporting errors in the data for individual units, incomplete coverage, nonresponse, imputations, and processing error. (See also Appendix III, pp. 905-919. The Bureau of the Census cannot accept the responsibility for the accuracy or limitations of the data presented here, other than those for which it collects. The responsibility for selection of the material and for proper presentation, however, rests with the Bureau.

For additional information on data presented.—Please consult the source publications available in local libraries or write to the agency indicated in the source notes. Write to the Bureau of the Census only if it is cited as the source.

Suggestions and comments.—Users of the *Statistical Abstract* and its supplements (see inside back cover) are urged to make their data needs known for consideration in planning future editions. Suggestions and comments for improving coverage and presentation of data should be sent to the Director, U.S. Bureau of the Census, Washington, DC 20233.

Contents

[Numbers following subjects are page numbers]

Contents

APPROXIMATE CONVERSION MEASURES

[For assistance on metric usage, call or write the Office of Metric Programs, U.S. Department of Commerce, Washington, DC 20230 (301-975-3689)]

Symbol	When you know conventional	Multiply by	To find metric	Symbol
in	inch	2.54	centimeter	cm
ft	foot	30.48	centimeter	cm
yd	yard	0.91	meter	m
mi	mile	1.61	kilometer	km
in^2	square inch	6.45	square centimeter	cm^2
ft^2	square foot	0.09	square meter	m^2
yd^2	square yard	0.84	square meter	m^2
mi^2	square mile	2.59	square kilometer	km^2
	acre	0.41	hectare	ha
oz	ounce [1]	28.35	gram	g
lb	pound[1]	.45	kilograms	kg
oz (troy)	ounce [2]	31.10	gram	g
	short ton (2,000 lbs)	0.91	metric ton	t
	long ton (2,240 lbs)	1.12	metric ton	t
fl oz	fluid ounce	29.57	milliliter	mL
c	cup	0.24	liter	L
pt	pint	0.47	liter	L
qt	quart	0.95	liter	L
gal	gallon	3.78	liter	L
ft^3	cubic foot	0.03	cubic meter	m^3
yd^3	cubic yard	0.76	cubic meter	m^3
F	degrees Fahrenheit (subtract 32)	0.55	degrees Celsius	C

Symbol	When you know metric	Multiply by	To find conventional	Symbol
cm	centimeter	0.39	inch	in
cm	centimeter	0.33	foot	ft
m	meter	1.09	yard	yd
km	kilometer	0.62	mile	mi
cm^2	square centimeter	0.15	square inch	in^2
m^2	square meter	10.76	square foot	ft^2
m^2	square meter	1.20	square yard	yd^2
km^2	square kilometer	0.39	square mile	mi^2
ha	hectare	2.47	acre	
g	gram	.035	ounce [1]	oz
kg	kilogram	2.21	pounds	lb[1]
g	gram	.032	ounce [2]	oz (troy)
t	metric ton	1.10	short ton (2,000 lbs)	
t	metric ton	0.98	long ton (2,240 lbs)	
mL	milliliter	0.03	fluid ounce	fl oz
L	liter	4.24	cup	c
L	liter	2.13	pint (liquid)	pt
L	liter	1.05	quart (liquid)	qt
L	liter	0.26	gallon	gal
m^3	cubic meter	35.32	cubic foot	ft^3
m^3	cubic meter	1.32	cubic yard	yd^3
C	degrees Celsius	1.80	degrees Fahrenheit (after subtracting 32)	F

[1] For weighing ordinary commodities.   [2] For weighing precious metals, jewels, etc.

Example of table structure:

No. 1002. Motor Vehicles—Registrations, Factory Sales, and Retail Sales: 1960 to 1990

[Minus sign (-) indicates decrease. For definition of average annual percent change, see Guide to Tabular Presentation. See also *Historical Statistics, Colonial Times to 1970*, series Q 148-155]

YEAR	REGISTRATION [1] (mil.) Total cars, trucks, buses	Pas-senger cars [2]	Trucks and buses	Motor-cycle regis-trat-ions [1] (1,000)	FACTORY SALES (1,000) Total cars, trucks, buses	Pas-senger cars	Trucks and buses [3]	RETAIL SALES (1,000) Passenger cars Total	Do-mestic	Im-ports	Trucks Total	Do-mestic	Im-ports
1960..	74	62	12	574	7,869	6,675	1,194	6,641	6,142	499	963	9,26	37
1965..	90	75	15	1,382	11,057	9,306	1,752	9,332	8,763	569	1,553	1,539	14
1970..	108	89	19	2,824	8,239	6,547	1,692	8,400	7,119	1,280	1,811	1,746	65
1975..	133	107	26	4,964	8,985	6,713	2,272	8,624	7,053	1,571	2,478	2,249	229
1976..	139	110	28	4,933	11,480	8,500	2,979	10,110	8,611	1,498	3,181	2,944	237
1977..	142	112	30	4,881	12,642	9,201	3,441	11,183	9,109	2,074	3,675	3,352	323
1978..	148	117	32	4,868	12,871	9,165	3,706	11,314	9,312	2,002	4,109	3,773	336
1979..	152	118	33	5,422	11,456	8,419	3,037	10,673	8,341	2,332	3,480	3,010	470
1980..	156	122	34	5,694	8,067	6,400	1,667	8,979	6,581	2,398	2,487	2,001	486
1981..	158	123	35	5,831	7,956	6,255	1,701	8,536	6,209	2,327	2,260	1,809	451
1982..	160	124	36	5,754	6,955	5,049	1,906	7,982	5,759	2,224	2,560	2,146	414
1983..	164	126	37	5,585	9,153	6,739	2,414	9,182	6,795	2,387	3,129	2,658	471
1984..	166	128	38	5,480	10,696	7,621	3,075	10,390	7,952	2,439	4,093	3,475	618
1985..	172	132	40	5,444	11,359	8,002	3,357	11,042	8,205	2,838	4,682	3,902	780
1986..	176	135	41	5,262	10,909	7,516	3,393	11,460	8,215	3,245	4,863	3,921	942
1987..	179	137	42	4,886	10,907	7,085	3,821	10,277	7,081	3,196	4,912	4,055	857
1988..	184	141	43	4,584	11,225	7,105	4,121	10,530	7,526	3,004	5,149	4,508	641
1989..	187	143	44	4,434	10,869	6,807	4,062	9,772	7,073	2,699	4,941	4,403	538
1990..	189	144	45	4,259	9,769	6,050	3,719	9,301	6,897	2,404	4,846	4,215	631

[1] Includes publicly owned vehicles. Excludes military vehicles.   [2] Includes taxis.   [3] Includes standard equipment.

Source: Registrations—U.S. Federal Highway Administration, *Selected Highway Statistics and Charts*, annual; sales—Motor Vehicle Manufacturers Association of the United States, Inc., Detroit, MI, *MVMA Motor Vehicle Facts and Figures*, annual.

Headnotes immediately below table titles provide information important for correct interpretation or evaluation of the table as a whole or for a major segment of it.

Footnotes below the bottom rule of tables give information relating to specific items or figures within the table.

Unit indicators show the *specified quantities* in which data items are presented. They are used for two primary reasons. Sometimes data are not available in absolute form and are estimates (as in the case of many surveys). In other cases we round the numbers in order to save space to show more data, as in the case above.

EXAMPLES OF UNIT INDICATOR INTERPRETATION FROM TABLE 1002

Year	Item	Unit Indicator	Number shown	Multiplier
1990.................	Car registrations...........	Millions............	144	1,000,000
1990.................	Sales.................	Thousands.........	6,050	1,000

To Determine the Figure it is Necessary to Multiply the Number Shown by the Unit Indicator:

Car registrations = 144 * 1,000,000 or 144,000,000 (144 million).

Sales = 6,050 * 1,000 or 6,050,000 (over 6 million).

When a table presents data with more than one unit indicator, they are found in the column headings or spanner (shown above), stub (table 64), or unit column (table 70). When the data in a table are shown in the same unit indicator, it is shown in boldface as the first part of the headnote (table 2). If no unit indicator is shown, data presented are in absolute form (table 1).

Heavy vertical rules are used to separate independent sections of a table, as shown above, or in tables where the stub is continued into one or more additional columns (table 4).

Averages. An average is a single number or value that is often used to represent the "typical value" of a group of numbers. It is regarded as a measure of "location" or "central tendency" of a group of numbers.

The *arithmetic mean* is the type of average used most frequently. It is derived by summing the individual item values of a particular group and dividing the total by the number of items. The arithmetic mean is often referred to as simply the "mean" or "average."

The *median* of a group of numbers is the middle number or value when each item in the group is arranged according to size (lowest to highest or visa versa); it generally has the same number of items above it as well as below it. If there is an even number if items in the group, the median is taken to be the average of the two middle numbers.

Per capita (or per person) quantities. A per capita figure represents an average computed for every person in a specified group (or population). It is derived by taking the total for an item (such as income, taxes, or retail sales) and dividing it by the number of persons in the specified population.

Index numbers. An index number is the measure of difference or change, usually expressed as a percent, relating one quantity (the variable) of a specified kind to another quantity of the same kind. Index numbers are widely used to express changes in prices over periods of time but may also be used to express differences between related subjects for a single point in time.

To compute a price index, a base year or period is selected. The base year price (of the commodity or service) is then designated as the base or reference price to which the prices for other years or periods are related. Many price indexes use the year 1982 as the base year; in tables this is shown as "1982=100". A method of expressing the price relationship is: The price of a set of one or more items for a related year (e.g. 1990) **divided by** the price of the same set of items for the base year (e.g. 1982). The result multiplied by 100 provides the index number. When 100 is subtracted from the index number, the result equals the percent change in price from the base year.

Average annual percent change. Unless otherwise stated in the *Abstract* (as in Section 1, Population), average annual percent change is computed by use of a *compound interest formula.* This formula assumes that the rate of change is constant throughout a specified compounding period (one year for average annual rates of change). The formula is similar to that used to compute the balance of a savings account which receives compound interest. According to this formula, at the end of a compounding period the amount of accrued change (e.g. school enrollment or bank interest) is added to the amount which existed at the beginning the period. As a result, over time (e.g., with each year or quarter), the same rate of change is applied to a larger and larger figure.

The *exponential formula,* which is based on continuous compounding, is often used to measure population change. It is preferred by population experts because they view population and population-related subjects as changing without interruption, ever ongoing. Both exponential and compound interest formulas assume a constant rate of change. The former, however, applies the amount of change continuously to the base rather than at the end of each compounding period. When the average annual rates are small (e.g., less than 5 percent) both formulas give virtually the same results. For an explanation of these two formulas as they relate to population, see U.S. Bureau of the Census, *The Methods and Materials of Demography,* vol. 2, 3d printing (rev.), 1975, pp. 372-381.

Current and constant dollars. Statistics in some tables in a number of sections are expressed in both current and constant dollars (see, for example, table 698 in section 14). Current dollar figures reflect actual prices or costs prevailing during the specified year(s). Constant dollar figures are estimates representing an effort to remove the effects of price changes from statistical series reported in dollar terms. In general, constant dollar series are derived by dividing current dollar estimates by the appropriate price index for the appropriate period (for example, the Consumer Price Index). The result is a series as it would presumably exist if prices were the same throughout, as in the base year—in other words as if the dollar had constant purchasing power. Any changes in this constant dollar series would reflect only changes in real volume of output, income, expenditures, or other measure.

Explanation of Symbols:

The following symbols, used in the tables throughout this book, are explained in condensed form in footnotes to the tables where they appear:

- Represents zero or rounds to less than half the unit of measurement shown.

B Base figure too small to meet statistical standards for reliability of a derived figure.

D Figure withheld to avoid disclosure pertaining to a specific organization or individual.

NA Data not enumerated, tabulated, or otherwise available separately.

NS Percent change irrelevant or insignificant.

S Figure does not meet publication standards for reasons other than that covered by symbol B, above.

X Figure not applicable because column heading and stub line make entry impossible, absurd, or meaningless.

Z Entry would amount to less than half the unit of measurement shown.

In many tables, details will not add to the totals shown because of rounding.

1990 Census Sample Data

No. 90-1. Selected Social Characteristics: 1990

[As of **April**. Based on sample data and subject to sampling variability; see technical documentation for Summary Tape File 3]

ITEM	Number	ITEM	Number
URBAN AND RURAL RESIDENCE		Lived in same house	122,796,970
Total population.	**248,709,873**	Lived in different house in U.S.	102,540,097
Urban population	187,051,543	Same State	80,954,800
Percent of total population	75.2	Same county	58,675,635
Rural population	61,658,330	Different county	22,279,165
Percent of total population	24.8	Different State.	21,585,297
Farm population	3,871,583	Lived abroad	5,108,710
SCHOOL ENROLLMENT		CHILDREN EVER BORN PER 1,000 WOMEN	
Persons 3 years and over enrolled		Women 15 to 24 years	305
in school	64,987,101	Women 25 to 34 years	1,330
Preprimary school	4,503,285	Women 35 to 44 years	1,960
Elementary or high school	42,566,788		
Percent in private school.	9.8	VETERAN STATUS	
College.	17,917,028	**Civilian veterans 16 years and over . . . . . .**	**27,481,055**
		65 years and over	7,158,654
EDUCATIONAL ATTAINMENT			
Persons 25 years and over	**158,868,436**	NATIVITY AND PLACE OF BIRTH	
Less than 9th grade	16,502,211	Native population	228,942,557
9th to 12th grade, no diploma.	22,841,507	Percent born in State of residence	67.1
High school graduate	47,642,763	Foreign-born population.	19,767,316
Some college, no degree	29,779,777	Entered the U.S. 1980 to 1990.	8,663,627
Associate degree	9,791,925		
Bachelor's degree.	20,832,567	LANGUAGE SPOKEN AT HOME	
Graduate or professional degree	11,477,686	**Persons 5 years and over. . . . .**	**230,445,777**
		Speak a language other than English	31,844,979
Percent high school graduate or higher.	75.2	Do not speak English "very well"	13,982,502
Percent bachelor's degree or higher.	20.3	Speak Spanish	17,345,064
		Do not speak English "very well"	8,309,995
RESIDENCE IN 1985		Speak Asian or Pacific Island language	4,471,621
Persons 5 years and over.	**230,445,777**	Do not speak English "very well"	2,420,355

Source: U.S. Bureau of the Census, *1990 Census of Population and Housing Data Paper Listing (CPH-L-80).*

No. 90-2. Selected Labor Force Characteristics: 1990

[See headnote, table 90-1]

ITEM	Number	ITEM	Number
LABOR FORCE STATUS		Females 16 years and over	99,803,358
Persons 16 years and over	**191,829,271**	With own children under 6 years	15,233,818
In labor force	125,182,378	Percent in labor force.	59.7
Percent in labor force.	65.3	With own children 6 to 17 years only	16,490,186
Civilian labor force	123,473,450	Percent in labor force.	75.0
Employed	115,681,202		
Unemployed	7,792,248	Own children under 6 years in families . . .	
Percent unemployed.	6.3	and subfamilies.	21,273,612
Armed Forces.	1,708,928	All parents present in household in labor force.	
Not in labor force	66,646,893	force.	12,043,581
Males 16 years and over.	92,025,913	Own children 6 to 17 years in families . . .	
In labor force	68,509,429	and subfamilies.	39,605,481
Percent in labor force.	74.4	All parents present in household in labor . . .	
Civilian labor force	66,986,201	force.	26,820,634
Employed	62,704,579		
Unemployed	4,281,622	Persons 16 to 19 years	14,315,448
Percent unemployed.	6.4	Not enrolled in school and not high school . . .	
Armed Forces.	1,523,228	graduate	1,605,494
Not in labor force	23,516,484	Employed or in Armed Forces	649,184
		Unemployed	274,320
Females 16 years and over	99,803,358	Not in labor force.	681,990
In labor force	56,672,949		
Percent in labor force.	56.8	COMMUTING TO WORK [1]	
Civilian labor force	56,487,249	**Workers 16 years and over. . . . .**	**115,070,274**
Employed	52,976,623	Percent drove alone	73.2
Unemployed	3,510,626	Percent in carpools.	13.4
Percent unemployed.	6.2	Percent using public transportation	5.3
Armed Forces.	185,700	Percent using other means.	1.3
Not in labor force	43,130,409	Percent walked or worked at home	6.9
		Mean travel time to work (minutes)	22.4

See footnotes at end of table.

No. 90-2. Selected Labor Force Characteristics: 1990—Continued
[See headnote, table 90-1]

ITEM	Number	ITEM	Number
OCCUPATION [2]		Manufacturing, durable goods	12,408,844
Executive, administrative, and managerial	14,227,916	Transportation	5,108,003
Professional specialty	16,305,666	Communications and other public utilities	3,097,059
Technicians and related support	4,257,235	Wholesale trade	5,071,026
Sales	13,634,686	Retail trade	19,485,666
Administrative support, including clerical	18,826,477		
Private household	521,154	Finance, insurance, and real estate	7,984,870
Protective service	1,992,852	Business and repair services.	5,577,462
Service, except protective and household	12,781,911	Personal services	3,668,696
		Entertainment and recreation services	1,636,460
Farming, forestry, and fishing	2,839,010	Health services.	9,682,684
Precision production, craft, and repair.	13,097,963	Educational services	9,633,503
Machine operators, assemblers, and		Other professional and related services	7,682,060
inspectors	7,904,197	Public administration	5,538,077
Transportation and material moving	4,729,001		
Handlers, equipment cleaners, helpers, and		CLASS OF WORKER [2]	
laborers	4,563,134	Private wage and salary workers	89,541,393
		Government workers	17,567,100
INDUSTRY [2]		Local government workers.	8,244,755
Agriculture, forestry, and fisheries	3,115,372	State government workers.	5,381,445
Mining.	723,423	Federal government workers	3,940,900
Construction.	7,214,763	Self-employed workers.	8,067,483
Manufacturing, nondurable goods	8,053,234	Unpaid family workers	505,226

[1] For workers at work during the reference week.   [2] For employed workers 16 years and over.
Source: U.S. Bureau of the Census, *1990 Census of Population and Housing Data Paper Listing (CPH-L-80).*

No. 90-3. Selected Income Characteristics: 1990
[See headnote, table 90-1]

ITEM	Number	ITEM	Number
INCOME IN 1989		Mean public assistance income (dollars) . . .	4,078
Households	91,993,582	With retirement income	14,353,202
Less than $5,000	5,684,517	Mean retirement income (dollars)	9,216
$5,000 to $9,999	8,529,980		
$10,000 to $14,999	8,133,273	NUMBER BELOW POVERTY LEVEL	
$15,000 to $24,999	16,123,742	IN 1989	
$25,000 to $34,999	14,575,125	All persons for whom poverty status is	
$35,000 to $49,999	16,428,455	determined	241,977,859
$50,000 to $74,999	13,777,883	Below poverty level.	31,742,864
$75,000 to $99,999	4,704,808		
$100,000 to $149,999	2,593,768	Persons 18 years and over.	179,372,340
$150,000 or more	1,442,031	Below poverty level.	20,313,948
Median household income (dollars)	30,056	Persons 65 years and over	29,562,647
		Below poverty level.	3,780,585
Families.	65,049,428		
Less than $5,000	2,582,206	Related children under 18 years	62,278,655
$5,000 to $9,999	3,636,361	Below poverty level.	11,161,836
$10,000 to $14,999	4,676,092	Related children under 5 years.	17,978,025
$15,000 to $24,999	10,658,345	Below poverty level.	3,617,099
$25,000 to $34,999	10,729,951	Related children 5 to 17 years	44,300,630
$35,000 to $49,999	13,270,930	Below poverty level.	7,544,737
$50,000 to $74,999	11,857,079		
$75,000 to $99,999	4,115,468	Unrelated individuals	36,672,001
$100,000 to $149,999	2,259,940	Below poverty level.	8,873,475
$150,000 or more	1,263,056	All families	65,049,428
Median family income (dollars)	35,225	Below poverty level.	6,487,515
		With related children under 18 years	33,536,660
Nonfamily households	26,944,154	Below poverty level.	4,992,845
Less than $5,000	3,311,694	With related children under 5 years.	14,250,048
$5,000 to $9,999	5,080,560	Below poverty level.	2,613,626
$10,000 to $14,999	3,593,796		
$15,000 to $24,999	5,577,805	Female householder families	10,381,654
$25,000 to $34,999	3,799,161	Below poverty level.	3,230,201
$35,000 to $49,999	2,979,107	With related children under 18 years	6,783,155
$50,000 to $74,999	1,685,327	Below poverty level.	2,866,941
$75,000 to $99,999	482,080	With related children under 5 years.	2,532,331
$100,000 to $149,999	274,043	Below poverty level.	1,452,618
$150,000 or more	160,581		
Median nonfamily household income (dollars) .	17,240	PERCENT BELOW POVERTY LEVEL IN 1989	
		All persons	13.1
Per capita income (dollars).	14,420	Persons 18 years and over	11.3
		Persons 65 years and over.	12.8
HOUSEHOLD INCOME TYPE IN 1989		Related children under 18 years	17.9
With wage and salary income	71,174,232	Related children under 5 years	20.1
Mean wage and salary income (dollars)	37,271	Related children 5 to 17 years	17.0
With nonfarm self-employment income	10,810,605	Unrelated individuals	24.2
Mean nonfarm self-employment income . . .			
(dollars)	20,218	All families.	10.0
With farm self-employment income	2,020,105	With related children under 18 years	14.9
Mean farm self-employment income (dol-		With related children under 5 years	18.3
lars)	10,064		
With Social Security income	24,210,922	Female householder families	31.1
Mean Social Security income (dollars)	7,772	With related children under 18 years	42.3
With public assistance income	6,943,269	With related children under 5 years	57.4

Source: U.S. Bureau of the Census, *1990 Census of Population and Housing Data Paper Listing (CPH-L-80).*

1990 Census Sample Data

No. 90-4. Selected Housing Characteristics: 1990

[See headnote, table 90-1]

ITEM	Number	ITEM	Number
Total housing units	**102,263,678**	VEHICLES AVAILABLE	
		Occupied housing units.	91,947,410
YEAR STRUCTURE BUILT		None	10,602,297
1989 to March 1990	2,169,436	One	31,038,711
1985 to 1988	9,024,365	Two	34,361,045
1980 to 1984	9,931,917	Three or more	15,945,357
1970 to 1979	22,291,826		
1960 to 1969	16,506,410	MORTGAGE STATUS AND SELECTED	
1950 to 1959	14,831,071	MONTHLY OWNER COSTS	
1940 to 1949	8,676,155	Specified owner-occupied housing units	45,550,059
1939 or earlier	18,832,498	With a mortgage	29,811,735
		Less than $300	1,455,511
BEDROOMS		$300 to $499	5,711,092
No bedroom	2,366,715	$500 to $699	6,635,180
One bedroom.	14,062,917	$700 to $999	7,497,193
Two bedrooms.	31,502,796	$1,000 to $1,499	5,294,990
Three bedrooms.	38,931,475	$1,500 to $1,999	1,847,081
Four bedrooms.	12,549,082	$2,000 or more	1,370,688
Five or more bedrooms	2,850,693	Median (dollars)	737
		Not mortgaged	15,738,324
SELECTED CHARACTERISTICS		Less than $100	960,802
Lacking complete plumbing facilities.	1,101,696	$100 to $199	6,372,610
Percent of total	1.08	$200 to $299	5,058,575
Lacking complete kitchen facilities.	1,109,626	$300 to $399	1,930,923
Condominium housing units	4,847,921	$400 or more	1,415,414
Percent of total	4.74	Median (dollars)	209
SOURCE OF WATER		SELECTED MONTHLY OWNER COSTS	
Public system or private company	86,068,766	AS A PERCENTAGE	
Individual drilled well	13,467,148	OF HOUSEHOLD INCOME IN 1989	
Individual dug well	1,664,543	Specified owner-occupied housing units	45,550,059
Some other source	1,063,221	Less than 20 percent	25,846,744
		20 to 24 percent	6,288,395
SEWAGE DISPOSAL		25 to 29 percent	4,280,439
Public sewer	76,455,211	30 to 34 percent	2,673,820
Septic tank or cesspool	24,670,877	35 percent or more	6,148,822
Other means	1,137,590	Not computed	311,839
Occupied housing units.	**91,947,410**	GROSS RENT	
		Specified renter-occupied housing units	32,170,036
HOUSE HEATING FUEL		Less than $200	2,815,090
Utility gas	46,850,923	$200 to $299	3,736,190
Bottled, tank, or LP gas	5,243,462	$300 to $499	11,814,251
Electricity	23,696,987	$500 to $749	8,471,363
Fuel oil, kerosene, etc.	11,243,727	$750 to $999	2,637,755
Coal or coke	358,965	$1,000 or more	1,276,044
Wood	3,609,323	No cash rent.	1,419,343
Solar energy	54,536	Median (dollars).	447
Other fuel	345,580		
No fuel used	543,907	GROSS RENT AS A PERCENTAGE OF	
		HOUSEHOLD INCOME IN 1989	
YEAR HOUSEHOLDER MOVED INTO UNIT		Specified renter-occupied housing units	32,170,036
1989 to March 1990	19,208,023	Less than 20 percent	9,647,452
1985 to 1988	25,963,818	20 to 24 percent	4,453,652
1980 to 1984	12,844,781	25 to 29 percent	3,664,975
1970 to 1979	17,102,506	30 to 34 percent	2,562,684
1960 to 1969	8,428,066	35 percent or more	9,864,161
1959 or earlier	8,400,216	Not computed	1,977,112
TELEPHONE			
No telephone in unit	4,817,457		

Source: U.S. Bureau of the Census, *1990 Census of Population and Housing Data Paper Listing (CPH-L-80).*

No. 90-5. Selected Social Characteristics and Commuting, by State: 1990

[See headnote, table 90-1]

DIVISION AND STATE	POPULATION			EDUCATIONAL ATTAINMENT[1], PERCENT COMPLETING—		Percent of persons 5 years old and over who lived in same house in 1985	FOREIGN-BORN POPULATION		PERSONS WHO SPEAK A LANGUAGE OTHER THAN ENGLISH[2]		COMMUTING TO WORK[3]		
	Total (1,000)	FARM POPULATION		High school	Bachelor's degree or higher		Number (1,000)	Percent of total	Number (1,000)	Percent	Percent drove alone	Percent in carpools	Percent using public transportation
		Number (1,000)	Percent of total										
U.S..	248,710	3,872	1.6	75.2	20.3	53.3	19,767	7.9	31,845	13.8	73.2	13.4	5.3
N.E.:													
ME...	1,228	11	0.9	78.8	18.8	55.6	36	3.0	105	9.2	74.3	14.0	0.9
NH...	1,109	6	0.5	82.2	24.4	50.7	41	3.7	89	8.7	78.2	12.3	0.7
VT...	563	12	2.1	80.8	24.3	51.9	18	3.1	30	5.8	72.2	12.9	0.7
MA...	6,016	9	0.2	80.0	27.2	58.4	574	9.5	852	15.2	72.1	10.7	8.3
RI...	1,003	1	0.1	72.0	21.3	57.4	95	9.5	159	17.0	78.1	12.1	2.5
CT...	3,287	5	0.2	79.2	27.2	57.4	279	8.5	466	15.2	77.7	11.2	3.9
M.A.:													
NY...	17,990	82	0.5	74.8	23.1	62.0	2,852	15.9	3,909	23.3	54.3	10.5	24.8
NJ...	7,730	17	0.2	76.7	24.9	60.1	967	12.5	1,406	19.5	71.6	12.4	8.8
PA...	11,882	117	1.0	74.7	17.9	63.4	369	3.1	807	7.3	71.4	12.9	6.4
E.N.C.:													
OH...	10,847	199	1.8	75.7	17.0	57.6	260	2.4	546	5.4	80.3	10.8	2.5
IN ...	5,544	188	3.4	75.6	15.6	55.6	94	1.7	246	4.8	78.9	12.8	1.3
IL....	11,431	207	1.8	76.2	21.0	55.7	952	8.3	1,499	14.2	69.9	12.2	10.1
MI...	9,295	120	1.3	76.8	17.4	56.9	355	3.8	570	6.6	81.5	10.5	1.6
WI...	4,892	196	4.0	78.6	17.7	57.3	122	2.5	264	5.8	74.5	11.5	2.5
W.N.C.:													
MN...	4,375	208	4.8	82.4	21.8	55.5	113	2.6	227	5.6	73.8	11.4	3.6
IA ...	2,777	257	9.2	80.1	16.9	58.2	43	1.6	100	3.9	73.4	11.9	1.2
MO...	5,117	180	3.5	73.9	17.8	54.3	84	1.6	178	3.8	77.4	13.3	2.0
ND...	639	60	9.4	76.7	18.1	57.3	9	1.5	47	7.9	71.4	10.7	0.6
SD...	696	76	10.9	77.1	17.2	55.5	8	1.1	42	6.5	72.0	10.1	0.3
NE...	1,578	118	7.5	81.8	18.9	55.9	28	1.8	70	4.8	76.1	11.2	1.2
KS...	2,478	108	4.4	81.3	21.1	51.7	63	2.5	132	5.7	78.8	11.5	0.6
S.A.:													
DE...	666	6	1.0	77.5	21.4	53.8	22	3.3	42	6.9	77.2	12.9	2.4
MD...	4,781	33	0.7	78.4	26.5	52.4	313	6.6	395	8.9	69.8	15.2	8.1
DC...	607	-	-	73.1	33.3	53.5	59	9.7	71	12.5	35.0	12.0	36.6
VA...	6,187	81	1.3	75.2	24.5	49.1	312	5.0	419	7.3	72.5	15.9	4.0
WV...	1,793	24	1.3	66.0	12.3	64.2	16	0.9	44	2.6	74.8	16.2	1.1
NC...	6,629	117	1.8	70.0	17.4	54.3	115	1.7	241	3.9	76.6	16.1	1.0
SC...	3,487	49	1.4	68.3	16.6	55.6	50	1.4	113	3.5	75.5	16.9	1.1
GA...	6,478	80	1.2	70.9	19.3	49.4	173	2.7	285	4.8	76.6	15.1	2.8
FL ...	12,938	47	0.4	74.4	18.3	44.9	1,663	12.9	2,098	17.3	77.1	14.1	2.0
E.S.C.:													
KY...	3,685	174	4.7	64.6	13.6	56.7	34	0.9	86	2.5	76.3	14.6	1.6
TN...	4,877	112	2.3	67.1	16.0	54.0	59	1.2	132	2.9	78.7	14.5	1.3
AL...	4,041	59	1.5	66.9	15.7	57.3	44	1.1	108	2.9	79.2	15.4	0.8
MS...	2,573	56	2.2	64.3	14.7	59.2	20	0.8	67	2.8	75.6	17.9	0.8
W.S.C.:													
AR...	2,351	64	2.7	66.3	13.3	54.3	25	1.1	61	2.8	77.3	15.5	0.5
LA...	4,220	40	1.0	68.3	16.1	59.3	87	2.1	392	10.1	75.3	15.0	3.0
OK...	3,146	83	2.6	74.6	17.8	52.1	65	2.1	146	5.0	78.5	13.9	0.6
TX...	16,987	192	1.1	72.1	20.3	49.2	1,524	9.0	3,970	25.4	76.5	14.9	2.2
Mt.:													
MT...	799	46	5.7	81.0	19.8	52.0	14	1.7	37	5.0	71.7	11.9	0.6
ID ...	1,007	45	4.5	79.7	17.7	50.5	29	2.9	59	6.4	74.8	12.0	1.9
WY...	454	16	3.5	83.0	18.8	49.5	8	1.7	24	5.7	73.8	13.5	1.4
CO...	3,294	45	1.4	84.4	27.0	45.2	142	4.3	321	10.5	74.3	12.8	2.9
NM...	1,515	15	1.0	75.1	20.4	51.8	81	5.3	494	35.5	74.6	15.2	1.0
AZ...	3,665	7	0.2	78.7	20.3	43.1	278	7.6	700	20.8	73.6	14.9	2.1
UT...	1,723	12	0.7	85.1	22.3	52.7	59	3.4	120	7.8	73.9	15.2	2.3
NV...	1,202	5	0.4	78.8	15.3	34.7	105	8.7	146	13.2	73.4	15.5	2.7
Pac.:													
WA ..	4,867	60	1.2	83.8	22.9	45.9	322	6.6	403	9.0	73.9	12.3	4.5
OR	2,842	60	2.4	81.5	20.6	46.1	139	4.9	192	7.3	73.3	12.8	3.4
CA...	29,760	151	0.5	76.2	23.4	44.4	6,459	21.7	8,619	31.5	71.6	14.6	4.9
AK...	550	1	0.2	86.6	23.0	40.6	25	4.5	60	12.1	62.5	15.3	2.4
HI ...	1,108	6	0.6	80.1	22.9	50.9	163	14.7	255	24.8	60.5	20.5	7.4

- Represents zero.   [1] Persons 25 years old and over.   [2] Persons 5 years old and over.   [3] Workers 16 years old and over.

Source: U.S. Bureau of the Census, *1990 Census of Population and Housing Data Paper Listing (CPH-L-80).*

1990 Census Sample Data

No. 90-6. Income and Poverty Status in 1989, by State: 1990

[See headnote, table 90-1]

DIVISION AND STATE	INCOME IN 1989				POVERTY STATUS IN 1989							
				Percent of house-holds with income $75,000 or more	Persons below poverty level		Related children below poverty level [1]		FAMILIES			
	Median house-hold income (dollars)	Median family income (dollars)	Per capita income (dollars)						All families below poverty level		Female householder families below poverty level [1]	
					Number (1,000)	Percent	Number (1,000)	Percent	Number (1,000)	Percent	Number (1,000)	Percent
U.S..	30,056	35,225	14,420	9.5	31,743	13.1	11,162	17.9	6,488	10.0	2,867	42.3
N.E.:												
ME. . .	27,854	32,422	12,957	5.5	128	10.8	40	13.2	26	8.0	12	41.6
NH. . .	36,329	41,628	15,959	10.7	69	6.4	19	7.0	13	4.4	5	25.4
VT . . .	29,792	34,780	13,527	6.8	53	9.9	16	11.5	10	6.9	5	36.4
MA. . .	36,952	44,367	17,224	14.6	519	8.9	171	12.9	103	6.7	60	39.4
RI . . .	32,181	39,172	14,981	9.7	93	9.6	30	13.5	18	6.8	10	41.7
CT . . .	41,721	49,199	20,189	18.4	217	6.8	77	10.4	44	5.0	27	34.0
M.A.:												
NY. . .	32,965	39,741	16,501	13.6	2,277	13.0	783	18.8	455	10.0	240	43.4
NJ . . .	40,927	47,589	18,714	18.3	573	7.6	195	11.0	114	5.6	61	32.8
PA . . .	29,069	34,856	14,068	7.9	1,284	11.1	422	15.4	259	8.2	119	42.4
E.N.C.:												
OH. . .	28,706	34,351	13,461	6.9	1,326	12.5	485	17.6	284	9.7	142	46.4
IN . . .	28,797	34,082	13,149	6.2	574	10.7	199	13.9	118	7.9	56	39.7
IL. . . .	32,252	38,664	15,201	10.5	1,327	11.9	486	16.8	264	9.0	136	43.2
MI . . .	31,020	36,652	14,154	9.2	1,191	13.1	440	18.2	252	10.2	142	48.1
WI . . .	29,442	35,082	13,276	6.2	509	10.7	184	14.6	97	7.6	50	43.3
W.N.C.:												
MN. . .	30,909	36,916	14,389	8.1	435	10.2	142	12.4	83	7.3	37	40.0
IA . . .	26,229	31,659	12,422	4.8	307	11.5	98	14.0	63	8.4	25	45.1
MO . . .	26,362	31,838	12,989	6.4	663	13.3	225	17.4	139	10.1	57	42.0
ND. . .	23,213	28,707	11,051	3.5	88	14.4	29	16.9	18	10.9	6	50.4
SD. . .	22,503	27,602	10,661	3.5	106	15.9	39	20.1	21	11.6	7	48.8
NE . . .	26,016	31,634	12,452	5.0	171	11.1	57	13.5	34	8.0	13	39.5
KS . . .	27,291	32,966	13,300	6.4	275	11.5	91	13.9	55	8.3	22	40.0
S.A.:												
DE . . .	34,875	40,252	15,854	11.0	56	8.7	19	11.7	11	6.1	6	31.8
MD. . .	39,386	45,034	17,730	15.6	385	8.3	124	10.9	75	6.0	42	29.1
DC. . .	30,727	36,256	18,881	14.2	96	16.9	28	25.0	16	13.3	10	33.0
VA . . .	33,328	38,213	15,713	11.8	612	10.2	192	13.0	127	7.7	57	36.4
WV . . .	20,795	25,602	10,520	3.5	345	19.7	113	25.9	80	16.0	23	55.0
NC. . .	26,647	31,548	12,885	6.0	830	13.0	267	16.9	180	9.9	81	41.1
SC. . .	26,256	30,797	11,897	5.6	518	15.4	188	20.8	111	11.9	54	45.8
GA. . .	29,021	33,529	13,631	8.4	923	14.7	336	19.8	198	11.5	98	44.3
FL . . .	27,483	32,212	14,698	7.9	1,604	12.7	512	18.3	320	9.0	133	38.6
E.S.C.:												
KY . . .	22,534	27,028	11,153	4.6	682	19.0	230	24.5	163	16.0	52	51.8
TN . . .	24,807	29,546	12,255	5.6	745	15.7	247	20.7	168	12.4	66	45.2
AL. . .	23,597	28,688	11,486	5.2	724	18.3	250	24.0	158	14.3	68	52.1
MS. . .	20,136	24,448	9,648	3.8	631	25.2	246	33.5	137	20.2	62	61.4
W.S.C.:												
AR. . .	21,147	25,395	10,520	3.7	437	19.1	153	25.0	97	14.8	34	52.1
LA . . .	21,949	26,313	10,635	5.2	967	23.6	377	31.2	213	19.4	99	60.1
OK. . .	23,577	28,554	11,893	5.0	510	16.7	175	21.4	113	13.0	41	48.3
TX . . .	27,016	31,553	12,904	8.0	3,001	18.1	1,140	24.0	618	14.1	208	43.6
Mt.:												
MT. . .	22,988	28,044	11,213	3.9	125	16.1	43	19.9	26	12.0	9	49.3
ID . . .	25,257	29,472	11,457	4.7	131	13.3	48	15.8	26	9.7	9	42.3
WY . . .	27,096	32,216	12,311	4.8	52	11.9	19	14.1	11	9.3	5	45.4
CO. . .	30,140	35,930	14,821	8.6	375	11.7	126	15.0	74	8.6	33	38.8
NM. . .	24,087	27,623	11,246	5.6	306	20.6	120	27.5	65	16.5	23	50.2
AZ . . .	27,540	32,178	13,461	7.5	564	15.7	207	21.7	109	11.4	39	40.0
UT . . .	29,470	33,246	11,029	6.0	192	11.4	76	12.2	35	8.6	13	38.9
NV . . .	31,011	35,837	15,214	8.3	120	10.2	36	12.8	23	7.3	10	31.1
Pac.:												
WA . .	31,183	36,795	14,923	8.5	518	10.9	171	14.0	100	7.8	48	39.5
OR. . .	27,250	32,336	13,418	6.2	345	12.4	107	15.2	66	0.7	27	40.0
CA. . .	35,798	40,559	16,409	14.7	3,628	12.5	1,336	17.8	671	9.3	276	36.1
AK. . .	41,408	46,581	17,610	18.6	48	9.0	18	10.9	9	6.8	4	28.0
HI . . .	38,829	43,176	15,770	15.8	88	8.3	30	11.1	16	6.0	6	29.8

[1] Related children under 18 years old.

Source: U.S. Bureau of the Census, *1990 Census of Population and Housing Data Paper Listing (CPH-L-80)*.

No. 90-7. Housing Units and Housing Characteristics, by State: 1990

[See headnote, table 90-1]

DIVISION AND STATE	Total housing units (1,000)	PERCENT OF UNITS BUILT 1980 to 1990	PERCENT OF UNITS BUILT 1939 or earlier	Percent condominium	Occupied housing units (1,000)	PERCENT OF HOUSEHOLDS WITH— Telephone	PERCENT OF HOUSEHOLDS WITH— No vehicles available	PERCENT OF HOUSEHOLDS WITH— 2 or more vehicles	PERCENT OF SPECIFIED UNITS WITH— Owner occupied With mortgages	PERCENT OF SPECIFIED UNITS WITH— Owner occupied Selected monthly costs of 35 percent or more[1]	PERCENT OF SPECIFIED UNITS WITH— Renter occupied, selected monthly costs of 35 percent or more[1]
U.S..	102,264	20.7	18.4	4.74	91,947	94.8	11.5	54.7	65.4	13.5	30.7
N.E.:											
ME...	587	20.7	34.9	1.83	465	96.3	8.7	57.1	60.9	13.2	28.6
NH...	504	27.7	27.1	6.90	411	96.6	6.3	61.7	72.2	19.1	28.2
VT...	271	22.4	36.5	5.33	211	95.5	8.0	58.0	65.3	14.7	30.6
MA...	2,473	13.8	38.9	6.38	2,247	97.9	14.3	49.3	68.1	16.4	30.9
RI ...	415	15.1	34.0	3.06	378	96.9	10.6	54.5	64.8	16.0	31.1
CT ...	1,321	15.7	25.5	9.08	1,230	97.4	10.0	58.6	69.1	16.9	29.6
M.A.:											
NY...	7,227	9.4	35.7	4.76	6,639	95.0	30.0	37.5	64.8	16.5	32.4
NJ ...	3,075	14.8	24.6	7.22	2,795	96.9	12.9	52.5	67.0	18.8	30.3
PA ...	4,938	12.4	35.1	2.09	4,496	97.4	15.2	49.5	53.9	11.6	30.2
E.N.C.:											
OH...	4,372	12.2	25.8	2.60	4,088	95.3	10.2	56.8	63.0	9.5	29.9
IN ...	2,246	14.5	24.2	1.39	2,065	94.1	8.5	59.1	64.4	8.3	27.1
IL....	4,506	11.7	27.1	5.38	4,202	95.4	14.0	50.9	63.9	11.0	30.6
MI ...	3,848	13.6	20.8	2.70	3,419	95.9	10.1	56.8	63.5	11.0	34.4
WI ...	2,056	14.5	28.5	1.69	1,822	97.2	9.3	57.8	61.0	9.8	28.4
W.N.C.:											
MN...	1,848	18.5	24.5	3.02	1,648	97.6	8.6	60.0	69.1	9.8	30.5
IA ...	1,144	10.0	35.0	1.17	1,064	96.6	7.1	61.7	55.8	8.4	26.4
MO ..	2,199	18.3	20.4	2.16	1,961	94.8	9.8	57.0	61.1	9.4	28.5
ND...	276	16.6	24.7	2.17	241	96.5	6.5	63.2	55.9	9.6	23.9
SD...	292	14.8	30.4	0.72	259	94.0	6.5	64.1	54.7	9.4	24.7
NE ..	661	12.9	30.7	1.17	602	96.4	7.2	62.5	58.7	8.8	24.2
KS ...	1,044	16.9	24.5	1.75	945	95.6	6.4	61.7	60.5	9.6	26.8
S.A.:											
DE...	290	24.3	14.3	3.58	247	96.9	8.2	59.3	67.4	9.7	26.4
MD...	1,892	21.6	15.5	6.14	1,749	96.8	12.3	56.0	72.2	11.9	27.5
DC...	278	5.5	37.7	10.28	250	95.8	37.4	21.2	63.8	14.6	28.6
VA...	2,496	26.3	11.0	4.92	2,292	94.6	9.0	59.8	71.5	13.5	27.7
WV...	781	17.7	23.7	0.58	689	89.7	13.7	50.4	44.4	9.0	30.6
NC...	2,818	28.6	9.9	2.82	2,517	92.9	9.6	59.2	61.8	11.8	26.3
SC...	1,424	29.0	8.5	4.05	1,258	90.9	10.9	57.2	61.9	12.3	25.8
GA...	2,638	32.1	8.1	2.76	2,367	91.7	10.3	58.8	70.3	13.4	28.9
FL ...	6,100	35.0	3.7	15.48	5,135	94.7	9.2	49.8	69.1	15.9	33.4
E.S.C.:											
KY...	1,507	20.0	15.9	1.37	1,380	89.8	11.5	56.0	58.0	9.9	26.7
TN...	2,026	24.2	10.2	2.19	1,854	92.9	9.8	58.2	61.5	11.9	26.8
AL...	1,670	23.5	9.3	1.39	1,507	91.3	10.3	58.7	59.9	11.9	27.4
MS...	1,010	24.1	8.6	0.65	911	87.4	12.1	54.2	59.5	15.6	30.4
W.S.C.:											
AR...	1,001	24.2	9.4	0.88	891	89.1	9.8	56.2	55.7	12.8	29.2
LA...	1,716	22.1	10.6	1.60	1,499	91.7	13.9	49.9	57.5	14.7	33.7
OK...	1,406	22.1	12.4	1.54	1,206	91.2	7.5	58.1	60.2	11.9	29.2
TX...	7,009	29.7	7.1	2.90	6,071	91.4	8.1	55.9	62.2	12.8	27.3
Mt.:											
MT...	361	17.5	21.8	1.70	306	93.1	6.7	63.5	59.2	11.1	28.6
ID ...	413	18.0	15.9	1.81	361	94.2	4.6	67.3	67.1	10.0	25.0
WY...	203	21.4	15.6	1.24	169	94.4	4.7	66.9	65.5	8.8	24.9
CO...	1,477	24.7	13.0	8.40	1,282	95.8	6.9	60.9	76.9	14.6	29.4
NM...	632	27.5	8.1	1.58	543	87.6	6.9	59.0	61.6	13.6	29.9
AZ...	1,659	37.8	3.2	6.26	1,369	91.5	7.8	53.3	73.4	15.9	32.5
UT...	598	24.4	13.5	5.55	537	96.0	5.4	66.1	69.9	10.9	26.0
NV...	519	40.1	2.9	7.38	466	94.6	7.8	54.8	81.3	16.1	30.7
Pac.:											
WA ..	2,032	23.1	15.7	3.08	1,872	96.5	7.5	61.4	71.0	10.0	29.0
OR...	1,194	16.6	16.8	1.76	1,103	95.5	8.0	59.9	68.4	12.4	29.7
CA...	11,183	22.9	10.7	7.66	10,381	97.0	8.9	57.9	77.3	21.1	36.4
AK...	233	38.0	3.0	5.25	189	91.7	11.9	54.0	76.4	13.7	24.2
HI ...	390	20.8	6.7	20.81	356	97.4	9.9	54.1	69.6	14.0	29.0

[1] Percent of household income in 1989.

Source: U.S. Bureau of the Census, *1990 Census of Population and Housing Data Paper Listing (CPH-L-80).*

Telephone Contacts List

To help *Abstract* users find more data and information about statistical publications, we are issuing this list of contacts for Federal agencies with major statistical programs. The intent is to give a single, first-contact point-of-entry for users of statistics. These agencies will provide general information on their statistical programs and publications, as well as specific information on how to order their publications.

Executive Office of the President

Office of Management and Budget
Administrator
Office of Information and Regulatory Affairs
Office of Management and Budget
Washington, DC 20503
Information: 202-395-3000
Publications: 202-395-7332

Department of Agriculture

Economic Research Service
Information Division
Economic Research Service
U.S. Department of Agriculture
Room 208
1301 New York Ave., N.W.
Washington, DC 20005-4788
Information and Publications: 202-219-0515

National Agricultural Statistics Service
National Agricultural Statistics Service
U.S. Department of Agriculture
14th St. and Independence Ave., S.W.
Washington, DC 20250
Information and Publications: 202-720-4020

Department of Commerce

U.S. Department of Commerce
Room 5058 Main Commerce
14th St. and Constitution Ave., N.W.
Washington, DC 20230
Newsroom: 202-377-4901

Bureau of the Census
Customer Services Branch
Data User Services Division
Bureau of the Census
U.S. Department of Commerce
Washington, DC 20233
Information and Publications: 301-763-4100

Bureau of Economic Analysis
Current Business Analysis Division, BE-53
Bureau of Economic Analysis
U.S. Department of Commerce
Washington, DC 20230
Information and Publications: 202-523-0777

Department of Commerce —Con.
International Trade Administration
Trade Statistics Division
Office of Trade and Investment Analysis
International Trade Administration
Room 2814 B
U.S. Department of Commerce
Washington, DC 20230
Information and Publications: 202-377-4211

National Oceanic and Atmospheric Administration
National Oceanic and Atmospheric Administration Library
U.S. Department of Commerce
6009 Executive Blvd.
Rockville, MD 20852
Library: 301-443-8330

Department of Defense

Department of Defense
Office of the Assistant Secretary of Defense (Public Affairs)
Attention: Directorate for Public Correspondence
The Pentagon, 2E777
Washington, DC 20301-1400
Information: 703-697-5737

Department of Education

Office of Information Services
Statistical Information Office
U.S. Department of Education
555 New Jersey Ave., N.W.
Washington, DC 20208-5641
Information and Publications: 202-219-1651; 1-800-424-1616

Department of Energy

Energy Information Administration
Office of Energy Information Services
Energy Information Administration
U.S. Department of Energy
Washington, DC 20585
Information and Publications: 202-586-8800

Department of Health and Human Services

Health Resources and Services Administration
Administrator for Health Resources and Services
Health Resources and Services Administration
U.S. Department of Health and Human Services
5600 Fishers Lane
42 Parklawn Building 14-05
Rockville, MD 20857
Information: 301-443-2216
Publications: 301-443-2086

Alcohol, Drug Abuse, and Mental Health Administration
U.S. Department of Health and Human Services
5600 Fishers Lane
Room 12C15
Rockville, MD 20857
Information: 301-443-3783
Publications: 301-468-2600

Centers for Disease Control
Office of Information
Centers for Disease Control
21600 Clifton Road, N.E.
Atlanta, GA 30333
Public Inquiries: 404-639-3534

Health Care Financing Administration
Office of Public Affairs
Health Care Financing Administration
U.S. Department of Health and Human Services
Room 428H, Humphrey Building
200 Independence Ave., S.W.
Washington, DC 20201
Information: 202-690-6145

National Center for Health Statistics
Scientific and Technical Information Branch
National Center for Health Statistics
U.S. Department of Health and Human Services
6525 Belcrest Rd. Rm. 1064
Hyattsville, MD 20782
Information and Publications: 301-436-8500

Social Security Administration
Publications Staff
Office of Research and Statistics
Social Security Administration
U.S. Department of Health and Human Services
Van Ness Centre, Room 209
4301 Connecticut Ave., N.W.
Washington, DC 20008
Information and Publications: 202-282-7138

Department of Housing and Urban Development

Assistant Secretary for Community Planning and Development
Office of the Assistant Secretary for Community Planning and Development
U.S. Department of Housing and Urban Development
451 7th St., S.W.
Washington, DC 20410-0555
Information: 202-708-2690
Publications: 301-251-5154

Department of the Interior

Bureau of Mines
Office of Public Information
Bureau of Mines
U.S. Department of the Interior
810 7th St., N.W.
Washington, DC 20241
Publications: 202-501-9649

Geological Survey
Public Inquiries Office
Geological Survey
U.S. Department of the Interior
507 National Center
Reston, VA 22092
Information and Publications: 703-648-6892

Department of Justice

Bureau of Justice Statistics
Statistics Division
Bureau of Justice Statistics
U.S. Department of Justice
633 Indiana Ave., N.W.
Washington, DC 20531
Information and Publications: 202-307-6100

National Criminal Justice Reference Service
Box 6000
Rockville, MD 20850
Information and Publications: 301-251-5500
Publications: 1-800-732-3277

Federal Bureau of Investigation
National Crime Information Center
Federal Bureau of Investigation
U.S. Department of Justice
9th St. and Pennsylvania Ave., N.W.
Washington, DC 20535
Information and Publications: 202-324-3691

Immigration and Naturalization Service
Statistics Branch
Immigration and Naturalization Service
U.S. Department of Justice
425 I St., N.W.
Washington, DC 20536
Attention: Tariff Rm. 235
Information and Publications: 202-376-3066

Department of Labor

Bureau of Labor Statistics
Office of Publications and Information Services
Bureau of Labor Statistics
U.S. Department of Labor
441 G St., N.W., Room 2831A
Washington, DC 20212
Information and Publications: 202-606-7828
Recording: CPI and PPI 202-523-9658

Employment and Training Administration
Office of Public Information
Employment and Training Administration
U.S. Department of Labor
200 Constitution Ave., N.W., Room S2322
Washington, DC 20210
Information and Publications: 202-523-6871

Department of Transportation

Federal Aviation Administration
Public Inquiry Center
APA 200
Federal Aviation Administration
U.S. Department of Transportation
800 Independence Ave., S.W.
Washington, DC 20591
Information and Publications: 202-267-3484

Federal Highway Administration
Office of Public Affairs
Federal Highway Administration
U.S. Department of Transportation
400 7th St., S.W.
Washington, DC 20590
Information and Publications: 202-366-0660

National Highway Traffic Safety Administration
Office of Public Affairs
National Highway Traffic Safety Administration
U.S. Department of Transportation
400 7th St., S.W.
Washington, DC 20590
Information: 202-366-0123
Publications: 202-366-2588

Department of the Treasury

Internal Revenue Service
Statistics of Income Division
Internal Revenue Service
U.S. Department of the Treasury
P.O. Box 2608
Washington, DC 20013
Information and Publications: 202-622-5000

Department of Veterans Affairs

Department of Veterans Affairs
Office of Public Affairs
Department of Veterans Affairs
810 Vermont Ave., N.W.
Washington, DC 20420
Information: 202-233-2741

Independent Agencies

Environmental Protection Agency
Public Information Center, PM-211B
Environmental Protection Agency
401 M St., S.W.
Washington, DC 20460
Information and Publications: 202-260-2080

Federal Reserve Board
Division of Research and Statistics
Federal Reserve Board
Washington, DC 20551
Information: 202-452-3301
Publications: 202-452-3245

National Science Foundation
Office of Public Information
National Science Foundation
1800 G St., N.W.
Washington, DC 20550
Information: 202-357-9498
Publications: 202-357-7861

Securities and Exchange Commission
Office of Public Affairs
Securities and Exchange Commission
450 5th St., N.W.
Washington, DC 20549
Information: 202-272-3100
Publications: 202-272-7460

Population

This section presents statistics on the growth, distribution, and characteristics of the U.S. population. The principal source of these data is the Bureau of the Census, which conducts a decennial census of population, a monthly population survey, a program of population estimates and projections, and a number of other periodic surveys relating to population characteristics. For a list of relevant publications, see the Guide to Sources of Statistics in Appendix I.

Decennial censuses.—The U.S. Constitution provides for a census of the population every 10 years, primarily to establish a basis for apportionment of members of the House of Representatives among the States. For over a century after the first census in 1790, the census organization was a temporary one, created only for each decennial census. In 1902, the Bureau of the Census was established as a permanent Federal agency, responsible for enumerating the population and also for compiling statistics on other subjects.

The census of population is a complete count. That is, an attempt is made to account for every person, for each person's residence, and for other characteristics (sex, age, family relationships, etc.). Since the 1940 census, in addition to the complete count information, some data have been obtained from representative samples of the population. In the 1990 census, variable sampling rates were employed. For most of the country, one in every six households (about 17 percent) received the long form or sample questionnaire; in governmental units estimated to have fewer than 2,500 inhabitants, every other household (50 percent) received the sample questionnaire to enhance the reliability of sample data for small areas. Exact agreement is not to be expected between sample data and the complete census count. Sample data may be used with confidence where large numbers are involved and assumed to indicate trends and relationships where small numbers are involved.

Three different census counts for the resident population in 1970 are shown in

In Brief

Total population, 1991	253 million
Northeast	*20 %*
Midwest	*24 %*
South	*35 %*
West	*21 %*
Total households, 1991	94 million
One-person households	*25 %*

the tables: 203,211,926; 203,235,298; and 203,302,031. The first is the initial tabulated count, the second is the official count, and the third contains the latest revisions. Breakdowns of the revised count of 203,302,031 are not available for demographic characteristics and may not be available for some levels of geography. The complete count data from the 1980 and 1990 censuses shown in this edition are consistent with figures published in the 1980 and 1990 census final reports, series PC80-1-A and series 1990 CP-1, respectively.

Census data presented here have not been adjusted for underenumeration. Results from the evaluation program for the 1980 census did not produce a definitive estimate of the undercount, but did show that coverage improved substantially over previous censuses. The 1980 Post-Enumeration Program (PEP) estimates of overall coverage ranged between a 1.0 percent overcount and a 2.1 percent undercount; Demographic Analysis (DA) estimated the net undercount at between 1.0 and 2.2 percent. Consistent estimates of census coverage for the censuses from 1940 to 1980 have been prepared by the method of demographic analysis. For one set of estimates, demographic analysis shows a net underenumeration of about 3.2 million persons in 1980, 6.1 million in 1970, and 6.2 million in 1960. Among the persons not counted in 1980 about 1.5 million were White-and-other races and 1.7 million were Black. The overall rate of net underenumeration in 1980, according to this set of estimates, was 1.4 percent. In 1970, the rate was 2.9 percent as compared with 3.3 percent in 1960 and 4.4 percent in 1950. The percent net undercount of Blacks—while still high relative to the rest of the population—dropped from 8.0 percent in 1970 to 5.9 percent in 1980. See *The Coverage of Population in the 1980 Census, Evaluation and Research Reports,* PHC80-E4, for a discussion of the various estimates of census coverage.

Current Population Survey (CPS).— This is a monthly nationwide survey of a scientifically selected sample representing the noninstitutional civilian population. The sample is located in 729 areas comprising 1,973 counties, independent cities, and minor civil divisions with coverage in every State and the District of Columbia and is subject to sampling error. At the present time, about 60,000 occupied households are eligible for interview every month; of these between 4 and 5 percent are, for various reasons, unavailable for interview.

While the primary purpose of the CPS is to obtain monthly statistics on the labor force, it also serves as a vehicle for inquiries on other subjects. Using CPS data, the Bureau issues a series of publications under the general title of Current Population Reports, which cover population characteristics (series P-20), consumer income (series P-60), special studies (series P-23), and other topics.

Estimates of population characteristics based on the CPS will not necessarily agree with the counts from the census because the CPS and the census use different procedures for collecting and processing the data for racial groups, the Hispanic population, and other topics. Caution should also be used when comparing estimates for 1980 and later, (for education data, 1981 and later), which reflect 1980 census-based population controls, to those for 1971 through 1979 (for education, to 1980), which reflect 1970 census-based population controls. This change in population controls had relatively little impact on derived measures such as means, medians, and percent distribution, but did have a significant impact on levels.

Population estimates and projections.— National population estimates are derived by using decennial census data as benchmarks and data available from various agencies as follows: Births and deaths (National Center for Health Statistics); immigrants (Immigration and Naturalization Service); Armed Forces (Department of Defense and Department of Transportation); net movement between Puerto Rico and the U.S. mainland (Puerto Rico Planning Board); and Federal employees abroad (Office of Personnel Management and Department of Defense). Estimates for States and smaller areas are based on data series such as births and deaths, school statistics from State departments of education and parochial school systems, and Federal income tax returns. These estimates contain estimated emigration of 160,000 per year since 1980 and net undocumented immigration of 200,000 per year. For further information, see *Current Population Reports,* series P-25, No. 1045.

Estimates of the population by age for April 1, 1990 (shown in table 19) are modified counts. The review of detailed 1990 information indicated that respondents tended to provide their age as of the date of completion of the questionnaire, not their age as of April 1, 1990. In addition, there may have been a tendency for respondents to round up their age if they were close to having a birthday. A detailed explanation of the age modification procedure appears in *1990 Census of Population and Housing Data Paper Listing* (CPH-L-74).

Population estimates and projections are published in the P-25 and P-26 series of *Current Population Reports.* These estimates and projections are generally consistent with official decennial census figures and do not reflect the amount of estimated census underenumeration. However, these estimates and projections by race have been modified and are not comparable to the census race categories (see section below under "race"). For details on methodology, see the sources cited below the individual tables.

Immigration.—The principal source of immigration data is the *Statistical Yearbook of the Immigration and Naturalization Service,* published annually by the Immigration and Naturalization Service (INS), a unit of the Department of Justice. Immigration statistics are prepared from entry visas and change of immigration status forms. Immigrants are aliens admitted for legal permanent residence in the United States. The procedures for admission depend on whether the alien is residing inside or outside the United States at the time of application for permanent residence. Eligible aliens residing outside the United States are issued immigrant visas by the U.S. Department of State. Eligible aliens residing in the United States are allowed to change their status from temporary to permanent residence at INS district offices. The category, immigrant, includes persons who may have entered the United States as nonimmigrants or refugees, but who subsequently changed their status to that of a permanent resident. Nonresident aliens admitted to the United States for a temporary period are nonimmigrants (tables 7 and 410). Refugees are considered nonimmigrants when initially admitted into the United States, but are not included in nonimmigrant admission data. A refugee is any person who is outside his or her country of nationality who is unable or unwilling to return to that country because of persecution or a well-founded fear of persecution.

U.S. immigration law gives preferential immigration status to aliens who are related to certain U.S. citizens or legal permanent residents, aliens with needed job skills, or aliens who qualify as refugees. Immigration to the United States can be divided into two general categories: (1) those subject to the annual worldwide limitation, and (2) those exempt from it. A maximum of 270,000 immigrants may be admitted annually under the current worldwide limitation. Visa allocation is determined by a system consisting of six preference categories, each with its own numerical limitation. The first, second, fourth, and fifth preferences are based on the alien's relationship with a U.S. citizen or legal permanent resident, and the third and sixth preferences are based on needed job skills (see table 6). Aliens not eligible for any of the six preferences may qualify for the nonpreference category. Heavy demand for preference visas has resulted in no nonpreference visas being issued since 1978. Additional visas have been issued under the nonpreference category since 1987 to persons from countries adversely affected by the Immigration Amendments of 1965. Those exempt from the worldwide limitation include immediate relatives of U.S.

citizens, refugees and asylees adjusting to permanent residence, and other various classes of special immigrants (see table 6).

Effective November 1966, Cubans admitted or paroled (i.e., admitted without an immigration visa) into the United States after January 1, 1959, and present in the United States for at least 2 years, may obtain permanent resident status. A court decision in September 1976 exempted Cuban refugees from numerical limitations, retroactive to 1968. The Refugee Act of 1980 changed the residency requirement from 2 years to 1 year. Beginning in fiscal year 1985, INS began adjusting eligible Cuban entrants who were admitted to the United States as part of the Mariel boat lift of 1980, which consisted of approximately 125,000 people.

Effective October 28, 1977, refugees from Vietnam, Laos, or Cambodia were eligible to apply for permanent resident status. Public Law 95-145 provided that Indochinese paroled into the United States after March 31, 1975, or physically present on that date, may become permanent residents after living for at least 2 years in the United States. This period was changed to one year under the Refugee Act of 1980. P.L. 95-145 expired on October 18, 1983. Indochinese refugees who entered the U.S. between March 1975 and April 1980 are eligible to adjust status under P.L. 95-412, the Act of October 5, 1978, which allows for the adjustment of refugee-parolees.

The Refugee Act of 1980, effective April 1, 1980, provides for a uniform admission procedure for refugees of all countries, based on the United Nations' definition of refugees. Authorized admission ceilings are set annually by the President in consultation with Congress. After one year of residence in the United States, refugees are eligible for immigrant status.

The Immigration Reform and Control Act of 1986 (IRCA) allows two groups of aliens to become temporary and then permanent residents of the United States: aliens who have been in the United States unlawfully since January 1, 1982, (legalization applicants) and aliens who were employed in seasonal agricultural work for a minimum period of time (Special Agricultural Worker (SAW) applicants). The application period for temporary residency for legalization applicants began on May 5, 1987, and ended on May 4, 1988, while the application period for SAW applicants began on June 1, 1987, and ended on November 30, 1988. Legalization applicants became eligible for permanent residence beginning in fiscal year 1989. The 1989 and 1990 immigrant data include temporary residents who were granted permanent residence under the legalization program of IRCA.

Metropolitan Areas.—The general concept of a metropolitan area is one of a large population nucleus together with adjacent communities which have a high degree of social and economic integration with that nucleus. Metropolitan statistical areas (MSA's), consolidated metropolitan statistical areas (CMSA's), and primary metropolitan statistical areas (PMSA's) are defined by the Office of Management and Budget as a standard for Federal agencies in the preparation and publication of statistics relating to metropolitan areas. The entire territory of the United States is classified as metropolitan (inside MSA's or CMSA's) or nonmetropolitan (outside MSA's or CMSA's). MSA's, CMSA's, and PMSA's are defined in terms of entire counties except in New England, where the definitions are in terms of cities and towns. To summarize data for New England that are available only by counties, New England County Metropolitan Areas (NECMA's) have been defined as a convenience for data users. From time to time, new metropolitan areas are created and the boundaries of others change. As a result, data for metropolitan areas over time may not be comparable and the analysis of historical trends must be made cautiously. For descriptive details and a listing of area titles and components of each metropolitan area, see Appendix II.

Urban and rural.—According to the 1990 census definition, the urban population comprises all persons living in (a) places of 2,500 or more inhabitants incorporated as cities, villages, boroughs (except in Alaska and New York), and towns (except in the New England States, New York, and Wisconsin), but excluding those persons living in the rural portions of extended cities (places

with low population density in one or more large parts of their area); (b) census designated places (previously termed unincorporated) of 2,500 or more inhabitants; and (c) other territory, incorporated or unincorporated, included in urbanized areas. An urbanized area comprises one or more places and the adjacent densely settled surrounding territory that together have a minimum population of 50,000 persons.

In censuses prior to 1950, the urban population comprised all persons living in incorporated places of 2,500 or more inhabitants and areas (usually minor civil divisions) classified as urban under special rules relating to population size and density. To improve its measure of the urban population, the Bureau of the Census in 1950 adopted the concept of the urbanized area and delineated boundaries for unincorporated places. The 1950 definition has continued substantially unchanged, except for minor modifications in 1960, the introduction of the extended city concept in 1970, and changes since the 1970 census in the criteria for defining urbanized areas so as to permit such areas to be defined around smaller centers. In all definitions, the population not classified as urban constitutes the rural population.

Residence.—In determining residence, the Bureau of the Census counts each person as an inhabitant of a usual place of residence (i.e., the place where one usually lives and sleeps). While this place is not necessarily a person's legal residence or voting residence, the use of these different bases of classification would produce the same results in the vast majority of cases.

Race.—The Bureau of the Census collects and publishes racial statistics as outlined in Statistical Policy Directive No. 15 issued by the U.S. Office of Management and Budget. This directive provides standards on ethnic and racial categories for statistical reporting to be used by all Federal agencies. According to the directive, the basic racial categories are American Indian or Alaska Native, Asian or Pacific Islander, Black, and White. (The directive identifies Hispanic origin as an ethnicity.) The concept of race the Bureau of the Census uses reflects self-identification by respondents; that is the individual's perception of his/her racial identity. The concept is not intended to reflect any biological or anthropological definition. Although the Bureau of the Census adheres to the overall guidelines of Directive No. 15, we recognize that there are persons who do not identify with a specific racial group. The 1990 census race question includes an "Other race" category with provisions for a write-in entry. Furthermore, the Bureau of the Census recognizes that the categories of the race item include both racial and national origin or socio-cultural groups.

Differences between the 1990 census and earlier censuses affect the comparability of data for certain racial groups and American Indian tribes. The lack of comparability is due to changes in the way some respondents reported their race as well as changes in 1990 census procedures related to the racial classification. (For a fuller explanation, see *1990 Census of Population, Volume I, General Population Characteristics* (1990 CP-1)).

Estimates of the population by race for April 1, 1990 (shown in tables 14 and 15) are modified counts and are not comparable to the 1990 census race categories. These estimates were computed using 1990 census data by race which had been modified to be consistent with the race categories used in the reporting of vital statistics by the U.S. National Center for Health Statistics. A detailed explanation of the race modification procedure appears in *1990 Census of Population and Housing Data Paper Listing* (CPH-L-74).

In the CPS and other household sample surveys in which data are obtained through personal interview, respondents are asked to classify their race as: (1) White, (2) Black, (3) American Indian, Aleut, or Eskimo, or (4) Asian or Pacific Islander. The procedures for classifying persons of mixed races who could not provide a single response to the race question are generally similar to those used in the census. For comments on comparability of 1980 CPS and census data, see section above on Current Population Survey.

Hispanic population.—In the 1990 census, the Bureau of the Census collected data on the Hispanic origin population in the United States by using a self-identification question. Persons of Spanish/Hispanic origin are those who classified themselves in one of the specific Hispanic origin categories listed on the questionnaire—Mexican, Puerto Rican, Cuban, or Other Spanish/Hispanic origin. The difference between the 1980 and the 1990 questionnaire was that in the 1980 census, a Hispanic origin question was used with prelisted categories for the largest Spanish origin groups and a residual Other Spanish/Hispanic category. For the 1990 census the questionnaire was modified by adding a space for the respondent to write-in the entry for the Other Spanish/Hispanic category. It should be noted that Hispanic persons may be of any race.

In the CPS information on Hispanic persons was gathered by using a self-identification question. Persons classified themselves in one of the Hispanic categories in response to the question: "What is the origin or descent of each person in this household?" Hispanic persons in the CPS were persons who reported themselves as Mexican-American, Chicano, Mexican, Puerto Rican, Cuban, Central or South American (Spanish countries), or other Hispanic origin.

Nativity.—The native population consists of all persons born in the United States, Puerto Rico, or an outlying area of the United States. It also includes persons born at sea or in a foreign country who have at least one American parent. All others are classified as "foreign born."

Mobility status.—The U.S. population is classified according to mobility status on the basis of a comparison between the place of residence of each individual at the time of the survey or census and the place of residence at a specified earlier date. Nonmovers are all persons who were living in the same house or apartment at the end of the period as at the beginning of the period. Movers are all persons who were living in a different house at the end of the period from that in which they were living at the beginning of the period. Movers from abroad include all persons, either citizens or aliens, whose place of residence was outside the United States at the beginning of the period; that is, in Puerto Rico, an outlying area under the jurisdiction of the United States, or a foreign country.

Living arrangements.—Living arrangements refer to residency in households or in group quarters. A "household" comprises all persons who occupy a "housing unit," that is, a house, an apartment or other group of rooms, or a single room that constitutes "separate living quarters." A household includes the related family members and all the unrelated persons, if any, such as lodgers, foster children, wards, or employees who share the housing unit. A person living alone or a group of unrelated persons sharing the same housing unit is also counted as a household. See text, section 26, Construction and Housing, for definition of housing unit.

All persons not living in households are classified as living in group quarters. These individuals may be institutionalized, e.g., under care or custody in juvenile facilities, jails, correctional centers, hospitals, or rest homes; or they may be residents in college dormitories, military barracks, rooming houses, etc. (see table 74).

Householder.—The householder is the first adult household member listed on the questionnaire. The instructions call for listing first the person (or one of the persons) in whose name the home is owned or rented. If a home is owned or rented jointly by a married couple, either the husband or the wife may be listed first. Prior to 1980, the husband was always considered the household head (householder) in married-couple households.

Family.—The term "family" refers to a group of two or more persons related by birth, marriage, or adoption and residing together in a household. A family includes among its members the householder.

Subfamily.—A subfamily consists of a married couple and their children, if any, or one parent with one or more never married children under 18 years old living in a household. Subfamilies are divided into "related" and "unrelated" subfamilies. A related subfamily is related to, but does not include, the householder. Members of a related subfamily are also members of the family with whom they live. The number of related subfamilies, therefore, is not included in the count of families. An unrelated subfamily may include persons such as guests, lodgers, or resident employees and their spouses and/or children; none of whom is related to the householder.

Married couple.—A "married couple" is defined as a husband and wife living together in the same household, with or without children and other relatives.

Unrelated individuals.—"Unrelated individuals" are persons (other than inmates of institutions) who are not members of families or subfamilies. An unrelated individual may be a nonfamily householder who lives alone or with nonrelatives only, or a secondary individual such as a guest, lodger, or resident employee. Persons in group quarters, except inmates of institutions, are classified as secondary individuals.

Statistical reliability.—For a discussion of statistical collection and estimation, sampling procedures, and measures of statistical reliability applicable to Census Bureau data, see Appendix III.

Historical statistics.—Tabular headnotes provide cross-references, where applicable, to *Historical Statistics of the United States, Colonial Times to 1970.* See Appendix IV.

Figure 1.1
Percent Change in State Population: 1980 to 1990

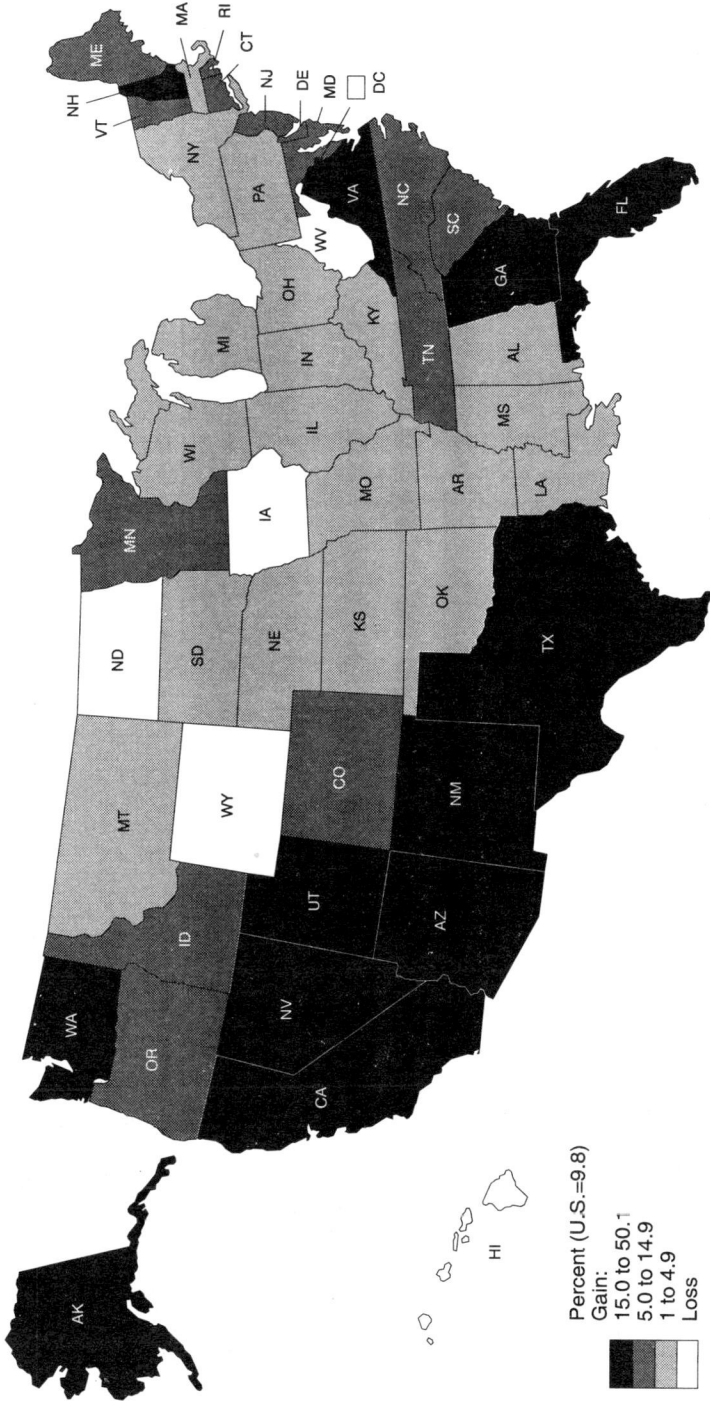

Percent (U.S.=9.8)
Gain:
15.0 to 50.1
5.0 to 14.9
1 to 4.9
Loss

Source: Chart prepared by U.S. Bureau of the Census. For data, see table 25.

Population

No. 1. Population and Area: 1790 to 1990

[Area figures represent area on indicated date including in some cases considerable areas not then organized or settled, and not covered by the census. Total area figures for 1790 to 1970 have been recalculated on the basis of the remeasurement of States and counties for the 1980 census. The land and water area figures for past censuses have not been adjusted and are not strictly comparable with the total area data for comparable dates because the land areas were derived from different base data, and these values are known to have changed with the construction of reservoirs, draining of lakes, etc. Density figures are based on land area measurements as reported in earlier censuses]

CENSUS DATE	RESIDENT POPULATION				AREA (square miles)		
	Number	Per square mile of land area	Increase over preceding census		Gross	Land	Water
			Number	Percent			
CONTERMINOUS U.S.[1]							
1790 (Aug. 2)	3,929,214	4.5	(X)	(X)	891,364	864,746	24,065
1800 (Aug. 4)	5,308,483	6.1	1,379,269	35.1	891,364	864,746	24,065
1810 (Aug. 6)	7,239,881	4.3	1,931,398	36.4	1,722,685	1,681,828	34,175
1820 (Aug. 7)	9,638,453	5.5	2,398,572	33.1	1,792,552	1,749,462	38,544
1830 (June 1)	12,866,020	7.4	3,227,567	33.5	1,792,552	1,749,462	38,544
1840 (June 1)	17,069,453	9.8	4,203,433	32.7	1,792,552	1,749,462	38,544
1850 (June 1)	23,191,876	7.9	6,122,423	35.9	2,991,655	2,940,042	52,705
1860 (June 1)	31,443,321	10.6	8,251,445	35.6	3,021,295	2,969,640	52,747
1870 (June 1)	[2]39,818,449	[2]13.4	8,375,128	26.6	3,021,295	2,969,640	52,747
1880 (June 1)	50,155,783	16.9	10,337,334	26.0	3,021,295	2,969,640	52,747
1890 (June 1)	62,947,714	21.2	12,791,931	25.5	3,021,295	2,969,640	52,747
1900 (June 1)	75,994,575	25.6	13,046,861	20.7	3,021,295	2,969,834	52,553
1910 (Apr. 15)	91,972,266	31.0	15,977,691	21.0	3,021,295	2,969,565	52,822
1920 (Jan. 1)	105,710,620	35.6	13,738,354	14.9	3,021,295	2,969,451	52,936
1930 (Apr. 1)	122,775,046	41.2	17,064,426	16.1	3,021,295	2,977,128	45,259
1940 (Apr. 1)	131,669,275	44.2	8,894,229	7.2	3,021,295	2,977,128	45,259
1950 (Apr. 1)	150,697,361	50.7	19,028,086	14.5	3,021,295	2,974,726	47,661
1960 (Apr. 1)	178,464,236	60.1	27,766,875	18.4	3,021,295	2,968,054	54,207
UNITED STATES							
1950 (Apr. 1)	151,325,798	42.6	19,161,229	14.5	3,618,770	3,552,206	63,005
1960 (Apr. 1)	[3]179,323,175	50.6	27,997,377	18.5	3,618,770	3,540,911	74,212
1970 (Apr. 1)	[3]203,302,031	[3]57.4	23,978,856	13.4	3,618,770	[3]3,540,023	[3]78,444
1980 (Apr. 1)	226,545,805	64.0	23,243,774	11.4	3,618,770	3,539,289	79,481
1990 (Apr. 1)	248,709,873	70.3	22,164,068	9.8	3,787,425	3,536,342	[4]251,083

X Not applicable.   [1] Excludes Alaska and Hawaii.   [2] Revised to include adjustments for underenumeration in southern States; unrevised number is 38,558,371 (13.0 per square mile).   [3] Figures corrected after 1970 final reports were issued.   [4] Comprises inland, coastal, Great Lakes, and territorial water. Data for prior years cover inland water only. For further explanation, see table 340.

Source: U.S. Bureau of the Census, *U.S. Census of Population: 1920* to *1990*, vol. I; and other reports and unpublished data. See also *Areas of the United States, 1940*, and *Area Measurement Reports, 1960*, series GE-20, No. 1.

No. 2. Population: 1900 to 1991

[In thousands, except percent. Estimates as of July 1. Prior to 1940, excludes Alaska and Hawaii. Total population includes Armed Forces abroad; civilian population excludes Armed Forces. For basis of estimates, see text, section 1. See also *Historical Statistics, Colonial Times to 1970*, series A 6-8]

YEAR	Resident population	YEAR	TOTAL		Resident population	Civilian population	YEAR	TOTAL		Resident population	Civilian population
			Population	Percent change				Population	Percent change		
1900. . . .	76,094	1952 . . .	157,553	1.73	156,393	153,892	1972 . . .	209,896	1.08	209,284	207,511
1905. . . .	83,822	1953 . . .	160,184	1.67	158,956	156,595	1973 . . .	211,909	0.96	211,357	209,600
1910. . . .	92,407	1954 . . .	163,026	1.77	161,884	159,695	1974 . . .	213,854	0.92	213,342	211,636
1915. . . .	100,546	1955 . . .	165,931	1.78	165,069	162,967	1975 . . .	215,973	0.99	215,465	213,789
1920. . . .	106,461	1956 . . .	168,903	1.79	168,088	166,055	1976 . . .	218,035	0.95	217,563	215,894
1925. . . .	115,829	1957 . . .	171,984	1.82	171,187	169,110	1977 . . .	220,239	1.01	219,760	218,106
1930. . . .	123,077	1958 . . .	174,882	1.68	174,149	172,226	1978 . . .	222,585	1.06	222,095	220,467
1935. . . .	127,250	1959 . . .	177,830	1.69	177,135	175,277	1979 . . .	225,055	1.11	224,567	222,969
1940. . . .	132,457	1960 . . .	180,671	1.60	179,979	178,140	1980 . . .	227,722	1.18	227,220	225,616
1941. . . .	133,669	1961 . . .	183,691	1.67	182,992	181,143	1981 . . .	229,958	0.98	229,457	227,809
1942. . . .	134,617	1962 . . .	186,538	1.55	185,771	183,677	1982 . . .	232,192	0.97	231,669	229,999
1943. . . .	135,107	1963 . . .	189,242	1.45	188,483	186,493	1983 . . .	234,321	0.92	233,806	232,111
1944. . . .	133,915	1964 . . .	191,889	1.40	191,141	189,141	1984 . . .	236,370	0.87	235,847	234,131
1945. . . .	133,434	1965 . . .	194,303	1.26	193,526	191,605	1985 . . .	238,492	0.90	237,950	236,245
1946. . . .	140,686	1966 . . .	196,560	1.16	195,576	193,420	1986 . . .	240,680	0.92	240,162	238,441
1947. . . .	144,083	1967 . . .	198,712	1.09	197,457	195,264	1987 . . .	242,836	0.90	242,321	240,582
1948. . . .	146,730	1968 . . .	200,706	1.00	199,399	197,113	1988 . . .	245,057	0.91	244,534	242,852
1949. . . .	149,304	1969 . . .	202,677	0.98	201,385	199,145	1989 . . .	247,343	0.93	246,820	245,132
1950. . . .	152,271	1970 . . .	205,052	1.17	203,984	201,895	1990 . . .	249,924	1.04	249,415	247,775
1951. . . .	153,982	1971 . . .	207,661	1.27	206,827	204,866	1991 . . .	252,688	1.11	252,177	250,566

Source: U.S. Bureau of the Census, *Current Population Reports*, series P-25, Nos. 311, 1045, and 1083.

No. 3. Center of Population: 1790 to 1990

["Center of population" is that point at which an imaginary flat, weightless, and rigid map of the United States would balance if weights of identical value were placed on it so that each weight represented the location of one person on the date of the census]

YEAR	North latitude			West longitude			Approximate location
	°	′	″	°	′	″	
1790 (August 2)	39	16	30	76	11	12	23 miles east of Baltimore, MD
1850 (June 1)	38	59	0	81	19	0	23 miles southeast of Parkersburg, WV
1900 (June 1)	39	9	36	85	48	54	6 miles southeast of Columbus, IN
1950 (April 1)	38	50	21	88	9	33	8 miles north–northwest of Olney, Richland County, IL
1960 (April 1)	38	35	58	89	12	35	In Clinton Co. about 6 1/2 miles northwest of Centralia, IL
1970 (April 1)	38	27	47	89	42	22	5.3 miles east–southeast of the Mascoutah City Hall in St. Clair County, IL
1980 (April 1)	38	8	13	90	34	26	1/4 mile west of De Soto in Jefferson County, MO
1990 (April 1)	37	52	20	91	12	55	9.7 miles southeast of Steelville, MO

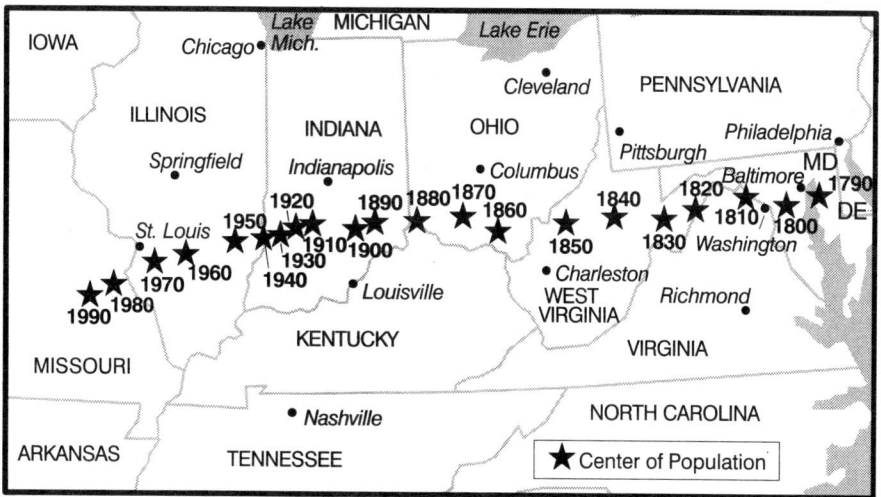

No. 4. U.S. Population Abroad, by Selected Area: 1992

[In thousands. As of June 3. Data compiled as part of noncombatant personnel evacuation requirements report]

AREA	Total[1]	Resident U.S. citizen	U.S. tourists	AREA	Total[1]	Resident U.S. citizen	U.S. tourists
Total[2]	14,285	6,269	6,674	Italy	155	102	28
Argentina	38	13	25	Japan	142	38	13
Australia	75	65	8	Jerusalem	28	26	2
Belgium	42	24	7	Martinique	221	(Z)	221
Brazil	46	34	11	Mexico	802	495	300
Canada	1,561	278	1,281	Netherlands	35	22	5
Costa Rica	31	25	4	Panama	36	8	1
Dominican Republic	97	87	9	Philippines	147	119	(Z)
Egypt	21	13	2	Portugal	47	31	12
France	224	126	91	Saudi Arabia	42	31	7
Germany	513	107	208	South Korea	72	8	38
Greece	70	38	30	Spain	60	27	31
Hong Kong	27	21	5	Switzerland	32	27	4
Ireland	71	43	28	United Kingdom	414	213	162
Israel	137	124	12	Venezuela	50	24	26

Z Less than 500. [1]Includes Dept. of Defense noncombatant employees, other U.S. government employees, and dependents of U.S. military and civilian employees, not shown separately. [2]Includes other areas not shown separately.
Source: U.S. Dept. of State, unpublished data.

Population

No. 5. Immigration: 1820 to 1990

[In thousands, except rate. For fiscal years ending in year shown, except as noted; see text, section 9. For definition of immigrants, see text, section 1. For 1820-1867, alien passengers arriving, 1868-1891 and 1895-1897, immigrants arriving; 1892-1894 and 1898 to the present, immigrants admitted. Rates based on Bureau of the Census estimates as of July 1 for resident population through 1929, and for total population thereafter (excluding Alaska and Hawaii prior to 1959). Population estimates for 1980 through 1989 reflect revisions based on the 1990 Census of Population. See also *Historical Statistics, Colonial Times to 1970*, series C 89]

PERIOD	Number	Rate [1]	PERIOD OR YEAR	Number	Rate [1]	YEAR	Number	Rate [1]
1820 to 1990....	56,994	3.4	1911 to 1920	5,736	5.7	1981	597	2.6
1820 to 1830 [2].....	152	1.2	1921 to 1930	4,107	3.5	1982	594	2.6
1831 to 1840 [3].....	599	3.9	1931 to 1940	528	0.4	1983	560	2.4
1841 to 1850 [4].....	1,713	8.4	1941 to 1950	1,035	0.7	1984	544	2.3
1851 to 1860 [4].....	2,598	9.3	1951 to 1960	2,515	1.5	1985	570	2.4
1861 to 1870 [5].....	2,315	6.4	1961 to 1970	3,322	1.7	1986	602	2.5
1871 to 1880.......	2,812	6.2	1971 to 1980	4,493	2.1	1987	602	2.5
1881 to 1890.......	5,247	9.2	1981 to 1990	7,338	3.1	1988	643	2.6
1891 to 1900.......	3,688	5.3	1970	373	1.8	1989 [6].........	1,091	4.4
1901 to 1910.......	8,795	10.4	1980	531	2.3	1990 [6].........	1,536	6.1

[1] Annual rate per 1,000 U.S. population. Rate computed by dividing sum of annual immigration totals by sum of annual U.S. population totals for same number of years. [2] Oct. 1, 1819, to Sept. 30, 1830. [3] Oct. 1, 1830, to Dec. 31, 1840. [4] Calendar years. [5] Jan. 1, 1861, to June 30, 1870. [6] Includes persons who were granted permanent residence under the legalization program of the Immigration Reform and Control Act of 1986.

No. 6. Immigrants Admitted, by Class of Admission: 1980 to 1990

[For fiscal year ending September 30. For definition of immigrants, see text, section 1. See also *Historical Statistics, Colonial Times to 1970*, series C 143-157]

CLASS OF ADMISSION	1980	1985	1986	1987	1988	1989	1990
Immigrants, total	**530,639**	**570,009**	**601,708**	**601,516**	**643,025**	**[1]1,090,924**	**[1]1,536,483**
Numerically limited	289,479	264,208	266,968	271,135	264,148	280,275	298,306
New arrivals	239,590	226,505	228,522	239,941	234,586	252,401	273,416
Adjustments	49,889	37,703	38,446	31,194	29,562	27,874	24,890
Exempt from numerical limitation.........	241,160	305,801	334,740	330,381	378,877	[1]810,649	[1]1,238,177
New arrivals	99,765	129,860	147,588	147,054	143,299	150,030	162,313
Adjustments	141,395	175,941	187,152	183,327	235,578	[1]660,619	[1]1,075,864
Numerically limited, total	289,479	264,208	266,968	271,135	264,148	280,275	298,306
Unmarried sons/daughters of U.S. citizens and their children (1st preference)	5,668	9,319	10,910	11,382	12,107	13,259	15,861
Spouses, unmarried sons/daughters of alien residents, and their children (2d pref.) ..	110,269	114,997	110,926	110,758	102,777	112,771	107,686
Professional or highly skilled immigrants (3d preference)	18,583	24,905	26,823	26,921	26,680	26,798	26,546
Married sons/daughters of U.S. citizens (4th preference) [2]	10,752	18,460	20,702	20,703	21,940	26,975	26,751
Brothers or sisters of U.S. citizens (5th preference) [2]	90,167	70,481	70,401	68,966	63,948	64,087	64,252
Needed skilled or unskilled workers (6th preference) [2]	25,786	25,990	26,802	26,952	26,927	25,957	27,183
Conditional entries by refugees [3]	12,222	(X)	(X)	(X)	(X)	(X)	(X)
Nonpreference	-	7	-	3,040	6,029	7,068	20,371
Recaptured Cuban numbers	15,913	(X)	(X)	(X)	(X)	(X)	(X)
Natives of under represented countries, PL. 100-658...................	(X)	(X)	(X)	(X)	(X)	(X)	8,790
Other........................	119	49	404	2,413	3,740	3,360	866
Exempt from numerical limitations	241,160	305,801	334,740	330,381	378,877	[1]810,649	[1]1,238,177
Immediate relatives	157,743	204,368	223,468	218,575	219,340	217,514	231,680
Spouses of U.S. citizens	96,854	129,790	137,597	132,452	130,977	125,744	125,426
Children of U.S. citizens............	27,207	35,592	40,639	40,940	40,863	41,276	46,065
Orphans...................	5,139	9,286	9,945	10,097	9,120	7,948	7,088
Parents of U.S. citizens	33,682	38,986	45,232	45,183	47,500	50,494	60,189
Refugee and asylee adjustments	75,835	95,040	104,383	91,840	81,719	84,288	97,364
Cuban Refugee Act, Nov. 1966.......	6,021	14,288	30,152	26,869	10,993	5,206	5,730
Indochinese Refugee Act, Oct. 1977	22,497	166	136	83	42	40	33
Refugee-Parolee Act, Oct. 1978	46,058	3,766	1,720	866	437	381	153
Asylees, Refugee Act of 1980.......	1,250	5,000	5,000	5,000	5,445	5,145	4,937
Refugees, Refugee Act of 1980	(X)	71,820	67,375	59,022	64,801	73,516	86,511
Other refugees.................	9	-	-	-	1	-	-
Special immigrants [2]	3,142	2,551	2,992	3,646	5,120	4,986	4,463
Ministers of religion [2]...........	1,529	1,853	2,060	2,041	2,207	2,595	2,786
Employees of U.S. Government abroad [2].	1,354	479	773	1,112	2,047	1,713	1,234
Foreign medical graduates, Act of Dec. 1981 [2]	(X)	87	48	28	7	11	2
Other special immigrants [2]	259	132	111	465	859	667	441
Aliens adjusted [4]	254	105	95	12,834	69,069	13,459	8,360
Children born abroad to resident aliens or subsequent to issuance of visa	4,059	3,508	3,554	3,269	3,082	2,806	2,630
Others not subject to numerical limitation..	127	229	248	217	547	[5]8,782	[5]13,308

- Represents zero. X Not applicable. [1] Includes 478,814 (for 1989) and 880,372 (for 1990) persons who were granted permanent residence under the legalization program of the Immigration Reform and Control Act (IRCA) of 1986. [2] Includes spouses and children. [3] In 1980, conditional entries were a 7th preference class. [4] Under sections 244 and 249, Immigration and Naturalization Act. Includes Cuban/Haitian entrants under the Act of November 1986. [5] Includes Amerasians under Public Law 100-202. Amerasians are aliens born in Vietnam between January 1, 1962 and January 1, 1976 who were fathered by U.S. citizens.

Source of tables 5 and 6: U.S. Immigration and Naturalization Service, *Statistical Yearbook*, annual.

No. 7. Nonimmigrants Admitted, by Class of Admission: 1970 to 1990

[In thousands, except as noted. For fiscal years ending in year shown; see text, section 9. Nonimmigrants are non-resident aliens (non-U.S. citizens) admitted to the United States for a temporary period. Included in this group are visitors for business and pleasure, students and their spouses and children, foreign government officials, exchange visitors and their spouses and children, international representatives, treaty traders and investors, representatives of foreign information media, fiances(ees) of U.S. citizens and their children, officials of the North Atlantic Treaty Organization (NATO) and aliens in transit. Most classes include spouses and unmarried minor (or dependent) children accompanying or following to join the alien. Excluded are border crossers, crewmen, and insular travelers. See also *Historical Statistics, Colonial Times to 1970,* series C 149-157]

CLASS OF ADMISSION	1970	1975	1985	1986	1987	1988	1989	1990
Nonimmigrants [1]	4,432	7,084	9,540	10,471	12,273	14,592	16,145	17,574
Temporary visitors, total	3,345	5,587	8,405	9,280	11,019	13,197	14,667	16,080
Percent of total	76	79	88	89	90	90	91	91
For pleasure	3,020	5,060	6,609	7,342	8,887	10,821	12,115	13,418
For business	325	527	1,797	1,938	2,132	2,376	2,553	2,661
Returning resident aliens [2]	494	800	(X)	(X)	(X)	(X)	(X)	(X)
Transit aliens [3]	232	273	237	244	264	299	293	306
Foreign government officials [4]	51	68	90	94	92	99	102	97
Treaty traders and investors [4]	19	35	97	104	114	126	140	148
Students [4]	107	118	286	288	289	338	361	355
Representatives to international organizations [4]	24	33	57	59	57	59	61	61
Temporary workers and industrial trainees	87	67	88	99	114	133	165	174
Workers of distinguished merit and ability	11	16	47	54	66	78	90	100
Performing services unavailable in U.S	69	38	25	28	29	33	49	41
Industrial trainees	5	4	3	3	3	3	2	3
Their spouses and children	1	11	13	14	16	20	24	29
Representatives of foreign information media [4]	5	6	17	17	18	22	21	20
Exchange visitors [4]	67	63	141	163	183	203	217	215
NATO officials [4]	2	4	8	7	7	9	9	8
Fiances(ees) of U.S. citizens [5]	(Z)	6	8	8	7	7	7	7
Intracompany transferees [4]	(Z)	22	107	108	107	102	101	103
Parolees [6]	(X)	(X)	64	67	63	95	107	90
Refugees	(X)	(X)	68	51	67	80	101	110

X Not applicable.   Z Less than 500.   [1] Includes nonimmigrants whose class of admission is unknown.   [2] For 1970 and 1975, returning resident aliens who had once been counted as immigrants were included with nonimmigrants. Since 1981, data no longer collected.   [3] Includes foreign government officials and their spouses and (unmarried minor or dependent) children, in transit.   [4] Includes spouses and children.   [5] Includes children of fiances(ees) of U.S. citizens.   [6] Aliens allowed to enter the United States for a temporary period of time on emergency conditions or when the entry is determined to be in the public interest (e.g., witness in court).

No. 8. Immigrants, by Country of Birth: 1961 to 1990

[In thousands. For fiscal years ending in year shown; see text, section 9. For definition of immigrants, see text, section 1]

COUNTRY OF BIRTH	1961-70, total	1971-80, total	1981-89, total	1990	COUNTRY OF BIRTH	1961-70, total	1971-80, total	1981-89, total	1990
All countries	3,321.7	4,493.3	5,801.6	1,536.5	Thailand	5.0	44.1	55.5	8.9
Europe [1]	1,238.6	801.3	593.2	112.4	Turkey	6.8	18.6	18.4	2.5
Czechoslovakia	21.4	10.2	10.1	1.4	Vietnam	4.6	179.7	352.6	48.8
France	34.3	17.8	20.3	2.8	**North America** [1]	1,351.1	1,645.0	2,167.4	957.6
Germany	200.0	66.0	62.6	7.5	Canada	286.7	114.8	102.4	16.8
Greece	90.2	93.7	26.4	2.7	Mexico	443.3	637.2	974.2	679.1
Hungary	17.3	11.6	8.1	1.7	Caribbean [1]	519.5	759.8	777.3	115.4
Ireland	42.4	14.1	22.5	10.3	Barbados	9.4	20.9	15.7	1.7
Italy	206.7	130.1	29.6	3.3	Cuba	256.8	276.8	148.6	10.6
Netherlands	27.8	10.7	10.5	1.4	Dominican				
Poland	73.3	43.6	76.9	20.5	Republic	94.1	148.0	209.6	42.2
Portugal	79.3	104.5	36.0	4.0	Haiti	37.5	58.7	119.9	20.3
Romania	14.9	17.5	34.3	4.6	Jamaica	71.0	142.0	188.8	25.0
Soviet Union	15.7	43.2	58.5	25.5	Trinidad and				
Spain	30.5	30.0	13.9	1.9	Tobago	24.6	61.8	32.8	6.7
Sweden	16.7	6.3	9.0	1.2	Central America [1]	97.7	132.4	312.5	146.2
Switzerland	16.3	6.6	6.2	0.8	Costa Rica	17.4	12.1	12.7	2.8
United Kingdom	230.5	123.5	126.2	15.9	El Salvador	15.0	34.4	134.4	80.2
Yugoslavia	46.2	42.1	16.4	2.8	Guatemala	15.4	25.6	55.6	32.3
Asia [1]	445.3	1,633.8	2,478.8	338.6	Honduras	15.5	17.2	37.5	12.0
Afghanistan	0.4	2.0	23.4	3.2	Nicaragua	10.1	13.0	32.5	11.6
Cambodia	1.2	8.4	111.4	5.2	Panama	18.4	22.7	25.6	3.4
China: Mainland	[2]96.7	[2]202.5	[2]341.8	31.8	**South America** [1]	228.3	284.4	370.1	85.8
Taiwan	([2])	([2])	([2])	15.2	Argentina	42.1	25.1	20.3	5.4
Hong Kong	25.6	47.5	53.6	9.4	Brazil	20.5	13.7	19.5	4.2
India	31.2	176.8	231.2	30.7	Chile	11.5	17.6	19.4	4.0
Iran	10.4	46.2	129.8	25.0	Colombia	70.3	77.6	100.2	24.2
Iraq	6.4	23.4	17.8	1.8	Ecuador	37.0	50.2	43.5	12.5
Israel	12.9	26.6	31.6	4.7	Guyana	7.1	47.5	84.0	11.4
Japan	38.5	47.9	37.5	5.7	Peru	18.6	29.1	48.7	15.7
Jordan	14.0	29.6	28.2	4.4	Venezuela	8.5	7.1	14.8	3.1
Korea	35.8	272.0	306.5	32.3	**Africa** [1]	39.3	91.5	156.4	35.9
Laos	0.1	22.6	135.2	10.4	Egypt	17.2	25.5	27.3	4.1
Lebanon	7.5	33.8	36.0	5.6	Nigeria	1.5	8.8	26.5	8.8
Pakistan	4.9	31.2	51.6	9.7	South Africa	4.5	11.5	13.7	2.0
Philippines	101.5	360.2	431.5	63.8	**Australia**	9.9	14.3	12.1	1.8
Syria	4.6	13.3	17.6	3.0	**Other countries** [3]	9.2	23.0	23.5	4.5

[1] Includes countries not shown separately.   [2] Data for Taiwan included with China: Mainland.   [3] Includes New Zealand and unknown countries.

Source of tables 7 and 8: U.S. Immigration and Naturalization Service, *Statistical Yearbook,* annual; and releases.

Population

No. 9. Immigrants Admitted as Permanent Residents Under Refugee Acts, by Country of Birth: 1961 to 1990

[For fiscal years ending in year shown; see text, section 9. Covers immigrants who were allowed to enter the United States under 1953 Refugee Relief Act and later acts; Hungarian parolees under July 1958 Act; refugee-escapee parolees under July 1960 Act; conditional entries by refugees under Oct. 1965 Act; Cuban parolees under Nov. 1966 Act; beginning 1978, Indochina refugees under Act of Oct. 1977; beginning 1980, refugee-parolees under the Act of Oct. 1978, and asylees under the Act of March 1980; and beginning 1981 refugees under the Act of March 1980]

COUNTRY OF BIRTH	1961-1970, total	1971-1980, total	1981-1989, total	1990	COUNTRY OF BIRTH	1961-1970, total	1971-1980, total	1981-1989, total	1990
Total	212,843	539,447	916,256	97,364	Iran	58	364	38,124	8,649
					Iraq	119	6,851	7,399	141
Europe	55,235	71,858	122,401	33,111	Korea	1,316	65	118	2
Austria	233	185	340	84	Laos	-	21,690	133,140	9,824
Bulgaria	1,799	1,238	1,019	178	Malaysia	9	192	1,218	59
Czechoslovakia	5,709	3,646	7,321	883	Philippines	100	216	3,113	290
Germany	665	143	697	154	Syria	383	1,336	1,752	393
Greece	586	478	1,093	315	Thailand	13	1,241	26,182	4,077
Hungary	4,044	4,358	4,074	868	Turkey	1,489	1,193	1,620	276
Italy	1,198	346	308	86	Vietnam	7	150,266	303,916	20,537
Netherlands	3,134	8	10	4	Other Asia	1,307	1,538	2,658	365
Poland	3,197	5,882	29,986	3,903	**North America**	132,068	252,633	111,930	9,910
Portugal	1,361	21	19	2	Cuba	131,557	251,514	105,699	7,668
Romania	7,158	6,812	26,612	3,186	El Salvador	1	45	1,138	245
Soviet Union	871	31,309	49,120	23,186	Nicaragua	3	36	3,896	1,694
Spain	4,114	5,317	652	84	Other N. America	507	1,038	1,197	303
Yugoslavia	18,299	11,297	301	23	**South America**	123	1,244	1,712	264
Other Europe	2,867	818	849	155	Chile	4	420	511	20
Asia	19,895	210,683	660,225	51,867	Other S. America	119	824	1,201	244
Afghanistan	-	542	20,802	2,144	**Africa**	5,486	2,991	19,937	2,212
Cambodia	-	7,739	109,345	4,719	Egypt	5,396	1,473	357	69
China [1]	5,308	13,760	7,595	333	Ethiopia	2	1,307	16,860	1,682
Hong Kong	2,128	3,468	1,886	30	Other Africa	88	211	2,720	461
Indonesia	7,658	222	1,357	28	**Other**	36	38	51	-

- Represents zero.   [1] Covers Mainland and Taiwan.
Source: U.S. Immigration and Naturalization Service, *Statistical Yearbook*, annual; and releases.

No. 10. Immigrants Admitted, by Leading States of Intended Residence and Country of Birth: 1990

[For year ending September 30. For definition of immigrants, see text, section 1]

COUNTRY OF BIRTH	Total [1]	California	New York	Texas	Illinois	Florida	New Jersey	Massachusetts	Arizona	Virginia
Total [2]	1,536,483	682,979	189,589	174,132	83,858	71,603	52,670	25,338	23,737	19,005
Europe [2]	112,401	21,417	26,392	2,828	12,358	6,021	8,016	6,118	866	1,556
Poland	20,537	961	4,647	212	7,776	419	2,172	557	85	107
Soviet Union	25,524	7,535	9,212	152	1,603	230	447	1,677	39	65
United Kingdom	15,928	3,761	2,062	847	459	1,841	788	579	227	467
Asia [2]	338,581	130,814	45,628	16,805	14,549	8,122	15,808	8,273	2,797	9,419
China:										
Mainland	31,815	11,494	9,721	1,010	914	460	1,030	1,189	234	380
Taiwan	15,151	6,806	1,783	1,034	456	267	970	284	123	308
India	30,667	5,794	4,931	1,956	3,431	822	3,927	671	167	805
Iran	24,977	14,344	1,735	1,400	391	587	469	456	203	922
Korea	32,301	9,951	4,475	1,202	1,523	524	1,619	350	222	1,480
Laos	10,446	4,851	126	216	175	102	16	267	38	91
Pakistan	9,729	1,532	2,553	1,026	934	444	690	112	44	582
Philippines	63,756	31,223	5,525	1,691	3,104	1,532	3,560	325	341	1,398
Vietnam	48,792	19,675	2,254	4,343	954	1,275	500	2,048	872	1,505
North America [2]	957,558	510,106	78,610	148,302	53,472	43,395	14,760	7,640	19,528	4,562
Canada	16,812	3,249	1,709	618	370	3,329	414	459	438	254
Mexico	679,068	420,377	7,099	130,813	48,618	6,210	1,441	273	18,350	899
Caribbean [2]	115,351	1,641	56,527	834	859	24,712	9,261	5,147	67	351
Cuba	10,645	424	401	87	97	8,519	559	31	10	13
Dominican Republic	42,195	155	26,457	95	83	1,694	4,044	2,153	6	58
Haiti	20,324	109	8,654	37	208	6,575	1,910	1,767	2	24
Jamaica	25,013	517	12,203	242	348	5,380	1,890	645	15	133
Central America [2]	146,202	84,812	13,264	16,023	3,623	9,136	3,641	1,758	672	3,051
El Salvador	80,173	51,009	5,601	12,033	751	1,061	1,609	774	265	2,324
Guatemala	32,303	21,868	2,324	1,739	1,908	945	688	538	231	307
Honduras	12,024	3,483	2,794	1,263	352	1,815	630	228	49	113
Nicaragua	11,562	4,979	596	478	73	3,976	258	35	69	171
South America [2]	85,819	12,105	31,251	2,837	2,188	12,827	11,354	1,487	257	1,803
Colombia	24,189	2,329	8,388	1,103	668	4,820	3,706	439	52	229
Ecuador	12,476	1,353	6,892	193	718	721	1,837	113	17	75
Guyana	11,362	246	8,227	88	43	577	1,037	100	4	54
Peru	15,726	3,620	3,522	505	356	2,150	2,960	206	69	520
Africa	35,893	5,344	7,424	3,162	1,223	1,114	2,670	1,747	207	1,597

[1] Includes other States, Puerto Rico and other outlying areas, not shown separately.   [2] Includes other countries and areas, not shown separately.
Source: U.S. Immigration and Naturalization Service, *Statistical Yearbook*, annual.

No. 11. Immigrants Admitted, by Leading Country of Birth and Metropolitan Area of Intended Residence: 1990

[For year ending September 30. Includes Puerto Rico. Includes new arrivals and persons adjusting their status. MSA-metropolitan statistical area; PMSA-primary metropolitan statistical area; and NECMA-New England county metropolitan area as defined by U.S. Office of Management and Budget, June 30, 1986. See text, section 1, and Appendix II]

METROPOLITAN AREA OF INTENDED RESIDENCE	Total [1]	Mexico	El Salvador	Philippines	Vietnam [2]	Dominican Republic	Guatemala	Korea	China: Mainland	India
Total [3]	1,536,483	679,068	80,173	63,756	48,662	42,195	32,303	32,301	31,815	30,667
Los Angeles-Long Beach, CA PMSA	374,773	231,267	42,172	11,644	4,745	86	18,446	6,059	3,525	1,440
New York, NY PMSA	164,330	6,436	2,853	4,750	1,155	25,430	1,895	3,586	9,030	3,530
Chicago, IL PMSA	73,107	41,848	631	2,655	742	70	1,839	1,238	802	3,024
Anaheim-Santa Ana, CA PMSA. . .	65,367	44,414	2,026	1,407	4,950	13	1,060	1,219	459	667
Houston, TX PMSA.	58,208	34,973	9,285	677	2,014	48	988	263	473	854
Miami-Hialeah, FL PMSA	37,677	1,273	706	292	56	1,342	650	64	157	139
San Diego, CA MSA	37,208	25,540	226	3,539	1,575	13	190	205	278	114
Riverside-San Bernardino, CA PMSA	35,616	27,159	998	1,224	505	2	581	373	136	269
Washington, DC-MD-VA MSA. . . .	32,705	1,056	4,956	1,228	2,188	277	620	1,940	802	1,465
San Francisco, CA PMSA	29,144	7,060	2,871	3,574	1,459	6	686	358	3,782	248
Dallas, TX PMSA.	28,533	19,391	1,595	270	1,015	15	377	391	248	523
San Jose, CA PMSA.	26,250	10,766	654	2,440	3,881	14	148	516	963	816
Oakland, CA PMSA	20,894	6,884	643	2,678	1,040	5	157	401	1,506	769
Boston-Lawrence-Salem-Lowell-Brockton, MA NECMA	20,776	215	698	246	1,435	2,093	494	241	1,115	501
Newark, NJ PMSA	16,089	127	521	883	197	538	235	195	226	813
Nassau-Suffolk, NY PMSA.	14,823	262	2,643	424	94	829	365	389	394	807
Phoenix, AZ MSA.	14,714	10,726	206	211	692	5	198	146	176	130
El Paso, TX MSA	14,476	14,009	25	33	5	1	15	59	18	20
Bergen-Passaic, NJ PMSA.	13,144	665	275	724	15	1,480	85	727	161	790
Philadelphia, PA-NJ PMSA.	11,440	382	64	577	1,228	126	37	909	439	931
Fresno, CA MSA	11,193	8,066	175	156	74	-	55	28	75	280
McAllen-Edinburg-Mission, TX MSA	9,937	9,719	29	10	-	2	27	7	2	1
Jersey City, NJ PMSA.	9,921	155	636	889	61	1,153	173	160	156	612
Fort Lauderdale-Hollywood-Pompano Beach, FL PMSA	9,906	349	112	127	87	111	67	58	92	145
Fort Worth-Arlington, TX PMSA . .	9,736	6,805	182	82	635	5	56	82	68	200
Oxnard-Ventura, CA PMSA	9,508	7,251	195	548	80	3	124	103	54	93
Sacramento, CA MSA	8,933	3,378	137	602	604	4	43	222	307	172
San Antonio, TX MSA	8,668	7,304	103	139	99	13	95	104	47	43
Atlanta, GA MSA	8,079	1,363	180	151	923	31	52	430	132	319
Seattle, WA PMSA	7,335	573	61	1,025	1,083	2	26	542	403	153
Bakersfield, CA MSA	7,246	6,094	194	344	10	-	63	39	17	83
Detroit, MI MSA	7,199	309	14	398	146	12	10	280	172	552
Honolulu, HI MSA.	6,706	44	6	3,051	537	-	-	678	511	16
Salinas-Seaside-Monterey, CA MSA	6,695	5,570	119	292	66	1	13	106	33	24
Middlesex-Somerset-Hunterdon, NJ PMSA.	6,414	177	68	433	46	636	51	205	222	1,093
San Juan, PR PMSA.	6,181	41	22	11	1	5,171	7	4	55	5
Brownsville-Harlingen, TX MSA. . .	6,175	5,883	75	38	-	-	22	1	6	1
Visalia-Tulare-Porterville, CA MSA .	5,925	4,846	62	175	3	-	20	11	10	56
Denver, CO PMSA	5,509	2,967	36	148	364	3	32	202	110	77
Santa Barbara-Santa Maria-Lompoc, CA MSA	5,489	4,483	43	178	28	1	127	49	24	27
Stockton, CA MSA	5,463	2,886	33	490	292	-	16	16	64	87
Minneapolis-St. Paul, MN-WI MSA.	5,439	193	15	156	559	6	15	246	106	145
Austin, TX MSA	5,044	3,496	183	37	195	1	27	70	60	53
West Palm Beach-Boca Raton-Delray Beach, FL MSA.	5,012	599	67	75	40	42	58	25	36	86
Las Vegas, NV MSA.	4,986	2,607	250	413	132	7	67	148	105	33
Tampa-St. Petersburg-Clearwater, FL MSA.	4,721	913	36	166	418	37	35	88	40	91
Bridgeport-Stamford-Norwalk-Danbury, CT NECMA	4,507	111	62	77	146	123	92	44	69	207
Portland, OR PMSA	4,493	1,071	39	147	654	1	33	283	190	50
Santa Cruz, CA MSA	4,396	3,963	31	69	15	3	7	8	44	11
Tucson, AZ MSA	4,232	3,338	34	50	159	-	19	36	41	23
Modesto, CA MSA	4,062	2,869	36	62	34	2	22	26	20	98
Baltimore, MD MSA	3,732	99	38	223	108	21	13	544	122	221
Merced, CA MSA	3,696	2,755	37	47	1	-	8	9	10	118
Hartford-New Britain-Middletown-Bristol, CT NECMA	3,673	35	17	55	223	47	11	66	68	151
Lake County, IL PMSA	3,587	2,429	98	157	4	-	45	94	24	126
Providence-Pawtucket-Woonsocket, RI NECMA	3,566	75	35	88	33	539	259	36	73	45
Vallejo-Fairfield-Napa, CA PMSA. .	3,510	1,756	99	983	61	1	22	45	24	80
Orlando, FL MSA	3,445	318	49	134	259	92	22	69	30	99
Aurora-Elgin, IL PMSA.	3,085	2,601	15	37	15	4	17	25	4	51
Albuquerque, NM MSA	2,878	2,264	27	35	154	1	34	38	27	35
Oklahoma City, OK MSA	2,741	1,391	5	55	364	1	39	78	31	51
Laredo, TX MSA	2,557	2,498	11	1	-	-	19	1	-	5

- Represents zero.   [1] Includes other countries, not shown separately.   [2] Data for immigrants admitted under the legalization program are not available separately for Vietnam and thus not included in this column.   [3] Includes other metropolitan areas, not shown separately.

Source: U.S. Immigration and Naturalization Service, *Statistical Yearbook*, annual.

No. 12. Total Population, by Age and Sex: 1980 to 1991

[In thousands, except as indicated. 1980, as of April 1, other years as of July 1. Includes Armed Forces abroad. For derivation of estimates, see text, section 1. For definition of median, see Guide to Tabular Presentation. See also Historical Statistics, Colonial Times to 1970, series A23-25 and A29-41]

YEAR AND SEX	Total, all ages	Under 5 years	5 to 9 years	10 to 14 years	15 to 19 years	20 to 24 years	25 to 29 years	30 to 34 years	35 to 39 years	40 to 44 years	45 to 49 years	50 to 54 years	55 to 59 years	60 to 64 years	65 to 74 years	75 years and over	5 to 13 years	14 to 17 years	18 to 24 years	16 years and over	65 years and over	Median age (yr.)
Total:																						
1980	227,061	16,348	16,700	18,242	21,226	21,529	19,629	17,629	14,010	11,688	11,095	11,711	11,615	10,088	15,581	9,969	31,159	16,249	30,289	171,711	25,549	30.0
1990	249,924	18,874	18,064	17,191	17,790	19,305	21,356	21,990	20,031	17,814	13,826	11,368	10,473	10,618	18,098	13,127	32,000	13,312	27,038	192,458	31,224	32.8
1991	252,688	19,222	18,237	17,671	17,242	19,372	20,844	22,242	20,573	18,779	14,101	11,646	10,423	10,582	18,280	13,474	32,500	13,423	26,599	194,265	31,754	33.1
Male:																						
1980	110,528	8,362	8,539	9,316	10,808	10,852	9,803	8,742	6,906	5,726	5,394	5,622	5,482	4,670	6,757	3,548	15,923	8,299	15,295	82,241	10,305	28.7
1990	122,049	9,658	9,247	8,805	9,141	9,897	10,764	10,974	9,951	8,800	6,782	5,521	5,004	4,947	7,932	4,624	16,384	6,843	13,863	92,624	12,557	31.6
1991	123,431	9,836	9,337	9,051	8,866	9,931	10,502	11,107	10,225	9,282	6,913	5,657	4,987	4,945	8,022	4,769	16,641	6,901	13,644	93,517	12,791	31.9
Female:																						
1980	116,533	7,986	8,161	8,926	10,418	10,677	9,826	8,887	7,105	5,961	5,702	6,089	6,133	5,418	8,824	6,420	15,237	7,950	14,995	89,470	15,245	31.2
1990	127,875	9,216	8,817	8,385	8,649	9,408	10,592	11,016	10,080	9,014	7,043	5,847	5,469	5,671	10,165	8,502	15,616	6,469	13,175	99,834	18,668	34.0
1991	129,257	9,386	8,900	8,620	8,376	9,440	10,341	11,135	10,349	9,498	7,188	5,989	5,436	5,637	10,258	8,705	15,859	6,522	12,955	100,748	18,962	34.3
PERCENT																						
Total:																						
1980	100.0	7.2	7.4	8.0	9.3	9.5	8.6	7.8	6.2	5.1	4.9	5.2	5.1	4.4	6.9	4.4	13.7	7.2	13.3	75.6	11.3	(X)
1990	100.0	7.6	7.2	6.9	7.1	7.7	8.5	8.8	8.0	7.1	5.5	4.5	4.2	4.2	7.2	5.3	12.8	5.3	10.8	77.0	12.5	(X)
1991	100.0	7.6	7.2	7.0	6.8	7.7	8.2	8.8	8.1	7.4	5.6	4.6	4.1	4.2	7.2	5.3	12.9	5.3	10.5	76.9	12.6	(X)
Male:																						
1980	100.0	7.6	7.7	8.4	9.8	9.8	8.9	7.9	6.2	5.2	4.9	5.1	5.0	4.2	6.1	3.2	14.4	7.5	13.8	74.4	9.3	(X)
1990	100.0	7.9	7.6	7.2	7.5	8.1	8.8	9.0	8.2	7.2	5.6	4.5	4.1	4.1	6.5	3.8	13.4	5.6	11.4	75.9	10.3	(X)
1991	100.0	8.0	7.6	7.3	7.2	8.0	8.5	9.0	8.3	7.5	5.6	4.6	4.0	4.0	6.5	3.9	13.5	5.6	11.1	75.8	10.4	(X)
Female:																						
1980	100.0	6.9	7.0	7.7	8.9	9.2	8.4	7.6	6.1	5.1	4.9	5.2	5.3	4.6	7.6	5.5	13.1	6.8	12.9	76.8	13.1	(X)
1990	100.0	7.2	6.9	6.6	6.8	7.4	8.3	8.6	7.9	7.0	5.5	4.6	4.3	4.4	7.9	6.6	12.2	5.1	10.3	78.1	14.6	(X)
1991	100.0	7.3	6.9	6.7	6.5	7.3	8.0	8.6	8.0	7.3	5.6	4.6	4.2	4.4	7.9	6.7	12.3	5.0	10.0	77.9	14.7	(X)

X Not applicable.

Source: U.S. Bureau of the Census, Current Population Reports, series P-25, No. 1045; and unpublished data.

No. 13. Total Population, by Sex and Age: 1991

[In thousands, except as indicated. As of July 1. Includes Armed Forces abroad. For derivation of estimates, see text, section 1]

AGE	Total	Male	Female	AGE	Total	Male	Female
Total	**252,688**	**123,431**	**129,257**	41 yrs. old	3,721	1,838	1,883
				42 yrs. old	3,634	1,793	1,841
Under 5 yrs. old	19,222	9,836	9,386	43 yrs. old	3,589	1,765	1,825
Under 1 yr. old	4,011	2,052	1,959	44 yrs. old	3,998	1,988	2,010
1 yr. old	3,969	2,030	1,938	45 to 49 yrs. old	14,101	6,913	7,188
2 yrs. old	3,806	1,949	1,857	45 yrs. old	2,834	1,394	1,440
3 yrs. old	3,718	1,902	1,816	46 yrs. old	2,823	1,385	1,437
4 yrs. old	3,717	1,902	1,815	47 yrs. old	2,850	1,394	1,456
5 to 9 yrs. old	18,237	9,337	8,900	48 yrs. old	2,857	1,397	1,459
5 yrs. old	3,702	1,897	1,806	49 yrs. old	2,737	1,343	1,395
6 yrs. old	3,681	1,884	1,797	50 to 54 yrs. old	11,646	5,657	5,989
7 yrs. old	3,575	1,829	1,746	50 yrs. old	2,528	1,234	1,294
8 yrs. old	3,512	1,797	1,715	51 yrs. old	2,340	1,140	1,200
9 yrs. old	3,767	1,930	1,836	52 yrs. old	2,298	1,116	1,182
				53 yrs. old	2,280	1,105	1,175
10 to 14 yrs. old	17,671	9,051	8,620	54 yrs. old	2,200	1,063	1,137
10 yrs. old	3,703	1,899	1,804	55 to 59 yrs. old	10,423	4,987	5,436
11 yrs. old	3,662	1,875	1,786	55 yrs. old	2,129	1,023	1,106
12 yrs. old	3,484	1,783	1,701	56 yrs. old	2,195	1,054	1,141
13 yrs. old	3,414	1,746	1,668	57 yrs. old	2,068	991	1,077
14 yrs. old	3,409	1,747	1,661	58 yrs. old	1,946	927	1,019
15 to 19 yrs. old	17,242	8,866	8,376	59 yrs. old	2,085	992	1,093
15 yrs. old	3,293	1,690	1,603	60 to 64 yrs. old	10,582	4,945	5,637
16 yrs. old	3,362	1,732	1,630	60 yrs. old	2,124	994	1,129
17 yrs. old	3,360	1,733	1,627	61 yrs. old	2,100	994	1,106
18 yrs. old	3,391	1,740	1,651	62 yrs. old	2,076	971	1,105
19 yrs. old	3,836	1,973	1,863	63 yrs. old	2,145	1,004	1,141
20 to 24 yrs. old	19,372	9,931	9,440	64 yrs. old	2,138	982	1,156
20 yrs. old	4,120	2,123	1,997	65 to 69 yrs. old	10,037	4,491	5,546
21 yrs. old	4,009	2,064	1,944	65 yrs. old	2,072	939	1,132
22 yrs. old	3,767	1,933	1,834	66 yrs. old	2,069	933	1,136
23 yrs. old	3,664	1,872	1,792	67 yrs. old	2,026	910	1,116
24 yrs. old	3,812	1,939	1,873	68 yrs. old	1,911	848	1,063
25 to 29 yrs. old	20,844	10,502	10,341	69 yrs. old	1,960	862	1,099
25 yrs. old	3,866	1,960	1,906	70 to 74 yrs. old	8,242	3,531	4,712
26 yrs. old	4,069	2,050	2,019	70 yrs. old	1,886	828	1,058
27 yrs. old	4,242	2,138	2,104	71 yrs. old	1,731	750	981
28 yrs. old	4,086	2,053	2,033	72 yrs. old	1,649	710	939
29 yrs. old	4,580	2,301	2,279	73 yrs. old	1,518	637	881
30 to 34 yrs. old	22,242	11,107	11,135	74 yrs. old	1,458	606	852
30 yrs. old	4,501	2,251	2,250	75 to 79 yrs. old	6,279	2,482	3,797
31 yrs. old	4,432	2,216	2,216	75 yrs. old	1,405	576	829
32 yrs. old	4,387	2,188	2,199	76 yrs. old	1,334	540	795
33 yrs. old	4,387	2,182	2,205	77 yrs. old	1,244	491	753
34 yrs. old	4,534	2,270	2,264	78 yrs. old	1,204	462	742
35 to 39 yrs. old	20,573	10,225	10,349	79 yrs. old	1,091	414	677
35 yrs. old	4,325	2,154	2,172	80 to 84 yrs. old	4,035	1,406	2,629
36 yrs. old	4,201	2,090	2,111	80 yrs. old	970	352	618
37 yrs. old	4,132	2,051	2,081	81 yrs. old	883	314	568
38 yrs. old	3,788	1,876	1,913	82 yrs. old	799	279	521
39 yrs. old	4,127	2,055	2,073	83 yrs. old	739	249	489
				84 yrs. old	644	211	433
40 to 44 yrs. old	18,779	9,282	9,498	85 yrs. old and over . . .	3,160	881	2,279
40 yrs. old	3,836	1,898	1,938	Median age (yr.)	33.1	31.9	34.3

Source: U.S. Bureau of the Census, unpublished data.

No. 14. Resident Population—Selected Characteristics: 1790 to 1991

[In thousands, except as indicated. Excludes Armed Forces abroad. For definition of median, see Guide to Tabular Presentation. See also *Historical Statistics, Colonial Times to 1970,* series A 73-81 and A 143-149]

DATE	SEX		RACE						RESIDENCE [2]		Median age (years)
	Male	Female	White	Black	Total	American Indians and Alaska Natives	Asian and Pacific Islanders	Hispanic origin [1]	Urban	Rural	
						Other					
1790 (Aug. 2) [3] . .	(NA)	(NA)	3,172	757	(NA)	(NA)	(NA)	(NA)	202	3,728	(NA)
1800 (Aug. 4) [3] . .	(NA)	(NA)	4,306	1,002	(NA)	(NA)	(NA)	(NA)	322	4,986	(NA)
1850 (June 1) [3] . .	11,838	11,354	19,553	3,639	(NA)	(NA)	(NA)	(NA)	3,544	19,648	18.9
1860 (June 1) [3] . .	16,085	15,358	26,923	4,442	79	(NA)	(NA)	(NA)	6,217	25,227	19.4
1870 (June 1) [3] . .	19,494	19,065	33,589	4,880	89	(NA)	(NA)	(NA)	9,902	28,656	20.2
1880 (June 1) [3] . .	25,519	24,637	43,403	6,581	172	(NA)	(NA)	(NA)	14,130	36,026	20.9
1890 (June 1) [3] . .	32,237	30,711	55,101	7,489	358	(NA)	(NA)	(NA)	22,106	40,841	22.0
1900 (June 1) [3] . .	38,816	37,178	66,809	8,834	351	(NA)	(NA)	(NA)	30,160	45,835	22.9
1910 (Apr. 15) [3] . .	47,332	44,640	81,732	9,828	413	(NA)	(NA)	(NA)	41,999	49,973	24.1
1920 (Jan. 1) [3] . .	53,900	51,810	94,821	10,463	427	(NA)	(NA)	(NA)	54,158	51,553	25.3
1930 (Apr. 1) [3] . .	62,137	60,638	110,287	11,891	597	(NA)	(NA)	(NA)	68,955	53,820	26.4
1940 (Apr. 1) [3] . .	66,062	65,608	118,215	12,866	589	(NA)	(NA)	(NA)	74,424	57,246	29.0
1950 (Apr. 1) [3] . .	74,833	75,864	134,942	15,042	713	(NA)	(NA)	(NA)	96,468	54,230	30.2
1950 (Apr. 1)	75,187	76,139	135,150	15,045	1,131	(NA)	(NA)	(NA)	96,847	54,479	30.2
1960 (Apr. 1)	88,331	90,992	158,832	18,872	1,620	(NA)	(NA)	(NA)	125,269	54,054	29.5
1970 (Apr. 1) [4] . . .	98,926	104,309	178,098	22,581	2,557	(NA)	(NA)	(NA)	149,647	53,565	28.0
1980 (Apr. 1) [5] . . .	110,053	116,493	194,713	26,683	5,150	1,420	3,729	14,609	167,051	59,495	30.0
1990 (Apr. 1) [5] . . .	121,239	127,471	208,704	30,483	9,523	2,065	7,458	22,354	187,053	61,656	32.8
1991 (July 1) [6] . . .	122,979	129,198	(NA)	(NA)	(NA)	(NA)	(NA)	(NA)	(NA)	(NA)	33.1

NA Not available. [1] Persons of Hispanic origin may be of any race. [2] Beginning 1950, current definition. For explanation of change, see text, section 1. [3] Excludes Alaska and Hawaii. [4] The revised 1970 resident population count is 203,302,031; which incorporates changes due to errors found after tabulations were completed. The race and sex data shown here reflect the official 1970 census count while the residence data come from the tabulated count; see text, section 1. [5] The race data shown have been modified; see text, section 1 for explanation. [6] Estimated.

Source: U.S. Bureau of the Census, *U.S. Census of Population: 1940,* vol. II, part 1, and vol. IV, part 1; *1950,* vol. II, part 1; *1960,* vol. I, part 1; *1970,* vol. I, part B; *Current Population Reports,* series P-25, No. 1045, and forthcoming report.

No. 15. Resident Population Characteristics—Percent Distribution: 1850 to 1991

[In percent. Excludes Armed Forces abroad]

DATE	SEX		RACE			RESIDENCE [1]	
	Male	Female	White	Black	Other	Urban	Rural
1850 (June 1) [2]	51.0	49.0	84.3	15.7	(NA)	15.3	84.7
1860 (June 1) [2]	51.2	48.8	85.6	14.1	0.3	19.8	80.2
1870 (June 1) [2]	50.6	49.4	87.1	12.7	0.2	25.7	74.3
1880 (June 1) [2]	50.9	49.1	86.5	13.1	0.3	28.2	71.8
1890 (June 1) [2]	51.2	48.8	87.5	11.9	0.6	35.1	64.9
1900 (June 1) [2]	51.1	48.9	87.9	11.6	0.5	39.7	60.3
1910 (Apr. 15) [2]	51.5	48.5	88.9	10.7	0.4	45.7	54.3
1920 (Jan. 1) [2]	51.0	49.0	89.7	9.9	0.4	51.2	48.8
1930 (Apr. 1) [2]	50.6	49.4	89.8	9.7	0.5	56.2	43.8
1940 (Apr. 1) [2]	50.2	49.8	89.8	9.8	0.4	56.5	43.5
1950 (Apr. 1) [2]	49.7	50.3	89.5	10.0	0.5	64.0	36.0
1950 (Apr. 1)	49.7	50.3	89.3	9.9	0.7	64.0	36.0
1960 (Apr. 1)	49.3	50.7	88.6	10.5	0.9	69.9	30.1
1970 (Apr. 1)	48.7	51.3	87.6	11.1	1.3	73.6	26.4
1980 (Apr. 1) [3]	48.6	51.4	85.9	11.8	2.3	73.7	26.3
1990 (Apr. 1) [3]	48.7	51.3	83.0	12.3	3.8	75.2	24.8
1991 (July 1) [4]	48.8	51.2	(NA)	(NA)	(NA)	(NA)	(NA)

NA Not available. [1] Beginning 1950, current definition. For explanation of change, see text, section 1. [2] Excludes Alaska and Hawaii. [3] The race data shown have been modified; see text, section 1 for explanation. [4] Estimated.

Source: U.S. Bureau of the Census, *U.S. Census of Population: 1940,* vol. II, part 1, and vol. IV, part 1; *1950,* vol. II, part 1; *1960,* vol. I, part 1; *1970,* vol. I, part B; *Current Population Reports,* series P-25, No. 1045, and forthcoming report.

No. 16. Resident Population, by Race and Hispanic Origin: 1980 and 1990

[As of **April 1**]

RACE AND HISPANIC ORIGIN	NUMBER (1,000)		PERCENT DISTRIBUTION		CHANGE, 1980-90	
	1980	1990	1980	1990	Number (1,000)	Percent
All persons	**226,546**	**248,710**	**100.0**	**100.0**	**22,164**	**9.8**
RACE						
White	188,372	199,686	83.1	80.3	11,314	6.0
Black	26,495	29,986	11.7	12.1	3,491	13.2
American Indian, Eskimo, or Aleut	1,420	1,959	0.6	0.8	539	37.9
American Indian	1,364	1,878	0.6	0.8	514	37.7
Eskimo	42	57	(Z)	(Z)	15	35.6
Aleut	14	24	(Z)	(Z)	10	67.5
Asian or Pacific Islander	[1]3,500	7,274	1.5	2.9	3,773	107.8
Chinese	806	1,645	0.4	0.7	839	104.1
Filipino	775	1,407	0.3	0.6	632	81.6
Japanese	701	848	0.3	0.3	147	20.9
Asian Indian	362	815	0.2	0.3	454	125.6
Korean	355	799	0.2	0.3	444	125.3
Vietnamese	262	615	0.1	0.2	353	134.8
Hawaiian	167	211	0.1	0.1	44	26.5
Samoan	42	63	(Z)	(Z)	21	50.1
Guamanian	32	49	(Z)	(Z)	17	53.4
Other Asian or Pacific Islander	(NA)	822	(NA)	0.3	(NA)	(NA)
Other race	6,758	9,805	3.0	3.9	3,047	45.1
HISPANIC ORIGIN						
Hispanic origin [2]	14,609	22,354	6.4	9.0	7,745	53.0
Mexican	8,740	13,496	3.9	5.4	4,755	54.4
Puerto Rican	2,014	2,728	0.9	1.1	714	35.4
Cuban	803	1,044	0.4	0.4	241	30.0
Other Hispanic	3,051	5,086	1.3	2.0	2,035	66.7
Not of Hispanic origin	211,937	226,356	93.6	91.0	14,419	6.8

NA Not available.   Z Less than .05 percent.   [1] Not entirely comparable with 1990 counts. The 1980 count shown here which is based on 100-percent tabulations includes only the nine specific Asian or Pacific Islander groups listed separately in the 1980 race item. The 1980 total Asian or Pacific Islander population of 3,726,440 from sample tabulations is comparable to the 1990 count; these figures include groups not listed separately in the race item on the 1980 census form.   [2] Persons of Hispanic origin may be any race.

Source: U.S. Bureau of the Census, press release CB91-216.

No. 17. Resident Population, by Age, Race, and Hispanic Origin—Percent Distribution: 1980 and 1990

[In percent. As of **April 1**]

RACE AND HISPANIC ORIGIN	TOTAL		UNDER 5 YEARS OLD		5 TO 17 YEARS OLD		18 TO 44 YEARS OLD		45 TO 64 YEARS OLD		65 YEARS OLD AND OVER	
	1980	1990	1980	1990	1980	1990	1980	1990	1980	1990	1980	1990
All persons	**100.0**	**100.0**	**100.0**	**100.0**	**100.0**	**100.0**	**100.0**	**100.0**	**100.0**	**100.0**	**100.0**	**100.0**
White	83.1	80.3	77.3	74.4	79.0	75.1	82.5	79.0	87.2	84.7	89.8	89.1
Black	11.7	12.1	14.9	15.2	14.7	15.0	11.7	12.4	9.4	9.9	8.2	8.0
American Indian, Eskimo, or Aleut .	0.6	0.8	0.9	1.1	0.9	1.1	0.6	0.8	0.4	0.6	0.3	0.4
Asian or Pacific Islander [1]	1.5	2.9	1.8	3.2	1.6	3.3	1.8	3.3	1.3	2.6	0.8	1.5
Other race	3.0	3.9	5.1	6.1	3.9	5.5	3.4	4.5	1.7	2.3	0.9	1.0
Hispanic origin [2]	6.4	9.0	10.2	13.0	8.4	11.9	6.8	9.8	4.4	6.3	2.8	3.7
Not of Hispanic origin	93.6	91.0	89.8	87.0	91.6	88.1	93.2	90.2	95.6	93.7	97.2	96.3

[1] 1980 data are not entirely comparable with 1990 counts. See footnote 1, table 16.   [2] Persons of Hispanic origin may be of any race.

Source: U.S. Bureau of the Census, *1980 Census of Population*, vol. 1, chapter B; and *1990 Census of Population and Housing Data Paper Listing* (CPH-L-74).

No. 18. Resident Population, by Age, Race, and Hispanic Origin: 1980 and 1990

[In thousands, except percent. As of April. Hispanic persons may be of any race]

YEAR AND SEX	Total, all years	Under 5 years	5-9 years	10-14 years	15-19 years	20-24 years	25-29 years	30-34 years	35-39 years	40-44 years	45-49 years	50-54 years	55-59 years	60-64 years	65-74 years	75 years and over	5-13 years	14-17 years	18-24 years
ALL RACES [1]																			
1980	226,546	16,348	16,700	18,242	21,168	21,319	19,521	17,561	13,965	11,669	11,089	11,710	11,615	10,088	15,187	9,969	31,159	16,247	30,022
1990	248,710	18,354	18,099	17,114	17,754	19,020	21,313	21,863	19,963	17,616	13,873	11,351	10,532	10,616	18,107	13,135	31,970	13,280	26,738
Male	121,239	9,392	9,263	8,767	9,103	9,676	10,696	10,877	9,902	8,692	6,811	5,515	5,034	4,947	7,942	4,624	16,367	6,824	13,616
Female	127,470	8,962	8,837	8,347	8,651	9,345	10,617	10,986	10,061	8,924	7,062	5,836	5,497	5,669	10,165	8,512	15,603	6,455	13,122
WHITE																			
1980	188,372	12,634	13,033	14,461	16,962	17,289	15,985	14,645	11,761	9,826	9,457	10,158	10,238	8,976	13,908	9,041	24,501	12,950	24,294
1990	199,686	13,649	13,616	12,854	13,343	14,524	16,639	17,352	16,082	14,506	11,586	9,505	8,968	9,211	16,026	11,826	24,036	9,942	20,358
Male	97,476	7,004	6,991	6,607	6,846	7,388	8,385	8,700	8,054	7,227	5,737	4,657	4,331	4,335	7,069	4,146	12,346	5,120	10,366
Female	102,210	6,645	6,626	6,247	6,497	7,136	8,254	8,652	8,027	7,279	5,849	4,847	4,638	4,876	8,957	7,680	11,690	4,823	9,992
BLACK																			
1980	26,495	2,436	2,491	2,673	2,985	2,725	2,321	1,889	1,458	1,251	1,143	1,179	1,037	871	1,341	746	4,596	2,364	3,914
1990	29,986	2,786	2,671	2,602	2,658	2,579	2,708	2,682	2,337	1,876	1,406	1,179	1,033	962	1,503	1,005	4,784	2,014	3,712
Male	14,170	1,408	1,350	1,314	1,342	1,259	1,286	1,251	1,083	866	642	532	457	414	618	348	2,418	1,023	1,825
Female	15,816	1,377	1,321	1,287	1,316	1,320	1,422	1,431	1,254	1,010	763	647	576	547	886	657	2,367	991	1,887
AMERICAN INDIAN, ESKIMO, ALEUT																			
1980	1,420	149	147	156	170	149	125	107	84	69	58	52	45	34	48	27	270	136	216
1990	1,959	202	199	188	181	166	176	171	150	126	97	77	62	51	72	42	352	143	238
Male	967	103	101	96	93	85	87	83	73	61	47	37	29	24	32	16	179	73	123
Female	992	99	98	92	87	81	88	88	76	65	50	40	32	27	40	26	173	70	116
ASIAN, PACIFIC ISLANDER																			
1980 [2]	3,500	293	302	280	289	320	369	371	277	221	181	158	130	98	138	74	527	224	439
1990	7,274	590	596	552	604	632	691	726	670	572	406	312	251	219	301	154	1,040	454	890
Male	3,558	301	302	281	312	326	343	350	317	267	195	152	114	94	134	71	528	234	459
Female	3,716	288	294	270	291	306	348	376	353	305	210	160	137	124	167	83	512	219	431
HISPANIC ORIGIN																			
1980	14,609	1,663	1,537	1,475	1,606	1,586	1,376	1,129	854	712	622	564	454	321	457	252	2,715	1,250	2,240
1990	22,354	2,388	2,194	2,002	2,054	2,304	2,341	2,062	1,661	1,284	954	756	639	554	723	438	3,813	1,557	3,184
Male	11,388	1,218	1,119	1,023	1,084	1,262	1,250	1,074	846	640	468	364	302	255	315	166	1,946	807	1,735
Female	10,966	1,169	1,075	978	970	1,043	1,091	988	815	644	486	392	337	299	408	272	1,867	750	1,449
PERCENT																			
Total, 1990 [1]	100.0	7.4	7.3	6.9	7.1	7.6	8.6	8.8	8.0	7.1	5.6	4.6	4.2	4.3	7.3	5.3	12.9	5.3	10.8
White	100.0	6.8	6.8	6.4	6.7	7.3	8.3	8.8	8.1	7.3	5.8	4.8	4.5	4.6	8.0	5.9	12.0	5.0	10.2
Black	100.0	9.3	8.9	8.7	8.9	8.6	9.0	8.9	7.8	6.3	4.7	3.9	3.4	3.2	5.0	3.4	16.0	6.7	12.4
American Indian, Eskimo, Aleut	100.0	10.3	10.2	9.6	9.2	8.5	9.0	8.7	7.7	6.4	5.0	3.9	3.2	2.6	3.7	2.1	18.0	7.3	12.2
Asian, Pacific Islander	100.0	8.1	9.8	7.6	8.3	8.7	9.5	10.0	9.2	7.9	5.6	4.3	3.5	3.0	4.1	2.1	14.3	6.2	12.2
Hispanic origin	100.0	10.7	9.8	9.0	9.2	10.3	10.5	9.2	7.4	5.7	4.3	3.4	2.9	2.5	3.2	2.0	17.1	7.0	14.2

[1] Includes other races, not shown separately.   [2] See footnote 1, table 16.

Source: U.S. Bureau of the Census, *1980 Census of Population*, vol. 1, chapter B; and *1990 Census of Population and Housing Data Paper Listing* (CPH-L-74).

No. 19. Resident Population, by Age and Sex: 1970 to 1991

[In thousands, except as indicated. Based on enumerated population as of April 1; 1991 based on estimated population as of July 1. Excludes Armed Forces overseas. For definition of median, see Guide to Tabular Presentation. See also *Historical Statistics, Colonial Times to 1970*, series A119-134]

YEAR AND SEX	Total, all years	Under 5 years	5-9 years	10-14 years	15-19 years	20-24 years	25-29 years	30-34 years	35-39 years	40-44 years	45-49 years	50-54 years	55-59 years	60-64 years	65-74 years	75 years and over	5-13 years	14-17 years	18-24 years	16 years and over	65 years and over	Median age (yr.)
1970, total[1]	203,235	17,163	19,969	20,804	19,084	16,383	13,486	11,437	11,113	11,988	12,124	11,111	9,979	8,623	12,443	7,530	36,675	15,851	23,714	141,268	19,972	28.0
Male	98,926	8,750	10,175	10,598	9,641	7,925	6,626	5,599	5,416	5,823	5,855	5,351	4,769	4,030	5,440	2,927	18,687	8,069	11,583	67,347	8,367	26.8
Female	104,309	8,413	9,794	10,206	9,443	8,458	6,859	5,838	5,697	6,166	6,269	5,759	5,210	4,593	7,002	4,603	17,987	7,782	12,131	73,920	11,605	29.3
1980, total	226,546	16,348	16,700	18,242	21,168	21,319	19,521	17,561	13,965	11,669	11,090	11,710	11,615	10,088	15,581	9,969	31,159	16,247	30,022	171,196	25,549	30.0
Male	110,053	8,362	8,539	9,316	10,755	10,663	9,705	8,677	6,862	5,708	5,388	5,621	5,482	4,670	6,757	3,548	15,923	8,298	15,054	81,766	10,305	28.8
Female	116,493	7,986	8,161	8,926	10,413	10,655	9,816	8,884	7,104	5,961	5,702	6,089	6,133	5,418	8,824	6,420	15,237	7,950	14,969	89,429	15,245	31.3
1990, total[2]	248,710	18,758	18,035	17,060	17,882	19,132	21,328	21,833	19,846	17,589	13,744	11,313	10,487	10,625	18,045	13,033	31,826	13,340	26,942	191,536	31,079	32.8
Male	121,239	9,599	9,232	8,739	9,173	9,743	10,702	10,862	9,833	8,676	6,739	5,493	5,008	4,947	7,907	4,586	16,295	6,857	13,734	91,964	12,493	31.6
Female	127,470	9,159	8,803	8,322	8,709	9,389	10,625	10,971	10,013	8,913	7,004	5,820	5,479	5,679	10,139	8,447	15,532	6,483	13,208	99,572	18,586	34.0
1991, total	252,177	19,222	18,237	17,671	17,205	19,194	20,718	22,159	20,518	18,754	14,094	11,645	10,423	10,582	18,280	13,474	32,500	13,423	26,385	193,754	31,754	33.1
Male	122,979	9,836	9,337	9,051	8,834	9,775	10,393	11,034	10,174	9,258	6,907	5,656	4,987	4,945	8,022	4,769	16,641	6,901	13,456	93,065	12,791	31.9
Female	129,198	9,386	8,900	8,620	8,371	9,419	10,325	11,125	10,344	9,496	7,188	5,989	5,436	5,637	10,258	8,705	15,859	6,522	12,929	100,689	18,962	34.3
Percent:																						
1970	100.0	8.4	9.8	10.2	9.4	8.1	6.6	5.6	5.5	5.9	6.0	5.5	4.9	4.2	6.1	3.7	18.0	7.8	11.7	69.5	9.8	(X)
1980[2]	100.0	7.2	7.4	8.1	9.3	9.4	8.6	7.8	6.2	5.2	4.9	5.2	5.1	4.5	6.9	4.4	13.8	7.2	13.3	75.6	11.3	(X)
1990	100.0	7.5	7.3	6.9	7.2	7.7	8.6	8.8	8.0	7.1	5.5	4.5	4.2	4.3	7.3	5.2	12.8	5.4	10.8	77.0	12.5	(X)
1991	100.0	7.6	7.2	7.0	6.8	7.6	8.2	8.8	8.1	7.4	5.6	4.6	4.1	4.2	7.2	5.3	12.9	5.3	10.5	76.8	12.6	(X)
Male	100.0	8.0	7.6	7.4	7.2	7.9	8.5	9.0	8.3	7.5	5.6	4.6	4.1	4.0	6.5	3.9	13.5	5.6	10.9	75.7	10.4	(X)
Female	100.0	7.3	6.9	6.7	6.5	7.3	8.0	8.6	8.0	7.4	5.6	4.6	4.2	4.4	7.9	6.7	12.3	5.0	10.0	77.9	14.7	(X)

X Not applicable. [1] Official count. The revised 1970 resident population count is 203,302,031; the difference of 66,733 is due to errors found after release of the official series. [2] The data shown have been modified from the official 1990 census counts. See text, section 1 for explanation.

Source: U.S. Bureau of the Census, *Current Population Reports*, series P-25, Nos. 917 and 1045; *1990 Census of Population and Housing Data Paper Listing* (CPH-L-74); and unpublished data.

No. 20. Ratio of Males to Females, by Age Group: 1940 to 1991

[**Number of males per 100 females**. As of **April 1**, except **1991**, as of **July 1**. Total resident population]

AGE	1940	1950	1960	1970	1980	1990	1991
All ages	**100.7**	**98.6**	**97.1**	**94.8**	**94.5**	**95.1**	**95.2**
Under 14 years	103.0	103.7	103.4	103.9	104.6	104.9	104.9
14 to 24 years	98.9	98.2	98.7	98.7	101.9	104.6	104.7
25 to 44 years	98.5	96.4	95.7	95.5	97.4	98.9	99.0
45 to 64 years	105.2	100.1	95.7	91.6	90.7	92.5	92.8
65 years and over	95.5	89.6	82.8	72.1	67.6	67.2	67.5

Source: U.S. Bureau of the Census, *U.S. Census of Population: 1940*, vol. II, part 1, and vol. IV, part 1; *1950*, vol. II, part 1; *1960*, vol. I, part 1; *1970*, vol. I, part B; *Current Population Reports*, series P-25, No. 1045; *1990 Census of Population and Housing Data Paper Listing* (CPH-L-74); and unpublished data.

No. 21. Annual Inmigration, Outmigration, and Net Migration for Regions: 1980 to 1990

[**In thousands**. As of **March**. For persons 1 year old and over. Excludes members of the Armed Forces except those living off post or with their families on post. Based on Current Population Survey; see text, section 1 and Appendix III. For composition of regions, see table 25. Minus sign (-) indicates net outmigration]

PERIOD	North-east	Mid-west	South	West	PERIOD	North-east	Mid-west	South	West
1980-1981: Inmigrants	464	650	1,377	871	**1986-1987:** Inmigrants	398	858	1,374	916
Outmigrants.	706	1,056	890	710	Outmigrants.	732	969	1,095	750
Net internal migration. . .	-242	-406	487	161	Net internal migration. . .	-334	-111	279	166
Movers from abroad	207	180	412	514	Movers from abroad	214	193	277	458
Net migration	-35	-226	899	675	Net migration	-120	82	556	624
1981-1982: Inmigrants	473	793	1,482	931	**1987-1988:** Inmigrants	430	715	1,338	613
Outmigrants.	685	1,163	1,012	819	Outmigrants.	671	818	886	721
Net internal migration. . .	-212	-370	470	112	Net internal migration. . .	-241	-103	452	-108
Movers from abroad	229	134	401	324	Movers from abroad	261	146	414	379
Net migration	17	-236	871	436	Net migration	20	43	866	271
1982-1983: Inmigrants	439	661	1,211	880	**1988-1989:** Inmigrants	370	777	1,318	791
Outmigrants.	625	947	973	645	Outmigrants.	714	703	1,071	637
Net internal migration. . .	-186	-286	238	235	Net internal migration. . .	-344	74	247	154
Movers from abroad	192	149	323	315	Movers from abroad	292	170	375	629
Net migration	6	-137	561	550	Net migration	-52	244	622	783
1983-1984: Inmigrants	487	820	1,399	834	**1989-1990:**				
Outmigrants.	578	1,102	973	887	Total inmigrants	461	908	1,428	964
Net internal migration. . .	-91	-282	426	-53	From Northeast.	(X)	139	445	174
Movers from abroad	213	141	383	341	From Midwest.	89	(X)	561	374
Net migration	122	-141	809	288	From South	246	536	(X)	416
1984-1985: Inmigrants	482	842	1,329	994	From West.	126	233	422	(X)
Outmigrants.	691	1,053	1,169	734	Total outmigrants	758	1,024	1,198	781
Net internal migration. . .	-209	-211	160	260	To Northeast	(X)	89	246	126
Movers from abroad	228	168	532	499	To Midwest	139	(X)	536	233
Net migration	19	-43	692	759	To South	445	561	(X)	422
1985-1986: Inmigrants	502	1,011	1,355	910	To West.	174	374	416	(X)
Outmigrants.	752	996	1,320	710	Net internal migration	-297	-116	230	183
Net internal migration. . .	-250	15	35	200	Movers from abroad	328	169	500	562
Movers from abroad	198	158	342	502	Net migration	30	53	730	745
Net migration	-52	173	377	702					

X Not applicable.

No. 22. Mobility Status of the Population, by Selected Characteristics: 1989 to 1990

[See headnote, table 21]

AGE AND REGION	Total (1,000)	Non-movers (same house)	PERCENT DISTRIBUTION						Movers from abroad
			Movers (different house in U.S.)						
			Total	Same county	Different county				
					Total	Same State	Different State		
Total	**242,208**	**82**	**17**	**11**	**7**	**3**	**3**	**1**
1 to 4 years old	14,948	76	23	15	8	4	4	1
5 to 9 years old	18,300	81	18	12	6	3	3	1
10 to 14 years old	17,168	85	14	9	5	2	3	1
15 to 19 years old	17,266	82	17	10	6	3	3	1
20 to 24 years old	17,988	62	36	23	14	7	6	2
25 to 29 years old	21,200	67	32	20	13	7	6	1
30 to 44 years old	59,236	81	18	11	7	3	4	1
45 to 54 years old	25,304	90	10	6	4	2	2	(Z)
55 to 64 years old	21,232	92	7	4	3	2	2	(Z)
65 to 74 years old	17,979	95	5	3	2	1	1	(Z)
75 years old and over	11,587	94	6	3	3	1	1	(Z)
Northeast	49,794	87	12	8	4	2	2	1
Midwest	58,499	84	16	10	6	3	3	(Z)
South	82,780	81	19	11	8	4	4	1
West	51,136	77	22	14	8	4	4	1

Z Less than 0.5 percent.

Source of tables 21 and 22: U.S. Bureau of the Census, *Current Population Reports*, series P-20, No. 456.

No. 23. U.S. Resident Population, by Region and Division: 1960 to 1991

[As of **April 1**; except **1985** and **1991**, as of **July 1**. For composition of divisions, see table 25]

REGION AND DIVISION	POPULATION (millions)						PERCENT DISTRIBUTION					
	1960	1970	1980	1985	1990	1991	1960	1970	1980	1985	1990	1991
United States	179.3	203.3	226.5	238.0	248.7	252.2	100.0	100.0	100.0	100.0	100.0	100.0
Northeast	44.7	49.1	49.1	49.9	50.8	51.0	24.9	24.1	21.7	21.0	20.4	20.2
New England	10.5	11.8	12.3	12.7	13.2	13.2	5.9	5.8	5.5	5.3	5.3	5.2
Middle Atlantic	34.2	37.2	36.8	37.1	37.6	37.8	19.1	18.3	16.2	15.6	15.1	15.0
Midwest	51.6	56.6	58.9	58.8	59.7	60.2	28.8	27.8	26.0	24.7	24.0	23.9
East North Central. . . .	36.2	40.3	41.7	41.4	42.0	42.4	20.2	19.8	18.4	17.4	16.9	16.8
West North Central . . .	15.4	16.3	17.2	17.4	17.7	17.8	8.6	8.0	7.6	7.3	7.1	7.1
South.	55.0	62.8	75.4	81.4	85.4	86.9	30.7	30.9	33.3	34.2	34.4	34.5
South Atlantic.	26.0	30.7	37.0	40.2	43.6	44.4	14.5	15.1	16.3	16.9	17.5	17.6
East South Central . . .	12.1	12.8	14.7	15.0	15.2	15.3	6.7	6.3	6.5	6.3	6.1	6.1
West South Central . . .	17.0	19.3	23.7	26.3	26.7	27.1	9.5	9.5	10.5	11.1	10.7	10.8
West	28.1	34.8	43.2	47.8	52.8	54.1	15.6	17.1	19.1	20.1	21.2	21.4
Mountain	6.9	8.3	11.4	12.7	13.7	14.0	3.8	4.1	5.0	5.4	5.5	5.6
Pacific.	21.2	26.5	31.8	35.1	39.1	40.0	11.8	13.1	14.0	14.8	15.7	15.9

Source: U.S. Bureau of the Census, *Census of Population: 1970*, vol. I; *1980 Census of Population*, vol. 1, chapter A (PC80-1-A); and press releases, CB91-289 and CB91-346.

No. 24. Resident Population, by Region, Race, and Hispanic Origin: 1990

[As of **April 1**. For composition of regions, see table 25]

RACE AND HISPANIC ORIGIN	POPULATION (1,000)					PERCENT DISTRIBUTION				
	United States	North-east	Midwest	South	West	United States	North-east	Midwest	South	West
Total.	248,710	50,809	59,669	85,446	52,786	100.0	20.4	24.0	34.4	21.2
White.	199,686	42,069	52,018	65,582	40,017	100.0	21.1	26.0	32.8	20.0
Black.	29,986	5,613	5,716	15,829	2,828	100.0	18.7	19.1	52.8	9.4
American Indian, Eskimo, Aleut	1,959	125	338	563	933	100.0	6.4	17.2	28.7	47.6
American Indian	1,878	122	334	557	866	100.0	6.5	17.8	29.7	46.1
Eskimo	57	2	2	3	51	100.0	2.9	3.5	4.9	88.8
Aleut	24	2	2	3	17	100.0	8.1	8.1	11.5	72.3
Asian or Pacific Islander [1].	7,274	1,335	768	1,122	4,048	100.0	18.4	10.6	15.4	55.7
Chinese	1,645	445	133	204	863	100.0	27.0	8.1	12.4	52.4
Filipino	1,407	143	113	159	991	100.0	10.2	8.1	11.3	70.5
Japanese	848	74	63	67	643	100.0	8.8	7.5	7.9	75.9
Asian Indian.	815	285	146	196	189	100.0	35.0	17.9	24.0	23.1
Korean	799	182	109	153	355	100.0	22.8	13.7	19.2	44.4
Vietnamese	615	61	52	169	334	100.0	9.8	8.5	27.4	54.3
Laotian	149	16	28	29	76	100.0	10.7	18.6	19.6	51.0
Cambodian	147	30	13	19	85	100.0	20.5	8.8	13.1	57.7
Thai	91	12	13	24	43	100.0	12.9	14.2	26.0	46.8
Hmong	90	2	37	2	50	100.0	1.9	41.3	1.8	55.0
Pakistani.	81	28	15	22	17	100.0	34.3	18.9	26.5	20.4
Hawaiian	211	4	6	12	189	100.0	2.0	2.6	5.8	89.6
Samoan	63	2	2	4	55	100.0	2.4	3.6	6.4	87.6
Guamanian	49	4	3	8	34	100.0	7.3	6.4	16.8	69.5
Other races	9,805	1,667	829	2,350	4,960	100.0	17.0	8.5	24.0	50.6
Hispanic origin [2]	22,354	3,754	1,727	6,767	10,106	100.0	16.8	7.7	30.3	45.2
Mexican	13,496	175	1,153	4,344	7,824	100.0	1.3	8.5	32.2	58.0
Puerto Rican	2,728	1,872	258	406	192	100.0	68.6	9.4	14.9	7.0
Cuban.	1,044	184	37	735	88	100.0	17.6	3.5	70.5	8.5
Other Hispanic	5,086	1,524	279	1,282	2,002	100.0	30.0	5.5	25.2	39.4
Not of Hispanic origin. . . .	226,356	47,055	57,942	78,679	42,680	100.0	20.8	25.6	34.8	18.9

[1] Includes other Asian and Pacific Islander races not shown separately.   [2] Persons of Hispanic origin may be of any race.

Source: U.S. Bureau of the Census, press release CB91-216.

Population

[As of **July 1**; except **1970, 1980, and 1990,** as of **April 1.** Insofar as possible, population shown for all years is that of
See *Historical Statistics, Colonial Times to 1970,* series A 172, for population by regions,

REGION, DIVISION, AND STATE	POPULATION (1,000)										
	1970	1980	1983	1984	1985	1986	1987	1988	1989	1990	1991
U.S.......	203,302	226,546	233,806	235,847	237,950	240,162	242,321	244,534	246,820	248,710	252,177
Northeast	49,061	49,135	49,540	49,723	49,874	50,077	50,308	50,591	50,757	50,809	50,976
N.E........	11,848	12,348	12,545	12,643	12,742	12,835	12,953	13,086	13,182	13,207	13,197
ME........	994	1,125	1,145	1,156	1,163	1,170	1,185	1,204	1,220	1,228	1,235
NH	738	921	958	977	997	1,025	1,054	1,083	1,105	1,109	1,105
VT........	445	511	523	527	530	534	540	550	558	563	567
MA	5,689	5,737	5,800	5,841	5,881	5,903	5,936	5,981	6,016	6,016	5,996
RI	950	947	956	962	969	977	990	997	1,001	1,003	1,004
CT........	3,032	3,108	3,163	3,180	3,201	3,224	3,248	3,272	3,283	3,287	3,291
M.A	37,213	36,787	36,995	37,080	37,132	37,243	37,355	37,505	37,575	37,602	37,779
NY	18,241	17,558	17,688	17,747	17,794	17,836	17,871	17,944	17,983	17,990	18,058
NJ........	7,171	7,365	7,468	7,516	7,566	7,623	7,672	7,713	7,726	7,730	7,760
PA........	11,801	11,864	11,838	11,816	11,772	11,784	11,812	11,847	11,866	11,882	11,961
Midwest....	56,589	58,866	58,695	58,781	58,826	58,855	59,025	59,263	59,468	59,669	60,225
E.N.C	40,262	41,682	41,369	41,397	41,423	41,460	41,595	41,727	41,873	42,009	42,414
OH	10,657	10,798	10,738	10,739	10,736	10,732	10,762	10,800	10,829	10,847	10,939
IN	5,195	5,490	5,451	5,459	5,460	5,455	5,474	5,493	5,524	5,544	5,610
IL	11,110	11,427	11,410	11,413	11,401	11,389	11,393	11,392	11,410	11,431	11,543
MI	8,882	9,262	9,048	9,050	9,077	9,129	9,189	9,219	9,253	9,295	9,368
WI	4,418	4,706	4,722	4,736	4,748	4,756	4,779	4,823	4,857	4,892	4,955
W.N.C......	16,327	17,183	17,326	17,384	17,404	17,395	17,430	17,536	17,595	17,660	17,811
MN	3,806	4,076	4,142	4,158	4,185	4,206	4,236	4,297	4,338	4,375	4,432
IA	2,825	2,914	2,871	2,859	2,830	2,792	2,767	2,769	2,771	2,777	2,795
MO	4,678	4,917	4,944	4,976	5,001	5,024	5,057	5,082	5,096	5,117	5,158
ND	618	653	677	681	677	670	661	655	646	639	635
SD	666	691	693	697	698	696	696	698	697	696	703
NE	1,485	1,570	1,584	1,589	1,585	1,575	1,567	1,572	1,575	1,578	1,593
KS........	2,249	2,364	2,416	2,424	2,428	2,433	2,446	2,462	2,473	2,478	2,495
South	62,812	75,372	79,454	80,425	81,418	82,438	83,219	83,903	84,700	85,446	86,916
S.A.........	30,678	36,959	38,853	39,496	40,163	40,868	41,625	42,324	43,008	43,567	44,421
DE	548	594	605	612	618	628	637	648	658	666	680
MD	3,924	4,217	4,314	4,366	4,414	4,488	4,566	4,659	4,727	4,781	4,860
DC	757	638	632	633	635	638	637	631	624	607	598
VA........	4,651	5,347	5,565	5,644	5,716	5,812	5,933	6,038	6,120	6,187	6,286
WV	1,744	1,950	1,945	1,928	1,907	1,883	1,858	1,830	1,807	1,793	1,801
NC	5,084	5,882	6,077	6,165	6,255	6,322	6,405	6,482	6,565	6,629	6,737
SC	2,591	3,122	3,234	3,272	3,304	3,343	3,381	3,413	3,457	3,487	3,560
GA	4,588	5,463	5,729	5,835	5,963	6,085	6,209	6,317	6,411	6,478	6,623
FL........	6,791	9,746	10,751	11,041	11,352	11,669	11,999	12,308	12,638	12,938	13,277
E.S.C	12,808	14,666	14,857	14,913	14,972	15,014	15,072	15,109	15,136	15,176	15,347
KY	3,221	3,661	3,695	3,696	3,695	3,688	3,684	3,681	3,677	3,685	3,713
TN	3,926	4,591	4,660	4,687	4,716	4,739	4,784	4,823	4,854	4,877	4,953
AL........	3,444	3,894	3,934	3,952	3,973	3,992	4,016	4,024	4,030	4,041	4,089
MS	2,217	2,521	2,568	2,578	2,588	2,594	2,589	2,581	2,574	2,573	2,592
W.S.C......	19,326	23,747	25,745	26,015	26,282	26,556	26,522	26,469	26,556	26,703	27,148
AR	1,923	2,286	2,306	2,320	2,327	2,332	2,343	2,343	2,346	2,351	2,372
LA........	3,645	4,206	4,396	4,401	4,409	4,407	4,345	4,289	4,253	4,220	4,252
OK	2,559	3,025	3,291	3,286	3,272	3,253	3,211	3,168	3,150	3,146	3,175
TX........	11,199	14,229	15,753	16,009	16,275	16,563	16,624	16,669	16,807	16,987	17,349
West.........	34,838	43,172	46,117	46,918	47,832	48,792	49,768	50,778	51,895	52,786	54,060
Mt	8,289	11,373	12,301	12,519	12,742	12,953	13,146	13,305	13,498	13,659	14,035
MT	694	787	814	821	822	814	805	800	800	799	808
ID	713	944	982	991	994	990	985	986	994	1,007	1,039
WY	332	470	510	505	500	496	477	465	458	454	460
CO	2,210	2,890	3,134	3,170	3,209	3,238	3,261	3,263	3,276	3,294	3,377
NM	1,017	1,303	1,394	1,417	1,439	1,463	1,479	1,491	1,504	1,515	1,548
AZ.......	1,775	2,718	2,969	3,067	3,184	3,309	3,438	3,536	3,622	3,665	3,750
UT.......	1,059	1,461	1,595	1,622	1,643	1,663	1,678	1,690	1,706	1,723	1,770
NV	489	800	902	925	951	981	1,024	1,075	1,137	1,202	1,284
Pac	26,549	31,800	33,817	34,399	35,090	35,839	36,622	37,473	38,397	39,127	40,025
WA	3,413	4,132	4,301	4,344	4,401	4,453	4,533	4,641	4,746	4,867	5,018
OR	2,092	2,633	2,653	2,667	2,673	2,684	2,701	2,742	2,791	2,842	2,922
CA	19,971	23,668	25,362	25,847	26,444	27,106	27,781	28,468	29,218	29,760	30,380
AK	303	402	488	514	533	544	539	542	547	550	570
HI........	770	965	1,013	1,028	1,040	1,052	1,068	1,080	1,095	1,108	1,135

X Not applicable.   [1] Persons per square mile were calculated on the basis of land area data from the 1990 census.

States: 1970 to 1991

present area of State; for area figures of States, see table 340. Minus sign (-) indicates decrease.
and A 195-198 for population and density, by States]

RANK				PERCENT CHANGE			POPULATION PER SQ. MILE OF LAND AREA [1]				REGION, DIVISION, AND STATE
1970	1980	1990	1991	1970-80	1980-90	1990-91	1970	1980	1990	1991	
(X)	(X)	(X)	(X)	11.4	9.8	1.4	57.5	64.1	70.3	71.3	**U.S.**
(X)	(X)	(X)	(X)	0.2	3.4	0.3	302.3	302.8	313.1	314.1	**Northeast**
(X)	(X)	(X)	(X)	4.2	7.0	-0.1	188.6	196.6	210.3	210.1	**N.E**
38	38	38	39	13.2	9.2	0.5	32.2	36.4	39.8	40.0	ME
41	42	40	41	24.8	20.5	-0.4	82.2	102.6	123.7	123.2	NH
48	48	48	49	15.0	10.0	0.7	48.1	55.3	60.8	61.3	VT
10	11	13	13	0.8	4.9	-0.3	725.8	732.0	767.6	765.0	MA
39	40	43	43	-0.3	5.9	0.1	908.8	906.4	960.3	961.1	RI
24	25	27	27	2.5	5.8	0.1	625.8	641.3	678.4	679.2	CT
(X)	(X)	(X)	(X)	-1.1	2.2	0.5	374.1	369.9	378.1	379.8	**M.A**
2	2	2	2	-3.7	2.5	0.4	386.3	371.8	381.0	382.4	NY
8	9	9	9	2.7	5.0	0.4	966.6	992.7	1,042.0	1,046.0	NJ
3	4	5	5	0.5	0.1	0.7	263.3	264.7	265.1	266.9	PA
(X)	(X)	(X)	(X)	4.0	1.4	0.9	75.3	78.3	79.4	80.1	**Midwest**
(X)	(X)	(X)	(X)	3.5	0.8	1.0	165.3	171.2	172.5	174.2	**E.N.C**
6	6	7	7	1.3	0.5	0.8	260.2	263.7	264.9	267.1	OH
11	12	14	14	5.7	1.0	1.2	144.8	153.1	154.6	156.4	IN
5	5	6	6	2.8	(Z)	1.0	199.8	205.5	205.6	207.6	IL
7	8	8	8	4.3	0.4	0.8	156.3	163.0	163.6	164.9	MI
16	16	16	17	6.5	4.0	1.3	81.3	86.6	90.1	91.2	WI
(X)	(X)	(X)	(X)	5.2	2.8	0.9	32.1	33.8	34.8	35.1	**W.N.C**
19	21	20	20	7.1	7.3	1.3	47.8	51.2	55.0	55.7	MN
25	27	30	30	3.1	-4.7	0.7	50.6	52.1	49.7	50.0	IA
13	15	15	15	5.1	4.1	0.8	67.9	71.4	74.3	74.9	MO
45	46	47	47	5.7	-2.1	-0.7	9.0	9.5	9.3	9.2	ND
44	45	45	45	3.7	0.8	1.0	8.8	9.1	9.2	9.3	SD
35	35	36	36	5.7	0.5	0.9	19.3	20.4	20.5	20.7	NE
28	32	32	32	5.1	4.8	0.7	27.5	28.9	30.3	30.5	KS
(X)	(X)	(X)	(X)	20.0	13.4	1.7	72.1	86.5	98.1	99.8	**South**
(X)	(X)	(X)	(X)	20.5	17.9	2.0	115.2	138.8	163.6	166.9	**S.A**
46	47	46	46	8.4	12.1	2.1	280.4	301.1	340.8	347.9	DE
18	18	19	19	7.5	13.4	1.6	401.4	431.4	489.2	497.2	MD
(X)	(X)	(X)	(X)	-15.6	-4.9	-1.4	12,321.6	10,394.6	9,882.8	9,742.9	DC
14	14	12	12	14.9	15.7	1.6	117.5	135.0	156.3	158.7	VA
34	34	34	34	11.8	-8.0	0.4	72.4	80.9	74.5	74.8	WV
12	10	10	10	15.7	12.7	1.6	104.4	120.7	136.1	138.3	NC
26	24	25	25	20.5	11.7	2.1	86.0	103.7	115.8	118.2	SC
15	13	11	11	19.1	18.6	2.2	79.2	94.3	111.9	114.3	GA
9	7	4	4	43.5	32.7	2.6	125.8	180.5	239.6	245.9	FL
(X)	(X)	(X)	(X)	14.5	3.5	1.1	71.7	82.1	85.0	85.9	**E.S.C**
23	23	23	24	13.7	0.7	0.8	81.1	92.1	92.8	93.5	KY
17	17	17	18	16.9	6.2	1.5	95.2	111.4	118.3	120.2	TN
21	22	22	22	13.1	3.8	1.2	67.9	76.7	79.6	80.6	AL
29	31	31	31	13.7	2.1	0.7	47.3	53.7	54.9	55.3	MS
(X)	(X)	(X)	(X)	22.9	12.4	1.7	45.3	55.7	62.6	63.7	**W.S.C**
32	33	33	33	18.9	2.8	0.9	36.9	43.9	45.1	45.5	AR
20	19	21	21	15.4	0.3	0.7	83.7	96.5	96.9	97.6	LA
27	26	28	28	18.2	4.0	0.9	37.3	44.0	45.8	46.2	OK
4	3	3	3	27.1	19.4	2.1	42.8	54.3	64.9	66.2	TX
(X)	(X)	(X)	(X)	23.9	22.3	2.4	19.9	24.6	30.1	30.9	**West**
(X)	(X)	(X)	(X)	37.2	20.1	2.8	9.7	13.3	16.0	16.4	**Mt**
43	44	44	44	13.3	1.6	1.2	4.8	5.4	5.5	5.6	MT
42	41	42	42	32.4	6.7	3.2	8.6	11.4	12.2	12.6	ID
49	49	50	50	41.3	-3.4	1.3	3.4	4.8	4.7	4.7	WY
30	28	26	26	30.8	14.0	2.5	21.3	27.9	31.8	32.6	CO
37	37	37	37	28.1	16.3	2.2	8.4	10.7	12.5	12.8	NM
33	29	24	23	53.1	34.8	2.3	15.6	23.9	32.3	33.0	AZ
36	36	35	35	37.9	17.9	2.7	12.9	17.8	21.0	21.5	UT
47	43	39	38	63.8	50.1	6.8	4.5	7.3	10.9	11.7	NV
(X)	(X)	(X)	(X)	19.8	23.0	2.3	29.7	35.5	43.7	44.7	**Pac**
22	20	18	16	21.1	17.8	3.1	51.3	62.1	73.1	75.4	WA
31	30	29	29	25.9	7.9	2.8	21.8	27.4	29.6	30.4	OR
1	1	1	1	18.5	25.7	2.1	128.0	151.7	190.8	194.8	CA
50	50	49	48	32.8	36.9	3.7	0.5	0.7	1.0	1.0	AK
40	39	41	40	25.3	14.9	2.4	119.9	150.2	172.5	176.7	HI

Source: U.S. Bureau of the Census, *Census of Population: 1970*, vol. I; and *1980 Census of Population*, vol. 1, chapter A (PC80-1-A) and chapter B (PC80-1-B); and press releases CB91-289 and CB91-346.

No. 26. Resident Population, by Race

[In thousands.

REGION, DIVISION, AND STATE	Total [1]	White	Black	AMERICAN INDIAN, ESKIMO, ALEUT				ASIAN, PACIFIC ISLANDER			
				Total	American Indian	Eskimo	Aleut	Total [2]	Chinese	Filipino	Japanese
U.S.	248,710	199,686	29,986	1,959	1,878	57	24	7,274	1,645	1,407	848
Northeast	50,809	42,069	5,613	125	122	2	2	1,335	445	143	74
N.E.	13,207	12,033	628	33	32	(Z)	(Z)	232	72	15	15
ME	1,228	1,208	5	6	6	(Z)	(Z)	7	1	1	1
NH	1,109	1,087	7	2	2	(Z)	(Z)	9	2	1	1
VT	563	555	2	2	2	(Z)	(Z)	3	1	(Z)	(Z)
MA	6,016	5,405	300	12	12	(Z)	(Z)	143	54	6	9
RI	1,003	917	39	4	4	(Z)	(Z)	18	3	2	1
CT	3,287	2,859	274	7	6	(Z)	(Z)	51	11	5	4
M.A	37,602	30,036	4,986	92	90	1	2	1,104	373	128	59
NY	17,990	13,385	2,859	63	61	1	1	694	284	62	35
NJ	7,730	6,130	1,037	15	15	(Z)	(Z)	273	59	53	17
PA	11,882	10,520	1,090	15	14	(Z)	(Z)	137	30	12	7
Midwest	59,669	52,018	5,716	338	334	2	2	768	133	113	63
E.N.C	42,009	35,764	4,817	150	147	1	1	573	103	97	50
OH	10,847	9,522	1,155	20	20	(Z)	(Z)	91	19	10	10
IN	5,544	5,021	432	13	12	(Z)	(Z)	38	7	5	5
IL	11,431	8,953	1,694	22	21	(Z)	(Z)	285	50	64	22
MI	9,295	7,756	1,292	56	55	(Z)	(Z)	105	19	14	11
WI	4,892	4,513	245	39	39	(Z)	(Z)	54	7	4	3
W.N.C	17,660	16,254	899	188	187	1	1	195	30	17	13
MN	4,375	4,130	95	50	49	(Z)	(Z)	78	9	4	4
IA	2,777	2,683	48	7	7	(Z)	(Z)	25	4	2	2
MO	5,117	4,486	548	20	20	(Z)	(Z)	41	9	6	3
ND	639	604	4	26	26	(Z)	(Z)	3	1	1	(Z)
SD	696	638	3	51	51	(Z)	(Z)	3	(Z)	1	(Z)
NE	1,578	1,481	57	12	12	(Z)	(Z)	12	2	1	2
KS	2,478	2,232	143	22	22	(Z)	(Z)	32	5	3	2
South	85,446	65,582	15,829	563	557	3	3	1,122	204	159	67
S.A.	43,567	33,391	8,924	172	170	1	1	631	114	108	39
DE	666	535	112	2	2	(Z)	(Z)	9	2	1	1
MD	4,781	3,394	1,190	13	13	(Z)	(Z)	140	31	19	7
DC	607	180	400	1	1	(Z)	(Z)	11	3	2	1
VA	6,187	4,792	1,163	15	15	(Z)	(Z)	159	21	35	8
WV	1,793	1,726	56	2	2	(Z)	(Z)	7	1	2	1
NC	6,629	5,008	1,456	80	80	(Z)	(Z)	52	9	5	5
SC	3,487	2,407	1,040	8	8	(Z)	(Z)	22	3	6	2
GA	6,478	4,600	1,747	13	13	(Z)	(Z)	76	13	6	6
FL	12,938	10,749	1,760	36	35	(Z)	(Z)	154	31	32	9
E.S.C	15,176	12,049	2,977	41	40	(Z)	(Z)	84	15	9	9
KY	3,685	3,392	263	6	6	(Z)	(Z)	18	3	2	3
TN	4,877	4,048	778	10	10	(Z)	(Z)	32	6	3	3
AL	4,041	2,976	1,021	17	16	(Z)	(Z)	22	4	2	2
MS	2,573	1,633	915	9	8	(Z)	(Z)	13	3	2	1
W.S.C	26,703	20,142	3,929	350	347	1	1	407	76	43	20
AR	2,351	1,945	374	13	13	(Z)	(Z)	13	2	2	1
LA	4,220	2,839	1,299	19	18	(Z)	(Z)	41	5	4	2
OK	3,146	2,584	234	252	252	(Z)	(Z)	34	5	3	2
TX	16,987	12,775	2,022	66	64	1	1	319	63	34	15
West	52,786	40,017	2,828	933	866	51	17	4,048	863	991	643
Mt	13,659	11,762	374	481	478	1	1	217	40	32	34
MT	799	741	2	48	48	(Z)	(Z)	4	1	1	1
ID	1,007	950	3	14	14	(Z)	(Z)	9	1	1	3
WY	454	427	4	9	9	(Z)	(Z)	3	1	(Z)	1
CO	3,294	2,905	133	28	27	(Z)	(Z)	60	9	5	11
NM	1,515	1,146	30	134	134	(Z)	(Z)	14	3	2	2
AZ	3,665	2,963	111	204	203	(Z)	(Z)	55	14	8	6
UT	1,723	1,616	12	24	24	(Z)	(Z)	33	5	2	7
NV	1,202	1,013	79	20	19	(Z)	(Z)	38	7	12	4
Pac	39,127	28,255	2,454	453	387	49	16	3,831	823	960	609
WA	4,867	4,309	150	81	78	2	2	211	34	44	34
OR	2,842	2,637	46	38	37	1	1	69	14	7	12
CA	29,760	20,524	2,209	242	236	3	4	2,846	705	732	313
AK	550	415	22	86	31	44	10	20	1	8	2
HI	1,108	370	27	5	5	(Z)	(Z)	685	69	169	247

Z Less than 500.   [1] Includes other races, not shown separately.   [2] Includes other Asian and Pacific Islander races not shown separately.

and Hispanic Origin—States: 1990

As of **April 1**]

ASIAN, PACIFIC ISLANDER-Con.						HISPANIC ORIGIN [3]					REGION, DIVISION, AND STATE
Asian Indian	Korean	Viet-nam-ese	Hawaiian	Samoan	Guama-nian	Total	Mexican	Puerto Rican	Cuban	Other Hispanic	
815	799	615	211	63	49	22,354	13,496	2,728	1,044	5,086	**U.S.**
285	182	61	4	2	4	3,754	175	1,872	184	1,524	**Northeast**
36	21	22	1	(Z)	1	568	29	316	16	207	**N.E**
1	1	1	(Z)	(Z)	(Z)	7	2	1	(Z)	3	ME
2	2	1	(Z)	(Z)	(Z)	11	2	3	1	5	NH
1	1	(Z)	(Z)	(Z)	(Z)	4	1	1	(Z)	2	VT
20	12	15	1	(Z)	(Z)	288	13	151	8	116	MA
2	1	1	(Z)	(Z)	(Z)	46	2	13	1	29	RI
12	5	4	(Z)	(Z)	(Z)	213	8	147	6	51	CT
249	161	39	3	1	3	3,186	146	1,556	167	1,317	**M.A**
141	96	16	1	1	2	2,214	93	1,087	74	960	NY
79	39	7	1	(Z)	1	740	29	320	85	306	NJ
28	27	16	1	(Z)	(Z)	232	24	149	7	52	PA
146	109	52	6	2	3	1,727	1,153	258	37	279	**Midwest**
123	80	26	3	1	2	1,438	944	244	30	220	**E.N.C**
21	11	5	1	(Z)	(Z)	140	58	46	4	32	OH
7	5	2	1	(Z)	(Z)	99	67	14	2	16	IN
64	42	10	1	(Z)	1	904	624	146	18	116	IL
24	16	6	1	(Z)	(Z)	202	138	19	5	40	MI
7	6	2	(Z)	(Z)	(Z)	93	58	19	2	15	WI
23	29	26	2	1	1	289	209	14	6	60	**W.N.C**
8	12	9	(Z)	(Z)	(Z)	54	35	3	2	14	MN
3	5	3	(Z)	(Z)	(Z)	33	24	1	(Z)	7	IA
6	6	4	1	1	(Z)	62	38	4	2	17	MO
(Z)	1	(Z)	(Z)	(Z)	(Z)	5	3	(Z)	(Z)	1	ND
(Z)	1	(Z)	(Z)	(Z)	(Z)	5	3	(Z)	(Z)	1	SD
1	2	2	(Z)	(Z)	(Z)	37	30	1	(Z)	6	NE
4	4	7	(Z)	(Z)	(Z)	94	76	4	1	13	KS
196	153	169	12	4	8	6,767	4,344	406	735	1,282	**South**
114	101	62	7	2	5	2,133	315	338	702	778	**S.A**
2	1	(Z)	(Z)	(Z)	(Z)	16	3	8	1	4	DE
28	30	9	1	(Z)	1	125	18	18	6	83	MD
2	1	1	(Z)	(Z)	(Z)	33	3	2	1	26	DC
20	30	21	1	(Z)	1	160	33	24	6	97	VA
2	1	(Z)	(Z)	(Z)	(Z)	8	3	1	(Z)	5	WV
10	7	5	1	(Z)	1	77	33	15	4	26	NC
4	3	2	(Z)	(Z)	(Z)	31	11	6	2	11	SC
14	15	8	1	(Z)	1	109	49	17	8	34	GA
31	12	16	2	1	1	1,574	161	247	674	492	FL
15	12	10	1	(Z)	1	95	39	13	5	39	**E.S.C**
3	3	2	(Z)	(Z)	(Z)	22	9	4	1	9	KY
6	5	2	1	(Z)	(Z)	33	14	4	2	13	TN
4	3	2	(Z)	(Z)	(Z)	25	10	4	1	10	AL
2	1	4	(Z)	(Z)	(Z)	16	7	1	(Z)	7	MS
67	40	97	4	1	3	4,539	3,990	55	28	466	**W.S.C**
1	1	2	(Z)	(Z)	(Z)	20	12	1	(Z)	6	AR
5	3	18	(Z)	(Z)	(Z)	93	23	6	9	55	LA
5	5	7	1	(Z)	(Z)	86	63	5	1	17	OK
56	32	70	3	1	2	4,340	3,891	43	18	388	TX
189	355	334	189	55	34	10,106	7,824	192	88	2,002	**West**
15	28	20	7	3	2	1,992	1,440	26	12	514	**Mt**
(Z)	1	(Z)	(Z)	(Z)	(Z)	12	8	(Z)	(Z)	3	MT
(Z)	1	1	(Z)	(Z)	(Z)	53	43	1	(Z)	9	ID
(Z)	(Z)	(Z)	(Z)	(Z)	(Z)	26	19	(Z)	(Z)	7	WY
4	11	7	1	(Z)	1	424	282	7	2	133	CO
2	1	1	(Z)	(Z)	(Z)	579	329	3	1	247	NM
6	6	5	2	(Z)	1	688	616	8	2	62	AZ
2	3	3	1	2	(Z)	85	57	2	(Z)	25	UT
2	4	2	2	(Z)	(Z)	124	85	4	6	29	NV
173	327	314	182	52	32	8,114	6,384	166	76	1,488	**Pac**
8	30	19	5	4	4	215	156	9	2	47	WA
4	9	9	2	1	1	113	86	3	1	23	OR
160	260	280	34	32	25	7.688	6.119	126	72	1,371	CA
(Z)	4	1	1	1	(Z)	18	9	2	(Z)	6	AK
1	24	5	139	15	2	81	14	26	1	41	HI

[3] Persons of Hispanic origin may be of any race.

U.S. Bureau of the Census, press release CB91-215.

No. 27. Resident Population, by Age and State: 1991

[In thousands, except percent. As of July 1. Includes Armed Forces stationed in area. See text, section 1 for basis of estimates. For explanation of methodology, contact source. See *Historical Statistics, Colonial Times to 1970*, series A 204-209 for decennial census data]

REGION, DIVISION, AND STATE	Total	Under 5 years	5 to 17 years	18 to 24 years	25 to 34 years	35 to 44 years	45 to 54 years	55 to 64 years	65 to 74 years	75 to 84 years	85 years and over	16 years and over	Percent 65 years and over
U.S. . . .	252,177	19,222	45,923	26,385	42,876	39,273	25,739	21,005	18,280	10,314	3,160	193,754	12.6
Northeast .	50,976	3,672	8,470	5,252	8,636	7,962	5,381	4,560	4,027	2,297	719	40,101	13.8
N.E.	13,197	951	2,153	1,410	2,313	2,104	1,366	1,112	1,004	587	197	10,409	13.6
ME . . .	1,235	86	224	123	200	201	127	107	93	55	19	957	13.4
NH . . .	1,105	85	195	112	197	188	114	86	73	41	14	852	11.6
VT. . . .	567	42	103	63	92	96	59	45	37	22	8	436	11.9
MA . . .	5,996	431	943	669	1,083	940	606	500	459	272	93	4,761	13.7
RI . . .	1,004	70	160	116	170	153	98	86	86	50	16	798	15.1
CT. . . .	3,291	237	527	327	571	526	362	289	256	147	48	2,605	13.7
M.A	37,779	2,721	6,317	3,842	6,323	5,858	4,016	3,448	3,023	1,711	522	29,692	13.9
NY. . . .	18,058	1,340	3,026	1,884	3,108	2,801	1,931	1,612	1,337	771	248	14,146	13.1
NJ. . . .	7,760	565	1,277	747	1,337	1,234	854	705	610	334	97	6,113	13.4
PA. . . .	11,961	816	2,014	1,211	1,878	1,823	1,231	1,131	1,077	605	176	9,433	15.5
Midwest. . .	60,225	4,487	11,327	6,202	9,895	9,248	6,103	5,106	4,415	2,584	858	46,061	13.0
E.N.C . . .	42,414	3,167	7,910	4,430	7,011	6,555	4,350	3,614	3,087	1,742	550	32,507	12.7
OH . . .	10,939	796	2,023	1,129	1,768	1,690	1,130	969	837	454	141	8,421	13.1
IN	5,610	406	1,059	609	906	859	582	480	407	228	73	4,305	12.6
IL	11,543	887	2,111	1,193	1,977	1,777	1,184	967	821	478	150	8,855	12.5
MI	9,368	717	1,767	994	1,546	1,466	963	784	662	357	110	7,147	12.1
WI	4,955	362	949	505	813	763	490	413	360	225	76	3,779	13.3
W.N.C . . .	17,811	1,320	3,417	1,772	2,884	2,693	1,754	1,493	1,328	843	307	13,554	13.9
MN . . .	4,432	338	851	433	768	702	440	344	297	188	70	3,359	12.5
IA	2,795	193	532	283	419	413	276	247	228	147	56	2,146	15.4
MO . . .	5,158	378	962	511	836	765	528	451	397	245	83	3,956	14.1
ND . . .	635	46	127	67	100	94	57	52	47	33	11	479	14.5
SD. . . .	703	54	146	69	107	101	63	59	55	35	14	523	14.7
NE. . . .	1,593	120	315	156	251	240	151	134	118	77	30	1,202	14.1
KS. . . .	2,495	190	482	252	403	378	238	205	186	117	43	1,889	13.9
South	86,916	6,526	15,978	9,250	14,661	13,356	8,904	7,300	6,356	3,557	1,029	66,800	12.6
S.A.	44,421	3,231	7,588	4,654	7,567	6,904	4,649	3,851	3,510	1,929	536	34,738	13.5
DE. . . .	680	51	117	75	120	104	70	60	51	25	7	528	12.2
MD . . .	4,860	377	824	487	898	810	537	398	320	162	48	3,775	10.9
DC. . . .	598	43	78	76	120	95	61	49	44	26	8	488	12.8
VA. . . .	6,286	461	1,078	704	1,139	1,033	684	505	409	211	62	4,907	10.9
WV . . .	1,801	106	331	187	256	282	193	174	156	89	26	1,418	15.1
NC . . .	6,737	485	1,158	776	1,140	1,050	713	589	492	261	73	5,274	12.3
SC. . . .	3,560	270	668	411	594	549	366	295	251	124	32	2,724	11.4
GA . . .	6,623	523	1,252	736	1,181	1,065	692	506	393	215	60	5,036	10.1
FL. . . .	13,277	915	2,083	1,202	2,120	1,916	1,333	1,276	1,395	817	221	10,587	18.3
E.S.C . . .	15,347	1,099	2,912	1,677	2,450	2,322	1,600	1,335	1,114	647	192	11,789	12.7
KY. . . .	3,713	256	703	401	602	571	389	321	270	154	47	2,863	12.7
TN. . . .	4,953	346	884	530	812	776	538	437	362	207	61	3,860	12.7
AL. . . .	4,089	295	776	447	644	610	425	363	303	176	50	3,140	12.9
MS . . .	2,592	202	549	299	393	364	249	213	180	110	33	1,925	12.4
W.S.C . . .	27,148	2,196	5,478	2,920	4,643	4,130	2,654	2,114	1,731	981	301	20,272	11.1
AR. . . .	2,372	170	456	241	354	340	246	212	196	121	36	1,816	14.9
LA. . . .	4,252	339	894	465	697	634	411	338	277	153	45	3,146	11.2
OK . . .	3,175	230	615	326	500	473	326	275	238	144	47	2,420	13.5
TX. . . .	17,349	1,457	3,512	1,888	3,091	2,684	1,671	1,289	1,021	563	172	12,889	10.1
West	54,060	4,538	10,149	5,681	9,684	8,707	5,351	4,039	3,482	1,875	554	40,791	10.9
Mt	14,035	1,149	2,844	1,430	2,356	2,217	1,378	1,080	941	500	139	10,440	11.3
MT . . .	808	59	165	72	119	133	84	68	61	36	11	609	13.4
ID . . .	1,039	82	236	103	152	160	102	79	71	42	12	755	12.0
WY . . .	460	34	102	44	72	78	46	35	28	15	5	338	10.6
CO . . .	3,377	258	625	338	607	602	351	255	200	106	34	2,580	10.1
NM . . .	1,548	130	328	154	254	240	151	122	100	54	15	1,136	10.9
AZ. . . .	3,750	310	700	390	637	557	358	301	298	159	40	2,840	13.2
UT. . . .	1,770	174	468	208	278	238	142	107	91	50	14	1,191	8.8
NV. . . .	1,284	101	220	121	238	209	144	112	93	38	8	992	10.8
Pac	40,025	3,388	7,305	4,251	7,328	6,490	3,973	2,959	2,540	1,376	415	30,351	10.8
WA . . .	5,018	383	932	489	859	856	526	383	341	190	58	3,832	11.8
OR . . .	2,922	209	539	273	452	501	311	235	228	133	40	2,251	13.7
CA. . . .	30,380	2,651	5,512	3,312	5,704	4,835	2,965	2,214	1,874	1,009	305	22,988	10.5
AK. . . .	570	57	123	56	112	110	57	31	16	6	1	406	4.2
HI	1,135	89	199	120	201	187	114	94	81	38	11	875	11.4

Source: U.S. Bureau of the Census, *Current Population Reports*, series P-25, forthcoming report.

No. 28. Urban and Rural Population, Housing Units, and Land Area: 1970 to 1990

[As of **April** 1. Total land area for the United States varies based on updated information and differences in measuring methods]

YEAR	Population (1,000)	Housing units (1,000)	Land area (1,000 sq. miles)	PERCENT DISTRIBUTION Population	PERCENT DISTRIBUTION Housing units	PERCENT DISTRIBUTION Land area
1970, total.	[1]203,302	[1]68,221	3,537	100.0	100.0	100.0
Urban.	149,647	50,143	54	73.6	73.0	1.5
Rural	53,565	18,536	3,483	26.4	27.0	98.5
1980, total.	[1]226,542	[1]88,411	3,539	100.0	100.0	100.0
Urban.	167,051	64,939	74	73.7	73.5	2.1
Rural	59,495	23,472	3,465	26.3	26.5	97.9
1990, total.	248,710	102,264	3,536	100.0	100.0	100.0
Urban.	187,053	76,212	87	75.2	74.5	2.5
Rural	61,656	26,052	3,449	24.8	25.5	97.5

[1] Total population and housing counts have been revised since the 1970 and 1980 census publications. Urban and rural numbers have not been corrected.

Source: U.S. Bureau of the Census, press release CB91-334.

No. 29. Urban and Rural Population—States: 1990

[**In thousands, except percent.** As of **April 1**. Resident population]

REGION, DIVISION, AND STATE	Total	URBAN Number	URBAN Percent	Rural	REGION, DIVISION, AND STATE	Total	URBAN Number	URBAN Percent	Rural
U.S.	248,710	187,053	75.2	61,656	DC.	607	607	100.0	-
					VA.	6,187	4,293	69.4	1,894
Northeast	50,809	40,092	78.9	10,717	WV	1,793	648	36.1	1,145
N.E.	13,207	9,829	74.4	3,378	NC	6,629	3,338	50.4	3,291
ME	1,228	548	44.6	680	SC.	3,487	1,905	54.6	1,581
NH	1,109	566	51.0	544	GA	6,478	4,097	63.2	2,381
VT.	563	181	32.2	382	FL.	12,938	10,967	84.8	1,971
MA	6,016	5,070	84.3	947	E.S.C	15,176	8,531	56.2	6,646
RI	1,003	863	86.0	140	KY.	3,685	1,910	51.8	1,775
CT.	3,287	2,602	79.1	686	TN.	4,877	2,970	60.9	1,907
M.A	37,602	30,263	80.5	7,340	AL.	4,041	2,440	60.4	1,601
NY.	17,990	15,164	84.3	2,826	MS	2,573	1,211	47.1	1,362
NJ.	7,730	6,910	89.4	820	W.S.C.	26,703	19,894	74.5	6,808
PA.	11,882	8,188	68.9	3,693	AR.	2,351	1,258	53.5	1,093
Midwest.	59,669	42,774	71.7	16,894	LA.	4,220	2,872	68.1	1,348
E.N.C	42,009	31,074	74.0	10,935	OK	3,146	2,130	67.7	1,015
OH	10,847	8,039	74.1	2,808	TX.	16,987	13,635	80.3	3,352
IN	5,544	3,598	64.9	1,946	West	52,786	45,531	86.3	7,255
IL	11,431	9,669	84.6	1,762	Mt	13,659	10,881	79.7	2,777
MI	9,295	6,556	70.5	2,739	MT	799	420	52.5	379
WI	4,892	3,212	65.7	1,680	ID	1,007	578	57.4	429
W.N.C.	17,660	11,700	66.3	5,959	WY	454	295	65.0	159
MN	4,375	3,056	69.9	1,319	CO	3,294	2,716	82.4	579
IA	2,777	1,683	60.6	1,094	NM	1,515	1,106	73.0	409
MO	5,117	3,516	68.7	1,601	AZ.	3,665	3,207	87.5	458
ND	639	340	53.3	298	UT.	1,723	1,499	87.0	224
SD.	696	348	50.0	348	NV.	1,202	1,061	88.3	140
NE.	1,578	,1,044	66.1	534	Pac	39,127	34,650	88.6	4,477
KS.	2,478	1,713	69.1	765	WA	4,867	3,718	76.4	1,149
South	85,446	58,656	68.6	26,790	OR	2,842	2,003	70.5	839
S.A.	43,567	30,231	69.4	13,336	CA.	29,760	27,571	92.6	2,189
DE.	666	487	73.0	180	AK.	550	371	67.5	179
MD	4,781	3,888	81.3	893	HI	1,108	986	89.0	122

- Represents zero.

Source: U.S. Bureau of the Census, press release CB91-334.

No. 30. Metropolitan and Nonmetropolitan Area Population: 1960 to 1990

[Metropolitan areas are as defined by U. S. Office of Management and Budget as of year shown, except as noted. See headnote, table 31]

ITEM	1960	1970	1980 [1] (SMSA's)	MSA's AND CMSA's [2] 1980	MSA's AND CMSA's [2] 1990
Metropolitan areas: Number of areas	212	243	318	284	284
Population (1,000)	112,885	139,480	169,431	172,678	192,726
Percent change over previous year shown . .	[3]33.0	23.6	21.5	(X)	11.6
Percent of total U.S. population.	63.0	68.6	74.8	76.2	77.5
Land area, percent of U.S. land area.	8.7	10.9	16.0	16.4	16.4
Nonmetropolitan areas, population (1,000)	66,438	63,822	57,115	53,864	55,984

X Not applicable.   [1] SMSA=standard metropolitan statistical area. Areas are as defined June 30, 1981.   [2] Areas are as defined June 30, 1990.   [3] Percent change from 1950.

Source: U.S. Bureau of the Census, *U.S. Census of Population: 1960* and *1970; 1980 Census of Population*, vol. 1, chapter A (PC80-1-A) and *Supplementary Report, Metropolitan Statistical Areas* (PC80-S1-18); and press release CB91-66.

No. 31. Number and Population of Metropolitan Areas, by Population Size-Class in 1990: 1970 to 1990

[As of **April 1**. Data exclude Puerto Rico. CMSA=consolidated metropolitan statistical area. MSA=metropolitan statistical area. PMSA=primary metropolitan statistical area. Areas are as defined by U.S. Office of Management and Budget, June 30, 1990. For definitions, see Appendix II. See also *Historical Statistics, Colonial Times to 1970*, series A 264-275]

LEVEL AND POPULATION SIZE-CLASS OF METROPOLITAN AREA IN 1990	CMSA's AND MSA's Number, 1990	CMSA's AND MSA's Population, 1970 (mil.)	CMSA's AND MSA's Population, 1980 (mil.)	CMSA's AND MSA's Population, 1990 Total (mil.)	CMSA's AND MSA's Population, 1990 Percent in each class	MSA's AND PMSA's Number, 1990	MSA's AND PMSA's Population, 1990 Total (mil.)	MSA's AND PMSA's Population, 1990 Percent in each class
Total, all metropolitan areas . . .	284	156.1	172.7	192.7	100	335	192.7	100
Level A (1,000,000 or more).	39	103.0	111.3	124.8	65	46	109.2	57
2,500,000 or more.	14	71.2	75.7	84.5	44	12	53.4	28
1,000,000 to 2,499,999	25	31.8	35.6	40.2	21	34	55.7	29
Level B (250,000 to 999,999)	95	35.8	41.4	46.4	24	120	58.7	31
500,000 to 999,999	34	19.0	22.0	24.9	13	45	32.4	17
250,000 to 499,999	61	16.8	19.4	21.5	11	75	26.3	14
Level C (100,000 to 249,999)	125	15.5	17.8	19.4	10	142	22.5	12
Level D (less than 100,000)	25	1.9	2.1	2.1	1	27	2.3	1

Source: U.S. Bureau of the Census, *1980 Census of Population, Supplementary Report, Metropolitan Statistical Areas* (PC80-S1-18); and press release CB91-66.

No. 32. Resident Population in Counties Within 50 Miles of Coastal Shorelines: 1960 to 1990

[Enumerated population as of **April 1**. Excludes Alaska and Hawaii. Covers 611 counties and independent cities which are entirely or substantially within 50 miles of U.S. coastal shorelines. Great Lakes region includes St. Lawrence River]

YEAR	Conterminous U.S., total	COUNTIES IN COASTAL REGIONS Total	COUNTIES IN COASTAL REGIONS Atlantic	COUNTIES IN COASTAL REGIONS Pacific	COUNTIES IN COASTAL REGIONS Great Lakes	COUNTIES IN COASTAL REGIONS Gulf of Mexico	Balance of conterminous U.S.
Land area, 1980 (1,000 sq. mi.)	2,962	467	122	118	134	94	2,495
POPULATION							
1960 (mil.).	178.5	92.7	41.7	16.8	26.4	7.8	85.7
1970 (mil.).	202.2	108.5	48.2	21.5	29.3	9.5	93.8
1980 (mil.).	225.2	118.4	50.7	25.4	29.8	12.6	106.7
1990 (mil.).	247.2	132.1	55.9	31.5	29.9	14.8	115.1
1960 (percent).	100	52	23	9	15	4	48
1970 (percent).	100	54	24	11	15	5	46
1980 (percent).	100	53	23	11	13	6	47
1990 (percent).	100	53	23	13	12	6	47

Source: U.S. Bureau of the Census, *U.S. Census of Population: 1960* and *1970; 1980 Census of Population*, vol. 1, chapter A (PC80-1-A-1), *U.S. Summary*, and *1990 Census of Population and Housing* (CPH1).

No. 33. Metropolitan and Nonmetropolitan Population—States: 1980 and 1990

[As of **April 1**. Excludes Armed Forces abroad. Metropolitan refers to 264 metropolitan statistical areas and 20 consolidated metropolitan statistical areas as defined by U.S. Office of Management and Budget, June 30, 1990; nonmetropolitan is the area outside metropolitan areas; see Appendix II. Minus sign (-) indicates decrease]

REGION, DIVISION, AND STATE	METRO Total (1,000) 1980	1990	Net change 1980-90 Number (1,000)	Percent	Pct of State 1980	1990	NONMETRO Total (1,000) 1980	1990	Net change 1980-90 Number (1,000)	Percent	Pct of State 1980	1990
U.S.	172,678	192,726	20,047	11.6	76.2	77.5	53,864	55,984	2,120	3.9	23.8	22.5
Northeast	43,439	44,791	1,352	3.1	88.4	88.2	5,698	6,018	320	5.6	11.6	11.8
N.E	10,020	10,598	579	5.8	81.1	80.2	2,329	2,609	280	12.0	18.9	19.8
ME	405	441	36	9.0	36.0	35.9	720	787	66	9.2	64.0	64.1
NH	511	622	111	21.8	55.5	56.1	410	487	77	18.9	44.5	43.9
VT	115	131	16	14.0	22.5	23.4	396	431	35	8.9	77.5	76.6
MA	5,231	5,438	207	3.9	91.2	90.4	506	578	73	14.4	8.8	9.6
RI	878	928	50	5.7	92.7	92.5	69	75	6	9.4	7.3	7.5
CT	2,879	3,038	158	5.5	92.7	92.4	228	250	21	9.3	7.3	7.6
M.A	33,420	34,193	773	2.3	90.8	90.9	3,368	3,409	41	1.2	9.2	9.1
NY	16,016	16,386	370	2.3	91.2	91.1	1,542	1,605	63	4.1	8.8	8.9
NJ	7,365	7,730	365	5.0	100.0	100.0	(X)	(X)	(X)	(X)	(X)	(X)
PA	10,038	10,077	39	0.4	84.6	84.8	1,826	1,805	-22	-1.2	15.4	15.2
Midwest	41,581	42,689	1,108	2.7	70.6	71.5	17,286	16,980	-306	-1.8	29.4	28.5
E.N.C	32,204	32,557	353	1.1	77.3	77.5	9,479	9,452	-27	-0.3	22.7	22.5
OH	8,521	8,567	47	0.5	78.9	79.0	2,277	2,280	3	0.1	21.1	21.0
IN	3,719	3,796	77	2.1	67.7	68.5	1,771	1,748	-23	-1.3	32.3	31.5
IL	9,340	9,450	110	1.2	81.7	82.7	2,088	1,981	-107	-5.1	18.3	17.3
MI	7,480	7,446	-35	-0.5	80.8	80.1	1,782	1,850	68	3.8	19.2	19.9
WI	3,145	3,298	154	4.9	66.8	67.4	1,561	1,593	32	2.1	33.2	32.6
W.N.C	9,376	10,132	755	8.1	54.6	57.4	7,808	7,528	-280	-3.6	45.4	42.6
MN	2,621	2,960	339	12.9	64.3	67.7	1,455	1,415	-40	-2.8	35.7	32.3
IA	1,223	1,223	(-Z)	(-Z)	42.0	44.0	1,691	1,554	-137	-8.1	58.0	56.0
MO	3,226	3,387	161	5.0	65.6	66.2	1,690	1,730	39	2.3	34.4	33.8
ND	234	257	23	9.8	35.9	40.3	418	381	-37	-8.8	64.1	59.7
SD	180	205	25	14.1	26.0	29.5	511	491	-20	-3.9	74.0	70.5
NE	708	766	58	8.2	45.1	48.5	862	812	-49	-5.7	54.9	51.5
KS	1,184	1,333	149	12.6	50.1	53.8	1,180	1,145	-36	-3.0	49.9	46.2
South	51,606	60,588	8,982	17.4	68.5	70.9	23,761	24,858	1,097	4.6	31.5	29.1
S.A	26,777	32,461	5,684	21.2	72.5	74.5	10,181	11,106	925	9.1	27.5	25.5
DE	398	442	44	11.0	67.0	66.3	196	224	28	14.3	33.0	33.7
MD	3,920	4,439	519	13.2	93.0	92.8	297	343	46	15.3	7.0	7.2
DC	638	607	-32	-4.9	100.0	100.0	(X)	(X)	(X)	(X)	(X)	(X)
VA	3,745	4,483	738	19.7	70.1	72.5	1,601	1,704	103	6.4	29.9	27.5
WV	718	653	-65	-9.1	36.8	36.4	1,232	1,140	-91	-7.4	63.2	63.6
NC	3,203	3,758	554	17.3	54.5	56.7	2,677	2,871	194	7.3	45.5	43.3
SC	1,866	2,113	247	13.2	59.8	60.6	1,254	1,374	119	9.5	40.2	39.4
GA	3,403	4,212	809	23.8	62.3	65.0	2,060	2,266	206	10.0	37.7	35.0
FL	8,884	11,754	2,870	32.3	91.2	90.8	863	1,184	321	37.3	8.8	9.2
E.S.C	8,023	8,513	490	6.1	54.7	56.1	6,643	6,663	21	0.3	45.3	43.9
KY	1,676	1,714	38	2.2	45.8	46.5	1,984	1,971	-13	-0.6	54.2	53.5
TN	3,048	3,300	252	8.3	66.4	67.7	1,543	1,577	34	2.2	33.6	32.3
AL	2,583	2,723	140	5.4	66.3	67.4	1,311	1,317	6	0.5	33.7	32.6
MS	716	776	60	8.3	28.4	30.1	1,805	1,798	-7	-0.4	71.6	69.9
W.S.C	16,806	19,614	2,808	16.7	70.8	73.5	6,937	7,089	151	2.2	29.2	26.5
AR	885	943	57	6.5	38.7	40.1	1,401	1,408	7	0.5	61.3	59.9
LA	2,893	2,935	42	1.5	68.8	69.5	1,313	1,285	-28	-2.1	31.2	30.5
OK	1,724	1,870	146	8.4	57.0	59.4	1,301	1,276	-26	-2.0	43.0	40.6
TX	11,304	13,867	2,563	22.7	79.5	81.6	2,921	3,119	198	6.8	20.5	18.4
West	36,052	44,658	8,606	23.9	83.5	84.6	7,119	8,128	1,009	14.2	16.5	15.4
Mt	7,340	9,179	1,838	25.0	64.6	67.2	4,031	4,480	449	11.1	35.4	32.8
MT	189	191	2	1.3	24.0	23.9	598	608	10	1.7	76.0	76.1
ID	173	206	33	18.9	18.3	20.4	771	801	30	3.9	81.7	79.6
WY	141	134	-6	-4.4	29.9	29.6	329	319	-10	-3.0	70.1	70.4
CO	2,326	2,686	360	15.5	80.5	81.5	563	608	45	8.0	19.5	18.5
NM	610	733	123	20.2	46.8	48.4	694	782	88	12.7	53.2	51.6
AZ	2,117	2,896	779	36.8	77.9	79.0	600	769	170	28.3	22.1	21.0
UT	1,128	1,336	207	18.4	77.2	77.5	333	387	54	16.3	22.8	22.5
NV	657	996	339	51.7	82.0	82.9	144	206	62	43.1	18.0	17.1
Pac	28,712	35,479	6,768	23.6	90.3	90.7	3,088	3,648	560	18.1	9.7	9.3
WA	3,322	3,976	654	19.7	80.4	81.7	810	891	81	10.0	19.6	18.3
OR	1,763	1,947	184	10.4	67.0	68.5	870	895	25	2.9	33.0	31.5
CA	22,689	28,493	5,805	25.6	95.9	95.7	979	1,267	288	29.4	4.1	4.3
AK	174	226	52	29.8	43.4	41.1	227	324	96	42.3	56.6	58.9
HI	763	836	74	9.7	79.0	75.5	202	272	70	34.6	21.0	24.5

X Not applicable.   Z Less than 500 or .05 percent.

Source: U.S. Bureau of the Census, unpublished data.

Population

No. 34. Metropolitan Areas—Population: 1970 to 1990

[As of **April 1**. Covers 20 consolidated metropolitan statistical areas (CMSA's), their 71 component primary metropolitan statistical areas (PMSA's), and the remaining 114 MSA's with 250,000 and over population in 1990 as defined by the U.S. Office of Management and Budget as of June 30, 1990. Figures for 1970 include corrections. Rank based on unrounded figures for CMSA's and MSA's only. For definitions and components of all MSA's and population of NECMA's (New England County Metropolitan Areas), see Appendix II. Minus sign (-) indicates decrease]

METROPOLITAN AREA	1970, total (1,000)	1980, total (1,000)	1990 Total (1,000)	1990 Rank	1990 Under 18 yrs. old (per-cent)	1990 65 yrs. old and over (per-cent)	PERCENT CHANGE 1970-80	PERCENT CHANGE 1980-90
Albany-Schenectady-Troy, NY MSA	811	836	874	48	23.3	14.2	3.1	4.6
Albuquerque, NM MSA	316	420	481	77	26.1	10.5	33.1	14.4
Allentown-Bethlehem-Easton, PA-NJ MSA	594	635	687	58	23.1	15.2	6.9	8.1
Appleton-Oshkosh-Neenah, WI MSA	277	291	315	114	26.7	11.9	5.2	8.2
Atlanta, GA MSA	1,684	2,138	2,834	12	25.9	7.9	27.0	32.5
Atlantic City, NJ MSA	235	276	319	112	22.7	16.2	17.8	15.6
Augusta, GA-SC MSA	291	346	397	91	27.9	9.9	18.8	14.7
Austin, TX MSA	360	537	782	52	25.3	7.4	48.9	45.6
Bakersfield, CA MSA	330	403	543	68	31.5	9.7	22.1	34.8
Baltimore, MD MSA	2,089	2,199	2,382	18	24.1	11.7	5.3	8.3
Baton Rouge, LA MSA	376	494	528	71	28.6	8.9	31.6	6.9
Beaumont-Port Arthur, TX MSA	348	373	361	102	27.6	13.1	7.4	-3.2
Binghamton, NY MSA	268	263	264	127	24.0	14.2	-1.8	0.4
Birmingham, AL MSA	794	884	908	46	25.4	13.2	11.3	2.7
Boston-Lawrence-Salem, MA-NH CMSA	3,939	3,972	4,172	7	22.2	12.4	0.8	5.0
Boston, MA PMSA	2,887	2,806	2,871	(X)	20.8	12.9	-2.8	2.3
Brockton, MA PMSA	163	183	189	(X)	25.5	11.3	12.4	3.6
Lawrence-Haverhill, MA-NH PMSA	301	339	394	(X)	26.4	11.6	12.7	16.1
Lowell, MA-NH PMSA	225	243	273	(X)	26.0	9.7	7.8	12.3
Nashua, NH PMSA	100	143	181	(X)	26.9	7.9	42.5	26.7
Salem-Gloucester, MA PMSA	263	258	264	(X)	21.0	14.9	-1.7	2.4
Brownsville-Harlingen, TX MSA	140	210	260	129	35.3	10.6	49.4	24.0
Buffalo-Niagara Falls, NY CMSA	1,349	1,243	1,189	33	23.6	15.2	-7.9	-4.3
Buffalo, NY PMSA	1,113	1,015	969	(X)	23.3	15.2	-8.8	-4.6
Niagara Falls, NY PMSA	236	227	221	(X)	24.9	15.2	-3.5	-2.9
Canton, OH MSA	394	404	394	93	25.3	14.4	2.7	-2.6
Charleston, SC MSA	336	430	507	73	27.6	8.6	28.1	17.8
Charleston, WV MSA	257	270	250	134	23.8	14.9	4.8	-7.1
Charlotte-Gastonia-Rock Hill, NC-SC MSA	840	971	1,162	34	24.7	10.9	15.6	19.6
Chattanooga, TN-GA MSA	371	426	433	82	24.8	13.0	15.0	1.6
Chicago-Gary-Lake County, IL-IN-WI CMSA	7,779	7,937	8,066	3	26.1	11.4	2.0	1.6
Aurora-Elgin, IL PMSA	277	316	357	(X)	29.8	9.2	13.8	13.1
Chicago, IL PMSA	6,093	6,060	6,070	(X)	25.4	11.8	-0.5	0.2
Gary-Hammond, IN PMSA	633	643	605	(X)	27.9	11.8	1.5	-5.9
Joliet, IL PMSA	274	355	390	(X)	29.6	9.0	29.4	9.7
Kenosha, WI PMSA	118	123	128	(X)	26.8	12.6	4.4	4.1
Lake County, IL PMSA	383	440	516	(X)	27.6	8.4	15.1	17.3
Cincinnati-Hamilton, OH-KY-IN CMSA	1,613	1,660	1,744	23	26.7	11.8	2.9	5.1
Cincinnati, OH-KY-IN PMSA	1,387	1,401	1,453	(X)	26.8	12.1	1.0	3.7
Hamilton-Middletown, OH PMSA	226	259	291	(X)	26.2	10.2	14.4	12.6
Cleveland-Akron-Lorain, OH CMSA	3,000	2,834	2,760	13	24.8	13.9	-5.5	-2.6
Akron, OH PMSA	679	660	658	(X)	24.4	12.9	-2.8	-0.4
Cleveland, OH PMSA	2,064	1,899	1,831	(X)	24.6	14.6	-8.0	-3.6
Lorain-Elyria, OH PMSA	257	275	271	(X)	27.4	11.6	7.0	-1.4
Colorado Springs, CO MSA	236	309	397	90	27.6	8.0	31.1	28.3
Columbia, SC MSA	323	410	453	79	25.0	9.3	27.0	10.6
Columbus, OH MSA	1,149	1,244	1,377	29	25.1	10.0	8.2	10.7
Corpus Christi, TX MSA	285	326	350	105	30.8	10.2	14.5	7.3
Dallas-Fort Worth, TX CMSA	2,352	2,931	3,885	9	27.3	8.0	24.6	32.6
Dallas, TX PMSA	1,556	1,957	2,553	(X)	27.2	7.7	25.8	30.4
Fort Worth-Arlington, TX PMSA	795	973	1,332	(X)	27.3	8.6	22.4	36.9
Davenport-Rock Island-Moline, IA-IL MSA	363	384	351	104	26.7	13.7	6.1	-8.8
Dayton-Springfield, OH MSA	975	942	951	44	25.3	12.4	-3.4	1.0
Daytona Beach, FL MSA	169	259	371	96	19.7	22.8	52.7	43.3
Denver-Boulder, CO CMSA	1,238	1,618	1,848	22	25.6	9.2	30.7	14.2
Boulder-Longmont, CO PMSA	132	190	225	(X)	23.0	7.6	43.8	18.8
Denver, CO PMSA	1,106	1,429	1,623	(X)	25.9	9.4	29.1	13.6
Des Moines, IA MSA	340	368	393	94	25.6	11.7	8.2	6.9
Detroit-Ann Arbor, MI CMSA	4,788	4,753	4,665	6	25.8	11.6	-0.7	-1.8
Ann Arbor, MI PMSA	234	265	283	(X)	21.6	7.5	13.1	6.9
Detroit, MI PMSA	4,554	4,488	4,382	(X)	26.1	11.8	-1.5	-2.4
El Paso, TX MSA	359	480	592	66	32.6	8.2	33.6	23.3
Erie, PA MSA	264	280	276	124	25.9	13.8	6.1	-1.5
Eugene-Springfield, OR MSA	215	275	283	119	24.5	13.1	27.8	2.8
Evansville, IN-KY MSA	255	276	279	121	25.4	14.0	8.5	1.0
Fayetteville, NC MSA	212	247	275	125	28.0	6.1	16.6	11.1
Flint, MI MSA	446	450	430	84	28.0	10.2	1.1	-4.4
Fort Myers-Cape Coral, FL MSA	105	205	335	110	19.6	24.8	95.1	63.3
Fort Pierce, FL MSA	79	151	251	133	20.9	23.6	91.7	66.1
Fort Wayne, IN MSA	335	354	364	100	27.9	11.5	5.8	2.7
Fresno, CA MSA	413	515	667	59	31.3	10.4	24.5	29.7

See footnotes at end of table.

No. 34. Metropolitan Areas—Population: 1970 to 1990—Continued

[See headnote, page 30]

METROPOLITAN AREA	1970, total (1,000)	1980, total (1,000)	1990				PERCENT CHANGE	
			Total (1,000)	Rank	Under 18 yrs. old (per-cent)	65 yrs. old and over (per-cent)	1970-80	1980-90
Grand Rapids, MI MSA.	539	602	688	57	28.6	10.5	11.6	14.4
Greensboro-Winston-Salem-High Point, NC MSA. . . .	743	851	942	45	23.0	12.2	14.6	10.6
Greenville-Spartanburg, SC MSA	473	570	641	62	24.3	12.1	20.4	12.4
Harrisburg-Lebanon-Carlisle, PA MSA	510	556	588	67	23.4	13.9	9.0	5.7
Hartford-New Britain-Middletown, CT CMSA	1,000	1,014	1,086	36	22.8	13.3	1.4	7.1
Bristol, CT PMSA	70	74	79	(X)	23.0	12.9	5.6	7.8
Hartford, CT PMSA	711	716	768	(X)	23.1	13.2	0.7	7.3
Middletown, CT PMSA	74	82	90	(X)	21.3	12.1	10.6	10.7
New Britain, CT PMSA	145	142	148	(X)	21.9	15.1	-2.1	4.2
Honolulu, HI MSA	631	763	836	51	24.5	11.1	20.9	9.7
Houston-Galveston-Brazoria, TX CMSA	2,169	3,100	3,711	10	28.9	7.3	42.9	19.7
Brazoria, TX PMSA	108	170	192	(X)	29.3	7.8	56.6	13.0
Galveston-Texas City, TX PMSA	170	196	217	(X)	27.6	10.5	15.3	11.1
Houston, TX PMSA	1,891	2,735	3,302	(X)	28.9	7.1	44.6	20.7
Huntington-Ashland, WV-KY-OH MSA	307	336	313	115	24.5	14.4	9.7	-7.1
Indianapolis, IN MSA	1,111	1,167	1,250	31	26.3	11.1	5.0	7.1
Jackson, MS MSA	289	362	395	92	28.1	10.5	25.4	9.2
Jacksonville, FL MSA	613	722	907	47	26.0	10.9	17.9	25.5
Johnson City-Kingsport-Bristol, TN-VA MSA	374	434	436	81	22.3	14.6	16.1	0.6
Kansas City, MO-KS MSA	1,373	1,433	1,566	25	26.4	11.6	4.4	9.3
Killeen-Temple, TX MSA	160	215	255	131	28.2	8.0	34.3	19.0
Knoxville, TN MSA	477	566	605	65	22.9	13.3	18.8	6.9
Lakeland-Winter Haven, FL MSA	229	322	405	87	24.1	18.6	40.8	26.0
Lancaster, PA MSA	320	362	423	85	26.5	13.1	13.2	16.7
Lansing-East Lansing, MI MSA	378	420	433	83	25.6	9.0	10.9	3.1
Las Vegas, NV MSA	273	463	741	53	24.5	10.5	69.5	60.1
Lexington-Fayette, KY MSA	267	318	348	106	23.9	10.3	19.1	9.7
Little Rock-North Little Rock, AR MSA	381	474	513	72	26.5	11.4	24.5	8.1
Los Angeles-Anaheim-Riverside, CA CMSA	9,981	11,498	14,532	2	26.6	9.8	15.2	26.4
Anaheim-Santa Ana, CA PMSA	1,421	1,933	2,411	(X)	24.4	9.2	36.0	24.7
Los Angeles-Long Beach, CA PMSA	7,042	7,477	8,863	(X)	26.2	9.7	6.2	18.5
Oxnard-Ventura, CA PMSA	378	529	669	(X)	27.4	9.4	39.8	26.4
Riverside-San Bernardino, CA PMSA	1,139	1,558	2,589	(X)	29.8	10.8	36.8	66.1
Louisville, KY-IN MSA	907	956	953	43	25.2	12.6	5.5	-0.4
Macon-Warner Robins, GA MSA	235	264	281	120	27.2	10.8	12.4	6.6
Madison, WI MSA	290	324	367	99	22.7	9.3	11.5	13.5
McAllen-Edinburg-Mission, TX MSA	182	283	384	95	36.6	10.0	56.1	35.4
Melbourne-Titusville-Palm Bay, FL MSA.	230	273	399	89	21.9	16.6	18.7	46.2
Memphis, TN-AR-MS MSA	834	913	982	41	27.8	10.3	9.5	7.5
Miami-Fort Lauderdale, FL CMSA	1,888	2,644	3,193	11	22.7	16.6	40.0	20.8
Fort Lauderdale-Hollywood-Pompano Beach, FL PMSA	620	1,018	1,255	(X)	20.4	20.8	64.2	23.3
Miami-Hialeah, FL PMSA	1,268	1,626	1,937	(X)	24.2	14.0	28.2	19.2
Milwaukee-Racine, WI CMSA.	1,575	1,570	1,607	24	26.4	12.4	-0.3	2.4
Milwaukee, WI PMSA	1,404	1,397	1,432	(X)	26.3	12.5	-0.5	2.5
Racine, WI PMSA	171	173	175	(X)	27.8	12.0	1.3	1.1
Minneapolis-St. Paul, MN-WI MSA	1,982	2,137	2,464	16	26.3	9.9	7.8	15.3
Mobile, AL MSA	377	444	477	78	28.0	12.5	17.7	7.5
Modesto, CA MSA	195	266	371	97	30.6	10.8	36.7	39.3
Montgomery, AL MSA.	226	273	293	117	27.4	11.4	20.7	7.3
Nashville, TN MSA.	699	851	985	40	25.1	10.6	21.6	15.8
New Haven-Meriden, CT MSA	489	500	530	69	22.6	14.1	2.4	5.9
New London-Norwich, CT-RI MSA	243	251	267	126	23.5	12.4	3.4	6.4
New Orleans, LA MSA	1,100	1,257	1,239	32	27.9	11.0	14.3	-1.4
New York-Northern New Jersey-Long Island, NY-NJ-CT CMSA	18,193	17,540	18,087	1	23.0	13.1	-3.6	3.1
Bergen-Passaic, NJ PMSA	1,358	1,293	1,278	(X)	21.7	14.5	-4.8	-1.1
Bridgeport-Milford, CT PMSA	444	439	444	(X)	23.2	14.7	-1.2	1.2
Danbury, CT PMSA	136	170	188	(X)	24.4	9.9	24.8	10.3
Jersey City, NJ PMSA	608	557	553	(X)	22.1	12.7	-8.4	-0.7
Middlesex-Somerset-Hunterdon, NJ PMSA	852	886	1,020	(X)	21.9	11.3	4.0	15.1
Monmouth-Ocean, NJ PMSA	670	849	986	(X)	23.6	17.3	26.7	16.1
Nassau-Suffolk, NY PMSA	2,556	2,606	2,609	(X)	23.3	12.4	2.0	0.1
New York, NY PMSA.	9,077	8,275	8,547	(X)	23.0	13.0	-8.8	3.0
Newark, NJ PMSA	1,937	1,879	1,824	(X)	23.5	12.5	-3.0	-2.9
Norwalk, CT PMSA	128	127	127	(X)	21.1	12.3	-0.7	0.5
Orange County, NY PMSA	222	260	308	(X)	27.6	10.4	17.1	18.5
Stamford, CT PMSA	206	199	203	(X)	20.8	14.1	-3.6	1.9
Norfolk-Virginia Beach-Newport News, VA MSA	1,059	1,160	1,396	28	26.4	9.0	9.6	20.3
Oklahoma City, OK MSA.	719	861	959	42	26.6	11.1	19.8	11.4

See footnotes at end of table.

Population

No. 34. Metropolitan Areas—Population: 1970 to 1990—Continued

[See headnote, page 30]

METROPOLITAN AREA	1970, total (1,000)	1980, total (1,000)	1990 Total (1,000)	1990 Rank	1990 Under 18 yrs. old (percent)	1990 65 yrs. old and over (percent)	PERCENT CHANGE 1970-80	PERCENT CHANGE 1980-90
Omaha, NE-IA MSA	556	585	618	63	27.8	10.6	5.2	5.7
Orlando, FL MSA	453	700	1,073	37	24.4	10.9	54.4	53.3
Pensacola, FL MSA	243	290	344	107	25.7	11.3	19.2	18.9
Peoria, IL MSA	342	366	339	108	26.4	13.8	7.0	-7.3
Philadelphia-Wilmington-Trenton, PA-NJ-DE-MD CMSA	5,749	5,681	5,899	5	24.3	13.3	-1.2	3.9
Philadelphia, PA-NJ PMSA	4,824	4,717	4,857	(X)	24.4	13.5	-2.2	3.0
Trenton, NJ PMSA	304	308	326	(X)	22.5	13.0	1.2	5.8
Vineland-Millville-Bridgeton, NJ PMSA	121	133	138	(X)	26.0	13.5	9.5	3.9
Wilmington, DE-NJ-MD PMSA	499	523	579	(X)	24.6	11.6	4.8	10.6
Phoenix, AZ MSA	971	1,509	2,122	20	26.2	12.5	55.4	40.6
Pittsburgh-Beaver Valley, PA CMSA	2,556	2,423	2,243	19	21.8	17.3	-5.2	-7.4
Beaver County, PA PMSA	208	204	186	(X)	23.3	16.9	-1.9	-9.0
Pittsburgh, PA PMSA	2,348	2,219	2,057	(X)	21.7	17.4	-5.5	-7.3
Portland-Vancouver, OR-WA CMSA	1,047	1,298	1,478	27	25.7	12.0	23.9	13.9
Portland, OR PMSA	919	1,106	1,240	(X)	25.1	12.2	20.3	12.1
Vancouver, WA PMSA	128	192	238	(X)	28.4	10.7	49.6	23.8
Poughkeepsie, NY MSA	222	245	259	130	23.9	11.4	10.2	5.9
Providence-Pawtucket-Fall River, RI-MA CMSA	1,065	1,083	1,142	35	22.8	15.1	1.7	5.4
Fall River, MA-RI PMSA	152	157	157	(X)	23.4	16.8	3.2	(Z)
Pawtucket-Woonsocket-Attleboro, RI-MA PMSA	301	307	329	(X)	24.1	14.2	2.2	7.2
Providence, RI PMSA	612	619	655	(X)	22.1	15.1	1.0	5.9
Provo-Orem, UT MSA	138	218	264	128	37.7	7.0	58.3	20.9
Raleigh-Durham, NC MSA	446	561	735	54	22.5	8.9	25.7	31.2
Reading, PA MSA	296	313	337	109	23.3	15.6	5.4	7.7
Reno, NV MSA	121	194	255	132	23.1	10.3	59.9	31.5
Richmond-Petersburg, VA MSA	676	761	866	49	24.3	11.3	12.6	13.7
Rochester, NY MSA	962	971	1,002	39	25.0	12.4	1.0	3.2
Rockford, IL MSA	272	280	284	118	26.4	12.6	2.7	1.5
Sacramento, CA MSA	848	1,100	1,481	26	26.2	10.8	29.8	34.7
Saginaw-Bay City-Midland, MI MSA	401	422	399	88	27.5	12.1	5.2	-5.3
St. Louis, MO-IL MSA	2,429	2,377	2,444	17	26.3	12.8	-2.2	2.8
Salem, OR MSA	187	250	278	122	26.4	14.4	33.9	11.3
Salinas-Seaside-Monterey, CA MSA	247	290	356	103	27.5	9.8	17.4	22.5
Salt Lake City-Ogden, UT MSA	684	910	1,072	38	35.5	8.4	33.1	17.8
San Antonio, TX MSA	888	1,072	1,302	30	29.0	10.3	20.7	21.5
San Diego, CA MSA	1,358	1,862	2,498	15	24.5	10.9	37.1	34.2
San Francisco-Oakland-San Jose, CA CMSA	4,754	5,368	6,253	4	23.1	11.1	12.9	16.5
Oakland, CA PMSA	1,628	1,762	2,083	(X)	24.3	10.7	8.2	18.2
San Francisco, CA PMSA	1,482	1,489	1,604	(X)	18.9	13.3	0.5	7.7
San Jose, CA PMSA	1,065	1,295	1,498	(X)	24.0	8.7	21.6	15.6
Santa Cruz, CA PMSA	124	188	230	(X)	23.8	11.3	52.0	22.1
Santa Rosa-Petaluma, CA PMSA	205	300	388	(X)	24.7	13.4	46.3	29.5
Vallejo-Fairfield-Napa, CA PMSA	251	334	451	(X)	27.4	10.2	33.2	34.9
Santa Barbara-Santa Maria-Lompoc, CA MSA	264	299	370	98	23.2	12.3	13.0	23.7
Sarasota, FL MSA	120	202	278	123	15.7	32.2	68.0	37.3
Scranton-Wilkes-Barre, PA MSA	696	729	734	55	22.3	18.2	4.7	0.7
Seattle-Tacoma, WA CMSA	1,837	2,093	2,559	14	24.6	10.7	14.0	22.3
Seattle, WA PMSA	1,425	1,608	1,973	(X)	23.8	10.7	12.8	22.7
Tacoma, WA PMSA	412	486	586	(X)	27.2	10.5	17.8	20.7
Shreveport, LA MSA	296	333	334	111	28.7	12.2	12.5	0.4
Spokane, WA MSA	287	342	361	101	26.4	13.3	18.9	5.7
Springfield, MA MSA	528	515	530	70	24.2	14.7	-2.4	2.8
Stockton, CA MSA	291	347	481	76	29.6	11.1	19.3	38.4
Syracuse, NY MSA	637	643	660	61	25.2	12.4	1.0	2.6
Tampa-St. Petersburg-Clearwater, FL MSA	1,106	1,614	2,068	21	20.4	21.6	46.0	28.2
Toledo, OH MSA	606	617	614	64	26.3	12.4	1.7	-0.4
Tucson, AZ MSA	352	531	667	60	24.9	13.7	51.1	25.5
Tulsa, OK MSA	526	657	709	56	26.8	11.6	25.0	7.9
Utica-Rome, NY MSA	340	320	317	113	24.5	15.7	-6.0	-1.1
Visalia-Tulare-Porterville, CA MSA	188	246	312	116	33.1	10.8	30.5	26.9
Washington, DC-MD-VA MSA	3,040	3,251	3,924	8	23.5	8.6	6.9	20.7
West Palm Beach-Boca Raton-Delray Beach, FL MSA	349	577	864	50	19.6	24.3	65.3	49.7
Wichita, KS MSA	417	442	485	75	27.8	11.9	6.2	9.7
Worcester, MA MSA	400	403	437	80	23.8	14.2	0.8	8.4
York, PA MSA	330	381	418	86	24.4	13.2	15.7	9.6
Youngstown-Warren, OH MSA	537	531	493	74	24.8	15.8	-1.1	-7.3

X Not applicable.   Z Less than .05 percent.

Source: U.S. Bureau of the Census, *1980 Census of Population, Supplementary Report, Metropolitan Statistical Areas*, (PC80-S1-18); press release CB91-66; and *1990 Census of Population and Housing*, Summary Tape File 1A.

No. 35. Metropolitan Areas With Large Numbers of Selected Racial Groups and of Hispanic Origin Population: 1990

[As of **April** 1. For Black, Hispanic origin, and Asian and Pacific Islander populations, areas selected had 100,000 or more of specified group; for American Indian, Eskimo, and Aleut population, areas selected are ten areas with largest number of that group. CMSA=consolidated metropolitan statistical area. MSA=metropolitan statistical area. For definitions and components of all metropolitan statistical areas, see Appendix II]

METROPOLITAN AREA	Number of specified group (1,000)	Percent of total metro.	METROPOLITAN AREA	Number of specified group (1,000)	Percent of total metro.
BLACK			**HISPANIC ORIGIN** [1]		
New York-Northern New Jersey-Long Island, NY-NJ-CT CMSA	3,289	18.2	Los Angeles-Anaheim-Riverside, CA CMSA .	4,779	32.9
Chicago-Gary-Lake County, IL-IN-WI CMSA .	1,548	19.2	New York-Northern New Jersey-Long Island, NY-NJ-CT CMSA	2,778	15.4
Los Angeles-Anaheim-Riverside, CA CMSA .	1,230	8.5	Miami-Fort Lauderdale, FL CMSA.	1,062	33.3
Philadelphia-Wilmington-Trenton, PA-NJ-DE-MD CMSA.	1,100	18.7	San Francisco-Oakland-San Jose, CA CMSA	970	15.5
Washington, DC-MD-VA MSA.	1,042	26.6	Chicago-Gary-Lake County, IL-IN-WI CMSA .	893	11.1
			Houston-Galveston-Brazoria, TX CMSA. . . .	772	20.8
Detroit-Ann Arbor, MI CMSA	975	20.9	San Antonio, TX MSA	620	47.6
Atlanta, GA MSA	736	26.0	Dallas-Fort Worth, TX MSA.	519	13.4
Houston-Galveston-Brazoria, TX CMSA	665	17.9	San Diego, CA MSA	511	20.4
Baltimore, MD MSA	616	25.9	El Paso, TX MSA	412	69.6
Miami-Fort Lauderdale, FL CMSA	591	18.5	Phoenix, AZ MSA	345	16.3
Dallas-Fort Worth, TX CMSA	555	14.3	McAllen-Edinburg-Mission, TX MSA	327	85.2
San Francisco-Oakland-San Jose, CA CMSA	538	8.6	Fresno, CA MSA	237	35.5
			Denver-Boulder, CO CMSA.	226	12.2
Cleveland-Akron-Lorain, OH CMSA	442	16.0	Philadelphia-Wilmington-Trenton, PA-NJ-DE-MD CMSA	226	3.8
New Orleans, LA MSA	430	34.7	Washington, DC-MD-VA MSA	225	5.7
St. Louis, MO-IL MSA	423	17.3	Brownsville-Harlingen, TX MSA	213	81.9
Memphis, TN-AR-MS MSA.	399	40.6	Boston-Lawrence-Salem, MA-NH CMSA . . .	193	4.6
Norfolk-Virginia Beach-Newport News, VA MSA	398	28.5	Corpus Christi, TX MSA	182	52.0
Richmond-Petersburg, VA MSA	252	29.2	Albuquerque, NM MSA.	178	37.1
Birmingham, AL MSA	246	27.1	Sacramento, CA MSA	172	11.6
			Tucson, AZ MSA.	163	24.5
Boston-Lawrence-Salem, MA-NH CMSA. . . .	239	5.7	Austin, TX MSA	160	20.5
Charlotte-Gastonia-Rock Hill, NC-SC MSA . .	232	19.9	Bakersfield, CA MSA	152	28.0
Milwaukee-Racine, WI CMSA	214	13.3	Tampa-St. Petersburg-Clearwater, FL MSA .	139	6.7
Cincinnati-Hamilton, OH-KY-IN CMSA	204	11.7	Laredo, TX MSA	125	93.9
Kansas City, MO-KS MSA	201	12.8	Visalia-Tulare-Porterville, CA MSA	121	38.8
Tampa-St. Petersburg-Clearwater, FL MSA . .	186	9.0	Salinas-Seaside-Monterey, CA MSA	120	33.6
Raleigh-Durham, NC MSA	183	24.9	Stockton, CA MSA	113	23.4
Greensboro—Winston-Salem—High Point, NC MSA.	182	19.3	**ASIAN AND PACIFIC ISLANDER**		
Jacksonville, FL MSA	181	20.0	Los Angeles-Anaheim-Riverside, CA CMSA .	1,339	9.2
Pittsburgh-Beaver Valley, PA CMSA	179	8.0	San Francisco-Oakland-San Jose, CA CMSA	927	14.8
Indianapolis, IN MSA	172	13.8	New York-Northern New Jersey-Long Island, NY-NJ-CT CMSA	873	4.8
Jackson, MS MSA	168	42.5	Honolulu, HI MSA	526	63.0
Columbus, OH MSA	165	12.0	Chicago-Gary-Lake County, IL-IN-WI CMSA .	256	3.2
San Diego, CA MSA	159	6.4	Washington, DC-MD-VA MSA	202	5.2
Baton Rouge, LA MSA	157	29.6	San Diego, CA MSA	198	7.9
Charleston, SC MSA.	153	30.2	Seattle-Tacoma, WA CMSA	164	6.4
Nashville, TN MSA	152	15.5	Houston-Galveston-Brazoria, TX CMSA. . . .	132	3.6
Columbia, SC MSA	138	30.4	Philadelphia-Wilmington-Trenton, PA-NJ-DE-MD CMSA	123	2.1
Orlando, FL MSA	133	12.4	Boston-Lawrence-Salem, MA-NH CMSA . . .	121	2.9
Mobile, AL MSA.	131	27.4	Sacramento, CA MSA	115	7.7
Dayton-Springfield, OH MSA	126	13.3			
Louisville, KY-IN MSA	125	13.1	**AMERICAN INDIAN, ESKIMO, ALEUT**		
Augusta, GA-SC MSA.	123	31.1	Los Angeles-Anaheim-Riverside, CA CMSA .	87	0.6
Seattle-Tacoma, WA CMSA	123	4.8	Tulsa, OK MSA.	48	6.8
Buffalo-Niagara Falls, NY CMSA.	122	10.3	New York-Northern New Jersey-Long Island, NY-NJ-CT CMSA	46	0.3
Shreveport, LA MSA.	117	35.0	Oklahoma City, OK MSA	46	4.8
Greenville-Spartanburg, SC MSA.	111	17.4	San Francisco-Oakland-San Jose, CA CMSA	41	0.7
West Palm Beach-Boca Raton-Delray Beach, FL MSA.	108	12.5	Phoenix, AZ MSA	38	1.8
Montgomery, AL MSA.	105	36.0	Seattle-Tacoma, WA CMSA	32	1.3
Sacramento, CA MSA	102	6.9	Minneapolis-St. Paul, MN-WI MSA	24	1.0
Little Rock-North Little Rock, AR MSA.	102	19.9	Tucson, AZ MSA.	20	3.0
Oklahoma City, OK MSA	101	10.5	San Diego, CA MSA	20	0.8

[1] Persons of Hispanic origin may be of any race.

Source: U.S. Bureau of the Census, press release CB91-229.

Population

No. 36. 75 Largest Metropolitan Areas—Racial and Hispanic Origin Populations: 1990

[As of **April 1**. Areas as defined by U.S. Office of Management and Budget, June 30, 1990. For definitions, see Appendix II]

METROPOLITAN AREA [1]	Total population (1,000)	PERCENT OF TOTAL METROPOLITAN POPULATION			
		Black	American Indian, Eskimo, Aleut	Asian and Pacific Islander	Hispanic origin [2]
New York-Northern New Jersey-Long Island, NY-NJ-CT CMSA ..	18,087	18.2	0.3	4.8	15.4
Los Angeles-Anaheim-Riverside, CA CMSA	14,532	8.5	0.6	9.2	32.9
Chicago-Gary-Lake County, IL-IN-WI CMSA	8,066	19.2	0.2	3.2	11.1
San Francisco-Oakland-San Jose, CA CMSA	6,253	8.6	0.7	14.8	15.5
Philadelphia-Wilmington-Trenton, PA-NJ-DE-MD CMSA.......	5,899	18.7	0.2	2.1	3.8
Detroit-Ann Arbor, MI CMSA	4,665	20.9	0.4	1.5	1.9
Boston-Lawrence-Salem, MA-NH CMSA.................	4,172	5.7	0.2	2.9	4.6
Washington, DC-MD-VA MSA...................	3,924	26.6	0.3	5.2	5.7
Dallas-Fort Worth, TX CMSA	3,885	14.3	0.5	2.5	13.4
Houston-Galveston-Brazoria, TX CMSA	3,711	17.9	0.3	3.6	20.8
Miami-Fort Lauderdale, FL CMSA	3,193	18.5	0.2	1.4	33.3
Atlanta, GA MSA	2,834	26.0	0.2	1.8	2.0
Cleveland-Akron-Lorain, OH CMSA	2,760	16.0	0.2	1.0	1.9
Seattle-Tacoma, WA CMSA....................	2,559	4.8	1.3	6.4	3.0
San Diego, CA MSA	2,498	6.4	0.8	7.9	20.4
Minneapolis-St. Paul, MN-WI MSA..............	2,464	3.6	1.0	2.6	1.5
St. Louis, MO-IL MSA................	2,444	17.3	0.2	1.0	1.1
Baltimore, MD MSA	2,382	25.9	0.3	1.8	1.3
Pittsburgh-Beaver Valley, PA CMSA	2,243	8.0	0.1	0.7	0.6
Phoenix, AZ MSA........................	2,122	3.5	1.8	1.7	16.3
Tampa-St. Petersburg-Clearwater, FL MSA.............	2,068	9.0	0.3	1.1	6.7
Denver-Boulder, CO CMSA	1,848	5.3	0.8	2.3	12.2
Cincinnati-Hamilton, OH-KY-IN CMSA	1,744	11.7	0.1	0.8	0.5
Milwaukee-Racine, WI CMSA	1,607	13.3	0.5	1.2	3.8
Kansas City, MO-KS MSA	1,566	12.8	0.5	1.1	2.9
Sacramento, CA MSA...................	1,481	6.9	1.1	7.7	11.6
Portland-Vancouver, OR-WA CMSA.............	1,478	2.8	0.9	3.5	3.4
Norfolk-Virginia Beach-Newport News, VA MSA...........	1,396	28.5	0.3	2.5	2.3
Columbus, OH MSA.....................	1,377	12.0	0.2	1.5	0.8
San Antonio, TX MSA..................	1,302	6.8	0.4	1.2	47.6
Indianapolis, IN MSA	1,250	13.8	0.2	0.8	0.9
New Orleans, LA MSA	1,239	34.7	0.3	1.7	4.3
Buffalo-Niagara Falls, NY CMSA.............	1,189	10.3	0.6	0.9	2.0
Charlotte-Gastonia-Rock Hill, NC-SC MSA	1,162	19.9	0.4	1.0	0.9
Providence-Pawtucket-Fall River, RI-MA CMSA...........	1,142	3.3	0.3	1.8	4.2
Hartford-New Britain-Middletown, CT CMSA	1,086	8.7	0.2	1.5	7.0
Orlando, FL MSA	1,073	12.4	0.3	1.9	9.0
Salt Lake City-Ogden, UT MSA.............	1,072	1.0	0.8	2.4	5.8
Rochester, NY MSA.................	1,002	9.4	0.3	1.4	3.1
Nashville, TN MSA...................	985	15.5	0.2	1.0	0.8
Memphis, TN-AR-MS MSA................	982	40.6	0.2	0.8	0.8
Oklahoma City, OK MSA	959	10.5	4.8	1.9	3.6
Louisville, KY-IN MSA..................	953	13.1	0.2	0.6	0.6
Dayton-Springfield, OH MSA	951	13.3	0.2	1.0	0.8
Greensboro—Winston-Salem—High Point, NC MSA	942	19.3	0.3	0.7	0.8
Birmingham, AL MSA	908	27.1	0.2	0.4	0.4
Jacksonville, FL MSA	907	20.0	0.3	1.7	2.5
Albany-Schenectady-Troy, NY MSA	874	4.7	0.2	1.2	1.8
Richmond-Petersburg, VA MSA	866	29.2	0.3	1.4	1.1
West Palm Beach-Boca Raton-Delray Beach, FL MSA	864	12.5	0.1	1.0	7.7
Honolulu, HI MSA....................	836	3.1	0.4	63.0	6.8
Austin, TX MSA....................	782	9.2	0.4	2.4	20.5
Las Vegas, NV MSA...................	741	9.5	0.9	3.5	11.2
Raleigh-Durham, NC MSA	735	24.9	0.3	1.9	1.2
Scranton—Wilkes-Barre, PA MSA	734	1.0	0.1	0.5	0.8
Tulsa, OK MSA	709	8.2	6.8	0.9	2.1
Grand Rapids, MI MSA	688	6.0	0.5	1.1	3.3
Allentown-Bethlehem, PA-NJ MSA	687	2.0	0.1	1.1	4.2
Fresno, CA MSA	667	5.0	1.1	8.6	35.5
Tucson, AZ MSA	667	3.1	3.0	1.8	24.5
Syracuse, NY MSA..................	660	5.9	0.6	1.2	1.4
Greenville-Spartanburg, SC MSA.................	641	17.4	0.1	0.7	0.8
Omaha, NE-IA MSA	618	8.3	0.5	1.0	2.6
Toledo, OH MSA	614	11.4	0.2	1.0	3.3
Knoxville, TN MSA	605	6.0	0.2	0.8	0.5
El Paso, TX MSA	592	3.7	0.4	1.1	69.6
Harrisburg-Lebanon-Carlisle, PA MSA	588	6.7	0.1	1.1	1.7
Bakersfield, CA MSA	543	5.5	1.3	3.0	28.0
New Haven-Meriden, CT MSA	530	12.1	0.2	1.6	6.2
Springfield, MA MSA..................	530	6.6	0.2	1.0	9.0
Baton Rouge, LA MSA	528	29.6	0.2	1.1	1.4
Little Rock-North Little Rock, AR MSA............	513	19.9	0.4	0.7	0.8
Charleston, SC MSA....................	507	30.2	0.3	1.2	1.5
Youngstown-Warren, OH MSA	493	11.1	0.2	0.4	1.5
Wichita, KS MSA	485	7.6	1.1	1.9	4.1

[1] Metropolitan areas are shown in rank order of total population of consolidated metropolitan statistical areas (CMSA) and metropolitan statistical areas (MSA). [2] Persons of Hispanic origin may be of any race.

Source: U.S. Bureau of the Census, press release CB91-229.

No. 37. Cities, by Population Size: 1960 to 1990

POPULATION SIZE	NUMBER OF CITIES				POPULATION (mil.)				PERCENT OF TOTAL			
	1960	1970	1980	1990	1960	1970	1980	1990	1960	1970	1980	1990
Total	18,088	18,666	19,097	19,289	115.9	131.9	140.3	152.9	100.0	100.0	100.0	100.0
1,000,000 or more. . . .	5	6	6	8	17.5	18.8	17.5	20.0	15.1	14.2	12.5	13.0
500,000 to 999,999 . . .	16	20	16	15	11.1	13.0	10.9	10.1	9.6	9.8	7.8	6.6
250,000 to 499,999 . . .	30	30	33	40	10.8	10.5	11.8	14.2	9.3	7.9	8.4	9.3
100,000 to 249,999 . . .	79	97	114	131	11.4	13.9	16.6	19.1	9.8	10.5	11.8	12.5
50,000 to 99,999.	180	232	250	309	12.5	16.2	17.6	21.2	10.8	12.2	12.3	13.9
25,000 to 49,999.	366	455	526	567	12.7	15.7	18.4	20.0	11.0	11.9	13.1	13.0
10,000 to 24,999.	978	1,127	1,260	1,290	15.1	17.6	19.8	20.3	13.1	13.3	14.1	13.3
Under 10,000	16,434	16,699	16,892	16,929	24.9	26.4	28.0	28.2	21.5	20.0	20.0	18.4

Source: U.S. Bureau of the Census, *Census of Population: 1970, 1980,* and *1990,* vol. I.

No. 38. Cities With 100,000 or More Inhabitants in 1990—Population, 1970 to 1990, and Land Area, 1990

[**Population**: As of **April 1**. Data refer to municipal limits as of January 1. Minus sign (-) indicates decrease]

CITY	POPULATION										Land area,[3] 1990 (square miles)
	1970,[1] total (1,000)	1980,[1] total (1,000)	1990								
			Total (1,000)	Rank	Per-cent change, 1980-90	Percent—				Per square mile	
						Black	American Indian, Eskimo, Aleut	Asian, Pacific Islander	His-panic [2]		
Abilene, TX	90	98	107	184	8.5	7.0	0.4	1.3	15.5	1,035	103.1
Akron, OH.	275	237	223	71	-6.0	24.5	0.3	1.2	0.7	3,586	62.2
Albany, NY	116	102	101	197	-0.6	20.6	0.3	2.3	3.1	4,721	21.4
Albuquerque, NM	245	332	385	38	15.6	3.0	3.0	1.7	34.5	2,910	132.2
Alexandria, VA.	111	103	111	168	7.7	21.9	0.3	4.2	9.7	7,281	15.3
Allentown, PA	110	104	105	189	1.3	5.0	0.2	1.3	11.7	5,934	17.7
Amarillo, TX	127	149	158	111	5.6	6.0	0.8	1.9	14.7	1,793	87.9
Anaheim, CA.	166	219	266	59	21.4	2.5	0.5	9.4	31.4	6,014	44.3
Anchorage, AK [4]	48	174	226	69	29.8	6.4	6.4	4.8	4.1	133	1,697.7
Ann Arbor, MI.	100	108	110	174	1.5	9.0	0.4	7.7	2.6	4,231	25.9
Arlington, VA [5].	174	153	171	100	12.0	10.5	0.3	6.8	13.5	6,605	25.9
Arlington, TX	90	160	262	61	63.5	8.4	0.5	3.9	8.9	2,814	93.0
Atlanta, GA	495	425	394	36	-7.3	67.1	0.1	0.9	1.9	2,990	131.8
Aurora, CO	75	159	222	72	40.1	11.4	0.6	3.8	6.6	1,676	132.5
Austin, TX.	254	346	466	27	34.6	12.4	0.4	3.0	23.0	2,138	217.8
Bakersfield, CA	70	106	175	97	65.5	9.4	1.1	3.6	20.5	1,904	91.8
Baltimore, MD	905	787	736	12	-6.4	59.2	0.3	1.1	1.0	9,108	80.8
Baton Rouge, LA	166	220	220	73	-0.4	43.9	0.1	1.7	1.6	2,969	74.0
Beaumont, TX	118	118	114	159	-3.2	41.3	0.2	1.7	4.3	1,427	80.1
Berkeley, CA	114	103	103	194	-0.6	18.8	0.6	14.8	8.4	9,783	10.5
Birmingham, AL.	301	284	266	60	-6.5	63.3	0.1	0.6	(Z)	1,791	148.5
Boise City, ID	75	102	126	148	23.0	0.6	0.6	1.6	2.7	2,726	46.1
Boston, MA.	641	563	574	20	2.0	25.6	0.3	5.3	10.8	11,860	48.4
Bridgeport, CT	157	143	142	125	-0.6	26.6	0.3	2.3	26.5	8,855	16.0
Buffalo, NY	463	358	328	50	-8.3	30.7	0.8	1.0	4.9	8,080	40.6
Cedar Rapids, IA	111	110	109	178	-1.4	2.9	0.2	1.0	1.1	2,034	53.5
Charlotte, NC	241	315	396	35	25.5	31.8	0.4	1.8	1.4	2,272	174.3
Chattanooga, TN	120	170	152	114	-10.1	33.7	0.2	1.0	0.6	1,287	118.4
Chesapeake, VA	90	114	152	115	32.7	27.4	0.3	1.2	1.3	446	340.7
Chicago, IL	3,369	3,005	2,784	3	-7.4	39.1	0.3	3.7	19.6	12,251	227.2
Chula Vista, CA	68	84	135	133	61.0	4.6	0.6	8.9	37.3	4,661	29.0
Cincinnati, OH	454	385	364	45	-5.5	37.9	0.2	1.1	0.7	4,714	77.2
Citrus Heights, CA [5] . . .	22	86	107	183	25.1	2.3	1.1	3.3	6.9	5,510	19.5
Cleveland, OH	751	574	506	23	-11.9	46.6	0.3	1.0	4.6	6,565	77.0
Colorado Springs, CO . . .	136	215	281	54	30.7	7.0	0.8	2.4	9.1	1,535	183.2
Columbus, GA	155	169	179	93	5.5	38.1	0.3	1.4	3.0	827	216.1
Columbus, OH.	540	565	633	16	12.0	22.6	0.2	2.4	1.1	3,315	190.9
Concord, CA	85	104	111	167	7.3	2.4	0.7	8.7	11.5	3,775	29.5
Corpus Christi, TX	205	232	257	64	10.9	4.8	0.4	0.9	50.4	1,907	135.0
Dallas, TX.	844	905	1,007	8	11.3	29.5	0.5	2.2	20.9	2,941	342.4
Dayton, OH.	243	194	182	89	-5.9	40.4	0.2	0.6	0.7	3,310	55.0
Denver, CO.	515	493	468	26	-5.1	12.8	1.2	2.4	23.0	3,051	153.3
Des Moines, IA	201	191	193	80	1.1	7.1	0.4	2.4	2.4	2,567	75.3
Detroit, MI.	1,514	1,203	1,028	7	-14.6	75.7	0.4	0.8	2.8	7,410	138.7
Durham, NC	95	101	137	132	35.1	45.7	0.2	2.0	1.2	1,972	69.3
East Los Angeles, CA. . .	105	110	126	146	14.9	1.4	0.4	1.3	94.7	16,828	7.5
Elizabeth, NJ.	113	106	110	172	3.6	19.8	0.3	2.7	39.1	8,929	12.3
El Monte, CA.	70	79	106	186	33.6	1.0	0.6	11.8	72.5	11,180	9.5
El Paso, TX.	322	425	515	22	21.2	3.4	0.4	1.2	69.0	2,100	245.4
Erie, PA	129	119	109	179	-8.7	12.0	0.2	0.5	2.4	4,944	22.0
Escondido, CA.	37	64	109	180	68.8	1.5	0.8	3.7	23.4	3,048	35.6
Eugene, OR	79	106	113	163	6.6	1.3	0.9	3.5	2.7	2,962	38.0
Evansville, IN	139	130	126	147	-3.2	9.5	0.2	0.6	0.6	3,102	40.7
Flint, MI	193	160	141	127	-11.8	47.9	0.7	0.5	2.9	4,161	33.8
Fort Lauderdale, FL	140	153	149	118	-2.5	28.1	0.2	0.9	7.2	4,763	31.4

See footnotes at end of table.

No. 38. Cities With 100,000 or More Inhabitants in 1990—Population, 1970 to 1990, and Land Area, 1990—Continued

[See headnote, p. 35]

CITY	1970, total[1] (1,000)	1980, total[1] (1,000)	POPULATION 1990 Total (1,000)	Rank	Percent change, 1980-90	Percent— Black	American Indian, Eskimo, Aleut	Asian, Pacific Islander	Hispanic[2]	Per square mile	Land area[3] 1990 (square miles)
Fort Wayne, IN	178	172	173	99	0.4	16.7	0.3	1.0	2.7	2,762	62.7
Fort Worth, TX.	393	385	448	28	16.2	22.0	0.4	2.0	19.5	1,592	281.1
Fremont, CA	101	132	173	98	31.4	3.8	0.7	19.4	13.3	2,250	77.0
Fresno, CA	166	217	354	47	62.9	8.3	1.1	12.5	29.9	3,573	99.1
Fullerton, CA	86	102	114	160	11.6	2.2	0.5	12.2	21.3	5,160	22.1
Garden Grove, CA	121	123	143	122	16.0	1.5	0.6	20.5	23.5	7,974	17.9
Garland, TX.	81	139	181	91	30.1	8.9	0.5	4.5	11.6	3,150	57.4
Gary, IN	175	152	117	158	-23.2	80.6	0.2	0.2	5.7	2,322	50.2
Glendale, AZ.	36	97	148	119	52.4	3.0	0.9	2.1	15.5	2,837	52.2
Glendale, CA.	133	139	180	92	29.5	1.3	0.3	14.1	21.0	5,882	30.6
Grand Rapids, MI	198	182	189	83	4.0	18.5	0.8	1.1	5.0	4,273	44.3
Greensboro, NC.	144	156	184	88	17.9	33.9	0.5	1.4	1.0	2,300	79.8
Hampton, VA.	121	123	134	135	9.1	38.9	0.3	1.7	2.0	2,582	51.8
Hartford, CT	158	136	140	129	2.5	38.9	0.3	1.4	31.6	8,077	17.3
Hayward, CA.	93	94	111	166	19.1	9.8	1.0	15.5	23.9	2,566	43.5
Hialeah, FL	102	145	188	85	29.4	1.9	0.1	0.5	87.6	9,772	19.2
Hollywood, FL	107	121	122	152	0.3	8.5	0.2	1.3	11.9	4,464	27.3
Honolulu, HI[5]	325	365	365	44	0.1	1.3	0.3	70.5	4.6	4,410	82.8
Houston, TX	1,234	1,595	1,631	4	2.2	28.1	0.3	4.1	27.6	3,020	539.9
Huntington Beach, CA.	116	171	182	90	6.5	0.9	0.6	8.3	11.2	6,871	26.4
Huntsville, AL	139	143	160	110	12.1	24.4	0.5	2.1	1.2	972	164.4
Independence, MO.	112	112	112	164	0.5	1.4	0.6	1.0	2.0	1,436	78.2
Indianapolis, IN	737	701	731	13	4.3	22.6	0.2	0.9	1.1	2,022	361.7
Inglewood, CA.	90	94	110	173	16.4	51.9	0.4	2.5	38.5	11,952	9.2
Irvine, CA	(6)	62	110	171	77.6	1.8	0.2	18.1	6.3	2,607	42.3
Irving, TX	97	110	155	113	41.0	7.5	0.6	4.6	16.3	2,293	67.6
Jackson, MS	154	203	197	78	-3.1	55.7	0.1	0.5	0.4	1,804	109.0
Jacksonville, FL.	504	541	635	15	17.9	25.2	0.3	1.9	2.6	837	758.7
Jersey City, NJ	260	224	229	67	2.2	29.7	0.3	11.4	24.2	15,359	14.9
Kansas City, KS.	168	161	150	116	-7.1	29.3	0.7	1.2	7.1	1,389	107.8
Kansas City, MO	507	448	435	31	-2.9	29.6	0.5	1.2	3.9	1,397	311.5
Knoxville, TN.	175	175	165	103	-5.7	15.8	0.2	1.0	0.7	2,137	77.3
Lakewood, CO.	93	114	126	145	11.1	1.0	0.7	1.9	9.1	3,100	40.8
Lansing, MI	131	130	127	144	-2.4	18.6	1.0	1.8	7.9	3,755	33.9
Laredo, TX	69	91	123	151	34.4	0.1	0.2	0.4	93.9	3,739	32.9
Las Vegas, NV.	126	165	258	63	56.9	11.4	0.9	3.6	12.5	3,101	83.3
Lexington-Fayette, KY[7].	108	204	225	70	10.4	13.4	0.2	1.6	1.1	792	284.5
Lincoln, NE.	150	172	192	81	11.7	2.4	0.6	1.7	2.0	3,033	63.3
Little Rock, AR	132	159	176	96	10.5	34.0	0.3	0.9	0.8	1,709	102.9
Livonia, MI	110	105	101	198	-3.8	0.3	0.2	1.3	1.3	2,823	35.7
Long Beach, CA.	359	361	429	32	18.8	13.7	0.6	13.6	23.6	8,585	50.0
Los Angeles, CA	2,812	2,969	3,485	2	17.4	14.0	0.5	9.8	39.9	7,426	469.3
Louisville, KY.	362	299	269	58	-9.9	29.7	0.2	0.7	0.7	4,332	62.1
Lowell, MA	94	92	103	193	11.9	2.4	0.2	11.1	10.1	7,506	13.8
Lubbock, TX	149	174	186	87	6.8	8.6	0.3	1.4	22.5	1,789	104.1
Macon, GA	122	117	107	185	-8.8	52.2	0.1	0.4	0.6	2,227	47.9
Madison, WI	172	171	191	82	12.1	4.2	0.4	3.9	2.0	3,311	57.8
Memphis, TN.	624	646	610	18	-5.5	54.8	0.2	0.8	0.7	2,384	256.0
Mesa, AZ	63	152	288	53	89.0	1.9	1.0	1.5	10.9	2,653	108.6
Mesquite, TX.	55	67	101	195	51.3	5.8	0.5	2.6	8.8	2,369	42.8
Metairie, LA[5]	136	164	149	117	-9.0	4.9	0.2	1.8	6.2	6,424	23.3
Miami, FL	335	347	359	46	3.4	27.4	0.2	0.6	62.5	10,080	35.6
Milwaukee, WI.	717	636	628	17	-1.3	30.5	0.9	1.9	6.3	6,537	96.1
Minneapolis, MN	434	371	368	42	-0.7	13.0	3.3	4.3	2.1	6,706	54.9
Mobile, AL	190	200	196	79	-2.1	38.9	0.2	1.0	1.0	1,663	118.0
Modesto, CA.	62	107	165	104	54.0	2.7	1.0	7.9	16.3	5,458	30.2
Montgomery, AL	133	178	187	86	5.2	42.3	0.2	0.7	0.8	1,386	135.0
Moreno Valley, CA	(6)	(6)	119	155	(X)	13.8	0.7	6.6	22.9	2,418	49.1
Nashville-Davidson, TN	426	456	488	25	6.9	24.3	0.2	1.4	0.9	1,032	473.3
Newark, NJ.	382	329	275	56	-16.4	58.5	0.2	1.2	26.1	11,554	23.8
New Haven, CT.	138	126	130	140	3.5	36.1	0.3	2.4	13.2	6,922	18.9
New Orleans, LA	593	558	497	24	-10.9	61.9	0.2	1.9	3.5	2,751	180.7
Newport News, VA.	138	145	170	101	17.4	33.6	0.3	2.3	2.8	2,488	68.3
New York, NY	7,896	7,072	7,323	1	3.5	28.7	0.4	7.0	24.4	23,701	309.0
Bronx Borough	1,472	1,169	1,204	(X)	(X)	37.3	0.5	3.0	43.5	28,641	42.0
Brooklyn Borough	2,602	2,231	2,301	(X)	(X)	37.9	0.3	4.8	20.1	32,620	70.5
Manhattan Borough	1,539	1,428	1,488	(X)	(X)	22.0	0.4	7.4	26.0	52,415	28.4
Queens Borough	1,987	1,891	1,952	(X)	(X)	21.7	0.4	12.2	19.5	17,839	109.4
Staten Island Borough	295	352	379	(X)	(X)	8.1	0.2	4.5	8.0	6,466	58.6
Norfolk, VA.	308	267	261	62	-2.2	39.1	0.4	2.6	2.9	4,859	53.8
Oakland, CA.	362	339	372	39	9.7	43.9	0.6	14.8	13.9	6,640	56.1
Oceanside, CA	40	77	128	143	67.4	7.9	0.7	6.1	22.6	3,157	40.7
Oklahoma City, OK.	368	404	445	29	10.1	16.0	4.2	2.4	5.0	731	608.2
Omaha, NE.	347	314	336	48	7.0	13.1	0.7	1.0	3.1	3,336	100.7
Ontario, CA.	64	89	133	136	49.9	7.3	0.7	3.9	41.7	3,624	36.8
Orange, CA.	77	91	111	169	21.0	1.4	0.5	7.9	22.8	4,741	23.3
Orlando, FL.	99	128	165	105	28.4	26.9	0.3	1.6	8.7	2,448	67.3
Overland Park, KS	78	82	112	165	36.7	1.8	0.3	1.9	2.0	2,007	55.7

See footnotes at end of table.

No. 38. Cities With 100,000 or More Inhabitants in 1990—Population, 1970 to 1990, and Land Area, 1990—Continued

[See headnote, p. 35]

CITY	1970, total [1] (1,000)	1980, total [1] (1,000)	POPULATION 1990 Total (1,000)	Rank	Percent change, 1980-90	Percent— Black	American Indian, Eskimo, Aleut	Asian, Pacific Islander	His- panic [2]	Per square mile	Land area, [3] 1990 (square miles)
Oxnard, CA . . .	71	108	142	123	31.4	5.2	0.8	8.6	54.4	5,819	24.4
Paradise, NV [5] .	24	85	125	150	47.0	4.9	0.6	4.0	10.5	2,616	47.7
Pasadena, CA	113	118	132	139	11.4	19.0	0.4	8.1	27.3	5,724	23.0
Pasadena, TX	90	113	119	154	6.0	1.0	0.5	1.6	28.8	2,727	43.8
Paterson, NJ	145	138	141	126	2.1	36.0	0.3	1.4	41.0	16,693	8.4
Peoria, IL	127	124	114	161	-8.6	20.9	0.2	1.7	1.6	2,776	40.9
Philadelphia, PA.	1,949	1,688	1,586	5	-6.1	39.9	0.2	2.7	5.6	11,734	135.1
Phoenix, AZ	584	790	983	9	24.5	5.2	1.9	1.7	20.0	2,342	419.9
Pittsburgh, PA	520	424	370	40	-12.8	25.8	0.2	1.6	0.9	6,649	55.6
Plano, TX	18	72	129	142	77.9	4.1	0.3	4.0	6.2	1,943	66.3
Pomona, CA	87	93	132	138	42.0	14.4	0.6	6.7	51.3	5,770	22.8
Portland, OR	380	368	437	30	18.8	7.7	1.2	5.3	3.2	3,508	124.7
Portsmouth, VA	111	105	104	191	-0.6	47.3	0.3	0.8	1.3	3,135	33.1
Providence, RI.	179	157	161	108	2.5	14.8	0.9	5.9	15.5	8,707	18.5
Raleigh, NC.	123	150	208	75	38.4	27.6	0.3	2.5	1.4	2,360	88.1
Rancho Cucamonga, CA .	([6])	55	101	196	63.5	5.9	0.6	5.4	20.0	2,682	37.8
Reno, NV	73	101	134	134	32.8	2.9	1.4	4.9	11.1	2,328	57.5
Richmond, VA	249	219	203	76	-7.4	55.2	0.2	0.9	0.9	3,377	60.1
Riverside, CA	140	171	227	68	32.8	7.4	0.8	5.2	26.0	2,916	77.7
Rochester, NY.	295	242	232	66	-4.2	31.5	0.5	1.8	8.7	6,474	35.8
Rockford, IL	147	140	139	130	-0.2	15.0	0.3	1.5	4.2	3,100	45.0
Sacramento, CA.	257	276	369	41	34.0	15.3	1.2	15.0	16.2	3,836	96.3
St. Louis, MO	622	453	397	34	-12.4	47.5	0.2	0.9	1.3	6,405	61.9
St. Paul, MN	310	270	272	57	0.7	7.4	1.4	7.1	4.2	5,157	52.8
St. Petersburg, FL	216	239	239	65	(-Z)	19.6	0.2	1.7	2.6	4,032	59.2
Salem, OR	69	89	108	182	21.0	1.5	1.6	2.4	6.1	2,595	41.5
Salinas, CA	59	80	109	177	35.2	3.0	0.9	8.1	50.6	5,839	18.6
Salt Lake City, UT	176	163	160	109	-1.9	1.7	1.6	4.7	9.7	1,467	109.0
San Antonio, TX.	654	786	936	10	19.1	7.0	0.4	1.1	55.6	2,810	333.0
San Bernardino, CA . . .	107	119	164	106	38.2	16.0	1.0	4.0	34.6	2,980	55.1
San Diego, CA.	697	876	1,111	6	26.8	9.4	0.6	11.8	20.7	3,428	324.0
San Francisco, CA	716	679	724	14	6.6	10.9	0.5	29.1	13.9	15,502	46.7
San Jose, CA	460	629	782	11	24.3	4.7	0.7	19.5	26.6	4,568	171.3
Santa Ana, CA	156	204	294	52	44.0	2.6	0.5	9.7	65.2	10,843	27.1
Santa Clarita, CA	([6])	([6])	111	170	(X)	1.5	0.6	4.2	13.4	2,733	40.5
Santa Rosa, CA	50	83	113	162	37.1	1.8	1.2	3.4	9.5	3,362	33.7
Savannah, GA	118	142	138	131	-2.9	51.3	0.2	1.1	1.4	2,198	62.6
Scottsdale, AZ.	68	89	130	141	46.8	0.8	0.6	1.2	4.8	706	184.4
Seattle, WA.	531	494	516	21	4.5	10.1	1.4	11.8	3.6	6,154	83.9
Shreveport, LA	182	206	199	77	-4.1	44.8	0.2	0.5	1.1	2,013	98.6
Simi Valley, CA	60	78	100	200	29.3	1.5	0.6	5.5	12.7	3,034	33.0
Sioux Falls, SD	72	81	101	199	23.9	0.7	1.6	0.7	0.6	2,238	45.1
South Bend, IN	126	110	106	187	-3.8	20.9	0.4	0.9	3.4	2,897	36.4
Spokane, WA	171	171	177	94	3.4	1.9	2.0	2.1	2.1	3,169	55.9
Springfield, IL	92	100	105	188	5.2	13.0	0.2	1.0	0.8	2,474	42.5
Springfield, MA	164	152	157	112	3.1	19.2	0.2	1.0	16.9	4,890	32.1
Springfield, MO	120	133	140	128	5.5	2.5	0.7	0.9	1.0	2,068	68.0
Stamford, CT.	109	102	108	181	5.5	17.8	0.1	2.6	9.8	2,865	37.7
Sterling Heights, MI	61	109	118	156	8.1	0.4	0.2	2.9	1.1	3,215	36.6
Stockton, CA.	110	150	211	74	42.3	9.6	1.0	22.8	25.0	4,013	52.6
Sunnyvale, CA.	96	107	117	157	10.0	3.4	0.5	19.3	13.2	5,353	21.9
Syracuse, NY	197	170	164	107	-3.7	20.3	1.3	2.2	2.9	6,528	25.1
Tacoma, WA	154	159	177	95	11.5	11.4	2.0	6.9	3.8	3,677	48.1
Tallahassee, FL	73	82	125	149	53.0	29.1	0.2	1.8	3.0	1,972	63.3
Tampa, FL	278	272	280	55	3.1	25.0	0.3	1.4	15.0	2,577	108.7
Tempe, AZ	64	107	142	124	32.7	3.2	1.3	4.1	10.9	3,590	39.5
Thousand Oaks, CA	36	77	104	190	35.4	1.2	0.4	4.8	9.6	2,106	49.6
Toledo, OH	383	355	333	49	-6.1	19.7	0.3	1.0	4.0	4,132	80.6
Topeka, KS.	125	119	120	153	1.0	10.6	1.3	0.8	5.8	2,173	55.2
Torrance, CA.	135	130	133	137	2.5	1.5	0.4	21.9	10.1	6,487	20.5
Tucson, AZ.	263	331	405	33	22.6	4.3	1.6	2.2	29.3	2,594	156.3
Tulsa, OK	330	361	367	43	1.8	13.6	4.7	1.4	2.6	2,001	183.5
Vallejo, CA.	72	80	109	175	36.0	21.2	0.7	23.0	10.8	3,613	30.2
Virginia Beach, VA	172	262	393	37	49.9	13.9	0.4	4.3	3.1	1,583	248.3
Waco, TX.	95	101	104	192	2.3	23.1	0.3	0.9	16.3	1,367	75.8
Warren, MI	179	161	145	120	-10.1	0.7	0.5	1.3	1.1	4,226	34.3
Washington, DC.	757	638	607	19	-4.9	65.8	0.2	1.8	5.4	9,883	61.4
Waterbury, CT	108	103	109	176	5.5	13.0	0.2	0.7	13.4	3,815	28.6
Wichita, KS.	277	280	304	51	8.6	11.3	1.2	2.6	5.0	2,640	115.1
Winston-Salem, NC	134	132	143	121	8.8	39.3	0.2	0.8	0.9	2,018	71.1
Worcester, MA.	177	162	170	102	4.9	4.5	0.3	2.8	9.6	4,520	37.6
Yonkers, NY	204	195	188	84	-3.7	14.1	0.2	3.0	16.7	10,403	18.1

X Not applicable.   Z Less than .05 percent.   [1] Population totals include corrections made after tabulations were completed.   [2] Hispanic persons may be of any race.   [3] As of January 1.   [4] Anchorage city consolidated with Anchorage Borough September 15, 1975.   [5] Data represent the census designated place as delineated by State and local authorities.   [6] Not incorporated.   [7] Lexington and Fayette County consolidated January 1, 1974.

Source: U.S. Bureau of the Census, *Census of Population: 1970*, vol. I, chapters A and B; *1980 Census of Population*, vol. 1, chapters A and B; *1990 Census of Population and Housing, Summary Population and Housing Characteristics*, (CPH-1).

No. 39. Population 65 Years Old and Over, by Age Group and Sex: 1970 to 1991

[As of **April 1**, except **1991**, as of **July 1**]

AGE GROUP AND SEX	NUMBER (1,000)				PERCENT DISTRIBUTION			
	1970	1980	1990	1991	1970	1980	1990	1991
Persons 65 yrs. and over	**19,980**	**25,549**	**31,079**	**31,754**	**100.0**	**100.0**	**100.0**	**100.0**
65 to 69 years old	6,998	8,782	10,066	10,037	35.0	34.3	32.4	31.6
70 to 74 years old	5,449	6,798	7,980	8,242	27.3	26.6	25.7	26.0
75 to 79 years old	3,838	4,794	6,103	6,279	19.2	18.8	19.6	19.8
80 to 84 years old	2,286	2,935	3,909	4,035	11.4	11.5	12.6	12.7
85 years old and over	1,409	2,240	3,021	3,160	7.1	8.8	9.7	10.0
Males, 65 yrs. and over	**8,369**	**10,305**	**12,493**	**12,791**	**100.0**	**100.0**	**100.0**	**100.0**
65 to 69 years old	3,125	3,903	4,508	4,491	37.3	37.8	36.1	35.1
70 to 74 years old	2,317	2,854	3,399	3,531	27.7	27.7	27.2	27.6
75 to 79 years old	1,562	1,848	2,389	2,482	18.7	18.0	19.1	19.4
80 to 84 years old	876	1,019	1,356	1,406	10.5	9.9	10.9	11.0
85 years old and over	489	682	841	881	5.8	6.6	6.7	6.9
Females, 65 yrs. and over	**11,610**	**15,245**	**18,586**	**18,962**	**100.0**	**100.0**	**100.0**	**100.0**
65 to 69 years old	3,873	4,880	5,558	5,546	33.4	31.9	29.9	29.2
70 to 74 years old	3,132	3,945	4,580	4,712	27.0	25.9	24.6	24.8
75 to 79 years old	2,276	2,946	3,714	3,797	19.6	19.3	20.0	20.0
80 to 84 years old	1,410	1,916	2,553	2,629	12.1	12.6	13.7	13.9
85 years old and over	919	1,559	2,180	2,279	7.9	10.3	11.7	12.0

Source: U.S. Bureau of the Census, *Current Population Reports*, series P-25, Nos. 917 and 1045; *1990 Census of Population and Housing Data Paper Listing* (CPH-L-74); and unpublished data.

No. 40. Persons 65 Years Old and Over—Characteristics, by Sex: 1970 to 1990

[As of **March, except as noted.** Covers civilian noninstitutional population, except 1970 includes institutional population. See headnote, table 41]

CHARACTERISTIC	TOTAL				MALE				FEMALE			
	1970	1980	1985	1990	1970	1980	1985	1990	1970	1980	1985	1990
Total [1] (million)	**19.9**	**24.2**	**26.8**	**29.6**	**8.3**	**9.9**	**11.0**	**12.3**	**11.5**	**14.2**	**15.8**	**17.2**
White (million)	18.2	21.9	24.2	26.5	7.6	9.0	9.9	11.0	10.6	12.9	14.3	15.4
Black (million)	1.5	2.0	2.2	2.5	0.7	0.8	0.9	1.0	0.9	1.2	1.3	1.5
Percent below poverty level [2]	25.3	15.2	12.4	11.4	20.2	11.1	8.7	7.8	29.2	17.9	15.0	13.9
PERCENT DISTRIBUTION												
Marital status:												
Single	7.6	5.5	5.2	4.6	7.5	4.9	5.3	4.2	7.7	5.9	5.1	4.9
Married	51.3	55.4	55.2	56.1	73.1	78.0	77.2	76.5	35.6	39.5	39.9	41.4
Spouse present	49.0	53.6	53.4	54.1	69.9	76.1	75.0	74.2	33.9	37.9	38.3	39.7
Spouse absent	2.3	1.8	1.8	2.0	3.2	1.9	2.2	2.3	1.7	1.7	1.6	1.7
Widowed	38.8	35.7	35.6	34.2	17.1	13.5	13.8	14.2	54.4	51.2	50.7	48.6
Divorced	2.3	3.5	4.0	5.0	2.3	3.6	3.7	5.0	2.3	3.4	4.3	5.1
Family status:												
In families [3]	67.1	67.6	67.3	66.7	79.2	83.0	82.4	81.9	58.5	56.8	56.7	55.8
Nonfamily householders	26.6	31.2	31.1	31.9	14.9	15.7	15.4	16.6	35.2	42.0	42.1	42.8
Secondary individuals	2.1	1.2	1.6	1.4	2.4	1.3	2.2	1.5	1.9	1.1	1.1	1.4
Residents of institutions	4.1	(NA)	(NA)	(NA)	3.6	(NA)	(NA)	(NA)	4.4	(NA)	(NA)	(NA)
Living arrangements:												
Living in household	95.2	99.8	99.6	99.7	95.5	99.9	99.5	99.9	95.0	99.7	99.6	99.5
Living alone	25.5	30.3	30.2	31.0	14.1	14.9	14.7	15.7	33.8	41.0	41.1	42.0
Spouse present	49.0	53.6	53.4	54.1	69.9	76.1	75.0	74.3	33.9	37.9	38.3	39.7
Living with someone else	20.7	15.9	15.9	14.6	11.5	8.9	9.8	9.9	27.4	20.8	20.2	17.8
Not in household [4]	4.8	0.2	0.4	0.3	4.5	0.1	0.5	0.1	5.0	0.3	0.4	0.5
Years of school completed:												
8 years or less	58.3	43.1	35.4	28.5	61.5	45.3	37.2	30.0	56.1	41.6	34.1	27.5
1 to 3 years of high school	13.4	16.2	16.5	16.1	12.6	15.5	15.7	15.7	13.9	16.7	17.0	16.4
4 years of high school	15.7	24.0	29.0	32.9	12.5	21.4	26.4	29.0	18.1	25.8	30.7	35.6
1 to 3 years of college	6.2	8.2	9.8	10.9	5.6	7.5	9.1	10.8	6.7	8.6	10.3	11.0
4 years or more of college	6.3	8.6	9.4	11.6	7.9	10.3	11.5	14.5	5.2	7.4	8.0	9.5
Labor force participation: [5]												
Employed	16.4	12.2	10.4	11.5	25.9	18.4	15.3	15.9	9.4	7.8	7.0	8.4
Unemployed	0.5	0.4	0.3	0.4	0.9	0.6	0.5	0.5	0.3	0.3	0.2	0.3
Not in labor force	83.0	87.5	89.2	88.1	73.2	81.0	84.2	83.6	90.3	91.9	92.7	91.3

NA Not available. [1] Includes other races, not shown separately. [2] Poverty status based on income in preceding year. [3] Beginning 1980, excludes those living in unrelated subfamilies. [4] In institutions (1970) and other group quarters. [5] Annual averages of monthly figures. Source: U.S. Bureau of Labor Statistics, *Employment and Earnings*, January issues.

Source: Except as noted, U.S. Bureau of the Census, *Current Population Reports*, series P-20, No. 450 and earlier reports; series P-23, No. 59; and series P-60, No. 168 and earlier reports; and unpublished data.

No. 41. Social and Economic Characteristics of the White and Black Populations: 1980 to 1991

[As of **March, except labor force status, annual average.** Excludes members of Armed Forces except those living off post or with their families on post. Based on Current Population Survey; see text, section 1, and Appendix III]

CHARACTERISTIC	NUMBER (1,000)									PERCENT DISTRIBU-TION, 1991	
	All races [1]			White			Black			White	Black
	1980	1990	1991	1980	1990	1991	1980	1990	1991	White	Black
Total persons	223,160	246,191	248,886	191,905	206,983	208,754	26,033	30,392	30,895	100.0	100.0
Under 5 years old	16,319	18,932	19,299	13,307	15,161	15,357	2,444	2,932	3,069	7.4	9.9
5 to 14 years old.	34,979	35,467	36,067	28,828	28,405	28,829	5,190	5,546	5,628	13.8	18.2
15 to 44 years old	103,493	115,690	116,395	88,570	96,656	97,075	12,247	14,660	14,809	46.5	47.9
45 to 64 years old	44,174	46,536	47,031	39,302	40,282	40,594	4,112	4,766	4,842	19.4	15.7
65 years old and over	24,194	29,566	30,093	21,898	26,479	26,898	2,040	2,487	2,547	12.9	8.2
YEARS OF SCHOOL COMPLETED											
Persons 25 years old and over	130,409	156,538	158,694	114,763	134,687	136,299	12,927	16,751	17,096	100.0	100.0
Elementary: 0 to 8 years.	22,817	17,591	16,849	18,739	14,131	13,527	3,559	2,701	2,607	9.9	15.2
High school: 1 to 3 years	18,086	17,461	17,379	15,064	14,080	13,882	2,748	2,969	3,085	10.2	18.0
4 years	47,934	60,119	61,272	43,149	52,449	53,250	3,980	6,239	6,448	39.1	37.7
College: 1 to 3 years	19,379	28,075	29,169	17,350	24,350	25,358	1,618	2,952	2,990	18.6	17.5
4 years or more	22,193	33,291	34,025	20,460	29,677	30,283	1,024	1,890	1,966	22.2	11.5
LABOR FORCE STATUS [2]											
Civilians 16 years old and over	167,745	188,049	189,765	146,122	160,415	161,511	17,824	21,300	21,615	100.0	100.0
Civilian labor force.	106,940	124,787	125,303	93,600	107,177	107,486	10,865	13,493	13,542	66.6	62.6
Employed.	99,303	117,914	116,877	87,715	102,087	101,039	9,313	11,966	11,863	62.6	54.9
Unemployed	7,637	6,874	8,426	5,884	5,091	6,447	1,553	1,527	1,679	4.0	7.8
Unemployment rate [3]	7.1	5.5	6.7	6.3	4.7	6.0	14.3	11.3	12.4	(X)	(X)
Not in labor force	60,806	63,262	64,462	52,523	53,237	54,025	6,959	7,808	8,074	33.4	37.4
FAMILY TYPE											
Total families	59,550	66,090	66,322	52,243	56,590	56,803	6,184	7,470	7,471	100.0	100.0
With own children [4]	31,022	32,289	32,401	26,474	26,718	26,794	3,820	4,378	4,380	47.2	58.6
Married couple	49,112	52,317	52,147	44,751	46,981	47,014	3,433	3,750	3,569	82.8	47.8
With own children [4]	24,961	24,537	24,397	22,415	21,579	21,531	1,927	1,972	1,884	37.9	25.2
Female householder, no spouse present.	8,705	10,890	11,268	6,052	7,306	7,512	2,495	3,275	3,430	13.2	45.9
With own children [4]	5,445	6,599	6,823	3,558	4,199	4,337	1,793	2,232	2,294	7.6	30.7
Male householder, no spouse present	1,733	2,884	2,907	1,441	2,303	2,276	256	446	472	4.0	6.3
With own children [4]	616	1,153	1,181	500	939	925	99	173	202	1.6	2.7
FAMILY INCOME IN PREVIOUS YEAR IN CONSTANT **(1990)** DOLLARS											
Total families	59,550	66,090	66,322	52,243	56,590	56,803	6,184	7,470	7,471	100.0	100.0
Less than $5,000	1,535	2,239	2,367	1,023	1,376	1,424	463	787	857	2.5	11.5
$5,000 to $9,999.	3,425	3,882	3,871	2,403	2,673	2,668	949	1,050	1,056	4.7	14.1
$10,000 to $14,999	4,533	5,065	4,973	3,593	3,955	3,985	852	942	843	7.0	11.3
$15,000 to $24,999	10,201	10,473	10,847	8,670	8,745	9,111	1,342	1,447	1,455	16.0	19.5
$25,000 to $34,999	9,956	10,521	10,716	8,915	9,209	9,379	886	1,030	1,047	16.5	14.0
$35,000 to $49,999	13,535	13,018	13,301	12,361	11,627	11,794	929	1,053	1,122	20.8	15.0
$50,000 or more	16,365	20,892	20,247	15,278	19,005	18,442	762	1,162	1,090	32.5	14.5
Median income (dol.) [5]	35,262	36,062	35,353	36,796	37,919	36,915	20,836	21,301	21,423	(X)	(X)
POVERTY [6]											
Families below poverty level	5,461	6,784	7,098	3,581	4,409	4,622	1,722	2,077	2,193	8.1	29.3
Persons below poverty level	26,072	31,528	33,585	17,214	20,785	22,326	8,050	9,302	9,837	10.7	31.9
HOUSING TENURE											
Total occupied units	80,776	93,347	94,312	70,766	80,163	80,968	8,586	10,486	10,671	100.0	100.0
Owner-occupied	54,891	59,846	60,395	49,913	54,094	54,527	4,173	4,445	4,526	67.3	42.4
Renter-occupied	24,421	31,895	32,218	19,581	24,685	24,976	4,257	5,862	5,945	30.8	55.7
No cash rent	1,464	1,606	1,698	1,272	1,384	1,466	156	178	200	1.8	1.9

X Not applicable.   [1] Includes other races not shown separately.   [2] Source: U.S. Bureau of Labor Statistics, *Employment and Earnings*, January issues.   [3] Total unemployment as percent of civilian labor force.   [4] Children under 18 years old.   [5] For definition of median, see Guide to Tabular Presentation.   [6] For explanation of poverty level, see text, section 14.

Source: Except as noted, U.S. Bureau of the Census, *Current Population Reports*, series P-20, No. 448; series P-60, Nos. 174 and 175; and unpublished data.

Population

No. 42. Social and Economic Characteristics of the Asian and Pacific Islander Population: 1991

[As of **March**. Excludes members of Armed Forces except those living off post or with their families on post. Based on Current Population Survey; see text, section 1 and Appendix III]

CHARACTERISTIC	Number (1,000)	Percent distribu-tion	CHARACTERISTIC	Number (1,000)	Percent distribu-tion
Total persons	**7,023**	100.0	FAMILY TYPE		
Under 5 years old	606	8.6	AND INCOME IN 1990		
5 to 14 years old	1,170	16.7	**Total families**	**1,536**	100.0
15 to 44 years old	3,494	49.8	Married couple	1,230	80.1
45 to 64 years old	1,240	17.6	Female householder,		
65 years old and over	514	7.3	no spouse present	194	12.7
			Male householder,		
YEARS OF			no spouse present	112	7.3
SCHOOL COMPLETED			Less than $5,000	60	3.9
Persons 25 years			$5,000 to $9,999	70	4.6
old and over	**4,158**	100.0	$10,000 to $14,999	88	5.7
Elementary: 0 to 8 years	515	12.4	$15,000 to $24,999	193	12.5
High school: 1 to 3 years	243	5.8	$25,000 to $34,999	197	12.8
4 years	1,186	28.5	$35,000 to $49,999	303	19.7
College: 1 to 3 years	591	14.2	$50,000 or more	626	40.7
4 years or more	1,623	39.0	Median income (dol.) [2]	42,245	(X)
			POVERTY [3]		
LABOR FORCE STATUS			Families below poverty level	169	11.0
Civilians 16 years			Persons below poverty level	858	12.2
old and over	**5,121**	100.0	HOUSING TENURE		
Civilian labor force	3,261	63.7	**Total occupied units**	**1,958**	100.0
Employed	3,054	59.6	Owner-occupied	995	50.8
Unemployed	207	4.0	Renter-occupied	947	48.4
Unemployment rate [1]	6.3	(X)	No cash rent	15	0.8
Not in labor force	1,860	36.3			

X Not applicable. [1] Total unemployment as percent of civilian labor force. [2] For definition of median, see Guide to Tabular Presentation. [3] For explanation of poverty level, see text, section 14.

Source: U.S. Bureau of the Census, *Current Population Reports*, series P-20, No. 459.

No. 43. American Indian, Eskimo, or Aleut Population—Population Living Inside and Outside Identified Areas, and Households, by Type: 1990

[**In thousands.** As of **April 1**. Households are based on race of householder]

IDENTIFIED AREA AND HOUSEHOLD TYPE	Total [1]	Oklahoma	California	Arizona	New Mexico	Alaska	Wash-ington
Total population	**1,959**	**252**	**242**	**204**	**134**	**86**	**81**
Inside identified areas	739	207	14	142	88	48	22
American Indian areas	692	207	14	142	88	1	22
Reservations [2]	411	6	13	142	68	1	21
Trust lands [3]	26	(X)	(Z)	(Z)	19	(X)	1
Tribal Jurisdiction Statistical Areas [4] . .	201	201	(X)	(X)	(X)	(X)	(X)
Tribal Designated Statistical Areas [5] .	54	(X)	(X)	(X)	(X)	(X)	(X)
Alaska Native Village Statistical Areas [6] .	47	(X)	(X)	(X)	(X)	47	(X)
Outside identified areas	1,220	45	229	61	47	37	60
Total households	**591**	**78**	**79**	**50**	**33**	**22**	**25**
Family households	442	59	56	41	28	16	18
Married couple family	284	43	37	24	16	10	11
With related children	179	25	21	18	13	7	6
With no related children	104	18	15	6	4	2	4
Male householder, no spouse present. . .	37	3	5	4	3	2	2
With related children	25	2	3	3	2	1	1
With no related children	12	1	2	1	1	1	(Z)
Female householder, no spouse present .	121	13	15	13	8	5	6
With related children	94	9	11	10	6	4	5
With no related children	27	3	4	3	2	1	1
Nonfamily households	149	19	23	9	6	6	7
One person households	116	16	16	7	5	5	5
Two or more person households	33	2	7	2	1	1	2

X Not applicable. Area not located within this State. Z Fewer than 500. [1] Includes other States not shown separately. [2] Federal American Indian reservations are areas with boundaries established by treaty, statute, and/or executive or court order, and recognized by the Federal Government as territory in which American Indian tribes have jurisdiction. State reservations are lands held in trust by State governments for the use and benefit of a given tribe. [3] Property associated with a particular American Indian reservation or tribe, held in trust by the Federal Government. These lands are located outside of a reservation boundary. [4] Areas delineated by federally-recognized tribes in Oklahoma without a reservation, for which the Census Bureau tabulates data. [5] Areas delineated outside Oklahoma by federally- and State- recognized tribes without a land base or associated trust lands, to provide statistical areas for which the Census Bureau tabulates data. [6] Alaska Native villages constitute tribes, bands, clans, groups, villages, communities, or associations in Alaska that are recognized pursuant to the Alaska Native Claims Settlement Act of 1972.

Source: U.S. Bureau of the Census, unpublished data.

No. 44. Social and Economic Characteristics of the Hispanic Population: 1991

[As of March, except labor force status, annual average. Excludes members of the Armed Forces except those living off post or with their families on post. Based on Current Population Survey; see text, section 1, and Appendix III]

CHARACTERISTIC	NUMBER (1,000)						PERCENT DISTRIBUTION					
	His-panic, total	Mexi-can	Puer-to Rican	Cuban	Central and South American	Other His-panic	His-panic, total	Mexi-can	Puer-to Rican	Cuban	Central and South American	Other His-panic
Total persons	21,437	13,421	2,382	1,055	2,951	1,628	100.0	100.0	100.0	100.0	100.0	100.0
Under 5 years old	2,370	1,592	262	59	318	139	11.1	11.9	11.0	5.6	10.8	8.5
5 to 14 years old	4,006	2,698	478	91	497	242	18.7	20.1	20.1	8.6	16.8	14.9
15 to 44 years old	10,993	6,936	1,178	463	1,612	806	51.3	51.7	49.5	43.9	54.6	49.5
45 to 64 years old	2,976	1,608	352	287	435	295	13.9	12.0	14.8	27.2	14.7	18.1
65 years old and over	1,091	587	112	156	89	146	5.1	4.4	4.7	14.8	3.0	9.0
YEARS OF SCHOOL COMPLETED												
Persons 25 years old and over.	11,208	6,518	1,261	784	1,658	986	100.0	100.0	100.0	100.0	100.0	100.0
Elementary: 0 to 8 years	3,761	2,609	306	223	456	166	33.6	40.0	24.3	28.4	27.5	16.8
High school: 1 to 3 years	1,695	1,067	224	83	201	119	15.1	16.4	17.8	10.6	12.1	12.1
4 years	3,285	1,747	416	220	533	370	29.3	26.8	33.0	28.1	32.1	37.5
College: 1 to 3 years	1,379	690	188	113	217	171	12.3	10.6	14.9	14.4	13.1	17.3
4 years or more	1,089	405	127	145	251	160	9.7	6.2	10.1	18.5	15.1	16.2
LABOR FORCE STATUS [1]												
Civilians 16 years old and over.	14,770	8,947	1,629	849	(NA)	(NA)	100.0	100.0	100.0	100.0	(NA)	(NA)
Civilian labor force	9,762	5,984	930	543	(NA)	(NA)	66.1	66.9	57.1	64.0	(NA)	(NA)
Employed.	8,799	5,363	822	499	(NA)	(NA)	59.6	59.9	50.5	58.8	(NA)	(NA)
Unemployed	963	621	108	44	(NA)	(NA)	6.5	6.9	6.6	5.2	(NA)	(NA)
Unemployment rate [2]	9.9	10.4	11.6	8.1	(NA)	(NA)	(X)	(X)	(X)	(X)	(NA)	(NA)
Not in labor force	5,008	2,963	699	306	(NA)	(NA)	33.9	33.1	42.9	36.0	(NA)	(NA)
FAMILY TYPE												
Total families	4,982	2,945	626	335	667	408	100.0	100.0	100.0	100.0	100.0	100.0
Married couple	3,454	2,164	328	255	441	266	69.3	73.5	52.4	76.1	66.1	65.1
Female householder, no spouse present	1,186	563	271	65	174	112	23.8	19.1	43.3	19.4	26.1	27.5
Male householder, no spouse present	342	218	27	15	52	30	6.9	7.4	4.3	4.5	7.8	7.3
FAMILY INCOME IN 1990												
Total families	4,982	2,945	626	335	667	408	100.0	100.0	100.0	100.0	100.0	100.0
Less than $5,000	312	167	69	19	35	22	6.3	5.7	11.0	5.7	5.2	5.4
$5,000 to $9,999	614	340	142	27	61	44	12.3	11.5	22.7	8.1	9.1	10.8
$10,000 to $14,999	629	402	63	30	92	41	12.6	13.7	10.1	9.0	13.8	10.0
$15,000 to $24,999	1,082	659	118	59	170	76	21.7	22.4	18.8	17.6	25.4	18.6
$25,000 to $34,999	826	520	71	66	105	64	16.6	17.7	11.3	19.7	15.7	15.7
$35,000 to $49,999	784	498	76	54	92	65	15.7	16.9	12.1	16.1	13.8	15.9
$50,000 or more	734	359	88	80	111	96	14.7	12.2	14.1	23.9	16.6	23.5
Median income (dol.) [3]	23,431	23,240	18,008	31,439	23,445	27,382	(X)	(X)	(X)	(X)	(X)	(X)
Families below poverty level [4] .	1,244	736	235	46	148	79	25.0	25.0	37.5	13.8	22.2	19.4
Persons below poverty level [4] .	6,006	3,764	966	178	748	350	28.1	28.1	40.6	16.9	25.4	21.5
HOUSING TENURE												
Total occupied units . . .	6,220	3,604	805	425	809	576	100.0	100.0	100.0	100.0	100.0	100.0
Owner-occupied	2,423	1,568	188	201	180	286	39.0	43.5	23.4	47.3	22.2	49.6
Renter-occupied [5]	3,797	2,036	617	224	630	290	61.0	56.5	76.6	52.5	77.8	50.3

NA Not available.   X Not applicable.   [1] Source: U.S. Bureau of Labor Statistics, *Employment and Earnings*, January 1992. [2] Total unemployment as percent of civilian labor force.   [3] For definition of median, see Guide to Tabular Presentation.   [4] For explanation of poverty level, see text, section 14.   [5] Includes no cash rent.

Source: Except as noted, U.S. Bureau of the Census, *Current Population Reports*, P-60, No. 174 and P-20, No. 455.

Population

No. 45. Native and Foreign-Born Population, by Place of Birth: 1920 to 1980

[In thousands, except percent. 1950 based on 20-percent sample; 1960 on 25-percent sample; 1970 on 15-percent sample. 1980 data are based on a sample from the 1980 census; see text, section 1. See source for sampling variability. See also *Historical Statistics, Colonial Times to 1970*, series C 1-10]

YEAR	Total population	NATIVE POPULATION							FOREIGN-BORN	
		Total	Born in State of residence	Born in other States		State of birth not reported	Born in outlying areas [1]	Born abroad or at sea of American parents		
				Number	Percent of native population				Number	Percent of total population
1920	106,022	92,001[2]	71,071	20,274	22.1	314	38	93	14,020	13.2
1930	123,203	108,919[2]	82,678	25,388	23.4	238	136	131	14,283	11.6
1940	132,165	120,508[2]	92,610	26,906	22.4	280	157	122	11,657	8.8
1950	150,845	140,413[2]	102,788	35,284	25.2	1,370	330	96	10,431	6.9
1960	179,326	169,588	119,293	44,691	26.4	4,541	660	402	9,738	5.4
1970	203,210	193,591	131,718	50,639	26.2	8,973	891	1,370	9,619	4.7
1980	226,546	212,466	144,871	65,452	30.8	(3)	1,088	1,055	14,080	6.2

[1] 1920-50, includes Alaska and Hawaii. Includes Puerto Rico. [2] Includes some persons born abroad of American parents, not shown separately. [3] Place of birth was allocated to those who did not report.

No. 46. Foreign-Born Population, by Place of Birth: 1980 and 1990

[As of **April 1**. Data for 1990 includes 1,864,285 persons born abroad of American parents. Data for 1980 excludes such persons. Based on a sample and subject to sampling variability, see text, section 1]

PLACE OF BIRTH	1980 (1,000)	1990 Number (1,000)	1990 Percent distribution	PLACE OF BIRTH	1980 (1,000)	1990 Number (1,000)	1990 Percent distribution
Total [1]	14,080	21,632	100.0	Thailand	55	120	0.6
				Turkey	52	65	0.3
Europe [2]	4,743	4,812	22.2	Vietnam	231	556	2.6
Austria	146	94	0.4	**Canada**	843	871	4.0
Belgium	36	41	0.2	**Caribbean [2]**	1,258	1,987	9.2
Czechoslovakia	113	90	0.4	Antigua-Barbuda	4	12	0.1
Denmark	43	38	0.2	Bahamas	14	24	0.1
Finland	29	24	0.1	Barbados	27	44	0.2
France	120	163	0.8	Cuba	608	751	3.5
Germany	849	1,163	5.4	Dominican Republic	169	357	1.7
Greece	211	189	0.9	Grenada	7	18	0.1
Hungary	144	112	0.5	Haiti	92	229	1.1
Ireland	198	177	0.8	Jamaica	197	343	1.6
Italy	832	640	3.0	Trinidad and Tobago	66	119	0.6
Latvia	34	26	0.1	**Central America [2]**	2,553	5,650	26.1
Lithuania	48	30	0.1	Belize	14	31	0.1
Netherlands	103	104	0.5	Costa Rica	30	48	0.2
Norway	63	46	0.2	El Salvador	94	473	2.2
Poland	418	397	1.8	Guatemala	63	233	1.1
Portugal	212	219	1.0	Honduras	39	115	0.5
Romania	67	93	0.4	Mexico	2,199	4,447	20.6
Spain	74	104	0.5	Nicaragua	44	172	0.8
Sweden	77	57	0.3	Panama	61	125	0.6
Switzerland	43	44	0.2	**South America [2]**	561	1,107	5.1
United Kingdom	669	765	3.5	Argentina	69	97	0.5
Yugoslavia	153	145	0.7	Bolivia	14	34	0.2
Soviet Union [3]	406	337	1.6	Brazil	41	94	0.4
Asia [2]	2,540	5,412	25.0	Chile	35	61	0.3
Afghanistan	4	29	0.1	Colombia	144	304	1.4
Burma	11	20	0.1	Ecuador	86	148	0.7
Cambodia	20	120	0.6	Guyana	49	123	0.6
China	286	543	2.5	Peru	55	152	0.7
Hong Kong	80	152	0.7	Uruguay	13	22	0.1
India	206	463	2.1	Venezuela	33	52	0.2
Indonesia	30	50	0.2	**Africa**	200	401	1.9
Iran	122	217	1.0	Cape Verde	10	15	0.1
Iraq	32	46	0.2	Egypt	43	69	0.3
Israel	67	97	0.4	Ethiopia	8	37	0.2
Japan	222	422	2.0	Ghana	8	22	0.1
Jordan	22	33	0.2	Kenya	6	16	0.1
Korea	290	663	3.1	Morocco	10	22	0.1
Laos	55	173	0.8	Nigeria	26	58	0.3
Lebanon	53	91	0.4	South Africa	16	38	0.2
Malaysia	10	35	0.2	**Oceania**	78	122	0.6
Pakistan	31	94	0.4	Australia	36	52	0.2
Philippines	501	998	4.6	Fiji	8	16	0.1
Saudi Arabia	17	17	0.1	New Zealand	11	18	0.1
Syria	22	38	0.2	Tonga	6	11	0.1
Taiwan	75	254	1.2	Western Samoa	13	13	0.1

[1] Includes persons whose place of birth was not reported. [2] Includes other areas not shown separately. [3] The former Soviet Union is now referred to as the following geopolitical entities: Armenia, Azerbaijan, Byelarus, Georgia, Kazakhstan, Kyrgyzstan, Moldova, Russia, Tajikistan, Turkmenistan, Ukraine, and Uzbekistan.

Source of tables 45 and 46: U.S. Bureau of the Census, *U.S. Census of Population: 1960*, vol. II, part 2A; *1970*, vol. I, parts C and D; *1980 Census of Population*, vol.1, chapter C (PC80-1-C) and chapter D (PC80-1-D); and *1990 Census of Population and Housing Data Paper Listing* (CPH-L-90).

No. 47. Population, by Selected Ancestry Group: 1980 and 1990

[As of **April 1**. Covers persons who reported single and multiple ancestry groups. Persons who reported a multiple ancestry group may be included in more than one category. Major classifications of ancestry groups do not represent strict geographic or cultural definitions. Ancestry data for 1980 are not entirely comparable with 1990 data. Based on a sample and subject to sampling variability; see text, section 1]

ANCESTRY GROUP	1980 (1,000)	1990 Number (1,000)	1990 Percent	ANCESTRY GROUP	1980 (1,000)	1990 Number (1,000)	1990 Percent
European: [1]				Slovene	126	124	0.1
Austrian	949	871	0.4	Swedish	4,345	4,681	1.9
Belgian	360	395	0.2	Swiss	982	1,045	0.4
British	(X)	1,119	0.4	Ukrainian	730	741	0.3
Croatian	253	544	0.2	Welsh	1,665	2,034	0.8
Czech	1,892	1,300	0.5	Yugoslavian	360	258	0.1
Czechoslovakian	(X)	315	0.1	West Indian: [1]			
Danish	1,518	1,635	0.7	Haitian	90	290	0.1
Dutch	6,304	6,227	2.5	Jamaican	253	435	0.2
English	49,598	32,656	13.1	West Indian	(X)	159	0.1
European	175	467	0.2	North Africa and			
Finnish	616	659	0.3	Southwest Asia:			
French	12,892	10,321	4.1	Arab	93	127	0.1
German	49,224	57,986	23.3	Armenian	213	308	0.1
Greek	960	1,110	0.4	Iranian	123	236	0.1
Hungarian	1,777	1,582	0.6	Lebanese	295	394	0.2
Irish	40,166	38,740	15.6	Syrian	107	130	0.1
Italian	12,184	14,715	5.9	Subsaharan Africa:			
Latvian	92	100	(Z)	African	204	246	0.1
Lithuanian	743	812	0.3	North America:			
Norwegian	3,454	3,869	1.6	Acadian	(X)	668	0.3
Polish	8,228	9,366	3.8	American	13,299	12,396	5.0
Portuguese	1,024	1,153	0.5	Canadian	456	561	0.2
Romanian	315	366	0.1	French Canadian	780	2,167	0.9
Russian	2,781	2,953	1.2	Pennsylvania German	(X)	306	0.1
Scandinavian	475	679	0.3	United States	(X)	644	0.3
Scotch-Irish	(X)	5,618	2.3				
Scottish	10,049	5,394	2.2				
Serbian	101	117	(Z)				
Slovak	777	1,883	0.8				

X Not applicable.   Z Less than .05 percent.   [1] Excludes Hispanic groups.

Source: U.S. Bureau of the Census, *1980 Census of Population, Supplementary Report,* series PC80-S1-10 and *1990 Census of Population and Housing Data Paper Listing* (CPH-L-89).

No. 48. Marital Status of the Population, by Sex and Age: 1991

[As of **March. Persons 18 years old and over.** Excludes members of Armed Forces except those living off post or with their families on post. Based on Current Population Survey; see text, section 1 and Appendix III. See *Historical Statistics, Colonial Times to 1970,* series A 160-171, for decennial census data]

SEX AND AGE	NUMBER OF PERSONS (1,000) Total	Single	Married	Widowed	Divorced	PERCENT DISTRIBUTION Total	Single	Married	Widowed	Divorced
Male	87,762	22,925	55,850	2,385	6,602	100.0	26.1	63.6	2.7	7.5
18 to 19 years old	3,436	3,320	116	-	1	100.0	96.6	3.4	-	-
20 to 24 years old	8,839	7,048	1,696	2	93	100.0	79.7	19.2	-	1.1
25 to 29 years old	10,331	4,827	4,997	7	500	100.0	46.7	48.4	0.1	4.8
30 to 34 years old	10,988	2,999	7,052	13	925	100.0	27.3	64.2	0.1	8.4
35 to 39 years old	10,066	1,769	7,202	18	1,077	100.0	17.6	71.5	0.2	10.7
40 to 44 years old	8,966	897	6,921	55	1,092	100.0	10.0	77.2	0.6	12.2
45 to 54 years old	12,428	920	9,950	123	1,435	100.0	7.4	80.1	1.0	11.5
55 to 64 years old	10,161	602	8,326	326	908	100.0	5.9	81.9	3.2	8.9
65 to 74 years old	8,156	381	6,594	751	430	100.0	4.7	80.8	9.2	5.3
75 years old and over	4,391	161	2,997	1,090	142	100.0	3.7	68.3	24.8	3.2
Female	95,833	18,542	56,840	11,289	9,161	100.0	19.3	59.3	11.8	9.6
18 to 19 years old	3,479	3,146	317	1	14	100.0	90.4	9.1	-	0.4
20 to 24 years old	9,148	5,862	3,035	7	243	100.0	64.1	33.2	0.1	2.7
25 to 29 years old	10,436	3,369	6,260	42	764	100.0	32.3	60.0	0.4	7.3
30 to 34 years old	11,160	2,086	7,861	82	1,121	100.0	10.7	70.5	0.7	10.0
35 to 39 years old	10,313	1,203	7,648	124	1,339	100.0	11.7	74.2	1.2	13.0
40 to 44 years old	9,320	818	6,857	185	1,459	100.0	8.8	73.6	2.0	15.7
45 to 54 years old	13,258	740	9,738	681	2,100	100.0	5.6	73.4	5.1	15.8
55 to 64 years old	11,184	417	7,867	1,704	1,196	100.0	3.7	70.3	15.2	10.7
65 to 74 years old	10,081	488	5,370	3,562	661	100.0	4.8	53.4	35.3	6.6
75 years old and over	7,464	412	1,885	4,902	264	100.0	5.5	25.3	65.7	3.6

- Represents or rounds to zero.

Source: U.S. Bureau of the Census, *Current Population Reports,* series P-20, No. 461.

No. 49. Marital Status of the Population, by Sex, Race, and Hispanic Origin: 1970 to 1991

[In millions, except percent. As of March, except as noted. Persons 18 years old and over, except as noted. Excludes members of Armed Forces except those living off post or with their families on post. Except as noted, based on Current Population Survey, see text, section 1 and Appendix III. See *Historical Statistics, Colonial Times to 1970*, series A 160-171, for decennial data]

MARITAL STATUS, RACE, AND HISPANIC ORIGIN	TOTAL				MALE				FEMALE			
	1970	1980	1990	1991	1970	1980	1990	1991	1970	1980	1990	1991
Total [1]	132.5	159.5	181.8	183.6	62.5	75.7	86.9	87.8	70.0	83.8	95.0	95.8
Single	21.4	32.3	40.4	41.5	11.8	18.0	22.4	22.9	9.6	14.3	17.9	18.5
Married	95.0	104.6	112.6	112.7	47.1	51.8	55.8	55.9	47.9	52.8	56.7	56.8
Widowed	11.8	12.7	13.8	13.7	2.1	2.0	2.3	2.4	9.7	10.8	11.5	11.3
Divorced	4.3	9.9	15.1	15.8	1.6	3.9	6.3	6.6	2.7	6.0	8.8	9.2
Percent of total	100.0	100.0	100.0	100.0	100.0	100.0	100.0	100.0	100.0	100.0	100.0	100.0
Single	16.2	20.3	22.2	22.6	18.9	23.8	25.8	26.1	13.7	17.1	18.9	19.3
Married	71.7	65.5	61.9	61.3	75.3	68.4	64.3	63.6	68.5	63.0	59.7	59.3
Widowed	8.9	8.0	7.6	7.4	3.3	2.6	2.7	2.7	13.9	12.8	12.1	11.8
Divorced	3.2	6.2	8.3	8.6	2.5	5.2	7.2	7.5	3.9	7.1	9.3	9.6
Percent standardized for age: [2]												
Single	14.1	16.5	20.6	21.4	16.5	18.7	23.3	24.0	12.1	14.5	18.2	19.0
Married	74.2	69.3	63.7	63.0	77.6	72.9	66.5	65.5	70.8	65.9	61.2	60.6
Widowed	8.3	7.6	6.9	6.7	3.3	2.7	2.7	2.7	13.0	12.1	10.8	10.4
Divorced	3.4	6.6	8.7	9.0	2.6	5.6	7.6	7.8	4.1	7.6	9.8	10.0
White, total	118.2	139.5	155.5	156.7	55.9	66.7	74.8	75.5	62.2	72.8	80.6	81.2
Single	18.4	26.4	31.6	32.2	10.2	15.0	18.0	18.3	8.2	11.4	13.6	13.9
Married	85.8	93.8	99.5	99.8	42.7	46.7	49.5	49.7	43.1	47.1	49.9	50.1
Widowed	10.3	10.9	11.7	11.5	1.7	1.6	1.9	2.0	8.6	9.3	9.8	9.6
Divorced	3.7	8.3	12.6	13.2	1.3	3.4	5.4	5.6	2.3	5.0	7.3	7.6
Percent of total	100.0	100.0	100.0	100.0	100.0	100.0	100.0	100.0	100.0	100.0	100.0	100.0
Single	15.6	18.9	20.3	20.5	18.2	22.5	24.1	24.2	13.2	15.7	16.9	17.1
Married	72.6	67.2	64.0	63.7	76.3	70.0	66.2	65.8	69.3	64.7	61.9	61.8
Widowed	8.7	7.8	7.5	7.4	3.1	2.5	2.6	2.6	13.8	12.8	12.2	11.8
Divorced	3.1	6.0	8.1	8.4	2.4	5.0	7.2	7.4	3.8	6.8	9.0	9.3
Black, total	13.0	16.6	20.3	20.6	5.9	7.4	9.1	9.3	7.1	9.2	11.2	11.4
Single	2.7	5.1	7.1	7.7	1.4	2.5	3.5	3.7	1.2	2.5	3.6	3.9
Married	8.3	8.5	9.3	9.0	3.9	4.1	4.5	4.3	4.4	4.5	4.8	4.7
Widowed	1.4	1.6	1.7	1.8	0.3	0.3	0.3	0.3	1.1	1.3	1.4	1.4
Divorced	0.6	1.4	2.1	2.2	0.2	0.5	0.8	0.9	0.4	0.9	1.3	1.3
Percent of total	100.0	100.0	100.0	100.0	100.0	100.0	100.0	100.0	100.0	100.0	100.0	100.0
Single	20.6	30.5	35.1	37.1	24.3	34.3	38.4	40.2	17.4	27.4	32.5	34.5
Married	64.1	51.4	45.8	43.6	66.9	54.6	49.2	46.7	61.7	48.7	43.0	41.0
Widowed	11.0	9.8	8.5	8.6	5.2	4.2	3.7	3.6	15.8	14.3	12.4	12.7
Divorced	4.4	8.4	10.6	10.8	3.6	7.0	8.8	9.5	5.0	9.5	12.0	11.8
Hispanic, [3] total	5.9	7.9	13.6	13.9	2.8	3.8	6.7	6.9	3.0	4.1	6.8	7.0
Single	1.7	1.9	3.7	3.8	0.9	1.0	2.2	2.2	0.8	0.9	1.5	1.6
Married	3.7	5.2	8.4	8.5	1.8	2.5	4.1	4.2	1.9	2.6	4.3	4.3
Widowed	0.3	0.4	0.5	0.6	0.1	0.1	0.1	0.1	0.2	0.3	0.4	0.5
Divorced	0.2	0.5	1.0	1.0	0.1	0.2	0.4	0.4	0.1	0.3	0.6	0.6
Percent of total	100.0	100.0	100.0	100.0	100.0	100.0	100.0	100.0	100.0	100.0	100.0	100.0
Single	29.3	24.1	27.2	27.3	32.2	27.3	32.1	32.2	26.5	21.1	22.5	22.4
Married	62.4	65.6	61.7	61.1	63.5	67.1	60.9	60.2	61.5	64.3	62.4	61.9
Widowed	4.9	4.4	4.0	4.3	2.0	1.6	1.5	1.5	7.6	7.1	6.5	7.1
Divorced	3.4	5.8	7.0	7.3	2.3	4.0	5.5	6.0	4.4	7.6	8.5	8.6

[1] Includes persons of other races, not shown separately. [2] 1960 age distribution used as standard; standardization improves comparability over time by removing effects of changes in age distribution of population. [3] Hispanic persons may be of any race. 1970 data as of April and covers persons 14 years old and over.

Source: U.S. Bureau of the Census, *Census of Population: 1970, Persons of Spanish Origin*, PC(2)1C; and *Current Population Reports*, series P-20, No. 461, and earlier reports.

No. 50. Divorced Persons per 1,000 Married Persons With Spouse Present, by Sex, Race, and Age: 1970 to 1991

[As of **March. 1970** and **1975**, persons **14** years old and over; beginning **1980, 15** years old and over. See headnote, table 49]

YEAR	Total	Male	Female	SEX AND YEAR	RACE		AGE			
					White	Black	15 to 29 years	30 to 44 years	45 to 64 years	65 years old and over
1970	47	35	60	Male: 1970	32	62	[1]28	33	40	32
1975	69	54	84	1980	74	149	78	104	70	48
1980	100	79	120	1990	112	208	88	146	124	67
1985	128	103	153	1991	117	239	94	155	134	61
1988	133	110	156	Female: 1970	56	104	[1]46	61	66	69
1989	138	114	161	1980	110	258	108	147	112	89
1990	142	118	166	1990	153	358	112	192	180	127
1991	148	124	172	1991	159	370	116	189	198	133

[1] 14 to 29 years.

Source: U.S. Bureau of the Census, *Current Population Reports*, series P-20, No. 461, and earlier reports.

No. 51. Single (Never-Married) Persons as Percent of Total Population, by Sex and Age: 1970 to 1991

[As of **March. Persons 18 years old and over.** Based on Current Population Survey; see headnote, table 48]

AGE	MALE					FEMALE				
	1970	1980	1985	1990	1991	1970	1980	1985	1990	1991
Total..............	**18.9**	**23.8**	**25.2**	**25.8**	**26.1**	**13.7**	**17.1**	**18.2**	**18.9**	**19.3**
18 to 19 years old	92.8	94.3	97.1	96.8	96.6	75.6	82.8	86.7	90.3	90.4
20 to 24 years old	54.7	68.8	75.6	79.3	79.7	35.8	50.2	58.5	62.8	64.1
25 to 29 years old	19.1	33.1	38.7	45.2	46.7	10.5	20.9	26.4	31.1	32.3
30 to 34 years old	9.4	15.9	20.8	27.0	27.3	6.2	9.5	13.5	16.4	18.7
35 to 39 years old	7.2	7.8	10.1	14.7	17.6	5.4	6.2	8.1	10.4	11.7
40 to 44 years old	6.3	7.1	8.6	10.5	10.0	4.9	4.8	5.3	8.0	8.8
45 to 54 years old	7.5	6.1	6.3	6.3	7.4	4.9	4.7	4.6	5.0	5.6
55 to 64 years old	7.8	5.3	6.1	5.8	5.9	6.8	4.5	3.7	3.9	3.7
65 years old and over......	7.5	4.9	5.3	4.2	4.3	7.7	5.9	5.1	4.9	5.1
65 to 74 years old.......	8.0	5.2	5.2	4.7	4.7	7.8	5.6	4.4	4.6	4.8
75 years old and over	6.6	4.2	5.3	3.4	3.7	7.5	6.3	6.2	5.4	5.5

No. 52. Unmarried Couples, by Selected Characteristics, 1980 to 1991, and by Marital Status of Partners, 1991

[**In thousands.** As of **March.** An "unmarried couple" is two unrelated adults of the opposite sex sharing the same household. See headnote, table 56]

PRESENCE OF CHILDREN AND AGE OF HOUSEHOLDER	1980	1985	1990	1991	MARITAL STATUS OF MALE	Total	MARITAL STATUS OF FEMALE			
							Never married	Divorced	Widowed	Married, husband absent
Unmarried couples ..	**1,589**	**1,983**	**2,856**	**3,039**	**Total, 1991**	**3,039**	**1,658**	**1,022**	**184**	**175**
No children under 15 yr ...	1,159	1,380	1,966	2,077	Never married..........	1,682	1,219	337	53	75
Some children under 15 yr .	431	603	891	962	Divorced	1,075	357	593	73	53
Under 25 yr. old	411	425	596	587	Widowed	95	19	25	48	4
25 to 44 yr. old.........	837	1,203	1,775	1,858	Married, wife absent.....	185	63	67	9	45
45 to 64 yr. old.........	221	239	358	453						
65 yr. old and over	119	116	127	141						

Source of tables 51 and 52: U.S. Bureau of the Census, *Current Population Reports*, series P-20, No. 461, and earlier reports.

No. 53. Black-White Married Couples: 1980 to 1991

[As of **March. Persons 15 years old and over.** Based on Current Population Survey; see headnote, table 48]

ITEM	NUMBER (1,000)			PERCENT		
	1980	1990	1991	1980	1990	1991
Total married couples	**49,714**	**53,256**	**53,227**	**100.0**	**100.0**	**100.0**
Black-White married couples, total	**167**	**211**	**231**	**0.3**	**0.4**	**0.4**
Husband Black, wife White	122	150	156	0.2	0.3	0.3
Wife Black, husband White	45	61	75	0.1	0.1	0.1

Source: U.S. Bureau of the Census, *Current Population Reports*, series P-20, No. 458 and earlier reports.

No. 54. Married-Couple Households, by Hispanic Origin Status of Husband and Wife: 1991

[**In thousands.** As of **March.** Based on Current Population Survey; see headnote, table 56]

ORIGIN OF HUSBAND	Total population	ORIGIN OF WIFE						
		Hispanic						Not Hispanic
		Total	Mexican	Puerto Rican	Cuban	Central and South American	Other Hispanic	
Total, all persons.............	**52,147**	**3,545**	**2,205**	**324**	**216**	**508**	**291**	**48,602**
Hispanic origin, total	3,462	2,930	1,893	261	185	408	183	531
Mexican....................	2,167	1,882	1,840	7	3	26	7	285
Puerto Rican..................	328	269	11	232	6	12	8	58
Cuban	255	214	8	7	170	24	6	41
Central and South American.......	442	379	24	8	5	341	2	63
Other Hispanic origin	270	186	11	7	2	6	160	84
Not of Hispanic origin.............	48,685	614	312	63	31	100	108	48,071

Source: U.S. Bureau of the Census, unpublished data.

Population

No. 55. Householder and Marital Status of Population, 15 Years Old and Over: 1991

[In thousands. As of March. See headnote, table 56]

HOUSEHOLDER AND MARITAL STATUS	Total, 15 yrs. and over[1]	MALE					FEMALE				
		Total[1]	20 to 24 years	25 to 44 years	45 to 64 years	65 yr. and over	Total[1]	20 to 24 years	25 to 44 years	45 to 64 years	65 yr. and over
Total persons	193,519	92,840	8,839	40,351	22,589	12,547	100,680	9,148	41,219	24,442	17,546
Householder.	94,312	63,279	2,540	29,719	19,725	11,100	31,033	1,902	11,909	7,549	9,427
Single	14,244	7,110	1,230	4,509	868	380	7,134	1,340	4,151	782	655
Married, spouse present .	52,147	48,222	1,218	22,126	16,206	8,605	3,925	248	2,123	1,099	430
Married, spouse absent. .	4,450	1,604	53	802	537	207	2,846	189	1,659	769	220
Widowed	11,688	1,921	-	66	392	1,462	9,766	1	372	2,089	7,303
Divorced.	11,783	4,422	39	2,214	1,722	446	7,362	123	3,605	2,809	819
Not householder.	99,208	29,561	6,299	10,632	2,864	1,447	69,647	7,246	29,311	16,893	8,119
Single	37,058	20,876	5,819	5,983	654	162	16,182	4,521	3,326	374	245
Married, spouse present .	54,307	5,005	347	2,576	1,319	717	49,302	2,479	24,400	15,570	6,536
Married, spouse absent. .	1,868	1,030	78	667	215	63	838	120	446	167	70
Widowed	1,987	464	2	27	56	379	1,522	5	61	296	1,161
Divorced.	3,988	2,186	54	1,379	620	127	1,803	120	1,077	487	107

- Represents or rounds to zero.   [1] Includes 15 to 19 year olds.

Source: U.S. Bureau of the Census, *Current Population Reports*, series P-20, No. 461.

No. 56. Households, Families, Subfamilies, Married Couples, and Unrelated Individuals: 1960 to 1991

[In thousands, except as indicated. As of March. Based on Current Population Survey; includes members of Armed Forces living off post or with their families on post, but excludes all other members of Armed Forces; see text, section 1 and Appendix III. For definition of terms, see text, section 1. Minus sign (-) indicates decrease. See also *Historical Statistics, Colonial Times to 1970*, series A 288-319]

TYPE OF UNIT	1960	1970	1975	1980	1985	1989	1990	1991	PERCENT CHANGE		
									1970-1980	1980-1990	1990-1991
Households.	52,799	63,401	71,120	80,776	86,789	92,830	93,347	94,312	27	16	1
Average size.	3.33	3.14	2.94	2.76	2.69	2.62	2.63	2.63	(X)	(X)	(X)
Family households	44,905	51,456	55,563	59,550	62,706	65,837	66,090	66,322	16	11	-
Married couple . . , ...	39,254	44,728	46,951	49,112	50,350	52,100	52,317	52,147	10	7	-
Male householder[1] . , ...	1,228	1,228	1,485	1,733	2,228	2,847	2,884	2,907	41	66	1
Female householder[1]	4,422	5,500	7,127	8,705	10,129	10,890	10,890	11,268	58	25	4
Nonfamily households	7,895	11,945	15,557	21,226	24,082	26,994	27,257	27,990	78	28	3
Male householder	2,716	4,063	5,912	8,807	10,114	11,874	11,606	12,150	117	32	5
Female householder.	5,179	7,882	9,645	12,419	13,968	15,120	15,651	15,840	58	26	1
One person	6,896	10,851	13,939	18,296	20,602	22,708	22,999	23,590	69	26	3
Families.	45,111	51,586	55,712	59,550	62,706	65,837	66,090	66,322	15	11	-
Average size.	3.67	3.58	3.42	3.29	3.23	3.16	3.17	3.18	(X)	(X)	(X)
Married couple	39,329	44,755	46,971	49,112	50,350	52,100	52,317	52,147	10	7	-
Male householder[1] . , ...	1,275	1,239	1,499	1,733	2,228	2,847	2,884	2,907	40	66	1
Female householder[1]	4,507	5,591	7,242	8,705	10,129	10,890	10,890	11,268	56	25	4
Unrelated subfamilies.	207	130	149	360	526	473	534	639	177	48	20
Married couple	75	27	20	20	46	49	68	94	(B)	(B)	(B)
Male reference persons[1] . , . .	47	11	14	36	85	26	45	41	(B)	(B)	(B)
Female reference persons[1] . .	85	91	115	304	395	398	421	504	234	39	20
Related subfamilies	1,514	1,150	1,349	1,150	2,228	2,278	2,403	2,546	-	109	6
Married couple	871	617	576	582	719	775	871	986	-6	50	13
Father-child[1]	115	48	69	54	116	103	153	142	(B)	(B)	-7
Mother-child[1]	528	484	705	512	1,392	1,400	1,378	1,418	6	169	3
Married couples.	40,200	45,373	47,547	49,714	51,114	52,924	53,256	53,227	10	7	-
With own household	39,254	44,728	46,951	49,112	50,350	52,100	52,317	52,147	10	7	-
Without own household	946	645	596	602	764	824	939	1,080	-7	56	15
Percent without	2.4	1.4	1.3	1.2	1.5	1.6	1.8	2.0	(X)	(X)	(X)
Unrelated individuals	11,092	14,988	19,100	26,426	30,518	34,499	35,384	36,298	76	34	3
Nonfamily householders.	7,895	11,945	15,557	21,226	24,082	26,994	27,257	27,990	78	28	3
Secondary individuals	3,198	3,043	3,543	5,200	6,436	7,505	8,127	8,308	71	56	2
Male	1,746	1,631	2,087	3,006	3,743	4,241	4,711	4,880	84	57	4
Female	1,451	1,412	1,456	2,194	2,693	3,264	3,416	3,428	55	56	-

- Represents or rounds to zero.   B Not shown; base less than 75,000.   X Not applicable.   [1] No spouse present.

Source: U.S. Bureau of the Census, *Current Population Reports*, series P-20, No. 458.

No. 57. Family and Nonfamily Households, by Race, Hispanic Origin, and Type: 1970 to 1991

[As of **March**, except as noted. Based on Current Population Survey, except as noted; see headnote, table 56. See also *Historical Statistics, Colonial Times to 1970*, series A 292-295 and A 320-334]

RACE, HISPANIC ORIGIN, AND TYPE	NUMBER (1,000)					PERCENT DISTRIBUTION				
	1970	1980	1985	1990	1991	1970	1980	1985	1990	1991
FAMILY HOUSEHOLDS										
White, total	46,166	52,243	54,400	56,590	56,803	100	100	100	100	100
Married couple	41,029	44,751	45,643	46,981	47,014	89	86	84	83	83
Male householder [1]	1,038	1,441	1,816	2,303	2,276	2	3	3	4	4
Female householder [1].	4,099	6,052	6,941	7,306	7,512	9	12	13	13	13
Black, total	4,856	6,184	6,778	7,470	7,471	100	100	100	100	100
Married couple	3,317	3,433	3,469	3,750	3,569	68	56	51	50	48
Male householder [1]	181	256	344	446	472	4	4	5	6	6
Female householder [1].	1,358	2,495	2,964	3,275	3,430	28	40	44	44	46
Asian or Pacific Islander, total [2] .	(NA)	818	(NA)	1,531	1,536	(NA)	100	(NA)	100	100
Married couple	(NA)	691	(NA)	1,256	1,230	(NA)	84	(NA)	82	80
Male householder [1]	(NA)	39	(NA)	86	112	(NA)	5	(NA)	6	7
Female householder [1].	(NA)	88	(NA)	188	194	(NA)	11	(NA)	12	13
Hispanic, total [3]	2,004	3,029	3,939	4,840	4,981	100	100	100	100	100
Married couple	1,615	2,282	2,824	3,395	3,454	81	75	72	70	69
Male householder [1]	82	138	210	329	342	4	5	5	7	7
Female householder [1].	307	610	905	1,116	1,186	15	20	23	23	24
NONFAMILY HOUSEHOLDS										
White, total	10,436	18,522	20,928	23,573	24,166	100	100	100	100	100
Male householder	3,406	7,499	8,608	9,951	10,312	33	40	41	42	43
Female householder.	7,030	11,023	12,320	13,622	13,853	67	60	59	58	57
Black, total	1,367	2,402	2,703	3,015	3,200	100	100	100	100	100
Male householder	564	1,146	1,244	1,313	1,531	41	48	46	44	48
Female householder.	803	1,256	1,459	1,702	1,670	59	52	54	56	52
Hispanic, total [3]	299	654	944	1,093	1,238	100	100	100	100	100
Male householder	150	365	509	587	669	50	56	54	54	54
Female householder.	148	289	435	506	569	49	44	46	46	46

NA Not available. [1] No spouse present. [2] 1980 data as of April and are from 1980 Census of Population. [3] Hispanic persons may be of any race. 1970 data as of April.

Source: U.S. Bureau of the Census, *Census of Population: 1970, Persons of Spanish Origin*, PC(2)-1C; and *Current Population Reports*, series P-20, No. 458, and earlier reports.

No. 58. Households, by Characteristic of Householder and Size of Household: 1970 to 1991

[As of **March**. Based on Current Population Survey; see headnote, table 56. See also *Historical Statistics, Colonial Times to 1970*, series A 335-349]

CHARACTERISTIC OF HOUSEHOLDER AND SIZE OF HOUSEHOLD	NUMBER (mil.)						PERCENT DISTRIBUTION					
	1970	1975	1980	1985	1990	1991	1970	1975	1980	1985	1990	1991
Total [1]	63.4	71.1	80.8	86.8	93.3	94.3	100	100	100	100	100	100
Age of householder:												
15 to 24 years old [2]	4.4	5.8	6.6	5.4	5.1	4.9	7	8	8	6	6	5
25 to 29 years old	6.1	7.8	9.3	9.6	9.4	9.2	10	11	12	11	10	10
30 to 34 years old	5.6	7.1	9.3	10.4	11.0	11.1	9	10	12	12	12	12
35 to 44 years old	11.8	11.9	14.0	17.5	20.6	21.3	19	17	17	20	22	23
45 to 54 years old	12.2	12.9	12.7	12.6	14.5	14.8	20	18	16	15	16	16
55 to 64 years old	10.8	11.3	12.5	13.1	12.5	12.5	17	16	16	15	13	13
65 to 74 years old	7.7	8.9	10.1	10.9	11.7	12.0	12	13	13	13	13	13
75 years old and over.	4.8	5.4	6.4	7.3	8.4	8.5	8	8	8	8	9	9
Male.	50.0	54.3	58.0	60.0	62.9	63.3	79	76	72	69	67	67
Female.	13.4	16.8	22.8	26.8	30.4	31.0	21	24	28	31	33	33
White	56.6	62.9	70.8	75.3	80.2	81.0	90	89	88	87	86	86
Black	6.2	7.3	8.6	9.5	10.5	10.7	10	10	11	11	11	11
Hispanic [3]	(NA)	(NA)	3.7	4.9	5.9	6.2	(NA)	(NA)	5	6	6	7
One person	10.9	13.9	18.3	20.6	23.0	23.6	17	20	23	24	25	25
Male	3.5	4.9	7.0	7.9	9.0	9.5	6	7	9	9	10	10
Female	7.3	9.0	11.3	12.7	14.0	14.1	12	13	14	15	15	15
Two persons	18.3	21.8	25.3	27.4	30.1	30.2	29	31	31	32	32	32
Three persons	10.9	12.4	14.1	15.5	16.1	16.1	17	17	18	18	17	17
Four persons	10.0	11.1	12.7	13.6	14.5	14.6	16	16	16	16	16	15
Five persons	6.5	6.4	6.1	6.1	6.2	6.2	10	9	8	7	7	7
Six persons	3.5	3.1	2.5	2.3	2.1	2.2	6	4	3	3	2	2
Seven persons or more	3.2	2.5	1.8	1.3	1.3	1.5	5	4	2	2	1	2

NA Not available. [1] Includes other races, not shown separately. [2] 1970 and 1975, persons 14 to 24 years old. [3] Hispanic persons may be of any race.

Source: U.S. Bureau of the Census, *Current Population Reports*, series P-20, No. 458, and earlier reports; and unpublished data.

No. 59. Household Characteristics, by Race, Hispanic Origin, and Type: 1991

[As of **March.** Based on Current Population Survey; see headnote, table 56. For composition of regions, see table 25]

CHARACTERISTIC	NUMBER OF HOUSEHOLDS (1,000)							PERCENT DISTRIBUTION							PERSONS PER HOUSEHOLD		
	Total	Black	His-panic[1]	Family: Total[2]	Family: Married couple	Family: Female house-holder[3]	Non-family house-holds	Total	Black	His-panic[1]	Family: Total[2]	Family: Married couple	Family: Female house-holder[3]	Non-family house-holds	Total	Black	His-panic[1]
Total	**94,312**	**10,671**	**6,220**	**66,322**	**52,147**	**11,268**	**27,990**	**100**	**100**	**100**	**100**	**100**	**100**	**100**	**2.63**	**2.87**	**3.44**
Age of householder:																	
15 to 24 years old	4,882	683	594	2,727	1,558	919	2,156	5	6	10	4	3	8	8	2.38	2.67	3.13
25 to 29 years old	9,246	1,199	845	6,260	4,552	1,309	2,986	10	11	14	9	9	12	11	2.64	2.90	3.52
30 to 34 years old	11,077	1,392	963	8,330	6,451	1,557	2,747	12	13	16	13	12	14	10	3.03	2.93	3.68
35 to 44 years old	21,304	2,578	1,524	17,078	13,245	3,074	4,226	23	24	25	26	25	27	15	3.28	3.35	3.98
45 to 54 years old	14,751	1,693	957	11,701	9,406	1,803	3,050	16	16	15	18	18	16	11	2.96	3.06	3.63
55 to 64 years old	12,524	1,337	682	9,326	7,898	1,118	3,198	13	13	11	14	15	10	11	2.35	2.72	2.98
65 to 74 years old	12,001	1,118	434	7,373	6,299	841	4,629	13	11	7	11	12	8	17	1.89	2.26	2.29
75 years old and over	8,526	672	220	3,527	2,737	646	4,998	9	6	4	5	5	6	18	1.56	1.93	1.96
Region:																	
Northeast	19,271	1,952	1,123	13,450	10,487	2,404	5,820	20	18	18	20	20	21	21	2.63	2.83	3.18
Midwest	23,223	2,121	408	16,119	12,910	2,547	7,104	25	20	7	24	25	23	25	2.58	2.82	3.43
South	32,312	5,737	1,982	23,279	18,106	4,232	9,034	34	54	32	35	35	38	32	2.63	2.96	3.34
West	19,506	862	2,706	13,474	10,645	2,084	6,032	21	8	44	20	20	19	22	2.71	2.53	3.62
Size of household:																	
One person	23,590	2,778	925	(X)	(X)	(X)	23,590	25	26	15	(X)	(X)	(X)	84	1.00	1.00	1.00
Two persons	30,181	2,685	1,354	26,620	20,433	4,793	3,560	32	25	22	40	39	43	13	2.00	2.00	2.00
Three persons	16,082	2,013	1,217	15,518	11,284	3,470	564	17	19	20	23	22	31	2	3.00	3.00	3.00
Four persons	14,556	1,674	1,167	14,356	12,160	1,796	200	15	16	19	22	23	16	1	4.00	4.00	4.00
Five persons	6,206	805	834	6,158	5,282	682	48	7	8	13	9	10	6	(Z)	5.00	5.00	5.00
Six persons	2,237	371	378	2,227	1,876	268	10	2	4	6	3	4	2	(Z)	6.00	6.00	6.00
Seven persons or more	1,459	346	345	1,442	1,111	259	17	2	3	6	2	2	2	(Z)	(NA)	(NA)	(NA)
Marital status of householder:																	
Single (never married)	14,244	2,807	1,057	3,742	(X)	2,722	10,502	15	26	17	6	(X)	24	38	(NA)	(NA)	(NA)
Married, spouse present	52,147	3,569	3,454	52,147	52,147	(X)	(X)	55	33	56	79	100	(X)	(X)	(NA)	(NA)	(NA)
Married, spouse absent	4,450	1,227	581	2,494	(X)	2,050	1,956	5	12	9	4	(X)	18	7	(NA)	(NA)	(NA)
Separated	3,448	1,062	430	2,000	(X)	1,663	1,448	4	10	7	3	(X)	15	5	(NA)	(NA)	(NA)
Widowed	11,688	1,433	423	2,852	(X)	2,436	8,836	12	13	7	4	(X)	22	32	(NA)	(NA)	(NA)
Divorced	11,783	1,635	705	5,087	(X)	4,060	6,696	13	15	11	8	(X)	36	24	(NA)	(NA)	(NA)
Tenure:																	
Owner occupied	60,395	4,526	2,423	47,293	40,728	4,951	13,102	64	42	39	71	78	44	47	2.75	3.14	3.56
Renter occupied	33,917	6,145	3,797	19,028	11,419	6,317	14,888	36	58	61	29	22	56	53	2.43	2.68	3.36

NA Not available.   X Not applicable.   Z Less than 0.5 percent.   [1] Hispanic persons may be of any race.   [2] Includes male householder, no spouse present.   [3] No spouse present.

Source: U.S. Bureau of the Census, *Current Population Reports*, series P-20, No. 458; and series P-60, No. 174.

No. 60. Households—States: 1970 to 1990

[As of **April 1**. For definitions of household and family, see text, section 1]

REGION, DIVISION, AND STATE	HOUSEHOLDS Number (1,000) 1970	1980	1990	Percent change 1970-80	1980-90	Persons per household 1980	1990	FAMILIES, 1990 (1,000) Total[1]	Married couple Total[2]	With related children[3]	One-parent[4]	NONFAMILY HOUSEHOLDS, 1990 (1,000) Total[5]	One-person
U.S....	63,450	80,390	91,947	26.7	14.4	2.75	2.63	64,518	50,708	24,552	8,551	27,429	22,580
Northeast .	15,483	17,471	18,873	12.8	8.0	2.74	2.61	13,071	10,089	4,688	1,655	5,802	4,828
N.E.....	3,645	4,362	4,943	19.7	13.3	2.74	2.58	3,404	2,692	1,254	396	1,538	1,225
ME ...	303	395	465	30.5	17.7	2.75	2.56	329	271	130	38	137	108
NH ...	225	323	411	43.5	27.1	2.75	2.62	293	245	122	29	119	90
VT....	132	178	211	35.0	18.1	2.75	2.57	145	119	59	17	66	49
MA ...	1,760	2,033	2,247	15.5	10.5	2.72	2.58	1,515	1,170	541	184	732	581
RI	292	339	378	16.0	11.6	2.70	2.55	259	202	92	31	119	99
CT....	933	1,094	1,230	17.2	12.5	2.76	2.59	864	685	309	98	366	297
M.A ..	11,837	13,109	13,930	10.7	6.3	2.74	2.62	9,667	7,397	3,434	1,259	4,263	3,603
NY....	5,914	6,340	6,639	7.2	4.7	2.70	2.63	4,489	3,316	1,563	670	2,150	1,806
NJ....	2,218	2,549	2,795	14.9	9.7	2.84	2.70	2,021	1,579	740	233	773	646
PA....	3,705	4,220	4,496	13.9	6.5	2.74	2.57	3,156	2,502	1,131	356	1,340	1,151
Midwest...	17,537	20,859	22,317	18.9	7.0	2.75	2.60	15,675	12,574	6,079	1,954	6,642	5,588
E.N.C ..	12,383	14,654	15,597	18.3	6.4	2.78	2.63	11,015	8,699	4,209	1,446	4,582	3,852
OH ...	3,289	3,834	4,088	16.5	6.6	2.76	2.59	2,895	2,294	1,099	374	1,192	1,020
IN	1,609	1,927	2,065	19.7	7.2	2.77	2.61	1,480	1,202	586	180	585	497
IL	3,502	4,045	4,202	15.5	3.9	2.76	2.65	2,925	2,272	1,111	392	1,277	1,081
MI....	2,653	3,195	3,419	20.4	7.0	2.84	2.66	2,439	1,883	909	356	980	809
WI....	1,329	1,652	1,822	24.3	10.3	2.77	2.61	1,275	1,048	505	144	547	444
W.N.C...	5,154	6,205	6,720	20.4	8.3	2.68	2.55	4,660	3,875	1,870	508	2,060	1,737
MN ...	1,154	1,445	1,648	25.2	14.0	2.74	2.58	1,131	943	468	119	517	414
IA ...	896	1,053	1,064	17.5	1.1	2.68	2.52	741	630	293	72	324	275
MO ...	1,521	1,793	1,961	17.9	9.4	2.67	2.54	1,368	1,105	522	169	593	511
ND ...	182	228	241	25.4	5.8	2.75	2.55	166	142	72	15	75	64
SD....	201	243	259	20.8	6.8	2.74	2.59	180	153	76	19	79	68
NE....	474	571	602	20.6	5.4	2.66	2.54	415	351	171	42	187	160
KS....	727	872	945	19.9	8.3	2.62	2.53	659	552	267	71	286	245
South	19,258	26,486	31,822	37.5	20.1	2.77	2.61	22,722	17,786	8,625	3,145	9,101	7,641
S.A.....	9,438	13,160	16,503	39.4	25.4	2.73	2.56	11,639	9,091	4,180	1,578	4,864	3,974
DE. ...	165	207	247	25.7	19.5	2.79	2.61	176	138	65	23	72	57
MD ...	1,175	1,461	1,749	24.3	19.7	2.82	2.67	1,246	949	462	179	503	395
DC...	263	253	250	-3.6	-1.4	2.40	2.26	122	63	26	36	128	104
VA....	1,391	1,863	2,292	34.0	23.0	2.77	2.61	1,629	1,302	640	198	662	524
WV ...	547	686	689	25.4	0.3	2.79	2.55	500	406	195	55	188	169
NC ...	1,510	2,043	2,517	35.4	23.2	2.78	2.54	1,812	1,424	668	242	705	597
SC....	734	1,030	1,258	40.3	22.1	2.93	2.68	928	710	354	141	330	281
GA ...	1,369	1,872	2,367	36.7	26.4	2.84	2.66	1,713	1,307	667	265	654	538
FL....	2,285	3,744	5,135	63.9	37.1	2.55	2.46	3,512	2,792	1,102	439	1,623	1,310
E.S.C ..	3,868	5,051	5,652	30.6	11.9	2.83	2.62	4,142	3,233	1,586	579	1,509	1,334
KY....	984	1,263	1,380	28.4	9.2	2.82	2.60	1,016	817	408	124	364	321
TN....	1,213	1,619	1,854	33.4	14.5	2.77	2.56	1,348	1,060	503	179	506	442
AL....	1,034	1,342	1,507	29.8	12.3	2.84	2.62	1,104	858	418	155	403	358
MS ...	637	827	911	29.9	10.2	2.97	2.75	674	498	257	121	237	213
W.S.C ...	5,952	8,276	9,668	39.0	16.8	2.80	2.69	6,941	5,462	2,860	988	2,727	2,332
AR....	615	816	891	32.6	9.2	2.74	2.57	652	527	248	82	240	214
LA....	1,052	1,412	1,499	34.2	6.2	2.91	2.74	1,090	803	428	195	409	356
OK ...	851	1,119	1,206	31.5	7.8	2.62	2.53	855	696	336	107	351	309
TX....	3,434	4,929	6,071	43.5	23.2	2.82	2.73	4,344	3,436	1,848	604	1,727	1,453
West	11,172	15,574	18,935	39.4	21.6	2.71	2.72	13,050	10,260	5,159	1,797	5,885	4,523
Mt	2,518	3,986	5,033	58.3	26.3	2.79	2.65	3,499	2,831	1,423	456	1,535	1,227
MT ...	217	284	306	30.6	7.9	2.70	2.53	212	177	86	25	94	80
ID	219	324	361	48.0	11.3	2.85	2.73	263	224	114	28	98	81
WY ...	105	166	169	58.3	1.9	2.78	2.63	120	101	53	14	49	41
CO ...	691	1,061	1,282	53.6	20.8	2.65	2.51	854	690	343	112	428	341
NM ...	289	441	543	52.6	22.9	2.90	2.74	391	304	161	62	151	125
AZ....	539	957	1,369	77.5	43.0	2.79	2.62	940	748	348	129	429	338
UT....	298	449	537	50.6	19.8	3.20	3.15	411	348	207	44	126	102
NV....	160	304	466	90.1	53.2	2.59	2.53	307	240	111	43	159	120
Pac	8,653	11,587	13,902	33.9	20.0	2.68	2.74	9,551	7,429	3,736	1,341	4,351	3,296
WA ...	1,106	1,541	1,872	39.3	21.5	2.81	2.50	1,265	1,020	490	161	607	476
OR ...	692	992	1,103	43.4	11.3	2.60	2.52	751	613	278	93	352	279
CA....	6,574	8,630	10,381	31.3	20.3	2.68	2.79	7,139	5,470	2,791	1,037	3,242	2,430
AK....	79	131	189	66.3	43.7	2.93	2.80	133	106	65	20	56	42
HI	203	294	356	44.8	21.2	3.15	3.01	263	210	111	30	93	69

[1] Includes other family types not shown separately. [2] Includes married couple families with no related children. [3] "Related children" in a family includes own children and all other persons under 18 years of age in the household, regardless of marital status, who are related to the householder, except the spouse of the householder. [4] Comprises male family householders with no wife present and with related children and female family householders with no husband present and with related children. [5] Includes nonfamily households with two or more persons.

Source: U.S. Bureau of the Census, *Census of Population: 1970; 1980 Census of Population*, vol. 1, chapter B; and unpublished data from *1990 Census of Population and Housing Summary Tape File 1C*.

Population

No. 61. Households, by Type—60 Largest Metropolitan Areas: 1990

[As of **April 1**. For definitions of household and family, see text, section 1. Areas as defined by U.S. Office of Management and Budget, June 30, 1990. For definitions, see Appendix II]

METROPOLITAN AREA [1]	HOUSEHOLDS [2]			FAMILIES (1,000)				One-person house-holds (1,000)
	Total (1,000)	Percent change, 1980 –90	Persons per house-hold	Total [3]	Married couple		One-par-ent [6]	
					Total [4]	With related chil-dren [5]		
New York-Northern New Jersey-Long Island, NY-NJ-CT CMSA.	6,621	4.8	2.67	4,554	3,353	1,563	652	1,748
Los Angeles-Anaheim-Riverside, CA CMSA.	4,901	18.3	2.91	3,410	2,568	1,366	510	1,126
Chicago-Gary-Lake County, IL-IN-WI CMSA.	2,908	5.1	2.72	2,029	1,526	768	294	736
San Francisco-Oakland-San Jose, CA CMSA.	2,330	14.1	2.61	1,512	1,167	562	201	604
Philadelphia-Wilmington-Trenton, PA-NJ-DE-MD CMSA	2,154	9.3	2.66	1,510	1,139	541	210	538
Detroit-Ann Arbor, MI CMSA.	1,723	4.8	2.67	1,216	898	434	194	421
Boston-Lawrence-Salem, MA-NH CMSA.	1,547	10.8	2.61	1,035	802	379	118	396
Washington, DC-MD-VA MSA	1,459	24.4	2.62	971	743	376	134	368
Dallas-Fort Worth, TX CMSA	1,450	36.8	2.64	1,001	789	423	138	367
Houston-Galveston-Brazoria, TX CMSA	1,332	21.5	2.75	938	723	409	143	328
Miami-Fort Lauderdale, FL CMSA	1,221	18.8	2.58	816	606	264	122	328
Atlanta, GA MSA	1,056	39.6	2.64	743	571	296	109	242
Cleveland-Akron-Lorain, OH CMSA	1,058	3.8	2.56	734	563	258	101	280
Seattle-Tacoma, WA CMSA	1,002	26.5	2.49	654	527	253	82	266
San Diego, CA MSA	887	32.4	2.69	599	469	229	82	203
Minneapolis-St. Paul, MN-WI MSA	936	21.5	2.58	630	512	261	75	234
St. Louis, MO-IL MSA	925	9.5	2.59	646	501	244	91	239
Baltimore, MD MSA.	880	14.9	2.64	621	459	218	98	207
Pittsburgh-Beaver Valley, PA CMSA.	892	0.8	2.46	615	484	205	66	246
Phoenix, AZ MSA	808	48.2	2.59	547	435	203	73	202
Tampa-St. Petersburg-Clearwater, FL MSA	869	32.4	2.32	574	463	167	66	243
Denver-Boulder, CO CMSA.	738	21.3	2.46	475	376	187	66	210
Cincinnati-Hamilton, OH-KY-IN CMSA.	653	11.3	2.61	458	359	182	64	167
Milwaukee-Racine, WI CMSA	601	7.4	2.61	417	321	152	62	151
Kansas City, MO-KS MSA	602	13.9	2.55	417	332	162	56	157
Sacramento, CA MSA	556	33.7	2.60	378	291	140	59	133
Portland-Vancouver, OR-WA CMSA	576	15.9	2.52	384	309	148	49	150
Norfolk-Virginia Beach-Newport News, VA MSA . .	494	27.9	2.69	358	277	146	54	104
Columbus, OH MSA	525	16.8	2.54	355	278	137	49	134
San Antonio, TX MSA	451	29.1	2.82	329	251	137	52	103
Indianapolis, IN MSA.	480	14.7	2.56	333	262	129	46	122
New Orleans, LA MSA.	455	3.6	2.67	316	219	114	64	120
Buffalo-Niagara Falls, NY CMSA	462	3.7	2.51	314	240	107	42	127
Charlotte-Gastonia-Rock Hill, NC-SC MSA	441	28.7	2.58	318	251	120	41	102
Providence-Pawtucket-Fall River, RI-MA CMSA . .	430	11.0	2.57	298	233	107	35	111
Hartford-New Britain-Middletown, CT CMSA	412	14.2	2.56	287	225	101	35	100
Orlando, FL MSA.	402	59.0	2.62	278	219	104	37	91
Salt Lake City-Ogden, UT MSA	348	20.1	3.04	260	216	128	31	72
Rochester, NY MSA	374	9.4	2.58	258	202	97	35	93
Nashville, TN MSA	376	24.5	2.54	265	208	102	36	93
Memphis, TN-AR-MS MSA	357	14.4	2.68	255	178	91	52	87
Oklahoma City, OK MSA	368	14.4	2.53	255	202	100	36	97
Louisville, KY-IN MSA	368	7.9	2.54	260	199	95	38	93
Dayton-Springfield, OH MSA.	364	7.1	2.55	258	203	95	35	91
Greensboro—Winston-Salem—High Point, NC MSA	372	21.2	2.47	263	208	94	33	93
Birmingham, AL MSA	345	9.1	2.58	250	192	93	35	85
Jacksonville, FL MSA.	344	32.3	2.57	240	186	93	36	84
Albany-Schenectady-Troy, NY MSA	336	11.1	2.51	225	178	83	26	90
Richmond-Petersburg, VA MSA.	332	23.2	2.53	229	174	84	35	83
West Palm Beach-Boca Raton-Delray Beach, FL MSA	366	56.0	2.32	242	199	66	25	100
Honolulu, HI MSA.	265	15.2	3.02	197	158	84	21	51
Austin, TX MSA	304	55.1	2.48	187	147	78	27	88
Las Vegas, NV MSA	287	65.1	2.54	189	144	65	28	73
Raleigh-Durham, NC MSA	288	44.4	2.44	187	147	71	25	77
Scranton—Wilkes-Barre, PA MSA	281	6.6	2.52	197	156	70	18	75
Tulsa, OK MSA	277	12.5	2.51	194	157	77	25	73
Grand Rapids, MI MSA	244	18.6	2.74	179	147	76	21	52
Allentown-Bethlehem, PA-NJ MSA.	260	12.8	2.57	187	155	69	17	61
Fresno, CA MSA	221	23.8	2.96	162	120	65	29	46
Tucson, AZ MSA	262	33.9	2.49	170	132	60	25	73

[1] Metropolitan areas are shown in rank order of total population of consolidated metropolitan statistical area (CMSA) and metropolitan statistical areas (MSA).   [2] Includes nonfamily households with two or more persons, not shown separately.   [3] Includes other family types not shown separately.   [4] Includes married couple families with no related children.   [5] "Related children" in a family includes own children and all other persons under 18 years of age in the household, regardless of marital status, who are related to the householder, except the spouse of the householder.   [6] Comprises male family householders with no wife present and with related children and female family householders with no husband present and with related children.

Source: U.S. Bureau of the Census, unpublished data from *1990 Census of Population and Housing Summary Tape File 1C*.

No. 62. Households, 1980 to 1991, and Persons in Households, 1991, by Type of Household and Presence of Children

[As of **March**. Based on Current Population Survey; see headnote, table 56. Minus sign (-) indicates decrease]

TYPE OF HOUSEHOLD AND PRESENCE OF CHILDREN	HOUSEHOLDS						PERSONS IN HOUSEHOLDS, 1991		Persons per household, 1991
	Number (1,000)			Percent change, 1980-1991	Percent distribution		Number (1,000)	Percent distribution	
	1980	1990	1991		1980	1991			
Total households.	80,776	93,347	94,312	17	100	100	248,464	100	2.63
Family households	59,550	66,090	66,322	11	74	70	214,244	86	3.23
With own children under 18	31,022	32,289	32,401	4	38	34	128,098	52	3.95
Without own children under 18	28,528	33,801	33,920	19	35	36	86,146	35	2.54
Married couple family.	49,112	52,317	52,147	6	61	55	170,101	68	3.26
With own children under 18	24,961	24,537	24,397	-2	31	26	101,839	41	4.17
Without own children under 18	24,151	27,780	27,750	15	30	29	68,262	27	2.46
Male householder, no spouse present. . .	1,733	2,884	2,907	68	2	3	9,033	4	3.11
With own children under 18	616	1,153	1,181	92	1	1	4,123	2	3.49
Without own children under 18	1,117	1,731	1,725	54	1	2	4,910	2	2.85
Female householder, no spouse present .	8,705	10,890	11,268	29	11	12	35,109	14	3.12
With own children under 18	5,445	6,599	6,823	25	7	7	22,136	9	3.24
Without own children under 18	3,261	4,290	4,445	36	4	5	12,973	5	2.92
Nonfamily households.	21,226	27,257	27,990	32	26	30	34,220	14	1.22
Living alone.	18,296	22,999	23,590	29	23	25	23,590	9	1.00
Male householder	8,807	11,606	12,150	38	11	13	16,039	6	1.32
Living alone.	6,966	9,049	9,450	36	9	10	9,450	4	1.00
Female householder	12,419	15,651	15,840	28	15	17	18,182	7	1.15
Living alone.	11,330	13,950	14,141	25	14	15	14,141	6	1.00

Source: U.S. Bureau of the Census, *Current Population Reports,* series P-20, No. 458, and earlier reports; and unpublished data.

No. 63. Living Arrangements of Persons 15 Years Old and Over, by Selected Characteristics: 1991

[As of **March**. Based on Current Population Survey which includes members of Armed Forces living off post or with families on post, but excludes other Armed Forces; see text, section 1 and Appendix III]

AGE AND SEX	ALL RACES [1]					WHITE PERSONS PERCENT LIVING—			BLACK PERSONS PERCENT LIVING—		
	Total (1,000)	Percent living—				Alone	With spouse	With other relatives	Alone	With spouse	With other relatives
		Alone	With spouse	With other relatives	With non-relatives						
Total.	193,519	12	55	26	6	12	58	23	13	33	48
15 to 19 years old.	16,839	1	3	93	4	1	3	92	1	1	96
20 to 24 years old.	17,986	6	24	56	15	6	26	52	5	11	76
25 to 34 years old.	42,905	10	57	23	11	10	61	19	10	33	49
35 to 44 years old.	38,665	9	70	16	6	9	73	13	11	45	38
45 to 54 years old.	25,686	10	73	13	4	10	75	11	15	50	29
55 to 64 years old.	21,345	14	73	10	3	13	76	8	20	45	26
65 years old and over	30,093	31	54	13	2	31	56	11	33	38	26
65 to 74 years old	18,238	25	64	10	2	24	66	9	31	44	21
75 years old and over. . .	11,855	41	39	17	3	42	41	15	36	28	34
Male.	92,840	10	57	25	8	10	60	22	13	37	41
15 to 19 years old.	8,513	1	1	95	3	1	2	94	1	1	96
20 to 24 years old.	8,839	7	18	60	16	7	19	58	6	11	74
25 to 34 years old.	21,319	12	53	21	14	12	56	19	12	33	40
35 to 44 years old.	19,032	11	70	12	8	10	73	10	14	50	25
45 to 54 years old.	12,428	10	76	8	5	10	78	8	16	59	16
55 to 64 years old.	10,161	11	79	6	4	10	82	5	19	52	14
65 years old and over	12,547	16	74	7	2	16	76	6	23	55	16
65 to 74 years old	8,156	13	79	6	2	13	81	5	23	57	13
75 years old and over. . .	4,391	21	66	11	3	21	67	9	23	51	22
Female.	100,680	14	53	28	5	15	56	24	13	30	54
15 to 19 years old.	8,326	1	4	91	4	1	5	90	(Z)	2	96
20 to 24 years old.	9,148	5	30	52	14	5	33	47	4	12	77
25 to 34 years old.	21,586	8	60	25	7	8	65	20	8	33	56
35 to 44 years old.	19,633	7	69	20	4	7	73	16	8	40	48
45 to 54 years old.	13,258	10	69	17	3	10	72	14	13	44	40
55 to 64 years old.	11,184	17	67	14	2	16	71	11	22	40	36
65 years old and over	17,546	42	40	16	2	43	41	14	39	27	33
65 to 74 years old	10,081	34	51	13	2	34	53	12	36	34	28
75 years old and over. . .	7,464	53	24	20	3	55	25	18	43	16	40

Z Less than .5 percent. [1] Includes other races not shown separately.

Source: U.S. Bureau of the Census, *Current Population Reports*, series P-20, No. 461.

Population

No. 64. Living Arrangements of Young Adults: 1970 to 1991

[1970 and 1980, as of April. Beginning 1985, as of March and based on Current Population Survey, see headnote, table 63]

LIVING ARRANGEMENTS AND SEX	PERSONS 18 TO 24 YEARS OLD					PERSONS 25 TO 34 YEARS OLD				
	1970	1980	1985	1990	1991	1970	1980	1985	1990	1991
Total (1,000)	22,357	29,122	27,844	25,310	24,902	24,566	36,796	40,857	43,240	42,905
Percent distribution:										
Child of householder [1]	47	48	54	53	54	8	9	11	12	12
Family householder or spouse . . .	38	29	24	22	22	83	72	68	65	64
Nonfamily householder	5	10	8	9	9	5	12	13	13	13
Other..................	10	13	14	16	16	4	7	9	11	11
Male (1,000)	10,398	14,278	13,695	12,450	12,275	11,929	18,107	20,184	21,462	21,319
Percent distribution:										
Child of householder [1]	54	54	60	58	60	10	11	13	15	15
Family householder or spouse . . .	30	21	16	15	14	79	66	60	56	55
Nonfamily householder	5	11	10	10	10	7	15	16	16	17
Other..................	10	13	14	17	16	5	8	11	13	14
Female (1,000)	11,959	14,844	14,149	12,860	12,627	12,637	18,689	20,673	21,779	21,586
Percent distribution:										
Child of householder [1]	41	43	48	48	49	7	7	8	8	9
Family householder or spouse . . .	45	36	32	30	29	86	78	76	73	72
Nonfamily householder	4	8	7	8	7	4	9	10	10	10
Other..................	10	13	13	15	15	4	6	7	9	9

[1] Includes unmarried college students living in dormitories.
Source: U.S. Bureau of the Census, *1970* and *1980 Census of Population*, PC(2)-4B and *Current Population Reports*, series P-20, No. 461, and earlier reports.

No. 65. Families, by Size and Presence of Children: 1980 to 1991

[In thousands, except as indicated. As of March. Excludes members of Armed Forces except those living off post or with their families on post. Based on Current Population Survey; see text, section 1 and Appendix III. For definition of families, see text, section 1]

CHARACTERISTIC	1980, total	1990, total	1991								
			All races [1]			White		Black		Hispanic [4]	
			Total [2]	Married couple	Female house-holder [3]	Total [2]	Married couple	Total [2]	Married couple	Total [2]	Married couple
Total.............	59,550	66,090	66,322	52,147	11,268	56,803	47,014	7,471	3,569	4,981	3,454
Size of family:											
Two persons	23,461	27,606	27,615	20,581	5,281	24,532	19,190	2,496	1,028	1,229	683
Three persons	13,603	15,353	15,298	11,330	3,274	12,928	10,185	1,941	831	1,188	731
Four persons	12,372	14,026	14,098	12,186	1,655	11,951	10,845	1,598	872	1,146	868
Five persons	5,930	5,938	5,965	5,229	618	4,929	4,538	788	477	777	634
Six persons	2,461	1,997	2,060	1,805	213	1,607	1,492	328	205	342	291
Seven or more persons . .	1,723	1,170	1,285	1,016	226	856	765	319	157	299	247
Average per family	3.29	3.17	3.18	3.24	3.00	3.12	3.19	3.51	3.65	3.82	4.03
Own children under age 18:											
None	28,528	33,801	33,920	27,750	4,445	30,009	25,483	3,091	1,685	1,778	1,180
One	12,443	13,530	13,303	9,319	3,283	10,955	8,181	1,847	762	1,105	727
Two	11,470	12,263	12,287	9,721	2,203	10,381	8,671	1,431	646	1,136	816
Three	4,674	4,650	4,835	3,840	908	3,972	3,392	691	312	596	453
Four or more	2,435	1,846	1,977	1,517	427	1,487	1,286	411	164	365	277
Own children under age 6:											
None	46,063	50,905	50,921	40,048	8,417	44,076	36,333	5,382	2,636	3,249	2,148
One	9,441	10,304	10,492	8,128	2,010	8,639	7,096	1,422	683	1,145	858
Two or more	4,047	4,882	4,909	3,971	841	4,088	3,585	667	250	587	447
PERCENT DISTRIBUTION											
Total.............	100	100	100	100	100	100	100	100	100	100	100
Size of family:											
Two persons	39	42	42	39	47	43	41	33	29	25	20
Three persons	23	23	23	22	29	23	22	26	23	24	21
Four persons	21	21	21	23	15	21	23	21	24	23	25
Five persons	10	9	9	10	5	9	10	11	13	16	18
Six persons	4	3	3	3	2	3	3	4	6	7	8
Seven or more persons . .	3	2	2	2	2	2	2	4	4	6	7
Own children under age 18:											
None	48	51	51	53	39	53	54	41	47	36	34
One	21	20	20	18	29	19	17	25	21	22	21
Two	19	19	19	19	20	18	18	19	18	23	24
Three	8	7	7	7	8	7	7	9	9	12	13
Four or more	4	3	3	3	4	3	3	6	5	7	8
Own children under age 6:											
None	77	77	77	77	75	78	77	72	74	65	62
One	16	16	16	16	18	15	15	19	19	23	25
Two or more	7	7	7	8	7	7	8	9	7	12	13

[1] Includes other races, not shown separately. [2] Includes other types of families, not shown separately. [3] No spouse present. [4] Hispanic persons may be of any race.
Source: U.S. Bureau of the Census, *Current Population Reports*, series P-20, No. 458 and earlier reports.

No. 66. Families, by Number of Own Children Under 18 Years Old: 1970 to 1991

[Except as noted, as of **March** and based on Current Population Survey; see headnote, table 65. See also *Historical Statistics, Colonial Times to 1970*, series A 353-358]

RACE, HISPANIC ORIGIN, AND YEAR	NUMBER OF FAMILIES (1,000)					PERCENT DISTRIBUTION					Average size of family
	Total	No children	One child	Two children	Three or more children	Total	No children	One child	Two children	Three or more children	
ALL FAMILIES [1]											
1970	51,586	22,774	9,398	8,969	10,445	100	44	18	17	20	3.58
1980	59,550	28,528	12,443	11,470	7,109	100	48	21	19	12	3.29
1985	62,706	31,594	13,108	11,645	6,359	100	50	21	19	10	3.23
1990	66,090	33,801	13,530	12,263	6,496	100	51	20	19	10	3.17
1991	66,322	33,920	13,303	12,287	6,812	100	51	20	19	10	3.18
Married couple	52,147	27,750	9,319	9,721	5,357	100	53	18	19	10	3.24
Male householder [2]	2,907	1,725	701	363	117	100	59	24	13	4	2.78
Female householder [2]	11,268	4,445	3,283	2,203	1,335	100	39	29	20	12	3.00
WHITE FAMILIES											
1970	46,261	20,719	8,437	8,174	8,931	100	45	18	18	19	3.52
1980	52,243	25,769	10,727	9,977	5,769	100	49	21	19	11	3.23
1985	54,400	28,169	11,174	9,937	5,120	100	52	21	18	9	3.16
1990	56,590	29,872	11,186	10,342	5,191	100	53	20	18	9	3.11
1991	56,803	30,009	10,955	10,381	5,459	100	53	19	18	10	3.12
BLACK FAMILIES											
1970	4,887	1,903	858	726	1,401	100	39	18	15	29	4.13
1980	6,184	2,364	1,449	1,235	1,136	100	38	23	20	18	3.67
1985	6,778	2,887	1,579	1,330	982	100	43	23	20	15	3.60
1990	7,470	3,093	1,894	1,433	1,049	100	41	25	19	14	3.46
1991	7,471	3,091	1,847	1,431	1,102	100	41	25	19	15	3.51
HISPANIC FAMILIES [3]											
1970	2,004	597	390	388	629	100	30	20	19	31	4.28
1980	3,029	946	680	698	706	100	31	22	23	23	3.90
1985	3,939	1,337	904	865	833	100	34	23	22	21	3.88
1990	4,840	1,790	1,095	1,036	919	100	37	23	21	19	3.83
1991	4,981	1,778	1,105	1,136	961	100	36	22	23	19	3.82

[1] Includes other races, not shown separately.   [2] No spouse present.   [3] Hispanic persons may be of any race. 1970 Hispanic data as of April and based on Census of Population.
Source: U.S. Bureau of the Census, *U.S. Census of Population, 1970* (PC-2-4A), and *Current Population Reports*, series P-20, No. 458, and earlier reports.

No. 67. Family Households With Own Children Under Age 18, by Type of Family, 1970 to 1991, and by Age of Householder, 1991

[As of **March**. Excludes members of Armed Forces except those living off post or with their families on post. Based on Current Population Survey; see text, section 1 and Appendix III]

FAMILY TYPE	1970	1980	1990	1991						
				Total	15 to 24 years old	25 to 34 years old	35 to 44 years old	45 to 54 years old	55 to 64 years old	65 years old and over
NUMBER (1,000)										
Family households with children	28,731	31,022	32,289	32,401	1,719	11,174	13,776	4,705	890	136
Married couple	25,532	24,961	24,537	24,397	821	8,114	10,780	3,842	742	99
Male householder [1]	341	616	1,153	1,181	75	380	494	185	38	9
Female householder [1]	2,858	5,445	6,599	6,823	824	2,679	2,502	679	110	29
PERCENT DISTRIBUTION										
Family households with children	100	100	100	100	100	100	100	100	100	100
Married couple	89	81	76	75	48	73	78	82	83	73
Male householder [1]	1	2	4	4	4	3	4	4	4	7
Female householder [1]	10	18	20	21	48	24	18	14	12	21
HOUSEHOLDS WITH CHILDREN, AS A PERCENT OF ALL FAMILY HOUSEHOLDS, BY TYPE										
Family households with children, total	56	52	49	49	63	77	81	40	10	1
Married couple	57	51	47	47	53	74	81	41	9	1
Male householder [1]	28	36	40	41	30	53	65	38	12	2
Female householder [1]	52	63	61	61	90	94	81	38	10	2

[1] No spouse present.
Source: U.S. Bureau of the Census, *Current Population Reports*, series P-20, No. 458, and earlier reports.

No. 68. Living Arrangements of Children Under 18 Years Old, by Selected Characteristic of Parent: 1991

[In thousands. As of March. Covers only those persons under 18 years old who are living with one or both parents. Characteristics are shown for the householder or reference person in married-couple situations. See also headnote, table 69]

CHARACTERISTIC OF PARENT	ALL RACES[1] Total	Both parents	Mother only	Father only	WHITE Total	Both parents	Mother only	Father only	BLACK Total	Both parents	Mother only	Father only	HISPANIC[2] Total	Both parents	Mother only	Father only
Children under 18 years old ...	**63,282**	**46,658**	**14,608**	**2,016**	**50,875**	**40,733**	**8,585**	**1,557**	**9,543**	**3,669**	**5,516**	**358**	**7,166**	**4,944**	**1,983**	**239**
Age:																
15 to 24 years old	3,821	1,371	2,311	139	2,421	1,140	1,169	112	1,255	147	1,085	23	654	306	315	34
25 to 29 years old	8,627	5,346	2,959	321	6,489	4,642	1,610	237	1,854	532	1,255	67	1,271	873	360	39
30 to 34 years old	14,241	10,426	3,446	370	11,678	9,365	2,018	295	2,101	719	1,327	55	1,670	1,158	457	55
35 to 39 years old	15,423	12,005	2,948	469	12,822	10,580	1,879	363	1,957	944	934	79	1,440	996	413	31
40 to 44 years old	12,096	9,926	1,778	393	10,115	8,653	1,154	308	1,291	680	543	68	1,090	813	228	49
45 to 54 years old	7,633	6,385	984	263	6,236	5,405	637	194	846	476	315	55	835	641	169	26
55 to 64 years old	1,265	1,068	147	51	998	869	90	39	195	135	49	12	191	150	35	5
65 years old and over	176	130	37	8	116	78	29	8	45	36	8	-	15	7	7	1
Educational attainment:																
Elementary: 0 to 8 years	4,576	3,214	1,143	220	3,732	2,742	826	164	507	229	239	39	2,422	1,756	580	86
High school: 1 to 3 years	7,822	4,101	3,470	251	5,370	3,450	1,745	175	2,162	449	1,646	67	1,520	904	584	33
4 years	24,427	17,289	6,287	850	19,310	15,071	3,568	671	4,323	1,634	2,538	151	1,931	1,295	554	82
College: 1 to 3 years	12,374	9,359	2,584	431	10,149	8,226	1,598	325	1,738	782	884	73	812	583	200	30
4 years	7,866	6,990	710	166	6,821	6,137	545	139	553	413	124	17	289	240	47	3
5 or more years	6,216	5,705	413	98	5,493	5,107	302	84	259	163	85	11	190	167	18	5
Employment status:[3]																
In the civilian labor force	53,350	42,557	8,983	1,811	44,666	37,593	5,641	1,431	6,453	3,115	3,046	291	5,379	4,271	884	224
Employed	49,487	40,122	7,777	1,588	41,845	35,538	5,063	1,244	5,570	2,862	2,443	265	4,750	3,805	748	197
Both parents employed	25,144	25,144	(X)	(X)	22,039	22,055	(X)	(X)	2,031	2,031	(X)	(X)	1,856	1,856	(X)	(X)
Unemployed	3,863	2,434	1,207	222	2,820	2,055	578	187	883	254	603	26	629	466	136	27
Not in the labor force	8,905	3,112	5,610	182	5,506	2,452	2,939	115	2,868	353	2,461	55	1,712	598	1,099	16
Family income:																
Under $5,000	3,541	545	2,856	140	1,939	417	1,438	84	1,467	65	1,363	41	566	159	394	13
$5,000 to $9,999	5,033	1,412	3,428	193	3,171	1,174	1,864	133	1,638	178	1,417	43	1,051	359	652	40
$10,000 to $14,999	4,921	2,431	2,279	211	3,579	2,054	1,348	178	1,147	254	865	28	1,075	713	326	35
$15,000 to $24,999	9,814	6,670	2,709	435	7,504	5,511	1,666	327	1,834	774	958	102	1,512	1,165	306	40
$25,000 to $29,999	4,857	3,725	921	211	4,113	3,326	623	164	545	244	270	31	625	508	104	13
$30,000 to $39,999	9,865	8,426	1,127	311	8,352	7,373	740	239	1,105	733	325	47	941	789	92	60
$40,000 to $49,999	7,970	7,214	535	220	6,999	6,414	407	179	684	534	114	37	618	558	47	13
$50,000 and over	17,280	16,234	752	293	15,218	14,464	500	253	1,122	888	205	29	778	690	63	24
Tenure:[4]																
Owned	39,352	33,524	4,790	1,037	34,189	30,015	3,315	859	3,612	2,164	1,309	139	2,552	2,111	350	91
Rented	23,930	13,134	9,818	979	16,686	10,718	5,271	698	5,930	1,505	4,207	219	4,614	2,833	1,633	148

- Represents or rounds to zero. X Not applicable. [1] Includes other races, not shown separately. [2] Persons of Hispanic origin may be of any race. [3] Excludes children whose parent is in the Armed Forces. [4] Refers to the tenure of the householder (who may or may not be the child's parent).

Source: U.S. Bureau of the Census, *Current Population Reports*, series P-20, No. 461.

No. 69. Children Under 18 Years Old, by Presence of Parents: 1970 to 1991

[As of **March**. Excludes persons under 18 years old who maintained households or family groups. Based on Current Population Survey; see headnote, table 65]

RACE, HISPANIC ORIGIN, AND YEAR	Number (1,000)	Both parents	PERCENT LIVING WITH—						
				Mother only				Father only	Neither parent
			Total	Divorced	Married, spouse absent	Single [1]	Wid-owed		
ALL RACES [2]									
1970	69,162	85	11	3	5	1	2	1	3
1980	63,427	77	18	8	6	3	2	2	4
1985	62,475	74	21	9	5	6	2	3	3
1990	64,137	73	22	8	5	7	2	3	3
1991	65,093	72	22	8	6	8	1	3	3
WHITE									
1970	58,790	90	8	3	3	(Z)	2	1	2
1980	52,242	83	14	7	4	1	2	2	2
1985	50,836	80	16	8	4	2	1	2	2
1990	51,390	79	16	8	4	3	1	3	2
1991	51,918	79	17	8	5	3	1	3	2
BLACK									
1970	9,422	59	30	5	16	4	4	2	10
1980	9,375	42	44	11	16	13	4	2	12
1985	9,479	40	51	11	12	25	3	3	7
1990	10,018	38	51	10	12	27	2	4	8
1991	10,209	36	54	10	11	31	2	4	7
HISPANIC [3]									
1970	[4]4,006	78	(NA)	(NA)	(NA)	(NA)	(NA)	(NA)	(NA)
1980	5,459	75	20	6	8	4	2	2	4
1985	6,057	68	27	7	11	7	2	2	3
1990	7,174	67	27	7	10	8	2	3	3
1991	7,462	66	27	7	10	9	2	3	4

NA Not available.   Z Less than 0.5 percent.   [1] Never married.   [2] Includes other races not shown separately.   [3] Hispanic persons may be of any race.   [4] All persons under 18 years old.

Source: U.S. Bureau of the Census, *Current Population Reports*, series P-20, No. 461, and earlier reports.

No. 70. Female Family Householders With No Spouse Present—Characteristics, by Race and Hispanic Origin: 1980 to 1991

[As of **March**. Covers persons 15 years old and over. Based on Current Population Survey; see headnote, table 65]

CHARACTERISTIC	Unit	WHITE			BLACK			HISPANIC ORIGIN [1]		
		1980	1990	1991	1980	1990	1991	1980	1990	1991
Female family householder .	1,000	6,052	7,306	7,512	2,495	3,275	3,430	610	1,116	1,186
Percent of all families.	Percent . . .	12	13	13	40	44	46	20	23	24
Median age [2].	Years	43.7	42.5	41.9	37.4	37.6	38.5	37.0	38.8	39.0
Marital status:										
Single (never married)	Percent . . .	11	15	17	27	39	41	23	27	27
Married, spouse absent	Percent . . .	17	16	18	29	21	19	32	29	31
Separated.	Percent . . .	14	14	14	27	19	16	29	23	24
Other.	Percent . . .	3	3	4	2	2	3	4	6	7
Widowed	Percent . . .	33	26	24	22	17	17	15	16	16
Divorced	Percent . . .	40	43	42	22	23	23	30	29	27
Presence of children under 18:										
No own children	Percent . . .	41	43	42	28	32	33	25	33	33
With own children	Percent . . .	59	58	58	72	68	67	75	67	67
One child	Percent . . .	28	30	30	26	30	28	28	25	26
Two children	Percent . . .	20	19	19	23	22	21	23	22	23
Three children	Percent . . .	7	7	7	11	9	11	15	13	11
Four or more children	Percent . . .	3	2	2	11	7	7	9	6	7
Children per family	Number . . .	1.03	0.95	0.95	1.51	1.26	1.27	1.56	1.37	1.37

[1] Persons of Hispanic origin may be of any race.   [2] For definition of median, see Guide to Tabular Presentation.

Source: U.S. Bureau of the Census, *Current Population Reports*, series P-20, No. 458, and earlier reports.

No. 71. Nonfamily Households, by Age of Householder and Presence of Nonrelatives: 1980 to 1991

[As of **March.** See headnote, table 65]

ITEM	NONFAMILY HOUSEHOLDS		MALE HOUSEHOLDER (1,000)					FEMALE HOUSEHOLDER (1,000)				
	Total (1,000)	Per-cent	Total	15 to 24 yr. old	25 to 44 yr. old	45 to 64 yr. old	65 yr. old and over	Total	15 to 24 yr. old	25 to 44 yr. old	45 to 64 yr. old	65 yr. old and over
1980, total	21,226	100	8,807	1,567	3,854	1,822	1,565	12,419	1,189	2,198	3,048	5,983
One person (living alone).	18,296	86	6,966	947	2,920	1,613	1,486	11,330	779	1,809	2,901	5,842
Nonrelatives present. . . .	2,930	14	1,841	620	934	209	79	1,089	410	389	147	141
1990, total	27,257	100	11,606	1,236	5,780	2,536	2,053	15,651	1,032	3,697	3,545	7,377
One person (living alone).	22,999	84	9,049	674	4,231	2,203	1,943	13,950	536	2,881	3,300	7,233
Nonrelatives present. . . .	4,258	16	2,557	560	1,551	334	112	1,701	497	817	245	143
1991, total	27,990	100	12,150	1,200	6,114	2,718	2,118	15,840	957	3,845	3,529	7,509
One person (living alone).	23,590	84	9,450	622	4,499	2,319	2,010	14,141	518	3,020	3,232	7,370
Nonrelatives present. . . .	4,400	16	2,700	578	1,615	399	108	1,700	438	825	298	139

Source: U.S. Bureau of the Census, *Current Population Reports,* series P-20, No. 461, and earlier reports; and unpublished data.

No. 72. Nonfamily Householders, by Sex and Marital Status: 1980 to 1991

[**In thousands.** As of **March.** Based on Current Population Survey; see headnote, table 65]

MARITAL STATUS	MALE HOUSEHOLDER						FEMALE HOUSEHOLDER					
	1980	1990	1991				1980	1990	1991			
			Total [1]	25 to 44 yr.	45 to 64 yr.	65 yr. old and over			Total [1]	25 to 44 yr.	45 to 64 yr.	65 yr. old and over
Total	8,807	11,606	12,150	6,114	2,718	2,118	12,419	15,651	15,840	3,845	3,529	7,509
Single	4,371	5,844	6,090	3,899	736	335	3,302	4,382	4,412	2,464	528	533
Married [2]	1,051	1,117	1,160	543	396	176	675	794	796	302	292	182
Widowed	1,177	1,417	1,505	30	256	1,219	6,569	7,428	7,330	62	1,169	6,098
Divorced	2,209	3,228	3,394	1,641	1,330	389	1,873	3,046	3,302	1,017	1,540	696

[1] Includes persons 15 to 24 years old not shown separately.　　[2] No spouse present.

Source: U.S. Bureau of the Census, *Current Population Reports,* series P-20, No. 461, and earlier reports; and unpublished data.

No. 73. Persons Living Alone, by Sex and Age: 1970 to 1991

[As of **March.** Based on Current Population Survey; see headnote, table 65]

SEX AND AGE	NUMBER OF PERSONS (1,000)						PERCENT DISTRIBUTION					
	1970	1975	1980	1985	1990	1991	1970	1975	1980	1985	1990	1991
Both sexes	10,851	13,939	18,296	20,602	22,999	23,590	100	100	100	100	100	100
15 to 24 years old [1] . . .	556	1,111	1,324	1,210	1,140	5	8	9	6	5	5
25 to 34 years old	[2]1,604	[2]2,744	[2]4,729	3,905	3,972	4,116	[2]15	[2]20	[2]26	19	17	17
35 to 44 years old	[2]	[2]	[2]	2,322	3,138	3,402	[2]	[2]	[2]	11	14	14
45 to 64 years old	3,622	4,076	4,514	4,939	5,502	5,550	33	29	25	24	24	24
65 to 74 years old	2,815	3,281	3,851	4,130	4,350	4,494	26	24	21	20	19	19
75 years old and over .	2,256	2,727	3,477	3,982	4,825	4,887	21	20	19	19	21	21
Male	3,532	4,918	6,966	7,922	9,049	9,450	33	35	38	39	39	40
15 to 24 years old [1] . . .	274	610	947	750	674	622	3	4	5	4	3	3
25 to 34 years old	[2]933	[2]1,689	[2]2,920	2,307	2,395	2,491	[2]9	[2]12	[2]16	11	10	11
35 to 44 years old	[2]	[2]	[2]	1,406	1,836	2,008	[2]	[2]	[2]	7	8	9
45 to 64 years old	1,152	1,329	1,613	1,845	2,203	2,319	11	10	9	9	10	10
65 to 74 years old	611	723	775	868	1,042	1,096	6	5	4	4	5	5
75 years old and over .	563	567	711	746	901	914	5	4	4	4	4	4
Female	7,319	9,021	11,330	12,680	13,950	14,141	68	65	62	62	61	60
15 to 24 years old [1] . . .	282	501	779	573	536	518	3	4	4	3	2	2
25 to 34 years old	[2]671	[2]1,055	[2]1,809	1,598	1,578	1,626	[2]6	[2]8	[2]10	8	7	7
35 to 44 years old	[2]	[2]	[2]	916	1,303	1,394	[2]	[2]	[2]	4	6	6
45 to 64 years old	2,470	2,747	2,901	3,095	3,300	3,232	23	20	16	15	14	14
65 to 74 years old	2,204	2,558	3,076	3,262	3,309	3,397	20	18	17	16	14	14
75 years old and over .	1,693	2,160	2,766	3,236	3,924	3,973	16	16	15	16	17	17

[1] 1970 and 1975, persons 14 to 24 years old.　　[2] Data for persons 35 to 44 years old included with persons 25 to 34 years old.

Source: U.S. Bureau of the Census, *Current Population Reports,* series P-20, No. 461, and earlier reports; and unpublished data.

No. 74. Population in Institutions and Other Group Quarters, by Type of Quarters and State: 1990

[As of **April** 1. See text, section 1 and Appendix III. See *Historical Statistics, Colonial Times to 1970*, series A 359-371, for inmates of institutions]

REGION, DIVISION, AND STATE	Group quarters population, total [1]	INSTITUTIONALIZED PERSONS Total [2]	INSTITUTIONALIZED PERSONS Correctional institutions	INSTITUTIONALIZED PERSONS Nursing homes	College dormitories	Military quarters	Emergency shelters for homeless persons	Persons visible in street locations
U.S.	6,697,744	3,334,018	1,115,111	1,772,032	1,953,558	589,700	190,406	49,734
Northeast	1,510,088	713,335	195,275	399,329	540,689	47,252	62,247	14,653
N.E.	445,031	179,333	33,227	119,646	198,866	20,349	12,454	970
ME	37,169	14,136	2,311	9,855	14,118	5,153	462	7
NH	32,151	11,466	1,991	8,202	17,025	923	404	8
VT.	21,642	6,161	807	4,809	13,435	-	261	16
MA	214,307	84,345	15,471	55,662	100,487	4,439	6,476	674
RI	38,595	14,801	2,645	10,156	18,898	2,851	502	44
CT.	101,167	48,424	10,002	30,962	34,903	6,983	4,349	221
M.A	1,065,057	534,002	162,048	279,683	341,823	26,903	49,793	13,683
NY.	545,265	267,122	90,025	126,175	165,925	12,875	33,228	10,732
NJ.	171,368	92,670	29,093	47,054	43,711	10,102	7,725	1,639
PA.	348,424	174,210	42,930	106,454	132,187	3,926	8,840	1,312
Midwest.	1,598,620	852,419	211,192	544,650	557,270	40,203	30,009	3,324
E.N.C	1,055,689	568,050	157,275	346,243	369,009	19,261	21,423	2,544
OH	261,451	152,331	41,618	93,769	88,785	449	4,773	188
IN	161,992	81,686	21,726	50,845	70,873	883	2,530	268
IL	286,956	149,842	37,334	93,662	86,777	16,091	8,017	1,755
MI	211,692	112,903	42,849	57,622	73,093	1,693	4,290	262
WI	133,598	71,288	13,748	50,345	49,481	145	1,813	71
W.N.C.	542,931	284,369	53,917	198,407	188,261	20,942	8,586	780
MN	117,621	63,279	9,969	47,051	39,280	24	2,483	138
IA	99,520	47,841	5,630	36,455	43,093	57	1,153	148
MO	145,397	80,854	19,975	52,060	44,033	6,424	2,393	215
ND	24,234	10,574	831	8,159	10,377	2,245	315	30
SD.	25,841	13,305	2,543	9,356	9,306	1,051	437	71
NE.	47,553	25,620	3,662	19,171	16,692	1,104	805	20
KS.	82,765	42,896	11,307	26,155	25,480	10,037	1,000	158
South	2,294,420	1,145,986	439,250	558,382	615,791	312,915	46,382	7,975
S.A.	1,243,962	577,690	231,369	270,930	322,299	213,816	27,052	5,025
DE.	20,071	8,662	3,347	4,596	8,806	1,164	349	19
MD	113,856	62,760	27,025	26,884	30,892	10,426	2,706	523
DC.	41,717	14,070	4,035	7,008	16,126	2,181	4,731	131
VA.	209,300	84,292	33,553	37,762	61,943	51,869	2,842	319
WV	36,911	19,469	4,439	12,591	15,083	32	579	33
NC	224,470	83,400	24,857	47,014	71,266	58,378	2,952	259
SC.	116,543	44,134	18,351	18,228	35,488	30,116	1,060	102
GA	173,633	87,266	40,803	36,549	39,723	30,261	4,122	450
FL.	307,461	173,637	74,959	80,298	42,972	29,339	7,711	3,189
E.S.C	392,424	194,314	63,082	102,900	131,846	38,432	5,733	922
KY.	101,176	47,609	13,948	27,874	30,600	15,228	1,474	118
TN.	129,129	65,389	21,335	35,192	43,683	11,126	2,094	357
AL.	92,402	51,583	19,226	24,031	28,859	6,085	1,657	364
MS	69,717	29,733	8,573	15,803	28,704	5,993	508	83
W.S.C	658,034	373,982	144,799	184,552	161,646	60,667	13,597	2,028
AR.	58,332	34,223	8,642	21,809	16,775	1,814	594	62
LA.	112,578	67,276	26,792	32,072	27,990	10,851	1,803	184
OK	93,677	51,211	15,108	29,666	24,924	8,712	2,335	340
TX.	393,447	221,272	94,257	101,005	91,957	39,290	8,865	1,442
West	1,294,616	622,278	269,394	269,671	239,808	189,330	51,768	23,782
Mt	297,687	144,834	60,762	65,842	77,782	27,269	9,807	3,215
MT	23,747	11,125	2,174	7,764	6,195	1,000	494	17
ID	21,490	10,478	2,871	6,318	6,676	740	539	19
WY	10,240	5,434	1,556	2,679	3,414	832	228	13
CO	79,472	35,976	13,446	18,506	22,749	12,895	2,721	393
NM	28,807	14,024	5,385	6,276	8,333	3,088	775	164
AZ.	80,683	41,508	22,636	14,472	18,459	6,071	3,014	1,897
UT.	29,048	12,739	4,252	6,222	10,156	1,046	974	276
NV.	24,200	13,550	8,442	3,605	1,800	1,597	1,062	436
Pac	996,929	477,444	208,632	203,829	162,026	162,061	41,961	20,567
WA	120,531	55,313	14,569	32,840	27,908	18,491	4,862	772
OR	66,205	33,378	10,912	18,200	18,970	122	3,505	564
CA.	751,860	376,374	178,199	148,362	108,880	115,334	32,063	18,081
AK.	20,701	4,574	2,630	1,202	1,310	8,807	604	79
HI	37,632	7,805	2,322	3,225	4,958	19,307	927	1,071

- Represents zero.   [1] Includes persons in other types of group quarters not shown separately.   [2] Includes other institutionalized persons not shown separately.

Source: U.S. Bureau of the Census, *1990 Census of Population and Housing Data Paper Listing* (CPH-L-22 through 72).

Population

No. 75. Religious Preference, Church Membership and Attendance: 1957 to 1990

[In percent. Covers civilian noninstitutional population, 18 years old and over. Data represent averages of the combined results of several surveys during year. Data are subject to sampling variability, see source]

YEAR	RELIGIOUS PREFERENCE					Church/ synagogue church membership mem- bers	Persons attending church/ synagogue [1]	AGE AND REGION	Church/ synagogue mem- bers, 1990
	Protestant	Catholic	Jewish	Other	None				
1957	66	26	3	1	3	[2]73	47	18-29 years old. . . .	57
1967	67	25	3	3	2	[3]73	43	30-49 years old. . . .	63
1975	62	27	2	4	6	71	41	50 years and over . .	74
1980	61	28	2	2	7	69	40	East [4]	65
1985	57	28	2	4	9	71	42	Midwest [5]	70
1989	56	28	2	4	10	69	43	South [6]	70
1990	56	25	2	6	11	65	40	West [7]	54

[1] Persons who attended a church or synagogue in the last seven days.   [2] 1952 data.   [3] 1965 data.   [4] ME, NH, RI, NY, CT, VT, MA, NJ, PA, WV, DE, MD, and DC.   [5] OH, IN, IL, MI, MN, WI, IA, ND, SD, KS, NE, and MO.   [6] KY, TN, VA, NC, SC, GA, FL, AL, MS, TX, AR, OK, and LA.   [7] AZ, NM, CO, NV, MT, ID, WY, UT, CA, WA, OR, AK, and HI.

Source: Princeton Religion Research Center, Princeton, NJ, "Emerging Trends," periodical. Based on surveys conducted by The Gallup Organization, Inc.

No. 76. Religious Bodies—Church Membership, 1960 to 1989, and Number of Churches, 1989

[Membership in thousands, except as indicated. See headnote, table 77. See also Historical Statistics, Colonial Times to 1970, series H 793-799]

RELIGIOUS BODY	MEMBERSHIP						Number of churches, 1989
	1960	1970	1975	1980	1985	1989	
Total	114,449	131,045	131,013	134,817	142,926	147,607	350,337
Members as percent of population [1]	64	63	61	59	60	60	(X)
Average members per local church	359	399	393	401	413	421	(X)
Buddhist Churches of America	20	100	60	60	100	19	67
Eastern Churches.	2,699	3,850	3,696	3,823	4,026	4,057	1,705
Jews [2]	5,367	5,870	6,115	5,920	5,835	5,944	3,416
Old Catholic, Polish National Catholic, and Armenian Churches.	590	848	846	924	1,024	980	442
The Roman Catholic Church	42,105	48,215	48,882	50,450	52,655	57,020	23,500
Protestants [3]	[4]63,669	71,713	71,043	73,479	79,096	79,387	320,039
Miscellaneous [5]	([4])	449	372	161	191	200	1,168

X Not applicable.   [1] Based on Bureau of the Census estimated total population as of July 1. Estimates for 1980's reflect results of 1990 census.   [2] Estimates of the Jewish community including those identified with Orthodox, Conservative and Reformed synagogues or temples.   [3] Includes nonprotestant bodies such as "Latter-day Saints" and "Jehovah's Witnesses."   [4] Data for "Miscellaneous" included with Protestants.   [5] Includes non-Christian bodies such as "Spiritualists," "Ethical Culture Movement," and "Unitarian-Universalists."

Source: National Council of the Churches of Christ in the United States of America, New York, NY, Yearbook of American and Canadian Churches, annual, (copyright).

No. 77. Religious Bodies—Selected Data

[Represents latest information available from religious bodies with memberships of 60,000 or more; excludes a few groups giving no data. Not all groups follow same calendar year nor count membership in same way; some groups give only approximate figures. Roman Catholics count all baptized persons, including infants; Jewish statistics are estimates of the number of persons living in Jewish households including as a consequence of intermarriage, approximately 7.4 percent non-Jewish persons. Eastern Orthodox Churches include all persons in their nationality or cultural groups; most Protestant bodies count only persons who have attained full membership, and previous estimates have indicated that all but a small minority of these are over 11 years of age; however, many Lutheran bodies and The Episcopal Church report all baptized persons, and not only those confirmed. Data which appear in italics are "noncurrent," i.e., they are reported for 1988 or earlier. All other data are "current" and were reported in 1989 or 1990]

RELIGIOUS BODY	Year	Churches reported	Membership (1,000)	Pastors serving parishes [1]	Sunday school enrollment [2] (1,000)
Total [3]	(X)	350,337	147,607	340,094	28,420
African Methodist Episcopal Church	1981	6,200	2,210	6,050	(NA)
African Methodist Episcopal Zion Church	1987	6,060	1,220	6,300	(NA)
American Baptist Association	1986	1,705	250	1,740	(NA)
American Baptist Churches in the U.S.A.	1989	5,833	1,549	5,390	308
Antiochian Orthodox Christian Archdiocese of North America, The . . .	1989	160	350	250	6
Apostolic Catholic Assyrian Church of the East, N. American Diocese .	1989	22	120	92	1
Armenian Apostolic Church of America	1990	30	180	24	1
Armenian Church of America, Diocese of the	1979	66	450	45	(NA)
Assemblies of God.	1989	11,192	2,138	16,028	1,366
Baptist Bible Fellowship, International	1986	3,449	1,406	3,400	(NA)
Baptist General Conference.	1990	792	134	1,200	78
Baptist Missionary Association of America	1989	1,339	229	1,350	98

See footnotes at end of table.

No. 77. Religious Bodies—Selected Data—Continued

[See headnote, page 58]

RELIGIOUS BODY	Year	Churches reported	Member- ship (1,000)	Pastors serving par- ishes [1]	Sunday school enrollment [2] (1,000)
Bulgarian Eastern Orthodox Church (Diocese of N. and S. America and Australia)............................	1971	13	86	(NA)	(NA)
Christian and Missionary Alliance, The......................	1989	1,829	266	1,766	189
Christian Brethren (a.k.a. Plymouth Brethren)	1984	1,150	98	(NA)	(NA)
Christian Church (Disciples of Christ)......................	1989	4,113	1,052	3,895	319
Christian Churches and Churches of Christ.................	1988	5,579	1,071	5,525	(NA)
Christian Congregation, Inc., The	1989	1,454	109	1,452	48
Christian Methodist Episcopal Church	1983	2,340	719	2,340	(NA)
Christian Reformed Church in North America	1989	712	226	624	(NA)
Church of God, The	1978	2,035	76	1,910	(NA)
Church of God (Anderson, IN)	1989	2,338	200	2,170	176
Church of God (Cleveland, TN)..........................	1989	5,763	582	6,207	509
Church of God in Christ, The	1982	9,982	3,710	9,204	(NA)
Church of God in Christ, International, The.................	1982	300	200	700	(NA)
Church of God of Prophecy, The.........................	1990	2,119	73	4,262	86
Church of Jesus Christ of Latter-day Saints, The	1989	9,049	4,175	27,147	3,329
Church of the Brethren	1989	1,102	150	1,911	(NA)
Church of the Nazarene	1989	5,158	561	4,313	865
Churches of Christ	1989	13,375	1,626	(NA)	(NA)
Community Churches, International Council of...............	1990	210	250	(NA)	(NA)
Congregational Christian Churches, National Association of.......	1990	400	90	400	(NA)
Conservative Baptist Association of America...............	1989	1,126	210	1,126	(NA)
Coptic Orthodox Church	1990	42	165	49	7
Cumberland Presbyterian Church	1989	743	91	590	41
Episcopal Church, The	1989	7,372	2,433	8,122	556
Evangelical Covenant Church, The	1989	592	89	821	73
Evangelical Free Church of America	1990	1,040	165	(NA)	(NA)
Evangelical Lutheran Church in America..................	1989	11,067	5,239	10,125	1,155
Free Methodist Church of North America	1989	1,066	76	(NA)	98
Free Will Baptists, National Association of	1989	2,517	204	2,800	160
Full Gospel Fellowship of Churches and Ministers, International.....	1985	450	65	850	(NA)
General Association of Regular Baptist Churches	1989	1,582	216	(NA)	(NA)
General Baptists (General Association of).................	1989	872	74	(NA)	(NA)
Greek Orthodox Archdiocese of North and South America	1977	535	1,950	610	(NA)
Independent Fundamental Churches of America	1990	705	74	820	71
International Church of the Foursquare Gospel	1989	1,404	203	(NA)	42
Jehovah's Witnesses	1989	9,141	826	-	-
Jews [4]	1989	3,416	5,944	(NA)	(NA)
Liberty Baptist Fellowship	1987	510	200	150	(NA)
Lutheran Church - Missouri Synod, The	1989	5,990	2,609	5,339	660
Mennonite Church	1989	1,034	93	1,504	(NA)
National Baptist Convention of America	1956	11,398	2,669	7,598	(NA)
National Baptist Convention, U.S.A., Inc..................	1958	26,000	5,500	26,000	(NA)
National Primitive Baptist Convention, Inc.................	1975	616	250	460	(NA)
North American Old Roman Catholic Church................	1986	133	63	109	(NA)
Old Order Amish Church................................	1989	785	71	3,140	(NA)
Orthodox Church in America	1978	440	1,000	457	(NA)
Pentecostal Church of God	1989	1,165	91	(NA)	(NA)
Pentecostal Holiness Church, International................	1989	1,475	119	1,583	133
Polish National Catholic Church of America	1960	162	282	141	(NA)
Presbyterian Church in America	1989	1,100	217	1,193	109
Presbyterian Church (U.S.A.)	1989	11,469	2,886	10,410	1,099
Primitive Baptists	1960	1,000	72	(NA)	(NA)
Progressive National Baptist Convention, Inc...............	1967	655	522	(NA)	(NA)
Reformed Church in America	1989	928	331	863	99
Reorganized Church of Jesus Christ of Latter-day Saints..........	1989	1,048	190	16,182	(NA)
Roman Catholic Church, The	1989	23,500	57,020	34,553	7,107
Romanian Orthodox Episcopate of America	1989	37	65	37	2
Salvation Army, The	1989	1,122	446	2,656	114
Serbian Eastern Orthodox Church in the U.S.A. and Canada	1986	68	67	60	(NA)
Seventh-day Adventist Church	1989	4,193	702	2,305	467
Southern Baptist Convention	1989	37,739	14,908	37,500	7,931
Ukrainian Orthodox Church in the U.S.A.	1966	107	88	107	(NA)
Unitarian Universalist Association	1989	1,010	182	1,181	46
United Church of Christ................................	1989	6,388	1,626	5,614	434
United Methodist Church, The	1988	37,514	8,979	20,844	(NA)
United Pentecostal Church, International	1990	3,592	500	(NA)	(NA)
Wesleyan Church, The	1989	1,650	110	1,848	179
Wisconsin Evangelical Lutheran Synod	1989	1,198	419	1,144	49

- Represents or rounds to zero. NA Not available. X Not applicable. [1] Includes other pastors performing pastoral duties. [2] Includes pupils, officers, and teachers. [3] Includes data for religious bodies with membership less than 60,000. [4] Estimate of size of Jewish community provided by American Jewish Yearbook. Estimates of the number of Jews holding membership in synagogues or temples of the four branches of Judaism amount to 4,750,000.

Source: National Council of the Churches of Christ in the United States of America, New York, NY, *Yearbook of American and Canadian Churches*, annual, (copyright).

No. 78. Christian Church Adherents, 1980, and Jewish Population, 1990—States

[Christian church adherents were defined as "all members, including full members, their children and the estimated number of other regular participants who are not considered as communicant, confirmed or full members." Data on Christian church adherents are based on reports of 111 church bodies and exclude 18 church bodies that reported more than 100,000 members to the *Yearbook of American and Canadian Churches*. Data on Jewish population are based primarily on a compilation of individual estimates made by local Jewish federations. Additionally, most large communities have completed Jewish demographic surveys from which the Jewish population can be determined]

REGION, DIVISION, AND STATE	CHRISTIAN ADHERENTS, 1980		JEWISH POPULATION, 1990		REGION, DIVISION, AND STATE	CHRISTIAN ADHERENTS, 1980		JEWISH POPULATION, 1990	
	Number (1,000)	Percent of population [1]	Number (1,000)	Percent of population [1]		Number (1,000)	Percent of population [1]	Number (1,000)	Percent of population [1]
U.S. . . .	111,736	49.3	5,981	2.4	VA . . .	2,221	41.5	68	1.1
Northeast.	27,029	55.0	3,029	6.0	WV . .	772	39.6	2	0.1
N.E.	7,381	59.8	426	3.3	NC . . .	3,169	53.9	16	0.3
ME. . .	461	41.0	8	0.7	SC . . .	1,603	51.3	9	0.3
NH. . .	407	44.2	7	0.6	GA. . .	2,560	46.9	72	1.1
VT . . .	244	47.7	5	0.9	FL . . .	3,707	38.0	567	4.6
MA. . .	3,669	64.0	276	4.7	E.S.C. . . .	8,079	55.1	42	0.3
RI . . .	710	75.0	16	1.6	KY . . .	1,979	54.1	12	0.3
CT . . .	1,890	60.8	113	3.5	TN . . .	2,485	54.1	19	0.4
M.A. . . .	19,649	53.4	2,604	6.9	AL . . .	2,230	57.3	9	0.2
NY . . .	8,548	48.7	1,843	10.3	MS. . .	1,385	54.9	2	0.1
NJ . . .	3,923	53.3	430	5.6	W.S.C .	13,189	55.5	132	0.5
PA . . .	7,177	60.5	330	2.8	AR . . .	1,282	56.1	2	0.1
Midwest. .	31,204	53.0	669	1.1	LA . . .	2,404	57.2	16	0.4
E.N.C . .	20,969	50.3	548	1.3	OK . . .	1,751	57.9	5	0.2
OH. . .	5,306	49.1	131	1.2	TX . . .	7,752	54.5	109	0.6
IN . . .	2,451	44.6	18	0.3	West . . .	15,986	37.0	1,127	2.2
IL. . . .	6,251	54.7	257	2.2	Mt.	5,241	46.1	153	1.1
MI . . .	3,932	42.5	107	1.2	MT. . .	348	44.2	(Z)	0.1
WI . . .	3,029	64.4	35	0.7	ID . . .	472	50.0	(Z)	0.1
W.N.C . .	10,235	59.6	121	0.7	WY . .	207	44.0	(Z)	0.1
MN. . .	2,644	64.9	30	0.7	CO. . .	1,052	36.4	50	1.5
IA . . .	1,781	61.1	6	0.2	NM. . .	767	58.9	6	0.4
MO . . .	2,613	53.1	62	1.2	AZ . . .	1,065	39.2	72	2.1
ND. . .	482	73.8	1	0.1	UT . . .	1,097	75.1	3	0.2
SD . . .	462	66.9	(Z)	0.1	NV . . .	233	29.1	20	1.9
NE . . .	990	63.1	7	0.5	Pac. . . .	10,745	33.8	974	2.6
KS . . .	1,262	53.4	14	0.6	WA . . .	1,275	30.9	33	0.7
South. . .	37,516	49.8	1,155	1.4	OR. . .	946	35.9	12	0.5
S.A.	16,247	44.0	981	2.3	CA. . .	8,082	34.1	920	3.2
DE . . .	238	40.1	9	1.4	AK . . .	123	30.6	2	0.5
MD. . .	1,673	39.7	211	4.6	HI . . .	319	33.1	7	0.6
DC. . .	304	47.6	25	4.2					

Z Fewer than 500. [1] Based on U.S. Bureau of the Census data for resident population enumerated as of April 1, 1980, and 1990.

Source: Christian church adherents-B. Quinn, H. Anderson, M. Bradley, P. Goetting, and P. Shriver, *Churches and Church Membership in the United States 1980*, Glenmary Research Center, Atlanta, GA, 1982, (copyright); Jewish population—American Jewish Committee and the Jewish Publication Society, New York, NY, *American Jewish Year Book, 1991*, (copyright).

No. 79. Religious Population of the World, by Region: 1991

[**In thousands, except percent**. Refers to adherents of all religions as defined and enumerated for each of the world's countries in *World Christian Encyclopedia* (1982), projected to mid-1991, adjusted for recent data]

RELIGION	Total	Percent distri- bution	Africa	Asia	Latin America	Northern America	Europe	Soviet Union	Oceania
Total population . . .	5,385,330	100.0	661,803	3,171,511	457,011	277,943	499,544	290,665	26,855
Christians	1,783,660	33.1	317,453	257,926	427,416	237,261	412,790	108,498	22,316
Roman Catholics.	1,010,352	18.8	119,244	121,311	397,810	96,315	262,026	5,551	8,095
Protestants	368,209	6.8	84,729	79,969	16,930	95,610	73,766	9,790	7,415
Orthodox	168,683	3.1	27,698	3,587	1,730	5,964	36,080	93,056	568
Anglicans.	73,835	1.4	26,063	694	1,275	7,284	32,879	(Z)	5,640
Other Christians	162,581	3.0	59,719	52,365	9,671	32,088	8,039	101	598
Muslims	950,726	17.7	269,959	625,194	1,326	2,642	12,545	38,959	101
Nonreligious [1]	884,468	16.4	1,840	700,523	16,828	25,265	52,289	84,477	3,246
Hindus	719,269	13.4	1,431	714,652	867	1,259	703	2	355
Buddhists	309,127	5.7	20	307,323	530	554	271	404	25
Atheists	236,809	4.4	307	158,429	3,162	1,310	17,563	55,511	527
Chinese folk-religionists [2].	183,646	3.4	12	183,361	71	121	60	1	20
New-religionists [3]	140,778	2.6	20	138,767	520	1,410	50	1	10
Tribal religionists	93,996	1.7	68,484	24,487	918	40	1	-	66
Sikhs	18,461	0.3	26	17,934	8	252	231	1	9
Jews	17,615	0.3	327	5,484	1,071	6,952	1,465	2,220	96
Shamanists	10,302	0.2	1	10,044	1	1	2	252	1
Confucians	5,917	0.1	1	5,883	2	26	2	2	1
Baha'is.	5,402	0.1	1,451	2,630	785	363	90	7	76
Jains	3,724	0.1	51	3,649	4	4	15	-	1
Shintoists	3,163	0.1	(Z)	3,160	1	1	1	(Z)	1
Other religionists	18,268	0.3	420	12,065	3,501	482	1,466	330	4

- Represents zero. Z Fewer than 500. [1] Persons professing no religion, nonbelievers, agnostics, freethinkers, and dereligionized secularists indifferent to all religion. [2] Followers of traditional Chinese religion (local deities, ancestor veneration, Confucian ethics, Taoism, etc.). [3] Followers of Asiatic 20th-century New Religions, New Religious movements, radical new crisis religions, and non-Christian syncretistic mass religions.

Source: Encyclopaedia Britannica, Inc., Chicago, IL, *1992 Britannica Book of the Year*. (Reprinted with permission. Copyright 1992.)

Vital Statistics

This section presents vital statistics data on births, deaths, abortions, fetal deaths, fertility, life expectancy, marriages and divorces. Vital statistics are compiled for the country as a whole by the National Center for Health Statistics (NCHS) and published in its annual report, *Vital Statistics of the United States,* in certain reports of the *Vital and Health Statistics* series, and in the *Monthly Vital Statistics Report.* Reports in this field are also issued by the various State bureaus of vital statistics. Data on fertility, on age of persons at first marriage, and on marital status and marital history are compiled by the Bureau of the Census from its Current Population Survey (CPS; see text, section 1) and published in *Current Population Reports,* series P-20. Data on abortions are published by the Alan Guttmacher Institute, New York, NY in selected issues of *Family Planning Perspectives.*

Registration of vital events.—The registration of births, deaths, fetal deaths, and other vital events in the United States is primarily a State and local function. The civil laws of every State provide for a continuous and permanent birth- and death-registration system. Many States also provide for marriage- and divorce-registration systems. Vital events occurring to U.S. residents outside the United States are not included in the data.

Births and deaths.—The live-birth, death, and fetal-death statistics prepared by NCHS are based on vital records filed in the registration offices of all States, of New York City, and of the District of Columbia. The annual collection of death statistics on a national basis began in 1900 with a national death-registration area of 10 States and the District of Columbia; a similar annual collection of birth statistics for a national birth-registration area began in 1915, also with 10 reporting States and the District of Columbia. Since 1933, the birth- and death-registration areas have comprised the entire United States, including Alaska (beginning 1959) and Hawaii (beginning 1960). National statistics on fetal deaths were

In Brief

1990:	
Births	4,179,000
Deaths	2,162,000
Marriages	2,448,000
Divorces	1,175,000
Leading causes of death:	
Heart disease	*725,000*
Cancer	*506,000*
Stroke	*145,340*
Accidents	*93,550*
Chronic lung disease	*88,989*

first compiled for 1918 and annually since 1922.

Prior to 1951, birth statistics came from a complete count of records received in the Public Health Service (now received in NCHS). From 1951 through 1971, they were based on a 50-percent sample of all registered births (except for a complete count in 1955 and a 20- to 50-percent sample in 1967). Beginning in 1972, they have been based on a complete count for States participating in the Vital Statistics Cooperative Program (VSCP) (for details, see the technical appendix in *Vital Statistics of the United States*) and on a 50-percent sample of all other areas. Beginning 1986 all reporting areas participated in the VSCP. Mortality data have been based on a complete count of records for each area (except for a 50-percent sample in 1972). Beginning in 1970, births to, and deaths of nonresident aliens of the United States and U.S. citizens outside the United States have been excluded from the data. Fetal deaths and deaths among Armed Forces abroad are excluded. Data based on samples are subject to sampling error; for details, see annual issues of *Vital Statistics of the United States.*

Mortality statistics by cause of death are compiled in accordance with World Health Organization regulations according to the *International Classification of Diseases* (ICD). The ICD is revised approximately every 10 years. The ninth revision of the ICD was employed beginning in 1979. Deaths for prior years were classified according to the revision of the

ICD in use at the time. Each revision of the ICD introduces a number of discontinuities in mortality statistics; for a discussion of those between the eighth and ninth revisions of the ICD, see *Monthly Vital Statistics Report,* vol. 28, No. 11, supplement.

Some of the tables present age-adjusted death rates in addition to crude death rates. Age-adjusted death rates shown in this section were prepared using the direct method, in which age-specific death rates for a population of interest are applied to a standard population distributed by age. Age adjustment eliminates the differences in observed rates between points in time or among compared population groups that result from age differences in population composition.

Abortions.—The U.S. Centers for Disease Control (CDC) collects data on abortions annually from States which have a central health agency with a statewide reporting system. The Alan Guttmacher Institute, New York, NY also issues data on the number of abortions based on its own surveys of hospitals and physicians. The Guttmacher Institute also publishes data on the characteristics of abortions after adjusting CDC data for changes in the number of States reporting each year.

Fertility and life expectancy.—The total fertility rate, defined as the number of births that 1,000 women would have in their lifetime if, at each year of age, they experienced the birth rates occurring in the specified year, is compiled and published by NCHS. Other data relating to social and medical factors which affect fertility rates, such as contraceptive use and birth expectations, are collected and made available by both NCHS and the Bureau of the Census. NCHS figures are based on information in birth and fetal death certificates and on the periodic National Surveys of Family Growth; Bureau of the Census data are based on decennial censuses and the CPS.

Data on life expectancy, the average remaining lifetime in years for persons who attain a given age, are computed and published by NCHS. For details, see the technical appendix in *Vital Statistics of the United States.*

Marriage and divorce.—The compilation of nationwide statistics on marriages and divorces in the United States began in 1887-88 when the National Office of Vital Statistics prepared estimates for the years 1867-86. Although periodic updates took place after 1888, marriage and divorce statistics were not collected and published annually until 1944 by that Office. In 1957 and 1958, respectively, the same Office established marriage- and divorce-registration areas. Beginning in 1957, the marriage-registration area comprised 30 States, plus Alaska, Hawaii, Puerto Rico, and the Virgin Islands; it currently includes 42 States and the District of Columbia. The divorce-registration area, starting in 1958 with 14 States, Alaska, Hawaii, and the Virgin Islands, currently includes a total of 31 States and the Virgin Islands. Procedures for estimating the number of marriages and divorces in the registration States are discussed in *Vital Statistics of the United States,* Vol. III—*Marriage and Divorce.* Total counts of events for registration and nonregistration States are gathered by collecting already summarized data on marriages and divorces reported by State offices of vital statistics and by county offices of registration.

Another important source of data on marriage and divorce trends in the United States is the March supplement to the Current Population Survey conducted by the Bureau of the Census. For information on marital status, see section 1.

Vital statistics rates.—Except as noted, vital statistics rates computed by NCHS are based on decennial census population figures as of April 1 for 1940, 1950, 1960, 1970, 1980, and 1990; and on midyear population figures for other years, as estimated by the Bureau of the Census (see text, section 1).

Race.—Data by race for births, deaths, marriages, and divorces from NCHS are based on information contained in the certificates of registration. The Census Bureau's Current Population Survey obtains information on race by asking respondents to classify their race as: (1) White, (2) Black, (3) American Indian, Eskimo, or Aleut, or (4) Asian or Pacific Islander.

Figure 2.1
Distribution of AIDS Deaths, by Age: 1982 through 1991

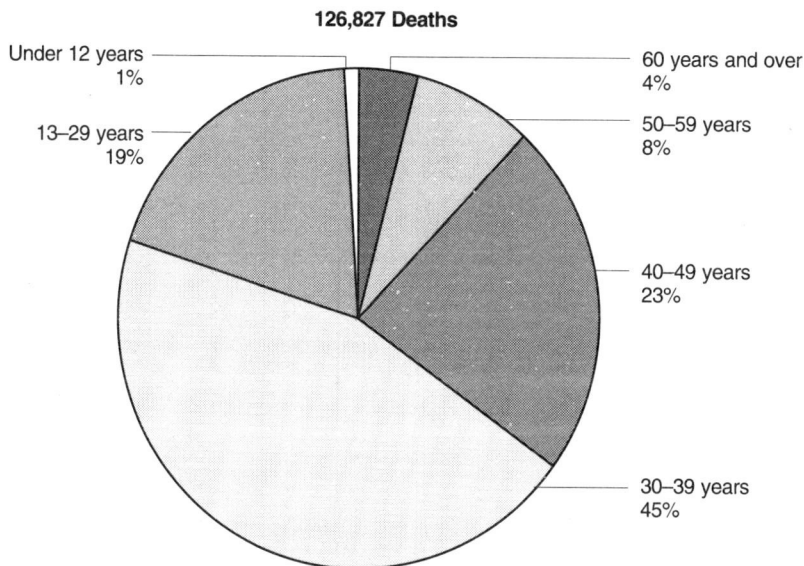

126,827 Deaths

Under 12 years
1%

13–29 years
19%

60 years and over
4%

50–59 years
8%

40–49 years
23%

30–39 years
45%

Source: Chart prepared by U.S. Bureau of the Census. For data, see table 119.

Figure 2.2
Distribution of First Cohabitations of Women, by Outcome: 1988

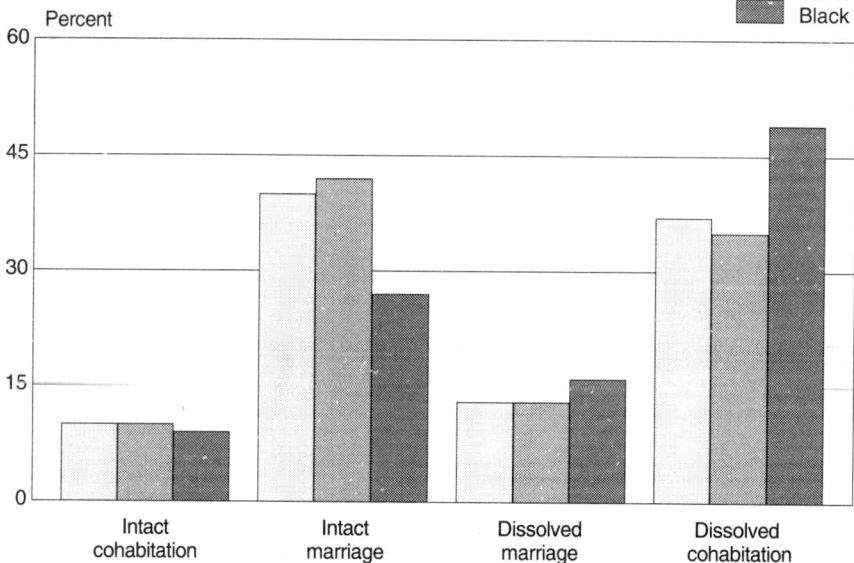

Total
White
Black

Percent

Intact cohabitation — Intact marriage — Dissolved marriage — Dissolved cohabitation

Source: Chart prepared by U.S. Bureau of the Census. For data, see table 133.

No. 80. Live Births, Deaths, Marriages, and Divorces: 1950 to 1990

[Prior to 1960, excludes Alaska and Hawaii. Beginning 1970, excludes births to and deaths of nonresidents of the United States. See Appendix III. See also *Historical Statistics, Colonial Times to 1970*, series B 1-5, B 142, B 167, and B 216]

YEAR	NUMBER (1,000)					RATE PER 1,000 POPULATION				
	Births [1]	Deaths		Mar-riages [3]	Divorc-es [4]	Births [1]	Deaths		Mar-riages [3]	Divorc-es [4]
		Total	Infant [2]				Total	Infant [2]		
1950	3,632	1,452	104	1,667	385	24.1	9.6	29.2	11.1	2.6
1955	4,097	1,529	107	1,531	377	25.0	9.3	26.4	9.3	2.3
1960	4,258	1,712	111	1,523	393	23.7	9.5	26.0	8.5	2.2
1965	3,760	1,828	93	1,800	479	19.4	9.4	24.7	9.3	2.5
1970	3,731	1,921	75	2,159	708	18.4	9.5	20.0	10.6	3.5
1971	3,556	1,928	68	2,190	773	17.2	9.3	19.1	10.6	3.7
1972	3,258	1,964	60	2,282	845	15.6	9.4	18.5	10.9	4.0
1973	3,137	1,973	56	2,284	915	14.8	9.3	17.7	10.8	4.3
1974	3,160	1,934	53	2,230	977	14.8	9.1	16.7	10.5	4.6
1975	3,144	1,893	51	2,153	1,036	14.6	8.8	16.1	10.0	4.8
1976	3,168	1,909	48	2,155	1,083	14.6	8.8	15.2	9.9	5.0
1977	3,327	1,900	47	2,178	1,091	15.1	8.6	14.1	9.9	5.0
1978	3,333	1,928	46	2,282	1,130	15.0	8.7	13.8	10.3	5.1
1979	3,494	1,914	46	2,331	1,181	15.6	8.5	13.1	10.4	5.3
1980	3,612	1,990	46	2,390	1,189	15.9	8.8	12.6	10.6	5.2
1981	3,629	1,978	43	2,422	1,213	15.8	8.6	11.9	10.6	5.3
1982	3,681	1,975	42	2,456	1,170	15.9	8.5	11.5	10.6	5.0
1983	3,639	2,019	41	2,446	1,158	15.5	8.6	11.2	10.5	4.9
1984	3,669	2,039	40	2,477	1,169	15.5	8.6	10.8	10.5	5.0
1985	3,761	2,086	40	2,413	1,190	15.8	8.7	10.6	10.1	5.0
1986	3,757	2,105	39	2,407	1,178	15.6	8.7	10.4	10.0	4.9
1987	3,809	2,123	38	2,403	1,166	15.7	8.7	10.1	9.9	4.8
1988	3,910	2,168	39	2,396	1,167	15.9	8.8	10.0	9.7	4.7
1989 [5]	4,041	2,050	40	[5]2,404	[5]1,163	16.3	8.7	9.8	[5]9.7	[5]4.7
1990 [5]	4,179	2,162	38	2,448	1,175	16.7	8.6	9.1	9.8	4.7

[1] Through 1955, adjusted for underregistration.   [2] Infants under 1 year, excluding fetal deaths; rates per 1,000 registered live births.   [3] Includes estimates for some States through 1965 and also for 1976 and 1977 and marriage licenses for some States for all years except 1973 and 1975. Beginning 1978, includes nonlicensed marriages in California.   [4] Includes reported annulments and some estimated State figures for all years.   [5] Preliminary.

Source: U.S. National Center for Health Statistics, *Vital Statistics of the United States*, annual, *Monthly Vital Statistics Report*, and unpublished data.

No. 81. Live Births and Deaths—20 Largest Metropolitan Areas: 1986

[Excludes births to and deaths of nonresidents of United States. Data are by place of residence. Metropolitan statistical areas (MSA's), consolidated metropolitan statistical areas (CMSA's), and New England County Metropolitan Areas (NECMA's) are as defined by the U.S. Office of Management and Budget as of June 30, 1987; see Appendix II for definitions and components]

METROPOLITAN AREA	NUMBER (1,000)			RATE PER 1,000 POPULATION		
	Births	Deaths		Births	Deaths	
		Total	Infant [1]		Total	Infant [1]
New York-Northern New Jersey-Long Island, NY-NJ-CT CMSA [2] .	261,869	171,369	2,744	15	9.6	10.5
Los Angeles-Anaheim-Riverside, CA CMSA	247,483	96,595	2,224	19	7.4	9.0
Chicago-Gary-Lake County (IL), IL-IN-WI CMSA.	130,021	68,677	1,641	16	8.5	12.6
San Francisco-Oakland-San Jose, CA CMSA	92,741	45,144	759	16	7.7	8.2
Philadelphia-Wilmington-Trenton, PA-NJ-DE-MD CMSA.	89,318	56,922	1,006	15	9.7	1.0
Detroit-Ann Arbor, MI CMSA	69,032	41,324	846	15	9.0	12.3
Boston-Lawrence-Salem-Lowell-Brockton, MA NECMA.	52,825	34,504	444	14	9.3	8.4
Dallas-Fort Worth, TX CMSA	71,880	23,784	727	20	6.5	10.1
Houston-Galveston-Brazoria, TX CMSA	67,600	20,862	643	19	5.7	9.5
Washington, DC-MD-VA MSA.	57,393	24,226	705	16	6.8	12.3
Miami-Fort Lauderdale, FL CMSA	44,247	30,480	487	15	10.5	11.0
Cleveland-Akron-Lorain, OH CMSA	39,589	26,899	439	14	9.7	11.1
Atlanta, GA MSA	42,210	17,325	494	16	6.7	11.7
St. Louis, MO-IL MSA	38,346	22,895	447	16	9.4	11.7
Pittsburgh-Beaver Valley, PA CMSA	28,301	25,737	294	12	11.1	10.4
Minneapolis-St. Paul, MN-WI MSA.	38,532	16,181	350	17	7.0	9.1
Seattle-Tacoma, WA CMSA	36,084	16,634	344	16	7.3	9.5
Baltimore, MD MSA	36,582	21,130	424	16	9.0	11.9
San Diego, CA MSA	39,044	15,608	356	18	7.1	9.1
Tampa-St. Petersburg-Clearwater, FL MSA.	24,557	23,879	278	13	12.5	11.3

[1] Infants under 1 year, excluding fetal deaths; rates per 1,000 registered live births.   [2] CT portion of CMSA covers all of Fairfield County.

Source: U.S. National Center for Health Statistics, *Vital Statistics of the United States*, annual; and unpublished data.

No. 82. Births and Birth Rates: 1970 to 1989

[Births in thousands and by race of child, except as indicated. Excludes births to nonresidents of United States. For population bases used to derive these data, see text, section 2. See Appendix III. Minus sign (-) indicates decrease. See also *Historical Statistics, Colonial Times to 1970,* series B 1, B 5-10, and B 12-20]

ITEM	1970	1980	1981	1982	1983	1984	1985	1986	1987	1988	1989
Live births [1]	3,731	3,612	3,629	3,681	3,639	3,669	3,761	3,757	3,809	3,910	4,041
Average annual percent change [2]	-0.2	2.8	0.5	1.4	-1.1	0.8	2.5	-0.1	1.4	2.6	3.4
White	3,091	2,899	2,909	2,942	2,904	2,924	2,991	2,970	2,992	3,046	3,132
Black	572	590	588	593	586	593	608	621	642	672	709
Male	1,915	1,853	1,860	1,886	1,866	1,879	1,928	1,925	1,951	2,002	2,069
Female	1,816	1,760	1,769	1,795	1,773	1,790	1,833	1,832	1,858	1,907	1,971
Males per 100 females	105.5	105.3	105.2	105.1	105.2	105.0	105.2	105.1	105.0	105.0	105.0
Age of mother:											
Under 20 years old	656	562	537	524	499	480	478	472	473	489	518
20 to 24 years old	1,419	1,226	1,212	1,206	1,160	1,142	1,141	1,102	1,076	1,067	1,078
25 to 29 years old	995	1,108	1,128	1,152	1,148	1,166	1,201	1,200	1,216	1,239	1,263
30 to 34 years old	428	550	581	605	625	658	696	721	761	804	842
35 to 39 years old	180	141	146	168	180	196	214	230	248	270	294
40 years old or more	53	24	25	26	27	28	29	31	36	41	46
Age of father:											
Under 20 years old	189	137	129	125	116	109	108	105	105	111	120
20 to 24 years old	1,015	803	785	768	722	696	685	651	627	617	613
25 to 29 years old	1,085	1,082	1,083	1,093	1,070	1,067	1,081	1,059	1,053	1,055	1,056
30 to 34 years old	599	739	768	780	782	806	837	845	872	904	922
35 to 39 years old	298	275	286	319	335	356	381	398	413	431	451
40 years old or more	214	139	141	149	153	160	167	174	191	205	221
Age not stated	330	437	437	447	461	475	502	524	549	585	659
Birth rate per 1,000 population	18.4	15.9	15.8	15.9	15.5	15.5	15.8	15.6	15.7	15.9	16.3
White	17.4	14.9	14.8	14.9	14.6	14.5	14.8	14.5	14.5	14.7	15.0
Black	25.3	22.1	21.6	21.4	20.9	20.8	21.1	21.2	21.6	22.2	23.1
Male	19.4	16.8	16.7	16.7	16.4	16.3	16.6	16.4	16.5	16.7	(NA)
Female	17.4	15.1	15.0	15.1	14.7	14.7	15.0	14.8	14.9	15.1	(NA)
Plural birth ratio [3]	[4]18.1	19.3	19.7	19.9	20.3	20.3	21.0	21.6	22.0	22.4	23.0
White	[4]17.3	18.5	18.8	19.2	19.6	19.8	20.4	21.2	21.6	22.0	[5]22.5
Black	[4]22.8	24.1	24.7	24.1	24.5	24.2	25.3	24.9	25.4	25.8	[5]26.9
Birth rate per 1,000 women	87.9	68.4	67.4	67.3	65.8	65.4	66.2	65.4	65.7	67.2	69.2
White [6]	84.1	64.7	63.9	63.9	62.4	62.2	63.0	61.9	62.0	63.0	64.7
Black [6]	115.4	88.1	85.4	84.1	81.7	81.4	82.2	82.4	83.8	86.6	90.4
Age of mother:											
10 to 14 years old	1.2	1.1	1.1	1.1	1.1	1.2	1.2	1.3	1.3	1.3	1.4
15 to 19 years old	68.3	53.0	52.7	52.9	51.7	50.9	51.3	50.6	51.1	53.6	58.1
20 to 24 years old	167.8	115.1	111.8	111.3	108.3	107.3	108.9	108.2	108.9	111.5	115.4
25 to 29 years old	145.1	112.9	112.0	111.0	108.7	108.3	110.5	109.2	110.8	113.4	116.6
30 to 34 years old	73.3	61.9	61.4	64.2	64.6	66.5	68.5	69.3	71.3	73.7	76.2
35 to 39 years old	31.7	19.8	20.0	21.1	22.1	22.8	23.9	24.3	26.2	27.9	29.7
40 to 44 years old	8.1	3.9	3.8	3.9	3.8	3.9	4.0	4.1	4.4	4.8	5.2
45 to 49 years old	0.5	0.2	0.2	0.2	0.2	0.2	0.2	0.2	0.2	0.2	0.2
Birth rate per 1,000 men [7]	71.5	57.0	56.3	56.4	55.3	55.0	55.7	54.9	55.0	55.9	57.3
White [7]	67.1	52.9	52.3	52.5	51.5	51.2	51.9	50.9	50.9	51.4	52.5
Black [7]	107.4	83.8	81.2	79.8	78.0	77.6	78.2	78.3	79.5	82.0	85.6
Age of father: [8]											
15 to 19 years old [9]	25.6	18.8	18.5	18.7	18.4	18.0	18.2	18.1	18.6	20.0	22.4
20 to 24 years old	146.6	92.0	88.0	86.1	83.5	81.9	82.8	82.3	83.0	85.5	89.2
25 to 29 years old	175.0	123.0	119.7	117.4	113.9	111.0	111.9	109.1	109.4	111.1	113.8
30 to 34 years old	112.3	91.0	88.6	90.4	88.7	88.8	89.7	88.7	89.3	91.0	92.3
35 to 39 years old	57.6	42.8	43.2	44.2	45.3	45.7	47.0	46.5	48.2	49.5	50.8
40 to 44 years old	24.9	17.1	16.9	17.6	17.2	17.8	18.1	18.4	19.1	20.0	20.6
45 to 49 years old	9.1	6.1	6.3	6.4	6.4	6.3	6.6	6.7	6.9	7.1	7.4
50 to 54 years old	3.1	2.2	2.3	2.4	2.3	2.4	2.5	2.5	2.5	2.6	2.7
55 years old and over	0.6	0.4	0.4	0.4	0.3	0.4	0.4	0.4	0.4	0.4	0.6

NA Not available. [1] Includes other races, not shown separately. [2] For explanation, see Guide to Tabular Presentation. For 1970, change from 1965. [3] Number of multiple births per 1,000 live births. [4] 1971. [5] Race of mother; data not directly comparable with prior years. [6] Per 1,000 women, 15 to 44 years old in specified group. [7] Rate computed by relating total births, regardless of age of father, to 1,000 men, 15 to 54 years old in specified group. [8] Rates by age of father computed using frequencies with age not stated distributed among all age groups. [9] Rate computed by relating births to fathers under 20 years of age to men 15 to 19 years old.

Source: U.S. National Center for Health Statistics, *Vital Statistics of the United States,* annual; and unpublished data.

No. 83. Live Births—Number and Rate, by State: 1970 to 1990

[Registered births. Excludes births to nonresidents of the United States, except as noted. See Appendix III]

REGION, DIVISION, AND STATE	NUMBER (1,000) By State of residence						By State of occur- rence[1]		RATE PER 1,000 POPULATION [2] By State of residence						By State of occur- rence[1]	
	1970	1980	1985	1987	1988	1989	1989	1990	1970	1980	1985	1987	1988	1989	1989	1990
U.S.	3,731	3,612	3,761	3,809	3,910	4,041	[3]4,021	[3]4,179	18.4	15.9	15.8	15.7	15.9	16.3	[3]16.2	[3]16.7
New England	200	162	179	187	193	200	202	204	16.9	13.1	14.2	14.6	14.9	15.3	15.5	15.5
Maine	18	16	17	17	17	17	17	16	17.9	14.6	14.5	14.2	14.3	14.3	13.8	13.1
New Hampshire . .	13	14	15	17	17	18	18	17	17.9	14.9	15.5	16.1	16.0	16.1	16.2	15.0
Vermont	8	8	8	8	8	8	8	8	18.8	15.4	15.0	14.8	14.6	15.0	14.0	14.0
Massachusetts . . .	95	73	82	84	88	92	96	95	16.6	12.7	14.1	14.4	15.0	15.5	16.3	16.0
Rhode Island	16	12	13	14	14	15	15	16	16.5	12.9	13.5	14.2	14.3	14.8	15.3	15.6
Connecticut	50	39	44	47	48	49	48	52	16.7	12.5	13.9	14.6	14.9	15.3	14.7	16.1
Middle Atlantic	630	495	526	548	564	582	578	595	16.9	13.4	14.1	14.6	15.0	15.4	15.3	15.7
New York	318	239	259	272	281	291	291	302	17.4	13.6	14.6	15.3	15.7	16.2	16.2	16.8
New Jersey	120	97	106	113	118	122	117	121	16.8	13.2	14.0	14.8	15.3	15.7	15.1	15.5
Pennsylvania	193	159	161	163	166	169	170	172	16.3	13.4	13.5	13.6	13.8	14.0	14.1	14.2
East North Central .	754	668	634	629	638	658	647	673	18.7	16.0	15.2	15.0	15.1	15.6	15.3	15.8
Ohio	200	169	160	158	161	164	163	166	18.7	15.7	14.9	14.6	14.8	15.0	14.9	15.1
Indiana	99	88	81	79	82	83	83	85	19.1	16.1	14.7	14.2	14.7	14.9	14.8	15.1
Illinois	205	190	181	181	185	190	187	193	18.5	16.6	15.7	15.6	15.9	16.3	16.0	16.4
Michigan	172	146	138	141	140	149	143	158	19.4	15.7	15.2	15.3	15.1	16.0	15.4	16.9
Wisconsin	78	75	74	71	71	72	72	72	17.6	15.9	15.4	14.8	14.6	14.8	14.8	14.8
West North Central.	284	288	275	262	265	268	266	276	17.4	16.8	15.6	14.9	14.9	15.0	14.9	15.3
Minnesota	68	68	67	65	67	68	67	68	18.0	16.6	16.1	15.3	15.5	15.5	15.3	15.5
Iowa	48	48	41	38	38	39	37	40	17.1	16.4	14.3	13.4	13.5	13.7	13.1	13.9
Missouri.	81	79	77	75	76	78	80	83	17.3	16.1	15.3	14.7	14.9	15.1	15.5	16.0
North Dakota	11	12	12	10	10	10	11	10	17.6	18.4	17.1	15.3	15.1	14.5	16.5	16.0
South Dakota	12	13	12	11	11	11	11	11	17.0	19.2	17.1	16.2	15.7	15.5	15.4	15.2
Nebraska.	26	27	26	24	24	24	24	24	17.3	17.4	15.9	14.9	14.9	15.0	15.1	15.0
Kansas	38	41	40	39	39	39	36	39	17.0	17.2	16.2	15.6	15.5	15.4	14.2	15.4
South Atlantic	574	547	599	629	654	683	679	705	18.7	14.8	14.9	15.1	15.4	15.8	15.7	16.1
Delaware.	11	9	10	10	10	11	11	12	19.2	15.8	15.5	15.4	15.8	15.9	17.1	17.1
Maryland	69	60	68	73	76	78	68	76	17.6	14.2	15.5	16.0	16.4	16.7	14.4	15.9
Dist. of Columbia. .	15	9	10	10	11	12	23	22	20.1	14.7	15.8	16.4	17.1	19.5	37.3	36.8
Virginia	86	78	86	90	93	97	93	97	18.6	14.7	15.1	15.3	15.5	15.9	15.3	15.6
West Virginia	31	29	24	22	22	22	23	23	17.8	15.1	12.5	11.8	11.6	11.9	12.4	12.6
North Carolina . . .	98	84	89	94	98	102	103	105	19.3	14.4	14.3	14.6	15.0	15.5	15.6	15.8
South Carolina . . .	52	52	52	53	55	57	55	57	20.1	16.6	15.6	15.4	15.9	16.3	15.7	15.9
Georgia.	97	92	96	103	106	110	110	115	21.1	16.9	16.1	16.5	16.7	17.1	17.1	17.6
Florida.	115	132	164	175	184	193	193	199	16.9	13.5	14.4	14.6	14.9	15.2	15.2	15.3
East South Central .	248	240	223	220	225	232	230	245	19.4	16.4	14.7	14.4	14.6	15.1	14.9	15.8
Kentucky.	60	60	53	51	51	53	53	57	18.7	16.3	14.2	13.8	13.7	14.3	14.1	15.2
Tennessee.	72	69	67	68	71	73	77	78	18.4	15.1	14.0	14.0	14.4	14.8	15.5	15.6
Alabama	67	64	60	60	61	63	58	67	19.4	16.3	14.9	14.6	14.8	15.2	14.2	16.2
Mississippi	49	48	43	41	42	43	42	43	22.1	19.0	16.6	15.7	16.1	16.4	16.1	16.4
West South Central.	386	445	478	458	460	464	452	484	20.0	18.7	18.0	17.0	17.1	17.2	16.7	17.8
Arkansas.	35	37	35	35	35	36	35	35	18.5	16.3	14.9	14.5	14.6	14.9	14.5	14.7
Louisiana.	74	82	81	74	74	73	69	72	20.4	19.5	18.2	16.6	16.8	16.6	15.7	16.5
Oklahoma	45	52	53	48	47	47	46	46	17.5	17.2	16.1	14.6	14.6	14.7	14.4	14.3
Texas	231	274	308	302	303	308	301	330	20.6	19.2	18.8	18.0	18.0	18.1	17.7	19.2
Mountain	172	226	234	232	235	237	236	243	20.7	19.9	18.4	17.6	17.6	17.5	17.4	17.7
Montana	13	14	13	12	12	12	11	11	18.2	18.1	16.4	15.1	14.5	14.5	14.1	14.2
Idaho	14	20	18	16	16	16	15	16	20.3	21.4	17.5	16.0	15.7	15.7	15.2	16.0
Wyoming	7	11	9	8	7	7	6	7	19.6	22.5	18.4	15.4	15.0	14.5	13.7	13.9
Colorado	42	50	55	54	53	53	53	53	18.8	17.2	17.0	16.3	16.2	15.9	15.9	16.0
New Mexico.	22	26	28	27	27	27	27	28	21.8	20.0	19.1	18.2	17.9	17.9	17.9	18.3
Arizona	38	50	59	63	66	67	68	69	21.3	18.4	18.6	18.7	18.8	18.9	19.0	18.9
Utah	27	42	37	35	36	36	36	37	25.5	28.6	22.8	21.0	21.3	20.8	21.2	21.6
Nevada	10	13	15	17	18	20	18	21	19.6	16.6	16.4	16.6	17.1	17.6	16.5	18.1
Pacific.	483	542	612	643	676	718	705	773	18.2	17.0	17.5	17.6	18.1	18.7	18.4	19.7
Washington	61	68	70	70	73	75	73	77	17.8	16.4	15.9	15.5	15.6	15.8	15.4	15.8
Oregon	35	43	39	39	40	41	44	46	16.8	16.4	14.7	14.2	14.5	14.6	15.5	15.9
California	363	403	471	503	533	570	557	618	18.2	17.0	17.9	18.2	18.9	19.2	18.7	20.7
Alaska.	8	10	13	12	11	12	12	12	25.1	23.7	24.6	22.2	21.4	22.1	21.9	21.8
Hawaii.	16	18	18	19	19	19	20	20	21.4	18.8	17.4	17.2	17.3	17.4	17.6	18.1

[1] Includes births to nonresidents. Provisional. [2] Based on population (excluding Armed Forces abroad enumerated as of April 1 for 1970, 1980, and 1990, and estimated as of July 1 for other years. [3] U.S. totals are based on monthly receipts corrected for observed differences between provisional and final monthly figures. State figures have not been corrected in this manner.

Source: U.S. National Center for Health Statistics, *Vital Statistics of the United States*, annual; and *Monthly Vital Statistics Report*.

No. 84. Total Fertility Rate and Intrinsic Rate of Natural Increase: 1960 to 1989

[Based on race of child and registered births only. Beginning 1970, excludes births to nonresidents of United States. The *total fertility rate* is the number of births that 1,000 women would have in their lifetime if, at each year of age, they experienced the birth rates occurring in the specified year. A total fertility rate of 2,110 represents "replacement level" fertility for the total population under current mortality conditions (assuming no net immigration). The *intrinsic rate of natural increase* is the rate that would eventually prevail if a population were to experience, at each year of age, the birth rates and death rates occurring in the specified year and if those rates remained unchanged over a long period of time. Minus sign (-) indicates decrease. See also Appendix III and *Historical Statistics, Colonial Times to 1970*, series B 11]

ANNUAL AVERAGE AND YEAR	TOTAL FERTILITY RATE			INTRINSIC RATE OF NATURAL INCREASE			ANNUAL AVERAGE AND YEAR	TOTAL FERTILITY RATE			INTRINSIC RATE OF NATURAL INCREASE		
	Total	White	Black and other	Total	White	Black and other		Total	White	Black and other	Total	White	Black and other
1960-64 ...	3,449	3,326	4,326	18.6	17.1	27.7	1977	1,790	1,703	2,279	-6.2	-8.1	3.2
1965-69 ...	2,622	2,512	3,362	8.2	6.4	18.6	1978	1,760	1,668	2,265	-6.8	-8.8	2.9
1970-74 ...	2,094	1,997	2,680	-0.7	-2.5	9.1	1979	1,808	1,716	2,310	-5.7	-7.7	3.8
1975-79 ...	1,774	1,685	2,270	-6.6	-8.5	3.0	1980	1,840	1,749	2,323	-5.1	-7.0	4.0
1980-84 ...	1,819	1,731	2,262	-5.4	-7.3	3.0	1981	1,815	1,726	2,275	-5.5	-7.4	3.3
1985-88 ...	1,870	1,769	2,339	-4.2	-6.3	4.3	1982	1,829	1,742	2,265	-5.2	-7.0	3.0
1970	2,480	2,385	3,067	6.0	4.5	14.4	1983	1,803	1,718	2,225	-5.7	-7.5	2.5
1971	2,267	2,161	2,920	2.6	0.8	12.6	1984	1,806	1,719	2,224	-5.6	-7.4	2.4
1972	2,010	1,907	2,628	-2.0	-3.9	8.6	1985	1,843	1,754	2,263	-4.8	-6.6	3.1
1973	1,879	1,783	2,443	-4.5	-6.5	5.7	1986	1,836	1,742	2,282	-4.9	-6.8	3.3
1974	1,835	1,749	2,339	-5.4	-7.2	4.0	1987	1,871	1,767	2,349	-4.2	-6.3	4.5
1975	1,774	1,686	2,276	-6.7	-8.6	3.0	1988	1,932	1,814	2,463	-3.0	-5.3	6.3
1976	1,738	1,652	2,223	-7.4	-9.3	2.1	1989	2,014	1,885	2,583	-1.4	-3.8	8.2

Source: U.S. National Center for Health Statistics, *Vital Statistics of the United States*, annual; and unpublished data.

No. 85. Birth Rates, by Live-Birth Order and Race: 1970 to 1989

[Births per 1,000 women 15 to 44 years old in specified racial group. Live-birth order refers to number of children born alive. Figures for births of order not stated are distributed. See also headnote, table 82, and *Historical Statistics, Colonial Times to 1970*, series B 20-27]

LIVE-BIRTH ORDER	ALL RACES [1]					WHITE					BLACK				
	1970	1980	1985	1988	1989	1970	1980	1985	1988	1989	1970	1980	1985	1988	1989
Total	87.9	68.4	66.2	67.2	69.2	84.1	64.7	63.0	63.0	64.7	115.4	88.1	82.2	86.6	90.4
First birth	34.2	29.5	27.6	27.6	28.4	32.9	28.4	26.5	26.2	26.9	43.3	35.2	32.4	33.5	34.7
Second birth	24.2	21.8	22.0	22.0	22.4	23.7	21.0	21.4	21.1	21.4	27.1	25.7	24.5	25.8	26.7
Third birth	13.6	10.3	10.4	10.9	11.3	13.3	9.5	9.7	10.1	10.5	16.1	14.5	13.9	15.1	15.9
Fourth birth	7.2	3.9	3.8	4.1	4.3	6.8	3.4	3.3	3.6	3.7	10.0	6.7	6.3	6.9	7.4
Fifth birth	3.8	1.5	1.4	1.5	1.6	3.4	1.3	1.1	1.2	1.3	6.4	3.0	2.7	2.9	3.1
Sixth and seventh	3.2	1.0	0.8	0.9	0.9	2.7	0.8	0.7	0.7	0.7	7.0	2.1	1.8	1.8	2.0
Eighth and over	1.8	0.4	0.3	0.3	0.3	1.2	0.3	0.2	0.2	0.2	5.6	0.9	0.6	0.5	0.6

[1] Includes other races not shown separately.

Source: U.S. National Center for Health Statistics, *Vital Statistics of the United States*, annual; and unpublished data.

No. 86. Cesarean Section Deliveries, by Age of Mother: 1970 to 1989

[Based on data collected from the National Hospital Discharge Survey, a sample survey of hospital records of patients discharged in year shown; subject to sampling variability]

AGE OF MOTHER	1970	1980	1981	1982	1983	1984	1985	1986	1987	1988 [1]	1989
Number of cesarean deliveries (1,000)	195	619	701	730	808	813	877	906	953	933	938
Rate: Mothers, all ages [2]	5.5	16.5	17.9	18.5	20.3	21.1	22.7	24.1	24.4	24.7	23.8
Under 20 years	3.9	14.5	13.2	13.4	15.0	16.5	16.1	18.3	18.5	19.5	18.1
20 to 24 years	4.9	15.8	16.0	17.6	19.0	19.6	21.2	21.9	22.9	20.1	21.1
25 to 29 years	5.9	16.7	19.4	19.9	20.5	20.8	22.9	25.3	23.7	26.7	24.8
30 to 34 years	7.5	18.0	21.3	20.4	24.6	24.6	26.6	26.2	28.3	28.0	26.6
35 years and over	8.3	20.6	24.4	23.6	25.4	28.7	30.7	32.6	31.6	32.1	30.3

[1] Beginning 1988, comparisons with data for earlier years should be made with caution as estimates of change may reflect improvements in the 1988 design rather than true changes in hospital use. [2] Cesarean rates are the number of cesarean deliveries per 100 total deliveries for specified category.

Source: U.S. National Center for Health Statistics, unpublished data.

No. 87. Live Births, by Race and Type of Hispanic Origin—Selected Characteristics: 1985 and 1989

[Represents registered births. Excludes births to nonresidents of the United States. Data are available on race of child from all States, but data on Hispanic origin of mother are available from only 23 States and the District of Columbia in 1985 and from 47 States and the District of Columbia in 1989. However, in 1985 approximately 90 percent of all births to Hispanic mothers occur to residents of the 23 States, and in 1989 this percent is approximately 99 percent]

RACE AND HISPANIC ORIGIN	NUMBER OF BIRTHS (1,000)		BIRTHS TO TEENAGE MOTHERS, PERCENT OF TOTAL		BIRTHS TO UNMAR-RIED MOTHERS, PERCENT OF TOTAL		PERCENT OF MOTHERS BEGINNING PRENATAL CARE DURING—				PERCENT OF BIRTHS WITH LOW BIRTH WEIGHT [1]	
							First trimester		Third trimester or no care			
	1985	1989	1985	1989	1985	1989	1985	1989	1985	1989	1985	1989
Total	3,761	4,041	12.7	12.8	22.0	27.1	76.2	75.5	5.7	6.4	6.8	7.0
White	2,991	3,132	10.8	10.7	14.5	19.0	79.4	79.0	4.7	5.2	5.6	5.7
Black	608	709	23.0	23.1	60.1	64.5	61.8	60.4	10.0	11.7	12.4	13.2
American Indian, Eskimo, Aleut.	43	49	19.1	18.8	40.7	[3]45.6	60.3	60.5	11.5	11.9	5.9	6.4
Asian and Pacific Islander [2]	116	147	5.5	6.1	10.1	[3]12.0	75.0	75.6	6.1	5.8	6.1	6.9
Filipino	21	26	5.8	6.4	12.1	[3]14.5	77.2	78.0	4.6	4.6	6.9	7.3
Chinese	18	23	1.1	1.2	3.7	[3]4.3	82.4	81.9	4.2	3.5	5.0	5.0
Japanese	10	11	2.9	2.9	7.9	[3]8.6	85.8	86.7	2.6	2.6	5.9	6.4
Hawaiian	7	8	15.9	16.4	(NA)	[3]35.9	(NA)	69.7	(NA)	7.6	6.4	7.2
Hispanic origin [3]	373	532	16.5	16.7	29.5	35.5	61.2	59.5	12.5	13.0	6.2	6.2
Mexican	243	327	17.5	17.4	25.7	31.7	59.9	56.7	12.9	14.6	5.8	5.6
Puerto Rican	35	56	20.9	21.9	51.1	55.2	58.3	62.7	15.5	11.3	8.7	9.5
Cuban	10	11	7.1	7.0	16.1	17.5	82.5	83.2	3.7	4.0	6.0	5.8
Central and South American	41	72	8.2	8.6	34.9	38.9	60.6	60.8	12.5	11.9	5.7	5.8

NA Not available. [1] Births less than 2,500 grams (5 lb.-8 oz.). [2] Includes races not shown separately. [3] 1988 data. [4] Hispanic persons may be of any race. Includes other types, not shown separately.

No. 88. Live Births, by Place of Delivery, Median and Low-Birth Weight, and Prenatal Care: 1970 to 1989

[Represents registered births. Excludes births to nonresidents of the United States. For total number of births, see table 80. See Appendix III]

YEAR	BIRTHS ATTENDED (1,000)				MEDIAN BIRTH WEIGHT			PERCENT OF BIRTHS WITH LOW BIRTH WEIGHT [4]			PERCENT OF BIRTHS BY PERIOD IN WHICH PRENA-TAL CARE BEGAN	
	In hos-pital [1]	Not in hospital			Total [3]	White	Black	Total [3]	White	Black	1st tri-mester	3d tri-mester or no prenatal care
		Physi-cian	Mid-wife and other [2]									
1970	3,708	5	18		7 lb.-4 oz. . .	7 lb.-5 oz. . .	6 lb.-14 oz. . .	7.9	6.8	13.9	68.0	7.9
1975	3,105	11	28		7 lb.-5 oz. . .	7 lb.-7 oz. . .	6 lb.-15 oz. . .	7.4	6.3	13.1	72.4	6.0
1980	3,576	12	24		7 lb.-7 oz. . .	7 lb.-8 oz. . .	7 lb.-0 oz. . .	6.8	5.7	12.5	76.3	5.1
1981	3,592	11	27		7 lb.-7 oz. . .	7 lb.-8 oz. . .	7 lb.-0 oz. . .	6.8	5.7	12.5	76.3	5.2
1982	3,642	10	28		7 lb.-7 oz. . .	7 lb.-8 oz. . .	7 lb.-0 oz. . .	6.8	5.6	12.4	76.1	5.5
1983	3,600	10	29		7 lb.-7 oz. . .	7 lb.-8 oz. . .	7 lb.-0 oz. . .	6.8	5.7	12.6	76.2	5.6
1984	3,631	10	28		7 lb.-7 oz. . .	7 lb.-9 oz. . .	7 lb.-0 oz. . .	6.7	5.6	12.4	76.5	5.6
1985	3,722	10	29		7 lb.-7 oz. . .	7 lb.-9 oz. . .	7 lb.-0 oz. . .	6.8	5.6	12.4	76.2	5.7
1986	3,720	9	27		7 lb.-7 oz. . .	7 lb.-9 oz. . .	7 lb.-0 oz. . .	6.8	5.6	12.5	75.9	6.0
1987	3,774	8	27		7 lb.-7 oz. . .	7 lb.-9 oz. . .	7 lb.-0 oz. . .	6.9	5.7	12.7	76.0	6.1
1988	3,872	9	28		7 lb.-7 oz. . .	7 lb.-9 oz. . .	7 lb.-0 oz. . .	6.9	5.6	13.0	75.9	6.1
1989	3,991	13	22		7 lb.-7 oz. . .	7 lb.-8 oz[5]. .	6 lb.-15 oz[5] .	7.0	5.7	13.2	73.9	6.3

[1] Includes all births in hospitals or institutions and in clinics. [2] Includes births with attendant not specified. [3] Includes other races not shown separately. [4] Through 1975, births of 2,500 grams (5 lb.-8 oz.) or less at birth; thereafter, less than 2,500 grams. [5] By race of mother; data not directly comparable with prior years.

Source of tables 87 and 88: U.S. National Center for Health Statistics, *Vital Statistics of the United States,* annual; *Monthly Vitals Statistics Report;* and unpublished data.

No. 89. Births to Unmarried Women, by Race of Child and Age of Mother: 1970 to 1989

[Excludes births to nonresidents of United States. Data for **1970** include estimates for States in which marital status data were not reported. Beginning in **1980**, marital status is inferred from a comparison of the child's and parents' surnames on the birth certificate for those States that do not report on marital status. No estimates included for misstatements on birth records or failures to register births. See also Appendix III and *Historical Statistics, Colonial Times to 1970*, series B 28-35]

RACE OF CHILD AND AGE OF MOTHER	1970	1980	1985	1988	1989	RACE OF CHILD AND AGE OF MOTHER	1970	1980	1985	1988	1989
NUMBER (1,000)						25 to 29 years	10	15	18	20	20
Total live births [1]	398.7	665.7	828.2	1,005.3	1,094.2	30 to 34 years	5	6	8	9	10
White	175.1	320.1	433.0	539.7	593.9	35 years and over	3	2	3	4	4
Black	215.1	325.7	365.5	426.7	457.5	BIRTHS TO UNMAR-					
Under 15 years	9.5	9.0	9.4	9.9	10.6	RIED WOMEN AS					
15 to 19 years	190.4	262.8	270.9	312.5	337.3	PERCENT OF ALL					
20 to 24 years	126.7	237.3	300.4	350.9	378.1	BIRTHS IN RACIAL					
25 to 29 years	40.6	99.6	152.0	196.4	215.5	GROUPS					
30 to 34 years	19.1	41.0	67.3	94.9	106.3	**Total** [1]	11	18	22	26	27
35 years and over	12.4	16.1	28.2	40.7	46.3	White	6	11	15	18	19
						Black	38	55	60	64	64
PERCENT DISTRIBUTION						BIRTH RATE [2]					
Total [1]	100	100	100	100	100	**Total** [1] [3]	26.4	29.4	32.8	38.6	41.8
White	44	48	52	54	54	White [3]	13.9	17.6	21.8	26.6	29.2
Black	54	49	44	42	42	Black [3]	95.5	82.9	78.8	88.9	93.1
Under 15 years	2	1	1	1	1	15 to 19 years	22.4	27.6	31.6	36.8	40.6
15 to 19 years	48	40	33	31	31	20 to 24 years	38.4	40.9	46.8	56.7	62.0
20 to 24 years	32	36	36	35	35	25 to 29 years	37.0	34.0	39.8	48.1	52.3
						30 to 34 years	27.1	21.1	25.0	31.7	34.4

[1] Includes other races not shown separately.   [2] Rate per 1,000 unmarried women (never-married, widowed, and divorced) estimated as of July 1.   [3] Covers women aged 15 to 44 years.

Source: U.S. National Center for Health Statistics, *Vital Statistics of the United States*, annual; *Monthly Vital Statistics Report;* and unpublished data.

No. 90. Low Birth Weight and Births to Teenage Mothers and to Unmarried Women—States: 1980 to 1989

[Represents registered births. Excludes births to nonresidents of the United States. Based on 100 percent of births in all States and the District of Columbia. See Appendix III]

DIVISION AND STATE	PERCENT OF BIRTHS WITH LOW BIRTH WEIGHT[1]		BIRTHS TO TEENAGE MOTHERS, PERCENT OF TOTAL		BIRTHS TO UNMAR- RIED WOMEN, PERCENT OF TOTAL		DIVISION AND STATE	PERCENT OF BIRTHS WITH LOW BIRTH WEIGHT[1]		BIRTHS TO TEENAGE MOTHERS, PERCENT OF TOTAL		BIRTHS TO UNMAR- RIED WOMEN, PERCENT OF TOTAL	
	1980	1989	1980	1988	1980	1989		1980	1989	1980	1988	1980	1989
U.S.	6.8	7.0	15.6	12.5	18.4	27.1	VA	7.5	7.1	15.5	11.2	19.2	25.2
							WV	6.7	6.6	20.1	16.9	13.1	23.5
N. Eng.	6.2	6.0	11.6	8.7	15.5	23.4	NC	7.9	8.1	19.2	16.0	19.0	27.7
ME	6.5	4.9	15.3	10.9	13.9	21.8	SC	8.6	9.2	19.8	16.8	23.0	31.6
NH	5.4	5.1	10.7	7.5	11.0	15.7	GA	8.6	8.4	20.7	16.5	23.2	31.7
VT	5.9	5.5	13.0	8.9	13.7	19.8	FL	7.6	7.7	18.2	13.7	23.0	30 2
MA	6.1	5.9	10.7	8.2	15.7	23.8	**E. So. Cent. . . .**	7.8	8.1	21.0	17.9	20.9	29.7
RI	6.3	6.2	12.3	10.3	[2]15.7	[2]24.9	KY	6.8	6.9	21.1	17.3	15.1	22.6
CT	6.7	6.9	11.4	8.6	[2]17.9	[2]26.3	TN	8.0	8.2	19.9	17.2	19.9	29.1
Mid. Atl.	7.1	7.4	12.6	9.8	21.3	29.1	AL	7.9	8.3	20.6	17.4	22.2	29.8
NY	7.4	7.7	11.8	9.4	[2]23.8	[2]31.9	MS	8.7	9.4	23.2	20.7	28.0	39.4
NJ	7.2	7.3	12.3	8.9	21.1	24.1	**W. So. Cent. . . .**	7.3	7.4	19.1	15.8	15.8	23.1
PA	6.5	7.1	13.9	10.9	17.7	27.9	AR	7.6	8.3	21.6	18.9	20.5	27.7
E. No. Cent. . . .	6.7	7.1	15.2	12.7	18.0	27.0	LA	8.6	9.1	20.1	16.8	23.4	35.3
OH	6.8	7.0	15.7	13.5	[2]17.8	28.0	OK	6.8	6.5	19.6	16.0	14.0	23.8
IN	6.3	6.6	17.3	14.1	15.5	23.8	TX	6.9	7.0	18.3	15.2	[2]13.3	[2]19.6
IL	7.2	7.7	15.7	12.5	22.5	30.9	**Mt. . . . .**	6.6	6.6	14.3	12.1	12.7	23.8
MI	6.9	7.6	14.0	12.5	[2]16.2	[2]24.5	MT	5.6	5.5	12.4	9.9	[2]12.5	21.7
WI	5.4	5.8	12.3	9.8	13.9	23.4	ID	5.3	5.5	13.1	11.6	7.9	16.1
W. No. Cent. . .	5.7	5.8	13.5	10.3	13.1	21.7	WY	7.3	7.3	15.5	12.0	8.2	18.5
MN	5.1	4.9	10.4	7.3	11.4	19.5	CO	8.2	7.8	13.3	10.7	13.0	20.5
IA	5.0	5.4	12.5	9.3	10.3	19.4	NM	7.6	7.0	18.2	15.7	16.1	34.5
MO	6.6	6.9	16.9	13.7	17.6	27.1	AZ	6.2	6.3	16.5	13.8	18.7	30.0
ND	4.9	5.0	10.9	7.6	9.2	16.9	UT	5.2	5.7	11.0	9.3	6.2	12.7
SD	5.1	5.4	13.5	10.6	13.4	21.8	NV	6.6	7.2	15.4	12.5	[2]13.5	23.5
NE	5.6	5.8	12.1	9.3	11.6	19.3	**Pac. . . . .**	5.8	6.0	13.6	10.9	19.6	28.8
KS	5.8	6.1	15.0	11.4	12.3	19.6	WA	5.1	5.6	12.5	10.6	13.6	23.4
So. Atl.	8.0	8.0	18.3	14.3	22.2	29.7	OR	4.9	5.2	13.3	11.4	14.8	25.3
DE	7.7	7.5	16.7	12.8	24.2	29.1	CA	5.9	6.1	13.9	11.1	[2]21.4	[2]30.0
MD	8.2	8.0	14.8	11.2	[2]25.2	28.9	AK	5.4	4.9	11.8	9.3	15.1	24.6
DC	12.8	15.9	20.7	17.6	56.5	64.3	HI	7.1	7.1	11.5	9.4	17.6	23.8

[1] Less than 2,500 grams (5 pounds-8 ounces).   [2] Marital status of mother is inferred.

Source: U.S. National Center for Health Statistics, *Vital Statistics of the United States*, annual; and *Monthly Vital Statistics Report*.

Vital Statistics

No. 91. Women Who Have Had a Child in the Last Year, by Age: 1980 to 1990

[As of **June.** See headnote, table 92]

AGE OF MOTHER	WOMEN WHO HAD A CHILD IN LAST YEAR (1,000)				TOTAL BIRTHS PER 1,000 WOMEN				FIRST BIRTHS PER 1,000 WOMEN			
	1980	1985	1988	1990 [1]	1980	1985	1988	1990 [1]	1980	1985	1988	1990 [1]
Total.........	3,247	3,497	3,667	3,913	71.1	68.6	69.7	67.0	28.5	27.1	24.4	26.4
18 to 29 years old....	2,476	2,512	2,384	2,568	103.7	101.4	99.3	90.8	48.6	47.1	42.0	43.2
18 to 24 years old ..	1,396	1,339	1,146	1,376	96.6	95.4	87.1	78.0	(NA)	53.5	47.7	41.4
25 to 29 years old ..	1,081	1,173	1,238	1,192	114.8	109.2	114.2	112.1	(NA)	38.7	35.2	46.2
30 to 44 years old....	770	984	1,283	1,346	35.4	37.6	44.9	44.7	6.3	8.0	9.6	10.6
30 to 34 years old ..	519	704	884	892	60.0	69.9	81.6	80.4	(NA)	15.8	20.3	21.9
35 to 39 years old ..	192	229	324	377	26.9	25.9	33.8	37.3	(NA)	5.2	5.1	6.5
40 to 44 years old ..	59	51	75	77	9.9	7.1	9.2	8.6	(NA)	0.8	0.5	1.2

NA Not available. [1] Data for 1990 reflect lowering of age limit to 15 years old.
Source: U.S. Bureau of the Census, *Current Population Reports,* series P-20, No. 454 and earlier reports.

No. 92. Social and Economic Characteristics of Women, 15 to 44 Years Old, Who Have Had a Child in the Last Year: 1990

[As of **June.** Covers civilian noninstitutional population. Since the number of women who had a birth during the 12-month period was tabulated and not the actual numbers of births, some small underestimation of fertility for this period may exist due to the omission of: (1) Multiple births, (2) Two or more live births spaced within the 12-month period (the woman is counted only once), (3) Women who had births in the period and who did not survive to the survey date, (4) Women who were in institutions and therefore not in the survey universe. These losses may be somewhat offset by the inclusion in the CPS of births to immigrants who did not have their children born in the United States and births to nonresident women. These births would not have been recorded in the vital registration system. Based on Current Population Survey (CPS); see text, section 1 and Appendix III]

CHARACTERISTIC	TOTAL, 15 TO 44 YEARS OLD			15 TO 29 YEARS OLD			30 TO 44 YEARS OLD		
	Num-ber of women (1,000)	Women who have had a child in the last year		Num-ber of women (1,000)	Women who have had a child in the last year		Num-ber of women (1,000)	Women who have had a child in the last year	
		Total births per 1,000 women	First births per 1,000 women		Total births per 1,000 women	First births per 1,000 women		Total births per 1,000 women	First births per 1,000 women
Total [1].................	58,381	67	26	28,274	91	43	30,107	45	11
White.......................	48,277	65	26	23,039	88	43	25,238	45	11
Black.......................	7,846	78	25	4,132	107	42	3,713	46	6
Asian or Pacific Islander	1,737	58	28	797	79	41	940	40	16
Hispanic [2].................	5,268	93	32	2,857	121	51	2,411	61	10
Married, spouse present...........	29,696	95	34	9,287	181	80	20,409	56	14
Married, spouse absent [3]........	2,397	73	22	913	137	49	1,484	34	6
Widowed or divorced	5,548	26	4	1,094	72	14	4,454	15	2
Single	20,739	37	21	16,980	40	25	3,759	22	7
Years of school completed:									
Not a high school graduate.......	12,385	66	23	8,607	78	32	3,778	39	4
High school, 4 years	21,939	72	29	9,852	119	56	12,086	35	6
College: 1-3 years	13,045	60	22	6,215	74	35	6,830	47	9
4 or more years.........	11,012	67	31	3,600	75	48	7,412	62	23
4 years.............	7,406	68	33	2,725	74	49	4,681	65	24
5 or more years.......	3,606	63	27	875	80	45	2,731	57	21
Labor force status: In labor force	41,648	50	22	19,149	67	37	22,499	35	10
Employed	38,840	49	21	17,306	66	36	21,534	35	10
Unemployed	2,808	62	32	1,842	73	43	965	40	11
Not in labor force	16,733	110	37	9,125	142	57	7,608	73	13
Occupation of employed women:									
Managerial-professional	9,837	49	22	3,133	62	38	6,704	43	14
Technical, sales, and admin. support.	17,311	51	23	8,300	68	38	9,010	36	10
Service workers	7,065	46	20	4,003	59	33	3,062	29	3
Farming, forestry, and fishing	463	40	12	210	67	21	253	18	4
Precision prod., craft, and repair ...	847	48	18	286	94	33	561	25	11
Operators, fabricators, and laborers .	3,318	44	14	1,375	82	30	1,943	18	3
Family income: Under $10,000	8,129	88	33	4,609	124	52	3,521	40	7
$10,000 to $14,999	5,224	76	29	2,987	107	48	2,238	35	9
$15,000 to $19,999	4,204	76	32	2,229	115	53	1,975	32	8
$20,000 to $29,999	9,630	64	22	4,792	88	36	4,838	41	7
$30,000 to $34,999	4,918	65	22	2,243	81	36	2,675	51	9
$35,000 to $49,999	10,394	62	29	4,580	86	52	5,814	43	12
$50,000 and over	12,034	56	25	4,960	54	32	7,074	57	20

[1] Includes women of other races and women with family income not reported, not shown separately. [2] Hispanic persons may be of any race. [3] Includes separated women.
Source: U.S. Bureau of the Census, *Current Population Reports,* series P-20, No. 454.

No. 93. Women Who Have Had a Child in the Last Year, by Age and Labor Force Status: 1976 to 1990

[See headnote, table 92. 1989 data not available]

YEAR	TOTAL, 18 TO 44 YEARS OLD				18 TO 29 YEARS OLD				30 TO 44 YEARS OLD			
	All women, percent in labor force	Number (1,000)	Women who have had a child in the last year		All women, percent in labor force	Number (1,000)	Women who have had a child in the last year		All women, percent in labor force	Number (1,000)	Women who have had a child in the last year	
			In the labor force				In the labor force				In the labor force	
			Number (1,000)	Percent			Number (1,000)	Percent			Number (1,000)	Percent
1976	60	2,797	865	31	(NA)	2,220	706	32	(NA)	577	159	28
1980	66	3,247	1,233	38	68	2,476	947	38	64	770	287	37
1981	67	3,381	1,411	42	69	2,499	1,004	40	66	881	407	46
1982	68	3,433	1,508	44	70	2,445	1,040	43	67	988	469	48
1983	69	3,625	1,563	43	71	2,682	1,138	42	68	942	425	45
1984	70	3,311	1,547	47	72	2,375	1,058	45	69	936	489	52
1985	71	3,497	1,691	48	71	2,512	1,204	48	70	984	488	50
1986	72	3,625	1,805	50	73	2,452	1,185	48	72	1,174	620	53
1987	73	3,701	1,881	51	73	2,521	1,258	50	73	1,180	623	53
1988	73	3,667	1,866	51	74	2,384	1,177	49	73	1,283	688	54
1990 [1]	71	3,913	2,068	53	68	2,568	1,275	50	75	1,346	793	59

NA Not available. [1] 15 to 44 years old.
Source: U.S. Bureau of the Census, *Current Population Reports*, series P-20, No. 454, and earlier reports.

No. 94. Childless Women and Children Ever Born, by Race, Age, and Marital Status: 1990

[See headnote, table 92]

CHARACTERISTIC	Total number of women (1,000)	WOMEN BY NUMBER OF CHILDREN EVER BORN (percent)				CHILDREN EVER BORN	
		Total	None	One	Two or more	Total number (1,000)	Per 1,000 women
ALL RACES [1]							
Women ever married.	37,642	100	19	23	58	66,124	1,757
15 to 19 years	433	100	45	42	13	311	718
20 to 24 years	3,521	100	39	34	28	3,495	993
25 to 29 years	7,340	100	29	28	42	9,752	1,329
30 to 34 years	9,118	100	17	23	60	16,305	1,788
35 to 39 years	9,035	100	12	18	69	18,507	2,048
40 to 44 years	8,194	100	11	17	72	17,754	2,167
Women never married.	20,739	100	82	10	8	6,707	323
15 to 19 years	8,049	100	94	5	1	546	68
20 to 24 years	5,633	100	81	12	8	1,759	312
25 to 29 years	3,297	100	71	14	16	1,828	555
30 to 34 years	1,972	100	67	14	19	1,318	668
35 to 39 years	1,076	100	64	15	21	797	741
40 to 44 years	711	100	70	13	17	457	644
WHITE							
Women ever married.	32,570	100	20	23	57	55,599	1,707
15 to 19 years	382	100	47	43	11	256	671
20 to 24 years	3,086	100	40	34	26	2,930	949
25 to 29 years	6,419	100	31	28	41	8,205	1,278
30 to 34 years	7,879	100	17	24	59	13,740	1,744
35 to 39 years	7,722	100	13	19	69	15,396	1,994
40 to 44 years	7,083	100	12	17	72	15,072	2,128
Women never married.	15,707	100	89	7	4	2,666	170
15 to 19 years	6,419	100	96	4	-	282	44
20 to 24 years	4,388	100	88	9	3	752	171
25 to 29 years	2,345	100	82	10	8	730	311
30 to 34 years	1,331	100	83	9	9	425	319
35 to 39 years	724	100	77	13	10	294	407
40 to 44 years	501	100	81	11	9	183	365
BLACK							
Women ever married.	3,657	100	13	21	66	7,927	2,168
15 to 19 years	36	100	35	05	30	38	1,039
20 to 24 years	312	100	26	31	43	434	1,390
25 to 29 years	657	100	15	27	58	1,198	1,824
30 to 34 years	894	100	12	19	69	1,960	2,192
35 to 39 years	942	100	9	17	75	2,321	2,464
40 to 44 years	816	100	10	20	70	1,977	2,422
Women never married.	4,189	100	53	20	26	3,890	929
15 to 19 years	1,308	100	85	11	3	245	187
20 to 24 years	1,015	100	50	23	27	958	943
25 to 29 years	804	100	34	25	41	1,081	1,344
30 to 34 years	568	100	29	28	43	863	1,519
35 to 39 years	315	100	34	21	46	480	1,525
40 to 44 years	178	100	36	23	41	263	1,477

- Represents or rounds to zero. [1] Includes other races, not shown separately.
Source: U.S. Bureau of the Census, *Current Population Reports*, series P-20, No. 454.

No. 95. Ability to Bear Children, Women 15 to 44 Years Old, by Age and Number of Prior Births: 1982 and 1988

[Based on the 1982 and 1988 National Survey of Family Growth]

AGE AND NUMBER OF PRIOR BIRTHS	ALL WOMEN (1,000)		PERCENT DISTRIBUTION							
			Surgically sterile [1]				Impaired fecundity [4]		Fecund [5]	
			Contraceptive [2]		Noncontraceptive [3]					
	1982	1988	1982	1988	1982	1988	1982	1988	1982	1988
All women.............	54,099	57,900	18.6	23.3	6.6	4.7	8.4	8.4	66.3	63.6
15 to 24 years old......	20,150	18,592	2.1	2.0	(B)	(B)	4.3	4.8	93.4	93.0
25 to 34 years old......	19,644	21,726	21.0	22.9	4.9	2.7	10.0	9.6	64.2	64.7
35 to 44 years old......	14,305	17,582	38.7	46.3	18.3	12.0	12.1	10.6	31.0	31.0
No prior births, total	22,941	25,129	1.7	2.8	1.4	1.5	8.4	8.8	88.5	86.9
15 to 24 years old......	15,547	14,978	(B)	(B)	-	-	4.1	4.1	95.8	95.7
25 to 34 years old......	5,628	7,252	(B)	3.1	(B)	(B)	14.7	13.4	80.2	82.0
35 to 44 years old......	1,766	2,899	(B)	15.8	12.7	9.2	25.7	21.4	51.3	53.6
One or more prior births, total	31,158	32,771	31.2	39.0	10.5	7.1	8.5	8.1	49.9	45.8
15 to 24 years old......	4,603	3,614	9.0	9.8	(B)	(B)	5.2	7.7	85.2	81.8
25 to 34 years old......	14,016	14,474	28.1	32.8	6.1	3.3	8.1	7.8	57.8	56.1
35 to 44 years old......	12,539	14,683	42.7	52.3	19.0	12.5	10.1	8.5	28.1	26.7

- Represents or rounds to zero.   B Base figure too small to meet statistical standards for reliability of a derived figure.
[1] Includes sterilization of the husband or the wife.   [2] Sterilization performed to prevent pregnancy.   [3] Includes women who had surgery to correct medical problems with their reproductive organs.   [4] Includes women who (a) said that it was impossible to have a baby for some reason other than a sterilization operation; (b) said that it was physically difficult for them to conceive or deliver a baby, or (c) were continuously married or cohabiting, had not used contraception, and had not become pregnant for 3 years or more.   [5] Includes women who are neither surgically sterile nor have impaired fecundity.
Source: U.S. National Center for Health Statistics, *Advance Data from Vital and Health Statistics*, No. 192.

No. 96. Lifetime Births Expected Per 1,000 Wives: 1971 to 1990

[As of **June.** See headnote, table 97]

YEAR	LIFETIME BIRTHS TO ALL WIVES [1] AGED—			LIFETIME BIRTHS TO WHITE WIVES AGED—			LIFETIME BIRTHS TO BLACK WIVES AGED—			LIFETIME BIRTHS TO HISPANIC [2] WIVES [1] AGED—		
	18 to 24 yrs. old	25 to 29 yrs. old	30 to 34 yrs. old	18 to 24 yrs. old	25 to 29 yrs. old	30 to 34 yrs. old	18 to 24 yrs. old	25 to 29 yrs. old	30 to 34 yrs. old	18 to 24 yrs. old	25 to 29 yrs. old	30 to 34 yrs. old
1971....	2,375	2,619	2,989	2,353	2,577	2,936	2,623	3,112	3,714	(NA)	(NA)	(NA)
1975....	2,173	2,260	2,610	2,147	2,233	2,564	2,489	2,587	3,212	2,223	2,607	3,238
1980....	2,134	2,166	2,248	2,130	2,146	2,223	2,155	2,426	2,522	2,428	2,495	2,909
1985....	2,183	2,236	2,167	2,177	2,227	2,139	2,242	2,259	2,521	2,367	2,628	2,712
1990....	2,244	2,285	2,277	2,218	2,272	2,257	2,509	2,443	2,579	2,404	2,482	2,824

NA Not available.   [1] Includes other races not shown separately.   [2] Hispanic persons may be of any race.

No. 97. Lifetime Births Expected by Women, 18 to 34 Years Old, by Selected Characteristics: 1990

[As of **June.** Covers women in the civilian noninstitutional population. Based on Current Population Survey; see text, section 1 and Appendix III]

CHARACTERISTIC	Women reporting on birth expectations (1,000)	RATE PER 1,000 WOMEN			PERCENTAGE EXPECTING—	
		Births to date	Future births expected	Lifetime births expected	No lifetime births	No future births
Total [1].....................	24,359	1,130	986	2,116	9.4	47.3
White............................	20,412	1,067	1,035	2,102	9.5	45.1
Black............................	3,085	1,585	649	2,234	8.4	62.2
Hispanic [2].....................	2,306	1,516	888	2,404	5.9	51.7
Not a high school graduate	3,774	1,785	654	2,439	6.9	62.2
High school, 4 years.............	9,920	1,255	823	2,077	8.9	53.6
College: 1 or more years..........	10,664	782	1,256	2,038	10.7	36.0
1 to 3 years	6,043	882	1,184	2,066	9.6	40.0
4 or more years	4,621	651	1,350	2,001	12.1	30.8
In labor force...................	17,742	903	1,096	1,999	10.8	43.2
Employed	16,510	884	1,105	1,989	10.9	42.7
Unemployed..................	1,232	1,154	976	2,130	8.5	50.2
Not in labor force...............	6,617	1,739	690	2,429	5.8	58.1
Managerial and professional........	3,946	699	1,278	1,977	10.8	34.8
Technical, sales, and admin. support ..	7,744	821	1,134	1,954	10.9	41.3
Service occupations	2,928	1,070	1,027	2,096	9.1	46.8
Farming, forestry, and fishing	180	1,338	831	2,169	16.1	58.2
Precision production, craft, and repairs.	335	1,168	678	1,846	12.4	59.4
Operators, fabricators and laborers ...	1,377	1,247	760	2,006	14.3	58.5

[1] Includes other races, not shown separately.   [2] Hispanic persons may be of any race.
Source of tables 96 and 97: U.S. Bureau of the Census, *Current Population Reports*, series P-20, No. 454.

No. 98. Contraceptive Use by Women, 15 to 44 Years Old, by Age, Race, Marital Status, and Method of Contraception: 1982 and 1988

[Based on the 1982 and 1988 National Survey of Family Growth; see Appendix III]

CONTRACEPTIVE STATUS AND METHOD	All women, 1982	1988								
		All women[1]	AGE			RACE		MARITAL STATUS		
			15-24 years	25-34 years	35-44 years	White	Black	Never married	Currently married	Formerly married
All women (1,000)	54,099	57,900	18,592	21,726	17,582	47,077	7,679	21,058	29,147	7,695
PERCENT DISTRIBUTION										
Sterile.	27.2	29.7	3.1	27.0	61.3	30.5	29.6	5.2	44.0	42.6
Surgically sterile	25.7	28.3	2.4	26.0	58.7	29.2	27.8	4.3	42.4	40.9
Noncontraceptively sterile [2] . .	6.6	4.7	0.2	2.7	12.0	4.7	5.7	0.9	6.2	9.7
Contraceptively sterile [3]	19.0	23.6	2.2	23.3	46.7	24.5	22.1	3.4	36.2	31.3
Nonsurgically sterile [4]	1.5	1.4	0.7	0.9	2.7	1.3	1.8	1.0	1.6	1.7
Pregnant, postpartum	5.0	4.8	5.0	7.6	1.1	4.8	5.0	2.4	7.1	2.5
Seeking pregnancy	4.2	3.8	2.7	5.8	2.4	3.7	3.9	1.3	6.0	2.0
Other nonusers	26.9	25.0	45.7	16.7	13.5	23.8	26.9	52.5	4.8	26.6
Not sexually active [5]	19.5	19.0	37.9	10.3	8.5	18.1	16.7	43.5	0.3	19.5
Sexually active [5]	7.4	6.5	7.8	6.4	5.0	5.7	10.2	9.0	4.5	7.1
Nonsurgical contraceptors	36.7	36.7	43.5	43.0	21.6	37.2	34.6	38.5	38.1	26.3
Pill	15.6	18.5	29.7	21.6	3.0	18.4	21.6	24.7	15.1	14.5
IUD.	4.0	1.2	0.1	1.4	2.1	1.1	1.7	0.6	1.5	2.1
Diaphragm	4.5	3.5	1.3	4.8	4.1	3.8	1.1	2.1	4.6	3.0
Condom	6.7	8.8	9.5	9.1	7.7	9.2	5.8	8.2	10.6	3.4
Foam.	1.3	0.6	0.3	0.8	0.8	0.6	0.6	0.2	1.0	0.5
Rhythm [6]	2.2	1.4	0.6	1.7	1.8	1.4	1.2	0.6	2.1	1.1
Other methods [7]	2.5	2.6	2.0	3.6	2.2	2.5	2.6	2.1	3.2	1.7

[1] Includes other races, not shown separately.   [2] Persons who had sterilizing operation and who gave as one reason that they had medical problems with their female organs.   [3] Includes all other sterilization operations and sterilization of the husband or current partner.   [4] Persons sterile from illness, accident, or congenital conditions.   [5] Those having intercourse in the last 3 months before the survey.   [6] Periodic abstinence and natural family planning.   [7] Withdrawal, douche, suppository, and less frequently used methods.

Source: U.S. National Center for Health Statistics, *Advance Data from Vital and Health Statistics*, No. 182, and unpublished data.

No. 99. Family Planning Visits—Number of Women: 1982 and 1988

[**For women 15 to 44 years old.** Number of family planning visits in the 12 months before the interview. Family planning services include (1) counseling for problems with or worries about sexual intercourse, and unwanted pregnancy or one that occured at a bad time, having a sterilizing operation, or birth control; (2) a checkup or medical test for corrct use, fit, or position of a birth control method, or health problems from using a birth control method; and (3) a visit to a physician or clinic to obtain a new method of birth control, or to renew a method already being used. Based on the 1982 and 1988 National Survey of Family Growth; see Appendix III]

AGE AND POVERTY LEVEL	ALL RACES [1]		WHITE		BLACK	
	1982	1988	1982	1988	1982	1988
AGE						
All ages	54,099	57,900	45,367	47,077	6,985	7,679
15 to 19 years old	9,521	9,179	7,815	7,313	1,416	1,409
20 to 24 years old	10,629	9,413	8,855	7,401	1,472	1,364
25 to 29 years old	10,263	10,796	8,569	8,672	1,335	1,459
30 to 34 years old	9,381	10,930	7,916	9,010	1,144	1,406
35 to 39 years old	7,893	9,583	6,697	7,936	884	1,170
40 to 44 years old	6,412	7,999	5,515	6,745	734	872
POVERTY LEVEL						
0 to 149 percent	13,843	13,561	10,093	9,052	3,338	3,601
150 percent or more	40,256	44,339	35,275	38,024	3,647	4,078

[1] Includes other races, not shown separately.

Source: U.S. National Center for Health Statistics, *Advance Data from Vital and Health Statistics*, No. 184.

No. 100. Abortions—Estimated Number, Rate, and Ratio, by Race: 1972 to 1988

[Refers to women 15 to 44 years old at time of abortion]

YEAR	ALL RACES				WHITE				BLACK AND OTHER			
	Women 15-44 years old (1,000)	Abortions			Women 15-44 years old (1,000)	Abortions			Women 15-44 years old (1,000)	Abortions		
		Num-ber (1,000)	Rate per 1,000 women	Ratio per 1,000 live births [1]		Num-ber (1,000)	Rate per 1,000 women	Ratio per 1,000 live births [1]		Num-ber (1,000)	Rate per 1,000 women	Ratio per 1,000 live births [1]
1972 ..	44,588	586.8	13.2	184	38,532	455.3	11.8	175	6,056	131.5	21.7	223
1975 ..	47,606	1,034.2	21.7	331	40,857	701.2	17.2	276	6,749	333.0	49.3	565
1976 ..	48,721	1,179.3	24.2	361	41,721	784.9	18.8	296	7,000	394.4	56.3	638
1977 ..	49,814	1,316.7	26.4	400	42,567	888.8	20.9	333	7,247	427.9	59.0	679
1978 ..	50,920	1,409.6	27.7	413	43,427	969.4	22.3	356	7,493	440.2	58.7	665
1979 ..	52,016	1,497.7	28.8	420	44,266	1,062.4	24.0	373	7,750	435.3	56.2	625
1980 ..	53,048	1,553.9	29.3	428	44,942	1,093.6	24.3	376	8,106	460.3	56.5	642
1981 ..	53,901	1,577.3	29.3	430	45,494	1,107.8	24.3	377	8,407	469.6	55.9	645
1982 ..	54,679	1,573.9	28.8	428	46,049	1,095.2	23.8	373	8,630	478.7	55.5	646
1983 ..	55,340	1,575.0	28.5	436	46,506	1,084.4	23.3	376	8,834	490.6	55.5	670
1984 ..	56,061	1,577.2	28.1	423	47,023	1,086.6	23.1	366	9,038	490.6	54.3	646
1985 ..	56,754	1,588.6	28.0	422	47,512	1,075.6	22.6	360	9,242	512.9	55.5	659
1986 [2]	57,483	1,574.0	27.4	416	48,010	1,044.7	21.8	350	9,473	529.3	55.9	661
1987 ..	57,964	1,559.1	27.1	405	48,288	1,017.3	21.1	338	9,676	541.8	56.0	648
1988 ..	58,192	1,590.8	27.3	401	48,325	1,025.7	21.2	333	9,867	565.1	57.3	638

[1] See headnote, table 102.   [2] Total abortions in 1986 have been estimated by interpolation between 1985 and 1987.

Source: 1972, U.S. Centers for Disease Control, Atlanta, GA, *Abortion Surveillance, Annual Summary, 1972,* 1974, and The Alan Guttmacher Institute; 1975-1988, S.K. Henshaw and J. Van Vort, eds., *Abortion Services in the United States, Each State and Metropolitan Area, 1987-1988,* The Alan Guttmacher Institute, New York, NY, 1992 (copyright).

No. 101. Abortions, by Selected Characteristics: 1973 to 1988

[Number of abortions from surveys conducted by source; characteristics from the U.S. Centers for Disease Control's (CDC) annual abortion surveillance summaries, with adjustments for changes in States reporting data to the CDC each year]

CHARACTERISTIC	NUMBER (1,000)				PERCENT DISTRIBUTION				ABORTION RATIO [1]			
	1973	1980	1985	1988	1973	1980	1985	1988	1973	1980	1985	1988
Total abortions	745	1,554	1,589	1,591	100	100	100	100	193	300	297	286
Age of woman:												
Less than 15 years old	12	15	17	14	2	1	1	1	476	607	624	553
15 to 19 years old	232	445	399	393	31	29	25	25	280	451	462	444
20 to 24 years old	241	549	548	520	32	35	35	33	181	310	328	327
25 to 29 years old	130	304	336	347	17	20	21	22	128	213	219	218
30 to 34 years old	73	153	181	197	10	10	11	12	165	213	203	194
35 to 39 years old	41	67	87	96	6	4	5	6	246	317	280	254
40 years old and over	17	21	21	24	2	1	1	2	334	461	409	361
Race of woman:												
White	549	1,094	1,076	1,026	74	70	68	65	178	274	265	250
Black and other	196	460	513	565	26	30	32	36	252	392	397	389
Marital status of woman:												
Married	216	320	281	277	29	21	18	17	74	98	88	87
Unmarried	528	1,234	1,307	1,314	71	79	82	83	564	649	605	556
Number of prior live births:												
None	411	900	872	814	55	58	55	51	242	365	358	333
One	115	305	349	379	15	20	22	24	108	208	219	227
Two	104	216	240	262	14	14	15	17	190	283	288	288
Three	61	83	85	93	8	5	5	6	228	288	281	276
Four or more	55	51	43	43	7	3	3	3	196	251	230	213
Number of prior induced abortions:												
None	(NA)	1,043	944	908	(NA)	67	60	57	(NA)	(NA)	(NA)	(NA)
One	(NA)	373	416	429	(NA)	24	26	27	(NA)	(NA)	(NA)	(NA)
Two or more	(NA)	138	228	254	(NA)	9	14	16	(NA)	(NA)	(NA)	(NA)
Weeks of gestation: [2]												
Less than 9 weeks	284	800	811	800	38	52	51	50	(NA)	(NA)	(NA)	(NA)
9-10 weeks	222	417	425	424	30	27	27	27	(NA)	(NA)	(NA)	(NA)
11-12 weeks	131	202	198	198	18	13	12	12	(NA)	(NA)	(NA)	(NA)
13 weeks or more	108	136	154	168	15	9	10	11	(NA)	(NA)	(NA)	(NA)

NA Not available.   [1] Number of abortions per 1,000 abortions and live births. Live births are those which occurred from July 1 of year shown through June 30 of the following year (to match time of conception with abortions).   [2] Beginning 1985, data not exactly comparable with prior years because of a change in the method of calculation.

Source: S.K. Henshaw and J. Van Vort, eds., *Abortion Services in the United States, Each State and Metropolitan Area, 1987-1988,* The Alan Guttmacher Institute, New York, NY, 1992 (copyright).

No. 102. Abortions—Number, Rate per 1,000 Women 15 to 44 Years Old, and Abortion/Live Birth Ratio, by State of Occurrence: 1980 to 1988

[Number of abortions are from surveys of hospitals, clinics, and physicians identified as providers of abortion services, conducted by The Alan Guttmacher Institute. Abortion rates are computed per 1,000 women 15 to 44 years of age on July 1 of specified year; abortion ratios are computed as the number of abortions per 1,000 live births from July 1 of year shown to June 30 of following year, by State of occurrence]

DIVISION, REGION, AND STATE	NUMBER OF ABORTIONS (1,000)			RATE PER 1,000 WOMEN, 15 TO 44 YEARS OLD			RATIO: ABORTIONS PER 1,000 LIVE BIRTHS		
	1980	1985	1988	1980	1985	1988	1980	1985	1988
United States	1,554	1,589	1,591	29.3	28.0	27.3	428	422	401
Northeast	396	407	387	34.9	(NA)	32.4	604	(NA)	495
New England.	84	85	87	28.9	28.6	27.9	530	504	433
Maine.	5	5	5	18.6	18.6	16.2	289	308	281
New Hampshire	5	7	5	21.1	29.0	17.5	347	419	259
Vermont	4	3	4	30.4	26.2	25.8	466	448	451
Massachusetts.	46	40	44	33.5	29.3	30.2	609	533	448
Rhode Island.	7	8	7	30.7	35.5	30.6	529	572	477
Connecticut.	19	22	24	25.6	29.3	31.2	561	550	506
Middle Atlantic	312	322	300	37.0	37.6	34.0	627	607	516
New York	188	195	184	45.8	47.4	43.3	780	746	629
New Jersey.	56	69	64	32.8	39.6	35.1	591	672	553
Pennsylvania.	69	57	52	26.1	21.3	18.9	423	348	300
Midwest.	318	289	292	23.3	(NA)	20.7	336	(NA)	319
East North Central.	243	221	223	24.9	22.1	22.4	369	356	343
Ohio	67	57	53	26.8	22.4	21.0	397	357	324
Indiana.	20	16	16	15.3	12.2	11.9	227	202	184
Illinois	69	65	73	25.9	23.8	26.4	374	372	392
Michigan.	65	64	63	29.7	28.7	28.5	457	486	442
Wisconsin	22	18	18	20.1	15.7	16.0	292	246	249
West North Central	75	68	69	19.2	16.7	16.7	260	252	261
Minnesota.	20	17	19	20.7	16.6	18.2	288	257	279
Iowa	9	10	9	14.3	15.0	14.6	195	248	252
Missouri	22	20	19	19.4	17.3	16.4	273	261	262
North Dakota.	3	3	2	21.5	18.5	14.9	235	230	197
South Dakota	1	2	1	9.0	10.6	5.7	103	140	81
Nebraska.	6	7	6	17.9	18.2	17.7	227	268	261
Kansas.	14	10	11	25.6	18.2	20.1	343	264	305
South	457	453	470	25.9	(NA)	23.4	369	(NA)	342
South Atlantic	255	257	277	29.4	27.1	27.7	462	429	408
Delaware	4	5	6	25.9	30.9	35.7	395	451	498
Maryland	31	30	33	29.2	26.9	28.6	571	480	462
District of Columbia	29	24	26	168.3	145.9	163.3	1,569	1,186	1,248
Virginia.	32	34	35	24.2	24.0	23.7	417	412	382
West Virginia.	3	5	3	6.9	10.1	7.5	104	185	140
North Carolina.	32	34	40	22.8	22.6	25.4	377	379	389
South Carolina.	14	11	14	18.2	13.7	16.7	274	228	257
Georgia	38	38	37	28.4	26.1	23.5	395	397	331
Florida	74	77	83	35.5	31.8	31.5	547	465	434
East South Central.	65	57	57	19.2	15.8	15.6	271	258	240
Kentucky	13	10	12	15.1	11.0	13.0	215	189	213
Tennessee	26	22	22	23.6	19.1	18.9	352	315	290
Alabama.	21	19	18	23.1	20.2	18.7	331	333	282
Mississippi	6	6	5	10.6	9.7	8.4	132	142	122
West South Central	137	139	136	24.5	21.8	21.3	308	290	297
Arkansas	6	5	6	12.3	10.1	11.6	173	159	180
Louisiana.	18	19	17	17.6	17.4	16.3	218	240	241
Oklahoma.	11	13	12	16.4	17.1	16.2	221	269	255
Texas.	102	101	101	30.0	25.5	24.8	367	320	331
West	383	440	442	36.8	(NA)	36.3	486	(NA)	492
Mountain	68	75	69	25.0	23.6	21.9	302	316	294
Montana.	4	4	3	20.1	19.0	16.5	265	288	263
Idaho.	3	3	2	12.7	11.1	8.2	141	155	124
Wyoming	1	1	1	9.5	7.9	5.1	107	125	89
Colorado.	23	24	19	31.4	28.8	22.4	447	438	350
New Mexico	8	6	7	27.0	17.4	19.1	358	219	249
Arizona.	16	22	23	25.0	29.9	28.8	310	373	348
Utah	4	4	5	12.3	11.1	12.8	97	116	138
Nevada	9	10	10	46.6	40.5	40.3	697	641	554
Pacific	315	365	372	41.0	42.8	41.5	561	594	562
Washington.	37	31	31	37.5	28.0	27.6	522	458	471
Oregon.	18	15	16	28.3	22.3	23.9	396	374	390
California.	250	304	312	43.7	47.9	45.9	598	640	594
Alaska	2	4	2	17.9	27.7	18.2	196	283	213
Hawaii	8	11	11	34.4	43.7	43.0	441	611	574

NA Not available.

Source: S.K. Henshaw and J. Van Vort, eds., *Abortion Services in the United States, Each State and Metropolitan Area, 1987-1988,* The Alan Guttmacher Institute, New York, NY, 1992 (copyright); and unpublished data.

No. 103. Expectation of Life at Birth, 1970 to 1990, and Projections, 1995 to 2010

[In years. Excludes deaths of nonresidents of the United States. See also *Historical Statistics, Colonial Times to 1970,* series B 107-115]

YEAR	TOTAL			WHITE			BLACK AND OTHER			BLACK		
	Total	Male	Female	Total	Male	Female	Total	Male	Female	Total	Male	Female
1970	70.8	67.1	74.7	71.7	68.0	75.6	65.3	61.3	69.4	64.1	60.0	68.3
1975	72.6	68.8	76.6	73.4	69.5	77.3	68.0	63.7	72.4	66.8	62.4	71.3
1976	72.9	69.1	76.8	73.6	69.9	77.5	68.4	64.2	72.7	67.2	62.9	71.6
1977	73.3	69.5	77.2	74.0	70.2	77.9	68.9	64.7	73.2	67.7	63.4	72.0
1978	73.5	69.6	77.3	74.1	70.4	78.0	69.3	65.0	73.5	68.1	63.7	72.4
1979	73.9	70.0	77.8	74.6	70.8	78.4	69.8	65.4	74.1	68.5	64.0	72.9
1980	73.7	70.0	77.4	74.4	70.7	78.1	69.5	65.3	73.6	68.1	63.8	72.5
1981	74.2	70.4	77.8	74.8	71.1	78.4	70.3	66.1	74.4	68.9	64.5	73.2
1982	74.5	70.9	78.1	75.1	71.5	78.7	71.0	66.8	75.0	69.4	65.1	73.7
1983	74.6	71.0	78.1	75.2	71.7	78.7	71.1	67.2	74.9	69.6	65.4	73.6
1984	74.7	71.2	78.2	75.3	71.8	78.7	71.3	67.4	75.0	69.7	65.6	73.7
1985	74.7	71.2	78.2	75.3	71.9	78.7	71.2	67.2	75.0	69.5	65.3	73.5
1986	74.8	71.3	78.3	75.4	72.0	78.8	71.2	67.2	75.1	69.4	65.2	73.5
1987	75.0	71.5	78.4	75.6	72.2	78.9	71.3	67.3	75.2	69.4	65.2	73.6
1988	74.9	71.5	78.3	75.6	72.3	78.9	71.2	67.1	75.1	69.2	64.9	73.4
1989	75.3	71.8	78.6	76.0	72.7	79.2	71.2	67.1	75.2	69.2	64.8	73.5
1990, prel.	75.4	72.0	78.8	76.0	72.6	79.3	72.4	68.4	76.3	70.3	66.0	74.5
Projections:[1] 1995 . .	76.3	72.8	79.7	76.8	73.4	80.2	(NA)	(NA)	(NA)	72.4	68.8	76.0
2000 . .	77.0	73.5	80.4	77.5	74.0	80.9	(NA)	(NA)	(NA)	73.5	69.9	77.1
2005 . .	77.6	74.2	81.0	78.1	74.6	81.5	(NA)	(NA)	(NA)	74.6	71.0	78.1
2010 . .	77.9	74.4	81.3	78.3	74.9	81.7	(NA)	(NA)	(NA)	75.0	71.4	78.5

. NA Not available. [1] Based on middle mortality assumptions; for details, see source. Source: U.S. Bureau of the Census, *Current Population Reports,* series P-25, No. 1018.

Source: Except as noted, U.S. National Center for Health Statistics, *Vital Statistics of the United States,* annual; *Monthly Vital Statistics Report;* and unpublished data.

No. 104. Selected Life Table Values: 1969 to 1989

[Beginning 1970, excludes deaths of nonresidents of the United States. See also *Historical Statistics, Colonial Times to 1970,* series B 116-125]

AGE AND SEX	TOTAL [1]				WHITE				BLACK		
	1969-1971	1979-1981	1985	1989	1969-1971	1979-1981	1985	1989	1979-1981	1985	1989
AVERAGE EXPECTATION OF LIFE IN YEARS											
At birth: Male.	67.0	70.1	71.2	71.8	67.9	70.8	71.9	72.7	64.1	65.3	64.8
Female.	74.6	77.6	78.2	78.3	75.5	78.2	78.7	79.2	72.9	73.5	73.5
Age 20: Male.	49.5	51.9	52.7	53.3	50.2	52.5	53.3	54	46.4	47.4	47.1
Female.	56.6	59.0	59.3	59.7	57.2	59.4	59.8	60.2	54.9	55.3	55.3
Age 40: Male.	31.5	33.6	34.3	35.1	31.9	34.0	34.7	35.6	29.5	30.2	30.4
Female.	37.6	39.8	40.1	40.5	38.1	40.2	40.4	40.9	36.3	36.6	36.8
Age 50: Male.	23.1	25.0	25.6	26.4	23.3	25.3	25.8	26.7	22.0	22.5	23.0
Female.	28.8	30.7	30.9	31.3	29.1	31.0	31.1	31.5	27.8	27.9	28.2
Age 65: Male.	13.0	14.2	14.6	15.2	13.0	14.3	14.6	15.2	13.3	13.3	13.6
Female.	16.8	18.4	18.6	18.8	16.9	18.6	18.7	19.0	17.1	17.0	17.0
ANNUAL DEATHS EXPECTED PER 1,000 ALIVE AT SPECIFIED AGE [2]											
At birth: Male.	22.5	13.9	12.0	10.9	20.1	12.3	10.6	9.1	23.0	19.9	20.0
Female.	17.5	11.2	9.4	8.8	15.3	9.7	8.0	7.2	19.3	16.5	17.2
Age 20: Male.	2.1	1.8	1.5	1.6	1.9	1.8	1.5	1.4	2.2	1.9	2.6
Female.	0.7	0.6	0.5	0.5	0.6	0.6	0.5	0.5	0.7	0.6	0.7
Age 40: Male.	4.0	3.0	2.9	3.1	3.4	2.6	2.5	2.6	6.9	6.7	7.7
Female.	2.3	1.6	1.4	1.4	1.9	1.4	1.3	1.2	3.2	2.9	3.2
Age 50: Male.	9.7	7.8	6.8	6.3	8.9	7.1	6.2	5.6	14.9	13.1	13.3
Female.	5.2	4.2	3.8	3.5	4.7	3.8	3.5	3.2	7.7	6.7	6.3
Age 65: Male.	34.6	28.2	25.7	23.7	33.9	27.4	24.9	22.8	38.5	36.1	34.3
Female	16.8	14.3	14.0	13.5	15.6	13.6	13.5	12.9	21.6	20.9	21.0
NUMBER SURVIVING TO SPECIFIED AGE PER 1,000 BORN ALIVE											
Age 20: Male.	961	973	977	978	965	975	979	981	961	967	964
Female.	973	982	985	985	976	984	986	987	972	976	975
Age 40: Male.	915	933	941	937	926	940	946	946	885	898	880
Female.	951	965	970	970	958	969	973	974	941	948	943
Age 50: Male.	861	890	902	899	877	901	912	911	801	819	799
Female.	919	941	948	949	929	947	953	956	896	908	903
Age 65: Male.	643	706	729	739	663	724	745	759	551	581	578
Female.	797	835	844	850	816	848	856	863	733	749	753

[1] Includes other races not shown separately. [2] See footnote 1, table 105.

Source: U.S. National Center for Health Statistics, *U.S. Life Tables and Actuarial Tables, 1969-71* and *1979-81; Vital Statistics of the United States,* annual; and unpublished data.

No. 105. Expectation of Life and Expected Deaths, by Race, Sex, and Age: 1989

| AGE IN 1989 (years) | EXPECTATION OF LIFE IN YEARS | | | | | EXPECTED DEATHS PER 1,000 ALIVE AT SPECIFIED AGE [1] | | | | |
| | Total | White | | Black | | Total | White | | Black | |
		Male	Female	Male	Female		Male	Female	Male	Female
At birth	75.3	72.7	79.2	64.8	73.5	9.86	9.08	7.15	20.04	17.17
1	75.0	72.3	78.8	65.2	73.8	0.69	0.69	0.53	1.18	0.91
2	74.1	71.4	77.8	64.2	72.9	0.52	0.50	0.41	0.91	0.75
3	73.1	70.4	76.9	63.3	71.9	0.40	0.38	0.32	0.72	0.61
4	72.1	69.5	75.9	62.3	71.0	0.33	0.32	0.27	0.59	0.49
5	71.1	68.5	74.9	61.4	70.0	0.29	0.29	0.23	0.51	0.40
6	70.2	67.5	73.9	60.4	69.0	0.26	0.27	0.21	0.45	0.32
7	69.2	66.5	73.0	59.4	68.0	0.24	0.26	0.19	0.40	0.27
8	68.2	65.5	72.0	58.5	67.1	0.21	0.23	0.17	0.34	0.23
9	67.2	64.5	71.0	57.5	66.1	0.18	0.20	0.15	0.28	0.22
10	66.2	63.6	70.0	56.5	65.1	0.16	0.17	0.13	0.24	0.23
11	65.2	62.6	69.0	55.5	64.1	0.17	0.17	0.13	0.24	0.25
12	64.3	61.6	68.0	54.5	63.1	0.22	0.24	0.16	0.34	0.27
13	63.3	60.6	67.0	53.5	62.1	0.32	0.39	0.22	0.55	0.30
14	62.3	59.6	66.0	52.6	61.2	0.47	0.59	0.30	0.83	0.33
15	61.3	58.6	65.1	51.6	60.2	0.63	0.82	0.39	1.16	0.37
16	60.4	57.7	64.1	50.7	59.2	0.79	1.03	0.48	1.47	0.42
17	59.4	56.8	63.1	49.8	58.2	0.91	1.21	0.53	1.78	0.48
18	58.5	55.8	62.1	48.8	57.3	0.99	1.31	0.55	2.07	0.54
19	57.5	54.9	61.2	47.9	56.3	1.03	1.37	0.53	2.33	0.62
20	56.6	54.0	60.2	47.1	55.3	1.06	1.42	0.50	2.61	0.70
21	55.6	53.0	59.2	46.2	54.4	1.10	1.47	0.48	2.89	0.79
22	54.7	52.1	58.3	45.3	53.4	1.13	1.51	0.47	3.10	0.88
23	53.8	51.2	57.3	44.4	52.4	1.15	1.53	0.47	3.23	0.95
24	52.8	50.3	56.3	43.6	51.5	1.17	1.55	0.49	3.28	1.03
25	51.9	49.4	55.3	42.7	50.6	1.18	1.55	0.50	3.32	1.10
26	50.9	48.4	54.4	41.9	49.6	1.20	1.56	0.52	3.38	1.18
27	50.0	47.5	53.4	41.0	48.7	1.23	1.58	0.54	3.50	1.28
28	49.1	46.6	52.4	40.2	47.7	1.27	1.62	0.56	3.69	1.39
29	48.1	45.7	51.5	39.3	46.8	1.32	1.67	0.59	3.94	1.51
30	47.2	44.7	50.5	38.5	45.9	1.38	1.73	0.62	4.20	1.65
31	46.2	43.8	49.5	37.6	44.9	1.45	1.79	0.66	4.47	1.78
32	45.3	42.9	48.6	36.8	44.0	1.51	1.86	0.70	4.78	1.91
33	44.4	42.0	47.6	36.0	43.1	1.59	1.93	0.73	5.14	2.02
34	43.5	41.0	46.6	35.1	42.2	1.66	2.02	0.76	5.53	2.13
35	42.5	40.1	45.7	34.3	41.3	1.75	2.11	0.80	5.96	2.25
36	41.6	39.2	44.7	33.5	40.4	1.85	2.22	0.85	6.39	2.37
37	40.7	38.3	43.7	32.7	39.5	1.94	2.32	0.91	6.79	2.53
38	39.8	37.4	42.8	32.0	38.6	2.04	2.42	0.99	7.11	2.71
39	38.8	36.5	41.8	31.2	37.7	2.14	2.52	1.09	7.40	2.92
40	37.9	35.6	40.9	30.4	36.8	2.25	2.63	1.20	7.69	3.16
41	37.0	34.7	39.9	29.7	35.9	2.38	2.76	1.33	8.02	3.40
42	36.1	33.8	39.0	28.9	35.0	2.53	2.93	1.46	8.38	3.65
43	35.2	32.9	38.0	28.1	34.1	2.71	3.13	1.59	8.78	3.90
44	34.3	32.0	37.1	27.4	33.3	2.92	3.38	1.73	9.23	4.15
45	33.4	31.1	36.1	26.6	32.4	3.15	3.66	1.89	9.69	4.43
46	32.5	30.2	35.2	25.9	31.5	3.41	3.98	2.07	10.19	4.74
47	31.6	29.3	34.3	25.1	30.7	3.71	4.33	2.29	10.80	5.07
48	30.7	28.4	33.4	24.4	29.8	4.05	4.71	2.54	11.53	5.43
49	29.8	27.5	32.4	23.7	29.0	4.43	5.12	2.84	12.37	5.83
50	28.9	26.7	31.5	23.0	28.2	4.85	5.58	3.16	13.30	6.27
51	28.1	25.8	30.6	22.3	27.3	5.31	6.10	3.51	14.25	6.75
52	27.2	25.0	29.7	21.6	26.5	5.84	6.73	3.90	15.21	7.30
53	26.4	24.2	28.8	20.9	25.7	6.43	7.49	4.31	16.14	7.91
54	25.6	23.3	28.0	20.3	24.9	7.08	8.35	4.76	17.07	8.59
55	24.7	22.5	27.1	19.6	24.1	7.79	9.29	5.24	18.04	9.31
56	23.9	21.7	26.2	18.9	23.4	8.55	10.29	5.77	19.09	10.09
57	23.1	21.0	25.4	18.3	22.6	9.37	11.37	6.34	20.27	11.01
58	22.3	20.2	24.6	17.7	21.8	10.27	12.55	6.97	21.61	12.12
59	21.6	19.4	23.7	17.1	21.1	11.23	13.81	7.64	23.10	13.38
60	20.8	18.7	22.9	16.4	20.4	12.27	15.18	8.39	24.68	14.76
61	20.1	18.0	22.1	15.9	19.7	13.37	16.63	9.18	26.36	16.17
62	19.3	17.3	21.0	15.3	19.0	14.52	18.12	10.02	28.15	17.51
63	18.6	16.6	20.5	14.7	18.3	15.69	19.62	10.91	30.07	18.72
64	17.9	15.9	19.7	14.1	17.7	16.91	21.18	11.84	32.12	19.85
65	17.2	15.2	19.0	13.6	17.0	18.20	22.80	12.85	34.31	21.00
70	13.9	12.1	15.3	11.0	13.9	27.31	34.77	20.03	47.63	29.38
75	10.9	9.4	11.9	8.8	11.0	41.31	53.66	31.61	65.79	42.53
80	8.3	7.1	8.9	6.9	8.5	63.71	82.84	51.62	94.32	65.05
85 and over	6.2	5.3	6.5	5.6	6.7	1,000.00	1,000.00	1,000.00	1,000.00	1,000.00

[1] Based on the proportion of the cohort who are alive at the beginning of an indicated age interval who will die before reaching the end of that interval. For example, out of every 1,000 people alive and exactly 50 years old at the beginning of the period, between 4 and 5 (4.85) will die before reaching their 51st birthdays.

Source: U.S. National Center for Health Statistics, *Vital Statistics of the United States*, annual; and unpublished data.

No. 106. Deaths and Death Rates, by Sex and Race: 1970 to 1990

[Rates are per 1,000 population for specified groups. Except as noted, excludes deaths of nonresidents of the United States. Excludes fetal deaths. For explanation of age-adjustment, see text, section 2. The standard population for this table is the total population of the United States enumerated in 1940. See Appendix III. See also *Historical Statistics, Colonial Times to 1970*, series B 167- 173 and B 181-192]

SEX AND RACE	1970	1980	1981	1982	1983	1984	1985	1986	1987	1988	1989	1990,[1] prel.
Deaths [2] (1,000)	**1,921**	**1,990**	**1,978**	**1,975**	**2,019**	**2,039**	**2,086**	**2,105**	**2,123**	**2,168**	**2,150**	**2,162**
Male [2] (1,000)	1,078	1,075	1,064	1,056	1,072	1,077	1,098	1,104	1,108	1,126	1,114	1,122
Female [2] (1,000)	843	915	914	918	947	963	989	1,001	1,015	1,042	1,036	1,040
White (1,000)	1,682	1,739	1,731	1,729	1,766	1,782	1,819	1,831	1,843	1,877	1,854	1,878
Male (1,000)	942	934	925	919	932	935	950	953	953	965	951	966
Female (1,000)	740	805	806	810	834	847	869	879	890	911	903	912
Black (1,000)	226	233	229	227	233	236	244	250	255	264	268	255
Male (1,000)	128	130	127	126	128	129	134	137	140	144	146	139
Female (1,000)	98	103	101	101	105	107	111	113	115	120	121	116
Death rates [2]	**9.5**	**8.8**	**8.6**	**8.5**	**8.6**	**8.6**	**8.7**	**8.7**	**8.7**	**8.8**	**8.7**	**8.6**
Male [2]	10.9	9.8	9.5	9.4	9.4	9.4	9.5	9.4	9.3	9.4	9.2	9.2
Female [2]	8.1	7.9	7.8	7.7	7.9	7.9	8.1	8.1	8.1	8.3	8.1	8.1
White	9.5	8.9	8.8	8.7	8.8	8.9	9.0	9.0	9.0	9.1	8.9	8.9
Male	10.9	9.8	9.7	9.5	9.6	9.5	9.6	9.5	9.5	9.5	9.3	9.4
Female	8.1	8.1	8.0	8.0	8.2	8.2	8.4	8.4	8.5	8.6	8.5	8.5
Black	10.0	8.8	8.4	8.2	8.3	8.3	8.5	8.5	8.6	8.7	8.7	8.2
Male	11.9	10.3	9.9	9.6	9.6	9.6	9.8	9.9	9.9	10.1	10.1	9.4
Female	8.3	7.3	7.1	6.9	7.1	7.1	7.3	7.3	7.4	7.5	7.5	7.1
Age-adjusted death rates [2]	**7.1**	**5.9**	**5.7**	**5.5**	**5.5**	**5.5**	**5.5**	**5.4**	**5.4**	**5.4**	**5.2**	**5.2**
Male [2]	9.3	7.8	7.5	7.3	7.3	7.2	7.2	7.1	7.0	7.0	6.8	6.7
Female [2]	5.3	4.3	4.2	4.1	4.1	4.1	4.1	4.1	4.0	4.0	4.0	3.9
White	6.8	5.6	5.4	5.3	5.3	5.2	5.2	5.2	5.1	5.1	5.0	4.9
Male	8.9	7.5	7.2	7.1	7.0	6.9	6.9	6.8	6.7	6.6	6.4	6.4
Female	5.0	4.1	4.0	3.9	3.9	3.9	3.9	3.9	3.8	3.8	3.7	3.7
Black	10.4	8.4	8.0	7.8	7.8	7.7	7.8	7.8	7.8	7.9	7.6	7.3
Male	13.2	11.1	10.7	10.4	10.2	10.1	10.2	10.3	10.2	10.4	10.3	9.6
Female	8.1	6.3	6.0	5.8	5.9	5.9	5.9	5.9	5.9	5.9	5.9	5.5

[1] Includes deaths of nonresidents of the United States. Based on a 10-percent sample of deaths.   [2] Includes other races, not shown separately.

No. 107. Death Rates, by Age, Sex, and Race: 1970 to 1990

[Number of deaths per 100,000 population in specified group. See headnote, table 106]

SEX, YEAR, AND RACE	All ages [1]	Under 1 yr. old	1-4 yr. old	5-14 yr. old	15-24 yr. old	25-34 yr. old	35-44 yr. old	45-54 yr. old	55-64 yr. old	65-74 yr. old	75-84 yr. old	85 yr. old and over
MALE [2]												
1970	1,090	2,410	93	51	189	215	403	959	2,283	4,874	10,010	17,822
1980	977	1,429	73	37	172	196	299	767	1,815	4,105	8,817	18,801
1985	945	1,197	58	32	141	178	278	669	1,693	3,788	8,504	18,325
1986	941	1,153	58	32	151	193	288	653	1,648	3,701	8,353	18,187
1987	935	1,129	58	32	146	193	292	644	1,624	3,618	8,232	18,031
1988	940	1,114	57	31	151	197	301	629	1,607	3,574	8,223	18,371
1989	921	1,107	54	30	147	201	307	618	1,565	3,439	7,329	17,616
1990, prel. [3]	917	1,038	49	29	156	206	306	601	1,508	3,359	7,950	17,522
White: 1970	1,087	2,113	84	48	171	177	344	883	2,203	4,810	10,099	18,552
1980	983	1,230	66	35	167	171	257	699	1,729	4,036	8,830	19,097
1985	960	1,039	52	30	136	157	241	609	1,614	3,717	8,500	18,789
1990, prel. [3]	937	909	44	28	141	179	266	547	1,455	3,316	7,976	17,973
Black: 1970	1,187	4,299	151	67	321	560	957	1,778	3,257	5,803	9,455	12,222
1980	1,034	2,587	111	47	209	407	690	1,480	2,873	5,131	9,232	16,099
1985	977	2,135	89	41	174	347	642	1,283	2,623	4,889	9,298	15,046
1990, prel. [3]	942	1,796	72	38	259	415	688	1,181	2,180	4,173	8,731	14,743
FEMALE [2]												
1970	808	1,864	75	32	68	102	231	517	1,099	2,580	6,678	15,518
1980	785	1,142	55	24	58	76	159	413	934	2,145	5,440	14,747
1985	807	932	45	21	50	69	138	373	919	2,095	5,220	14,343
1986	809	906	46	20	52	72	140	365	906	2,091	5,152	14,298
1987	813	902	45	19	52	74	139	360	900	2,063	5,118	14,261
1988	827	898	45	20	52	74	140	351	905	2,056	5,173	14,508
1989	814	898	44	20	52	75	139	340	882	2,011	5,050	14,034
1990, prel. [3]	809	831	39	19	51	73	138	333	878	2,002	4,942	13,728
White: 1970	813	1,615	66	30	62	84	193	463	1,015	2,471	6,699	15,980
1980	806	963	49	23	56	65	138	373	876	2,067	5,402	14,980
1985	837	787	40	19	48	59	121	340	864	2,020	5,171	14,579
1990, prel. [3]	848	715	36	18	48	61	119	308	825	1,957	4,921	13,994
Black: 1970	829	3,369	129	44	112	231	533	1,044	1,986	3,861	6,692	10,707
1980	733	2,124	84	31	71	150	324	768	1,561	3,057	6,212	12,367
1985	728	1,757	71	28	60	136	278	654	1,502	2,926	6,252	12,155
1990, prel. [3]	711	1,505	62	23	67	152	290	551	1,424	2,674	5,764	11,831

[1] Includes unknown age.   [2] Includes other races not shown separately.   [3] Includes deaths of nonresidents. Based on a 10-percent sample of deaths.

Sources of tables 106 and 107: U.S. National Center for Health Statistics, *Vital Statistics of the United States*, annual; *Monthly Vital Statistics Report;* and unpublished data.

No. 108. Deaths and Death Rates, by State: 1970 to 1990

[Excludes deaths of nonresidents of the United States, except as noted. See Appendix III]

REGION, DIVISION, AND STATE	NUMBER OF DEATHS (1,000)								RATE PER 1,000 POPULATION							
	By State of residence						By State of occur-rence [1]		By State of residence						By State of occur-rence [1]	
	1970	1980	1985	1987	1988	1989	1989, prel.	1990, prel.	1970	1980	1985	1987	1988	1989	1989, prel.	1990, prel.
United States . .	1,921	1,990	2,086	2,123	2,168	2,150	2,155	2,162	9.5	8.8	8.7	8.7	8.8	8.7	8.7	8.6
New England	116	115	118	118	120	116	117	116	9.8	9.3	9.3	9.2	9.2	8.9	9.0	8.9
Maine	11	11	11	11	12	11	11	11	11.1	9.6	9.8	9.5	9.6	9.2	9.0	9.0
New Hampshire . .	7	8	8	8	9	8	8	8	10.0	8.3	8.5	8.0	8.1	7.7	7.6	7.3
Vermont	4	5	5	5	5	5	5	5	10.0	9.0	8.7	8.7	8.4	8.1	7.9	8.2
Massachusetts . . .	57	55	56	56	56	54	55	56	10.1	9.6	9.6	9.5	9.6	9.1	9.4	9.4
Rhode Island	9	9	10	10	10	10	10	10	10.0	9.8	10.0	9.8	9.8	9.6	9.8	9.5
Connecticut	26	27	28	28	29	28	28	27	8.6	8.8	8.9	8.8	8.8	8.7	8.7	8.3
Middle Atlantic	383	365	367	371	376	367	363	359	10.3	9.9	9.9	9.9	10.0	9.7	9.6	9.5
New York	188	173	172	174	176	172	170	167	10.3	9.8	9.7	9.7	9.8	9.6	9.5	9.3
New Jersey	68	69	71	72	73	71	69	69	9.5	9.4	9.4	9.4	9.5	9.2	9.0	8.9
Pennsylvania	127	124	124	125	126	124	124	123	10.8	10.4	10.4	10.5	10.5	10.3	10.3	10.2
East North Central .	377	365	370	372	379	372	370	370	9.4	8.8	8.9	8.9	9.0	8.8	8.7	8.7
Ohio	100	98	99	99	100	98	98	99	9.4	9.1	9.2	9.2	9.2	9.0	9.0	9.0
Indiana	49	47	48	49	50	49	49	50	9.3	8.6	8.8	8.8	9.0	8.8	8.8	8.9
Illinois	111	103	102	102	105	103	102	101	10.0	9.0	8.9	8.8	9.1	8.9	8.7	8.6
Michigan	76	75	79	80	80	79	78	78	8.6	8.1	8.7	8.7	8.7	8.5	8.4	8.4
Wisconsin	41	41	41	42	43	42	43	43	9.2	8.7	8.7	8.8	8.9	8.7	8.8	8.7
West North Central.	164	159	162	162	164	161	164	165	10.1	9.2	9.2	9.2	9.3	9.0	9.2	9.2
Minnesota	34	33	35	35	35	34	34	35	8.9	8.2	8.3	8.1	8.2	7.9	7.9	8.0
Iowa	29	27	28	27	28	27	25	28	10.4	9.3	9.7	9.6	9.8	9.6	8.9	9.8
Missouri	52	50	50	51	51	50	56	53	11.1	10.1	10.0	9.9	9.9	9.8	10.8	10.2
North Dakota	6	6	6	5	6	6	6	6	9.1	8.6	8.2	8.2	8.5	8.3	8.9	9.2
South Dakota	7	7	7	7	7	7	7	6	9.9	9.5	9.3	9.4	9.2	9.2	9.1	8.9
Nebraska	15	14	15	15	15	15	15	15	10.1	9.2	9.3	9.3	9.3	9.2	9.5	9.2
Kansas	22	22	22	22	23	22	22	22	9.7	9.3	9.0	8.9	9.2	8.9	8.6	8.6
South Atlantic	290	330	364	379	389	391	394	397	9.5	8.9	9.0	9.1	9.2	9.1	9.1	9.1
Delaware	5	5	5	6	6	6	6	6	9.0	8.5	8.8	8.7	8.7	8.7	8.9	8.6
Maryland	33	34	37	38	39	38	38	38	8.4	8.1	8.3	8.4	8.4	8.2	8.1	8.1
Dist. of Col.	9	7	7	7	8	8	10	10	11.7	11.1	11.2	11.9	12.4	12.7	16.5	16.0
Virginia	39	43	45	47	48	47	46	48	18.4	8.0	7.9	7.9	7.9	7.7	7.6	7.7
West Virginia	20	19	19	20	20	20	19	20	11.5	9.9	10.0	10.4	10.6	10.5	10.5	10.6
North Carolina . . .	45	48	53	55	58	57	58	58	8.8	8.2	8.5	8.6	8.9	8.7	8.8	8.7
South Carolina . . .	23	25	27	28	29	30	29	29	8.8	8.1	8.1	8.3	8.5	8.4	8.2	8.1
Georgia	42	44	49	50	52	52	54	53	9.1	8.1	8.1	8.1	8.1	8.1	8.4	8.2
Florida.	75	105	121	127	131	133	134	136	11.0	10.7	10.7	10.6	10.6	10.5	10.6	10.4
East South Central .	128	134	140	142	145	145	143	149	10.0	9.1	9.3	9.3	9.5	9.4	9.3	9.6
Kentucky	33	34	35	35	36	35	34	35	10.3	9.2	9.4	9.3	9.6	9.5	9.1	9.4
Tennessee	38	41	43	45	46	45	47	48	9.7	8.9	9.1	9.3	9.4	9.2	9.6	9.7
Alabama	34	36	38	38	39	39	37	41	9.8	9.1	9.3	9.2	9.5	9.5	9.1	10.0
Mississippi	23	24	25	25	25	25	24	24	10.5	9.4	9.4	9.4	9.5	9.7	9.3	9.3
West South Central.	175	195	209	210	215	217	215	220	9.1	8.2	7.9	7.8	8.0	8.0	8.0	8.1
Arkansas	21	23	24	24	25	25	25	25	10.7	9.9	10.2	10.2	10.4	10.2	10.2	10.2
Louisiana	33	36	37	36	38	38	36	37	9.2	8.5	8.3	8.2	8.5	8.6	8.3	8.5
Oklahoma	27	28	30	29	30	30	29	29	10.5	9.3	9.0	9.0	9.3	9.2	8.9	9.1
Texas	94	108	118	120	123	125	126	128	8.4	7.6	7.2	7.1	7.3	7.4	7.4	7.5
Mountain	66	80	88	92	95	95	97	99	8.0	7.0	6.9	7.0	7.1	7.1	7.2	7.2
Montana	7	7	7	7	7	7	7	7	9.5	8.5	8.2	8.2	8.4	8.4	8.3	8.5
Idaho	6	7	7	7	8	7	7	7	8.6	7.2	7.1	7.4	7.7	7.4	7.1	7.1
Wyoming	3	3	3	3	3	3	3	3	8.8	6.9	6.4	6.2	6.8	6.9	6.5	6.5
Colorado	17	19	20	21	21	21	22	22	7.9	6.6	6.3	6.4	6.5	6.4	6.6	6.6
New Mexico	7	9	10	10	10	11	11	11	7.3	7.0	6.7	6.9	6.9	6.9	6.9	7.1
Arizona	15	21	25	27	28	28	29	29	8.4	7.9	7.7	8.0	7.9	7.9	8.1	8.1
Utah	7	8	9	9	9	9	9	10	6.7	5.6	5.5	5.4	5.5	5.4	5.6	5.6
Nevada	4	6	7	8	8	9	9	10	7.9	7.4	7.7	7.8	8.0	7.8	8.2	8.3
Pacific	221	247	268	277	285	286	290	287	8.3	7.8	7.7	7.6	7.6	7.5	7.6	7.3
Washington	30	32	35	35	36	36	36	37	8.8	7.7	7.8	7.7	7.8	7.6	7.6	7.5
Oregon	20	22	24	24	25	25	27	26	9.3	8.3	8.9	8.9	9.0	8.8	9.7	9.0
California	166	187	202	209	215	217	217	215	8.3	7.9	7.7	7.6	7.6	7.5	7.5	7.2
Alaska.	1	2	2	2	2	2	2	2	4.8	4.3	4.0	3.9	3.9	4.0	3.9	4.2
Hawaii.	4	5	6	6	6	7	7	7	5.2	5.2	5.5	5.7	5.5	5.8	6.0	6.3

[1] Includes deaths of nonresidents.

Source: U.S. National Center for Health Statistics, *Vital Statistics of the United States*, annual; *Monthly Vital Statistics Report*; and unpublished data.

No. 109. Infant, Maternal, and Neonatal Mortality Rates; and Fetal Mortality Ratios, by Race: 1970 to 1989

[Deaths per 1,000 live births, except as noted. Excludes deaths of nonresidents of U.S. See also Appendix III and *Historical Statistics, Colonial Times to 1970*, series B 136-147]

ITEM	1970	1975	1979	1980	1981	1982	1983	1984	1985	1986	1987	1988	1989
Infant deaths [1]	20.0	16.1	13.1	12.6	11.9	11.5	11.2	10.8	10.6	10.4	10.1	10.0	9.8
White	17.8	14.2	11.4	11.0	10.5	10.1	9.7	9.4	9.3	8.9	8.6	8.5	8.2
Black and other	30.9	24.2	19.8	19.1	17.8	17.3	16.8	16.1	15.8	15.7	15.4	15.0	15.2
Black	32.6	26.2	21.8	21.4	20.0	19.6	19.2	18.4	18.2	18.0	17.9	17.6	17.7
Maternal deaths [2]	21.5	12.8	9.6	9.2	8.5	7.9	8.0	7.8	7.8	7.2	6.6	8.4	7.9
White	14.4	9.1	6.4	6.7	6.3	5.8	5.9	5.4	5.2	4.9	5.1	5.9	5.6
Black and other	55.9	29.0	22.7	19.8	17.3	16.4	16.3	16.9	18.1	16.0	12.0	17.4	16.5
Black	59.8	31.3	25.1	21.5	20.4	18.2	18.3	19.7	20.4	18.8	14.2	19.5	18.4
Fetal deaths [3]	14.2	10.7	9.4	9.2	9.0	8.9	8.5	8.2	7.9	7.7	7.7	7.5	7.5
White	12.4	9.5	8.4	8.2	8.0	7.9	7.5	7.4	7.0	6.8	6.7	6.4	6.4
Black and other	22.6	16.0	13.8	13.4	12.8	12.7	12.4	11.5	11.3	11.2	11.5	11.4	11.4
Neonatal deaths [4]	15.1	11.6	8.9	8.5	8.0	7.7	7.3	7.0	7.0	6.7	6.5	6.3	6.2
White	13.8	10.4	7.9	7.5	7.1	6.8	6.4	6.2	6.1	5.8	5.5	5.4	5.2
Black and other	21.4	16.8	12.9	12.5	11.8	11.3	10.8	10.2	10.3	10.1	10.0	9.7	9.6
Black	22.8	18.3	14.3	14.1	13.4	13.1	12.4	11.8	12.1	11.7	11.7	11.5	11.3

[1] Represents deaths of infants under 1 year old, exclusive of fetal deaths. [2] Per 100,000 live births from deliveries and complications of pregnancy, childbirth, and the puerperium. Beginning 1979, deaths are classified according to the ninth revision of the *International Classification of Diseases;* for the earlier years classified according to the revision in use at the time; see text, section 2. [3] Includes only those deaths with stated or presumed period of gestation of 20 weeks or more. [4] Represents deaths of infants under 28 days old, exclusive of fetal deaths.

No. 110. Fetal and Infant Deaths—Number and Percent Distribution: 1970 to 1989

[State requirements for reporting of fetal deaths vary. Most States require reporting of fetal deaths of gestations of 20 weeks or more. There is substantial evidence that not all fetal deaths for which reporting is required are reported. For details of methodology, see Appendix III and source]

	NUMBER						PERCENT DISTRIBUTION					
		Fetal deaths		Infant deaths				Fetal deaths		Infant deaths		
YEAR	Total	Early [1]	Late [2]	Neonatal		Post-neo-natal [5]	Total	Early [1]	Late [2]	Neonatal		Post-neo-natal [5]
				Early [3]	Late [4]					Early [3]	Late [4]	
1970	127,628	17,170	35,791	50,821	5,458	18,388	100.0	13.5	28.0	39.8	4.3	14.4
1980	78,879	10754	22,599	25,492	5,126	14,908	100.0	13.6	28.7	32.3	6.5	18.9
1981	75,901	11126	21,470	24,384	4,737	14,184	100.0	14.7	28.3	32.1	6.2	18.7
1982	75,095	11,028	21,666	23,706	4,629	14,066	100.0	14.7	28.9	31.6	6.2	18.7
1983	71,379	10,933	19,819	22,315	4,192	14,120	100.0	15.3	27.8	31.3	5.9	19.8
1984	69,679	10,963	19,136	21,566	4,125	13,889	100.0	15.7	27.5	31.0	5.9	19.9
1985	69,691	10,958	18,703	21,865	4,314	13,851	100.0	15.7	26.8	31.4	6.2	19.9
1986	67,863	11,100	17,872	21,053	4,159	13,679	100.0	16.4	26.3	31.0	6.1	20.2
1987	67,757	11,656	17,693	20,471	4,156	13,781	100.0	17.2	26.1	30.2	6.1	20.3
1988	68,352	11,833	17,609	20,471	4,219	14,220	100.0	17.3	25.8	29.9	6.2	20.8
1989	70,124	12,397	18,072	20,796	4,372	14,487	100.0	17.7	25.8	29.7	6.2	20.7

[1] 20-27 weeks gestation. [2] 28 weeks or more gestation. [3] Less than 7 days. [4] 7-27 days. [5] 28 days-11 months.

No. 111. Infant Deaths and Infant Mortality Rates, by Cause of Death: 1980 to 1989

[Excludes deaths of nonresidents of U.S. Deaths classified according to ninth revision of *International Classification of Diseases*. See also Appendix III]

CAUSE OF DEATH	NUMBER			PERCENT DISTRIBUTION			INFANT MORTALITY RATE [1]		
	1980	1985	1989	1980	1985	1989	1980	1985	1989
Total	45,526	40,030	39,655	100.0	100.0	100	1,260.3	1,064.5	981.3
Congenital anomalies	9,220	8,561	8,120	20.3	21.4	20.5	255.2	227.7	200.9
Sudden infant death syndrome	5,510	5,315	5,634	12.1	13.3	14.2	152.5	141.3	139.4
Respiratory distress syndrome	4,989	3,691	3,631	11.0	9.2	9.9	138.1	98.2	89.9
Disorders relating to short gestation and unspecified low birthweight	3,648	3,257	3,931	8.0	8.1	9.2	101.0	86.6	97.3
Newborn affected by maternal complications of pregancy	1,572	1,335	1,534	3.5	3.3	3.9	43.5	35.5	38.0
Intrauterine hypoxia and birth asphyxia	1,497	1,158	725	3.3	2.9	2.5	41.4	30.8	17.9
Infections specific to the perinatal period	971	955	892	2.1	2.4	2.5	26.9	25.4	22.1
Accidents and adverse effects	1,166	890	996	2.6	2.2	2.2	32.3	23.7	24.6
Newborn affected by complications of placenta, cord, and membranes	985	891	984	2.2	2.2	1.8	27.3	23.7	24.4
Pneumonia and influenza	1,012	705	636	2.2	1.8	1.6	28.0	18.7	15.7
All other causes	14,956	13,272	12,572	32.9	33.2	31.7	414.1	352.9	311.1

[1] Deaths of infants under 1 year old per 100,000 live births.

Source of tables 109-111: U.S. National Center for Health Statistics, *Vital Statistics of the United States*, annual; and *Monthly Vital Statistics Report*.

No. 112. Infant Mortality Rates, by Race—States: 1980 to 1988

[Deaths per 1,000 live births, by place of residence. Represents deaths of infants under 1 year old, exclusive of fetal deaths. Excludes deaths of nonresidents of the United States. See appendix III and *Historical Statistics, Colonial Times to 1970*, series B 143-147, for U.S. total by race]

DIVISION AND STATE	TOTAL[1] 1980	1985	1988	WHITE 1980	1988	BLACK 1980	1988
U.S ...	12.6	10.6	10.0	11.0	8.5	21.4	17.6
N.E.	10.5	9.2	8.1	10.1	7.6	17.7	15.2
ME	9.2	9.1	7.9	9.4	8.0	-	-
NH	9.9	9.3	8.3	9.9	8.4	[2]22.5	[2]13.4
VT	10.7	8.5	6.8	10.7	6.7	-	-
MA	10.5	9.1	7.9	10.1	7.3	16.8	15.4
RI	11.0	8.2	8.2	10.9	7.5	[2]17.4	[2]13.8
CT	11.2	10.0	8.9	10.2	8.0	19.1	15.5
M.A.	12.8	10.8	10.3	11.1	8.4	21.1	18.6
NY	12.5	10.8	10.8	10.8	8.9	20.0	18.1
NJ	12.5	10.6	9.9	10.3	7.9	21.9	18.5
PA	13.2	11.0	9.9	11.9	8.1	23.1	19.8
E.N.C.	13.0	10.6	10.5	10.9	8.7	24.4	19.6
OH	12.8	10.3	9.7	11.2	8.6	23.0	15.9
IN	11.9	10.9	11.0	10.5	9.9	23.4	19.7
IL	14.8	11.7	11.3	11.7	8.7	26.3	20.7
MI	12.8	11.4	11.1	10.6	8.6	24.2	21.9
WI	10.3	9.1	8.4	9.7	7.5	18.5	16.4
W.N.C	11.3	9.5	8.9	10.5	8.1	21.3	17.1
MN	10.0	8.8	7.8	9.6	7.2	20.0	19.5
IA	11.8	9.5	8.7	11.5	8.3	27.2	19.9
MO	12.4	10.2	10.1	11.1	9.0	20.7	16.2
ND	12.1	8.5	10.5	11.7	10.0	[2]27.5	-
SD	10.9	9.9	10.1	9.0	9.7	-	-
NE	11.5	9.6	9.0	10.7	8.1	25.2	22.4
KS	10.4	9.3	8.0	9.5	7.0	20.6	16.5
S.A.	14.5	12.1	11.6	11.6	8.8	21.6	18.5
DE	13.9	14.8	11.8	9.8	9.1	27.9	21.1
MD	14.0	11.9	11.3	11.6	8.5	20.4	17.8
DC	25.0	20.8	23.2	17.8	19.9	26.7	26.0

DIVISION AND STATE	TOTAL[1] 1980	1985	1988	WHITE 1980	1988	BLACK 1980	1988
VA	13.6	11.5	10.4	11.9	8.1	19.8	17.9
WV	11.8	10.7	9.0	11.4	8.5	21.5	21.6
NC	14.5	11.8	12.5	12.1	9.6	20.0	19.5
SC	15.6	14.2	12.3	10.8	9.6	22.9	16.6
GA	14.5	12.7	12.6	10.8	9.2	21.0	18.9
FL	14.6	11.3	10.6	11.8	8.5	22.8	17.4
E.S.C.	14.5	12.1	11.4	11.8	9.1	21.8	17.2
KY	12.9	11.2	10.7	12.0	10.0	22.0	17.4
TN	13.5	11.4	10.8	11.9	8.2	19.3	18.6
AL	15.1	12.6	12.1	11.6	9.3	21.6	17.2
MS	17.0	13.7	12.3	11.1	8.7	23.7	16.1
W.S.C.	12.7	10.4	9.4	11.1	8.5	19.8	14.4
AR	12.7	11.6	10.7	10.3	8.7	20.0	17.4
LA	14.3	11.9	11.0	10.5	9.0	20.6	14.3
OK	12.7	10.9	9.0	12.1	9.3	21.8	12.6
TX	12.2	9.8	9.0	11.2	8.3	18.8	14.2
Mt.	11.0	9.8	9.2	10.7	9.0	[2]19.5	[2]15.5
MT	12.4	10.3	8.7	11.8	8.8	-	[2]12.8
ID	10.7	10.4	8.8	10.7	8.5	-	[2]25.0
WY	9.8	12.2	8.9	9.3	8.8	[2]25.9	[2]16.8
CO	10.1	9.4	9.6	9.8	9.6	19.1	12.0
NM	11.5	10.6	10.0	11.3	9.7	[2]23.1	[2]14.2
AZ	12.4	9.7	9.7	11.8	9.4	18.4	17.9
UT	10.4	9.6	8.0	10.5	7.9	[2]27.3	[2]6.2
NV	10.7	8.5	8.4	10.0	7.5	20.6	18.7
Pac.	11.2	9.7	8.6	10.9	8.3	17.8	15.9
WA	11.8	10.7	9.0	11.5	8.7	16.4	16.1
OR	12.2	9.9	8.6	12.2	8.5	[2]15.9	[2]14.7
CA	11.1	9.5	8.6	10.6	8.2	18.0	15.9
AK	12.3	10.8	11.6	9.4	9.8	[2]19.5	[2]20.2
HI	10.3	8.8	7.2	11.6	7.2	[2]11.8	[2]9.0

- Represents zero.   [1] Includes other races, not shown separately.   [2] Based on a frequency of less than 20 infant deaths.

No. 113. Age-Adjusted Death Rates, by Selected Causes: 1970 to 1989

[Rates per 100,000 population. For explanation of age-adjustment, see text, section 2. The standard population for this table is the total population of the United States enumerated in 1940. See also headnote, table 114]

CAUSE OF DEATH	1970	1980	1989
All causes	714.3	585.8	523.0
Major cardiovascular diseases	340.1	256.0	194.2
Diseases of heart	253.6	202.0	155.9
Rheumatic fever and rheumatic heart disease	6.3	2.6	1.5
Hypertensive heart disease[1]	4.9	6.8	5.3
Ischemic heart disease	228.1	149.8	105.1
Other diseases of endocardium	2.3	2.0	2.4
All other forms of heart disease	12.0	40.8	41.5
Hypertension[1]	2.9	2.0	1.8
Cerebrovascular diseases	66.3	40.8	28.0
Atherosclerosis	8.4	5.7	2.9
Other	8.8	5.5	5.4
Malignancies[2]	129.9	132.8	133.0
Of respiratory and intrathoracic organs	28.4	36.4	40.3
Of digestive organs and peritoneum	35.2	33.0	30.0
Of genital organs	15.6	13.6	13.1
Of breast	12.6	12.5	12.5
Of urinary organs	5.7	5.2	5.0
Leukemia	5.8	5.4	4.9
Accidents and adverse effects	53.7	42.3	33.8
Motor vehicle	27.4	22.9	18.9
All other	26.3	19.5	14.9
Chronic obstructive pulmonary diseases and allied conditions[3]	11.6	15.9	19.4
Bronchitis, chronic and unspecified	2.1	1.0	0.8
Emphysema	8.4	4.0	3.7
Asthma	1.0	1.0	1.4
Other	(4)	9.9	13.5
Pneumonia and influenza	22.1	12.9	13.7
Pneumonia	20.8	12.4	13.4
Influenza	1.3	0.5	0.3
Diabetes mellitus	14.1	10.1	11.5
Suicide	11.8	11.4	11.3
Chronic liver disease and cirrhosis	14.7	12.2	8.9
Nephritis, nephrotic syndrome, and nephrosis	3.5	4.5	4.4
Homicide and legal intervention	9.1	10.8	9.4
Septicemia	1.4	2.6	4.1
Other infective and parasitic diseases	2.8	1.8	10.8
Benign neoplasms[5]	2.0	2.0	1.7
Ulcer of stomach and duodenum	3.2	1.7	1.3
Hernia of abdominal cavity and intestinal obstruction[6]	2.6	1.4	1.1
Anemias	1.3	0.9	0.9
Cholelithiasis and other disorders of gallbladder	1.3	0.8	0.6
Nutritional deficiencies	0.8	0.5	0.5
Infections of kidney	2.8	0.7	0.3
Tuberculosis	2.2	0.6	0.6
Meningitis	0.8	0.6	0.4
Viral hepatitis	0.5	0.3	0.5
Acute bronchitis and bronchiolitis	0.5	0.2	0.1
Hyperplasia of prostate	0.6	0.2	0.1
Symptoms, signs, and ill-defined conditions	10.4	9.8	8.1
All other causes	44.0	36.8	38.6

[1] With or without renal disease.   [2] Includes other types of malignancies not shown separately.   [3] Prior to 1980, data are shown for bronchitis, emphysema, and asthma.   [4] Included in "all other causes." Comparable data not available separately. [5] Includes neoplasms of unspecified nature; beginning 1980 also includes carcinoma in situ.   [6] Without mention of hernia.

Source of tables 112 and 113: U.S. National Center for Health Statistics, *Vital Statistics of the United States*, annual; and unpublished data.

82

Vital Statistics

No. 114. Deaths and Death Rates, by Selected Causes: 1970 to 1990

[Excludes deaths of nonresidents of the U.S., except as noted. Beginning 1979, deaths classified according to ninth revision of *International Classification of Diseases;* for earlier years, classified according to revision in use at that time. See also Appendix III and *Historical Statistics, Colonial Times to 1970,* series B 149-166]

CAUSE OF DEATH	DEATHS (1,000)					CRUDE DEATH RATE PER 100,000 POPULATION [2]				
	1970	1980	1985	1989	1990 [1] prel.	1970	1980	1985	1989	1990, [1] prel.
All causes	1,921.0	1,989.8	2,086.4	2,150.5	2,162.0	945.3	878.3	873.9	866.3	861.9
Major cardiovascular diseases	1,008.0	988.5	977.9	931.8	920.4	496.0	436.4	409.6	375.4	366.9
Diseases of heart	735.5	761.1	771.2	733.9	725.0	362.0	336.0	323.0	295.6	289.0
Percent of total	38.3	38.3	37.0	34.1	33.5	38.3	38.3	37.0	34.1	33.5
Rheumatic fever and rheumatic heart disease	14.9	7.8	6.6	6.1	6.3	7.3	3.5	2.8	2.5	2.5
Hypertensive heart disease [3]	15.0	24.8	23.7	23.3	23.6	7.4	10.9	9.9	9.4	9.4
Ischemic heart disease	666.7	565.8	536.8	498.0	489.3	328.1	249.7	224.8	200.6	195.1
Other diseases of endocardium . . .	6.7	7.2	9.5	12.2	12.3	3.3	3.2	4.0	4.9	4.9
All other forms of heart disease . . .	32.3	155.5	194.6	194.2	193.5	15.9	68.7	81.5	78.2	77.1
Hypertension [3]	8.3	7.8	7.8	8.8	9.2	4.1	3.5	3.2	3.5	3.7
Cerebrovascular diseases	207.2	170.2	153.1	145.6	145.3	101.9	75.1	64.1	58.6	57.9
Atherosclerosis	31.7	29.4	23.9	19.4	16.5	15.6	13.0	10.0	7.8	6.6
Other	25.3	20.0	22.0	24.3	24.4	12.5	8.8	9.2	9.8	9.7
Malignancies [4]	330.7	416.5	461.6	496.2	506.0	162.8	183.9	193.3	199.9	201.7
Percent of total	17.2	20.9	22.1	23.1	23.4	17.2	20.9	22.1	23.1	23.4
Of respiratory and intrathoracic organs	69.5	108.5	127.3	142.3	143.8	34.2	47.9	53.3	57.3	57.3
Of digestive organs and peritoneum . .	94.7	110.6	116.6	119.7	121.3	46.6	48.8	48.8	48.2	48.4
Of genital organs	41.2	46.4	49.7	55.0	58.0	20.3	20.5	20.8	22.1	23.1
Of breast	29.9	35.9	40.4	43.1	45.1	14.7	15.8	16.9	17.4	18.0
Of urinary organs	15.5	17.8	18.9	20.2	20.4	7.6	7.9	7.9	8.2	8.1
Leukemia	14.5	16.5	17.3	18.2	18.7	7.1	7.3	7.3	7.4	7.4
Accidents and adverse effects	114.6	105.7	93.5	95.0	93.6	56.4	46.7	39.1	38.3	37.3
Motor vehicle	54.6	53.2	45.9	47.6	47.9	26.9	23.5	19.2	19.2	19.1
All other	60.0	52.5	47.6	47.5	45.7	29.5	23.3	19.9	19.1	18.2
Chronic obstructive pulmonary diseases and allied conditions [5] . . .	30.9	56.1	74.7	84.3	89.0	15.2	24.7	31.3	34.0	35.5
Bronchitis, chronic and unspecified . .	5.8	3.7	3.6	3.8	3.4	2.9	1.6	1.5	1.5	1.3
Emphysema	22.7	13.9	14.2	15.5	16.5	11.2	6.1	5.9	6.2	6.6
Asthma	2.3	2.9	3.9	4.9	4.6	1.1	1.3	1.6	2.0	1.8
Other	([6])	35.6	53.0	60.2	64.6	([6])	15.7	22.2	24.3	25.7
Pneumonia and influenza	62.7	54.6	67.6	76.6	78.6	30.9	24.1	28.3	30.8	31.3
Pneumonia	59.0	51.9	65.6	75.0	76.7	29.0	22.9	27.5	30.2	30.6
Influenza	3.7	2.7	2.1	1.6	1.9	1.8	1.2	0.9	0.6	0.8
Diabetes mellitus	38.3	34.9	37.0	46.8	48.8	18.9	15.4	15.5	18.9	19.5
Suicide	23.5	26.9	29.5	30.2	30.8	11.6	11.9	12.3	12.2	12.3
Chronic liver disease and cirrhosis	31.4	30.6	26.8	26.7	25.6	15.5	13.5	11.2	10.8	10.2
Other infective and parasitic diseases . .	6.9	5.1	8.1	29.2	32.2	3.4	2.2	3.4	11.8	12.8
Human immunodeficiency virus (HIV) infection (AIDS)	([7])	([7])	([7])	22.1	24.1	([7])	([7])	([7])	8.9	9.6
Homicide and legal intervention	16.8	24.3	19.9	22.9	25.7	8.3	10.7	8.3	9.2	10.2
Nephritis, nephrotic syndrome, and nephrosis	8.9	16.8	21.3	21.1	20.9	4.4	7.4	8.9	8.5	8.3
Septicemia	3.5	9.4	17.2	19.3	19.8	1.7	4.2	7.2	7.8	7.9
Certain conditions originating in the perinatal period	43.2	22.9	19.2	18.8	17.5	21.3	10.1	8.1	7.6	7.0
Congenital anomalies	16.8	13.9	12.8	12.9	13.4	8.3	6.2	5.4	5.2	5.3
Benign neoplasms [8]	4.8	6.2	6.7	6.7	7.0	2.4	2.7	2.8	2.7	2.8
Ulcer of stomach and duodenum	8.6	6.1	6.6	6.5	6.2	4.2	2.7	2.8	2.6	2.5
Hernia of abdominal cavity and intestinal obstruction [9]	7.2	5.4	5.4	5.5	5.6	3.6	2.4	2.2	2.2	2.2
Anemias	3.4	3.2	3.7	4.0	4.2	1.7	1.4	1.5	1.6	1.7
Cholelithiasis and other disorders of gall bladder	4.0	3.3	3.0	3.0	3.0	2.0	1.5	1.2	1.2	1.2
Nutritional deficiencies	2.5	2.4	2.9	3.0	3.1	1.2	1.0	1.2	1.2	1.2
Tuberculosis	5.2	2.0	1.8	2.0	1.8	2.6	0.9	0.7	0.8	0.7
Infections of kidney	8.2	2.7	2.0	1.4	1.1	4.0	1.2	0.8	0.6	0.4
Viral hepatitis	1.0	0.8	0.9	1.5	1.7	0.5	0.4	0.4	0.6	0.7
Meningitis	1.7	1.4	1.2	1.1	1.2	0.8	0.6	0.5	0.4	0.5
Acute bronchitis and bronchiolitis	1.3	0.6	0.6	0.6	0.6	0.6	0.3	0.3	0.3	0.2
Hyperplasia of prostate	2.2	0.8	0.5	0.4	0.3	1.1	0.3	0.2	0.2	0.1
Symptoms, signs, and ill-defined conditions	25.8	28.8	31.0	27.0	26.3	12.7	12.7	13.0	10.9	10.5
All other causes	108.8	120.0	153.0	171.5	174.1	53.5	53.0	64.4	69.1	69.4

[1] Based on a 10-percent sample of deaths. Includes deaths of nonresidents. [2] 1970, 1980, and 1990 based on resident population enumerated as of Apr. 1; 1985 and 1989 estimated as of July 1. Estimates do not reflect revisions based on the 1990 Census of Population. [3] With or without renal disease. [4] Includes other types of malignancies not shown separately. [5] Prior to 1980, data are shown for bronchitis, emphysema, and asthma. [6] Included in "all other causes." Comparable data not available separately. [7] Data are included in several other categories. [8] Includes neoplasms of unspecified nature; beginning 1980 also includes carcinoma in situ. [9] Without mention of hernia.

Source: U.S. National Center for Health Statistics, *Vital Statistics of the United States,* annual; *Monthly Vital Statistics Report;* and unpublished data.

No. 115. Deaths, by Selected Cause and Selected Characteristics: 1989

[In thousands. Excludes deaths of nonresidents of the U.S. Deaths classified according to ninth revision of *International Classification of Diseases.* See also Appendix III]

AGE, SEX, AND RACE	Total[1]	Diseases of heart	Malignant neoplasms	Accidents and adverse effects	Cerebrovascular diseases	Chronic obstructive pulmonary diseases[2]	Pneumonia, flu	Suicide	Chronic liver disease, cirrhosis	Diabetes mellitus	Homicide and legal intervention
ALL RACES[3]											
Both sexes, total[4]	2,150.5	733.9	496.2	95.0	145.6	84.3	76.6	30.2	26.7	46.8	22.9
Under 15 years old	55.9	1.4	1.8	7.9	0.3	0.2	1.0	0.2	(Z)	0.1	1.2
15 to 24 years old	36.5	0.9	1.9	16.7	0.2	0.2	0.3	4.9	0.1	0.1	6.2
25 to 34 years old	60.5	3.5	5.3	16.6	0.9	0.3	0.9	6.6	1.0	0.7	7.1
35 to 44 years old	80.9	11.8	15.7	11.9	2.4	0.6	1.4	5.3	3.6	1.4	4.0
45 to 54 years old	118.3	30.9	39.1	7.5	4.6	2.3	1.7	3.6	4.7	2.8	1.9
55 to 64 years old	260.1	81.4	96.1	7.6	10.5	10.7	3.9	3.3	6.8	6.9	1.1
65 to 74 years old	481.2	165.8	155.0	8.8	26.3	27.1	10.4	3.3	6.5	13.2	0.7
75 to 84 years old	599.2	234.3	130.6	10.3	50.7	30.6	24.0	2.3	3.3	14.2	0.4
85 years old and over	457.4	203.9	50.6	7.8	49.6	12.3	33.0	0.7	0.7	7.5	0.1
Male, total[4]	1,114.2	368.2	263.3	63.9	57.3	48.2	35.7	24.1	17.3	19.7	17.7
Under 15 years old	31.9	0.7	1.0	4.9	0.1	0.1	0.6	0.2	(Z)	(Z)	0.7
15 to 24 years old	27.2	0.6	1.1	12.6	0.1	0.1	0.1	4.1	(Z)	0.1	5.1
25 to 34 years old	44.2	2.4	2.6	12.9	0.5	0.2	0.5	5.3	0.7	0.4	5.6
35 to 44 years old	55.3	8.8	6.9	9.0	1.3	0.3	0.9	4.1	2.7	0.9	3.1
45 to 54 years old	74.8	23.1	19.7	5.5	2.4	1.1	1.1	2.7	3.4	1.6	1.5
55 to 64 years old	159.6	56.2	53.6	5.3	5.7	6.0	2.5	2.5	4.5	3.4	0.8
65 to 74 years old	278.4	101.6	87.4	5.3	13.3	15.8	6.4	2.7	3.9	5.9	0.5
75 to 84 years old	292.7	112.3	69.3	5.2	20.8	18.0	12.1	1.9	1.7	5.4	0.2
85 years old and over	149.7	62.4	21.8	3.0	13.1	6.6	11.5	0.6	0.3	2.0	0.1
Female, total[4]	1,036.3	365.7	232.8	31.1	88.2	36.2	40.8	6.1	9.4	27.1	5.2
Under 15 years old	24.0	0.6	0.8	2.9	0.1	0.1	0.4	0.1	(Z)	(Z)	0.6
15 to 24 years old	9.3	0.3	0.8	4.1	0.1	0.1	0.1	0.8	(Z)	0.1	1.1
25 to 34 years old	16.4	1.1	2.7	3.7	0.5	0.1	0.4	1.2	0.3	0.3	1.5
35 to 44 years old	25.6	2.9	8.8	2.8	1.1	0.3	0.5	1.2	0.9	0.5	0.9
45 to 54 years old	43.4	7.9	19.4	2.0	2.2	1.1	0.6	0.9	1.3	1.2	0.4
55 to 64 years old	100.4	25.1	42.5	2.3	4.8	4.8	1.4	0.8	2.2	3.6	0.3
65 to 74 years old	202.8	64.2	67.7	3.5	13.0	11.3	4.1	0.6	2.6	7.2	0.3
75 to 84 years old	306.5	122.0	61.3	5.0	29.9	12.7	11.9	0.4	1.6	8.7	0.2
85 years old and over	307.6	141.5	28.8	4.8	36.5	5.7	21.4	0.1	0.4	5.4	0.1
WHITE											
Both sexes, total[4]	1,853.8	648.9	434.2	79.1	125.5	77.9	67.9	27.4	22.2	38.1	11.3
Under 15 years old	37.6	0.9	1.4	5.7	0.2	0.1	0.6	0.2	(Z)	(Z)	0.6
15 to 24 years old	27.2	0.6	1.5	14.3	0.2	0.1	0.2	4.1	(Z)	0.1	2.5
25 to 34 years old	43.4	2.3	4.3	13.6	0.6	0.2	0.5	5.7	0.6	0.5	3.3
35 to 44 years old	58.9	8.6	12.6	9.4	1.5	0.4	0.8	4.8	2.5	1.1	2.1
45 to 54 years old	91.6	23.9	31.9	6.0	3.0	1.9	1.2	3.4	3.7	2.0	1.2
55 to 64 years old	215.4	67.1	82.1	6.2	7.8	9.6	3.0	3.2	5.7	5.1	0.7
65 to 74 years old	418.5	144.4	136.6	7.6	21.6	25.1	8.9	3.1	5.8	10.6	0.5
75 to 84 years old	539.1	211.8	117.6	9.2	44.9	28.9	21.8	2.2	3.1	12.0	0.3
85 years old and over	421.7	189.1	46.0	7.1	45.9	11.6	30.8	0.7	0.7	6.6	0.1
BLACK											
Both sexes, total[4]	267.6	77.4	55.6	13.4	18.0	5.7	7.6	2.2	3.9	8.0	11.0
Under 15 years old	16.3	0.4	0.3	1.8	0.1	0.1	0.3	(Z)	(Z)	(Z)	0.5
15 to 24 years old	8.2	0.3	0.3	1.9	0.1	0.1	0.1	0.5	(Z)	(Z)	3.5
25 to 34 years old	15.6	1.1	0.9	2.5	0.3	0.1	0.3	0.7	0.3	0.1	3.6
35 to 44 years old	20.1	3.0	2.7	2.1	0.8	0.2	0.6	0.4	0.9	0.3	1.7
45 to 54 years old	24.1	6.4	6.4	1.3	1.4	0.4	0.5	0.2	0.9	0.7	0.7
55 to 64 years old	40.5	13.1	12.6	1.2	2.5	1.0	0.8	0.1	0.9	1.6	0.4
65 to 74 years old	57.0	19.6	16.6	1.1	4.3	1.8	1.4	0.1	0.6	2.3	0.3
75 to 84 years old	54.0	20.3	11.7	0.9	5.2	1.5	1.9	(Z)	0.2	1.9	0.1
85 years old and over	31.7	13.2	4.1	0.6	3.3	0.5	1.8	(Z)	0.3	0.8	0.1

Z Fewer than 50. [1] Includes other causes, not shown separately. [2] Includes allied conditions. [3] Includes other races, not shown separately. [4] Includes those deaths with age not stated.

Source: U.S. National Center for Health Statistics, *Vital Statistics of the United States,* annual.

Vital Statistics

No. 116. Deaths, by Age and Leading Cause: 1989

[Excludes deaths of nonresidents of the United States. Deaths classified according to ninth revision of *International Classification of Diseases*. See also appendix III and *Historical Statistics, Colonial Times to 1970*, series B 149-166]

AGE AND LEADING CAUSE OF DEATH	NUMBER OF DEATHS (1,000)			DEATH RATE PER 100,000 POPULATION		
	Total	Male	Female	Total	Male	Female
ALL AGES [1]						
All races [2]	2,150.5	1,114.2	1,036.3	866.3	921.0	814.3
White	1,853.8	950.9	903.0	887.2	930.2	846.0
Black	267.6	146.4	121.2	873.0	1,006.5	752.4
Leading causes of death:						
Heart disease	733.8	368.2	365.7	295.6	304.3	287.3
Malignant neoplasms (cancer)	496.2	263.3	232.8	199.9	217.6	183.0
Stroke (cerebrovascular disease)	145.5	57.3	88.2	58.6	47.4	69.3
Accidents	95.0	63.9	31.1	38.3	52.8	24.5
Chronic obstructive pulmonary disease	84.3	48.2	36.2	34.0	39.8	28.4
Pneumonia	76.6	35.7	40.8	30.8	29.5	32.1
Diabetes	46.8	19.7	27.1	18.9	16.3	21.3
Suicide	30.2	24.1	6.1	12.2	19.9	4.8
Chronic liver disease, cirrhosis	26.7	17.3	9.4	10.8	14.3	7.4
Homicide and legal intervention	22.9	17.7	5.2	9.2	14.6	4.1
1 TO 14 YEARS OLD						
All causes	16.2	9.5	6.7	32.4	37.3	27.4
Leading causes of death:						
Accidents	6.9	4.4	2.5	13.7	17.2	10.1
Malignant neoplasms (cancer)	1.7	0.9	0.7	3.3	3.6	3.0
Congenital anomalies	1.4	0.7	0.7	2.8	2.7	2.9
Homicide and legal intervention	0.9	0.5	0.4	1.8	2.0	1.6
Heart disease	0.6	0.3	0.3	1.2	1.2	1.1
Pneumonia and influenza	0.4	0.2	0.2	0.7	0.7	0.7
15 TO 24 YEARS OLD						
All causes	36.5	27.2	9.3	99.9	147.2	51.6
Leading causes of death:						
Accidents	16.7	12.6	4.1	45.8	68.5	22.7
Motor vehicle	12.9	9.4	3.5	35.4	51.1	19.5
Homicide and legal intervention	6.2	5.1	1.1	16.9	27.7	5.9
Suicide	4.9	4.1	0.8	13.3	22.2	4.2
Malignant neoplasms (cancer)	1.9	1.1	0.8	5.1	5.8	4.3
Heart disease	0.9	0.6	0.3	2.6	3.2	1.9
HIV infection [3]	0.6	0.5	0.1	1.7	2.7	0.6
25 TO 44 YEARS OLD						
All causes	141.4	99.5	42.0	176.1	248.9	103.9
Leading causes of death:						
Accidents	28.4	21.9	6.5	35.4	54.8	16.2
Motor vehicle	16.6	12.2	4.4	20.6	30.4	10.9
Malignant neoplasms (cancer)	21.1	9.5	11.5	26.2	23.8	28.6
HIV infection [3]	16.3	14.6	1.7	20.3	36.6	4.2
Heart disease	15.2	11.2	4.0	19.0	28.0	10.0
Suicide	11.9	9.4	2.4	14.8	23.6	6.1
Homicide and legal intervention	11.2	8.8	2.4	13.9	22.0	5.8
45 TO 64 YEARS OLD						
All causes	378.3	234.4	143.9	813.3	1,050.8	595.1
Leading causes of death:						
Malignant neoplasms (cancer)	135.2	73.3	62.0	290.9	328.5	256.2
Heart disease	112.3	79.3	33.0	241.5	355.4	136.4
Stroke (cerebrovascular disease)	15.1	8.1	7.0	32.5	36.4	28.9
Accidents	15.0	10.8	4.2	32.4	48.4	17.5
Chronic obstructive pulmonary disease	13.0	7.1	5.9	28.0	32.0	24.4
Chronic liver disease and cirrhosis	11.5	7.9	3.6	24.7	35.4	14.8
Diabetes	9.7	4.9	4.8	20.9	22.1	19.8
65 YEARS OLD AND OVER						
All causes	1,537.8	720.8	817.0	4,963.0	5,704.4	4,452.4
Leading causes of death:						
Heart disease	604.0	276.3	327.6	1,949.2	2,186.8	1,785.6
Malignant neoplasms (cancer)	336.2	178.4	157.8	1,085.1	1,412.1	859.9
Stroke (cerebrovascular disease)	126.7	47.2	79.5	408.8	373.6	433.0
Chronic obstructive pulmonary disease	70.0	40.3	29.7	225.8	319.0	161.6
Pneumonia and influenza	67.4	30.0	37.4	217.5	237.2	204.0
Diabetes	34.8	13.4	21.4	112.3	106.0	116.6
Accidents	26.8	13.5	13.3	86.6	107.0	72.5

[1] Includes those deaths with age not stated.   [2] Includes other races, not shown separately.   [3] Human immunodeficiency virus.

Source: U.S. National Center for Health Statistics, *Vital Statistics of the United States*, annual; and unpublished data.

No. 117. Death Rates, by Selected Causes and Selected Characteristics: 1970 to 1989

[Deaths per 100,000 population in specified group. Except as noted, excludes deaths of nonresidents of United States. See headnote, tables 113 and 114]

YEAR AND CHARACTERISTIC	Total [1]	Diseases of heart	Malignant neoplasms	Accidents and adverse effects	Cerebrovascular diseases	Chronic obstructive pulmonary diseases [2]	Pneumonia, flu	Suicide	Chronic liver disease, cirrhosis	Diabetes mellitus	Homicide and legal intervention
ALL RACES [3]											
Both sexes:											
1970, age-adjusted . . .	714.3	253.6	129.9	53.7	66.3	([4])	22.1	11.8	14.7	14.1	9.1
1980, age-adjusted . . .	585.8	202.0	132.8	42.3	40.8	15.9	12.9	11.4	12.2	10.1	10.8
1985, age-adjusted . .	546.1	180.5	133.6	34.7	32.3	18.7	13.4	11.5	9.6	9.6	8.3
1989, age-adjusted [5] . .	523.0	155.9	133.0	33.8	28.0	19.4	13.7	11.3	8.9	11.5	9.4
15 to 24 years old . .	99.9	2.6	5.1	45.8	0.6	0.5	0.7	13.3	0.2	0.4	16.9
25 to 34 years old . .	138.1	7.9	12.1	37.8	2.1	0.7	2.0	15.0	2.2	1.6	16.3
35 to 44 years old . .	221.7	32.3	43.1	32.5	6.4	1.7	3.9	14.6	9.9	3.9	11.0
45 to 54 years old . .	475.0	124.2	157.2	30.1	18.4	9.2	6.9	14.6	19.0	11.2	7.6
55 to 64 years old . .	1,204.4	376.7	445.1	35.0	48.8	49.8	18.0	15.5	31.3	32.1	5.0
65 to 74 years old . .	2,646.7	911.8	852.6	48.5	144.7	148.9	57.3	18.0	35.7	72.4	4.1
75 to 84 years old . .	6,138.8	2,400.6	1,338.1	105.1	519.8	313.8	246.1	23.1	34.2	145.1	4.2
85 years old and over	15,034.8	6,701.6	1,662.3	255.2	1,631.0	403.5	1,083.3	22.8	23.1	245.6	4.3
Male:											
1970, age-adjusted	931.6	348.5	157.4	80.7	73.2	([4])	28.8	17.3	20.2	13.5	14.9
1980, age-adjusted	777.2	280.4	165.5	64.0	44.9	26.1	17.4	18.0	17.1	10.2	17.4
1985, age-adjusted [5]	716.8	247.7	164.5	51.8	35.2	27.9	18.2	18.8	13.6	9.9	12.8
1989, age-adjusted [5] . . .	678.7	210.2	162.4	49.5	30.4	26.4	17.9	18.6	12.8	12.0	14.7
15 to 24 years old. . . .	147.2	3.2	5.8	68.5	0.6	0.5	0.8	22.2	0.2	0.4	27.7
25 to 34 years old. . . .	201.2	10.8	11.8	58.6	2.1	0.8	2.4	24.3	3.1	1.9	25.7
35 to 44 years old. . . .	307.0	49.1	38.4	50.1	7.1	1.9	5.2	22.8	15.1	4.9	17.5
45 to 54 years old. . . .	617.9	190.3	162.8	45.5	20.0	9.4	9.0	22.4	27.9	12.8	12.2
55 to 64 years old. . . .	1,564.8	551.3	525.3	51.9	55.9	58.8	24.1	24.6	44.3	33.2	8.0
65 to 74 years old. . . .	3,439.2	1,255.3	1,079.1	65.7	164.3	194.7	78.6	33.0	48.6	73.1	5.8
75 to 84 years old. . . .	7,929.3	3,043.5	1,877.3	141.3	564.0	486.5	327.3	51.3	46.9	147.3	5.8
85 years old and over .	17,615.9	7,338.2	2,563.3	351.8	1,539.2	774.6	1,356.8	66.7	35.5	240.1	7.6
Female:											
1970, age-adjusted	532.5	175.2	108.8	28.2	60.8	([4])	16.7	6.8	9.8	14.4	3.7
1980, age-adjusted	432.6	140.3	109.2	21.8	37.6	8.9	9.8	5.4	7.9	10.0	4.5
1985, age-adjusted	409.4	127.3	111.4	18.6	30.0	12.5	10.1	4.9	6.1	9.4	3.9
1989, age-adjusted [5]	395.3	112.3	111.7	18.9	26.2	14.7	10.7	4.5	5.5	11.0	4.1
15 to 24 years old. . . .	51.6	1.9	4.3	22.7	0.6	0.4	0.7	4.2	0.2	0.4	5.9
25 to 34 years old. . . .	74.8	5.0	12.4	17.0	2.1	0.7	1.6	5.6	1.4	1.3	6.8
35 to 44 years old. . . .	138.5	15.9	47.7	15.3	5.9	1.6	2.6	6.6	4.8	2.9	4.7
45 to 54 years old. . . .	339.8	61.6	151.9	15.5	16.9	8.9	4.8	7.3	10.5	9.6	3.2
55 to 64 years old. . . .	881.7	220.5	373.3	19.8	42.5	41.7	12.5	7.3	19.6	31.2	2.4
65 to 74 years old. . . .	2,010.7	636.1	670.9	34.6	128.9	112.1	40.2	5.9	25.3	71.8	2.7
75 to 84 years old. . . .	5,050.0	2,009.6	1,010.2	83.1	493.0	208.7	196.7	6.0	26.5	143.7	3.2
85 years old and over .	14,033.9	6,454.7	1,312.9	217.8	1,666.6	259.5	977.3	5.8	18.3	247.7	3.0
WHITE											
Both sexes:											
1970, age-adjusted . . .	679.6	249.1	127.8	51.0	61.8	([4])	19.8	12.4	13.4	12.9	4.7
1980, age-adjusted . . .	559.4	197.6	129.6	41.5	38.0	16.3	12.2	12.1	11.0	9.1	6.9
1985, age-adjusted . . .	523.1	176.1	130.7	34.1	30.1	19.2	12.8	12.3	8.9	8.6	5.4
1989, age-adjusted . . .	496.1	151.0	130.2	32.9	25.9	19.8	13.0	12.0	8.3	10.3	5.4
Male:											
1970, age-adjusted	893.4	347.6	154.3	76.2	68.3	([4])	26.0	18.2	18.8	12.7	7.3
1980, age-adjusted	745.3	277.5	160.5	62.3	41.9	26.7	16.2	18.9	15.7	9.5	10.9
1985, age-adjusted	688.7	244.5	159.2	50.4	32.8	28.5	17.4	19.9	12.6	9.2	8.1
1989, age-adjusted	644.2	205.9	157.2	47.8	28.0	26.8	16.9	19.6	11.9	11.0	8.1
Female:											
1970, age-adjusted	501.7	167.8	107.6	27.2	56.2	([4])	15.0	7.2	8.7	12.8	2.2
1980, age-adjusted	411.1	134.6	107.7	21.4	35.2	9.2	9.4	5.7	7.0	8.7	3.2
1985, age-adjusted	390.6	121.7	110.3	18.4	27.9	12.9	9.8	5.3	5.6	8.1	2.9
1989, age-adjusted	374.9	106.6	110.7	18.5	24.1	15.2	10.3	4.8	5.0	9.6	2.8
BLACK											
Both sexes:											
1970, age-adjusted . . .	1,044.0	307.6	156.7	74.4	114.5	([4])	40.4	6.1	24.8	26.5	46.1
1980, age-adjusted . . .	842.5	255.7	172.1	51.2	68.5	12.5	19.2	6.4	21.6	20.3	40.6
1985, age-adjusted . . .	779.9	236.2	173.0	41.8	55.0	15.0	18.5	6.4	16.1	19.7	29.0
1989, age-adjusted . . .	783.1	216.4	172.7	42.7	49.0	16.6	19.8	7.1	13.9	23.7	35.7
Male:											
1970, age-adjusted	1,318.6	375.9	198.0	119.5	122.5	([4])	53.8	9.9	33.1	21.2	82.1
1980, age-adjusted	1,112.8	327.3	229.9	82.0	77.5	20.9	28.0	11.1	30.6	17.7	71.9
1985, age-adjusted	1,024.0	301.0	231.6	66.7	60.8	23.9	26.8	11.3	23.4	17.7	49.9
1989, age-adjusted	1,032.1	272.6	230.6	67.3	54.1	24.9	27.9	12.5	20.5	22.6	61.5
Female:											
1970, age-adjusted	814.4	251.7	123.5	35.3	107.9	([4])	29.2	2.9	17.8	30.9	15.0
1980, age-adjusted	631.1	201.1	129.7	25.1	61.7	6.3	12.7	2.4	14.4	22.1	13.7
1985, age-adjusted	589.1	186.8	130.4	20.7	50.3	8.7	12.4	2.1	10.1	21.1	10.8
1989, age-adjusted	585.6	172.9	130.9	21.6	44.9	10.9	13.8	2.4	8.5	24.2	12.5

[1] Includes other causes, not shown separately.   [2] Includes allied conditions.   [3] Includes other races not shown separately. [4] Data not available on a comparable basis with later years.   [5] Includes persons under 15 years old, not shown separately. Source: U.S. National Center for Health Statistics, *Monthly Vital Statistics Report* and *Vital Statistics of the United States*, annual.

No. 118. Death Rates, by Cause—States

[Deaths per 100,000 resident population estimated as of July 1. By place of residence. Excludes nonresidents of the United States. Causes of death classified according to ninth revision of *International Classification of Diseases*]

DIVISION AND STATE	Total [1] 1989	Diseases of heart 1989	Malignant neoplasms 1989	Cerebro-vascular diseases 1989	Accidents and adverse effects 1989	Suicide 1989	Chronic obstructive pulmonary diseases [2] 1988	Pneumonia, flu 1988	Diabetes mellitus 1988	Chronic liver disease and cirrhosis 1988	Athero-sclerosis 1988	Homicide and legal intervention 1988	HIV [3] infection 1988
U.S. . . .	**866.3**	**295.6**	**199.9**	**58.6**	**38.3**	**12.2**	**33.7**	**31.6**	**16.4**	**10.7**	**9.0**	**9.0**	**6.8**
N.E.	**888.9**	**300.4**	**224.5**	**56.8**	**29.6**	**9.8**	**34.6**	**36.6**	**17.6**	**11.5**	**10.1**	**4.2**	**4.7**
ME.	915.3	312.1	230.4	59.4	35.3	13.9	46.1	29.5	22.9	10.5	14.4	3.0	1.4
NH	765.3	254.6	195.8	51.1	32.7	11.4	33.3	28.2	16.4	11.1	9.9	2.6	2.2
VT	808.8	260.1	192.9	52.6	39.9	16.6	45.2	33.4	16.7	11.0	8.8	2.5	1.1
MA	911.9	301.6	230.5	58.0	27.4	8.3	34.4	43.0	15.7	12.4	10.7	4.1	5.4
RI	957.6	342.4	245.4	60.7	28.8	10.0	34.3	26.1	28.6	13.1	9.4	4.5	4.2
CT	872.0	303.5	220.3	55.2	28.9	9.4	29.3	34.1	16.4	10.2	7.9	5.6	6.2
M.A.	**972.4**	**355.8**	**226.1**	**55.6**	**31.8**	**9.2**	**32.2**	**35.4**	**19.7**	**12.8**	**8.6**	**9.0**	**14.9**
NY	956.4	361.1	212.2	50.9	30.2	8.5	31.0	38.7	18.1	14.2	8.7	12.8	22.3
NJ	923.7	314.3	232.5	53.1	27.4	6.5	29.3	31.1	19.8	13.5	8.0	5.4	15.0
PA	1027.5	374.5	242.6	64.2	36.9	12.1	36.0	33.3	21.9	10.3	8.7	5.6	3.9
E.N.C.	**879.6**	**312.5**	**204.9**	**60.0**	**34.9**	**11.2**	**33.6**	**31.3**	**17.8**	**9.9**	**10.3**	**7.8**	**2.6**
OH	901.9	324.2	212.9	57.6	33.4	11.3	37.5	29.9	19.7	8.9	9.4	5.2	2.1
IN	877.8	306.0	203.1	67.9	36.7	12.1	37.4	28.8	22.0	8.3	12.1	5.9	2.0
IL	886.7	314.9	205.3	58.9	35.0	10.0	30.4	33.1	15.8	10.8	9.1	9.8	4.0
MI	850.4	303.0	197.7	56.1	35.3	11.3	31.4	29.1	16.5	11.7	12.9	11.5	2.3
WI	870.2	305.9	201.7	66.6	35.2	12.3	32.7	37.1	16.2	8.1	8.7	3.5	1.2
W.N.C.	**902.3**	**310.4**	**207.0**	**68.0**	**39.1**	**11.8**	**37.3**	**39.0**	**15.2**	**7.0**	**12.0**	**4.6**	**2.1**
MN	788.1	249.9	184.2	65.4	35.4	11.8	30.1	35.7	12.9	6.8	9.8	2.9	1.7
IA	957.6	340.9	217.9	75.4	40.4	11.1	42.5	44.4	16.2	6.8	17.6	1.9	0.8
MO	977.4	343.2	225.3	67.1	42.0	12.9	40.5	37.7	16.0	7.3	8.6	8.5	3.6
ND	834.8	283.9	205.6	61.1	33.6	10.6	30.4	31.5	17.2	8.7	14.7	2.4	0.4
SD	915.9	335.8	202.0	71.5	45.9	12.6	33.7	43.2	13.3	7.3	9.7	4.5	0.7
NE	918.7	318.3	205.3	71.8	38.0	10.8	36.4	45.7	15.5	6.4	16.1	3.4	1.7
KS	886.9	307.8	199.4	64.5	38.8	11.3	40.4	38.1	16.4	7.1	13.5	4.0	2.2
S.A.	**906.1**	**303.2**	**212.2**	**62.1**	**42.6**	**13.8**	**34.2**	**27.9**	**16.8**	**11.2**	**7.5**	**11.5**	**7.2**
DE	868.2	291.4	212.3	48.0	37.1	14.1	30.2	22.9	22.3	9.7	5.8	4.7	3.9
MD	817.1	257.9	202.3	48.7	30.1	11.2	30.4	27.9	16.7	9.8	6.4	10.6	5.4
DC	1266.4	326.7	282.0	73.8	36.6	8.4	23.5	44.7	22.0	34.7	3.7	49.9	40.0
VA	773.6	258.7	184.7	54.4	36.3	13.3	27.3	29.0	12.5	9.0	6.8	8.2	4.3
WV	1053.2	394.8	235.9	63.4	48.1	12.4	48.1	36.7	20.8	8.8	11.1	5.8	0.9
NC	874.7	288.8	197.5	70.2	48.3	13.3	32.3	29.7	20.4	10.8	6.4	9.0	3.4
SC	843.3	272.1	184.9	70.1	52.7	12.1	27.4	21.5	15.9	9.4	5.2	10.0	3.3
GA	812.0	260.3	173.2	58.3	46.9	13.3	29.0	26.1	14.4	9.2	6.2	12.8	7.5
FL	1047.8	365.4	257.1	66.4	42.1	16.4	43.1	27.3	17.3	13.6	9.8	13.9	11.7
E.S.C.	**942.8**	**328.0**	**209.6**	**70.3**	**50.7**	**12.7**	**35.9**	**31.6**	**18.7**	**8.8**	**9.0**	**9.8**	**2.1**
KY	949.8	328.8	221.5	67.4	46.2	12.9	41.1	35.9	22.7	8.7	10.2	6.0	1.2
TN	920.1	313.1	205.5	71.9	47.3	13.2	35.6	33.2	15.1	8.4	8.8	10.4	2.1
AL	947.2	320.1	209.0	69.7	53.6	12.3	35.1	28.8	19.3	9.8	9.3	11.5	2.2
MS	968.6	367.3	201.0	72.2	58.9	12.0	30.7	27.1	19.0	8.1	7.5	11.8	2.8
W.S.C.	**803.6**	**266.9**	**178.2**	**56.2**	**41.5**	**12.3**	**27.2**	**26.7**	**14.4**	**8.2**	**7.9**	**11.9**	**5.7**
AR	1024.4	346.7	229.7	84.6	53.7	10.2	36.2	41.7	17.5	7.0	8.7	10.6	2.2
LA	859.5	291.1	194.2	56.4	43.7	12.4	25.9	23.2	19.6	7.4	8.5	13.2	5.6
OK	924.8	331.8	207.2	70.8	41.4	12.9	37.2	36.0	16.6	8.9	12.0	8.1	2.4
TX	735.0	237.1	161.3	49.3	39.2	12.5	24.3	23.7	12.2	8.4	6.9	12.4	6.9
Mt.	**705.1**	**212.1**	**158.0**	**42.9**	**41.7**	**17.7**	**38.6**	**28.2**	**14.3**	**10.3**	**8.4**	**6.9**	**3.5**
MT	838.1	253.2	195.8	53.5	44.5	20.0	47.6	30.9	19.0	10.8	10.9	4.2	0.6
ID	736.5	228.3	164.9	56.9	47.3	15.8	40.2	34.2	16.3	6.5	8.3	3.7	1.1
WY	685.1	203.8	158.7	35.8	44.4	17.3	41.1	31.1	14.6	8.6	6.1	2.7	0.6
CO	637.4	184.0	141.8	39.9	33.3	16.6	39.3	29.8	11.2	8.3	10.8	5.8	5.1
NM	691.9	197.3	147.2	36.8	53.3	19.5	31.3	24.3	17.1	12.8	7.0	11.1	2.1
AZ	793.4	246.6	181.6	46.1	45.9	18.9	41.9	28.6	15.6	12.9	9.1	9.3	4.3
UT	541.2	159.8	108.8	37.4	32.5	12.4	22.1	24.3	13.1	4.8	4.4	3.2	2.0
NV	778.5	245.6	187.2	40.5	43.0	23.1	52.8	25.0	11.7	17.1	6.4	9.9	6.1
Pac.	**747.8**	**237.4**	**169.1**	**55.0**	**37.6**	**13.1**	**34.8**	**31.7**	**12.6**	**13.4**	**8.7**	**9.4**	**9.5**
WA	759.6	235.2	183.1	56.4	35.8	13.6	39.7	28.3	14.1	9.8	10.2	5.9	4.4
OR	883.6	269.1	206.4	71.8	44.3	16.7	43.2	33.4	16.0	10.4	14.0	5.4	3.6
CA	745.3	239.5	165.7	54.2	37.1	12.7	34.2	33.0	12.0	14.7	8.3	10.7	11.2
AK	397.5	90.3	83.5	18.4	70.6	16.9	13.5	8.8	7.6	8.6	1.0	5.2	1.3
HI	584.7	179.3	141.5	44.2	27.2	9.8	17.5	17.9	13.4	7.2	3.5	3.2	5.6

[1] Includes other causes not shown separately.   [2] Includes allied conditions.   [3] Human immunodeficiency virus.

Source: U.S. National Center for Health Statistics, *Monthly Vital Statistics Report*.

No. 119. Acquired Immunodeficiency Syndrome (AIDS) Deaths, by Selected Characteristics: 1982 to 1991

[Data are shown by year of death and are subject to retrospective changes. For data on AIDS cases reported, see table 192. Based on reporting by State health departments]

| CHARACTERISTIC | NUMBER | | | | | | | | | PERCENT DISTRIBUTION | |
	Total, 1982-1991 [1]	1984	1985	1986	1987	1988	1989	1990	1991	Total	1991
Total [2]	126,827	3,266	6,404	10,965	14,612	18,248	25,045	26,389	19,718	100	100
Age:											
Under 5 years old.	1,430	45	92	118	213	223	271	271	147	1	1
5 to 12 years old	294	4	12	24	46	42	58	62	44	(Z)	(Z)
13 to 29 years old	23,922	679	1,291	2,176	2,864	3,531	4,598	4,745	3,574	19	18
30 to 39 years old	57,062	1,467	2,882	4,974	6,535	8,091	11,380	11,927	8,830	45	45
40 to 49 years old	29,120	704	1,342	2,354	3,116	4,054	5,800	6,383	4,903	23	25
50 to 59 years old	10,339	277	555	881	1,186	1,538	2,052	2,098	1,560	8	8
60 years old and over . . .	4,660	90	230	438	652	769	886	903	660	4	3
Sex:											
Male	113,948	3,000	5,915	10,022	13,178	16,334	22,392	23,498	17,628	90	89
Female.	12,879	266	489	943	1,434	1,914	2,653	2,891	2,090	10	11
Race/ethnicity:											
White, non-Hispanic	71,259	1,893	3,807	6,507	8,250	10,044	13,653	14,584	11,378	56	58
Black, non-Hispanic	37,558	895	1,705	2,904	4,283	5,564	7,635	8,053	5,815	30	29
Hispanic	16,791	454	852	1,465	1,954	2,462	3,498	3,494	2,292	13	12

Z Less than 0.5 percent.   [1] Includes deaths prior to 1982.   [2] Includes other race/ethnicity groups not shown separately.

Source: U.S. Centers for Disease Control, Atlanta, GA, unpublished data.

No. 120. Death Rates From Heart Disease, by Sex, Age, and Selected Type: 1970 to 1989

[Deaths per 100,000 population in specified age groups. Excludes deaths of nonresidents of the United States. Beginning 1980, deaths classified according to the ninth revision of the *International Classification of Diseases*. For earlier years, classified according to the revision in use at the time; see text, section 2. See Appendix III]

| AGE AT DEATH AND SELECTED TYPE OF HEART DISEASE | MALE | | | | | FEMALE | | | | |
	1970	1980	1985	1988	1989	1970	1980	1985	1988	1989
Total U.S. rate [1]	422.5	368.6	342.8	321.9	304.3	304.5	305.1	304.3	301.2	287.3
25 to 34 years	15.2	11.4	11.5	11.3	10.8	7.7	5.3	5.0	5.1	5.0
35 to 44 years	103.2	68.7	58.4	52.2	49.1	32.2	21.4	18.3	16.8	15.9
45 to 54 years	376.4	282.6	236.9	199.8	190.3	109.9	84.5	73.8	66.7	61.6
55 to 64 years	987.2	746.8	651.9	584.7	551.3	351.6	272.1	250.3	237.0	220.5
65 years old and over	3,258.0	2,778.6	2,519.3	2,336.1	2,186.8	2,268.2	2,027.5	1,938.0	1,881.3	1,785.6
65 to 74 years	2,170.3	1,728.0	1,508.4	1,358.1	1,255.3	1,082.7	828.6	745.3	685.6	636.1
75 to 84 years	4,534.8	3,834.3	3,498.0	3,239.1	3,043.5	3,120.8	2,497.0	2,245.2	2,122.4	2,009.6
85 years old and over	8,426.2	8,752.7	8,123.7	7,830.9	7,338.2	7,591.8	7,350.5	6,935.7	6,810.1	6,454.7
Persons 45 to 54 years old:										
Ischemic heart	338.0	217.3	169.9	134.5	129.1	84.0	52.2	43.3	36.8	34.2
Rheumatic heart	11.4	3.1	1.9	1.5	1.2	10.6	4.3	2.7	2.1	1.9
Hypertensive heart [2]	4.6	8.3	8.4	7.5	7.5	4.0	5.4	4.6	4.2	4.2
Persons 55 to 64 years old:										
Ischemic heart	904.6	581.1	474.6	401.3	385.1	299.1	189.0	163.3	147.1	139.1
Rheumatic heart	21.5	6.2	4.2	3.4	3.3	20.8	9.2	6.3	5.6	4.6
Hypertensive heart [2]	11.7	21.8	19.6	18.6	19.0	9.1	13.3	12.2	11.6	10.5
Persons 65 to 74 years old:										
Ischemic heart	2,010.0	1,355.5	1,110.8	956.9	900.9	978.0	605.3	514.1	453.1	428.1
Rheumatic heart	31.9	11.8	8.6	7.3	6.6	30.2	18.6	13.3	12.5	11.2
Hypertensive heart [2]	30.6	44.3	38.2	34.9	32.8	24.8	36.2	29.0	26.3	24.9
Persons 75 to 84 years old:										
Ischemic heart	4,222.7	2,953.7	2,544.9	2,277.5	2,181.1	2,866.3	1,842.7	1,547.5	1,413.1	1,359.6
Rheumatic heart	04.8	16.7	14.7	13.6	13.8	34.3	25.4	24.1	24.6	23.3
Hypertensive heart [2]	80.8	90.7	79.5	69.6	69.4	83.9	101.1	80.4	74.3	73.6
Persons 85 years old and over:										
Ischemic heart	7,781.5	6,501.6	5,658.9	5,236.2	5,042.5	6,951.5	5,280.6	4,642.8	4,374.2	4,242.2
Rheumatic heart	34.7	19.5	17.7	21.1	19.8	39.2	25.8	27.2	29.9	30.1
Hypertensive heart [2]	182.0	180.3	150.7	148.8	142.9	223.5	250.8	213.9	199.4	205.1

[1] Includes persons under 25 years old, not shown separately.   [2] With or without renal disease.

Source: U.S. National Center for Health Statistics, *Vital Statistics of the United States*, annual; and unpublished data.

No. 121. Death Rates From Cancer, by Sex, Age, and Selected Type: 1970 to 1989

[Deaths per 100,000 population in the specified age groups. See headnote, table 120]

AGE AT DEATH AND SELECTED TYPE OF CANCER	MALE					FEMALE				
	1970	1980	1985	1988	1989	1970	1980	1985	1988	1989
Total U.S. rate [1]	182.1	205.3	212.6	215.5	217.6	144.4	163.6	175.1	180.0	183.0
25 to 34 years	16.3	13.4	13.0	11.7	11.8	16.7	14.0	13.1	12.2	12.4
35 to 44 years	53.0	44.0	42.3	39.7	38.4	65.6	53.1	49.1	48.5	47.7
45 to 54 years	183.5	188.7	174.5	166.3	162.8	181.5	171.8	164.0	154.9	151.9
55 to 64 years	511.8	520.8	531.1	526.7	525.3	343.2	361.7	379.1	376.6	373.3
65 years old and over	1,221.2	1,371.6	1,389.8	1,398.6	1,412.1	708.3	767.8	813.8	840.5	859.9
65 to 74 years	1,006.8	1,093.2	1,085.6	1,072.7	1,079.1	557.9	607.1	644.6	659.2	670.9
75 to 84 years	1,588.3	1,790.5	1,840.2	1,861.0	1,877.3	891.9	903.1	948.3	982.6	1,010.2
85 years old and over	1,720.8	2,369.5	2,413.7	2,527.9	2,563.3	1,096.7	1,255.7	1,262.9	1,292.8	1,312.9
Persons, 35 to 44 years old:										
Respiratory, intrathoracic	17.0	12.6	10.6	9.6	9.0	6.5	6.8	5.8	5.6	5.5
Digestive organs, peritoneum	11.4	9.5	9.0	9.1	8.4	8.6	6.5	5.8	5.6	5.4
Breast	0.1	-	0.1	0.1	(B)	20.4	17.9	17.5	17.6	17.7
Genital organs	1.4	0.7	0.7	0.5	0.7	13.6	8.3	7.1	6.9	6.9
Lymphatic and hematopoietic tissues, excl. leukemia	5.6	4.3	4.6	4.4	4.7	3.2	2.4	2.3	2.4	2.3
Urinary organs	1.9	1.4	1.6	1.4	1.4	1.0	0.6	0.9	0.7	0.7
Lip, oral cavity, and pharynx	1.7	1.8	1.4	1.2	1.2	0.7	0.5	0.6	0.4	0.5
Leukemia	3.4	3.2	3.0	3.0	2.7	2.8	2.6	2.1	2.1	2.0
Persons, 45 to 54 years old:										
Respiratory, intrathoracic	72.1	79.8	70.7	65.7	64.1	22.2	34.8	35.9	35.0	34.2
Digestive organs, peritoneum	45.9	44.3	41.7	39.5	38.9	32.5	27.8	25.7	22.4	22.0
Breast	0.4	0.2	0.3	0.3	0.2	52.6	48.1	46.7	45.3	44.7
Genital organs	3.4	3.4	3.1	3.1	2.9	34.4	24.1	20.4	18.5	18.5
Lymphatic and hematopoietic tissues, excl. leukemia	12.8	10.2	10.0	10.5	10.5	8.3	6.6	6.4	6.1	6.1
Urinary organs	8.0	7.4	7.5	7.0	7.0	3.5	3.3	3.0	2.9	3.1
Lip, oral cavity, and pharynx	7.9	8.2	6.8	6.6	5.9	2.8	2.6	2.0	1.9	1.8
Leukemia	6.6	6.2	5.7	5.5	5.3	4.9	4.4	4.3	3.9	3.9
Persons, 55 to 64 years old:										
Respiratory, intrathoracic	202.3	223.8	231.1	229.5	227.1	38.9	74.5	93.9	102.2	104.3
Digestive organs, peritoneum	139.0	129.3	129.3	125.9	124.5	86.0	79.1	74.7	69.8	68.2
Breast	0.6	0.7	0.6	0.4	0.6	77.6	80.5	83.6	81.8	78.6
Genital organs	22.8	23.5	24.3	25.1	27.0	58.2	46.8	42.8	41.3	39.5
Lymphatic and hematopoietic tissues, excl. leukemia	27.1	24.4	25.0	25.6	26.2	17.7	16.8	17.5	16.5	17.5
Urinary organs	26.4	22.9	22.2	21.4	22.7	9.4	8.9	8.5	8.5	8.9
Lip, oral cavity, and pharynx	20.1	17.9	15.8	15.4	15.6	6.2	6.0	5.4	4.9	5.4
Leukemia	15.4	14.7	14.6	13.9	14.6	9.0	9.3	9.2	8.5	9.1
Persons, 65 to 74 years old:										
Respiratory, intrathoracic	340.7	422.0	424.8	425.4	425.5	45.6	106.1	145.1	164.1	175.9
Digestive organs, peritoneum	293.3	284.1	272.7	257.3	261.8	185.8	173.6	162.7	155.6	154.5
Breast	1.4	1.1	1.0	1.1	1.1	93.8	101.1	107.7	109.4	111.1
Genital organs	103.7	107.6	108.3	111.8	113.7	85.6	73.6	71.2	71.3	70.1
Lymphatic and hematopoietic tissues, excl. leukemia	50.3	48.1	52.2	52.0	53.4	34.6	34.4	36.6	38.5	39.2
Urinary organs	60.3	56.9	51.1	50.0	50.1	20.1	19.7	19.7	19.7	19.4
Lip, oral cavity, and pharynx	26.8	25.4	23.7	20.9	20.2	6.7	8.8	8.6	8.3	8.0
Leukemia	35.3	35.3	34.0	32.7	35.1	19.3	18.7	19.2	17.8	19.1
Persons, 75 to 84 years old:										
Respiratory, intrathoracic	354.2	511.5	559.0	579.8	581.3	56.5	98.0	137.2	169.9	187.7
Digestive organs, peritoneum	507.5	496.6	476.2	456.8	458.9	353.3	326.3	312.2	297.1	301.2
Breast	2.7	2.1	2.3	2.3	2.2	127.4	126.4	137.7	143.1	147.5
Genital organs	299.4	315.4	321.4	333.9	340.5	104.9	95.7	93.8	94.5	93.6
Lymphatic and hematopoietic tissues, excl. leukemia	74.0	80.0	92.8	96.7	101.0	49.4	57.8	64.2	69.4	72.5
Urinary organs	112.2	112.4	106.2	102.5	106.6	44.0	37.4	36.8	36.9	38.1
Lip, oral cavity, and pharynx	36.6	31.4	27.6	26.0	24.0	10.8	10.9	10.0	11.0	10.6
Leukemia	68.3	71.5	70.1	71.8	71.9	39.6	38.5	38.5	37.7	37.2
Persons, 85 years and over:										
Respiratory, intrathoracic	215.3	386.3	450.2	492.8	500.7	56.5	96.3	102.7	125.7	128.1
Digestive organs, peritoneum	583.7	705.8	656.8	658.1	670.1	465.0	504.3	490.4	483.3	485.4
Breast	2.9	2.6	3.9	4.0	4.1	157.1	169.3	175.9	183.9	185.8
Genital organs	434.2	612.3	605.0	663.6	698.0	107.3	115.9	104.6	106.8	109.7
Lymphatic and hematopoietic tissues, excl. leukemia	58.1	93.2	113.1	126.8	128.8	41.7	63.0	72.6	78.7	82.8
Urinary organs	140.5	177.0	182.7	165.0	174.1	59.9	63.8	62.3	64.8	63.3
Lip, oral cavity, and pharynx	47.0	40.2	32.2	33.0	28.7	19.2	16.0	15.8	14.4	16.1
Leukemia	83.3	117.1	113.1	110.1	100.0	50.9	61.1	63.0	62.4	63.5

- Represents zero. B Base figure too small to meet statistical standards for reliability of a derived figure. [1] Includes persons under 25 years of age and malignant neoplasms of other and unspecified sites, not shown separately.

Source: U.S. National Center for Health Statistics, *Vital Statistics of the United States*, annual; and unpublished data.

No. 122. Death Rates From Accidents and Violence: 1970 to 1989

[Rates are per 100,000 population. Excludes deaths of nonresidents of the United States. Beginning 1980, deaths classified according to the ninth revision of the *International Classification of Diseases*. For earlier years, classified according to the revisions in use at the time; see text, section 2. See Appendix III]

CAUSE OF DEATH AND AGE	WHITE						BLACK					
	Male			Female			Male			Female		
	1970	1980	1989	1970	1980	1989	1970	1980	1989	1970	1980	1989
Total [1]	101.9	97.1	81.1	42.4	36.3	32.8	183.2	154.0	138.6	51.7	42.6	39.4
Motor vehicle accidents.	39.1	35.9	27.0	14.8	12.8	12.1	44.3	31.1	28.3	13.4	8.3	9.3
All other accidents	38.2	30.4	24.5	18.3	14.4	12.7	63.3	46.0	37.0	22.5	18.6	15.0
Suicide.	18.0	19.9	21.4	7.1	5.9	5.2	8.0	10.3	12.2	2.6	2.2	2.4
Homicide	6.8	10.9	8.2	2.1	3.2	2.8	67.6	66.6	61.1	13.3	13.5	12.9
15 to 24 years old	130.7	138.6	107.1	34.9	37.3	32.7	234.3	162.0	188.0	45.5	35.0	33.9
25 to 34 years old	96.6	118.4	96.0	23.8	29.0	26.6	384.4	256.9	205.9	76.0	49.4	47.4
35 to 44 years old	85.7	94.1	80.4	25.8	29.2	24.7	345.2	218.1	184.9	77.2	43.2	40.8
45 to 54 years old	87.5	90.8	73.8	30.4	31.8	25.5	303.3	207.3	144.0	65.5	40.2	30.8
55 to 64 years old	101.5	92.3	80.1	36.3	33.8	28.7	242.4	188.5	130.6	56.0	47.3	37.3
65 years old and over	216.9	163.9	151.9	122.4	87.2	81.4	220.0	215.8	187.1	107.9	102.9	87.8
65 to 74 years old.	128.0	116.7	101.4	57.7	46.4	42.2	217.4	182.2	146.3	81.5	68.7	56.0
75 to 84 years old.	229.3	209.2	197.5	149.0	101.5	92.0	236.0	261.4	230.2	140.1	137.5	101.5
85 years old and over	466.7	438.5	431.9	391.4	268.1	228.0	271.8	379.2	404.2	214.3	235.7	222.4

[1] Includes persons under 15 years old, not shown separately.

No. 123. Deaths and Death Rates From Accidents, by Type: 1970 to 1989

[See headnote, table 122; and Appendix III. See also *Historical Statistics, Colonial Times to 1970*, series B 163-165]

TYPE OF ACCIDENT	DEATHS (number)					RATE PER 100,000 POPULATION				
	1970	1980	1985	1988	1989	1970	1980	1985	1988	1989
Accidents and adverse effects.	114,638	105,718	93,457	97,100	95,028	56.4	46.7	39.1	39.5	38.3
Motor-vehicle accidents	54,633	53,172	45,901	49,078	47,575	26.9	23.5	19.2	20.0	19.2
Traffic	53,493	51,930	44,822	48,024	46,586	26.3	22.9	18.8	19.5	18.8
Nontraffic	1,140	1,242	1,079	1,054	989	0.6	0.5	0.5	0.4	0.4
Water-transport accidents.	1,651	1,429	1,111	979	866	0.8	0.6	0.5	0.4	0.3
Air and space transport accidents . .	1,612	1,494	1,428	1,012	1,123	0.8	0.7	0.6	0.4	0.5
Railway accidents	852	632	551	571	608	0.4	0.3	0.2	0.2	0.2
Accidental falls	16,926	13,294	12,001	12,096	12,151	8.3	5.9	5.0	4.9	4.9
Fall from one level to another. . . .	4,798	3,743	3,365	3,317	3,062	2.4	1.7	1.4	1.3	1.2
Fall on the same level.	828	415	411	433	476	0.4	0.2	0.2	0.2	0.2
Fracture, cause unspecified, and other unspecified falls	11,300	9,136	8,225	8,346	8,613	5.6	4.0	3.4	3.4	3.5
Accidental drowning.	6,391	6,043	4,407	4,199	4,015	3.1	2.7	1.8	1.7	1.6
Accidents caused by—										
Fires and flames	6,718	5,822	4,938	4,965	4,716	3.3	2.6	2.1	2.0	1.9
Firearms.	2,406	1,955	1,649	1,501	1,489	1.2	0.9	0.7	0.6	0.6
Electric current	1,140	1,095	802	714	702	0.6	0.5	0.3	0.3	0.3
Accidental poisoning by—										
Drugs and medicines	2,505	2,492	3,612	4,865	5,035	1.2	1.1	1.5	2.0	2.0
Other solid and liquid substances .	1,174	597	479	488	568	0.6	0.3	0.2	0.2	0.2
Gases and vapors	1,620	1,242	1,079	873	921	0.8	0.5	0.5	0.4	0.4
Complications due to medical procedures	3,581	2437	2,852	3,038	2,992	1.8	1.1	1.2	1.2	1.2
Inhalation and ingestion of objects . .	2,753	3,249	3,551	3,805	3,578	1.4	1.4	1.5	1.5	1.4

No. 124. Suicides, by Sex and Method Used: 1970 to 1989

[Excludes deaths of nonresidents of the United States. Beginning 1979, deaths classified according to the ninth revision of the *International Classification of Diseases*. For earlier years, classified according to the revision in use at the time; see text, section 2. See also *Historical Statistics, Colonial Times to 1970*, series H 979-986]

METHOD	MALE							FEMALE						
	1970	1980	1984	1986	1987	1988	1989	1970	1980	1985	1986	1987	1988	1989
Total	16,629	20,505	23,145	24,226	24,272	24,078	24,102	6,851	6,364	6,308	6,070	6,524	6,320	6,130
Firearms [1]	9,704	12,937	14,809	15,518	15,539	15,656	15,680	2,068	2,459	2,554	2,635	2,597	2,513	2,498
Percent of total.	58.4	63.1	64.0	64.1	64.0	65.0	65.1	30.2	38.6	40.5	39.5	39.8	39.7	40.8
Poisoning [2]	3,299	2,997	3,319	3,516	3,790	3,403	3,211	3,285	2,456	2,385	2,520	2,531	2,422	2,232
Hanging and strangulation [3] .	2,422	2,997	3,532	3,761	3,478	3,588	3,708	831	694	732	845	757	787	776
Other [4]	1,204	1,574	1,485	1,431	1,465	1,431	1,503	667	755	637	678	639	607	624

[1] Includes explosives in 1970.   [2] Includes solids, liquids, and gases.   [3] Includes suffocation.   [4] Beginning 1980, includes explosives.

Source of tables 122-124: U.S. National Center for Health Statistics, *Vital Statistics of the United States*, annual; and unpublished data.

No. 125. Suicide Rates, by Sex, Race, and Age Group: 1970 to 1989
[See headnote, tables 117 and 122]

AGE	TOTAL [1]			MALE						FEMALE					
				White			Black			White			Black		
	1970	1980	1989	1970	1980	1989	1970	1980	1989	1970	1980	1989	1970	1980	1989
All ages [2]	**11.6**	**11.9**	**12.2**	**18.0**	**19.9**	**21.4**	**8.0**	**10.3**	**12.2**	**7.1**	**5.9**	**5.2**	**2.6**	**2.2**	**2.4**
10 to 14 years old. . . .	0.6	0.8	1.4	1.1	1.4	2.2	0.3	0.5	1.7	0.3	0.3	0.7	0.4	0.1	(B)
15 to 19 years old. . . .	5.9	8.5	11.3	9.4	15.0	19.4	4.7	5.6	10.3	2.9	3.3	4.5	2.9	1.6	2.3
20 to 24 years old. . . .	12.2	16.1	15.3	19.3	27.8	26.8	18.7	20.0	23.7	5.7	5.9	4.3	4.9	3.1	3.4
25 to 34 years old. . . .	14.1	16.0	15.0	19.9	25.6	24.9	19.2	21.8	22.0	9.0	7.5	5.9	5.7	4.1	3.7
35 to 44 years old. . . .	16.9	15.4	14.6	23.3	23.5	23.8	12.6	15.6	18.1	13.0	9.1	7.1	3.7	4.6	3.9
45 to 54 years old. . . .	20.0	15.9	14.6	29.5	24.2	24.2	13.8	12.0	10.9	13.5	10.2	8.0	3.7	2.8	3.0
55 to 64 years old. . . .	21.4	15.9	15.5	35.0	25.8	26.6	10.6	11.7	10.4	12.3	9.1	7.9	2.0	2.3	2.5
65 years and over. . . .	20.8	17.8	20.1	41.1	37.5	43.5	8.7	11.4	15.7	8.5	6.5	6.3	2.6	1.4	1.8
65 to 74 years over .	20.8	16.9	18.0	38.7	32.5	35.1	8.7	11.1	15.4	9.6	7.0	6.4	2.9	1.7	(B)
75 to 84 years over .	21.2	19.1	23.1	45.5	45.5	55.3	8.9	10.5	14.7	7.2	5.7	6.3	1.7	1.4	(B)
85 years and over . .	19.0	19.2	22.8	45.8	52.8	71.9	8.7	18.9	(B)	5.8	5.8	6.2	2.8	-	(B)

- Represents or rounds to zero. B Base figure too small to meet statistical standards for reliability of a derived figure.
[1] Includes other races, not shown separately. [2] Includes other age groups, not shown separately.

No. 126. Firearm Mortality Among Children, Youth, and Young Adults, 1 to 34 Years Old: 1988
[**Death rate per 100,000 population.** Deaths classified according to the ninth revision of the *International Classification of Diseases*]

ITEM	All ages [1]	Under 5 years	5 to 9 years	10 to 14 years	15 to 19 years	20 to 24 years	25 to 29 years	30 to 34 years
MALE								
Natural causes:								
White	867.3	210.8	11.2	12.3	19.5	29.7	51.6	87.5
Black	866.4	477.3	16.6	14.7	28.9	62.7	132.5	267.4
Firearms:								
White	20.2	0.6	0.7	4.2	21.7	29.8	27.1	23.5
Black	49.8	1.8	1.9	7.8	79.5	119.2	103.2	84.3
Accidents: White	1.0	0.3	0.4	1.8	2.6	1.8	0.9	1.0
Black	1.6	0.7	0.8	2.1	3.4	2.5	2.0	1.1
Suicide: White	14.2	(X)	(X)	1.2	12.7	17.2	15.9	14.0
Black	7.1	(X)	(X)	0.7	6.8	12.3	10.7	13.6
Homicide: White.	4.9	0.3	0.3	0.8	6.0	10.2	9.9	8.2
Black	41.1	1.1	1.1	4.5	67.9	103.6	89.5	69.1
FEMALE								
Natural causes:								
White	825.9	166.3	10.0	9.2	12.4	18.2	27.3	41.5
Black	713.5	403.5	14.2	15.0	23.2	42.7	76.9	131.1
Firearms:								
White	3.7	0.3	0.4	1.1	3.8	4.5	5.6	5.2
Black	7.5	0.9	0.9	3.6	8.4	13.9	16.0	12.8
Accidents: White	0.1	0.1	0.1	0.3	0.2	0.1	0.2	0.1
Black	0.3	0.3	0.1	0.6	0.4	0.4	0.1	0.4
Suicide: White	2.2	(X)	(X)	0.4	2.3	2.0	2.6	2.8
Black	1.1	(X)	(X)	0.4	0.9	1.5	1.5	1.5
Homicide: White.	1.4	0.2	0.3	0.4	1.3	2.3	2.6	2.1
Black	6.2	0.6	0.7	2.5	7.1	11.9	14.2	10.8

X Not applicable. [1] Includes 35 years old and over, not shown separately.
Source: U.S. National Center for Health Statistics, *Monthly Vital Statistics Report*, Vol. 39, No. 11, and unpublished data.

No. 127. Marriages and Divorces: 1970 to 1988
[See also *Historical Statistics, Colonial Times to 1970*, series B 214-217]

YEAR	MARRIAGES [1]						DIVORCES AND ANNULMENTS		
	Number (1,000)	Rate per 1,000 population					Number (1,000)	Rate per 1,000 population	
		Total	Men, 15 yrs. old and over	Women 15 yrs. old and over	Unmarried women			Total	Married women 15 yrs. old and over
					15 yrs. old and over	15 to 44 yrs. old			
1970	2,159	10.6	31.1	28.4	76.5	140.2	708	3.5	14.9
1975	2,153	10.0	27.9	25.6	66.9	118.5	1,036	4.8	20.3
1980	2,390	10.6	28.5	26.1	61.4	102.6	1,189	5.2	22.6
1981	2,422	10.6	28.4	26.1	61.7	103.1	1,213	5.3	22.6
1982	2,456	10.6	28.4	26.1	61.4	101.9	1,170	5.0	21.7
1983	2,440	10.5	28.0	25.7	59.9	99.3	1,158	4.9	21.3
1984	2,477	10.5	28.1	25.8	59.5	99.0	1,169	5.0	21.5
1985	2,413	10.1	26.9	24.8	57.0	94.9	1,190	5.0	21.7
1986	2,407	10.0	26.5	24.5	56.2	93.9	1,178	4.9	21.2
1987	2,403	9.9	26.2	24.2	55.7	92.4	1,166	4.8	20.8
1988	2,396	9.7	25.9	23.9	54.6	91.0	1,167	4.7	20.7

[1] Beginning 1980, includes nonlicensed marriages registered in California.
Sources of tables 125 and 127: U.S. National Center for Health Statistics, *Vital Statistics of the United States*, annual; *Monthly Vital Statistics Report*; and unpublished data.

No. 128. Percent Distribution of Marriages, by Marriage Order: 1970 to 1988

[Beginning 1980, excludes Iowa. Excludes marriages with marriage order not stated. See headnote, table 129]

MARRIAGE ORDER	1970	1980	1981	1982	1983	1984	1985	1986	1987	1988
Total.........................	100.0	100.0	100.0	100.0	100.0	100.0	100.0	100.0	100.0	100.0
First marriage of bride and groom..........	68.6	56.2	54.7	54.8	54.4	54.4	54.3	53.9	53.9	54.1
First marriage of bride, remarriage of groom ...	7.6	11.3	11.8	11.6	11.6	11.5	11.5	11.3	11.3	11.1
Remarriage of bride, first marriage of groom ...	7.3	9.8	10.1	10.3	10.5	10.7	10.9	11.2	11.3	11.4
Remarriage of bride and groom	16.5	22.7	23.4	23.3	23.5	23.4	23.4	23.6	23.5	23.4

No. 129. Percent Distribution of Marriages, by Age, Sex, and Previous Marital Status: 1980 to 1988

[Data cover marriage registration area; see text, section 2. Based on a sample and subject to sampling variability; for details, see source]

SEX AND PREVIOUS MARITAL STATUS	Total	Under 20 years old	20-24 years old	25-29 years old	30-34 years old	35-44 years old	45-64 years old	65 years old and over
WOMEN								
All marriages: [1]								
1980	100.0	21.1	37.1	18.7	9.3	7.8	5.0	1.0
1985	100.0	13.9	34.4	22.1	12.0	11.1	5.4	1.0
1988 ...., ...	100.0	11.8	31.5	24.1	13.2	12.6	5.8	1.0
First marriages: [2]								
1980	100.0	30.4	47.3	16.0	4.0	1.6	0.6	0.1
1985	100.0	20.8	46.3	22.4	6.9	2.8	0.6	0.1
1988 ...., ...	100.0	17.7	43.3	26.1	8.5	3.7	0.7	0.1
Remarriages: [2][3]								
1980	100.0	1.7	15.3	24.4	20.6	20.8	14.3	2.9
1985	100.0	0.9	11.1	21.6	21.9	27.1	14.6	2.9
1988	100.0	0.7	9.1	20.5	21.9	29.5	15.4	2.8
Previously divorced: [4] 1980.	100.0	1.7	16.7	26.7	22.5	21.6	10.0	0.6
1988.	100.0	0.8	9.8	22.2	23.3	30.7	12.5	0.6
MEN								
All marriages: [1]								
1980	100.0	8.5	35.7	23.8	12.3	10.5	7.4	1.8
1985	100.0	5.3	30.1	26.2	14.4	14.0	8.2	1.9
1988 ...., ...	100.0	4.5	26.9	27.2	15.8	15.1	8.6	1.9
First marriages: [2]								
1980	100.0	12.7	50.0	25.7	7.5	2.9	1.1	0.1
1985	100.0	8.1	43.4	31.5	11.0	4.7	1.1	0.1
1988 ...., ...	100.0	6.9	38.7	33.9	13.6	5.8	1.1	0.1
Remarriages: [2][3]								
1980	100.0	0.2	7.2	20.1	21.9	25.6	20.0	5.1
1985	100.0	0.1	4.9	16.0	20.6	31.6	21.6	5.2
1988	100.0	0.1	4.0	14.4	20.1	33.1	23.1	5.2
Previously divorced: [4] 1980.	100.0	0.2	7.7	21.7	24.1	27.7	17.3	1.4
1988.	100.0	0.1	4.3	15.6	21.8	35.3	21.3	1.6

[1] Includes marriage order not stated. [2] Excludes data for Iowa. [3] Includes remarriages of previously widowed. [4] Excludes remarriages in Michigan, Ohio, and South Carolina.

No. 130. Marriage Rates and Median Age of Bride and Groom, by Previous Marital Status: 1970 to 1988

[Data cover marriage registration area; see text, section 2. Beginning 1977, excludes Iowa. Figures for previously divorced and previously widowed exclude data for Michigan and Ohio for all years, for South Carolina beginning 1975, and for the District of Columbia for 1970. Based on a sample and subject to sampling variability; for details, see source. For definition of median, see Guide to Tabular Presentation. See also *Historical Statistics, Colonial Times to 1970*, series A 158-159]

YEAR	MARRIAGE RATES [1]						MEDIAN AGE AT MARRIAGE (years)					
	Women			Men			Women			Men		
	Single	Divorced	Wid-owed	Single	Divorced	Wid-owed	First mar-riage	Remarriage		First mar-riage	Remarriage	
								Divorced	Widowed		Divorced	Widowed
1970	93.4	123.3	10.2	80.4	204.5	40.6	20.6	30.1	51.2	22.5	34.5	58.7
1975	75.9	117.2	8.3	61.5	189.8	40.4	20.8	30.2	52.4	22.7	33.6	59.4
1977	69.2	107.3	7.6	56.7	173.4	35.3	21.1	30.2	53.1	23.0	33.6	60.1
1978	68.2	105.0	7.1	56.4	168.6	32.7	21.4	30.5	52.6	23.2	33.8	59.7
1979	67.8	104.0	7.7	56.3	165.6	35.3	21.6	30.8	55.2	23.4	33.9	61.7
1980	66.0	91.3	6.7	54.7	142.1	32.2	21.8	31.0	53.6	23.6	34.0	61.2
1981	64.9	96.3	6.5	53.8	150.8	30.8	22.0	31.2	53.6	23.9	34.4	61.0
1982	66.0	94.4	6.1	53.1	146.9	32.1	22.3	31.6	54.1	24.1	34.9	61.7
1983	63.8	91.6	6.2	51.8	142.1	30.7	22.5	32.0	54.0	24.4	35.3	62.0
1984	63.5	87.3	5.8	51.6	132.7	28.7	22.8	32.5	54.2	24.6	35.9	62.4
1985	61.5	81.8	5.7	50.1	121.6	27.7	23.0	32.8	54.6	24.8	36.1	62.7
1986	59.7	79.5	5.5	49.1	117.8	26.8	23.3	33.1	54.3	25.1	36.6	62.9
1987	58.9	80.7	5.4	48.8	115.7	26.1	23.6	33.3	53.9	25.3	36.7	62.8
1988	58.4	78.6	5.3	48.3	109.7	25.1	23.7	33.6	53.9	25.5	37.0	63.0

[1] Rate per 1,000 population 15 years old and over in specified group.
Source of tables 128-130: U.S. National Center for Health Statistics, *Vital Statistics of the United States*, annual; *Monthly Vital Statistics Report*; and unpublished data.

No. 131. First Marriage Dissolution and Years Until Remarriage for Women, by Race and Hispanic Origin: 1988

[For women 15 to 44 years old. Based on 1988 National Survey of Family Growth; see appendix III. Marriage dissolution includes death of spouse, separation because of marital discord, and divorce]

ITEM	Number (1,000)	YEARS UNTIL REMARRIAGE (cummulative percent)					
		All	1	2	3	4	5
ALL RACES [1]							
Year of dissolution of first marriage:							
All years	11,577	56.8	20.6	32.8	40.7	46.2	49.7
1980-84	3,504	47.5	16.3	28.1	36.4	[2]41.1	[2]45.4
1975-79	3,235	65.3	21.9	36.0	44.7	52.7	55.4
1970-74	1,887	83.2	24.9	38.6	47.9	56.4	61.2
1965-69	1,013	89.9	32.6	48.7	60.2	65.0	72.8
WHITE							
Year of dissolution of first marriage:							
All years	10,103	59.9	21.9	35.2	43.5	49.4	53.0
1980-84	3,030	51.4	18.2	31.1	40.3	[2]45.2	[2]49.8
1975-79	2,839	69.5	23.2	38.5	46.9	55.6	58.4
1970-74	1,622	87.5	24.9	39.8	49.8	59.3	64.3
1965-69	893	91.0	34.7	52.3	64.9	69.3	76.9
BLACK							
Year of dissolution of first marriage:							
All years	1,166	34.0	[3]10.9	[3]16.5	[3]19.6	[3]22.7	[3]25.0
1980-84	380	19.7	[3]4.7	[3]10.6	[3]12.9	[2]14.8	[2]14.8
1975-79	301	32.3	[3]11.4	[3]15.6	18.5	22.2	24.9
1970-74	227	59.0	[3]22.3	29.4	35.3	38.7	42.3
1965-69	98	81.2	[3]20.9	[3]27.3	[3]31.3	40.8	52.1
Hispanic, [4] all years	942	44.7	12.5	16.6	22.7	27.8	29.9

[1] Includes other races.   [2] The percent having remarried is biased downward because the women had not completed the indicated number of years since dissolution of first marriage at the time of the survey.   [3] Figure does not meet standard of reliability or precision.   [4] Hispanic persons may be of any race.
Source: National Center for Health Statistics, *Advance Data From Vital and Health Statistics*, No. 194.

No. 132. Divorces and Annulments—Median Duration of Marriage, Median Age at Divorce, and Children Involved: 1970 to 1988

[Data cover divorce-registration area; see text, section 2. Based on a sample and subject to sampling variability; for details, see source. Median age computed on data by single years of age. See also *Historical Statistics, Colonial Times to 1970*, series B 218]

DURATION OF MARRIAGE, AGE AT DIVORCE, AND CHILDREN INVOLVED	1970	1975	1980	1981	1982	1983	1984	1985	1986	1987	1988
Median duration of marriage (years)	6.7	6.5	6.8	7.0	7.0	7.0	6.9	6.8	6.9	7.0	7.1
Median age at divorce:											
Men (years)	32.9	32.2	32.7	33.1	33.6	34.0	34.3	34.4	34.6	34.9	35.1
Women (years)	29.8	29.5	30.3	30.6	31.1	31.5	31.7	31.9	32.1	32.5	32.6
Estimated number of children involved in divorce (1,000)	870	1,123	1,174	1,180	1,108	1,091	1,081	1,091	1,064	1,038	1,044
Avg. number of children per decree	1.22	1.08	0.98	0.97	0.94	0.94	0.92	0.92	0.90	0.89	0.89
Rate per 1,000 children under 18 years of age.	12.5	16.7	17.3	18.7	17.6	17.4	17.2	17.3	16.8	16.3	16.4

Source: U.S. National Center for Health Statistics, *Vital Statistics of the United States*, annual, *Monthly Vital Statistics Report*, and unpublished data.

No. 133. Cohabitation of Women, 15-44 Years Old, by Race and Hispanic Origin: 1988

[In percent, except where indicated. Based on the 1988 National Survey of Family Growth; see Appendix III. Cohabitation: not married but living with a partner or boyfriend]

ITEM	Total [1]	White	Black	Hispanic [2]
ALL WOMEN				
Number (1,000)	57,900	47,077	7,679	5,557
Ever married	63.6	66.8	47.1	62.1
Marital status:				
Married	50.3	54.0	28.6	45.2
Cohabiting [3]	5.2	5.4	4.6	6.9
Single:				
Never married	33.3	30.0	49.9	33.8
Separated	2.8	2.2	6.5	5.3
Divorced	7.8	7.7	9.5	7.8
Widowed	0.7	0.6	1.0	0.9
Occurence of cohabitation:				
Cohabited before first marriage [4]	25.4	25.0	29.3	25.5
Ever cohabited [5]	33.5	33.6	35.0	32.9
Outcome of first cohabitation:				
Intact cohabitation	10.0	10.3	9.2	12.6
Marriage	52.8	54.4	42.1	48.6
Intact	39.7	41.7	26.5	37.3
Dissolved	13.1	12.7	15.6	11.3
Dissolved cohabitation	37.2	35.3	48.7	38.8
WOMEN EVER-MARRIED				
Number (1,000)	36,842	31,465	3,614	3,452
Cohabited with first husband before marriage	25.7	24.9	31.7	24.0
Ever cohabited [5]	39.9	39.5	45.6	37.1

[1] Includes other races not shown separately.   [2] Hispanic persons may be of any race.   [3] Includes women who are separated, divorced, and widowed.   [4] Includes women who had cohabited but had not married.   [5] Includes women who cohabited sometime after their first marriage ended.
Source: U.S. National Center for Health Statistics, *Advance Data from Vital and Health Statistics*, No. 194, and unpublished data.

No. 134. Marriages and Divorces—Number and Rate, by State: 1980 to 1990

[By place of occurrence]

REGION, DIVISION, AND STATE	MARRIAGES [1] Number (1,000)			Rate per 1,000 population [2]			DIVORCES [3] Number (1,000)			Rate per 1,000 population [2]		
	1980	1985	1990, prel.	1980	1985	1990, prel.	1980	1985	1990, prel.	1980	1985	1990, prel.
U.S.	2,390.3	2,412.6	[4]2,448.0	10.6	10.1	[4]9.8	1,189.0	[5]1,190.0	[5]1,175.0	5.2	[5]5.0	[5]4.7
New England	106.3	114.3	112.2	8.6	9.0	8.5	49.0	49.9	44.0	4.0	3.9	3.4
Maine	12.0	12.2	11.8	10.7	10.5	9.5	6.2	6.1	5.3	5.5	5.2	4.3
New Hampshire	9.3	11.4	10.6	10.0	11.4	9.4	5.3	4.9	5.3	5.7	4.9	4.7
Vermont	5.2	5.5	6.1	10.2	10.4	10.7	2.6	2.4	2.6	5.1	4.4	4.5
Massachusetts	46.3	49.8	47.8	8.1	8.6	8.1	17.9	21.6	16.8	3.1	3.7	2.8
Rhode Island	7.5	8.0	8.1	7.9	8.3	8.1	3.6	3.7	3.8	3.8	3.8	3.7
Connecticut	26.0	27.3	27.8	8.4	8.6	8.6	13.5	11.2	10.3	4.3	3.5	3.2
Middle Atlantic	294.0	314.3	314.1	8.0	8.5	8.3	124.7	137.1	121.6	3.4	3.7	3.2
New York	144.5	164.0	169.3	8.2	9.2	9.4	62.0	67.6	57.9	3.5	3.8	3.2
New Jersey	55.8	61.2	58.0	7.6	8.1	7.5	27.8	29.3	23.6	3.8	3.9	3.0
Pennsylvania	93.7	89.1	86.8	7.9	7.5	7.2	34.9	40.2	40.1	2.9	3.4	3.3
East North Central . . .	395.5	[6]362.2	[7]267.4	9.5	[6]8.7	[7]8.7	212.4	[6]192.6	[7]109.0	5.1	[6]4.6	[7]4.3
Ohio	99.8	[6]94.4	95.8	9.2	[6]8.8	8.7	58.8	[6]53.0	51.0	5.4	[6]4.9	4.7
Indiana	57.9	51.1	54.3	10.5	9.3	9.6	[8]40.0	[8]35.3	(NA)	[8]7.3	[8]6.4	(NA)
Illinois	109.8	97.7	(NA)	9.6	8.5	(NA)	51.0	48.9	(NA)	4.5	4.2	(NA)
Michigan	86.9	79.0	76.1	9.4	8.7	8.2	45.0	38.8	40.2	4.9	4.3	4.3
Wisconsin	41.1	40.0	41.2	8.7	8.4	8.4	17.5	16.6	17.8	3.7	3.5	3.6
West North Central . .	173.7	158.3	156.1	10.1	9.0	8.7	79.6	74.3	76.9	4.6	4.2	4.3
Minnesota	37.6	35.1	33.7	9.2	8.4	7.7	15.4	14.8	15.4	3.8	3.5	3.5
Iowa	27.5	24.6	24.8	9.4	8.5	8.7	11.9	10.5	11.1	4.1	3.7	3.9
Missouri	54.6	49.5	49.3	11.1	9.8	9.5	27.6	25.0	26.4	5.6	5.0	5.1
North Dakota	6.1	5.4	4.8	9.3	7.9	7.3	2.1	2.3	2.3	3.3	3.4	3.6
South Dakota	8.8	7.8	7.7	12.7	11.0	10.8	2.8	2.6	2.6	4.1	3.6	3.7
Nebraska	14.2	12.7	12.5	9.1	7.9	7.7	6.4	6.4	6.5	4.1	4.0	4.0
Kansas	24.8	23.3	23.4	10.5	9.5	9.2	13.4	12.8	12.6	5.7	5.2	5.0
South Atlantic	413.1	438.8	455.4	11.2	10.9	10.4	206.3	210.5	226.6	5.6	5.2	5.2
Delaware	4.4	5.4	5.6	7.5	8.6	8.2	2.3	3.0	3.0	3.9	4.8	4.4
Maryland	46.3	46.1	46.1	11.0	10.5	9.7	17.5	16.2	16.1	4.1	3.7	3.4
Dist. of Columbia . . .	5.2	5.0	4.7	8.1	8.1	7.9	4.7	2.7	3.3	7.3	4.3	5.5
Virginia	60.2	66.5	71.3	11.3	11.7	11.5	23.6	24.1	27.3	4.4	4.2	4.4
West Virginia	17.4	14.6	13.2	8.9	7.5	7.2	10.3	9.9	9.7	5.3	5.1	5.3
North Carolina	46.7	50.5	52.1	7.9	8.1	7.8	28.1	30.2	34.0	4.8	4.8	5.1
South Carolina	53.9	52.8	55.8	17.3	15.8	15.7	13.6	13.5	16.1	4.4	4.0	4.5
Georgia	70.6	72.3	64.4	12.9	12.1	9.8	34.7	33.4	35.7	6.4	5.6	5.5
Florida	108.3	125.5	142.3	11.1	11.0	10.9	71.6	77.5	81.7	7.3	6.8	6.3
East South Central . . .	[6]168.8	171.8	185.5	[6]11.5	11.4	12.0	[6]87.5	[6]86.2	93.8	[6]6.0	[6]5.7	6.1
Kentucky	[6]32.7	46.0	51.3	[6]8.9	12.3	13.8	[6]16.7	18.3	21.8	[6]4.6	4.9	5.8
Tennessee	59.2	55.0	66.6	12.9	11.5	13.4	30.2	29.9	32.3	6.6	6.3	6.5
Alabama	49.0	46.1	43.3	12.6	11.5	10.5	26.7	25.0	25.3	6.9	6.2	6.1
Mississippi	27.9	24.8	24.3	11.1	9.5	9.3	13.8	[6]13.0	14.4	5.2	[6]5.0	5.5
West South Central . .	298.2	308.6	292.9	12.6	11.6	10.8	[6]155.0	[6]160.9	[7]136.8	[6]6.5	(NA)	[7]6.0
Arkansas	26.5	31.7	35.7	11.6	13.4	14.8	[6]15.9	[6]16.5	16.8	[6]6.9	[6]7.0	6.9
Louisiana	43.5	39.4	41.2	10.3	8.8	9.4	[6]18.1	[6]17.6	(NA)	[6]4.3	(NA)	(NA)
Oklahoma	46.5	35.9	33.2	15.4	10.9	10.3	24.2	26.4	24.9	8.0	8.0	7.7
Texas	181.8	201.6	182.8	12.8	12.3	10.7	96.8	100.4	95.1	6.8	6.1	5.5
Mountain	241.7	233.7	[7]127.6	21.3	18.3	[7]10.2	86.1	89.9	87.0	7.6	7.0	6.3
Montana	8.3	7.2	7.0	10.6	8.7	8.7	4.9	4.3	4.1	6.3	5.2	5.1
Idaho	13.4	12.3	15.0	14.2	12.2	14.6	6.6	6.2	6.6	7.0	6.2	6.5
Wyoming	6.9	5.4	4.8	14.6	10.6	10.3	4.0	3.8	3.1	8.5	7.5	6.6
Colorado	34.9	33.6	31.5	12.1	10.4	9.4	18.6	19.2	18.4	6.4	5.9	5.5
New Mexico	16.6	[9]15.5	13.2	12.8	[9]10.7	8.5	10.4	[10]13.2	7.7	8.0	[10]9.1	4.9
Arizona	30.2	35.7	37.0	11.1	11.2	10.2	19.9	21.2	25.1	7.3	6.6	6.9
Utah	17.0	17.5	19.0	11.6	10.6	11.0	7.8	8.8	8.8	5.3	5.3	5.1
Nevada	114.3	106.5	(NA)	142.8	113.7	(NA)	13.8	13.3	13.3	17.3	14.2	11.4
Pacific	298.8	310.6	334.4	9.4	8.9	8.5	187.9	188.5	[7]52.7	5.9	5.4	[7]5.6
Washington	47.7	43.8	48.6	11.6	9.9	10.0	28.6	26.3	28.8	6.9	6.0	5.9
Oregon	23.0	22.4	25.2	8.7	8.3	8.8	17.8	15.7	15.9	6.7	5.9	5.5
California [11]	210.9	222.8	236.7	8.9	8.5	7.9	133.5	[12]137.5	(NA)	5.6	[12]5.2	(NA)
Alaska	5.4	6.2	5.7	13.3	11.8	10.8	3.5	4.0	2.9	8.8	7.7	5.5
Hawaii	11.9	15.4	18.1	12.3	14.7	16.1	4.4	4.9	5.2	4.6	4.6	4.6

NA Not available. [1] Data are counts of marriages performed, except as noted. [2] Based on total population residing in area; population enumerated as of April 1 for 1980; estimated as of July 1 for all other years. [3] Includes annulments. [4] Estimate for United States is based on monthly reports adjusted for observed differences from final monthly figures. State figures are not adjusted in this manner. [5] Estimated. [6] Data are incomplete. [7] Excludes figures for States shown below as not available. [8] Includes divorce petitions filed for some counties. [9] Premarital health forms issued. [10] Divorce petitions filed. [11] Marriage data include nonlicensed marriages registered. [12] Data include legal separations.

Source: U.S. National Center for Health Statistics, *Vital Statistics of the United States*, annual; and *Monthly Vital Statistics Reports*.

Figure 3.1
Personal Health Care Expenses: 1970 to 1990

1970
1980
1990

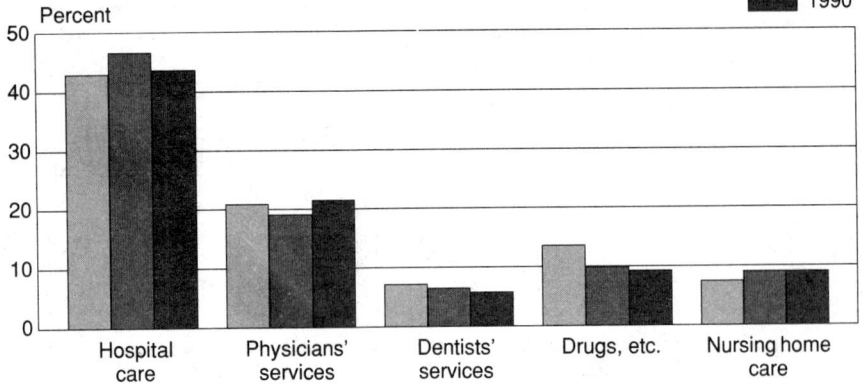

Figure 3.2
**Consumer Price Indexes—
Medical Services: 1970 to 1991**

1970
1980
1991

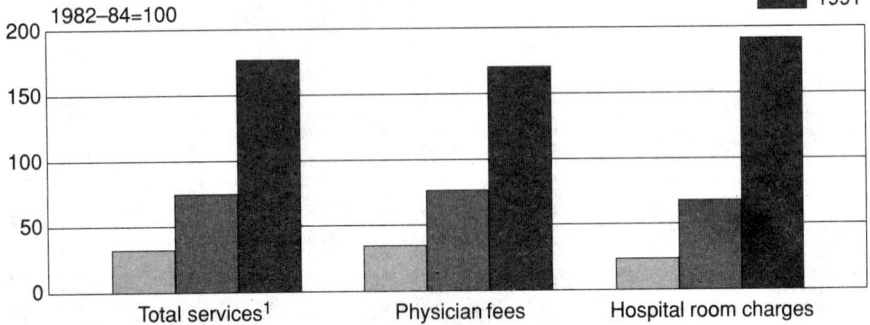

[1]Includes other medical care services.

Figure 3.3
**Per Capita Meat Consumption,
by Selected Products: 1970 to 1990**

1970
1980
1990

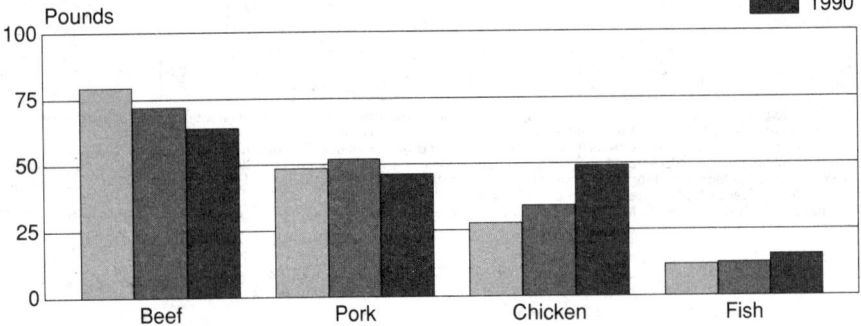

Source: Charts prepared by U.S. Bureau of the Census.
For figure 3.1 data, see table 137; figure 3.2 data, see table 151; figure 3.3 data, see table 205.

Health and Nutrition

This section presents statistics on health expenditures and insurance coverage, including Medicare and Medicaid; medical personnel; hospitals; nursing homes and other care facilities; incidence of acute and prevalence of chronic conditions; nutritional intake of the population; and food consumption. Summary statistics showing recent trends on health care and discussions of selected health issues are published annually by the U.S. National Center for Health Statistics (NCHS) in *Health, United States.* Data on national health expenditures, medical costs, and insurance coverage are compiled by the U.S. Health Care Financing Administration (HCFA) and appear in the quarterly *Health Care Financing Review* and in the *Annual Medicare Program Statistics* series. Statistics on health insurance are also collected by NCHS and are published in series 10 of *Vital and Health Statistics.* The Census Bureau also publishes data on insurance coverage in *Current Population Reports,* series P-70. Statistics on health facilities are collected by NCHS and are published in series 14 of *Vital and Health Statistics.* Statistics on hospitals are published annually by the American Hospital Association, Chicago, IL, in *Hospital Statistics.* Primary sources for data on nutrition are the quarterly *National Food Review* and the annual *Food Consumption, Prices, and Expenditures,* both issued by the U.S. Department of Agriculture. NCHS also conducts periodic surveys of nutrient levels in the population and clinical signs of malnutrition.

National health expenditures.—HCFA compiles estimates of national health expenditures (NHE) to measure spending for health care in the United States. With the publication of the 1988 estimates, major revisions to the NHE back to 1960 have been incorporated into the accounts. The NHE accounts are structured to show spending by type of expenditure (i.e., hospital care, physician care, dental care, and other professional care; home health; drugs and other medical nondurables; vision products and other medical durables; nursing home care and other personal health expenditures; plus nonpersonal health expenditures for such items as public health, research, construction of medical

In Brief	
In 1990:	
34 million with no health insurance.	
Hospital surgeries— percent outpatient:	
1980	*16*
1990	*51*
Per capita consumption of chicken:	
1980	*34 pounds*
1990	*49 pounds*

facilities, and administration) and by source of funding (e.g., private health insurance, out-of-pocket payments, and a range of public programs including Medicare, Medicaid, and those operated by the Department of Veterans Affairs (VA)).

In all cases except private insurance (HCFA conducts its own survey of part of the health insurance industry), data used to estimate health expenditures come from existing sources which are tabulated for other purposes. The type of expenditure estimates rely upon statistics produced by such groups as the American Hospital Association, the Internal Revenue Service, the Department of Commerce, and the Department of Health and Human Services (HHS). Source of funding estimates are constructed using administrative and statistical records from the Medicare and Medicaid programs, the Department of Defense and VA medical programs, the Social Security Administration, Census Bureau's *Governmental Finances,* State and local governments, other HHS agencies, and other nongovernment sources. Detailed descriptions of sources and methods, along with the most recent analysis of health care expenditure estimates, are published in the *Health Care Financing Review's* annual article on national health expenditures.

Medicare and Medicaid.—Since July 1966, the Federal Medicare program has provided two coordinated plans for nearly all people age 65 and over: (1) A hospital insurance plan which covers hospital and related services and (2) a voluntary supplementary medical insurance plan, financed partially by monthly premiums paid by participants, which partly covers physicians' and related medical services. Such insurance also applies, since July 1973, to disabled beneficiaries of any age after 24 months of entitlement to cash benefits under the social security or railroad retirement programs and to persons with end stage renal disease.

Under Medicaid, all States (except Arizona) offer basic health services to certain very poor people: Individuals who are pregnant, aged, disabled or blind, and families with dependent children. Medicaid eligibility is automatic for almost all cash welfare recipients in these States. Thirty-one States also extend Medicaid to certain other persons who qualify, except for incomes above regular eligibility levels; those persons include those who have medical expenses which, when subtracted from their income, spend down to a State "medically needy" level or those who meet the higher "medically needy" income restrictions. Within Federal guidelines, each State determines its own Medicaid eligibility criteria and the health services to be provided under Medicaid. The cost of providing Medicaid services is jointly shared by the Federal Government and the States.

Health resources.—Hospital statistics based on data from the American Hospital Association's yearly survey are published annually in *Hospital Statistics,* and cover all hospitals accepted for registration by the Association. To be accepted for registration, a hospital must meet certain requirements relating to number of beds, construction, equipment, medical and nursing staff, patient care, clinical records, surgical and obstetrical facilities, diagnostic and treatment facilities, laboratory services, etc. Data obtained from NCHS cover all U.S. hospitals which meet certain criteria for inclusion. The criteria are published in *Vital and Health Statistics* reports, series 13. NCHS defines a hospital as a non-Federal short-term general or special facility with six or more inpatient beds with an average stay of less than 60 days.

Statistics on the demographic characteristics of persons employed in the health occupations are compiled by the U.S. Bureau of Labor Statistics and reported in *Employment and Earnings* (monthly) (see table 629, section 13). Data based on surveys of health personnel and utilization of health facilities providing long-term care, ambulatory care, and hospital care are presented in NCHS series 13 and series 14, *Data on Health Resources Utilization* and *Data on Health Resources: Manpower and Facilities.* Statistics on patient visits to health care providers, as reported in health interviews, appear in NCHS series 10, *National Health Interview Survey Data.*

The HCFA's *Health Care Financing Review* and *Health Care Financing Program Statistics* present data for hospitals and nursing homes as well as extended care facilities and home health agencies. These data are based on records of the Medicare program and differ from those of other sources because they are limited to facilities meeting Federal eligibility standards for participation in Medicare.

Data on patients in hospitals for the mentally ill and on mental health facilities are collected by the National Institute of Mental Health (NIMH) and appear in *Mental Health, U.S.,* the *Mental Health Statistics* reports, (series CN), and the Mental Health Statistical Note series.

Disability and illness.—General health statistics, including morbidity, disability, injuries, preventive care, and findings from physiological testing are collected by NCHS in its National Health Interview Survey and its National Health and Nutrition Examination Surveys and appear in *Vital and Health Statistics,* series 10 and 11, respectively. The Department of Labor compiles statistics on industrial injuries (see section 13). Annual incidence data on notifiable diseases are compiled by the Public Health Service (PHS) at its Centers for Disease Control in Atlanta, Georgia, and are published as a supplement to its *Morbidity and Mortality Weekly Report.* The list of diseases is revised annually and includes those which, by mutual agreement of the States and PHS, are communicable diseases of national importance.

Nutrition.—Statistics on annual per capita consumption of food and its nutrient value are estimated by the U.S. Department of Agriculture and published quarterly in *National Food Review.* Historical data can be found in *Food Consumption, Prices, and Expenditures,* issued annually.

Statistical reliability.—For discussion of statistical collection, estimation, and sampling procedures and measures of reliability applicable to data from NCHS and HCFA, see Appendix III.

Historical statistics.—Tabular headnotes provide cross-references, where applicable, to *Historical Statistics of the United States, Colonial Times to 1970.* See Appendix IV.

No. 135. National Health Expenditures: 1960 to 1990

[Includes Puerto Rico and outlying areas]

YEAR	TOTAL[1]			HEALTH SERVICES AND SUPPLIES						
				Private				Public		
				Out-of-pocket payments			Insurance premiums[4] (bil.dol.)		Medical payments	
	Total (bil.dol.)	Per capita (dol.)	Percent of GNP[2]	Total[3] (bil.dol.)	Total (bil.dol.)	Percent of total private		Total (bil.dol.)	Medicare (bil. dol.)	Public assistance (bil. dol.)
1960	27.1	143	5.3	19.8	13.3	67.5	5.9	5.7	–	0.5
1965	41.6	204	5.9	29.9	19.0	63.7	10.0	8.3	–	1.7
1970	74.4	346	7.3	44.1	25.6	58.0	16.7	24.9	7.6	6.3
1971	82.3	379	7.5	48.2	27.1	56.2	19.1	28.2	8.5	7.7
1972	92.3	421	7.6	54.0	29.8	55.2	21.9	31.8	9.3	8.9
1973	102.5	464	7.5	59.9	32.9	54.8	24.6	35.9	10.7	10.2
1974	116.1	521	7.9	66.1	35.6	53.8	27.8	42.8	13.5	11.9
1975	132.9	592	8.3	74.5	38.5	51.8	32.9	50.2	16.4	14.5
1976	152.2	672	8.5	86.3	42.5	49.2	39.7	56.9	19.8	16.4
1977	172.0	753	8.6	98.6	46.3	46.9	47.8	64.6	22.8	18.8
1978	193.7	839	8.6	110.4	50.2	45.5	55.0	73.6	26.8	20.9
1979	217.2	932	8.7	123.2	54.1	43.9	63.2	84.1	31.1	24.0
1980	250.1	1,063	9.2	140.7	59.5	42.3	73.4	98.1	37.5	28.0
1981	290.2	1,221	9.5	163.3	67.2	41.1	86.9	114.2	45.2	32.6
1982	326.1	1,358	10.3	185.2	74.2	40.1	100.5	127.0	52.6	34.5
1983	358.6	1,479	10.5	204.1	81.4	39.9	111.4	139.5	59.9	37.9
1984	389.6	1,592	10.3	223.3	87.7	39.3	123.7	150.8	65.9	40.7
1985	422.6	1,710	10.5	241.9	94.4	39.0	134.1	165.4	72.2	44.6
1986	454.8	1,822	10.7	258.5	100.9	39.0	143.2	180.3	77.4	48.3
1987	494.1	1,961	10.9	279.1	108.8	39.0	154.8	197.7	83.4	53.9
1988	546.0	2,146	11.2	311.0	119.3	38.4	174.4	215.1	90.5	58.2
1989	602.8	2,346	11.6	342.1	126.1	36.9	196.4	240.0	102.6	65.9
1990	666.2	2,566	12.2	374.8	136.1	36.3	216.8	268.6	111.2	79.4

– Represents zero. [1] Includes medical research and medical facilities construction. [2] GNP=Gross national product; see table 676. [3] Includes other sources of funds not shown separately. [4] See footnote 2, table 136.
Source: U. S. Health Care Financing Administration, *Health Care Financing Review,* fall 1991.

No. 136. National Health Expenditures, by Type: 1970 to 1990

[In millions of dollars, except percent. Includes Puerto Rico and outlying areas. See also *Historical Statistics, Colonial Times to 1970*, series B 248-261]

TYPE OF EXPENDITURE	1970	1980	1984	1985	1986	1987	1988	1989	1990
Total	74,377	250,126	389,637	422,619	454,814	494,098	546,014	602,792	666,187
Average annual percent change [1] ..	12.3	13.5	8.7	8.5	7.6	8.6	10.5	10.4	10.5
Private expenditures.	46,703	144,966	230,025	247,851	264,586	285,734	318,874	350,237	383,567
Health services and supplies	44,148	140,736	223,344	241,863	258,544	279,080	311,036	342,055	374,758
Out-of-pocket payments	25,606	59,500	87,711	94,390	100,913	108,823	119,293	126,087	136,108
Insurance premiums [2]	16,743	73,407	123,744	134,060	143,167	154,760	174,426	196,418	216,828
Other	1,798	7,829	11,889	13,413	14,464	15,497	17,318	19,550	21,822
Medical research	215	274	493	501	714	725	744	779	827
Medical facilities construction......	2,341	3,956	6,188	5,488	5,328	5,929	7,094	7,402	7,982
Public expenditures	27,674	105,159	159,612	174,768	190,228	208,364	227,140	252,555	282,620
Percent Federal of public	64.1	68.4	70.6	70.7	69.9	69.1	69.0	69.3	69.1
Health services and supplies	24,908	98,114	150,838	165,361	180,311	197,745	215,133	240,045	268,623
Medicare [3]	7,633	37,533	65,917	72,161	77,383	83,402	90,525	102,590	111,195
Public assistance medical payments [4]	6,310	28,007	40,721	44,585	48,276	53,870	58,185	65,908	79,358
Temporary disability insurance [5].	66	52	55	55	55	57	62	67	72
Workers' compensation (medical) [5] .	1,409	5,177	6,971	8,036	9,069	10,757	12,353	13,935	15,553
Defense Dept. hospital, medical....	1,784	4,346	6,624	7,634	8,427	9,303	9,766	10,404	11,513
Maternal, child health programs....	425	892	1,103	1,262	1,434	1,607	1,694	1,814	1,913
Public health activities	1,385	7,219	10,794	12,306	13,486	14,600	16,571	18,293	19,318
Veterans' hospital, medical care ...	1,764	5,934	8,382	8,613	9,087	9,620	10,011	10,647	11,390
Medical vocational rehabilitation....	158	298	385	401	425	468	500	525	555
State and local hospitals [6]	3,173	5,589	6,717	7,030	9,119	10,336	11,443	12,093	13,012
Other [7]	803	3,067	3,169	3,282	3,550	3,725	4,024	3,768	4,742
Medical research	1,741	5,170	6,626	7,294	7,826	8,304	9,596	10,268	11,537
Medical facilities construction......	1,025	1,875	2,148	2,112	2,092	2,315	2,411	2,242	2,460

[1] Change from prior year shown; for 1970, change from 1965. For explanation of average annual percent change, see Guide to Tabular Presentation. [2] Covers insurance benefits and amount retained by insurance companies for expenses, additions to reserves, and profits (net cost of insurance). [3] Represents expenditures for benefits and administrative cost from Federal hospital and medical insurance trust funds under old-age, survivors, disability, and health insurance programs; see text, section 12. [4] Payments made directly to suppliers of medical care (primarily Medicaid). [5] Includes medical benefits paid under public law by private insurance carriers and self-insurers. [6] Expenditures not offset by other revenues. [7] Covers expenditures for Alcohol, Drug Abuse, and Mental Health Administration; Indian Health Service; school health and other programs.

Source: U.S. Health Care Financing Administration, *Health Care Financing Review*, fall 1991.

No. 137. National Health Expenditures, by Object: 1970 to 1990

[See headnote, table 136. See also *Historical Statistics, Colonial Times to 1970*, series B 221-235]

OBJECT OF EXPENDITURE	EXPENDITURE (bil.dol.)							PERCENT		
	1970	1980	1985	1987	1988	1989	1990	1970	1980	1990
Total	74.4	250.1	422.6	494.1	546.0	602.8	666.2	100.0	100.0	100.0
Spent by—										
Consumers	42.3	132.9	228.5	263.6	293.7	322.5	352.9	56.9	53.1	53.0
Government.................	27.7	105.2	174.8	208.4	227.1	252.6	282.6	37.2	42.0	42.4
Other [1]	4.4	12.1	19.4	22.2	25.2	27.7	30.6	5.9	4.8	4.6
Spent for—										
Health services and supplies..........	69.1	238.9	407.2	476.8	526.2	582.1	643.4	92.8	95.5	96.6
Personal health care expenses........	64.9	219.4	369.7	439.3	482.8	529.9	585.3	87.3	87.7	87.9
Hospital care	27.9	102.4	168.3	194.2	212.0	232.6	256.0	37.6	40.9	38.4
Physicians' services...........	13.6	41.9	74.0	93.0	105.1	113.6	125.7	18.3	16.7	18.9
Dentists' services	4.7	14.4	23.3	27.1	29.4	31.6	34.0	6.3	5.7	5.1
Other professional services [2].	1.5	8.7	16.6	21.1	23.8	27.1	31.6	2.0	3.5	4.7
Home health care	0.1	1.3	3.8	4.1	4.5	5.6	6.9	0.2	0.5	1.0
Drugs/other medical nondurables ...	8.8	21.6	36.2	43.2	46.3	50.6	54.6	11.8	8.6	8.2
Vision products/other med. durables [3]	2.0	4.6	7.1	9.1	10.1	11.4	12.1	2.7	1.8	1.8
Nursing home care	4.9	20.0	34.1	39.7	42.8	47.7	53.1	6.5	8.0	8.0
Other health services	1.4	4.6	6.4	7.8	8.7	9.7	11.3	1.8	1.8	1.7
Net cost of insurance and admin. [4]	2.8	12.2	25.2	22.9	26.8	33.9	38.7	3.7	4.9	5.8
Government public health activities	1.4	7.2	12.3	14.6	16.6	18.3	19.3	1.9	2.9	2.9
Medical research	2.0	5.4	7.8	9.0	10.3	11.0	12.4	2.6	2.2	1.9
Medical facilities construction	3.4	5.8	7.6	8.2	9.5	9.6	10.4	4.5	2.3	1.6

[1] Includes nonpatient revenues, privately funded construction, and industrial inplant. [2] Includes services of registered and practical nurses in private duty, visiting nurses, podiatrists, optometrists, physical therapists, clinical psychologists, chiropractors, naturopaths, and Christian Science practitioners. [3] Includes expenditures for eyeglasses, hearing aids, orthopedic appliances, artificial limbs, crutches, wheelchairs, etc. [4] Includes administrative expenses of federally financed health programs.

Source: U.S. Health Care Financing Administration, *Health Care Financing Review*, fall 1991.

No. 138. Health Services and Supplies—Per Capita National and Private Consumer Expenditures, by Object: 1970 to 1990

[In dollars, except percent. Based on Social Security Administration estimates of total U.S. population as of July 1, including Armed Forces and Federal employees abroad and civilian population of outlying areas. Excludes research and construction. See also *Historical Statistics, Colonial Times to 1970*, series B 222-232]

OBJECT OF EXPENDITURE	1970	1975	1980	1984	1985	1986	1987	1988	1989	1990
Total, national	321	555	1,015	1,529	1,648	1,759	1,892	2,068	2,265	2,479
Average annual percent change [1]	11.4	11.5	14.1	7.9	7.8	6.7	7.6	9.3	9.5	9.4
Hospital care	130	233	435	643	681	720	771	833	905	986
Physicians' services	63	104	178	274	299	329	369	413	442	484
Dentists' services	22	37	61	87	94	99	108	116	123	131
Other professional services [2]	7	16	37	61	67	75	84	93	105	122
Home health care	1	2	6	14	16	16	16	18	22	27
Drugs and other medical nondurables	41	58	92	137	146	159	171	182	197	210
Vision products and other medical durables [2]	9	14	19	25	29	32	36	40	45	47
Nursing home care	23	44	85	127	138	147	157	168	186	205
Other health services	6	12	19	24	26	28	31	34	38	44
Net cost of insurance and administration [2]	13	23	52	90	102	98	91	105	132	149
Government public health activities	6	14	31	44	50	54	58	65	71	74
Total, private consumer [3]	197	318	565	864	924	978	1,046	1,154	1,255	1,360
Hospital care	56	100	182	266	276	288	309	340	371	394
Physicians' services	49	75	124	188	202	218	244	275	288	315
Dentists' services	21	35	58	85	92	97	105	113	120	128
Other professional services [2]	5	10	26	43	46	51	58	65	72	83
Home health care	-	-	1	3	3	3	3	3	4	5
Drugs and other medical nondurables	39	54	85	126	134	145	155	164	177	187
Vision products and other medical durables [2]	9	13	17	20	23	25	28	31	35	36
Nursing home care	11	19	38	62	68	74	77	83	83	94
Net cost of insurance	7	14	35	71	81	78	68	80	104	118

- Represents or rounds to zero.   [1] Change from prior year shown; for 1970, change from 1965. For explanation of average annual percent change, see Guide to Tabular Presentation.   [2] See footnotes for corresponding objects in table 137.   [3] Represents out-of-pocket payments and private health insurance.
Source: U.S. Health Care Financing Administration, *Health Care Financing Review*, fall 1991.

No. 139. Personal Health Care—Third Party Payments and Private Consumer Expenditures: 1970 to 1990

[In billions of dollars, except percent. See headnote, table 140]

ITEM	1970	1975	1980	1984	1985	1986	1987	1988	1989	1990
Personal health care expenditures	64.9	116.6	219.4	341.2	369.7	400.8	439.3	482.8	529.9	585.3
Third party payments, total	39.3	78.0	159.9	253.5	275.3	299.9	330.5	363.5	403.8	449.2
Percent of personal health care	60.5	66.9	72.9	74.3	74.5	74.8	75.2	75.3	76.2	76.7
Private insurance payments	15.2	29.9	65.3	106.3	114.0	123.8	137.7	154.1	169.6	186.1
Government expenditures	22.4	45.3	87.1	135.7	148.4	162.1	177.8	192.6	215.2	241.8
Other [1]	1.7	2.9	7.6	11.4	12.9	14.0	15.0	16.8	19.0	21.3
Private consumer expenditures [2]	40.8	68.4	124.8	194.0	208.4	224.7	246.5	273.4	295.7	322.2
Percent met by private insurance	37.2	43.7	52.3	54.8	54.7	55.1	55.9	56.4	57.4	57.8
Hospital care	12.1	22.4	42.8	65.0	68.3	71.8	77.8	86.6	95.3	102.2
Percent met by private insurance	79.2	80.4	87.5	87.5	87.1	88.1	88.8	87.1	87.3	87.5
Physicians' services	10.6	16.8	29.2	46.0	49.8	54.5	61.5	70.0	74.1	81.7
Percent met by private insurance	45.1	54.5	61.5	65.9	67.7	68.7	69.1	70.2	71.3	71.2

[1] Includes nonpatient revenues and industrial inplant health services.   [2] Includes expenditures not shown separately. Represents out-of-pocket payments and private health insurance benefits. Excludes net cost of insurance.
Source: U.S. Health Care Financing Administration, *Health Care Financing Review*, fall 1991.

No. 140. Personal Health Care Expenditures, by Object and Source of Payment: 1990

[In millions of dollars, except as indicated. Includes Puerto Rico and outlying areas. Covers all expenditures for health services and supplies, except net cost of insurance and administration, government public health activities, and expenditures of philanthropic agencies for fund raising activities]

SOURCE	Total	Hospital care	Physicians' services	Dentiots' services	Other professional services [1]	Home health care	Drugs and other medical nondurables	Vision products and other medical durables [1]	Nursing home care	Other personal health care
Total	585,328	256,009	125,655	33,985	31,608	6,918	54,566	12,138	53,146	11,302
Out of pocket payments	136,108	12,821	23,497	18,000	8,761	837	40,154	8,175	23,863	-
Third party payments	449,220	243,188	102,158	15,985	22,847	6,081	14,412	3,963	29,283	11,302
Private health insurance	186,132	89,391	58,166	15,132	12,762	502	8,341	1,262	576	-
Government	241,819	139,972	43,944	853	6,449	5,087	6,071	2,701	27,689	9,052
Other [2]	21,268	13,824	48	-	3,635	493	-	-	1,018	2,250
Private [3]	343,508	116,037	81,711	33,132	25,158	1,831	48,495	9,437	25,458	2,250

- Represents or rounds to zero.   [1] See footnotes for corresponding objects on table 137.   [2] Includes nonpatient revenues and industrial inplant.   [3] Covers out-of-pocket payments, private health insurance, nonpatient revenues and industrial inplant.
Source: U.S. Health Care Financing Administration, *Health Care Financing Review*, fall 1991.

No. 141. Government Expenditures for Health Services and Supplies: 1980 and 1990

[In millions of dollars, except percent. Includes Puerto Rico and outlying areas. Excludes medical research and construction]

YEAR AND TYPE OF SERVICE	TOTAL [1]		FEDERAL		State and local	Medi- care [2] (OASDHI)	Public assis- tance [3]	OTHER HEALTH SERVICES		
	Amount	Percent distribu- tion	Total	Percent of total				Vet- erans	Defense Dept. [4]	Workers' compen- sation [5]
1980, total [1]	**98,114**	**100.0**	**66,762**	**68.0**	**31,352**	**37,533**	**28,007**	**5,934**	**4,346**	**5,177**
Hospital care.	54,599	55.6	41,344	75.7	13,255	26,373	10,933	4,918	3,737	2,007
Physicians' services	12,626	12.9	9,668	76.6	2,959	7,948	2,424	59	261	1,667
Nursing home care.	10,525	10.7	6,139	58.3	4,386	411	9,752	361	-	-
Drugs and other medical nondurables.	1,661	1.7	819	49.3	842	-	1,536	13	13	78
Administration	3,839	3.9	2,063	53.7	1,776	1,118	1,318	49	37	1,225
Public health activities. . .	7,219	7.4	1,246	17.3	5,973	-	-	-	-	-
1990, total [1]	**268,623**	**100.0**	**184,335**	**68.6**	**84,287**	**111,195**	**79,358**	**11,390**	**11,513**	**15,553**
Hospital care.	139,972	52.1	104,625	74.7	35,347	68,333	31,119	9,516	9,112	7,388
Physicians' services	43,944	16.4	35,141	80.0	8,803	29,985	5,742	114	1,450	6,156
Nursing home care.	27,689	10.3	17,166	62.0	10,522	2,473	24,174	1,041	-	-
Drugs and other medical nondurables.	6,071	2.3	3,000	49.4	3,072	-	5,654	9	83	289
Administration	7,485	2.8	4,772	63.8	2,284	2,284	3,835	37	165	985
Public health activities. . .	19,318	7.2	2,339	12.1	16,979	-	-	-	-	-

- Represents zero. [1] Includes other items not shown separately. [2] Covers hospital and medical insurance payments and administrative costs under old-age, survivors, disability and health insurance program. [3] Covers Medicaid and other medical public assistance. Includes funds paid into Medicare trust fund by States to cover premiums for public assistance recipients and medically indigent persons. [4] Includes care for retirees and military dependents. [5] Medical benefits.

Source: U.S. Health Care Financing Administration, *Health Care Financing Review*, fall 1991.

No. 142. Expenditures for Health Services and Supplies, by Type of Payer: 1970 to 1990

[In billions of dollars]

TYPE OF PAYER	1970	1975	1980	1983	1984	1985	1986	1987	1988	1989	1990
Total expenditures	69.1	124.7	238.9	343.6	374.2	407.2	438.9	476.8	526.2	582.1	643.4
Private.	50.1	86.2	162.1	233.5	256.1	278.9	302.9	327.2	362.8	397.5	430.4
Business	15.1	28.8	64.8	97.9	105.0	115.0	127.3	133.6	153.1	169.7	186.2
Contribution of private health insurance premiums	11.2	20.9	48.4	74.2	78.6	85.4	93.6	96.7	112.9	125.7	139.1
Households [1]	33.6	54.9	90.3	125.4	140.5	152.0	162.7	179.8	194.3	210.3	224.7
Contribution of private health insurance premiums	4.6	8.9	16.2	21.1	26.4	28.4	28.9	35.3	34.9	39.2	42.6
Out-of-pocket spending	25.6	38.5	59.5	81.4	87.7	94.4	100.9	108.8	119.3	126.1	136.1
Non-patient revenues [2]	1.5	2.5	7.0	10.2	10.6	12.0	12.9	13.8	15.4	17.5	19.6
Public.	18.9	38.5	76.7	110.1	118.1	128.3	135.9	149.6	163.4	184.6	212.9
Federal government.	10.4	21.3	42.5	60.0	63.4	69.0	70.4	77.3	84.2	96.2	113.9
State/local government	8.5	17.2	34.2	50.1	54.7	59.3	65.5	72.3	79.1	88.4	99.1

[1] Includes other items not shown separately. [2] Includes philanthropy.

Source: U.S. Health Care Financing Administration, *Health Care Financing Review*, winter 1991.

No. 143. Benefit Expenditures of Private Health Insurance Organizations: 1970 to 1987

[In millions of dollars]

TYPE OF PLAN	1970	1980	1982	1983	1984	1985	1986	1987			
								Total	Hos- pital care	Physi- cians serv- ices	Dental care and other
Total	**15,320**	**67,504**	**89,929**	**97,990**	**105,280**	**111,994**	**124,622**	**139,090**	**73,589**	**43,392**	**22,109**
Blue Cross-Blue Shield . .	7,060	25,467	32,144	34,398	35,522	37,290	41,258	44,525	27,913	11,874	4,738
Insurance companies . . .	7,104	25,774	36,424	40,109	41,547	42,680	45,810	51,549	26,892	16,675	7,982
Independent plans	1,156	16,264	21,360	23,483	28,211	32,024	37,554	43,016	18,783	14,843	9,390

Source: U.S. Health Care Financing Administration, *Health Care Financing Review*, winter 1988, and unpublished data.

No. 144. Medicare Program—Enrollment and Payments: 1970 to 1990

[Enrollment as of **July 1**; payments for calendar year. Benefit payments represent trust fund outlays. Includes Puerto Rico, outlying areas, and enrollees in foreign countries. See text, section 3, for explanation of coverage]

TYPE OF INSURANCE	Unit	1970	1975	1980	1984	1985	1986	1987	1988	1989	1990
HOSPITAL AND/OR MEDICAL INSURANCE											
Enrollment, total.	1,000 .	20,491	24,959	28,478	30,455	31,083	31,750	32,411	32,980	33,579	34,203
Benefit payments	Mil. dol	7,099	15,588	35,699	62,918	70,527	75,997	80,316	86,487	98,305	108,707
HOSPITAL INSURANCE											
Enrollment, total.	1,000 .	20,361	24,640	28,067	29,996	30,589	31,216	31,853	32,413	33,040	33,719
Persons 65 and over . .	1,000 .	20,361	22,472	25,104	27,112	27,683	28,257	28,822	29,312	29,869	30,464
Disabled persons [1] . . .	1,000 .	(X)	2,168	2,963	2,884	2,907	2,959	3,031	3,101	3,171	3,255
Benefit payments	Mil. dol	5,124	11,315	25,064	43,257	47,580	49,758	49,496	52,517	60,011	66,239
MEDICAL INSURANCE											
Enrollment, total.	1,000 .	19,584	23,904	27,400	29,415	29,989	30,590	31,170	31,617	32,099	32,629
Persons 65 and over . .	1,000 .	19,584	21,945	24,680	26,764	27,311	27,863	28,382	28,780	29,216	29,686
Disabled persons [1] . . .	1,000 .	(X)	1,959	2,719	2,651	2,678	2,727	2,788	2,837	2,883	2,943
Benefit payments	Mil. dol	1,975	4,273	10,635	19,661	22,947	26,239	30,820	33,970	38,294	42,468

X Not applicable.   [1] Age under 65; includes persons enrolled because of end-stage renal disease (ESRD) only.
Source: U.S. Health Care Financing Administration. Published in U.S. Social Security Administration, *Annual Statistical Supplement* to the *Social Security Bulletin.*

No. 145. Medicare—Persons Served and Reimbursements: 1980 to 1989

[Persons served are enrollees who use covered services, incurred expenses greater than the applicable deductible amounts and for whom Medicare paid benefits. Reimbursements are amounts paid to providers for covered services. Excluded are retroactive adjustments resulting from end of fiscal year cost settlements and certain lump-sum interim payments. Also excluded are beneficiary (or third party payor) liabilities for applicable deductibles, coinsurance amounts, and charges for non-covered services. Includes data for enrollees living in outlying territories and foreign countries]

TYPE OF COVERAGE AND SERVICE	Unit	PERSONS 65 YEARS OLD AND OVER				DISABLED PERSONS [1]			
		1980	1985	1988	1989	1980	1985	1988	1989
Persons served, total [2]	1,000 . .	**16,271**	**20,347**	**22,942**	**23,868**	**1,760**	**1,944**	**2,182**	**2,287**
Hospital insurance [2]	1,000 . .	6,024	6,058	6,082	6,155	728	662	649	659
Inpatient hospital	1,000 . .	5,951	5,714	5,779	5,725	721	636	625	627
Skilled-nursing services.	1,000 . .	248	304	371	613	9	10	13	23
Home health services [3]	1,000 . .	675	1,448	1,485	1,580	51	101	97	105
Supplementary medical insurance [2] . .	1,000 . .	16,099	20,186	22,808	23,746	1,723	1,916	2,156	2,263
Physicians' and other medical services	1,000 . .	15,627	19,590	22,270	23,283	1,631	1,820	2,041	2,159
Outpatient services	1,000 . .	6,629	9,889	12,795	13,291	909	1,096	1,357	1,415
Home health services [3]	1,000 . .	302	27	32	36	25	-	-	-
Persons served per 1,000 enrollees, total [2]	Rate . .	**638**	**722**	**768**	**785**	**594**	**669**	**704**	**721**
Hospital insurance [2]	Rate . .	240	219	208	206	246	228	209	208
Inpatient hospital	Rate . .	237	206	197	192	243	219	202	198
Skilled-nursing services.	Rate . .	10	11	13	21	3	4	4	7
Home health services [3]	Rate . .	27	52	51	53	17	35	31	33
Supplementary medical insurance [2] .	Rate . .	652	739	793	813	634	716	760	785
Physicians' and other medical services	Rate . .	633	717	774	797	600	680	720	749
Outpatient services	Rate . .	269	362	445	455	334	409	478	491
Home health services [3]	Rate . .	12	1	1	1	9	-	-	-
Reimbursements, total.	Mil. dol.	**29,134**	**56,199**	**72,900**	**82,222**	**4,478**	**7,495**	**8,980**	**10,363**
Hospital insurance	Mil. dol.	20,353	37,360	45,703	50,448	2,765	4,785	5,436	6,253
Inpatient hospital	Mil. dol.	19,583	35,313	43,112	45,439	2,714	4,638	5,264	5,936
Skilled-nursing services.	Mil. dol.	331	464	811	2,806	13	17	33	143
Home health services [3]	Mil. dol.	440	1,583	1,781	2,202	38	130	140	173
Supplementary medical insurance [2] . .	Mil. dol.	8,781	18,839	27,196	31,774	1,713	2,709	3,544	4,111
Physicians' and other medical services	Mil. dol.	7,361	15,309	21,311	25,310	997	1,712	2,162	2,623
Outpatient services	Mil. dol.	1,261	3,499	5,843	6,407	701	997	1,383	1,489
Home health services [3]	Mil. dol.	159	31	43	57	16	-	1	4
Reimbursements, per person served, total.	Dollars.	**1,791**	**2,762**	**3,178**	**3,445**	**2,544**	**3,855**	**4,115**	**4,531**
Hospital insurance	Dollars .	3,379	6,167	7,515	8,196	3,798	7,224	8,373	9,482
Inpatient hospital	Dollars .	3,291	6,181	7,461	7,937	3,765	7,295	8,418	9,455
Skilled-nursing services.	Dollars .	1,336	1,525	2,184	4,580	1,571	1,681	2,529	6,107
Home health services [3]	Dollars .	652	1,093	1,199	1,394	733	1,288	1,449	1,645
Supplementary medical insurance . . .	Dollars .	545	933	1,192	1,338	994	1,414	1,644	1,817
Physicians' and other medical services.	Dollars .	471	781	957	1,087	611	941	1,059	1,215
Outpatient services	Dollars .	190	354	457	482	771	909	1,019	1,051
Home health services [3]	Dollars .	526	1,122	1,359	1,614	619	1,598	123	230

- Represents or rounds to zero.   [1] Age under 65; includes persons enrolled because of end-stage renal disease (ESRD) only.   [2] Persons are counted once for each type of covered service used, but are not double counted in totals.   [3] Beginning 1982, a change in legislation resulted in virtually all home health services being paid under hospital insurance.

Source: U.S. Health Care Financing Administration, *Medicare Program Statistics*, annual; and unpublished data.

No. 146. Medicare—Hospital Utilization and Hospital and Physician Charges: 1970 to 1990

[Data reflect date expense was incurred based on bills submitted for payment and recorded in Health Care Financing Administration central records through May 1991. Includes Puerto Rico, Virgin Islands, Guam, other outlying areas, and enrollees in foreign countries]

ITEM	Unit	PERSONS 65 YEARS OLD AND OVER					DISABLED PERSONS [1]				
		1970	1980	1985	1989, prel.	1990, prel.	1975	1980	1985	1989, prel.	1990, prel.
Hospital inpatient care:											
Admissions [2]	1,000...	6,141	9,258	9,751	7,876	9,252	822	1,271	1,319	1,056	1,262
Per 1,000 enrollees [3]	Rate ...	302	369	352	264	304	379	429	454	333	388
Covered days of care.	Millions	79	98	80	79	82	9	13	11	11	11
Per 1,000 enrollees [3]	Rate ...	3,902	3,885	2,882	2,635	2,702	4,198	4,549	3,739	3,526	3,464
Per admission	Days ..	12.9	10.5	8.2	10.0	8.9	11.1	10.6	8.2	10.6	8.7
Hospital covered charges	Mil. dol.	5,968	28,615	49,236	78,840	90,846	1,371	4,087	6,582	10,337	11,910
Per covered day.	Dollars..	75	293	617	1,002	1,104	151	303	606	925	1,057
Percent of covered charges reimbursed [4]	Percent .	78.0	70.0	65.6	50.7	47.5	73.6	68.6	64.4	50.4	46.5
Physician allowed charges	Mil. dol.	2,310	9,011	17,743	26,274	30,447	367	1,112	1,823	2,477	2,907
Percent reimbursed	Percent .	71.9	78.0	78.8	78.4	76.9	76.1	78.7	78.8	78.0	75.7

[1] Disabled persons under age 65 and persons enrolled solely because of end-stage renal disease. [2] Beginning 1990, represents number of discharges. [3] Based on Hospital Insurance (HI) enrollment as of July 1. [4] Billing reimbursements exclude: (1) PPS pass-through amounts for capital, direct medical education, kidney acquisitions, and bad debts by Medicare patients; (2) certain lump-sum interim payments; and (3) retroactive adjustments resulting from end-of-fiscal year cost reports.

Source: U.S. Health Care Financing Administration, unpublished data.

No. 147. Medicare and Medicaid—Summary, by State and Other Areas: 1990

[Data are preliminary estimates]

REGION, DIVISION, AND STATE	MEDICARE		MEDICAID [3]		REGION, DIVISION, AND STATE	MEDICARE		MEDICAID [3]	
	Enroll-ment [1] (1,000)	Pay-ments [2] (mil.dol.)	Recipi-ents [4] (1,000)	Pay-ments [2] (mil. dol.)		Enroll-ment [1] (1,000)	Pay-ments [2] (mil.dol.)	Recipi-ents [4] (1,000)	Pay-ments [2] (mil. dol.)
Total	34,203	108,707	25,255	64,859	WV	308	844	250	361
U.S. [5]	33,498	108,150	24,014	64,709	NC......	892	2,326	563	1,426
NE........	7,446	26,697	5,323	22,264	SC......	442	1,126	317	743
N.E........	1,890	6,185	1,250	5,206	GA......	732	2,347	651	2,076
ME......	183	501	133	432	FL	2,339	7,677	1,038	2,361
NH......	137	344	45	243	E.S.C.	2,174	6,762	1,866	3,335
VT......	75	188	60	153	KY......	534	1,582	468	977
MA......	867	3,152	591	2,730	TN......	692	2,231	613	1,163
RI	159	489	171	442	AL......	582	1,854	352	609
CT......	469	1,511	250	1,205	MS......	366	1,096	433	586
M.A......	5,557	20,512	4,073	17,059	W.S.C.	3,197	10,482	2,564	5,383
NY......	2,509	9,619	2,329	11,877	AR......	391	1,125	264	599
NJ	1,092	3,485	567	2,298	LA......	531	1,984	585	1,315
PA......	1,956	7,408	1,177	2,883	OK......	451	1,346	273	688
Midwest	8,420	25,504	5,555	14,430	TX......	1,824	6,027	1,442	2,781
E.N.C.	5,786	18,495	4,076	10,342	West	6,107	19,377	5,044	9,886
OH......	1,543	4,844	1,221	3,132	Mt.	1,637	4,627	621	1,578
IN	762	2,249	347	1,343	MT......	117	317	61	171
IL......	1,534	4,770	1,067	2,424	ID	132	323	55	162
MI	1,233	4,618	1,048	2,195	WY......	52	155	29	59
WI	714	2,014	393	1,248	CO......	358	926	191	516
W.N.C..	2,634	7,010	1,479	4,088	NM......	179	474	130	275
MN......	588	1,314	380	1,410	AZ......	498	1,565	(X)	(X)
IA	457	1,183	240	620	UT......	160	429	108	247
MO	781	2,391	448	897	NV......	141	437	47	149
ND......	98	257	49	194	Pac........	4,470	14,750	4,423	8,309
SD.....	110	272	49	166	WA......	615	1,650	448	952
NE......	237	553	119	309	OR......	424	998	227	519
KS	363	1,040	194	491	CA......	3,279	11,751	3,624	6,507
South......	11,512	36,562	8,092	18,129	AK......	25	89	39	139
S.A......	6,142	19,318	3,662	9,411	HI	127	262	85	191
DE......	88	282	41	123	PR	429	509	1,230	146
MD......	541	2,177	330	1,090	Outlying areas.....	8	22	[6]11	[6]4
DC......	78	398	93	246	Foreign .	268	36	(X)	(X)
VA......	722	2,140	379	985					

X Not applicable. [1] Hospital and/or medical insurance enrollment as of July 1. [2] Payments are for calendar year and represent disbursements from Federal hospital and medical insurance trust funds. Estimates of distribution by State based on preliminary billing data. [3] For fiscal year ending Sept. 30. [4] Persons receiving Medicaid at any time during the year. [5] Includes data for enrollees with residence unknown. [6] Virgin Islands only.

Source: U.S. Health Care Financing Administration, unpublished data.

No. 148. Medicaid—Selected Utilization Measures, by Type of Facility: 1975 to 1990

[In thousands. For fiscal years ending in year shown. Includes Virgin Islands. See text, section 3. Excludes Arizona which has no Title XIX (Medicaid) program]

MEASURE	1975	1980	1984	1985	1986	1987	1988	1989	1990
General hospitals:									
Total discharges	3,031	3,203	3,414	3,616	3,713	3,558	3,905	3,734	3,932
Recipients discharged	2,336	2,255	2,263	2,390	2,564	2,525	2,640	2,701	2,758
Total days of care	22,941	24,089	23,185	29,562	29,517	23,124	24,022	22,754	22,059
Skilled nursing facility:									
Total recipients	630	606	559	547	571	537	579	563	586
Total days of care	78,111	102,832	100,265	72,119	116,044	112,466	119,806	118,222	125,591
Intermediate care facilities: [1]									
Total recipients	69	121	141	147	145	140	145	147	138
Total days of care	9,060	250,124	46,310	47,324	48,418	45,611	46,825	50,276	46,509
Intermediate care facilities: [2]									
Total recipients	582	789	796	828	828	834	866	875	771
Total days of care	121,604	170,665	202,158	205,877	217,972	216,292	224,887	249,006	212,526

[1] Mentally retarded.   [2] General.

Source: U.S. Health Care Financing Administration, unpublished data.

No. 149. Medicaid—Selected Characteristics of Persons Covered: 1980 to 1990

[In thousands, except percent. Represents number of persons as of March of following year who were enrolled at any time in year shown. Person did not have to receive medical care paid for by Medicaid in order to be counted. See headnote, table 566]

POVERTY STATUS	1980	1985	1988	1990							
				Total [1]	White	Black	His-panic [2]	Under 18 years old	18-44 years old	45-64 years old	65 years and over
Persons covered, total	18,966	19,204	21,185	24,261	15,078	7,809	3,912	12,094	7,284	2,302	2,582
Below poverty level	11,113	12,652	13,325	15,175	8,758	5,686	2,686	8,313	4,490	1,261	1,112
Above poverty level	7,854	6,552	7,860	9,086	6,320	2,123	1,226	3,781	2,794	1,041	1,470
Percent of total population .	8.4	8.1	8.6	9.7	7.2	25.3	18.3	18.5	6.8	4.9	8.6
Below poverty level	39.1	39.7	42.3	45.2	39.2	57.8	44.7	61.9	36.1	31.0	30.4
Above poverty level	4.0	3.2	3.7	4.2	3.4	10.2	7.9	7.3	3.0	2.4	5.6

[1] Includes other races not shown separately.   [2] Persons of Hispanic origin may be of any race.

Source: U.S. Bureau of the Census, *Current Population Reports*, series P-60, No. 155, earlier reports and unpublished data.

No. 150. Medical Assistance (Medicaid)—Recipients and Payments, by Basis of Eligibility and Type of Service: 1980 to 1990

[For fiscal year ending in year shown; see text, section 3. Includes Puerto Rico and outlying areas. Excludes Arizona, which has no Title XIX (Medicaid) program. Medical vendor payments are those made directly to suppliers of medical care]

BASIS OF ELIGIBILITY AND TYPE OF SERVICE	RECIPIENTS (1,000)					PAYMENTS (mil. dol.)				
	1980	1985	1988	1989	1990	1980	1985	1988	1989	1990
Total [1] **. . . . .**	21,605	21,814	22,907	23,511	25,255	23,311	37,508	48,710	54,500	64,859
Age 65 and over	3,440	3,061	3,159	3,132	3,202	8,739	14,096	17,135	18,558	21,508
Blindness	92	80	86	95	83	124	249	344	409	434
Disabled [2]	2,819	2,937	3,401	3,496	3,635	7,497	13,203	18,250	20,476	23,969
AFDC [3] program	14,210	15,275	15,541	16,036	17,230	6,354	9,160	11,731	13,788	17,690
Other and unknown	1,499	1,214	1,343	1,175	1,105	596	798	1,250	1,268	1,257
Inpatient services in—										
General hospital	3,680	3,434	3,832	4,170	4,593	6,412	9,453	12,076	13,378	16,674
Mental hospital	66	60	60	90	92	775	1,192	1,375	1,470	1,714
Intermediate care facilities:										
Mentally retarded	121	147	145	148	147	1,989	4,731	6,022	6,649	7,354
Other	789	828	866	888	860	4,202	6,516	7,923	8,871	9,667
Skilled nursing facility	609	547	579	564	601	3,685	5,071	6,354	6,660	8,026
Physicians	13,765	14,387	15,265	15,686	17,078	1,875	2,346	2,953	3,408	4,018
Dental	4,652	4,672	5,072	4,214	4,552	402	450	577	408	593
Other practitioner	3,234	3,357	3,480	3,555	3,873	198	251	284	317	372
Outpatient hospital	9,705	10,072	10,533	11,344	12,370	1,101	1,789	2,413	2,837	3,324
Clinic	1,531	2,121	2,256	2,391	2,804	320	714	1,105	1,249	1,688
Laboratory [4]	3,212	6,354	7,579	7,759	8,959	121	337	543	590	721
Home health	392	535	569	609	719	332	1,120	2,015	2,572	3,404
Prescribed drugs	13,707	13,921	15,323	15,916	17,294	1,318	2,315	3,294	3,689	4,420
Family planning	1,129	1,636	1,525	1,564	1,752	81	195	206	227	265

[1] Recipient data do not add due to small number of recipients that are reported in more than one category. Includes recipients of and payments for other care not shown separately.   [2] Permanently and totally.   [3] Aid to families with dependent children.
[4] Includes radiological services.

Source: U.S. Health Care Financing Administration, *Health Care Financing Review*, quarterly.

No. 151. Indexes of Medical Care Prices: 1970 to 1991

[1982-1984 = 100. Indexes are annual averages of monthly data based on components of consumer price index for all urban consumers; for explanation, see text, section 15. See *Historical Statistics, Colonial Times to 1970,* series B 262-272 for similar data]

YEAR	Index, total	MEDICAL CARE SERVICES				Medical care commodities [2]	ANNUAL PERCENT CHANGE					Medical care commodities [2]
		Total [1]	Professional services		Hospital room		Total [1]	Medical care services				
			Total [1]	Physicians	Dental				Total [1]	Physicians	Dental	Hospital room
1970	34.0	32.3	37.0	34.5	39.2	23.6	46.5	[3]6.6	[3]7.0	[3]7.5	[3]5.7	[3]12.9	[3]2.4
1975	47.5	46.6	50.8	48.1	53.2	38.3	53.3	12.0	12.6	12.1	10.4	17.1	8.3
1978	61.8	61.2	64.5	63.4	65.1	54.0	64.4	8.4	8.5	8.4	7.1	11.1	7.0
1979	67.5	67.2	70.1	69.2	70.5	60.1	69.0	9.2	9.8	9.1	8.3	11.3	7.1
1980	74.9	74.8	77.9	76.5	78.9	68.0	75.4	11.0	11.3	10.5	11.9	13.1	9.3
1981	82.9	82.8	85.9	84.9	86.5	78.1	83.7	10.7	10.7	11.0	9.6	14.9	11.0
1982	92.5	92.6	93.2	92.9	93.1	90.4	92.3	11.6	11.8	9.4	7.6	15.7	10.3
1983	100.6	100.7	99.8	100.1	99.4	100.6	100.2	8.8	8.7	7.8	6.8	11.3	8.6
1984	106.8	106.7	107.0	107.0	107.5	109.0	107.5	6.2	6.0	6.9	8.1	8.3	7.3
1985	113.5	113.2	113.5	113.3	114.2	115.4	115.2	6.3	6.1	5.9	6.2	5.9	7.2
1986	122.0	121.9	120.8	121.5	120.6	122.3	122.8	7.5	7.7	7.2	5.6	6.0	6.6
1987	130.1	130.0	128.8	130.4	128.8	131.1	131.0	6.6	6.6	7.3	6.8	7.2	6.7
1988	138.6	138.3	137.5	139.8	137.5	143.3	139.9	6.5	6.4	7.2	6.8	9.3	6.8
1989	149.3	148.9	146.4	150.1	146.1	158.1	150.8	7.7	7.7	7.4	6.3	10.3	7.8
1990	162.8	162.7	156.1	160.8	155.8	175.4	163.4	9.0	9.3	7.1	6.6	10.9	8.4
1991	177.0	177.1	165.7	170.5	167.4	191.9	176.8	8.7	8.9	6.0	7.4	9.4	8.2

[1] Includes other services, not shown separately.   [2] Prior to 1978, covers drugs and prescriptions only.   [3] Change from 1969.
Source: U.S. Bureau of Labor Statistics, *CPI Detailed Report,* January 1992, and unpublished data.

No. 152. Average Annual Expenditures of Consumer Units for Health Care, 1984 to 1990, and by Selected Characteristics, 1990

[In dollars, except percent. See text, section 14, and headnote, table 693. For composition of regions, see table 25]

ITEM	HEALTH CARE, TOTAL		Health insurance	Medical services	Drugs and medical supplies [1]	PERCENT DISTRIBUTION			
	Amount	Percent of total expenditures				Health care, total	Health insurance	Medical services	Drugs and medical supplies
1984........................	1,049	4.8	370	454	225	100.0	35.3	43.3	21.4
1985........................	1,108	4.7	375	496	238	100.0	33.8	44.8	21.5
1986........................	1,135	4.8	371	502	261	100.0	32.7	44.2	23.0
1987........................	1,135	4.6	392	467	276	100.0	34.5	41.1	24.3
1988........................	1,298	5.0	474	529	294	100.0	36.5	40.8	22.7
1989........................	1,407	5.1	537	542	327	100.0	38.2	38.5	23.2
1990	**1,480**	5.2	581	562	337	100.0	39.3	38.0	22.8
Age of reference person:									
Under 25 years old...........	403	2.4	106	190	106	100.0	26.3	47.1	26.3
25 to 34 years old	981	3.5	391	391	199	100.0	39.9	39.9	20.3
35 to 44 years old	1,415	4.0	485	646	283	100.0	34.3	45.7	20.0
45 to 54 years old	1,597	4.3	583	664	349	100.0	36.5	41.6	21.9
55 to 64 years old	1,791	6.1	700	654	436	100.0	39.1	36.5	24.3
65 to 74 years old	2,197	10.5	1014	656	528	100.0	46.2	29.9	24.0
75 years old and over.........	2,223	14.4	960	674	589	100.0	43.2	30.3	26.5
Region of residence:									
Northeast..................	1,396	4.7	553	559	285	100.0	39.6	40.0	20.4
Midwest...................	1,336	5.2	550	457	330	100.0	41.2	34.2	24.7
South.....................	1,600	5.9	637	573	390	100.0	39.8	35.8	24.4
West......................	1,544	4.8	558	676	310	100.0	36.1	43.8	20.1
Size of consumer unit:									
One person................	977	5.7	389	356	231	100.0	39.8	36.4	23.6
Two persons...............	1,796	6.2	729	629	439	100.0	40.6	35.0	24.4
Two or more persons	1,677	5.1	657	642	377	100.0	39.2	38.3	22.5
Three persons	1,618	4.8	627	638	354	100.0	38.8	39.4	21.9
Four persons	1,581	4.2	618	648	316	100.0	39.1	41.0	20.0
Five persons or more........	1,555	4.3	548	682	325	100.0	35.2	43.9	20.9
Income before taxes:									
Complete income reporters [2]	1,497	5.2	585	565	347	100.0	39.1	37.7	23.2
Quintiles of income:									
Lowest 20 percent	1,012	7.8	407	334	272	100.0	40.2	33.0	26.9
Second 20 percent........	1,420	7.9	582	451	386	100.0	41.0	31.8	27.2
Third 20 percent	1,409	5.7	614	484	312	100.0	43.6	34.4	22.1
Fourth 20 percent	1,560	4.6	610	595	354	100.0	39.1	38.1	22.7
Highest 20 percent........	2,080	3.8	710	958	412	100.0	34.1	46.1	19.8
Incomplete reporters of income ..	1,390	5.6	562	544	285	100.0	40.4	39.1	20.5

[1] Includes prescription and non-prescription drugs.   [2] A complete reporter is a consumer unit providing values for at least one of the major sources of income.
Source: Bureau of Labor Statistics, *Consumer Expenditure Survey,* annual.

No. 153. Health Insurance Coverage Status, by Selected Characteristics: 1985 to 1990

[Data represents monthly averages for **first quarter**. Government health insurance includes Medicare, Medicaid, and military plans. Based on Survey of Income and Program Participation; see text, section 14]

CHARACTERISTIC	NUMBER (mil.)						PERCENT				
		Covered by private or Government health insurance				Not cov-ered by health insur-ance		Covered by private or Government health insurance			Not cov-ered by health insur-ance
	Total	Total [1]	Private insurance		Cov-ered by Medi-caid		Total	Total [1]	Private	Cov-ered by Medi-caid	
			Total	Related to employ-ment [2]							
1985 [3]	234.0	199.4	174.6	141.3	16.1	34.6	100.0	85.2	74.6	6.9	14.8
1986	236.7	202.6	177.5	144.1	16.7	34.2	100.0	85.6	75.0	7.1	14.4
1987	238.9	206.0	180.6	146.3	18.0	32.9	100.0	86.2	75.6	7.5	13.8
1988	241.4	210.6	186.6	150.4	17.7	30.8	100.0	87.2	77.3	7.4	12.8
1989	243.6	212.0	187.2	151.8	17.7	31.7	100.0	87.0	76.8	7.3	13.0
1990, total [4]	**246.2**	**212.6**	**186.2**	**150.5**	**18.5**	**33.6**	**100.0**	**86.4**	**75.6**	**7.5**	**13.6**
Male	119.8	101.7	90.7	75.1	6.8	18.1	100.0	84.9	75.7	5.7	15.1
Female	126.4	110.9	95.4	75.4	11.7	15.5	100.0	87.7	75.5	9.3	12.3
White	207.5	181.0	163.9	131.9	10.8	26.4	100.0	87.2	79.0	5.2	12.7
Black	30.4	24.7	17.0	14.3	6.6	5.6	100.0	81.3	55.9	21.7	18.4
Hispanic origin [5]	20.7	14.2	10.4	8.8	3.3	6.5	100.0	68.6	50.2	15.9	31.4
Under 16 years	57.7	49.3	40.9	34.4	8.0	8.5	100.0	85.4	70.9	13.9	14.7
16 to 24 years	32.0	25.0	22.3	17.5	2.4	7.0	100.0	78.1	69.7	7.5	21.9
25 to 34 years	43.3	35.2	31.8	28.7	2.7	8.1	100.0	81.3	73.4	6.2	18.7
35 to 44 years	37.1	32.2	30.2	27.5	1.4	4.8	100.0	86.8	81.4	3.8	12.9
45 to 54 years	25.2	22.3	21.0	18.4	1.0	3.0	100.0	88.5	83.3	4.0	11.9
55 to 64 years	21.3	19.1	17.2	13.8	1.0	2.1	100.0	89.7	80.8	4.7	9.9
65 years and over	29.6	29.5	22.8	10.1	2.3	0.1	100.0	99.7	77.0	7.8	0.3

[1] Includes other Government insurance, not shown separately. [2] Related to current or prior employment of self or other family members. [3] Revised since originally published. [4] Includes other races, not shown separately. [5] Persons of Hispanic origin may be of any race.

Source: U.S. Bureau of the Census, *Current Population Reports*, series P-70, No. 29, and unpublished data.

No.154. Health Insurance Coverage, by Selected Characteristic: 1985 to 1987

[Data represent persons covered by Government or private health insurance coverage during a 28 month period, from February 1985 through May 1987. For composition of regions, see table 25]

CHARACTERISTIC	All per-sons (mil.)	COVERED BY INSURANCE (mil.)						PERCENT COVERED BY INSURANCE			
		Government or private			Private			Government or private			Private for entire period
		For entire period	For part of the period	No cov-erage	For entire period	For part of the period	No cov-erage	For entire period	For part of the period	No cov-erage	
Total	226.5	162.8	53.8	9.8	138.9	61.3	26.3	71.9	23.8	4.3	61.3
Under 18 years old	63.0	41.3	18.5	3.2	36.0	17.6	9.4	65.5	29.5	5.1	57.1
Under 6 years old	21.8	14.2	6.6	1.0	11.8	6.3	3.7	65.0	30.4	4.6	54.2
18 to 24 years old	26.6	12.8	12.2	1.6	11.4	12.3	2.9	48.1	45.9	6.0	43.0
25 to 44 years old	69.9	50.5	16.2	3.2	47.3	16.3	6.3	72.3	23.2	4.5	67.7
45 to 64 years old	43.2	34.6	6.7	1.8	31.0	8.1	4.2	80.1	15.5	4.3	71.7
65 years old and over	23.8	23.6	0.1	(Z)	13.1	7.1	3.6	99.3	0.6	0.1	55.3
Male	109.0	76.5	27.0	5.5	67.0	29.6	12.4	70.2	24.8	5.0	61.5
Female	117.5	86.4	26.8	4.3	71.9	31.6	14.0	73.5	22.8	3.7	61.2
White	192.2	141.5	42.9	7.8	124.4	49.7	18.4	73.6	22.3	4.0	64.6
Black	27.0	16.8	8.6	1.6	10.9	9.2	6.9	62.3	31.7	5.9	40.5
Hispanic [1]	15.7	7.5	6.4	1.8	5.5	6.1	4.1	48.0	40.6	11.3	34.9
Residence:											
Northeast	45.9	35.8	9.2	0.9	30.0	11.0	4.9	77.9	20.2	1.9	65.2
Midwest	61.0	46.2	12.6	2.2	41.4	14.0	5.5	75.8	20.7	3.6	68.0
South	76.4	51.5	20.4	4.5	42.7	23.4	10.4	67.4	26.6	5.9	55.8
West	43.2	29.3	11.6	2.2	24.8	12.9	5.5	67.9	26.9	5.2	57.5
Educational attainment: [2]											
Less than 12 years	38.8	27.6	8.5	2.6	16.9	12.8	9.2	71.2	21.9	6.8	43.5
12 to 15 years	92.8	67.9	21.5	3.4	61.3	24.8	6.8	73.2	23.0	3.7	66.0
16 years or more	28.4	24.3	3.7	0.4	23.3	4.6	0.6	85.6	12.9	1.5	81.8
Work-status: [3] Worked entire 28 months—											
Full time	51.7	44.4	6.2	1.1	44.0	6.5	1.2	86.0	12.1	2.0	85.1
Part time	4.9	3.6	0.9	0.3	3.4	0.9	0.5	74.6	18.7	6.8	70.5
Had at least one work interruption	62.9	34.8	24.2	3.9	32.1	24.4	6.4	55.3	38.4	6.2	51.0

Z Less than 50,000. [1] Persons of Hispanic origin may be of any race. [2] For persons 19 years old and over. [3] For **wage** and salary workers.

Source: U.S. Bureau of the Census, *Current Population Reports*, series P-70, No. 17.

No. 155. Persons Without Health Insurance Coverage, by Selected Characteristic: 1989

[In percent, except as indicated. Annual average of monthly figures. Based on Current Population Survey; see text, section 1 and Appendix III]

CHARACTERISTIC	Total	UNDER 65 YEARS OLD					65 years and over
		Total	Under 18 years	18 to 24 years	25 to 44 years	45 to 64 years	
All persons (1,000)	243,532	214,313	64,003	25,401	78,795	46,114	29,219
Persons not covered [1]	13.9	15.7	14.9	27.4	15.5	10.5	1.2
SEX							
Male	15.1	16.7	15.1	31.3	17.6	9.6	1.3
Female.	12.7	14.6	14.7	23.7	13.6	11.2	1.2
RACE							
White	12.8	14.5	14.0	26.3	14.4	9.4	1.0
Black	20.2	21.9	18.9	34.3	22.5	17.5	2.5
Other	19.7	20.4	18.9	27.8	20.7	17.5	8.4
EDUCATION [2]							
Less than 12 years	20.8	30.1	(X)	42.1	35.5	19.9	1.5
12 years	14.4	16.6	(X)	29.8	16.8	8.5	0.7
More than 12 years	8.4	9.2	(X)	16.0	9.0	5.8	1.3
EMPLOYMENT STATUS [2]							
Currently employed.	13.9	14.3	(X)	26.6	13.6	9.0	1.5
Unemployed	38.3	39.2	(X)	44.5	40.8	26.5	(X)
Not in labor force	10.8	18.5	(X)	26.0	21.2	12.8	1.2
FAMILY INCOME							
Less than $5,000	27.1	31.3	25.5	27.3	42.4	35.5	1.5
$5,000 to $9,999	27.7	36.9	31.6	43.5	43.5	32.2	1.6
$10,000 to $19,999	24.3	30.1	30.2	37.5	32.0	21.3	1.1
$20,000 to $34,999	10.6	11.6	10.9	22.1	11.8	6.8	1.0
$35,000 to $49,999	5.8	6.0	4.0	18.4	5.8	3.9	0.8
$50,000 or more	3.6	3.7	2.3	12.9	3.7	1.9	1.6

X Not applicable. [1] Excludes 9.7 million persons for whom insurance coverage was unknown. Includes persons whose demographic coverage was unknown. [2] Excludes persons under 18 years old.

Source: U.S. National Center for Health Statistics, *Advance Data from Vital and Health Statistics*, No. 201, June 18, 1991.

No. 156. Health Maintenance Organizations (HMO)—Number and Enrollment, by Type and Size of Organization: 1976 to 1991

[As of **June 30**, except as noted. Under the Health Maintenance Organization Act, an HMO must have four characteristics: (1) an organized system for providing health care in a geographic area, for which the HMO is responsible for providing or otherwise assuring its delivery; (2) an agreed upon set of basic and supplemental health maintenance and treatment services; (3) a voluntarily enrolled group of people; and (4) community rating. A **group HMO** contracts with one or more medical groups to provide services to members and generally provides all services except hospital care under one roof. Data for group model HMO's include staff model HMO's (a model in which the HMO hires its own physicians) and network HMO's (an HMO that provides comprehensive health services to members in two or more distinct geographic areas). **Individual practice association (IPA) HMO** contracts with a physician organization that in turn contracts with individual physicians. IPA physicians provide care to HMO members from their private offices and continue to see their fee-for-service patients. An **open-ended product line** allows enrollees to receive services from health care providers outside the HMO network for additional out-of-pocket fee (typically a deductible and coinsurance are imposed)]

TYPE OF PRACTICE AND SIZE	1976	1980	1984 (Dec.31)	1985	1986	1987	1988	1989 (Jan.1)	1990 (July 1)	1991 (Jan.1)
NUMBER OF PLANS										
Total	175	236	337	393	595	662	643	607	[1]556	[1]556
Group	134	139	195	212	250	245	231	220	206	208
I.P.A	41	97	142	181	345	417	412	387	350	348
Less than 15,000 members . .	128	144	143	171	315	325	271	229	179	171
15,000-24,999 members	15	36	45	56	63	86	98	102	94	107
25,000-49,999 members	12	28	78	79	107	100	114	112	125	121
50,000-99,999 members	7	15	40	51	67	89	86	89	72	72
100,000 members or more. . .	10	13	31	36	47	62	74	74	84	85
ENROLLMENT (1,000)										
Total	6,016	9,100	16,743	18,894	23,664	28,587	[2]31,366	[2]31,940	[2]33,622	[2]34,072
Group	5,627	7,406	13,075	14,247	15,210	17,261	17,883	18,371	19,743	20,415
I.P.A	390	1,694	3,667	4,646	8,454	11,326	13,483	13,569	13,879	13,657
Less than 15,000 members . .	620	870	975	1,020	1,514	1,797	1,794	1,591	1,317	1,242
15,000-24,999 members	297	732	867	1,101	1,220	1,681	1,933	2,044	1,793	2,064
25,000-49,999 members	365	907	2,699	2,813	3,791	3,564	4,011	3,927	4,249	4,188
50,000-99,999 members	525	976	2,577	3,315	4,828	6,343	6,041	6,274	5,121	5,132
100,000 members or more. . .	4,210	5,615	9,625	10,646	12,311	15,202	17,587	18,104	21,142	21,446
HMO'S WITH OPEN-ENDED PRODUCT LINE										
Number of plans	(X)	(X)	(X)	(X)	(X)	(X)	48	70	96	116
Enrollment (1,000)	(X)	(X)	(X)	(X)	(X)	(X)	482	617	1,041	1,191

X Not applicable. [1] Includes three HMO's containing only open-ended members, not distributed by enrollment size. [2] Excludes enrollees participating in open-ended plans.

Source: Interstudy, Excelsior, MN, *The Interstudy Edge*, 1990, vol. 2, and earlier publications (copyright) and Group Health Association of America, Inc., Washington, DC, releases.

No. 157. Children—Health Insurance and Medical Care: 1988

[Based on the National Health Interview Survey; see Appendix III]

CHARACTERISTIC	Total	AGE GROUP					
		Under 1 year	1 to 4 years	5 to 7 years	8 to 11 years	12 to 14 years	15 to 17 years
All children (1,000) [1]	63,569	3,850	14,536	11,037	13,635	9,872	10,639
PERCENT COVERED BY HEALTH INSURANCE							
All children	83.1	80.1	83.7	83.3	83.8	83.0	82.3
Sex: Male	83.5	80.4	83.5	83.7	83.8	84.3	83.1
Female	82.7	79.7	84.0	83.0	83.8	81.4	81.3
Race: White	83.7	80.7	84.4	84.3	83.6	83.7	83.5
Black	80.9	81.2	80.5	79.7	84.1	81.7	77.6
Hispanic origin: Hispanic	70.0	62.2	75.2	76.3	65.0	68.1	68.3
Non-Hispanic	84.9	82.8	85.2	84.3	86.3	85.1	83.8
Family income: Under $10,000	71.8	74.0	75.3	73.9	71.0	69.7	64.4
$10,000 to $24,999	76.1	75.1	76.9	78.2	75.3	73.5	76.6
$25,000 to $39,999	89.8	85.6	90.5	89.4	92.1	90.2	87.4
$40,000 or more	92.4	93.3	93.2	91.7	92.0	93.2	91.6
PERCENT WHO VISITED A DOCTOR FOR HEALTH CARE [2]							
All children	63.9	93.8	81.5	66.0	49.6	54.8	53.9
Sex: Male	64.1	94.4	81.3	65.9	49.4	57.6	52.5
Female	63.7	93.1	81.7	66.0	49.9	51.6	55.3
Race: White	63.7	95.1	81.4	65.7	47.9	56.0	54.0
Black	65.0	87.6	82.6	66.6	55.7	51.7	55.7
Hispanic origin: Hispanic	63.4	93.5	82.3	70.4	49.5	51.9	45.5
Non-Hispanic	63.6	93.5	81.1	65.2	49.5	55.0	54.8
Family income: Under $10,000	62.9	87.4	78.9	65.6	49.5	53.5	45.9
$10,000 to $24,999	61.6	96.1	80.4	62.8	43.7	47.9	52.6
$25,000 to $39,999	64.3	94.9	82.5	67.7	47.1	54.3	56.9
$40,000 or more	68.0	97.2	85.8	70.0	56.3	62.5	58.4
Covered by health insurance	66.8	96.1	83.4	68.6	52.6	58.6	57.7
Not covered by health insurance	56.9	91.8	79.3	58.9	39.0	42.1	44.3
PERCENT WITH REGULAR SOURCE OF HEALTH CARE [3]							
All children	88.0	89.9	92.3	90.8	86.9	85.0	82.9
Sex: Male	87.6	90.1	92.0	89.9	86.0	85.1	82.6
Female	88.5	89.6	92.6	91.7	87.9	84.9	83.3
Race: White	88.6	92.1	93.0	91.3	87.2	85.1	83.4
Black	86.5	79.8	90.3	87.9	86.4	86.2	82.9
Hispanic origin: Hispanic	81.1	88.2	89.2	82.1	81.6	72.6	72.2
Non-Hispanic	88.9	89.8	92.9	91.9	87.6	86.6	84.2
Family income: Under $10,000	83.8	82.4	88.3	88.8	80.8	83.2	74.8
$10,000 to $24,999	86.0	92.7	92.5	88.3	83.7	77.4	81.1
$25,000 to $39,999	91.1	91.3	94.6	94.6	89.4	89.3	86.1
$40,000 or more	92.4	94.4	96.5	94.7	93.0	90.5	87.0
Covered by health insurance	91.9	93.0	94.9	94.0	90.9	90.0	88.2
Not covered by health insurance	79.0	85.7	88.5	83.4	75.6	70.3	70.7
PERCENT WITH REGULAR SOURCE OF HEALTH CARE—CLINIC [4]							
All children	15.5	22.0	18.6	14.8	13.1	14.3	13.3
Sex: Male	15.1	23.9	17.9	13.6	13.4	13.2	12.9
Female	15.9	19.8	19.3	16.0	12.8	15.6	13.7
Race: White	11.2	16.0	14.1	9.9	9.8	10.1	9.1
Black	35.2	46.5	40.8	37.0	29.3	33.5	30.3
Hispanic origin: Hispanic	26.2	47.6	27.8	21.1	23.2	25.2	23.6
Non-Hispanic	14.2	18.7	17.3	14.1	11.9	13.0	12.3
Family income: Under $10,000	36.5	35.9	39.5	34.9	36.7	35.9	33.0
$10,000 to $24,999	22.4	32.2	27.9	20.0	20.0	19.6	16.1
$25,000 to $39,999	9.2	11.9	9.8	9.1	7.3	8.8	10.2
$40,000 or more	5.7	4.2	6.6	4.4	3.3	5.7	8.9
Covered by health insurance	13.0	18.1	16.2	12.0	10.5	11.7	11.6
Not covered by health insurance	32.3	40.2	32.7	32.9	32.1	33.3	25.7

[1] Includes other races and unknown income. [2] For routine health care within the past year. [3] Includes private physicians, private clinics HMO's, prepaid practices and sources listed in footnote 4. [4] Includes hospital outpatient clinics and emergency rooms, walk-in and emergency care centers and other clinics.

Source: U.S. National Center for Health Statistics, *Advance Data from Vital and Health Statistics*, No. 188, October 1, 1990.

No. 158. Physicians, Dentists, and Nurses: 1970 to 1989

[Physicians, dentists, and nurses as of **end of year,** except as noted. Data for physicians include Puerto Rico and outlying areas. See also *Historical Statistics, Colonial Times to 1970,* series B 275-290]

ITEM	Unit	1970	1975	1980	1983	1984	1985	1986	1987	1988	1989
Physicians, number [1]	1,000...	348	409	487	542	(NA)	577	595	612	629	645
Rate per 100,000 population [2]	Rate...	171	190	214	232	(NA)	243	248	253	257	261
Doctors of medicine [3]	1,000...	334	394	468	520	(NA)	553	569	586	601	615
Active non-Federal [4]	1,000...	281	312	397	447	(NA)	476	484	500	516	527
Rate per 100,000 population [4][5]	Rate...	139	146	176	193	(NA)	202	203	208	212	215
Active foreign medical school graduates [4][6]	1,000...	54	(NA)	82	100	(NA)	105	107	111	115	116
Doctors of osteopathy [7]	1,000...	14	15	19	22	23	24	25	27	28	30
Medical and osteopathic schools [7]	Number.	110	123	141	142	142	142	142	142	142	142
Students [7]	1,000...	42.6	59.3	70.1	73.5	73.6	73.2	72.8	72.3	71.9	71.6
Graduates [7]	1,000...	8.8	13.9	16.2	17.1	17.6	17.8	17.7	17.4	17.5	17.2
Newly licensed physicians, total [6][8]	1,000...	11.0	16.9	18.2	20.6	18.3	18.3	19.6	20.3	21.2	20.1
Percent of total active M.D.'s [9]	Percent.	3.5	4.6	4.2	4.3	(NA)	3.6	3.8	3.8	3.8	3.6
Graduates of—											
U.S. and Canadian medical schools	1,000...	8.0	10.9	14.9	15.8	14.2	15.3	16.7	17.1	18.0	17.4
Foreign medical schools	1,000...	3.0	6.0	3.3	4.8	4.1	3.0	2.9	3.2	3.2	2.7
Percent of total newly licensed.	Percent.	27.3	35.4	18.2	23.1	22.3	16.7	15.0	15.9	15.2	13.7
Dentists, number.	1,000...	116	127	141	150	153	156	158	161	164	168
Active (exc. in Federal service) [5]	1,000...	96	107	121	130	133	136	138	140	142	144
Rate per 100,000 population [5]	Rate...	48	50	54	56	57	58	58	58	58	59
Dental schools [10]	Number.	53	59	60	60	60	60	59	58	58	58
Students [10]	1,000...	16.6	20.8	22.8	21.4	20.6	19.6	18.7	17.9	17.1	16.2
Graduates [10]	1,000...	3.7	5.0	5.3	5.8	5.3	5.4	5.0	4.7	4.6	4.3
Nurses, number (active registered).	1,000...	750	961	1,273	1,439	1,486	1,544	1,585	1,627	1,648	1,666
Rate per 100,000 population [2]	Rate...	368	446	560	616	630	649	662	671	674	675
Nursing programs [11]	Number.	1,343	1,360	1,385	1,466	1,477	1,473	1,469	1,465	1,442	1,457
Students [11]	1,000...	165	250	231	251	237	218	194	183	185	201
Graduates [11]	1,000...	44	75	76	77	80	82	77	71	65	62

NA Not available.   [1] Includes not classified, inactive, and Federal physicians. Data for 1988 and 1989 as of January 1 the following year.   [2] Based on Bureau of the Census estimated resident population as of July 1. Estimates reflect revisions based on the 1990 Census of Population.   [3] Excludes non-Federal physicians with temporary foreign addresses; see headnote, table 159.   [4] Excludes nonclassified physicians.   [5] Based on Bureau of the Census estimated civilian population as of July 1. Estimates reflect revisions based on the 1990 Census of Population.   [6] Foreign medical graduates exclude graduates of Canadian schools.   [7] Number of schools and students as of fall of prior year; graduates for academic year ending in year shown.   [8] Based on data from annual surveys conducted by the Association of American Medical Colleges and the American Association of Colleges of Medicine.   [8] Source: American Medical Association, Chicago, IL, *U.S. Medical Licensure Statistics, 1991* and prior issues and *License Requirements, 1991,* and prior issues and *Physician Characteristics and Distribution in the U.S.,* annual. (Copyright.)   [9] Excludes M.D.'s with unknown addresses. Includes those not classified.   [10] See footnote 7. Based on data from the American Dental Association, Council on Dental Education, *Annual Report on Dental Education.*   [11] Number of programs and students are as of October 15 and number of graduates are for academic year ending in year shown; from National League for Nursing, *NLN Data Book,* annual issues and *State-Approved Schools of Nursing, RN,* annual issues.

Source: Except as noted, U.S. Dept. of Health and Human Services, Health Resources and Services Administration, unpublished data. Prior to 1980, data were published by U.S. National Center for Health Statistics in *Health Resources Statistics,* annual.

No. 159. Physicians, by Type of Practice: 1970 to 1989

[As of **December 31,** except 1988 and 1989 for MD's as of January 1 of the following year. Includes Puerto Rico and outlying areas. Excludes 4,148 non-Federal physicians with temporary foreign addresses in 1970, 5,559 in 1975, 6,755 in 1980, 6,259 in 1981, 174 in 1982, 7,039 in 1983, 7,514 in 1985, 8,072 in 1986, 8,947 in 1987, 8,947 in 1988 and 9,059 in 1989]

TYPE OF PRACTICE	NUMBER (1,000)									PERCENT DISTRIBUTION			
	1970	1975	1980	1983	1985	1986	1987	1988	1989	1970	1980	1985	1989
All physicians [1]	348.3	409.0	486.5	541.1	576.7	594.7	612.4	629.1	645.0	100	100	100	100
Doctors of medicine [1]	334.0	393.7	467.7	519.5	552.7	569.2	585.6	600.8	615.4	96	96	96	95
Active M.D.'s [2]	311.2	366.4	435.5	479.4	511.0	519.4	534.7	549.2	560.0	89	90	89	87
Non-Federal [3]	301.3	359.7	443.5	496.9	528.2	544.3	561.0	577.6	592.2	87	91	92	92
Patient care	255.0	287.8	361.9	408.1	431.5	444.7	461.2	477.2	487.8	73	74	75	76
Office based [4]	188.9	213.3	271.2	308.3	329.0	325.8	337.5	350.1	359.9	54	56	57	56
General practice [5]	50.8	46.3	47.7	51.4	53.9	53.6	55.1	56.3	57.6	15	10	9	9
Specialty	138.1	167.0	223.5	257.0	275.2	272.1	282.4	293.7	302.4	40	46	48	47
Training programs [6]	45.8	53.5	59.6	70.6	72.2	85.4	87.5	88.4	89.9	13	12	13	14
Full-time hospital staff	20.3	21.0	31.0	29.2	30.3	33.5	36.2	38.8	38.0	6	6	5	6
Other professional activity	26.3	24.3	35.2	39.3	44.0	39.1	38.4	39.2	39.0	8	7	8	6
Retired, not in practice	19.6	21.4	25.7	36.9	38.6	46.8	48.0	48.8	52.7	6	5	7	8
Federal [7]	29.5	28.2	17.8	19.4	21.6	21.9	21.7	20.4	20.4	8	4	4	3
Patient care [7]	23.5	24.1	14.6	15.3	17.3	17.4	17.3	15.9	16.1	7	3	3	2
Full-time hospital staff	14.6	17.7	11.0	11.1	12.9	12.9	13.0	12.4	12.8	4	2	2	2
Other professional activity	6.0	4.1	3.2	4.0	4.3	4.5	4.5	4.4	4.4	2	1	1	1
Doctors of osteopathy [8]	14.3	15.4	18.8	21.6	24.0	25.5	26.8	28.3	29.6	4	4	4	5

[1] Includes physicians with unknown addresses and those not classified, not shown separately.   [2] Excludes physicians of unknown addresses.   [3] Includes physicians inactive and not classified. Excludes unknown addresses.   [4] Covers all physicians rendering patient care (or patient services by pathologists) in solo, partnership, group practice, or other industry, insurance companies, health depts., laboratories, etc.   [5] Includes family practice.   [6] Includes 7,828 clinical fellows in 1986, 7,987 in 1987 and 8,338 in 1988 and 8,249 on 1989.   [7] Includes Federal physicians in office-based practice and training programs.   [8] Total DO's. For 1990 the number of total DO's is 30,900; for 1991, 32,300. Source: American Osteopathic Association, Chicago, IL.

Source: Except as noted, 1970 and 1975, U.S. National Center for Health Statistics, *Health Resources Statistics,* annual; thereafter, American Medical Association, Chicago, IL, *Physician Characteristics and Distribution in the U.S.,* annual (copyright).

No. 160. Active Non-Federal Physicians and Dentists, 1990, and Nurses, 1989—States

[As of **Dec. 31, except as noted.** Excludes doctors of osteopathy, Federally employed persons, and physicians with addresses unknown. Includes all physicians not classified according to activity status]

REGION, DIVISION, AND STATE	PHYSICIANS, 1990 [1]		DENTISTS, 1990		NURSES, 1989		REGION, DIVISION, AND STATE	PHYSICIANS, 1990 [1]		DENTISTS, 1990		NURSES, 1989	
	Total	Rate[2]	Total	Rate[2]	Total	Rate[2]		Total	Rate[2]	Total	Rate[2]	Total	Rate[2]
U.S.	**532,638**	**216**	**145,500**	**59**	**1,666,200**	**676**	DC..	3,674	615	600	100	9,500	1591
North-							VA..	12,615	213	3,210	53	34,400	580
east ...	**141,690**	**280**	**36,660**	**72**	**428,400**	**846**	WV..	3,086	166	850	47	11,200	603
N.E ...	**38,031**	**293**	**9,220**	**70**	**131,000**	**1008**	NC..	12,262	190	2,730	42	40,500	626
ME..	2,155	178	580	48	10,200	841	SC..	5,541	161	1,410	41	15,900	461
NH..	2,199	200	650	59	10,100	917	GA..	11,144	175	2,950	46	35,800	562
VT..	1,432	253	320	57	5,200	917	FL..	26,123	208	6,230	49	84,100	669
MA..	19,910	337	4,470	74	68,000	1153	**E.S.C.**	**25,740**	**168**	**7,370**	**49**	**82,500**	**539**
RI..	2,515	254	560	56	9,300	938	KY..	6,202	168	2,020	55	18,400	498
CT..	9,820	305	2,640	81	28,200	875	TN..	9,619	196	2,660	55	29,100	591
M.A...	**103,659**	**275**	**27,440**	**73**	**297,400**	**790**	AL..	6,464	158	1,700	42	22,800	557
NY..	56,395	315	14,200	79	143,300	800	MS..	3,455	133	990	39	12,200	469
NJ..	18,971	246	5,740	74	53,400	692	**W.S.C.**	**45,916**	**171**	**12,740**	**48**	**127,400**	**475**
PA..	28,293	235	7,500	63	100,700	837	AR..	3,595	150	970	41	12,000	501
Midwest .	**114,273**	**190**	**35,510**	**60**	**438,900**	**731**	LA..	8,173	188	2,050	49	18,700	430
E.N.C .	**81,124**	**192**	**25,200**	**60**	**300,500**	**712**	OK..	4,697	147	1,580	51	15,100	473
OH..	21,379	196	6,110	56	81,600	749	TX..	29,451	175	8,140	48	81,600	484
IN...	8,764	157	2,710	49	37,900	678							
IL...	24,680	212	7,310	64	83,600	719	**West ...**	**113,761**	**222**	**31,780**	**61**	**317,900**	**620**
MI ..	17,129	185	5,860	63	62,900	679	**Mt....**	**24,690**	**184**	**7,790**	**57**	**84,500**	**631**
WI ..	9,172	189	3,210	66	34,500	709	MT..	1,263	158	520	65	5,300	662
W.N.C.	**33,149**	**186**	**10,310**	**59**	**138,400**	**779**	ID...	1,259	125	550	55	5,300	525
MN..	9,574	220	2,930	67	34,300	788	WY..	654	139	260	58	2,800	594
IA...	4,280	151	1,610	58	23,100	814	CO..	6,894	211	2,320	71	23,400	715
MO..	10,100	196	2,790	54	38,900	756	NM..	2,768	183	700	47	7,300	482
ND..	1,102	170	320	51	6,000	923	AZ..	6,961	197	1,790	49	23,700	671
SD..	992	140	350	51	5,900	833	UT..	3,145	185	1,150	67	8,500	500
NE..	2,741	172	1,030	66	12,200	763	NV..	1,746	159	500	42	8,200	746
KS..	4,360	175	1,280	52	18,000	723	**Pac...**	**89,071**	**235**	**23,990**	**62**	**233,400**	**617**
							WA..	10,006	213	3,140	65	35,800	761
South ...	**162,914**	**192**	**41,550**	**49**	**480,800**	**568**	OR..	5,778	205	1,970	69	21,100	749
S.A ...	**91,258**	**215**	**21,440**	**50**	**270,900**	**637**	CA..	70,062	244	17,680	60	167,900	584
DE..	1,329	199	290	44	6,000	898	AK..	734	146	340	65	2,700	538
MD..	15,484	334	3,170	67	33,500	722	HI...	2,491	236	850	81	5,900	559

[1] As of January 1, 1990.   [2] Per 100,000 civilian population. Based on U.S. Bureau of the Census estimates as of July 1 for 1989 for physicians and nurses; July 1, 1990 for dentists. Estimates do not reflect revisions based on the 1990 Census of Population.
Source: Physicians: American Medical Association, Chicago, IL, *Physician Characteristics and Distribution in the U.S.,* annual (copyright); Dentists and nurses: U.S. Dept. of Health and Human Services, Health Resources and Services Administration, unpublished data. Dentists: Based on data supplied by American Dental Association, Bureau of Economic and Behavioral Research.

No. 161. Federal and Non-Federal Physicians, by Sex, Specialty, and Major Professional Activity: 1970 to 1990

[**In thousands, except percent.** As of **December 31 through 1985; 1990** as of **January 1.** Includes Puerto Rico and outlying areas]

SPECIALTY	1970		1975	1980	1985	1990						
						Total		Patient care				Other profes- sional [2]
	Total	Per- cent				Num- ber	Per- cent	Total	Office based	Hospital based		
										Full time	Resi- dents [1]	
Total [3]	**334.5**	**100.0**	**393.7**	**467.7**	**552.7**	**615.4**	**100.0**	**503.9**	**360.9**	**50.8**	**92.1**	**43.4**
Male	(NA)	(NA)	358.1	413.4	472.0	511.2	83.1	417.5	311.7	40.5	65.3	36.5
Female	(NA)	(NA)	35.6	54.3	80.7	104.2	16.9	86.4	49.2	10.3	26.8	6.9
General practice [4]	57.9	17.3	54.6	60.0	67.1	70.5	11.5	68.3	58.0	4.2	6.0	2.2
Internal medicine	41.9	12.5	54.3	71.5	90.4	98.3	16.0	88.7	58.0	7.6	23.1	9.6
Pediatrics	17.9	5.4	21.7	28.3	35.6	40.9	6.6	37.6	26.6	3.6	7.3	3.4
General surgery	29.8	8.9	31.6	34.0	38.2	38.4	6.2	36.8	24.5	2.9	9.4	1.6
Obstetrics, gynecology	18.9	5.7	21.7	26.3	30.9	33.7	5.5	32.5	25.5	1.9	5.2	1.1
Orthopedic surgery	9.6	2.9	11.4	14.0	17.2	19.1	3.1	18.7	14.2	1.1	3.4	0.4
Ophthalmology	9.9	3.0	11.1	13.0	14.9	16.1	2.6	15.6	13.1	0.6	1.9	0.5
Psychiatry	21.1	6.3	23.9	27.5	32.3	35.2	5.7	31.8	20.1	6.0	5.6	3.4
Anesthesiology	10.1	3.0	12.8	14.0	20.0	26.0	4.2	24.9	17.8	3.0	4.1	1.1
Pathology	10.3	3.1	11.7	13.4	15.5	16.2	2.6	13.0	7.3	3.2	2.5	3.2
Radiology	10.5	3.1	11.5	11.7	16.1	8.5	1.4	7.9	6.1	1.2	0.7	0.5

NA Not available.   [1] Includes interns and clinical fellows.   [2] Medical teaching, administration, research, and other. [3] Includes other specialties not shown separately. Beginning 1975, also Includes physicians who are inactive, not classified, or with address unknown, not shown separately.   [4] Includes general practice.
Source: American Medical Association, Chicago, IL, *Distribution of Physicians in the United States, 1970, Physician Distribution and Medical Licensure in the U.S., 1975;* and, beginning 1980, *Physician Characteristics and Distribution in the U.S.,* annual, (copyright).

No. 162. Physician and Dental Visits, by Patient Characteristics: 1970 to 1989

[See headnote, table 188. Based on National Health Interview Survey; see Appendix III]

TYPE OF VISIT AND YEAR	TOTAL VISITS (mil.)				VISITS PER PERSON PER YEAR									
	Sex		Race [1]		Sex		Race [1]		Age (years)					
	Male	Fe-male	White	Black	Male	Fe-male	White	Black	Under 6	6 to 16	17 to 24	25 to 44	45 to 64	65 and over
Physicians: 1970..	396	531	832	87	4.1	5.1	4.8	3.9	5.9	2.9	4.6	4.6	5.2	6.3
1980..........	426	610	903	115	4.0	5.4	4.8	4.5	6.7	3.2	4.0	4.6	5.1	6.4
1985..........	498	733	1,074	132	4.4	6.1	5.4	4.7	[2]6.3	3.1	4.2	4.9	6.1	8.3
1987..........	523	765	1,118	140	4.5	6.2	5.5	4.9	[2]6.7	[3]3.3	[4]4.4	4.8	6.4	8.9
1988..........	530	774	1,139	136	4.5	6.2	5.6	4.6	[2]7.0	[3]3.4	[4]3.8	5.1	6.1	8.7
1989..........	552	771	1,148	140	4.7	6.1	5.6	4.7	[2]6.7	[3]3.5	[4]3.9	5.1	6.1	8.9
Dentists: 1970 ...	133	171	283	17	1.4	1.7	1.6	0.8	0.5	1.9	1.8	1.7	1.5	1.1
1980..........	158	207	333	26	1.5	1.8	1.8	1.0	0.5	2.3	1.6	1.7	1.8	1.4
1983..........	183	239	382	31	1.6	2.0	1.9	1.1	0.5	2.6	1.6	1.9	2.0	1.5
1986..........	210	256	416	37	1.9	2.2	2.1	1.4	[2]0.7	[3]2.4	[4]1.7	2.0	2.2	2.1
1989..........	221	271	441	34	1.9	2.2	2.1	1.1	[2]0.5	[3]2.4	[4]1.6	2.0	2.4	2.0

[1] See footnote 2, table 188.   [2] Under 5 years.   [3] 5 to 17 years.   [4] 18 to 24 years.
Source: U.S. National Center for Health Statistics, *Vital and Health Statistics*, series 10, and unpublished data.

No. 163. Physician Contacts, by Place of Contact and Selected Patient Characteristic: 1984 and 1989

[Based on the National Health Interview Survey; see Appendix III. Data are age-adjusted]

CHARACTERISTIC	PHYSICIAN CONTACTS PER PERSON (Number)		PERCENT BY PLACE OF CONTACT									
			Doctor's office		Hospital [1]		Telephone		Home		Other [2]	
	1984	1989	1984	1989	1984	1989	1984	1989	1984	1989	1984	1989
Total [3]	5.0	5.3	56.0	59.6	14.3	13.2	15.1	12.3	1.6	1.4	13.1	13.4
Sex: Male	4.4	4.8	55.1	58.1	15.9	15.0	13.2	11.2	1.6	1.2	14.3	14.5
Female	5.6	5.9	56.5	60.5	13.2	12.1	16.2	12.9	1.6	1.6	12.5	12.9
Race: White	5.1	5.5	57.6	60.9	12.8	12.2	15.8	12.9	1.5	1.4	12.3	12.7
Black	4.8	4.9	43.9	50.6	25.4	20.4	10.2	9.3	2.2	2.0	18.4	17.8
Income: [4]												
Less than $14,000....	5.8	6.3	46.7	48.5	19.7	18.0	12.0	10.8	2.5	2.4	19.1	20.3
$14,000 to $24,999 ...	4.8	5.2	53.4	58.9	16.7	14.3	14.3	12.9	0.9	1.4	14.7	12.5
$25,000 to $34,999 ...	4.9	5.5	59.2	61.0	13.5	12.1	14.8	12.4	0.8	0.8	11.7	13.7
$35,000 to $49,999 ...	5.2	5.2	60.8	63.1	10.9	12.1	17.5	12.9	1.0	0.6	9.8	11.4
$50,000 or more	5.5	6.0	60.5	63.4	10.5	10.7	16.8	13.6	1.7	1.7	10.6	10.7

[1] Includes hospital outpatient department, emergency room, and other hospital contacts.   [2] Includes clinics and places outside a hospital.   [3] Includes other races and unknown family income.   [4] Catagories shown are for 1989. Catagories for 1984 are: less than $10,000; $10,000 to $18,999; $19,000 to $29,999; and $40,000 or more.

Source: U.S. National Center for Health Statistics, *Health, U.S.,* 1990.

No. 164. Physicians' Mean Net Income and Liability Premiums, by Selected Specialty: 1982 to 1989

[In thousands of dollars. Based on a sample telephone survey of 4,000 nonfederal office and hospital based patient care physicians, excluding residents, with a response rate of 69.1% in 1990. For details, see source. For definition of mean, see Guide to Tabular Presentation]

SPECIALTY	1982	1983	1984	1985	1986	1987	1988	1989
MEAN NET INCOME								
All physicians [1]	97.7	104.1	108.4	112.2	119.5	132.3	144.7	155.8
General/Family practice......	71.4	66.9	71.6	77.9	80.3	91.5	94.6	95.9
Internal medicine...........	86.9	94.6	104.2	102.0	109.4	121.8	130.9	146.5
Surgery...................	128.6	144.3	151.0	155.0	162.4	187.9	207.5	220.5
Pediatrics.................	70.5	70.8	73.7	76.2	81.8	85.3	94.9	104.7
Obstetrics/Gynecology.......	112.3	118.1	118.8	124.3	135.9	163.2	180.7	194.3
MEAN LIABILITY PREMIUM								
All physicians [1]	5.8	6.9	8.4	10.5	12.8	15.0	15.9	15.5
General/Family practice......	3.5	4.2	4.6	6.8	7.3	8.9	9.4	9.0
Internal medicine...........	3.7	4.5	4.9	5.8	7.1	8.4	9.0	8.2
Surgery...................	9.9	11.0	13.3	16.6	21.3	24.5	26.5	25.8
Pediatrics.................	2.9	3.9	3.4	4.7	6.3	7.1	9.3	7.8
Obstetrics/Gynecology.......	10.8	14.0	19.0	23.5	29.3	35.3	35.3	37.0

[1] Includes other specialties, not shown separately.

Source: American Medical Association, Chicago IL, *Socioeconomic Characteristics of Medical Practice, 1990/1991* (copyright).

No. 172. Facilities and Services Provided by Community Hospitals: 1990

[Community hospitals are non-federal short-stay (average length of stay fewer than 30 days) excluding hospital units of institutions. Data are for hospitals responding to that portion of the questionnaire—5,056 of a total of 5,384 hospitals]

SERVICE	Hospitals with service	Percent of total	SERVICE	Hospitals with service	Percent of total
Alcoholism/chemical dependency			Psychiatric services:		
outpatient services	1,035	20.5	Emergency	1,699	33.6
Birthing rooms.	3,292	65.1	Outpatient	989	19.6
Blood bank.	3,493	69.1			
Cardiac catheterization	1,390	27.5	Radiation therapy:		
Computed tomographic (CT) scanner . .	3,544	70.1	X-ray	983	19.4
Emergency department.	4,728	93.5	Megavoltage (mil. volts).	994	19.7
			Radio-active implants	1,262	25.0
Extracorporeal shock wave			Radio isotope facilities:		
lithotripter	319	6.3	Diagnostic	3,173	62.8
Genetic counseling services	495	9.8	Therapeutic	1,279	25.3
Geriatric services.	3,072	60.8	Rehabilitation outpatient		
Hemodialysis	1,347	26.6	department	2,606	51.5
Histopathology laboratory	3,272	64.7	Reproductive health services	2,129	42.1
Home health services.	1,801	35.6			
Hospice	817	16.2	Therapy services:		
Hospital auxiliary	4,152	82.1	Occupational therapy services.	2,510	49.6
Magnetic resonance imaging (MRI)	919	18.2	Physical therapy services	4,271	84.5
Open-heart surgery facilities	847	16.8	Recreational therapy services	1,656	32.8
Organ tissue transplant.	526	10.4	Respiratory therapy services.	4,579	90.6
			Trauma center.	651	12.9
Outpatient department	4,309	85.2	Ultrasound	4,262	84.3
Outpatient surgery services	4,788	94.7	Volunteer services department.	3,427	67.8
Patient representative services.	2,688	53.2	Women's center	1,045	20.7

Source: American Hospital Association, Chicago, IL, *Hospital Statistics, 1991-1992*, (copyright).

No. 173. Hospital Utilization Rates, by Sex, 1970 to 1989, and Selected Characteristics, 1989

[Represents estimates of inpatients discharged from noninstitutional, short-stay hospitals, exclusive of Federal hospitals. Excludes newborn. Based on sample data collected from the National Hospital Discharge Survey, a sample survey of hospital records of patients discharged in year shown; subject to sampling variability. For methodological details, see source. For composition of regions, see table 25]

SELECTED CHARACTERISTIC	Patients discharged (1,000)	PATIENTS DISCHARGED PER 1,000 PERSONS [1]			DAYS OF CARE PER 1,000 PERSONS [1]			AVERAGE STAY (days)			Beds used per day [2]
		Total	Male	Female	Total	Male	Female	Total	Male	Female	
1970.	29,127	144	118	169	1,122	982	1,251	8.0	8.7	7.6	321
1980.	37,832	168	139	194	1,217	1,068	1,356	7.3	7.7	7.0	337
1983.	38,783	167	139	193	1,155	1,024	1,278	6.9	7.4	6.6	316
1984.	37,162	159	132	184	1,044	924	1,155	6.6	7.0	6.3	286
1985.	35,056	148	124	171	954	849	1,053	6.5	6.9	6.2	261
1986.	34,256	143	121	164	913	817	1,003	6.4	6.8	6.1	250
1987	33,387	138	116	159	889	806	968	6.4	6.9	6.1	244
1988 [3].	31,146	128	107	147	834	757	907	6.5	7.1	6.2	228
1989, [3] total	**30,947**	**126**	**105**	**145**	**815**	**741**	**884**	**6.5**	**7.0**	**6.1**	**223**
Age:											
Under 1 year old	791	201	233	166	1,210	1,346	1,068	6.0	5.8	6.4	332
1 to 4 years old	819	55	66	45	195	233	155	3.5	3.5	3.5	53
5 to 14 years old	987	28	31	25	142	162	120	5.0	5.3	4.7	39
15 to 24 years old	3,617	101	47	154	410	272	547	4.1	5.7	3.5	112
25 to 34 years old	4,969	115	56	173	523	370	673	4.5	6.6	3.9	143
35 to 44 years old	3,262	90	76	103	502	474	529	5.6	6.2	5.1	138
45 to 64 years old	6,271	135	143	128	904	962	850	6.7	6.7	6.6	248
65 to 74 years old	4,678	257	281	238	2,116	2,232	2,022	8.2	7.9	8.5	580
75 years old and over . . .	5,552	434	485	405	4,087	4,507	3,861	9.4	7.3	9.5	1,120
Region:											
Northeast	7,044	139	123	154	1,070	986	1,146	7.7	8.0	7.4	293
Midwest	7,676	128	109	146	817	747	884	6.4	6.9	6.1	224
South.	10,960	130	106	152	815	728	896	6.3	6.9	5.9	223
West	5,268	103	84	121	559	519	597	5.4	6.2	4.9	153

[1] Based on Bureau of the Census estimated civilian population as of July 1. Estimates do not reflect revisions based on the 1990 Census of Population.   [2] Average daily number of beds occupied per 100,000 civilian population.   [3] Comparisons of 1988 and 1989 data with data for earlier years should be made with caution as estimates of change may reflect improvements in the design rather than true changes in hospital use.

Source: U.S. National Center for Health Statistics, *Vital Health Statistics*, series 13, and unpublished data.

No. 174. Hospital Discharges and Days of Care, by Sex, Age, and Diagnosis: 1989

[See headnote, table 173]

AGE AND FIRST-LISTED DIAGNOSIS	DISCHARGES Number (1,000)	DISCHARGES Per 1,000 persons [1]	Days of care per 1,000 persons [1]	Average stay (days)	AGE AND FIRST-LISTED DIAGNOSIS	DISCHARGES Number (1,000)	DISCHARGES Per 1,000 persons [1]	Days of care per 1,000 persons [1]	Average stay (days)
MALE					FEMALE				
All ages	**12,583**	**105.3**	**740.7**	**7.0**	**All ages**	**18,364**	**144.5**	**883.9**	**6.1**
					Delivery	3,937	31.0	90.2	2.9
Diseases of heart	1,892	15.8	107.3	6.8	Diseases of heart	1,642	12.9	93.5	7.2
Malignant neoplasms	770	6.4	59.3	9.2	Malignant neoplasms	838	6.6	61.1	9.3
Pneumonia, all forms	544	4.6	35.5	7.8	Fractures, all sites	541	4.3	39.9	9.4
Fractures, all sites	480	4.0	30.3	7.5	Pneumonia, all forms	489	3.8	32.3	8.4
Cerebrovascular diseases	344	2.9	29.6	10.3					
					Under 15 years [2]	1,077	40.9	198.6	4.9
Under 15 years [2]	1,521	55.1	268.3	4.9	Pneumonia, all forms	95	3.6	16.7	4.6
Acute respiratory infection	137	5.0	17.1	3.4	Acute respiratory infection	78	3.0	10.4	3.5
Pneumonia, all forms	126	4.6	18.7	4.1	Bronchitis, emphysema [3]	64	2.4	6.8	2.8
Bronchitis, emphysema [3]	115	4.2	12.2	2.9	Congenital anomalies	53	2.0	12.6	6.2
Congenital anomalies	83	3.0	14.5	4.8	Chronic disease of tonsils and				
Fractures, all sites	77	2.8	15.0	5.4	adenoids	48	1.8	2.1	1.2
15 to 44 years [2]	3,405	59.8	371.5	6.2	15 to 44 years [2]	8,443	144.9	588.2	4.1
Fractures, all sites	241	4.2	25.8	6.1	Delivery	3,926	67.4	196.2	2.9
Psychoses	217	3.8	51.3	13.5	Pregnancy w/abortive outcome	227	3.9	9.0	2.3
Diseases of heart	146	2.6	13.9	5.4	Psychoses	197	3.4	48.4	14.3
Lacerations and open wounds	124	2.2	8.1	3.7	Benign neoplasms	161	2.8	11.5	4.2
Intervertebral disc disorders	122	2.1	9.4	4.4	Cholelithiasis	142	2.4	11.4	4.7
45 to 64 years [2]	3,179	142.8	962.1	6.7	45 to 64 years [2]	3,092	127.9	850.0	6.6
Diseases of heart	730	32.8	195.4	6.0	Diseases of heart	386	16.0	95.4	6.0
Malignant neoplasms	240	10.8	96.8	9.0	Malignant neoplasms	273	11.3	92.2	8.2
Cerebrovascular diseases	88	4.0	34.2	8.7	Benign neoplasms	108	4.4	21.2	4.8
Fractures, all sites	80	3.6	32.2	9.0	Cholelithiasis	107	4.4	23.7	5.4
Intervertebral disc disorders	78	3.5	18.1	5.2	Psychoses	104	4.3	64.0	14.9
65 years old and older [2]	4,478	354.4	3,047.0	8.6	65 years old and older [2]	5,752	313.5	2,850.1	9.1
Diseases of heart	1,007	79.7	603.6	7.6	Diseases of heart	1,170	63.8	497.8	7.8
Malignant neoplasms	447	35.4	335.6	9.5	Malignant neoplasms	431	23.5	247.7	10.6
Pneumonia, all forms	271	21.4	200.8	9.4	Cerebrovascular disease	368	20.1	205.1	10.2
Cerebrovascular disease	238	18.9	207.7	11.0	Fractures, all sites	329	17.9	206.0	11.5
Hyperplasia of prostate	193	15.3	84.2	5.5	Pneumonia, all forms	261	14.2	139.6	9.8

[1] See footnote 1, table 173. [2] Includes other first-listed diagnoses, not shown separately. [3] Includes asthma.

Source: U.S. National Center for Health Statistics, *Health, United States*, 1990, and unpublished data.

No. 175. Surgery Performed in Hospitals: 1980 to 1990

[In thousands, except percent]

TYPE OF HOSPITAL	1980	1983	1984	1985	1986	1987	1988	1989	1990	Percent change 1980-90
OUTPATIENT SURGERIES (1,000)										
All hospitals	3,198	4,969	5,803	7,309	8,705	9,758	10,586	10,953	11,678	265.2
Ownership:										
Non federal hospitals	3,063	4,735	5,549	6,984	8,272	9,145	10,038	10,362	11,085	261.9
Community hospitals [1]	3,054	4,715	5,530	6,951	8,247	9,126	10,028	10,351	11,070	262.5
Non governmental nonprofit	2,416	3,677	4,319	5,392	6,265	6,903	7,577	7,834	8,389	247.2
Federal hospitals	135	235	254	325	434	612	548	591	593	339.2
Size of hospital: 6 to 99 beds	354	506	591	752	966	1,146	1,229	1,241	1,303	268.0
100 to 199 beds	571	864	1,092	1,502	1,811	2,030	2,252	2,360	2,498	337.8
200 to 299 beds	630	996	1,168	1,521	1,836	2,023	2,297	2,383	2,543	303.4
300 to 499 beds	977	1,438	1,727	2,069	2,368	2,617	2,845	2,920	3,172	224.8
500 beds or more	666	1,167	1,225	1,465	1,725	1,942	1,963	2,049	2,162	224.4
OUTPATIENT SURGERIES AS PERCENT OF TOTAL										
All hospitals	16.4	23.9	27.8	34.5	40.3	44.2	47.0	48.7	50.6	(X)
Ownership:										
Non federal hospitals	16.3	23.8	27.8	34.5	40.3	43.9	46.8	48.5	50.5	(X)
Community hospitals [1]	16.3	23.8	27.8	34.6	40.3	43.8	46.8	48.5	50.5	(X)
Non governmental nonprofit	17.1	24.6	28.8	35.5	40.8	44.2	47.0	48.6	50.7	(X)
Federal hospitals	18.6	26.7	28.1	33.9	40.7	49.9	49.7	51.5	51.8	(X)
Size of hospital: 6 to 99 beds	17.9	25.6	29.6	36.5	44.7	49.4	52.8	54.1	56.2	(X)
100 to 199 beds	15.4	22.9	28.2	36.3	42.9	47.2	50.3	52.3	55.0	(X)
200 to 299 beds	16.7	25.2	29.1	36.4	42.0	45.7	49.2	50.7	52.9	(X)
300 to 499 beds	17.2	24.1	28.6	34.4	40.0	43.1	46.5	48.0	48.8	(X)
500 beds or more	15.1	23.0	24.9	30.4	35.2	39.2	39.6	41.6	43.9	(X)

X Not applicable. [1] For definition of comminity hospital, see footnotes 1 and 2, table 167.

Source: American Hospital Association, Chicago IL, *Hospital Statistics*, annual (copyright) and unpublished data from the Annual Survey of Hospitals.

No. 176. Procedures for Inpatients Discharged From Short-Stay Hospitals: 1980 to 1989

[Excludes newborn infants and discharges from Federal hospitals. See headnote, table 173]

SEX AND TYPE OF PROCEDURE	NUMBER OF PROCEDURES (1,000)					RATE PER 1,000 POPULATION [2]				
	1980	1985	1987	1988 [1]	1989 [1]	1980	1985	1987	1988 [1]	1989 [1]
BOTH SEXES										
Surgical procedures, total [3]	24,494	24,799	25,655	25,625	[4]23,370	108.6	104.6	106.2	105.0	[4]94.8
Procedures to assist delivery [4]	2,391	2,494	2,938	3,131	2,446	10.6	10.5	12.2	12.8	9.9
Cesarean section	619	877	953	933	938	2.7	3.7	3.9	3.8	3.8
Cardiac catheterization	348	681	866	930	958	1.5	2.9	3.6	3.8	3.9
Reduction of fracture [5]	605	681	685	639	671	2.7	2.9	2.8	2.6	2.7
Repair of current obstetric laceration . .	355	548	660	690	762	1.6	2.3	2.7	2.8	3.1
Hysterectomy	649	670	655	578	541	2.9	2.8	2.7	2.4	2.2
Diagnostic and other non-surgical procedures [6]	6,918	11,961	13,463	13,567	16,672	30.7	50.5	55.7	55.6	67.6
CAT scan [7]	306	1,378	1,646	1,613	1,519	1.4	5.8	6.8	6.6	6.2
Diagnostic ultrasound	318	1,234	1,596	1,562	1,558	1.4	5.2	6.6	6.4	6.3
Angiocardiography and arteriography [8] .	569	1,117	1,448	1,624	1,620	2.5	4.7	6.0	6.7	6.6
Radioisotope scan	525	838	759	704	635	2.3	3.5	3.1	2.9	2.6
Cystoscopy	867	645	593	542	487	3.8	2.7	2.5	2.2	2.0
MALE										
Surgical procedures, total [3]	8,505	8,805	9,073	9,069	8,886	78.1	76.8	77.6	76.7	74.4
Cardiac catheterization	228	439	533	598	601	2.1	3.8	4.6	5.1	5.0
Prostatectomy	335	367	410	358	376	3.1	3.2	3.5	3.0	3.1
Reduction of fracture [5]	325	339	367	367	342	3.0	3.0	3.1	2.8	2.9
Repair of inguinal hernia	483	370	290	261	220	4.4	3.2	2.5	2.2	1.8
Diagnostic and other non-surgical procedures [6]	3,386	5,889	6,643	6,665	7,202	31.1	51.4	56.8	56.4	60.3
Angiocardiography and arteriography [8] .	355	693	868	995	1,000	3.3	6.0	7.4	8.4	8.4
CAT scan [7]	152	671	814	775	721	1.4	5.9	7.0	6.6	6.0
FEMALE										
Surgical procedures, total [3]	15,989	15,994	16,583	16,555	14,484	137.1	130.6	133.0	131.5	114.0
Procedures to assist delivery [4]	2,391	2,494	2,938	3,131	2,446	20.5	20.4	23.6	24.9	19.2
Cesarean section	619	877	953	933	938	5.3	7.2	7.6	7.4	7.4
Repair of current obstetric laceration . .	355	548	660	690	762	3.0	4.5	5.3	5.5	6.0
Hysterectomy	649	670	655	578	541	5.6	5.5	5.3	4.6	4.3
Diagnostic and other non-surgical procedures [6]	3,532	6,072	6,820	6,902	9,471	30.3	49.6	54.7	54.8	74.5
Diagnostic ultrasound	204	756	981	963	930	1.7	6.2	7.9	7.6	7.3
CAT scan [7]	154	707	833	838	798	1.3	5.8	6.7	6.7	6.3

[1] Comparisons of 1988 and 1989 data with data for earlier years should be made with caution as estimates of change may reflect improvements in the design rather than true changes in hospital use.   [2] Based on Bureau of the Census estimated civilian population as of July 1. Population estimates do not reflect revised estimates based on the 1990 Census of Population.   [3] Includes other types of surgical procedures not shown separately.   [4] Beginning in 1989, the definition of some surgical and diagnostic and other non-surgical procedures was revised, causing a discontinuity in the trends for some totals.   [5] Excluding skull, nose, and jaw.   [6] Includes other non-surgical procedures not shown separately.   [7] Computerized axial tomography.   [8] Using contrast material.

Source: U.S. National Center for Health Statistics, *Vital and Health Statistics*, series 13, and unpublished data.

No. 177. Organ Transplants and Grafts: 1981 to 1990

[As of end of year. Based on reports of procurement programs and transplant centers in the United States]

PROCEDURE	NUMBER OF PROCEDURES							NUMBER OF CENTERS		Number of people waiting, as of 1990	One-year survival rates, 1989 (percent)
	1981	1985	1986	1987	1988	1989	1990	1981	1990		
Transplant:											
Heart	62	719	1,368	1,512	1,647	1,673	1,998	8	148	1,796	82
Liver	26	602	924	1,199	1,680	2,160	2,534	1	85	1,248	65
Kidney	4,883	7,095	076	8,967	9,123	8,890	9,433	157	232	17,955	92
Heart-lung	5	30	45	41	74	67	52	(NA)	79	226	55
Lung	-	2	-	11	31	89	187	(NA)	68	309	45
Pancreas/Islet cell	(NA)	130	140	180	243	413	529	(NA)	83	474	45
Cornea grafts	15,500	26,300	28,000	35,930	36,900	38,464	40,631	(NA)	[1]107	(NA)	[2]95
Bone grafts	(NA)	(NA)	200,000	250,000	300,000	(NA)	350,000	(NA)	75	(NA)	(NA)
Skin grafts	(NA)	(NA)	2,000	5,000	5,200	(NA)	5,500	(NA)	25	(NA)	(NA)

- Represents zero.   NA Not available.   [1] Eye banks.   [2] Success rate.

Source: U.S. Department of Health and Human Services, Public Health Service, Division of Organ Transplantation, American Association of Tissue Banks, McLean, VA, and Eye Bank Association of America, Washington, DC, and unpublished data.

No. 178. Patients Discharged From Hospitals—Principal Source of Expected Payment, by Selected Characteristic: 1989

[Covers non-Federal short-stay hospitals. Discharges excludes newborn infants. Based on the National Hospital Discharge Survey. See headnote, table 173. For composition of regions, see table 25]

CHARACTERISTIC	Total discharges [1] (1,000)	PRINCIPAL SOURCE OF EXPECTED PAYMENT— PERCENT DISTRIBUTION								
		Private insurance	Government					Self-pay	No charge	Other [2]
			Medicare	Medicaid	Worker's compensation	Other				
AGE										
All ages	30,947	38.9	34.2	10.4	1.8	2.2	5.6	0.4	3.8
Under 15 years old	2,597	51.4	4.1	24.0	(X)	3.2	8.5	1.1	5.0
15 to 44 years old	11,848	54.8	3.4	16.7	2.6	3.2	9.5	0.6	5.5
45 to 64 years old	6,271	61.1	13.3	7.8	2.3	2.9	5.1	0.3	4.2
65 years old and over	10,230	3.6	90.4	1.1	1.1	0.4	0.7	(³)	1.3
SEX										
Male, all ages	12,583	36.8	37.6	7.3	3.1	2.2	6.1	0.5	3.7
Under 15 years old	1,521	50.7	4.8	24.1	(X)	3.2	8.7	1.1	4.7
15 to 44 years old	3,405	50.6	5.7	9.9	6.8	3.6	13.0	0.9	5.1
45 to 64 years old	3,179	60.8	15.2	5.3	3.1	2.7	5.3	0.3	4.5
65 years old and over	4,478	4.5	88.9	0.9	1.3	0.5	0.6	(³)	1.6
Female, all ages	18,364	40.3	31.9	12.5	0.9	2.2	5.3	0.3	3.9
Under 15 years old	1,077	52.3	3.0	23.8	(X)	3.2	8.3	1.2	5.3
15 to 44 years old	8,443	56.5	2.5	19.4	0.9	3.0	8.2	0.4	5.6
45 to 64 years old	3,092	61.5	11.4	10.4	1.4	3.0	4.9	0.3	3.9
65 years old and over	5,752	2.8	91.6	1.2	0.9	0.3	0.7	(³)	1.1
RACE										
White	22,678	40.8	37.4	6.8	2.0	1.8	4.7	0.3	3.7
All other	4,867	30.3	22.1	25.7	1.2	3.6	8.6	1.3	4.2
Not stated	3,402	38.6	30.5	12.3	1.5	3.2	7.5	(³)	3.9
GEOGRAPHIC REGION										
Northeast	7,044	39.4	33.4	11.1	2.1	1.2	6.0	0.3	4.3
Midwest	7,676	39.5	34.3	9.9	2.3	1.7	4.3	0.3	5.4
South	10,960	38.6	34.8	10.1	1.5	2.6	6.5	0.7	1.7
West	5,268	37.8	33.9	10.7	1.4	3.4	5.0	(³)	5.0

X Not applicable.   [1] Includes discharges for whom expected source of payment was unknown.   [2] Includes all other nonprofit source of payment such as church, welfare, or United Way.   [3] Figure does not meet standards of reliability or precision.

Source: U.S. National Center for Health Statistics, unpublished data.

No. 179. Nursing and Related Care Facilities: 1971 to 1989

ITEM	Unit	1971	1973	1976	1978	1980	1982	1984	1986	1989
Nursing and related care: [1]										
Facilities	Number	22,004	21,834	20,468	[2]18,722	[3]23,065	[4]25,849	(NA)	[4]25,648	(NA)
Beds	1,000	1,202	1,328	1,415	[2]1,349	[3]1,537	[4]1,642	(NA)	[4]1,709	(NA)
Resident patients	1,000	1,076	1,198	1,293	[2]1,240	[3]1,396	[4]1,493	(NA)	[4]1,553	(NA)
Employees, full-time	1,000	568	636	653	[2]664	[3]798	(NA)	(NA)	(NA)	(NA)
Per 1,000 patients	Rate	528	531	505	[2]535	[3]571	(NA)	(NA)	(NA)	(NA)
Skilled nursing facilities [5]	Number	4,277	3,970	3,922	4,745	5,052	5,408	5,952	6,897	8,198
Beds	1,000	307	287	309	408	436	488	530	(NA)	491
Per 1,000 Medicare enrollees [6]	Rate	15.1	13.5	13.7	17.3	17.7	19.1	19.9	(NA)	16.8

NA Not available.   [1] Covers nursing homes with 3 beds or more and all other places providing some form of nursing, personal, or domiciliary care; standards vary widely among States. Includes skilled nursing facilities. 1971-1984 based on National Master Facility Inventory. Some changes in data beginning 1976 may be due to dependence on State collection. 1986 data based on the 1986 Inventory of Long Term Care Places. Data may not be strictly comparable with previous years.   [2] Includes 1976 data for California, District of Columbia, New York, and North Carolina.   [3] Excludes hospital-based nursing homes and includes 1978 data for Alaska and South Dakota.   [4] Excludes hospital-based nursing homes.   [5] Source: Through 1976, U.S. Social Security Administration, *Health Insurance Statistics* and unpublished data. Beginning 1978, U.S. Health Care Financing Administration, *Medicare Participating Providers and Suppliers of Health Services, 1980;* and unpublished data. Covers facilities and beds certified for participation under Medicare as of mid-year. Includes facilities which have transfer agreements with one or more participating hospitals, and are engaged primarily in providing skilled nursing care and related services for the rehabilitation of injured, disabled, or sick persons.   [6] Based on number of aged persons residing in United States who were enrolled in the Medicare hospital insurance program as of July 1 of year stated.

Source: Except as noted, U.S. National Center for Health Statistics, *Health Resources Statistics,* annual through 1976 and 1978; 1982 and 1986, *Advance Data from Vital and Health Statistics,* No. 111 and No. 147, and unpublished data.

No. 180. Nursing and Related Care Facilities—Selected Characteristics: 1986

[Excludes hospital-based nursing homes. Based on the 1986 Inventory of Long-Term Care Places. For composition of regions, see table 25]

CHARACTERISTIC	TOTAL FACILITIES				NURSING HOMES [1]				RESIDENTIAL FACILITIES [2]			
	Homes	Beds (1,000)	Average number of beds	Occu-pancy rate	Homes	Beds (1,000)	Average number of beds	Occu-pancy rate	Homes	Beds (1,000)	Average number of beds	Occu-pancy rate
Total	25,646	1709.2	67	91.0	16,388	1,507.4	92	91.7	9,258	201.8	22	85.4
Northeast	4,863	373.8	77	93.7	2,948	317.5	108	94.8	1,915	56.3	29	87.6
Midwest	7,474	539.8	72	90.7	5,393	506.7	94	91.2	2,081	33.1	16	84.4
South	7,311	516.5	71	90.1	5,008	464.0	93	90.5	2,303	52.5	23	86.4
West	5,998	279.1	47	89.4	3,039	219.2	72	91.1	2,959	59.9	20	83.1
Government........	1,045	106.6	102	93.0	789	99.7	126	93.6	256	6.8	27	85.3
Proprietary........	20,223	1235.4	61	90.5	12,336	1,079.0	87	91.3	7,887	156.5	20	85.1
Nonprofit.........	4,378	367.2	84	91.8	3,263	328.7	101	92.4	1,115	38.5	35	86.5
3 to 9 beds	5,918	32.6	6	82.8	1,340	7.2	5	82.6	4,578	25.5	6	82.9
10 to 24 beds	3,695	58.1	16	86.3	1,069	18.2	17	87.6	2,626	39.9	15	85.7
25 to 49 beds	3,135	115.5	37	89.5	2,061	77.8	38	90.8	1,074	37.6	35	86.8
50 to 74 beds	3,470	208.7	60	92.2	3,037	182.7	60	92.8	433	26.0	60	87.6
75 to 99 beds	2,526	221.6	88	92.1	2,335	205.4	88	92.5	191	16.3	85	86.5
100 to 199 beds ...	5,755	756.2	131	91.1	5,468	717.6	131	91.5	287	38.6	135	84.8
200 to 299 beds....	858	198.2	231	90.8	804	186.1	231	91.3	54	12.1	225	82.9
300 to 499 beds....	239	84.9	355	91.2	225	80.1	356	92.1	14	4.8	340	76.9
500 beds or more....	50	33.4	667	95.0	49	32.3	659	94.8	1	1.1	1050	99.7
Certification: Medicare or Medicaid (skilled nursing facility)	8,045	984.1	122	92.9	8,045	984.1	122	92.9	-	-	-	-
Medicaid (intermediate care facility) [3]	5,375	411.5	77	90.3	5,375	411.5	77	90.3	-	-	-	-
Not certified nursing home	2,968	111.8	38	86.3	2,968	111.8	38	86.3	-	-	-	-
Residential facilities .	9,258	201.8	22	85.4	(X)	(X)	(X)	(X)	9,258	201.8	22	85.4

- Represents zero.   X Not applicable.   [1] These facilities have three or more beds and provide to adults who require it either (a) nursing care or (b) personal care (such as help with bathing, eating, using toilet facilities, or dressing) and/or supervision over such activities as money management, walking, and shopping.   [2] These facilities offer no nursing services and provide only personal care or supervisory care.   [3] Facilities certified as both skilled nursing facilities and intermediate care facilities have been classified as skilled nursing facilities.

Source: U.S. National Center for Health Statistics, *Advance Data From Vital and Health Statistics,* No. 147 and unpublished data.

No. 181. Residential Facilities for Persons with Mental Retardation: 1970 to 1989

[For years ending **June 30.** Persons with mental retardation refers to those who have been so designated by State governments in the process of placing them into residential facilities]

ITEM	STATE OPERATED FACILITIES [1]					PRIVATE FACILITIES [3]			
	1970	1980 [2]	1985 [2]	1988 [2]	1989 [2]	1977	1982	1988	1989
Number of facilities [4]	190	394	881	1,177	1,305	10,219	14,605	35,365	38,657
Residents beginning of year.........	189,956	148,734	117,101	102,390	99,267	(NA)	(NA)	(NA)	(NA)
Admissions [5]...................	14,985	14,064	7,713	6,928	6,518	22,363	22,431	(NA)	(NA)
Deaths in institutions..............	3,496	2,142	1,537	1,373	1,205	891	920	(NA)	(NA)
Live releases [6]...................	14,702	16,225	10,310	7,683	7,479	12,384	12,999	(NA)	(NA)
Residents end of year.............	186,743	140,230	112,183	99,327	94,268	89,120	115,032	171,275	180,023
Rate per 100,000 population [7]......	92.5	62.2	47.5	40.9	38.5	40.9	50.0	70.5	73.4
Average daily residents	187,897	136,304	111,791	99,095	96,171	(NA)	(NA)	(NA)	(NA)
Maintenance expenditures per day per average daily resident (dollars) [8].....	13	68	122	157	184	[9]19	[9]37	(NA)	(NA)

NA Not available.   [1] Data as submitted by many State agencies; figures reflect some estimates. Resident patients at the end of a year do not equal the number at the beginning of a succeeding year. Includes estimates for underreporting.   [2] Includes data for 142 facilities in 1980, 121 facilities in 1985, 122 in 1988, and 123 in 1989 operated as mental hospitals or other care facilities and which have residents with mental retardation. The average daily number of residents with mental retardation in these facilities was 8,240 in 1980, 5,602 in 1985, 1,933 in 1988, and 1,605 in 1989.   [3] A privately-operated living quarter which provides 24-hour, 7-days-a-week responsibility for room, board, and supervision of mentally retarded persons. Excludes single-family homes providing services to a relative; and nursing homes, boarding homes, and foster homes not formally licensed or contracted as mental retardation service providers.   [4] Beginning 1985, reflects the development of a large number of community based State-operated facilities which were developed in the early 1980's.   [5] Includes readmissions and excludes transfers. Excludes people entering newly opened facilities.   [6] 1970, represents excess of residents released alive from facility over those returning to facility. Beginning 1980, total live releases.   [7] Based on Bureau of the Census estimated civilian population as of July 1. Estimates reflect revisions based on 1990 Census of Population.   [8] Reporting facilities only; includes salaries and wages, purchased provisions, fuel, light, water, etc.   [9] Represents average daily reimbursement rate per resident.

Source: State-operated facilities: 1970, U.S. Office of Human Development Services, *Residents in Public Institutions for the Mentally Retarded,* annual, and unpublished data; 1980 through 1988, Center for Residential Services and Community Living (CRSCL), Institute on Community Integration, UAP, University of Minnesota, Minneapolis, MN, White, Lakin, Hill, Wright, and Bruininks, Report No. 30; 1989: MN, White, MN, White, Lakin, Bruininks, and Li, Report No. 33; 1989: Private facilities: CRSCL, Lakin, White, Prouty, Bruininks and Kimm, Brief Report No. 35, and unpublished data.

Health and Nutrition

No. 182. Mental Retardation Facilities—Summary, by Selected Characteristics: 1986

[Mental retardation (MR) facilities include intermediate care facilities (ICF-MR), foster homes, group residences, semi-independent living programs, State institutions and other kinds of MR places. Based on the 1986 Inventory of Long-Term Care Places. For an explanation of mental retardation, see table 181. For details, see source. For composition of regions, see table 25]

CHARACTERISTIC	FACILITIES		BEDS		RESIDENTS						Average number of residents
					Number			Percent distribution			
	Number	Percent distribution	Number	Percent distribution	Total [1]	Black	Hispanic [2]	Total [1]	Black	Hispanic [2]	
Total	**14,639**	**100.0**	**269,954**	**100.0**	**250,472**	**29,442**	**10,181**	**100.0**	**100.0**	**100.0**	**17**
BED SIZE											
1 to 5 beds..........	5,115	34.9	17,099	6.3	15,234	1,726	623	6.1	5.9	6.1	3
6 to 9 beds..........	5,491	37.5	37,318	13.8	34,815	3,159	1,587	13.9	10.7	15.6	6
10 to 15 beds	2,097	14.3	24,991	9.3	23,444	1,950	937	9.4	6.6	9.2	11
16 to 99 beds	1,531	10.5	58,050	21.5	54,090	5,485	2,333	21.6	18.6	22.9	35
100 beds or more.....	405	2.8	132,496	49.1	122,889	17,122	4,701	49.1	58.2	46.2	303
100 to 199 beds	198	1.4	26,206	9.7	24,539	3,698	995	9.8	12.6	9.8	124
200 to 499 beds	126	0.9	41,331	15.3	38,322	4,904	1,465	15.3	16.7	14.4	304
500 beds or more	81	0.6	64,959	24.1	60,028	8,520	2,241	24.0	28.9	22.0	741
GEOGRAPHIC REGION											
Northeast	3,806	26.0	65,812	24.4	61,707	5,634	1,578	24.6	19.1	15.5	16
Midwest	4,741	32.4	83,067	30.8	77,193	6,438	1,079	30.8	21.9	10.6	16
South..............	2,380	16.3	71,887	26.6	66,767	14,538	2,668	26.7	49.4	26.2	28
West	3,712	25.4	49,188	18.2	44,805	2,832	4,856	17.9	9.6	47.7	12
TYPE OF OWNERSHIP											
Profit	6,330	43.2	66,536	24.6	60,560	6,503	3,495	24.2	22.1	34.3	10
Nonprofit	6,396	43.7	78,935	29.2	75,193	6,938	2,316	30.0	23.6	22.7	12
Government	1,913	13.1	124,483	46.1	114,719	16,001	4,370	45.8	54.3	42.9	6

[1] Includes races not shown separately.   [2] Persons of Hispanic origin may be of any race.

Source: U.S. National Center for Health Statistics, *Advance Data*, No. 143, September 1987.

No. 183. Mental Health Facilities—Summary by Type of Facility: 1988

[Facilities, beds and inpatients as of **yearend 1988**; other data are for calendar year or fiscal year ending in a month other than December since facilities are permitted to report on either a calendar or fiscal year basis. Excludes private psychiatric office practice and psychiatric service modes of all types in hospitals or outpatient clinics of Federal agencies other than Veterans Administration. Excludes data from Puerto Rico, Virgin Islands, Guam, and other territories]

TYPE OF FACILITY	Number of facilities	INPATIENT BEDS		INPATIENTS		Average daily inpatients (1,000)	Inpatient care episodes [2] (1,000)	EXPENDITURES		Patient care staff [4] (1,000)
		Total (1,000)	Rate [1]	Total (1,000)	Rate [1]			Total (mil. dol.)	Per capita [3] (dol.)	
Total.........	**4,941**	**272.0**	**112.0**	**228.0**	**93.9**	**227.9**	**2,232.3**	**23,071**	**95**	**382.0**
Mental hospitals:										
State and county	286	106.8	44.0	100.3	41.3	99.5	407.5	6,990	29	116.9
Private [5]..........	886	67.6	27.8	52.9	21.8	52.9	457.6	5,915	24	87.0
General hospitals [6]...	1,486	48.5	20.0	34.9	14.4	36.0	914.0	3,617	15	61.8
Veterans Administration [7].	138	25.7	10.6	19.5	8.0	19.6	265.7	1,290	5	21.6
Free-standing psychiatric outpatient services [8] ...	757	(X)	(X)	(X)	(X)	(X)	(X)	668	3	11.1
Other [9]	1,388	23.4	9.6	20.4	8.4	19.9	187.5	4,591	19	83.6

X Not applicable.   [1] Rate per 100,000 population. Based on Bureau of Census estimated civilian population as of July 1. Estimates reflect revisions based on the 1990 Census of Population.   [2] "Inpatient care episodes" is defined as the number of residents in inpatient facilities at the beginning of the year plus the total additions to inpatient facilities during the year.   [3] Based on Bureau of the Census estimated civilian population as of July 1. Estimates reflect revisions based on the 1990 Census of Population.   [4] Full-time equivalent.   [5] Includes residential treatment centers for emotionally disturbed children.   [6] Non-Federal hospitals with separate psychiatric services.   [7] Includes Veterans Administration (VA) neuropsychiatric hospitals, VA general hospitals with separate psychiatric settings and VA freestanding psychiatric outpatient clinics.   [8] Includes mental health facilities which provide only psychiatric outpatient services.   [9] Includes other multiservice mental health facilities with two or more settings, which are not elsewhere classified, as well as freestanding partial care facilities which only provide psychiatric partial care services. Number of facilities, expenditures, and staff data also include freestanding psychiatric partial care facilities.

Source: U.S. National Institute of Mental Health, *Statistical Note* series; and unpublished data. (Data collected biennially.)

No. 184. Persons Injured, by Sex, 1970 to 1988, and by Age and Place, 1989

[Covers civilian noninstitutional population and comprises incidents leading to restricted activity and/or medical attention. Beginning 1982, data not strictly comparable with other years. See headnote, table 188. Based on National Health Interview Survey; see Appendix III]

YEAR	PERSONS INJURED (millions)			RATE PER 100 POPULATION			AGE AND PLACE	PERSONS INJURED (millions)			RATE PER 100 POPULATION		
	Total	Male	Female	Total	Male	Female		Total	Male	Female	Total	Male	Female
1970 ..	56.0	31.8	24.2	28.0	33.0	23.3	**1989, total** [1].	58.0	31.7	26.3	23.8	26.9	20.9
1975 ..	71.9	39.4	32.5	34.4	39.1	30.0	Under 5 years...	4.2	(NA)	(NA)	22.2	(NA)	(NA)
1978 ..	67.5	38.1	29.4	31.6	36.9	26.6	5 to 17 years ...	12.8	(NA)	(NA)	28.4	(NA)	(NA)
1979 ..	69.1	40.2	28.9	32.0	38.6	25.9	18 to 44 years...	28.9	16.1	12.7	27.7	31.6	23.9
1980 ..	68.1	39.0	29.1	31.2	37.1	25.8	45 years and over	12.1	5.2	7.0	16.1	15.1	16.9
1982 ..	60.0	32.4	27.6	26.4	29.6	23.4	Home	17.6	9.2	8.3	7.2	7.8	6.7
1983 ..	61.1	33.0	28.1	26.6	29.8	23.7	Street or						
1984 ..	61.1	33.7	27.4	26.4	30.1	22.9	highway	8.3	4.2	4.1	3.4	3.6	3.2
1985 ..	62.6	34.6	28.0	26.8	30.6	23.1	Industrial	8.3	6.0	2.3	3.4	5.1	1.8
1986 ..	62.4	34.0	28.4	26.4	29.8	23.3	Other........	14.2	8.6	5.7	5.9	7.3	4.5
1987 ..	62.1	33.6	28.4	26.0	29.1	23.1							
1988 ..	59.2	32.4	26.8	24.6	27.7	21.6							

NA Not available.   [1] Includes unknown place of accident, not shown separately.
Source: U.S. National Center for Health Statistics, *Vital and Health Statistics*, series 10, No. 176, and unpublished data.

No. 185. Injuries Associated With Consumer Products: 1988 and 1989

[Estimates calculated from a representative sample of hospitals with emergency treatment departments in the United States and its territories. Product involvement does not necessarily mean the product caused the accident. Data were selected from the U.S. Consumer Product Safety Commission's National Electronic Injury Surveillance System]

PRODUCT	1988	1989	PRODUCT	1988	1989
Home maintenance:			Housewares:		
Noncaustic cleaning equip. [1]	19,338	19,328	Cookware, pots, pans..........	29,226	29,888
Cleaning agents (except soap)....	36,344	35,673	Cutlery, knives, unpowered	337,464	335,083
Drain, oven cleaners, caustics	(NA)	10,006	Drinking glasses	114,923	114,682
Paints, solvents, lubricants	21,928	17,649	Scissors	19,566	21,144
Misc. household chemicals	14,348	17,126	Small kitchen appliances........	35,484	36,945
Home workshop equipment:			Tableware and accessories......	114,628	106,400
Batteries	12,080	11,967	Misc. housewares	51,383	48,685
Hoists, lifts, jacks...........	15,165	10,899	General household appliances:		
Power home tools, except saws...	24,208	22,002	Cooking ranges, ovens etc	41,442	41,727
Power home workshop saws....	64,232	71,074	Irons, clothes steamers.......	18,805	18,193
Welding, soldering, cutting tools...	13,940	15,276	Refrigerators, freezers........	26,615	31,630
Wires, cords, not specified	14,298	11,361	Washers, dryers	19,075	19,108
Workshop manual tools	99,016	88,813	Misc. household appliances......	22,124	26,356
Misc. workshop equipment	33,726	33,561	Heating, cooling equipment: [5]		
Yard and garden equipment:			Chimneys, fireplaces	14,682	14,355
Chains and saws............	36,145	37,278	Fans (except stove)	19,384	15,866
Hand garden tools	35,427	29,988	Heating stoves, space heaters....	30,992	32,458
Trimmers, small power tools [2]	(NA)	12,150	Pipes, heating and plumbing	24,188	24,744
Hatchets, axes	16,458	15,013	Radiators	17,976	18,103
Lawn and garden care equipment.....	39,421	38,636	Home entertainment equipment:		
Lawn mowers	53,830	61,864	Pet supplies, equipment	13,576	17,845
Other power lawn equipment....	15,300	13,556	Sound recording equip [6]	37,440	35,006
Household packaging and containers:			Television sets	31,754	34,949
Cans, other containers	183,023	179,484	Misc. hobby equipment........	11,868	11,955
Glass bottles, jars	67,439	71,058	Personal use items:		
Paper, cardboard, plastic products .	34,174	32,670	Cigarettes, lighters, fuels........	20,878	21,092
Home furnishing: [3]			Clothing	115,058	102,397
Bathtub, shower structures	121,600	125,829	Grooming devices	25,680	27,013
Beds, mattresses, pillows	299,222	302,190	Holders for personal items	14,895	12,799
Carpets, rugs	82,235	87,739	Jewelry	43,087	43,868
Chairs, sofas, sofa beds	291,446	305,896	Paper money, coins	29,418	28,745
Desks, cabinets, shelves, racks ...	166,661	164,451	Pencils, pens, other desk supplies .	42,130	42,407
Electric fixtures, lamps, equipment .	40,517	38,787	Razors, shavers, razor blades	36,122	35,401
Ladders, stools	128,818	131,551	Sewing equipment	29,996	27,629
Mirrors, mirror glass	23,013	21,630	Sports and recreation equipment:		
Sinks, toilets..............	42,016	43,162	Barbecue grills, stoves, equipment .	13,239	13,324
Tables..................	269,255	265,268	Bicycles, accessories	525,027	514,738
Misc. covers, fabrics..........	14,545	(NA)	Exercise equipment	65,029	67,028
Other misc. accessories	39,417	40,287	Horseback riding	43,820	(NA)
Home structures, construction: [4]			Mopeds, minibikes, ATV's [7].....	112,571	106,792
Cabinets or door hardware	17,209	17,993	Nonpowder guns, BB's, pellets. ...	22,240	24,044
Ceilings, walls, inside panels	186,328	189,317	Playground equipment	204,726	210,236
Counters, counter tops	23,088	27,121	Skateboards	80,242	65,819
Fences	113,331	105,919	Toboggans, sleds, snow disks, etc .	28,818	35,008
Glass doors, windows, panels	176,393	182,725	Trampolines	13,944	15,866
Handrails, railings, banisters	35,899	37,284	Miscellaneous products:		
Nails, carpet tacks, etc.........	220,640	214,123	Dollies, carts..............	32,604	35,563
Nonglass doors, panels	281,649	281,310	Elevators, other lifts..........	11,539	14,198
Porches, open side floors, etc	92,508	92,840	Fireworks, flares	10,330	9,800
Stairs, ramps, landings, floors	1,477,887	1,450,421	Gasoline and diesel fuels	15,964	13,534
Window, door sills, frames.......	41,457	44,373	Toys	141,755	147,898
Misc. construction materials......	59,829	67,711			

NA Not available.   [1] Includes detergent.   [2] Includes garden tools.   [3] Includes accessories.   [4] Includes materials.
[5] Includes ventilating equipment.   [6] Includes reproducing equipment.   [7] All-terrain vehicles.
Source: National Safety Council, Itasca, IL, *Accident Facts*, annual, (copyright).

No. 186. Costs of Accidents: 1990

[Covers costs for accidents in which deaths or disabling injuries beyond the day of the accident occurred, together with vehicle accidents and fires]

COST	AMOUNT (bil. dol.)					PERCENT DISTRIBUTION				
	Total [1]	Motor vehicle	Work	Home	Other	Total [1]	Motor vehicle	Work	Home	Other
Total	173.8	89.0	63.8	23.5	13.4	100.0	100.0	100.0	100.0	100.0
Wage loss [2]	48.2	25.2	10.2	7.9	7.2	27.7	28.3	16.0	33.6	53.7
Medical expense	28.4	6.2	8.7	10.0	4.1	16.3	7.0	13.6	42.6	30.6
Insurance administration [3]	30.1	22.3	10.3	1.0	0.7	17.3	25.1	16.1	4.3	5.2
Fire loss	9.7	(NA)	3.7	4.6	1.4	5.6	(NA)	5.8	19.6	10.4
Motor vehicle property damage	28.2	28.2	1.7	(NA)	(NA)	16.2	31.7	2.7	(NA)	(NA)
Uninsured work loss [4]	29.2	7.1	29.2	(NA)	(NA)	16.8	8.0	45.8	(NA)	(NA)

NA Not available. [1] Excludes duplication between work and motor vehicle ($15.9 billion). [2] Actual wage losses, the present value of future earnings lost, and the replacement-cost value of household services of employed persons and householders. [3] The difference between premiums paid to companies and the claims paid by them. [4] The value of time lost by noninjured workers (e.g. giving first aid).

Source: National Safety Council, Itasca, IL, *Accident Facts, 1991,* (copyright).

No. 187. Injury, Medical Care, Morbidity, and Mortality Costs, by Sex, Age, and Cause: 1985

[An injury consists of damage to tissue caused by the exchange of kinetic, thermal, chemical, electrical or radiation energy at levels intolerable to tissue, or the deprivation of oxygen due to suffocation. For explanation of methodology, see source]

AGE, CAUSE, AND SEX	Number injured [1] (1,000)	INJURY MEDICAL CARE AND MORBIDITY LOSSES					INJURY MORTALITY LOSSES				
		Life years lost [2]		Lifetime costs [4][5]		Deaths, number [6] (1,000)	Life years lost [2]		Lifetime costs [5][7]	
		Total (1,000)	Rate [3]	Total (mil. dol.)	Per injured person (dol.)		Total (1,000)	Per death	Total (mil. dol.)	Per death (dol.)
Total	56,716	5,086	9.0	108,241	1,908	155,665	5,285	34.0	49,374	317,189
Age: Under 4 years old	4,066	470	11.6	3,152	775	4,434	320	72.2	976	220,081
5 to 14 years old	10,184	822	8.1	8,028	788	5,992	337	56.2	1,670	278,754
15 to 24 years old	12,721	1,388	10.9	24,266	1,908	33,896	1,658	48.9	14,876	438,884
25 to 44 years old	18,015	1,314	7.3	40,930	2,272	51,579	2,045	39.6	24,891	482,583
45 to 64 years old	7,344	476	6.5	17,833	2,428	27,854	625	22.4	6,138	220,375
65 years old and over	4,386	616	14.0	14,031	3,199	31,910	300	9.4	822	25,771
Cause: Motor vehicles	5,326	1,173	22.0	30,245	5,679	52,375	1,952	37.3	18,438	352,042
Falls	12,276	363	3.0	35,638	2,903	16,470	436	26.5	1,642	99,669
Firearms	236	188	79.8	2,238	9,483	32,586	1,162	35.7	12,172	373,520
Poisonings	1,691	18	1.0	4,104	2,427	11,894	275	23.1	4,433	372,691
Fires/burns	1,457	1,259	86.4	2,407	1,652	5,710	258	45.2	1,424	249,367
Drownings/near drownings	32	161	511.3	175	5,469	6,287	206	32.8	2,278	362,292
Other	35,698	1,924	5.4	33,433	937	30,340	995	32.8	8,989	296,266
Male	32,014	3,059	9.6	67,909	2,121	111,867	3,827	34.2	40,086	358,344
Age: Under 4 years old	2,454	262	10.7	1,914	780	2,618	182	69.5	617	235,664
5 to 14 years old	5,981	563	9.4	5,576	932	3,986	219	54.9	1,198	300,607
15 to 24 years old	8,003	950	11.9	16,931	2,116	26,502	1,272	48.0	12,205	460,550
25 to 44 years old	10,907	890	8.2	29,458	2,701	40,327	1,561	38.7	20,850	517,012
45 to 64 years old	3,445	255	7.4	10,641	3,089	20,245	431	21.3	4,786	236,423
65 years old and over	1,223	137	11.2	3,388	2,770	18,189	162	8.9	430	23,614
Cause: Motor vehicles	2,426	737	30.4	18,891	7,787	36,836	1,362	37.0	14,437	391,921
Falls	5,626	212	3.8	19,724	3,506	9,136	280	30.6	1,317	144,143
Firearms	190	126	66.4	1,761	9,268	27,289	945	34.6	10,567	387,235
Poisonings	681	11	1.6	2,300	3,377	7,621	218	28.6	3,289	431,608
Fires/burns	794	636	80.2	1,809	2,278	3,477	170	48.9	992	285,300
Drownings/near drownings	30	100	332.6	124	4,133	5,067	120	23.7	1,994	393,464
Other	22,267	1,238	5.6	23,300	1,046	22,439	733	32.7	7,490	333,803
Female	24,702	2,027	8.2	40,331	1,633	43,798	1,458	33.3	9,288	212,075
Age: Under 4 years old	1,612	208	12.9	1,237	767	1,816	138	76.0	359	199,617
5 to 14 years old	4,203	259	6.2	2,452	583	2,006	118	58.8	472	235,331
15 to 24 years old	4,717	438	9.3	7,334	1,555	7,394	386	52.2	2,671	361,227
25 to 44 years old	7,108	424	6.0	11,473	1,614	11,252	484	43.0	4,042	359,190
45 to 64 years old	3,900	221	5.7	7,191	1,844	7,609	194	25.5	1,352	177,677
65 years old and over	3,162	478	15.1	10,643	3,366	13,721	138	10.1	393	28,630
Cause: Motor vehicles	2,900	436	15.0	11,354	3,915	15,539	590	38.0	4,001	257,506
Falls	6,650	151	2.3	15,914	2,393	7,334	156	21.3	325	44,267
Firearms	46	62	134.6	477	10,370	5,297	217	41.0	1,604	302,860
Poisonings	1,010	7	0.7	1,805	1,787	4,273	57	13.3	1,143	267,610
Fires/burns	663	622	93.8	599	903	2,233	88	39.4	432	193,416
Drownings/near drownings	2	62	3,780.9	51	25,500	1,220	86	70.5	284	232,825
Other	13,431	686	5.1	10,132	754	7,901	262	33.2	1,499	189,660

[1] Excludes 142,568 deaths in 1985. [2] Number of years person would have been productive in absence of injury, disability, or impairment. [3] Per 100 injured persons. [4] Value of goods and services not produced because of injury related illnesses and disability ($64.9 billion) and cost of medical services ($43.3 billion). [5] Cost estimates based on the person's age, sex, life expectancy at the time of death, annual earnings, labor force participation rates, value of homemaking services, and at 6 percent discount rate by which to convert to present worth the potential aggregate earnings lost over the years. Includes costs incurred in the first year injury occurs as well as costs in later years (e.g. rehabilitation). [6] Includes 13,097 deaths in later years due to injuries sustained in 1985. [7] Value of lifetime earnings lost by persons who are fatally injured and die prematurely, discounted at 6 percent.

Source: Institute for Health and Aging, University of California, San Francisco, CA and the Injury Prevention Center, The Johns Hopkins University, Baltimore, MD, *Cost of Injury in the United States: A Report to Congress, 1989.*

No. 188. Days of Disability, by Type and Selected Characteristitcs: 1970 to 1989

[Covers civilian noninstitutional population. Beginning 1985, the levels of estimates may not be comparable to estimates for 1970-1980 because the later data are based on a revised questionnaire and field procedures; for further information, see source. Based on National Health Interview Survey; see Appendix III. For composition of regions, see table 25]

ITEM	TOTAL DAYS OF DISABILITY (millions)						DAYS PER PERSON					
	1970	1980	1985	1987	1988	1989	1970	1980	1985	1987	1988	1989
Restricted-activity days [1] . .	2,913	4,165	3,453	3,448	3,536	3,693	14.6	19.1	14.8	14.5	14.7	15.2
Male	1,273	1,802	1,442	1,464	1,487	1,558	13.2	17.1	12.8	12.7	12.7	13.2
Female	1,640	2,363	2,011	1,984	2,049	2,135	15.8	21.0	16.6	16.1	16.5	17.0
White [2]	2,526	3,518	2,899	2,896	2,969	3,087	14.4	18.7	14.5	14.3	14.6	15.0
Black [2]	365	580	489	475	487	511	16.2	22.7	17.4	16.4	16.6	17.1
Hispanic [3]	(NA)	(NA)	228	226	253	278	(NA)	(NA)	13.2	12.0	13.0	13.2
Under 65 years	2,331	3,228	2,557	2,594	2,657	2,774	12.9	16.6	12.4	12.3	12.5	12.9
65 years and over	582	937	895	854	879	919	30.7	39.2	33.1	30.3	30.6	31.5
Northeast	709	862	689	684	667	669	14.5	17.9	13.8	13.6	13.5	13.7
Midwest	691	989	744	746	762	812	12.4	17.2	12.7	13.0	12.8	13.6
South	996	1,415	1,308	1,220	1,328	1,392	15.9	19.8	16.3	15.0	16.1	16.7
West	518	899	712	797	779	820	15.6	22.0	15.7	16.0	15.6	15.8
Family income:												
Under $10,000	(NA)	(NA)	893	756	754	694	(NA)	(NA)	25.8	24.2	26.6	26.5
$10,000 to $19,999 . . .	(NA)	(NA)	781	750	751	768	(NA)	(NA)	16.7	16.9	17.8	18.7
$20,000 to $34,999 . . .	(NA)	(NA)	791	761	734	752	(NA)	(NA)	12.1	12.3	12.3	13.3
$35,000 or more	(NA)	(NA)	568	685	726	798	(NA)	(NA)	9.9	9.9	9.7	9.9
Bed-disability days [4]	1,222	1,520	1,436	1,474	1,519	1,579	6.1	7.0	6.1	6.2	6.3	6.5
Male	503	616	583	595	607	652	5.2	5.9	5.2	5.2	5.2	5.5
Female	720	904	852	879	912	927	6.9	8.0	7.1	7.1	7.3	7.4
Under 65 years	959	1,190	1,064	1,081	1,107	1,164	5.3	6.1	5.1	5.1	5.2	5.4
65 years and over	263	330	371	394	412	415	13.8	13.8	13.7	14.0	14.4	14.2
Work-loss days [5]	417	485	575	603	609	659	5.4	5.0	5.3	5.4	5.3	5.6
Male	243	271	287	299	307	322	5.0	4.9	4.8	4.8	4.8	5.0
Female	175	215	288	304	302	337	5.9	5.1	6.0	6.1	5.8	6.4
School-loss days [6]	222	204	217	198	222	260	4.9	5.3	4.8	4.4	4.9	5.7
Male	108	95	100	96	107	129	4.7	4.8	4.4	4.2	4.6	5.6
Female	114	109	117	102	115	131	5.1	5.7	5.3	4.6	5.2	5.9

NA Not available.   [1] A day when a person cuts down on his usual activities for more than half a day because of illness or injury. Includes bed-disability, work-loss, and school-loss days. Total includes other races and unknown income, not shown separately.   [2] Beginning 1980 race was determined by asking the household respondent to report his race. In earlier years the racial classification of respondents was determined by interviewer observation.   [3] Persons of Hispanic origin may be of any race.   [4] A day when a person stayed in bed more than half a day because of illness or injury. Includes those work-loss and school-loss days actually spent in bed.   [5] A day when a person lost more than half a workday because of illness or injury. Computed for persons 17 years of age and over (beginning 1985, 18 years of age and over) in the currently employed population, defined as those who were working or had a job or business from which they were not on layoff during the 2-week period preceding the week of interview.   [6] Child's loss of more than half a school day because of illness or injury. Computed for children 6-16 years of age. Beginning 1985, children 5-17 years old.

Source: U.S. National Center for Health Statistics, *Vital and Health Statistics*, series 10, No. 176; and unpublished data.

No. 189. Percent of Children Immunized Against Specified Diseases, by Age-Group: 1980 to 1985

[Covers civilian noninstitutional population. Data are estimates from the Immunization Survey which is a supplemental questionnaire submitted to a subsample of households interviewed for the Current Population Survey (see text, section 1 and Appendix III). Subject to sampling variability; see source]

DISEASE	ALL RESPONDENTS										RESPON-DENTS CON-SULTING RECORDS, [1] 1985	
	1 to 4 years old					5 to 14 years old						
			1985					1985			1 to 4 years old	5 to 14 years old
	1980, total	1984, total	Total	White	Black and other	1980, total	1984, total	Total	White	Black and other		
Diptheria-tetanus-pertussis [2]	66.3	65.7	64.9	68.7	48.7	74.0	73.8	73.7	76.0	64.0	87.0	93.0
Polio [2]	58.8	54.8	55.3	58.9	40.1	70.0	70.2	69.7	72.6	57.5	75.7	88.4
Measles	63.5	62.8	60.8	63.6	48.8	71.0	73.5	71.5	73.6	62.6	76.9	87.6
Rubella	63.5	60.9	58.9	61.6	47.7	74.0	72.4	70.2	72.3	61.4	73.8	85.3
Mumps	56.6	58.7	58.9	61.8	47.0	63.2	70.9	71.6	73.6	63.2	75.5	87.1

[1] Data are based only on the 29 percent of White respondents and the 15 percent of Black and other respondents who consulted records for some or all vaccination questions.   [2] Three or more doses.

Source: U.S. Centers for Disease Control, Atlanta, GA, *United States Immunization Survey*, annual.

No. 190. Specified Reportable Diseases—Cases Reported: 1970 to 1990

[Figures should be interpreted with caution. Although reporting of some of these diseases is incomplete, the figures are of value in indicating trends of disease incidence. Includes cases imported from outside the United States. See *Historical Statistics, Colonial Times to 1970,* series B 291-303, for related data]

DISEASE	1970	1980	1983	1984	1985	1986	1987	1988	1989	1990
AIDS [1]	(NA)	(NA)	2,117	4,445	8,249	13,166	21,070	31,001	33,722	41,595
Amebiasis	2,888	5,271	6,658	5,252	4,433	3,532	3,123	2,860	3,217	3,328
Aseptic meningitis	6,480	8,028	12,696	8,326	10,619	11,374	11,487	7,234	10,274	11,852
Botulism [2]	12	89	133	123	122	109	82	84	89	92
Brucellosis (undulant fever)	213	183	200	131	153	106	129	96	95	85
Chickenpox (1,000)	([3])	190.9	177.5	222.0	178.2	183.2	213.2	192.9	185.4	173.1
Diphtheria	435	3	5	1	3	-	3	2	3	4
Encephalitis:										
Primary infectious [4]	1,580	1,362	1,761	1,257	1,376	1,302	1,418	882	981	1,341
Post infectious [4]	370	40	34	108	161	124	121	121	88	105
Hepatitis: B (serum) (1,000)	8.3	19.0	24.3	26.1	26.6	26.1	25.9	23.2	23.4	21.1
A (infectious) (1,000)	56.8	29.1	21.5	22.0	23.2	23.4	25.3	28.5	35.8	31.4
Unspecified (1,000)	([3])	11.9	7.1	5.5	5.5	3.9	3.1	2.5	2.3	1.7
Non-A, non-B (1,000)	([3])	([3])	3.5	3.9	4.2	3.6	3.0	2.6	2.5	2.6
Legionellosis	([3])	([3])	852	750	830	948	1,038	1,085	1,190	1,370
Leprosy	129	223	259	290	361	270	238	184	163	198
Leptospirosis	47	85	61	40	57	41	43	54	93	77
Malaria	3,051	2,062	813	1,007	1,049	1,123	944	1,099	1,277	1,292
Measles (1,000)	47.4	13.5	1.5	2.6	2.8	6.3	3.7	3.4	18.2	27.8
Meningococcal infections	2,505	2,840	2,736	2,746	2,479	2,594	2,930	2,964	2,727	2,451
Mumps (1,000)	105.0	8.6	3.4	3.0	3.0	7.8	12.8	4.9	5.7	5.3
Pertussis [5] (1,000)	4.2	1.7	2.5	2.3	3.6	4.2	2.8	3.5	4.2	4.6
Plague	13	18	40	31	17	10	12	15	4	2
Poliomyelitis, acute	33	9	15	8	7	8	6	9	5	7
Psittacosis	35	124	142	172	119	224	98	114	116	113
Rabies, animal	3,224	6,421	5,878	5,567	5,565	5,504	4,658	4,651	4,724	4,826
Rabies, human	3	-	2	3	1	-	1	-	1	1
Rheumatic fever, acute [6]	3,227	432	88	117	90	147	141	158	144	108
Rubella [7] (1,000)	56.6	3.9	1.0	1.0	0.6	0.6	0.3	0.2	0.4	1.1
Salmonellosis [8] (1,000)	22.1	33.7	44.3	40.9	65.3	50.0	50.9	48.9	47.8	48.6
Shigellosis [9] (1,000)	13.8	19.0	19.7	17.4	17.1	17.1	23.9	30.6	25.0	27.1
Tetanus	148	95	91	74	83	64	48	53	53	64
Toxic-shock syndrome	([3])	([3])	502	482	384	412	372	390	400	322
Trichinosis	109	131	45	68	61	39	40	45	30	129
Tuberculosis [10] (1,000)	37.1	27.7	23.8	22.3	22.2	22.8	22.5	22.4	23.5	25.7
Tularemia	172	234	310	291	177	170	214	201	152	152
Typhoid fever	346	510	507	390	402	362	400	436	460	552
Typhus fever:										
Flea-borne (endemic-murine)	27	81	62	53	37	67	49	54	41	50
Tick-borne (Rocky Mt. spotted fever)	380	1,163	1,126	838	714	760	604	609	623	651
Venereal diseases (civilian cases):										
Gonorrhea (1,000)	600	1,004	900	879	911	901	781	720	733	690
Syphilis (1,000)	91	69	75	70	68	68	87	103	111	134
Other (1,000)	2.2	1.0	1.2	1.0	2.3	4.2	5.3	5.2	4.9	4.6

- Represents zero.   NA Not available.   [1] Acquired immunodeficiency syndrome was not a notifiable disease until 1984. Figures are shown for years in which cases were reported to the CDC.   [2] Beginning in 1980, includes foodborne, infant, wound, and unspecified cases.   [3] Disease was not notifiable.   [4] Beginning 1980, reported data reflect new diagnostic categories. [5] Whooping cough.   [6] Based on reports from States: 38 in 1970, 37 in 1980, 36 in 1983 and 1984, 31 in 1985, 29 in 1986 and 1988, 25 in 1987, 28 in 1989, and 30 in 1990.   [7] German measles.   [8] Excludes typhoid fever.   [9] Bacillary dysentery. [10] Newly reported active cases. New diagnostic standards introduced in 1980.

Source: U.S. Centers for Disease Control, Atlanta, GA, *Summary of Notifible Diseases, United States, Morbidity and Mortality Weekly Report,* vol. 39, No. 53, October 1991.

No. 191. Selected Measures of Hospital Utilization for Patients Discharged With the Diagnosis of AIDS: 1984 to 1989

[Based on National Hospital Discharge Survey; see source for details]

MEASURE OF UTILIZATION	Unit	1984	1985	1986	1987	1988 [1]	1989 [1]
Number of patients discharged	1,000	10	23	37	50	71	96
Rate of patient discharges [2]	Rate	0.4	1.0	1.6	2.1	2.9	3.9
Number of days of care	1,000	123	387	606	783	983	1,303
Rate of days of care [2]	Rate	5.2	16.3	25.3	32.4	40.3	52.8
Average length of stay [3]	Days	12.1	17.1	16.2	15.7	13.8	13.6

[1] Comparisons of 1988 and 1989 data with data for earlier years should be made with caution as estimates of change may reflect improvements in the design rather than true changes in hospital use.   [2] Per 10,000 population. Based on Bureau of the Census estimated civilian population as of July 1. Population estimates do not reflect revised estimates based on the 1990 Census of Population.   [3] For similar data on all patients, see table 173.

Source: National Center for Health Statistics, *Health, United States, 1990.*

No. 192. AIDS Cases Reported, by Patient Characteristic: 1981 to 1991

[**Provisional.** For cases reported in the year shown. For data on AIDS deaths, see table 120. Data are subject to retrospective changes and may differ from those data in table 190]

CHARACTERISTIC	NUMBER OF CASES										PERCENT DISTRIBU- TION	
	Total	1981-1983	1984	1985	1986	1987	1988	1989	1990	1991	1981-1983	1991
Total	199,516	2,920	4,442	8,215	13,150	21,109	30,754	33,638	41,616	43,672	100.0	100.0
Age:												
Under 5 years old	2,656	44	47	113	155	266	444	494	579	514	1.5	1.2
5 to 12 years old.	623	2	3	17	28	56	127	102	144	144	0.1	0.3
13 to 29 years old. . . .	39,547	655	956	1,684	2,822	4,365	6,358	6,736	8,113	7,858	22.4	18.0
30 to 39 years old. . . .	91,571	1,338	2,115	3,852	6,104	9,632	14,131	15,539	18,929	19,931	45.8	45.6
40 to 49 years old. . . .	44,675	625	919	1,714	2,703	4,513	6,529	7,331	9,696	10,645	21.4	24.4
50 to 59 years old. . . .	14,438	221	319	631	964	1,566	2,148	2,424	2,923	3,242	7.6	7.4
60 years old and over .	6,006	35	83	204	374	711	1,017	1,012	1,232	1,338	1.2	3.1
Sex:												
Male	178,033	2,704	4,146	7,630	12,101	19,276	27,467	29,978	36,736	37,995	92.6	87.0
Female	21,483	216	296	585	1,049	1,833	3,287	3,660	4,880	5,677	7.4	13.0
Race/ethnic group:												
White, non-Hispanic. . .	110,343	1,647	2,689	4,969	7,841	12,973	17,093	18,600	22,322	22,209	56.4	50.9
Black, non-Hispanic. . .	59,975	826	1,123	2,087	3,386	5,384	9,117	10,302	13,202	14,548	28.3	33.3
Hispanic	27,159	436	609	1,097	1,802	2,548	4,267	4,356	5,645	6,399	14.9	14.7
Other/unknown.	2,039	11	21	62	121	204	277	380	447	516	0.4	1.2
Leading States: [1]												
New York	42,619	1,318	1,583	2,482	3,768	3,945	6,968	6,001	8,390	8,164	45.1	18.7
California	38,329	591	1,008	1,979	2,658	4,893	5,709	6,440	7,342	7,709	20.2	17.7
Florida.	19,464	222	314	551	1,029	1,643	2,677	3,456	4,021	5,551	7.6	12.7
Texas	14,475	109	250	482	937	1,667	2,216	2,385	3,342	3,087	3.7	7.1
New Jersey	12,671	199	282	468	767	1,510	2,450	2,228	2,462	2,305	6.8	5.3
Illinois	6,313	57	100	188	346	629	990	1,136	1,276	1,591	2.0	3.6
Georgia	5,700	38	56	191	304	517	838	1,095	1,227	1,434	1.3	3.3
Pennsylvania	5,648	55	90	200	309	654	853	1,072	1,193	1,222	1.9	2.8
Massachusetts	4,307	47	86	164	282	452	711	753	842	970	1.6	2.2
Maryland	4,110	32	54	149	188	457	544	715	994	977	1.1	2.2
District of Columbia . . .	3,438	23	90	178	226	464	495	495	740	727	0.8	1.7
Louisiana	3,048	18	55	104	165	336	401	508	704	757	0.6	1.7
Ohio	2,906	14	31	54	212	336	506	488	665	600	0.5	1.4
Washington	2,788	7	59	110	168	324	342	512	710	556	0.2	1.3
Virginia	2,742	27	40	109	160	243	349	391	743	680	0.9	1.6
Michigan	2,588	12	32	61	150	211	455	506	577	584	0.4	1.3
Missouri.	2,487	8	27	50	74	238	411	442	582	655	0.3	1.5
Connecticut	2,428	28	57	86	175	252	412	431	423	564	1.0	1.3
North Carolina	2,255	9	15	66	81	209	276	444	565	590	0.3	1.4
Colorado	2,025	26	38	62	166	226	325	387	360	435	0.9	1.0
Percent of total . .	90.4	97.3	96.1	94.1	92.5	91.0	90.8	88.8	89.3	89.7	(X)	(X)

X Not applicable. [1] States with at least 2,000 total cases reported 1991.
Source: U.S. Centers for Disease Control, Atlanta, GA, unpublished data.

No. 193. AIDS Cases, and Appropriations for AIDS, by Category and Leading States: 1984 to 1991

[**For fiscal years, except as indicated.** Based on survey of State budget analysts, commissioners of health and AIDS coordinators, and other State agencies with AIDS programs, (e.g. Departments of Education)]

ITEM	Unit	1984-1991, total	1985	1986	1987	1988	1989	1990	1991
State government appropriations [1] . .	Mil. dol .	1,125.9	9.6	27.5	66.7	156.3	247.0	278.9	330.6
Number of States.	Number	(X)	9	21	28	37	47	51	51
Appropriations for—									
Education/information	Percent.	(X)	(NA)	25	19	21	26	28	25
Patient care [2]	Percent.	(X)	(NA)	4	15	16	25	[3]45	[3]51
Support services [2].	Percent.	(X)	(NA)	12	11	19	13	(3)	(3)
Research.	Percent.	(X)	(NA)	41	27	17	8	1	2
Testing/counseling	Percent.	(X)	(NA)	3	11	12	18	14	12
Leading areas by appropriations: [4]									
California	$1,000 .	284,325	4,094	16,020	31,515	58,033	76,877	46,649	47,738
New York	$1,000 .	273,922	2,800	4,500	9,500	39,920	52,884	68,576	90,493
Florida.	$1,000 .	76,919	32	576	5,557	12,630	17,765	19,432	20,994
Massachusetts	$1,000 .	66,279	1,500	1,604	4,073	7,591	14,754	18,517	18,242
New Jersey	$1,000 .	59,216	920	1,969	4,963	7,907	13,012	15,469	14,446
Percent of total . . .	Percent.	69.0	97.4	89.6	83.3	80.6	70.0	60.0	58.0

NA Not available. X Not applicable. [1] Includes DC. Includes appropriations from State governments direct general revenue funds only; excludes Medicaid expenditures. Includes appropriations for other activities, not shown separately. [2] Beginning 1989, hospice care included in patient care, rather than support services. [3] Beginning 1990, patient care and support services were combined. [4] Areas with over $7 million appropriations for 1989.
Source: AIDS Policy Center, Intergovernmental Health Policy Project, The George Washington University, Washington, DC, *Intergovernmental AIDS Reports*, vol. 4, Special Edition.

No. 194. Acute Conditions, by Type, 1970 to 1989, and by Selected Characteristics, 1989

[Covers civilian noninstitutional population. Estimates include only acute conditions which were medically attended or caused at least one day of restricted activity. Based on National Health Interview Survey; see Appendix III. See headnote, table 188. For composition of regions, see table 25]

YEAR AND CHARACTERISTIC	NUMBER OF CONDITIONS (mil.)					RATE PER 100 POPULATION				
	Infective and parasitic	Respiratory Upper	Respiratory Other	Digestive system	Injuries	Infective and parasitic	Respiratory Upper	Respiratory Other	Digestive system	Injuries
1970.	48.2	127.3	92.5	23.0	59.2	24.1	63.7	46.3	11.5	29.6
1975.	47.6	124.0	109.0	21.6	76.2	22.8	59.3	52.1	10.3	36.4
1980.	53.6	124.2	129.0	24.9	72.7	24.6	57.0	59.2	11.4	33.4
1985.	47.8	95.1	108.4	16.3	64.0	20.5	40.7	46.4	7.0	27.4
1986.	54.4	85.2	143.6	15.0	64.3	23.0	36.1	60.8	6.3	27.2
1987.	55.3	84.7	106.4	15.0	64.5	23.2	35.5	44.6	6.3	27.0
1988.	53.8	90.7	118.7	15.1	59.2	22.3	37.6	49.3	6.3	24.6
1989, total [1]	48.9	92.5	139.3	14.3	59.2	20.1	38.0	57.2	5.9	24.3
Under 5 years old	10.0	18.0	15.0	2.1	4.3	53.2	96.2	79.7	11.0	22.7
5 to 17 years old	18.7	21.8	41.0	2.9	13.1	43.4	48.1	90.6	6.3	28.9
18 to 24 years old	3.9	11.9	13.5	1.6	7.1	15.4	46.9	53.2	6.5	28.0
25 to 44 years old	10.6	26.2	44.5	3.6	22.4	13.5	33.2	56.5	4.5	28.4
45 to 64 years old	4.0	9.9	17.8	1.9	7.4	8.6	21.4	38.6	4.1	16.2
65 years old and over	1.7	4.7	7.5	2.2	4.9	5.9	16.2	25.8	7.6	16.8
Male	21.6	42.0	63.6	6.8	32.1	18.3	35.6	53.9	5.8	27.2
Female	27.3	50.5	75.7	7.5	27.1	21.8	40.2	60.3	5.9	21.6
White	43.5	80.4	123.0	11.3	50.9	21.2	39.2	59.9	5.5	24.8
Black	4.3	9.8	11.5	2.3	7.1	14.3	32.6	38.6	7.8	23.8
Northeast	9.3	17.1	18.9	2.0	9.8	19.1	34.9	38.7	4.1	19.9
Midwest	9.3	21.2	38.4	3.1	16.0	15.7	35.6	64.5	5.2	26.8
South	21.7	30.1	38.7	5.5	20.8	26.1	36.2	46.5	6.7	25.1
West	8.5	24.1	43.3	3.6	12.6	16.4	46.4	83.4	6.9	24.3
Family income:										
Under $10,000	3.9	12.7	16.1	2.3	7.7	14.9	48.6	61.3	8.9	29.3
$10,000 to $19,999	7.9	13.7	20.6	3.2	9.8	19.4	33.3	50.2	7.7	23.9
$20,000 to $34,999	12.7	21.7	36.6	2.9	15.7	22.4	38.3	64.6	5.2	27.7
$35,000 or more	17.7	32.0	46.5	3.9	18.9	22.0	39.9	57.9	4.9	23.6

[1] Includes other races and unknown income, not shown separately.
Source: U.S. National Center for Health Statistics, *Vital and Health Statistics*, series 10, No. 176 and unpublished data.

No. 195. Prevalence of Selected Reported Chronic Conditions, by Age and Sex: 1980 and 1989

[Covers civilian noninstitutional population. Conditions classified according to ninth revision of International Classification of Diseases. Based on National Health Interview Survey; see Appendix III. See headnote, table 188]

CHRONIC CONDITION	1980 Number of conditions (1,000)	1980 Rate [1]	1989 Number of conditions (1,000)	1989 Total	1989 Under 18 yrs.	1989 18-44 yrs.	1989 45-64 yrs.	1989 65-74 yrs.	1989 75 yrs. and over	1989 Male	1989 Female
Heart conditions	16,434	75.4	18,493	75.9	17.1	36.1	118.9	231.6	353.0	73.9	77.9
High blood pressure (Hypertension)	24,919	114.3	27,664	113.6	2.2	56.0	229.1	383.8	375.6	97.9	128.3
Varicose veins of lower extremities	5,930	27.2	7,536	30.9	-	24.8	57.8	72.6	86.6	12.5	48.3
Hemorrhoids	8,616	39.5	11,489	47.2	[2]0.7	57.2	74.9	77.4	57.5	41.8	52.2
Chronic bronchitis	7,869	36.1	11,974	49.2	50.5	44.5	53.7	54.2	57.6	37.7	60.0
Asthma	6,803	31.2	11,621	47.7	61.0	41.3	41.5	57.3	42.3	47.4	48.0
Chronic sinusitis	31,956	145.0	33,683	138.3	68.9	161.1	173.5	151.8	155.8	120.5	155.1
Hay fever, allergic rhinitis without asthma	17,433	80.0	21,166	86.9	59.7	108.8	87.4	69.4	65.5	85.4	88.4
Dermatitis, including eczema	9,139	41.9	8,420	34.6	35.7	36.0	30.6	33.5	32.9	29.8	39.1
Diseases of sebaceous glands [3]	5,046	23.2	5,692	23.4	[2]3.1	32.4	13.1	9.3	[2]5.7	21.7	24.9
Arthritis	27,773	127.4	30,999	127.3	[2]1.4	48.9	253.8	437.3	554.5	95.8	156.9
Trouble with—											
Ingrown nails	[4]4,503	[4]19.8	5,726	23.5	9.1	23.7	28.1	36.1	64.8	18.3	28.4
Corns and calluses	[4]4,811	[4]21.2	4,342	17.8	[2]0.2	14.6	31.5	41.0	54.3	12.0	23.3
Dry (itching) skin	[4]3,698	[4]16.3	4,289	17.6	9.9	17.1	22.9	23.4	35.5	17.1	18.1
Diabetes	5,665	26.0	6,489	26.6	[2]1.8	10.7	58.2	89.7	85.7	23.7	29.4
Migraine	5,630	25.8	9,978	41.0	15.5	57.2	51.2	29.8	[2]11.8	23.2	57.7
Diseases of urinary system [5]	5,444	25.0	6,938	28.5	4.9	30.1	38.1	57.4	62.2	14.8	41.4
Visual impairments	7,984	36.6	7,881	32.4	9.0	27.2	45.1	69.3	101.7	40.6	24.6
Cataracts	[4]5,124	[4]22.6	5,698	23.4	[2]0.2	3.5	16.1	107.4	234.3	16.0	30.3
Hearing impairments	17,370	79.7	20,246	83.1	15.6	47.8	127.7	239.4	360.3	98.5	68.7
Tinnitus	[4]5,130	[4]22.6	5,867	24.1	[2]1.7	14.4	45.8	76.4	68.9	24.3	23.9
Deformities or orthopedic impairments	18,504	84.9	27,993	114.9	29.3	138.3	155.5	141.4	177.0	113.7	116.1
Hernia of abdominal cavity	[4]4,900	[4]21.6	4,576	18.8	4.1	9.6	36.9	57.3	52.0	18.5	19.1
Frequent indigestion	[4]5,360	[4]23.6	5,418	22.2	[2]1.9	24.5	35.5	34.9	42.8	23.1	21.5
Frequent constipation	[4]4,431	[4]19.5	4,529	18.6	8.2	11.9	20.9	42.2	92.2	10.9	27.1

- Represents or rounds to zero. [1] Conditions per 1,000 persons. [2] Figure does not meet standards of reliability or precision. [3] Acne and sebaceous skin cyst. [4] 1982 data. [5] Includes kidney trouble and bladder disorders.
Source: U.S. National Center for Health Statistics, *Vital and Health Statistics*, series 10 and unpublished data.

No. 196. Alcoholism and Drug Abuse Treatment Facilities and Clients, by Facility Location and Ownership: 1989

[As of September 30. Based on the National Drug and Alcoholism Treatment Unit Survey (NDATUS), a census of all known drug abuse and alcholism treatment facilities in the U.S. Data collected in cooperation with State agencies which defined what constitutes a facility for reporting purposes]

FACILITY LOCATION AND OWNERSHIP	TOTAL			ALCOHOLISM TREATMENT			DRUG ABUSE TREATMENT		
	Units reporting [1][2]	Clients in treatment [2]	Budgeted capacity	Units reporting [2]	Clients in treatment [2]	Budgeted capacity	Units reporting [2]	Clients in treatment [2]	Budgeted capacity
Total	7,642	718,966	903,250	6,374	374,437	469,603	6,170	344,529	433,647
Community mental health center	956	107,613	123,145	883	68,627	75,665	848	38,986	47,480
Hospital [3]	1,353	88,921	127,397	1,244	45,637	64,291	1,150	43,284	63,106
Correctional facility	113	13,753	21,480	82	3,657	6,020	104	10,096	15,460
Halfway house	745	18,293	23,455	705	11,933	14,851	451	6,360	8,604
Other residential facility . . .	1,049	50,089	66,245	789	20,506	28,959	863	29,583	37,286
Outpatient facility	2,977	366,834	459,983	2,347	197,153	249,603	2,389	169,681	210,380
Other location.	449	73,463	81,545	324	26,924	30,214	365	46,539	51,331
Private for-profit	1,258	91,632	145,110	1,129	53,167	81,013	1,047	38,465	64,097
Private nonprofit	4,958	431,576	529,576	4,132	221,242	272,044	4,025	210,334	257,532
State and local government	1,236	171,907	199,105	942	84,691	97,657	967	87,216	101,448
Federal government.	190	23,851	29,459	171	15,337	18,889	131	8,514	10,570

[1] Unduplicated count. [2] Excludes data from 117 units which did not report budgeted capacity. With these data included, total number of clients in treatment was 734,955 (383,525 alcoholism clients and 351,430 drug abuse clients). [3] Includes general hospitals, alcoholism hospitals, mental/psychiatric hospitals, and other specialized hospitals.

Source: U.S. National Institute on Drug Abuse and U.S. National Institute on Alcohol Abuse and Alcoholism, *1989 National Drug and Alcoholism Treatment Unit Survey: Final Report.*

No. 197. Drug Use, by Type of Drug and Age Group: 1974 to 1991

[In percent. Current users are those who used drugs at least once within month prior to this study. Based on national samples of respondents residing in households. Subject to sampling variability; see source]

AGE AND TYPE OF DRUG	EVER USED						CURRENT USER					
	1974	1979	1982	1985	1988	1991	1974	1979	1982	1985	1988	1991
12 TO 17 YEARS OLD												
Marihuana.	23.0	30.9	26.7	23.6	17.4	13.0	12.0	16.7	11.5	12.0	6.4	4.3
Cocaine	3.6	5.4	6.5	4.9	3.4	2.4	1.0	1.4	1.6	1.5	1.1	0.4
Inhalants	8.5	9.8	(NA)	9.2	8.8	7.0	0.7	2.0	(NA)	3.4	2.0	1.8
Hallucinogens	6.0	7.1	5.2	3.3	3.5	3.4	1.3	2.2	1.4	1.2	0.8	0.8
Heroin	1.0	0.5	(NA)	(NA)	0.6	0.3	(NA)	(NA)	(NA)	(NA)	(NA)	0.1
Stimulants [1]	5.0	3.4	6.7	5.6	4.2	3.0	1.0	1.2	2.6	1.6	1.2	0.5
Sedatives [1]	5.0	3.2	5.8	4.1	2.4	2.4	1.0	1.1	1.3	1.0	0.6	0.5
Tranquilizers [1]	3.0	4.1	4.9	4.8	0.2	2.1	1.0	0.6	0.9	0.6	0.2	0.3
Analgesics [1]	(NA)	3.2	4.2	5.8	4.2	4.4	(NA)	0.6	0.7	1.6	0.9	1.1
Alcohol.	54.0	70.3	65.2	55.5	50.2	46.4	34.0	37.2	30.2	31.0	25.2	20.3
Cigarettes	52.0	54.1	49.5	45.2	42.3	37.9	25.0	12.1	14.7	15.3	11.8	10.8
18 TO 25 YEARS OLD												
Marihuana.	52.7	68.2	64.1	60.3	56.4	50.5	25.2	35.4	27.4	21.8	15.5	13.0
Cocaine	12.7	27.5	28.3	25.2	19.7	17.9	3.1	9.3	6.8	7.6	4.5	2.0
Inhalants	9.2	16.5	(NA)	12.4	12.5	10.9	(NA)	1.2	(NA)	0.8	1.7	1.5
Hallucinogens	16.6	25.1	21.1	11.3	13.8	13.2	2.5	4.4	1.7	1.9	1.9	1.2
Heroin	4.5	3.5	1.2	1.2	0.4	0.8	(NA)	(NA)	(NA)	(NA)	(NA)	0.1
Stimulants [1]	17.0	18.2	18.0	17.1	11.3	9.4	3.7	3.5	4.7	3.7	2.4	0.8
Sedatives [1]	15.0	17.0	18.7	11.0	5.5	4.3	1.6	2.8	2.6	1.6	0.9	0.6
Tranquilizers [1]	10.0	15.8	15.1	12.0	7.8	7.5	1.2	2.1	1.6	1.6	1.0	0.6
Analgesics [1]	(NA)	11.8	12.1	11.3	9.4	10.2	(NA)	1.0	1.0	1.8	1.5	1.5
Alcohol.	81.6	95.3	94.6	92.6	90.3	90.2	69.3	75.9	70.9	71.4	65.3	63.6
Cigarettes	68.8	82.8	76.9	75.6	75.0	71.2	48.8	42.6	39.5	36.8	35.2	32.2
26 YEARS OLD AND OVER												
Marihuana.	9.9	19.6	23.0	27.2	30.7	32.9	2.0	6.0	6.6	6.1	3.9	3.3
Cocaine	0.9	4.3	8.5	9.5	9.9	11.8	(NA)	0.9	1.2	2.0	0.9	0.8
Inhalants	1.2	3.9	(NA)	5.0	3.9	4.4	(NA)	0.5	(NA)	0.5	0.2	0.3
Hallucinogens	1.3	4.5	6.4	6.2	6.6	8.0	(NA)	(NA)	(NA)	(NA)	(NA)	0.1
Heroin	0.5	1.0	1.1	1.1	1.1	1.7	(NA)	(NA)	(NA)	(NA)	(NA)	(NA)
Stimulants [1]	3.0	5.8	6.2	7.9	6.6	7.1	(NA)	0.5	0.6	0.7	0.5	0.2
Sedatives [1]	2.0	3.5	4.8	5.2	3.3	4.5	(NA)	(NA)	(NA)	0.6	0.3	0.3
Tranquilizers [1]	2.0	3.1	3.6	7.2	4.6	5.7	(NA)	(NA)	(NA)	1.0	0.6	0.4
Analgesics [1]	(NA)	2.7	3.2	5.6	4.5	5.5	(NA)	(NA)	(NA)	0.9	0.4	0.5
Alcohol.	73.2	91.5	88.2	89.4	88.6	88.7	54.5	61.3	59.8	60.6	54.8	52.5
Cigarettes	65.4	83.0	78.7	80.5	79.6	77.6	39.1	36.9	34.6	32.8	29.8	28.8

NA Not available. [1] Nonmedical use.

Source: U.S. National Institute on Drug Abuse, *National Household Survey on Drug Abuse: 1991.*

Health and Nutrition

No. 198. Users of Selected Drugs, by User Characteristic: 1991

[In percent. See headnote, table 197. For composition of regions, see table 25]

SUBSTANCE AND AGE GROUP	Total [1]	SEX		RACE/ETHNICITY			REGION			
		Male	Female	White [2]	Black [2]	His-panic	North-east	Mid-west	South	West
CURRENT USERS										
Cigarettes: Total	27.0	28.7	25.5	27.3	27.9	24.7	26.9	28.1	27.3	25.4
12 to 17 years old	10.8	11.8	9.8	12.7	4.3	8.7	11.6	12.4	10.2	9.5
18 to 25 years old	32.2	32.0	32.3	35.7	22.0	24.7	35.7	33.4	30.3	30.8
26 to 34 years old	32.9	34.8	31.0	33.2	36.8	28.6	32.6	34.3	35.8	26.9
35 years old and over	26.6	28.8	24.7	25.8	32.6	27.7	25.2	27.6	27.0	26.2
Alcohol: Total	50.9	58.1	44.3	52.7	43.7	47.5	56.3	52.3	44.0	56.3
12 to 17 years old	20.3	22.3	18.2	20.4	20.1	22.5	19.0	21.9	19.8	20.7
18 to 25 years old	63.6	69.7	57.8	67.2	56.0	52.8	71.1	65.2	57.7	65.7
26 to 34 years old	61.7	70.8	52.8	63.8	57.1	57.2	66.3	64.5	55.9	63.5
35 years old and over	49.5	57.4	42.5	50.9	40.3	47.8	55.3	50.5	41.1	57.2
Marijuana: Total	4.8	6.3	3.4	4.5	7.2	4.3	5.2	4.6	4.2	5.8
12 to 17 years old	4.3	5.0	3.7	4.4	4.5	4.6	3.7	4.6	3.9	5.5
18 to 25 years old	13.0	15.7	10.5	13.7	14.6	9.1	14.7	11.5	12.1	14.8
26 to 34 years old	7.0	9.5	4.5	6.6	11.9	4.2	6.2	7.6	5.6	9.2
35 years old and over	2.1	3.0	1.3	1.9	3.5	2.3	2.8	2.0	1.7	2.3
Cocaine: Total	0.9	1.3	0.6	0.7	1.8	1.6	0.9	0.9	0.8	1.3
12 to 17 years old	0.4	0.5	0.3	0.3	0.5	1.3	0.5	(NA)	0.6	0.4
18 to 25 years old	2.0	2.8	1.3	1.7	3.1	2.7	1.5	2.1	1.8	3.0
26 to 34 years old	1.8	2.6	1.1	1.6	2.7	2.0	2.1	1.7	1.4	2.4
35 years old and over	0.5	0.6	0.3	0.2	1.3	1.0	0.4	0.6	0.4	0.6
Smokeless tobacco: Total	3.4	6.4	0.6	3.9	2.0	0.8	1.1	3.0	5.4	2.5
12 to 17 years old	3.0	5.3	0.5	3.8	0.8	1.1	0.9	3.7	3.7	2.5
18 to 25 years old	5.8	11.6	0.4	7.5	1.2	1.7	2.4	4.7	8.0	6.5
26 to 34 years old	3.5	7.0	0.2	4.3	1.5	0.8	0.7	2.9	6.0	3.0
35 years old and over	2.8	5.2	0.7	3.0	2.8	0.4	1.0	2.6	4.8	1.3
EVER USED										
Crack: Total	1.9	2.6	1.3	1.5	4.3	2.1	1.8	2.0	1.5	2.6
12 to 17 years old	0.9	0.7	1.0	0.8	1.1	1.3	0.6	0.4	0.9	1.7
18 to 25 years old	3.7	4.7	2.8	3.7	4.7	3.3	4.6	3.1	3.0	5.0
26 to 34 years old	3.7	5.1	2.3	2.8	9.2	3.7	2.8	3.3	3.5	5.2
35 years old and over	1.0	1.6	0.6	0.8	3.0	1.1	1.0	1.6	0.6	1.3
Inhalants: Total	5.6	7.1	4.1	5.8	3.8	4.9	4.9	4.6	4.9	8.4
12 to 17 years old	7.0	7.1	7.0	7.7	5.1	6.6	5.1	6.8	7.6	7.9
18 to 25 years old	10.9	12.3	9.6	12.8	4.4	6.6	9.8	9.7	9.8	15.4
26 to 34 years old	9.2	12.2	6.4	10.4	4.7	6.3	7.8	6.6	9.1	13.5
35 years old and over	2.7	3.9	1.7	2.6	2.9	2.8	2.8	2.4	1.8	4.8
Hallucinogens: Total	8.2	10.3	6.4	9.1	4.1	6.5	7.9	8.0	6.1	12.7
12 to 17 years old	3.4	3.3	3.4	3.9	1.2	3.5	2.9	3.8	3.1	3.9
18 to 25 years old	13.2	15.4	11.0	15.8	5.4	7.5	11.7	12.1	10.5	21.0
26 to 34 years old	15.6	18.9	12.4	18.0	6.0	9.1	15.2	15.1	12.5	21.3
35 years old and over	5.4	7.2	3.8	5.7	3.7	5.6	5.4	5.5	3.4	9.0
Stimulants: [3] Total	7.0	8.2	5.9	7.9	3.3	4.8	4.4	6.2	6.5	11.5
12 to 17 years old	3.0	2.5	3.4	3.5	0.8	2.1	1.5	3.0	3.5	3.3
18 to 25 years old	9.4	9.8	8.9	11.3	3.3	5.1	5.0	10.5	9.1	13.2
26 to 34 years old	12.2	14.1	10.4	14.3	5.0	6.3	7.9	10.3	12.6	17.8
35 years old and over	5.4	6.8	4.2	5.8	3.3	4.7	3.6	4.5	4.5	10.1
Sedatives: [3] Total	4.3	4.8	3.8	4.6	3.0	3.0	3.3	3.6	3.9	6.7
12 to 17 years old	2.4	2.0	2.9	2.7	1.2	2.2	1.8	2.4	2.7	2.5
18 to 25 years old	4.3	4.5	4.1	5.1	2.4	2.3	2.1	5.5	4.4	5.0
26 to 34 years old	7.5	8.7	6.3	8.6	3.8	3.4	6.2	5.9	8.1	9.3
35 years old and over	3.5	4.0	3.1	3.5	3.4	3.3	2.8	2.7	2.7	6.8
Tranquilizers: [3] Total	5.6	6.0	5.2	6.2	3.1	3.9	4.2	4.8	5.6	7.9
12 to 17 years old	2.1	1.8	2.5	2.6	1.1	1.0	1.4	1.9	2.6	2.0
18 to 25 years old	7.5	7.6	7.4	8.9	3.9	3.7	6.2	7.9	7.9	7.6
26 to 34 years old	10.1	11.0	9.1	11.5	5.7	5.4	9.1	8.9	11.0	10.7
35 years old and over	4.2	4.6	3.9	4.4	2.4	4.2	2.5	3.2	3.8	7.9
Analgesics: [3] Total	6.1	6.8	5.4	6.5	4.7	4.0	4.0	6.8	5.3	8.7
12 to 17 years old	4.4	4.3	4.6	4.8	3.9	3.6	2.7	5.0	5.0	4.4
18 to 25 years old	10.2	10.6	9.8	11.4	6.8	6.5	6.0	11.6	9.7	13.9
26 to 34 years old	9.8	11.1	8.5	11.1	6.8	4.1	7.6	8.7	11.0	10.9
35 years old and over	4.1	4.8	3.5	4.2	3.3	3.0	2.6	5.3	2.4	7.4

NA Not available. [1] Includes other races, not shown separately. [2] Non-Hispanic. [3] Nonmedical use.

Source: U.S. National Institute on Drug Abuse, *National Household Survey on Drug Abuse, 1991.*

No. 199. Cigarette Smoking by Age, Sex, Race, and Educational Attainment: 1965 to 1988

[In percent, except total population in millions. For persons 20 years old and over. Based on the National Health Interview Survey; see Appendix III]

CHARACTERISTIC	1965	1970	1974	1976	1978	1979	1980	1983	1985	1987	1988
Total 20 years old and over [1]	109.0	120.4	123.8	125.1	137.8	139.5	143.7	158.7	160.3	162.2	167.9
PRESENT SMOKERS											
Age:											
20 to 24 years old.	47.8	41.5	39.6	39.6	35.3	35.9	36.1	36.9	31.8	29.5	27.6
25 to 44 years old.	49.5	44.5	44.6	42.5	39.5	39.3	38.0	36.3	34.8	33.2	32.9
45 to 64 years old.	39.9	38.5	37.7	37.8	37.1	35.3	36.3	33.3	31.6	30.9	29.4
65 years old and over	17.1	16.2	17.2	17.0	16.4	16.5	17.3	16.7	16.0	15.2	14.9
Sex:											
Male.	50.2	44.3	43.4	42.1	39.0	38.4	38.5	35.5	33.2	31.5	30.9
Female	31.9	30.8	31.4	31.3	29.6	29.2	29.0	28.7	28.0	26.2	25.3
Race:											
White	40.0	36.5	36.1	35.6	33.6	33.2	32.9	31.4	29.9	28.3	27.5
Black	43.0	41.4	44.0	41.2	38.2	36.8	37.2	36.6	36.0	33.5	32.3
Educational attainment:											
Less than high school	(NA)	34.8	36.5	35.8	35.3	34.9	35.5	34.7	35.7	33.9	32.8
High school graduate.	(NA)	38.3	37.6	37.8	36.5	35.4	35.7	35.6	34.2	32.9	32.6
Some college.	(NA)	36.7	36.9	36.4	32.7	33.3	31.2	30.0	28.1	25.8	25.4
College graduate.	(NA)	28.1	28.3	27.4	23.8	23.4	24.6	19.9	18.4	16.1	15.6
QUIT RATIO [2]											
Age:											
20 to 24 years old.	17.8	20.8	20.9	22.0	22.8	22.6	22.2	21.4	26.0	23.8	27.5
25 to 44 years old.	23.6	29.8	29.3	29.4	31.9	31.8	33.0	34.3	38.2	37.2	36.8
45 to 64 years old.	30.9	36.1	39.7	40.4	40.1	42.4	40.9	46.4	49.7	49.2	52.8
65 years old and over	48.7	56.9	57.8	59.6	62.4	61.7	61.0	64.7	68.0	69.2	69.8
Sex:											
Male.	31.4	37.9	39.3	39.9	41.3	41.5	41.5	44.1	49.0	46.4	47.3
Female	24.6	29.2	30.8	32.1	33.8	34.0	34.0	37.6	40.0	41.4	43.4
Race:											
White	30.5	36.7	38.0	38.4	39.9	40.3	40.4	43.3	46.7	46.6	48.0
Black	22.8	23.2	21.8	26.3	27.5	28.0	27.7	29.3	31.8	32.0	32.8
Educational attainment:											
Less than high school	(NA)	38.1	38.0	39.5	38.7	40.8	39.4	42.1	41.3	44.3	46.3
High school graduate.	(NA)	33.6	35.2	35.0	36.3	36.7	36.5	38.7	40.5	41.1	41.6
Some college.	(NA)	34.9	36.6	37.2	41.0	37.5	40.6	41.2	46.0	45.5	46.4
College graduate.	(NA)	48.2	47.9	46.1	49.7	50.6	48.7	54.9	61.1	59.1	60.6

NA Not available. [1] Includes other races, not shown separately. [2] Percent of persons who have ever smoked who are former smokers.

Source: U.S. Centers for Disease Control, Office of Smoking and Health, *Reducing the Health Consequences of Smoking, 1989* and unpublished data.

No. 200. Cancer—Estimated New Cases, 1991, and Survival Rates, 1974-76 to 1981-87

[The 5-year relative survival rate, which is derived by adjusting the observed survival rate for expected mortality, represents the liklihood that a person will not die from causes directly related to their cancer within five years. Survival data shown are based on those patients diagnosed while residents of an area listed below during the time periods shown. Data are based on information collected as part of the National Cancer Institute's Surveillance, Epidemiology and End Results (SEER) program, a collection of population-based registries in Connecticut, New Mexico, Utah, Iowa, Hawaii, Atlanta, Detroit, Seattle-Puget Sound, and San Francisco-Oakland]

SITE	ESTIMATED NEW CASES, [1] 1991 (1,000)			5 YEAR RELATIVE SURVIVAL RATES (percent)								
				All races [2]			White			Black		
	Total	Male	Fe-male	1974-1976	1977-1980	1981-1987	1974-1976	1977-1980	1981-1987	1974-1976	1977-1980	1981-1987
All sites [3]	1,100	545	555	49.1	49.4	51.1	50.0	50.5	52.5	38.6	38.8	38.4
Lung	161	101	60	12.2	13.1	13.1	12.3	13.3	13.4	11.3	11.6	10.8
Breast [4]	176	1	175	74.1	77.4	77.0	74.7	75.1	78.2	62.6	63.0	63.1
Colon.	112	54	58	49.9	52.5	57.0	50.1	52.7	57.8	45.5	47.7	47.3
Prostate	122	122	(X)	66.5	70.7	74.1	67.4	71.8	75.6	57.7	62.2	63.0
Bladder	50	37	13	72.3	74.7	78.1	73.5	75.6	79.0	47.5	54.7	59.2
Rectum	46	25	21	48.2	49.6	54.3	48.5	50.6	55.1	41.2	36.8	44.1
Corpus uteri	33	(X)	33	88.2	84.3	82.9	89.0	85.6	84.4	62.2	56.2	55.5
Non-Hodgkin's lymphoma [5] . .	37	20	18	47.0	48.3	50.8	47.4	48.5	51.4	47.8	49.2	44.5
Oral cavity and pharynx.	31	21	10	53.0	52.2	51.2	54.8	54.2	53.6	35.3	34.3	31.2
Leukemia [5]	28	16	12	33.5	35.5	35.2	34.2	36.3	36.3	30.5	29.6	29.0
Melanoma of skin.	32	17	15	79.3	81.2	81.5	79.5	81.5	81.7	68.6	50.6	69.5
Pancreas	28	14	15	2.6	2.5	3.1	2.7	2.3	2.8	2.2	5.1	4.3
Kidney	25	16	10	51.4	51.7	53.0	51.5	51.3	53.2	48.9	56.5	52.1
Stomach.	24	15	9	15.0	16.5	17.0	14.3	15.6	16.0	16.1	16.4	17.4
Ovary.	21	(X)	21	36.4	38.1	38.8	36.2	37.5	38.7	40.8	39.6	36.1
Cervix uteri [6]	13	(X)	13	68.3	67.4	65.9	69.1	68.3	67.5	63.0	61.9	57.4

X Not applicable. [1] Estimates provided by American Cancer Society are based on rates from the National Cancer Institute's SEER program 1984-87. [2] Includes other races, not shown separately. [3] Includes other sites, not shown separately. [4] Survival rates for female only. [5] All types combined. [6] Invasive cancer only.

Source: U.S. National Institutes of Health, National Cancer Institute, *Cancer Statistics Review: 1973-1988*, 1991.

No. 201. Women Who Have Had a Mammogram, Breast Physical Exam or Who Perform Breast Self Exams (BSE): 1987

[For **women 40 years old and over.** Based on the National Health Interview Survey and subject to sampling error; for details see source and Appendix III]

AGE AND RACE	Total women (1,000)	PERCENT HAVING A—						PERCENT PERFORMING BSE—		
		Mammogram			Breast physical exam			At least once a week	Once a month to less than once a week	Less than once a month
		Ever	In the past—		Ever	In the past—				
			11 months	12-36 months		11 months	12-36 months			
Total [1]	47,676	38.1	14.8	14.3	81.3	33.2	30.4	14.5	32.8	20.0
40 to 54 years old	19,597	42.2	16.8	16.1	86.7	39.0	32.3	13.4	37.4	24.5
40 to 44 years old	7,664	38.8	14.7	15.3	87.3	39.4	32.5	9.7	42.0	27.4
45 to 49 years old	6,344	43.5	18.1	16.7	86.6	39.1	30.4	15.8	35.2	22.8
50 to 54 years old	5,588	45.5	18.3	16.6	86.1	38.5	34.3	16.1	33.2	22.3
55 to 64 years old	11,749	41.1	16.9	13.6	83.1	31.9	32.4	14.8	35.0	18.6
55 to 59 years old	5,814	43.2	17.6	14.9	85.9	34.5	33.6	14.3	35.5	19.4
60 to 64 years old	5,935	38.7	16.1	12.1	80.0	28.9	31.1	15.4	34.4	17.7
65 to 74 years old	9,665	35.2	12.9	14.3	76.8	30.7	26.3	15.7	30.4	17.2
65 to 69 years old	5,436	37.5	14.7	14.0	79.8	33.3	26.0	15.9	33.6	16.4
70 to 74 years old	4,229	32.1	10.5	14.7	72.7	27.1	26.9	15.6	26.1	18.3
75 years old and over	6,665	24.8	8.0	9.9	68.2	21.8	26.7	15.3	18.8	13.1
75 to 79 years old	3,418	30.0	[2]9.6	12.4	73.1	23.6	27.7	13.7	23.0	14.6
80 to 85 years old	2,008	20.4	[2]5.1	9.4	65.5	20.1	29.6	18.6	17.7	10.7
85 years and over	1,239	17.5	[2]7.9	[2]3.6	58.8	19.7	19.4	14.5	9.2	12.9
White	41,877	39.2	15.3	14.8	82.8	33.6	30.9	13.5	33.5	20.9
40 to 54 years old	16,757	43.9	17.6	16.8	88.6	39.5	32.9	11.9	38.2	26.1
55 to 64 years old	10,311	42.2	17.1	14.1	84.8	32.5	33.2	13.7	36.0	19.0
65 to 74 years old	8,715	36.5	13.4	14.9	78.3	31.0	26.9	15.1	31.3	17.8
75 years old and over	6,094	25.5	8.3	10.3	70.2	22.7	27.3	14.9	19.2	13.8
Black	4,830	31.2	12.9	10.4	73.7	33.4	25.8	21.9	30.1	14.5
40 to 54 years old	2,272	33.7	13.7	11.5	79.6	39.8	27.4	20.5	35.1	16.3
55 to 64 years old	1,205	36.4	[2]7.9	[2]10.7	78.0	31.2	28.0	23.5	32.3	16.5
65 to 74 years old	824	24.7	[2]8.4	[2]10.0	65.7	30.4	[2]21.7	[2]23.7	21.4	[2]12.1
75 years old and over	529	17.1	[2]3.4	[2]5.2	47.6	[2]12.7	[2]19.7	[2]22.1	[2]14.5	[2]4.4

[1] Includes other races, not shown separately.   [2] Relative standard error exceeds 30 percent of the estimate.

Source: U.S. National Center for Health Statistics, *Vital and Health Statistics*, series 10, No. 172.

No. 202. Personal Health Practices, by Selected Characteristic: 1985

[**In percent.** For persons 18 years of age and over. Based on National Health Interview Survey; see Appendix III]

CHARACTERISTIC	Sleeps 6 hours or less	Never eats breakfast	Snacks every day	Less physically active [1]	Had 5 or more drinks on any day [2]	Current smoker	30 percent or more above weight [3]
All persons [4]	22.0	24.3	39.0	16.4	37.5	30.1	13.0
Age: 18 to 29 years old	19.8	30.4	42.2	17.1	54.4	31.9	7.5
30 to 44 years old	24.3	30.1	41.4	18.3	39.0	34.5	13.6
54 to 64 years old	22.7	21.4	37.9	15.3	24.6	31.6	18.1
65 years old and over	20.4	7.5	30.7	13.5	12.2	16.0	13.2
65 to 74 years old	19.7	9.0	32.4	15.8	(NA)	19.7	14.9
75 years old and over	21.5	5.1	27.8	9.8	(NA)	10.0	10.3
Sex: Male	22.7	25.2	40.7	16.5	49.3	32.6	12.1
Female	21.4	23.6	37.5	16.3	23.3	27.8	13.7
Race: White	21.3	24.5	39.4	16.7	38.3	29.6	12.4
All other	26.6	23.2	36.3	14.3	29.9	33.1	16.4
Black	27.8	23.6	37.2	13.9	29.3	34.9	18.7
Other	21.4	21.5	32.6	16.5	33.3	24.8	6.7
Education level: Less than 12 years	23.3	22.6	37.8	12.3	35.9	35.4	17.5
12 years	21.9	26.5	39.6	16.5	38.9	33.4	13.4
More than 12 years	21.2	23.3	39.2	19.1	36.8	23.1	9.4

NA Not available.   [1] Less than contemporaries.   [2] Percent of drinkers who had 5 or more drinks on any one day in the past year.   [3] Above desirable weight. Based on 1960 Metropolitan Life Insurance Company standards. Data are self-reported.
[4] Excludes persons whose health practices are unknown.

Source: U.S. National Center for Health Statistics, *Health Promotion and Disease Prevention, United States 1985, Vital and Health Statistics*, series 10, No. 163 and unpublished data.

No. 203. Medical Device Implants, by Age, Sex, and Race: 1988

[In thousands, except percent. Based in the National Health Interview Survey; for details, see Appendix III]

DEVICE	Total [1]	PERCENT DISTRIBUTION							
		Age				Sex		Race	
		Under 18 years old	18-44 years old	45-64 years old	65 years old and over	Male	Female	White	Black
Artificial joints [2]	1,625	[3]0.6	13.0	24.6	61.7	39.9	60.1	92.3	6.2
Hip joints	816	[3]0.5	6.5	26.3	66.7	37.5	62.4	93.5	5.5
Knee joints	521	-	10.9	20.5	68.5	41.8	58.2	88.1	10.0
Fixation devices [4]	4,890	3.9	44.3	28.4	23.4	57.2	42.8	91.7	6.6
Head	351	[3]4.3	67.8	22.8	[3]5.4	57.3	42.7	93.2	[3]4.8
Torso	563	[3]5.3	49.6	31.8	13.3	62.7	37.5	92.2	[3]6.9
Upper extremities	646	[3]3.7	55.9	25.4	15.0	70.4	29.7	91.6	[3]5.6
Lower extremities	2,690	3.0	39.6	27.9	29.4	52.8	47.2	91.1	7.7
Other	622	[3]6.4	34.4	34.1	25.1	57.9	42.1	93.6	[3]3.7
Other devices:									
Ear vent tubes	1,494	[5]25.8	[6]27.0	[7]34.6	[8]12.6	39.9	61.1	92.3	6.2
Silicone implants	620	[3]0.5	73.1	23.7	[3]2.9	8.2	91.8	97.6	[3]0.8
Breast implants	544	[3]0.6	73.0	24.1	[3]2.6	[3]2.0	98.0	98.5	-
Shunt or catheter	321	24.3	24.3	22.1	29.3	50.5	49.2	85.7	[3]12.5
Dental implants	275	[3]2.2	57.8	27.3	[3]12.7	56.4	43.6	93.8	[3]4.0
Heart valve	279	(NA)	[9]14.7	35.5	49.8	52.3	47.8	89.2	10.0
Pacemaker	460	(NA)	(NA)	[10]13.5	86.7	50.4	49.6	93.7	[3]5.2
Eye lens	3,765	(NA)	(NA)	[10]18.7	81.3	37.6	62.4	95.6	3.5

- Represents or rounds to zero.   NA Not available.   [1] Includes other races, not shown separately.   [2] Includes other devices, not shown separately.   [3] Figure does not meet standards of reliability or precision.   [4] Includes sites unknown. Each device represents a single body part regardless of the number of pins, screws, nails, wires, rods or plates.   [5] Under 3 years old.   [6] 3 to 5 years old.   [7] 6 to 17 years old.   [8] 18 years old and over.   [9] Under 45 years old.   [10] Under 65 years old.

Source: U.S. National Center for Health Statistics, *National Health Interview Survey*, 1988, unpublished data.

No. 204. Cumulative Percent Distribution of Population by Height and Sex: 1976-80

[For persons 18 to 74 years old. Height was measured without shoes. Based on sample and subject to sampling variability; see source]

HEIGHT	MALES						FEMALES					
	18-24 years	25-34 years	35-44 years	45-54 years	55-64 years	65-74 years	18-24 years	25-34 years	35-44 years	45-54 years	55-64 years	65-74 years
Percent under—												
4'8"	-	-	-	-	-	-	0.05	-	0.10	0.28	0.46	1.04
4'9"	-	-	-	-	-	-	0.43	0.23	0.34	0.35	1.07	2.27
4'10"	-	-	-	-	-	-	0.94	0.64	0.95	1.22	3.02	4.23
4'11"	-	-	-	-	-	-	2.22	1.65	1.94	4.20	6.43	9.33
5'	0.18	0.05	0.27	-	0.27	0.24	4.22	3.65	4.56	8.88	11.40	17.20
5'1"	0.18	0.31	0.34	0.19	0.72	1.22	9.13	8.60	7.75	16.16	19.70	29.00
5'2"	0.34	0.42	0.87	0.70	0.92	2.66	17.75	19.11	18.24	27.68	31.71	44.34
5'3"	0.61	0.54	2.07	1.50	2.78	5.97	29.06	32.96	33.11	39.83	45.87	59.15
5'4"	2.37	1.55	3.68	2.55	5.28	10.53	41.81	47.43	49.90	57.21	63.89	76.44
5'5"	3.85	4.36	6.36	5.72	9.29	18.31	58.09	61.36	63.88	70.47	77.44	86.97
5'6"	8.24	9.51	12.39	11.39	17.54	29.42	74.76	74.92	78.07	84.64	88.91	94.63
5'7"	16.18	15.25	17.63	21.24	29.10	41.63	85.37	85.65	87.95	91.21	94.56	97.86
5'8"	26.68	26.69	26.40	33.56	43.53	57.75	92.30	93.28	93.43	96.28	97.70	99.20
5'9"	38.89	39.68	42.52	50.39	58.21	69.96	96.23	97.19	97.18	98.17	99.36	99.81
5'10"	53.66	55.35	57.01	63.38	71.51	81.95	98.34	99.49	99.19	99.58	99.78	99.92
5'11"	68.25	69.67	70.70	76.94	83.09	89.59	99.38	99.68	99.39	99.84	99.81	100.00
6'	80.14	81.58	81.15	85.83	90.99	94.52	-	-	-	-	-	-
6'1"	88.54	89.95	90.04	93.43	96.28	97.82	-	-	-	-	-	-
6'2"	92.74	95.57	95.05	98.01	97.66	99.17	-	-	-	-	-	-
6'3"	96.17	97.98	97.82	99.35	98.90	99.86	-	-	-	-	-	-
6'4"	98.40	99.23	99.19	99.70	99.79	100.00	-	-	-	-	-	-

- Represents or rounds to zero.

Source: U.S. National Center for Health Statistics, *Vital and Health Statistics*, series 11, No. 238.

Health and Nutrition

No. 205. Per Capita Consumption of Major Food Commodities: 1970 to 1990

[In pounds, retail weight except as indicated. Consumption represents the residual after exports, nonfood use and ending stocks are subtracted from the sum of beginning stocks, domestic production, and imports. Based on Bureau of the Census estimated population. Estimates reflect revisions based on the 1990 Census of Population. For similar but unrevised data, see *Historical Statistics, Colonial Times to 1970*, series G 881-915]

COMMODITY	1970	1975	1980	1985	1986	1987	1988	1989	1990
Red meat, total (boneless, trimmed weight) [1][2]	132.0	125.3	126.4	124.9	122.2	117.4	119.5	115.9	112.3
Beef	79.6	83.0	72.1	74.6	74.4	69.5	68.6	65.4	64.0
Veal	2.0	2.8	1.3	1.5	1.6	1.3	1.1	1.0	0.9
Lamb and mutton	2.1	1.3	1.0	1.1	1.0	1.0	1.0	1.1	1.1
Pork (excluding lard)	48.2	38.2	52.1	47.7	45.2	45.6	48.8	48.4	46.3
Fish and shellfish (edible weight) [3]	11.8	12.2	12.5	15.1	15.5	16.2	15.2	15.6	15.5
Fresh and frozen	6.9	7.5	7.9	9.8	9.8	10.7	10.0	10.2	10.1
Canned	4.5	4.3	4.3	5.0	5.4	5.2	4.9	5.1	5.1
Tuna	2.5	2.9	3.0	3.3	3.6	3.5	3.6	3.9	3.7
Cured	0.4	0.4	0.3	0.3	0.3	0.3	0.3	0.3	0.3
Poultry products: (boneless weight) [2][4]	34.1	34.2	42.6	49.4	51.3	55.5	57.4	60.8	63.6
Chicken	27.7	27.5	34.3	39.9	40.7	43.4	44.7	47.3	49.3
Turkey	6.4	6.7	8.3	9.6	10.6	12.1	12.6	13.5	14.4
Eggs (farm weight) (number)	309	276	271	255	254	254	246	236	233
Dairy products:									
Total (milk equivalent) [5]	563.8	539.1	543.3	593.7	591.5	601.3	583.2	565.3	570.6
Fluid milk and cream [6]	275.1	261.4	245.6	241.0	240.5	238.5	234.6	236.4	233.2
Beverage milks	269.1	254.0	237.4	229.7	228.6	226.5	222.3	224.3	221.5
Plain whole milk	213.5	174.9	141.7	119.7	112.9	108.5	102.4	94.5	87.6
Plain lowfat milk	29.8	53.2	70.1	83.3	88.1	89.6	89.9	96.3	98.2
Plain skim milk	11.6	11.5	11.6	12.6	13.5	14.0	16.1	20.2	22.9
Flavored whole milk	5.6	6.3	4.7	3.7	3.5	3.4	3.3	3.1	2.8
Flavored lowfat and skim milks	3.0	3.3	5.3	6.0	6.3	6.6	6.6	6.5	6.6
Buttermilk	5.5	4.7	4.1	4.4	4.2	4.3	4.1	3.7	3.5
Yogurt	0.8	2.1	2.6	4.1	4.4	4.4	4.7	4.3	4.1
Cream [7]	3.8	3.3	3.4	4.4	4.7	4.7	4.6	4.8	4.6
Sour cream and dip	1.1	1.6	1.8	2.3	2.4	2.4	2.5	2.5	2.5
Condensed and evaporated milk:									
Whole milk	7.0	5.2	3.8	3.6	3.6	3.7	3.5	3.1	3.1
Skim milk	5.0	3.5	3.3	3.8	4.3	4.2	4.2	4.7	4.8
Cheese [8]	11.4	14.3	17.5	22.5	23.1	24.1	23.7	23.9	24.7
American	7.0	8.2	9.6	12.2	12.1	12.4	11.4	11.1	11.1
Cheddar	5.9	6.0	6.9	9.8	9.8	10.6	9.5	9.2	9.2
Italian	2.1	3.2	4.4	6.5	7.0	7.6	8.1	8.5	9.1
Mozzarella	1.2	2.1	3.0	4.6	5.2	5.6	6.0	6.4	6.9
Other [9]	2.3	2.9	3.4	3.9	4.0	4.1	4.1	4.3	4.4
Swiss	0.9	1.1	1.3	1.3	1.3	1.2	1.3	1.2	1.4
Cream and Neufchatel	0.6	0.7	1.0	1.2	1.3	1.4	1.5	1.6	1.7
Cottage cheese	5.2	4.7	4.5	4.1	4.1	3.9	3.9	3.6	3.4
Ice cream	17.8	18.6	17.5	18.1	18.4	18.4	17.3	16.1	15.7
Ice milk	7.7	7.6	7.1	6.9	7.2	7.4	8.0	8.4	7.7
Fats and oils:									
Total, fat content only [10]	52.6	52.6	57.2	64.3	64.3	62.9	63.0	61.1	62.7
Butter (product weight)	5.4	4.7	4.5	4.9	4.6	4.7	4.5	4.4	4.4
Margarine (product weight)	10.8	11.0	11.3	10.8	11.4	10.5	10.3	10.2	10.9
Lard (direct use)	4.6	3.2	2.6	1.8	1.7	1.8	1.8	1.8	2.2
Edible tallow (direct use)	(NA)	(NA)	1.1	1.9	1.8	0.9	0.8	0.9	0.8
Shortening	17.3	17.0	18.2	22.9	22.1	21.4	21.5	21.5	22.2
Salad and cooking oils	15.4	17.9	21.2	23.5	24.2	25.4	25.8	24.0	24.2
Other edible fats and oils	2.3	2.0	1.5	1.6	1.7	1.4	1.3	1.3	1.2
Flour and cereal products	135.1	138.8	145.5	158.0	163.9	173.4	172.9	175.0	185.4
Wheat flour [11]	110.9	114.5	116.9	124.7	125.7	129.9	130.0	129.2	137.8
Rye flour	1.2	1.0	0.7	0.7	0.6	0.6	0.6	0.6	0.6
Rice, milled [12]	6.7	7.6	9.5	9.1	11.7	13.9	14.4	15.6	16.6
Corn products	11.1	10.8	12.9	17.8	19.8	22.5	20.7	21.8	22.1
Oat products	4.2	4.2	4.6	4.8	5.1	5.5	6.2	6.9	7.4
Barley products	1.0	1.0	1.0	0.9	0.9	0.9	0.9	0.9	0.9
Caloric sweeteners, total [13]	122.6	117.9	123.9	130.0	129.1	132.6	133.2	134.3	137.5
Sugar, refined cane and beet	101.8	89.2	83.6	62.7	60.0	62.4	62.1	62.5	64.2
Corn sweeteners (dry weight)	19.3	27.4	39.1	65.9	67.7	68.9	69.7	70.3	71.9
Low-calorie sweeteners (sugar sweetness equivalent) [14]	5.8	6.1	7.7	18.1	18.5	19.1	20.0	(NA)	(NA)
Saccharin	5.8	6.1	7.7	6.0	5.5	5.5	6.0	(NA)	(NA)
Aspartame	-	-	-	12.1	13.0	13.6	14.0	(NA)	(NA)
Other:									
Cocoa beans	3.9	3.2	3.4	4.6	4.8	4.8	4.8	4.9	5.2
Coffee (green beans)	13.6	12.2	10.3	10.5	10.5	10.2	9.8	10.3	10.2
Peanuts (shelled)	5.5	6.0	4.8	6.3	6.4	6.4	6.9	7.0	6
Tree nuts (shelled)	1.8	2.0	1.8	2.4	2.3	2.2	2.3	2.3	2.5

- Represents or rounds to zero. NA Not available. [1] Excludes edible offals. [2] Excludes shipments to Puerto Rico and the other U.S. possessions. [3] Excludes consumption from recreational fishing, approximately 3 to 4 pounds per capita. [4] Includes backs, necks, skin, and giblets. [5] Includes other products, not shown separately. [6] Fluid milk figures are aggregates of commercial sales and milk produced and consumed on farms. [7] Heavy cream, light cream, and half and half. [8] Excludes cottage, pot, and baker's cheese. [9] Includes other cheeses, not shown separately. [10] The fat content of butter and margarine is 80 percent of product weight. [11] White, whole wheat, semolina, and durum flour. [12] For crop year beginning in previous year. [13] Dry weight. Includes edible syrups (maple, molasses, etc.) and honey, not shown separately. [14] Assumes saccharin is 300 times as sweet as sugar and aspartame 200 times as sweet as sugar.

Source: U.S. Department of Agriculture, Economic Research Service, *Food Consumption, Prices, and Expenditures*, annual.

No. 206. Per Capita Utilization of Selected Commercially Produced Fresh Fruits and Vegetables: 1970 to 1990

[In pounds, farm weight. Domestic food use of fresh fruits and vegetables reflects the fresh-market share of commodity production plus imports and minus exports. All data are on a calendar year basis except for citrus fruits, October or November; apples, August; grapes and pears, July; prior to years indicated. See headnote, table 205]

COMMODITY	1970	1975	1980	1982	1983	1984	1985	1986	1987	1988	1989	1990
Fresh fruits, total	79.4	85.0	90.0	87.6	93.2	91.7	89.3	95.9	101.1	99.2	99.2	92.3
Noncitrus	50.6	55.6	61.2	62.9	63.7	67.6	66.7	69.8	75.4	72.7	74.3	69.8
Bananas	17.4	17.6	20.8	22.6	21.3	22.2	23.5	25.8	25.0	24.3	24.7	24.4
Apples	17.0	19.5	19.2	17.7	18.5	18.6	17.5	18.2	21.3	20.0	21.6	19.8
Grapes	2.5	3.2	3.8	6.2	6.0	6.5	7.5	7.3	7.6	8.2	8.4	7.8
Peaches	5.8	5.0	5.7	4.0	4.1	5.4	4.0	4.7	4.7	5.1	4.2	3.7
Pears	1.9	2.7	2.6	2.9	3.0	2.6	2.8	3.1	3.6	3.3	3.4	3.2
Strawberries	1.7	1.8	2.0	2.4	2.4	3.1	3.1	3.0	3.3	3.5	3.5	3.3
Pineapples	0.7	1.0	1.5	1.7	1.7	1.5	1.5	1.8	1.7	1.8	2.0	2.1
Plums	1.5	1.3	1.6	1.1	1.5	2.0	1.5	1.4	2.1	1.8	1.6	1.5
Nectarines	0.6	0.9	1.6	1.4	1.5	1.5	1.7	1.4	1.5	1.5	1.5	1.5
Other [1]	1.5	2.5	2.3	3.0	3.8	4.2	3.5	3.3	4.5	3.2	3.4	2.4
Citrus	28.8	29.4	28.9	24.8	29.5	24.0	22.6	26.1	25.8	26.4	24.9	22.6
Oranges	16.2	15.9	15.8	12.7	16.1	12.8	12.3	14.5	14.0	14.7	13.0	13.4
Grapefruit	8.2	8.3	8.0	7.5	8.2	6.4	5.8	6.6	6.7	6.8	6.9	4.5
Other [2]	4.4	5.2	5.0	4.5	5.2	4.8	4.5	4.9	5.0	5.0	5.0	4.7
Selected melons	21.7	17.7	17.9	22.0	19.6	23.9	24.1	24.6	24.3	23.7	26.3	25.2
Watermelons	13.5	11.4	10.7	12.5	11.3	14.4	13.5	12.8	13.0	13.5	13.4	14.1
Cantaloups	7.2	5.2	5.8	7.7	6.5	7.7	8.5	9.4	9.1	7.9	10.4	9.1
Honeydews	1.0	1.1	1.4	1.8	1.8	1.8	2.1	2.4	2.2	2.3	2.5	2.0
Selected fresh vegetables	88.8	89.9	92.7	95.9	92.6	100.3	100.2	99.3	105.7	109.6	112.9	111.0
Asparagus	0.4	0.4	0.3	0.4	0.4	0.4	0.5	0.6	0.6	0.6	0.6	0.6
Broccoli	0.5	1.0	1.4	2.0	2.0	2.5	2.6	3.0	3.1	3.8	3.8	3.4
Cabbage	11.4	9.1	8.1	9.2	8.5	9	9.2	8.2	8.0	8.7	8.4	8.7
Carrots	6.0	6.4	6.1	6.6	6.4	6.9	6.5	6.5	8.3	7.2	7.8	8.0
Cauliflower	0.7	0.9	1.1	1.3	1.4	1.8	1.8	2.2	2.1	2.2	2.2	2.2
Celery	7.3	6.9	7.5	7.6	7.2	7.3	7.0	6.6	6.7	7.2	7.5	7.2
Corn	7.8	7.8	6.5	6.0	6.1	6.4	6.4	6.0	6.3	5.7	6.4	6.4
Cucumbers	2.9	2.9	3.9	3.9	3.9	4.1	3.9	4.6	5.0	4.8	4.8	4.6
Iceberg lettuce	22.4	23.5	25.6	24.9	22.4	24.9	23.7	21.9	25.7	27.0	28.7	27.8
Onions	12.4	13.4	13.3	15.4	15.0	15.9	16.4	16.7	16.3	17.6	17.7	18.6
Snap beans	1.5	1.4	1.3	1.3	1.2	1.3	1.3	1.3	1.2	1.2	1.2	1.1
Green peppers	2.2	2.5	2.9	3.0	3.3	3.6	3.8	4.0	4.2	4.5	4.7	4.6
Tomatoes	12.1	12.0	12.8	12.5	12.6	14.2	14.8	15.8	15.8	16.8	16.7	15.4
Other fresh [3]	1.2	1.7	1.9	1.8	2.2	2.0	2.3	1.9	2.4	2.3	2.4	2.4
Potatoes	121.7	122.2	114.3	114.8	118.4	121.9	122.4	125.7	125.7	122.2	126.7	127.2
Fresh	61.8	52.6	51.1	47.1	49.8	48.3	46.3	48.8	47.9	49.6	49.6	45.4
For freezing	28.5	37.1	35.4	38.6	39.2	43.7	45.4	46.2	47.8	43.2	46.5	49.9
For chips/shoestrings	17.4	15.5	16.6	17.1	17.8	18	17.6	18.2	17.6	17.2	17.5	17.3
For dehydrating	12.0	14.7	9.4	10.2	9.8	10.1	11.2	10.7	10.6	10.2	11.1	12.8
For canning	2.0	2.0	1.9	1.9	1.9	1.8	1.9	1.8	1.8	1.9	2.0	1.9
Sweet potatoes [4]	5.4	5.4	4.4	5.5	4.6	4.9	5.4	4.4	4.4	4.1	4.1	4.7
Mushrooms	1.3	1.9	2.7	3.0	3.5	3.5	3.6	3.8	3.5	3.5	3.5	3.7
For fresh	0.3	0.7	1.2	1.4	1.6	1.8	1.8	1.9	1.9	2.0	2.0	2.0
For processing	1.0	1.2	1.5	1.5	1.8	1.8	1.8	1.9	1.6	1.6	1.5	1.7

[1] Includes apricots, avocados, cherries, cranberries, figs, kiwifruit, mangos, olives, papayas, persimmons, and pomegranates.   [2] Includes tangerines, tangelos, lemons, and limes.   [3] Includes artichokes, garlic, and eggplant.   [4] Fresh and processed.

Source: U.S. Dept. of Agriculture, Economic Research Service, *Food Consumption, Prices and Expenditures,* annual; and unpublished data.

No. 207. Per Capita Consumption of Selected Beverages, by Type: 1970 to 1990

[In gallons. See headnote, table 205]

COMMODITY	1970	1975	1980	1983	1984	1985	1986	1987	1988	1989	1990
Nonalcoholic [1]	95.8	95.8	101.7	100.4	101.1	102.1	102.5	104.5	105.1	106.6	105.8
Milk (plain and flavored)	31.2	29.5	27.6	26.3	26.4	26.7	26.5	26.3	25.8	26	25.7
Whole	25.4	21.0	17.0	15.1	14.7	14.3	13.5	13.0	12.3	11.3	10.5
Lowfat	4.5	7.1	9.2	9.9	10.3	10.9	11.5	11.7	11.7	12.4	12.6
Skim	1.3	1.3	1.3	1.2	1.3	1.5	1.6	1.6	1.9	2.3	2.7
Tea	6.0	7.5	7.3	7.0	7.1	7.1	7.1	7.0	7.1	7.1	6.9
Coffee	33.4	31.4	26.7	26.3	26.8	27.4	27.5	26.7	25.7	26.9	26.7
Soft drinks	20.8	22.2	35.0	35.2	36.0	35.7	35.8	39.2	41.1	41.8	42.5
Citrus juice	3.6	5.2	5.1	5.6	4.8	5.2	5.5	5.3	5.4	4.8	4.0
Alcoholic (adult population)	35.7	39.7	42.8	41.7	41.1	40.5	40.6	40.0	39.5	38.9	39.5
Beer	30.6	33.9	36.6	35.6	35.0	34.4	34.7	34.4	34.1	33.7	34.4
Wine	2.2	2.7	3.2	3.3	3.4	3.5	3.5	3.3	3.2	3.0	2.9
Distilled spirits	3.0	3.1	3.0	2.7	2.6	2.5	2.4	2.3	2.2	2.1	2.2

[1] Excludes vegetable juices, noncitrus fruit juices and drinks, canned concentrated citrus juices, and chilled-fresh citrus juices produced for local sale. Includes chilled citrus juices produced commercially from fresh fruit in Florida.

Source: U.S. Dept. of Agriculture, Economic Research Service, *Food Consumption, Prices, and Expenditures,* annual; and unpublished data.

No. 208. Nutrition—Nutrients in Foods Available for Civilian Consumption per Capita per Day and Percent Change: 1955 to 1988

[Based on estimates of per capita food consumption at the retail level, on imputed consumption data for foods no longer reported, and on estimates of quantities of home grown produce. Food supply estimates do not reflect loss of food or nutrients from further marketing or home processing. Enrichment and fortification levels of iron, thiamin, riboflavin, niacin, vitamin A, vitamin B$_6$, vitamin B$_{12}$, and ascorbic acid are included. Minus sign (-) indicates decrease. See *Historical Statistics, Colonial Times to 1970,* series G 851-856 for related details]

NUTRIENT	Unit	1955-59	1965-69	1975-79	1985-88	PERCENT CHANGE, 1985-88 FROM		
						1955-59	1965-69	1975-79
Food energy	Calories	3,100	3,200	3,300	3,600	13.9	11.1	8.3
Protein	Grams	94	97	99	104	9.6	6.7	4.8
Total fat [1]	Grams	142	154	157	169	16.0	8.9	7.1
Saturated	Grams	60	62	58	61	1.6	-1.6	4.9
Monounsaturated	Grams	56	62	63	67	16.4	7.5	6.0
Polyunsaturated	Grams	19	23	29	34	44.1	32.4	14.7
Cholesterol	Milligrams	510	490	450	440	-15.9	-11.4	-2.3
Carbohydrate	Grams	380	380	390	420	9.5	9.5	7.1
Vitamin A	Retinol equivalents	1,320	1,350	1,540	1,630	19.0	17.2	5.5
Carotenes	Retinol equivalents	430	430	600	750	42.7	42.7	20.0
Vitamin E	Milligram α-TE [2]	11.3	12.7	14.5	16.3	30.7	22.1	11.0
Ascorbic acid	Milligrams	100	96	111	116	13.8	17.2	4.3
Thiamin	Milligrams	1.9	1.9	2.1	2.2	13.6	13.6	4.5
Riboflavin	Milligrams	2.3	2.2	2.4	2.4	4.2	8.3	0.0
Niacin	Milligrams	20	22	24	26	23.1	15.4	7.7
Vitamin B$_6$	Milligrams	1.9	2.0	2.1	2.1	9.5	4.8	0.0
Folacin	Micrograms	282	267	277	283	0.4	5.7	2.1
Vitamin B$_{12}$	Micrograms	9.4	10.0	10.0	9.2	-2.2	-8.7	-8.7
Calcium	Milligrams	920	850	850	900	-2.2	5.6	5.6
Phosphorus	Milligrams	1,470	1,460	1,470	1,530	3.9	4.6	3.9
Magnesium	Milligrams	320	310	310	330	3.0	6.1	6.1
Iron	Milligrams	13.8	14.3	15.1	17.0	18.8	15.9	11.2
Zinc	Milligrams	11.8	12.3	12.5	12.6	6.3	2.4	0.8
Copper	Milligrams	1.6	1.5	1.6	1.6	0.0	6.3	0.0
Potassium	Milligrams	3,530	3,380	3,370	3,460	-2.0	2.3	2.6

[1] Includes other types of fat, not shown separately.   [2] Alpha-Tocopherol equivalents.
Source: U.S. Dept. of Agriculture, Human Nutrition Information Service. Data published by Economic Research Service in *Food Consumption, Prices, and Expenditures,* annual; and *National Food Review,* quarterly.

No. 209. Persons Using Vitamin-Mineral Products, by Selected Characteristic: 1986

[Based on the National Health Interview Survey and subject to sampling error; for details, see Appendix III and source]

CHARACTERISTIC	PERSONS (1,000)					PERCENT USING VITAMIN-MINERAL PRODUCTS				
	Adults 18 years old and over				Children 2-6 yrs. old	Adults 18 years old and over				Children 2-6 yrs. old
	Total	18-44	45-64	65 and over		Total	18-44	45-64	65 and over	
Total [1]	169,587	97,541	44,660	27,386	18,162	36.4	34.4	39.8	38.2	43.3
Sex: Male	81,804	49,225	21,289	11,290	9,252	31.2	30.2	32.7	32.2	44.4
Female	87,783	48,316	23,371	16,096	8,910	41.3	38.6	46.2	42.4	42.2
Race/ethnicity:										
White	145,842	82,172	39,064	24,607	14,805	38.5	36.2	42.2	40.1	46.3
Black	18,583	11,821	4,477	2,286	2,711	21.5	22.7	22.2	14.2	30.3
Other	5,162	3,549	1,120	493	646	32.0	31.1	26.3	52.3	30.7
Hispanic origin [2]	10,495	7,456	2,282	758	2,014	28.7	26.7	31.5	40.6	37.6
Mexican	5,309	3,969	1,029	312	1,207	23.5	22.8	24.8	(B)	36.9
Puerto Rican	1,140	729	343	(B)	(B)	28.0	(B)	(B)	(B)	(B)
Cuban	927	516	292	(B)	(B)	21.9	(B)	(B)	(B)	(B)
Years of school completed: [3]										
Less than 12 years	41,599	15,785	12,356	13,459	2,680	25.5	20.3	26.3	30.7	26.9
12 years	64,954	38,599	18,388	7,967	6,572	36.0	31.2	45.3	45.3	40.1
13 years or more	62,013	42,764	13,690	5,558	8,865	44.3	42.6	49.3	47.3	51.0
Family income:										
Less than $7,000	14,889	8,135	2,676	4,077	1,928	27.3	26.6	27.8	30.2	22.8
$7,000 to $14,999	24,752	12,257	5,176	7,318	2,674	32.5	30.6	30.4	37.0	38.6
$15,000 to $24,999	33,138	19,272	8,250	5,615	3,691	34.8	32.2	35.1	43.1	44.2
$25,000 to $39,999	41,161	26,819	10,874	3,467	4,847	38.8	36.6	43.2	42.6	51.2
$40,000 or more	33,806	20,737	11,151	1,918	3,200	44.8	41.7	50.6	44.3	50.3

B Base figure too small to meet statistical standards of a reliable figure.   [1] Includes persons with education and income unknown.   [2] Includes persons of other Hispanic origin. Persons of Hispanic origin may be of any race.   [3] For children, education of responsible adult.
Source: U.S. National Center for Health Statistics, *Advance Data from Vital and Health Statistics,* No. 174.

Education

This section presents data primarily concerning formal education as a whole, at various levels, and for public and private schools. Data shown relate to the school-age population and school enrollment, educational attainment, education personnel, and financial aspects of education. In addition, data are shown for libraries and computer usage in schools. The chief sources are the decennial census of population and the Current Population Survey (CPS), both conducted by the Bureau of the Census (see text, section 1); annual, biennial, and other periodic surveys conducted by the National Center for Education Statistics, a part of the U.S. Department of Education; and surveys conducted by the National Education Association.

The censuses of population have included data on school enrollment since 1840 and on educational attainment since 1940. The CPS has reported on school enrollment annually since 1945 and on educational attainment periodically since 1947.

The National Center for Education Statistics is continuing the pattern of statistical studies and surveys conducted by the U.S. Office of Education since 1870. The annual *Digest of Education Statistics* provides summary data on pupils, staff, finances, including government expenditures, and organization at the elementary, secondary, and higher education levels. It is also a primary source for detailed information on Federal funds for education, projections of enrollment, graduates, and teachers. *The Condition of Education,* issued annually, presents a summary of information on education of particular interest to policymakers.

Other sources of data include special studies by the National Center for Education Statistics and annual or biennial reports of education agencies in individual States. The census of governments, conducted by the Bureau of the Census every 5 years (for the years ending in "2" and "7"), provides data on school district finances and State and local government expenditures for education. Reports pub-

In Brief

The enrollment rate of 3 to 5 year olds in preprimary school:

1970	*37 percent*
1990	*59 percent*

Persons 25 years old and over completing college:

1970	*11 percent*
1991	*21 percent*

Engineering and math doctoral students, nonresident aliens:

1988-89	48 percent of total

lished by the Bureau of Labor Statistics contain data relating civilian labor force experience to educational attainment (see also tables 611, 616, 631, and 637 in section 13).

Types and sources of data.—The statistics in this section are of two general types. One type, exemplified by data from the Bureau of the Census, is based on direct interviews with individuals to obtain information about their own and their family members' education. Data of this type relate to school enrollment and level of education attained, classified by age, sex, and other characteristics of the population. The school enrollment statistics reflect attendance or enrollment in any regular school within a given period; educational attainment statistics reflect the highest grade completed by an individual.

For enrollment data starting in October 1981, the CPS used 1980 census population controls; for years 1971 through 1980, 1970 census population controls had been used. This change had little impact on summary measures (e.g., medians) and proportional measures (e.g., enrollment rates); however, use of the controls may have significant impact on absolute numbers.

Beginning with data for 1986, a new edit and tabulation package for school enrollment has been introduced. The data produced increased the estimates of high school enrollment for 1986 by 200,000 and college enrollment by 300,000. See table 218 which presents both earlier and revised estimates. In other enrollment tables, revised estimates are shown. In 1988, a new edit and tabulation package was introduced for educational attainment data.

The second type, generally exemplified by data from the National Center for Education Statistics and the National Education Association, is based on reports from administrators of educational institutions and of State and local agencies having jurisdiction over education. Data of this type relate to enrollment, attendance, staff, and finances for the Nation, individual States, and local areas.

Unlike the National Center for Education Statistics, the Census Bureau does not regularly include specialized vocational, trade, business, or correspondence schools in its surveys. The National Center for Education Statistics includes nursery schools and kindergartens that are part of regular grade schools in their enrollment figures. The Census Bureau includes all nursery schools and kindergartens. At the higher education level, the statistics of both agencies are concerned with institutions granting degrees or offering work acceptable for degree-credit, such as junior colleges.

School attendance.—All States require that children attend school. While State laws vary as to the ages and circumstances of compulsory attendance, generally they require that formal schooling begin by age 6 and continue to age 16.

Schools.—The National Center for Education Statistics defines a *school* as "a division of the school system consisting of students composing one or more grade groups or other identifiable groups, organized as one unit with one or more teachers to give instruction of a defined type, and housed in a school plant of one or more buildings. More than one school may be housed in one school plant, as is the case when the elementary and secondary programs are housed in the same school plant."

Regular schools are those which advance a person toward a diploma or degree.

They include public and private nursery schools, kindergartens, graded schools, colleges, universities, and professional schools.

Public schools are schools controlled and supported by local, State, or Federal governmental agencies; *private* schools are those controlled and supported mainly by religious organizations or by private persons or organizations.

The Bureau of the Census defines *elementary* schools as including grades 1 through 8; *high* schools as including grades 9 through 12; and *colleges* as including junior or community colleges, regular 4-year colleges, and universities and graduate or professional schools. Statistics reported by the National Center for Education Statistics and the National Education Association by type of organization, such as elementary level and secondary level, may not be strictly comparable with those from the Bureau of the Census because the grades included at the two levels vary, depending on the level assigned to the middle or junior high school by the local school systems.

School year.—Except as otherwise indicated in the tables, data refer to the school year which, for elementary and secondary schools, generally begins in September of the preceding year and ends in June of the year stated. For the most part, statistics concerning school finances are for a 12-month period, usually July 1 to June 30. Enrollment data generally refer to a specific point in time, such as fall, as indicated in the tables.

Statistical reliability.—For a discussion of statistical collection, estimation, and sampling procedures and measures of statistical reliability applicable to Census Bureau and the National Center for Education Statistics data, see Appendix III.

Historical statistics.—Tabular headnotes provide cross-references, where applicable, to *Historical Statistics of the United States, Colonial Times to 1970.* See Appendix IV.

Figure 4.1
School Enrollment: 1970 to 2000

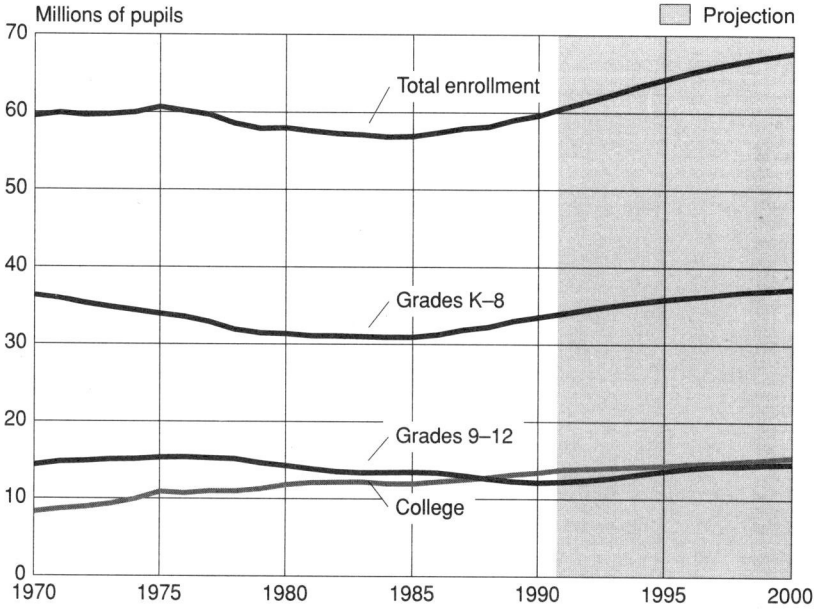

Source: Chart prepared by U.S. Bureau of the Census. For data, see table 215.

Figure 4.2
Percentage of Persons 25 Years Old and Over Completing High School or More: 1970 to 1991

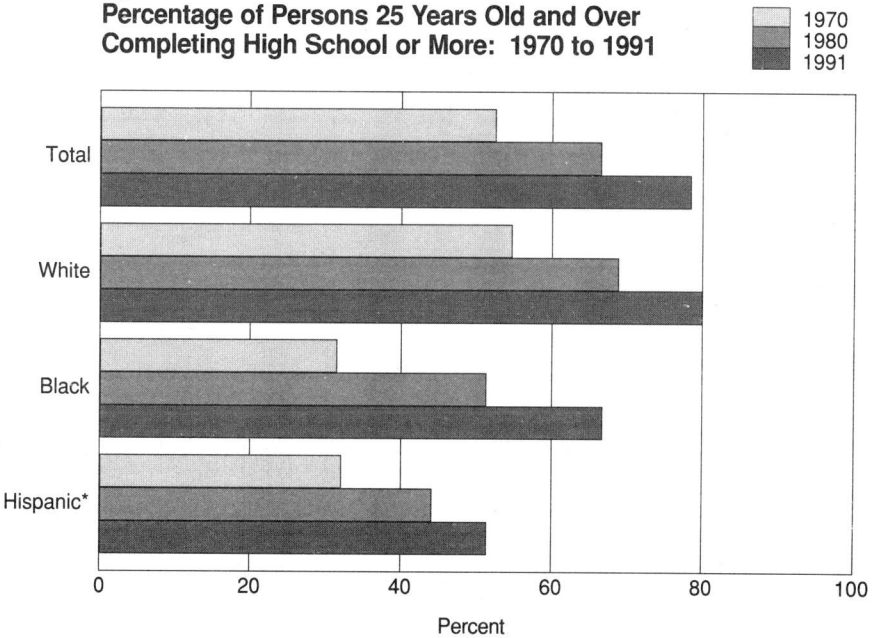

.*Persons of Hispanic origin may be of any race.
Source: Chart prepared by U.S. Bureau of the Census. For data, see table 220.

Education

No. 210. School Enrollment, 1955 to 1990, With Projections to 2002, and Number of Schools, 1955 to 1988

[**In thousands.** Enrollment and number of schools as of fall. See also *Historical Statistics, Colonial Times to 1970,* series H421-429]

ITEM AND YEAR	TOTAL		ELEMENTARY [1]		SECONDARY		COLLEGE	
	Public	Private	Public	Private	Public	Private	Public	Private
Enrollment: [2]								
1955	32,164	5,777	22,159	3,800	8,521	800	[3]1,484	1,177
1965	46,039	8,251	26,604	4,900	15,465	1,400	3,970	1,951
1970	52,322	7,516	27,492	4,052	18,402	1,311	6,428	2,153
1971	52,875	7,344	27,682	3,900	18,389	1,300	6,804	2,144
1972	52,797	7,144	27,312	3,700	18,414	1,300	7,071	2,144
1973	52,864	7,183	26,443	3,700	19,001	1,300	7,420	2,183
1974	53,062	7,235	26,394	3,700	18,679	1,300	7,989	2,235
1975	53,655	7,350	25,656	3,700	19,164	1,300	8,835	2350
1976	52,964	7,526	25,427	3,825	18,884	1,342	8,653	2,359
1977	52,424	7,579	24,954	3,797	18,623	1,343	8,847	2,439
1978	51,338	7,559	25,018	3,732	17,534	1,353	8,786	2,474
1979	50,688	7,533	24,547	3,700	17,104	1,300	9,037	2,533
1980	50,334	7,971	24,196	3,992	16,681	1,339	9,457	2,640
1981	49,691	8,225	24,087	4,100	15,957	1,400	9,647	2,725
1982	49,261	8,330	23,823	4,200	15,742	1,400	9,696	2,730
1983	48,935	8,497	23,949	4,315	15,303	1,400	9,683	2,782
1984	48,685	8,465	24,095	4,300	15,113	1,400	9,477	2,765
1985	48,901	8,325	24,229	4,195	15,193	1,362	9,479	2,768
1986	49,467	8,242	24,150	4,116	15,603	1,336	9,714	2,790
1987	49,980	8,272	24,304	4,232	15,703	1,247	9,973	2,793
1988	50,350	8,136	24,415	4,036	15,774	1,206	10,161	2,894
1989	51,041	8,298	24,620	4,162	15,906	1,193	10,515	2,943
1990, est.	51,767	8,165	25,614	4,066	15,412	1,129	10,741	2,970
2000, proj.	58,759	9,339	28,175	4,516	18,364	1,351	12,220	3,472
2002, proj.	59,546	9,480	28,238	4,545	18,830	1,383	12,478	3,552
Schools: [4]								
1955	(X)	(X)	104.4	12.4	26.0	3.9	0.7	1.2
1965	(X)	(X)	73.2	15.3	26.6	4.6	0.8	1.4
1970	(X)	(X)	65.8	14.4	25.4	3.8	(NA)	(NA)
1976 [5]	(X)	(X)	62.6	16.4	25.4	5.9	1.5	1.6
1978	(X)	(X)	62.0	16.1	24.5	5.8	1.5	1.7
1980	(X)	(X)	61.1	16.8	24.4	5.7	1.5	1.7
1984	(X)	(X)	58.8	(NA)	23.9	(NA)	1.5	1.8
1986	(X)	(X)	60.8	(NA)	23.4	(NA)	1.5	1.9
1987	(X)	(X)	61.5	(NA)	22.9	(NA)	1.6	2.0
1988	(X)	(X)	61.5	(NA)	22.8	(NA)	1.6	2.0

NA Not available. X Not applicable. [1] Enrollment includes kindergarten. [2] For regular schools. [3] Degree-credit enrollment only. [4] Excludes schools not reported by level, such as special education. Schools with both elementary and secondary programs are included under elementary and also secondary. [5] Beginning 1976, branch campuses of college institutions counted separately.

Source: U.S. National Center for Education Statistics, *Digest of Education Statistics,* annual and *Projections of Education Statistics,* annual.

No. 211. School Expenditures, by Type of Control and Level of Instruction in Constant (1989-90) Dollars: 1960 to 1991

[**In millions of dollars. For school years ending in year shown.** Total expenditures for public elementary and secondary schools include current expenditures, interest on school debt and capital outlay. See also Appendix III. See *Historical Statistics, Colonial Times to 1970,* series H 494, 499, and 500 for related but not comparable data, and H 513-519 for private schools]

YEAR	Total	ELEMENTARY AND SECONDARY SCHOOLS			COLLEGES AND UNIVERSITIES		
		Total	Public	Private [1]	Total	Public	Private [1]
1960	103,100	72,224	67,471	4,754	30,886	16,869	14,016
1970	230,115	145,155	136,751	8,403	84,960	54,569	30,391
1975	266,404	168,785	158,978	9,807	97,619	66,112	31,507
1979	274,911	172,411	160,733	11,678	102,500	68,789	33,712
1980	270,896	168,729	156,953	11,776	102,167	67,768	34,398
1981	260,021	164,646	152,627	12,020	103,375	68,247	35,128
1982	266,882	162,565	150,017	12,548	104,317	68,559	35,758
1983	274,366	166,529	153,204	13,325	107,837	70,296	37,541
1984	285,177	173,403	159,057	14,346	111,773	72,510	39,263
1985	297,316	179,357	164,471	14,886	117,959	76,478	41,481
1986	314,453	188,799	173,396	15,403	125,654	81,761	43,893
1987	333,123	199,995	183,671	16,324	133,128	85,626	47,502
1988	343,081	205,739	188,969	16,770	137,342	88,236	49,106
1989 prel.	356,853	215,830	198,857	16,973	141,023	90,208	50,814
1990 [1]	365,100	220,600	203,300	17,300	144,500	93,100	51,400
1991 [1]	371,900	224,400	207,000	17,500	147,300	95,100	52,200

[1] Estimated.

Source: U.S. National Center for Education Statistics, *Digest Education Statistics,* annual.

No. 212. School Enrollment, Faculty, Graduates, and Finances, 1985 to 1990, and Projections, 1992 to 2000

[As of **fall, except as indicated**]

ITEM	Unit	1985	1988	1989	1990	1992	1993	1994	1995	2000
ELEMENTARY AND SECONDARY SCHOOLS										
School-age population: [1] Total	1,000. . .	44,975	45,388	45,331	45,817	47,112	47,807	47,615	49,320	51,629
5 to 13 years old	1,000. . .	30,110	31,406	31,835	32,527	33,402	33,934	33,310	34,673	36,044
14 to 17 years old	1,000. . .	14,865	13,982	13,496	13,290	13,710	13,873	14,305	14,647	15,585
School enrollment: Total	1,000. . .	44,979	45,430	45,881	46,221	47,601	48,410	49,279	50,054	52,406
Public	1,000. . .	39,422	40,189	40,526	41,026	42,250	42,971	43,749	44,442	46,539
Private	1,000. . .	5,557	5,241	5,355	5,195	5,351	5,439	5,530	5,612	5,867
Elementary	1,000. . .	28,424	28,451	28,782	29,680	30,442	30,800	31,130	31,460	32,691
Public	1,000. . .	24,229	24,415	24,620	25,614	26,250	26,550	26,830	27,115	28,175
Private	1,000. . .	4,195	4,036	4,162	4,066	4,192	4,250	4,300	4,345	4,516
Secondary	1,000. . .	16,555	16,980	17,099	16,541	17,159	17,610	18,149	18,594	19,715
Public	1,000. . .	15,193	15,774	15,906	15,412	16,000	16,421	16,919	17,327	18,364
Private	1,000. . .	1,362	1,206	1,193	1,129	1,159	1,189	1,230	1,267	1,351
Classroom teachers: Total	1,000. . .	2,550	2,668	2,734	2,744	2,791	2,847	2,902	2,958	3,181
Public	1,000. . .	2,207	2,323	2,356	2,391	2,433	2,482	2,530	2,579	2,774
Private	1,000. . .	343	345	377	353	358	365	372	379	408
Elementary	1,000. . .	1,483	1,604	1,664	1,632	1,645	1,674	1,704	1,736	1,866
Public	1,000. . .	1,237	1,353	1,389	1,379	1,389	1,414	1,439	1,467	1,576
Private	1,000. . .	246	251	275	253	255	260	264	269	289
Secondary	1,000. . .	1,067	1,064	1,070	1,112	1,146	1,173	1,198	1,222	1,316
Public	1,000. . .	970	970	968	1,012	1,043	1,067	1,090	1,112	1,198
Private	1,000. . .	97	94	102	100	103	105	108	110	118
Projected demand for new teachers.	1,000. . .	(NA)	(NA)	237	216	218	242	239	240	261
High school graduates, total [2]	1,000. . .	2,643	2,724	2,592	2,465	2,470	2,464	2,563	2,615	2,943
Public	1,000. . .	2,383	2,456	2,324	2,210	2,215	2,209	2,298	2,345	2,639
Public schools: [2]										
Average daily attendance (ADA). .	1,000. . .	36,523	37,282	37,511	37,974	39,107	39,774	40,494	41,136	43,077
Constant (**1988-89**) dollars:										
Teachers' average salary	Dol.	28,061	29,567	30,145	30,629	31,821	32,513	33,076	33,654	35,541
Current school expenditures . . .	Bil. dol . .	152.8	168.6	174.4	178.3	190.1	195.9	202.4	209.0	237.7
HIGHER EDUCATION										
Enrollment, total	1,000. . .	12,247	13,055	13,458	13,931	14,235	14,366	14,512	14,621	15,692
Male	1,000. . .	5,818	6,002	6,155	6,419	6,516	6,531	6,549	6,575	6,922
Female	1,000. . .	6,429	7,053	7,302	7,512	7,719	7,835	7,963	8,046	8,770
Full-time.	1,000. . .	7,075	7,437	7,627	7,828	7,871	7,895	7,949	7,988	8,770
Part-time	1,000. . .	5,172	5,619	5,830	6,103	6,364	6,471	6,563	6,633	6,922
Public	1,000. . .	9,479	10,161	10,515	10,844	11,083	11,187	11,305	11,393	12,220
Private.	1,000. . .	2,768	2,894	2,943	3,087	3,152	3,179	3,207	3,228	3,472
2-year institutions.	1,000. . .	4,531	4,875	5,083	5,193	5,312	5,376	5,446	5,501	5,882
4-year institutions.	1,000. . .	7,716	8,180	8,374	8,738	8,923	8,990	9,066	9,120	9,810
Full-time equivalent	1,000. . .	8,943	9,467	9,734	10,033	10,171	10,232	10,321	10,385	11,270
Public.	1,000. . .	6,668	7,097	7,337	7,529	7,628	7,675	7,743	7,794	8,456
Private	1,000. . .	2,276	2,370	2,397	2,504	2,543	2,558	2,578	2,592	2,813
Faculty, total	1,000. . .	715	804	824	834	868	876	883	891	955
Public	1,000. . .	503	559	577	586	605	611	617	622	667
Private.	1,000. . .	212	245	247	248	263	265	267	269	290
Degrees conferred, total [2]	1,000. . .	1,830	1,869	1,916	1,974	2,042	2,054	2,062	2,068	2,203
Associate's.	1,000. . .	446.0	435.2	445.0	470.0	476.0	478.0	480.0	487.0	529.0
Bachelor's	1,000. . .	987.8	1,017.7	1,043.0	1,064.0	1,101.0	1,100.0	1,100.0	1,098.0	1,164.0
Master's.	1,000. . .	288.6	300.8	310.0	327.0	343.0	350.0	354.0	354.0	376.0
Doctorates	1,000. . .	33.7	35.8	38.0	38.7	39.8	40.0	40.2	40.4	41.4
First-professional	1,000. . .	73.9	70.8	71.0	73.8	82.6	85.5	87.8	88.1	92.9

NA Not available. [1] As of July. [2] For school year ending June the following year.

Source: U.S. National Center for Education Statistics, *Projections of Educational Statistics*, biennial.

No. 213. Federal Funds for Education and Related Programs, by Level of Education or Activity, Agency, and Program: 1980 to 1991

[In millions of dollars, except percent. For fiscal years ending in June. To the extent possible, amounts represent outlays]

LEVEL, AGENCY, AND PROGRAM	1980	1985	1990	1991 [1]
Total, all programs	**34,317.1**	**38,809.9**	**50,439.5**	**54,638.1**
Percent of Federal budget outlays	5.8	5.0	4.9	5.1
Elementary/secondary education programs	**16,027.7**	**16,901.3**	**21,525.1**	**24,436.2**
Department of Education	6,629.1	7,296.7	9,681.3	11,192.2
Grants for the disadvantaged	3,204.7	4,206.8	4,494.1	5,335.4
School improvement programs	788.9	526.4	1,189.2	1,555.7
Indian education	93.4	82.3	69.5	69.1
Education for the handicapped	821.8	1,018.0	1,616.6	2,317.2
Vocational and adult education	860.7	658.3	1,306.7	906.5
Department of Agriculture [2]	4,064.5	4,134.9	5,529.0	6,186.5
Child nutrition programs	3,377.1	3,664.6	4,977.1	5,635.2
Agricultural Marketing Service—commodities [3]	388.0	336.5	350.4	350.9
Special milk program [3]	159.3	16.0	18.7	23.0
Department of Defense [2]	370.8	831.6	1,097.9	1,175.8
Overseas dependents schools	338.8	613.4	865.0	916.3
Section VI schools [4]		162.6	193.6	222.2
Department of Energy	77.6	23.0	15.6	16.4
Energy conservation for school buildings	77.2	22.7	15.2	15.0
Department of Health and Human Services	1,077.0	1,531.1	1,937.6	2,552.1
Head Start	735.0	1,075.1	1,447.8	2,055.5
Social security student benefits	342.0	456.0	489.8	496.6
Department of the Interior [2]	318.2	389.8	445.3	429.4
Mineral Leasing Act and other funds	111.6	186.4	226.3	188.9
Indian Education	206.2	202.9	218.4	240.0
Department of Justice	23.9	36.1	66.0	83.0
Inmate programs	18.9	27.8	63.9	79.5
Department of Labor	1,849.8	1,945.3	2,505.5	2,584.2
Job Corps	469.8	604.7	739.4	800.2
Department of Veterans Affairs	545.8	344.8	155.4	126.3
Vocational rehab for disabled veterans	88.0	107.5	136.8	120.9
Other agencies and programs	1,071.0	368.1	91.8	90.3
Higher education programs [5]	**10,939.5**	**10,956.5**	**13,399.1**	**13,702.0**
Department of Education [2]	5,682.2	8,202.5	11,176.0	11,168.5
Student financial assistance	3,682.8	4,162.7	5,920.3	5,970.2
Guaranteed student loans	1,408.0	3,534.8	4,372.4	4,201.2
Department of Agriculture	10.5	17.7	31.3	32.3
Department of Defense	545.0	1,041.7	625.3	644.0
Tuition assistance for military personnel	(NA)	77.1	106.1	99.5
Service academies [3]	106.1	196.4	120.6	132.1
Senior ROTC	[6]	354.0	174.6	154.8
Professional development education	[6]	414.2	224.0	257.6
Department of Energy [2]	57.7	19.5	25.5	42.0
University laboratory cooperative program	2.8	6.5	9.4	20.9
Energy conservation for buildings—higher education	53.5	12.7	7.5	7.4
Department of Health and Human Services [2]	2,235.7	298.2	337.2	404.7
Health professions training programs	460.7	212.2	230.6	269.6
National Health Service Corps scholarships	70.7	2.3	4.8	27.0
Alcohol, drug abuse, and mental health training programs	122.1	43.6	81.4	83.6
Social security postsecondary students' benefits	1,559.0	25.0	-	-
Department of the Interior	80.2	125.2	135.5	165.6
Shared revenues, Mineral Leasing Act and other receipts—estimated education share	35.4	72.0	70.0	80.0
Indian programs	44.8	53.3	65.5	85.5
Department of Transportation	12.5	55.6	46.0	49.0
Department of Veterans Affairs [2]	1,803.8	944.1	599.8	697.9
Vietnam-era veterans	1,580.0	694.2	47.0	-
Post-Vietnam veterans	0.9	82.6	161.5	160.0
All-volunteer-force educational assistance	-	0.2	269.9	423.2
Other agencies and programs [2]	511.9	252.0	422.5	498.0
National Endowment for the Humanities	56.5	49.1	50.9	54.9
National Science Foundation	64.6	60.1	161.9	213.4
United States Information Agency	51.1	124.0	181.2	193.4
Other education programs [2]	**1,548.7**	**2,107.6**	**3,382.9**	**3,670.5**
Department of Education [2]	747.7	1,173.1	2,251.8	2,450.2
Administration	187.3	284.9	328.3	365.5
Libraries	129.1	85.7	137.3	154.8
Rehabilitative services and handicapped research	426.9	798.3	1,780.4	1,921.1
Department of Agriculture	271.1	336.4	352.5	382.7
Department of Health and Human Services	37.8	47.2	78.0	87.3
Department of Justice	27.6	25.5	26.9	31.0
Department of State	25.0	23.8	47.5	40.3
Department of Transportation	10.2	3.8	1.5	1.6
Department of the Treasury	14.6	16.2	41.5	46.5
Other agencies and programs [2]	44.7	481.7	583.1	630.9
Agency for International Development	99.7	141.8	170.4	167.5
Library of Congress	151.9	169.3	189.8	215.1
National Endowment for the Arts	0.2	1.1	0.9	1.5
National Endowment for the Humanities	85.8	76.3	89.7	96.8
Research programs at universities and related institutions	**5,801.2**	**8,844.6**	**12,132.4**	**12,829.4**
Department of Agriculture	216.4	293.3	346.0	364.0
Department of Defense	644.5	1,245.9	1,668.9	1,693.1
Department of Energy	1,470.2	2,205.3	2,482.8	2,595.5
Department of Health and Human Services	2,087.1	3,228.0	4,735.9	4,979.6
National Aeronautics and Space Administration	254.6	485.8	1,092.2	1,234.8
National Science Foundation	743.8	1,087.0	1,417.4	1,588.4

- Represents or rounds to zero. NA Not available. [1] Estimated. [2] Includes other programs and agencies, not shown separately. [3] Purchased under Section 32 of the Act of August 1935 for use in child nutrition programs. [4] Includes stateside schools on military installations for free education of dependents. [5] Instructional costs only including academics, audiovisual, academic computing center faculty training, military training, physical education, and libraries. [6] Included in total above.

Source: U.S. National Center for Education Statistics, Digest of Education Statistics, 1991.

No. 214. School Expenditures, by Source of Funds in Constant (1989-90) Dollars: 1970 to 1988

[For school years ending in year shown. Includes nursery, kindergarten, and special programs when provided by school system. All nonpublic school data and all data beginning 1980 are estimates. Due to revised methodology, data for 1970 are not comparable to later years or to table 211]

SOURCE OF FUNDS AND TYPE OF SCHOOL	TOTAL (bil. dol.)									PERCENT		
	1970	1980	1982	1983	1984	1985	1986	1987	1988	1970	1980	1988
Total	236.6	270.9	266.9	274.4	285.2	297.3	314.5	333.1	343.1	100.0	100.0	100.0
Federal.	25.2	30.9	25.0	24.2	24.6	25.6	27.5	28.8	29.2	10.7	11.4	8.5
State	74.6	105.2	102.9	105.2	108.5	115.4	123.0	129.4	132.7	31.5	38.8	38.7
Local	76.0	70.7	70.0	71.7	75.0	76.0	79.1	83.8	86.8	32.1	26.1	25.3
All other	60.8	64.0	68.9	73.2	77.1	80.3	84.9	91.1	94.4	25.7	23.6	27.5
Public	190.9	224.7	218.6	223.6	231.6	240.9	255.2	269.3	277.2	80.7	82.9	80.8
Federal	19.5	24.3	18.9	18.4	18.4	19.0	20.2	20.7	21.0	8.2	9.0	6.1
State	74.3	104.5	102.3	104.5	107.8	114.6	122.2	128.4	131.5	31.4	38.6	38.3
Local.	75.6	70.5	69.8	71.4	74.7	75.7	78.8	83.6	86.5	32.0	26.0	25.2
All other.	21.5	25.5	27.7	29.2	30.6	31.6	34.0	36.8	38.1	9.1	9.4	11.1
Private	45.7	46.2	48.3	50.8	53.6	56.4	59.3	63.8	65.9	19.3	17.1	19.2
Federal	5.7	6.7	6.1	6.0	6.2	6.6	7.2	8.1	8.1	2.4	2.5	2.4
State and local	0.7	1.0	0.9	0.9	1.0	1.1	1.2	1.3	1.5	0.3	0.4	0.4
All other.	39.3	38.5	41.4	44.0	46.5	48.7	50.9	54.3	56.1	16.6	14.2	16.4
Elementary and secondary	153.6	168.7	162.6	166.5	173.4	179.4	188.0	200.0	205.7	100.0	100.0	100.0
Federal	11.4	15.4	11.1	10.9	10.8	10.9	11.6	11.8	11.9	7.4	9.1	5.8
State.	53.1	73.1	71.2	73.1	75.7	80.1	85.4	91.0	93.3	34.6	43.3	45.4
Local.	72.9	68.0	67.2	68.8	72.1	72.9	75.9	80.4	83.2	47.5	40.3	40.4
All other.	16.1	12.2	13.0	13.8	14.8	15.4	15.9	16.9	17.3	10.5	7.2	8.4
Public	137.8	157.0	150.0	153.2	159.1	164.5	173.4	183.7	189.0	89.7	93.1	91.9
Federal	11.4	15.4	11.1	10.9	10.8	10.9	11.6	11.8	11.9	7.4	9.1	5.8
State	53.1	73.1	71.2	73.1	75.7	80.1	85.4	91.0	93.3	34.6	43.3	45.4
Local	72.9	68.0	67.2	68.8	72.1	72.9	75.9	80.4	83.2	47.5	40.3	40.4
All other	0.3	0.5	0.4	0.5	0.5	0.5	0.5	0.6	0.5	0.2	0.3	0.2
Private	15.8	11.8	12.5	13.3	14.3	14.9	15.4	16.3	16.8	10.3	7.0	8.2
Higher education	83.0	102.2	104.3	107.9	111.8	118.0	125.7	133.1	137.3	100.0	100.0	100.0
Federal	13.8	15.6	13.9	13.3	13.8	14.7	15.9	17.0	17.2	16.6	15.3	12.5
State	21.5	32.1	31.7	32.2	32.8	35.3	37.6	38.5	39.6	25.9	31.4	28.8
Local.	3.0	2.8	2.8	2.8	2.9	3.1	3.2	3.4	3.5	3.6	2.7	2.5
All other	44.7	51.7	56.0	59.5	62.3	65.0	69.0	74.2	77.1	53.9	50.6	56.2
Public	53.1	67.8	68.5	70.2	72.5	76.5	81.8	85.6	88.2	64.0	66.3	64.2
Federal	8.1	8.9	7.8	7.5	7.6	8.1	8.6	8.9	9.1	9.8	8.7	6.6
State	21.2	31.4	31.0	31.4	32.1	34.5	36.8	37.4	38.3	25.5	30.7	27.9
Local	2.7	2.5	2.6	2.6	2.6	2.8	2.9	3.1	3.2	3.3	2.4	2.3
All other	21.2	25.0	27.3	28.8	30.2	31.1	33.5	36.2	37.6	25.5	24.5	27.4
Private	29.9	34.4	35.8	37.5	39.3	41.5	43.9	47.5	49.1	36.0	33.7	35.8
Federal	5.7	6.7	6.1	6.0	6.2	6.6	7.2	8.1	8.1	6.9	6.6	5.9
State and local.	0.7	1.0	0.9	0.9	1.0	1.1	1.2	1.3	1.5	0.8	1.0	1.1
All other	23.5	26.7	28.9	30.7	32.1	33.8	35.5	38.0	39.3	28.3	26.1	28.6

Source: U.S. National Center for Education Statistics, *Digest of Education Statistics,* annual.

No. 215. Enrollment in Public and Private Schools, by Control and Level, 1970 to 1990, and Projections, 1991 to 2000

[In thousands. As of fall. Data are for regular day schools and exclude independent nursery schools and kindergartens, residential schools for exceptional children, subcollegiate departments of colleges, Federal schools for Indians, and federally operated schools on Federal installations. College data include degree-credit and nondegree-credit enrollment]

CONTROL OF SCHOOL AND LEVEL	1970	1980	1984	1985	1986	1987	1988	1989	1990, est.	1991, proj.	1995, proj.	2000, proj.
Total	59,838	58,306	57,151	57,226	57,710	58,253	58,486	59,339	59,931	60,947	64,675	68,098
Public.	52,322	50,335	48,686	48,901	49,468	49,981	50,350	51,041	51,767	52,557	55,835	58,759
Private	7,516	7,971	8,465	8,325	8,242	8,272	8,136	8,298	8,165	8,390	8,840	9,339
Kindergarten through 8 . .	36,610	31,639	31,205	31,229	31,536	32,163	32,535	33,311	33,808	34,313	36,127	37,548
Public	32,558	27,647	26,905	27,034	27,420	27,931	28,499	29,149	29,742	30,186	31,782	33,032
Private	4,052	3,992	4,300	4,195	4,116	4,232	4,036	4,162	4,066	4,127	4,345	4,516
Grades 9 through 12. . . .	14,647	14,570	13,704	13,750	13,669	13,324	12,896	12,570	12,413	12,529	13,927	14,858
Public	13,336	13,231	12,304	12,388	12,333	12,077	11,690	11,377	11,284	11,389	12,660	13,507
Private	1,311	1,339	1,400	1,362	1,336	1,247	1,206	1,193	1,129	1,140	1,267	1,351
College.	8,581	12,097	12,242	12,247	12,504	12,767	13,055	13,458	13,710	14,105	14,621	15,692
Public	6,428	9,457	9,477	9,479	9,714	9,973	10,161	10,515	10,741	10,982	11,393	12,220
Private	2,153	2,640	2,765	2,768	2,790	2,794	2,894	2,943	2,970	3,123	3,228	3,472

Source: U.S. National Center for Education Statistics, *Projections of Education Statistics,* annual; *Digest of Education Statistics,* annual; and unpublished data.

No. 216. School Enrollment, by Age, Race, and Hispanic Origin: 1970 to 1991

[As of **October**. Covers civilian noninstitutional population enrolled in nursery school and above. Based on Current Population Survey, see text, section 1. *See Historical Statistics, Colonial Times to 1970*, series H 442-476 for enrollment 5-34 years old]

AGE, RACE, AND HISPANIC ORIGIN	ENROLLMENT (1,000)						RATE					
	1970	1980	1985	1989	1990	1991	1970	1980	1985	1989	1990	1991
Total 3 to 34 years old [1]	60,357	57,348	58,013	59,235	60,588	61,276	56.4	49.7	48.3	49.1	50.2	50.7
3 and 4 years old	1,461	2,280	2,801	2,898	3,292	3,068	20.5	36.7	38.9	39.1	44.4	40.5
5 and 6 years old	7,000	5,853	6,697	6,990	7,207	7,178	89.5	95.7	96.1	95.2	96.5	95.4
7 to 13 years old	28,943	23,751	22,849	24,431	25,016	25,445	99.2	99.3	99.2	99.3	99.6	99.7
14 and 15 years old	7,869	7,282	7,362	6,493	6,555	6,634	98.1	98.2	98.1	98.8	99.0	98.8
16 and 17 years old	6,927	7,129	6,654	6,254	6,098	6,155	90.0	89.0	91.7	92.7	92.5	93.3
18 and 19 years old	3,322	3,788	3,716	4,125	4,044	3,969	47.7	46.4	51.6	56.0	57.3	59.6
20 and 21 years old	1,949	2,515	2,708	2,630	2,852	3,041	31.9	31.0	35.3	38.5	39.7	42.0
22 to 24 years old.	1,410	1,931	2,068	2,207	2,231	2,365	14.9	16.3	16.9	19.9	21.0	22.2
25 to 29 years old.	1,011	1,714	1,942	1,960	2,013	2,045	7.5	9.3	9.2	9.3	9.7	10.2
30 to 34 years old.	466	1,105	1,218	1,248	1,281	1,377	4.2	6.4	6.1	5.7	5.8	6.2
35 years old and over . . .	(NA)	1,290	1,766	2,230	2,439	2,620	(NA)	1.4	1.7	2.0	2.1	2.2
White: Total 3 to 34 years old	51,719	47,673	47,452	47,923	48,899	49,156	56.2	48.9	47.8	48.4	49.5	50.0
3 and 4 years old	1,181	1,844	2,250	2,370	2,700	2,502	19.9	36.3	38.6	39.4	44.9	41.3
5 and 6 years old	5,899	4,781	5,437	5,598	5,750	5,727	90.3	95.8	96.4	95.2	96.5	95.3
7 to 13 years old	24,564	19,585	18,464	19,638	20,076	20,325	99.2	99.2	99.3	99.3	99.6	99.6
14 and 15 years old	6,761	6,038	6,007	5,197	5,265	5,311	98.2	98.3	98.1	98.8	99.1	98.7
16 and 17 years old	6,008	5,937	5,449	4,993	4,858	4,902	90.6	88.6	91.6	92.3	92.5	93.3
18 and 19 years old	2,924	3,199	3,105	3,392	3,271	3,197	48.7	46.3	52.4	56.4	57.1	59.7
20 and 21 years old	1,750	2,206	2,318	2,208	2,402	2,517	33.1	31.9	36.1	39.5	41.0	43.2
22 to 24 years old.	1,305	1,669	1,744	1,841	1,781	1,910	15.7	16.4	17.0	20.0	20.2	21.7
25 to 29 years old.	910	1,473	1,635	1,659	1,706	1,646	7.7	9.2	9.2	9.4	9.9	9.9
30 to 34 years old.	416	942	1,043	1,028	1,090	1,119	4.2	6.3	6.2	5.6	5.9	6.0
35 years old and over . . .	(NA)	1,104	1,533	1,956	2,096	2,219	(NA)	1.3	1.7	2.0	2.1	2.2
Black: Total 3 to 34 years old	7,829	8,251	8,444	8,707	8,854	9,031	57.4	53.9	50.9	51.3	51.9	52.5
3 and 4 years old	250	371	469	407	452	428	22.7	38.2	42.7	38.9	41.6	37.2
5 and 6 years old	999	904	1,030	1,084	1,129	1,108	84.9	95.4	95.7	94.9	96.3	95.8
7 to 13 years old	3,998	3,598	3,549	3,761	3,832	3,941	99.3	99.4	99.1	99.2	99.8	99.7
14 and 15 years old	1,025	1,088	1,106	1,023	1,023	1,032	97.6	97.9	97.9	99.4	99.2	99.1
16 and 17 years old	837	1,047	994	1,033	962	959	85.7	90.6	91.7	93.7	91.7	91.7
18 and 19 years old	352	494	472	541	596	578	40.1	45.7	44.1	50.2	55.2	55.6
20 and 21 years old	174	242	298	309	305	329	22.8	23.4	27.7	30.7	28.4	30.0
22 to 24 years old.	84	196	215	253	274	249	8.0	13.6	13.7	17.2	20.0	18.2
25 to 29 years old.	68	187	192	168	162	229	4.8	8.8	7.4	6.4	6.1	8.7
30 to 34 years old.	41	124	119	130	119	177	3.4	6.8	5.1	4.9	4.4	6.5
35 years old and over . . .	(NA)	186	233	167	238	289	(NA)	1.8	1.9	1.5	2.1	2.5
Hispanic: [2] **Total 3 to 34 years old**	(NA)	4,263	5,070	5,722	6,073	6,306	(NA)	49.8	47.7	45.8	47.4	47.9
3 and 4 years old	(NA)	172	213	202	249	299	(NA)	28.5	27.0	23.8	29.8	30.6
5 and 6 years old	(NA)	491	662	785	835	850	(NA)	94.5	94.5	92.8	94.8	92.4
7 to 13 years old	(NA)	2,009	2,322	2,637	2,794	2,909	(NA)	99.2	99.0	98.7	99.4	99.7
14 and 15 years old	(NA)	568	606	706	739	732	(NA)	94.3	96.1	96.5	99.0	97.2
16 and 17 years old	(NA)	454	562	554	592	532	(NA)	81.8	84.5	86.4	85.4	82.6
18 and 19 years old	(NA)	226	238	327	329	394	(NA)	37.8	41.8	44.6	44.1	47.9
20 and 21 years old	(NA)	111	137	152	213	215	(NA)	19.5	24.0	18.8	27.2	26.4
22 to 24 years old.	(NA)	93	125	153	121	144	(NA)	11.7	11.6	12.0	9.9	11.6
25 to 29 years old.	(NA)	84	120	129	130	140	(NA)	6.9	6.6	6.6	6.3	6.9
30 to 34 years old.	(NA)	54	83	76	72	93	(NA)	5.1	5.7	3.8	3.6	4.5
35 years old and over . . .	(NA)	(NA)	(NA)	136	145	148	(NA)	(NA)	(NA)	2.1	2.1	2.0
Mexican: [2] **Total 3 to 34 years old**	(NA)	2,698	3,180	3,743	4,017	4,171	(NA)	49.0	47.5	44.7	46.8	47.7
3 and 4 years old	(NA)	104	137	148	165	215	(NA)	27.0	26.0	22.7	27.4	32.3
5 and 6 years old	(NA)	327	458	553	619	581	(NA)	93.2	95.3	91.8	94.7	92.1
7 to 13 years old	(NA)	1,378	1,526	1,768	1,815	1,957	(NA)	99.5	99.2	98.9	99.7	99.7
14 and 15 years old	(NA)	361	367	481	499	475	(NA)	92.1	97.7	95.7	99.5	97.6
16 and 17 years old	(NA)	257	358	356	403	351	(NA)	76.1	83.8	85.3	83.8	81.0
18 and 19 years old	(NA)	113	127	176	213	282	(NA)	32.0	35.2	40.9	40.9	47.0
20 and 21 years old	(NA)	55	61	79	121	132	(NA)	15.6	16.4	14.6	23.6	24.8
22 to 24 years old.	(NA)	40	55	77	70	70	(NA)	7.5	7.8	8.9	8.3	8.2
25 to 29 years old.	(NA)	41	56	64	64	61	(NA)	5.4	5.0	5.0	4.9	4.8
30 to 34 years old.	(NA)	22	36	41	47	48	(NA)	3.3	4.5	3.3	3.6	3.7
35 years old and over . . .	(NA)	(NA)	(NA)	73	81	89	(NA)	(NA)	(NA)	2.0	2.1	2.2

NA Not available.   [1] Includes other races, not shown separately.   [2] Persons of Hispanic origin may be of any race.

Source: U.S. Bureau of the Census, *Current Population Reports*, series P-20, No. 460, and earlier reports; and unpublished data.

No. 217. Enrollment in Public and Private Schools: 1960 to 1991

[In millions, except percent. As of October. For civilian noninstitutional population. For 1960, 5 to 34 years old; for 1970 to 1985, 3 to 34 years old; beginning 1986, for 3 years old and over]

YEAR	PUBLIC						PRIVATE					
	Total	Nur-sery	Kinder-garten	Ele-mentary	High School	College	Total	Nur-sery	Kinder-garten	Ele-mentary	High School	College
1960	39.0	(NA)	(¹)	27.5	9.2	2.3	7.2	(NA)	(¹)	4.9	1.0	1.3
1970	52.2	0.3	2.6	30.0	13.5	5.7	8.1	0.8	0.5	3.9	1.2	1.7
1980	(NA)	0.6	2.7	24.4	(NA)	(NA)	(NA)	1.4	0.5	3.1	(NA)	(NA)
1985	49.0	0.9	3.2	23.8	12.8	8.4	9.0	1.6	0.6	3.1	1.2	2.5
1989 [2]	52.5	0.9	3.3	25.9	12.1	10.3	8.9	1.9	0.6	2.7	0.8	2.9
1990 [2]	53.8	1.2	3.3	26.6	11.9	10.7	9.2	2.2	0.6	2.7	0.9	2.9
1991 [2]	54.5	1.1	3.5	26.6	12.2	11.1	9.4	1.8	0.6	3.0	1.0	3.0
Percent White:												
1960	85.7	(NA)	(¹)	84.3	88.2	92.2	95.7	(NA)	(¹)	95.3	96.7	96.3
1970	84.5	59.5	84.4	83.1	85.6	90.7	93.4	91.1	88.2	94.1	96.1	92.8
1980	(NA)	68.2	80.7	80.9	(NA)	(NA)	(NA)	89.0	87.0	90.7	(NA)	(NA)
1990	79.8	71.7	78.3	78.9	79.2	84.1	87.4	89.6	83.2	88.2	89.4	85.0
1991	79.3	74.0	78.3	78.6	78.4	82.8	86.7	89.0	81.8	87.9	88.8	84.3

NA Not available.   ¹ Included in elementary school.   ² See table 260 for college enrollment 35 years old and over. See also footnote 2, table 218.

Source: U.S. Bureau of the Census, *Current Population Reports*, series P-20, No. 460, and earlier reports; and unpublished data.

No. 218. School Enrollment, by Sex and Level: 1960 to 1991

[In millions. As of Oct. For the civilian noninstitutional population. For **1960**, persons 5 to 34 years old; **1970**, 3 to 34 years old; thereafter, 3 years old and over. Elementary includes kindergarten and grades 1-8; high school, grades 9-12; and college, 2-year and 4-year colleges, universities, and graduate and professional schools. Data for college represent degree-credit enrollment]

YEAR	ALL LEVELS [1]			ELEMENTARY			HIGH SCHOOL			COLLEGE		
	Total	Male	Female	Total	Male	Female	Total	Male	Female	Total	Male	Female
1960	46.3	24.2	22.0	32.4	16.7	15.7	10.2	5.2	5.1	3.6	2.3	1.2
1970	60.4	31.4	28.9	37.1	19.0	18.1	14.7	7.4	7.3	7.4	4.4	3.0
1980	58.6	29.6	29.1	30.6	15.8	14.9	14.6	7.3	7.3	11.4	5.4	6.0
1985	59.8	30.0	29.7	30.7	15.7	15.0	14.1	7.2	6.9	12.5	5.9	6.6
1986	60.1	30.4	29.7	31.1	16.1	15.0	14.0	7.1	6.9	12.4	5.8	6.6
1986 [2]	60.5	30.6	30.0	31.1	16.1	15.0	14.2	7.2	7.0	12.7	6.0	6.7
1987	60.6	30.7	29.9	31.6	16.3	15.3	13.8	7.0	6.8	12.7	6.0	6.7
1988	61.1	30.7	30.5	32.2	16.6	15.6	13.2	6.7	6.4	13.1	5.9	7.2
1989	61.5	30.8	30.7	32.5	16.7	15.8	12.9	6.6	6.3	13.2	6.0	7.2
1990	63.0	31.5	31.5	33.2	17.1	16.0	12.8	6.5	6.4	13.6	6.2	7.4
1991	63.9	32.1	31.8	33.8	17.3	16.4	13.1	6.8	6.4	14.1	6.4	7.6

¹ Beginning 1970, includes nursery schools, not shown separately.   ² Revised. Data beginning 1986, based on a revised edit and tabulation package.

Source: U.S. Bureau of the Census, *Current Population Reports*, series P-20, No. 460, and earlier reports; and unpublished data.

No. 219. Years of School Completed, by Age and Race: 1950 to 1991

[In percent, except median. Through **1980**, as of **April 1**; **1990** and **1991** as of **March**. Excludes Armed Forces, except members living off post or with families on post. Beginning 1980, excludes inmates of institutions. 1950 based on 20-percent sample; 1960 on 25-percent sample; 1970 on 20-percent sample; and 1980 on 17-percent sample; 1990 and 1991 based on Current Population Survey; see text, section 1. For definition of median, see Guide to Tabular Presentation]

ITEM	PERSONS 25 YEARS OLD AND OVER						PERSONS 25 TO 29 YEARS OLD					
	1950	1960	1970	1980	1990	1991	1950	1960	1970	1980	1990	1991
All persons: Not high school graduates	65.7	58.9	47.7	33.5	22.4	21.6	47.2	39.3	26.2	15.5	14.3	14.6
With less than 5 years of school	11.1	8.3	5.5	3.6	2.4	2.4	4.7	2.8	1.7	1.1	1.2	1.0
High school graduates of more . . .	34.3	41.1	52.3	66.5	77.6	78.4	52.8	60.7	73.8	84.5	85.7	85.4
College or more	6.2	7.7	10.7	16.2	21.3	21.4	7.7	11.1	16.3	22.1	23.2	23.2
Median school years completed . .	9.3	10.6	12.1	12.5	12.7	12.7	12.0	12.3	12.6	12.9	12.9	12.9
Black persons: Not high school graduates	87.1	79.9	68.6	48.8	33.8	33.3	77.8	62.3	44.6	24.8	18.4	18.3
With less than 5 years of school	32.9	23.8	14.6	8.2	5.1	4.7	16.8	7.0	3.2	1.1	1.0	0.6
High school graduates of more . . .	12.9	20.1	31.4	51.2	66.2	66.7	22.2	37.7	55.4	75.2	81.7	81.7
College or more	2.1	3.1	4.4	8.4	11.3	11.5	2.7	4.8	6.0	11.4	13.4	11.0
Median school years completed . .	6.8	8.0	9.8	12.0	12.4	12.4	8.6	9.9	12.1	12.6	12.7	12.7

Source: U.S. Bureau of the Census, *U.S. Census of Population, 1950, 1960, 1970*, and *1980*, vol. I; and *Current Population Reports*, series P-20, No. 462.

No. 220. Years of School Completed, by Race, Hispanic Origin, and Sex: 1970 and 1991

[**Persons 25 years old and over.** Persons of Hispanic origin may be of any race. For definition of median, see Guide to Tabular Presentation. See headnote, table 219. See also *Historical Statistics, Colonial Times to 1970*, series H 602-617]

YEAR, RACE, HISPANIC ORIGIN, AND SEX	Popula-tion (1,000)	PERCENT OF POPULATION COMPLETING—							Median school years com-pleted
		Elementary school			High school		College		
		1 to 4 years	5 to 7 years	8 years	1 to 3 years	4 years	1 to 3 years	4 years or more	
1970, total persons [1]	109,899	5.5	10.0	12.8	19.4	31.1	10.6	10.7	12.1
White	98,246	4.5	9.1	13.0	18.8	32.2	11.1	11.3	12.1
Male	46,527	4.8	9.7	13.3	18.2	28.5	11.1	14.4	12.1
Female	51,718	4.1	8.6	12.8	19.4	35.5	11.1	8.4	12.1
Black	10,375	14.6	18.7	10.5	24.8	21.2	5.9	4.4	9.8
Male	4,714	17.7	19.1	10.2	22.9	20.0	6.0	4.2	9.4
Female	5,661	12.0	18.3	10.8	26.4	22.2	5.8	4.6	10.0
Hispanic	3,946	19.5	18.6	11.5	18.2	21.1	6.5	4.5	9.1
Male	1,897	19.1	18.0	11.3	18.1	19.9	7.6	5.9	9.3
Female	2,050	19.9	19.2	11.6	18.3	22.3	5.4	3.2	8.9
1991, total persons [1]	158,694	2.4	3.8	4.4	11.0	38.6	18.4	21.4	12.7
White	136,299	2.0	3.4	4.5	10.2	39.1	18.6	22.2	12.8
Male	65,394	2.2	3.6	4.5	9.9	36.1	18.4	25.4	12.8
Female	70,905	1.8	3.3	4.5	10.5	41.8	18.8	19.3	12.7
Black	17,096	4.7	6.4	4.1	18.0	37.7	17.5	11.5	12.4
Male	7,626	6.5	6.3	4.3	16.3	38.3	17.0	11.4	12.4
Female	9,470	3.3	6.6	3.9	19.4	37.2	17.9	11.6	12.4
Hispanic	11,208	12.5	14.8	6.3	15.1	29.3	12.3	9.7	12.0
Male	5,509	12.9	14.8	6.1	14.7	28.5	13.0	10.0	12.1
Female	5,699	12.1	14.7	6.5	15.5	30.1	11.7	9.4	12.0

[1] Includes other races, not shown separately.

Source: U.S. Bureau of the Census, *U.S. Census of Population: 1970*, vols. I and II; and *Current Population Reports*, series P-20, No. 462.

No. 221. Years of School Completed, by Selected Characteristic: 1991

[**For persons 25 years old and over.** As of **March.** In percent, except number of persons. For composition of regions, see table 25]

CHARACTERISTIC	Population (1,000)	PERCENT OF POPULATION WITH—		
		4 years of high school or more	1 or more years of col-lege	4 or more years of col-lege
Total persons	158,694	78.4	39.8	21.4
Age:				
25 to 34 years old	42,905	86.1	45.3	23.7
35 to 44 years old	38,665	87.7	50.2	27.5
45 to 54 years old	25,686	81.2	41.1	23.2
55 to 64 years old	21,346	71.9	31.4	16.9
65 to 74 years old	18,237	63.5	25.3	13.2
75 years old or over	11,855	49.0	20.8	10.5
Sex: Male	75,487	78.5	42.5	24.3
Female	83,207	78.3	37.4	18.8
Race: White	136,299	79.9	40.8	22.2
Black	17,096	66.7	29.0	11.5
Other	5,299	78.7	49.0	33.5
Hispanic origin: Hispanic	11,208	51.3	22.0	9.7
Non-Hispanic	147,486	80.5	41.2	22.3
Region: Northeast	33,293	80.3	39.7	23.7
Midwest	38,230	80.7	38.0	20.0
South	54,217	74.2	36.9	19.4
West	32,954	80.9	46.9	24.3
Marital Status:				
Never married	22,091	81.6	47.4	27.7
Married spouse present	101,706	81.4	41.7	23.0
Married spouse absent	5,820	66.8	28.8	12.3
Separated	4,349	68.2	27.8	10.9
Widowed	13,665	53.6	19.6	8.3
Divorced	15,413	80.5	38.7	17.1
Civilian labor force status:				
Employed	97,874	87.3	48.4	27.3
Unemployed	6,203	73.1	30.0	12.6
Not in the labor force	53,844	62.6	25.1	11.7

Source: U.S. Bureau of the Census, Current *Population Reports*, series P-20, No. 462.

No. 222. Percent of Population With Less Than 12 Years of School and With 4 Years of College or More, by Race and Hispanic Origin: 1970 to 1991

[Persons 25 years old and over. As of April 1970 and 1980, and March beginning 1985]

RACE AND HISPANIC ORIGIN	LESS THAN 12 YEARS OF SCHOOL						4 YEARS OF COLLEGE OR MORE					
	1970	1980	1985	1989	1990	1991	1970	1980	1985	1989	1990	1991
All races [1]	47.7	33.5	26.1	23.1	22.4	21.6	10.7	16.2	19.4	21.1	21.3	21.4
White	45.5	31.2	24.5	21.6	20.9	20.1	11.3	17.1	20.0	21.8	22.0	22.2
Black	68.6	48.8	40.2	35.4	33.8	33.3	4.4	8.4	11.1	11.8	11.3	11.5
Hispanic origin [2]	67.9	56.0	52.1	49.1	49.2	48.7	4.5	7.6	8.5	9.9	9.2	9.7
Mexican	75.8	62.4	58.7	57.3	55.9	56.4	2.5	4.9	5.5	6.1	5.5	6.2
Puerto Rican	76.6	59.9	53.7	46.0	44.5	42.1	2.2	5.6	7.0	9.8	9.6	10.1
Cuban	56.1	44.7	48.9	37.0	36.5	39.0	11.1	16.2	16.7	19.8	20.2	18.5
Other [3]	55.1	42.6	35.8	34.9	37.9	35.6	7.0	12.4	16.4	15.7	15.5	15.6

[1] Includes races not shown separately.   [2] Persons of Hispanic origin may be of any race.   [3] Includes Central and South American and other Hispanic origin.

Source: U.S. Bureau of the Census, *Census of Population: 1970*, vols. I and II; *1980 Census of Population*, vol. I, chapter C, *Current Population Reports*, series P-20, No. 455, and earlier reports; and unpublished data.

No. 223. Highest Degree Earned, by Selected Characteristic: 1987

[For persons 18 years old and over. Based on the Survey of Income and Program Participation; see source for details]

CHARACTERISTIC	Total persons	LEVEL OF DEGREE								
		Not a high school grad- uate	High school grad- uate only	Some college, no degree	Voca- tional	Asso- ciate	Bache- lor's	Mas- ter's	Profes- sional	Doc- torate
NUMBER (1,000) All persons [1]	176,405	39,679	64,636	31,045	3,743	7,393	21,018	6,192	1,723	977
Age: 18 to 24 years old . .	26,148	4,203	10,596	8,043	389	928	1,912	77	-	-
25 to 34 years old	42,858	5,032	16,202	8,248	987	2,574	7,623	1,575	499	117
35 to 44 years old	34,352	4,921	12,101	5,931	862	2,208	5,359	2,114	509	347
45 to 54 years old	23,052	5,394	9,048	3,208	478	763	2,508	1,211	232	210
55 to 64 years old	21,726	6,668	8,364	2,690	457	473	1,928	656	285	205
65 years old and over .	28,268	13,462	8,324	2,924	571	446	1,687	558	198	98
Sex: Male	84,106	19,341	28,494	15,160	1,273	3,376	10,909	3,416	1,344	792
Female	92,299	20,338	36,141	15,884	2,471	4,017	10,109	2,776	379	184
Race: White	151,882	31,875	56,240	26,981	3,415	6,538	18,850	5,486	1,605	891
Male	72,862	15,552	24,687	13,404	1,211	3,028	9,982	2,978	1,307	713
Female	79,020	16,323	31,553	13,577	2,205	3,510	8,868	2,508	298	178
Black	19,290	6,406	6,911	3,069	245	706	1,445	440	37	33
Male	8,696	3,127	3,176	1,252	41	261	583	221	8	26
Female	10,594	3,279	3,735	1,817	203	445	861	219	29	7
MEAN MONTHLY INCOME [2] (dol.) All persons [1]	1,325	761	1,135	1,283	1,417	1,630	2,109	2,776	4,323	4,118
Age: 18 to 24 years old . .	649	422	683	573	1,249	859	1,033	(B)	(B)	(B)
25 to 34 years old	1,360	741	1,126	1,391	1,166	1,581	1,836	2,294	3,449	(B)
35 to 44 years old	1,695	876	1,298	1,624	1,534	1,947	2,319	2,834	5,725	4,703
45 to 54 years old	1,778	962	1,494	1,999	1,744	2,033	2,838	3,786	4,781	3,178
55 to 64 years old	1,433	847	1,262	1,439	1,616	1,547	2,753	2,678	4,639	5,901
65 years old and over .	993	708	971	1,310	1,354	1,337	2,079	2,064	(B)	(B)
Sex: Male	1,810	1,046	1,578	1,693	1,917	2,133	2,777	3,327	4,840	4,493
Female	883	489	785	892	1,159	1,206	1,388	2,098	2,494	(B)
Race: White	1,382	799	1,174	1,318	1,474	1,654	2,159	2,825	4,370	4,224
Black	915	559	877	1,072	835	1,361	1,596	2,181	(B)	(B)

— Less than .05 percent.   B Base figure too small to meet statistical standards for reliability of a derived figure.   [1] Includes other races, not shown separately.   [2] For definition of mean, see Guide to Tabular Presentation.

Source: U.S. Bureau of the Census, *Current Population Reports*, series P-70, No. 21.

Education

No. 224. Preprimary School Enrollment—Summary: 1970 to 1991

[As of **October.** Civilian noninstitutional population. Includes public and nonpublic nursery school and kindergarten programs. Excludes 5 year olds enrolled in elementary school. Based on Current Population Survey; see text, section 1]

ITEM	1970	1975	1980	1985	1986	1987	1988	1989	1990	1991
NUMBER OF CHILDREN (1,000)										
Population, 3 to 5 years old	**10,949**	**10,183**	**9,284**	**10,733**	**10,866**	**10,872**	**10,994**	**11,038**	**11,207**	**11,370**
Total enrolled [1] **. . . . .**	**4,104**	**4,954**	**4,878**	**5,865**	**5,971**	**5,932**	**5,977**	**6,026**	**6,659**	**6,334**
Nursery	1,094	1,745	1,981	2,477	2,545	2,555	2,621	2,825	3,378	2,824
Public.	332	570	628	846	829	819	852	930	1,202	996
Private	762	1,174	1,353	1,631	1,715	1,736	1,770	1,894	2,177	1,827
Kindergarten	3,010	3,211	2,897	3,388	3,426	3,377	3,356	3,201	3,281	3,510
Public.	2,498	2,682	2,438	2,847	2,859	2,842	2,875	2,704	2,767	2,968
Private	511	528	459	541	567	535	481	496	513	543
White	3,443	4,105	3,994	4,757	4,851	4,748	4,891	4,911	5,389	5,104
Black	586	731	725	919	892	893	814	872	964	928
Hispanic [2]	(NA)	(NA)	370	496	593	587	544	520	642	675
3 years old.	454	683	857	1,035	1,041	1,022	1,028	1,005	1,205	1,075
4 years old.	1,007	1,418	1,423	1,765	1,772	1,717	1,768	1,882	2,086	1,993
5 years old.	2,643	2,852	2,598	3,065	3,157	3,192	3,183	3,139	3,367	3,266
ENROLLMENT RATE										
Total enrolled [1] **. . . . .**	**37.5**	**48.6**	**52.5**	**54.6**	**55.0**	**54.6**	**54.4**	**54.6**	**59.4**	**59.4**
White	37.8	48.6	52.7	54.7	55.2	54.1	55.4	55.0	59.7	56.2
Black	34.9	48.1	51.8	55.8	54.1	54.2	48.2	54.2	57.8	53.1
Hispanic [2]	(NA)	(NA)	43.3	43.3	47.8	45.5	44.2	41.6	49.0	46.4
3 years old.	12.9	21.5	27.3	28.8	28.9	28.6	27.6	27.1	32.6	28.2
4 years old.	27.8	40.5	46.3	49.1	49.0	47.7	49.1	51.0	56.0	53.0
5 years old.	69.3	81.3	84.7	86.5	86.7	86.1	86.6	86.4	88.8	86.0

NA Not available.   [1] Includes races not shown separately.   [2] Persons of Hispanic origin may be of any race. The method of identifying Hispanic children was changed in 1980 from allocation based on status of mother to status reported for each child. The number of Hispanic children using the new method is larger.
Source: U.S. Bureau of the Census, *Current Population Reports*, series P-20, No. 460; and unpublished data.

No. 225. Preprimary School Enrollment, by Level of Enrollment and Labor Force Status of Mother: 1978 and 1991

[See headnote table 224]

RACE AND LABOR FORCE STATUS	ALL CHILDREN (1,000)		PERCENT ENROLLED IN—							PERCENT NOT ENROLLED	
			Nursery school				Kindergarten				
			Total		Full day		Total		Full day, 1991		
	1978	1991	1978	1991	1978	1991	1978	1991	1991	1978	1991
TOTAL [1]											
Children 3 to 5 years old .	9,110	11,370	20.0	24.8	6.9	8.2	30.3	30.9	13.0	49.7	44.3
Living with mother	8,883	10,602	19.8	25.3	6.8	8.3	30.4	30.8	12.8	49.8	43.9
Mother in labor force	4,097	6,146	22.1	28.5	11.4	11.8	31.0	31.6	14.1	47.0	39.9
Employed	3,737	5,568	22.5	29.2	11.7	12.2	31.0	31.8	14.1	46.5	39.0
Full time	2,446	3,860	22.3	27.3	15.2	14.2	31.2	31.7	14.8	46.5	41.0
Part time	1,291	1,709	23.0	33.5	5.2	7.7	30.5	31.9	12.3	46.4	34.6
Unemployed	360	578	17.4	21.6	7.8	8.0	30.6	30.1	14.2	52.0	48.3
Mother not in labor force	4,786	4,456	17.9	20.9	2.9	3.5	29.9	29.8	11.1	52.2	49.3
WHITE											
Children 3 to 5 years old .	7,460	9,083	19.5	26.0	5.2	7.4	30.1	30.0	11.3	50.5	44.0
Living with mother	7,301	8,574	19.4	26.5	5.1	7.5	30.1	30.2	11.3	50.5	43.3
Mother in labor force	3,235	4,939	21.1	27.9	9.2	10.7	30.4	30.8	12.4	48.5	41.3
Employed	3,014	4,578	21.3	29.9	9.4	11.0	30.7	30.8	12.4	48.0	39.3
Full time	1,877	3,037	20.1	27.9	12.6	13.1	31.0	30.7	13.1	48.9	41.4
Part time	1,137	1,541	23.3	33.0	4.1	6.7	30.2	31.0	11.1	46.5	35.2
Unemployed	220	360	17.9	21.9	6.4	6.7	27.1	30.8	12.2	55.0	47.3
Mother not in labor force	4,067	3,635	18.0	22.6	1.9	3.3	29.8	29.4	9.8	52.2	48.0
BLACK											
Children 3 to 5 years old .	1,410	1,747	22.1	19.3	15.3	12.0	31.0	33.8	21.2	46.9	46.9
Living with mother	1,347	1,529	21.7	19.7	15.5	12.4	31.3	33.8	20.9	47.1	46.5
Mother in labor force	731	933	25.9	24.4	20.6	17.0	32.5	35.7	22.6	41.6	39.9
Employed	598	750	28.0	24.7	22.8	18.4	31.7	37.3	23.6	40.3	38.0
Full time	469	641	29.6	24.0	24.8	19.0	32.0	35.7	22.9	38.4	40.3
Part time	128	111	22.3	27.9	15.8	14.4	30.7	45.9	27.0	47.0	26.2
Unemployed	133	182	16.7	24.2	10.6	11.5	35.7	29.1	18.7	47.6	46.7
Mother not in labor force	616	596	16.6	12.2	9.4	5.2	29.8	31.0	18.3	53.5	56.8
HISPANIC [2]											
Children 3 to 5 years old .	720	1,456	11.8	14.2	5.0	5.7	29.1	32.1	12.4	59.1	53.7
Living with mother	713	1,348	11.7	22.8	5.0	8.8	28.9	52.2	20.2	59.4	25.0
Mother in labor force	296	573	16.3	17.8	7.1	10.1	27.5	33.2	13.6	56.2	49.0
Employed	263	494	17.1	19.4	6.7	10.5	26.0	32.6	13.4	56.9	48.0
Full time	196	395	16.9	18.0	7.5	10.1	25.9	32.4	12.2	57.2	49.6
Part time	67	99	(B)	25.3	(B)	12.1	(B)	32.3	18.2	(B)	42.4
Unemployed	33	79	(B)	7.6	(B)	7.6	(B)	38.0	15.2	(B)	54.4
Mother not in labor force	417	776	8.4	11.1	3.5	1.9	29.9	31.1	11.5	61.7	57.8

B Base figure too small to meet statistical standards for reliability of derived figure.   [1] Includes races not shown separately.   [2] Persons of Hispanic origin may be of any race.
Source: U.S. Bureau of the Census, *Current Population Reports*, series P-20, No. 460; and unpublished data.

No. 226. Public Elementary and Secondary Schools—Summary: 1980 to 1991

[For school year ending in year shown, except as indicated. Data are estimates]

ITEM	Unit	1980	1985	1986	1987	1988	1989	1990	1991
School districts, total.	Number .	16,044	15,812	15,739	15,684	15,571	15,530	15,449	15,344
ENROLLMENT									
Population 5-17 years old [1] . .	1,000. . .	48,041	44,942	44,975	45,148	45,291	45,388	45,330	45,166
Percent of resident population	Percent .	21.4	19.0	18.8	18.7	18.6	18.5	18.3	18.2
Fall enrollment [2]	1,000. . .	41,778	39,354	39,595	39,763	40,020	40,218	40,525	41,196
Percent of population 5-17 years old	Percent .	87.0	87.6	87.9	88.3	88.6	88.8	89.4	91.2
Elementary [3]	1,000. . .	24,397	23,830	24,241	24,503	25,222	25,759	26,396	27,037
Secondary [4]	1,000. . .	17,381	15,524	15,354	15,260	14,798	14,459	14,128	14,159
Average daily:									
Attendance (ADA)	1,000. . .	38,411	36,530	36,681	36,905	37,066	37,174	37,534	38,215
Membership (ADM)	1,000. . .	40,812	38,751	38,724	38,988	(NA)	(NA)	(NA)	(NA)
High school graduates	1,000. . .	2,762	2,424	2,388	2,429	2,497	2,467	2,331	2,273
INSTRUCTIONAL STAFF									
Total [5]	1,000. . .	2,521	2,473	2,519	2,563	2,604	2,651	2,688	2,728
Classroom teachers.	1,000. . .	2,211	2,175	2,215	2,249	2,284	2,324	2,365	2,400
Average salaries:									
Instructional staff.	Dollar . .	16,715	24,666	26,362	27,706	29,235	30,904	32,700	34,413
Classroom teachers.	Dollar . .	15,970	23,600	25,199	26,569	28,023	29,566	31,361	33,021
REVENUES									
Revenue receipts	Mil. dol. .	97,635	141,013	153,807	163,767	175,959	193,144	206,754	222,661
Federal	Mil. dol. .	9,020	9,533	10,351	10,553	11,325	12,375	13,277	13,737
State.	Mil. dol. .	47,929	69,107	75,935	81,542	86,921	94,329	100,546	108,884
Local	Mil. dol. .	40,686	62,373	67,521	71,672	77,713	86,440	92,930	100,039
Percent of total:									
Federal	Percent .	9.2	6.8	6.7	6.4	6.4	6.4	6.4	6.2
State.	Percent .	49.1	49.0	49.4	49.8	49.4	48.8	48.6	48.9
Local	Percent .	41.7	44.2	43.9	43.8	44.2	44.8	44.9	44.9
EXPENDITURES									
Total	Mil. dol. .	96,105	139,382	152,187	163,091	175,606	191,379	208,528	225,693
Current expenditures (day schools)	Mil. dol. .	85,661	127,230	138,067	147,476	158,612	171,728	186,383	200,786
Other current expenditures [6]	Mil. dol. .	1,859	2,109	2,385	2,597	2,478	2,911	3,288	3,332
Capital outlay	Mil. dol. .	6,504	7,529	9,066	10,161	11,528	13,299	14,959	17,297
Interest on school debt . . .	Mil. dol. .	2,081	2,514	2,670	2,857	2,989	3,440	3,898	4,278
Percent of total:									
Current expenditures (day schools)	Percent .	89.1	91.3	90.8	90.5	90.6	90.3	89.8	89.0
Other current expenditures [6]	Percent .	1.9	1.5	1.6	1.6	1.6	1.5	1.5	1.5
Capital outlay	Percent .	6.8	5.4	5.9	6.2	6.1	6.5	7.0	7.7
Interest on school debt . . .	Percent .	2.2	1.8	1.8	1.7	1.7	1.7	1.7	1.9
In current dollars:									
Revenue receipts per pupil in—									
ADA.	Dollar . .	2,542	3,860	4,193	4,438	4,747	5,196	5,508	5,827
ADM	Dollar . .	2,392	3,639	3,972	4,200	(NA)	(NA)	(NA)	(NA)
Current expenditures per pupil in—									
ADA.	Dollar . .	2,230	3,483	3,764	3,996	4,279	4,620	4,966	5,254
ADM	Dollar . .	2,099	3,283	3,565	3,783	(NA)	(NA)	(NA)	(NA)
In constant **(1991)** dollars: [7]									
Revenue receipts per pupil in—									
ADA.	Dollar . .	4,385	4,888	5,160	5,343	5,488	5,741	5,810	5,827
ADM	Dollar . .	4,127	4,607	4,888	5,057	(NA)	(NA)	(NA)	(NA)
Current expenditures per pupil in—									
ADA.	Dollar . .	3,847	4,410	4,632	4,811	4,947	5,105	5,237	5,254
ADM	Dollar . .	3,621	4,157	4,388	4,554	(NA)	(NA)	(NA)	(NA)

NA Not available.   [1] Estimated resident population as of July 1 of the previous year, except 1990 enumerated population as of April 1. Estimates do not reflect revisions based on the 1990 Census of Population.   [2] Fall enrollment of the previous year.   [3] Kindergarten through grade 6.   [4] Grades 7 through 12.   [5] Full-time equivalent.   [6] Current expenses for summer schools, adult education, post-high school vocational education, personnel retraining, etc., when operated by local school districts and not part of regular public elementary and secondary day-school program.   [7] Compiled by U.S. Bureau of the Census. Deflated by the Consumer Price Index, all wage earners (for school year) supplied by U.S. National Center for Education Statistics.

Source: Except as noted, National Education Association, Washington, DC, *Estimates of School Statistics*, annual (copyright) and *Rankings of the States*, annual (copyright); and unpublished data.

No. 227. Public and Private Elementary and Secondary Schools—Enrollment and Teachers, 1960 to 1990, and Projections, 1991 to 2000

[In thousands, except percent. As of fall. Schools are classified by type of organization, rather than by grade group; elementary includes kindergarten and secondary includes junior high. Minus sign (-) indicates decrease]

ITEM	TOTAL				PUBLIC [2]			PRIVATE		
	Total	Percent change [1]	Elementary	Secondary	Total	Elementary	Secondary	Total	Elementary	Secondary
Enrollment: 1960	42,181	3.6	29,150	13,031	36,281	24,350	11,931	5,900	4,800	1,100
1965	48,369	2.8	31,504	16,865	42,069	26,604	15,465	6,300	4,900	1,400
1970	51,257	1.1	31,544	19,713	45,894	27,492	18,402	5,363	4,052	1,311
1974	50,073	-0.7	30,094	19,979	45,073	26,394	18,679	5,000	3,700	1,300
1975	49,819	-0.6	29,356	20,464	44,819	25,656	19,164	5,000	3,700	1,300
1980	46,208	-1.5	28,188	18,020	40,877	24,196	16,681	5,331	3,992	1,339
1985	44,979	-0.6	28,424	16,555	39,422	24,229	15,193	5,557	4,195	1,362
1986	45,205	0.5	28,266	16,939	39,753	24,150	15,603	5,452	4,116	1,336
1987	45,486	0.6	28,537	16,950	40,007	24,304	15,703	5,479	4,232	1,247
1988	45,430	-0.1	28,451	16,980	40,189	24,415	15,774	5,241	4,036	1,206
1989	45,881	1.0	28,782	17,099	40,526	24,620	15,906	5,355	4,162	1,193
1990, est.	46,221	0.7	29,680	16,541	41,026	25,614	15,412	5,195	4,066	1,129
1991, proj.	46,841	1.3	30,070	16,772	41,575	25,943	15,632	5,266	4,127	1,140
1992, proj.	47,601	1.6	30,442	17,159	42,250	26,250	16,000	5,351	4,192	1,159
1993, proj.	48,410	1.7	30,800	17,610	42,971	26,550	16,421	5,439	4,250	1,189
1995, proj.	50,054	3.4	31,460	18,594	44,442	27,115	17,327	5,612	4,345	1,267
2000, proj.	52,406	4.7	32,691	19,715	46,539	28,175	18,364	5,867	4,516	1,351
Teachers: 1960	1,600	4.5	991	609	1,408	858	550	192	133	59
1965	1,933	3.9	1,112	822	1,710	965	746	223	147	76
1970	2,292	3.4	1,283	1,009	2,059	1,130	929	233	153	80
1974	2,410	1.6	1,330	1,078	2,165	1,166	997	245	164	81
1975	2,453	1.4	1,353	1,100	2,198	1,181	1,017	255	172	83
1980	2,485	0.3	1,401	1,084	2,184	1,189	995	301	212	89
1985	2,549	0.5	1,482	1,067	2,206	1,236	970	343	246	97
1986	2,592	1.7	1,517	1,075	2,244	1,267	977	348	250	98
1987	2,631	1.5	1,554	1,077	2,279	1,297	982	353	257	95
1988	2,668	1.4	1,604	1,064	2,323	1,353	970	345	251	94
1989	2,734	2.5	1,664	1,070	2,356	1,389	968	377	275	102
1990, est.	2,744	0.4	1,632	1,112	2,391	1,379	1,012	353	253	100
1991, proj.	2,826	3.0	1,631	1,194	2,465	1,378	1,087	360	253	107
1992, proj.	2,791	-1.2	1,645	1,146	2,433	1,389	1,043	358	255	103
1993, proj.	2,847	2.0	1,674	1,173	2,482	1,414	1,067	365	260	105
1995, proj.	2,958	3.9	1,736	1,222	2,579	1,467	1,112	379	269	110
2000, proj.	3,181	7.5	1,866	1,316	2,774	1,576	1,198	408	289	118

[1] Average from prior year shown; for 1960, change from 1955. For explanation of average annual change, see Guide to Tabular Presentation.   [2] Data beginning 1970 are estimated.

Source: U.S. National Center for Education Statistics, *Digest of Education Statistics*, annual; and *Projections of Education Statistics*, annual.

No. 228. Public Elementary and Secondary Schools, by Type and Size of School: 1989-90

[Data reported by schools, rather than school districts]

ENROLLMENT SIZE OF SCHOOL	NUMBER OF SCHOOLS					ENROLLMENT (1,000)				
	Total	Elementary [1]	Secondary [2]	Combined [3]	Other [4]	Total	Elementary [1]	Secondary [2]	Combined [3]	Other [4]
Total	83,425	59,757	20,359	2,280	1,029	40,502	25,784	13,647	917	154
PERCENT DISTRIBUTION [5]										
Total	100.00	100.00	100.00	100.00	100.00	100.00	100.00	100.00	100.00	100.00
Under 100 students	8.92	6.56	11.10	26.32	60.93	0.92	0.74	0.94	2.97	17.33
100 to 199 students	10.88	10.59	10.96	14.61	17.01	3.32	3.66	2.41	5.23	16.08
200 to 299 students	12.23	13.45	9.16	10.09	9.14	6.23	7.69	3.39	6.16	14.53
300 to 399 students	14.53	17.08	8.29	9.17	5.15	10.30	13.54	4.32	7.98	11.86
400 to 499 students	13.70	16.00	8.29	8.16	2.53	12.46	16.26	5.57	9.04	7.45
500 to 599 students	11.49	13.16	7.65	7.54	1.07	12.74	16.32	6.27	10.22	4.00
600 to 699 students	8.31	9.01	7.03	5.35	0.68	10.88	13.17	6.81	8.59	2.94
700 to 799 students	5.65	5.74	5.84	3.99	0.58	8.54	9.69	6.53	7.42	2.90
800 to 999 students	6.37	5.46	9.24	6.58	0.97	11.45	10.91	12.31	14.55	5.68
1,000 to 1,499 students	5.41	2.71	13.26	6.27	1.55	13.08	7.06	24.09	18.46	12.35
1,500 to 1,999 students	1.60	0.21	5.70	1.40	0.29	5.56	0.78	14.59	5.89	3.25
2,000 to 2,999 students	0.80	0.03	3.08	0.39	0.10	3.78	0.15	10.76	2.29	1.63
3,000 or more students	0.10	0.01	0.39	0.13	(Z)	0.74	0.04	2.02	1.21	(Z)
Average enrollment [5]	(X)	(X)	(X)	(X)	(X)	493	441	670	402	150

X Not applicable.   Z Represents or rounds to zero.   [1] Includes schools beginning with grade 6 or below and with no grade higher than 8.   [2] Includes schools with no grade lower than 7.   [3] Includes schools with both elementary and secondary grades.   [4] Includes special education, alternative, and other schools not classified by grade span.   [5] Data for those schools reporting enrollment.

Source: U.S. National Center for Education Statistics, unpublished data from "Common Core of Data" survey.

No. 229. Public Elementary and Secondary School Enrollment, by State: 1980 and 1989

[As of **fall**. Includes unclassified students]

STATE	ENROLLMENT (1,000) K through Grade 8		Grades 9 through 12		ENROLLMENT RATE [1]		STATE	ENROLLMENT (1,000) K through Grade 8		Grades 9 through 12		ENROLLMENT RATE [1]	
	1980	1989	1980	1989	1980	1989		1980	1989	1980	1989	1980	1989
U.S.	27,647	29,149	13,231	11,377	86.5	89.4	MO	567	576	277	232	83.8	86.3
AL	528	526	231	198	87.6	89.2	MT	106	110	50	41	92.9	95.7
AK	60	82	26	28	94.0	99.3	NE	189	194	91	77	86.6	88.8
AZ	357	451	157	156	88.9	90.6	NV	101	137	49	49	93.4	97.8
AR	310	311	138	124	90.3	91.4	NH	112	124	55	47	85.3	88.0
CA	2,730	3,471	1,347	1,301	88.0	91.3	NJ	820	766	426	310	81.5	83.7
CO	374	408	172	155	92.2	93.5	NM	186	203	85	93	89.5	92.5
CT	364	338	168	123	83.3	86.8	NY	1,838	1,784	1,033	782	80.8	84.3
DE	62	71	37	27	79.5	82.2	NC	786	770	343	311	90.0	91.7
DC	71	61	29	21	91.8	89.3	ND	77	85	40	33	85.9	91.3
FL	1,042	1,303	468	469	84.4	89.3	OH	1,312	1,242	645	525	84.8	86.8
GA	742	828	327	298	86.9	87.6	OK	399	421	179	158	92.9	93.5
HI	110	123	55	46	83.4	85.2	OR	319	340	145	132	88.5	93.9
ID	144	157	59	58	95.4	95.5	PA	1,231	1,148	678	507	80.4	81.2
IL	1,335	1,280	649	517	82.6	83.0	RI	98	98	51	37	79.7	83.8
IN	708	671	347	283	88.0	89.6	SC	426	444	193	172	88.1	89.3
IA	351	338	183	140	88.4	92.2	SD	86	94	42	34	87.4	90.9
KS	283	314	133	117	88.7	92.1	TN	602	590	252	230	87.8	89.6
KY	464	452	206	179	83.7	88.1	TX	2,049	2,443	851	885	92.4	95.8
LA	544	582	234	201	80.3	86.0	UT	250	323	93	115	98.2	95.9
ME	153	152	70	62	91.5	97.2	VT	66	69	29	26	87.9	93.8
MD	493	507	258	192	83.9	87.0	VA	703	712	307	273	90.7	94.8
MA	676	590	346	235	88.6	89.3	WA	515	586	242	224	91.0	94.3
MI	1,227	1,128	570	449	90.1	89.5	WV	270	227	113	100	92.6	92.8
MN	482	529	272	211	87.2	92.3	WI	528	549	303	234	82.1	87.1
MS	330	370	147	133	79.6	88.7	WY	70	70	28	27	97.3	97.2

[1] Percent of persons 5-17 years old. Based on estimated resident population as of July 1 of year shown and enumerated population as of April 1, 1980. Population data not adjusted for revisions based of the 1990 Census of Population.

Source: U.S. National Center for Education Statistics, *Digest of Education Statistics*, annual.

No. 230. Public Elementary and Secondary School Enrollment, 1990, and Projections, 1991 and 1992

[**In thousands**. As of fall. Includes unclassified students]

STATE	K THROUGH GRADE 8			GRADES 9 THROUGH 12			STATE	K THROUGH GRADE 8			GRADES 9 THROUGH 12		
	1990	1991	1992	1990	1991	1992		1990	1991	1992	1990	1991	1992
U.S.	29,742	30,186	30,663	11,284	11,389	11,587	MO	588	594	601	222	232	237
AL	529	531	533	199	195	197	MT	109	108	108	43	43	42
AK	82	84	84	30	28	29	NE	197	197	196	77	77	78
AZ	475	495	513	115	165	172	NV	145	151	158	52	54	56
AR	314	315	316	121	123	125	NH	130	136	141	41	46	48
CA	3,611	3,728	3,850	1,352	1,373	1,410	NJ	783	800	824	300	300	302
CO	414	421	428	155	155	159	NM	208	212	216	92	93	95
CT	349	357	367	120	120	120	NY	1,813	1,831	1,854	750	768	779
DE	74	76	76	26	27	29	NC	782	796	815	301	302	306
DC	61	61	62	19	20	19	ND	85	84	83	32	33	34
FL	1,364	1,426	1,488	498	467	479	OH	1,256	1,262	1,268	514	514	519
GA	854	875	898	298	304	310	OK	422	418	415	157	156	158
HI	126	129	133	45	47	49	OR	342	345	347	143	137	141
ID	155	155	152	66	60	62	PA	1,174	1,188	1,201	494	493	500
IL	1,288	1,294	1,305	515	517	521	RI	101	102	105	37	37	37
IN	681	682	682	275	280	285	SC	451	456	462	171	171	174
IA	339	336	330	145	141	145	SD	95	96	96	34	35	36
KS	319	322	323	117	120	125	TN	597	602	608	225	225	227
KY	451	445	440	179	177	181	TX	2,468	2,493	2,516	885	887	892
LA	577	573	570	202	194	197	UT	322	319	316	123	126	133
ME	154	157	160	62	60	60	VT	71	71	72	25	26	26
MD	529	549	571	186	190	196	VA	733	755	782	265	269	274
MA	606	621	637	223	225	226	WA	607	620	632	225	232	240
MI	1,145	1,153	1,161	432	436	440	WV	223	216	210	100	97	95
MN	543	552	558	209	215	222	WI	563	567	569	228	235	241
MS	366	364	362	134	132	135	WY	69	67	66	29	27	27

Source: U.S. National Center for Education Statistics, *Projections of Education Statistics*, annual.

150 Education

No. 231. Public Elementary and Secondary School Enrollment, by Grade: 1960 to 1989

[1960, for school year; thereafter, as of fall of year. Beginning 1975, kindergarten includes nursery schools. For 1960, enrollment figures are prorated and 12th grade includes postgraduates. See also *Historical Statistics, Colonial Times to 1970*, series H 420-424]

GRADE	ENROLLMENT (1,000)										PERCENT DISTRIBUTION		
	1960	1970	1975	1980	1984	1985	1986	1987	1988	1989	1960	1980	1989
Pupils enrolled . .	36,087	45,894	44,819	40,877	39,208	39,422	39,753	40,007	40,189	40,526	100.0	100.0	100.0
Kindergarten and													
grades 1-8	27,602	32,558	30,515	27,647	26,905	27,034	27,420	27,930	28,499	29,149	76.5	67.6	71.9
Kindergarten.	1,923	2,564	2,971	2,689	3,009	3,192	3,310	3,388	3,433	3,489	5.3	6.6	8.6
First	3,733	3,817	3,238	2,894	3,113	3,239	3,358	3,407	3,460	3,485	10.3	7.1	8.6
Second	3,436	3,654	3,027	2,800	2,904	2,941	3,054	3,173	3,223	3,289	9.5	6.8	8.1
Third	3,302	3,663	3,038	2,893	2,765	2,895	2,933	3,046	3,167	3,235	9.2	7.1	8.0
Fourth	3,146	3,675	3,112	3,107	2,772	2,771	2,896	2,938	3,051	3,182	8.7	7.6	7.9
Fifth	3,118	3,635	3,281	3,130	2,761	2,776	2,775	2,901	2,945	3,067	8.6	7.7	7.6
Sixth	3,070	3,598	3,476	3,038	2,831	2,789	2,806	2,811	2,937	2,987	8.5	7.4	7.4
Seventh	3,173	3,662	3,619	3,085	3,036	2,938	2,899	2,910	2,905	3,027	8.8	7.5	7.5
Eighth	2,701	3,601	3,636	3,086	3,186	2,982	2,870	2,839	2,853	2,853	7.5	7.5	7.0
Unclassified [1]	(X)	690	1,116	924	527	511	520	519	525	534	(X)	2.3	1.3
Grades 9-12	8,485	13,336	14,304	13,231	12,304	12,388	12,333	12,077	11,690	11,377	23.5	32.4	28.1
Ninth	2,412	3,654	3,879	3,377	3,441	3,439	3,256	3,143	3,106	3,124	6.7	8.3	7.7
Tenth	2,258	3,458	3,723	3,368	3,145	3,230	3,215	3,020	2,895	2,867	6.3	8.2	7.1
Eleventh	2,063	3,128	3,354	3,195	2,819	2,866	2,954	2,936	2,749	2,629	5.7	7.8	6.5
Twelfth	1,752	2,775	2,986	2,925	2,599	2,550	2,601	2,681	2,650	2,473	4.8	7.2	6.1
Unclassified [1]	(X)	321	362	366	300	303	308	297	290	284	(X)	0.9	0.7

X Not applicable.   [1] Includes ungraded and special education.
Source: U.S. National Center for Education Statistics, *Digest of Education Statistics*, annual.

No. 232. Public Elementary and Secondary School Teachers—Selected Characteristics: 1988

[For school year ending in year shown. Based on survey and subject to sampling error; for details, see source. See table 246 for similar data on private school teachers]

CHARACTERISTIC	Unit	AGE				SEX		RACE/ETHNICITY			LEVEL OF CONTROL	
		Under 30 years old	30 to 39 years old	40 to 49 years old	Over 50 years old	Male	Fe-male	White	Black	His-pan-ic [1]	Ele-men-tary	Sec-ondary
Total [2]	1,000. . .	311	813	752	417	681	1,631	2,050	190	67	1,182	1,142
Highest degree held:												
Bachelor's	Percent .	82.9	53.3	44.2	42.3	44.2	55.5	52.4	50.1	60.9	56.8	47.3
Master's	Percent .	15.4	40.6	46.0	45.5	44.9	37.9	39.9	41.9	29.6	36.9	43.2
Education specialist . .	Percent .	1.1	5.2	7.8	9.3	7.5	5.7	6.2	5.9	6.7	5.6	7.0
Doctorate	Percent .	(B)	0.5	1.3	1.6	1.6	0.6	0.8	1.4	(B)	0.6	1.3
Full-time teaching experience:												
Less than 3 years	Percent .	36.5	6.0	2.3	1.2	6.2	8.7	8.1	6.4	11.9	8.4	7.6
3 to 9 years	Percent .	63.2	33.6	14.0	5.7	19.5	28.8	26.7	19.6	33.2	27.4	24.6
10 to 20 years	Percent .	(B)	60.2	55.0	27.9	44.3	44.6	44.3	46.0	40.9	44.3	44.7
20 years or more.	Percent .	(B)	(B)	28.6	65.0	29.9	17.8	20.8	27.9	13.9	19.8	23.0
Salary:												
Total.	Dol.	21,228	26,359	30,635	32,550	32,436	26,345	28,199	27,821	27,235	26,660	29,717
Base	Dol.	19,257	24,447	28,556	30,826	28,244	25,350	26,236	25,965	25,103	25,578	26,879
School year supplement:												
Teachers receiving . . .	Percent .	37.9	32.0	30.8	21.8	52.2	22.6	31.3	21.0	28.7	17.5	43.7
Salary	Dol.	1,881	2,127	2,142	2,387	2,691	1,620	2,031	3,271	2,877	1,818	2,264
Summer school supplement:												
Teachers receiving . . .	Percent .	17.4	16.3	16.3	11.9	19.8	13.8	15.3	18.5	19.9	13.1	18.1
Salary	Dol.	1,880	1,761	1,779	1,955	2,152	1,608	1,738	2234	2,581	1,646	1,934
Teachers with other employment:												
School year only	Percent .	5.2	5.0	5.8	5.0	8.8	3.8	5.3	4.6	3.9	3.7	6.8
Summer only	Percent .	16.9	6.7	5.1	3.8	10.5	5.5	7.0	6.7	6.8	5.7	8.4
All year	Percent .	11.3	8.8	9.5	6.6	18.6	4.9	9.2	7.3	6.6	5.8	12.2

B Base too small to meet statistical reliability of a derived figure.   [1] Persons of Hispanic origin may be of any race.   [2] Includes teachers with no degrees, not shown separately.
Source: U.S. National Center for Education Statistics, *Digest of Education Statistics*, 1990.

No. 233. Public Elementary and Secondary Schools—Number and Average Salary of Classroom Teachers, 1960 to 1991, and by State, 1991

[Estimates for school year ending in **June** of year shown. Schools classified by type of organization rather than by grade-group; elementary includes kindergarten]

YEAR AND STATE	TEACHERS [1] (1,000)			AVG. SALARY ($1,000)			YEAR AND STATE	TEACHERS [1] (1,000)			AVG. SALARY ($1,000)		
	Total	Ele-men-tary	Sec-ondary	All teach-ers	Ele-men-tary	Sec-ondary		Total	Ele-men-tary	Sec-ondary	All teach-ers	Ele-men-tary	Sec-ondary
1960.....	1,355	834	521	5.0	4.8	5.3	KY.....	36.7	25.0	11.6	29.1	28.4	30.6
1970.....	2,008	1,109	899	8.6	8.4	8.9	LA......	43.6	29.2	14.4	26.2	26.2	26.2
1975.....	2,171	1,169	1,001	11.7	11.3	12.0	ME......	14.5	9.7	4.7	28.5	27.9	29.9
1979.....	2,199	1,189	1,010	15.0	14.7	15.4	MD......	42.1	22.0	20.1	38.4	37.0	39.8
1980.....	2,211	1,206	1,005	16.0	15.6	16.5	MA......	54.0	23.2	30.8	36.1	36.1	36.1
1981.....	2,192	1,196	996	17.6	17.2	18.1	MI	80.9	54.8	26.1	38.3	38.2	38.6
1982.....	2,158	1,200	959	19.3	18.9	19.8	MN......	43.6	23.6	20.0	33.1	32.4	34.0
1983.....	2,134	1,182	952	20.7	20.2	21.3	MS......	27.8	16.7	11.1	24.4	23.9	25.0
1984.....	2,144	1,189	955	21.9	21.5	22.6	MO	51.3	26.6	24.7	28.5	27.6	29.5
1985.....	2,175	1,212	963	23.6	23.2	24.2	MT......	9.6	6.8	2.8	26.7	26.1	28.2
1986.....	2,215	1,242	973	25.2	24.7	25.8	NE......	18.4	10.4	8.1	26.6	26.6	26.6
1987.....	2,249	1,274	975	26.6	26.1	27.2	NV......	10.4	6.2	4.2	32.2	31.2	33.7
1988.....	2,283	1,309	974	28.0	27.5	28.8	NH......	10.5	7.1	3.4	31.3	31.3	31.3
1989.....	2,324	1,354	970	29.6	29.0	30.2	NJ......	79.9	50.0	29.9	38.4	37.6	39.7
1990.....	2,365	1,391	973	31.4	30.8	32.0	NM......	16.2	11.3	4.9	26.2	25.5	26.9
							NY......	186.0	91.4	94.6	42.1	40.4	43.7
1991, U.S.	**2,400**	**1,425**	**974**	**33.0**	**32.4**	**33.8**	NC......	63.9	38.8	25.0	29.2	29.0	29.4
AL......	40.0	20.7	19.4	27.3	27.3	27.3	ND......	7.5	4.9	2.6	23.6	23.5	23.7
AK......	6.6	4.6	2.0	43.4	43.3	44.1	OH......	103.0	57.3	45.7	32.6	31.7	33.8
AZ......	34.5	26.6	7.9	30.8	30.8	31.3	OK......	36.8	19.6	17.2	24.3	23.5	25.2
AR......	25.6	12.6	13.0	23.0	22.4	23.7	OR......	26.2	16.2	10.0	32.3	31.6	33.3
CA......	214.3	157.4	56.9	39.6	38.7	41.1	PA......	100.3	49.1	51.2	36.1	35.4	36.7
CO......	32.3	16.5	15.8	31.8	31.1	32.6	RI	9.4	5.5	4.0	37.7	37.2	38.4
CT......	35.3	23.6	11.6	43.8	43.3	45.0	SC......	36.2	24.3	11.8	28.3	27.7	29.5
DE......	6.0	3.0	2.9	35.2	34.0	36.2	SD......	8.3	5.8	2.6	22.4	22.1	23.0
DC......	6.1	3.9	2.2	39.6	39.6	39.6	TN......	43.6	30.9	12.7	28.2	27.8	29.4
FL......	108.1	58.6	49.5	30.6	30.5	30.2	TX......	206.4	111.0	95.4	28.3	27.7	28.9
GA......	68.9	47.0	21.8	29.2	29.2	29.2	UT......	17.4	9.7	7.7	25.0	24.6	25.6
HI	9.8	5.5	4.3	32.5	32.5	32.5	VT......	7.1	3.7	3.4	31.0	30.3	31.6
ID	11.3	6.1	5.1	25.5	25.0	26.0	VA......	64.0	38.0	26.0	32.4	31.3	33.9
IL.......	108.4	76.2	32.3	34.6	33.1	38.3	WA	41.9	25.0	16.9	33.1	32.4	34.0
IN	54.5	29.2	25.3	32.0	31.7	32.4	WV	21.5	11.9	9.5	26.0	25.6	26.4
IA	31.1	15.0	16.2	28.0	26.9	29.0	WI	47.7	28.5	19.1	33.1	31.8	34.3
KS......	29.1	17.3	11.8	29.8	29.8	29.8	WY	6.6	2.9	3.7	29.0	28.8	29.1

[1] Full-time equivalent.

Source: National Education Association, Washington, DC, *Estimates of School Statistics, 1990-91,* and earlier issues. (Copyright by the National Education Association. All rights reserved.)

No. 234. Average Starting Salaries of Public School Teachers Compared With Salaries in Private Industry, by Selected Position: 1975 to 1991

[Except as noted, salaries represent what corporations plan to offer graduates graduating in the year shown with bachelors' degrees. Based on a survey of approximately 200 companies]

ITEM AND POSITION	1975	1980	1984	1985	1986	1987	1988	1989	1990	1991
SALARIES (dollars)										
Teachers [1]	8,233	10,764	14,500	15,460	16,500	17,500	19,400	(NA)	20,486	21,542
College graduates:										
Engineering	12,744	20,136	26,844	26,880	28,512	28,932	29,856	30,852	32,304	34,236
Accounting............	11,880	15,720	20,172	20,628	21,216	22,512	25,140	25,908	27,408	27,924
Sales—marketing	10,344	15,936	19,620	20,616	20,688	20,232	23,484	27,768	27,828	26,580
Business administration ...	9,768	14,100	19,416	19,896	21,324	21,972	23,880	25,344	26,496	26,256
Liberal arts [2]	9,312	13,296	19,344	18,828	21,060	20,508	23,508	25,608	26,364	25,560
Chemistry	11,904	17,124	24,192	24,216	24,264	27,048	27,108	27,552	29,088	29,700
Mathematics—statistics ...	10,980	17,604	22,416	22,704	23,976	25,548	25,548	28,416	28,944	29,244
Economics—finance	10,212	14,472	20,484	20,964	22,284	21,984	23,928	25,812	26,712	26,424
Computer science	(NA)	17,712	24,864	24,156	26,172	26,280	26,904	28,608	29,100	30,924
INDEX (1975=100)										
Teachers [1]	100	131	176	187	200	213	236	(NA)	249	262
College graduates:										
Engineering	100	158	211	211	224	227	234	242	253	268
Accounting............	100	132	170	174	179	189	212	218	230	235
Sales—marketing	100	154	190	199	200	196	227	268	269	256
Business administration ...	100	144	199	204	218	225	244	259	271	268
Liberal arts [2]	100	143	208	202	226	220	252	275	283	274
Chemistry	100	144	203	203	204	227	228	231	244	249
Mathematics—statistics ...	100	160	204	207	218	233	233	258	263	266
Economics—finance	100	142	201	205	218	215	234	252	261	258
Computer science [3]	(NA)	125	176	171	185	186	190	202	205	218

NA Not available. [1] Estimate. Minimum mean salary. Source: National Education Association, Washington, DC, unpublished data. [2] Excludes Chemistry, Mathematics, Economics, and Computer Science. [3] Computer science index (1978=100).

Source: Except as noted, Northwestern University Placement Center, Evanston, IL, *The Northwestern Lindquist-Endicott Report,* (copyright).

No. 235. Average Salary and Wages Paid in Public School Systems, by Selected Positions: 1975 to 1991

[In dollars. For school year ending in year shown. Data reported by a stratified sample of school systems enrolling 300 or more pupils. Data represent unweighted means of average salaries paid school personnel reported by each school system]

POSITION	1975	1980	1985	1986	1987	1988	1989	1990	1991
ANNUAL SALARY									
Central office administrators:									
Superintendent (contract salary). . . .	30,338	39,344	56,954	60,707	64,580	68,147	71,190	75,425	79,874
Deputy/assoc. superintendent.	30,074	37,440	52,877	57,190	60,222	63,872	66,214	69,623	72,428
Assistant superintendent	26,460	33,452	48,003	51,209	53,656	56,894	59,655	62,698	66,553
Administrators for—									
Finance and business	21,850	27,147	40,344	43,200	45,259	47,330	49,933	52,354	55,097
Instructional services	22,608	29,790	43,452	46,110	48,810	50,838	53,716	56,359	59,162
Public relations/information	21,470	24,021	35,287	37,329	38,925	41,305	43,402	44,926	47,938
Staff personnel services	21,470	29,623	44,182	46,269	48,627	51,421	53,972	56,344	59,271
Subject area supervisors	18,601	23,974	34,422	36,797	38,763	41,086	43,555	45,929	48,366
School building administrators:									
Principals:									
Elementary	19,061	25,165	36,452	39,024	41,536	43,664	45,909	48,431	51,453
Junior high/middle	21,136	27,625	39,650	42,365	44,861	47,078	49,427	52,163	55,083
Senior high	22,894	29,207	42,094	44,986	47,896	50,512	52,987	55,722	59,106
Assistant principals:									
Elementary	15,968	20,708	30,496	32,895	34,347	36,364	38,360	40,916	43,548
Junior high/middle	17,868	23,507	33,793	36,094	37,958	40,093	42,292	44,570	46,981
Senior high	18,939	24,816	35,491	37,616	39,758	41,839	44,002	46,486	49,009
Classroom teachers.	11,507	15,913	23,587	25,276	26,731	28,230	29,608	31,278	32,915
Auxiliary professional personnel:									
Counselors.	14,479	18,847	27,593	29,388	31,132	32,896	34,244	35,979	38,024
Librarians.	12,546	16,764	24,981	26,668	28,390	30,046	31,645	33,469	35,417
School nurses	10,673	13,788	19,944	21,339	22,219	23,692	24,804	26,090	27,713
Secretarial/clerical personnel:									
Central office:									
Secretaries/stenographers.	7,318	10,331	15,343	16,383	17,182	18,220	19,045	20,238	21,303
Accounting/payroll clerks	7,588	10,479	15,421	16,604	17,273	18,229	19,143	20,088	21,202
Clerk-typists	6,089	8,359	12,481	13,208	13,729	14,651	15,192	16,125	16,859
School building level:									
Secretaries/stenographers.	6,046	8,348	12,504	13,233	13,947	14,749	15,364	16,184	16,953
Library clerks.	5,052	6,778	9,911	10,412	10,641	11,234	11,751	12,151	12,696
HOURLY WAGE RATE									
Other support personnel:									
Teacher aides:									
Instructional	2.91	4.06	5.89	6.20	6.43	6.72	7.05	7.43	7.77
Noninstructional.	2.81	3.89	5.60	5.91	6.14	6.45	6.69	7.08	7.43
Custodians.	3.54	4.88	6.90	7.28	7.51	7.82	8.19	8.54	9.05
Cafeteria workers	2.61	3.78	5.42	5.76	5.92	6.23	6.56	6.77	7.19
Bus drivers.	3.75	5.21	7.27	7.72	8.06	8.31	8.78	9.21	9.52

Source: Educational Research Service, Arlington, VA, *National Survey of Salaries and Wages in Public Schools*, annual, vols. 2 and 3. (All rights reserved. copyright.)

No. 236. Public School Employment, by Occupation, Sex, and Race: 1982 and 1990

[In thousands. Covers full-time employment. 1982 excludes Hawaii, District of Columbia, and New Jersey. Based on sample survey of school districts with 250 or more students. 1990 based on sample survey of school districts with 100 or more employees; see source for sampling variability]

OCCUPATION	1982					1990				
	Total	Male	Female	White [1]	Black [1]	Total	Male	Female	White [1]	Black [1]
All occupations	3,082	1,063	2,019	2,498	432	3,181	914	2,267	2,502	463
Officials, administrators	41	31	10	36	3	43	28	15	37	4
Principals and assistant										
principals	90	72	19	76	11	90	56	34	70	13
Classroom teachers [2]	1,680	534	1,146	1,435	186	1,746	468	1,278	1,469	192
Elementary schools	798	129	669	667	98	875	128	747	722	103
Secondary schools.	706	363	343	619	67	662	304	358	570	66
Other professional staff	235	91	144	193	35	227	58	170	187	30
Teachers aides [3]	215	14	200	146	45	324	54	270	208	69
Clerical, secretarial staff.	210	4	206	177	19	226	5	221	181	24
Service workers [4]	611	316	295	434	132	524	245	279	348	129

[1] Excludes individuals of Hispanic origin. [2] Includes other classroom teachers, not shown separately. [3] Includes technicians. [4] Includes craftworkers and laborers.

Source: U.S. Equal Employment Opportunity Commission, *Elementary-Secondary Staff Information (EEO-5)*, biennial.

No. 237. Public Elementary and Secondary School Price Indexes: 1975 to 1989

[1983 = 100. For years ending June 30. Reflects prices paid by public elementary-secondary schools. For explanation of average annual percent change, see Guide to Tabular Presentation]

YEAR	Index, total	Average annual percent change [1]	PERSONNEL COMPENSATION				CONTRACTED SERVICES, SUPPLIES AND EQUIPMENT						
			Total	Professional salaries	Non-professional salaries	Fringe benefits	Total	Services	Supplies and materials	Equipment replacement	Library materials and textbooks	Utilities	Fixed costs
1975 ..	52.7	(X)	53.3	56.0	55.6	40.2	50.6	55.7	58.0	53.7	53.8	35.9	45.0
1976 ..	57.1	8.3	57.6	60.2	59.7	45.7	55.2	59.5	62.5	58.9	60.6	39.9	50.5
1977 ..	60.8	6.5	61.2	63.4	63.2	50.7	59.2	63.4	65.4	62.3	64.7	44.3	56.6
1978 ..	64.6	6.3	64.9	67.2	67.6	52.8	63.8	67.6	69.2	66.7	72.1	48.4	62.6
1979 ..	70.3	8.8	70.4	71.9	72.6	62.5	69.9	71.5	75.8	72.2	76.7	56.2	69.8
1980 ..	76.5	8.8	75.7	76.7	77.8	69.8	79.6	77.4	85.9	79.6	82.1	73.2	77.6
1981 ..	85.7	12.0	84.4	85.1	85.9	80.2	90.4	85.7	95.7	88.0	86.9	92.8	86.9
1982 ..	93.7	9.4	92.6	92.8	94.4	90.3	97.8	94.6	101.1	95.5	91.6	102.2	94.1
1983 ..	100.0	6.7	100.0	100.0	100.0	100.0	100.0	100.0	100.0	100.0	100.0	100.0	100.0
1984 ..	105.6	5.6	106.2	105.7	104.5	109.4	103.5	106.2	102.2	103.0	107.3	98.2	106.9
1985 ..	112.6	6.6	114.2	113.4	111.3	120.3	106.4	112.3	103.5	105.6	113.0	96.5	111.8
1986 ..	119.6	6.2	122.7	121.4	117.6	132.6	107.6	118.8	102.5	108.7	119.0	88.3	117.8
1987 ..	125.7	5.1	129.9	128.4	121.9	143.5	109.8	122.8	103.9	111.3	126.8	83.2	124.6
1988 ..	132.7	5.5	137.6	135.5	127.5	155.4	113.7	125.3	110.3	111.3	145.2	78.6	131.2
1989 ..	139.7	5.3	145.1	142.2	134.0	166.6	119.5	132.2	118.8	116.3	157.0	77.1	137.0

X Not applicable.　[1] Change from immediate prior year shown.

Source: Research Associates of Washington, Washington, DC, *Inflation Measures for Schools and Colleges*, annual.

No. 238. Finances of Public Elementary and Secondary School Systems, by Enrollment-Size Group: 1988-89

[In millions of dollars, except as indicated. Data are estimates subject to sampling variability. For details, see source. See also Appendix III]

ITEM	All school systems	ENROLLMENT SIZE						
		50,000 or more	25,000 to 49,999	15,000 to 24,999	7,500 to 14,999	5,000 to 7,499	3,000 to 4,999	Under 3,000
Enrollment, fall 1988 (1,000)	40,228	7,346	3,756	3,710	6,111	3,584	4,681	11,040
General revenue [1]	193,572	37,114	17,068	16,062	27,407	16,332	21,831	57,758
Intergovernmental	107,020	20,912	9,827	9,478	15,316	8,235	10,605	32,647
From Federal government.......	1,321	290	80	79	146	94	118	514
From States.................	103,052	20,392	9,458	9,175	14,860	7,962	10,186	31,019
Federal aid distributed by State governments	10,071	2,528	999	826	1,347	739	950	2,682
From local governments........	2,648	231	289	224	310	180	301	1,114
From own sources	86,552	16,202	7,240	6,584	12,091	8,097	11,226	25,111
Taxes...................	58,459	7,738	4,883	4,456	8,158	5,878	8,190	19,155
Property	56,965	7,423	4,747	4,402	7,926	5,720	7,954	18,793
Contribution from parent government.................	16,020	6,502	1,179	912	1,938	1,153	1,597	2,739
Charges and miscellaneous	12,072	1,961	1,178	1,216	1,995	1,066	1,439	3,217
Current charges.............	5,532	1,029	480	539	826	475	624	1,559
School lunch sales	3,273	452	281	304	521	324	429	963
Interest earnings	3,410	565	326	307	497	297	395	1,023
Other...................	3,130	367	372	370	672	294	419	635
Employee-retirement revenue	869	615	236	-	18	-	-	-
General expenditure [1]	193,618	36,768	17,201	16,067	27,253	16,276	21,804	58,249
Intergovernmental	563	30	29	46	99	60	78	220
Direct......................	193,056	36,738	17,172	16,020	27,153	16,217	21,726	58,029
Current operation	176,019	34,042	15,403	14,300	24,394	14,815	19,714	53,350
Salaries and wages	113,028	22,706	10,406	9,749	16,438	9,791	12,966	30,971
Capital outlay	13,838	2,218	1,432	1,411	2,233	1,108	1,615	3,821
Construction	8,574	1,369	845	878	1,446	720	1,050	2,265
Interest on debt	3,100	478	336	310	527	293	396	858
Employee-retirement expenditure	279	175	100	-	-	-	-	-
Debt outstanding [2]	48,568	7,631	4,781	4,529	7,583	4,451	6,340	13,254
Long-term...................	46,173	7,390	4,628	4,421	7,312	4,269	5,914	12,240
Short-term..................	2,395	241	153	108	272	182	425	1,013
Long-term debt issued	7,951	1,544	538	593	1,262	680	1,180	2,154
Long-term debt retired	4,074	546	443	376	646	358	532	1,173
Cash and security holdings	44,003	9,819	4,764	2,959	5,160	3,114	4,287	13,900
Employee-retirement holdings.	5,458	3,757	1,612	-	88	-	-	-

- Represents or rounds to zero.　[1] Excludes interschool system transactions.　[2] As of end of fiscal year.

Source: U.S. Bureau of the Census, *Public Education Finances: 1988-89*, GF-89-10.

No. 239. Public Elementary and Secondary Estimated Finances, 1970 to 1991, and by State, 1991

[In millions of dollars, except as noted. For school years ending in June of year shown]

YEAR AND STATE	RECEIPTS						EXPENDITURES					
		Revenue receipts				Non-revenue receipts [1]			Current expenditures			
	Total	Total	Source				Total [2]	Per capita [3] (dol.)	Elementary and secondary day schools	Average per pupil in ADA [4]		Capital outlay
			Federal	State	Local					Amount (dol.)	Rank	
1970	41,621	38,192	2,767	15,628	19,797	3,429	39,091	194	32,683	773	(X)	4,158
1975	66,319	63,047	5,089	27,472	30,486	3,273	62,340	292	53,333	1,286	(X)	5,409
1980	101,724	97,635	9,020	47,929	40,686	4,089	96,105	428	85,661	2,230	(X)	6,504
1982	117,776	113,999	8,419	54,573	51,007	3,777	113,005	492	102,048	2,753	(X)	6,404
1983	125,179	120,486	8,691	57,449	54,346	4,693	119,159	514	108,773	2,960	(X)	6,131
1984	133,373	128,875	9,005	61,611	58,259	4,498	127,014	543	116,295	3,185	(X)	6,373
1985	146,976	141,013	9,533	69,107	62,373	5,963	139,382	591	127,230	3,483	(X)	7,529
1986	161,118	153,807	10,351	75,935	67,521	7,311	152,187	640	138,067	3,764	(X)	9,066
1987	170,651	163,767	10,553	81,542	71,672	6,884	163,091	679	147,476	3,996	(X)	10,161
1988	183,835	175,959	11,325	86,921	77,713	7,876	175,606	725	158,612	4,280	(X)	11,528
1989	202,104	193,144	12,375	94,329	86,440	8,960	191,379	783	171,728	4,620	(X)	13,299
1990	215,848	206,754	13,277	100,546	92,930	9,094	208,528	845	186,383	4,975	(X)	14,959
1991, total	232,985	222,661	13,737	108,884	100,039	10,325	225,693	907	200,786	5,261	(X)	17,297
Alabama	2,531	2,421	319	1,612	490	110	2,806	694	2,487	3,648	47	267
Alaska	1,016	916	116	583	217	100	894	1,626	798	7,887	5	36
Arizona	3,305	2,867	144	1,239	1,483	438	3,270	892	2,533	4,231	41	563
Arkansas	1,687	1,578	149	946	482	109	1,571	668	1,365	3,334	48	164
California	27,512	27,022	1,900	18,079	7,043	490	27,323	918	24,024	4,826	31	2,094
Colorado	3,326	2,871	133	1,131	1,607	454	2,771	841	2,510	4,809	32	170
Connecticut	3,773	3,772	151	1,569	2,052	1	3,783	1,151	3,559	7,914	4	138
Delaware	616	590	50	401	139	26	593	891	557	6,016	10	20
District of Columbia	608	575	57	-	518	33	613	1,010	579	8,210	3	10
Florida	11,196	10,615	682	5,500	4,433	581	11,156	862	9,166	5,154	22	1,757
Georgia	5,498	5,382	326	2,871	2,185	116	5,568	859	5,129	4,860	29	374
Hawaii	932	932	80	851	1	-	869	784	797	5,008	28	43
Idaho	808	775	51	478	246	33	730	725	614	3,200	50	40
Illinois	9,988	9,534	719	3,500	5,316	454	9,009	788	7,960	5,062	23	403
Indiana	4,786	4,732	240	2,669	1,823	55	5,130	925	4,324	5,051	24	457
Iowa	2,384	2,263	125	1,164	974	120	2,350	846	2,198	4,839	30	132
Kansas	2,248	2,204	109	971	1,125	44	2,244	906	1,941	5,009	27	213
Kentucky	2,909	2,711	260	1,865	585	198	2,673	725	2,499	4,390	37	116
Louisiana	3,287	3,147	310	1,777	1,060	140	3,198	758	2,872	4,012	42	190
Maine	1,261	1,167	75	596	497	94	1,303	1,062	1,172	5,894	12	97
Maryland	4,612	4,549	220	1,723	2,606	62	4,514	944	4,092	6,184	9	312
Massachusetts	5,380	5,332	275	1,966	3,090	49	5,209	866	4,898	6,351	8	195
Michigan	8,664	8,208	373	2,907	4,929	455	8,604	926	7,653	5,257	19	514
Minnesota	4,745	4,330	177	2,386	1,767	415	4,330	990	3,729	5,260	18	426
Mississippi	1,719	1,653	275	885	493	66	1,726	671	1,575	3,322	49	115
Missouri	4,232	3,917	218	1,522	2,177	315	3,795	742	3,230	4,415	36	440
Montana	736	736	68	340	328	-	786	983	708	5,184	21	62
Nebraska	1,225	1,182	77	305	800	43	1,195	757	1,116	4,381	38	59
Nevada	1,159	971	37	403	530	189	1,206	1,004	851	4,564	34	317
New Hampshire	1,087	1,023	27	77	919	64	977	881	870	5,504	15	46
New Jersey	9,600	9,496	335	3,641	5,520	104	9,452	1,223	9,207	9,159	1	88
New Mexico	1,246	1,230	147	937	146	16	1,387	915	1,133	4,446	35	199
New York	21,870	21,270	1,067	8,933	11,270	600	21,340	1,186	19,600	8,500	2	1,275
North Carolina	5,488	5,370	332	3,579	1,459	118	5,392	814	4,850	4,802	33	511
North Dakota	464	451	33	219	199	13	459	719	416	3,685	46	34
Ohio	9,950	9,141	513	3,908	4,720	809	9,338	861	8,555	5,639	14	519
Oklahoma	2,591	2,426	196	1,490	740	165	2,441	776	2,033	3,742	43	345
Oregon	2,575	2,497	151	668	1,679	77	2,628	925	2,371	5,291	17	193
Pennsylvania	13,072	11,887	561	5,554	5,772	1,185	10,568	889	9,827	6,534	7	326
Rhode Island	854	854	34	350	469	-	895	892	870	6,989	6	11
South Carolina	2,958	2,754	234	1,443	1,077	204	2,911	835	2,480	4,327	39	306
South Dakota	552	536	60	144	332	17	498	716	448	3,730	44	44
Tennessee	3,047	2,931	296	1,391	1,244	116	3,015	618	2,841	3,707	45	75
Texas	16,095	15,270	1,078	6,822	7,370	825	15,380	905	13,444	4,238	40	1,383
Utah	1,437	1,395	88	796	511	42	1,426	828	1,246	2,993	51	120
Vermont	679	662	33	245	384	18	558	992	507	5,740	13	24
Virginia	5,362	5,291	255	1,876	3,160	71	5,825	941	4,996	5,360	16	627
Washington	5,077	4,568	248	3,370	950	509	5,327	1,095	3,953	5,045	26	1,146
West Virginia	1,639	1,637	132	1,095	410	2	1,583	883	1,500	5,046	25	33
Wisconsin	4,635	4,467	168	1,826	2,472	169	4,538	928	4,159	5,946	11	234
Wyoming	567	554	31	281	241	13	535	1,178	485	5,255	20	35

- Represents or rounds to zero. X Not applicable. [1] Amount received by local education agencies from the sales of bonds and real property and equipment, loans, and proceeds from insurance adjustments. [2] Includes interest on school debt and other current expenditures not shown separately. [3] Based on Bureau of the Census estimated resident population, as of July 1, the previous year, except 1991 as of enumerated population as of April 1, 1990. Estimates reflect revisions based on the 1990 Census of Population. [4] Average daily attendance.

Source: National Education Association, Washington, DC, *Estimates of School Statistics,* annual (copyright); and unpublished data.

No. 240. Microcomputers for Student Instruction in Elementary and Secondary Schools: 1981 to 1990

[As of fall for public schools; as of mid-winter of the previous year for private schools. Public school data based on surveys of every school district and all public schools. Private school data based on surveys of all Catholic and private schools. For details, see source]

YEAR	PUBLIC SCHOOLS										PRIVATE SCHOOLS			
	Number of schools (1,000)				Percent with micros				Number of micros [2] (1,000)	Students per micro [3]	Number of schools (1,000)	Percent with micros	Number of micros [2] (1,000)	Students per micro [3]
	Total [1]	Elementary	Junior	Senior	Total	Elementary	Junior	Senior						
1981	84.2	53.3	10.1	15.6	18.2	11.1	25.6	42.7	(NA)	(NA)	(NA)	(NA)	(NA)	(NA)
1982	82.4	51.9	9.9	15.3	30.0	20.2	39.8	57.8	(NA)	(NA)	(NA)	(NA)	(NA)	(NA)
1983	81.5	51.3	9.8	15.2	68.4	62.4	80.5	86.1	324.4	92.3	22.8	23.8	(NA)	(NA)
1984	81.1	51.0	9.8	15.2	85.1	82.2	93.1	94.6	569.8	63.5	24.4	53.0	62.2	56.2
1985	80.8	50.8	9.7	15.1	92.2	91.0	97.3	97.4	842.6	45.5	23.4	70.3	101.2	41.6
1986	80.5	50.7	9.7	15.1	95.6	94.9	98.5	98.7	1,081.9	36.5	22.7	77.1	129.2	33.7
1987	80.6	50.9	9.7	15.0	96.4	96.0	98.6	99.0	1,354.0	30.8	22.7	78.7	151.1	28.8
1988	80.8	51.0	9.8	15.0	97.1	96.8	98.8	99.1	1,522.9	26.9	22.3	82.8	185.5	23.5
1989	81.7	49.5	11.5	13.7	97.0	96.8	98.5	99.1	1,706.4	24.1	23.4	81.8	222.8	20.1
1990, total . . .	82.0	49.7	11.7	13.8	97.2	97.3	98.4	98.8	2,028.7	20.9	22.3	88.2	241.8	19.5
Number of micros [2] . .	2,028.7	863.0	369.8	646.5	(X)	(X)	(X)	(X)	(X)	(X)	241.8	(X)	(X)	(X)
Students per micro [3] .	20.9	25.6	19.2	16.4	(X)	(X)	(X)	(X)	(X)	(X)	19.5	(X)	(X)	(X)

NA Not available.   X Not applicable.   [1] Includes other schools, not shown separately.   [2] Includes estimates for schools not reporting number of micros.   [3] For schools reporting number of micros.

Source: Market Data Retrieval, Shelton, CT, *Microcomputers in Schools, 1986-87,* (copyright); and unpublished data.

No. 241. Instructional Use of Computers in Elementary and Secondary Schools, 1985 and 1989, and by Level, 1989

[Includes microcomputers and terminals used by students or teachers. Based on stratified, probability sample of 1,416 public, private, and parochial schools surveyed in spring 1989]

ITEM	Unit	Total, 1985	1989, BY SCHOOL LEVEL [1]			
			Total [2]	Elementary	Middle grades	High school
ALL SCHOOLS						
Computers used for instruction	1,000	1,034	2,355	897	583	895
Schools using computers	Percent . . .	86	96	96	95	98
Schools with 15 or more computers	Percent . . .	24	57	49	60	68
SCHOOLS USING COMPUTERS FOR INSTRUCTION						
Mean number of computers	Number . . .	10	26	19	26	45
Median [3]	Number . . .	8	19	16	20	31
Students per computer, median [3]	Number . . .	42	20	23	18	14
Percent of all instructional computers in—						
Classrooms	Percent . . .	37	36	43	28	32
Computer labs	Percent . . .	49	50	42	58	55
Other locations	Percent . . .	14	14	15	14	13
Percent of all instructional computers used—						
Usually every day	Percent . . .	(NA)	71	67	68	77
Less than every week for instruction or not used at all	Percent . . .	(NA)	10	10	11	9
Hours of use per week (in rooms with greatest number of, computers)median [3]	Number . . .	17	20	20	20	22
Percent of all student computer use: [4]						
Learning math	Percent . . .	(NA)	14	19	12	8
Word processing (how to use)	Percent . . .	(NA)	14	12	14	15
Keyboarding (how to)	Percent . . .	(NA)	13	13	15	12
Learning English	Percent . . .	(NA)	13	18	11	8
Programming	Percent . . .	(NA)	8	4	9	12
Recreational use	Percent . . .	(NA)	8	10	9	5
Tools, e.g., spreadsheets	Percent . . .	(NA)	7	4	8	11
Learning science	Percent . . .	(NA)	6	7	7	6
Learning social studies	Percent . . .	(NA)	5	8	5	3
Business education [5]	Percent . . .	(NA)	5	2	4	10
Industrial arts	Percent . . .	(NA)	3	1	3	5
Fine arts	Percent . . .	(NA)	2	2	2	2
Learning foreign languages	Percent . . .	(NA)	1	1	2	2
Other	Percent . . .	(NA)	1	1	1	1

NA Not available.   [1] Schools encompassing more than one level are apportioned among the appropriate levels rather than included more than once.   [2] 1989 data do not include schools that have only students below grade 4.   [3] For definition of median, see Guide to Tabular Presentation.   [4] Estimates supplied by each school's most informed computer-using teacher.   [5] Other than keyboarding or word processing instruction.

Source: Center for Social Organization of Schools, Johns Hopkins University, Baltimore, MD, International Computers-in-Education Survey, International Association for the Evaluation of Educational Achievement (I.E.A.), unpublished data.

Education

No. 242. Student Use of Computers, by Level of Instruction and Selected Characteristics: 1989

[**In percent**, except as indicated. As of **October**. Based on Current Population Survey and subject to sampling error; for details see Appendix III]

CHARACTERISTIC	Total	Prekinder-garten and kinder-garten	Grades 1 thru 8	Grades 9 thru 12	1 thru 4 years of college	5 years of college or more
Total students (1,000)	61,465	6,745	28,662	12,878	10,661	2,520
PERCENT USING COMPUTERS AT SCHOOL						
Sex: Male	43.5	13.9	52.9	38.7	42.1	47.0
Female	41.9	15.6	51.7	39.8	36.8	34.9
Race: White [1]	45.7	17.0	58.4	40.6	40.0	39.5
Black [1]	32.5	7.5	35.7	36.0	35.1	34.4
Hispanic	42.5	8.5	46.9	41.0	43.5	58.0
Other [1]	35.0	9.8	40.3	33.5	33.1	42.1
Household income: Under $5,000	36.7	8.5	40.4	35.6	40.1	53.5
$5,000 to $9,999	36.1	9.2	40.3	32.7	40.5	60.2
$10,000 to $14,999	38.4	14.6	44.4	39.1	30.8	55.2
$15,000 to $19,999	41.5	11.9	50.9	34.8	39.6	44.0
$20,000 to $24,999	42.4	14.6	51.8	40.1	32.5	44.4
$25,000 to $29,999	46.1	16.1	56.4	43.8	40.4	42.1
$30,000 to $34,999	44.2	17.4	56.8	37.8	37.1	33.3
$35,000 to $39,999	45.2	16.1	58.3	41.5	34.5	45.3
$40,000 to $49,999	44.7	15.4	59.7	36.7	38.1	35.4
$50,000 to $59,999	48.4	17.0	61.2	46.1	43.6	35.3
$60,000 to $74,999	45.3	15.1	58.9	42.9	43.2	28.3
$74,999 or more	51.2	21.2	67.0	45.8	49.6	31.0
Control of school: Public	43.3	16.4	51.9	39.0	37.5	41.3
Private	38.9	11.8	56.6	42.6	46.3	39.7
PERCENT USING COMPUTERS AT HOME						
Sex: Male	20.7	11.0	18.7	23.9	25.4	36.0
Female	17.0	9.3	16.9	17.4	18.1	31.1
Race: White [1]	22.6	12.3	22.3	25.3	23.6	35.4
Black [1]	7.3	3.7	6.8	8.5	9.1	18.2
Hispanic	19.0	9.9	16.6	22.5	23.5	24.7
Other [1]	7.4	2.9	6.6	7.8	11.7	30.2
Household income: Under $5,000	8.4	4.5	4.1	6.6	17.7	29.4
$5,000 to $9,999	5.4	1.0	2.7	4.4	14.2	28.4
$10,000 to $14,999	7.2	1.9	6.2	6.5	11.8	26.5
$15,000 to $19,999	11.3	3.2	9.2	13.6	15.8	33.6
$20,000 to $24,999	12.9	6.8	11.6	13.6	16.9	32.2
$25,000 to $29,999	17.0	11.9	16.5	17.1	19.2	29.6
$30,000 to $34,999	17.7	8.0	17.6	20.2	19.4	30.7
$35,000 to $39,999	21.4	8.7	22.2	25.1	22.1	26.5
$40,000 to $49,999	25.7	14.8	27.5	27.7	21.7	40.7
$50,000 to $59,999	31.1	20.0	31.2	34.7	29.9	43.2
$60,000 to $74,999	32.2	21.4	37.4	33.9	25.0	38.9
$74,999 or more	43.8	25.2	50.9	53.4	33.9	41.4
Control of school: Public	17.9	8.3	16.8	19.7	20.7	32.2
Private	24.4	13.4	27.7	35.9	23.8	35.9
PERCENT USING COMPUTERS AT HOME FOR SCHOOL WORK						
Sex: Male	9.5	0.6	6.3	13.6	16.0	25.9
Female	8.3	0.6	6.2	10.8	11.7	22.0
Race: White [1]	10.7	0.6	7.7	15.2	15.1	25.4
Black [1]	3.4	0.9	2.7	4.0	6.2	12.3
Hispanic	9.1	-	5.8	13.2	15.4	14.8
Other [1]	3.6	-	2.8	4.4	6.6	27.6
Household income: Under $5,000	5.0	-	1.5	4.1	12.6	23.8
$5,000 to $9,999	3.2	-	0.6	2.6	10.3	26.5
$10,000 to $14,999	3.5	0.7	1.8	3.6	8.1	19.3
$15,000 to $19,999	4.5	-	2.1	5.2	9.3	30.2
$20,000 to $24,999	5.7	0.3	3.8	7.6	10.5	23.8
$25,000 to $29,999	6.4	0.3	4.1	8.2	12.3	19.7
$30,000 to $34,999	8.0	0.1	5.7	12.0	12.8	19.8
$35,000 to $39,999	10.5	1.2	7.9	15.0	15.9	18.7
$40,000 to $49,999	11.9	0.7	9.7	17.1	14.3	29.4
$50,000 to $59,999	15.7	0.7	12.6	21.9	20.0	31.5
$60,000 to $74,999	14.6	0.9	13.0	20.4	14.7	25.6
$74,999 or more	22.0	2.4	21.9	34.2	21.2	22.2
Control of school: Public	8.5	0.6	5.9	11.5	13.1	22.2
Private	11.4	0.5	9.4	23.6	15.8	27.2

- Represents or rounds to zero.   [1] Non-Hispanic.

Source: U.S. National Center for Education Statistics, *Digest of Education Statistics*, 1990.

No. 243. Handicapped Children and Youth in Educational Programs for the Handicapped, by Type of Handicap: 1980 to 1990

[For school year ending in year shown. **For persons under 22 years old, except as noted.** Represents children under 20 served under Chapter 1 of the Elementary and Secondary Education Act (ESEA), State Operated Programs (SOP), and children 3 to 21 served under Education for the Handicapped, Part B (EHA-B). Excludes outlying areas]

ITEM	1980	1982	1983	1984	1985	1986	1987	1988 [1]	1989 [1]	1990 [1]
All conditions (1,000)	4,005	4,198	4,255	4,298	4,315	4,317	4,374	4,128	4,173	4,261
PERCENT DISTRIBUTION										
Learning disabled	31.9	38.6	40.9	42.0	42.4	43.1	43.6	47.0	47.8	48.5
Speech impaired.	29.6	27.0	26.6	26.2	26.1	26.1	25.8	23.2	23.1	22.9
Mentally retarded	21.7	18.7	17.8	16.9	16.1	15.3	15.0	14.6	13.8	13.3
Emotionally disturbed.	8.2	8.1	8.3	8.4	8.6	8.7	8.7	9.1	8.9	9.0
Hard of hearing and deaf	2.0	1.8	1.7	1.7	1.6	1.5	1.5	1.4	1.4	1.4
Orthopedically handicapped	1.6	1.4	1.3	1.3	1.3	1.3	1.3	1.1	1.1	1.1
Other health impaired	2.6	1.9	1.2	1.2	1.6	1.3	1.2	1.1	1.2	1.2
Visually handicapped.	0.8	0.7	0.7	0.7	0.7	0.6	0.6	0.6	0.5	0.5
Multihandicapped	1.5	1.7	1.5	1.5	1.6	2.0	2.2	1.9	2.0	2.1
Deaf-blind	0.1	0.1	0.1	0.1	0.1	(Z)	(Z)	(Z)	(Z)	(Z)

Z Less than .05 percent.   [1] For children 6 to 21 years old; total number of children served under 22 years old was 4,494,280 in school year 1987-88, 4,568,118 in school year 1988-89, and 4,687,620 in 1989-90.

Source: U.S. Dept. of Education, Office of Special Education Programs, *Annual Report to Congress*.

No. 244. Handicapped Children and Youth 3 to 21 Years Old, by Age and Educational Environment: 1988

[For school year ending in year shown. Covers children 3 to 21 served under Chapter 1 of ESEA (SOP) and EHA-B; see headnote, table 243. Includes 40,237 children in Puerto Rico, American Samoa, and Guam]

ENVIRONMENT		NUMBER (1,000)				PERCENT DISTRIBUTION			
	Total	3-5 years old	6-11 years old	12-17 years old	18-21 years old	3-5 years old	6-11 years old	12-17 years old	18-21 years old
Total	**4,389.7**	**306.2**	**2,094.8**	**1,756.3**	**222.4**	**100.0**	**100.0**	**100.0**	**100.0**
Regular class [1]	1,299.0	122.8	832.2	315.1	28.7	40.1	39.7	17.9	12.9
Resource room [2]	1,671.2	43.1	747.0	803.1	78.3	14.1	35.6	45.7	35.2
Separate class [3]	1,093.5	87.3	431.0	502.4	72.7	28.5	20.6	28.6	32.7
Separate school facility:									
Public	169.2	25.1	47.6	70.2	26.2	8.2	2.3	4.0	11.8
Private	75.8	20.1	23.1	26.0	6.5	6.5	1.1	1.5	2.9
Separate residential facility:									
Public	21.6	1.0	4.5	12.1	4.3	0.3	0.2	0.7	1.9
Private	12.8	0.4	2.7	7.5	2.0	0.1	0.1	0.4	0.9
Correctional facility	10.9	(NA)	(NA)	(NA)	(NA)	(NA)	(NA)	(NA)	(NA)
Home/hospital	35.2	6.1	6.2	19.4	3.4	2.0	0.3	1.1	1.6

NA Not available.   [1] Receives special education and related services less than 21 percent of the school day.   [2] Receives services between 21 and 60 percent of the school day.   [3] Receives services for more than 60 percent of the school day.

Source: U.S. Dept. of Education, Office of Special Education Programs, Data Analysis Systems (DANS), unpublished data.

No. 245. Catholic Elementary and Secondary Schools: 1960 to 1990

[As of **October 1**. Regular sessions only. See also *Historical Statistics, Colonial Times to 1970*, series H 535-544]

ITEM	Unit	1960	1970	1975	1980	1985	1986	1987	1988	1989	1990
Elementary schools. . .	Number	10,501	9,362	8,340	8,043	7,806	7,693	7,601	7,501	7,395	7,291
Pupils enrolled	1,000. .	4,373	3,359	2,525	2,269	2,057	1,998	1,942	1,912	1,893	1,884
Teachers, total	1,000. .	108	112	99	97	97	94	93	94	94	91
Religious.	1,000. .	79	52	35	25	18	17	15	14	12	11
Lay	1,000. .	29	60	64	72	79	77	78	80	82	80
Secondary schools . . .	Number	2,392	1,981	1,653	1,516	1,430	1,409	1,391	1,362	1,324	1,296
Pupils enrolled	1,000. .	880	1,008	890	837	762	728	681	639	606	592
Teachers, total	1,000. .	44	54	50	49	50	48	47	44	43	40
Religious.	1,000. .	33	28	20	14	11	10	10	8	8	6
Lay	1,000. .	11	26	30	35	39	38	37	36	35	34

Source: National Catholic Educational Association, Washington, DC, *A Statistical Report on Catholic Elementary and Secondary Schools for the Years 1967-68 to 1969-70*, and *U.S. Catholic Schools, 1973-74*, and National Catholic Educational Association/Ganley's, *Catholic Schools in America*, annual, (copyright).

No. 246. Private Elementary and Secondary School Teachers—Selected Characteristics: 1988

[For school year ending in year shown. Based on survey and subject to sampling error; for details, see source. See table 232 for similar data on public school teachers]

CHARACTERISTIC	Unit	AGE				SEX		RACE/ETHNICITY			LEVEL OF CONTROL	
		Under 30 years old	30 to 39 years old	40 to 49 years old	Over 50 years old	Male	Fe-male	White	Black	His-pan-ic [1]	Ele-men-tary	Sec-ondary
Total [2]............	1,000...	66	104	83	49	67	240	288	7	9	160	147
Highest degree held:												
Bachelor's.........	Percent .	83.4	59.3	51.9	52.4	50.9	64.2	61.3	70.5	60.8	70.9	50.9
Master's	Percent .	11.4	31.4	39.1	34.7	38.2	27.4	29.9	15.3	19.7	21.0	39.2
Education specialist ..	Percent .	(B)	3.1	3.1	5.1	3.6	2.7	2.9	(B)	(B)	2.1	3.7
Doctorate	Percent .	(B)	(B)	2.6	(B)	5.0	0.8	1.6	(B)	(B)	(B)	3.1
Full-time teaching experience:												
Less than 3 years	Percent .	47.3	15.6	8.0	4.0	18.5	18.4	18.3	27.1	21.3	18.4	18.5
3 to 9 years	Percent .	51.4	45.4	31.6	11.1	28.9	39.8	37.4	40.9	40.2	40.5	34.0
10 to 20 years	Percent .	(B)	38.2	44.0	27.5	33.7	28.8	29.9	21.2	25.0	28.7	31.0
20 years or more.....	Percent .	(B)	(B)	15.4	56.8	18.6	12.1	13.6	(B)	(B)	11.8	15.4
Salary:												
Total.............	Dol.....	15,708	18,340	20,044	19,215	23,273	16,924	18,249	16,837	18,360	16,122	21,017
Base	Dol.....	13,755	16,719	18,271	17,630	19,606	15,693	16,519	15,267	16,385	14,957	18,540

B Base too small to meet statistical standards of reliability for a derived figure.   [1] Persons of Hispanic origin may be of any race.   [2] Includes teachers with no degrees, not shown separately.
Source: U.S. National Center for Education Statistics, *Digest of Education Statistics*, 1990.

No. 247. Private Elementary and Secondary Enrollment, Schools, and Tuition Paid, by Orientation and Tuition Levels: 1988

[For school year ending in year shown. Based on survey and subject to sampling error; for details see source]

ORIENTATION AND TUITION LEVEL	ENROLLMENT (1,000)				SCHOOLS				AVERAGE ANNUAL TUITION (dol.)			
	Total	Ele-men-tary	Sec-ondary	Com-bined	Total	Ele-men-tary	Sec-ondary	Com-bined	Total	Ele-men-tary	Sec-ondary	Com-bined
Total.............	5,479	3,175	896	1,408	26,807	17,087	2,425	7,296	1,915	1,357	2,552	2,767
Catholic schools..........	2,902	2,097	732	73	9,527	7,760	1,420	348	1,327	1,005	2,045	3,382
Less than $1,000.......	1,230	1,187	(B)	(B)	4,860	4,619	(B)	(B)	(X)	(X)	(X)	(X)
$1,000 to $2,499	1,456	882	556	(B)	4,113	3,017	1,037	(B)	(X)	(X)	(X)	(X)
$2,500 or more	215	(B)	(B)	(B)	554	(B)	(B)	(B)	(X)	(X)	(X)	(X)
Other religious schools	1,715	768	93	853	12,132	6,859	501	4,771	1,941	1,619	3,592	2,052
Less than $1,000.......	283	170	(B)	111	4,407	2,794	(B)	1,601	(X)	(X)	(X)	(X)
$1,000 to $2,499	1,034	481	(B)	537	6,377	3,497	(B)	2,751	(X)	(X)	(X)	(X)
$2,500 or more	397	118	74	205	1,347	568	360	419	(X)	(X)	(X)	(X)
Non-sectarian schools	863	310	71	482	5,148	2,468	504	2,177	3,839	3,091	6,391	3,941
Less than $1,000.......	96	(B)	(B)	74	805	(B)	(B)	619	(X)	(X)	(X)	(X)
$1,000 to $2,499	214	73	(B)	140	1,388	836	(B)	520	(X)	(X)	(X)	(X)
$2,500 or more	552	219	66	267	2,984	1,518	428	1,038	(X)	(X)	(X)	(X)

B Base figure too small to meet statistical standards of reliability for a derived figure.   X Not applicable.
Source: U.S. National Center for Education Statistics, *Digest of Education Statistics*, 1990.

No. 248. Private Elementary and Secondary Schools—Enrollment Size and Minority Enrollment, by Orientation: 1988

[For school year ending in year shown. Based on survey and subject to sampling error; for details see source]

CHARACTERISTIC	ENROLLMENT (1,000)				SCHOOLS			
	Total	Catholic	Other religious	Non-sectarian	Total	Catholic	Other religious	Non-sectarian
Total [1]...................	5,479.4	2,901.8	1,714.9	862.7	26,807	9,527	12,132	5,148
School enrollment:								
Less than 150 students...........	841.3	177.7	450.0	213.6	13,122	1,820	8,058	3,245
150 to 299 students	1,744.4	938.1	559.4	247.0	8,125	4,225	2,697	1,203
300 to 499 students	1,291.8	837.4	318.5	135.9	3,454	2,211	868	374
500 to 749 students	784.0	467.3	189.7	127.0	1,319	801	315	203
750 or more students	817.9	481.3	197.4	(B)	758	470	193	(B)
Percent minority students:								
Less than 5 percent	44.4	43.4	50.9	34.8	46	45.2	55.8	26.4
5 percent, less than 20 percent	28.7	26.4	29.4	35.2	28	24.2	27.0	36.0
20 percent, less than 50 percent.....	12.3	13.1	8.9	16.2	12	12.4	8.6	19.8
50 percent or more.............	14.6	17.1	10.8	13.9	14	18.2	8.6	17.8

B Base too small to meet statistical standards of reliability of a derived figure.   [1] Includes enrollment size class not specified.
Source: U.S. National Center for Education Statistics, *Digest of Education Statistics*, 1991.

No. 249. Scholastic Aptitude Test (SAT) Scores and Characteristics of College-Bound Seniors: 1967 to 1991

[For school year ending in year shown]

TYPE OF TEST AND CHARACTERISTIC	Unit	1967	1970	1975	1980	1985	1986	1987	1988	1989	1990	1991
TEST SCORES [1]												
Verbal, total [2]	Point . . .	466	460	434	424	431	431	430	428	427	424	422
Male	Point . . .	463	459	437	428	437	437	435	435	434	429	426
Female	Point . . .	468	461	431	420	425	426	425	422	421	419	418
Math, total [2]	Point . . .	492	488	472	466	475	475	476	476	476	476	474
Male	Point . . .	514	509	495	491	499	501	500	498	500	499	497
Female	Point . . .	467	465	449	443	452	451	453	455	454	455	453
PARTICIPANTS												
Total	1,000 . . .	(NA)	(NA)	996	992	977	1,001	1,080	1,134	1,088	1,026	1,033
Male	Percent	(NA)	(NA)	49.9	48.2	48.3	48.1	48.2	47.0	47.9	47.8	47.7
White	Percent	(NA)	(NA)	86.0	82.1	81.0	(NA)	78.2	77.0	74.7	73.0	72.0
Black	Percent	(NA)	(NA)	7.9	9.1	7.5	(NA)	8.7	9.2	9.6	10.0	10.0
Obtaining scores [1] of—												
600 or above:												
Verbal	Percent .	(NA)	(NA)	7.9	7.2	7.9	7.9	8.1	7.3	7.8	7.4	7.2
Math	Percent .	(NA)	(NA)	15.6	15.1	17.1	17.9	18.3	17.6	18.0	18.4	17.8
Below 400:												
Verbal	Percent .	(NA)	(NA)	37.8	41.8	39.4	38.2	39.8	39.4	40.4	41.2	42.4
Math	Percent .	(NA)	(NA)	28.5	30.2	28.2	28.0	28.3	27.8	28.0	28.4	29.1
Selected intended area of study:												
Business and commerce	Percent .	(NA)	(NA)	11.5	18.6	21.0	(NA)	23.1	23.0	22.3	21.0	19.0
Engineering	Percent .	(NA)	(NA)	6.7	11.1	11.7	(NA)	11.1	10.1	10.1	10.0	10.0
Social science	Percent .	(NA)	(NA)	7.7	7.8	7.5	(NA)	10.9	11.7	12.6	13.0	12.0
Education	Percent .	(NA)	(NA)	9.1	6.1	4.7	(NA)	6.0	6.6	7.1	7.0	8.0
SAT average [1] by high school rank:												
Top tenth	Point . . .	(NA)	(NA)	(NA)	539	547	547	552	550	550	549	548
Second tenth	Point . . .	(NA)	(NA)	(NA)	470	482	481	484	483	483	481	480
Second fifth	Point . . .	(NA)	(NA)	(NA)	431	442	440	440	440	440	438	437
Third fifth	Point . . .	(NA)	(NA)	(NA)	386	396	396	395	395	394	392	391

NA Not available.   [1] Minimum score 200; maximum score, 800.   [2] 1967 and 1970 are estimates based on total number of persons taking SAT.

Source: College Entrance Examination Board, New York, NY, *National College-Bound Senior*, annual, (copyright).

No. 250. American College Testing (ACT) Program Scores and Characteristics of College-Bound Students: 1967 to 1991

[For academic year ending in year shown. Except as indicated, test scores and characteristics of college-bound students. Through 1985, data based on 10 percent sample; thereafter, based on all ACT tested seniors]

TYPE OF TEST AND CHARACTERISTIC	Unit	1967	1970	1975	1980	1985	1986	1987	1988	1989	1990 [1]	1991 [1]
TEST SCORES [2]												
Composite	Point . . .	19.9	18.6	18.5	18.5	18.6	18.8	18.7	18.8	18.6	20.6	20.6
Male	Point . . .	20.3	19.5	19.5	19.3	19.4	19.6	19.5	19.5	19.3	21.0	20.9
Female	Point . . .	19.4	17.8	17.9	17.8	17.9	18.1	18.1	18.1	18.0	20.3	20.4
English	Point . . .	18.5	17.7	17.9	17.8	18.1	18.5	18.4	18.5	18.4	20.5	20.3
Male	Point . . .	17.6	17.1	17.3	17.3	17.6	17.9	17.9	18.0	17.8	20.1	19.8
Female	Point . . .	19.4	18.3	18.3	18.2	18.6	18.9	18.9	19.0	18.9	20.9	20.7
Math	Point . . .	20.0	17.6	17.4	17.3	17.2	17.3	17.2	17.2	17.1	19.9	20.0
Male	Point . . .	21.1	19.3	18.9	18.9	18.6	18.8	18.6	18.4	18.3	20.7	20.6
Female	Point . . .	18.8	16.2	16.2	16.0	16.0	16.0	16.1	16.1	16.1	19.3	19.4
Reading [3]	Point . . .	19.7	17.4	17.2	17.2	17.4	17.6	17.5	17.4	17.2	(NA)	21.2
Male	Point . . .	20.3	18.7	18.2	18.3	18.3	18.6	18.4	18.4	18.1	(NA)	21.3
Female	Point . . .	19.0	16.4	16.4	16.4	16.6	16.9	16.7	16.6	16.4	(NA)	21.1
Science reasoning [4]	Point . . .	20.8	21.1	21.1	21.0	21.2	21.4	21.4	21.4	21.2	(NA)	20.7
Male	Point . . .	21.6	22.4	22.4	22.3	22.6	22.7	22.8	22.6	22.6	(NA)	21.3
Female	Point . . .	20.0	20.0	20.0	20.0	20.0	20.1	20.2	20.1	20.0	(NA)	20.1
PARTICIPANTS [5]												
Total	1,000 . . .	788	714	822	836	739	730	730	777	842	855	817	796
Male	Percent .	52	46	45	45	46	46	46	46	46	46	46	45
White	Percent .	(NA)	77	83	83	82	82	81	81	80	79	79
Black	Percent .	4	7	8	8	8	8	8	9	9	9	9
Obtaining composite scores [6]												
of— 27 or above	Percent .	14	14	13	13	14	14	14	14	14	12	11
18 or below	Percent .	21	33	33	33	32	31	31	31	32	35	35
Planned educational major:												
Business [7]	Percent .	18	21	20	19	21	22	23	23	22	20	18
Engineering	Percent .	8	6	8	10	9	9	8	9	9	9	10
Social science [8]	Percent .	10	9	6	6	7	8	9	10	11	10	10
Education	Percent .	16	12	9	7	6	7	8	8	8	8	10

NA Not available.   [1] Beginning 1990, not comparable with previous years because a new version of the ACT was introduced. Estimated average composite scores for prior years: 1989, 20.6; 1988, 1987, and 1986, 20.8.   [2] Minimum score, 1; maximun core, 36.   [3] Prior to 1990, social studies; data not comparable with previous years.   [4] Prior to 1990, natural sciences; data not comparable with previous years.   [5] Beginning 1985, data are for seniors who graduated in year shown and had taken the ACT in their junior or senior years.   [6] Prior to 1990, 26 or above and 15 or below.   [7] Includes political and persuasive (e.g. sales) fields through 1975; thereafter, business and commerce.   [8] Includes religion through 1975.

Source: The American College Testing Program, Iowa City, IA, *High School Profile Report*, annual.

No. 251. Proficiency Test Scores for Selected Subjects, by Characteristic: 1977 to 1990

[Based on The National Assessment of Educational Progress Tests which are administered to a representative sample of students in public and private schools. Test scores can range from 0 to 500. For details, see source]

TEST AND YEAR	Total	SEX		RACE			PARENTAL EDUCATION				
		Male	Female	White [1]	Black [1]	His-panic	Less than high school	High school	More than high school		
									Total	Some college	College grad-uate
READING											
9 year olds:											
1979 to 1980	215	210	220	221	189	190	194	213	226	(NA)	(NA)
1983 to 1984	211	208	214	218	186	187	195	209	223	(NA)	(NA)
1989 to 1990	209	204	215	217	182	189	193	209	218	(NA)	(NA)
13 year olds:											
1979 to 1980	259	254	263	264	232	237	239	254	271	(NA)	(NA)
1983 to 1984	257	253	262	263	236	240	240	253	268	(NA)	(NA)
1989 to 1990	257	251	263	262	242	238	241	251	267	(NA)	(NA)
17 year olds:											
1979 to 1980	286	282	290	293	243	261	262	277	299	(NA)	(NA)
1983 to 1984	289	284	294	296	264	268	269	281	301	(NA)	(NA)
1989 to 1990	290	284	297	297	267	275	270	283	300	(NA)	(NA)
MATHEMATICS											
9 year olds:											
1977 to 1978	219	217	220	224	192	203	200	219	(NA)	230	231
1981 to 1982	219	217	221	224	195	204	199	218	(NA)	225	229
1989 to 1990	230	229	230	235	208	214	210	226	(NA)	236	238
13 year olds:											
1977 to 1978	264	264	265	272	230	238	245	263	(NA)	273	284
1981 to 1982	269	269	268	274	240	252	251	263	(NA)	275	282
1989 to 1990	270	271	270	276	249	255	253	263	(NA)	277	280
17 year olds:											
1977 to 1978	300	304	297	306	268	276	280	294	(NA)	305	317
1981 to 1982	299	302	296	304	272	277	279	293	(NA)	304	312
1989 to 1990	305	306	303	310	289	284	285	294	(NA)	308	316
SCIENCE											
9 year olds:											
1976 to 1977	220	222	218	230	192	175	199	223	(NA)	237	232
1981 to 1982	221	221	221	229	189	187	198	218	(NA)	229	231
1989 to 1990	229	230	227	238	196	206	210	226	(NA)	238	236
13 year olds:											
1976 to 1977	247	251	244	256	208	213	224	245	(NA)	260	267
1981 to 1982	250	256	245	257	217	226	225	243	(NA)	259	264
1989 to 1990	255	259	252	264	226	232	233	247	(NA)	263	268
17 year olds:											
1976 to 1977	290	297	282	298	262	240	265	284	(NA)	296	309
1981 to 1982	283	292	275	293	249	235	259	275	(NA)	290	300
1989 to 1990	290	296	285	301	253	262	261	276	(NA)	297	306

NA Not available.   [1] Non-Hispanic.

Source: U.S. National Center for Education Statistics, *Digest of Education Statistics*, annual.

No. 252. High School Dropouts, by Race and Hispanic Origin: 1973 to 1990

[In percent. As of October]

ITEM	1973	1975	1980	1982	1983	1984	1985	1986	1987 [1]	1988 [1]	1989 [1]	1990 [1]
EVENT DROPOUTS [2]												
Total [3]	6.3	5.9	6.2	5.6	5.3	5.3	5.3	4.8	4.2	4.9	4.5	4.1
White, non-Hispanic	5.5	5.0	5.3	4.9	4.5	4.6	4.4	3.7	3.7	4.2	3.5	3.4
Male	6.2	4.6	5.7	5.1	4.8	5.0	4.6	3.8	4.2	4.3	3.7	3.6
Female	4.9	5.4	4.9	4.7	4.1	4.2	4.1	3.7	3.2	4.1	3.3	3.2
Black, non-Hispanic	9.9	8.5	8.4	8.0	7.2	6.0	8.1	5.6	6.5	5.9	7.9	5.1
Male	12.0	8.4	7.8	9.1	7.2	6.2	8.5	5.2	6.2	6.5	7.0	4.3
Female	8.0	8.7	8.9	6.9	7.3	5.8	7.7	6.0	6.7	5.2	8.7	5.8
Hispanic	9.9	11.1	11.8	9.6	10.2	11.6	9.9	12.1	5.8	10.6	7.8	8.1
Male	8.2	10.4	17.7	9.9	14.0	13.0	9.5	12.6	5.2	12.5	7.8	8.9
Female	11.5	11.8	6.8	9.2	6.3	10.4	10.3	11.5	6.4	8.4	7.8	7.4
STATUS DROPOUTS [4]												
Total [3]	14.1	13.9	14.1	13.9	13.7	13.1	12.6	12.2	12.7	12.9	12.6	12.1
White, non-Hispanic	11.6	11.4	11.3	11.4	11.2	11.0	10.4	9.7	10.4	9.6	9.4	9.0
Male	11.5	10.9	12.2	12.0	12.2	12.0	11.0	10.2	10.8	10.3	10.3	9.3
Female	11.8	11.8	10.5	10.8	10.1	10.1	9.9	9.1	10.0	8.9	8.5	8.7
Black, non-Hispanic	22.2	22.8	19.2	18.4	18.0	15.5	15.2	14.1	14.2	14.3	13.9	13.2
Male	21.5	22.9	20.8	21.1	20.0	16.9	16.1	14.7	14.9	15.0	14.9	11.9
Female	22.8	22.8	17.8	15.9	16.2	14.3	14.4	13.5	13.3	13.7	13.0	14.4
Hispanic	33.5	29.2	35.2	31.7	31.6	29.8	27.6	30.1	28.6	35.8	33.0	32.4
Male	30.4	26.7	37.2	30.5	34.3	30.6	29.9	32.8	29.1	36.0	34.4	34.3
Female	36.4	31.6	33.2	32.8	29.1	29.0	25.2	27.2	28.1	35.4	31.6	30.3

[1] Beginning 1987 reflects new editing procedures for cases with missing data on school enrollment.   [2] Percent of students who drop out in a single year without completing high school. For grades 10 to 12.   [3] Includes other races, not shown separately.   [4] Percent of the population who have not completed high school and are not enrolled, regardless of when they dropped out. For persons 16 to 24 years old.

Source: U.S. National Center for Education Statistics, *Dropout Rates in the United States, 1990.*

No. 253. High School Dropouts 14 to 24 Years Old, by Age, Race, and Hispanic Origin: 1970 to 1991

[As of **October**. See headnote, table 255 for definition of dropouts]

AGE AND RACE	NUMBER OF DROPOUTS (1,000)								PERCENT OF POPULATION			
	1970	1980	1985	1987	1988	1989	1990	1991	1970	1980	1985	1991
Total dropouts [1][2]	4,670	5,212	4,456	4,349	4,300	4,109	3,854	3,964	12.2	12.0	10.6	10.5
16 to 17 years	617	709	505	500	482	395	418	395	8.0	8.8	7.0	6.0
18 to 21 years	2,138	2,578	2,095	1,966	2,081	2,128	1,921	1,960	16.4	15.8	14.1	14.1
22 to 24 years	1,770	1,798	1,724	1,785	1,668	1,516	1,458	1,526	18.7	15.2	14.1	14.3
White [2]	3,577	4,169	3,583	3,522	3,480	3,314	3,127	3,229	10.8	11.3	10.3	10.5
16 to 17 years	485	619	424	401	411	328	334	312	7.3	9.2	7.1	5.9
18 to 21 years	1,618	2,032	1,678	1,577	1,670	1,690	1,516	1,558	14.3	14.7	13.6	13.9
22 to 24 years	1,356	1,416	1,372	1,465	1,342	1,236	1,235	1,287	16.3	14.0	13.3	14.6
Black [2]	1,047	934	748	706	709	648	611	631	22.2	16.0	12.6	11.3
16 to 17 years	125	80	70	77	67	61	73	77	12.8	6.9	6.5	7.4
18 to 21 years	500	486	376	338	368	363	345	354	30.5	23.0	17.5	16.6
22 to 24 years	397	346	279	273	263	220	185	191	37.8	24.0	17.8	14.0
Hispanic [2][3]	(NA)	919	820	941	1,177	1,168	1,122	1,262	(NA)	29.5	23.3	29.5
16 to 17 years	(NA)	92	97	76	123	80	89	102	(NA)	16.6	14.6	15.8
18 to 21 years	(NA)	470	335	410	552	538	502	574	(NA)	40.3	29.3	35.1
22 to 24 years	(NA)	323	365	439	494	524	523	565	(NA)	40.6	33.9	45.7

NA Not available.   [1] Includes other groups not shown separately.   [2] Includes persons 14 to 15 years, not shown separately.
[3] Persons of Hispanic origin may be of any race.
Source: U.S. Bureau of the Census, *Current Population Reports*, series P-20, No. 460, and earlier reports; and unpublished data.

No. 254. Enrollment Status, by Race, Hispanic Origin, and Sex: 1975 and 1991

[As of **October**. For persons 18 to 21 years old. For the civilian noninstitutional population. Based on the Current Population Survey; see text, section 1 and Appendix III]

CHARACTERISTIC	TOTAL PERSONS 18 TO 21 YEARS OLD (1,000)		PERCENT DISTRIBUTION									
			Enrolled in high school		High school graduates						Not high school graduates	
					Total		In college		Not in college			
	1975	1991	1975	1991	1975	1991	1975	1991	1975	1991	1975	1991
Total [1]	15,693	13,906	5.7	8.2	78.0	77.7	33.5	42.2	44.5	35.5	16.3	14.1
White	13,448	11,187	4.7	6.9	80.6	79.1	34.6	44.1	46.0	35.0	14.7	13.9
Black	1,997	2,138	12.5	14.2	60.4	69.3	24.9	28.3	35.6	41.0	27.0	16.6
Hispanic [2]	899	1,637	12.0	13.4	57.2	51.6	24.4	23.9	32.8	27.7	30.8	35.1
Male [1]	7,584	6,772	7.4	10.5	76.6	75.0	35.4	40.1	41.3	34.9	15.9	14.6
White	6,545	5,459	6.2	8.9	79.7	76.1	36.9	41.4	42.8	34.7	14.1	15.0
Black	911	1,026	15.9	18.9	55.0	66.3	23.9	26.8	31.1	39.5	29.0	14.7
Hispanic [2]	416	826	17.3	13.9	54.6	45.3	25.2	17.8	29.3	27.5	27.9	41.0
Female [1]	8,109	7,134	4.2	6.0	79.2	80.3	31.8	44.2	47.4	36.1	16.6	13.6
White	6,903	5,728	3.2	5.0	81.4	82.1	32.4	46.8	49.0	35.3	15.3	12.8
Black	1,085	1,112	9.7	9.6	65.0	71.9	25.8	29.7	39.2	42.3	25.4	18.4
Hispanic [2]	484	812	7.6	12.8	59.3	58.1	23.6	30.0	35.7	28.1	33.1	29.1

[1] Includes other races not shown separately.   [2] Persons of Hispanic origin may be of any race.
Source: U.S. Bureau of the Census, *Current Population Reports*, series P-20, No. 460, and forthcoming report.

No. 255. Employment Status of High School Graduates Not Enrolled in College and School Dropouts, by Sex and Race: 1980 to 1990

[**In thousands, except percent**. As of **October**. For civilian noninstitutional population 16 to 24 years old. High school graduates: Persons not enrolled in college who have completed 4 years of high school only. Dropouts: Persons not in regular school and who have not completed the 12th grade nor received a general equivalency degree. Based on Current Population Survey; see text, section 1, and Appendix III]

EMPLOYMENT STATUS, SEX, AND RACE	GRADUATES					DROPOUTS				
	1980	1985	1988	1989	1990	1980	1985	1988	1989	1990
Civilian population.	11,622	10,381	8,999	8,645	8,370	5,254	4,323	4,231	4,042	3,800
In labor force	9,795	8,825	7,638	7,266	7,107	3,549	2,920	2,763	2,703	2,506
Percent of population	84.3	85.0	84.9	84.1	84.9	67.5	67.5	65.3	66.9	66.0
Employed [1]	8,567	7,707	6,932	6,552	6,279	2,651	2,165	2,235	2,147	1,993
Percent of labor force	87.5	87.3	90.8	90.2	88.3	74.7	74.1	80.9	79.4	79.5
Male...................	4,462	4,001	3,648	3,534	3,435	1,780	1,475	1,482	1,491	1,304
Female...............	4,105	3,706	3,284	3,018	2,845	871	690	753	656	689
White	7,638	6,732	5,899	5,543	5,334	2,310	1,888	1,924	1,861	1,761
Black	817	865	894	853	794	305	226	238	223	178
Unemployed [1]	1,228	1,118	706	714	828	898	755	528	555	513
Percent of labor force	12.5	12.7	9.2	9.8	11.7	25.3	25.9	19.1	20.6	20.5
Male...................	695	569	376	364	428	548	462	331	343	301
Female...............	532	549	330	350	400	350	293	197	213	212
White	924	729	488	478	526	636	582	394	397	361
Black	289	360	205	224	279	239	160	127	148	136
Not in labor force	1,827	1,556	1,361	1,379	1,262	1,705	1,403	1,468	1,339	1,294
Percent of population	15.7	15.0	15.1	16.0	15.1	32.5	32.5	34.7	33.1	34.1

[1] Includes other races not shown separately.
Source: U.S. Bureau of Labor Statistics, Bulletin 2307; and unpublished data.

Education

No. 256. Public High School Graduates, by State, 1980 to 1990, and Projections, 1991 to 1993

[In thousands. For school year ending in year shown]

STATE	1980	1985	1986	1987	1988	1989	1990, est.	1991, proj.	1992, proj.	1993, proj.
U.S.	2,747.7	2,414.0	2,382.6	2,428.8	2,500.2	2,456.2	2,324.0	2,210.0	2,193.0	2,215.0
AL	45.2	40.0	39.6	42.5	43.8	43.4	36.6	39.8	38.5	38.9
AK	5.2	5.2	5.5	5.7	5.9	5.6	5.4	5.3	5.3	5.3
AZ	28.6	27.9	27.5	29.5	29.8	31.9	32.1	28.2	29.2	29.7
AR	29.1	26.3	26.2	27.1	27.8	27.9	27.3	25.9	25.8	25.5
CA	249.2	225.4	229.0	237.4	249.6	244.6	229.4	227.1	234.9	243.5
CO	36.8	32.3	32.6	34.2	36.0	35.5	33.0	31.3	30.4	31.4
CT	37.7	32.1	33.6	31.1	32.4	30.9	30.0	26.2	26.0	25.7
DE	7.6	5.9	5.8	5.9	6.0	6.1	6.1	5.2	5.3	5.4
DC	5.0	3.9	3.9	3.8	3.9	3.6	3.6	3.1	3.2	2.8
FL	87.3	81.1	83.0	82.2	89.2	90.8	89.0	86.8	87.8	78.6
GA	61.6	58.7	59.1	60.0	61.8	61.9	56.6	57.5	57.3	58.6
HI	11.5	10.1	10.0	10.4	10.6	10.4	9.9	9.6	9.2	9.5
ID	13.2	12.1	12.1	12.2	12.4	12.5	11.6	11.6	12.2	12.3
IL	135.6	117.0	114.3	116.1	119.1	116.7	108.1	102.0	101.0	102.3
IN	73.1	63.3	59.8	60.4	64.0	63.6	59.4	56.9	54.5	56.8
IA	43.4	36.1	34.3	34.6	35.2	34.3	31.8	29.5	29.5	30.9
KS	30.9	26.0	25.6	26.9	27.0	26.8	25.1	24.5	24.3	25.2
KY	41.2	38.0	37.3	36.9	39.5	38.9	38.7	34.8	33.1	34.1
LA	46.3	39.7	40.0	39.1	39.1	37.2	35.9	34.6	33.1	33.6
ME	15.4	13.9	13.0	13.7	13.8	13.9	13.3	12.5	12.2	12.3
MD	54.3	48.3	46.7	46.1	47.2	45.8	41.6	39.2	38.4	38.7
MA	73.8	63.4	60.4	61.0	59.5	54.9	55.0	49.0	48.0	46.3
MI	124.3	105.9	101.0	102.7	106.2	101.8	93.0	88.1	86.5	86.0
MN	64.9	53.4	52.0	53.5	54.6	53.1	48.5	46.6	47.0	48.5
MS	27.6	25.3	25.1	26.2	27.9	24.2	25.0	23.5	23.0	23.2
MO	62.3	51.3	49.2	50.8	51.3	52.0	48.5	46.5	46.1	46.9
MT	12.1	10.0	9.8	10.1	10.3	10.5	9.4	9.0	9.1	9.2
NE	22.4	18.0	17.8	18.1	18.3	18.7	18.6	16.5	16.8	17.4
NV	8.5	8.6	8.8	9.5	9.4	9.5	9.5	9.3	9.6	9.9
NH	11.7	11.1	10.6	10.8	11.7	11.3	10.4	9.7	9.7	9.4
NJ	94.6	81.5	78.8	79.4	80.9	76.3	68.4	64.7	63.0	62.1
NM	18.4	15.6	15.5	15.7	15.9	15.5	14.9	14.8	15.1	15.4
NY	204.1	166.8	162.2	163.8	165.4	154.6	142.4	132.6	130.2	131.6
NC	70.0	67.2	65.9	65.4	67.8	69.3	64.5	62.2	60.1	60.7
ND	9.9	8.1	7.6	7.8	8.4	8.1	7.7	7.6	7.4	7.5
OH	144.2	122.3	119.6	121.1	124.5	125.0	114.5	107.7	104.6	107.1
OK	39.3	34.6	34.5	35.5	36.1	36.8	35.6	32.8	32.3	30.3
OR	29.9	26.9	26.3	27.2	28.1	26.9	25.6	24.5	25.0	25.5
PA	146.5	127.2	122.9	121.2	124.4	118.9	109.6	103.9	100.6	101.7
RI	10.9	9.2	8.9	8.8	8.9	8.6	7.7	7.5	7.5	7.3
SC	38.7	34.5	34.5	36.0	36.1	37.0	34.6	33.4	32.6	33.1
SD	10.7	8.2	7.9	8.1	8.4	8.2	7.7	7.3	7.3	7.7
TN	49.8	43.3	43.3	44.7	47.9	48.6	47.5	43.7	43.5	43.7
TX	171.4	159.2	161.2	168.4	171.4	177.0	182.1	169.7	169.9	174.7
UT	20.0	19.9	19.8	20.9	22.2	22.9	22.5	23.3	24.2	24.9
VT	6.7	5.8	5.8	6.0	6.2	6.0	5.7	5.2	5.2	5.2
VA	66.6	61.0	63.1	65.0	65.7	65.0	61.3	57.7	57.0	56.5
WA	50.4	45.4	45.8	49.9	51.8	49.4	46.9	44.7	45.3	46.3
WV	23.4	22.3	21.9	22.4	22.4	22.9	21.9	21.3	20.6	20.3
WI	69.3	58.9	58.3	56.9	58.4	55.0	55.0	50.2	49.3	50.0
WY	6.1	5.7	5.6	5.9	6.1	6.1	5.8	5.6	5.6	5.7

Source: U.S. National Center for Education Statistics, *Projections of Education Statistics to 2002,* annual.

No. 257. General Educational Development (GED) Credentials Issued, by Age: 1974 to 1989

[In percent, except number issued]

YEAR	GED'S issued (1,000)	PERCENT DISTRIBUTION BY AGE OF TEST TAKER				
		Under 19 years old	20 to 24 years old	25 to 29 years old	30 to 34 years old	35 years old or over
1974	294	35	27	13	9	17
1975	340	33	26	14	9	18
1979	426	37	28	12	13	11
1980	479	37	27	13	8	15
1981	489	37	27	13	8	14
1982	486	37	28	13	8	15
1983	465	34	29	14	8	15
1984	427	32	28	15	9	16
1985	413	32	26	15	10	16
1986	428	32	26	15	10	17
1987	444	33	24	15	10	18
1988	410	35	22	14	10	18
1989	357	36	22	14	10	17

Source: U.S. National Center for Education Statistics, *Digest of Education Statistics,* 1991.

No. 258. College Enrollment and Percent of High School Graduates Enrolled in or Completed 1 or More Years of College, by Sex, Race, and Hispanic Origin: 1960 to 1991

[As of **October**, except as noted. Covers civilian noninstitutional population 14 to 24 years old, except as noted]

ITEM AND YEAR	ALL PERSONS				MALE			FEMALE		
	Total [1]	White	Black	His-panic origin [2]	White	Black	His-panic origin [2]	White	Black	His-panic origin [2]
College enrollment (1,000): 1960 [3]	2,279	2,138	[4]141	(NA)	1,297	[4]68	(NA)	841	[4]73	(NA)
1970	6,065	5,535	437	(NA)	3,213	202	(NA)	2,322	236	(NA)
1975	7,228	6,368	699	308	3,437	308	148	2,931	392	160
1980	7,475	6,546	718	325	3,303	292	156	3,243	426	168
1982	7,932	6,810	789	353	3,403	340	147	3,405	448	206
1983	7,737	6,677	772	366	3,422	343	162	3,256	430	205
1984	7,844	6,735	826	367	3,479	383	156	3,256	443	210
1985	7,799	6,729	755	391	3,374	355	178	3,357	400	211
1986	7,613	6,426	820	455	3,206	350	230	3,221	471	226
1987	7,932	6,677	855	463	3,386	390	250	3,289	464	213
1988	7,973	6,796	785	463	3,310	303	237	3,486	482	228
1989	7,987	6,778	867	470	3,286	332	216	3,493	535	255
1990	8,142	6,767	929	448	3,355	442	226	3,413	486	222
1991	8,304	6,917	846	526	3,311	382	216	3,607	461	310
Percent of high school graduates enrolled: 1960 [3]	23.8	24.3	[4]18.7	(NA)	31.1	[4]21.1	(NA)	18.1	[4]16.9	(NA)
1970	33.3	33.9	26.7	(NA)	42.9	29.5	(NA)	26.3	24.7	(NA)
1975	33.1	33.0	32.5	36.2	36.9	33.4	37.9	29.4	32.0	34.8
1980	32.3	32.5	28.3	30.3	34.3	27.0	31.2	30.9	29.2	29.4
1982	33.5	33.6	28.2	30.1	34.9	28.6	28.0	32.3	27.9	31.8
1983	33.1	33.5	27.7	32.3	35.9	27.9	33.1	31.3	27.5	31.8
1984	33.7	34.2	28.0	30.0	36.8	29.6	28.2	31.8	26.8	31.5
1985	34.3	35.0	26.5	27.5	36.6	28.2	26.4	33.6	25.1	28.4
1986	32.9	33.0	28.7	30.6	35.1	28.5	33.6	31.1	28.8	28.2
1987	36.9	37.1	30.6	28.7	39.2	32.3	31.1	35.2	29.4	26.4
1988	37.6	38.4	28.6	31.3	39.6	25.1	32.2	37.3	31.3	30.5
1989	38.5	39.1	31.5	29.4	39.7	27.5	26.2	38.6	34.7	30.5
1990	39.6	39.8	33.7	29.4	40.7	35.1	29.4	38.9	32.4	29.5
1991	41.4	42.0	31.8	34.6	41.9	32.2	29.7	42.1	31.4	39.2
Percent of high school graduates enrolled in college or completed 1 or more years of college: 1960 [3]	40.4	41.0	[4]32.5	(NA)	47.1	[4]33.5	(NA)	35.6	[4]31.8	(NA)
1970	52.3	53.4	39.4	(NA)	60.9	41.4	(NA)	47.2	39.3	(NA)
1975	52.5	52.7	48.1	50.8	56.6	50.5	55.4	49.1	46.4	46.7
1980	51.1	51.4	45.9	47.3	51.8	44.1	49.5	50.9	47.4	45.4
1982	52.7	53.1	45.5	47.3	53.2	44.5	44.8	52.9	46.3	49.2
1983	52.8	53.4	45.0	48.4	53.5	43.6	47.4	53.4	46.3	49.7
1984	53.0	53.8	45.2	46.0	54.2	45.2	45.7	53.4	45.1	46.6
1985	54.3	55.3	43.8	46.7	55.5	43.6	44.9	55.2	44.0	48.0
1986	55.0	55.5	47.8	45.6	55.1	44.4	44.4	55.8	50.4	46.8
1987	56.5	57.1	48.7	44.2	56.7	48.3	45.1	57.5	48.9	43.2
1988	57.5	58.6	46.6	47.1	57.9	42.8	48.4	59.2	49.6	46.0
1989 [5]	57.9	58.9	49.1	43.6	58.5	45.8	42.7	59.2	51.8	44.5
1990 [5]	58.9	60.1	48.0	44.7	58.7	48.9	46.5	61.4	47.3	43.0
1991 [5]	60.7	62.3	46.1	47.6	59.9	46.1	42.2	64.5	47.0	52.4

NA Not available. [1] Includes other races, not shown separately. [2] Persons of Hispanic origin may be of any race. [3] As of April. [4] Black and other races. [5] Population 15 to 24 years old.

Source: U.S. Bureau of the Census, *U.S. Census of Population: 1960*, vol. I, *Characteristics of the Population*, part 1; *Current Population Reports*, series P-20, No. 460, and earlier reports; and unpublished data.

No. 259. Enrollment in Institutions of Higher Education, by Sex, Age, and Attendance Status, 1970 to 1989, and Projections, 1997 and 2002

[As of **fall**]

SEX AND RACE	NUMBER (1,000)						PART-TIME					
	1970	1980	1985	1989, est.	1997, proj.	2002, proj.	1970	1980	1985	1989, est.	1997, proj.	2002, proj.
Total	8,581	12,097	12,247	13,458	14,978	16,030	2,766	4,999	5,172	5,813	6,766	6,995
Male	5,044	5,874	5,818	6,155	6,691	7,052	1,540	2,185	2,211	2,428	2,767	2,818
14 to 17 years old. . . .	130	99	121	71	78	82	5	15	19	13	15	16
18 and 19 years old. . .	1,349	1,375	1,230	1,338	1,410	1,525	84	146	122	112	153	176
20 and 21 years old. . .	1,005	1,250	1,216	1,103	1,300	1,453	105	154	189	195	229	285
22 to 24 years old	964	1,064	1,048	1,084	1,046	1,164	314	377	318	363	367	412
25 to 29 years old	783	993	991	1,031	946	871	456	615	596	633	594	546
30 to 34 years old	308	576	574	599	586	553	236	447	424	436	429	404
35 years old and over .	415	507	639	851	1,324	1,405	340	430	542	677	982	979
Female.	3,537	6,223	6,429	7,302	8,287	8,978	1,225	2,813	2,961	3,403	3,999	4,177
14 to 17 years old. . . .	129	148	113	101	118	128	12	17	12	13	19	20
18 and 19 years old. . .	1,250	1,526	1,370	1,506	1,600	1,806	110	174	156	183	221	266
20 and 21 years old. . .	786	1,165	1,166	1,246	1,316	1,602	128	209	218	211	244	300
22 to 24 years old	493	925	885	1,098	1,162	1,336	262	438	388	467	466	523
25 to 29 years old	291	878	962	1,044	1,089	1,019	212	646	662	726	776	711
30 to 34 years old	179	667	687	745	784	771	151	531	527	559	573	552
35 years old and over .	409	914	1,246	1,563	2,217	2,318	349	799	998	1,244	1,700	1,806

Source: U.S. National Center for Education Statistics, *Projections of Education Statistics*, annual.

Education

No. 260. College Enrollment, by Sex, Age, Race, and Hispanic Origin: 1972 to 1991

[**In thousands**. As of **October** for civilian noninstitutional population, 14 years old and over. Based on Current Population Survey; see text, section 1 and Appendix III]

SEX, AGE, AND RACE	1972	1975	1980	1983	1984	1985	1986 [1]	1987	1988	1989	1990	1991
Total [2]	9,095	10,880	11,387	12,367	12,305	12,524	12,651	12,719	13,116	13,180	13,621	14,057
Male [3]	5,218	5,911	5,430	6,038	5,989	5,906	5,957	6,030	5,950	5,950	6,192	6,439
18 to 24 years.	3,534	3,693	3,604	3,820	3,929	3,749	3,702	3,867	3,770	3,717	3,922	3,954
25 to 34 years.	1,178	1,521	1,325	1,576	1,492	1,464	1,545	1,421	1,395	1,443	1,412	1,605
35 years old and over	365	569	405	535	476	561	628	625	727	716	772	832
Female [3]	3,877	4,969	5,957	6,329	6,316	6,618	6,694	6,689	7,166	7,231	7,427	7,618
18 to 24 years.	2,724	3,243	3,625	3,657	3,662	3,788	3,775	3,826	4,021	4,085	4,042	4,218
25 to 34 years.	581	947	1,378	1,510	1,522	1,599	1,559	1,564	1,568	1,637	1,749	1,680
35 years old and over	418	614	802	1,009	969	1,100	1,240	1,176	1,452	1,396	1,546	1,636
White	8,147	9,547	9,926	10,607	10,522	10,782	10,707	10,731	11,140	11,243	11,488	11,686
Male	4,723	5,263	4,804	5,187	5,111	5,101	5,074	5,104	5,078	5,136	5,235	5,304
Female	3,427	4,285	5,123	5,420	5,410	5,681	5,632	5,627	6,063	6,107	6,253	6,382
Black	727	1,099	1,163	1,227	1,274	1,208	1,359	1,351	1,321	1,287	1,393	1,477
Male	384	523	476	537	590	518	580	587	494	480	587	629
Female	343	577	686	690	684	689	779	764	827	807	807	848
Hispanic origin [4]	242	411	443	579	563	665	794	739	747	754	748	830
Male	126	218	222	273	248	301	377	390	355	353	364	347
Female	117	193	221	306	315	363	417	349	391	401	384	483

[1] Revised. See footnote 2, table 218. [2] Includes other races not shown separately. [3] Includes persons 14 to 17 years old, not shown separately. [4] Persons of Hispanic origin may be of any race.

Source: U.S. Bureau of the Census, *Current Population Reports*, series P-20, No. 460, and earlier reports; and unpublished data.

No. 261. College Enrollment, by Selected Characteristics: 1980 to 1988

[**In thousands**. As of **fall**. Totals may differ from other tables because of adjustments to underreported and nonreported racial/ethnic data. Nonresident alien students are not distributed among racial/ethnic groups. Minus sign (-) indicates decrease]

CHARACTERISTIC	1980	1984	1988	Percent change 1980-1988	CHARACTERISTIC	1980	1984	1988	Percent change 1980-1988
Total	12,086.8	12,233.1	13,043.1	7.9	2-year	255.1	288.8	383.9	50.5
Male	5,868.1	5,858.3	5,998.2	2.2	4-year	216.6	246.1	296.0	36.7
Female.	6,218.7	6,374.7	7,044.9	13.3	Undergraduate.	433.1	495.2	631.2	45.7
Public.	9,456.4	9,456.4	10,156.4	7.4	Graduate	32.1	31.7	39.5	23.1
Private	2,630.4	2,776.6	2,886.7	9.7	Professional	6.5	8.0	9.3	43.1
2-year	4,521.4	4,526.9	4,868.1	7.7	American Indian [1] . .	83.9	83.6	92.5	10.3
4-year	7,565.4	7,706.1	8,175.0	8.1	Male	37.8	37.4	39.1	3.4
Undergraduate.	10,469.0	10,610.8	11,304.2	8.0	Female.	46.1	46.1	53.4	15.8
Graduate	1,340.9	1,343.7	1,471.9	9.8	Public.	74.2	72.1	91.1	22.8
Professional	276.8	278.5	267.1	-3.5	Private	9.7	11.4	11.5	18.6
White [1]	9,833.0	9,814.7	10,283.2	4.6	2-year	47.0	45.5	50.4	7.2
Male	4,772.9	4,689.9	4,711.6	-1.3	4-year	36.9	38.1	42.1	14.1
Female.	5,060.1	5,124.7	5,571.6	10.1	Undergraduate.	77.9	77.8	85.9	10.3
Public.	7,656.1	7,542.4	7,963.8	4.0	Graduate	5.2	4.8	5.6	7.7
Private	2,176.9	2,272.3	2,319.4	6.5	Professional	0.8	1.0	1.1	37.5
2-year	3,558.5	3,514.3	3,701.5	4.0	Asian [1]	286.4	389.5	496.7	73.4
4-year	6,274.5	6,300.4	6,581.6	4.9	Male	151.3	210.0	259.2	71.3
Undergraduate.	8,480.7	8,484.0	8,906.7	5.0	Female.	135.2	179.5	237.5	75.7
Graduate	1,104.7	1,087.3	1,153.2	4.4	Public.	239.7	322.7	405.7	69.3
Professional	247.7	243.4	223.2	-9.9	Private	46.7	66.8	91.0	94.9
Black [1]	1,106.8	1,075.8	1,129.6	2.1	2-year	124.3	167.1	199.3	60.3
Male	463.7	436.8	442.7	-4.5	4-year	162.1	222.4	297.4	83.5
Female.	643.0	639.0	686.9	6.8	Undergraduate.	248.7	343.0	436.6	75.6
Public.	876.1	844.0	881.1	0.6	Graduate	31.6	37.1	45.7	44.6
Private	230.7	231.8	248.5	7.7	Professional	6.1	9.3	14.4	136.1
2-year	472.5	458.7	473.3	0.2	Nonresident alien [1] .	305.0	334.6	361.2	18.4
4-year	634.3	617.0	656.3	3.5	Male	210.8	230.4	235.3	11.6
Undergraduate.	1,018.8	994.9	1,038.8	2.0	Female.	94.2	104.1	125.9	33.7
Graduate	75.1	67.4	76.5	1.9	Public.	204.1	219.0	237.8	16.5
Professional	12.8	13.4	14.3	11.7	Private	100.8	115.5	123.3	22.3
Hispanic	471.7	534.9	680.0	44.2	2-year	64.1	52.5	59.6	-7.0
Male	231.6	253.8	310.3	34.0	4-year	240.9	282.1	301.5	25.2
Female.	240.1	281.2	369.6	53.9	Undergraduate.	209.9	215.8	205.0	-2.3
Public.	406.2	456.1	586.9	44.5	Graduate	92.2	115.3	151.4	64.2
Private	65.5	78.9	93.1	42.1	Professional	2.9	3.4	4.7	62.1

[1] Non-Hispanic.

Source: U.S. National Center for Education Statistics, *Digest of Education Statistics*, 1990.

No. 262. Higher Education—Summary: 1970 to 1989

[Institutions, staff, and enrollment as of fall. Finances for fiscal year ending in the following year. Covers universities, colleges, professional schools, junior and teachers colleges, both publicly and privately controlled, regular session. Includes estimates for institutions not reporting. See also appendix III, and *Historical Statistics, Colonial Times to 1970*, series H 680, H 699-705, and H 710]

ITEM	Unit	1970	1980	1983	1984	1985	1986	1987	1988	1989 [1]
Institutions [2]	Number.	2,556	3,231	3,284	3,331	3,340	3,406	3,587	3,565	3,535
4-year	Number .	1,665	1,957	2,013	2,025	2,029	2,070	2,135	2,129	2,127
2-year	Number .	891	1,274	1,271	1,306	1,311	1,336	1,452	1,436	1,408
Instructional staff	1,000. . .	474	686	724	717	715	722	[3]793	804	824
Percent full-time	Percent .	78	66	65	64	64	64	66	(NA)	64
Total enrollment [4]	1,000. . .	8,581	12,097	12,465	12,242	12,247	12,504	12,767	13,055	13,458
Male	1,000. . .	5,044	5,874	6,024	5,864	5,818	5,885	5,932	6,002	6,155
Female	1,000. . .	3,537	6,223	6,441	6,378	6,429	6,619	6,835	7,053	7,302
4-year institutions.	1,000. . .	6,262	7,571	7,741	7,711	7,716	7,824	7,990	8,180	8,374
2-year institutions.	1,000. . .	2,319	4,526	4,723	4,531	4,531	4,680	4,776	4,875	5,083
Full time.	1,000. . .	5,815	7,098	7,261	7,098	7,075	7,120	7,231	7,437	7,627
Part time	1,000. . .	2,766	4,999	5,204	5,144	5,172	5,384	5,536	5,619	5,831
Public	1,000. . .	6,428	9,457	9,683	9,477	9,479	9,714	9,973	10,161	10,515
Private	1,000. . .	2,153	2,640	2,782	2,765	2,768	2,790	2,793	2,894	2,943
Undergraduate [5]	1,000. . .	7,376	10,475	10,846	10,618	10,597	10,798	11,046	11,317	11,666
Men	1,000. . .	4,254	5,000	5,158	5,007	4,962	5,018	5,068	5,138	5,278
Women.	1,000. . .	3,122	5,475	5,688	5,611	5,635	5,780	5,978	6,179	6,388
First-time freshmen	1,000. . .	2,063	2,588	2,444	2,357	2,292	2,219	2,246	2,379	2,353
First professional	1,000. . .	173	278	279	279	274	270	268	267	274
Men	1,000. . .	159	199	188	185	180	174	170	167	168
Women.	1,000. . .	15	78	90	94	94	97	98	100	105
Graduate [5]	1,000. . .	1,031	1,343	1,340	1,345	1,376	1,435	1,452	1,472	1,518
Men	1,000. . .	630	675	677	672	677	693	693	697	709
Women.	1,000. . .	400	670	663	673	700	742	759	774	809
Current funds revenues [6]	Mil. dol .	23,879	65,585	84,417	92,473	100,438	108,810	117,340	128,502	139,635
Tuition and fees	Mil. dol. .	5,021	13,773	19,715	21,283	23,117	25,706	27,837	30,807	33,926
Federal government.	Mil. dol. .	3,198	9,748	10,406	11,509	12,705	13,904	14,772	15,894	17,255
State government	Mil. dol. .	6,595	20,106	24,707	27,583	29,912	31,309	33,517	36,031	38,349
Auxiliary enterprises	Mil. dol. .	3,125	7,287	9,456	10,100	10,674	11,364	11,948	12,856	13,938
Plant funds	Mil. dol. .	(NA)	4,774	6,238	6,737	7,713	(NA)	(NA)	(NA)	(NA)
Increase in fund balance [8] . . .	Mil. dol. .	498	2,793	2,410	4,653	7,239	(NA)	(NA)	(NA)	(NA)
Current funds expenditures [6] .	Mil. dol	23,375	64,053	81,993	89,951	97,536	105,764	113,786	123,867	134,656
Educational and general [9] . .	Mil. dol. .	17,616	50,074	63,741	70,061	76,128	82,956	89,157	96,803	105,585
Auxiliary enterprises [10]	Mil. dol. .	2,988	7,288	9,250	10,012	10,528	11,037	11,400	12,280	13,204
Gross addition to plant value . .	Mil. dol. .	4,165	6,471	7,604	8,306	10,149	(NA)	(NA)	(NA)	(NA)
Value of plant	Mil. dol. .	46,054	88,761	107,640	114,764	122,261	(NA)	(NA)	(NA)	(NA)
Endowment (book value)	Mil. dol. .	11,341	20,941	29,502	33,399	38,698	(NA)	(NA)	(NA)	(NA)

NA Not available. [1] Preliminary. [2] Beginning 1980, number of institutions includes count of branch campuses. Due to revised survey procedures, data beginning 1987 are not comparable with previous years. [3] Due to revised survey methods, data not comparable with previous years. [4] Beginning 1980, branch campuses counted according to actual status, e.g., 2-year branch in 2-year category; previously a 2-year branch included in university category. [5] Includes unclassified students. (Students taking courses for credit, but are not candidates for degrees.) [6] Includes items not shown separately. [7] Annual net increase in plant funds. [8] Includes endowment and, beginning 1980, annuity and student loans. [9] Data for 1970 are not strictly comparable with later years. [10] Includes activities.

Source: U.S. National Center for Education Statistics, *Digest of Education Statistics*, annual; and unpublished data.

No. 263. Junior (2-Year) Colleges—Summary: 1970 to 1989

[Institutions and their enrollment as of fall; financial data for fiscal year ending the following year. Prior to 1975, excludes 2-year branches of universities and other 4-year institutions. Beginning 1980, includes schools accredited by the National Association of Trade and Technical Schools. See *Historical Statistics, Colonial Times to 1970*, series H 690-692 and H 705, for related but not comparable data. See also Appendix III]

ITEM	Unit	1970	1975	1980	1983	1984	1985	1986	1987	1988	1989 [1]
Institutions [2]	Number.	891	1,128	1,274	1,271	1,306	1,311	1,336	1,452	1,436	1,408
Public	Number.	654	897	945	916	935	932	960	992	984	968
Private	Number.	237	231	329	355	371	379	376	460	452	440
Enrollment.	1,000. . .	2,223	3,970	4,526	4,723	4,531	4,531	4,680	4,776	4,875	5,083
Public	1,000. . .	2,102	3,836	4,329	4,459	4,279	4,270	4,414	4,541	4,615	4,821
Private	1,000. . .	121	134	198	264	252	261	266	235	260	263
Male	1,000. . .	1,317	2,165	2,047	2,131	2,016	2,002	2,061	2,073	2,090	2,187
Female	1,000. . .	006	1,805	2,479	2,592	2,514	2,529	2,619	2,704	2,785	2,896
Current funds revenue [3] . . .	Mil. dol .	2,504	5,304	8,505	10,590	11,449	12,293	13,136	14,060	15,387	(NA)
Tuition and fees	Mil. dol. .	413	896	1,618	2,316	2,469	2,618	2,844	3,057	3,376	(NA)
State government	Mil. dol. .	926	2,248	3,961	4,773	5,189	5,659	5,982	6,350	6,898	(NA)
Local government	Mil. dol. .	701	1,187	1,623	1,706	1,860	2,027	2,200	2,352	2,662	(NA)
Current funds expenditures.	Mil. dol	2,327	5,092	8,212	10,314	11,207	11,976	12,779	13,644	14,726	(NA)
Education and general [4] . . .	Mil. dol. .	2,073	4,736	7,608	9,530	10,374	11,118	11,875	12,701	13,676	(NA)
Instruction.	Mil. dol. .	1,205	2,401	3,764	4,715	5,075	5,398	5,729	6,082	6,617	(NA)

NA Not available. [1] Preliminary. [2] See footnote 2, table 262. [3] Includes items not shown separately. [4] Includes mandatory transfers.

Source: U.S. National Center for Education Statistics, *Digest of Education Statistics*, annual; and *Financial Statistics of Institutions of Higher Education*, annual.

No. 264. Institutions of Higher Education—Number, 1990, and Enrollment 1980 and 1990, and by Selected Characteristics, 1990—States and Other Areas

[Number of institutions for academic year beginning 1990. Opening fall enrollment of resident and extension students attending full-time or part-time. Excludes students taking courses for credit by mail, radio, or TV, and students in branches of U.S. institutions operated in foreign countries. See Appendix III]

STATE OR OTHER AREA	Total enroll-ment, 1980 (1,000)	Num-ber of insti-tu-tions [1]	1990 Enrollment (1,000)							Minority enrollment			
			Total	Male	Female	Public	Private	Full-time	White [2]	Total [3]	Black [2]	His-panic	Foreign
U.S.	12,097	3,559	13,710	6,239	7,472	10,741	2,969	7,780	10,675	2,639	1,223	758	397
Northeast. . .	2,587	859	2,782	1,245	1,537	1,644	1,138	1,680	2,223	454	221	126	105
N.E.	766	256	819	364	455	431	388	492	709	79	32	21	31
ME.	43	31	57	24	33	42	16	32	55	1	(Z)	(Z)	1
NH.	47	28	60	27	32	32	27	37	57	2	1	(Z)	1
VT.	31	22	36	16	21	21	15	25	34	2	(Z)	(Z)	1
MA.	418	116	419	188	231	185	234	262	350	48	18	13	21
RI	67	12	78	36	43	42	36	50	70	6	3	2	2
CT	160	47	169	73	95	109	59	85	143	20	10	6	5
M.A.	1,822	603	1,963	881	1,082	1,213	750	1,189	1,514	375	189	105	74
NY	992	324	1,035	458	577	608	428	645	749	239	112	75	47
NJ	322	59	324	145	178	262	62	163	242	70	33	22	12
PA	508	220	604	278	326	343	261	381	523	66	44	8	15
Midwest. . . .	3,044	917	3,499	1,600	1,899	2,763	736	2,013	2,974	438	258	85	84
E.N.C	2,169	562	2,437	1,117	1,320	1,941	496	1,366	2,020	359	217	72	56
OH. . . .	489	154	555	260	295	426	129	338	481	60	45	5	14
IN	247	80	283	134	149	223	60	183	251	24	15	4	7
IL	644	170	729	331	398	551	178	365	541	173	89	49	15
MI	520	97	570	256	314	487	82	289	476	80	57	9	14
WI	269	61	300	136	164	254	46	191	271	22	11	5	6
W.N.C. . . .	875	355	1,062	483	579	822	240	647	954	79	41	13	28
MN. . . .	207	78	254	114	139	199	55	153	235	13	4	2	5
IA	140	58	171	80	91	118	53	120	155	9	4	2	7
MO	234	93	289	131	159	200	89	163	251	32	23	3	7
ND	34	20	38	19	19	35	3	30	34	2	(Z)	(Z)	1
SD. . . .	33	19	34	15	19	27	8	24	31	2	(Z)	(Z)	1
NE	90	34	113	51	62	95	18	63	105	6	3	2	2
KS	137	53	163	73	90	149	14	94	143	15	7	4	5
South.	3,437	1,153	4,219	1,896	2,323	3,504	715	2,512	3,178	939	589	235	103
S.A.	1,724	580	2,123	946	1,177	1,686	436	1,216	1,611	457	322	78	55
DE. . . .	33	10	42	18	24	34	8	25	35	6	5	1	1
MD. . . .	226	57	260	113	147	222	39	121	191	61	44	5	8
DC. . . .	87	17	81	38	43	13	68	50	41	31	25	2	9
VA	281	83	353	158	195	291	62	196	281	67	50	5	6
WV	82	28	85	38	47	74	11	58	79	4	3	(Z)	2
NC	288	125	352	155	197	285	67	223	274	73	62	3	5
SC	132	64	159	69	90	131	28	109	123	34	31	1	2
GA	184	95	252	115	137	196	55	167	189	57	49	3	6
FL	412	101	538	242	296	440	99	267	398	124	53	58	16
E.S.C.	614	282	745	330	414	627	117	503	603	129	118	3	13
KY. . . .	143	62	178	75	103	147	31	114	163	13	10	1	2
TN. . . .	205	87	226	103	123	175	51	147	187	35	31	1	4
AL	164	87	218	99	119	196	22	149	167	46	43	1	5
MS. . . .	102	46	123	53	69	109	14	93	86	35	34	(Z)	2
W.S.C.	1,099	291	1,352	620	731	1,190	161	793	964	353	149	154	35
AR. . . .	78	35	90	39	52	79	12	65	75	14	12	(Z)	1
LA	160	36	187	81	106	158	28	134	130	52	45	3	5
OK. . . .	160	48	173	80	93	151	22	103	141	27	12	3	5
TX	701	172	901	421	481	802	99	492	618	260	80	148	24
West	2,978	621	3,163	1,457	1,706	2,783	380	1,528	2,261	798	148	312	109
Mt.	658	186	880	411	469	784	95	456	720	139	21	78	22
MT	35	19	36	17	19	32	4	26	32	3	(Z)	(Z)	1
ID	43	11	52	24	28	41	11	35	48	3	(Z)	1	1
WY	21	9	31	14	18	31	1	17	29	2	(Z)	1	1
CO. . . .	163	57	227	106	121	201	26	121	191	31	7	17	5
NM. . . .	58	28	86	38	48	83	2	45	53	32	2	24	1
AZ	203	38	265	123	142	249	16	116	206	52	8	30	7
UT	94	15	121	62	59	86	35	78	110	6	1	2	5
NV	41	9	62	27	35	61	(Z)	18	51	10	3	3	1
Pac.	2,321	435	2,284	1,046	1,237	1,998	285	1,072	1,541	659	127	234	87
WA	304	57	263	116	147	228	36	150	225	33	7	6	4
OR. . . .	157	46	167	79	88	145	21	95	146	13	2	3	8
CA. . . .	1,791	310	1,770	814	956	1,555	215	785	1,130	574	115	223	66
AK. . . .	21	7	30	12	18	28	2	11	24	5	1	1	5
HI	47	15	54	25	29	43	11	31	16	34	2	1	4
U.S. military [4].	50	9	47	41	7	47	-	47	40	8	6	1	(Z)
Other:													
American Samoa	1	1	1	1	1	1	-	1	(Z)	1	(Z)	(Z)	(Z)
Guam	3	2	5	2	2	5	-	2	(Z)	4	(Z)	(Z)	(Z)
No. Marianas . .	-	1	-	(Z)	(Z)	1	-	1	(Z)	(Z)	(Z)	(Z)	(Z)
Puerto Rico . .	131	58	151	58	93	56	95	119	(Z)	151	(Z)	151	(Z)
Virgin Islands .	2	2	2	1	2	2	-	1	(Z)	2	(Z)	(Z)	(Z)

- Represents zero.   Z Less than 500 or 50.   [1] Branch campuses counted as separate institutions.   [2] Non-Hispanic.   [3] Includes other races not shown separately.   [4] Military academies.

Source: U.S. National Center for Education Statistics, *Digest of Education Statistics*, annual.

No. 265. Higher Education Price Indexes: 1965 to 1989

[1983 = 100. For years ending June 30. Reflects prices paid by colleges and universities]

YEAR	Index, total	Average annual percent change [1]	PERSONNEL COMPENSATION				CONTRACTED SERVICES, SUPPLIES, AND EQUIPMENT					
			Total	Professional salaries	Nonprofessional salaries	Fringe benefits	Total	Services	Supplies and materials	Equipment	Library acquisitions	Utilities
1965 ..	29.8	4.1	30.5	34.9	31.0	13.0	27.6	35.8	33.8	36.0	19.3	15.7
1970 ..	39.5	6.7	42.1	47.7	38.8	24.7	31.9	42.8	37.6	41.9	25.7	16.3
1971 ..	42.1	6.4	44.8	50.1	41.8	28.0	34.1	45.1	39.0	43.5	30.8	18.0
1972 ..	44.3	5.3	47.1	52.0	44.9	31.1	36.0	47.8	39.8	45.1	34.9	19.2
1973 ..	46.7	5.3	49.8	54.3	47.6	34.7	37.6	49.9	41.1	46.5	37.7	20.2
1974 ..	49.9	6.9	52.8	57.2	50.6	38.6	41.4	52.2	46.5	49.4	41.6	24.8
1975 ..	54.3	8.8	56.3	60.3	54.6	42.9	48.5	56.8	58.0	58.3	46.7	31.8
1976 ..	57.9	6.7	60.0	63.5	59.0	47.8	51.8	60.0	60.7	61.7	53.7	34.4
1977 ..	61.7	6.6	63.5	66.4	63.1	52.8	56.1	63.5	63.8	64.8	58.6	40.5
1978 ..	65.8	6.6	67.6	69.9	68.1	58.4	60.4	67.0	66.6	69.3	64.3	45.9
1979 ..	70.6	7.3	72.4	74.1	73.4	64.5	65.2	71.0	71.7	74.7	71.4	50.3
1980 ..	77.5	9.8	78.4	79.4	80.2	72.6	75.0	76.5	84.6	81.6	79.5	64.1
1981 ..	85.9	10.8	85.8	86.3	87.7	81.8	86.2	85.3	95.6	89.6	89.3	79.7
1982 ..	94.0	9.4	93.5	93.7	94.6	91.5	95.3	94.8	100.4	96.4	95.5	92.4
1983 ..	100.0	6.4	100.0	100.0	100.0	100.0	100.0	100.0	100.0	100.0	100.0	100.0
1984 ..	104.7	4.7	105.4	104.7	105.2	108.3	102.8	104.7	103.1	102.2	103.8	100.8
1985 ..	110.5	5.5	112.0	111.4	109.1	117.7	106.1	109.2	105.4	104.8	108.5	103.0
1986 ..	115.6	4.6	118.8	118.2	113.0	127.7	106.2	114.3	104.2	106.9	117.2	95.5
1987 ..	120.3	4.1	125.4	125.0	116.4	137.5	105.2	117.8	103.5	108.8	129.9	84.4
1988 ..	125.8	4.5	131.6	130.9	120.4	147.2	108.4	122.1	107.9	110.9	138.7	84.4
1989 ..	133.1	5.8	139.5	138.7	125.2	159.0	114.0	129.0	116.9	115.8	149.9	85.2

[1] Change from immediate prior year.

Source: Research Associates of Washington, Washington, DC, *Inflation Measures for Schools and Colleges,* annual.

No. 266. Institutions of Higher Education—Finances: 1975 to 1990

[In millions of dollars. For fiscal years ending in year shown. For coverage, see headnote, table 262. See also Appendix III and *Historical Statistics, Colonial Times to 1970,* series H 729-738 and H 747-749]

ITEM	1975	1980	1985	1986	1987	1988	1989	1990		
								Total	Public	Private
Current funds revenues	35,364	58,520	92,473	100,438	108,810	117,340	128,502	139,635	88,911	50,724
Tuition and fees.	7,233	11,930	21,283	23,117	25,706	27,837	30,807	33,926	13,820	20,106
Federal government	4,692	8,902	11,509	12,705	13,904	14,772	15,894	17,255	9,171	8,083
State government.	10,857	18,378	27,583	29,912	31,309	33,517	36,031	38,349	37,052	1,297
Local government	1,424	1,588	2,387	2,545	2,799	3,006	3,364	3,640	3,264	376
Endowment earnings	718	1,177	2,096	2,276	2,378	2,586	2,914	3,144	462	2,682
Private gifts, grants, and contracts [1]	1,745	2,808	4,896	5,411	5,953	6,359	7,061	7,781	3,369	4,413
Educational activities [2]	555	1,239	2,127	2,373	2,642	2,918	3,316	3,632	2,424	1,208
Auxiliary enterprises	4,066	6,481	10,100	10,674	11,364	11,948	12,856	13,938	8,473	5,465
Other funds revenues [3]	4,073	6,015	10,490	11,426	12,755	14,397	16,260	17,970	10,875	7,094
Current funds expenditures [4] . . .	34,735	56,914	89,951	97,536	105,764	113,786	123,867	134,656	85,771	48,885
Educational and general	27,250	44,543	70,061	76,128	82,956	89,157	96,803	105,585	69,164	36,421
Instruction	11,720	18,497	28,777	31,032	33,711	35,834	38,813	42,146	29,257	12,889
Institutional support	2,964	5,054	8,588	9,351	10,085	10,774	11,529	12,674	7,490	5,184
Research	3,126	5,099	7,552	8,437	9,162	10,351	11,432	12,506	8,542	3,964
Plant operation [5].	2,738	4,700	7,345	7,605	7,819	8,231	8,740	9,458	6,334	3,125
Academic support	2,240	3,876	6,075	6,667	7,305	8,142	8,904	9,438	6,535	2,903
Libraries	998	1,624	2,362	2,551	2,441	2,836	3,010	3,254	2,103	1,152
Student services	1,404	2,567	4,178	4,563	4,976	5,397	5,781	6,388	4,021	2,367
Scholarships and fellowships	1,429	2,200	3,670	4,160	4,776	5,325	5,919	6,656	2,386	4,269
Unrestricted funds	611	905	1,962	2,285	2,645	2,941	3,283	3,854	1,099	2,754
Restricted funds	818	1,296	1,709	1,875	2,131	2,384	2,636	2,802	1,287	1,515
Public service	1,098	1,817	2,861	3,120	3,448	3,786	4,227	4,690	3,689	1,001
Mandatory transfers.	532	732	1,016	1,192	1,212	1,318	1,458	1,630	909	721
Auxiliary enterprises [4]	4,059	6,486	10,012	10,528	11,037	11,400	12,280	13,204	8,282	4,922
Hospitals [4]	2,341	4,757	8,011	8,692	9,173	10,406	11,825	12,679	8,114	4,565
Independent operations [4]	1,086	1,128	1,868	2,187	2,598	2,823	2,959	3,187	210	2,977

[1] Private grants represent nongovernmental revenue for sponsored research and other sponsored programs; includes private contracts.   [2] Sales and service of educational departments only.   [3] Includes sales and services of hospitals, federally funded research and development centers, and others sources.   [4] Includes mandatory transfers which are primarily current expenditures for plant.   [5] Includes maintenance.

Source: U.S. National Center for Education Statistics, *Digest of Education Statistics,* annual.

Education

No. 267. Major Federal Student Financial Assistance Programs—Number of Recipients and Funds Utilized, by Type of Program: 1970 to 1992

[For award years July 1 of year shown to the following June 30, except as indicated. Funds utilized exclude operating costs, etc., and represent funds given to students]

PROGRAM	Unit	1970	1980	1985	1987	1988, est.	1989, est.	1990, est.	1991, est.	1992, est.
Pell Grants:										
Number of recipients...	1,000...	(X)	2,858	2,910	3,002	3,341	3,473	3,276	3,421	3,017
Funds utilized........	Mil. dol. .	(X)	2,387	3,572	3,746	4,471	4,768	4,712	5,077	5,760
Average grant	Dollars..	(X)	835	1,227	1,248	1,338	1,373	1,438	1,484	1,909
Supplemental Educational Opportunity Grants: [1]										
Number of recipients...	1,000...	253.4	716.5	686.0	635.3	678.8	727.6	728.0	835.0	899.0
Funds utilized........	Mil. dol. .	134	368	410	419	423	466	488	584	643
Average grant	Dollars..	527	513	598	659	622	641	670	700	715
Perkins Loans: [2]										
Number of recipients...	1,000...	452.0	813.4	700.9	673.5	692.0	695.9	660.0	688.0	566.0
Loan funds utilized [3]...	Mil. dol. .	241	694	703	805	874	903	824	860	707
Average loan	Dollars..	532	853	1,003	1,195	1,263	1,297	1,250	1,250	1,250
Loans in default [4]	Mil. dol. .	(NA)	612.0	690.0	771.0	736.0	741.0	727.5	(NA)	(NA)
Default rate	Percent .	(NA)	11.6	8.3	8.2	7.2	6.8	6.2	(NA)	(NA)
College Work-Study:										
Number of recipients...	1,000...	425.0	819.1	728.4	685.5	672.7	676.7	841.0	827.0	752.0
Funds utilized [3]	Mil. dol. .	200	660	656	635	625	664	791	782	710
Average annual earnings	Dollars..	470	806	901	926	930	980	940	945	945
Stafford Loans: [5]										
Number of loans......	1,000...	1,017	2,904	3,730	4,381	4,584	4,558	3,978	3,958	4,140
Loan funds utilized [6] ...	Mil. dol. .	1,015	6,200	8,839	11,385	11,965	12,166	10,871	10,979	11,700
Average loan .. , ...	Dollars..	998	2,135	2,369	2,599	2,610	2,669	2,733	2,774	2,826
Loans in default [7]	Mil. dol. .	(NA)	1,440	4,256	6,963	8,457	10,454	13,134	16,561	19,452
Default rate [8]........	Percent .	(NA)	10.1	8.9	9.4	9.2	9.6	10.4	12.2	12.9

NA Not available.   X Not applicable.   [1] For 1970, data represents Educational Opportunity Grants Program.   [2] Formerly National Direct Student Loans.   [3] Includes institutional matching funds.   [4] Loans in default represents all loans in institutions' portfolio.   [5] Formerly Guaranteed Student Loans. Beginning with 1985, data include activity under the PLUS (Parent Loans for Undergraduate Students), FISL (Federally Insured Student Loans), and SLS (Supplemental Loans for Students) programs.   [6] Represents dollar amount of commitments.   [7] As of September 30 of year shown.   [8] Cumulative dollar amount of default claims to lenders, minus cumulative collections as a percent of all loans that have ever gone into repayment.

Source: U.S. Dept. of Education, Office of Postsecondary Education, unpublished data.

No. 268. Finances of Public Institutions of Higher Education, 1986 to 1989, and by State, 1989

[For academic years ending in year shown. Data provided by the State higher education finance officers]

YEAR AND STATE	FTE [1] enrollment (1,000)	APPROPRIATIONS FOR CURRENT OPERATIONS [2] Total (mil. dol.)	APPROPRIATIONS FOR CURRENT OPERATIONS [2] Per FTE [1] student (dol.)	NET TUITION REVENUES [3] Total (mil. dol.)	NET TUITION REVENUES [3] Per FTE [1] student (dol.)	YEAR AND STATE	FTE [1] enrollment (1,000)	APPROPRIATIONS FOR CURRENT OPERATIONS [2] Total (mil. dol.)	APPROPRIATIONS FOR CURRENT OPERATIONS [2] Per FTE [1] student (dol.)	NET TUITION REVENUES [3] Total (mil. dol.)	NET TUITION REVENUES [3] Per FTE [1] student (dol.)
Total, 1986 ..	6,974.3	26,028.0	3,732	7,875.0	1,129	MN	169.4	716.8	4,231	226.8	1,339
Total, 1987 ..	7,048.2	27,705.0	3,931	8,467.0	1,201	MS	84.5	282.5	3,343	123.6	1,463
Total, 1988 ..	7,231.1	29,363.0	4,071	9,233.0	1,280	MO	138.9	496.9	3,577	209.0	1,505
						MT	26.6	92.8	3,491	21.2	797
Total, 1989	**7,436.9**	**31,255.0**	**4,203**	**10,165.0**	**1,367**	NE.......	62.3	198.9	3,191	72.1	1,157
AL........	144.3	557.8	3,865	215.7	1,495	NV.......	25.9	106.3	4,100	28.5	1,099
AK........	13.9	137.3	9,879	20.4	1,468	NH	24.6	68.4	2,782	84.4	3,432
AZ........	139.1	548.6	3,944	198.4	1,426	NJ........	161.1	910.1	5,648	250.2	1,553
AR........	58.6	220.7	3,767	81.4	1,389	NM	59.2	261.0	4,405	56.6	955
CA........	1055.2	5,177.7	4,907	546.3	518	NY........	420.5	2,495.3	5,934	512.9	1,220
CO	122.8	350.4	2,853	249.0	2,027	NC	205.2	1,042.7	5,082	170.5	831
CT........	61.3	388.7	6,345	97.7	1,595	ND	31.1	87.1	2,803	44.9	1,445
DE........	21.1	98.0	4,649	82.0	3,890	OH	323.3	1,096.5	3,392	672.2	2,079
DC........	9.7	74.3	7,695	6.3	653	OK	103.6	382.9	3,698	115.2	1,113
FL........	258.9	1,290.6	4,984	274.8	1,061	OR	98.5	373.8	3,796	132.0	1,340
GA	170.7	722.9	4,235	209.7	1,229	PA	270.4	1,080.7	3,996	738.5	2,731
HI	27.9	201.6	7,229	20.0	717	RI	27.5	121.1	4,402	52.6	1,912
ID	31.5	139.5	4,431	21.5	683	SC.......	108.2	409.9	3,790	170.0	1,572
IL	353.8	1,291.3	3,650	369.5	1,044	SD.......	18.2	56.9	3,122	33.2	1,821
IN	161.2	627.8	3,894	324.0	2,010	TN.......	129.5	545.3	4,210	181.0	1,397
IA	96.6	401.4	4,155	184.6	1,911	TX.......	584.4	1,700.5	2,910	560.9	960
KS.......	98.8	367.9	3,722	124.6	1,261	UT.......	57.1	233.0	4,079	69.1	1,210
KY.......	101.2	368.5	3,643	137.7	1,361	VT.......	15.2	35.5	2,337	83.4	5,491
LA.......	120.0	316.2	2,634	199.2	1,660	VA.......	198.9	772.6	3,885	347.0	1,745
ME	29.5	152.4	5,167	44.0	1,492	WA	149.6	644.4	4,307	160.9	1,075
MD	153.1	613.9	4,011	253.6	1,657	WV.......	55.6	162.2	2,918	65.1	1,171
MA	124.9	658.6	5,273	187.5	1,501	WI........	188.2	757.9	4,028	333.3	1,771
MI	325.0	1,293.5	3,980	785.4	2,417	WY	20.5	123.4	6,028	16.4	801

[1] Full-time equivalent (FTE). Credit and non-credit program enrollment including summer session. Excludes medical enrollments. [2] State and local appropriations. Includes aid to students attending in-State public institutions. Excludes sums for research, agriculture stations and cooperative extension, and hospitals and medical schools. [3] Excludes appropriated aid to students attending in-State public institutions.

Source: Research Associates of Washington, Washington, DC, *State Profiles: Financing Public Higher Education*, annual.

No. 269. Institutions of Higher Education—Charges: 1975 to 1990

[In dollars. Estimated. Data are for the entire academic year ending in year shown. Figures are average charges per full-time equivalent student. Room and board are based on full-time students]

ACADEMIC CONTROL AND YEAR	TUITION AND REQUIRED FEES [1]				BOARD RATES [2]				DORMITORY CHARGES			
	All institutions	2-yr. colleges	4-yr. colleges	Other 4-yr. schools	All institutions	2-yr. colleges	4-yr. colleges	Other 4-yr. schools	All institutions	2-yr. colleges	4-yr. colleges	Other 4-yr. schools
Public:												
1975	432	277	599	448	625	638	634	613	506	424	527	497
1980	583	355	840	662	867	893	898	833	715	574	750	703
1985	971	584	1,386	1,117	1,241	1,302	1,276	1,201	1,196	921	1,237	1,200
1988	1,218	706	1,726	1,407	1,454	1,417	1,482	1,434	1,378	943	1,410	1,409
1989	1,285	730	1,846	1,515	1,533	1,488	1,576	1,504	1,457	965	1,483	1,506
1990, prel. .	1,367	758	2,006	1,631	1,638	1,609	1,720	1,572	1,516	958	1,563	1,554
Private:												
1975	2,117	1,367	2,614	1,954	700	660	771	666	586	564	691	536
1980	3,130	2,062	3,811	3,020	955	923	1,078	912	827	766	1,001	768
1985	5,315	3,485	6,843	5,135	1,462	1,294	1,647	1,405	1,426	1,424	1,753	1,309
1988	6,988	4,161	8,771	6,574	1,775	1,537	2,060	1,687	1,748	1,380	2,244	1,593
1989	7,461	4,817	9,451	7,172	1,880	1,609	2,269	1,762	1,849	1,540	2,353	1,686
1990, prel. .	8,174	5,324	10,400	7,815	1,951	1,800	2,345	1,825	1,931	1,648	2,420	1,783

[1] For in-State students. [2] Beginning 1988, rates reflect 20 meals per week, rather than meals served 7 days a week.
Source: U.S. National Center for Education Statistics, *Digest of Education Statistics*, annual.

No. 270. Voluntary Financial Support of Higher Education: 1970 to 1990

[For school years ending in years shown; enrollment as of fall of preceding year. Voluntary support, as defined in Gift Reporting Standards, excludes income from endowment and other invested funds as well as all support received from Federal, State, and local governments and their agencies]

ITEM	Unit	1970	1980	1984	1985	1986	1987	1988	1989	1990
Estimated support, total [1]	**Mil. dol**	**1,780**	**3,800**	**5,600**	**6,320**	**7,400**	**8,500**	**8,200**	**8,925**	**9,800**
Individuals	Mil. dol.	822	1,757	2,621	2,876	3,606	4,412	3,969	4,369	4,770
Alumni	Mil. dol.	381	910	1,305	1,460	1,825	2,346	2,042	2,292	2,540
Business corporations	Mil. dol.	269	696	1,271	1,574	1,702	1,819	1,853	1,947	2,170
Foundations	Mil. dol.	434	903	1,081	1,175	1,363	1,513	1,607	1,742	1,920
Religious denominations.	Mil. dol.	102	155	190	208	211	204	197	237	240
Current operations.	Mil. dol.	951	2,250	3,405	3,800	4,022	4,420	4,666	5,045	5,440
Capital purposes.	Mil. dol.	829	1,550	2,195	2,520	3,378	4,080	3,534	3,880	4,360
Enrollment, higher education . . .	1,000. .	8,094	11,570	12,465	12,242	12,247	12,504	12,768	13,043	13,087
Support per student.	Dollars.	220	328	449	516	604	680	642	684	749
In **1989-90** dollars	Dollars.	733	537	561	620	706	776	704	717	749
Expenditures, higher education . .	Bil. dol.	24.7	62.5	89.6	98.3	105.7	115.9	123.7	131.4	143.2
Expenditures per student	Dollars.	3,052	5,402	7,188	8,030	8,631	9,268	9,688	10,074	10,942
In **1989-90** dollars	Dollars.	10,173	8,841	8,974	9,651	10,083	10,580	10,623	10,560	10,942
Institutions reporting support	Number	1,045	1,019	1,118	1,114	1,194	1,174	1,142	1,132	1,056
Total support reported	**Mil. dol**	**1,472**	**3,055**	**4,686**	**5,295**	**6,332**	**7,323**	**7,041**	**7,546**	**8,214**
Private 4-year institutions	Mil. dol.	1,154	2,178	3,146	3,522	4,164	4,844	4,466	4,847	5,072
Public 4-year institutions.	Mil. dol.	292	856	1,504	1,728	2,104	2,413	2,506	2,625	3,056
2-year colleges	Mil. dol.	26	20	35	45	64	65	69	74	85

[1] Includes other contributions not shown separately.
Source: Council for Aid to Education, New York, NY, *Voluntary Support of Education*, annual.

No. 271. Institutions of Higher Education—Average Salaries and Fringe Benefits for Faculty Members, by Type of Control: 1970 to 1991

[In thousands of dollars. For academic year ending in year shown. Figures are for 9 months teaching for full-time faculty members in 4-year colleges and universities]

TYPE OF CONTROL AND ACADEMIC RANK	1970	1975	1980	1984	1985	1986	1987	1988	1989	1990	1991
AVERAGE SALARIES											
Public: All ranks	13.1	16.6	22.1	29.4	31.2	33.4	35.8	37.2	39.6	41.9	44.0
Professor	17.3	21.7	28.8	37.1	39.6	42.3	45.3	47.2	50.1	53.2	55.8
Associate professor.	13.2	16.7	21.9	28.4	30.2	32.2	34.2	35.6	37.9	40.3	42.2
Assistant professor	10.9	13.7	18.0	23.5	25.0	26.7	28.5	29.6	31.7	33.5	35.2
Instructor.	9.1	11.2	14.8	19.1	19.5	20.9	21.8	22.2	23.9	25.0	26.3
Private: [1] All ranks	13.1	16.6	22.1	31.1	33.0	35.4	37.8	39.7	42.4	45.1	47.0
Professor	17.8	22.4	30.1	41.5	44.1	47.0	50.3	52.2	55.9	59.6	61.6
Associate professor.	12.6	16.0	21.0	29.4	30.9	32.9	34.9	36.6	38.8	41.2	43.2
Assistant professor	10.3	13.0	17.0	23.7	25.0	26.8	28.3	30.1	31.9	34.0	35.5
Instructor.	8.6	10.9	13.3	18.4	19.0	19.8	20.4	22.7	24.1	26.0	26.2
AVERAGE FRINGE BENEFITS											
All ranks combined:											
Public.	1.9	2.5	3.9	6.0	7.0	7.3	7.8	8.2	9.0	9.8	10.5
Private [1]	2.2	2.8	4.1	6.4	7.2	8.0	8.6	9.2	10.0	10.9	11.6

[1] Excludes church-related colleges and universities.
Source: Maryse Eymonerie Associates/American Association of University Professors, Washington, DC, *AAUP Annual Report on the Economic Status of the Profession.*

Education

No. 272. Institutions of Higher Education—Tenure Status of Full-Time Faculty, by Type and Control of Institution and Rank and Sex of Faculty: 1990

[In percent. Data are for those institutions of higher education reporting tenure status. Excludes schools with no tenure]

TYPE OF INSTITUTION AND CONTROL	Total faculty	ACADEMIC RANK						SEX	
		Profes-sor	Asso-ciate pro-fessor	Assis-tant pro-fessor	Instruc-tor	Lecturer	No aca-demic rank	Male	Female
All institutions.	63.5	95.6	81.0	19.7	6.9	7.8	68.7	69.7	48.5
4-year	62.3	95.7	80.6	17.0	4.5	6.7	17.9	68.8	44.6
University	65.0	96.9	85.0	9.7	3.8	2.5	0.3	71.2	43.6
Other 4-year	60.4	94.7	77.7	21.2	4.7	10.5	29.4	67.0	45.1
2-year	71.6	94.2	85.6	52.0	17.1	36.6	75.7	76.7	64.4
Public institutions	65.9	96.2	83.9	22.9	8.7	9.3	70.3	71.9	51.4
4-year	64.6	96.4	83.7	19.3	5.8	8.0	10.2	71.0	46.7
University	66.0	97.1	87.9	10.3	4.2	2.6	0.3	72.2	44.4
Other 4-year	63.5	95.9	80.4	25.5	6.5	12.2	20.7	70.1	48.0
2-year	72.0	94.4	85.9	52.9	17.5	36.8	76.0	77.0	65.0
Private institutions.	57.0	93.9	73.8	12.7	1.7	1.6	41.4	63.7	40.3
4-year	57.1	93.9	73.8	12.5	1.6	1.6	32.8	63.7	40.3
University	62.2	96.3	75.9	8.3	2.1	2.1	(NA)	68.2	41.3
Other 4-year	54.6	92.3	72.8	14.3	1.5	0.8	39.1	61.2	39.9
2-year	51.5	87.9	70.4	27.3	6.8	(NA)	63.3	61.1	41.8

NA Not available.

Source: U.S. National Center for Education Statistics, *Digest of Education Statistics*, 1991.

No. 273. College Freshmen—Summary Characteristics: 1970 to 1991

[In percent. As of fall for first-time full-time freshmen. Based on sample survey and subject to sampling error; see source]

CHARACTERISTIC	1970	1980	1984	1985	1986	1987	1988	1989	1990	1991
Sex: Male	55	49	48	48	48	47	46	46	46	47
Female.	45	51	52	52	52	53	54	54	54	53
Average grade in high school:										
A- to A+.	16	21	20	21	23	21	24	23	23	24
B- to B+.	58	60	58	59	56	59	58	59	58	57
C to C+.	27	19	21	20	20	19	19	17	19	19
D	1	1	1	1	1	1	1	-	-	-
Political orientation:										
Liberal	34	20	20	21	22	22	22	22	23	(NA)
Middle of the road	45	60	58	57	56	56	54	54	55	(NA)
Conservative.	17	17	19	19	19	18	20	21	20	(NA)
Probable field of study:										
Arts and humanities.	16	9	8	8	9	9	10	9	9	8
Biological sciences	4	4	4	4	4	4	4	4	4	4
Business	16	24	26	27	26	27	26	25	21	18
Education.	11	7	7	7	8	9	9	9	10	9
Engineering	9	12	11	11	11	10	10	10	8	10
Physical science	2	3	3	2	2	2	2	2	2	2
Social science.	14	7	7	8	8	9	9	10	10	8
Professional.	4	15	14	13	12	11	12	13	15	18
Technical.	(NA)	6	5	5	4	3	2	3	4	4
Data processing/computer programming	(NA)	2	2	2	2	1	1	1	1	1
Other [1]	(NA)	(NA)	16	16	15	16	16	15	16	17
Communications.	(NA)	2	2	2	2	3	3	3	2	2
Computer science.	(NA)	1	3	2	2	2	2	2	2	2
Recipient of financial aid:										
Pell grant.	(NA)	33	20	19	17	17	20	22	23	23
Supplemental educational opportunity grant	(NA)	8	6	5	5	6	6	6	7	7
State scholarship or grant.	(NA)	16	14	14	14	16	14	15	16	13
College grant	(NA)	13	17	19	18	13	20	20	22	22
Federal guaranteed student loan	(NA)	21	23	23	25	22	22	23	23	22
Perkins loan [2]	(NA)	9	6	6	7	5	3	2	8	7
College loan	(NA)	4	4	4	4	4	5	6	6	5
College work-study grant.	(NA)	15	9	10	10	10	10	10	10	11
Attitudes—agree or strongly agree:										
Activities of married women are best confined to home and family.	48	27	23	22	20	26	26	26	25	26
Capital punishment should be abolished	56	34	26	27	26	24	23	21	22	21
Legalize marijuana	38	39	23	22	21	20	19	17	19	21
There is too much concern for the rights of criminals.	52	66	(NA)	(NA)	(NA)	68	69	69	(NA)	65
Abortion should be legalized	(NA)	54	54	55	59	59	57	65	65	63

- Represents or rounds to zero.   NA Not available.   [1] Includes other fields of study and undecided, not shown separately.
[2] National Direct Student Loan prior to 1990.

Source: The Higher Education Research Institute, University of California, Los Angeles, CA, *The American Freshman: National Norms*, annual.

No. 274. Freshman Enrollment in Remedial Courses, by Institutional Characteristic: 1989

[In percent, except number of freshmen. As of fall. Remedial courses are those developed for students lacking skills necessary to perform college-level work as required by the institution. Based on survey and subject to sampling error; for details, see source]

INSTITUTIONAL CHARACTERISTIC	Number of freshmen (1,000)	INSTITUTIONS OFFERING COURSES				FRESHMEN TAKING COURSES			
		Total	Reading	Writing	Math	Total	Reading	Writing	Math
All institutions	2,242	74	58	65	68	30	13	16	21
Control: Public	1,784	91	82	87	89	32	13	17	23
Private	457	58	34	44	47	22	12	11	12
Type: 2-year	1,069	90	82	84	84	36	16	20	26
4-year	1,173	64	41	53	57	24	9	12	15
Size of institution:									
Fewer than 1,000	109	60	76	47	48	26	9	15	18
1,000 to 4,999	650	78	64	69	75	33	16	17	22
5,000 or more	1,483	87	76	81	81	29	11	15	20

Source: U.S. National Center for Education Statistics, "College Level Remedial Education in the Fall of 1989," FRSS-38.

No. 275. Foreign (Nonimmigrant) Student Enrollment in Institutions of Higher Education, by Region of Origin, 1976 to 1991, and by Field of Study, 1980 and 1990

[For fall of the previous year]

REGION OF ORIGIN	ENROLLMENT (1,000)									PERCENT ENROLLED IN—					
	1976	1980	1985	1986	1987	1988	1989	1990	1991	Engineering		Science[1]		Business	
										1980	1990	1980	1990	1980	1990
All regions	179	286	342	344	350	356	366	387	408	25	19	8	9	16	19
Africa	25	36	40	34	32	28	26	25	24	20	15	9	8	19	20
Nigeria	11	16	18	13	12	8	6	4	4	19	12	9	5	22	20
Asia [2]	97	165	200	210	218	224	232	245	263	32	23	8	10	16	18
China: Taiwan.	11	18	23	24	26	27	29	31	34	17	26	15	10	17	17
Hong Kong	12	10	10	11	11	11	11	11	13	22	17	9	6	26	33
India	10	9	15	16	18	21	23	26	29	31	35	16	11	21	16
Indonesia	1	2	7	8	9	9	9	9	10	27	20	7	4	21	37
Iran	20	51	17	14	12	10	9	7	6	45	29	7	14	11	7
Japan	7	12	13	13	15	18	24	30	37	7	5	5	3	19	21
Malaysia	2	4	22	23	22	19	16	14	14	13	30	14	4	22	28
Saudi Arabia.	3	10	8	7	6	5	5	4	4	30	26	4	4	14	14
South Korea.	3	5	16	19	20	21	21	22	23	17	19	11	12	15	15
Thailand	7	7	7	7	6	6	7	7	7	17	14	6	4	26	35
Europe	14	23	33	34	36	39	43	46	50	15	12	9	8	14	21
Latin America [3]	30	42	49	45	43	45	45	48	48	20	14	8	6	14	19
Mexico	5	6	6	5	5	6	6	7	7	16	13	7	8	11	18
Venezuela	5	10	10	7	5	4	3	3	3	30	17	8	7	11	19
North America	10	16	16	16	16	16	17	19	19	8	8	6	6	13	15
Canada	10	15	15	15	16	16	16	18	18	8	8	6	6	12	14
Oceania	3	4	4	4	4	4	4	4	4	5	5	7	6	16	18

[1] Physical and life sciences.   [2] Includes countries not shown separately.   [3] Includes Central America, Caribbean, and South America.

Source: Institute of International Education, New York, NY, *Open Doors*, annual, (copyright).

No. 276. Higher Education Registrations in Foreign Languages: 1960 to 1990

[As of fall]

ITEM	1960	1965	1968	1970	1974	1977	1980	1983	1986	1990
Registrations [1] (1,000)	[2]647.1	1,034.9	1,127.4	1,111.5	946.6	933.5	924.8	966.0	1,003.2	1,183.5
Index (1960=100).	100.0	159.9	174.2	171.8	146.3	144.3	142.9	149.3	155.0	182.9
By selected language (1,000):										
Spanish	178.7	310.3	364.9	389.2	362.2	376.7	379.4	386.2	411.3	533.6
French	228.8	371.6	388.1	359.3	253.1	246.1	248.4	270.1	275.3	272.6
German	146.1	213.0	216.0	202.6	152.1	135.4	126.9	128.2	121.0	133.4
Italian	11.1	22.9	30.4	34.2	33.0	33.3	34.8	38.7	40.9	49.7
Japanese	1.7	3.4	4.3	6.6	9.6	10.7	11.5	16.1	23.5	45.7
Russian	30.6	33.7	40.7	36.1	32.5	27.8	24.0	30.4	34.0	44.4
Latin	[2]25.7	39.6	35.0	27.6	25.2	24.4	25.0	24.2	25.0	28.2
Chinese	1.8	3.4	5.1	6.2	10.6	9.8	11.4	13.2	16.9	19.5
Ancient Greek	[2]12.7	19.5	19.3	16.7	24.4	25.8	22.1	19.4	17.6	16.4
Hebrew	3.8	8.1	10.2	16.6	22.4	19.4	19.4	18.2	15.6	13.0
Portuguese	1.0	3.0	4.0	5.1	5.1	5.0	4.9	4.4	5.1	6.1
Arabic	0.5	0.9	1.1	1.3	2.0	3.1	3.5	3.4	3.4	3.5
12 languages as percent of total.	99.3	99.6	99.3	99.1	98.5	98.3	98.5	98.6	98.6	98.5

[1] Includes other foreign languages, not shown separately.   [2] Estimated.

Source: Association of Departments of Foreign Languages, New York, NY, *ADFL Bulletin*, vol. 23, No. 3, and earlier issues, (copyright).

No. 277. Salary Offers to Candidates for Degrees, by Field of Study: 1980 to 1991

[**In dollars.** Data are average beginning salaries based on offers made by business, industrial, government, and nonprofit and educational employers to graduating students. Data from representative colleges throughout the United States]

FIELD OF STUDY	BACHELOR'S				MASTER'S [1]				DOCTOR'S			
	Monthly, 1980	Annual			Monthly, 1980	Annual			Monthly, 1980	Annual		
		1989	1990	1991		1989	1990	1991		1989	1990	1991
Accounting	1,293	25,290	26,391	26,642	1,517	28,874	29,647	30,996	(NA)	(NA)	(NA)	(NA)
Business, general [2] . .	1,218	22,274	23,529	24,019	1,795	33,903	36,175	35,241	(NA)	(NA)	(NA)	(NA)
Marketing [3]	1,145	22,523	23,543	23,713	1,794	34,462	35,440	43,182	(NA)	(NA)	(NA)	(NA)
Engineering:												
Civil	1,554	26,735	28,136	29,658	1,753	30,723	32,336	34,551	2,089	37,214	44,481	43,060
Chemical	1,801	32,949	35,122	37,492	1,947	36,131	37,862	40,457	2,452	47,853	50,524	52,992
Computer.	(NA)	30,413	31,490	32,280	(NA)	37,183	35,748	38,348	(NA)	53,380	50,526	56,584
Electrical [4]	1,690	30,661	31,778	33,190	1,912	36,435	37,526	38,804	2,534	48,666	53,147	54,612
Mechanical	1,703	30,539	32,064	33,999	1,893	35,260	36,506	38,114	2,426	45,893	49,887	46,866
Nuclear [5]	1,668	31,281	31,750	32,175	1,831	34,024	36,728	38,086	(NA)	(NA)	(NA)	(NA)
Petroleum	1,987	32,987	35,202	38,882	(NA)	38,475	38,412	43,608	(NA)	(NA)	(NA)	(NA)
Engineering tech. .	1,585	28,310	29,318	30,098	(NA)	(NA)	(NA)	(NA)	(NA)	(NA)	(NA)	(NA)
Chemistry	1,459	26,698	27,494	26,836	1,688	32,157	32,320	33,575	2,261	43,215	45,356	47,911
Mathematics [6]	1,475	26,789	27,032	27,370	1,685	31,498	30,069	30,061	2,199	37,500	42,775	41,146
Physics.	(NA)	28,296	28,002	29,227	(NA)	29,889	31,480	35,207	2,303	42,632	41,486	39,913
Humanities	1,074	23,010	23,213	23,567	1,309	25,799	(NA)	(NA)	(NA)	(NA)	(NA)	(NA)
Social sciences [7] . . .	1,072	20,205	21,627	21,375	1,298	23,814	(NA)	(NA)	(NA)	(NA)	(NA)	(NA)
Computer science . .	1,558	28,557	29,804	30,696	1,858	35,823	36,849	37,894	(NA)	50,049	54,788	58,300

NA Not available.   [1] Candidates with 1 year or less of full-time nonmilitary employment.   [2] For master's degree, offers are after nontechnical undergraduate degree.   [3] Includes distribution.   [4] Includes computer engineering for 1988.   [5] Includes engineering physics.   [6] Beginning 1989, excludes actuarial.   [7] Excludes economics.

Source: College Placement Council, Inc., Bethlehem, PA, Salary Survey, *A Study of Beginning Offers*, annual, (copyright).

No. 278. Earned Degrees Conferred, by Level of Degree and Sex, 1950 to 1989 and Projections, 1990 and 1995

[**In thousands, except percent.** Beginning 1960, includes Alaska and Hawaii. See *Historical Statistics, Colonial Times to 1970*, series H-751-763 for similar data. See also Appendix III]

YEAR ENDING	DEGREES		ASSOCIATE'S		BACHELOR'S		MASTER'S		FIRST PROFES- SIONAL		DOCTOR'S	
	Total	Percent male	Male	Female	Male	Female	Male	Female	Male	Female	Male	Female
1950 [1]	497	75.7	(NA)	(NA)	329	103	41	17	(NA)	(NA)	6	1
1960 [1]	477	65.8	(NA)	(NA)	254	138	51	24	(NA)	(NA)	9	1
1965	664	61.6	(NA)	(NA)	289	213	78	40	27	1	15	2
1970	1,271	59.2	117	89	451	341	126	83	33	2	26	4
1971	1,393	59.0	144	108	476	364	138	92	36	2	28	5
1972	1,509	58.7	166	126	501	387	150	102	41	3	28	5
1973	1,586	58.1	175	141	518	404	154	109	46	4	29	6
1974	1,653	57.5	189	155	527	418	158	119	49	5	27	6
1975	1,666	56.1	191	169	505	418	162	131	49	7	27	7
1976	1,726	55.7	210	181	505	421	167	145	53	10	26	8
1977	1,741	54.7	211	196	496	424	168	149	52	12	25	8
1978	1,744	53.3	205	208	487	434	161	150	52	14	24	8
1979	1,727	52.1	192	211	477	444	153	148	53	16	24	9
1980	1,731	51.1	184	217	474	456	151	147	53	17	23	10
1981	1,752	50.3	189	228	470	465	147	149	53	19	23	10
1982	1,788	49.8	197	238	473	480	146	150	52	20	22	10
1983	1,822	49.6	207	249	479	490	145	145	51	22	22	11
1984	1,819	49.6	203	250	482	492	144	141	51	23	22	11
1985	1,828	49.3	203	252	483	497	143	143	50	25	22	11
1986	1,830	49.0	196	250	486	502	144	145	49	25	22	12
1987	1,825	48.4	192	246	481	510	141	148	47	25	22	12
1988	1,834	48.0	190	245	477	518	145	154	45	25	23	12
1989	1,870	47.3	185	250	483	535	149	161	45	26	23	13
1990, proj.	1,916	46.2	185	260	485	558	149	170	43	28	24	14
1995, proj.	2,062	46.3	203	277	510	590	165	189	53	35	24	16

NA Not available.   [1] First-professional degrees are included with bachelor's degrees.

Source: U.S. National Center for Education Statistics, *Digest of Education Statistics*, annual.

No. 279. Earned Degrees Conferred, by Field of Study and Level of Degree: 1971 to 1989

LEVEL AND FIELD OF STUDY	1971	1980	1985	1986	1987	1988	1989	PERCENT FEMALE	
								1971	1989
Bachelor's, total	839,730	929,417	979,477	987,823	991,339	994,829	1,017,667	43.4	52.5
Agriculture and natural resources	12,672	22,802	18,107	16,823	14,991	14,222	13,488	4.2	31.1
Architecture and environmental design	5,570	9,132	9,325	9,119	8,922	8,603	9,191	11.9	39.3
Area and ethnic studies	2,582	2,840	2,867	3,060	3,340	3,453	3,949	52.4	59.2
Business and management	114,865	185,361	233,351	238,160	241,156	243,725	246,659	9.1	46.7
Communications [1]	10,802	28,616	42,083	43,091	45,408	46,726	48,625	35.3	60.4
Computer and information sciences	2,388	11,154	38,878	41,889	39,664	34,523	30,637	13.6	30.7
Education	176,614	118,169	88,161	87,221	87,115	91,287	96,988	74.5	77.7
Engineering [1]	50,046	68,893	96,105	95,953	93,074	88,706	85,273	0.8	13.6
Foreign languages	19,945	11,133	9,954	10,102	10,184	10,045	10,774	74.6	73.3
Health sciences	25,190	63,607	64,513	64,535	63,206	60,754	59,111	77.1	84.9
Home economics	11,167	18,411	15,555	15,288	14,942	14,855	14,717	97.3	90.6
Law	545	683	1,157	1,197	1,178	1,303	1,976	5.0	60.3
Letters	64,933	33,497	34,091	35,434	37,133	39,551	43,323	65.5	67.1
Liberal/general studies	5,461	20,069	19,191	19,248	21,365	21,790	23,459	29.0	57.2
Library and archival sciences	1,013	398	202	157	139	123	122	92.0	86.9
Life sciences	35,743	46,370	38,445	38,524	38,114	36,755	36,079	29.1	50.2
Mathematics	24,801	11,378	15,146	16,306	16,489	15,904	15,237	38.0	46.0
Military sciences	357	251	299	256	383	350	419	0.3	9.8
Multi/interdisciplinary studies	8,306	14,404	15,727	15,700	16,402	17,353	18,213	28.4	53.8
Parks and recreation	1,621	5,753	4,593	4,433	4,107	4,078	4,171	34.7	59.0
Philosophy, religion, and theology	11,890	13,276	12,439	11,841	11,686	11,526	11,733	25.5	29.9
Physical sciences	21,412	23,410	23,732	21,731	19,974	17,806	17,204	13.8	29.7
Psychology	37,880	41,962	39,811	40,521	42,868	45,003	48,516	44.5	70.8
Protective services	2,045	15,015	12,510	12,704	12,930	13,367	14,626	9.2	38.0
Public affairs [2]	6,252	18,422	13,838	13,878	14,161	14,294	15,254	60.2	67.6
Social sciences [2]	155,236	103,519	91,461	93,703	96,185	100,288	107,714	36.8	44.4
Visual and performing arts	30,394	40,892	37,936	36,949	36,223	36,638	37,781	59.7	61.5
Unclassified	-	-	-	-	-	-	1,801	2,428	41.9
Master's, total	230,509	298,081	286,251	288,567	289,557	299,317	309,762	40.1	51.9
Agriculture and natural resources	2,457	3,976	3,928	3,801	3,523	3,479	3,245	5.9	31.2
Architecture and environmental design	1,705	3,139	3,275	3,260	3,142	3,159	3,378	13.8	35.1
Area and ethnic studies	1,032	852	879	927	851	903	978	38.3	49.2
Business and management	26,481	55,006	67,527	67,137	67,496	69,655	73,154	3.9	33.6
Communications [1]	1,856	3,082	3,669	3,823	3,937	3,925	4,233	34.6	59.6
Computer and information sciences	1,588	3,647	7,101	8,070	8,491	9,197	9,392	10.3	27.9
Education	88,952	103,951	76,137	76,353	75,501	77,867	82,238	56.2	75.3
Engineering [1]	16,443	16,243	21,557	21,661	22,693	23,388	24,541	1.1	13.0
Foreign languages	4,755	2,236	1,724	1,721	1,746	1,844	1,911	65.5	68.5
Health sciences	5,445	15,068	17,383	18,624	18,426	18,665	19,255	55.9	78.1
Home economics	1,452	2,690	2,383	2,298	2,070	2,053	2,174	93.9	85.7
Law	955	1,817	1,796	1,924	1,943	1,880	2,098	4.8	28.9
Letters	11,148	6,807	5,934	6,291	6,123	6,194	6,608	60.2	65.6
Liberal/general studies	549	1,373	1,180	1,154	1,126	1,354	1,408	44.3	64.8
Library and archival sciences	7,001	5,374	3,893	3,626	3,815	3,713	3,940	81.3	79.3
Life sciences	5,728	6,510	5,059	5,013	4,954	4,784	4,933	33.6	49.6
Mathematics	5,191	2,860	2,882	3,159	3,321	3,442	3,424	29.2	39.9
Military sciences	2	46	119	83	83	49	-	-	-
Multi/interdisciplinary studies	1,157	3,579	3,184	3,104	3,041	3,098	3,225	30.9	39.0
Parks and recreation	218	647	544	495	476	461	460	29.8	53.7
Philosophy, religion, and theology	4,036	5,126	5,519	5,630	5,989	5,913	5,899	27.1	36.3
Physical sciences	6,367	5,219	5,796	5,902	5,652	5,733	5,737	13.3	26.7
Psychology	4,431	7,806	8,408	8,293	8,204	7,872	8,579	37.2	67.4
Protective services	194	1,805	1,235	1,074	1,019	1,024	1,046	10.3	31.0
Public affairs [2]	8,215	18,413	16,045	16,300	17,032	17,290	17,928	49.2	64.3
Social sciences [2]	16,476	12,101	10,380	10,428	10,397	10,294	10,854	28.5	40.2
Visual and performing arts	6,675	8,708	8,714	8,416	8,506	7,937	8,234	47.4	56.3
Unclassified	-	-	-	-	-	4,144	890	44.3	
Doctorate's, total	32,107	32,615	32,943	33,653	34,120	34,870	35,759	14.3	36.5
Agriculture and natural resources	1,086	991	1,213	1,158	1,049	1,142	1,184	2.9	19.6
Architecture and environmental design	36	79	89	73	92	98	86	8.3	26.7
Area and ethnic studies	144	151	137	157	132	140	110	16.7	48.2
Business and management	807	792	866	969	1,098	1,109	1,150	2.9	26.6
Communications [1]	145	193	234	223	275	234	248	13.1	44.8
Computer and information sciences	128	240	248	344	374	428	538	2.3	15.1
Education	6,403	7,941	7,151	7,110	6,909	6,553	6,783	21.2	57.3
Engineering [1]	3,638	2,507	3,230	3,410	3,820	4,191	4,533	0.6	8.8
Foreign languages	781	549	437	448	441	411	422	38.0	60.0
Health sciences	459	771	1,199	1,241	1,213	1,261	1,439	16.3	57.5
Home economics	123	192	276	311	207	309	263	61.0	77.6
Law	20	40	105	54	120	89	76	0.0	39.5
Letters	1,857	1,500	1,239	1,215	1,181	1,172	1,238	28.0	54.8
Life sciences	3,645	3,636	3,432	3,358	3,423	3,629	3,533	16.3	36.7
Mathematics	1,199	724	699	742	725	750	882	7.8	19.4
Multi/interdisciplinary studies	80	295	285	319	261	261	257	13.8	38.5
Philosophy, religion, and theology	866	1,693	1,608	1,660	1,658	1,604	1,629	5.8	16.3
Physical sciences	4,390	3,089	3,403	3,551	3,672	3,809	3,852	5.6	19.7
Psychology	1,782	2,768	2,908	3,088	3,123	2,987	3,263	24.0	56.2
Public affairs [2]	185	372	431	385	398	470	417	23.8	50.1
Social sciences [2]	3,659	3,219	2,851	2,955	2,916	2,781	2,878	13.9	32.6
Visual and performing arts	621	655	693	722	792	725	755	22.2	41.3
Other and unclassified	53	218	209	160	136	717	223	28.3	35.4

- Represents zero. [1] Includes technologies. [2] Includes history.
Source: U.S. National Center for Education Statistics, *Digest of Education Statistics*, annual.

No. 280. Degrees Conferred in Selected Professions: 1960 to 1989

[First professional degrees. See Appendix III]

TYPE OF DEGREE AND SEX OF RECIPIENT	1960	1970	1975	1980	1983	1984	1985	1986	1987	1988	1989 [1]
Medicine (M.D.):											
Institutions conferring degrees..	79	86	104	112	118	119	120	120	122	122	124
Degrees conferred, total......	7,032	8,314	12,447	14,902	15,484	15,813	16,041	15,938	15,620	15,358	15,454
Men.................	6,645	7,615	10,818	11,416	11,350	11,359	11,167	11,022	10,566	10,278	10,326
Women	387	699	1,629	3,486	4,134	4,454	4,874	4,916	5,054	5,080	5,128
Percent of total.........	5.5	8.4	13.1	23.4	26.7	28.2	30.4	30.8	32.4	33.1	33.2
Dentistry (D.D.S. or D.M.D.):											
Institutions conferring degrees..	45	48	52	58	59	60	59	59	58	57	58
Degrees conferred, total......	3,247	3,718	4,773	5,258	5,585	5,353	5,339	5,046	4,741	4,477	4,247
Men.................	3,221	3,684	4,627	4,558	4,631	4,302	4,233	3,907	3,603	3,300	3,139
Women	26	34	146	700	954	1,051	1,106	1,139	1,138	1,177	1,108
Percent of total.........	0.8	0.9	3.1	13.3	17.1	19.6	20.7	22.6	24.0	26.3	26.1
Law (LL.B. or J.D.):											
Institutions conferring degrees..	134	145	154	179	177	179	181	181	180	180	182
Degrees conferred, total......	9,240	14,916	29,296	35,647	36,853	37,012	37,491	35,844	36,172	35,397	35,567
Men.................	9,010	14,115	24,881	24,893	23,550	23,382	23,070	21,874	21,643	21,067	21,048
Women	230	801	4,415	10,754	13,303	13,630	14,421	13,970	14,529	14,330	14,519
Percent of total.........	2.5	5.4	15.1	30.2	36.1	36.8	38.5	39.0	40.2	40.5	40.8
Theological (B.D., M.Div., M.H.L.):											
Institutions conferring degrees..	(NA)	(NA)	(NA)	(NA)	(NA)	(NA)	(NA)	(NA)	(NA)	(NA)	(NA)
Degrees conferred, total......	(NA)	5,298	5,095	7,115	6,494	6,878	7,221	7,283	7,181	6,466	6,005
Men.................	(NA)	5,175	4,748	6,133	5,395	5,673	5,886	5,865	5,794	5,080	4,639
Women	(NA)	123	347	982	1,099	1,205	1,335	1,418	1,387	1,386	1,366
Percent of total.........	(NA)	2.3	6.8	13.8	16.9	17.5	18.5	19.5	19.3	21.4	22.7

NA Not available.　　[1] Preliminary.

Source: U.S. National Center for Education Statistics, *Digest of Education Statistics*, annual.

No. 281. Graduate Student Enrollment and Degrees Conferred in Selected Fields, by Race/Ethnicity: 1988-89

ITEM	NUMBER				PERCENT DISTRIBUTION			
	Total	Minority [1]	White [2]	Non-resident alien [3]	Total	Minority [1]	White [2]	Non-resident alien [3]
Graduate enrollment (1,000).....	1,472	167	1,153	151	100.0	11.3	78.3	10.3
Degrees conferred: [4]								
Masters................	308,872	33,193	241,607	34,072	100.0	10.7	78.2	11.0
Doctorates..............	35,692	3,117	24,895	7,680	100.0	8.7	69.7	21.5
SELECTED FIELD								
Agriculture and natural resources:								
Masters................	3,245	168	2,222	855	100.0	5.2	68.5	26.3
Doctorates..............	1,184	65	677	442	100.0	5.5	57.2	37.3
Business and management:								
Masters................	73,154	7,817	57,445	7,892	100.0	10.7	78.5	10.8
Doctorates..............	1,150	93	746	311	100.0	8.1	64.9	27.0
Computer and info. systems:								
Masters................	9,392	1,400	5,290	2,702	100.0	14.9	56.3	28.8
Doctorates..............	538	48	285	205	100.0	8.9	53.0	38.1
Engineering:								
Masters................	24,541	3,089	14,206	7,246	100.0	12.6	57.9	29.5
Doctorates..............	4,533	402	1,947	2,184	100.0	8.9	43.0	48.2
Mathematics:								
Masters................	3,424	282	2,123	1,019	100.0	8.2	62.0	29.8
Doctorates..............	882	49	413	420	100.0	5.6	46.8	47.6
Physical sciences:								
Masters................	5,737	469	3,962	1,306	100.0	8.2	69.1	22.8
Doctorates..............	3,852	284	2,436	1,132	100.0	7.4	63.2	29.4
Social sciences:								
Masters................	10,854	1,026	7,678	2,150	100.0	9.5	70.7	19.8
Doctorates..............	2,878	279	1,874	725	100.0	9.7	65.1	25.2

[1] American Indian/Alaskan native, non-Hispanic Black, Asian/Pacific Islander and Hispanic.　[2] Non-Hispanic.　[3] A person who is not a citizen or national of the U.S. who is in the country on a temporary basis and does not have the right to remain indefinitely.　[4] Includes degrees conferred in fields not shown separately. Excludes 890 masters degrees and 67 doctorate degrees for which racial/ethnic group was not available.

Source: U.S. National Center for Education Statistics, *Digest of Education Statistics*, 1991. (Data are collected biennially.)

No. 282. Earned Degrees Below Bachelor's, by Curriculum: 1984 to 1990

[Covers associate degrees and other awards based on post-secondary curriculums of less than 4 years in institutions of higher education]

FIELD OF STUDY	1984	1985	1986	1987	1988	1989	1990	PERCENT FEMALE 1984	PERCENT FEMALE 1990
All degrees..............	610,332	614,749	604,634	590,683	601,713	601,280	640,098	54.3	57.0
Agriculture and natural resources. ...	10,641	10,466	9,263	8,680	8,769	7,541	9,321	28.9	29.7
Architecture and environmental design.....................	1,927	1,939	2,016	2,260	2,520	2,452	2,528	84.3	86.9
Area and ethnic studies	64	69	115	266	172	208	242	60.9	72.7
Business and management.........	166,238	170,170	168,168	161,813	158,844	153,072	153,248	66.5	73.0
Communications [1].............	4,162	4,580	4,528	4,561	4,414	5,300	4,570	43.2	41.3
Computer and information sciences	16,111	15,896	13,307	11,972	11,936	10,321	13,373	49.1	54.2
Education	8,503	8,551	8,354	8,095	7,958	8,314	8,827	72.2	72.7
Engineering [1]...............	100,080	100,146	97,609	97,731	104,036	94,655	93,467	7.9	8.5
Foreign languages	372	427	526	484	584	629	707	.5	61.8
Health sciences	107,142	107,248	104,051	96,261	96,119	96,884	109,398	87.0	85.1
Home economics	14,344	14,966	14,760	14,333	15,142	15,286	18,511	75.0	76.3
Law	2,551	2,948	3,259	3,728	4,661	6,068	7,935	83.1	83.5
Letters	822	681	812	574	574	626	774	64.8	65.5
Liberal/general studies	109,451	107,814	109,529	109,764	114,882	119,577	129,783	54.9	58.8
Library and archival sciences	260	253	208	203	165	204	215	86.2	89.8
Life sciences	1,297	1,205	1,080	1,136	980	1,050	1,197	52.4	54.5
Mathematics	821	813	705	691	695	664	813	36.4	36.2
Military sciences	87	34	[2]1,000	[2]1,009	141	164	129	4.6	11.6
Multi/interdisciplinary studies	8,398	8,697	9,873	9,842	11,053	11,444	11,916	54.5	55.7
Parks and recreation	819	893	787	660	717	678	593	50.9	36.3
Philosophy, religion, and theology ...	1,740	1,830	1,810	1,371	1,427	1,502	1,593	44.3	45.9
Physical sciences	2,990	2,296	2,230	2,179	1,998	2,079	2,295	34.7	38.0
Psychology	1,147	1,032	1,005	1,068	1,105	1,143	1,143	67.0	74.3
Protective services	15,554	16,057	15,592	17,786	17,832	17,901	20,174	23.8	24.3
Public affairs	5,812	6,230	6,245	6,478	7,007	8,765	10,471	47.2	32.6
Social sciences	2,755	2,613	2,753	2,782	2,915	2,962	3,131	57.1	55.1
Visual and performing arts	26,244	24,358	24,015	24,327	23,107	21,438	22,790	32.7	33.7
Undistributed	-	2,537	1,034	629	1,960	10,353	10,954	(X)	47.7

- Represents zero. X Not applicable. [1] includes technologies. [2] Includes a certificate program.

Source: U.S. National Center for Education Statistics, *Digest of Education Statistics*, annual.

No. 283. High School Graduates Completing College: 1976 to 1986

[Cumulative percent of 1972, 1980, and 1982 high school graduates completing college. For highest level of degree attained. Based on survey and subject to sampling error, see source]

STUDENT CHARACTERISTIC	1972 HIGH SCHOOL SENIORS 1-2 year degrees by June—			1972 HIGH SCHOOL SENIORS Bachelor's degrees by June—			1980 HIGH SCHOOL SENIORS 1-2 year degrees by Feb.—		1980 HIGH SCHOOL SENIORS Bachelor's degrees by Feb. 1986	1982 high school seniors, 1-2 year degrees by Feb. 1986
	1976	1982	1986	1976	1980	1986	1984	1986		
Total	6.4	11.8	16.6	14.3	25.1	27.7	8.8	12.5	18.8	7.9
Sex:										
Male	5.6	10.8	15.8	13.3	27.5	30.1	7.7	10.8	18.4	5.9
Female.	7.2	12.6	17.3	15.3	22.9	25.4	9.9	14.1	19.2	9.6
Race/ethnicity:										
White [1]	6.9	12.1	17.0	15.6	27.0	29.4	9.0	12.5	20.8	7.9
Black [1]...............	2.1	9.4	14.6	7.8	14.7	19.2	6.4	10.4	10.1	7.1
Hispanic...............	3.3	9.1	13.7	3.1	9.7	10.9	9.2	14.7	6.8	9.5
Asian [1]...............	8.0	21.0	27.7	5.8	5.8	18.5	11.8	15.7	28.7	5.3
American Indian [1]	4.1	20.1	26.2	29.2	53.2	56.1	16.9	20.3	9.2	5.8
High school average:										
A.....................	7.9	13.5	19.0	41.9	59.3	60.7	8.2	11.3	49.0	3.9
A to B	7.4	13.0	17.0	23.5	39.3	42.4	12.6	15.9	28.5	7.1
B.....................	7.1	11.7	17.8	12.3	24.9	28.0	9.7	14.0	18.5	9.5
B to C	6.8	12.8	18.2	6.0	14.3	17.5	9.7	12.5	9.0	8.5
C.....................	2.6	7.7	12.8	2.4	6.1	7.7	5.4	10.0	2.5	7.2
D.....................	3.2	7.0	9.7	1.1	3.6	4.5	3.0	7.6	1.3	6.2
High school program:										
General	5.4	10.1	14.7	5.6	12.0	14.2	8.5	12.0	10.0	8.5
Academic	8.0	15.0	20.9	27.5	45.6	49.1	10.2	14.0	37.4	6.8
Vo/tech	4.7	7.9	10.9	1.3	4.3	5.4	9.1	12.6	3.4	9.2

[1] Non-Hispanic.

Source: U.S. National Center for Education Statistics, *Digest of Education Statistics*, 1989.

No. 284. Libraries—Number, by Type: 1980 to 1990

TYPE	1980	1985	1990 Total	1990 Per-cent	TYPE	1980	1985	1990 Total	1990 Per-cent
Total [1]	31,564	32,323	34,613	100.0	Academic.	4,591	5,034	4,593	13.3
					Junior college	1,191	1,188	1,233	3.6
United States.	28,638	29,843	30,761	88.9	Colleges, universities.	3,400	3,846	3,360	9.7
Public	8,717	8,849	9,060	26.2	Departmental	1,489	1,824	1,454	4.2
Public branches	5,936	6,330	5,833	16.9	Law, medicine,				
Special [2]	7,649	7,530	9,051	26.1	religious.	269	531	501	1.4
Medicine.	1,674	1,667	1,861	5.4	Government	1,260	1,574	1,735	5.0
Religious.	913	839	946	2.7	Armed Forces.	485	526	489	1.4
Law	417	435	647	1.9	Outlying areas	113	114	110	0.3

[1] Includes public libraries with annual incomes of less than $2,000 or book funds of less than $500, law libraries with less than 10,000 volumes each, Canadian libraries, and libraries in regions administered by the U. S., not shown separately. [2] Includes other types of special libraries, not shown separately. Increase between 1985 and 1990 is due mainly to revised criteria for identifying special libraries and improved methods of counting.

Source: R.R. Bowker Co., New York, NY, *The Bowker Annual: Library and Book Trade Almanac* and *American Library Directory*, annual. (Copyright by Reed Publishing.)

No. 285. College and University Libraries—Summary 1975 to 1988

[For school year ending in year shown, except enrollment as of fall. Prior to 1982, includes outlying areas]

ITEM	1975	1976	1977	1979	1982	1985	1988
Number of libraries	2,972	2,987	3,058	3,122	3,104	3,322	3,438
Total enrollment	10,322	11,291	11,121	11,392	12,372	12,242	12,767
COLLECTIONS (1,000)							
Number of volumes	447,059	468,033	481,442	519,895	567,826	631,727	718,504
Volumes added during year.	23,242	22,977	22,367	21,608	19,507	20,658	21,907
Number of serial subscriptions.	4,434	4,618	4,670	4,775	4,890	6,317	6,416
STAFF							
Total.	56,836	56,852	57,087	58,416	58,476	58,476	67,251
Librarians and professional	23,530	23,104	23,308	23,676	23,816	21,822	25,115
OPERATING EXPENDITURES (mil. dol.)							
Total [1].	1,091,784	1,180,128	1,259,637	1,502,158	1,943,769	2,404,524	2,770,075
Salaries	592,568	649,374	698,090	824,438	1,081,894	1,156,138	1,451,551
Collection	327,904	357,544	373,699	450,180	561,199	750,282	891,281

[1] Includes other expenditures, not shown separately.

Source: U.S. National Center for Education Statistics, *Digest of Education Statistics*, 1991.

No. 286. Large College and University Libraries—Selected Statistics: 1985

[**Staff as of fall; expenditures for school year.** For the largest 15 college and university libraries by collection-size]

INSTITUTION	Number of volumes (1,000)	STAFF [1] Total	STAFF [1] Profes-sional	OPERATING EXPENDITURES ($1,000) Total	OPERATING EXPENDITURES ($1,000) Sala-ries/ wages [2]	OPERATING EXPENDITURES ($1,000) Books and other mate-rial [3]	OPERATING EXPENDITURES ($1,000) Binding and re-binding	OPERATING EXPENDITURES ($1,000) Other
Harvard University.	10,930	1,001	310	30,452	17,905	6,872	621	5,054
Yale University	8,192	595	176	18,982	11,242	4,916	279	2,544
University of Illinois-Urbana Campus	6,808	551	122	15,500	8,932	4,724	228	1,616
University of California-Berkeley	6,611	721	170	26,024	17,603	5,115	520	2,786
University of Michigan, Ann Arbor	5,802	544	143	14,795	10,072	3,335	275	1,112
Columbia University, Main Division.	5,461	559	128	18,340	11,316	4,260	393	2,370
University of California-Los Angeles	5,453	692	190	27,586	16,805	5,850	614	4,317
University of Texas at Austin.	5,402	593	131	19,441	11,261	6,539	182	1,458
Stanford University (Calif).	5,318	590	155	25,202	16,377	5,755	351	2,720
Univeristy of North Carolina at Chapel Hill. . . .	4,851	370	109	12,639	6,475	4,228	246	1,690
University of Chicago.	4,661	334	77	12,433	6,942	2,980	247	2,265
University of Wisconsin-Madison	4,495	519	132	17,179	9,936	4,141	218	2,885
University of Washington	4,416	483	125	14,833	8,445	4,313	373	1,702
Indiana University at Bloomington	4,366	495	109	12,092	7,399	3,516	210	967
University of Minnesota, Minneapolis-St. Paul .	4,229	412	109	15,138	9,255	3,570	382	1,932

[1] Full-time equivalent. [2] Includes salary equivalents of contributed services, fringe benefits of total staff, and wages of student assistants charged to library budgets. [3] Includes expenses of book stock, periodicals, audiovisual materials, and other library materials.

Source: U.S. National Center for Education Statistics, *Digest of Education Statistics*, 1988.

Law Enforcement, Courts, and Prisons

This section presents data on crimes committed, victims of crimes, arrests, and data related to criminal violations, and the criminal justice system. The major sources of these data are the Bureau of Justice Statistics (BJS) and the Federal Bureau of Investigation (FBI). BJS issues several reports, including *Sourcebook of Criminal Justice Statistics, Criminal Victimization in the United States, Prisoners in State and Federal Institutions, Children in Custody, National Survey of Courts, Census of State Correctional Facilities* and *Survey of Prison Inmates, Census of Jails* and *Survey of Jail Inmates, Parole in the United States, Capital Punishment,* and the annual *Expenditure and Employment Data for the Criminal Justice System.* The Federal Bureau of Investigation's major annual report is *Crime in the United States,* which presents data on reported crimes as gathered from State and local law enforcement agencies.

Other major sources of these data include: *Annual Report of the Director, Federal Court Management Statistics, Federal Offenders,* and *Sentences Imposed Chart* issued by the Administrative Office of the U.S. Courts; *Governmental Finances and Public Employment,* issued annually by the Bureau of the Census; and the *Statistical Report,* issued annually by the Federal Bureau of Prisons.

Legal jurisdiction and law enforcement.—Law enforcement is, for the most part, a function of State and local officers and agencies. The U.S. Constitution reserves general police powers to the States. By act of Congress, Federal offenses include only offenses against the U.S. Government and against or by its employees while engaged in their official duties, and offenses which involve the crossing of State lines or an interference with interstate commerce. Excluding the military, there are 52 separate criminal law jurisdictions in the United States: 1 in each of the 50 States, 1 in the District of Columbia, and the Federal jurisdiction. Each of these has its own criminal law and procedure and its own

In Brief

Violent crimes up 10.4 % in 1990 from 1989

Reported rapes up 8.1 % to 102,600 in 1990 compared to 1989

Prisoner population (738,894 in 1990) grew 58,000 from 1989

law enforcement agencies. While the systems of law enforcement are quite similar among the States, there are often substantial differences in the penalties for like offenses.

Law enforcement can be divided into three parts: Investigation of crimes and arrests of persons suspected of committing them; prosecution of those charged with crime; and the punishment or treatment of persons convicted of crime.

Crime.—There are two major approaches taken in determining the extent of crime. One perspective is provided by the FBI through its Uniform Crime Reporting Program (UCR). The FBI receives monthly and annual reports from law enforcement agencies throughout the country, currently representing 98 percent of the national population. Each month, city police, sheriffs, and State police file reports on the number of index offenses that become known to them. The FBI Crime Index offenses are as follows: *Murder and nonnegligent manslaughter,* is based on police investigations, as opposed to the determination of a medical examiner or judicial body, includes willful felonious homicides, and excludes attempts and assaults to kill, suicides, accidental deaths, justifiable homicides, and deaths caused by negligence; *forcible rape* includes forcible rapes and attempts; *robbery* includes stealing or taking anything of value by force or violence or threat of force or violence and includes attempted robbery; *aggravated assault* includes assault with intent to kill; *burglary* includes any unlawful entry to commit a felony or a theft and includes attempted burglary and burglary followed by larceny; *larceny* includes theft of property or articles of value without use of force and violence or fraud and excludes embezzlement, "con games," forgery, etc.; *motor vehicle theft* includes all cases where vehicles are driven away and abandoned, but excludes vehicles taken for temporary use and returned by the taker. Arson was added as the eighth Index offense in April 1979 following a Congressional mandate. *Arson* includes any willful or malicious burning or attempt to burn with or without intent to defraud, a dwelling house, public building, motor vehicle or aircraft, personal property of another, etc. The monthly Uniform Crime Reports also contain data on crimes cleared by arrest and on characteristics of persons arrested for all criminal offenses. In summarizing and publishing crime data, the FBI depends primarily on the adherence to the established standards of reporting for statistical accuracy, presenting the data as information useful to persons concerned with the problem of crime and criminal-law enforcement.

National Crime Survey (NCS).—A second perspective on crime is provided by the National Crime Survey (NCS) of the Bureau of Justice Statistics. Details about the crimes come directly from the victims. No attempt is made to validate the information against police records or any other source. The NCS measures rape, robbery, assault, household and personal larceny, burglary, and motor vehicle theft. The NCS includes offenses reported to the police, as well as those not reported. Police reporting rates (percent of victimizations) varied by type of crime. In 1990, for instance, 54 percent of the rapes were reported; 50 percent of the robberies; 47 percent of assaults; 25 percent of personal larcenies without contact; 51 percent of the household burglaries; and 75 percent of motor vehicle thefts.

Murder and kidnaping are not covered. Commercial burglary and robbery were dropped from the program during 1977. The so-called victimless crimes, such as drunkenness, drug abuse, and prostitution, also are excluded, as are crimes for which it is difficult to identify knowledgeable respondents or to locate data records.

Crimes of which the victim may not be aware also cannot be measured effectively. Buying stolen property may fall into this category, as may some instances of embezzlement. Attempted crimes of many types probably are under recorded for this reason. Events in which the victim has shown a willingness to participate in illegal activity also are excluded.

In any encounter involving a personal crime, more than one criminal act can be committed against an individual. For example; a rape may be associated with a robbery; or a household offense, such as a burglary, can escalate into something more serious in the event of a personal confrontation. In classifying the survey-measured crimes, each criminal incident has been counted only once—by the most serious act that took place during the incident and ranked in accordance with the seriousness classification system used by the Federal Bureau of Investigation. The order of seriousness for crimes against persons is as follows: Rape, robbery, assault, and larceny. Consequently, if a person were both robbed and assaulted, the event would be classified as robbery; if the victim suffered physical harm, the crime would be categorized as robbery with injury. Personal crimes take precedence over household offenses.

A *victimization,* basic measure of the occurrence of a crime, is a specific criminal act as it affects a single victim. The number of victimizations is determined by the number of victims of such acts. Victimization counts serve as key elements in computing rates of victimization. For crimes against persons, the rates are based on the total number of individuals age 12 and over or on a portion of that population sharing a particular characteristic or set of traits. As general indicators of the danger of having been victimized during the reference period, the rates are not sufficiently refined to represent true measures of risk for specific individuals or households.

An *incident* is a specific criminal act involving one or more victims; therefore, the number of incidents of personal crimes lower than that of victimizations.

Courts.—Statistics on criminal offenses and the outcome of prosecutions are incomplete for the country as a whole, although data are available for many States individually. The only national compilations of such statistics were made by the Bureau of the Census for 1932 to 1945 covering a maximum of 32 States, and by the Bureau of Justice Statistics for 1986 based on a nationally representative sample survey.

The bulk of civil and criminal litigation in the country is commenced and determined in the various State courts. Only when the U.S. Constitution and acts of Congress specifically confer jurisdiction upon the Federal courts may civil litigation be heard and decided by them. Generally, the Federal courts have jurisdiction over the following types of cases: Suits or proceedings by or against the United States; civil actions between private parties arising under the Constitution, laws, or treaties of the United States; civil actions between private litigants who are citizens of different States; civil cases involving admiralty, maritime, or prize jurisdiction; and all matters in bankruptcy.

There are several types of courts with varying degrees of legal jurisdiction. These jurisdictions include original, appellate, general, and limited or special. A *court of original jurisdiction* is one having the authority initially to try a case and pass judgment on the law and the facts; a *court of appellate jurisdiction* is one with the legal authority to review cases and hear appeals; a *court of general jurisdiction* is a trial court of unlimited original jurisdiction in civil and/or criminal cases, also called a "major trial court"; a *court of limited or special jurisdiction* is a trial court with legal authority over only a particular class of cases, such as probate, juvenile, or traffic cases.

The 94 Federal courts of original jurisdiction are known as the U.S. district courts. One or more of these courts is established in every State and one each in the District of Columbia, Puerto Rico, the Virgin Islands, the Northern Mariana Islands, and Guam. Appeals from the district courts are taken to intermediate appellate courts of which there are 13,

known as U.S. courts of appeals and the United States Court of Appeals for the Federal Circuit. The Supreme Court of the United States is the final and highest appellate court in the Federal system of courts.

Juvenile offenders.—For statistical purposes, the FBI and most States classify as juvenile offenders persons under the age of 18 years who have committed a crime or crimes.

Delinquency cases are all cases of youths referred to a juvenile court for violation of a law or ordinance or for seriously "antisocial" conduct. Several types of facilities are available for those adjudicated delinquent, ranging from the short-term physically unrestricted environment to the long-term very restrictive atmosphere.

Prisoners.—Data on prisoners in Federal and State prisons and reformatories were collected annually by the Bureau of the Census until 1950, by the Federal Bureau of Prisons until 1971, transferred then to the Law Enforcement Assistance Administration, and, in 1979, to the Bureau of Justice Statistics. Adults convicted of criminal activity may be given a prison or jail sentence. A *prison* is a confinement facility having custodial authority over adults sentenced to confinement of more than one year. A *jail* is a facility, usually operated by a local law enforcement agency, holding persons detained pending adjudication and/or persons committed after adjudication to one year or less. Nearly every State publishes annual data either for its whole prison system or for each separate State institution.

Statistical reliability.—For discussion of statistical collection, estimation, and sampling procedures and measures of statistical reliability pertaining to the National Crime Survey and Uniform Crime Reporting Program, see Appendix III.

Historical statistics.—Tabular headnotes provide cross-references, where applicable, to *Historical Statistics of the United States, Colonial Times to 1970*. See Appendix IV.

No. 287. Crimes and Crime Rates, by Type: 1980 to 1990

[Data refer to offenses known to the police. Rates are based on Bureau of the Census estimated resident population as of **July 1**, except 1980, enumerated as of **April, 1**. Annual totals for years prior to 1984 were adjusted in 1984 and may not be consistent with those in prior editions. See source for details. Minus sign (-) indicates decrease. For definitions of crimes, see text, section 5. See *Historical Statistics, Colonial Times to 1970*, series H 952-961 for related data]

ITEM AND YEAR	Total	VIOLENT CRIME						PROPERTY CRIME			
		Total	Mur-der[1]	Forci-ble rape	Rob-bery	Aggra-vated assault		Total	Bur-glary	Larce-ny—theft	Mortor vehi-cle theft
Number of offenses (1,000):											
1980	13,408	1,345	23.0	83.0	566	673		12,064	3,795	7,137	1,132
1981	13,424	1,362	22.5	82.5	593	664		12,062	3,780	7,194	1,088
1982	12,974	1,322	21.0	78.8	553	669		11,652	3,447	7,143	1,062
1983	12,109	1,258	19.3	78.9	507	653		10,851	3,130	6,713	1,008
1984	11,882	1,273	18.7	84.2	485	685		10,609	2,984	6,592	1,032
1985	12,431	1,329	19.0	88.7	498	723		11,103	3,073	6,926	1,103
1986	13,212	1,489	20.6	91.5	543	834		11,723	3,241	7,257	1,224
1987	13,509	1,484	20.1	91.1	518	855		12,025	3,236	7,500	1,289
1988	13,923	1,566	20.7	92.5	543	910		12,357	3,218	7,706	1,433
1989	14,251	1,646	21.5	94.5	578	952		12,605	3,168	7,872	1,565
1990	14,476	1,820	23.4	102.6	639	1,055		12,656	3,074	7,946	1,636
Percent change, number of offenses:											
1980 to 1990	8.0	35.3	1.7	23.6	12.9	56.8		4.9	-19.0	11.3	44.5
1985 to 1990	16.5	36.9	23.2	15.7	28.3	45.9		14.0	0.0	14.7	48.3
1989 to 1990	1.6	10.6	8.8	8.6	10.6	10.8		0.4	-3.0	0.9	4.5
Rate per 100,000 population:											
1980	5,950	597	10.2	36.8	251	299		5,353	1,684	3,167	502
1981	5,858	594	9.8	36.0	259	290		5,264	1,650	3,140	475
1982	5,604	571	9.1	34.0	239	289		5,033	1,489	3,085	459
1983	5,175	538	8.3	33.7	217	279		4,637	1,338	2,869	431
1984	5,031	539	7.9	35.7	205	290		4,492	1,264	2,791	437
1985	5,207	557	7.9	37.1	209	303		4,651	1,287	2,901	462
1986	5,480	618	8.6	37.9	225	346		4,863	1,345	3,010	508
1987	5,550	610	8.3	37.4	213	351		4,940	1,330	3,081	529
1988	5,664	637	8.4	37.6	221	370		5,027	1,309	3,135	583
1989	5,741	663	8.7	38.1	233	383		5,078	1,276	3,171	630
1990	5,820	732	9.4	41.2	257	424		5,089	1,236	3,195	658
Percent change, rate per 100,000 population:											
1980 to 1990	-2.2	22.6	-7.8	12.0	2.4	41.8		-4.9	-26.6	0.9	31.1
1985 to 1990	11.8	31.4	19.0	11.1	23.0	39.9		9.4	-4.0	10.1	42.4
1989 to 1990	1.4	10.4	8.0	8.1	10.3	10.7		0.2	-3.1	0.8	4.4

[1] Includes nonnegligent manslaughter.

Source: U.S. Federal Bureau of Investigation, *Crime in the United States*, annual.

No. 288. Crimes and Crime Rates, by Type and Area: 1989 and 1990

[**In thousands, except rate.** Rate per 100,000 population; see headnote, table 292. Estimated totals based on reports from city and rural law enforcement agencies representing 96 percent of the national population. For definitions of crimes, see text, section 5]

TYPE OF CRIME	1989						1990					
	MSA's[1]		Other cities		Rural areas		MSA's[1]		Other cities		Rural areas	
	Total	Rate	Total	Rate	Total	Rate	Total	Rate	Total	Rate	Total	Rate
Total	12,430	6,496	1,149	5,034	673	1,974	12,605	6,547	1,188	5,303	683	2,022
Violent crime	1,492	780	90	394	64	189	1,648	856	102	458	70	207
Murder and nonnegligent manslaughter	19	10	1	5	2	5	20	11	1	5	2	6
Forcible rape	81	42	6	27	7	21	88	46	7	33	8	22
Robbery	560	293	13	58	5	16	620	322	14	63	5	16
Aggravated assault	832	435	69	304	50	147	920	478	80	357	55	163
Property crime	10,938	5,716	1,059	4,640	608	1,785	10,957	5,691	1,085	4,845	613	1,815
Burglary	2,702	1,412	237	1,040	229	673	2,611	1,356	236	1,053	227	671
Larceny-theft	6,762	3,534	771	3,380	339	995	6,803	3,533	797	3,559	346	1,024
Motor vehicle theft	1,474	771	50	221	40	117	1,543	801	52	232	41	121

[1] For definition, see Appendix II.

Source: U.S. Federal Bureau of Investigation, *Crime in the United States*, annual.

No. 289. Crime Rates by State, 1985 to 1990, and by Type, 1990

[**Offenses known to the police per 100,000 population.** Based on Bureau of the Census estimated resident population as of July 1. For definitions of crimes, see text, section 5]

REGION, DIVISION, AND STATE	1985, total	1989, total	1990 Total	Violent crime Total	Murder[1]	Forcible rape	Robbery	Aggravated assault	Property crime Total	Burglary	Larceny—theft	Motor vehicle theft
United States.....	5,207	5,741	5,820	732	9.4	41	257	424	5,088	1,236	3,195	658
Northeast............	4,627	5,072	5,193	757	8.6	29	353	366	4,437	1,020	2,598	818
New England........	4,487	4,854	4,996	536	3.9	30	172	330	4,460	1,094	2,645	721
Maine..............	3,672	3,584	3,698	143	2.4	20	25	96	3,555	823	2,555	177
New Hampshire	3,252	3,596	3,645	132	1.9	35	27	68	3,514	735	2,534	244
Vermont	3,888	4,089	4,341	127	2.3	26	12	87	4,214	1,087	2,918	208
Massachusetts......	4,758	5,136	5,298	736	4.0	34	217	481	4,562	1,113	2,525	924
Rhode Island	4,723	5,225	5,353	432	4.8	25	122	280	4,921	1,271	2,695	954
Connecticut........	4,705	5,270	5,387	554	5.1	28	235	286	4,833	1,228	2,874	731
Middle Atlantic.......	4,675	5,147	5,263	834	10.2	29	416	379	4,429	995	2,582	852
New York	5,589	6,293	6,364	1,181	14.5	30	625	512	5,183	1,161	2,979	1,043
New Jersey	5,094	5,269	5,447	648	5.6	30	301	311	4,800	1,017	2,843	940
Pennsylvania	3,037	3,360	3,476	431	6.7	26	176	222	3,045	729	1,811	506
Midwest............	4,674	4,949	5,102	594	7.0	43	199	346	4,508	983	3,024	501
East North Central	4,939	5,150	5,322	662	8.1	47	234	373	4,660	1,008	3,086	566
Ohio..............	4,187	4,733	4,843	506	6.1	47	189	265	4,337	983	2,864	491
Indiana............	3,914	4,440	4,683	474	6.2	38	101	328	4,209	943	2,827	439
Illinois [3].........	5,384	5,639	5,935	967	10.3	39	394	524	4,968	1,063	3,262	643
Michigan..........	6,366	5,968	5,995	790	10.4	78	234	468	5,204	1,143	3,347	714
Wisconsin	4,017	4,165	4,395	265	4.6	21	113	127	4,130	751	2,963	416
West North Central ...	4,046	4,473	4,579	432	4.4	31	114	282	4,147	925	2,876	346
Minnesota.........	4,134	4,383	4,539	306	2.7	34	93	177	4,233	907	2,960	366
Iowa..............	3,943	4,081	4,101	300	1.9	18	39	240	3,801	808	2,823	170
Missouri	4,366	5,127	5,121	715	8.8	32	216	458	4,405	1,066	2,800	539
North Dakota.......	2,679	2,561	2,922	74	0.8	18	8	47	2,848	427	2,289	133
South Dakota.......	2,641	2,685	2,909	163	2.0	34	12	114	2,747	527	2,109	110
Nebraska	3,695	4,092	4,213	330	2.7	30	51	246	3,883	724	2,981	178
Kansas............	4,375	4,983	5,193	448	4.0	40	118	286	4,745	1,167	3,244	335
South..............	5,256	6,205	6,334	766	11.8	45	237	472	5,567	1,498	3,471	598
South Atlantic	5,375	6,425	6,546	857	11.4	45	277	523	5,689	1,525	3,589	576
Delaware..........	4,961	4,865	5,360	655	5.0	88	165	397	4,705	970	3,291	444
Maryland..........	5,373	5,563	5,830	919	11.5	46	364	498	4,912	1,120	3,083	709
District of Columbia [2]..	8,007	10,293	10,774	2,458	77.8	50	1,214	1,117	8,316	1,983	4,997	1,336
Virginia	3,779	4,211	4,441	351	8.8	31	123	188	4,090	731	3,031	327
West Virginia	2,253	2,363	2,503	169	5.7	24	38	102	2,334	657	1,523	154
North Carolina......	4,121	5,254	5,486	624	10.7	34	152	426	4,862	1,530	3,048	284
South Carolina.....	4,841	5,619	6,045	977	11.2	54	152	759	5,069	1,380	3,302	386
Georgia...........	5,110	7,073	6,764	756	11.8	54	263	427	6,007	1,619	3,714	674
Florida	7,574	8,804	8,811	1,244	10.7	52	417	764	7,566	2,171	4,570	826
East South Central....	3,651	4,085	4,389	557	10.2	39	131	376	3,833	1,098	2,374	360
Kentucky..........	2,947	3,317	3,299	390	7.2	29	69	285	2,909	767	1,943	199
Tennessee	4,167	4,514	5,051	670	10.5	50	191	419	4,381	1,264	2,545	572
Alabama	3,942	4,628	4,915	709	11.6	33	144	521	4,207	1,103	2,755	348
Mississippi.........	3,266	3,515	3,869	340	12.2	44	86	198	3,529	1,251	2,070	208
West South Central ...	5,991	7,064	7,092	738	13.5	49	233	443	6,354	1,682	3,902	770
Arkansas	3,585	4,556	4,867	532	10.3	43	113	365	4,335	1,211	2,834	289
Louisiana	5,564	6,241	6,487	898	17.2	42	270	569	5,588	1,438	3,549	602
Oklahoma	5,425	5,503	5,599	547	8.0	47	122	370	5,051	1,447	3,002	602
Texas.............	6,569	7,927	7,827	761	14.1	52	261	435	7,065	1,852	4,305	909
West	6,405	6,550	6,405	808	9.1	45	263	491	5,597	1,304	3,515	778
Mountain	6,183	6,250	6,268	517	6.0	42	109	360	5,751	1,286	3,979	486
Montana	4,549	3,998	4,502	159	4.9	24	22	108	4,343	709	3,391	243
Idaho	3,908	3,931	4,057	276	2.7	27	15	231	3,781	813	2,803	165
Wyoming..........	4,015	3,889	4,211	301	4.9	30	16	251	3,909	631	3,129	149
Colorado..........	6,919	6,039	6,054	526	4.2	46	91	385	5,528	1,209	3,891	428
New Mexico........	6,486	6,574	6,684	780	9.2	50	115	606	5,904	1,739	3,828	337
Arizona...........	7,116	8,060	7,889	652	7.7	41	161	443	7,236	1,670	4,703	863
Utah..............	5,317	5,682	5,660	284	3.0	38	57	186	5,376	881	4,258	238
Nevada...........	6,575	6,272	6,064	601	9.7	62	238	291	5,463	1,367	3,503	593
Pacific.............	6,486	6,656	6,452	910	10.2	46	317	536	5,543	1,310	3,352	880
Washington........	6,529	6,504	6,220	502	4.9	64	130	303	5,721	1,263	4,011	447
Oregon...........	6,730	6,161	5,646	507	3.8	47	144	312	5,139	1,135	3,545	459
California..........	6,518	6,763	6,604	1,045	11.9	43	377	614	5,558	1,345	3,198	1,016
Alaska	5,877	4,780	5,153	525	7.5	73	77	367	4,628	894	3,168	565
Hawaii	5,201	6,270	6,107	281	4.0	32	91	153	5,826	1,228	4,217	381

[1] Includes nonnegligent manslaughter.   [2] Includes offenses reported by the police at the National Zoo.   [3] Forcible rape figures for 1989 and 1990 were estimated using the national rate of forcible rapes when grouped by like agencies as figures submitted were not in accordance with national Uniform Crime Reporting program guidelines.

Source: U.S. Federal Bureau of Investigation, *Crime in the United States,* annual.

Law Enforcement, Courts, and Prisons

No. 290. Crime Rates, by Type—Selected Large Cities: 1990

[**Offenses known to the police per 100,000 population.** Based on Bureau of the Census estimated resident population as of July 1. For definitions of crimes, see text, section 5]

CITY RANKED BY POPULATION SIZE, 1990 [1]	Crime index, total	VIOLENT CRIME					PROPERTY CRIME			
		Total	Mur-der	Forci-ble rape	Rob-bery	Aggra-vated assault	Total	Bur-glary	Larce-ny—theft	Motor vehicle theft
New York, NY	9,699	2,384	31	43	1,370	941	7,316	1,638	3,668	2,009
Los Angeles, CA	9,225	2,405	28	58	1,036	1,283	6,821	1,477	3,519	1,825
Chicago, IL	(2)	(2)	31	(2)	1,335	1,477	8,220	1,803	4,670	1,747
Houston, TX	11,338	1,388	35	82	792	479	9,950	2,636	4,808	2,506
Philadelphia, PA	7,192	1,349	32	46	808	463	5,843	1,523	2,689	1,632
San Diego, CA	9,145	1,085	12	40	390	643	8,061	1,503	4,375	2,183
Detroit, MI	12,192	2,699	57	161	1,266	1,216	9,493	2,536	4,002	2,955
Dallas, TX	15,520	2,438	44	134	1,049	1,211	13,082	3,275	7,372	2,435
Phoenix, AZ	10,756	1,085	13	52	344	675	9,672	2,510	5,381	1,782
San Antonio, TX	12,477	612	22	46	306	238	11,865	2,780	7,495	1,590
San Jose, CA	4,869	601	5	53	132	411	4,269	735	2,996	538
Baltimore, MD	10,596	2,438	41	93	1,288	1,015	8,158	2,004	4,807	1,347
Indianapolis, IN	6,749	1,287	12	112	340	824	5,462	1,629	2,833	1,000
San Francisco, CA	9,662	1,711	14	58	974	665	7,951	1,467	4,915	1,569
Jacksonville, FL	10,463	1,830	28	111	622	1,070	8,633	2,753	4,931	949
Columbus, OH	9,907	1,110	14	102	560	434	8,798	2,343	5,117	1,338
Milwaukee, WI	9,299	1,000	25	79	660	237	8,299	1,482	4,709	2,108
Memphis, TN	9,872	1,488	32	136	680	640	8,384	2,544	3,763	2,078
Washington, DC	10,774	2,458	78	50	1,214	1,117	8,316	1,983	4,997	1,336
Boston, MA	11,851	2,379	25	94	1,049	1,212	9,472	1,783	5,162	2,527
Seattle, WA	12,601	1,507	10	93	522	882	11,094	2,166	7,656	1,273
El Paso, TX	11,239	992	7	50	268	668	10,248	1,856	7,298	1,094
Cleveland, OH	9,115	1,818	33	167	973	645	7,297	2,017	3,024	2,256
New Orleans, LA	12,436	2,259	61	73	1,217	908	10,177	2,742	4,992	2,443
Nashville-Davidson, TN	7,879	1,378	13	111	433	821	6,501	1,780	4,027	694
Denver, CO	7,756	899	14	80	281	524	6,857	1,997	3,591	1,269
Austin, TX	11,714	714	10	60	314	331	11,000	2,442	7,722	836
Fort Worth, TX	14,977	1,748	29	97	626	997	13,229	3,418	7,754	2,057
Oklahoma City, OK	10,611	1,082	15	95	314	658	9,529	2,572	5,769	1,187
Portland, OR	11,101	1,792	8	97	581	1,106	9,309	2,050	5,930	1,328
Kansas City, MO	12,953	2,550	28	119	1,033	1,370	10,403	2,678	5,344	2,381
Long Beach, CA	9,572	1,957	25	69	976	886	7,615	2,017	3,937	1,662
Tucson, AZ	11,879	908	7	72	223	606	10,972	1,951	8,412	609
St. Louis, MO	14,671	3,449	45	83	1,187	2,134	11,222	2,907	6,192	2,123
Charlotte, NC	12,594	2,303	24	97	810	1,373	10,290	2,751	6,858	682
Atlanta, GA	19,236	4,085	59	176	1,550	2,300	15,151	3,939	8,380	2,832
Virginia Beach, VA	5,779	230	4	38	108	80	5,550	1,012	4,208	330
Albuquerque, NM	10,064	1,331	9	58	268	997	8,733	2,468	5,752	513
Oakland, CA	10,906	1,570	39	139	868	524	9,335	2,284	5,125	1,927
Pittsburgh, PA	(2)	(2)	(2)	(2)	(2)	(2)	(2)	(2)	(2)	(2)
Sacramento, CA	9,127	1,077	12	57	485	524	8,050	1,886	4,391	1,773
Minneapolis, MN	(2)	(2)	(2)	(2)	(2)	(2)	(2)	(2)	(2)	(2)
Tulsa, OK	9,534	1,334	16	104	419	795	8,201	2,233	3,900	2,069
Honolulu, HI	6,102	288	4	33	106	145	5,814	1,170	4,247	397
Cincinnati, OH	7,556	1,230	14	107	443	666	6,327	1,620	4,246	461
Miami, FL	19,024	4,353	36	83	2,279	1,954	14,671	3,767	8,233	2,671
Fresno, CA	10,530	1,242	19	73	450	701	9,288	2,015	5,258	2,015
Omaha, NE	7,050	935	3	65	180	687	6,115	1,248	4,466	401
Toledo, OH	9,610	1,064	11	127	525	401	8,546	1,883	5,278	1,386
Buffalo, NY	8,893	1,608	11	108	662	826	7,286	2,488	3,719	1,079
Wichita, KS	8,928	720	6	106	355	254	8,208	2,049	5,444	714
Santa Ana, CA	7,589	907	15	25	529	338	6,682	1,217	4,132	1,334
Mesa, AZ	7,086	598	3	33	96	467	6,488	1,348	4,272	868
Colorado Springs, CO	7,476	421	3	72	92	255	7,055	1,446	5,198	411
Tampa, FL	17,125	3,326	22	131	1,130	2,044	13,799	4,316	7,131	2,352
Newark, NJ	16,256	3,882	41	119	2,188	1,535	12,374	2,449	4,555	5,369
St Paul, MN	8,134	1,015	7	99	287	623	7,119	1,864	4,404	851
Louisville, KY	6,424	848	15	45	405	383	5,576	1,771	3,228	577
Anaheim, CA	7,168	676	8	35	366	268	6,492	1,583	3,664	1,245
Birmingham, AL	11,262	1,577	47	100	676	753	9,685	2,616	5,162	1,907
Arlington, TX	8,524	717	3	53	224	437	7,807	1,719	5,041	1,048
Norfolk, VA	10,254	1,091	24	84	533	451	9,163	1,608	6,485	1,070
Corpus Christi, TX	10,307	624	11	93	173	347	9,683	2,381	6,816	485
St. Petersburg, FL	12,289	2,351	13	73	860	1,405	9,938	2,575	6,275	1,088
Rochester, NY	11,039	1,237	17	76	541	602	9,802	2,506	6,378	918
Jersey City, NJ	9,176	1,877	12	50	1,050	765	7,299	2,027	3,071	2,201
Anchorage, AK	5,747	588	4	90	155	339	5,159	910	3,571	678
Lexington-Fayette, KY	7,208	785	9	63	201	513	6,423	1,410	4,676	337
Akron, OH	7,845	1,159	8	87	347	717	6,686	1,575	4,363	748
Aurora, CO	8,030	1,437	4	77	179	1,178	6,593	1,359	4,728	506
Baton Rouge, LA	12,384	1,855	21	48	354	1,432	10,529	2,633	6,544	1,353
Stockton, CA	11,503	1,245	24	80	619	523	10,258	2,404	6,180	1,674
Raleigh, NC	6,657	567	12	46	187	323	6,090	1,373	4,433	379
Shreveport, LA	10,741	1,272	33	67	445	727	9,469	2,578	6,462	430

[1] Data are not available for Pittsburgh, PA and Minneapolis, MN. [2] The rates for forcible rape, violent crime, and crime index are not shown because the forcible rape figures were not in accordance with national Uniform Crime Reporting guidelines.

No. 291. Murder—Circumstances and Weapons Used or Cause of Death: 1980 to 1990

[Based solely on police investigation. For definition of murder, see text, section 5]

CHARACTERISTIC	1980	1985	1989	1990	CHARACTERISTIC	1980	1985	1989	1990
Murders, total	21,860	17,545	18,954	20,045	Other motives.	20.6	18.1	19.0	19.5
Percent distribution . .	100.0	100.0	100.0	100.0	Unknown	15.1	22.8	23.7	24.7
CIRCUMSTANCES					TYPE OF WEAPON				
Felonies, total.	17.7	17.9	21.4	20.5	OR CAUSE OF DEATH				
Robbery	10.8	9.2	9.1	9.2	Guns.	62.4	58.7	62.4	64.1
Narcotics	1.7	2.9	7.4	6.5	Handguns	45.8	43.0	47.6	49.5
Sex offenses	1.5	1.5	1.1	1.1	Cutting or stabbing . . .	19.3	21.1	18.2	17.5
Other felonies	3.7	4.3	3.8	3.7	Blunt objects [1]	5.0	5.5	6.0	5.4
Suspected felonies . . .	6.7	2.0	0.8	0.7	Personal weapons [2]. . .	5.9	6.7	5.5	5.5
Argument, total	39.9	39.3	35.2	34.5	Strangulations,				
Property or money . .	2.6	2.7	2.9	2.6	asphyxiations.	2.3	2.4	2.5	2.0
Romantic triangle . . .	2.3	2.3	2.0	2.0	Fire.	1.3	1.4	1.2	1.4
Other arguments . . .	35.0	34.3	30.3	29.9	All other [3]	3.8	4.2	4.1	4.1

[1] Refers to club, hammer, etc.   [2] Hands, fists, feet, etc.   [3] Includes poison, drowning, explosives, narcotics, and unknown.

Source: U.S. Federal Bureau of Investigation, *Crime in the United States,* annual.

No. 292. Homicide Victims, by Race and Sex: 1970 to 1989

[**Rates per 100,000 resident population in specified group.** Excludes deaths to nonresidents of United States Beginning 1980, deaths classified according to the ninth revision of the *International Classification of Diseases;* for earlier years, classified according to revision in use at the time; see text, section 2. See also *Historical Statistics, Colonial Times to 1970,* series H 971-978]

YEAR	HOMICIDE VICTIMS					HOMICIDE RATE [2]				
	Total [1]	White		Black		Total [1]	White		Black	
		Male	Female	Male	Female		Male	Female	Male	Female
1970.	16,848	5,865	1,938	7,265	1,569	8.3	6.8	2.1	67.6	13.3
1975.	21,310	8,222	2,751	8,092	1,929	9.9	9.0	2.9	69.0	14.9
1980.	24,278	10,381	3,177	8,385	1,898	10.7	10.9	3.2	66.6	13.5
1981.	23,646	9,941	3,125	8,312	1,825	10.3	10.4	3.1	64.8	12.7
1982.	22,358	9,260	3,179	7,730	1,743	9.6	9.6	3.1	59.1	12.0
1983.	20,191	8,355	2,880	6,822	1,672	8.6	8.6	2.8	51.4	11.3
1984.	19,796	8,171	2,956	6,563	1,677	8.4	8.3	2.9	48.7	11.2
1985.	19,893	8,122	3,041	6,616	1,666	8.3	8.2	2.9	48.4	11.0
1986.	21,731	8,567	3,123	7,634	1,861	9.0	8.6	3.0	55.0	12.1
1987.	21,103	7,979	3,149	7,518	1,969	8.7	7.9	3.0	53.3	12.6
1988.	22,032	7,994	3,072	8,314	2,089	9.0	7.9	2.9	58.0	13.2
1989.	22,909	11,308	2,971	8,888	2,074	9.2	8.2	2.8	61.1	12.9

[1] Includes races not shown separately.   [2] Rate based on enumerated population figures as of April 1 for 1970 and 1980; July 1 estimates for other years.

Source: U.S. National Center for Health Statistics, *Vital Statistics of the United States,* annual, and unpublished data.

No. 293. Forcible Rape—Number and Rate, by Selected Characteristic: 1970 to 1990

[For definition of rape, see text, section 5]

ITEM	1970	1975	1980	1982	1983	1984	1985	1986	1987	1988	1989	1990
NUMBER												
Total	37,990	56,090	82,990	78,770	78,920	84,230	88,670	91,460	91,110	92,490	94,500	102,560
By force	26,888	41,501	63,599	59,967	61,019	66,367	71,060	73,453	73,456	75,441	78,411	86,541
Attempt	11,102	14,589	19,391	18,803	17,901	17,863	17,610	18,007	17,654	17,049	16,089	16,019
RATE												
Per 100,000 population . .	18.7	26.3	36.8	34.0	33.7	35.7	37.1	37.9	37.4	37.6	38.1	41.2
Per 100,000 females. . . .	30.4	51.3	71.6	66.2	65.6	69.4	72.3	73.9	73.0	73.4	74.3	80.5
Per 100,000 females 12 years old and over . . .	46.3	62.9	86.3	79.3	78.5	83.0	86.6	88.6	87.5	88.1	89.3	96.6
AVERAGE ANNUAL PERCENT CHANGE IN RATE [1]												
Per 100,000 population . .	(NA)	0.4	6.1	−5.6	−0.9	5.9	3.9	2.2	−1.3	0.5	1.3	8.1
Per 100,000 females 12 years old and over . . .	(NA)	−0.3	6.0	−5.7	−1.0	5.7	4.3	2.3	−1.2	0.7	1.4	8.2

NA Not available.   [1] Represents annual average from prior year shown except for 1975, from 1974; for 1980, from 1979; and for 1982, from 1981.

Source: U.S. Federal Bureau of Investigation, *Population-at-Risk Rates and Selected Crime Indicators,* annual.

No. 294. Robbery and Property Crimes, by Type and Selected Characteristic: 1980 to 1990

[For definition of crime, see text, section 5]

ITEM	NUMBER OF OFFENSES (1,000)				RATE PER 100,000 INHABITANTS				AVERAGE VALUE LOST (dol.)	
	1980	1985	1989	1990	1980	1985	1989	1990	1989	1990
Robbery, total [1]	566	498	578	639	251.1	208.5	233.0	257.0	701	783
Type of crime:										
Street or highway	293	273	318	359	130.1	114.4	128.0	144.2	538	633
Commercial house	78	60	68	73	34.6	25.3	27.5	29.5	1,214	1,341
Gas station	23	17	16	18	10.4	7.0	6.6	7.1	455	442
Convenience store	38	29	36	39	17.0	12.0	14.7	15.6	364	341
Residence	60	51	57	62	26.8	21.5	22.9	25.1	902	1,049
Bank	8	7	8	9	3.8	2.8	3.2	3.8	3,591	3,244
Weapon used:										
Firearm	228	176	192	234	101.3	73.6	77.3	94.1	(NA)	(NA)
Knife or cutting instrument	73	66	77	76	32.3	27.7	31.2	30.7	(NA)	(NA)
Other dangerous weapon	51	46	61	61	22.8	19.2	24.5	24.5	(NA)	(NA)
Strongarm	214	210	248	268	94.8	88.0	100.0	107.7	(NA)	(NA)
Burglary, total	3,795	3,073	3,168	3,074	1,684.1	1,287.3	1,276.3	1,235.9	1,060	1,133
Forcible entry	2,789	2,148	2,212	2,150	1,237.5	899.6	891.1	864.5	(NA)	(NA)
Unlawful entry	711	668	697	678	315.6	280.0	280.7	272.8	(NA)	(NA)
Attempted forcible entry	295	257	259	245	131.0	107.8	104.5	98.7	(NA)	(NA)
Residence	2,525	2,046	2,096	2,033	1,120.6	857.0	844.4	817.4	1,080	1,143
Nonresidence	1,270	1,027	1,072	1,041	563.5	430.3	431.9	418.5	1,023	1,110
Occurred during the night	1,508	1,177	1,170	1,135	669.0	493.1	471.2	456.4	(NA)	(NA)
Occurred during the day	1,263	1,025	1,134	1,151	560.3	429.2	456.8	462.8	(NA)	(NA)
Larceny-theft, total	7,137	6,926	7,872	7,946	3,167.0	2,901.2	3,171.3	3,194.8	462	480
Pocket picking	85	79	78	81	37.9	32.9	31.6	32.4	303	355
Purse snatching	107	83	89	82	47.5	35.0	35.8	32.8	244	278
Shoplifting	773	968	1,230	1,291	343.0	405.3	495.3	519.1	102	115
From motor vehicles	1,231	1,369	1,729	1,744	546.4	573.3	696.5	701.3	502	541
Motor vehicle accessories	1,366	1,158	1,227	1,185	606.2	485.2	494.3	476.3	315	319
Bicycles	715	566	431	443	317.5	237.3	173.7	178.2	204	215
From buildings	1,187	1,078	1,155	1,118	526.9	451.6	465.4	449.4	747	791
From coin-operated machines	58	60	65	63	25.8	24.9	26.2	25.4	153	147
Other	1,613	1,565	1,868	1,940	715.7	655.7	752.3	780.0	668	671
Motor vehicles, total	1,132	1,103	1,565	1,636	502.2	507.8	630.4	657.8	5,222	5,032
Automobiles	845	832	1,232	1,304	374.8	348.5	496.4	524.3	(NA)	(NA)
Trucks and buses	149	156	232	238	66.1	65.4	93.6	95.5	(NA)	(NA)

NA Not available.   [1] Includes other crimes not shown separately.   [2] Includes other types of motor vehicles not shown separately.

Source: U.S. Federal Bureau of Investigation, *Population-at-Risk Rates and Selected Crime Indicators*, annual.

No. 295. Number and Rate of Victimizations for Crimes Against Persons and Households, by Type: 1973 to 1990

[Data based on National Crime Survey; see text, section 5, and Appendix III]

YEAR	PERSONAL SECTOR								HOUSEHOLD SECTOR			
	Total	Violent crimes						Larce-ny—theft	Total	Bur-glary	Lar-ceny	Motor vehicle theft
		Total	Rape	Rob-bery	Assault							
					Total	Aggra-vated	Simple					
NUMBER (1,000)												
1973	20,322	5,351	156	1,108	4,087	1,655	2,432	14,971	15,340	6,459	7,537	1,344
1975	21,867	5,573	154	1,147	4,272	1,631	2,641	16,294	17,400	6,744	9,223	1,433
1980	21,430	6,130	174	1,209	4,747	1,707	3,041	15,300	18,821	6,973	10,468	1,381
1985	19,296	5,823	138	985	4,699	1,605	3,094	13,474	15,568	5,594	8,703	1,270
1986	18,751	5,515	130	1,009	4,376	1,543	2,833	13,235	15,368	5,557	8,455	1,356
1987	19,371	5,796	148	1,046	4,602	1,587	3,014	13,575	15,966	5,705	8,788	1,473
1988	19,966	5,910	127	1,048	4,734	1,741	2,993	14,056	15,830	5,777	8,419	1,634
1989	19,691	5,861	135	1,092	4,634	1,665	2,969	13,829	16,128	5,352	8,955	1,820
1990 [1]	18,984	6,009	130	1,150	4,729	1,601	3,128	12,975	15,419	5,148	8,304	1,968
RATE [1]												
1973	123.6	32.6	1.0	6.7	24.9	10.1	14.8	91.1	217.8	91.7	107.0	19.1
1975	128.9	32.8	0.9	6.8	25.2	9.6	15.6	96.0	236.5	91.7	125.4	19.5
1980	116.3	33.3	0.9	6.6	25.8	9.3	16.5	83.0	227 4	84.3	126.5	16.7
1985	99.4	30.0	0.7	5.1	24.2	8.3	15.9	69.4	174.4	62.7	97.5	14.2
1986	95.6	28.1	0.7	5.1	22.3	7.9	14.4	67.5	170.0	61.5	93.5	15.0
1987	98.0	29.3	0.8	5.3	23.3	8.0	15.2	68.7	173.9	62.1	95.7	16.0
1988	100.1	29.6	0.7	5.3	23.7	8.7	15.0	70.5	169.6	61.9	90.2	17.5
1989	97.8	29.1	0.7	5.4	23.0	8.3	14.7	68.7	169.9	56.4	94.4	19.2
1990	93.4	29.6	0.6	5.7	23.3	7.9	15.4	63.8	161.0	53.8	86.7	20.5

- Represents zero or rounds to zero.   [1] Rate per 1,000 persons, 12 years old and over; and per 1,000 households.

Source: U.S. Bureau of Justice Statistics, *Criminal Victimization in the United States*, annual.

No. 296. Victimization Rates for Crimes Against Persons: 1973 to 1990

[Rates per 1,000 persons, 12 years old and over. Includes attempted crimes. Data based on National Crime Survey; see text, section 5, and Appendix III. Totals exclude personal larceny]

YEAR	Total [1]	White	Black	His-panic [2]	MALE White	MALE Black	MALE His-panic [2]	FEMALE White	FEMALE Black	FEMALE His-panic [2]	VICTIM-OFFENDER RELATIONSHIP Stranger	VICTIM-OFFENDER RELATIONSHIP Non-stranger
1973	33	32	42	36	43	53	53	21	32	22	22	11
1980	33	32	41	40	43	53	54	22	31	27	21	12
1981	35	33	50	39	44	61	53	23	40	26	23	12
1982	34	33	44	40	42	57	49	25	33	32	22	12
1983	31	30	41	38	39	50	48	21	33	29	18	13
1984	31	30	41	35	38	51	45	22	33	26	17	14
1985	30	29	38	30	38	47	33	21	31	27	18	12
1986	28	28	33	27	35	39	39	21	29	15	16	12
1987	29	28	42	39	36	52	44	20	34	35	17	13
1988	30	28	40	35	34	47	(NA)	22	35	(NA)	18	12
1989	29	28	36	39	35	50	50	22	25	28	18	12
1990	30	28	40	37	36	53	50	21	28	25	18	12

NA Not available.   [1] Includes races not shown separately.   [2] Hispanic persons may be of any race.

No. 297. Crime Incidents, by Place and Time of Occurrence and Injury: 1990

INCIDENT CHARACTERISTICS	Rape	ROBBERY Total	ROBBERY Completed	ROBBERY Attempted	ASSAULT Total	ASSAULT Aggravated	ASSAULT Simple assault	Personal larceny with contact
Incidents, total	**124,480**	**1,036,840**	**724,950**	**311,890**	**4,089,660**	**1,282,850**	**2,806,810**	**632,010**
PERCENT DISTRIBUTION								
Place of occurrence	100.0	100.0	100.0	100.0	100.0	100.0	100.0	100.0
Inside own home.................	35.0	9.4	10.8	6.3	13.4	11.8	14.1	[1]1.8
Near own home, on the street near home	[1]12.3	7.4	6.5	9.4	11.9	12.2	11.8	6.4
Friend's, relative's, or neighbor's home . .	[1]10.5	4.8	4.3	6.1	8.2	10.1	7.3	[1]1.7
Inside commercial property	9.4	4.9	6.4	[1]1.5	13.7	11.9	14.5	26.5
In parking lot or garage	3.4	12.7	11.4	15.8	7.9	9.6	7.1	6.5
Inside school, on school property......	0.0	4.8	4.0	6.7	11.4	6.2	13.8	5.4
In park, field, or playground..........	[1]0.5	3	3.3	[1]2.5	4	4.8	3.6	[1]0.8
On street not near own or friend's home .	17.9	41.2	42.8	37.3	20.0	22.1	19.1	23.0
Other	[1]11.0	11.7	10.6	14.5	9.6	11.2	8.7	27.8
Time of occurrence:								
Daytime (6 a.m. to 6 p.m.)	27.0	44.0	42.5	47.5	48.6	41.7	51.7	65.6
Nighttime.....................	73.0	54.4	57.0	51.9	51.0	57.8	47.9	31.8
Percent of incidents:								
Involving the presence of a weapon	17.2	49.6	50.5	47.5	28.8	91.8	(X)	(X)
Resulting in victim injury	(NA)	34.5	34.1	31.6	33.0	39.2	29.8	(X)

NA Not available.   X Not applicable.   [1] Estimate based on about ten or fewer sample cases.
Source of tables 296 and 297: U.S. Bureau of Justice Statistics, *Criminal Victimization in the United States,* annual.

No. 298. Weapons Used in Crime Incidents by Armed Offenders, by Type of Weapon and Crime: 1989

RELATIONSHIP AND TYPE OF INCIDENT	Number of weapons used [1]	PERCENT DISTRIBUTION Total	Firearm Total	Firearm Hand gun	Firearm Other gun	Firearm Gun type un-known [2]	Knife	Sharp object	Blunt object	Other	Type un-known
Crimes of violence	1,875,880	100.0	31.7	26.6	5.0	0.2	26.7	3.3	17.7	15.0	5.4
Completed	787,900	100.0	27.1	24.7	2.2	0.3	26.9	4.9	17.6	18.5	5.0
Attempted	1,087,970	100.0	35.1	27.9	7.0	0.2	26.6	2.2	17.9	12.5	5.7
Rape [3]...........	28,470	100.0	26.4	26.4	-	-	39.7	6.3	14.0	13.6	-
Robbery..........	497,130	100.0	39.7	38.2	[2]1.5	-	32.8	3.8	12.1	8.8	[2]2.8
Aggravated assault ..	1,350,260	100.0	28.9	22.3	6.3	0.3	24.2	3.1	19.9	17.4	6.5
Involving strangers:											
Crimes of violence...	1,301,160	100.0	35.5	29.9	5.4	0.1	25.4	3.7	15.9	13.8	5.7
Rape [3].........	26,070	100.0	19.6	19.6	-	-	43.4	6.8	15.3	14.9	-
Robbery	430,950	100.0	42.3	41.1	[2]1.3	-	31.2	4.4	12.2	6.6	[2]3.3
Aggravated assault .	844,130	100.0	32.5	24.6	7.7	0.2	21.9	3.3	17.8	17.4	7.1
Involving nonstrangers:											
Crimes of violence...	574,720	100.0	23.3	18.9	4.0	0.4	29.7	[2]2.4	21.9	17.8	4.9
Rape [3].........	2,400	100.0	100.0	100.0	-	-	-	-	-	-	-
Robbery	66,180	100.0	[2]22.8	[2]19.6	[2]3.3	-	43.0	[2]0	[2]11.1	[2]23.1	[2]0
Aggravated assault .	506,130	100.0	23.0	18.4	4.1	0.4	28.1	[2]2.8	23.4	17.2	5.5

- Represents zero.   [1] Some respondents may have cited more than one weapon present.   [2] Based on about 10 or fewer sample cases.

Source: U.S. Bureau of Justice Statistics, *Criminal Victimization in the United States, 1989.*

No. 299. Households Touched by Crime, 1981 and 1990, and by Characteristic, 1990

[A household is considered "touched by crime" if during the year it experienced a burglary, auto theft or household theft or if a household member was raped, robbed, or assaulted, or a victim of personal theft, no matter where the crime occurred. Data based on the National Crime Survey; see text, section 5, and Appendix III]

TYPE OF CRIME	1981		1989, prel.						
	Num- ber (1,000)	Percent touched	Num- ber (1,000)	Percent touched					
				Total [1]	White	Black	Urban	Sub- urban	Rural
Total [2]	24,863	30.0	22,652	23.7	23.1	27.8	29.6	22.7	16.9
Violent crime	4,850	5.9	4,478	4.7	4.6	5.4	6.1	4.2	3.6
Rape.	165	0.2	104	0.1	0.1	0.1	0.2	0.1	0.1
Robbery.	1,117	1.3	967	1.0	0.8	2.2	1.8	0.7	0.4
Assault	3,890	4.7	3,591	3.8	3.8	3.6	4.4	3.5	3.2
Theft	17,705	21.4	15,905	16.7	16.6	17.0	20.3	16.5	11.6
Burglary	6,101	7.4	4,557	4.8	4.3	7.9	6.7	3.9	3.7
Motor vehicle theft	1,285	1.6	1,825	1.9	1.7	3.2	2.9	1.8	0.7

[1] Includes other races not shown separately.   [2] Types of crime will not add to "total" since each household may report as many crime categories as experienced.

Source: U.S. Bureau of Justice Statistics, 1981, *Households Touched by Crime;*1990, *Crime and the Nation's Households, 1990.*

No. 300. Reported Child Neglect and Abuse Cases, by Division: 1980 to 1987

[Represents total number of child maltreatment reports documented within the States, including substantiated and unsubstantiated reports. Derived from data provided by State child protective services personnel to the National Study on Child Neglect and Abuse Reporting, conducted by the American Association for Protecting Children, a division of the American Humane Association, and funded through the National Center on Child Abuse and Neglect, OHDS, DHHS. Also the figures embody the variation among States with respect to whether they use individual child reports or reports which indicate all involved children in the family. Data for 1988 are not available as no survey was taken. For composition of divisions, see fig. I, inside front cover]

YEAR	U.S., total	New England	Middle Atlantic	East North Central	West North Central	South Atlantic	East South Central	West South Central	Moun- tain	Pacific
Total number of reports (1,000):										
1980	785.1	48.3	91.8	105.3	77.7	154.5	58.2	69.7	37.7	141.8
1981	846.2	39.0	101.9	110.5	85.7	174.8	66.1	88.4	37.3	142.5
1982	924.1	49.9	105.5	126.0	96.8	182.1	75.4	95.8	41.5	151.0
1983	1,001.4	58.5	101.0	141.6	93.8	228.5	62.3	103.0	49.5	163.3
1984	1,155.6	55.2	145.6	182.7	107.9	205.4	93.0	116.0	60.0	189.8
1985	1,299.4	59.9	152.2	208.7	107.7	225.0	121.6	128.3	77.6	218.4
1986	1,973.4	95.8	228.1	313.5	207.9	299.2	123.6	188.1	98.9	418.3
1987	2,025.2	99.8	242.5	334.6	180.6	293.4	127.5	174.9	128.2	443.7
Reports per 1,000 population:										
1980	3.5	3.9	2.5	2.5	4.5	4.2	4.0	2.9	3.3	4.4
1981	3.7	3.1	2.8	2.6	5.0	4.6	4.5	3.6	3.2	4.4
1982	4.0	4.0	2.9	3.0	5.6	4.8	5.1	3.8	3.4	4.6
1983	4.3	4.7	2.7	3.4	5.4	5.9	4.2	4.0	4.0	4.8
1984	4.9	4.4	3.9	4.4	6.2	5.2	6.2	4.4	4.8	5.5
1985	5.4	4.7	4.1	5.0	6.1	5.6	8.0	4.8	6.1	6.2
1986	8.2	7.5	6.1	7.5	11.8	7.3	8.1	7.0	7.6	11.7
1987	8.3	7.8	6.5	8.0	10.2	7.0	8.3	6.5	9.7	12.1

Source: American Humane Association, Denver, CO, *National Analysis of Official Child Neglect and Abuse Reporting,* annual; and unpublished data.

No. 301. Child Maltreatment Cases Reported—Summary: 1976 to 1986

[In percent, except as indicated. Total number of children reported is generally a duplicate count in that a child may be reported and therefore enumerated more than once each year. Because of differences in enumeration methods, a relatively small number of States (5 to 10) can provide only unduplicated reports, whereas most States provide only duplicated counts]

ITEM	1976	1977	1978	1979	1980	1981	1982	1983	1984	1985	1986
Number of children reported (1,000).	669	838	836	988	1,154	1,225	1,262	1,477	1,727	1,928	2,086
Rate per 10,000 children	101	128	129	154	181	194	201	236	273	306	328
Type of maltreatment:											
Deprivation of necessities	70.7	64.0	62.9	63.1	60.7	59.4	62.5	58.4	54.6	53.6	54.9
Minor physical injury	18.9	20.8	21.2	15.4	19.8	20.4	16.8	18.5	17.7	17.8	13.9
Sexual maltreatment	3.2	6.1	6.6	5.8	6.8	7.5	6.9	8.5	13.3	13.8	15.7
Emotional maltreatment	21.6	25.4	23.8	14.9	13.5	11.9	10.0	10.1	11.2	11.5	8.3
Other maltreatment	11.2	11.6	11.3	15.8	14.7	19	16.3	16.7	16.5	13.8	21.6
Characteristics of child involved:											
Age, average (years)	7.7	7.6	7.4	7.5	7.3	7.2	7.1	7.1	7.2	7.2	7.2
Sex: Male	50.0	49.9	49.4	49.5	49.8	49.2	49.5	48.9	48.0	47.6	47.5
Female	50.0	50.1	50.6	50.5	50.2	50.5	50.5	51.1	52.0	52.4	52.5
Characteristics of perpetrator:											
Age, average (years)	32.3	31.7	31.7	32.0	31.4	31.4	32.1	31.3	31.5	31.6	31.7
Sex: Male	39.0	39.2	39.0	38.1	41.2	39.3	38.6	40.4	43.0	44.1	44.1
Female	61.0	60.8	61.0	61.9	58.8	60.7	61.4	59.6	57.0	55.9	55.9

Source: American Humane Association, Denver, CO, *National Study on Child Neglect and Abuse Reporting,* annual.

No. 302. Persons Arrested, by Charge, Sex, and Age: 1990

[Represents arrests (not charges) reported by 10,206 agencies (reporting 12 months) with a total 1990 population of 194 million as estimated by FBI]

CHARGE	Total (1,000)	PERCENT DISTRIBUTION							
		Male	Under 15 years	Under 18 years	18-24 years	25-44 years	45-54 years	55-64 years	65 yr. and over
Total arrests	**11,250**	**81.6**	**5.3**	**15.6**	**30.1**	**47.0**	**4.9**	**1.8**	**0.7**
Serious crimes [1]	**2,328**	**78.1**	**11.3**	**28.1**	**28.4**	**37.7**	**3.5**	**1.4**	**0.9**
Murder and nonnegligent manslaughter	18	89.6	1.5	14.0	37.7	40.8	4.7	1.8	1.0
Forcible rape	31	98.9	5.2	14.9	29.3	48.7	4.7	1.7	0.7
Robbery	136	91.7	6.5	24.2	37.4	36.8	1.3	0.3	0.1
Aggravated assault	377	86.7	3.9	13.6	28.7	50.2	5.0	1.8	0.7
Burglary [2]	341	91.2	13.0	33.0	32.0	32.9	1.6	0.4	0.1
Larceny—theft	1,241	68.0	13.5	30.0	26.0	37.0	4.0	1.8	1.2
Motor vehicle theft	168	90.0	12.0	43.3	31.2	23.9	1.2	0.3	0.1
Arson	15	87.0	28.7	43.8	19.7	30.6	3.9	1.5	0.6
All other nonserious crimes:									
Other assaults	801	83.9	5.8	14.9	27.6	51.0	4.5	1.5	0.6
Forgery and counterfeiting	74	65.4	1.6	9.1	34.6	51.5	3.7	0.8	0.3
Fraud	280	55.8	0.9	3.4	28.3	59.9	6.1	1.7	0.6
Embezzlement	12	58.8	0.7	7.2	36.7	49.2	5.0	1.4	0.4
Stolen property [3]	132	88.0	7.0	25.9	36.1	34.5	2.5	0.7	0.2
Vandalism	257	89.2	19.7	40.4	28.6	28.2	1.9	0.6	0.3
Weapons (carrying, etc.)	176	92.6	4.7	18.2	35.1	40.1	4.3	1.7	0.7
Prostitution and commercialized vice	91	36.0	0.2	1.4	28.9	64.6	3.5	1.1	0.5
Sex offenses [4]	85	92.3	8.0	15.9	20.9	49.3	7.8	3.9	2.1
Drug abuse violations	869	83.2	1.0	7.4	33.1	55.6	3.1	0.6	0.2
Gambling	15	86.2	1.0	5.2	16.8	45.3	17.1	10.7	4.9
Offenses against family and children	66	82.2	1.2	4.0	24.1	63.9	6.0	1.5	0.6
Driving while intoxicated	1,391	87.2	(Z)	1.1	25.0	61.1	8.3	3.3	1.2
Liquor laws	552	81.3	1.9	22.1	55.2	18.6	2.6	1.1	0.4
Drunkenness	717	90.0	0.3	2.7	24.0	58.3	9.3	4.1	1.6
Disorderly conduct	580	80.9	5.1	16.6	34.4	43.2	3.9	1.4	0.6
Vagrancy	31	87.4	2.5	8.1	22.5	56.3	8.6	3.4	1.0
Suspicion	18	85.0	6.2	17.4	28.1	50.1	3.4	0.8	0.3
Curfew, loitering (juveniles)	65	72.0	28.9	100.0	(X)	(X)	(X)	(X)	(X)
Runaways (juveniles)	138	43.6	43.8	100.0	(X)	(X)	(X)	(X)	(X)
All other offenses, except traffic	2,572	83.4	2.8	9.7	32.0	51.3	4.8	1.6	0.7

X Not applicable. Z Less than .05 percent. [1] Includes arson arrests, a newly established index offense in 1979. [2] Breaking or entering. [3] Buying, receiving, possessing. [4] Excludes forcible rape and prostitution, shown separately.

Source: U.S. Federal Bureau of Investigation, *Crime in the United States*, annual.

No. 303. Drug Use Among Persons Arrested—Percent Testing Positive, by Sex and Selected City: 1990 and 1991

[Based on the Drug Use Forecasting System, which measures drug use among persons arrested for primarily serious nondrug crimes. The program obtains voluntary, confidential urinalysis specimens from a new sample of arrestees each quarter]

CITY	MALES					FEMALES				
	July-Sept. 1990	Oct.-Dec. 1990	Jan.-Mar. 1991	Apr.-June 1991	July-Sept. 1991	July-Sept. 1990	Oct.-Dec. 1990	Jan.-Mar. 1991	Apr.-June 1991	July-Sept. 1991
Birmingham, AL	56	60	66	61	57	74	58	67	66	54
Chicago, IL	75	72	77	75	68	(NA)	(NA)	(NA)	(NA)	(NA)
Cleveland, OH	49	57	57	56	53	(NA)	71	86	78	75
Dallas, TX	51	50	52	56	55	51	56	64	52	57
Denver, CO	35	46	56	54	(NA)	53	52	57	54	48
Detroit, MI	45	56	58	57	49	67	77	68	70	66
Ft. Lauderdale, FL	56	57	65	60	60	66	54	65	60	63
Houston, TX	60	55	68	64	62	49	53	52	60	58
Indianapolis, IN	33	38	53	39	43	28	26	57	52	56
Kansas City, MO	39	42	56	49	(NA)	56	69	67	67	(NA)
Los Angeles, CA	66	56	62	62	60	71	69	76	77	70
New Orleans, LA	62	58	54	63	62	55	56	47	58	44
New York, NY	80	75	75	79	69	70	(NA)	74	74	84
Omaha, NE	22	23	42	40	23	(NA)	(NA)	(NA)	(NA)	(NA)
Philadelphia, PA	73	72	76	77	70	74	69	74	75	76
Phoenix, AZ	45	44	49	50	42	55	47	68	60	59
Portland, OR	57	70	65	56	61	57	56	65	72	71
St. Louis, MO	42	48	57	57	57	52	46	58	62	38
San Antonio, TX	43	44	52	46	44	43	45	56	39	52
San Diego, CA	79	74	79	76	74	75	72	75	71	74
San Jose, CA	49	54	65	56	57	48	61	56	56	45
Washington, DC	58	55	61	63	59	72	58	74	78	70

NA Not available.

Source: U.S. National Institute of Justice, *Drug Use Forecasting*, quarterly.

No. 304. Drug Arrest Rates for Drug Abuse Violations, 1980 to 1990, and by Region, 1990

[Rate per 100,000 inhabitants. Based on Bureau of the Census estimated resident population as of July 1, except 1980 and 1990, enumerated as of April 1. For composition of regions, see fig. 1 inside front cover]

OFFENSE	1980	1985	1987	1988	1989	1990				
						Total	North-east	Mid-west	South	West
									Region	
Drug arrest rate, total	256.0	346.2	400.9	423.4	526.8	437.5	522.6	228.4	395.2	614.4
Sale and/or manufacture	57.9	82.0	103.6	118.8	170.8	140.4	219.7	72.3	112.2	171.7
Heroin or cocaine [1]	10.8	27.8	56.7	75.1	101.0	94.3	184.8	26.2	76.5	102.6
Marijuana	28.4	36.4	28.1	23.6	33.0	26.6	25.0	16.4	25.1	39.7
Synthetic or manufactured drugs	2.8	2.6	3.5	3.5	3.8	2.8	2.8	1.7	4.1	2.0
Other dangerous nonnarcotic drugs ..	15.9	15.2	15.3	16.7	33.1	16.6	7.0	28.1	6.5	27.5
Possession	198.1	264.1	297.2	304.6	356.0	297.2	302.9	156.1	283.0	442.7
Heroin or cocaine [1]	22.2	74.4	126.2	147.2	183.0	145.0	174.9	44.9	121.1	243.6
Marijuana	146.2	156.1	133.8	118.5	121.1	104.0	110.0	83.1	125.2	90.9
Synthetic or manufactured drugs	6.7	5.6	7.0	7.9	7.4	6.7	5.8	3.4	11.8	3.8
Other dangerous nonnarcotic drugs ..	23.0	28.1	30.3	31.0	44.4	41.5	12.1	24.7	24.9	104.3

[1] Includes other derivatives such as morphine, heroin, and codeine.
Source: U.S. Federal Bureau of Investigation, *Crime in the United States*, annual.

No. 305. Drug Removals, Laboratory Seizures, and Persons Indicted, by DEA: 1985 to 1990

[Represents domestic drug removals. 1 kg=.454 lbs; du=dosage unit. Minus sign (-) indicates decrease]

ITEM	Unit	1985	1986	1987	1988	1989	1990	PERCENT CHANGE	
								1985-90	1989-90
Domestic drug removals:									
Heroin	kg	447	382	382	829	629	637	42.5	1.3
Cocaine	kg	18,129	26,954	37,405	57,113	82,438	72,881	302.0	-11.6
Cannabis (Marijuana)	1,000 kg.	745	711	649	602	336	149	-80.0	-55.7
Dangerous drugs.	mil. du ..	26	32	34	114	109	147	465.4	34.9
Clandestine laboratory seizures ..	Number .	338	509	682	810	852	549	62.4	-35.6
Narcotic Title III intercepts	Number .	136	79	93	129	192	235	72.8	22.4
Asset removals:									
Total seizures.	$1,000..	246,344	401,415	504,397	671,290	975,884	1,068,268	333.6	9.5
DEA seizures.	$1,000..	171,888	310,730	402,071	483,355	659,802	862,361	401.7	30.7
Seizures through interagency cooperation	$1,000..	74,456	90,684	102,308	187,936	316,082	205,907	176.5	-34.9
Arrests	Number .	15,727	18,687	21,869	23,994	25,718	22,800	45.0	-11.3
Convictions	Number .	10,519	12,028	12,427	13,091	15,917	15,529	47.6	-2.4

Source: Drug Enforcement Administration, unpublished data.

No. 306. Authorized Intercepts of Communication-Summary: 1970 to 1990

[Data for jurisdictions with statutes authorizing or approving interception of wire or oral communication]

ITEM	1970	1975	1980	1981	1982	1983	1984	1985	1986	1987	1988	1989	1990
Jurisdictions: [1]													
With wiretap statutes	19	24	28	29	29	31	31	32	32	33	34	37	40
Reporting interceptions	12	18	22	22	22	20	24	22	24	22	23	25	25
Intercept applications authorized..	596	701	564	589	578	648	801	784	754	673	738	763	872
Intercept installations	582	676	524	562	518	602	773	722	676	634	678	720	812
Federal	179	106	79	106	129	205	277	235	247	233	286	305	321
State.	403	570	445	456	389	397	496	487	429	401	392	415	491
Intercepted communications, avg. [2] .	655	654	1,058	848	1,082	1,107	1,209	1,320	1,328	1,299	1,251	1,656	1,487
Incriminating	295	305	315	190	209	229	298	275	253	230	316	337	321
Persons arrested [3]	1,874	2,234	1,871	1,735	1,725	1,716	2,393	2,469	2,410	2,226	2,486	2,804	2,057
Convictions [3]	151	336	259	248	453	521	649	660	761	506	543	706	420
Major offense specified:													
Gambling	325	408	199	156	150	157	186	206	189	135	126	111	116
Drugs.	127	178	282	318	333	360	483	434	348	379	435	471	520
Homicide and assault	21	16	13	33	31	31	30	25	34	18	14	20	21
Other	123	99	70	82	64	100	102	119	183	141	163	161	204

[1] Jurisdictions include Federal Government, States, and beginning 1975, District of Columbia.　[2] Average per authorized installation.　[3] Based on information received from intercepts installed in year shown; additional arrests/convictions will occur In subsequent years but are not shown here.
Source: Administrative Office of the U.S. Courts, *Report on Applications for Orders Authorizing or Approving the Interception of Wire, Oral or Electronic Communications*, (Wiretap Report), annual.

No. 307. Aliens Expelled and Immigration Violations: 1970 to 1991

[For fiscal years ending in year shown. See text, section 9. See also *Historical Statistics, Colonial Times to 1970*, series C 144, C 149, and C 158-160]

ITEM	Unit	1970	1975	1980	1985	1986	1987	1988	1989	1990	1991
Aliens expelled.	1,000	320	679	737	1,062	1,608	1,113	934	860	1,045	1,091
Deported	1,000	17	23	17	21	22	22	23	30	26	28
Required to depart	1,000	303	656	719	1,041	1,586	1,091	911	830	1,019	1,063
Prosecutions disposed of	Number . .	6,034	14,172	14,863	17,688	23,405	18,894	18,360	18,580	20,079	18,882
Immigration violations	Number. . .	5,510	13,947	14,498	16,976	22,751	18,200	17,590	17,992	19,351	18,297
Nationality violations.	Number. . .	524	225	365	712	654	694	770	588	728	585
Convictions	Number . .	5,497	12,811	12,935	9,833	15,259	11,996	12,208	12,561	12,719	11,509
Immigration violations	Number. . .	4,991	12,676	12,678	9,635	15,104	11,786	11,929	12,379	12,515	11,392
Nationality violations.	Number. . .	506	135	257	198	155	210	279	182	204	117

No. 308. Immigration Border Patrol and Investigation Activities: 1985 to 1991

[**In thousands, except where indicated.** For fiscal years ending in year shown. See text, section 9]

ITEM	1985	1989	1990	1991	ITEM	1985	1989	1990	1991
BORDER PATROL					Other.	37.8	55.5	42.8	31.1
					Number of seizures. . . .	7,827	10,789	17,275	14,693
Border patrol agents:					Value of seizures				
Authorized (number). .	3,228	4,804	4,852	4,968	(mil. dol.)	122.0	1,212.7	843.6	950.2
On duty (number) . .	3,023	3,857	4,360	4,312	Narcotics (mil. dol.) . .	119.8	1,191.5	797.8	910.1
Border patrol obligations					**INVESTIGATION**				
(mil. dol.)	141.9	246.4	261.1	295.5	Deportable aliens				
Persons apprehended [1] .	1,272.4	906.5	1,123.2	1,152.7	located	83.9	61.1	64.1	63.6
Deportable aliens					Mexican.	48.3	33.1	35.8	35.5
located [2]	1,262.4	893.0	1,103.4	1,132.9	Canadian	1.1	0.5	0.4	0.5
Mexican.	1,218.7	832.2	1,054.8	1,095.1	Other.	34.5	28.5	30.0	29.7
Canadian	5.9	5.3	5.7	6.7					

[1] Covers deportable aliens located and U.S. citizens engaged in smuggling or other immigration violations.   [2] Beginning 1988, includes apprehension by the antismuggling unit.   [3] Includes types not shown separately.

Source of tables 307 and 308: U.S. Immigration and Naturalization Service, *Statistical Yearbook*, annual; and unpublished data.

No. 309. Law Enforcement Officers Killed, by Division, or Assaulted, by Type of Weapon Used: 1980 to 1990

[Covers officers killed feloniously and accidentally in line of duty; includes Federal officers. 1988 excludes Florida and Kentucky. For composition of regions, see fig. I, inside front cover. See also *Historical Statistics, Colonial Times to 1970*, series H 987-998]

ITEM	1980	1982	1983	1984	1985	1986	1987	1988	1989	1990
OFFICERS KILLED										
Total killed.	[1]165	[2]164	[3]152	147	[4]148	133	148	[5]155	[6]145	132
Northeast	31	17	20	21	19	15	24	17	23	13
Midwest	23	41	26	22	23	20	31	18	22	20
South.	72	75	64	69	64	63	51	77	68	68
West	32	27	34	32	29	29	40	39	23	23
Puerto Rico.	6	3	6	3	10	6	2	-	8	8
ASSAULTS										
Population (1,000) [8]	182,288	176,563	198,341	195,794	198,935	196,030	190,025	186,418	189,641	199,065
Number of—										
Agencies represented	9,235	8,829	9,908	10,002	9,906	9,755	8,957	8,866	9,213	9,483
Police officers.	345,554	319,101	377,620	372,268	389,808	380,249	378,977	369,743	380,232	412,314
Total assaulted.	57,847	55,775	62,324	60,153	61,724	64,259	63,842	58,752	62,172	71,794
Firearm	3,295	2,642	3,067	2,654	2,793	2,852	2,789	2,759	3,154	3,662
Knife or cutting instrument . . .	1,653	1,452	1,829	1,662	1,715	1,614	1,561	1,367	1,379	1,641
Other dangerous weapon . . .	5,415	4,879	5,527	5,148	5,263	5,721	5,685	5,573	5,778	7,390
Hands, fists, feet, etc	47,484	46,802	51,901	50,689	51,953	54,072	53,807	49,053	51,861	59,101

- Represents zero.   [1] Includes one officer in Virgin Islands.   [2] Includes one officer in Mariana Islands.   [3] Includes one officer each in Guam and Mariana Islands.   [4] Includes one officer in Guam and two in foreign locations.   [5] Includes one officer in American Samoa and two in foreign locations.   [6] Includes one officer killed in Guam and one Federal officer killed in Peru.   [7] Represents the number of persons covered by agencies shown.

Source: U.S. Federal Bureau of Investigation, *Law Enforcement Officers Killed and Assaulted*, annual.

No. 310. Criminal Justice System—Public Expenditures and Employment, by Activity and Level of Government: 1988

[Based on a sample survey of local governments. Data for State governments were compiled from State financial records and for the Federal Government from the *Budget of the United States Government*]

TYPE OF GOVERNMENT	Total	Percent change from 1985	ACTIVITY					
			Police protection	Judicial	Legal services	Public defense	Correc- tions	Other justice
TOTAL EXPENDITURES [1] (mil. dol.)								
All governments [2]	60,980	33.7	27,956	7,618	4,229	1,398	19,119	591
Federal government. . . . . . . ;	7,794	33.9	3,555	1,158	1,022	385	1,226	447
State and local government [2]	53,517	34.0	24,401	6,460	3,277	1,013	17,962	384
State government.	22,120	38.1	4,513	3,071	1,076	428	12,671	361
Local government	33,535	32.2	20,333	3,688	2,237	618	6,530	131
FULL-TIME EQUIVALENT EMPLOYMENT (1,000)								
All governments [2]	1,601	16.9	784	209	104	14	483	6
Federal government. . . . . . ;	118	9.4	65	18	16	(Z)	17	(Z)
State and local government [2]	1,483	17.7	719	191	88	13	465	6
State government.	518	20.1	115	67	28	6	297	4
Local government	965	16.4	604	124	60	7	168	2

Z Fewer than 500.   [1] Covers direct and intergovernmental expenditures.   [2] Totals are adjusted to exclude duplication from intergovernmental expenditures.

Source: U.S. Bureau of Justice Statistics, *Justice Expenditure and Employment in the U.S., 1988*, July 1990.

No. 311. General Purpose Law Enforcement Agencies—Number, Employment, and Expenditures: 1987

[Includes both full-time and part-time employees. State police data are based on the 49 main State police agencies; Hawaii does not have a State police agency. Expenditure data cover fiscal years ending in year stated]

TYPE OF AGENCY	Number of agencies[1]	NUMBER OF EMPLOYEES			EXPENDITURES (mil. dol.)		
		Total	Sworn	Civilian	Total	Operating	Capital
NUMBER							
Total	15,118	757,508	555,364	202,144	28,071.1	26,334.4	1,736.6
Local police	11,989	493,930	376,023	117,907	18,011.3	17,161.4	849.9
Sheriff.	3,080	189,234	128,728	60,506	6,857.8	6,200.2	657.6
State police	49	74,344	50,613	23,731	3,202.0	2,972.9	229.1
PERCENT							
Total	100.0	100.0	100.0	100.0	100.0	100.0	100.0
Local police	79.3	65.2	67.7	58.3	64.2	65.2	48.9
Sheriff.	20.4	25.0	23.2	29.9	24.4	23.5	37.9
State police	0.3	9.8	9.1	11.7	11.4	11.3	13.2

[1] The number of agencies reported here is the result of a weighted sample and not an exact enumeration.

Source: U.S. Bureau of Justice Statistics, *Profile of State and Local Law Enforcement Agencies, 1987*, March 1989.

No. 312. Special Functions of Local Police Agencies: 1987

[Special functions are those functions that go beyond such traditional law enforcement functions as traffic enforcement, accident investigation, crime investigation, patrol, fingerprinting, and communications]

POPULATION SERVED	PERCENT OF ALL AGENCIES THAT REPORTED HAVING PRIMARY RESPONSIBILITY FOR—								
	Animal control	Emer- gency medical services	Court security	Civil defense	Civil process- serving	Jail oper- ations	Training academy operation	Labora- tory test- ing for drugs	Ballistics work
All sizes.	49.9	25.3	21.8	21.1	17.7	12.4	6.5	4.3	2.2
1,000,000 or more . .	-	30.6	7.6	30.8	7.6	15.4	84.7	76.9	76.9
500,000-999,999 . . .	6.9	20.6	10.4	20.6	6.9	10.4	82.8	48.2	55.2
250,000-499,999 . . .	16.7	9.5	11.9	14.3	7.1	23.8	85.7	45.3	47.6
100,000-249,999 . . .	28.6	17.6	19.1	14.2	8.1	33.0	49.9	16.9	13.9
50,000-99,999	50.0	27.1	33.7	28.6	9.3	25.5	25.7	17.1	3.5
25,000-49,999	51.2	26.4	27 8	21.5	9.2	25.6	9.8	9.6	0.8
10,000-24,999	54.2	27.9	24.6	23.0	11.7	20.8	6.9	4.2	2.1
2,500-9,999.	55.2	27.4	23.1	21.5	16.3	12.5	5.2	3.0	1.0
Under 2,500	44.7	22.4	17.9	19.6	23.9	5.1	2.8	2.5	2.1

- Represents zero.

Source: U.S. Bureau of Justice Statistics, *Profile of State and Local Law Enforcement Agencies, 1987*, March 1989.

No. 313. State and Local Government Police Protection and Correction—Employment and Expenditures: 1988

[Employment as of **October.** Expenditures for fiscal years ending between **July 1987** and **June 1988.** Local government data are estimates subject to sampling variation; see Appendix III and source. For composition of regions, see fig. I, inside front cover]

REGION, DIVISION, AND STATE	FULL-TIME EQUIVALENT EMPLOYMENT					EXPENDITURES			
	Total	Police protection	Correction	Per 10,000 population [1]		Total [2] (mil. dol.)	Per capita [1] (dol.)	Police protection (mil. dol.)	Correction (mil. dol.)
				Police protection	Correction				
United States ...	1,106,891	671,654	435,237	27.3	17.7	56,453	230	26,277	18,963
Northeast	261,433	162,186	99,247	32.1	19.6	13,876	274	6,432	4,542
New England.	52,863	36,796	16,067	28.4	12.4	2,833	219	1,421	790
Maine.	4,228	2,777	1,451	23.0	12.0	171	142	79	59
New Hampshire. . . .	3,823	2,756	1,067	25.4	9.8	192	177	95	49
Vermont	1,801	1,224	577	22.0	10.4	81	145	39	22
Massachusetts.	25,295	17,881	7,414	30.4	12.6	1,443	245	716	409
Rhode Island.	3,999	2,803	1,196	28.2	12.0	201	203	102	52
Connecticut.	13,717	9,355	4,362	28.9	13.5	745	230	390	199
Middle Atlantic	208,570	125,390	83,180	33.3	22.1	11,043	294	5,011	3,752
New York	118,463	66,261	52,202	37.0	29.1	6,865	383	3,032	2,500
New Jersey.	46,736	30,476	16,260	39.5	21.1	2,125	275	1,054	629
Pennsylvania.	43,371	28,653	14,718	23.9	12.3	2,053	171	926	623
Midwest.	232,156	153,034	79,122	25.6	13.2	11,363	190	5,660	3,384
East North Central. . .	169,564	112,153	57,411	26.6	13.6	8,520	202	4,250	2,577
Ohio	38,432	24,947	13,485	23.0	12.4	2,126	196	964	729
Indiana.	19,074	12,306	6,768	22.1	12.2	727	131	342	239
Illinois	54,485	38,541	15,944	33.2	13.7	2,435	210	1,370	604
Michigan.	39,440	23,463	15,977	25.4	17.3	2,292	248	1,052	770
Wisconsin.	18,133	12,896	5,237	26.6	10.8	940	194	521	234
West North Central . .	62,592	40,881	21,711	23.0	12.2	2,843	160	1,410	807
Minnesota.	12,949	8,564	4,385	19.9	10.2	801	186	383	230
Iowa	8,317	5,713	2,604	20.2	9.2	409	144	196	108
Missouri	21,186	13,665	7,521	26.6	14.6	837	163	442	246
North Dakota.	1,784	1,303	481	19.5	7.2	82	123	37	20
South Dakota	2,212	1,497	715	21.0	10.0	91	127	46	25
Nebraska	5,826	3,619	2,207	22.6	13.8	226	141	113	65
Kansas.	10,318	6,520	3,798	26.1	15.2	397	159	193	113
South	378,897	218,604	160,293	25.8	18.9	16,229	192	7,541	5,720
South Atlantic	210,522	116,902	93,620	27.6	22.1	9,517	224	4,332	3,484
Delaware	3,349	1,769	1,580	26.8	23.9	171	260	76	55
Maryland	25,305	14,041	11,264	30.4	24.4	1,232	267	551	462
District of Columbia .	8,291	4,594	3,697	73.4	59.1	591	958	231	255
Virginia.	27,646	14,136	13,510	23.5	22.5	1,227	204	553	449
West Virginia	4,511	3,184	1,327	17.0	7.1	169	90	81	43
North Carolina.	26,889	15,728	11,161	24.2	17.2	1,149	177	511	463
South Carolina.	16,004	8,335	7,669	24.0	22.1	560	161	230	255
Georgia	29,158	16,532	12,626	26.1	19.9	1,186	187	529	459
Florida	69,369	38,583	30,786	31.3	25.0	3,231	262	1,570	1,043
East South Central. . .	54,880	33,814	21,066	22.0	13.7	2,154	140	993	736
Kentucky	11,941	7,326	4,615	19.7	12.4	523	140	228	178
Tennessee	19,927	11,435	8,492	23.4	17.3	771	157	343	298
Alabama.	14,699	9,556	5,143	23.3	12.5	595	145	274	192
Mississippi	8,313	5,497	2,816	21.0	10.7	266	101	147	69
West South Central . .	113,495	67,888	45,607	25.2	17.0	4,558	170	2,216	1,501
Arkansas	7,416	4,782	2,634	20.0	11.0	246	103	125	72
Louisiana	20,021	12,090	7,931	27.4	18.0	850	193	426	253
Oklahoma	13,262	8,632	4,630	26.6	14.3	485	149	229	176
Texas.	72,796	42,384	30,412	25.2	18.1	2,978	177	1,437	1,000
West	234,405	137,830	96,575	27.2	19.1	14,985	296	6,644	5,317
Mountain	60,676	37,186	23,490	27.9	17.6	3,186	239	1,493	1,047
Montana.	2,824	1,811	1,013	22.5	12.6	123	153	62	30
Idaho	3,383	2,434	949	24.3	9.5	148	147	75	42
Wyoming	2,365	1,633	732	34.1	15.3	109	227	58	27
Colorado.	13,724	8,941	4,783	27.1	14.5	768	233	383	225
New Mexico	7,734	4,438	3,296	29.4	21.9	318	211	147	112
Arizona.	18,929	10,232	8,697	29.3	24.9	1,045	300	480	354
Utah	5,391	3,596	1,795	21.3	10.6	288	170	137	91
Nevada	6,326	4,101	2,225	38.9	21.1	307	367	150	167
Pacific	173,729	100,644	73,085	26.9	19.6	11,799	316	5,151	4,270
Washington.	17,917	10,081	7,836	21.7	16.9	938	202	428	318
Oregon.	10,346	6,174	4,172	22.3	15.1	588	212	284	173
California	138,148	79,868	58,280	28.2	20.6	9,709	343	4,211	3,614
Alaska	2,803	1,562	1,241	29.8	23.7	293	559	109	93
Hawaii	4,515	2,959	1,556	26.9	14.2	273	248	118	72

[1] Based on resident population as of July 1. [2] Includes judicial and legal, not shown separately.

Source: U.S. Bureau of the Census, *Public Employment,* series GE No. 1, annual, and *Government Finances,* series GF, No. 5, annual.

No. 314. Lawyers—Selected Characteristics: 1960 to 1988

[See headnote, table 315. See also *Historical Statistics, Colonial Times to 1970,* series H 1028-1062]

CHARACTERISTIC	1960	1963	1966	1970	1980	1985	1988
All lawyers [1]	285,933	296,069	316,656	355,242	542,205	655,191	723,189
Lawyers reporting [2]	252,385	268,782	289,404	324,818	(X)	(X)	(X)
Male	245,897	261,639	281,336	315,715	498,019	569,649	606,768
Female	6,488	7,143	8,068	9,103	44,185	85,542	116,421
Status in practice: [3]							
Government	25,621	29,314	31,280	35,803	50,490	53,035	57,742
Federal	13,045	15,113	16,284	18,710	20,132	19,989	23,042
State	4,316	6,486	7,416	9,293	30,358	33,046	34,700
City or county	8,260	7,715	7,580	7,800	(4)	(4)	(4)
Judicial [5]	8,180	8,748	9,712	10,349	19,160	21,677	19,071
Federal	599	707	800	878	2,611	3,003	2,551
State and county	5,301	5,712	6,823	7,548	16,549	18,674	16,520
City	2,280	2,329	2,089	1,923	(4)	(4)	(4)
Private practice	192,353	200,586	212,662	236,085	370,111	460,206	519,941
Individual	116,911	113,127	113,273	118,963	179,923	216,336	240,141
Partner	60,709	70,064	78,544	92,442	144,279	177,392	194,976
Associate [6]	14,733	17,395	20,845	24,680	45,908	66,478	84,824
Salaried	25,198	29,510	33,222	40,486	73,862	83,843	85,671
Private industry	22,533	26,492	29,405	33,593	54,626	63,622	66,627
Educational institutions	1,798	2,100	2,717	3,732	6,606	7,254	7,575
Other private employment	867	918	1,100	3,161	12,630	12,967	11,469
Inactive or retired [5]	10,887	12,024	14,881	16,812	28,582	36,430	40,762

X Not applicable.   [1] 1960 to 1970 includes lawyers not reporting and an adjustment (subtraction) for duplications; 1980, 1985, and 1988 weighted to account for non-reporters and duplicate listings.   [2] 1960 to 1970 includes duplications; 1980, 1985, and figures are weighted to adjust for duplication of entries.   [3] 1960 to 1970, in cases where more than one subentry was applicable, the individual was tabulated in each. In 1980 and 1985 lawyers who were in both private practice and government service are coded in private practice.   [4] Data no longer available separately; included with category above.   [5] Beginning 1988, "senior" judges are included in "Retired" rather than "Judicial."   [6] Associates are lawyers designated as such by their employers.

Source: American Bar Foundation, Chicago, IL, 1960 to 1970, *The 1971 Lawyer Statistical Report,* 1971 (copyright); 1980, *The Lawyer Statistical Report: A Statistical Profile of the U.S. Legal Profession in the 1980's,* 1985 (copyright); 1985 and 1988, *Supplement to The Lawyer Statistical Report: The U.S. Legal Profession in 1988,* 1991 and similar report for 1985 (copyright).

No. 315. Lawyers, by State: 1970 to 1988

[Data based on 1971, 1980, and 1988 editions of *Martindale-Hubbell Law Directory.* Represents all persons who are members of the bar, including those in industries, educational institutions, etc., and those inactive or retired]

STATE	1970 [1]	1980 [2]	1988 Total [2]	1988 In private practice [2]	1988 Population per lawyer [3]	STATE	1970 [1]	1980 [2]	1988 Total [2]	1988 In private practice [2]	1988 Population per lawyer [3]
U.S. [4]	324,818	542,205	723,189	519,941	340	MO	7,230	10,731	13,463	9,495	382
AL	3,291	5,466	7,261	5,276	565	MT	978	1,617	2,161	1,606	373
AK	443	1,355	1,940	1,355	270	NE	2,481	3,722	4,473	3,022	358
AZ	2,618	5,657	8,859	6,222	394	NV	739	1,771	2,489	1,723	423
AR	1,969	3,188	3,939	2,746	608	NH	791	1,678	2,613	1,922	415
CA	31,580	64,840	93,054	70,496	304	NJ	11,126	18,400	27,308	19,647	283
CO	4,197	8,652	12,253	9,006	269	NM	1,201	2,508	3,503	2,620	430
CT	5,398	8,930	13,144	8,629	246	NY	48,312	62,745	81,698	60,651	219
DE	733	1,332	1,813	1,078	364	NC	4,367	7,459	10,238	7,324	634
DC	15,501	25,465	32,114	15,524	19	ND	728	1,101	1,286	904	519
FL	10,917	23,521	33,259	24,634	371	OH	15,349	23,949	28,290	20,269	384
GA	5,517	11,087	15,314	11,528	414	OK	4,637	7,034	8,853	6,443	366
HI	857	2,027	3,130	2,310	351	OR	2,996	5,803	7,743	5,582	357
ID	803	1,706	2,242	1,551	447	PA	13,557	22,872	30,319	23,061	396
IL	20,404	32,421	40,743	29,044	285	RI	1,284	2,070	2,654	2,095	374
IN	5,447	8,443	10,091	7,265	551	SC	2,236	4,195	5,482	4,177	633
IA	3,820	5,550	6,159	4,266	460	SD	812	1,125	1,385	992	515
KS	3,126	4,759	5,978	4,113	417	TN	4,770	7,802	9,515	6,771	514
KY	3,625	6,200	7,517	5,447	496	TX	17,217	30,151	43,455	32,580	388
LA	5,089	8,752	11,515	9,244	383	UT	1,309	2,480	3,640	2,720	464
ME	1,068	2,062	2,922	2,105	412	VT	581	1,095	1,537	1,099	362
MD	6,619	10,648	14,608	9,689	316	VA	6,401	10,895	14,916	9,846	403
MA	11,316	18,537	24,218	18,506	243	WA	4,466	8,468	12,925	9,555	360
MI	10,569	17,443	21,644	15,630	427	WV	1,719	2,566	3,016	2,238	622
MN	5,481	9,433	12,723	8,714	339	WI	6,177	9,117	10,829	7,681	448
MS	2,517	3,850	4,384	3,316	598	WY	449	927	1,168	793	410

[1] Represents lawyers reporting only. Includes an estimated adjustment (subtraction) to account for duplications. Based on reporting from approximately 90 percent of all lawyers.   [2] Weighted to account for non-reporters and duplicate listings.   [3] Based on Bureau of the Census estimated resident population, including Armed Forces station in area as of July 1, 1988.   [4] Total for U.S. counts each lawyer only once regardless of the number of offices maintained by the lawyer. If, however, a lawyer maintains an office in more than one State, the lawyer is included in the total shown for each State in which the lawyer maintains an office.

Source: American Bar Foundation, Chicago, IL, *The 1971 Lawyer Statistical Report,* 1971 (copyright); 1980, *The Lawyer Statistical Report: A Statistical Profile of the U.S. Legal Profession in the 1980s,* 1985 (copyright); and 1985, *Supplement to The Lawyer Statistical Report: The U.S. Legal Profession in 1985,* 1986 (copyright).

No. 316. U.S. Supreme Court—Cases Filed and Disposition: 1970 to 1990

[Statutory term of court begins first Monday in **October**. See *Historical Statistics, Colonial Times to 1970*, series H 1063-1078, for related but not comparable data]

ACTION	1970	1975	1980	1984	1985	1986	1987	1988	1989	1990
Total cases on docket	**4,212**	**4,761**	**5,144**	**5,006**	**5,158**	**5,123**	**5,268**	**5,657**	**5,746**	**6,316**
Appellate cases on docket............	1,903	2,352	2,749	2,575	2,571	2,547	2,577	2,587	2,416	2,351
From prior term...................	325	431	527	539	400	476	440	446	384	365
Docketed during present term........	1,578	1,921	2,222	2,036	2,171	2,071	2,137	2,141	2,032	1,986
Cases acted upon [2]...............	1,613	1,900	2,324	2,253	2,185	2,189	2,224	2,271	2,096	2,042
Granted review	214	244	167	167	166	152	157	130	103	114
Denied, dismissed, or withdrawn.....	1,285	1,538	1,999	1,953	1,863	1,876	1,919	1,973	1,881	1,802
Summarily decided..............	114	118	90	59	78	71	66	75	44	81
Cases not acted upon	290	452	425	322	386	358	353	316	320	309
Pauper cases on docket	2,289	2,395	2,371	2,416	2,577	2,564	2,675	3,056	3,316	3,951
Cases acted upon [2]...............	1,802	1,997	2,027	2,087	2,189	2,250	2,263	2,638	2,891	3,436
Granted review	41	28	17	18	20	15	23	17	19	27
Denied, dismissed, or withdrawn.....	1,683	1,903	1,968	2,050	2,136	2,186	2,210	2,577	2,824	3,369
Summarily decided..............	78	66	32	14	24	38	21	32	35	28
Cases not acted upon	487	398	344	329	388	314	412	418	425	515
Original cases on docket.............	20	14	24	15	10	12	16	14	14	14
Cases disposed of during term	7	7	7	8	2	1	5	2	2	3
Total cases available for argument...............	**267**	**280**	**264**	**271**	**276**	**270**	**280**	**254**	**204**	**201**
Cases disposed of	160	181	162	184	175	179	175	173	147	131
Cases argued....................	151	179	154	175	171	175	167	170	146	125
Cases dismissed or remanded without argument...............	9	2	8	9	4	4	8	3	1	6
Cases remaining	107	99	102	87	101	91	105	81	57	70
Cases decided by signed opinion	126	160	144	159	161	164	151	156	143	121
Cases decided by per curiam opinion.....	22	16	8	11	10	10	9	12	3	4
Number of signed opinions	109	138	123	139	146	145	139	133	129	112

- Represents zero. [1] Beginning 1980, includes cases granted review and carried over to next term, not shown separately.
Source: Office of the Clerk, Supreme Court of the United States, unpublished data.

No. 317. U.S. Courts of Appeals—Cases Commenced and Disposition: 1970 to 1990

[For years ending **June 30**. See also *Historical Statistics, Colonial Times to 1970*, series H 1079-1096]

ITEM	1970	1975	1980	1984	1985	1986	1987	1988	1989	1990
Cases commenced [1].	**11,662**	**16,658**	**23,200**	**31,490**	**33,360**	**34,292**	**35,176**	**37,524**	**39,734**	**40,898**
Criminal	2,660	4,187	4,405	4,881	4,989	5,134	5,260	6,012	8,020	9,493
U.S. civil........	2,167	2,981	4,654	6,259	6,744	6,415	6,292	6,210	6,349	6,626
Private civil......	4,834	6,511	10,200	15,466	16,827	17,876	19,246	20,464	20,626	20,490
Administrative appeals	1,522	2,290	2,950	3,045	3,179	3,187	2,723	3,043	2,965	2,578
Cases terminated [1]..	**10,699**	**16,000**	**20,887**	**31,185**	**31,387**	**33,774**	**34,444**	**35,888**	**37,372**	**38,520**
Criminal	2,581	4,005	3,993	4,876	4,892	5,134	5,039	5,284	6,297	7,509
U.S. civil........	1,912	3,094	4,346	6,074	6,363	6,535	6,227	6,386	6,127	6,379
Private civil......	4,367	6,252	8,942	15,309	15,743	17,276	18,338	19,798	20,313	20,369
Administrative appeals	1,407	1,909	2,643	3,212	2,760	3,235	3,237	2,625	2,914	2,582
Cases disposed of [2] .	**6,139**	**9,077**	**10,607**	**14,327**	**16,369**	**18,199**	**18,502**	**19,178**	**19,322**	**21,006**
Affirmed or granted .	4,626	6,763	8,017	10,961	12,286	13,398	13,681	14,953	15,240	16,629
Reversed or denied .	1,280	1,632	1,845	2,382	2,770	3,249	2,924	2,664	2,617	2,565
Other...........	233	682	745	984	1,313	1,552	1,897	1,561	1,465	1,812
Median months [3]	8.2	7.4	8.9	8.3	10.3	10.3	10.3	10.1	10.3	10.1

[1] Includes original proceedings and bankruptcy appeals not shown separately. [2] Terminated on the merits after hearing or submission. Beginning 1975, data not comparable with 1970 due to changes in criteria. [3] Prior to 1985, the figure is from filing of complete record to final disposition; beginning 1985, figure is from filing notice of appeal to final disposition. For definition of median, see Guide to Tabular Presentation.

No. 318. U.S. District Courts—Civil and Criminal Cases: 1970 to 1990

[In thousands, except percent. For years ending **June 30**. See also *Historical Statistics, Colonial Times to 1970*, series H 1097-1111]

ITEM	1970	1975	1980	1984	1985	1986	1987	1988	1989	1990
Civil cases: Commenced	87.3	117.3	168.8	261.5	273.7	254.8	239.0	239.6	233.5	217.9
Cases terminated [1]	79.5	103.8	155.0	241.8	268.6	265.8	237.5	238.1	234.6	213.4
No court action	31.1	39.2	68.7	113.9	129.4	122.2	97.8	79.6	64.3	51.6
Court action, total........	48.4	64.6	86.2	127.9	139.2	143.6	139.7	158.6	170.4	161.8
Before pretrial.........	29.4	40.3	53.8	86 1	95.6	101.9	95.3	114.7	129.7	127
Pretrial	11.0	15.6	22.4	29.6	31.1	29.9	32.5	32.2	29.5	25.5
Trials	8.0	8.7	10.1	12.1	12.6	11.7	11.9	11.6	11.2	9.2
Percent reaching trial . . .	10.0	8.4	6.5	5.0	4.7	4.4	5.0	4.9	4.8	4.3
Criminal cases: Commenced [2].	38.1	41.1	28.0	35.9	38.5	40.4	42.2	43.5	44.9	48.0
Defendants disposed of [3]	36.4	49.2	36.6	44.5	47.4	50.0	54.2	52.8	54.6	56.5
Not convicted	8.2	11.8	8.0	8.4	8.8	9.3	10.2	9.9	10.1	9.8
Convicted.............	28.2	37.4	28.6	36.1	38.5	40.7	43.9	42.9	44.5	46.7
Imprisonment	12.4	17.3	13.2	17.7	18.7	20.6	23.3	22.5	24.9	27.8
Probation.............	11.4	17.9	11.1	13.9	14.4	15.2	16.0	16.1	15.0	14.2
Fine and other	4.4	2.2	4.4	4.5	5.4	4.9	4.6	4.4	4.7	4.7

[1] Excludes land condemnation cases. [2] Excludes transfers. [3] Beginning 1975, includes DC; beginning 1980, includes Guam, Virgin Islands, and Northern Mariana Islands; 1980 through 1982 includes Canal Zone.
Source of tables 317 and 318: Administrative Office of the U.S. Courts, *Annual Report of the Director*.

No. 319. U.S. District Courts—Civil Cases Commenced and Pending: 1980 to 1990

[For years ending June 30]

TYPE OF CASE	CASES COMMENCED				CASES PENDING			
	1980	1985	1989	1990	1980	1985	1989	1990
Cases total	168,789	273,513	233,529	217,879	186,113	254,114	242,433	242,346
Contract actions [1]	49,052	102,642	61,975	46,039	40,521	65,983	49,000	43,490
Recovery of overpayments [2] . . .	15,588	58,160	16,467	10,878	6,696	22,576	6,419	5,177
Real property actions	11,067	10,118	11,217	9,505	15,436	9,324	8,764	8,853
Tort actions.	32,539	41,593	42,090	43,759	41,062	57,243	68,391	72,933
Personal injury	27,517	37,560	38,361	40,593	34,994	52,608	64,105	69,033
Personal injury product liability	(NA)	12,507	13,408	18,679	9,118	22,111	34,837	41,933
Asbestos	(NA)	4,239	8,230	13,687	(NA)	11,194	25,419	33,182
Other personal injury.	27,517	25,053	24,953	21,914	25,876	30,497	29,268	25,148
Personal property damage	5,022	4,033	3,729	3,166	6,068	4,635	4,286	3,900
Actions under statutes [1]	75,574	119,160	118,131	118,465	88,534	121,295	115,215	113,254
Civil rights [1]	12,944	19,553	19,378	18,793	18,819	26,148	24,174	24,059
Employment	5,017	8,082	9,000	8,413	8,893	12,187	11,815	8,459
Bankruptcy suits	1,688	6,331	5,228	5,056	1,443	4,866	3,777	4,062
Commerce (ICC rates, etc.). . . .	1,105	912	1,339	2,401	6,194	747	949	1,460
Environmental matters	557	652	938	958	751	912	1,395	1,558
Prisoner petitions	23,287	33,468	41,481	42,630	18,008	29,982	33,854	36,325
Forfeiture and penalty	3,019	4,908	4,920	6,193	2,282	3,658	4,175	4,946
Labor laws	8,640	11,749	13,328	13,841	9,045	11,002	11,840	12,252
Protected property rights [3]	3,783	5,412	5,977	5,700	4,014	5,151	5,595	5,497
Securities commodities and exchanges	1,694	3,266	2,608	2,629	3,255	5,082	4,561	4,636
Social Security laws.	9,043	19,771	10,206	7,439	13,154	20,302	10,779	8,068
Tax suits	3,262	2,966	2,402	2,604	3,075	2,972	2,868	2,850
Freedom of information	627	565	307	407	617	555	385	451

NA Not available. [1] Includes other types not shown separately. [2] Includes enforcement of judgments in student loan cases, and overpayments of veterans benefits. [3] Includes copyright, patent, and trademark rights.

No. 320. U.S. District Courts—Trials: 1970 to 1990

[For years ending June 30. A trial is defined as a contested proceeding (other than a hearing on a motion) before either court or jury in which evidence is introduced and final judgment sought See also *Historical Statistics, Colonial Times to 1970*, series H 1112-1118]

TYPE OF TRIAL	1970	1975	1980	1984	1985	1986	1987	1988	1989	1990
Total	16,032	19,236	19,825	20,830	20,729	20,242	19,985	19,901	20,102	20,433
Civil trials	9,449	11,603	13,191	14,374	14,254	13,276	13,162	12,536	12,085	11,502
Nonjury	6,078	7,903	9,254	9,037	8,817	8,054	7,597	7,088	6,878	6,737
Jury	3,371	3,700	3,937	5,337	5,437	5,222	5,565	5,448	5,207	4,765
Criminal trials.	6,583	7,633	6,634	6,456	6,475	6,966	6,823	7,365	8,017	8,931
Nonjury	2,357	2,726	3,216	2,823	2,778	3,066	2,912	3,215	3,553	3,870
Jury	4,226	4,907	3,418	3,633	3,697	3,900	3,911	4,150	4,464	5,061

No. 321. U.S. District Courts—Criminal Cases Commenced and Defendants Disposed of, by Nature of Offense: 1989 and 1990

[For years ending June 30]

NATURE OF OFFENSE	1989		DISPOSITION OF DEFENDANTS, 1990									
	Cases commenced [1]	Defendants disposed of	Cases commenced, [1] 1990	Total defendants disposed of	Not convicted		Convicted [2]			Sentenced		
					Total	Acquitted	Total	Guilty plea [3]	By court or jury	Imprisonment	Probation	Fine and other
Total	44,891	54,643	47,962	56,519	9,794	1,601	46,725	39,734	6,273	27,796	14,196	4,733
General offenses:												
Homicide	174	166	176	162	33	8	129	90	37	106	11	12
Robbery.	1,309	1,206	1,379	1,340	111	26	1,229	1,060	165	1,207	21	1
Assault	567	579	562	559	173	42	386	279	105	254	106	26
Burglary	107	103	104	122	9	2	113	101	12	99	12	2
Larceny-theft.	3,474	4,065	3,391	3,574	675	70	2,899	2,640	220	1,088	1,571	240
Embezzlement and fraud	8,958	10,982	9,579	10,774	1,202	183	9,572	8,759	756	4,134	5,113	325
Auto theft.	233	462	243	319	47	10	272	243	28	198	72	2
Forgery [4]	1,505	1,733	1,514	1,774	217	18	1,557	1,444	105	805	729	23
Sex offenses.	324	348	433	333	62	16	271	223	47	185	83	3
DAPCA [5]	11,858	16,834	12,592	19,271	3,083	473	16,188	13,036	3,121	13,838	2,135	215
Misc. general offenses	16,385	18,165	13,265	12,504	3,323	627	9,181	7,437	1,243	3,212	2,514	3,455

[1] Excludes transfers. [2] Convicted and sentenced. [3] Includes nolo contendere. [4] Includes counterfeiting. [5] All marijuana, narcotics, and controlled substances prosecutions under the Drug Abuse, Prevention and Control Act.
Source of tables 324-326: Administrative Office of the U.S. Courts, *Annual Report of the Director.*

No. 322. U.S. District Courts—Offenders Convicted and Sentenced to Prison, 1980 and 1990, and Length of Sentence, 1990

MOST SERIOUS OFFENSE OF CONVICTION	OFFENDERS CONVICTED		CONVICTED OFFENDERS SENTENCED TO PRISON		Length of sentence, 1990 (mo.)	MOST SERIOUS OFFENSE OF CONVICTION	OFFENDERS CONVICTED		CONVICTED OFFENDERS SENTENCED TO PRISON		Length of sentence, 1990 (mo.)
	1980	1990, prel.	1980	1990, prel.			1980	1990, prel.	1980	1990, prel.	
Total [1]	29,943	48,730	13,766	29,430	57.4	Possession . . .	502	1,446	115	457	13.1
Violent offenses .	2,134	2,281	1,770	1,999	89.8	Trafficking and					
Property offenses	10,780	13,396	4,630	5,775	22.3	manufacturing.	4,633	14,631	3,560	13,297	83.5
Fraudulent offenses [2] . . .	6,733	9,979	2,825	4,391	22.3	Public-order offenses	11,893	14,891	3,690	6,427	27.7
Embezzle- ment	1,605	1,834	460	515	17.7	Regulatory offenses	1,828	1,977	484	757	26.3
Fraud [3]	3,307	6,749	1,384	3,180	23.9	Other offenses .	10,065	12,914	3,206	5,670	27.8
Forgery . . .	1,180	895	610	387	17.1	Weapons . . .	980	2,332	578	1,802	47.5
Other offenses [2]	4,047	3,417	1,805	1,384	22.5	Immigration. .	2,200	2,622	1,017	1,903	10.5
Larceny	3,026	2,676	1,180	914	18.7	Tax law					
Drug offenses [2] . .	5,135	16,077	3,675	13,754	81.2	violations [4]	1,407	1,147	487	498	25.1

[1] For 1990, includes 2,085 offenders convicted and 1,475 convited offenders sentenced for whom offense category could not be determined. [2] Includes offenses not shown separately. [3] Excludes tax fraud. [4] Includes tax fraud.
Source: U.S. Bureau of Justice Statistics, *Federal Criminal Case Processing, 1980-89*, October 1991.

No. 323. U.S. District Courts—Defendants Charged With Violations of Drug Abuse Prevention and Control Act: 1980 to 1990

[For years ending June 30]

ITEM	MARIJUANA				DRUGS				CONTROLLED SUBSTANCES (prescribed drugs)			
	1980	1985	1989	1990	1980	1985	1989	1990	1980	1985	1989	1990
Defendants disposed of . . .	1,690	3,984	4,547	5,139	3,290	5,595	10,717	12,649	1,363	1,598	1,570	1,483
Not convicted	569	854	898	1,011	749	868	1,548	1,850	276	246	249	222
Dismissed [1]	483	709	798	915	620	692	1,280	1,506	234	200	221	189
Convicted	1,121	3,130	3,649	4,128	2,541	4,727	9,169	10,799	1,087	1,352	1,321	1,261
By guilty plea and nolo contendere	772	2,523	3,227	3,624	1,830	3,839	7,356	8,423	848	1,138	1,103	1,020
Imprisonment, total [2]	754	2,036	2,448	3,004	1,945	3,701	8,151	9,804	780	1,049	1,027	1,030
Regular sentence.	555	1,512	2,249	2,931	1,410	2,885	7,649	9,551	582	810	940	980
Avg. sentence (mo.).	47.2	53.2	52.7	48.9	60.8	77.8	86.2	46.5	69.3	92.0	79.3	
Other sentences to prison[2] . .	199	524	199	73	535	816	502	253	198	239	87	50
Probation, total	341	938	1,145	1,054	588	960	942	874	303	287	271	207
Avg. sentence (mo.).	37.9	31.2	25.1	25.1	39.9	39.7	41.8	40.0	37.2	40.5	33.6	32.3
Fine only	20	83	39	39	4	3	14	17	3	6	8	8
Other [3]	6	73	17	31	4	63	62	104	1	10	15	16

[1] Includes defendants committed under 28 USC 2902, Narcotic Addict Rehabilitation Act of 1966. [2] Split or mixed sentences of prison and probation in the same case as well as indeterminate and Youth Corrections Act sentences are included under total imprisonment and other sentences to prison. [3] Includes deportation, suspended sentences, imprisonment for four days or less or for time already served, remitted and suspended fines and life sentences.
Source: Administrative Office of the U.S. Courts, *Annual Report of the Director*.

No. 324. Federal Prosecutions of Public Corruption: 1975 to 1990

[As of Dec. 31. Prosecution of persons who have corrupted public office in violation of Federal Criminal Statutes]

PROSECUTION STATUS	1975	1979	1980	1981	1982	1983	1984	1985	1986	1987	1988	1989	1990
Total: [1] Indicted	255	666	721	878	729	1,073	936	1,182	1,193	1,340	1,274	1,349	1,176
Convicted	179	536	552	730	671	972	934	997	1,026	1,081	1,067	1,149	1,084
Awaiting trial	27	178	213	231	186	222	269	256	246	368	288	375	300
Federal officials: Indicted.	53	114	123	198	158	[2]460	408	563	596	651	629	695	615
Convicted	43	102	131	159	147	[2]424	429	470	523	545	529	610	583
Awaiting trial	5	21	16	23	38	58	77	90	83	118	86	126	103
State officials: Indicted . .	36	56	72	87	49	81	58	79	88	102	66	71	96
Convicted	18	32	51	66	43	65	52	66	71	76	69	54	79
Awaiting trial	5	28	28	36	18	26	21	20	24	26	14	18	28
Local officials: Indicted . .	139	211	247	244	257	270	203	248	232	246	276	269	257
Convicted	94	151	168	211	232	226	196	221	207	204	229	201	225
Awaiting trial	15	63	82	102	58	61	74	49	55	89	79	122	98

[1] Includes individuals who are neither public officials nor employees but who were involved with public officials or employees in violating the law, not shown separately. [2] Increases in the number indicted and convicted between 1982 and 1983 resulted from a greater focus on federal corruption nationwide and more consistent reporting of cases involving lower-level employees.
Source: U.S. Department of Justice, *Federal Prosecutions of Corrupt Public Officials, 1970-1980* and *Report to Congress on the Activities and Operations of the Public Integrity Section*, annual.

No. 325. Delinquency Cases Disposed, by Juvenile Courts: 1975 to 1989

YEAR	CASES DISPOSED		Case rate [1]	YEAR	CASES DISPOSED		Case rate [1]
	Total (1,000)	Per-cent change			Total (1,000)	Per-cent change	
1975	1,050	(NA)	33.8	1983	1,030	-4.0	38.3
1976	1,077	2.6	35.1	1984	1,034	0.4	38.7
1977	1,076	-0.1	35.8	1985	1,112	7.5	42.2
1978	1,023	-4.9	34.6	1986	1,150	3.4	44.2
1979	1,048	2.4	36.2	1987	1,145	-0.4	44.5
1980	1,093	4.3	38.3	1988	1,151	0.5	45.2
1981	1,100	0.6	39.1	1989	1,189	3.3	47.0
1982	1,073	-2.5	39.1				

NA Not available.　[1] Number of cases disposed per 1,000 youth (ages 10 to 17) at risk.
Source: National Center for Juvenile Justice, Pittsburgh, PA, *Juvenile Court Statistics*, annual.

No. 326. Delinquency Cases Disposed by Juvenile Courts, by Reason for Referral, 1982 to 1989

[In thousands. A delinquency offense is an act committed by a juvenile for which an adult could be prosecuted in a criminal court. Disposition of a case involves taking a definite action such as transferring the case to criminal court, dismissing the case, placing the youth on probation, placing the youth in a facility for delinquents, or such actions as fines, restitution, and community service]

REASON FOR REFERRAL	1982	1983	1984	1985	1986	1987	1988	1989
All delinquency offense	1,073	1,030	1,034	1,112	1,150	1,145	1,151	1,189
Violent offenses	57	55	61	67	71	65	68	77
Criminal homicide	2	1	1	1	2	2	2	2
Forcible rape	3	3	3	4	5	4	4	4
Robbery	26	24	22	26	26	22	21	23
Aggravated assault	27	27	35	36	39	38	41	48
Property offenses	475	451	442	489	498	500	502	514
Burglary	158	145	129	139	141	134	131	131
Larceny	278	270	276	307	308	313	310	309
Motor vehicle theft	34	31	31	36	42	48	55	67
Arson	5	5	6	7	6	6	7	7
Delinquency offenses	541	524	530	555	582	580	581	599
Simple assault	86	81	73	92	96	100	102	108
Vandalism	64	64	69	84	85	84	82	83
Drug law violations	62	57	65	76	73	73	80	78
Obstruction of justice	47	55	63	68	78	79	78	82
Other [1]	282	268	260	235	250	245	239	248

[1] Includes such offenses as stolen property offenses, trespassing, weapons offenses, other sex offenses, liquor law violations, disorderly conduct, and miscellaneous offenses.
Source: U.S. National Center for Juvenile Justice, Pittsburgh, PA, *Juvenile Court Statistics*, annual.

No. 327. Juveniles Held in Public and Private Custody—Residents and Facilities: 1985 to 1989

[Public and private facilities for juveniles includes detention centers, shelters, reception and diagnostic centers, training schools, halfway houses, group homes, ranches, forestry camps, and farms]

CHARACTERISTIC	Unit	PUBLIC CUSTODY			PRIVATE CUSTODY		
		1985	1987	1989	1985	1987	1989
Number of residents [1][2]	Number	51,402	56,097	58,303	34,112	38,184	37,845
Juvenile [3]	Number	49,322	53,503	56,123	34,080	38,143	37,822
Average age [4]	Years	15.4	15.8	16.0	14.9	14.8	14.9
Male	Number	42,549	46,272	49,443	23,844	26,339	26,602
Female	Number	6,773	7,231	6,680	10,236	11,804	11,220
White	Number	29,969	31,103	30,705	23,999	26,839	25,696
Black	Number	18,269	21,057	24,003	9,204	10,357	11,076
Number of admissions (all residents) [5][6]	Number	527,759	597,624	624,597	101,007	126,102	141,907
Number of departures (all residents) [5][6]	Number	520,903	592,229	614,430	96,006	120,071	135,319
Average daily residents [6]	Number	49,480	54,036	56,595	33,121	38,172	37,944
Facilities, total [2][7]	Number	1,040	1,107	1,100	1,996	2,195	2,167
Occupancy less than 70 percent	Percent	35	28	24	20	18	16
70 to 100 percent	Percent	55	57	57	79	79	82
More than 100 percent	Percent	10	15	18	1	3	2
Personnel, total [2][8]	Number	(NA)	62,249	58,775	(NA)	49,144	49,334
Operating costs [5]	Mil. dol.	1,247.9	1,458.7	1,674.0	805.5	1,060.0	1,186.8
Per resident operating cost [9]	$1,000	25.2	27.0	29.6	24.3	27.8	31.3

NA Not available.　[1] Includes adults.　[2] Data for February 1, 1985, February 2, 1987, and February 15, 1989.
[3] Includes races not reported and races not shown.　[4] Based on juvenile residents only.　[5] Data are for calendar years 1984, 1986, and 1988.　[6] Juvenile and adult.　[7] Occupancy is calculated on the average daily resident population.　[8] 1987 personnel includes full, part-time, and volunteer and 1989 includes full and part-time only.　[9] Based on average daily residents.
Source: 1985, U.S. Bureau of Justice Statistics, *Census of Public and Private Juvenile Detention, Correctional, and Shelter Facilities, 1975-85*; thereafter, U.S. Office of Juvenile Justice and Delinquency Prevention, *1987* and *1989 Census of Public and Private Juvenile Custody Facilities*, and *1987 Children in Custody* and *Juvenile Taken Into Custody: fiscal Year 1990 Report*.

No. 328. Jail Inmates, by Race and Detention Status: 1978 to 1990

[Excludes Federal and State prisons or other correctional institutions; institutions exclusively for juveniles; State-operated jails in Alaska, Connecticut, Delaware, Hawaii, Rhode Island, and Vermont; and other facilities which retain persons for less than 48 hours. As of **June 30**. For 1978, 1983, and 1988, data based on National Jail Census; for other years, based on sample survey and subject to sampling variability]

CHARACTERISTIC	1978	1983	1984	1985	1986	1987	1988	1989	1990
Total inmates [1]	158,394	223,552	234,500	256,615	274,444	295,873	343,569	395,553	405,320
Percent of rated capacity	65	85	90	94	96	98	101	108	104
Percent of operational capacity	64	81	(NA)	(NA)	(NA)	(NA)	(NA)	(NA)	(NA)
Male	148,839	207,783	216,275	235,909	251,235	270,172	313,158	356,050	368,002
Female	9,555	15,769	16,743	19,077	21,501	23,920	30,411	37,253	37,318
White	89,418	130,118	138,355	151,403	159,178	168,647	166,302	201,732	186,989
Black	65,104	87,508	93,800	102,646	112,522	124,267	141,979	185,910	174,335
Other races	3,872	5,926	2,345	2,566	2,744	2,959	3,932	7,911	5,321
Hispanic [2]	16,349	31,297	30,485	35,926	38,422	41,422	51,455	55,377	57,449
Non-Hispanic	142,045	192,254	204,015	220,689	236,022	254,451	292,114	340,176	347,871
Adult [3]	156,783	221,815	233,018	254,986	272,736	294,092	341,893	393,303	403,019
Awaiting arraignment or trial	77,453	113,984	116,331	127,059	142,112	150,101	175,669	204,291	207,358
Convicted	75,438	107,660	113,491	123,409	127,067	139,394	166,224	189,012	195,661
Juvenile [4]	1,611	1,736	1,482	1,629	1,708	1,781	1,676	2,250	2,301

NA Not available. [1] For 1984 to 1987 and 1989, includes juveniles not shown separately by sex, and for 1988 and 1990 includes 31,356 and 38,671 persons, respectively, of unknown race not shown separately. [2] Hispanic persons may be of any race. [3] Includes inmates not classified by conviction status. [4] Juveniles are persons whose age makes them initially subject to juvenile court authority although they are sometimes tried as adults in criminal court.

Source: U.S. Bureau of Justice Statistics, *Profile of Jail Inmates, 1978 and 1989; Jail Inmates*, annual; and *1988 Census of Local Jails.*

No. 329. Federal and State Prisoners: 1960 to 1990

[Based on Bureau of the Census estimated resident population, as of **July 1**. Prior to 1970, excludes State institutions in Alaska. Beginning 1980, includes all persons under jurisdiction of Federal and State authorities rather than those in the custody of such authorities. Represents inmates sentenced to maximum term of more than a year. See also *Historical Statistics, Colonial Times to 1970*, series H 1135-1140]

YEAR	PRESENT AT END OF YEAR						RECEIVED FROM COURTS					
	All institutions		Federal		State		All institutions		Federal		State	
	Number	Rate [1]	Number	Rate [1]	Number	Rate [1]	Number	Rate [1]	Number	Rate [1]	Number	Rate [1]
1960....	212,953	118.6	23,218	12.9	189,735	105.7	88,575	49.3	13,723	7.6	74,852	41.7
1970....	196,429	96.7	20,038	9.8	176,391	86.8	79,351	39.1	12,047	5.9	67,304	33.1
1975....	240,593	113.3	24,131	11.4	216,462	102.0	129,573	61.0	16,770	7.9	112,803	53.1
1980....	315,974	139.2	20,611	9.1	295,363	130.1	142,122	62.7	10,907	4.8	131,215	57.9
1982....	395,516	170.6	23,652	10.2	371,864	160.4	177,109	76.1	12,461	5.4	164,648	70.7
1983....	419,346	179.0	26,331	11.2	393,015	167.8	187,408	80.1	14,119	6.0	173,289	74.1
1984....	443,398	187.5	27,602	12.0	415,796	175.8	180,418	76.0	13,491	5.7	166,927	70.3
1985....	480,568	216.5	32,695	13.6	447,873	187.6	198,499	82.7	15,368	6.4	183,131	76.3
1986....	522,084	230.4	36,531	15.0	485,553	201.4	219,382	91.0	16,067	7.0	203,315	84.0
1987....	560,812	229.0	39,523	16.0	521,289	214.2	241,887	99.0	16,260	7.0	225,627	92.0
1988....	603,732	244.0	42,738	17.0	560,994	227.0	261,242	106.0	15,932	6.4	245,310	99.3
1989....	680,907	274.3	47,168	19.0	633,739	255.3	316,215	127.4	18,388	7.4	297,827	120.0
1990....	738,894	294.5	50,810	20.3	688,084	274.3	(NA)	(NA)	(NA)	(NA)	323,069	128.8

NA Not available. [1] Rate per 100,000 estimated population.

Source: U.S. Bureau of Justice Statistics, *Prisoners in State and Federal Institutions on December 31*, annual, and *Correctional Populations in the United States*, annual.

No. 330. State Prison Inmates—Selected Characteristics: 1979 and 1986

[Based on a sample survey of about 13,711 inmates in 1986 and 11,397 inmates in 1979; subject to sampling variability]

CHARACTERISTIC	NUMBER 1979	NUMBER 1986	PERCENT OF PRISON INMATES 1979	PERCENT OF PRISON INMATES 1986
Total [1]	274,564	450,416	100.0	100.0
Under 18 years old	2,220	2,057	0.8	0.5
18 to 24 years old	97,860	120,384	35.6	26.7
25 to 34 years old	116,284	205,817	42.4	45.7
35 to 44 years old	37,926	87,502	13.8	19.4
45 to 54 years old	13,987	23,524	5.1	5.2
55 to 64 years old	4,786	8,267	1.7	1.8
65 years old and over	1,499	2,808	0.5	0.6
Male	263,484	430,604	96.0	95.6
Female	11,080	19,812	4.0	4.4
White	136,295	223,648	49.6	49.7
Black	131,329	211,021	47.8	46.9
Other races	6,939	15,412	2.6	3.4

CHARACTERISTIC	NUMBER 1979	NUMBER 1986	PERCENT OF PRISON INMATES 1979	PERCENT OF PRISON INMATES 1986
Never married	142,414	241,707	51.9	53.7
Married	61,420	91,492	22.4	20.3
Widowed	6,248	8,343	2.3	1.9
Divorced	46,314	81,263	16.9	18.1
Separated	18,168	26,985	6.6	6.0
Years of school:				
Less than 12 years	144,771	276,309	52.7	61.6
12 years or more	129,792	172,385	47.3	38.4
Pre-arrest employment status:				
Employed	192,800	309,364	70.5	69.0
Not employed	80,663	138,773	29.5	31.0
Looking for work	38,230	80,508	14.0	18.0
Not looking for work	42,433	58,265	15.5	13.0

[1] For 1986, includes data not reported for all characteristics except sex.

Source: U.S. Bureau of Justice Statistics, *Profile of State Prison Inmates, 1986*, January 1988.

No. 331. Prisoners Under Jurisdiction of State and Federal Correctional Authorities—Summary, by State: 1980 to 1990

[For years ending **December 31**]

SEX, REGION, DIVISION, AND STATE	1980	1985	1988	1989	1990	SENTENCED TO MORE THAN 1 YEAR			1990	
						1985	1988	1989	Total	Rate per 100,000 population [1]
United States . .	329,821	503,271	627,588	712,364	774,375	481,393	603,720	680,907	738,894	292
Male	316,401	480,147	594,996	671,752	730,141	459,934	573,587	643,643	698,410	278
Female.	13,420	23,124	32,592	40,612	44,234	21,459	30,133	37,264	40,484	16
Federal institutions [2]	24,363	40,223	49,928	59,171	67,432	32,695	42,738	47,168	50,810	20
State institutions . . .	305,458	463,048	577,660	653,193	706,943	448,698	560,982	633,739	688,084	272
Northeast	45,796	75,706	99,180	113,970	123,392	72,656	94,522	109,399	119,063	232
N.E.	9,926	15,432	19,784	22,830	25,079	12,490	15,143	18,270	20,759	158
ME	814	1,226	1,277	1,455	1,523	967	1,214	1,432	1,480	118
NH	326	683	1,019	1,166	1,342	683	1,019	1,166	1,342	117
VT [3]	480	677	820	905	1,049	443	553	626	681	117
MA [4]	3,185	5,390	6,757	7,524	8,273	[5]5,390	6,455	[5]7,268	[5]7,899	132
RI [3]	813	1,307	1,906	2,479	2,392	964	1,179	1,469	1,586	157
CT [3]	4,308	6,149	8,005	9,301	10,500	4,043	4,723	6,309	7,771	238
M.A	35,870	60,274	79,396	91,140	98,313	60,166	79,379	91,129	98,304	260
NY.	21,815	34,712	44,560	51,232	54,895	34,712	44,560	51,232	54,895	304
NJ.	[6]5,884	[6]11,335	16,936	19,439	21,128	11,335	16,936	19,439	21,128	271
PA.	8,171	14,227	17,900	20,469	22,290	14,119	17,883	20,458	22,281	183
Midwest.	66,211	95,704	120,382	136,342	145,791	95,245	120,077	136,046	145,478	239
E.N.C	51,175	72,599	92,914	106,018	113,703	[5]72,280	92,751	[5]105,884	[5]113,555	267
OH	13,489	20,864	26,462	30,538	31,822	[5]20,864	26,462	[5]30,538	[5]31,822	289
IN [4]	6,683	9,904	11,406	12,341	12,736	9,615	11,271	12,220	12,615	223
IL [4]	11,899	18,634	21,081	24,712	27,516	[5]18,634	21,081	[5]24,712	[5]27,516	234
MI [4]	15,124	17,755	27,612	31,639	34,267	17,755	27,612	31,639	34,267	366
WI	3,980	5,442	6,353	6,788	7,362	5,412	6,325	6,775	7,335	149
W.N.C	15,036	23,105	27,468	30,324	32,088	22,965	27,326	30,162	31,923	207
MN	2,001	2,343	2,799	3,103	3,176	[5]2,343	2,799	[5]3,103	[5]3,176	72
IA [4]	2,481	2,832	3,034	3,584	3,967	[5]2,832	3,034	[5]3,584	[5]3,967	139
MO	5,726	9,915	12,176	13,921	14,943	[5]9,915	12,176	[5]13,921	[5]14,943	287
ND	253	422	466	451	483	375	414	404	435	67
SD.	635	1,047	1,020	1,256	1,341	[5]1,035	1,020	[5]1,256	[5]1,341	187
NE.	1,446	1,814	2,156	2,393	2,403	1,733	2,066	2,278	2,286	140
KS.	2,494	4,732	5,817	5,616	5,775	[5]4,732	5,817	[5]5,616	[5]5,775	227
South	146,358	202,926	233,907	262,270	284,029	195,868	226,735	252,769	275,217	316
S.A.	78,815	108,228	126,428	141,997	152,886	101,620	119,642	133,142	144,713	330
DE [3]	1,474	2,553	3,197	3,458	3,471	1,759	2,207	2,284	2,241	323
MD	7,731	13,005	14,276	16,514	17,848	12,303	13,572	15,378	16,734	348
DC [3] [4]	3,145	6,404	8,831	9,954	9,947	4,604	6,628	6,650	6,798	1148
VA.	8,920	12,073	14,184	16,477	17,593	11,717	13,928	16,273	17,418	279
WV	1,257	1,725	1,455	1,536	1,565	[5]1,725	1,455	[5]1,536	[5]1,565	85
NC [4]	15,513	17,344	17,078	17,454	18,411	16,007	16,251	16,628	17,764	265
SC.	7,862	10,510	13,888	15,720	17,319	9,908	12,902	14,808	16,208	451
GA [4]	12,178	16,014	18,787	20,885	22,345	15,115	18,018	19,619	21,605	327
FL [4]	20,735	28,600	34,732	39,999	44,387	28,482	34,681	39,966	44,380	336
E.S.C	21,055	30,335	34,833	40,737	43,451	29,885	34,447	40,194	42,860	278
KY.	3,588	5,801	7,119	8,289	9,023	[5]5,801	7,119	[5]8,289	[5]9,023	241
TN.	7,022	[6]7,127	[6]7,720	[9]10,630	[9]10,388	[5]7,127	7,720	[5]10,630	[5]10,388	207
AL.	6,543	11,015	12,610	13,907	15,665	10,749	12,357	13,575	15,365	370
MS	3,902	6,392	7,384	7,911	8,375	6,208	7,251	7,700	8,084	307
W.S.C	46,488	64,363	72,646	79,536	87,692	64,363	72,646	79,433	87,644	323
AR.	2,911	[6]4,611	[6]5,519	6,649	6,766	[5]4,611	5,519	[5]6,546	[5]6,718	277
LA.	8,889	13,890	16,242	17,257	18,599	[5]13,890	16,242	[5]17,257	[5]18,599	427
OK	4,796	8,330	10,448	11,608	12,285	[5]8,330	10,448	[5]11,608	[5]12,285	381
TX [4]	29,892	37,532	40,437	44,022	50,042	[5]37,532	40,437	[5]44,022	[5]50,042	290
West	47,093	88,712	124,191	140,611	153,731	84,929	119,648	135,525	148,326	277
Mt	13,141	22,798	31,325	35,027	36,780	22,329	30,689	34,438	36,158	264
MT	739	1,129	1,272	1,328	1,425	[5]1,129	1,272	[5]1,328	[5]1,425	176
ID	817	1,294	1,581	1,850	1,961	[5]1,294	1,581	[5]1,850	[5]1,961	190
WY	534	758	[6]945	1,026	1,110	758	945	1,026	1,110	237
CO	2,629	3,369	5,765	6,908	7,018	[5]3,369	5,765	[5]6,908	[5]7,018	209
NM	1,279	[6]2,313	2,825	3,158	3,187	2,112	2,723	3,120	3,067	196
AZ [4]	4,372	8,531	12,095	13,251	14,261	8,273	11,578	12,726	13,781	375
UT.	932	1,633	1,961	2,394	2,496	1,623	1,944	2,368	2,474	142
NV.	1,839	3,771	4,881	5,112	5,322	3,771	4,881	5,112	5,322	444
Pac	33,952	65,914	92,866	105,584	116,951	62,600	88,959	101,087	112,168	286
WA	[6]4,399	6,909	5,816	6,928	7,995	6,909	5,816	6,928	7,995	162
OR	3,177	4,454	5,991	6,156	6,492	4,454	5,991	6,156	6,492	223
CA [4]	24,569	50,111	76,171	87,297	97,309	48,279	73,780	84,338	94,122	311
AK [3]	822	2,329	2,588	2,744	2,622	1,530	1,862	1,908	1,851	348
HI [3]	985	2,111	2,300	2,459	2,533	1,428	1,510	1,757	1,708	150

[1] Based on resident population estimated as of July 1, 1989.   [2] Includes persons held under other jurisdiction, not shown separately.   [3] Includes both jail and prison inmates (State has combined jail and prison system).   [4] Numbers are custodial, not jurisdictional counts.   [5] Includes an undetermined number of prisoners with sentences shorter than 1 year.   [6] Jurisdiction counts exclude prisoners held in jail because of crowding.

Source: U.S. Bureau of Justice Statistics, *Prisoners in 1990,* and earlier reports.

No. 332. Adults Under Correctional Supervision: 1989

[In thousands except rate. As of **Dec. 31.** Excludes juveniles, persons incarcerated in mental health institutions in lieu of prison, persons held by the armed services, persons held on Indian reservations, parolees under county jurisdiction, parolees whose sentences were for 1 year or less, and court probationers (those not placed under the supervisory authority of a probation agency)]

REGION, DIVISION, AND STATE	Total [1]	Rate [2]	Prison [3]	Parole [4]	Proba-tion [5]	REGION, DIVISION, AND STATE	Total [1]	Rate [2]	Prison [3]	Parole [4]	Proba-tion [5]
U.S...	**4,053.9**	**220.1**	**683.4**	**456.8**	**2,520.5**	DC ...	26.1	562.2	9.2	4.9	10.4
						VA ...	51.5	111.5	14.4	7.4	19.1
Northeast ..	**729.7**	**188.6**	**109.3**	**110.5**	**443.8**	WV ...	9.5	68.4	1.6	0.9	5.0
N.E	**195.4**	**195.5**	**22.3**	**6.1**	**158.8**	NC ...	104.6	212.1	17.7	7.6	72.3
ME ...	9.9	107.7	1.4	0.0	6.9	SC ...	52.5	205.4	14.9	3.6	29.7
NH ...	5.5	66.8	1.1	0.5	3.0	GA ...	182.6	393.5	20.9	17.4	125.4
VT ...	6.5	152.9	0.9	0.2	5.4	FL ...	266.7	272.2	39.6	2.3	192.5
MA ...	106.4	232.6	7.6	4.7	88.5	**E.S.C ...**	**157.9**	**139.6**	**35.0**	**22.9**	**72.8**
RI ...	15.1	196.8	2.5	0.4	12.2	KY ...	23.6	85.6	6.9	3.1	8.1
CT ...	51.9	209.5	8.8	0.3	42.8	TN ...	60.9	165.3	7.8	10.7	30.9
M.A	**534.3**	**186.2**	**86.9**	**104.4**	**285.0**	AL ...	51.5	171.2	13.6	5.8	26.5
NY ...	245.7	180.7	51.2	36.7	128.7	MS ...	21.8	117.9	6.8	3.3	7.3
NJ ...	116.1	196.7	16.0	20.1	66.8	**W.S.C ...**	**600.8**	**311.7**	**72.7**	**106.0**	**365.3**
PA ...	172.5	187.5	19.7	47.7	89.5	AR ...	28.5	162.5	5.8	3.5	17.6
						LA ...	67.0	215.5	13.1	9.2	32.3
Midwest ...	**791.5**	**177.5**	**136.2**	**55.9**	**542.8**	OK ...	39.0	164.4	9.8	2.0	24.2
E.N.C	**573.2**	**182.9**	**105.7**	**38.8**	**385.6**	TX ...	466.2	387.3	44.0	91.3	291.2
OH ...	124.0	153.3	30.3	6.5	78.2						
IN ...	84.1	203.4	12.4	3.5	61.9	**West......**	**813.5**	**214.9**	**139.3**	**84.9**	**488.3**
IL ...	144.4	166.4	24.7	14.6	93.9	**Mt ....**	**148.0**	**153.4**	**34.5**	**10.0**	**82.4**
MI ...	173.7	254.3	31.6	9.9	121.4	MT ...	6.6	113.1	1.3	0.8	3.5
WI ...	47.0	130.2	6.7	4.4	30.2	ID ...	7.6	107.6	1.6	0.2	4.0
W.N.C ...	**218.3**	**164.8**	**30.5**	**17.2**	**157.1**	WY ...	4.1	121.7	1.0	0.3	2.4
MN ...	67.0	207.9	3.1	1.7	58.6	CO ...	39.6	161.5	6.4	1.8	26.4
IA ...	21.3	99.7	3.6	1.9	13.7	NM ...	12.0	112.0	3.0	1.2	5.7
MO ...	71.4	185.2	13.9	7.6	45.3	AZ ...	49.1	190.7	13.3	2.0	27.7
ND ...	2.6	53.8	0.5	0.1	1.7	UT ...	10.8	100.1	2.4	1.3	5.5
SD ...	4.9	95.1	1.3	0.5	2.7	NV ...	18.1	217.2	5.4	2.4	7.3
NE ...	16.9	142.3	2.4	0.5	12.6	**Pac ......**	**665.5**	**235.9**	**104.8**	**75.0**	**405.9**
KS ...	34.3	184.8	5.6	4.8	22.5	WA ...	98.7	278.5	7.0	9.8	74.3
						OR ...	46.8	220.2	5.7	5.8	31.9
South	**1,585.2**	**251.6**	**245.3**	**184.0**	**986.5**	CA ...	498.6	233.5	87.3	57.5	285.0
S.A	**826.6**	**254.9**	**137.6**	**55.1**	**548.5**	AK ...	6.5	179.4	2.5	0.5	3.3
DE ...	13.8	273.6	3.1	1.0	9.7	HI ...	15.0	181.3	2.3	1.3	11.4
MD ...	119.3	337.6	16.2	9.9	84.5						

[1] Includes persons in jail not shown separately.　[2] Rate per 10,000 persons 18 years old and over.　[3] Includes all inmates of Federal and State institutions.　[4] Includes all adults under State parole supervision whether released from prison via parole board decision or mandatory release, who were sentenced to more than one year in prison.　[5] Includes all adults who, as part of a State, or local court order, have been placed under the supervisory authority of a probation agency.

Source: U.S. Bureau of Justice Statistics, *Probation and Parole*, annual; *Prisoners in State and Federal Institutions on December 31*, annual; and *Correctional Populations in the United States*, annu al.

No. 333. Prisoners Under Sentence of Death: 1980 to 1990

[As of **December 31.** Excludes prisoners under sentence of death who remained within local correctional systems pending exhaustion of appellate process or who had not been committed to prison]

CHARACTERISTIC	1980	1985	1988	1989	1990	CHARACTERISTIC	1980	1985	1988	1989	1990
Total [1]	**688**	**1,575**	**2,117**	**2,243**	**2,356**	Marital status:					
						Never married	268	655	898	956	998
White	418	896	1,235	1,308	1,375	Married	229	487	594	610	632
Black and other	270	679	882	935	981	Divorced [2]	217	449	632	684	726
Under 20 years	11	13	11	6	8	Time elapsed since					
20 to 24 years	173	212	195	191	168	sentencing:					
25 to 34 years	334	804	1,048	1,080	1,110	Less than 12 months .	185	273	293	231	231
35 to 54 years	186	531	823	917	1,006	12 to 47 months	389	739	812	809	753
55 years and over.....	10	31	47	56	64	48 to 71 months	102	303	408	408	438
Years of school						72 months and over..	38	276	610	802	934
completed:											
7 years or less	68	147	180	183	178	Legal status at arrest:					
8 years	74	159	184	178	186	Not under sentence ..	384	861	1,207	1,301	1,345
9 to 11 years	204	483	692	739	775	Parole or probation ..	115	350	[3]545	[3]585	578
12 years..........	162	440	657	695	729	Prison or escaped ...	45	81	00	94	128
More than 12 years ..	43	127	180	192	209	Unknown	170	299	279	270	305
Unknown	163	235	231	263	279						

[1] For 1980 to 1989, revisions to the total number of prisoners were not carried to the characteristics except for race.　[2] Includes persons married but separated, widows, widowers, and unknown.　[3] Includes prisoners on mandatory conditional release, work release, leave, AWOL, or bail. Covers 20 prisoners in 1985 and 24 in 1988 and 1989.

Source: U.S. Bureau of Justice Statistics, *Capital Punishment*, annual.

No. 334. Movement of Prisoners Under Sentence of Death: 1980 to 1990

[Prisoners reported under sentence of death by civil authorities. The term "under sentence of death" begins when the court pronounces the first sentence of death for a capital offense. As a result of a major procedural change, beginning 1980, all data except executions are not strictly comparable to corresponding data in 1975. See source for explanation]

STATUS	1980	1981	1982	1983	1984	1985	1986	1987	1988	1989	1990
Under sentence of death, Jan.1 . .	595	688	856	1,063	1,209	1,420	1,575	1,800	1,967	2,117	2,243
Received death sentence [1] [2]	203	250	287	263	296	281	297	299	296	251	244
White	125	131	166	156	173	165	164	190	196	133	147
Black	77	115	117	105	119	114	123	106	91	114	94
Dispositions other than executions [2]	101	82	76	117	108	108	73	90	128	102	108
Executions	-	1	2	5	21	18	18	25	11	16	23
Under sentence of death, Dec. 31 [1]	688	856	1,063	1,209	1,420	1,575	1,800	1,967	2,117	2,243	2,356
White	425	499	615	694	809	896	1,006	1,128	1,238	1,308	1,375
Black	268	357	446	508	595	664	750	813	853	898	943

- Represents zero.　[1] Includes races other than White or Black.　[2] Revisions to total number of prisoners under death sentence not carried to this category.

Source: U.S. Bureau of Justice Statistics, *Capital Punishment,* annual.

No. 335. Prisoners Executed Under Civil Authority: 1930 to 1990

[Excludes executions by military authorities. The Army (including the Air Force) carried out 160 (148 between 1942 and 1950, 3 each in 1954, 1955, and 1957, and 1 each in 1958, 1959, and 1961). Of the total, 106 were executed for murder (including 21 involving rape), 53 for rape, and 1 for desertion. The Navy carried out no executions during the period. See also *Historical Statistics, Colonial Times to 1970,* series H 1155-1167]

YEAR OR PERIOD	Total [1]	White	Black	EXECUTED FOR MURDER			EXECUTED FOR RAPE			EXECUTED, OTHER OFFENSES [2]		
				Total [1]	White	Black	Total [1]	White	Black	Total [1]	White	Black
All years	4,002	1,838	2,122	3,477	1,751	1,686	455	48	405	70	39	31
1930 to 1939.	1,667	827	816	1,514	803	687	125	10	115	28	14	14
1940 to 1949.	1,284	490	781	1,064	458	595	200	19	179	20	13	7
1950 to 1959.	717	336	376	601	316	280	102	13	89	14	7	7
1960 to 1967.	191	98	93	155	87	68	28	6	22	8	5	3
1968 to 1976.	-	-	-	-	-	-	-	-	-	-	-	-
1977 to 1980.	3	3	-	3	3	-	-	-	-	-	-	-
1981	1	1	-	1	1	-	-	-	-	-	-	-
1982	2	1	1	2	1	1	-	-	-	-	-	-
1983	5	4	1	5	4	1	-	-	-	-	-	-
1984	21	13	8	21	13	8	-	-	-	-	-	-
1985	18	11	7	18	11	7	-	-	-	-	-	-
1986	18	11	7	18	11	7	-	-	-	-	-	-
1987	25	13	12	25	13	12	-	-	-	-	-	-
1988	11	6	5	11	6	5	-	-	-	-	-	-
1989	16	8	8	16	8	8	-	-	-	-	-	-
1990	23	16	7	23	16	7	-	-	-	-	-	-

- Represents zero.　[1] Includes races other than White or Black.　[2] Includes 25 armed robbery, 20 kidnapping, 11 burglary, 8 espionage (6 in 1942 and 2 in 1953), and 6 aggravated assault.

Source: Through 1978, U.S. Law Enforcement Assistance Administration; thereafter, U.S. Bureau of Justice Statistics, *Correctional Populationss in the United States,* annual.

No. 336. Prisoners Under Sentence of Death and Executed Under Civil Authority, by States: 1950 to 1990

[No executions took place in Maine, Michigan, Minnesota, New Hampshire, North Dakota, Rhode Island, and Wisconsin from 1940 to 1987. Maine, Minnesota, and Wisconsin never authorized the death penalty during the period. New Hampshire and Rhode Island authorized it for most of the 4 decades but did not apply it. Michigan abolished the penalty in 1963, and North Dakota allowed the punishment statute to lapse in 1975. Alaska and Hawaii could enter these data after receiving statehood in 1959, but neither has authorized the death penalty]

STATE	1950 to 1959	1960 to 1969	1970 to 1979	1980 to 1989	1990	STATE	1950 to 1959	1960 to 1969	1970 to 1979	1980 to 1989	1990	STATE	1950 to 1959	1960 to 1969	1970 to 1979	1980 to 1989	1990
U.S.[1]	717	191	3	117	23	IA	1	2	-	-	-	OH . . .	32	7	-	-	-
						KS	5	5	-	-	-	OK . . .	7	6	-	-	1
AL. . . .	20	5	-	7	1	KY . . .	16	1	-	-	-	OR . . .	4	1	-	-	-
AZ . . .	8	4	-	-	-	LA. . . .	27	1	-	18	1	PA . . .	31	3	-	-	-
AR . . .	18	9	-	-	2	MD . . .	6	1	-	-	-	SC . . .	26	8	-	2	1
CA . . .	74	30	-	-	-	MA . . .	-	-	-	-	-	SD . . .	-	-	-	-	-
CO . . .	3	6	-	-	-	MS . . .	36	10	-	4	-	TN . . .	8	1	-	-	-
CT . . .	5	1	-	-	-	MO . . .	7	4	-	1	4	TX . . .	74	29	-	33	4
DE . . .	-	-	-	-	-	MT . . .	-	-	-	-	-	UT . . .	6	1	1	2	-
DC . . .	4	-	-	-	-	NE . . .	2	-	-	-	-	VT . . .	2	-	-	-	-
FL. . . .	49	12	1	20	4	NV . . .	9	2	1	3	1	VA . . .	23	6	-	-	3
GA . . .	85	14	-	14	-	NJ. . . .	17	3	-	-	-	WA . . .	6	2	-	-	-
ID . . .	3	-	-	-	-	NM . . .	3	1	-	-	-	WV . . .	9	-	-	-	-
IL	9	2	-	-	1	NY . . .	52	10	-	-	-	WY . . .	-	1	-	-	-
IN	2	1	-	2	-	NC . . .	19	1	-	3	-						

- Represents zero.　[1] Includes 23 Federal executions not shown by State (1940 to 1949, 13; 1950 to 1959, 9; and 1960 to 1969, 1).

Source: Through 1978, U.S. Law Enforcement Assistance Administration; thereafter, U.S. Bureau of Justice Statistics, *Capital Punishment,* annual.

No. 337. Fire Losses—Total and Per Capita: 1960 to 1990

[1960 excludes Alaska and Hawaii. Includes allowance for uninsured and unreported losses but excludes losses to government property and forests. Represents incurred losses]

YEAR	Total (mil. dol.)	Per capita [1]	YEAR	Total (mil. dol.)	Per capita [1]	YEAR	Total (mil. dol.)	Per capita [1]
1960.	1,108	6.19	1973.	2,639	12.49	1982.	5,894	25.41
1965.	1,456	7.51	1974.	3,190	14.95	1983.	6,320	26.98
1966.	1,497	7.64	1975.	3,190	14.81	1984.	7,602	32.15
1967.	1,707	8.66	1976.	3,558	16.35	1985.	7,753	32.47
1968.	1,830	9.20	1977.	3,764	17.13	1986.	8,488	35.21
1969.	1,952	9.71	1978.	4,008	18.05	1987.	8,634	35.44
1970.	2,328	11.41	1979.	4,851	21.60	1988.	9,626	39.11
1971.	2,316	11.20	1980.	5,579	24.55	1989.	9,514	38.33
1972.	2,304	11.01	1981.	5,625	24.50	1990.	8,609	34.61

[1] Based on Bureau of the Census estimated resident population as of July 1.

Source: 1960, National Board of Fire Underwriters, New York, NY, *Report of the Committee on Statistics and Origin of Losses;* thereafter, Insurance Information Institute, New York, NY, *Insurance Facts,* annual.

No. 338. Fires—Number and Loss, by Type and Property Use: 1980 to 1990

[Based on annual sample survey of fire departments. No adjustments were made for unreported fires and losses. Property loss includes direct property loss only]

TYPE AND PROPERTY USE	NUMBER (1,000)					PROPERTY LOSS (mil. dol.)				
	1980	1985	1988	1989	1990	1980	1985	1988	1989	1990
Fires, total	**2,988**	**2,371**	**2,437**	**2,115**	**2,019**	**6,254**	**7,324**	**8,352**	**8,655**	**7,818**
Structure.	1,065	860	745	688	624	5,454	6,437	7,188	7,518	6,713
Outside of structure [1]	87	51	63	55	52	61	63	185	132	90
Brush and rubbish	1,115	832	1,009	819	787	-	-	-	-	-
Vehicle.	472	456	478	435	436	685	792	941	963	967
Other.	249	172	142	118	120	54	32	38	42	48
Structure by property use:										
Public assembly	29	24	20	18	17	326	462	297	286	317
Educational	20	13	10	9	9	101	114	112	116	136
Institutional	28	23	14	12	11	25	17	23	43	33
Stores and offices	62	49	38	35	31	645	654	754	703	603
Residential.	758	622	552	513	467	3,042	3,774	4,020	3,998	4,253
1-2 family units [3]	591	502	432	402	359	2,447	3,217	3,349	3,335	3,534
Apartments	143	104	106	96	95	401	476	548	541	623
Hotels and motels	12	8	8	7	6	154	56	100	87	66
Other residential	12	8	6	8	7	40	25	168	35	30
Storage [4].	65	52	50	44	40	512	683	[5]735	[6]673	534
Industry, utility, defense [4] . .	55	36	27	25	22	672	572	[5]1,079	[6]1,406	623
Special structures	48	41	34	32	27	131	161	168	293	214

- Represents zero. [1] Includes outside storage, crops,timber, etc. [2] Includes two prison fires totalling $120 million. [3] Includes mobile homes. [4] Data underreported as some incidents were handled by private fire brigades or fixed suppression systems which do not report. [4] Data underreported as some incidents were handled by private fire brigades or fixed suppression systems which do not report. [5] Includes three industrial fires totaling $464 million. [6] Includes one large industrial fire totaling $750 million.

Source: National Fire Protection Association, Quincy, MA, "Fire Loss in the United States During 1990", *NFPA Journal,* September 1991, and prior issues, (copyright 1991)

No. 339. Fires and Property Loss for Incendiary and Suspicious Fires and Civilian Fire Deaths and Injuries, by Selected Property Type: 1980 to 1990

[Based on sample survey of fire departments]

ITEM	1980	1985	1989	1990	ITEM	1980	1985	1989	1990
NUMBER (1,000)					**CIVILIAN FIRE DEATHS**				
					Deaths, total [2]	6,505	6,185	5,410	5,195
Structure fires, total . . .	1,065	860	688	624	Residential property.	5,446	5,025	4,435	4,115
Structure fires of incendiary					One- and two-family				
or suspicious origin . . .	146	117	97	97	dwellings	4,175	4,020	3,545	3,370
Fires of incendiary origin .	92	69	59	58	Apartments	1,025	865	790	680
Fires of suspicious origin .	54	48	38	39	Vehicles	740	825	685	695
PROPERTY LOSS [1] (mil. dol.)					**CIVILIAN FIRE INJURIES**				
					Injuries, total [2]	30,200	28,425	28,250	28,600
Structure fires, total . . .	5,454	6,437	7518	6713	Residential property.	21,000	19,825	20,750	20,650
Structure fires of incendiary					One- and two-family				
or suspicious origin . . .	1,760	1,670	1558	1394	dwellings	16,100	15,250	15,225	15,250
Fires of incendiary origin .	1,158	1,069	1057	875	Apartments	3,600	3,925	5,050	4,975
Fires of suspicious origin .	602	601	501	519	Vehicles	4,075	3,600	3,025	3,350

[1] Direct property loss only. [2] Includes other not shown separately.

Source: National Fire Protection Association, Quincy, MA, "Fire Loss in the United States during 1990", *NFPA Journal,* September 1991, and prior issues, (copyright 1991).

Figure 6.1
Hazardous Waste Sites: June 1991

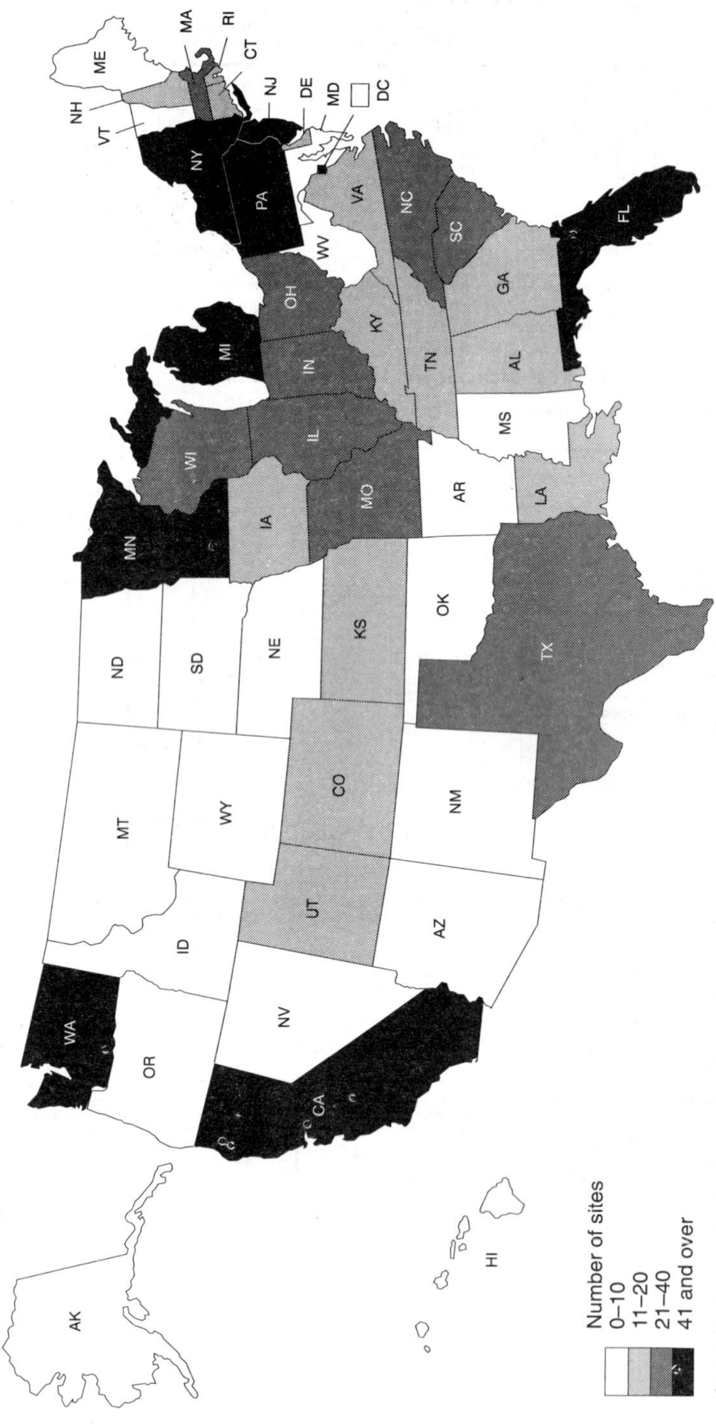

Number of sites
0–10
11–20
21–40
41 and over

Source: Chart prepared by U.S. Bureau of the Census. For data, see table 357.

Geography and Environment

This section presents a variety of information on the physical environment of the United States, starting with basic area measurement data and ending with climatic data for selected weather stations around the country. The subjects covered between those poir.ts are mostly concerned with environmental trends, but include such related subjects as land use and ownership, water consumption, hazardous waste sites, threatened and endangered wildlife, and expenditures for pollution abatement and control.

The information in this section is selected from a wide range of Federal agencies that compile the data for various administrative or regulatory purposes, such as the Environmental Protection Agency, Geological Survey, National Oceanic and Atmospheric Administration, and General Services Administration. Other agencies include the Bureau of the Census, which presents nationwide area measurement information; the Council on Environmental Quality (CEQ), which presents data on environmental conditions and pollutants in its annual report; and the Bureau of Economic Analysis, which compiles data on pollution abatement and control expenditures.

For the 1990 census, area measurements were calculated by computer based on the information contained in a single, consistent geographic data base, the TIGER File (described below), rather than relying on historical and local information. This especially affects inland water areas in 1990, which had only covered those bodies of water of least 40 acres and those steams with a width of at least one-eighth of a statute mile from 1940 to 1980. Inland water areas in 1990 increased because the data reflected any body of water or stream that appeared in the TIGER data base; however, water areas shown in the 1990 census data files reflect all water whereas water area measurements reported in the previous censuses were only for inland water.

Geography.—The Geological Survey conducts investigations, surveys, and research in the fields of geography, geology, topography, geographic information

In Brief

Pollution abatement expenditures, 1989	$91 bil.
Superfund hazardous waste sites, 1991	1,211
Municipal solid waste per person	4 lb. per day

systems, mineralogy, hydrology, and geothermal energy resources as well as natural hazards. In cooperation with State and local agencies, the Geological Survey prepares and publishes topographic, land use/land cover, geologic, and hydrologic maps and data compilations. The Geological Survey provides United States cartographic data through the Earth Sciences Information Center, water resources data through a multi-volume *Catalog of Information on Water Data,* and a variety of research and Open-File reports which are announced monthly in *New Publications of the Geological Survey.* In a joint project with the Census Bureau, the Geological Survey has provided the basic information on geographic features for input into a national geographic and cartographic data base being prepared by the Census Bureau, called the TIGER (Topologically Integrated Geographic Encoding and Referencing) System.

Maps prepared by the Bureau of the Census show names and boundaries of various types of legal and statistical areas, such as places, county subdivisions, census tracts, and urbanized areas, and are available as of the specific decennial census. An inventory of most of these areas is available for the 1990 census both in printed and tape form in the *Geographic Identification Code Scheme* and for the 1987 economic censuses in the *Geographic Reference Manual* (EC87-R-1). The Census Bureau maintains a current inventory of governmental units and their legal boundaries through its annual Boundary and Annexation Survey. The TIGER data base contains information on the legal and statistical entities used by the Census Bureau, as well as on both man-made and natural features, such as streets, roads, railroads, rivers, and lakes; information is available to the public in form of machine-readable TIGER extract files.

An inventory of the Nation's land resources by type of use/cover was conducted by the Soil Conservation Service in 1982 and 1987. The results, published in the *1987 National Inventory of Land Resources,* cover all non-Federal land in Puerto Rico, the Virgin Islands, and the U.S. except Alaska.

Environment.—The CEQ is responsible for overseeing the environmental assessment process, recommending national environmental policies, analyzing changes and trends in the environment, and for reviewing Federal programs affecting the environment. It reports on environmental conditions, trends, programs and activities in its annual publication, *Environmental Quality.* The principal Federal agency responsible for pollution abatement and control activities is the Environmental Protection Agency (EPA). It is responsible for establishing and monitoring national air quality standards, water quality activities, solid and hazardous waste disposal, and control of toxic substances.

National Ambient Air Quality Standards (NAAQS) for suspended particulate matter, sulfur dioxide, photochemical oxidants, carbon monoxide, and nitrogen dioxide were originally set by the EPA in April 1971. Every 5 years each of the NAAQS are reviewed and revised if new health or welfare data indicates that a change is necessary. The standard for photochemical oxidants now called ozone was revised in February 1979. Also, a new NAAQS for lead was promulgated in October 1978 and for suspended particulate matter in 1987. Table 352 gives some of the health-related standards for the six air pollutants having NAAQS. Responsibility for demonstrating compliance with or progress toward achieving these standards lies with the State agencies. In 1990 there were 1,279 nonFederal sampling stations for particulates, 741 for sulfur dioxide, 491 for carbon monoxide, 812 for ozone, 330

for nitrogen dioxide, and 406 for lead. Data from these State networks are periodically submitted to EPA's National Aerometric Data Bank for summarization in annual reports on the nationwide status and trends in air quality; for details, see *National Air Quality and Emissions Trends Report, 1990.*

Pollution abatement and control expenditures.—Data on expenditures for pollution abatement and control are compiled and published by the U.S. Bureau of Economic Analysis (BEA), the U.S. Bureau of the Census, and the CEQ as part of ongoing programs. BEA conducts surveys on national expenditures for pollution abatement and control and presents the data in its *Survey of Current Business.* The U.S. Bureau of the Census collects data on State and local government and industry expenditures on control activities. Data on government expenditures are reported in an annual series of publications, *Government Finances,* which covers expenditures on sewage and sanitation outlays. Industry data are reported annually in *Current Industrial Reports.* CEQ publishes some expenditure data in *Environmental Quality.*

Climate.—NOAA, through the National Weather Service and the National Environmental Satellite, Data and Information Service, is responsible for data on climate. NOAA maintains about 11,600 weather stations, of which over 3,000 produce autographic precipitation records, about 600 take hourly readings of a series of weather elements, and the remainder record data once a day. These data are reported monthly in the *Climatological Data* (published by State), and monthly and annually in the *Local Climatological Data* (published by location for major cities).

The climatological temperature, precipitation, and degree day normals listed in this publication are derived for comparative purposes and are averages for the 30-year period, 1961-90. For stations that did not have continuous records for the entire 30 years from the same instrument site, the normals have been adjusted to provide representative values for the current location. The information in all other tables is based on data from the beginning of the record at that location through 1990, except as noted.

No. 340. Land and Water Area of States and Other Areas: 1990

[One square mile = 2.59 square kilometers. See *Historical Statistics of the United States, Colonial Times to 1970*, series A 210-263, for land area]

REGION, DIVISON, STATE, AND OTHER AREA	Year admitted to state-hood	TOTAL AREA Rank	TOTAL AREA Sq. mi.	TOTAL AREA Sq. km.	LAND AREA Sq. mi.	LAND AREA Sq. km.	WATER AREA Sq. mi.	WATER AREA Sq. km
United States	(X)	(X)	3,787,425	9,809,431	3,536,342	9,159,125	251,083	650,306
Northeast	(X)	(X)	181,252	469,442	162,274	420,289	18,978	49,152
New England	(X)	(X)	71,997	186,472	62,812	162,682	9,185	23,790
Maine	1820	39	35,387	91,653	30,865	79,939	4,523	11,714
New Hampshire	¹1788	46	9,351	24,219	8,969	23,231	382	988
Vermont	¹1791	45	9,615	24,903	9,249	23,956	366	947
Massachusetts	¹1788	44	10,555	27,337	7,838	20,300	2,717	7,037
Rhode Island	¹1790	50	1,545	4,002	1,045	2,706	500	1,295
Connecticut	¹1788	48	5,544	14,358	4,845	12,550	698	1,808
Middle Atlantic	(X)	(X)	109,255	282,970	99,462	257,607	9,792	25,362
New York	¹1788	27	54,475	141,089	47,224	122,310	7,251	18,779
New Jersey	¹1787	47	8,722	22,590	7,419	19,215	1,303	3,375
Pennsylvania	¹1787	33	46,058	119,291	44,820	116,083	1,239	3,208
Midwest	(X)	(X)	821,872	2,128,648	751,521	1,946,440	70,350	182,208
East North Central	(X)	(X)	301,479	780,830	243,539	630,766	57,940	150,064
Ohio	1803	34	44,828	116,103	40,953	106,067	3,875	10,036
Indiana	1816	38	36,420	94,328	35,870	92,904	550	1,424
Illinois	1818	25	57,918	150,007	55,593	143,987	2,325	6,021
Michigan	1837	11	96,810	250,738	56,809	147,136	40,001	103,603
Wisconsin	1848	23	65,503	169,653	54,314	140,673	11,190	28,981
West North Central	(X)	(X)	520,393	1,347,817	507,982	1,315,674	12,410	32,143
Minnesota	1858	12	86,943	225,182	79,617	206,207	7,326	18,974
Iowa	1846	26	56,276	145,754	55,875	144,716	401	1,038
Missouri.	1821	21	69,709	180,546	68,898	178,446	811	2,100
North Dakota	1889	19	70,704	183,123	68,994	178,695	1,710	4,428
South Dakota	1889	17	77,121	199,745	75,898	196,575	1,224	3,169
Nebraska	1867	16	77,358	200,358	76,878	199,113	481	1,245
Kansas	1861	15	82,282	213,110	81,823	211,922	459	1,189
South	(X)	(X)	919,937	2,382,636	871,070	2,256,071	48,867	126,565
South Atlantic	(X)	(X)	292,993	758,853	266,220	689,510	26,773	69,343
Delaware	¹1787	49	2,489	6,447	1,955	5,062	535	1,385
Maryland	¹1788	42	12,407	32,135	9,775	25,316	2,633	6,819
District of Columbia . . .	(X)	(X)	68	177	61	159	7	18
Virginia	¹1788	35	42,769	110,771	39,598	102,558	3,171	8,213
West Virginia	1863	41	24,231	62,759	24,087	62,384	145	375
North Carolina	¹1789	28	53,821	139,397	48,718	126,180	5,103	13,217
South Carolina	¹1788	40	32,007	82,898	30,111	77,988	1,896	4,911
Georgia	¹1788	24	59,441	153,953	57,919	150,010	1,522	3,943
Florida	1845	22	65,758	170,313	53,997	139,852	11,761	30,461
East South Central	(X)	(X)	183,414	475,042	178,616	462,615	4,798	12,427
Kentucky	1792	37	40,411	104,665	39,732	102,907	679	1,758
Tennessee	1796	36	42,146	109,158	41,220	106,759	926	2,400
Alabama	1819	30	52,423	135,775	50,750	131,443	1,673	4,332
Mississippi	1817	32	48,434	125,443	46,914	121,506	1,520	3,937
West South Central	(X)	(X)	443,530	1,148,742	426,234	1,103,946	17,296	44,795
Arkansas	1836	29	53,182	137,742	52,075	134,875	1,107	2,867
Louisiana	1812	31	51,843	134,275	43,566	112,836	8,277	21,439
Oklahoma	1907	20	69,903	181,049	68,679	177,877	1,224	3,171
Texas	1845	2	268,601	695,676	261,914	678,358	6,687	17,319
West	(X)	(X)	1,864,365	4,828,706	1,751,477	4,536,325	112,888	292,381
Mountain	(X)	(X)	863,614	2,236,760	856,122	2,217,356	7,492	19,403
Montana	1809	4	147,046	380,850	145,556	376,991	1,490	3,859
Idaho	1890	14	83,574	216,456	82,751	214,325	823	2,131
Wyoming	1890	10	97,818	253,349	97,105	251,501	714	1,848
Colorado	1876	8	104,100	269,620	103,730	268,660	371	960
New Mexico	1912	5	121,598	314,939	121,365	314,334	234	605
Arizona	1912	6	114,006	295,276	113,642	294,333	364	943
Utah	1896	13	84,904	219,902	82,168	212,816	2,736	7,086
Nevada	1864	7	110,567	286,368	109,806	284,397	761	1,971
Pacific	(X)	(X)	1,000,751	2,591,946	895,355	2,318,968	105,397	272,978
Washington	1889	18	71,303	184,674	66,582	172,447	4,721	12,227
Oregon	1859	9	98,386	254,819	96,003	248,647	2,383	6,172
California	1850	3	163,707	424,002	155,973	403,970	7,734	20,031
Alaska.	1959	1	656,424	1,700,139	570,374	1,477,267	86,051	222,871
Hawaii	1959	43	10,932	28,313	6,423	16,636	4,508	11,676
Other areas:								
Puerto Rico.	(X)	(X)	3,515	9,104	3,459	8,959	56	145
American Samoa	(X)	(X)	77	199	77	199	-	-
Guam.	(X)	(X)	209	541	209	541	-	-
No. Mariana Islands	(X)	(X)	184	477	184	477	-	-
Palau.	(X)	(X)	192	497	192	497	-	-
Virgin Islands of the U.S .	(X)	(X)	132	342	132	342	1	3

- Represents zero. X Not applicable. ¹ Year of ratification of Constitution; one of the original 13 States.
Source: U.S. Bureau of the Census, *1990 Census of Population and Housing*, series CPH-1.

No. 341. Territorial Expansion of the United States and Acquisitions of Other Areas

[One square mile=2.59 square kilometers. Boundaries of all territories listed under "United States" were indefinite, at least in part, at time of acquisition. Area figures shown here represent precise determinations of specific territories which have been marked upon maps, based upon interpretations of the several treaties of cession, which are necessarily debatable. See also *Historical Statistics, Colonial Times to 1970*, series J 1–2]

ACCESSION	Acquisition date	GROSS AREA (land and water)		ACCESSION	Acquisition date	GROSS AREA (land and water)	
		Sq. ml.	Sq. km.			Sq. ml.	Sq. km.
Total	(X)	**3,791,748**	**9,820,629**	Alaska	1867	570,374	1,477,267
				Hawaii	1898	6,423	16,636
United States[1]	(X)	3,787,318	9,809,155				
Territory in 1790 [2]	(X)	917,815	2,377,141	Other areas:			
Louisiana Purchase	1803	909,380	2,355,294	Puerto Rico	[3]1898	5,325	9,086
Purchase of Florida	1819	58,666	151,945	Guam	[4]1898	571	562
Texas	1845	388,687	1,006,699	American Samoa	[5]1899	583	233
Oregon	1846	286,541	742,141	Virgin Islands of the U.S.	1917	737	443
Mexican Cession	1848	529,189	1,370,600	Palau	[6]1947	630	624
Gadsden Purchase	1853	29,670	76,845	N. Mariana Islands	[7]1947	1,950	490

X Not applicable. [1] Based on 1990 Census; sum of areas listed will not equal these figures. [2] Includes that part of drainage basin of Red River of the North, south of 49th parallel, sometimes considered part of Louisiana Purchase. [3] Ceded by Spain in 1898, ratified in 1899, and became Commonwealth of Puerto Rico by Act of Congress on July 25, 1952. [4] Acquired 1898; ratified 1899. [5] Acquired 1899; ratified 1900. [6] Remaining portion of the Trust Territory of the Pacific Islands (TTPI), under U. N. trusteeship since 1947. The Federated States of Micronesia and the Marshall Islands, also formerly part of the TTPI, became freely associated States in 1986 and are not included in the table. [7] Attained Commonwealth status in 1986, separate from the TTPI, of which it had been a part since 1947.

Source: U.S. Geological Survey, *Boundaries of the United States and the Several States,* Paper 909, 1976; and U.S. Bureau of the Census, unpublished data.

Figure 6.2

Territorial Expansion of the United States and Acquisitions of Other Principal Areas

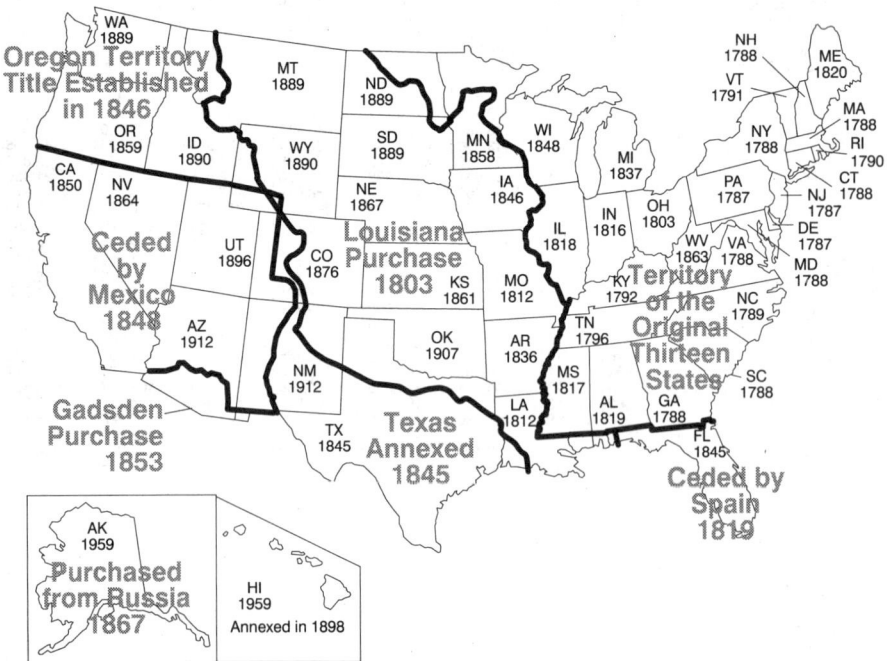

Source: Chart prepared by U.S. Bureau of the Census. For data, see table 341.

No. 342. Area and Acquisition of the Federal Public Domain: 1781 to 1989

[In millions of acres. Areas of acquisitions are as computed in 1912, and do not agree with figures in square miles shown in table 348 which include later adjustments and reflect subsequent remeasurement. Excludes outlying areas of the United States amounting to 645,949 acres in 1978. See also *Historical Statistics, Colonial Times to 1970,* series J 3-6]

YEAR	Land area, total [1]	YEAR	LAND AREA [1]			YEAR AND ACQUISITION	ACREAGE		
			Total	Public domain	Acquired		Total	Land	Inland water
1802....	200.0	1975...	760.4	702.9	57.5	**Aggregate**	**1,837.8**	**1,804.7**	**33.1**
1850....	1,200.0	1976...	762.2	702.8	59.4				
1880....	900.0	1977...	741.5	683.3	58.2	1781-1802 (State Cessions)......	236.8	233.4	3.4
1912....	600.0	1978...	775.2	712.0	63.3	1803, Louisiana Purchase [2]......	529.9	523.4	6.5
1946....	413.0	1979...	744.1	684.3	59.8	1819, Cession from Spain........	46.1	43.3	2.8
1950....	412.0	1980...	719.5	648.0	71.5	Red River Basin [3].......	29.6	29.1	0.5
1955....	407.9	1981...	730.8	668.7	62.2	1846, Oregon Compromise	183.4	180.6	2.7
1959....	768.6	1982...	729.8	670.0	59.8	1848, Mexican Cession [2].......	338.7	334.5	4.2
1960....	771.5	1983...	732.0	672.4	59.6	1850, Purchase from Texas......	78.9	78.8	0.1
1965....	765.8	1984...	726.6	658.9	67.7	1853, Gadsden Purchase	19.0	19.0	(Z)
1970....	761.3	1985...	726.7	656.2	70.5	1867, Alaska Purchase.........	375.3	362.5	12.8
1971....	760.2	1986...	727.1	662.7	64.4				
1972....	760.7	1987...	724.3	661.0	63.3				
1973....	761.0	1988...	688.2	623.2	65.0				
1974....	760.5	1989...	662.2	597.9	64.3				

Z Less than 50,000.   [1] Owned by Federal Government. Comprises original public domain plus acquired lands. Estimated from imperfect data available for indicated years. Prior to 1959, excludes Alaska, and 1960, Hawaii. Source: Beginning 1955, U.S. General Services Administration, *Inventory Report on Real Property Owned by the United States Throughout the World,* annual. [2] Data for Louisiana Purchase exclude areas eliminated by Treaty of 1819 with Spain. Such areas are included in figures for Mexican Cession. [3] Represents drainage basin of Red River of the North, south of 49th parallel. Authorities differ as to method and date of its acquisition. Some hold it as part of the Louisiana Purchase; others, as acquired from Great Britain.

Source: Except as noted, U.S. Dept. of the Interior. Estimated area, Bureau of Land Management; all other data, Office of the Secretary, *Areas of Acquisitions to the Territory of the U.S.,* 1922.

No. 343. Total and Federally Owned Land, 1960 to 1989, and by State, 1989

[As of **end of fiscal year;** see text, section 9. Total land area figures are not comparable with those in table 340]

REGION, DIVISION AND STATE	Total (1,000 acres)	Not owned by Federal Government (1,000 acres)	OWNED BY FEDERAL GOVERNMENT [1]		REGION, DIVISION AND STATE	Total (1,000 acres)	Not owned by Federal Government (1,000 acres)	OWNED BY FEDERAL GOVERNMENT [1]	
			Acres (1,000)	Percent				Acres (1,000)	Percent
1960........	2,273,407	1,501,894	771,512	33.9	**South.......**	**561,238**	**531,149**	**30,090**	**5.4**
1965........	2,271,343	1,505,546	765,797	33.7	**S.A.......**	**171,325**	**159,847**	**11,478**	**6.7**
1970........	2,271,343	1,510,042	761,301	33.5	DE......	1,266	1,236	30	2.4
1975........	2,271,343	1,510,929	760,414	33.5	MD.....	6,319	6,122	197	3.1
1980........	2,271,343	1,551,822	719,522	31.7	DC.....	39	28	11	27.8
1985........	2,271,343	1,544,658	726,686	32.0	VA.....	25,496	23,578	1,918	7.5
1987........	2,271,343	1,547,277	724,066	31.9	WV	15,411	13,311	2,099	13.6
1988........	2,271,343	1,583,090	688,253	30.3	NC.....	31,403	30,262	1,141	3.6
					SC.....	19,374	18,940	434	2.2
1989, total.	**2,271,343**	**1,609,185**	**662,158**	**29.2**	GA.....	37,295	35,003	2,292	6.1
Northeast....	**104,699**	**102,337**	**2,363**	**2.3**	FL......	34,721	31,366	3,356	9.7
N.E.......	**40,401**	**39,037**	**1,363**	**3.4**	**E.S.C......**	**115,141**	**110,207**	**4,934**	**4.3**
ME......	19,848	19,695	153	0.8	KY......	25,512	24,121	1,391	5.5
NH......	5,769	5,015	754	13.1	TN......	26,728	25,406	1,322	4.9
VT......	5,937	5,582	355	6.0	AL......	32,678	32,129	550	1.7
MA......	5,035	4,952	83	1.6	MS......	30,223	28,552	1,671	5.5
RI......	677	672	5	0.7	**W.S.C.....**	**274,773**	**261,095**	**13,678**	**5.0**
CT......	3,135	3,121	14	0.4	AR......	33,599	30,178	3,421	10.2
M.A.......	**64,299**	**63,299**	**1,000**	**1.6**	LA......	28,868	22,330	6,538	22.6
NY......	30,681	30,458	223	0.7	OK......	44,088	43,214	874	2.0
NJ......	4,814	4,678	136	2.8	TX......	168,218	165,373	2,845	1.7
PA......	28,804	28,164	641	2.2	**West.......**	**1,122,535**	**510,279**	**612,257**	**54.5**
Midwest.....	**482,870**	**465,421**	**17,449**	**3.6**	**Mt........**	**548,449**	**287,756**	**260,693**	**47.5**
E.N.C	**156,679**	**149,923**	**6,756**	**4.3**	MT......	93,271	67,409	25,863	27.7
OH......	26,222	25,900	322	1.2	ID......	52,933	19,811	33,122	62.6
IN......	23,158	22,689	470	2.0	WY.....	62,343	31,936	30,407	48.8
IL......	35,795	35,301	494	1.4	CO.....	66,486	43,838	22,648	34.1
MI......	36,492	32,927	3,565	9.8	NM.....	77,766	52,019	25,747	33.1
WI......	35,011	33,105	1,906	5.4	AZ......	72,688	41,197	31,491	43.3
W.N.C	**326,191**	**315,498**	**10,693**	**3.3**	UT......	52,697	19,086	33,611	63.8
MN......	51,206	48,819	2,387	4.7	NV.....	70,264	12,461	57,803	82.3
IA	35,860	35,701	159	0.4	**Pac.......**	**574,087**	**222,523**	**351,564**	**61.2**
MO......	44,248	42,218	2,031	4.6	WA	42,694	30,321	12,373	29.0
ND......	44,453	42,488	1,965	4.4	OR.....	61,599	31,930	29,669	48.2
SD......	48,882	46,138	2,744	5.6	CA.....	100,207	39,164	61,043	60.9
NE......	49,032	48,313	719	1.5	AK.....	365,482	117,679	247,802	67.8
KS......	52,511	51,821	690	1.3	HI	4,106	3,429	677	16.5

[1] Excludes trust properties.

Source: U.S. General Services Administration, *Inventory Report on Real Property Owned by the United States Throughout the World,* annual.

No. 344. Land Cover/Use, by State: 1987

[In thousands of acres. Excludes Alaska and District of Columbia]

STATE	Total surface area [1]	Federal land	NONFEDERAL LAND Total	Developed [2]	Rural Total	Cropland	Pasture land	Rangeland	Forest land	Minor cover/ use
United States ..	1,937,726	404,069	1,484,156	77,305	1,406,851	422,416	129,021	401,685	393,904	59,826
Northeast	108,080	2,392	100,778	9,611	91,166	14,532	7,669	-	64,246	4,720
New England	42,670	1,332	38,609	3,005	35,604	2,311	1,248	-	30,307	1,739
Maine	21,290	161	19,517	508	19,009	943	419	-	16,933	714
New Hampshire . .	5,938	729	4,971	372	4,599	163	115	-	4,052	269
Vermont	6,153	335	5,556	208	5,348	653	388	-	4,184	122
Massachusetts . . .	5,302	89	4,849	1,063	3,786	291	179	-	2,937	379
Rhode Island	776	4	661	161	500	22	37	-	404	37
Connecticut	3,212	14	3,056	693	2,362	239	110	-	1,797	218
Middle Atlantic	65,410	1,060	62,168	6,606	55,562	12,221	6,422	-	33,939	2,981
New York	31,429	234	29,782	2,485	27,297	5,774	3,686	-	16,650	1,187
New Jersey	4,984	148	4,563	1,325	3,239	673	229	-	1,890	447
Pennsylvania	28,997	677	27,823	2,796	25,027	5,774	2,507	-	15,398	1,348
Midwest	490,474	17,883	460,128	23,789	436,339	233,455	40,718	71,859	71,637	18,670
East North Central .	159,066	6,269	148,602	12,368	136,233	72,743	12,982	-	42,482	8,027
Ohio	26,451	347	25,686	2,925	22,762	12,537	2,444	-	6,426	1,354
Indiana	23,159	487	22,302	1,780	20,522	13,930	2,073	-	3,698	821
Illinois	36,061	492	34,792	2,792	32,000	25,121	2,689	-	3,447	744
Michigan	37,457	3,130	33,051	2,921	30,130	9,484	2,735	-	15,483	2,429
Wisconsin	35,938	1,813	32,770	1,951	30,820	11,671	3,041	-	13,428	2,680
West North Central.	331,408	11,615	311,527	11,421	300,105	160,713	27,736	71,859	29,155	10,643
Minnesota	54,017	3,390	47,077	2,136	44,941	22,990	3,425	157	13,952	4,417
Iowa	36,016	172	35,387	1,688	33,699	27,031	3,866	-	1,841	961
Missouri.	44,606	2,060	41,655	2,165	39,491	15,090	12,606	56	10,959	781
North Dakota	45,250	1,882	42,255	1,242	41,013	28,064	1,206	9,933	428	1,382
South Dakota	49,354	2,873	45,467	1,064	44,403	17,819	2,354	22,152	565	1,513
Nebraska.	49,507	652	48,218	1,250	46,967	20,601	1,957	22,900	728	782
Kansas	52,658	587	51,467	1,876	49,592	29,119	2,324	16,660	681	808
South	575,044	26,391	527,041	30,657	496,384	233,455	67,937	113,837	189,507	17,571
South Atlantic	178,469	12,757	156,196	13,346	142,849	26,495	16,165	3,592	88,408	8,190
Delaware.	1,309	33	1,213	165	1,048	521	30	-	357	141
Maryland	6,695	159	6,048	936	5,111	1,795	514	-	2,415	388
Virginia	26,091	2,368	22,812	1,663	21,150	3,309	3,315	-	13,622	904
West Virginia	15,508	1,116	14,227	532	13,695	1,053	1,892	-	10,466	284
North Carolina . . .	33,708	2,309	28,622	2,487	26,135	6,548	1,992	-	16,528	1,067
South Carolina . . .	19,912	1,340	17,785	1,422	16,363	3,371	1,177	-	11,073	742
Georgia	37,702	2,062	34,664	2,375	32,289	6,307	3,040	-	21,860	1,083
Florida.	37,545	3,369	30,825	3,766	27,059	3,592	4,205	3,592	12,088	3,583
East South Central .	116,446	5,116	108,068	5,705	102,363	22,870	18,493	96	58,115	2,789
Kentucky	25,862	1,169	24,023	1,224	22,799	5,818	5,955	-	10,054	972
Tennessee.	26,972	1,369	24,759	1,669	23,090	5,765	5,019	-	11,601	706
Alabama	33,091	904	31,230	1,640	29,591	4,210	3,595	96	21,017	673
Mississippi	30,521	1,674	28,056	1,172	26,884	7,078	3,924	-	15,443	439
West South Central.	280,129	8,518	262,778	11,606	251,172	58,167	33,279	110,149	42,984	6,593
Arkansas	34,040	3,129	29,904	1,232	28,672	8,182	5,678	164	14,268	380
Louisiana	30,561	1,174	26,472	1,455	25,016	6,484	2,276	234	12,736	3,286
Oklahoma	44,772	1,176	42,431	1,716	40,715	11,557	7,590	14,546	6,505	517
Texas	170,756	3,040	163,971	7,203	156,768	31,944	17,735	95,204	9,476	2,410
West	764,128	357,403	396,209	13,247	382,962	66,896	12,697	215,989	68,514	18,865
Mountain	552,680	266,171	280,033	5,964	274,069	44,235	7,828	182,653	27,532	11,822
Montana	94,109	27,074	65,682	999	64,682	17,881	3,169	36,769	5,253	1,611
Idaho	53,481	33,190	19,628	477	19,152	6,532	1,354	6,596	4,071	600
Wyoming	62,598	29,457	32,576	501	32,075	2,362	928	26,784	984	1,017
Colorado	66,618	23,833	42,320	1,375	40,945	10,967	1,266	23,427	4,079	1,207
New Mexico	77,819	26,423	51,144	698	50,445	2,297	186	40,782	4,685	2,496
Arizona	72,960	30,647	41,994	1,116	40,878	1,306	81	31,867	4,912	2,712
Utah	54,336	35,476	16,440	465	15,975	2,002	563	8,507	3,194	1,711
Nevada	70,759	60,071	10,250	333	9,916	889	282	7,921	356	469
Pacific.	211,448	91,232	116,176	7,283	108,893	22,662	4,869	33,337	40,982	7,043
Washington	43,608	12,471	29,947	1,564	28,383	7,758	1,421	5,574	12,634	997
Oregon	62,127	32,305	28,918	941	27,977	4,348	1,916	9,152	11,857	705
California.	101,572	46,014	53,654	4,621	49,033	10,209	1,501	17,719	15,073	4,531
Hawaii.	4,141	443	3,657	157	3,500	348	31	891	1,419	811

- Represents zero.   [1] Includes water area not shown separately.   [2] Includes urban and built-up areas in units of 10 acres or greater, and rural transportation.

Source: U.S. Dept. of Agriculture, Soil Conservation Service, and Iowa State University, Statistical Laboratory; Statistical Bulletin No. 790, *Summary Report, 1987 National Resources Inventory*, December 1989.

No. 345. Extreme and Mean Elevations States and Other Areas

[1 foot = .305 meter]

STATE OR OTHER AREA	HIGHEST POINT Name	Elevation Feet	Elevation Meters	LOWEST POINT Name	Elevation Feet	Elevation Meters	APPROXIMATE MEAN ELEVATION Feet	APPROXIMATE MEAN ELEVATION Meters
U.S.	Mt. McKinley (AK)	20,320	6,198	Death Valley (CA)	−282	−86	2,500	763
AL	Cheaha Mountain	2,405	733	Gulf of Mexico	([1])	([1])	500	153
AK	Mount McKinley	20,320	6,198	Pacific Ocean	([1])	([1])	1,900	580
AZ	Humhreys Peak	12,633	3,853	Colorado River	70	21	4,100	1,251
AR	Magazine Mountain	2,753	840	Ouachita River	55	17	650	198
CA	Mount Whitney	14,494	4,419	Death Valley	−282	−86	2,900	885
CO	Mt. Elbert	14,433	4,402	Arkansas River	3,350	1,022	6,800	2,074
CT	Mt. Frissell on South slope	2,380	726	Long Island Sound	([1])	([1])	500	153
DE	Ebright Road, New Castle County	442	135	Atlantic Ocean	([1])	([1])	60	18
DC	Tenleytown	410	125	Potomac River	1	(Z)	150	46
FL	Sec. 30, T6N, R20W, Walton County	345	105	Atlantic Ocean	([1])	([1])	100	31
GA	Brasstown Bald	4,784	1,459	Atlantic Ocean	([1])	([1])	600	183
HI	Puu Wekiu	13,796	4,208	Pacific Ocean	([1])	([1])	3,030	924
ID	Borah Peak	12,662	3,862	Snake River	710	217	5,000	1,525
IL	Charles Mound	1,235	377	Mississippi River	279	85	600	183
IN	Franklin Twp., Wayne Co .	1,257	383	Ohio River	320	98	700	214
IA	Sec. 29, T100N, R41W, Osceola County [2]	1,670	509	Mississippi River	480	146	1,100	336
KS	Mount Sunflower	4,039	1,232	Verdigris River	679	207	2,000	610
KY	Black Mountain	4,139	2,162	Mississippi River	257	78	750	229
LA	Driskill Mountain	535	163	New Orleans	−8	−2	100	31
ME	Mount Katahdin	5,267	1,606	Atlantic Ocean	([1])	([1])	600	183
MD	Backbone Mountain	3,360	1,025	Atlantic Ocean	([1])	([1])	350	107
MA	Mount Greylock	3,487	1,064	Atlantic Ocean	([1])	([1])	500	153
MI	Mount Arvon	1,979	604	Lake Erie	571	174	900	275
MN	Eagle Mountain, Cook Co .	2,301	702	Lake Superior	600	183	1,200	366
MS	Woodall Mountain	806	246	Gulf of Mexico	([1])	([1])	300	92
MO	Taum Sauk Mountain	1,772	540	St. Francis River	230	70	800	244
MT	Granite Peak	12,799	3,904	Kootenai River	1,800	549	3,400	1,037
NE	Johnson Twp., Kimball Co.	5,424	1,654	Missouri River	840	256	2,600	793
NV	Boundary Peak	13,140	4,007	Colorado River	479	146	5,500	1,678
NH	Mount Washington	6,288	1,918	Atlantic Ocean	([1])	([1])	1,000	305
NJ	High Point	1,803	550	Atlantic Ocean	([1])	([1])	250	76
NM	Wheeler Peak	13,161	4,014	Red Bluff Reservoir	2,842	867	5,700	1,739
NY	Mount Marcy	5,344	1,630	Atlantic Ocean	([1])	([1])	1,000	305
NC	Mount Mitchell	6,684	2,039	Atlantic Ocean	([1])	([1])	700	214
ND	White Butte, Slope Co . . .	3,506	1,069	Red River	750	229	1,900	580
OH	Campbell Hill	1,549	472	Ohio River	455	139	850	259
OK	Black Mesa	4,973	1,517	Little River	289	88	1,300	397
OR	Mount Hood	11,239	3,428	Pacific Ocean	([1])	([1])	3,300	1,007
PA	Mount Davis	3,213	980	Delaware River	([1])	([1])	1,100	336
RI	Jerimoth Hill	812	248	Atlantic Ocean	([1])	([1])	200	61
SC	Sassafras Mountain	3,560	1,086	Atlantic Ocean	([1])	([1])	350	107
SD	Harney Peak	7,242	2,209	Big Stone Lake	966	295	2,200	671
TN	Clingmans Dome	6,643	2,026	Mississippi River	178	54	900	275
TX	Guadalupe Peak	8,749	2,668	Gulf of Mexico	([1])	([1])	1,700	519
UT	Kings Peak	13,528	4,126	Beaverdam Wash	2,000	610	6,100	1,861
VT	Mount Mansfield	4,393	1,340	Lake Champlain	95	29	1,000	305
VA	Mount Rogers	5,729	1,747	Atlantic Ocean	([1])	([1])	950	290
WA	Mount Rainier	14,410	4,395	Pacific Ocean	([1])	([1])	1,700	519
WV	Spruce Knob	4,861	1,483	Potomac River	240	73	1,500	458
WI	Timms Hill	1,951	595	Lake Michigan	579	177	1,050	320
WY	Gannett Peak	13,804	4,210	Belle Fourche River	3,099	945	6,700	2,044
Other areas: Puerto Rico	Cerro de Punta	4,390	1,339	Atlantic Ocean	([1])	([1])	1,800	549
American Samoa . .	Lata Mountain	3,160	964	Pacific Ocean	([1])	([1])	1,300	397
Guam	Mount Lamlam	1,332	406	Pacific Ocean	([1])	([1])	330	101
Virgin Is.. .	Crown Mountain	1,556	475	Atlantic Ocean	([1])	([1])	750	229

Z Less than 0.5 meter.   [1] Sea level.   [2] "Sec." denotes section; "T," township; "R," range; "N," north; "W," west.

Source: U.S. Geological Survey, for highest and lowest points, *Elevations and Distances in the United States, 1990*; for mean elevations, 1983 edition.

No. 346. Flows of Largest U.S. Rivers—Length, Discharge, and Drainage Area

RIVER	Location of mouth	Source stream (name and location)	Length (miles) [1]	Average discharge at mouth (1,000 cubic ft. per second)	Drainage area (1,000 sq. mi.)
Mississippi	Louisiana.	Mississippi River, MN.	[2]2,340	[3]593	[4][5]1,150
St. Lawrence.	Canada.	North River, MN	1,900	348	[5]396
Ohio	Illinois-Kentucky . . .	Allegheny River, PA.	1,310	281	203
Columbia	Oregon-Washington.	Columbia River, Canada.	1,240	265	[5]250
Yukon	Alaska.	McNeil River, Canada	1,980	225	[5]328
Missouri	Missouri.	Red Rock Creek, MT	2,540	76.2	[5]529
Tennessee	Kentucky	Courthouse Creek, NC	886	68	40.9
Mobile	Alabama	Tickanetley Creek, GA	774	67.2	44.6
Kuskokwim	Alaska.	South Fork Kuskokwim River, AK.	724	67	48
Copper.	Alaska.	Copper River, AK	286	59	24.4
Atchafalaya [6].	Louisiana.	Tierra Blanca Creek, NM	1,420	58	95.1
Snake	Washington	Snake River, WY.	1,040	56.9	108
Red.	Louisiana.	Tierra Blanca Creek, NM	1,290	56	93.2
Stikine	Alaska.	Stikine River, Canada.	379	56	[5]20
Susitna.	Alaska.	Susitna River, AK	313	51	20
Tanana.	Alaska.	Nabesna River, AK	659	41	44.5
Arkansas	Arkansas	East Fork Arkansas River, CO. . .	1,460	41	161
Susquehanna	Maryland	Hayden Creek, NY.	447	38.2	27.2
Willamette.	Oregon	Middle Fork Williamette River, OR	309	37.4	11.4
Nushagak	Alaska.	Nushagak River, AK	285	36	13.4
Alabama.	Alabama	Tickanetley Creek, GA	729	34.6	22.8
Wabash	Indiana-Illinois. . . .	Wabash River, OH.	512	31	32.9
White	Arkansas	White River, AR	722	30.5	27.8
Pend Oreille	Canada.	Blacktail Creek, MT	531	30.4	[5]26.3
Alsek	Alaska.	Aishihik River, Canada	290	30	[5]10.7

[1] From source to mouth. [2] The length from the source of the Missouri River to the Mississippi River and thence to the Gulf of Mexico is about 3,710 miles. [3] Includes about 167,000 cubic ft. per second diverted from the Mississippi into the Atchafalaya River but excludes the flow of the Red River. [4] Excludes the drainage areas of the Red and Atchafalaya Rivers. [5] Drainage area includes both the U.S. and Canada. [6] In east-central Louisiana, the Red River flows into the Atchafalaya River, a distributary of the Mississippi River. Data on average discharge, length, and drainage area include the Red River, but exclude all water diverted into the Atchafalaya from the Mississippi River.

Source: U.S. Geological Survey, *Largest Rivers in the United States*, Open File Report 87-242, August 1987.

No. 347. Water Area, Other Than Inland Water—States

[Includes only that portion of body of water under the jurisdiction of the United States, excluding Alaska and Hawaii. Excludes inland waters; see footnote 2, table 1. One square mile=2.59 square kilometers]

BODY OF WATER	AREA		BODY OF WATER	AREA	
	Sq. mi.	Sq. km.		Sq. mi.	Sq. km.
Total	**74,364**	**192,603**	Gulf of Mexico coastal water	3,837	9,938
			Alabama	560	1,450
Atlantic coastal water	2,298	5,952	Florida	1,698	4,398
Florida	37	96	Louisiana	1,016	2,631
Georgia.	48	124	Mississippi	556	1,440
Maine.	1,102	2,854	Texas	7	18
Massachusetts.	959	2,484			
Rhode Island	14	36	Lake Michigan.	22,178	57,441
South Carolina	138	357	Illinois	1,526	3,952
			Indiana	228	591
Chesapeake Bay	3,237	8,384	Michigan	13,037	33,766
Maryland.	1,726	4,470	Wisconsin	7,387	19,132
Virginia	1,511	3,913			
			New York Harbor.	92	238
Delaware Bay	665	1,722	New Jersey	69	179
Delaware.	350	907	New York	23	60
New Jersey	315	816	Lake Ontario: New York	3,033	78
Lake Erie	5,002	12,955	Pacific coastal water	343	888
Michigan.	216	559	California.	69	179
New York	594	1,538	Oregon	48	124
Ohio.	3,457	8,954	Washington	226	585
Pennsylvania	735	1,904			
			Puget Sound: Washington	561	1,453
Straits of Georgia and Juan de Fuca:			Lake St. Clair: Michigan	116	300
Washington	1,610	4,170			
Lake Huron: Michigan.	8,975	23,245	Lake Superior	21,118	54,696
Long Island Sound.	1,298	3,364	Michigan	16,231	42,038
Connecticut	573	1,484	Minnesota	2,212	5,729
New York	726	1,880	Wisconsin	2,675	6,928

Source: U.S. Bureau of the Census, *Areas of the United States: 1940.*

No. 348. Water Withdrawals and Consumptive Use—States and Other Areas: 1985

[In millions of gallons per day, except as noted. Figures may not add due to rounding. Withdrawal signifies water physically withdrawn from a source. Includes fresh and saline water]

| STATE OR OTHER AREA | Total [1] | Per capita (gal. per day) fresh | WATER WITHDRAWN | | | | | | Con-sumptive use,[4] fresh water |
| | | | Source | | Selected major uses | | | | |
			Ground water	Surface water	Irriga-tion	Public supply [2]	Indus-trial [3]	Thermo-electric	
United States	399,000	1,400	74,000	325,000	137,000	39,900	29,300	187,000	92,300
Alabama	8,600	2,140	347	8,250	69	654	851	6,920	541
Alaska	406	727	72	334	-	86	133	30	27
Arizona	6,430	1,960	3,100	3,330	5,520	645	133	58	3,700
Arkansas	5,910	2,500	3,810	2,100	3,870	317	175	1,090	3,210
California	49,700	1,420	15,100	34,600	30,600	5,450	1,160	12,200	21,100
Colorado	13,600	4,190	2,340	11,200	12,400	754	211	110	4,850
Connecticut	3,780	375	144	3,640	3	401	147	3,210	106
Delaware	1,650	222	79	1,580	27	87	410	1,120	39
District of Columbia	348	556	-	348	-	218	-	130	24
Florida	17,000	554	4,050	13,000	2,910	1,940	679	11,400	2,730
Georgia	5,450	899	1,000	4,440	453	935	656	3,330	838
Hawaii	2,150	1,100	655	1,490	906	215	20	970	132
Idaho	22,300	22,200	4,800	17,500	20,600	301	334	-	5,290
Illinois	14,500	1,250	968	13,500	71	1,910	639	11,700	686
Indiana	8,030	1,470	635	7,400	47	714	2,750	4,480	454
Iowa	2,770	960	671	2,090	67	415	260	1,810	473
Kansas	5,670	2,310	4,800	866	4,730	358	95	415	4,710
Kentucky	4,200	1,130	205	3,990	8	451	266	3,410	260
Louisiana	10,400	2,210	1,440	8,980	1,480	675	2,100	5,960	2,090
Maine	1,520	733	66	1,460	2	127	250	1,070	203
Maryland	6,710	321	219	6,490	34	834	371	5,429	423
Massachusetts	9,660	1,070	315	9,340	16	802	153	8,450	316
Michigan	11,400	1,270	600	10,800	210	1,370	1,380	8,390	611
Minnesota	2,830	676	685	2,150	209	604	457	1,470	768
Mississippi	2,510	885	1,580	933	886	328	236	670	661
Missouri	6,110	1,210	640	5,470	306	699	116	4,930	504
Montana	8,650	10,500	203	8,450	8,300	174	60	67	1,900
Nebraska	10,000	6,250	5,590	4,450	7,270	272	167	2,210	4,910
Nevada	3,740	3,860	908	2,830	3,350	300	35	23	1,890
New Hampshire	894	688	84	810	1	111	239	543	76
New Jersey	6,940	307	668	6,270	132	1,110	1,140	4,550	279
New Mexico	3,280	2,320	1,510	1,780	2,820	264	83	59	1,530
New York	15,200	508	1,100	14,100	38	3,050	1,080	10,900	1,400
North Carolina	8,760	1,260	435	8,320	132	764	539	7,270	439
North Dakota	1,160	1,690	127	1,040	154	84	13	892	201
Ohio	12,700	1,180	730	12,000	17	1,560	540	10,500	396
Oklahoma	1,270	386	568	707	445	547	113	134	576
Oregon	6,540	2,450	660	5,880	5,710	496	301	12	2,600
Pennsylvania	14,300	1,210	799	13,500	11	1,780	2,210	10,200	589
Rhode Island	409	152	27	381	3	122	20	261	23
South Carolina	6,820	2,040	214	6,610	34	421	1,130	5,190	340
South Dakota	675	956	249	425	460	96	49	4	361
Tennessee	8,450	1,770	444	8,010	9	697	1,610	6,060	275
Texas	25,300	1,230	7,410	17,900	8,120	3,100	2,760	11,000	8,650
Utah	4,320	2,540	815	3,500	3,590	453	213	28	2,130
Vermont	126	235	37	89	1	65	55	1	26
Virginia	7,250	853	341	6,910	52	691	673	5,760	269
Washington	7,030	1,600	1,220	5,810	4,940	1,050	559	427	4,700
West Virginia	5,440	2,810	227	5,210	4	172	1,030	4,210	877
Wisconsin	6,740	1,400	570	6,170	84	659	461	5,440	321
Wyoming	6,220	12,200	526	5,700	5,660	111	184	236	2,670
Puerto Rico	2,600	176	175	2,430	167	409	18	2,010	163
Virgin Islands	124	68	2	123	-	6	14	103	1

- Represents zero.   [1] Includes self-supplied withdrawals for commercial use (1.2 mil. gallons) and livestock (4.4 mil. gallons) that are not shown separately under "major uses."   [2] Includes domestic withdrawals for normal household purposes. [3] Includes water used in mining.   [4] Water that has been evaporated, transpired, or incorporated into products, plant or animal tissue; and therefore, is not available for immediate reuse.

Source: U.S. Geological Survey, *Estimated Use of Water in the United States in 1985*, circular 1004.

No. 349. U.S. Water Withdrawals and Consumptive Use Per Day, by End Use: 1940 to 1985

[Includes Puerto Rico. Withdrawal signifies water physically withdrawn from a source. Includes fresh and saline water; excludes water used for hydroelectric power. See also *Historical Statistics, Colonial Times to 1970*, series J 92-103]

YEAR	Total (bil. gal.)	Per capita [1] (gal.)	Irrigation (bil. gal.)	PUBLIC SUPPLY [2]		Rural [4] (bil. gal.)	Industrial and misc. [5] (bil. gal.)	Steam electric utilities (bil. gal.)
				Total (bil. gal.)	Per capita[3] (gal.)			
WITHDRAWALS								
1940.........................	140	1,027	71	10	75	3.1	29	23
1950.........................	180	1,185	89	14	145	3.6	37	40
1955.........................	240	1,454	110	17	148	3.6	39	72
1960.........................	270	1,500	110	21	151	3.6	38	100
1965.........................	310	1,602	120	24	155	4.0	46	130
1970.........................	370	1,815	130	27	166	4.5	47	170
1975.........................	420	1,972	140	29	168	4.9	45	200
1980.........................	450	1,953	150	34	183	5.6	45	210
1985.........................	400	1,650	140	38	189	7.8	30	190
CONSUMPTIVE USE								
1960.........................	61	339	52	3.5	25	2.8	3.0	0.2
1965.........................	77	403	66	5.2	34	3.2	3.4	0.4
1970.........................	87	427	73	5.9	36	3.4	4.1	0.8
1975.........................	96	451	80	6.7	38	3.4	4.2	1.9
1980.........................	100	440	83	7.1	38	3.9	5.0	3.2
1985.........................	92	380	74	([6])	([6])	[7]9.2	6.1	6.2

[1] Based on the Bureau of the Census resident population as of July 1.   [2] Includes commercial water withdrawals.   [3] Based on population served.   [4] Rural farm and nonfarm household and garden use, and water for farm stock and dairies.   [5] For 1940 to 1960, includes manufacturing and mineral industries, rural commercial industries, air-conditioning, resorts, hotels, motels, military and other State and Federal agencies, and miscellaneous; thereafter, includes manufacturing, mining and mineral processing, ordnance, construction, and miscellaneous.   [6] Public supply consumptive use included in end-use categories.   [7] Includes public supply consumptive use for domestic and commercial purposes.

Source: 1940-1960, U.S. Bureau of Domestic Business Development, based principally on committee prints, *Water Resources Activities in the United States*, for the Senate Committee on National Water Resources, U.S. Senate, thereafter, U.S. Geological Survey, *Estimated Use of Water in the United States in 1985*, circular 1004, and previous quinquennial issues.

No. 350. National Ambient Water Quality in Rivers and Streams—Violation Rate: 1980 to 1990

[In percent. Violation level based on U.S. Environmental Protection Agency water quality criteria. Violation rate represents the proportion of all measurements of a specific water quality pollutant which exceeds the "violation level" for that pollutant. "Violation" does not necessarily imply a legal violation. Data based on U.S. Geological Survey's National Stream Quality Accounting Network (NASQAN) data system; for details, see source. Years refer to water years. A water year begins in Oct. and ends in Sept. μg=micrograms; mg=milligrams. For metric conversion, see page IX]

POLLUTANT	VIOLATION LEVEL	1980	1983	1984	1985	1986	1987	1988	1989	1990
Fecal coliform bacteria ...	Above 200 cells per 100 ml .	31	34	30	28	24	23	22	30	26
Dissolved oxygen	Below 5 mg per liter	5	4	3	3	3	2	2	3	2
Phosphorus, total, as phosporous	Above 1.0 mg per liter	4	3	4	3	3	3	4	2	3
Lead, dissolved	Above 50 μg per liter......	5	5	(Z)	(Z)	(Z)	(Z)	(Z)	(Z)	(Z)
Cadmium, dissolved	Above 10 μg per liter......	1	1	(Z)	(Z)	(Z)	(Z)	(Z)	(Z)	(Z)

Z Less than 1.

Source: U.S. Geological Survey, national-level data, unpublished; State-level data, *Water-Data Report*, annual series prepared in cooperation with the State governments.

No. 351. Oil Polluting Incidents Reported in and Around U.S. Waters: 1973 to 1990

YEAR	Incidents	Gallons	YEAR	Incidents	Gallons
1973.................	11,054	15,289,188	1985................	7,740	8,465,055
1974.................	12,083	15,739,792	1986................	6,539	4,613,387
1975.................	10,998	21,528,444	1987................	6,352	3,887,004
1976.................	11,066	18,517,384	1988................	6,791	6,645,985
1977.................	10,979	8,188,398	1989................	8,225	13,615,706
1978.................	12,174	11,035,890			
1979.................	11,556	10,051,271	1990, prel............	7,114	4,255,308
1980.................	9,886	12,638,848	Tankships...........	245	886,216
1981.................	9,589	8,919,789	Tank barges	409	2,514,025
1982.................	9,416	10,404,646	Other vessels	2,657	423,514
1983.................	10,530	8,378,719	Nonvessels...........	3,803	431,553
1984.................	10,089	19,007,332			

Source: U.S. Coast Guard. Based on unpublished data from the *Marine Safety Information System*, December 30, 1991.

No. 352. National Ambient Air Pollutant Concentrations: 1982 to 1990

[Data represent annual composite averages of pollutant based on daily 24-hour averages of monitoring stations, except carbon monoxide is based on the second-highest, non-overlapping, 8-hour average; ozone, average of the second-highest daily maximum one hour value; and lead, quarterly average of ambient lead levels. Based on data from the National Aerometric Data Bank. $\mu g/m^3$ = micrograms of pollutant per cubic meter of air; ppm = parts per million]

POLLUTANT	Unit	Monitoring stations, number	Air quality standard [1]	1982	1983	1984	1985	1986	1987	1988	1989	1990
Carbon monoxide	ppm	248	[2]9	7.95	7.82	7.74	6.99	7.11	6.67	6.42	6.32	5.89
Ozone	ppm	388	[3].12	0.125	0.137	0.125	0.123	0.119	0.125	0.136	0.116	0.114
Sulfur dioxide . .	ppm	374	.03	0.010	0.009	0.010	0.009	0.009	0.009	0.009	0.008	0.008
Total suspended particulates . .	$\mu g/m^3$	1,750	75	48.7	48.4	49.9	47.7	47.6	48.6	49.7	48	47.3
Nitrogen dioxide .	ppm	116	.053	0.024	0.023	0.024	0.024	0.024	0.024	0.024	0.023	0.022
Lead	$\mu g/m^3$	139	[4]1.5	0.484	0.413	0.381	0.258	0.151	0.108	0.087	0.074	0.070

[1] Refers to the primary National Ambient Air Quality Standard that protects the public health.   [2] Based on 8-hour standard of 9 ppm.   [3] Based on 1-hour standard of .12 ppm.   [4] Based on 3-month standard of 1.5 $\mu g/m^3$

Source: U.S. Environmental Protection Agency, *National Air Quality and Emissions Trends Report*, annual.

No. 353. National Air Pollutant Emissions: 1940 to 1990

[In millions of metric tons, except lead in thousands of metric tons. Metric ton = 1.1023 short tons. PM = Particulate matter, SO_x = Sulfur oxides, NO_x = Nitrogen oxides, VOC = volatile organic compound, CO = Carbon monoxide, Pb = Lead. NA Not available]

YEAR	EMISSIONS						PERCENT CHANGE FROM PRIOR YEAR					
	PM	SO_x	NO_x	VOC	CO	Pb	PM	SO_x	NO_x	VOC	CO	Pb
1940	23.1	17.6	6.9	15.2	82.6	(NA)	(NA)	(NA)	(NA)	(NA)	(NA)	(NA)
1950	24.9	19.8	9.4	18.1	87.6	(NA)	7.8	12.5	36.2	19.1	6.1	(NA)
1960	21.6	19.7	13.0	21.0	89.7	(NA)	-13.3	-0.5	38.3	16.0	2.4	(NA)
1970	18.5	28.3	18.5	25.0	101.4	203.8	-14.4	43.7	42.3	19.0	13.0	(NA)
1980	8.5	23.4	20.9	21.1	79.6	70.6	-54.1	-17.3	13.0	-15.6	-21.5	-65.4
1981	8.0	22.6	20.9	19.8	77.4	56.4	-5.9	-3.4	0.0	-6.2	-2.8	-20.1
1982	7.1	21.4	20.0	18.4	72.4	54.4	-11.3	-5.3	-4.3	-7.1	-6.5	-3.5
1983	7.1	20.7	19.3	19.3	74.5	46.4	0.0	-3.3	-3.5	4.9	2.9	-14.7
1984	7.4	21.5	19.8	20.3	71.8	40.1	4.2	3.9	2.6	5.2	-3.6	-13.6
1985	7.2	21.1	19.9	20.1	68.7	20.1	-2.7	-1.9	0.5	-1.0	-4.3	-49.9
1986	6.7	20.9	19.1	19.0	63.2	8.4	-6.9	-0.9	-4.0	-5.5	-8.0	-58.2
1987	6.9	20.5	19.4	19.3	63.4	8.0	3.0	-1.9	1.6	1.6	0.3	-4.8
1988	7.5	20.6	20.0	19.4	64.7	7.6	8.7	0.5	3.1	0.5	-2.1	-5.0
1989	7.2	20.8	19.8	18.5	60.4	7.2	-4.0	1.0	-1.0	-4.6	-6.6	-5.3
1990	7.5	21.2	19.6	18.7	60.1	7.1	4.2	1.9	-1.0	1.1	-0.5	-1.4

No. 354. Air Pollutant Emissions, by Pollutant and Source: 1970 to 1990

[In millions of metric tons, except lead in thousands of metric tons. Metric ton = 1.1023 short tons]

YEAR AND POLLUTANT	Total emissions	CONTROLLABLE EMISSIONS							Misc. uncontrollable	PERCENT OF TOTAL		
		Transportation		Fuel combustion [1]		Industrial processes	Solid waste disposal			Transportation	Fuel combustion [1]	Industrial
		Total	Road vehicles	Total	Electric utilities							
1970: Carbon monoxide	101.4	74.4	65.3	4.5	0.2	8.9	6.4		7.2	73.4	4.4	8.8
Sulfur oxides	28.4	0.6	0.3	21.3	15.8	6.4	-		0.1	2.1	75.0	22.5
Volatile organic compounds . .	25.0	10.3	9.1	0.6	-	8.9	1.8		3.3	41.2	2.4	35.6
Particulates	18.5	1.2	0.9	4.6	2.3	10.5	1.1		1.1	6.5	24.9	56.8
Nitrogen oxides	18.5	8.0	6.3	9.1	4.4	0.7	0.4		0.3	43.2	49.2	3.8
Lead	203.8	163.6	156.0	9.6	0.3	23.9	6.7		-	80.3	4.7	11.7
1980: Carbon monoxide	79.6	56.1	48.7	7.4	0.3	6.3	2.2		7.6	70.5	9.3	7.9
Sulfur oxides	23.4	0.9	0.4	18.7	15.5	3.8	-		0.0	3.8	79.9	16.2
Volatile organic compounds . .	21.1	7.5	6.2	0.9	-	9.2	0.6		2.9	35.5	4.3	43.6
Particulates	8.5	1.3	1.1	2.4	0.8	3.3	0.4		1.1	15.3	28.2	38.8
Nitrogen oxides	20.9	9.8	7.9	10.1	6.1	0.7	0.1		0.2	46.9	48.3	3.3
Lead	70.6	59.4	56.4	3.9	0.1	3.6	3.7		-	84.1	5.5	5.1
1990: Carbon monoxide	60.1	37.6	30.3	7.5	0.3	4.7	1.7		8.6	62.6	12.5	7.8
Sulfur oxides	21.2	0.9	0.6	17.1	14.2	3.1	-		-	4.2	80.7	14.6
Volatile organic compounds . .	18.7	6.4	5.1	0.9	-	8.1	0.6		2.7	34.2	4.8	43.3
Particulates	7.5	1.5	1.3	1.7	0.4	2.8	0.3		1.2	20.0	22.7	37.3
Nitrogen oxides	19.6	7.5	5.6	11.2	7.3	0.6	0.1		0.3	38.3	57.1	3.1
Lead	7.1	2.2	2.0	0.5	0.1	2.2	2.2		-	31.0	7.0	31.0

- Represents zero.   [1] Stationary sources.

Source of tables 353 and 354: U.S. Environmental Protection Agency, *National Air Pollutant Emission Estimates, 1940-1990*, March 1992.

No. 355. Metropolitan Areas Failing to Meet National Ambient Air Quality Standards for Carbon Monoxide—Number of Days Exceeding Standards: 1989 and 1990

[Areas generally represent the officially defined metropolitan area, but may, in some cases, not have all the counties identified as part of the area; see *Federal Register*, 40 CFR, part 81, *Air Quality Designations: Final Rule*, Nov. 6, 1991. Nonattainment status was as of October 29, 1991]

METROPOLITAN AREA	1989	1990	METROPOLITAN AREA	1989	1990	METROPOLITAN AREA	1989	1990
Albuquerque, NM	6	3	Hartford, CT CMSA	1	-	Phoenix, AZ	9	4
Anchorage, AK	3	12	Klamath County, OR [1]	2	-	Portland, OR-WA CMSA	2	2
Baltimore, MD	-	1	Lake Tahoe S. Shore, CA	(NA)	5	Provo-Orem, UT	12	11
Boston, MA-NH CMSA	-		Las Vegas, NV	26	17	Raleigh-Durham, NC	2	2
Chico, CA	1	1	Longmont, CO	(NA)	-	Reno, NV	2	7
Cleveland, OH CMSA	1	-	Los Angeles, CA CMSA	72	47	Sacramento, CA	18	11
Colorado Springs, CO	1	-	Medford, OR	15	-	San Diego, CA	4	-
Denver-Boulder, CO CMSA	6	3	Memphis, TN-AR-MS	2	1	San Francisco, CA CMSA	6	2
Duluth, MN	2	-	Minneapolis-St. Paul, MN-WI	2	1	Seattle-Tacoma, WA CMSA	2	2
El Paso, TX	5	4	Missoula County, MT [1]	2	1	Spokane, WA	11	6
Fairbanks, AK [1]	3	2	Modesto, CA	8	2	Stockton, CA	4	2
Fort Collins, CO	1	-	New York, NY-NJ-CT CMSA	16	4	Syracuse, NY	2	1
Fresno, CA	13	1	Ogden, UT	(NA)	3	Washington, DC-MD-VA	1	-
Grant Pass, OR [1]	(NA)	1	Philadelphia, PA-NJ-DE-MD CMSA	2	-			
Greensboro-Winston-Salem, NC	(NA)	-						

- Represents zero.   NA Not available.   [1] Not a metropolitan area.

No. 356. Metropolitan Areas Failing to Meet National Ambient Air Quality Standards for Ozone—Number of Days Exceeding Standards: 1988 to 1990

[See headnote, table 355. Nonattainment status was as of October 29, 1991]

METROPOLITAN AREA	1988-1990, avg.	1990	METROPOLITAN AREA	1988-1990, avg.	1990
Albany-Schenectady-Troy, NY	3.8	-	Louisville, KY-IN	3.5	2.1
Allentown-Bethlehem-Easton, PA-NJ	2.4	-	Los Angeles South Coast Air, CA [5]	124.8	103.6
Altoona, PA	1.3	-	Manchester, NH	1.7	1.0
Atlanta, GA	5.7	11.3	Manitowoc Co, WI	6.3	2.3
Atlantic City, NJ	4.1	5.3	Memphis, TN-AR-MS	1.4	-
Baltimore, MD	8.7	5.6	Miami-Fort Lauderdale, FL CMSA	1.0	1.0
Baton Rouge, LA	5.8	6.1	Milwaukee-Racine, WI CMSA	8.6	2.3
Beaumont-Port Arthur, TX	5.0	3.2	Monterey Bay, CA [6]	4.3	-
Birmingham, AL	2.7	4.1	Muskegon, MI	6.8	3.1
Boston-Lawrence-Salem, MA-NH CMSA [1]	10.0	2.0	Nashville, TN	6.5	5.8
Buffalo-Niagara Falls, NY CMSA	3.1	-	New York, NY-NJ-CT CMSA [7]	12.7	5.1
Canton, OH	1.7	-	Norfolk-Virginia Beach-Newport News, VA	1.3	-
Charleston, WV	2.3	-	Owensboro, KY	4.4	3.0
Charlotte-Gastonia-Rock Hill, NC-SC [3]	2.7	1.0	Parkersburg-Marietta, WV-OH	5.5	-
Cherokee County, SC [3]	1.6	-	Philadelphia, PA-NJ-DE-MD CMSA	7.0	5.0
Chicago-Gary-Lake County, IL-IN-WI CMSA	8.6	2.3	Phoenix, AZ	6.0	6.0
Cincinnati-Hamilton, OH-KY-IN CMSA	4.7	4.0	Pittsburgh-Beaver Valley, PA CMSA	5.6	-
Cleveland-Akron-Lorain, OH CMSA	4.0	1.2	Portland-Vancouver, OR-WA CMSA	2.2	4.2
Columbus, OH	1.7	1.0	Portland, ME	9.1	6.3
Dallas-Fort Worth, TX CMSA	3.5	4.0	Portsmouth-Dover-Rochester, NH-ME	4.1	1.0
Dayton-Springfield, OH	2.7	-	Poughkeepsie, NY	1.3	-
Detroit-Ann Arbor, MI CMSA	3.7	-	Providence, RI [8]	5.7	6
Door County, WI [3]	1.8	3.5	Raleigh-Durham, NC	3.4	-
Edmonson County, KY [3]	1.7	-	Reading, PA	3.1	-
El Paso, TX	4.2	4.1	Reno, NV	2.0	2.0
Erie, PA	2.6	-	Richmond-Petersburg, VA	3.1	1.0
Essex County, NY [3]	1.8	-	Sacramento, CA	9.9	6.1
Evansville, IN-KY	1.1	-	St. Louis, MO-IL	3.8	2.1
Grand Rapids, MI	3.7	2.0	Salt Lake City-Ogden, UT	2	1.0
Greater Connecticut, CT [4]	7.4	6.1	San Diego, CA	10.1	26.0
Greenbrier County, WV [3]	1.4	-	San Joaquin Valley, CA [6]	36.6	24.5
Greensboro-Winston-Salem-High Point, NC	7.2	1.1	San Francisco-Bay area, CA	2.4	1.0
Hancock and Waldo counties, ME [3]	2.5	-	Santa Barbara-Santa Maria-Lompoc, CA	1.6	2.0
Harrisburg-Lebanon-Carlisle, PA	1.8	1.0	Scranton-Wilkes-Barre, PA	2.7	-
Houston-Galveston-Brazoria, TX CMSA	16.2	24.0	Seattle-Tacoma, WA	3.3	3.3
Huntington-Ashland, WV-KY-OH	5.3	4.6	Sheboygan, WI	5.4	-
Indianapolis, IN	1.0	1.0	Smyth County, VA [3]	3.8	(NA)
Jefferson County, NY [3]	2.0	-	South Bend-Mishawaka, IN	1.1	-
Jersey Co., IL [3]	3.1	2.0	Southeast Desert Modified AQMD, CA [9]	56.2	43
Johnstown, PA	2.5	-	Springfield, MA	7.7	3.0
Kansas City, MO-KS	1.2	1.3	Sussex County, DE [3]	3.7	1.1
Kent County and Queen Anne's Co., MD [3]	1.6	1.0	Tampa-St. Petersburg-Clearwater, FL	1	-
Kewaunee County, WI [3]	3.5	-	Toledo, OH	2.4	-
Knox Co. and Lincoln counties, ME [3]	8.5	1.3	Ventura County, CA	35.8	14.0
Knoxville, TN	2.1	1.0	Walworth County, WI	1.3	-
Lake Charles, LA	2.0	2.0	Washington, DC-MD-VA	3.3	3.4
Lancaster, PA	1.0	-	York, PA	1.9	1
Lewiston-Auburn, ME	1.5	-	Youngstown-Warren, OH [10]	1.8	1
Lexington-Fayette, KY	2.0	1.0			

- Represents zero.   NA Not available.   [1] Includes both the Worcester, MA and New Bedford, MA MSA's.   [2] Excludes York Co., SC.   [3] Not a metropolitan area.   [4] Primarily represents Hartford-New Haven area.   [5] Primarily represents Los Angeles and Orange counties.   [6] Primarily represents Monterey, Santa Cruz, and San Benito counties.   [7] Excludes the Connecticut portion.   [8] Covers entire State of Rhode Island.   [9] Represents primarily San Joaquin, Turlock, Merced, Madera, Fresno, Kings, Tulare, and Kern counties.   [10] Includes Sharon, PA.

Source: U.S. Environmental Protection Agency, press release, November 1991.

No. 357. Hazardous Waste Sites on the National Priority List, by State: 1991

[Includes both proposed and final sites listed on the National Priorities List for the Superfund program as authorized by the Comprehensive Environmental Response, Compensationa, and Liability Act of 1980 and the Superfund Amendments and Reauthorization Act of 1986]

STATE	Total sites	Rank	Percent distribution	Federal	Non-Federal	STATE	Total sites	Rank	Percent distribution	Federal	Non-Federal
Total	1,211	(X)	(X)	119	1,091	Missouri	22	16	1.8	3	19
						Montana	8	39	0.7	-	8
United States	1,201	(X)	100.0	118	1,082	Nebraska	8	39	0.7	1	7
Alabama	12	27	1.0	2	10	Nevada.	1	50	0.1	-	1
Alaska	6	43	0.5	4	2	New Hampshire	17	22	1.4	1	16
Arizona.	10	32	0.8	3	7	New Jersey	109	1	9.1	6	103
Arkansas.	10	32	0.8	-	10	New Mexico.	10	32	0.8	2	8
California.	91	3	7.6	20	71	New York	84	4	7.0	4	80
Colorado.	16	23	1.3	3	13	North Carolina	22	16	1.8	1	21
Connecticut	15	24	1.2	1	14	North Dakota	2	47	0.2	-	2
Delaware.	20	18	1.7	1	19	Ohio.	33	11	2.7	3	30
District of Columbia.	-	(X)	0.0	-	-	Oklahoma	10	32	0.8	1	9
Florida	52	6	4.3	4	48	Oregon	8	39	0.7	1	7
Georgia.	13	26	1.1	2	11	Pennsylvania	97	2	8.1	4	93
Hawaii	2	47	0.2	2	-	Rhode Island	12	27	1.0	2	10
Idaho	9	37	0.7	2	7	South Carolina	23	15	1.9	1	22
Illinois	37	10	3.1	4	33	South Dakota	4	45	0.3	1	3
Indiana	33	11	2.7	-	33	Tennessee	14	25	1.2	2	12
Iowa	20	18	1.7	1	19	Texas.	29	13	2.4	4	25
Kansas.	11	30	0.9	1	10	Utah.	12	27	1.0	4	8
Kentucky.	19	21	1.6	-	19	Vermont	8	39	0.7	-	8
Louisiana.	11	30	0.9	1	10	Virginia	20	18	1.7	1	19
Maine.	9	37	0.7	2	7	Washington	49	7	4.1	15	34
Maryland.	10	32	0.8	2	8	West Virginia	5	44	0.4	-	5
Massachusetts.	25	14	2.1	3	22	Wisconsin	39	9	3.2	-	39
Michigan	77	5	6.4	-	77	Wyoming.	3	46	0.2	1	2
Minnesota	42	8	3.5	2	40	Guam	1	(X)	(X)	-	1
Mississippi.	2	47	0.2	-	2	Puerto Rico	9	(X)	(X)	1	8

- Represents zero. X Not applicable.

U.S. Environmental Protection Agency, press release, July 1991. Also in the *Federal Register*.

No. 358. State and Local Government Expenditures for Solid Waste Management and Sewerage, by State: 1990

[In millions of dollars, except as indicated]

STATE	TOTAL EXPENDITURES [1] Total	Per cap- ita [2] (dol.)	Solid waste man- age- ment	Sew- erage	CAPITAL EXPENDI- TURES Solid waste man- age- ment	Sew- erage	STATE	TOTAL EXPENDITURES [1] Total	Per cap- ita [2] (dol.)	Solid waste man- age- ment	Sew- erage	CAPITAL EXPENDI- TURES Solid waste man- age- ment	Sew- erage
U.S.	28,452.7	114	10,143.8	18,308.9	1,818.4	8,355.9	MS . .	165.4	64	43.4	122.0	2.3	74.1
							MO . .	339.8	66	60.3	279.5	6.2	135.3
							MT . .	41.4	52	19.7	21.6	2.1	4.7
AL. . .	230.5	57	106.1	124.4	6.4	47.6	NE. . .	83.2	53	23.1	60.1	3.8	18.9
AK. . .	92.6	168	25.0	67.5	1.8	29.3	NV. . .	86.0	72	2.2	83.9	0.3	33.6
AZ. . .	395.6	108	116.3	279.2	22.8	189.5	NH . .	146.0	132	60.9	85.1	10.3	40.0
AR. . .	132.3	56	51.9	80.5	4.4	25.2	NJ . . .	1,639.5	212	703.7	935.8	84.3	407.8
CA. . .	3,596.8	121	816.4	2,780.4	76.5	1,299.5	NM . .	146.8	97	55.1	91.7	12.7	0.0
CO . .	290.5	88	59.7	230.8	28.4	67.8	NY . . .	3,386.8	188	1,921.3	1,465.5	575.8	871.8
CT . . .	549.4	167	309.9	239.5	35.3	111.0	NC . .	622.5	94	244.3	378.1	41.9	179.5
DE. . .	97.0	146	43.1	53.9	1.9	13.2	ND . .	31.8	50	13.2	18.6	0.9	10.6
DC. . .	169.7	280	40.9	128.9	0.7	45.7	OH . .	1,137.5	105	267.7	869.9	26.1	388.4
FL. . .	1,611.1	125	892.8	718.4	186.7	349.4	OK . .	227.1	72	85.8	141.3	3.4	64.7
GA . .	560.3	86	213.6	346.7	36.5	172.2	OR . .	247.6	87	43.6	204.0	3.9	94.9
HI . . .	182.7	165	78.8	103.9	34.9	61.7	PA. . .	1,321.6	111	497.3	824.4	97.9	251.1
ID . . .	78.1	78	26.3	51.8	1.7	21.4	RI . . .	125.1	125	28.9	96.3	0.4	40.6
IL . . .	1,114.3	97	268.8	845.5	16.8	334.3	SC. . .	208.6	77	104.2	164.3	11.1	89.3
IN . . .	432.4	78	65.0	367.4	3.9	119.0	SD. . .	31.7	45	8.1	23.6	1.0	10.4
IA . . .	259.2	93	65.4	193.8	4.1	105.2	TN. . .	407.4	84	132.3	275.1	19.1	147.6
KS. . .	119.1	48	38.4	80.7	2.9	15.5	TX. . .	1,622.1	95	414.2	1,207.9	29.7	586.9
KY. . .	243.4	66	79.5	163.9	3.7	48.3	UT. . .	145.0	84	42.8	102.2	4.1	52.5
LA. . .	421.0	100	129.6	291.4	11.3	149.2	VT. . .	57.0	101	15.8	41.2	1.8	24.2
ME . .	141.8	115	52.5	89.3	3.2	41.1	VA. . .	753.4	122	256.8	496.6	37.1	175.1
MD . .	620.2	130	222.3	397.9	18.9	148.6	WA . .	805.5	166	437.6	367.9	229.7	164.3
MA . .	871.6	145	250.7	620.9	31.0	373.1	WV . .	104.1	58	26.2	77.9	2.2	20.3
MI . . .	1,014.5	109	310.8	703.7	26.3	206.3	WI . . .	726.6	149	185.7	540.9	16.0	287.9
MN . .	490.0	112	137.5	352.4	12.3	147.5	WY . .	68.9	152	48.2	20.7	22.1	8.2

[1] Includes capital expenditures. [2] Based on resident population estimated as of July 1, 1990.

Source: U.S. Bureau of the Census, *Governmental Finances, 1989-1990*, series GF, No. 5.

No. 359. Municipal Solid Waste Generation, Recovery, and Disposal: 1960 to 1988

[In millions of tons, except as indicated. Covers post-consumer residential and commercial solid wastes which comprise the major portion of typical municipal collections. Excludes mining, agricultural and industrial processing, demolition and construction wastes, sewage sludge, and junked autos and obsolete equipment wastes. Based on material-flows estimating procedure and wet weight as generated. NA Not available]

ITEM AND MATERIAL	1960	1965	1970	1975	1980	1985	1986	1987	1988
Waste generated	87.8	103.4	121.9	128.0	149.6	161.6	167.4	174.1	179.6
Per person per day (lb.)	2.66	3.00	3.27	3.26	3.61	3.71	3.80	3.92	4.00
Materials recovered.	5.9	6.8	8.6	9.9	14.5	16.4	18.3	20.1	23.5
Per person per day (lb.)	0.18	0.19	0.23	0.25	0.35	0.38	0.42	0.45	0.52
Combustion for energy recovery	(NA)	0.2	0.4	0.7	2.7	7.6	9.6	16.0	24.5
Per person per day (lb.)	(NA)	0.01	0.02	0.02	0.06	0.17	0.22	0.36	0.59
Combustion without energy recovery .	27.0	26.8	24.7	17.8	11.0	4.1	3.0	2.0	1.0
Per person per day (lb.)	0.82	0.75	0.66	0.45	0.27	0.10	0.07	0.05	0.02
Landfilled, other disposal	54.9	69.6	88.2	99.7	121.4	133.5	136.5	136.0	130.5
Per person per day (lb.)	1.67	2.05	2.37	2.54	2.93	3.06	3.09	3.06	2.87
Percent distribution of generation:									
Paper and paperboard	34.1	36.8	36.3	33.6	36.6	38.1	39.2	40.0	40.0
Glass.	7.6	8.4	10.4	10.5	10.0	8.2	7.8	7.1	7.0
Metals.	12.0	10.7	11.6	11.2	9.7	8.8	8.7	8.5	8.5
Plastics	0.5	1.4	2.5	3.5	5.2	7.2	7.3	7.7	8.0
Rubber and leather	2.3	2.5	2.6	3.0	2.9	2.4	2.6	2.5	2.5
Textiles	1.9	1.8	1.6	1.7	1.7	1.7	1.6	2.1	2.1
Wood	3.4	3.4	3.3	3.4	3.3	3.3	3.4	3.4	3.6
Food wastes.	13.9	12.3	10.5	10.5	8.8	8.2	7.9	7.6	7.4
Yard wastes	22.8	20.9	19.0	19.7	18.4	18.6	18.0	17.8	17.6
Other wastes	1.6	1.8	2.2	2.9	3.4	3.6	3.5	3.3	3.2

No. 360. Generation and Recovery of Selected Materials in Municipal Solid Waste: 1960 to 1988

[In millions of tons, except as indicated. Covers post-consumer residential and commercial solid wastes which comprise the major portion of typical municipal collections. Excludes mining, agricultural and industrial processing, demolition and construction wastes, sewage sludge, and junked autos and obsolete equipment wastes. Based on material-flows estimating procedure and wet weight as generated]

ITEM AND MATERIAL	1960	1965	1970	1975	1980	1985	1986	1987	1988
Waste generated, total	**87.8**	**103.4**	**121.9**	**128.1**	**149.6**	**161.6**	**167.4**	**174.1**	**179.6**
Paper and paperboard	29.9	38.0	44.2	43.0	54.7	61.5	65.6	69.6	71.8
Ferrous metals	9.9	10.1	12.6	12.3	11.6	10.9	11.1	11.3	11.6
Aluminum.	0.4	0.5	0.8	1.1	1.8	2.3	2.4	2.4	2.5
Other nonferrous metals	0.2	0.5	0.7	0.9	1.1	1.0	1.0	1.1	1.1
Glass.	6.7	8.7	12.7	13.5	15.0	13.2	13.0	12.3	12.5
Plastics	0.4	1.4	3.1	4.5	7.8	11.6	12.2	13.4	14.4
Yard waste	20.0	21.6	23.2	25.2	27.5	30.0	30.2	31.0	31.6
Other wastes	20.3	22.6	24.6	27.6	30.1	31.1	31.9	33.0	34.1
Materials recovered, total	**5.9**	**6.8**	**8.6**	**9.9**	**14.5**	**16.4**	**18.3**	**20.1**	**23.5**
Paper and paperboard	5.4	5.7	7.4	8.2	11.9	13.1	14.8	16.3	18.4
Ferrous metals	0.1	0.1	0.1	0.2	0.4	0.4	0.4	0.4	0.7
Aluminum.	0.0	0.0	0.0	0.1	0.3	0.6	0.6	0.7	0.8
Other nonferrous metals	0.0	0.3	0.3	0.4	0.5	0.5	0.6	0.6	0.7
Glass.	0.1	0.1	0.2	0.4	0.8	1.0	1.1	1.3	1.5
Plastics	0.0	0.0	0.0	0.0	0.0	0.1	0.1	0.1	0.2
Yard waste.	0.0	0.0	0.0	0.0	0.0	0.0	0.0	0.0	0.5
Other wastes	0.3	0.6	0.6	0.6	0.6	0.7	0.7	0.7	0.7
Percent of generation recovered, total	**6.7**	**6.6**	**7.1**	**7.7**	**9.7**	**10.1**	**10.9**	**11.5**	**13.1**
Paper and paperboard	18.1	15.0	16.7	19.1	21.8	21.3	22.6	23.4	25.6
Ferrous metals	1.0	1.0	0.8	1.6	3.4	3.7	3.6	3.5	5.8
Aluminum.	0.0	0.0	0.0	9.1	16.7	26.1	25.0	29.2	31.7
Other nonferrous metals	0.0	60.0	42.9	44.4	45.5	50.0	60.0	54.5	65.1
Glass.	1.5	1.1	1.6	3.0	5.3	7.6	8.5	10.6	12.0
Plastics	0.0	0.0	0.0	0.0	0.0	0.9	0.8	0.7	1.1
Yard waste.	0.0	0.0	0.0	0.0	0.0	0.0	0.0	0.0	1.6
Other wastes	1.5	2.7	2.4	2.2	2.0	2.3	2.2	2.1	2.1

Source of tables 359 and 360: Franklin Associates, Ltd., Prairie Village, KS, *Characterization of Municipal Solid Waste in the United States: 1990 Update*. Prepared for the U.S. Environmental Protection Agency.

No. 361. Synthetic Organic Pesticides—Production and Sales: 1970 to 1990

[Includes a small quantity of soil conditioners. 1 kg.—.454 lbs]

ITEM	Unit	1970	1980	1981	1982	1983	1984	1985	1986	1987	1988	1989	1990
Production, total	**Mil. kg.**	**469**	**666**	**649**	**505**	**461**	**539**	**560**	**535**	**472**	**528**	**572**	**557**
Herbicides	Mil. kg.	183	366	380	283	259	325	343	329	252	318	316	317
Insecticides.	Mil. kg.	222	229	203	172	147	159	168	155	172	160	192	175
Fungicides	Mil. kg.	63	71	65	50	56	56	49	51	48	50	50	44
All other pesticides [1] . .	Mil. kg.	(NA)	(NA)	(NA)	(NA)	(NA)	(NA)	(NA)	(NA)	(NA)	(NA)	14	22
Sales, total	**Mil. kg.**	**400**	**638**	**585**	**520**	**461**	**502**	**463**	**426**	**413**	**424**	**461**	**442**
Sales value	Mil. dol	870	4,078	4,652	4,432	4,054	4,730	4,437	4,234	4,171	4,354	5,203	4,774

NA Not available. [1] Beginning 1989, may include some former insecticides along with new products.

Source: U.S. International Trade Commission, *Synthetic Organic Chemicals*, annual.

No. 362. Pollution Abatement and Control Expenditures in Current and Constant (1982) Dollars, 1980 to 1989, and by Media, 1989

[In millions of dollars, except percent. Excludes agricultural production of crops and livestock except feedlots]

ITEM	1980	1983	1984	1985	1986	1987	1988	1989 Total [1]	1989 Air	1989 Water	1989 Solid waste
CURRENT DOLLARS											
Total expenditures	53,538	61,779	68,929	74,636	78,717	81,486	86,063	91,348	32,657	36,009	23,227
Pollution abatement	50,491	58,060	65,230	70,945	74,612	77,319	81,588	86,571	30,217	34,962	22,642
Personal consumption	6,589	9,771	10,767	11,839	12,188	10,872	12,043	10,635	10,635	-	-
Business	32,283	37,589	42,191	45,097	46,832	49,620	52,190	57,046	19,265	23,540	15,837
Government	11,620	10,700	12,273	14,009	15,593	16,827	17,355	18,889	317	11,422	6,806
Federal	494	795	944	1,225	1,346	1,237	1,402	1,381	70	731	300
State and local	2,778	3,547	3,886	4,324	4,793	5,356	6,149	7,076	12	493	6,506
Govt. enterprise fixed capital	8,347	6,358	7,443	8,460	9,454	10,235	9,804	10,433	235	10,197	-
Regulation and monitoring	1,296	1,385	1,362	1,279	1,532	1,519	1,695	1,803	490	670	400
Research and development . . .	1,751	2,335	2,337	2,412	2,573	2,648	2,781	2,974	1,950	377	184
CONSTANT (1982) DOLLARS											
Total expenditures	62,046	60,007	64,713	68,121	72,071	71,502	73,622	74,381	28,251	29,581	17,166
Pollution abatement	58,421	56,453	61,326	64,846	68,488	67,963	69,970	70,658	26,326	28,780	16,723
Personal consumption	7,164	9,731	10,565	11,336	12,147	10,305	11,042	9,184	9,184	-	-
Business	37,885	36,533	39,495	41,282	43,066	43,782	45,168	47,053	16,872	19,914	11,703
Government	13,372	10,188	11,266	12,228	13,275	13,876	13,760	14,422	270	8,867	5,021
Regulation and monitoring	1,533	1,315	1,230	1,104	1,291	1,234	1,337	1,347	366	501	296
Research and development . . .	2,092	2,239	2,157	2,171	2,292	2,306	2,315	2,376	1,560	300	147

- Represents zero. [1] Includes "other and unallocated" expenditures (such as for noise, radiation, and pesticide pollution and business expenditures not assigned to media) which may be either positive or negative; therefore, data may not add.

Source: U.S. Bureau of Economic Analysis, *Survey of Current Business*, November 1991, and prior issues.

No. 363. Air and Water Pollution Abatement Expenditures in Constant (1982) Dollars: 1980 to 1989

[In millions of dollars. See headnote, table 362]

YEAR	AIR Total	Mobile sources [1] Total	Cars	Trucks	Stationary sources Total [2]	Industrial Facilities	Industrial Oper-ations [3]	WATER Total [4]	Industrial Facilities	Industrial Oper-ations [3]	Public sewer systems [5] Facilities	Public sewer systems [5] Oper-ations [3]
1980	24,744	11,764	8,818	2,946	12,980	5,946	6,304	24,647	3,725	4,081	8,942	4,694
1981	25,850	13,401	10,564	2,837	12,448	5,446	6,299	21,984	3,259	4,180	6,882	4,880
1982	24,961	13,464	10,530	2,934	11,496	5,086	5,675	21,199	3,080	4,022	6,148	5,156
1983	26,367	15,581	12,274	3,307	10,785	4,104	5,990	21,543	2,811	4,509	5,551	5,475
1984	28,591	17,561	13,481	4,081	11,030	4,115	6,260	23,257	2,900	4,795	6,387	5,649
1985	29,665	18,697	14,209	4,488	10,968	3,935	6,452	24,724	2,995	5,035	7,005	6,016
1986	30,788	19,508	14,804	4,704	11,280	3,884	6,892	26,449	2,854	5,379	7,774	6,691
1987	28,065	16,770	12,392	4,378	11,295	3,955	6,874	27,962	3,119	5,988	8,248	7,116
1988	29,112	18,117	(NA)	(NA)	10,995	3,876	6,684	27,192	2,849	5,906	7,691	7,553
1989, prel. .	26,326	14,930	(NA)	(NA)	11,396	4,168	6,802	28,780	3,553	6,370	7,923	7,817

NA Not available. [1] Excludes expenditures to reduce emissions from sources other than cars and trucks. [2] Includes other expenditures not shown separately. [3] Operation of facilities. [4] Includes nonpoint sources not shown separately. [5] Includes expenditures for private connectors to sewer systems, by owners of animal feedlots, and by government enterprises.

Source: U.S. Bureau of Economic Analysis, *Survey of Current Business*, November 1991, and prior issues.

No. 364. Pollution Abatement Capital Expenditures and Operating Costs of Manufacturing Establishments, 1980 to 1989, and by Selected Industry Group, 1989

[In millions of dollars. Based on probability sample of about 20,000 manufacturing establishments. Excludes apparel and other textile establishments and establishments with less than 20 employees. Data for 1987 are not available as no survey was conducted]

YEAR AND INDUSTRY GROUP	POLLUTION ABATEMENT CAPITAL EXPENDITURES					POLLUTION ABATEMENT GROSS OPERATING COSTS [1]				
				Solid waste					Solid waste	
	Total	Air	Water	Hazard-ous	Non-hazard-ous	Total	Air	Water	Hazard-ous	Non-hazard-ous
1980.	3,502.9	2,105.5	1,146.5	(NA)	[2]251.0	8,141.8	3,297.8	3,193.1	(NA)	[2]1,650.6
1985.	2,809.7	1,292.3	1,017.9	326.2	172.9	11,677.9	4,330.2	4,609.5	943.0	1,795.3
1986.	2,846.9	1,462.8	1,038.7	168.7	176.0	12,258.1	4,261.0	4,820.2	1,135.5	2,041.4
1988.	3,423.3	1,524.1	1,289.5	332.1	277.5	14,008.6	4,466.5	5,276.0	1,687.0	2,579.0
All industries, 1989 [3] .	**4,309.0**	**1,819.0**	**1,824.5**	**304.9**	**360.6**	**15,625.6**	**4,694.2**	**5,853.4**	**2,074.1**	**3,004.0**
Food and kindred products.	260.6	51.7	183.6	3.8	21.4	1,056.2	137.4	663.6	17.0	238.3
Paper and allied products. .	808.2	392.4	261.0	13.2	141.6	1,449.0	388.1	686.8	31.4	342.8
Chemical and allied products	1,194.8	380.3	598.6	128.9	87.0	3,509.2	794.0	1,613.8	560.1	541.3
Petroleum and coal products	417.6	146.5	230.4	33.7	7.0	2,170.0	1,258.2	578.8	163.5	169.4
Rubber, miscellaneous plastic products	78.2	50.3	16.0	3.2	8.8	403.3	85.3	99.6	56.9	161.5
Stone, clay, glass products.	97.3	73.2	17.1	1.4	5.6	591.7	328.4	85.0	38.9	139.4
Primary metal industries. . .	407.0	216.3	138.7	23.7	28.4	1,931.1	883.1	574.2	201.0	272.7
Fabricated metals products	151.0	50.5	71.3	17.2	12.1	895.7	123.8	389.5	212.6	169.8
Machinery, exc. electrical. .	169.5	99.8	54.8	8.3	6.6	571.9	80.6	170.5	149.4	171.4
Electrical, electronic equipment	188.7	66.6	94.3	23.5	4.3	729.1	100.9	308.9	198.6	120.7
Transportation equipment. .	286.8	156.0	84.6	31.7	14.7	1,000.3	212.2	318.1	226.7	243.4

- Represents zero.   D Withheld to avoid disclosing operations of individual companies.   NA Not available.   [1] Includes payments to governmental units.   [2] Hazardous and nonhazardous solid waste were not collected separately prior to 1983. [3] Includes industries not shown separately; excludes Major Group 23, Apparel and Other Textile Products.

Source: U.S. Bureau of the Census, *Current Industrial Reports*, series MA-200, annual.

No. 365. Threatened and Endangered Wildlife and Plant Species—Number: 1991

[As of **March 31**. Endangered species: One in danger of becoming extinct throughout all or a significant part of its natural range. Threatened species: One likely to become endangered in the foreseeable future]

ITEM	Mam-mals	Birds	Rep-tiles	Amphib-ians	Fishes	Snails	Clams	Crusta-ceans	Insects	Arach-nids	Plants
Endangered species, total	**304**	**226**	**80**	**14**	**64**	**8**	**41**	**8**	**14**	**3**	**210**
U.S. only	36	57	8	6	51	7	39	8	12	3	203
U.S. and foreign	19	16	8	-	2	-	-	-	1	-	6
Foreign only [1]	249	153	64	8	11	1	2	-	1	-	1
Threatened species, total	**30**	**12**	**32**	**5**	**34**	**6**	**2**	**2**	**9**	**-**	**63**
U.S. only	5	7	14	4	28	6	2	2	9	-	52
U.S. and foreign	3	5	4	1	6	-	-	-	-	-	9
Foreign only [1]	22	-	14	-	-	-	-	-	-	-	2

- Represents zero.   [1] Species outside United States and outlying areas as determined by Fish and Wildlife Service.

Source: U.S. Fish and Wildlife Service, *Endangered Species Technical Bulletin*, April 1991, vol. XV, No. 4.

No. 366. Tornadoes, Floods, and Tropical Cyclones: 1980 to 1990

[See also *Historical Statistics, Colonial Times to 1970*, series J 268-278]

ITEM	1980	1981	1982	1983	1984	1985	1986	1987	1988	1989	1990
Tornadoes, number [1]	866	783	1,046	931	907	684	764	656	702	856	1,133
Lives lost, total	28	24	64	34	122	94	15	59	32	50	53
Most in a single tornado. . .	5	5	10	3	16	18	3	30	5	21	29
Property loss of $500,000 and over	92	55	92	95	125	69	75	38	48	60	91
Floods: Lives lost	97	90	155	200	126	304	80	82	29	81	(NA)
Property loss (mil. dol.)	1,500	1,000	3,500	4,100	4,000	3,000	4,000	1,490	114	415	(NA)
North Atlantic tropical cyclones and hurricanes: [2]											
Number reaching U.S. coast. .	2	2	1	2	2	11	6	7	12	4	-
Hurricanes only.	1	-	-	1	1	7	4	2	5	3	-
Lives lost in U.S.	2	-	-	22	4	9	-	-	-	56	13

- Represents zero.   NA Not available.   [1] A violent, rotating column of air descending from a cumulonimbus cloud in the form of a tubular- or funnel-shaped cloud, usually characterized by movements along a narrow path and wind speeds from 100 to over 300 miles per hour. Also known as a "twister" or "waterspout."   [2] Tropical cyclones have maximum winds of 39 to 73 miles per hour; hurricanes have maximum winds of 74 miles per hour or higher.

Source: U.S. National Oceanic and Atmospheric Administration, 1966-1980, *Climatological Data: National Summary*, monthly with annual summary; thereafter, *Storm Data*, monthly.

No. 367. Normal Daily Mean Temperature—Selected Cities

[In **Fahrenheit degrees.** Airport data except as noted. Based on standard 30-year period, 1961 through 1990. See *Historical Statistics, Colonial Times to 1970*, series J 110-136 and J 164-267, for related data]

STATE	STATION	Jan.	Feb.	Mar.	Apr.	May	June	July	Aug.	Sept.	Oct.	Nov.	Dec.	Annual avg.
AL	Mobile	49.9	53.2	60.5	67.8	74.5	80.4	82.3	81.8	77.9	68.4	59.8	53.0	67.5
AK	Juneau	24.2	28.4	32.7	39.7	47.0	53.0	56.0	55.0	49.4	42.2	32.0	27.1	40.6
AZ	Phoenix	53.6	57.7	62.2	69.9	78.8	88.2	93.5	91.5	85.6	74.5	61.9	54.1	72.6
AR	Little Rock	39.1	43.6	53.1	62.1	70.2	78.4	81.9	80.6	74.1	63.0	52.1	42.8	61.8
CA	Los Angeles	56.8	57.6	58.0	60.1	62.7	65.7	69.1	70.5	69.9	66.8	61.6	56.9	63.0
	Sacramento	45.2	50.7	53.6	58.3	65.3	71.6	75.7	75.1	71.5	64.2	53.3	45.3	60.8
	San Diego	57.4	58.6	59.6	62.0	64.1	66.8	71.0	72.6	71.4	67.7	62.0	57.4	64.2
	San Francisco	48.7	52.2	53.3	55.6	58.1	61.5	62.7	63.7	64.5	61.0	54.8	49.4	57.1
CO	Denver	29.7	33.4	39.0	48.2	57.2	66.9	73.5	71.4	62.3	51.4	39.0	31.0	50.3
CT	Hartford	24.6	27.5	37.5	48.7	59.6	68.5	73.7	71.6	63.3	52.2	41.9	29.5	49.9
DE	Wilmington	30.6	33.4	42.7	52.2	62.5	71.5	76.4	75.0	68.0	56.2	46.3	35.8	54.2
DC	Washington	34.6	37.5	47.2	56.5	66.4	75.6	80.0	78.5	71.3	59.7	49.8	39.4	58.0
FL	Jacksonville	52.4	55.2	61.1	67.0	73.4	79.1	81.6	81.2	78.1	69.8	61.9	55.1	68.0
	Miami	67.2	68.5	71.7	75.2	78.7	81.4	82.6	82.8	81.9	78.3	73.6	69.1	75.9
GA	Atlanta	41.0	44.8	53.5	61.5	69.2	76.0	78.8	78.1	72.7	62.3	53.1	44.5	61.3
HI	Honolulu	72.9	73.0	74.4	75.8	77.5	79.4	80.5	81.4	81.0	79.6	77.2	74.1	77.2
ID	Boise	29.0	35.9	42.4	49.1	57.5	66.5	74.0	72.5	62.6	51.8	39.9	30.1	50.9
IL	Chicago	21.0	25.4	37.2	48.6	58.9	68.6	73.2	71.7	64.4	52.8	40.0	26.6	49.0
	Peoria	21.6	26.3	39.0	51.4	61.9	71.5	75.5	73.1	66.1	54.0	41.2	27.0	50.7
IN	Indianapolis	25.5	29.6	41.4	52.4	62.8	71.9	75.4	73.2	66.6	54.7	43.0	30.9	52.3
IA	Des Moines	19.4	24.7	37.3	50.9	62.3	71.8	76.6	73.9	65.1	53.5	39.0	24.4	49.9
KS	Wichita	29.5	34.8	45.4	56.4	65.6	75.7	81.4	79.3	70.3	58.6	44.7	33.0	56.2
KY	Louisville	31.7	35.7	46.3	56.3	65.3	73.2	77.2	75.8	69.5	57.6	47.1	36.9	56.1
LA	New Orleans	51.3	54.3	61.6	68.5	74.8	80.0	81.9	81.5	78.1	69.1	61.1	54.5	68.1
ME	Portland	20.8	23.3	33.0	43.3	53.3	62.4	68.6	67.3	59.1	48.5	38.7	26.5	45.4
MD	Baltimore	31.8	34.8	44.1	53.4	63.4	72.5	77.0	75.6	68.5	56.6	46.8	36.7	55.1
MA	Boston	28.6	30.3	38.6	48.1	58.2	67.7	73.5	71.9	64.8	54.8	45.3	33.6	51.3
MI	Detroit	22.9	25.4	35.7	47.3	58.4	67.6	72.3	70.5	63.2	51.2	40.2	28.3	48.6
	Sault Ste. Marie	12.9	14.0	24.0	38.2	50.5	58.0	63.8	62.6	55.1	45.3	33.0	19.0	39.7
MN	Duluth	7.0	12.3	24.4	38.6	50.8	59.8	66.1	63.7	54.2	43.7	28.4	12.8	38.5
	Minneapolis-St. Paul	11.8	17.9	31.0	46.4	58.5	68.2	73.6	70.5	60.5	48.8	33.2	17.9	44.9
MS	Jackson	44.1	47.9	56.7	64.6	72.0	78.8	81.5	80.9	75.9	64.7	55.8	47.8	64.2
MO	Kansas City	25.7	31.2	42.7	54.5	64.1	73.2	78.5	76.1	67.5	56.6	43.1	30.4	53.6
	St. Louis	29.3	33.9	45.1	56.7	66.1	75.4	79.8	77.6	70.2	58.4	46.2	33.9	56.1
MT	Great Falls	21.2	27.4	33.3	43.6	53.1	61.6	68.2	66.9	56.6	47.5	33.9	23.9	44.8
NE	Omaha	21.1	26.9	38.6	51.9	62.4	72.1	76.9	74.1	65.1	53.4	39.0	25.1	50.6
NV	Reno	32.9	38.0	42.8	48.6	56.5	65.1	71.6	69.6	60.4	50.8	40.3	32.7	50.8
NH	Concord	18.6	21.8	32.4	43.9	55.2	64.2	69.5	67.3	58.8	47.8	37.1	24.3	45.1
NJ	Atlantic City	30.9	33.0	41.5	50.0	60.4	69.4	74.7	73.4	66.1	54.9	45.8	35.8	53.0
NM	Albuquerque	34.2	40.0	46.9	55.2	64.2	74.2	78.5	75.9	68.6	57.0	44.3	35.3	56.2
NY	Albany	20.6	23.5	34.3	46.4	57.6	66.9	71.8	69.6	61.3	50.2	39.7	26.5	47.4
	Buffalo	23.6	24.5	33.8	45.2	56.6	65.9	71.1	69.0	61.9	51.1	40.5	29.1	47.7
	New York [1]	31.5	33.6	42.4	52.5	62.7	71.6	76.8	75.5	68.2	57.5	47.6	36.6	54.7
NC	Charlotte	39.3	42.5	50.9	59.4	67.4	75.7	79.3	78.3	72.4	61.3	52.1	42.6	60.1
	Raleigh	38.9	42.0	50.4	59.0	67.0	74.3	78.1	77.1	71.1	60.1	51.2	42.6	59.3
ND	Bismarck	9.2	15.7	28.2	43.0	55.0	64.4	70.4	68.3	57.0	45.7	28.6	14.0	41.6
OH	Cincinnati	28.1	31.8	43.0	53.2	62.9	71.0	75.1	73.5	67.3	55.1	44.3	33.5	53.2
	Cleveland	24.8	27.2	37.3	47.6	58.0	67.6	71.9	70.4	63.9	52.8	42.6	30.9	49.6
	Columbus	26.4	29.6	40.9	51.0	61.2	69.2	73.2	71.5	65.5	53.7	42.9	31.9	51.4
OK	Oklahoma City	35.9	40.9	50.3	60.4	68.4	76.7	82.0	81.1	73.0	62.0	49.6	39.3	60.0
OR	Portland	39.6	43.6	47.3	51.0	57.1	63.5	68.2	68.6	63.3	54.5	46.1	40.2	53.6
PA	Philadelphia	30.4	33.0	42.4	52.4	62.9	71.8	76.7	75.5	68.2	56.4	46.4	35.8	54.3
	Pittsburgh	26.1	28.7	39.4	49.6	59.5	67.9	72.1	70.5	63.9	52.4	42.3	31.5	50.3
RI	Providence	27.9	29.7	37.4	47.4	57.3	66.9	72.7	71.3	64.1	53.6	44.0	32.8	50.4
SC	Columbia	43.8	46.8	55.2	63.0	70.9	77.4	80.8	79.7	74.2	63.3	54.6	46.9	63.1
SD	Sioux Falls	13.8	19.7	32.5	46.9	58.4	68.3	74.3	71.4	60.9	48.6	33.0	18.3	45.5
TN	Memphis	39.7	44.2	53.1	62.9	71.2	79.1	82.6	81.0	74.2	63.1	52.5	43.7	62.3
	Nashville	36.2	40.4	50.2	59.2	67.7	75.6	79.3	78.1	71.8	60.4	50.0	40.5	59.1
TX	Dallas-Fort Worth	43.4	47.9	56.7	65.5	72.8	81.0	85.3	84.9	77.4	67.2	56.2	46.9	65.4
	El Paso	42.8	48.1	55.1	63.4	71.8	80.4	82.3	80.1	74.4	64.0	52.4	44.1	63.2
	Houston	50.4	53.9	60.6	68.3	74.5	80.4	82.6	82.3	78.2	69.6	61.0	53.5	67.9
UT	Salt Lake City	27.9	34.1	41.8	49.7	58.8	69.1	77.9	75.6	65.2	53.2	40.8	29.7	52.0
VT	Burlington	16.3	18.2	30.7	43.9	56.3	65.2	70.5	67.9	58.9	47.8	36.8	23.0	44.6
VA	Norfolk	39.1	41.0	48.6	57.0	66.1	74.1	78.2	77.2	71.9	61.2	52.5	43.8	59.2
	Richmond	35.7	38.7	48.0	57.3	66.0	73.9	78.0	76.0	70.0	58.6	49.6	40.1	57.7
WA	Seattle-Tacoma	40.1	43.5	45.6	49.2	55.1	60.9	65.2	65.5	60.6	52.8	45.3	40.5	52.0
	Spokane	27.1	33.3	38.7	45.9	53.9	62.0	68.8	68.4	58.9	47.3	35.1	27.8	47.3
WV	Charleston	32.1	35.5	45.9	54.8	63.5	71.4	75.1	73.9	67.7	56.2	46.8	37.0	55.0
WI	Milwaukee	18.9	23.0	33.3	44.4	54.6	65.0	70.9	69.3	61.7	50.3	37.7	24.4	46.1
WY	Cheyenne	26.5	29.3	33.6	42.5	52.0	61.3	68.4	66.4	57.4	47.0	35.2	27.8	45.6
PR	San Juan	77.0	77.1	78.0	79.4	80.9	82.3	82.6	82.7	82.5	81.9	80.0	78.1	80.2

[1] City office data.

Source: U.S. National Oceanic and Atmospheric Administration, *Climatography of the United States*, No.81.

No. 368. Normal Daily Maximum Temperature—Selected Cities

[In Fahrenheit degrees. Airport data except as noted. Based on standard 30-year period, 1961 through 1990]

STATE	STATION	Jan.	Feb.	Mar.	Apr.	May	June	July	Aug.	Sept.	Oct.	Nov.	Dec.	Annual avg.
AL	Mobile	59.7	63.6	70.9	78.5	84.6	90.0	91.3	90.5	86.9	79.5	70.3	62.9	77.4
AK	Juneau	29.4	34.1	38.7	47.2	55.1	60.9	63.9	62.7	55.9	47.1	36.7	31.6	46.9
AZ	Phoenix	65.9	70.7	75.5	84.5	93.6	103.5	105.9	103.7	98.3	88.1	74.9	66.2	85.9
AR	Little Rock	49.0	53.9	64.0	73.4	81.3	89.3	92.4	91.4	84.6	75.1	62.7	52.5	72.5
CA	Los Angeles	65.7	65.9	65.5	67.4	69.0	71.9	75.3	76.6	76.6	74.4	70.3	65.9	70.4
	Sacramento	52.7	60.0	64.0	71.1	80.3	87.8	93.2	92.1	87.3	77.9	63.1	52.7	73.5
	San Diego	65.9	66.5	66.3	68.4	69.1	71.6	76.2	77.8	77.1	74.6	69.9	66.1	70.8
	San Francisco	55.6	59.4	60.8	63.9	66.5	70.3	71.6	72.3	73.6	70.1	62.4	56.1	65.2
CO	Denver	43.2	46.6	52.2	61.8	70.8	81.4	88.2	85.8	76.9	66.3	52.5	44.5	64.2
CT	Hartford	33.2	36.4	46.8	59.9	71.6	80.0	85.0	82.7	74.8	63.7	51.0	37.5	60.2
DE	Wilmington	38.7	41.9	52.1	62.6	72.9	81.4	85.6	84.1	77.7	66.6	55.5	43.9	63.6
DC	Washington	42.3	45.9	56.5	66.7	76.2	84.7	88.5	86.9	80.1	69.1	58.3	47.0	66.9
FL	Jacksonville	64.2	67.0	73.0	79.1	84.7	89.3	91.4	90.7	87.2	80.2	73.6	66.8	78.9
	Miami	75.2	76.5	79.1	82.4	85.3	87.6	89.0	89.0	87.8	84.5	80.4	76.7	82.8
GA	Atlanta	50.4	55.0	64.3	72.7	79.6	85.8	88.0	87.1	81.8	72.7	63.4	54.0	71.2
HI	Honolulu	80.1	80.5	81.6	82.8	84.7	86.5	87.5	88.7	88.5	86.9	84.1	81.2	84.4
ID	Boise	36.4	44.2	52.9	61.4	71.0	80.9	90.2	88.1	77.0	64.6	48.7	37.7	62.8
IL	Chicago	29.0	33.5	45.8	58.6	70.1	79.6	83.7	81.8	74.8	63.3	48.4	34.0	58.6
	Peoria	29.9	34.9	48.1	62.0	72.8	82.2	85.7	83.1	76.9	64.8	49.8	34.6	60.4
IN	Indianapolis	33.7	38.3	50.9	63.3	73.8	82.7	85.5	83.6	77.6	65.8	51.9	38.5	62.1
IA	Des Moines	28.1	33.7	46.9	61.8	73.0	82.2	86.7	84.2	75.6	64.3	48.0	32.6	59.8
KS	Wichita	39.8	45.9	57.2	68.3	76.9	86.8	92.8	90.7	81.4	70.6	55.3	43.0	67.4
KY	Louisville	40.3	44.8	56.3	67.3	76.0	83.5	87.0	85.7	80.3	69.2	56.8	45.1	66.0
LA	New Orleans	60.8	64.1	71.6	78.5	84.4	89.2	90.6	90.2	86.6	79.4	71.1	64.3	77.6
ME	Portland	30.3	33.1	41.4	52.3	63.2	72.7	78.8	77.4	69.3	58.7	47.0	35.1	54.9
MD	Baltimore	40.2	43.7	54.0	64.3	74.2	83.2	87.2	85.4	78.5	67.3	56.5	45.2	65.0
MA	Boston	35.7	37.5	45.8	55.9	66.6	76.3	81.8	79.8	72.8	62.7	52.2	40.4	59.0
MI	Detroit	30.3	33.3	44.4	57.7	69.6	78.9	83.3	81.3	73.9	61.5	48.1	35.2	58.1
	Sault Ste. Marie	21.1	23.2	32.8	48.0	62.6	70.5	76.3	73.8	65.9	54.3	40.0	26.2	49.6
MN	Duluth	16.2	21.7	32.9	48.2	61.9	71.0	77.1	73.9	63.8	52.3	35.2	20.7	47.9
	Minneapolis-St. Paul	20.7	26.6	39.2	56.5	69.4	78.8	84.0	80.7	70.7	58.8	41.0	25.5	54.3
MS	Jackson	55.6	60.1	69.3	77.4	84.0	90.6	92.4	92.0	88.0	79.1	69.2	59.5	76.4
MO	Kansas City	34.7	40.6	52.8	65.1	74.3	83.3	88.7	86.4	78.1	67.5	52.6	38.8	63.6
	St. Louis	37.7	42.6	54.6	66.9	76.1	85.2	89.3	87.3	79.9	68.5	54.7	41.7	65.4
MT	Great Falls	30.6	37.5	43.7	55.3	65.2	74.6	83.3	81.6	69.6	59.3	43.5	33.1	56.4
NE	Omaha	31.3	37.1	49.4	63.8	74.0	83.7	87.9	85.2	76.5	65.6	49.3	34.6	61.5
NV	Reno	45.1	51.7	56.3	63.7	72.9	83.1	91.9	89.6	79.5	68.6	53.8	45.5	66.8
NH	Concord	29.8	33.0	42.8	56.3	68.9	77.3	82.4	79.8	71.6	60.7	47.1	34.2	57.0
NJ	Atlantic City	40.4	42.5	51.6	60.7	71.2	80.0	84.5	83.3	76.6	66.0	55.7	45.3	63.2
NM	Albuquerque	46.8	53.5	61.4	70.8	79.7	90.0	92.5	89.0	81.9	71.0	57.3	47.5	70.1
NY	Albany	30.2	33.2	44.0	57.5	69.7	79.0	84.0	81.4	73.2	61.8	48.7	34.9	58.1
	Buffalo	30.2	31.6	41.7	54.2	66.1	75.3	80.2	77.9	70.8	59.4	47.1	35.3	55.8
	New York [1]	37.6	40.3	50.0	61.2	71.7	80.1	85.2	83.7	76.2	65.3	54.0	42.5	62.3
NC	Charlotte	49.0	53.0	62.3	71.2	78.3	85.8	88.9	87.7	81.9	72.0	62.6	52.3	70.4
	Raleigh	48.9	52.6	62.1	71.7	78.6	85.0	88.0	86.8	81.1	71.6	62.6	52.7	70.1
ND	Bismarck	20.2	26.4	38.5	54.9	67.8	77.1	84.4	82.7	70.8	58.7	39.3	24.5	53.8
OH	Cincinnati	36.6	40.8	53.0	64.2	74.0	82.0	85.5	84.1	77.9	66.0	53.3	41.5	63.2
	Cleveland	31.9	35.0	46.3	57.9	68.6	78.3	82.4	80.5	73.6	62.1	50.0	37.4	58.7
	Columbus	34.1	38.0	50.5	62.0	72.3	80.4	83.7	82.1	76.2	64.5	51.4	39.2	61.2
OK	Oklahoma City	46.7	52.1	62.0	71.9	79.1	87.3	93.4	92.5	83.8	73.6	60.4	49.9	71.1
OR	Portland	45.4	51.0	56.0	60.6	67.1	74.0	79.9	80.3	74.6	64.0	52.6	45.6	62.6
PA	Philadelphia	37.9	41.0	51.6	62.6	73.1	81.7	86.1	84.6	77.6	66.3	55.1	43.4	63.4
	Pittsburgh	33.7	36.9	49.0	60.3	70.6	78.9	82.6	80.8	74.3	62.5	50.4	38.6	59.9
RI	Providence	36.6	38.3	46.1	57.0	67.3	76.9	82.1	80.7	74.3	64.1	53.0	41.2	59.8
SC	Columbia	55.3	59.3	68.2	76.5	83.5	88.8	91.6	90.1	85.1	76.3	67.8	58.8	75.1
SD	Sioux Falls	24.3	29.6	42.3	59.0	70.7	80.5	86.3	83.3	73.1	61.2	43.4	28.0	56.8
TN	Memphis	48.5	53.5	63.2	73.3	81.0	89.3	92.3	90.8	83.9	74.3	62.3	52.5	72.1
	Nashville	45.9	50.8	61.2	70.8	78.8	86.5	89.5	88.4	82.5	72.5	60.4	50.2	69.8
TX	Dallas-Fort Worth	54.1	58.9	67.8	76.3	82.9	91.9	96.5	96.2	87.8	78.5	66.8	57.5	76.3
	El Paso	56.1	62.2	69.9	78.7	87.1	96.5	96.1	93.5	87.1	78.4	66.4	57.5	77.5
	Houston	61.0	65.3	71.1	78.4	84.6	90.1	92.7	92.5	88.4	81.6	72.4	64.7	78.6
UT	Salt Lake City	36.4	43.6	52.2	61.3	71.9	82.8	92.2	89.4	79.2	66.1	50.8	37.8	63.6
VT	Burlington	25.1	27.5	39.3	53.6	67.2	75.8	81.2	77.9	69.0	57.0	44.0	30.4	54.0
VA	Norfolk	47.3	49.7	57.9	66.9	75.3	82.9	86.4	85.1	79.6	69.5	61.2	52.2	67.8
	Richmond	45.7	49.2	59.5	70.0	77.8	85.1	88.4	87.1	80.9	70.7	61.3	50.2	68.8
WA	Seattle-Tacoma	45.0	49.5	52.7	57.2	63.9	69.9	75.2	75.2	69.3	59.7	50.5	45.1	59.4
	Spokane	33.2	40.6	47.7	57.0	65.8	74.7	83.1	82.5	72.0	58.6	41.4	33.8	57.5
WV	Charleston	41.2	45.3	56.7	66.8	75.5	83.1	85.7	84.4	78.8	68.2	57.3	46.0	65.8
WI	Milwaukee	26.1	30.1	40.4	52.9	64.3	74.9	79.9	77.8	70.6	58.7	44.7	31.2	54.3
WY	Cheyenne	37.7	40.5	44.9	54.7	64.6	74.4	82.2	80.0	71.1	60.0	46.8	38.8	58.0
PR	San Juan	83.2	83.6	84.4	85.8	87.2	88.6	88.5	88.7	88.8	88.3	85.9	83.8	86.4

[1] City office data.

Source: U.S. National Oceanic and Atmospheric Administration, *Climatography of the United States*, No. 81.

No. 369. Normal Daily Minimum Temperature—Selected Cities

[In Fahrenheit degrees. Airport data except as noted. Based on standard 30-year period, 1961 through 1990]

STATE	STATION	Jan.	Feb.	Mar.	Apr.	May	June	July	Aug.	Sept.	Oct.	Nov.	Dec.	Annual avg.
AL	Mobile........	40.0	42.7	50.1	57.1	64.4	70.7	73.2	72.9	68.7	57.3	49.1	43.1	57.4
AK	Juneau	19.0	22.7	26.7	32.1	38.9	45.0	48.1	47.3	42.9	37.2	27.2	22.6	34.1
AZ	Phoenix........	41.2	44.7	48.8	55.3	63.9	72.9	81.0	79.2	72.8	60.8	48.9	41.8	59.3
AR	Little Rock.......	29.1	33.2	42.2	50.7	59.0	67.4	71.5	69.8	63.5	50.9	41.5	33.1	51.0
CA	Los Angeles......	47.8	49.3	50.5	52.8	56.3	59.5	62.8	64.2	63.2	59.2	52.8	47.9	55.5
	Sacramento......	37.7	41.4	43.2	45.5	50.3	55.3	58.1	58.0	55.7	50.4	43.4	37.8	48.1
	San Diego	48.9	50.7	52.8	55.6	59.1	61.9	65.7	67.3	65.6	60.9	53.9	48.8	57.6
	San Francisco	41.8	45.0	45.8	47.2	49.7	52.6	53.9	55.0	55.2	51.8	47.1	42.7	49.0
CO	Denver	16.1	20.2	25.8	34.5	43.6	52.4	58.6	56.9	47.6	36.4	25.4	17.4	36.2
CT	Hartford........	15.8	18.6	28.1	37.5	47.6	56.9	62.2	60.4	51.8	40.7	32.8	21.3	39.5
DE	Wilmington.......	22.4	24.8	33.1	41.8	52.2	61.6	67.1	65.9	58.2	45.7	37.0	27.6	44.8
DC	Washington	26.8	29.1	37.7	46.4	56.6	66.5	71.4	70.0	62.5	50.3	41.1	31.7	49.2
FL	Jacksonville	40.5	43.3	49.2	54.9	62.1	69.1	71.9	71.8	69.0	59.3	50.2	43.4	57.1
	Miami	59.2	60.4	64.2	67.8	72.1	75.1	76.2	76.7	75.9	72.1	66.7	61.5	69.0
GA	Atlanta	31.5	34.5	42.5	50.2	58.7	66.2	69.5	69.0	63.5	51.9	42.8	35.0	51.3
HI	Honolulu	65.6	65.4	67.2	68.7	70.3	72.2	73.5	74.2	73.5	72.3	70.3	67.0	70.0
ID	Boise	21.6	27.5	31.9	36.7	43.9	52.1	57.7	56.8	48.2	39.0	31.1	22.5	39.1
IL	Chicago........	12.9	17.2	28.5	38.6	47.7	57.5	62.6	61.6	53.9	42.2	31.6	19.1	39.5
	Peoria	13.2	17.7	29.8	40.8	50.9	60.7	65.4	63.1	55.2	43.1	32.5	19.3	41.0
IN	Indianapolis	17.2	20.9	31.9	41.5	51.7	61.0	65.2	62.8	55.6	43.5	34.1	23.2	42.4
IA	Des Moines	10.7	15.6	27.6	40.0	51.5	61.2	66.5	63.6	54.5	42.7	29.9	16.1	40.0
KS	Wichita	19.2	23.7	33.6	44.5	54.3	64.6	69.9	67.9	59.2	46.6	33.9	23.0	45.0
KY	Louisville.......	23.2	26.5	36.2	45.4	54.7	62.9	67.3	65.8	58.7	45.8	37.3	28.6	46.0
LA	New Orleans	41.8	44.4	51.6	58.4	65.2	70.8	73.1	72.8	69.5	58.7	51.0	44.8	58.5
ME	Portland........	11.4	13.5	24.5	34.1	43.4	52.1	58.3	57.1	48.9	38.3	30.4	17.8	35.8
MD	Baltimore........	23.4	25.9	34.1	42.5	52.6	61.8	66.8	65.7	58.4	45.9	37.1	28.2	45.2
MA	Boston	21.6	23.0	31.3	40.2	49.8	59.1	65.1	64.0	56.8	46.9	38.3	26.7	43.6
MI	Detroit.........	15.6	17.6	27.0	36.8	47.1	56.3	61.3	59.6	52.5	40.9	32.2	21.4	39.0
	Sault Ste. Marie . . .	4.6	4.8	15.3	28.4	38.4	45.5	51.3	51.3	44.3	36.2	25.9	11.8	29.8
MN	Duluth.........	-2.2	2.8	15.7	28.9	39.6	48.5	55.1	53.3	44.5	35.1	21.5	4.9	29.0
	Minneapolis-St. Paul	2.8	9.2	22.7	36.2	47.6	57.6	63.1	60.3	50.3	38.8	25.2	10.2	35.3
MS	Jackson........	32.7	35.7	44.1	51.9	60.0	67.1	70.5	69.7	63.7	50.3	42.3	36.1	52.0
MO	Kansas City	16.7	21.8	32.6	43.8	53.9	63.1	68.2	65.7	56.9	45.7	33.6	21.9	43.7
	St. Louis	20.8	25.1	35.5	46.4	56.0	65.7	70.4	67.9	60.5	48.3	37.7	26.0	46.7
MT	Great Falls.......	11.6	17.2	22.8	31.9	40.9	48.6	53.2	52.2	43.5	35.8	24.3	14.6	33.1
NE	Omaha	10.9	16.7	27.7	39.9	50.9	60.4	65.9	62.9	53.6	41.2	28.7	15.6	39.5
NV	Reno	20.7	24.2	29.2	33.3	40.1	46.9	51.3	49.6	41.3	32.9	26.7	19.9	34.7
NH	Concord	7.4	10.4	22.1	31.5	41.4	51.2	56.5	54.7	46.0	34.9	27.0	14.4	33.1
NJ	Atlantic City	21.4	23.5	31.3	39.3	49.6	58.7	64.8	63.5	55.5	43.7	35.8	26.3	42.8
NM	Albuquerque......	21.7	26.4	32.2	39.6	48.6	58.3	64.4	62.6	55.2	43.0	31.2	23.1	42.2
NY	Albany.........	11.0	13.8	24.5	35.1	45.4	54.6	59.6	57.8	49.4	38.6	30.7	18.2	36.6
	Buffalo	17.0	17.4	25.9	36.2	47.0	56.5	61.9	60.1	53.0	42.7	33.9	22.9	39.5
	New York [1]	25.3	26.9	34.8	43.8	53.7	63.0	68.4	67.3	60.1	49.7	41.1	30.7	47.1
NC	Charlotte	29.6	31.9	39.4	47.5	56.4	65.6	69.6	68.9	62.9	50.6	41.5	32.8	49.7
	Raleigh	28.8	31.3	38.7	46.2	55.3	63.6	68.1	67.5	61.1	48.4	39.7	32.4	48.4
ND	Bismarck	-1.7	5.1	17.8	31.0	42.2	51.6	56.4	53.9	43.1	32.5	17.8	3.3	29.4
OH	Cincinnati........	19.5	22.7	33.1	42.2	51.8	60.0	64.8	62.9	56.6	44.2	35.3	25.3	43.2
	Cleveland	17.6	19.3	28.2	37.3	47.3	56.8	61.4	60.3	54.2	43.5	35.0	24.5	40.5
	Columbus	18.5	21.2	31.2	40.0	50.1	58.0	62.7	60.8	54.8	42.9	34.3	24.6	41.6
OK	Oklahoma City	25.2	29.6	38.5	48.8	57.7	66.1	70.6	69.6	62.2	50.4	38.6	28.6	48.8
OR	Portland........	33.7	36.1	38.6	41.3	47.0	52.9	56.5	56.9	52.0	44.9	39.5	34.8	44.5
PA	Philadelphia	22.8	24.8	33.2	42.1	52.7	61.8	67.2	66.3	58.7	46.4	37.6	28.1	45.1
	Pittsburgh	18.5	20.3	29.8	38.8	48.4	56.9	61.6	60.2	53.5	42.3	34.1	24.4	40.7
RI	Providence.......	19.1	20.9	28.8	37.7	47.3	56.8	63.2	61.9	53.8	43.0	34.9	24.4	41.0
SC	Columbia	32.1	34.2	42.2	49.4	58.2	66.0	70.0	69.2	63.2	50.1	41.5	34.9	50.9
SD	Sioux Falls.......	3.3	9.7	22.6	34.8	45.9	56.1	62.3	59.4	48.7	36.0	22.6	8.6	34.2
TN	Memphis	30.9	34.8	43.0	52.4	61.2	68.9	72.9	71.1	64.5	51.9	42.7	34.8	52.4
	Nashville	26.5	29.9	39.1	47.5	56.6	64.7	68.9	67.7	61.1	48.3	39.6	30.9	48.4
TX	Dallas-Fort Worth ..	32.7	36.9	45.6	54.7	62.6	70.0	74.1	73.6	66.9	55.8	45.4	36.3	54.6
	El Paso	29.4	33.9	40.2	48.0	56.5	64.3	68.4	66.6	61.6	49.6	38.4	30.7	49.0
	Houston	39.7	42.6	50.0	58.1	64.4	70.6	72.4	72.0	67.9	57.6	49.6	42.2	57.3
UT	Salt Lake City.....	19.3	24.6	31.4	37.9	45.6	55.4	63.7	61.8	51.0	40.2	30.9	21.6	40.3
VT	Burlington	7.5	8.9	22.0	34.2	45.4	54.6	59.7	57.9	48.8	38.6	29.6	15.5	35.2
VA	Norfolk	30.9	32.3	39.3	47.1	56.8	65.2	70.0	69.4	64.2	52.9	43.8	35.4	50.6
	Richmond	25.7	28.1	36.3	44.6	54.2	62.7	67.5	66.4	59.0	46.5	37.9	29.0	46.6
WA	Seattle-Tacoma ...	35.2	37.4	38.5	41.2	46.3	51.0	55.2	55.7	51.9	45.8	40.1	35.8	44.6
	Spokane	20.8	25.9	29.6	34.7	41.9	49.2	54.4	54.3	45.8	36.0	28.8	21.7	36.9
WV	Charleston	23.0	25.7	35.0	42.8	51.5	59.8	64.4	63.4	56.5	44.2	36.3	28.0	44.2
WI	Milwaukee	11.6	15.9	26.2	35.8	44.8	55.0	62.0	60.8	52.8	41.8	30.7	17.5	37.9
WY	Cheyenne	15.2	18.1	22.1	30.1	39.4	48.3	54.6	52.8	43.7	33.9	23.7	16.7	33.2
PR	San Juan........	70.8	70.6	71.6	72.9	74.5	76.1	76.8	76.7	76.2	75.5	74.0	72.4	74.0

[1] City office data.

Source: U.S. National Oceanic and Atmospheric Administration, *Climatography of the United States*, No. 81.

No. 370. Highest Temperature of Record—Selected Cities

[**In Fahrenheit degrees.** Airport data, except as noted. For period of record through 1990]

STATE	STATION	Length of record (yr.)	Jan.	Feb.	Mar.	Apr.	May	June	July	Aug.	Sept.	Oct.	Nov.	Dec.	Annual
AL	Mobile.........	49	84	82	90	94	100	102	104	102	99	93	87	81	104
AK	Juneau	46	57	55	59	71	82	86	90	83	72	61	56	54	90
AZ	Phoenix........	53	88	92	100	105	113	122	118	116	118	107	93	88	122
AR	Little Rock......	49	83	85	91	95	98	105	112	108	106	97	86	80	112
CA	Los Angeles......	55	88	92	95	102	97	104	97	98	110	106	101	94	110
	Sacramento	40	70	76	88	93	105	115	114	109	108	101	87	72	115
	San Diego	50	88	88	93	98	96	101	95	98	111	107	97	88	111
	San Francisco	63	72	78	85	92	97	106	105	98	103	99	85	75	106
CO	Denver	56	73	76	84	89	96	104	104	101	97	88	79	75	104
CT	Hartford........	36	65	73	87	96	97	100	102	101	99	91	81	74	102
DE	Wilmington.......	43	75	78	86	94	95	99	102	101	100	91	85	74	102
DC	Washington	49	79	82	89	95	97	101	104	103	101	94	86	75	104
FL	Jacksonville	49	85	88	91	95	100	103	105	102	100	96	88	84	105
	Miami	48	88	89	92	96	95	98	98	98	97	95	89	87	98
GA	Atlanta	42	79	80	85	93	95	101	105	102	98	95	84	77	105
HI	Honolulu	21	87	88	88	89	93	92	92	93	94	94	93	89	94
ID	Boise	51	63	70	81	92	98	109	111	110	102	91	74	65	111
IL	Chicago.........	32	65	71	88	91	93	104	102	100	99	91	78	71	104
	Peoria	51	70	72	86	92	93	105	103	103	100	90	81	71	105
IN	Indianapolis	51	71	74	85	89	93	102	104	102	100	90	81	74	104
IA	Des Moines	51	65	73	91	93	98	103	105	108	101	95	76	69	108
KS	Wichita	38	75	84	89	96	100	110	113	110	107	95	85	83	113
KY	Louisville	43	77	77	86	91	95	102	105	101	104	92	84	76	105
LA	New Orleans	44	83	85	89	92	96	100	101	102	101	92	87	84	102
ME	Portland........	50	64	64	86	85	94	97	99	103	95	88	74	69	103
MD	Baltimore........	40	75	79	87	94	98	100	104	105	100	92	83	77	105
MA	Boston	39	63	70	81	94	95	100	102	102	100	90	78	73	102
MI	Detroit.........	32	62	65	81	89	93	104	102	100	98	91	77	68	104
	Sault Ste. Marie ...	50	45	47	75	85	89	93	97	98	95	80	67	60	98
MN	Duluth.........	49	52	55	78	88	90	93	97	97	95	86	70	55	97
	Minneapolis-St. Paul	52	58	60	83	95	96	102	105	102	98	89	75	63	105
MS	Jackson........	27	82	85	89	94	99	105	106	102	104	95	88	84	106
MO	Kansas City	18	69	76	86	93	92	105	107	109	102	92	82	70	109
	St. Louis	33	76	85	89	93	93	102	107	107	104	94	85	76	107
MT	Great Falls.......	53	62	68	78	89	92	103	101	105	106	98	91	76	106
NE	Omaha	54	69	78	89	97	99	105	114	110	104	96	80	72	114
NV	Reno	49	70	75	83	89	96	103	104	105	101	91	77	70	105
NH	Concord	49	68	66	85	95	97	98	102	101	98	90	80	68	102
NJ	Atlantic City	47	78	75	87	94	99	106	104	102	99	90	84	75	106
NM	Albuquerque......	51	69	76	85	89	98	105	105	101	100	91	77	72	105
NY	Albany.........	44	62	67	86	92	94	99	100	99	100	89	82	71	100
	Buffalo	47	72	65	81	94	90	96	97	99	98	87	80	74	99
	New York [1]	122	72	75	86	96	99	101	106	104	102	94	84	72	106
NC	Charlotte	51	78	81	90	93	100	103	103	103	104	98	85	77	104
	Raleigh	46	79	84	92	95	97	104	105	105	104	98	88	79	105
ND	Bismarck........	51	62	68	81	93	98	107	109	109	105	95	75	65	109
OH	Cincinnati.......	29	69	73	84	89	93	102	103	102	98	88	81	75	103
	Cleveland	49	73	69	83	88	92	104	103	102	101	90	82	77	104
	Columbus	51	74	73	85	89	94	102	100	101	100	90	80	76	102
OK	Oklahoma City	37	80	84	93	100	104	105	109	110	102	96	87	86	110
OR	Portland........	50	63	71	80	87	100	100	107	107	105	92	73	64	107
PA	Philadelphia	49	74	74	87	94	96	100	104	101	100	96	81	72	104
	Pittsburgh	38	69	69	82	89	91	98	103	100	97	87	82	74	103
RI	Providence.......	37	66	72	80	98	94	97	100	104	100	86	78	70	104
SC	Columbia	43	84	84	91	94	101	107	107	107	101	101	90	83	107
SD	Sioux Falls......	45	66	70	87	94	100	110	108	108	104	94	76	61	110
TN	Memphis	49	78	81	85	94	99	104	108	105	103	95	85	81	108
	Nashville	51	78	84	86	91	97	106	107	104	105	94	84	79	107
TX	Dallas-Fort Worth ..	37	88	88	96	95	103	113	110	108	106	102	89	88	113
	El Paso........	51	80	83	89	98	104	111	112	108	104	96	87	80	112
	Houston	21	84	91	91	95	97	103	104	107	102	94	89	83	107
UT	Salt Lake City.....	62	62	69	78	85	93	104	107	104	100	89	75	67	107
VT	Burlington	47	63	62	84	91	93	97	99	101	94	85	75	65	101
VA	Norfolk	42	78	81	88	97	97	101	103	104	99	95	86	80	104
	Richmond	61	80	83	93	96	100	104	105	102	103	99	86	80	105
WA	Seattle-Tacoma ...	46	64	70	75	85	93	96	98	99	98	89	74	63	99
	Spokane	43	59	61	71	90	96	100	103	108	98	86	67	56	108
WV	Charleston......	43	79	78	89	94	93	98	104	101	102	92	85	80	104
WI	Milwaukee	50	62	65	82	91	92	101	101	103	98	89	77	63	103
WY	Cheyenne	55	66	71	74	82	90	100	100	96	93	83	73	69	100
PR	San Juan........	36	92	96	96	97	96	97	95	97	97	98	96	94	98

[1] City office data.

Source: U.S. National Oceanic and Atmospheric Administration, *Comparative Climatic Data*, annual.

No. 371. Lowest Temperature of Record—Selected Cities

[**In Fahrenheit degrees.** Airport data, except as noted. For period of record through 1990]

STATE	STATION	Length of record (yr.)	Jan.	Feb.	Mar.	Apr.	May	June	July	Aug.	Sept.	Oct.	Nov.	Dec.	Annual
AL	Mobile.........	49	3	11	21	32	43	49	60	59	42	32	22	8	3
AK	Juneau	46	−22	−22	−15	6	25	31	36	27	23	11	−5	−21	−22
AZ	Phoenix.........	53	17	22	25	32	40	50	61	60	47	34	25	22	17
AR	Little Rock	49	−4	−5	11	28	40	46	54	52	37	29	17	−1	−5
CA	Los Angeles......	55	23	32	34	39	43	48	49	51	47	41	34	32	23
	Sacramento	40	23	23	26	32	36	41	48	49	43	36	26	18	18
	San Diego	50	29	36	39	41	48	51	55	57	51	43	38	34	29
	San Francisco	63	24	25	30	31	36	41	43	42	38	34	25	20	20
CO	Denver	56	−25	−30	−11	−2	22	30	43	41	17	3	−8	−25	−30
CT	Hartford.........	36	−26	−21	−6	9	28	37	44	36	30	17	1	−14	−26
DE	Wilmington.......	43	−14	−6	2	18	30	41	48	43	36	24	14	−7	−14
DC	Washington	49	−5	4	11	24	34	47	54	49	39	29	16	1	−5
FL	Jacksonville	49	7	19	23	34	45	47	61	63	48	36	21	11	7
	Miami	48	30	32	32	46	53	60	69	68	68	51	39	30	30
GA	Atlanta	42	−8	5	10	26	37	46	53	55	36	28	3	-	−8
HI	Honolulu	21	53	53	55	57	60	65	66	67	66	64	57	54	53
ID	Boise	51	−17	−15	6	19	22	31	35	37	23	11	−3	−25	−25
IL	Chicago.........	32	−27	−17	−8	7	24	36	40	41	28	17	1	−25	−27
	Peoria	51	−25	−18	−10	14	25	39	47	41	26	19	−2	−23	−25
IN	Indianapolis	51	−22	−21	−7	16	28	39	44	41	28	17	−2	−23	−23
IA	Des Moines	51	−24	−20	−22	9	30	38	47	40	26	14	−3	−22	−24
KS	Wichita	38	−12	−21	−2	15	31	43	51	48	31	21	1	−16	−21
KY	Louisville	43	−20	−19	−1	22	31	42	50	46	33	23	−1	−15	−20
LA	New Orleans	44	14	19	25	32	41	50	60	60	42	35	24	11	11
ME	Portland.........	50	−26	−39	−21	8	23	33	40	33	23	15	3	−21	−39
MD	Baltimore........	40	−7	−3	6	20	32	40	50	45	35	25	13	-	−7
MA	Boston	39	−12	−4	6	16	34	45	50	47	38	28	15	−7	−12
MI	Detroit..........	32	−21	−15	−4	10	25	36	41	38	29	17	9	−10	−21
	Sault Ste. Marie ...	50	−36	−35	−24	−2	18	26	36	29	25	16	−10	−25	−36
MN	Duluth	49	−39	−33	−29	−5	17	27	35	32	22	8	−23	−34	−39
	Minneapolis-St. Paul	52	−34	−28	−32	2	18	34	43	39	26	15	−17	−29	−34
MS	Jackson.........	27	2	11	15	27	38	47	51	55	35	29	17	4	2
MO	Kansas City	18	−17	−19	−10	12	30	42	52	43	33	21	1	−23	−23
	St. Louis	33	−18	−10	−5	22	31	43	51	47	36	23	1	−16	−18
MT	Great Falls.......	53	−37	−35	−29	−6	15	31	40	35	21	−9	−25	−43	−43
NE	Omaha	54	−23	−21	−16	5	27	38	44	43	25	13	−9	−23	−23
NV	Reno	49	−16	−16	−2	13	18	25	33	24	20	8	1	−16	−16
NH	Concord	49	−33	−37	−16	8	21	30	35	29	21	10	−5	−22	−37
NJ	Atlantic City	47	−10	−11	5	12	25	37	42	40	32	20	10	−7	−11
NM	Albuquerque......	51	−17	−5	8	19	28	40	52	52	37	25	−7	−7	−17
NY	Albany..........	44	−28	−21	−21	10	26	36	40	34	24	16	5	−22	−28
	Buffalo	47	−16	−20	−7	12	26	35	43	38	32	20	9	−10	−20
	New York [1]	122	−6	−15	3	12	32	44	52	50	39	28	5	−13	−15
NC	Charlotte........	51	−5	5	4	24	32	45	53	53	39	24	11	2	−5
	Raleigh	46	−9	5	11	23	31	38	48	46	37	19	11	4	−9
ND	Bismarck	51	−44	−39	−31	−12	15	30	35	33	11	5	−30	−43	−44
OH	Cincinnati.......	29	−25	−11	−11	17	27	39	47	43	33	16	1	−20	−25
	Cleveland	49	−19	−15	−5	10	25	31	41	38	32	19	3	−15	−19
	Columbus	51	−19	−13	−6	14	25	35	43	39	31	20	5	−17	−19
OK	Oklahoma City	37	−4	−3	3	20	37	47	53	51	36	22	11	−8	−8
OR	Portland.........	50	−2	−3	19	29	29	39	43	44	34	26	13	6	−3
PA	Philadelphia	49	−7	−4	7	19	28	44	51	44	35	25	15	1	−7
	Pittsburgh	38	−18	−12	−1	14	26	34	42	39	31	16	−1	−12	−18
RI	Providence.......	37	−13	−7	1	14	29	41	48	40	33	20	6	−10	−13
SC	Columbia	43	−1	5	4	26	34	44	54	53	40	23	12	4	−1
SD	Sioux Falls......	45	−36	−31	−23	5	17	33	38	34	22	9	−17	−28	−36
TN	Memphis	49	−4	−11	12	29	38	48	52	48	36	25	9	−13	−13
	Nashville	51	−17	−13	2	23	34	42	51	47	36	26	−1	−10	−17
TX	Dallas-Fort Worth ..	37	4	7	15	29	41	51	59	56	43	29	20	−1	−1
	El Paso	51	−8	8	14	23	31	46	57	56	41	25	1	5	−8
	Houston	21	12	20	22	31	44	52	62	62	48	32	19	7	7
UT	Salt Lake City.....	62	−22	−30	2	14	25	35	40	37	27	16	−14	−21	−30
VT	Burlington	47	−30	−30	−20	2	24	33	39	35	25	15	−2	2C	−30
VA	Norfolk	42	−3	8	18	28	36	45	54	49	45	27	20	7	−3
	Richmond	61	−12	−10	11	23	31	40	51	46	35	21	10	−1	−12
WA	Seattle-Tacoma ...	46	-	1	11	29	28	38	43	44	35	28	6	6	-
	Spokane	43	−22	−17	−7	17	24	33	37	35	24	11	−21	−25	−25
WV	Charleston.......	43	−15	−6	-	19	26	33	46	41	34	17	6	−12	−15
WI	Milwaukee	50	−26	−19	−10	12	21	33	40	44	28	18	−5	−20	−26
WY	Cheyenne	55	−29	−34	−21	−8	16	25	38	36	8	2	−14	−28	−34
PR	San Juan........	36	61	62	60	64	66	69	69	70	69	67	66	63	60

- Represents zero.   [1] City office data.

Source: U.S. National Oceanic and Atmospheric Administration, *Comparative Climatic Data*, annual.

No. 372. Normal Monthly and Annual Precipitation—Selected Cities

[In inches. Airport data, except as noted. Based on standard 30-year period, 1961 through 1990. See *Historical Statistics, Colonial Times to 1970*, series J 164-267, for related data]

STATE	STATION	Jan.	Feb.	Mar.	Apr.	May	June	July	Aug.	Sept.	Oct.	Nov.	Dec.	Annual
AL	Mobile.........	4.76	5.46	6.41	4.48	5.74	5.04	6.85	6.96	5.91	2.94	4.10	5.31	63.96
AK	Juneau........	4.54	3.75	3.28	2.77	3.42	3.15	4.16	5.32	6.73	7.84	4.91	4.44	54.31
AZ	Phoenix........	0.67	0.68	0.88	0.22	0.12	0.13	0.83	0.96	0.86	0.65	0.66	1.00	7.66
AR	Little Rock......	3.42	3.61	4.91	5.49	5.17	3.57	3.60	3.26	4.05	3.75	5.20	4.83	50.86
CA	Los Angeles......	2.40	2.51	1.98	0.72	0.14	0.03	0.01	0.15	0.31	0.34	1.76	1.66	12.01
	Sacramento......	3.73	2.87	2.57	1.16	0.27	0.12	0.05	0.07	0.37	1.08	2.72	2.51	17.52
	San Diego......	1.80	1.53	1.77	0.79	0.19	0.07	0.02	0.10	0.24	0.37	1.45	1.57	9.90
	San Francisco	4.35	3.17	3.06	1.37	0.19	0.11	0.03	0.05	0.20	1.22	2.86	3.09	19.70
CO	Denver.........	0.50	0.57	1.28	1.71	2.40	1.79	1.91	1.51	1.24	0.98	0.87	0.64	15.40
CT	Hartford........	3.41	3.23	3.63	3.85	4.12	3.75	3.19	3.65	3.79	3.57	4.04	3.91	44.14
DE	Wilmington.......	3.03	2.91	3.43	3.39	3.84	3.55	4.23	3.40	3.43	2.88	3.27	3.48	40.84
DC	Washington.....	2.72	2.71	3.17	2.71	3.66	3.38	3.80	3.91	3.31	3.02	3.12	3.12	38.63
FL	Jacksonville......	3.31	3.93	3.68	2.77	3.55	5.69	5.60	7.93	7.05	2.90	2.19	2.72	51.32
	Miami..........	2.01	2.08	2.39	2.85	6.21	9.33	5.70	7.58	7.63	5.64	2.66	1.83	55.91
GA	Atlanta........	4.75	4.81	5.77	4.26	4.29	3.56	5.01	3.66	3.42	3.05	3.86	4.33	50.77
HI	Honolulu........	3.55	2.21	2.20	1.54	1.13	0.50	0.59	0.44	0.78	2.28	3.00	3.80	22.02
ID	Boise.........	1.45	1.07	1.29	1.24	1.08	0.81	0.35	0.43	0.80	0.75	1.48	1.36	12.11
IL	Chicago........	1.53	1.36	2.69	3.64	3.32	3.78	3.66	4.22	3.82	2.41	2.92	2.47	35.82
	Peoria	1.51	1.42	2.91	3.77	3.70	3.99	4.20	3.10	3.87	2.65	2.69	2.44	36.25
IN	Indianapolis	2.32	2.46	3.79	3.70	4.00	3.49	4.47	3.64	2.87	2.63	3.23	3.34	39.94
IA	Des Moines	0.96	1.11	2.33	3.36	3.66	4.46	3.78	4.20	3.53	2.62	1.79	1.32	33.12
KS	Wichita	0.79	0.96	2.43	2.38	3.81	4.31	3.13	3.02	3.49	2.22	1.59	1.20	29.33
KY	Louisville........	2.86	3.30	4.66	4.23	4.62	3.46	4.51	3.54	3.16	2.71	3.70	3.64	44.39
LA	New Orleans	5.05	6.01	4.90	4.50	4.56	5.84	6.12	6.17	5.51	3.05	4.42	5.75	61.88
ME	Portland........	3.53	3.33	3.67	4.08	3.62	3.44	3.09	2.87	3.09	3.90	5.17	4.55	44.34
MD	Baltimore........	3.05	3.12	3.38	3.09	3.72	3.67	3.69	3.92	3.41	2.98	3.32	3.41	40.76
MA	Boston	3.59	3.62	3.69	3.60	3.25	3.09	2.84	3.24	3.06	3.30	4.22	4.01	41.51
MI	Detroit........	1.76	1.74	2.55	2.95	2.92	3.61	3.18	3.43	2.89	2.10	2.67	2.82	32.62
	Sault Ste. Marie ...	2.42	1.74	2.30	2.35	2.71	3.14	2.71	3.61	3.69	3.23	3.45	2.88	34.23
MN	Duluth........	1.22	0.80	1.91	2.25	3.03	3.82	3.61	3.99	3.84	2.49	1.80	1.24	30.00
	Minneapolis-St. Paul	0.95	0.88	1.94	2.42	3.39	4.05	3.53	3.62	2.72	2.19	1.55	1.08	28.32
MS	Jackson.........	5.24	4.70	5.82	5.57	5.05	3.18	4.51	3.77	3.55	3.26	4.81	5.91	55.37
MO	Kansas City	1.09	1.10	2.51	3.12	5.04	4.72	4.38	4.01	4.86	3.29	1.92	1.58	37.62
	St. Louis	1.81	2.12	3.58	3.50	3.97	3.72	3.85	2.85	3.12	2.68	3.28	3.03	37.51
MT	Great Falls.......	0.91	0.57	1.10	1.41	2.52	2.39	1.24	1.54	1.24	0.78	0.66	0.85	15.21
NE	Omaha	0.74	0.77	2.04	2.66	4.52	3.87	3.51	3.24	3.72	2.28	1.49	1.02	29.86
NV	Reno	1.07	0.99	0.71	0.38	0.69	0.46	0.28	0.32	0.39	0.38	0.87	0.99	7.53
NH	Concord	2.51	2.53	2.72	2.91	3.14	3.15	3.23	3.32	2.81	3.23	3.66	3.16	36.37
NJ	Atlantic City	3.46	3.06	3.62	3.56	3.33	2.64	3.83	4.14	2.93	2.82	3.58	3.32	40.29
NM	Albuquerque......	0.44	0.46	0.54	0.52	0.50	0.59	1.37	1.64	1.00	0.89	0.43	0.50	8.88
NY	Albany.........	2.36	2.27	2.93	2.99	3.41	3.62	3.18	3.47	2.95	2.83	3.23	2.93	36.17
	Buffalo	2.70	2.31	2.68	2.87	3.14	3.55	3.08	4.17	3.49	3.09	3.83	3.67	38.58
	New York [1]	3.42	3.27	4.08	4.20	4.42	3.67	4.35	4.01	3.89	3.56	4.47	3.91	47.25
NC	Charlotte........	3.71	3.84	4.43	2.68	3.82	3.39	3.92	3.73	3.50	3.36	3.23	3.48	43.09
	Raleigh........	3.48	3.69	3.77	2.59	3.92	3.68	4.01	4.02	3.19	2.86	2.98	3.24	41.43
ND	Bismarck........	0.45	0.43	0.77	1.67	2.18	2.72	2.14	1.72	1.49	0.90	0.49	0.51	15.47
OH	Cincinnati........	2.59	2.69	4.24	3.75	4.28	3.84	4.24	3.35	2.88	2.86	3.46	3.15	41.33
	Cleveland.......	2.04	2.19	2.91	3.14	3.49	3.70	3.52	3.40	3.44	2.54	3.17	3.09	36.63
	Columbus.......	2.18	2.24	3.27	3.21	3.93	4.04	4.31	3.72	2.96	2.15	3.22	2.86	38.09
OK	Oklahoma City	1.13	1.56	2.71	2.77	5.22	4.31	2.61	2.60	3.84	3.23	1.98	1.40	33.36
OR	Portland........	5.35	3.85	3.56	2.39	2.06	1.48	0.63	1.09	1.75	2.67	5.34	6.13	36.30
PA	Philadelphia	3.21	2.79	3.46	3.62	3.75	3.74	4.28	3.80	3.42	2.62	3.34	3.38	41.41
	Pittsburgh	2.54	2.39	3.41	3.15	3.59	3.71	3.75	3.21	2.97	2.36	2.85	2.92	36.85
RI	Providence.......	3.88	3.61	4.05	4.11	3.76	3.33	3.18	3.63	3.48	3.69	4.43	4.38	45.53
SC	Columbia........	4.42	4.12	4.82	3.28	3.68	4.80	5.50	6.09	3.67	3.04	2.90	3.59	49.91
SD	Sioux Falls.......	0.51	0.64	1.64	2.52	3.03	3.40	2.68	2.85	3.02	1.78	1.09	0.70	23.86
TN	Memphis........	3.73	4.35	5.41	5.46	4.98	3.55	3.79	3.43	3.53	3.01	5.10	5.74	52.10
	Nashville........	3.58	3.81	4.85	4.37	4.88	3.57	3.97	3.46	3.46	2.62	4.12	4.61	47.30
TX	Dallas-Fort Worth ..	1.83	2.18	2.77	3.50	4.88	2.98	2.31	2.21	3.39	3.52	2.29	1.84	33.70
	El Paso.........	0.40	0.41	0.29	0.20	0.25	0.67	1.54	1.58	1.70	0.76	0.44	0.57	8.81
	Houston........	3.29	2.96	2.92	3.21	5.24	4.96	3.60	3.49	4.89	4.27	3.79	3.45	46.07
UT	Salt Lake City.....	1.11	1.23	1.91	2.12	1.80	0.93	0.81	0.86	1.28	1.44	1.29	1.40	16.18
VT	Burlington	1.82	1.63	2.23	2.76	3.12	3.47	3.65	4.06	3.30	2.88	3.13	2.42	34.47
VA	Norfolk........	3.78	3.47	3.70	3.06	3.81	3.82	5.06	4.81	3.90	3.15	2.85	3.23	44.64
	Richmond	3.24	3.16	3.61	2.96	3.84	3.62	5.03	4.40	3.34	3.53	3.17	3.26	43.16
WA	Seattle-Tacoma ...	5.38	3.99	3.54	2.33	1.70	1.50	0.76	1.14	1.88	3.23	5.83	5.91	37.19
	Spokane	1.98	1.49	1.49	1.18	1.41	1.26	0.67	0.72	0.73	0.99	2.15	2.42	16.49
WV	Charleston.......	2.91	3.04	3.63	3.31	3.94	3.59	4.99	4.01	3.24	2.89	3.59	3.39	42.53
WI	Milwaukee.......	1.60	1.45	2.67	3.50	2.84	3.24	3.47	3.53	3.38	2.41	2.51	2.33	32.93
WY	Cheyenne	0.40	0.39	1.03	1.37	2.39	2.08	2.09	1.69	1.27	0.74	0.53	0.42	14.40
PR	San Juan........	2.81	2.15	2.35	3.76	5.93	4.00	4.37	5.32	5.28	5.71	5.94	4.72	52.34

[1] City office data.

Source: U.S. National Oceanic and Atmospheric Administration, *Climatography of the United States*, No. 81.

No. 373. Average Number of Days With Precipitaion of .01 Inch or More—Selected Cities

[Airport data, except as noted. For period of record through 1990, except as noted]

STATE	STATION	Length of record (yr.	Jan.	Feb.	Mar.	Apr.	May	June	July	Aug.	Sept.	Oct.	Nov.	Dec.	Annual
AL	Mobile.	49	11	10	10	7	8	11	16	14	10	6	8	10	122
AK	Juneau [1]	46	18	17	18	17	17	16	17	17	20	24	20	21	220
AZ	Phoenix.	51	4	4	4	2	1	1	4	5	3	3	3	4	36
AR	Little Rock.	48	9	9	10	10	10	8	8	7	7	7	8	9	104
CA	Los Angeles.	55	6	6	6	3	1	(Z)	1	(Z)	1	2	4	5	35
	Sacramento	51	10	9	9	5	3	1	(Z)	(Z)	1	3	7	9	57
	San Diego	50	7	6	7	5	2	1	(Z)	1	1	2	5	6	42
	San Francisco	63	11	10	10	6	3	1	(Z)	(Z)	1	4	7	10	62
CO	Denver	56	6	6	9	9	11	9	9	9	6	5	5	5	89
CT	Hartford.	36	11	10	11	11	12	11	10	10	9	8	11	12	127
DE	Wilmington.	43	11	10	11	11	12	10	9	9	8	8	9	10	116
DC	Washington	49	10	9	11	10	11	9	10	9	8	7	8	9	112
FL	Jacksonville	49	8	8	8	6	8	12	15	14	13	9	6	8	115
	Miami	48	6	6	6	6	10	15	16	17	17	14	8	7	129
GA	Atlanta	56	11	10	11	9	9	10	12	9	8	6	8	10	115
HI	Honolulu	41	10	9	9	9	7	6	7	6	7	9	9	10	99
ID	Boise	51	12	10	10	8	8	6	2	3	4	6	10	11	90
IL	Chicago.	32	11	10	12	12	11	10	10	9	9	9	11	11	126
	Peoria.	51	9	8	11	12	11	10	9	8	9	8	9	10	113
IN	Indianapolis	51	12	10	13	12	12	10	9	9	8	8	10	12	125
IA	Des Moines	51	7	7	10	10	11	11	9	9	9	8	7	8	107
KS	Wichita	37	5	5	8	8	11	9	7	8	8	6	5	6	86
KY	Louisville	43	11	11	13	12	12	10	11	8	8	8	10	11	124
LA	New Orleans	42	10	9	9	7	8	11	15	13	10	6	7	10	114
ME	Portland.	50	11	10	11	12	13	11	10	9	8	9	12	11	128
MD	Baltimore.	40	10	9	11	11	11	9	9	10	7	7	9	9	113
MA	Boston	39	11	10	12	11	12	11	9	10	9	9	11	12	126
MI	Detroit.	32	13	11	13	13	11	10	9	9	10	10	12	14	135
	Sault Ste. Marie	49	19	15	13	11	11	12	10	11	13	13	17	20	166
MN	Duluth	49	12	10	11	10	12	13	11	11	12	9	11	12	134
	Minneapolis-St. Paul	52	9	7	10	10	11	12	10	10	9	8	8	9	114
MS	Jackson.	27	11	9	10	8	9	8	10	10	8	6	8	10	109
MO	Kansas City	18	7	7	10	10	11	10	7	9	8	8	8	8	104
	St. Louis	33	8	8	11	11	11	9	9	8	8	8	9	9	111
MT	Great Falls.	53	9	8	9	9	12	12	7	8	7	6	7	8	101
NE	Omaha	54	6	7	9	9	12	11	9	9	8	7	6	6	98
NV	Reno	48	6	6	6	4	4	3	2	2	2	3	5	6	51
NH	Concord	49	11	10	11	12	12	11	10	10	9	9	11	11	125
NJ	Atlantic City	47	11	10	11	11	10	9	9	9	8	7	9	10	112
NM	Albuquerque.	51	4	4	5	3	4	4	9	9	6	5	3	4	61
NY	Albany.	44	12	11	12	12	13	11	10	10	10	9	12	12	134
	Buffalo	47	20	17	16	14	12	11	10	11	11	12	16	20	169
	New York [2]	121	11	10	11	11	11	10	11	10	8	8	9	10	121
NC	Charlotte	51	10	10	11	9	10	10	11	10	7	7	8	10	111
	Raleigh	46	10	10	10	9	10	9	11	10	8	7	8	9	112
ND	Bismarck	51	8	7	8	8	10	12	9	9	7	6	6	8	96
OH	Cincinnati.	43	12	11	13	12	11	11	10	9	8	8	11	12	129
	Cleveland	49	16	14	15	14	13	11	10	10	10	10	14	16	156
	Columbus	51	13	12	14	13	13	11	11	9	8	9	11	13	137
OK	Oklahoma City	51	5	6	7	8	10	9	6	6	7	6	5	5	82
OR	Portland.	50	18	16	17	14	12	9	4	5	8	13	18	19	152
PA	Philadelphia	50	11	9	11	11	11	10	9	9	8	8	9	10	117
	Pittsburgh	38	16	14	16	14	13	12	11	10	9	11	13	16	154
RI	Providence.	37	11	10	12	11	11	11	9	9	8	9	11	12	124
SC	Columbia	43	10	10	11	8	9	9	12	11	8	6	7	9	109
SD	Sioux Falls.	45	6	6	9	9	11	11	9	9	8	6	6	6	97
TN	Memphis	40	10	10	11	10	9	8	8	9	8	6	9	10	106
	Nashville	49	11	11	12	11	11	9	10	9	8	7	9	11	119
TX	Dallas-Fort Worth	37	7	7	7	8	9	6	5	5	7	6	6	6	78
	El Paso	51	4	3	2	2	2	3	8	8	5	4	3	4	48
	Houston	21	10	8	9	7	8	9	9	9	9	7	9	9	104
UT	Salt Lake City.	62	10	9	10	9	8	5	5	6	5	6	8	9	90
VT	Burlington	47	14	12	13	12	13	13	12	12	12	12	14	15	154
VA	Norfolk	42	10	10	11	10	10	9	11	11	8	8	8	9	115
	Richmond	53	10	9	11	9	11	9	11	10	8	7	8	9	113
WA	Seattle-Tacoma	46	19	16	17	14	10	9	5	6	9	13	18	19	156
	Spokane	43	14	11	11	9	9	8	4	5	6	8	13	15	113
WV	Charleston.	43	15	14	15	14	13	11	13	11	9	10	12	14	151
WI	Milwaukee	50	11	10	12	12	12	11	10	9	9	9	10	11	125
WY	Cheyenne	55	6	6	9	10	12	11	11	10	7	6	6	6	99
PR	San Juan.	35	17	13	12	13	17	16	19	19	17	17	18	19	196

Z Less than 1/2 day. [1] For period of record through 1988. [2] City office data.

Source: U.S. National Oceanic and Atmospheric Administration, *Comparative Climatic Data,* annual.

No. 374. Snow and Ice Pellets—Selected Cities

[**In inches.** Airport data, except as noted. For period of record through 1990. T denotes trace]

STATE	STATION	Length of record (yr.)	Jan.	Feb.	Mar.	Apr.	May	June	July	Aug.	Sept.	Oct.	Nov.	Dec.	Annual
AL	Mobile	49	0.1	0.2	-	T	-	-	T	-	-	-	T	0.1	0.4
AK	Juneau	46	25.9	18.8	15.5	3.7	-	T	-	-	T	1	12.3	22.2	99.4
AZ	Phoenix	53	T	-	T	T	-	-	-	-	-	-	-	-	T
AR	Little Rock	48	2.5	1.5	0.5	T	-	-	-	-	-	-	0.2	0.7	5.4
CA	Los Angeles	55	T	T	T	-	-	-	-	-	-	-	-	T	T
	Sacramento	42	T	-	T	-	-	-	-	-	-	-	-	T	T
	San Diego	50	T	-	T	-	-	-	-	-	-	-	T	T	T
	San Francisco	63	-	T	T	-	-	-	-	-	-	-	-	-	T
CO	Denver	56	7.9	7.5	12.8	9.0	1.7	-	T	T	1.6	3.7	8.2	7.4	59.8
CT	Hartford	36	12.3	11.6	9.5	1.6	-	-	-	-	-	0.1	2.1	10.6	47.8
DE	Wilmington	43	6.8	6.2	3.2	0.2	T	-	T	-	-	0.1	1	3.5	21.0
DC	Washington	47	5.5	5.4	2.1	-	T	-	T	-	-	-	0.9	3.2	17.1
FL	Jacksonville	49	T	-	-	-	-	-	T	-	-	-	-	-	T
	Miami	48	-	-	-	-	-	-	-	-	-	-	-	-	-
GA	Atlanta	56	0.9	0.5	0.4	T	-	-	-	-	-	-	-	0.2	2
HI	Honolulu	44	-	-	-	-	-	-	-	-	-	-	-	-	-
ID	Boise	51	6.8	3.6	1.8	0.7	0.1	T	T	T	-	0.1	2.2	6	21.3
IL	Chicago	32	10.7	8.5	6.6	1.7	0.1	-	-	T	T	0.5	2.0	8.6	38.7
	Peoria	47	6.5	5.5	4.1	0.9	-	-	T	-	-	0.1	2.0	6.0	25.1
IN	Indianapolis	59	6.1	5.8	3.5	0.5	-	-	-	T	-	0.2	1.8	5.0	22.9
IA	Des Moines	51	8.1	7.3	6.5	2	-	-	-	-	T	0.2	2.7	6.9	33.7
KS	Wichita	37	4.7	4.4	2.6	0.3	T	T	-	-	-	-	1.2	3.4	16.6
KY	Louisville	43	5.4	4.4	3.3	0.1	T	-	-	-	-	-	1.1	2.2	16.5
LA	New Orleans	44	-	0.1	T	T	T	-	-	-	-	-	-	0.1	0.2
ME	Portland	50	19.4	17.5	12.4	2.9	0.2	-	-	-	T	0.2	3.1	14.7	70.4
MD	Baltimore	40	6.1	6.7	3.7	0.1	T	-	-	-	-	-	1.1	3.6	21.3
MA	Boston	55	12.2	11.4	7.4	0.9	-	-	-	-	-	-	1.4	7.4	40.7
MI	Detroit	32	10.0	9.1	6.8	1.7	T	-	-	-	T	0.2	3.1	10.6	41.5
	Sault Ste. Marie	49	28.6	19.3	15.2	5.5	0.5	T	-	T	0.1	2.3	15.3	30	116.8
MN	Duluth	47	16.9	11.3	13.8	6.4	0.7	-	T	-	T	1.3	11	15.5	76.9
	Minneapolis-St. Paul	52	9.9	8.4	10.9	3	0.1	T	-	-	-	0.4	7.1	9.4	49.2
MS	Jackson	27	0.6	0.2	0.2	-	-	-	-	-	-	-	-	-	1
MO	Kansas City	56	5.7	4.4	3.7	0.7	T	T	-	-	-	-	1	4.5	20
	St. Louis	54	5.3	4.5	4.3	0.4	T	T	-	-	-	T	1.4	4	19.9
MT	Great Falls	53	9.9	8.5	10.4	7.3	1.8	0.3	T	T	1.6	3.1	7.5	8.9	59.3
NE	Omaha	55	7.3	6.8	6.6	0.8	0.1	T	-	-	T	0.3	2.5	5.7	30.1
NV	Reno	48	5.8	5.2	4.6	1.3	0.9	-	-	-	-	0.4	2.2	4.3	24.7
NH	Concord	49	18.1	14.7	10.6	2.3	0.1	-	-	-	-	0.1	4.0	13.7	63.6
NJ	Atlantic City	46	5.3	5.5	2.7	0.4	T	-	-	-	-	T	0.4	2.3	16.6
NM	Albuquerque	51	2.5	2.2	1.9	0.6	-	T	T	-	T	0.1	1.1	2.6	11.0
NY	Albany	44	16.5	14.3	10.9	2.8	0.1	-	T	-	T	0.2	4.3	15.2	64.3
	Buffalo	47	23.8	18.5	11.1	3.2	0.3	T	-	-	T	0.2	11.4	22.8	91.3
	New York [1]	122	7.6	8.5	5.0	0.9	T	-	T	-	-	0.9	5.5	-	28.4
NC	Charlotte	51	2.1	1.8	1.3	-	-	-	-	-	-	-	0.1	0.5	5.8
	Raleigh	46	2.4	2.7	1.4	-	-	-	-	-	-	-	0.1	0.8	7.4
ND	Bismarck	51	7.2	6.7	8.3	3.8	0.8	T	T	T	0.3	1.3	5.8	6.9	41.1
OH	Cincinnati	43	7.0	5.4	4.3	0.5	-	-	-	-	-	0.2	2.1	4.0	23.5
	Cleveland	49	12.3	11.7	10.3	2.4	0.1	-	-	-	T	0.6	5.0	11.9	54.3
	Columbus	43	8.3	6.2	4.5	1	-	T	-	-	T	-	2.3	5.7	28.0
OK	Oklahoma City	51	3.1	2.6	1.4	-	T	-	-	-	-	T	0.5	1.8	9.4
OR	Portland	50	3.4	0.9	0.5	T	-	T	-	T	T	-	0.5	1.4	6.7
PA	Philadelphia	48	6.6	6.5	3.6	0.3	T	-	-	-	-	-	0.7	3.6	21.3
	Pittsburgh	38	11.6	9.4	8.1	1.8	0.1	T	-	-	T	0.2	3.4	8.2	42.8
RI	Providence	37	9.8	9.8	7.4	0.7	0.2	-	-	-	-	0.1	1.1	7.1	36.2
SC	Columbia	43	0.5	0.9	0.2	T	-	-	-	-	-	-	T	0.2	1.8
SD	Sioux Falls	45	6.5	8.0	9.7	2.3	-	T	-	-	-	0.5	5.2	7.4	39.6
TN	Memphis	40	2.5	1.4	0.9	T	T	-	-	-	-	-	T	0.7	5.6
	Nashville	49	4.0	3.1	1.4	-	-	-	-	T	-	-	0.5	1.6	10.6
TX	Dallas-Fort Worth	37	1.3	1.0	0.2	T	T	-	-	-	-	-	0.1	0.3	2.9
	El Paso	51	1.3	0.9	0.4	0.4	T	-	T	-	-	-	1.0	1.7	5.7
	Houston	56	0.2	0.2	-	-	-	T	-	-	-	-	-	T	0.4
UT	Salt Lake City	62	13.0	9.5	9.9	5.0	0.6	T	-	-	0.1	1.3	6.4	12	57.8
VT	Burlington	47	18.8	16.5	12	3.6	0.2	-	T	-	T	0.2	6.8	18.7	76.8
VA	Norfolk	42	2.8	3.0	1.1	-	-	T	-	-	-	-	-	0.9	7.8
	Richmond	53	5.1	4.2	2.5	0.1	T	-	-	-	-	T	0.4	2.0	14.3
WA	Seattle-Tacoma	46	5.3	1.7	1.4	0.1	T	-	T	-	T	-	1.3	2.5	12.3
	Spokane	43	16.3	7.8	4.1	0.7	0.1	T	-	-	T	0.4	6.2	15.0	50.6
WV	Charleston	43	10.6	8.8	4.6	0.9	-	T	T	T	T	0.1	2.2	5.0	32.2
WI	Milwaukee	50	12.9	9.8	8.7	1.8	0.1	-	T	T	T	0.2	3.0	10.5	47.0
WY	Cheyenne	55	6.2	5.9	12.4	9.0	3.5	0.2	T	T	0.8	3.6	6.8	6.2	54.6
PR	San Juan	35	-	-	-	-	-	-	-	-	-	T	-	-	T

- Represents zero or rounds to zero.   [1] City office data.

Source: U.S. National Oceanic and Atmospheric Administration, *Comparative Climatic Data*, annual.

No. 375. Sunshine, Average Wind Speed, Mean Number of Days Minimum Temperature Below 32 Degrees Fahrenheit, and Average Relative Humidity—Selected Cities

[Airport data, except as noted. For period of record through 1990, except as noted. M=morning. A=afternoon]

STATE	STATION	AVERAGE PERCENTAGE OF POSSIBLE SUNSHINE — Length of record (yr.)	Annual	AVERAGE WIND SPEED (m.p.h.) — Length of record (yr.)	Annual	Jan.	July	MINIMUM TEMPERATURE 32 DEGREES OR LESS — Length of record (yr.)	Mean number (days)	AVERAGE RELATIVE HUMIDITY (percent) — Length of record (yr.)	Annual M	Annual A	Jan. M	Jan. A	July M	July A
AL	Mobile	[1]40	[1]59	42	9.0	10.4	7.0	28	23	28	86	57	81	61	89	60
AK	Juneau	33	30	45	8.3	8.3	7.5	46	142	24	84	73	80	77	83	70
AZ	Phoenix	95	86	45	6.3	5.3	7.2	30	8	30	51	23	66	32	45	20
AR	Little Rock	32	62	48	7.8	8.6	6.7	30	60	30	84	57	80	61	88	56
CA	Los Angeles	32	73	42	7.5	6.7	7.8	31	(Z)	31	79	64	69	59	86	68
	Sacramento	42	78	41	7.9	7.2	9.0	40	17	30	82	46	90	70	76	28
	San Diego	50	68	50	6.9	5.9	7.4	30	(Z)	30	76	62	70	56	82	66
	San Francisco	38	66	63	10.6	7.2	13.6	31	2	31	84	61	86	66	86	59
CO	Denver	41	70	42	8.7	8.7	8.3	30	157	30	67	40	63	49	68	34
CT	Hartford	36	57	36	8.5	9.0	7.5	31	135	31	76	52	71	56	78	51
DE	Wilmington	(NA)	(NA)	42	9.1	9.8	7.8	43	100	43	78	55	75	60	79	54
DC	Washington	42	56	42	9.4	10.0	8.2	30	71	30	74	53	69	55	76	53
FL	Jacksonville	39	63	41	8.0	8.2	7.1	49	15	54	88	56	87	57	88	58
	Miami	14	73	41	9.3	9.5	7.9	26	(Z)	26	84	61	84	59	84	63
GA	Atlanta	55	61	52	9.1	10.5	7.6	30	54	30	82	56	78	59	88	60
HI	Honolulu	38	69	41	11.4	9.7	13.3	21	-	21	72	56	81	62	67	51
ID	Boise	48	64	51	8.8	8.0	8.4	51	124	51	69	43	80	70	54	22
IL	Chicago	10	55	32	10.3	11.6	8.2	32	133	32	80	60	76	67	82	57
	Peoria	47	57	47	10.0	11.2	7.8	31	129	31	83	61	79	68	86	59
IN	Indianapolis	46	55	42	9.6	10.9	7.4	31	118	31	83	62	80	70	87	60
IA	Des Moines	40	59	41	10.9	11.7	9.0	29	135	29	79	60	75	67	82	57
KS	Wichita	37	65	37	12.3	12.2	11.3	37	111	37	80	55	79	62	78	48
KY	Louisville	43	56	43	8.4	9.7	6.7	30	89	30	81	58	76	64	85	58
LA	New Orleans	17	60	42	8.2	9.4	6.1	44	13	42	87	63	85	66	91	66
ME	Portland	50	57	50	8.8	9.2	7.6	50	157	50	79	59	76	61	80	59
MD	Baltimore	40	57	40	9.2	9.7	8.0	40	97	37	77	54	71	57	81	53
MA	Boston	55	58	33	12.5	13.9	11.0	26	98	26	72	58	67	57	74	57
MI	Detroit	25	53	32	10.4	12.0	8.5	32	136	32	81	60	80	69	82	53
	Sault Ste. Marie	49	47	49	9.3	9.8	7.8	49	181	49	85	67	81	75	89	61
MN	Duluth	40	52	41	11.1	11.6	9.4	29	185	29	81	63	76	65	85	59
	Minneapolis-St. Paul	52	58	52	10.6	10.5	9.4	31	156	31	78	59	74	67	80	54
MS	Jackson	26	60	27	7.4	8.6	5.9	27	50	27	91	58	87	64	93	59
MO	Kansas City	18	62	18	10.8	11.5	9.4	18	110	18	81	60	76	63	84	57
	St. Louis	31	57	41	9.7	10.6	8.0	30	100	30	83	59	81	65	85	56
MT	Great Falls	46	61	49	12.8	15.3	10.1	29	157	29	66	45	66	60	65	29
NE	Omaha	54	60	54	10.6	10.9	8.9	26	141	26	81	59	78	65	84	57
NV	Reno	42	79	48	6.6	5.6	7.0	27	174	27	70	32	79	51	63	18
NH	Concord	49	54	48	6.7	7.2	5.7	25	173	25	81	54	75	58	84	52
NJ	Atlantic City	30	56	32	10.1	11.0	8.5	26	110	26	81	56	77	58	83	57
NM	Albuquerque	51	76	3	11.8	11.7	10.6	30	119	30	60	29	70	40	60	27
NY	Albany	52	52	52	8.9	9.8	7.4	25	149	25	80	57	77	63	81	55
	Buffalo	47	49	51	12.0	14.3	10.3	30	133	30	80	63	79	72	78	55
	New York [2]	104	58	58	9.4	10.7	7.6	77	80	61	72	56	68	60	75	55
NC	Charlotte	40	63	41	7.5	7.9	6.6	30	67	30	83	54	78	55	87	57
	Raleigh	36	59	41	7.8	8.5	6.7	26	78	26	85	54	78	55	89	58
ND	Bismarck	51	59	51	10.2	10.0	9.2	31	186	31	80	56	74	63	83	47
OH	Cincinnati	7	52	43	9.1	10.7	7.1	28	108	28	81	59	78	67	85	57
	Cleveland	47	49	49	10.6	12.3	8.6	30	124	30	79	62	77	69	81	57
	Columbus	39	49	41	8.5	10.1	6.6	31	119	31	80	59	76	67	85	56
OK	Oklahoma City	36	68	42	12.4	12.8	10.9	25	77	25	79	54	77	59	80	49
OR	Portland	41	48	42	7.9	9.9	7.6	50	43	50	86	60	86	76	82	45
PA	Philadelphia	48	56	50	9.5	10.3	8.1	31	97	31	76	55	73	59	79	54
	Pittsburgh	38	46	38	9.1	10.7	7.2	31	123	30	78	57	75	65	83	54
RI	Providence	37	58	37	10.6	11.2	9.5	27	119	27	75	55	70	56	77	56
SC	Columbia	37	64	42	6.9	7.2	6.3	24	61	24	87	51	82	54	89	54
SD	Sioux Falls	[3]48	[3]63	42	11.1	11.1	9.8	27	168	27	81	60	76	67	82	53
TN	Memphis	35	64	42	8.9	10.1	7.5	49	57	51	81	57	78	63	84	57
	Nashville	48	56	49	8.0	9.2	6.5	25	76	25	84	57	79	63	89	54
TX	Dallas-Fort Worth	12	64	37	10.8	11.2	9.6	27	40	27	82	56	79	59	80	48
	El Paso	48	83	48	8.9	8.4	8.3	30	65	30	57	27	65	34	62	29
	Houston	21	56	21	7.9	8.3	7.0	21	21	21	90	59	85	63	92	58
UT	Salt Lake City	52	66	61	8.9	7.7	9.6	31	125	31	67	43	70	69	52	22
VT	Burlington	47	49	47	8.9	9.7	7.9	26	156	25	77	59	71	63	78	53
VA	Norfolk	26	61	42	10.7	11.5	9.0	42	54	42	78	57	74	58	82	59
	Richmond	40	62	42	7.7	8.1	6.8	61	85	56	83	53	80	57	85	56
WA	Seattle-Tacoma	24	46	42	9.0	9.8	8.3	31	31	31	83	62	81	74	82	49
	Spokane	42	54	43	8.9	8.8	6.4	31	139	31	77	52	85	78	64	27
WV	Charleston	[4]47	[4]40	43	6.3	7.5	5.0	43	100	43	83	56	77	62	90	60
WI	Milwaukee	50	54	50	11.6	12.7	9.7	30	141	30	81	64	76	68	82	61
WY	Cheyenne	51	65	33	13.0	15.4	10.3	31	171	31	65	44	57	50	70	38
PR	San Juan	35	66	35	8.4	8.5	9.6	35	-	35	79	65	81	64	79	66

- Represents zero.   Z Less than one-half a day.   NA Not available.   [1] Recording site is in Montgomery, AL.   [2] City office data.   [3] Recording site is in Rapid City, SD.   [4] Recording site is Elkins, WV.

Source: U.S. National Oceanic and Atmospheric Administration, *Comparative Climatic Data*, annual.

No. 376. Normal Monthly and Seasonal Heating Degree Days, 65 Degree Base—Selected Cities

[Airport data, except as noted. Based on standard 30-year period, 1961 through 1990. Degree day normals are used to determine relative estimates of heating requirements for buildings. Each day that the average temperature for a day is below 65 degrees F. produces one heating degree day]

STATE	STATION	Jan.	Feb.	Mar.	Apr.	May	June	July	Aug.	Sept.	Oct.	Nov.	Dec.	Seasonal
AL	Mobile..........	492	344	177	48	-	-	-	-	-	52	196	393	1,702
AK	Juneau	1,265	1,025	1,001	759	558	360	279	310	468	707	990	1,175	8,897
AZ	Phoenix.........	362	227	182	75	8	-	-	-	-	17	134	345	1,350
AR	Little Rock.......	803	599	384	133	25	-	-	-	8	128	387	688	3,155
CA	Los Angeles.....	258	215	224	158	96	54	9	5	22	32	127	258	1,458
	Sacramento	614	400	357	230	80	12	-	-	16	78	351	611	2,749
	San Diego	245	189	177	113	73	51	13	-	19	24	109	243	1,256
	San Francisco	505	358	363	287	218	121	92	68	79	135	306	484	3,016
CO	Denver	1,094	885	806	504	253	71	-	-	144	429	780	1,054	6,020
CT	Hartford.........	1,252	1,050	853	489	194	20	-	6	96	397	693	1,101	6,151
DE	Wilmington.......	1,066	885	691	384	122	-	-	-	35	288	561	905	4,937
DC	Washington	942	770	552	264	60	-	-	-	14	195	456	794	4,047
FL	Jacksonville	421	296	169	37	-	-	-	-	-	31	149	331	1,434
	Miami	88	51	14	-	-	-	-	-	-	-	6	41	200
GA	Atlanta	744	566	365	138	27	-	-	-	10	138	367	636	2,991
HI	Honolulu	-	-	-	-	-	-	-	-	-	-	-	-	-
ID	Boise	1,116	815	701	477	242	75	6	20	160	414	753	1,082	5,861
IL	Chicago.........	1,364	1,109	862	492	235	35	5	19	84	391	750	1,190	6,536
	Peoria..........	1,345	1,084	806	408	183	11	-	9	54	356	714	1,178	6,148
IN	Indianapolis	1,225	991	732	378	165	5	-	6	58	338	660	1,057	5,615
IA	Des Moines	1,414	1,128	859	428	165	10	-	11	71	372	780	1,259	6,497
KS	Wichita	1,101	846	608	278	102	5	-	-	29	221	609	992	4,791
KY	Louisville.......	1,032	820	580	273	105	6	-	-	36	254	537	871	4,514
LA	New Orleans	450	316	162	28	-	-	-	-	-	30	178	349	1,513
ME	Portland.........	1,370	1,168	992	651	363	100	11	39	189	512	789	1,194	7,378
MD	Baltimore........	1,029	846	648	348	108	-	-	-	29	276	546	877	4,707
MA	Boston	1,128	972	818	507	221	32	-	6	72	321	591	973	5,641
MI	Detroit..........	1,305	1,109	908	531	243	38	-	16	102	435	744	1,138	6,569
	Sault Ste. Marie ...	1,615	1,428	1,271	804	457	224	92	128	300	611	960	1,426	9,316
MN	Duluth..........	1,798	1,476	1,259	792	445	170	60	113	329	660	1,098	1,618	9,818
	Minneapolis-St. Paul	1,649	1,319	1,054	558	244	41	11	22	167	502	954	1,460	7,981
MS	Jackson.........	656	485	285	87	7	-	-	-	6	104	295	542	2,467
MO	Kansas City	1,218	946	691	325	135	7	-	6	56	279	657	1,073	5,393
	St. Louis	1,107	871	617	266	111	-	-	-	21	237	564	964	4,758
MT	Great Falls.......	1,358	1,053	983	642	372	156	37	91	299	543	933	1,274	7,741
NE	Omaha	1,361	1,067	818	398	164	14	-	9	80	372	780	1,237	6,300
NV	Reno	995	756	688	492	274	76	13	20	178	440	741	1,001	5,674
NH	Concord	1,438	1,210	1,011	633	312	70	13	39	196	533	837	1,262	7,554
NJ	Atlantic City	1,057	896	729	450	167	12	-	-	53	324	576	905	5,169
NM	Albuquerque......	955	700	561	301	89	-	-	-	18	259	621	921	4,425
NY	Albany..........	1,376	1,162	952	558	247	34	-	12	141	459	759	1,194	6,894
	Buffalo	1,283	1,134	967	594	279	59	5	17	130	431	735	1,113	6,747
	New York[1]	1,039	879	701	375	125	-	-	-	34	250	522	880	4,805
NC	Charlotte........	797	630	437	183	42	-	-	-	6	161	391	694	3,341
	Raleigh	809	644	458	193	47	-	-	-	9	189	414	694	3,457
ND	Bismarck........	1,730	1,380	1,141	660	324	116	15	69	262	598	1,092	1,581	8,968
OH	Cincinnati........	1,144	930	682	354	151	11	-	-	51	327	621	977	5,248
	Cleveland	1,246	1,058	859	522	250	40	-	11	99	387	672	1,057	6,201
	Columbus	1,197	991	747	420	187	23	-	12	81	361	663	1,026	5,708
OK	Oklahoma City	902	675	464	176	31	-	-	-	15	137	462	797	3,659
OR	Portland.........	787	599	549	420	249	91	28	35	102	326	567	769	4,522
PA	Philadelphia	1,073	896	701	378	123	5	-	-	32	283	558	905	4,954
	Pittsburgh	1,206	1,016	794	462	214	36	6	14	100	400	681	1,039	5,968
RI	Providence.......	1,150	988	856	528	246	31	-	8	90	359	630	998	5,884
SC	Columbia........	665	514	317	108	18	-	-	-	5	138	323	561	2,649
SD	Sioux Falls.......	1,587	1,268	1,008	543	240	50	10	22	165	508	960	1,448	7,809
TN	Memphis	784	582	383	127	25	-	-	-	10	131	380	660	3,082
	Nashville	893	689	469	193	59	-	-	-	21	195	450	760	3,729
TX	Dallas-Fort Worth ..	670	484	286	75	-	-	-	-	-	51	275	566	2,407
	El Paso.........	688	473	316	110	7	-	-	-	-	88	378	648	2,708
	Houston	468	322	187	36	-	-	-	-	-	31	181	374	1,599
UT	Salt Lake City.....	1,150	865	719	464	215	51	-	-	108	373	726	1,094	5,765
VT	Burlington	1,510	1,310	1,063	633	282	58	6	29	199	533	846	1,302	7,771
VA	Norfolk	803	672	508	249	51	-	-	-	11	164	380	657	3,495
	Richmond	908	736	527	241	61	-	-	-	23	233	462	772	3,963
WA	Seattle-Tacoma ...	772	602	601	474	307	144	58	65	156	378	591	760	4,908
	Spokane	1,175	888	815	573	344	139	30	56	223	549	897	1,153	6,842
WV	Charleston.......	1,020	826	592	312	129	10	-	-	44	299	546	868	4,646
WI	Milwaukee.......	1,429	1,176	983	618	338	82	14	27	123	456	819	1,259	7,324
WY	Cheyenne	1,194	1,000	973	675	403	150	31	44	251	558	894	1,153	7,326
PR	San Juan........	-	-	-	-	-	-	-	-	-	-	-	-	-

- Represents zero.   [1] City office data.

Source: U.S. National Oceanic and Atmospheric Administration, *Climatography of the United States*, No. 81.

No. 377. Normal Monthly and Seasonal Cooling Degree Days, 65 Degree Base—Selected Cities

[Airport data, except as noted. Based on standard 30-year period, 1961 through 1990. Degree day normals are used to determine relative estimates of heating requirements for buildings. Each day that the average temperature for a day is above 65 degrees F. produces one cooling degree day]

STATE	STATION	Jan.	Feb.	Mar.	Apr.	May	June	July	Aug.	Sept.	Oct.	Nov.	Dec.	Annual avg.
AL	Mobile	24	14	38	132	295	462	536	521	387	157	40	21	2,627
AK	Juneau	-	-	-	-	-	-	-	-	-	-	-	-	
AZ	Phoenix	8	22	95	222	436	696	884	822	618	311	41	7	4,162
AR	Little Rock	-	-	15	46	187	402	524	484	281	66	-	-	2,005
CA	Los Angeles	-	8	7	11	25	75	136	176	169	88	25	7	727
	Sacramento	-	-	-	29	89	210	332	313	211	53	-	-	1,237
	San Diego	9	10	9	23	45	105	199	240	211	107	19	7	984
	San Francisco	-	-	-	5	-	16	21	28	64	11	-	-	145
CO	Denver	-	-	-	-	11	128	267	203	63	7	-	-	679
CT	Hartford	-	-	-	-	27	125	270	210	45	-	-	-	677
DE	Wilmington	-	-	-	-	44	199	353	310	125	15	-	-	1,046
DC	Washington	-	-	-	9	104	318	465	419	203	31	-	-	1,549
FL	Jacksonville	31	22	48	97	260	423	515	502	393	179	56	25	2,551
	Miami	156	149	221	306	425	492	546	552	507	412	264	168	4,198
GA	Atlanta	-	-	8	33	157	330	428	406	241	54	10	-	1,667
HI	Honolulu	245	224	291	324	388	432	481	508	480	453	366	282	4,474
ID	Boise	-	-	-	-	9	120	285	252	88	-	-	-	754
IL	Chicago	-	-	-	-	46	143	259	226	66	12	-	-	752
	Peoria	-	-	-	-	87	206	326	261	87	15	-	-	982
IN	Indianapolis	-	-	-	-	96	212	322	260	106	18	-	-	1,014
IA	Des Moines	-	-	-	5	81	214	360	287	74	15	-	-	1,036
KS	Wichita	-	-	-	20	121	326	508	443	188	22	-	-	1,628
KY	Louisville	-	-	-	12	115	252	378	335	171	25	-	-	1,288
LA	New Orleans	25	17	56	133	304	450	524	512	393	157	61	23	2,655
ME	Portland	-	-	-	-	-	22	123	111	12	-	-	-	268
MD	Baltimore	-	-	-	-	59	227	372	329	134	16	-	-	1,137
MA	Boston	-	-	-	-	10	113	264	220	66	5	-	-	678
MI	Detroit	-	-	-	-	38	116	231	186	48	7	-	-	626
	Sault Ste. Marie	-	-	-	-	8	14	55	54	-	-	-	-	131
MN	Duluth	-	-	-	-	-	14	94	72	-	-	-	-	180
	Minneapolis-St. Paul	-	-	-	-	43	137	278	192	32	-	-	-	682
MS	Jackson	8	6	28	75	224	414	512	493	333	94	19	9	2,215
MO	Kansas City	-	-	-	10	107	253	419	350	131	18	-	-	1,288
	St. Louis	-	-	-	17	145	312	459	391	177	33	-	-	1,534
MT	Great Falls	-	-	-	-	-	54	137	150	47	-	-	-	388
NE	Omaha	-	-	-	5	84	227	369	292	83	12	-	-	1,072
NV	Reno	-	-	-	-	10	79	217	162	40	-	-	-	508
NH	Concord	-	-	-	-	8	46	153	111	10	-	-	-	328
NJ	Atlantic City	-	-	-	-	25	144	301	260	86	10	-	-	826
NM	Albuquerque	-	-	-	7	64	279	419	338	126	11	-	-	1,244
NY	Albany	-	-	-	-	18	91	213	155	30	-	-	-	507
	Buffalo	-	-	-	-	19	86	194	141	37	-	-	-	477
	New York [1]	-	-	-	-	54	203	366	326	130	17	-	-	1,096
NC	Charlotte	-	-	-	15	116	321	443	412	228	47	-	-	1,582
	Raleigh	-	-	6	13	109	279	406	375	192	37	-	-	1,417
ND	Bismarck	-	-	-	-	14	98	183	171	22	-	-	-	488
OH	Cincinnati	-	-	-	-	86	191	313	266	120	20	-	-	996
	Cleveland	-	-	-	-	33	118	218	178	66	8	-	-	621
	Columbus	-	-	-	-	69	149	258	214	96	11	-	-	797
OK	Oklahoma City	-	-	9	38	136	351	527	499	255	44	-	-	1,859
OR	Portland	-	-	-	-	-	46	127	147	51	-	-	-	371
PA	Philadelphia	-	-	-	-	58	209	363	326	128	17	-	-	1,101
	Pittsburgh	-	-	-	-	44	123	227	184	67	9	-	-	654
RI	Providence	-	-	-	-	7	88	239	203	63	6	-	-	606
SC	Columbia	8	-	13	48	201	372	490	456	281	86	11	-	1,966
SD	Sioux Falls	-	-	-	-	35	149	298	220	42	-	-	-	744
TN	Memphis	-	-	14	64	217	423	546	496	286	72	-	-	2,118
	Nashville	-	-	10	19	143	318	443	406	225	52	-	-	1,616
TX	Dallas-Fort Worth	-	5	29	90	246	480	629	617	372	119	11	5	2,603
	El Paso	-	-	10	62	217	462	536	468	282	57	-	-	2,094
	Houston	16	11	50	135	295	462	546	536	396	174	61	18	2,700
UT	Salt Lake City	-	-	-	-	23	174	400	329	114	7	-	-	1,047
VT	Burlington	-	-	-	-	13	64	176	119	16	-	-	-	388
VA	Norfolk	-	-	-	9	85	277	409	378	218	46	-	-	1,422
	Richmond	-	-	-	10	92	270	403	366	173	34	-	-	1,348
WA	Seattle-Tacoma	-	-	-	-	-	21	64	81	24	-	-	-	190
	Spokane	-	-	-	-	-	49	148	161	40	-	-	-	398
WV	Charleston	-	-	-	6	83	202	313	276	125	26	-	-	1,031
WI	Milwaukee	-	-	-	-	16	82	197	160	24	-	-	-	479
WY	Cheyenne	-	-	-	-	-	39	136	87	23	-	-	-	285
PR	San Juan	372	339	403	432	493	519	546	549	525	524	450	406	5,558

- Represents zero.   [1] City office data.

Source: U.S. National Oceanic and Atmospheric Administration, *Climatography of the United States*, No. 81.

Figure 7.1
Participation in 10 Most Popular Sports Activities, by Sex: 1990

Male
Female

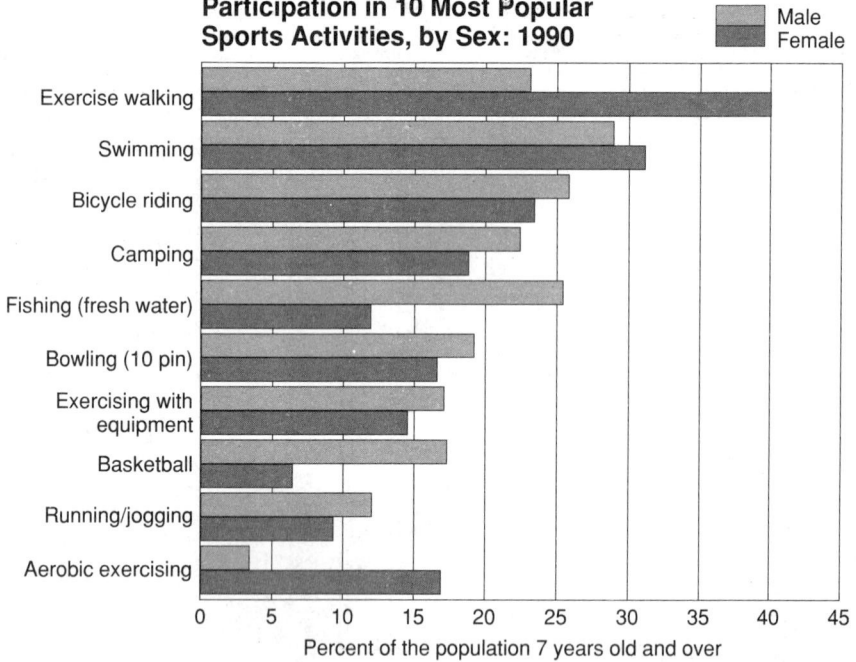

Percent of the population 7 years old and over

Source: Chart prepared by U.S. Bureau of the Census. For data, see table 396.

Figure 7.2
Foreign Visitors for Pleasure Admitted, by Country of Last Residence—Top 10 Countries: 1990

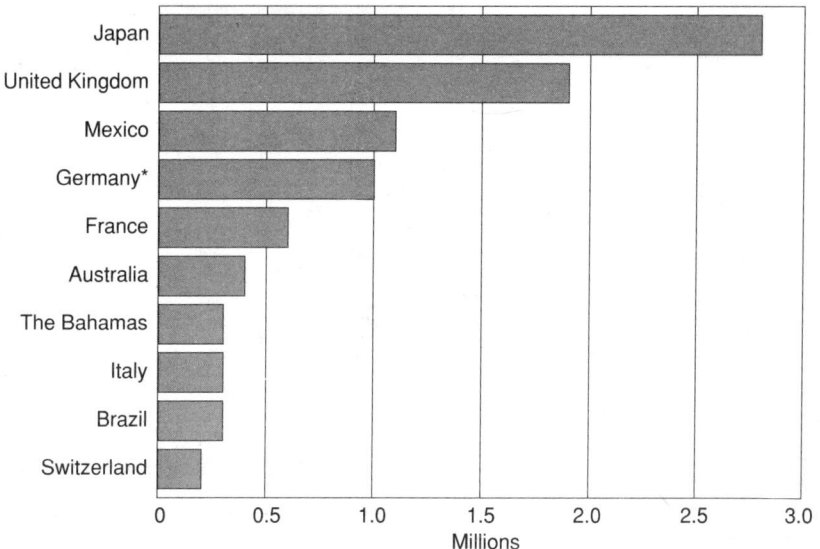

Millions

*Former West Germany (prior to unification).
Source: Chart prepared by U.S. Bureau of the Census. For data, see table 410.

Parks, Recreation, and Travel

This section presents data on national parks and forests, State parks, recreational activities, the arts and humanities, and domestic and foreign travel.

Parks and recreation.—The Department of the Interior has responsibility for administering the national parks. As part of this function, it issues reports relating to the usage of public parks for recreation purposes. The National Park Service publishes information on visits to national park areas in its annual report, *National Park Statistical Abstract. The National Parks: Index (year)* is a biannual report which has appeared under a variety of *Index* titles prior to 1985. Beginning with the 1985 edition, the report has appeared under the current title. The *Index* contains brief descriptions, with acreages, of each area administered by the Service, plus certain "related" areas. A statistical summary of Service-administered areas is also presented. The annual *Federal Recreation Fee Report* summarizes the prior year's recreation fee receipts and recreation visitation statistics for seven Federal land managing agencies.

Statistics for State parks are compiled by the National Association of State Park Directors which issues its annual *Information Exchange.* The Bureau of Land Management, in its *Public Land Statistics,* also issues data on recreational use of its lands. The Department of Agriculture's Forest Service, in its *Report of the Forest Service,* issues data on recreational uses of the national forests.

Visitation.—Data on visitation to reporting areas are collected by several different agencies and groups. The methodology used to collect these results may vary accordingly, from visual counts and estimates to the use of electromagnetic traffic counters. In using and comparing these data, one should also be aware of several different definitions that follow: Recreation visit, which is the entry of any person into an area for recreation purposes; nonrecreation visits, which include visits going to and from inholdings, through traffic, tradespeople and personnel with business in the area; and visitor hour, which constitutes the presence of a person in a recreation area or site for recreational purposes for periods of time aggregating 60 minutes.

In Brief

Sales between 1990 and 1991:
*Compact disks up 16 percent
Cassettes down 19 percent.*

1990 attendance at major league sports:
Baseball games	55.5 million
Football games	17.6 million
Hockey games	12.6 million

Recreation and leisure activities.—Statistics on the participation in various recreation and leisure time activities are based on several sample surveys. Data on participation in fishing, hunting, and other forms of wildlife-associated recreation are published every 5 years by the U.S. Department of Interior, Fish and Wildlife Service. The most recent data are from the 1985 survey. Data on participation in various sports recreation activities are published by the National Sporting Goods Association.

Travel.—Information on foreign travel and personal expenditures abroad, as well as expenditures by foreign citizens traveling in the United States, is compiled annually by the U.S. Bureau of Economic Analysis and published in selected issues of the monthly *Survey of Current Business.* Statistics on arrivals to the United States are reported by the U.S. Travel and Tourism Administration (USTTA), in cooperation with the U.S. Immigration and Naturalization Service, and are published in *Summary and Analysis of International Travel to the United States.* Sources of statistics on departures from the United States include USTTA's in-flight survey, the Department of Transportation's *International Air Travel Statistics* and other sources. Data on domestic travel, business receipts and employment of the travel industry, and travel expenditures are published by the U.S. Travel Data Center, the national nonprofit center for travel and tourism research which is located in Washington, DC. Other data on household transportation characteristics may be found in section 21.

Historical statistics.—Tabular headnotes provide cross-references, where applicable, to *Historical Statistics of the United States, Colonial Times to 1970.* See Appendix IV.

No. 378. Visitation to Federal Recreation Areas, by Administering Federal Agency: 1978 to 1990

[In **millions of visitor hours.** For years ending **September 30,** except as indicated. Covers persons entering and using a recreation area over a specified period of time. For definition of visitor hour, see text, section 7]

ADMINISTERING FEDERAL AGENCY	1978	1980	1982	1983	1984	1985	1986	1987	1988	1989	1990
All areas	**7,094**	**6,367**	**6,640**	**6,668**	**6,252**	**6,403**	**6,858**	**7,332**	**7,419**	**7,475**	**7,620**
Fish and Wildlife Service.	84	17	12	63	60	65	67	72	81	45	53
Forest Service.	2,622	2,819	2,801	2,733	2,731	2,705	2,718	2,861	2,908	3,030	3,157
U.S. Army Corps of Engineers [1].	2,071	1,926	1,632	1,638	1,652	1,721	2,068	2,176	2,290	2,296	2,280
National Park Service	1,154	1,042	1,216	1,276	1,240	1,298	1,348	1,394	1,376	1,315	1,322
Bureau of Land Management [2]. .	634	68	341	596	208	246	284	515	461	493	518
Bureau of Reclamation	431	407	558	285	282	289	296	306	294	286	280
Tennessee Valley Authority [3] . . .	97	87	80	78	79	79	77	8	9	10	10

[1] Beginning 1986, not comparable with previous years.   [2] Data not comparable for all years.   [3] Beginning in 1989, the TVA discontinued reporting visitation to non-fee charging areas. Data for 1987 and 1988 have been adjusted to reflect this policy.

Source: 1978 and 1980, U.S. Heritage Conservation and Recreation Service, *Federal Recreation Fee Report*, annual; thereafter, U.S. National Park Service.

No. 379. National Park System—Summary: 1982 to 1990

[**For fiscal years ending in year shown, except as noted;** see text, section 10. Includes data for five areas in Puerto Rico and Virgin Islands, one area in American Samoa, and one area in Guam. See also *Historical Statistics, Colonial Times to 1970,* series H 806-828]

ITEM	1982	1983	1984	1985	1986	1987	1988	1989	1990
Finances (mil. dol.): [1]									
Expenditures reported	709.7	779.6	843.6	848.1	818.3	909.3	922.9	1,036.8	986.1
Salaries and wages	310.6	343.8	354.6	369.4	372.2	401.5	423.9	441.4	459.1
Improvements, maintenance	98.3	102.4	136.4	127.4	119.6	144.1	154.7	197.5	160.0
Construction.	73.0	87.5	93.3	84.7	125.9	102.6	86.3	85.2	108.5
Other	227.8	245.9	259.3	266.6	200.6	261.1	258.0	312.7	258.5
Funds available	1,024.4	1,191.7	1,215.8	1,248.2	1,271.5	1,276.0	1,338.4	1,440.0	1,505.5
Appropriations	715.2	828.9	785.9	821.6	769.3	846.2	874.6	996.7	1,052.5
Other [2]	309.2	362.8	429.9	426.6	502.2	429.8	463.8	443.3	453.0
Revenue from operations.	25.5	33.1	36.2	50.6	50.7	70.8	77.2	86.3	78.6
Recreation visits (millions): [3]									
All areas	244.1	243.6	248.6	263.4	281.1	287.2	282.5	269.4	258.7
National parks [4]	49.6	50.0	49.7	50.0	53.5	56.6	56.4	57.4	57.7
National monuments	16.2	16.2	15.8	15.9	21.2	23.5	23.2	23.7	23.9
National historical, commemorative, archaeological [5]	62.3	57.3	63.6	61.9	65.5	68.6	61.2	63.9	57.5
National parkways	36.1	37.7	37.9	40.0	41.6	39.3	42.0	31.2	29.1
National recreation areas [4]	49.7	48.9	45.7	49.4	54.8	56.5	54.5	49.6	47.2
National seashores and lakeshores .	17.2	19.0	21.2	25.3	23.0	21.9	23.2	21.9	23.3
National Capital Parks	5.3	6.3	7.2	8.3	6.9	8.1	9.0	8.9	7.5
Miscellaneous other areas	7.7	8.2	7.5	12.6	14.5	12.7	12.9	12.8	12.5
Recreation overnight stays (millions) [3]	16.4	15.7	16.0	15.8	16.0	17.1	17.0	17.4	17.6
In commercial lodgings.	3.3	3.3	3.5	3.5	3.5	3.7	3.8	3.9	3.9
In Park Service campgrounds	8.8	7.8	7.7	7.3	7.2	8.0	7.9	7.8	7.9
In tents.	4.2	3.6	3.7	3.6	3.5	4.0	3.9	3.9	4.1
In recreation vehicles	4.6	4.2	3.9	3.8	3.8	4.0	3.9	3.9	3.8
In backcountry	2.4	2.6	2.0	1.7	1.6	1.6	1.6	1.6	1.7
Other	1.9	2.0	2.8	3.2	3.6	3.8	3.7	4.1	4.2
Land (1,000 acres): [6]									
Total	74,800	74,846	74,913	75,749	75,863	75,970	76,176	76,331	76,362
Parks	45,414	45,427	45,454	45,739	45,791	45,875	45,955	46,081	46,089
Recreation areas.	3,313	3,317	3,322	3,335	3,337	3,339	3,339	3,342	3,344
Other	26,073	26,102	26,137	26,675	26,735	26,756	26,882	26,907	26,929
Acquisition, gross	40	50	44	34	177	134	38	73	21
By purchase.	37	43	42	29	69	27	37	14	18
By gift.	3	1	(Z)	2	20	(Z)	(Z)	58	2
By transfer or exchange	(Z)	6	2	3	88	107	1	1	3
Exclusion	(Z)	2	2	(Z)	4	(Z)	(Z)	1	1
Acquisition, net	40	48	42	34	173	134	38	71	21

Z Less than 500 acres.   [1] Financial data are those associated with the National Park System. Certain other functions of the National Park Service (principally the activities absorbed from the former Heritage Conservation and Recreation Service in 1981) are excluded.   [2] Includes funds carried over from prior years.   [3] For calendar year.   [4] Combined data for North Cascades National Park and two adjacent National Recreation Areas are included in National Parks total.   [5] Includes military areas.   [6] Federal land only, as of Dec. 31. Federal land acreages, in addition to National Park Service administered lands, also include lands within national park system area boundaries but under the administration of other agencies. Year-to-year changes in the federal lands figures include changes in the acreages of these other lands and hence often differ from "net acquisition."

Source: U.S. National Park Service, Visits, *National Park Statistical Abstract*, annual; and unpublished data. Other data are unpublished.

No. 380. National Forest Recreation Use—Summary, 1980 to 1990, and by Activity and States and Other Areas, 1990

[For year ending September 30. Estimated. Represents recreational use of National Forest land and water in States which have a Forest Service recreation program. See also *Historical Statistics, Colonial Times to 1970,* series H 829-835]

YEAR AND ACTIVITY	Recreation visitor-days [1] (1,000)	Per-cent	STATE	Recreation visitor-days [1], 1990 (1,000)	STATE OR OTHER AREA	Recreation visitor-days [1], 1990 (1,000)
1980	233,549	100.0	U.S. ...	263,051	NV.......	3,278
1981	235,709	100.0			NH.......	2,676
1982	233,438	100.0	AL.......	698	NM.......	7,704
1983	227,708	100.0	AK.......	5,414	NY.......	72
1984	227,554	100.0	AZ.......	19,039	NC.......	5,472
1985	225,407	100.0	AR.......	2,441	ND.......	169
1986	226,533	100.0	CA.......	61,007	OH.......	504
1987	238,458	100.0	CO.......	25,204	OK.......	387
1988	242,316	100.0	FL.......	2,961	OR.......	21,036
1989	252,495	100.0	GA.......	2,833	PA.......	2,631
			ID.......	11,819	SC.......	816
1990, total	**263,051**	**100.0**	IL.......	1,638	SD.......	2,966
			IN.......	569	TN.......	2,826
Mechanized travel and viewing scenery ...	89,196	33.9	KS.......	61	TX.......	2,155
Camping, picnicking and swimming	74,145	28.2	KY.......	2,447	UT.......	12,744
Hiking, horseback riding and water travel ..	22,543	8.6	LA.......	527	VT.......	1,369
Winter sports......................	16,143	6.1	MA.......	58	VA.......	3,900
Hunting	15,913	6.1	MI.......	4,916	WA.......	22,451
Fishing..........................	15,616	5.9	MN.......	5,399	WV.......	1,234
Resorts, cabins and organization camps. ...	15,106	5.7	MS.......	1,177	WI.......	2,095
Nature studies....................	2,115	0.8	MO	1,713	WY	6,609
Other [2]...........................	12,274	4.7	MT.......	9,704		
			NE.......	149	PR.......	186

[1] One recreation visitor-day is the recreation use of National Forest land or water that aggregates 12 visitor-hours. This may entail 1 person for 12 hours, 12 persons for 1 hour, or any equivalent combination of individual or group use, either continuous or intermittent.   [2] Includes team sports, gathering forest products, attending talks and programs, and other uses.

Source: U.S. Forest Service, unpublished data.

No. 381. Recreational Use of Public Lands Administered by Bureau of Land Management, 1982 to 1990, and by State, 1990

[In thousands. For year ending Sept. 30. Beginning 1987, increase due to an estimated longer length of stay per visit, especially in California. See text, section 7]

YEAR AND STATE	Number of visits	Total	Off-road vehicle travel	Other motor-ized travel	Non-motor-ized travel	Camp-ing	Hunting	Other	Fishing	Boating	Other	Snow-and ice-based recreational activity, winter sports
1982.......	58,135	316,959	19,471	32,646	11,237	63,928	108,996	44,587	19,287	10,101	1,043	5,663
1983.......	56,270	334,010	24,397	35,534	12,237	84,066	92,974	39,734	20,290	16,869	4,992	2,917
1984.......	59,228	271,373	21,348	25,433	9,579	73,032	73,898	37,650	14,263	11,184	2,092	2,894
1985.......	51,739	244,612	36,995	24,053	10,047	65,397	51,842	23,098	14,254	11,710	2,193	5,023
1986.......	54,253	284,142	49,688	25,866	14,397	95,196	35,570	19,331	18,227	15,891	3,951	6,025
1987.......	56,427	514,716	123,325	34,325	19,172	195,315	57,624	38,412	22,932	15,140	5,212	3,259
1988.......	57,460	492,756	122,014	35,748	19,761	178,703	55,285	38,340	21,617	13,294	4,979	3,015
1989.......	60,957	493,214	65,808	74,075	36,676	173,597	46,760	45,871	23,392	18,491	5,425	3,119
1990, total....	**71,820**	**523,753**	**63,016**	**83,445**	**41,316**	**165,366**	**47,053**	**57,958**	**28,664**	**20,806**	**8,313**	**7,816**
AK........	234	4,351	41	208	83	3,035	358	97	305	149	4	71
AZ........	9,368	72,776	662	107	2,570	48,282	2,306	9,883	938	5,553	2,175	300
CA........	26,459	233,704	45,308	47,965	23,604	59,216	10,682	31,941	5,158	3,785	3,034	3,011
CO........	3,101	19,932	981	3,264	557	4,762	6,135	721	1,835	1,374	41	262
ID........	2,117	20,261	759	1,009	673	4,892	5,288	1,265	2,073	1,502	497	2,303
MT [1]........	4,129	23,044	3,642	2,059	905	6,324	4,451	524	3,381	1,031	106	621
NV........	2,778	18,040	3,454	1,940	1,364	5,502	2,748	868	1,695	214	154	101
NM........	3,078	13,653	2,391	844	726	3,024	2,930	1,701	1,212	772	51	2
OR [2]......	12,099	58,924	1,385	11,632	5,298	15,314	4,501	6,494	7,625	3,896	2,124	655
UT........	7,248	49,031	4,060	13,349	5,247	13,145	4,773	2,965	3,061	2,261	76	94
WY	1,209	10,037	333	1,068	289	1,870	2,881	1,499	1,381	269	51	396

[1] Includes North Dakota and South Dakota.   [2] Includes Washington.

Source: U.S. Bureau of Land Management, *Public Land Statistics,* annual.

No. 382. State Parks and Recreation Areas—States: 1990

[For year ending June 30. Data are shown as reported by State park directors. In some States, park agency has under its control forests, fish and wildlife areas and/or other areas. In other States, agency is responsible for State parks only]

DIVISION AND STATE	Acreage (1,000)	VISITORS (1,000) Total [1]	VISITORS (1,000) Day	REVENUE Total ($1,000)	REVENUE Percent of operating budget	DIVISION AND STATE	Acreage (1,000)	VISITORS (1,000) Total [1]	VISITORS (1,000) Day	REVENUE Total ($1,000)	REVENUE Percent of operating budget
U.S.	11,238	722,819	664,888	401,800	37.9	WV. . . .	201	8,470	7,829	11,968	49.6
						NC. . . .	129	8,549	8,264	1,377	15.0
N.E:						SC. . . .	79	7,236	6,236	9,698	57.9
ME. . . .	74	2,188	1,979	1,504	36.8	GA. . . .	57	14,924	11,224	11,546	45.7
NH	33	2,759	2,567	7,554	92.5	FL	426	14,124	13,097	16,878	40.0
VT	171	916	546	4,129	94.0	E.S.C:					
MA. . . .	271	12,695	11,941	9,314	50.4	KY	42	26,704	25,693	35,642	64.5
RI. . . .	9	5,321	5,038	2,525	47.2	TN	133	26,093	24,919	18,275	50.5
CT	171	7,331	6,943	2,096	25.2	AL	50	5,800	4,721	22,303	83.1
M.A:						MS	23	3,703	3,079	4,817	45.0
NY	259	58,884	55,864	27,752	25.4	W.S.C:					
NJ	302	10,503	10,061	5,459	22.0	AR	48	6,765	6,178	10,494	55.3
PA	277	38,399	36,773	6,675	15.0	LA	38	1,090	784	1,756	30.9
E.N.C:						OK	94	16,613	14,351	12,399	59.5
OH. . . .	208	63,740	61,369	11,255	25.4	TX	433	21,112	18,773	12,003	34.2
IN.	57	9,450	7,800	8,281	65.8	Mt:					
IL	333	36,457	35,978	2,491	7.8	MT	52	697	539	852	25.4
MI	263	22,556	17,334	19,105	76.4	ID.	42	2,463	2,197	1,480	41.3
WI	121	11,495	10,154	7,265	62.1	WY. . . .	120	1,732	1,294	351	12.9
W.N.C:						CO. . . .	233	8,179	7,736	8,046	85.0
MN. . . .	200	7,753	6,932	6,448	37.6	NM. . . .	123	4,410	1,764	8,728	106.8
IA. . . .	83	11,784	11,274	1,245	14.6	AZ	39	2,122	1,758	2,148	32.0
MO. . . .	110	14,464	13,375	2,787	15.8	UT	116	5,062	4,540	3,544	27.5
ND	17	982	837	759	45.7	NV	142	2,721	2,524	811	19.0
SD	92	5,739	5,365	3,488	61.5	Pac:					
NE	149	9,004	7,670	4,548	58.2	WA. . . .	236	40,118	37,852	6,022	22.9
KS	296	3,994	2,596	2,350	33.3	OR	88	40,201	38,034	7,714	31.0
S.A:						CA	1,299	77,811	71,429	43,170	26.8
DE	12	2,748	2,454	3,477	45.2	AK	3,169	5,961	5,256	706	14.1
MD. . . .	226	7,495	7,008	5,108	24.2	HI. . . .	25	19,813	19,727	1,292	17.7
VA	67	3,688	3,235	2,164	23.2						

[1] Includes overnight visitors.

Source: National Association of State Park Directors, Austin, TX, *1991 Annual Information Exchange.*

No. 383. Personal Consumption Expenditures for Recreation in Constant (1987) Dollars: 1970 to 1990

[In billions of dollars, except percent. Represents market value of purchases of goods and services by individuals and nonprofit institutions]

TYPE OF PRODUCT OR SERVICE	1970	1980	1984	1985	1986	1987	1988	1989	1990
Total recreation expenditures.	91.3	149.1	183.8	195.5	208.4	223.7	240.0	251.3	256.6
Percent of total personal consumption [1]	5.0	6.1	6.7	6.8	7.0	7.3	7.6	7.8	7.9
Books and maps	10.5	10.2	11.6	11.4	11.7	13.0	14.1	14.7	15.4
Magazines, newspapers, and sheet music	13.2	18.4	18.5	17.9	18.0	18.8	19.9	20.3	20.8
Nondurable toys and sport supplies.	9.5	17.4	21.3	22.3	23.6	25.5	26.2	27.5	28.3
Wheel goods, sports and photographic equipment [2]	10.3	20.2	23.4	24.4	26.3	28.3	28.9	29.0	27.7
Video and audio products, computer equipment, and musical instruments	8.8	17.6	25.5	29.7	35.4	39.0	45.5	49.5	52.5
Radio and television repair.	2.7	3.5	3.1	3.3	3.2	3.3	3.4	3.4	3.4
Flowers, seeds, and potted plants.	4.0	5.9	6.9	7.0	7.6	8.5	9.2	9.7	9.6
Admissions to specified spectator amusements	8.2	9.9	10.9	10.2	10.1	10.2	10.5	10.6	11.2
Motion picture theaters.	4.2	3.8	4.0	3.6	3.6	3.5	3.4	3.4	3.4
Legitimate theaters and opera, and entertainments of nonprofit institutions [3]	1.3	2.7	2.9	2.9	3.0	3.2	3.4	3.5	4.1
Spectator sports [4]	2.8	3.4	4.0	3.7	3.6	3.5	3.7	3.7	3.7
Clubs and fraternal organizations except insurance [5] . . .	3.8	4.0	5.3	6.3	6.6	7.0	7.2	7.4	7.8
Commercial participant amusements [6]	6.3	12.5	15.3	16.1	16.4	17.3	18.5	19.0	19.2
Pari-mutuel net receipts.	2.8	3.6	3.2	3.2	3.2	3.3	3.2	3.1	3.1
Other [7]	11.3	25.8	38.9	43.5	46.3	49.3	53.4	57.0	57.7

[1] See table 681. [2] Includes boats and pleasure aircraft. [3] Except athletic. [4] Consists of admissions to professional and amateur athletic events and to racetracks, including horse, dog, and auto. [5] Consists of dues and fees excluding insurance premiums. [6] Consists of billiard parlors; bowling alleys; dancing, riding, shooting, skating, and swimming places; amusement devices and parks; golf courses; sightseeing buses and guides; private flying operations; casino gambling and other commercial participant amusements. [7] Consists of net receipts of lotteries and expenditures for purchases of pets and pet care services, cable TV, film processing, photographic studios, sporting and recreation camps, video cassette rentals, and recreational services, not elsewhere classified.

Source: U.S. Bureau of Economic Analysis, *The National Income and Product Accounts of the United States: Volume 2, 1959-88* and *Survey of Current Business,* July issues.

No. 384. Average Annual Expenditures of All Consumer Units for Entertainment and Reading, 1984 to 1990, and by Selected Characteristics, 1990

[In dollars, except as indicated. Based on Consumer Expenditure Survey; see text, section 14, for description of survey. See also headnote, table 693. For composition of regions, see table 25]

YEAR AND CHARACTERISTIC	ENTERTAINMENT AND READING		ENTERTAINMENT				Reading
	Total	Percent of total expenditures	Total	Fees and admissions	Television, radios, and sound equipment	Other equipment and services [1]	
1984	1,187	5.4	1,055	313	322	420	132
1985	1,311	5.6	1,170	320	371	479	141
1986	1,289	5.4	1,149	308	371	470	140
1987	1,335	5.5	1,193	323	379	491	142
1988	1,479	5.7	1,329	353	416	560	150
1989	1,581	5.7	1,424	377	429	618	157
1990, all consumer units.	**1,575**	**5.6**	**1,422**	**371**	**454**	**597**	**153**
Age of reference person:							
Under 25 years old	908	5.5	833	218	344	272	75
25 to 34 years old	1,606	5.7	1,472	342	503	628	134
35 to 44 years old	2,025	5.7	1,837	527	583	726	188
45 to 54 years old	2,150	5.8	1,966	438	592	937	184
55 to 64 years old	1,670	5.7	1,507	365	390	752	163
65 to 74 years old	1,070	5.1	914	329	307	277	156
75 years old and over	535	3.5	423	153	161	109	112
Region of residence: Northeast	1,502	5.1	1,331	398	429	505	171
Midwest	1,516	5.8	1,356	347	433	576	160
South	1,397	5.2	1,266	306	439	521	131
West	2,017	6.2	1,853	482	528	842	164
Size of consumer unit: One person. .	950	5.5	841	235	290	316	109
Two persons	1,819	5.6	1,649	424	518	708	170
Two or more persons	1,629	5.6	1,461	382	428	651	168
Three persons	1,737	5.2	1,572	376	527	670	165
Four persons	2,160	5.8	1,975	510	642	824	185
Five persons or more.	2,032	5.6	1,866	507	591	767	166
Income before taxes:							
Complete income reporters [2]	1,607	5.5	1,451	375	461	613	156
Under $5,000	550	4.4	491	121	216	154	59
$5,000 to $9,999.	643	4.9	579	87	204	288	64
$10,000 to $14,999	702	4.3	612	123	278	211	90
$15,000 to $19,999	928	4.5	821	191	319	312	107
$20,000 to $29,999	1,269	5.2	1,127	301	404	422	142
$30,000 to $39,999	1,684	5.4	1,502	400	527	576	182
$40,000 to $49,999	2,443	6.4	2,241	536	639	1,066	202
$50,000 and over	3,435	6.1	3,137	902	843	1,391	298

[1] Other equipment and services includes pets, toys, and playground equipment, and sports, exercise, and photographic equipment.   [2] A complete reporter is a consumer unit providing values for at least one of the major sources of income.

Source: U.S. Bureau of Labor Statistics, *Consumer Expenditure Survey*, annual.

No. 385. Quantity of Books Sold and Value of U.S. Domestic Consumer Expenditures, by Type of Publication and Market Area: 1982 to 1990

[Includes all titles released by publishers in the United States and imports which appear under the imprints of American publishers. Multi-volume sets, such as encyclopedias, are counted as one unit]

TYPE OF PUBLICATION AND MARKET AREA	UNITS SOLD (mil.)						CONSUMER EXPENDITURES (mil. dol.)					
	1982	1985	1987	1988	1989	1990	1982	1985	1987	1988	1989	1990
Total [1]	1,723	1,788	1,804	1,871	2,003	2,005	9,889	12,611	14,671	16,111	18,036	19,043
Hardbound, total	646	694	738	757	826	824	6,190	7,969	9,326	10,055	11,243	11,789
Softbound, total	1,077	1,094	1,066	1,114	1,177	1,181	3,699	4,642	5,345	6,056	6,793	7,254
Trade	459	553	577	610	685	705	2,484	3,660	5,070	6,040	6,498	6,498
Adult	315	360	357	365	404	403	2,028	2,871	3,399	3,806	4,520	4,777
Juvenile	144	193	220	244	281	301	456	789	1,054	1,264	1,520	1,721
Religious	144	134	128	121	124	130	706	926	1,104	1,168	1,274	1,362
Professional	106	110	120	125	128	131	1,630	2,043	2,350	2,573	2,769	2,957
Bookclubs	133	130	121	112	109	108	510	582	660	671	684	705
Elhi text.	233	234	207	202	213	209	1,067	1,415	1,633	1,716	1,000	1,048
College text	115	110	119	130	136	137	1,388	1,575	1,803	1,998	2,144	2,319
Mail order publications	134	121	128	138	152	138	581	650	679	720	822	752
Mass market paperbacks-rack sized	382	382	391	419	441	433	1,102	1,244	1,411	1,556	1,693	1,775
General retailers	756	829	864	914	994	1,010	3,743	5,103	6,117	6,875	7,914	8,465
College stores	224	225	230	243	253	255	1,910	2,309	2,636	2,904	3,164	3,403
Libraries and institutions [2] . . .	80	80	81	82	87	88	888	1,090	1,252	1,361	1,500	1,592
Schools [2]	262	260	236	233	246	244	1,313	1,685	1,946	2,065	2,290	2,365
Direct to consumers	319	300	299	302	316	304	1,889	2,214	2,477	2,638	2,859	2,901
Other	82	94	95	97	108	104	146	210	244	267	309	316

[1] Types of publications include university press publications and subscription reference works, not shown separately.   [2] Elhi libraries included in schools.

Source: Book Industry Study Group, Inc., New York, NY, *Book Industry Trends*, annual, (copyright).

No. 386. New Books and Editions Published, 1980 to 1991, and Imports, by Subject, 1980 to 1990

[Covers listings in Bowker's Weekly Record in year shown, plus titles issued in that year which were listed in following 6 months. Comprises new books (published for first time) and new editions (with changes in text or format). Excludes government publications; books sold only by subscription; dissertations; periodicals and quarterlies; and pamphlets under 49 pages. See also *Historical Statistics, Colonial Times to 1970*, series R 191-216]

SUBJECT	NEW BOOKS AND NEW EDITIONS						IMPORTS					
	1980	1985	1988	1989	1990	1991, prel.	1980	1985	1987	1988	1989	1990, prel.
Total	42,377	[1]50,070	55,483	53,446	46,738	41,223	5,390	7,304	8,229	8,722	7,315	6,414
Agriculture	461	536	666	562	514	468	104	118	135	129	104	86
Art	1,691	1,545	1,602	1,569	1,262	1,119	157	166	128	154	128	94
Biography	1,891	1,953	2,250	2,193	1,957	1,890	126	216	173	190	144	115
Business	1,185	1,518	1,647	1,569	1,191	1,298	74	196	154	194	152	134
Education	1,011	1,085	1,113	1,054	1,039	973	133	211	276	239	233	234
Fiction..........	2,835	5,105	5,564	5,941	5,764	4,199	71	171	291	287	119	166
General works	1,643	2,905	2,475	2,332	1,760	1,684	132	329	382	372	322	266
History	2,220	2,327	3,260	2,563	2,243	2,107	296	395	482	509	376	329
Home economics	879	1,228	1,057	949	758	721	40	41	39	36	31	19
Juvenile.	2,859	3,801	4,954	5,413	5,172	4,555	58	92	109	104	101	103
Language	529	632	628	586	649	521	134	216	201	206	182	202
Law	1,102	1,349	1,343	1,096	896	967	112	170	225	191	156	138
Literature..........	1,686	1,964	2,272	2,298	2,049	1,903	183	267	295	330	275	242
Medicine	3,292	3,579	3,900	3,447	3,014	2,710	671	598	757	779	712	588
Music	357	364	329	375	289	275	35	70	66	74	78	52
Philosophy, psychology .	1,429	1,559	1,955	2,058	1,683	1,611	218	267	331	275	348	284
Poetry and drama	1,179	1,166	1,270	1,128	874	821	120	220	180	224	147	119
Religion	2,055	2,564	2,746	2,586	2,285	2,059	94	173	163	162	173	176
Science...........	3,109	3,304	3,743	3,288	2,742	2,427	1,069	1,242	1,302	1,396	1,187	1,030
Sociology, economics ..	7,152	7,441	8,247	7,971	7,042	5,508	1,050	1,559	1,736	1,825	1,575	1,368
Sports, recreation	971	1,154	1,099	1,077	973	893	85	107	97	97	94	75
Technology	2,337	2,526	2,694	2,690	2,092	2,089	373	419	651	897	638	546
Travel	504	465	669	701	495	425	55	61	56	52	39	48

[1] Increase is due largely to a major improvement in the recording of paperbound books.

Source: R. R. Bowker Co., New York, NY, *Publishers Weekly*. (Copyright by Reed Publishing.)

No. 387. Average (Mean) Retail Prices—Books, 1980 to 1990 and Periodicals, 1980 to 1991

[See headnote, table 386. For definition of mean, see Guide to Tabular Presentation]

SUBJECT	BOOKS (per vol.)				SUBJECT	PERIODICALS [3]			
	1980	1985	1989	1990, prel.		1980	1985	1990	1991
Hardcover [1]	24.64	31.46	40.61	39.91	**Total. ....**	34.54	59.70	93.45	104.36
Agriculture	27.55	36.77	51.17	52.88	Agriculture	15.24	26.05	42.43	42.36
Art.................	27.70	35.15	50.30	41.17	Business and economics.....	25.42	44.41	63.25	70.87
Biography...........	19.77	22.20	27.34	27.50	Chemistry and physics	137.45	238.43	412.66	472.84
Business............	22.45	28.84	37.94	45.18	Children's periodicals	7.85	13.31	17.51	18.38
Education	17.01	27.28	37.62	38.39	Education...............	23.45	37.81	56.33	62.43
Fiction.............	12.46	15.29	18.69	20.02	Engineering	49.15	84.38	138.84	160.13
General reference	29.84	37.91	49.73	55.07	Fine and applied arts	18.67	27.03	36.89	38.61
History	22.78	27.02	37.95	35.60	History.................	15.77	25.55	35.51	38.35
Home economics......	13.31	17.50	22.17	24.35	Home economics..........	24.63	41.04	64.49	74.11
Juvenile	8.16	9.95	13.01	13.08	Industrial arts	20.70	35.09	54.69	60.96
Language	22.16	28.68	47.35	38.43	Journalism, communications ..	27.34	46.08	60.85	62.81
Law	33.25	41.70	58.62	55.09	Labor and industrial relations ..	18.84	34.75	52.74	57.59
Literature...........	18.70	24.53	32.74	35.01	Law...................	23.00	35.15	50.32	53.30
Medicine.	34.28	44.36	69.87	67.46					
Music..............	21.79	28.79	41.73	41.30	Library and information science.	23.25	40.66	57.34	62.73
Philosophy, psychology ..	21.70	28.11	36.55	39.65	Literature and languages.....	15.30	24.18	30.63	32.99
Poetry and drama......	17.85	22.14	31.12	30.87	Mathmatics, botany, geology,				
Religion	17.61	19.13	28.12	31.27	and general science	67.54	116.93	188.19	209.55
Science	37.45	55.19	68.90	71.48	Medicine	73.37	137.92	217.87	249.94
Sociology, economics ...	31.76	33.33	41.26	41.25	Philosophy and religion......	14.73	24.30	30.76	32.91
Sports, recreation......	15.92	23.43	29.42	30.08	Physical education and				
Technology..........	33.64	50.37	71.04	75.78	recreation	13.83	23.72	32.20	34.64
Travel	16.80	24.66	31.37	29.87	Political science.	19.30	32.72	49.67	52.81
					Psychology.............	41.95	76.34	125.31	135.40
Paperbacks:					Sociology and anthropology..	27.56	50.87	77.61	88.69
Mass market [2]	(NA)	3.63	4.32	4.47	Zoology	44.58	90.75	153.78	172.56
Trade or other	8.60	13.98	17.16	16.62	General interest periodicals ...	19.87	26.41	31.24	32.25

NA Not available. [1] Excludes publications of the United States and other governmental units, books sold only by subscription, and dissertations. [2] "Pocket-sized" books sold primarily through magazine and news outlets, supermarkets, variety stores, etc. [3] Average annual subscription prices.

Source: R. R. Bowker Co., New York, NY. Books, *Publishers Weekly*, March 1990; *Bowker Annual: Library and Book Trade Almanac*; Periodicals, *Library Journal*, April 15, 1990, and earlier issues. (Copyright by Reed Publishing.)

No. 388. Phonograph Records and Other Recording Media—Manufacturers' Shipments and Value: 1975 to 1991

[Domestic shipments based on reports of manufacturers representing more than 85 percent of the market. Domestic value data based on list prices of records and other media. Minus sign (-) indicates returns greater than shipments]

TYPE OF MEDIA	UNIT SHIPMENTS [1] (mil.)					MANUFACTUERS' VALUE (mil. dol.)				
	1975	1980	1985	1990	1991	1975	1980	1985	1990	1991
Total	531.8	683.7	652.9	865.7	801.0	2,378.3	3,862.4	4,387.8	7,541.1	7,834.2
Phonograph records . . .	421.0	487.1	287.7	39.3	26.8	1,696.5	2,559.6	1,561.5	180.9	93.3
Long-playing albums [2] .	257.0	322.8	167.0	11.7	4.8	1,485.0	2,290.3	1,280.5	86.5	29.4
Singles	164.0	164.3	120.7	27.6	22.0	211.5	269.3	281.0	94.4	63.9
Pre-recorded	110.8	196.6	342.6	529.6	429.1	681.8	1,302.8	2,436.8	3,730.3	3,250.0
8-track cartridges	94.6	86.4	3.5	-		583.0	526.4	25.3	(X)	(X)
Cassettes	16.2	110.2	339.1	442.2	360.1	98.8	776.4	2,411.5	3,472.4	3,019.6
Cassette singles	(X)	(X)	(X)	87.4	69.0	(X)	(X)	(X)	257.9	230.4
Compact disks (CD's) . . .	(X)	(X)	22.6	286.5	333.3	(X)	(X)	389.5	3,451.6	4,337.7
CD singles	(X)	(X)	(X)	1.1	5.7	(X)	(X)	(X)	6.0	35.1
Music video	(X)	(X)	(X)	9.2	6.1	(X)	(X)	(X)	172.3	118.1

- Rounds to zero.   X Not applicable.   [1] Units net after returns.   [2] Includes extended play albums.
Source: Recording Industry Association of America, Inc., Washington, DC, *Inside the Recording Industry: A Statistical Overview: 1991*, and earlier issues.

No. 389. Household Camera and Video Equipment Use, by Selected Characteristic: 1985 and 1988

[**As of January, except as indicated.** Based on surveys and subject to sampling error; for details, see source]

CHARACTERISTIC	TOTAL HOUSE-HOLDS [1] (1,000)		PERCENT OWNING—						PERCENT USING VIDEO TRANSFER SERVICE [2]	
			Camera		Video equipment					
					Video cassette recorder		Video camera/ camcorder			
	1985	1988	1985	1988	1985	1988	1985	1988	1985	1988
Total	85,407	89,479	85.1	91.9	20.9	66.5	2.2	7.2	1.2	5.5
Age of householder:										
Under 25 years old	2,985	4,255	93.0	95.1	18.2	66.9	-	3.6	-	4.9
25 to 34 years old	17,841	24,698	92.3	95.5	24.7	74.5	3.4	7.9	0.8	4.8
35 to 44 years old	17,638	20,056	94.5	96.0	34.2	81.0	4.2	10.2	2.7	7.1
45 to 54 years old	14,042	13,569	90.7	94.5	23.7	69.8	1.0	9.3	1.0	7.9
55 years old and over	32,901	26,900	74.2	83.5	10.5	45.3	1.2	3.9	0.8	3.7
Educational attainment of householder:										
Some high school or less	11,329	6,249	72.5	81.2	6.6	46.0	1.1	3.2	1.2	2.4
High school graduate	33,240	27,466	83.0	90.2	17.8	58.6	1.2	6.8	0.4	4.0
Some college.	18,384	25,978	90.4	93.1	24.0	69.4	3.0	5.9	1.8	4.8
College graduate or more.	22,454	29,787	90.0	94.8	29.6	75.4	3.9	9.8	1.5	8.0
Household income:										
Under $10,000	14,178	14,373	65.6	79.7	6.7	30.8	-	1.8	1.0	1.9
$10,000 to $19,999	15,467	17,705	82.9	90.1	7.0	50.5	0.4	0.9	-	3.2
$20,000 to $29,999	13,635	16,634	87.1	94.1	17.9	72.5	0.5	5.6	0.5	5.4
$30,000 to $44,999	18,723	19,223	93.5	95.8	38.0	78.4	4.7	10.0	1.4	5.9
$45,000 or more.	23,404	21,544	89.2	96.1	26.1	85.9	3.8	14.6	2.3	9.4

- Represents or rounds to zero.   [1] As of March the prior year.   [2] Anytime during the prior year.
Source: Photo Marketing Association International, Jackson, MI, *Consumer Photographic Survey, 1985* and *1988*, (copyright).

No. 390. Household Participation in Lawn and Garden Activities—Summary: 1985 to 1990

[Based on national sample survey conducted by the Gallup Organization. For the 1989 survey, a total of 2,053 households were personally interviewed at home. For composition of regions, see table 25. Subject to sampling variability; see source]

ACTIVITY	1985	1987	1988	1989	1990	CHARACTERISTIC OF RESPONDENT	1990, PERCENT DISTRIBUTION	
							House-holds	Sales
Number of households (mil.). .	87.9	89.5	91.1	92.8	93.3	Total	100	100
Percent of households engaged in—						18 to 29 years old	21	17
Lawn care	64	59	58	57	66	30 to 49 years old	42	48
Indoor houseplants	42	41	41	37	43	50 years old and over	37	35
Flower gardening	41	43	42	41	48			
Vegetable gardening	37	33	34	32	37	Northeast.	22	23
Shrub care.	30	33	34	29	38	Midwest.	26	24
Insect control	27	30	32	29	39	South	32	31
Landscaping.	23	24	22	22	31	West.	20	22
Tree care.	20	25	23	23	31			
Flower bulbs	19	27	24	23	31	City.	23	20
Fruit trees	17	18	16	14	19	Suburb	34	36
Raising transplants [1]	11	15	11	11	15	Small town.	11	9
Growing berries	7	9	8	7	9	Rural.	32	34
Ornamental gardening	7	8	6	5	7			
Herb gardening.	(NA)	7	5	7	9			
Container gardening	(NA)	12	11	11	15			
Total retail sales (mil. dol.). . .	12,026	17,491	15,518	16,285	20,802			

NA Not available.   [1] Starting plants in advance of planting in ground.
Source: The National Gardening Association, Burlington, VT, *National Gardening Survey*, annual, (copyright).

No. 391. Sport Fishing and Hunting Licenses—Number and Cost: 1970 to 1990

[In millions, except as indicated. For fiscal years ending in year shown; see text, section 9. See also *Historical Statistics, Colonial Times to 1970,*series H 875-876]

ITEM	1970	1975	1980	1983	1984	1985	1986	1987	1988	1989	1990
Fishing licenses: Sales.	**31.1**	**34.7**	**35.2**	**37.8**	**36.1**	**35.7**	**35.9**	**36.5**	**36.8**	**36.6**	**36.9**
Resident	26.8	30.0	30.1	32.5	31.0	30.5	30.4	31.0	31.3	31.0	31.0
Nonresident	4.3	4.7	5.1	5.3	5.1	5.2	5.4	5.6	5.5	5.6	5.9
Paid license holders [1]	24.4	27.5	28.0	29.1	29.0	29.7	30.4	30.3	31.4	30.3	30.7
Cost to anglers (mil. dol.) . . .	91	142	196	244	260	282	302	315	330	341	363
Hunting licenses: Sales	**22.2**	**25.9**	**27.0**	**28.9**	**28.5**	**27.7**	**27.9**	**28.8**	**30.0**	**29.3**	**29.7**
Resident	21.0	24.7	25.6	27.2	26.8	26.1	26.3	27.1	27.7	27.3	27.5
Nonresident	1.2	1.3	1.4	1.7	1.7	1.6	1.7	1.7	2.0	2.0	2.2
Paid license holders [1]	15.4	16.6	16.3	16.4	16.0	15.9	15.8	15.8	15.9	15.9	15.8
Cost to hunters (mil. dol). . . .	102	155	222	277	292	301	323	345	381	400	422
Federal duck stamps sold (1,000)	**2,072**	**2,222**	**2,090**	**1,926**	**1,868**	**1,914**	**1,780**	**1,794**	**1,663**	**1,395**	**1,406**

[1] Resident and nonresident. Includes multiple counting of license holders who bought nonresident licenses as well as a home State license. "Licenses" includes licenses, tags, permits and stamps.

Source: U.S. Fish and Wildlife Service, *Federal Aid in Fish and Wildlife Restoration,* annual.

No. 392. Household Pet Ownership: 1983 and 1987

[Based on a sample survey of 40,000 households in 1987 and 20,000 in 1983; for details, see source]

ITEM	Unit	DOG		CAT		PET BIRD		HORSE	
		1983	1987	1983	1987	1983	1987	1983	1987
Households owning companion pets [1]	Million . .	36.1	34.7	24.2	27.7	4.2	5.2	2.4	2.6
Percent of all households	Percent .	42.5	38.2	28.4	30.5	5.0	5.7	2.8	2.8
Average number owned.	Number .	1.5	1.5	2.2	2.0	2.5	2.5	3.0	2.6
Total companion pet population [1]	Million . .	55.6	52.4	52.2	54.6	10.4	12.9	7.0	6.6
Households obtaining veterinary care [2] . . .	Percent .	74	78	47	60	8	8	43	47
Average visits per year	Number .	1.8	2.4	1.0	1.6	0.1	0.2	1.4	1.9
Average annual cost	Dollars . .	66.87	82.86	36.83	54.26	(NA)	4.47	(NA)	120.75
Total expenditures.	Mil. dol. .	2,564	3,012	955	1,573	(NA)	26	180	330
PERCENT DISTRIBUTION OF HOUSEHOLDS OWNING PETS									
Annual household income: Under $10,000 .	Percent .	19	14	20	14	21	17	16	14
$10,000 to $19,999	Percent .	53	19	53	20	54	20	53	22
$20,000 to $29,999	Percent .	([3])	18	([3])	19	([3])	18	([3])	20
$30,000 to $44,999	Percent .	28	23	27	22	25	21	31	21
$45,000 and over	Percent .	([4])	26	([4])	25	([4])	24	([4])	23
Family size: [1] One person	Percent .	12	13	15	16	13	14	8	10
Two persons	Percent .	30	30	30	30	24	24	26	27
Three persons	Percent .	22	23	20	21	20	20	24	23
Four or more persons	Percent .	36	34	35	33	43	42	42	40

NA Not available. [1] As of December for 1987; as of May for 1983. [2] During 1987 for 1987; for 1983, between May 1982-83. [3] Income range for 1983—$10,000 to $29,999. [4] Income range for 1983—over $30,000.

Source: American Veterinary Medical Association, Schaumburg, IL, *The Veterinary Services Market for Companion Animals,* July 1983 and *August 1988,* (copyright).

No. 393. Boy Scouts and Girl Scouts—Membership and Units: 1970 to 1990

[In thousands. Boy Scouts as of Dec. 31; Girl Scouts as of Sept. 30. Current age requirements for each category are in parentheses. Includes Puerto Rico and outlying areas]

ITEM	1970	1975	1980	1982	1983	1984	1985	1986	1987	1988	1989	1990
BOY SCOUTS OF AMERICA												
Membership	**6,287**	**5,318**	**4,318**	**4,542**	**4,689**	**4,755**	**4,845**	**5,171**	**5,347**	**5,364**	**5,356**	**5,446**
Boys	4,683	3,933	3,207	3,425	3,567	3,657	3,755	4,037	4,180	4,228	4,247	4,293
Tiger cubs (6 yr. old)	(X)	(X)	(X)	84	124	145	169	260	291	314	332	346
Cub Scouts (7 to 10 yr. old)	2,438	1,997	1,696	1,609	1,569	1,493	1,499	1,714	1,819	1,834	1,824	1,832
Boy Scouts (11 to 17 yr. old)	1,916	1,503	1,064	1,126	1,116	1,078	1,063	1,042	1,032	1,025	1,008	1,018
Explorers (14 to 20 yr. old) [1]	329	434	447	606	758	941	1,024	1,021	1,037	1,055	1,083	1,097
Adults	1,604	1,385	1,110	1,117	1,122	1,098	1,090	1,134	1,168	1,136	1,109	1,153
Total units (packs, troops, posts)	157	150	129	132	134	135	134	132	131	131	130	131
GIRL SCOUTS OF THE U.S.A.												
Membership	**3,922**	**3,234**	**2,784**	**2,819**	**2,888**	**2,871**	**2,802**	**2,917**	**2,947**	**3,052**	**3,166**	**3,269**
Girls [2]	3,248	2,723	2,250	2,247	2,281	2,247	2,172	2,248	2,274	2,345	2,415	2,480
Daisies (5 to 6 yr. old).	(X)	(X)	(X)	(X)	(X)	(X)	61	114	137	162	175	186
Brownies (6 to 8 yr. old)	1,259	1,160	1,115	1,120	1,163	1,172	1,128	1,166	1,167	1,243	1,276	1,288
Juniors (8 to 11 yr. old)	1,509	1,188	894	874	847	801	735	725	705	739	759	786
Cadettes (11 to 14 yr. old).	395	301	172	169	176	170	151	143	132	144	150	163
Seniors (14 to 17 yr. old)	85	74	46	41	40	40	40	41	38	43	42	44
Adults	674	511	534	572	607	624	630	669	673	707	751	788
Total units (troops, groups)	164	159	154	160	165	166	166	174	180	189	196	202

X Not applicable. [1] Both girls and boys are members. [2] Beginning 1980, also includes girls without age-level program information, not shown separately.

Source: Boy Scouts of America, National Council, Irving, TX, *Annual Report;* and Girl Scouts of the United States of America, New York, NY, *Annual Report.*

No. 394. Selected Spectator Sports: 1980 to 1990

[See also *Historical Statistics, Colonial Times to 1970,* series H 865-870 and H 872]

SPORT	Unit	1980	1983	1984	1985	1986	1987	1988	1989	1990
Baseball, major leagues: [1]										
Attendance.	1,000 . .	43,746	46,269	45,262	47,742	48,452	53,182	53,800	55,910	55,509
Regular season	1,000 . .	43,014	45,540	44,742	46,824	47,506	52,011	52,999	55,173	54,824
National League	1,000 . .	21,124	21,549	20,781	22,292	22,333	24,734	24,499	25,324	24,492
American League.	1,000 . .	21,890	23,991	23,961	24,532	25,173	27,277	28,500	29,849	30,332
Playoffs.	1,000 . .	407	425	248	591	624	784	541	514	476
World Series	1,000 . .	325	304	272	327	322	387	260	223	209
Players' salaries: [2]										
Average	$1,000 .	144	289	329	371	413	412	439	497	598
Basketball: [3] [4]										
Men's:										
College:										
Teams.	Number.	1,258	1,266	1,260	1,266	1,265	1,270	1,277	1,264	1,313
Attendance.	1,000 . .	30,692	31,471	31,684	32,057	31,645	31,911	32,504	33,020	33,660
Women's:										
College:										
Teams.	Number.	(NA)	1,114	1,147	1,166	1,188	1,188	1,190	1,190	1,195
Attendance.	1,000 . .	(NA)	2,502	2,870	2,944	3,020	3,121	3,301	3,577	3,898
Pro: [5]										
Teams	Number.	22	23	23	23	23	23	23	25	27
Attendance, total [6]	1,000 . .	10,697	10,262	11,128	11,534	12,210	13,190	14,070	16,586	18,586
Regular season	1,000 . .	9,938	9,638	10,015	10,506	11,215	12,065	12,654	15,465	17,369
Average per game	Number.	11,017	10,220	10,620	11,141	11,893	12,765	13,419	15,088	15,690
Playoffs	1,000 . .	740	606	1,096	985	979	1,091	1,397	1,077	1,203
Players' salaries:										
Average.	$1,000 .	170	249	275	325	375	440	510	603	817
Football:										
College: [4]										
Teams	Number.	642	651	654	661	666	667	673	673	673
Attendance	1,000 . .	35,541	36,302	36,652	36,312	36,388	36,463	35,581	36,406	36,627
National Football League: [7]										
Teams	Number.	28	28	28	28	28	28	28	28	28
Attendance, total [8]	1,000 . .	14,092	13,953	14,053	14,058	17,304	[9]15,180	17,024	17,400	17,666
Regular season	1,000 . .	13,392	13,277	13,398	13,345	13,588	[9]11,406	13,539	13,626	13,960
Average per game	Number.	59,787	59,273	59,813	59,567	60,663	[9]54,315	60,446	60,829	62,321
Postseason games [10]	1,000 . .	700	676	655	711	734	656	658	686	848
Players' salaries: [11]										
Average	$1,000 .	79	134	177	194	198	204	239	300	350
Median base salary	$1,000 .	70	90	110	140	150	175	180	200	236
National Hockey league: [12]										
Regular season attendance . . .	1,000 . .	10,534	11,021	11,359	11,633	11,621	12,116	12,418	12,423	12,578
Playoffs attendance	1,000 . .	977	1,008	1,107	1,109	1,152	1,336	1,323	1,322	1,356
Players' salaries: [13]										
Average	$1,000 .	108	130	145	150	158	172	188	210	254
Horseracing: [14] [15]										
Racing days	Number.	13,133	13,545	13,683	13,745	13,853	14,208	14,285	14,240	13,841
Attendance.	1,000 . .	74,690	75,693	74,076	73,346	70,580	70,105	69,949	69,551	63,803
Pari-mutuel turnover	Mil. dol .	11,218	11,733	12,032	12,222	12,421	13,122	13,616	13,867	7,162
Revenue to government	Mil. dol .	713	639	650	625	587	608	596	585	611
Greyhound: [14]										
Total performances	Number.	5,855	8,257	8,661	9,590	10,654	11,156	12,904	13,393	14,915
Attendance.	1,000 . .	20,874	22,140	22,076	23,853	25,759	26,215	26,477	33,818	28,660
Pari-mutuel turnover	Mil. dol .	2,064	2,306	2,421	2,702	3,005	3,193	3,291	3,278	3,388
Revenue to government	Mil. dol .	152	170	177	201	215	221	230	239	235
Jai alai: [14]										
Total performances	Number.	1,616	2,795	2,721	2,736	2,761	2,906	3,615	3,835	3,620
Games played.	Number.	25,349	44,425	42,842	32,260	36,276	38,476	47,716	(NA)	(NA)
Attendance	1,000 . .	3,939	4,829	4,878	4,722	6,757	6,816	6,414	5,227	5,329
Pari-mutuel turnover	Mil. dol .	(NA)	619.8	665.9	664.0	667.6	707.5	663.6	553.0	545.5
Revenue to government	Mil. dol .	35	45	48	50	50	51	44	39	39
Professional rodeo: [16]										
Rodeos	Number.	631	650	643	617	616	637	707	741	754
Performances	Number.	1,921	1,964	1,936	1,887	1,868	1,832	2,037	2,128	2,159
Members	Number.	5,114	5,353	5,324	5,239	5,603	5,342	5,479	5,560	5,693
Permit-holders (rookies)	Number.	4,038	2,929	2,911	2,534	2,700	2,746	3,310	3,584	3,290

NA Not available. [1] Source: The National League of Professional Baseball Clubs, New York, NY, *National League Green Book,* and The American League of Professional Baseball Clubs, New York, NY, *American League Red Book.* [2] Source: Major League Baseball Players Association, New York, NY. [3] Season ending in year shown. [4] Source: National Collegiate Athletic Assn., Overland Park, KS. For women's attendance total, excludes double-headers with men's teams. [5] Source: National Basketball Assn., New York, NY. [6] Includes All-Star game, not shown separately. [7] Source: National Football League, New York, NY. [8] Beginning 1986, includes preseason attendance, not shown separately. [9] Season was interrupted by a strike. [10] Includes Pro Bowl, a non-championship game and Super Bowl. [11] Source: National Football League Players Association, Washington, DC. [12] Source: National Hockey League, Montreal, Quebec. [13] Source: National Hockey League Players Association, Toronto, Canada. [14] Source: Association of Racing Commissioners International, Inc., Lexington, KY. [15] Includes thoroughbred, harness, quarter horse, and fairs. [16] Source: Professional Rodeo Cowboys Association, Colorado Springs, CO, *Official Professional Rodeo Media Guide,* annual, (copyright).

Source: Compiled from sources listed in footnotes.

No. 395. Selected Recreational Activities: 1970 to 1990

[See also *Historical Statistics, Colonial Times to 1970*, series H 862-864, H 871, H 874, and H 877]

ACTIVITY	Unit	1970	1975	1980	1985	1986	1987	1988	1989	1990
Softball, amateur: [1]										
Total participants [2]	Million. .	16	26	30	41	41	41	41	41	41
Youth participants	1,000 . .	255	450	650	712	717	720	722	900	1,000
Adult teams [3]	1,000 . .	29	66	110	152	172	178	182	188	199
Youth teams [3]	1,000 . .	2	9	18	31	35	38	40	46	251
Golfers (one round or more) [4] [5]	1,000 . .	11,245	13,036	15,112	17,520	19,900	21,200	23,000	24,200	27,800
Golf rounds played [5]	1,000 . .	266,169	308,562	357,701	414,777	419,000	431,000	484,000	469,000	502,000
Golf facilities	Number.	10,188	11,370	12,005	12,346	12,384	12,407	12,582	12,658	12,846
Classification:										
Private	Number.	4,619	4,770	4,839	4,861	4,885	4,898	4,897	4,862	4,810
Daily fee	Number.	4,248	5,014	5,372	5,573	5,587	5,583	5,748	5,833	6,024
Municipal	Number.	1,321	1,586	1,794	1,912	1,912	1,926	1,937	1,963	2,012
Tennis: [6]										
Players	1,000 . .	10,655	[7][8]29,201	(NA)	[9]18,951	[9]18,017	[9]16,911	[9]17,314	[9]18,844	[9]18,401
Courts	1,000 . .	(NA)	130	(NA)	220	220	220	220	220	220
Indoor	1,000 . .	(NA)	8	(NA)	14	14	14	14	14	14
Tenpin bowling:										
Participants, total [10]	Million. .	51.8	62.5	72.0	67.0	67.0	68.0	68.0	71.0	71.0
Male	Million. .	24.8	29.9	34.0	32.0	32.0	33.1	33.1	35.4	35.4
Female	Million. .	27.0	32.6	38.0	35.0	35.0	34.9	34.9	35.6	35.6
Establishments [11]	Number.	9,140	8,577	8,591	8,275	8,149	8,031	7,923	7,671	7,544
Lanes [11]	1,000 . .	141	141	154	155	153	151	150	147	146
Membership, total [11] [12]	1,000 . .	7,733	8,751	9,595	8,064	7,839	7,421	7,167	6,570	6,357
American Bowling Congress	1,000 . .	4,210	4,300	4,688	3,657	3,625	3,424	3,313	3,036	2,922
Women's Bowling Congress	1,000 . .	2,988	3,692	4,118	3,714	3,551	3,351	3,189	2,859	2,742
Young American Bowling Alliance [13]	1,000 . .	535	759	789	693	663	646	665	675	693
Motion picture theaters [14] [15]	1,000 . .	14	15	18	21	23	24	23	23	24
Four-wall	1,000 . .	10	11	14	18	20	21	22	22	23
Drive-in	1,000 . .	4	4	4	3	3	3	2	1	1
Receipts, box office	Mil. dol.	1,225	2,115	2,749	3,749	3,778	4,253	4,458	5,033	5,022
Admission, average price . .	Dollars .	1.55	2.05	2.69	3.55	3.71	3.91	4.11	4.45	4.75
Attendance	Million. .	921	1,033	1,022	1,056	1,017	1,089	1,085	1,133	1,058
Bicycles: [16]										
Domestic shipments	Million. .	5.0	5.6	6.9	5.8	5.3	5.2	4.5	5.3	6.0
Imports	Million. .	1.9	1.7	2.0	5.6	7.0	7.4	5.4	5.4	4.8
Boating: [17]										
Recreational boats owned .	Million. .	8.8	9.7	11.8	13.8	14.3	14.5	15.1	15.6	16.0
Outboard boats	Million. .	5.2	5.7	6.8	7.4	7.6	7.5	7.7	7.9	7.9
Inboard boats	Million. .	0.6	0.8	1.2	1.4	1.5	1.7	1.8	2.0	2.1
Sailboats	Million. .	0.6	0.8	1.0	1.2	1.2	1.2	1.3	1.3	1.3
Canoes	Million. .	2.4	2.4	1.3	1.8	1.9	2.0	2.1	2.2	2.3
Rowboats and other	Million. .	([18])	([18])	1.5	1.8	1.9	2.1	2.2	2.1	2.2
Expenditures, total [19]	Bil. dol .	3.4	4.8	7.4	13.3	14.5	16.5	17.9	17.1	13.7
Outboard motors in use . . .	1,000 . .	7,215	7,649	8,241	9,733	10,081	10,469	10,860	11,225	11,524
Motors sold	1,000 . .	430	435	315	392	410	444	460	430	352
Value, retail	Mil. dol .	281	411	554	1,319	1,464	1,726	1,828	1,764	1,546
Outboard boats sold	1,000 . .	276	328	290	305	314	342	355	291	227
Value, retail	Mil. dol .	177	263	408	759	835	1,001	1,225	1,134	978
Inboard/outdrive boats sold	1,000 . .	43	70	56	115	120	144	148	133	97
Value, retail	Mil. dol .	182	420	616	1,663	1,861	2,450	2,585	2,354	1,794
All terrain vehicles:										
Vehicles in use or owned [20]	1,000 . .	(NA)	(NA)	(NA)	2,000	2,300	2,475	2,517	2,309	2,240
Imports [21]	1,000 . .	(NA)	(NA)	(NA)	683	498	317	209	121	100

NA Not available. [1] Source: Amateur Softball Association, Oklahoma City, OK. [2] Amateur Softball Association teams and other amateur softball teams. [3] Amateur Softball Association teams only. [4] Source: National Golf Foundation, Jupiter, FL. [5] Beginning 1986, based on persons 12 years of age and over; prior years, for persons 5 years of age and over. [6] Source: U.S. Tennis Association, Princeton, NJ. [7] Survey by A. C. Nielsen Co. [8] 1976 data. [9] Based on National Sporting Goods Association Sports Participation Survey. [10] For season ending in year shown. Persons 5 years old and over. Source: National Bowling Council, Washington, DC. [11] Source: American Bowling Congress, Greendale, WI. Season ending in year shown. [12] Membership totals are for U.S., Canada and for U.S. military personnel worldwide. [13] Prior to 1985, represents American Jr. Bowling Congress and ABC/WIBC Collegiate Division. [14] Source: Motion Picture Association of America, Inc., New York, NY. [15] Prior to 1975, figures represent theaters; thereafter, screens. [16] Source: Bicycle Manufacturers Association of America, Inc., Washington, DC. [17] Source: National Marine Manufacturers Association, Chicago, IL. [18] Included in canoes. [19] Represents estimated expenditures for new and used boats, motors, accessories, safety equipment, fuel, insurance, docking, maintenance, storage, repairs, and other expenses. [20] Source: Specialty Vehicle Institute of America, Irvine, CA. [21] Source: Motorcycle Industry Council, Inc., Irvine, CA.

Source: Compiled from sources listed in footnotes.

No. 396. Participation in Sports Activities, by Selected Characteristics: 1990

[In thousands, except rank. For persons 7 years of age or older. Except as indicated, a participant plays a sport more than once in the year. Based on a sampling of 10,000 households]

ACTIVITY	ALL PERSONS Number	Rank	SEX Male	Female	AGE 7-11 yrs.	12-17 yrs.	18-24 yrs.	25-34 yrs.	35-44 yrs.	45-54 yrs.	55-64 yrs.	65 yrs. and over	HOUSEHOLD INCOME (dol) Under 15,000	15,000- 24,999	25,000- 34,999	35,000- 49,999	Over 50,000
Total	**224,648**	**(X)**	**109,059**	**115,588**	**18,243**	**20,042**	**26,141**	**43,950**	**37,912**	**25,477**	**21,343**	**31,540**	**53,047**	**38,439**	**33,332**	**44,188**	**55,640**
Number participated in:																	
Aerobic exercising [1]	23,252	10	3,717	19,535	708	1,874	4,588	7,903	4,284	1,816	1,225	855	3,772	3,390	3,516	4,594	7,980
Backpacking/wilderness camping [1]	10,809	24	6,634	4,175	1,123	1,241	1,643	3,426	1,949	772	532	122	2,198	1,693	1,788	2,192	2,939
Baseball	15,576	17	12,603	2,974	4,805	4,588	2,463	1,984	1,289	305	41	101	3,033	2,062	2,648	3,140	4,694
Basketball	26,315	8	18,898	7,417	4,860	8,289	4,488	5,525	2,463	439	173	76	4,597	3,844	4,030	5,648	8,195
Bicycle riding [1]	55,245	3	28,152	27,093	11,843	9,020	6,416	11,239	7,632	3,767	2,868	2,460	10,469	8,546	8,869	11,492	15,869
Bowling	40,117	6	20,919	19,198	4,180	5,026	7,217	10,214	6,524	3,260	1,834	1,861	7,057	6,401	6,864	8,760	11,034
Calisthenics [1]	13,185	19	6,176	7,009	1,210	2,140	1,828	3,722	1,751	933	733	868	2,795	1,572	2,098	2,633	4,086
Camping (vacation/overnight) [1]	46,177	4	24,391	21,787	6,707	5,480	5,399	11,104	8,911	3,987	2,778	1,810	8,506	7,872	7,724	9,773	12,302
Exercise walking [1]	71,431	1	25,146	46,286	2,334	3,385	6,592	14,721	14,317	10,344	8,977	10,761	15,964	11,656	10,743	14,231	18,837
Exercising with equipment [1]	35,329	7	18,620	16,708	556	3,250	6,526	10,454	6,871	3,312	2,297	2,063	5,728	4,430	5,212	7,408	12,551
Fishing—fresh water	41,495	5	27,719	13,776	5,000	4,372	5,229	9,775	7,165	4,359	2,850	2,745	9,390	7,372	7,144	8,717	8,872
Fishing—salt water	12,281	21	8,807	3,474	528	1,332	1,668	2,794	2,290	1,377	1,214	1,080	2,549	2,151	1,424	2,149	4,007
Football	14,451	18	12,441	2,010	2,822	5,101	3,239	2,251	692	271	42	33	3,044	2,251	2,271	2,933	3,953
Golf	22,959	12	17,275	5,684	638	1,579	2,918	6,071	4,607	2,669	2,165	2,313	2,140	2,764	2,919	5,448	9,688
Hiking	22,042	13	11,443	10,598	2,289	1,895	2,254	5,751	4,743	2,300	1,609	1,201	4,466	3,610	3,164	4,731	6,069
Hunting with firearms	18,512	15	16,169	2,343	422	2,133	2,959	5,195	3,445	2,074	1,398	886	3,801	3,610	3,041	4,342	3,718
Racquetball	8,070	25	5,955	2,115	231	627	2,346	3,033	1,214	503	65	50	1,260	1,423	760	1,753	2,874
Running/jogging [1]	23,817	9	13,060	10,756	2,747	4,576	4,497	6,147	3,747	1,091	611	400	4,700	3,116	3,309	5,025	7,666
Skiing—alpine/downhill	11,354	22	6,665	4,689	611	2,053	2,713	3,098	1,805	1,752	275	47	801	1,187	1,286	2,170	5,910
Skiing—cross country	5,134	26	2,637	2,496	306	500	563	1,336	1,089	640	593	105	446	504	824	1,011	2,349
Soccer	10,920	23	7,015	3,905	4,661	3,745	1,059	885	419	123	23	-	1,573	1,323	1,931	2,494	3,600
Softball	20,076	14	11,535	8,541	3,333	3,869	3,521	5,982	2,598	436	298	40	3,614	3,326	3,267	3,712	6,158
Swimming [1]	67,469	2	31,543	35,925	10,989	10,579	9,947	13,985	9,949	4,952	3,663	3,406	11,951	10,053	10,411	14,686	20,367
Target shooting	12,825	20	10,134	2,691	716	1,591	2,565	3,617	2,483	1,049	602	203	2,152	2,443	2,253	3,153	2,824
Tennis	18,401	16	10,317	8,084	1,324	3,680	4,012	4,760	2,408	1,161	763	292	2,184	2,243	2,711	3,271	7,992
Volleyball	23,195	11	11,182	12,014	1,830	5,717	4,804	6,594	3,150	795	223	83	4,551	3,395	3,474	4,846	6,929

- Represents or rounds to zero. X Not applicable. [1] Participant engaged in activity at least six times in the year.

Source: National Sporting Goods Association, Mt. Prospect, IL, *Sports Participation in 1990: Series I,* (copyright).

No. 397. Sporting Goods Sales, by Product Category: 1980 to 1991

[**In millions of dollars, except percent.** Based on a sample survey of consumer purchases of 80,000 households, except recreational transport, which was provided by industry associations. Excludes Alaska and Hawaii]

SELECTED PRODUCT CATEGORY	1980	1982	1983	1984	1985	1986	1987	1988	1989	1990	1991, proj.
Sales, all products	16,691	18,684	23,111	26,401	27,446	30,614	33,942	42,093	45,184	44,140	45,056
Annual percent change [1] . .	-1.4	5.8	23.7	14.2	4.0	11.5	10.9	24.0	7.3	-2.3	2.1
Percent of retail sales . , . .	1.7	1.7	2.0	2.1	2.0	2.1	2.2	2.5	2.6	2.4	(NA)
Athletic and sport clothing [2] . .	3,127	3,014	3,226	3,432	3,376	3,931	4,645	10,736	11,557	11,382	11,871
Athletic and sport footwear [3] .	1,731	1,900	2,189	2,381	2,610	3,199	3,524	3,772	5,763	6,437	6,803
Walking shoes	(NA)	(NA)	(NA)	(NA)	263	368	512	752	1,237	1,509	1,690
Gym shoes, sneakers	465	659	639	669	656	642	693	783	1,125	1,177	1,212
Jogging and running shoes. . .	397	421	557	591	572	476	475	460	515	645	677
Tennis shoes	359	287	340	371	470	448	367	353	508	582	599
Aerobic shoes	(NA)	10	29	54	178	333	401	327	425	389	373
Basketball shoes	86	81	119	159	185	187	169	226	293	428	462
Golf shoes.	68	99	115	110	109	120	130	128	129	157	170
Athletic and sport equipment [3]	6,487	7,114	7,925	8,317	8,922	9,477	9,900	10,705	11,503	12,073	12,534
Firearms and hunting.	1,351	1,567	1,666	1,620	1,699	1,675	1,804	1,894	2,139	2,295	2,364
Exercise equipment.	(NA)	723	960	1,055	1,216	1,206	1,191	1,452	1,748	1,797	1,833
Golf	386	493	633	630	730	828	946	1,111	1,167	1,204	1,252
Camping	646	735	790	699	724	833	858	945	996	1,072	1,136
Bicycles (10-12-15-18+ speed)	(NA)	656	761	765	975	1,089	930	819	906	1,092	1,147
Fishing tackle.	539	586	606	616	681	773	830	766	769	813	837
Snow skiing	379	332	386	502	593	622	661	710	606	606	613
Tennis	237	277	293	315	273	260	238	264	315	291	294
Archery.	149	168	179	212	212	214	224	235	261	265	275
Baseball and softball.	158	154	173	153	176	180	173	174	206	217	225
Water skis	123	106	133	146	125	132	148	160	96	88	88
Bowling accessories	107	103	106	108	106	114	129	129	143	155	160
Recreational transport	5,345	6,656	9,771	12,271	12,539	14,007	15,873	16,880	16,360	14,248	13,848
Pleasure boats	2,718	3,684	4,612	6,209	6,753	7,372	8,906	9,637	9,319	7,524	7,524
Recreational vehicles	1,178	1,701	3,368	4,082	3,515	3,940	4,507	4,839	4,481	4,007	3,486
Bicycles and supplies	1,233	1,148	1,638	1,840	2,109	2,518	2,272	2,131	2,259	2,423	2,544
Snowmobiles	216	123	153	140	162	177	188	273	301	294	294

NA Not available.   [1] Represents change from immediate prior year.   [2] Category expanded in 1988; not comparable with earlier years.   [3] Includes other products not shown separately.

Source: National Sporting Goods Association, Mt. Prospect, IL, *The Sporting Goods Market in 1991*, and prior issues, (copyright).

No. 398. Consumer Purchases of Sporting Goods, by Consumer Characteristics: 1990

[**In percent.** Based on sample survey of consumer purchases of 80,000 households. Excludes Alaska and Hawaii]

CHARACTERISTIC	Total house-holds	FOOTWEAR				EQUIPMENT					
		Aero-bic shoes	Gym shoes/ sneak-ers	Jog-ging/ run-ning shoes	Walk-ing shoes	Bicy-cles	Camp-ing equip-ment	Exer-cise equip-ment	Rifles	Shot-guns	Golf equip-ment
Total.	100.0	100.0	100.0	100.0	100.0	100.0	100.0	100.0	100.0	100.0	100.0
Age of user:											
Under 14 years old	20.3	6.9	37.3	9.0	1.8	20.1	11.0	1.0	1.3	3.3	2.0
14 to 17 years old.	5.4	5.6	13.7	7.2	1.8	8.0	5.0	2.0	4.0	2.2	3.0
18 to 24 years old.	10.7	10.2	7.8	8.1	2.7	11.2	9.0	5.0	10.2	6.8	6.0
25 to 34 years old.	17.7	26.9	15.1	23.6	11.2	20.6	26.0	23.0	31.4	30.2	22.0
35 to 44 years old.	14.7	24.2	10.3	26.6	18.9	17.3	23.0	26.0	26.8	29.8	21.0
45 to 64 years old.	18.7	19.3	11.7	20.0	36.5	10.1	14.0	28.0	22.0	25.7	31.0
65 years old and over	12.5	6.9	4.1	5.5	27.1	1.3	2.0	7.0	4.3	2.0	12.0
Multiple ages	-	-	-	-	-	11.4	10.0	8.0	-	-	4.0
Sex of user:											
Male.	48.8	15.1	51.6	59.9	49.7	56.1	64.0	45.0	97.3	96.4	83.0
Female.	51.2	84.9	48.4	40.1	50.3	31.9	24.0	45.0	2.7	3.6	13.0
Both sexes	-	-	-	-	-	12.0	13.0	9.0	-	-	4.0
Education of household head:											
Less than high school	12.7	7.5	9.8	6.5	4.2	4.6	7.0	7.0	8.5	8.7	3.0
High school	30.5	25.7	29.5	21.1	20.3	17.7	26.0	22.0	26.3	36.0	16.0
Some college.	27.2	28.0	28.1	29.7	32.4	32.6	33.0	32.0	44.0	29.4	27.0
College graduate	29.6	38.8	32.6	42.7	43.1	45.1	35.0	39.0	21.2	25.9	54.0
Annual household income:											
Under $15,000	24.9	12.4	15.1	10.6	13.4	9.0	13.0	9.0	14.8	11.9	4.0
$15,000 to $24,999.	18.2	15.2	16.7	14.2	8.8	13.2	16.0	10.0	12.8	14.9	9.0
$25,000 to $34,999.	16.1	17.7	16.4	16.6	11.7	17.4	17.0	14.0	14.8	16.4	16.0
$35,000 to $49,999.	18.8	24.3	22.0	23.8	23.5	23.4	24.0	23.0	27.4	30.6	21.0
$50,000 and over	22.0	30.4	29.8	34.8	42.6	37.0	30.0	45.0	30.2	26.2	50.0

- Represents or rounds to zero.   [1] 10-12-15-18+ speed.

Source: National Sporting Goods Association, Mt. Prospect, IL, *The Sporting Goods Market in 1991*, and prior issues, (copyright).

No. 399. Performing Arts—Selected Data: 1970 to 1989

[Receipts and expenditures in millions of dollars. For season ending in year shown, except as indicated]

ITEM	1970	1975	1980	1982	1983	1984	1985	1986	1987	1988	1989
Legitimate theater: [1]											
Broadway shows:											
New productions	62	59	67	53	50	36	31	33	40	31	29
Playing weeks [2][3]	1,047	1,101	1,541	1,461	1,259	1,119	1,062	1,049	1,031	1,114	1,097
Number of tickets sold (1,000)	(NA)	(NA)	9,380	10,694	8,102	7,898	7,156	6,527	6,968	8,142	7,968
Gross box office receipts....	53.3	57.4	143.4	221.2	263.1	226.5	208.0	190.6	207.2	253.4	262.0
Road shows:											
Playing weeks [3]	1,024	799	1,351	1,317	990	1,057	993	983	901	893	869
Gross box office receipts....	48.0	50.9	181.2	249.5	184.3	206.2	225.9	235.6	224.2	222.9	255.5
Nonprofit professional theatres: [4]											
Comapnies reporting	(NA)	39	147	123	189	230	217	201	188	189	192
Gross income	(NA)	34.5	113.6	142.5	186.0	226.6	234.7	263.8	271.2	276.4	349.0
Earned income	(NA)	21.8	67.3	89.5	117.2	145.7	146.1	160.8	165.2	167.0	224.6
Contributed income	(NA)	12.7	46.3	53.0	68.8	80.9	88.6	103.0	106.0	109.4	124.4
Gross expenses	(NA)	34.3	113.6	144.3	189.0	230.3	239.3	263.3	272.8	277.9	349.2
Productions	(NA)	398	1,852	2,081	2,616	3,434	2,710	2,944	2,427	2,369	2,469
Performances	(NA)	11,952	42,109	36,727	47,195	56,735	52,341	57,727	46,768	46,149	53,263
Total attendence (mil.)	(NA)	5.4	14.2	13.1	13.7	15.5	14.2	14.8	14.6	13.9	18.7
Opera companies [5]	648	807	986	993	1,031	1,051	1,123	1,176	1,224	1,250	1,285
Major [6]	35	54	109	133	144	154	168	170	174	187	209
Expenditures	36.5	(NA)	133.6	191.1	212.4	236.7	256.5	270.3	321.1	352.3	403.8
Other companies	266	335	458	416	488	491	576	602	658	654	658
Workshops [7]	347	418	419	444	399	406	379	404	392	409	418
Opera performances	4,779	6,428	9,391	9,510	10,693	10,421	10,642	11,080	11,794	12,361	15,098
Operas performed...	341	387	497	571	590	576	578	660	622	658	731
Musical performances [8]	(NA)	(NA)	1,397	2,233	2,749	2,787	4,983	6,993	7,759	8,836	9,825
Musicals performed [8]	(NA)	(NA)	104	122	120	129	242	301	278	296	279
World premieres	17	16	79	94	96	101	121	116	129	141	165
Attendance (mil.)	4.6	8.0	10.7	10.1	12.7	13.0	14.1	14.4	16.4	17.7	21.4
Symphony orchestras [9]	1,441	1,463	1,572	1,572	1,572	1,572	1,572	1,572	1,572	1,572	1,666
College [10]	298	300	385	385	386	380	371	371	365	350	422
Community [11]	1,019	1,003	926	919	920	937	946	927	936	903	924
Urban	24	41	85	94	101	89	89	93	92	103	103
Metropolitan	72	90	115	110	98	96	96	107	102	123	121
Regional	([12])	([12])	29	34	37	40	40	43	45	57	59
Major	28	29	32	30	30	30	30	31	32	36	37
Concerts	6,599	14,171	22,229	19,204	19,167	19,086	19,969	20,272	20,059	17,774	(NA)
Attendance (mil.)	12.7	18.3	22.6	22.0	22.0	23.2	23.7	25.4	25.1	23.6	(NA)
Gross income	73.3	124.5	246.3	325.5	348.9	379.0	435.4	480.5	523.6	561.8	(NA)
Earned income	43.1	70.9	141.2	187.6	201.8	220.2	250.7	282.4	305.9	332.9	(NA)
Contributed income	30.2	53.6	105.1	137.9	147.1	158.8	184.7	198.1	217.7	228.9	(NA)
Gross expenses	76.4	129.5	252.1	315.3	352.2	389.8	441.8	491.2	525.4	571.3	612.9

NA Not available.   [1] Source: *Variety*, New York, NY, various June issues (copyright).   [2] All shows (new productions and holdovers from previous seasons).   [3] Eight performances constitute one playing week.   [4] Source: Theatre Communications Group, New York, NY. For years ending on or prior to Aug.30.   [5] Source: Central Opera Service, New York, NY, *Central Opera Service Bulletin*, periodic.   [6] Companies with budgets of over $100,000 and issue American Guild of Musical Artists (AGMA) contracts to soloists.   [7] Workshops are primarily college and university opera groups.   [8] Covers not-for-profit companies only.   [9] Source: American Symphony Orchestra League, Inc., Washington, DC. For years ending Aug. 31. Orchestras other than college groups are principally defined by their annual budgets: For 1987 and 1988, community, under $135,000; urban, $135,000-$280,000; metropolitan, $280,000-$1,000,000; regional, $1,000,000-$3,600,000; and major, over $3,600,000. Prior to 1987, other budget classifications were in effect.   [10] Includes youth orchestras.   [11] Beginning 1980, includes youth and chamber groups with budgets under $70,000.   [12] Classification began in 1976.

Source: Compiled from sources listed in footnotes.

No. 400. Financial Support of the Arts by Private Corporate Business—Summary: 1984 to 1988

[In millions of dollars]

TYPE OF ART CATEGORY	1984	1985	1988	TYPE OF ART CATEGORY	1984	1985	1988
Direct cash support	**482.4**	**559.0**	**634.0**	Historic and cultural preservation projects	9.7	11.3	(NA)
Museums	104.5	133.2	101.4	Libraries	4.8	8.8	14.4
Symphony orchestra	66.8	79.8	101.4	Commercial TV and radio, cultural			
Performing arts and cultural facilities	52.0	60.4	31.7	programming	6.5	5.6	(NA)
Theaters	67.2	49.5	76.1	Public TV and radio, general support	16.5	4.5	25.4
Art funds—general support	28.5	37.9	(NA)	Crafts	2.3	1.8	(NA)
Other music	25.3	30.2	44.4	Artist-in-residence programs	1.1	1.0	(NA)
Dance	20.7	25.4	50.7	Poetry and writing	1.4	1.0	(NA)
Public TV and radio, program				Video projects (non-commercial)	0.2	0.2	(NA)
underwriting	17.9	23.6	25.4	Folk art	-	-	(NA)
Opera	24.8	22.7	50.7	Other (excluding commercial			
Films (non-commercial)	15.7	13.2	(NA)	activities)	12.7	38.0	63.4
Arts-in-education programs	3.8	11.8	19.0				

- Represents or rounds to zero.   NA Not available.

Source: Business Committee for the Arts, New York, NY, press release.

No. 401. Arts and Humanities—Selected Federal Aid Programs: 1970 to 1990

[In millions of dollars, except as indicated. For fiscal years ending in year shown, see text, section 9]

TYPE OF FUND AND PROGRAM	1970	1975	1980	1984	1985	1986	1987	1988	1989	1990
National Endowment for the Arts:										
Funds available [1]	15.7	86.9	188.1	169.9	171.7	167.1	170.9	171.1	166.7	170.8
Program appropriation	6.3	67.3	97.0	119.0	118.7	115.7	120.8	122.2	123.5	124.3
Matching funds [2]	2.0	7.5	42.9	27.4	29.5	30.0	29.3	32.9	23.6	32.4
Grants awarded (number)	556	3,071	5,505	5,056	4,801	4,484	4,542	4,628	4,604	4,475
Funds obligated	12.9	81.7	166.4	147.4	149.4	146.6	151.4	156.3	148.3	157.6
Music	2.5	14.9	13.6	15.2	15.3	14.6	15.1	15.3	15.3	16.5
State programs	1.9	14.7	22.1	24.6	24.4	23.8	24.6	24.9	25.5	26.1
Museums	(NA)	10.8	11.2	12.5	11.9	11.5	11.5	12.6	12.7	12.1
Theater	2.8	6.4	8.4	10.7	10.6	10.2	10.8	10.7	10.7	10.6
Dance	1.7	6.1	8.0	9.1	9.0	9.0	9.1	9.2	9.5	9.6
Media arts	0.2	5.4	8.4	9.5	9.9	12.3	12.9	12.4	12.7	13.9
Challenge [3]	(X)	(X)	50.8	18.8	20.7	20.7	20.8	24.8	15.4	19.7
Visual arts	1.0	3.2	7.3	6.6	6.2	5.7	6.2	6.0	6.1	5.9
Other	2.8	20.1	36.6	40.6	41.3	38.8	40.4	40.4	40.2	43.1
National Endowment for the Humanities:										
Funds available [1]	13.0	86.0	186.2	127.3	125.6	121.1	128.4	125.2	137.1	141.0
Program appropriation	6.1	67.3	100.3	97.8	95.2	[4]91.9	[4]95.8	96.7	108.3	114.2
Matching funds [2]	2.0	6.5	38.4	29.5	30.4	27.3	28.5	28.5	28.7	26.3
Grants awarded (number)	542	1,330	2,917	2,523	2,241	2,297	2,888	2,113	2,285	2,195
Funds obligated	10.5	73.1	185.5	127.6	125.7	121.1	128.4	125.2	137.1	141.0
Education programs	4.2	17.1	18.3	19.3	17.9	14.8	16.4	16.6	16.5	16.3
State programs	(X)	(X)	26.0	26.0	24.4	24.4	25.0	25.3	29.0	29.6
Research grants	2.0	13.4	32.0	24.1	24.4	21.0	21.7	21.9	22.1	22.5
Fellowship program	1.7	10.9	18.0	15.0	15.3	14.4	15.3	15.3	15.3	15.3
Challenge [3]	(X)	(X)	53.5	18.3	19.6	16.2	16.5	16.5	16.7	14.6
General programs	(X)	(X)	(X)	24.3	24.1	24.7	25.4	24.9	25.1	25.4
Preservation [5]	(X)	(X)	(X)	(X)	(X)	4.1	4.1	4.7	12.3	17.5
National Capital Arts and Cultural Affairs Program	(X)	(X)	(X)	(X)	(X)	1.9	4.0	(X)	(X)	(X)
Other	2.6	31.8	37.7	0.7	(X)	(X)	(X)	(X)	(X)	(X)

NA Not available. X Not applicable. [1] Includes other funds, not shown separately. Excludes administrative funds. Gifts are included through 1980; excluded thereafter. [2] Represents Federal funds appropriated only upon receipt or certification by Endowment of matching non-Federal gifts. [3] Program designed to stimulate new sources and higher levels of giving to institutions for the purpose of guaranteeing long-term stability and financial independence. Program requires a match of at least 3 private dollars to each Federal dollar. Funds for challenge grants are not allocated by program area because they are awarded on a grant-by-grant basis. [4] Excludes National Capital Arts and Cultural Affairs Program. [5] Program designed to support projects which preserve and guarantee access to print and nonprint media in danger of disintegration or deterioration.
Source: U.S. National Endowment for the Arts, *Annual Report;* and U.S. National Endowment for the Humanities, *Annual Report.*

No. 402. State Legislative Appropriations for State Arts Agencies: 1988 to 1991

[In thousands of dollars, except as indicated. For fiscal years ending in year shown. Fiscal years for most States ended June 30; see text, section 9]

STATE OR AREA	1988	1989	1990	1991 Total	1991 Per capita [1] (dol.)	STATE OR AREA	1988	1989	1990	1991 Total	1991 Per capita [1] (dol.)
Total	242,842	270,652	292,304	273,823	1.08	NE.	608	868	1,025	1,048	0.66
						NV.	270	269	353	359	0.30
AL.	1,319	1,476	1,949	1,579	0.39	NH.	451	474	497	519	0.47
AK.	1,275	1,692	1,217	1,432	2.60	NJ	20,101	22,760	19,722	11,703	1.51
AZ.	1,323	1,545	[2]2,570	[2]2,068	0.56	NM.	706	710	906	1,119	0.74
AR.	1,016	1,021	1,016	973	0.41	NY	53,564	53,529	59,484	50,981	2.83
CA.	13,677	15,682	16,795	16,958	0.57	NC.	4,505	4,996	4,978	[6]5,428	0.82
CO.	1,041	1,108	1,308	1,536	0.47	ND.	222	214	263	274	0.43
CT.	2,000	2,119	2,148	2,197	0.67	OH.	9,591	9,980	12,075	12,130	1.12
DE.	686	785	1,207	1,313	1.97	OK.	1,679	2,670	3,377	3,195	1.02
DC.	3,544	3,544	2,537	3,200	5.27	OR.	1,293	1,431	1,359	1,537	0.54
FL.	17,340	24,179	23,635	23,386	1.81	PA	9,780	12,753	12,814	11,704	0.99
GA.	3,024	3,248	3,413	3,338	0.52	RI	1,070	1,440	1,383	1,010	1.01
HI	3,902	6,747	8,777	12,065	10.89	SC	2,801	3,159	3,534	3,633	1.04
ID	198	339	434	665	0.66	SD.	330	338	348	405	0.58
IL.	7,581	7,509	10,705	10,348	0.91	TN	1,523	3,506	3,783	4,299	0.88
IN	1,969	1,970	2,317	2,812	0.51	TX	3,383	2,680	3,437	3,386	0.20
IA	[3]729	[4]825	[5]1,442	[5]1,249	0.45	UT	1,518	1,603	2,869	4,284	2.49
KS	583	1,072	1,238	1,072	0.43	VT	350	457	509	479	0.85
KY	2,032	2,368	2,387	3,302	0.90	VA	3,017	3,771	5,392	4,016	0.65
LA	931	996	909	936	0.22	WA	1,704	2,063	2,232	2,396	0.49
ME.	515	636	702	755	0.61	WV	1,811	[7]1,133	[7]1,675	[7]2,384	1.33
MD.	5,157	5,971	6,332	7,442	1.56	WI	1,276	[8]1,725	2,254	2,422	0.50
MA.	21,148	19,539	17,685	12,624	2.10	WY	203	206	235	351	0.77
MI	12,611	12,466	12,233	9,152	0.98	Am. Samoa . .	30	-	-	48	1.02
MN.	3,030	3,184	4,208	4,213	0.96	Guam.	339	561	458	620	4.65
MS.	421	496	497	514	0.20	No. Marianas .	60	101	115	114	2.63
MO	4,660	4,913	5,008	4,480	0.88	PR	8,111	11,013	13,549	13,335	3.79
MT.	730	726	781	780	0.98	VI	104	85	231	257	2.52

- Represents zero. [1] Based on enumerated resident population as of April 1, 1990. [2] Includes $1,000,000 to be generated by the Arizona Arts Trust Fund. [3] Includes $250,000 one-time appropriation. [4] Includes $140,000 one-time lottery funds. [5] Includes $220,000 lottery funds. [6] Includes $522,000 one-time appropriation. [7] Excludes administrative expenses. [8] Includes $250,000 one-time Governor's Award.
Source: National Assembly of State Arts Agencies, Washington, DC, unpublished data.

No. 403. Travel by U.S. Residents, by Selected Trip Characteristics: 1985 to 1990

[In millions. See headnote, table 404]

CHARACTERISTIC	TRIPS					PERSON TRIPS [1]				
	1985	1987	1988	1989	1990	1985	1987	1988	1989	1990
Total..............	558.4	636.3	656.1	664.3	661.1	1,077.6	1,191.1	1,232.5	1,260.1	1,274.5
Purpose:										
Visit friends and relatives	206.8	210.5	213.8	231.4	246.0	430.8	437.1	425.8	476.5	523.3
Other pleasure	177.6	234.4	241.5	225.9	214.5	376.0	464.6	502.1	469.3	447.5
Business or convention	133.3	157.5	155.6	169.7	155.6	185.2	206.2	211.7	232.0	209.5
Other	40.7	33.9	45.2	37.3	45.0	85.6	83.2	92.9	82.3	94.2
Mode of transport:										
Auto, truck, recreation vehicle ..	376.1	433.7	472.6	479.8	483.9	797.7	889.4	952.2	982.7	1,011.3
Airplane................	140.5	160.7	154.6	154.6	144.9	217.3	239.9	238.6	234.3	214.5
Other	41.8	41.9	28.9	29.9	32.3	62.6	61.8	41.7	43.1	48.7
Vacation trip.............	339.8	366.2	396.2	416.7	422.3	728.7	775.2	830.9	878.3	883.9
Weekend trip..............	224.0	274.4	271.7	282.4	280.0	470.1	559.4	560.0	582.1	580.2

[1] A count of times each person (child or adult) goes on a trip.

Source: U.S. Travel Data Center, Washington, DC, *National Travel Survey*, annual, (copyright).

No. 404. Characteristics of Business Trips and Pleasure Trips: 1980 to 1990

[Represents trips to places 100 miles or more from home by one or more household members traveling together. Based on a monthly telephone survey of 1,500 U.S. adults. For details, see source]

CHARACTERISTIC	Unit	BUSINESS TRIPS				PLEASURE TRIPS			
		1980	1985	1989	1990	1980	1985	1989	1990
Total trips...........................	Millions .	97.1	133.3	169.7	155.6	342.8	384.4	457.3	460.5
Average household members on trip	Number .	1.5	1.4	1.4	1.4	2.2	2.1	2.0	2.1
Average nights per trip [1].................	Nights ..	(NA)	3.6	3.2	3.7	(NA)	5.6	4.4	4.4
Average miles per trip [2].................	Miles....	(NA)	1,180	1,090	1,020	(NA)	1,010	950	867
Traveled primarily by auto/truck/RV [3]									
rental car........................	Percent .	56	51	57	58	80	73	76	77
Traveled primarily by air	Percent .	42	44	39	37	16	21	19	18
Used a rental car while on trip	Percent .	25	20	16	14	7	6	7	7
Stayed in a hotel while on trip	Percent .	66	62	65	71	34	39	38	37
Used a travel agent	Percent .	21	28	20	21	10	13	12	12
Also a vacation trip..................	Percent .	10	13	17	17	75	80	81	82
Male travelers	Percent .	(NA)	67	72	71	(NA)	48	49	49
Female travelers	Percent .	(NA)	33	28	29	(NA)	52	51	51
Household income:									
Less than $40,000..................	Percent .	(NA)	58	44	42	(NA)	73	65	63
$40,000 or more...................	Percent .	(NA)	42	56	56	(NA)	27	35	38

NA Not available. [1] Includes no overnight stays. [2] U.S. only. [3] Recreational vehicle.

Source: U.S. Travel Data Center, Washington, DC, *National Travel Survey*, annual, (copyright).

No. 405. Domestic Travel Expenditures, by State: 1989

[Represents U.S. spending on domestic overnight trips and day trips of 100 miles or more away from home. Excludes spending by foreign visitors and by U.S. residents in U.S. territories and abroad]

STATE	Total (mil. dol.)	Share of total (percent)	Rank	STATE	Total (mil. dol.)	Share of total (percent)	Rank	STATE	Total (mil. dol.)	Share of total (percent)	Rank
U.S. total .	272,027	100.0	(X)	KS	2,176	0.8	34	ND	702	0.3	49
				KY	2,901	1.1	30	OH	7,253	2.7	10
AL	3,150	1.2	27	LA	4,161	1.5	22	OK	2,362	0.9	32
AK	1,000	0.4	45	ME	1,357	0.5	40	OR	3,141	1.2	28
AZ	4,370	1.6	20	MD	4,273	1.6	21	PA	8,664	3.2	8
AR	2,065	0.8	36	MA	6,252	2.3	14	RI	621	0.2	51
CA	38,241	14.1	1	MI	6,427	2.4	12	SC	3,937	1.4	23
CO	4,844	1.8	18	MN	3,587	1.3	25	SD	679	0.2	50
CT	3,022	1.1	29	MS	1,821	0.7	38	TN	5,530	2.0	15
DE	748	0.3	48	MO	5,393	2.0	17	TX	15,543	5.7	4
DC	2,714	1.0	31	MT	1,179	0.4	42	UT	2,117	0.8	35
FL	21,437	0.0	2	NE	1,509	0.6	39	VT	889	0.3	47
GA	7,054	2.6	11	NV	9,753	3.6	6	VA	7,827	2.9	9
HI	5,492	2.0	16	NH	1,120	0.4	44	WA	4,451	1.6	19
ID	1,179	0.4	41	NJ	8,974	3.3	7	WV	1,161	0.4	43
IL	10,865	4.0	5	NM	2,007	0.7	37	WI	3,647	1.3	24
IN	3,493	1.3	26	NY	18,301	6.7	3	WY	990	0.4	46
IA	2,341	0.9	33	NC	6,306	2.3	13				

X Not applicable.

Source: U.S. Travel Data Center, Washington, DC, *Impact of Travel on State Economies, 1989*, (copyright).

No. 406. Business Receipts and Employment of Selected Travel Industry Sectors: 1975 to 1990

| | BUSINESS RECEIPTS (mil. dol.) | | | | | | | EMPLOYMENT (1,000) | | | | | |
| YEAR | Travel indus- try, total | Transportation [1] | | | Motel, hotel | Eating and drink- ing places | Amuse- ment and recre- ation ser- vices | Travel indus- try, total | Transportation | | Eating and drink- ing places | Hotels, motels, and tourist courts | Amuse- ment and recre- ation serv- ices |
		Air [2]	Bus	Rail [3]					Intercity highway pas- sengers	Air			
1975	94,549	10,301	1,172	247	13,002	51,067	18,760	5,228.5	39.9	362.8	3,379.5	849.5	596.8
1980	163,015	23,405	1,709	382	26,832	90,058	20,629	6,918.3	37.9	453.4	4,625.8	1,037.7	763.5
1981	180,774	25,598	1,809	429	31,572	98,118	23,248	7,102.2	38.1	454.6	4,749.5	1,076.4	783.6
1982	189,433	25,488	1,854	436	32,749	104,593	24,313	7,205.6	38.8	443.6	4,831.2	1,092.8	799.2
1983	205,228	27,519	1,965	481	35,897	113,281	26,085	7,481.3	35.5	455.2	5,041.8	1,131.1	817.7
1984	221,931	31,437	2,035	524	38,917	121,321	27,697	7,938.7	37.3	488.5	5,388.0	1,221.3	803.6
1985	235,437	33,343	1,989	563	41,837	127,949	29,756	8,396.4	34.9	522.0	5,709.2	1,289.9	840.4
1986	251,213	33,846	1,890	592	43,300	139,415	32,170	8,717.6	33.2	566.7	5,916.2	1,337.6	863.9
1987	276,157	37,555	1,826	639	48,200	153,461	34,476	9,058.7	30.1	603.3	6,105.8	1,427.0	892.5
1988	301,817	41,963	2,036	738	52,400	166,860	37,820	9,377.0	29.0	644.3	6,281.8	1,503.0	918.3
1989	320,348	45,320	2,185	842	58,138	173,894	39,969	9,760.0	30.8	683.9	6,439.0	1,561.3	1,045.1
1990	334,881	45,324	2,000	888	60,490	182,044	44,135	0,027.0	26.1	751.3	6,565.2	1,595.4	1,088.8

[1] Passenger transport service.   [2] U.S. certificated carriers in domestic service.   [3] Covers fiscal years October 1 through September 30.
Source: U.S. Travel Data Center, Washington, DC, *The 1990-91 Economic Review of Travel in America*, (copyright).

No. 407. International Travelers and Expenditures—Summary: 1970 to 1991

[For coverage, see tables 408 and 409. Beginning 1984, receipts, payments, and fares not comparable with previous years. See source for details. Minus sign (-) indicates deficit. See also *Historical Statistics, Colonial Times to 1970*, series H 921, 928, 941, and 945]

| YEAR | TRAVEL AND PASSENGER FARE (mil. dol.) | | | | U.S. net travel and passen- ger payments (mil. dol.) | U.S. travelers abroad [2] (1,000) | Foreign visitors to the U.S. [2] (1,000) |
| | Payments by U.S. travelers | | Receipts from foreign visitors | | | | |
	Total [1]	Expenditures abroad	Total [1]	Travel receipts			
1970	5,195	3,980	2,708	2,331	-2,487	(NA)	12,362
1975	8,680	6,417	5,464	4,697	-3,216	(NA)	15,698
1980	14,004	10,397	12,650	10,588	-1,354	[2]22,365	22,326
1982	17,166	12,394	15,085	12,393	-2,081	[2]23,148	21,667
1983	19,152	13,149	14,044	10,947	-5,108	[2]24,853	21,652
1984	29,183	23,305	21,064	17,050	-8,119	34,388	26,913
1985	31,805	25,155	21,986	17,663	-9,819	35,257	25,417
1986	33,412	26,746	25,730	20,273	-7,682	37,684	26,158
1987	37,433	30,022	30,232	23,366	-7,201	39,996	29,489
1988	41,030	33,098	37,706	28,935	-3,324	41,247	34,238
1989	42,935	34,548	45,547	35,173	2,612	41,643	36,605
1990	47,634	38,671	52,830	40,579	5,196	43,558	39,089
1991, est. . .	48,707	39,418	59,387	45,551	10,680	42,320	42,114

NA Not available.   [1] Includes passenger fares not shown separately.   [2] Mexico visitation data are under-reported.
Source: Travelers and visitors: U.S Travel and Tourism Administration (USTTA), unpublished data. Fares and Payments: Through 1988, U.S. Bureau of Economic Analysis, *Survey of Current Business*, June 1990, and earlier issues; beginning 1989, USTTA, based on data from the Bureau of Economic Analysis.

No. 408. U.S. Travel to Foreign Countries—Travelers and Expenditures: 1984 to 1991

[Travelers in thousands; expenditures in millions of dollars. Covers residents of the United States, its territories and possessions. See source for details. See also *Historical Statistics, Colonial Times to 1970*, series H 921-940]

ITEM AND AREA	1984	1985	1986	1987	1988	1989	1990	1991, est.
Total travelers	34,388	35,257	37,684	39,996	41,247	41,643	43,558	42,320
Canada	11,706	12,100	14,134	13,306	13,341	12,689	12,668	12,540
Mexico	10,992	10,461	11,512	13,074	13,463	14,163	14,900	15,365
Total overseas	11,690	12,696	12,038	13,616	14,443	14,791	15,990	14,415
Europe	5,623	6,780	5,887	6,114	7,438	7,233	8,043	(NA)
Latin America [1]	1,040	977	1,011	1,049	1,184	1,301	1,519	(NA)
Other	5,027	4,939	5,140	6,453	5,821	6,257	6,428	(NA)
Expenditures abroad	23,305	25,155	26,746	30,022	33,098	34,548	38,671	39,418
Canada	2,228	2,503	3,030	2,935	3,228	3,390	3,499	3,681
Mexico	3,358	3,280	3,579	3,975	4,828	5,657	5,999	6,747
Total overseas	17,719	19,372	20,137	23,112	25,042	25,501	29,173	28,990
Europe	7,917	9,382	9,186	10,229	11,313	11,924	14,403	14,270
Latin America [1]	1,759	1,706	1,771	2,178	2,591	2,416	2,411	2,434
Other	8,043	8,284	9,180	10,725	11,138	11,161	12,359	12,286
Fares to foreign carriers	5,878	6,650	6,666	7,411	7,932	8,387	8,963	9,289

NA Not available.   [1] Includes Central and South America.
Source: Travelers: U.S Travel and Tourism Administration (USTTA), unpublished data. Expenditures: Through 1988, U.S. Bureau of Economic Analysis, *Survey of Current Business*, June 1990, and earlier issues; beginning 1989, USTTA, based on data from the Bureau of Economic Analysis.

No. 409. Foreign Travel to the United States—Travelers and Receipts: 1984 to 1991

[**Travelers in thousands; receipts in millions of dollars.** Includes travelers for business and pleasure, foreigners in transit through the United States, and students; excludes travel by foreign government personnel and foreign businessmen employed in the United States. See source for details. See also *Historical Statistics, Colonial Times to 1970*, series H 946-951]

AREA OF ORIGIN	1984	1985	1986	1987	1988	1989	1990	1991
International travelers.	26,913	25,416	26,158	29,489	34,238	36,605	39,089	42,114
Canada	10,982	10,880	10,943	12,418	13,843	15,366	17,262	18,927
Mexico	8,403	6,999	6,355	6,637	7,883	7,240	6,768	7,032
Total overseas	7,528	7,537	8,860	10,434	12,512	13,999	15,059	16,155
Europe.	2,981	2,905	3,722	4,663	5,772	6,251	6,659	7,360
Latin America [1]	1,065	1,068	1,255	1,265	1,363	1,518	1,740	2,019
Other	3,482	3,564	3,883	4,506	5,377	6,230	6,660	6,776
Total receipts.	17,050	17,663	20,273	23,366	28,935	35,173	40,579	45,551
Canada	2,612	2,571	2,689	3,294	3,986	4,852	5,690	6,572
Mexico	1,905	2,013	1,942	2,040	2,652	3,398	4,004	4,572
Total overseas	12,533	13,079	15,642	18,032	22,297	26,923	30,885	34,407
Europe.	4,411	4,772	5,836	7,585	9,762	10,987	12,635	14,347
Latin America [1]	2,236	2,065	2,519	2,504	2,724	3,250	3,856	4,416
Other	5,886	6,242	7,287	7,943	9,811	12,686	14,394	15,644
Fares to U.S. carriers	4,014	4,323	5,457	6,866	8,771	10,374	12,251	13,836

[1] Includes Central and South America.

Source: Travelers: U.S Travel and Tourism Administration (USTTA), unpublished data. Receipts: Through 1988, U.S. Bureau of Economic Analysis, *Survey of Current Business*, June 1990, and earlier issues; beginning 1989, USTTA, based on data from the Bureau of Economic Analysis.

No. 410. Foreign Visitors for Pleasure Admitted, by Country of Last Residence: 1985 to 1990

[**In thousands. For years ending September 30.** See headnote, table 7, section 1]

COUNTRY	1985	1988	1989	1990	COUNTRY	1985	1988	1989	1990
Total [1]	6,609	10,821	12,115	13,418	Africa [2]	101	103	108	105
					Egypt.	16	16	16	16
Europe [2]	2,048	4,459	4,967	5,383	Nigeria	25	15	14	11
Austria	34	85	82	87	Oceania [2]	282	430	497	562
Belgium	39	82	80	95	Australia	195	265	324	380
Denmark.	36	78	86	75	New Zealand.	74	138	144	153
Finland.	24	50	67	83					
France	226	473	497	566	North America	1,664	2,013	2,293	2,463
Greece.	34	42	43	43	Canada	79	84	101	119
Ireland	55	94	91	81	Mexico . . . .·.	773	820	999	1,061
Italy	155	271	276	308	Caribbean [2]	584	824	899	963
Netherlands	82	176	190	214	Bahamas, the	211	310	316	332
Norway.	41	76	81	80	Barbados.	17	28	32	34
Poland	40	43	52	55	Cayman Islands	18	27	28	31
Soviet Union	2	19	38	53	Dominican Republic. . .	57	90	114	137
Spain	64	130	160	183	Haiti	56	63	63	57
Sweden	71	168	207	230	Jamaica.	74	121	134	132
Switzerland	110	227	221	236	Netherlands Antilles. . .	27	24	26	31
United Kingdom	598	1,397	1,790	1,899	Trinidad and Tobago. . .	71	77	82	81
West Germany.	373	942	897	969	Central America [2]	228	285	294	320
					Costa Rica.	41	46	50	62
Asia [2]	1,866	2,985	3,317	3,830	El Salvador	38	40	46	46
China (Mainland China					Guatemala	53	78	86	91
and Taiwan).	83	105	136	187	Panama.	38	46	41	43
Hong Kong	64	84	97	111	South America [2]	606	796	896	1,016
India	52	73	73	75	Argentina	66	98	106	136
Israel	80	119	121	128	Brazil	148	233	272	300
Japan.	1,277	2,247	2,483	2,846	Chile	28	43	57	54
Korea.	26	35	75	120	Colombia	123	119	122	122
Philippines	59	73	69	76	Ecuador	42	46	52	57
Saudi Arabia	31	31	33	33	Peru.	44	63	74	97
Singapore	23	30	30	32	Venezuela.	122	137	162	199

[1] Includes countries unknown or not reported.   [2] Includes countries not shown separately.

Source: U.S. Immigration and Naturalization Service, *Statistical Yearbook*, annual.

Figure 8.1

Congressional Representation in 1990 and Changes Since 1980, by State

(Changes shown in parentheses)

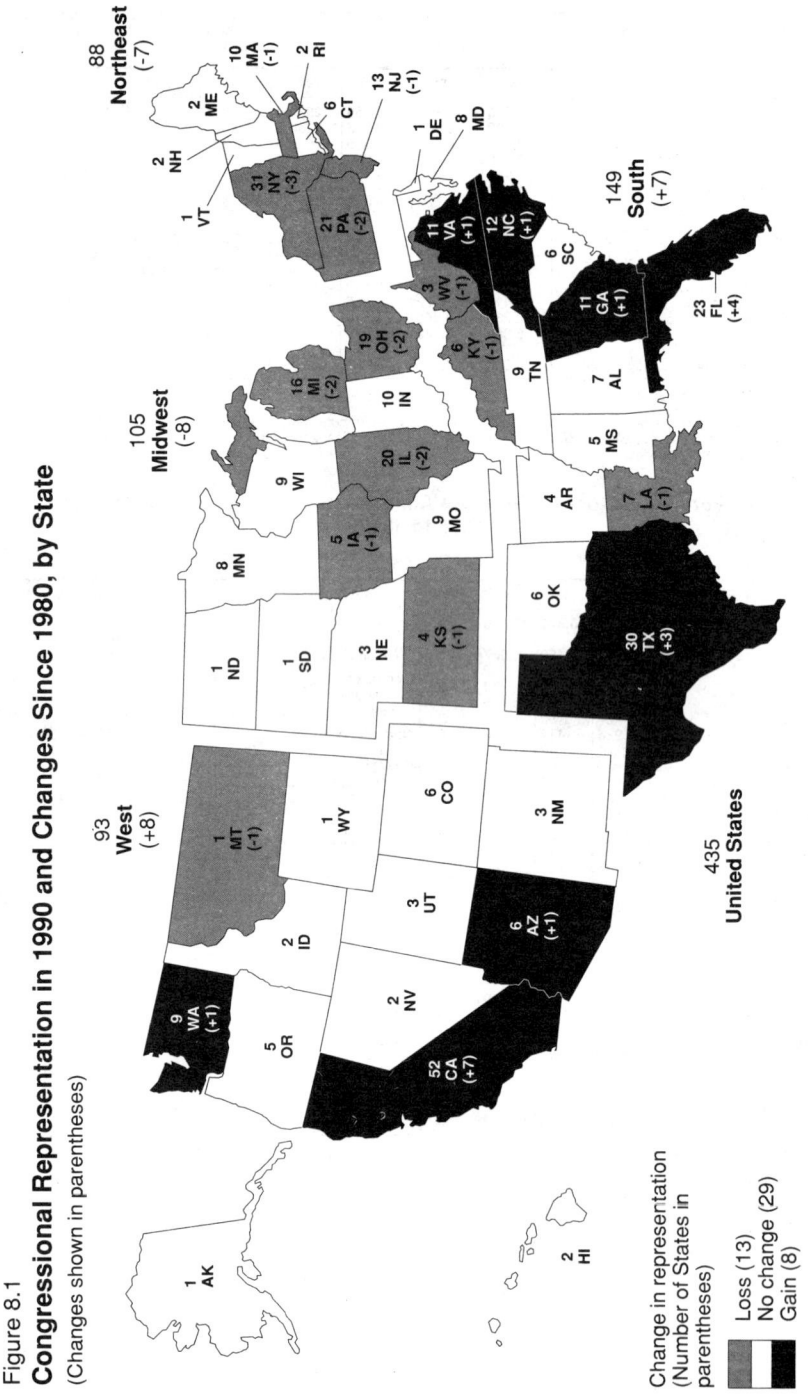

Change in representation
(Number of States in
parentheses)

Loss (13)
No change (29)
Gain (8)

Source: Chart prepared by U.S. Bureau of the Census. For data, see table 417.

Elections

This section relates primarily to Presidential, congressional, and gubernatorial elections. Also presented are summary tables on congressional legislation; State legislatures; Black, Hispanic, and female officeholders; population of voting age; voter participation; and campaign finances.

Official statistics on Federal elections, collected by the Clerk of the House, are published biennially in *Statistics of the Presidential and Congressional Election* and *Statistics of the Congressional Election*. Federal and State elections data appear also in *America Votes*, a biennial volume of the Elections Research Center, Chevy Chase, MD. Federal elections data also appear in the U.S. Congress, *Congressional Directory*, and in official State documents. Data on reported registration and voting for social and economic groups are obtained by the U.S. Bureau of the Census as part of the Current Population Survey (CPS) and are published in *Current Population Reports*, series P-20 (see text, section 1).

Almost all Federal, State, and local governmental units in the United States conduct elections for political offices and other purposes. The conduct of elections is regulated by State laws or, in some cities and counties, by local charter. An exception is that the U.S. Constitution prescribes the basis of representation in Congress and the manner of electing the President, and grants to Congress the right to regulate the times, places, and manner of electing Federal officers. Amendments to the Constitution have prescribed national criteria for voting eligibility. The 15th Amendment, adopted in 1870, gave all citizens the right to vote regardless of race, color, or previous condition of servitude. The 19th Amendment, adopted in 1919, further extended the right to vote to all citizens regardless of sex. The payment of poll taxes as a prerequisite to voting in Federal elections was banned by the 24th Amendment in 1964. In 1971, as a result of the 26th Amendment, eligibility to vote in national elections was extended to all citizens, 18 years old and over.

In Brief

Projected voting-age population in November 1992: 189 million

Persons with grade school education in 1990:

Strong or weak Democrats	*54%*
Strong or weak Republicans	*11%*

Persons with college education in 1990:

Strong or weak Democrats	*34%*
Strong or weak Republicans	*31%*

Presidential election.—The Constitution specifies how the President and Vice President are selected. Each State elects, by popular vote, a group of electors equal in number to its total of members of Congress. The 23d Amendment, adopted in 1961, grants the District of Columbia three presidential electors, a number equal to that of the least populous State. Subsequent to the election, the electors meet in their respective States to vote for President and Vice President. Usually, each elector votes for the candidate receiving the most popular votes in his or her State. A majority vote of all electors is necessary to elect the President and Vice President. If no candidate receives a majority, the House of Representatives, with each State having one vote, is empowered to elect the President and Vice President, again, with a majority of votes required.

The 22d Amendment to the Constitution, adopted in 1951, limits presidential tenure to two elective terms of 4 years each, or to one elective term for any person who, upon succession to the Presidency, has held the office or acted as President for more than 2 years.

Congressional election.—The Constitution provides that Representatives be apportioned among the States according to their population; that a census of population be taken every 10 years as a basis for apportionment; and that each State have at least one Representative. At the time of each apportionment, Congress decides what the total number of

Representatives will be. Since 1912, the total has been 435, except during 1960 to 1962 when it increased to 437, adding one Representative each for Alaska and Hawaii. The total reverted to 435 after reapportionment following the 1960 census. Members are elected for 2-year terms, all terms covering the same period. The District of Columbia, American Samoa, Guam, and the Virgin Islands each elect one nonvoting Delegate and Puerto Rico elects a nonvoting Resident Commissioner.

The Senate is composed of 100 members, two from each State, who are elected to serve for a term of 6 years. One-third of the Senate is elected every 2 years. Senators were originally chosen by the State legislatures. The 17th Amendment to the Constitution, adopted in 1913, prescribed that Senators be elected by popular vote.

Voter eligibility and participation.—The Census Bureau publishes estimates of the population of voting age and the percent casting votes in each State for Presidential and congressional election years. These voting-age estimates include a number of persons who meet the age requirement but are not eligible to vote, (e.g. aliens and some institutionalized persons). In addition, since 1964, voter participation and voter characteristics data have been collected during November of election years as part of the CPS. These survey data include noncitizens in the voting age population estimates, but exclude members of the Armed Forces and the institutional population.

Statistical reliability.—For a discussion of statistical collection and estimation, sampling procedures, and measures of statistical reliability applicable to Census Bureau data, see Appendix III.

Historical statistics.—Tabular headnotes provide cross-references, where applicable, to *Historical Statistics of the United States, Colonial Times to 1970.* See Appendix IV.

Figure 8.2
Popular Vote Cast for President, by Major Party: 1968 to 1988

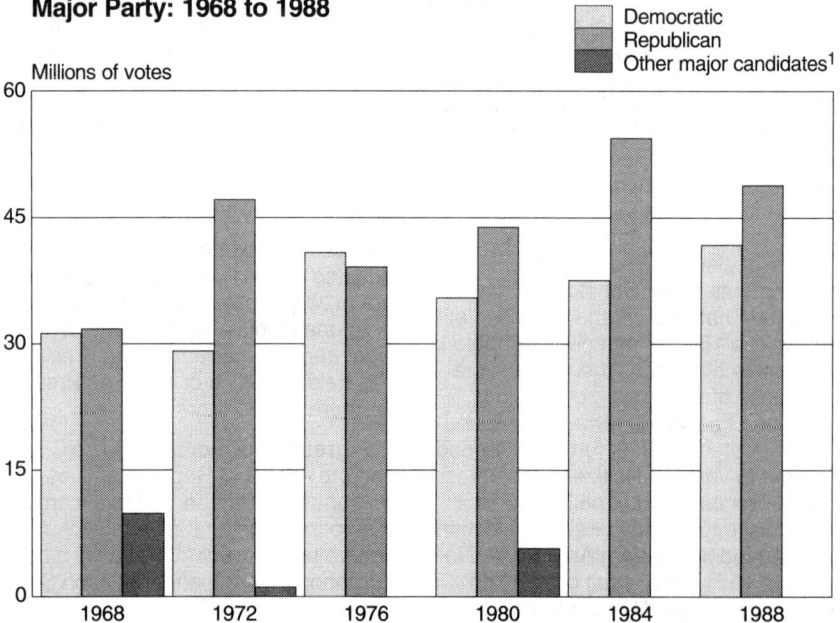

[1]1968–American Independent, George Wallace; 1972–American, John Schmitz; 1980–Independent, John Anderson.
Souurce: Chart prepared by U.S. Bureau of the Census. For data, see tables 411 and 412.

No. 411. Vote Cast for President, by Major Political Party: 1932 to 1988

[Prior to 1960, excludes Alaska and Hawaii; prior to 1964, excludes DC. Vote cast for major party candidates include the votes of minor parties cast for those candidates. See also *Historical Statistics, Colonial Times to 1970*, series Y 79-83 and Y 135]

YEAR	CANDIDATES FOR PRESIDENT		VOTE CAST FOR PRESIDENT						
			Total popular vote [1] (1,000)	Democratic			Republican		
	Democratic	Republican		Popular vote		Elec-toral vote	Popular vote		Elec-toral vote
				Number (1,000)	Per-cent		Number (1,000)	Per-cent	
1932	F. D. Roosevelt. .	Hoover	39,759	22,830	57.4	472	15,761	39.6	59
1936	F. D. Roosevelt. .	Landon	45,655	27,757	60.8	523	16,684	36.5	8
1940	F. D. Roosevelt. .	Willkie	49,900	27,313	54.7	449	22,348	44.8	82
1944	F. D. Roosevelt. .	Dewey.	47,977	25,613	53.4	432	22,018	45.9	99
1948	Truman	Dewey.	48,794	24,179	49.6	303	21,991	45.1	189
1952	Stevenson	Eisenhower.	61,551	27,315	44.4	89	33,936	55.1	442
1956	Stevenson	Eisenhower.	62,027	26,023	42.0	73	35,590	57.4	457
1960	Kennedy	Nixon.	68,838	34,227	49.7	303	34,108	49.5	219
1964	Johnson.	Goldwater	70,645	43,130	61.1	486	27,178	38.5	52
1968	Humphrey	Nixon.	73,212	31,275	42.7	191	31,785	43.4	301
1972	McGovern	Nixon.	77,719	29,170	37.5	17	47,170	60.7	520
1976	Carter	Ford	81,556	40,831	50.1	297	39,148	48.0	240
1980	Carter	Reagan	86,515	35,484	41.0	49	43,904	50.7	489
1984	Mondale.	Reagan	92,653	37,577	40.6	13	54,455	58.8	525
1988	Dukakis	Bush	91,595	41,809	45.6	111	48,886	53.4	426

[1] Include votes for minor party candidates, independents, unpledged electors, and scattered write-in votes.

No. 412. Vote Cast for Leading Minority Party Candidates for President: 1932 to 1988

[See headnote, table 411]

YEAR	Candidate	Party	Popular vote (1,000)	Candidate	Party	Popular vote (1,000)
1932 . .	Norman Thomas . . .	Socialist	885	William Z. Foster . . .	Communist	103
1936 . .	William Lemke.	Union	892	Norman Thomas . . .	Socialist	188
1940 . .	Norman Thomas . . .	Socialist	116	Roger Babson	Prohibition	59
1944 . .	Norman Thomas . . .	Socialist	79	Claude Watson	Prohibition.	75
1948 . .	Strom Thurmond . . .	States' Rights	1,176	Henry Wallace	Progressive	1,157
1952 . .	Vincent Hallinan. . . .	Progressive	140	Stuart Hamblen	Prohibition	73
1956 . .	T. Coleman Andrews.	States' Rights	111	Eric Hass	Socialist Labor	44
1960 . .	Eric Hass	Socialist Labor	48	Rutherford Decker . .	Prohibition	46
1964 . .	Eric Hass	Socialist Labor	45	Clifton DeBerry	Socialist Workers . . .	33
1968 . .	George Wallace . . .	American Independent.	9,906	Henning Blomen . . .	Socialist Labor	53
1972 . .	John Schmitz.	American.	1,099	Benjamin Spock. . . .	People's	79
1976 . .	Eugene McCarthy. . .	Independent	757	Roger McBride	Libertarian	173
1980 . .	John Anderson	Independent	5,720	Ed Clark	Libertarian	921
1984 . .	David Bergland	Libertarian	228	Lyndon H. LaRouche.	Independent	79
1988 . .	Ron Paul	Libertarian	432	Lenora B. Fulani . . .	New Alliance	217

Source of tables 411 and 412: Elections Research Center, Chevy Chase, MD, *America at the Polls 2*, 1965, and *America Votes*, biennial, (copyright).

No. 413. Democratic and Republican Percentages of Two-Party Presidential Vote, by Selected Characteristics of Voters: 1984 and 1988

[In percent. Covers citizens of voting-age living in private housing units in the contiguous United States. Percentages for Democratic Presidential vote are computed by subtracting the percentage Republican vote from 100 percent; third party votes are not included as valid data. Data are from the National Election Studies and are based on a sample (for 1988, 2,040 respondents) and subject to sampling variability; for details, see source]

CHARACTERISTIC	1984		1988		CHARACTERISTIC	1984		1988	
	Demo-cratic	Repub-lican	Demo-cratic	Repub-lican		Demo-cratic	Repub-lican	Demo-cratic	Repub-lican
Total [1]	**42**	**58**	**47**	**53**	Race:				
Year of birth:					White.	37	63	41	59
1959 or later	42	58	48	52	Black	91	9	92	8
1943 to 1958.	41	59	47	53					
1927 to 1942.	40	60	49	51	Education:				
1911 to 1926.	44	56	44	56	Grade school.	62	38	61	39
1895 to 1910.	42	58	47	53	High school.	42	58	51	49
					College.	38	62	42	58
Sex:									
Male	38	62	44	57	Union household.	57	43	59	41
Female.	45	55	50	50	Non-union household. .	37	63	44	56

[1] Includes other characteristics, not shown separately.

Source: Center for Political Studies, University of Michigan, Ann Arbor, MI. Data are published in Warren E. Miller and Santa A. Traugott, *American National Election Studies Data Sourcebook, 1952-1986*, Harvard University Press, Cambridge, MA, 1989 (copyright).

No. 414. Electoral Vote Cast for President, by Major Political Party—States: 1948 to 1988

[D = Democratic, R = Republican. For composition of regions, see table 25. See also *Historical Statistics, Colonial Times to 1970*, series Y 84-134]

REGION, DIVISION, AND STATE	1948 [1]	1952	1956 [2]	1960 [3]	1964	1968 [4]	1972 [5]	1976 [6]	1980	1984	1988 [7]
Democratic......	303	89	73	303	486	191	17	297	49	13	111
Republican......	189	442	457	219	52	301	520	240	489	525	426
Northeast: Democratic .	20	-	-	121	126	102	14	86	4	-	53
Republican..	118	133	133	12	-	24	108	36	118	113	60
Midwest: Democratic ..	101	-	13	71	149	31	-	58	10	10	29
Republican...	54	153	140	82	-	118	145	87	135	127	108
South: Democratic	117	89	60	101	121	45	3	149	31	3	8
Republican	11	77	105	50	47	77	165	20	138	174	168
West: Democratic.....	65	-	-	10	90	13	-	4	4	-	21
Republican.....	6	79	79	75	5	82	102	97	98	111	90
New England: ME	R-5	R-5	R-5	R-5	D-4	D-4	R-4	R-4	R-4	R-4	R-4
NH	R-4	R-4	R-4	R-4	D-4	R-4	R-4	R-4	R-4	R-4	R-4
VT	R-3	R-3	R-3	R-3	D-3	R-3	R-3	R-3	R-3	R-3	R-3
MA	D-16	R-16	R-16	D-16	D-14	D-14	D-14	D-14	R-14	R-13	D-13
RI	D-4	R-4	R-4	D-4	D-4	D-4	R-4	D-4	D-4	R-4	D-4
CT	R-8	R-8	R-8	D-8	D-8	D-8	R-8	R-8	R-8	R-8	R-8
Middle Atlantic: NY ...	R-47	R-45	R-45	D-45	D-43	D-43	R-41	D-41	R-41	R-36	D-36
NJ	R-16	R-16	R-16	D-16	D-17	R-17	R-17	R-17	R-17	R-16	R-16
PA	R-35	R-32	R-32	D-32	D-29	D-29	R-27	D-27	R-27	R-25	R-25
East North Central: OH	D-25	R-25	R-25	R-25	D-26	R-26	R-25	D-25	R-25	R-23	R-23
IN	R-13	R-13	R-13	R-13	D-13	R-13	R-13	R-13	R-13	R-12	R-12
IL	D-28	R-27	R-27	D-27	D-26	R-26	R-26	R-26	R-26	R-24	R-24
MI	R-19	R-20	R-20	D-20	D-21	D-21	R-21	R-21	R-21	R-20	R-20
WI	D-12	R-12	R-12	R-12	D-12	D-12	R-11	D-11	R-11	R-11	D-11
West North Central: MN	D-11	R-11	R-11	D-11	D-10	D-10	R-10	D-10	D-10	D-10	D-10
IA	D-10	R-10	R-10	R-10	D-9	R-9	R-8	R-8	R-8	R-8	D-8
MO	D-15	R-13	D-13	D-13	D-12	R-12	R-12	D-12	D-12	R-11	R-11
ND	R-4	R-4	R-4	R-4	D-4	R-4	R-3	R-3	R-3	R-3	R-3
SD	R-4	R-4	R-4	R-4	D-4	R-4	R-4	R-4	R-4	R-3	R-3
NE	R-6	R-6	R-6	R-6	D-5	R-5	R-5	R-5	R-5	R-5	R-5
KS	R-8	R-8	R-8	R-8	D-7	R-7	R-7	R-7	R-7	R-7	R-7
South Atlantic: DE....	R-3	R-3	R-3	D-3	D-3	R-3	R-3	D-3	R-3	R-3	R-3
MD	R-8	R-9	R-9	D-9	D-10	D-10	R-10	D-10	D-10	R-10	R-10
DC	(X)	(X)	(X)	(X)	D-3	D-3	D-3	D-3	D-3	D-3	D-3
VA	D-11	R-12	R-12	R-12	D-12	R-12	[5]R-11	R-12	R-12	R-12	R-12
WV	D-8	D-8	R-8	D-8	D-7	D-7	R-6	D-6	D-6	R-6	[7]D-5
NC	D-14	D-14	D-14	D-14	D-13	[4]R-12	R-13	D-13	R-13	R-13	R-13
SC	([1])	D-8	D-8	D-8	R-8	R-8	R-8	D-8	R-8	R-8	R-8
GA	D-12	D-12	D-12	D-12	R-12	([4])	R-12	D-12	D-12	R-12	R-12
FL	D-8	R-10	R-10	R-10	D-14	R-14	R-17	D-17	R-17	R-21	R-21
East South Central: KY	D-11	D-10	R-10	R-10	D-9	R-9	R-9	D-9	R-9	R-9	R-9
TN	[1]D-11	R-11	R-11	R-11	D-11	R-11	R-10	D-10	R-10	R-11	R-11
AL	([1])	D-11	[2]D-10	[3]D-5	R-10	([4])	R-9	D-9	R-9	R-9	R-9
MS	([1])	D-8	D-8	([3])	R-7	([4])	R-7	D-7	R-7	R-7	R-7
West South Central: AR	D-9	D-8	D-8	D-8	D-6	([4])	R-6	D-6	R-6	R-6	R-6
LA	([1])	D-10	R-10	D-10	R-10	([4])	R-10	D-10	R-10	R-10	R-10
OK	D-10	R-8	R-8	[3]R-7	D-8	R-8	R-8	R-8	R-8	R-8	R-8
TX	D-23	R-24	R-24	D-24	D-25	D-25	R-26	D-26	R-26	R-29	R-29
Mountain: MT	D-4	R-4	R-4	R-4	D-4	R-4	R-4	R-4	R-4	R-4	R-4
ID	D-4	R-4	R-4	R-4	D-4	R-4	R-4	R-4	R-4	R-4	R-4
WY	D-3	R-3	R-3	R-3	D-3	R-3	R-3	R-3	R-3	R-3	R-3
CO	D-6	R-6	R-6	R-6	D-6	R-6	R-7	R-7	R-7	R-8	R-8
NM	D-4	R-4	R-4	D-4	D-4	R-4	R-4	R-4	R-4	R-5	R-5
AZ	D-4	R-4	R-4	R-4	R-5	R-5	R-6	R-6	R-6	R-7	R-7
UT	D-4	R-4	R-4	R-4	D-4	R-4	R-4	R-4	R-4	R-5	R-5
NV	D-3	R-3	R-3	D-3	D-3	R-3	R-3	R-3	R-3	R-4	R-4
Pacific: WA.........	D-8	R-9	R-9	R-9	D-9	D-9	R-9	[6]R-8	R-9	R-10	D-10
OR	R-6	R-6	R-6	R-6	D-6	R-6	R-6	R-6	R-6	R-7	D-7
CA	D-25	R-32	R-32	R-32	D-40	R-40	R-45	R-45	R-45	R-47	R-47
AK	(X)	(X)	(X)	R-3	D-3	R-3	R-3	R-3	R-3	R-3	R-3
HI	(X)	(X)	(X)	D-3	D-4	D-4	D-4	D-4	D-4	R-4	D-4

- Represents zero. X Not applicable. [1] Excludes 39 electoral votes cast for States' Rights Democratic candidates as follows: AL 11, LA 10, MS 9, SC 8, and TN 1. [2] Excludes one electoral vote cast for Walter B. Jones in Alabama. [3] Excludes 15 electoral votes cast for Harry F. Byrd as follows: AL 6, MS 8, and OK 1. [4] Excludes 46 electoral votes cast for American Independent George C. Wallace as follows: AL 10, AR 6, GA 12, LA 10, MS 7, and NC 1. [5] Excludes one electoral vote cast for Libertarian John Hospers in Virginia. [6] Excludes one electoral vote cast for Ronald Reagan in Washington. [7] Excludes one electoral vote cast for Lloyd Bentsen for President in West Virginia.

Source: 1948-1972, U.S. Congress, Clerk of the House, *Statistics of the Presidential and Congressional Election*, quadrennial; 1976-1988, Elections Research Center, Chevy Chase, MD, *America Votes*. biennial, (copyright.)

No. 415. Popular Vote Cast for President, by Political Party—States: 1980 to 1988

[In thousands, except percent. D=Democratic, R=Republican. Leading party vote refers to the party vote representing either a majority or a plurality for the victorious party in the area shown. See also *Historical Statistics, Colonial Times to 1970*, series Y 135-186]

REGION, DIVISION, AND STATE	1980				1984				1988			
	Total [1]	Demo-cratic Party	Repub-lican Party	Per-cent for leading party	Total [1]	Demo-cratic Party	Repub-lican Party	Per-cent for leading party	Total [1]	Demo-cratic Party	Repub-lican Party	Percent for leading party
United States . .	86,515	35,484	43,904	R-50.7	92,653	37,577	54,455	R-58.8	91,595	41,809	48,886	R-53.4
Northeast	19,206	8,019	9,147	R-47.6	20,483	9,046	11,336	R-55.3	19,852	9,689	9,961	R-50.2
N.E.	5,467	2,206	2,446	R-44.7	5,614	2,437	3,153	R-56.2	5,730	2,826	2,836	R-49.5
ME	523	221	239	R-45.6	553	215	337	R-60.8	555	244	307	R-55.3
NH	384	109	222	R-57.7	389	120	267	R-68.6	451	164	282	R-62.4
VT.	213	82	95	R-44.4	235	96	136	R-57.9	243	116	124	R-51.1
MA	2,524	1,054	1,058	R-41.9	2,559	1,240	1,311	R-51.2	2,633	1,401	1,195	D-53.2
RI	416	198	155	D-47.7	410	197	212	R-51.7	405	225	178	D-55.6
CT.	1,406	542	677	R-48.2	1,467	570	891	R-60.7	1,443	677	750	R-52.0
M.A	13,739	5,813	6,703	R-48.8	14,870	6,609	8,183	R-55.0	14,121	6,863	7,125	R-50.5
NY.	6,202	2,728	2,894	R-46.7	6,807	3,120	3,665	R-53.8	6,486	3,348	3,082	D-51.6
NJ.	2,976	1,147	1,547	R-52.0	3,218	1,261	1,934	R-60.1	3,100	1,320	1,743	R-56.2
PA.	4,562	1,938	2,262	R-49.6	4,845	2,228	2,584	R-53.3	4,536	2,195	2,300	R-50.7
Midwest.	25,178	10,291	12,827	R-50.9	25,441	10,511	14,761	R-58.0	24,663	11,556	12,915	R-52.4
E.N.C	17,458	7,221	8,825	R-50.5	17,613	7,279	10,213	R-58.0	16,982	7,819	9,038	R-53.2
OH	4,284	1,752	2,207	R-51.5	4,548	1,825	2,679	R-58.9	4,394	1,940	2,417	R-55.0
IN	2,242	844	1,256	R-56.0	2,233	841	1,377	R-61.7	2,169	861	1,298	R-59.8
IL	4,750	1,981	2,358	R-49.6	4,819	2,086	2,707	R-56.2	4,559	2,216	2,311	R-50.7
MI	3,910	1,662	1,915	R-49.0	3,802	1,530	2,252	R-59.2	3,669	1,676	1,965	R-53.6
WI	2,273	982	1,089	R-47.9	2,212	996	1,199	R-54.2	2,192	1,127	1,047	D-51.4
W.N.C.	7,719	3,070	4,002	R-51.8	7,828	3,232	4,548	R-58.1	7,681	3,737	3,877	R-50.5
MN	2,052	954	873	D-46.5	2,084	1,036	1,033	D-49.7	2,097	1,109	962	D-52.9
IA	1,318	509	676	R-51.3	1,320	606	703	R-53.3	1,226	671	545	D-54.7
MO	2,100	931	1,074	R-51.2	2,123	849	1,274	R-60.0	2,094	1,002	1,085	R-51.8
ND	302	79	194	R-64.2	309	104	200	R-64.8	297	128	167	R-56.0
SD.	328	104	198	R-60.5	318	116	200	R-63.0	313	146	165	R-52.8
NE.	641	167	420	R-65.5	652	188	460	R-70.6	661	259	398	R-60.2
KS.	980	326	567	R-57.9	1,022	333	677	R-66.3	993	423	554	R-55.8
South	25,813	11,554	13,118	R-50.8	28,833	10,998	17,699	R-61.4	28,558	12,004	16,327	R-57.2
S.A	12,589	5,698	6,198	R-49.2	14,124	5,519	8,565	R-60.6	14,234	5,927	8,207	R-57.7
DE.	236	106	111	R-47.2	255	102	152	R-59.8	250	109	140	R-55.9
MD	1,540	726	681	D-47.1	1,676	788	880	R-52.5	1,714	826	876	R-51.1
DC.	175	131	24	D-74.8	211	180	29	D-85.4	193	159	28	D-82.6
VA.	1,866	752	990	R-53.0	2,147	796	1,337	R-62.3	2,192	860	1,309	R-59.7
WV	738	367	334	D-49.8	736	328	405	R-55.1	653	341	310	D-52.2
NC	1,856	876	915	R-49.3	2,175	824	1,346	R-61.9	2,134	890	1,237	R-58.0
SC.	894	430	442	R-49.4	969	344	616	R-63.6	986	371	606	R-61.5
GA	1,597	891	654	D-55.8	1,776	707	1,069	R-60.2	1,810	715	1,081	R-59.8
FL.	3,687	1,419	2,047	R-55.5	4,180	1,449	2,730	R-65.3	4,302	1,657	2,619	R-60.9
E.S.C	5,147	2,465	2,518	R-48.9	5,464	2,155	3,267	R-59.8	5,269	2,174	3,055	R-58.0
KY.	1,295	616	635	R-49.1	1,369	540	822	R-60.0	1,323	580	734	R-55.5
TN.	1,618	783	788	R-48.7	1,712	712	990	R-57.8	1,636	680	947	R-57.9
AL.	1,342	637	654	R-48.8	1,442	552	873	R-60.5	1,378	550	816	R-59.2
MS	893	429	441	R-49.4	941	352	582	R-61.9	932	364	558	R-59.9
W.S.C	8,078	3,389	4,403	R-54.5	9,244	3,325	5,867	R-63.5	9,054	3,903	5,065	R-55.9
AR.	838	398	403	R-48.1	884	339	535	R-60.5	828	349	467	R-56.4
LA.	1,549	708	793	R-51.2	1,707	652	1,037	R-60.8	1,628	717	884	R-54.3
OK	1,150	402	696	R-60.5	1,256	385	862	R-68.6	1,171	483	678	R-57.9
TX.	4,542	1,881	2,511	R-55.3	5,398	1,949	3,433	R-63.6	5,427	2,353	3,037	R-56.0
West	16,318	5,620	8,813	R-54.0	17,895	7,022	10,659	R-59.6	18,522	8,560	9,683	R-52.3
Mt	4,346	1,251	2,637	R-60.7	4,736	1,546	3,131	R-66.1	5,014	2,043	2,887	R-57.6
MT	364	118	207	R-56.8	384	147	232	R-60.5	366	169	190	R-52.1
ID	437	110	291	R-66.5	411	109	298	R-72.4	409	147	254	R-62.1
WY	177	49	111	R-62.6	189	53	133	R-70.5	177	67	107	R-60.5
CO	1,184	368	652	R-55.1	1,295	455	822	R-63.4	1,372	621	728	R-53.1
NM	457	168	251	R-54.9	514	202	307	R-59.7	521	244	270	R-51.9
AZ.	874	247	530	R-60.6	1,026	334	681	R-66.4	1,172	454	703	R-60.0
UT.	604	124	440	R-72.8	630	155	469	R-74.5	647	207	428	R-66.2
NV.	248	67	155	R-62.5	287	92	189	R-65.8	350	133	206	R-58.9
Pac	11,973	4,369	6,177	R-51.6	13,159	5,476	7,528	R-57.2	13,509	6,517	6,797	R-50.3
WA	1,742	650	865	R-49.7	1,884	807	1,052	R-55.8	1,865	934	904	D-50.0
OR	1,182	457	571	R-48.3	1,227	536	686	R-55.9	1,202	616	560	D-51.3
CA.	8,587	3,084	4,525	R-52.7	9,505	3,923	5,467	R-57.5	9,887	4,702	5,055	R-51.1
AK.	158	42	86	R-54.3	208	62	138	R-66.7	200	73	119	R-59.6
HI	303	136	130	D-44.8	336	147	185	R-55.1	354	192	159	D-54.3

[1] Includes other parties.

Source: Elections Research Center, Chevy Chase, MD, *America Votes*, biennial, (copyright.)

No. 416. Vote Cast for United States Senators, 1988 and 1990, and Incumbent Senators, 1991—States

[In thousands, except percent. D=Democrat; R=Republican]

DIVISION AND STATE	1988 Total	1988 Percent for leading party	1990 Total	1990 Percent for leading party	INCUMBENT SENATORS AND YEAR TERM EXPIRES Name, party and year	Name, party and year
N.E.:						
ME	557	D-81.2	520	R-61.3	George J. Mitchell (D) 1995	William S. Cohen (R) 1997
NH	(X)	(X)	291	R-65.1	Warren B. Rudman (R) 1993	Robert C. Smith (R) 1997
VT	240	R-68.0	(X)	(X)	Patrick J. Leahy (D) 1993	James M. Jeffords (R) 1995
MA	2,606	D-65.0	2,316	D-57.1	Edward M. Kennedy (D) 1995	John Kerry (D) 1997
RI	398	R-54.6	364	D-61.8	Claiborne Pell (D) 1997	John H. Chafee (R) 1995
CT	1,384	D-49.8	(X)	(X)	Christopher J. Dodd (D) 1993	Joseph Lieberman (D) 1995
M.A.:						
NY	6,041	D-67.0	(X)	(X)	Daniel Moynihan (D) 1995	Alfonse D'Amato (R) 1993
NJ	2,988	D-53.6	1,938	D-50.4	Bill Bradley (D) 1997	Frank Lautenberg (D) 1995
PA	4,367	R-66.5	[1]3,383	[1]D-55.0	Harris Wofford (D) 1995	Arlen Specter (R) 1993
E.N.C.:						
OH	4,353	D-57.0	(X)	(X)	John Glenn (D) 1993	Howard Metzenbaum (D) 1995
IN	2,099	R-68.1	[2]1,504	[2]R-53.6	Daniel R. Coats (R) 1993	Richard G. Lugar (R) 1995
IL	(X)	(X)	3,251	D-65.1	Alan J. Dixon (D) 1993	Paul Simon (D) 1997
MI	3,506	D-60.4	2,560	D-57.5	Carl Levin (D) 1997	Donald Riegle Jr. (D) 1995
WI	2,168	D-52.1	(X)	(X)	Herb Kohl (D) 1995	Bob Kasten (R) 1993
W.N.C.:						
MN	2,094	R-56.2	1,808	D-50.4	Paul Wellstone (D) 1997	Dave Durenberger (R) 1995
IA	(X)	(X)	984	D-54.5	Tom Harkin (D) 1997	Charles Grassley (R) 1993
MO	2,079	R-67.7	(X)	(X)	Christopher S. Bond (R) 1993	John C. Danforth (R) 1995
ND	289	D-59.4	(X)	(X)	Quentin N. Burdick (D) 1995	Kent Conrad (D) 1993
SD	(X)	(X)	259	R-52.4	Tom Daschle (D) 1993	Larry Pressler (R) 1997
NE	668	D-56.7	594	D-58.9	Jim Exon (D) 1997	Bob Kerrey (D) 1995
KS	(X)	(X)	786	R-73.6	Bob Dole (R) 1993	Nancy Kassebaum (R) 1997
S.A.:						
DE	243	R-62.1	180	D-62.7	Joseph R. Biden Jr. (D) 1997	William Roth Jr. (R) 1995
MD	1,617	D-61.8	(X)	(X)	Barbara A. Mikulski (D) 1993	Paul S. Sarbanes (D) 1995
VA	2,069	D-71.2	1,084	R-80.9	Charles S. Robb (D) 1995	John W. Warner (R) 1997
WV	635	D-64.8	404	D-68.3	Robert C. Byrd (D) 1995	John Rockefeller IV (D) 1997
NC	(X)	(X)	2,070	R-52.5	Terry Sanford (D) 1993	Jesse Helms (R) 1997
SC	(X)	(X)	751	R-64.2	Ernest F. Hollings (D) 1993	Strom Thurmond (R) 1997
GA	(X)	(X)	1,034	D-100.0	Wyche Fowler Jr. (D) 1993	Sam Nunn (D) 1997
FL	4,068	R-50.4	(X)	(X)	Bob Graham (D) 1993	Connie Mack (R) 1995
E.S.C.:						
KY	(X)	(X)	916	R-52.2	Wendell H. Ford (D) 1993	Mitch McConnell (R) 1997
TN	1,567	D-65.1	784	D-67.7	Al Gore (D) 1997	Jim Sasser (D) 1995
AL	(X)	(X)	1,186	D-60.5	Howell Heflin (D) 1997	Richard C. Shelby (D) 1993
MS	947	R-53.9	274	R-100.0	Thad Cochran (R) 1997	Trent Lott (R) 1995
W.S.C.:						
AR	(X)	(X)	495	D-99.8	Dale Bumpers (D) 1993	David Pryor (D) 1997
LA	(X)	(X)	[3]1,396	[3]D-56.5	John B. Breaux (D) 1993	J. Bennett Johnston (D) 1997
OK	(X)	(X)	884	D-83.2	David L. Boren (D) 1997	Don Nickles (R) 1993
TX	5,323	D-59.2	3,822	R-60.2	Lloyd Bentsen (D) 1995	Phil Gramm (R) 1997
Mt.:						
MT	365	R-51.9	319	D-68.1	Max Baucus (D) 1997	Conrad Burns (R) 1995
ID	(X)	(X)	316	R-61.3	Larry E. Craig (R) 1997	Steve Symms (R) 1993
WY	181	R-50.4	158	R-63.9	Alan K. Simpson (R) 1997	Malcolm Wallop (R) 1995
CO	(X)	(X)	1,022	R-55.7	Tim Wirth (D) 1993	Hank Brown (R) 1997
NM	509	D-63.3	407	R-72.9	Jeff Bingaman (D) 1995	Pete V. Domenici (R) 1997
AZ	1,165	D-56.7	(X)	(X)	Dennis DeConcini (D) 1995	John McCain (R) 1993
UT	641	R-67.1	(X)	(X)	Jake Garn (R) 1993	Orrin G. Hatch (R) 1995
NV	350	D-50.2	(X)	(X)	Harry Reid (D) 1993	Richard H. Bryan (D) 1995
Pac.:						
WA	1,849	R-51.1	(X)	(X)	Brock Adams (D) 1993	Slade Gorton (R) 1995
OR	(X)	(X)	1,099	R-53.7	Mark O. Hatfield (R) 1997	Bob Packwood (R) 1993
CA	9,744	R-52.8	(X)	(X)	Alan Cranston (D) 1993	John Seymour (R) 1995 [4]
AK	(X)	(X)	190	R-66.2	Frank H. Murkowski (R) 1993	Ted Stevens (R) 1997
HI	324	D-76.6	[5]350	[5]D-54.0	Daniel K. Akaka (D) 1995	Daniel K. Inouye (D) 1993

X Not applicable.   [1] Special election in November 1991 to fill vacancy caused by death of Senator John Heinz.   [2] Special election to fill the unexpired term of Vice-President Quayle.   [3] Louisiana holds an open-primary election with candidates from all parties running on the same ballot. Any candidate who receives a majority is elected. In 1990 J. Bennett Johnston received more than 50 percent of the vote in the October open-primary.   [4] Appointed by the Governor to fill the vacancy caused by the resignation of Senator Pete Wilson. Will serve until a successor is elected in November 1992.   [5] Special election to fill the unexpired term of Senator Matsunaga.

Source: Elections Research Center, Chevy Chase, MD, *America Votes,* biennial, (copyright.)

No. 417. Apportionment of Membership in House of Representatives, by State: 1790 to 1990

[Total membership includes Representatives assigned to newly admitted States after the apportionment acts. Population figures used for apportionment purposes are those determined for States by each decennial census. No reapportionment based on 1920 population census. For method of calculating apportionment and a short history of apportionment, see House Report 91-1314, 91st Congress, 2d session, *The Decennial Population Census and Congressional Apportionment*. See also *Historical Statistics, Colonial Times to 1970*, series Y 220-271]

MEMBERSHIP BASED ON CENSUS OF—

STATE	1790	1800	1810	1820	1830	1840	1850	1860	1870	1880	1890	1900	1910	1930	1940	1950	1960	1970	1980	1990
U.S.	106	142	186	213	242	232	237	243	293	332	357	391	435	435	435	437	435	435	435	435
Northeast .	57	76	97	105	112	94	92	87	95	95	99	108	123	122	120	115	108	104	95	88
N.E.	29	35	41	39	38	31	29	27	28	26	27	29	32	29	28	28	25	25	24	23
ME ...	(X)	(X)	(X)	7	8	7	6	5	5	4	4	4	4	3	3	3	2	2	2	2
NH ...	4	5	6	6	5	4	3	3	3	2	2	2	2	2	2	2	2	2	2	2
VT	2	4	6	5	5	4	3	3	3	2	2	2	2	1	1	1	1	1	1	1
MA ...	14	17	20	13	12	10	11	10	11	12	13	14	16	15	14	14	12	12	11	10
RI	2	2	2	2	2	2	2	2	2	2	2	2	3	2	2	2	2	2	2	2
CT....	7	7	7	6	6	4	4	4	4	4	4	4	5	5	6	6	6	6	6	6
M.A.	28	41	56	66	74	63	63	60	67	69	72	79	91	93	92	87	83	79	71	65
NY....	10	17	27	34	40	34	33	31	33	34	34	37	43	45	45	43	41	39	34	31
NJ....	5	6	6	6	6	5	5	5	7	7	8	10	12	14	14	14	15	15	14	13
PA....	13	18	23	26	28	24	25	24	27	28	30	32	36	34	33	30	27	25	23	21
Midwest...	(X)	1	8	19	32	50	59	75	98	117	128	136	143	137	131	129	125	121	113	105
E.N.C. ..	(X)	1	8	18	30	43	48	56	69	74	78	82	86	90	87	87	88	86	80	74
OH ...	(X)	[1]1	6	14	19	21	21	19	20	21	21	21	22	24	23	23	24	23	21	19
IN ...	(X)	(X)	[1]1	3	7	10	11	11	13	13	13	13	13	12	11	11	11	11	10	10
IL	(X)	(X)	[1]1	1	3	7	9	14	19	20	22	25	27	27	26	25	24	24	22	20
MI	(X)	(X)	(X)	(X)	[1]1	3	4	6	9	11	12	12	13	17	17	18	19	19	18	16
WI	(X)	(X)	(X)	(X)	(X)	[1]2	3	6	8	9	10	11	11	10	10	10	10	9	9	9
W.N.C. ..	(X)	(X)	(X)	1	2	7	11	19	29	43	50	54	57	47	44	42	37	35	33	31
MN ...	(X)	(X)	(X)	(X)	(X)	(X)	[1]2	2	3	5	7	9	10	9	9	9	8	8	8	8
IA ...	(X)	(X)	(X)	(X)	(X)	[1]2	2	6	9	11	11	11	11	9	8	8	7	6	6	5
MO ...	(X)	(X)	(X)	1	2	5	7	9	13	14	15	16	16	13	13	11	10	10	9	9
ND ...	(X)	(X)	(X)	(X)	(X)	(X)	(X)	(X)	(X)	[1]1	1	2	3	2	2	2	2	1	1	1
SD ...	(X)	(X)	(X)	(X)	(X)	(X)	(X)	(X)	(X)	[1]2	2	2	3	2	2	2	2	2	1	1
NE ...	(X)	(X)	(X)	(X)	(X)	(X)	(X)	[1]1	1	3	6	6	6	5	4	4	3	3	3	3
KS ...	(X)	(X)	(X)	(X)	(X)	(X)	(X)	1	3	7	8	8	8	7	6	6	5	5	5	4
South	49	65	81	89	98	86	83	76	93	107	112	126	136	133	135	134	133	134	142	149
S.A.	46	56	62	61	61	47	43	36	43	49	50	53	56	54	56	60	63	65	69	75
DE...	1	1	2	1	1	1	1	1	1	1	1	1	1	1	1	1	1	1	1	1
MD...	8	9	9	9	8	6	6	5	6	6	6	6	6	6	6	7	7	8	8	8
VA...	19	22	23	22	21	15	13	11	9	10	10	10	10	9	9	10	10	10	10	11
WV...	(X)	(X)	(X)	(X)	(X)	(X)	(X)	(X)	3	4	4	5	6	6	6	6	5	4	4	3
NC ...	10	12	13	13	13	9	8	7	8	9	9	10	10	11	12	12	11	11	11	12
SC...	6	8	9	9	9	7	6	4	5	7	7	7	7	6	6	6	6	6	6	6
GA...	2	4	6	7	9	8	8	7	9	10	11	11	12	10	10	10	10	10	10	11
FL...	(X)	(X)	(X)	(X)	(X)	[1]1	1	1	2	2	2	3	4	5	6	8	12	15	19	23
E.S.C ...	3	9	18	25	33	32	32	28	34	36	37	38	39	34	35	32	29	27	28	27
KY....	2	6	10	12	13	10	10	9	10	11	11	11	11	9	9	8	7	7	7	6
TN....	[1]1	3	6	9	13	11	10	8	10	10	10	10	10	9	10	9	9	8	9	9
AL....	(X)	(X)	[1]1	3	5	7	7	6	8	8	9	9	10	9	9	9	8	7	7	7
MS ...	(X)	(X)	[1]1	2	4	5	5	5	6	7	7	8	8	7	7	6	5	5	5	5
W.S.C ...	(X)	(X)	1	3	4	7	8	12	16	22	25	35	41	45	44	42	41	42	45	47
AR....	(X)	(X)	(X)	(X)	[1]1	1	2	3	4	5	6	7	7	7	7	6	4	4	4	4
LA....	(X)	(X)	[1]1	3	3	4	4	5	6	6	6	7	8	8	8	8	8	8	8	7
OK ...	(X)	(X)	(X)	(X)	(X)	(X)	(X)	(X)	(X)	(X)	(X)	[1]5	8	9	8	6	6	6	6	6
TX ...	(X)	(X)	(X)	(X)	(X)	[1]2	2	4	6	11	13	16	18	21	21	22	23	24	27	30
West	(X)	(X)	(X)	(X)	(X)	2	3	5	7	13	18	21	33	43	49	59	69	76	85	93
Mt	(X)	(X)	(X)	(X)	(X)	(X)	(X)	1	2	5	7	8	14	14	16	16	17	19	24	24
MT ...	(X)	(X)	(X)	(X)	(X)	(X)	(X)	(X)	(X)	[1]1	1	1	2	2	2	2	2	2	2	1
ID ...	(X)	(X)	(X)	(X)	(X)	(X)	(X)	(X)	(X)	[1]1	1	1	2	2	2	2	2	2	2	2
WY ...	(X)	(X)	(X)	(X)	(X)	(X)	(X)	(X)	(X)	[1]1	1	1	1	1	1	1	1	1	1	1
CO ...	(X)	(X)	(X)	(X)	(X)	(X)	(X)	(X)	[1]1	1	2	3	4	4	4	4	4	5	6	6
NM ...	(X)	(X)	(X)	(X)	(X)	(X)	(X)	(X)	(X)	(X)	(X)	(X)	[2]1	1	2	2	2	2	3	3
AZ ...	(X)	(X)	(X)	(X)	(X)	(X)	(X)	(X)	(X)	(X)	(X)	(X)	[2]1	1	2	2	3	4	5	6
UT....	(X)	(X)	(X)	(X)	(X)	(X)	(X)	(X)	(X)	(X)	[1]1	1	2	2	2	2	2	2	3	3
NV ...	(X)	(X)	(X)	(X)	(X)	(X)	(X)	[1]1	1	1	1	1	1	1	1	1	1	1	2	2
Pac	(X)	(X)	(X)	(X)	(X)	2	3	4	5	8	11	13	19	29	33	43	52	57	61	69
WA ...	(X)	(X)	(X)	(X)	(X)	(X)	(X)	(X)	(X)	[1]1	2	3	5	6	6	7	7	7	8	9
OR ...	(X)	(X)	(X)	(X)	(X)	(X)	[1]1	1	1	1	2	2	3	3	4	4	4	4	5	5
CA....	(X)	(X)	(X)	(X)	(X)	[1]2	2	3	4	6	7	8	11	20	23	30	38	43	45	52
AK....	(X)	(X)	(X)	(X)	(X)	(X)	(X)	(X)	(X)	(X)	(X)	(X)	(X)	(X)	(X)	[1]1	1	1	1	1
HI	(X)	(X)	(X)	(X)	(X)	(X)	(X)	(X)	(X)	(X)	(X)	(X)	(X)	(X)	(X)	[1]1	2	2	2	2

X Not applicable.   [1] Assigned after apportionment.   [2] Included in apportionment in anticipation of statehood.

Source: U.S. Bureau of the Census, press release CB90-232.

No. 418. Representatives Elected, by Percent of Vote Cast for Winner and Major Party, 1970 to 1990, and by State, 1990

YEAR, REGION, DIVISION, AND STATE	TOTAL REPRESENTATIVES ELECTED				DEMOCRATS ELECTED				REPUBLICANS ELECTED				REPRESENTATIVES ELECTED WITH NO MAJOR PARTY OPPOSITION		
	Total	Percentage of vote			Total	Percentage of vote			Total	Percentage of vote			Total	Demo-crats	Repub-licans
		Under 55	55-59.9	60 and over		Under 55	55-59.9	60 and over		Under 55	55-59.9	60 and over			
1970	435	59	64	312	255	28	26	201	180	31	38	111	63	58	5
1980	435	78	63	294	243	35	35	173	192	43	28	121	64	39	15
1982	435	76	73	286	269	40	33	196	166	36	40	90	56	46	10
1984	435	58	56	321	253	33	38	182	182	25	18	139	68	54	14
1986	435	46	41	348	258	22	18	218	177	24	23	130	75	57	18
1988	435	37	34	364	260	21	15	224	175	16	19	140	80	60	20
1990, total	¹435	¹52	71	312	267	29	40	198	167	22	31	114	85	49	36
Northeast	¹95	¹14	17	64	56	10	9	37	38	3	8	27	19	12	7
N.E	¹24	¹7	3	14	16	4	1	11	7	2	2	3	5	5	-
ME	2	1	-	1	1	-	-	1	1	1	-	-	-	-	-
NH	2	1	1	-	1	1	-	-	1	-	1	-	-	-	-
VT	¹1	¹1	-	-	-	-	-	-	-	-	-	-	-	-	-
MA	11	2	-	9	10	2	-	8	1	-	-	1	5	5	-
RI	2	-	2	-	1	-	1	-	1	-	1	-	-	-	-
CT	6	2	-	4	3	1	-	2	3	1	-	2	-	-	-
M.A	71	7	14	50	40	6	8	26	31	1	6	24	14	7	7
NY	34	1	7	26	21	1	4	16	13	-	3	10	6	4	2
NJ	14	5	2	7	8	5	1	2	6	-	1	5	2	2	-
PA	23	1	5	17	11	-	3	8	12	1	2	9	6	1	5
Midwest	113	12	16	85	68	6	9	53	45	6	7	32	13	7	6
E.N.C	80	6	11	63	49	4	6	39	31	2	5	24	10	5	5
OH	21	1	3	17	11	1	1	9	10	-	2	8	1	1	-
IN	10	2	3	5	8	2	2	4	2	-	1	1	1	-	-
IL	22	1	2	19	15	1	2	12	7	-	-	7	5	2	3
MI	18	-	3	15	11	-	1	10	7	-	2	5	1	1	-
WI	9	2	-	7	4	-	-	4	5	2	-	3	3	1	2
W.N.C	33	6	5	22	19	2	3	14	14	4	2	8	3	2	1
MN	8	1	-	7	6	1	-	5	2	-	-	2	-	-	-
IA	6	1	-	5	2	-	-	2	4	1	-	3	3	2	1
MO	9	3	3	3	6	1	2	3	3	2	1	-	-	-	-
ND	1	-	-	1	1	-	-	1	-	-	-	-	-	-	-
SD	1	-	-	1	1	-	-	1	-	-	-	-	-	-	-
NE	3	1	1	1	1	-	1	-	2	1	-	1	-	-	-
KS	5	-	1	4	2	-	-	2	3	-	1	2	-	-	-
South	142	13	21	108	95	9	14	72	47	4	7	36	47	28	19
S.A	69	8	16	45	45	5	10	30	24	3	6	15	15	9	6
DE	1	-	-	1	1	-	-	1	-	-	-	-	-	-	-
MD	8	-	3	5	5	-	1	4	3	-	2	1	-	-	-
VA	10	2	1	7	6	1	-	5	4	1	1	2	5	5	-
WV	4	1	1	2	4	1	1	2	-	-	-	-	1	1	-
NC	11	1	4	6	7	-	4	3	4	1	-	3	-	-	-
SC	6	-	1	5	4	-	1	3	2	-	-	2	3	2	1
GA	10	2	2	6	9	1	2	6	1	1	-	-	-	-	-
FL	19	2	4	13	9	2	1	6	10	-	3	7	6	1	5
E.S.C	28	3	1	24	20	2	1	17	8	1	-	7	11	6	5
KY	7	1	-	6	4	1	-	3	3	-	-	3	3	1	2
TN	9	1	1	7	6	1	1	4	3	-	-	3	4	2	2
AL	7	1	-	6	5	-	-	5	2	1	-	1	3	2	1
MS	5	-	-	5	5	-	-	5	-	-	-	-	1	1	-
W.S.C	45	2	4	39	30	2	3	25	15	-	1	14	21	13	8
AR	4	-	-	4	3	-	-	3	1	-	-	1	-	-	-
LA	8	-	-	8	4	-	-	4	4	-	-	4	8	4	4
OK	6	-	1	5	4	-	-	4	2	-	1	1	-	-	-
TX	27	2	3	22	19	2	3	14	8	-	-	8	13	9	4
West	85	13	17	55	48	4	8	36	37	9	9	19	6	2	4
Mt	24	3	5	16	11	1	2	8	13	2	3	8	2	-	2
MT	2	-	-	2	1	-	-	1	1	-	-	1	-	-	-
ID	2	1	-	1	2	1	-	1	-	-	-	-	-	-	-
WY	1	-	1	-	-	-	-	-	1	-	1	-	-	-	-
CO	6	1	-	5	3	-	-	3	3	1	-	2	-	-	-
NM	3	-	-	3	1	-	-	1	2	-	-	2	1	-	1
AZ	5	-	1	4	1	-	-	1	4	-	1	3	1	-	1
UT	3	1	2	-	2	-	2	-	1	1	-	-	-	-	-
NV	2	-	1	1	1	-	-	1	1	-	1	-	-	-	-
Pac	61	10	12	39	37	3	6	28	24	7	6	11	4	2	2
WA	8	3	2	3	5	2	-	3	3	1	2	-	-	-	-
OR	5	-	-	5	4	-	-	4	1	-	-	1	1	1	-
CA	45	6	10	29	26	1	6	19	19	5	4	10	3	1	2
AK	1	1	-	-	-	-	-	-	1	-	-	1	-	-	-
HI	2	-	-	2	2	-	-	2	-	-	-	-	-	-	-

- Represents zero.   ¹ Includes one Representative elected as an Independent.

Source: Compiled by U.S. Bureau of the Census from Elections Research Center, Chevy Chase, MD, *America Votes*, biennial, (copyright).

No. 419. Vote Cast for United States Representatives, by Major Political Party—States: 1986 to 1990

[In thousands, except percent. In each State, totals represent the sum of votes cast in each Congressional District or votes cast for Representative at Large in States where only one member is elected. In all years there are numerous districts within the State where either the Republican or Democratic party had no candidate. In some States the Republican and Democratic vote includes votes cast for the party candidate by endorsing parties. See also *Historical Statistics, Colonial Times to 1970*, series Y 211-214]

REGION, DIVISION, AND STATE	1986				1988				1990			
	Total[1]	Democratic	Republican	Percent for leading party	Total[1]	Democratic	Republican	Percent for leading party	Total[1]	Democratic	Republican	Percent for leading party
U.S. [2] ...	59,619	32,540	26,532	D-54.6	81,786	43,662	37,175	D-53.4	61,513	32,565	27,648	D-52.9
Northeast ...	12,405	6,820	5,363	D-55.0	17,806	9,490	7,989	D-53.3	12,792	6,483	5,868	D-50.7
N.E.	3,641	2,122	1,433	D-58.3	5,327	3,086	2,066	D-57.4	4,453	2,523	1,742	D-56.7
ME.....	422	165	249	R-59.1	555	276	278	R-50.2	517	284	233	D-55.0
NH.....	241	84	156	R-64.9	429	176	252	R-58.6	291	141	149	R-51.2
VT.....	189	-	168	R-89.1	240	45	99	R-41.2	210	6	83	[3] I-56.0
MA.....	1,503	1,198	250	D-79.7	2,371	1,787	509	D-75.4	2,051	1,420	567	D-69.2
RI.....	306	130	176	R-57.6	391	140	251	R-64.1	347	182	165	D-52.5
CT.....	980	545	434	D-55.6	1,341	660	677	R-50.5	1,037	489	546	R-52.6
M.A.	8,764	4,698	3,930	D-53.6	12,479	6,403	5,923	D-51.3	8,339	3,959	4,126	R-47.1
NY [4] ...	3,904	2,132	1,665	D-54.6	5,506	2,950	2,441	D-53.6	3,662	1,830	1,662	D-50.0
NJ.....	1,554	803	739	D-51.7	2,776	1,336	1,412	R-50.9	1,827	837	911	R-49.9
PA.....	3,306	1,763	1,526	D-53.3	4,197	2,117	2,070	D-50.4	2,851	1,293	1,552	R-54.5
Midwest	16,981	8,954	7,968	D-52.7	23,539	12,270	11,205	D-52.1	17,484	9,370	7,970	D-53.6
E.N.C.	11,350	5,969	5,331	D-52.6	16,111	8,360	7,715	D-51.9	11,699	6,202	5,363	D-53.0
OH.....	3,067	1,512	1,536	R-50.1	4,155	2,087	2,068	D-50.2	3,418	1,807	1,590	D-52.9
IN.....	1,556	788	756	D-50.7	2,120	1,097	1,023	D-51.7	1,514	831	683	D-54.9
IL.....	3,017	1,623	1,393	D-53.8	4,344	2,317	2,023	D-53.3	3,077	1,646	1,349	D-53.5
MI.....	2,327	1,342	977	D-57.7	3,456	1,824	1,605	D-52.8	2,434	1,321	1,089	D-54.3
WI.....	1,383	704	669	D-50.9	2,035	1,035	997	D-50.9	1,256	597	652	R-51.9
W.N.C.....	5,631	2,985	2,637	D-53.0	7,429	3,910	3,490	D-52.6	5,785	3,168	2,607	D-54.8
MN.....	1,393	832	558	D-59.7	1,969	1,149	810	D-58.3	1,781	1,042	736	D-58.5
IA.....	890	428	461	R-51.9	1,189	580	607	R-51.0	792	401	385	D-50.6
MO.....	1,430	828	600	D-57.9	2,070	1,148	910	D-55.5	1,353	728	625	D-53.8
ND.....	286	216	67	D-75.5	300	213	84	D-70.9	234	153	81	D-65.2
SD.....	290	171	118	D-59.2	312	224	88	D-71.7	257	174	83	D-67.6
NE.....	555	197	358	R-64.5	656	230	426	R-64.9	587	277	309	R-52.7
KS.....	787	313	475	R-60.3	932	367	565	R-60.6	781	394	387	D-50.4
South [2]	16,451	9,819	6,519	D-59.7	22,979	12,951	9,826	D-56.4	17,180	9,691	7,265	D-56.4
S.A. [2]	8,284	4,991	3,249	D-60.2	12,121	6,660	5,420	D-54.9	9,409	5,222	4,063	D-55.5
DE.....	161	106	54	D-66.2	235	158	76	D-67.5	177	116	58	D-65.5
MD.....	1,063	669	394	D-62.9	1,561	937	624	D-60.0	1,091	566	517	D-51.9
DC.....	127	102	18	D-80.1	171	122	22	D-71.3	160	98	42	D-61.7
VA.....	1,043	545	467	D-52.2	1,891	802	1,077	R-57.0	1,153	663	411	D-57.5
WV.....	396	299	97	D-75.5	569	437	132	D-76.8	375	251	123	D-67.1
NC.....	1,573	890	682	D-56.6	1,985	1,108	876	D-55.8	2,011	1,076	935	D-53.5
SC.....	717	453	261	D-63.2	991	550	439	D-55.4	670	383	275	D-57.2
GA [5][6] ...	1,062	773	289	D-72.8	1,672	1,115	557	D-66.7	1,394	855	539	D-61.3
FL [5][6] ...	2,142	1,154	987	D-53.9	3,047	1,431	1,616	R-53.0	2,378	1,213	1,163	D-51.0
E.S.C.....	3,375	2,006	1,346	D-59.4	4,611	2,707	1,841	D-58.7	2,866	1,712	1,070	D-59.7
KY.....	630	375	253	D-59.5	1,105	534	564	R-51.1	764	353	397	R-52.0
TN.....	1,105	636	449	D-57.6	1,409	844	536	D-59.9	717	369	289	D-51.5
AL.....	1,116	679	436	D-60.8	1,178	722	432	D-61.3	1,017	690	315	D-67.9
MS.....	524	316	208	D-60.3	918	607	308	D-66.1	369	299	69	D-81.2
W.S.C. ...	4,792	2,822	1,924	D-58.9	6,248	3,583	2,565	D-57.3	4,906	2,758	2,132	D-56.2
AR [5][7] ...	666	387	268	D-58.1	606	353	253	D-58.3	665	369	296	D-55.5
LA [8] ...	391	288	102	D-73.8	205	89	116	R-56.8	106	106	-	D-100.0
OK [5][9] ...	725	430	291	D-59.4	767	406	362	D-52.9	857	519	338	D-60.6
TX.....	3,010	1,717	1,263	D-57.0	4,670	2,736	1,834	D-58.6	3,278	1,763	1,498	D-53.8
West	13,786	6,949	6,680	D-50.4	17,461	8,952	8,155	D-51.3	14,057	7,022	6,545	D-50.0
Mt.....	3,748	1,591	2,142	R-57.2	4,793	2,062	2,664	R-55.6	3,872	1,783	2,043	R-52.8
MT.....	318	172	146	D-54.1	365	193	172	D-52.9	317	157	160	R-50.5
ID.....	376	163	208	R-55.4	407	198	203	R-49.9	315	183	131	D-58.2
WY.....	160	49	111	R-69.5	178	57	118	R-66.6	158	71	87	R-55.1
CO.....	1,018	450	566	R-55.6	1,315	645	667	R-50.7	1,001	504	487	D-50.3
NM.....	386	179	207	R-53.6	449	209	236	R-52.6	359	146	214	R-59.5
AZ.....	804	260	540	R-67.2	1,125	322	766	R-68.1	966	345	621	R-64.3
UT.....	429	197	230	R-53.6	609	260	341	R-56.0	442	234	191	D-52.9
NV.....	257	121	134	R-52.0	344	177	160	D-51.4	313	144	151	R-48.2
Pac.....	10,038	5,358	4,538	D-53.4	12,669	6,891	5,492	D-54.4	10,185	5,239	4,502	D-51.4
WA.....	1,295	768	527	D-59.3	1,731	988	743	D-57.1	1,313	696	596	D-53.0
OR.....	1,032	505	440	D-50.7	1,024	665	358	D-64.9	1,053	667	342	D-63.4
CA.....	7,200	3,744	3,328	D-52.0	9,381	4,945	4,174	D-52.7	7,287	3,568	3,347	D-49.0
AK.....	180	74	102	R-56.5	193	72	121	R-62.5	192	92	99	R-51.7
HI.....	331	187	135	D-56.4	340	221	97	D-64.1	341	216	118	D-63.3

- Represents zero. [1] Includes vote cast for minor parties. [2] Includes vote cast for non-voting Delegate at Large in District of Columbia. [3] Leading party candidate was Independent. [4] Includes votes cast by other endorsing parties for Democratic and Republican candidates. [5] State law does not require tabulation of votes for unopposed candidates. [6] In 1986 Districts 3, 4, 5, 7, 8, 15, and 17 were unopposed; in 1988 Districts 3, 5, 7, 12, 17, and 18 were unopposed; in 1990 Districts 8, 10, 12, 13, and 16 were unopposed. [7] In 1988 District 1 was unopposed. [8] 1986 data are for general election runoffs in two districts. 1986 open primary totals: total, 755,680; Democratic, 599,291; Republican, 148,007. 1988 data are for a general election runoff in one district. 1988 open primary totals: total, 550,370; Democratic 337,724; Republican, 212,646. 1990 data are for a general election runoff in one district. 1990 open primary totals: total, 1,186,253; Democratic, 706,004; Republican, 450,867. [9] In 1986 District 6 was unopposed; in 1988 Districts 3 and 4 were unopposed.

Source: Elections Research Center, Chevy Chase, MD, *America Votes,* biennial, (copyright).

No. 420. Vote Cast for United States Representatives, by Major Political Party—Congressional Districts: 1990

[In some States the Democratic and Republican vote includes votes cast for the party candidate by endorsing parties]

STATE AND DIS-TRICT	Total vote cast (1,000)	DEMOCRATIC CANDIDATE Name	Per-cent of total	REPUBLICAN CANDIDATE Name	Per-cent of total
AL	**1,017**	(X)	68	(X)	31
1st ...	83	(¹)	(¹)	Callahan ..	100
2d ...	171	Baggiano ..	49	Dickinson..	51
3d ...	138	Browder. .	74	Sledge ...	26
4th ...	130	Bevill.....	100	(¹).	(¹)
5th ...	168	Cramer ...	67	McDonald .	33
6th ...	146	Erdreich..	92	(¹).	(¹)
7th....	181	Harris	71	Barker....	29
AK	**192**	Devens...	48	Young....	52
AZ	**966**	(X)	36	(X)	64
1st...	167	(¹).	(¹)	Rhodes...	100
2d ...	116	Udall.....	66	Sweeney..	34
3d ...	237	Hartstone.	43	Stump....	57
4th ...	231	Ivey	39	Kyl	61
5th ...	215	Phillips ...	35	Kolbe....	65
AR	**665**	(X)	56	(X)	45
1st...	157	Alexander.	64	Hayes....	36
2d ...	171	Thornton..	60	Keet.....	40
3d ...	184	Ivy	30	Hammer-schmidt	71
4th...	152	Anthony...	72	Rood....	28
CA	**7,287**	(X)	49	(X)	46
1st...	230	Bosco.....	42	Riggs....	43
2d ...	209	Rush.....	31	Herger...	64
3d ...	219	Matsui...	60	Landowski.	35
4th ...	210	Fazio	55	Baughman .	39
5th ...	156	Pelosi....	77	Nichols ...	23
6th ...	202	Boxer	68	Boerum ...	32
7th ...	200	Miller....	61	Payton ...	40
8th ...	195	Dellums...	61	Galewski..	39
9th ...	162	Stark.....	58	Romero...	42
10th ..	131	Edwards...	63	Patrosso..	37
11th ..	159	Lantos....	66	Quraishi. .	29
12th ..	206	Palmer....	34	Campbell..	61
13th ..	168	Mineta....	58	Smith	36
14th ..	249	Malberg...	49	Doolittle..	52
15th ..	147	Condit....	66	Burris....	34
16th ..	181	Panetta...	74	Reiss	22
17th ..	151	Dooley....	55	Pashayan..	46
18th ..	99	Lehman ..	100	(¹).	(¹)
19th ..	173	Ferguson..	44	Lagomar-sino	55
20th ..	189	M.Thomas.	35	W.Thomas.	60
21st ..	203	Freiman...	34	Gallegly...	59
22d ..	181	Bayer....	34	Moorhead.	60
23d ..	167	Beilenson.	62	Salomon..	34
24th ..	104	Waxman...	69	Cowles...	26
25th ..	69	Roybal....	70	Renshaw...	25
26th ..	128	Berman...	61	Dahlson...	35
27th ..	156	Levine....	58	Cohen....	37
28th ..	96	Dixon	73	Adams....	22
29th ..	65	Waters....	79	DeWitt....	19
30th ..	78	Martinez...	58	Franco...	37
31st ..	84	Dymally...	67	Sato....	33
32d ..	111	Anderson..	62	Kahn....	39
33d ..	159	Webb	31	Dreier....	64
34th ..	92	Torres....	61	Eastman..	39
35th ..	201	Norton....	33	Lewis	61
36th ..	137	Brown....	53	Hammock.	47
37th ..	232	Waite	45	McCand-less ...	50
38th ..	104	Jackson. . .	42	Dornan ...	58
39th ..	174	Hoffman...	31	Danne-meyer ..	65
40th ..	210	Gratz	32	Cox	68
41st ..	215	Kripke	44	Lowery ...	49
42d ..	184	Kim-brough ..	37	Rohra-bacher ...	59
43d ..	222	(¹).	(¹)	Packard...	68
44th ..	109	Bates	45	Cunning-ham....	46
45th ..	170	(¹).	(¹)	Hunter....	73
CO	**1,001**	(X)	50	(X)	49
1st...	129	Schroeder .	64	Roemer...	36
2d ...	173	Skaggs ...	61	Lewis	39
3d ...	177	Campbell..	72	Ellis	28
4th...	165	Bond.....	46	Allard	54
5th ...	192	Johnston..	30	Hefley...	66
6th...	163	Jarrett....	36	Schaefer..	65
CT	**1,037**	(X)	47	(X)	53
1st...	177	Kennelly ..	71	Garvey ...	29
2d ...	176	Gejden-son ...	60	Ragsdale..	40
3d ...	174	DeLauro ..	52	Scott.....	48
4th ...	138	Smith ...	23	Shays....	77
5th ...	182	Moffett ...	47	Franks....	52
6th ...	190	Kulas ...	26	Johnson...	74
DE	**177**	Carper....	66	Williams...	32
FL	**2,378**	(X)	51	(X)	49
1st...	169	Hutto	52	Ketchel...	48
2d ...	181	Peterson ..	57	Grant	43
3d ...	116	Bennett...	73	Sullivan...	27
4th ...	216	Hughes ...	44	James....	56
5th ...	158	Fletcher...	40	McCollum .	60
6th ...	234	Johnson...	41	Stearns...	59
7th ...	147	Gibbons...	68	Prout....	32
8th ...	(NA)	(¹).	(¹)	Young	(NA)
9th ...	245	Knapp....	42	Bilirakis...	58
10th ..	(NA)	(¹).	(¹)	Ireland....	(NA)
11th ..	233	Bacchus ..	52	Tolley....	48
12th ..	(NA)	(¹).	(¹)	Lewis	(NA)
13th ..	(NA)	(¹).	(¹)	Goss.....	(NA)
14th ..	236	Johnston..	66	Shore	34
15th ..	107	(¹).	(¹)	Shaw	98
16th ..	(NA)	L. Smith..	(NA)	(¹).	(¹)
17th ..	102	Lehman ...	78	Rodney ...	21
18th ..	93	Anscher...	40	Ros-Lehtinen .	60
19th ..	141	Fascell ...	62	Allen.....	38
GA	**1,394**	(X)	61	(X)	39
1st...	113	Thomas...	71	Meredith..	29
2d ...	107	Hatcher...	73	Waters....	27
3d ...	116	Ray	63	Broun ...	37
4th ...	184	Jones	53	Linder....	48
5th ...	114	Lewis	76	Tibbs....	24
6th ...	157	Worley ...	50	Gingrich [2]	50
7th ...	159	Darden ...	60	Beverly...	40
8th ...	118	Rowland ..	69	Cunning-ham....	31
9th ...	172	Jenkins ...	56	Hoffman ..	44
10th ..	154	Barnard...	58	Jones	42
HI	**341**	(X)	63	(X)	35
1st...	163	Aber-crombie .	61	Liu	39
2d ...	178	Mink....	66	Poepoe ...	31
ID	**315**	(X)	58	(X)	42
1st...	160	LaRocco ..	53	Smyser ...	47
2d ...	154	Stallings ..	64	McDevitt..	36
IL	**3,077**	(X)	54	(X)	44
1st...	108	Hayes....	94	Peyton ...	6
2d ...	103	Savage...	78	Hespel...	22
3d ...	156	Russo....	71	Klein.....	29
4th...	131	Sangmeis-ter....	59	Hoffman ..	41
5th ...	111	Lipinski...	66	Shestokas.	31
6th ...	145	Cassidy...	33	Hyde.....	67
7th ...	100	Collins....	80	Dooley ...	20
8th ...	89	Rosten-kowski ..	79	(¹).	(¹)
9th ...	136	Yates....	71	Sohn.....	29
10th ..	154	McNamara.	31	Porter	68
11th ..	154	Annunzio ..	54	Dudycz...	45
12th ..	138	(¹).	(¹)	Crane....	82
13th ..	176	Thomas...	34	Fawell....	66

See footnotes at end of table.

No. 420. Vote Cast for United States Representatives, by Major Political Party—Congressional Districts: 1990—Continued

[See headnote, p. 258]

STATE AND DISTRICT	Total vote cast (1,000)	DEMOCRATIC CANDIDATE Name	Percent of total	REPUBLICAN CANDIDATE Name	Percent of total
IL-Con.					
14th..	168	Westphal..	33	Hastert ...	67
15th..	120	([1])......	([1])	Madigan ..	100
16th..	152	Cox	55	Hallock ...	45
17th..	153	Evans	67	Lee......	34
18th..	107	([1])......	([1])	Michel....	98
19th..	172	Bruce	66	Kerans ...	32
20th..	197	Durbin....	66	Jurgens...	34
21st..	144	Costello...	66	Gaffner ...	34
22d ..	165	Poshard...	84	([1]).......	([1])
IN.....	**1,514**	(X)......	55	(X)	45
1st..	104	Visclosky..	66	Costas	34
2d ...	157	Sharp	59	Pence....	41
3d ...	159	Roemer....	51	Hiler	49
4th...	164	Long.....	61	Hawks....	39
5th...	153	Jontz	53	Johnson ...	47
6th...	183	Fadely....	37	Burton....	64
7th...	155	Riley.....	42	Myers	57
8th...	178	McCloskey.	55	Mourdock..	45
9th...	156	Hamilton ..	69	Coates ...	31
10th..	104	Jacobs ...	66	Horvath...	34
IA.....	**792**	(X)......	51	(X)......	49
1st..	90	([1]).......	([1])	Leach	100
2d ...	166	Tabor	49	Nussle....	50
3d ...	102	Nagle	99	([1]).......	([1])
4th...	131	Smith	98	([1]).......	([1])
5th...	147	Powell....	32	Lightfoot ..	68
6th...	156	Earll	28	Grandy ...	72
KS	**781**	(X)......	50	(X)......	50
1st...	164	West.....	37	Roberts...	63
2d ...	158	Slattery...	63	Morgan ...	37
3d ...	148	Jones	40	Meyers ...	60
4th...	158	Glickman..	71	Grund	29
5th...	153	Wingert...	41	Nichols ...	59
KY	**764**	(X)......	46	(X)......	52
1st...	98	Hubbard ..	87	([1]).......	([1])
2d ...	117	Natcher...	66	Tori......	34
3d ...	140	Mazzoli...	61	Brown....	39
4th...	147	Martin ...	31	Bunning...	69
5th...	65	([1]).......	([1])	Rogers ...	100
6th...	77	([1]).......	([1])	Hopkins...	100
7th...	121	Perkins ...	51	Scott.....	49
LA [3] ...	**(NA)**	(X).....	(X)	(X)......	(X)
1st...	(X)	(X).....	(X)	Livingston [4].	(X)
2d ...	106	Jefferson [5].	100	(X)......	(X)
3d ...	(X)	Tauzin [4]...	(X)	(X)......	(X)
4th...	(X)	(X).....	(X)	McCrery [4] .	(X)
5th...	(X)	Huckaby [4] .	(X)	(X)......	(X)
6th...	(X)	(X).....	(X)	Baker [4] ...	(X)
7th...	(X)	Hayes [4]...	(X)	(X)......	(X)
8th...	(X)	(X).....	(X)	Holloway [4].	(X)
ME	**517**	(X)......	55	(X)......	45
1st...	279	Andrews ..	60	Emery....	40
2d ...	239	McGowan .	49	Snowe....	51
MD	**1,091**	(X)......	52	(X)......	47
1st...	156	Dyson....	43	Gilchrest .	57
2d ...	155	Bowers ...	26	Bentley ...	74
3d ...	118	Cardin....	70	Nichols ...	30
4th...	145	McMillen .	59	Duckworth .	41
5th...	105	Hoyer	81	Breuer....	19
6th...	163	Byron	65	Fiotes	35
7th...	70	Mfume....	85	Kondner ...	15
8th...	177	Walker ...	22	Morella ...	74
MA	**2,051**	(X)......	69	(X)......	28
1st...	195	Arden	22	Conte	78
2d ...	134	Neal	100	([1]).......	([1])
3d ...	152	Early.....	99	([1]).......	([1])
4th...	219	Frank	66	Soto	35
5th...	211	Atkins	52	MacGovern	48
6th...	230	Mavroules .	65	Kelley	35
7th...	156	Markey ...	100	([1]).......	([1])
8th...	174	Kennedy ..	72	Fiscus....	23
9th...	177	Moakley...	70	([1]).......	([1])
10th..	258	Studds ...	53	Bryan	47
11th..	146	Donnelly ..	100	([1]).......	([1])
MI.....	**2,434**	(X)......	54	(X)......	45
1st...	86	Conyers...	89	Shoulders .	9
2d ...	150	White	33	Pursell....	64
3d ...	142	Wolpe....	58	Haskins...	42
4th...	131	McFarland .	42	Upton	58
5th...	167	Trzybinski .	25	Henry	75
6th...	98	Carr	100	([1]).......	([1])
7th...	132	Kildee	68	Morrill	32
8th...	144	Traxler ...	69	White	31
9th...	163	Greene ...	45	Vander Jagt....	55
10th..	154	Dennison..	33	Camp	65
11th..	154	Gould	39	Davis	61
12th..	152	Bonior....	65	Dingeman .	34
13th..	68	Collins....	80	Edwards ..	17
14th..	123	Hertel	64	McNealy ..	33
15th..	112	Ford	61	Adkins....	37
16th..	134	Dingell....	67	Beaumont .	32
17th..	132	Levin.....	70	Lankford ..	30
18th..	191	Briggs	34	Broomfield.	66
MN	**1,781**	(X)......	59	(X)......	41
1st...	201	Penny	78	Andersen..	22
2d ...	204	Stone	38	Weber....	62
3d ...	293	DeMars ...	33	Ramstad...	67
4th...	221	Vento	65	Maitland ..	35
5th...	199	Sabo.....	73	Gilbertson .	27
6th...	255	Sikorski...	65	Anderson..	35
7th...	200	Peterson..	54	Stangeland....	46
8th...	207	Oberstar ..	73	Shuster ...	27
MS	**369**	(X)......	81	(X)......	19
1st...	67	Whitten ...	65	Bowlin....	35
2d ...	71	Espy.....	84	Benford...	16
3d ...	49	Montgomery....	100	([1]).......	([1])
4th...	71	Parker....	81	Parks	19
5th...	111	Taylor....	81	Smith	19
MO	**1,353**	(X)......	54	(X)......	46
1st...	103	Clay	61	Piotrowski .	39
2d ...	189	Horn [6]...	50	Buechner..	50
3d ...	157	Gephardt .	57	Holekamp .	43
4th...	171	Skelton ...	62	Eyerly	38
5th...	116	Wheat....	62	Gardner...	38
6th...	152	McClure...	48	Coleman ..	52
7th...	160	Deaton ...	48	Hancock ..	52
8th...	142	Carnahan..	43	Emerson..	57
9th...	164	Volkmer...	58	Curtis	43
MT	**317**	(X)......	50	(X)......	51
1st...	164	Williams...	61	Johnson ..	39
2d ...	153	Burris	37	Marlenee..	63
NE	**587**	(X)......	47	(X)......	53
1st...	200	Hall......	35	Bereuter ..	65
2d ...	193	Hoagland..	58	Milder....	42
3d ...	193	Scofield...	49	Barrett....	51
NV	**313**	(X)......	46	(X)......	48
1st...	138	Bilbray....	61	Dickinson. .	34
2d ...	175	Wisdom...	34	Vucanovich....	59
NH	**291**	(X)......	49	(X)......	51
1st...	148	Keefe	45	Zeliff.....	55
2d ...	142	Swett	53	Douglas...	47

See footnotes at end of table.

No. 420. Vote Cast for United States Representatives, by Major Political Party—Congressional Districts: 1990—Continued

[See headnote, p. 258]

STATE AND DISTRICT	Total vote cast (1,000)	DEMOCRATIC CANDIDATE Name	Percent of total	REPUBLICAN CANDIDATE Name	Percent of total
NJ	1,827	(X)	46	(X)	50
1st...	134	Andrews	54	Mangini	43
2d...	111	Hughes	88	(1)	(1)
3d...	159	Pallone	49	Kapalko	47
4th..	159	Setaro	35	Smith	63
5th..	156	Olsen	22	Roukema	76
6th..	126	Dwyer	56	Daniel-czyk	46
7th..	134	Bergen	23	Rinaldo	75
8th..	73	Roe	77	(1)	(1)
9th..	155	Torricelli	53	Russo	45
10th..	52	Payne	81	Berkeley	17
11th..	144	Gordon	33	Gallo	65
12th..	168	Chandler	31	Zimmer	64
13th..	171	Adler	39	Saxton	58
14th..	85	Guarini	66	Theemling	29
NM	359	(X)	41	(X)	60
1st...	139	Vigil-Giron	30	Schiff	70
2d...	81	(1)	(1)	Skeen	100
3d...	140	Richardson	75	Archuletta	26
NY	3,662	(X)	50	(X)	45
1st...	134	Hochbrueckner	56	Creighton	35
2d...	102	Downey	55	Bugler	36
3d...	137	Mrazek	53	Previdi	43
4th...	130	Goban	32	Lent	61
5th...	132	Epstein	41	McGrath	55
6th...	61	Flake	73	Sampol	22
7th...	51	Ackerman	100	(1)	(1)
8th...	78	Scheuer	72	Reifenkugel	28
9th...	55	Manton	64	Darby	24
10th...	76	Schumer	80	Kinsella	20
11th...	39	Towns	93	(1)	(1)
12th...	43	Owens	95	(1)	(1)
13th...	59	Solarz	80	Ramos	20
14th...	98	Pocchia	36	Molinari	60
15th...	90	Reiter	37	Green	59
16th...	57	Rangel	97	(1)	(1)
17th...	98	Weiss	81	Koeppel	15
18th...	41	Serrano	93	Chiavaro	3
19th...	75	Engel	61	Gouldman	23
20th...	131	Lowey	63	Belitto	27
21st...	140	Barbuto	24	Fish	71
22d...	139	Dow	27	Gilman	69
23d...	183	McNulty	64	Buhrmaster	36
24th...	178	Lawrence	32	Solomon	68
25th...	109	(1)	(1)	Boehlert	84
26th...	97	(1)	(1)	Martin	100
27th...	151	Murray	35	Walsh	63
28th...	151	McHugh	65	Krieger	35
29th...	141	Eber	25	Horton	63
30th...	165	Slaughter	59	Regan	41
31st...	160	Gaughan	43	Paxon	57
32d...	124	LaFalce	55	Waring	31
33d...	110	Nowak	78	Kepfer	17
34th...	129	Leahey	29	Houghton	70
NC	2,011	(X)	54	(X)	47
1st...	163	Jones	65	Moye	35
2d...	175	Valentine	75	Sharpe	25
3d...	142	Lancaster	59	Davis	41
4th...	240	Price	58	Carrington	42
5th...	193	Neal	59	Bell	41
6th...	188	Allegrone	33	Coble	67
7th...	145	Rose	66	Anderson	34
8th...	180	Hefner	55	Blanton	45
9th...	213	McKnight	38	McMillan	62
10th...	172	Green	38	Ballenger	62
11th...	201	Clarke	49	Taylor	51
ND	234	Dorgan	65	Schafer	35
OH	3,418	(X)	53	(X)	47
1st...	164	Luken	51	Blackwell	49
2d...	161	Yates	36	Gradison	64
3d...	117	Hall	100	(1)	(1)
4th...	168	Burkhart	38	Oxley	62
5th...	166	Mange	25	Gillmor	69
6th...	165	Mitchell	29	McEwen	71
7th...	156	Schira	38	Hobson	62
8th...	164	Jolivette	39	Boehner	61
9th...	151	Kaptur	78	Lammers	22
10th...	168	Buchanan	37	Miller	63
11th...	170	Eckart	66	Mueller	34
12th...	181	Gelpi	28	Kasich	72
13th...	165	Pease	57	Nielsen	37
14th...	164	Sawyer	60	Bender	40
15th...	168	Erney	41	Wylie	59
16th...	172	Mendenhall	41	Regula	59
17th...	171	Traficant	78	DeJulio	22
18th...	163	Applegate	74	Hales	26
19th...	205	Feighan	65	Lawko	35
20th...	149	Oakar	73	Smith	27
21st...	129	Stokes	80	Roski	20
OK	857	(X)	61	(X)	39
1st...	135	Glassco	44	Inhofe	56
2d...	148	Synar	61	Gorham	39
3d...	134	Brewster	80	Miller	20
4th...	137	McCurdy	74	Bell	26
5th...	165	Baggett	30	Edwards	70
6th...	138	English	80	Burns	20
OR	1,053	(X)	63	(X)	33
1st...	238	AuCoin	63	Molander	30
2d...	188	Smiley	32	Smith	68
3d...	210	Wyden	81	Mooney	19
4th...	189	DeFazio	86	(1)	(1)
5th...	227	Kopetski	55	Smith	45
PA	2,851	(X)	45	(X)	55
1st...	92	Foglietta	79	Jackson	21
2d...	103	Gray	92	Bakove	8
3d...	150	Borski	60	McColgan	40
4th...	133	Kolter	56	Johnston	44
5th...	131	Stretton	39	Schulze	57
6th...	130	Yatron	57	Hicks	43
7th...	162	Innelli	35	Weldon	65
8th...	150	Kostmayer	57	Schaller	43
9th...	107	(1)	(1)	Shuster	100
10th...	113	(1)	(1)	McDade	100
11th...	88	Kanjorski	100	(1)	(1)
12th...	131	Murtha	62	Choby	38
13th...	149	Tomkin	40	Coughlin	60
14th...	108	Coyne	72	Caligiuri	28
15th...	127	Orloski	39	Ritter	61
16th...	129	Guyll	34	Walker	66
17th...	110	(1)	(1)	Gekas	100
18th...	167	Walgren	49	Santorum	51
19th...	96	(1)	(1)	Goodling	100
20th...	125	Gaydos	66	Lee	34
21st...	93	(1)	(1)	Ridge	100
22d...	124	Murphy	63	Hayden	37
23d...	132	Shannon	41	Clinger	59
RI	347	(X)	53	(X)	48
1st...	163	Wolf	45	Machtley	55
2d...	184	Reed	59	Coxe	41
SC	670	(X)	57	(X)	41
1st...	124	Platt	35	Ravenel	66
2d...	102	(1)	(1)	Spence	89
3d...	125	Derrick	58	Haskett	42
4th...	134	Patterson	61	Haskins	38
5th...	92	Spratt	100	(1)	(1)
6th...	95	Tallon	100	(1)	(1)

See footnotes at end of table.

No. 420. Vote Cast for United States Representatives, by Major Political Party—Congressional Districts: 1990—Continued

[See headnote, p. 258]

STATE AND DISTRICT	Total vote cast (1,000)	DEMOCRATIC CANDIDATE Name	Percent of total	REPUBLICAN CANDIDATE Name	Percent of total
SD	257	Johnson ..	68	Frankenfeld	32
TN	717	(X)	52	(X)	40
1st...	48	(¹)	(¹)	Quillen ...	100
2d ...	78	(¹)	(¹)	Duncan ...	81
3d ...	94	Lloyd....	53	Rhoden...	39
4th...	77	Cooper ...	67	Sanders...	30
5th...	77	Clement.	72	(¹)	(¹)
6th...	91	Gordon ...	67	Cochran ..	29
7th...	107	Blood-worth	38	Sundquist .	62
8th...	62	Tanner ..	100	(¹)	(¹)
9th...	84	Ford	58	Davis	31
TX	3,278	(X)	54	(X)	46
1st...	146	Chapman..	61	Hodges ...	39
2d ...	139	Wilson...	56	Peterson ..	44
3d ...	154	(¹)	(¹)	Bartlett ...	100
4th...	109	Hall.....	100	(¹)	(¹)
5th...	109	Bryant...	60	Rucker ...	38
6th...	188	Welch....	33	Barton....	67
7th...	114	(¹)	(¹)	Archer....	100
8th...	61	(¹)	(¹)	Fields	100
9th...	138	Brooks ...	58	Meyers ...	42
10th..	235	Pickle	65	Beilharz...	31
11th..	138	Edwards ..	54	Shine	47
12th..	137	Geren	71	McGinn ...	29
13th..	145	Sarpalius ..	57	Waterfield .	44
14th..	164	Laughlin ..	54	Dial......	46
15th..	72	de la Garza..	100	(¹)	(¹)
16th..	65	Coleman ..	96	(¹)	(¹)
17th..	104	Stenholm..	100	(¹)	(¹)
18th..	55	Washing-ton	100	(¹)	(¹)
19th..	84	(¹)	(¹)	Combest ..	100
20th..	56	Gonzalez..	100	(¹)	(¹)
21st..	193	Roberts ...	25	Smith	75
22d ..	131	Director...	29	DeLay....	71
23d ..	112	Busta-mante ..	64	Gonzales..	37
24th..	86	Frost.....	100	(¹)	(¹)
25th..	67	Andrews ..	100	(¹)	(¹)
26th..	210	Caton	30	Armey....	70
27th..	63	Ortiz	100	(¹)	(¹)
UT	442	(X)	53	(X)	43
1st...	159	Brunsdale .	44	Hansen...	52
2d ...	148	Owens ...	58	Atwood ...	40
3d ...	136	Orton	58	Snow	36
VT⁷ ...	210	Sandoval..	3	Smith	40
VA	1,153	(X)	58	(X)	36
1st...	141	Fox......	49	Bateman ..	51
2d ...	74	Pickett....	75	(¹)	(¹)
3d ...	118	Starke....	31	Bliley.....	65
4th...	91	Sisisky...	78	(¹)	(¹)
5th...	67	Payne....	99	(¹)	(¹)
6th...	112	Olin	83	(¹)	(¹)
7th...	141	Smith	42	Slaughter..	58
8th...	171	Moran	52	Parris	45
9th...	69	Boucher ..	97	(¹)	(¹)
10th..	169	Canter....	34	Wolf	62
WA	1,313	(X)	53	(X)	45
1st...	193	Sullivan ..	48	Miller.....	52
2d ...	184	Swift.....	51	Smith	42
3d ...	178	Unsoeld..	54	Williams...	46
4th...	151	Hougen ...	29	Morrison ..	71
5th...	160	Foley	69	Derby	31
6th...	129	Hicks	61	Mueller ...	39
7th...	148	McDer-mott....	72	Penberthy .	24
8th...	171	Giles.....	44	Chandler..	56
WV	375	(X)	67	(X)	33
1st...	109	Mollohan ..	67	Tuck.....	33
2d ...	114	Staggers ..	56	Luck.....	45
3d ...	75	Wise.....	100	(¹)	(¹)
4th...	77	Rahall....	52	Brewster ..	48
WI	1,256	(X)	48	(X)	52
1st...	95	Aspin	99	(¹)	(¹)
2d ...	182	Kasten-meier ..	47	Klug	53
3d ...	155	Ziegeweid .	39	Gunderson.	61
4th...	140	Kleczka ..	69	Cook.....	31
5th...	114	Moody....	68	Hammer-smith ...	27
6th...	112	(¹)	(¹)	Petri	100
7th...	161	Obey.....	62	McEwen ..	38
8th...	179	Sistine...	46	Roth.....	54
9th...	118	(¹)	(¹)	Sensen-brenner .	100
WY	158	Maxfield..	45	Thomas...	55

NA Not available.   X Not applicable.   [1] No candidate.   [2] The winning Republican candidate received 78,768 votes; the Democratic candidate, 77,794.   [3] Louisiana holds an open-primary election with candidates from all parties running on the same ballot. Any candidate who receives a majority is elected; if no candidate receives 50 percent, there is a run-off election in November between the top two finishers.   [4] Candidate listed won seat in open-primary.   [5] Both candidates in run-off election were Democrats.   [6] The winning Democratic candidate received 94,378 votes; the Republican candidate, 94,324.   [7] The winning candidate was Sanders, an Independent, who received 56 percent of the vote.

Source: Elections Research Center, Chevy Chase, MD, *America Votes*, biennial, (copyright).

Elections

No. 421. Composition of Congress, by Political Party: 1961 to 1991

[D=Democratic, R=Republican. Data for beginning of first session of each Congress (as of January 3). Excludes vacancies at beginning of session. See also *Historical Statistics, Colonial Times to 1970*, series Y 204-210]

YEAR	Party and President	Congress	HOUSE			SENATE		
			Majority party	Minority party	Other	Majority party	Minority party	Other
1961	D (Kennedy).	87th	D-263	R-174	-	D-65	R-35	-
1963	D (Kennedy).	88th	D-258	R-177	-	D-67	R-33	-
1965	D (Johnson).	89th	D-295	R-140	-	D-68	R-32	-
1967	D (Johnson).	90th	D-247	R-187	-	D-64	R-36	-
1969	R (Nixon).	91st	D-243	R-192	-	D-57	R-43	-
1971 [1]	R (Nixon).	92d.	D-254	R-180	-	D-54	R-44	2
1973 [1] [2]	R (Nixon).	93d.	D-239	R-192	1	D-56	R-42	2
1975 [3]	R (Ford)	94th	D-291	R-144	-	D-60	R-37	2
1977 [4]	D (Carter)	95th	D-292	R-143	-	D-61	R-38	1
1979 [4]	D (Carter)	96th	D-276	R-157	-	D-58	R-41	1
1981 [4]	R (Reagan).	97th	D-243	R-192	-	R-53	D-46	1
1983	R (Reagan).	98th	D-269	R-165	-	R-54	D-46	-
1985	R (Reagan).	99th	D-252	R-182	-	R-53	D-47	-
1987	R (Reagan).	100th	D-258	R-177	-	D-55	R-45	-
1989	R (Bush)	101st	D-259	R-174	-	D-55	R-45	-
1991 [5]	R (Bush)	102nd	D-267	R-167	1	D-56	R-44	-

- Represents zero. [1] Senate had one Independent and one Conservative-Republican. [2] House had one Independent-Democrat. [3] Senate had one Independent, one Conservative-Republican, and one undecided (New Hampshire). [4] Senate had one Independent. [5] House had one Independent-Socialist.

Source: U.S. Congress, Joint Committee on Printing, *Congressional Directory*, annual; beginning 1977, biennial.

No. 422. U.S. Congress—Measures Introduced and Enacted and Time in Session: 1973 to 1990

[Excludes simple and concurrent resolutions. See also *Historical Statistics, Colonial Times to 1970*, series Y 189-198]

ITEM	93d Cong., 1973-74	94th Cong., 1975-76	95th Cong., 1977-78	96th Cong., 1979-80	97th Cong., 1981-82	98th Cong., 1983-84	99th Cong., 1985-86	100th Cong., 1987-88	101st Cong., 1989-90
Measures introduced	23,396	21,096	19,387	12,583	11,490	11,156	9,885	9,588	6,664
Bills.	21,950	19,762	18,045	11,722	10,582	10,134	8,697	8,515	5,977
Joint resolutions	1,446	1,334	1,342	861	908	1,022	1,188	1,073	687
Measures enacted	774	729	803	736	529	677	483	761	666
Public	651	588	633	613	473	623	466	713	650
Private.	123	141	170	123	56	54	17	48	16
HOUSE OF REPRESENTATIVES									
Number of days	318	311	323	326	303	266	281	298	281
Number of hours.	1,487	1,788	1,898	1,876	1,420	1,705	1,794	1,659	1,688
Number of hours per day	4.7	5.7	5.9	5.8	4.7	6.4	6.4	5.6	6.0
SENATE									
Number of days	334	320	337	333	312	281	313	307	274
Number of hours.	2,028	2,210	2,510	2,324	2,158	1,951	2,531	2,341	2,254
Number of hours per day	6.1	6.9	7.4	7.0	6.9	6.9	8.1	7.6	8.2

Source: U.S. Congress, *Congressional Record* and *Daily Calendar*, selected issues.

No. 423. Congressional Bills Vetoed: 1961 to 1990

[See also *Historical Statistics, Colonial Times to 1970*, series Y 199-203]

PERIOD	President	Total vetoes	Regular vetoes	Pocket vetoes	Vetoes sustained	Bills passed over veto
1961-63	Kennedy	21	12	9	21	
1963-69	Johnson	30	16	14	30	-
1969-74	Nixon	42	24	18	36	6
1974-77	Ford	72	53	19	60	12
1977-81	Carter	31	13	18	29	2
1981-89	Reagan	78	39	39	69	9
1989-90	Bush.	11	8	3	11	-

- Represents zero.

Source: U.S. Congress, Senate Library, *Presidential Vetoes ... 1789-1968*; U.S. Congress, *Calendars of the U.S. House of Representatives and History of Legislation*, annual.

No. 424. Composition of Congress, by Political Party Affiliation—States: 1985 to 1991

[Figures are for the beginning of the first session (as of January 3). Dem. = Democratic; Rep. = Republican]

REGION, DIVISION, AND STATE	REPRESENTATIVES								SENATORS							
	99th Cong.,[1] 1985		100th Cong., 1987		101st Cong.,[1][2] 1989		102nd Cong.,[3] 1991		99th Cong., 1985		100th Cong., 1987		101st Cong., 1989		102nd Cong., 1991	
	Dem.	Rep.	Dem.	Rep.	Dem.	Rep.	Dem.	Rep.	Dem.	Rep.	Dem.	Rep.	Dem.	Rep.	Dem.	Rep.
U.S.	252	182	258	177	259	174	267	167	47	53	55	45	55	45	56	44
Northeast	54	41	55	40	55	40	56	38	9	9	9	9	10	8	10	8
N.E.	14	10	15	9	14	10	16	7	6	6	6	6	7	5	7	5
ME	-	2	1	1	1	1	1	1	1	1	1	1	1	1	1	1
NH	-	2	-	2	-	2	1	1	-	2	-	2	-	2	-	2
VT	-	1	-	1	-	1	-	-	1	1	1	1	1	1	1	1
MA	10	1	10	1	10	1	10	1	2	-	2	-	2	-	2	-
RI	1	1	1	1	-	2	1	1	1	1	1	1	1	1	1	-
CT	3	3	3	3	3	3	3	3	1	1	1	1	2	-	2	-
M.A.	40	31	40	31	41	30	40	31	3	3	3	3	3	3	3	3
NY	19	15	20	14	21	13	21	13	1	1	1	1	1	1	1	1
NJ	8	6	8	6	8	6	8	6	2	-	2	-	2	-	2	-
PA	13	10	12	11	12	11	11	12	-	2	-	2	-	2	-	2
Midwest	61	51	62	51	64	48	68	45	12	12	13	11	13	11	14	10
E.N.C	44	35	46	34	47	32	49	31	7	3	7	3	7	3	7	3
OH	11	10	11	10	11	10	11	10	2	-	2	-	2	-	2	-
IN	4	5	6	4	6	3	8	2	-	2	-	2	-	2	-	2
IL	13	9	13	9	14	8	15	7	2	-	2	-	2	-	2	-
MI	11	7	11	7	11	7	11	7	2	-	2	-	2	-	2	-
WI	5	4	5	4	5	4	4	5	1	1	1	1	1	1	1	1
W.N.C	17	16	16	17	17	16	19	14	5	9	6	8	6	8	7	7
MN	5	3	5	3	5	3	6	2	-	2	-	2	-	2	1	1
IA	2	4	2	4	2	4	2	4	1	1	1	1	1	1	1	1
MO	6	3	5	4	5	4	6	3	1	1	-	2	-	2	-	2
ND	1	-	1	-	1	-	1	-	1	1	2	-	2	-	2	-
SD	1	-	1	-	1	-	1	-	-	2	1	1	1	1	1	1
NE	-	3	-	3	1	2	1	2	2	-	2	-	2	-	2	-
KS	2	3	2	3	2	3	2	3	-	2	-	2	-	2	-	2
South	93	49	96	46	95	46	95	47	18	14	23	9	22	10	22	10
S.A.	44	25	48	21	47	22	45	24	7	9	11	5	11	5	11	5
DE	1	-	1	-	1	-	1	-	1	1	1	1	1	1	1	1
MD	6	2	6	2	6	2	5	3	1	1	2	-	2	-	2	-
VA	4	6	5	5	5	5	6	4	-	2	-	2	1	1	1	1
WV	4	-	4	-	4	-	4	-	2	-	2	-	2	-	2	-
NC	6	5	8	3	8	3	7	4	-	2	1	1	1	1	1	1
SC	3	3	4	2	4	2	4	2	1	1	1	1	1	1	1	1
GA	8	2	8	2	9	1	9	1	1	1	2	-	2	-	2	-
FL	12	7	12	7	10	9	9	10	1	1	2	-	1	1	1	1
E.S.C	18	10	19	9	18	9	20	8	5	3	6	2	5	3	5	3
KY	4	3	4	3	4	3	4	3	1	1	1	1	1	1	1	1
TN	6	3	6	3	6	3	6	3	2	-	2	-	2	-	2	-
AL	5	2	5	2	4	2	5	2	1	1	2	-	2	-	2	-
MS	3	2	4	1	4	1	5	-	1	1	1	1	-	2	-	2
W.S.C	31	14	29	16	30	15	30	15	6	2	6	2	6	2	6	2
AR	3	1	3	1	3	1	3	1	2	-	2	-	2	-	2	-
LA	6	2	5	3	4	4	4	4	2	-	2	-	2	-	2	-
OK	5	1	4	2	4	2	4	2	1	1	1	1	1	1	1	1
TX	17	10	17	10	19	8	19	8	1	1	1	1	1	1	1	1
West	44	41	45	40	45	40	48	37	8	18	10	16	10	16	10	16
Mt	7	17	9	15	9	15	11	13	5	11	6	10	6	10	6	10
MT	1	1	1	1	1	1	1	1	2	-	2	-	1	1	1	1
ID	1	1	1	1	1	1	2	-	-	2	-	2	-	2	-	2
WY	-	1	-	1	-	1	-	1	-	2	-	2	-	2	-	2
CO	2	4	3	3	3	3	3	3	1	1	1	1	1	1	1	1
NM	1	2	1	2	1	2	1	2	1	1	1	1	1	1	1	1
AZ	1	4	1	4	1	4	1	4	1	1	1	1	1	1	1	1
UT	-	3	1	2	1	2	2	1	-	2	-	2	-	2	-	2
NV	1	1	1	1	1	1	1	1	-	2	1	1	2	-	2	-
Pac	37	24	36	25	36	25	37	24	3	7	4	6	4	6	4	6
WA	5	3	5	3	5	3	5	3	-	2	1	1	1	1	1	1
OR	3	2	3	2	3	2	4	1	-	2	-	2	-	2	1	1
CA	27	18	27	18	27	18	26	19	1	1	1	1	1	1	1	1
AK	-	1	-	1	-	1	-	1	-	2	-	2	-	2	-	2
HI	2	-	1	1	1	1	2	-	2	-	2	-	2	-	2	-

- Represents zero. [1] Indiana had one vacancy. [2] Alabama had one vacancy. [3] Vermont had one Independent-Socialist Representative.

Source: U.S. Congress, Joint Committee on Printing, *Congressional Directory*, biennial; and unpublished data.

No. 425. Members of Congress—Incumbents Re-elected: 1966 to 1990

ITEM	PRESIDENTIAL-YEAR ELECTIONS						MIDTERM ELECTIONS						
	1968	1972	1976	1980	1984	1988	1966	1970	1974	1978	1982	1986	1990
Representatives:													
Incumbent candidates	409	390	384	398	412	409	411	401	391	382	393	394	407
Re-elected	396	365	368	361	393	402	362	379	343	358	354	385	391
Percent of candidates	96.8	93.6	95.8	90.7	95.4	98.3	88.1	94.5	87.7	93.7	90.1	97.7	96.1
Defeated: In primaries. . .	4	12	3	6	3	1	8	10	8	5	[1]10	3	1
In general elections . . .	9	13	13	31	16	6	41	12	40	19	29	6	15
Senators:													
Incumbent candidates	28	27	25	29	29	27	32	31	27	25	30	28	32
Re-elected	20	20	16	16	26	23	28	24	23	15	28	21	31
Percent of candidates	71.4	74.1	64.0	55.2	89.7	85.2	87.5	77.4	85.2	60.0	93.3	75.0	96.9
Defeated: In primaries. . .	4	2	-	4	-	-	3	1	2	3	-	-	-
In general elections. . .	4	5	9	9	3	4	1	6	2	7	2	7	1

- Represents zero.   [1] Six incumbents defeated in primaries by other incumbents due to redistricting.

Source: Ornstein, Norman J., Thomas E. Mann, and Michael J. Malbin, *Vital Statistics on Congress, 1991-1992*, Congressional Quarterly, Inc., Washington, DC, 1991 and Congressional Quarterly, Inc., Washington, DC, *Congressional Quarterly Weekly Report*, vol. 46, No. 18, May 6, 1989, and selected prior issues, (copyright).

No. 426. Members of Congress—Selected Characteristics: 1977 to 1991

[As of beginning of first session of each Congress, (January 3). Figures for Representatives exclude vacancies]

MEMBERS OF CONGRESS AND YEAR	Male	Fe-male	Black	His-panic [1]	AGE (in years)						SENIORITY [2]				
					Under 40	40 to 49	50 to 59	60 to 69	70 to 79	80 and over	Less than 2 years	2 to 9 years	10 to 19 years	20 to 29 years	30 years or more
REPRESENTATIVES															
95th Cong., 1977	417	18	16	5	81	121	147	71	15	-	71	207	116	33	8
96th Cong., 1979	417	16	16	5	86	125	145	63	14	-	80	206	105	32	10
97th Cong., 1981	416	19	17	6	94	142	132	54	12	1	77	231	96	23	8
98th Cong., 1983	413	21	21	8	86	145	132	57	13	1	83	224	88	28	11
99th Cong., 1985	412	22	20	10	71	154	131	59	17	2	49	237	104	34	10
100th Cong., 1987	412	23	23	11	63	153	137	56	24	2	51	221	114	37	12
101st Cong., 1989	408	25	24	10	41	163	133	74	20	2	39	207	139	35	13
102d Cong., 1991	407	28	25	11	39	152	134	86	20	4	55	178	147	44	11
SENATORS															
95th Cong., 1977	100	-	1	-	6	26	35	21	10	2	18	41	24	12	5
96th Cong., 1979	99	1	-	-	10	31	33	17	8	1	20	41	23	12	4
97th Cong., 1981	98	2	-	-	9	35	36	14	6	-	19	51	17	11	2
98th Cong., 1983	98	2	-	-	7	28	39	20	3	3	5	61	21	10	3
99th Cong., 1985	98	2	-	-	4	27	38	25	4	2	8	56	27	7	2
100th Cong., 1987	98	2	-	-	5	30	36	22	5	2	14	41	36	7	2
101st Cong., 1989	98	2	-	-	-	30	40	22	6	2	23	22	43	10	2
102d Cong., 1991	98	2	-	-	-	23	46	24	5	2	5	34	47	10	4

- Represents zero.   [1] Source: National Association of Latino Elected and Appointed Officials, Washington, DC, *National Roster of Hispanic Elected Officials*, annual.   [2] Represents consecutive years of service.

Source: Except as noted, compiled by U.S. Bureau of the Census from data published in *Congressional Directory*, biennial.

No. 427. Congressional Staff, by Location of Employment: 1967 to 1989

[Excludes those persons employed in Congressional support agencies such as the U.S. General Accounting Office, the Library of Congress, and the Congressional Budget Office]

YEAR	PERSONAL STAFF		YEAR	STANDING COMMITTEE STAFF		LOCATION OF EMPLOYMENT	1981	1983	1985	1987	1989
	House	Senate		House	Senate						
1967 . .	4,055	1,749	1970. .	702	635	Total.	17,422	17,963	18,136	18,124	17,306
1972 . .	5,280	2,426	1976. .	1,680	1,201						
1976 . .	6,939	3,251	1977. .	1,776	1,028	House of Representatives. . .	11,217	11,537	11,636	11,703	11,184
1977 . .	6,942	3,554	1978. .	1,844	1,151	Committee staff [2]	1,917	2,068	2,146	2,136	2,267
1978 . .	6,944	3,268	1979. .	1,909	1,269	Personal staff	7,487	7,606	7,528	7,584	7,569
1979 . .	7,067	3,593	1980. .	1,917	1,191	Leadership staff.	127	135	144	138	133
1980 . .	7,371	3,746	1981. .	1,843	1,022	Officers of House, staff . . .	1,686	1,728	1,818	1,845	1,215
1981 . .	7,487	3,945	1982. .	1,839	1,047						
1982 . .	7,511	4,041	1983. .	1,970	1,075	Senate	6,079	6,303	6,369	6,289	5,984
1983 . .	7,606	4,059	1984. .	1,944	1,095	Committee staff [2]	1,150	1,176	1,178	1,207	1,116
1984 . .	7,385	3,949	1985. .	2,009	1,080	Personal staff	3,945	4,059	4,097	4,075	3,837
1985 . .	7,528	4,097	1986. .	1,954	1,075	Leadership staff.	106	120	118	103	105
1986 . .	[1]7,920	[1]3,774	1987. .	2,024	1,074	Officers of Senate, staff . .	878	948	976	904	926
1987 . .	7,584	4,075	1988. .	1,976	970						
1989 . .	7,569	3,837	1989. .	1,986	1,013	Joint committee staff	126	123	131	132	138

[1] House figure is average for year and Senate figure only covers period following implementation of Gramm-Rudman budget reductions.   [2] Covers standing, select and special committees.

Source: Ornstein, Norman J., Thomas E. Mann, and Michael J. Malbin, *Vital Statistics on Congress, 1991-1992*, Congressional Quarterly, Inc., Washington, DC, 1991, (copyright).

No. 428. Number of Governors, by Political Party Affiliation: 1970 to 1992

[Reflects results of elections in previous year and holdover incumbents]

YEAR	Demo-cratic	Re-pub-lican	Inde-pen-dent	YEAR	Demo-cratic	Re-pub-lican	Inde-pen-dent	YEAR	Demo-cratic	Re-pub-lican	Inde-pen-dent
1970......	18	32	-	1983......	34	16	-	1988......	27	23	-
1975......	36	13	1	1984......	35	15	-	1989......	28	22	-
1980......	31	19	-	1985......	34	16	-	1990......	29	21	-
1981......	27	23	-	1986......	34	16	-	1991 [1].....	28	20	2
1982......	27	23	-	1987......	26	24	-	1992......	27	21	2

- Represents zero.   [1] Reflects result of runoff election in Arizona in February 1991.
Source: National Governors' Association, Washington, DC, *Directory of Governors of the American States, Commonwealths & Territories*, annual, (copyright).

No. 429. Vote Cast for and Governor Elected, by State: 1984 to 1990

[In thousands, except percent. D=Democratic, R=Republican, I=Independent]

DIVISION AND STATE	1984 Total vote [1]	1984 Percent leading party	1986 Total vote [1]	1986 Percent leading party	1988 Total vote [1]	1988 Percent leading party	1990 Total vote [1]	1990 Percent leading party	Candidate elected at most recent election
N.E.:									
ME........	(X)	(X)	427	R-39.9	(X)	(X)	522	R-46.7	John R. McKernan Jr.
NH........	384	R-66.8	251	R-53.7	442	R-60.4	295	R-60.3	Judd Gregg
VT........	234	D-50.0	197	D-47.0	243	D-55.4	211	R-51.8	Richard A. Snelling
MA........	(X)	(X)	1,684	D-68.7	(X)	(X)	2,343	R-50.2	William F. Weld
RI........	408	R-60.0	323	R-64.7	401	R-50.8	357	D-74.1	Bruce Sundlun
CT........	(X)	(X)	994	D-57.9	(X)	(X)	1,141	I-40.4	Lowell P. Weicker Jr.
M.A.:									
NY [2]........	(X)	(X)	4,294	D-64.6	(X)	(X)	4,057	D-53.2	Mario M. Cuomo
NJ [2]........	1,973	R-69.6	(X)	(X)	2,254	D-61.2	(X)	(X)	James J. Florio
PA........	(X)	(X)	3,388	D-50.7	(X)	(X)	3,053	D-67.7	Robert P. Casey
E.N.C.:									
OH........	(X)	(X)	3,067	D-60.6	(X)	(X)	3,478	R-55.7	George V. Voinovich
IN........	2,198	R-52.2	(X)	(X)	2,141	D-53.2	(X)	(X)	Evan Bayh
IL........	(X)	(X)	3,144	R-52.7	(X)	(X)	3,257	R-50.7	Jim Edgar
MI........	(X)	(X)	2,397	D-68.1	(X)	(X)	2,565	R-49.8	John Engler
WI........	(X)	(X)	1,527	R-52.7	(X)	(X)	1,380	R-58.2	Tommy G. Thompson
W.N.C.:									
MN........	(X)	(X)	1,416	D-55.8	(X)	(X)	1,807	R-49.6	Arne Carlson
IA........	(X)	(X)	911	R-51.9	(X)	(X)	976	R-60.6	Terry E. Branstad
MO........	2,108	R-56.7	(X)	(X)	2,086	R-64.2	(X)	(X)	John Ashcroft
ND........	314	D-55.3	(X)	(X)	299	D-59.9	(X)	(X)	George Sinner
SD........	(X)	(X)	294	R-51.8	(X)	(X)	257	R-58.9	George S. Mickelson
NE........	(X)	(X)	564	R-52.9	(X)	(X)	587	D-49.9	Ben Nelson
KS........	(X)	(X)	841	R-51.9	(X)	(X)	783	D-48.6	Joan Finney
S.A.:									
DE........	244	R-55.5	(X)	(X)	240	R-70.7	(X)	(X)	Michael N. Castle
MD [2]........	(X)	(X)	1,101	D-82.4	(X)	(X)	1,111	D-59.8	William Donald Schaefer
VA [2]........	1,343	D-55.2	(X)	(X)	1,789	D-50.1	(X)	(X)	L. Douglas Wilder
WV........	742	R-53.3	(X)	(X)	650	D-58.9	(X)	(X)	Gaston Caperton
NC........	2,227	R-54.3	(X)	(X)	2,180	R-56.1	(X)	(X)	James G. Martin
SC........	(X)	(X)	754	R-51.0	(X)	(X)	761	R-69.5	Carroll A. Campbell Jr.
GA........	(X)	(X)	1,175	D-70.5	(X)	(X)	1,450	D-52.9	Zell Miller
FL........	(X)	(X)	3,386	R-54.6	(X)	(X)	3,531	D-56.5	Lawton Chiles
E.S.C.:									
KY [3]........	1,031	D-54.5	781	D-64.6	(X)	(X)	835	D-64.7	Brereton C. Jones
TN........	(X)	(X)	1,210	D-54.2	(X)	(X)	790	D-60.8	Ned McWherter
AL........	(X)	(X)	1,236	R-56.3	(X)	(X)	1,216	R-52.1	Guy Hunt
MS [3]........	743	D-55.1	722	D-53.4	(X)	(X)	711	R-50.8	Kirk Fordice
W.S.C.:									
AR........	887	D-62.6	689	D-63.9	(X)	(X)	696	D-57.5	Bill Clinton
LA........	[4]1,616	[4]62.3	[4]1,559	[4]33.1	(X)	(X)	[5]1,728	[5]D-61.2	Edwin W. Edwards
OK........	(X)	(X)	910	R-47.5	(X)	(X)	911	D-57.4	David Walters
TX........	(X)	(X)	3,441	R-52.7	(X)	(X)	3,893	D-49.5	Ann W. Richards
Mt.:									
MT........	379	D-70.3	(X)	(X)	367	R-51.9	(X)	(X)	Stan Stephens
ID........	(X)	(X)	387	D-49.9	(X)	(X)	321	D-68.2	Cecil D. Andrus
WY........	(X)	(X)	165	D-54.0	(X)	(X)	160	D-65.4	Mike Sullivan
CO........	(X)	(X)	1,059	D-58.2	(X)	(X)	1,011	D-61.9	Roy Romer
NM........	(X)	(X)	395	D-50.0	(X)	(X)	411	D-54.0	Bruce King
AZ........	(X)	(X)	867	R-39.7	(X)	(X)	[6]941	[6]R-52.4	Fife Symington
UT........	630	R-55.9	(X)	(X)	649	R-40.1	(X)	(X)	Norman H. Bangerter
NV........	(X)	(X)	260	D-71.9	(X)	(X)	321	D-64.8	Robert J. Miller
Pac.:									
WA........	1,889	D-53.3	(X)	(X)	1,875	D-62.2	(X)	(X)	Booth Gardner
OR........	(X)	(X)	1,060	D-51.9	(X)	(X)	1,113	D-45.7	Barbara Roberts
CA........	(X)	(X)	7,444	R-60.5	(X)	(X)	7,699	R-49.2	Pete Wilson
AK........	(X)	(X)	180	D-47.3	(X)	(X)	195	I-38.9	Walter J. Hickel
HI........	(X)	(X)	334	D-52.0	(X)	(X)	340	D-59.8	John Waihee III

X Not applicable.   [1] Includes minor party and scattered votes.   [2] Voting years 1985 and 1989.   [3] Voting years 1983, 1987, and 1991.   [4] Primary elections in Oct. 1983 and Oct. 1987, held on a non-party basis. Winner was Democratic. Runner-up in 1987 withdrew from runoff.   [5] Result of runoff election in 1991.   [6] Result of runoff election in February 1991.
Source: Elections Research Center, Chevy Chase, MD, *America Votes*, biennial and unpublished data, (copyright).

No. 430. Composition of State Legislatures, by Political Party Affiliation: 1984 to 1990

[Data reflect election results in year shown for most States; and except as noted, results in previous year for other States. Figures reflect immediate results of elections, including holdover members in State houses which do not have all of their members running for re-election. Dem.=Democrat, Rep.=Republican. In general, Lower House refers to body consisting of State Representatives; Upper House, of State Senators]

STATE	LOWER HOUSE								UPPER HOUSE							
	1984 [1] [2]		1986 [3] [4]		1988 [5] [6]		1990 [7] [8]		1984 [1] [9]		1986 [3] [10]		1988 [5] [11]		1990 [7] [12]	
	Dem.	Rep.	Dem.	Rep.	Dem.	Rep.	Dem.	Rep.	Dem.	Rep.	Dem.	Rep.	Dem.	Rep.	Dem.	Rep.
U.S.	3,136	2,316	3,294	2,164	3,277	2,176	3,273	2,174	1,187	753	1,177	762	1,192	751	1,209	731
AL [13]	87	12	89	16	85	17	83	22	28	4	30	5	28	6	28	7
AK [14]	21	18	24	16	23	17	23	17	9	11	8	12	8	12	10	10
AZ [15]	22	38	24	36	26	34	27	33	12	18	11	19	13	17	17	13
AR [14]	91	9	91	9	88	11	91	9	31	4	31	4	31	4	31	4
CA [14]	47	33	44	36	46	33	47	32	25	15	23	15	24	15	26	11
CO [14]	18	47	25	40	26	39	27	38	11	24	10	25	11	24	12	23
CT [15]	66	85	92	59	88	63	89	62	12	24	25	11	23	13	20	16
DE [14]	19	22	19	22	18	23	17	24	13	8	13	8	13	8	15	6
FL [14]	77	43	75	45	73	47	74	46	32	8	25	15	23	17	23	17
GA [15]	154	26	153	27	144	36	145	35	47	9	46	10	45	11	45	11
HI [14]	40	11	40	10	45	6	45	6	21	4	20	5	22	3	22	3
ID [15]	17	67	20	64	20	64	28	56	14	28	16	26	19	23	21	21
IL [14]	67	51	67	51	67	51	72	46	31	28	31	28	31	28	31	28
IN [14]	39	61	48	52	50	50	52	48	20	30	19	30	24	26	24	26
IA [14]	60	40	58	42	61	39	55	45	29	21	30	20	30	20	28	22
KS [14]	49	76	51	74	58	67	63	62	16	24	16	24	18	22	18	22
KY [14]	74	26	71	29	72	28	68	32	28	10	29	9	30	8	27	11
LA [13]	91	14	87	15	86	17	84	17	38	1	34	5	34	5	33	6
ME [15]	85	66	86	65	97	54	97	54	24	11	20	15	20	15	22	13
MD [13]	124	17	124	17	125	16	117	24	41	6	40	7	40	7	38	9
MA [15]	126	34	127	33	128	32	121	38	32	8	32	8	32	8	26	14
MI [14]	57	53	64	46	61	49	61	49	18	19	18	20	18	20	18	20
MN [14]	65	69	83	51	80	53	80	54	42	24	47	20	44	23	46	21
MS [13]	116	6	113	9	112	9	102	19	49	3	45	7	44	8	44	8
MO [14]	108	55	111	52	104	58	97	65	21	13	21	13	22	12	23	11
MT [14]	50	50	49	51	52	48	61	39	28	22	25	25	23	27	29	21
NE.	(16)	(16)	(16)	(16)	(16)	(16)	(16)	(16)	(16)	(16)	(16)	(16)	(16)	(16)	(16)	(16)
NV [14]	17	25	29	13	30	12	22	20	13	8	9	12	8	13	11	10
NH [15]	102	297	132	268	119	281	128	270	6	18	8	16	8	16	11	13
NJ [14]	30	50	39	41	44	36	43	37	23	17	24	16	22	17	22	17
NM [14]	42	28	47	23	45	25	49	21	21	21	21	21	26	16	26	16
NY [15]	94	56	92	56	92	58	95	55	26	35	25	36	27	34	26	35
NC [15]	82	38	84	36	74	46	81	39	38	12	40	10	37	13	36	14
ND [14]	42	64	45	61	45	61	48	58	24	29	27	26	32	21	27	26
OH [14]	58	40	60	39	59	40	61	38	15	18	15	18	14	19	12	21
OK [14]	69	32	70	31	68	32	69	32	34	14	30	17	33	15	37	11
OR [14]	34	26	31	29	32	28	28	32	18	12	17	13	19	11	20	10
PA [14]	103	100	103	100	104	99	107	96	23	27	23	26	23	27	24	26
RI [15]	77	21	80	20	83	17	89	11	38	12	38	12	41	9	45	5
SC [14]	96	27	92	32	87	37	80	41	36	10	36	10	35	11	34	11
SD [15]	13	57	22	48	24	46	24	46	10	25	11	24	15	20	17	18
TN [14]	62	37	61	38	59	40	56	43	23	10	23	10	22	11	20	13
TX [14]	98	52	94	56	93	57	92	56	25	6	25	6	23	8	22	8
UT [14]	14	61	27	48	28	47	31	44	6	23	8	21	7	22	10	19
VT [15]	72	78	74	75	74	76	73	75	18	12	19	11	16	14	16	14
VA [14]	65	33	64	35	59	39	59	39	31	8	30	10	30	10	30	10
WA [14]	53	45	61	37	63	35	58	40	27	22	25	24	24	25	24	25
WV [14]	73	27	78	22	81	19	74	26	30	4	27	7	29	5	33	1
WI [14]	52	47	54	45	56	43	58	41	19	14	20	11	20	13	19	14
WY [14]	18	46	20	44	23	41	22	42	11	19	11	19	11	19	19	10

[1] Status as of Jan. 1985, except for NJ and VA which are as of Jan. 1986 and reflect elections held in 1985. [2] Excludes one Independent for RI; two Independents for VA; five Independents for AL; one Libertarian for AK; and one vacancy each for AL, NH, OH, RI, and SC. [3] Status as of Jan. 1, 1987, except for KY, LA, MS, NJ, and VA which are as of Jan. 1988 and reflect elections held in 1987. [4] Excludes one Independent each for VT and VA; two Liberals for NY; one vacancy each for HI and KY; and three vacancies for LA. [5] Status as of Jan. 1989, except for NJ and VA which are as of Jan. 1990. [6] Excludes one Independent for AR; two Independents for VA; one Independent Democrat for MS; one vacancy each for CA, MN, MO and OK; two vacancies for LA; and three vacancies for AL. [7] For LA and MS reflects election results in 1987 and for NJ and VA reflects election results in 1989. [8] Excludes one Independent each for LA, MA, and SC; one Independent Democrat for MO; two Independents each for VT and VA; one vacancy each for CA and MO; two vacancies each for SC and TX; three vacancies for LA. [9] Excludes three Independents for AL, and one vacancy each for MI, MN, and VA. [10] Excludes one Independent for CA; one vacancy each for CA, IN, OK, and PA; and two vacancies for WI. [11] Excludes one Independent for CA and one vacancy each for AL and NJ. [12] Excludes one Independent for CA; one vacancy each for NJ, SC, and TX; and two vacancies for CA. [13] Members of both houses serve 4-year terms. [14] Upper House members serve 4-year terms and Lower House members serve 2-year terms. [15] Members of both houses serve 2-year terms. [16] Single chamber (unicameral body) of 49 members, elected without party designation.

Source: The Council of State Governments, Lexington, KY, 1984, *Book of the States*, biennial; beginning 1986, *State Elective Officials and the Legislatures*, biennial, (copyright).

No. 431. Political Party Control of State Legislatures, by Party: 1961 to 1992

[As of beginning of year. Until 1972 there were two non-partisan legislatures in Minnesota and Nebraska. Since then only Nebraska has had a non-partisan legislature]

YEAR	LEGISLATURES UNDER—			YEAR	LEGISLATURES UNDER—			YEAR	LEGISLATURES UNDER—		
	Democratic control	Split control or tie	Republican control		Democratic control	Split control or tie	Republican control		Democratic control	Split control or tie	Republican control
1961...	27	6	15	1973...	27	6	16	1985...	27	11	11
1963...	25	7	16	1975...	37	7	5	1987...	28	12	9
1965...	32	10	6	1977...	36	8	5	1989 [2]	28	13	8
1967...	24	8	16	1979...	30	7	12	1990...	29	11	9
1969...	20	8	20	1981...	28	6	15	1992...	29	14	6
1971...	23	9	16	1983 [1]	34	4	11				

[1] Two 1984 mid-term recall elections resulted in a change in control of the Michigan State senate. At the time of the 1984 election, therefore, Democrats controlled 33 legislatures.   [2] A party change during the year by a Democratic representative broke the tie in the Indiana House of Representatives, giving the Republicans control of both chambers.

Source: National Conference of State Legislatures, Denver, CO, *State Legislatures*, periodic.

No. 432. Black Elected Officials, by Office, 1970 to 1991, and by Region and State, 1991

[As of **January 1991**, no Black elected officials had been identified in Hawaii, Idaho, Montana, or North Dakota]

REGION, DIVISION, AND STATE	Total	U.S. and State legislatures [1]	City and county offices [2]	Law enforcement [3]	Education [4]	REGION, DIVISION, AND STATE	Total	U.S. and State legislatures [1]	City and county offices [2]	Law enforcement [3]	Education [4]
1970 (Feb.)..	1,479	179	719	213	368	IA	12	1	6	1	4
1975 (Apr.)..	3,522	299	1,885	387	951	MO	175	18	120	15	22
1977 (July)..	4,342	316	2,509	451	1,066	SD	2	-	2	-	-
1978 (July)..	4,544	316	2,616	458	1,154	NE	4	1	1	-	2
1979 (July)..	4,636	315	2,675	491	1,155	KS	20	4	7	2	7
1980 (July)..	4,963	326	2,871	534	1,232	**South .....**	**5,037**	**262**	**3,377**	**474**	**924**
1981 (July)..	5,109	343	2,914	559	1,293	**S.A .....**	**2,086**	**143**	**1,486**	**131**	**326**
1982 (July)..	5,241	342	3,017	573	1,309	DE	26	3	14	3	6
1983 (July)..	5,719	386	3,283	620	1,430	MD	132	32	71	23	6
1984 (Jan.)..	5,865	396	3,367	657	1,445	DC	209	[5]4	198	-	7
1985 (Jan.)..	6,312	407	3,689	685	1,531	VA	151	11	127	13	-
1986 (Jan.)..	6,384	410	3,800	676	1,498	WV	25	2	19	4	-
1987 (Jan.)..	6,646	428	3,949	727	1,542	NC	443	19	324	24	76
1988 (Jan.)..	6,793	424	4,089	738	1,542	SC	405	21	246	12	126
1989 (Jan.)..	7,191	441	4,388	760	1,602	GA	511	37	360	26	88
1990 (Jan.)..	7,335	440	4,481	769	1,645	FL	184	14	127	26	17
						E.S.C	**1,630**	**65**	**1,146**	**183**	**236**
1991 (Jan.)..	**7,445**	**476**	**4,493**	**847**	**1,629**	KY	71	3	54	6	8
Northeast ..	**744**	**83**	**280**	**116**	**265**	TN	163	14	100	25	24
N.E	**115**	**29**	**62**	**2**	**22**	AL	706	24	530	68	84
ME	1	-	1	-	-	MS	690	24	462	84	120
NH	2	2	-	-	-	**W.S.C .....**	**1,321**	**54**	**745**	**160**	**362**
VT	2	2	-	-	-	AR	350	12	195	39	104
MA	31	6	17	1	7	LA	551	20	305	83	143
RI	12	8	3	-	1	OK	122	6	93	2	21
CT	67	11	41	1	14	TX	298	16	152	36	94
M.A	**629**	**54**	**218**	**114**	**243**	**West......**	**346**	**34**	**94**	**104**	**114**
NY	277	26	51	66	134	**Mt .....**	**50**	**12**	**10**	**16**	**12**
NJ	213	9	120	-	84	WY	2	1	-	-	1
PA	139	19	47	48	25	CO	17	4	2	9	2
Midwest ...	**1,318**	**97**	**742**	**153**	**326**	NM	4	-	1	2	1
E.N.C	**1,092**	**72**	**604**	**128**	**288**	AZ	17	4	4	3	6
OH	214	14	126	29	45	UT	1	-	-	1	-
IN	74	9	53	4	8	NV	9	3	3	1	2
IL	476	25	298	23	130	**Pac .....**	**296**	**22**	**84**	**88**	**102**
MI	305	18	117	68	102	WA	20	2	8	6	4
WI	23	6	10	4	3	OR	14	3	6	4	1
W.N.C ...	**226**	**25**	**138**	**25**	**38**	CA	259	16	68	78	97
MN	13	1	2	7	3	AK	3	1	2	-	-

- Represents zero.   [1] Includes elected State administrators.   [2] County commissioners and councilmen, mayors, vice mayors, aldermen, regional officials, and other.   [3] Judges, magistrates, constables, marshalls, sheriffs, justices of the peace, and other.   [4] Members of State education agencies, college boards, school boards, and other.   [5] Includes two shadow senators and one shadow representative.

Source: Joint Center for Political Studies, Washington, DC, *Black Elected Officials: A National Roster*, annual, (copyright).

No. 433. Hispanic Public Officials, by Office, 1984 to 1991, and by State, 1991

[For States not shown, no Hispanic public officials had been identified]

REGION, DIVISION, AND STATE	Total	State executives and legislators	County and municipal officials	Judicial and law enforcement	Education and school boards	REGION, DIVISION, AND STATE	Total	State executives and legislators	County and municipal officials	Judicial and law enforcement	Education and school boards
1984 (July)	[1]3,063	110	1,276	495	1,173	NE	3	-	3	-	-
1985 (Sept.)	[1]3,147	119	1,316	517	1,185	KS	6	4	1	-	1
1986 (Sept.)	[1]3,202	122	1,352	530	1,188	South	[1]2,043	38	914	376	710
1987 (Sept.)	[1]3,317	127	1,412	568	1,199	S.A	[1]63	11	39	10	2
1988 (Sept.)	[1]3,360	124	1,425	574	1,226	DE	1	-	1	-	-
1989 (Sept.)	[1]3,783	133	1,724	575	1,341	MD	1	-	1	-	-
1990 (Sept.)	[1]4,004	134	1,819	583	1,458	SC	1	-	1	-	-
						FL	[1]60	11	36	10	2
1991 (Sept.). .	[1]4,202	143	1,865	596	1,587	W.S.C.	[1]1,980	27	875	366	708
Northeast	[1]149	14	40	11	83	AR	1	-	-	-	1
N.E	22	5	9	-	8	LA	8	-	-	8	-
MA	4	1	-	-	3	OK	2	-	1	-	1
RI	1	1	-	-	-	TX	[1]1,969	27	874	358	706
CT	17	3	9	-	5	West........	[1]1,826	78	859	200	684
M.A	[1]127	9	31	11	75	Mt	[1]1,184	69	638	147	328
NY	[1]76	7	9	10	49	MT	2	-	-	1	1
NJ	42	1	19	-	22	ID	2	-	2	-	-
PA	9	1	3	1	4	WY	5	-	5	-	-
Midwest	184	13	52	9	110	CO	213	10	145	9	49
E.N.C	171	7	47	8	109	NM	[1]672	47	354	93	177
OH	8	-	5	2	1	AZ	[1]283	11	128	43	100
IN	9	1	6	1	1	UT	3	-	3	-	-
IL	139	3	30	3	103	NV	4	1	1	1	1
MI	12	-	6	2	4	Pac	[1]642	9	221	53	356
WI	3	3	-	-	-	WA	15	2	6	1	6
W.N.C	13	6	5	1	1	OR	8	-	5	2	1
MN	3	2	-	1	-	CA	[1]617	7	208	50	349
MO	1	-	1	-	-	AK	2	-	2	-	-

- Represents zero.   [1] Includes U.S. Representatives, not shown separately.

Source: National Association of Latino Elected and Appointed Officials, Washington, DC, *National Roster of Hispanic Elected Officials,* annual.

No. 434. Women Holding State and Local Public Offices, by Office and State: 1985 to 1992

[For data on women in U.S. Congress, see table 426]

STATE	Statewide elective executive office,[1][2] 1992	State legislature,[1] 1992	County governing boards, 1988	Mayors and municipal council members, 1985	STATE	Statewide elective executive office,[1][2] 1992	State legislature,[1] 1992	County governing boards, 1988	Mayors and municipal council members, 1985
United States ..	60	1,375	1,653	14,672	Missouri.	1	31	17	-
Alabama	1	8	7	281	Montana	2	31	18	110
Alaska.	-	14	17	233	Nebraska.	2	9	27	241
Arizona	2	31	8	87	Nevada.	3	12	10	15
Arkansas	2	10	71	365	New Hampshire ..	-	131	8	113
California	2	22	56	465	New Jersey	-	15	15	451
Colorado	3	31	18	315	New Mexico	1	16	17	86
Connecticut	2	43	(X)	240	New York	-	27	131	797
Delaware	1	8	2	57	North Carolina ...	-	25	45	337
Dist. of Columbia. .	(X)	(X)	(X)	7	North Dakota	2	23	11	174
Florida.	1	30	51	311	Ohio.	[3]1	20	25	1,129
Georgia.	-	34	28	251	Oklahoma	[3]3	13	5	312
Hawaii.	-	21	8	3	Oregon	3	22	20	344
Idaho	1	36	14	141	Pennsylvania	-	24	35	-
Illinois	1	33	152	-	Rhode Island . . .	1	25	(X)	30
Indiana	2	26	10	-	South Carolina ...	1	22	36	184
Iowa	3	22	35	732	South Dakota ...	2	26	16	149
Kansas	2	45	24	445	Tennessee.	-	15	117	144
Kentucky.	-	8	17	-	Texas	[3]3	23	30	786
Louisiana.	2	10	32	183	Utah	-	12	2	137
Maine	-	60	3	243	Vermont	-	56	(X)	87
Maryland	-	44	21	133	Virginia	1	17	49	211
Massachusetts ...	-	37	5	217	Washington	-	48	15	341
Michigan	1	22	123	2,779	West Virginia	-	28	11	202
Minnesota	2	42	37	542	Wisconsin	1	32	241	-
Mississippi.	-	12	8	176	Wyoming	2	23	5	86

- Represents zero.   X Not applicable.   [1] As of April.   [2] Excludes women elected to the judiciary, women appointed to State cabinet-level positions, women elected to executive posts by the legislature, and elected members of university Board of Trustees or board of education.   [3] Includes one official who was appointed to an elective position.

Source: Center for the American Woman and Politics, Eagleton Institute of Politics, Rutgers University, New Brunswick, NJ, information releases.

No. 435. Voting-Age Population, Percent Reporting Registered, and Voted: 1976 to 1990

[As of **November.** Covers civilian noninstitutional population 18 years old and over. Includes aliens. Figures are based on Current Population Survey (see text, section 1, and Appendix III) and differ from those in table 437 based on population estimates and official vote counts]

CHARACTERISTIC	VOTING-AGE POPULATION (mil.)								PERCENT REPORTING THEY REGISTERED								PERCENT REPORTING THEY VOTED							
									Presidential election years				Congressional election years				Presidential election years				Congressional election years			
	1976	1978	1980	1982	1984	1986	1988	1990	1976	1980	1984	1988	1978	1982	1986	1990	1976	1980	1984	1988	1978	1982	1986	1990
Total [1]	**146.5**	**151.6**	**157.1**	**165.5**	**170.0**	**173.9**	**178.1**	**182.1**	**66.7**	**66.9**	**68.3**	**66.6**	**62.6**	**64.1**	**64.3**	**62.2**	**59.2**	**59.2**	**59.9**	**57.4**	**45.9**	**48.5**	**46.0**	**45.0**
18 to 20 years old	12.1	12.6	12.3	12.1	11.2	10.7	10.7	10.8	47.1	44.7	47.0	44.9	34.7	35.0	35.4	35.0	38.0	35.7	36.7	33.2	20.1	19.8	18.6	18.4
21 to 24 years old	14.8	15.5	15.9	16.7	16.7	15.7	14.8	14.0	54.8	52.7	54.3	50.6	45.1	47.8	46.6	43.3	45.6	43.1	43.5	38.3	26.2	28.4	24.2	22.0
25 to 34 years old	31.7	33.4	35.7	38.8	40.3	41.9	42.7	42.7	62.3	62.0	63.3	57.8	55.5	57.1	55.8	53.0	55.4	54.6	54.5	48.0	38.0	40.4	35.1	33.8
35 to 44 years old	22.8	24.2	25.6	28.1	30.7	33.0	35.2	37.9	69.8	70.6	70.9	69.3	66.7	67.5	67.9	65.5	63.3	64.4	63.5	61.3	50.1	52.2	49.3	48.4
45 to 64 years old	43.3	43.4	43.6	44.3	44.3	44.2	45.9	46.9	75.5	75.8	76.6	75.5	74.3	75.6	74.8	75.5	68.7	69.3	69.8	67.9	58.5	59.9	60.9	55.8
65 years old and over	22.0	23.0	24.1	25.6	26.7	27.7	28.8	29.9	71.4	74.6	76.9	78.4	72.8	75.2	76.9	76.5	62.2	65.1	67.7	68.8	55.9	59.9	60.9	60.3
Male	69.0	71.5	74.1	78.0	80.3	82.4	84.5	86.6	67.1	66.6	67.3	65.2	62.6	63.7	63.4	61.2	59.6	59.1	59.0	56.4	46.6	48.7	45.8	44.6
Female	77.6	80.2	83.0	87.4	89.6	91.5	93.6	95.5	66.4	67.1	69.3	67.8	62.5	64.4	65.0	63.1	58.8	59.4	60.8	58.3	45.3	48.4	46.1	45.4
White	129.3	133.4	137.7	143.6	146.8	149.9	152.9	155.6	68.3	68.4	69.6	67.9	63.8	65.6	65.3	63.8	60.9	60.9	61.4	59.1	47.3	49.9	47.0	46.7
Black	14.9	15.6	16.4	17.6	18.4	19.0	19.7	20.4	58.5	60.0	66.3	64.5	57.1	59.1	64.0	58.8	48.7	50.5	55.8	51.5	37.2	43.0	43.2	39.2
Hispanic [2]	6.6	6.8	8.2	8.8	9.5	11.8	12.9	13.8	37.8	36.3	40.1	35.5	32.9	35.3	35.9	32.3	31.8	29.9	32.6	28.8	23.5	25.3	24.2	21.0
Region: [3]																								
Northeast	33.9	35.1	35.5	36.4	36.9	37.3	37.9	38.1	65.9	64.8	66.6	64.8	62.3	62.5	62.0	61.0	59.5	58.5	59.7	57.4	48.1	49.8	44.4	45.2
Midwest	39.2	40.3	41.5	41.9	42.1	42.8	43.3	43.9	72.3	73.8	74.6	72.5	68.1	71.1	70.7	61.3	65.1	65.8	65.7	62.9	50.5	54.7	49.5	48.6
South	47.1	48.8	50.6	55.4	57.6	59.2	60.7	62.4	64.6	64.8	66.9	65.6	60.1	61.7	63.0	61.3	54.9	55.6	56.8	54.5	39.6	41.8	43.0	42.4
West	26.2	27.5	29.5	31.9	33.4	34.6	36.2	37.7	63.2	63.3	64.7	63.0	59.1	60.6	60.8	57.7	57.5	57.2	58.5	55.6	47.5	50.7	48.4	45.0
School years completed:																								
8 years or less	24.9	23.6	22.7	22.4	20.6	19.6	19.1	17.7	54.4	53.0	53.4	47.5	53.2	52.3	50.5	44.0	44.1	42.6	42.9	36.7	34.6	35.7	32.7	27.7
High school: 1 to 3 years	22.2	22.3	22.5	22.3	22.1	21.4	21.1	21.0	55.6	54.6	54.9	52.8	52.9	53.3	52.4	47.9	47.2	45.6	44.4	41.3	35.1	37.7	33.8	30.9
4 years	55.7	58.4	61.2	65.2	67.8	68.6	70.0	71.5	66.9	66.4	67.3	64.6	62.0	62.9	62.9	60.0	59.4	58.9	58.7	54.7	45.3	47.1	44.1	42.2
College: 1 to 3 years	23.6	25.1	26.7	28.8	30.9	33.0	34.3	36.3	75.2	74.4	75.7	73.5	68.7	70.0	70.0	68.7	68.1	67.2	67.5	64.5	51.5	53.3	49.9	50.0
4 years or more	20.2	22.2	24.0	26.9	28.6	31.3	33.6	35.6	83.7	84.3	83.8	83.1	76.9	79.4	77.8	77.3	79.8	79.9	79.1	77.6	63.9	66.5	62.5	62.5
Employed	86.0	93.2	95.0	97.2	104.2	108.5	113.8	115.5	68.8	68.7	69.4	67.1	63.0	65.5	64.4	62.6	62.0	61.8	61.6	58.4	46.7	50.0	49.9	45.1
Unemployed	6.4	4.9	6.9	10.8	7.4	6.6	5.8	6.7	52.1	50.3	54.3	44.1	44.1	49.8	50.6	44.6	43.7	41.2	44.0	38.6	27.4	34.1	31.2	27.9
Not in labor force	54.1	53.5	55.2	57.5	58.4	58.8	58.5	59.9	65.2	65.8	68.1	67.2	63.4	64.3	65.4	63.4	56.5	57.0	58.9	57.3	46.2	48.7	48.2	46.7

[1] Includes other races not shown separately.   [2] Hispanic persons may be of any race.   [3] For composition of regions, see table 25.

Source: U.S. Bureau of the Census, *Current Population Reports*, series P-20, No. 453, and earlier reports.

Elections

No. 436. Political Party Identification of the Adult Population, by Degree of Attachment, 1960 to 1990, and by Selected Characteristics, 1990

[In percent. Covers citizens of voting-age living in private housing units in the contiguous United States. Data are from the National Election Studies and are based on a s and subject to sampling variablity; for details, see source]

YEAR AND SELECTED CHARACTERISTIC	Total	Strong Demo-crat	Weak Demo-crat	Inde-pendent Demo-crat	Inde-pendent	Inde-pendent Repub-lican	Weak Repub-lican	Strong Repub-lican	Apolitical
1960.	100	20	25	6	10	7	14	16	3
1964.	100	27	25	9	8	6	14	11	1
1968.	100	20	25	10	11	9	15	10	1
1970.	100	20	24	10	13	8	15	9	1
1972.	100	15	26	11	13	10	13	10	1
1976.	100	15	25	12	15	10	14	9	1
1980.	100	18	23	11	13	12	14	9	2
1984.	100	17	20	11	11	12	15	12	2
1986.	100	18	22	10	12	11	15	10	2
1988.	100	18	18	12	11	13	14	14	2
1990, total [1]	**100**	**20**	**19**	**12**	**11**	**12**	**15**	**10**	**2**
Year of birth:									
1959 or later (Under 32 years old) .	100	11	17	15	15	14	16	9	2
1943 to 1958 (32 to 47 years old). .	100	20	22	14	10	10	15	8	2
1927 to 1942 (48 to 63 years old). .	100	24	17	11	9	14	13	10	1
1911 to 1926 (64 to 79 years old). .	100	30	22	7	6	10	13	13	1
1895 to 1910 (80 to 95 years old). .	100	43	14	9	5	2	19	9	(Z)
Sex:									
Male .	100	18	18	14	9	13	16	11	1
Female .	100	22	20	11	12	11	14	9	2
Race:									
White.	100	17	19	11	11	13	16	11	1
Black.	100	40	23	16	8	7	3	2	2
Education:									
Grade school .	100	37	17	9	13	6	7	4	5
High school .	100	19	21	13	13	11	13	9	2
College .	100	17	17	12	7	15	19	12	(Z)

Z Less than 0.5 percent. [1] Includes other characteristics, not shown separately.

Source: Center for Political Studies, University of Michigan, Ann Arbor, MI, unpublished data. Data prior to 1988 published in Warren E. Miller and Santa A. Traugott, *American National Election Studies Data Sourcebook, 1952-1986,* Harvard University Press, Cambridge, MA, 1989, (copyright).

No. 437. Participation in Elections for President and U.S. Representatives: 1932 to 1990

[As of **November.** Estimated resident population 21 years old and over, 1932-70, except as noted, and 18 years old and over thereafter; includes Armed Forces. Prior to 1960, excludes Alaska and Hawaii. District of Columbia is included in votes cast for President beginning 1964 and in votes cast for Representative beginning 1972]

YEAR	Resident popula-tion (incl. aliens) of voting age [1] (1,000)	VOTES CAST For Presi-dent [2] (1,000)	Per-cent of vot-ing-age popu-lation	For U.S. Repre-senta-tives (1,000)	Per-cent of vot-ing-age popu-lation	YEAR	Resident popula-tion (incl. aliens) of voting age [1] (1,000)	VOTES CAST For Presi-dent [2] (1,000)	Per-cent of vot-ing-age popu-lation	For U.S. Repre-senta-tives (1,000)	Per-cent of vot-ing-age popu-lation
1932. . . .	75,768	39,758	52.5	37,657	49.7	1962. . . .	112,952	(X)	(X)	51,267	45.4
1934. . . .	77,997	(X)	(X)	32,256	41.4	1964. . . .	114,090	70,645	61.9	65,895	57.8
1936. . . .	80,174	45,654	56.9	42,886	53.5	1966. . . .	116,638	(X)	(X)	52,908	45.4
1938. . . .	82,354	(X)	(X)	36,236	44.0	1968. . . .	120,285	73,212	60.9	66,288	55.1
1940. . . .	84,728	49,900	58.9	46,951	55.4	1970. . . .	124,498	(X)	(X)	54,173	43.5
1942. . . .	86,465	(X)	(X)	28,074	32.5	1972. . . .	140,777	77,719	55.2	71,430	50.7
1944. . . .	85,654	47,977	56.0	45,103	52.7	1974. . . .	146,338	(X)	(X)	52,495	35.9
1946. . . .	92,659	(X)	(X)	34,398	37.1	1976. . . .	152,308	81,556	53.5	74,422	48.9
1948. . . .	95,573	48,794	51.1	45,933	48.1	1978. . . .	158,369	(X)	(X)	55,332	34.9
1950. . . .	98,134	(X)	(X)	40,342	41.1	1980. . . .	164,595	86,515	52.6	77,995	47.4
1952. . . .	99,929	61,551	61.6	57,571	57.6	1982. . . .	169,936	(X)	(X)	64,514	38.0
1954. . . .	102,075	(X)	(X)	42,580	41.7	1984. . . .	174,468	92,653	53.1	83,231	47.7
1956. . . .	104,515	62,027	59.3	58,426	55.9	1986. . . .	178,566	(X)	(X)	59,619	33.4
1958. . . .	106,447	(X)	(X)	45,818	43.0	1988. . . .	182,779	91,595	50.1	81,786	44.7
1960. . . .	109,672	68,838	62.8	64,133	58.5	1990. . . .	185,812	(X)	(X)	61,513	33.1

X Not applicable. [1] Population 18 and over in Georgia, 1944-70, and in Kentucky, 1956-70; 19 and over in Alaska and 20 and over in Hawaii, 1960-70. [2] Source: 1932-58, U.S. Congress, Clerk of the House, *Statistics of the Presidential and Congressional Election,* biennial.

Source: Except as noted, U.S. Bureau of the Census, *Current Population Reports,* series P-25, No. 1085; and Elections Research Center, Chevy Chase, MD, *America Votes,* biennial, (copyright).

No. 438. Voter Registration—Registered Voters, 1984 to 1990, and Registration Deadlines and Residency Requirements, 1990

[Registration figures are based on final and official registration statistics provided by Secretaries of State and State Registrars. The accuracy of registration figures varies according to the stringency of purges conducted in each State and locality. There is, therefore, some inflation in these figures, although the trends between years are likely to be accurate]

STATE	1984		1988		1990							
							Registered voters				Votes cast	
							Total[3]		Percent of total registered			
	Registered voters (1,000)	Percent registered of voting age population	Registered voters (1,000)	Percent registered of voting age population	Registration deadline[1] (days)	Residency requirement[2] (days)	Number (1,000)	Percent of voting age population	Democrats	Republicans	Number (1,000)	Percent registered voters
U.S ...	126,997[4]	73[4]	129,800[4]	71[4]	(X)	(X)	121,273[4]	67[4]	(NA)	(NA)	66,237	55
AL.	2,343	81	2,380	79	10	(5)	2,375	78	(NA)	(NA)	1,216	51
AK.	305	88	294	76	30	30	300	82	19	21	195	65
AZ.	1,463	65	1,798	69	29	50	1,860	69	42	47	1,055	57
AR.	1,268	74	1,203	68	20	(5)	1,219	68	(NA)	(NA)	696	57
CA.	13,074	69	14,005	67	29	29	13,478	62	50	39	7,699	57
CO.	1,621	69	2,030	82	25	32	1,922	78	34	31	1,022	53
CT.	1,806	75	1,784	72	21	(6)	1,703	68	39	27	1,141	67
DE.	314	69	318	65	(7)	(6)	299	58	43	38	180	60
DC.	275	56	300	61	30	(5)	308	65	78	9	169	55
FL.	5,574	65	6,047	63	30	(6)	6,031	59	52	41	3,531	59
GA	2,732	65	2,941	63	30	(6)	2,773	57	(NA)	(NA)	1,450	52
HI	419	55	444	54	30	(6)	453	53	(NA)	(NA)	350	77
ID	582	85	572	82	10	30	540	76	(NA)	(NA)	321	59
IL	6,470	77	6,357	74	28	30	6,032	69	(NA)	(NA)	3,257	54
IN	3,054	76	2,866	71	29	30	2,765	66	(NA)	(NA)	1,513	55
IA	1,729	82	1,690	82	10	(5)	1,580	75	38	31	984	62
KS.	1,291	72	1,266	69	15	(5)	1,205	65	30	44	786	65
KY.	2,023	75	2,026	74	30	30	1,854	67	67	30	916	49
LA	2,262	72	2,228	70	24	(5)	2,169	70	74	18	1,391	64
ME	811	95	855	96	(8)	(6)	872	94	(NA)	(NA)	522	60
MD	2,253	69	2,310	66	29	(6)	2,135	59	63	29	1,111	52
MA	3,254	73	3,275	72	28	(6)	3,214	70	42	14	2,343	73
MI	5,889	89	5,953	88	30	30	5,892	86	(NA)	(NA)	2,565	44
MN	2,893	95	2,917	92	(8)	20	2,871	88	(NA)	(NA)	1,808	63
MS	1,670	93	1,596	86	30	30	1,593	85	(NA)	(NA)	369	23
MO	2,969	80	2,942	77	20	(5)	2,748	71	(NA)	(NA)	1,353	49
MT	527	90	506	86	30	30	436	75	(NA)	(NA)	319	73
NE.	903	77	899	77	(9)	(5)	891	75	42	50	594	67
NV.	356	52	445	57	30	30	516	60	45	43	321	62
NH	544	74	650	79	10	10	659	77	29	39	295	45
NJ.	4,073	71	4,011	68	29	30	3,718	62	(NA)	(NA)	1,938	52
NM.	651	65	675	61	28	(6)	658	60	59	35	411	62
NY.	9,044	68	8,612	64	30	30	8,202	60	(NA)	(NA)	4,057	49
NC.	3,271	71	3,432	70	10[10]21	30	3,348	66	64	31	2,071	62
ND.	(11)	(11)	(11)	(11)	(11)	30	(11)	(11)	(11)	(11)	(NA)	(X)
OH.	6,358	81	6,323	79	29	(6)	5,834	72	(NA)	(NA)	3,478	60
OK.	1,950	81	2,199	92	10	(6)	2,011	86	65	33	911	45
OR.	1,609	81	1,524	74	21	20	1,477	69	39	47	1,113	75
PA.	6,194	69	5,876	65	30	30	5,659	61	51	44	3,053	54
RI	542	74	549	72	30	30	537	70	(NA)	(NA)	364	68
SC.	1,396	58	1,438	57	30	30	1,355	52	(NA)	(NA)	761	56
SD.	443	88	440	87	15	(6)	420	81	43	49	259	62
TN.	2,580	74	2,417	66	29	20	2,460	65	(NA)	(NA)	772	31
TX.	7,900	69	8,202	67	30	30	7,701	63	(NA)	(NA)	3,893	51
UT.	840	82	807	75	20	30	781	72	(NA)	(NA)	442	57
VT.	322	82	348	85	17	(5)	350	82	(NA)	(NA)	211	60
VA.	2,552	60	2,877	63	31	(6)	2,738	58	(NA)	(NA)	1,153	42
WA	2,458	76	2,499	73	30	30	2,225	62	(NA)	(NA)	1,313	59
WV	1,025	72	969	69	30	30	885	64	66	31	404	46
WI	(12)	(12)	(12)	(12)	(8)	10	(12)	(12)	(12)	(12)	(NA)	(X)
WY	240	68	226	64	30	(9)	222	68	35	57	160	72

NA Not available. X Not applicable. [1] Number of days prior to a general election by which a prospective voter must register with State or local election officials. [2] Number of days a prospective voter must reside in a State to vote in a general election. [3] Includes voters registered with other parties and with no party (independents), not shown separately. [4] Estimate based on actual registration statistics from the States which keep registration records. Percentages are the actual percentages of the voting age population who registered in the States, for which actual registration figures are available. The estimates are derived from applying that percentage to the national voting age population figure. [5] No residency requirements. [6] No durational requirement. To varying degrees, States without durational residency requirements may call for proof of residency or sworn certification of resident status; enforcement of such residency certification often left to discretion of local registration officials. [7] Third Saturday in October. [8] Election day. [9] Second Friday before election day. [10] Business days. [11] North Dakota does not require registration. [12] Wisconsin does not keep statewide registration statistics.

Source: Committee for the Study of the American Electorate, Washington, DC, *Non-Voter Study,* '84-'85, '88-'89, and '90-'91.

No. 439. Resident Population of Voting Age and Percent Casting Votes—States: 1984 to 1990, and Projections, 1992

[As of **November.** Estimated population, 18 years old and over. Includes Armed Forces stationed in each State, aliens, and institutional population]

REGION, DIVISION, AND STATE	VOTING-AGE POPULATION 1984 (1,000)	1986 (1,000)	1988 (1,000)	1990 (1,000)	1992, proj. Total (1,000)	Percent Black	Percent female	PERCENT CASTING VOTES FOR— Presidential electors 1984	1988	U.S. Representatives 1984	1986	1988	1990
U.S.	174,468	178,566	182,779	185,812	189,044	11.4	52.0	53.1	50.1	47.7	33.4	44.7	33.1
Northeast	37,582	38,064	38,590	38,838	38,824	10.9	52.8	54.5	51.4	51.0	32.6	46.1	32.9
N.E	9,567	9,748	9,950	10,137	10,143	4.6	52.5	58.7	57.6	55.5	37.4	53.5	43.9
ME	855	875	908	924	944	0.3	52.2	64.7	61.1	63.4	48.2	61.1	56.0
NH	732	775	817	835	852	0.6	51.3	53.1	55.2	51.0	31.1	52.5	34.8
VT	392	403	420	422	429	0.2	52.0	59.9	57.9	57.7	46.9	57.1	49.7
MA	4,447	4,502	4,565	4,646	4,607	4.9	53.0	57.5	57.7	52.8	33.4	51.9	44.1
RI	735	751	765	776	776	3.7	53.1	55.8	52.9	53.1	40.7	51.1	44.7
CT	2,405	2,442	2,476	2,534	2,535	7.8	52.3	61.0	58.3	59.5	40.1	54.2	40.9
M.A	28,015	28,315	28,640	28,701	28,681	13.1	52.9	53.1	49.3	49.5	31.0	43.6	29.1
NY	13,331	13,447	13,574	13,683	13,609	16.1	53.0	51.1	47.8	46.6	29.0	40.6	26.8
NJ	5,695	5,811	5,894	5,927	5,943	13.1	52.5	56.5	52.6	52.5	26.7	47.1	30.8
PA	8,989	9,057	9,171	9,091	9,129	8.7	53.1	53.9	49.5	51.8	36.5	45.8	31.4
Midwest	43,240	43,704	44,403	44,160	44,656	9.0	52.3	58.8	55.5	55.9	38.9	53.0	39.6
E.N.C	30,373	30,723	31,204	31,133	31,482	10.8	52.4	58.0	54.4	54.7	36.9	51.6	37.6
OH	7,875	7,946	8,059	8,066	8,146	10.0	52.8	57.8	54.5	55.0	38.6	51.6	42.4
IN	3,995	4,040	4,111	4,105	4,176	7.3	52.4	55.9	52.8	54.6	38.5	51.6	36.9
IL	8,448	8,517	8,636	8,495	8,568	13.9	52.2	57.0	52.8	54.2	35.4	50.3	36.2
MI	6,568	6,699	6,805	6,851	6,923	13.2	52.3	57.9	53.9	52.6	34.7	50.8	35.5
WI	3,487	3,522	3,593	3,616	3,669	4.3	51.8	63.4	61.0	59.5	39.3	56.6	34.7
W.N.C	12,867	12,981	13,199	13,027	13,174	4.7	52.1	60.8	58.2	58.7	43.4	56.3	44.4
MN	3,057	3,115	3,201	3,222	3,278	1.9	51.7	68.2	65.5	64.6	44.7	61.5	55.3
IA	2,125	2,105	2,125	2,061	2,075	1.5	52.5	62.1	57.7	59.7	42.3	56.0	38.4
MO	3,709	3,772	3,840	3,813	3,858	9.8	52.8	57.2	54.5	55.0	37.9	53.9	35.5
ND	494	488	484	462	458	0.4	50.7	62.6	61.4	62.6	58.6	62.0	50.6
SD	509	511	518	498	502	0.2	51.6	62.5	60.4	62.1	56.8	60.2	51.7
NE	1,174	1,171	1,183	1,152	1,167	3.3	52.2	55.5	55.9	55.4	47.4	55.5	50.9
KS	1,800	1,818	1,848	1,819	1,836	5.4	51.7	56.8	53.7	55.2	43.3	50.4	42.9
South	59,257	61,004	62,470	63,821	65,411	17.1	52.3	48.7	45.7	38.7	27.0	36.8	26.9
S.A	29,710	30,896	32,069	33,312	34,320	18.8	52.4	47.5	44.4	38.7	26.8	37.8	28.2
DE	459	477	498	507	525	16.4	52.4	55.6	50.2	52.9	33.8	47.2	35.0
MD	3,259	3,372	3,498	3,640	3,719	24.4	52.4	51.4	49.0	45.9	31.5	44.6	30.0
DC	490	486	472	481	459	64.3	54.5	43.1	40.9	33.1	26.1	36.2	33.2
VA	4,234	4,392	4,568	4,716	4,842	17.8	51.7	50.7	48.0	43.4	23.7	41.4	24.4
WV	1,424	1,412	1,398	1,349	1,350	2.9	53.0	51.7	46.7	49.4	28.0	40.7	27.8
NC	4,586	4,731	4,880	5,061	5,217	20.2	52.4	47.4	43.7	47.1	33.2	40.7	39.7
SC	2,382	2,458	2,531	2,587	2,672	27.1	52.4	40.7	39.0	39.0	29.2	39.2	25.9
GA	4,224	4,421	4,593	4,791	4,950	24.9	52.4	42.0	39.4	36.0	24.0	36.4	29.1
FL	8,651	9,146	9,632	10,180	10,586	11.8	52.4	48.3	44.7	[1]28.2	[1]23.4	[1]31.6	[1]23.4
E.S.C	10,879	11,065	11,254	11,252	11,479	17.7	52.9	50.2	46.8	41.6	30.5	41.0	25.5
KY	2,695	2,720	2,752	2,740	2,779	6.7	52.5	50.8	48.1	44.1	23.2	40.2	27.9
TN	3,489	3,569	3,660	3,685	3,783	14.6	52.8	49.1	44.7	37.7	31.0	38.5	19.5
AL	2,892	2,947	2,997	2,995	3,056	22.9	53.1	49.9	46.0	39.7	37.9	39.3	34.0
MS	1,803	1,827	1,845	1,832	1,861	32.0	53.3	52.2	50.5	48.2	28.7	49.8	20.1
W.S.C	18,668	19,044	19,148	19,257	19,612	13.7	51.8	49.5	47.3	36.9	25.2	32.6	25.5
AR	1,707	1,732	1,750	1,737	1,768	13.7	52.8	51.8	47.3	[1]27.1	38.5	[1]34.6	38.3
LA	3,131	3,153	3,112	2,988	2,992	28.5	52.8	54.5	52.3	[2]20.5	[2]12.4	[2]6.6	[2]3.5
OK	2,410	2,396	2,366	2,310	2,328	6.7	52.1	52.1	49.6	46.1	[1]30.3	[1]32.4	37.1
TX	11,420	11,764	11,919	12,222	12,524	11.5	51.3	47.3	45.5	41.0	25.6	39.2	26.8
West.	34,389	35,795	37,316	38,993	40,153	5.3	50.6	52.0	49.6	49.4	38.5	46.8	36.0
Mt	8,920	9,260	9,548	9,856	10,157	2.6	50.9	53.1	52.5	50.8	40.5	50.2	39.3
MT	591	587	586	579	586	0.2	51.2	65.0	62.4	62.8	54.2	62.3	54.8
ID	687	693	703	707	740	0.4	50.8	59.8	58.2	59.0	54.3	57.9	44.5
WY	355	349	339	319	322	0.6	50.0	53.2	52.1	53.0	45.8	52.5	49.5
CO	2,350	2,407	2,440	2,447	2,501	3.9	50.9	55.1	56.2	53.1	42.3	53.9	40.9
NM	1,001	1,041	1,065	1,075	1,104	1.8	51.6	51.3	48.9	50.0	37.1	42.2	33.4
AZ	2,226	2,400	2,543	2,696	2,749	2.8	51.2	46.1	46.1	42.4	33.5	44.2	35.8
UT	1,021	1,048	1,067	1,104	1,142	0.7	51.3	61.7	60.6	58.9	40.9	57.1	40.1
NV	688	734	804	929	1,013	5.9	49.1	41.7	43.5	39.4	35.0	42.8	33.7
Pac	25,469	26,536	27,768	29,137	29,996	6.2	50.4	51.7	48.6	48.9	37.8	45.6	35.0
WA	3,226	3,329	3,491	3,650	3,818	2.8	50.9	58.4	53.4	56.0	38.9	49.6	36.0
OR	1,984	2,022	2,096	2,140	2,226	1.5	51.5	61.8	57.3	60.6	51.0	48.9	49.2
CA	19,152	20,043	21,006	22,124	22,668	7.4	50.3	49.6	47.1	46.8	35.9	44.7	32.9
AK	350	358	359	382	395	3.8	47.6	59.4	55.7	58.9	50.3	53.8	50.2
HI	757	784	815	841	889	2.1	49.9	44.4	43.5	36.5	42.2	41.7	40.5

[1] State law does not require tabulation of votes for unopposed candidates.   [2] See footnote 8, table 419.

Source: Compiled by U.S. Bureau of the Census. Population data from U.S. Bureau of the Census, *Current Population Reports,* series P-25, No. 1085; votes cast from Elections Research Center, Chevy Chase, MD, *America Votes,* biennial (copyright).

No. 440. Political Party Financial Activity, by Major Political Party: 1981 to 1990

[In millions of dollars. Covers financial activity during 2-year calendar period indicated. Some political party financial activities, such as building funds and state and local election spending, are not reported to the source. Also excludes contributions earmarked to federal candidates through the party organizations, since some of those funds never passed through the committees' accounts]

YEAR AND TYPE OF COMMITTEE	DEMOCRATIC				REPUBLICAN			
	Receipts, net [1]	Dis- burse- ments, net [1]	Contribu- tions to candi- dates	Monies spent on behalf of party's nomi- nees [2]	Receipts, net [1]	Dis- burse- ments, net [1]	Contribu- tions to candi- dates	Monies spent on behalf of party's nomi- nees [2]
1981-82.	39.3	40.1	1.7	3.3	215.0	214.0	5.6	14.3
1983-84.	98.5	97.4	2.6	9.0	297.9	300.8	4.9	20.1
1985-86, total	64.8	65.9	1.7	9.0	255.2	258.9	3.4	14.3
National committee	17.2	17.4	(Z)	0.3	83.8	86.7	0.4	(Z)
Senatorial committee	13.4	13.5	0.6	6.1	84.4	83.7	0.6	10.0
Congressional committee	12.3	12.6	0.6	1.5	39.8	40.8	1.7	4.1
Conventions, other national.	7.9	8.1	(Z)	-	0.2	0.2	-	-
State and local	14.0	14.3	0.5	1.0	47.0	47.4	0.8	0.3
1987-88, total	135.2	129.1	1.8	17.9	267.1	261.0	3.4	22.7
National committee	52.3	47.0	0.1	8.1	91.0	89.9	0.3	8.3
Senatorial committee	16.3	16.3	0.4	6.2	65.9	63.3	0.8	10.2
Congressional committee	12.5	12.5	0.7	2.4	34.7	33.7	1.6	4.1
Conventions, other national.	19.2	19.2	-	-	9.6	9.6	-	-
State and local	35.0	34.1	0.6	1.2	65.9	64.5	0.7	0.1
1989-90, total	85.8	90.9	1.5	8.7	206.3	213.5	2.9	10.7
National committee	14.5	18.5	0.1	0.1	68.7	70.4	0.3	0.1
Senatorial committee	17.5	17.6	0.4	4.5	65.1	67.6	0.7	7.7
Congressional committee	9.1	9.1	0.4	2.9	33.2	34.4	0.9	2.8
Conventions, other national.	8.8	9.2	-	-	-	-	-	-
State and local	35.8	36.4	0.5	1.2	39.3	41.1	1.0	0.2

- Represents zero. Z Less than $50,000. [1] Excludes monies transferred between affiliated committees. [2] Monies spent in the general election.

Source: U.S. Federal Election Commission, *FEC Reports on Financial Activity, Final Report, Party and Non-Party Political Committees,* biennial.

No. 441. Independent Expenditures for Presidential and Congressional Campaigns: 1981 to 1990

[In thousands of dollars. Covers campaign finance activity during 2-year calendar period indicated. An "independent expenditure" is money spent to support or defeat a clearly identified candidate. According to Federal election law, such an expenditure must be made without cooperation or consultation with the candidate or his/her campaign. Independent expenditures are not limited as are contributions]

TYPE OF OFFICE AND YEAR	ALL PARTIES			DEMOCRATS		REPUBLICANS		OTHERS	
	Total	For	Against	For	Against	For	Against	For	Against
TOTAL									
1981-82	7,282	2,135	5,147	1,252	4,597	883	550	-	-
1983-84	23,420	19,951	3,468	1,693	1,016	18,257	2,453	1	-
1985-86	10,205	8,832	1,373	3,450	888	5,376	485	6	-
1987-88	21,341	16,654	4,687	2,865	4,248	13,784	439	6	-
1989-90	5,774	4,177	1,597	1,530	735	2,645	862	2	-
PRESIDENTIAL									
1981-82	185	184	1	92	1	92	-	-	-
1983-84	17,468	16,638	831	806	487	15,830	344	1	-
1985-86	841	795	45	76	28	719	17	-	-
1987-88	14,127	10,628	3,499	568	3,352	10,054	146	6	-
1989-90	497	322	174	5	169	318	5	-	-
SENATE									
1981-82	4,875	724	4,150	426	3,667	298	484	-	-
1983-84	4,627	2,134	2,493	326	110	1,808	2,082	-	-
1985-86	5,312	4,331	980	988	632	3,343	348	-	-
1987-88	4,401	3,641	761	831	617	2,810	143	(Z)	-
1989-90	3,506	2,362	1,144	756	428	1,604	716	2	-
HOUSE OF REPRESENTATIVES									
1981-82	2,221	1,226	995	734	929	492	66	-	-
1983-84	1,325	1,180	145	561	118	619	27	-	-
1985-86	4,053	3,706	347	2,386	227	1,314	120	6	-
1987-88	2,813	2,385	427	1,466	279	920	149	(Z)	-
1989-90	1,772	1,493	279	770	138	723	141	-	-

- Represents zero. Z Less than $500.

Source: U.S. Federal Election Commission, *FEC Index of Independent Expenditures, 1987-88,* May 1989 and press release of May 19, 1989, and unpublished data.

No. 442. Political Action Committees—Number, by Committee Type: 1980 to 1991

[As of **December 31**]

COMMITTEE TYPE	1980	1985	1986	1987	1988	1989	1990	1991
Total	2,551	3,992	4,157	4,165	4,268	4,178	4,172	4,094
Corporate	1,206	1,710	1,744	1,775	1,816	1,796	1,795	1,738
Labor	297	388	384	364	354	349	346	338
Trade/membership/health	576	695	745	865	786	777	774	742
Non-connected	374	1,003	1,077	957	1,115	1,060	1,062	1,083
Cooperative	42	54	56	59	59	59	59	57
Corporation without stock	56	142	151	145	138	137	136	136

Source: U.S. Federal Election Commission, press release of January 20, 1992.

No. 443. Political Action Committees—Financial Activity Summary by Committee Type: 1985 to 1990

[**In millions of dollars.** Covers financial activity during 2-year calendar period indicated. Data have not been adjusted for transfers between affiliated committees]

COMMITTEE TYPE	RECEIPTS			DISBURSEMENTS [1]			CONTRIBUTIONS TO CANDIDATES		
	1985-86	1987-88	1989-90	1985-1986	1987-88	1989-90	1985-1986	1987-88	1989-90
Total	353.4	384.6	372.1	340.0	364.2	357.6	139.8	159.2	159.1
Corporate	82.0	96.9	106.5	79.3	89.8	101.1	49.6	56.2	58.1
Labor	65.3	78.5	88.9	57.9	74.1	84.6	31.0	35.5	34.7
Trade/membership/health	75.4	89.5	92.5	73.3	83.7	88.1	34.6	41.2	44.8
Non-connected	118.6	106.3	71.6	118.4	104.9	71.4	19.4	20.3	15.1
Cooperative	4.7	4.9	5.0	4.7	4.5	4.8	2.7	2.7	2.9
Corporation without stock	7.4	8.5	7.6	6.4	7.2	7.7	2.6	3.3	3.4

[1] Comprises contributions to candidates, independent expenditures, and other disbursements.

Source: U.S. Federal Election Commission, *FEC Reports on Financial Activity, Final Report, Party and Non-Party Political Committees,* biennial.

No. 444. Presidential Campaign Finances—Federal Funds for General Election: 1980 to 1988

[**In millions of dollars.** Based on FEC certifications, audit reports, and Dept. of Treasury reports]

1980		1984		1988	
Candidate	Amount	Candidate	Amount	Candidate	Amount
Total	62.7	Total	80.3	Total	92.2
Anderson [1]	4.2	Mondale	40.2	Bush	46.1
Carter	29.4	Reagan	40.1	Dukakis	46.1
Reagan	29.2				

[1] John Anderson, as the candidate of a new party, was permitted to raise funds privately. Total receipts for the Anderson campaign, including Federal funds, were $17.6 million, and total expenditures were $15.6 million.

Source: U.S. Federal Election Commission, press releases of November 15, 1981, June 4, 1986, and April 9, 1989.

No. 445. Presidential Campaign Finances—Primary Campaign Receipts and Disbursements: 1979 to 1988

[**In millions of dollars.** Covers campaign finance activity during 2-year calendar period indicated. Covers candidates who received Federal matching funds or who had significant financial activity]

ITEM	TOTAL			DEMOCRATIC			REPUBLICAN		
	1979-80	1983-84 [1]	1987-88 [2]	1979-80	1983-84	1987-88	1979-80	1983-84	1987-88
Receipts, total [3]	94.2	105.0	213.8	35.6	77.5	91.9	58.5	27.1	116.0
Individual contributions	61.0	62.8	141.1	23.9	46.2	59.4	37.1	16.4	76.8
Federal matching funds	30.9	34.9	65.7	10.3	24.6	30.1	20.5	10.1	34.7
Disbursements	92.3	103.6	210.7	35.6	77.4	90.2	56.7	25.9	114.6

[1] Includes Citizens Party candidate, not shown separately. [2] Includes a minor party candidate who sought several party nominations and a Democratic candidate who did not receive Federal matching funds, but who had significant financial activity. [3] Includes other types of receipts, not shown separately.

Source: U.S. Federal Election Commission, *FEC Reports on Financial Activity, Final Report, Presidential Pre-Nomination Campaigns,* quadrennial.

No. 446. Congressional Campaign Finances—Receipts and Disbursements: 1985 to 1990

[Covers all campaign finance activity during 2-year calendar period indicated for primary, general, run-off, and special elections. For 1985-86 relates to 1,611 House of Representatives candidates and 262 Senate candidates; for 1987-88 to 1,582 House of Representatives candidates and 210 Senate candidates; for 1989-90 to 1,580 House of Representatives candidates and 179 Senate candidates. Data have been adjusted to eliminate transfers between all committees within a campaign. For further information on legal limits of contributions, see Federal Election Campaign Act of 1971, as amended]

ITEM	HOUSE OF REPRESENTATIVES						SENATE					
	Amount (mil. dol.)			Percent distribution			Amount (mil. dol.)			Percent distribution		
	1985-86	1987-88	1989-90	1985-86	1987-88	1989-90	1985-86	1987-88	1989-90	1985-86	1987-88	1989-90
Total receipts [1]	257.7	278.3	285.4	100	100	100	214.4	199.3	186.3	100	100	100
Individual contributions	127.6	129.9	129.9	50	47	46	140.1	128.1	119.6	65	64	64
Other committees	87.4	102.2	108.5	34	37	38	45.3	45.7	41.2	21	23	22
Candidate loans	20.9	23.2	20.9	8	8	7	6.2	8.2	10.0	3	4	5
Candidate contributions	4.8	4.9	4.8	2	2	2	1.9	6.8	2.4	1	3	1
Democrats	139.9	160.3	163.4	54	58	57	91.8	107.7	89.5	43	54	48
Republicans	117.7	117.0	120.9	46	42	42	122.5	91.3	96.8	57	46	52
Others	0.1	1.0	1.1	(Z)	(Z)	(Z)	0.1	0.3	(Z)	(Z)	(Z)	(Z)
Incumbents	149.7	175.6	181.9	58	63	64	90.3	98.3	118.7	42	49	64
Challengers	49.2	52.5	47.7	19	19	17	67.2	56.3	54.8	31	28	29
Open seats [2]	58.8	50.2	55.9	23	18	20	56.9	44.7	12.8	27	22	7
Total disbursements	239.3	257.6	265.8	100	100	100	211.6	201.4	180.4	100	100	100
Democrats	128.7	145.6	151.0	54	57	57	89.0	107.9	87.6	42	54	49
Republicans	110.5	111.0	113.7	46	43	43	122.6	93.1	92.9	58	46	52
Others	0.1	1.0	1.1	(Z)	(Z)	(Z)	(Z)	0.3	(Z)	(Z)	(Z)	(Z)
Incumbents	132.5	156.6	163.4	55	61	62	89.3	101.2	113.5	42	50	63
Challengers	48.8	51.7	47.0	20	20	18	66.2	56.1	54.9	31	28	30
Open seats [2]	58.0	49.3	55.4	24	19	21	56.1	44.1	12.1	27	22	7

Z Less than $50,000 or 0.5 percent.   [1] Includes other types of receipts, not shown separately.   [2] Elections in which an incumbent did not seek re-election.

Source: U.S. Federal Election Commission, *FEC Reports on Financial Activity, Final Report, U.S. Senate and House Campaigns*, biennial.

No. 447. Contributions to Congressional Campaigns by Political Action Committees (PAC), by Type of Committee: 1979 to 1990

[In millions of dollars. Cover amounts given to candidates in primary, general, run-off, and special elections during the 2-year calendar period indicated. For number of political action committees, see table 442]

TYPE OF COMMITTEE	HOUSE OF REPRESENTATIVES						SENATE					
	Total	Demo-crats	Repub-licans	Incum-bents	Chal-lengers	Open seats [1]	Total	Demo-crats	Repub-licans	Incum-bents	Chal-lengers	Open seats [1]
1979-80	37.9	20.5	17.2	24.9	7.9	5.1	17.3	8.4	9.0	8.6	6.6	2.1
1981-82	61.1	34.2	26.8	40.8	10.9	9.4	22.6	11.2	11.4	14.3	5.2	3.0
1983-84, total [2]	75.7	46.3	29.3	57.2	11.3	7.2	29.7	14.0	15.6	17.9	6.3	5.4
Corporate	23.4	10.4	13.1	18.8	2.6	2.0	12.0	3.2	8.8	8.8	1.1	2.2
Trade association [3]	20.4	10.5	9.9	16.5	2.1	1.7	6.3	2.7	3.7	4.5	0.9	1.0
Labor	19.8	18.8	1.0	14.3	3.5	2.0	5.0	4.7	0.3	1.6	2.3	1.2
Nonconnected [4]	9.1	4.7	4.4	4.9	2.9	1.3	5.4	3.0	2.4	2.4	2.0	1.0
1985-86, total [2]	87.4	54.7	32.6	65.9	9.1	12.4	45.3	20.2	25.1	23.7	10.2	11.4
Corporate	26.9	12.9	14.0	22.9	1.0	3.0	19.2	4.8	14.4	11.7	2.7	4.9
Trade association [3]	23.4	12.3	11.2	19.3	1.3	2.8	9.5	3.8	5.7	5.7	1.6	2.1
Labor	22.6	21.1	1.6	14.7	4.3	3.6	7.2	6.6	0.6	2.2	3.2	1.9
Nonconnected [4]	11.1	6.6	4.5	6.1	2.4	2.6	7.7	4.2	3.4	3.1	2.4	2.2
1987-88, total [2]	102.2	67.4	34.7	82.2	10.0	10.0	45.7	24.2	21.5	28.7	8.0	9.0
Corporate	31.6	16.3	15.4	28.6	1.1	1.9	18.8	7.2	11.6	12.7	2.4	3.7
Trade association [3]	28.6	16.5	12.0	24.6	1.5	2.5	10.4	4.8	5.6	7.1	1.3	2.0
Labor	26.8	24.8	2.0	18.3	5.1	3.3	7.1	6.5	0.5	3.6	2.2	1.3
Nonconnected [4]	11.4	7.4	3.9	7.3	2.2	1.9	7.8	4.8	3.0	4.2	2.0	1.6
1989-90, total [2]	108.5	72.2	36.2	87.5	7.3	13.6	41.2	20.2	21.0	29.5	8.2	3.5
Corporate	35.4	18.7	16.7	30.8	1.4	3.2	18.0	6.1	11.9	13.0	3.5	1.5
Trade association [3]	32.5	19.3	13.3	27.5	1.4	3.6	10.0	4.2	5.8	7.2	1.8	0.9
Labor	27.6	25.8	1.8	19.8	3.2	4.5	6.0	5.6	0.4	3.9	1.7	0.4
Nonconnected [4]	8.5	5.5	2.9	5.5	1.1	1.8	5.7	3.5	2.2	4.2	1.1	0.5

[1] Elections in which an incumbent did not seek re-election.   [2] Includes other types of political action committees not shown separately.   [3] Includes membership organizations and health organizations.   [4] Represents "ideological" groups as well as other issue groups not necessarily ideological in nature.

Source: U.S. Federal Election Commission, *FEC Reports on Financial Activity, Final Report, U.S. Senate and House Campaigns*, biennial.

State and Local Government Finances and Employment

This section presents data on revenues, expenditures, debt, and employment of State and local governments. Nationwide statistics relating to State and local governments, their numbers, finances, and employment, are compiled primarily by the Bureau of the Census through a program of censuses and surveys. Every fifth year (for years ending in "2" and "7") the Bureau conducts a Census of Governments involving collection of data for all governmental units in the United States. In addition, the Bureau conducts annual surveys which cover all the State governments and a sample of local governments.

Publications issued annually by the Bureau of the Census include a report on finances which presents figures for the Federal Government, nationwide totals for State and local governments by type and State-local data by States. Also issued annually are a series of publications on State, city, county, and school finances, and on city, county, and other public employment. Financial data are published in the GF publication series, employment data in the GE series. There is also a series of quarterly reports covering tax revenue and finances of major public employee retirement systems, as well as a series (GSS) of special studies.

Basic information for Census Bureau statistics on governments is obtained by mail canvass from State and local officials; however, financial data for each of the State governments and for many of the large local governments are compiled from their official records and reports by Census Bureau personnel. In over half of the States, all or part of local government financial data are obtained through central collection arrangements with State governments. Financial data on the Federal Government is based on the *Budget* published by the Office of Management and Budget (see page 311).

Governmental units.—The governmental structure of the United States includes, in addition to the Federal Government and the States, thousands of

In Brief

State government revenue (from own sources) in 1990: $505,843 million

Taxes	*59%*
Insurance trust funds	*21%*
Charges	*8%*
Interest earnings	*5%*
Utility and liquor stores	*1%*

State government direct expenditures in 1990: $397,291 million

Public welfare	*21%*
Education	*19%*
Insurance trust funds	*14%*
Highways	*9%*

local governments—counties, municipalities, townships, school districts, and numerous kinds of "special districts." As shown by table 448, almost 83,200 local governments were identified by the 1987 Census of Governments. As defined by the census, governmental units include all agencies or bodies having an organized existence, governmental character, and substantial autonomy. While most of these governments can impose taxes, many of the special districts—such as independent public housing authorities, the New York Port Authority, and numerous local irrigation, power, and other types of districts—are financed from rentals, charges for services, benefit assessments, grants from other governments, toll charges, and other nontax sources. The count of governments excludes semi-autonomous agencies through which States, cities, and counties sometimes provide for certain functions—for example, "dependent" school systems, State institutions of higher education, and certain other "authorities" and special agencies which are under the administrative or fiscal control of an established governmental unit.

Finances.—Unless otherwise stated, financial data relate to fiscal years ending in the year shown. Most States end their fiscal year June 30; however, Alabama and Michigan end their fiscal year Sept. 30; New York, March 31; and Texas, Aug. 31. The Federal Government ended the fiscal year June 30 until 1976 when its fiscal year, by an act of Congress, was revised to extend from Oct. 1 to Sept. 30. A 3-month quarter (July 1 to Sept. 30, 1976) bridged the transition. Beginning 1963, local government figures are for fiscal years which close at various dates during the 12 months ended June 30 of the year specified (exceptions are school districts in Alabama, which close Sept. 30 of the specified year; school districts in Texas, which close Aug. 31 of year cited; and Washington, DC which ends its fiscal year Sept. 30); figures for 1962 and earlier years are for fiscal years ended during the calendar year.

Nationwide government finance statistics have been classified and presented in terms of uniform concepts and categories, rather than according to the highly diverse terminology, organization, and fund structure utilized by individual governments. Accordingly, financial statistics which appear here for the Federal Government and for individual States or local governments have been standardized and may not agree directly with figures appearing in the original sources.

Statistics on governmental finances distinguish among general government, utilities, liquor stores, and insurance trusts. *General government* comprises all activities except utilities, liquor stores, and insurance trusts. Utilities include government water supply, electric light and power, gas supply, and transit systems. Liquor stores are operated by 17 States and by local governments in 5 States. Insurance trusts relate to employee retirement, unemployment compensation, and other social insurance systems administered by the Federal, State, and local governments.

Data for cities relate only to municipal corporations and their dependent agencies and do not include amounts for other local governments overlying city areas. Therefore, expenditure figures for "education" do not include spending by the separate school districts which administer public schools within most municipal areas. Variations in the assignment of governmental responsibility for public assistance, health, hospitals, public housing, and other functions to a lesser degree also have an important effect upon reported amounts of city expenditure, revenue, and debt. Therefore, any intercity comparisons based upon these figures should be made with caution and with due recognition of variations that exist among urban areas in the relative role of the municipal corporation.

Employment and payrolls.—These data are based mainly on mail canvassing of State and local governments. Payroll includes all salaries, wages, and individual fee payments for the month specified, and employment relates to all persons on governmental payrolls during a pay period of the month covered—including paid officials, temporary help, and (unless otherwise specified) part-time as well as full-time personnel. Beginning 1986, statistics for full-time equivalent employment have been computed with a formula using hours worked by part-time employees. A payroll based formula was used prior to 1985. Full-time equivalent employment statistics were not computed for 1985. Figures shown for individual governments cover major dependent agencies such as institutions of higher education, as well as the basic central departments and agencies of the government.

Statistical reliability.—For a discussion of statistical collection and estimation, sampling procedures, and measures of statistical reliability applicable to Census Bureau data, see Appendix III.

Historical statistics.—Tabular headnotes provide cross-references, where applicable, to *Historical Statistics of the United States, Colonial Times to 1970.* See Appendix IV.

Figure 9.1

State Government Tax Collections, by Type: 1970 and 1990

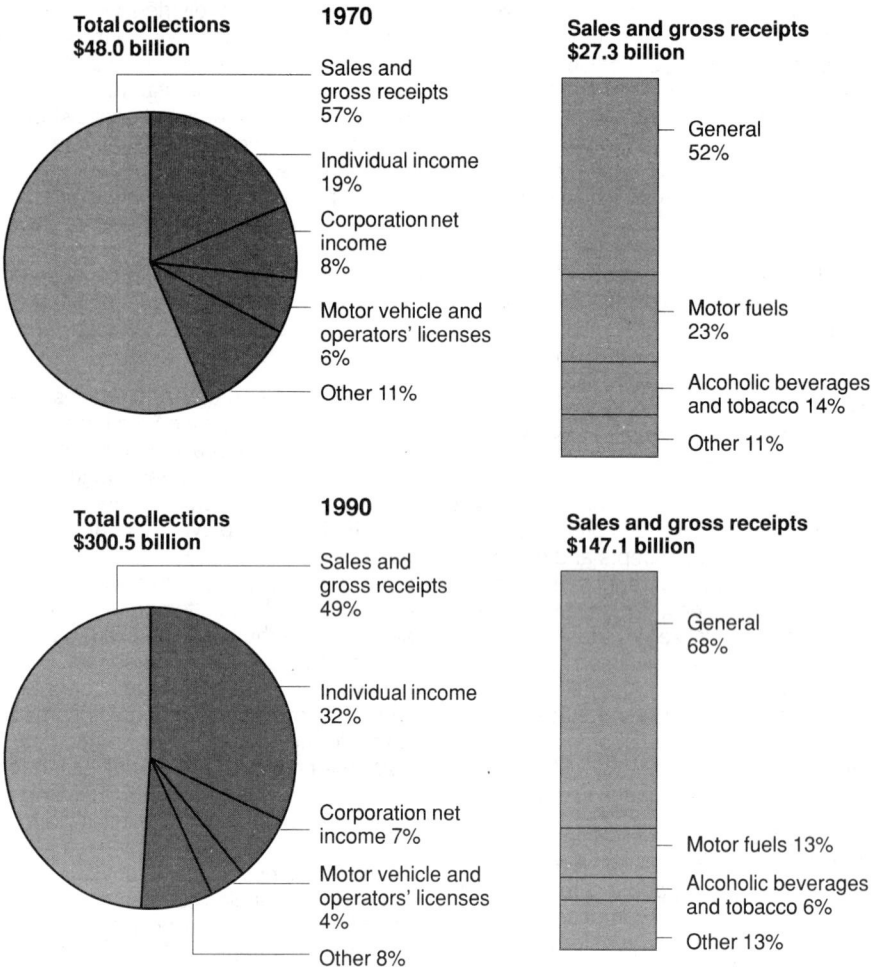

1970

Total collections
$48.0 billion

Sales and
gross receipts
57%

Individual income
19%

Corporation net
income
8%

Motor vehicle and
operators' licenses
6%

Other 11%

Sales and gross receipts
$27.3 billion

General
52%

Motor fuels
23%

Alcoholic beverages
and tobacco 14%

Other 11%

1990

Total collections
$300.5 billion

Sales and
gross receipts
49%

Individual income
32%

Corporation net
income 7%

Motor vehicle and
operators' licenses
4%

Other 8%

Sales and gross receipts
$147.1 billion

General
68%

Motor fuels 13%

Alcoholic beverages
and tobacco 6%

Other 13%

Source: Chart prepared by U.S. Bureau of the Census. For data, see table 463.

No. 448. Number of Governmental Units, by Type of Government: 1942 to 1987

TYPE OF GOVERNMENT	1942	1952[1]	1957[1]	1962	1967	1972	1977	1982	1987
Total	155,116	116,807	102,392	91,237	81,299	78,269	79,913	81,831	83,237
U.S. Government	1	1	1	1	1	1	1	1	1
State government	48	50	50	50	50	50	50	50	50
Local governments	155,067	166,756	102,341	91,186	81,248	78,218	79,862	81,780	83,186
County	3,050	3,052	3,050	3,043	3,049	3,044	3,042	3,041	3,042
Municipal	16,220	16,807	17,215	18,000	18,048	18,517	18,862	19,076	19,200
Township and town	18,919	17,202	17,198	17,142	17,105	16,991	16,822	16,734	16,691
School district	108,579	67,355	50,454	34,678	21,782	15,781	15,174	14,851	14,721
Special district	8,299	12,340	14,424	18,323	21,264	23,885	25,962	28,078	29,532

[1] Adjusted to include units in Alaska and Hawaii which adopted statehood in 1959.
Source: U.S. Bureau of the Census, *Census of Governments*: 1967, vol. 1, No. 1, *Governmental Organization, 1982*, vol. 6, No. 4, *Historical Statistics on Governmental Finances and Employment* (GC82(6)–4), and *Census of Governments*, 1987, vol. 1, No. 1, *Governmental Organization*.

No. 449. All Governments—Revenue, Expenditure, and Debt: 1980 to 1990

[For fiscal year ending in year shown; see text, section 9. Local government amounts are estimates subject to sampling variation; see Appendix III and source. See also *Historical Statistics, Colonial Times to 1970*, series Y 505-637 and Y 652-848]

ITEM AND YEAR	All govern-ments (bil. dol.)	FEDERAL [1] Total (bil. dol.)	FEDERAL [1] Per-cent of total	STATE AND LOCAL (bil. dol.) Total	State	Local	AVERAGE ANNUAL PERCENT CHANGE[2] Fed-eral	State	Local	PER CAPITA [3] (dollars) Total	Fed-eral	State and local
Revenue: [4] 1980	[5]932	565	60.7	[5]452	277	258	10.6	12.0	11.2	[5]4,115	2,496	1,993
1985	[5]1,419	807	56.9	[5]720	439	402	7.4	9.7	9.3	[5]5,943	3,379	3,015
1989	[5]1,917	1,093	57.0	[5]954	587	532	7.9	8.3	7.5	[5]7,724	4,402	3,841
1990	[5]2,047	1,155	56.4	[5]1,032	632	580	5.7	7.8	9.1	[5]8,230	4,642	4,150
Intergovernmental: 1980	(X)	2	(X)	[5]83	64	102	(X)	12.3	13.3	(X)	8	367
1985	(X)	2	(X)	[5]106	90	138	1.6	6.9	6.2	(X)	8	445
1989	(X)	3	(X)	[5]126	116	175	1.5	8.0	7.7	(X)	12	507
1990	(X)	3	(X)	[5]137	126	191	0.3	9.1	8.8	(X)	12	550
General, own sources:												
1980	717	417	58.2	299	169	130	9.8	11.4	9.7	3,163	1,842	1,321
1985	1,050	559	53.2	492	276	216	6.0	10.3	10.7	4,400	2,339	2,059
1989	1,400	740	52.9	660	367	293	7.4	8.4	8.1	5,642	2,983	2,659
1990	1,493	780	52.3	713	391	322	5.4	6.7	9.7	6,004	3,138	2,866
Taxes: [4] 1980	574	351	61.1	223	137	86	9.2	11.1	8.3	2,535	1,548	986
1985	804	454	56.4	350	215	134	5.3	9.5	9.3	3,369	1,902	1,465
1989	1,085	616	56.8	469	284	184	9.5	7.6	7.5	4,369	2,481	1,888
1990	1,134	632	55.8	502	300	201	2.7	5.8	9.0	4,559	2,542	2,017
Property: 1980	68	(X)	(X)	68	3	66	(X)	10.2	7.1	302	(X)	302
1985	104	(X)	(X)	104	4	100	(X)	6.6	8.8	435	(X)	435
1989	143	(X)	(X)	143	5	137	(X)	7.3	7.8	574	(X)	574
1990	156	(X)	(X)	156	6	150	(X)	8.0	9.2	626	(X)	626
Individual income:												
1980	286	244	85.3	42	37	5	10.4	15.0	11.9	1,263	1,077	186
1985	401	331	82.5	70	64	6	6.3	11.5	5.3	1,681	1,386	294
1989	543	446	82.0	98	89	9	11.1	10.8	9.4	2,189	1,795	394
1990	573	467	81.6	106	96	10	4.8	8.2	6.4	2,302	1,877	425
Corporate income:												
1980	78	65	82.9	13	13	-	7.0	13.6	-	344	285	59
1985	80	61	76.2	19	18	2	-1.0	5.8	(X)	337	257	80
1989	129	103	79.9	26	24	2	9.7	10.0	0.2	521	416	104
1990	117	94	79.9	24	22	2	-9.5	-8.9	-11.9	471	376	95
Sales or gross receipts:												
1980	112	[6]32	28.6	80	68	12	5.8	9.6	14.7	494	[6]141	353
1985	176	[6]49	28.0	126	105	21	8.9	9.2	11.7	735	[6]206	529
1989	219	[6]53	24.0	166	139	28	-0.2	6.2	6.3	880	[6]212	669
1990	232	[6]54	23.3	178	147	31	2.8	6.4	11.0	932	[6]217	715
Current charges and miscellaneous: 1980	142	67	46.7	76	32	44	14.3	12.9	13.3	629	294	335
1985	246	104	42.5	142	60	82	9.4	13.3	13.3	1,031	438	594
1989	316	125	39.4	191	83	109	-2.0	11.3	9.2	1,273	502	771
1990	359	148	41.3	211	91	120	19.0	9.8	10.7	1,445	596	849
Expenditures: [4] 1980	[5]959	617	64.4	[5]434	258	261	11.5	11.7	10.9	[5]4,232	2,724	1,916
1985	[5]1,581	1,032	65.3	[5]658	391	391	10.8	8.7	8.4	[5]6,622	4,323	2,756
1989	[5]2,031	1,270	62.6	[5]891	525	533	4.6	8.3	7.4	[5]8,180	5,116	3,589
1990	[5]2,219	1,393	62.8	[5]976	572	581	9.7	9.0	9.0	[5]8,921	5,601	3,924
Intergovernmental: 1980	(X)	91	(X)	[5]2	85	2	14.6	11.3	10.8	(X)	401	8
1985	(X)	107	(X)	[5]2	122	4	3.4	7.6	18.1	(X)	449	8
1989	(X)	127	(X)	3	165	5	7.0	9.1	-5.0	(X)	513	12
1990	(X)	147	(X)	3	175	6	15.5	5.8	19.1	(X)	591	13
Direct: [4] 1980	959	526	54.9	432	173	259	11.0	11.9	10.9	4,232	2,323	1,908
1985	1,581	925	58.5	656	269	387	11.9	9.2	8.4	6,622	3,874	2,748
1989	2,031	1,143	56.3	888	360	528	4.3	7.9	7.6	8,180	4,603	3,577
1990	2,219	1,246	58.5	973	397	575	9.0	10.5	8.9	8,921	5,010	3,911
Current operation: 1980	517	209	40.5	308	108	200	7.8	13.3	11.6	2,282	923	1,359
1985	833	360	43.3	473	172	300	11.5	9.7	8.5	3,488	1,509	1,979
1989	1,073	432	40.3	641	233	408	-0.8	9.3	7.8	4,322	1,741	2,580
1990	1,190	490	41.2	700	258	442	13.4	10.8	8.5	4,785	1,970	2,815
Capital outlay: 1980	99	36	36.7	63	23	40	7.4	5.8	9.2	439	161	278
1985	157	77	49.1	80	31	49	16.1	5.6	4.5	657	323	335
1989	212	100	47.1	112	43	69	6.7	6.0	8.1	853	402	451
1990	221	98	44.3	123	46	78	-1.9	5.6	12.7	888	394	495
Debt outstanding: [7] 1980	1,250	914	73.2	336	122	214	9.4	11.3	7.7	5,517	4,036	1,481
1985	2,396	1,827	76.3	571	212	359	14.9	11.7	10.8	10,036	7,655	2,393
1989	3,679	2,881	78.3	798	296	503	10.2	6.8	5.2	14,822	11,606	3,216
1990	4,127	3,266	79.2	861	318	542	13.4	7.7	7.9	16,592	13,132	3,460

- Represents or rounds to zero.   X Not applicable.   [1] Data adjusted to system for reporting State and local data and therefore differ from figures in section 10 tables.   [2] Percent change from prior year, except for 1980, change from 1970 and 1985, change from 1980. For explanation, see Guide to Tabular Presentation. Minus sign (-) indicates decrease.   [3] 1980 and 1990 based on enumerated resident population as of April 1; all other years based on estimated resident population as of July 1. Estimates do not reflect revisions based on the 1990 Census of Population. Excludes intergovernmental amounts.   [4] Includes amounts, not shown separately.   [5] Excludes duplicative transactions between levels of government; see source.   [6] Includes customs.   [7] End of fiscal year.

Source: U.S. Bureau of the Census, *Historical Statistics on Governmental Finances and Employment (GC 82(6)-4)*; and *Government Finances*, series GF, No. 5, annual.

No. 450. All Governments—Revenue and Expenditure, by Level of Government: 1990

[For fiscal year ending in year shown, see text, section 9. Local government amounts are estimates subject to sampling variation; see source and appendix III. See also *Historical Statistics, Colonial Times to 1970*, series Y 505-637 and Y 652-848]

SOURCE OF REVENUE AND TYPE OF EXPENDITURE	All governments (mil. dol.)	Federal (mil. dol.)	State (mil. dol.)	Local (mil. dol.)	PERCENT Federal	PERCENT State and local	PER CAPITA[1] (dol.) Federal	PER CAPITA[1] (dol.) State and local
Revenue	2,046,998	1,154,596	632,172	580,193	100.0	100.0	4,642	4,150
Intergovernment revenue	(2)	2,911	126,329	190,723	0.3	26.2	12	550
Revenue from own sources	2,046,998	1,151,685	505,843	389,470	99.8	73.8	4,631	3,600
General revenue from own sources	1,493,179	780,479	391,101	321,599	67.6	58.8	3,138	2,866
Percent of total revenue	73	68	62	55	(X)	(X)	(X)	(X)
Taxes[3]	1,133,886	632,267	300,489	201,130	54.8	41.4	2,542	2,017
Property	155,613	(X)	5,848	149,765	(X)	12.8	(X)	626
Individual income	572,524	466,884	96,076	9,563	40.4	8.7	1,877	425
Corporation income	117,073	93,507	21,751	1,815	8.1	1.9	376	95
Sales and gross receipts	231,855	53,970	147,069	30,815	4.7	14.7	217	715
Customs duties	16,810	16,810	(X)	(X)	1.5	(X)	68	(X)
General sales and gross receipts	121,287	(X)	99,702	21,585	(X)	10.0	(X)	488
Selective sales and gross receipts[3]	93,758	37,160	47,367	9,231	3.2	4.7	149	228
Motor fuel	33,120	13,077	19,379	664	1.1	1.7	53	81
Alcoholic beverages	9,223	5,753	3,191	279	0.5	0.3	23	14
Tobacco products	10,002	4,268	5,541	193	0.4	0.5	17	23
Public utilities	17,892	6,476	6,514	4,903	0.6	0.9	26	46
Motor vehicle and operators' licenses	11,444	(X)	10,675	769	(X)	0.9	(X)	46
Death and gift	15,355	11,500	3,832	23	1.0	0.3	46	16
Charges and misc. general revenue[3]	359,293	148,212	90,612	120,469	12.8	17.4	596	849
Current charges[3]	204,418	88,877	42,745	72,795	7.7	9.5	357	465
National defense and international relations	8,268	8,268	(X)	(X)	0.7	(X)	33	(X)
Postal service	38,202	38,202	(X)	(X)	3.3	(X)	54	(X)
Education[3]	32,840	-	23,585	9,256	-	2.7	-	132
School lunch sales	3,454	-	13	3,441	-	0.3	-	14
Higher education	26,339	-	23,224	3,115	-	2.2	-	106
Natural resources	29,205	27,385	1,347	473	2.4	0.2	110	7
Hospitals	31,191	77	9,388	21,726	(Z)	2.6	(Z)	125
Sewerage and sanitation	17,647	(X)	224	17,423	(X)	1.5	(X)	71
Parks and recreation	3,456	100	748	2,608	(Z)	0.3	(Z)	13
Housing and community development	5,843	2,997	190	2,656	0.3	0.2	12	11
Air transportation	5,193	20	556	4,617	(Z)	0.4	14	21
Water transport and terminals	2,394	906	355	1,133	0.1	0.1	4	6
Special assessments	2,427	(X)	146	2,281	(X)	0.2	(X)	10
Sale of property	5,270	3,967	246	1,057	0.4	0.1	16	5
Interest earnings	70,037	11,313	27,370	31,353	1.0	4.8	45	236
Utility revenue	55,202	(X)	3,305	51,897	(X)	4.6	(X)	222
Liquor stores	3,441	(X)	2,907	533	(X)	0.3	(X)	14
Insurance trust revenue	495,176	371,206	108,530	15,441	32.2	10.2	1,493	498
Expenditure	2,218,793	1,393,121	572,318	581,207	100.0	100.0	5,601	3,924
Intergovernment expenditure	(2)	146,990	175,028	5,836	10.6	15.7	591	13
Direct expenditure	2,218,793	1,246,131	397,291	575,371	89.5	84.3	5,010	3,911
General expenditure	1,686,774	855,234	333,256	498,284	61.4	72.1	3,439	3,343
Percent of total expenditure	76	61	58	86	(X)	(X)	(X)	(X)
Education[3]	305,552	17,404	75,497	212,652	1.3	25.0	70	1,159
Elementary and secondary education	202,009	-	1,798	200,211	-	17.5	-	812
Higher education	73,418		60,978	12,441	-	6.4	-	295
Public welfare	140,734	33,447	83,336	23,951	2.4	9.3	134	431
Health and hospitals	92,487	17,852	35,543	39,092	1.3	6.5	72	300
Highways	61,913	856	36,464	24,593	0.1	5.3	3	245
Police protection	35,921	5,344	4,487	26,090	0.4	2.7	21	123
Fire protection	13,186	(X)	(X)	13,186	(X)	1.1	(X)	53
Corrections[4]	26,229	1,594	15,898	8,737	0.1	2.1	6	99
Natural resources[4]	96,922	70,266	11,906	14,750	5.1	2.3	283	107
Sewerage and sanitation	28,453	(X)	1,527	26,926	(X)	1.3	(X)	114
Housing and community development	32,430	16,951	1,724	13,756	1.2	1.3	68	62
Governmental administration	57,546	12,710	17,707	27,130	0.9	3.9	51	180
Interest on general debt	237,691	187,952	21,532	28,207	13.5	4.7	756	200
Other	557,710	490,858	27,635	39,214	35.2	5.8	1,974	269
Utility expenditure	74,875	(X)	7,131	67,744	(X)	6.5	(X)	301
Liquor stores expenditure	2,926	(X)	2,452	474	(X)	0.3	(X)	12
Insurance trust expenditure	454,218	390,897	54,452	8,870	28.1	5.5	1,572	255
By character and object:								
Current operation	1,190,147	490,016	258,046	442,084	35.2	60.7	1,970	2,815
Capital outlay	220,960	97,891	45,524	77,545	7.0	10.7	394	495
Construction	98,536	9,422	34,803	54,310	0.7	7.7	38	358
Equip., land and existing structures	122,424	88,469	10,721	23,235	6.4	2.9	356	137
Assistance and subsidies	106,602	79,375	16,902	10,325	5.7	2.4	319	109
Interest on debt (general and utility)	246,866	187,952	22,367	36,547	13.5	5.1	756	237
Insurance benefits and repayments	454,218	390,897	54,452	8,870	28.1	5.5	1,572	255
Expenditure for salaries and wages	487,594	146,436	101,338	239,820	10.5	29.6	589	1,372

- Represents zero or rounds to zero.   X Not applicable.   Z Less than .05 percent or $.50.   [1] Based on enumerated resident population as of April 1.   [2] Aggregates exclude duplicative transactions between levels of government; see source.   [3] Includes amounts not shown separately.   [4] Includes parks and recreation.

Source: U.S. Bureau of the Census, *Government Finances*, series GF, No. 5, annual.

No. 451. All Governments—Expenditure for Capital Outlay, by Level of Government and by Function: 1970 to 1990

[In millions of dollars, except percent. For fiscal years ending in year shown; see text, section 9. Except for 1982 and 1987, local government data are estimates subject to sampling variation; see Appendix III. See also *Historical Statistics, Colonial Times to 1970*, series Y 523-524, Y 673-674, Y 740-741, and Y 787-788]

LEVEL AND FUNCTION	1970	1975	1980	1984	1985	1986	1987	1988	1989	1990
Total	**47,519**	**66,622**	**99,386**	**143,094**	**156,912**	**176,096**	**195,713**	**197,844**	**211,734**	**220,960**
Federal Government:										
Total	17,869	21,798	36,492	72,456	77,014	85,647	96,871	93,531	99,790	97,891
Annual percent change [1]	-6.0	4.1	10.9	-10.3	6.3	11.2	13.1	-3.4	6.7	-1.9
As percent of direct expenditure	9.7	7.5	6.9	8.7	8.3	8.7	9.3	7.7	8.7	7.9
By function:										
National defense [2]	14,027	14,507	28,161	60,382	64,154	71,995	78,222	74,790	78,891	75,624
Education	9	2	97	58	39	5	13	7	9	41
Highways.............	9	70	132	187	121	204	173	173	165	181
Health and hospitals	166	311	673	1,016	916	1,160	1,327	1,228	1,403	1,096
Natural resources	1,691	3,416	4,046	4,435	4,092	3,651	4,058	3,581	3,786	4,698
Housing [3]	853	1,059	317	1,471	1,935	2,515	3,642	5,180	5,032	4,343
Air transportation	234	363	151	249	785	391	494	407	658	664
Water transportation [4]	285	251	1,003	482	583	245	315	370	306	385
All other	595	1,819	1,912	4,176	4,389	5,481	8,627	7,792	9,540	10,859
State and local governments:										
Total	29,650	44,824	62,894	70,638	79,898	90,449	98,842	104,313	111,944	123,069
Annual percent change [1]	5.0	8.6	7.0	4.3	13.1	13.2	9.3	5.5	7.3	9.9
As percent of direct expenditure	20.0	16.7	14.5	11.8	12.2	12.6	12.7	12.6	12.6	12.7
By function:										
Education [5]	7,621	9,861	10,737	11,596	13,477	15,490	17,803	18,529	21,854	25,997
Higher education	2,705	2,834	2,972	3,855	4,629	5,217	6,141	6,397	6,851	7,441
Elementary and secondary..	4,658	6,532	7,362	7,258	8,358	10,009	11,355	11,789	14,584	18,057
Highways.............	10,762	13,646	19,133	20,269	23,900	26,807	28,352	31,635	32,754	33,867
Health and hospitals	790	1,781	2,443	2,366	2,709	2,810	3,029	3,436	3,445	3,848
Natural resources	789	1,113	1,052	1,414	1,736	1,803	2,157	1,894	2,019	2,545
Housing [3]	1,319	1,821	2,248	3,104	3,217	3,516	3,394	3,619	3,765	3,997
Air transportation	691	852	1,391	1,814	1,875	2,183	2,632	2,896	2,965	3,434
Water transportation [4]	258	419	623	585	717	911	869	911	943	924
Sewerage	1,385	3,569	6,272	5,664	5,926	6,461	7,483	8,300	8,343	8,356
Parks and recreation [6]	684	1,261	2,023	1,962	2,196	2,554	2,838	3,142	3,350	3,877
Utilities [6]	2,437	4,846	9,933	12,599	13,435	15,340	15,638	14,782	15,371	16,601
Water...............	1,201	2,111	3,335	3,438	4,160	5,134	6,135	6,052	6,372	6,873
Electric..............	820	1,485	4,572	5,153	5,247	6,127	5,086	4,473	4,291	3,976
Transit..............	366	1,203	1,921	3,873	3,830	3,830	4,165	3,998	4,430	5,443
Gas................	50	48	105	135	198	250	253	259	279	310
Other	2,915	5,656	7,039	9,265	10,711	12,573	14,645	15,172	17,135	19,623

[1] Change from prior year shown. 1970, change from 1969. For definition of average annual percent change, see Guide to Tabular Presentation. [2] Includes international relations and U.S. service schools. [3] Includes community development. [4] Includes terminals. [5] Includes other education. [6] Beginning 1980, includes outlays by State governments.

Source: U.S. Bureau of the Census, *Census of Governments: 1977, 1982* and *1987*, Vol. 6, No. 4, *Historical Statistics on Governmental Finances and Employment;* and *Government Finances,* series GF No. 5, annual.

No. 452. Federal, State, and Local Government Spending on Public Works: 1980 to 1990

[In millions of dollars. Public works include expenditures on highways, airports, water transport and terminals, sewerage, solid waste management, water supply, and mass transit systems. Represents direct expenditures excluding intergovernmental grants]

LEVEL AND TYPE OF EXPENDITURE	Total	Highways	Airport transportation	Water transport and terminals	Sewerage	Solid waste management	Water supply	Mass transit
1980: Total	72,177	33,745	5,071	3,278	9,892	3,322	9,228	7,641
Federal	5,114	434	2,570	2,110	-	-	-	-
State.	22,832	20,661	360	360	334	-	91	1,026
Local	44,231	12,650	2,141	808	9,558	3,322	9,137	6,615
Capital expenditures (percent) ...	48	50	50	50	63	11	36	25
1985: Total	101,925	45,856	7,153	3,353	12,186	5,212	14,298	13,867
Federal	6,103	834	3,409	1,860	-	-	-	-
State.	31,821	27,167	473	534	328	-	69	3,250
Local	64,001	17,854	3,271	959	11,858	5,214	14,228	10,617
Capital expenditures (percent) ...	42	52	37	39	49	14	29	28
1990: Total	146,762	61,913	10,983	4,524	18,309	10,144	22,101	18,788
Federal	7,911	856	4,499	2,556	-	-	-	-
State.	43,787	36,464	635	504	636	891	136	4,521
Local	95,064	24,593	5,848	1,464	17,673	9,253	21,966	14,267
Capital expenditures (percent) ...	42	55	37	29	46	18	31	29

- Represents or rounds to zero.

Source: U.S. Bureau of the Census, *Government Finances,* series GF, No. 5, annual.

No. 453. Federal Grants-in-Aid Summary: 1970 to 1993

[For fiscal year ending in year shown; see text, section 9. Minus sign (-) indicates decrease]

YEAR	CURRENT DOLLARS							CONSTANT (1982) DOLLARS	
	Total grants (bil. dol.)	Average annual percent change [1]	Grants to individuals		Grants as percent of—			Total grants (bil. dol.)	Average annual percent change [1]
			Total (bil. dol.)	Percent of total grants	State-local govt. outlays [2]	Federal outlays	Gross national product		
1970	24.0	17.2	8.6	35.8	19.0	12.3	2.4	61.2	11.6
1975	49.8	15.7	16.4	33.0	22.6	15.0	3.3	87.1	7.3
1980	91.5	10.4	31.9	34.9	25.8	15.5	3.4	105.9	-0.7
1985	105.9	8.5	48.1	45.4	20.9	11.2	2.7	94.0	4.2
1987	108.4	-3.5	56.4	52.0	18.2	10.8	2.4	90.7	-6.5
1988	115.3	6.4	61.0	52.9	18.2	10.8	2.4	92.5	2.0
1989	121.8	5.6	65.9	54.1	17.3	10.7	2.4	93.4	1.1
1990	136.9	12.2	78.6	57.5	17.9	10.9	2.5	100.9	7.7
1991, estimate. . . .	158.6	15.8	94.7	59.7	(NA)	11.2	2.8	110.4	9.4
1992, projection. . . .	171.0	7.8	106.2	62.1	(NA)	11.8	2.9	113.9	3.2
1993, projection. . . .	184.1	7.7	117.7	63.9	(NA)	12.7	2.9	117.8	3.4

NA Not available. [1] Average annual percent change from prior year shown. For explanation, see Guide to Tabular Presentation. 1970, change from 1965. [2] Outlays as defined in the national income and product accounts.

Source: Advisory Commission on Intergovernmental Relations, Washington, DC, *Significant Features of Fiscal Federalism, 1991 Edition*, vol. II, based on *Budget of the United States Government, FY 92*, Table 12.1.

No. 454. Federal Aid to State and Local Governments: 1970 to 1991

[In millions of dollars. For fiscal year ending in year shown; see text, section 9. Includes trust funds. Minus sign (-) indicates previously disbursed funds returned to the Federal Government. See *Historical Statistics, Colonial Times to 1970*, series Y 638-651, for related data]

TYPE OF AID, FUNCTION, AND MAJOR PROGRAM	1970	1975	1980	1985	1988	1989	1990	1991
Grant-in-aid shared revenue [1]	[2]24,065	49,791	91,451	105,897	115,382	121,976	135,377	152,017
National defense	37	74	93	157	188	253	241	185
Natural resources and environment	411	2,437	5,363	4,069	3,747	3,606	3,745	4,040
Environmental Protection Agency.	194	2,025	4,603	3,197	2,895	2,797	2,874	3,071
Energy.	25	43	499	529	457	420	461	457
Agriculture	604	404	569	2,420	2,069	1,359	1,285	1,220
Transportation [1]	4,599	5,864	13,087	17,055	18,083	18,225	19,225	19,878
Airports	83	292	590	789	825	1,135	1,220	1,541
Highways.	4,395	4,702	9,209	12,841	13,926	13,349	14,172	14,418
Railroads.	-	(Z)	54	36	22	15	14	2
Urban mass transit	105	689	3,129	3,304	3,228	3,500	3,730	3,821
Community and regional development [1]	1,780	2,842	6,486	5,221	4,266	4,074	4,965	4,273
Appalachian development.	184	306	335	198	141	104	124	157
Community development block grants.	(X)	38	3,902	3,817	3,050	2,948	2,818	2,976
Education, employment, training, social services [1]	6,417	12,133	21,862	17,817	19,882	21,987	23,101	26,020
Compensatory education for the disadvantaged [3]	1,470	2,184	3,370	4,194	4,016	4,165	4,437	5,193
School improvement programs [3]	86	332	523	479	384	846	1,080	1,243
Bilingual and immigrant education [3]	-	93	166	111	130	132	152	148
Federally affected areas impact aid	622	577	622	629	694	735	799	747
Vocational and adult education	285	653	854	633	1,261	824	1,287	1,038
Libraries	105	210	158	79	94	131	127	132
Work programs	81	304	383	274	90	86	7	-
Social services-block grants to States.	574	2,047	2,763	2,743	2,666	2,671	2,749	2,822
Human development services	390	803	1,548	1,807	1,997	2,571	2,267	2,920
Training and employment assistance	954	2,504	6,191	2,775	2,958	3,020	3,042	2,985
Health [1]	3,849	8,810	15,758	24,451	32,586	36,679	43,890	55,783
Alcohol, drug abuse, and mental health [4] . . .	146	590	679	501	720	666	1,241	1,744
Medicaid [4]	2,727	6,840	13,957	22,655	30,462	34,604	41,103	52,533
Income security [1]	5,795	9,352	18,495	27,153	31,620	32,523	35,447	36,856
Family support payments to States (AFDC and CSE) [4]	4,142	5,121	7,273	9,169	10,764	11,166	12,246	13,520
Food stamps-administration	559	136	412	886	1,113	1,167	1,199	1,406
Child nutrition and special milk programs [4]. . .	379	1,565	3,388	3,479	4,159	4,455	4,871	5,418
Housing assistance [4]	436	1,326	3,435	6,407	8,618	8,515	9,516	7,903
Veterans benefits and services.	18	32	90	91	106	127	134	141
Administration of justice	42	725	529	95	427	520	574	940
General government [5].	479	7,072	8,616	6,838	1,950	2,204	2,309	2,224

- Represents zero. X Not applicable. Z Less than $500,000. [1] Includes items not shown separately. [2] Includes $5 million for international affairs subsequently provided to a private institution. [3] The 1983 Budget proposed dismantlement of the Dept. of Education (DED). Budget data for elementary and secondary education previously performed by DED are included in the Foundation for Education Assistance under compensatory education for the disadvantaged, school improvement (formerly titled "Special programs and populations") programs and bilingual and immigrant education. [4] Includes grants for payments to individuals. [5] Includes general purpose fiscal assistance.

Source: U.S. Office of Management and Budget, *Historical Tables, Budget of the United States Government*, annual, and *Budget of the United States Government*, annual.

No. 455. Federal Aid to State and Local Governments—Selected Programs, by State: 1990

[In millions of dollars, except per capita. For fiscal year ending Sept. 30]

DIVISION AND STATE	FEDERAL AID [1]		OE [3] compensatory education [4]	EPA [5] waste treatment facilities construction	HHS [6]		HUD [8]		ETA [10] employment/ training	Dept. of Transportation, highway trust fund
	Total	Per capita [2] (dol.)			Family Support Administration [7]	Medicaid	Lower income housing assistance [9]	Community development		
Total [11]	134,457	533	4,437	2,294	15,140	40,857	7,372	2,818	5,735	13,686
New England:										
Maine	762	621	23	14	86	283	52	11	29	66
New Hampshire	427	385	11	14	30	121	33	9	19	56
Vermont	377	670	11	12	41	105	20	5	14	55
Massachusetts	3,857	641	109	87	469	1,570	323	83	130	181
Rhode Island	773	770	16	22	67	246	91	13	29	126
Connecticut	1,973	600	48	42	192	613	162	39	72	391
Middle Atlantic:										
New York	15,761	876	461	310	3,150	6,301	852	274	430	604
New Jersey	3,977	514	139	127	416	1,261	336	115	172	354
Pennsylvania	6,125	515	214	104	616	1,814	364	206	271	759
East North Central:										
Ohio	5,388	497	144	108	607	1,957	322	140	250	404
Indiana	2,423	437	68	57	185	945	112	54	120	259
Illinois	5,280	462	213	101	520	1,276	393	149	288	502
Michigan	4,751	511	171	82	794	1,506	190	108	284	356
Wisconsin	2,538	519	63	46	438	893	110	49	113	222
West North Central:										
Minnesota	2,366	541	51	46	281	790	134	49	89	281
Iowa	1,289	464	35	41	128	414	45	33	55	186
Missouri	2,177	425	69	50	182	576	127	61	108	272
North Dakota	471	737	10	10	35	134	22	6	22	70
South Dakota	511	734	13	10	33	122	33	7	20	95
Nebraska	779	494	21	5	75	210	32	13	29	103
Kansas	1,021	412	32	20	93	304	42	23	42	162
South Atlantic:										
Delaware	313	470	15	7	25	68	28	6	17	40
Maryland	2,350	491	69	98	197	620	163	45	97	365
District of Columbia	1,718	2,831	22	17	96	217	54	15	34	67
Virginia	2,237	361	81	56	181	548	150	46	91	316
West Virginia	1,009	562	39	35	102	287	52	20	45	108
North Carolina	2,942	444	98	43	208	1,020	156	55	130	386
South Carolina	1,892	542	64	19	121	642	78	26	71	161
Georgia	3,136	484	118	50	256	1,002	176	68	107	387
Florida	4,576	354	194	116	346	1,427	233	123	188	478
East South Central:										
Kentucky	2,044	555	75	23	156	753	117	35	89	161
Tennessee	2,717	557	85	27	181	970	142	45	110	271
Alabama	2,101	520	88	32	75	601	117	37	107	292
Mississippi	1,595	620	80	17	107	510	80	35	60	124
West South Central:										
Arkansas	1,250	532	53	6	61	474	60	26	59	128
Louisiana	2,658	630	101	20	200	1,041	118	48	96	302
Oklahoma	1,568	498	41	13	122	515	95	28	65	175
Texas	6,889	406	311	86	505	1,954	312	170	287	1,026
Mountain:										
Montana	591	740	13	4	48	133	36	8	25	96
Idaho	569	565	15	12	32	124	21	9	31	126
Wyoming	568	1,253	7	6	24	44	11	3	17	111
Colorado	1,429	434	41	15	113	306	85	24	65	250
New Mexico	959	633	33	4	53	213	53	13	36	96
Arizona	1,620	442	52	11	126	408	92	35	81	186
Utah	838	487	16	11	71	224	21	16	42	121
Nevada	442	368	9	2	32	74	29	8	28	90
Pacific:										
Washington	2,568	528	60	35	387	704	93	43	126	401
Oregon	1,708	601	45	20	176	369	69	22	78	150
California	13,932	468	486	133	2,494	3,870	675	248	670	1,344
Alaska	717	1,303	16	14	50	89	41	6	34	160
Hawaii	598	540	12	17	59	121	28	8	24	125

[1] Includes other amounts not shown separately.   [2] Based on Bureau of the Census enumerated resident population as of April 1.   [3] Office of Education.   [4] For the disadvantaged.   [5] Environmental Protection Agency.   [6] Department of Health and Human Services.   [7] Includes work incentives, family support payments (Aid to Families with Dependent Children), community service block grant, low income home energy assistance, refugee assistance, and assistance for legalized aliens.   [8] Department of Housing and Urban Development.   [9] Includes public housing, housing payments (section 8) to public agencies, and college housing.   [10] Employment and Training Administration, Job Training Partnership Act.   [11] Includes outlying areas and undistributed amounts, not shown separately.

Source: U.S. Bureau of the Census, *Federal Expenditures by State for Fiscal Year 1990.*

No. 456. State and Local Governments—Summary of Finances: 1980 to 1990

[For fiscal year ending in year shown, see text, section 9. Local government amounts includes here are estimates subject to sampling variations; see Appendix III and source. See also *Historical Statistics, Colonial Times to 1970*, series Y 652-709]

SOURCE OF REVENUE AND TYPE OF EXPENDITURE	TOTAL (mil. dol.)			PER CAPITA (dol.) [1]			PERCENT DISTRIBUTION		
	1980	1985	1990	1980	1985	1990	1980	1985	1990
Revenue [2]	451,537	719,686	1,032,115	1,993	3,015	4,150	100	100	100
From Federal Government	83,029	106,193	136,802	366	445	550	18	15	13
Public welfare	24,921	39,081	59,961	110	164	241	6	5	6
Highways	8,980	12,993	14,368	40	54	58	2	2	1
Education..................	14,435	16,758	23,233	64	70	93	3	2	2
Employment security administration .	2,056	2,690	3,024	9	11	12	1	(Z)	(Z)
Revenue sharing	6,844	4,556	-	30	19	-	2	1	-
Other and unallocable	25,793	30,115	36,216	114	126	146	6	4	4
From State and local sources.	368,509	613,492	895,313	1,627	2,570	3,600	82	85	87
General, net intergovernmental	299,293	491,525	712,700	1,321	2,059	2,866	66	68	69
Taxes....................	223,463	349,793	501,619	986	1,465	2,017	50	49	49
Property.................	68,499	103,757	155,613	302	435	626	15	14	15
Sales and gross receipts......	79,927	126,281	177,885	353	529	715	18	18	17
Individual income..........	42,080	70,097	105,640	186	294	425	9	10	10
Corporation income........	13,321	19,158	23,566	59	80	95	3	3	2
Other.................	19,636	30,500	38,915	87	128	156	4	4	4
Charges and miscellaneous	75,830	141,732	211,081	335	594	849	17	20	21
Utility and liquor stores	25,560	44,814	58,642	113	188	236	6	6	6
Water supply system..........	6,766	11,980	17,674	30	50	71	2	2	2
Electric power system	11,387	21,781	29,268	50	91	118	3	3	3
Transit system	2,397	4,244	5,216	11	18	21	1	1	1
Gas supply system	1,809	3,573	3,043	8	15	12	(Z)	1	(Z)
Liquor stores	3,201	3,235	3,441	14	14	14	1	1	(Z)
Insurance trust revenue [3]	43,656	77,153	123,970	193	323	498	10	11	12
Employee retirement..........	25,441	53,195	94,268	112	223	379	6	7	9
Unemployment compensation....	13,529	17,640	18,441	60	74	74	3	3	2
Direct expenditure.........	432,328	656,188	972,662	1,908	2,749	3,911	100	100	100
By function:									
Direct general expenditure [3]	367,340	552,197	831,540	1,621	2,313	3,343	85	84	86
Education [3]	133,211	192,686	288,148	588	807	1,159	31	29	30
Elementary and secondary									
education	92,930	131,987	202,009	410	553	812	22	20	21
Higher education	33,919	52,316	73,418	150	219	295	8	8	8
Highways	33,311	45,022	61,057	147	189	245	8	7	6
Public welfare	45,552	69,577	107,287	201	291	431	11	11	11
Health	8,387	13,711	24,223	37	57	97	2	2	3
Hospitals................	23,787	36,000	50,412	105	151	203	6	6	5
Police protection............	13,494	20,956	30,577	60	88	123	3	3	3
Fire protection	5,718	8,917	13,186	25	37	53	1	1	1
Natural resources	5,509	8,357	12,330	24	35	50	1	1	1
Sanitation and sewerage	13,214	17,398	28,453	58	73	114	3	3	3
Housing and community									
development	6,062	10,373	15,479	27	43	62	1	2	2
Parks and recreation..........	6,520	9,160	14,326	29	38	58	2	1	2
Financial administration	6,719	10,448	16,217	30	44	65	2	2	2
General control	8,697	14,314	22,976	38	60	92	2	2	2
Interest on general debt [4]	14,747	32,427	49,739	65	136	200	3	5	5
Utility and liquor stores [4]	36,191	59,800	77,801	160	250	313	8	9	8
Water supply system..........	9,228	14,298	22,101	41	60	89	2	2	2
Electric power system	15,016	25,344	30,997	66	106	125	4	4	3
Transit system	7,641	13,867	18,788	34	58	76	2	2	2
Gas supply system	1,715	3,468	2,989	8	15	12	(Z)	1	(Z)
Liquor stores	2,591	2,823	2,926	11	12	12	1	(Z)	(Z)
Insurance trust expenditure [3]	28,797	44,191	63,321	127	185	255	7	7	7
Employee retirement..........	14,008	24,414	38,355	62	102	154	3	4	4
Unemployment compensation....	12,070	14,995	16,499	53	63	66	3	2	2
By character and object:									
Current operation..............	307,811	472,543	700,131	1,359	1,979	2,815	71	72	72
Capital outlay	62,894	79,930	123,069	278	335	495	15	12	13
Construction	51,492	60,685	89,114	227	254	358	12	9	9
Equipment, land and existing									
structures	11,402	19,245	33,955	50	81	137	3	3	4
Assistance and subsidies	15,222	20,707	27,227	67	87	109	4	3	3
Interest on debt (general and utility) .	17,604	38,817	58,914	78	163	237	4	6	6
Insurance benefits and repayments. .	28,797	44,191	63,321	127	185	255	7	7	7
Expenditure for salaries and wages ...	*163,896*	*236,877*	*341,158*	*723*	*992*	*1,372*	*38*	*36*	*35*
Debt outstanding, end of year .	335,603	571,351	860,584	1,481	2,393	3,460	100	100	100
Long-term..................	322,456	551,768	841,278	1,423	2,311	3,383	96	97	98
Short-term..................	13,147	19,583	19,306	58	82	78	4	3	2
Long-term debt:									
Issued	42,364	101,164	108,468	187	424	436	(X)	(X)	(X)
Retired	17,404	43,565	64,831	77	182	261	(X)	(X)	(X)

- Represents zero. X Not applicable. Z Less than .5 percent. [1] 1980 and 1990 based on enumerated resident population as of April 1. 1985 based on estimated resident population as of July 1 and do not reflect revisions based on the 1990 Census of Population. [2] Aggregates exclude duplicative transaction between State and local governments; see source. [3] Includes amounts not shown separately. [4] Interest on utility debt included in "utility expenditure." For total interest on debt, see "Interest on debt (general and utility)."

Source: U.S. Bureau of the Census, *Census of Governments: 1982, Historical Statistics on Governmental Finances and Employment (GC 82(6)-4)* and *Government Finances*, series GF, No. 5, annual.

No. 457. State and Local Government Receipts and Expenditures in the National Income and Product Accounts: 1970 to 1990

[In billions of dollars. For explanation of national income, see text, section 14]

ITEM	1970	1980	1983	1984	1985	1986	1987	1988	1989	1990
Receipts	129.0	361.4	443.4	492.2	528.7	571.2	594.3	631.8	677.0	724.5
Personal tax and nontax receipts [1]	16.7	56.2	76.2	87.1	94.0	101.6	111.8	117.6	131.5	138.8
Income taxes	10.9	42.6	58.3	67.5	72.1	77.4	86.0	89.9	101.4	106.1
Nontaxes	1.4	5.0	7.6	8.7	9.9	11.4	11.9	12.7	14.1	15.5
Corporate profits tax accruals	3.7	14.5	15.9	18.8	20.2	22.7	23.9	26.0	24.1	23.2
Indirect business tax and nontax accruals [1]	74.8	172.3	226.6	251.7	271.4	292.0	306.5	324.5	349.1	373.4
Sales taxes	31.6	82.9	107.4	121.1	131.1	140.4	149.8	161.4	171.4	181.4
Property taxes	36.7	68.8	91.9	99.7	107.0	114.5	121.1	127.6	140.8	152.1
Contributions for social insurance	9.2	29.7	37.7	40.2	42.8	47.3	49.2	51.9	54.1	57.0
Federal grants-in-aid	24.4	88.7	87.0	94.4	100.3	107.6	102.8	111.3	118.2	132.2
Expenditures	127.2	336.6	403.2	434.1	472.6	517.0	554.2	593.0	635.9	698.8
Purchases	112.6	298.0	360.3	389.9	428.1	465.3	496.6	531.7	570.0	618.0
Compensation of employees	71.1	193.5	243.9	261.9	283.2	305.9	327.3	351.9	379.1	409.8
Transfer payments to persons	20.1	65.7	85.9	93.5	101.2	110.9	119.6	130.0	143.3	163.5
Net interest paid [2]	−1.8	−19.3	−30.9	−34.0	−38.7	−40.4	−41.2	−44.2	−49.9	−53.7
Less: Dividends received	0.2	1.9	3.4	3.9	4.5	5.1	5.9	6.9	8.1	9.0
Subsidies [3]	−3.6	−5.8	−8.7	−11.4	−13.5	−13.5	−14.9	−17.5	−19.5	−20.0
Surplus	1.8	24.8	40.3	58.1	56.1	54.3	40.1	38.4	41.1	25.7

[1] Includes other items not shown separately.   [2] Interest paid less interest received.   [3] Less current surplus of government.

Source: U.S. Bureau of Economic Analysis, *Survey of Current Business*, March 1992, and unpublished data.

No. 458. New Issues of Long-Term State and Local Government Securities: 1970 to 1990

[In billions of dollars. Beginning 1983, includes outlying areas]

ITEM	1970	1980	1983	1984	1985	1986	1987	1988	1989	1990
All issues, new capital and refunding	18.2	48.5	85.1	108.0	222.2	151.2	105.7	116.8	125.1	128.0
General obligations	11.9	14.1	21.5	26.7	54.1	42.7	30.5	29.4	37.2	40.4
Revenue	6.1	34.3	63.6	81.3	168.1	108.5	75.2	87.4	87.9	87.6
Type of issuer:										
State	4.2	5.3	9.2	9.1	13.1	14.7	9.8	9.3	11.7	14.9
Special district and statutory authority	5.6	27.0	48.6	64.5	138.6	85.1	61.6	68.3	69.6	69.7
Municipalities, counties, townships [1]	8.4	16.1	27.3	34.3	70.5	51.4	34.3	39.2	44.0	43.4
Issues for new capital, total	18.1	46.7	71.1	95.2	160.0	80.8	55.3	77.2	81.1	93.4
Use of proceeds:										
Education	5.0	4.6	8.2	7.9	16.6	11.4	9.1	13.5	13.8	17.3
Transportation	3.2	2.6	4.4	7.6	12.1	7.8	3.9	7.1	9.0	10.9
Roads, bridges	1.5	1.1	1.3	2.0	4.7	4.2	1.7	2.4	2.9	2.9
Utilities and conservation	3.5	8.0	18.0	27.0	13.1	110.6	9.8	9.8	12.8	12.8
Electric and gas	0.9	3.4	6.3	6.8	10.9	5.1	1.8	0.7	2.3	2.9
Social welfare	1.2	19.4	25.4	29.4	63.3	12.5	10.5	16.6	14.8	19.2
Public housing	0.5	15.5	17.4	19.3	37.2	8.7	7.0	10.9	7.1	8.4
Industrial aid	0.1	1.7	3.6	15.7	14.1	4.7	2.4	2.5	3.4	2.8
Other	5.1	10.4	16.0	16.6	26.9	31.3	18.8	27.7	27.3	30.4

[1] Includes school districts.

Source: Public Securities Association, New York, NY, IDD/PSA Municipal Database.

No. 459. State and Local Governments—Indebtedness: 1980 to 1990

[In billions of dollars, except per capita. As of end of fiscal year; see text, section 9. Local government amounts are estimates subject to sampling variation; see source and Appendix III. See *Historical Statistics, Colonial Times to 1970*, series Y 680, Y 747, and Y 794, for debt outstanding]

ITEM	DEBT OUTSTANDING						LONG-TERM		
	Total	Per capita [1] (dol.)	Long-term			Short-term	Net long-term	Debt issued	Debt retired
			Local schools [2]	Utilities	All other				
1980: Total	335.6	1,482	32.3	55.2	235.0	13.1	262.9	42.4	17.4
State	122.0	540	3.8	4.6	111.5	2.1	79.8	16.4	5.7
Local	213.6	942	28.5	50.6	123.5	11.0	183.1	25.9	11.7
1985: Total	568.6	2,382	43.8	90.8	414.5	19.6	430.5	101.2	43.5
State	211.9	890	6.7	8.6	193.8	2.8	110.4	41.7	16.4
Local	356.7	1,494	37.1	82.2	220.6	16.8	320.1	59.5	27.2
1989: Total	798.4	3,216	52.7	127.5	600.2	18.0	445.5	102.2	63.8
State	295.5	1,190	3.7	12.2	277.4	2.3	118.2	42.0	26.9
Local	502.9	2,026	49.0	115.3	322.8	15.7	327.2	60.2	36.8
1990: Total	860.6	3,460	60.4	134.8	646.1	19.3	477.0	108.5	64.8
State	318.3	1,280	4.4	12.3	298.8	2.8	125.5	43.5	22.9
Local	542.3	2,181	56.0	122.4	347.4	16.5	351.5	65.0	42.0

[1] 1980 and 1990 based on enumerated resident population as of April 1; 1985 and 1989 based on estimated resident population as of July 1 and do not reflect revisions based on the 1990 Census of Population.   [2] Includes debt for education activities other than higher education.

Source: U.S. Bureau of the Census, *Government Finances*, series GF, No. 5, annual, and unpublished data.

No. 460. State Governments—Revenue,

[In millions of dollars, except as indicated. Data will not match other tables due to later revisions.

YEAR, DIVISION, AND STATE	Total revenue [1]	GENERAL REVENUE								DEBT OUTSTANDING Total
		Total		Per capita [2]		Intergovernmental revenue		Taxes	Charges and miscellaneous	
		Amount	Rank	Total (dol.)	Rank	From Federal Government	From local governments			
1970	88,939	77,755	(X)	384	(X)	12,252	995	47,962	9,545	42,008
1980	276,962	233,592	(X)	1,034	(X)	61,892	2,434	137,075	32,190	121,958
1985	439,416	365,835	(X)	1,536	(X)	84,434	5,453	215,893	60,055	211,917
1986	481,279	393,475	(X)	1,636	(X)	92,666	5,908	228,053	66,848	247,715
1987	517,217	419,487	(X)	1,728	(X)	95,463	6,918	246,933	70,173	265,551
1988	541,426	445,138	(X)	1,815	(X)	100,478	6,763	264,146	73,751	276,786
1989	586,931	482,721	(X)	1,948	(X)	108,235	7,530	284,413	82,543	295,500
U.S., 1990	**625,473**	**517,443**	**(X)**	**2,086**	**(X)**	**118,353**	**7,995**	**300,489**	**90,607**	**318,237**
New England:										
Maine	3,246	2,848	40	2,319	16	691	5	1,561	591	2,125
New Hampshire . . .	1,922	1,563	48	1,410	50	374	57	595	538	3,338
Vermont.	1,592	1,433	49	2,545	11	394	(Z)	666	373	1,259
Massachusetts . . .	17,034	15,774	10	2,622	8	3,307	293	9,369	2,805	18,715
Rhode Island	3,034	2,484	41	2,568	9	667	44	1,233	540	3,616
Connecticut	9,591	8,636	20	2,627	7	1,753	4	5,268	1,611	10,988
Middle Atlantic:										
New York.	64,253	52,441	2	2,915	5	12,902	4,234	28,615	6,690	46,547
New Jersey	22,624	18,275	9	2,364	13	3,644	132	10,434	4,065	18,908
Pennsylvania	27,223	21,951	4	1,847	37	5,269	65	13,220	3,397	10,926
East North Central:										
Ohio	28,516	19,968	7	1,841	38	4,767	217	11,436	3,548	11,209
Indiana	11,456	10,702	17	1,930	29	2,255	75	6,102	2,270	4,140
Illinois	24,313	20,840	5	1,823	39	4,489	103	12,891	3,357	15,262
Michigan	23,405	19,708	8	2,120	21	4,181	507	11,343	3,676	9,170
Wisconsin	13,388	10,975	16	2,244	18	2,365	80	6,558	1,972	6,119
West North Central:										
Minnesota	13,162	10,991	15	2,512	12	2,274	117	6,819	1,782	3,764
Iowa	6,728	5,829	29	2,099	23	1,291	69	3,313	1,156	1,875
Missouri.	9,343	8,012	21	1,566	48	1,804	15	4,939	1,253	5,250
North Dakota	1,810	1,629	47	2,549	10	443	19	677	489	872
South Dakota	1,494	1,310	50	1,882	33	451	7	500	352	1,787
Nebraska.	3,073	2,856	39	1,810	40	681	17	1,513	645	1,361
Kansas	5,136	4,386	33	1,770	41	958	17	2,669	741	306
South Atlantic:										
Delaware	2,316	2,104	43	3,159	4	307	3	1,130	665	2,978
Maryland	12,195	10,445	18	2,185	19	2,095	93	6,450	1,806	6,644
Virginia	13,607	11,630	12	1,880	34	2,105	185	6,600	2,739	6,083
West Virginia	4,435	3,814	37	2,127	20	942	6	2,230	636	2,471
North Carolina	14,485	12,345	11	1,862	36	2,648	240	7,865	1,592	3,071
South Carolina	8,750	6,930	26	1,987	27	1,728	90	3,934	1,178	3,894
Georgia	13,108	11,190	14	1,727	44	2,877	56	7,078	1,179	3,117
Florida.	23,868	20,626	6	1,594	47	3,999	155	13,289	3,182	9,950
East South Central:										
Kentucky	8,593	7,347	24	1,994	26	1,794	12	4,261	1,279	5,295
Tennessee.	9,110	7,987	22	1,638	46	2,479	42	4,245	1,223	2,618
Alabama	9,041	7,595	23	879	35	2,060	65	3,820	1,650	3,979
Mississippi	5,344	4,523	32	1,758	42	1,492	13	2,396	622	1,343
West South Central:										
Arkansas	4,511	4,056	35	1,725	45	1,143	5	2,261	647	1,747
Louisiana	10,096	8,924	19	2,115	22	2,399	16	4,087	2,423	12,770
Oklahoma	7,201	5,977	27	1,900	31	1,345	41	3,477	1,114	3,714
Texas	30,975	25,959	3	1,528	49	6,499	36	14,717	4,707	7,864
Mountain:										
Montana	2,225	1,829	45	2,289	17	548	15	858	409	1,396
Idaho	2,417	1,994	44	1,980	28	494	15	1,139	346	977
Wyoming	1,900	1,657	46	3,649	2	504	22	612	519	938
Colorado	7,527	5,783	30	1,756	43	1,362	30	3,069	1,322	2,422
New Mexico	4,731	4,072	34	2,688	6	779	58	2,014	1,221	1,830
Arizona	8,598	6,983	25	1,905	30	1,293	247	4,377	1,067	2,193
Utah	4,302	3,530	38	2,049	25	966	36	1,768	759	1,790
Nevada	3,266	2,270	42	1,889	32	366	15	1,583	306	1,573
Pacific:										
Washington	14,999	11,496	13	2,362	14	2,246	56	7,423	1,771	5,686
Oregon	7,001	5,830	28	2,051	24	1,638	30	2,786	1,376	6,558
California	88,704	69,251	1	2,327	15	16,051	327	43,419	9,454	28,866
Alaska	5,500	4,842	31	8,804	1	623	5	1,546	2,668	5,536
Hawaii.	4,326	3,842	36	3,467	3	610	5	2,335	892	3,396

X Not applicable.   Z Less than $500,000.   [1] Includes liquor stores, utilities, and insurance trust activities, not shown separately.   [2] 1970, 1980, and 1990 based on enumerated resident population as of April 1. All other years based on estimated resident population as of July 1; estimates do not reflect revisions based on the 1990 Census of Population.

Debt, and Expenditure 1970 to 1990, and by State, 1990

For fiscal year ending in year shown; see text, section 9]

DEBT OUTSTANDING—Con. Per capita [2] Total (dol.)	Rank	Total expenditures [1]	GENERAL EXPENDITURES Total [3] Amount	Per capita [2] Total (dol.)	Rank	Educa-tion	Public welfare	High-ways	Health and hospitals	Natural re-sources	YEAR, DIVISION, AND STATE
207	(X)	85,055	77,642	383	(X)	30,865	13,206	13,483	5,355	2,223	1970
540	(X)	257,812	228,223	1,010	(X)	87,939	44,219	25,044	17,855	4,346	1980
89	(X)	390,742	345,047	1,449	(X)	128,604	67,264	33,154	27,595	6,758	1985
1,030	(X)	424,205	376,429	1,565	(X)	140,189	72,464	36,661	30,131	7,312	1986
1,094	(X)	455,700	403,942	1,664	(X)	149,901	78,454	38,273	32,131	7,816	1987
1,129	(X)	484,667	432,179	1,763	(X)	159,500	84,235	40,681	34,872	8,310	1988
1,194	(X)	525,077	469,269	1,895	(X)	173,184	92,750	42,694	38,602	9,070	1989
1,283	**(X)**	**571,909**	**507,875**	**2,047**	**(X)**	**184,529**	**104,971**	**44,249**	**42,662**	**9,909**	**U.S., 1990**
											N.E.:
1,731	16	3,044	2,743	2,234	16	942	689	244	162	73	ME
2,793	8	1,972	1,676	1,512	48	401	328	207	143	33	NH
2,236	13	1,565	1,466	2,603	9	516	274	147	66	42	VT
3,111	5	18,736	17,039	2,832	5	3,496	4,604	616	1,635	149	MA
3,605	3	3,014	2,658	2,741	7	782	547	189	256	23	RI
3,343	4	9,886	8,880	2,702	8	2,178	1,701	985	955	71	CT
											M.A.:
2,587	9	59,139	49,697	2,763	6	14,266	14,820	2,228	5,018	378	NY
2,446	11	21,454	18,041	2,334	15	5,390	3,456	1,324	1,237	201	NJ
920	36	24,531	21,234	1,787	37	6,975	5,186	2,275	1,667	331	PA
											E.N.C.:
1,033	29	25,237	20,489	1,889	32	7,720	5,058	1,700	1,585	237	OH
747	40	10,414	9,992	1,802	36	4,235	1,930	974	714	124	IN
1,335	21	22,072	20,055	1,754	41	6,488	4,437	2,190	1,393	279	IL
987	31	23,098	19,561	2,104	19	6,418	4,543	1,355	2,491	255	MI
1,251	23	11,416	10,499	2,146	17	3,685	2,221	796	692	196	WI
											W.N.C.:
860	38	11,355	10,407	2,379	12	3,774	2,064	1,001	815	256	MN
675	43	6,317	5,935	2,137	18	2,418	1,112	738	532	145	IA
1,026	30	8,326	7,703	1,505	49	3,274	1,377	779	676	188	MO
1,365	20	1,755	1,587	2,483	11	592	226	202	86	73	ND
2,568	10	1,344	1,281	1,841	33	377	187	186	90	51	SD
863	37	2,885	2,815	1,784	39	907	498	409	288	98	NE
124	50	4,705	4,329	1,747	42	1,845	732	544	380	121	KS
											S.A.:
4,471	2	2,128	1,994	2,994	4	709	228	191	147	33	DE
1,390	18	11,296	9,832	2,057	21	2,865	1,864	1,241	831	235	MD
983	33	12,632	11,850	1,920	30	4,723	1,484	1,680	1,265	169	VA
1,378	19	4,212	3,530	1,969	25	1,454	632	451	192	85	WV
463	48	13,493	12,555	1,894	31	5,966	1,833	1,335	960	278	NC
1,117	27	7,910	6,775	1,943	28	2,843	1,078	487	787	143	SC
481	47	12,213	11,393	1,759	40	5,048	2,125	1,008	955	288	GA
769	39	21,723	20,558	1,589	47	7,829	3,529	1,733	1,786	616	FL
											E.S.C.:
1,437	17	7,772	7,101	1,927	29	2,945	1,419	718	441	211	KY
537	45	8,403	7,879	1,616	46	2,821	1,675	1,029	646	110	TN
985	32	8,108	7,400	1,831	34	3,380	1,049	716	893	143	AL
522	46	4,838	4,394	1,708	44	1,883	696	411	340	129	MS
											W.S.C.:
743	41	4,223	3,930	1,672	45	1,686	788	420	328	106	AR
3,026	7	9,420	8,524	2,020	23	3,177	1,342	740	848	207	LA
1,181	25	6,515	5,612	1,784	38	2,369	1,090	662	531	96	OK
463	49	26,027	23,630	1,391	50	10,973	4,189	2,730	1,818	364	TX
											Mt.:
1,747	15	2,007	1,651	2,066	20	576	276	252	97	86	MT
970	34	2,047	1,831	1,818	35	751	228	288	80	87	ID
2,067	14	1,641	1,485	3,270	2	524	110	250	93	85	WY
735	42	6,510	5,627	1,708	43	2,491	902	628	372	131	CO
1,208	24	4,172	3,891	2,568	10	1,681	436	386	319	77	NM
598	44	8,265	7,535	2,056	22	2,759	1,077	1,469	316	117	AZ
1,039	28	3,857	3,471	2,014	24	1,663	458	349	334	80	UT
1,308	22	2,929	2,366	1,060	20	848	219	295	94	56	NV
											Pac.:
1,168	26	13,567	11,389	2,340	14	5,082	2,098	864	798	350	WA
2,308	12	6,352	5,563	1,957	27	1,730	934	651	502	185	OR
970	35	78,867	70,189	2,359	13	26,906	16,421	3,512	5,520	1,775	CA
10,065	1	4,688	4,284	7,790	1	1,057	368	464	176	208	AK
3,065	6	3,832	3,547	3,201	3	1,113	431	202	311	134	HI

[3] Includes amounts not shown separately.

Source: U.S. Bureau of the Census, *State Government Finances*, series GF, No. 3; and *Census of Governments: 1977* and *1987, Vol. 6, Historical Statistics on Governmental Finances and Employment*.

No. 461. State Governments—Summary of Finances: 1980 to 1990

[For fiscal years ending in year shown; see text section 9. See also *Historical Statistics, Colonial Times to 1970*, series Y 710-782]

ITEM	TOTAL (mil. dol.)			PER CAPITA [1] (dol.)			PERCENT DISTRIBUTION		
	1980	1985	1990	1980	1985	1990	1980	1985	1990
Borrowing and revenue	293,356	476,501	672,637	1,299	2,001	2,684	100	100	100
Borrowing.	16,394	37,547	40,465	73	158	163	6	8	6
Revenue	276,962	438,954	632,172	1,226	1,843	2,521	94	92	94
General revenue.	233,592	365,344	517,429	1,034	1,534	2,086	80	77	78
Taxes	137,075	215,320	300,489	607	904	1,211	47	45	45
Sales and gross receipts	67,855	105,325	147,069	300	442	593	23	22	22
General	43,168	69,629	99,702	191	292	402	15	15	15
Motor fuels.	9,722	13,352	19,379	43	56	78	3	3	3
Alcoholic beverages.	2,478	3,031	3,191	11	13	13	1	1	1
Tobacco products	3,738	4,247	5,541	17	18	22	1	1	1
Other.	8,750	15,066	19,256	39	63	78	3	3	3
Licenses	8,690	13,546	18,842	38	57	76	3	3	3
Motor vehicles.	4,936	7,045	9,848	22	30	40	2	2	2
Corporations in general. . . .	1,388	2,767	3,099	6	12	12	1	1	1
Other.	2,366	3,734	5,895	10	16	22	1	1	1
Individual income	37,089	63,644	96,076	164	267	387	13	13	14
Corporation net income	13,321	17,637	21,751	59	74	88	5	4	3
Property	2,892	3,984	5,848	13	17	24	1	1	1
Other	7,227	11,184	10,903	32	47	44	3	2	2
Charges and miscellaneous. . . .	32,190	60,102	90,612	142	252	365	11	13	14
Intergovernmental revenue	64,326	89,922	126,329	285	378	509	22	19	19
From Federal Government . . .	61,892	84,469	118,353	274	355	477	21	18	18
Public welfare	24,680	38,664	59,397	109	162	239	8	8	9
Education.	12,765	15,307	21,271	57	64	86	4	3	3
Highways	8,860	12,702	13,931	39	53	56	3	3	2
Other.	15,587	17,796	23,754	69	75	96	5	4	4
From local governments.	2,434	5,453	7,976	11	23	32	1	1	1
Utility revenue	1,304	2,948	3,305	6	12	13	(Z)	1	1
Liquor stores revenue	2,765	2,753	2,907	12	12	12	1	1	(Z)
Insurance trust revenue [2]	39,301	67,907	108,530	174	285	410	13	14	15
Employee retirement	21,146	43,993	78,898	94	185	291	7	9	11
Unemployment compensation . .	13,468	17,596	18,370	60	74	74	5	4	3
Expenditure and debt redemption	263,494	402,536	592,194	1,166	1,691	2,385	100	100	100
Debt redemption	5,682	11,708	19,876	25	49	80	2	3	3
Expenditure [3]	257,812	390,828	572,318	1,141	1,641	2,305	98	97	97
General expenditure	228,223	345,133	508,284	1,010	1,449	2,047	87	86	86
Education.	87,939	128,604	184,935	389	540	744	33	32	31
Public welfare	44,219	67,317	104,971	196	283	423	17	17	18
Highways	25,044	33,186	44,249	111	139	178	10	8	8
Health and hospitals.	17,855	27,595	42,665	79	116	172	7	7	7
Corrections.	4,449	9,171	17,266	20	39	70	2	2	3
Natural resources	4,346	6,758	9,909	19	28	40	2	2	2
General control	3,232	5,231	8,384	14	22	34	1	1	1
Financial administration.	3,031	4,996	8,616	13	21	35	1	1	2
Police protection	2,263	3,518	5,166	10	15	21	1	1	1
Employment security	2,001	2,606	3,003	9	11	12	1	1	1
Housing and community development	601	1,540	2,856	3	6	12	(Z)	(Z)	1
Misc. and unallocable.	33,242	54,611	76,264	147	229	307	13	14	13
Utility expenditure	2,401	5,364	7,131	11	23	29	1	1	1
Liquor stores expenditure	2,206	2,391	2,452	10	10	10	1	1	(Z)
Insurance trust expenditure [2]	24,981	37,940	54,452	111	159	219	10	9	9
Employee retirement	10,256	18,230	29,562	45	77	119	4	5	5
Unemployment compensation . .	12,006	14,928	16,423	53	63	66	5	4	3
By character and object:									
Intergovernmental expenditure . . .	84,504	121,571	175,028	374	511	706	32	30	30
Direct expenditure	173,307	269,257	397,291	767	1,131	1,599	66	67	67
Current operation.	108,131	172,210	258,046	479	723	1,038	41	43	44
Capital outlay	23,325	30,657	45,524	103	129	183	9	8	8
Construction	19,736	23,877	34,803	87	100	140	8	6	6
Land and existing structures . .	1,345	1,833	3,471	6	8	14	1	1	1
Equipment.	2,243	4,947	7,250	10	21	29	1	1	1
Assistance and subsidies	9,818	12,842	16,902	43	54	68	4	3	3
Interest on debt.	7,052	15,608	22,367	31	66	90	3	4	4
Insurance benefits [4]	24,981	37,940	54,452	111	159	219	10	9	9
Debt outstanding, end of year.	121,958	211,904	318,237	540	890	1,283	100	100	100
Long-term.	119,821	209,112	315,473	530	878	1,272	98	99	99
Full-faith and credit	49,364	60,432	74,965	219	254	302	41	29	24
Nonguaranteed.	70,457	148,680	240,508	312	624	969	58	70	76
Short-term.	2,137	2,792	2,764	9	12	11	2	1	1
Net long-term	79,810	110,348	125,507	353	463	506	65	52	39
Full-faith and credit only.	39,357	47,779	63,475	174	201	256	32	23	20

Z Less than .05 percent. [1] 1980 and 1990 based on enumerated resident population as of April 1. 1985 based on estimated resident population as of July 1 and do not reflect revisions based on the 1990 Census of Population. [2] Includes other items not shown separately. [3] Intergovernmental and direct. [4] Includes repayments.

Source: U.S. Bureau of the Census, *1982 Census of Governments: Historical Statistics on Governmental Finances and Employment* (GC82(6)-4) and *State Government Finances*, series GF, No. 3, annual.

No. 462. State Resources, Expenditures, and Balances: 1990 to 1992

[Fiscal year data; see text; section 9. **General funds** exclude special funds earmarked for particular purposes, such as highway trust funds and federal funds; they support most on-going broad-based State services, and are available for appropriation to support any governmental activity. Minus sign (-) indicates deficit]

STATE	EXPENDITURES BY FUND SOURCE					STATE GENERAL FUND					
	Total, 1990 (mil. dol.)	1991 [1]				Resources [3][4]		Expenditures [4]		Balance [5]	
		Total [2] (mil. dol.)	General fund (percent)	Federal funds (percent)	Other State funds (percent)	1991 (mil. dol.)	1992 [1] (mil. dol.)	1991 (mil. dol.)	1992 [1] (mil. dol.)	1991 (mil. dol.)	1992 [1] (mil. dol.)
United States ...	501,193	550,102	52	23	22	295,512	307,353	292,498	307,020	3,057	325
New England:											
Maine..........	2,651	2,915	56	24	15	1,585	1,519	1,581	1,518	4	1
New Hampshire....	1,392	1,454	43	27	27	618	699	643	703	-25	-4
Vermont.........	1,223	1,291	48	28	21	577	608	643	659	-65	-51
Massachusetts.....	17,196	17,174	42	20	33	13,870	13,694	13,633	13,577	237	117
Rhode Island......	2,246	2,293	64	23	9	1,450	1,757	1,446	1,747	4	[6]1
Connecticut.......	9,446	9,662	68	14	12	5,661	6,956	6,626	6,956	-966	-
Middle Atlantic:											
New York........	46,361	49,177	57	22	17	28,898	29,824	28,898	29,824	-	-
New Jersey.......	16,408	18,073	68	22	7	12,188	14,972	12,187	14,569	1	403
Pennsylvania......	21,814	24,650	51	25	21	11,967	13,637	12,421	13,635	-454	2
East North Central:											
Ohio	21,105	23,082	43	24	30	12,863	13,271	12,727	13,280	135	-8
Indiana..........	9,011	9,930	60	26	13	5,933	5,830	5,823	5,778	109	52
Illinois	18,845	20,590	54	16	26	11,602	12,105	11,502	11,995	100	110
Michigan.........	17,511	18,423	42	25	33	7,560	7,058	7,729	7,843	-169	-785
Wisconsin........	11,019	11,805	54	21	24	6,478	6,704	6,364	6,586	114	118
West North Central:											
Minnesota........	9,986	11,096	63	19	16	7,459	6,752	6,904	6,496	555	256
Iowa	7,001	7,419	43	21	36	3,142	3,210	3,131	3,202	11	8
Missouri	8,020	8,566	50	21	29	4,281	4,369	4,241	4,335	40	34
North Dakota......	1,519	1,503	35	36	27	628	654	523	587	105	67
South Dakota	1,162	1,306	37	39	24	534	570	523	570	11	-
Nebraska	2,750	3,376	44	21	35	1,634	1,675	1,460	1,534	174	141
Kansas..........	4,761	5,187	48	20	31	2,657	2,619	2,495	2,495	162	125
South Atlantic:											
Delaware	2,203	2,283	54	12	26	1,327	1,346	1,213	1,238	114	108
Maryland	11,312	11,734	53	18	24	6,199	6,152	6,199	6,139	-	13
Virginia..........	12,298	13,130	48	16	34	6,331	6,289	6,331	6,261	-	28
West Virginia......	3,680	4,042	47	25	25	1,977	2,009	1,888	1,985	89	24
North Carolina.....	11,765	12,617	61	21	18	7,562	7,983	7,562	7,883	-	101
South Carolina.....	7,683	8,422	42	27	28	3,524	3,447	3,462	3,385	62	62
Georgia.........	11,817	12,616	60	22	15	7,408	7,455	7,373	7,455	35	-
Florida	22,812	27,076	39	17	41	11,085	11,127	10,943	11,127	142	-
East South Central:											
Kentucky	7,740	9,814	44	24	24	4,358	4,640	4,188	4,613	170	27
Tennessee	7,549	8,186	49	31	17	3,870	3,874	3,863	3,860	7	14
Alabama........	7,383	8,025	43	50	6	3,387	3,338	3,386	3,338	1	-
Mississippi	4,082	4,717	42	34	24	1,949	1,928	1,945	1,928	4	1
West South Central:											
Arkansas	4,555	4,789	39	26	35	1,879	1,928	1,879	1,928	-	-
Louisiana........	8,483	9,505	47	28	23	4,938	4,466	4,520	4,466	418	-
Oklahoma........	5,920	6,694	45	24	31	3,246	3,400	3,067	3,184	179	216
Texas..........	23,531	26,324	58	23	17	16,243	17,040	15,514	17,469	729	-428
Mountain:											
Montana.........	1,764	2,002	23	26	48	509	536	450	520	59	16
Idaho...........	1,815	2,050	46	31	24	951	997	917	997	34	-
Wyoming........	1,366	1,406	29	22	48	480	395	434	393	46	3
Colorado.........	5,292	5,441	50	25	26	2,690	2,859	2,673	2,783	16	76
New Mexico	3,834	3,828	50	22	27	1,884	2,073	1,928	2,074	(6)	-1
Arizona..........	5,985	7,159	47	31	19	3,381	3,517	3,336	3,512	45	5
Utah	3,212	3,479	50	21	27	1,776	1,876	1,742	1,851	34	24
Nevada	(NA)	(NA)	(NA)	(NA)	(NA)	991	1,044	928	1,001	64	43
Pacific:											
Washington.......	11,350	13,380	54	19	24	7,492	7,569	7,024	7,667	468	-98
Oregon..........	6,987	7,570	31	15	54	2,744	2,977	2,364	2,687	380	290
California	67,247	75,896	55	28	12	39,005	42,374	40,264	43,718	-1,259	-1,344
Alaska	3,726	3,755	66	20	14	3,598	3,078	2,807	2,901	791	177
Hawaii	4,375	5,190	54	12	15	3,146	3,151	2,799	2,769	347	382

- Represents zero. NA Not available. [1] Estimated. [2] Includes bonds not shown separately. [3] Includes funds budgeted, adjustments, and balances from previous year. [4] May or may not include budget stabilization fund transfers, depending on State accounting practices. [5] Resources less expenditures. [6] Ending balance is held in a budget stabilization fund.

Source: National Association of State Budget Officers, Washington, DC, *State Expenditure Report 1991*, and National Governors' Association and NASBO, *Fiscal Survey of the States*, semi-annual (copyright).

No. 463. State Government Tax Collections and Excise Taxes, 1970-90, and by State, 1990

[Tax collections for **fiscal years ending in year shown**; see text, section 9. Excise tax rates as of **September 1**. Collections include local shares of State-imposed taxes. 1990 tax collections preliminary]

YEAR, REGION, DIVISION, AND STATE	STATE TAX COLLECTIONS (mil. dol.)									EXCISE TAX RATES		
	Total [1]	Sales and gross receipts				Indi-vidual income	Corpo-ration net income	Motor vehicle and opera-tors' li-censes	General sales and gross receipts (percent) [2]	Ciga-rettes (cents per pack-age)	Gaso-line (cents per gal.)
		Total [1]	Gen-eral sales and gross receipts	Motor fuels	Alcoholic bever-ages and tobacco products						
1970 [3]	47,962	27,254	14,177	6,283	3,728	9,183	3,738	2,728	(X)	(X)	(X)
1975 [3]	80,155	43,346	24,780	8,255	5,249	18,819	6,642	3,941	(X)	(X)	(X)
1980 [3]	137,075	67,855	43,168	9,722	6,216	37,089	13,321	5,325	(X)	(X)	(X)
1985 [3]	215,893	105,419	69,633	13,344	7,393	63,908	17,631	7,780	(X)	(X)	(X)
1990 [3]	**300,489**	**147,069**	**99,702**	**19,379**	**8,732**	**96,076**	**21,751**	**10,675**	**(X)**	**(X)**	**(X)**
Northeast	**70,961**	**29,696**	**18,960**	**2,659**	**1,937**	**28,282**	**5,935**	**2,151**	**(X)**	**(X)**	**(X)**
New England	**18,692**	**8,337**	**5,441**	**956**	**591**	**6,820**	**1,832**	**709**	**(X)**	**(X)**	**(X)**
Maine	1,561	773	509	138	77	581	58	55	5 F&D	31	17
New Hampshire	595	271	(X)	81	50	41	127	58	(X)	25	16
Vermont	666	321	136	54	26	251	27	39	4 F&D	17	16
Massachusetts	9,369	2,852	1,956	302	223	4,910	871	319	5 F&D	26	17
Rhode Island	1,233	645	397	73	49	427	69	40	7 F&D	37	20
Connecticut	5,268	3,475	2,443	308	166	610	680	198	8 F&D	40	22
Middle Atlantic	**52,269**	**21,359**	**13,519**	**1,703**	**1,346**	**21,462**	**4,103**	**1,442**	**(X)**	**(X)**	**(X)**
New York	28,615	9,368	6,003	544	733	15,289	1,885	604	[4]4 F&D	39	8
New Jersey	10,434	5,444	3,291	414	256	2,952	1,123	363	7 F&D	40	10.5
Pennsylvania	13,220	6,547	4,225	745	357	3,221	1,095	475	6 F&D	18	12
Midwest	**68,760**	**32,842**	**21,964**	**5,451**	**1,988**	**24,454**	**5,439**	**2,924**	**(X)**	**(X)**	**(X)**
East North Central	**48,330**	**23,004**	**15,389**	**3,721**	**1,376**	**17,055**	**4,176**	**1,927**	**(X)**	**(X)**	**(X)**
Ohio	11,436	5,752	3,589	971	285	4,125	643	411	[4]5 F&D	18	20
Indiana	6,102	3,372	2,551	565	148	2,090	341	178	5 F&D	15.5	15
Illinois	12,891	6,468	4,077	916	385	4,288	939	651	[5]6.25	30	19
Michigan	11,343	4,414	3,188	740	377	3,927	1,816	509	4 F&D	25	15
Wisconsin	6,558	2,998	1,984	529	181	2,625	437	178	[4]5 F&D	30	21.5
West North Central	**20,430**	**9,838**	**6,575**	**1,730**	**612**	**7,399**	**1,263**	**997**	**(X)**	**(X)**	**(X)**
Minnesota	6,819	2,966	1,870	461	209	2,877	482	339	[4]6 F&D	38	20
Iowa	3,313	1,471	944	334	98	1,272	200	221	4 F&D	31	20
Missouri	4,939	2,509	1,899	355	102	1,791	221	213	[4]4.225 D	13	11
North Dakota	677	380	231	67	20	106	47	41	5 F&D	30	17
South Dakota	500	403	250	80	23	(X)	31	21	[4]4 D	23	18
Nebraska	1,513	827	508	209	54	496	72	59	[4]5 F&D	27	21.9
Kansas	2,669	1,282	873	224	106	857	210	103	[4]4.25 D	24	16
South [3]	**87,840**	**51,452**	**33,871**	**7,769**	**3,108**	**19,898**	**4,410**	**3,250**	**(X)**	**(X)**	**(X)**
South Atlantic [3]	**48,576**	**26,069**	**17,741**	**3,713**	**1,549**	**14,557**	**2,879**	**1,516**	**(X)**	**(X)**	**(X)**
Delaware	1,130	159	(X)	64	17	456	118	24	(X)	19	16
Maryland	6,450	2,712	1,572	450	86	2,864	293	156	5 F&D	13	18.5
Dist. of Col. [3]	23,110	674	467	30	15	638	140	18	6 F&D	17	18
Virginia	6,600	2,644	1,353	622	100	3,082	306	264	[4]3.5 D	2.5	17.5
West Virginia	2,230	1,193	765	209	41	517	222	76	6 D	17	15.5
North Carolina	7,865	3,192	1,773	793	166	3,390	612	262	[4]3 D	2	21.5
South Carolina	3,934	2,137	1,448	358	144	1,380	151	89	5 D	7	16
Georgia	7,078	3,454	2,639	441	204	2,868	478	100	[4]4 D	12	[6]7.5
Florida	13,289	10,578	8,191	776	791	(X)	699	545	[4]6 F&D	33.9	4
East South Central	**14,722**	**8,751**	**5,559**	**1,592**	**467**	**2,864**	**911**	**530**	**(X)**	**(X)**	**(X)**
Kentucky	4,261	1,911	1,088	360	64	1,210	279	154	[4]6 F&D	3	15
Tennessee	4,245	3,268	2,344	630	143	103	332	172	[4]5.5 D	13	20
Alabama	3,820	2,003	1,038	294	176	1,121	180	137	[4]4 D	16.5	11
Mississippi	2,396	1,569	1,089	308	84	430	120	67	6 D	18	18
West South Central	**24,542**	**16,632**	**10,571**	**2,464**	**1,092**	**2,477**	**620**	**1,204**	**(X)**	**(X)**	**(X)**
Arkansas	2,261	1,210	839	219	87	739	130	80	[4]4 D	21	13.5
Louisiana	4,087	2,035	1,263	399	111	737	394	80	[7]4 D	20	20
Oklahoma	3,477	1,541	844	331	127	1,001	96	275	[4]4.5 D	23	17
Texas	14,717	11,846	7,625	1,515	767	(X)	(X)	769	[4]6.25 F&D	41	15
West	**72,929**	**33,082**	**24,908**	**3,498**	**1,698**	**23,443**	**5,968**	**2,348**	**(X)**	**(X)**	**(X)**
Mountain	**15,420**	**8,279**	**5,633**	**1,324**	**362**	**4,097**	**612**	**726**	**(X)**	**(X)**	**(X)**
Montana	858	183	(X)	112	25	280	80	39	(X)	18	20
Idaho	1,139	559	383	108	27	403	73	60	5 D	18	18
Wyoming	612	217	162	37	6	(X)	(X)	43	[4]3 D	12	9
Colorado	3,069	1,337	825	325	81	1,342	123	122	[4]3 F&D	20	20
New Mexico	2,014	1,136	836	165	35	361	62	105	[4]5	15	16.2
Arizona	4,377	2,575	1,918	333	87	1,064	180	237	[4]5 F&D	15	17
Utah	1,768	915	707	132	38	647	94	48	[4]5 D	23	19
Nevada	1,583	1,357	802	112	63	(X)	(X)	72	[4]5.75 F&D	35	16.25
Pacific	**57,509**	**24,803**	**19,275**	**2,174**	**1,336**	**19,346**	**5,356**	**1,622**	**(X)**	**(X)**	**(X)**
Washington	7,423	5,564	4,471	484	252	(X)	(X)	191	6.5 F&D	34	22
Oregon	2,786	394	(X)	236	89	1,827	148	232	(X)	28	18
California	43,419	17,270	13,627	1,359	909	16,824	4,928	1,158	[4]5 F&D	35	14
Alaska	1,546	91	(X)	42	23	(X)	185	21	(X)	29	8
Hawaii	2,335	1,484	1,177	53	63	695	95	20	4 D	([8])	[9]11

X Not applicable.   [1] Includes amounts for types not shown separately.   [2] F=food exempt from sales tax; D=prescription drugs exempt from sales tax.   [3] DC excluded from total.   [4] Local sales tax rates are additional.   [5] Food and prescription drugs are subject to a 1 percent State tax. In addition, these items may be subject to a 1 percent local tax.   [6] An additional tax is levied at the rate of 3 percent of the retail sales price, less than the current 7.5 cents per gallon tax.   [7] Food products subject to a 2 percent State tax.   [8] Tax is 40 percent of wholesale price.   [9] Combined State and county rates are: Hawaii 19.8 cents; Honolulu 27.5 cents; Kauai 21 cents, and Maui 20 cents.

Source: U.S. Bureau of the Census, *State Government Tax Collections*, series GF, No. 1, annual.

No. 464. State Government Individual Income Taxes: 1990

[As of October 1990. Only basic rates, brackets and exemptions are shown. Local income tax rates, even those mandated by the State, are not included. Taxable income rates and brackets listed below apply to single individuals and married taxpayers filing "combined separate" returns (in States where this is permitted). Alaska, Florida, Nevada, South Dakota, Texas, Washington, and Wyoming have no State income tax]

STATE	Taxable income rates (range in percent)	TAXABLE INCOME BRACKETS		PERSONAL EXEMPTIONS			SIZE OF STANDARD DEDUCTION [1]			Federal income tax deduct-ible [2]
		Lowest: amount under	Highest: amount over	Single	Married-joint return	Depen-dents	Percent	Single	Married-joint return	
AL [3] [4] ..	2.0-5.0	$500	$3,000	$1,500	$3,000	$300	20	$2,000	$4,000	Yes
AZ [5] ...	3.8-7.0	10,000	150,000	2,000	4,000	2,000	(X)	3,500	7,000	No
AR [6] ...	1.0-7.0	3,000	25,000	[6]20	[6]40	[6]20	10	1,000	1,000	No
CA [5] ...	1.0-9.3	4,213	27,646	[6]58	[6]116	[6]58	(X)	2,169	4,339	No
CO ...				5% of modified Federal taxable income						No
CT ...				Limited income tax [7]						No
DE [3] ...	3.2-7.7	[8]5,000	40,000	1,250	2,500	1,250	(X)	1,300	1,600	No
DC	6.0-9.5	10,000	20,000	1,270	2,540	1,270	(X)	2,000	2,000	No
GA	1.0-6.0	750	7,000	1,500	3,000	1,500	(X)	2,300	3,000	No
HI....	2.0-10.0	1,500	20,500	1,040	2,080	1,040	(X)	1,500	1,900	No
ID....	2.0-8.2	1,000	20,000		Same as Federal [9]					No
IL	3.0		Flat rate	1,000	2,000	1,000	(X)	(X)	(X)	No
IN [3] ..	3.4		Flat rate	1,000	2,000	1,000	(X)	(X)	(X)	No
IA [3] [5] ..	.4-9.98	[10]1,038	[10]46,710	[6]20	[6]40	[6]15	(X)	1,260	3,100	Yes
KS [3] ..	[11]4.5-5.95	[11]27,500	[11]27,500	2,000	4,000	2,000	(X)	3,000	5,000	Yes
KY [3] ...	2.0-6.0	3,000	8,000	[6]20	[6]40	[6]20	(X)	650	650	Yes
LA	2.0-6.0	10,000	50,000	[12]4,500	[12]9,000	[12]1,000		Combined with exemptions [12]		Yes
ME	2.0-8.5	4,050	16,200	2,050	4,100	2,050	(X)	3,250	5,450	No
MD [3] [13] ..	2.0-5.0	1,000	3,000	1,200	2,400	1,200	15	2,000	4,000	No
MA [3] ..	5.0-10.0		Flat rate [14]	2,200	4,400	1,000	(X)	(X)	(X)	No
MI [3] [15] ..	4.6		Flat rate	2,100	4,200	2,100	(X)	(X)	(X)	No
MN [5] ..	6.0-8.0	13,000	13,000		Same as Federal [9]					No
MS	3.0-5.0	5,000	10,000	6,000	9,500	1,500	15	2,300	3,400	No
MO [3] [16] ..	1.5-6.0	1,000	9,000	1,200	2,400	400	(X)	Same as Federal [9]		Yes
MT [5] ..	2.0-11.0	1,600	55,000	1,260	2,520	1,260	20	2,360	4,720	Yes
NE	2.0-6.41	1,800	27,000	1,230	2,460	[17]1,230	(X)	Same as Federal [9]		No
NH				Limited income tax [17]						No
NJ	2.0-3.5	[18]20,000	50,000	1,000	2,000	1,000	(X)	(X)	(X)	No
NM [5] ..	1.8-8.5	[19]5,200	64,000	2,000	4,000	2,000	(X)	Same as Federal [9]		No
NY [3] ..	4.0-7.875	5,500	13,000	-	-	1,000	(X)	6,000	9,500	No
NC	[20]6.0-7.0 [21]2.67-	12,750	12,750	2,000	4,000	2,000	(X)	3,000	5,000	No
ND [3] ..	12.0	[21]3,000	[21]50,000		Same as Federal [9]					Yes
OH [3] ..	.743-6.9	5,000	100,000	650	1,300	650	(X)	(X)	(X)	No
OK [5] ..	[22]5.7-0	[22]1,000	[22]10,000	1,000	2,000	1,000	15	2,000	2,000	Yes [22]
OR [5] ..	5.0-9.0	2,000	5,000	98	196	98	(X)	1,800	3,000	Yes [23]
PA [3] ..	2.1		Flat rate	(X)	(X)	(X)	(X)	(X)	(X)	No
RI.				22.96% of Federal income tax liability						No
SC [5] ..	2.75-7.0	2,030	10,150		Same as Federal [9]					No
TN				Limited income tax [24]						No
UT	2.55-7.2	750	3,750	75% of Federal exemption				Same as Federal [9]		Yes [25]
VT				28% of Federal income tax liability						No
VA	2.0-5.75	3,000	17,000	800	1,600	800	(X)	3,000	5,000	No
WV....	3.0-6.5	10,000	60,000	2,000	4,000	2,000	(X)	(X)	(X)	No
WI	4.9-6.93	7,500	15,000	-	-	[6]50	(X)	5,200	8,900	No

- Represents zero. X Not applicable. [1] The lesser of either (a) the percentage indicated, multiplied by adjusted gross income (AGI) or (b) the dollar value listed. [2] A State provision that allows the taxpayer to deduct fully the Federal income tax payment; reduces the effective marginal tax rate for persons in the highest State and Federal tax brackets by approximately 30% of the nominal tax rate—the deduction is of a lesser benefit to other taxpayers. [3] States in which one or more local governments levy a local income tax. [4] Social Security (FICA) taxes are included in itemized deductions. [5] Indexed by an inflation factor. [6] Tax credit per dependent. [7] There is an income tax on interest, capital gains, and dividend income only. The rate of this tax ranges from 1% of interest and dividend income for taxpayers with an AGI of $54,000 to $57,999 to 12% of such income of taxpayers with an AGI over $100,000. Capital gains are taxed at 7% after an exemption of $100 is applied. [8] Lowest personal income tax rate (3.2%) applies to income in the $2,000-$5,000 bracket. Taxable income under $2,000 is not subject to tax. [9] Personal exemptions on the 1990 return are $2,150 each; standard deduction for single is $3,400 and for those filing joint returns, $5,700. [10] Tax cannot reduce after-tax income of taxpayer to below $5,000 (single) or $7,500 (married-joint return). [11] Income below $27,500 taxed at 4.5% rate, income above $27,500 taxed at 5.95% rate. [12] Personal exemption and standard deduction are combined. [13] All counties have a local income tax surcharge of at least 20% of State tax liability; most counties have a surcharge of 50%. Single taxpayers have a minimum standard deduction of $1,500 and married taxpayers a minimum standard deduction of $3,000. [14] 10% (flat rate) imposed on capital gains, interest, and dividends of residents, and Massachusetts business income of nonresidents. All other net income taxed at 5%. No taxes are imposed on a single person with gross income of $8,000 or less ($12,000 married). [15] Persons who can be claimed as a dependent on someone else's return get an exemption of $1,000. If their AGI is $1,500 or less, they owe no tax. [16] FICA taxes deductible when itemizing deductions. [17] There is a 5% tax on dividend and interest income (excluding income from savings bank deposits) in excess of $1,200 ($2,400 married). [18] No taxpayer is subject to tax if gross income is $3,000 or less ($1,500 married, filing separately). [19] Several rebates are available for lower income taxpayers. [20] Taxable income brackets are for single taxpayers. Breaking point for higher marginal tax rate varies according to filing status. [21] Applies to the long-form method. As an alternative, taxpayers may use the short-form method where the tax is 14% of the adjusted federal income tax liability. [22] These tax rates and brackets apply to single persons not deducting Federal income tax. For individuals deducting Federal income tax, rates range from .5% of the first $1,000 to 10% on income over $16,000. [23] Federal income tax deduction limited to $3,000 ($1,500 married, filing separately). [24] Interest and dividends taxed at 6%. [25] One-half of federal tax liability is deductible.

Source: Advisory Commission on Intergovernmental Relations, Washington, DC, *Significant Features of Fiscal Federalism,* 1991 Edition, Volume 1.

No. 465. State Fiscal Capacity and Effort: 1988

[**Fiscal capacity:** the ability of a government to raise revenues. **Representative Tax System:** fiscal capacity is the dollar amount of revenue that each State would raise if it were to apply a set of tax rates based on all States' average behavior to a common set of tax bases. **Representative Revenue System:** similar to the RTS, also measures ability to raise major non-tax revenues. **Effort:** extent to which a State government is utilizing the revenue bases available]

STATE	Representative Tax System		Representative Revenue System [3]	
	Capacity [1]	Effort [2]	Capacity	Effort
United States	100	100	100	100
Alabama	76	84	77	95
Alaska	159	127	255	122
Arizona	99	96	97	97
Arkansas	74	84	74	86
California	116	94	115	98
Colorado	107	89	106	94
Connecticut	143	90	142	83
Delaware	124	84	120	94
District of Columbia	123	154	126	137
Florida	104	82	103	87
Georgia	94	89	93	98
Hawaii	114	112	111	111
Idaho	76	93	76	98
Illinois	99	102	100	95
Indiana	87	93	88	96
Iowa	83	113	84	118
Kansas	91	104	91	104
Kentucky	81	88	80	89
Louisiana	83	90	84	97
Maine	98	105	97	99
Maryland	109	108	111	102
Massachusetts	129	94	131	89
Michigan	95	112	96	112
Minnesota	104	112	103	117
Mississippi	65	94	65	108
Missouri	90	86	89	86
Montana	85	102	84	102
Nebraska	90	98	89	106
Nevada	135	69	129	75
New Hampshire	126	66	123	66
New Jersey	124	101	126	95
New Mexico	83	99	88	103
New York	109	152	110	141
North Carolina	91	93	89	91
North Dakota	86	91	85	107
Ohio	91	97	92	98
Oklahoma	89	89	87	95
Oregon	91	99	91	104
Pennsylvania	94	97	95	93
Rhode Island	99	104	100	99
South Carolina	79	96	78	102
South Dakota	78	95	78	95
Tennessee	84	83	84	89
Texas	96	88	95	89
Utah	78	106	76	109
Vermont	105	100	102	100
Virginia	104	91	104	90
Washington	98	102	98	105
West Virginia	78	88	76	90
Wisconsin	90	119	90	117
Wyoming	123	94	118	105

[1] Based on a nationwide standard tax system of rates and bases that is representative of actual state-local tax systems. It includes all taxes of State and local governments broken down into 27 categories. Tax capacity effort estimate is divided by population, then indexed to the national average to provide a standardized basis for comparison. For example, California's RTS index of 116 means that, in 1988, the state's capacity to generate tax revenues was 16 percent above the per capita national average. Similarly, Wisconsin's RTS capacity index of 90 means that it would have collected 10 percent less per capita than the average state had it used an average tax system.   [2] Calculated by dividing a States' actual revenues by its calculated capacity. For example, California's actual revenue of $1,948 per capita is 94% of its per capita tax capacity, $2,062. Notice, tax effort is not indexed to a national standard but is a simple ratio of revenue to capacity.   [3] See footnotes 1 and 2. Includes non-tax own-source revenues such as user charges, rents, and royalties, as well as all taxes included in the RTS.

Source: Advisory Commission on Intergovernmental Relations, Washington, DC, *1988 State Fiscal Capacity and Index,* (M-170).

No. 466. Gross Revenue of Selected States From Parimutuel and Amusement Taxes and Lotteries, by State: 1990

[In millions of dollars, except percent. For fiscal years; see text, section 9]

YEAR AND STATE	Gross revenue	Parimutuel taxes	Amuse-ment taxes [1]	LOTTERY REVENUE Total [2]	Apportionment of funds (percent) Prizes	Administra-tion	Proceeds available from ticket sales
Total [3]	20,099.7	658.2	622.9	[4]18,818.6	53.9	6.0	39.8
Alabama	4.9	4.9	0.1	(X)	(X)	(X)	(X)
Alaska	1.6	-	1.6	(X)	(X)	(X)	(X)
Arizona	280.8	9.3	0.8	270.7	50.6	8.0	41.3
Arkansas	19.1	19.1	-	(X)	(X)	(X)	(X)
California	2,486.3	136.2	-	2,350.1	52.9	7.8	39.3
Colorado	140.8	8.3	0.9	131.6	55.6	14.5	29.8
Connecticut	577.0	59.5	19.8	497.7	53.1	5.1	41.7
Delaware	62.3	0.1	-	62.3	56.2	3.5	40.3
District of Columbia	141.5	-	-	141.5	52.1	9.0	38.9
Florida	2,049.0	102.7	2.5	1,943.8	52.2	6.2	41.6
Idaho	67.7	1.4	-	66.3	48.4	15.1	36.5
Illinois	1,477.7	45.1	8.4	1,424.2	55.6	3.6	40.8
Indiana	378.6	-	(Z)	378.6	57.7	7.3	35.0
Iowa	161.1	8.8	-	152.3	59.6	12.6	27.7
Kansas	62.0	-	0.8	61.2	47.2	18.5	34.3
Kentucky	198.8	11.1	0.3	187.4	57.5	9.9	32.6
Louisiana	24.0	22.6	1.4	(X)	(X)	(X)	(X)
Maine	100.0	1.5	-	98.5	53.6	9.5	36.9
Maryland	774.0	3.0	1.4	769.6	52.8	3.4	43.8
Massachusetts	1,493.9	31.7	9.6	1,452.6	63.7	4.7	31.6
Michigan	1,115.8	20.6	-	1,095.2	53.7	4.2	42.1
Minnesota	66.1	2.1	-	64	53.6	33.8	12.5
Missouri	210.9	-	-	210.9	55.6	11.5	33.0
Montana	21.7	0.2	-	21.5	47.4	26.5	26.0
Nebraska	7.9	0.7	7.2	(X)	(X)	(X)	(X)
Nevada	317.7	-	317.7	(X)	(X)	(X)	(X)
New Hampshire	104.4	10.4	1.5	92.5	57.0	9.9	33.2
New Jersey	1,393.4	7.9	228.8	1,156.7	51.5	3.5	45.0
New Mexico	0.8	0.8	(Z)	(X)	(X)	(X)	(X)
New York	1,963.5	78.4	0.8	1,884.3	52.0	3.4	44.6
North Dakota	4.9	-	4.9	(X)	(X)	(X)	(X)
Ohio	1,536.7	13.6	-	1,523.1	54.3	5.9	39.8
Oklahoma	8.3	8.3	(Z)	(X)	(X)	(X)	(X)
Oregon	158.5	4.9	0.1	153.6	56.4	16.6	27.0
Pennsylvania	1,451.7	9.1	0.5	1,442.1	55.8	2.7	41.5
Rhode Island	71.1	12.2	0.2	58.7	51.1	4.9	44.1
South Carolina	12.8	-	12.8	(X)	(X)	(X)	(X)
South Dakota	29.4	0.6	-	28.8	33.7	14.9	51.0
Vermont	40.9	0.2	-	40.7	58.0	15.5	26.8
Virginia	454.3	-	0.1	454.2	55.6	9.6	34.9
Washington	256.7	10.4	(Z)	246.3	47.4	14.2	38.4
West Virginia	75.3	11.5	(Z)	63.8	49.5	15.8	34.8
Wisconsin	295.2	0.8	0.6	293.8	53.9	9.0	37.0

- Represents or rounds to zero. X Not applicable. Z Less than $50,000. [1] Represents nonlicense taxes. [2] Excludes commissions. [3] Includes States whose gross revenues were less than $1,000,000 not shown separately. [4] Total excludes Washington DC.
Source: U.S. Bureau of the Census, *State Government Finances*, series GF, No. 3, annual.

No. 467. State Government Revenue From Severance Taxes, by State: 1985 to 1990

[In millions of dollars. For fiscal years; see text, section 9. **Severance taxes** are taxes imposed distinctively on the removal of natural products, such as oil, gas, other minerals, timber, and fish; from land or water and measured by value and/or quantity of products removed or sold. See source for information on particular taxes (including changes in tax rates) and additional analytical detail]

REGION AND STATE	1985	1988	1989	1990	REGION AND STATE	1985	1988	1989	1990
Total	7,211	4,331	4,145	4,683	Nebraska	4.6	2.6	2.3	2.7
					Nevada [2]	0.1	10.7	0.4	22.9
Alabama	89.6	60.6	61.7	59.2	New Hampshire	0.1	-0.1	0.1	0.2
Alaska	1,389.3	818.7	698.9	1,103.8	New Mexico	390.8	291.9	256.2	292.7
Arkansas	26.0	16.3	14.5	15.6	North Carolina	1.5	1.6	1.5	1.5
California	19.1	26.1	29.3	30.9	North Dakota	176.3	93.3	79.5	79.6
Colorado	30.4	15.3	13.8	14.4	Ohio	8.2	0.4	0.0	9.5
Florida [1]	173.2	75.0	60.6	65.9	Oklahoma	708.8	386.7	371.6	395.3
Idaho	0.7	0.7	0.4	0.5	Oregon	31.8	32.0	37.5	52.2
Indiana	1.5	0.7	1.0	0.8	South Dakota	4.5	8.1	9.2	8.6
Kansas	111.9	81.8	79.7	86.6	Tennessee	2.8	1.8	1.6	1.5
Kentucky	228.0	210.0	195.1	213.9	Texas	2,175.3	1,058.8	1,172.2	1,087.9
Louisiana	745.2	474.9	411.5	429.1	Utah	49.4	29.2	30.6	30.1
Michigan	75.7	43.6	40.5	45.6	Virginia	1.6	1.7	1.5	1.6
Minnesota	80.0	7.8	6.4	2.1	Washington [3]	36.2	45.8	58.9	69.3
Mississippi	92.9	53.2	45.1	54.8	West Virginia [3]	(X)	128.5	135.7	162.7
Missouri	(Z)	(Z)	(Z)	(Z)	Wisconsin	1.0	0.9	0.9	0.9
Montana	150.7	112.8	85.5	95.7	Wyoming	404.0	230.3	231.7	254.0

X Not applicable. Z Less than $50,000. [1] Beginning 1986, corporate excise tax was reclassified to corporate net income tax. [2] Taxation of mineral proceeds changed via constitutional amendment effective May 24, 1989. [3] Severance tax replaced the business and occupation tax for specified firms engaged in natural resource activities effective July 1, 1987.
Source: U.S. Bureau of the Census, *State Government Tax Collections*, series GF, No. 1, annual.

No. 468. State Government Intergovernmental Expenditures, 1980 to 1990, and by State, 1990

[For **fiscal year**, see text, section 9]

YEAR, DIVISION, AND STATE	Total (mil. dol.)	Per capita [1] (dol.)	Rank	As per-cent of general expendi-ture	YEAR, DIVISION, AND STATE	Total (mil. dol.)	Per capita [1] (dol.)	Rank	As per-cent of general expendi-ture
1980	84,504	374	(X)	37	MI	6,314	679	7	32
1985	121,571	511	(X)	35	MN	4,277	978	13	41
1986	131,966	549	(X)	35	MS	1,691	657	29	38
1987	141,279	582	(X)	35	MO	2,561	501	18	33
1988	151,662	619	(X)	35	MT	420	525	44	25
1989	165,506	668	(X)	35	NE	772	489	39	27
					NV	949	790	37	40
1990, U.S.	175,096	704	(X)	34	NH	220	199	49	13
AL	2,015	499	23	27	NJ	5,819	753	9	32
AK	909	1,653	38	21	NM	1,463	966	32	38
AZ	2,433	664	19	32	NY	19,441	1,081	2	39
AR	1,177	500	34	30	NC	5,085	767	10	40
CA	35,174	1,182	1	50	ND	370	579	45	23
CO	1,816	551	28	32	OH	7,386	681	3	36
CT	1,858	565	27	21	OK	1,637	520	30	29
DE	359	538	46	18	OR	1,479	520	31	27
FL	7,205	557	5	35	PA	6,921	583	6	33
GA	3,667	566	15	32	RI	488	487	43	18
HI	101	92	50	3	SC	1,885	541	26	28
ID	585	581	41	32	SD	242	348	48	19
IL	5,856	512	8	29	TN	2,211	453	22	28
IN	3,385	611	17	34	TX	7,343	432	4	31
IA	1,946	701	24	33	UT	981	569	35	28
KS	1,312	529	33	30	VT	265	472	47	18
KY	1,913	519	25	27	VA	3,472	561	16	29
LA	2,331	552	21	27	WA	3,767	774	14	33
ME	664	540	40	24	WV	960	535	36	27
MD	2,420	506	20	25	WI	4,316	882	12	41
MA	4,649	773	11	27	WY	584	1,287	42	39

X Not applicable. [1] 1980 and 1990 based on enumerated resident population as of April 1; all other years based on estimated resident population as of July 1; estimates do not reflect revisions based on the 1990 Census of Population.
Source: U.S. Bureau of the Census, *Census of Governments: 1987*, vol. 6, No. 4; *Historical Statistics on Governmental Finances and Employment* (GC82(6)-4); and *State Government Finances*, series GF, No. 3, annual.

No. 469. Local Government General Revenue, by Source, 1980 to 1990, and by State, 1990

[**In millions of dollars**, for **fiscal year**, see text, section 9. Data are estimates based on sample and subject to sampling variability; see source and Appendix III]

YEAR, DIVISION, AND STATE	Total [1]	INTERGOVERN-MENTAL FROM— Federal	INTERGOVERN-MENTAL FROM— State	FROM OWN SOURCES Total	FROM OWN SOURCES Taxes	YEAR, DIVISION, AND STATE	Total [1]	INTERGOVERN-MENTAL FROM— Federal	INTERGOVERN-MENTAL FROM— State	FROM OWN SOURCES Total	FROM OWN SOURCES Taxes
1980	232,453	21,136	81,289	130,027	86,387	DC	4,405	1,599	(X)	2,806	2,310
1985	354,119	21,724	116,380	216,014	134,473	VA	10,809	367	3,290	7,152	5,127
1989	468,549	17,588	157,652	293,308	184,478	WV	2,090	52	881	1,157	572
1990, U.S.	512,322	18,449	172,274	321,599	201,130	NC	11,286	412	4,725	6,149	3,239
N.E.	23,518	931	7,589	14,999	11,767	SC	4,946	162	1,803	2,981	1,512
ME	1,802	66	600	1,137	863	GA	12,570	455	3,561	8,554	4,589
NH	1,786	52	224	1,510	1,279	FL	27,660	872	8,077	18,711	9,304
VT	825	27	239	559	465	**E.S.C.**	22,687	857	9,213	12,617	6,232
MA	11,528	563	4,362	6,603	4,827	KY	4,388	182	1,782	2,424	1,250
RI	1,405	60	406	939	810	TN	9,002	283	3,970	4,750	2,578
CT	6,172	163	1,758	4,251	3,523	AL	5,361	192	1,903	3,266	1,548
M.A.	101,873	2,864	33,212	65,796	48,053	MS	3,936	200	1,558	2,177	856
NY	62,417	1,604	20,275	40,538	30,150	**W.S.C.**	44,073	1,405	12,081	30,588	18,241
NJ	17,454	389	5,436	11,629	9,038	AR	2,603	87	1,087	1,429	732
PA	22,002	871	7,501	13,629	8,865	LA	6,918	306	2,228	4,385	2,504
E.N.C.	78,021	2,654	25,360	50,009	33,845	OK	4,423	154	1,497	2,772	1,478
OH	19,231	762	6,431	12,038	8,230	TX	30,129	858	7,269	22,002	13,527
IN	9,204	242	3,435	5,528	2,942	**Mt**	26,903	1,074	9,273	16,558	9,569
IL	21,628	938	5,483	15,208	11,132	MT	1,394	78	416	901	576
MI	17,965	482	5,812	11,671	7,876	ID	1,449	59	572	818	432
WI	9,993	230	4,199	5,564	3,665	WY	1,292	29	504	759	389
W.N.C.	32,375	1,311	10,257	20,803	12,266	CO	7,208	231	1,821	5,157	3,273
MN	11,056	537	4,291	6,227	3,263	NM	2,575	157	1,292	1,126	546
IA	5,033	186	1,689	3,158	1,912	AZ	7,589	318	2,703	4,568	2,664
MO	7,042	319	1,990	4,733	2,999	UT	2,660	93	944	1,622	958
ND	966	53	348	564	325	NV	2,736	109	1,021	1,607	737
SD	928	52	205	670	507	**Pac**	99,155	2,975	40,121	56,060	29,689
NE	2,865	97	569	2,198	1,351	WA	9,613	376	3,746	5,490	2,909
KS	4,485	67	1,165	3,253	1,909	OR	5,739	360	1,408	3,971	2,711
S.A.	83,713	4,377	25,170	54,167	31,466	CA	80,298	2,058	34,048	44,193	22,837
DE	918	41	402	476	241	AK	2,202	91	815	1,297	691
MD	9,029	417	2,431	6,181	4,572	HI	1,303	90	104	1,109	541

X Not applicable. [1] Excludes duplicative intergovernmental transactions.
Source: U.S. Bureau of the Census, *Census of Governments: 1982*, vol. 6, No. 4; *Historical Statistics on Governmental Finances and Employment* (GC82(6)-4); and *Government Finances*, series GF, No. 5, annual.

No. 470. State Aid to Local Governments: 1982, 1988, and 1989

[In millions of dollars. Fiscal year data; see text, section 9. Expenditures are from State resources only, federal dollars for particular programs which may be passed along to local governments are excluded. For additional data on State general fund resources and expenditures; see table 462. For data on Federal aid to State and local governments; see tables 454 and 455]

STATE	TOTAL AID [1]			RESTRICTED AID [2]			UNRESTRICTED AID [3]		
	1982	1988	1989	1982	1988	1989	1982	1988	1989
United States	88,129	142,532	153,320	78,427	126,531	136,678	9,703	16,001	16,643
New England:									
Maine	318	612	642	297	553	580	21	59	62
New Hampshire.	95	136	187	35	85	135	59	51	51
Vermont.	86	183	238	86	183	238	1	(Z)	(Z)
Massachusetts	1,698	3,178	3,339	1,234	2,125	2,247	464	1,053	1,092
Rhode Island	193	364	392	176	312	339	16	52	52
Connecticut	733	1,483	1,940	594	1,365	1,826	138	117	114
Middle Atlantic:									
New York.	10,755	18,403	20,409	9,696	17,125	19,114	1,059	1,278	1,295
New Jersey.	2,928	4,589	5,048	2,048	3,490	3,889	880	1,099	1,159
Pennsylvania.	3,461	5,459	5,745	3,401	5,362	5,740	60	97	5
East North Central:									
Ohio	4,625	8,230	8,214	4,477	7,699	7,572	148	531	642
Indiana.	1,844	2,875	3,136	1,821	2,851	3,115	23	24	21
Illinois	3,379	4,665	4,895	2,447	3,191	3,378	932	1,474	1,517
Michigan	2,875	4,871	5,257	2,437	4,032	4,152	438	839	1,106
Wisconsin.	1,993	3,369	3,510	1,225	2,257	2,384	767	1,112	1,126
West North Central:									
Minnesota	2,550	3,386	3,560	2,499	3,343	3,503	52	43	57
Iowa	908	1,283	1,414	889	1,263	1,414	19	20	-
Missouri	1,038	2,190	2,171	983	2,062	2,038	56	127	132
North Dakota	333	324	320	277	278	274	56	46	46
South Dakota	64	91	93	59	86	87	4	6	6
Nebraska	299	276	312	299	245	277	-	31	35
Kansas	659	949	1,089	535	761	863	124	189	226
South Atlantic:									
Delaware	197	339	352	194	326	347	3	12	5
Maryland	1,460	2,225	2,360	1,380	2,107	2,241	80	118	119
Virginia.	1,384	2,548	2,735	1,311	2,441	2,627	73	106	108
West Virginia.	649	872	912	635	861	899	14	11	13
North Carolina.	2,186	4,117	4,520	2,170	4,022	4,294	16	95	227
South Carolina [4]	760	1,341	1,419	685	1,183	1,241	74	158	178
Georgia	1,590	2,702	2,878	1,530	2,612	2,818	60	90	60
Florida	3,728	8,147	7,988	2,956	6,457	6,441	771	1,689	1,546
East South Central:									
Kentucky	1,003	1,546	1,585	964	1,546	1,585	40	-	-
Tennessee	981	1,574	1,679	745	1,177	1,252	236	398	427
Alabama.	860	1,286	1,527	690	1,032	1,293	170	254	235
Mississippi	666	1,031	1,167	483	774	856	182	257	311
West South Central:									
Arkansas	497	840	879	454	791	831	43	48	48
Louisiana	1,301	1,308	1,666	1,023	1,135	1,495	278	173	171
Oklahoma.	736	935	1,031	712	915	1,011	24	20	21
Texas	4,186	5,426	5,741	4,186	5,426	5,698	-	-	43
Mountain:									
Montana.	186	280	285	171	260	266	15	21	19
Idaho.	329	469	502	294	424	449	34	45	53
Wyoming	319	394	347	151	310	249	168	84	98
Colorado	785	1,153	1,249	767	1,136	1,249	18	17	(Z)
New Mexico	909	1,245	1,283	714	882	889	195	362	394
Arizona	957	1,909	2,127	801	1,583	1,774	157	326	353
Utah	447	741	912	447	741	757	1	(Z)	155
Nevada	346	604	(NA)	169	262	(NA)	178	342	(NA)
Pacific:									
Washington	2,011	2,826	2,971	1,769	2,743	2,882	241	83	90
Oregon	795	1,058	1,283	611	808	961	184	250	322
California	17,479	27,986	31,268	16,470	25,339	28,520	1,006	2,647	2,749
Alaska	531	682	703	424	569	589	107	112	114
Hawaii	18	33	42	(5)	(5)	4	18	33	38

- Represents or rounds to zero. NA Not available. Z Less than $500,000. [1] State resources given to local governments for public service delivery, either for specific programs or for general purpose government. [2] Funds must be spent by the receiving local units on programs identified by the State government; most common programs are in the following areas: education, human services, transportation, criminal justice, environmental protection, housing/community development, natural resources, and economic development. [3] Funds granted to local governments without stipulating the use of these funds; most commonly in the form of payments in lieu of taxes; shared sales, income, and cigarette taxes; other shared taxes and fees; and direct State appropriations. [4] South Carolina has two shared revenue programs that are distributed directly to local governments but are not considered part of State budget. [5] Restricted aid is zero because State provides many of these services directly.

Source: National Association of State Budget Officers, Washington, DC, *State Aid to Local Governments 1990*, (copyright).

No. 471. Number of Local Governments, by Type—States: 1982 and 1987

[Governments in existence in January. Limited to governments actually in existence. Excludes, therefore, a few counties and numerous townships and "incorporated places" existing as areas for which statistics can be presented as to population and other subjects, but lacking any separate organized county, township, or municipal government]

STATE	1982			1987					Special district governments			
	All local govern-mental units [1]	School district govern-ments	Special district govern-ments	All local govern-mental units	County govern-ments [2]	Munic-ipal govern-ments [2]	Town-ship govern-ments [2]	School district govern-ments	Total [1]	Natural re-sources	Fire pro-tection	Hous-ing and com-munity devel-opment
U.S.	**81,780**	**14,851**	**28,078**	**83,186**	**3,042**	**19,200**	**16,691**	**14,721**	**29,532**	**6,360**	**5,070**	**3,464**
AL	1,018	127	390	1,053	67	436	-	129	421	69	4	156
AK	156	-	6	172	9	149	-	14	14	-	-	13
AZ	452	232	130	576	15	81	-	227	253	82	116	-
AR	1,424	372	505	1,396	75	483	-	333	505	245	33	130
CA	4,102	1,111	2,506	4,331	57	442	-	1,098	2,734	521	389	93
CO	1,544	185	1,030	1,593	62	266	-	180	1,085	188	213	56
CT	479	16	281	477	-	31	149	16	281	1	55	91
DE	217	19	139	281	3	57	-	19	202	197	-	3
DC	2	-	1	2	-	1	-	-	1	-	-	-
FL	969	95	417	965	66	390	-	95	414	133	48	98
GA	1,268	187	390	1,286	158	532	-	186	410	28	6	208
HI	18	-	14	18	3	1	-	-	14	14	-	-
ID	1,018	117	659	1,065	44	198	-	118	705	169	119	13
IL	6,467	1,049	2,602	6,627	102	1,279	1,434	1,029	2,783	913	801	114
IN	2,865	305	897	2,806	91	567	1,008	304	836	129	-	45
IA	1,871	456	361	1,877	99	955	-	451	372	234	69	15
KS	3,795	326	1,370	3,803	105	627	1,360	324	1,387	271	-	101
KY	1,241	180	517	1,303	119	437	-	178	569	127	85	24
LA	468	66	39	452	61	301	-	66	24	2	-	-
ME	806	98	195	800	16	22	471	88	203	13	-	28
MD	439	-	264	401	23	155	-	-	223	165	-	20
MA	798	81	354	836	12	39	312	82	391	16	20	249
MI	2,643	599	184	2,699	83	534	1,242	590	250	85	1	-
MN	3,529	436	356	3,555	87	855	1,798	441	374	119	-	169
MS	858	169	315	853	82	293	-	171	307	227	-	59
MO	3,117	557	1,195	3,147	114	930	325	561	1,217	155	145	172
MT	1,029	399	450	1,243	54	128	-	547	514	117	128	18
NE	3,324	1,069	1,157	3,152	93	534	454	952	1,119	110	427	134
NV	184	17	134	197	16	18	-	17	146	29	15	14
NH	517	160	113	524	10	13	221	160	120	9	15	22
NJ	1,591	548	454	1,625	21	320	247	551	486	16	172	84
NM	319	89	101	331	33	98	-	88	112	73	-	7
NY	3,249	726	923	3,302	57	618	929	720	978	2	898	-
NC	905	-	321	916	100	495	-	-	321	142	1	108
ND	2,795	325	692	2,787	53	366	1,355	310	703	83	279	34
OH	3,393	669	377	3,377	88	940	1,318	621	410	100	30	55
OK	1,702	638	406	1,802	77	591	-	636	498	110	17	119
OR	1,454	352	825	1,502	36	240	-	350	876	213	270	23
PA	5,198	514	2,050	4,956	66	1,022	1,548	515	1,805	5	1	88
RI	122	3	80	125	-	8	31	3	83	3	39	26
SC	645	92	242	707	46	269	-	92	300	46	86	43
SD	1,767	196	199	1,762	64	309	984	193	212	102	31	38
TN	913	15	469	904	94	334	-	14	462	124	-	94
TX	4,180	1,124	1,681	4,415	254	1,156	-	1,113	1,892	399	70	396
UT	504	40	211	530	29	225	-	40	236	71	13	11
VT	664	273	83	673	14	55	237	272	95	20	19	9
VA	407	-	83	430	95	229	-	-	106	43	-	-
WA	1,734	300	1,130	1,779	39	266	-	297	1,177	161	411	48
WV	633	55	292	630	55	230	-	55	290	15	-	32
WI	2,592	408	263	2,719	72	580	1,268	433	366	150	-	204
WY	395	56	225	424	23	95	-	56	250	114	44	-

- Represents zero. [1] Includes other types of governments not shown separately. [2] Includes "town" governments in the six New England States and in Minnesota, New York, and Wisconsin.

Source: U.S. Bureau of the Census, *Census of Governments: 1982* and *1987, Vol. 1, No. 1, Government Organization.*

No. 472. County, Municipal, and Township Governments, 1987, and Their Population, 1986, by Population-Size Group

[Number of governments as of **January 1987**; population estimated as of **July 1, 1986**, and do not reflect revisions based on the 1990 Census of Population. Consolidated city-county governments are classified as municipal rather than county governments. Township governments include "towns" in the six New England States, Minnesota, New York, and Wisconsin]

POPULATION-SIZE GROUP	COUNTY GOVERNMENTS			MUNICIPAL GOVERNMENTS			TOWNSHIP GOVERNMENTS		
	Number, 1987	Population, **1986**		Number, 1987	Population, **1986**		Number, 1987	Population, **1986**	
		Number (1,000)	Per-cent		Number (1,000)	Per-cent		Number (1,000)	Per-cent
Total	3,042	217,397	100.0	19,200	149,864	100.0	16,691	52,065	100.0
250,000 or more	167	113,164	52.1	61	44,059	29.4	4	1,744	3.4
100,000 to 249,999	231	35,559	16.4	122	17,882	11.9	29	4,015	7.7
50,000 to 99,999	387	27,279	12.6	285	19,522	13.0	74	4,989	9.6
25,000 to 49,999	616	21,807	10.0	561	19,386	13.0	233	7,832	15.1
10,000 to 24,999	943	15,580	7.2	1,303	20,425	13.6	706	10,899	20.9
5,000 to 9,999	[1]698	[1]4,007	[1]1.9	1,544	10,950	7.3	1,005	7,021	13.5
2,500 to 4,999	(NA)	(NA)	(NA)	2,151	7,646	5.1	1,775	6,215	11.9
1,000 to 2,499	(NA)	(NA)	(NA)	3,804	6,061	4.1	3,722	5,958	11.4
Less than 1,000	(NA)	(NA)	(NA)	9,369	3,933	2.6	9,143	3,392	6.5

NA Not available. [1] For population-size group less than 9,999.

Source: U.S. Bureau of the Census, *Census of Governments: 1987, Vol. 1, No. 1, Government Organization.*

No. 473. County Governments—Summary of Finances, 1980 to 1990, and Per Capita, by Population-Size Group, 1990

[Covers fiscal years ending between **July 1** of preceding year and **June 30** of year stated. Represents all counties and their dependent agencies (including dependent school systems where applicable). Per capita based on estimated resident population as of **July 1**. Population estimates do not reflect revisions based on the 1990 Census of Population]

ITEM	ALL COUNTIES (mil. dol.) [1]			PER CAPITA (dollars), **1990**								
				All counties		Counties with **1988** population (1,000) of—						
	1980	1985	1990	Total (3,043) [2]	Per-cent distri-bution	Less than 100 [3] (2,631)	100 to 149.9 (133)	150 to 199.9 (66)	200 to 299.9 (74)	300 to 499.9 (62)	500 to 999.9 (52)	1,000 or more (24)
General revenue	54,573	85,500	135,775	612	100	625	488	542	499	504	743	649
Intergovernmental revenue [4]	24,746	32,614	53,953	243	40	299	181	183	165	168	237	271
From State governments	18,969	26,716	49,225	222	36	281	163	164	147	153	211	242
From Federal government	4,948	4,708	2,780	13	2	11	12	12	11	10	13	16
Tax revenue [4]	18,813	30,898	48,750	220	36	181	168	234	181	212	324	229
Property	14,300	23,193	35,723	161	26	130	122	162	131	155	226	183
Charges and miscellaneous	11,014	21,988	33,072	149	24	146	138	125	153	125	183	149
General expenditure	54,291	80,948	127,626	575	100	507	486	550	493	509	755	637
Capital outlay	6,505	7,603	13,467	61	11	48	48	59	49	54	97	64
Other	47,786	73,345	114,159	514	90	459	438	491	444	455	659	573
Public welfare	8,591	12,237	18,114	82	14	46	69	62	76	79	110	124
Education	8,412	11,683	18,395	83	14	106	94	135	57	84	118	17
Highways	5,227	7,008	9,415	42	7	64	38	41	37	32	35	27
Hospitals	5,975	9,005	13,018	59	10	61	44	24	52	31	59	85
General control [5]	3,374	5,566	9,149	39	7	47	21	22	23	25	36	52
Police protection	2,661	4,392	6,693	30	5	25	24	34	24	25	35	39
Financial administration .	1,521	2,410	3,363	15	3	16	12	17	15	14	17	15
General public buildings .	1,072	1,489	2,182	10	2	9	8	9	10	9	16	7
Health	2,806	4,794	8,791	40	7	36	36	36	39	35	43	48
Correction	1,759	3,466	6,590	30	5	15	19	22	27	27	44	47
Natural resources	687	1,033	1,314	6	1	5	3	3	3	4	6	11
Parks and recreation . . .	1,094	1,506	2,487	11	2	5	5	10	8	13	23	14
Interest on general debt	1,542	4,652	7,976	36	6	27	28	30	26	29	56	46
Other and unallocable . .	9,570	11,709	20,139	93	16	46	86	104	95	102	160	105
Debt outstanding, end of year	32,993	72,260	118,608	534	100	434	426	442	387	459	789	639
Long-term	31,543	69,192	115,392	520	97	430	416	440	376	447	772	605
Short-term	1,450	3,068	3,216	14	3	4	10	2	11	13	16	34

[1] Data for counties under 100,000 population are estimates subject to sampling variation; see Appendix III and source. [2] Figures in parentheses represent number of counties in each size group. [3] Estimated. [4] Includes other revenues not shown separately. [5] Includes judicial and legal as well as other administrative expenditures.

Source: U.S. Bureau of the Census, *County Government Finances*, series GF, No. 8, annual.

No. 474. City Governments—Summary of Finances: 1980 to 1990

[For fiscal years ending in year shown; see text, section 9. Data revised since originally published and may not agree, therefore, with table 476. Represents all municipalities and their dependent agencies (including dependent school systems where applicable); excludes other local governments overlying city areas. Includes sample-based estimates for cities of less than 50,000; thus subject to sampling variation. See Appendix III and source]

ITEM	TOTAL (mil. dol.)			PER CAPITA [1] (dol.)			PERCENT DISTRIBUTION		
	1980	1985	1990	1980	1985	1990	1980	1985	1990
Revenue	94,862	147,672	202,393	672	1,007	1,323	100	100	100
General revenue	76,056	114,649	158,301	539	781	1,035	80	78	78
Intergovernmental revenue	28,270	35,859	45,306	200	244	296	30	24	22
From State governments only	15,939	23,103	34,243	113	157	224	17	16	17
Taxes	31,256	47,647	68,788	222	325	450	33	32	34
Property	16,859	23,459	35,024	119	160	229	18	16	17
Percent of total taxes	53.9	49.2	50.9	(X)	(X)	(X)	(X)	(X)	(X)
Sales and gross receipts	8,208	13,877	19,190	58	95	125	9	9	10
General	5,096	8,569	11,645	36	58	76	5	6	6
Selective	3,112	5,307	7,545	22	36	49	3	4	4
Income, licenses and other	6,189	10,312	14,574	44	70	95	7	7	7
Charges and miscellaneous	16,530	31,142	44,207	117	212	289	17	21	22
Current charges only	9,875	16,514	25,265	70	113	165	10	11	13
Utility and liquor store revenue	15,719	26,471	33,266	111	180	217	17	18	16
Water system	4,989	8,504	11,578	35	58	76	5	6	6
Electric power system	8,007	13,363	17,312	57	91	113	8	9	9
Gas supply system	1,444	2,796	2,335	10	19	15	2	2	1
Transit system	1,032	1,548	1,766	7	11	12	1	1	1
Liquor stores	247	260	275	2	2	2	-	-	-
Insurance trust revenue	3,088	6,552	10,827	22	45	71	3	4	5
Expenditure	93,699	140,000	198,790	664	954	1,299	100	100	100
General expenditure	72,433	105,652	153,684	513	720	1,004	77	76	77
Police protection	8,200	12,574	18,183	58	86	119	9	9	9
Fire protection	4,535	6,798	9,487	32	46	62	5	5	5
Highways	5,977	8,709	12,106	42	59	79	6	6	6
Sewerage and other sanitation	7,907	11,446	16,476	56	78	108	8	8	8
Public welfare	3,801	5,762	7,890	27	39	52	4	4	4
Education	9,284	11,433	17,368	66	78	114	10	8	9
Libraries	883	1,304	1,906	6	9	12	1	1	1
Health and hospitals	4,457	6,575	9,141	32	45	60	5	5	5
Parks and recreation	3,433	4,993	7,584	24	34	50	4	4	4
Housing and community develop	3,459	5,105	7,661	25	35	50	4	4	4
Airports	1,100	1,694	2,878	8	12	19	1	1	2
Financial administration	1,843	2,703	3,695	13	18	25	2	2	2
General control [2]	2,015	3,401	5,274	14	23	34	2	2	3
General public buildings	1,090	1,483	1,767	8	10	12	1	1	1
Interest on general debt	3,054	6,859	11,317	22	47	74	3	5	6
Other and unallocable	11,395	14,814	20,751	81	101	136	12	11	10
Utility and liquor store expenditure	18,274	29,534	38,436	130	201	251	20	21	19
Water system	5,933	9,601	13,579	42	65	89	6	7	7
Electric power system	8,596	13,588	17,490	61	93	114	9	10	9
Gas supply system	1,334	2,724	2,263	9	19	15	1	2	1
Transit system	2,189	3,381	4,855	16	23	32	2	2	3
Liquor stores	222	240	250	2	2	2	-	-	-
Insurance trust expenditure	2,993	4,814	6,669	21	33	44	3	3	3
By character and object:									
Direct expenditure	91,692	136,601	193,900	650	931	1,267	98	98	98
Current operation	66,687	99,301	138,818	473	677	907	71	71	70
Capital outlay	16,285	21,374	31,747	115	146	207	17	15	16
Construction	13,341	16,638	22,811	95	113	149	14	12	12
Land and existing structures [3]	2,944	4,736	8,935	21	32	58	3	3	5
Assistance payments	1,546	2,060	2,212	11	14	14	2	2	1
Interest on debt	4,182	9,052	14,455	30	62	94	5	7	7
Insurance benefits, repayments	2,992	4,814	6,669	21	33	44	3	3	3
Intergovernmental expenditure	2,007	3,399	4,890	14	23	32	2	2	3
Total salaries and wages [4]	*34,709*	*48,050*	*66,973*	*246*	*328*	*438*	*37*	*34*	*34*
Debt outstanding, year end	86,019	141,139	212,919	610	961	1,392	100	100	100
Long-term	82,346	135,912	207,487	584	926	1,356	96	96	98
Full faith and credit	39,570	46,345	68,510	280	316	448	46	33	32
Nonguaranteed	42,776	89,567	138,977	303	611	908	50	64	65
Short-term	3,673	5,227	5,432	26	36	36	4	4	3
Net long-term debt outstanding	72,528	124,516	139,109	514	849	909	84	88	65
Long-term debt issued	12,582	25,683	27,991	89	175	183	(X)	(X)	13
Long-term debt retired	5,541	11,397	17,980	39	78	118	(X)	(X)	8

- Represents or rounds to zero.   X Not applicable.   [1] 1980 and 1990 based on enumerated resident population as of April 1; 1985 data based on estimated resident population as of July 1 and do not reflect revisions based on the 1990 Census of Population.   [2] Includes judicial and legal as well as other governmental administration.   [3] Includes equipment.   [4] Included in items shown above.

Source: U.S. Bureau of the Census, *City Government Finances*, series GF No. 4, annual.

No. 475. City Governments—Total and Per Capita Revenue, Expenditure, and Debt for Largest Cities: 1990

[For **fiscal year** closed in the 12 months ending **June 30, 1990.** Cities ranked by size of population estimated as of April 1, 1990, except Honolulu and Baton Rouge ranked by county population. Data reflect inclusion of fiscal activity of dependent school systems, where applicable. Intercity comparisons should be made with caution due to variations in responsibilities among urban areas; for details see text, section 9, and source]

CITIES RANKED BY 1990 POPULATION	GENERAL REVENUE		INTERGOV REVENUE		TAXES		GENERAL EXPENDITURE		GROSS DEBT OUTSTANDING	
	Total (mil. dol.)	Per capita [1] (dol.)	Total (mil. dol.)	Per capita [1] (dol.)	Total (mil. dol.)	Per capita [1] (dol.)	Total (mil. dol.)	Per capita [1] (dol.)	Total (mil. dol.)	Per capita [1] (dol.)
New York City, NY [2]	32,056	4,360	12,334	1,677	15,171	2,063	31,292	4,256	26,005	3,537
Los Angeles, CA	3,519	1,050	439	131	1,739	519	3,228	963	6,278	1,873
Chicago, IL	3,033	1,019	752	253	1,597	536	2,865	962	4,298	1,443
Houston, TX [2]	1,296	763	57	34	692	408	1,387	817	3,611	2,126
Philadelphia, PA [2]	2,587	1,571	611	371	1,588	964	2,579	1,566	3,796	2,305
San Diego, CA	1,087	1,016	195	182	348	325	868	811	1,406	1,314
Detroit, MI	1,517	1,465	673	650	522	503	1,458	1,408	1,450	1,400
Dallas, TX	812	822	38	39	475	481	785	795	1,570	1,590
Phoenix, AZ	958	1,036	314	339	317	343	1,153	1,246	2,062	2,228
San Antonio, TX	534	566	96	102	201	214	688	730	4,035	4,278
San Jose, CA [2]	605	819	79	107	308	418	680	921	1,043	1,412
Baltimore, MD [2]	1,655	2,203	802	1,068	640	852	1,495	1,989	1,257	1,673
Indianapolis, IN [2]	866	1,191	257	353	388	533	899	1,237	953	1,311
San Francisco, CA [2]	2,342	3,202	740	1,011	867	1,185	1,886	2,577	2,392	3,269
Jacksonville, FL [2]	673	1,060	143	225	223	352	695	1,094	4,297	6,768
Columbus, OH	476	835	72	127	261	459	486	853	1,072	1,882
Milwaukee, WI	559	932	277	463	154	258	551	920	516	860
Memphis, TN	750	1,162	469	728	154	239	717	1,112	736	1,141
Washington, DC [2]	4,080	6,612	1,306	2,117	2,310	3,744	4,142	6,713	3,423	5,548
Boston, MA [2]	1,603	2,775	746	1,292	576	996	1,498	2,593	854	1,478
Seattle, WA	630	1,255	93	186	320	637	546	1,088	904	1,800
El Paso, TX	244	472	25	48	111	216	233	453	451	874
Cleveland, OH	521	1,000	130	250	268	514	501	960	713	1,367
New Orleans, LA [2]	634	1,193	127	238	272	511	662	1,245	1,128	2,122
Nashville-Davidson, TN [2]	916	1,903	183	380	455	946	843	1,752	2,331	4,842
Denver, CO [2]	939	1,907	205	417	359	730	910	1,849	1,266	2,573
Austin, TX	534	1,148	64	138	170	366	541	1,164	3,188	6,860
Fort Worth, TX	401	941	80	188	191	448	389	913	942	2,208
Oklahoma City, OK	328	756	28	64	163	375	315	725	504	1,161
Portland, OR	392	932	73	174	205	488	370	878	639	1,518
Kansas City, MO	517	1,177	50	114	309	703	496	1,129	616	1,403
Long Beach, CA	573	1,382	98	235	153	369	583	1,406	749	1,804
Tucson, AZ	350	896	120	309	130	332	352	902	773	1,982
St. Louis, MO [2]	513	1,271	74	184	287	712	529	1,310	709	1,756
Charlotte, NC	383	1,026	104	278	136	365	432	1,158	706	1,893
Atlanta, GA	680	1,618	166	394	209	497	582	1,385	1,069	2,544
Virginia Beach, VA [2]	680	1,861	253	693	335	916	643	1,761	508	1,390
Albuquerque, NM	461	1,219	162	429	121	318	495	1,307	1,264	3,339
Oakland, CA	476	1,335	75	209	202	566	482	1,350	1,110	3,111
Pittsburgh, PA	357	952	89	238	222	592	353	940	604	1,609
Sacramento, CA	272	803	27	80	143	424	272	803	309	913
Minneapolis, MN	584	1,693	165	477	190	553	621	1,801	1,980	5,745
Tulsa, OK	379	1,029	20	55	152	411	362	982	1,451	3,939
Honolulu, HI [2]	1,018	1,215	116	138	387	462	726	866	805	960
Cincinnati, OH	483	1,305	100	271	220	593	478	1,290	231	622
Miami, FL	309	832	66	177	163	440	324	874	560	1,510
Fresno, CA	209	681	39	126	99	322	182	593	260	849
Omaha, NE	217	614	41	116	131	372	213	602	179	507
Toledo, OH	235	689	45	133	126	370	242	711	194	569
Buffalo, NY	639	2,037	441	1,407	123	393	686	2,188	384	1,223
Wichita, KS	246	833	41	139	73	247	203	687	559	1,892
Santa Ana, CA	170	711	30	124	97	404	156	652	329	1,375
Mesa, AZ	172	613	56	201	43	153	187	668	534	1,903
Colorado Springs, CO	231	817	21	76	81	287	237	837	430	1,517
Tampa, FL	329	1,169	54	192	111	395	361	1,282	1,217	4,317
Newark, NJ	316	1,005	174	555	84	269	349	1,113	150	478
St. Paul, MN	422	1,628	156	604	87	336	392	1,513	986	3,807
Louisville, KY	222	788	39	138	141	500	315	1,118	359	1,274
Anaheim, CA	261	1,066	40	165	108	442	262	1,072	669	2,733
Birmingham, AL	225	812	31	112	141	509	258	931	730	2,634
Arlington, TX	148	575	10	40	84	328	153	594	422	1,639
Norfolk, VA [2]	540	1,885	220	767	199	694	559	1,950	540	1,885
Las Vegas, NV	275	1308	90	428	55	261	216	1025	89	421
Corpus Christi, TX	139	532	10	40	69	263	138	530	424	1,626
St. Petersburg, FL	225	955	23	100	79	335	226	958	543	2,306
Rochester, NY	568	2,470	317	1,380	155	674	532	2,317	213	927
Jersey City, NJ	177	815	70	321	88	405	222	1,019	172	792
Riverside, CA	182	865	22	106	74	350	181	857	627	2979
Anchorage, AK [2]	648	2,968	278	1,271	173	790	620	2,837	1,008	4,614
Lexington-Fayette, KY [2]	205	910	33	145	96	428	209	925	429	1,901
Akron, OH	179	809	25	115	89	404	180	813	131	591
Aurora, CO	150	684	12	56	82	375	148	678	464	2,123
Baton Rouge, LA [2]	350	970	41	114	172	477	344	955	766	2,126
Stockton, CA	134	704	22	116	64	338	122	638	176	924
Raleigh, NC	165	878	58	311	67	356	153	816	97	515

[1] Based on 1988 estimated population as of July 1. Estimates do not reflect revisions based on the 1990 Census of Population. [2] Represents, in effect, city-county consolidated government.

Source: U.S. Bureau of the Census, *City Government Finances*, series GF, No. 4, annual.

No. 476. City Governments—Finances,
[In millions of dollars. For fiscal year closed

CITIES RANKED BY 1990 [1] POPULATION	REVENUE							Utility and liquor store revenue	Gross debt out-stand-ing
	Total [2]	General revenue							
		Total [2]	Intergovernmental		Taxes				
			From State and local govts	From Federal Government	Total [2]	Prop-erty	Sales and gross receipts		
New York City, NY [3]	37,807	32,056	11,339	994	15,171	6,589	3,554	1,840	26,005
Los Angeles, CA	6,585	3,519	370	69	1,739	632	773	2,162	6,278
Chicago, IL	3,777	3,033	486	266	1,597	627	831	207	4,298
Houston, TX [3]	1,702	1,296	26	31	692	376	296	227	3,611
Philadelphia, PA [3]	3,380	2,587	459	152	1,588	311	34	558	3,796
San Diego, CA	1,296	1,087	129	66	348	138	186	131	1,406
Detroit, MI	2,021	1,517	560	113	522	182	50	157	1,450
Dallas, TX	1,120	812	19	19	475	278	184	101	1,570
Phoenix, AZ	1,115	958	226	88	317	117	185	112	2,062
San Antonio, TX	1,434	534	57	39	201	111	84	868	4,035
San Jose, CA	700	605	72	7	308	117	137	6	1,043
Baltimore, MD [3]	1,865	1,655	741	61	640	437	45	48	1,257
Indianapolis, IN [3]	892	866	186	71	388	314	16	8	953
San Francisco, CA [3]	2,914	2,342	639	101	867	464	185	185	2,392
Jacksonville, FL [3]	1,399	673	94	48	223	173	41	638	4,297
Columbus, OH	547	476	46	26	261	22	6	71	1,072
Milwaukee, WI	781	559	235	42	154	143	4	39	516
Memphis, TN [3]	1,689	750	455	14	154	115	29	806	736
Washington, DC [3]	4,323	4,080	73	1,234	2,310	727	674	52	3,423
Boston, MA [3]	1,805	1,603	675	71	576	533	28	58	854
Seattle, WA	1,011	630	66	27	320	106	141	321	904
El Paso, TX	303	244	11	14	111	56	52	34	451
Cleveland, OH	677	521	57	73	268	50	3	156	713
New Orleans, LA [3]	716	634	39	88	272	123	130	49	1,128
Nashville-Davidson, TN [3]	1,547	916	169	14	455	261	162	591	2,331
Denver, CO [3]	1,088	939	160	46	359	99	218	86	1,266
Austin, TX	1,033	534	55	9	170	103	63	453	3,188
Fort Worth, TX	501	401	30	50	191	130	57	56	942
Oklahoma City, OK	370	328	4	24	163	25	134	30	504
Portland, OR	441	392	53	20	205	144	30	44	639
Kansas City, MO	620	517	25	25	309	56	132	41	616
Long Beach, CA	740	573	65	33	153	67	71	166	749
Tucson, AZ	437	350	94	27	130	26	98	70	773
St. Louis, MO [3]	645	513	31	43	287	36	120	30	709
Charlotte, NC	422	383	85	19	136	121	5	30	706
Atlanta, GA [3]	801	680	95	70	209	113	64	62	1,069
Virginia Beach, VA [3]	717	680	167	86	335	202	106	37	508
Albuquerque, NM [3]	505	461	109	53	121	43	73	44	1,264
Baton Rouge, LA [3]	386	350	23	18	172	53	108	3	766
Oakland, CA	503	476	49	26	202	100	60	-	1,110
Pittsburgh, PA	391	357	64	25	222	102	22	-	604
Sacramento, CA	327	272	27	614	143	45	84	19	309
Minneapolis, MN	730	584	134	31	190	147	34	24	1,980
Tulsa, OK [3]	437	379	13	7	152	18	130	38	1,451
Honolulu, HI [3]	1,095	1,018	50	66	387	302	54	77	805
Cincinnati, OH	640	483	61	39	220	37	4	54	231
Miami, FL	372	309	36	29	163	120	35	-	560
Fresno, CA	266	209	26	12	99	35	48	17	260
Omaha, NE	247	217	31	9	131	60	63	-	179
Toledo, OH	254	235	32	13	126	13	-	20	194
Buffalo, NY	656	639	388	53	123	108	10	17	384
Wichita, KS	304	246	41	-	73	49	21	20	559
Santa Ana, CA	188	170	27	3	97	44	42	18	329
Mesa, AZ	240	172	50	7	43	4	35	68	534
Colorado Springs, CO	498	231	13	8	81	16	64	267	430
Tampa, FL	429	329	39	15	111	44	58	24	1,217
Newark, NJ	344	316	162	12	84	50	8	26	150
St. Paul, MN	461	422	99	57	87	66	16	24	986
Louisville, KY	277	222	11	28	141	53	18	55	359
Anaheim, CA	475	261	38	2	108	38	62	215	669
Birmingham, AL	259	225	23	8	141	26	46	-	730
Arlington, TX	178	148	1	9	84	48	35	30	422
Norfolk, VA [3]	593	540	159	61	199	113	65	33	540
Las Vegas, NV	275	275	85	90	55	21	12	-	89
Corpus Christi, TX	189	139	4	6	69	38	29	50	424
St. Petersburg, FL	278	225	18	5	79	48	27	39	543
Rochester, NY	591	568	255	62	155	142	10	23	213
Jersey City, NJ	201	177	70	70	88	86	-	18	172
Riverside, CA	327	182	20	2	74	23	41	145	627
Anchorage, AK [3]	763	648	271	7	173	163	5	90	1,008
Lexington-Fayette, KY [3]	219	205	15	18	96	19	16	1	429
Akron, OH	204	179	13	12	89	15	-	24	131
Aurora, CO	173	150	9	3	82	14	65	24	464
Stockton, CA	139	134	21	2	64	15	37	5	176
Raleigh, NC	181	165	50	8	67	58	2	16	97

- Represents zero. Z Less than $50,000. [1] Based on enumerated resident population as of April 1. [2] Includes other categories, not shown separately. [3] Represents, in effect, city-county consolidated government.

Largest Cities: 1990

in the 12 months ending **June 30, 1990.** See headnote, table 475]

	EXPENDITURE									
	General expenditure								Utility and liquor store	CITIES RANKED BY **1990** [1] POPULATION
Total [2]	Total [2]	Education	Housing and community development	Public welfare	Health and hospitals	Police protection	Fire protection	Highways		
37,630	31,292	7,040	2,287	5,803	3,378	1,760	743	867	3,985	New York City, NY [3]
6,448	3,228	12	229	-	8	618	240	173	2,670	Los Angeles, CA
3,408	2,865	1	128	83	79	535	210	327	193	Chicago, IL
1,660	1,387	-	18	-	49	238	132	91	213	Houston, TX
3,498	2,579	16	137	191	246	305	114	65	652	Philadelphia, PA [3]
1,080	868	-	78	1	1	137	57	53	172	San Diego, CA
1,946	1,458	3	41	-	91	287	78	131	259	Detroit, MI
989	785	-	12	-	16	141	72	87	121	Dallas, TX
1,348	1,153	4	57	1	2	153	79	152	174	Phoenix, AZ
1,687	688	1	28	5	16	96	59	59	988	San Antonio, TX
721	680	-	62	-	-	91	48	60	9	San Jose, CA
1,611	1,495	493	65	2	52	142	77	134	42	Baltimore, MD [3]
952	899	(Z)	47	59	155	166	32	49	22	Indianapolis, IN [3]
2,519	1,886	52	37	239	410	139	95	27	435	San Francisco, CA [3]
1,396	695	-	37	13	29	74	48	33	672	Jacksonville, FL [3]
597	486	-	5	-	20	88	57	41	111	Columbus, OH
649	551	-	43	-	10	114	56	46	34	Milwaukee, WI
1,587	717	372	8	-	14	63	53	18	814	Memphis, TN
4,513	4,142	674	247	672	443	276	98	124	86	Washington, DC [3]
1,726	1,498	463	55	3	198	157	88	43	62	Boston, MA [3]
945	546	-	23	-	11	71	48	61	346	Seattle, WA
293	233	-	5	-	12	42	19	113	49	El Paso, TX
708	501	-	45	-	16	114	57	40	207	Cleveland, OH
750	662	-	63	18	11	56	28	49	60	New Orleans, LA [3]
1,505	843	263	6	12	66	54	33	29	629	Nashville-Davidson, TN [3]
1,031	910	-	13	98	111	84	46	115	100	Denver, CO [3]
1,012	541	(Z)	5	2	109	45	31	72	448	Austin, TX
501	389	-	6	-	9	49	31	37	92	Fort Worth, TX
371	315	-	8	-	1	47	38	28	49	Oklahoma City, OK
441	370	(Z)	28	(Z)	1	74	47	22	42	Portland, OR
571	496	24	8	(Z)	44	69	38	50	49	Kansas City, MO
775	583	-	62	-	13	81	53	23	191	Long Beach, CA
473	352	-	24	2	1	50	23	59	113	Tucson, AZ
607	529	1	21	7	43	89	29	16	29	St. Louis, MO [3]
508	432	-	9	(Z)	2	34	26	55	72	Charlotte, NC
741	582	17	20	2	-	68	37	27	102	Atlanta, GA
679	643	293	5	13	17	39	19	79	13	Virginia Beach, VA [3]
577	495	-	15	1	6	55	24	36	82	Albuquerque, NM
368	344	-	10	1	27	39	18	14	5	Baton Rouge, LA [3]
523	482	2	52	1	(Z)	55	37	27	-	Oakland, CA
401	353	-	8	(Z)	7	42	36	40	14	Pittsburgh, PA
310	272	(Z)	(Z)	-	1	57	33	24	21	Sacramento, CA
716	621	(Z)	76	-	10	51	27	41	22	Minneapolis, MN
415	362	-	6	-	7	37	30	21	50	Tulsa, OK
909	726	-	71	-	8	96	40	40	182	Honolulu, HI [3]
577	478	-	56	-	35	57	45	58	51	Cincinnati, OH
355	324	(Z)	22	1	(Z)	80	41	11	-	Miami, FL
233	182	-	7	-	-	36	17	19	30	Fresno, CA
222	213	(Z)	14	(Z)	-	33	24	33	-	Omaha, NE
267	242	-	10	-	6	44	30	28	9	Toledo, OH
704	686	329	68	-	1	46	36	25	17	Buffalo, NY
237	203	-	(Z)	-	1	23	15	30	20	Wichita, KS
172	156	-	28	-	1	40	20	18	16	Santa Ana, CA
257	187	-	4	(Z)	-	37	17	18	70	Mesa, AZ
525	237	-	7	-	79	30	18	34	288	Colorado Springs, CO
436	361	-	6	-	4	42	19	17	50	Tampa, FL
387	349	-	16	35	6	56	47	3	31	Newark, NJ
432	392	-	58	-	7	31	23	60	22	St. Paul, MN
370	315	-	17	3	4	36	21	7	54	Louisville, KY
495	262	-	43	-	3	46	17	14	233	Anaheim, CA
273	258	3	17	-	3	32	26	17	-	Birmingham, AL
176	153	-	12	-	1	22	15	23	23	Arlington, TX
605	559	195	63	26	27	30	19	25	32	Norfolk, VA [3]
216	216	-	4	(Z)	1	32	26	62	-	Las Vegas, NV
176	138	-	1	-	5	21	11	17	38	Corpus Christi, TX
286	226	-	4	-	5	34	13	20	48	St. Petersburg, FL
547	532	255	29	-	-	36	24	18	14	Rochester, NY
253	222	-	10	6	9	47	33	7	27	Jersey City, NJ
128	122	-	3	-	1	27	20	9	7	Stockton, CA
736	620	270	-	-	28	35	21	42	110	Anchorage, AK [3]
220	209	-	14	6	10	19	19	11	5	Lexington-Fayette, KY [3]
201	180	-	9	-	9	25	18	22	21	Akron, OH
182	148	-	5	-	(Z)	27	15	15	34	Aurora, CO
347	181	-	15	-	1	31	14	18	166	Riverside, CA
181	153	-	8	1	(Z)	20	14	25	28	Raleigh, NC

Source: U.S. Bureau of the Census, *City Government Finances,* series GF, No. 4, annual.

No. 477. City Governments—Finances, by Population-Size Groups: 1990

[For fiscal year closed in the 12 months ending June 30, 1990. Represents all municipalities and their dependent agencies, including dependent school systems where applicable. Size classifications based on 1988 population estimates; municipalities selected according to their 1988 estimated populations. Population data do not reflect revisions based on the 1990 Census of Population]

ITEM	All cities [1]	CITIES HAVING A 1988 POPULATION OF—						
		Less than 75,000 [1]	75,000 to 99,999	100,000 to 199,999	200,000 to 299,999	300,000 to 499,000	500,000 to 999,999	1,000,000 or more
Number of cities, 1990.	19,265	18,986	93	109	25	27	18	7
Population, 1988 (1,000)	153,001	82,063	8,108	14,842	6,078	10,418	12,358	19,134
FINANCES, 1990 (mil. dol.)								
General revenue [2]	**158,301**	**53,226**	**7,340**	**14,528**	**6,661**	**12,491**	**18,960**	**45,095**
Taxes [2]	68,788	21,661	3,300	6,109	2,575	5,251	8,235	21,657
Property.	35,024	12,522	2,127	3,741	1,281	2,312	4,186	8,855
Percent of total taxes	51	58	64	61	50	44	51	41
Sales and gross receipts.	19,190	6,093	902	1,694	838	1,939	1,999	5,725
Intergovernmental [2].	45,306	13,862	1,813	3,921	1,832	2,985	5,831	15,062
From State governments.	34,243	10,433	1,476	2,987	1,283	1,809	3,316	12,939
From Federal Government	7,545	1,782	247	552	386	795	2,091	1,692
Current charges	25,265	10,015	1,249	2,546	1,224	2,384	2,515	5,332
Water supply and other utilities revenue [3]	33,266	16,132	1,459	3,476	1,329	1,957	3,629	5,284
General expenditure [2]	**153,684**	**50,450**	**7,227**	**14,933**	**6,664**	**12,387**	**18,344**	**43,679**
Police and fire protection	27,670	10,999	1,510	2,974	1,236	2,368	3,129	5,454
Education	17,368	3,060	1,111	2,237	899	931	2,059	7,071
Sewerage and sanitation	16,476	7,263	728	1,515	651	1,373	1,826	3,120
Highways	12,106	5,902	651	1,222	557	990	1,077	1,707
Health and hospitals	9,141	2,316	271	541	215	522	1,423	3,853
Public welfare	7,890	276	51	218	78	176	1,013	6,078
Housing and community development . .	7,661	1,835	335	675	413	576	908	2,919
Interest on general debt.	11,317	3,768	519	1,148	709	1,407	1,422	2,344
Water supply and other utilities expenditure [3]	38,436	16,931	1,570	3,598	1,477	2,301	4,415	8,144
Gross debt outstanding.	**212,919**	**71,082**	**9,553**	**20,967**	**12,821**	**23,442**	**28,209**	**46,845**
Long term	207,487	69,011	9,307	20,694	12,652	23,056	27,954	44,813
Short term	5,432	2,073	246	273	169	385	255	2,031
PERCENT DISTRIBUTION								
General revenue [2]	**100**	**100**	**100**	**100**	**100**	**100**	**100**	**100**
Taxes [2]	44	41	45	42	39	42	43	48
Property.	22	24	29	26	19	19	22	20
Sales and gross receipts.	12	11	12	12	13	16	11	13
Intergovernmental.	29	26	25	27	28	24	31	33
Current charges	16	19	17	18	18	19	13	12
General expenditure [2]	**100**	**100**	**100**	**100**	**100**	**100**	**100**	**100**
Police and fire protection	18	22	21	20	19	19	17	13
Education	11	6	15	15	14	8	11	16
Sewerage and sanitation	11	14	10	10	10	11	10	7
Highways	8	12	9	8	8	8	6	4
Health and hospitals	6	5	4	4	3	4	8	9
Public welfare	5	1	1	2	1	1	6	14
Housing and community development . .	5	4	5	5	6	5	5	7
Interest on general debt.	7	7	7	8	11	11	8	5
PER CAPITA [4] (dollars)								
General revenue [2]	**1,035**	**649**	**905**	**979**	**1,096**	**1,199**	**1,534**	**2,357**
Taxes [2]	450	264	407	412	424	504	666	1,132
Property.	229	153	262	252	211	222	339	463
Sales and gross receipts.	126	74	111	114	138	186	162	299
Intergovernmental [2].	296	169	224	264	302	287	472	787
From State governments.	224	127	182	201	211	174	268	676
From Federal Government	49	22	31	37	64	76	169	89
Current charges	165	122	154	172	201	229	204	279
Water supply and other utilities revenue [3]	218	197	180	234	219	188	294	276
General expenditure [2]	**1,005**	**615**	**891**	**1,006**	**1,097**	**1,189**	**1,484**	**2,283**
Police and fire protection	181	134	186	200	203	227	253	285
Education	114	37	137	151	148	89	167	370
Sewerage and sanitation	108	89	90	102	107	132	148	163
Highways	79	72	80	82	92	95	87	89
Health and hospitals	60	28	34	37	35	50	115	201
Public welfare	52	3	6	15	13	17	82	318
Housing and community development . .	50	22	41	46	68	55	74	153
Interest on general debt.	74	46	64	77	117	135	115	123
Water supply and other utilities expenditure [3]	251	206	194	243	243	221	357	426
Gross debt outstanding.	**1,392**	**866**	**1,178**	**1,413**	**2,110**	**2,250**	**2,283**	**2,448**
Long term	1,356	841	1,148	1,394	2,082	2,213	2,262	2,342
Short term.	36	25	30	18	28	37	21	106

[1] Data are estimates subject to sampling variation, see source and Appendix III.　　[2] Includes items not shown separately.
[3] Include liquor stores.　　[4] Based on 1988 estimated resident population as of July 1.

Source: U.S. Bureau of the Census, *City Government Finances*, series GF, No. 4, annual.

No. 478. Estimated State and Local Taxes Paid by a Family of Four in Selected Large Cities, by Income Level: 1990

[Preliminary. Data based on average family of four (two wage earners and two school age children) owning their own home and living in a city where taxes apply. Comprises State and local sales, income, auto, and real estate taxes. For definition of median, see Guide to Tabular Presentation]

CITY	TOTAL TAXES PAID BY GROSS FAMILY INCOME LEVEL (dol.)				PERCENT OF INCOME BY INCOME LEVEL			
	$25,000	$50,000	$75,000	$100,000	$25,000	$50,000	$75,000	$100,000
Albuquerque, NM	1,998	4,081	6,839	9,608	8.0	8.2	9.1	9.6
Atlanta, GA	2,707	5,445	8,909	11,842	10.8	10.9	11.9	11.8
Baltimore, MD	2,826	5,748	8,849	11,726	11.3	11.5	11.8	11.7
Bridgeport, CT	2,966	5,304	8,982	11,585	11.9	10.6	12.0	11.6
Burlington, VT	2,196	4,448	7,587	10,438	8.8	8.9	10.1	10.4
Charleston, WV	1,749	3,653	6,499	8,984	7.0	7.3	8.7	9.0
Charlotte, NC	2,129	4,603	7,531	10,066	8.5	9.2	10.0	10.1
Chicago, IL	2,160	4,241	6,604	8,657	8.6	8.5	8.8	8.7
Cleveland, OH	2,484	5,195	8,282	11,413	9.9	10.4	11.0	11.4
Columbia, SC	2,312	5,208	8,728	11,620	9.2	10.4	11.6	11.6
Des Moines, IA	2,556	5,254	8,261	10,946	10.2	10.5	11.0	10.9
Detroit, MI	2,980	6,112	9,570	13,458	11.9	12.2	12.8	13.5
Honolulu, HI	2,112	4,665	7,681	10,501	8.4	9.3	10.2	10.5
Indianapolis, IN	2,203	3,912	6,491	8,378	8.8	7.8	8.7	8.4
Jackson, MS	1,880	4,068	6,937	9,280	7.5	8.1	9.2	9.3
Louisville, KY	2,411	5,035	7,922	10,548	9.6	10.1	10.6	10.5
Memphis, TN	1,787	3,039	4,567	5,845	7.1	6.1	6.1	5.8
Milwaukee, WI	3,436	7,411	11,474	15,156	13.7	14.8	15.3	15.2
Newark, NJ	2,800	5,609	8,733	11,892	11.2	11.2	11.6	11.9
New York City, NY	2,647	6,323	10,608	14,480	10.6	12.6	14.1	14.5
Norfolk, VA	2,167	4,704	7,921	10,438	8.7	9.4	10.6	10.4
Omaha, NE	2,938	5,033	8,530	11,455	11.8	10.1	11.4	11.5
Philadelphia, PA	3,192	6,071	8,940	11,661	12.8	12.1	11.9	11.7
Portland, ME	2,118	4,934	8,941	12,083	8.5	9.9	11.9	12.1
Portland, OR	3,457	7,310	11,484	15,189	13.8	14.6	15.3	15.2
Providence, RI	2,641	5,232	8,885	11,894	10.6	10.5	11.8	11.9
St. Louis, MO	2,063	4,408	6,985	9,188	8.3	8.8	9.3	9.2
Salt Lake City, UT	2,304	4,940	7,816	10,365	9.2	9.9	10.4	10.4
Sioux Falls, SD	2,106	3,658	5,487	6,980	8.4	7.3	7.3	7.0
Washington, DC	2,372	5,126	8,405	11,539	9.5	10.3	11.2	11.5
Median [1]	2,112	4,448	7,531	10,066	8.4	8.9	10.0	10.1

[1] Median of all 51 cities. For complete list of cities, see table 479.

Source: Government of the District of Columbia, Department of Finance and Revenue, *Tax Rates and Tax Burdens in the District of Columbia: A Nationwide Comparison,* annual.

No. 479. Residential Property Tax Rates in Selected Large Cities: 1990

CITY	EFFECTIVE TAX RATE PER $100		Assessment level (percent)	Nominal rate per $100	CITY	EFFECTIVE TAX RATE PER $100		Assessment level (percent)	Nominal rate per $100
	Rank	Rate				Rank	Rate		
Detroit, MI	1	4.40	49.3	8.92	New Orleans, LA	26	1.46	10.0	14.65
Milwaukee, WI	2	3.78	98.5	3.84	Billings, MT	27	1.44	3.9	37.27
Portland, OR	3	3.32	100.0	3.32	Wilmington, DE	28	1.31	77.7	1.69
Des Moines, IA	4	3.10	79.5	3.90	Phoenix, AZ	29	1.31	10.0	13.08
Newark, NJ	5	2.96	17.4	16.99	Seattle, WA	30	1.30	95.7	1.36
Philadelphia, PA	6	2.64	32.0	8.26	Columbia, SC	31	1.26	4.0	31.42
Omaha, NE	7	2.63	90.0	2.92	Norfolk, VA	32	1.24	90.0	1.38
Providence, RI	8	2.55	100.0	2.55	Louisville, KY	33	1.20	92.0	1.30
Baltimore, MD	9	2.46	40.0	6.16	Wichita, KS	34	1.17	7.8	14.97
Manchester, NH	10	2.36	21.0	11.22	Charlotte, NC	35	1.15	86.0	1.34
Sioux Falls, IA	11	2.27	90.0	2.52	St. Louis, MO	36	1.15	19.0	6.03
Houston, TX	12	2.19	100.0	2.19	Denver, CO	37	1.12	16.6	6.76
Jacksonville, FL	13	2.18	100.0	2.18	Minneapolis, MN	38	1.11	10.9	10.16
Bridgeport, CT	14	2.10	34.9	6.03	Salt Lake City, UT	39	1.08	60.0	1.80
Atlanta, GA	15	2.08	40.0	5.20	Oklahoma City, OK	40	1.04	11.0	9.45
Cleveland, OH	16	2.00	35.0	5.70	Albuquerque, NM	41	1.04	33.3	3.11
Boise City, ID	17	1.92	98.1	1.96	Washington, DC	42	0.96	94.6	1.01
Fargo, ND	18	1.78	4.5	39.59	Little Rock, AR	43	0.95	18.7	5.08
Memphis, TN	19	1.77	25.0	7.09	Las Vegas, NV	44	0.88	35.0	2.50
Anchorage, AK	20	1.76	95.0	1.85	Boston, MA	45	0.85	100.0	0.85
Portland, ME	21	1.74	46.4	3.75	New York City, NY	46	0.79	8.0	9.84
Burlington, VT	22	1.65	72.0	2.29	Casper, WY	47	0.71	9.5	7.50
Chicago, IL	23	1.63	16.0	10.20	Birmingham, AL	48	0.70	10.0	6.95
Indianapolis, IN	24	1.62	15.0	10.79	Los Angeles, CA	49	0.63	61.2	1.03
Jackson, MS	25	1.47	10.0	14.73	Charleston, WV	50	0.61	35.3	1.73
					Honolulu, HI	51	0.48	100.0	0.48

Source: Government of the District of Columbia, Department of Finance and Revenue, *Tax Rates and Tax Burdens in the District of Columbia: A Nationwide Comparison,* annual.

No. 480. Gross Assessed Value of Property and Government Revenue From Property Taxes: 1975 to 1990

[In billions of dollars, except percent. Data are estimates subject to sampling variability; see Appendix III and source]

ITEM	1975	1979	1981	1984	1985	1986	1987	1988	1989	1990
Gross assessed value of property [1]	1,096.3	1,678.8	2,958.2	4,053.1	(NA)	4,817.8	(NA)	(NA)	6,013.2	(NA)
State assessed	74.8	113.5	159.2	200.1	(NA)	242.9	(NA)	(NA)	257.2	(NA)
Locally assessed	1,021.5	1,565.3	2,799.0	3,853.0	(NA)	4,574.9	(NA)	(NA)	5,756.0	(NA)
Real property	881.6	1,358.5	2,514.9	3,446.5	(NA)	4,104.5	(NA)	(NA)	5,219.7	(NA)
Percent of locally assessed . . .	86.3	86.8	89.8	89.4	(NA)	89.7	(NA)	(NA)	90.7	(NA)
Net assessed value of locally taxable property [2]	1,062.9	1,607.3	2,837.5	3,868.8	(NA)	4,619.7	(NA)	(NA)	5,791.1	(NA)
Percent of gross assessed	97.0	95.7	95.9	95.5	(NA)	95.9	(NA)	(NA)	96.3	(NA)
REVENUE FROM PROPERTY TAXES										
Total revenue, State and local	51.5	64.9	75.0	96.5	103.8	111.7	121.2	132.2	142.5	155.6
Percent of general revenue	22.6	18.9	17.7	17.8	17.4	17.4	17.7	18.2	18.1	18.3
Percent of tax revenue	36.4	31.6	30.7	30.1	29.7	29.9	29.9	30.4	30.4	31.0
Revenue, State governments.	1.5	2.5	2.9	3.9	4.0	4.4	4.6	5.0	5.4	5.8
Percent of general revenue	0.9	1.0	0.9	1.0	0.9	0.9	0.9	1.1	1.1	1.1
Percent of tax revenue	1.8	2.0	2.0	2.0	1.9	1.9	1.9	1.9	1.9	1.9
Revenue, local governments	50.0	62.5	72.0	92.6	99.8	107.4	116.6	127.2	137.1	149.8
Annual average percent change from prior year shown	[3]6.6	5.7	7.3	7.9	7.8	7.6	8.6	9.1	7.8	9.3
Percent of general revenue	32.2	26.6	25.0	25.3	24.8	24.7	24.8	29.3	29.3	29.2
Percent of tax revenue	81.6	77.5	76.0	75.0	74.2	74.0	73.7	74.1	74.3	74.5

NA Not available.   [1] Gross assessed value amounts may include prior year components for those states unable to report data for indicated year at time of publication. See sources for definitions of terms and limitations of data.   [2] Value subject to local general property taxation, including State-assessed property, after deduction of partial exemptions.   [3] Change from 1971.

Source: U.S. Bureau of the Census, *Census of Governments: 1982* and *1987*, vol. 2; *Property Values Subject to Local General Property Taxation in the United States: 1975* and *1979*, series GSS Nos. 80, 92, and 98; and *Government Finances*, series GF, No. 5, annual.

No. 481. Governmental Employment and Payrolls: 1970 to 1990

[For **October.** Covers both full-time and part-time employees. Except for 1987, local government data are estimates subject to sampling variation; see source and Appendix III. See also *Historical Statistics, Colonial Times to 1970*, series Y 272-307]

TYPE OF GOVERNMENT	1970	1975	1980	1983	1984	1985	1986	1987	1988	1989	1990
EMPLOYEES (1,000)											
Total	13,028	14,973	16,213	16,034	16,436	16,690	16,933	17,212	17,588	17,879	18,369
Federal (civilian) [1]	2,881	2,890	2,898	2,875	2,942	3,021	3,019	3,091	3,112	3,114	3,105
State and local	10,147	12,084	13,315	13,159	13,494	13,669	13,913	14,121	14,476	14,765	15,263
Percent of total	77.9	80.7	82.1	82.1	82.1	81.9	82.2	82.0	82.3	82.6	83.1
State	2,755	3,271	3,753	3,816	3,898	3,984	4,068	4,116	4,236	4,365	4,503
Local	7,392	8,813	9,562	9,344	9,595	9,685	9,846	10,005	10,240	10,400	10,760
Counties.	1,229	1,563	1,853	1,811	1,872	1,891	1,926	1,963	2,024	2,085	2,167
Municipalities	2,244	2,506	2,561	2,424	2,434	2,467	2,494	2,493	2,570	2,569	2,642
School districts	3,316	3,969	4,270	4,211	4,387	4,416	4,502	4,627	4,679	4,774	4,950
Townships	330	392	394	379	386	392	400	393	415	405	418
Special districts	275	383	484	519	516	519	524	529	552	568	585
OCTOBER PAYROLLS (mil. dol.)											
Total	8,334	13,224	19,935	24,525	26,904	28,945	30,670	32,669	34,203	36,763	39,228
Federal (civilian) [1]	2,428	3,584	5,205	6,301	7,137	7,580	7,561	7,924	7,976	8,636	8,999
State and local	5,906	9,640	14,730	18,224	19,767	21,365	23,109	24,745	26,227	28,127	30,229
Percent of total	70.9	72.9	73.9	74.3	73.5	73.8	75.3	75.7	76.7	76.5	77.1
State	1,612	2,653	4,285	5,346	5,815	6,329	6,810	7,263	7,842	8,443	9,083
Local	4,294	6,987	10,445	12,878	13,952	15,036	16,298	17,482	18,385	19,684	21,146
Counties.	640	1,183	1,936	2,387	2,596	2,819	3,009	3,270	3,532	3,855	4,192
Municipalities	1,361	2,129	2,951	3,640	3,872	4,191	4,407	4,770	4,979	5,274	5,564
School districts	2,032	3,160	4,683	5,729	6,283	6,746	7,517	7,961	8,298	8,852	9,551
Townships	122	215	330	398	421	446	474	522	556	599	642
Special districts	140	300	546	724	780	834	892	959	1,020	1,104	1,197

[1] Includes employees outside the United States.

Source: U.S. Bureau of the Census, *1982* and *1987 Census of Governments*, vol. 6, No. 5; *Historical Statistics on Governmental Finances and Employment;* and *Public Employment*, series GE, No. 1, annual.

No. 482. Governmental Employment and Payrolls, by Level of Government and Function: 1990

[For **October.** Covers both full-time and part-time employees. Local government data are estimates subject to sampling variation; see source and Appendix III]

FUNCTION	EMPLOYEES (1,000)					OCTOBER PAYROLLS (mil. dol.)				
	Total	Federal (civil-ian)[1]	State and local			Total	Federal (civil-ian)[1]	State and local		
			Total	State	Local			Total	State	Local
Total	18,369	3,105	15,263	4,503	10,760	39,228	8,999	30,229	9,083	21,146
National defense [2]	1,038	1,038	(X)	(X)	(X)	2,998	2,998	(X)	(X)	(X)
Postal Service	816	816	(X)	(X)	(X)	2,321	2,321	(X)	(X)	(X)
Space research and technology.	25	25	(X)	(X)	(X)	103	103	(X)	(X)	(X)
Education	7,971	13	7,958	1,984	5,974	15,116	37	15,078	3,426	11,652
Teachers	4,545	(X)	4,544	614	3,931	10,637	(X)	10,637	1,576	9,061
Highways	573	4	569	261	308	1,199	14	1,184	596	588
Health and hospitals.	1,793	291	1,502	730	772	3,820	826	2,993	1,522	1,472
Public welfare	499	10	489	217	272	954	33	922	455	467
Police protection	832	79	754	89	664	2,134	275	1,860	257	1,603
Fire protection	327	(X)	327	(X)	327	739	(X)	739	(X)	739
Sanitation and sewerage	238	(X)	238	2	236	489	(X)	489	4	484
Parks and recreation.	336	24	311	45	266	464	58	406	70	336
Natural resources.	427	225	202	164	38	1,074	673	400	335	66
Financial administration	488	140	349	147	202	1,045	357	687	326	362
Other government administration.	388	28	361	53	308	618	83	535	122	413
Judicial and legal	348	43	305	110	195	880	142	738	325	413
All other	2,269	369	1,899	701	1,198	5,277	1,079	4,199	1,646	2,553

X Not applicable. [1] Includes employees outside United States. [2] Includes international relations.

Source: U.S. Bureau of the Census, *Public Employment,* series GE, No. 1.

No. 483. State and Local Government—Full-Time Employment and Salary, by Sex and Race/Ethnic Group: 1973 to 1990

[**As of June 30.** Excludes school systems and educational institutions. Based on reports from State governments (44 in 1973, 48 in 1975 and 1976, 47 in 1977, 45 in 1978, 48 in 1979, 42 in 1980, 49 in 1981, 47 in 1983, 49 in 1984 through 1987, and 50 in 1989 and 1990) and a sample of county, municipal, township, and special district jurisdictions employing 15 or more nonelected, nonappointed full-time employees. Data for 1982 and 1988 not available. For definition of median, see Guide to Tabular Presentation]

YEAR AND OCCUPATION	EMPLOYMENT (1,000)							MEDIAN ANNUAL SALARY ($1,000)					
	Total	Male	Fe-male	White[1]	Minority			Male	Fe-male	White[1]	Minority		
					Total[2]	Black[1]	His-panic[3]				Total[1]	Black[2]	His-panic[3]
1973	3,809	2,486	1,322	3,115	693	523	125	9.6	7.0	8.8	7.5	7.4	7.4
1975	3,899	2,436	1,464	3,102	797	602	147	11.3	8.2	10.2	8.8	8.6	8.9
1976	4,369	2,724	1,645	3,490	880	664	165	11.8	8.6	10.7	9.2	9.1	9.4
1977	4,415	2,737	1,678	3,480	935	705	175	12.4	9.1	11.3	9.7	9.5	9.9
1978	4,447	2,711	1,736	3,481	966	723	181	13.3	9.7	12.0	10.4	10.1	10.7
1979	4,576	2,761	1,816	3,568	1,008	751	192	14.1	10.4	12.8	10.9	10.6	11.4
1980	3,987	2,350	1,637	3,146	842	619	163	15.2	11.4	13.8	11.8	11.5	12.3
1981	4,665	2,740	1,925	3,591	1,074	780	205	17.7	13.1	16.1	13.5	13.3	14.7
1983	4,492	2,674	1,818	3,423	1,069	768	219	20.1	15.3	18.5	15.9	15.6	17.3
1984	4,580	2,700	1,880	3,458	1,121	799	233	21.4	16.2	19.6	17.4	16.5	18.4
1985	4,742	2,789	1,952	3,563	1,179	835	248	22.3	17.3	20.6	18.4	17.5	19.2
1986	4,779	2,797	1,982	3,549	1,230	865	259	23.4	18.1	21.5	19.6	18.7	20.2
1987	4,849	2,818	2,031	3,600	1,249	872	268	24.2	18.9	22.4	20.9	19.3	21.1
1989	5,257	3,030	2,227	3,863	1,394	961	308	26.1	20.6	24.1	22.1	20.7	22.7
1990, total . .	5,374	3,071	2,302	3,918	1,456	994	327	27.3	21.8	25.2	23.3	22.0	23.8
Officials/adminis-trators	299	206	94	254	45	30	10	42.5	35.0	40.2	38.0	37.9	38.1
Professionals. . .	1,192	598	594	935	257	157	50	34.7	29.7	31.9	30.6	29.5	31.7
Technicians. . . .	502	298	204	383	119	74	29	28.0	22.2	25.5	25.1	22.8	25.0
Protective service	884	768	116	681	203	140	52	26.3	24.0	27.9	31.2	25.7	30.7
Paraprofession-als	392	109	284	244	148	120	21	20.3	18.4	19.2	21.0	18.0	19.6
Admin. support .	972	123	849	683	289	191	73	20.8	18.9	18.9	19.8	19.4	19.6
Skilled craft. . . .	456	436	19	347	109	69	30	25.0	20.1	24.7	26.0	24.8	26.2
Service/mainte-nance	676	534	142	392	284	211	61	20.3	16.4	19.8	20.1	18.4	19.8

[1] Non-Hispanic. [2] Includes other minority groups, not shown separately. [3] Hispanic persons may be of any race.

Source: U.S. Equal Employment Opportunity Commission, *State and Local Government Information Report,* annual.

No. 484. State and Local Government—Employee Benefits: 1990

[In percent. For January through July. Covers full-time employees in State and local governments. Covers only benefits for which the employer pays part or all of the premium or expenses involved, except unpaid maternity and paternity leave, and long-term care insurance. Based on sample survey of establishments. For data on employee benefits in firms, see table 662]

TYPE OF EMPLOYEE BENEFIT	All employees	Regular employees [1]	Teachers [2]	Police and fire fighters	TYPE OF EMPLOYEE BENEFIT	All employees	Regular employees [1]	Teachers [2]	Police and fire fighters
Paid: Vacations	67	87	10	98	Accident/sickness.	21	23	16	17
Holidays	74	89	33	94	Noncontributory.	17	19	15	14
Jury duty leave	94	94	97	82	Long-term disability	27	26	32	20
Funeral leave	63	63	62	75	Noncontributory.	18	17	23	12
Rest time.	56	69	22	49	Retirement and savings plans:				
Military leave	81	83	74	86	Defined benefit pension	90	89	94	92
Sick leave	95	93	97	95	Noncontributory	23	23	23	21
Personal leave	39	33	57	25	Defined contribution.	9	8	11	13
Lunch time.	11	8	13	39	Money purchase pension [4].	8	7	10	12
Unpaid: Maternity leave.	51	49	57	45	Additional benefits:				
Unpaid paternity leave	33	33	35	29	Child care	9	10	7	7
Insurance plans:					Educational assistance:				
Medical	93	93	91	97	Job related	63	66	53	69
Dental	62	62	64	63	Not job related.	18	20	13	16
Extended care facility	74	74	72	80	Eldercare.	4	4	4	3
Home health care.	76	76	76	83	Employee assistance				
Hospital/room & board . . .	93	93	91	97	program.	59	64	45	71
In HMO's [3]	21	21	19	24	Financial counseling	7	8	7	6
Inpatient surgery	93	93	91	97	Flexible benefits plans	5	4	7	(Z)
Mental health care:					In-house infirmary	18	19	17	11
Inpatient	92	92	90	95	Long-term care insurance. . .	2	2	3	(Z)
Outpatient	88	89	84	94	Nonproduction bonuses,				
Vision.	32	31	32	35	cash	35	38	23	59
Alcohol abuse treatment:					Parking	81	79	87	82
In detoxification.	91	92	90	95	Prepaid legal services	8	8	6	17
In rehabilitation	76	78	71	81	Recreation facilities	15	13	19	22
Outpatient	70	72	64	80	Reimbursement accounts [5] . .	31	31	30	26
Drug abuse treatment:					Relocation allowance	13	16	6	11
In detoxification.	91	91	89	95	Severance pay	27	26	28	32
In rehabilitation	74	76	67	79	Subsidized commuting	7	8	1	18
Outpatient	69	71	62	77	Subsidized meals	7	8	5	4
Life.	88	88	87	89	Travel accident insurance. . .	14	14	13	13
Noncontributory	77	77	78	80	Wellness programs	29	31	22	32

Z Less than 0.5 percent. [1] Includes all white-collar employees (professional, administrative, technical, clerical) and blue-collar employees (production, service) except those classified as teachers or police and firefighters. [2] Includes all personnel in primary and secondary schools, junior colleges, colleges, and universities whose primary duty is teaching or closely related activities. [3] For definition, see table 156. [4] Fixed contributions are periodically placed in an employee's account and benefits are based on how much money has accumulated at retirement. [5] Account which is used throughout the year to pay for plan premiums or to reimburse the employee for benefit related expenses. Account may be financed by employer, employee, or both.

Source: U.S. Bureau of Labor Statistics, *Employee Benefits in State and Local Governments, 1990.*

No. 485. State and Local Government Major Collective Bargaining Agreements— Average Percent Changes in Wage and Compensation Rates Negotiated: 1984 to 1990

[In percent, except as indicated. Averages presented are means; for definition of mean, see Guide to Tabular Presentation]

ITEM	1984	1985	1986	1987	1988	1989	1990
Compensation rate changes, [1] all settlements:							
First year	5.2	4.2	6.2	4.9	5.4	5.1	5.1
Over life of contract [2]	5.4	5.1	6.0	4.8	5.3	4.9	5.1
State government: First year	4.3	4.8	6.8	4.3	5.3	4.9	4.4
Over life of contract [2]	4.0	4.8	6.0	4.3	4.9	4.6	3.9
Local government, first year	6.0	3.7	5.6	5.4	5.5	5.6	5.4
Over life of contract [2]	6.6	5.5	6.0	5.1	5.8	5.5	5.8
Wage rate changes, [3] all settlements:							
First year	4.8	4.6	5.7	4.9	5.1	5.1	4.9
Over life of contract [2]	5.1	5.4	5.7	5.1	5.3	5.1	5.0
State government: First year	3.6	4.8	6.3	4.1	5.3	5.0	4.7
Over life of contract [2]	3.8	4.9	6.0	4.2	5.0	4.7	4.2
Local government: First year	5.4	4.4	5.3	5.3	5.0	5.2	5.0
Over life of contract [2]	5.9	5.7	5.6	5.5	5.5	5.4	5.2
Number of workers affected (mil.) [4]	0.7	1.5	0.9	1.3	1.1	1.1	0.9
State government.	0.3	0.5	0.3	0.5	0.4	0.5	0.2
Local government.	0.5	0.9	0.6	0.8	0.7	0.6	0.7
Wage rate changes, all agreements [5].	5.0	5.7	5.5	4.9	4.7	5.1	4.6
Source: Current settlements	1.9	4.1	2.4	2.7	2.3	2.5	2.0
Prior settlements	3.1	1.6	3.0	2.2	2.4	2.6	2.6
Cost-of-living adjustments	(Z)	(Z)	(Z)	(Z)	(Z)	(Z)	(Z)
State government	5.4	4.5	5.6	4.3	4.1	4.0	4.7
Local government	4.7	6.5	5.4	5.3	5.1	5.9	4.6

Z Less than .05 percent. [1] Data relate to settlements of 5,000 workers or more in each calendar year, whether wages and benefits were changed or not. [2] Average annual rate of change. [3] Data relate to settlements covering 1,000 workers or more in each calendar year but exclude possible changes in wages under cost-of-living adjustment (COLA) clauses, except increases guaranteed by the contract. Includes all settlements, whether wages were changed or not. [4] Number of workers covered by settlements reached in each calendar year. [5] Data relate to all wage changes implemented in the year stemming from settlements reached in the year, deferred from prior year agreements, and cost-of-living clauses.

Source: U.S. Bureau of Labor Statistics, *Current Wage Developments,* monthly.

No. 486. State and Local Government Employment (Full-Time Equivalent), by Selected Function, 1970 to 1990, and by State, 1990

[In thousands, for **October.** Full-time equivalent employment not available for 1985. Except 1987, local government data are estimates subject to sampling variation; see source and Appendix III]

| YEAR, REGION, DIVISION, AND STATE | EDUCATION | | | | HEALTH AND HOSPITALS | | HIGHWAYS | | POLICE AND FIRE PROTECTION | | PUBLIC WELFARE | |
| | Total | | Higher education | | | | | | | | | |
	State	Local	State	Local	State	Local	State	Local	State[1]	Local	State	Local
1970.	803.0	3,454.6	722.2	119.4	482.0	469.0	296.8	271.4	55.8	583.7	97.3	152.5
1980 [2].	1,062.8	4,278.3	947.7	212.1	649.8	646.4	255.3	277.4	75.5	745.0	171.5	200.4
1986 [2].	1,256.4	4,595.3	1,140.4	212.8	652.5	643.9	249.7	284.4	78.5	813.8	186.6	223.1
1987.	1,252.3	4,726.7	1,137.4	215.5	659.9	650.4	248.1	266.0	84.8	796.7	190.1	220.6
1988.	1,309.5	4,815.5	1,192.7	230.6	673.8	662.6	251.0	288.9	84.3	838.3	198.1	230.9
1989.	1,359.8	4,937.5	1,235.1	238.1	682.6	682.8	255.2	285.2	88.7	840.1	200.9	240.6
1990	**1,418.5**	**5,067.5**	**1,289.2**	**250.5**	**695.6**	**695.6**	**256.7**	**293.3**	**88.1**	**864.5**	**212.9**	**252.1**
Northeast	**181.0**	**1,014.0**	**157.4**	**35.1**	**176.4**	**113.2**	**53.5**	**73.5**	**21.3**	**200.0**	**44.3**	**96.3**
New England	**63.9**	**248.6**	**56.3**	**-**	**47.2**	**12.8**	**16.4**	**14.9**	**5.4**	**53.8**	**19.0**	**6.3**
Maine	7.2	29.6	5.8	-	2.9	1.2	2.8	1.5	0.6	3.5	2.0	0.2
New Hampshire . .	5.5	20.2	5.2	-	1.8	0.3	1.9	1.5	0.4	4.0	1.1	2.3
Vermont	4.7	13.5	4.4	-	1.2	-	1.2	0.9	0.5	1.0	1.2	-
Massachusetts . .	23.0	106.7	22.1	-	23.9	9.5	5.0	6.0	1.9	28.5	8.7	1.8
Rhode Island	7.0	16.5	6.0	-	3.0	-	1.0	0.9	0.3	4.8	1.9	0.1
Connecticut	16.5	62.1	12.8	-	14.4	1.8	4.5	4.1	1.7	12.0	4.1	1.9
Middle Atlantic	**117.1**	**765.4**	**101.6**	**35.1**	**129.2**	**100.4**	**37.1**	**58.6**	**15.9**	**146.2**	**25.3**	**90.0**
New York	52.8	385.4	47.2	19.5	81.3	82.9	14.8	37.1	5.8	81.6	7.8	60.1
New Jersey	31.7	169.2	24.2	8.2	22.7	11.3	8.9	10.8	4.7	34.3	7.2	11.4
Pennsylvania	32.6	210.8	30.2	7.4	25.2	6.2	13.4	10.7	5.4	30.3	10.3	18.5
Midwest	**402.7**	**1,210.0**	**381.9**	**61.5**	**140.8**	**153.9**	**51.6**	**77.9**	**18.1**	**192.2**	**55.3**	**65.2**
East North Central .	**270.4**	**827.4**	**257.0**	**42.9**	**88.7**	**105.3**	**28.9**	**47.7**	**12.2**	**142.7**	**35.5**	**48.6**
Ohio	67.2	200.1	64.8	4.1	23.1	28.5	8.7	13.1	2.2	35.7	2.1	22.7
Indiana	48.2	111.0	43.6	-	12.5	22.3	4.9	6.0	1.8	16.7	5.3	3.0
Illinois	53.7	218.2	50.7	17.7	24.5	22.8	9.1	10.6	4.2	49.0	13.2	7.6
Michigan	66.3	195.5	64.3	11.7	19.8	21.6	4.2	8.8	3.2	25.2	13.8	2.8
Wisconsin	35.0	102.6	33.6	9.4	8.8	10.1	2.02	9.2	0.8	16.1	1.1	12.5
West North Central.	**132.3**	**382.6**	**124.9**	**18.6**	**52.1**	**48.6**	**22.7**	**30.2**	**5.9**	**49.5**	**19.8**	**16.6**
Minnesota	37.5	85.2	35.8	1.3	9.7	15.3	5.1	7.5	0.9	10.2	1.8	9.5
Iowa	27.7	66.9	26.6	5.7	9.5	9.5	2.8	5.5	0.9	6.9	3.7	1.7
Missouri	23.5	101.2	21.3	4.5	15.6	10.8	6.8	6.2	1.9	17.1	6.4	2.6
North Dakota	7.1	12.8	6.7	-	2.3	0.2	1.1	1.1	0.2	1.4	0.4	0.8
South Dakota . . .	4.5	16.0	4.1	-	2.1	0.6	1.2	1.5	0.3	1.6	1.1	-
Nebraska.	11.3	36.4	10.7	2.2	4.8	4.4	2.2	3.1	0.7	4.2	2.8	1.2
Kansas	20.7	64.1	19.7	4.9	8.4	7.7	3.5	5.3	1.0	8.1	3.6	0.8
South	**506.8**	**1,869.5**	**461.5**	**75.8**	**277.7**	**281.1**	**104.8**	**91.8**	**29.2**	**291.5**	**85.2**	**36.8**
South Atlantic	**238.6**	**910.1**	**217.8**	**42.9**	**139.3**	**141.2**	**58.3**	**39.2**	**17.1**	**158.0**	**34.2**	**27.7**
Delaware	6.9	11.5	6.7	-	3.7	-	1.4	0.5	0.7	1.4	1.7	-
Maryland	27.0	92.6	24.9	9.2	13.8	3.2	5.3	5.7	2.4	18.5	6.8	1.8
Dist. of Columbia . .	(X)	12.8	(X)	1.6	(X)	8.1	(X)	1.0	(X)	7.3	(X)	1.9
Virginia	43.9	131.4	40.9	-	25.0	8.5	12.8	4.0	2.4	18.9	2.2	7.0
West Virginia	13.4	41.3	11.9	-	3.2	4.0	5.5	1.0	0.9	3.0	2.1	-
North Carolina . . .	41.1	146.0	38.1	12.3	17.2	22.5	11.5	3.3	3.1	18.9	1.1	10.7
South Carolina . . .	30.4	70.5	27.4	-	17.2	13.3	5.1	2.3	1.7	9.3	5.1	0.5
Georgia	37.1	141.7	31.9	0.3	28.2	44.0	6.5	7.4	2.1	24.1	7.3	0.7
Florida.	38.8	262.3	36.1	19.5	31.0	37.6	10.2	14.0	3.8	56.6	7.9	5.1
East South Central .	**113.0**	**307.8**	**101.0**	**4.6**	**50.0**	**63.6**	**18.2**	**21.4**	**5.5**	**44.4**	**18.1**	**5.4**
Kentucky	31.9	75.9	27.7	-	7.2	7.4	6.1	3.0	1.7	8.4	4.6	0.6
Tennessee.	31.5	86.9	29.5	-	14.8	21.1	4.7	7.0	1.8	16.0	5.7	3.4
Alabama	34.1	80.0	29.9	-	17.2	19.7	4.1	7.1	1.0	13.2	4.4	1.1
Mississippi	15.5	65.0	13.9	4.6	10.8	15.4	3.3	4.3	1.0	6.8	3.4	0.3
West South Central.	**155.2**	**651.6**	**142.6**	**28.3**	**88.4**	**76.3**	**28.2**	**31.2**	**6.6**	**89.1**	**32.9**	**3.7**
Arkansas	15.6	51.1	13.0	-	8.0	4.4	3.9	3.2	0.9	5.9	3.3	0.3
Louisiana	29.6	94.2	26.2	0.1	22.4	10.3	5.4	5.1	1.0	14.5	5.5	0.7
Oklahoma	24.7	71.5	22.7	-	10.8	8.6	3.7	5.4	1.7	10.5	7.7	0.2
Texas	85.3	434.8	80.7	28.2	47.2	53.0	15.2	17.5	3.0	58.2	16.4	2.5
West	**327.5**	**973.4**	**288.4**	**77.8**	**100.2**	**147.4**	**46.8**	**50.1**	**19.7**	**180.8**	**28.1**	**53.5**
Mountain	**113.0**	**293.6**	**105.9**	**11.3**	**27.3**	**32.7**	**17.0**	**16.3**	**5.2**	**45.4**	**11.6**	**7.4**
Montana	6.6	23.8	5.9	0.2	1.6	1.4	1.8	1.3	0.4	2.0	1.2	0.9
Idaho	8.3	22.8	7.7	0.9	1.6	4.1	1.6	1.3	0.4	2.8	0.7	0.1
Wyoming	3.3	14.9	3.2	1.6	1.5	2.9	1.7	0.8	0.3	1.7	0.5	-
Colorado	30.3	68.5	29.1	1.2	6.1	10.6	2.9	4.7	0.9	11.3	1.5	3.9
New Mexico	16.8	35.7	15.9	0.9	6.6	2.6	2.6	1.7	0.5	5.2	2.0	0.3
Arizona	21.6	75.1	19.2	6.5	3.1	6.1	3.2	4.0	1.7	12.4	2.6	1.6
Utah	19.0	32.7	18.1	-	5.2	1.4	1.8	1.4	0.6	4.3	2.1	0.4
Nevada	7.1	20.1	6.8	-	1.6	3.6	1.4	1.1	0.4	5.6	0.9	0.1
Pacific	**214.5**	**679.8**	**182.5**	**66.5**	**72.9**	**114.7**	**29.8**	**33.8**	**14.5**	**135.4**	**16.5**	**46.1**
Washington	40.1	83.4	38.3	-	13.2	9.9	5.8	5.7	1.8	14.0	6.3	0.7
Oregon	19.1	60.6	18.1	6.2	7.2	4.8	3.3	3.4	1.1	8.5	4.1	0.9
California	118.3	524.5	113.5	60.3	45.7	99.2	17.7	22.9	11.2	106.5	3.4	44.3
Alaska.	7.5	11.3	4.2	-	1.1	0.6	2.9	0.7	0.4	1.7	1.6	0.1
Hawaii.	29.5	-	8.4	-	5.7	0.2	0.1	1.1	-	4.7	1.1	0.1

- Represents or rounds to zero.   X Not applicable.   [1] For State government, represents police protection only.

[2] Beginning 1986, data not comparable with previous years due to a change in how full-time equivalent is calculated; see text, section 9.

Source: U.S. Bureau of the Census, *1987 Census of Governments*, vol. 3. No. 2, and *Public Employment*, series GE, No. 1, annual.

No. 487. State and Local Government Employment and Average Earnings, by State: 1986 and 1990

[For **October**]

REGION, DIVISION, AND STATE	TOTAL FULL-TIME EQUIVALENT EMPLOYMENT (1,000)				FULL-TIME EQUIVALENT EMPLOYMENT PER 10,000 POPULATION [2]				AVERAGE OCTOBER EARNINGS [3] (dol.)			
	State		Local [1]		State		Local [1]		State		Local [1]	
	1986	1990	1986	1990	1986	1990	1986	1990	1986	1990	1986	1990
U.S.	3,437	3,840	8,415	9,239	143	154	349	371	2,052	2,472	1,992	2,364
Northeast	704	748	1,823	1,945	141	147	365	383	2,180	2,774	2,137	2,651
New England	212	223	390	414	166	169	306	313	2,053	2,627	2,005	2,530
Maine	20	22	36	42	168	179	307	345	1,714	2,352	1,590	1,978
New Hampshire	18	16	29	33	172	145	285	301	1,759	2,352	1,701	2,215
Vermont	11	13	15	18	211	233	270	312	1,842	2,302	1,653	2,090
Massachusetts	88	93	192	196	151	155	329	325	2,034	2,541	2,082	2,554
Rhode Island	19	21	24	27	195	205	245	266	2,041	2,586	2,215	2,656
Connecticut	56	58	95	98	175	178	297	299	2,336	3,018	2,089	2,854
Middle Atlantic	492	524	1,433	1,531	132	139	384	407	2,233	2,835	2,173	2,684
New York	272	285	810	866	153	158	456	482	2,355	2,997	2,266	2,795
New Jersey	96	112	283	304	126	145	372	393	2,278	2,859	2,146	2,698
Pennsylvania	124	127	340	361	104	107	286	304	1,915	2,437	1,976	2,403
Midwest	812	892	2,016	2,155	137	150	340	361	2,007	2,510	2,008	2,307
East North Central	529	584	1,414	1,497	127	139	339	356	2,189	2,593	2,057	2,375
Ohio	122	139	365	385	113	128	340	355	1,984	2,510	1,911	2,236
Indiana	75	89	182	196	136	161	330	354	2,056	2,496	1,686	2,036
Illinois	130	145	385	416	113	127	333	364	2,165	2,520	2,166	2,463
Michigan	128	144	315	316	140	155	344	340	2,541	2,858	2,329	2,646
Wisconsin	74	67	168	183	154	136	351	375	2,128	2,503	2,035	2,372
West North Central	283	309	602	658	161	175	342	373	1,863	2,352	1,892	2,152
Minnesota	61	70	137	163	145	160	326	374	2,428	2,936	2,318	2,552
Iowa	57	57	101	107	199	207	355	387	2,049	2,936	1,735	2,024
Missouri	66	74	157	171	130	145	310	334	1,621	1,965	1,826	2,052
North Dakota	15	15	22	20	222	234	318	314	1,805	2,057	2,017	2,138
South Dakota	13	13	23	24	177	192	330	349	1,684	1,979	1,441	1,733
Nebraska	29	29	65	68	184	186	407	430	1,509	2,075	1,785	2,089
Kansas	43	50	96	104	174	200	390	421	1,687	2,077	1,700	1,979
South	1,238	1,414	2,887	3,236	149	165	348	379	1,803	2,145	1,711	2,014
South Atlantic	609	717	1,436	1,639	149	165	351	376	1,834	2,197	1,810	2,194
Delaware	17	21	16	17	272	314	252	250	1,795	2,245	1,991	2,458
Maryland	80	89	143	159	178	186	321	333	2,046	2,609	2,233	2,776
District of Columbia	(X)	(X)	51	57	(X)	(X)	817	939	(X)	(X)	2,594	3,024
Virginia	102	117	195	221	177	188	336	356	1,895	2,267	1,787	2,248
West Virginia	34	34	61	59	180	188	317	326	1,574	1,919	1,625	1,862
North Carolina	93	107	216	244	147	161	341	368	1,935	2,372	1,662	2,065
South Carolina	69	79	109	116	204	227	322	333	1,705	1,956	1,558	1,848
Georgia	91	112	239	270	149	173	391	418	1,811	2,037	1,589	1,872
Florida	124	160	407	497	106	123	348	384	1,748	2,095	1,872	2,247
East South Central	247	281	486	542	162	185	320	357	1,706	2,076	1,512	1,769
Kentucky	63	75	102	114	170	204	275	310	1,651	2,141	1,596	1,823
Tennessee	71	79	157	175	147	163	327	358	1,746	2,055	1,554	1,883
Alabama	70	79	131	148	174	196	324	367	1,884	2,196	1,532	1,749
Mississippi	42	47	95	105	161	183	364	407	1,430	1,824	1,324	1,543
West South Central	381	416	964	1,055	142	156	359	395	1,817	2,101	1,665	1,866
Arkansas	39	43	71	78	163	182	299	330	1,724	1,922	1,388	1,545
Louisiana	86	85	151	155	191	200	337	368	1,673	2,047	1,494	1,713
Oklahoma	64	65	109	116	195	208	329	369	1,733	1,975	1,595	1,761
Texas	193	223	633	706	115	131	379	415	1,927	2,192	1,748	1,952
West	684	787	1,689	1,902	135	149	334	360	2,356	2,735	2,321	2,770
Mountain	219	247	457	512	168	181	351	375	1,976	2,288	1,964	2,276
Montana	16	17	29	35	192	211	349	434	1,864	2,072	1,727	1,959
Idaho	18	19	33	37	175	186	332	372	1,766	2,100	1,535	1,772
Wyoming	11	11	25	24	213	239	494	539	1,924	2,045	1,967	2,110
Colorado	50	54	122	130	155	165	375	395	2,368	2,765	2,017	2,292
New Mexico	34	40	49	57	231	262	332	379	1,792	2,100	1,680	1,783
Arizona	43	50	119	136	128	137	358	370	2,126	2,384	2,185	2,540
Utah	33	37	47	51	197	216	283	294	1,654	2,000	1,900	2,092
Nevada	15	19	33	42	154	160	343	348	1,990	2,502	2,140	2,574
Pacific	465	539	1,231	1,390	124	138	328	355	2,530	2,936	2,456	2,952
Washington	79	91	143	164	177	187	320	336	2,231	2,459	2,134	2,515
Oregon	44	52	91	100	163	184	338	353	1,975	2,302	2,018	2,322
California	279	325	965	1,091	104	109	358	367	2,751	3,209	2,535	3,073
Alaska	21	22	20	21	393	401	377	385	3,228	3,543	3,324	3,491
Hawaii.	41	49	12	13	389	445	113	120	1,844	2,317	2,010	2,536

X Not applicable.   [1] Estimates subject to sampling variation; see source and Appendix III.   [2] 1986 based on Bureau of the Census estimated resident population as of July 1. Estimates do not reflect revisions based on the Census of Population. 1990 based on enumerated population as of April 1.   [3] For full-time employees.

Source: U.S. Bureau of the Census, *Public Employment*, series GE, No. 1, annual.

No. 488. City Government Employment and Payrolls: 1970 to 1990

[For **October**. Includes only those school systems operated as part of the city government. Represents average for period of intervals shown; for 1970, change from 1960. 1972, 1977, 1982, and 1987 based on complete census of all cities; other years based on sample and subject to sampling variation. For explanation of average annual percent change, see Guide to Tabular Presentation. Minus sign (-) indicates decrease]

YEAR	ALL EMPLOYEES, FULL-TIME AND PART-TIME (1,000)		OCTOBER PAYROLLS (mil. dol.)		AVERAGE ANNUAL PERCENT CHANGE		FULL-TIME EQUIVALENT EMPLOYMENT [1] (1,000)			AVERAGE EARNINGS IN OCTOBER, FULL-TIME EMPLOYEES (dollars)	
	Total	Excl. education	Total	Excl. education	All employees	October payroll	Total	Education	Other	Education	Other
1970	2,244	1,815	1,361	1,062	2.9	8.8	1,922	359	1,563	838	681
1975	2,506	2,074	2,129	1,725	0.6	7.3	2,142	376	1,767	1,130	972
1976	2,443	2,021	2,235	1,804	-2.5	5.0	2,107	360	1,747	1,207	1,035
1977	2,511	2,084	2,415	1,959	2.8	8.0	2,168	358	1,812	1,280	1,087
1978	2,511	2,086	2,537	2,059	(Z)	5.1	2,165	361	1,804	1,341	1,148
1979	2,553	2,121	2,729	2,215	1.7	7.6	2,189	364	1,825	1,414	1,231
1980	2,561	2,130	2,942	2,403	0.3	7.8	2,166	360	1,806	1,501	1,338
1981	2,469	2,056	3,222	2,640	-3.6	9.5	2,111	346	1,765	1,686	1,500
1982	2,396	2,015	3,428	2,861	-2.9	6.4	2,088	317	1,770	1,791	1,625
1983	2,423	2,051	3,640	3,059	1.1	6.2	2,060	300	1,760	1,962	1,739
1984	2,434	2,070	3,872	3,268	0.4	6.4	2,090	300	1,790	2,033	1,831
1985	2,467	2,102	4,191	3,536	1.4	8.2	(NA)	(NA)	(NA)	2,117	1,953
1986	2,494	2,126	4,407	3,724	1.1	5.1	2,181	320	1,860	2,186	2,044
1987	2,493	2,110	4,770	3,977	(Z)	8.2	2,223	337	1,885	2,406	2,163
1988	2,570	2,188	4,979	4,136	3.1	4.4	2,251	342	1,910	2,566	2,220
1989	2,569	2,190	5,274	4,405	(Z)	5.9	2,268	341	1,927	2,669	2,343
1990	2,642	2,237	5,564	4,675	2.8	5.5	2,295	338	1,957	2,683	2,449

NA Not available. Z Less than .05 percent. [1] Beginning 1986, data not comparable to previous years due to a change in how full-time equivalent is calculated; see text, section 9.

Source: U.S. Bureau of the Census, *Census of Governments, 1972, 1977, 1982,* and *1987,* Vol. 3, No. 2, *Compendium of Public Employment,* and *City Employment,* series GE, No. 2, annual.

No. 489. City Government Employment and Payrolls—All Cities and Cities With 75,000 Population or More, by Function: 1980 to 1990

[For **October**]

ITEM	EMPLOYEES (1,000)				Cities with 75,000 population or more,[2] 1990	OCTOBER PAYROLLS (mil. dol.)				Cities with 75,000 population or more,[2] 1990
	All cities [1]					All cities [1]				
	1980	1986	1989	1990		1980	1986	1989	1990	
Total	2,561	2,494	2,569	2,642	1,556	2,942	4,407	5,274	5,564	3,772
Full-time	2,071	2,050	2,111	2,149	1,370	2,826	4,231	5,043	5,334	3,654
Part-time	489	445	458	493	186	116	175	231	229	117
Full-time equivalent [3]	2,166	2,181	2,268	2,295	1,437	(X)	(X)	(X)	(X)	(X)
Education [4]	360	320	341	338	269	539	683	869	889	722
Percent of total...........	17	15	15	15	19	18	15	16	16	19
Instructional staff...........	266	233	238	264	212	436	553	687	754	615
Others..................	94	87	103	74	57	102	130	182	134	107
Highways...................	121	127	128	133	57	141	223	252	274	133
Public welfare...............	41	50	55	57	51	47	91	109	118	109
Hospitals..................	131	124	122	124	80	143	211	259	282	202
Health....................	35	38	41	42	34	47	73	86	93	80
Police protection.............	365	391	401	412	226	550	858	1,020	1,093	666
Fire protection	190	194	197	199	115	300	478	551	579	369
Sewerage..................	60	67	71	74	37	74	122	143	155	85
Solid waste management	104	92	87	86	50	118	163	172	174	118
Parks and recreation	103	112	118	121	72	116	170	197	211	128
Housing and community development.....................	44	46	46	46	39	57	92	100	104	89
Correction	18	25	32	35	33	27	63	85	90	87
Libraries	34	43	45	45	28	38	63	76	80	52
Financial administration	69	71	73	74	35	85	130	153	164	87
Judicial, legal, other governmental administration	112	113	123	129	72	147	230	284	314	189
Local utilities [5]	209	226	227	226	144	306	493	569	594	429
Water supply..............	93	99	101	101	50	116	182	210	219	123
Electric power.............	44	50	50	51	28	67	119	136	142	88
Transit...................	66	70	68	66	62	115	178	208	217	210
All other functions...........	171	141	160	154	94	208	267	349	350	226

X Not applicable. [1] Data are estimates subject to sampling variation; see source and Appendix III. [2] Based on enumerated resident population as of April 1. [3] Beginning 1986, data not directly comparable with previous years due to a change in how full-time equivalent is calculated. See text, section 9. [4] City-operated schools and colleges only. [5] Includes gas supply, not shown below.

Source: U.S. Bureau of the Census, *City Employment,* series GE, No. 2, annual.

No. 490. City Government Employment and Payroll—Largest Cities: 1980 and 1990

[For Oct. See text, section 9. See footnote 3, table 476, for those areas representing city/county consolidated governments]

CITIES RANKED BY 1990 POPULATION	TOTAL EMPLOYMENT (1,000)		FULL-TIME EQUIVALENT EMPLOYMENT [1]				OCTOBER PAYROLL (mil. dol.)		AVERAGE EARNINGS IN OCTOBER, FULL-TIME EMPLOYEES (dol.)	
			Total (1,000)		Per 10,000 population [2]					
	1980	1990	1980	1990	1980	1990	1980	1990	1980	1990
New York, NY [3][4]	364	[5]456	319	[5]374	451	[5]537	504	[5]1,092	1,587	[5]2,783
Los Angeles, CA	42	51	41	51	138	150	73	177	1,806	3,488
Chicago, IL	47	42	45	42	150	139	71	125	1,569	3,002
Houston, TX	18	20	18	20	111	115	26	40	1,499	2,061
Philadelphia, PA	33	32	32	32	189	194	51	89	1,611	2,843
San Diego, CA	8	10	7	10	81	91	12	29	1,773	3,019
Detroit, MI	22	22	22	21	179	204	40	50	1,852	2,663
Dallas, TX	14	[6]15	14	[6]15	153	[6]147	20	[6]28	1,465	[6]1,945
Phoenix, AZ	9	12	9	11	114	123	14	32	1,517	2,876
San Antonio, TX	10	13	10	13	128	136	13	28	1,282	2,227
San Jose, CA [3][9]	[7]4	[8]6	[7]4	[8]5	[7]60	[8]66	[7]7	[8]16	[7]1,714	[8]3,453
Baltimore, MD [3][9]	44	30	40	29	514	387	47	73	1,172	2,540
Indianapolis, IN	13	13	12	12	174	202	13	23	1,098	1,910
San Francisco, CA	21	26	21	26	310	351	37	94	1,761	3,648
Jacksonville, FL	[10]11	11	[10]11	10	[10]202	154	[10]11	24	[10]1,031	2,582
Columbus, OH	8	8	7	7	122	131	10	18	1,498	2,416
Milwaukee, WI	10	[8]9	9	[8]9	145	[8]143	15	[8]21	1,631	[8]2,431
Memphis, TN [3]	25	22	22	21	342	327	29	48	1,335	2,287
Washington, DC [3][4]	45	[11]50	42	[11]48	651	[11]776	73	[11]139	1,761	[11]2,930
Boston, MA [3]	[7]28	[12]21	[7]25	[12]21	[7]444	[12]361	[7]35	[12]50	[7]1,398	[12]2,391
Seattle, WA	10	11	9	10	188	204	77	32	1,830	3,274
El Paso, TX	5	5	4	5	104	94	3	9	942	1,973
Cleveland, OH	10	9	9	8	160	158	13	21	1,460	2,521
New Orleans, LA	[13]13	[14]10	[13]13	[14]10	[13]225	[14]181	[13]11	[14]16	[13]919	[14]1,623
Nashville-Davidson, TN [3]	[15]18	18	[15]17	16	[15]374	352	[15]22	42	[15]1,295	2,510
Denver, CO	13	13	12	12	244	241	18	31	1,540	2,649
Austin, TX	8	10	7	10	199	206	10	21	1,515	2,186
Fort Worth, TX	[10]5	5	[10]5	5	[10]120	123	[10]5	11	[10]1,198	2,171
Oklahoma City, OK	5	5	4	4	104	103	6	11	1,323	2,430
Portland, OR	5	5	4	5	115	107	8	15	1,916	3,305
Kansas City, MO	7	6	7	6	145	144	9	15	1,368	2,390
Long Beach, CA	[7]5	7	[7]4	5	[7]122	130	[7]7	18	[7]1,678	3,413
Tucson, AZ	4	5	4	5	124	120	6	12	1,474	2,528
St. Louis, MO	13	[14]8	13	[14]7	280	[14]183	15	[14]17	1,279	[14]2,363
Charlotte, NC	4	5	4	5	125	130	5	11	1,290	2,399
Atlanta, GA	8	8	8	8	187	192	10	18	1,230	2,286
Virginia Beach, VA [3]	10	14	9	13	346	359	11	28	1,204	2,232
Albuquerque, NM	[10]4	7	[10]4	6	[10]119	164	[10]4	12	[10]1,135	2,040
Baton Rouge, LA	[13]4	6	[13]4	5	[13]106	142	[13]3	11	[13]908	2,235
Oakland, CA	4	5	4	4	109	115	7	15	2,011	3,948
Pittsburgh, PA	[13]6	[8]6	[13]6	[8]6	[13]135	[8]149	[13]6	[8]12	[13]1,116	[8]2,240
Sacramento, CA	3	4	3	4	119	115	6	11	1,762	3,021
Minneapolis, MN	6	[14]6	5	[14]6	136	[14]165	9	[14]15	1,821	[14]2,815
Tulsa, OK	[7]4	4	[7]4	4	[7]115	115	[7]5	11	[7]1,184	2,555
Honolulu, HI	9	9	9	9	117	110	12	24	1,401	2,600
Cincinnati, OH	7	[14]7	7	[14]6	174	[14]170	10	[14]16	1,527	[14]2,634
Miami, FL	4	6	4	4	118	109	6	15	1,408	3,771
Fresno, CA	3	3	3	3	115	89	4	8	1,607	2,944
Omaha, NE	3	3	3	2	92	77	5	8	1,684	3,051
Toledo, OH	4	3	3	3	96	89	6	9	1,758	2,847
Buffalo, NY [3]	14	13	13	13	348	397	18	31	1,475	2,596
Wichita, KS	3	[8]3	3	[8]3	111	[8]90	4	[8]5	1,327	[8]2,083
Santa Ana, CA	2	2	1	2	68	71	2	7	1,819	4,144
Mesa, AZ	1	2	1	2	89	83	2	7	1,592	2,898
Colorado Springs, CO	4	6	3	5	158	186	5	13	1,445	2,618
Tampa, FL	5	4	5	4	165	150	5	10	1,178	2,505
Newark, NJ [16]	12	[17]5	12	[17]5	374	[17]156	17	[17]8	1,387	[17]1,698
St. Paul, MN	4	4	3	3	125	130	6	10	1,734	3,265
Louisville, KY	6	5	6	4	186	152	7	9	1,358	2,180
Anaheim, CA	2	4	2	3	91	107	3	9	1,616	3,728
Birmingham, AL	4	4	4	4	128	138	5	8	1,333	2,243
Arlington, TX [3]	[10]1	2	[10]1	2	[10]63	69	[10]1	5	[10]1,180	2,538
Norfolk, VA [3]	11	10	10	10	380	343	12	22	1,222	2,268

[1] 1990 data not comparable with 1980 due to a change in how full-time equivalent is calculated. See text, section 9.   [2] 1980 based on enumerated resident population as of April 1, 1980; 1990 based on 1988 estimated resident population as of July 1.   [3] Includes city-operated elementary and secondary schools.   [4] Includes city-operated university or college.   [5] Fashion Institute of Technology data are for 1989.   [6] 1984 data.   [7] 1979 data.   [8] 1988 data.   [9] Prior to 1990, includes data for city operated college.   [10] 1978 data.   [11] Elementary and secondary school data are for 1989.   [12] Noneducation data are for 1986.   [13] 1977 data.   [14] 1989 data.   [15] Noneducation data are for 1979.   [16] Prior to 1983, city-operated elementary and secondary schools.   [17] 1983 data.

Source: U.S. Bureau of the Census, City Employment, series GE, No. 2, annual.

Federal Government Finances and Employment

This section presents statistics relating to the financial structure and the civilian employment of the Federal Government. The fiscal data cover taxes, other receipts, outlays, and debt. The principal sources of fiscal data are *The Budget of the United States Government* and related documents, published annually by the Office of Management and Budget (OMB), and the Department of the Treasury's *United States Government Annual Report* and its *Appendix.* Detailed data on tax returns and collections are published annually by the Internal Revenue Service. Personnel data relating to staffing and payrolls for the various public functions and agencies, to employee characteristics, and to civil service status; are published by the Office of Personnel Management and the Bureau of Labor Statistics (see p. 314). The primary source for data on public lands is *Public Land Statistics,* published annually by the Bureau of Land Management, Department of the Interior. Data on federally owned land and real property are collected by the General Services Administration and presented in its annual *Inventory Report on Real Property Owned by the United States Throughout the World.*

Budget concept.—Under the unified budget concept, all Federal monies are included in one comprehensive budget. These monies comprise both Federal funds and trust funds. Federal funds are derived mainly from taxes and borrowing and are not restricted by law to any specific government purpose. Trust funds, such as the Unemployment Trust Fund, collect certain taxes and other receipts for use in carrying out specific purposes or programs in accordance with the terms of the trust agreement or statute. Fund balances include both cash balances with Treasury and investments in U.S. securities. Part of the balance is obligated, part unobligated. Prior to 1985, the budget totals, under provisions of law, excluded some Federal activities—including the Federal Financing Bank, the Postal Service, the Synthetic Fuels Corporation, and the lending activities of

In Brief	
	1992
Gross Federal debt	$4 tril.
Net interest outlays	$199 bil.

the Rural Electrification Administration. The Balanced Budget and Emergency Deficit Control Act of 1985 (P.L.99-177) repealed the off-budget status of these entities and placed social security (Federal old-age and survivors insurance and the Federal disability insurance trust funds) off-budget. Though social security is now off-budget and, by law, excluded from coverage of the congressional budget resolutions, it continues to be a Federal program.

Receipts arising from the Government's sovereign powers are reported as governmental receipts; all other receipts, i.e., from business-type or market-oriented activities, are offset against outlays. Outlays are reported on a checks-issued (net) basis (i.e., outlays are recorded at the time the checks to pay bills are issued).

Debt concept.—For most of U.S. history, the total debt consisted of debt borrowed by the Treasury (i.e., public debt). The present debt series includes both public debt and agency debt. The *gross Federal debt* includes money borrowed by the Treasury and by various Federal agencies; it is the broadest generally used measure of the Federal debt. *Total public debt* is covered by a statutory debt limitation and includes only borrowing by the Treasury.

Treasury receipts and outlays.—All receipts of the Government, with a few exceptions, are deposited to the credit of the U.S. Treasury regardless of ultimate disposition. Under the Constitution, no money may be withdrawn from the Treasury unless appropriated by the Congress.

The day-to-day cash operations of the Federal Government clearing through the accounts of the U.S. Treasury are reported in the *Daily Treasury Statement.* Extensive detail on the public debt is published in the *Monthly Statement of the Public Debt of the United States.*

Budget receipts such as taxes, customs duties, and outlays represented by checks issued and cash payments made by disbursing officers as well as government agencies are reported in the *Daily Treasury Statement of Receipts and Outlays of the United States Government* and in the Treasury's *United States Government Annual Report* and its *Appendix.* These deposits in and payments from accounts maintained by Government agencies are on the same basis as the unified budget.

The quarterly *Treasury Bulletin* contains data on fiscal operations and related Treasury activities, including financial statements of Government corporations and other business-type activities.

Income tax returns and tax collections.—Tax data are compiled by the Internal Revenue Service of the Treasury Department. The *Annual Report of the Commissioner and Chief Counsel of the Internal Revenue Service* gives a detailed account of tax collections by kind of tax and by regions, districts, and States. The agency's annual *Statistics of Income* reports present detailed data from individual income tax returns and corporation income tax returns. The quarterly *Statistics of Income Bulletin* has, in general, replaced the supplemental *Statistics of Income* publications which presented data on such diverse subjects as tax-exempt organizations, unincorporated businesses, fiduciary income tax and estate tax returns, sales of capital assets by individuals, international income and taxes reported by corporations and individuals, and estate tax wealth.

Employment and payrolls.—The Office of Personnel Management collects employment and payroll data from all departments and agencies of the Federal Government, except the Central Intelligence Agency, the National Security Agency, and the Defense Intelligence Agency. Employment figures represent the number of persons who occupied civilian positions at the end of the report month shown and who are paid for personal services rendered for the Federal Government, regardless of the nature of appointment or method of payment.

Federal payrolls include all payments for personal services rendered during the report month and payments for accumulated annual leave of employees who separate from the service. Since most Federal employees are paid on a biweekly basis, the calendar month earnings are partially estimated on the basis of the number of work days in each month where payroll periods overlap.

Federal employment and payroll figures are published by the Office of Personnel Management in its *Federal Civilian Workforce Statistics—Employment and Trends.* It also publishes biennial employment data for minority groups, data on occupations of white- and blue-collar workers, and data on employment by geographic area; reports on salary and wage distribution of Federal employees are published annually. General schedule is primarily white-collar; wage system primarily blue-collar. Data on Federal employment are also issued by the Bureau of Labor Statistics in its *Monthly Labor Review* and in *Employment and Earnings* and by the Bureau of the Census in its annual *Public Employment.*

Public lands.—These data refer to transactions which involve the disposal, under public land laws, of Federal public lands to non-Federal owners. In general, original entries and selections are applications to secure title to public lands which have been accepted as properly filed (i.e., allowed). Some types of applications, however, are not reported until issuance of the final certificate, which passes equitable title to the land to the applicant. Applications are approved when full compliance with the requirements of the laws is shown and become final entries (perfected entries) upon issuance of a final certificate. Patents are Government deeds which pass legal title to the land to the applicant. Certifications are issued in lieu of patents in connection with certain State selections.

Historical statistics.—Tabular headnotes provide cross-references, where applicable, to *Historical Statistics of the United States, Colonial Times to 1970.* See Appendix IV.

Figure 10.1
The Government of the United States
(As of July 1, 1991)

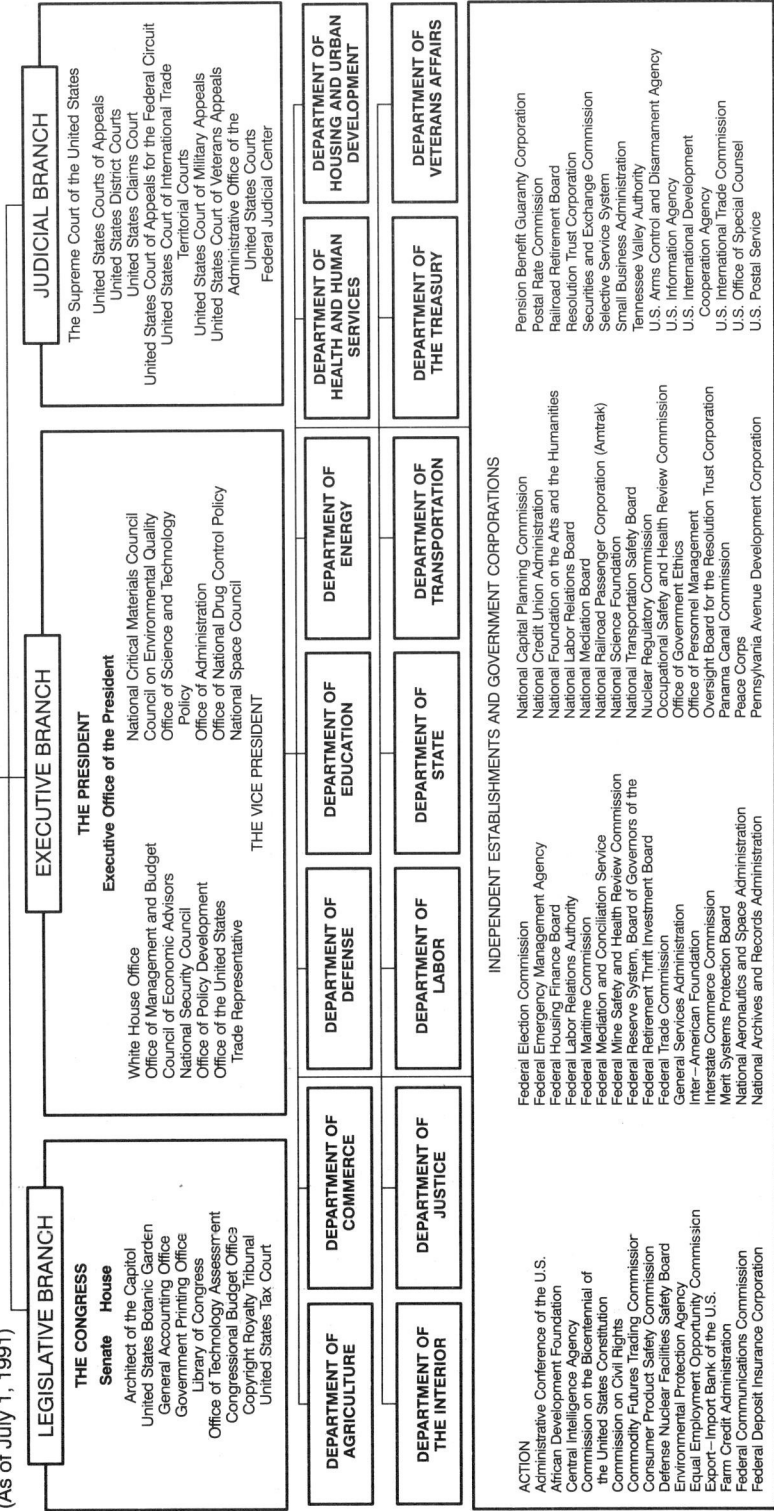

THE CONSTITUTION

LEGISLATIVE BRANCH

THE CONGRESS

Senate   House

Architect of the Capitol
United States Botanic Garden
General Accounting Office
Government Printing Office
Library of Congress
Office of Technology Assessment
Congressional Budget Office
Copyright Royalty Tribunal
United States Tax Court

EXECUTIVE BRANCH

THE PRESIDENT

Executive Office of the President

White House Office
Office of Management and Budget
Council of Economic Advisors
National Security Council
Office of Policy Development
Office of the United States
Trade Representative

National Critical Materials Council
Council on Environmental Quality
Office of Science and Technology
Policy
Office of Administration
Office of National Drug Control Policy
National Space Council

THE VICE PRESIDENT

JUDICIAL BRANCH

The Supreme Court of the United States
United States Courts of Appeals
United States District Courts
United States Claims Court
United States Court of Appeals for the Federal Circuit
United States Court of International Trade
Territorial Courts
United States Court of Military Appeals
United States Court of Veterans Appeals
Administrative Office of the
United States Courts
Federal Judicial Center

DEPARTMENT OF AGRICULTURE

DEPARTMENT OF THE INTERIOR

DEPARTMENT OF COMMERCE

DEPARTMENT OF JUSTICE

DEPARTMENT OF DEFENSE

DEPARTMENT OF LABOR

DEPARTMENT OF EDUCATION

DEPARTMENT OF STATE

DEPARTMENT OF ENERGY

DEPARTMENT OF TRANSPORTATION

DEPARTMENT OF HEALTH AND HUMAN SERVICES

DEPARTMENT OF THE TREASURY

DEPARTMENT OF HOUSING AND URBAN DEVELOPMENT

DEPARTMENT OF VETERANS AFFAIRS

INDEPENDENT ESTABLISHMENTS AND GOVERNMENT CORPORATIONS

ACTION
Administrative Conference of the U.S.
African Development Foundation
Central Intelligence Agency
Commission on the Bicentennial of
the United States Constitution
Commission on Civil Rights
Commodity Futures Trading Commission
Consumer Product Safety Commission
Defense Nuclear Facilities Safety Board
Environmental Protection Agency
Equal Employment Opportunity Commission
Export–Import Bank of the U.S.
Farm Credit Administration
Federal Communications Commission
Federal Deposit Insurance Corporation

Federal Election Commission
Federal Emergency Management Agency
Federal Housing Finance Board
Federal Labor Relations Authority
Federal Maritime Commission
Federal Mediation and Conciliation Service
Federal Mine Safety and Health Review Commission
Federal Reserve System, Board of Governors of the
Federal Retirement Thrift Investment Board
Federal Trade Commission
General Services Administration
Inter–American Foundation
Interstate Commerce Commission
Merit Systems Protection Board
National Aeronautics and Space Administration
National Archives and Records Administration

National Capital Planning Commission
National Credit Union Administration
National Foundation on the Arts and the Humanities
National Labor Relations Board
National Mediation Board
National Railroad Passenger Corporation (Amtrak)
National Science Foundation
National Transportation Safety Board
Nuclear Regulatory Commission
Occupational Safety and Health Review Commission
Office of Government Ethics
Office of Personnel Management
Oversight Board for the Resolution Trust Corporation
Panama Canal Commission
Peace Corps
Pennsylvania Avenue Development Corporation

Pension Benefit Guaranty Corporation
Postal Rate Commission
Railroad Retirement Board
Resolution Trust Corporation
Securities and Exchange Commission
Selective Service System
Small Business Administration
Tennessee Valley Authority
U.S. Arms Control and Disarmament Agency
U.S. Information Agency
U.S. International Development
Cooperation Agency
U.S. International Trade Commission
U.S. Office of Special Counsel
U.S. Postal Service

Source: Chart prepared by U.S. Bureau of the Census.

Figure 10.2
**Federal Budget—Receipts, Outlays and
Surplus or Deficit: 1970 to 1992**

Billions of dollars

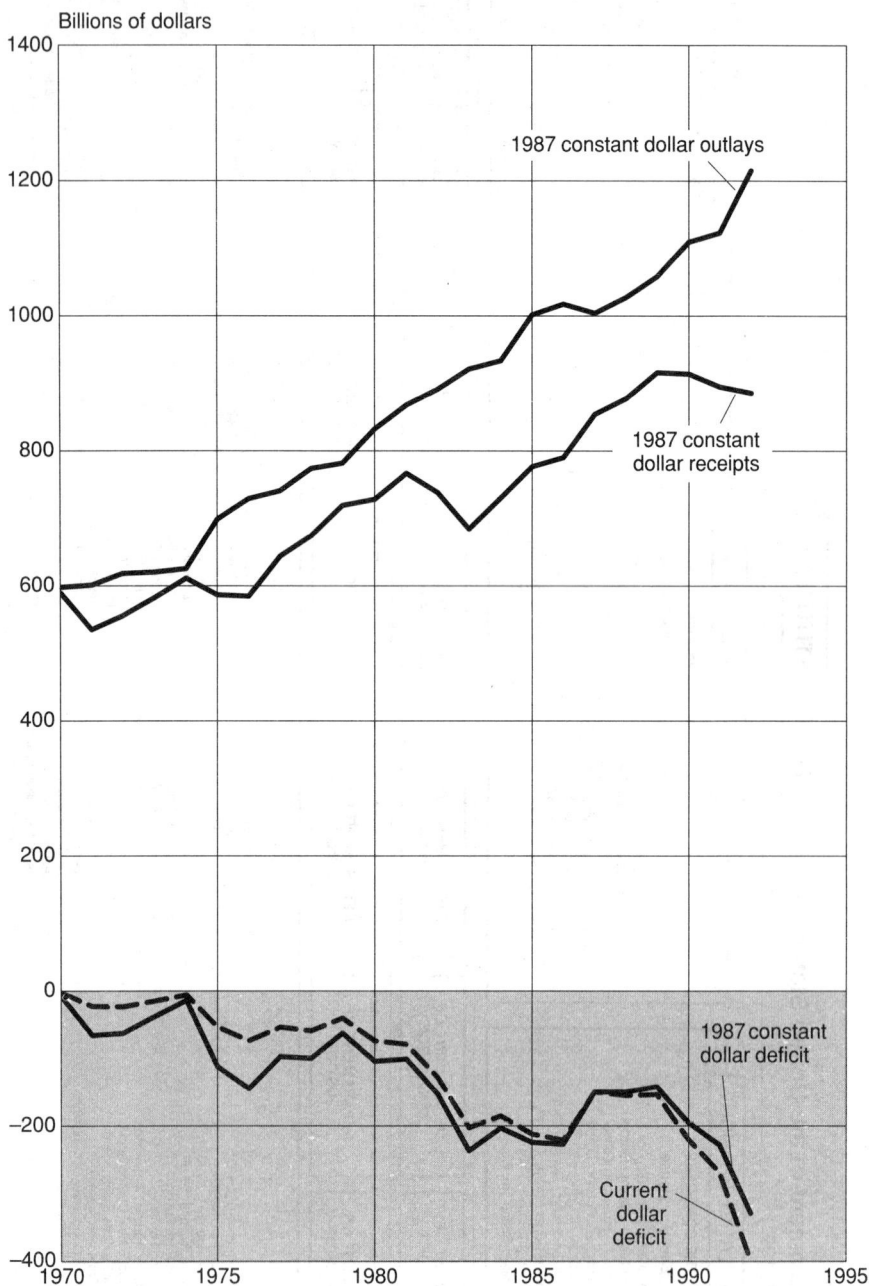

Note: Data for 1992 is projected.
Source: Chart prepared by U.S. Bureau of the Census. For data, see tables 491,494 and 496.

No. 491. Federal Budget—Summary: 1945 to 1992

[In millions of dollars, except percent. For fiscal years ending in year shown; see text, section 9. The Balanced Budget and Emergency Deficit Control Act of 1985 put all the previously off-budget Federal entities into the budget and moved Social Security off-budget. Minus sign (-) indicates deficit or decrease]

YEAR	Receipts	OUTLAYS[1] Total	Human resources	National defense	Percent of GNP[2]	Surplus or deficit (-)	GROSS FEDERAL DEBT[3] Total	Held by— Federal Gov't Account	Held by— The public	Federal Reserve System	As percent of GNP[2]	ANNUAL PERCENT CHANGE[4] Receipts	Outlays	Gross Federal debt[3]	Outlays, off-budget
1945	45,159	92,712	1,859	82,965	43.6	-48,720	260,123	24,941	235,182	21,792	122.5	3.2	1.5	27.3	0.1
1950	39,443	42,562	14,221	13,724	16.0	-4,702	256,853	37,830	219,023	18,331	96.3	0.1	9.6	1.7	0.5
1955	65,451	68,444	14,908	42,729	17.7	-4,091	274,366	47,751	226,616	23,607	71.0	-6.0	-3.4	1.3	4.0
1960	92,492	92,191	26,184	48,130	18.2	510	290,525	53,686	236,840	26,523	57.3	16.7	0.1	1.1	10.9
1965	116,817	118,228	36,576	50,620	17.6	-1,605	322,318	61,540	260,778	39,100	47.9	3.7	-0.3	2.0	16.5
1966	130,835	134,532	43,257	58,111	18.2	-3,068	328,498	64,784	263,714	42,169	44.5	12.0	13.8	1.9	19.7
1967	148,822	157,464	51,272	71,417	19.8	-12,620	340,445	73,819	266,626	46,719	42.8	13.7	17.0	3.6	20.4
1968	152,973	178,134	59,375	81,926	19.8	-27,742	368,685	79,140	289,545	52,230	43.4	2.8	13.1	8.3	22.3
1969	186,882	183,640	66,410	82,497	19.8	-507	365,769	87,661	278,108	54,095	39.4	22.2	3.1	-0.8	25.2
1970	192,807	195,649	75,349	81,692	19.8	-8,694	380,921	97,723	283,198	57,714	38.5	3.2	6.5	4.1	27.6
1971	187,139	210,172	91,901	78,872	19.9	-26,052	408,176	105,140	303,037	65,518	38.7	-2.9	7.4	7.2	32.8
1972	207,309	230,681	107,211	79,174	19.9	-26,052	435,936	113,559	322,377	71,426	37.8	10.8	9.8	6.8	36.9
1973	230,799	245,707	119,522	76,681	19.0	-15,403	466,291	125,381	340,910	75,181	36.4	11.3	6.5	7.0	45.6
1974	263,224	269,359	135,783	79,347	19.2	-7,971	483,893	140,194	343,699	80,648	34.2	14.0	9.6	3.8	52.1
1975	279,090	332,332	173,245	86,509	21.8	-55,260	541,925	147,225	394,700	84,993	35.6	6.0	23.4	12.0	60.4
1976	298,060	371,779	203,594	89,619	21.9	-70,499	628,970	151,566	477,404	94,714	37.0	6.8	11.9	16.1	69.6
1976[5]	81,232	95,973	52,065	22,269	21.4	-13,336	643,561	148,052	495,509	96,702	35.9	(X)	(X)	(X)	19.4
1977	355,559	409,203	221,895	97,241	21.2	-49,745	706,398	157,295	549,103	105,004	36.5	19.3	10.1	12.3	80.7
1978	399,561	458,729	242,329	104,495	21.1	-54,902	776,602	169,477	607,125	115,480	35.8	12.4	12.1	9.9	89.7
1979	463,302	503,464	267,574	116,342	20.6	-38,178	828,923	189,162	639,761	115,594	33.9	16.0	9.8	6.7	100.0
1980	517,112	590,920	313,374	133,995	22.1	-72,689	908,503	199,212	709,291	120,846	34.0	11.6	17.4	9.6	114.3
1981	599,272	678,249	362,022	157,513	22.7	-73,916	994,298	209,507	784,791	124,466	33.3	15.9	14.8	9.4	135.2
1982	617,766	745,755	388,681	185,309	23.8	-120,003	1,136,798	217,560	919,238	134,497	36.2	3.1	10.0	14.3	151.4
1983	600,562	808,380	426,003	209,903	24.3	-207,977	1,371,164	240,114	1,131,049	155,527	41.3	-2.8	8.4	20.6	147.1
1984	666,457	851,846	432,042	227,413	23.8	-185,586	1,564,110	264,159	1,299,951	155,122	42.4	11.0	5.4	14.1	165.8
1985	734,057	946,391	471,822	252,748	23.8	-221,623	1,816,974	317,612	1,499,362	169,806	46.0	10.1	11.1	16.2	176.8
1986	769,091	990,336	481,594	273,375	23.5	-237,898	2,120,082	383,919	1,736,163	190,855	50.7	4.6	4.6	16.7	183.5
1987	854,143	1,003,911	502,196	281,999	22.5	-169,257	2,345,578	457,444	1,888,134	212,040	53.0	11.1	1.4	10.6	193.8
1988	908,954	1,064,140	533,404	290,361	22.1	-193,897	2,600,760	550,507	2,050,252	229,218	54.4	6.4	6.0	10.3	202.7
1989	990,691	1,144,169	568,668	303,559	22.1	-206,132	2,867,538	677,214	2,190,324	220,088	55.9	9.0	7.5	10.9	210.9
1990	1,031,308	1,251,778	619,327	299,331	22.9	-220,470	3,206,347	795,906	2,410,441	234,410	58.7	4.1	9.4	11.8	225.1
1991	1,054,264	1,323,011	689,691	273,292	23.5	-268,746	3,598,993	911,751	2,687,242	258,591	64.0	2.2	5.7	12.2	241.7
1992, est.	1,075,706	1,475,439	776,900	307,304	25.2	-399,733	4,077,510	1,000,227	3,077,283	(NA)	69.5	2.0	11.5	13.3	251.5

NA Not available. X Not applicable. [1] Includes off-budget receipts, outlays, and interfund transactions. [2] Gross national product as of fiscal year; for calendar year GNP, see table 701. [3] See text, section 10 for discussion of debt concept. [4] Change from previous year. For explanation of average annual percent change, see Guide to Tabular Presentation. [5] Represents transition quarter, July-Sept.

Source: U.S. Office of Management and Budget, *Budget of the United States Government*, annual.

No. 492. Federal Receipts, by Source: 1980 to 1992

[In millions of dollars. For fiscal years ending in year shown; see text, section 9. Receipts reflect collections. Covers both Federal funds and trust funds (see text, section 10). Excludes government-sponsored but privately-owned corporations, Federal Reserve System, District of Columbia government, and money held in suspense as deposit funds. See *Historical Statistics, Colonial Times to 1970*, series Y 343-351, and Y 472-487 for related data]

SOURCE	1980	1985	1989	1990	1991	1992, est.	PERCENT DISTRIBUTION 1980	PERCENT DISTRIBUTION 1992, est.
Total receipts [1]	517,112	734,057	990,691	1,031,308	1,054,264	1,075,706	100.0	100.0
Individual income taxes	244,069	334,531	445,690	466,884	467,827	478,749	47.2	44.5
Corporation income taxes	64,600	61,331	103,291	93,507	98,086	89,031	12.5	8.3
Social insurance	157,803	265,163	359,416	380,047	396,016	410,863	30.5	38.2
Employment taxes and contributions	138,748	234,646	332,859	353,891	370,526	383,663	26.8	35.7
Old-age and survivors insurance	96,581	169,822	240,595	255,031	265,503	271,784	18.7	25.3
Disability insurance	16,628	16,348	23,071	26,625	28,382	29,138	3.2	2.7
Hospital insurance	23,217	44,871	65,396	68,556	72,842	79,007	4.5	7.3
Railroad retirement/ pension fund	2,323	2,213	2,391	2,292	2,371	2,329	0.4	0.2
Railroad social security equivalent account	-	1,391	1,407	1,387	1,428	1,405	-	0.1
Unemployment insurance	15,336	25,758	22,011	21,635	20,922	22,547	3.0	2.1
Other retirement contributions	3,719	4,759	4,546	4,522	4,568	4,653	0.7	0.4
Excise taxes	24,329	35,992	34,386	35,345	42,402	46,098	4.7	4.3
Federal funds	15,563	19,097	13,147	15,591	18,275	21,170	3.0	2.0
Alcohol	5,601	5,562	5,661	5,695	7,364	8,219	1.1	0.8
Tobacco	2,443	4,779	4,378	4,081	4,706	4,897	0.5	0.5
Windfall profits	6,934	6,348	-	-	-	-	1.3	-
Ozone depletion	-	-	-	360	562	662	-	0.1
Other taxes	585	261	317	2,460	2,549	4,343	0.1	0.4
Trust funds [1]	8,766	16,894	21,239	19,754	24,127	24,928	1.7	2.3
Highways	6,620	13,015	15,628	13,867	16,979	17,387	1.3	1.6
Airport and airway	1,874	2,851	3,664	3,700	4,910	5,193	0.4	0.5
Black lung disability	272	581	563	665	652	627	0.1	0.1
Hazardous substance response	-	273	883	818	810	825	-	0.1
Aquatic resources	-	126	187	218	260	278	-	-
Leaking underground storage	-	-	168	122	123	145	-	-
Vaccine injury compensations	-	-	99	159	81	120	-	-
Oil spill liability	-	-	-	143	254	283	-	-
Estate and gift taxes	6,389	6,422	8,745	11,500	11,138	12,063	1.2	1.1
Customs duties	7,174	12,079	16,334	16,707	15,949	17,260	1.4	1.6
Federal Reserve deposits	11,767	17,059	19,604	24,319	19,158	18,507	2.3	1.7

- Represents or rounds to zero.   [1] Totals reflect interfund and intragovernmental transactions and/or other functions, not shown separately.

Source: U.S. Office of Management and Budget, *Budget of the United States Government*, annual.

No. 493. Federal Trust Fund Receipts, Outlays, and Balances: 1989 to 1992

[In billions of dollars. For fiscal ending in yeay shown; see text section 9. Receipts deposited. Outlays on a checks-issued basis, less refunds collected. Balances: That which have not been spent. See text, section 10 for discussion of the budget concept and trust funds]

DESCRIPTION	INCOME 1989	INCOME 1991	INCOME 1992, est.	OUTLAYS 1989	OUTLAYS 1991	OUTLAYS 1992, est.	BALANCES [1] 1989	BALANCES [1] 1991	BALANCES [1] 1992, est.
Total [2]	509.8	631.1	658.9	386.3	518.8	560.3	690.9	896.8	995.3
Airport and airway trust fund	4.7	6.2	6.5	2.9	5.3	5.8	22.5	15.3	16.0
Federal employees retirement funds	49.6	57.2	60.1	29.6	33.7	34.5	243.2	269.0	294.7
Federal old-age, survivors and disablity insurance trust funds	(NA)	325.9	336.9	(NA)	272.4	286.7	(NA)	268.4	318.6
Foreign military sales trust fund	8.2	12.5	11.4	8.4	11.5	11.3	4.7	6.8	6.9
Health insurance trust funds	118.9	133.2	146.3	96.6	117.7	131.8	94.7	125.6	140.0
Highway trust funds	16.9	18.5	19.0	14.5	15.7	17.4	16.7	20.7	22.2
Military retirement trust funds	34.0	36.0	36.5	20.2	23.1	24.3	65.2	90.5	102.7
Railroad retirement trust funds	10.1	11.3	11.2	9.4	10.1	10.5	8.6	10.4	11.2
Unemployment trust funds	25.5	25.5	26.3	18.7	28.4	35.7	45.1	47.8	38.4
Veterans life insurance trust funds	1.4	1.5	1.5	1.1	1.2	1.3	12.1	12.7	12.9
Other trust funds [3]	5.0	6.8	6.5	1.9	3.1	4.5	21.4	29.6	31.6

NA Not available.   [1] Balances available on a çash basis (rather than an authorization basis) at the end of the year. Balances are primarily invested in Federal debt securities.   [2] Includes funds not shown separately.   [3] Outlays include the Federal Deposit Insurance Corporation (FDIC) through August 8, 1989. Effective August 9, 1989, the permanent insurance fund of the FDIC was classified under law as a Federal fund.

Source: U.S. Office of Management and Budget, *Budget of the United States Government*, annual.

No. 494. Federal Budget Outlays—Defense, Human and Physical Resources, and Net Interest Payments: 1940 to 1992

[In millions of dollars.]

YEAR	Outlays, total	National defense	HUMAN RESOURCES — Total	Social Security	Income security	Medical care	Health	Education[1]	Veterans benefits	PHYSICAL RESOURCES — Total[2]	Transportation	Commerce and housing	Net interest	Other	Undistributed
1940	9,468	1,660	4,139	28	1,514	(NA)	55	1,972	570	2,312	392	550	899	775	-317
1945	92,712	82,965	1,859	267	1,137	(NA)	211	134	110	1,747	3,654	-2,630	3,112	4,418	-1,389
1950	42,562	13,724	14,221	781	4,097	(NA)	268	241	8,834	3,667	967	1,035	4,812	7,955	-1,817
1955	68,444	42,729	14,908	4,427	5,071	(NA)	291	445	4,675	2,732	1,246	92	4,850	6,718	-3,493
1960	92,191	48,130	26,184	11,602	7,378	(NA)	795	968	5,441	7,991	4,126	1,618	6,947	7,760	-4,820
1964	118,528	54,757	35,294	16,620	9,641	(NA)	1,788	1,563	5,682	9,528	5,242	1,157	8,199	16,458	-5,708
1965	118,228	50,620	36,576	17,460	9,455	(NA)	1,791	2,146	5,723	11,264	5,730	3,245	8,591	17,086	-5,908
1966	134,532	58,111	43,257	20,694	9,662	64	2,543	4,372	5,923	13,410	5,936	3,979	9,386	16,911	-6,542
1967	157,464	71,417	51,212	21,725	10,248	2,748	3,351	6,458	6,743	14,674	6,316	4,280	10,268	17,126	-7,294
1968	178,134	81,926	59,375	23,854	11,798	4,649	4,390	7,642	7,042	16,002	6,526	-119	11,090	17,786	-8,045
1969	183,640	82,497	66,410	27,298	13,066	5,695	5,126	7,548	7,642	11,869	7,008	2,112	12,699	18,151	-7,986
1970	195,649	81,692	75,349	30,270	15,645	6,213	5,907	8,634	8,679	15,574	8,052	2,366	14,380	17,286	-8,632
1971	210,172	78,872	91,901	35,872	22,936	6,622	6,843	9,849	9,778	18,286	9,066	2,222	14,841	16,379	-10,107
1972	230,681	79,174	107,211	40,157	27,638	7,479	8,674	12,529	10,732	19,574	9,172	931	15,478	18,828	-9,583
1973	245,707	76,681	119,522	49,090	28,264	8,052	9,356	12,745	12,015	20,614	10,918	4,705	17,349	24,950	-13,409
1974	269,359	79,347	135,783	55,867	33,699	9,639	10,733	12,457	13,388	25,106	13,739	9,947	21,449	24,423	-16,749
1975	332,332	86,509	173,245	64,658	50,160	12,875	12,930	16,022	16,599	35,449	13,739	7,619	23,244	27,487	-13,602
1976	371,792	89,619	203,594	73,899	60,784	15,834	15,734	18,910	18,433	39,188	13,739	931	26,727	27,050	-14,386
1976[3]	95,975	22,269	52,065	19,763	14,981	4,264	3,924	5,169	3,963	9,512	3,358	3,093	6,949	9,388	-14,206
1977	409,218	97,241	221,895	85,061	61,044	19,345	17,302	21,104	18,038	40,746	14,829	6,254	29,901	34,315	-14,879
1978	458,746	104,495	242,329	93,861	61,488	26,768	18,524	26,710	18,978	52,591	15,521	4,686	35,458	39,594	-15,720
1979	503,485	116,342	267,574	104,073	66,359	26,495	20,494	30,223	19,931	54,013	17,532	9,390	42,636	40,396	-17,476
1980	590,947	133,995	313,374	118,547	86,540	32,090	23,169	31,843	21,185	65,985	21,329	8,206	52,538	44,996	-19,942
1981	678,249	157,513	362,022	139,584	99,723	39,149	26,866	33,709	22,991	70,886	23,379	6,256	68,774	47,095	-28,041
1982	745,755	185,309	388,681	155,964	107,717	46,567	27,445	27,029	23,958	61,752	20,625	6,681	85,044	51,069	-26,099
1983	808,380	209,903	426,003	170,724	122,598	52,588	28,641	26,606	24,846	57,600	21,334	6,917	89,828	59,023	-33,976
1984	851,846	227,413	432,042	178,223	112,668	57,540	30,417	27,579	25,614	57,938	23,669	4,229	111,123	55,287	-31,957
1985	946,391	252,748	471,822	188,623	128,200	65,822	33,542	29,342	26,352	56,789	25,838	4,890	129,504	68,227	-32,698
1986	990,336	273,375	481,594	198,757	119,796	70,164	35,936	30,585	26,356	58,614	28,117	6,182	136,047	73,713	-33,007
1987	1,003,911	281,999	502,196	207,353	123,250	75,120	39,967	29,724	26,782	54,932	26,222	18,815	138,652	62,588	-36,455
1988	1,064,140	290,361	533,404	219,341	129,332	78,878	44,487	31,938	29,428	68,283	27,272	29,211	151,838	57,822	-36,967
1989	1,144,169	303,559	568,668	232,542	136,031	84,964	48,390	36,674	30,066	82,065	27,608	67,142	169,266	57,822	-37,212
1990	1,251,778	299,331	619,327	248,623	147,277	89,102	57,716	38,497	29,112	124,619	29,485	75,639	184,221	60,896	-36,615
1991	1,323,011	273,292	689,691	269,015	170,846	104,489	71,183	42,809	31,349	133,762	31,099	87,149	194,541	71,081	-39,356
1992, est.	1,475,439	307,304	776,900	286,732	198,093	118,638	94,593	45,025	33,819	152,969	34,031	(NA)	198,820	78,207	-38,761

NA Not available. [1] Also includes training, employment, and social services. [2] Includes outlays not shown separately. [3] Transition quarter, July to September.

Source: U. S. Office of Management and Budget, *Budget of the United States Government*, annual.

No. 495. Federal Outlays, by Detailed Function: 1980 to 1992

[In millions of dollars. For fiscal years ending in year shown; outlays stated in terms of checks issued or cash payments. See headnote, table 492]

FUNCTION	1980	1985	1989	1990	1991	1992, est.	PERCENT DISTRIBUTION 1980	PERCENT DISTRIBUTION 1992, est.
Total outlays	590,920	946,316	1,144,069	1,251,778	1,323,011	1,475,439	100.00	100.00
On-budget.	476,591	769,509	933,258	1,026,713	1,081,324	1,223,909	80.65	82.95
Off-budget.	114,329	176,807	210,911	225,065	241,687	251,530	19.35	17.05
National defense	133,995	252,748	303,559	299,331	273,292	307,304	22.68	20.83
Dept. of Defense—Military.	130,912	245,154	294,880	289,755	262,389	294,039	22.15	19.93
Military personnel	40,897	67,842	80,676	75,622	83,439	79,289	6.92	5.37
Operation and maintenance	44,788	72,371	87,001	88,340	101,769	97,828	7.58	6.63
Procurement	29,021	70,381	81,620	80,972	82,028	73,952	4.91	5.01
R and D, test, and evaluation	13,127	27,103	37,002	37,458	34,589	36,145	2.22	2.45
Military construction	2,450	4,260	5,275	5,080	3,497	4,541	0.41	0.31
Family housing.	1,680	2,642	3,257	3,501	3,296	3,404	0.28	0.23
Other	−1,050	553	50	−1,218	−46,229	−521	−0.18	−0.04
Atomic energy defense activities	2,878	7,098	8,119	8,988	10,004	11,685	0.49	0.79
Defense related activities	206	495	560	587	899	980	0.03	0.07
International affairs	12,714	16,176	9,573	13,764	15,851	17,811	2.15	1.21
International development and humanitarian assistance.	3,626	5,409	4,836	5,498	5,141	6,154	0.61	0.42
Conduct of foreign affairs	1,366	2,043	2,886	3,050	3,282	3,560	0.23	0.24
Foreign information and exchange activities	534	805	1,106	1,103	1,253	1,343	0.09	0.09
International financial programs activities	2,425	−1,471	−722	−4,539	−3,648	−1,029	-	−0
International security assistance.	4,763	9,391	1,467	8,652	9,823	7,783	0.81	0.53
Income security	86,540	128,200	136,031	147,277	170,846	198,093	14.64	13.43
General retirement and disability insurance	5,083	5,617	5,650	5,148	4,945	5,538	0.86	0.38
Federal employee retirement and disability	26,594	38,591	49,151	51,981	56,106	57,718	4.50	3.91
Housing assistance	5,632	25,263	14,715	15,891	17,200	19,438	0.95	1.32
Food and nutrition assistance	14,016	18,540	21,192	23,964	28,481	33,561	2.37	2.27
Other income security.	17,163	22,715	29,706	31,404	37,030	45,145	2.90	3.06
Unemployment compensation	18,051	17,475	15,616	18,889	27,084	36,693	3.05	2.49
Health	23,169	33,542	48,390	57,716	71,183	94,593	3.92	6.41
Health care services.	18,003	26,984	39,164	47,642	60,723	82,810	3.05	5.61
Health research.	3,442	4,908	7,325	8,611	8,899	10,058	0.58	0.68
Consumer and occupational health and safety	1,006	1,182	1,356	1,462	1,560	1,724	0.17	0.12
Medicare.	32,090	65,822	84,964	98,102	104,489	118,638	5.43	8.04
Social Security	118,547	188,623	232,542	248,623	269,015	286,732	20.06	19.43
On-budget	675	5,189	5,069	3,625	2,619	6,078	0.11	0.41
Off-budget	117,872	183,434	227,473	244,998	266,395	280,654	19.95	0.00
Veterans benefits and services	21,185	26,292	30,066	29,112	31,349	33,819	3.59	2.29
Income security for veterans	11,688	14,714	16,544	15,241	16,961	17,193	1.98	1.17
Educ., training, and rehab	2,342	1,059	459	278	427	696	0.40	0.05
Hospital and medical care.	6,515	9,547	11,343	12,134	12,889	13,727	1.10	0.93
Housing for veterans	(Z)	214	878	517	85	1,153	0.00	0.08
Other.	665	758	843	943	987	1,050	0.11	0.07
Education, training, employment, and social services.	31,843	29,342	36,674	38,497	42,809	45,025	5.39	3.05
Elementary, secondary, and vocational education.	6,893	7,598	9,150	9,918	11,372	13,052	1.17	0.88
Higher education	6,723	8,156	10,584	11,107	11,961	11,140	1.14	0.76
Research and general educ. aids	1,212	1,229	1,509	1,577	1,773	1,966	0.21	0.13
Training and employment	10,345	4,972	5,292	5,361	5,388	5,792	1.75	0.39
Other labor services.	551	678	786	810	788	871	0.09	0.06
Social services	6,119	6,710	9,354	9,723	11,526	12,204	1.04	0.83

See footnotes at end of table.

No. 495. Federal Outlays, by Detailed Function: 1980 to 1992—Continued

[In millions of dollars. See headnote, table 492]

SOURCE OR FUNCTION	1980	1985	1989	1990	1991	1992, est.	PERCENT DISTRIBUTION	
							1980	1992, est.
Commerce and housing credit........	9,390	4,229	29,211	67,142	75,639	87,149	1.59	5.91
Mortgage credit................	5,887	3,054	4,978	3,845	5,362	3,201	1.00	0.22
Postal Service.................	1,246	1,351	127	2,116	1,828	1,335	0.21	0.09
Deposit insurance	−285	−2,198	21,996	58,081	66,394	80,185	−0.05	5.43
Other commerce	2,542	2,022	2,109	3,100	2,054	2,427	0.43	0.16
Transportation	21,329	25,838	27,608	29,485	31,099	34,031	3.61	2.31
Ground transportation...........	15,274	17,606	17,946	18,954	19,545	21,086	2.58	1.43
Air transportation..............	3,723	4,895	6,622	7,234	8,184	9,042	0.63	0.61
Water transportation...........	2,229	3,201	2,916	3,151	3,148	3,633	0.38	0.25
Other transportation...........	104	137	124	146	223	270	0.02	0.02
Natural resources and environment	13,858	13,357	16,182	17,067	18,552	20,231	2.35	1.37
Water resources	4,223	4,122	4,271	4,401	4,366	4,729	0.71	0.32
Conservation and land management..	1,043	1,481	3,324	3,553	4,047	4,374	0.18	0.30
Recreational resources..........	1,677	1,621	1,817	1,876	2,137	2,474	0.28	0.17
Pollution control and abatement.....	5,510	4,465	4,878	5,156	5,853	6,131	0.93	0.42
Other natural resources	1,405	1,668	1,890	2,080	2,148	2,522	0.24	0.17
Energy	10,156	5,685	3,702	2,428	1,662	4,026	1.72	0.27
Supply	8,367	2,615	2,226	1,062	1,170	3,000	1.42	0.20
Conservation.................	569	491	333	365	386	463	0.10	0.03
Emergency preparedness	342	1,838	621	442	−235	336	0.06	0.02
Information, policy, and regs	878	740	521	559	340	226	0.15	0.02
Community/regional develop	11,252	7,680	5,362	8,498	6,811	7,533	1.90	0.51
Community development..........	4,907	4,598	3,693	3,530	3,543	3,911	0.83	0.27
Area and regional development	4,303	3,117	1,894	2,868	2,743	3,144	0.73	0.21
Disaster relief and insurance	2,043	(Z)	−226	2,100	525	478	0.35	0.03
Agriculture....................	8,839	25,565	16,919	11,958	15,183	17,219	1.50	1.17
Farm income stabilization	7,441	23,751	14,817	9,761	12,924	14,670	1.26	0.99
Research and services	1,398	1,813	2,102	2,197	2,259	2,550	0.24	0.17
Net interest	52,538	129,504	169,266	184,221	194,541	198,820	8.89	13.48
On-budget	*54,877*	*133,622*	*180,661*	*200,212*	*214,763*	*222,673*	*9.29*	*15.09*
Off-budget	*−2,339*	*−4,118*	*−11,395*	*−15,991*	*−20,222*	*−23,853*	*0.39*	*−1.62*
Interest on the public debt.........	74,808	178,898	240,963	264,820	286,004	292,992	12.66	19.86
Other interest	−10,224	−23,438	−19,755	−18,191	−20,266	−16,948	−1.73	−1.15
General science, space, and technology.	5,832	8,627	12,838	14,444	16,111	16,373	0.99	1.11
Gen. science and basic research	1,381	2,019	2,642	2,835	3,154	3,612	0.23	0.24
General government	13,028	11,588	9,017	10,734	11,661	12,838	2.20	0.87
Legislative functions.............	1,038	1,355	1,652	1,763	1,916	2,230	0.18	0.15
Exec. direction and manag't.	97	113	129	160	190	197	0.02	0.01
Central fiscal operations	2,612	3,492	5,517	6,004	6,097	6,790	0.44	0.46
General property and records management	327	96	−396	31	657	704	0.06	0.05
General purpose fiscal assistance....	8,582	6,353	2,061	2,161	2,100	2,158	1.45	0.15
Other general government.	569	521	814	800	1,280	1,505	0.10	0.10
Deductions, offsetting receipts	−351	−506	−893	−361	−718	−914	−0.06	−0.06
Administration of justice............	4,584	6,270	9,474	9,995	12,276	14,061	0.78	0.95
Federal law enforcement.	2,239	3,520	4,719	4,648	5,661	6,422	0.38	0.44
Federal litigative and judicial	1,347	2,064	3,255	3,579	4,352	5,029	0.23	0.34
Federal correctional activities.......	342	537	1,044	1,291	1,600	1,901	0.06	0.13
Criminal justice assistance.	656	150	455	477	663	709	0.11	0.05
Undistributed offsetting receipts	*−19,942*	*−32,698*	*−37,212*	*−36,615*	*−39,356*	*−38,761*	*−3.37*	*−2.63*
On-budget	*−18,738*	*−30,189*	*−32,354*	*−31,048*	*−33,553*	*−32,665*	*−3.17*	*−2.21*
Off-budget	*−1,204*	*−2,509*	*−4,858*	*−5,567*	*−5,804*	*−6,095*	*−0.20*	*−0.41*
Employer share, employee retirement .	*−15,842*	*−27,157*	*−34,283*	*−33,611*	*−36,206*	*−36,478*	*−2.68*	*−2.47*
Rents and royalties [1]	*−4,101*	*−5,542*	*−2,929*	*−3,004*	*−3,150*	*−2,282*	*−0.69*	*−0.15*

- Represents zero.   Z Less than $500,000.   [1] On Outer Continental Shelf.

Source: U.S. Office of Management and Budget, *Budget of the United States Government,* annual.

No. 496. Federal Budget Outlays in Constant (1987) Dollars: 1940 to 1992

[Dollar amounts in billions of dollars. For fiscal years ending in year shown; see text, section 9. Given the inherent imprecision in deflating outlays, the in constant dollars present a reasonable perspective—not precision. The deflators and the categories that are deflated are as comparable over time as feasible. See headnote, table 491. Minus sign (-) indicates decrease]

OUTLAYS	1940	1950	1960	1970	1980	1985	1986	1987	1988	1989	1990	1991	1992, est.
Outlays, total	**95.8**	**250.1**	**389.5**	**597.8**	**832.1**	**1,001.3**	**1,017.3**	**1,003.9**	**1,027.1**	**1,057.9**	**1,109.4**	**1,122.9**	**1,214.7**
National defense	18.1	94.6	217.9	264.4	187.1	261.3	276.4	282.0	283.3	285.5	271.1	238.5	258.8
Nondefense outlays	77.8	155.5	171.7	333.5	645.0	740.1	740.8	721.9	743.8	772.7	838.3	884.3	955.8
Payments for individuals	14.0	63.0	87.8	183.8	394.9	458.6	467.5	471.5	480.0	490.8	510.6	542.6	593.1
Direct payments	11.5	57.3	78.8	159.0	348.6	405.6	411.4	413.5	420.2	429.2	443.2	467.6	500.1
Grants to State and local gov't's	2.5	5.8	9.0	24.7	46.3	53.0	56.2	57.8	59.9	61.7	67.4	75.0	93.0
Other grants	6.2	6.7	20.1	48.7	81.2	59.8	59.6	50.5	50.8	50.3	52.0	53.8	56.7
Net interest	8.2	24.2	26.6	41.6	74.4	137.3	140.1	138.7	146.5	156.4	163.5	166.1	164.7
All other	53.0	74.2	60.4	87.0	122.9	118.7	107.6	97.9	102.4	109.4	144.5	155.0	173.1
Undistributed offsetting receipts	-3.7	-12.5	-23.1	-29.0	-28.5	-34.3	-34.0	-36.5	-35.8	-34.3	-32.4	-33.2	-31.7
PERCENT OF GDP													
Outlays, total	9.9	16.0	18.2	19.9	22.3	23.8	23.5	22.5	22.1	22.1	22.9	23.5	25.2
National defense	1.7	5.2	9.5	8.3	5.1	6.4	6.5	6.3	6.0	5.5	5.5	4.9	5.2
Nondefense outlays	8.2	10.9	8.7	11.6	17.3	17.5	17.0	16.2	16.1	16.3	17.4	18.7	19.9
Payments for individuals	1.7	5.1	4.8	6.6	10.5	10.8	10.7	10.6	10.4	10.4	10.7	11.6	12.5
Direct payments	1.4	4.7	4.3	5.7	9.3	9.5	9.4	9.3	9.1	9.1	9.3	10.0	10.5
Grants to State and local gov't's	0.3	0.5	0.5	0.9	1.2	1.2	1.3	1.3	1.3	1.3	1.4	1.6	2.0
Other grants	0.6	0.4	0.9	1.6	2.2	1.4	1.4	1.1	1.1	1.1	1.1	1.1	1.1
Net interest	0.9	1.8	1.4	1.5	2.0	3.3	3.2	3.1	3.2	3.3	3.4	3.5	3.4
All other	5.0	4.2	2.6	2.9	3.3	2.8	2.5	2.2	2.2	2.3	3.0	3.2	3.6
Undistributed offsetting receipts	-0.3	-0.7	-1.0	-0.9	-0.8	-0.8	-0.8	-0.8	-0.8	-0.7	-0.7	-0.7	-0.7
PERCENT OF OUTLAYS													
Outlays, total	100.0	100.0	100.0	100.0	100.0	100.0	100.0	100.0	100.0	100.0	100.0	100.0	100.0
National defense	17.5	32.2	52.2	41.8	22.7	26.7	27.6	28.1	27.3	26.5	23.9	20.7	20.8
Nondefense outlays	82.5	67.8	47.8	58.2	77.3	73.3	72.4	71.9	72.7	73.5	76.1	79.3	79.2
Payments for individuals	17.5	32.1	26.2	33.1	47.1	45.2	45.6	46.9	47.0	46.8	46.7	49.2	49.5
Direct payments	14.4	29.2	23.5	28.7	41.6	39.9	40.1	41.2	41.2	41.0	40.5	42.4	41.8
Grants to State and local gov't's	3.1	2.3	2.7	4.5	5.5	5.2	5.5	5.8	5.9	5.9	6.2	6.8	7.8
Other grants	6.1	2.3	4.9	7.4	9.9	6.0	5.9	5.0	5.0	4.8	4.6	4.7	4.6
Net interest	9.5	11.3	7.5	7.4	8.9	13.7	13.7	13.8	14.3	14.8	14.7	14.7	13.5
All other	52.8	26.3	15.5	14.4	14.8	11.9	10.6	9.8	10.0	10.3	13.0	13.8	14.2
Undistributed offsetting receipts	-3.4	-4.3	-5.2	-4.4	-3.4	-3.5	-3.3	-3.6	-3.5	-3.3	-2.9	-3.0	-2.6

Source: U.S. Office of Management and Budget, *Budget of the United States Government*, annual.

No. 497. Revenue Losses—Estimates for Selected "Tax Expenditures," by Function: 1989 to 1993

[In millions of dollars. For years ending, Sept. 30, except as noted. Tax expenditures are defined as *revenue losses attributable to provisions of the Federal tax laws which allow a special exclusion, exemption, or deduction from gross income or which provide a special credit, a preferential rate of tax, or a deferral of liability*. Represents tax expenditures of **$1 billion or more in** 1993]

DESCRIPTION	1989	1990	1991	1992	1993, est.
National defense:					
Exclusion of benefits and allowances to Armed Forces personnel	1,900	1,965	2,345	2,400	2,460
International affairs:					
Exclusion of income earned abroad by United States citizens . .	1,155	1,205	2,480	2,630	2,810
Inventory property sales source rules exception	2,000	2,200	4,230	4,440	4,660
Natural resources and environment:					
Exclusion of interest on state and local IDB [1]					
for pollution control and sewage and waste disposal facilities .	1,575	1,515	2,000	1,985	1,985
Commerce and housing credit:					
Exclusion of interest on—					
Small issue IDB [1]	2,600	2,445	1,725	1,680	1,615
Life insurance savings.	6,230	6,920	9,455	9,790	10,265
State and local housing bonds for owner-occupied housing . .	1,895	1,775	2,730	2,745	2,575
State and local debt for rental housing.	1,220	1,150	1,505	1,490	1,475
Exclusion of capital gains on home sales for persons					
age 55 and over	3,190	3,230	4,255	4,280	4,395
Deductibility of—					
Mortgage interest on owner-occupied homes	34,190	39,785	40,690	42,000	42,900
Property tax on owner-occupied homes	10,065	11,240	10,735	11,610	12,605
Step-up basis of capital gains at death	(NA)	(NA)	32,750	36,025	46,120
Investment credit, other than ESOP [2]	6,655	4,520	(NA)	(NA)	(NA)
Accelerated depreciation of machinery and equip. [3]	28,805	23,525	18,725	17,205	19,505
Reduced rates on the first $100,000 of corporate incomes:					
Pre-1983 budget method	2,875	3,235	4,310	4,450	4,820
Exception from passive loss rules for $25,000 rental losses. .	4,210	5,475	7,635	7,995	8,315
Education:					
Deductibility of—					
Charitable contributions (education).	1,570	1,720	1,805	1,920	2,030
Other charitable contributions other than education	10,590	11,730	12,285	13,135	14,045
Credit for child and dependent care expenses.	3,710	3,895	3,265	3,605	3,605
Health:					
Exclusion of employer contrib. for medical insurance					
premiums and medical care.	26,550	29,820	45,500	49,495	54,150
Deductibility of medical expenses.	2,690	2,860	3,025	3,170	3,365
Exclusion of interest on State and local debt for private					
nonprofit health facilities.	2,430	2,370	1,650	1,730	1,830
Deductibility of charitable contributions (health)	1,415	1,555	1,635	1,750	1,875
Social Security and medicare:					
Exclusion of Social Security benefits:					
Disability insurance benefits	1,105	1,145	1,320	1,440	1,555
OASI benefits for retired workers	14,840	15,680	1,695	18,140	19,375
Benefits for dependents and survivors	2,940	3,110	3,170	3,355	3,560
Income security:					
Exclusion of workmen's compensation benefits	2,760	2,980	3,230	3,505	3,720
Net exclusion of pension contributions and earnings:					
Employer plans	42,805	45,085	60,715	64,450	68,310
Individual Retirement Accounts.	5,440	5,960	8,290	7,720	7,160
Keoghs	1,325	1,470	3,520	3,615	3,750
Exclusion of other employee benefits:					
Premiums on group term life insurance	2,460	2,565	3,685	3,880	4,000
Additional deduction for the elderly [4]	1,260	1,505	1,680	1,840	2,000
Veterans benefits and services:					
Exclusion of veterans disability compensation	1,490	1,500	1,655	1,705	1,760
General purpose fiscal assistance:					
Exclusion of interest on public purpose State and local debt. . .	11,110	11,290	13,925	14,800	15,585
Deductibility of nonbusiness State and local taxes other					
than on owner-occupied homes	18,495	20,290	20,940	22,075	23,810
Tax credit for corporations receiving income from doing					
business in United States possessions	1,910	2,100	3,180	3,485	3,815

NA Not available. [1] Industrial development bonds. [2] Employee stock ownership plans. Includes investment credit for rehabilitation of structures, energy property, and reforestation expenditures. [3] Pre-1983 budget method. [4] Data on calendar year basis.

Source: U.S. Office of Management and Budget, *Budget of the United States Government,* annual.

No. 498. Federal Budget Outlays, by Agency: 1980 to 1992

[In billions of dollars. For fiscal year ending in year shown; see text, section 9]

DEPARTMENT OR OTHER UNIT	1980	1985	1986	1987	1988	1989	1990	1991	1992, est.
Total	590.9	946.3	990.3	1,003.9	1,064.1	1,144.2	1,251.8	1,323.0	1,475.4
Legislative branch	1.2	1.6	1.7	1.8	1.9	2.1	2.2	2.3	2.8
The Judiciary.	0.6	1.0	1.1	1.2	1.3	1.5	1.6	2.0	2.4
Funds appropriated to President [1]. . . .	8.5	11.9	11.0	10.4	7.3	4.3	10.1	11.7	11.5
Departments:									
Agriculture	34.8	55.5	58.7	49.6	44.0	48.3	46.0	54.1	61.8
Commerce	3.1	2.1	2.1	2.1	2.3	2.6	3.7	2.6	2.9
Defense	146.1	263.9	285.7	294.7	304.0	318.3	314.7	288.5	322.3
Education	14.8	16.7	17.7	16.8	18.2	21.6	23.1	25.3	26.5
Energy	6.5	10.6	11.0	10.7	11.2	11.4	12.1	12.5	15.7
Health and Human Services	194.2	315.5	333.9	351.3	373.6	399.8	438.7	484.4	544.1
Housing and Urban Development. . .	12.7	28.7	14.1	15.5	18.9	19.7	20.2	22.8	24.2
Interior	4.5	4.8	4.8	5.1	5.1	5.2	5.8	6.1	7.1
Justice	2.6	3.6	3.8	4.3	5.4	6.2	6.5	8.2	9.4
Labor [2]	29.7	23.9	24.1	23.5	21.9	22.7	25.3	34.0	44.4
State.	1.9	2.6	2.9	2.8	3.4	3.7	4.0	4.3	4.5
Transportation	19.8	25.0	27.4	25.4	26.4	26.6	28.6	30.5	33.4
Treasury	76.5	164.9	179.2	180.3	202.5	230.7	255.3	276.9	291.9
Veterans Affairs	21.1	26.3	26.5	27.0	29.3	30.0	29.0	31.2	33.6
Independent agencies:									
Environmental Protection Agency. . .	5.6	4.5	4.9	4.9	4.9	4.9	5.1	5.8	5.9
General Services Administration . . .	0.2	(-Z)	0.4	0.1	-0.3	-0.5	-0.1	0.5	0.4
NASA [3]	5.0	7.3	7.4	7.6	9.1	11.0	12.4	13.9	13.8
Office of Personnel Management. . .	15.1	23.7	24.0	27.0	29.2	29.1	31.9	34.8	36.1
Small Business Administration	2.0	0.7	0.6	-0.1	-0.1	0.1	0.6	0.6	0.5
Other independent agencies	16.1	10.0	12.2	14.3	23.5	33.9	73.6	80.5	96.2
Undistributed offsetting receipts	-32.0	-58.7	-65.0	-72.3	-78.9	-89.2	-99.0	-110.6	-116.0

Z Less than $50 million.   [1] Represents international affairs funds mainly.   [2] Includes Pension Benefit Guaranty Corporation.   [3] National Aeronautics and Space Administration.

Source: U.S. Office of Management and Budget, *Budget of the United States Government*, annual.

No. 499. Federal Securities—Interest Bearing Debt, by Type and Debt Holder: 1970 to 1991

[In billions of dollars. As of end of fiscal year; see text, section 9. The Export-Import Bank was moved within the budget effective October 1, 1976. Adjustments are made to include totals for the period it was outside the budget (1970-76). Also adjustments are made to reflect certain Export-Import Bank borrowing now classified as agency debt.]

YEAR	Federal securities, total [1]	Interest-bearing debt, total	TYPE								DEBT HOLDER		
			Marketable				Nonmarketable				U.S. Govt. account	Federal reserve banks [3]	Private investors
			Total	Bills	Notes	Treasury bonds	Total [1]	U.S. savings bonds	Govt. account series [2]				
1970. . . .	383	369	233	76	94	63	136	51	76		95	58	216
1975. . . .	544	532	316	129	150	37	217	65	124		145	85	302
1980. . . .	914	906	595	200	311	84	312	73	190		198	121	588
1985. . . .	1,827	1,821	1,360	384	776	200	461	77	314		317	170	1,335
1988. . . .	2,615	2,600	1,803	398	1,090	300	797	106	536		550	229	1,820
1989. . . .	2,881	2,836	1,893	407	1,133	338	944	114	664		677	221	1,939
1990. . . .	3,266	3,211	2,093	482	1,218	377	1,118	122	779		796	233	2,183
1991. . . .	3,683	3,663	2,391	565	1,388	423	1,272	134	908		920	265	2,478

[1] Includes items not shown separately.   [2] 1970 known as U.S. Treasury special issues.   [3] Public Issues.

Source: U.S. Dept. of the Treasury, *Treasury Bulletin*, quarterly.

No. 500. Interest-Bearing Government Securities Outstanding: 1970 to 1991

[In billions of dollars, except percent. As of end of fiscal year; see text, section 9. Par values, except U.S. savings bonds series, E, F, J, and U.S. savings notes, which are included at current redemption values]

TYPE OF SECURITY	1970	1975	1980	1983	1984	1985	1986	1987	1988	1989	1990	1991
State and local govts.[1]	139	214	329	447	493	551	655	698	748	805	827	848
Taxable [2]	306	419	723	1,146	1,304	1,511	1,761	1,911	2,076	(NA)	(NA)	(NA)
Government account series [3]	76	124	190	235	260	314	366	441	536	664	779	908
By issuer:												
U.S. Treasury	369	532	906	1,376	1,560	1,821	2,123	2,348	2,600	2,836	3,211	3,663
Agency securities	13	11	7	5	4	4	4	4	12	24	33	18
State and local govts.[1]	139	214	329	447	493	551	655	698	748	805	827	848

NA Not available.   [1] Source: Board of Governors, Federal Reserve System, unpublished data. Includes some partially taxable debt.   [2] Interest is subject to both normal and surtax rates of Federal income tax.   [3] Prior to July 1, 1974, known as U.S. Treasury special issues.

Source: Except as noted, U.S. Dept. of the Treasury, through 1980, *Statistical Appendix* to the *Annual Report of the Secretary of the Treasury on the State of the Finances;* thereafter, *Treasury Bulletin*, quarterly.

No. 501. Federal Participation in Domestic Credit Markets: 1980 to 1992

[In billions of dollars, except percent. See headnote, table 502. Federal credit programs are primarily in three forms: direct loans from the Federal Government, Federal guarantees of private lending, and lending by privately-owned government-sponsored enterprises]

TYPE OF PARTICIPATION	1980	1985	1986	1987	1988	1989	1990	1991	1992
Total funds loaned in U.S. credit markets,									
excluding equities [1]	327.0	767.0	878.6	780.0	795.0	711.0	656.0	496.0	**(NA)**
Federal and federally assisted lending	79.9	110.3	129.1	149.2	109.4	128.6	133.5	105.3	144.8
Federal participation rate (percent).	24.4	14.4	14.7	19.1	13.8	18.1	20.4	21.2	(NA)
Direct loans.	24.2	28.0	11.2	−19.0	−13.4	−14.6	2.8	−7.5	4.6
Guaranteed loans.	31.6	21.6	34.6	60.4	40.3	41.7	40.7	22.1	36.8
Government-sponsored enterprise loans	24.1	60.7	83.3	107.8	82.5	101.5	90.0	90.7	103.4
Total funds borrowed in U.S. credit markets [1] . . .	327.0	767.0	878.6	780.0	795.0	711.0	656.0	496.0	**(NA)**
Federal and federally assisted borrowing.	122.5	278.9	374.5	324.0	289.4	305.0	376.2	423.5	540.8
Federal participation rate (percent).	37.5	36.4	42.6	41.5	36.4	42.9	57.4	85.4	(NA)
Federal borrowing from public	69.5	199.4	236.8	152.0	162.1	140.1	220.1	276.8	392.5
Borrowing for guaranteed loans	31.6	21.6	34.6	60.4	40.3	41.7	40.7	22.1	36.8
Government-sponsored enterprise borrowing . .	21.4	57.9	103.2	111.7	87.1	123.2	115.4	124.6	111.5

NA Not available.   [1]Funds loaned to and borrowed by nonfinancial sectors, excluding equities.

Source: U.S. Office of Management and Budget, *Special Analyses, Budget of the United States Government*, annual.

No. 502. Federal Direct and Guaranteed Loans: 1970 to 1989

[In billions of dollars. As of end of fiscal year; see text, section 9. Government guaranteed loans are not included in Federal budget outlays. They constitute contingent liabilities not resulting in outlays, except in event of default. See headnote, table 501]

ITEM	1970	1975	1980	1982	1983	1984	1985	1986	1987	1988	1989
Direct loans, amount: [1]											
Gross (new) loans dispersed	12.4	28.8	49.3	37.1	43.8	41.4	64.4	42.2	35.2	33.7	26.0
Net loan outlays	3.0	12.8	24.2	23.4	15.3	6.3	28.0	11.2	−19.0	−13.4	−14.6
Direct loans outstanding	51.1	74.1	163.9	207.8	223.0	229.3	257.4	251.6	234.2	222.0	207.0
Guaranteed loans: [2]											
Primary [3]	27.5	31.2	66.2	59.6	78.0	73.3	55.5	89.6	151.7	96.4	96.3
Net loans	8.4	8.7	31.6	20.9	34.1	20.1	21.6	34.6	60.4	40.3	41.7
Outstanding loans	125.1	198.3	298.5	331.2	363.8	386.7	410.4	449.8	507.0	550.0	588.6

[1] Includes loans from "off-budget" government accounts.   [2] Includes capital subscriptions to international financial institutions. To avoid double counting, secondary guaranteed loans and guaranteed loans held as direct loans are excluded.   [3] Gross loan guarntees minus both secondary guaranteed loans, and guaranteed loans held as direct loans by the Government—by either on- or off-budget accounts.

Source: U.S. Office of Management and Budget, *Budget of the United States Government*, annual.

No. 503. U.S. Savings: 1970 to 1991

[In billions of dollars, except percent. As of end of fiscal year, see text section 9. See *Historical Statistics, Colonial Times to 1970*, series Y 500, for similar but not exactly comparable data]

ITEM	1970	1975	1980	1984	1985	1986	1987	1988	1989	1990	1991
Amounts outstanding, total [1]	51.8	65.5	72.7	73.1	77.3	85.8	97.3	106.5	114.3	122.5	133.8
Funds from sales	4.7	6.8	4.8	3.9	5.0	8.3	10.3	7.3	7.7	7.8	9.2
Accrued discounts	1.0	3.3	4.2	5.3	5.2	5.6	6.1	7.9	7.5	8.0	9.9
Redemptions [2]	6.3	6.5	16.7	6.1	5.7	5.1	4.9	5.9	7.3	7.5	7.5
Percent of total outstanding. . .	12.2	10.0	23.0	8.3	7.4	6.0	5.1	5.6	6.3	6.1	5.6

[1] Interest-bearing debt only for amounts and end of period or end of year.   [2] Matured and unmatured bonds.

Source: U.S. Dept. of the Treasury, *Treasury Bulletin*, quarterly.

No. 504. Government-Sponsored Enterprise Securities and Guarantees Outstanding: 1970 to 1990

[As of December 31. In billions of dollars]

ENTERPRISE	1970	1980	1989	1990	ENTERPRISE	1970	1980	1989	1990
Total.	38.9	176.9	866.7	980.1	Mortgage-backed securities . .	(X)	(X)	228.2	299.8
Farm credit system:					Freddie Mac: [2]				
Farm credit banks	11.4	51.8	42.4	41.9	Debt	(X)	4.7	24.1	28.4
Banks for cooperatives	1.9	8.6	12.6	13.3	Mortgage-backed securities . .	(X)	17.0	272.9	316.4
Farmer Mac [1]	(X)	(X)	(X)	(X)	Fed. home loan bank system . .	10.5	37.3	136.8	117.9
Fannie Mae: [1]					Sallie Mae [3]	(X)	2.7	33.6	39.0
Debt	15.2	54.9	116.1	123.4					

X Not applicable.   [1] Federal National Mortgage Association.   [2] Federal Home Loan Mortgage Corporation.   [3] Student Loan Mortgage Association.

Source: Congressional Budget Office, *Controlling the Risks of Government-Sponsored Enterprises*, April 1991.

No. 505. Federal Funds—Summary Distribution, by State: 1990

[In millions of dollars. For year ending Sept. 30. Data for grants, salaries and wages and direct payments to individuals are on an expenditures basis; procurement is on obligation basis]

REGION, DIVISION, AND STATE	FEDERAL FUNDS		Defense	Non-defense	Direct payments to individuals	Procurement	Grants to State and local governments	Salaries and wages
	Total [1]	Per capita [2] (dol.)						
U.S	993,418	3,994	224,286	769,125	494,011	187,551	130,861	145,165
Northeast	203,330	4,002	35,976	167,354	110,207	32,411	34,032	20,896
New England	59,091	4,474	17,064	42,028	27,526	15,330	8,169	5,935
Maine..............	4,925	4,011	1,243	3,682	2,566	942	762	561
New Hampshire.......	3,559	3,209	902	2,657	1,925	430	427	692
Vermont............	1,772	3,148	153	1,619	1,025	107	377	210
Massachusetts........	29,778	4,949	8,909	20,869	13,253	8,808	3,857	2,647
Rhode Island.........	4,318	4,303	957	3,361	2,291	600	773	558
Connecticut..........	14,739	4,484	4,900	9,840	6,466	4,443	1,973	1,267
Middle Atlantic	144,239	3,836	18,912	125,326	82,681	17,081	25,863	14,961
New York...........	70,493	3,918	8,344	62,149	37,595	8,621	15,761	6,423
New Jersey..........	28,322	3,664	5,205	23,116	16,271	4,307	3,977	3,396
Pennsylvania.........	45,424	3,823	5,363	40,061	28,815	4,153	6,125	5,142
Midwest..............	206,360	3,458	29,549	176,807	118,451	25,150	28,964	22,477
East North Central......	135,664	3,229	15,726	119,936	83,541	13,571	20,380	14,106
Ohio	37,920	3,496	6,411	31,509	21,785	6,038	5,388	3,922
Indiana.............	16,915	3,051	2,656	14,258	10,024	1,971	2,423	1,800
Illinois	36,696	3,210	3,158	33,538	22,687	2,601	5,280	4,755
Michigan............	29,205	3,142	2,175	27,029	19,671	1,698	4,751	2,432
Wisconsin...........	14,928	3,052	1,326	13,602	9,374	1,263	2,538	1,197
West North Central	70,696	4,003	13,823	56,871	34,910	11,579	8,584	8,371
Minnesota...........	15,073	3,445	2,117	12,956	7,544	2,078	2,336	1,348
Iowa	9,962	3,587	687	9,275	5,704	700	1,289	733
Missouri	24,258	4,741	7,490	16,768	10,791	6,961	2,177	2,858
North Dakota........	2,910	4,555	423	2,486	1,277	164	471	511
South Dakota	2,863	4,114	298	2,565	1,385	119	511	503
Nebraska	6,092	3,448	901	5,191	3,146	426	779	953
Kansas.............	9,538	3,850	1,907	7,630	5,063	1,131	1,021	1,465
South	348,226	4,075	82,399	265,825	170,424	58,534	40,995	66,142
South Atlantic..........	195,919	4,497	50,413	145,504	91,501	33,361	20,173	43,821
Delaware	2,149	3,226	336	1,812	1,269	138	313	384
Maryland	27,118	5,671	7,235	19,883	9,816	6,694	2,350	6,101
District of Columbia	17,353	28,592	2,358	14,995	1,961	2,936	1,718	9,439
Virginia............	36,346	5,874	17,380	18,967	12,525	10,168	2,237	10,303
West Virginia........	6,609	3,685	416	6,193	4,472	325	1,009	600
North Carolina.......	20,172	3,043	4,219	15,953	11,540	1,592	2,942	3,564
South Carolina.......	13,664	3,919	3,136	10,527	6,197	2,664	1,892	2,407
Georgia	21,149	3,265	4,958	16,190	10,839	2,228	3,136	4,427
Florida	51,359	3,970	10,375	40,984	32,882	6,616	4,576	6,596
East South Central	58,900	3,881	10,167	48,733	30,579	10,322	8,457	8,187
Kentucky	13,524	3,670	1,720	11,804	7,267	2,010	2,044	1,918
Tennessee	18,049	3,701	2,075	15,974	9,470	3,308	2,717	2,225
Alabama............	17,261	4,272	3,921	13,340	8,589	3,388	2,101	2,756
Mississippi	10,066	3,912	2,451	7,615	5,253	1,616	1,595	1,288
West South Central	93,407	3,498	21,819	71,588	48,344	14,851	12,365	14,134
Arkansas	8,250	3,509	997	7,253	5,286	391	1,250	930
Louisiana	15,116	3,582	2,858	12,258	7,667	2,384	2,658	1,863
Oklahoma...........	11,804	3,753	2,387	9,417	6,529	873	1,568	2,281
Texas..............	58,237	3,428	15,577	42,660	28,862	11,203	6,889	9,060
West................	212,506	4,026	60,566	151,941	94,186	49,681	26,539	35,500
Mountain	58,041	4,249	15,009	43,033	24,804	14,513	7,016	9,581
Montana...........	3,345	4,186	295	3,050	1,644	167	591	523
Idaho..............	3,888	3,862	324	3,564	1,803	862	569	508
Wyoming	1,855	4,089	231	1,624	770	146	568	315
Colorado...........	14,586	4,428	5,063	9,523	5,687	4,043	1,429	2,757
New Mexico	8,640	5,703	1,622	7,018	2,852	3,256	959	1,358
Arizona............	15,072	4,112	4,860	10,212	7,382	3,667	1,620	2,047
Utah	6,511	3,779	1,891	4,620	2,490	1,543	838	1,427
Nevada	4,144	3,448	723	3,422	2,176	829	442	646
Pacific.............	154,465	3,948	45,557	108,908	69,382	35,168	19,523	25,919
Washington..........	20,149	4,140	5,362	14,787	9,328	3,943	2,568	3,584
Oregon............	9,826	3,457	779	9,047	5,960	649	1,708	1,186
California	115,802	3,891	35,467	80,335	51,448	29,500	13,932	17,746
Alaska	3,227	5,867	1,345	1,882	612	529	717	1,237
Hawaii	5,461	4,927	2,604	2,857	2,034	547	598	2,166
Undistributed	22,996	(X)	15,799	7,196	745	21,775	302	150

X Not applicable.   [1] Includes other programs not shown separately.   [2] Based on Bureau of the Census resident population as of April 1, 1990.

Source: U.S. Bureau of the Census, *Federal Expenditures by State for Fiscal Year,* annual.

No. 506. Tax Returns Filed—Examination Coverage: 1970 to 1990

[In thousands, except as indicated. Identification of returns with either schedule C (nonfarm sale proprietorships) or schedule F (farm proprietorships) for audit examination purposes was based in the largest source of income on the return and certain other characteristics. Therefore, the number with schedule C is not comparable to the number of nonfarm sale proprietorships returns in table 829]

YEAR AND ITEM	Returns filed [1]	RETURNS EXAMINED					AVERAGE TAX AND PENALTY—DOLLARS PER RETURN		
		Total	Percent of returns filed	By—			Revenue agents	Tax auditors	Service centers
				Revenue agents	Tax auditors	Service centers			
INDIVIDUAL RETURNS									
1970	76,431	1,672	2.2	(NA)	(NA)	-	(NA)	(NA)	-
1975	81,272	1,839	2.3	355.2	1,483.4	-	2,609	219	-
1980	90,727	1,834	2.0	292.5	1,346.3	195.1	1,335	602	39
1984	95,541	1,216	1.3	276.2	859.4	80.4	11,584	1,314	692
1985	96,497	1,266	1.3	332.6	810.9	122.1	10,854	1,539	496
1986	99,529	1,091	1.1	298.9	732.5	59.6	14,052	1,945	862
1987	101,751	1,109	1.1	317.5	610.4	181.3	12,235	2,107	4,084
1988	103,251	1,061	1.0	352.8	532.3	175.7	9,750	2,190	4,195
1989	107,029	985	0.9	243.0	542.7	199.0	11,347	1,827	2,393
1990, total	**109,868**	**883**	**0.8**	**202.8**	**517.2**	**163.2**	**16,248**	**1,963**	**3,817**
1040A, income under $25,000	42,116	186	0.4	12.3	138.9	34.8	17,958	1,378	4,716
Non 1040A, income: [2]									
Under $25,000	20,465	115	0.6	16.5	79.1	19.7	6,243	1,269	1,131
$25,000 - $49,999, simple	26,359	196	0.7	28.0	138.1	29.8	7,278	1,690	3,524
$50,000 - $99,999, complex	11,167	121	1.1	27.0	78.0	22.5	9,512	1,896	2,398
$100,000 and over	2,555	120	4.7	47.8	28.4	44.3	25,735	4,760	5,345
Schedule C-TGR: [3]									
Under $25,000	2,168	29	1.4	9.4	18.9	1.1	6,959	2,237	1,348
$25,000 - $99,999	2,667	50	1.9	20.8	25.5	3.5	9,697	3,787	1,682
$100,000 and over	1,464	50	3.4	33.1	9.8	6.6	27,608	7,308	4,735
Schedule F-TGR: [3]									
Under $100,000	638	8	1.3	3.2	4.7	0.4	5,964	1,133	789
$100,000 and over	269	7	2.7	4.9	1.8	0.4	16,560	2,183	3,712
1989 —OTHER RETURNS									
Fiduciary	2,625	3	0.1	2.6	-	-	42,992	-	-
Partnerships	1,663	13	0.8	13.2	-	-	193,925	-	-
Corporations, total	2,752	71	2.6	71.3	-	-	193,925	-	-
Estate, total	56	12	21.1	11.8	-	-	15,525	-	-
Gift	124	2	1.3	1.6	-	-	150,526	-	-
Excise	887	41	4.7	41.3	-	-	5,313	-	-
Employment	28,893	70	0.2	48.7	2.3	-	6,886	1,003	-
Windfall profit	-	3	-	0.5	-	-	972,264	-	18,283
Miscellaneous	-	1	-	0.1	-	2.5	445	-	-
Service center corrections	-	274	-	-	-	274.3	-	-	1,526

- Represents zero.   NA Not available.   [1] Returns filed in previous calendar year.   [2] Income from positive sources only.   [3] Total gross receipts.

Source: U.S. Internal Revenue Service, *Annual Report of the Commissioner and Chief Counsel of the Internal Revenue Service.*

No. 507. Internal Revenue Gross Collections, by Source: 1970 to 1990

[For fiscal year ending in year shown; see text section 9. See also *Historical Statistics, Colonial Times to 1970,* series Y 35

SOURCE OF REVENUE	COLLECTIONS (bil. dol.)						PERCENT OF TOTAL				
	1970	1980	1985	1987	1988	1989	1970	1980	1985	1989	1990
All taxes	**195.8**	**519.4**	**742.9**	**886.3**	**935.1**	**1,013.5**	**1,056.3**	**100.0**	**100.0**	**100.0**	**100.0**
Individual income taxes	103.7	287.5	396.7	465.4	473.7	515.7	540.2	54.9	53.4	50.9	51.1
Withheld by employers	77.4	223.8	299.0	322.5	341.5	361.4	388.4	43.1	40.2	35.7	36.8
Employment taxes [1]	37.4	128.3	225.2	277.0	318.0	345.6	367.2	24.7	30.2	34.1	34.8
Old-age and disability insurance	35.7	122.5	215.6	266.6	307.6	336.8	357.5	23.6	29.0	33.2	33.8
Unemployment insurance	0.8	3.3	5.7	6.2	6.2	4.7	5.5	0.6	0.8	0.5	0.5
Corporation income taxes	35.0	72.4	77.4	102.8	109.7	117.0	110.0	13.9	10.4	11.5	10.4
Estate and gift taxes	3.7	6.5	6.6	7.7	7.8	9.0	11.8	1.3	0.9	0.9	1.1
Excise taxes	15.9	24.6	37.0	33.3	25.9	26.0	27.1	4.7	5.0	2.6	2.6
Alcohol and tobacco	6.8	8.1	9.9	10.4	10.3	10.1	10.1	1.6	1.3	1.0	1.0
Manufactures	6.7	6.5	10.0	10.2	10.6	11.2	11.0	1.3	1.3	1.1	1.0
Windfall profits tax	(X)	3.1	5.1	(Z)	(Z)	(Z)	(Z)	0.6	0.7	(Z)	(Z)
Other	2.4	10.0	17.0	12.0	5.0	4.7	6.0	1.9	2.3	0.5	0.6

X Not applicable.   Z Less than $50 million or .05 percent.   [1] Includes railroad retirement, not shown separately.

Source: U.S. Internal Revenue Service, *Annual Report of the Commissioner and Chief Counsel of the Internal Revenue Service.*

No. 508. Federal Individual Income Tax Returns With Adjusted Gross Income (AGI)—Summary: 1980 to 1989

[Includes Puerto Rico and Virgin Islands. Includes returns of resident aliens, based on a sample of unaudited returns as filed. Data are not comparable for all years because of tax changes and other changes, as indicated. See Statistics of Income, Individual Income Tax Returns publications for a detailed explanation. See Appendix III. See Historical Statistics, Colonial Times to 1979, series Y 393-411, for related data]

ITEM	NUMBER OF RETURNS (1,000)				AMOUNT (mil. dol.)				AVERAGE AMOUNT DOLLARS (dollars)			
	1980	1985	1988	1989	1980	1985	1988	1989	1980	1985	1988	1989
Total returns	93,902	101,660	109,708	112,136	1,613,731	2,305,951	3,083,020	3,256,358	17,185	22,683	28,102	29,039
Form 1040	57,123	67,006	71,359	71,563	1,310,088	1,938,263	2,614,128	2,725,119	22,935	28,927	36,633	38,080
Salaries and wages	83,802	87,198	93,257	95,488	1,349,843	1,928,201	2,337,984	2,449,531	16,108	22,113	25,070	25,653
Interest received	49,020	64,526	69,421	69,882	102,009	182,109	186,982	220,116	2,081	2,822	2,693	3,150
Dividends in AGI	10,739	15,528	22,903	23,080	38,761	55,046	77,330	81,309	3,600	3,545	3,376	3,523
Business or profession profit less loss	8,881	11,900	13,571	14,161	55,129	78,773	126,323	132,738	6,207	6,620	9,308	9,373
Sales of capital assets, net gain less loss, in AGI	9,971	11,126	14,286	15,060	30,029	67,694	153,786	145,631	3,012	6,084	10,763	9,670
Pensions and annuities in AGI	7,374	13,133	16,481	16,817	43,340	95,096	138,786	147,358	5,878	7,241	8,420	8,762
Rents and royalties, net income less loss	8,208	9,964	9,986	10,131	4,105	-10,946	-1,279	928	500	-1,099	-128	92
Partnerships and S Corporations, profit less loss	3,910	5,488	5,889	5,928	10,099	-2,527	100,743	63,092	2,583	-460	17,107	10,643
Farm profit less loss	2,608	2,621	2,368	2,360	-1,792	-12,005	-1,177	-214	-687	-4,580	-497	-91
Statutory adjustments, total	13,149	37,763	10,747	9,927	28,614	95,082	28,202	24,573	2,176	2,518	2,624	2,475
Individual Retirement Arrangements	2,564	16,206	6,361	5,825	3,431	38,212	11,882	10,829	1,338	2,358	1,867	1,859
Self-employed retirement (Keogh) plan	569	676	815	822	2,008	5,182	6,627	6,326	3,529	7,666	8,131	7,696
Married couples who both work	(NA)	24,835	(NA)	(NA)	(NA)	24,615	(NA)	(NA)	(NA)	991	(NA)	(NA)
Exemptions, total [2]	227,925	244,180	221,884	223,756	227,569	253,720	430,771	447,130	998	1,039	1,941	1,998
Age 65 or older	11,847	16,749	(NA)	(NA)	(NA)	(NA)	(NA)	(NA)	(NA)	(NA)	(NA)	(NA)
Blind	185	327	(NA)	(NA)	(NA)	(NA)	(NA)	(NA)	(NA)	(NA)	(NA)	(NA)
Standard and itemized deductions, total [3]	88,105	96,849	108,375	111,311	362,776	554,734	684,780	740,409	4,118	5,728	6,318	6,652
Itemized deductions, total [3]	28,950	39,848	31,903	31,972	218,028	405,024	395,216	430,978	7,531	10,164	12,388	13,480
Medical and dental expenses	19,458	10,777	4,810	5,128	14,972	22,926	17,994	20,921	769	2,127	3,740	4,080
Taxes paid	28,747	39,548	31,328	31,393	69,404	128,085	120,628	131,300	2,414	3,239	3,850	4,182
Interest paid	26,677	36,287	29,631	29,438	91,187	180,095	179,738	193,186	3,418	4,963	6,065	6,562
Contributions	26,601	36,162	29,111	29,132	25,810	47,963	50,949	55,459	970	1,326	1,750	1,904
Taxable income [4]	88,105	96,124	90,124	92,314	1,279,985	1,820,741	2,069,967	2,173,346	14,528	18,942	22,928	23,543
Income tax before credits	76,136	85,994	90,219	92,246	256,294	332,165	418,889	438,240	3,366	3,863	4,643	4,751
Tax credits, total [2]	19,674	20,995	14,099	12,035	7,216	10,248	7,047	6,131	367	488	499	509
Child care	4,231	8,418	9,023	6,028	956	3,128	3,813	2,439	226	372	422	405
Elderly and disabled	562	463	357	320	135	109	69	64	240	235	193	200
Residential energy	4,670	2,979	(NA)	(NA)	562	812	(NA)	(NA)	120	273	(NA)	(NA)
Foreign tax	393	454	559	642	1,342	783	1,087	1,312	3,415	1,725	1,944	2,044
General business credit [5]	(NA)	4,614	365	332	(NA)	4,791	718	593	(NA)	1,038	1,967	1,736
Income tax, total [6]	73,906	82,846	87,735	89,178	250,341	325,710	412,870	432,940	3,387	3,932	4,705	4,855

NA Not available.   [1] Represents corporations with no more than 35 shareholders (10 in 1980), most of which are individuals electing to be taxed at the shareholder level.   [2] Includes items not shown separately.   [3] For 1985, includes charitable deduction for nonitemizers. Starting 1988 includes additional standard deductions for age 65 or older or for blindness.   [4] For 1980 and 1985, includes amounts "taxed" at zero percent.   [5] Includes investment credit.   [6] Includes minimum tax or alternative tax.

Source: U.S. Internal Revenue Service, Statistics of Income Bulletin, and Statistics of Income, Individual Income Tax Returns, annual.

No. 509. Individual Income Tax Returns—Number, Income Tax, and Average Tax, by Size of Adjusted Gross Income: 1988 and 1989

[Number in thousands; money amounts in billions of dollars, except as indicated]

SIZE OF ADJUSTED GROSS INCOME	NUMBER OF RETURNS 1988	NUMBER OF RETURNS 1989, prel.	ADJUSTED GROSS INCOME (AGI) 1988	ADJUSTED GROSS INCOME (AGI) 1989, prel.	TAXABLE INCOME 1988	TAXABLE INCOME 1989, prel.	INCOME TAX TOTAL [1] 1988	INCOME TAX TOTAL [1] 1989, prel.	TAX AS PERCENT OF AGI 1988	TAX AS PERCENT OF AGI 1989, prel.	AVERAGE TAX ($1,000) 1988	AVERAGE TAX ($1,000) 1989, prel.
Total	109,708	112,136	3,083.0	3,256.4	2,070.0	2,173.3	412.9	432.9	13.8	13.6	4.7	4.9
Less than $1,000 [2]	3,962	3,866	-39.3	-40.7	0.2	0.2	0.1	0.1	(X)	(X)	0.2	0.2
$1,000-$2,999	7,456	7,331	14.7	14.4	1.0	1.0	0.2	0.2	4.6	4.6	0.1	0.1
$3,000-$4,999	6,467	6,396	25.7	25.4	2.5	2.3	0.4	0.4	4.4	3.9	0.2	0.2
$5,000-$6,999	6,218	6,080	37.4	36.3	6.4	5.2	0.9	0.8	3.9	3.5	0.2	0.2
$7,000-$8,999	6,191	6,038	49.4	48.2	12.1	11.4	1.8	1.7	5.8	5.2	0.5	0.5
$9,000-$10,999	5,850	5,955	58.4	59.6	18.4	17.5	2.5	2.5	6.5	6.3	0.6	0.6
$11,000-$12,999	5,430	5,846	65.2	70.2	25.0	26.4	3.4	3.6	7.0	6.8	0.8	0.8
$13,000-$14,999	5,428	5,391	75.8	75.3	33.8	32.2	4.5	4.3	7.4	7.2	1.0	1.0
$15,000-$16,999	4,966	4,914	79.4	78.6	39.6	38.5	5.5	5.3	7.5	7.3	1.2	1.2
$17,000-$18,999	4,653	4,680	83.6	84.2	44.2	45.1	6.4	6.5	7.9	7.7	1.4	1.4
$19,000-$21,999	6,093	6,118	124.6	125.1	71.3	70.7	10.4	10.5	8.5	8.4	1.7	1.8
$22,000-$24,999	5,328	5,359	125.0	125.6	76.2	75.1	11.3	11.2	9.1	8.9	2.1	2.1
$25,000-$29,999	7,518	7,615	206.2	209.2	130.6	131.9	20.4	20.7	9.9	9.7	2.7	2.7
$30,000-$39,999	11,957	12,100	415.3	420.2	274.6	278.3	44.1	45.6	10.7	10.7	3.8	3.8
$40,000-$49,999	8,265	8,590	369.1	383.7	255.1	263.1	42.8	44.0	11.6	11.4	5.1	5.1
$50,000-$74,999	8,904	9,921	532.7	594.4	383.1	424.6	74.3	81.3	14.0	13.3	8.2	8.2
$75,000-$99,999	2,520	3,059	214.2	261.1	159.6	193.0	35.7	42.7	16.7	15.9	14.0	14.0
$100,000-$199,999	1,778	2,090	236.1	276.3	183.3	212.2	47.8	54.5	20.3	19.0	26.1	26.1
$200,000-$499,999	548	613	161.9	179.1	134.7	146.4	38.7	41.6	23.9	23.3	68.0	68.0
$500,000-$999,999	115	116	77.9	78.5	67.6	66.9	19.2	18.9	24.6	24.3	167.1	163.5
$1,000,000 or more	62	58	169.6	151.5	150.8	131.4	42.4	36.6	25.0	24.7	684.5	636.6

X Not applicable. [1] Consists of income after credits, and alternative minimum tax, and minimum tax. [2] In addition to low income taxpayers, this size class (and others) includes taxpayers with tax preferences," not reflected in adjusted gross income or taxable income which are subject to the "alternative minimum tax" (included in total income tax).
Source: U.S. Internal Revenue Service, *Statistics of Income Bulletin*, quarterly and *Statistics of Income, Individual Income Tax Returns*, annual.

No. 510. Individual Income Tax Returns—Itemized Deductions and Statutory Adjustments, by Size of Adjusted Gross Income: 1989

[Preliminary]

ITEM	Unit	Total	Under $10,000	$10,000 to $19,999	$20,000 to $29,999	$30,000 to $39,999	$40,000 to $49,999	$50,000 to $99,999	$100,000 and over
Returns with itemized deductions:									
Number	1,000	31,972	792	2,576	4,289	5,364	5,424	10,782	2,745
Amount	Mil. dol.	430,978	7,032	21,092	35,788	49,201	56,658	149,852	111,355
Medical and dental expenses:									
Returns	1,000	5,128	494	1,274	1,216	859	593	633	59
Amount	Mil. dol	20,921	2,925	5,438	3,952	2,489	2,088	3,204	825
Taxes paid: Returns, total	1,000	31,393	664	2,398	4,172	5,312	5,385	10,729	2,734
State, local income taxes	1,000	26,415	329	1,678	3,487	4,493	4,665	9,363	2,400
Real estate taxes	1,000	27,999	549	1,977	3,482	4,641	4,841	9,933	2,577
Amount, total	Mil. dol	131,300	852	3,443	7,713	12,471	15,915	47,243	43,661
State, local income taxes	Mil. dol	80,905	141	1,008	3,330	6,276	8,714	28,170	33,267
Real estate taxes	Mil. dol	45,211	657	2,203	3,905	5,557	6,485	17,065	9,337
Interest paid: Returns	1,000	29,438	545	2,083	3,895	5,038	5,143	10,248	2,486
Amount	Mil. dol	193,186	2,474	8,242	16,632	24,773	27,890	70,990	42,185
Home mortgages interest:									
Returns	1,000	25,684	448	1,663	3,233	4,377	4,558	9,229	2,176
Amount	Mil. dol	162,714	2,216	7,275	14,589	21,792	24,718	62,253	29,872
Contributions: Returns	1,000	29,132	534	2,101	3,720	4,817	5,015	10,302	2,645
Amount	Mil. dol	55,459	398	2,286	4,238	5,767	6,643	18,099	18,028
Employee business expense:									
Returns	1,000	9,927	768	1,647	1,950	1,740	1,338	1,620	783
Amount	Mil.	24,573	873	2,283	3,332	3,298	2,343	5,298	6,940
Returns with statutory adjustments: [1]									
Returns	1,000	5,825	301	946	1,364	1,232	964	725	275
Amount of adjustments	Mil. dol	10,829	451	1,554	2,398	2,259	1,526	1,808	799
Payments to IRA's: [2] Returns	1,000	822	15	36	57	67	75	291	278
Amount	Mil. dol	6,326	10	63	140	214	230	1,553	4,109
Payments to Keogh plans:									
Returns	1,000	8,306	67	389	1,083	1,429	1,545	3,160	632
Amount	Mil. dol	20,708	117	730	2,168	2,807	2,980	8,161	3,746
Alimony paid: Returns	1,000	601	29	64	93	84	60	172	86
Amount	Mil.dol.	4,514	154	284	444	423	273	1,237	1,591

[1] Includes disability income exclusion, employee business expenses, moving expenses, forfeited interest penalty, alimony paid, deduction for expense of living abroad, and other data not shown separately. [2] Individual Retirement Account.

Source: U.S. Internal Revenue Service, *Statistics of Income, Individual Income Tax Returns*, annual.

No. 511. Federal Individual Income Tax Returns—Adjusted Gross Income (AGI), by Source of Income and Income Class for Taxable Returns: 1989

[In millions of dollars, except as indicated. Minus sign (-) indicates net loss was greater than net income. See headnote, table 508]

ITEM	Total [1]	Under $10,000	$10,000 to $19,999	$20,000 to $29,999	$30,000 to $39,999	$40,000 to $49,999	$50,000 to $99,999	$100,000 and over
Number of returns(1,000)	89,180	14,322	21,702	16,716	12,047	8,560	12,960	2,873
Source of income:								
Adjusted gross income (AGI)	3,158,294	79,682	326,530	412,669	418,393	382,363	854,215	684,441
Salaries and wages	2,337,830	63,128	244,972	336,713	349,694	316,072	684,843	342,408
Interest received	204,278	9,478	29,083	24,290	20,118	18,417	43,977	58,915
Dividends in AGI	77,815	1,980	5,702	5,827	5,662	5,232	18,293	35,119
Business; prof., net profit less loss	128,906	2,317	10,456	13,108	12,122	11,814	35,364	43,725
Pensions and annuities in AGI	138,668	4,428	28,292	24,788	20,019	16,979	31,530	12,633
Sales of property, net [2]	140,542	2,087	1,794	3,241	3,585	4,589	19,916	105,332
Rents, royalties, net [3]	928	-2,098	134	-1,111	-849	-660	-2,095	7,606
Other sources, net [4]	129,327	-1,638	6,097	5,813	8,042	9,920	22,387	78,703
Percent of all returns:								
Number of returns	79.5	12.8	19.4	14.9	10.7	7.6	11.6	2.6
Adjusted gross income	96.9	2.6	10.0	12.7	12.8	11.7	26.2	21.0
Salaries and wages	95.4	2.6	10.0	9.8	14.3	12.9	28.0	14.0
Interest received	92.8	4.3	13.2	11.0	9.1	8.4	20.0	26.8
Dividends in AGI	95.7	2.4	7.0	7.2	6.9	6.4	22.6	43.2
Business; prof., net profit less loss	97.1	1.7	7.9	9.9	9.1	8.9	26.6	32.9
Pensions and annuities in AGI	94.1	3.0	19.2	16.8	13.6	11.5	21.4	8.6
Sales of property [2]	95.8	1.4	1.2	2.2	2.4	3.1	13.6	71.8

[1] Includes a small number of taxable returns with no adjusted gross income.   [2] Includes sales of capital assets and other property; net gain less loss.   [3] Excludes rental passive losses disallowed in the compilation of AGI; net income less loss. [4] Includes statutory adjustments of $28,201 million for 1989.

Source: U.S. Internal Revenue Service, *Statistics of Income, Individual Income Tax Returns*, 1989.

No. 512. Federal Individual Income Tax Returns, Income, and Taxes, 1970 to 1989, and by State, 1989

YEAR, DIVISION, STATE	Number of returns [1] (1,000)	Adjusted gross income (AGI) [2]	INCOME TAX Total [3] (mil. dol.)	INCOME TAX Per capita [4] (dol.)	YEAR, DIVISION, STATE	Number of returns [1] (1,000)	Adjusted gross income (AGI) [2]	INCOME TAX Total [3] (mil. dol.)	INCOME TAX Per capita [4] (dol.)
1970	74,278	631,626	82,880	406	S.A.	19,819	562,088	77,210	1,791
1975	82,229	947,785	124,526	578	DE	324	9,842	1,352	2,009
1980	93,902	1,613,731	250,341	1,102	MD	2,314	76,934	10,720	2,284
1985	102,037	2,289,333	336,638	1,410	DC	323	10,030	1,514	2,507
1987	107,402	2,772,620	386,357	1,587	VA	2,864	88,220	12,067	1,978
1988	110,348	3,064,260	431,416	1,755	WV	688	16,192	1,997	1,075
					NC	3,002	77,689	9,998	1,522
U.S., 1989	113,242	3,250,669	453,494	1,827	SC	1,513	36,549	4,410	1,256
Northeast	24,017	778,391	113,916	2,244	GA	2,820	76,936	10,117	1,572
N.E.	6,499	212,270	31,399	2,407	FL	5,971	169,688	25,035	1,976
ME	568	14,338	1,808	1,480	E.S.C.	6,297	151,485	19,457	1,263
NH	553	17,146	2,464	2,226	KY	1,497	36,216	4,644	1,246
VT	268	7,103	936	1,651	TN	2,134	53,532	7,222	1,461
MA	2,956	96,340	14,139	2,391	AL	1,670	40,953	5,159	1,252
RI	476	13,698	1,885	1,889	MS	996	20,784	2,432	927
CT	1,678	63,645	10,167	3,139	W.S.C.	11,137	281,273	39,228	1,453
M.A.	17,518	566,121	82,517	2,187	AR	953	20,693	2,507	1,041
NY	8,180	275,423	40,309	2,246	LA	1,647	38,354	5,018	1,145
NJ	3,832	137,227	20,772	2,685	OK	1,299	31,060	4,012	1,244
PA	5,506	153,471	21,436	1,780	TX	7,238	191,166	27,691	1,629
Midwest	27,078	750,969	103,005	1,713	West	23,797	706,100	98,097	1,894
E.N.C.	19,170	542,956	75,102	1,776	Mt.	5,953	154,499	20,258	1,499
OH	5,017	133,502	17,740	1,626	MT	350	7,518	980	1,216
IN	2,490	65,785	8,743	1,563	ID	410	9,650	1,201	1,184
IL	5,296	162,701	24,166	2,073	WY	200	5,220	739	1,555
MI	4,145	121,711	16,807	1,812	CO	1,533	42,448	5,772	1,740
WI	2,222	59,257	7,646	1,571	NM	643	14,548	1,772	1,159
W.N.C.	7,908	208,013	27,903	1,563	AZ	1,573	41,173	5,300	1,490
MN	1,994	57,354	7,644	1,756	UT	661	16,767	1,932	1,131
IA	1,249	30,584	3,972	1,399	NV	583	17,175	2,562	2,306
MO	2,269	59,896	8,125	1,575	Pac.	17,844	551,601	77,839	2,033
ND	280	6,155	799	1,211	WA	2,232	65,107	9,351	1,964
SD	305	6,490	859	1,201	OR	1,271	33,361	4,328	1,534
NE	722	17,773	2,350	1,459	CA	13,486	428,913	60,680	2,087
KS	1,098	29,761	4,154	1,653	AK	313	8,368	1,302	2,470
South	37,253	994,846	135,895	1,589	HI	542	15,852	2,178	1,958

[1] Beginning 1985, includes returns filled by nonresident aliens and certain self-employment tax returns. [2] Less deficit. [3] Includes additional tax for tax preferences, self-employment tax, tax from investment credit recapture and other income-related taxes. Total is before earned income credit. [4] Based on resident population as of July 1.

Source: U.S. Internal Revenue Service, *Statistics of Income Bulletin*, spring 1990.

No. 513. Federal Individual Income Tax—Effective (Average) and Marginal Tax Rates, for Selected Income Groups: 1970 to 1990

[Refers to income after exclusions. Effective rate represents tax liability divided by stated income. The marginal tax rate is the percentage of the first additional dollar of income which would be paid in income tax. Computations assume the low income allowance, standard deduction, zero bracket amount, or itemized deductions equal to 10 percent of adjusted gross income, whichever is greatest. Excludes self employment tax. See Historical Statistics, Colonial Times to 1970, series 412-439, for similar data on net income]

CURRENT DOLLARS — TAX LIABILITY (dol.)

ADJUSTED GROSS INCOME [1]	1970[2]	1979-80	1985	1988	1989	1990
Single person, no dependents:						
$5,000	683	250	177	8	20	25
$10,000	1,778	1,177	888	758	735	705
$20,000	5,030	3,837	2,854	2,258	2,235	2,205
$25,000	7,144	5,484	4,125	3,294	3,161	2,988
$35,000	11,904	9,194	6,916	5,954	5,835	5,718
$50,000	19,695	16,032	12,067	9,794	9,629	9,498
$75,000	34,019	29,487	22,195	17,154	16,959	16,718
Married couple, 2 dependents [3]:						
$5,000	275	[4]-500	[4]-550	[4]-700	[4]-700	[4]-700
$10,000	1,122	374	[4]-132	[4]-858	[4]-910	[4]-953
$20,000	3,213	2,265	1,682	1,080	1,020	953
$25,000	4,490	3,497	2,566	1,830	1,770	1,703
$35,000	7,677	6,571	4,916	3,330	3,270	3,203
$50,000	13,674	12,118	9,086	6,549	6,281	5,960
$75,000	25,594	23,404	17,649	12,849	12,636	12,386

CURRENT DOLLARS — EFFECTIVE RATE (percent)

ADJUSTED GROSS INCOME	1970[2]	1979-80	1985	1988	1989	1990
Single person, no dependents:						
$5,000	13.7	5.0	3.5	0.2	0.4	0.5
$10,000	17.8	11.8	8.9	7.6	7.4	7.1
$20,000	25.2	19.2	14.3	11.3	11.2	11.0
$25,000	28.6	21.9	16.5	13.2	12.6	12.0
$35,000	34.0	26.3	19.8	17.0	17.1	16.3
$50,000	39.4	32.1	24.1	19.5	19.3	19.0
$75,000	45.4	39.3	29.6	22.9	22.6	22.3
Married couple, 2 dependents [3]:						
$5,000	5.5	[4]-10.0	[4]-11.0	[4]-14.0	[4]-14.0	[4]-14.0
$10,000	11.2	3.7	[4]-1.3	[4]-8.6	[4]-9.1	[4]-9.5
$20,000	16.1	11.3	8.4	5.4	5.1	4.8
$25,000	18.0	14.0	10.3	7.3	7.1	6.8
$35,000	21.9	18.8	14.0	9.5	9.3	9.2
$50,000	27.3	24.2	18.2	13.1	12.6	11.9
$75,000	34.1	31.2	23.5	17.1	16.8	16.5

CURRENT DOLLARS — MARGINAL TAX RATE (percent)

ADJUSTED GROSS INCOME	1970[2]	1979-80	1985	1988	1989	1990
Single person, no dependents:						
$5,000	19.5	16	12	15	15	15
$10,000	28.7	21	16	15	15	15
$20,000	43.1	34	26	28	28	28
$25,000	49.2	39	26	28	28	28
$35,000	54.3	44	34	28	28	28
$50,000	61.5	55	42	28	28	28
$75,000	65.6	63	48	33	33	33
Married couple, 2 dependents [3]:						
$5,000	15.0	[4]-	[4]24.2	[4]-14	[4]-14	[4]-14
$10,000	19.5	[4]12.5	[4]23.2	[4]10	[4]10	[4]10
$20,000	25.6	16	16	15	15	15
$25,000	32.8	21	18	15	15	15
$35,000	40.0	28	25	28	28	28
$50,000	49.2	37	33	28	28	28
$75,000	56.4	54	42	28	33	28

CURRENT INCOME EQUIVALENT TO CONSTANT INCOME (dol.) / CONSTANT (1988) DOLLARS

	1970[2]	1980	1985	1988	1989	1990
Single person, no dependents:						
$5,000	1,730	3,490	4,490	5,000	5,230	5,480
$10,000	3,450	6,970	8,990	10,000	10,460	10,950
$20,000	6,910	13,950	17,970	20,000	20,920	21,900
$25,000	8,640	17,430	22,460	25,000	26,150	27,380
$35,000	12,090	24,400	31,450	35,000	36,610	38,330
$50,000	17,270	34,860	44,930	50,000	52,290	54,750
$75,000	25,910	52,290	67,390	75,000	78,440	82,130
Married couple, 2 dependents [3]:						
$5,000	1,730	3,490	4,490	5,000	5,230	5,480
$10,000	3,450	6,970	8,990	10,000	10,460	10,950
$20,000	6,910	13,950	17,970	20,000	20,920	21,900
$25,000	8,640	17,430	22,460	25,000	26,150	27,380
$35,000	12,090	24,400	31,450	35,000	36,610	38,330
$50,000	17,270	34,860	44,930	50,000	52,290	54,750
$75,000	25,910	52,290	67,390	75,000	78,440	82,130

CONSTANT (1988) DOLLARS — EFFECTIVE RATE (percent)

	1970[2]	1980	1985	1988	1989	1990
Single person, no dependents:						
$5,000	4.1	0.8	2.6	0.2	0.4	0.5
$10,000	10.9	8.6	8.2	7.6	7.7	7.7
$20,000	15.4	14.9	13.3	11.3	11.3	11.4
$25,000	16.8	17.4	15.6	13.2	13.3	13.4
$35,000	19.3	21.7	18.6	17.0	17.1	17.1
$50,000	23.2	26.2	22.7	19.5	19.5	19.5
$75,000	29.2	32.8	28.1	22.9	22.9	22.9
Married couple, 2 dependents [3]:						
$5,000	-	[4]-10.0	[4]-11.0	[4]-14.0	[4]-14.0	[4]-14.0
$10,000	2.5	[4]-5.4	[4]-1.2	[4]-8.6	[4]-8.5	[4]-8.5
$20,000	6.7	7.5	7.6	5.4	5.5	5.7
$25,000	10.2	9.9	9.4	7.3	7.4	7.5
$35,000	12.4	13.6	12.8	9.5	9.6	9.7
$50,000	15.0	18.7	16.9	13.1	13.2	13.3
$75,000	18.4	24.9	22.1	17.1	17.2	17.3

CONSTANT (1988) DOLLARS — MARGINAL TAX RATE (percent)

	1970[2]	1980	1985	1988	1989	1990
Single person, no dependents:						
$5,000	15.0	14	[4]11	15	15	15
$10,000	19.5	18	15	15	15	15
$20,000	25.6	26	23	28	28	28
$25,000	32.8	30	26	28	28	28
$35,000	40.0	34	30	28	28	28
$50,000	45.4	44	38	28	28	28
$75,000	51.3	55	48	33	33	33
Married couple, 2 dependents [3]:						
$5,000	14.0	[4]-10	[4]-11	[4]-14	[4]-14	[4]-14
$10,000	17.9	[4]12.5	[4]23.2	[4]10	[4]10	[4]10
$20,000	19.5	18	16	15	15	15
$25,000	22.6	21	18	15	15	15
$35,000	25.6	28	25	28	28	28
$50,000	32.8	37	33	28	28	28
$75,000	40.0	49	38	28	33	28

- Represents zero.   [1] See headnote, table 508.   [2] Includes tax surcharge.   [3] Only one spouse is assumed to work.   [4] Refundable earned income credit.

Source: U.S. Dept. of the Treasury, unpublished data.

No. 514. Federal Civilian Employment, by Branch, and Agency: 1970 to 1990

[As of September 30]

AGENCY	1970	1980	1985	1987	1988	1989	1990
Total, all agencies	**2,866,313**	**2,875,866**	**3,020,531**	**3,090,699**	**3,112,823**	**3,123,731**	**3,128,267**
Legislative Branch, total [1]	29,939	39,710	38,764	37,918	37,547	37,690	37,495
Congress [1]	11,428	19,096	19,656	19,364	19,200	19,504	19,474
U.S. Senate	(NA)	7,195	7,294	7,311	7,200	7,401	7,369
House of Representatives	(NA)	11,888	12,351	12,038	11,985	12,090	12,089
Architect of the Capitol	1,636	2,168	2,145	2,157	2,158	2,161	2,235
Judicial Branch	6,879	15,178	18,225	20,244	21,502	21,915	23,605
Supreme Court	(NA)	331	337	342	341	327	332
U.S. Courts	(NA)	14,847	17,888	19,902	21,161	21,588	23,221
Executive Branch, total	2,829,495	2,820,978	2,963,542	3,032,537	3,053,774	3,064,126	3,067,167
Executive Office of the President [1]	997	1,886	1,526	1,553	1,554	1,577	1,731
White House Office	333	406	367	366	366	371	396
Office of Management and Budget	604	616	566	550	552	527	574
Office of Administration	(NA)	166	194	193	212	202	205
Council of Economic Advisors	60	35	30	30	29	32	34
Executive Departments	1,772,363	1,716,970	1,789,270	1,806,101	1,804,057	2,065,038	2,065,542
State	40,042	23,497	25,254	25,483	25,634	25,327	25,288
Treasury	90,683	124,663	130,084	149,187	160,516	152,548	158,655
Defense	1,169,173	960,116	1,084,549	1,090,018	1,049,619	1,075,437	1,034,152
Justice	40,075	56,327	64,433	70,696	76,515	79,667	83,932
Interior	71,671	77,357	77,485	76,719	78,216	77,545	77,679
Agriculture	114,309	129,139	117,750	116,993	120,869	122,062	122,594
Commerce	36,124	48,563	35,150	34,826	52,819	45,091	69,920
Labor	10,928	23,400	18,260	17,976	18,178	18,125	17,727
Health & Human Services	110,186	155,662	140,151	127,039	123,270	122,259	123,959
Housing & Urban Development	15,046	16,964	12,289	13,033	13,342	13,544	13,596
Transportation	66,970	72,361	62,227	62,488	63,506	65,615	67,364
Energy	7,156	21,557	16,749	16,749	17,031	17,130	17,731
Education	-	7,364	4,889	4,894	4,542	4,696	4,771
Veterans Affairs [2]	169,241	228,285	247,156	250,013	245,467	245,992	248,174
Independent agencies [1]	1,056,135	1,102,122	1,172,746	1,224,883	1,248,163	997,511	999,894
Environmental Protection Agency	-	14,715	13,788	15,173	15,309	15,590	17,123
Equal Employment Opportunity Comm. .	797	3,515	3,222	3,278	3,229	2,743	2,880
Federal Deposit Insurance Corporation . .	2,462	3,520	6,723	9,219	8,249	9,031	17,641
Fed. Emergency Managmt Agency	-	3,427	3,133	2,700	2,610	3,048	3,137
General Services Administration [3]	37,661	37,654	25,782	21,878	20,070	20,063	20,277
National Aeronautics & Space Admin . .	30,674	23,714	22,562	22,950	23,130	24,165	24,872
Nuclear Regulatory Commission	-	3,283	3,605	3,426	3,341	3,288	3,353
Office of Personnel Management	5,513	8,280	6,353	6,078	6,673	6,859	6,636
Small Business Administration	4,397	5,804	4,960	4,846	4,588	4,653	5,128
Smithsonian Institution, Summary	2,547	4,403	4,757	5,028	5,034	5,158	5,092
Tennessee Valley Authority	23,785	51,714	32,035	32,738	28,290	26,676	28,392
U.S. Information Agency	10,156	8,138	8,851	8,896	8,821	8,723	8,555
U.S. International Development Cooperation Agency	14,493	6,152	5,054	4,803	4,836	4,816	4,698
U.S. Postal Service	721,183	660,014	750,021	797,851	831,956	826,310	816,886

- Represents zero.   NA Not available   [1] Includes other branches, or other agencies, not shown separately.   [2] Formerly Veterans Administration.   [3] 1980 figure includes the National Archives and Records Administration which became an independent agency in 1985.

Source: U.S. Office of Personnel Management, *Federal Civilian Workforce Statistics—Employment and Trends*, bimonthly.

No. 515. Federal White Collar Civilian Employment, by Sex and Grade: 1970 to 1989

[**1970, as of Oct. 31; thereafter as of Sept. 30.** Represents full-time white-collar employment]

GRADE [1]	TOTAL (1,000)					PERCENT WOMEN				
	1970	1980	1985	1987	1989	1970	1980	1985	1987	1989
Total employment [2]	**1,885**	**1,985**	**2,156**	**2,203**	**(NA)**	**33.1**	**38.6**	**47.4**	**48.2**	**(NA)**
General Schedule and equivalent pay system . . .	1,259	1,473	1,561	1,585	1,608	40.3	45.1	47.7	48.4	48.7
Grades 1-6 ($10,581-$23,628)	521	561	563	549	518	72.2	74.1	74.5	74.9	74.8
Grades 7-10 ($20,195-$35,369)	302	357	377	389	388	33.4	46.3	50.3	51.4	53.5
Grades 11-12 ($29,891-$46,571)	264	335	388	407	434	9.5	19.3	27.5	30	32.9
Grades 13-15 ($42,601-$76,982)	164	217	231	239	267	3	8.2	12.1	14.2	17
Grades 16-18 ($69,451-$78,200) [3]	8	3	1	1	1	1.4	4.4	6.1	6.9	9.1
Postal pay system [4]	521	483	553	600	(NA)	(NA)	26.8	33.2	36.2	(NA)

NA Not available. [1] Pay ranges shown for General Schedule grades are as of January 31, 1990.   [2] Includes other systems, not shown separately.   [3] Beginning 1980, change in number reflects shift of senior level employees to Senior Executive Service.   [4] Source: U.S. Postal Service, *National Payroll Hours*, annual.

Source: Except as noted, U.S. Office of Personnel Management, *Occupations of Federal White-Collar and Blue-Collar Workers*, biennial, and *The Pay Structure of the Federal Civil Service*, annual.

No. 516. Federal Civilian Employment and Annual Payroll, by Branch: 1970 to 1990

[Annual employment: **For fiscal year ending in year shown;** see text, section 9. Includes employees in U.S. territories and in foreign countries. Data represent employees in active-duty status, including intermittent employees. Annual employment figures are averages of monthly figures. Excludes Central Intelligence Agency, National Security Agency, and, as of November 1984, the Defense Intelligence Agency. See also *Historical Statistics, Colonial Times to 1970*, series Y 308-317]

YEAR	EMPLOYMENT						PAYROLL (mil. dol.)				
	Total (1,000)	Percent of U.S. employed [1]	Executive		Legisla-tive (1,000)	Judicial (1,000)	Total	Executive		Legisla-tive	Judi-cial
			Total (1,000)	Defense (1,000)				Total	Defense		
1970 [2]	2,997	3.7	[2]2,961	1,263	29	7	[2]27,322	[2]26,894	11,264	338	89
1975	2,877	3.4	2,830	1,044	37	10	39,126	38,423	13,418	549	154
1979	2,897	2.9	2,844	974	40	13	53,590	52,513	18,065	817	260
1980 [3]	2,987	3.0	[3]2,933	971	40	14	[3]58,012	[3]56,841	18,795	883	288
1981	2,909	2.9	2,855	986	40	15	63,793	62,510	21,227	922	360
1982	2,871	2.9	2,816	1,019	39	16	65,503	64,125	22,226	980	398
1983	2,878	2.9	2,823	1,033	39	16	69,878	68,420	23,406	1,013	445
1984	2,935	2.8	2,879	1,052	40	17	74,616	73,084	25,253	1,081	451
1985	3,001	2.8	2,944	1,080	39	18	80,599	78,992	28,330	1,098	509
1986	3,047	2.8	2,991	1,089	38	19	82,598	80,941	29,272	1,112	545
1987	3,075	2.7	3,018	1,084	38	19	85,543	83,797	29,786	1,153	593
1988	3,113	2.7	3,054	1,073	38	21	88,841	86,960	29,609	1,226	656
1989	3,133	2.7	3,074	1,067	38	22	92,847	90,870	30,301	1,266	711
1990	[4]3,233	2.7	3,173	1,060	38	23	99,138	97,022	31,990	1,329	787

[1] Civilian only. See table 612.   [2] Includes 33,000 temporary census workers.   [3] Includes 81,116 temporary census workers.   [4] Includes 111,020 temporary census workers.

Source: U.S. Office of Personnel Management, *Federal Civilian Workforce Statistics—Employment and Trends*, bimonthly; and unpublished data.

No. 517. Federal Civilian Employment—Summary: 1970 to 1990

[**In thousands. As of Dec. 31.** Excludes U.S. Territories and foreign countries, Central Intelligence Agency, National Security Agency, and the Defense Intelligence Agency. Partially estimated]

CHARACTERISTICS	UNITED STATES							WASHINGTON, DC [1]			
	1970	1975	1980	1985	1988	1989	1990	1980	1985	1989	1990
Paid employment	2,645	2,741	2,782	2,902	2,981	2,974	2,940	366	353	358	358
Male	1,931	1,896	1,806	1,769	1,730	1,722	1,685	202	191	183	183
Female	714	845	976	1,133	1,251	1,252	1,255	164	162	175	175
Full-time	2,516	2,496	2,504	2,589	2,648	2,673	2,632	342	335	342	342
Other	129	245	278	313	333	301	308	24	18	16	16
Competitive service [2]	2,393	1,714	1,692	1,710	1,707	1,733	1,694	258	246	249	248
Permanent appointment	2,281	1,647	1,622	1,628	1,632	1,662	1,637	247	234	241	241
Temp. and indef. appointment	112	67	70	82	75	71	57	11	12	8	7
Excepted and Senior Executive Services (SES) [3]	252	1,027	1,091	1,191	1,275	1,241	1,246	107	108	109	109
Permanent appointment	164	860	917	1,015	1,070	1,049	1,029	70	73	76	76
Temp. and indef. appointment	88	167	174	176	205	192	217	37	35	33	33
White-collar [4]	2,113	2,254	2,324	2,478	2,596	2,588	2,576	335	327	336	336
Blue-collar [4]	532	487	458	424	385	386	364	31	26	22	22

[1] Through June 30, 1980, represents SMSA; thereafter, MSA.   [2] In 1971, under Postal Reorganization Act of 1970, U.S. Postal Service employees were changed from competitive service to excepted service.   [3] Excepted from competitive requirements of Civil Service Act. Prior to 1980 SES was not included in total.   [4] Through 1980, based on full-time employment; beginning 1985, based on total workforce.

No. 518. Accessions to and Separations From Paid Civilian Employment in the Federal Government: 1970 to 1991

[**In thousands, except rate. For fiscal year ending in year shown;** see text, section 9. Includes accessions and separations of full-time, part-time and intermittent employees]

ITEM	UNITED STATES							WASHINGTON, DC [1]				
	1970 [2]	1975	1980 [2]	1985	1989	1990	Oct. 1990-July 1991	1980 [2]	1985	1989	1990	Oct. 1990 July 1991
Accessions, total	727	606	995	630	636	898	501	94	63	67	59	55
Monthly rate [3]	2.2	1.9	2.9	1.9	1.8	2.5	1.7	2.3	1.6	1.7	1.5	1.6
Separations, total	797	589	1,004	530	606	889	489	89	58	58	52	36
Monthly rate [3]	2.4	1.8	3.0	1.6	1.7	2.4	1.7	2.2	1.5	1.5	1.3	1.1
Quit [4]	334	213	228	218	205	191	116	33	25	26	23	13

[1] See footnote 1, table 517.   [2] Includes temporary census enumerators.   [3] Per 100 employees.   [4] Represents voluntary resignations by employees or separations by agency if employee declines new assignment, abandons position, joins military, or fails to return from military furlough.

Source of tables 517 and 518: U.S. Office of Personnel Management, *Federal Civilian Workforce Statistics—Employment and Trends*, bimonthly; and unpublished data.

No. 519. Paid Civilian Employment in the Federal Government: 1989

[As of December 31. Excludes members and employees of Congress, Central Intelligence Agency, Defense Intelligence Agency, employees overseas, temporary census enumerators, seasonal and on-call employees, temporary Christmas help of the U.S. Postal Service, and National Security Agency]

DIVISION AND STATE	Total (1,000)	Percent defense	DIVISION AND STATE	Total (1,000)	Percent defense
U.S.	2,906	31.4	DC	212	8.1
			VA	161	66.2
Northeast	481	26.3	WV	15	11.0
N.E.	124	26.6	NC	46	33.0
ME.	17	58.8	SC	32	59.0
NH.	8	19.4	GA.	88	41.2
VT	5	12.5	FL.	112	29.4
MA.	60	19.5	E.S.C.	173	32.5
RI	10	41.8	KY.	35	35.4
CT	24	20.7	TN.	56	13.9
M.A.	357	26.2	AL.	57	44.5
NY.	152	11.8	MS.	24	43.6
NJ	75	34.6	W.S.C	275	35.0
PA.	129	38.1	AR.	19	25.6
Midwest	492	24.7	LA.	34	25.7
E.N.C	320	26.4	OK.	45	50.2
OH.	91	37.8	TX.	177	33.9
IN	41	37.0	West	642	37.4
IL.	104	19.4	Mt.	193	31.2
MI	56	20.1	MT.	11	11.6
WI	27	11.5	ID .	10	13.5
W.N.C.	173	21.7	WY	6	17.0
MN.	32	9.0	CO.	53	26.0
IA	18	8.0	NM.	26	36.5
MO	66	28.9	AZ.	39	26.0
ND.	8	25.8	UT.	36	57.9
SD.	9	15.3	NV.	11	18.9
NE.	15	26.7	Pac.	449	40.0
KS.	25	27.3	WA	65	43.8
South.	1,254	33.9	OR.	29	10.2
S.A.	806	33.8	CA.	315	39.5
DE.	5	32.7	AK.	15	32.2
MD.	133	31.0	HI	25	75.6

[1] Preliminary. Includes employees not specified by State.

Source: U.S. Office of Personnel Management, *Biennial Report of Employment by Geographic Area*

No. 520. Paid Full-Time Federal Civilian Employment, All Areas: 1980 to 1990

[As of March 31. Excludes employees of Congress and Federal courts, maritime seamen of Dept. of Commerce, and small number for whom rates were not reported. See text, section 10 for explanation of general schedule and wage system. See also *Historical Statistics, Colonial Times to 1970*, series Y 318-331]

COMPENSATION AUTHORITY	EMPLOYEES (1,000)					AVERAGE PAY				
	1980	1985	1988	1989	1990	1980	1985	1988	1989	1990
Total.	2,498	2,590	2,014	2,016	2,036	19,447	26,139	28,211	29,618	31,174
General Schedule.	1,402	1,450	1,480	1,494	1,506	19,910	26,186	28,114	29,655	31,239
Wage System .	456	418	383	374	369	17,970	23,288	24,965	25,462	26,565
Postal pay system [1] .	527	586	(NA)	(NA)	(NA)	18,344	26,559	(NA)	(NA)	(NA)
Other.	113	136	151	148	161	24,825	34,413	37,393	39,764	41,149

NA Not available.   [1] Source: U.S. Postal Service, *National Payroll Hours*, annual.

Source: Except as noted, U.S. Office of Personnel Management, *Pay Structure of the Federal Civil Service*, annual.

No. 521. Federal General Schedule Employee Pay Increases: 1965 to 1992

[Percent change from prior year shown, except 1965, change from 1964. Represents legislated pay increases. For some years data based on range; for details see source]

EFFECTIVE DATE	Average increase	EFFECTIVE DATE	Average increase	EFFECTIVE DATE	Average increase
Oct. 1, 1965	3.6	Oct. 1, 1974	5.5	Jan. 1, 1985	3.5
July 1, 1966	2.9	Oct. 1, 1975	5.0	Jan. 1, 1986	-
Oct. 1, 1967	4.5	Oct. 1, 1976	5.2	Jan. 1, 1987	3.0
July 1, 1968	4.9	Oct. 1, 1977	7.0	Jan. 1, 1988	2.0
July 1, 1969	9.1	Oct. 1, 1978	5.5	Jan. 1, 1989	4.1
Dec. 27, 1969	6.0	Oct. 1, 1979	7.0	Jan. 1, 1990	3.6
Jan. 1, 1971	6.0	Oct. 1, 1980	9.1	Jan. 1, 1991	4.1
Jan. 1, 1972	5.5	Oct. 1, 1981	4.8	Jan. 1, 1992	4.2
Oct. 1, 1972	5.1	Oct. 1, 1982	4.0		
Oct. 1, 1973	4.8	Jan. 1, 1984	4.0		

- Represents zero.

Source: U.S. Office of Personnel Management, *Pay Structure of the Federal Civil Service*, annual.

No. 522. Federal Government Employment, by Race and National Origin and, by Pay System: 1982 and 1990

[As of Sept. 30. Covers total employment for only Executive Branch agencies participating in OPM's Central Personnel Data File (CPDF). Excludes foreign nationals abroad and U.S. Postal Service]

PAY SYSTEM	1982					1990				
	Total employ-ees (1,000)	Race/National origin				Total employ-ees (1,000)	Race/National origin			
		Total [1] (1,000)	Per-cent of total	Black non-His-panic (1,000)	His-panic (1,000)		Total [1] (1,000)	Per-cent of total	Black non-His-panic (1,000)	His-panic (1,000)
All pay systems, total [2]...	2,008.6	484.0	24.1	311.1	90.0	2,150.4	587.5	27.3	356.9	115.2
General Schedule and equivalent [3]..	1,508.3	336.1	22.3	222.0	59.0	1,655.5	437.3	26.4	272.7	83.1
Grades 1-4 ($10,581-$18,947)....	303.6	101.9	33.6	71.0	16.1	228.1	96.1	42.1	65.1	15.7
Grades 5-8 ($16,305-$29,081)....	464.9	126.5	27.2	90.2	20.2	506.1	168.7	33.3	115.0	28.7
Grades 9-12 ($24,705-$46,571) ..	530.0	87.6	16.5	50.1	18.7	648.2	137.9	21.3	75.0	31.6
Grades 13-15 ($42,601-$76,982) ..	209.8	20.1	9.6	10.7	4.0	273.1	34.6	12.7	17.6	7.1
Executive, total..............	7.8	0.6	7.7	0.3	0.1	10.1	0.8	7.9	0.5	0.2
Wage pay system	414.0	134.6	32.5	83.5	28.0	368.8	124.6	33.8	72.8	26.9
Other pay systems [4]...........	69.3	10.1	14.6	3.7	2.3	115.2	24.7	21.4	11.0	4.8

[1] Includes American Indians, Alaska Natives, Asians, and Pacific Islanders, not shown separately.   [2] Due to the inclusion of unspecified employee records, the pay systems listed do not add to the total.   [3] Pay rates as of January 1990 for general schedule. Each grade (except Executive) includes several salary steps. Range is from lowest to highest step of grades shown.   [4] Includes white-collar employment in other than General Schedule and Equivalent or Executive pay plans.
Source: U.S. Office of Personnel Management, *1989 Affirmative Employment Statistics*, biennial.

No. 523. Federal Land and Buildings Owned and Leased, and Predominant Land Usage: 1970 to 1989

[For fiscal years ending in years shown; see text section 9. Covers Federal real property throughout the world, except as noted. Cost of land figures represent total cost of property owned in year shown. For further details see source. For data on Federal land by State, see table 343]

ITEM AND AGENCY	Unit	1970	1975	1980	1984	1985	1986	1987	1988	1989
Federally owned: Land	Mil. acres.	762	761	720	727	727	727	724	688	662
Buildings, number [1]	1,000 ...	418	405	403	438	454	429	412	442	451
Buildings, floor area [1]........	Mil. sq/ft .	2,542	2,502	2,522	2,725	2,860	2,731	2,700	2,780	2,806
Cost of land, buildings, etc.[2]	Bil. dol. ..	79	91	107	147	148	158	165	164	164
Federally leased: Land	Mil. acres.	1.6	1.2	1.4	1.8	1.3	1.3	1.6	1.6	1.5
Buildings, floor area [1]........	Mil. sq/ft .	182	210	214	203	237	246	246	248	254
Rental property, cost	Mil. dol ..	451	664	1,054	1,547	1,681	1,774	1,893	2,001	2,127
Predominant usage (U.S. only)	Mil. acres.	761	760	720	727	727	727	724	688	662
Forest and wildlife.............	Mil. acres.	503	502	422	430	431	431	431	400	375
Grazing	Mil. acres.	164	164	162	153	155	155	154	151	151
Parks and historic sites	Mil. acres.	25	25	93	91	94	96	96	99	98
Other	Mil. acres.	70	69	43	52	48	46	43	38	39

[1] Excludes data for Dept. of Defense military functions outside United States.   [2] Includes other uses not shown separately.
Source: U.S. General Services Administration, *Inventory Report on Real Property Owned by the United States Throughout the World*, annual.

No. 524. Public Lands—Disposal: 1980 to 1990

[For fiscal year ending in year shown: see text, section 9. Period figures are totals, not annual averages. See also *Historical Statistics, Colonial Times to 1970*, series J 10-15 and J 28-32]

ITEM	Unit	1980	1985	1986	1987	1988	1989	1990
Applications, entries, and selections allowed [1]	1,000 acres .	1,167	1,404	4	1	1	1	1
Applications, entries, and selections approved [1]	1,000 acres .	175	6,491	683	1,812	1,387	579	238
Patents and certificates [1]........	1,000 acres .	2,495	4,217	3,704	3,000	5,419	780	1052
Mineral class, total	Number....	106,125	119,419	105,513	89,789	82,585	83,762	81,354
Leases [2].................	Number....	105,963	119,101	105,226	89,546	82,450	83,656	81,248
Permits [2].................	Number....	132	316	246	231	121	96	96
Licenses	Number....	30	2	41	12	14	10	5
Grazing Leases [3].............	Number....	7,700	7,387	7,218	7,164	7,197	7,263	7,105
Permits [4]	Number....	14,741	12,493	12,394	12,368	12,537	12,362	12,153

[1] Excludes Indian fee and reissue trusts and corrective patents.   [2] Excludes free-use permits for disposition of mineral materials.   [3] Beginning 1985, as of September 30.   [4] Licenses and permits within grazing districts.
Source: U.S. Bureau of Land Management, *Public Land Statistics*, annual.

Figure 11.1
Cumulative Arms Transfers: 1985 to 1989

Billions of dollars

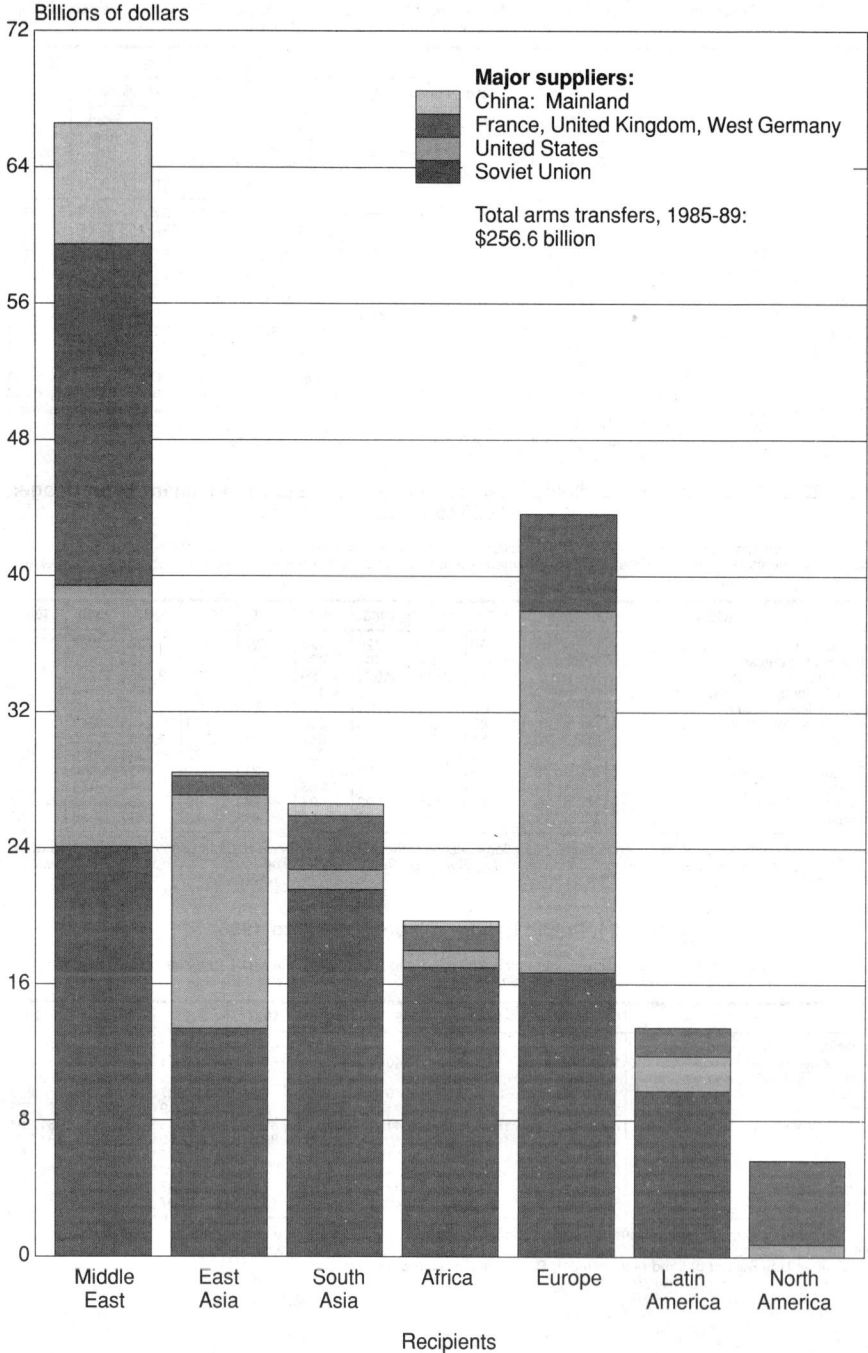

Major suppliers:
China: Mainland
France, United Kingdom, West Germany
United States
Soviet Union

Total arms transfers, 1985-89:
$256.6 billion

Recipients

Source: Chart prepared by U.S. Bureau of the Census. For data, see table 534.

National Defense and Veterans Affairs

This section presents data on national defense and its human and financial costs; active and reserve military personnel; ships, equipment and aircraft; and federally sponsored programs and benefits for veterans. The principal sources of these data are the annual *Selected Manpower Statistics* and the *Atlas/Data Abstract for the United States and Selected Areas* issued by the Office of the Secretary of Defense; *Annual Report of Secretary of Veterans Affairs, Department of Veterans Affairs,* and *The Budget of the United States Government,* Office of Management and Budget. For more data on expenditures, personnel, and ships, see section 31.

Department of Defense (DOD).—DOD is responsible for providing military forces of the United States. The President serves as Commander in Chief of the Armed Forces; from him, the authority flows to the Secretary of Defense and through the Joint Chiefs of Staff to the commanders of unified and specified commands (e.g., Strategic Air Command).

Reserve components.—Reserve personnel of the Armed Forces consist of the Army National Guard, Army Reserve, Naval Reserve, Marine Corps Reserve, Air National Guard, Air Force Reserve, and Coast Guard Reserve. They provide trained personnel available for active duty in the Armed Forces in time of war or national emergency and at such other times as authorized by law. The National Guard has dual Federal-State responsibilities and uses jointly provided equipment, facilities, and budget support. The President is empowered to mobilize the National Guard and to use such of the Armed Forces as he considers necessary to enforce Federal authority in any State.

The ready reserve includes selected reservists who are intended to assist active forces in a war and the individual ready reserve who, in a major war, would be used to fill out active and reserve units and later would be a source of combat replacements; a portion of the ready reserve serves in an active status. The

> **In Brief**
>
> 1992 National
> defense outlays $307.3 bil.

standby reserve cannot be called to active duty unless the Congress gives explicit approval. The retired reserve represents a low potential for mobilization.

Department of Veterans Affairs.—The Department of Veterans Affairs administers laws authorizing benefits for eligible former and present members of the Armed Forces and for the beneficiaries of deceased members. Veterans benefits available under various acts of Congress include compensation for service-connected disability or death; pensions for nonservice-connected disability or death; vocational rehabilitation, education, and training; home loan insurance; life insurance; health care; special housing and automobiles or other conveyances for certain disabled veterans; burial and plot allowances; and educational assistance to families of deceased or totally disabled veterans, servicemen missing in action, or prisoners of war. Since these benefits are legislated by Congress, the dates they were enacted and the dates they apply to veterans may be different from the actual dates the conflicts occurred.

VA estimates of veterans cover all persons with active duty service during periods of war or armed conflict and until 1982 include those living outside the United States. Veteran population estimates for September 1982 are for the 50 States, the District of Columbia and Puerto Rico. Veterans whose active duty service was entirely during periods of peacetime are eligible for some veterans benefits and, where appropriate, are included in VA estimates.

Historical statistics.—Tabular headnotes provide cross-references, where applicable, to *Historical Statistics of the United States, Colonial Times to 1970.* See Appendix IV.

National Defense and Veterans Affairs

No. 525. National Defense Outlays and Veterans Benefits: 1960 to 1992

[For fiscal year ending in year shown; see text, section 9. Includes outlays of Department of Defense, Department of Veterans Affairs, and other agencies for activities primarily related to national defense and veterans programs. For explanation of average annual percent change, see Guide to Tabular Presentation. Minus sign (-) indicates decline. See Historical Statistics, Colonial Times to 1970, series Y 472, 473 and Y 476, for related data]

Year	NATIONAL DEFENSE AND VETERANS OUTLAYS				ANNUAL PERCENT CHANGE [1]				DEFENSE OUTLAYS, PERCENT OF—		
		Defense outlays				Defense outlays					
	Total outlays (bil. dol.)	Current dollars	Constant (1982) dollars (bil. dol.)	Veterans outlays (bil. dol.)	Total outlays	Current dollars	Constant (1982) dollars	Veterans outlays	Federal outlays	Gross national product [2]	
1960	53.5	48.1	192.1	5.4	2.5	2.4	-1.9	3.1	52.2	9.5	
1962	58.0	52.3	202.2	5.6	4.0	4.3	2.6	1.7	49.0	9.4	
1963	58.9	53.4	197.1	5.5	1.6	2.0	-2.5	-1.9	48.0	9.1	
1964	60.4	54.8	198.8	5.7	2.6	2.5	0.9	2.9	46.2	8.7	
1965	56.3	50.6	181.4	5.7	-6.8	-7.6	-8.8	0.7	42.8	7.5	
1966	64.0	58.1	197.9	5.9	13.7	14.8	9.1	3.5	43.2	7.9	
1967	78.2	71.4	235.1	6.7	22.1	22.9	18.8	13.8	45.4	9.0	
1968	89.0	81.9	254.8	7.0	13.8	14.7	8.4	4.4	46.0	9.6	
1969	90.1	82.5	243.4	7.6	1.3	0.7	-4.5	8.5	44.9	8.9	
1970	90.4	81.7	225.6	8.7	0.3	-1.0	-7.3	13.6	41.8	8.3	
1971	88.7	78.9	202.7	9.8	-1.9	-3.5	-10.2	12.7	37.5	7.5	
1972	89.9	79.2	190.9	10.7	1.4	0.4	-5.8	9.8	34.3	6.9	
1973	88.7	76.7	175.1	12.0	1.3	-3.1	-8.3	12.0	31.2	6.0	
1974	92.7	79.3	163.3	13.4	4.6	3.5	-6.7	11.4	29.5	5.6	
1975	103.1	86.5	159.8	16.6	11.2	9.0	-2.1	24.0	26.0	5.7	
1976	108.1	89.6	153.6	18.4	4.8	3.6	-3.9	11.0	24.1	5.3	
1976, TQ [3]	26.2	22.3	37.1	4.0	(X)	(X)	(X)	(X)	23.2	5.0	
1977	115.3	97.2	154.3	18.0	6.7	8.5	0.5	-2.1	23.8	5.0	
1978	123.5	104.5	155.0	19.0	7.1	7.5	0.5	5.2	22.8	4.8	
1979	136.3	116.3	159.1	19.9	10.4	11.3	2.6	5.0	23.1	4.8	
1980	155.2	134.0	164.0	21.2	13.9	15.2	3.1	6.3	22.7	5.0	
1981	180.5	157.5	171.4	23.0	16.3	17.6	4.5	8.5	23.2	5.3	
1982	209.3	185.3	185.3	24.0	15.9	17.6	8.1	4.2	24.9	5.9	
1983	234.7	209.9	201.3	24.8	12.1	13.3	8.6	3.3	26.0	6.3	
1984	253.0	227.4	211.3	25.6	7.8	8.3	5.0	3.2	26.7	6.2	
1985	279.0	252.7	230.0	26.3	10.3	11.1	8.8	2.7	26.7	6.4	
1986	299.7	273.4	244.0	26.4	7.4	8.2	6.1	0.4	27.6	6.5	
1987	308.8	282.0	251.0	26.8	3.0	3.1	2.9	1.5	28.1	6.4	
1988	319.8	290.4	252.8	29.4	3.6	3.0	0.7	9.7	27.3	6.1	
1989	333.7	303.6	256.6	30.1	4.3	4.5	1.5	2.4	26.2	5.9	
1990	328.4	299.3	271.1	29.1	-1.6	-1.4	5.7	-3.3	23.9	5.5	
1991	304.6	273.3	238.5	31.3	-7.2	-8.7	-12.0	7.6	20.7	4.9	
1992	341.1	307.3	258.8	33.8	12.0	12.4	8.5	8.0	20.8	5.2	

X Not applicable. [1] Change from prior year shown; for 1960, change from 1955. [2] Represents fiscal year GNP; for definition, see text, section 14. [3] Transition quarter, July-Sept.

Source: U.S. Office of Management and Budget, *Budget of the United States Government,* annual.

No. 526. Federal Budget Outlays for National Defense Functions: 1970 to 1992

[In billions of dollars, except percent. For fiscal year ending in year shown; see text, section 9. Minus sign (-) indicates decline. See Historical Statistics, Colonial Times to 1970, series Y 473, for total]

DEFENSE FUNCTION	1970	1980	1983	1984	1985	1986	1987	1988	1989	1990	1991	1992, est.
Total.	81.7	134.0	209.9	227.4	252.7	273.4	282.0	290.4	303.6	299.3	273.3	307.3
Percent change [1]	10.1	15.2	13.3	8.3	11.1	8.2	3.1	3.0	4.5	-1.4	-8.7	12.4
Defense Dept., military	80.1	130.9	204.4	220.9	245.2	265.5	274.0	281.9	294.9	289.8	262.4	294.6
Military personnel	29.0	40.9	60.9	64.2	67.8	71.5	72.0	76.3	80.7	75.6	83.4	79.3
Percent of military	36.2	31.2	29.8	29.0	27.7	26.9	26.3	27.1	27.0	-1.7	-9.5	12.3
Operation, maintenance	21.6	44.8	64.9	67.4	72.4	75.3	76.2	84.5	87.0	88.3	101.8	97.8
Procurement	21.6	29.0	53.6	61.9	70.4	76.5	80.7	77.2	81.6	81.0	82.0	74.0
Research and development . .	7.2	13.1	20.6	23.1	27.1	32.3	33.6	34.8	37.0	37.5	34.6	36.1
Military construction	1.2	2.5	3.5	3.7	4.3	5.1	5.9	5.9	5.3	5.1	3.5	4.5
Family housing	0.6	1.7	2.1	2.4	2.6	2.8	2.9	3.1	3.3	3.5	3.3	3.4
Other [2]	-1.1	-1.1	-1.2	-1.7	0.6	2.0	2.6	0.2	0.1	-1.2	-46.2	-0.5
Atomic energy activities [3]	1.4	2.9	5.2	6.1	7.1	7.4	7.5	7.9	8.1	9.0	10.0	11.7
Defense-related activities [4] . . .	0.2	0.2	0.3	0.4	0.5	0.5	0.6	0.5	0.6	0.6	0.9	1.0

[1] Change from immediate prior year; for 1970, change from 1965. [2] Revolving and management funds, trust funds, special foreign currency program, allowances, and offsetting receipts. [3] Defense activities only. [4] Includes civil defense activities.

Source: U.S. Office of Management and Budget, *Budget of the United States Government,* annual.

No. 527. National Defense—Budget Authority and Outlays: 1975 to 1992

[In billions of dollars, except percent. For fiscal year ending in year shown, except as noted; see text, section 9. See *Historical Statistics, Colonial Times to 1970*, series Y 458-460 for outlays]

ITEM	1975	1980	1983	1984	1985	1986	1987	1988	1989	1990	1991	1992, est.
Budget authority [1]	87.6	143.9	245.0	265.2	294.7	289.1	287.4	292.0	299.6	303.3	303.6	289.2
Department of Defense-Military [2]	85.8	140.6	238.9	258.2	286.8	281.4	279.5	283.8	290.8	293.0	290.0	276.2
Atomic energy [1][3]	1.8	3.2	6.2	7.0	7.8	7.7	8.0	8.3	8.7	10.3	12.7	12.9
Unobligated balances [1][4]	15.1	23.3	35.1	44.0	52.2	62.1	60.4	42.8	41.7	(NA)	(NA)	(NA)
Department of Defense-Military	15.1	23.0	34.6	43.4	51.6	61.5	60.0	42.3	41.2	(NA)	(NA)	(NA)
Atomic energy [1][3]	(NA)	0.3	0.6	0.6	0.6	0.6	0.4	0.5	0.5	(NA)	(NA)	(NA)
Outlays (Defense) [1]	86.5	134.0	209.9	227.4	252.7	273.4	282.0	290.4	303.6	299.3	273.3	307.3
Department of Defense-Military	84.9	130.9	204.4	220.9	245.2	265.5	274.0	281.9	294.9	289.7	262.4	294.6
Atomic energy [1][3]	1.7	3.1	5.5	6.5	7.6	7.9	8.0	8.4	8.7	9.0	10.0	11.7

NA Not available.   [1] Includes defense budget authority, balances, and outlays by other departments.   [2] Excluding accruals.   [3] Includes other defense related activities.   [4] Start of year.

Source: U.S. Office of Management and Budget, *Budget of the United States Government,* annual.

No. 528. Employment—Defense-Related Agencies: 1970 to 1990

[In thousands, except percent. Annual averages]

EMPLOYMENT	1970	1980	1984	1985	1986	1987	1988	1989	1990
Total U.S. employment [1]	80,796	100,907	106,702	108,856	111,303	114,177	116,677	119,030	119,550
Federal	4,763	4,386	4,521	4,608	4,601	4,709	4,690	4,662	4,577
Resident Armed Forces	2,118	1,604	1,697	1,706	1,706	1,737	1,709	1,688	1,637
Civilian personnel [2]	2,645	2,782	2,824	2,902	2,895	2,972	2,981	2,974	2,940
Federal defense-related agencies, excluding Armed Forces [3]	1,211	948	1,033	1,073	1,059	1,079	1,041	(NA)	1,024
Percent of Federal civilian personnel.	44.3	33.1	36.8	37.3	36.5	36.3	34.9	(NA)	34.8
Federal defense-related agencies [1]	3,329	2,552	2,730	2,779	2,765	2,816	2,750	(NA)	2,661
Percent of total Federal [1]	68.7	57.1	60.6	60.7	60.0	59.8	58.6	(NA)	58.1
Percent of total U.S. [1]	4.1	2.5	2.6	2.6	2.5	2.5	2.4	(NA)	2.2

NA Not available.   [1] Includes resident Armed Forces.   [2] See table 517.   [3] Source: Beginning 1980, U.S. Dept. of Defense, *Civilian Manpower Statistics,* annual (Sept. issues).

Source: Except as noted, U.S. Bureau of Labor Statistics, *Employment and Earnings,* monthly.

No. 529. Military and Civilian Personnel and Expenditures: 1985 to 1990

UNIT	1985	1986	1987	1988	1989	1990
Personnel, total (mil. dol.)	3,808	3,936	3,934	3,864	3,885	3,693
Active duty military	1,354	1,378	1,377	1,338	1,342	1,185
Civilian	976	960	979	937	965	931
Reserve and National Guard.	1,478	1,597	1,578	1,588	1,578	1,577
Expenditures, total (mil. dol.)	216,045	217,740	217,719	211,195	212,509	209,904
Payroll outlays	75,949	81,714	84,457	85,428	92,593	88,650
Active duty military pay	29,818	31,300	34,002	34,483	38,221	33,705
Civilian Pay	24,815	28,156	26,328	27,299	27,960	28,230
Retired military pay	17,029	17,633	18,658	18,573	20,591	21,159
Reserve and National Guard pay	4,287	4,624	5,468	5,073	5,821	5,556
Prime contract awards over $25,000 (mil. dol.)	140,096	136,026	133,262	125,767	119,917	121,254
Supply contracts	92,375	86,626	79,006	72,634	67,540	66,895
Service contracts	24,224	24,637	26,978	25,109	24,347	28,540
R and D contracts	18,752	19,545	21,540	22,364	22,996	21,955
Construction contracts	3,245	3,810	4,102	3,795	3,668	2,088
Civil function contracts	1,500	1,409	1,636	1,866	1,365	1,775
Major area of work (mil. dol.):						
Aircraft, fixed wing	11,683	10,085	8,048	5,324	5,335	6,329
Gas Turbines and jet engines	2,848	2,842	1,766	1,521	1,630	1,856
Guided Missiles	(NA)	1,067	882	869	886	928
Guided missile handling and servicing equip.	(NA)	(NA)	(NA)	(NA)	875	446
Major location of expenditures (mil. dol.):						
Arlington VA	(NA)	2,263	2,413	2,449	2,314	2,527
Bethpage, NY	2,699	2,875	3,261	2,760	(NA)	2,377
Denver, CO	(NA)	(NA)	(NA)	(NA)	(NA)	2,506
Fort Worth, TX	3,912	4,889	3,709	3,681	4,122	3,594
Los Angeles, CA	7,125	5,704	2,696	(NA)	2,339	2,459
Newport News, VA	(NA)	(NA)	2,355	5,423	(NA)	2,745
Norfolk, VA	2,200	2,464	2,523	2,689	2,597	2,741
San Diego, CA	4,027	4,043	4,668	4,208	4,534	4,820
St. Louis, MO.	7,412	5,556	5,793	5,109	5,965	5,616
Washington, DC	(NA)	(NA)	(NA)	2,687	2,352	2,771

NA Not available.

Source: U.S. Dept. of Defense, *Atlas/Data abstract for the United States and Selected Areas,* annual.

No. 530. Military Prime Contract Awards to All Businesses, by Program: 1980 to 1991

[In billions of dollars. Net values for fiscal year ending in year shown; see text, section 9. Includes all new prime contracts; debit or credit changes in contracts are also included. Actions cover official awards, amendments, or other changes in prime contracts to obtain military supplies, services, or construction. Excludes term contracts and contracts which do not obligate a firm total dollar amount or fixed quantity, but includes job orders, task orders, and delivery orders against such contracts]

DOD PROCUREMENT PROGRAM	1980	1984	1985	1986	1987	1988	1989	1990	1991
Total	83.7	146.0	163.7	158.8	156.5	151.4	139.3	144.7	150.9
Intragovernmental [1]	10.2	10.1	12.4	9.9	8.8	8.9	9.6	10.0	11.9
For work outside the U.S.	5.4	8.3	8.6	9.1	8.9	8.2	6.4	7.1	9.2
Educ. and nonprofit institutions	1.5	2.7	3.1	3.4	3.5	3.5	3.3	3.5	3.6
With business firms for work in the U.S. [2]	66.7	124.9	139.6	136.5	135.3	130.8	120.0	123.8	125.9
Major hard goods	41.0	86.3	98.1	92.8	93.0	85.9	79.9	79.1	74.1
Aircraft	12.5	29.2	34.6	32.3	27.7	25.0	24.2	24.0	23.6
Electronics and communication equip.	9.6	19.7	22.0	19.7	22.6	17.8	18.1	18.5	15.2
Missiles and space systems	7.9	16.7	18.7	19.4	19.8	19.7	18.7	17.1	16.4
Ships	6.0	9.4	10.4	9.4	11.5	13.7	9.6	10.3	9.3
Tanks, ammo. and weapons	5.1	11.4	12.5	12.0	11.6	9.7	9.2	9.2	9.6
Services	5.9	8.5	9.1	10.4	11.0	12.0	11.7	14.6	16.9

[1] Covers only purchases from other Federal agencies and reimbursable purchases on behalf of foreign governments.
[2] Includes Department of Defense. Includes other business not shown separately. Contracts awarded for work in U.S. possessions, and other areas subject to complete sovereignty of U.S.; contracts in a classified location; and any intragovernmental contracts entered into overseas.

Source: U.S. Dept. of Defense, Prime Contract Awards, semiannual.

No. 531. Department of Defense Contract Awards, Payroll, and Civilian and Military Personnel—States: 1990

[For years ending Sept. 30. Contracts refer to awards made in year specified; expenditures relating to awards may extend over several years. Civilian employees include United States citizen and foreign national direct hire civilians subject to Office of Management and Budget (OMB) ceiling controls and civilian personnel involved in civil functions in the United States. Excludes indirect hire civilians and those direct hire civilians not subject to OMB ceiling controls. Military personnel include active duty personnel based ashore. Excludes personnel temporarily shore-based in a transient status, or afloat. Payroll outlays include the gross earnings of civilian and active duty military personnel for services rendered to the government and for cash allowances for benefits. Excludes employer's share of employee benefits, accrued military retirement benefits and most permanent change of station costs]

STATE	Contract awards (mil. dol.)	Payroll (mil. dol.)	PERSONNEL (1,000) Civilian	PERSONNEL (1,000) Military	STATE	Contract awards (mil. dol.)	Payroll (mil. dol.)	PERSONNEL (1,000) Civilian	PERSONNEL (1,000) Military
U.S.	124,119	96,970	911.2	1,263.4	DC	1,516	1,190	17.1	13.9
					VA	6,781	10,507	105.2	94.0
Northeast	27,191	9,253	126.4	67.2	WV	152	206	1.7	0.6
N.E.	13,889	3,064	32.4	25.0	NC	1,561	3,774	17.5	98.0
ME.	1,065	667	9.3	5.3	SC	985	2,622	19.1	38.3
NH.	427	219	1.4	0.3	GA	1,984	3,793	37.3	60.0
VT.	71	81	0.7	0.1	FL	5,166	6,003	32.4	75.0
MA.	6,933	1,016	11.7	8.5	E.S.C.	6,275	5,906	59.4	79.3
RI.	413	422	4.3	3.6	KY	591	1,807	14.2	38.7
CT.	4,979	659	5.0	7.0	TN	2,059	944	7.9	9.3
M.A.	13,302	6,190	94.0	42.2	AL	1,834	2,093	26.0	18.6
NY.	6,860	1,867	17.8	24.9	MS.	1,792	1,062	11.3	12.8
NJ.	3,493	1,634	25.8	11.3	W.S.C.	12,557	11,282	92.9	173.8
PA.	2,949	2,689	50.5	5.9	AR	306	718	4.9	8.7
Midwest	20,960	11,023	123.0	127.6	LA	1,246	1,414	9.2	26.4
E.N.C.	11,045	6,359	85.8	58.3	OK	779	1,893	22.0	26.2
OH.	4,760	2,125	35.4	11.7	TX	10,225	7,258	56.7	112.5
IN.	2,190	1,043	15.3	5.6	West	34,729	27,876	235.5	398.3
IL.	1,791	1,837	19.9	31.8	Mt.	7,131	7,136	58.7	106.0
MI.	1,337	927	11.7	8.3	MT.	82	232	1.2	4.4
WI.	968	427	3.6	1.0	ID.	78	282	1.4	4.4
W.N.C.	9,915	4,665	37.2	69.3	WY	63	173	1.1	3.6
MN.	1,780	363	3.0	1.0	CO.	2,664	2,172	13.6	38.7
IA	458	205	1.5	0.4	NM.	682	999	9.7	15.3
MO	6,298	1,556	18.7	14.1	AZ	2,511	1,658	9.9	23.8
ND.	149	332	1.9	10.0	UT.	802	1,026	19.7	6.1
SD.	125	272	1.4	6.7	NV.	250	594	1.9	9.6
NE.	253	685	4.0	12.6	Pac.	27,599	20,740	176.9	292.4
KS.	852	1,250	6.8	24.4	WA	1,760	3,209	28.8	36.4
South.	41,239	48,816	426.2	670.3	OR.	317	431	2.9	1.1
S.A.	22,406	31,628	274.0	417.1	CA.	24,265	13,952	121.3	188.7
DE.	133	262	1.8	4.5	AK.	560	903	4.9	23.3
MD.	4,129	3,271	41.9	32.7	HI	697	2,245	19.0	42.9

[1] Military awards for supplies, services, and construction. Net value of contracts of over $25,000 for work in each State and DC. Figures reflect impact of prime contracting on State distribution of defense work. Often the State in which a prime contractor is located in is not the State where the subcontracted work is done. See also headnote, table 530. Undistributed civilians and military personnel, their payrolls and prime contract awards for performance in classified locations are excluded.
Source: U.S. Dept. of Defense, Atlas/Data Abstract for the United States and Selected Areas, annual.

No. 532. Worldwide Military Expenditures: 1980 to 1989

[For military expenditures and Armed Forces by country, see section 31. GNP=Gross national product]

COUNTRY GROUP	1980	1981	1982	1983	1984	1985	1986	1987	1988	1989
Current dollars, total [1] ...	**602**	**682**	**764**	**821**	**869**	**925**	**956**	**990**	**1,016**	**1,035**
United States............	144	170	196	218	237	266	281	288	293	304
Percent of total........	23.9	24.9	25.7	26.5	27.3	28.8	29.4	29.1	28.9	29.4
Developed countries [2]......	490	553	616	663	706	709	792	827	853	867
Developing countries [2]......	113	129	148	158	163	166	165	164	163	168
NATO countries [3].........	239	276	312	342	367	402	421	435	444	462
Constant (1988) dollars, total	**887**	**916**	**965**	**999**	**1,018**	**1,053**	**1,061**	**1,065**	**1,058**	**1,035**
United States............	212	228	248	265	278	303	312	310	305	304
Percent of total..........	23.9	24.9	25.7	26.5	27.3	28.8	29.4	29.1	28.8	29.4
Developed countries [2]......	721	743	778	807	827	864	878	889	888	867
Developing countries [2]......	166	173	187	192	191	189	183	176	170	168
NATO countries [3].........	352	370	395	416	430	458	467	468	462	462
Percent of GNP...........	**5.3**	**5.4**	**5.7**	**5.7**	**5.6**	**5.6**	**5.5**	**5.4**	**5.1**	**4.9**
United States............	5.3	5.6	6.2	6.4	6.3	6.6	6.6	6.4	6.0	5.8
Developed countries [2]......	5.3	5.3	5.6	5.6	5.6	5.6	5.6	5.5	5.3	5.0
Developing countries [2]......	5.5	5.7	6.1	6.2	6.0	5.7	5.3	4.9	4.5	4.3
NATO countries [3].........	4.3	4.5	4.8	4.9	4.9	5.0	5.0	4.9	4.6	4.5

[1] Includes countries not shown separately.   [2] Twenty-eight developed countries; see table 533 for selected countries; for complete list, see source.   [3] North Atlantic Treaty Organization.

No. 533. Arms Trade in Constant (1989) Dollars—Selected Countries: 1987 to 1989

[In millions of dollars, except percent. Because some countries exclude arms imports or exports from their trade statistics and their "total" imports and exports are therefore understated and because arms traansfers maybe estimated independently of trade data, the ratio of arms to total imports or exports maybe overstated and may even exceed 100 percent]

COUNTRY	1987	1988	1989 Total	1989 Arms imports as percent of total imports	COUNTRY	1987	1988	1989 Total	1989 Arms imports as percent of total imports
World total [1]....	**62,690**	**55,430**	**45,430**	**(NA)**	RECIPIENTS				
					Developing [1]	**50,190**	**41,180**	**34,630**	**4.7**
					Afghanistan.......	1,506	2,707	3,800	462.3
EXPORTERS					Algeria	753	885	575	6.5
					Angola	1,828	1,457	750	30.0
Canada..........	645	677	410	0.2	Argentina........	151	312	40	1.0
China: Mainland	1,936	2,707	2,000	0.2	Cuba............	1,936	1,770	1,200	14.8
Czechoslovakia.....	1,398	963	875	3.5	Egypt	1,828	807	600	8.1
France	3,227	2,394	2,700	0.1	El Salvador.......	54	62	70	6.4
Poland	1,398	1,249	400	2.6	Ethiopia.........	1,076	729	925	97.3
Soviet Union.......	24,310	22,490	19,600	0.8	Greece..........	333	489	2,000	12.4
United Kingdom	5,055	1,666	3,000	0.3	India...........	3,764	3,539	3,500	17.1
United States......	15,380	15,410	11,200	0.3	Iran............	2,151	2,394	1,300	12.4
West Germany	1,613	1,249	1,200	0.3	Iraq............	5,808	5,101	1,900	15.8
					Israel...........	1,936	2,082	725	5.0
					Jordan..........	355	468	190	8.9
IMPORTERS					Kuwait..........	172	219	490	7.8
					Libya...........	672	625	975	15.7
Developed [1].....	**2,154**	**2,347**	**2,390**	**0.4**	Morocco	441	135	40	0.7
Australia	780	1,353	675	1.5	Nicaragua	538	573	430	78.2
Canada..........	183	219	190	0.2	North Korea.......	452	1,041	525	(NA)
Czechoslovakia.....	995	219	460	3.5	Oman	118	31	60	2.7
East Germany	333	1,041	825	(NA)	Pakistan	344	437	460	6.4
Hungary..........	430	125	30	0.2	Peru............	473	31	180	7.5
Italy	215	291	300	0.2	Saudi Arabia.......	7,529	2,811	4,200	21.2
Japan	1,076	1,249	1,400	0.7	South Korea.......	672	703	370	0.6
Poland	887	1,041	625	2.6	Spain...........	1,076	1,041	750	1.0
Romania	129	21	20	(NA)	Syria...........	2,151	1,353	1,000	47.7
Soviet Union.......	1,398	1,249	900	0.8	Turkey..........	1,022	1,015	1,100	7.0
United Kingdom	592	677	650	0.3	Venezuela	108	135	80	1.0
United States......	2,366	2,602	1,600	0.3	Vietnam..........	2,044	1,561	1,300	(NA)
West Germany	672	1,145	875	0.3	Yemen (Sanaa).....	430	448	420	(NA)

NA Not available.   [1] Includes countries not shown separately.
Source of tables 532 and 533: U.S. Arms Control and Disarmament Agency, *World Military Expenditures and Arms Transfers*, annual.

National Defense and Veterans Affairs

No. 534. Arms Transfers—Cumulative Value for Period 1985-89, by Major Supplier and Recipient Country

[In millions of dollars]

RECIPIENT	Total [1]	SUPPLIER					
		Soviet Union	United States	France	United Kingdom	China: Mainland	West Germany
World, total.	256,585	102,465	60,480	18,075	14,095	8,360	6,190
Africa [1].	24,390	17,005	990	935	300	315	185
Algeria	3,260	2,700	50	20	40	-	-
Angola	6,000	5,500	-	80	-	-	-
Ethiopia	3,805	3,600	-	-	-	20	-
Libya	5,080	3,200	-	-	-	30	10
Morocco.	770	-	240	150	-	20	-
Mozambique	850	825	-	5	5	-	-
Nigeria	705	30	50	110	120	-	130
Sudan	330	-	100	-	-	50	-
East Asia [1]	31,815	13,385	13,720	250	570	215	300
China: Mainland.	2,205	500	210	120	260	(X)	40
Taiwan.	3,885	-	3,000	-	-	-	-
North Korea	2,770	2,700	-	-	-	40	-
Malaysia.	710	-	270	20	10	-	-
South Korea	2,645	-	2,600	10	30	-	-
Thailand.	1,430	-	1,000	-	20	170	120
Vietnam	8,230	8,200	-	-	-	-	-
South Asia [1]	28,305	21,565	1,155	1,980	700	720	490
Afghanistan.	9,730	9,700	-	-	-	-	-
India	16,080	11,800	210	1,900	650	-	470
Pakistan	2,000	5	925	80	40	410	20
Europe [1].	54,000	16,705	21,250	1,705	1,110	-	2,890
Belgium	1,460	-	1,400	60	-	-	-
Bulgaria	3,600	3,100	-	-	-	-	20
Czechoslovakia	3,440	3,300	-	-	-	-	-
Denmark.	570	-	500	20	20	-	-
East Germany	4,425	3,500	-	-	-	-	-
France	980	-	900	(X)	10	-	-
Greece.	3,210	90	1,800	1,000	-	-	210
Hungary	800	500	-	-	-	-	-
Italy	1,220	-	1,200	-	-	-	-
Netherlands	2,560	-	2,200	-	10	-	330
Norway.	1,275	-	675	10	-	-	60
Poland	4,780	4,500	-	-	-	-	-
Soviet Union	5,910	(X)	-	-	-	-	-
Spain	3,335	-	2,800	70	210	-	10
Sweden	540	-	420	20	30	-	40
Switzerland	2,210	-	450	30	350	-	1,200
Turkey	3,970	-	2,500	20	360	-	1,000
United Kingdom.	3,200	-	3,200	(X)	-	-	-
West Germany.	3,530	-	2,600	360	60	-	(X)
Yugoslavia	855	675	150	-	-	-	-
Latin America [1]	16,905	9,730	2,065	830	150	-	680
Argentina	730	-	70	30	-	-	370
Chile	485	-	10	60	30	-	10
Colombia	290	-	80	-	20	-	5
Cuba	8,690	7,300	-	-	-	-	-
Ecuador	315	-	60	70	60	-	-
Peru.	855	220	40	340	-	-	30
Venezuela.	920	-	500	60	-	-	60
Middle East [1].	84,535	24,075	15,350	11,045	8,405	7,100	645
Egypt.	5,800	575	2,900	675	170	190	40
Iran	10,250	-	10	75	100	2,800	50
Iraq	22,750	13,000	-	1,700	20	1,600	90
Israel	6,100	-	6,100	-	-	-	-
Jordan	2,070	1,200	460	110	40	-	10
Kuwait	1,345	180	150	450	110	-	-
Saudi Arabia	23,040	-	5,000	7,000	7,700	2,500	40
Syria	7,160	6,100	-	20	-	10	-
Yemen (Sanaa)	1,765	1,600	20	-	-	-	5
North America.	10,755	-	735	1,300	2,700	10	900
Canada	825	-	735	-	-	-	-
United States	9,930	-	(X)	1,300	2,700	10	900

- Represents $2.5 million or less.   X Not applicable.   [1] Includes countries not shown separately.

Source: U.S. Arms Control and Disarmament Agency, *World Military Expenditures and Arms Transfers,* annual.

No. 535. Arms Delivered, by Selected Supplier and Major Weapon Type: 1985-89

[The suppliers included are the five largest single exporters of major weapons in terms of magnitude of deliveries as well as other countries of the two major alliances; excluded are Albania, Bulgaria, Greece, Malta, Spain, Turkey, and Yugoslavia]

TYPE OF WEAPON	Total [1]	United States [2]	France	United Kingdom	China: Mainland
Land armaments: Tanks.	7,302	971	38	70	560
Anti-air artillery [3]	2,432	2	25	-	820
Field artillery [4]	8,717	612	85	50	2,535
Armored personnel carriers.	13,718	1,052	505	12	1,300
Naval craft: Major surface combatants [5]	50	-	-	6	2
Other surface combatants [6]	528	23	39	37	16
Submarines	24	-	-	-	-
Missile attack boats.	8	-	-	-	4
Aircraft: Combat aircraft (supersonic)	1,534	412	118	66	85
Combat aircraft (subsonic)	261	24	12	41	31
Other aircraft [7]	1,301	162	68	11	34
Helicopters.	1,582	193	235	23	-
Missiles (surface-to-air)	22,282	1,176	930	81	705

- Represents $2.5 million or less. [1] Includes other countries not shown separately. [2] United States data are by fiscal years, while other suppliers' data are by calendar years. [3] Includes weapons over 23 millimeters. [4] Includes mobile rocket launchers mortars, and recoilless rifles over 100 millimeters. [5] Includes aircraft carriers, cruisers, destroyers, destroyer escorts, and frigates. [6] Includes motor torpedo boats, subchasers, and minesweepers. [7] Includes reconnaissance aircraft, trainers, transports, and utility aircraft.
Source: U.S. Arms Control and Disarmament Agency, *World Military Expenditures and Arms Transfers,* annual.

No. 536. Estimates of Total Dollar Costs of American Wars

[**In millions of dollars, except percent.** Service-connected veterans' benefits estimated at 40 percent of total veterans benefits, except as noted]

ITEM	World War II	Vietnam Conflict	Korean Conflict	World War I	Civil War: Union	Civil War: Confederacy	Spanish American War	American Revolution	War of 1812	Mexican War
Original incremental, direct costs: [1]										
Current dollars	360,000	140,600	50,000	32,700	2,300	1,000	270	100-140	89	82
Constant (1967) dollars	816,300	148,800	69,300	100,000	8,500	3,700	1,100	400-680	170	300
Percent 1 year's GNP	188	14	15	43	74	123	2	104	14	4
Service-connected benefits [2]	96,666	32,288	19,512	19,580	3,290	-	2,111	28	20	26
Interest, pmts. on war loans [3]	(4)	(4)	(4)	(4)	11,000	1,200	(4)	60	20	10
Current cost to 1990 [5]	466,000	179,000	72,000	63,500	6,790	(4)	2,441	170	120	120

- Represents zero. [1] Figures are rounded and taken from Claudia D. Goldin, Encyclopedia of American Economic History, p. 938. [2] Total cost to Oct. 1, 1990. For World War I and later wars, benefits are actual service-connected figures from Annual Report of Veterans Administration. For earlier wars, service-connected veterans' benefits are estimated at 40 percent of total, the approximate ratio of service-connected to total benefits since World War I. [3] Total cost to 1990. Interest payments are a very rough approximation based on the percentage of the original costs of each war financed by money creation and debt, the difference between the level of public debt at the beginning of the war and at its end, and the approximate time required to pay off the war debts. [4] Unknown. [5] Figures are rounded estimates.
Source: Originally presented in U.S. Congress, Joint Economic Committee, *The Military Budget and National Economic Priorities,* Part 1, 91st Congress, 1st session (statement of James L. Clayton); subsequently revised and updated by James L. Clayton, University of Utah, Salt Lake City, Utah.

No. 537. U.S. Military Sales and Assistance to Foreign Governments: 1950 to 1990

[**In millions of dollars,** except as indicated. **For fiscal year ending in year shown;** see text section 9. Department of Defense (DOD) sales deliveries cover deliveries against DOD sales orders authorized under Arms Export Control Act, as well as earlier and applicable legislation. For details regarding individual programs, see source]

ITEM	1950-81 [1]	1982	1983	1984	1985	1986	1987	1988	1989	1990
Military sales agreements	91,066	16,558	14,444	12,872	10,559	6,540	6,449	11,739	10,747	13,948
Weapons and ammunition	38,699	6,651	7,697	5,936	3,433	2,208	1,838	5,058	4,386	5,341
Support equipment [2]	11,513	3,631	1,048	1,847	1,720	664	783	997	997	1,843
Spare parts and mods	20,066	3,263	3,036	2,544	2,371	1,544	1,626	3,125	2,534	2,806
Support services	20,788	3,013	2,663	2,545	3,035	2,124	2,202	2,559	2,830	3,958
Military construction sales agreements.	14,569	86	22	404	958	69	133	208	74	234
Military sales deliveries [3]	104,701	10,547	12,048	9,650	8,173	7,882	11,399	9,212	7,313	7,533
Military sales financing	24,849	3,884	5,107	5,716	4,940	4,947	4,053	4,049	4,273	4,813
Military assistance programs [4]	54,178	395	413	700	812	841	976	702	542	137
Military assist. program deliveries [5]	53,804	416	173	129	76	76	84	56	53	29
IMET program/deliveries [5]	1,999	44	47	52	54	51	54	46	46	47
Students trained (1,000).	506	6	7	6	7	6	6	6	5	5

[1] Includes transition quarter, July-September 1976. [2] Includes aircraft, ships, support vehicles, communications equipment, and other supplies. [3] Includes military construction sales deliveries. [4] Also includes Military Assistance Service Funded (MASF) program data, Section 506(a) drawdown authority, and MAP Merger Funds. [5] Includes Military Assistance Service Funded (MASF) program data and Section 506(a) drawdown authority.

Source: U.S. Defense Security Assistance Agency, *Foreign Military Sales, Foreign Military Construction Sales, and Military Assistance Facts,* annual; and unpublished data.

No. 538. U.S. Military Sales Deliveries to Foreign Governments, by Country: 1950 to 1990

[In millions of dollars. For fiscal years ending in year shown; see text, section 9. Represents Department of Defense military sales]

COUNTRY	1950-1982 [1]	1983	1984	1985	1986	1987	1988	1989	1990 Total	1990 Percent distribution
Total [2]	75,307	12,948	9,659	8,473	7,882	11,399	9,212	7,313	7,533	100.00
Australia............	2,109	322	395	515	399	601	856	390	275	3.64
Belgium	1,189	273	196	119	28	27	222	153	186	2.47
Canada	1,588	111	139	73	114	127	213	154	111	1.47
China: Taiwan	1,965	389	275	339	247	373	488	350	574	7.62
Egypt..............	1,596	1,006	313	599	618	992	506	325	472	6.27
Germany	7,141	323	336	222	206	324	324	561	399	5.30
Greece.............	1,565	157	105	115	73	79	129	138	115	1.52
Israel..............	8,014	258	214	479	190	1,295	750	232	159	2.11
Italy...............	802	26	54	55	66	75	62	64	66	0.88
Japan..............	1,174	385	333	389	152	237	213	170	231	3.07
Jordan.............	964	256	77	122	61	53	55	60	44	0.58
Morocco............	535	50	69	49	37	43	74	33	24	0.32
Netherlands	1,464	513	401	339	283	425	299	383	378	5.02
Norway............	1,023	251	191	30	43	77	119	98	128	1.70
Saudi Arabia	39,623	5,989	3,573	2,270	2,787	3,472	1,356	981	1,158	15.37
Singapore...........	913	83	33	22	135	143	193	38	48	0.64
South Korea	4,505	298	258	258	344	353	335	328	298	3.96
Spain..............	3,682	68	66	93	262	823	637	687	155	2.06
Thailand............	2,200	157	163	118	116	95	300	212	177	2.35
Turkey.............	4,490	150	305	389	280	279	730	668	710	9.43
United Kingdom.......	5,497	478	447	386	361	198	180	131	206	2.73
Venezuela...........	798	33	129	195	67	50	27	13	20	0.27

[1] Includes transactions for the transition quarter, July-September 1976.   [2] Includes countries not shown.

Source: U.S. Defense Security Assistance Agency, *Foreign Military Sales, Foreign Military Construction Sales,* and *Military Assistance Facts,* annual.

No. 539. Summary of Active and Reserve Military Personnel and Forces: 1989 to 1991

ITEM	1989	1990, est.	1991, est.	ITEM	1989	1990, est.	1991, est.
Military personnel (1,000):				Total naval vessels.........	566	551	546
Active	2,130	2,076	2,039	Aircraft carriers	14	14	14
Guard and Reserve	1,171	1,155	1,152	Battleships	4	4	2
Strategic forces:				Nuclear attack submarines....	96	91	86
Intercontinental ballistic missiles:				Amphibious assault ships.....	65	64	66
Peacekeeper.............	50	50	50	Sealift fleet...............	69	68	66
Minuteman	950	950	950				
Poseidon-Trident	576	608	656	Air Forces:			
Strategic bomber squadrons	21	19	19	Air Force fighter wings (equiv.):			
General purpose forces:				Active	25	24	24
Land forces:				Navy attack wings: Active	13	13	13
Army divisions (Active)	18	18	16	Marine Corps wings: Active ...	3	3	3
Marine divisions...........	3	3	3	Air Force B-52 squadrons	3	2	3
Naval forces (total):				Strategic airlift squadrons	20	20	20

Source: U.S. Office of Management and Budget, *Budget of the United States Government,* annual.

No. 540. Intercontinental Ballistic Missiles (ICBM's): 1980 to 1989

WEAPONS SYSTEM	1980	1983	1984	1985	1986	1987	1988	1989
ICBM's:								
United States [1]	1,052	1,040	1,030	1,017	999	996	1,000	1,000
Minuteman II	450	450	450	450	450	450	450	450
Minuteman III................	550	550	550	550	534	514	500	500
Peacekeeper (MX).............	-	-	-	-	-	32	50	50
Soviet Union	1,398	1,398	1,398	1,398	1,418	1,389	1,348	(NA)
SS-11	640	520	520	448	440	420	400	350
SS-13	60	60	60	60	60	60	60	60
SS-17	150	150	150	150	150	145	125	75
SS-18	308	308	308	308	308	308	308	308
SS-19	240	360	360	360	360	350	330	300
SS-24	-	-	-	-	-	6	12	60
SS-25	-	-	-	72	100	100	125	220

- Represents zero.   NA Not available.   [1] Includes weapons not shown separately.

Source: The Congress of the United States, Library of Congress, Congressional Research Service, *U.S./Soviet Military Balance, Statistical Trends, 1980-1990,* July 1990.

No. 541. Department of Defense Manpower: 1950 to 1991

[In thousands. As of **end of fiscal year;** see text, section 9. Includes National Guard, Reserve, and retired regular personnel on extended or continuous active duty. Excludes Coast Guard. Other officer candidates are included under enlisted personnel. See also *Historical Statistics, Colonial Times to 1970*, series Y 904-916]

YEAR	Total [1] [2]	ARMY			NAVY [3]			MARINE CORPS			AIR FORCE		
		Total [2]	Offic-ers	Enlist-ed	Total [2]	Offic-ers	Enlist-ed	Total [2]	Offic-ers	Enlist-ed	Total [2]	Offic-ers	Enlist-ed
1950	1,459	593	73	519	381	45	333	74	7	67	411	57	354
1955	2,935	1,109	122	986	661	75	583	205	18	187	960	137	823
1960	2,475	873	101	770	617	70	545	171	16	154	815	130	683
1961	2,483	859	100	757	626	70	552	177	16	161	821	129	690
1962	2,806	1,066	116	949	664	75	585	191	17	174	884	135	746
1963	2,699	976	108	866	664	76	584	190	17	173	869	134	733
1964	2,686	973	111	861	666	76	585	190	17	173	857	133	721
1965	2,654	969	112	855	670	78	588	190	17	173	825	132	690
1966	3,092	1,200	118	1,080	743	80	659	262	21	241	887	131	753
1967	3,375	1,442	144	1,297	750	82	664	285	24	262	897	135	759
1968	3,546	1,570	166	1,402	764	85	674	307	25	283	905	140	762
1969	3,458	1,512	173	1,337	774	85	684	310	26	284	862	135	723
1970	3,065	1,323	167	1,153	691	81	606	260	25	235	791	130	657
1971	2,713	1,124	149	972	622	75	542	212	22	191	755	126	625
1972	2,322	811	121	687	587	73	511	198	20	178	726	122	600
1973	2,252	801	116	682	564	71	490	196	19	177	691	115	572
1974	2,162	783	106	674	546	67	475	189	19	170	644	110	529
1975	2,128	784	103	678	535	66	466	196	19	177	613	105	503
1976	2,082	779	99	678	525	64	458	192	19	174	585	100	481
1977	2,075	782	98	680	530	63	462	192	19	173	571	96	470
1978	2,062	772	98	670	530	63	463	191	18	172	570	95	470
1979	2,027	759	97	657	523	62	457	185	18	167	559	96	459
1980	2,051	777	99	674	527	63	460	188	18	170	558	98	456
1981	2,083	781	102	675	540	65	470	191	18	172	570	99	467
1982	2,109	780	103	673	553	67	481	192	19	173	583	102	476
1983	2,123	780	106	669	558	68	485	194	20	174	592	105	483
1984	2,138	780	108	668	565	69	491	196	20	176	597	106	486
1985	2,151	781	110	667	571	71	495	198	20	178	602	108	489
1986	2,169	781	110	667	581	72	504	199	20	179	608	109	495
1987	2,174	781	108	668	587	72	510	200	20	179	607	107	495
1988	2,138	772	107	660	593	72	516	197	20	177	576	105	467
1989	2,130	770	107	658	593	72	516	197	20	177	571	104	463
1990	2,044	732	104	624	579	72	503	197	20	177	535	100	431
1991	1,986	711	104	603	570	71	495	194	20	174	510	97	409

[1] Beginning 1980, excludes Navy Reserve personnel on active duty for Training and Administration of Reserves (TARS). From 1969, includes the full-time Guard and Reserve. [2] Includes Cadets. [3] Prior to 1980, includes Navy Reserve personnel on active duty for Training and Administration of Reserves (TARS).

Source: U.S. Dept. of Defense, *Selected Manpower Statistics*, annual.

No. 542. Military Personnel on Active Duty, by Location: 1970 to 1991

[In thousands. 1970 and 1975, as of Dec. 31; thereafter, **as of end of fiscal year;** see text, section 9]

ITEM	1970	1975	1980	1984	1985	1986	1987	1988	1989	1990	1991
Total	3,066	2,128	2,051	2,138	2,151	2,169	2,174	2,138	2,130	2,044	1,986
Shore-based [1]	2,798	1,912	1,840	1,908	1,920	1,929	1,928	1,891	1,884	1,794	1,743
Afloat [2]	268	216	211	230	231	240	246	248	246	252	243
United States [3]	2,033	1,643	1,562	1,628	1,636	1,644	1,650	1,598	1,620	1,437	1,539
Foreign countries	1,033	485	488	510	516	526	524	541	510	609	448

[1] Includes Navy personnel temporarily on shore. [2] Includes Marine Corps. [3] Includes outlying areas.

Source: U.S. Dept. of Defense, *Selected Manpower Statistics*, annual; and unpublished data.

No. 543. Military Personnel on Active Duty in Foreign Countries: 1991

[As of end of fiscal year]

COUNTRY	1991	COUNTRY	1991	COUNTRY	1991
Total	447,572	E. Asia and Pac. [1]	104,781	Saudi Arabia	14,617
Ashore	396,014	Australia.	707	United Arab Emirates . . .	39
Afloat	51,558	China.	33	Afloat.	17,266
Western Europe [1]	284,939	Hong Kong	31	Western Hemisphere [1] . . .	19,456
Austria	32	Indonesia	40	Antigua.	74
Denmark.	64	Japan.	44,566	Bahamas, The.	44
France	81	New Zealand.	58	Bermuda.	1,178
Germany	203,423	Philippines	7,761	Brazil	46
Greece.	1,375	Rep. of Korea	40,062	Canada	513
Greenland.	163	Singapore	68	Colombia	43
Iceland.	3,209	Thailand.	111	Costa Rica	12
Italy	13,389	Afloat.	11,300	Cuba (Guantanamo)	2,323
Netherlands	2,635	Africa, Near East,		El Salvador	96
Norway.	225	and South Asia [1]	35,335	Honduras	1,005
Portugal	2,031	Bahrain	255	Mexico	28
Spain.	6,166	Egypt.	1,135	Panama	10,568
Switzerland	29	India	29	Peru.	31
Turkey	6,343	Israel	438	Venezuela.	34
U.S.S.R.	56	Kenya	28	Afloat.	3,234
United Kingdom	23,442	Morocco.	40	Antarctica.	61
Afloat.	19,758	Pakistan	31		

[1] Includes areas not shown separately.

Source: U.S. Department of Defense, *Selected Manpower Statistics,* annual.

No. 544. Coast Guard Personnel on Active Duty: 1970 to 1990

[As of **end of fiscal year;** see text, section 9]

YEAR	Total	Officers	Cadets	Enlisted	YEAR	Total	Officers	Cadets	Enlisted
1970.	37,689	5,512	653	31,524	1984.	38,705	6,790	759	31,156
1975.	36,788	5,630	1,177	29,981	1985.	38,595	6,775	733	31,087
1979.	38,559	6,340	806	31,413	1986.	37,284	6,577	754	29,953
1980.	39,381	6,463	877	32,041	1987.	38,576	6,644	859	31,073
1981.	39,760	6,519	981	32,260	1988.	37,723	6,530	887	30,306
1982.	38,248	6,431	902	30,915	1989.	37,474	6,611	869	29,994
1983.	39,708	6,535	811	32,362	1990.	36,939	6,876	927	29,136

Source: U.S. Dept. of Transportation, *Annual Report of the Secretary of Transportation.*

No. 545. Vietnam Conflict—U.S. Military Forces in Vietnam and Combat Area Casualties: 1957 to 1989

[Military forces as of **Dec. 31.** All U.S. forces withdrawn by Jan. 27, 1973]

ITEM	Unit	1957-1989, total [1]	1957-1964	1965	1966	1967	1968	1969	1970	1971	1972	1973-1989
Military forces [2]	1,000. . .	(X)	[3]23.3	184.3	385.3	485.6	536.1	475.2	234.6	156.8	24.2	-
Battle deaths [4]	Number .	47,355	279	1,432	5,047	9,463	14,623	9,426	4,230	1,376	361	1,118
Killed	Number .	38,498	197	1,124	4,142	12,624	7,525	8,117	3,486	1,082	205	-
Died of wounds . . .	Number .	5,210	10	111	579	979	1,598	1,168	555	160	28	22
Died while missing [5] .	Number .	3,647	72	197	326	959	401	141	189	134	128	1,068

- Represents zero. X Not applicable. [1] Number in this column indicates 28 more deaths than a tally of the number by time period, due to the inclusion of Cambodia, Thailand, Laos and China. [2] Source: U.S. Dept. of Defense, *Selected Manpower Statistics,* annual. [3] For 1964 only. [4] Casualties from enemy action. Deaths exclude 10,796 servicemen who died in accidents or from disease. [5] Includes servicemen who died while captured.

Source: Except as indicated, National Archives and Records Administration, unpublished data from Combat Area Casualties database, as of October 1989.

No. 546. Armed Forces Personnel—Summary of Major Conflicts

[For Revolutionary War, number of personnel serving not known, but estimates range from 184,000 to 250,000; for War of 1812, 286,730 served; for Mexican War, 78,718 served. Dates of the major conflicts may differ from those specified in various laws providing benefits for veterans. See table 563 for data on Vietnam conflict. See also *Historical Statistics, Colonial Times to 1970*, series Y 856-903]

ITEM	Unit	Civil War [1]	Spanish-American War	World War I	World War II	Korean conflict	Vietnam conflict
Personnel serving [2]	1,000 . . .	2,213	307	4,735	[3]16,113	[4]5,720	[5]8,744
Average duration of service	Months . .	20	8	12	33	.19	23
Service abroad: Personnel serving	Percent. .	(NA)	[6]29	53	73	[7]56	(NA)
Average duration [8]	Months . .	(NA)	1.5	6	16	13	(NA)
Casualties: [9] Battle deaths [2]	1,000 . . .	140	(Z)	53	292	34	[10]47
Wounds not mortal [2]	1,000 . . .	282	2	204	671	103	[10]153
Draftees: Classified	1,000 . . .	777	(X)	24,234	36,677	9,123	[5]75,717
Examined	1,000 . . .	522	(X)	3,764	17,955	3,685	[5]8,611
Rejected	1,000 . . .	160	(X)	803	6,420	1,189	[5]3,880
Inducted	1,000 . . .	46	(X)	2,820	10,022	1,560	[5]1,759

NA Not available. X Not applicable. Z Fewer than 500. [1] Union forces only. Estimates of the number serving in Confederate forces range from 600,000 to 1.5 million. [2] Source U.S. Department of Defense, *Selected Manpower Statistics, FY 1988*, annual. [3] Covers Dec. 1, 1941, to Dec. 31, 1946. [4] Covers June 25, 1950, to July 27, 1953. [5] Covers Aug. 4, 1964, to Jan. 27, 1973. [6] Army and Marines only. [7] Excludes Navy. Covers July 1950 through Jan. 1955. Far East area only. [8] During hostilities only. [9] For periods covered, see footnotes 3, 4, and 5. [10] Covers Jan. 1, 1961, to Jan. 27, 1973. Includes known military service personnel who have died from combat related wounds.

Source: Except as noted, the President's Commission on Veterans' Pensions, Veterans' *Benefits in the United States*, vol. I, 1956; and U.S. Dept. of Defense, unpublished data.

No. 547. Enlisted Military Personnel Accessions: 1980 to 1990

[In thousands. For years ending Sept. 30]

BRANCH OF SERVICE	1980	1985	1989	1990	BRANCH OF SERVICE	1980	1985	1989	1990
Total	582	529	530	461	**Marine Corps**	58	57	49	48
Army	265	201	224	182	First enlistments	42	36	33	33
First enlistments	163	117	112	85	Reenlistments	15	19	16	14
Reenlistments	97	84	111	97	**Air Force**	132	133	102	104
Navy	127	139	155	135	First enlistments	76	68	44	37
First enlistments	75	67	74	62	Reenlistments	56	64	58	68
Reenlistments	36	50	62	59					

Source: U.S. Dept. of Defense, *Selected Manpower Statistics*, annual.

No. 548. Military Personnel on Active Duty and Monthly Basic Pay: 1985 to 1990

[Personnel as of Sept. 30; basic pay as of January, except as noted]

RANK/GRADE	PERSONNEL (1,000)				MONTHLY BASIC PAY (dollars)			
	1985	1988	1989	1990	1985	1988	1989	1990
Total [1]	2,151.0	2,138.2	2,130.2	2,043.7	(X)	(X)	(X)	(X)
Recruit—E-1	127.6	119.6	128.9	97.6	594	634	674	684
Private—E-2	140.6	145.1	151.9	140.3	689	750	775	803
Pvt. 1st class—E-3	336.3	304.7	281.6	280.1	747	806	832	871
Corporal—E-4	444.4	458.9	456.8	427.8	866	949	977	1,014
Sergeant—E-5	356.2	360.9	362.1	361.5	1,036	1,141	1,185	1,245
Staff Sgt.—E-6	237.8	244.5	245.7	239.1	1,260	1,380	1,433	1,480
Sgt. 1st class—E-7	131.9	133.0	134.0	134.1	1,525	1,662	1,722	1,784
Master Sgt.—E-8	38.5	38.3	37.9	38	1,826	1,980	2,047	2,117
Sgt. Major—E-9	15.1	15.2	15.1	15.3	2,234	2,429	2,504	2,583
Warrant Officer—W-1	2.4	2.7	3.2	3.2	1,403	1,565	1,618	1,686
Chief Warrant—W-4	3.2	3.2	3.1	3	2,491	2,705	2,818	2,943
2d Lt.—0-1	39.7	35.3	34.0	31.9	1,275	1,382	1,426	1,485
1st Lt.—0-2	42.7	42.4	42.0	37.9	1,737	1,896	1,982	2,056
Captain—0-3	104.4	105.8	106.2	106.6	2,230	2,436	2,520	2,618
Major—0-4	53.3	53.2	53.6	53.2	2,708	2,966	3,070	3,196
Lt. Colonel—0-5	32.8	32.9	32.4	32.3	3,279	3,594	3,737	3,894
Colonel—0-6	14.7	14.4	14.0	14	4,039	4,400	4,561	4,758
Brig. General—0-7	0.5	0.5	0.5	0.5	4,928	5,333	5,526	5,751
Major General—0-8	0.4	0.4	0.4	0.4	5,667	[2]6,042	6,291	6,516
Lt. General—0-9	0.1	0.1	0.1	0.1	[2]5,725	[2]6,042	[2]6,292	6,516
General—0-10	(Z)	(Z)	(Z)	(Z)	[2]5,725	[2]6,042	[2]6,292	6,516

X Not applicable. Z Fewer than 50. [1] Includes cadets and midshipmen and warrant officers, W-2 and W-3. [2] Statutory limitation.

Source: U.S. Dept. of Defense, *Selected Manpower Statistics*, annual, and Office of the Comptroller, unpublished data.

No. 549. Military Reserve Personnel: 1970 to 1989

[**In thousands.** As of **end of fiscal year**; see text, section 9. Excludes U.S. Coast Guard Reserve. The ready reserve includes selected reservists who are intended to assist active forces in a war and the individual ready reserve who, in a major war, would be used to fill out active and reserve units and later would be a source of combat replacements; a portion of the ready reserve serves in an active status. The standby reserve cannot be called to active duty unless the Congress gives its explicit approval. The retired reserve represents a low potential for mobilization]

RESERVE STATUS AND BRANCH OF SERVICE	1970	1975	1979	1980	1981	1982	1983	1984	1985	1986	1987	1988	1989
Total reserves	3,639	2,656	2,109	2,169	2,267	2,250	2,295	2,310	2,370	2,434	2,455	2,538	2,540
Ready reserve	2,574	1,529	1,203	1,263	1,317	1,359	1,419	1,491	1,566	1,613	1,620	1,642	1,631
Standby reserve	492	412	103	86	65	52	44	44	44	41	38	34	29
Retired reserve	573	715	803	821	885	839	832	775	760	780	798	862	879
Army	2,221	1,631	1,173	1,218	1,337	1,360	1,408	1,428	1,481	1,508	1,509	1,525	1,530
Navy	808	521	427	438	436	415	423	425	431	464	471	525	522
Air Force.	610	504	509	514	494	476	463	457	459	462	475	488	488

Source: U.S. Dept. of Defense, *Official Guard and Reserve Manpower Strengths and Statistics*, quarterly.

No. 550. Ready Reserve Personnel Profile—Race, Age, and Sex: 1989 and 1990

ITEM	RACE					PERCENT DISTRIBUTION			
	Total	White	Black	Asian	American Indian	White	Black	Asian	American Indian
1989, total . . .	1,676,105	1,282,456	372,765	13,237	7,647	76.5	22.2	0.8	0.5
Male	1,357,453	1,139,498	199,771	11,573	6,611	68.0	11.9	0.7	0.4
Officers	214,783	200,325	12,487	1,664	307	12.0	0.7	0.1	(Z)
Enlisted	1,142,670	939,173	187,284	9,909	6,304	56.0	11.2	0.6	0.4
Female.	318,652	142,958	172,994	1,664	1,036	8.5	10.3	0.1	0.1
Officers	35,717	28,760	6,580	313	64	1.7	0.4	(Z)	(Z)
Enlisted	282,935	114,198	166,414	1,351	972	6.8	9.9	0.1	0.1
1990, total . . .	1,558,867	1,269,278	271,470	14,608	3,511	81.4	17.4	0.9	0.2
Male	1,362,014	1,137,557	209,360	12,724	2,373	73.0	13.4	0.8	0.2
Officers	218,033	203,061	12,851	1,794	327	13.0	0.8	0.1	(Z)
Enlisted	1,143,981	934,496	196,509	10,930	2,046	59.9	12.6	0.7	0.1
Female.	196,845	131,721	62,110	1,884	1,130	8.4	4.0	0.1	0.1
Officers	18,277	11,785	6,095	339	58	0.8	0.4	(Z)	(Z)
Enlisted	178,568	119,936	56,015	1,545	1,072	7.7	3.6	0.1	0.1

Z Less than .05 percent.

Source: U.S. Dept. of Defense, *Official Guard and Reserve Manpower Strengths and Statistics*, annual.

No. 551. Military Reserve Costs: 1970 to 1990

[**In millions of dollars.** As of **end of fiscal year**; see text, section 9. Army and Air Force data include National Guard]

TYPE OF COST	1970	1980	1982	1983	1984	1985	1986	1987	1988	1989	1990
Total.	2,597	7,969	10,464	11,910	11,886	19,414	19,640	18,947	19,234	20,630	22,081
Operations and maintenance . . .	994	3,526	4,716	5,137	5,128	5,734	5,770	6,168	6,670	6,765	6,757
Personnel.	1,133	2,456	3,912	4,633	5,065	7,703	8,500	8,382	8,837	9,129	9,106
Procurement.	187	1,459	971	1,471	984	5,009	4,383	3,316	2,533	3,520	4,914
Active-duty support	234	408	556	386	408	566	616	601	610	611	638
Construction	49	120	309	283	301	402	371	480	584	605	666

Source: U.S. Dept. of Defense, unpublished data.

No. 552. National Guard—Summary: 1970 to 1990

[As of **end of fiscal year**; see text, section 9. Includes Puerto Rico]

ITEM	Unit	1970	1975	1980	1984	1985	1986	1987	1988	1989	1990
Army National Guard: Units .	Number . .	3,052	3,245	3,379	4,351	4,353	5,712	6,125	5,982	5,715	4,055
Personnel [1]	1,000	410	403	368	434	438	446	452	455	457	444
Funds obligated [2]	Mil. dol . . .	752	1,322	1,802	3,093	4,387	4,825	4,955	5,258	5,354	5,187
Value of equipment	Mil. dol . . .	1,600	4,100	7,600	14,300	18,800	19,700	22,300	27,390	30,129	29,010
Air National Guard: Units . . .	Number . .	958	1,106	1,054	1,202	1,184	1,229	1,281	1,272	1,339	1,339
Personnel [1]	1,000	90	95	96	105	109	113	115	115	116	118
Funds obligated [2]	Mil. dol . . .	467	890	1,678	2,488	2,813	2,809	2,886	3,072	3,183	3,192
Value of equipment (est.) [3] .	Mil. dol . . .	(NA)	3,100	5,200	17,500	21,400	26,100	23,668	25,683	27,481	26,356

NA Not available. [1] Officers and enlisted personnel. [2] Federal funds; includes personnel, operations, maintenance, and military construction. [3] Beginning 1984, increase due to repricing of aircraft to current year dollars to reflect true replacement value.

Source: National Guard Bureau, *Annual Review of the Chief, National Guard Bureau;* and unpublished data.

No. 553. Wartime Veterans—States: 1991

[Estimates in thousands. As of end of fiscal year; see text, section 9. Data were estimated starting with veteran's place of residence as of **April 1, 1980**, based on 1980 Census of Population data, extended to later years on the basis of estimates of veteran interstate migration, separations from the Armed Forces, and mortality; not directly comparable with earlier estimates previously published by the VA. Excludes 423,000 veterans whose only active-duty military service occurred since September 8, 1980, and who failed to satisfy the minimum service requirement. Also excludes a small indeterminate number of National Guard personnel or reservists who incurred service-connected disabilities while on an initial tour of active duty for training only]

STATE	Total [1]	World War I	World War II [2][3]	KOREAN CONFLICT Total [2][3][4]	KOREAN CONFLICT No prior wartime service [4]	VIETNAM ERA Total [2][4][5]	VIETNAM ERA No prior wartime service	PERSIAN GULF WAR Total [5][6]	PERSIAN GULF WAR No prior wartime service
U.S.	20,280	65	8,443	4,693	3,859	8,269	7,697	263	216
Northeast	4,225	13	1,933	957	834	1,460	1,407	46	37
N.E.	1,146	3	508	266	224	423	402	11	9
ME	116	-	47	27	22	48	45	2	1
NH	110	-	41	25	21	50	47	1	1
VT	46	-	18	10	9	20	19	1	1
MA	495	2	233	115	97	168	160	4	3
RI	90	-	42	21	17	33	30	1	1
CT	289	1	127	68	58	104	101	2	2
M.A.	3,079	10	1,425	691	610	1,037	1,005	35	28
NY	1,305	5	601	293	264	431	422	16	13
NJ	653	2	308	153	133	215	205	5	4
PA	1,121	3	516	245	213	391	378	14	11
Midwest	4,924	18	1,953	1,089	968	1,990	1,925	70	61
E.N.C.	3,404	11	1,361	742	665	1,360	1,324	49	43
OH	933	3	389	201	179	363	351	14	12
IN	450	1	171	100	89	187	182	7	6
IL	891	3	372	199	178	336	328	11	10
MI	726	2	275	155	141	305	298	11	10
WI	404	2	154	87	78	169	165	6	5
W.N.C.	1,520	7	592	347	303	630	601	21	18
MN	363	2	134	81	72	156	152	5	4
IA	237	1	87	51	47	101	98	4	3
MO	470	2	192	110	93	189	178	6	5
ND	47	-	17	10	10	20	20	1	1
SD	57	-	22	15	13	22	21	1	1
NE	131	1	52	32	28	53	49	2	2
KS	215	1	88	48	40	89	83	2	2
South	6,932	21	2,898	1,639	1,285	2,952	2,652	98	77
S.A.	3,684	11	1,618	890	682	1,510	1,334	49	38
DE	59	-	24	13	11	25	23	1	1
MD	404	1	164	101	79	171	156	5	4
DC	41	-	19	11	8	14	13	1	-
VA	497	1	199	135	99	227	193	7	5
WV	160	1	71	34	29	61	57	2	2
NC	523	1	223	123	103	210	191	7	6
SC	270	1	109	66	52	121	105	4	3
GA	498	1	177	116	92	245	221	7	6
FL	1,232	5	632	291	209	436	375	15	11
E.S.C.	1,136	4	459	271	225	473	434	18	14
KY	265	1	105	61	53	108	102	4	4
TN	395	1	155	88	74	173	161	6	4
AL	304	1	123	79	64	125	112	5	4
MS	172	1	76	43	34	67	59	3	2
W.S.C.	2,112	6	821	478	378	969	884	31	25
AR	185	1	79	42	33	78	70	3	3
LA	311	1	130	69	56	130	120	5	4
OK	290	1	115	67	53	129	118	4	3
TX	1,326	3	497	300	236	632	576	19	15
West	4,199	11	1,658	1,006	771	1,871	1,710	50	40
Mt.	1,179	2	455	273	213	539	491	16	13
MT	74	-	28	15	13	32	31	1	1
ID	81	-	30	18	15	36	34	2	1
WY	40	-	12	8	7	21	20	1	1
CO	299	1	100	71	55	153	139	4	3
NM	130	-	50	30	23	60	54	2	2
AZ	332	1	148	76	57	137	122	4	3
UT	109	-	43	25	20	48	45	1	1
NV	114	-	44	30	23	52	46	1	1
Pac.	3,020	9	1,203	733	558	1,332	1,219	34	27
WA	456	1	165	107	80	225	204	6	5
OR	267	1	103	54	44	121	115	4	3
CA	2,171	7	894	542	411	919	840	22	18
AK	49	-	12	10	8	31	29	1	-
HI	77	-	29	20	15	36	31	1	1

- Represents or rounds to zero. [1] Includes one living Spanish-American War veteran and an indeterminate number of Mexican Border period veterans. Veterans who served in more than one wartime period are counted only once. [2] Includes 269,000 who served in the Vietnam era, Korean conflict, and World War II. [3] Includes 649,000 who served in both World War II and the Korean conflict. [4] Includes 339,000 who served in both the Korean conflict and the Vietnam era. [5] Excludes reservists. [6] Includes 47,000 who served in both the Vietnam-era and the Persian Gulf War.

Source: U.S. Dept. of Veterans Affairs, Management Sciences Service (008B2), *Annual Report of the Secretary of Veterans Affairs,* Fiscal Year 1991.

No. 554. Veterans Living in the United States and Puerto Rico, by Age and Service: 1991

[In thousands, except as indicated. As of Sept. 30. Estimated. Excludes 487,000 veterans whose only active duty military service occurred since Sept. 30, 1980. See headnote, table 553. See *Historical Statistics, Colonial Times to 1970*, series Y 943-956, for all veterans]

AGE	Total veterans	WARTIME VETERANS							PEACETIME VETERANS	
		Total [1]	Vietnam era		Korean conflict		World War II [3][4]	World War I	Total	Post-Vietnam era [5]
			Total [2][3]	No prior wartime service	Total [2][3][4]	No prior wartime service [2]				
All ages	[6]26,629	20,370	8,303	7,730	4,726	3,889	8,469	65	6,259	3,043
Under 30 years old . . .	1,132	180	-	-	-	-	-	-	953	953
30 to 34 years old. . . .	1,458	158	131	131	-	-	-	-	1,299	1,299
35 to 39 years old. . . .	1,787	1,198	1,190	1,190	-	-	-	-	590	590
40 to 44 years old. . . .	3,268	3,119	3,117	3,117	-	-	-	-	149	131
45 to 49 years old. . . .	2,952	2,434	2,434	2,434	-	-	-	-	518	35
50 to 54 years old. . . .	2,378	845	707	685	161	161	-	-	1,532	20
55 to 59 years old. . . .	2,815	1,951	305	132	1,812	1,810	8	-	864	11
60 to 64 years old. . . .	3,194	3,027	228	30	2,023	1,792	1,204	-	167	3
65 years old and over .	7,646	7,458	192	10	730	126	7,257	65	187	(Z)

- Represents zero.   Z Less than 500.   [1] Veterans who served in more than one wartime period are counted only once.
[2] Includes Vietnam era (no prior wartime service), Korean conflict (no prior wartime service), World War II, and World War I.
[2] Includes 339,000 who served in both the Korean conflict and the Vietnam era.   [3] Includes 269,000 who served in the Vietnam era, Korean conflict, and World War II.   [4] Includes 649,000 who served in both World War II and the Korean conflict.   [5] Service only after May 7, 1975.   [6] There is also one living Spanish-American War veteran and an estimated 65 living Mexican Border conflict veterans.

Source: U.S. Dept. of Veterans Affairs, Office of Information Management and Statistics, Veteran Population, annual.

No. 555. Disabled Veterans Receiving Compensation: 1970 to 1990

[In thousands, except as indicated. As of end of fiscal year; see text, section 9. Represents veterans receiving compensation for service-connected disabilities. Totally disabled refers to veterans with any disability, mental or physical, deemed to be total and permanent which prevents the individual from maintaining a livelihood and are rated for disability at 100 percent]

MILITARY SERVICE	1970	1975	1980	1984	1985	1986	1987	1988	1989	1990
Disabled, all periods [1]	2,092	2,220	2,274	2,251	2,240	2,225	2,212	2,199	2,192	2,184
Peace-time	185	194	262	335	352	367	382	398	421	444
World War I [1]	85	55	30	15	12	10	18	6	5	3
World War II.	1,416	1,309	1,193	1,080	1,049	1,015	982	947	912	876
Korea	239	240	236	226	223	220	218	215	212	209
Vietnam.	167	423	553	595	604	613	623	633	643	652
Totally disabled, all periods [1] .	124	123	121	137	136	133	132	131	131	131
Peace-time	16	16	20	25	26	26	26	26	26	27
World War I [1]	11	6	3	1	1	1	1	1	(Z)	(Z)
World War II.	63	58	51	56	54	51	49	47	45	43
Korea	16	16	16	17	17	16	16	16	16	16
Vietnam.	18	26	31	38	38	39	40	41	43	44
Compensation (mil. dol.) . . .	2,393	3,797	6,104	8,041	8,270	8,379	8,434	8,721	8,937	9,284

Z Less than 500.   [1] Includes Spanish-American War and Mexican Border service, not shown separately.

Source: U.S. Dept. of Veterans Affairs, *Annual Report of the Secretary of Veterans Affairs;* and unpublished data.

No. 556. Veterans Benefits—Expenditures, by Program: 1970 to 1989

[In millions of dollars. For fiscal years ending in year shown; see text, section 9. On an accrued expenditure basis]

PROGRAM	1970	1975	1980	1984	1985	1986	1987	1988	1989
Total [1]	10,201	18,003	23,187	28,494	30,119	31,556	32,365	33,791	30,041
Compensation and pensions [2]	5,330	7,551	11,257	13,942	14,234	14,399	14,399	14,880	15,008
Educ'al asst. and readjustm't benefits.	1,047	4,529	2,383	1,043	1,169	907	916	998	1,027
Medical services; administ. expenses .	[3]2,009	3,919	6,647	9,123	9,992	10,269	10,641	11,299	10,745
Hospital; domiciliary constr'n [4]	75	136	342	486	557	567	589	634	657
Insurance and indemnities	1,181	1,345	1,637	1,750	1,853	2,008	1,689	1,734	2,013
Loan guaranty revolving fund	249	423	445	1,511	1,626	2,667	3,333	3,635	3,771
Direct loans	180	84	49	8	8	9	9	6	2

[1] Excludes expenditures from personal funds of patients. Includes expenditures from VA Revolving Supply Fund and insurance trust funds and miscellaneous expenditures   [2] Includes expenditures for statutory burial awards, special clothing allowance, mortgage life insurance, invalid lifts, headstones and markers, and other expenses.   [3] Includes National Cancer Institute expenditures (transfer to Dept. of Veterans Affairs).   [4] Includes construction grants for State extended care facilities. Beginning 1975, includes expenditures for health manpower training facilities.

Source: U.S. Dept. of Veterans Affairs, *Annual Report of the Secretary of Veterans Affairs.*

No. 557. Veterans Compensation and Pension Benefits—Number on Rolls and Average Payment, by Period of Service and Status: 1980 to 1990

[As of **Sept. 30**. Living refers to veterans receiving compensation for disability incurred or aggravated while on active duty and war veterans receiving pension and benefits for nonservice connected disabilities. Deceased refers to deceased veterans whose dependents were receiving pensions and compensation benefits. See also *Historical Statistics, Colonial Times to 1970*, series Y 998-999]

PERIOD OF SERVICE AND VETERAN STATUS	VETERANS ON ROLLS (1,000)					AVERAGE PAYMENT (annual basis) [1] (dol.)				
	1980	1985	1988	1989	1990	1980	1985	1988	1989	1990
Total	4,646	4,006	3,725	3,654	3,584	2,370	3,505	3,949	4,111	4,335
Living veterans	3,195	2,931	2,804	2,776	2,746	2,600	3,666	4,003	4,126	4,320
Service connected	2,273	2,240	2,199	2,192	2,184	2,669	3,692	3,967	4,078	4,250
Nonservice connected	922	690	606	584	562	2,428	3,581	4,133	4,308	4,591
Deceased veterans	1,451	1,075	921	878	838	1,863	3,066	3,787	4,062	4,382
Service connected	358	336	325	323	320	3,801	5,836	6,649	6,992	7,349
Nonservice connected	1,093	739	595	555	518	1,228	1,809	2,224	2,358	2,548
Prior to World War I.	14	7	5	4	4	1,432	1,855	2,226	2,388	2,616
Living.	(Z)	(Z)	(Z)	(Z)	(Z)	2,634	4,436	9,149	8,411	10,502
World War I	692	381	261	228	198	1,683	2,461	2,986	3,181	3,435
Living.	198	68	32	24	18	2,669	4,439	5,759	6,316	6,922
World War II.	2,520	2,097	1,869	1,797	1,723	2,307	3,317	3,724	3,851	4,052
Living. . . . . . [2]	1,849	1,575	1,407	1,352	1,294	2,462	3,460	3,823	3,936	4,123
Korean conflict [2]	446	399	392	391	390	2,691	4,114	4,618	4,836	5,105
Living.	317	309	307	306	305	2,977	4,260	4,658	4,852	5,103
Peace-time	312	404	449	472	495	3,080	3,973	4,023	4,042	4,132
Living. . . . . . [3]	262	352	398	421	444	2,828	3,589	3,613	3,621	3,709
Vietnam era [3]	662	716	749	762	774	2,795	4,021	4,463	4,683	4,945
Living.	569	626	661	673	685	2,709	3,849	4,229	4,416	4,671

Z Fewer than 500.   [1] Averages calculated by multiplying average monthly payment by 12.   [2] Service during period June 27, 1950, to Jan. 31, 1955.   [3] Service from Aug. 5, 1964, to May 7, 1975.

Source: U.S. Dept. of Veterans Affairs, *Annual Report of the Secretary of Veterans Affairs;* and unpublished data.

No. 558. Veterans Administration Health Care Summary: 1980 to 1990

[For years ending **Sept. 30**]

ITEM	Unit	1980	1985	1990	ITEM	Unit	1980	1985	1990
Facilities operating:	. . . . .				Prescriptions dispensed .	Millions	36.7	48.1	58.6
Hospitals	Number	172	172	172	Laboratory.	Millions	215	173	188
Domiciliaries	Number	16	16	32	Radiology examinations .	Millions	5.7	5.4	5.5
Outpatient clinics	Number	226	226	(NA)	Inpatients treated [3]	1,000. .	1,359	1,435	1,113
Nursing home units . .	Number	92	115	126	Average daily	1,000. .	105	100	87
Employment [1]	1,000. .	194	203	202	Outpatient visits	Millions	18.0	19.6	22.6
Obligations [2]	Mil. dol.	6,215	9,258	11,840					

NA Not available.   [1] Net full-time equivalent.   [2] 1980, cost basis; thereafter, obligation basis.   [3] Based on the number of discharges and deaths during the fiscal year, plus the number on the rolls (bed occupants and patients on authorized leave of absence) at the end of the fiscal year. Excludes interhospital transfers.

Source: U.S. Dept. of Veterans Affairs, *Annual Report of the Secretary of Veterans Affairs; Directory of VA Facilities*, biennial; and unpublished data.

No. 559. Veterans Assistance to Persons in Education and Training Programs: 1980 to 1990

[In thousands, except where indicated. For fiscal years ending in year shown; see text, section 9. Represents persons in training during year]

PROGRAM	1980	1984	1985	1986	1987	1988	1989	1990
Post-Korea Education Assistance [1]	1,107	528	402	308	239	203	164	86
Institutions of higher education	842	421	326	257	203	176	144	77
Resident schools other than college	149	78	54	35	26	19	13	6
Correspondence schools	42	10	7	6	4	4	3	2
On-the-job training.	74	19	15	9	7	4	3	2
Children's Educational Assistance.	82.6	63.6	55.3	48.4	43.4	40.9	38.7	37.5
Institutions of higher education	75.5	57.1	50.0	43.9	39.7	37.8	36.2	35.3
Schools other than college	6.5	6.2	5.2	4.3	3.6	3.0	2.4	2.1
Special restorative training	0.1	0.1	(Z)	(Z)	(Z)	(Z)	(Z)	(Z)
On-the-job training.	0.5	0.2	0.2	0.1	0.1	0.1	0.1	0.1
Spouses, Widows/Widowers Educational Assistance Program	13.0	7.6	6.6	5.9	5.3	5.0	4.6	4.5
Institutions of higher education	10.8	6.5	5.7	5.0	4.5	4.3	4.1	4.1
Schools other than college	2.2	1.1	1.0	0.9	0.7	0.6	0.5	0.4
Vocational Rehab. Program for Disabled Vets	25.5	29.0	26.9	25.8	24.6	24.7	27.0	27.8
Guaranteed and insured loans, (1,000). . . .	297.4	251.6	178.9	313.8	479.5	234.7	189.7	196.6
Guaranteed and insured loans, (mil. dol.) . .	14,815	15,612	11,452	21,966	34,900	17,302	14,416	15,779
Guaranty and insurance (mil. dol.)	6,370	6,034	4,363	7,896	12,237	6,172	5,211	5,561

Z Fewer than 50.   [1] Includes some Post-Vietnam veterans.

Source: U.S. Dept. of Veterans Affairs, *Annual Report of the Secretary of Veterans Affairs;* and unpublished data.

Figure 12.1
Percentage of Persons Receiving Monthly Social Security Benefits, by Type of Beneficiary: 1990

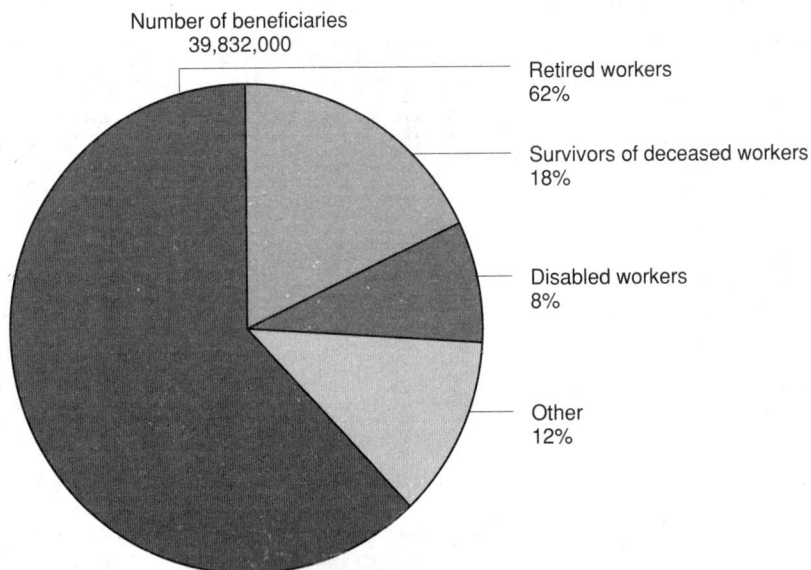

Number of beneficiaries
39,832,000

Retired workers
62%

Survivors of deceased workers
18%

Disabled workers
8%

Other
12%

Source: Chart prepared by U.S. Bureau of the Census. For data, see table 573.

Figure 12.2
Adult Population Doing Volunteer Work: 1989

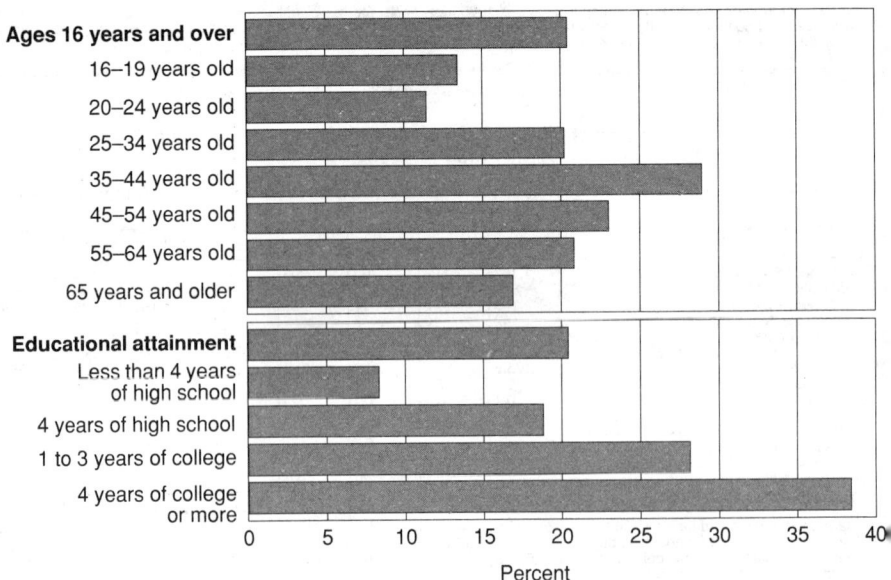

Ages 16 years and over
16–19 years old
20–24 years old
25–34 years old
35–44 years old
45–54 years old
55–64 years old
65 years and older

Educational attainment
Less than 4 years of high school
4 years of high school
1 to 3 years of college
4 years of college or more

Percent

Source: Chart prepared by U.S. Bureau of the Census. For data, see table 601.

Social Insurance and Human Services

This section presents data related to governmental expenditures for social welfare; governmental programs for old-age, survivors, disability, and health insurance (OASDHI); governmental employee retirement; Individual Retirement Account, Keogh account and private pension plans; government unemployment and temporary disability insurance; Federal supplemental security income payments and aid to the needy; child and other welfare services; and Federal food programs. Also included here are selected data on workers' compensation, including black lung benefits; vocational rehabilitation; child support; child care; and philanthropic trusts and foundations.

The principal source for these data is the Department of Health and Human Services' (HHS) quarterly *Social Security Bulletin* which presents current data on many of the programs and summary data in annual statistical supplements. Current data on employment security are published annually in the Department of Labor's *Unemployment Insurance, Financial Data.* Statistics on aid to families with dependent children (AFDC) are presented in the U.S. Family Support Administration's annual publication, *Quarterly Public Assistance Statistics.*

Social insurance under the Social Security Act.—Programs established by the Social Security Act provide protection against wage loss resulting from retirement, prolonged disability, death, or unemployment, and protection against the cost of medical care during old age and disability. The Federal OASDHI program provides cash benefits to retired or disabled insured workers and their dependents and to survivors of insured workers. To be eligible, a worker must have had a specified period of employment in which OASDHI taxes were paid. A worker becomes eligible for full benefits at age 65, although reduced benefits may be obtained up to 3 years earlier; the worker's spouse is under the same limitations. Survivor benefits are payable to dependents of deceased insured

In Brief

In 1990, households below poverty level receiving:

Medicaid	46%
Food stamps	43%

Social Security beneficiaries, 1990:

Total	40 million
Retired workers	25 million

workers. Disability benefits are payable to an insured worker under age 65 with a prolonged disability and to the disabled worker's dependents on the same basis as dependents of retired workers. Also, disability benefits are provided at age 50 to the disabled widow or widower of a deceased worker who was fully insured at the time of death. A lump-sum benefit is generally payable on the death of an insured worker to a spouse or minor children. For information on the Medicare program, see section 3.

Retirement, survivors, disability, and hospital insurance benefits are funded by a payroll tax on annual earnings (up to a maximum of earnings set by law) of workers, employers, and the self-employed. The maximum taxable earnings are adjusted annually to reflect increasing wage levels (see table 571). Tax receipts and benefit payments are administered through Federal trust funds. Special benefits for uninsured persons; hospital benefits for persons 65 and over with specified amounts of Social Security coverage less than that required for cash benefit eligibility; and that part of the cost of supplementary medical insurance not financed by contributions from participants are financed from Federal general revenues.

Unemployment insurance is presently administered by the U.S. Employment and Training Administration and each State's employment security agency. By agreement with the U.S. Secretary of Labor, State agencies also administer unemployment compensation for eligible ex-service members and Federal employees, unemployment assistance under the Disaster Relief Act of 1970, and workers assistance and relocation allowances under the Trade Act. Under State unemployment insurance laws, benefits related to the individual's past earnings are paid to unemployed eligible workers. State laws vary concerning the length of time benefits are paid and their amount. In most States, benefits are payable for 26 weeks and, during periods of high unemployment, extended benefits are payable under a Federal-State program to those who have exhausted their regular State benefits. The basic benefit can vary among States by over 100 percent. Some States also supplement the basic benefit with allowances for dependents. Unemployment insurance is funded by a Federal unemployment tax levied on the taxable payrolls of most employers. Taxable payroll under the Federal Act and most State laws is the first $7,000 in wages paid each worker during a year. Employers are allowed a percentage credit of taxable payroll for contributions paid to States under State unemployment insurance laws. The remaining percent of the Federal tax finances administrative costs, the Federal share of extended benefits, and advances to States. About 97 percent of wage and salary workers are covered by unemployment insurance.

Retirement Programs for Government Employees.—The Civil Service Retirement System (CSRS) and the Federal Employees' Retirement System (FERS) are the two major programs providing age and service, disability, and survivor annuities for Federal civilian employees. In general, employees hired after December 31, 1983, are covered under FERS and the social security program (OASDHI), and employees on staff prior to that date are members of CSRS and are covered under Medicare. CSRS employees were offered the option of transferring to FERS during 1987. There are separate retirement systems for the uniformed services (supplementing OASDHI) and for certain special groups of Federal employees. State and local government employees are covered for the most part by State and local retirement systems similar to the Federal civil service retirement system. In many

jurisdictions these benefits supplement OASDHI coverage.

Workers' compensation.—All States provide protection against work-connected injuries and deaths, although some States exclude certain workers (e.g., domestic help). Federal laws cover Federal employees, private employees in the District of Columbia, and longshoremen and harbor workers. In addition, the Social Security Administration and the Department of Labor administer a "black lung" benefits program for coal miners disabled by pneumoconiosis and for specified dependents and survivors. Specified occupational diseases are compensable to some extent. In most States, benefits are related to the worker's salary. The benefits may or may not be augmented by dependents' allowances or automatically adjusted to prevailing wage levels.

Public aid.—State-administered public assistance programs (Aid to Families with Dependent Children (AFDC), emergency assistance and general assistance) and the Federal Supplemental Security Income (SSI) program administered by the Social Security Administration provide benefits to persons who qualify. AFDC and emergency assistance are in part federally funded while the costs of general assistance are met entirely with State and local funds. The SSI program replaced Federal grants for aid to the aged, blind, and disabled in the 50 States and the District of Columbia in 1974. Residents of the Northern Mariana Islands became eligible in 1978. Federal grants continue for aid to the aged, blind, and disabled in Guam, Puerto Rico, and the Virgin Islands. The SSI program provides a minimum income for the aged, blind, and disabled and establishes uniform national basic eligibility requirements and payment standards. Most States supplement the basic SSI payment.

Federal Food Stamp program.—Under the Food Stamp program, single persons and those living in households meeting nationwide standards for income and assets may receive coupons redeemable for food at most retail food stores. The monthly amount of coupons a unit receives is determined by household size and income. Households without income receive the determined monthly cost of a nutritionally adequate diet for their household size. This amount is updated to account for food price increases. Households with income receive the difference between the amount of a nutritionally adequate diet and 30 percent of their income, after certain allowable deductions.

To qualify for the program, a household must have less than $2,000 in disposable assets ($3,000 if one member is aged 60 or older), gross income below 130 percent of the official poverty guidelines, and net income below 100 percent of the poverty guidelines. Households with a person aged 60 or older or a disabled person receiving SSI, Social Security, or veterans' disability benefits may have gross income exceeding 130 percent of the poverty guidelines. All households must meet these requirements, even those receiving other Federal assistance payments. Households are certified for varying lengths of time, depending on their income sources and individual circumstances.

Health and welfare services.—Programs providing health and welfare services are aided through Federal grants to States for child welfare services, vocational rehabilitation, activities for the aged, maternal and child health services, maternity and infant care projects,

comprehensive health services, and a variety of public health activities. For information about the Medicaid program, see section 3.

Noncash benefits.—The Bureau of the Census annually collects data on the characteristics of recipients of noncash (in-kind) benefits to supplement the collection of annual money income data in the Current Population Survey (see text, section 1 and section 15). Noncash benefits are those benefits received in a form other than money which serve to enhance or improve the economic well-being of the recipient. As for money income, the data for noncash benefits are for the calendar year prior to the date of the interview. The major categories of noncash benefits covered are public transfers (e.g. food stamps, school lunch, public housing, and Medicaid) and employer or union-provided benefits to employees.

Statistical reliability.—For discussion of statistical collection, estimation, and sampling procedures and measures of statistical reliability applicable to HHS and Census Bureau data, see Appendix III.

Historical statistics.—Tabular headnotes provide cross-references, where applicable, to *Historical Statistics of the United States, Colonial Times to 1970.* See Appendix IV.

354 Social Insurance and Human Services

No. 560. Social Welfare Expenditures Under Public Programs: 1970 to 1989

[In billions of dollars, except percent. **For fiscal years ending in year shown;** see text, section 9. Represents outlays from trust funds (mostly social insurance funds built up by earmarked contributions from insured persons, their employers, or both) and budgetary outlays from general revenues. Includes administrative expenditures, capital outlay, and some expenditures and payments outside U.S. See table 561 for program detail. See *Historical Statistics, Colonial Times to 1970*, series H 1-47, for related but not comparable data]

YEAR	SOCIAL WELFARE OUTLAYS Total	Percent change [1]	Social insurance	Public aid	Health and medical programs [2]	Vet-erans pro-grams	Educa-tion	Housing	Other social welfare	All health and medical care [3]
					TOTAL					
1970	146	14.6	55	16	10	9	51	1	4	25
1975	289	21.2	123	41	17	17	81	3	7	51
1980	492	14.6	230	72	27	21	121	7	14	100
1985	731	8.0	370	97	39	27	172	13	14	172
1986	781	6.8	391	103	44	27	189	12	14	186
1987	833	6.7	413	111	48	28	205	13	15	204
1988	886	6.4	434	118	53	29	219	17	15	218
1989	956	7.9	468	127	57	30	239	18	17	242
					FEDERAL					
1970	77	13.2	45	10	5	9	6	1	2	16
1975	167	22.0	100	27	8	17	9	3	4	33
1980	302	15.0	191	49	13	21	13	6	9	69
1985	449	7.0	310	62	18	27	14	11	8	122
1986	471	4.9	326	66	19	27	15	10	8	131
1987	496	5.3	343	69	21	28	16	11	9	141
1988	525	5.8	360	74	23	29	17	14	8	149
1989	563	7.2	387	80	24	30	19	15	8	166
					STATE AND LOCAL					
1970	68	16.3	9	7	5	(Z)	45	(Z)	2	9
1975	122	20.0	23	14	9	(Z)	72	1	3	18
1980	190	13.7	39	23	14	(Z)	108	1	5	31
1985	282	9.7	59	35	21	(Z)	158	2	6	49
1986	309	9.8	65	37	25	(Z)	174	2	6	55
1987	337	8.9	70	42	27	(Z)	188	2	7	63
1988	361	7.2	74	44	30	(Z)	202	3	7	69
1989	393	8.8	81	48	33	(Z)	220	3	8	76
					PERCENT OF TOTAL EXPENDITURES, BY TYPE					
1970	100	(X)	38	11	7	6	35	1	3	17
1980	100	(X)	47	15	6	4	25	1	3	20
1985	100	(X)	51	13	5	4	24	2	2	24
1987	100	(X)	50	13	6	3	25	2	2	25
1988	100	(X)	49	13	6	3	25	2	2	25
1989	100	(X)	49	13	6	3	25	2	2	25
					PERCENT FEDERAL OF TOTAL					
1970	53	(X)	83	59	48	99	12	83	55	65
1980	62	(X)	83	68	47	99	11	91	65	69
1985	62	(X)	84	64	46	99	8	88	56	71
1987	60	(X)	83	62	43	99	8	84	56	69
1988	59	(X)	83	63	43	99	8	85	52	68
1989	59	(X)	83	63	43	99	8	84	51	69
					PER CAPITA (Current dollars) [4]					
1970	698	13.2	262	79	46	43	244	3	20	120
1980	2,122	13.2	990	311	118	92	523	33	59	434
1985	3,004	6.5	1,516	400	161	111	708	52	56	706
1987	3,358	5.7	1,662	449	195	112	826	53	62	824
1988	3,540	5.4	1,731	474	212	116	878	66	62	873
1989	3,783	6.9	1,849	506	226	119	946	72	66	958
					PER CAPITA (Constant (1989) dollars) [4][5]					
1970	2,113	8.1	794	240	140	131	740	10	60	365
1980	3,184	2.2	1,485	467	177	138	785	50	88	650
1985	3,496	3.1	1,765	466	187	129	825	60	65	822
1987	3,648	1.0	1,805	487	211	122	897	58	67	895
1988	3,703	1.5	1,811	496	222	122	918	69	65	913
1989	3,783	2.2	1,849	506	226	119	946	72	66	958

X Not applicable.   Z Less than $500 million.   [1] Percent change from immediate preceding year.   [2] Excludes program parts of social insurance, public aid, veterans, and other social welfare.   [3] Combines "Health and medical programs" with medical services included in social insurance, public aid, veterans, vocational rehabilitation, and antipoverty programs.   [4] Excludes payments within foreign countries for education, veterans, OASDHI, and civil service retirement.   [5] Constant dollar figures are based on implicit price deflators for personal consumption expenditures published by U.S. Bureau of Economic Analysis in *Survey of Current Business*, July 1991.

Source: U.S. Social Security Administration, *Social Security Bulletin*, May 1991 and unpublished data.

No. 561. Social Welfare Expenditures, by Source of Funds and Public Program: 1980 to 1989

[In millions of dollars. See headnote, table 560, and *Historical Statistics, Colonial Times to 1970*, series H 1-47, for related but not comparable data]

PROGRAM	FEDERAL				STATE AND LOCAL			
	1980	1985	1988	1989	1980	1985	1988	1989
Total	302,438	449,296	525,225	563,191	189,548	281,777	360,948	392,676
Social insurance	**191,162**	**310,175**	**360,265**	**387,290**	**38,592**	**59,420**	**73,783**	**80,765**
Old-age, survivors, disability, health	152,110	257,535	300,048	324,109	(X)	(X)	(X)	(X)
Health insurance (Medicare)	34,992	71,384	83,610	94,552	(X)	(X)	(X)	(X)
Public employee retirement[1]	26,983	40,504	47,606	50,248	12,507	22,540	30,442	33,546
Railroad employee retirement	4,769	6,276	6,676	6,971	(X)	(X)	(X)	(X)
Unemployment insurance and employment services[2]	4,408	2,604	2,965	2,893	13,919	15,740	13,152	13,488
Other railroad employee insurance[3]	224	189	100	109	(X)	(X)	(X)	(X)
State temporary disability insurance[4]	(X)	(X)	(X)	(X)	1,377	1,944	2,754	2,886
Workers' compensation[5]	2,668	3,067	2,869	2,960	10,789	19,197	27,435	30,844
Hospital and medical benefits	130	280	367	410	3,596	6,800	10,743	12,415
Public aid[6]	**48,666**	**61,985**	**74,137**	**79,852**	**23,309**	**35,200**	**44,358**	**47,623**
Public assistance[6]	23,542	33,523	43,431	47,828	21,522	32,965	41,345	44,269
Medical vendor payments (Medicaid)[7]	14,550	22,677	30,771	34,858	13,020	21,449	27,858	30,316
Social services	1,757	2,057	2,025	2,003	586	686	675	668
Supplemental security income	6,440	9,605	11,674	12,469	1,787	2,235	3,013	3,354
Food stamps	9,083	12,513	13,071	13,589	(X)	(X)	(X)	(X)
Other[8]	9,601	6,344	5,961	5,964	(X)	(X)	(X)	(X)
Health and medical programs	**12,840**	**18,029**	**22,894**	**24,215**	**14,423**	**21,024**	**30,064**	**32,651**
Hospital and medical care	6,636	9,877	12,751	12,881	5,667	6,688	11,190	12,288
Civilian programs	2,438	2,455	3,081	2,723	5,667	6,688	11,190	12,288
Defense Department[9]	4,198	7,422	9,670	10,158	(X)	(X)	(X)	(X)
Maternal and child health programs	351	422	468	494	519	800	1,197	1,297
Medical research	4,428	5,992	7,839	8,548	496	899	1,293	1,361
Medical facilities construction	210	339	-	261	1,450	1,336	1,444	1,572
Other	1,215	1,399	1,836	2,031	6,291	11,301	14,940	16,133
Veterans programs	**21,254**	**26,704**	**28,845**	**29,638**	**212**	**338**	**409**	**466**
Pensions and compensation	11,306	14,333	14,914	15,279	(X)	(X)	(X)	(X)
Health and medical programs	6,204	9,493	11,331	11,663	(X)	(X)	(X)	(X)
Hospital and medical care	5,750	8,809	10,152	10,782	(X)	(X)	(X)	(X)
Hospital construction	323	458	964	646	(X)	(X)	(X)	(X)
Medical and prosthetic research	131	227	215	235	(X)	(X)	(X)	(X)
Education	2,401	1,171	653	647	(X)	(X)	(X)	(X)
Life insurance[10]	665	796	963	1,002	(X)	(X)	(X)	(X)
Welfare and other	679	912	984	1,047	212	338	409	466
Education[11]	**13,452**	**13,796**	**16,966**	**18,520**	**107,597**	**158,251**	**202,416**	**220,111**
Elementary and secondary[12]	7,430	7,278	8,826	9,684	79,720	113,419	159,009	173,487
Construction[13]	41	23	46	18	6,483	8,335	11,743	14,566
Higher	4,468	5,102	6,492	7,404	21,708	36,028	43,406	46,624
Construction	42	32	1	22	1,486	2,314	3,198	3,290
Vocational and adult[13]	1,207	1,087	1,288	1,069	6,169	8,804	(12)	(12)
Housing	**6,278**	**11,059**	**14,006**	**15,184**	**601**	**1,540**	**2,550**	**2,943**
Other social welfare	**8,786**	**7,548**	**8,112**	**8,492**	**4,813**	**6,004**	**7,368**	**8,117**
Vocational rehabilitation	1,006	1,187	1,489	1,560	245	350	416	439
Medical services and research	237	275	343	390	56	85	101	110
Institutional care[14]	74	121	138	141	408	259	393	446
Child nutrition[15]	4,209	4,349	4,956	5,197	643	960	1,294	1,448
Child welfare[16]	57	200	239	247	743	(NA)	(NA)	(NA)
Special CSA and ACTION programs[17]	2,303	504	153	163	(X)	(X)	(X)	(X)
Welfare, not elsewhere classified[18]	1,137	1,188	1,137	1,184	2,774	4,435	5,264	5,784

- Represents zero. NA Not available. X Not applicable. [1] Excludes refunds to those leaving service. Federal data include military retirement. [2] Includes compensation for Federal employees and ex-servicemen, trade adjustment and cash training allowance, and payments under extended, emergency, disaster, and special unemployment insurance programs. [3] Unemployment and temporary disability insurance. [4] Cash and medical benefits in five areas. Includes private plans where applicable. [5] Benefits paid by private insurance carriers, State funds, and self-insurers. Federal includes black lung benefit programs. [6] Includes payments under State general assistance programs and work incentive activities, not shown separately. [7] Medical vendor payments are those made directly to suppliers of medical care. [8] Refugee assistance, surplus food for the needy, and work-experience training programs under the Comprehensive Employment and Training Act. Beginning 1985, includes low-income energy assistance program. [9] Includes medical care for military dependent families. [10] Excludes servicemen's group life insurance. [11] Federal expenditures include administrative costs (Department of Education) and research, not shown separately. [12] Beginning 1986, all state and local vocational education costs included with elementary-secondary. [13] Construction costs of vocational and adult education programs included under elementary-secondary expenditures. [14] Federal expenditures represent primarily surplus foods for nonprofit institutions. [15] Surplus food for schools and programs under National School Lunch and Child Nutrition Acts. [16] Represents primarily child welfare services under Title V of the Social Security Act. [17] Includes domestic volunteer programs under ACTION and community action and migrant workers programs under Community Services Administration. Beginning 1988, represents ACTION funds only. [18] Federal expenditures include administrative expenses of the Secretary of Health and Human Services; Indian welfare and guidance; and aging and juvenile delinquency activities. State and local include antipoverty and manpower programs, child care and adoption services, legal assistance, and other unspecified welfare services.

Source: U.S. Social Security Administration, *Social Security Bulletin*, May 1991; and unpublished data.

No. 562. Social Welfare Expenditures Under Public Programs as Percent of GNP and Total Government Outlays: 1970 to 1989

[See headnote, table 560]

YEAR	TOTAL EXPENDITURES				FEDERAL				STATE AND LOCAL GOVERNMENT			
	Total (bil. dol.)	Percent change[1]	Percent of—		Total (bil. dol.)	Percent change[1]	Percent of—		Total (bil. dol.)	Percent change[1]	Percent of—	
			Total GNP[2]	Total govt. outlays			Total GNP[2]	Total Federal outlays			Total GNP[2]	Total State and local outlays
1970....	146	14.6	14.7	46.5	77	13.2	7.8	40.0	68	16.3	6.9	57.9
1975....	289	21.2	19.0	56.6	167	22.0	11.0	53.6	122	20.0	8.0	61.6
1980....	492	14.6	18.4	57.1	302	15.0	11.3	54.2	190	13.7	7.1	62.9
1985....	731	8.0	18.5	52.2	449	7.0	11.4	48.6	282	9.7	7.1	60.2
1987....	833	6.7	18.8	53.4	496	5.3	11.2	50.0	337	8.9	7.6	60.0
1988....	886	6.4	18.5	52.8	525	5.8	11.0	49.3	361	7.2	7.5	59.7
1989....	956	7.9	18.6	53.0	563	7.2	11.0	49.3	393	8.8	7.7	60.2

[1] Percent change from immediate prior year. [2] Gross national product.
Source: U.S. Social Security Administration, *Social Security Bulletin*, May 1991; and unpublished data.

No. 563. Private Expenditures for Social Welfare, by Type: 1980 to 1989

[In millions of dollars, except percent]

TYPE	1980	1983	1984	1985	1986	1987	1988	1989
Total expenditures	244,375	356,958	392,558	440,566	489,007	517,872	566,457	614,875
Percent of gross national product .	8.9	10.5	10.4	11.0	11.6	11.5	11.6	11.8
Health	145,000	211,000	230,000	247,900	264,600	285,700	318,900	350,200
Income maintenance..............	51,169	82,423	93,235	116,207	140,803	140,461	145,380	151,847
Private pension plan payments[1][2]	37,560	66,683	76,683	98,450	122,209	120,442	124,546	129,662
Short-term sickness and disability[2]...	6,280	6,993	7,497	8,026	8,046	8,924	9,636	9,829
Long-term disability[2]	1,282	1,817	1,874	1,937	2,263	2,293	2,295	2,892
Life insurance and death[3]	5,075	6,519	6,899	7,489	7,797	8,166	8,418	9,063
Supplemental unemployment[2].....	972	411	282	305	488	636	485	401
Education	26,751	35,911	38,872	42,634	46,061	49,865	55,232	60,144
Welfare and other services.........	21,455	27,624	30,451	33,825	37,543	41,846	46,945	52,684

[1] Covers benefits paid for solely by employers and all benefits of employment-related pension plans to which employee contributions are made. Excludes individual savings plans such as IRA's and Keogh plans. Pension plan benefits include monthly benefits and lump-sum distributions to retired and disabled employees and their dependents and to survivors of deceased employees. Also includes preretirement lump-sum distributions. [2] Covers wage and salary workers in private industry. [3] Covers all wage and salary workers.
Source: U.S. Social Security Administration, *Annual Statistical Supplement* to the *Social Security Bulletin*, annual.

No. 564. Cash and Noncash Benefits for Persons With Limited Income—Average Monthly Recipients: 1985 to 1990

[In thousands. For years ending September 30, except as noted. See headnote, table 565]

PROGRAM	1985	1989	1990	PROGRAM	1985	1989	1990
MEDICAL CARE				Interest reduction payments[15]...	528	528	531
Medicaid[1]	21,814	23,511	25,255	Rural rental housing loans[15].....	26	16	16
Veterans[2][3]	504	569	585	EDUCATION AID			
Indian Health Services[4]	931	1,100	1,100	Stafford loans[16][17]	3,477	3,682	3,624
Community health centers[4].....	5,200	5,350	5,350	Pell grants[16]	2,797	3,198	3,434
CASH AID				Head Start	448	451	541
A.F.D.C.[5]	10,813	10,935	11,439	College Work-Study Program[16]..	737	785	835
Supplemental Security Income...	4,305	4,753	4,913	Supplemental Educational			
Earned income tax credit[6]	17,313	33,444	33,693	Opportunity Grants[16]	720	660	633
Pensions for needy veterans[7][8]..	1,489	1,139	1,080	JOBS AND TRAINING			
General assistance[6]	1,323	1,091	1,205	Training for disadvantaged adults			
FOOD BENEFITS				and youth[18][19]............	350	397	416
Food stamps[9]	21,400	20,200	21,500	Job Corps[18]...............	41	41	40
School lunch program[10][11]..	11,500	11,700	11,600	Summer youth employment			
Women, infants and children[12]..	3,138	4,100	4,500	program[18][20]	785	605	625
Nutrition program for elderly[4][13].	3,630	3,538	3,548	Work incentive program[21].....	1,013	1,700	444
HOUSING BENEFITS				Senior community service			
Lower-income housing asst.				employment program[22]......	64	66	65
(Sec. 8)[14]............	2,010	2,420	2,500	ENERGY AID			
Low-rent public housing[14]	1,355	1,404	1,405	Low-income energy assistance[23].	6,800	5,900	5,800
Rural housing loans[15]........	41	25	25				

[1] Unduplicated annual number. [2] See footnote 4, table 565. [3] For 1985, estimated number of patients discharged from hospital during year. For other years, estimated number of inpatients. [4] Annual numbers. [5] See footnote 6, table 565. [6] Estimated. [7] See footnote 8, table 565. [8] Estimate as of September. [9] See footnote 9, table 565. [10] See footnote 10, table 565. [11] Estimated daily average. [12] See footnote 12, table 565. [13] See footnote 13, table 565. [14] Units eligible for payment at end of year. [15] Represents total families or dwelling units during year. [16] Total numbers for the school year ending in year shown. [17] See footnote 15, table 565. [18] See footnote 18, table 565. [19] Average monthly enrollment for program year. [20] Total participants (June-August). [21] New registrants only. [22] Annual number of jobs authorized. [23] Number of households that received heating and winter crisis aid.
Source: Library of Congress, Congressional Research Service, "Cash and Noncash Benefits for Persons With Limited Income: Eligibility Rules, Recipient and Expenditure Data, FY 1988-90," Report No. 91-741 EPW, September 1991 and earlier reports.

No. 565. Cash and Noncash Benefits for Persons With Limited Income—Expenditures: 1985 to 1990

[In millions of dollars. For years ending September 30, except as noted. Programs covered provide cash, goods, or services to persons who make no payment and render no service in return. In case of job and training programs and some educational benefits, recipients must work or study for wages, training allowances, stipends, grants, or loans. Most of the programs base eligibility on individual, household, or family income, but some use group or area income tests; and a few offer help on the basis of presumed need]

PROGRAM	TOTAL EXPENDITURES [1]				FEDERAL EXPENDITURES			
	1985	1988	1989	1990	1985	1988	1989	1990
Total	143,606	172,508	186,449	210,630	105,064	125,047	134,715	152,166
Medical care [2]	49,752	66,644	73,554	86,197	27,880	38,608	42,393	50,211
Medicaid [3]	41,258	54,304	60,896	72,228	22,844	30,567	34,384	41,195
Veterans [4][5]	3,053	5,855	5,678	6,458	3,053	5,855	5,678	6,458
General assistance [5]	3,125	3,966	4,300	4,600	-	-	-	-
Indian Health Services	862	1,006	1,082	1,250	862	1,006	1,082	1,250
Maternal and child health services	783	860	903	907	478	527	554	554
Community health centers.	383	396	435	478	383	396	435	478
Cash aid [2]	37,636	45,707	49,652	55,136	24,486	30,314	33,163	37,044
A.F.D.C. [3][6].	16,736	19,016	19,662	21,196	8,909	10,319	10,647	11,505
Supplemental Security Income [3].	11,857	14,684	15,757	17,232	[7]9,603	[7]11,648	[7]12,417	[7]13,606
Earned income tax credit (refunded portion) . . .	1,162	2,930	4,257	5,902	1,162	2,930	4,257	5,902
Pensions for needy veterans [8]	3,842	3,935	4,024	3,954	3,842	3,935	4,024	3,954
General assistance	2,499	2,624	2,819	3,184	-	-	-	-
Food benefits [2]	20,391	21,355	21,997	25,257	19,362	20,216	20,835	24,011
Food stamps [3][9]	13,470	14,369	14,916	17,702	12,599	13,289	13,815	16,517
School lunch program [10][11]	2,665	2,937	3,082	3,250	2,665	2,937	3,082	3,250
Women, infants and children [12]	1,500	1,800	1,924	2,119	1,500	1,800	1,924	2,119
Nutrition program for elderly [13].	614	561	582	578	456	502	521	517
Housing benefits [2]	14,113	14,701	15,925	17,544	14,113	14,701	15,925	17,544
Lower-income housing asst. (Sec. 8)	6,818	9,133	9,918	10,577	6,818	9,133	9,918	10,577
Low-rent public housing	3,408	2,526	3,043	3,918	3,408	2,526	3,043	3,918
Rural housing loans [14]	1,790	1,271	1,267	1,311	1,790	1,271	1,267	1,311
Interest reduction payments.	619	628	611	630	619	628	611	630
Rural rental housing loans [14]	903	555	555	572	903	555	555	572
Education aid [2]	9,970	11,691	13,029	14,375	9,516	11,147	12,484	13,746
Stafford loans [15]	3,888	3,775	5,012	5,648	3,888	3,775	5,012	5,648
Pell grants [16]	2,800	4,187	4,260	4,484	2,800	4,187	4,260	4,484
Head Start	1,309	1,508	1,544	1,940	1,047	1,206	1,235	1,552
College Work-Study Program [16]	555	593	588	610	555	593	588	610
Supplemental Educational Opportunity Grants [16].	375	413	408	438	375	413	408	438
Services [2].	5,476	5,659	5,671	5,801	3,551	3,559	3,571	3,661
Social services (Title 20) [17]	4,650	4,800	4,800	4,902	2,725	2,700	2,700	2,762
Community services block grant	372	382	381	389	372	382	381	389
Jobs and training [2]	3,976	3,820	3,912	4,215	3,895	3,748	3,815	3,966
Training for disadvantaged adults and youth [18][19]	1,886	1,810	1,788	1,745	1,886	1,810	1,788	1,745
Job Corps [18][19]	617	716	742	803	617	716	742	803
Summer youth employment program [18][19]	725	718	709	700	725	718	709	700
Work incentive program	297	103	186	452	267	93	148	265
Senior community service employment program [19]	362	368	382	408	326	331	344	367
Energy assistance [2]	2,292	2,001	1,809	1,802	2,261	1,824	1,629	1,680
Low-income energy assistance [3][20]	2,095	1,840	1,648	1,641	2,070	1,663	1,468	1,519
Other [21]	(X)	930	900	303	(X)	930	900	303

- Represents zero.   X Not applicable.   [1] Includes State and local government expenditures not shown separately.   [2] Includes other programs not shown separately.   [3] Includes administrative expenses.   [4] Medical care for veterans with a non-service-connected disability.   [5] Estimated.   [6] Aid to Families with Dependent Children program. Excludes data for foster care program and child support operations (cost and collections).   [7] Excludes Federal sums spent for SSI (State supplements) to Indochinese refugees.   [8] Includes dependents and survivors.   [9] Includes Puerto Rico's nutritional assistance program.   [10] Free and reduced-price segments.   [11] Includes estimate of commodity assistance.   [12] Special supplemental food program for women, infants and children.   [13] No income test required but preference given to those with greatest need.   [14] Amount of loans obligated.   [15] Formerly Guaranteed Student Loans.   [16] Appropriation available for school year ending the fiscal year named.   [17] Non-Federal expenditure data are rough estimates.   [18] Programs represent specific titles under the Job Training and Partnership Act (JTPA).   [19] Federal funds are appropriations.   [20] Federal funds include amounts transferred to other programs serving the needy. State spending includes funds received as "oil overcharge" settlements.   [21] Represents State Legalization Impact Assistance Grants, offered between 1988 and 1992, to offset State and local costs of welfare, health care, and education provided to legalized aliens.

Source: Library of Congress, Congressional Research Service, "Cash and Noncash Benefits for Persons With Limited Income: Eligibility Rules, Recipient and Expenditure Data, FY 1988-90," Report No. 91-741 EPW, September 30, 1991, and earlier reports.

No. 566. Households Receiving Means-Tested Noncash Benefits: 1980 to 1990

[In thousands, except percent. Households as of **March** of following year. Covers civilian noninstitutional population, including persons in the Armed Forces living off post or with their families on post. A means-tested benefit program requires that the household's income and/or assets fall below specified guidelines in order to qualify for benefits. The means-tested noncash benefits covered are food stamps, free or reduced-price school lunches, public or subsidized housing, and Medicaid. There are general trends toward under-estimation of noncash beneficiaries. Households are classified according to poverty status of family or nonfamily householder; for explanation of poverty level, see text, section 14. Based on Current Population Survey; see text, section 1, and Appendix III]

TYPE OF BENEFIT RECEIVED	1980	1985	1987	1989	1990			
					Total	Below poverty level		Above poverty level
						Number	Percent distribution	
Total households	82,368	88,458	91,066	93,347	94,312	12,227	100	82,085
Receiving at least one noncash benefit. .	14,266	14,466	14,277	15,012	16,098	7,671	63	8,427
Not receiving cash public assistance . .	7,860	7,860	7,730	8,342	8,819	3,169	26	5,650
Receiving cash public assistance [1] . . .	6,407	6,607	6,547	6,669	7,279	4,502	37	2,777
Total households receiving—								
Food stamps	6,769	6,779	6,351	6,508	7,163	5,193	43	1,970
School lunch	5,532	5,752	5,778	5,943	6,252	3,195	26	3,057
Public housing	2,777	3,799	3,983	4,085	4,339	2,637	22	1,702
Medicaid.	8,287	8,178	8,314	9,180	10,321	5,609	46	4,712

[1] Households receiving money from Aid to Families with Dependent Children program, Supplemental Security Income program or other public assistance programs.

Source: U.S. Bureau of the Census, *Current Population Reports*, series P-60, No. 155 and earlier reports and unpublished data.

No. 567. Public Income-Maintenance Programs—Cash Benefit Payments: 1970 to 1990

[Includes payments outside the United States and benefits to dependents, where applicable]

PROGRAM	PAYMENTS (bil. dol.)										PERCENT		
	1970	1980	1983	1984	1985	1986	1987	1988	1989	1990	1970	1980	1989
Total [1]	**60.5**	**228.1**	**298.6**	**309.1**	**335.2**	**356.6**	**372.0**	**393.8**	**418.9**	**(NA)**	**100**	**100**	**100**
Percent of personal income [2]	7.3	10.1	10.5	9.9	9.9	10.1	9.8	9.7	9.6	(NA)	(X)	(X)	(X)
OASDI [3]	31.6	120.3	166.9	175.5	186.1	196.1	204.7	216.4	229.6	245.6	52	53	55
Public employee retirement [4]	9.2	40.6	55.0	59.0	63.0	66.9	72.1	78.0	83.8	(NA)	15	18	20
Railroad retirement.	1.8	4.9	6.0	6.1	6.3	6.4	6.5	6.7	6.9	7.2	3	2	2
Veterans' pensions, compensation.	5.5	11.4	13.7	13.8	14.1	14.3	14.3	14.7	15.0	15.5	9	5	4
Unemployment benefits [5]	4.2	18.9	19.2	13.6	14.4	16.0	14.4	13.2	13.5	16.5	7	8	3
Temporary disability benefits	0.7	1.4	1.6	1.8	1.8	2.1	2.5	2.8	2.9	(NA)	1	1	1
Workers' compensation [6]	2.0	9.7	11.9	13.3	22.3	24.7	27.1	30.3	33.8	(NA)	3	4	8
Public assistance [7]	4.9	12.1	13.9	14.6	15.3	16.1	16.5	17.0	17.6	18.8	8	5	4
Supplemental Security Income [7] . .	(X)	7.9	9.5	10.4	11.1	12.9	13.6	14.7	15.8	16.3	(X)	3	4

NA Not available.   X Not applicable.   [1] Includes lump sum death benefits, not shown separately. Lump sum death benefits for State and local goverment employee retirement systems are not available beginning 1987.   [2] For base data, see table 682.   [3] Old-age, survivors, and disability insurance under Federal Social Security Act; see text, section 12.   [4] Excludes refunds of contributions to employees who leave service.   [5] Beginning 1981, covers State unemployment insurance, Ex-Servicemen's Compensation Act and railroad unemployment insurance only.   [6] Includes black lung benefits.   [7] Beginning 1975, Federal grants to States for aid to aged, blind, and disabled replaced by Supplemental Security Income programs; see text, section 12.

Source: U.S. Social Security Administration, *Social Security Bulletin*, monthly and unpublished data.

No. 568. Estimated Workers Under Social Insurance Programs: 1970 to 1990

[In millions. As of **December**, except as noted. See also *Historical Statistics, Colonial Times to 1970*, series H 51-56]

EMPLOYMENT AND COVERAGE STATUS	1970	1980	1982	1983	1984	1985	1986	1987	1988	1989	1990
Total labor force [1][2]	**86.3**	**109.1**	**112.7**	**113.5**	**115.7**	**117.5**	**119.8**	**122.0**	**123.8**	**125.7**	**126.2**
Paid civilian population	77.8	98.9	98.4	102.2	105.5	107.7	110.2	113.3	115.6	117.4	117.0
Unpaid family workers	0.9	0.6	0.5	0.6	0.5	0.4	0.3	0.4	0.4	0.3	0.3
Unemployed	4.7	7.4	11.6	9.0	8.0	7.7	7.5	6.5	6.1	6.3	7.3
Armed Forces [2]	3.0	2.1	2.2	1.7	1.7	1.7	1.8	1.8	1.7	1.7	1.6
Civilian population covered by:											
Public retirement programs	75.2	96.4	95.7	99.5	104.4	106.6	109.1	112.2	114.5	116.3	116.0
OASDHI [3]	69.1	89.3	88.9	92.7	98.0	100.3	102.9	106.0	108.4	110.1	109.8
Railroad retirement	0.6	0.5	0.4	0.4	0.4	0.3	0.3	0.3	0.3	0.3	0.3
Public employees retirement [4]	5.5	6.6	6.4	6.4	6.0	6.0	5.9	5.9	5.8	5.9	5.9
Unemployment insurance	55.8	87.2	87.9	91.3	95.8	98.2	100.2	103.7	106.9	109.1	110.8
Workers' compensation	59.0	79.1	78.1	80.5	83.4	85.1	87.2	90.0	92.8	95.3	96.7
Temporary disability insurance	14.6	18.4	18.1	18.7	19.3	19.8	20.3	21.6	21.8	22.2	(NA)

NA Not available.   [1] Data from U.S. Bureau of Labor Statistics and based on U.S. Bureau of the Census' Current Population Survey; see text, section 1, and Appendix III.   [2] Excludes Armed Forces overseas beginning 1983.   [3] OASDHI=Old-age, survivors, disability, and health insurance. Excludes members of Armed Forces and railroad employees.   [4] Data represent yearly averages. Excludes State and local government employees covered by both OASDHI and their own retirement program.

Source: U.S. Social Security Administration, *Annual Statistical Supplement* to the *Social Security Bulletin*.

No. 569. Selected Social Insurance Programs—Estimated Payrolls of Covered Employment in Relation to Wages and Salaries: 1970 to 1989

[In billions of dollars, except percent. Data for Federal civilian and military personnel cover all areas. Gross amount before deduction of social insurance contributions. OASDHI: Old-age, survivors, disability, and health insurance programs under Social Security Act; see text, section 12. See also *Historical Statistics, Colonial Times to 1970*, series H 57-69]

PROGRAM	1970	1980	1982	1983	1984	1985	1986	1987	1988	1989
Total earnings [1]	615	1,553	1,717	1,867	2,073	2,232	2,377	2,573	2,785	2,952
All wages and salaries [1]	549	1,372	1,586	1,676	1,839	1,975	2,094	2,250	2,431	2,573
Civilian	528	1,342	1,546	1,634	1,794	1,928	2,044	2,198	2,378	2,518
Payrolls covered by—										
Retirement programs [2]	528	1,318	1,529	1,614	1,775	1,896	2,011	2,157	2,345	2,496
OASDHI [3][4]	480	1,229	1,423	1,502	1,665	1,782	1,896	2,042	2,227	2,373
Railroad retirement [3]	6	13	13	12	13	13	12	12	12	12
Federal civil service	26	52	59	62	65	70	72	74	80	88
State and local government	53	123	143	153	162	175	190	203	219	235
Unemployment insurance [3]	389	1,303	1,500	1,583	1,739	1,870	1,983	2,046	2,215	2,348
Workers' compensation program [5]	441	1,136	1,301	1,382	1,516	1,618	1,725	1,845	1,997	2,115
Net earnings in self-employment covered by OASDHI	48	98	99	109	117	130	139	156	182	196
Percent of civilian payrolls covered by—										
OASDHI [3][6]	90.9	92.6	93.1	92.6	92.9	92.4	92.8	92.9	93.7	94.2
Railroad retirement [3]	1.2	1.0	0.8	0.7	0.7	0.7	0.6	0.5	0.5	0.5
Federal civil service retirement	5.0	3.9	3.9	3.8	3.7	3.6	3.5	3.4	3.4	3.5
State and local government retirement	10.1	9.2	9.2	9.4	9.0	9.1	9.3	9.2	9.2	9.3
Unemployment insurance [3]	73.7	97.1	97.0	96.9	97.0	97.0	97.0	93.1	93.1	93.2
Workers' compensation programs [5]	83.6	84.6	84.1	84.6	84.5	83.9	84.4	84.0	84.0	84.0

[1] Data from U.S. Bureau of Economic Analysis. Earnings include self-employed; wages and salaries represent civilian and military pay in cash and in kind. [2] Adjusted for duplication in coverage by both OASDHI and State and local government retirement systems. [3] Taxable plus estimated nontaxable wages and salaries. [4] Includes Armed Forces in all areas. [5] Payrolls of employers insured with private carriers, State funds, or self-insured, and pay covered by Federal programs in all areas. [6] Percent computed after excluding Armed Forces payroll covered by OASDHI.

No. 570. Selected Social Insurance Programs—Source of Funds From Contributions and Transfers: 1980 to 1990

[In billions of dollars]

PROGRAM AND SOURCE OF FUNDS	1980	1983	1984	1985	1986	1987	1988	1989	1990
Social Security trust funds:									
Old-age and survivors insurance (OASI)	104.0	143.9	167.1	182.4	194.3	206.0	233.2	252.7	270.3
Employer	49.7	63.9	78.1	83.7	90.3	95.5	107.4	117.6	125.3
Employee	49.4	63.7	74.0	83.4	89.8	95.1	106.9	116.8	124.5
Self-employed	4.3	5.0	6.6	7.7	8.8	10.1	13.1	13.5	15.9
Government [1]	0.5	11.2	0.9	2.5	0.5	0.4	0.3	0.3	-1.6
Tax credits [2]	(X)	(X)	4.6	1.8	1.6	1.6	2.1	2.1	1.4
Taxation of benefits [3]	(X)	(X)	2.8	3.2	3.4	3.3	3.4	2.4	4.8
Disability insurance (DI)	13.4	19.1	16.1	18.4	18.6	19.7	22.1	24.1	27.9
Employer	6.3	8.4	7.5	8.1	8.7	9.3	10.3	11.3	13.4
Employee	6.3	8.3	7.1	8.1	8.7	9.3	10.3	11.2	13.3
Self-employed	0.7	0.8	0.7	0.8	0.9	1.0	1.3	1.3	1.6
Government [1]	0.1	1.6	0.1	1.0	(Z)	(Z)	(Z)	(Z)	-0.7
Tax credits [2]	(X)	(X)	0.4	0.2	0.2	0.2	0.2	0.2	0.1
Taxation of benefits [3]	(X)	(X)	0.2	0.2	0.2	(-Z)	0.1	0.1	0.1
Hospital insurance (HI) [4]	25.0	41.3	43.6	48.0	55.6	59.6	63.4	69.4	71.9
Employer	11.6	18.2	20.4	22.6	26.0	27.8	29.2	32.3	33.9
Employee	11.5	18.1	20.4	22.5	25.9	27.6	29.1	32.0	33.6
Self-employed	0.7	0.9	1.4	2.0	2.3	2.8	3.6	3.5	4.1
Government [1]	0.9	3.6	0.9	(Z)	0.7	0.6	0.6	0.7	-0.5
Tax credits [2]	(X)	(X)	0.2	0.4	0.4	0.5	0.6	0.5	0.4
Supplementary medical insurance (SMI) [5]	10.5	19.1	22.2	23.9	23.5	31.0	35.0	41.6	44.4
Aged	2.7	3.8	4.7	5.1	5.2	6.7	8.0	9.8	10.3
Disabled	0.3	0.4	0.4	0.5	0.5	0.7	0.8	1.0	1.0
Government	7.5	14.9	17.1	18.3	17.8	23.6	26.2	30.9	33.0
Railroad retirement [6]	2.6	3.6	[4]4.8	[4]5.0	[4]4.8	[4]3.9	[4]4.6	[4]4.1	[4]4.5
Employer	1.7	2.0	2.4	2.4	2.4	2.4	2.7	2.5	2.5
Employee	0.6	0.8	1.0	1.1	1.1	1.1	1.3	1.2	1.2
Government [1]	0.3	0.7	1.1	1.1	0.9	0.3	0.4	0.3	0.6
Federal civil service	20.0	25.1	25.6	27.2	27.7	27.8	28.8	29.9	31.9
Employer (Federal and DC govt.)	16.2	20.7	20.9	22.5	23.0	23.1	24.3	25.4	?7.4
Employee [7]	3.8	4.5	4.7	4.7	4.7	4.6	4.5	4.5	4.5
State and local government [8]	25.7	32.8	34.3	37.5	39.2	41.6	46.7	44.0	(NA)
Employer (government)	18.8	24.1	25.3	27.7	28.6	30.4	34.9	31.2	(NA)
Employee	6.9	8.7	9.0	9.8	10.6	11.2	11.8	12.8	(NA)

NA Not available. X Not applicable. Z Less than $50 million. [1] Represents cost of gratuitous military service wage credits and, for OASI only, Federal payments for special age-72 benefits. For HI only, also includes transfers of appropriations for HI payments of persons not insured for cash benefits under OASI, DI, or railroad retirement and transfers for Professional Standards Review Organization expenditures. Beginning 1983, includes taxes on deemed wage credits for military service performed after 1956. Minus sign (-) represents repayments to Government for previous overpayments. [2] See footnotes 5 and 6, table 571. [3] Revenues arising from application of income tax to up to half of the social security benefits of beneficiaries who have substantial amounts of other income. Minus sign (-) indicates tax refunds. [4] Includes other sources not shown separately. [5] Includes premiums paid on behalf of eligibles by State governments under "buy-in" arrangements. [6] Excludes HI contributions and includes employer contributions to supplement benefit account. [7] Includes voluntary contributions to purchase additional annuity. [8] Estimated.

Source of tables 569 and 570: U.S. Social Security Administration, *Annual Statistical Supplement* to the *Social Security Bulletin*.

No. 571. Social Security—Covered Employment, Earnings, and Contribution Rates: 1970 to 1990

[Includes Puerto Rico, Virgin Islands, American Samoa, and Guam. Represents all reported employment. Data are estimated. OASDHI=Old-age, survivors, disability, and health insurance; SMI=Supplementary medical insurance. See also *Historical Statistics, Colonial Times to 1970*, series H 172-185]

ITEM	Unit	1970	1980	1983	1984	1985	1986	1987	1988	1989	1990
Workers with insured status [1]....	Million ...	105.7	137.4	145.0	147.0	148.7	150.6	152.7	155.4	158.0	160.4
Male..................	Million ...	61.9	75.4	78.4	78.8	79.7	80.7	81.5	82.6	83.7	84.7
Female...............	Million ...	43.8	62.0	66.6	68.2	69.0	69.9	71.2	72.8	74.3	75.7
Under 25 years old	Million ...	17.7	25.5	24.4	23.1	22.3	21.9	21.3	21.3	21.1	20.9
25 to 34 years old..........	Million ...	22.3	34.9	38.0	39.7	39.9	40.0	40.6	41.0	41.3	41.4
35 to 44 years old..........	Million ...	19.0	22.4	25.9	27.2	28.5	29.8	31.2	32.3	33.5	34.8
45 to 54 years old..........	Million ...	19.0	18.6	18.6	18.8	19.0	19.3	19.8	20.5	21.4	22.1
55 to 59 years old..........	Million ...	7.8	9.2	9.2	9.1	9.1	9.0	8.9	8.8	8.7	8.7
60 to 64 years old..........	Million ...	6.3	7.9	8.4	8.6	8.7	8.8	8.7	8.7	8.7	8.6
65 to 69 years old..........	Million ...	5.1	6.7	7.1	7.1	7.3	7.5	7.6	7.7	7.9	8.0
70 years old and over	Million ...	8.5	12.1	13.4	13.4	13.9	14.3	14.7	15.0	15.4	15.8
Workers reported with—											
Taxable earnings [2]	Million ...	93	112	112	116	120	123	125	130	133	134
Maximum earnings [2]	Million ...	24	10	7	7	7	7	7	8	8	8
Earnings in covered employment .	Bil. dol...	532	1,326	1,608	1,772	1,912	2,035	2,198	2,411	2,593	2,722
Reported taxable [2]	Bil. dol...	416	1,176	1,454	1,609	1,724	1,844	1,960	2,101	2,243	2,370
Percent of total	Percent ..	78.2	88.7	90.4	90.8	90.2	90.6	89.2	87.1	86.5	87.1
Average per worker:											
Total earnings [2]	Dollars...	5,711	11,817	14,345	15,260	15,955	16,587	17,584	18,610	19,494	20,373
Taxable earnings [2]	Dollars...	4,464	10,500	12,982	13,871	14,367	14,992	15,680	16,215	16,863	17,739
Annual maximum taxable earnings	Dollars...	7,800	25,900	35,700	[3]37,800	39,600	42,000	43,800	45,000	48,000	51,300
Maximum tax.............	Dollars...	374	1,588	2,392	[3]2,533	2,792	3,003	3,132	3,380	3,605	3,924
Contribution rates for OASDHI: [4]											
Each employer and employee ..	Percent ..	4.80	6.13	6.70	[5]7.00	7.05	7.15	7.15	[6]7.51	[6]7.51	7.65
Self-employed...........	Percent ..	6.90	8.10	9.35	[6]14.00	[6]14.10	[6]14.30	[6]14.30	[6]15.02	[6]15.02	[6]15.30
SMI, monthly premium [7]	Dollars...	5.30	9.60	12.20	14.60	15.50	15.50	17.90	24.80	31.90	28.60

[1] Fully insured for retirement and/or survivor benefits as of beginning of year.   [2] Includes self-employment.   [3] Employee's maximum tax; see footnote 5.   [4] As of January 1, 1991 each employee and employer pays 7.65 percent and the self-employed pay 15.3 percent.   [5] Employee pays 6.7 percent. Employee's additional .3 percent is supplied from general revenues. [6] Self-employed pays 11.3 percent in 1984, 11.8 percent in 1985, 12.3 percent in 1986 and 1987, and 13.02 percent in 1988 and 1989. The additional amount is supplied from general revenues. Beginning 1990, self-employed pays 15.3 percent, and half of the tax is deductible for income tax purposes and for computing self-employment income subject to social security tax. [7] 1970-82, as of July 1; beginning 1983, as of January 1. As of January 1, 1991 the monthly premium is $29.90.

Source: U.S. Social Security Administration, *Annual Statistical Supplement* to the *Social Security Bulletin*, and unpublished data.

No. 572. Social Security Trust Funds: 1980 to 1990

[**In billions of dollars, except percent.** See also *Historical Statistics, Colonial Times to 1970*, series H 238-242]

TYPE OF TRUST FUND	1980	1983	1984	1985	1986	1987	1988	1989	1990
Old-age and survivors insurance (OASI):									
Net contribution income [1]	103.5	138.3	167.0	180.2	194.2	206.0	233.2	252.6	272.4
Interest received [2].	1.8	6.7	2.6	1.9	3.1	4.7	7.6	12.0	16.4
Benefit payments [3].	105.1	149.2	157.8	167.2	176.8	[4]183.6	[4]195.5	208.0	223.0
Assets, end of year ...	22.8	[5]19.7	[5]27.1	[5]35.8	39.1	62.1	102.9	155.1	214.2
Disability insurance (DI):									
Net contribution income [1]	13.3	18.0	16.1	17.4	18.6	19.7	22.1	24.1	28.7
Interest received [2].	0.5	1.6	1.2	0.9	0.8	0.6	0.6	0.7	0.9
Benefit payments [3].	15.5	17.5	17.9	18.8	19.9	[4]20.5	[4]21.7	22.9	24.8
Assets, end of year ...	3.6	[5]5.2	[5]4.0	[5]6.3	7.8	6.7	6.9	7.9	11.1
Hospital insurance (HI):									
Net contribution income [1][7]	23.9	38.2	42.5	47.7	54.7	58.8	62.6	68.5	71.1
Interest received [2].	1.1	2.6	3.0	3.4	3.6	4.5	5.8	7.3	8.5
Benefit payments.	25.1	39.3	43.3	47.5	49.8	49.5	52.5	60.0	66.2
Assets, end of year ...	13.7	[8]12.9	[8]15.7	[8]20.5	40.0	53.7	69.6	85.6	98.9
Supplementary medical insurance (SMI):									
Net premium income	3.0	4.2	5.2	5.6	5.7	7.4	8.8	10.8	11.3
Transfers from general revenue ...	7.5	14.9	17.1	18.3	17.8	23.6	26.2	30.9	33.0
Interest received	0.4	0.7	1.0	1.2	1.1	0.9	0.9	1.1	1.6
Benefit payments	10.6	18.1	19.7	22.9	26.2	30.8	34.0	38.4	42.5
Assets, end of year	4.5	7.1	9.7	10.9	8.3	8.4	9.0	12.2	15.5

[1] Includes deposits by States and deductions for refund of estimated employee-tax overpayment. Beginning in 1983, includes government contributions on deemed wage credits for military service in 1957 and later. Beginning 1984 includes tax credits on wages paid in 1984 and net earnings from self-employment in 1984-89; and taxation of benefits (OASI and DI, only). [2] Beginning in 1983, includes interest on advance tax transfers and interest on reimbursement for unnegotiated checks. Data for 1983 and 1984 reflect interest on deemed wage credits for military service performed after 1956. Data for 1983-1986 reflect interest on interfund borrowing. [3] Includes payments for vocational rehabilitation services furnished to disabled persons receiving benefits because of their disabilities. Beginning in 1983, amounts reflect deductions for unnegotiated benefit checks. [4] Data adjusted to reflect 12 months of benefit payments. [5] Includes $18 billion borrowed from the DI and HI Trust Funds. Repayments on Jan. 31, 1985, reduced such amounts to $13.2 billion. [6] Excludes $5 billion lent to the OASI Trust Fund. Repayment on Jan. 31, 1985, reduced the total to $2.5 billion. [7] Includes premiums from aged ineligibles enrolled in HI. [8] Excludes $12 billion lent to the OASI Trust Fund. Repayment on Jan. 31, 1985, reduced the total to $10.6 billion.

Source: U.S. Social Security Administration, *Annual Report of Board of Trustees, OASI, DI, HI, and SMI Trust Funds*. Also published in *Social Security Bulletin*, monthly.

No. 573. Social Security (OASDI)—Benefits, by Type of Beneficiary: 1970 to 1990

[A person eligible to receive more than one type of benefit is generally classified or counted only once as a retired-worker beneficiary. OASDI=Old-age, survivors, and disability insurance. See also headnote, table 571; Appendix III; and *Historical Statistics, Colonial Times to 1970*, series H 197-229]

TYPE OF BENEFICIARY	1970	1980	1983	1984	1985	1986	1987	1988	1989	1990
	BENEFITS IN CURRENT-PAYMENT STATUS[1] (end of year)									
Number of benefits (1,000)...	26,229	35,585	36,085	36,479	37,058	37,703	38,190	38,627	39,151	39,829
Retired workers [2] (1,000).	13,349	19,562	21,419	21,906	22,432	22,980	23,440	23,858	24,327	24,838
Disabled workers [3] (1,000)	1,493	2,859	2,569	2,597	2,657	2,728	2,786	2,830	2,895	3,011
Wives and husbands [2][4] (1,000)...	2,952	3,477	3,347	3,355	3,375	3,387	3,381	3,367	3,367	3,367
Children (1,000)	4,122	4,607	3,593	3,408	3,319	3,295	3,244	3,204	3,165	3,187
Under age 18	3,315	3,423	2,812	2,729	2,699	2,665	2,604	2,534	2,488	2,497
Disabled children [5]	271	450	488	506	526	545	561	574	586	600
Students [6]	537	733	293	173	94	84	79	96	91	89
Of retired workers	546	639	512	477	457	450	439	432	423	422
Of deceased workers	2,688	2,610	2,146	2,010	1,917	1,878	1,837	1,809	1,780	1,776
Of disabled workers	889	1,358	936	921	945	966	968	963	962	989
Widowed mothers [7] (1,000)	523	562	400	382	372	351	329	318	312	304
Widows and widowers [2][8] (1,000).	3,227	4,411	4,694	4,779	4,863	4,928	4,984	5,029	5,071	5,111
Parents [2] (1,000)	29	15	11	10	10	9	8	7	6	6
Special benefits [9] (1,000)	534	93	51	40	32	25	19	14	10	7
Average monthly benefit, current dollars:										
Retired workers [2]	118	341	441	461	479	489	513	537	567	603
Retired worker and wife [2]	199	567	743	780	814	831	873	914	966	1,027
Disabled workers [3]	131	371	456	471	484	488	508	530	556	587
Wives and husbands [2][4]	59	164	217	227	236	241	253	265	281	298
Children of retired workers	45	140	176	186	198	204	216	228	242	259
Children of deceased workers	82	240	298	314	330	337	352	368	385	406
Children of disabled workers	39	110	136	139	142	141	146	151	157	164
Widowed mothers [7]	87	246	309	322	332	338	353	368	388	409
Widows and widowers, nondisabled [2]	102	311	396	415	433	444	468	493	522	557
Parents [2]	103	276	350	364	378	386	407	428	454	482
Special benefits [9]	45	105	129	134	138	140	145	151	158	167
Average monthly benefit, constant (1990) dollars:[10]										
Retired workers [2]	397	529	582	586	586	591	595	596	602	603
Retired worker and wife [2]	669	879	981	991	996	1,006	1,012	1,015	1,025	1,027
Disabled workers [3]	440	575	602	598	592	591	589	588	590	587
Wives and husbands [2][4]	198	254	287	288	289	292	293	294	298	298
Children of deceased workers	276	372	394	399	405	408	409	409	409	406
Widowed mothers [7]	292	381	408	409	406	409	409	409	412	409
Widows and widowers, nondisabled [2]	343	482	523	527	530	538	543	547	554	556
	BENEFITS AWARDED DURING YEAR (1,000)									
Number of benefits	3,722	4,215	3,756	3,691	3,796	3,853	3,734	3,681	3,646	3,717
Retired workers [2]	1,338	1,620	1,670	1,607	1,690	1,734	1,682	1,654	1,657	1,665
Disabled workers [3]	350	389	311	362	377	417	416	409	426	468
Wives and husbands [2][4]	436	469	436	425	440	441	411	391	380	379
Children	1,091	1,174	753	722	714	701	685	706	675	695
Widowed mothers [7]	112	108	82	74	72	69	65	63	60	58
Widows and widowers [2][8]	363	452	502	500	502	491	475	458	449	452
Parents [2]	2	1	(Z)	(Z)	(Z)	(Z)	(Z)	(Z)	(Z)	(Z)
Special benefits [9]	30	1	1	1	1	(Z)	(Z)	(Z)	(Z)	(Z)
	BENEFIT PAYMENTS DURING YEAR (bil. dol.)									
Total amount [11]	31.9	120.5	167.0	175.8	186.2	196.7	204.2	217.2	230.9	247.8
Monthly benefits [12]	31.6	120.1	166.8	175.6	186.0	196.5	204.0	217.0	230.6	247.6
Retired workers [2]	18.4	70.4	103.6	110.0	116.8	123.6	128.5	137.0	146.0	156.8
Disabled workers [3]	2.4	12.8	15.2	15.6	16.5	17.4	18.1	19.2	20.3	22.1
Wives and husbands [2][4]	2.2	7.0	9.9	10.4	11.1	11.7	12.1	12.8	13.6	14.5
Children	3.5	10.5	10.8	10.7	10.7	10.9	11.0	11.3	11.5	12.0
Under age 18	2.7	7.4	8.3	8.4	8.5	8.7	8.5	8.7	8.7	9.0
Disabled children [5]	0.3	1.0	1.4	1.6	1.8	2.0	2.0	2.2	2.3	2.5
Students [6]	0.6	2.1	1.0	0.6	0.4	0.3	0.4	0.5	0.5	0.5
Of retired workers	0.3	1.1	1.1	1.1	1.1	1.2	1.2	1.2	1.2	1.3
Of deceased workers	2.8	7.4	7.9	7.8	7.8	7.8	7.8	8.1	8.3	8.6
Of disabled workers	0.5	2.0	1.7	1.7	1.8	1.9	1.9	2.0	2.0	2.2
Widowed mothers [7]	0.6	1.6	1.8	1.5	1.5	1.5	1.4	1.4	1.4	1.4
Widows and widowers [2][8]	4.1	17.6	25.4	27.3	29.3	31.3	32.8	35.2	37.7	40.7
Parents [2]	(Z)	0.1	0.1	0.1	0.1	(Z)	(Z)	(Z)	(Z)	(Z)
Special benefits [9]	0.3	0.1	0.1	0.1	0.1	(Z)	(Z)	(Z)	(Z)	(Z)
Lump sum	0.3	0.4	0.2	0.2	0.2	0.2	0.2	0.2	0.2	0.2

Z Fewer than 500 or less than $50 million.   [1] Benefit payment actually being made at a specified time with no deductions or with deductions amounting to less than a month's benefits; i.e., the benefits actually being received.   [2] 62 years and over.   [3] Disabled workers under age 65.   [4] Includes wife beneficiaries with entitled children in their care and entitled divorced wives.   [5] 18 years old and over. Disability began before age 18 and, beginning 1973, before age 22.   [6] Full-time students aged 18-21 through 1984 and aged 18 and 19 beginning 1985.   [7] Includes surviving divorced mothers with entitled children in their care and, beginning June 1975, widowed fathers with entitled children in their care.   [8] Includes widows aged 60-61, surviving divorced wives aged 60 and over, disabled widows and widowers aged 50 and over; and beginning Jan. 1973, widowers aged 60-61.   [9] Benefits for persons aged 72 and over not insured under regular or transitional provisions of Social Security Act.   [10] Constant dollar figures are based on the consumer price index for December as published by the U.S. Bureau of Labor Statistics.   [11] Represents total disbursements of benefit checks by the U.S. Dept. of the Treasury during the years specified.   [12] Distribution by type estimated.

Source: U.S. Social Security Administration, *Annual Statistical Supplement* to the *Social Security Bulletin*, and unpublished data.

No. 574. Social Security—Beneficiaries, Annual Payments, and Average Monthly Benefit, 1970 to 1990, and by State and Other Areas, 1990

[Number of beneficiaries in current-payment status and average monthly benefit as of **December**. See also headnote, table 573, and Appendix III]

YEAR, DIVISION, STATE, AND OTHER AREA	NUMBER OF BENEFICIARIES (1,000)				ANNUAL PAYMENTS (mil.dol.)				AVERAGE MONTHLY BENEFIT (dol.)		
	Total	Retired workers and dependents[1]	Survivors	Disabled workers and dependents	Total	Retired workers and dependents[1]	Survivors[2]	Disabled workers and dependents	Retired workers[3]	Disabled workers	Widows and widowers[4]
1970.	26,229	17,093	6,470	2,665	31,863	21,076	7,721	3,067	118	131	102
1980.	35,585	23,309	7,598	4,678	120,472	78,025	27,010	15,437	341	371	311
1985.	37,058	25,989	7,162	3,907	186,195	128,536	38,824	18,836	479	484	433
1986.	37,703	26,541	7,166	3,995	196,692	135,949	40,896	19,847	489	488	444
1987.	38,190	26,988	7,157	4,045	204,156	141,329	42,315	20,512	513	508	468
1988.	38,627	27,390	7,163	4,074	217,214	150,526	44,996	21,692	537	530	493
1989.	39,151	27,853	7,170	4,129	230,850	160,352	47,625	22,873	567	556	522
1990, total	**39,829**	**28,367**	**7,197**	**4,266**	**247,796**	**172,042**	**50,951**	**24,803**	**603**	**587**	**557**
United States	**38,889**	**27,800**	**6,986**	**4,103**	**244,020**	**169,934**	**49,937**	**24,150**	**606**	**590**	**560**
New England	**2,142**	**1,613**	**332**	**196**	**13,843**	**10,156**	**2,517**	**1,167**	**(NA)**	**(NA)**	**(NA)**
Maine	215	155	36	24	1,246	866	247	132	555	534	526
New Hampshire.	162	123	24	15	1,032	761	183	87	605	583	578
Vermont.	88	63	15	9	542	379	110	53	589	578	561
Massachusetts.	970	727	152	91	6,224	4,521	1,159	545	605	577	586
Rhode Island	181	137	26	18	1,150	855	195	99	601	555	578
Connecticut	527	408	79	40	3,649	2,774	623	251	661	590	621
Middle Atlantic	**6,299**	**4,639**	**1,086**	**573**	**42,173**	**30,267**	**8,286**	**3,619**	**(NA)**	**(NA)**	**(NA)**
New York	2,832	2,077	474	281	19,034	13,692	3,578	1,764	645	613	598
New Jersey.	1,229	921	202	106	8,462	6,224	1,561	676	659	610	612
Pennsylvania.	2,237	1,641	410	186	14,677	10,351	3,147	1,179	621	608	587
East North Central. . . .	**6,798**	**4,827**	**1,258**	**713**	**44,724**	**30,798**	**9,558**	**4,366**	**(NA)**	**(NA)**	**(NA)**
Ohio	1,803	1,253	355	196	11,616	7,763	2,672	1,181	618	613	585
Indiana.	913	645	166	102	5,929	4,088	1,241	599	628	606	589
Illinois	1,753	1,265	322	166	11,760	8,273	2,456	1,031	641	612	601
Michigan	1,490	1,045	277	168	10,010	6,797	2,144	1,068	643	644	600
Wisconsin.	838	619	139	81	5,409	3,877	1,045	487	618	594	584
West North Central . . .	**3,024**	**2,217**	**537**	**270**	**18,656**	**13,205**	**3,890**	**1,561**	**(NA)**	**(NA)**	**(NA)**
Minnesota	669	503	114	53	4,101	2,955	842	304	587	572	556
Iowa	524	388	93	43	3,292	2,355	686	251	605	579	567
Missouri	914	648	165	101	5,582	3,833	1,165	584	589	576	548
North Dakota	113	82	22	9	653	456	148	49	567	556	524
South Dakota	128	93	24	11	739	514	164	61	557	533	524
Nebraska	268	200	47	21	1,664	1,192	352	121	595	569	570
Kansas	407	303	72	33	2,625	1,900	533	191	617	570	579
South Atlantic.	**7,148**	**5,091**	**1,262**	**795**	**43,252**	**30,042**	**8,570**	**4,638**	**(NA)**	**(NA)**	**(NA)**
Delaware	104	76	18	11	691	494	134	63	627	603	585
Maryland	609	442	115	52	3,875	2,706	829	340	601	606	568
District of Columbia . .	77	55	15	7	430	295	94	41	515	525	474
Virginia.	834	577	158	99	4,928	3,302	1,063	563	567	572	516
West Virginia.	370	228	84	58	2,247	1,330	576	340	595	627	527
North Carolina.	1,075	739	197	139	6,250	4,207	1,259	784	561	551	487
South Carolina	541	359	104	78	3,117	2,053	627	437	561	559	482
Georgia	884	572	181	131	5,066	3,224	1,116	725	560	559	492
Florida	2,653	2,043	390	220	16,648	12,431	2,872	1,345	602	598	574
East South Central . . .	**2,630**	**1,678**	**553**	**399**	**14,812**	**9 230**	**3,453**	**2,128**	**(NA)**	**(NA)**	**(NA)**
Kentucky	646	403	137	106	3,656	2,198	880	578	553	584	496
Tennessee	825	547	164	113	4,763	3,088	1,055	620	561	556	497
Alabama	709	452	155	102	4,019	2,503	971	544	555	560	480
Mississippi	451	276	97	78	2,374	1,441	547	386	520	538	449
West South Central . . .	**3,847**	**2,581**	**823**	**443**	**22,465**	**14,633**	**5,436**	**2,394**	**(NA)**	**(NA)**	**(NA)**
Arkansas	470	310	90	69	2,581	1,664	560	358	539	553	477
Louisiana	652	391	158	103	3,689	2,146	1,002	540	560	595	509
Oklahoma.	532	375	105	53	3,165	2,151	715	298	575	570	529
Texas	2,193	1,505	470	218	13,030	8,672	3,159	1,198	583	579	538
Mountain	**1,948**	**1,412**	**324**	**211**	**11,906**	**8,408**	**2,275**	**1,221**	**(NA)**	**(NA)**	**(NA)**
Montana.	138	97	24	16	846	574	173	98	588	602	559
Idaho.	157	116	26	15	953	681	186	87	586	593	558
Wyoming	62	44	11	7	388	274	78	36	604	580	568
Colorado	422	300	73	48	2,551	1,754	520	276	588	582	559
New Mexico	219	149	42	28	1,243	829	269	145	568	572	518
Arizona	591	440	90	61	3,701	2,681	647	373	610	619	581
Utah	192	140	33	19	1,175	848	228	99	611	575	581
Nevada	168	127	24	17	1,049	767	174	109	604	616	579
Pacific	**5,054**	**3,742**	**810**	**502**	**32,193**	**23,192**	**5,951**	**3,050**	**(NA)**	**(NA)**	**(NA)**
Washington.	714	534	111	70	4,633	3,367	842	424	624	602	591
Oregon	492	374	75	43	3,170	2,339	564	267	614	600	581
California	3,665	2,695	596	374	23,293	16,661	4,359	2,273	615	591	581
Alaska	34	22	7	4	204	132	47	24	602	584	537
Hawaii	149	117	21	10	893	693	139	62	593	582	530
Puerto Rico	564	316	110	139	2,146	1,111	479	556	384	480	346
Guam	5	3	1	(Z)	21	11	8	2	438	471	403
American Samoa . .	4	2	1	1	12	4	5	2	384	430	310
Virgin Islands	10	6	2	1	47	30	12	5	509	529	479
Abroad	358	239	97	22	1,550	952	510	88	434	521	430

NA Not available.   Z Less than 500.   [1] Includes special benefits; see footnote 9, table 573.   [2] Includes lump-sum payments to survivors of deceased workers.   [3] Excludes persons with special benefits.   [4] Nondisabled only.
Source: U.S. Social Security Administration. Quarterly in *Social Security Bulletin.*

No. 575. Pension Plan Coverage of Workers, by Selected Characteristics: 1990

[Covers workers as of **March** of following year who had earnings in year shown. Based on Current Population Survey; see text, section 1 and Appendix III]

SEX AND AGE	NUMBER WITH COVERAGE (1,000)				PERCENT OF TOTAL WORKERS			
	Total [1]	White	Black	Hispanic [2]	Total [1]	White	Black	Hispanic [2]
Total	**53,120**	**45,817**	**5,757**	**2,639**	**40**	**40**	**41**	**26**
Male	30,664	26,887	2,893	1,537	42	43	42	26
Under 65 years old	29,987	26,275	2,838	1,515	43	43	42	26
15 to 24 years old	1,626	1,368	217	162	13	13	17	12
25 to 44 years old	18,060	15,738	1,786	939	47	48	46	28
45 to 64 years old	10,301	9,169	835	414	55	55	53	37
65 years old and over	677	612	55	22	25	24	29	23
Female	22,456	18,930	2,864	1,102	36	36	40	27
Under 65 years old	21,990	18,524	2,818	1,095	37	36	41	27
15 to 24 years old	1,341	1,119	185	86	12	11	14	10
25 to 44 years old	13,509	11,266	1,824	691	42	41	46	31
45 to 64 years old	7,140	6,139	809	318	46	45	50	36
65 years old and over	466	406	46	7	22	22	22	12

[1] Includes other races, not shown separately.　[2] Hispanic persons may be of any race.

Source: U.S. Bureau of the Census, unpublished data.

No. 576. Private Pension Plans—Summary, by Type of Plan: 1975 to 1988

["Pension plan" is defined by the Employee Retirement Income Security Act (ERISA) as "any plan, fund, or program which was heretofore or is hereafter established or maintained by an employer or an employee organization, or by both, to the extent that such plan (a) provides retirement income to employees, or (b) results in a deferral of income by employees for periods extending to the termination of covered employment or beyond, regardless of the method of calculating the contributions made to the plan, the method of calculating the benefits under the plan, or the method of distributing benefits from the plan." A defined benefit plan provides a definite benefit formula for calculating benefit amounts - such as a flat amount per year of service or a percentage of salary or a percentage of salary times years of service. A defined contribution plan is a pension plan in which the contributions are made to an individual account for each employee. The retirement benefit is dependent upon the account balance at retirement. The balance depends upon amounts contributed, investment experience, and, in the case of profit sharing plans, amounts which may be allocated to the account due to forfeitures by terminating employees. Employee Stock Ownership Plans (ESOP)(see table 855) and 401(k) plans are included among defined contribution plans. Data are based on Form 5500 series reports filed with the Internal Revenue Service]

ITEM	Unit	TOTAL				DEFINED CONTRIBUTION PLAN				DEFINED BENEFIT PLAN			
		1975	1980	1985	1988	1975	1980	1985	1988	1975	1980	1985	1988
Number of plans [1]	1,000	311.1	488.9	632.1	729.9	207.7	340.8	462.0	584.0	103.3	148.1	170.2	146.0
Total participants [2][3]	Million	44.5	57.9	74.7	77.7	11.5	19.9	35.0	37.0	33.0	38.0	39.7	40.7
Active participants [2][4]	Million	38.4	49.0	62.3	62.4	11.2	18.9	33.2	34.5	27.2	30.1	29.0	27.9
Contributions	Bil. dol.	37.1	66.2	95.1	91.2	12.8	23.5	53.1	64.9	24.2	42.0	42.0	26.3
Benefits [5]	Bil. dol.	19.1	35.3	101.9	118.6	6.2	13.1	47.4	58.2	12.9	22.1	54.5	60.4

[1] Excludes all plans covering only one participant.　[2] Includes double counting of workers in more than one plan.　[3] Total participants include active participants, vested separated workers, and retirees.　[4] Any workers currently in employment covered by a plan and who are earning or retaining credited service under a plan. Includes any nonvested former employees who have not yet incurred breaks in service.　[5] Benefits paid directly from trust and premium payments made from plan to insurance carriers. Excludes benefits paid directly by insurance carriers.

Source: U.S. Dept. of Labor, Pension and Welfare Benefits Administration, *Trends in Pensions*, 1989 and unpublished data.

No. 577. Assets of Private and Public Pension Funds, by Type of Fund: 1980 to 1991

[In billions of dollars. As of **end of year**. Except for corporate equities, represents book value. Excludes Social Security trust funds, see table 572]

TYPE OF PENSION FUND	1980	1983	1984	1985	1986	1987	1988	1989	1990	1991
Total, all types	**916**	**1,350**	**1,498**	**1,795**	**2,063**	**2,182**	**2,451**	**2,848**	**2,963**	**3,473**
Private funds	642	926	1,011	1,241	1,424	1,476	1,637	1,884	1,961	2,320
Insured	172	286	332	400	477	549	628	714	798	893
Noninsured [1]	470	640	680	841	947	928	1,009	1,171	1,163	1,427
Corporate equities [2]	231	309	295	393	454	453	506	625	585	781
U.S. Government securities	51	98	115	136	147	142	146	163	171	194
Corporate bonds [3]	78	66	78	92	96	92	94	103	107	120
Time deposits	25	49	63	74	88	82	92	97	97	107
Public funds	275	423	487	554	639	706	814	964	1,002	1,153
State and local government	198	311	357	405	469	517	606	735	752	877
Corporate bonds [3]	95	107	118	129	140	125	146	182	188	199
Corporate equities [2]	44	90	97	120	150	170	220	300	296	373
U.S. Government securities	40	88	111	124	144	169	185	198	220	250
Other	19	27	31	32	35	54	56	54	47	55
U.S. Government	76	112	130	149	170	188	208	229	251	276
Civil service [4]	74	111	127	145	163	182	200	220	241	266
Railroad retirement	3	1	3	4	6	7	8	9	9	11

[1] Covers all pension funds of corporations, nonprofit organizations, unions, and multi-employer groups. Also includes deferred profit-sharing plans and Federal Employees Retirement System (FERS) Thrift Savings Fund. Excludes health, welfare, and bonus plans. Includes other types of assets not shown separately.　[2] Includes mutual fund shares.　[3] Includes foreign bonds.　[4] Includes U.S. Foreign Service Retirement and Disability Trust Fund and the Federal Employees Retirement System.

Source: Board of Governors of the Federal Reserve System, *Annual Statistical Digest*, and unpublished data.

No. 578. Individual Retirement Accounts (IRA) Plans—Value, by Type of Holder: 1981 to 1990
[As of **December 31**. Estimated]

TYPE OF HOLDER	AMOUNT (bil. dol.)										PERCENT DISTRIBUTION	
	1981	1982	1983	1984	1985	1986	1987	1988	1989	1990	1981	1990
Total..............	26	52	91	132	200	277	334	393	465	529	100	100
Savings institutions........	14	20	32	43	56	69	77	90	98	92	54	17
Commercial banks........	6	14	27	37	52	67	77	88	99	119	22	22
Mutual funds...........	3	6	11	17	32	54	72	86	112	127	10	24
Self directed............	(NA)	6	8	15	29	45	59	68	82	105	(NA)	20
Life insurance companies....	3	6	9	13	17	22	26	36	49	57	13	11
Credit unions...........	(Z)	2	5	8	14	21	23	25	26	29	1	5

NA Not available.   Z Less than $500 million.
Source: Investment Company Institute, Washington, DC, *Mutual Fund Fact Book*, annual, (copyright).

No. 579. Public Employee Retirement Systems—Beneficiaries and Benefits: 1970 to 1989
[Number of beneficiaries as of end of year]

YEAR	Unit	Total	LEVEL OF GOVERNMENT				TYPE OF BENEFIT			
			Federal			State and local	Age and service	Disability	Survivor	
			Total [1]	Civil service	Armed Forces				Monthly	Lump-sum
Beneficiaries:										
1970.................	1,000..	3,050	1,759	958	773	1,291	2,204	419	427	(X)
1980.................	1,000..	5,659	3,052	1,675	1,330	2,607	4,200	708	751	(X)
1985.................	1,000..	6,890	3,512	1,971	1,487	3,378	5,271	745	874	(X)
1987.................	1,000..	7,323	3,625	2,032	1,535	3,698	5,768	658	897	(X)
1988.................	1,000..	7,422	3,714	2,089	1,567	3,708	5,765	698	959	(X)
Benefits:										
1970.................	Mil. dol.	9,355	6,075	2,820	3,133	3,280	7,210	1,312	645	189
1980.................	Mil. dol.	41,060	28,042	15,065	12,478	13,018	32,416	5,371	2,896	377
1985.................	Mil. dol.	63,413	40,912	22,840	17,416	22,501	50,562	7,623	4,684	544
1987.................	Mil. dol.	71,412	44,026	25,163	18,061	27,386	58,178	7,812	5,366	[2]56
1988.................	Mil. dol.	77,242	47,518	27,638	18,991	29,724	62,704	8,379	6,072	[2]87
1989.................	Mil. dol.	82,929	50,188	29,128	20,063	32,741	(NA)	(NA)	(NA)	(NA)
Average annual benefit per annuitant, current dollars:										
1970.................	Dollars.	3,005	3,440	(NA)	(NA)	2,413	3,271	3,136	1,512	(X)
1980.................	Dollars.	7,190	9,181	(NA)	(NA)	4,859	7,719	7,588	3,855	(X)
1985.................	Dollars.	9,137	11,659	(NA)	(NA)	6,512	9,592	10,232	5,556	(X)
1988.................	Dollars.	10,395	12,771	(NA)	(NA)	8,016	10,877	12,001	6,330	(X)
Average annual benefit per annuitant, constant (1988) dollars: [3]										
1970.................	Dollars.	8,700	9,959	(NA)	(NA)	6,986	9,470	9,079	4,377	(X)
1980.................	Dollars.	10,312	13,167	(NA)	(NA)	6,969	11,070	11,070	5,529	(X)
1985.................	Dollars.	10,169	12,975	(NA)	(NA)	7,247	10,675	11,387	6,183	(X)
1988.................	Dollars.	10,395	12,771	(NA)	(NA)	8,016	10,877	12,001	6,330	(X)

NA Not available.   X Not applicable.   [1] Includes other Federal agencies, not shown separately.   [2] Lump-sum payments for State and local government are not available.   [3] Constant dollar figures are based on implicit price deflators for personal consumption expenditures supplied by U.S. Bureau of Economic Analysis.
Source: U.S. Social Security Administration, *Social Security Bulletin*, June 1990 and unpublished data.

No. 580. Federal Civil Service Retirement: 1970 to 1990
[As of **end of fiscal year** or **for fiscal year ending in year shown**; see text, section 9. See also *Historical Statistics, Colonial Times to 1970*, series H 262-270]

ITEM	Unit	1970	1980	1984	1985	1986	1987	1988	1989	1990
Employees covered [1]...........	1,000 ..	2,650	2,720	2,660	2,750	2,800	2,810	2,800	2,880	2,950
Annuitants, total................	1,000 ..	958	1,675	1,910	1,955	2,008	2,032	2,089	2,120	2,143
Age and service.............	1,000 ..	477	905	1,082	1,122	1,166	1,186	1,237	1,267	1,288
Disability.................	1,000 ..	185	343	338	332	326	318	311	305	297
Survivors.................	1,000 ..	296	427	490	501	516	528	541	548	558
Receipts, total [2]..............	Mil. dol	4,683	24,389	36,734	40,790	43,216	43,640	46,696	49,302	52,689
Employee contributions........	Mil. dol	1,740	3,686	4,608	4,679	4,714	4,641	4,544	4,491	4,501
Federal government contributions..	Mil. dol	1,952	15,562	20,848	22,301	22,980	23,144	24,258	25,367	27,368
Disbursements, total [3]...........	Mil. dol	2,752	14,977	21,951	23,203	24,694	25,772	28,306	29,713	31,416
Age and service annuitants [4].....	Mil. dol	2,129	12,639	18,403	19,414	20,702	21,678	23,889	25,095	26,495
Survivors.................	Mil. dol	389	1,912	2,943	3,158	3,304	3,485	3,749	4,033	4,366
Average monthly benefit:										
Age and service.............	Dollars .	362	992	1,149	1,189	1,197	1,267	1,263	1,310	1,369
Disability.................	Dollars .	221	723	851	881	881	893	930	966	1,003
Survivors.................	Dollars .	116	392	501	528	536	552	583	616	653
Cash and security holdings........	Bil. dol .	22.4	73.7	124.7	142.3	160.8	178.7	197.1	216.7	238.0

[1] Excludes employees in Leave Without Pay status.   [2] Includes interest on investments.   [3] Includes refunds, death claims, and administration.   [4] Includes disability annuitants.
Source: U.S. Office of Personnel Management, *Compensation Report*, annual.

No. 581. State and Local Government Retirement Systems—Beneficiaries and Finances: 1970 to 1989

[In millions of dollars, except as indicated. For fiscal years closed during the 12 months ending June 30]

YEAR AND LEVEL OF GOVERNMENT	Number of beneficiaries (1,000)	RECEIPTS					BENEFITS AND WITHDRAWALS			Cash and security holdings
		Total	Employee contributions	Government contributions		Earnings on investments	Total	Benefits	Withdrawals	
				State	Local					
1970: All systems	(NA)	9,848	2,788	2,046	2,554	2,460	3,638	3,037	601	54,918
State-administered	(NA)	7,184	2,149	1,978	1,237	1,821	2,382	1,913	469	39,966
Locally administered . .	(NA)	2,664	639	67	1,318	639	1,256	1,124	132	14,952
1980: All systems	(NA)	37,313	6,466	7,581	9,951	13,315	14,008	12,207	1,801	185,226
State-administered	(NA)	28,603	5,285	7,399	5,611	10,308	10,257	8,809	1,448	144,682
Locally administered . .	(NA)	8,710	1,180	181	4,340	3,008	3,752	3,399	353	40,544
1985: All systems	3,378	71,411	9,468	12,227	15,170	34,546	24,413	21,999	2,414	374,433
State-administered	2,661	55,960	7,901	11,976	8,944	27,139	18,230	16,183	2,047	296,951
Locally administered . .	716	15,451	1,567	251	6,226	7,407	6,183	5,816	367	77,481
1989: All systems	3,911	100,125	12,862	13,249	18,037	55,978	35,114	32,992	2,122	628,778
State-administered	3,120	81,090	10,813	13,155	11,202	45,919	26,979	25,277	1,702	503,074
Locally administered . .	791	19,036	2,048	94	6,835	10,059	8,136	7,716	420	125,704

NA Not available.

Source: U.S. Bureau of the Census, *Finances of Employee-Retirement Systems of State and Local Governments*, series GF, No. 2, annual.

No. 582. State Unemployment Insurance—Summary: 1980 to 1990

[See headnote, table 583]

ITEM	Unit	1980	1982	1983	1984	1985	1986	1987	1988	1989	1990
Insured unemployment, avg. weekly . .	1,000 . .	3,350	4,061	3,396	2,476	2,611	2,641	2,330	2,081	2,157	2,522
Percent of covered employment [1] . .	Percent	3.9	4.6	3.9	2.8	2.9	2.8	2.3	2.0	2.1	2.4
Percent of civilian unemployed. . . .	Percent	43.9	38.0	31.7	29.0	31.4	32.1	31.4	31.0	33.0	36.0
Unemployment benefits, avg. weekly .	Dollars .	99	119	124	123	127	135	140	145	152	162
Percent of weekly wage	Percent	37.5	37.2	37.6	35.8	35.3	35.8	35.3	34.9	35.4	36.0
Weeks compensated.	Million .	149.0	185.3	155.5	111.6	119.3	121.4	105.2	94.2	97.6	116.0
Beneficiaries, first payments [2]	1,000 . .	10,001	11,648	8,907	7,765	8,350	8,361	7,205	6,861	7,369	8,628
Average duration of benefits [2]	Weeks . .	14.9	15.9	17.5	14.4	14.3	14.5	14.6	13.7	13.2	13.4
Claimants exhausting benefits.	1,000 . .	3,072	4,175	4,180	2,600	2,575	2,688	2,409	1,979	1,940	2,323
Percent of first payment [3]	Percent	33.2	38.5	38.4	34.1	31.3	30.6	28.5	28.0	29.4	
Contributions collected [4]	Bil. dol.	11.4	12.2	14.6	18.8	19.3	18.1	17.6	17.7	16.5	15.2
Benefits paid	Bil. dol.	13.8	20.7	17.8	12.6	14.0	15.4	14.2	13.2	13.6	18.1
Funds available for benefits [5]	Bil. dol.	11.4	7.5	7.3	11.6	16.0	19.6	23.2	31.1	37.5	38.4
Average employer contribution rate [6] .	Percent	2.5	2.5	2.8	3.2	3.1	2.7	2.6	2.5	2.2	2.0

[1] Insured unemployment as percent of average covered employment in preceding year.   [2] Weeks compensated divided by first payment.   [3] Based on first payments for 12-month period ending June 30.   [4] Contributions from employers; also employees in States which tax workers.   [5] End of year. Sum of balances in State clearing accounts, benefit-payment accounts, and State accounts in Federal unemployment trust funds.   [6] As percent of taxable wages.

No. 583. State Unemployment Insurance, by State and Other Areas: 1990

[Includes unemployment compensation for State and local government employees where covered by State law. For State data on insured unemployment, see table 641. See also *Historical Statistics, Colonial Times to 1970*, series H 305-317]

STATE	Beneficiaries, first payments (1,000)	Benefits paid (mil.dol.)	Avg. weekly unemployment benefits (dol.)	STATE	Beneficiaries, first payments (1,000)	Benefits paid (mil.dol.)	Avg. weekly unemployment benefits (dol.)	STATE	Beneficiaries, first payments (1,000)	Benefits paid (mil.dol.)	Avg. weekly unemployment benefits (dol.)
Total .	8,628	18,057	162	KY	131	194	136	OH. . . .	338	665	155
AL	169	182	116	LA	85	127	102	OK. . . .	61	106	150
AK	40	91	163	ME. . . .	59	115	159	OR. . . .	126	256	162
AZ	83	147	135	MD	119	267	170	PA	472	1,225	189
AR	91	140	133	MA	303	1,143	217	RI. . . .	62	171	194
CA	1,210	2,232	131	MI	466	1,166	204	SC. . . .	115	135	130
CO	71	144	168	MN	133	362	190	SD	7	9	120
CT	155	443	201	MS	77	103	111	TN	261	254	113
DE	22	42	176	MO	179	295	135	TX	346	784	162
DC	24	89	213	MT	24	38	137	UT	33	58	163
FL	254	468	146	NE	27	36	120	VT	26	53	149
GA	251	318	143	NV	46	91	162	VA	169	189	146
HI. . . .	22	48	196	NH	49	60	128	WA. . . .	188	426	169
ID. . . .	39	59	145	NJ	325	1,052	207	WV	54	99	146
IL	352	946	170	NM	27	54	126	WI	196	362	171
IN	139	147	107	NY	615	1,873	181	WY	10	20	159
IA	82	146	161	NC	299	323	152	PR	118	130	79
KS	67	152	171	ND	14	24	136	VI.	1	2	127

Source of tables 582 and 583: U.S. Employment and Training Administration, *Unemployment Insurance Data Summary*, annual.

No. 584. Workers' Compensation Payments: 1970 to 1989

[In billions of dollars, except as indicated. See headnote, table 585. See also *Historical Statistics, Colonial Times to 1970*, series H 332-345]

ITEM	1970	1980	1981	1982	1983	1984	1985	1986	1987	1988	1989
Workers covered [1] (mil.)	59	79	78	77	78	82	84	86	89	91	94
Premium amounts paid. . . .	**4.9**	**22.3**	**23.0**	**22.8**	**23.0**	**25.1**	**29.2**	**34.0**	**38.1**	**43.3**	**48.0**
Private carriers.	3.6	15.7	16.2	15.4	15.4	16.6	19.5	22.8	25.4	28.5	31.9
State funds	0.7	3.0	2.9	2.6	2.7	3.0	3.5	4.5	5.3	6.7	7.2
Federal programs [2].	0.2	1.1	1.2	1.5	1.5	1.6	1.7	1.8	1.8	1.9	2.0
Self-insurers	0.5	2.4	2.8	3.2	3.5	3.9	4.5	4.9	5.5	6.2	6.9
Annual benefits paid	**3.0**	**13.6**	**15.1**	**16.4**	**17.6**	**19.7**	**22.2**	**24.6**	**27.4**	**30.7**	**34.3**
By private carriers [3]	1.8	7.0	7.9	8.6	9.3	10.6	12.3	13.8	15.5	17.5	19.9
From State funds [4]	0.8	4.3	4.6	4.8	5.1	5.4	5.7	6.2	6.8	7.5	8.0
Employers' self-insurance [5]	0.4	2.3	2.6	3.0	3.2	3.7	4.1	4.6	5.2	5.7	6.4
Type of benefit:											
Medical/hospitalization	1.1	3.9	4.4	5.1	5.7	6.4	7.5	8.7	9.9	11.5	13.4
Compensation payments.	2.0	9.7	10.6	11.3	11.9	13.3	14.7	16.0	17.5	19.2	20.9
Disability	1.8	8.4	9.2	9.9	10.4	11.7	13.1	14.3	15.8	17.6	19.2
Survivor	0.2	1.3	1.4	1.5	1.5	1.6	1.7	1.6	1.6	1.6	1.7
Percent of covered payroll:											
Workers' compensation costs [6][7] .	1.11	1.96	1.85	1.75	1.67	1.64	1.80	1.97	2.06	2.16	2.27
Benefits [7].	0.66	1.07	1.08	1.16	1.17	1.21	1.30	1.37	1.43	1.49	1.58

[1] Estimated per month.   [2] Includes Federal employer compensation program and that portion of Federal black lung benefits program financed from employer contributions.   [3] Net cash and medical benefits paid under standard workers' compensation policies.   [4] Net cash and medical benefits paid by competitive and exclusive State funds and by Federal workers' compensation programs, including black lung benefit program.   [5] Cash and medical benefits paid by self-insurers, plus value of medical benefits paid by employers carrying workers' compensation policies that exclude standard medical coverage.   [6] Premiums written by private carriers and State funds, and benefits paid by self-insurers increased by 5-10 percent to allow for administrative costs. Also includes benefits paid and administrative costs of Federal system for government employees.   [7] Excludes programs financed from general revenue—black lung benefits and supplemental pensions in some States.

Source: U.S. Social Security Administration, *Annual Statistical Supplement* to the *Social Security Bulletin.*

No. 585. Workers' Compensation Payments, by State: 1980 to 1989

[In millions of dollars. Calendar-year data, except fiscal-year data for Federal civilian and other programs and for a few States with State funds. Payments represent cash and medical benefits and include insurance losses paid by private insurance carriers (compiled from the *Spectator (Insurance by States . . . of Casualty Lines),* from reports of State insurance commissions, and from A. M. Best Co.); net disbursements of State funds (from the *Spectator,* from *Argus Casualty and Surety Chart,* and from State reports), estimated for some states; and self-insurance payments, estimated from available State data. Includes benefit payments under Longshoremen's and Harbor Workers' Compensation Act and Defense Bases Compensation Act for States in which such payments are made]

STATE	1980	1985	1987	1988	1989	STATE	1980	1985	1987	1988	1989
Total	**13,618**	**22,224**	**27,390**	**30,733**	**34,316**	Nebraska	42	68	88	103	112
						Nevada	69	123	180	219	250
Alabama.	112	203	274	311	380	New Hampshire	48	91	128	143	154
Alaska	60	109	139	122	113	New Jersey.	316	501	627	682	761
Arizona.	120	198	222	301	324	New Mexico	54	140	146	196	226
Arkansas	83	129	160	177	196	New York	637	985	1,207	1,345	1,528
California	1,628	3,243	4,251	4,716	5,242	North Carolina	131	236	272	328	386
Colorado.	114	284	402	474	532	North Dakota.	17	33	44	44	50
Connecticut.	147	305	434	496	587	Ohio	776	1,387	1,562	1,716	1,816
Delaware	21	41	51	57	68	Oklahoma.	127	289	289	306	313
						Oregon.	275	396	510	556	576
District of Columbia .	69	74	87	81	84	Pennsylvania	572	998	1,272	1,484	1,820
Florida	362	815	1,178	1,422	1,732	Rhode Island.	55	97	143	168	200
Georgia	185	360	510	581	661	South Carolina.	79	152	186	208	240
Hawaii	60	133	137	151	180	South Dakota.	13	26	36	40	44
Idaho	37	66	70	87	93	Tennessee	129	204	289	341	390
Illinois	699	912	1,068	1,277	1,432	Texas	701	1,564	2,074	2,462	2,843
Indiana.	110	152	202	245	297	Utah	39	80	126	116	142
Iowa	99	121	141	169	190	Vermont	15	30	41	44	55
Kansas	84	142	175	197	220	Virginia.	182	276	354	409	465
Kentucky	161	225	274	293	326	Washington.	324	619	678	755	811
						West Virginia	176	285	355	363	375
Louisiana	301	466	544	565	586	Wisconsin.	170	287	369	422	487
Maine.	81	194	277	314	342	Wyoming	22	47	45	46	47
Maryland	187	306	374	397	437						
Massachusetts.	296	510	734	859	1,078	Federal programs:					
Michigan.	626	769	885	1,035	1,120	Civilian employees.	776	1,055	1,146	1,253	1,274
Minnesota.	260	453	490	470	497	Black lung					
Mississippi	60	98	137	155	171	benefits [1]	1,739	1,603	1,545	1,499	1,479
Missouri	124	237	320	379	423	Other [2]	8	7	8	8	8
Montana.	41	102	138	150	153						

[1] Includes payments by Social Security Administration and by Department of Labor.   [2] Primarily payments made to dependents of reservists who died while on active duty in the Armed Forces.

Source: U.S. Social Security Administration, *Social Security Bulletin,* Spring 1992 and selected prior issues.

No. 586. Black Lung Benefit Program—Beneficiaries and Payments: 1975 to 1990

[In thousands, except as indicated. Benefits payable to miners disabled because of pneumoconiosis and to their dependents and survivors as a result of Federal Coal Mine Health and Safety Act of 1969 and subsequent amendments and revisions. Claims by miners or their survivors are handled by the Social Security Administration (SSA) or the Department of Labor, depending upon the date the claim was filed. Claims filed by a miner by June 30, 1973, and those filed by survivors by December 31, 1973, were processed by SSA. Benefits under the program as administered by SSA are paid out of Federal general tax revenues. Claims filed by a miner between July 1 and December 31, 1973, and all claims filed after December 1973 were processed by Department of Labor and are paid by either a responsible mine operator or the Department of Labor]

TYPE OF BENEFICIARY	SOCIAL SECURITY ADMINISTRATION						DEPARTMENT OF LABOR					
	1975	1980	1985	1988	1989	1990	1975	1980	1985	1988	1989	1990
Beneficiaries, total [1]	482	399	295	242	226	211	(NA)	139	160	149	144	138
Miners	165	120	78	57	51	46	(NA)	53	61	54	52	49
Widows	139	147	138	127	123	119	(NA)	27	38	42	43	44
Dependents [2]	177	133	79	57	51	46	(NA)	59	61	52	49	45
Payments (mil. dol.)	950	1,030	1,025	905	885	863	10	707	574	595	591	571

NA Not available.   [1] As of end of year.   [2] Dependent wife or child or surviving child, parent, brother, or sister.

Source: U.S. Social Security Administration, *Social Security Bulletin*, monthly; and U.S. Department of Labor, Employment Standards Administration, *Black Lung Benefits Act, Annual Report.*

No. 587. Persons With Work Disability, by Selected Characteristics: 1990

[In thousands, except percent. As of **March.** Covers civilian noninstitutional population and members of Armed Forces living off post or with their families on post. Persons are classified as having a work disability if they (1) have a health problem or disability which prevents them from working or which limits the kind or amount of work they can do; (2) have a service-connected disability or ever retired or left a job for health reasons; (3) did not work in survey reference week or previous year because of long-term illness or disability; or (4) are under age 65, and are covered by Medicare or receive Supplemental Security Income. Based on Current Population Survey; see text, section 1 and Appendix III]

AGE AND PARTICIPATION STATUS IN ASSISTANCE PROGRAMS	Total [1]	Male	Female	White	Black	Hispanic [2]
Persons with work disability	**14,164**	**7,234**	**6,930**	**11,266**	**2,528**	**1,106**
16 to 24 years old	1,147	576	571	852	247	93
25 to 34 years old	2,459	1,283	1,177	1,911	473	229
35 to 44 years old	2,902	1,559	1,344	2,352	463	246
45 to 54 years old	2,958	1,512	1,446	2,350	548	246
55 to 64 years old	4,697	2,305	2,393	3,801	797	291
Percent work disabled of total population.	**8.9**	**9.3**	**8.6**	**8.4**	**13.4**	**8.4**
16 to 24 years old	3.6	3.6	3.5	3.3	5.3	2.8
25 to 34 years old	5.7	6.0	5.4	5.3	8.7	5.5
35 to 44 years old	7.8	8.5	7.1	7.4	11.4	8.9
45 to 54 years old	11.7	12.3	11.1	10.8	20.6	14.5
55 to 64 years old	22.1	23.0	21.3	20.5	37.8	24.1
Percent of work disabled—						
Receiving Social Security income	28.2	29.9	26.5	28.4	28.5	20.3
Receiving food stamps	19.0	15.5	22.5	15.5	33.8	30.5
Covered by Medicaid	25.4	20.4	30.6	21.0	43.1	36.7
Residing in public housing	4.5	3.4	5.7	2.5	12.9	6.9
Residing in subsidized housing	3.1	1.9	4.4	2.7	4.6	4.1

[1] Includes other races not shown separately.   [2] Hispanic persons may be of any race.

Source: U.S. Bureau of the Census, unpublished data.

No. 588. Vocational Rehabilitation—Summary: 1980 to 1990

[For fiscal years ending in year shown; see text, section 9. Includes Puerto Rico, Guam, Virgin Islands, American Samoa, Northern Mariana Islands, and Trust Territory of the Pacific Islands. Vocational rehabilitation of the disabled defined as restoration, preservation, or development of the ability to function in productive activity. Rehabilitation services provided by State vocational rehabilitation agencies with matching State and Federal funds include medical restoration, training, counseling, guidance, and placement services. See also *Historical Statistics, Colonial Times to 1970*, series H 392-397]

ITEM	Unit	1980	1983	1984	1985	1986	1987	1988	1989	1990
Federal and State expenditures [1]	Mil. dol.	[2]1,076	1,254	1,366	1,452	1,506	1,649	1,776	1,867	1,910
Federal expenditures	Mil. dol.	[2]817	937	1,038	1,100	1,144	1,275	1,373	1,446	1,525
Applicants processed for program eligibility.	1,000	717	602	594	594	594	597	606	623	625
Percent accepted into program	Percent	58	58	59	60	58	58	58	58	57
Total persons rehabilitated [3]	1,000	277	216	226	228	223	220	218	220	216
Rehabilitation rate [4]	Percent	64	62	63	64	64	63	63	63	62
Severely disabled persons rehabilitated [3][5]	1,000	143	124	133	135	135	136	141	147	146
Rohabilitation rato [4]	Percent	61	59	61	62	62	62	62	62	62
Percent of total persons rehabilitated	Percent	51	57	59	59	61	62	65	67	68
Persons served, total [6]	1,000	1,095	939	936	932	924	917	919	929	938
Persons served, severely disabled [5][6]	1,000	606	562	565	581	580	584	604	625	640
Percent of total persons served	Percent	55	60	60	62	63	64	66	67	68

[1] Includes expenditures only under the basic support provisions of the Rehabilitation Act.   [2] Estimates based on amounts appropriated.   [3] Persons successfully placed into gainful employment.   [4] Persons rehabilitated as a percent of all active case closures (whether rehabilitated or not).   [5] Severely disabled individuals fall into any of the following three categories: (a) clients with specified major disabling conditions such as blindness and deafness; (b) clients who at any time in the vocational rehabilitation process had been Social Security disability beneficiaries or recipients of Supplemental Security Income; and (c) other individuals with substantial loss in conducting certain specified activities.   [6] Includes active cases accepted for rehabilitation services during year plus active cases on hand at beginning of year.

Source: U.S. Dept. of Education, Rehabilitation Services Administration, *Caseload Statistics of State Vocational Rehabilitation Agencies in Fiscal Years*, and *State Vocational Rehabilitation Agency Program Data in Fiscal Years*, both annual.

No. 589. Protection Against Short-Term Sickness Income Loss: 1980 to 1989

[In millions of dollars, except percent. "Short-term sickness" refers to short-term or temporary nonwork-connected disability (lasting not more than 6 months) and the first 6 months of long-term disability. See also *Historical Statistics, Colonial Times to 1970*, series H 115-124]

ITEM	1980	1982	1983	1984	1985	1986	1987	1988	1989
Short-term sickness: Income loss	38,529	45,201	48,565	54,419	59,143	62,982	68,153	73,841	78,286
Total protection provided [1]	14,426	16,252	16,395	17,904	19,587	20,278	22,486	23,973	25,369
Protection as percent of loss.	37.4	36.0	33.8	32.9	33.1	32.2	33.0	32.5	32.4
Benefits provided by protection:									
Individual insurance.	1,280	1,595	1,152	1,410	1,796	1,774	2,062	2,057	2,451
Group benefits to workers in private employment	7,633	8,498	8,614	9,115	9,897	10,011	11,377	12,237	12,577
Private cash insurance [2]	3,271	2,931	2,708	2,507	2,601	2,268	2,713	2,901	2,727
Publicly operated cash sickness funds [3] . . .	770	987	1,008	968	1,179	1,255	1,696	1,779	1,907
Sick leave.	3,593	4,581	4,899	5,640	6,116	6,488	6,969	7,557	7,944
Sick leave for government employees.	5,338	6,026	6,490	7,218	7,736	8,299	8,827	9,472	10,116

[1] Provided by individual insurance, group benefits to workers in private employment, and sick leave for government employees. Includes benefits for the sixth month of disability payable under old-age, survivors, disability, and health insurance program, not shown separately. [2] Group accident and sickness insurance and self-insurance privately written either on a voluntary basis or in compliance with State temporary disability insurance laws in CA, HI, NJ, and NY. Includes a small but undetermined amount of group disability insurance benefits paid to government workers and to self-employed persons through farm, trade, or professional associations. [3] Includes State-operated plans in RI, CA, and NJ; State Insurance Fund and special fund for disabled unemployed in New York; and provisions of Railroad Unemployment Insurance Act.
Source: U.S. Social Security Administration, *Social Security Bulletin*, May 1986 and unpublished data.

No. 590. Federal Food Programs: 1980 to 1990

[For fiscal years ending in year shown; see text, section 9. Program data include Puerto Rico, Virgin Islands, Guam, American Samoa, Northern Marianas, and the former Trust Territory when a Federal food program was operated in these areas. Participation data are average monthly figures except as noted. Participants are not reported for the special milk program, the nutrition program for the elderly, and the commodity distribution programs. Cost data are direct Federal benefits to recipients; they exclude Federal administrative payments and applicable State and local contributions. Federal costs for commodities and cash-in-lieu of commodities are shown separately from direct cash benefits for those programs receiving both]

PROGRAM	Unit	1980	1984	1985	1986	1987	1988	1989	1990
Food Stamp:									
Participants	Million . .	21.1	20.9	19.9	19.4	19.1	18.6	18.8	20.1
Federal cost.	Mil. dol. .	8,721	10,696	10,744	10,605	10,500	11,149	11,676	14,205
Nutrition assistance program									
for Puerto Rico: [1]									
Federal cost.	Mil. dol. .	(X)	825	825	820	853	879	908	937
National school lunch program (NSLP): [2]									
Free lunches served	Million . .	1,671	1,702	1,657	1,678	1,656	1,651	1,627	1,662
Reduced-price lunches served.	Million . .	308	248	255	257	259	262	263	273
Children participating [3]	Million . .	26.6	23.4	23.6	23.7	23.9	24.2	24.2	24.1
Federal cost.	Mil. dol. .	2,279	2,508	2,578	2,715	2,797	2,916	3,006	3,214
School breakfast (SB): [3]									
Children participating [3].	Million . .	3.6	3.4	3.4	3.5	3.6	3.7	3.8	4.1
Federal cost.	Mil. dol. .	288	364	379	406	447	482	513	596
Special school milk:									
Quantity reimbursed	Mil. 1/2 pt	1,795	174	167	162	162	194	189	181
Federal cost.	Mil. dol. .	145	16	16	15	15	19	19	19
Special supplemental food									
program (WIC): [4]									
Participants	Million . .	1.9	3.0	3.1	3.3	3.4	3.6	4.1	4.5
Federal cost.	Mil. dol. .	584	1,117	1,193	1,264	1,345	1,435	1,489	1,637
Commodity supplemental food program: [5]									
Participants	Million . .	0.1	0.2	0.2	0.2	0.2	0.2	0.2	0.3
Federal cost.	Mil. dol. .	19	41	42	40	47	52	62	71
Child and adult care (CC): [6]									
Participants [7]	Million . .	0.7	1.0	1.0	1.1	1.2	1.3	1.4	1.5
Federal cost.	Mil. dol. .	207	348	390	427	476	538	612	720
Summer feeding (SF): [8]									
Children participating [9].	Million . .	1.9	1.4	1.5	1.5	1.6	1.6	1.7	1.7
Federal cost.	Mil. dol. .	104	88	103	106	114	113	132	145
Needy family commodity:									
Participants	Million . .	0.1	0.1	0.1	0.1	0.1	0.1	0.1	0.1
Federal cost.	Mil. dol. .	24	40	47	49	49	47	51	51
Nutrition program for the elderly:									
Meals served	Million . .	166	213	225	228	232	240	243	246
Federal cost.	Mil. dol .	75	127	134	137	139	146	146	142
Federal cost of commodities donated to [10]—									
Child nutrition (NSLP, CC, SF									
and SB)	Mil. dol. .	930	853	840	869	919	853	795	729
Charitable institutions,									
summer camps	Mil. dol. .	71	190	170	240	158	158	136	104
Emergency feeding [11]	Mil. dol. .	(X)	1,032	973	846	846	593	266	286

X Not applicable. [1] Puerto Rico was included in the food stamp program until June 30, 1982. [2] See headnote, table 591. [3] Nine month (September through May) average daily meals (lunches or breakfasts) served divided by the ratio of average daily attendance to enrollment. [4] WIC serves women, infants, and children. [5] Program provides commodities to women, infants, children, and the elderly. [6] Program provides year-round subsidies to feed preschool children in child care centers and family day care homes. Certain care centers serving disabled or elderly adults also receive meal subsidies. [7] Quarterly average daily attendance at participating institutions. [8] Program provides free meals to children in poor areas during summer months. [9] Peak month (July) average daily attendance at participating institutions. [10] Includes the Federal cost of commodity entitlements, cash-in-lieu of commodities, and bonus foods. [11] Provides free commodities to needy persons for home consumption through food banks, hunger centers, soup kitchens, and similar non-profit agencies. Includes the Emergency Food Assistance Program and the commodity purchases for soup kitchens program.
Source: U.S. Dept. of Agriculture, Food and Nutrition Service. In "Annual Historical Review of FNS Programs" and unpublished data.

No. 591. Federal Food Stamp and National School Lunch Programs, by State: 1980 to 1990

[Cost data for years ending Sept. 30. Food stamp participants, as of Sept. 30; food stamp households, average monthly number participating in year ending Sept. 30. Data on pupils participating in National School Lunch Program are for month in which most pupils participated nationwide. For National School Lunch Program, covers public and private elementary and secondary schools and residential child care institutions. National School Lunch Program costs include Federal cash reimbursements at rates set by law for each meal served but do not include the value of USDA donated commodities utilized in this program]

REGION, DIVISION, AND STATE	FOOD STAMP PROGRAM								NATIONAL SCHOOL LUNCH PROGRAM					
	Households participating, 1990		Persons (1,000)			Cost (mil. dol.)			Persons (1,000)			Cost (mil. dol.)		
	Number (1,000)	Percent of all households	1980	1985	1990	1980	1985	1990	1980	1985	1990	1980	1985	1990
Total [1]	8,013	(NA)	22,028	19,198	20,498	8,721	10,744	14,205	27,011	24,051	24,589	2,279	2,578	3,214
U.S.	8,005	8.7	20,115	19,148	20,472	7,859	10,702	14,172	26,384	23,400	24,019	2,200	2,466	3,098
Northeast	1,626	8.6	4,379	3,910	3,717	1,686	2,112	2,470	4,969	4,057	4,033	426	432	489
N.E.	322	6.5	945	711	735	361	367	426	1,366	1,008	991	104	90	95
ME	43	9.2	139	109	98	60	62	63	146	115	108	13	12	11
NH	15	3.6	53	26	35	22	15	20	101	86	91	7	6	6
VT	18	8.5	46	41	39	18	20	22	59	46	47	5	4	4
MA	158	7.0	446	329	348	171	173	207	703	479	454	49	42	44
RI	30	7.9	87	69	70	31	35	42	69	56	60	7	7	7
CT	58	4.7	174	139	146	59	62	72	288	226	231	23	20	23
M.A.	1,304	9.4	3,434	3,199	2,982	1,325	1,745	2,044	3,603	3,048	3,042	322	342	393
NY	720	10.8	1,804	1,753	1,594	726	938	1,086	1,593	1,486	1,546	171	192	232
NJ	157	5.6	600	440	396	226	260	289	679	551	507	58	57	60
PA	427	9.5	1,030	1,005	992	373	547	670	1,331	1,012	990	93	93	102
Midwest	1,980	8.9	4,340	4,955	4,900	1,609	2,915	3,568	6,767	5,666	5,806	457	513	619
E.N.C.	1,506	9.7	3,382	3,907	3,695	1,261	2,341	2,767	4,401	3,615	3,687	310	357	421
OH	473	11.6	928	1,113	1,114	382	697	861	1,156	910	919	79	96	109
IN	112	5.4	399	385	320	154	242	226	717	621	635	39	41	54
IL	432	10.3	915	1,096	1,041	394	713	835	1,129	918	932	91	110	131
MI	393	11.5	903	949	940	263	541	663	866	723	733	69	73	82
WI	95	5.2	237	364	281	68	148	180	533	444	468	32	36	45
W.N.C	474	7.1	958	1,048	1,205	348	574	801	2,366	2,050	2,119	146	157	197
MN	111	6.7	188	220	268	62	105	165	558	465	489	33	33	42
IA	68	6.4	156	203	170	54	107	109	439	391	392	24	26	31
MO	171	8.7	364	337	441	142	212	312	664	539	547	47	49	58
ND	14	5.8	28	31	37	9	16	25	93	94	94	5	6	8
SD	17	6.6	46	48	50	18	26	35	101	89	102	7	9	12
NE	37	6.1	72	95	94	25	44	59	203	187	191	11	14	18
KS	55	5.8	104	113	145	38	64	96	308	286	302	19	21	29
South	3,044	9.6	8,396	7,362	8,203	3,438	4,189	5,936	10,464	9,786	9,890	952	1,050	1,334
S.A.	1,196	7.2	3,811	2,925	3,084	1,547	1,670	2,228	4,846	4,474	4,454	443	466	558
DE	13	5.3	53	34	35	21	22	25	68	55	59	5	5	6
MD	117	6.7	335	273	275	140	171	208	434	347	347	36	34	40
DC	28	11.2	104	68	64	41	40	43	57	48	47	8	9	10
VA	148	6.5	412	340	356	158	189	247	717	610	586	51	53	60
WV	97	14.1	216	267	259	87	159	192	245	227	198	20	26	29
NC	171	6.8	592	449	438	234	237	282	887	814	749	90	82	91
SC	96	7.6	444	353	270	181	194	240	489	478	451	51	57	60
GA	210	8.9	658	524	561	264	290	382	894	890	908	80	88	106
FL	315	6.1	997	616	826	421	368	609	1,055	1,006	1,110	102	113	158
E.S.C.	723	12.8	2,283	2,064	1,951	938	1,194	1,388	2,252	2,128	2,085	215	241	281
KY	163	11.8	485	533	449	211	332	334	567	510	498	48	53	61
TN	212	11.4	674	496	542	282	280	372	648	611	590	55	60	68
AL	169	11.2	606	545	460	246	318	330	607	592	570	62	69	77
MS	178	19.5	518	490	500	199	264	352	430	415	428	50	59	76
W.S.C	1,126	11.6	2,302	2,373	3,168	952	1,325	2,320	3,366	3,184	3,351	294	343	495
AR	85	9.5	301	233	231	122	126	151	356	298	292	31	34	41
LA	252	16.8	584	648	721	243	365	549	767	726	694	67	80	104
OK	107	8.9	214	250	270	73	134	186	408	368	362	30	34	46
TX	681	11.2	1,203	1,241	1,946	514	701	1,429	1,835	1,793	2,003	166	195	304
West	1,355	7.2	3,000	2,922	3,652	1,126	1,485	2,199	4,184	3,892	4,289	365	470	657
Mt.	373	7.4	818	742	1,025	339	446	726	1,352	1,249	1,362	98	118	170
MT	20	6.5	45	52	56	18	31	41	104	87	84	6	7	10
ID	20	5.5	65	53	57	29	36	40	120	122	131	7	10	14
WY	10	5.9	15	25	27	6	15	21	51	57	57	3	4	5
CO	89	6.9	173	168	226	71	94	156	299	284	282	21	24	31
NM	54	10.0	191	145	158	81	88	117	174	171	179	19	23	30
AZ	120	8.8	227	195	348	97	121	239	291	264	331	23	29	47
UT	36	6.7	65	74	101	22	40	71	233	209	233	14	16	24
NV	23	4.9	37	31	53	15	22	41	80	55	67	5	5	8
Pac.	982	7.1	2,182	2,180	2,627	787	1,039	1,473	2,832	2,644	2,927	267	353	487
WA	144	7.7	260	274	341	90	140	190	354	322	361	26	32	43
OR	90	8.2	213	214	209	80	142	168	277	230	234	18	22	26
CA	707	6.8	1,571	1,571	1,975	530	639	1,009	2,006	1,906	2,147	210	279	396
AK	9	4.8	32	24	26	27	25	25	33	39	39	4	6	8
HI	31	8.7	106	96	76	60	93	81	162	147	145	9	14	14

NA Not available. [1] Includes Puerto Rico, other outlying areas and Dept. of Defense overseas. After July 1, 1982, Puerto Rico was dropped from Food Stamp program and transferred to a nutrition assistance program.

Source: U.S. Dept. of Agriculture, Food and Nutrition Service. In "Annual Historical Review of FNS Programs" and unpublished data.

No. 592. Public Aid—Recipients and Average Monthly Cash Payments Under Supplemental Security Income (SSI) and Public Assistance: 1975 to 1990

[As of **December**, except as noted. Public assistance data for all years include Puerto Rico, Guam, and Virgin Islands; SSI data are for federally administered payments only. See text, section 12. Excludes payments made directly to suppliers of medical care. See also Appendix III and *Historical Statistics, Colonial Times to 1970*, series H 355-367]

PROGRAM	RECIPIENTS (1,000)					AVG. MONTHLY PAYMENTS (dol.)				
	1975	1980	1985	1989	1990	1975	1980	1985	1989	1990
SSI, total..................	4,314	4,142	4,138	4,593	4,817	114	168	226	275	299
Aged......................	2,307	1,808	1,504	1,439	1,454	91	128	164	199	213
Blind......................	74	78	82	83	84	147	213	274	320	342
Disabled..................	1,933	2,256	2,551	3,071	3,279	141	198	261	309	337
Old-age assistance [1]...........	18	19	18	17	17	21	39	36	37	36
Aid to the blind [1].............	(Z)	(Z)	(Z)	(Z)	(Z)	15	36	39	40	42
Aid to permanently, totally disabled [1].	17	21	23	25	26	15	35	38	39	40
AFDC: [2] Families..............	3,568	3,843	3,721	3,875	4,218	229	288	341	383	392
Recipients [3]................	11,404	11,101	10,924	11,175	12,160	72	100	118	133	136
Children.................	8,106	7,599	7,247	7,558	8,233	(NA)	(NA)	(NA)	(NA)	(NA)
General assistance cases........	692	796	1,051	937	1,060	144	161	(NA)	(NA)	(NA)

NA Not available.   Z Fewer than 500.   [1] Average monthly recipients and payments for the year.   [2] Aid to Families with Dependent Children program.   [3] Includes the children and one or both parents, or one caretaker relative other than a parent, in families where the needs of such adults were considered in determining the amount of assistance.

No. 593. Public Aid Payments: 1975 to 1990

[**In millions of dollars**. See headnote, table 592. Supplemental Security Income data cover federally- and State-administered payments. See also Appendix III and *Historical Statistics, Colonial Times to 1970*, series H 346-354]

PROGRAM	1975	1980	1982	1983	1984	1985	1986	1987	1988	1989	1990
Payments, total [1]	16,313	21,994	21,979	23,385	25,035	26,431	28,311	29,556	30,910	32,762	36,034
Supplemental Security Income [2] ..	5,878	7,941	8,981	9,404	10,371	11,060	12,081	12,951	13,786	14,980	16,599
Aged...................	2,605	2,734	2,824	2,814	2,973	3,035	3,096	3,194	3,299	3,476	3,736
Blind...................	131	190	217	229	249	264	277	291	302	316	334
Disabled................	3,142	5,014	5,909	6,357	7,143	7,755	8,700	9,458	10,177	11,180	12,521
Public assistance [1]..........	10,434	14,048	12,998	13,981	14,664	15,371	16,230	16,605	17,124	17,782	19,435
Old-age assistance	5	9	8	8	8	8	8	7	7	7	7
Blind...................	(Z)	(Z)	(Z)	(Z)	(Z)	(Z)	(Z)	(Z)	(Z)	(Z)	(Z)
Permanently, totally disabled ...	3	9	10	10	10	10	11	11	11	12	12
Families with dependent children.	9,211	12,475	12,878	13,838	14,505	15,196	16,033	16,373	16,827	17,466	19,067
Emergency assistance	78	113	102	125	141	157	178	214	279	297	349
General assistance	1,138	1,442	(NA)	(NA)	(NA)	(NA)	(NA)	(NA)	(NA)	(NA)	(NA)

NA Not available.   Z Less than $500,000.   [1] Beginning 1982, excludes general assistance payments.   [2] Includes data not available by reason for eligibility.

Source of tables 592 and 593: U.S. Social Security Administration, *Social Security Bulletin,* quarterly and *Annual Statistical Supplement* to the *Social Security Bulletin,* and U.S. Administration for Children and Families, *Quarterly Public Assistance Statistics,* annual.

No. 594. Public Aid Recipients as Percent of Population, by State: 1980 and 1990

[Total recipients as of **June** of Aid to Families with Dependent Children and of Federal Supplemental Security Income as percent of resident population. Based on estimated resident population as of July 1 for 1980 and as of April 1 for 1990]

DIVISION AND STATE	1980	1990	DIVISION AND STATE	1980	1990	DIVISION AND STATE	1980	1990	DIVISION AND STATE	1980	1990
U.S ...	6.5	6.5	IL	7.0	7.1	WV	6.0	8.8	**Mt**	3.5	4.2
			MI......	8.9	8.6	NC	5.8	5.7	MT	3.4	4.9
N.E	6.9	5.6	WI......	6.1	6.6	SC	7.6	5.8	ID......	3.1	2.7
ME	7.4	6.6	**W.N.C**	4.5	4.8	GA	6.9	7.1	WY	1.9	3.8
NH	3.0	2.2	MN	4.2	4.9	FL	4.4	4.6	CO	3.7	4.3
VT	6.4	5.7	IA	4.6	4.7	**E.S.C**	7.9	7.9	NM	6.1	5.8
MA	8.3	6.4	MO	5.9	5.8	KY	7.2	7.9	AZ	3.0	4.7
RI	7.2	6.4	ND	3.0	3.6	TN	6.4	7.2	UT	3.2	3.3
CT	5.2	4.7	SD	4.2	4.2	AL	8.1	6.5	NV	2.3	2.9
M.A	7.6	6.7	NE	3.2	3.7	MS	11.4	11.4	**Pac**	7.9	8.4
NY	8.4	7.7	KS	3.8	4.1				WA	4.9	6.0
NJ	7.4	5.3	**S.A**	6.8	5.4	**W.S.C**	5.2	6.2	OR	4.9	4.3
PA	6.7	6.0	DE	6.6	4.4	AR	7.2	6.3	CA	8.8	9.4
E.N.C	6.6	7.0	MD	6.1	5.1	LA	8.3	9.8	AK	4.6	4.6
OH	6.0	7.3	DC	15.5	10.9	OK	5.2	5.6	HI	7.3	5.2
IN	3.7	3.9	VA	4.6	3.9	TX	4.0	5.4			

Source: Compiled by U.S. Bureau of the Census. Data from U.S. Social Security Administration, *Social Security Bulletin,* quarterly, and U.S. Administration for Children and Families, *Quarterly Public Assistance Statistics,* annual.

No. 595. Aid to Families With Dependent Children (AFDC) and Supplemental Security Income (SSI)—Recipients and Payments, by State and Other Areas: 1980 to 1990

[Recipients as of **December**. Data for SSI cover Federal SSI payments and/or federally-administered State supplementation, except as noted. For explanation of methodology, see Appendix III]

DIVISION AND STATE OR OTHER AREA	AFDC Recipients (1,000)			AFDC Payments for year (mil. dol.)			Average monthly payment per family		SSI Recipients (1,000)		SSI Payments for year (mil. dol.)	
	1980	1989	1990	1980	1989	1990	1989	1990	1980	1990	1980	1990
Total	11,101	11,175	12,160	12,475	17,466	19,067	$383	$392	[2]4,142	[2]4,817	[3]7,715	16,133
U.S.	10,923	10,979	11,960	12,409	17,388	18,984	388	396	4,142	4,817	7,690	16,133
New England	647	505	577	910	1,098	1,250	503	517	198	209	356	652
ME	58	53	62	60	90	104	394	425	22	24	29	56
NH	24	15	21	27	26	35	429	415	[4]5	[4]7	[4]8	[4]19
VT	24	21	25	32	43	51	493	518	9	10	16	31
MA	348	256	282	510	600	647	507	510	124	119	241	397
RI	54	44	52	72	88	104	499	508	15	17	25	53
CT	140	117	135	209	252	309	559	593	[4]23	[4]32	[4]39	[4]96
Middle Atlantic	2,216	1,779	1,902	2,954	3,330	3,612	437	463	615	711	1,259	2,533
NY	1,110	964	1,031	1,623	2,146	2,326	498	530	366	415	791	1,557
NJ	469	308	323	560	441	459	357	364	86	105	156	340
PA	637	508	549	771	743	827	367	391	163	191	312	635
East North Central	2,419	2,274	2,398	2,838	3,459	3,612	375	384	466	622	827	2,021
OH	572	623	657	561	837	896	326	323	119	156	200	483
IN	170	149	164	139	163	174	267	271	[4]41	[4]60	[4]60	[4]174
IL	691	623	656	722	789	868	306	329	[4]124	[4]177	[4]207	[4]593
MI	753	641	684	1,063	1,223	1,232	489	500	114	143	237	483
WI	232	237	236	353	442	441	456	459	68	86	124	288
West North Central	614	619	648	697	925	955	363	363	190	216	270	584
MN	146	164	177	207	343	355	496	496	[4]32	[4]40	[4]42	[4]110
IA	111	97	96	144	149	154	364	378	26	33	34	86
MO	216	207	218	182	223	237	271	275	[4]84	[4]85	[4]128	[4]237
ND	13	16	16	16	24	24	370	377	[4]6	[4]7	[4]9	[4]18
SD	19	19	19	19	22	22	282	290	8	10	10	26
NE	38	41	44	42	57	60	334	329	[4]14	[4]16	[4]19	[4]42
KS	72	77	77	87	107	103	359	328	20	25	28	65
South Atlantic	1,463	1,467	1,654	1,125	1,640	1,843	265	274	744	847	1,173	2,370
DE	34	21	22	32	26	30	291	293	7	8	11	22
MD	220	181	198	214	272	304	366	371	48	60	82	185
DC	82	44	54	92	79	87	359	398	15	16	31	54
VA	176	150	158	160	169	181	257	267	[4]81	[4]95	[4]120	[4]257
WV	80	109	109	60	109	112	245	243	[4]41	[4]47	[4]72	[5]146
NC	202	216	255	154	225	257	243	242	[4]141	[4]149	[4]210	[4]403
SC	156	105	118	72	93	97	209	209	[4]83	[4]90	[4]124	[4]234
GA	234	285	320	138	295	333	255	260	155	159	233	415
FL	279	356	420	203	371	443	248	269	174	222	291	653
East South Central	704	686	743	366	454	510	166	172	470	501	716	1,371
KY	175	171	204	136	161	185	227	219	[4]94	[4]115	[4]151	[4]337
TN	174	207	231	85	146	176	181	193	131	140	199	384
AL	178	130	132	84	61	63	114	121	[4]134	[4]133	[4]195	[4]351
MS	176	188	176	61	85	86	121	124	112	114	171	300
West South Central	716	1,038	1,155	401	743	812	183	183	543	564	793	1,478
AR	85	71	73	51	55	57	193	193	78	76	107	187
LA	219	281	279	124	186	188	168	169	137	133	221	378
OK	92	105	129	92	125	135	294	299	[4]67	[4]60	[4]100	[4]158
TX	320	581	673	134	377	431	169	166	[5]262	[5]295	[5]365	[5]755
Mountain	302	402	455	274	477	524	287	294	116	162	188	476
MT	20	32	29	19	40	40	335	343	7	10	11	29
ID	20	16	17	24	19	20	265	282	[4]8	[4]10	[4]11	[4]29
WY	7	14	16	9	19	20	306	352	[4]2	[4]3	[4]3	[4]9
CO	81	100	109	81	133	138	316	316	[4]31	[4]38	[4]46	[4]110
NM	56	55	67	42	55	66	222	264	[4]25	[4]32	[4]41	[4]90
AZ	60	117	144	40	122	146	266	264	[4]30	[4]45	[4]53	[4]139
UT	44	45	47	48	64	65	345	353	[4]8	13	[4]11	38
NV	14	23	25	11	25	28	277	275	7	11	11	33
Pacific	1,843	2,208	2,427	2,844	5,263	5,867	609	610	798	984	2,108	4,646
WA	173	225	237	251	424	447	440	449	45	62	85	208
OR	94	87	99	147	139	150	389	368	[4]22	[4]32	[4]35	[4]95
CA	1,498	1,833	2,023	2,328	4,553	5,107	642	640	718	873	1,962	4,278
AK	16	19	24	27	55	62	690	720	[4]3	[4]5	[4]6	[4]14
HI	61	44	44	91	92	100	563	590	10	14	20	51
PR	170	189	193	60	72	74	102	103	(X)	(X)	(X)	(X)
GU	5	4	4	3	3	6	243	487	(X)	(X)	(X)	(X)
VI	3	3	3	2	3	3	267	267	(X)	(X)	(X)	(X)
N. Mariana	(X)	(X)	(X)	(X)	(X)	(X)	(X)	(X)	[5]1	[5]1	[5]1	[5]2

X Not applicable.   [1] See footnote 3, table 592.   [2] Includes small number of recipients whose residence was "unknown." [3] 1980 figures include payments to Indochina refugees (total, $24 million) which were not available by State.   [4] Data for persons with Federal SSI payments only; State has State-administered supplementation.   [5] Data for persons with Federal SSI payments only; State supplementary payments not made.

Source: U.S. Social Security Administration, *Social Security Bulletin*, quarterly, and *Annual Statistical Supplement* to the *Social Security Bulletin*; and U.S. Administration for Children and Families, *Quarterly Public Assistance Statistics*, annual.

No. 596. Child Support—Award and Recipiency Status of Women: 1981 to 1989

[Women with own children under 21 years of age present from absent fathers. For 1989, women 15 years old and over as of April 1990; for previous years, women 18 years old and over as of April of following year. Covers civilian noninstitutional population. Based on Current Population Survey; see text, section 1 and Appendix III]

AWARD AND RECIPIENCY STATUS	ALL WOMEN						WOMEN BELOW THE POVERTY LEVEL					
	Number (1,000)			Percent distribution			Number (1,000)			Percent distribution		
	1981	1985	1989	1981	1985	1989	1981	1985	1989	1981	1985	1989
Total	8,387	8,808	9,955	100	100	100	2,566	2,797	3,206	100	100	100
Payments awarded.	4,969	5,396	5,748	59	61	58	1,018	1,130	1,387	40	40	43
Supposed to receive payments .	4,043	4,381	4,953	48	50	50	806	905	1,190	31	32	37
Not supposed to receive payments	926	1,015	795	11	12	8	212	225	197	8	8	6
Payments not awarded	3,417	3,411	4,207	41	39	42	1,547	1,668	1,819	60	60	57
Supposed to receive payments .	4,043	4,381	4,953	100	100	100	806	905	1,190	100	100	100
Actually received payments	2,902	3,243	3,725	72	74	75	495	595	813	61	66	68
Received full amount	1,888	2,112	2,546	47	48	51	(NA)	(NA)	(NA)	(NA)	(NA)	(NA)
Received partial amount	1,014	1,131	1,179	25	26	24	(NA)	(NA)	(NA)	(NA)	(NA)	(NA)
Did not receive payments	1,140	1,138	1,228	28	26	25	311	310	377	39	34	32

NA Not available.

Source: U.S. Bureau of the Census, *Current Population Reports*, series P-23, No. 173.

No. 597. Child Support and Alimony—Selected Characteristics of Women: 1989

[See headnote, table 596. Alimony data are for ever-divorced and currently separated women. For definition of mean, see Guide to Tabular Presentation]

RECIPIENCY STATUS OF WOMEN	Unit	Total [1]	AGE			RACE		His-panic [2]	CURRENT MARITAL STATUS			
			18 to 29 years	30 to 39 years	40 years and over	White	Black		Divorced	Married [3]	Single [4]	Separated
CHILD SUPPORT												
All women, total.	1,000 . .	9,955	3,086	4,175	2,566	6,905	2,770	1,112	3,056	2,531	2,950	1,352
Payments awarded.	1,000 . .	5,748	1,408	2,685	1,632	4,661	955	452	2,347	1,999	704	648
Percent of total	Percent.	58	46	64	64	68	35	41	77	79	24	48
Supposed to receive child support in 1989.	1,000 . .	4,953	1,208	2,413	1,309	4,048	791	364	2,123	1,685	583	527
Percent received payment.	Percent.	75	76	74	76	77	70	70	77	72	72	72
Mean child support	Dollars .	2,995	1,981	3,032	3,903	3,132	2,263	2,965	3,322	2,931	1,888	3,060
Percent of total income .	Percent.	19	20	18	19	19	16	20	17	20	20	21
Women with incomes below the poverty level in 1989.	1,000 . .	3,206	1,531	1,189	434	1,763	1,314	536	820	176	1,590	612
Payments awarded.	1,000 . .	1,387	608	568	195	962	384	177	577	127	389	288
Percent of total	Percent.	43	40	48	45	55	29	33	70	72	25	47
Supposed to receive child support in 1989.	1,000 . .	1,190	507	500	168	827	325	148	525	106	334	221
Percent received payment.	Percent.	68	68	67	72	68	70	64	66	67	69	74
Mean child support	Dollars .	1,889	1,515	2,167	2,316	1,972	1,674	1,824	2,112	2,275	1,553	1,717
Percent of total income .	Percent.	37	33	36	56	39	32	37	38	52	34	35
ALIMONY												
All women, total.	1,000 . .	20,610	2,464	6,093	12,051	17,245	2,863	1,499	8,888	7,738	(X)	2,790
Number awarded payments. . .	1,000 . .	3,189	184	610	2,394	2,801	305	171	1,472	1,170	(X)	316
Percent of total	Percent.	16	8	10	20	16	11	11	17	15	(X)	11
Supposed to receive payments	1,000 . .	922	85	267	569	787	98	63	567	170	(X)	164
Women with incomes below the poverty level in 1989.	1,000 . .	3,692	726	1,206	1,758	2,640	931	477	1,860	420	(X)	1,147
Number awarded payments. . .	1,000 . .	429	60	96	273	340	76	31	223	55	(X)	110
Percent of total	Percent.	12	8	8	16	13	8	6	12	13	(X)	10
Supposed to receive payments	1,000 . .	178	43	56	79	149	26	21	112	11	(X)	54

X Not applicable.   [1] Includes other items, not shown separately.   [2] Hispanic women may be of any race.   [3] Remarried women whose previous marriage ended in divorce.   [4] Never-married women.

Source: U.S. Bureau of the Census, *Current Population Reports*, series P-23, No. 173.

No. 598. Child Support Enforcement Program—Caseload and Collections: 1980 to 1990

[For years ending Sept. 30. Includes Puerto Rico, Guam, and the Virgin Islands. The Child Support Enforcement program locates absent parents, establishes paternity of children born out-of-wedlock, and establishes and enforces support orders. By law, these services are available to all families that need them. The program is operated at the State and local government level but 68 percent of administrative costs are paid by the Federal government. Child support collected for families not receiving Aid to Families with Dependent Children (AFDC) goes to the family to help it remain self-sufficient. Most of the child support collected on behalf of AFDC families goes to Federal and State governments to offset AFDC payments. Based on data reported by State agencies. Minus sign (-) indicates net outlay]

ITEM	Unit	1980	1984	1985	1986	1987	1988	1989	1990
Total cases...................	1,000...	5,432	7,999	8,401	9,724	10,635	11,078	11,877	12,796
AFDC and AFDC arrears only caseload	1,000...	(NA)	(NA)	(NA)	7,220	7,655	7,501	7,610	7,953
AFDC cases...............	1,000...	4,583	6,136	6,242	5,749	5,776	5,703	5,709	5,872
AFDC arrears only cases [1]......	1,000...	(NA)	(NA)	(NA)	1,472	1,879	1,798	1,901	2,082
Non-AFDC cases.............	1,000...	849	1,863	2,159	2,503	2,981	3,577	4,266	4,843
Cases for which a collection was made:									
AFDC cases................	1,000...	503	647	684	582	609	621	658	701
AFDC arrears only cases [1].......	1,000...	(NA)	(NA)	(NA)	158	196	181	202	224
Non-AFDC cases.............	1,000...	243	547	654	786	934	1,083	1,247	1,363
Percentage of cases with collections:									
AFDC cases...............	Percent..	11.0	10.5	11.0	10.1	10.5	10.9	11.5	11.9
AFDC arrears only cases [1]	Percent..	(NA)	(NA)	(NA)	10.8	10.5	10.1	10.6	10.8
Non-AFDC cases.............	Percent..	28.7	29.4	30.3	31.4	31.3	30.3	29.2	28.1
Absent parents located, total.......	1,000...	643	875	878	1,046	1,145	1,388	1,629	2,062
Paternities established, total........	1,000...	144	219	232	245	269	307	339	393
Support obligations established, total..	1,000...	374	573	669	731	812	870	938	1,022
FINANCES									
Collections, total	Mil. dol..	1,478	2,378	2,694	3,249	3,917	4,613	5,250	6,018
AFDC collections	Mil. dol..	603	1,000	1,090	1,225	1,348	1,486	1,593	1,754
State share................	Mil. dol..	274	448	415	424	473	523	563	622
Incentive payments to States....	Mil. dol..	72	134	145	158	185	221	266	264
Federal share............. [2]....	Mil. dol..	246	402	341	369	413	445	458	535
Payments to AFDC families [2]..	Mil. dol..	10	17	189	275	278	298	307	334
Non-AFDC collections	Mil. dol..	874	1,378	1,604	2,023	2,569	3,128	3,656	4,264
Administrative expenditures, total	Mil. dol..	466	723	814	941	1,066	1,171	1,363	1,606
State share	Mil. dol..	117	216	243	308	316	366	426	545
Federal share	Mil. dol..	349	507	571	633	750	804	938	1,061
Program savings, total..........	Mil. dol..	127	260	86	9	5	18	-77	-186
State share	Mil. dol..	230	366	317	274	342	378	403	340
Federal share	Mil. dol..	-103	-105	-231	-264	-337	-360	-480	-526
Total fees and costs recovered for non-AFDC cases	Mil. dol..	5	3	3	6	7	7	7	22
Percentage of AFDC payments recovered	Percent.	5.2	7.0	7.3	8.6	9.1	9.8	10.0	10.3

NA Not available. [1] Reflects cases that are no longer receiving AFDC but still have outstanding child support due.
[2] Beginning 1985, States were required to pass along to the family the first $50 of any current child support collected each month.

Source: U.S. Department of Health and Human Services, Office of Child Support Enforcement, *Annual Report to Congress.*

No. 599. Adoptions, by Relationship of Petitioner, 1960 to 1986, and Foreign Adoptions, 1980 to 1991

[Data on foreign adoptions for **year ending September 30.** Estimated. Data on total adoptions for 1960- 1975 are generally based on material shown by Penelope Maza in "Adoption Trends: 1944-1975", Child Welfare Research Notes #9, issued by the U.S. Dept. of Health and Human Services, Administration for Children, Youth and Families. Data on domestic adoptions for 1982 and 1986 are based on data collected by the National Committee for Adoption from various State health, welfare, adoption, and statistical offices. For further comments, see source]

YEAR	TOTAL ADOPTIONS						FOREIGN ADOPTIONS [1]			
	Total	Related petitioners	Unrelated petitioners by type of agency making placement				Year	Number	Country of origin of adoptee	Number
			Total	Public agency	Private agency	Inde-pendent				
1960	107,000	49,200	57,800	13,300	20,800	23,700	1980.....	5,139	1991, total [2]...	9,008
1965	142,000	65,300	76,700	20,700	32,200	23,800	1985.....	9,286	Romania........	2,552
1970	175,000	85,800	89,200	29,500	40,100	19,600	1987.....	10,097	Korea..........	1,817
1975	129,000	81,300	47,700	18,600	18,100	11,000	1988.....	9,120	Peru..........	722
1982 [3]....	141,861	91,141	50,720	19,428	14,549	16,743	1989.....	7,948	Colombia	527
1986 [3]....	104,088	52,931	51,157	20,064	15,053	16,040	1990.....	7,088	India	448

[1] Source: U.S. Immigration and Naturalization Service, *Statistical Yearbook of Immigration and Naturalization Service.*
[2] Includes other countries, not shown separately. [3] Domestic adoptions only.

Source: Except as noted, National Committee for Adoption, Inc., Washington, DC, *Adoption Factbook II, 1989* (copyright); and unpublished data.

No. 600. Primary Child Care Arrangements Used by Employed Mothers for Children Under 5 Years Old: 1977 to 1988

[Data were obtained for the three youngest children in the household, except as noted. Based on the Survey of Income and Program Participation; see text, section 14]

TYPE OF ARRANGEMENT	1977, [1] June	1984-85, winter	1986, fall	1987, fall	1988, fall
Children under 5 years old, total (1,000) . .	**4,370**	**8,168**	**8,849**	**9,124**	**9,483**
PERCENT DISTRIBUTION					
Care in child's home	33.9	31.0	28.7	29.9	28.2
By father	14.4	15.7	14.5	15.3	15.1
By grandparent	(2)	5.7	5.2	5.1	5.7
By other relative	[2]12.6	3.7	3.4	3.3	2.2
By nonrelative	7.0	5.9	5.5	6.2	5.3
Care in another home	40.7	37.0	40.7	35.6	36.8
By grandparent	(NA)	10.2	10.2	8.7	8.2
By other relative	18.3	4.5	6.5	4.6	5.0
By nonrelative	22.4	22.3	24.0	22.3	23.6
Organized child care facilities	13.0	23.1	22.4	24.4	25.8
Day/group care center	(NA)	14.0	14.9	16.1	16.6
Nursery school/preschool	(NA)	9.1	7.5	8.3	9.2
School-based activity.	(NA)	(NA)	(NA)	(NA)	0.2
Child cares for self	0.4	-	-	0.3	0.1
Mother cares for child at work [3]	11.4	8.1	7.4	8.9	7.6
Other arrangements [4]	0.6	0.8	0.8	1.0	1.3

- Represents or rounds to zero.   NA Not available.   [1] Data only for the two youngest children under 5 years of age.   [2] Data for grandparents included in other relative.   [3] Includes mothers working at home or away from home.   [4] Includes children in kindergarten/grade school.

Source: U.S. Bureau of the Census, *Current Population Reports,* series P-70, No. 30.

No. 601. Percent of Adult Population Doing Volunteer Work: 1989

[**For year ending in May.** Covers civilian noninstitutional population, 16 years old and over. A volunteer is a person who performed unpaid work for an organization such as a church, the Boy or Girl Scouts, a school, Little League, etc. during the year. Persons who did work on their own such as helping out neighbors or relatives are excluded. Based on Current Population Survey; see text, section 1 and Appendix III]

CHARACTERISTIC	VOLUNTEER WORKERS		PERCENT DISTRIBUTION OF VOLUNTEERS, BY TYPE OF ORGANIZATION [1]							
	Number (1,000)	Per-cent of popu-lation	Total	Churches, other religious organi-zations	Schools, other educa-tional insti-tutions	Civic or political organi-zations	Hospi-tals, other health organi-zations	Social or welfare organi-zations	Sport or recrea-tional organi-zations	Other organi-zations
Total [2]	**38,042**	**20.4**	**100.0**	**37.4**	**15.1**	**13.2**	**10.4**	**9.9**	**7.8**	**6.3**
16 to 19 years old	1,902	13.4	100.0	34.4	26.8	8.9	9.2	7.0	8.2	5.5
20 to 24 years old	2,064	11.4	100.0	30.5	18.5	12.7	11.9	11.6	8.0	6.8
25 to 34 years old	8,680	20.2	100.0	34.9	18.3	13.3	9.1	9.3	8.9	6.1
35 to 44 years old	10,337	28.9	100.0	33.1	20.3	12.6	7.4	8.5	12.1	6.1
45 to 54 years old	5,670	23.0	100.0	40.8	11.8	15.1	10.1	8.8	7.1	6.3
55 to 64 years old	4,455	20.8	100.0	45.7	6.7	16.1	12.4	10.9	2.5	5.7
65 years old and over.	4,934	16.9	100.0	43.3	4.3	11.1	17.8	14.5	1.8	7.2
Male	16,681	18.8	100.0	35.9	10.5	17.2	7.0	10.1	11.8	7.5
Female.	21,361	21.9	100.0	38.5	18.8	10.1	13.1	9.7	4.6	5.3
White.	34,823	21.9	100.0	36.6	15.1	13.5	10.7	9.8	8.0	6.3
Black	2,505	11.9	100.0	50.4	12.4	9.6	7.0	10.4	4.6	5.6
Hispanic origin [3]	1,289	9.4	100.0	42.2	18.3	9.6	8.5	8.9	6.9	5.6
Educational attainment: [4]										
Less than 4 years of high school	2,939	8.3	100.0	48.4	6.6	10.0	10.0	13.1	4.8	7.0
4 years of high school	11,105	18.8	100.0	41.5	12.5	11.2	11.1	8.8	8.2	6.7
1 to 3 years of college. . . .	7,572	28.1	100.0	36.8	14.7	13.3	10.8	10.1	8.0	6.3
4 years of college or more .	12,459	38.4	100.0	32.9	17.4	16.4	9.7	10.1	7.8	5.7

[1] Organization for which most of the work was done.   [2] Includes other races, not shown separately.   [3] Persons of Hispanic origin may be of any race.   [4] Persons 25 years old and over.

Source: U.S. Bureau of Labor Statistics, *News,* USDL 90-154, March 29, 1990.

No. 602. Charity Contributions—Average Dollar Amount and Percent of Household Income, by Age of Respondent and Household Income: 1989

[Estimates cover households' contribution activity for the year and are based on respondents' replies as to contribution and volunteer activity of household. Based on a sample survey conducted during March to May 1990 and subject to sampling variability; see source]

AGE	ALL CONTRIBUTING HOUSEHOLDS		CONTRIBUTORS AND VOLUNTEERS		HOUSEHOLD INCOME	ALL CONTRIBUTING HOUSEHOLDS		CONTRIBUTORS AND VOLUNTEERS	
	Average amount (dol.)	Percent of household income	Average amount (dol.)	Percent of household income		Average amount (dol.)	Percent of household income	Average amount (dol.)	Percent of household income
Total	978	2.5	1,192	2.9	Under $10,000 . . .	379	5.5	363	5.5
18 to 24 years	484	1.2	635	1.5	$10,000-$19,999 . .	485	3.2	640	4.1
25 to 34 years	893	2.1	1,056	2.6	$20,000-$29,999 . .	728	2.9	926	3.7
35 to 44 years	956	2.2	1,158	2.6	$30,000-$39,999 . .	894	2.6	987	2.8
45 to 54 years	1,098	2.3	1,418	2.8	$40,000-$49,999 . .	831	1.8	971	2.2
55 to 64 years	1,420	3.6	1,950	4.7	$50,000-$59,999 . .	941	1.7	1,144	2.1
65 to 74 years	1,070	4.4	951	3.7	$60,000-$74,999 . .	1,250	1.8	1,551	2.3
75 years and over. .	698	3.2	1,005	4.5	$75,000-$99,999 . .	2,793	3.2	3,961	4.5
					$100,000 and over.	2,893	2.9	2,138	2.1

No. 603. Charity Contributions—Percent of Households Contributing, by Dollar Amount, Type of Charity, and Percentage of Income Contributed: 1989

[See headnote, table 602]

ANNUAL AMOUNT OF HOUSEHOLD CONTRIBUTIONS	PERCENT DISTRIBUTION		TYPE OF CHARITY	Percentage of households	Average contribution per contributing household	PERCENTAGE OF HOUSEHOLD INCOME CONTRIBUTED	PERCENT DISTRIBUTION		Percentage of respondents volunteering
	All households	Givers					All households	Contributing households	
None	24.9	(X)	Arts, culture, humanities .	9.6	193	Total	100.0	(X)	54.4
Givers	75.1	100.0	Education	19.1	291	Noncontributors. . .	24.9	(X)	25.7
$1 to $100. . . .	16.3	27.0	Environment.	13.4	88	Contributors	75.1	(X)	63.9
$101 to $200 . .	8.1	13.4	Health.	32.4	143	Reporting dollar			
$201 to $300 . .	4.8	8.0	Human services	23.0	263	amount and			
$301 to $400 . .	4.6	7.6	International	4.2	202	income	59.6	100.0	63.6
$401 to $500 . .	3.1	5.1	Private, community			Less than 1			
$501 to $600 . .	2.6	4.3	foundations.	6.4	116	percent.	28.9	48.4	54.6
$601 to $700 . .	1.5	2.5	Public, societal benefit . .	11.2	120	1-1.99 percent. . .	10.9	18.3	66.7
$701 to $999 . .	4.8	7.9	Recreation - adults	6.2	135	2-2.99 percent. . .	5.8	9.8	66.0
$1,000 or more.	14.5	24.0	Religion.	53.2	896	3-4.99 percent. . .	5.0	8.4	81.1
Amount not			Youth development	21.6	129	5 percent or			
reported.	14.7	(X)				more	9.0	15.1	77.5

X Not applicable.
Source: Hodgkinson, Virginia, Murray Weitzman, and the Gallup Organization, Inc., *Giving and Volunteering in the United States: 1990 Edition*. (Copyright and published by INDEPENDENT SECTOR, Washington, DC, Fall 1990.)

No. 604. Private Philanthropy Funds, by Source and Allocation: 1970 to 1990

[In billions of dollars. Estimates for sources of funds based on U.S. Internal Revenue Service reports of corporate and foundation tax returns and individual charitable deductions; econometric formula utilizing Commerce Department data on personal income, Standard & Poor's 500 Composite Index, Census population data; and surveys conducted by the source and by Council for Aid to Education, The Conference Board, The Foundation Center, and other research organizations. Estimates for allocation of funds based on surveys of recipient organizations conducted by source and other groups. Because of changes in estimation procedures over time, data by type of allocation may not be comparable for all years. See *Historical Statistics, Colonial Times to 1970*, series H 398-411, for similar but not comparable data]

SOURCE AND ALLOCATION	1970	1975	1980	1981	1982	1983	1984	1985	1986	1987	1988	1989	1990
Total funds.	21.0	28.6	48.7	55.6	59.8	64.7	70.7	80.1	90.9	93.4	104.6	115.9	122.6
Individuals	16.2	23.5	40.7	46.4	48.5	53.5	58.6	65.9	74.6	75.9	86.5	96.8	101.8
Foundations.	1.9	1.7	2.8	3.1	3.2	3.6	3.9	4.9	5.4	5.9	6.2	6.6	7.1
Corporations	0.8	1.2	2.4	2.5	2.9	3.6	4.1	4.5	5.2	5.0	5.4	5.6	5.9
Charitable bequests	2.1	2.2	2.6	3.6	5.2	3.9	4.0	4.8	5.7	6.6	6.6	7.0	7.8
Allocation:													
Religion	9.3	12.8	22.2	25.1	28.1	31.8	35.6	38.2	41.7	48.7	55.6	62.5	65.8
Health	2.4	3.6	5.3	5.8	6.2	6.7	6.8	7.7	8.4	9.2	9.6	9.9	9.9
Education.	2.6	2.8	5.0	5.8	6.0	6.7	7.3	8.2	9.4	9.8	10.2	11.0	12.4
Human service	2.9	2.9	4.9	5.6	6.3	7.2	7.9	8.5	9.1	9.8	10.5	11.4	11.8
Arts, culture and humanities. . .	0.7	1.6	3.2	3.7	5.0	4.2	4.5	5.1	5.8	6.3	6.8	7.5	7.9
Public/society benefit	0.5	0.8	1.5	1.8	1.7	1.9	1.9	2.2	2.5	2.9	3.2	3.8	4.9
Environment/wildlife.	(¹)	(¹)	(¹)	(¹)	(¹)	(¹)	(¹)	(¹)	(¹)	(¹)	1.3	1.5	2.3
International	(¹)	(¹)	(¹)	(¹)	(¹)	(¹)	(¹)	(¹)	(¹)	(¹)	2.2	2.0	2.2
All other.	2.6	4.1	6.7	7.9	6.6	6.2	6.7	10.2	14.0	3.1	5.3	6.3	5.3

¹ Included in "All other."
Source: AAFRC Trust for Philanthropy, New York, NY, *Giving USA*, annual, (copyright).

No. 605. Foundations—Number and Finances, by Asset Size

[Figures are for latest year reported by foundations, usually **1988** or **1989**. Covers nongovernment nonprofit organizations with funds and programs managed by their own trustees or directors, whose goal was to maintain or aid social, educational, religious, or other activities deemed to serve the common good. Excludes organizations which make general appeals to the public for funds, act as trade associations for industrial or other special groups, or do not currently award grants]

ASSET SIZE	Number	Assets (mil. dol.)	Gifts received (mil. dol.)	Expen-ditures (mil. dol.)	Grants (mil. dol.)	PERCENT DISTRIBUTION				
						Number	Assets	Gifts received	Expen-ditures	Grants
Total	31,996	137,553	5,524	9,345	7,912	100.0	100.0	100.0	100.0	100.0
Under $50,000.	8,005	147	202	272	252	25.1	0.1	3.7	2.9	3.1
$50,000-$99,999	3,443	251	65	101	92	10.8	0.2	1.2	1.1	1.2
$100,000-$249,999.	5,472	894	171	218	196	17.1	0.6	3.1	2.3	2.5
$250,000-$499,999.	3,987	1,422	185	237	208	12.5	1.0	3.4	2.5	2.6
$500,000-$999,999.	3,530	2,516	276	340	294	11.0	1.8	5.0	3.6	3.7
$1,000,000-$4,999,999	4,963	10,922	1,060	1,208	1,047	15.5	7.9	19.2	12.9	13.2
$5,000,000-$9,999,999	1,119	7,937	543	736	616	3.5	5.8	9.8	7.9	7.8
$10,000,000-$49,999,999 . . .	1,115	22,849	1,276	1,879	1,574	3.5	16.6	23.1	20.1	19.9
$50,000,000-$99,999,999 . . .	192	13,395	523	894	712	0.6	9.7	9.5	9.6	9.0
$100,000,000-$249,999,999. .	97	15,365	508	915	800	0.3	11.2	9.2	9.8	10.1
$250,000,000 or more.	73	61,855	715	2,545	2,120	0.2	45.0	12.9	27.2	26.8

Source: The Foundation Center, New York, NY, *The National Data Book of Foundations*, 15th Edition, 1991.

No. 606. Foundations—Grants Reported, by Subject Field and Recipient Organization: 1990

[Covers grants of $10,000 or more in size, up from $5,000 in 1989. Based on reports of 832 foundations. Grant sample totaling $4.47 billion represented about 57 percent of all grant dollars awarded by private foundations. For definition of foundation, see headnote, table 605]

SUBJECT FIELD	NUMBER OF GRANTS		DOLLAR VALUE OF GRANTS		RECIPIENT ORGANIZATION [1]	NUMBER OF GRANTS		DOLLAR VALUE OF GRANTS	
	Num-ber	Per-cent distri-bution	Amount (mil. dol.)	Per-cent distri-bution		Num-ber	Per-cent distri-bution	Amount (mil. dol.)	Per-cent distri-bution
Total	57,443	100.0	4,475	100.0	Community improvement				
Arts and culture	9,053	15.8	639	14.3	organizations.	2,630	4.6	151	3.4
Education	13,319	23.2	1,150	25.7	Educational institutions.	17,766	30.9	1,733	38.7
Environment & animals. . . .	2,583	4.5	208	4.7	Colleges & universities . . .	10,953	19.1	1,255	28.0
					Educational support				
Health.	7,275	12.7	752	16.8	agencies	2,538	4.4	177	4.0
Human services	12,360	21.5	645	14.4	Schools	2,623	4.6	143	3.2
International affairs,					Federated funds	1,961	3.4	195	4.4
development & peace. . .	1,622	2.8	140	3.1	Hospitals/medical care				
					facilities	3,050	5.3	300	6.7
Public/society benefit. . . .	6,649	11.6	491	11.0	Human service agencies. . . .	9,689	16.9	472	10.5
Science and technology . . .	2,074	3.6	223	5.0	International organizations . .	1,523	2.7	116	2.6
Social sciences.	1,049	1.8	133	3.0	Museums/historical societies.	2,832	4.9	277	6.2
Religion.	1,238	2.2	85	1.9	Performing arts groups.	3,443	6.0	188	4.2
Other	221	0.4	7	0.2	Professional societies &				
					associations	3,028	5.3	193	4.3

[1] Grants may be awarded to multiple types of recipient organizations and would thereby be double-counted.

Source: The Foundation Center, New York, NY, *Foundation Grants Index, 1992*, 20th Edition, 1991.

No. 607. Corporate Philanthropy—Donations, by Type of Beneficiary: 1975 to 1989

[**In millions of dollars.** Based on a sample of corporations that gave at least $100,000; see source]

BENEFICIARY	1975	1980	1982	1983	1984	1985	1986	1987	1988	1989
Total [1]	436.8	994.6	1,281.6	1,278.4	1,444.3	1,694.7	1,673.7	1,658.4	1,645.7	1,820.1
Health and human services [1]	180.0	337.9	397.3	367.6	399.9	494.1	468.6	450.5	480.2	481.0
Federated drives	104.6	170.7	182.4	(NA)	193.9	(NA)	225.9	203.6	234.0	218.3
Other local health, human										
services.	20.5	41.7	44.6	(NA)	71.2	(NA)	(NA)	215.9	(NA)	(NA)
Education [1]	158.4	375.8	522.2	498.8	561.7	650.0	718.0	610.1	614.1	699.8
Dept. and research grants [2]	23.8	64.7	114.6	(NA)	175.3	(NA)	198.5	(NA)	(NA)	(NA)
Employee matching gifts [2]	14.0	45.4	71.2	(NA)	72.2	(NA)	98.7	108.5	108.2	115.0
Unrestricted operating grants [2] . .	29.1	56.0	57.4	(NA)	38.7	(NA)	70.0	(NA)	(NA)	(NA)
Culture and art	33.0	108.7	145.8	145.2	154.7	187.5	198.7	178.6	183.6	201.2
Civic, community activities [1]	45.2	116.8	149.3	188.8	271.6	279.5	220.5	236.1	212.2	253.5
Community improvement.	15.2	47.0	48.2	(NA)	30.5	(NA)	12.6	53.4	51.3	87.0
Environment; ecology	7.5	10.8	13.8	(NA)	97.1	(NA)	35.9	44.0	17.3	11.7

NA Not available. [1] Includes other beneficiaries not shown separately. [2] Higher education institutions.

Source: The Conference Board, New York, NY, *Annual Survey of Corporate Contributions*, (copyright).

Labor Force, Employment, and Earnings

This section presents statistics on the labor force; its distribution by occupation and industry affiliation; and the supply of, demand for, and conditions of labor. The chief source of these data is the Current Population Survey conducted by the U.S. Bureau of the Census. Comprehensive historical data are published by the Bureau of Labor Statistics (BLS) in *Labor Force Statistics Derived From the Current Population Survey, 1948-87, BLS Bulletin 2307.* These data are supplemented on a current basis by the BLS monthly publications *Employment and Earnings* and the *Monthly Labor Review.* Detailed data on the labor force are also available from the Census Bureau's decennial census of population.

Types of data.—Most statistics in this section are obtained by two methods: household interviews or questionnaires, and reports of establishment payroll records. Each method provides data which the other cannot suitably supply. Population characteristics, for example, are readily obtainable only from the household survey, while detailed industrial classifications can be readily derived only from establishment records.

Household data are obtained from a monthly sample survey of the population. The Current Population Survey (CPS) is used to gather data for the calendar week including the 12th of the month and provides current comprehensive data on the labor force (see text, section 1). The CPS provides information on the work status of the population without duplication since each person is classified as employed, unemployed, or not in the labor force. Employed persons holding more than one job are counted only once, according to the job at which they worked the most hours during the survey week.

Monthly data from the CPS are published by the Bureau of Labor Statistics in *Employment and Earnings* and the related reports mentioned above. Data presented include national totals of the number of persons in the civilian labor force by sex, race, Hispanic origin, and age; the number employed; hours of work; industry and

In Brief	
Labor force participation rate of married women with children under 6 years old:	
1960	18.8
1970	30.3
1980	45.1
1991	59.9
Projected job growth 1988-2000:	
Home health aides	up 92%
Medical assistants	up 74%
Typists/word processors	down 11%
Farmers	down 21%

occupational groups; and the number unemployed, reasons for, and duration of unemployment. Monthly data from the CPS are also presented for regions and 11 large States. Annual data shown in this section are averages of monthly figures for each calendar year, unless otherwise specified.

In addition to monthly data, the CPS also produces annual estimates of employment and unemployment for each State, 50 large metropolitan statistical areas, and selected cities. These estimates are published by BLS in its annual *Geographic Profile of Employment and Unemployment.* More detailed geographic data (e.g., for counties and cities) are provided by the decennial population censuses.

Data based on establishment records are compiled by BLS and cooperating State agencies as part of an ongoing Current Employment Statistics Program. Data, gathered from a sample of employers who voluntarily complete mail questionnaires monthly, are supplemented by data from other government agencies and adjusted at intervals to data from government social insurance program reports. The estimates exclude proprietors of unincorporated firms, self-employed persons, private household workers, unpaid family workers, agricultural workers, and the Armed Forces. In March 1990, reporting establishments employed 9 million manufacturing workers (48 percent of the total manufacturing employment at the time), 18 million workers in nonmanufacturing industries (25 percent of the total in nonmanufacturing), and 14 million Federal, State, and local government employees (75 percent of total government).

The establishment survey counts workers each time they appear on a payroll during the reference week (as with the CPS, the week including the 12th of the month). Thus, unlike the CPS, a person with two jobs is counted twice. The establishment survey is designed to provide detailed industry information for the Nation, States, and metropolitan areas on nonfarm wage and salary employment, average weekly hours, and average hourly and weekly earnings. Establishment survey data are published in *Employment and Earnings* and the *Monthly Labor Review,* cited above. Historical national and geographic data are published in *BLS Bulletin 2370, Employment, Hours, and Earnings, United States, 1909-90* and *Bulletin 2320, Employment, Hours, and Earnings, States and Areas, 1972-87,* updated annually.

Labor force.—According to the CPS definitions, the civilian labor force comprises all civilians in the noninstitutional population 16 years and over classified as "employed" or "unemployed" according to the criteria below: Employed civilians comprise (a) all civilians, who, during the reference week, did any work for pay or profit (minimum of an hour's work) or worked 15 hours or more as unpaid workers in a family enterprise, and (b) all civilians who were not working but who had jobs or businesses from which they were temporarily absent for noneconomic reasons (illness, weather conditions, vacation, labor-management dispute, etc.) whether they were paid for the time off or were seeking other jobs. Unemployed persons comprise all civilians who had no employment during the reference week, who made specific efforts to find a job within the previous 4 weeks (such as applying directly to an employer, or to a public employment service, or checking with friends), and who were available for work during that week, except for temporary illness. Persons on layoff from a job or waiting to report to a new job within 30 days are also classified as unemployed if they were available for work. All other civilian persons, 16 years old and over, are "not in the labor force." The total labor force includes, in addition to the civilian

employed and unemployed, members of the Armed Forces stationed in the United States. They are also included in the employed totals.

Beginning in 1982, changes in the estimation procedures and the introduction of 1980 census data caused substantial increases in the population and estimates of persons in all labor force categories. Rates on labor force characteristics, however, were essentially unchanged. In order to avoid major breaks in series, some 30,000 labor force series were adjusted back to 1970. The effect of the 1982 revisions on various data series and an explanation of the adjustment procedure used are described in "Revisions in the Current Population Survey in January 1982," in the February 1982 issue of *Employment and Earnings.* The revisions did not, however, smooth out the breaks in series occurring between 1972 and 1979, and data users should make allowances for them in making certain data comparisons.

Beginning in January 1985, the CPS estimation procedure was revised due to the implementation of a new sample design. A description of the changes and an indication of their effect on the national estimates of labor force characteristics appear in "Changes in the Estimation Procedure in the Current Population Survey Beginning in January 1985" in the February 1985 issue of *Employment and Earnings.* Overall, the revisions had only a slight effect on most estimates. The greatest impact was on estimates of persons of Hispanic origin, which were revised to the extent possible, back to January 1980.

Beginning in January 1986, the CPS estimation procedure was revised to reflect an explicit estimate of the number of undocumented immigrants (largely Hispanic) since 1980 and an improved estimate of the number of legal foreign-born emigrants for the same time period. The revisions had a comparatively small effect on the total population and labor force estimates, but their effect on the estimates of persons of Hispanic origin was more pronounced. As a result, data for Hispanics, to the extent possible, were again revised back to January 1980. An explanation of the changes and their effect on estimates of labor force characteristics appears in "Changes in the Estimation Procedure in the Current Population Survey Beginning in January 1986" in the February 1986 issue of *Employment and Earnings.*

Hours and earnings.—Average hourly earnings, based on establishment data, are gross earnings (i.e., earnings before payroll deductions) and include overtime premiums; they exclude irregular bonuses and value of payments in kind. Hours are those for which pay was received. Wages and salaries from the CPS consist of total monies received for work performed by an employee during the income year. It includes wages, salaries, commissions, tips, piece-rate payments, and cash bonuses earned before deductions were made for taxes, bonds, union dues, etc. Persons who worked 35 hours or more are classified as working full time (see table 626).

Industrial and occupational groups.— Establishments responding to the establishment survey are classified into industries on the basis of their principal product or activity (determined by annual sales volume) in accordance with the *Standard Industrial Classification (SIC) Manual,* Office of Management and Budget. The SIC is a classification structure for the entire national economy. The structure provides data on a division and industry code basis, according to the level of industrial detail. For example, manufacturing is a major industrial division; food and kindred products (code 20) is one of its major groups. One of the ways this group is further divided is into meat products (code 201) and meat packing plants (code 2011). Periodically, the SIC is revised to reflect changes in the industrial composition of the economy. The *1987 SIC Manual* has been issued; the previous was the *1972 SIC Manual.* Tables shown in this *Abstract* indicate which *SIC Manual* the data shown are based on.

Industry data derived from the CPS for 1983-91 utilize the 1980 census industrial classification developed from the 1972 SIC. CPS data from 1971 to 1982 were based on the 1970 census classification system which was developed from the 1967 SIC. Most of the industry categories were not affected by the change in classification.

The occupational classification system used in the 1980 census and in the CPS for 1983-91 evolved from the 1980 Standard Occupational Classification (SOC) system, first introduced in 1977.

Occupational categories used in the 1980 census classification system are so radically different from the 1970 census system used in the CPS through 1982, that their implementation represented a break in historical data series. In cases where data have not yet been converted to the 1980 classifications and still reflect the 1970 classifications (e.g., table 657), comparisons between the two systems should not be made. To help users bridge the data gap, a limited set of estimates was developed for the 1972-82 period based on the new classifications. The estimates were developed by means of applying conversion factors created by double coding a 20-percent sample of CPS occupational records for 6 months during 1981-82. For further details, contact BLS.

Productivity.—The Bureau of Labor Statistics (BLS) publishes data on productivity as measured by output per hour (labor productivity), output per combined unit of labor and capital input (multifactor productivity), and, for manufacturing industries, output per combined unit of capital, labor, energy, materials, and purchased service inputs. Labor productivity and related indexes are published for the business sector as a whole and its major subsectors: nonfarm business, manufacturing, nonfinancial corporations, 146 specific industries, and various functional areas of the Federal civilian government. Multifactor productivity and related measures are published for the private business sector and its major subsectors. Productivity indexes which take into account capital, labor, energy, materials, and service inputs are published for the 20 major two-digit industry groups which comprise the manufacturing sector and for the steel and motor vehicle industries. The major sector data are published in the BLS quarterly news release, *Productivity and Costs* and in the annual *Multifactor Productivity Measures* release. The specific industry productivity measures are published annually in the BLS Bulletin, *Productivity Measures for Selected Industries,* and the *Handbook of Labor Statistics.* Detailed information on methods, limitations, and data sources appears in the *BLS Handbook of Methods,* BLS Bulletin 2285 (1988), chapters 10 and 11.

Unions.—As defined here, unions include traditional labor unions and employee associations similar to labor unions. Data on union membership status provided by

BLS are for employed wage and salary workers and relate to their principal job. Earnings by union membership status are usual weekly earnings of full-time wage and salary workers. The information is collected through the Current Population Survey. For a full description of the method of collection and comparability with earlier data, see "New Data on Union Members and Their Earnings" in the January 1985 issue of *Employment and Earnings,* and "Changing Employment Patterns of Organized Workers" in the February 1985 issue of the *Monthly Labor Review.* Collective bargaining settlements data are available for bargaining situations involving 1,000 or more workers in private industry and State and local government.

Work stoppages.—Work stoppages include all strikes and lockouts known to BLS which last for at least one full day or shift and involve 1,000 or more workers. All stoppages, whether or not authorized by a union, legal or illegal, are counted. Excluded are work slowdowns and instances where employees report to work late, or leave early, to attend mass meetings or mass rallies.

Seasonal adjustment.—Many economic statistics reflect a regularly recurring seasonal movement which can be estimated on the basis of past experience. By eliminating that part of the change which can be ascribed to usual seasonal variation (e.g., climate or school openings and closings), it is possible to observe the cyclical and other nonseasonal movements in the series. However, in evaluating deviations from the seasonal pattern—that is, changes in a seasonally adjusted series— it is important to note that seasonal adjustment is merely an approximation based on past experience. Seasonally adjusted estimates have a broader margin of possible error than the original data on which they are based, since they are subject not only to sampling and other errors, but also are affected by the uncertainties of the adjustment process itself.

Statistical reliability.—For discussion of statistical collection, estimation, sampling procedures, and measures of statistical reliability applicable to Census Bureau and BLS data, see Appendix III.

Historical statistics.—Tabular headnotes provide cross-references, where applicable, to *Historical Statistics of the United States, Colonial Times to 1970.* See Appendix IV.

Figure 13.1
10 Fastest Growing Occupations: 1990 to 2005

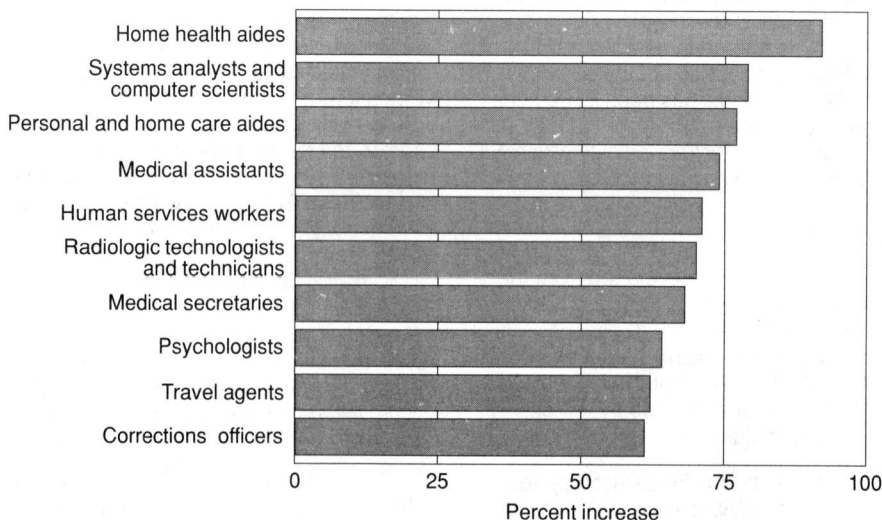

Percent increase

Source: Chart prepared by U.S. Bureau of the Census. For data, see table 630.

No. 608. Employment Status of the Noninstitutional Population 16 Years Old and Over: 1950 to 1991

[In thousands, except as indicated. Annual averages of monthly figures. Based on Current Population Survey; see text, section 1 and Appendix III. See also *Historical Statistics, Colonial Times to 1970*, series D 11-19 and D 85-86]

YEAR	Noninstitutional population	LABOR FORCE Number	Employed Total	Employed Civilian Resident Armed Forces	Employed Civilian Total	Employed Civilian Agriculture	Employed Civilian Nonagricultural industries	Unemployed Number	Unemployed Percent of labor force [1]	Not in labor force
1950	106,164	63,377	60,087	1,169	58,918	7,160	51,758	3,288	5.2	42,787
1960	119,106	71,489	67,639	1,861	65,778	5,458	60,318	3,852	5.4	47,617
1970	139,203	84,889	80,796	2,118	78,678	3,463	75,215	4,093	4.8	54,315
1975	154,831	95,453	87,524	1,678	85,846	3,408	82,438	7,929	8.3	59,377
1980	169,349	108,544	100,907	1,604	99,303	3,364	95,938	7,637	7.0	60,806
1981	171,775	110,315	102,042	1,645	100,397	3,368	97,030	8,273	7.5	61,460
1982	173,939	111,872	101,194	1,668	99,526	3,401	96,125	10,678	9.5	62,067
1983	175,891	113,226	102,510	1,676	100,834	3,383	97,450	10,717	9.5	62,665
1984	178,080	115,241	106,702	1,697	105,005	3,321	101,685	8,539	7.4	62,839
1985	179,912	117,167	108,856	1,706	107,150	3,179	103,971	8,312	7.1	62,744
1986	182,293	119,540	111,303	1,706	109,597	3,163	106,434	8,237	6.9	62,752
1987	184,490	121,602	114,177	1,737	112,440	3,208	109,232	7,425	6.1	62,888
1988	186,322	123,378	116,677	1,709	114,968	3,169	111,800	6,701	5.4	62,944
1989	188,081	125,557	119,030	1,688	117,342	3,199	114,142	6,528	5.2	62,523
1990	189,686	126,424	119,550	1,637	117,914	3,186	114,728	6,874	5.4	63,262
1991	191,329	126,867	118,440	1,564	116,877	3,233	113,644	8,426	6.6	64,462
PERCENT DISTRIBUTION										
1950	100.0	59.7	56.6	1.1	55.5	6.7	48.8	3.1	(X)	40.3
1960	100.0	60.0	56.8	1.6	55.2	4.6	50.6	3.2	(X)	40.0
1970	100.0	61.0	58.0	1.5	56.5	2.5	54.0	2.9	(X)	39.0
1980	100.0	64.1	59.6	0.9	58.6	2.0	56.7	4.5	(X)	35.9
1990	100.0	66.6	63.0	0.9	62.2	1.7	60.5	3.6	(X)	33.4
1991	100.0	66.3	61.9	0.8	61.1	1.7	59.4	4.4	(X)	33.7

X Not applicable. [1] Unemployment as a percent of the labor force, including resident Armed Forces.

Source: U.S. Bureau of Labor Statistics, Bulletin 2307; and *Employment and Earnings*, monthly.

No. 609. Civilian Labor Force and Participation Rates by Race, Hispanic Origin, Sex, and Age, 1970 to 1991, and Projections, 2000 and 2005

[For civilian noninstitutional population 16 years old and over. Annual averages of monthly figures. Rates are based on annual average civilian noninstitutional population of each specified group and represent proportion of each specified group in the civilian labor force. Based on Current Population Survey; see text, section 1 and Appendix III. See also *Historical Statistics, Colonial Times to 1970*, series D 42-48]

RACE, SEX, AND AGE	CIVILIAN LABOR FORCE (millions) 1970	1980	1985	1990	1991	2000	2005	PARTICIPATION RATE (percent) 1970	1980	1985	1990	1991	2000	2005
Total [1]	82.8	106.9	115.5	124.8	125.3	142.9	150.7	60.4	63.8	64.8	66.4	66.0	68.7	69.0
White	73.6	93.6	99.9	107.2	107.5	120.3	125.8	60.2	64.1	65.0	66.8	66.6	69.3	69.7
Male	46.0	54.5	56.5	59.3	59.3	64.5	66.8	80.0	78.2	77.0	76.9	76.4	76.7	76.2
Female	27.5	39.1	43.5	47.9	48.2	55.8	58.9	42.6	51.2	54.1	57.5	57.4	62.3	63.5
Black [2]	9.2	10.9	12.4	13.5	13.5	16.5	17.8	61.8	61.0	62.9	63.3	62.6	65.7	65.6
Male	5.2	5.6	6.2	6.7	6.8	8.1	8.7	76.5	70.3	70.8	70.1	69.5	71.0	70.2
Female	4.0	5.3	6.1	6.8	6.8	8.4	9.1	49.5	53.1	56.5	57.8	57.0	61.2	61.7
Hispanic [3]	(NA)	6.1	7.7	9.6	9.8	14.2	16.8	(NA)	64.0	64.6	67.0	66.1	69.3	69.9
Male	(NA)	3.8	4.7	5.8	5.9	8.4	9.9	(NA)	81.4	80.3	81.2	80.1	81.8	81.6
Female	(NA)	2.3	3.0	3.8	3.9	5.8	6.9	(NA)	47.4	49.3	53.0	52.3	56.6	58.0
Male	51.2	61.5	64.4	68.2	68.4	75.9	79.3	79.7	77.4	76.3	76.1	75.5	76.0	75.4
16 to 19 years	4.0	5.0	4.1	3.9	3.6	4.4	4.6	56.1	60.5	56.8	55.7	53.2	57.4	57.7
16 and 17 years	1.8	2.1	1.7	1.5	1.4	1.8	1.9	47.0	50.1	45.1	43.7	41.2	47.3	47.9
18 and 19 years	2.2	2.9	2.5	2.4	2.2	2.6	2.6	66.7	71.3	68.9	67.0	65.3	68.0	68.0
20 to 24 years	5.7	8.6	8.3	7.3	7.3	7.2	8.0	83.3	85.9	85.0	84.3	83.4	85.5	86.1
25 to 34 years	11.3	17.4	18.8	19.8	19.6	17.3	17.0	96.4	95.2	94.7	94.2	93.7	93.9	93.6
35 to 44 years	10.5	11.8	14.5	17.3	17.9	20.4	19.2	96.9	95.5	95.0	94.4	94.2	93.7	93.4
45 to 54 years	10.4	9.9	9.9	11.2	11.5	16.5	18.6	94.3	91.2	91.0	90.7	90.5	90.5	90.3
55 to 64 years	7.1	7.2	7.1	6.8	6.7	7.8	9.7	83.0	72.1	67.9	67.7	66.9	68.2	67.9
65 years and over	2.2	1.9	1.9	2.0	2.0	2.2	2.3	26.8	19.0	15.8	16.4	15.8	15.8	16.0
Female	31.5	45.5	51.1	56.6	56.9	67.0	71.4	43.3	51.5	54.5	57.5	57.3	62.0	63.0
16 to 19 years	3.2	4.4	3.8	3.5	3.3	4.1	4.2	44.0	52.9	52.1	51.8	50.2	54.1	54.3
16 and 17 years	1.3	1.8	1.5	1.4	1.3	1.7	1.7	34.9	43.6	42.1	41.9	40.1	45.3	45.4
18 and 19 years	1.9	2.6	2.3	2.2	2.0	2.4	2.5	53.6	61.9	61.7	60.5	59.8	62.9	63.2
20 to 24 years	4.9	7.3	7.4	6.6	6.4	6.6	7.3	57.7	68.9	71.8	71.6	70.4	74.3	75.3
25 to 34 years	5.7	12.3	14.7	16.0	15.8	14.8	14.7	45.0	65.5	70.9	73.6	73.3	78.2	79.7
35 to 44 years	6.0	8.6	11.6	14.6	15.1	18.4	17.8	51.1	65.5	71.8	76.5	76.6	83.3	85.3
45 to 54 years	6.5	7.0	7.5	9.3	9.7	15.0	17.2	54.4	59.9	64.4	71.2	72.0	79.0	81.5
55 to 64 years	4.2	4.7	4.9	5.1	5.1	6.5	8.4	43.0	41.3	42.0	45.3	45.3	51.9	54.3
65 years and over	1.1	1.2	1.2	1.5	1.5	1.6	1.8	9.7	8.1	7.3	8.7	8.6	8.6	8.8

NA Not available. [1] Beginning 1980, includes other races not shown separately. [2] For 1970, Black and other. [3] Persons of Hispanic origin may be of any race.

Source: U.S. Bureau of Labor Statistics, Bulletin 2307; *Employment and Earnings*, monthly, January issues; *Monthly Labor Review*, November 1991; and unpublished data.

No. 610. Hispanic Persons—Civilian Labor Force Participation: 1990 and 1991

[For civilian noninstitutional population, 16 years old and over. Annual averages of monthly figures. Based on Current Population Survey; see text, section 1 and Appendix III]

ITEM	1990					1991				
	Total	Mex-ican	Puerto Rican	Cuban	Other His-panic origin [1]	Total	Mex-ican	Puerto Rican	Cuban	Other His-panic origin [1]
Total (1,000).............	14,927	8,742	1,546	847	3,162	14,770	8,947	1,629	849	3,345
Percent in labor force: Male.......	81.2	82.9	71.9	74.8	82.1	80.1	81.2	71.8	75.7	82.0
Female........	53.0	52.8	42.8	55.9	58.0	52.3	51.5	45.9	52.8	57.4
Employed (1,000)...............	8,808	5,478	780	512	2,038	8,799	5,363	822	499	2,115
Percent.....................	100.0	100.0	100.0	100.0	100.0	100.0	100.0	100.0	100.0	100.0
Managerial and professional.....	12.6	10.1	15.6	23.3	15.4	13.0	10.4	17.9	25.1	15.1
Tech., sales, and admin. suppport.	24.1	21.9	30.5	34.1	25.0	24.5	22.5	32.0	33.1	24.8
Services...................	20.1	19.1	18.1	14.3	25.0	20.3	18.9	17.5	12.0	27.0
Precision production, craft, and repair..............	13.2	14.1	12.9	10.8	11.3	12.9	13.9	10.7	12.8	11.3
Operators, fabricators and laborers.................	24.6	26.9	21.2	16.4	21.7	23.5	25.9	20.7	15.6	20.1
Farming, forestry, and fishing	5.5	7.9	1.7	1.2	1.7	5.7	8.4	1.2	1.4	1.8
Percent of labor force unemployed:										
Male.....................	7.8	7.9	9.3	6.9	7.2	10.1	10.6	12.4	7.7	8.5
Female...................	8.3	8.8	8.9	7.5	7.2	9.5	10.0	10.7	8.6	7.8

[1] Includes Central or South American and other Hispanic origin.
Source: U.S. Bureau of Labor Statistics, *Employment and Earnings*, monthly, January issues.

No. 611. Civilian Labor Force and Participation Rates, by Educational Attainment, Sex, and Race: 1970 to 1991

[As of **March**, except as noted. For civilian noninstitutional population 25 to 64 years of age. See headnote, table 609]

ITEM	CIVILIAN LABOR FORCE					PARTICIPATION RATE [1]				
	Total (1,000)	Percent distribution				Total	Less than high school	High school grad-uate	College	
		Less than high school	High School grad-uate	College						
				1-3 years	4 years or more				1-3 years	4 years or more
Total: [2] 1970........	61,765	36.1	38.1	11.8	14.1	70.3	65.5	70.2	73.8	82.3
1975.............	67,774	27.5	39.7	14.4	18.3	70.5	61.6	70.5	75.7	84.5
1980.............	78,010	20.6	39.8	17.6	22.0	73.9	60.7	74.2	79.5	86.1
1985.............	88,424	15.9	40.2	19.0	24.9	76.2	59.9	75.9	81.6	87.7
1988.............	94,870	14.7	39.9	19.7	25.7	77.5	60.8	76.9	82.5	88.4
1989.............	97,318	14.0	39.6	20.0	26.4	78.2	60.5	77.9	83.3	88.4
1990 [3]............	99,981	13.3	39.4	20.8	26.5	78.9	61.4	78.4	83.5	88.6
1991 [3]............	101,171	12.8	39.2	21.3	26.7	78.8	61.0	78.2	83.4	88.3
Male: 1970	39,303	37.5	34.5	12.2	15.7	93.5	89.3	96.3	95.8	96.1
1975.............	41,628	28.9	36.1	14.8	20.2	90.3	82.6	93.2	93.3	95.7
1980.............	45,417	22.2	35.7	17.7	24.3	89.4	78.8	91.9	92.4	95.3
1985.............	49,647	17.7	36.9	18.3	27.1	88.6	72.2	90.0	91.2	94.6
1988.............	52,616	16.5	37.3	18.5	27.8	88.6	76.4	89.5	91.3	94.4
1989.............	53,668	15.7	36.9	19.2	28.2	88.8	75.9	89.6	91.8	94.5
1990 [3]............	55,049	14.9	37.3	19.8	28.0	89.3	76.4	90.1	92.1	94.6
1991 [3]............	55,554	14.5	37.1	20.3	28.2	88.9	75.9	89.4	91.9	94.3
Female: 1970	22,462	33.5	44.3	10.9	11.2	49.0	43.0	51.3	50.9	60.9
1975.............	26,146	26.5	45.5	13.9	14.1	52.3	44.1	53.9	57.3	62.7
1980.............	32,593	18.4	45.4	17.4	18.7	59.5	43.7	61.2	66.4	73.4
1985.............	38,779	13.7	44.4	19.9	22.0	64.7	44.3	65.0	72.5	78.6
1988.............	42,254	12.4	43.3	21.2	23.1	67.1	45.4	66.9	74.7	80.8
1989.............	43,650	11.9	42.9	20.9	24.3	68.3	45.5	68.5	75.4	81.1
1990 [3]............	44,932	11.2	42.1	22.1	24.6	69.1	46.5	68.8	75.7	81.3
1991 [3]............	45,617	10.7	41.8	22.5	25.0	69.3	46.0	68.9	75.8	81.3
White: 1970	55,044	33.7	39.3	12.2	14.8	70.1	65.2	69.7	73.3	81.9
1975.............	60,026	25.7	40.6	14.7	19.0	70.7	61.9	70.1	75.3	84.5
1980.............	68,509	19.1	40.2	17.7	22.9	74.2	61.4	73.7	79.2	86.0
1985.............	76,739	14.7	40.7	19.1	25.6	76.6	60.7	75.8	81.1	87.7
1988.............	81,886	13.8	40.1	19.7	26.4	78.1	62.2	76.9	82.2	88.6
1989.............	83,694	13.0	39.7	20.0	27.2	78.7	61.6	77.8	83.2	88.5
1990 [3]............	85,882	12.5	39.4	20.8	27.3	79.5	63.0	78.6	83.4	88.6
1991 [3]............	86,776	12.1	39.1	21.3	27.5	79.5	62.6	78.5	83.4	88.5
Black: 1970	6,721	55.5	28.2	8.0	8.3	72.0	67.1	76.8	81.0	87.4
1975.............	7,586	41.9	33.1	12.4	12.6	69.8	60.9	75.1	79.7	85.1
1980.............	7,731	34.7	38.1	16.3	11.0	71.5	58.1	79.2	82.0	90.1
1985.............	9,157	26.2	39.5	19.2	15.0	73.4	57.0	77.2	85.6	89.9
1988.............	9,985	22.6	43.0	19.2	15.2	74.3	56.2	77.9	85.8	90.6
1989.............	10,358	21.7	42.3	20.5	15.6	74.9	56.7	78.9	83.9	90.4
1990 [3]............	10,711	19.4	43.0	21.8	15.8	75.4	55.7	78.6	84.6	91.0
1991 [3]............	10,863	18.4	43.0	22.5	16.0	75.0	55.1	77.4	84.6	90.4

[1] Percent of the civilian population in each group in the civilian labor force.   [2] Includes other races, not shown separately. For 1970, White and Black races only.   [3] Not strictly comparable with previous years. Annual averages of monthly figures.
Source: U.S. Bureau of Labor Statistics, Bulletin 2307; and unpublished data.

No. 612. Employment Status of the Civilian Noninstitutional Population 16 Years Old and Over, by Sex, Race, and Hispanic Origin: 1960 to 1991

[In thousands, except as indicated. Annual averages of monthly figures. Based on Current Population Survey; see text, section 1, and Appendix III. See also *Historical Statistics, Colonial Times to 1970*, series D 11-19 and D 85-86]

YEAR, SEX, RACE, AND HISPANIC ORIGIN	Civilian noninstitutional population	CIVILIAN LABOR FORCE						NOT IN LABOR FORCE	
		Total	Percent of population	Employed	Employment/ population ratio [1]	Unemployed			
						Number	Percent of labor force	Number	Percent of population
Total: [2]									
1960	117,245	69,628	59.4	65,778	56.1	3,852	5.5	47,617	40.6
1970	137,085	82,771	60.4	78,678	57.4	4,093	4.9	54,315	39.6
1980	167,745	106,940	63.8	99,303	59.2	7,637	7.1	60,806	36.2
1985	178,206	115,461	64.8	107,150	60.1	8,312	7.2	62,744	35.2
1987	182,753	119,865	65.6	112,440	61.5	7,425	6.2	62,888	34.4
1988	184,613	121,669	65.9	114,968	62.3	6,701	5.5	62,944	34.1
1989	186,393	123,869	66.5	117,342	63.0	6,528	5.3	62,523	33.5
1990	188,049	124,787	66.4	117,914	62.7	6,874	5.5	63,262	33.6
1991	189,765	125,303	66.0	116,877	61.6	8,426	6.7	64,462	34.0
Male:									
1960	55,662	46,388	83.3	43,904	78.9	2,486	5.4	9,274	16.7
1970	64,304	51,228	79.7	48,990	76.2	2,238	4.4	13,076	20.3
1980	79,398	61,453	77.4	57,186	72.0	4,267	6.9	17,945	22.6
1985	84,469	64,411	76.3	59,891	70.9	4,521	7.0	20,058	23.7
1987	86,899	66,207	76.2	62,107	71.5	4,101	6.2	20,692	23.8
1988	87,857	66,927	76.2	63,273	72.0	3,655	5.5	20,930	23.8
1989	88,762	67,840	76.4	64,315	72.5	3,525	5.2	20,923	23.6
1990	89,650	68,234	76.1	64,435	71.9	3,799	5.6	21,417	23.9
1991	90,552	68,411	75.5	63,593	70.2	4,817	7.0	22,141	24.5
Female:									
1960	61,582	23,240	37.7	21,874	35.5	1,366	5.9	38,343	62.3
1970	72,782	31,543	43.3	29,688	40.8	1,855	5.9	41,239	56.7
1980	88,348	45,487	51.5	42,117	47.7	3,370	7.4	42,861	48.5
1985	93,736	51,050	54.5	47,259	50.4	3,791	7.4	42,686	45.5
1987	95,853	53,658	56.0	50,334	52.5	3,324	6.2	42,195	44.0
1988	96,756	54,742	56.6	51,696	53.4	3,046	5.6	42,014	43.4
1989	97,630	56,030	57.4	53,027	54.3	3,003	5.4	41,601	42.6
1990	98,399	56,554	57.5	53,479	54.3	3,075	5.4	41,845	42.5
1991	99,214	56,893	57.3	53,284	53.7	3,609	6.3	42,321	42.7
White:									
1960	105,282	61,915	58.8	58,850	55.9	3,065	5.0	43,367	41.2
1970	122,174	73,556	60.2	70,217	57.5	3,339	4.5	48,618	39.8
1980	146,122	93,600	64.1	87,715	60.0	5,884	6.3	52,523	35.9
1985	153,679	99,926	65.0	93,736	61.0	6,191	6.2	53,753	35.0
1987	156,958	103,290	65.8	97,789	62.3	5,501	5.3	53,669	34.2
1988	158,194	104,756	66.2	99,812	63.1	4,944	4.7	53,439	33.8
1989	159,338	106,355	66.7	101,584	63.8	4,770	4.5	52,983	33.3
1990	160,415	107,177	66.8	102,087	63.6	5,091	4.7	53,237	33.2
1991	161,511	107,486	66.6	101,039	62.6	6,447	6.0	54,025	33.4
Black:									
1973	14,917	8,976	60.2	8,128	54.5	846	9.4	5,941	39.8
1980	17,824	10,865	61.0	9,313	52.2	1,553	14.3	6,959	39.0
1985	19,664	12,364	62.9	10,501	53.4	1,864	15.1	7,299	37.1
1987	20,352	12,993	63.8	11,309	55.6	1,684	13.0	7,359	36.2
1988	20,692	13,205	63.8	11,658	56.3	1,547	11.7	7,487	36.2
1989	21,021	13,497	64.2	11,953	56.9	1,544	11.4	7,524	35.8
1990	21,300	13,493	63.3	11,966	56.2	1,527	11.3	7,808	36.7
1991	21,615	13,542	62.6	11,863	54.9	1,679	12.4	8,074	37.4
Hispanic: [3]									
1980	9,598	6,146	64.0	5,527	57.6	620	10.1	3,451	36.0
1985	11,915	7,698	64.6	6,888	57.8	811	10.5	4,217	35.4
1986	12,344	8,076	65.4	7,219	58.5	857	10.6	4,268	34.6
1988	13,325	8,982	67.4	8,250	61.9	732	8.2	4,342	32.6
1989	13,791	9,323	67.6	8,573	62.2	750	8.0	4,468	32.4
1990	14,297	9,576	67.0	8,808	61.6	769	8.0	4,721	33.0
1991	14,770	9,762	66.1	8,799	59.6	963	9.9	5,008	33.9
Mexican:									
1986	7,377	4,941	67.0	4,387	59.5	555	11.2	2,436	33.0
1989	8,295	5,740	69.2	5,247	63.3	493	8.6	2,555	30.8
1990	8,742	5,970	68.3	5,478	62.7	492	8.2	2,773	31.7
1991	8,947	5,984	66.9	5,363	59.9	621	10 4	2,963	33.1
Puerto Rican:									
1986	1,494	804	53.8	691	46.3	113	14.0	690	46.2
1989	1,545	889	57.5	803	52.0	86	9.6	656	42.5
1990	1,546	859	55.6	780	50.5	79	9.1	687	44.4
1991	1,629	930	57.1	822	50.5	108	11.6	699	42.9
Cuban:									
1986	842	570	67.7	533	63.3	36	6.4	272	32.3
1989	886	562	63.5	531	59.9	31	5.6	324	36.6
1990	847	552	65.1	512	60.4	40	7.2	295	34.8
1991	849	543	63.9	499	58.8	44	8.1	306	36.0

[1] Civilian employed as a percent of the civilian noninstitutional population. [2] Includes other races, not shown separately. [3] Persons of Hispanic origin may be of any race. Includes persons of other Hispanic origin, not shown separately.

Source: U.S. Bureau of Labor Statistics, Bulletin 2307; and *Employment and Earnings*, monthly, January issues.

No. 613. Characteristics of the Civilian Labor Force, by State: 1991

[**In thousands, except ratio and rate.** For civilian noninstitutional population, 16 years old and over. Annual averages of monthly figures. Because of separate processing and weighting procedures, the totals for the United States may differ from results obtained by aggregating totals for regions and States]

REGION, DIVISION AND STATE	TOTAL		EMPLOYED		Employed/popula-tion ratio [1]	UNEMPLOYED					PARTICIPA-TION RATE [3]	
						Total		Rate [2]				
	Num-ber	Fe-male	Total	Fe-male		Num-ber	Fe-male	Total	Male	Fe-male	Male	Female
United States...	125,303	56,893	116,877	53,284	61.6	8,426	3,609	6.7	7.0	6.3	75.5	57.3
Northeast.........	**25,566**	**11,635**	**23,716**	**10,891**	**60.2**	**1,850**	**744**	**7.2**	**7.9**	**6.4**	**74.8**	**56.0**
New England.....	**7,033**	**3,304**	**6,474**	**3,074**	**63.7**	**560**	**230**	**8.0**	**8.8**	**7.0**	**77.8**	**61.5**
Maine..........	647	302	598	283	62.8	49	19	7.5	8.6	6.3	75.5	61.0
New Hampshire ...	634	288	589	269	68.0	46	19	7.2	7.8	6.5	81.6	65.3
Vermont	311	145	291	138	65.5	20	7	6.4	7.7	4.7	76.3	63.8
Massachusetts....	3,127	1,478	2,847	1,364	61.6	280	114	9.0	10.1	7.7	76.5	59.9
Rhode Island.....	513	241	469	223	60.8	44	18	8.5	9.3	7.6	75.5	58.5
Connecticut......	1,801	850	1,679	798	66.9	121	53	6.7	7.2	6.2	80.7	63.9
Middle Atlantic.....	**18,533**	**8,331**	**17,243**	**7,817**	**59.0**	**1,290**	**514**	**7.0**	**7.6**	**6.2**	**73.8**	**54.1**
New York	8,583	3,839	7,967	3,594	57.7	616	245	7.2	7.8	6.4	72.9	52.6
New Jersey......	4,018	1,806	3,752	1,701	62.3	266	105	6.6	7.3	5.8	76.9	57.4
Pennsylvania.....	5,933	2,685	5,524	2,521	58.7	409	164	6.9	7.5	6.1	73.0	54.1
Midwest...........	**30,869**	**14,146**	**28,892**	**13,321**	**63.2**	**1,977**	**825**	**6.4**	**6.9**	**5.8**	**76.8**	**59.1**
East North Central..	**21,402**	**9,734**	**19,902**	**9,110**	**61.8**	**1,500**	**623**	**7.0**	**7.5**	**6.4**	**76.0**	**57.7**
Ohio...........	5,440	2,474	5,094	2,330	61.3	346	144	6.4	6.8	5.8	75.0	56.8
Indiana........	2,798	1,320	2,632	1,247	61.7	166	73	5.9	6.3	5.5	75.2	57.4
Illinois.........	6,029	2,723	5,598	2,546	62.8	431	177	7.1	7.7	6.5	77.9	58.3
Michigan.......	4,543	2,023	4,125	1,851	58.8	418	173	9.2	9.7	8.5	74.4	55.7
Wisconsin......	2,592	1,194	2,453	1,136	66.2	140	58	5.4	5.9	4.8	77.1	63.1
West North Central .	**9,467**	**4,412**	**8,990**	**4,211**	**66.7**	**477**	**201**	**5.0**	**5.4**	**4.6**	**78.8**	**62.5**
Minnesota......	2,431	1,157	2,307	1,110	69.5	124	47	5.1	6.1	4.0	80.5	66.6
Iowa..........	1,516	704	1,447	676	66.9	70	29	4.6	5.0	4.1	78.8	62.2
Missouri	2,689	1,254	2,511	1,176	63.8	177	78	6.6	6.9	6.2	77.5	60.2
North Dakota.....	317	146	304	140	65.0	13	6	4.1	4.3	3.8	76.3	59.9
South Dakota.....	361	167	349	161	67.2	12	6	3.4	3.3	3.6	76.8	62.7
Nebraska	857	395	834	385	69.4	23	10	2.7	2.9	2.6	79.8	63.4
Kansas.........	1,295	588	1,238	563	66.3	57	26	4.4	4.4	4.4	79.2	60.4
South............	**42,434**	**19,488**	**39,618**	**18,181**	**60.9**	**2,816**	**1,306**	**6.6**	**6.6**	**6.7**	**74.6**	**56.8**
South Atlantic.....	**22,075**	**10,307**	**20,669**	**9,647**	**61.6**	**1,406**	**660**	**6.4**	**6.3**	**6.4**	**74.3**	**58.2**
Delaware.......	364	168	342	159	64.8	23	8	6.2	7.2	5.0	78.3	60.7
Maryland.......	2,554	1,185	2,403	1,115	66.0	151	70	5.9	5.9	5.9	78.0	62.8
District of Columbia.	282	141	260	130	60.6	22	11	7.7	7.8	7.6	70.3	61.6
Virginia........	3,306	1,567	3,113	1,473	66.7	193	94	5.8	5.7	6.0	78.3	64.0
West Virginia	783	326	701	296	49.5	82	30	10.5	11.5	9.1	67.6	44.2
North Carolina	3,445	1,602	3,246	1,510	64.1	198	92	5.8	5.8	5.7	76.3	60.5
South Carolina ...	1,744	821	1,635	772	62.1	108	49	6.2	6.4	6.0	73.7	59.5
Georgia.........	3,166	1,500	3,008	1,421	62.3	158	79	5.0	4.8	5.2	75.2	57.4
Florida.........	6,431	2,999	5,961	2,771	57.6	471	228	7.3	7.1	7.6	70.6	54.6
East South Central..	**7,236**	**3,278**	**6,710**	**3,036**	**57.6**	**526**	**243**	**7.3**	**7.2**	**7.4**	**72.4**	**53.1**
Kentucky.......	1,744	787	1,615	729	57.5	128	57	7.4	7.4	7.3	72.2	52.9
Tennessee	2,416	1,080	2,256	1,009	59.1	160	71	6.6	6.7	6.6	73.8	53.9
Alabama.......	1,894	854	1,758	789	56.6	135	65	7.2	6.8	7.6	71.4	51.8
Mississippi.......	1,183	557	1,081	508	56.6	102	50	8.6	8.3	8.9	71.1	54.1
West South Central .	**13,123**	**5,902**	**12,239**	**5,498**	**61.6**	**884**	**404**	**6.7**	**6.7**	**6.8**	**76.3**	**56.7**
Arkansas.......	1,118	510	1,036	472	57.4	82	38	7.3	7.2	7.5	71.3	53.6
Louisiana	1,933	888	1,796	819	57.3	137	69	7.1	6.6	7.8	72.1	52.7
Oklahoma.......	1,517	694	1,416	643	59.1	101	42	6.7	7.1	6.2	73.5	54.3
Texas..........	8,555	3,818	7,991	3,563	63.8	564	255	6.6	6.5	6.7	78.6	58.7
West.............	**26,433**	**11,624**	**24,650**	**10,890**	**62.2**	**1,783**	**734**	**6.7**	**7.1**	**6.3**	**76.4**	**57.5**
Mountain.........	**6,775**	**3,079**	**6,396**	**2,917**	**63.6**	**379**	**161**	**5.6**	**5.9**	**5.2**	**76.0**	**59.3**
Montana.......	403	186	375	174	62.7	28	12	6.9	7.4	6.4	74.3	60.8
Idaho..........	504	218	473	205	63.5	31	13	6.1	6.3	5.8	77.7	57.8
Wyoming........	240	105	228	100	66.7	12	5	5.1	5.2	5.0	78.7	61.8
Colorado........	1,755	820	1,667	780	67.0	87	39	5.0	5.1	4.8	78.2	63.3
New Mexico.....	715	319	665	298	59.4	49	21	6.9	7.2	6.5	73.5	54.8
Arizona.........	1,704	786	1,608	747	59.4	96	40	5.7	6.2	5.0	71.1	55.6
Utah...........	805	358	765	340	67.3	39	18	4.9	4.8	5.0	80.9	61.2
Nevada.........	649	287	614	273	66.5	36	14	5.5	6.1	4.7	79.3	61.6
Pacific..........	**19,658**	**8,545**	**18,254**	**7,973**	**61.8**	**1,404**	**573**	**7.1**	**7.5**	**6.7**	**76.6**	**56.8**
Washington......	2,498	1,131	2,340	1,071	63.1	157	61	6.3	7.1	5.4	75.8	59.3
Oregon.........	1,508	660	1,418	617	63.1	90	43	6.0	5.6	6.5	76.8	58.4
California........	14,833	6,369	13,714	5,916	61.2	1,119	453	7.5	7.9	7.1	76.6	56.0
Alaska.........	258	120	236	111	64.8	22	8	8.5	9.9	6.9	80.5	64.9
Hawaii	561	265	546	258	66.8	15	7	2.8	2.7	2.8	76.4	61.7

[1] Civilian employment as a percent of civilian noninstitutional population.   [2] Percent unemployed of the civilian labor force.
[3] Percent of civilian noninstitutional population of each specified group in the civilian labor force.

Source: U.S. Bureau of Labor Statistics, *Geographic Profile of Employment and Unemployment, 1991.*

No. 614. Civilian Labor Force Status, by Selected Metropolitan Area: 1990

[In thousands, except rate. For the civilian noninstitutional population 16 years old and over. Annual averages of monthly figures. Except as noted, data are derived from the Local Area Unemployment Statistics Program. For composition of metropolitan areas, see Appendix II]

METROPOLITAN AREAS RANKED BY LABOR FORCE SIZE, 1990	Em-ployed	UNEMPLOYED		METROPOLITAN AREAS RANKED BY LABOR FORCE SIZE, 1990	Em-ployed	UNEMPLOYED	
		Total	Rate [1]			Total	Rate [1]
U.S. total	117,914	6,874	5.5	San Francisco, CA PMSA.	844.3	28.9	3.3
Los Angeles-Long Beach, CA PMSA [2]	4,173.0	255.0	5.8	Kansas City, MO-Kansas City, KS, MSA	810.2	42.3	5.0
New York, NY PMSA.	3,759.9	250.6	6.2	San Jose, CA PMSA	780.7	32.9	4.0
Chicago, IL MSA.	3,099.1	195.5	5.9	Cincinnati, OH-KY-IN PMSA	754.1	32.8	4.2
Philadelphia, PA-NJ PMSA	2,332.8	113.7	4.6	Milwaukee, WI PMSA	730.2	28.9	3.8
Washington, DC-MD-VA MSA . . .	2,134.4	75.4	3.4	Columbus, OH MSA	706.9	32.6	4.4
Detroit, MI PMSA.	1,990.0	160.7	7.5	Sacramento, CA MSA	703.6	35.5	4.8
Houston, TX PMSA.	1,634.2	89.2	5.2	Fort Worth-Arlington, TX PMSA. .	695.5	38.4	5.2
Boston, MA PMSA	1,481.6	79.2	5.1	Bergen-Passaic, NJ PMSA	674.6	32.1	4.5
Atlanta, GA MSA	1,444.7	77.2	5.1	Portland, OR PMSA	655.2	28.7	4.2
Dallas, TX PMSA	1,359.3	73.6	5.1	Indianapolis, IN MSA.	642.7	28.0	4.2
Minneapolis-St. Paul, MN-WI MSA	1,350.2	60.0	4.3	Fort Lauderdale-Hollywood-Pompano Beach, FL PMSA.	624.0	36.2	5.5
Nassau-Suffolk, NY PMSA	1,349.2	53.6	3.8	Charlotte-Gastonia-Rock Hill, NC-SC MSA	624.1	22.6	3.5
Anaheim-Santa Ana, CA PMSA. .	1,336.4	46.4	3.4	Orlando, FL MSA	606.5	34.0	5.3
St. Louis, MO-IL MSA [3]	1,197.0	75.2	5.9	Norfolk-Virginia Beach-Newport News, VA MSA	594.4	29.5	4.7
Baltimore, MD MSA.	1,152.9	61.6	5.1	San Antonio, TX MSA	563.9	41.8	6.9
San Diego, CA MSA	1,121.6	52.8	4.5	Middlesex-Somerset-Hunterdon, NJ PMSA	568.3	22.0	3.7
Seattle, WA PMSA	1,086.6	39.2	3.5	New Orleans, LA MSA.	544.4	33.1	5.7
Oakland, CA PMSA.	1,046.4	45.9	4.2	Nashville, TN MSA	511.6	21.1	4.0
Phoenix, AZ MSA	1,028.1	46.4	4.3	Greensboro-Winston-Salem-High Point, NC MSA	501.6	19.4	3.7
Riverside-San Bernardino, CA PMSA.	1,001.0	70.6	6.6	Louisville, KY-IN MSA	494.1	26.6	5.1
Tampa-St. Petersburg-Clearwater, FL MSA	965.8	52.1	5.1	Salt Lake City-Ogden, UT MSA . .	490.1	21.0	4.1
Pittsburgh, PA PMSA.	944.0	47.8	4.8	Rochester, NY MSA	491.1	18.9	3.7
Cleveland, OH PMSA	909.1	45.7	4.8	Oklahoma City, OK MSA	473.2	26.8	5.4
Newark, NJ PMSA	901.4	51.1	5.4				
Miami-Hialeah, FL PMSA	888.5	63.8	6.7				
Denver, CO PMSA	853.2	41.1	4.6				

[1] Percent unemployed of the civilian labor force.   [2] Derived from the Current Population Survey.   [3] Excludes part of Sullivan City in Crawford County, Missouri.

Source: U.S. Bureau of Labor Statistics, *Employment and Earnings,* May 1991.

No. 615. Civilian Labor Force—Percent Distribution, by Sex and Age: 1960 to 1991

[For civilian noninstitutional population 16 years old and over. Annual averages of monthly figures. Based on Current Population Survey; see text, section 1 and Appendix III. See *Historical Statistics, Colonial Times to 1970,* series D 29-41, for similar but not exactly comparable data]

YEAR AND SEX	Civilian labor force (1,000)	PERCENT DISTRIBUTION						
		16 to 19 years	20 to 24 years	25 to 34 years	35 to 44 years	45 to 54 years	55 to 64 years	65 yrs. and over
Total: 1960	69,628	7.0	9.6	20.7	23.4	21.3	13.5	4.6
1970	82,771	8.8	12.8	20.6	19.9	20.5	13.6	3.9
1975	93,775	9.5	14.7	24.4	18.0	18.2	12.1	3.2
1980	106,940	8.8	14.9	27.3	19.1	15.8	11.2	2.9
1985	115,461	6.8	13.6	29.1	22.6	15.0	10.4	2.5
1987	119,865	6.7	12.5	29.4	23.7	15.2	9.9	2.6
1988	121,669	6.6	11.9	29.2	24.2	15.7	9.7	2.7
1989	123,869	6.4	11.4	29.0	24.7	16.1	9.6	2.8
1990	124,787	5.9	11.1	28.7	25.5	16.4	9.5	2.8
1991	125,303	5.5	10.9	28.2	26.3	16.9	9.4	2.8
Male: 1960	46,388	6.0	8.9	22.1	23.6	20.6	13.8	4.9
1970	51,228	7.8	11.2	22.1	20.4	20.3	13.9	4.2
1975	56,299	8.5	13.4	25.2	18.5	18.5	12.5	3.4
1980	61,453	8.1	14.0	27.6	19.3	16.1	11.8	3.1
1985	64,411	6.4	12.9	29.2	22.5	15.3	11.0	2.7
1987	66,207	6.2	11.8	29.7	23.5	15.4	10.5	2.9
1988	66,927	6.2	11.3	29.5	24.0	15.8	10.2	2.9
1989	67,840	6.1	11.0	29.3	24.5	16.1	10.0	3.0
1990	68,234	5.7	10.7	29.0	25.3	16.4	9.9	3.0
1991	68,411	5.2	10.6	28.6	26.1	16.8	9.8	2.9
Female: 1960	23,240	8.8	11.1	17.8	22.8	22.7	12.8	3.9
1970	31,543	10.3	15.5	18.1	18.9	20.7	13.2	3.3
1975	37,475	10.8	16.5	23.1	17.4	17.8	11.5	2.8
1980	45,487	9.6	16.1	26.9	19.0	15.4	10.4	2.6
1985	51,050	7.4	14.6	28.9	22.7	14.6	9.7	2.3
1987	53,658	7.2	13.3	29.0	24.0	15.0	9.2	2.3
1988	54,742	7.1	12.6	28.8	24.4	15.6	9.1	2.4
1989	56,030	6.8	12.0	28.5	25.0	16.1	9.1	2.6
1990	56,554	6.3	11.6	28.3	25.8	16.5	9.0	2.7
1991	56,893	5.9	11.3	27.7	26.6	17.0	8.9	2.7

Source: U.S. Bureau of Labor Statistics, Bulletin 2307, and *Employment and Earnings,* monthly, January issues.

No. 616. Civilian Labor Force—Years of School Completed, by Sex and Race: 1991

[In thousands. Annual averages of monthly figures. For civilian noninstitutional population 25 years and over. Based on Current Population Survey; see text, section 1 and Appendix III]

EMPLOYMENT STATUS, SEX, AND RACE	Population, 25 years and over (1,000)	ELEMENTARY SCHOOL		HIGH SCHOOL		COLLEGE		
		Less than 5 years	5-8 years	1-3 years	4 years	1-3 years	4 years	5 years or more
Total [1]	**158,533**	**3,551**	**12,937**	**17,210**	**61,077**	**29,393**	**20,216**	**14,149**
Civilian labor force	104,676	1,070	4,272	8,518	40,833	22,089	16,144	11,749
Employed	99,016	963	3,841	7,601	38,458	21,039	15,644	11,471
Unemployed.	5,660	107	431	918	2,375	1,050	501	278
Not in labor force	53,857	2,480	8,665	8,692	20,244	7,304	4,071	2,400
Male, total.	75,093	1,781	6,160	7,897	26,870	13,762	10,374	8,249
Civilian labor force	57,553	733	2,807	5,044	21,168	11,575	9,059	7,167
Employed	54,293	665	2,521	4,490	19,831	11,007	8,779	7,000
Unemployed.	3,260	68	286	554	1,337	568	279	167
Not in labor force	17,541	1,048	3,353	2,853	5,702	2,187	1,316	1,082
Female, total	83,439	1,770	6,777	9,314	34,207	15,631	9,841	5,900
Civilian labor force	47,123	337	1,465	3,474	19,665	10,514	7,086	4,581
Employed	44,723	299	1,319	3,111	18,628	10,032	6,864	4,470
Unemployed.	2,400	39	146	363	1,038	482	221	111
Not in labor force	36,316	1,432	5,312	5,839	14,542	5,117	2,756	1,318
White, total	136,153	2,560	10,726	13,846	52,991	25,542	17,802	12,686
Civilian labor force	89,945	884	3,551	6,791	35,058	18,992	14,144	10,525
Employed	85,538	794	3,197	6,137	33,208	18,189	13,729	10,283
Unemployed.	4,407	89	354	654	1,851	802	415	242
Not in labor force	46,208	1,676	7,175	7,055	17,933	6,550	3,659	2,161
Black, total	17,049	691	1,753	2,961	6,549	3,027	1,333	736
Civilian labor force	11,125	109	534	1,502	4,737	2,473	1,155	615
Employed	10,078	99	475	1,265	4,277	2,262	1,105	596
Unemployed.	1,047	11	60	237	459	212	50	19
Not in labor force	5,924	582	1,219	1,459	1,812	553	178	121
Hispanic [2], total	11,300	1,368	2,458	1,665	3,254	1,475	670	410
Civilian labor force	7,634	640	1,427	1,035	2,432	1,207	547	346
Employed	6,992	567	1,257	906	2,259	1,146	522	335
Unemployed.	642	73	171	129	172	62	24	12
Not in labor force	3,666	728	1,030	630	822	268	123	63

[1] Includes other races, not shown separately. [2] Persons of Hispanic origin may be of any race.

Source: U.S. Bureau of Labor Statistics, unpublished data.

No. 617. School Enrollment and Labor Force Status of Civilians 16 to 24 Years Old, by Selected Characteristics: 1980 and 1990

[In thousands, except percent. As of October. Civilian noninstitutional population. Based on Current Population Survey; see text, section 1 and Appendix III]

CHARACTERISITC	POPULATION		CIVILIAN LABOR FORCE			EMPLOYED		UNEMPLOYED		
	1980	1990	1980, total	1990		1980	1990	1980, total	1990	
				Total	Percent [1]				Total	Rate [2]
Total, 16 to 24 years [3]	**37,103**	**31,421**	**24,918**	**20,679**	**65.8**	**21,454**	**18,317**	**3,464**	**2,363**	**11.4**
Enrolled in school [3]	15,713	15,210	7,454	7,301	48.0	6,433	6,527	1,021	774	10.6
16 to 19 years	11,126	10,118	4,836	4,244	42.0	4,029	3,645	807	599	14.1
20 to 24 years	4,587	5,092	2,618	3,057	60.0	2,404	2,882	214	174	5.7
Male.	7,997	7,704	3,825	3,635	47.2	3,259	3,215	566	420	11.6
Female	7,716	7,507	3,629	3,666	48.8	3,174	3,312	455	353	9.6
College level	7,664	8,139	3,996	4,542	55.8	3,632	4,231	364	311	6.9
Full-time	6,396	6,810	2,854	3,376	49.6	2,554	3,117	300	259	7.7
White	13,242	12,308	6,687	6,294	51.1	5,889	5,705	798	588	9.4
Below college	6,566	5,535	3,095	2,374	42.9	2,579	2,021	516	354	14.9
College level	6,678	6,772	3,592	3,919	57.9	3,310	3,685	282	234	6.0
Black	2,028	2,129	595	718	33.7	406	576	189	142	19.7
Below college	1,282	1,207	294	306	25.4	174	212	120	94	30.8
College level	747	922	300	411	44.6	230	364	70	47	11.5
Not enrolled [3]	21,390	16,210	17,464	13,379	82.5	15,021	11,789	2,443	1,589	11.9
White	18,103	13,317	15,121	11,276	84.7	13,318	10,193	1,803	1,083	9.6
Black	2,864	2,441	2,055	1,752	71.8	1,451	1,298	604	454	25.9

[1] Percent of civilian noninstitutional population. [2] Percent of civilian labor force in each category. [3] Includes other races, not shown separately.

Source: U.S. Bureau of Labor Statistics, Bulletin 2307; News, USDL 91-264, June 6, 1991; and unpublished data.

No. 618. Labor Force Participation Rates, by Marital Status, Sex, and Age: 1960 to 1991

[Annual averages of monthly figures. See table 613 for definition of participation rate. Based on Current Population Survey; see text, section 1 and Appendix III]

MARITAL STATUS AND YEAR	MALE PARTICIPATION RATE							FEMALE PARTICIPATION RATE						
	Total	16-19 years	20-24 years	25-34 years	35-44 years	45-64 years	65 and over	Total	16-19 years	20-24 years	25-34 years	35-44 years	45-64 years	65 and over
Single:														
1960...	69.8	42.6	80.3	91.5	88.6	80.1	31.2	58.6	30.2	77.2	83.4	82.9	79.8	24.3
1970...	65.5	54.6	73.8	87.9	86.2	75.7	25.2	56.8	44.7	73.0	81.4	78.6	73.0	19.7
1975...	68.7	57.9	77.9	86.7	83.2	69.9	21.0	59.8	49.6	72.5	80.8	78.6	68.3	15.8
1980...	72.6	59.9	81.3	89.2	82.2	66.9	16.8	64.4	53.6	75.2	83.3	76.9	65.6	13.9
1985...	73.8	56.3	81.5	89.4	84.6	65.5	15.6	66.6	52.3	76.3	82.4	80.8	67.9	9.8
1986...	74.2	55.8	82.6	89.4	85.3	63.9	15.5	67.2	53.1	76.9	82.3	80.9	65.7	9.9
1987...	74.2	55.6	82.1	89.7	84.9	63.9	17.1	67.4	53.5	76.9	82.6	81.3	62.8	9.6
1988...	74.7	56.5	82.1	89.6	84.5	62.7	15.8	67.7	53.7	76.5	82.8	81.9	65.7	10.4
1989...	75.5	57.4	82.5	90.0	84.6	64.6	18.2	68.0	54.1	76.4	82.2	81.6	66.3	11.4
1990...	74.9	55.1	81.5	89.9	84.6	67.1	15.7	66.9	51.8	74.7	81.2	81.0	66.1	12.2
1991...	74.2	52.6	80.6	89.6	84.8	66.8	14.0	66.5	50.3	73.5	80.3	81.2	68.4	12.7
Married: [1]														
1960...	89.2	91.5	97.1	98.8	98.6	93.7	36.6	31.9	27.2	31.7	28.8	37.2	36.0	6.7
1970...	86.1	92.3	94.7	98.0	98.1	91.2	29.9	40.5	37.8	47.9	38.8	46.8	44.0	7.3
1975...	83.0	92.9	95.3	97.4	97.1	86.8	23.3	44.3	46.2	57.0	48.4	52.0	43.8	7.0
1980...	80.9	91.3	96.9	97.5	97.2	84.3	20.5	49.8	49.3	61.4	58.8	61.8	46.9	7.3
1985...	78.7	91.0	95.6	97.4	96.8	81.7	16.8	53.8	49.6	65.7	65.8	68.1	49.4	6.6
1986...	78.6	90.2	96.1	97.2	96.6	81.6	17.0	54.9	50.3	65.5	66.8	69.5	50.6	7.2
1987...	78.7	88.5	96.1	97.3	96.6	81.8	17.5	55.9	51.7	67.1	67.7	71.3	51.8	7.2
1988...	78.6	91.1	95.9	97.1	96.7	82.1	17.8	56.7	51.8	66.8	68.1	72.3	53.5	7.6
1989...	78.5	93.7	95.9	97.2	96.8	82.4	17.8	57.8	51.9	65.7	69.0	73.5	55.5	8.1
1990...	78.2	92.3	95.6	96.9	96.8	82.5	17.6	58.4	50.0	66.5	69.8	74.0	56.5	8.5
1991...	77.8	93.2	95.4	96.6	96.6	82.3	16.8	58.5	48.7	65.0	70.1	74.3	57.1	8.3
Other: [2]														
1960...	63.1	(B)	96.9	95.2	94.4	83.2	22.7	41.6	43.5	58.0	63.1	70.0	60.0	11.4
1970...	60.7	(B)	90.4	93.7	91.1	78.5	19.3	40.3	48.6	60.3	64.6	68.8	61.9	10.0
1975...	63.4	(B)	88.8	92.4	89.4	73.4	15.4	40.1	47.6	65.3	68.6	69.2	59.0	8.3
1980...	67.5	(B)	92.6	94.1	91.9	73.3	13.7	43.6	50.0	68.4	76.5	77.1	60.2	8.2
1985...	68.7	(B)	95.1	93.7	91.8	72.8	11.4	45.1	51.9	66.2	76.9	81.6	61.0	7.5
1986...	68.2	(B)	94.3	93.9	91.3	72.4	11.7	45.6	52.8	69.7	77.1	82.6	61.9	7.3
1987...	67.3	(B)	92.2	93.9	90.9	72.5	11.6	45.7	46.9	67.4	77.6	82.7	62.7	7.3
1988...	67.2	(B)	92.5	93.4	90.8	72.5	11.7	46.2	54.2	66.2	77.2	82.1	63.6	7.9
1989...	67.9	(B)	91.1	93.6	90.9	74.2	11.7	47.0	48.2	65.8	78.3	82.2	64.7	8.3
1990...	68.3	(B)	93.1	93.0	90.8	74.6	12.0	47.2	54.4	65.6	77.3	82.3	65.0	8.5
1991...	67.7	(B)	93.9	92.1	90.5	73.5	12.3	46.8	45.8	63.3	74.8	82.1	65.2	8.4

B For 1960, percentage not shown where base is less than 50,000; beginning 1970, 35,000.   [1] Spouse present.
[2] Widowed, divorced, and married (spouse absent).
Source: U.S. Bureau of Labor Statistics, Bulletins 2217 and 2340; and unpublished data.

No. 619. Marital Status of Women in the Civilian Labor Force: 1960 to 1991

[Annual averages of monthly figures. For civilian noninstitutional population 16 years old and over. Based on Current Population Survey; see text, section 1 and Appendix III. See also *Historical Statistics, Colonial Times to 1970*, series D 49-62]

YEAR	FEMALE LABOR FORCE (1,000)				PERCENT DISTRIBUTION, FEMALE LABOR FORCE			FEMALE LABOR FORCE AS PERCENT OF FEMALE POPULATION			
	Total	Single	Married [1]	Other [2]	Single	Married [1]	Other [2]	Total	Single	Married [1]	Other [2]
1960	23,240	5,410	12,893	4,937	23.3	55.5	21.2	37.7	58.6	31.9	41.6
1965	26,200	5,976	14,829	5,396	22.8	56.6	20.6	39.3	54.5	34.9	40.7
1970	31,543	7,265	18,475	5,804	23.0	58.6	18.4	43.3	56.8	40.5	40.3
1974	36,211	8,671	20,868	6,672	23.9	57.6	18.4	45.7	59.5	43.3	40.2
1975	37,475	9,125	21,484	6,866	24.3	57.3	18.3	46.3	59.8	44.3	40.1
1976	38,983	9,689	22,139	7,156	24.9	56.8	18.4	47.3	61.0	45.3	40.5
1977	40,613	10,311	22,776	7,526	25.4	56.1	18.5	48.4	62.1	46.4	41.5
1978	42,631	11,067	23,539	8,025	26.0	55.2	18.8	50.0	63.7	47.8	42.8
1979	44,235	11,597	24,378	8,260	26.2	55.1	18.7	50.9	64.6	49.0	43.1
1980	45,487	11,865	24,980	8,643	26.1	54.9	19.0	51.5	64.4	49.9	43.6
1981	46,696	12,124	25,428	9,144	26.0	54.5	19.6	52.1	64.5	50.5	44.6
1982	47,755	12,460	25,971	9,324	26.1	54.4	19.5	52.6	65.1	51.1	44.8
1983	48,503	12,650	26,408	9,376	26.1	54.6	19.3	52.9	65.0	51.8	44.4
1984	49,709	12,867	27,199	9,644	25.9	54.7	19.4	53.6	65.6	52.8	44.7
1985	51,050	13,163	27,894	9,993	25.8	54.6	19.6	54.5	66.6	53.8	45.1
1986	52,413	13,512	28,623	10,277	25.8	54.6	19.6	55.3	67.2	54.9	45.6
1987	53,658	13,885	29,381	10,393	25.9	54.8	19.4	56.0	67.4	55.9	45.7
1988	54,742	14,194	29,921	10,627	25.9	54.7	19.4	56.6	67.7	56.7	46.2
1989	56,030	14,377	30,548	11,104	25.7	54.5	19.8	57.4	68.0	57.8	47.0
1990	56,554	14,229	30,970	11,354	25.2	54.8	20.1	57.5	66.9	58.4	47.2
1991	56,893	14,295	31,175	11,423	25.1	54.8	20.1	57.3	66.5	58.5	46.8

[1] Husband present.   [2] Widowed, divorced, or separated.
Source: U.S. Bureau of Labor Statistics, Bulletin 2307; and unpublished data.

No. 620. Women in the Civilian Labor Force, by Marital Status and Presence and Age of Children: 1960 to 1991

[As of **March**. For 1960, civilian noninstitutional persons 14 years old and over, thereafter 16 years old and over. Based on Current Population Survey; see text, section 1 and Appendix III]

ITEM	TOTAL			WITH ANY CHILDREN								
				Total			Children 6 to 17 only			Children under 6		
	Single	Mar-ried [1]	Other [2]	Single	Mar-ried [1]	Other	Single	Mar-ried[1]	Other	Single	Mar-ried [1]	Other [2]
IN LABOR FORCE (mil.)												
1960	5.4	12.3	4.9	(NA)	6.6	1.5	(NA)	4.1	1.0	(NA)	2.5	0.4
1970	7.0	18.4	5.9	(NA)	10.2	1.9	(NA)	6.3	1.3	(NA)	3.9	0.6
1980	11.2	24.9	8.8	0.6	13.7	3.6	0.2	8.4	2.6	0.3	5.2	1.0
1985	12.9	27.7	10.3	1.1	14.9	4.0	0.4	8.5	2.9	0.7	6.4	1.1
1986	13.1	28.2	10.4	1.2	15.3	4.1	0.4	8.8	2.9	0.8	6.6	1.2
1987	13.5	29.2	10.4	1.4	16.0	4.1	0.5	9.0	2.9	0.9	7.0	1.1
1988	13.8	29.7	10.6	1.4	16.2	4.0	0.5	9.3	2.9	0.8	7.0	1.1
1989	14.0	30.5	10.7	1.5	16.4	4.0	0.6	9.4	2.8	1.0	7.0	1.1
1990	14.0	31.0	11.2	1.5	16.5	4.2	0.6	9.3	3.0	0.9	7.2	1.2
1991	14.1	31.1	11.1	1.7	16.6	4.1	0.6	9.1	3.0	1.1	7.4	1.2
PARTICIPATION RATE [3]												
1960	44.1	30.5	40.0	(NA)	27.6	56.0	(NA)	39.0	65.9	(NA)	18.6	40.5
1970	53.0	40.8	39.1	(NA)	39.7	60.7	(NA)	49.2	66.9	(NA)	30.3	52.2
1980	61.5	50.1	44.0	52.0	54.1	69.4	67.6	61.7	74.6	44.1	45.1	60.3
1985	65.2	54.2	45.6	51.6	60.8	71.9	64.1	67.8	77.8	46.5	53.4	59.7
1986	65.3	54.6	45.9	52.9	61.3	73.6	65.9	68.4	78.2	47.5	53.8	64.6
1987	65.1	55.8	45.7	54.1	63.8	73.4	64.1	70.6	78.6	49.9	56.8	62.7
1988	65.4	56.6	46.1	51.6	65.0	72.0	66.7	72.5	77.5	44.9	57.1	60.6
1989	66.0	57.6	46.0	54.7	65.6	72.0	69.0	73.4	78.2	48.9	57.4	60.1
1990	66.4	58.2	46.8	55.2	66.3	74.2	69.7	73.6	79.7	48.7	58.9	63.6
1991	65.1	58.5	46.2	53.6	66.8	72.7	64.8	73.6	79.5	48.8	59.9	59.8
EMPLOYMENT (mil.)												
1960	5.1	11.6	4.6	(NA)	6.2	1.3	(NA)	3.9	0.9	(NA)	2.3	0.4
1970	6.5	17.5	5.6	(NA)	9.6	1.8	(NA)	6.0	1.2	(NA)	3.6	0.6
1980	10.1	23.6	8.2	0.4	12.8	3.3	0.2	8.1	2.4	0.2	4.8	0.9
1985	11.6	26.1	9.4	0.9	13.9	3.5	0.3	8.1	2.6	0.5	5.9	0.9
1986	11.7	26.7	9.6	0.9	14.4	3.7	0.4	8.3	2.6	0.5	6.1	1.0
1987	12.1	27.8	9.6	1.0	15.1	3.7	0.4	8.6	2.7	0.6	6.5	1.0
1988	12.6	28.5	9.9	1.1	15.4	3.6	0.4	8.9	2.7	0.6	6.5	1.0
1989	12.8	29.4	10.1	1.2	15.8	3.6	0.5	9.1	2.6	0.7	6.7	1.0
1990	12.9	29.9	10.5	1.2	15.8	3.8	0.5	8.9	2.7	0.7	6.9	1.1
1991	12.9	29.7	10.4	1.4	15.7	3.7	0.5	8.8	2.7	0.8	6.9	1.0
UNEMPLOY-MENT RATE [4]												
1960	6.0	5.4	6.2	(NA)	6.0	8.4	(NA)	4.9	6.8	(NA)	7.8	12.5
1970	7.1	4.8	4.8	(NA)	6.0	7.2	(NA)	4.8	5.9	(NA)	7.9	9.8
1980	10.3	5.3	6.4	23.2	5.9	9.2	15.6	4.4	7.9	29.2	8.3	12.8
1985	10.2	5.7	8.5	23.8	6.6	12.1	15.4	5.5	10.6	28.5	8.0	16.1
1986	10.5	5.4	7.8	28.5	6.0	10.5	17.7	4.8	8.8	34.6	7.6	14.7
1987	10.2	4.5	7.5	25.6	5.4	10.1	17.6	4.9	8.4	29.9	5.9	14.5
1988	8.6	4.0	5.9	22.4	4.8	8.1	17.8	3.8	6.6	25.3	6.1	12.0
1989	8.1	3.4	5.7	21.3	3.8	8.4	14.3	3.7	7.2	25.3	4.1	11.3
1990	8.2	3.5	5.7	18.4	4.2	8.5	14.5	3.8	7.7	20.8	4.8	10.2
1991	8.8	4.6	6.8	17.9	5.3	9.1	10.7	4.2	7.7	22.0	6.7	12.7

NA Not available.   [1] Husband present.   [2] Widowed, divorced or separated.   [3] Percent of women in each specific category in the labor force.   [4] Unemployed as a percent of civilian labor force in specified group.

Source: U.S. Bureau of Labor Statistics, Bulletin 2307; and unpublished data.

No. 621. Labor Force Participation Rates for Wives, Husband Present, by Age of Own Youngest Child: 1975 to 1991

[As of **March**, except as indicated. For civilian noninstitutional population, 16 years old and over. For definition of participation rate, see table 620. Based on Current Population Survey; see text, section 1 and Appendix III]

PRESENCE AND AGE OF CHILD	TOTAL				WHITE				BLACK			
	1975	1985	1990	1991	1975	1985	1990	1991	1975	1985	1990	1991
Wives, total . . .	44.4	54.2	58.2	58.5	43.6	53.3	57.6	57.9	54.1	63.8	64.7	66.1
No children under 18. .	43.8	48.2	51.1	51.2	43.6	47.5	50.8	50.9	47.6	55.2	52.9	54.8
With children under 18.	44.9	60.8	66.3	66.8	43.6	59.9	65.6	66.2	58.4	71.7	75.6	76.5
Under 6, total	36.7	53.4	58.9	59.9	34.7	52.1	57.8	59.0	54.9	69.6	73.1	73.4
Under 3	32.7	50.5	55.5	56.8	30.7	49.4	54.9	55.9	50.1	66.2	67.5	70.3
1 year or under .	30.8	49.4	53.9	55.8	29.2	48.6	53.3	54.9	50.0	63.7	64.4	66.9
2 years	37.1	54.0	60.9	60.6	35.1	52.7	60.3	58.9	56.4	69.9	75.4	77.8
3 to 5 years	42.2	58.4	64.1	64.7	40.1	56.6	62.5	64.0	61.2	73.8	80.4	77.3
3 years	41.2	55.1	63.1	62.2	39.0	52.7	62.3	61.2	62.7	72.3	74.5	81.0
4 years	41.2	59.7	65.1	65.5	38.7	58.4	63.2	64.9	64.9	70.6	80.6	74.1
5 years	44.4	62.1	64.5	67.1	43.8	59.9	62.0	66.5	56.3	79.1	86.2	79.1
6 to 13 years	51.8	68.2	73.0	72.8	50.7	67.7	72.6	72.4	65.7	73.3	77.6	80.1
14 to 17 years. . . .	53.5	67.0	75.1	75.7	53.4	66.6	74.9	76.0	52.3	74.4	78.8	77.6

Source: U.S. Bureau of Labor Statistics, Bulletin 2340; and unpublished data.

No. 622. Civilian Labor Force—Employment Status, by Sex, Race, and Age: 1991

[For civilian noninstitutional population 16 years old and over. Annual averages of monthly figures. Based on Current Population Survey; see text, section 1 and Appendix III]

AGE AND RACE	CIVILIAN LABOR FORCE			MALE (1,000)			FEMALE (1,000)			PERCENT OF LABOR FORCE			
	Total (1,000)	Percent by age		Total	Em-ployed	Un-em-ployed	Total	Em-ployed	Un-em-ployed	Employed		Unemployed	
		Male	Fe-male							Male	Fe-male	Male	Fe-male
All workers [1].	125,303	100.0	100.0	68,411	63,593	4,817	56,893	53,284	3,609	93.0	93.7	7.0	6.3
16 to 19 years . . .	6,918	5.2	5.9	3,588	2,879	709	3,330	2,749	581	80.2	82.6	19.8	17.4
20 to 24 years . . .	13,710	10.6	11.3	7,270	6,421	849	6,440	5,812	628	88.3	90.2	11.7	9.8
25 to 34 years . . .	35,330	28.6	27.7	19,548	18,188	1,360	15,782	14,726	1,057	93.0	93.3	7.0	6.7
35 to 44 years . . .	32,975	26.1	26.6	17,854	16,883	971	15,121	14,402	718	94.6	95.3	5.4	4.7
45 to 54 years . . .	21,118	16.8	17.0	11,461	10,909	552	9,657	9,255	402	95.2	95.8	4.8	4.2
55 to 64 years . . .	11,752	9.8	8.9	6,699	6,389	310	5,052	4,879	173	95.4	96.6	4.6	3.4
65 years and over .	3,500	2.9	2.7	1,990	1,923	66	1,511	1,461	50	96.7	96.7	3.3	3.3
White	107,486	100.0	100.0	59,332	55,557	3,775	48,154	45,482	2,672	93.6	94.5	6.4	5.5
16 to 19 years . . .	5,966	5.2	6.0	3,094	2,552	542	2,872	2,436	436	82.5	84.8	17.5	15.2
20 to 24 years . . .	11,575	10.4	11.3	6,148	5,522	626	5,427	4,990	436	89.8	92.0	10.2	8.0
25 to 34 years . . .	29,896	28.2	27.3	16,754	15,695	1,059	13,142	12,403	740	93.7	94.4	6.3	5.6
35 to 44 years . . .	28,293	26.2	26.5	15,547	14,769	777	12,747	12,195	551	95.0	95.7	5.0	4.3
45 to 54 years . . .	18,288	16.9	17.1	10,035	9,593	442	8,253	7,928	325	95.6	96.1	4.4	3.9
55 to 64 years . . .	10,314	10.0	9.1	5,940	5,667	272	4,375	4,231	143	95.4	96.7	4.6	3.3
65 years and over .	3,154	3.1	2.8	1,815	1,758	57	1,339	1,298	41	96.9	96.9	3.1	3.1
Black	13,542	100.0	100.0	6,754	5,880	874	6,788	5,983	805	87.1	88.1	12.9	11.9
16 to 19 years . . .	744	5.8	5.2	390	247	142	354	227	128	63.5	63.9	36.5	36.1
20 to 24 years . . .	1,673	12.9	11.8	870	675	195	802	636	166	77.6	79.3	22.4	20.7
25 to 34 years . . .	4,199	31.2	30.8	2,110	1,858	252	2,089	1,809	280	88.1	86.6	11.9	13.4
35 to 44 years . . .	3,507	24.9	26.9	1,680	1,519	162	1,827	1,688	139	90.4	92.4	9.6	7.6
45 to 54 years . . .	2,057	14.9	15.5	1,003	917	86	1,054	989	65	91.4	93.8	8.6	6.2
55 to 64 years . . .	1,087	8.4	7.7	565	537	28	522	502	20	95.0	96.2	5.0	3.8
65 years and over .	275	2.0	2.1	135	127	8	140	133	6	94.1	95.7	5.9	4.3
Hispanic [2] . . .	9,762	100.0	100.0	5,873	5,278	595	3,890	3,521	368	89.9	90.5	10.1	9.5
16 to 19 years . . .	653	6.5	7.0	379	290	90	273	213	60	76.3	78.0	23.7	22.0
20 to 24 years . . .	1,476	16.0	13.8	939	830	109	537	474	63	88.4	88.3	11.6	11.7
25 to 34 years . . .	3,204	33.9	31.2	1,991	1,807	185	1,213	1,102	111	90.7	90.8	9.3	9.2
35 to 44 years . . .	2,363	23.5	25.3	1,379	1,261	118	984	909	75	91.4	92.4	8.6	7.6
45 to 54 years . . .	1,307	12.5	14.7	736	678	58	571	525	46	92.1	91.9	7.9	8.1
55 to 64 years . . .	653	6.5	6.9	383	352	31	270	259	11	91.9	95.9	8.1	4.1
65 years and over .	107	1.1	1.1	65	60	5	42	39	3	92.3	92.9	7.7	7.1

[1] Includes other races not shown separately.   [2] Persons of Hispanic origin may be of any race.

Source: U.S. Bureau of Labor Statistics, *Employment and Earnings*, monthly, January 1992.

No. 623. Employed Civilians and Weekly Hours, by Selected Characteristics: 1970 to 1991

[In thousands, except as indicated. For civilian noninstitutional population 16 years old and over. Annual averages of monthly figures. Based on Current Population Survey; see text, section 1 and Appendix III]

AGE, SEX, AND MARITAL STATUS	1970	1980	1985	1986	1987	1988	1989	1990	1991
Total employed	78,678	99,303	107,150	109,597	112,440	114,968	117,342	117,914	116,877
Age:									
16 to 19 years.	6,144	7,710	6,434	6,472	6,640	6,805	6,759	6,261	5,628
20 to 24 years.	9,731	14,087	13,980	13,790	13,524	13,244	12,962	12,622	12,233
25 to 34 years.	16,318	24,082	27,204	31,208	32,201	33,105	33,574	34,045	32,914
35 to 44 years.	15,922	19,523	24,732	25,861	27,179	28,269	29,443	30,543	31,286
45 to 54 years.	16,473	16,234	16,509	16,440	17,487	18,447	19,279	19,765	20,164
55 to 64 years.	10,974	11,586	11,474	11,405	11,465	11,433	11,499	11,464	11,268
65 years and over	3,118	2,960	2,813	2,919	3,041	3,197	3,355	3,428	3,384
Sex: Male	48,990	57,186	59,891	60,892	62,107	63,273	64,315	64,435	63,593
Female	29,688	42,117	47,259	48,706	50,334	51,696	53,027	53,479	53,284
Marital status:									
Married, spouse present	55,554	62,536	65,584	66,802	68,372	69,228	70,164	70,624	70,196
Single (never married).	15,039	24,082	26,780	27,478	28,355	29,500	30,113	29,761	29,278
Widowed, divorced, separated	8,087	12,684	14,786	15,318	15,713	16,242	17,066	17,531	17,403
Class of worker:									
Nonagriculture.	75,215	95,938	103,971	106,434	109,232	111,800	114,142	114,728	113,644
Wage and salary worker.	69,491	88,525	95,871	98,299	100,771	103,021	105,259	105,715	104,520
Self-employed	5,221	7,000	7,811	7,881	8,201	8,519	8,605	8,760	8,899
Unpaid family workers	502	413	289	255	260	260	279	252	225
Agriculture	3,463	3,364	3,179	3,163	3,208	3,169	3,199	3,186	3,233
Wage and salary worker.	1,154	1,425	1,535	1,547	1,632	1,621	1,665	1,679	1,673
Self-employed	1,810	1,642	1,458	1,447	1,423	1,398	1,403	1,400	1,442
Unpaid family workers	499	297	185	169	153	150	131	107	118
Weekly hours:									
Nonagriculture:									
Wage and salary workers	38.3	38.1	38.7	38.8	38.7	39.1	39.3	39.2	39.0
Self-employed	45.0	41.2	41.1	41.1	41.0	41.0	41.1	40.8	40.4
Unpaid family workers	37.9	34.7	35.1	35.5	36.3	36.0	35.1	33.9	35.4
Agriculture:									
Wage and salary workers	40.0	41.6	40.8	40.9	40.6	41.3	41.8	41.3	41.0
Self-employed	51.0	49.3	48.2	48.4	47.8	47.5	47.9	46.9	46.8
Unpaid family workers	40.0	38.6	38.5	39.7	39.9	39.7	39.4	38.5	40.3

Source: U.S. Bureau of Labor Statistics, *Employment and Earnings*, monthly, January issues; and unpublished data.

No. 624. Self-Employed Workers, by Selected Characteristics: 1970 to 1991

[In thousands. For civilian noninstitutional population 16 years old and over. Annual averages of monthly figures. Based on Current Population Survey; see text, section 1, and Appendix III]

ITEM	1970	1975	1980	1985	1987	1988	1989	1990	1991
Total self-employed..............	7,031	7,427	8,642	9,269	9,624	9,917	10,008	10,160	10,341
Industry:									
Agriculture.........................	1,810	1,722	1,642	1,458	1,423	1,398	1,403	1,400	1,442
Nonagriculture	5,221	5,705	7,000	7,811	8,201	8,519	8,605	8,760	8,899
Mining	14	16	28	20	27	28	26	24	23
Construction	687	839	1,173	1,301	1,384	1,427	1,423	1,463	1,447
Manufacturing	264	273	358	347	354	394	406	429	420
Transportation and public utilities	196	223	282	315	335	345	323	302	318
Trade........................	1,667	1,709	1,899	1,792	1,841	1,823	1,882	1,859	1,879
Finance, insurance, and real estate......	254	335	458	558	597	624	621	635	619
Services......................	2,140	2,310	2,804	3,477	3,663	3,878	3,924	4,048	4,193
Occupation:									
Managerial and professional specialty.....	(NA)	(NA)	(NA)	2,585	2,714	2,929	3,059	3,067	3,117
Technical, sales, and administrative support. .	(NA)	(NA)	(NA)	2,059	2,139	2,155	2,195	2,252	2,245
Service occupations...............	(NA)	(NA)	(NA)	980	1,058	1,159	1,146	1,213	1,273
Precision production, craft, and repair......	(NA)	(NA)	(NA)	1,611	1,680	1,674	1,648	1,680	1,697
Operators, fabricators, and laborers	(NA)	(NA)	(NA)	568	595	604	585	568	584
Farming, forestry, and fishing	(NA)	(NA)	(NA)	1,465	1,438	1,395	1,376	1,380	1,427

NA Not available.
Source: U.S. Bureau of Labor Statistics, Bulletin 2307; *Employment and Earnings*, monthly, January issues; and unpublished data.

No. 625. Persons With a Job But Not at Work: 1970 to 1991

[In thousands, except percent. For civilian noninstitutional population 16 years old and over. Annual averages of monthly figures. Based on Current Population Survey; see text, section 1 and Appendix III. See *Historical Statistics, Colonial Times to 1970*, series D 116-126, for related but not comparable data]

REASON FOR NOT WORKING	1970	1975	1980	1985	1986	1987	1988	1989	1990	1991 Total	1991 Male	1991 Female
All industries, number	4,645	5,221	5,881	5,789	5,741	5,910	5,831	6,170	6,157	5,909	2,780	3,130
Percent of employed...	5.9	6.1	5.9	5.4	5.2	5.3	5.1	5.3	5.2	5.1	4.4	5.9
Reason for not working:												
Vacation...............	2,341	2,815	3,320	3,338	3,234	3,421	3,236	3,437	3,531	3,297	1,520	1,777
Illness	1,324	1,343	1,426	1,308	1,292	1,320	1,364	1,405	1,341	1,302	650	653
Bad weather	128	139	155	141	128	92	122	133	89	118	105	13
Industrial dispute	156	95	105	42	56	34	30	63	24	17	12	5
All other.............	696	829	876	960	1,030	1,043	1,080	1,132	1,172	1,175	492	682

Source: U.S. Bureau of Labor Statistics, *Employment and Earnings*, monthly, January issues; and unpublished data.

No. 626. Employed and Unemployed Workers, by Work Schedules, Sex, and Age: 1980 to 1991

[In thousands. See headnote, table 610]

CHARACTERISTIC	EMPLOYED 1980	EMPLOYED 1985	EMPLOYED 1990	EMPLOYED 1991	CHARACTERISTIC	UNEMPLOYED 1980	UNEMPLOYED 1985	UNEMPLOYED 1990	UNEMPLOYED 1991
Total........	99,303	107,150	117,914	116,877	Total..........	7,637	8,312	6,874	8,426
Full-time[1]	82,562	88,534	97,994	96,575	Looking for full-time work.	6,269	6,793	5,541	6,932
Male	51,717	53,862	57,982	56,936	Male	3,703	3,925	3,264	4,211
16 to 19 years old.	2,017	1,437	1,343	1,085	16 to 19 years old..	537	446	328	363
20 to 24 years old.	6,533	6,078	5,452	5,115	20 to 24 years old..	994	857	582	736
25 to 54 years old.	35,644	39,207	44,229	43,947	25 to 54 years old..	1,923	2,329	2,098	2,795
55 years and over.	7,521	7,139	6,959	6,789	55 years and over..	250	292	255	317
Female	30,845	34,672	40,011	39,638	Female...........	2,564	2,868	2,277	2,721
16 to 19 years old.	1,456	1,069	975	785	16 to 19 years old..	430	331	233	258
20 to 24 years old.	5,098	4,903	4,386	4,079	20 to 24 years old..	636	636	439	481
25 to 54 years old.	20,395	24,838	30,485	30,696	25 to 54 years old..	1,363	1,727	1,491	1,830
55 years and over.	3,897	3,862	4,166	4,079	55 years and over..	135	173	115	152
Part-time[1]	16,740	18,615	19,920	20,302	Looking for part-time				
Male	5,471	6,028	6,452	6,657	work	1,369	1,519	1,332	1,494
16 to 19 years old.	2,068	1,891	1,894	1,795	Male	563	596	535	607
20 to 24 years old.	999	1,261	1,174	1,306	16 to 19 years old..	377	360	301	346
25 to 54 years old.	1,092	1,568	1,842	2,033	20 to 24 years old..	81	87	84	113
55 years and over.	1,314	1,308	1,543	1,523	25 to 54 years old..	54	79	89	88
Female	11,270	12,587	13,468	13,645	55 years and over..	52	70	61	60
16 to 19 years old.	2,169	2,036	2,049	1,964	Female...........	806	923	797	888
20 to 24 years old.	1,456	1,738	1,611	1,733	16 to 19 years old..	326	330	286	323
25 to 54 years old.	5,827	6,837	7,584	7,687	20 to 24 years old..	124	158	116	147
55 years and over.	1,815	1,976	2,224	2,261	25 to 54 years old..	299	359	323	347
					55 years and over..	57	75	72	71

[1] Full-time workers include employed persons on full-time (35 hours or more per week) schedules and those working part-time (between 1 and 34 hours) for economic reasons who usually work full-time. Part-time workers include employed persons working part-time voluntarily and those working part-time for economic reasons, who usually work part-time. Employed persons with a job but not at work are distributed according to whether they usually work full- or part-time.
Source: U.S. Bureau of Labor Statistics, Bulletin 2307; and *Employment and Earnings*, monthly, January issues.

No. 627. Job Accessions, by Selected Charactertics: 1987 to 1989

[In percent, except as indicated. For the civilian noninstitutionalized population. A job accession is the report of a person indicating he/she did not have a job in one month but obtained one the following month. Based on the Survey of Income and Program Participation; see source for details]

ITEM	Total	16 to 19 years old	20 to 24 years old	25 to 34 years old	35 years old and over
Total accessions (1,000)	41,485	9,571	7,899	10,463	13,553
Sex: Male	44.8	50.4	44.8	41.4	43.4
Female	55.2	49.6	55.2	58.6	56.6
Number of accessions: One only	67.1	49.9	64.9	73.1	75.8
Two only	24.4	33.4	25.1	20.9	20.2
Three or more	8.6	16.7	10.0	6.0	4.0
Industry: Agriculture, forestry, fisheries	3.5	4.0	2.8	3.2	3.8
Mining	0.6	0.2	0.1	0.9	0.8
Construction	6.7	4.0	8.1	7.9	6.8
Manufacturing	12.9	9.9	11.9	14.8	14.3
Transportation, public utilities [1]	4.0	2.6	2.7	5.2	4.8
Wholesale trade	2.9	2.0	2.4	3.7	3.3
Retail trade	26.2	43.4	25.4	22.1	17.6
Finance, insurance, real estate	5.2	2.7	6.5	5.6	5.9
Business and repair	8.1	7.2	9.8	8.7	7.4
Personal services	5.9	5.7	6.0	4.0	7.3
Entertainment and recreation	2.2	3.7	2.1	1.2	2.1
Professional and related	19.5	11.9	21.0	21.4	22.7
Public administisration	2.3	2.7	1.2	1.4	3.3
Occupation: Executive, admin., managerial	4.8	0.1	4.0	6.4	7.2
Professional specialty	8.8	3.0	9.8	10.3	11.2
Technical/related support	2.0	0.3	2.6	3.3	1.7
Sales	14.5	19.3	12.9	12.5	13.4
Admin. support, inc. clerical	16.7	14.5	18.8	16.0	17.5
Private households	1.6	0.8	1.5	1.5	2.2
Protective service	1.0	1.8	0.7	0.3	1.2
Service workers	19.4	28.3	20.4	17.7	13.9
Farm, forestry and fishery	3.5	4.7	2.6	3.3	3.5
Precision production, craft/repair	8.2	4.5	9.0	10.4	8.5
Machine operators, assemblers	7.1	5.4	6.6	7.8	8.0
Transportation/material moving	4.0	2.5	2.5	4.5	5.6
Handlers and laborers	8.4	14.4	8.6	6.0	6.0
Paid by the hour [2] (1,000)	31,856	8,881	6,331	7,705	8,938
Hourly earnings (dol.): Total	5.63	4.33	5.33	6.33	6.54
Male	6.38	4.54	5.65	7.72	8.30
Female	5.07	4.11	5.06	5.43	5.51
Not paid by the hour [2] (1,000)	7,672	496	1,357	2,182	3,637
Weekly earnings (dol.): Total	336	101	238	325	411
Male	430	77	310	403	525
Female	233	127	184	244	266

[1] Includes communications.   [2] As of the first job accession. Excludes a small number of persons who reported having a job for a given period, but no earnings.

Source: U.S. Bureau of the Census, *Current Population Reports*, series P-70, No. 27.

No. 628. Multiple Jobholders, by Industry and Occupation: 1991

[As of May. Multiple jobholders are employed persons who, either 1) had jobs as wage or salary workers with two employers or more; 2) were self-employed and also held a wage and salary job; or 3) were unpaid family workers on their primary jobs but also held wage and salary job. Based on the Current Population Survey; see text, section 1, and Appendix III]

CHARACTERISTIC	TOTAL Em- ployed	TOTAL Multiple jobholders Number	TOTAL Multiple jobholders Rate [1]	MALE Em- ployed	MALE Multiple jobholders Number	MALE Multiple jobholders Rate [1]	FEMALE Em- ployed	FEMALE Multiple jobholders Number	FEMALE Multiple jobholders Rate [1]
Total, 16 years and over	116,626	7,183	6.2	63,499	4,054	6.4	53,127	3,129	5.9
Industry and class of worker of primary job:									
Agriculture	3,466	179	5.2	2,737	139	5.1	728	41	5.6
Nonagricultural industries	113,160	7,003	6.2	60,762	3,915	6.4	52,399	3,088	5.9
Wage and salary workers	104,193	6,691	6.4	55,063	3,733	6.8	49,129	2,958	6.0
Mining	737	25	3.4	592	17	2.8	145	8	5.8
Construction	5,745	271	4.7	5,231	239	4.6	514	33	6.4
Manufacturing	19,993	1,044	5.2	13,497	798	5.9	6,496	245	3.8
Durable goods	11,669	628	5.4	8,562	506	5.9	3,107	122	3.9
Nondurable goods	8,324	416	5.0	4,935	292	5.9	3,390	123	3.6
Transportation and public utilities	7,848	487	6.2	5,526	356	6.4	2,321	131	5.6
Wholesale trade	4,255	261	6.1	3,010	190	6.3	1,246	70	5.7
Retail trade	17,250	914	5.3	8,354	444	5.3	8,896	470	5.3
Finance, insurance, and real estate . . .	7,066	414	5.9	2,860	187	6.5	4,206	227	5.4
Services	35,592	2,747	7.7	12,719	1,125	8.8	22,873	1,622	7.1
Public administration	5,709	528	9.3	3,274	376	11.5	2,434	152	6.2
Self-employed workers	8,733	306	3.5	5,663	182	3.2	3,070	123	4.0
Unpaid family workers	235	7	2.9	36	-	-	199	7	3.4
Occupation of primary job:									
Managerial and professional specialty . . .	31,154	2,259	7.3	16,678	1,269	7.6	14,476	990	6.8
Technical, sales, and admin. support . . .	36,002	2,154	6.0	12,584	803	6.4	23,418	1,351	5.8
Service occupations	15,534	1,063	6.8	6,252	527	8.4	9,282	536	5.8
Precision production, craft, and repair . . .	13,115	652	5.0	12,019	608	5.1	1,096	44	4.0
Operators, fabricators, and laborers	17,065	851	5.0	12,804	682	5.3	4,261	169	4.0
Farming, forestry, and fishing	3,756	203	5.4	3,162	164	5.2	594	39	6.6

- Represents or rounds to zero.   [1] Multiple jobholders as a percent of all employed persons in specified group.

Source: U.S. Bureau of Labor Statistics, *News*, USDL 91-547, October 28, 1991.

No. 629. Employed Civilians, by Occupation, Sex, Race, and Hispanic Origin: 1983 and 1991

[For civilian noninstitutional population 16 years old and over. Annual average of monthly figures. Based on Current Population Survey; see text, section 1 and Appendix III. Persons of Hispanic origin may be of any race]

OCCUPATION	1983				1991			
	Total employed (1,000)	Percent of total			Total employed (1,000)	Percent of total		
		Female	Black	His-panic		Female	Black	His-panic
Total.................................	100,834	43.7	9.3	5.3	116,877	45.6	10.1	7.5
Managerial and professional specialty ...	23,592	40.9	5.6	2.6	31,012	46.3	6.3	3.7
Executive, administrative, and managerial [1]	10,772	32.4	4.7	2.8	14,954	40.6	5.7	4.0
Officials and administrators, public	417	38.5	8.3	3.8	511	45.9	11.3	3.6
Financial managers	357	38.6	3.5	3.1	481	44.7	4.0	3.2
Personnel and labor relations managers............	106	43.9	4.9	2.6	126	57.6	5.7	3.1
Purchasing managers.......................	82	23.6	5.1	1.4	112	33.9	2.9	2.2
Managers, marketing, advertising and public relations...	396	21.8	2.7	1.7	514	30.6	2.1	2.9
Administrators, education and related fields	415	41.4	11.3	2.4	541	55.2	8.5	4.2
Managers, medicine and health	91	57.0	5.0	2.0	199	65.0	6.2	4.1
Managers, properties and real estate..............	305	42.8	5.5	5.2	448	46.0	6.3	5.8
Management-related occupations [1]...............	2,966	40.3	5.8	3.5	3,951	50.8	7.4	4.4
Accountants and auditors....................	1,105	38.7	5.5	3.3	1,446	51.5	7.6	3.7
Professional specialty [1]......................	12,820	48.1	6.4	2.5	16,058	51.6	6.7	3.4
Architects .,..........................	103	12.7	1.6	1.5	127	17.1	2.1	4.4
Engineers [1]............................	1,572	5.8	2.7	2.2	1,846	8.2	3.6	2.4
Aerospace engineers......................	80	6.9	1.5	2.1	103	8.7	1.9	3.1
Chemical engineers......................	67	6.1	3.0	1.4	81	9.3	3.2	2.3
Civil engineers........................	211	4.0	1.9	3.2	223	5.6	4.0	2.5
Electrical and electronic....................	450	6.1	3.4	3.1	562	8.6	4.9	2.8
Industrial engineers......................	210	11.0	3.3	2.4	201	13.6	4.3	2.5
Mechanical	259	2.8	3.2	1.1	311	4.9	3.4	1.5
Mathematical and computer scientists [1]...........	463	29.6	5.4	2.6	923	36.8	6.3	2.9
Computer systems analysts, scientists	276	27.8	6.2	2.7	675	33.7	5.8	2.6
Operations and systems researchers and analysts ...	142	31.3	4.9	2.2	201	43.0	8.2	3.9
Natural scientists [1].......................	357	20.5	2.6	2.1	438	26.1	3.3	3.6
Chemists, except biochemists	98	23.3	4.3	1.2	127	29.9	5.2	4.6
Geologists and geodesists	65	18.0	1.1	2.6	57	10.5	0.7	0.6
Biological and life scientists	55	40.8	2.4	1.8	98	37.9	5.2	5.2
Health diagnosing occupations [1]...............	735	13.3	2.7	3.3	849	18.1	2.6	3.6
Physicians...........................	519	15.8	3.2	4.5	575	20.1	3.2	4.4
Dentists............................	126	6.7	2.4	1.0	150	10.1	1.5	2.7
Health assessment and treating occupations.........	1,900	85.8	7.1	2.2	2,376	86.2	7.2	2.9
Registered nurses......................	1,372	95.8	6.7	1.8	1,712	94.8	7.1	2.4
Pharmacists..........................	158	26.7	3.8	2.6	187	36.8	3.4	3.2
Dietitians .,.........................	71	90.8	21.0	3.7	71	93.7	19.1	6.8
Therapists [1].........................	247	76.3	7.6	2.7	340	77.9	7.2	4.8
Inhalation therapists	69	69.4	6.5	3.7	68	63.0	10.3	7.6
Physical therapists	55	77.0	9.7	1.5	101	77.5	5.8	5.4
Speech therapists	51	90.5	1.5	-	72	88.2	1.3	3.4
Physicians' assistants	51	36.3	7.7	4.4	67	37.1	8.0	3.7
Teachers, college and university...............	606	36.3	4.4	1.8	773	40.8	4.8	2.9
Teachers, except college and university [1]...........	3,365	70.9	9.1	2.7	4,029	74.3	8.6	3.7
Prekindergarten and kindergarten.............	299	98.2	11.8	3.4	445	98.7	12.4	5.8
Elementary school......................	1,350	83.3	11.1	3.1	1,524	85.9	8.9	3.3
Secondary school......................	1,209	51.8	7.2	2.3	1,222	54.7	7.3	3.4
Special education	81	82.2	10.2	2.3	282	83.7	9.5	3.4
Counselors, educational and vocational	184	53.1	13.9	3.2	222	64.4	15.5	3.7
Librarians, archivists, and curators..............	213	84.4	7.8	1.6	212	81.1	5.8	2.6
Librarians...........................	193	87.3	7.9	1.8	194	83.0	6.1	2.4
Social scientists and urban planners [1]	261	46.8	7.1	2.1	386	53.5	6.7	3.5
Economists	98	37.9	6.3	2.7	116	45.7	5.1	3.2
Psychologists........................	135	57.1	8.6	1.1	230	60.3	7.8	3.8
Social, recreation, and religious workers [1].........	831	43.1	12.1	3.8	1,124	51.0	15.1	5.9
Social workers........................	407	64.3	18.2	6.3	603	68.0	21.9	7.2
Recreation workers.....................	65	71.9	15.7	2.0	106	76.3	16.3	7.2
Clergy.............................	293	5.6	4.9	1.4	331	9.3	5.4	4.3
Lawyers and judges	651	15.8	2.7	1.0	772	18.9	2.8	1.6
Lawyers............................	612	15.3	2.6	0.9	744	19.0	2.6	1.6
Writers, artists, entertainers, and athletes [1].........	1,544	42.7	4.8	2.9	1,957	46.7	5.0	4.1
Authors	62	46.7	2.1	0.9	91	53.2	1.4	1.0
Technical writers.......................	(²)	(²)	(²)	(²)	62	50.0	5.3	1.8
Designers	393	52.7	3.1	2.7	527	53.4	2.9	4.3
Musicians and composers..................	155	28.0	7.9	4.4	156	31.1	7.6	6.2
Actors and directors	60	30.8	6.6	3.4	87	33.2	10.5	4.8
Painters, sculptors, craft-artists, and artist printmakers..........................	186	47.4	2.1	2.3	208	55.3	2.7	3.2
Photographers	113	20.7	4.0	3.4	136	23.0	7.7	4.4
Editors and reporters	204	48.4	2.9	2.1	279	51.1	4.5	2.8
Public relations specialists	157	50.1	6.2	1.9	173	56.2	8.3	3.1
Announcers..........................	(²)	(²)	(²)	(²)	60	21.3	6.2	5.2
Athletes............................	58	17.6	9.4	1.7	77	24.7	7.5	4.2

See footnotes at end of table.

No. 629. Employed Civilians, by Occupation, Sex, Race, and Hispanic Origin: 1983 and 1991—Continued

[See headnote, page 392]

OCCUPATION	1983				1991			
	Total em- ployed (1,000)	Percent of total			Total em- ployed (1,000)	Percent of total		
		Fe- male	Black	His- panic		Fe- male	Black	His- panic
Technical, sales, and administrative support..........	31,265	64.6	7.6	4.3	36,086	64.7	9.3	6.0
Technicians and related support	3,053	48.2	8.2	3.1	3,794	49.4	8.9	4.6
Health technologists and technicians [1]..........	1,111	84.3	12.7	3.1	1,379	82.9	12.9	5.5
Clinical laboratory technologists and technicians.....	255	76.2	10.5	2.9	317	75.7	13.4	6.8
Dental hygienists.........................	66	98.6	1.6	-	84	99.8	1.1	3.3
Health record technologists and technicians	([2])	([2])	([2])	([2])	67	93.9	13.4	5.2
Radiologic technicians	101	71.7	8.6	4.5	140	74.5	7.9	8.8
Licensed practical nurses	443	97.0	17.7	3.1	445	95.0	16.5	4.4
Engineering and related technologists and technicians [1].	822	18.4	6.1	3.5	947	18.4	7.2	4.4
Electrical and electronic technicians	260	12.5	8.2	4.6	350	13.6	9.3	4.7
Drafting occupations	273	17.5	5.5	2.3	264	17.4	5.4	4.2
Surveying and mapping technicians	([2])	([2])	([2])	([2])	67	10.1	2.9	3.9
Science technicians [1]	202	29.1	6.6	2.8	241	29.8	6.6	5.6
Biological technicians......................	52	37.7	2.9	2.0	64	38.2	5.9	5.6
Chemical technicians	82	26.9	9.5	3.5	88	26.0	7.9	6.0
Technicians, except health, engineering, and science [1].	917	35.3	5.0	2.7	1,227	39.4	6.2	3.6
Airplane pilots and navigators	69	2.1	-	1.6	101	3.4	1.5	2.9
Computer programmers	443	32.5	4.4	2.1	546	34.0	5.7	2.6
Legal assistants	128	74.0	4.3	3.6	219	83.0	6.7	4.9
Sales occupations........................	11,818	47.5	4.7	3.7	13,958	48.8	6.6	5.5
Supervisors and proprietors	2,958	28.4	3.6	3.4	3,739	34.3	4.3	4.9
Sales representatives, finance and business services [1]..	1,853	37.2	2.7	2.2	2,344	42.1	5.0	3.7
Insurance sales........................	551	25.1	3.8	2.5	588	31.1	5.3	3.1
Real estate sales	570	48.9	1.3	1.5	712	51.5	3.8	3.4
Securities and financial services sales	212	23.6	3.1	1.1	312	28.9	3.8	4.1
Advertising and related sales................	124	47.9	4.5	3.3	140	53.1	4.2	4.1
Sales representatives, commodities, except retail......	1,442	15.1	2.1	2.2	1,601	22.4	2.6	3.5
Sales workers, retail and personal services..........	5,511	69.7	6.7	4.8	6,200	66.9	9.7	7.2
Cashiers	2,009	84.4	10.1	5.4	2,500	80.9	12.9	8.4
Sales-related occupations	54	58.7	2.8	1.3	74	66.9	4.0	1.2
Administrative support, including clerical	16,395	79.9	9.6	5.0	18,334	80.0	11.4	6.6
Supervisors...........................	676	53.4	9.3	5.0	777	58.4	12.3	7.2
Computer equipment operators.................	605	63.9	12.5	6.0	746	66.3	13.9	6.5
Computer operators.....................	597	63.7	12.1	6.0	741	66.3	13.9	6.5
Secretaries, stenographers, and typists [1]	4,861	98.2	7.3	4.5	4,427	98.5	9.1	5.0
Secretaries............................	3,891	99.0	5.8	4.0	3,791	99.0	7.9	4.8
Typists	906	95.6	13.8	6.4	591	95.1	16.8	6.2
Information clerks........................	1,174	88.9	8.5	5.5	1,515	89.5	9.0	7.4
Receptionists	602	96.8	7.5	6.6	875	97.1	8.1	7.1
Records processing occupations, except financial [1]	866	82.4	13.9	4.8	891	80.5	14.9	7.9
Order clerks	188	78.1	10.6	4.4	230	78.8	17.1	7.7
Personnel clerks, except payroll and time keeping ...	64	91.1	14.9	4.6	69	86.4	18.1	5.7
Library clerks..........................	147	81.9	15.4	2.5	151	77.0	8.8	5.6
File clerks	287	83.5	16.7	6.1	297	80.9	16.3	9.9
Records clerks	157	82.8	11.6	5.6	125	84.0	13.1	8.2
Financial records processing [1]	2,457	89.4	4.6	3.7	2,389	91.0	6.2	5.6
Bookkeepers, accounting, and auditing clerks	1,970	91.0	4.3	3.3	1,912	91.5	5.0	5.2
Payroll and time keeping clerks	192	82.2	5.9	5.0	170	90.6	9.0	6.3
Billing clerks..........................	146	88.4	6.2	3.9	170	90.7	11.8	7.9
Cost and rate clerks	96	75.6	5.9	5.3	81	80.7	12.3	5.3
Duplicating, mail and other office machine operators ...	68	54.6	16.6	6.1	71	61.7	14.2	10.7
Communications equipment operators	256	89.1	17.0	4.4	225	87.2	19.1	6.8
Telephone operators	244	90.4	17.0	4.3	213	89.2	19.5	6.4
Mail and message distributing occupations	799	31.6	18.1	4.5	923	37.8	21.1	5.7
Postal clerks, except mail carriers	248	36.7	26.2	5.2	278	48.3	27.7	6.3
Mail carrier, postal service	259	17.1	12.5	2.7	332	27.8	17.1	3.0
Mail clerks, except postal service..............	170	50.0	15.8	5.9	174	48.9	20.6	8.8
Messengers...........................	122	26.2	16.7	5.2	140	26.9	18.3	7.0
Material recording, scheduling, and distributing [1][3]	1,562	37.5	10.9	6.6	1,784	42.6	12.7	8.6
Dispatchers	157	45.7	11.4	4.3	217	51.3	11.0	6.6
Production coordinators	182	44.0	6.1	2.2	186	51.0	7.8	4.0
Traffic, shipping, and receiving clerks	421	22.6	9.1	11.1	550	29.6	13.8	10.9
Stock and inventory clerks	532	38.7	13.3	5.5	565	43.9	13.4	8.6
Weighers, measurers, and checkers.............	79	47.2	16.9	5.8	64	49.7	15.9	11.0
Expediters	112	57.5	8.4	4.3	131	64.7	9.6	7.4
Adjusters and investigators	675	69.9	11.4	5.1	1,178	76.0	13.1	6.3
Insurance adjusters, examiners, and investigators	199	65.0	11.5	3.3	352	77.1	12.2	5.7
Investigators and adjusters, except insurance........	301	70.1	11.3	4.8	568	76.1	12.5	6.2
Eligibility clerks, social welfare................	69	88.7	12.9	9.4	91	90.0	17.3	6.5
Bill and account collectors	106	66.4	8.5	6.5	167	66.0	14.5	7.7
Miscellaneous administrative support [1].............	2,397	85.2	12.5	5.9	3,408	84.1	12.9	7.9
General office clerks	648	80.6	12.7	5.2	765	80.9	12.7	8.2
Bank tellers	480	91.0	7.5	4.3	481	90.3	10.7	6.5
Data entry keyers	311	93.6	18.6	5.6	517	86.0	16.0	9.0
Statistical clerks	96	75.7	7.5	3.4	77	75.1	10.2	6.0
Teachers' aides	348	93.7	17.8	12.6	486	93.1	13.0	12.4

See footnotes at end of table.

No. 629. Employed Civilians, by Occupation, Sex, Race, and Hispanic Origin: 1983 and 1991—Continued

[See headnote, page 392]

OCCUPATION	1983				1991			
	Total em- ployed (1,000)	Percent of total			Total em- ployed (1,000)	Percent of total		
		Fe- male	Black	His- panic		Fe- male	Black	His- panic
Service occupations	13,857	60.1	16.6	6.8	15,986	59.8	17.2	11.2
Private household [1]	980	96.1	27.8	8.5	787	96.0	21.0	21.0
Child care workers	408	96.9	7.9	3.6	340	96.7	10.5	14.1
Cleaners and servants	512	95.8	42.4	11.8	403	95.8	29.3	26.3
Protective service	1,672	12.8	13.6	4.6	2,071	15.2	16.8	6.2
Supervisors, protective service	127	4.7	7.7	3.1	182	9.0	11.1	5.1
Supervisors, police and detectives	58	4.2	9.3	1.2	95	9.4	11.1	6.5
Firefighting and fire prevention	189	1.0	6.7	4.1	220	2.3	8.6	4.4
Firefighting occupations	170	1.0	7.3	3.8	200	1.4	8.9	4.7
Police and detectives	645	9.4	13.1	4.0	870	14.0	15.5	5.8
Police and detectives, public service	412	5.7	9.5	4.4	485	10.3	11.3	6.5
Sheriffs, bailiffs, and other law enforcement officers	87	13.2	11.5	4.0	116	18.3	15.2	7.9
Correctional institution officers	146	17.8	24.0	2.8	269	18.7	23.3	3.6
Guards	711	20.6	17.0	5.6	799	21.6	21.7	7.5
Guards and police, except public service	602	13.0	18.9	6.2	685	15.9	23.5	7.7
Service except private household and protective	11,205	64.0	16.0	6.9	13,128	64.6	17.1	11.4
Food preparation and service occupations [1]	4,860	63.3	10.5	6.8	5,370	59.3	12.4	12.2
Bartenders	338	48.4	2.7	4.4	290	54.0	2.0	4.7
Waiters and waitresses	1,357	87.8	4.1	3.6	1,355	81.6	4.2	7.1
Cooks, except short order	1,359	50.8	16.0	6.8	1,779	46.9	18.3	14.4
Short-order cooks	93	38.5	12.9	2.4	82	28.9	23.3	11.7
Food counter, fountain, and related occupations	326	76.0	9.1	6.7	329	71.0	10.9	7.9
Kitchen workers, food preparation	138	77.0	13.7	8.1	131	70.6	16.6	13.8
Waiters' and waitresses' assistants	364	38.8	12.6	14.2	380	38.5	15.3	20.6
Health service occupations	1,739	89.2	23.5	4.8	2,178	88.6	26.4	6.9
Dental assistants	154	98.1	6.1	5.7	177	98.2	5.6	6.4
Health aides, except nursing	316	86.8	16.5	4.8	494	83.1	19.6	7.3
Nursing aides, orderlies, and attendants	1,269	88.7	27.3	4.7	1,506	89.2	31.2	6.9
Cleaning and building service occupations [1]	2,736	38.8	24.4	9.2	3,068	43.1	22.8	16.0
Maids and housemen	531	81.2	32.3	10.1	718	82.9	27.2	19.7
Janitors and cleaners	2,031	28.6	22.6	8.9	2,126	30.9	21.0	15.4
Personal service occupations [1]	1,870	79.2	11.1	6.0	2,512	81.6	11.9	7.7
Barbers	92	12.9	8.4	12.1	104	18.3	16.7	8.2
Hairdressers and cosmetologists	622	88.7	7.0	5.7	745	90.2	8.6	7.5
Attendants, amusement and recreation facilities	131	40.2	7.1	4.3	145	38.8	9.5	7.4
Public transportation attendants	63	74.3	11.3	5.9	85	83.0	11.1	5.9
Welfare service aides	77	92.5	24.2	10.5	121	94.7	25.0	16.0
Child care workers, except private household	633	96.8	12.6	5.2	972	96.0	11.7	7.1
Precision production, craft, and repair	**12,328**	**8.1**	**6.8**	**6.2**	**13,162**	**8.6**	**7.8**	**8.6**
Mechanics and repairers	4,158	3.0	6.8	5.3	4,427	3.7	7.7	7.0
Mechanics and repairers, except supervisors [1]	3,906	2.8	7.0	5.5	4,176	3.4	7.8	7.0
Vehicle and mobile equipment mechanics/repairers [1]	1,683	0.8	6.9	6.0	1,778	1.1	6.7	8.4
Automobile mechanics	800	0.5	7.8	6.0	864	0.8	7.3	9.5
Aircraft engine mechanics	95	2.5	4.0	7.6	133	4.0	7.2	9.3
Electrical and electronic equipment repairers [1]	674	7.4	7.3	4.5	711	9.6	9.9	4.9
Data processing equipment repairers	98	9.3	6.1	4.5	152	14.8	11.8	3.8
Telephone installers and repairers	247	9.9	7.8	3.7	64	6.5	7.9	7.6
Construction trades	4,289	1.8	6.6	6.0	4,808	1.8	7.3	9.1
Construction trades, except supervisors	3,784	1.9	7.1	6.1	4,198	1.9	7.7	9.6
Carpenters	1,160	1.4	5.0	5.0	1,277	1.3	4.7	8.2
Extractive occupations	196	2.3	3.3	6.0	145	3.1	5.3	7.2
Precision production occupations	3,685	21.5	7.3	7.4	3,782	23.2	8.5	10.0
Operators, fabricators, and laborers	**16,091**	**26.6**	**14.0**	**8.3**	**17,172**	**25.2**	**15.0**	**12.0**
Machine operators, assemblers, and inspectors [1]	7,744	42.1	14.0	9.4	7,696	40.1	14.8	13.4
Textile, apparel, and furnishings machine operators [1]	1,414	82.1	18.7	12.5	1,234	76.9	23.7	18.6
Textile sewing machine operators	806	94.0	15.5	14.5	676	89.2	20.0	22.7
Pressing machine operators	141	66.4	27.1	14.2	128	64.5	25.8	23.5
Fabricators, assemblers, and hand working occupations	1,715	33.7	11.3	8.7	1,868	32.8	11.9	11.7
Production inspectors, testers, samplers, and weighers	794	53.8	13.0	7.7	768	52.0	13.9	10.9
Transportation and material moving occupations	4,201	7.8	13.0	5.9	4,878	9.0	15.6	8.5
Motor vehicle operators	2,978	9.2	13.5	6.0	3,680	10.6	16.3	8.5
Trucks, heavy and light	2,195	3.1	12.3	5.7	2,666	4.2	14.5	8.4
Transportation occupations, except motor vehicles	212	2.4	6.7	3.0	176	2.3	11.0	6.9
Material moving equipment operators	1,011	4.8	12.9	6.3	1,022	4.2	14.1	8.7
Industrial truck and tractor operators	369	5.6	19.6	8.2	436	7.0	20.5	11.0
Handlers, equipment cleaners, helpers, and laborers [1]	4,147	16.8	15.1	8.6	4,597	17.5	14.5	13.5
Freight, stock, and material handlers	1,488	15.4	15.3	7.1	1,688	18.0	14.9	10.1
Laborers, except construction	1,024	19.4	16.0	8.6	1,257	19.1	14.6	13.6
Farming, forestry, and fishing	**3,700**	**16.0**	**7.5**	**8.2**	**3,459**	**16.1**	**6.4**	**14.6**
Farm operators and managers	1,450	12.1	1.3	0.7	1,250	16.5	1.1	1.5
Other agricultural and related occupations	2,072	19.9	11.7	14.0	2,038	16.8	9.5	23.0
Farm workers [1]	1,149	24.8	11.6	15.9	883	21.4	8.6	26.8
Forestry and logging occupations	126	1.4	12.8	2.1	112	5.6	11.7	10.4
Fishers, hunters, and trappers	53	4.5	1.8	2.5	59	3.6	2.8	7.3

- Represents or rounds to zero.   [1] Includes other occupations, not shown separately.   [2] Level of total employment below 50,000.   [3] Includes clerks.

Source: U.S. Bureau of Labor Statistics, *Employment and Earnings*, monthly, January issues.

No. 630. Civilian Employment in Occupations with the Largest Job Growth and in the Fastest Growing and Fastest Declining Occupations: 1990 and 2005

[In thousands, except percent. For occupations employing 100,000 or more in 1990. Includes wage and salary jobs, self-employed and unpaid family members. Estimates based on the Current Employment Statistics estimates and the Occupational Employment Statistics estimates. See source for methodological assumptions. Minus sign (-) indicates decrease]

OCCUPATION	EMPLOYMENT				PERCENT CHANGE 1990-2005		
	1990	2005 [1]			Low	Mod-erate	High
		Low	Mod-erate	High			
Total [2]	122,573	136,806	147,191	154,543	12	20	26
LARGEST JOB GROWTH [3]							
Salespersons, retail	3,619	4,180	4,506	4,728	15	24	31
Registered nurses	1,727	2,318	2,494	2,648	34	44	53
Cashiers	2,633	3,094	3,318	3,474	18	26	32
General office clerks	2,737	3,149	3,407	3,597	15	24	31
Truck drivers light and heavy	2,362	2,767	2,979	3,125	17	26	32
General managers and top executives	3,086	3,409	3,684	3,871	10	19	25
Janitors and cleaners [4]	3,007	3,332	3,562	3,728	11	18	24
Nursing aides, orderlies, and attendants	1,274	1,700	1,826	1,934	33	43	52
Food counter, fountain, and related workers	1,607	2,067	2,158	2,229	29	34	39
Waiters and waitresses	1,747	2,110	2,196	2,262	21	26	29
Teachers, secondary school	1,280	1,575	1,717	1,849	23	34	45
Receptionists and information clerks	900	1,228	1,322	1,394	36	47	55
Systems analysts and computer scientists	463	769	829	864	66	79	87
Food preparation workers	1,156	1,442	1,521	1,585	25	32	37
Child care workers	725	1,027	1,078	1,123	42	49	55
Gardeners and groundskeepers, except farm	874	1,158	1,222	1,275	33	40	46
Accountants and auditors	985	1,235	1,325	1,385	25	34	41
Computer programmers	565	811	882	923	44	56	63
Teachers, elementary	1,362	1,538	1,675	1,803	13	23	32
Guards	883	1,094	1,181	1,238	24	34	40
Teacher aides and educational assistants	808	999	1,086	1,165	24	34	44
Licensed practical nurses	644	849	913	968	32	42	50
Clerical supervisors and managers	1,218	1,373	1,481	1,559	13	22	28
Home health aides	287	512	550	582	78	92	103
Cooks, restaurant	615	840	872	898	37	42	46
Maintenance repairers, general utility	1,128	1,283	1,379	1,447	14	22	28
Secretaries, except legal and medical	3,064	3,065	3,312	3,488	-	8	14
Cooks, short order and fast food	743	953	989	1,018	28	33	37
Stock clerks, sales floor	1,242	1,343	1,451	1,524	8	17	23
Lawyers	587	745	793	830	27	35	42
Marketing, advertising, and public relations managers	427	582	630	659	36	47	54
Food service and lodging managers	595	762	793	819	28	33	38
Physicians	580	730	776	818	26	34	41
Financial managers	701	828	894	939	18	28	34
Teachers, preschool and kindergarten	425	555	598	636	31	41	50
Automotive mechanics	757	861	923	969	14	22	28
Medical secretaries	232	363	390	415	57	68	79
Dining room and cafeteria attendants and bar helpers	461	592	619	641	28	34	39
Electricians	548	652	706	748	19	29	36
Carpenters	1,057	1,134	1,209	1,274	7	14	20
FASTEST GROWING							
Home health aides	287	512	550	582	78	92	103
Systems analysts and computer scientists	463	769	829	864	66	79	87
Personal and home care aides	103	170	183	194	64	77	87
Medical assistants	165	268	287	306	62	74	85
Human services workers	145	231	249	264	59	71	82
Radiologic technologists and technicians	149	234	252	268	58	70	80
Medical secretaries	232	363	390	415	57	68	79
Psychologists	125	193	204	214	55	64	72
Travel agents	132	199	214	224	51	62	70
Correction officers	230	342	372	400	49	61	74
Flight attendants	101	146	159	168	45	59	67
Computer programmers	565	811	882	923	44	56	63
Management analysts	151	218	230	240	44	52	58
Child care workers	725	1,027	1,078	1,123	42	49	55
FASTEST DECLINING							
Electrical and electronic equipment assemblers, precision	171	78	90	92	-55	-48	-46
Electrical and electronic assemblers	232	112	128	131	-52	-45	-44
Child care workers, private household	314	176	190	200	-44	-40	-36
Textile draw-out and winding machine operators [5]	199	116	138	142	-41	-31	-29
Telephone and cable TV line installers and repairers	133	85	92	98	-36	-30	-26
Machine tool cutting operators and tenders [6]	145	93	104	107	-36	-29	-26
Cleaners and servants, private household	411	287	310	326	-30	-25	-21
Machine forming operators and tenders [6]	174	119	131	137	-32	-25	-21
Switchboard operators	246	175	189	198	-29	-23	-19
Farmers	1,074	822	850	876	-23	-21	-18
Sewing machine operators, garment	585	368	469	478	-37	-20	-18
Farm workers	837	723	745	766	-14	-11	-8
Typists and word processors	972	805	869	916	-17	-11	-6

- Represents or rounds to zero.   [1] Based on low, moderate, or high trend assumptions.   [2] Includes other occupations, not shown separately.   [3] In descending order, based on absolute employment change 1990 to 2005 (moderate growth).   [4] Includes maids and housekeepers.   [5] Includes tenders.   [6] Metal and plastic.

Source: U.S. Bureau of Labor Statistics, *Monthy Labor Review*, November 1991.

No. 631. Occupation of Employed Civilians, by Sex, Race, and Educational Attainment: 1991

[In thousands. Annual averages of monthly figures. For civilian noninstitutional population 25 years and over. Based on Current Population Survey; see text, section 1 and Appendix III]

SEX, RACE, AND YEARS OF SCHOOL	Total employed	Mana-gerial/ profes-sional	Tech./ sales/ adminis-trative	Service [1]	Precision produc-tion [2]	Opera-tors/ fabrica-tors [3]	Farming, forestry, fishing
Male, total [4]	54,293	15,849	10,649	4,508	10,696	10,249	2,341
Less than 4 years of high school	7,676	413	595	986	2,038	2,827	816
4 years of high school only	19,831	2,313	3,453	1,974	5,674	5,435	980
1 to 3 years of college	11,007	2,744	3,113	1,067	2,267	1,499	317
4 years of college or more	15,779	10,378	3,489	480	716	488	228
White	47,483	14,464	9,425	3,449	9,640	8,396	2,109
Less than 4 years of high school	6,420	367	511	729	1,818	2,302	693
4 years of high school only	17,248	2,130	3,082	1,479	5,151	4,507	898
1 to 3 years of college	9,648	2,513	2,735	856	2,045	1,203	296
4 years of college or more	14,168	9,453	3,096	385	627	384	222
Black	4,957	758	819	832	810	1,566	173
Less than 4 years of high school	1,014	30	59	202	180	447	96
4 years of high school only	2,101	127	298	396	413	808	60
1 to 3 years of college	1,051	167	287	173	164	246	13
4 years of college or more	791	435	175	60	53	65	3
Female, total [4]	44,723	13,300	18,856	7,321	1,030	3,739	476
Less than 4 years of high school	4,729	244	1,016	1,905	220	1,238	105
4 years of high school only	18,628	2,486	9,583	3,758	549	2,013	239
1 to 3 years of college	10,032	2,831	5,336	1,238	176	370	81
4 years of college or more	11,335	7,739	2,921	419	85	119	52
White	38,055	11,799	16,455	5,591	854	2,909	447
Less than 4 years of high school	3,709	214	903	1,346	186	968	92
4 years of high school only	15,960	2,249	8,537	2,912	459	1,576	227
1 to 3 years of college	8,541	2,523	4,530	992	139	280	78
4 years of college or more	9,844	6,813	2,485	341	70	85	51
Black	5,121	1,061	1,845	1,431	119	647	17
Less than 4 years of high school	825	22	85	486	22	203	8
4 years of high school only	2,176	183	854	710	63	358	8
1 to 3 years of college	1,211	240	672	197	27	74	2
4 years of college or more	909	617	234	38	7	13	-

- Represents or rounds to zero.   [1] Includes private household workers.   [2] Includes craft and repair.   [3] Includes laborers.
[4] Includes other races, not shown separately.
Source: U.S. Bureau of Labor Statistics, unpublished data.

No. 632. Employment by Industry, 1970 to 1991, and by Selected Characteristics, 1991

[In thousands, except percent. See headnote, table 610. Data from 1985 forward not strictly comparable with earlier years due to changes in industrial classification]

INDUSTRY	1970	1980	1985	1989	1990	1991 Total	1991 Percent Female	1991 Percent Black	1991 Percent Hispanic[1]
Total employed	78,678	99,303	107,150	117,342	117,914	116,877	45.6	10.1	7.5
Agriculture	3,463	3,364	3,179	3,199	3,186	3,233	21.1	5.0	14.0
Mining	516	979	939	719	730	733	17.6	5.4	6.6
Construction	4,818	6,215	6,987	7,680	7,696	7,087	8.5	6.6	8.4
Manufacturing	20,746	21,942	20,879	21,652	21,184	20,434	32.7	10.3	8.5
Transportation, communication, and other public utilities	5,320	6,525	7,548	8,094	8,136	8,204	28.8	13.9	6.1
Wholesale and retail trade	15,008	20,191	22,296	24,230	24,269	24,055	46.9	7.9	8.4
Wholesale trade	2,672	3,920	4,341	4,611	4,651	4,640	29.0	5.6	7.3
Retail trade	12,336	16,270	17,955	19,618	19,618	19,415	51.2	8.5	8.6
Finance, insurance, real estate	3,945	5,993	7,005	7,988	8,021	7,786	59.1	8.7	5.6
Banking and other finances	1,697	2,568	3,135	3,447	3,434	3,287	64.1	9.6	6.3
Insurance and real estate	2,248	3,425	3,870	4,542	4,587	4,500	55.4	8.1	5.2
Services [2]	20,385	28,752	33,322	38,227	39,084	39,705	61.9	11.4	6.8
Business services [2]	1,403	2,361	3,999	5,288	5,288	5,325	47.3	10.7	7.4
Advertising	147	191	263	282	277	255	48.7	4.7	4.1
Services to dwellings and buildings	(NA)	370	571	801	813	833	51.3	17.5	18.5
Personnel supply services	(NA)	235	590	786	704	658	67.9	18.1	5.4
Business management/consulting	(NA)	307	395	557	604	610	47.8	6.4	3.5
Computer and data processing	(NA)	221	549	797	799	847	36.5	5.1	2.8
Detective/protective services	(NA)	213	318	364	373	399	19.7	25.1	9.1
Automobile services	600	952	1,322	1,391	1,429	1,435	12.3	8.7	11.8
Personal services [2]	4,276	3,839	4,352	4,664	4,667	4,675	70.4	14.3	12.3
Private households	1,782	1,257	1,254	1,108	1,023	1,000	85.9	21.4	18.9
Hotels and lodging places	979	1,149	1,451	1,695	1,780	1,813	63.4	14.5	12.7
Entertainment and recreation	717	1,047	1,278	1,440	1,503	1,570	39.7	9.1	7.7
Professional and related services [2]	12,904	19,853	21,563	24,609	25,335	25,835	69.0	11.5	5.2
Hospitals	2,843	4,036	4,269	4,568	4,690	4,839	77.3	16.0	5.5
Health services, except hospitals	1,628	3,345	3,641	4,542	4,757	4,978	78.0	12.4	5.9
Elementary, secondary schools	6,126	5,550	5,431	5,970	6,028	6,116	73.4	11.2	5.4
Colleges and universities	(³)	2,108	2,281	2,514	2,609	2,570	52.7	9.0	4.3
Social services	828	1,590	1,682	2,110	2,234	2,350	80.2	16.3	6.8
Legal services	429	776	995	1,207	1,217	1,274	55.2	5.2	4.0
Public administration [4]	4,476	5,342	4,995	5,553	5,608	5,639	41.8	15.2	5.6

NA Not available.   [1] Persons of Hispanic origin may be of any race.   [2] Includes industries not shown separately.
[3] Included with el/sec schools.   [4] Includes workers involved in uniquely governmental activities, e.g., judicial and legislative.
Source: U.S. Bureau of Labor Statistics, *Employment and Earnings*, monthly, January issues.

No. 633. Employment by Selected Industry, 1975 to 1990, and Projections, 2005

[**In thousands, except percent.** Figures may differ from those in other tables since these data exclude establishments not elsewhere classified (SIC 99); in addition, agriculture services (SIC 074, 5, 8) are included in agriculture, not services. See source for details. N.e.c. means not elsewhere classified. Minus sign (-) indicates decrease]

1987 SIC [1] code	INDUSTRY	EMPLOYMENT			ANNUAL AVERAGE RATE OF CHANGE	
		1975	1990	2005 [2]	1975-1990	1990-2005 [2]
(X)	Total	87,666	122,570	147,190	2.3	1.2
(X)	Nonfarm wage and salary	76,680	109,319	132,647	2.4	1.3
(X)	Goods-producing (excluding agriculture)	22,600	24,958	25,241	0.7	0.1
10-14	Mining	752	711	668	-0.4	-0.4
15,16,17	Construction	3,525	5,136	6,059	2.5	1.1
20-39	Manufacturing	18,323	19,111	18,514	0.3	-0.2
24,25,32-39	Durable manufacturing	10,662	11,115	10,517	0.3	-0.4
24	Lumber and wood products	627	741	722	1.1	-0.2
25	Furniture and fixtures	417	510	618	1.4	1.3
32	Stone, clay and glass products	598	557	516	-0.5	-0.5
33	Primary metal industries	1,139	756	643	-2.7	-1.1
331	Blast furnaces/basic steel products	548	275	222	-4.5	-1.4
34	Fabricated metal products	1,453	1,423	1,238	-0.1	-0.9
35	Industrial machinery and equipment	2,076	2,095	1,941	0.1	-0.5
3571,2,5,7	Computer equipment	210	396	345	4.3	-0.9
36	Electronic and other electric equipment [3]	1,442	1,673	1,567	1.0	-0.4
3661	Telephone and telegraph apparatus	148	128	110	-1.0	-1.0
3674	Semiconductors and related devices	122	238	235	4.6	-0.1
37	Transportation equipment	1,700	1,980	1,889	1.0	-0.3
371	Motor vehicles and equipment	792	809	744	0.1	-0.6
38	Instruments and related products [3]	804	1,004	1,018	1.5	0.1
382	Measuring/controlling devices, watches	326	334	271	0.2	-1.4
3841-3	Medical instruments and supplies	109	206	282	4.3	2.1
39	Miscellaneous manufacturing industries	407	377	364	-0.5	-0.2
20-23,26-31	Nondurable manufacturing	7,661	7,995	7,998	0.3	-
20	Food and kindred products	1,658	1,668	1,560	-	-0.4
21	Tobacco manufactures	76	49	34	-2.9	-2.5
22	Textile mill products	868	691	596	-1.5	-1.0
23	Apparel and other textile products	1,243	1,043	848	-1.2	-1.4
26	Paper and allied products	633	699	727	0.7	0.3
27	Printing and publishing	1,083	1,574	1,900	2.5	1.3
28	Chemicals and allied products	1,015	1,093	1,098	0.5	-
29	Petroleum and coal products	194	158	122	-1.4	-1.7
30	Rubber/misc. plastics products	643	889	1,043	2.2	1.1
31	Leather and leather products	248	132	72	-4.1	-4.0
(X)	Service producing	54,080	84,363	107,405	3.0	1.6
40-42,44-49	Transportation, communications, utilities	4,542	5,826	6,689	1.7	0.9
40-42,44-47	Transportation	2,634	3,554	4,427	2.0	1.5
48	Communications	1,176	1,311	1,143	0.7	-0.9
49	Electric, gas, and sanitary services	733	961	1,119	1.8	1.0
50,51	Wholesale trade	4,430	6,205	7,210	2.3	1.0
52-59	Retail trade	12,630	19,683	24,804	3.0	1.6
58	Eating and drinking places	3,380	6,565	8,712	4.5	1.9
60-67	Finance, insurance, and real estate	4,165	6,739	8,129	3.3	1.3
70-87,89	Services	13,627	27,588	39,058	4.8	2.3
70	Hotels and other lodging places	898	1,649	2,174	4.1	1.9
72	Personal services	782	1,113	1,338	2.4	1.2
73	Business services [3]	1,697	5,241	7,623	7.8	2.5
731	Advertising	122	238	345	4.6	2.5
734	Services to buildings	391	809	995	5.0	1.4
736	Personnel supply services	242	1,559	2,068	13.2	1.9
737	Computer and data processing services	143	784	1,494	12.0	4.4
75	Auto repair, services, and garages	439	928	1,245	5.1	2.0
76	Miscellaneous repair shops	218	390	480	4.0	1.4
78	Motion pictures	206	408	476	4.7	1.0
784	Video tape rental	(NA)	132	150	(NA)	0.8
79	Amusement and recreation services	613	1,089	1,428	3.9	1.8
80	Health services	4,134	7,844	11,519	4.4	2.6
801,2,3,4	Offices of health practitioners	936	2,180	3,470	5.8	3.1
805	Nursing and personal care facilities	759	1,420	2,182	4.3	2.9
806	Hospitals, private	2,274	3,547	4,605	3.0	1.8
807,8,9	Health services, n.e.c.	165	697	1,262	10.1	4.0
81	Legal services	341	919	1,427	6.8	3.0
02	Educational services	1,001	1,652	2,326	3.4	2.3
83	Social services	690	1,811	2,874	6.6	3.1
84,86,8733	Museums, zoos, and membership organizations	1,573	2,149	2,488	2.1	1.0
87,89	Engineering, management, and services n.e.c. [4]	(NA)	2,396	3,660	(NA)	2.9
(X)	Government	14,686	18,322	21,515	1.5	1.1
(X)	Federal government	2,748	3,085	3,184	0.8	0.2
(X)	State and local government	11,937	15,237	18,331	1.6	1.2
01,02,07,08,09	Agriculture	3,459	3,276	3,080	-0.4	-0.4
88	Private households	1,362	1,014	700	-1.9	-2.4
(X)	Nonag. self-employed and unpaid family	6,165	8,961	10,763	2.5	1.2

- Represents or rounds to zero.   NA Not available.   X Not applicable.   [1] 1987 Standard Industrial Classification; see text, section 13.   [2] Based on assumptions of moderate growth; see source.   [3] Includes other industries, not shown separately. [4] Excludes SIC 8733.

Source: U.S. Bureau of Labor Statistics, *Monthly Labor Review*, November 1991.

Labor Force, Employment, and Earnings

No. 634. High Technology Employment and Average Pay, by Industry: 1989

[For wage and salary workers. Based on surveys and subject to sampling error; for details see source]

1987 SIC [1] code	INDUSTRY	HIGH TECH EMPLOYMENT				Average annual pay (dol.)
		Total (1,000)	R&D employment			
			Total (1,000)	Percent of total employed	Percent distribution	
(X)	All high technology industries [2]	10,012.5	312.6	3.1	100.0	$34,626
(X)	Level 1 industries [3]	8,666.9	299.9	3.5	86.6	35,597
131	Crude Petroleum and Natural Gas operations	193.1	3.1	1.6	1.9	45,822
211	Cigarettes.	38.4	0.6	1.6	0.4	46,273
281	Industrial inorganic chemicals	134.1	5.1	3.8	1.3	39,611
282	Plastics materials and synthetics	183.2	6.3	3.4	1.8	38,432
283	Drugs	231.3	21.6	9.2	2.3	39,986
284	Soap, cleaners, and toilet goods	159.9	5.1	3.1	1.6	32,781
285	Paints and allied products	63.1	3.4	5.2	0.6	30,536
286	Industrial organic chemicals.	149.0	14.4	9.6	1.5	43,519
287	Agricultural chemicals.	52.5	0.8	1.5	0.5	33,167
289	Miscellaneous chemical products	100.2	3.7	3.7	1.0	33,101
291	Petroleum refining	118.5	4.6	3.9	1.2	43,452
299	Miscellaneous petroleum and coal products.	11.9	0.2	2.0	0.1	30,758
335	Nonferrous rolling and drawing.	176.7	2.0	1.2	1.8	31,462
355	Special industry machinery	161.9	2.3	1.4	1.6	30,388
357	Computer and office equipment	455.0	15.3	3.4	4.5	40,409
362	Electrical industrial apparatus.	177.1	2.9	1.6	1.8	27,028
366	Communications equipment.	270.6	8.1	3.0	2.7	24,238
367	Electronic components and accessories.	614.0	9.0	1.5	6.1	29,387
371	Motor vehicles and equipment	847.1	19.3	2.2	8.5	37,191
372	Aircraft and parts.	708.6	8.6	1.2	7.1	37,216
376	Guided missiles, space vehicles, parts. .	195.0	9.4	4.8	1.9	39,540
381	Search and navigation equipment.	302.5	9.3	3.1	3.0	38,491
382	Measuring and controlling devices	331.1	8.8	2.7	3.3	30,940
384	Medical instruments and supplies	238.8	6.3	2.6	2.4	28,836
386	Photographic equipment and supplies . .	104.3	1.5	1.4	1.0	40,755
737	Computer and data-processing services.	732.7	31.4	4.9	7.3	35,787
871	Engineering and architectural services. .	774.9	20.6	2.8	7.7	35,438
873	Research and testing services	528.6	68.6	14.5	5.3	32,088
874	Management and public relations	577.2	7.1	1.5	5.8	35,280
899	Services, n.e.c. [4]	35.6	0.5	1.7	0.4	41,649
(X)	Level II industries [5]	1,345.7	12.7	0.9	13.4	28,373
229	Miscellaneous textile goods.	52.1	0.5	0.9	0.5	23,035
261	Pulp mills	16.8	0.2	1.1	0.2	39,800
267	Miscelleanous converted paper products	240.1	2.4	1.0	2.4	27,697
348	Ordinance and accessories, n.e.c. [4] . . .	75.1	0.6	0.8	0.8	29,766
351	Engines and turbines	90.8	1.0	1.1	0.9	36,549
356	General industry machinery	243.3	2.1	0.9	2.4	29,223
359	Industrial machines, n.e.c. [4]	321.7	2.8	0.9	3.2	26,303
365	Household audio and video equipment .	87.2	0.8	0.9	0.9	28,595
369	Miscellaneous electrical equipment and supplies	170.8	1.8	1.0	1.7	28,315
379	Miscellaneous transportation equipment.	47.9	0.5	1.0	0.5	25,278

X Not applicable.   [1] 1987 Standard Industrial Classification; see text, section 13.   [2] Those industries whose proportion of R&D employment is at least equal to the average proportion of all industries surveyed.   [3] Industries whose proportion of R&D employment is at least 50 percent higher than the average of all industries surveyed.   [4] N.e.c. means not elsewhere classified.   [5] Industries whose proportion of R&D employment is at least equal to the average of all industries surveyed, but less than 50 percent higher than the average.

Source: U.S. Bureau of Labor Statistics, *Monthly Labor Review,* July 1991; and unpublished data.

No. 635. Unemployed Workers—Summary: 1980 to 1991

[In thousands, except as Indicated. For civilian noninstitutional population 16 years old and over. Annual averages of monthly figures. For data on unemployment insurance, see table 582. See also *Historical Statistics, Colonial Times to 1970*, series D 87-101]

ITEM AND CHARACTERISTIC	1980	1984	1985	1986	1987	1988	1989	1990	1991
UNEMPLOYED									
Total [1]	**7,637**	**8,539**	**8,312**	**8,237**	**7,425**	**6,701**	**6,528**	**6,874**	**8,426**
Labor force time lost [2] (percent)	7.9	8.6	8.1	7.9	7.1	6.3	5.9	6.2	7.6
16 to 19 years old	1,669	1,499	1,468	1,454	1,347	1,226	1,194	1,149	1,290
20 to 24 years old	1,835	1,838	1,738	1,651	1,453	1,261	1,218	1,221	1,477
25 to 44 years old	2,964	3,709	3,681	3,761	3,410	3,095	3,010	3,273	4,106
45 to 64 years old	1,075	1,394	1,331	1,279	1,135	1,032	1,016	1,124	1,437
65 years and over	94	97	93	91	78	87	91	107	116
Male	4,267	4,744	4,521	4,530	4,101	3,655	3,525	3,799	4,817
16 to 19 years old	913	812	806	779	732	667	658	629	709
20 to 24 years old	1,076	1,023	944	899	779	676	660	666	849
25 to 44 years old	1,619	2,050	1,950	2,054	1,858	1,657	1,572	1,774	2,331
45 to 64 years old	600	806	766	741	684	606	585	668	862
65 years and over	58	53	55	58	49	49	49	61	66
Female	3,370	3,794	3,791	3,707	3,324	3,046	3,003	3,075	3,609
16 to 19 years old	755	687	661	675	616	558	536	519	581
20 to 24 years old	760	815	794	752	674	585	558	555	628
25 to 44 years old	1,345	1,659	1,732	1,708	1,552	1,439	1,437	1,498	1,775
45 to 64 years old	473	589	566	539	453	427	430	456	575
65 years and over	36	45	39	33	30	38	41	46	50
White [3]	5,884	6,372	6,191	6,140	5,501	4,944	4,770	5,091	6,447
16 to 19 years old	1,291	1,116	1,074	1,070	995	910	863	856	977
20 to 24 years old	1,364	1,282	1,235	1,149	1,017	874	856	844	1,063
Black [3]	1,553	1,914	1,864	1,840	1,684	1,547	1,544	1,527	1,679
16 to 19 years old	343	353	357	347	312	288	300	258	270
20 to 24 years old	426	504	455	453	397	349	322	335	362
Hispanic [3][4]	620	800	811	857	751	732	750	769	963
16 to 19 years old	145	149	141	141	136	148	132	131	149
20 to 24 years old	138	164	171	183	152	145	158	135	172
Full-time workers	6,269	7,057	6,793	6,708	5,979	5,357	5,211	5,541	6,932
Part-time workers	1,369	1,481	1,519	1,529	1,446	1,343	1,317	1,332	1,494
UNEMPLOYMENT RATE (percent) [5]									
Total [1]	**7.1**	**7.5**	**7.2**	**7.0**	**6.2**	**5.5**	**5.3**	**5.5**	**6.7**
16 to 19 years old	17.8	18.9	18.6	18.3	16.9	15.3	15.0	15.5	18.6
20 to 24 years old	11.5	11.5	11.1	10.7	9.7	8.7	8.6	8.8	10.8
25 to 44 years old	6.0	6.4	6.2	6.1	5.4	4.8	4.5	4.8	6.0
45 to 64 years old	3.7	4.8	4.5	4.3	3.8	3.3	3.2	3.5	4.4
65 years and over	3.1	3.3	3.2	3.0	2.5	2.7	2.6	3.0	3.3
Male	6.9	7.4	7.0	6.9	6.2	5.5	5.2	5.6	7.0
16 to 19 years old	18.3	19.6	19.5	19.0	17.8	16.0	15.9	16.3	19.8
20 to 24 years old	12.5	11.9	11.4	11.0	9.9	8.9	8.8	9.1	11.7
25 to 44 years old	5.6	6.3	5.9	6.0	5.3	4.6	4.3	4.8	6.2
45 to 64 years old	3.5	4.8	4.5	4.4	4.0	3.5	3.3	3.7	4.7
65 years and over	3.1	3.0	3.1	3.2	2.6	2.5	2.4	3.0	3.3
Female	7.4	7.6	7.4	7.1	6.2	5.6	5.4	5.4	6.3
16 to 19 years old	17.2	18.0	17.6	17.6	15.9	14.4	14.0	14.7	17.4
20 to 24 years old	10.4	10.9	10.7	10.3	9.4	8.5	8.3	8.5	9.8
25 to 44 years old	6.4	6.6	6.6	6.2	5.5	4.9	4.8	4.9	5.7
45 to 64 years old	4.0	4.9	4.6	4.2	3.5	3.2	3.1	3.2	3.9
65 years and over	3.1	3.8	3.3	2.8	2.4	2.9	2.9	3.1	3.3
White [3]	6.3	6.5	6.2	6.0	5.3	4.7	4.5	4.7	6.0
16 to 19 years old	15.5	16.0	15.7	15.6	14.4	13.1	12.7	13.4	16.4
20 to 24 years old	9.9	9.3	9.2	8.7	8.0	7.1	7.2	7.2	9.2
Black [3]	14.3	15.9	15.1	14.5	13.0	11.7	11.4	11.3	12.4
16 to 19 years old	38.5	42.7	40.2	39.3	34.7	32.4	32.4	31.1	36.3
20 to 24 years old	23.6	26.1	24.5	24.1	21.8	19.6	18.0	19.9	21.6
Hispanic [3][4]	10.1	10.7	10.5	10.6	8.8	8.2	8.0	8.0	9.9
16 to 19 years old	22.5	24.1	24.3	24.7	22.3	22.0	19.4	19.5	22.9
20 to 24 years old	12.1	12.4	12.6	12.9	10.6	9.8	10.7	9.1	11.6
Experienced workers [6]	6.9	7.1	6.8	6.6	5.8	5.2	5.0	5.3	6.5
Women maintaining families [1]	9.2	10.4	10.5	9.9	9.3	8.2	8.1	8.2	9.1
White	7.3	7.8	8.1	7.8	6.8	6.0	6.1	6.3	7.2
Black	14.0	16.7	16.4	15.4	15.4	13.7	13.0	13.1	13.9
Married men, wife present [1]	4.2	4.6	4.3	4.4	3.9	3.3	3.0	3.4	4.4
White	3.9	4.3	4.0	4.0	3.6	3.0	2.8	3.1	4.2
Black	7.4	8.1	8.0	8.0	6.5	5.8	5.8	6.2	6.5
Percent without work for—									
Less than 5 weeks	43.1	39.2	42.1	41.9	43.7	46.0	48.6	46.1	40.1
5 to 10 weeks	23.4	20.6	22.2	22.6	21.6	22.2	22.2	23.5	22.9
11 to 14 weeks	9.0	8.1	8.0	8.4	7.9	7.8	8.1	8.6	9.5
15 to 26 weeks	13.8	12.9	12.3	12.7	12.7	12.0	11.2	11.8	14.5
27 weeks and over	10.7	19.1	15.4	14.4	14.0	12.1	9.9	10.1	13.0
Unemployment duration, average (weeks)	11.9	18.2	15.6	15.0	14.5	13.5	11.9	12.1	13.8

[1] Includes other races, not shown separately. [2] Aggregate hours lost by the unemployed and persons on part time for economic reasons as a percent of potentially available labor force hours. [3] Includes other ages, not shown separately. [4] Persons of Hispanic origin may be of any race. [5] Unemployed as percent of civilian labor force in specified group. [6] Wage and salary workers.

Source: U.S. Bureau of Labor Statistics, *Employment and Earnings*, monthly, January issues; and unpublished data.

No. 636. Unemployed Persons, by Sex and Reason, 1980 to 1991, and by Duration, 1991

[In thousands, except as indicated. For civilian noninstitutional population 16 years old and over. Annual averages of monthly figures. Based on Current Population Survey; see text, section 1 and Appendix III]

SEX AND REASON UNEMPLOYED	1980	1983	1984	1985	1986	1987	1988	1989	1990	1991 Total	Less than 5 weeks	5 to 14 weeks	15 weeks or more
											Duration of unemployment (percent)		
Male.	4,267	6,260	4,744	4,521	4,530	4,101	3,655	3,525	3,799	4,817	36.5	32.4	31.1
Job losers	2,649	4,331	2,976	2,749	2,725	2,432	2,078	1,975	2,208	3,105	32.0	33.0	35.0
Job leavers. . . .	438	386	375	409	520	494	503	495	511	492	42.3	32.7	25.0
Reentrants	776	953	867	876	805	761	697	726	782	865	44.2	31.0	24.7
New entrants . .	405	589	526	487	480	413	376	328	298	356	49.4	30.1	20.5
Female.	3,370	4,457	3,794	3,791	3,707	3,324	3,046	3,003	3,075	3,609	44.9	32.2	22.9
Job losers	1,297	1,926	1,445	1,390	1,308	1,134	1,014	1,008	1,114	1,503	34.5	33.9	31.6
Job leavers. . . .	453	444	449	468	494	471	480	529	503	487	50.5	31.4	18.1
Reentrants	1,152	1,459	1,317	1,380	1,355	1,213	1,112	1,117	1,101	1,222	52.0	30.6	17.4
New entrants . .	468	627	584	552	549	506	440	349	357	398	55.8	31.7	12.6

Source: U.S. Bureau of Labor Statistics, *Employment and Earnings*, monthly, January issues; Bulletin 2307; and unpublished data.

No. 637. Unemployment Rates, by Educational Attainment, Sex, and Race: 1970 to 1991

[In percent. As of March, except as indicated. Civilian noninstitutional population 25 to 64 years of age. Based on Current Population Survey; see text, section 1 and Appendix III]

ITEM	1970	1975	1980	1982	1983	1984	1985	1986	1987	1988	1989	1990[1]	1991[1]
Total.	3.3	6.9	5.0	7.6	9.0	6.6	6.1	6.1	5.7	4.7	4.4	4.4	5.5
Less than 4 years of high school[2]	4.6	10.7	8.4	12.5	15.8	12.1	11.4	11.6	11.1	9.6	9.1	8.5	11.0
4 years of high school, only	2.9	6.9	5.1	8.5	10.0	7.2	6.9	6.9	6.3	5.4	4.8	4.9	5.9
College: 1-3 years	2.9	5.5	4.3	6.4	7.3	5.3	4.7	4.7	4.5	3.7	3.4	3.7	4.8
4 years or more	1.3	2.5	1.9	3.0	3.5	2.7	2.4	2.3	2.3	1.7	2.2	2.2	2.8
Male: Total.	2.9	6.7	4.9	7.9	9.8	6.9	6.1	6.2	6.0	5.1	4.7	4.4	5.8
Less than 4 years of high school[2]	4.0	10.5	8.2	12.7	16.1	12.3	11.2	11.7	11.2	10.1	9.7	8.2	11.0
4 years of high school, only	2.4	6.7	5.3	9.3	11.9	8.1	7.2	7.4	6.7	6.2	5.4	5.1	6.4
College: 1-3 years	2.7	5.1	4.4	6.8	8.4	5.2	4.5	4.7	5.0	3.9	3.2	3.7	4.9
4 years or more	1.1	2.2	1.7	2.9	3.4	2.7	2.4	2.3	2.5	1.6	2.3	2.1	2.8
Female: Total.	4.0	7.4	5.0	7.2	7.9	6.1	6.0	5.8	5.2	4.2	4.0	4.4	5.2
Less than 4 years of high school[2]	5.7	10.5	8.9	12.2	15.3	11.7	11.7	11.4	10.9	8.9	8.4	9.0	10.9
4 years of high school, only	3.6	7.1	5.0	7.8	8.0	6.3	6.5	6.3	5.8	4.6	4.2	4.6	5.4
College: 1-3 years	3.1	6.3	4.1	5.3	6.0	5.3	4.8	4.8	4.0	3.4	3.7	3.7	4.7
4 years or more	1.9	3.4	2.2	3.3	3.7	2.7	2.5	2.4	2.1	1.9	2.0	2.3	2.8
White: Total.	3.1	6.5	4.4	6.8	8.0	5.7	5.3	5.5	5.0	4.0	3.8	3.8	5.0
Less than 4 years of high school[2]	4.5	10.1	7.8	12.2	15.0	10.9	10.6	10.9	10.2	8.3	7.4	7.6	10.3
4 years of high school, only	2.7	6.5	4.6	7.6	8.9	6.4	6.1	6.2	5.5	4.6	4.2	4.2	5.4
College: 1-3 years	2.8	5.1	3.9	5.4	6.5	4.6	3.9	4.2	4.1	3.2	3.0	3.2	4.2
4 years or more	1.3	2.4	1.8	2.8	3.1	2.4	2.1	2.2	2.2	1.5	2.0	2.1	2.7
Black: Total[3]	4.7	10.9	9.6	13.9	16.8	13.3	12.0	10.7	10.6	10.0	9.2	8.6	9.6
Less than 4 years of high school[2]	5.2	13.5	11.7	14.4	19.9	17.4	15.3	15.3	14.8	15.7	15.9	13.3	14.7
4 years of high school, only	5.2	10.7	9.5	16.4	18.9	14.5	13.0	11.7	11.7	11.2	9.2	9.5	9.9
College: 1-3 years	3.5	9.8	9.0	12.5	13.3	9.7	10.6	8.7	7.6	7.4	6.9	6.8	8.8
4 years or more	0.9	3.9	4.0	7.1	8.1	6.2	5.4	3.2	4.2	3.3	4.7	3.0	4.1

[1] Not strictly comparable with data for earlier years. Annual averages of monthly figures.   [2] Includes persons reporting no school years completed.   [3] For 1970 and 1975, data refer to Black and other workers.
Source: U.S. Bureau of Labor Statistics, Bulletin 2307; and unpublished data.

No. 638. Unemployment Rates, by Industry, 1975 to 1991, and by Sex, 1980 and 1991

[In percent. For civilian noninstitutional population 16 years old and over. Annual averages of monthly figures. Rate represents unemployment as a percent of labor force in each specified group. Beginning 1985, data not strictly comparable with earlier years due to changes in industrial classification]

INDUSTRY	1975	1980	1985	1988	1989	1990	1991	MALE 1980	MALE 1991	FEMALE 1980	FEMALE 1991
All unemployed[1]	8.5	7.1	7.2	5.5	5.3	5.5	6.7	6.9	7.0	7.4	6.3
Industry:[2]											
Agriculture.	10.4	11.0	13.2	10.6	9.6	9.7	11.6	9.7	11.6	15.1	11.8
Mining.	4.1	6.4	9.5	7.9	5.8	4.8	7.7	6.7	8.6	4.5	3.4
Construction.	18.0	14.1	13.1	10.6	10.0	11.1	15.4	14.6	15.9	8.9	10.1
Manufacturing.	10.9	8.5	7.7	5.3	5.1	5.8	7.2	7.4	6.5	10.8	8.6
Transportation and public utilities . . .	5.6	4.9	5.1	3.9	3.9	3.8	5.3	5.1	5.5	4.4	4.6
Wholesale and retail trade	8.7	7.4	7.6	6.2	6.0	6.4	7.6	6.6	7.2	8.3	8.0
Finance, insurance, and real estate . .	4.9	3.4	3.5	3.0	3.1	3.0	4.0	3.2	3.8	3.5	4.0
Services	7.1	5.9	6.2	4.9	4.8	5.0	5.7	6.3	6.4	5.8	5.3
Government.	4.1	4.1	3.9	2.8	2.7	2.6	3.2	3.9	3.3	4.3	3.1

[1] Includes the self-employed, unpaid family workers, and persons with no previous work experience, not shown separately.
[2] Covers unemployed wage and salary workers.
Source: U.S. Bureau of Labor Statistics, *Employment and Earnings*, monthly, January issues.

No. 639. Unemployment and Unemployment Rates by Occupation, 1983 to 1991, and by Sex, 1991

[For civilian noninstitutional population 16 years old and over. Beginning 1985, annual averages of monthly data; 1983 data estimated, see text, section 13. Rate represents unemployment as a percent of the labor force for each specified group. Based on Current Population Survey; see text, section 1 and Appendix III]

OCCUPATION	NUMBER (1,000)			UNEMPLOYMENT RATE				
	1983	1985	1991	1983	1985	1991		
						Total	Male	Female
Total [1]	10,717	8,312	8,426	9.6	7.2	6.7	7.0	6.3
Managerial and professional specialty	795	645	886	3.3	2.4	2.8	2.7	2.9
Executive, administrative, and managerial	396	329	494	3.5	2.6	3.2	3.0	3.5
Professional specialty	399	316	393	3.0	2.3	2.4	2.4	2.4
Technical sales, and administrative support	2,116	1,694	1,941	6.3	4.9	5.1	4.7	5.3
Technicians and related support	152	110	132	4.7	3.3	3.4	3.8	2.9
Sales occupations	850	702	838	6.7	5.3	5.7	4.4	7.0
Administrative support, including clerical	1,114	882	971	6.4	4.9	5.0	5.7	4.9
Service occupations	1,697	1,386	1,292	10.9	8.8	7.5	8.0	7.1
Private household	79	69	55	7.4	6.4	6.5	10.4	6.3
Protective service	120	85	99	6.7	4.7	4.6	4.4	5.3
Service except private household and protective. .	1,498	1,233	1,139	11.8	9.5	8.0	9.3	7.3
Precision production, craft, and repair	1,466	1,038	1,130	10.6	7.2	7.9	7.9	7.8
Mechanics and repairers	344	225	242	7.6	4.8	5.2	5.2	4.6
Construction trades	709	531	644	14.2	10.1	11.8	11.8	12.0
Other precision production, craft, and repair.	412	281	244	9.6	6.4	5.9	5.2	8.0
Operators, fabricators, and laborers.	2,955	2,140	2,011	15.5	11.3	10.5	10.3	11.1
Machine operators, assemblers, inspectors	1,411	980	883	15.4	11.1	10.3	9.5	11.4
Transportation and material moving occupations. .	596	422	392	12.4	8.5	7.4	7.5	6.4
Handlers, equipment cleaners, helpers, laborers. .	948	739	736	18.6	14.3	13.8	14.1	12.5
Construction laborers	207	186	198	25.8	21.3	22.1	22.0	(B)
Farming, forestry, and fishing	407	315	286	9.9	8.3	7.6	7.6	8.1

B Base is less than 35,000.   [1] Includes persons with no previous work experience and those whose last job was in the Armed Forces.

Source: U.S. Bureau of Labor Statistics, *Employment and Earnings*, monthly, January issues..

No. 640. Range of Unemployment Measures Based on Varying Definitions of Unemployment and the Labor Force: 1970 to 1991

[In percent. Annual averages of monthly figures. Based on Current Population Survey, see text, section 1 and Appendix III]

MEASURE	1970	1975	1980	1984	1985	1986	1987	1988	1989	1990	1991
Persons unemployed 15 weeks or longer as a percent of the civilian labor force	0.8	2.7	1.7	2.4	2.0	1.9	1.7	1.3	1.1	1.2	1.9
Job losers as a percent of the civilian labor force . .	2.2	4.7	3.7	3.9	3.6	3.4	3.0	2.5	2.4	2.7	3.7
Unemployed persons 25 years and over as a percent of the 25 and over civilian labor force.	3.3	6.0	5.1	5.8	5.6	5.4	4.8	4.3	4.0	4.4	5.4
Unemployed full-time jobseekers as a percent of the full-time civilian labor force	4.5	8.1	6.9	7.2	6.8	6.6	5.8	5.2	4.9	5.2	6.5
Total unemployed as a percent of the labor force, including the resident Armed Forces [1]	4.8	8.3	7.0	7.4	7.1	6.9	6.1	5.4	5.2	5.4	6.6
Total unemployed as a percent of the civilian labor force [1]	4.9	8.5	7.1	7.5	7.2	7.0	6.2	5.5	5.3	5.5	6.7
Total full-time jobseekers plus 1/2 part-time jobseekers plus 1/2 total on part-time for economic reasons as a percent of the civilian labor force less 1/2 of the part-time labor force	6.3	10.5	9.2	10.1	9.6	9.4	8.5	7.6	7.2	7.6	9.2
Total full-time jobseekers plus 1/2 part-time jobseekers plus 1/2 total on part-time for economic reasons plus discouraged workers as a percent of the civilian labor force plus discouraged workers less 1/2 of the part-time labor force	7.1	11.6	10.1	11.2	10.6	10.3	9.3	8.4	7.9	8.2	10.0

[1] Current unemployment rate definition.

Source: U.S. Bureau of Labor Statistics, Bulletin 2307; *Employment Situation,* monthly news release; and unpublished data.

No. 641. Total Unemployed and Insured Unemployed—States: 1980 to 1990

[For civilian noninstitutional population 16 years old and over. Annual averages of monthly figures. Total unemployment estimates based on the Current Population Survey (CPS); see text, section 1, and Appendix III. U.S. totals derived by independent population controls; therefore State data may not add to U.S. totals. See table 613 for 1991 unemployment data]

| DIVISION AND STATE | TOTAL UNEMPLOYED | | | | | | | | | | INSURED UNEMPLOYED [2] | | | |
| | Number (1,000) | | | | | Percent [1] | | | | | Number (1,000) | | Percent [3] | |
	1980	1985	1988	1989	1990	1980	1985	1988	1989	1990	1989	1990	1989	1990
U.S.	7,637	8,312	6,701	6,528	6,874	7.1	7.2	5.5	5.3	5.5	[4]2,158	[4]2,522	[4]2.1	[4]2.4
N.E.: ME	39	30	22	25	33	7.8	5.4	3.8	4.1	5.1	11.5	17.3	2.2	3.4
NH	22	21	15	21	36	4.7	3.9	2.4	3.5	5.6	5.4	11.1	1.1	2.2
VT	16	13	8	11	15	6.4	4.8	2.8	3.7	5.0	5.0	8.0	2.0	3.2
MA	162	121	103	127	189	5.6	3.9	3.3	4.0	6.0	84.4	112.8	2.8	3.8
RI	34	25	16	21	35	7.2	4.9	3.1	4.1	6.7	14.1	20.0	3.1	4.5
CT	94	83	52	64	91	5.9	4.9	3.0	3.7	5.1	28.6	45.0	1.8	2.8
M.A.: NY	597	544	358	442	451	7.5	6.5	4.2	5.1	5.2	180.1	219.1	2.3	2.7
NJ	259	218	151	163	202	7.2	5.7	3.8	4.1	5.0	81.4	104.6	2.3	3.0
PA	425	442	294	264	318	7.8	8.0	5.1	4.5	5.4	126.9	150.1	2.6	3.1
E.N.C.: OH	426	455	320	300	307	8.4	8.9	6.0	5.5	5.7	86.0	98.7	1.9	1.6
IN	252	215	150	136	150	9.6	7.9	5.3	4.7	5.3	29.3	34.3	1.2	1.4
IL	458	513	392	359	371	8.3	9.0	6.8	6.0	6.2	104.6	120.0	2.1	2.4
MI	534	433	348	326	344	12.4	9.9	7.6	7.1	7.1	109.4	121.6	2.9	3.2
WI	167	171	110	114	113	7.2	7.2	4.3	4.4	4.4	46.1	49.4	2.2	1.7
W.N.C.: MN	125	133	94	102	116	5.9	6.0	4.0	4.3	4.8	37.0	41.0	1.9	2.1
IA	82	113	67	65	63	5.8	8.0	4.5	4.3	4.2	17.8	19.9	1.6	1.7
MO	167	159	148	143	151	7.2	6.4	5.7	5.5	5.7	46.1	52.0	2.1	2.4
ND	15	20	16	14	13	5.0	5.9	4.8	4.3	3.9	4.5	4.0	2.0	1.7
SD	16	18	14	15	13	4.9	5.1	3.9	4.2	3.7	2.7	2.1	1.1	0.8
NE	31	44	29	25	18	4.1	5.5	3.6	3.1	2.2	7.5	7.3	1.1	1.1
KS	53	62	61	52	57	4.5	5.0	4.8	4.0	4.4	19.8	19.0	2.0	1.9
S.A.: DE	22	17	11	13	19	7.7	5.3	3.2	3.5	5.1	4.0	4.8	1.2	1.4
MD	140	103	110	93	118	6.5	4.6	4.5	3.7	4.6	28.9	37.6	1.5	1.9
DC	24	27	17	16	20	7.3	8.4	5.0	5.0	6.6	7.4	8.4	1.7	1.9
VA	128	161	120	123	137	5.0	5.6	3.9	3.9	4.3	21.7	27.9	0.9	1.1
WV	74	100	74	66	64	9.4	13.0	9.9	8.6	8.3	16.1	16.3	2.8	2.9
NC	187	167	121	119	139	6.6	5.4	3.6	3.5	4.1	41.2	56.0	1.4	1.9
SC	96	107	76	80	81	6.9	6.8	4.5	4.7	4.7	22.9	26.9	1.6	1.9
GA	163	187	185	177	175	6.4	6.5	5.8	5.5	5.4	39.4	46.7	1.4	1.7
FL	251	319	305	348	378	5.9	6.0	5.0	5.6	5.9	58.1	76.7	1.1	1.5
E.S.C.: KY	133	161	134	108	103	8.0	9.5	7.9	6.2	5.8	27.3	30.6	2.1	2.3
TN	152	180	136	121	125	7.3	8.0	5.8	5.1	5.2	41.5	51.3	2.0	2.5
AL	147	160	136	134	128	8.8	8.9	7.2	7.0	6.8	32.4	35.7	2.2	2.4
MS	79	115	96	91	88	7.5	10.3	8.4	7.8	7.5	21.9	23.4	2.5	2.7
W.S.C.: AR	76	91	86	82	78	7.6	8.7	7.7	7.2	6.9	24.7	26.4	2.9	3.1
LA	121	229	209	151	117	6.7	11.5	10.9	7.9	6.2	36.3	30.0	2.5	2.1
OK	66	112	102	85	86	4.8	7.1	6.7	5.6	5.6	17.0	17.3	1.6	1.6
TX	352	564	606	567	521	5.2	7.0	7.3	6.7	6.2	107.1	111.6	1.6	1.7
Mt.: MT	23	31	27	24	23	6.1	7.7	6.8	5.9	5.8	7.1	7.6	2.7	2.8
ID	34	37	28	25	29	7.9	7.9	5.8	5.1	5.8	10.8	11.3	3.1	3.2
WY	9	18	15	15	13	4.0	7.1	6.3	6.3	5.4	3.5	3.1	2.0	1.7
CO	88	101	109	98	87	5.9	5.9	6.4	5.8	4.9	22.9	21.8	1.6	1.5
NM	42	57	54	46	44	7.5	8.8	7.8	6.7	6.3	10.9	10.4	2.1	2.0
AZ	83	96	104	89	92	6.7	6.5	6.3	5.2	5.3	23.8	26.7	1.7	1.9
UT	40	43	37	37	34	6.3	5.9	4.9	4.6	4.3	8.1	8.2	1.3	1.3
NV	27	41	30	30	31	6.2	8.0	5.2	5.0	4.9	9.2	12.0	1.6	2.1
Pac.: WA	157	171	141	151	122	7.9	8.1	6.2	6.2	4.9	58.5	61.1	3.0	3.1
OR	108	117	82	84	82	8.3	8.8	5.8	5.7	5.5	31.9	37.2	2.8	3.2
CA	790	931	743	737	823	6.8	7.2	5.3	5.1	5.6	321.1	377.3	2.5	3.0
AK	18	24	23	17	18	9.7	9.7	9.3	6.7	6.9	9.1	11.2	4.4	5.5
HI	21	27	16	13	15	4.9	5.6	3.2	2.6	2.8	5.1	5.5	1.1	1.2

[1] Total unemployment as percent of civilian labor force.　[2] Source: U.S. Employment and Training Administration, *Unemployment Insurance, Financial Data*, annual updates.　[3] Insured unemployment as percent of average covered employment in the previous year.　[4] Includes 39,900 in Puerto Rico and the Virgin Islands in 1989 and 43,700 in 1990.

Source: Except as noted, U.S. Bureau of Labor Statistics, *Geographic Profile of Employment and Unemployment*, annual.

No. 642. U.S. Employment Service Job Openings and Placements, and Index of Help-Wanted Advertising: 1970 to 1990

[In thousands, except as indicated. Openings 1970-1983, for years ending Sept. 30; beginning 1985, for years ending June 30]

ITEM	1970	1980	1982	1983	1984	1985	1986	1987	1988	1989
Job openings: [1] Received	6,130	8,122	6,494	[2]5,144	7,529	6,950	6,968	7,240	6,998	6,791
Average per month	511	677	541	[2]572	627	579	581	603	583	566
Nonagricultural placements [1]	4,604	5,610	3,012	[2]2,297	3,270	4,856	4,516	4,503	4,284	3,713
Index of help-wanted advertising in newspapers [3] (1967=100) ...	93	128	95	130	138	138	153	157	151	128

[1] As reported by State employment agencies. Beginning 1985, all placements. Placements include duplication for individuals placed more than once.　[2] Data for nine months from October 1, 1983 through June 30, 1984.　[3] Source: The Conference Board, New York, NY, *The Statistical Bulletin*. Further reproduction prohibited without permission. Index based on number of advertisements in classified sections of 51 newspapers, each in a major employment area.

Source: Except as noted, U.S. Employment and Training Administration, unpublished data.

No. 643. Nonfarm Establishments, Employees, Hours, and Earnings, by Industry: 1960 to 1991

[Based on data from establishment reports. Includes all full- and part-time employees who worked during, or received pay for, any part of the pay period reported. Excludes proprietors, the self-employed, farm workers, unpaid family workers, private household workers, and Armed Forces. Establishment data shown here conform to industry definitions in the 1987 Standard Industrial Classification Manual and are adjusted to March 1990 employment benchmarks; consequently, may not be comparable with previously published data. Based on the Current Employment Statistics Program; see Appendix III. See also *Historical Statistics, Colonial Times to 1970*, series D 127-141 and D 803, 878, 881, 884, and 890]

ITEM AND YEAR	Total	GOODS-PRODUCING				SERVICE-PRODUCING						
		Total	Mining	Construction	Manufacturing	Total	Transportation and public utilities	Wholesale trade	Retail trade	Finance, insurance, and real estate	Services	Government
EMPLOYEES (1,000)												
1960	54,189	20,434	712	2,926	16,796	33,755	4,004	3,153	8,238	2,628	7,378	8,353
1965	60,765	21,926	632	3,232	18,062	38,839	4,036	3,477	9,239	2,977	9,036	10,074
1970	70,880	23,578	623	3,588	19,367	47,302	4,515	4,006	11,034	3,645	11,548	12,554
1975	76,945	22,600	752	3,525	18,323	54,345	4,542	4,430	12,630	4,165	13,892	14,686
1980	90,406	25,658	1,027	4,346	20,285	64,748	5,146	5,292	15,018	5,160	17,890	16,241
1985	97,519	24,859	927	4,673	19,260	72,660	5,238	5,736	17,336	5,955	21,999	16,394
1986	99,525	24,558	777	4,816	18,965	74,967	5,255	5,774	17,909	6,283	23,053	16,693
1987	102,200	24,708	717	4,967	19,024	77,492	5,372	5,865	18,462	6,547	24,235	17,010
1988	105,536	25,173	713	5,110	19,350	80,363	5,527	6,055	19,077	6,649	25,669	17,386
1989	108,329	25,322	693	5,187	19,442	83,007	5,644	6,221	19,549	6,695	27,120	17,779
1990	109,971	24,958	711	5,136	19,111	85,014	5,826	6,205	19,683	6,739	28,240	18,322
1991	108,981	23,819	697	4,696	18,426	85,163	5,824	6,072	19,346	6,708	28,779	18,433
PERCENT DISTRIBUTION												
1960	100.0	37.7	1.3	5.4	31.0	62.3	7.4	5.8	15.2	4.8	13.6	15.4
1965	100.0	36.1	1.0	5.3	29.7	63.9	6.6	5.7	15.2	4.9	14.9	16.6
1970	100.0	33.3	0.9	5.1	27.3	66.7	6.4	5.7	15.6	5.1	16.3	17.7
1975	100.0	29.4	1.0	4.6	23.8	70.6	5.9	5.8	16.4	5.4	18.1	19.1
1980	100.0	28.4	1.1	4.8	22.4	71.6	5.7	5.9	16.6	5.7	19.8	18.0
1985	100.0	25.5	1.0	4.8	19.7	74.5	5.4	5.9	17.8	6.1	22.6	16.8
1986	100.0	24.7	0.8	4.8	19.1	75.3	5.3	5.8	18.0	6.3	23.2	16.8
1987	100.0	24.2	0.7	4.9	18.6	75.8	5.3	5.7	18.1	6.4	23.7	16.6
1988	100.0	23.9	0.7	4.8	18.3	76.1	5.2	5.7	18.1	6.3	24.3	16.5
1989	100.0	23.4	0.6	4.8	17.9	76.6	5.2	5.7	18.0	6.2	25.0	16.4
1990	100.0	22.7	0.6	4.7	17.4	77.3	5.3	5.6	17.9	6.1	25.7	16.7
1991	100.0	21.9	0.6	4.3	16.9	78.1	5.3	5.6	17.8	6.2	26.4	16.9
WEEKLY HOURS [1]												
1960	38.6	(NA)	40.4	36.7	39.7	(NA)	(NA)	40.5	38.0	37.2	(NA)	(NA)
1965	38.8	(NA)	42.3	37.4	41.2	(NA)	41.3	40.8	36.6	37.2	35.9	(NA)
1970	37.1	(NA)	42.7	37.3	39.8	(NA)	40.5	39.9	33.8	36.7	34.4	(NA)
1975	36.1	(NA)	41.9	36.4	39.5	(NA)	39.7	38.6	32.4	36.5	33.5	(NA)
1980	35.3	(NA)	43.3	37.0	39.7	(NA)	39.6	38.4	30.2	36.2	32.6	(NA)
1985	34.9	(NA)	43.4	37.7	40.5	(NA)	39.5	38.4	29.4	36.4	32.5	(NA)
1986	34.8	(NA)	42.2	37.4	40.7	(NA)	39.2	38.3	29.2	36.4	32.5	(NA)
1987	34.8	(NA)	42.4	37.8	41.0	(NA)	39.2	38.1	29.2	36.3	32.5	(NA)
1988	34.7	(NA)	42.3	37.9	41.1	(NA)	38.8	38.1	29.1	35.9	32.6	(NA)
1989	34.6	(NA)	43.0	37.9	41.0	(NA)	38.9	38.0	28.9	35.8	32.6	(NA)
1990	34.5	(NA)	44.1	38.2	40.8	(NA)	38.9	38.1	28.8	35.8	32.6	(NA)
1991	34.3	(NA)	44.4	38.1	40.7	(NA)	38.6	38.1	28.6	35.8	32.5	(NA)
HOURLY EARNINGS [1]												
1960	$2.09	(NA)	$2.60	$3.07	$2.26	(NA)	(NA)	$2.24	$1.52	$2.02	(NA)	(NA)
1965	2.46	(NA)	2.92	3.70	2.61	(NA)	$3.03	2.60	1.82	2.39	$2.05	(NA)
1970	3.23	(NA)	3.85	5.24	3.35	(NA)	3.85	3.43	2.44	3.07	2.81	(NA)
1975	4.53	(NA)	5.95	7.31	4.83	(NA)	5.88	4.72	3.36	4.06	4.02	(NA)
1980	6.66	(NA)	9.17	9.94	7.27	(NA)	8.87	6.95	4.88	5.79	5.85	(NA)
1985	8.57	(NA)	11.98	12.32	9.54	(NA)	11.40	9.15	5.94	7.94	7.90	(NA)
1986	8.76	(NA)	12.46	12.48	9.73	(NA)	11.70	9.34	6.03	8.36	8.18	(NA)
1987	8.98	(NA)	12.54	12.71	9.91	(NA)	12.03	9.59	6.12	8.73	8.49	(NA)
1988	9.28	(NA)	12.80	13.08	10.19	(NA)	12.26	9.98	6.31	9.06	8.88	(NA)
1989	9.66	(NA)	13.26	13.54	10.48	(NA)	12.60	10.39	6.53	9.53	9.38	(NA)
1990	10.02	(NA)	13.69	13.78	10.83	(NA)	12.96	10.79	6.76	9.97	9.83	(NA)
1991	10.34	(NA)	14.21	14.01	11.18	(NA)	13.23	11.16	7.00	10.42	10.24	(NA)
WEEKLY EARNINGS [1]												
1960	$81	(NA)	$105	$113	$90	(NA)	(NA)	$91	$58	$75	(NA)	(NA)
1965	95	(NA)	124	138	100	(NA)	£125	106	67	89	$74	(NA)
1970	120	(NA)	164	195	133	(NA)	156	137	82	113	97	(NA)
1975	164	(NA)	249	266	191	(NA)	233	182	109	148	135	(NA)
1980	235	(NA)	397	368	289	(NA)	351	267	147	210	191	(NA)
1985	299	(NA)	520	464	386	(NA)	450	351	175	289	256	(NA)
1986	305	(NA)	526	467	396	(NA)	459	358	176	304	266	(NA)
1987	313	(NA)	532	480	406	(NA)	472	365	179	316	276	(NA)
1988	322	(NA)	541	496	419	(NA)	476	380	184	325	289	(NA)
1989	334	(NA)	570	513	430	(NA)	490	395	189	341	306	(NA)
1990	346	(NA)	604	526	442	(NA)	504	411	195	357	320	(NA)
1991	355	(NA)	631	534	455	(NA)	511	425	200	373	333	(NA)

NA Not available.   [1] Average hours and earnings. Private production and related workers in mining, manufacturing, and construction; nonsupervisory employees in other industries.

Source: U.S. Bureau of Labor Statistics, *Employment and Earnings*, monthly, March issues.

No. 644. Employees in Nonfarm Establishments—States: 1980 to 1991

[In thousands. For coverage, see headnote, table 643. National totals differ from the sum of the State figures because of differing benchmarks among States and differing industrial and geographic stratification. Based on 1987 *Standard Industrial Classification Manual*, see text, section 13]

DIVISION AND STATE	1980	1985	1989	1990	1991 Total [1]	Construction	Manufacturing	Transportation and public utilities	Wholesale and retail trade	Finance, insurance, and real estate	Services	Government
U.S....	90,406	97,519	108,329	109,971	108,981	4,696	18,426	5,824	25,418	6,708	28,779	18,433
Northeast .	20,502	21,962	23,647	23,389	22,497	796	3,731	1,171	4,960	1,730	6,492	3,581
N.E....	5,481	6,067	6,572	6,364	6,040	195	1,138	259	1,381	446	1,752	866
ME ...	418	458	542	535	513	22	96	22	127	25	126	96
NH ...	385	466	529	508	480	17	98	17	119	31	126	72
VT....	200	225	262	258	248	12	44	11	57	12	68	44
MA ...	2,652	2,926	3,103	2,979	2,817	79	485	124	650	204	890	385
RI....	398	429	462	451	423	13	92	15	89	26	127	61
CT....	1,427	1,562	1,674	1,633	1,558	51	323	70	340	148	415	209
M.A. ...	15,021	15,896	17,075	17,025	16,456	601	2,593	912	3,579	1,284	4,740	2,714
NY....	7,207	7,751	8,247	8,213	7,886	275	1,057	419	1,603	755	2,326	1,447
NJ....	3,060	3,414	3,690	3,642	3,493	122	560	230	820	228	964	567
PA...	4,753	4,730	5,139	5,170	5,077	204	976	263	1,157	301	1,451	701
Midwest...	23,634	23,995	26,580	27,028	26,766	1,006	5,457	1,370	6,452	1,545	6,574	4,275
E.N.C ...	16,728	16,841	18,669	18,954	18,699	705	4,077	909	4,467	1,073	4,556	2,848
OH ...	4,367	4,373	4,817	4,882	4,811	176	1,068	211	1,155	257	1,201	727
IN	2,130	2,169	2,479	2,522	2,502	117	616	132	594	125	533	377
IL	4,850	4,755	5,214	5,288	5,220	199	947	303	1,253	379	1,355	766
MI	3,443	3,562	3,922	3,970	3,875	129	899	157	927	189	934	632
WI....	1,938	1,983	2,236	2,292	2,291	84	546	107	539	124	543	346
W.N.C..	6,905	7,154	7,911	8,074	8,067	301	1,380	461	1,984	472	2,008	1,428
MN ...	1,770	1,865	2,087	2,130	2,136	76	396	110	518	128	559	343
IA	1,110	1,074	1,200	1,226	1,237	46	232	55	312	72	297	220
MO ...	1,970	2,095	2,315	2,345	2,295	88	415	152	549	136	579	371
ND ...	245	252	260	266	271	10	18	17	72	13	71	66
SD. ...	238	249	276	289	297	12	35	14	79	17	75	63
NE. ...	628	651	708	730	736	28	99	48	187	49	180	146
KS. ...	945	968	1,064	1,089	1,095	42	184	65	269	58	248	219
South	29,147	32,390	35,989	36,816	36,525	1,761	5,986	2,008	8,603	1,980	8,939	6,833
S.A. ...	14,695	16,789	19,433	19,773	19,382	979	3,002	1,013	4,590	1,097	4,989	3,639
DE. ...	259	293	345	348	341	18	70	15	74	33	84	48
MD ...	1,712	1,888	2,155	2,171	2,097	130	193	100	507	131	619	415
DC. ...	616	629	681	686	677	11	15	23	58	35	256	280
VA. ...	2,157	2,455	2,862	2,896	2,831	154	411	148	639	153	731	581
WV ...	646	597	615	630	629	27	83	38	144	25	151	128
NC ...	2,380	2,651	3,074	3,118	3,070	147	826	154	704	135	599	500
SC. ...	1,189	1,296	1,500	1,545	1,514	90	368	65	341	66	297	285
GA ...	2,159	2,570	2,941	2,992	2,942	125	542	196	732	164	638	538
FL....	3,576	4,410	5,261	5,387	5,280	276	494	274	1,391	357	1,615	866
E.S.C ...	5,142	5,384	6,121	6,235	6,221	264	1,408	325	1,414	277	1,324	1,153
KY....	1,210	1,250	1,433	1,471	1,470	63	280	81	351	62	335	265
TN. ...	1,747	1,868	2,167	2,192	2,175	87	501	116	510	104	500	351
AL....	1,356	1,427	1,601	1,636	1,639	79	380	83	356	73	324	333
MS ...	829	839	919	937	937	35	246	45	197	39	166	204
W.S.C...	9,311	10,217	10,436	10,808	10,923	518	1,576	670	2,599	606	2,626	2,040
AR. ...	742	797	893	924	937	36	234	56	206	38	198	164
LA. ...	1,579	1,591	1,539	1,590	1,617	96	187	110	372	79	381	334
OK ...	1,138	1,165	1,164	1,193	1,202	39	169	69	284	61	272	266
TX....	5,851	6,663	6,840	7,101	7,167	347	987	434	1,736	428	1,774	1,277
West	17,578	19,486	22,185	22,813	22,604	1,052	3,257	1,208	5,354	1,390	6,142	4,048
Mt	4,502	5,110	5,621	5,812	5,904	288	629	338	1,421	322	1,656	1,151
MT ...	280	279	291	297	302	11	22	20	81	14	77	71
ID	330	336	366	385	398	20	63	20	101	21	86	85
WY ...	210	207	193	199	203	12	10	15	46	7	40	55
CO ...	1,251	1,419	1,482	1,521	1,542	67	186	98	375	97	420	282
NM ...	465	520	562	580	583	28	42	29	138	26	152	151
AZ....	1,014	1,279	1,455	1,486	1,498	78	177	81	373	93	412	271
UT....	551	624	691	724	745	32	106	42	178	36	189	154
NV....	400	446	581	621	633	41	26	33	129	29	281	81
Pac	13,076	14,376	16,564	17,001	16,700	764	2,628	870	3,933	1,067	4,486	2,897
WA ...	1,608	1,710	2,052	2,152	2,171	117	351	112	525	117	534	411
OR ...	1,045	1,030	1,209	1,252	1,251	52	212	65	315	83	297	226
CA...	9,849	10,979	12,570	12,830	12,497	551	2,026	628	2,911	819	3,445	2,079
AK....	169	231	227	238	243	11	18	22	47	11	52	71
HI	405	426	506	528	539	34	20	43	136	38	158	109

[1] Includes mining, not shown separately.

Source: U.S. Bureau of Labor Statistics, Bulletin 2320; and *Employment and Earnings*, monthly, May issues. Compiled from data supplied by cooperating State agencies.

No. 645. Nonfarm Industries—Number of Employees and Number and Earnings of Production Workers: 1980 to 1991

[Annual averages of monthly figures. Covers all full- and part-time employees who worked during, or received pay for, any part of the pay period including the 12th of the month. For mining and manufacturing, data refer to production and related workers; for construction, to employees engaged in actual construction work; and for other industries, to nonsupervisory employees and working supervisors. See also headnote, table 643. See *Historical Statistics, Colonial Times to 1970*, series D 127-151, D 802-810, and D 877-892, for related data]

1987 SIC [1] code	INDUSTRY	ALL EMPLOYEES TOTAL (1,000)			PRODUCTION WORKERS					
					Total (1,000)			Average hourly earnings (dollars)		
		1980	1990	1991	1980	1990	1991	1980	1990	1991
(X)	Total...............	90,406	109,971	108,981	(NA)	(NA)	(NA)	(NA)	(NA)	(NA)
(X)	Private sector [2].........	74,166	91,649	90,548	60,331	74,254	73,238	6.66	10.02	10.34
(B)	Mining..................	1,027	711	697	762	510	496	9.17	13.69	14.21
10	Metal mining............	98	59	59	74	46	47	10.26	14.07	14.92
12	Coal mining.............	246	148	139	204	120	113	10.86	16.72	17.11
13	Oil and gas extraction.......	560	394	392	389	260	257	8.59	12.94	13.53
14	Nonmetallic minerals, except fuels....	123	111	107	96	84	80	7.52	11.57	11.88
(C)	Construction...............	4,346	5,136	4,696	3,421	3,987	3,584	9.94	13.78	14.01
15	General building contractors........	1,173	1,308	1,173	900	944	832	9.22	13.02	13.28
16	Heavy construction, except building...	895	763	703	720	637	581	9.20	13.36	13.80
17	Special trade contractors.........	2,278	3,065	2,821	1,802	2,405	2,170	10.63	14.26	14.36
(D)	Manufacturing..............	20,285	19,111	18,426	14,214	12,974	12,447	7.27	10.83	11.18
(X)	Durable goods............	12,159	11,115	10,556	8,472	7,371	6,962	7.75	11.35	11.76
24	Lumber and wood products [3]......	705	741	697	587	610	571	6.57	9.09	9.28
241	Logging..................	88	85	80	71	70	66	8.64	11.23	11.15
242	Sawmills and planing mills........	215	200	190	190	174	164	6.70	9.23	9.42
243	Millwork, plywood, and structural members.................	207	264	244	170	213	195	6.44	9.05	9.30
244	Wood containers............	43	45	44	37	38	37	4.95	6.64	6.70
2451	Mobile homes..............	46	42	41	36	34	33	6.08	8.67	9.01
25	Furniture and fixtures [3]...........	466	510	482	376	403	378	5.49	8.52	8.77
251	Household furniture...........	301	291	276	253	243	229	5.12	7.87	8.15
252	Office furniture............	51	69	64	40	52	47	5.91	9.63	9.54
254	Partitions and fixtures..........	63	80	77	47	57	56	6.68	9.77	10.04
32	Stone, clay, and glass products [3]....	629	557	522	486	433	402	7.50	11.11	11.36
321	Flat glass................	18	17	15	14	13	12	9.65	15.15	15.80
322	Glass and glassware, pressed and blown.................	124	83	80	105	71	69	7.97	12.41	12.80
323	Products of purchased glass......	45	60	56	32	46	42	6.50	9.75	9.74
324	Cement, hydraulic............	31	18	18	25	14	14	10.55	13.90	14.13
325	Structural clay products........	46	36	32	34	28	25	6.14	9.55	9.72
326	Pottery and related products.....	47	39	36	39	30	29	6.25	9.62	9.81
327	Concrete, gypsum, and plaster.....	204	208	193	157	158	145	7.45	10.77	10.98
33	Primary metal industries [3]........	1,142	756	720	878	574	543	9.77	12.92	13.33
331	Blast furnaces and basic steel products.................	512	275	261	396	211	198	11.39	14.81	15.34
332	Iron and steel foundries........	209	132	126	167	105	99	8.20	11.55	11.85
333	Primary nonferrous metals.......	71	46	45	53	34	34	10.63	14.36	14.63
335	Nonferrous rolling and drawing....	211	172	166	151	124	119	8.81	12.29	12.72
336	Nonferrous foundries (castings)....	90	84	80	72	66	63	7.30	10.21	10.57
34	Fabricated metal products [3]......	1,609	1,423	1,359	1,194	1,048	994	7.45	10.83	11.20
341	Metal cans and shipping containers .	75	50	49	63	43	42	9.84	14.28	14.66
342	Cutlery, handtools, and hardware...	164	131	123	125	96	90	7.02	10.78	11.11
343	Plumbing and heating, exc. electric..	71	60	57	52	43	40	6.59	9.75	9.95
344	Fabricated structural metal products.................	507	427	409	351	303	287	7.27	10.16	10.51
345	Screw machine products........	109	96	91	84	74	70	6.96	10.70	11.09
346	Metal forgings and stampings	261	226	215	205	179	169	8.56	12.71	13.22
35	Industrial machinery and equipment [3] .	2,517	2,095	1,993	1,614	1,259	1,186	8.00	11.78	12.17
351	Engines and turbines..........	135	89	88	87	58	56	9.73	14.55	15.31
352	Farm and garden machinery.....	169	106	101	116	78	73	8.78	10.97	11.26
353	Construction and related machinery .	389	228	214	255	140	129	8.60	11.92	12.40
354	Metalworking machinery.........	399	330	313	290	236	221	8.13	12.27	12.62
355	Special industry machinery......	195	159	148	125	94	85	7.53	11.91	12.34
356	General industrial machinery......	300	248	241	196	159	153	7.95	11.32	11.75
357	Computer and office equipment....	421	440	419	181	137	135	6.75	11.52	12.16
358	Refrigeration and service machinery...............	175	177	167	120	124	115	7.23	10.94	11.17
36	Electronic and other elec. equip. [3]....	1,771	1,673	1,591	(4)	1,055	1,001	(4)	10.30	10.73
361	Electric distribution equipment....	117	97	92	82	68	64	6.96	10.17	10.67
362	Electrical industrial apparatus......	232	169	161	163	118	112	(1)	10.01	10.23
363	Household appliances..........	162	125	121	128	100	96	6.95	10.25	10.36
364	Electric lighting and wiring equip....	188	189	178	157	136	128	6.43	10.11	10.51
365	Household audio and video equip....	109	83	79	79	57	53	6.42	9.71	10.59
366	Communications equipment.......	(4)	263	249	(4)	133	126	(4)	11.04	11.52
367	Electronic components and accessories..............	539	581	551	325	328	313	6.05	10.01	10.46
37	Transportation equipment [3]........	1,881	1,980	1,856	1,220	1,218	1,148	9.35	14.10	14.79
371	Motor vehicles and equipment.....	789	809	776	575	615	592	9.85	14.59	15.32
372	Aircraft and parts............	636	706	651	344	342	315	9.28	14.78	15.60
373	Ship and boat building and repairing...............	221	187	176	176	141	135	8.22	10.92	11.44
374	Railroad equipment...........	71	33	31	53	25	22	9.93	13.41	14.02
376	Guided missiles, space vehicles, and parts	111	186	170	35	57	49	9.22	14.39	14.90

See footnotes at end of table.

No. 645. Nonfarm Industries—Number of Employees and Number and Earnings of Production Workers: 1980 to 1991—Continued

[See headnote, p. 405]

1987 SIC [1] code	INDUSTRY	ALL EMPLOYEES TOTAL (1,000)			PRODUCTION WORKERS					
					Total (1,000)			Average hourly earnings (dollars)		
		1980	1990	1991	1980	1990	1991	1980	1990	1991
(X)	**Durable goods—Continued**									
38	Instruments and related products	1,022	1,004	970	([4])	498	475	([4])	11.31	11.71
381	Search and navigation equipment . . .	([4])	284	261	([4])	94	82	([4])	14.66	15.28
382	Measuring and controlling devices . .	([4])	324	308	([4])	180	167	([4])	10.69	11.18
384	Medical instruments and supplies . . .	([4])	244	252	([4])	143	146	([4])	9.86	10.24
385	Ophthalmic goods	44	42	40	31	29	27	5.30	8.19	8.50
386	Photographic equipment and supplies	135	100	100	67	43	44	8.83	14.11	14.55
387	Watches, clocks, watchcases, and parts	22	11	10	17	8	8	5.24	7.70	7.92
39	Misc. manufacturing industries [3]	418	377	366	313	274	263	5.46	8.61	8.85
391	Jewelry, silverware, and plated ware	56	53	52	40	37	37	5.76	9.23	9.41
394	Toys and sporting goods	117	104	103	88	76	75	5.01	7.94	8.20
395	Pens, pencils, office and art supplies	37	34	32	27	24	23	5.58	8.89	9.31
396	Costume jewelry and notions	([4])	33	31	([4])	25	22	([4])	7.40	7.62
(X)	**Nondurable goods**	8,127	7,995	7,870	5,798	5,603	5,486	6.56	10.12	10.44
20	Food and kindred products [3]	1,708	1,668	1,674	1,175	1,200	1,210	6.85	9.61	9.88
201	Meat products	358	426	438	298	362	374	6.99	7.94	8.10
202	Dairy products	175	155	152	96	95	94	6.86	10.56	10.84
203	Preserved fruits and vegetables	246	247	245	202	206	205	5.94	8.95	9.39
204	Grain mill products	144	127	127	99	88	89	7.67	11.54	11.87
205	Bakery products	230	212	210	139	133	132	7.14	10.86	11.23
206	Sugar and confectionery products . . .	108	101	106	81	80	83	6.56	10.23	10.61
207	Fats and oils	44	31	31	32	22	21	7.03	10.11	10.26
208	Beverages	234	186	183	105	78	77	8.12	13.48	13.82
21	Tobacco products	69	49	48	54	36	36	7.74	16.29	16.89
211	Cigarettes	46	35	35	35	26	26	9.23	19.57	20.36
22	Textile mill products [3]	848	691	667	737	593	572	5.07	8.02	8.30
221	Broadwoven fabric mills, cotton	150	91	88	135	82	78	5.25	8.31	8.60
222	Broadwoven fabric mills, synthetics . .	116	77	73	104	68	64	5.30	8.63	8.90
223	Broadwoven fabric mills, wool	19	17	17	16	14	14	5.21	8.61	8.84
224	Narrow fabric mills	23	24	24	20	20	20	4.63	7.39	7.85
225	Knitting mills	224	206	200	194	180	174	4.77	7.37	7.64
226	Textile finishing, except wool	74	61	61	62	50	50	5.39	8.45	8.80
227	Carpets and rugs	54	62	59	44	51	48	5.20	8.25	8.38
228	Yarn and thread mills	125	101	94	113	90	84	4.76	7.68	7.97
23	Apparel and other textile products [3] . . .	1,264	1,043	1,024	1,079	874	856	4.56	6.57	6.75
231	Men's and boys' suits and coats . . .	77	50	49	67	42	41	5.34	7.33	7.41
232	Men's and boys' furnishings	362	275	273	310	236	234	4.23	6.05	6.28
233	Women's and misses outerwear	417	331	327	360	276	273	4.61	6.26	6.48
234	Women's and children's undergarments	90	63	61	76	52	50	4.15	6.18	6.47
236	Girls' and children's outerwear	64	57	56	55	48	48	4.20	5.95	6.15
26	Paper and allied products [3]	685	699	691	519	524	520	7.84	12.30	12.70
262	Papermills	179	179	178	133	135	135	9.05	15.10	15.56
263	Paperboard mills	65	52	50	51	40	39	9.28	15.26	15.71
265	Paperboard containers and boxes . . .	205	210	208	157	162	161	6.94	10.39	10.75
267	Misc. converted paper products	220	244	241	163	176	174	6.89	10.79	11.14
27	Printing and publishing [3]	1,252	1,574	1,537	699	873	846	7.53	11.25	11.50
271	Newspapers	420	476	463	164	166	161	7.72	11.19	11.45
272	Periodicals	90	129	126	16	48	45	7.16	11.95	12.28
273	Books	101	122	120	52	66	65	6.76	10.10	10.33
275	Commercial printing	410	553	540	304	402	390	7.85	11.52	11.76
278	Blankbooks and bookbinding	62	72	69	51	56	52	5.78	8.83	9.05
28	Chemicals and allied products [3]	1,107	1,093	1,090	626	603	585	8.30	13.55	14.07
281	Industrial inorganic chemicals	161	142	139	88	72	67	9.07	14.70	15.16
282	Plastics materials and synthetics . . .	205	181	179	137	116	111	8.21	13.98	14.81
283	Drugs	196	238	247	97	105	108	7.69	12.92	13.54
284	Soap, cleaners, and toilet goods . .	141	160	157	86	99	96	7.67	11.72	12.05
285	Paints and allied products	65	62	60	33	31	30	7.39	12.02	12.57
286	Industrial organic chemicals	174	155	154	88	86	80	9.67	15.98	16.54
287	Agricultural chemicals	72	56	57	45	34	34	8.12	13.73	14.18
29	Petroleum and coal products [3]	198	158	159	125	103	103	10.10	16.23	17.02
291	Petroleum refining	155	118	120	93	75	76	10.94	17.58	18.51
295	Asphalt paving and roofing materials	31	27	26	24	21	19	7.69	12.85	12.84
30	Rubber and misc. plastics products [3] . .	765	889	859	588	688	660	6.58	9.77	10.10
301	Tires and inner tubes	115	86	84	81	63	62	9.74	15.42	16.09
302	Rubber and plastics footwear	22	11	11	20	9	9	4.43	6.66	6.87
31	Leather and leather products [3]	233	132	121	197	109	98	4.58	6.90	7.16
311	Leather tanning and finishing	19	15	14	16	12	11	6.10	9.03	9.49
314	Footwear, except rubber	144	74	67	123	63	56	4.42	6.61	6.78
316	Luggage	16	11	9	12	8	6	4.90	6.91	6.99
317	Handbags and personal leather goods	30	15	13	25	12	10	4.33	6.08	6.32

See footnotes at end of table.

No. 645. Nonfarm Industries—Number of Employees and Number and Earnings of Production Workers: 1980 to 1991—Continued

[See headnote, p. 405]

1987 SIC[1] code	INDUSTRY	ALL EMPLOYEES TOTAL (1,000)			PRODUCTION WORKERS Total (1,000)			PRODUCTION WORKERS Average hourly earnings (dollars)		
		1980	1990	1991	1980	1990	1991	1980	1990	1991
(E)	**Transp. and public utilities [3]**	5,146	5,826	5,824	4,293	4,835	4,839	8.87	12.96	13.23
40	Railroad transportation...........	532	280	269	([4])	([4])	([4])	([4])	([4])	([4])
4011	Class I railroads [5]	482	241	231	(4)	([4])	([4])	[6]9.92	[6]16.08	[6]15.68
41	Local and interurban passenger transit .	265	343	361	244	313	331	6.34	9.19	9.46
42	Trucking and warehousing	1,280	1,638	1,638	1,121	1,427	1,424	9.13	11.72	11.90
44	Water transportation	211	174	174	([4])	([4])	([4])	([4])	([4])	([4])
45	Transportation by air	453	751	750	([4])	([4])	([4])	([4])	([4])	([4])
46	Pipelines, except natural gas	21	19	19	15	14	14	10.50	17.04	17.61
47	Transportation services	198	350	352	([4])	([4])	([4])	([4])	([4])	([4])
48	Communication [3]	1,357	1,311	1,292	1,014	978	976	8.50	13.51	13.98
481	Telephone communication........	1,072	910	892	779	654	651	8.72	14.14	14.64
483	Radio and television broadcasting..	192	236	232	154	195	193	7.44	12.72	13.44
484	Cable and other pay television services..................	([4])	128	132	([4])	107	112	([4])	10.50	10.72
49	Electric, gas, and sanitary services [3] .	829	961	970	678	762	766	8.90	15.24	15.78
491	Electric services	391	457	455	316	353	352	9.12	15.82	16.36
492	Gas production and distribution	168	165	165	138	129	129	8.27	14.28	14.92
493	Combination utility services	197	193	192	162	156	152	9.64	17.59	18.57
495	Sanitary services	50	117	127	44	101	109	7.16	11.55	11.77
(F)	**Wholesale trade ....**	5,292	6,205	6,072	4,328	4,985	4,868	6.95	10.79	11.16
(G)	**Retail trade [3] ....**	15,018	19,683	19,346	13,484	17,434	17,079	4.88	6.76	7.00
53	General merchandise stores........	2,245	2,516	2,357	2,090	2,357	2,212	4.77	6.84	7.04
54	Food stores..................	2,384	3,229	3,227	2,202	2,968	2,961	6.24	7.36	7.60
55	Automotive dealers and service stations	1,689	2,081	2,037	1,430	1,734	1,693	5.66	8.92	9.08
56	Apparel and accessory stores......	957	1,178	1,120	820	987	924	4.30	6.26	6.67
57	Furniture and home furnishings stores .	606	825	804	502	675	655	5.53	8.56	8.96
58	Eating and drinking places	4,626	6,565	6,571	4,256	5,957	5,945	3.69	4.97	5.18
(H)	**Finance, insurance, real estate .**	5,160	6,709	6,708	3,907	4,884	4,845	5.79	9.97	10.42
60	Depository institutions	([4])	2,278	2,255	([4])	1,652	1,632	([4])	8.45	8.79
61	Nondepository institutions	([4])	374	375	([4])	271	274	([4])	10.40	10.92
62	Security and commodity brokers	227	427	425	([4])	([4])	([4])	([4])	([4])	([4])
63	Insurance carriers..............	1,224	1,453	1,463	854	976	985	6.29	11.19	11.76
64	Insurance, agents, brokers, service ...	464	665	666	([4])	([4])	([4])	([4])	([4])	([4])
65	Real estate	989	1,319	1,294	([4])	([4])	([4])	([4])	([4])	([4])
67	Holding and other investment offices ..	115	223	230	([4])	([4])	([4])	([4])	([4])	([4])
(I)	**Services [3] ....**	17,890	28,240	28,779	15,921	24,646	25,081	5.85	9.83	10.24
70	Hotels and other lodging places	1,076	1,649	1,610	([4])	([4])	([4])	([4])	([4])	([4])
701	Hotels and motels	1,038	1,595	1,555	954	1,413	1,373	4.45	6.99	7.21
72	Personal services [3]	818	1,113	1,120	([4])	([4])	([4])	([4])	([4])	([4])
721	Laundry, cleaning, garment services .	356	433	431	318	385	381	4.47	6.83	7.06
723	Beauty shops	284	373	383	264	334	344	4.26	7.10	7.26
73	Business services [3]	2,564	5,241	5,301	([4])	4,610	4,643	([4])	9.48	9.78
731	Advertising	153	238	232	116	171	164	8.07	13.52	13.98
736	Personnel supply services	543	1,559	1,522	([4])	([4])	([4])	([4])	([4])	([4])
7361	Employment agencies	([4])	263	254	([4])	([4])	([4])	([4])	([4])	([4])
7363	Help supply services	([4])	1,296	1,268	([4])	1,253	1,222	([4])	8.08	8.28
737	Computer and data processing services..................	304	784	835	254	612	655	7.16	15.10	15.53
7372	Prepackaged software	([4])	113	126	([4])	([4])	([4])	([4])	([4])	([4])
7374	Data processing and preparation ..	([4])	200	209	([4])	([4])	([4])	([4])	([4])	([4])
75	Auto repair, services, and parking	571	928	916	488	768	754	6.10	8.79	9.02
753	Automotive repair shops	350	533	526	297	437	428	6.52	9.67	9.86
78	Motion pictures	([4])	408	399	([4])	344	329	([4])	10.95	11.83
783	Motion picture theaters	124	112	110	([4])	([4])	([4])	([4])	([4])	([4])
79	Amusement and recreation services. ..	([4])	1,089	1,125	([4])	955	984	([4])	8.14	8.13
80	Health services [3]	5,278	7,844	8,237	4,712	6,974	7,324	5.68	10.41	10.97
801	Offices and clinics of medical doctors..................	802	1,353	1,432	([4])	1,117	1,180	([4])	10.60	11.18
805	Nursing and personal care facilities. .	997	1,420	1,508	898	1,283	1,361	4.17	7.25	7.56
806	Hospitals	2,750	3,547	3,653	2,522	3,247	3,351	6.06	11.79	12.51
808	Home health care services	([4])	289	332	([4])	267	307	([4])	8.71	9.38
81	Legal services	498	919	927	427	758	757	7.35	14.21	14.67
82	Educational services	1,138	1,652	1,668	([4])	([4])	([4])	([4])	([4])	([4])
83	Social services................	1,134	1,811	1,946	([4])	([4])	([4])	([4])	([4])	([4])
86	Membership organizations	1,539	1,937	1,946	([4])	([4])	([4])	([4])	([4])	([4])
87	Engineering and management services.	([4])	2,503	2,468	([4])	1,905	1,878	([4])	13.57	14.11
(J)	**Government ....**	16,241	18,322	18,433	(NA)	(NA)	(NA)	(NA)	(NA)	(NA)
(X)	Federal government	2,866	3,085	2,966	(NA)	(NA)	(NA)	(NA)	(NA)	(NA)
(X)	State government.............	3,610	4,303	4,345	(NA)	(NA)	(NA)	(NA)	(NA)	(NA)
(X)	Local government.............	9,765	10,934	11,123	(NA)	(NA)	(NA)	(NA)	(NA)	(NA)

NA Not available. X Not applicable. [1] 1987 Standard Industrial Classification, see text, section 13. [2] Excludes government. [3] Includes industries not shown separately. [4] Included in totals; not available separately. [5] For changes in "Class I" classification, see text, section 21. [6] Includes all employees except executives, officials, and staff assistants who received pay during the month.

Source: U.S. Bureau of Labor Statistics, Bulletin 2370, supplement to Employment and Earnings, July 1991; and *Employment and Earnings*, monthly, March 1992.

No. 646. Indexes of Output per Hour for All Employees—Selected Industries: 1975 to 1990

[See text, section 13. Minus sign (-) indicates decrease. See also *Historical Statistics, Colonial Times to 1970*, series W 14, 17, and 19, W 30-54, and 62-65]

1987 SIC [1] code	INDUSTRY	INDEXES (1982=100)							AVERAGE ANNUAL PERCENT CHANGE [2]	
		1975	1980	1985	1987	1988	1989	1990, prel.	1975-1990	1985-1990
(B)	**Mining:**									
1011	Iron (usable ore)	120.0	125.6	187.2	245.3	254.4	243.9	221.3	6.3	4.5
1021	Copper (recoverable metal)	66.5	78.8	163.0	174.3	191.2	187.7	183.3	7.8	1.8
12	Coal	88.2	94.2	129.3	151.8	168.6	179.1	180.8	5.9	7.4
1311	Crude petroleum, natural gas	183.3	125.1	106.9	128.0	128.9	125.1	123.4	-2.3	2.7
14	Nonmetallic minerals [3]	101.5	108.1	120.0	127.8	130.5	131.8	134.8	1.6	2.5
(D)	**Manufacturing:**									
2011, 2013	Red meat products	75.2	95.3	108.4	108.7	111.4	102.7	(NA)	[4]2.4	[4]-0.7
2015	Poultry dressing/processing plants . . .	69.9	84.2	106.2	108.2	104.9	111.6	(NA)	[4]3.2	[4]1.3
203	Preserved fruits, vegetables	86.8	93.5	105.5	111.6	112.1	113.2	(NA)	[4]1.9	[4]1.6
204	Grain mill products	72.1	87.0	115.9	123.5	123.6	123.2	(NA)	[4]4.3	[4]1.8
2051, 2052	Bakery products	90.4	90.7	106.3	111.4	103.4	103.0	106.7	1.3	-0.9
2086	Bottled, canned soft drinks	78.5	93.7	111.5	126.9	137.2	137.6	146.7	4.0	5.5
2211, 21	Cotton, synthetic broadwoven fabric . .	77.1	93.4	110.9	118.2	115.9	120.3	127.4	3.4	2.0
2421	Sawmills, planing mills	84.3	89.0	115.8	125.4	126.1	127.7	123.6	3.4	0.9
251	Household furniture	93.2	95.5	107.0	113.1	114.1	114.9	116.3	1.6	1.4
2611,21,31	Paper, paperboard, pulp mills	77.8	94.4	110.6	124.0	127.2	128.1	130.2	3.4	3.0
2653	Corrugated, solid fiber boxes	86.0	99.1	109.4	110.2	113.1	109.9	112.7	1.9	0.3
281	Industrial inorganic chemicals	100.2	109.2	123.9	143.9	138.4	130.6	(NA)	[4]1.8	[4]1.6
2823, 2824	Synthetic fibers.............	81.3	111.3	130.7	151.6	158.5	155.3	156.0	4.4	3.6
2834	Pharmaceuticals	86.4	99.0	110.7	114.0	115.4	111.6	111.5	1.9	-0.1
2869	Industrial organic chemicals, n.e.c . .	97.8	113.4	129.1	150.6	162.9	167.5	(NA)	[4]3.1	[4]7.2
2911	Petroleum refining	111.7	118.7	128.8	143.5	150.1	156.0	155.7	2.0	3.7
3011	Tires, inner tubes	71.6	79.9	119.0	134.9	132.3	136.9	135.1	4.9	2.6
308	Miscellaneous plastics	78.3	86.9	102.6	117.0	116.0	114.6	115.4	2.6	2.5
314	Footwear..................	95.2	93.1	101.0	100.6	101.6	100.7	98.7	0.5	-0.5
3271, 72	Concrete products	101.0	99.3	110.7	113.8	117.0	122.7	123.0	1.2	2.0
3273	Ready-mixed concrete	107.7	102.7	107.7	115.5	126.6	117.2	(NA)	[4]0.6	[4]3.1
331	Steel....................	102.7	113.2	153.4	167.6	174.8	179.4	185.4	4.3	4.3
3321	Gray ductile iron foundries	103.6	96.9	110.1	114.7	120.7	119.4	117.9	1.1	1.6
3353, 54, 55	Aluminum rolling, drawing	88.2	100.8	116.5	125.9	124.8	121.8	120.3	2.0	0.2
3441	Fabricated structural metal	97.9	102.6	118.3	118.8	118.1	112.3	(NA)	[4]1.5	[4]-1.1
3442	Metal doors, sash, and trim.......	93.0	94.3	110.7	108.0	105.1	103.7	(NA)	[4]0.9	[4]-1.6
3465, 6, 9	Metal stampings	95.0	101.9	106.6	117.6	120.4	119.4	(NA)	[4]1.5	[4]3.2
352	Farm, garden machinery.........	103.0	98.3	106.2	113.8	123.0	126.8	133.8	1.4	5.1
3531	Construction machinery, equipment . .	105.6	109.6	119.2	123.1	131.8	130.0	124.7	1.2	1.1
3585	Refrigeration, heating equipment . . .	89.8	93.7	103.8	105.5	109.0	111.9	(NA)	[4]1.1	[4]2.2
3621	Motors, generators	90.9	94.4	105.6	110.1	116.2	112.7	117.9	1.6	2.2
3631,2,3,9	Major household appliances	86.2	97.4	114.8	123.3	127.0	128.8	127.4	2.9	2.2
3645,46,47,48	Lighting fixtures	98.0	102.5	118.2	122.7	126.0	122.2	122.4	1.5	0.3
3674	Semiconductors	28.3	75.6	105.1	152.3	166.7	193.5	206.8	12.0	15.9
371	Motor vehicles, equipment	90.5	93.7	125.4	133.7	137.4	136.9	136.2	3.0	2.0
3825	Instruments to measure electricity . .	80.4	90.9	104.1	111.4	118.8	121.7	(NA)	[4]3.2	[4]3.7
3861	Photographic equipment and supplies .	86.2	102.3	110.5	122.5	130.0	139.2	(NA)	[4]2.8	[4]5.7
(E, G, H, I)	**Transportation, utilities, trade:**									
4011	RR transport (revenue traffic) [5]	77.3	92.6	139.7	178.3	195.6	208.2	218.4	7.6	9.7
Pts. of 411, 13, 14	Bus carriers [6]	98.2	102.1	88.3	91.9	99.2	96.1	(NA)	[4]-0.5	[4]2.9
4213	Trucking, except local [7]	82.6	99.7	120.5	128.7	135.4	140.8	(NA)	[4]3.3	[4]4.0
Pts. of 4512, 13,22	Air transportation [7]	76.2	92.5	118.7	127.0	122.7	118.3	113.9	3.0	-0.8
4612, 13	Petroleum pipelines [7]	107.3	104.4	118.5	118.7	124.3	122.4	121.3	1.0	0.6
481	Telephone communications.......	66.5	91.5	116.1	128.6	135.3	141.9	142.7	5.2	4.3
491, 92, 93	Gas and electric utilities	106.0	107.8	101.5	104.2	109.5	111.2	111.1	-0.1	2.3
5093	Scrap and wasted materials [8]	[9]97.0	105.0	124.2	133.1	130.5	118.7	(NA)	[10]2.4	[10]-0.9
5251	Hardware stores [8]	89.6	102.3	102.2	106.3	115.5	121.3	123.7	2.0	4.0
5311	Department stores............	79.8	92.4	115.5	124.0	123.5	120.7	119.4	3.1	0.4
5331	Variety stores [8]	108.4	95.3	97.6	75.6	74.1	87.0	100.0	-0.9	0.9
54	Food stores [8]	103.4	105.1	99.9	97.3	95.5	92.2	91.6	-0.8	-1.9
5511	New, used car dealers	94.6	99.2	112.3	112.5	116.1	117.2	121.6	1.6	1.4
5531	Auto, home supply stores [8]	83.8	99.6	112.3	117.8	123.1	120.8	121.0	2.5	1.9
5541	Gasoline service stations [8]	76.3	94.0	121.5	129.7	129.7	129.7	125.4	3.6	0.3
56	Apparel, accessory stores [8]	83.1	93.3	116.6	114.2	114.4	115.7	115.2	2.9	-0.7
57	Furniture, furnishings, equip. stores [8] .	84.2	98.4	118.3	126.1	130.7	129.6	(NA)	[4]3.4	[4]2.2
58	Eating, drinking places [8]	104.0	102.9	92.8	96.3	98.3	96.3	96.5	-0.7	0.7
5912	Drug, proprietary stores [8]	87.3	99.1	98.9	97.5	98.3	99.0	98.5	0.6	0.0
592	Liquor stores [8]	89.1	94.5	100.7	87.3	85.5	87.6	87.0	-0.2	-2.6
602	Commercial banking	96.6	99.5	117.7	124.9	129.1	126.0	(NA)	[4]1.8	[4]2.1
7011	Hotels, motels, tourist courts [8]	101.0	107.0	112.4	110.9	109.6	101.8	97.0	-0.2	2.8
721	Laundry, cleaning services [8]	106.6	100.4	98.0	94.7	93.6	95.8	95.4	-1.1	-0.4
7231, 7241	Beauty and barber shops [8]	91.1	95.0	102.7	108.4	106.1	112.0	109.3	1.4	1.4
753	Automotive repair shops [8]	116.6	109.7	108.4	108.8	114.7	117.2	114.6	-0.3	1.9

NA Not available.   [1] 1987 Standard Industrial Classification; see text, section 13.   [2] For explanation of average annual percent change, see source.   [3] Excludes fuels.   [4] Change from 1975 to 1989 and 1985 to 1989.   [5] Class 1 line-haul railroads and switching and terminal companies.   [6] Class 1 interstate carriers regulated by the ICC.   [7] Refers to output per employee.   [8] Data relate to all persons (paid employees, unpaid family workers, and the self-employed).   [9] 1977 data.   [10] Change from 1977 to 1989 and 1985 to 1989.

Source: U.S. Bureau of Labor Statistics, Bulletin 2406, *Productivity Measures for Selected Industries and Government Services*, April 1992; and unpublished data.

No. 647. Productivity and Related Measures: 1960 to 1991

[See text, section 13. Minus sign (-) indicates decrease. See also *Historical Statistics, Colonial Times to 1970*, series D 689-704 and W 22-25]

ITEM	1960	1970	1975	1980	1985	1987	1988	1989	1990	1991
INDEXES (1982 = 100)										
Output per hour, business sector	65.6	87.0	95.4	98.6	106.1	109.4	110.4	109.5	109.7	110.0
Nonfarm business	70.0	88.6	96.6	99.0	105.4	108.3	109.2	108.2	108.1	108.4
Manufacturing	(NA)	(NA)	(NA)	94.4	108.0	117.2	122.0	122.5	125.7	127.5
Output, [1] business sector.	52.3	75.9	85.0	100.5	116.7	124.8	130.1	132.4	132.9	131.0
Nonfarm business	51.9	75.8	84.9	100.8	116.8	125.0	130.6	132.8	133.2	131.1
Manufacturing	(NA)	(NA)	(NA)	103.8	115.5	124.6	133.4	134.6	135.0	132.0
Hours, [2] business sector	79.7	87.2	89.1	101.9	109.9	114.1	117.9	120.9	121.2	119.1
Nonfarm business	74.2	85.6	88.0	101.8	110.8	115.4	119.5	122.7	123.1	120.9
Manufacturing	(NA)	(NA)	(NA)	109.9	107.0	106.2	109.4	109.8	107.4	103.5
Compensation per hour, [3] business sector .	21.1	36.7	54.5	85.0	113.0	122.7	128.0	132.5	139.6	145.1
Nonfarm business	22.2	37.0	54.8	84.9	112.6	122.1	127.2	131.5	138.3	143.8
Manufacturing	(NA)	(NA)	(NA)	83.1	111.0	118.0	122.6	127.5	134.3	140.0
Real hourly compensation, [3] business sector	68.7	91.2	97.7	99.5	101.3	104.3	104.4	103.1	103.1	102.8
Nonfarm business	72.3	92.0	98.3	99.4	101.0	103.7	103.8	102.3	102.1	101.9
Manufacturing	(NA)	(NA)	(NA)	97.4	99.5	100.2	100.0	99.2	99.2	99.2
Unit labor costs, [4] business sector	32.1	42.2	57.1	86.2	106.5	112.2	116.0	121.0	127.2	131.9
Nonfarm business	31.7	41.8	56.7	85.7	106.8	112.8	116.4	121.5	127.9	132.6
Manufacturing	(NA)	(NA)	(NA)	88.1	102.8	100.7	100.5	104.0	106.9	109.8
ANNUAL PERCENT CHANGE [5]										
Output per hour, business sector	1.6	1.3	2.3	-0.7	1.4	1.0	0.9	-0.7	0.2	0.2
Nonfarm business	1.0	0.9	2.2	-0.9	0.8	0.8	0.9	-0.9	-0.1	0.3
Manufacturing	(NA)	(NA)	(NA)	-1.9	2.3	4.1	4.0	0.5	2.5	1.4
Output, [1] business sector.	1.7	-0.6	-1.9	-1.6	3.6	4.1	4.3	1.8	0.4	-1.5
Nonfarm business	1.6	-0.7	-2.0	-1.7	3.4	4.1	4.4	1.7	0.3	-1.6
Manufacturing	(NA)	(NA)	(NA)	-6.5	1.5	4.9	7.1	0.9	0.3	-2.3
Hours, [2] business sector	0.1	-1.9	-4.1	-0.9	2.1	3.1	3.3	2.6	0.2	-1.7
Nonfarm business	0.6	-1.6	-4.2	-0.8	2.5	3.3	3.5	2.7	0.3	-1.8
Manufacturing	(NA)	(NA)	(NA)	-4.7	-0.8	0.7	2.9	0.4	-2.2	-3.7
Compensation per hour, [3] business sector .	4.3	7.6	10.0	10.7	4.5	3.5	4.3	3.5	5.4	3.9
Nonfarm business	4.4	7.2	9.9	10.7	4.2	3.4	4.1	3.4	5.2	4.0
Manufacturing	(NA)	(NA)	(NA)	12.0	5.0	2.2	3.9	4.0	5.3	4.2
Real hourly compensation, [3] business sector	2.6	1.7	0.8	-2.4	0.9	-0.1	0.1	-1.2	-	-0.3
Nonfarm business	2.6	1.4	0.7	-2.4	0.6	-0.2	-	-1.4	-0.2	-0.2
Manufacturing	(NA)	(NA)	(NA)	-1.3	1.4	-1.4	-0.2	-0.8	-0.1	-
Unit labor costs, [4] business sector	2.7	6.2	7.5	11.5	3.0	2.5	3.3	4.3	5.2	3.7
Nonfarm business	3.3	6.3	7.5	11.7	3.3	2.6	3.2	4.3	5.3	3.7
Manufacturing	(NA)	(NA)	(NA)	14.2	2.7	-1.8	-0.1	3.5	2.7	2.7

- Represents zero. NA Not available. [1] Refers to gross domestic product originating in the sector, in 1987 prices.
[2] Hours at work of all persons engaged in the business and nonfarm business sectors (employees, proprietors, and unpaid family workers); employees' and proprietors' hours in manufacturing. [3] Wages and salaries of employees plus employers' contributions for social insurance and private benefit plans. Also includes an estimate of same for self-employed. Real compensation deflated by the consumer price index for all urban consumers, see text, section 15. [4] Hourly compensation divided by output per hour. [5] All changes are from the immediate prior year.

Source: U.S. Bureau of Labor Statistics, *Employment and Earnings*, monthly; and unpublished data.

No. 648. Computer Use On the Job, Sex, and Educational Attainment, by Selected Computer Activity: 1989

[As of October. In percent. Based on Current Population Survey and subject to sampling error; for details, see Appendix III]

EDUCATIONAL ATTAINMENT AND SEX	Persons using computers at work [1]	COMPUTER ACTIVITY [2]				
		Word processing	Book-keeping	Inventory control	Communications	Data bases
Total	**38.3**	**41.1**	**26.5**	**25.5**	**25.1**	**27.3**
Not a high school graduate	8.4	17.7	20.0	37.4	13.2	11.7
High school graduate	29.8	32.2	27.7	29.7	21.0	20.0
Some college.	50.0	40.0	28.2	27.3	26.7	27.2
Four years of college	59.6	46.5	26.6	22.7	29.8	32.6
More than four years of college.	59.9	57.4	22.5	15.9	31.3	37.7
Male	32.3	37.4	24.1	30.9	20.1	20.8
Not a high school graduate	6.2	12.1	12.3	41.4	10.4	9.0
High school graduate	20.2	19.8	20.5	41.9	19.7	17.7
Some college.	40.6	31.8	24.4	34.6	28.0	29.1
Four years of college	59.0	45.6	28.3	27.1	32.3	35.6
More than four years of college.	60.4	56.8	24.2	17.8	34.6	40.1
Female	46.0	44.4	28.7	20.7	24.0	25.1
Not a high school graduate	12.1	22.6	26.6	33.9	15.7	14.1
High school graduate	40.6	39.1	31.7	22.9	21.7	21.3
Some college.	60.7	46.3	31.1	21.8	25.7	25.7
Four years of college	60.3	47.7	24.4	16.9	26.5	28.7
More than four years of college.	59.0	58.5	19.6	12.8	25.9	33.6

[1] Unduplicated count.   [2] Persons may be included on more than one activity.

Source: U.S. National Center for Education Statistics, *Digest of Education Statistics*, 1990.

No. 649. Average Annual Total Compensation and Wages and Salaries per Full-Time Equivalent Employee, by Industry: 1980 to 1990

[In dollars. Wage and salary payments include executives' compensation, bonuses, tips, and payments-in-kind; total compensation includes, in addition to wages and salaries, employer contributions for social insurance, employer contributions to private pension and welfare funds, director' fees, jury and witness fees, etc. Through 1985, based on 1972 Standard Industrial Classification Code (SIC); beginning 1988, based on the 1987 SIC. See text, section 13]

INDUSTRY	ANNUAL TOTAL COMPENSATION					ANNUAL WAGES AND SALARIES				
	1980	1985	1988	1989	1990	1980	1985	1988	1989	1990
Domestic industries	18,815	25,266	28,736	29,702	31,101	15,757	21,079	24,032	24,766	25,889
Agriculture, forestry, and fisheries	9,836	12,833	14,086	15,249	17,104	8,596	11,086	12,453	13,452	15,004
Mining	28,181	38,367	42,794	44,443	46,514	23,405	32,035	35,001	36,247	37,829
Construction	22,033	27,581	30,466	31,465	32,836	18,571	22,768	25,872	26,647	27,713
Manufacturing	22,023	29,999	33,765	34,937	36,503	17,954	24,549	27,639	28,490	29,648
Transportation	25,029	30,895	33,004	33,717	35,197	20,850	25,305	27,058	27,542	28,795
Communication	28,341	39,980	44,197	45,905	47,393	22,079	31,381	35,528	36,618	38,007
Electric, gas, and sanitary services	27,358	39,429	44,005	46,343	47,822	21,701	31,669	35,979	37,725	38,996
Wholesale trade	21,598	28,853	34,048	35,138	36,857	18,822	25,013	29,208	30,055	31,435
Retail trade	12,490	15,625	17,443	17,886	18,462	10,953	13,602	15,135	15,484	15,941
Finance, insurance, and real estate	18,968	28,014	34,443	35,327	36,679	15,871	23,724	29,682	30,329	31,529
Services	15,236	21,395	25,309	26,271	27,791	13,460	18,743	22,159	22,936	24,218
Government and government enterprises.	19,681	27,821	32,044	33,548	35,334	15,911	22,062	25,150	26,238	27,604

Source: U.S. Bureau of Economic Analysis, *The National Income and Product Accounts of the United States, Volume 2, 1958-88;* and *Survey of Current Business,* July issues.

No. 650. Average Hourly and Weekly Earnings in Current and Constant (1982) Dollars, by Private Industry Group: 1970 to 1991

[Average earnings include overtime. Data are for production and related workers in mining, manufacturing, and construction, and nonsupervisory employees in other industries. Excludes agriculture. See headnote, table 643. See also *Historical Statistics, Colonial Times to 1970,* series D 877-892]

PRIVATE INDUSTRY GROUP	CURRENT DOLLARS						CONSTANT (1982) DOLLARS [1]					
	1970	1980	1985	1989	1990	1991	1970	1980	1985	1989	1990	1991
Average hourly earnings	3.23	6.66	8.57	9.66	10.02	10.34	8.03	7.78	7.77	7.64	7.53	7.46
Manufacturing	3.35	7.27	9.54	10.48	10.83	11.18	8.33	8.49	8.65	8.28	8.14	8.07
Mining	3.85	9.17	11.98	13.26	13.69	14.21	9.58	10.71	10.86	10.48	10.29	10.25
Construction	5.24	9.94	12.32	13.54	13.78	14.01	13.03	11.61	11.17	10.70	10.35	10.11
Transportation, public utilities	3.85	8.87	11.40	12.60	12.96	13.23	9.58	10.36	10.34	9.96	9.74	9.55
Wholesale trade	3.43	6.95	9.15	10.39	10.79	11.16	8.53	8.12	8.30	8.21	8.11	8.05
Retail trade	2.44	4.88	5.94	6.53	6.76	7.00	6.07	5.70	5.39	5.16	5.08	5.05
Finance, insurance, real estate	3.07	5.79	7.94	9.53	9.97	10.42	7.64	6.76	7.20	7.53	7.49	7.52
Services	2.81	5.85	7.90	9.38	9.83	10.24	6.99	6.83	7.16	7.42	7.39	7.39
Average weekly earnings. . . .	120	235	299	334	346	355	298	275	271	264	260	256
Manufacturing	133	289	386	430	442	455	332	337	350	340	332	328
Mining	164	397	520	570	604	631	409	464	471	451	454	455
Construction	195	368	464	513	526	534	486	430	421	406	395	385
Transportation, public utilities	156	351	450	490	504	511	388	410	408	387	379	368
Wholesale trade	137	267	351	395	411	425	341	312	318	312	309	307
Retail trade	82	147	175	189	195	200	205	172	158	149	146	144
Finance, insurance, real estate	113	210	289	341	357	373	281	245	262	270	268	269
Services	97	191	257	306	320	333	240	223	233	242	241	240

[1] Earnings in current dollars divided by the Consumer Price Index (CPI-W) on a 1982 base; see text, section 15.

Source: U.S. Bureau of Labor Statistics, Bulletin 2370, supplement to *Employment and Earnings,* July 1991; and *Employment and Earnings,* monthly.

No. 651. Annual Percent Changes in Earnings and Compensation: 1980 to 1991

[Annual percent change from immediate prior year. Minis sign (-) indicates decrease]

ITEM	1980	1983	1984	1985	1986	1987	1988	1989	1990	1991
Current dollars:										
Hourly earnings, total [1]	8.1	4.4	3.7	3.0	2.2	2.5	3.3	4.1	3.7	3.2
Hourly earnings, manufacturing	8.5	4.0	4.1	3.8	2.0	1.8	2.8	2.8	3.3	3.2
Compensation per employee-hour [1]	10.6	3.9	3.9	4.1	4.9	3.4	4.1	3.4	5.1	4.0
Constant (1982) dollars:										
Hourly earnings, total [1]	-4.8	1.4	0.1	-0.4	0.5	-1.0	-0.5	-0.7	-1.4	-0.9
Hourly earnings, manufacturing	-4.5	0.9	0.6	0.3	0.3	-1.6	-1.2	-1.9	-1.7	-0.9
Compensation per employee-hour [1] .	-2.5	0.6	-0.4	0.5	2.9	-0.2	0.0	-1.4	-0.2	-0.2
Consumer Price Index [2]	13.5	3.2	4.3	3.6	1.9	3.6	4.1	4.8	5.4	4.2

[1] Nonfarm business sector.   [2] See text, section 15.

Source: U.S. Bureau of Labor Statistics, *Monthly Labor Review.*

No. 652. Average Annual Pay, by State: 1988 to 1990

[In dollars except percent change. For workers covered by State unemployment insurance laws and for Federal civilian workers covered by unemployment compensation for Federal employees, approximately 90 percent of total civilian employment. Excludes most agricultural workers on small farms, all Armed Forces, elected officials in most States, railroad employees, most domestic workers, employees of certain nonprofit organizations and most self-employed individuals. Pay includes bonuses, cash value of meals and lodging, and tips and other gratuities]

STATE	AVERAGE ANNUAL PAY			PERCENT CHANGE		STATE	AVERAGE ANNUAL PAY			PERCENT CHANGE	
	1988	1989	1990 [1]	1988-1989	1989-1990		1988	1989	1990 [1]	1988-1989	1989-1990
U.S. . .	21,872	22,563	23,602	3.2	4.6	MO.	20,295	20,900	21,716	3.0	3.9
AL	19,003	19,593	20,468	3.1	4.5	MT	16,957	17,224	17,895	1.6	3.9
AK	28,033	29,704	29,946	6.0	0.8	NE	17,190	17,690	18,577	2.9	5.0
AZ	20,383	20,809	21,443	2.1	3.0	NV	20,548	21,333	22,358	3.8	4.8
AR	17,023	17,418	18,204	2.3	4.5	NH	20,749	21,553	22,609	3.9	4.9
CA	24,126	24,917	26,180	3.3	5.1	NJ	25,748	26,780	28,449	4.0	6.2
CO	21,472	21,940	22,908	2.2	4.4	NM	18,259	18,667	19,347	2.2	3.6
CT	26,234	27,500	28,995	4.8	5.4	NY	26,347	27,303	28,873	3.6	5.8
DE	21,977	23,268	24,423	5.9	5.0	NC	18,636	19,321	20,220	3.7	4.7
DC	30,253	32,106	33,717	6.1	5.0	ND	16,508	16,932	17,626	2.6	4.1
FL	19,523	20,072	21,032	2.8	4.8	OH	21,501	21,986	22,843	2.3	3.9
GA	20,504	21,072	22,114	2.8	4.9	OK	19,098	19,533	20,288	2.3	3.9
HI	20,444	21,624	23,167	5.8	7.1	OR	19,637	20,303	21,332	3.4	5.1
ID	17,648	18,146	18,991	2.8	4.7	PA	21,485	22,313	23,457	3.9	5.1
IL	23,608	24,212	25,312	2.6	4.5	RI	21,206	21,128	22,388	4.6	6.0
IN	20,437	20,931	21,699	2.4	3.7	SC	18,009	18,797	19,669	4.4	4.6
IA	17,928	18,420	19,224	2.7	4.4	SD	15,424	15,810	16,430	2.5	3.9
KS	19,030	19,475	20,238	2.3	3.9	TN	19,209	19,712	20,611	2.6	4.6
KY	18,545	19,001	19,947	2.5	5.0	TX	21,130	21,740	22,700	2.9	4.4
LA	19,330	19,750	20,646	2.2	4.5	UT	18,910	19,362	20,074	2.4	3.7
ME	18,347	19,202	20,154	4.7	5.0	VT	18,640	19,497	20,532	4.6	5.3
MD	22,515	23,469	24,730	4.2	5.4	VA	21,053	21,882	22,750	3.9	4.0
MA	24,143	25,233	26,689	4.5	5.8	WA	20,806	21,617	22,646	3.9	4.8
MI	24,193	24,767	25,376	2.4	2.5	WV	19,341	19,788	20,715	2.3	4.7
MN	21,481	22,155	23,126	3.1	4.4	WI	19,743	20,204	21,101	2.3	4.4
MS	16,522	17,047	17,718	3.2	3.9	WY	19,097	19,230	20,049	0.7	4.3

[1] Preliminary.

Source: U.S. Bureau of Labor Statistics, *Employment and Wages, Annual Averages 1990, Bulletin 2393;* and USDL News Release 91-390, *Average Annual Pay by State and Industry, 1990.*

No. 653. Average Annual Pay, by Selected Metropolitan Areas: 1988 to 1990

[In dollars. Metropolitan areas ranked by population size 1988. For composition of metropolitan areas, see Appendix II. See also headnote table 652. For civilian labor force data, see table 614]

METROPOLITAN AREA	1988	1989	1990 [1]	METROPOLITAN AREA	1988	1989	1990 [1]
U.S. total.	21,872	22,563	23,602	Kansas City, MO-KS MSA	21,598	22,219	23,199
U.S. metropolitan total	22,831	23,566	24,675	Milwaukee-Racine, WI CMSA . . .	21,738	22,298	23,244
New York-Northern New Jersey-				Portland-Vancouver, OR-WA,			
Long Island, NY-NJ-CT CMSA . . .	28,104	29,208	31,047	CMSA	21,227	22,014	23,178
Los Angeles-Anaheim-Riverside, CA				Sacramento, CA MSA	21,933	23,002	24,405
CMSA	24,944	25,682	26,932	Norfolk-Virginia Beach-Newport			
Chicago-Gary-Lake County (IL),				News, VA MSA	18,983	19,446	20,218
IL-IN-WI CMSA	25,033	25,703	26,887	Columbus, OH MSA	21,301	21,835	22,869
San Francisco-Oakland-San Jose,				San Antonio, TX MSA	19,325	19,677	20,212
CA CMSA.	26,674	27,568	29,001	New Orleans, LA MSA.	20,389	20,695	21,595
Philadelphia-Wilmington-Trenton,				Indianapolis, IN MSA.	21,877	22,345	23,337
PA-NJ-DE-MD CMSA	23,997	25,070	26,626	Buffalo-Niagara Falls, NY CMSA . .	20,396	21,080	22,161
Detroit-Ann Arbor, MI CMSA.	26,467	27,164	27,820	Charlotte-Gastonia-Rock Hill,			
Dallas-Fort Worth, TX CMSA	23,553	24,298	25,422	NC-SC MSA	20,697	21,618	22,803
Boston-Lawrence-Salem-Lowell-				Hartford-New Britain-Middletown-			
Brockton, MA NECMA	25,731	26,915	28,484	CT NECMA	25,787	27,224	28,767
Washington, DC-MD-VA MSA	26,784	28,041	29,384	Salt Lake City-Ogden, UT MSA . . .	19,498	20,014	20,781
Houston-Galveston-Brazoria,				Rochester, NY MSA	23,469	24,550	25,414
TX CMSA.	24,274	25,023	26,253	Memphis, TN-AR-MS MSA	20,371	20,877	21,964
Miami-Fort Lauderdale, FL CMSA . .	21,551	21,919	23,036	Nashville, TN MSA	20,469	21,203	22,083
Cleveland-Akron-Lorain, OH CMSA .	22,802	23,382	24,326	Orlando, FL MSA	19,930	20,373	21,259
Atlanta, GA MSA	23,445	24,075	25,301	Louisville, KY-IN MSA	20,048	20,579	21,376
St. Louis, MO-IL MSA	22,735	23,409	24,256	Oklahoma City, OK MSA	19,998	20,447	20,988
Seattle-Tacoma, WA CMSA	22,709	23,608	24,991	Dayton-Springfield, OH MSA.	21,981	22,320	23,019
Minneapolis-St. Paul, MN-WI MSA . .	23,618	24,372	25,405	Greensboro-Winston-Salem-			
San Diego, CA MSA	22,183	22,956	23,942	High Point, NC MSA	20,204	20,950	21,348
Baltimore, MD MSA.	22,261	23,110	24,459	Birmingham, AL MSA	20,775	21,542	22,588
Pittsburgh-Beaver Valley, PA CMSA. .	21,811	22,435	23,684	Providence-Pawtucket-			
Phoenix, AZ MSA	21,438	21,955	22,660	Woonsocket, RI NECMA	20,089	21,059	22,381
Tampa-St. Petersburg-Clearwater,				Jacksonville, FL MSA	19,987	20,571	21,520
FL MSA	18,714	19,456	20,320	Albany-Schenectady-Troy, NY			
Denver-Boulder, CO CMSA	23,368	23,898	25,031	MSA	21,779	22,807	23,834
Cincinnati-Hamilton, OH-KY-IN,				Richmond-Petersburg, VA MSA. . . .	21,293	22,351	23,376
CMSA	21,933	22,512	23,590	Honolulu, HI MSA	21,196	22,399	24,054

[1] Preliminary.

Source: U.S. Bureau of Labor Statistics, USDL News Release 91-417, *Average Annual Pay Levels in Metropolitan Areas, 1990,* and earlier issues.

No. 654. Full-Time Wage and Salary Workers—Number and Median Weekly Earnings, by Selected Characteristics: 1983 to 1991

[In current dollars of usual weekly earnings. Data represent annual averages of quarterly data. See text, section 13 for a discussion of occupational data. Based on Current Population Survey; see text, section 1, and Appendix III. For definition of median, see Guide to Tabular Presentation]

CHARACTERISTIC	NUMBER OF WORKERS (1,000)				MEDIAN WEEKLY EARNINGS (dol.)			
	1983	1985	1990	1991	1983	1985	1990	1991
All workers [1]	70,976	77,002	85,082	83,525	313	343	415	430
Male	42,309	45,589	49,015	47,910	378	406	485	497
16 to 24 years old	6,702	6,956	6,313	5,714	223	240	283	286
25 years old and over	35,607	38,632	42,702	42,197	406	442	514	525
Female	28,667	31,414	36,068	35,615	252	277	348	368
16 to 24 years old	5,345	5,621	5,001	4,488	197	210	254	267
25 years old and over	23,322	25,793	31,066	31,127	267	296	370	388
White	61,739	66,481	72,637	71,176	319	355	427	446
Male	37,378	40,030	42,563	41,482	387	417	497	509
Female	24,361	26,452	30,075	29,694	254	281	355	374
Black	7,373	8,393	9,642	9,498	261	277	329	348
Male	3,883	4,367	4,909	4,832	293	304	360	374
Female	3,490	4,026	4,733	4,665	231	252	308	323
Hispanic origin [2]	(NA)	(NA)	6,993	6,887	(NA)	(NA)	307	315
Male	(NA)	(NA)	4,410	4,332	(NA)	(NA)	322	328
Female	(NA)	(NA)	2,583	2,554	(NA)	(NA)	280	293
Family relationship:								
Husbands	28,720	30,260	31,326	30,793	410	455	532	558
Wives	14,884	16,270	18,666	18,726	257	285	363	381
Women who maintain families	3,948	4,333	5,007	5,062	256	278	339	362
Men who maintain families	1,331	1,313	1,786	1,694	377	396	444	448
Other persons in families:								
Men	5,518	6,173	6,434	6,008	219	238	296	299
Women	4,032	4,309	4,475	4,110	201	213	271	285
All other men [3]	6,740	7,841	9,468	9,416	350	380	442	458
All other women [3]	5,803	6,503	7,920	7,716	274	305	376	395
Occupation, male:								
Managerial and professional	10,312	11,078	12,263	12,254	516	583	731	753
Exec., admin., managerial	5,344	5,835	6,401	6,402	530	593	742	758
Professional specialty	4,967	5,243	5,863	5,853	506	571	720	748
Technical, sales, and administrative support	8,125	8,803	9,596	9,363	385	420	496	509
Tech. and related support	1,428	1,563	1,747	1,719	424	472	570	576
Sales	3,853	4,227	4,666	4,556	389	431	505	518
Admin. support, incl. clerical	2,844	3,013	3,183	3,088	362	391	440	459
Service	3,723	3,947	4,476	4,492	255	272	320	330
Private household	11	13	12	14	(B)	(B)	(B)	(B)
Protective	1,314	1,327	1,523	1,587	355	391	477	502
Other service	2,398	2,607	2,942	2,892	217	230	273	283
Precision production [4]	9,180	10,026	10,169	9,762	387	408	488	494
Mechanics and repairers	3,418	3,752	3,669	3,604	377	400	477	489
Construction trades	2,966	3,308	3,603	3,323	375	394	480	484
Other	2,796	2,966	2,897	2,835	408	433	510	512
Operators, fabricators and laborers	9,833	10,585	11,257	10,801	308	325	378	387
Machine operators, assemblers, and inspectors	4,138	4,403	4,510	4,272	319	341	391	396
Transportation and material moving	3,199	3,459	3,721	3,703	335	369	418	423
Handlers, equipment cleaners, helpers, and laborers	2,496	2,724	3,027	2,826	251	261	308	315
Farming, forestry, fishing	1,137	1,150	1,253	1,238	200	216	263	269
Occupation, female:								
Managerial and professional	7,139	8,302	10,595	10,854	357	399	511	527
Exec., admin., managerial	2,772	3,492	4,764	4,918	339	383	485	504
Professional specialty	4,367	4,810	5,831	5,936	367	408	534	559
Technical, sales, and administrative support	13,517	14,622	16,202	15,779	247	269	332	350
Tech. and related support	1,146	1,200	1,470	1,453	299	331	417	445
Sales	2,460	2,929	3,531	3,317	204	226	292	308
Admin. support, incl. clerical	9,911	10,494	11,202	11,009	248	270	332	348
Service	3,598	3,963	4,531	4,416	173	185	230	244
Private household	267	330	298	292	116	130	171	163
Protective	139	156	216	232	250	278	405	421
Other service	3,193	3,477	4,017	3,892	176	188	231	245
Precision production [4]	784	906	893	880	256	268	316	341
Mechanics and repairers	120	144	139	144	337	392	459	506
Construction trades	45	53	50	42	(B)	265	394	(B)
Other	619	709	704	694	244	253	300	318
Operators, fabricators, and laborers	3,486	3,482	3,675	3,528	204	216	262	273
Machine operators, assemblers, and inspectors	2,853	2,778	2,840	2,731	202	216	260	270
Transportation and material moving	159	189	227	240	253	252	314	339
Handlers, equipment cleaners, helpers and laborers	474	514	608	556	211	209	250	261
Farming, forestry, fishing	143	138	171	159	169	185	216	224

B Data not shown where base is less than 50,000.   NA Not available.   [1] Includes other races, not shown separately. [2] Persons of Hispanic origin may be of any race.   [3] The majority of these persons are living alone or with nonrelatives. Also included are persons in families where the husband, wife or other person maintaining the family is in the Armed Forces, and persons in unrelated subfamilies.   [4] Includes craft and repair.

Source: U.S. Bureau of Labor Statistics, Bulletin 2307, and *Employment and Earnings*, monthly, January issues.

No. 655. Median Weekly Earnings of Families, by Type of Family, Number of Earners, Race, and Hispanic Origin: 1980 to 1991

[In current dollars of usual weekly earnings. Annual averages of quarterly figures based on Current Population Survey; see text, section 1, and Appendix III. For families with wage and salary earners]

CHARACTERISTIC	NUMBER OF FAMILIES (1,000)					MEDIAN WEEKLY EARNINGS (dollars)				
	1980	1985	1989	1990	1991	1980	1985	1989	1990	1991
TOTAL										
Total families with earners [1]	**41,162**	**41,616**	**43,525**	**43,759**	**43,530**	**400**	**522**	**624**	**653**	**669**
Married-couple families	33,825	33,459	34,125	34,219	33,930	433	582	701	732	754
One earner.	14,797	13,347	12,139	12,166	12,177	303	385	430	455	455
Husband	12,127	10,346	9,175	8,994	8,784	336	440	502	520	532
Wife	2,059	2,243	2,236	2,407	2,636	159	217	251	267	279
Other family member	611	758	727	764	757	163	204	253	280	278
Two or more earners [2]	19,028	20,112	21,987	22,053	21,753	535	715	845	880	911
Husband and wife only	12,990	14,019	15,761	15,934	15,923	507	684	808	844	884
Husband and other family member(s) .	2,369	2,159	1,811	1,751	1,637	557	689	801	825	838
Wife and other family member(s)	426	514	519	527	557	350	454	521	557	589
Other family members only	139	176	169	176	163	356	468	558	554	617
Families maintained by women	5,690	6,470	7,295	7,323	7,441	222	297	347	363	385
One earner	4,022	4,397	4,929	4,983	5,090	184	234	273	288	306
Householder	3,104	3,432	3,898	3,937	4,045	188	243	282	296	315
Other family member	918	965	1,031	1,045	1,045	168	200	234	254	270
Two or more earners	1,668	2,073	2,366	2,340	2,351	370	487	566	607	622
Families maintained by men	1,647	1,688	2,104	2,218	2,159	360	450	506	514	514
One earner	1,016	1,031	1,216	1,352	1,337	283	346	382	396	404
Two or more earners	631	656	888	866	822	502	625	718	778	736
WHITE										
Total families with earners [1]	**35,786**	**35,848**	**36,981**	**37,239**	**36,978**	**411**	**543**	**651**	**681**	**695**
Married-couple families	30,316	29,899	30,233	30,361	30,069	438	589	712	745	767
One earner [2]	13,437	12,097	10,815	10,856	10,851	311	395	449	473	474
Husband	11,152	9,496	8,310	8,162	7,953	343	452	511	535	549
Wife	1,740	1,925	1,879	2,044	2,252	160	218	254	270	280
Two or more earners	16,878	17,802	19,418	19,505	19,218	542	723	854	892	922
Husband and wife only	11,448	12,394	13,944	14,148	14,098	511	691	817	855	895
Families maintained by women	4,140	4,616	5,114	5,127	5,209	233	311	363	382	399
Families maintained by men	1,331	1,333	1,634	1,751	1,701	374	475	522	539	529
BLACK										
Total families with earners [1]	**4,503**	**4,668**	**5,133**	**5,082**	**5,098**	**299**	**378**	**447**	**459**	**484**
Married-couple families	2,802	2,671	2,782	2,724	2,735	366	487	579	601	625
One earner [2]	1,103	902	929	893	897	210	257	299	304	313
Husband	769	580	576	527	503	244	292	360	345	366
Wife	279	257	282	290	312	151	206	230	243	272
Two or more earners	1,700	1,769	1,853	1,831	1,838	472	622	730	748	776
Husband and wife only	1,238	1,258	1,348	1,297	1,362	461	603	706	713	756
Families maintained by women	1,438	1,703	1,984	1,986	2,003	192	259	303	314	339
Families maintained by men	263	294	367	372	360	307	360	430	397	401
HISPANIC ORIGIN [3]										
Total families with earners [1]	**(NA)**	**(NA)**	**3,542**	**3,624**	**3,636**	**(NA)**	**(NA)**	**480**	**496**	**495**
Married-couple families	(NA)	(NA)	2,619	2,599	2,599	(NA)	(NA)	520	555	546
One earner [2]	(NA)	(NA)	1,044	1,050	1,102	(NA)	(NA)	310	322	322
Husband	(NA)	(NA)	858	814	850	(NA)	(NA)	332	356	355
Wife	(NA)	(NA)	126	164	176	(NA)	(NA)	220	236	235
Two or more earners	(NA)	(NA)	1,574	1,549	1,497	(NA)	(NA)	667	716	732
Husband and wife only	(NA)	(NA)	977	924	917	(NA)	(NA)	630	672	713
Families maintained by women	(NA)	(NA)	633	691	701	(NA)	(NA)	337	326	343
Families maintained by men	(NA)	(NA)	291	334	337	(NA)	(NA)	467	468	462

NA Not available.   [1] Excludes families in which there is no wage or salary earner or in which the husband, wife, or other person maintaining the family is either self-employed or in the Armed Forces.   [2] Includes other earners, not shown separately.   [3] Persons of Hispanic origin may be of any race.

Source: U.S. Bureau of Labor Statistics, Bulletin 2307; and *Employment and Earnings*, monthly, January issues.

No. 656. Number of Workers With Earnings and Median Earnings, by Occupation of Longest Job Held and Sex: 1990

[Covers civilians 15 years old and over as of **March 1991**. Based on Current Population Survey; see text, section 1, and Appendix III. For definition of median, see Guide to Tabular Presentation]

MAJOR OCCUPATION OF LONGEST JOB HELD	ALL WORKERS				YEAR ROUND FULL-TIME					
	Women		Men		Women		Men		Ratio: Women to men	
	Number (1,000)	Median earnings	Number (1,000)	Median earnings	Number (1,000)	Median earnings	Number (1,000)	Median earnings	Number	Median earnings
Total [1]	**61,732**	**$12,250**	**72,348**	**$21,522**	**31,682**	**$19,822**	**49,171**	**$27,678**	**0.64**	**0.72**
Executive, administrators, and managerial.	6,577	22,551	9,244	37,010	4,857	25,858	7,873	40,541	0.62	0.64
Professional specialty	8,814	23,113	8,035	36,942	4,982	29,181	6,192	41,100	0.80	0.71
Technical and related support . .	2,044	20,312	2,053	28,042	1,284	23,992	1,595	30,897	0.81	0.78
Sales	8,393	7,307	7,871	22,955	3,223	16,986	5,594	29,652	0.58	0.57
Admin. support, incl. clerical. . . .	16,728	14,292	4,141	20,287	9,760	18,475	2,835	26,192	3.44	0.71
Precision production, craft and repair	1,395	13,377	13,448	22,149	795	18,739	9,412	26,506	0.08	0.71
Machine operators, assemblers, and inspectors	3,773	10,983	5,389	19,389	2,103	14,652	3,736	22,345	0.56	0.66
Transportation and material moving	511	10,805	5,056	20,053	174	16,003	3,241	24,559	0.05	0.65
Handlers, equipment cleaners, helpers, and laborers	995	8,270	4,885	9,912	412	13,650	2,065	18,426	0.20	0.74
Service workers	11,722	5,746	7,801	10,514	3,769	12,139	4,106	18,550	0.92	0.65
Private household	1,007	2,166	43	(B)	183	7,309	9	(B)	20.33	(X)
Service, except private household.	10,716	6,173	7,758	10,549	3,586	12,288	4,097	18,574	0.88	0.66
Farming, forestry, and fishing . . .	680	3,810	3,548	7,881	241	10,007	1,736	14,452	0.14	0.69

B Base less than 75,000.   X Not applicable.   [1] Includes persons whose longest job was in the Armed Forces.
Source: U.S. Bureau of the Census, *Current Population Reports*, series P-60, No. 174.

No. 657. Employment Cost Index (ECI), by Industry and Occupation: 1982 to 1991

[As of **December**. The ECI is a measure of the rate of change in employee compensation (wages, salaries, and employer costs for employee benefits). Data are not seasonally adjusted: 1982-1985 based on 1970 Census of Population; thereafter, based on fixed employment counts from the 1980 Census of Population]

ITEM	INDEXES (June 1989 = 100)							PERCENT CHANGE FOR 12 MONTHS ENDING—				
	1982	1985	1987	1988	1989	1990	1991	1985	1988	1989	1990	1991
Civilian workers [1]	**74.8**	**86.8**	**93.1**	**97.7**	**102.6**	**107.6**	**112.2**	**4.3**	**4.9**	**5.0**	**4.9**	**4.3**
Workers, by occupational group:												
White-collar workers	72.9	85.8	92.7	97.6	102.9	108.3	112.8	4.9	5.3	5.4	4.2	5.2
Blue-collar workers	78.2	88.4	93.8	97.8	102.0	106.5	111.1	3.3	4.3	4.4	4.4	4.3
Service workers	74.3	87.2	93.1	98.2	102.8	108.0	113.1	3.9	5.5	4.7	5.1	4.7
Workers, by industry division:												
Manufacturing	76.9	87.8	93.4	97.6	102.0	107.2	112.2	3.3	4.5	4.5	5.1	4.7
Nonmanufacturing.	73.9	86.4	92.9	97.7	102.8	107.8	112.3	4.7	5.2	5.2	4.9	4.2
Services.	70.5	84.1	92.3	97.9	103.7	110.2	114.6	4.7	6.1	5.9	6.3	4.0
Public administration [2]	71.9	85.4	93.8	97.8	103.2	108.7	112.6	4.9	4.3	5.5	5.3	3.6
Private industry workers [3]	**75.8**	**87.3**	**93.1**	**97.6**	**102.3**	**107.0**	**111.7**	**3.9**	**4.8**	**4.8**	**4.6**	**4.4**
Workers, by occupational group:												
White-collar workers	73.7	86.4	92.7	97.3	102.4	107.4	112.2	4.9	5.0	5.2	4.9	4.5
Blue-collar workers	78.4	88.5	93.7	97.9	101.9	106.4	111.0	3.1	4.5	4.1	4.4	4.3
Service workers	76.3	88.4	93.3	98.2	102.5	107.3	112.4	3.0	5.3	4.4	4.7	4.8
Workers, by industry division:												
Manufacturing	76.9	87.8	93.4	97.6	102.0	107.2	112.2	3.3	4.5	4.5	5.1	4.7
Nonmanufacturing.	75.1	87.0	92.9	97.5	102.3	106.9	111.5	4.3	5.0	4.9	4.5	4.3
Services.	(NA)	84.1	92.2	97.5	102.9	109.3	114.0	(NA)	5.7	5.5	6.2	4.3
Business services	(NA)	(NA)	92.5	97.2	101.3	107.4	111.1	(NA)	5.1	4.2	6.0	3.4
Health services	(NA)	83.7	91.5	97.0	103.7	110.8	116.5	(NA)	6.0	6.9	6.8	5.1
Hospitals	(NA)	(NA)	91.0	96.6	103.5	110.7	116.1	(NA)	6.2	7.1	7.0	4.9
Workers by bargaining status:												
Union	79.6	90.1	04.5	98.2	101.8	106.2	111.1	2.6	3.9	3.7	4.3	4.6
Nonunion	74.3	86.3	92.7	97.4	102.4	107.3	111.9	4.6	5.1	5.1	4.8	4.3
State and local government workers	**70.8**	**84.6**	**93.0**	**98.2**	**104.3**	**110.4**	**114.4**	**5.6**	**5.6**	**6.2**	**5.8**	**3.6**
Workers, by occupational group:												
White-collar workers	70.4	84.2	92.8	98.3	104.6	110.9	114.6	5.8	5.9	6.4	6.0	3.3
Blue-collar workers	73.9	86.7	94.3	97.5	103.7	108.7	112.9	5.3	3.4	6.4	4.8	3.9
Workers, by industry division:												
Services	70.0	84.0	92.5	98.5	104.7	111.3	115.3	5.9	6.5	6.3	6.3	3.6
Schools	69.0	83.6	92.7	98.7	105.3	111.6	115.6	6.2	6.5	6.7	6.0	3.6
Elementary and secondary	68.6	83.6	92.9	99.1	105.5	112.1	116.2	6.4	6.7	6.7	6.3	3.7
Services, excluding schools [4]	73.1	85.2	92.2	97.8	103.2	110.2	114.4	4.7	6.1	5.5	6.8	3.8
Public administration [2]	71.9	85.4	93.8	97.8	103.2	108.7	112.6	4.9	4.3	5.5	5.3	3.6

NA Not available.   [1] Includes private industry and State and local government workers and excludes farm, household, and Federal government workers.   [2] Consists of legislative, judicial, administrative, and regulatory activities.   [3] Excludes farm and household workers.   [4] Includes library, social, and health services. Formerly called hospitals and other services.
Source: U.S. Bureau of Labor Statistics, *News, Employment Cost Index*, quarterly.

No. 658. Effective Federal Minimum Hourly Wage Rates, 1950 to 1992, and Coverage in 1990

[Employee estimates as of **September 1990**, except as indicated. The Fair Labor Standards Act of 1938 and subsequent amendments provide for minimum wage coverage applicable to specified nonsupervisory employment categories. Exempt from coverage are executives and administrators or professionals]

IN EFFECT	MINIMUM RATES FOR NONFARM			Minimum rates for farm workers [4]	SEX, RACE, AND INDUSTRY	NONSUPERVISORY EMPLOYEES, **1990**				
	Laws prior to 1986 [1]	Percent, avg. earnings [2]	1966 and later [3]			Total (1,000)	Subject to minimum wage rates			
							Total (1,000)	Percent of total	Prior to 1966 [6][7] (1,000)	1966 and later [3][7] (1,000)
Jan. 25, 1950. . . .	$0.75	54	(X)	(X)	**Total. . . . .**	92,857	82,050	88.4	51,379	30,671
Mar. 1, 1956	1.00	52	(X)	(X)						
Sept. 3, 1961. . . .	1.15	50	(X)	(X)	Male	47,093	41,467	88.1	27,626	13,841
Sept. 3, 1963	1.25	51	(X)	(X)	Female	45,764	40,583	88.7	23,753	16,830
Feb. 1, 1967	1.40	50	$1.00	$1.00	White.	81,689	71,921	88.0	45,882	26,039
Feb. 1, 1968	1.60	54	1.15	1.15	Black and other.	11,168	10,129	90.7	5,497	4,632
Feb. 1, 1969	([5])	51	1.30	1.30	Black only	10,161	9,216	90.7	5,013	4,203
Feb. 1, 1970	([5])	49	1.45	([5])						
Feb. 1, 1971	([5])	46	1.60	([5])	**Private industry . .**	81,688	70,881	86.8	51,379	19,502
					Agriculture [8]	1,704	654	38.4	-	654
May 1, 1974	2.00	46	1.90	1.60	Mining	653	649	99.4	649	-
Jan. 1, 1975	2.10	45	2.00	1.80	Construction	4,898	4,823	98.5	4,096	727
Jan. 1, 1976	2.30	46	2.20	2.00	Manufacturing	16,916	16,448	97.2	16,345	103
Jan. 1, 1977	([5])	42	2.30	2.20	Transp., public utilities	5,243	5,209	99.4	5,130	79
Jan. 1, 1978	2.65	44	2.65	2.65	Wholesale trade	5,474	4,370	79.8	4,104	266
Jan. 1, 1979	2.90	45	2.90	2.90	Retail trade.	17,894	16,205	90.6	7,999	8,206
Jan. 1, 1980	3.10	44	3.10	3.10	Finance, insurance,					
Jan. 1, 1981	3.35	43	3.35	3.35	real estate.	5,868	4,449	75.8	4,275	174
Apr. 1, 1990.	3.80	35	3.80	3.80	Service [9]	21,705	17,174	79.1	8,781	8,393
Apr. 1, 1991.	4.25	38	4.25	4.25	Private households. . . .	1,333	900	67.5	-	900
Apr. 1, 1992.	([5])	37	([5])	([5])	**Government [9][10] . .**	11,169	11,169	100.0	-	11,169

- Represents zero. X Not applicable. [1] Applies to workers covered prior to 1961 Amendments and, after Sept. 1965, to workers covered by 1961 Amendments. Rates set by 1961 Amendments were: Sept. 1961, $1.00; Sept. 1964, $1.15; and Sept. 1965, $1.25. [2] Percent of gross average hourly earnings of production workers in manufacturing. [3] Applies to workers newly covered by Amendments of 1966, 1974, and 1977, and Title IX of Education Amendments of 1972. [4] Included in coverage as of 1966, 1974, and 1977 Amendments. [5] No change in rate. [6] Includes workers in retail-service establishments with less than $250,000 in gross annual sales which are part of enterprises covered under criteria in effect prior to the 1966 Amendments. These workers became subject under the 1974 Amendments. [7] Currently employed workers subject to provisions. [8] Estimates based on average employment for the ten-month active season. [9] Estimates for educational services in private industry and government relate to October. [10] Federal, State, and local employees.
Source: U.S. Department of Labor, Employment Standards Administration, *Minimum Wage and Maximum Hours Standards Under the Fair Labor Standards Act*, 1981, annual; and unpublished data.

No. 659. Workers Paid Hourly Rates, by Selected Characteristics: 1992

[Average of the four quarters ending in the first quarter of 1992; for employed wage and salary workers. Based on Current Population Survey, see text, section 1, and Appendix III]

CHARACTERISTIC	NUMBER OF WORKERS [1] (1,000)				PERCENT DISTRIBUTION				PERCENT OF ALL WORKERS PAID HOURLY RATES		
	Total paid hourly rates	At or below $4.25			Total paid hourly rates	At or below $4.25			At or below $4.25		
		Total	At $4.25	Below $4.25		Total	At $4.25	Below $4.25	Total	At $4.25	Below $4.25
Total, 16 years and over [2]	61,782	5,716	3,365	2,351	100.0	100.0	100.0	100.0	9.3	5.4	3.8
16 to 24 years	14,135	2,915	1,760	1,155	22.9	51.0	52.3	49.1	20.6	12.5	8.2
16 to 19 years	4,984	1,660	1,033	627	8.1	29.0	30.7	26.7	33.3	20.7	12.6
25 years and over	47,647	2,801	1,604	1,197	77.1	49.0	47.7	50.9	5.9	3.4	2.5
Male, 16 years and over	31,010	2,082	1,301	781	50.2	36.4	38.7	33.2	6.7	4.2	2.5
16 to 24 years	7,335	1,248	788	460	11.9	21.8	23.4	19.6	17.0	10.7	6.3
16 to 19 years	2,506	732	480	252	4.1	12.8	14.3	10.7	29.2	19.2	10.1
25 years and over	23,675	834	513	321	38.3	14.6	15.2	13.7	3.5	2.2	1.4
Women, 16 years and over . .	30,771	3,634	2,064	1,570	49.8	63.6	61.3	66.8	11.8	6.7	5.1
16 to 24 years	6,800	1,667	972	695	11.0	29.2	28.9	29.6	24.5	14.3	10.2
16 to 19 years	2,477	928	553	375	4.0	16.2	16.4	16.0	37.5	22.3	15.1
25 years and over	23,972	1,967	1,091	876	38.8	34.4	32.4	37.3	8.2	4.6	3.7
White	51,776	4,673	2,691	1,982	83.8	81.8	80.0	84.3	9.0	5.2	3.8
Black	7,927	074	561	313	12.8	15.3	16.7	13.3	110	71	39
Hispanic origin [3]	5,908	655	474	181	9.6	11.5	14.1	7.7	11.1	8.0	3.1
Full-time workers	45,854	2,146	1,358	788	74.2	37.5	40.4	33.5	4.7	3.0	1.7
Part-time workers [4]	15,928	3,570	2,006	1,564	25.8	62.5	59.6	66.5	22.4	12.6	9.8
Private sector	53,607	5,319	3,102	2,217	86.8	93.1	92.2	94.3	9.9	5.8	4.1
Goods-producing industries [5]	17,783	709	481	228	28.8	12.4	14.3	9.7	4.0	2.7	1.3
Service-producing industries [6]	35,822	4,610	2,620	1,990	58.0	80.7	77.9	84.6	12.9	7.3	5.6
Public sector	8,169	397	263	134	13.2	6.9	7.8	5.7	4.9	3.2	1.6

[1] Excludes the incorporated self-employed. [2] Includes races not shown separately. [3] Persons of Hispanic origin may be of any race. [4] Working fewer than 35 hours per week. [5] Includes agriculture, mining, construction, and manufacturing. [6] Includes transportation and public utilities; wholesale trade; finance, insurance, and real estate; private households; and other service industries, not shown separately.
Source: U.S. Bureau of Labor Statistics, unpublished data.

No. 660. Employer Costs for Employee Compensation per Hour Worked, 1988 and 1991, and by Industry, 1991

[As of March, for private industry workers. Based on a sample of establishments; see source for details]

COMPENSATION COMPONENT	COST (dol.)						PERCENT DISTRIBUTION					
	1988	1991					1988	1991				
		Total	Goods producing [1]	Service producing [2]	Manufacturing	Nonmanufacturing		Total	Goods producing [1]	Service producing [2]	Manufacturing	Nonmanufacturing
Total compensation....	13.79	15.40	18.48	14.31	18.22	14.67	100.0	100.0	100.0	100.0	100.0	100.0
Wages and salaries	10.02	11.14	12.70	10.58	12.40	10.81	72.7	72.3	68.7	74.0	68.1	73.7
Total benefits	3.77	4.27	5.78	3.72	5.81	3.86	27.3	27.7	31.3	26.0	31.9	26.3
Paid leave	0.97	1.05	1.27	0.97	1.38	0.96	7.0	6.8	6.9	6.8	7.6	6.6
Vacation........	0.48	0.52	0.66	0.47	0.71	0.47	3.5	3.4	3.6	3.3	3.9	3.2
Holiday..........	0.33	0.35	0.46	0.32	0.50	0.31	2.4	2.3	2.5	2.2	2.8	2.1
Sick............	0.12	0.13	0.11	0.14	0.12	0.13	0.9	0.8	0.6	1.0	0.7	0.9
Other...........	0.04	0.05	0.05	0.05	0.05	0.04	0.3	0.3	0.3	0.3	0.3	0.3
Supplemental pay	0.33	0.36	0.63	0.26	0.67	0.28	2.4	2.3	3.4	1.8	3.7	1.9
Premium pay......	0.17	0.17	0.35	0.11	0.36	0.13	1.2	1.1	1.9	0.8	2.0	0.9
Nonproduction bonuses	0.12	0.13	0.20	0.11	0.21	0.11	0.8	0.9	1.1	0.8	1.2	0.8
Shift pay.........	0.04	0.05	0.08	0.04	0.09	0.04	0.3	0.3	0.4	0.3	0.5	0.3
Insurance.........	0.78	1.01	1.41	0.86	1.51	0.88	5.6	6.5	7.6	6.0	8.3	6.0
Pensions and savings .	0.45	0.44	0.66	0.36	0.60	0.40	3.3	2.9	3.6	2.5	3.3	2.7
Pensions	0.38	0.35	0.50	0.29	0.44	0.32	2.8	2.2	2.7	2.0	2.4	2.2
Savings and thrift...	0.07	0.10	0.15	0.07	0.16	0.08	0.5	0.6	0.8	0.5	0.9	0.5
Legally required [3]	1.22	1.40	1.78	1.26	1.62	1.34	8.8	9.1	9.7	8.8	8.9	9.1
Social Security.....	0.81	0.92	1.09	0.86	1.08	0.88	5.9	6.0	5.9	6.0	5.9	6.0
Federal unemployment	0.03	0.03	0.03	0.03	0.03	0.03	0.2	0.2	0.2	0.2	0.2	0.2
State unemployment.	0.12	0.09	0.12	0.08	0.11	0.09	0.8	0.6	0.6	0.6	0.6	0.6
Workers compensation	0.24	0.33	0.54	0.25	0.39	0.31	1.7	2.1	2.9	1.8	2.2	2.1
Other benefits [4]	0.02	(Z)	0.03	(Z)	0.04	(Z)	0.2	(Z)	0.2	(Z)	0.2	(Z)

Z Represents or rounds to zero.   [1] Mining, construction, and manufacturing.   [2] Transportation, communications, public utilities, wholesale trade, retail trade, finance, insurance, real estate, and services.   [3] Includes railroad retirement, railroad unemployment, railroad supplemental unemployment, and other legally required benefits, not shown separately.   [4] Includes severance pay, and supplemental unemployment benefits.

Source: U.S. Bureau of Labor Statistics, *News, Employer Costs for Employee Compensation*, June 1991, USDL 91-292.

No. 661. Employees With Employer- or Union-Provided Pension Plans or Group Health Plans, by Occupation and Selected Characteristic: 1990

[In thousands, except percent. For civilian wage and salary workers 15 years old and over as of March 1991. Based on Current Population Survey; see text, section 1, and Appendix III]

OCCUPATION	Total	WITH PENSION PLANS		WITH GROUP HEALTH PLANS		CHARACTERISTIC	Total	WITH PENSION PLANS		WITH GROUP HEALTH PLANS	
		Number	Percent	Number	Percent			Number	Percent	Number	Percent
Total	134,325	53,120	39.5	70,251	52.3	**AGE**					
Executive, admin., managerial	15,842	8,050	50.8	10,672	67.4	Total........	134,325	53,120	39.5	70,251	52.3
						15 to 24 years	24,260	2,967	12.2	5,843	24.1
Prof. specialty ...	16,849	10,009	59.4	11,380	67.5	25 to 44 years	70,610	31,568	44.7	41,311	58.5
Tech./related support	4,099	2,259	55.0	2,873	70.1	45 to 64 years	34,544	17,442	50.5	21,079	61.0
						65 years and over .	4,911	1,143	23.3	2,018	41.1
Sales workers ...	16,289	4,125	25.3	6,707	41.2	**WORK EXPERIENCE**					
Admin. support, inc. clerical....	20,959	9,598	45.8	11,991	57.2	Worked	133,353	52,379	39.3	70,127	52.6
						Full-time	104,471	49,088	47.0	65,590	62.8
Precision prod., craft/repair....	14,851	6,191	41.7	8,634	58.1	50 weeks or more.	80,043	42,840	53.5	56,321	70.4
						27 to 49 weeks ..	14,720	4,778	32.5	7,072	48.0
Mach. operators, assemblers [1]..	9,167	3,949	43.1	5,775	63.0	26 weeks or fewer.	9,708	1,471	15.2	2,198	22.6
						Part-time	28,883	3,291	11.4	4,537	15.7
Transportation/ material moving.	5,570	2,088	37.5	3,123	56.1	50 weeks or more.	11,595	2,025	17.5	2,596	22.4
						27 to 49 weeks ..	7,078	810	11.4	1,190	16.8
Handlers, equip. cleaners [2].....	5,889	1,614	27.4	2,335	39.6	26 weeks or fewer.	10,210	456	4.5	752	7.4
						EMPLOYER SIZE					
Service workers ..	19,535	4,162	21.3	5,847	29.9	Under 25	41,059	4,648	11.3	11,000	26.8
Pvt. households.	1,050	21	2.0	40	3.8	25 to 99	17,206	5,235	30.4	8,907	51.8
Other........	18,485	4,141	22.4	5,807	31.4	100 to 499.......	18,697	8,458	45.2	11,776	63.0
Farming, forestry and fishing ...	4,300	347	8.1	811	18.9	500 to 999.......	7,145	3,866	54.1	4,807	67.3
Armed Forces ...	976	729	74.7	102	10.4	Over 1,000.......	50,219	30,913	61.6	33,760	67.2

[1] Includes inspectors.   [2] Includes helpers and laborers.

Source: U.S. Bureau of the Census, unpublished data.

No. 662. Employee Benefits in Medium and Large Firms, 1989 and Small Firms, 1990

[Covers full-time employees in private industry. Medium and large firms exclude establishments with fewer than 100 workers, executive and traveling operating employees, and Alaska and Hawaii. Small firms include those with fewer than 100 employees. Covers only benefits for which the employer pays part or all of the premium or expenses involved, except unpaid parental leave and long-term care insurance. Based on a sample survey of establishments; for details, see sources. For data on employee benefits in State and local governments, see table 484]

MEDIUM AND LARGE FIRMS, 1989	All employees	Professional and administrative	Technical and clerical	Production and service	SMALL FIRMS, 1990	All employees	Professional, technical and related	Clerical and sales	Production and service
Percent of employees participating in—					Percent of employees participating in—				
Paid: Vacations	97	98	99	95	Paid: Vacations	88	94	93	83
Holidays	97	97	96	97	Holidays	84	95	91	75
Jury duty leave	90	95	92	87	Jury duty leave	54	72	62	43
Funeral leave	84	87	86	80	Funeral leave	47	57	54	38
Rest time	71	57	69	80	Rest time	48	42	46	51
Military leave	53	61	57	45	Military leave	21	29	26	15
Sick leave	68	93	87	44	Sick leave	47	70	61	29
Personal leave	22	28	30	14	Personal leave	11	17	13	7
Lunch time	10	4	4	16	Lunch time	8	7	7	7
Maternity leave	3	4	2	3	Maternity leave	2	3	3	1
Paternity leave	1	2	1	1	Paternity leave	(Z)	(Z)	(Z)	(Z)
Unpaid: Maternity leave	37	39	37	35	Unpaid: Maternity leave	17	26	20	12
Paternity leave	18	20	17	17	Paternity leave	8	13	8	5
Insurance plans:					Insurance plans:				
Medical care	92	93	91	93	Medical care	69	82	75	60
Noncontributory	48	45	41	54	Noncontributory	40	46	40	37
Hospital/room and board	90	91	89	91	Hospital/room and board	69	82	75	60
Inpatient surgery	90	91	89	91	Inpatient surgery	69	82	75	60
					Mental health care:				
Mental health care	89	91	88	90	Inpatient	68	80	74	59
Private duty nursing	79	82	80	78	Outpatient	66	77	72	58
Dental	66	69	66	65	Dental	30	38	35	24
Extended care facility	74	75	74	74	Extended care facility	57	66	63	49
Home health care	69	74	72	65	Home health care	55	66	62	45
Hospice care	39	46	43	33	Hospice care	35	40	40	30
Vision	32	33	33	33	Vision	8	7	8	8
In HMO's	16	20	18	11	In HMO's	10	12	8	9
Alcohol abuse treatment	89	90	88	89	Alcohol abuse treatment	(NA)	(NA)	(NA)	(NA)
Inpatient detoxification	(NA)	(NA)	(NA)	(NA)	Inpatient detoxification	67	80	73	58
Inpatient rehabilitation	(NA)	(NA)	(NA)	(NA)	Inpatient rehabilitation	54	64	58	47
Outpatient	(NA)	(NA)	(NA)	(NA)	Outpatient	50	60	54	43
Drug abuse treatment	88	90	87	89	Drug abuse treatment	(NA)	(NA)	(NA)	(NA)
Inpatient detoxification	(NA)	(NA)	(NA)	(NA)	Inpatient detoxification	65	77	71	56
Inpatient rehabilitation	(NA)	(NA)	(NA)	(NA)	Inpatient rehabilitation	50	60	55	44
Outpatient	(NA)	(NA)	(NA)	(NA)	Outpatient	47	55	51	41
Life	94	95	94	93	Life	64	79	70	55
Noncontributory	82	82	81	83	Noncontributory	53	69	60	43
Accident/sickness	43	29	29	58	Accident/sickness	26	25	24	27
Noncontributory	36	22	22	51	Noncontributory	17	14	15	19
Long-term disability	45	65	57	27	Long-term disability	19	36	25	9
Noncontributory	35	50	43	23	Noncontributory	16	30	21	8
Retirement and savings plans:					Retirement and savings plans:				
Defined benefit pension	63	64	63	63	Defined benefit pension	20	20	23	18
Earnings-based formula [1]	47	59	54	38	Earnings-based formula [1]	14	17	19	9
Defined contribution	48	59	52	40	Defined contribution	31	40	36	24
Savings and thrift	30	41	35	21	Savings and thrift	10	16	15	5
Employee stock ownership	3	4	3	3	Employee stock ownership	1	1	1	(Z)
Deferred profit sharing	15	13	13	16	Deferred profit sharing	15	17	17	13
Money purchase pension	5	8	6	3	Money purchase pension	6	9	6	6
Additional benefits:					Additional benefits:				
Parking	90	85	86	94	Parking	86	84	85	88
Educational assistance	69	81	75	59	Educational assistance	39	58	46	30
Travel accident insurance	53	69	60	39	Travel accident insurance	15	24	19	9
Severance pay	39	54	46	27	Severance pay	19	30	26	12
Relocation allowance	36	68	29	21	Relocation allowance	12	22	15	6
Recreation facilities	28	36	26	24	Recreation facilities	6	12	6	4
Nonproduction bonuses, cash	27	26	28	28	Nonproduction bonuses, cash	45	42	47	44
Child care	5	6	6	3	Child care	1	2	2	1
Flexible benefits plans	9	14	15	3	Flexible benefits plans	1	3	2	1
Reimbursement accounts [2]	23	36	31	11	Reimbursement accounts [2]	8	13	9	4
Eldercare	3	4	3	2	Eldercare	2	5	1	1
Long-term care insurance	3	3	3	2	Long-term care insurance	1	(Z)	1	1
Wellness programs	23	30	25	19	Wellness programs	6	10	8	4
Employee assistance programs	49	57	50	44	Employee assistance programs	15	21	17	11

NA Not available.   Z Represents or rounds to zero.   [1] Earnings-based formulas pay a percent of employee's annual earnings (usually earnings in the final years of employment) per year of service.   [2] Account which is used throughout the year to pay for plan premiums or to reimburse the employee for benefit related expenses. Account may be financed by employer, employee, or both.

Source: U.S. Bureau of Labor Statistics, Employee Benefits in Medium and Large Firms, 1989, Bulletin 2363; and Employee Benefits in Small Private Establishments, 1990, Bulletin 2388.

No. 663. Major Collective Bargaining Agreements—Average Percent Wage Rate Changes Under All Agreements: 1970 to 1991

[In percent, except as indicated. Data represent all wage rate changes implemented under the terms of private nonfarm industry agreements affecting 1,000 workers or more. Series covers production and related workers in manufacturing and nonsupervisory workers in nonmanufacturing industries. Data measure all wage rate changes effective in the year stemming from settlements reached in the year, deferred from prior year settlements, and cost-of-living adjustment (COLA) clauses]

CHANGES	1970	1975	1980	1984	1985	1986	1987	1988	1989	1990	1991
Average wage rate change (prorated over all workers)	8.8	8.7	9.9	3.7	3.3	2.3	3.1	2.6	3.2	3.5	3.6
Source:											
Current settlements.	5.1	2.8	3.6	0.8	0.7	0.5	0.7	0.7	1.2	1.3	1.1
Prior settlements	3.1	3.7	3.5	2.0	1.8	1.7	1.8	1.3	1.3	1.5	1.9
COLA provisions.	0.6	2.2	2.8	0.9	0.7	0.2	0.5	0.6	0.7	0.7	0.5
Industry:											
Manufacturing	7.1	8.5	10.2	4.3	2.8	1.5	3.4	2.8	3.5	4.4	3.7
Nonmanufacturing.	10.5	8.9	9.7	3.3	3.6	2.9	2.9	2.5	3.0	3.0	3.5
Construction	(NA)	8.1	9.9	2.9	3.0	3.0	3.1	2.9	3.1	3.4	3.4
Transportation and public utilities	(NA)	9.7	10.8	3.0	3.6	2.7	2.7	2.1	2.3	2.2	3.3
Wholesale and retail trade.	(NA)	9.2	7.6	3.4	3.3	2.9	2.0	2.3	3.2	3.6	3.5
Services.	(NA)	6.4	8.1	4.9	5.1	3.7	3.8	3.5	5.3	4.3	4.9
Nonmanufacturing, excluding construction	(NA)	9.3	9.6	3.4	3.7	2.9	2.8	2.4	3.0	2.9	3.6
Average wage rate increase for workers receiving an increase	9.4	9.0	10.1	4.7	4.2	3.4	3.8	3.4	4.0	4.2	4.0
Source:											
Current settlements.	11.9	10.2	9.4	3.9	4.1	3.1	3.5	3.3	4.2	4.1	4.2
Prior settlements	5.8	5.2	5.6	4.1	3.7	3.9	3.3	3.1	3.4	3.3	3.7
COLA provisions.	3.7	4.8	7.7	2.7	2.2	1.0	2.6	2.7	3.3	2.7	2.0
Total number of workers receiving a wage rate increase (mil.)	10.2	9.7	8.9	6.0	5.5	5.1	5.3	4.7	4.8	4.9	5.1
Source (mil.):											
Current settlements.	4.7	2.7	3.5	1.7	1.4	1.7	1.5	1.4	1.7	1.9	1.5
Prior settlements	5.7	7.3	5.6	3.6	3.4	2.8	3.5	2.6	2.3	2.7	3.0
COLA provisions.	1.8	4.7	3.4	2.5	2.3	1.4	1.3	1.3	1.3	1.4	1.3
Number of workers not receiving a wage rate increase (mil.).	0.6	0.4	0.2	1.3	1.5	1.4	1.0	1.3	1.2	1.0	0.5

NA Not available.

Source: U.S. Bureau of Labor Statistics, *Compensation and Working Conditions*, monthly.

No. 664. Major Collective Bargaining Settlements—Average Percent Changes in Wage and Compensation Rates Negotiated: 1970 to 1991

[In percent, except as indicated. Data represent private nonfarm industry settlements affecting production and related workers in manufacturing and nonsupervisory workers in nonmanufacturing industries. Wage data cover units with 1,000 workers or more. Compensation data relate to units of 5,000 or more. Data relate to contracts negotiated in each calendar year but exclude possible changes in wage rates under cost-of-living adjustment (COLA) clauses, except increases guaranteed by the contract. Includes all settlements, whether wage and benefit rates were changed or not. Minus sign (-) indicates decrease]

CHANGES	1970	1975	1980	1983	1984	1985	1986	1987	1988	1989	1990	1991
Compensation rates:												
First year	13.1	11.4	10.4	3.4	3.6	2.6	1.1	3.0	3.1	4.5	4.6	4.1
Over life of contract [1].	9.1	8.1	7.1	3.0	2.8	2.7	1.6	2.6	2.5	3.4	3.2	3.4
Wage rates:												
All industries:												
First year	11.9	10.2	9.5	2.6	2.4	2.3	1.2	2.2	2.5	4.0	4.0	3.6
Contracts with COLA	(NA)	12.2	8.0	1.9	2.9	1.6	1.9	2.3	2.4	3.9	3.4	3.4
Contracts without COLA	(NA)	9.1	11.7	3.3	2.1	2.7	0.9	2.1	2.7	4.0	4.4	3.7
Over life of contract [1]	8.9	7.8	7.1	2.8	2.4	2.7	1.8	2.1	2.4	3.4	3.2	3.2
Contracts with COLA	(NA)	7.1	5.0	2.0	1.8	2.5	1.7	1.5	1.8	2.8	1.9	3.0
Contracts without COLA	(NA)	8.3	10.3	3.7	2.7	2.8	1.8	2.5	2.8	3.5	4.0	3.3
Manufacturing:												
First year	8.1	9.8	7.4	0.4	2.3	0.8	-1.2	2.1	2.2	3.9	3.7	3.9
Over life of contract [1].	6.0	8.0	5.4	2.1	1.5	1.8	0.2	1.3	2.1	3.2	2.1	3.1
Nonmanufacturing:												
First year	15.2	10.4	10.9	3.8	2.5	3.3	2.0	2.3	2.8	4.0	4.3	3.4
Over life of contract [1].	11.5	7.8	8.3	3.2	2.9	3.3	2.3	2.7	2.5	3.4	4.0	3.3
Number of workers affected (mil.) . .	4.7	2.9	3.8	3.1	2.3	2.2	2.5	2.0	1.8	1.9	2.0	1.8
Manufacturing (mil.)	2.2	0.8	1.6	1.1	0.9	0.9	0.6	0.9	0.7	0.4	0.9	0.6
Nonmanufacturing (mil.).	2.5	2.1	2.2	2.0	1.4	1.3	1.9	1.1	1.1	1.5	1.1	1.2

NA Not available.   [1] Average annual rate of change.

Source: U.S. Bureau of Labor Statistics, *Compensation and Working Conditions*, monthly.

No. 665. Workers Killed or Disabled on the Job, 1960 to 1990, and by Industry Group, 1990

[Data for 1990 are preliminary estimates. Estimates based on data from the U.S. National Center for Health Statistics, State Departments of Health, and State industrial commissions. Numbers of workers based on data from the U.S. Bureau of Labor Statistics]

YEAR	DEATHS						Dis-abling injur-ies [2]	YEAR AND INDUSTRY GROUP	DEATHS		Dis-abling injur-ies [2]
	Total		Manufacturing		Nonmanu-facturing				Number (1,000)	Rate [1]	
	Number (1,000)	Rate [1]	Number (1,000)	Rate [1]	Number (1,000)	Rate [1]	(1,000)				(1,000)
1960....	13.8	21	1.7	10	12.1	25	1,950	1990, total.......	10.5	9	1,800
1965....	14.1	20	1.8	10	12.3	24	2,100	Agriculture [3].........	1.3	42	120
1970....	13.8	18	1.7	9	12.1	21	2,200	Mining and quarrying [4]..	0.3	43	30
1975....	13.0	15	1.6	9	11.4	17	2,200	Construction..........	2.1	33	210
1980....	13.2	13	1.7	8	11.5	15	2,200	Manufacturing........	1.1	6	360
1984....	11.5	11	1.1	6	10.4	12	1,900	Transportation and utilities	1.3	22	120
1985....	11.5	11	1.2	6	10.3	12	2,000	Trade [5]............	1.2	4	330
1986....	11.1	10	1.0	5	10.1	11	1,800	Services [6]..........	1.6	4	340
1987....	11.3	10	1.0	5	10.3	11	1,800	Government.........	1.6	9	290
1988....	11.0	10	1.1	6	9.9	10	1,800				
1989....	10.7	9	1.1	6	9.6	10	1,700				
1990....	10.5	9	1.1	6	9.4	10	1,800				

[1] Per 100,000 workers. [2] Disabling injury defined as one which results in death, some degree of physical impairment, or renders the person unable to perform regular activities for a full day beyond the day of the injury. [3] Includes forestry and fishing. [4] Includes oil and gas extraction. [5] Includes wholesale and retail trade. [6] Includes finance, insurance and real estate.

Source: National Safety Council, Itasca, IL, *Accident Facts*, annual, (copyright).

No. 666. Worker Deaths and Injuries and Production Time Lost: 1985 to 1990

ITEM	DEATHS (1,000)			DISABLING INJURIES [1] (mil.)			PRODUCTION TIME LOST (mil. days)					
							In the current year			In future years [2]		
	1985	1989	1990	1985	1989	1990	1985	1989	1990	1985	1989	1990
All accidents........	46.3	48.2	47.3	4.6	4.6	4.6	100.0	95.0	95.0	380.0	370.0	380.0
On the job.............	11.4	10.7	10.5	1.9	1.8	1.8	40.0	35.0	35.0	110.0	90.0	100.0
Off the job.............	34.9	37.5	36.8	2.7	2.8	2.8	60.0	60.0	60.0	270.0	280.0	280.0
Motor vehicle..........	22.2	23.7	23.2	0.9	0.9	0.9	(NA)	(NA)	(NA)	(NA)	(NA)	(NA)
Public nonmotor vehicle...	6.9	6.9	6.9	0.9	0.9	0.9	(NA)	(NA)	(NA)	(NA)	(NA)	(NA)
Home...............	5.8	6.9	6.7	0.9	1.0	1.0	(NA)	(NA)	(NA)	(NA)	(NA)	(NA)

NA Not available. [1] See footnote 2, table 665. [2] Based on an average of 5,850 days lost in future years per fatality and 565 days lost in future years per permanent injury.

Source: National Safety Council, Itasca, IL, *Accident Facts*, 1991, (copyright).

No. 667. Industries with the Highest Occupational Illness and Injury Rates: 1989 and 1990

[Rates per full-time employees. Industries shown are those with highest rates in 1990. See headnote, table 668]

1987 SIC [1] code	INDUSTRY	1989	1990	1987 SIC [1] code	INDUSTRY	1989	1990
(X)	Private sector, total..........	8.6	8.8	3316	Cold finishing of steel shapes......	22.8	24.3
3731	Ship building and repairing........	45.8	46.2	3639	Household appliances, n.e.c........	20.8	24.2
2011	Meat packing plants	35.1	42.4	3341	Secondary nonferrous metals......	23.7	24.1
3431	Metal sanitary ware............	(NA)	31.5	2522	Office furniture, except wood.......	20.9	24.1
3321	Gray and ductile iron foundries.....	27.7	30.5	3715	Truck trailers.................	27.6	24.0
3465	Automotive stampings...........	27.6	29.3	3211	Flat glass....................	21.9	24.0
2015	Poultry slaughtering and processing..	22.8	26.9	3441	Fabricated structural metal........	24.4	23.6
3711	Motor vehicles and car bodies......	26.6	26.8	3325	Steel foundries, n.e.c. [2]..........	24.8	23.5
3334	Primary aluminum..............	23.9	26.4	3364	Nonferrous die-casting exc. aluminum.	19.2	23.3
2061	Raw cane sugar...............	22.1	26.3	3443	Fabricated plate work (boiler shops)..	24.0	22.8
2452	Prefabricated wood buildings......	27.9	25.8	2013	Sausages and other prepared meats .	22.6	22.7
3412	Metal barrels, drums, and pails.....	24.0	25.4	2045	Prepared flour mixes and doughs....	21.6	22.6
2451	Mobile homes.................	23.9	25.4	3322	Malleable iron foundries..........	20.3	22.5
2429	Special product sawmills, n.e.c. [2]...	25.6	25.2	2092	Fresh or frozen prepared fish......	24.3	22.5
2439	Structural wood members, n.e.c. [2]...	30.4	24.5	3462	Iron and steel forgings...........	23.5	22.4

NA Not available. X Not applicable. [1] 1987 Standard Industrial Classification; see text, section 13. [2] N.e.c. means not elsewhere classified.

Source: U.S. Bureau of Labor Statistics, *Occupational Injuries and Illnesses in the United States by Industry*, annual.

No. 668. Occupational Injury and Illness Incidence Rates, by Selected Industries: 1989 and 1990

[Rates per 100 full-time employees. For nonfarm employment data, see table 645. Rates refer to any occupational injury or illness resulting in (1) fatalities, (2) lost workday cases, or (3) nonfatal cases without lost workdays. Incidence rates were calculated as: Number of injuries and illnesses or lost workdays divided by total hours worked by all employees during year multiplied by 200,000 as base for 100 full-time equivalent workers (working 40 hours per week, 50 weeks a year)]

1987 SIC [1] code	INDUSTRY	1989	1990	1987 SIC [1] code	INDUSTRY	1989	1990
(X)	**Private sector** [2]	**8.6**	**8.8**	31	Leather and leather products	13.6	12.1
A	**Agriculture, forestry, fishing** [2]	**10.9**	**11.6**	E	**Transportation and public utilities**	**9.2**	**9.6**
B	**Mining**	**8.5**	**8.3**	40	Railroad transportation	7.7	7.5
10	Metal mining	8.5	6.8	41	Local passenger transit [3]	9.6	9.7
11	Anthracite mining	(NA)	(NA)	42	Trucking and warehousing	13.5	14.3
12	Coal mining	11.6	10.8	44	Water transportation	12.1	11.9
13	Oil and gas extraction	7.6	8.0	45	Transportation by air	14.2	15.1
14	Nonmetallic minerals, exc. fuels	7.9	7.1	46	Pipelines, except natural gas	3.5	3.4
C	**Construction**	**14.3**	**14.2**	47	Transportation services	4.3	3.9
15	General building contractors	13.9	13.4	48	Communications	3.1	3.3
16	Heavy construction, except			49	Electric, gas, sanitary services	8.0	8.2
	building	13.8	13.8	F, G	**Wholesale and retail trade**	**8.0**	**7.9**
17	Special trade contractors	14.6	14.7	F	Wholesale trade	7.7	7.4
D	**Manufacturing**	**13.1**	**13.2**	G	Retail trade	8.1	8.1
(X)	Durable goods	14.1	14.2	H	**Finance, insurance, real estate** [4]	**2.0**	**2.4**
24	Lumber and wood products	18.4	18.1	60	Depository institutions	1.4	2.1
25	Furniture and fixtures	16.1	16.9	62	Security and commodity brokers	(NA)	0.9
32	Stone, clay, and glass products	15.5	15.4	63	Insurance carriers	1.7	2.1
33	Primary metal industries	18.7	19.0	64	Insurance agents, brokers, and		
34	Fabricated metal products	18.5	18.7		service	1.0	1.3
35	Industrial machinery and equipment	12.1	12.0	65	Real estate	4.8	4.8
36	Electronic and other electric			I	**Services** [4]	**5.5**	**6.0**
	equipment	9.1	9.1	70	Hotels and other lodging places	10.8	10.7
37	Transportation equipment	17.7	17.8	72	Personal services	3.6	3.6
38	Instruments and related products	5.6	5.9	73	Business services	4.7	5.0
39	Miscellaneous manufacturing			75	Auto repair, services, and		
	industries	11.1	11.3		parking	6.7	7.4
(X)	Nondurable goods	11.6	11.7	76	Miscellaneous repair services	8.6	8.4
20	Food and kindred products	18.5	20.0	78	Motion pictures	(NA)	3.6
21	Tobacco products	8.7	7.7	79	Amusement and recreation		
22	Textile mill products	10.3	9.6		services	8.6	9.0
23	Apparel and other textile			80	Health services	7.3	8.4
	products	8.6	8.8	81	Legal services	0.5	0.6
26	Paper and allied products	12.7	12.1	82	Educational services	3.5	3.8
27	Printing and publishing	6.9	6.9	83	Social services	5.7	6.5
28	Chemicals and allied products	7.0	6.5	84	Museums, botanical, zoological		
29	Petroleum and coal products	6.6	6.6		gardens	6.2	7.4
30	Rubber and misc. plastics			87	Engineering and management		
	products	16.2	16.2		services	1.9	2.1

NA Not available.   X Not applicable.   [1] 1987 Standard Industrial Classification; see text, section 13.   [2] Excludes farms with fewer than 11 employees.   [3] Includes interurban.   [4] Includes categories not shown separately.

Source: U.S. Bureau of Labor Statistics, *Occupational Injuries and Illnesses in the United States by Industry*, annual.

No. 669. Work Stoppages: 1960 to 1991

[Excludes work stoppages involving fewer than 1,000 workers and lasting less than 1 day. Information is based on reports of labor disputes appearing in daily newspapers, trade journals, and other public sources. The parties to the disputes are contacted by telephone, when necessary, to clarify details of the stoppages]

YEAR	Number of work stoppages [1]	Workers involved [2] (1,000)	DAYS IDLE		YEAR	Number of work stoppages [1]	Workers involved [2] (1,000)	DAYS IDLE	
			Number [3] (1,000)	Percent estimated working time [4]				Number [3] (1,000)	Percent estimated working time [4]
1960	222	896	13,260	0.09	1980	187	795	20,844	0.09
1965	268	999	15,140	0.10	1981	145	729	16,908	0.07
1969	412	1,576	29,397	0.29	1982	96	656	9,061	0.04
1970	381	2,468	52,761	0.29	1983	81	909	17,461	0.08
1971	298	2,516	35,538	0.19	1984	62	376	8,499	0.04
1972	250	975	16,764	0.09	1985	54	324	7,079	0.03
1973	317	1,400	16,260	0.08	1986	69	533	11,861	0.05
1974	424	1,796	31,809	0.16	1987	46	174	[5]4,469	0.02
1975	235	965	17,563	0.09	1988	40	118	4,364	0.02
1976	231	1,519	23,962	0.12	1989	51	452	16,996	0.07
1977	298	1,212	21,258	0.10	1990	44	185	5,926	0.02
1978	219	1,006	23,774	0.11	1991	40	392	4,584	0.02
1979	235	1,021	20,409	0.09					

[1] Beginning in year indicated.   [2] Workers counted more than once if involved in more than one stoppage during the year.   [3] Resulting from all stoppages in effect in a year, including those that began in an earlier year.   [4] Agricultural and government employees are included in the total working time; private household and forestry and fishery employees are excluded.   [5] Revised since originally published.

Source: U.S. Bureau of Labor Statistics, *Compensation and Working Conditions*, monthly.

No. 670. U.S. Membership in AFL-CIO Affiliated Unions, by Selected Union: 1979 to 1991

[In thousands. Figures represent the labor organizations as constituted in 1989 and reflect past merger activity. Membership figures based on average per capita paid membership to the AFL-CIO for the 2-year period ending in June of the year shown and reflect only actively-employed members. Labor unions shown had a membership of 50,000 or more in 1991]

LABOR ORGANIZATION	1979	1985	1989	1991	LABOR ORGANIZATION	1979	1985	1989	1991
Total [1]	13,621	13,109	14,100	13,933	Machinists and Aerospace				
Actors and Artistes	75	100	97	99	(IAM) [2]	688	537	517	534
Allied Industrial Workers	92	63	60	53	Marine Engineers				
Automobile, Aerospace and					Beneficial Assn.	23	22	48	53
Agriculture (UAW)	(X)	974	917	840	Mine Workers	(X)	(X)	(X)	82
Bakery, Confectionery and					Office and Professional				
Tobacco	131	115	103	101	Employees	83	90	84	89
Boiler Makers, Iron Ship-					Oil, Chemical, Atomic				
builders [2][3]	129	110	75	66	Workers (OCAW)	146	108	71	90
Bricklayers	106	95	84	84	Painters	160	133	128	124
Carpenters [2]	626	616	613	494	Paperworkers Int'l	262	232	210	202
Clothing and Textile Workers					Plumbing and Pipefitting	228	226	220	220
(ACTWU) [2]	308	228	180	154	Postal Workers	245	232	213	228
Communication Workers					Retail, Wholesale Depart-				
(CWA)	485	524	492	492	ment Store	122	106	137	128
Electrical Workers (IBEW)	825	791	744	730	Rubber, Cork, Linoleum,				
Electronic, Electrical and					Plastic	158	106	92	89
Salaried [2][4]	243	198	171	160	Seafarers	84	80	80	80
Operating Engineers	313	330	330	330	Service Employees				
FireFighters	150	142	142	151	(SEIU) [2][5]	537	688	762	881
Food and Commercial					Sheet Metal Workers	120	108	108	108
Workers (UFCW) [2]	1,123	989	999	997	Stage Employees, Moving				
Garment Workers (ILGWU)	314	210	153	143	Picture Machine Operators	50	50	50	50
Glass, Molders, Pottery, and					State, County, Municipal				
Plastics [2]	50	104	86	80	(AFSCME) [5]	889	997	1,090	1,191
Government, American					Steelworkers	964	572	481	459
Federation (AFGE)	236	199	156	151	Teachers (AFT)	423	470	544	573
Graphic Communications [2]	171	141	124	113	Teamsters [6]	(X)	(X)	1,161	1,379
Hotel Employees and					Transit Union	94	94	96	98
Restaurant Employees	373	327	278	269	Transport Workers	85	85	85	85
Ironworkers	146	140	111	101	Transportation/Communica-				
Laborers	475	383	406	406	tions International	127	102	86	73
Letter Carriers (NALC)	151	186	201	210	Transportation Union, United	121	88	(X)	64
Longshoreman's Association	63	65	62	60	Utility Workers	53	52	51	55

X Not applicable. [1] Includes other AFL-CIO affiliated unions, not shown separately. [2] Figures reflect mergers with one or more unions since 1979. For details see source. [3] Includes Blacksmiths, Forgers and Helpers. [4] Includes Machine and Furniture Workers. [5] Excludes Hospital and Health Care Employees which merged into both unions on June 1, 1989, (membership of 23,000 in 1985; 60,000 in 1987; and 58,000 in 1989). [6] Includes Chauffeurs, Warehousemen, and Helpers.
Source: American Federation of Labor and Congress of Industrial Organizations, Washington, DC, *Report of the AFL-CIO Executive Council*, biannual.

No. 671. U.S. Union Membership in Manufacturing, by State: 1984 to 1989

[Data represent annual average dues-paying full-time equivalent membership derived from financial records. Excludes unemployed members. In general, annual per capita revenues received by the parent organization were divided by the per capita rate to yield membership. For unions with multiple dues structures or other structures, other methods were used. See source for details. A right-to-work State has laws which prohibit collective bargaining contracts from including clauses requiring union membership as a condition of employment. Data for DC not available]

STATE	MANUFACTURING— UNION MEMBERSHIP (1,000)			PERCENT OF EMPLOYED [1]			STATE	MANUFACTURING— UNION MEMBERSHIP (1,000)			PERCENT OF EMPLOYED [1]		
	1984	1988	1989	1984	1988	1989		1984	1988	1989	1984	1988	1989
U.S.	5,285.9	4,771.1	4,603.1	27.3	24.9	23.8	MT	5.6	5.2	4.9	24.9	25.0	22.8
AL [2]	72.2	57.4	55.1	20.1	15.3	14.3	NE [2]	11.1	9.1	8.6	12.3	9.9	8.7
AK	4.3	3.7	3.6	38.1	25.5	24.6	NV [2]	1.6	1.5	1.4	7.6	6.2	5.4
AZ [2]	9.2	7.2	7.0	5.3	3.8	3.7	NH	9.9	8.2	7.8	8.0	6.7	6.7
AR [2]	28.6	27.3	26.3	13.4	12.0	11.2	NJ	184.9	165.6	160.8	25.4	24.8	24.4
CA	510.5	488.4	481.3	24.7	22.6	22.2	NM	5.6	4.2	3.9	15.3	10.4	9.5
CO	21.2	18.8	18.3	10.9	10.0	9.5	NY	668.2	588.0	561.7	50.4	48.2	47.2
CT	70.2	58.7	56.7	16.9	15.6	15.3	NC [2]	41.4	39.7	38.3	5.0	4.6	4.4
DE [2]	13.8	14.1	13.8	19.6	20.5	19.4	ND [2]	2.1	1.7	1.7	13.6	10.4	10.1
FL [2]	43.3	48.2	48.9	8.6	8.9	9.0	OH	469.0	450.4	438.8	41.6	40.9	39.6
GA [2]	77.3	67.8	66.3	14.1	11.9	11.7	OK	30.6	26.9	26.2	17.5	17.1	15.9
HI	9.0	9.1	9.0	41.3	41.4	41.0	OR	49.9	45.2	44.1	24.8	21.4	20.3
ID [3]	7.3	4.9	4.5	13.3	8.6	7.3	PA	457.1	428.3	413.4	40.7	40.7	39.3
IL	407.7	314.8	201.0	40.0	33.3	20.8	RI	13.0	12.8	12.4	10.7	11.1	11.1
IN [2]	248.7	237.8	234.7	40.1	37.6	37.0	SC [2]	14.6	11.8	11.1	3.9	3.1	2.9
IA [2]	65.3	46.8	43.5	30.8	20.8	18.5	SD [2]	1.1	0.8	0.7	3.8	2.7	2.4
KS [2]	22.6	20.6	20.1	12.8	11.4	10.9	TN [2]	78.4	67.2	65.0	15.8	13.5	12.7
KY	69.6	62.6	60.4	27.0	23.0	21.5	TX [2]	159.8	142.6	134.1	15.9	15.1	13.8
LA [2]	36.8	34.5	33.4	20.2	20.4	19.4	UT [2]	6.8	4.9	4.6	7.2	5.0	4.4
ME	23.8	20.1	19.7	21.5	18.7	18.4	VT	5.5	4.1	3.9	11.2	8.3	8.1
MD	71.2	62.0	60.2	32.5	30.0	29.2	VA [2]	48.5	52.1	50.6	11.5	12.2	11.9
MA	128.8	115.8	111.8	19.2	19.9	19.6	WA	99.7	93.6	90.7	34.6	28.2	25.3
MI	487.8	500.6	486.9	50.7	53.6	51.6	WV	34.9	25.7	24.4	38.1	29.8	28.1
MN	96.2	70.1	65.5	25.7	18.1	16.4	WI	161.4	133.3	127.8	31.1	24.3	23.0
MS [2]	19.0	19.0	18.4	8.7	8.1	7.6	WY [2]	1.6	1.3	1.2	20.0	15.9	13.0
MO	179.2	136.5	127.8	41.3	32.4	29.6							

[1] Employed in manufacturing. [2] Right-to-work State. [3] Right-to-work State beginning 1988.
Source: Grant/Thornton, Chicago, IL, *Manufacturing Climates Study*, annual.

No. 672. Union Members, by Selected Characteristics: 1983 and 1991

[Annual averages of monthly data. Covers employed wage and salary workers 16 years old and over. Excludes self-employed workers whose businesses are incorporated although they technically qualify as wage and salary workers. Based on Current Population Survey, see text, section 1, and Appendix III]

CHARACTERISTIC	EMPLOYED WAGE AND SALARY WORKERS										MEDIAN USUAL WEEKLY EARNINGS[3] (dol.)							
	Total (1,000)		Union members[1] (1,000)		Represented by unions[2] (1,000)		Percent union members		Percent represented by union		Total		Union members[1]		Represented by unions[2]		Not represented by unions	
	1983	1991	1983	1991	1983	1991	1983	1991	1983	1991	1983	1991	1983	1991	1983	1991	1983	1991
Total	88,290	102,786	17,717	16,568	20,532	18,734	20.1	16.1	23.3	18.2	313	430	388	526	383	522	288	404
16 to 24 years old	19,305	17,340	1,749	1,142	2,145	1,341	9.1	6.6	11.1	7.7	210	278	281	356	275	347	203	272
25 to 34 years old	25,978	30,106	5,097	4,228	5,990	4,824	19.6	14.0	23.1	16.0	321	417	382	496	376	491	304	403
35 to 44 years old	18,722	27,056	4,648	5,339	5,362	6,040	24.8	19.7	28.6	22.3	369	499	411	557	407	555	339	479
45 to 54 years old	13,150	16,863	3,554	3,743	4,014	4,163	27.0	22.2	30.5	24.7	366	507	404	581	402	580	335	480
55 to 64 years old	9,201	9,116	2,474	1,919	2,788	2,138	26.9	21.1	30.3	23.5	346	469	392	534	390	529	316	427
65 years and over	1,934	2,305	196	198	234	228	10.1	8.6	12.1	9.9	260	381	338	522	330	526	238	348
Men	47,856	53,931	11,809	10,430	13,270	11,494	24.7	19.3	27.7	21.3	378	497	416	568	414	567	349	473
Women	40,433	48,856	5,908	6,138	7,262	7,240	14.6	12.6	18.0	14.8	252	368	309	467	307	462	237	348
White	77,046	87,981	14,844	13,587	17,182	15,331	19.3	15.4	22.3	17.4	319	446	396	544	391	539	295	415
Men	42,168	46,586	10,134	8,754	11,364	9,604	24.0	18.8	26.9	20.6	387	509	423	581	421	581	362	488
Women	34,877	41,395	4,710	4,833	5,818	5,726	13.5	11.7	16.7	13.8	254	374	314	477	313	473	240	355
Black	8,979	11,318	2,440	2,425	2,850	2,759	27.2	21.4	31.7	24.4	261	348	331	461	324	452	222	314
Men	4,477	5,502	1,420	1,355	1,615	1,524	31.7	24.6	36.1	27.7	293	374	366	489	360	485	244	330
Women	4,502	5,816	1,020	1,070	1,235	1,236	22.7	18.4	27.4	21.2	231	323	292	420	287	414	209	302
Hispanic[4]	(NA)	8,193	(NA)	1,275	(NA)	1,447	(NA)	15.6	(NA)	17.7	(NA)	315	(NA)	439	(NA)	438	(NA)	295
Men	(NA)	4,860	(NA)	823	(NA)	906	(NA)	16.9	(NA)	18.6	(NA)	328	(NA)	481	(NA)	482	(NA)	305
Women	(NA)	3,333	(NA)	451	(NA)	541	(NA)	13.5	(NA)	16.2	(NA)	293	(NA)	374	(NA)	376	(NA)	278
Full-time workers	70,976	83,525	16,271	15,179	18,745	17,095	22.9	18.2	26.4	20.5	313	430	388	526	383	522	288	404
Part-time workers	17,314	19,261	1,446	1,390	1,787	1,639	8.4	7.2	10.3	8.5	(X)	(X)	(X)	(X)	(X)	(X)	(X)	(X)
Managerial and professional specialty	19,657	26,018	3,354	3,802	4,307	4,611	17.1	14.6	21.9	17.7	437	627	423	634	421	630	446	626
Technical, sales, and admin. support	28,024	32,649	3,377	3,395	4,199	4,035	12.1	10.4	15.0	12.4	281	394	350	480	341	474	270	382
Service occupations	12,875	14,649	1,971	2,037	2,306	2,261	15.3	13.9	17.9	15.4	205	280	305	448	299	437	182	253
Precision, production, craft, and repair	10,542	11,189	3,466	2,899	3,760	3,105	32.9	25.9	35.7	27.8	377	483	456	598	450	593	322	430
Operators, fabricators, and laborers	15,416	16,492	5,452	4,345	5,839	4,619	35.4	26.3	37.9	28.0	275	351	366	480	361	475	226	310
Farming, forestry, and fishing	1,775	1,790	98	90	122	103	5.5	5.0	6.9	5.7	196	263	292	414	287	405	189	256
Agricultural wage and salary workers	1,446	1,517	49	32	55	36	3.4	2.1	3.8	2.4	198	267	(B)	(B)	(B)	(B)	195	264
Private nonagr. wage and salary workers	71,225	83,294	11,933	9,909	13,369	10,907	16.8	11.9	18.8	13.1	307	415	389	510	385	506	286	400
Mining	869	676	180	101	201	114	20.7	15.0	23.1	16.9	481	596	470	588	470	589	488	598
Construction	4,109	4,624	1,131	977	1,207	1,034	27.5	21.1	29.4	22.4	348	468	518	679	510	665	296	412
Manufacturing	19,066	19,590	5,303	3,976	5,812	4,269	27.8	20.3	30.5	21.8	335	444	370	485	368	484	315	425
Transportation and public utilities	5,142	6,082	2,182	1,895	2,376	2,036	42.4	31.2	46.2	33.5	417	532	449	595	445	589	386	501
Wholesale and retail trade, total	18,081	21,015	1,568	1,406	1,775	1,552	8.7	6.7	9.8	7.4	252	334	353	416	348	413	242	326
Finance, insurance, and real estate	5,559	6,694	160	161	228	221	2.9	2.4	4.1	3.3	296	449	284	463	285	454	297	448
Services	18,400	24,613	1,410	1,392	1,770	1,681	7.7	5.7	9.6	6.8	272	394	303	431	303	436	268	390
Government	15,618	17,975	5,735	6,627	7,109	7,791	36.7	36.9	45.5	43.3	351	506	386	560	381	554	316	461

B Data not shown where base is less than 50,000. NA Not available. X Not applicable. [1] Members of a labor union or an employee association similar to a labor union. [2] Members of a labor union or an employee association similar to a union as well as workers who report no union affiliation but whose jobs are covered by a union or an employee association contract. [3] For full-time employed wage and salary workers; 1983 revised since originally published. [4] Persons of Hispanic origin may be of any race.

Source: U.S. Bureau of Labor Statistics, Employment and Earnings, January issues.

Income, Expenditures, and Wealth

This section presents data on gross domestic product (GDP), gross national product (GNP), national and personal income, saving and investment, money income, poverty, and national and personal wealth. The data on income and expenditures measure two aspects of the U.S. economy. One aspect relates to the national income and product accounts (NIPA), a summation reflecting the entire complex of the Nation's economic income and output and the interaction of its major components; the other relates to the distribution of money income to families and individuals, or consumer income.

The primary source for data on GDP, GNP, national and personal income, and gross saving and investment is the *Survey of Current Business,* published monthly, with supplements, by the Department of Commerce, Bureau of Economic Analysis (BEA). A comprehensive revision to the NIPA was completed in December 1991. A discussion of the revision appears in the August through October, 1991 and the December 1992 issues of *Survey of Current Business.* Detailed historical data appear in *The National Income and Product Accounts of the United States, volume 2, 1959-88* and the January and July 1992 issues of *Survey of Current Business*; detailed data for the most recent years are normally published each July in the *Survey.*

Sources of income distribution data are the decennial censuses of population and the Current Population Survey (CPS), both products of the Bureau of the Census (see text, section 1). Annual data on income of families, individuals, and households, by income class, are presented in *Current Population Reports-Consumer Income,* series P-60.

Data on individuals' saving and assets are published by the Board of Governors of the Federal Reserve System in the quarterly *Flow of Funds Accounts;* and detailed information on personal wealth is published periodically by the Internal Revenue Service (IRS) in *SOI Bulletin.*

In Brief

Gross domestic product
annual percent change:

1988-89	2.5
1980-90	1.0
1990-91	-0.7

Median household income
in 1990: $29,943

Poverty status of persons in 1990:
*Number below poverty level:
33.6 million
Percent below poverty level: 13.5*

National income and product.—*Gross domestic product* is the total national output of goods and services valued at market prices. GDP can be viewed in terms of expenditure categories which comprise purchases of goods and services by consumers and government, gross private domestic investment, and net exports of goods and services. The goods and services included are largely those bought for final use (excluding illegal transactions) in the market economy. A number of inclusions, however, represent imputed values, the most important of which is rental value of owner-occupied housing. GDP, in this broad context, measures the output attributable to the factors of production located in the United States. *Gross State product* (GSP) is the gross market value of the goods and services attributable to labor and property located in a State. It is the State counterpart of the Nation's gross domestic product.

Gross national product measures the output attributable to all labor and property supplied by United States residents. GNP differs from "national income" mainly in that GNP includes allowances for depreciation and for indirect business taxes (sales and property taxes); see table 677.

In December 1991, the Bureau of Economic Analysis began featuring gross domestic product rather than gross national product as the primary measure of

United States production. GDP is now the standard measure of growth because it is the appropriate measure for much of the short term monitoring and analysis of the economy. In addition, the use of GDP facilitates comparisons of economic activity in the United States with that in other countries. GDP is the primary measure of production in the System of National Accounts, the set of international guidelines for economic accounting that the U.S. economic accounts will be moving toward in the mid-1990's. Virtually all other countries have already adopted GDP as their primary measure of production. The dollar levels of GDP and GNP differ little, but percentage changes sometimes differ. The annual rates of growth of real GNP have been slightly less than the annual rates of growth of real GDP in most years of the 1980's. The quarterly differences are greater; they are larger, and they also fluctuate.

National income is the aggregate of labor and property earnings which arises in the current production of goods and services. It is the sum of employee compensation, proprietors' income, rental income of persons, corporate profits, and net interest. It measures the total factor costs of the goods and services produced by the economy. Income is measured before deduction of taxes on income.

Capital consumption adjustment for corporations, nonfarm sole proprietorships, and partnerships is the difference between capital consumption claimed on income tax returns and capital consumption allowances that are measured at straightline depreciation, consistent service lives, and replacement cost. The tax return data are valued at historical costs and reflect changes over time in service lives and depreciation patterns as permitted by tax regulations. *Inventory valuation adjustment* represents the difference between the book value of inventories used up in production and the cost of replacing them.

Personal income is the current income received by persons from all sources minus their personal contributions for social insurance. Classified as "persons" are individuals (including owners of unincor-

porated firms), nonprofit institutions serving individuals, private trust funds, and private noninsured welfare funds. Personal income includes transfers (payments not resulting from current production) from government and business such as Social Security benefits, public assistance, etc., but excludes transfers among persons. Also included are certain nonmonetary types of income-chiefly estimated net rental value to owner-occupants of their homes and the value of services furnished without payment by financial intermediaries.

Disposable personal income is personal income less personal tax and nontax payments. It is the income available to persons for spending and saving. Personal tax and nontax payments are tax payments (net of refunds) by persons (except personal contributions for social insurance) that are not chargeable to business expense, and certain personal payments to general government that are treated like taxes. Personal taxes include income, estate and gift, and personal property taxes and motor vehicle licenses. Nontax payments include passport fees, fines and penalties, and donations.

Consumer Expenditure Survey.—The Consumer Expenditure Survey program was begun in late 1979. The principal objective of the survey is to collect current consumer expenditure data which provide a continuous flow of data on the buying habits of American consumers. The data are necessary for future revisions of the Consumer Price Index.

The survey conducted by the Bureau of the Census for the Bureau of Labor Statistics, consists of two components: (1) An interview panel survey in which the expenditures of consumer units are obtained in five interviews conducted every 3 months; and (2) a diary or record-keeping survey completed by participating households for two consecutive 1-week periods.

Each component of the survey queries an independent sample of consumer units representative of the U.S. total population. Over 52 weeks of the year, 5,000 consumer units are sampled for the diary survey. Each consumer unit keeps a diary for two 1-week periods yielding approximately 10,000 diaries a year. The interview sample is selected on a rotating panel basis, targeted at 5,000 consumer units per quarter. Data are collected in 88 urban and 16 rural areas of the country that are representative of the U.S. total population. The survey includes students in student housing.

The Diary survey is designed to obtain expenditures on small, frequently purchased items which are normally difficult for respondents to recall. Detailed records of expenses are kept for food and beverages, both at home and in eating places, tobacco, housekeeping supplies, nonprescription drugs, and personal care products and services.

The Interview survey is designed to obtain data on the types of expenditures which respondents can be expected to recall for a period of 3 months or longer. In general, these include relatively large expenditures, such as those for property, automobiles, and major appliances, or expenditures which occur on a fairly regular basis, such as rent, utilities, or insurance premiums. Including "global estimates" for food, it is estimated that about 95 percent of expenditures are covered in the interview. Excluded are nonprescription drugs, household supplies, and personal care items. The interview survey also provides data on expenditures incurred while on trips. Both surveys exclude all business related expenditures for which the family is reimbursed.

In contrast to previous publications from the survey which have presented data from the diary and quarterly interview surveys separately, the tables in the most recently published *Consumer Expenditure Survey* combine, or integrate, data from the two surveys. Integration is necessary to permit analysis of total family expenditures because neither the diary nor quarterly interview survey was designed to collect a complete account of consumer spending.

Distribution of money income to families and individuals.—Money income statistics are based on data collected in various field surveys of income conducted since 1936. Since 1947, the Bureau of the Census has collected the data on an annual basis and published them in *Current Population Reports,* series P-60. In each of the surveys, field

representatives interview of the population with respect to income received during the previous year. Money income as defined by the Bureau of the Census differs from the BEA concept of "personal income."

Data on consumer income collected in the CPS by the Bureau of the Census cover money income received (exclusive of certain money receipts such as capital gains) before payments for personal income taxes, Social Security, union dues, Medicare deductions, etc. Therefore, money income does not reflect the fact that some families receive part of their income in the form of noncash benefits (see section 12) such as food stamps, health benefits, and subsidized housing; that some farm families receive noncash benefits in the form of rent-free housing and goods produced and consumed on the farm; or that noncash benefits are also received by some nonfarm residents which often take the form of the use of business transportation and facilities, full or partial payments by business for retirement programs, medical and educational expenses, etc. These elements should be considered when comparing income levels. For data on noncash benefits, see section 12. None of the aggregate income concepts (GDP, national income, or personal income) is exactly comparable with money income, although personal income is the closest.

Several changes were made in the collection and presentation of data from the March 1980 CPS. The changes include (1) the use of a more detailed income questionnaire for all sample households, (2) the use of an expanded sample, (3) the implementation of the "householder" concept rather than the traditional "head" concept, (4) the exclusion of a small number of "secondary families" from the count of all families, (5) the use of more detailed income intervals in the upper range of the income distribution, (6) the introduction of the new farm definition, and (7) the restriction of the population with income to persons 15 years old and over. For more information on the impact and comparability, see the source.

Beginning in the March 1981 Current Population Survey, 1980 census population controls were used; for income years

1971 through 1979, 1970 census population controls had been used. This change had little impact on income summary measures (means and medians) and proportional measures (percent distributions and poverty rates); however, use of the controls may have significant impact on the absolute numbers.

Income and poverty data for 1986 are the first estimates based entirely on households selected from the 1980 census-based sample design. Estimates by type of residence categories such as metropolitan, nonmetropolitan, farm, and nonfarm reflect metropolitan areas defined as of June 1984. In addition, the March 1987 CPS income supplement was revised to allow for the coding of larger earnings amounts on the questionnaire. A description of this change and its effect on estimates in this report can be found in *Current Population Reports,* series P-60, No. 157.

A new computer processing system was introduced to the March 1989 CPS income supplement. The system in use before this year was first introduced in 1976 but was never fully updated to reflect questionnaire changes. In addition, the programs used to process the CPS file were written in a language which was phased out of Census. The March 1988 file was reprocessed based on the new procedures to better evaluate the new processing procedures and allow year to year comparisons to be made using a consistent processing system. A description of this change and its effect on estimates in this report can be found in *Current Population Reports,* series P-60, No. 166.

In October 1983, the Census Bureau began to collect data under the new Survey of Income and Program Participation (SIPP). The information supplied by this survey is expected to provide better measures of the status and changes in income distribution and poverty of households and persons in the United States. The data collected in SIPP will be used to study Federal and State aid programs (such as food stamps, welfare, Medicaid, and subsidized housing), to estimate program costs and coverage, and to assess the effects of proposed changes in program eligibility rules or

benefit levels. The core questions are repeated at each interview and cover labor force activity, the types and amounts of income received, and participation status in various programs. The core also contains questions covering attendance in postsecondary schools and private health insurance coverage. Various supplements or topical modules covering areas such as educational attainment, assets and liabilities, and pension plan coverage are periodically included.

Poverty.—Families and unrelated individuals are classified as being above or below the poverty level using the poverty index originated at the Social Security Administration in 1964 and revised by Federal Interagency Committees in 1969 and 1980. The poverty index is based solely on money income and does not reflect the fact that many low-income persons receive noncash benefits such as food stamps, Medicaid, and public housing. The index is based on the Department of Agriculture's 1961 Economy Food Plan and reflects the different consumption requirements of families based on their size and composition. The poverty thresholds are updated every year to reflect changes in the Consumer Price Index. The following technical changes to the thresholds were made in 1981: (1) distinctions based on sex of householder have been eliminated; (2) separate thresholds for farm families have been dropped; and (3) the matrix has been expanded to families of nine or more persons from the old cutoff of seven or more persons. These changes have been incorporated in the calculation of poverty data beginning with 1981. The following table shows the average thresholds used for selected years between 1970 and 1988. See *Current Population Reports,* series P-60, No. 175 for more details.

In the recent past, the Bureau of the Census has published a number of technical papers that presented experimental poverty estimates based on income definitions that counted the value of selected government noncash benefits. The Census Bureau has also published annual reports on after-tax income. The *Current Population Reports,* series P-60, No. 176-RD brings together the benefit and tax data that previously appeared in the separate reports. This report shows the distribution of income among households and the prevalence of poverty under the official definition of money income and under definitions that add income components or subtract taxes. The types of income that are included in one or more of the definitions: (1) money income excluding capital gains or lump-sum payments, (2) capital gains, (3) the value of employer contributions to health insurance plans, (4) the value of food stamps, (5) the subsidy value of school lunches, (6) the subsidy value of housing assistance, (7) the fungible values of Medicare and Medicaid coverage (that is, the benefits are counted as income to the extent that they free up resources that could have been spent on medical care), and (8) the imputed net return on equity in own home. The types of taxes accounted for are Federal and State income taxes and payroll taxes.

The poverty statistics presented by the Bureau of the Census and Congressional Budget Office in tables 727 and 729 reflect alternative adjustments for inflation. The study used a variation of the Consumer Price Index to adjust poverty thresholds for the effects of changing prices since 1967. The alternative measure of inflation uses estimates of the cost of renting equivalent housing to assess homeownership costs;

this methodology has been used in the official Consumer Price Index since 1983. See text, section 15, and source for more details.

Personal wealth.—Personal wealth estimates, issued by the IRS, are based on a sample of Federal estate tax returns which must be filed for deceased persons. Estimates are weighted to adjust for age, sex, and "social class" (as determined by the IRS through insurance holdings). Gross estate is the gross value of all assets, including the full face value of life insurance (reduced by policy loans), before reduction by the amount of debts. The level of gross estate or gross assets required for filing estate tax returns increased from $60,000 in 1972 to $120,000 in 1976. Net worth is one's level of worth after all debts have been removed.

Statistical reliability.—For a discussion of statistical collection and estimation, sampling procedures, and measures of statistical reliability pertaining to Census Bureau data, see Appendix III.

Historical statistics.—Tabular headnotes provide cross-references, where applicable, to *Historical Statistics of the United States, Colonial Times to 1970.* See Appendix IV.

Weighted Average Poverty Thresholds Based on Money Income for Families and Unrelated Individuals: 1980 to 1990

SIZE OF UNIT	1980[1]	1983	1984	1985	1986	1987	1988	1989	1990
1 person (unrelated individual)	$4,190	$5,061	$5,278	$5,469	$5,572	$5,778	$6,024	$6,311	$6,652
Under 65 years	4,290	5,180	5,400	5,593	5,701	5,909	6,155	6,451	6,800
65 years and over	3,949	4,775	4,979	5,156	5,255	5,447	5,674	5,947	6,268
2 persons	5,363	6,483	6,762	6,998	7,138	7,397	7,704	8,076	8,509
Householder under 65 years	5,537	6,697	6,983	7,231	7,372	7,641	7,958	8,343	8,794
Householder 65 years and over ..	4,983	6,023	6,282	6,503	6,630	6,872	7,158	7,501	7,905
3 persons	6,565	7,938	8,277	8,573	8,737	9,056	9,436	9,885	10,419
4 persons	8,414	10,178	10,609	10,989	11,203	11,611	12,092	12,675	13,359
5 persons	9,966	12,049	12,566	13,007	13,259	13,737	14,305	14,990	15,792
6 persons	11,269	13,630	14,207	14,696	14,986	15,509	16,149	16,921	17,839
7 persons	(NA)	15,500	16,096	16,656	17,049	17,649	18,248	19,162	20,241
8 persons	(NA)	17,170	17,961	18,512	18,791	19,515	20,279	21,328	22,582
9 or more persons	(NA)	20,310	21,247	22,083	22,497	23,105	24,133	25,480	26,848

NA Not available. [1]Poverty levels for nonfarrm families.
Source: U.S. Bureau of the Census, Current Population Reports, P–60, No. 175.

No. 673. GDP in Current and Constant (1987) Dollars: 1959 to 1991

[In billions of dollars. For explanation of gross domestic product, see text, section 14]

ITEM	1959	1960	1965	1970	1975	1979	1980	1981	1982
CURRENT DOLLARS									
Gross domestic product (GDP)	**494.2**	**513.4**	**702.7**	**1,010.7**	**1,585.9**	**2,488.6**	**2,708.0**	**3,030.6**	**3,149.6**
Personal consumption expenditures	**318.1**	**332.4**	**444.6**	**646.5**	**1,024.9**	**1,583.7**	**1,748.1**	**1,926.2**	**2,059.2**
Durable goods.	42.8	43.5	63.5	85.3	134.3	214.2	212.5	228.5	236.5
Nondurable goods	148.5	153.1	191.9	270.4	416.0	613.3	682.9	744.2	772.3
Services.	126.8	135.9	189.2	290.8	474.5	756.2	852.7	953.5	1,050.4
Gross private domestic investment	**78.8**	**78.7**	**118.0**	**150.3**	**226.0**	**480.2**	**467.6**	**558.0**	**503.4**
Fixed investment	74.6	75.5	108.3	148.1	231.7	467.5	477.1	532.5	519.3
Nonresidential	46.5	49.2	74.1	106.7	169.0	326.4	353.8	410.0	413.7
Residential	28.1	26.3	34.2	41.4	62.7	141.0	123.3	122.5	105.7
Change in business inventories . . .	4.2	3.2	9.7	2.3	−5.7	12.8	−9.5	25.4	−15.9
Net exports of goods and services.	**−1.7**	**2.4**	**3.9**	**1.2**	**13.6**	**−23.8**	**−14.7**	**−14.7**	**−20.6**
Exports	20.6	25.3	35.4	57.0	136.3	228.9	279.2	303.0	282.6
Imports	22.3	22.8	31.5	55.8	122.7	252.7	293.9	317.7	303.2
Government purchases	**99.0**	**99.8**	**136.3**	**212.7**	**321.4**	**448.5**	**507.1**	**561.1**	**607.6**
Federal	57.1	55.3	69.5	100.1	129.4	179.3	209.1	240.8	266.6
National defense	46.4	45.3	51.0	76.8	89.6	121.9	142.7	167.5	193.8
State and local	41.8	44.5	66.8	112.6	192.0	269.2	298.0	320.3	341.1
CONSTANT (1987) DOLLARS									
Gross domestic product (GDP)	**1,928.8**	**1,970.8**	**2,470.5**	**2,873.9**	**3,221.7**	**3,796.8**	**3,776.3**	**3,843.1**	**3,760.3**
Personal consumption expenditures	**1,178.9**	**1,210.8**	**1,497.0**	**1,813.5**	**2,097.5**	**2,448.4**	**2,447.1**	**2,476.9**	**2,503.7**
Durable goods.	114.4	115.4	156.2	183.7	226.8	289.0	262.7	264.6	262.5
Nondurable goods	518.5	526.9	616.7	717.2	767.1	862.8	860.5	867.9	872.2
Services.	546.0	568.5	724.1	912.5	1,103.6	1,296.5	1,323.9	1,344.4	1,368.9
Gross private domestic investment	**296.4**	**290.8**	**413.0**	**429.7**	**437.6**	**669.7**	**594.4**	**631.1**	**540.5**
Fixed investment	282.8	282.7	387.9	423.8	451.5	656.1	602.7	606.5	558.0
Nonresidential	165.2	173.3	250.6	292.0	316.8	448.8	437.8	455.0	433.9
Residential	117.6	109.4	137.3	131.8	134.7	207.4	164.8	151.6	124.1
Change in business inventories . . .	13.6	8.1	25.1	5.9	−13.9	13.6	−8.3	24.6	−17.5
Net exports of goods and services.	**−21.8**	**−7.6**	**−6.4**	**−35.2**	**23.1**	**−10.6**	**30.7**	**22.0**	**−7.4**
Exports	73.8	88.4	118.1	161.3	232.9	293.5	320.5	326.1	296.7
Imports	95.6	96.1	124.5	196.4	209.8	304.1	289.9	304.1	304.1
Government purchases	**475.3**	**476.9**	**566.9**	**665.8**	**663.5**	**689.3**	**704.2**	**713.2**	**723.6**
Federal	265.7	259.0	282.1	315.0	262.7	271.7	284.8	295.8	306.0
National defense	-	-	-	-	184.9	185.1	194.2	206.4	221.4
State and local	209.6	217.9	284.8	350.9	400.8	417.6	419.4	417.4	417.6

	1983	1984	1985	1986	1987	1988	1989	1990	1991
CURRENT DOLLARS									
Gross domestic product (GDP)	**3,405.0**	**3,777.2**	**4,038.7**	**4,268.6**	**4,539.9**	**4,900.4**	**5,244.0**	**5,513.8**	**5,672.6**
Personal consumption expenditures	**2,257.5**	**2,460.3**	**2,667.4**	**2,850.6**	**3,052.2**	**3,296.1**	**3,517.9**	**3,742.6**	**3,889.1**
Durable goods.	275.0	317.9	352.9	389.6	403.7	437.1	459.8	465.9	445.2
Nondurable goods	817.8	873.0	919.4	952.2	1,011.1	1,073.8	1,146.9	1,217.7	1,251.9
Services.	1,164.7	1,269.4	1,395.1	1,508.8	1,637.4	1,785.2	1,911.2	2,059.0	2,191.9
Gross private domestic investment	**546.7**	**718.9**	**714.5**	**717.6**	**749.3**	**793.6**	**837.6**	**802.6**	**726.7**
Fixed investment	552.2	647.8	689.9	709.0	723.0	777.4	801.6	802.7	745.2
Nonresidential	400.2	468.9	504.0	492.4	497.8	545.4	570.7	587.0	550.1
Residential	152.0	178.9	185.9	216.6	225.2	232.0	230.9	215.7	195.1
Change in business inventories . . .	−5.5	71.1	24.6	8.6	26.3	16.2	36.0	-	−18.5
Net exports of goods and services.	**−51.4**	**−102.7**	**−115.6**	**−132.5**	**−143.1**	**−108.0**	**−82.9**	**−74.4**	**−30.7**
Exports	276.7	302.4	302.1	319.2	364.0	444.2	504.9	550.4	591.3
Imports	328.1	405.1	417.6	451.7	507.1	552.2	587.8	624.8	622.0
Government purchases	**652.3**	**700.8**	**772.3**	**833.0**	**881.5**	**918.7**	**971.4**	**1,042.9**	**1,087.5**
Federal	292.0	310.9	344.3	367.8	384.9	387.0	401.4	424.9	445.1
National defense	214.4	233.1	258.6	276.7	292.1	295.6	300.0	313.4	323.5
State and local	360.3	389.9	428.1	465.3	496.6	531.7	570.0	618.0	642.4
CONSTANT (1987) DOLLARS									
Gross domestic product (GDP)	**3,906.6**	**4,148.5**	**4,279.8**	**4,404.5**	**4,540.0**	**4,718.6**	**4,836.9**	**4,884.9**	**4,848.8**
Personal consumption expenditures	**2,619.4**	**2,746.1**	**2,865.8**	**2,969.1**	**3,052.2**	**3,162.4**	**3,223.1**	**3,262.6**	**3,259.0**
Durable goods.	297.7	338.5	370.1	402.0	403.7	428.7	440.8	438.9	412.5
Nondurable goods	900.3	934.6	958.7	991.0	1,011.1	1,035.1	1,049.3	1,050.8	1,043.0
Services.	1,421.4	1,473.0	1,537.0	1,576.1	1,637.4	1,698.5	1,732.9	1,773.0	1,803.4
Gross private domestic investment	**599.5**	**757.5**	**745.9**	**735.1**	**749.3**	**773.4**	**789.2**	**744.5**	**673.7**
Fixed investment	595.1	689.6	723.8	726.5	723.0	753.4	756.6	744.2	687.6
Nonresidential	420.8	490.2	521.8	500.3	497.8	530.8	542.4	548.8	512.4
Residential	174.2	199.3	202.0	226.2	225.2	222.7	214.2	195.5	175.2
Change in business inventories . . .	4.4	67.9	22.1	8.5	26.3	19.9	32.6	0.2	−13.9
Net exports of goods and services.	**−56.1**	**−122.0**	**−145.3**	**−155.1**	**−143.0**	**−104.0**	**−75.7**	**−51.3**	**−20.9**
Exports	285.9	305.7	309.2	329.6	364.0	421.6	469.2	505.7	537.8
Imports	342.1	427.7	454.6	484.7	507.1	525.7	544.9	557.0	558.7
Government purchases	**743.8**	**766.9**	**813.4**	**855.4**	**881.5**	**886.8**	**900.4**	**929.1**	**937.1**
Federal	320.8	331.0	355.2	373.0	384.9	377.3	375.0	380.9	384.9
National defense	234.2	245.8	265.6	280.6	292.1	287.0	280.7	281.3	281.4
State and local	423.0	436.0	458.2	482.4	496.6	509.6	525.3	548.2	552.2

- Represents or rounds to zero.

Source: U.S. Bureau of Economic Analysis, *Survey of Current Business,* March 1992; and unpublished data.

No. 674. Gross National Product, by Industry, in Current and Constant (1982) Dollars: 1980 to 1989

[In billions of dollars, except percent. Based on the *1972 Standard Industrial Classification Manual;* see text, section 13. Data include non-factor charges (capital consumption allowances and indirect business taxes, etc.) as well as factor charges against gross product corporate profits and capital consumption allowances have been shifted from a company to an establishment basis. These data are not fully consistent with other gross domestic product tables because they do not yet reflect the results of the comprehensive National Income and Product Accounts revision; see text, section 14]

INDUSTRY	CURRENT DOLLARS				CONSTANT (1982) DOLLARS			
	1980	1985	1988	1989	1980	1985	1988	1989
Gross national product	2,732	4,015	4,874	5,201	3,187	3,619	4,017	4,118
Domestic industries (gross domestic product) . .	2,684	3,974	4,840	5,163	3,132	3,582	3,989	4,088
Private industries	2,357	3,502	4,296	4,561	2,743	3,200	3,620	3,711
Agriculture, forestry, and fisheries.	77	92	104	113	76	96	97	100
Mining.	107	114	80	80	144	139	130	127
Construction	138	187	237	248	153	166	178	179
Manufacturing [1]	581	790	941	966	674	779	917	929
Durable goods [1]	352	459	527	541	408	472	571	584
Lumber and wood products	19	22	31	32	21	20	26	26
Furniture and fixtures	9	14	15	16	10	12	12	12
Stone, clay, and glass products	19	25	26	26	21	22	23	24
Primary metal industries	44	35	43	44	48	33	38	37
Fabricated metal products	46	58	65	68	54	56	66	66
Machinery, except electrical	77	83	96	97	86	124	164	175
Electric and electronic equipment	55	82	90	97	63	74	88	91
Motor vehicles and equipment	27	54	53	50	35	50	50	47
Instruments and related products	19	26	30	31	22	24	28	27
Nondurable goods.	229	331	414	425	265	308	347	345
Food and kindred products	52	70	81	81	60	65	68	70
Tobacco manufactures	7	12	14	16	10	6	4	3
Textile mill products	15	17	20	21	16	16	17	17
Apparel and other textile products.	17	21	24	25	21	20	22	22
Paper and allied products	23	33	46	47	26	30	35	33
Printing and publishing	32	53	66	68	37	43	47	45
Chemicals and allied products	45	64	96	99	50	59	78	76
Petroleum and coal products	17	32	35	34	23	39	44	45
Rubber and misc. plastic products.	17	26	30	31	19	27	30	31
Leather and leather products	4	3	3	3	4	3	3	3
Transportation and public utilities	241	374	444	461	294	331	395	402
Transportation	106	138	165	172	117	132	154	156
Railroad transportation	21	22	22	21	23	23	27	28
Local and interurban passenger transit. . . .	5	7	9	10	6	7	6	6
Trucking and warehousing	44	59	70	73	50	61	67	69
Water transportation	7	8	8	8	8	4	4	4
Transportation by air.	18	27	38	40	17	23	32	32
Pipelines, except natural gas	5	5	4	4	5	5	5	6
Transportation services	6	10	14	15	7	10	12	12
Communications	67	110	129	134	80	90	108	109
Telephone and telegraph.	60	98	114	117	71	82	98	99
Radio and television broadcasting.	6	11	15	16	8	8	10	11
Electric, gas, and sanitary services.	68	127	150	156	97	109	134	137
Wholesale trade	194	281	317	339	200	267	291	305
Retail trade	245	377	460	486	282	354	399	412
Finance, insurance, and real estate	401	640	827	897	469	528	590	604
Banking.	51	79	100	119	57	62	62	63
Credit agencies other than banks.	6	12	16	20	5	7	8	8
Security and commodity brokers	10	24	42	44	11	19	36	38
Insurance carriers	37	41	62	60	39	39	37	37
Insurance agents and brokers	14	22	35	37	16	18	21	22
Real estate	282	449	562	607	335	374	413	424
Holding and other investment companies . . .	1	12	10	8	6	9	11	11
Services [1]	374	648	885	971	451	539	623	652
Hotels and other lodging places.	19	30	41	44	22	26	31	32
Personal services	19	30	39	43	22	25	29	30
Business services	69	146	202	223	84	121	148	159
Auto repair, services, and garages	21	33	41	44	25	29	28	29
Motion pictures	5	9	14	15	6	7	9	10
Amusement and recreation services	12	20	27	30	13	18	22	23
Health services.	108	185	250	273	134	149	161	164
Legal services	23	46	69	75	31	34	41	42
Educational services	16	26	32	36	19	22	23	24
Social services and membership organizations.	26	38	51	56	30	33	39	41
Private households	7	9	10	10	7	9	9	10
Government and government enterprises	322	477	573	619	003	401	423	431
Federal.	115	171	192	208	138	146	152	152
State and local	207	306	380	411	245	254	272	278
Statistical discrepancy	5	-5	-28	-17	6	-4	-24	-14
Rest of the world	48	41	33	38	56	37	28	30

[1] Includes items not shown separately.

Source: U.S. Bureau of Economic Analysis, *Survey of Current Business,* April, 1991.

No. 675. GDP Components—Average Annual Percent Change in Current and Constant (1987) Dollars: 1959 to 1991

[In percent. GDP = Gross domestic product. Minus sign (-) indicates decrease]

ITEM	1959-1960	1969-1970	1979-1980	1984-1985	1985-1986	1986-1987	1987-1988	1988-1989	1989-1990	1990-1991
CURRENT DOLLARS										
Gross domestic product...	3.9	5.3	8.8	6.9	5.7	6.4	7.9	7.0	5.1	2.9
Personal consumption expenditures	4.5	7.1	10.4	8.4	6.9	7.1	8.0	6.7	6.4	3.9
Durable goods............	1.6	-1.0	-0.8	11.0	10.4	3.6	8.3	5.2	1.3	-4.4
Nondurable goods..........	3.1	7.2	11.3	5.3	3.6	6.2	6.2	6.8	6.2	2.8
Services.................	7.2	9.6	12.8	9.9	8.1	8.5	9.0	7.1	7.7	6.5
Gross private domestic investment	-0.1	-3.2	-2.6	-0.6	0.4	4.4	5.9	5.5	-4.2	-9.5
Fixed investment..........	1.2	1.8	2.1	6.5	2.8	2.0	7.5	3.1	0.1	-7.2
Nonresidential..........	5.8	3.7	8.4	7.5	-2.3	1.1	9.6	4.6	2.9	-6.3
Residential.............	-6.4	-2.8	-12.6	3.9	16.5	4.0	3.0	-0.5	-6.6	-9.6
Exports of goods and services..	22.8	15.6	22.0	-0.1	5.7	14.0	22.0	13.7	9.0	7.4
Imports of goods and services..	2.2	10.5	16.3	3.1	8.2	12.3	8.9	6.4	6.3	-0.4
Government purchases	0.8	5.4	13.1	10.2	7.9	5.8	4.2	5.7	7.4	4.3
Federal	-3.2	-0.4	16.6	10.7	6.8	4.6	0.5	3.7	5.9	4.8
State and local	6.5	11.2	10.7	9.8	8.7	6.7	7.1	7.2	8.4	3.9
CONSTANT (1987) DOLLARS										
Gross domestic product...	2.2	-	-0.5	3.2	2.9	3.1	3.9	2.5	1.0	-0.7
Personal consumption expenditures	2.7	2.4	-0.1	4.4	3.6	2.8	3.6	1.9	1.2	-0.1
Durable goods............	0.9	-3.7	-9.1	9.3	8.6	0.4	6.2	2.8	-0.4	-6.0
Nondurable goods	1.6	2.0	-0.3	2.6	3.4	2.0	2.4	1.4	0.1	-0.7
Services................	4.1	4.0	2.1	4.3	2.5	3.9	3.7	2.0	2.3	1.7
Gross private domestic investment	-1.9	-6.9	-11.2	-1.5	-1.4	1.9	3.2	2.0	-5.7	-9.5
Fixed investment	-	-2.9	-8.1	5.0	0.4	-0.5	4.2	0.4	-1.6	-7.6
Nonresidential	4.9	-1.5	-2.5	6.4	-4.1	-0.5	6.6	2.2	1.2	-6.6
Residential.............	-7.0	-5.9	-20.5	1.4	12.0	-0.4	-1.1	-3.8	-8.7	-10.4
Exports of goods and services..	19.8	9.1	9.2	1.1	6.6	10.4	15.8	11.3	7.8	6.3
Imports of goods and services..	0.5	3.8	-4.7	6.3	6.6	4.6	3.7	3.7	2.2	0.3
Government purchases	0.3	-2.4	2.2	6.1	5.2	3.1	0.6	1.5	3.2	0.9
Federal	-2.6	-7.4	4.8	7.3	5.0	3.2	-2.0	-0.6	1.6	1.1
State and local	4.0	2.6	0.4	5.1	5.3	2.9	2.6	3.1	4.4	0.7

- Represents or rounds to zero.

Source: U.S. Bureau of Economic Analysis, *Survey of Current Business*, March 1992; and unpublished data.

No. 676. Gross Domestic Product, by Type of Product and Sector: 1970 to 1991

[In billions of dollars]

ITEM	1970	1980	1984	1985	1986	1987	1988	1989	1990	1991
Gross domestic product...	1,010.7	2,708.0	3,777.2	4,038.7	4,268.6	4,539.9	4,900.4	5,244.0	5,513.8	5,672.6
MAJOR TYPE OF PRODUCT										
Goods..................	467.8	1,176.2	1,591.9	1,652.6	1,705.3	1,794.5	1,942.0	2,098.1	2,167.6	2,193.2
Services................	434.3	1,215.4	1,770.7	1,939.0	2,097.3	2,267.2	2,460.9	2,634.7	2,834.0	3,012.9
Structures...............	108.6	316.4	414.7	447.1	466.0	478.2	497.5	511.3	512.2	466.5
SECTOR										
Business................	858.7	2,328.9	3,251.1	3,473.5	3,665.7	3,890.8	4,201.0	4,490.7	4,699.4	4,803.3
Households and institutions	32.4	89.3	132.0	141.7	153.3	170.5	187.6	205.0	225.1	246.4
Government...............	119.5	289.8	394.1	423.6	449.6	478.7	511.7	548.3	589.2	622.9

Source: U.S. Bureau of Economic Analysis, *Survey of Current Business*, March 1992, and unpublished data.

No. 677. Relation of GDP, GNP, Net National Product, National Income, Personal Income, Disposable Personal Income, and Personal Saving: 1970 to 1990

[In billions of dollars. For definitions, see text, section 14]

ITEM	1970	1980	1984	1985	1986	1987	1988	1989	1990
Gross domestic product	1,010.7	2,708.0	3,777.2	4,038.7	4,268.6	4,539.9	4,900.4	5,244.0	5,513.8
Plus: Receipts of factor income from the rest of the world [1]	13.0	80.6	108.1	97.3	96.0	105.1	128.7	145.4	147.7
Less: Payments of factor income to the rest of the world [2]	6.6	46.5	83.8	82.4	86.9	100.5	120.8	141.2	137.0
Gross national product	1,017.1	2,742.1	3,801.5	4,053.6	4,277.7	4,544.5	4,908.2	5,248.2	5,524.5
Less: Consumption of fixed capital . . .	88.8	311.9	433.2	454.5	478.6	502.2	534.0	574.5	594.8
Equals: Net national product [3]	928.3	2,430.2	3,368.3	3,599.1	3,799.2	4,042.4	4,374.2	4,673.7	4,929.8
Less: Indirect business tax and nontax liability.	94.3	212.0	309.5	329.9	345.5	365.0	385.3	411.0	439.2
Plus: Subsidies [4]	2.6	4.8	9.5	6.4	9.7	14.1	10.9	6.1	4.8
Equals: National income [3]	833.5	2,198.2	3,058.3	3,268.4	3,437.9	3,692.3	4,002.6	4,244.7	4,459.6
Less: Corporate profits [5]	77.5	177.7	264.2	280.8	271.6	319.8	365.0	351.7	319.0
Net interest	40.0	191.2	307.9	326.2	350.2	360.4	387.7	452.6	490.1
Contributions for social insurance. . .	62.2	216.6	325.0	353.8	379.8	400.7	442.3	473.4	501.7
Plus: Personal interest income	69.2	274.0	461.9	498.1	531.7	548.1	583.2	669.0	721.3
Personal dividend income.	23.5	57.1	78.8	87.9	104.7	100.4	108.4	119.8	124.8
Government transfer payments to persons	81.8	312.6	437.8	468.1	497.1	521.3	555.9	602.0	661.7
Business transfer payments	2.8	8.8	15.1	17.8	20.7	20.8	20.8	22.4	23.2
Equals: Personal income	831.0	2,265.4	3,154.6	3,379.8	3,590.4	3,802.0	4,075.9	4,380.2	4,679.8
Less: Personal tax and nontax payments	109.0	312.4	395.1	436.8	459.0	512.5	527.7	591.7	621.0
Equals: Disposable personal income	722.0	1,952.9	2,759.5	2,943.0	3,131.5	3,289.5	3,548.2	3,788.6	4,058.8
Less: Personal outlays	664.5	1,799.1	2,537.5	2,753.7	2,944.0	3,147.5	3,392.5	3,622.4	3,853.1
Equals: Personal saving	57.5	153.8	222.0	189.3	187.5	142.0	155.7	166.1	205.8

[1] Consists largely of receipts by U.S. residents of interest and dividends and reinvested earnings of foreign affiliates of U.S. corporations.   [2] Consists largely of payments to foreign residents of interest and dividends and reinvested earnings of U.S. affiliates of foreign corporations.   [3] Includes items not shown separately.   [4] Less current surplus of government enterprises.   [5] With inventory valuation and capital consumption adjustments.

Source: U.S. Bureau of Economic Analysis, *Survey of Current Business,* March 1992; and unpublished data.

No. 678. Selected Per Capita Income and Product Items: 1959 to 1991

[Based on Bureau of the Census estimated population including Armed Forces abroad; based on quarterly averages. Prior to 1960, excludes Alaska and Hawaii]

YEAR	CURRENT DOLLARS					CONSTANT (1987) DOLLARS			
	Gross domestic product	Gross national product	Personal income	Disposable personal income	Personal consumption expenditures	Gross domestic product	Gross national product	Disposable personal income	Personal consumption expenditures
1959	2,791	2,807	2,209	1,958	1,796	10,907	10,968	7,256	6,658
1960	2,840	2,858	2,264	1,994	1,839	10,916	10,982	7,264	6,698
1961	2,894	2,914	2,321	2,048	1,869	11,024	11,097	7,382	6,740
1962	3,063	3,086	2,430	2,137	1,953	11,414	11,496	7,583	6,931
1963	3,186	3,210	2,516	2,210	2,030	11,717	11,803	7,718	7,089
1964	3,376	3,403	2,661	2,369	2,149	12,209	12,301	8,140	7,384
1965	3,616	3,643	2,845	2,527	2,287	12,727	12,822	8,508	7,703
1966	3,915	3,942	3,061	2,699	2,450	13,338	13,425	8,822	8,005
1967	4,097	4,125	3,253	2,861	2,562	13,536	13,624	9,114	8,163
1968	4,430	4,461	3,536	3,077	2,785	13,953	14,047	9,399	8,506
1969	4,733	4,763	3,816	3,274	2,978	14,191	14,280	9,606	8,737
1970	4,928	4,959	4,052	3,521	3,152	14,022	14,109	9,875	8,842
1971	5,283	5,320	4,302	3,779	3,372	14,249	14,345	10,111	9,022
1972	5,750	5,791	4,671	4,042	3,658	14,801	14,904	10,414	9,425
1973	6,368	6,428	5,184	4,521	4,002	15,422	15,564	11,013	9,752
1974	6,819	6,893	5,637	4,893	4,337	15,185	15,346	10,832	9,602
1975	7,343	7,404	6,053	5,329	4,745	14,917	15,037	10,906	9,711
1976	8,109	8,187	6,632	5,796	5,241	15,502	15,646	11,192	10,121
1977	8,961	9,055	7,269	6,316	5,772	16,039	16,201	11,406	10,425
1978	10,029	10,127	8,121	7,042	6,384	16,635	16,795	11,851	10,744
1979	11,055	11,198	9,032	7,787	7,035	16,007	17,082	12,039	10,876
1980	11,892	12,040	9,948	8,576	7,677	16,584	16,790	12,005	10,746
1981	13,177	13,321	11,021	9,455	8,375	16,710	16,890	12,156	10,770
1982	13,564	13,694	11,589	9,989	8,868	16,194	16,348	12,146	10,782
1983	14,531	14,657	12,216	10,642	9,634	16,672	16,813	12,349	11,179
1984	15,978	16,081	13,345	11,673	10,408	17,549	17,659	13,029	11,617
1985	16,933	16,995	14,170	12,339	11,184	17,944	18,007	13,258	12,015
1986	17,735	17,773	14,917	13,010	11,843	18,299	18,337	13,552	12,336
1987	18,694	18,712	15,655	13,545	12,568	18,694	18,713	13,545	12,568
1988	19,994	20,026	16,630	14,477	13,448	19,252	19,284	13,890	12,903
1989	21,196	21,213	17,705	15,313	14,219	19,550	19,566	14,030	13,027
1990	22,056	22,099	18,720	16,236	14,971	19,540	19,579	14,154	13,051
1991	22,450	22,502	19,133	16,695	15,392	19,190	19,235	13,990	12,898

Source: U.S. Bureau of the Census, *Survey of Current Business,* April 1992; and unpublished data.

No. 679. National Income, by Type of Income: 1970 to 1991

[In billions of dollars]

TYPE OF INCOME	1970	1980	1985	1986	1987	1988	1989	1990	1991
National income.	**833.5**	**2,198.2**	**3,268.4**	**3,437.9**	**3,692.3**	**4,002.6**	**4,244.7**	**4,459.6**	**4,542.5**
Compensation of employees.	618.3	1,644.4	2,382.8	2,523.8	2,698.7	2,921.3	3,101.3	3,290.3	3,388.2
Wages and salaries	551.5	1,376.6	1,986.3	2,105.4	2,261.2	2,443.0	2,585.8	2,738.9	2,808.2
Government.	117.1	261.4	373.7	395.7	421.8	449.0	478.6	514.0	540.5
Other	434.3	1,115.2	1,612.6	1,709.8	1,839.4	1,994.0	2,107.2	2,224.9	2,267.7
Supplements to wages and salaries. . .	66.8	267.8	396.5	418.4	437.4	478.3	515.5	551.4	580.0
Employer contributions for social insurance	34.3	127.9	204.7	217.7	227.1	247.8	261.7	277.3	289.4
Other labor income	32.5	139.8	191.8	200.7	210.4	230.5	253.7	274.0	290.6
Proprietors' income [1]	79.9	171.8	259.9	283.7	310.2	324.3	347.0	373.2	379.7
Farm	14.6	11.5	21.5	22.3	31.3	30.9	41.4	42.5	35.1
Nonfarm. . . . . [2] . . .	65.3	160.3	238.4	261.5	279.0	293.4	305.5	330.7	344.5
Rental income of persons [2].	17.8	13.2	18.7	8.7	3.2	4.3	-12.9	-12.7	-12.7
Corporate profits [1] [3].	77.5	177.7	280.8	271.6	319.8	365.0	351.7	319.0	307.1
Corporate profits [3]	71.8	197.8	225.3	227.6	273.4	320.3	327.0	318.2	315.8
Profits before tax.	78.4	240.9	225.0	217.8	287.9	347.5	344.5	332.3	312.7
Profits tax liability	34.4	84.8	96.5	106.5	127.1	137.0	138.0	135.3	124.6
Profits after tax	44.0	156.1	128.5	111.3	160.8	210.5	206.6	197.0	188.1
Dividends.	23.7	59.0	92.4	109.8	106.2	115.3	127.9	133.7	137.8
Undistributed profits.	20.3	97.1	36.1	1.6	54.6	95.2	78.7	63.3	50.3
Inventory valuation adjustment.	-6.6	-43.0	0.2	9.7	-14.5	-27.3	-17.5	-14.2	3.1
Capital consumption adjustment	5.6	-20.2	55.5	44.1	46.4	44.7	24.7	0.8	-8.7
Net interest	40.0	191.2	326.2	350.2	360.4	387.7	452.6	490.1	480.2
Addenda:									
Corporate profits after tax [1]	43.1	92.9	184.2	165.1	192.8	228.0	213.7	183.6	182.5
Net cash flow [1]. . . . . . [1].	70.9	218.9	369.7	349.6	394.2	440.3	436.3	415.4	428.3
Undistributed profits [1]	19.4	33.9	91.9	55.4	86.5	112.6	85.8	49.9	44.7
Consumption of fixed capital	51.5	185.1	277.8	294.2	307.7	327.6	350.5	365.5	383.6
Less: Inventory valuation adjustment	-6.6	-43.0	0.2	9.7	-14.5	-27.3	-17.5	-14.2	3.1
Equals: Net cash flow	77.5	262.0	369.5	339.8	408.7	467.5	453.9	429.5	425.2

[1] With inventory valuation and capital consumption adjustments.   [2] With capital consumption adjustment.   [3] With inventory valuation adjustment.

Source: U.S. Bureau of Economic Analysis, *Survey of Current Business*, March 1992; and unpublished data.

No. 680. National Income, by Sector: 1970 to 1990

[In billions of dollars]

SECTOR	1970	1980	1984	1985	1986	1987	1988	1989	1990
National income.	**833.5**	**2,198.2**	**3,058.3**	**3,268.4**	**3,437.9**	**3,692.3**	**4,002.6**	**4,244.7**	**4,459.6**
Domestic business	675.1	1,785.0	2,507.9	2,688.3	2,825.9	3,038.5	3,295.4	3,487.2	3,634.5
Corporate business.	482.2	1,320.8	1,838.0	1,963.8	2,057.2	2,210.2	2,399.6	2,532.1	2,608.3
Compensation of employees.	401.0	1,121.4	1,516.5	1,621.3	1,717.0	1,817.7	1,965.8	2,078.5	2,186.8
Corporate profits [1].	70.4	142.7	233.0	250.0	238.7	280.3	315.9	297.8	258.8
Net interest	10.8	56.7	88.5	92.6	101.5	112.2	118.0	155.8	162.7
Sole proprietorships and partnerships .	134.7	308.9	428.6	464.6	497.8	540.0	584.4	630.1	678.4
Compensation of employees.	49.2	102.9	126.7	133.1	136.2	159.3	177.3	186.0	199.5
Proprietors' income [1].	79.5	170.5	234.1	258.2	282.2	308.6	322.5	345.0	374.1
Net interest	6.0	35.4	67.8	73.3	79.4	72.1	84.6	99.1	104.7
Other private business [2]	45.3	122.1	195.5	210.3	218.9	232.7	250.9	261.2	279.2
Compensation of employees.	3.2	7.8	12.1	13.9	15.8	17.1	18.6	19.9	21.2
Proprietors' income [1]	0.4	1.3	1.9	1.7	1.6	1.6	1.8	1.9	-0.9
Rental income of persons [3].	17.8	13.2	23.3	18.7	8.7	3.2	4.3	-7.9	-12.9
Net interest	23.9	99.8	158.2	176.0	192.8	210.8	226.2	247.2	271.8
Government enterprises [4].	12.9	33.2	45.7	49.6	52.0	55.6	60.4	63.7	68.7
Households and institutions [5]	32.4	89.3	132.0	141.7	153.3	170.5	187.6	205.0	225.1
General government [4]	119.5	289.8	394.1	423.6	449.6	478.7	511.7	548.3	589.2
Rest of the world	6.4	34.1	24.3	14.8	9.1	4.6	7.9	4.2	10.8

[1] With inventory valuation and capital consumption adjustments.   [2] Consist of all business activities reported on the individual income tax return in Schedule E—Supplemental Income Schedule; tax-exempt cooperatives; and owner-occupied nonfarm housing and buildings and equipment owned and used by nonprofit institutions servicing individuals, which are considered to be business activities selling their current services to their owners.   [3] With capital consumption adjustment.   [4] Compensation of employees.   [5] Compensation of employees in private households; nonprofit social and athletic clubs; labor organizations; nonprofit schools and hospitals; religious, charitable, and welfare organizations; and all other nonprofit organizations serving individuals.

Source: U.S. Bureau of Economic Analysis, *Survey of Current Business*, January 1992; and unpublished data.

No. 681. Personal Consumption Expenditures, by Type of Expenditure in Current and Constant (1987) Dollars: 1970 to 1990

[In billions of dollars]

TYPE OF EXPENDITURE	CURRENT DOLLARS				CONSTANT (1987) DOLLARS			
	1970	1980	1985	1990	1970	1980	1985	1990
Personal consumption expenditures	646.5	1,748.1	2,667.4	3,742.6	1,813.5	2,447.1	2,865.8	3,262.6
Food and tobacco [1]	152.9	362.6	482.8	639.8	431.0	487.5	519.4	548.2
Food purchased for off-premise consumption	104.4	241.7	309.5	396.8	283.6	307.5	329.5	341.8
Purchased meals and beverages [2] . . .	34.9	93.4	132.9	187.5	105.8	132.3	144.1	163.9
Tobacco products	10.8	20.9	31.7	43.9	33.5	38.7	36.4	32.4
Clothing, accessories, and jewelry [1]	57.6	131.8	185.9	259.7	107.8	157.1	195.5	230.0
Shoes	7.8	17.4	22.8	31.5	14.4	19.9	23.4	28.2
Clothing	39.8	89.8	129.3	177.1	66.3	106.0	135.3	159.1
Jewelry and watches	4.1	15.0	21.4	30.7	8.4	16.8	23.2	25.0
Personal care	11.8	26.9	39.9	59.1	34.0	38.0	42.4	52.2
Housing [1]	94.0	255.2	392.5	547.1	269.3	399.4	435.9	474.5
Owner-occupied nonfarm dwellings-space rent	61.3	178.4	271.0	379.7	174.4	278.7	301.3	326.8
Tenant-occupied nonfarm dwellings-rent	26.0	61.8	101.0	140.8	75.1	98.2	112.2	125.2
Household operation [1]	84.8	233.6	342.3	434.2	239.2	315.3	348.4	406.4
Furniture [3]	8.6	20.7	28.6	37.6	17.8	25.8	29.9	35.6
Semidurable house furnishings [4]	4.9	10.6	15.7	21.1	12.2	14.9	16.7	19.7
Cleaning and polishing preparations . .	8.2	22.9	36.7	51.4	26.4	31.2	38.8	45.4
Household utilities	22.7	81.1	119.3	135.9	92.3	111.7	116.5	123.8
Electricity	9.6	37.2	59.3	70.6	33.3	54.0	59.9	66.2
Gas	5.6	19.1	29.4	26.6	27.0	27.6	26.7	26.0
Water and other sanitary services . .	3.2	9.4	16.5	26.2	11.7	16.2	18.4	21.7
Fuel oil and coal	4.4	15.4	14.1	12.5	20.2	14.0	11.5	10.0
Telephone and telegraph	10.1	27.6	42.8	52.7	19.9	41.1	43.4	54.1
Medical care [1]	60.0	207.2	364.7	593.0	208.7	346.5	404.3	482.0
Drug preparations and sundries [5]	8.1	21.8	38.9	59.9	23.5	38.8	44.3	48.9
Physicians	14.0	42.8	76.3	133.5	52.7	72.9	87.9	108.3
Dentists	4.9	13.7	22.1	32.2	16.0	22.4	24.9	26.7
Hospitals and nursing homes [6]	23.4	98.7	170.4	269.2	87.1	164.0	187.4	217.8
Health insurance	4.4	12.8	22.7	34.2	13.9	23.0	22.6	25.6
Medical care [7]	2.1	7.6	19.1	28.6	10.0	17.7	18.4	20.3
Personal business [1]	32.0	101.6	184.9	289.2	119.5	175.5	216.3	248.3
Expense of handling life insurance [8] . .	7.1	23.4	38.8	55.1	22.6	37.8	45.0	47.5
Legal services	4.9	13.6	28.6	49.2	21.7	26.6	32.8	41.6
Funeral and burial expenses	2.3	4.6	6.6	8.2	8.2	8.8	7.5	7.2
Transportation [1]	81.1	235.7	363.3	458.1	219.5	274.8	368.6	405.4
User-operated transportation [1]	74.2	214.9	333.5	419.3	198.8	247.4	338.8	372.2
New autos	21.9	46.4	87.4	96.6	47.4	60.2	94.5	91.5
Net purchases of used autos	4.8	10.8	24.3	35.8	20.9	20.8	27.9	33.4
Tires, tubes, accessories, etc.	6.1	14.9	18.1	22.4	10.8	15.3	18.3	21.3
Repair, greasing, washing, parking, storage, rental, and leasing	12.3	33.7	57.7	88.6	39.3	48.3	63.0	77.9
Gasoline and oil	21.9	86.7	96.9	106.8	62.9	72.0	79.2	85.0
Purchased local transportation	3.0	4.8	7.4	8.7	8.8	7.8	8.1	7.7
Mass transit systems	1.8	2.9	4.4	5.7	5.3	5.3	4.9	5.1
Taxicab	1.2	1.9	2.9	3.0	3.5	2.5	3.2	2.6
Purchased intercity transportation [1] . . .	4.0	16.1	22.4	30.0	11.9	19.7	21.6	25.5
Railway (commutation)	0.2	0.3	0.4	0.7	0.8	0.5	0.5	0.6
Bus	0.5	1.4	1.6	1.5	2.3	2.4	1.8	1.3
Airline	3.1	13.5	18.7	25.2	8.1	15.2	17.6	21.3
Recreation [1][9]	43.1	117.6	187.9	280.2	91.3	149.1	195.5	256.6
Magazines, newspapers, and sheet music	4.1	12.0	16.6	23.7	13.2	18.4	17.9	20.8
Nondurable toys and sport supplies . .	5.5	14.6	21.5	31.6	9.5	17.4	22.3	28.3
Radio and television receivers, records, and musical instruments . . .	8.5	19.9	32.1	48.8	8.8	17.6	29.7	52.5
Education and research	12.5	33.6	54.5	86.7	41.6	51.7	59.6	74.5
Religious and welfare activities	12.1	38.6	63.3	103.8	35.4	51.3	67.7	92.0

[1] Includes other expenditures not shown separately. [2] Consists of purchases (including tips) of meals and beverages from retail, service, and amusement establishments, hotels, dining and buffet cars, schools, school fraternities, institutions, clubs, and industrial lunch rooms. Includes meals and beverages consumed both on and off-premise. [3] Includes mattresses and bedsprings. [4] Consist largely of textile house furnishings including piece goods allocated to house furnishing use. Also includes lamp shades, brooms, and brushes. [5] Excludes drug preparations and related products dispensed by physicians, hospitals, and other medical services. [6] Consists of (1) current expenditures (including consumption of fixed capital) of nonprofit hospitals and nursing homes, and (2) payments by patients to proprietary and government hospitals and nursing homes. [7] Consist of (1) premiums, less benefits and dividends, for health, hospitalization and accidental death and dismemberment insurance provided by commercial insurance carriers, and (2) administrative expenses (including consumption of fixed capital) of Blue Cross and Blue Shield plans and of other independent prepaid and self-insured health plans. [8] Consist of (1) operating expenses of life insurance carriers and private noninsured pension plans, and (2) premiums, less benefits and dividends, of fraternal benefit societies. Excludes expenses allocated by commercial carriers to accident and health insurance. [9] For additional details, see table 383.

Source: U.S. Bureau of Economic Analysis, *Survey of Current Business*, January 1992; and unpublished data.

No. 682. Personal Income and Its Disposition: 1970 to 1991

[In billions of dollars, except percent. For definition of personal income, see text, section 14]

ITEM	1970	1980	1985	1988	1989	1990	1991
Personal income	831.0	2,265.4	3,379.8	4,075.9	4,380.2	4,679.8	4,834.4
Wage and salary disbursements	551.5	1,376.6	1,986.5	2,443.0	2,585.8	2,738.9	2,808.3
Commodity-producing industries [1]	203.7	471.9	612.2	699.1	723.8	745.4	738.7
Manufacturing	158.4	355.7	461.3	524.5	542.1	555.8	556.5
Distributive industries [2]	131.2	336.4	475.9	575.3	607.5	634.6	641.2
Service industries [3]	99.4	306.9	524.5	719.6	775.9	845.0	887.8
Government	117.1	261.4	373.9	449.0	478.6	514.0	540.6
Other labor income	32.5	139.8	191.8	230.5	253.7	274.0	290.6
Proprietors' income [4]	79.9	171.8	259.9	324.3	347.0	373.2	379.7
Rental income of persons [5]	17.8	13.2	18.7	4.3	-7.9	-12.9	-12.7
Personal dividend income	23.5	57.1	87.9	108.4	119.8	124.8	128.5
Personal interest income	69.2	274.0	498.1	583.2	669.0	721.3	718.6
Transfer payments to persons	84.6	321.5	485.9	576.7	624.4	684.9	759.5
Old-age, survivors, disability, and health insurance benefits	38.5	154.2	253.4	300.4	325.1	352.0	380.0
Gov't unemployment insurance benefits	4.0	16.1	15.7	13.4	14.4	17.9	26.6
Veterans benefits	7.7	15.0	16.7	16.9	17.3	17.8	18.4
Gov't employees retirement benefits	10.2	43.0	66.6	82.2	87.2	93.1	99.7
Other transfer payments	24.3	93.2	133.5	163.7	180.4	203.9	234.8
Less: Personal contributions for social insurance	*27.9*	*88.6*	*149.1*	*194.5*	*211.7*	*224.3*	*238.0*
Less: Personal tax and nontax payments	*109.0*	*312.4*	*436.8*	*527.7*	*591.7*	*621.0*	*616.1*
Equals: Disposable personal income	**722.0**	**1,952.9**	**2,943.0**	**3,548.2**	**3,788.6**	**4,058.8**	**4,218.4**
Less: Personal outlays	*664.5*	*1,799.1*	*2,753.7*	*3,392.5*	*3,622.4*	*3,853.1*	*3,999.1*
Personal consumption expenditures	646.5	1,748.1	2,667.4	3,296.1	3,517.9	3,742.6	3,889.1
Interest paid by persons	16.8	49.4	83.6	93.7	101.6	107.5	106.8
Personal transfer payments to foreigners (net)	1.2	1.6	2.7	2.7	2.9	2.9	3.2
Equals: Personal saving	**57.5**	**153.8**	**189.3**	**155.7**	**166.1**	**205.8**	**219.3**
Percent of disposable personal income	8.0	7.9	6.4	4.4	4.4	5.1	5.2
Disposable personal income, 1987 dollars	2,025.3	2,733.6	3,162.1	3,404.3	3,471.2	3,538.3	3,534.9
PERCENT DISTRIBUTION							
Personal income	**100.0**	**100.0**	**100.0**	**100.0**	**100.0**	**100.0**	**100.0**
Wage and salary disbursements	66.4	60.8	58.8	59.9	59.0	58.5	58.1
Other labor income	3.9	6.2	5.7	5.7	5.8	5.9	6.0
Proprietors' income [4]	9.6	7.6	7.7	8.0	7.9	8.0	7.9
Rental income of persons [5]	2.1	0.6	0.6	0.1	-0.2	-0.3	-0.3
Personal dividend income	2.8	2.5	2.6	2.7	2.7	2.7	2.7
Personal interest income	8.3	12.1	14.7	14.3	15.3	15.4	14.9
Transfer payments	10.2	14.2	14.4	14.1	14.3	14.6	15.7
Less: Personal contributions for social insurance	*-3.4*	*-3.9*	*-4.4*	*-4.8*	*-4.8*	*-4.8*	*-4.9*

[1] Comprises agriculture, forestry, fisheries, mining, construction, and manufacturing.   [2] Comprises transportation; communication; electric, gas and sanitary services; and trade.   [3] Comprises finance, insurance, and real estate; services; and rest of world.   [4] With capital consumption and inventory valuation adjustments.   [5] With capital consumption adjustment.

Source: U.S. Bureau of Economic Analysis, *Survey of Current Business,* March 1992; and unpublished data.

No. 683. Gross Saving and Investment: 1970 to 1991

[In billions of dollars]

ITEM	1970	1980	1984	1985	1986	1987	1988	1989	1990	1991
Gross saving	**155.2**	**465.4**	**633.9**	**610.4**	**574.6**	**619.0**	**704.0**	**743.4**	**710.9**	**715.5**
Gross private saving	165.8	499.6	742.7	735.7	721.4	730.7	802.3	826.5	850.4	887.0
Personal saving	57.5	153.8	222.0	189.3	187.5	142.0	155.7	166.1	205.8	219.3
Undistributed corporate profits [1]	19.4	33.9	87.5	91.9	55.4	86.5	112.6	85.8	49.9	44.7
Undistributed profits	20.3	97.1	63.8	36.1	1.6	54.6	95.2	78.7	63.3	50.3
Inventory valuation adjustment	-6.6	-43.0	-4.1	0.2	9.7	-14.5	-27.3	-17.5	-14.2	3.1
Capital consumption adjustment	5.6	-20.2	27.8	55.5	44.1	46.4	44.7	24.7	0.8	-8.7
Corporate consumption of fixed capital	51.5	185.1	265.9	277.8	294.2	307.7	327.6	350.5	365.5	383.6
Noncorporate consumption of fixed capital	37.3	126.8	167.4	176.7	184.4	194.4	206.4	224.0	229.3	239.3
Government surplus or deficit (-) [2]	-11.5	-35.3	-108.8	-125.3	-146.8	-111.7	-98.3	-83.0	-139.5	-171.5
Federal	-13.3	-60.1	-166.9	-181.4	-201.0	-151.8	-136.6	-124.2	-165.3	-201.5
State and local	1.8	24.8	58.1	56.1	54.3	40.1	38.4	41.1	25.7	30.0
Capital grants received by the U.S. (net)	0.9	1.2	-	-	-	-	-	-	-	-
Gross investment	**155.2**	**479.1**	**624.9**	**596.5**	**575.9**	**594.2**	**675.6**	**740.7**	**719.0**	**734.3**
Gross private domestic investment	150.3	467.6	718.9	714.5	717.6	749.3	793.6	837.0	802.6	726.7
Net foreign investment	4.9	11.5	-94.0	-118.1	-141.7	-155.1	-118.0	-96.8	-83.6	7.6
Statistical discrepancy	**-**	**13.6**	**-9.0**	**-13.9**	**1.2**	**-24.8**	**-28.4**	**-2.7**	**8.1**	**18.8**

- Represents or rounds to zero.   [1] With inventory valuation and capital consumption adjustments.   [2] National income and product accounts basis.

Source: U.S. Bureau of Economic Analysis, *Survey of Current Business,* March 1992; and unpublished data.

No. 684. Gross State Product: 1980 to 1989

[In billions of dollars. For definition of gross state product, see text, section 14]

DIVISION AND STATE	CURRENT DOLLARS						CONSTANT (1982) DOLLARS					
	1980	1985	1986	1987	1988	1989	1980	1985	1986	1987	1988	1989
U.S. . . .	2,670	3,966	4,186	4,484	4,854	5,165	3,115	3,590	3,712	3,847	4,032	4,130
N.E.	139	224	248	275	301	312	162	203	217	233	248	249
ME	10	16	18	20	22	23	12	14	15	17	18	18
NH	9	17	19	22	24	25	11	15	17	19	20	20
VT	5	8	9	10	11	12	6	7	8	8	9	9
MA	66	106	116	128	141	145	76	96	102	109	117	116
RI	9	14	15	17	18	19	11	12	13	14	15	15
CT	40	64	71	78	86	89	46	58	61	66	70	70
M.A.	430	650	701	758	828	872	500	577	604	632	668	676
NY	215	332	359	385	420	441	251	292	306	317	335	338
NJ	89	145	159	175	193	203	103	129	137	146	155	157
PA	126	173	184	199	215	228	146	156	161	169	178	182
E.N.C.	482	661	701	743	802	849	559	604	622	641	675	691
OH	122	168	177	186	201	212	141	154	158	162	171	173
IN	60	80	85	91	98	105	69	73	76	79	83	86
IL	144	197	208	222	241	256	166	179	184	190	201	207
MI	104	143	153	161	173	182	122	131	136	138	145	148
WI	53	72	77	82	89	94	61	67	69	72	75	77
W.N.C.	199	278	290	305	325	349	229	254	259	264	272	281
MN	49	71	76	81	87	94	56	66	68	70	73	76
IA	35	42	43	45	48	53	40	39	39	39	41	43
MO	53	79	84	89	95	100	62	71	74	75	78	79
ND	8	11	10	10	10	11	10	10	9	9	9	9
SD	7	9	9	10	10	11	8	8	8	8	8	9
NE	18	25	26	27	29	31	21	23	23	23	24	25
KS	28	41	42	44	47	49	33	37	38	39	40	40
S.A.	386	625	680	742	808	865	448	552	587	616	648	665
DE	7	11	11	13	14	15	8	10	10	11	11	12
MD	44	71	77	85	93	99	52	62	66	70	74	76
DC	19	29	31	33	37	39	22	25	25	27	28	28
VA	58	96	106	116	127	136	68	84	90	95	100	103
WV	19	24	24	25	27	28	22	22	22	23	24	24
NC	59	95	104	112	121	130	69	83	89	93	97	99
SC	27	42	46	50	54	60	31	38	40	42	45	48
GA	56	95	105	113	123	130	64	85	91	95	99	101
FL	96	162	177	195	213	227	111	143	153	162	170	174
E.S.C.	139	203	215	231	249	264	161	185	191	200	209	214
KY	37	52	54	57	62	66	43	47	48	50	52	54
TN	45	68	73	81	87	92	52	62	65	69	72	74
AL	35	53	56	60	64	68	41	48	49	51	54	55
MS	22	31	32	33	36	38	25	29	29	30	31	32
W.S.C.	327	470	446	455	484	509	395	444	428	426	436	440
AR	20	30	31	33	35	37	24	27	28	29	30	30
LA	64	82	72	72	77	79	79	79	73	71	72	72
OK	38	50	47	47	50	52	45	48	46	45	45	45
TX	205	308	295	303	322	340	247	290	282	282	289	293
Mt.	140	208	213	223	238	254	163	189	191	193	199	205
MT	9	11	11	12	12	13	11	11	11	10	10	11
ID	10	13	13	14	15	16	11	11	11	12	12	13
WY	11	13	11	11	11	11	13	13	11	11	11	11
CO	37	56	58	60	62	66	43	51	51	51	52	53
NM	17	24	22	23	24	25	20	22	21	21	22	22
AZ	30	49	54	58	62	65	34	44	47	49	51	51
UT	15	24	24	25	26	28	17	21	21	21	22	23
NV	12	18	19	21	25	28	14	16	17	18	19	21
Pac.	427	647	693	752	819	891	498	581	612	642	677	709
WA	51	70	76	82	88	96	59	62	66	69	72	76
OR	30	38	40	44	48	52	35	34	35	37	39	41
CA	319	501	539	589	642	697	372	449	473	500	529	552
AK	14	21	18	17	18	20	18	21	21	19	20	21
HI	13	18	19	21	23	26	15	15	16	17	18	19

Source: U.S. Bureau of Economic Analysis, Survey of Current Business, December 1991; and unpublished data.

No. 685. Gross State Product, by Industry: 1989

[**In billions of dollars.** For definition of gross state product, see text, section 14. Industries based on *1972 Standard Industrial Classification Manual;* see text, section 13]

DIVISION AND STATE	Total [1]	Farms, forestry, and fisheries [2]	Construction	Manufacturing	Transportation and public utilities	Wholesale trade	Retail trade	Finance, insurance, and real estate	Services	Government [3]
U.S. ...	5,165	113	248	966	461	339	486	897	971	604
N.E.	312	3	16	63	22	21	31	58	68	29
ME	23	1	2	5	2	1	3	4	4	3
NH	25	(Z)	1	6	2	1	3	5	5	2
VT	12	(Z)	1	2	1	1	1	2	2	1
MA	145	1	8	27	10	11	14	24	36	13
RI	19	(Z)	1	4	1	1	2	3	4	2
CT	89	1	4	19	7	6	9	19	17	8
M.A.	872	7	42	149	78	64	73	181	186	90
NY	441	3	20	62	37	33	35	102	99	49
NJ	203	1	11	37	19	17	17	42	40	19
PA	228	3	10	49	23	14	21	37	47	22
E.N.C.	849	16	35	216	75	57	79	141	146	81
OH	212	3	8	58	19	13	20	34	36	20
IN	105	3	5	30	10	6	10	16	15	9
IL	256	5	12	51	26	21	23	45	50	23
MI	182	2	7	50	13	11	17	31	31	18
WI	94	4	3	26	7	6	8	16	14	9
W.N.C.	349	19	13	69	35	24	33	59	57	37
MN	94	4	3	20	8	7	9	17	16	9
IA	53	5	2	11	4	3	5	10	8	5
MO	100	2	4	23	11	7	10	15	18	10
ND	11	1	1	1	1	1	1	2	2	1
SD	11	1	(Z)	1	1	1	1	2	2	1
NE	31	4	1	4	3	2	3	5	5	4
KS	49	3	2	9	6	3	5	8	7	6
S.A.	865	17	49	145	78	54	88	135	161	132
DE	15	(Z)	1	4	1	1	1	3	2	2
MD	99	1	6	11	8	6	11	17	22	17
DC	39	(Z)	3	1	2	1	2	3	12	16
VA	136	2	9	22	12	7	12	22	24	25
WV	28	(Z)	1	4	4	1	2	5	4	3
NC	130	3	5	39	11	8	13	18	17	16
SC	60	1	2	15	5	3	6	10	8	9
GA	130	2	6	25	14	12	13	20	21	16
FL	227	6	16	23	20	16	28	38	51	28
E.S.C.	264	7	11	64	24	15	25	39	39	34
KY	66	2	3	15	6	3	6	10	9	8
TN	92	2	4	22	7	6	10	14	15	11
AL	68	2	2	16	7	4	6	10	10	10
MS	38	1	2	11	4	2	4	5	5	5
W.S.C.	509	12	21	86	57	32	46	76	83	58
AR	37	2	2	9	4	2	4	5	5	4
LA	79	1	4	12	9	4	7	12	12	8
OK	52	2	2	7	6	3	5	7	8	8
TX	340	7	14	57	38	23	30	51	57	39
Mt.	254	8	15	29	26	13	26	40	51	35
MT	13	1	1	1	1	1	1	2	2	2
ID	16	2	(Z)	3	2	1	2	2	3	2
WY	11	(Z)	1	(Z)	2	(Z)	1	2	1	1
CO	66	2	3	9	7	4	7	10	14	9
NM	25	1	1	2	3	1	2	4	5	5
AZ	65	2	5	8	6	3	7	11	13	9
UT	28	1	1	5	3	2	3	4	5	4
NV	28	(Z)	3	1	2	1	3	4	10	3
Pac.	891	23	45	146	66	59	86	168	179	107
WA	96	4	6	16	8	7	11	14	16	14
OR	52	2	2	10	5	4	5	9	9	6
CA	697	16	34	118	49	46	66	139	146	78
AK	20	1	1	1	2	(Z)	1	2	2	4
HI	26	1	2	1	3	1	3	4	6	5

Z Less than $500 million.　[1] Includes mining, not shown separately.　[2] Includes agricultural services.　[3] Includes Federal civilian and military, State and local government.

Source: U.S Bureau of Economic Analysis, *Survey of Current Business,* December 1991.

No. 686. Disposable Personal Income Per Capita in Current and Constant (1987) Dollars—States: 1980 to 1991

REGION, DIVISION, AND STATE	CURRENT DOLLARS				Income rank		CONSTANT (1987) DOLLARS			
	1980	1985	1990	1991 [1]	1980	1991 [1]	1980	1985	1990	1991 [1]
United States	8,424	11,902	15,898	16,318	(X)	(X)	11,603	12,757	13,824	13,632
Northeast	8,965	13,121	18,341	18,782	(X)	(X)	12,348	14,063	15,949	15,691
New England	8,936	13,432	18,800	19,132	(X)	(X)	12,309	14,397	16,348	15,983
Maine	7,218	10,418	14,975	15,093	39	28	9,942	11,166	13,022	12,609
New Hampshire	8,523	13,485	18,475	18,710	15	5	11,740	14,453	16,065	15,631
Vermont	7,410	10,662	14,896	15,121	35	27	10,207	11,428	12,953	12,632
Massachusetts	8,926	13,543	19,051	19,385	13	3	12,295	14,516	16,566	16,195
Rhode Island	8,130	12,035	15,870	16,024	26	18	11,198	12,899	13,800	13,387
Connecticut	10,198	15,188	21,447	21,967	2	1	14,047	16,279	18,650	18,352
Middle Atlantic	8,974	13,014	18,180	18,659	(X)	(X)	12,361	13,949	15,809	15,588
New York	8,966	12,984	18,178	18,631	10	6	12,350	13,916	15,807	15,565
New Jersey	9,822	15,015	21,328	21,884	4	2	13,529	16,093	18,546	18,282
Pennsylvania	8,460	11,773	16,136	16,609	16	15	11,653	12,618	14,031	13,876
Midwest	8,407	11,712	15,533	15,913	(X)	(X)	11,580	12,553	13,507	13,294
East North Central	8,544	11,806	15,734	16,122	(X)	(X)	11,769	12,654	13,682	13,469
Ohio	8,275	11,345	15,025	15,396	24	24	11,398	12,160	13,065	12,862
Indiana	7,874	10,743	14,441	14,773	31	32	10,846	11,514	12,557	12,342
Illinois	9,151	12,836	17,510	17,908	8	9	12,605	13,758	15,226	14,961
Michigan	8,622	11,890	15,560	15,938	14	19	11,876	12,744	13,530	13,315
Wisconsin	8,315	11,436	14,958	15,438	20	23	11,453	12,257	13,007	12,897
West North Central	8,076	11,490	15,054	15,416	(X)	(X)	11,124	12,315	13,090	12,879
Minnesota	8,410	11,908	15,553	15,869	17	20	11,584	12,763	13,524	13,257
Iowa	8,012	11,063	14,647	14,873	27	30	11,036	11,857	12,737	12,425
Missouri	7,954	11,530	14,956	15,331	28	25	10,956	12,358	13,005	12,808
North Dakota	7,339	10,725	13,416	14,157	37	38	10,109	11,495	11,666	11,827
South Dakota	7,322	10,167	14,308	14,831	38	31	10,085	10,897	12,442	12,390
Nebraska.	7,873	11,491	15,153	15,466	32	22	10,844	12,316	13,177	12,921
Kansas	8,388	11,776	15,398	15,849	18	21	11,554	12,622	13,390	13,241
South	7,614	10,829	14,460	14,910	(X)	(X)	10,488	11,607	12,574	12,456
South Atlantic	7,782	11,300	15,373	15,735	(X)	(X)	10,719	12,111	13,368	13,145
Delaware	8,259	12,134	16,435	16,732	25	13	11,376	13,005	14,291	13,978
Maryland	8,942	13,351	18,172	18,477	12	7	12,317	14,310	15,802	15,436
District of Columbia	10,290	14,395	19,351	20,231	(X)	(X)	14,174	15,429	16,827	16,901
Virginia	8,296	12,255	16,698	17,038	23	11	11,427	13,135	14,520	14,234
West Virginia	6,773	8,937	11,946	12,381	46	49	9,329	9,579	10,388	10,343
North Carolina	6,819	9,895	13,925	14,295	45	36	9,393	10,606	12,109	11,942
South Carolina	6,505	9,302	12,880	13,166	48	44	8,960	9,970	11,200	10,999
Georgia	7,088	10,567	14,354	14,694	41	33	9,763	11,326	12,482	12,276
Florida	8,384	11,941	15,859	16,254	19	17	11,548	12,798	13,790	13,579
East South Central	6,692	9,269	12,865	13,358	(X)	(X)	9,218	9,935	11,187	11,160
Kentucky	6,952	9,348	12,879	13,338	43	43	9,576	10,019	11,199	11,143
Tennessee	6,991	9,903	13,857	14,328	42	35	9,629	10,614	12,050	11,970
Alabama	6,574	9,210	12,806	13,360	47	41	9,055	9,871	11,136	11,161
Mississippi	5,953	8,090	11,054	11,528	50	50	8,200	8,671	9,612	9,631
West South Central	7,920	10,998	13,871	14,439	(X)	(X)	10,909	11,788	12,062	12,063
Arkansas	6,479	9,296	12,370	12,917	49	47	8,924	9,964	10,757	10,791
Louisiana.	7,406	10,004	12,764	13,349	36	42	10,201	10,722	11,099	11,152
Oklahoma	7,939	9,993	12,579	12,951	30	46	10,935	10,711	10,938	10,820
Texas	8,298	11,713	14,590	15,187	22	26	11,430	12,554	12,687	12,688
West	9,245	12,691	16,292	16,711	(X)	(X)	12,734	13,602	14,167	13,961
Mountain	8,096	10,983	14,116	14,602	(X)	(X)	11,152	11,772	12,275	12,199
Montana	7,692	9,709	13,318	14,079	33	39	10,595	10,406	11,581	11,762
Idaho	7,451	9,605	13,390	13,527	34	40	10,263	10,295	11,643	11,301
Wyoming	9,420	10,919	13,871	14,675	6	34	12,975	11,703	12,062	12,260
Colorado	8,944	12,642	16,030	16,640	11	14	12,320	13,550	13,939	13,901
New Mexico	7,138	9,769	12,398	12,961	40	45	9,832	10,471	10,781	10,828
Arizona	7,943	11,184	13,826	14,232	29	37	10,941	11,987	12,023	11,890
Utah	6,874	9,160	12,012	12,492	44	48	9,468	9,818	10,445	10,436
Nevada	9,714	12,275	16,142	16,382	5	16	13,380	13,156	14,037	13,686
Pacific	9,656	13,311	17,050	17,451	(X)	(X)	13,300	14,267	14,826	14,579
Washington	9,013	12,492	16,252	16,967	7	12	12,690	13,389	14,132	14,175
Oregon	8,304	10,856	14,546	14,997	21	29	11,438	11,636	12,649	12,529
California	9,875	13,688	17,384	17,705	3	10	13,602	14,671	15,117	14,791
Alaska.	11,572	15,977	18,932	19,320	1	4	15,939	17,124	16,463	16,140
Hawaii.	9,065	12,123	17,107	18,161	9	8	12,486	12,994	14,876	15,172

X Not applicable.   [1] Preliminary.

Source: U.S. Bureau of Economic Analysis, *Survey of Current Business,* August issues; and unpublished data.

Income, Expenditures, and Wealth

No. 687. Personal Income in Current and Constant (1987) Dollars—States: 1980 to 1991

[In billions of dollars, except percent. Represents a measure of income received from all sources during the calendar year by the residents of each State. Data exclude Federal employees overseas and, for 1980, U.S. residents employed by private U.S. firms on temporary foreign assignment. Totals may differ from those in tables 677, 678, and 682. See text, section 14. Minus sign (-) indicates decrease]

REGION, DIVISION, AND STATE	CURRENT DOLLARS				CONSTANT (1987) DOLLARS				Average annual percent change [2]		Percent distribution	
	1980	1985	1990	1991 [1]	1980	1985	1990	1991 [1]	1980-1991 [1]	1990-1991 [1]	1980	1991 [1]
United States	2,254.1	3,317.5	4,664.1	4,812.1	3,104.8	3,555.8	4,055.7	4,020.1	2.4	-0.9	100.0	100.0
Northeast.........	521.5	776.4	1,105.3	1,127.1	718.3	832.2	961.2	941.6	2.5	-2.0	23.1	23.4
New England......	130.4	202.0	292.4	296.0	179.6	216.5	254.2	247.2	2.9	-2.7	5.8	6.2
Maine..........	9.3	13.9	21.2	21.4	12.8	14.9	18.4	17.8	3.1	-3.0	0.4	0.4
New Hampshire . .	9.0	15.3	23.1	23.1	12.5	16.4	20.1	19.3	4.1	-3.7	0.4	0.5
Vermont	4.4	6.6	9.9	10.1	6.1	7.1	8.6	8.4	3.0	-2.3	0.2	0.2
Massachusetts....	60.9	95.0	135.8	137.3	83.9	101.8	118.1	114.7	2.9	-2.9	2.7	2.9
Rhode Island	9.0	13.3	18.9	18.9	12.4	14.3	16.4	15.8	2.2	-3.8	0.4	0.4
Connecticut......	37.7	57.9	83.5	85.2	51.9	62.0	72.7	71.2	2.9	-2.1	1.7	1.8
Middle Atlantic.....	391.1	574.4	813.0	831.2	538.7	615.7	706.9	694.4	2.3	-1.8	17.4	17.3
New York	188.3	280.3	398.4	405.5	259.4	300.4	346.4	338.8	2.5	-2.2	8.4	8.4
New Jersey	85.4	133.3	192.5	196.9	117.6	142.9	167.4	164.5	3.1	-1.7	3.8	4.1
Pennsylvania	117.4	160.8	222.1	228.8	161.8	172.4	193.2	191.1	1.5	-1.1	5.2	4.8
Midwest..........	584.4	803.3	1,089.3	1,119.3	805.0	861.0	947.3	935.1	1.4	-1.3	25.9	23.3
East North Central..	420.3	570.4	776.0	797.3	578.9	611.4	674.8	666.1	1.3	-1.3	18.6	16.6
Ohio...........	105.0	142.0	190.8	196.0	144.7	152.2	165.9	163.7	1.1	-1.3	4.7	4.1
Indiana	50.8	68.3	94.0	96.6	69.9	73.2	81.7	80.7	1.3	-1.3	2.3	2.0
Illinois.........	124.0	170.0	233.8	240.4	170.8	182.2	203.3	200.8	1.5	-1.2	5.5	5.0
Michigan	94.1	127.2	171.2	175.0	129.6	136.4	148.8	146.2	1.1	-1.8	4.2	3.6
Wisconsin	46.4	62.9	86.3	89.4	63.9	67.4	75.0	74.7	1.4	-0.5	2.1	1.9
West North Central .	164.1	232.8	313.3	322.0	226.1	249.6	272.5	269.0	1.6	-1.3	7.3	6.7
Minnesota.......	41.1	59.3	82.2	84.7	56.6	63.5	71.5	70.8	2.0	-1.0	1.8	1.8
Iowa...........	27.8	36.2	48.1	48.9	38.3	38.8	41.8	40.9	0.6	-2.3	1.2	1.0
Missouri	45.8	66.7	89.6	92.0	63.1	71.5	77.9	76.9	1.8	-1.3	2.0	1.9
North Dakota.....	5.6	8.2	9.8	10.2	7.7	8.8	8.5	8.5	0.9	0.3	0.2	0.2
South Dakota.....	5.7	7.8	11.1	11.5	7.8	8.4	9.6	9.6	1.9	0.1	0.3	0.2
Nebraska.......	14.6	20.8	27.6	28.4	20.1	22.3	24.0	23.8	1.5	-1.2	0.6	0.6
Kansas........	23.6	33.8	44.9	46.2	32.5	36.2	39.0	38.6	1.6	-1.2	1.0	1.0
South.............	677.4	1,032.4	1,448.3	1,506.2	933.1	1,106.5	1,259.4	1,258.3	2.8	-0.1	30.1	31.3
South Atlantic	340.6	535.0	793.5	819.5	469.2	573.4	690.0	684.6	3.5	-0.8	15.1	17.0
Delaware........	6.1	9.1	13.4	13.8	8.4	9.8	11.7	11.6	2.9	-1.1	0.3	0.3
Maryland.......	45.6	70.2	105.0	107.3	62.8	75.2	91.3	89.6	3.3	-1.8	2.0	2.2
District of Columbia.	7.9	11.1	14.2	14.6	10.8	11.9	12.3	12.2	1.1	-1.0	0.3	0.3
Virginia	52.8	82.5	122.4	125.6	72.7	88.4	106.4	104.9	3.4	-1.4	2.3	2.6
West Virginia	15.5	19.5	24.6	25.5	21.3	20.9	21.4	21.3	0.0	-0.3	0.7	0.5
North Carolina	47.2	73.0	108.2	112.1	65.0	78.2	94.1	93.7	3.4	-0.5	2.1	2.3
South Carolina	23.8	35.8	53.0	54.9	32.8	38.3	46.1	45.9	3.1	-0.5	1.1	1.1
Georgia........	45.8	75.4	110.9	115.0	63.1	80.8	96.4	96.1	3.9	-0.3	2.0	2.4
Florida	96.1	158.4	241.8	250.7	132.3	169.8	210.3	209.4	4.3	-0.4	4.3	5.2
East South Central..	113.9	160.9	226.6	236.8	156.9	172.5	197.0	197.8	2.1	0.4	5.1	4.9
Kentucky.......	29.4	40.1	55.3	57.7	40.5	43.0	48.1	48.2	1.6	0.2	1.3	1.2
Tennessee	37.0	53.6	77.5	80.9	50.9	57.5	67.4	67.5	2.6	0.2	1.6	1.7
Alabama.......	30.1	43.0	60.7	63.7	41.4	46.1	52.8	53.2	2.3	0.8	1.3	1.3
Mississippi.......	17.5	24.2	33.0	34.6	24.1	25.9	28.7	28.9	1.7	0.6	0.8	0.7
West South Central .	222.9	336.5	428.2	449.9	307.0	360.6	372.4	375.8	1.9	0.9	9.9	9.3
Arkansas.......	17.1	24.8	33.4	35.0	23.5	26.6	29.0	29.2	2.0	0.8	0.8	0.7
Louisiana	36.7	50.7	61.2	64.4	50.5	54.3	53.2	53.8	0.6	1.1	1.6	1.3
Oklahoma.......	28.6	40.2	48.6	50.2	39.4	43.1	42.3	42.0	0.6	-0.7	1.3	1.0
Texas..........	140.5	220.7	285.1	300.2	193.5	236.6	247.9	250.8	2.4	1.2	6.2	6.2
West	470.8	705.5	1,021.1	1,059.4	648.4	756.2	887.9	885.1	2.9	-0.3	20.9	22.0
Mountain.........	108.1	162.5	225.4	237.3	149.0	174.2	196.0	198.2	2.6	1.2	4.8	4.9
Montana	7.0	9.1	12.2	13.0	9.7	9.7	10.6	10.8	1.0	1.9	0.3	0.3
Idaho	8.1	10.9	15.4	16.0	11.2	11.6	13.4	13.4	1.6	-0.3	0.4	0.3
Wyoming........	5.4	6.5	7.4	7.9	7.4	7.0	6.4	6.6	-1.1	2.6	0.2	0.2
Colorado........	30.8	47.5	62.3	65.6	42.5	50.9	54.2	54.8	2.4	1.3	1.4	1.4
New Mexico......	10.7	16.2	21.7	23.0	14.7	17.4	18.8	19.2	2.4	1.9	0.5	0.5
Arizona........	25.1	41.0	58.9	61.5	34.6	43.9	51.2	51.4	3.7	0.3	1.1	1.3
Utah..........	11.7	17.5	24.2	25.7	16.1	18.8	21.0	21.5	2.6	2.2	0.5	0.5
Nevada.........	9.3	13.8	23.3	24.6	12.7	14.8	20.3	20.6	4.4	1.4	0.4	0.5
Pacific...........	362.6	543.0	795.7	822.1	499.5	582.0	691.9	686.8	2.9	-0.7	16.1	17.1
Washington	44.6	62.0	92.2	97.6	61.4	66.5	80.2	81.5	2.6	1.7	2.0	2.0
Oregon.........	26.1	34.0	49.2	51.4	35.9	36.4	42.7	42.9	1.6	0.5	1.2	1.1
California........	276.1	422.6	619.8	636.5	380.3	453.0	538.9	531.8	3.1	-1.3	12.2	13.2
Alaska	5.6	9.8	11.9	12.5	7.7	10.5	10.4	10.5	2.8	0.7	0.2	0.2
Hawaii	10.3	14.6	22.7	24.2	14.2	15.6	19.7	20.2	3.3	2.5	0.5	0.5

[1] Preliminary.   [2] For definition of average annual percent change, see Guide to Tabular Presentation.

Source: U.S. Bureau of Economic Analysis, *Survey of Current Business*, August issues; and unpublished data.

No. 688. Personal Income Per Capita in Current and Constant (1987) Dollars—States: 1980 to 1991

[See headnote, table 687]

REGION, DIVISION, AND STATE	CURRENT DOLLARS					CONSTANT (1987) DOLLARS					Income rank	
	1980	1985	1989	1990	1991 [1]	1980	1985	1989	1990	1991 [1]	1980	1991 [1]
United States	9,919	13,942	17,738	18,696	19,082	13,663	14,943	16,229	16,257	15,942	(X)	(X)
Northeast	10,603	15,567	20,661	21,736	22,111	14,605	16,685	18,903	18,901	18,472	(X)	(X)
New England	10,542	15,852	21,371	22,111	22,425	14,521	16,990	19,553	19,227	18,734	(X)	(X)
Maine	8,218	11,913	16,455	17,183	17,306	11,320	12,768	15,055	14,942	14,458	39	30
New Hampshire	9,788	15,389	20,334	20,773	20,951	13,482	16,494	18,604	18,063	17,503	23	9
Vermont	8,577	12,490	16,895	17,506	17,747	11,814	13,387	15,457	15,223	14,826	35	26
Massachusetts	10,612	16,145	21,853	22,555	22,897	14,617	17,304	19,994	19,613	19,129	12	3
Rhode Island	9,518	13,746	18,089	18,809	18,840	13,110	14,733	16,550	16,356	15,739	27	19
Connecticut	12,112	18,083	24,422	25,395	25,881	16,683	19,382	22,344	22,083	21,622	2	1
Middle Atlantic	10,624	15,470	20,412	21,604	22,001	14,634	16,581	18,675	18,786	18,380	(X)	(X)
New York	10,721	15,751	20,881	22,129	22,456	14,767	16,882	19,104	19,243	18,760	10	4
New Jersey	11,573	17,622	23,628	24,881	25,372	15,941	18,887	21,618	21,636	21,196	4	2
Pennsylvania	9,891	13,661	17,608	18,679	19,128	13,624	14,642	16,110	16,243	15,980	18	16
Midwest	9,919	13,655	17,305	18,227	18,586	13,663	14,636	15,833	15,850	15,527	(X)	(X)
East North Central	10,077	13,771	17,541	18,444	18,799	13,880	14,760	16,048	16,038	15,705	(X)	(X)
Ohio	9,723	13,224	16,646	17,568	17,916	13,393	14,174	15,230	15,277	14,967	25	23
Indiana	9,245	12,516	16,124	16,921	17,217	12,734	13,415	14,752	14,714	14,383	31	32
Illinois	10,837	14,908	19,335	20,433	20,824	14,927	15,979	17,690	17,768	17,397	7	10
Michigan	10,165	14,018	17,660	18,378	18,679	14,001	15,025	16,148	15,981	15,605	15	20
Wisconsin	9,845	13,247	16,724	17,590	18,046	13,561	14,198	15,301	15,296	15,076	20	22
West North Central	9,534	13,379	16,744	17,711	18,079	13,132	14,340	15,319	15,401	15,104	(X)	(X)
Minnesota	10,062	14,165	17,852	18,731	19,107	13,860	15,182	16,333	16,288	15,962	16	17
Iowa	9,537	12,797	16,307	17,301	17,505	13,136	13,716	14,919	15,044	14,624	26	28
Missouri	9,298	13,344	16,687	17,479	17,842	12,807	14,302	15,267	15,199	14,906	29	25
North Dakota	8,538	12,085	14,116	15,355	16,088	11,760	12,953	12,915	13,352	13,440	37	38
South Dakota	8,217	11,182	14,492	15,890	16,392	11,318	11,985	13,259	13,817	13,694	40	36
Nebraska	9,274	13,129	16,382	17,490	17,852	12,774	14,072	14,988	15,209	14,914	30	24
Kansas	9,941	13,930	16,962	18,104	18,511	13,693	14,930	15,519	15,743	15,464	17	21
South	8,944	12,680	15,965	16,892	17,329	12,320	13,591	14,607	14,689	14,477	(X)	(X)
South Atlantic	9,171	13,320	17,273	18,126	18,449	12,632	14,277	15,803	15,762	15,413	(X)	(X)
Delaware	10,249	14,726	19,282	20,095	20,349	14,117	15,783	17,641	17,474	17,000	14	11
Maryland	10,790	15,895	20,856	21,857	22,080	14,862	17,036	19,081	19,006	18,446	8	5
District of Columbia	12,322	17,499	22,083	23,603	24,439	16,972	18,756	20,204	20,524	20,417	(X)	(X)
Virginia	9,827	14,438	18,891	19,701	19,976	13,536	15,475	17,284	17,131	16,688	21	12
West Virginia	7,915	10,227	12,751	13,744	14,174	10,902	10,961	11,666	11,951	11,841	46	49
North Carolina	7,999	11,669	15,422	16,266	16,642	11,018	12,507	14,110	14,144	13,903	44	34
South Carolina	7,589	10,831	13,969	15,141	15,420	10,453	11,609	12,780	13,166	12,882	48	43
Georgia	8,348	12,643	16,223	17,045	17,364	11,499	13,551	14,843	14,822	14,506	38	29
Florida	9,764	13,954	17,851	18,539	18,880	13,449	14,956	16,332	16,121	15,773	24	18
East South Central	7,752	10,749	14,017	14,909	15,429	10,678	11,521	12,824	12,964	12,890	(X)	(X)
Kentucky	8,022	10,852	14,021	14,992	15,539	11,050	11,631	12,828	13,037	12,982	43	42
Tennessee	8,030	11,374	15,009	15,868	16,325	11,061	12,191	13,732	13,798	13,638	42	37
Alabama	7,704	10,830	14,058	14,998	15,567	10,612	11,608	12,862	13,042	13,005	47	41
Mississippi	6,926	9,340	12,077	12,830	13,343	9,540	10,011	11,049	11,157	11,147	50	50
West South Central	9,326	12,802	14,956	16,000	16,571	12,846	13,721	13,683	13,913	13,844	(X)	(X)
Arkansas	7,465	10,672	13,296	14,176	14,753	10,282	11,438	12,165	12,327	12,325	49	47
Louisiana	8,682	11,495	13,338	14,528	15,143	11,959	12,320	12,203	12,633	12,651	34	45
Oklahoma	9,393	12,298	14,501	15,451	15,827	12,938	13,181	13,267	13,436	13,222	28	40
Texas	9,798	13,562	15,682	16,717	17,305	13,496	14,536	14,348	14,537	14,457	22	31
West	10,843	14,750	18,271	19,226	19,598	14,935	15,809	16,716	16,718	16,373	(X)	(X)
Mountain	9,445	12,755	15,553	16,428	16,907	13,010	13,671	14,239	14,285	14,124	(X)	(X)
Montana	8,924	11,056	14,520	15,304	16,043	12,292	11,850	13,285	13,308	13,403	33	39
Idaho	8,569	10,933	14,276	15,250	15,401	11,803	11,718	13,061	13,261	12,866	36	44
Wyoming	11,339	13,081	14,921	16,283	17,118	15,618	14,020	13,651	14,159	14,301	6	33
Colorado	10,598	14,805	17,815	18,860	19,440	14,598	15,868	16,299	16,400	16,241	13	14
New Mexico	8,169	11,288	13,452	14,254	14,844	11,252	12,099	12,307	12,395	12,401	41	46
Arizona	9,172	12,866	15,366	16,006	16,401	12,634	13,790	14,059	13,918	13,702	32	35
Utah	7,952	10,658	13,056	13,985	14,529	10,953	11,423	11,945	12,161	12,138	45	40
Nevada	11,421	14,510	18,380	19,049	19,175	15,731	15,552	16,816	16,564	16,019	5	15
Pacific	11,343	15,474	19,223	20,200	20,541	15,624	16,585	17,587	17,565	17,160	(X)	(X)
Washington	10,725	14,096	17,790	18,777	19,442	14,773	15,108	16,276	16,328	16,242	9	13
Oregon	9,866	12,702	16,258	17,182	17,592	13,590	13,614	14,875	14,941	14,697	19	27
California	11,603	15,981	19,734	20,689	20,952	15,982	17,129	18,055	17,990	17,504	3	8
Alaska	13,835	18,405	20,585	21,646	21,932	19,056	19,727	18,833	18,823	18,322	1	6
Hawaii	10,617	14,030	18,659	20,361	21,306	14,624	15,038	17,071	17,705	17,799	11	7

X Not applicable.   [1] Preliminary.

Source: U.S. Bureau of Economic Analysis, *Survey of Current Business,* August issues; and unpublished data.

No. 689. Personal Income and Personal Income Per Capita for Selected Metropolitan Areas: 1985 to 1990

[As defined **June 30, 1991**, CMSA=Consolidated Metropolitan Statistical Area; NECMA= New England County Metropolitan Area; MSA=Metropolitan Statistical Area. See text, section and Appendix II]

METROPOLITAN AREA, RANKED BY 1990 POPULATION	PERSONAL INCOME				PER CAPITA PERSONAL INCOME			
	1985 (mil. dol.)	1989 (mil. dol.)	1990 (mil. dol.)	Annual percent change, 1989-90	1985 (dol.)	1989 (dol.)	1990 (dol.)	Percent of national average, 1990
United States [1]	3,317,545	4,378,166	4,664,057	6.5	13,942	17,738	18,696	(X)
New York-Northern New Jersey-Long Island, NY-NJ-CT CMSA [2]	317,259	431,586	456,336	5.7	17,850	24,040	25,405	135.9
Los Angeles-Anaheim-Riverside, CA CMSA	205,721	283,232	302,747	6.9	16,057	19,871	20,691	110.7
Chicago-Gary-Lake County (IL), IL-IN-WI CMSA	126,297	167,142	177,562	6.2	15,828	20,782	21,982	117.6
San Francisco-Oakland-San Jose, CA CMSA	110,314	145,543	157,260	8.1	18,959	23,565	25,037	133.9
Philadelphia-Wilmington-Trenton, PA-NJ-DE-MD CMSA	88,854	119,779	127,045	6.1	15,530	20,375	21,499	115.0
Detroit-Ann Arbor, MI CMSA	71,792	92,292	96,214	4.2	15,576	19,836	20,595	110.2
Boston-Lawrence-Salem-Lowell-Brockton, MA NECMA	64,539	89,097	92,019	3.3	17,272	23,524	24,315	130.1
Washington, DC-MD-VA MSA	66,042	94,613	99,953	5.6	18,658	24,393	25,363	135.7
Dallas-Fort Worth, TX MSA	58,213	72,027	77,518	7.6	16,618	18,873	19,821	106.0
Houston-Galveston-Brazoria, TX CMSA . .	54,355	64,490	70,878	9.9	15,020	17,551	19,028	101.8
Miami-Fort Lauderdale, FL CMSA	43,484	59,245	62,982	6.3	14,937	18,893	19,606	104.9
Atlanta, GA MSA	38,186	54,098	57,798	6.8	15,539	19,439	20,263	108.4
Cleveland-Akron-Lorain, OH CMSA	40,581	51,307	54,216	5.7	14,628	18,576	19,640	105.0
Seattle-Tacoma, WA CMSA	35,455	49,782	54,514	9.5	15,786	20,027	21,087	112.8
San Diego, CA MSA	32,190	46,217	49,344	6.8	15,139	18,944	19,588	104.8
Minneapolis-St. Paul, MN-WI MSA	37,089	49,590	52,835	6.5	16,399	20,411	21,330	114.1
St. Louis, MO-IL MSA	36,565	47,038	49,451	5.1	15,224	19,307	20,200	108.0
Baltimore, MD MSA	35,204	48,143	51,284	6.5	15,657	20,373	21,461	114.8
Pittsburgh-Beaver Valley, PA CMSA	31,972	39,394	42,168	7.0	13,732	17,467	18,827	100.7
Phoenix, AZ MSA.	26,491	36,279	38,470	6.0	14,515	17,317	18,042	96.5
Tampa-St. Petersburg-Clearwater, FL MSA	25,862	35,713	38,056	6.6	13,868	17,620	18,274	97.7
Denver-Boulder, CO CMSA	30,067	36,303	38,806	6.9	16,598	19,738	20,950	112.1
Cincinnati-Hamilton, OH-KY-IN CMSA . . .	23,017	30,528	32,577	6.7	13,710	17,605	18,632	99.7
Milwaukee-Racine, WI CMSA	23,266	29,875	31,695	6.1	14,939	18,717	19,665	105.2
Kansas City, MO-KS MSA	22,370	28,896	30,614	5.9	15,152	18,600	19,482	104.2
Sacramento, CA MSA	18,253	26,063	28,651	9.9	14,444	18,024	19,180	102.6
Portland-Vancouver, OR-WA CMSA.	18,979	25,877	28,213	9.0	14,058	17,908	18,938	101.3
Norfolk-Virginia Beach-Newport News, VA MSA	16,717	22,023	23,302	5.8	13,198	15,975	16,613	88.9
Columbus, OH MSA	17,699	23,747	25,328	6.7	13,714	17,408	18,319	98.0
San Antonio, TX MSA	15,487	19,155	20,310	6.0	12,808	14,921	15,517	83.0
Indianapolis, IN MSA	16,885	22,883	24,478	7.0	14,117	18,456	19,522	104.4
New Orleans, LA MSA	16,981	19,161	20,465	6.8	13,058	15,331	16,560	88.6
Buffalo-Niagara Falls, NY CMSA	16,033	20,088	21,386	6.5	13,346	16,823	17,997	96.3
Charlotte-Gastonia-Rock Hill, NC-SC MSA	13,935	19,949	21,565	8.1	13,166	17,425	18,455	98.7
Providence-Pawtucket-Woonsocket, RI NECMA	12,048	16,386	17,129	4.5	13,639	17,939	18,665	99.8
Hartford-New Britain-Middletown-Bristol, CT NECMA	18,716	26,278	27,503	4.7	17,298	23,442	24,444	130.7
Orlando, FL MSA	11,829	17,849	19,246	7.8	13,468	17,192	17,737	94.9
Salt Lake City-Ogden, UT MSA	11,909	14,962	16,182	8.2	11,734	14,101	15,033	80.4
Rochester, NY MSA	14,943	19,390	20,399	5.2	15,100	19,349	20,338	108.8
Nashville, TN MSA	12,187	17,151	18,146	5.8	13,518	17,617	18,339	98.1
Memphis, TN-AR-MS MSA	11,910	16,367	17,512	7.0	12,633	16,760	17,797	95.2
Oklahoma City, OK MSA	13,214	15,002	15,840	5.6	13,499	15,676	16,501	88.3
Louisville, KY-IN MSA	12,473	16,307	17,421	6.8	13,107	17,159	18,263	97.7
Dayton-Springfield, OH MSA	12,746	16,219	17,114	5.5	13,700	17,099	17,965	96.1
Greensboro-Winston-Salem-High Point, NC MSA	12,110	16,713	17,604	5.3	13,566	17,904	18,621	99.6
Birmingham, AL MSA	11,166	14,809	15,893	7.3	12,531	16,363	17,479	93.5
Jacksonville, FL MSA	10,911	15,057	16,134	7.2	13,469	16,926	17,675	94.5
Albany-Schenectady-Troy, NY MSA.	11,782	15,972	16,985	6.3	13,835	18,306	19,404	103.8

X Not applicable.   [1] Includes other areas not listed separately.   [2] Includes Bridgeport-Stamford-Norwalk-Danbury, CT NECMA.

Source: U.S. Bureau of Economic Analysis, *Survey of Current Business,* April issues; and unpublished data.

No. 690. Percent Distribution of Shares of National Income, by Type: 1970 to 1991

TYPE OF INCOME	1970	1980	1984	1985	1986	1987	1988	1989	1990	1991
National income, total.	100.0	100.0	100.0	100.0	100.0	100.0	100.0	100.0	100.0	100.0
Compensation of employees	74.2	74.8	72.8	72.9	73.4	73.1	73.0	73.1	73.8	74.6
Wages and salaries.	66.2	62.6	60.5	60.8	61.2	61.2	61.0	60.9	61.4	61.8
Supplements to wages, salaries . .	8.0	12.2	12.3	12.1	12.2	11.8	11.9	12.1	12.4	12.8
Proprietors' income [1]	9.6	7.8	7.7	8.0	8.3	8.4	8.1	8.2	8.4	8.4
Farm	1.8	0.5	0.7	0.7	0.6	0.8	0.8	1.0	1.0	0.8
Nonfarm	7.8	7.3	7.0	7.3	7.6	7.6	7.3	7.2	7.4	7.6
Rental income of persons [2]	2.1	0.6	0.8	0.6	0.3	0.1	0.1	-0.2	-0.3	-0.3
Corporate profits [1]	9.3	8.1	8.6	8.6	7.9	8.7	9.1	8.3	7.2	6.8
Profits before tax	9.4	11.0	7.9	6.9	6.3	7.8	8.7	8.1	7.5	6.9
Profits after tax	5.3	7.1	4.8	3.9	3.2	4.4	5.3	4.9	4.4	4.1
Inventory valuation adjustment . . .	-0.8	-2.0	-0.1	0.0	0.3	-0.4	-0.7	-0.4	-0.3	0.1
Capital consumption adjustment . .	0.7	-0.9	0.9	1.7	1.3	1.3	1.1	0.6	(Z)	-0.2
Net interest	4.8	8.7	10.1	10.0	10.2	9.8	9.7	10.7	11.0	10.6

Z Less than .05.   [1] With inventory valuation and capital consumption adjustments.   [2] With capital consumption adjustment.

Source: Compiled by U.S. Bureau of the Census; based on data from U.S. Bureau of Economic Analysis, *Survey of Current Business*, March 1992; and unpublished data.

No. 691. Flow of Funds Accounts—Composition of Individuals' Savings: 1970 to 1991

[In billions of dollars. Combined statement for households, farm and nonfarm, noncorporate business, nonprofit organizations, and personal trusts. Minus sign (-) indicates decrease. See *Historical Statistics, Colonial Times to 1970*, series F 566-594, for similar but not exactly comparable data]

COMPOSITION OF SAVINGS	1970	1980	1985	1986	1987	1988	1989	1990	1991
Increase in financial assets	80.1	326.1	573.4	576.0	456.9	544.1	580.9	479.9	478.5
Checkable deposits and currency.	7.4	9.2	34.1	99.2	7.8	7.3	23.5	21.1	67.7
Time and savings deposits	43.5	124.9	129.9	98.3	118.1	152.6	101.1	11.9	-58.8
Money market fund shares	-	24.5	8.7	39.6	28.1	27.0	86.1	46.7	33.4
Securities.	0.9	11.5	109.9	22.5	141.3	67.6	70.4	120.4	85.4
U.S. savings bonds.	0.3	-7.3	5.3	13.6	7.8	8.5	8.2	8.5	11.9
Other U.S. Treasury securities	-10.4	29.3	1.7	-20.0	-2.2	39.1	22.3	53.2	1.9
U.S. Government agency securities.	4.6	9.3	25.1	-35.0	56.7	76.6	95.5	39.3	4.0
Tax-exempt obligations	-0.1	0.7	81.0	-1.2	93.1	54.1	61.7	22.6	4.4
Corporate and foreign bonds	9.2	-13.8	-16.8	44.8	6.4	-32.2	-26.5	-23.4	-21.0
Open-market paper	-2.2	3.8	59.4	13.9	7.6	41.6	-1.1	17.1	-35.1
Mutual fund shares.	2.2	1.7	73.5	141.5	71.8	2.3	41.9	52.7	133.6
Other corporate equities	-2.8	-12.3	-119.4	-135.0	-99.8	-122.4	-131.6	-49.5	-14.2
Private life insurance reserves	5.2	9.7	10.4	17.2	25.7	24.9	25.9	25.3	31.8
Private insured pension reserves	2.9	22.3	63.4	82.5	62.7	85.0	80.6	84.4	95.2
Private noninsured pension reserves.	7.2	51.2	77.2	52.9	-48.7	17.0	32.6	10.2	81.7
Government insurance and pension reserves .	8.9	35.3	72.3	78.7	73.9	84.9	93.3	88.0	82.9
Miscellaneous financial assets.	4.1	37.5	67.6	85.1	47.9	77.9	67.5	71.9	59.2
Gross investment in tangible assets.	151.6	410.1	651.3	709.0	734.7	778.9	813.9	805.7	745.9
Owner-occupied homes	29.8	116.3	157.4	180.6	202.7	222.9	234.7	216.7	191.1
Other fixed assets [1]	37.0	87.6	134.4	139.7	133.1	128.8	117.2	121.2	113.8
Consumer durables	85.3	212.5	352.9	389.6	403.7	437.1	459.8	465.9	445.1
Inventories [1].	-0.6	-6.3	6.7	-0.9	-4.8	-10.0	2.2	1.9	-4.2
Capital consumption allowances	103.4	314.3	435.4	464.1	496.7	532.3	575.5	610.3	646.7
Owner-occupied homes	13.5	47.0	64.4	67.1	70.0	73.0	76.0	79.4	83.9
Other fixed assets [1]	24.1	81.1	113.9	118.9	125.9	134.8	149.5	151.7	158.3
Consumer durables	65.8	186.2	257.1	278.2	300.8	324.5	350.1	379.2	404.5
Net investment in tangible assets	48.2	95.8	215.9	244.9	237.9	246.6	238.3	195.4	99.2
Owner-occupied homes	16.3	69.4	93.0	113.6	132.7	150.0	158.7	137.4	107.2
Other fixed assets [1]	12.9	6.4	20.4	20.8	7.1	-6.0	-32.3	-44.5	
Consumer durables	19.6	26.3	95.8	111.4	102.9	112.6	109.7	86.7	40.7
Inventories [1].	-0.6	-6.3	6.7	-0.9	-4.8	-10.0	2.2	1.9	-4.2
Net increase in liabilities [2].	39.3	209.5	436.3	392.3	362.2	393.0	364.8	291.2	172.3
Mortgage debt on nonfarm homes	13.6	96.5	156.3	216.8	234.0	230.7	218.6	216.9	139.3
Other mortgage debt [1]	16.5	57.5	102.3	71.0	65.7	62.7	48.1	16.3	1.8
Consumer credit	4.6	2.6	82.5	58.0	33.5	50.4	43.1	14.3	-16.5
Security credit.	-1.3	7.3	18.9	6.7	-16.3	1.7	-1.0	-3.7	11.2
Policy loans	2.3	6.7	-0.1	-0.1	(Z)	1.1	3.7	4.6	5.7
Other liabilities [1]	3.7	38.9	76.5	39.9	45.4	46.4	52.3	42.8	30.7
Individuals' saving	89.1	212.3	353.1	428.6	332.6	397.7	454.4	384.2	405.4
Less: Government insurance and pension reserve	8.9	35.3	72.3	78.7	73.9	84.9	93.3	88.0	82.9
Net investment in consumer durables	19.6	26.3	95.8	111.4	102.9	112.6	109.7	86.7	40.7
Net saving by farm corporations	(Z)	0.5	0.9	0.6	0.9	1.4	1.8	2.2	1.6
Equals: Personal saving, flow of funds basis.	60.6	150.3	184.1	237.9	154.9	198.8	249.6	207.4	280.2
Personal saving, NIPA basis.	57.0	154.3	189.7	187.8	142.7	156.2	166.9	206.6	221.1
Difference [3].	3.0	-4.0	-5.6	50.1	12.2	42.6	82.6	0.8	59.1

- Represents or rounds to zero.   Z Less than $50 million.   [1] Includes corporate farms.   [2] Includes items not shown separately.   [3] Personal saving on national income account basis measures personal saving as income less taxes and consumption; flow-of-funds basis measures the same concept from acquisition of assets less borrowing.

Source: Board of Governors of the Federal Reserve System, *Flow of Funds Accounts,* quarterly.

No. 692. Average Annual Income

[In dollars. Based on Consumer Expenditure Survey, integrated data from the Interview and Diary surveys; see text, section for the noninstitutional population. Second, expenditures reported here are

Line no.	CHARACTERISTIC	Income before taxes [1]	Total expenditures	Food, total	FOOD AT HOME					Food away from home	Alcoholic beverages
					Total [2]	Cereal, bakery products	Meats, poultry, fish, eggs	Dairy products	Fruits and vegetables		
1	All consumer units.	31,889	28,369	4,296	2,485	368	668	295	408	1,811	293
	Age of reference person:										
2	Under 25 years old	14,089	16,518	2,761	1,285	183	296	156	188	1,476	318
3	25 to 34 years old	32,325	28,107	4,100	2,340	332	628	292	366	1,760	365
4	35 to 44 years old	41,208	35,579	5,380	3,134	475	801	377	490	2,246	370
5	45 to 54 years old	43,451	36,996	5,490	3,008	440	850	345	468	2,482	324
6	55 to 64 years old	35,309	29,244	4,430	2,601	378	747	291	447	1,830	254
7	65 to 74 years old	21,501	20,895	3,305	2,106	324	598	247	392	1,199	166
8	75 years old and over	15,435	15,448	2,406	1,654	268	405	201	347	752	71
	Region of residence:										
9	Northeast.	35,521	29,489	4,623	2,599	407	751	313	444	2,024	332
10	Midwest.	29,012	25,919	4,022	2,313	347	591	280	372	1,709	293
11	South	29,599	27,011	4,077	2,381	345	655	271	380	1,696	249
12	West.	35,385	32,445	4,658	2,749	392	700	337	459	1,909	328
	Size of consumer unit:										
13	One person	18,678	17,126	2,302	1,130	169	272	134	206	1,172	261
14	Two or more persons.	37,187	32,768	5,077	3,016	446	823	359	486	2,061	306
15	Two persons	32,790	28,836	4,295	2,393	339	666	267	423	1,902	340
16	Three persons	37,719	33,672	5,119	2,977	440	834	346	469	2,142	308
17	Four persons.	43,545	37,477	5,879	3,565	552	910	450	541	2,314	309
18	Five or more persons	40,602	36,260	6,183	4,135	622	1,144	520	625	2,048	199
	Single consumers:										
19	No earner	11,193	11,817	1,774	1,233	198	313	146	240	540	66
20	One earner	22,838	20,125	2,592	1,074	154	251	128	188	1,518	367
	Consumer units of two or more persons:										
21	No earner	17,180	18,960	3,494	2,493	366	725	311	449	1,001	151
22	One earner	27,891	27,999	4,562	2,902	437	795	342	492	1,660	238
23	Two earners	43,405	35,878	5,177	2,896	417	765	345	457	2,282	366
24	Three or more	52,010	43,422	6,810	3,986	614	1,137	466	600	2,824	334
	Husband and wife consumer units:										
25	Total	41,599	35,992	5,422	3,167	471	851	377	511	2,255	309
26	Husband and wife only.	36,196	31,509	4,567	2,507	356	697	276	445	2,061	337
	Husband and wife with children:										
27	Oldest child under 6	40,687	35,009	4,660	2,972	424	751	389	459	1,687	266
28	Oldest child 6 to 17	44,628	38,779	6,187	3,660	575	925	454	550	2,527	289
29	Oldest child 18 or over	50,200	42,785	6,887	4,034	610	1,157	474	611	2,853	341
30	One parent, at least one child under 18 . .	17,415	19,230	3,539	2,397	359	693	289	362	1,142	164
31	Single person and other	21,123	19,160	2,779	1,506	220	398	178	263	1,273	289
	Occupation of reference person:										
32	Self employed workers.	37,508	35,795	5,083	2,745	414	741	333	446	2,338	348
	Wage and salary earners:										
33	Managers and professionals.	51,359	41,901	5,571	2,796	432	669	329	473	2,775	433
34	Technical, sales, and clerical	33,487	29,047	4,424	2,453	347	689	282	384	1,972	319
35	Service workers	21,798	21,253	3,524	2,177	301	630	264	328	1,347	251
36	Construction workers/mechanics . . .	33,587	28,100	4,231	2,571	364	725	319	380	1,660	329
37	Operators, fabricators and laborers . .	28,692	25,465	4,197	2,652	394	721	314	414	1,546	275
38	Retired	18,188	18,144	2,968	2,007	310	546	247	368	961	137
	Income before taxes:										
39	Complete reporters of income [1]	31,889	29,050	4,352	2,509	370	667	301	412	1,843	309
	Quintiles of income:										
40	Lowest 20 percent.	5,637	12,908	2,401	1,609	232	469	193	272	792	127
41	Second 20 percent	14,115	17,924	3,113	2,063	305	549	256	343	1,050	196
42	Third 20 percent	24,500	24,673	3,859	2,326	337	636	290	377	1,533	281
43	Fourth 20 percent	38,376	34,247	5,256	3,038	439	798	367	483	2,218	385
44	Highest 20 percent	76,660	55,411	7,127	3,509	538	882	401	585	3,618	554
45	Incomplete reporting of income	([1])	24,616	4,080	2,386	359	673	272	390	1,694	232

[1] Income values derived from "complete income reporters" only. Represents the combined income of all consumer unit members 14 years or over during the 12 months preceding the interview. A complete reporter is a consumer unit providing values for at least one of the major sources of income. [2] Includes other amounts not shown separately. [3] Includes household equipment.

and Expenditures of All Consumer Units: 1990

14 for description. In interpreting the expenditure data, several factors should be considered. First the data are averages out-of-pocket expenditures]

	HOUSING				Ap-parel and serv-ices	TRANSPORTATION			Health care	Per-sonal insur-ance and pen-sions	Other expen-di-tures [5]	Per-sonal taxes	Line no.
Total	Shel-ter	Fuel, utili-ties, public serv-ices	House-hold oper-ations, furnish-ings [3]	House-keeping sup-plies		Vehi-cle pur-chases	Gaso-line, motor oil	All other trans-porta-tion [4]					
8,886	**5,032**	**1,890**	**1,557**	**406**	**1,617**	**2,129**	**1,047**	**1,946**	**1,480**	**2,592**	**4,080**	**2,952**	**1**
4,845	3,025	906	736	178	1,034	1,591	722	1,185	403	972	2,687	843	2
9,349	5,667	1,684	1,631	368	1,571	2,421	1,080	1,914	981	2,761	3,566	2,954	3
11,354	6,528	2,153	2,180	494	2,310	2,523	1,245	2,313	1,415	3,700	4,966	4,471	4
10,719	6,130	2,357	1,748	483	2,165	2,967	1,391	2,692	1,597	3,847	5,804	4,070	5
8,610	4,390	2,160	1,572	488	1,557	2,014	1,134	2,151	1,791	2,958	4,345	3,507	6
6,591	3,339	1,838	1,051	362	972	1,163	792	1,511	2,197	1,071	3,127	1,378	7
5,527	2,857	1,515	882	273	489	921	396	815	2,223	261	2,338	829	8
9,789	5,855	1,981	1,527	426	1,808	1,920	867	2,026	1,396	2,690	4,038	3,094	9
7,837	4,217	1,838	1,392	390	1,357	2,068	1,000	1,726	1,336	2,408	3,874	2,426	10
8,000	4,177	2,000	1,443	380	1,549	2,275	1,152	1,884	1,600	2,395	3,831	2,715	11
10,699	6,592	1,681	1,979	447	1,852	2,174	1,115	2,240	1,544	3,042	4,792	3,791	12
6,012	3,865	1,198	748	200	886	888	556	1,216	977	1,293	2,735	1,970	13
10,010	5,488	2,161	1,874	486	1,903	2,614	1,239	2,233	1,677	3,101	4,608	3,346	14
8,941	4,930	1,925	1,641	446	1,564	2,026	1,065	2,042	1,796	2,575	4,190	3,145	15
10,025	5,447	2,175	1,924	480	2,016	3,085	1,247	2,304	1,618	3,375	4,574	3,236	16
11,448	6,275	2,366	2,247	559	2,233	3,157	1,443	2,521	1,581	3,744	5,163	4,475	17
11,104	6,089	2,544	1,959	512	2,257	2,824	1,447	2,274	1,555	3,305	5,113	2,551	18
4,954	2,801	1,237	699	217	449	317	330	648	1,395	106	1,780	729	19
6,615	4,473	1,175	775	191	1,128	1,215	685	1,539	738	1,970	3,277	2,660	20
5,953	2,903	1,762	934	354	819	1,668	667	1,198	2,169	212	2,628	695	21
9,100	4,869	2,036	1,723	472	1,741	2,013	1,027	1,726	1,518	2,179	3,895	2,185	22
11,244	6,351	2,164	2,229	500	2,051	2,806	1,345	2,443	1,535	3,942	4,967	4,356	23
11,344	6,238	2,739	1,808	559	2,560	3,953	1,807	3,407	1,963	4,743	6,503	4,600	24
10,842	5,896	2,280	2,128	538	2,032	2,993	1,362	2,456	1,898	3,546	5,130	3,890	25
9,593	5,186	2,040	1,877	489	1,657	2,381	1,137	2,229	2,091	2,875	4,641	3,650	26
12,723	7,060	2,033	3,160	470	1,881	2,767	1,190	2,272	1,551	3,795	3,905	3,635	27
11,672	6,375	2,367	2,336	594	2,373	3,411	1,454	2,298	1,597	4,011	5,487	4,152	28
11,171	5,934	2,775	1,841	621	2,450	3,907	1,797	3,289	1,969	4,226	6,747	4,152	29
7,007	3,980	1,598	1,156	271	1,502	1,028	615	1,066	629	1,157	2,524	1,032	30
6,460	4,009	1,401	818	232	1,039	1,113	682	1,382	1,037	1,507	2,871	1,996	31
10,673	6,090	2,278	1,861	444	1,921	2,584	1,192	2,317	2,192	3,867	5,617	2,825	32
13,372	7,885	2,225	2,724	537	2,557	2,990	1,289	2,886	1,685	4,747	6,373	5,907	33
9,254	5,395	1,859	1,599	401	1,659	1,910	1,076	2,192	1,276	2,942	3,993	3,271	34
6,518	3,736	1,596	882	303	1,343	1,613	878	1,558	903	1,809	2,857	1,639	35
8,460	4,775	1,915	1,383	386	1,514	2,576	1,466	1,900	1,116	2,766	3,743	2,900	36
7,311	4,055	1,826	1,078	351	1,348	2,455	1,233	1,750	1,030	2,402	3,464	2,176	37
5,993	3,016	1,684	967	325	709	1,307	640	1,199	2,058	436	2,697	1,027	38
8,895	5,036	1,870	1,559	430	1,663	2,171	1,054	1,974	1,497	2,920	4,215	2,952	39
4,440	2,413	1,214	578	236	667	798	521	722	1,012	327	1,893	83	40
5,866	3,257	1,558	769	281	961	1,355	747	1,136	1,420	867	2,264	686	41
7,616	4,294	1,844	1,114	365	1,335	1,842	1,068	1,700	1,409	2,054	3,510	1,822	42
9,910	5,563	2,076	1,745	526	1,958	2,722	1,321	2,420	1,560	3,795	4,920	3,326	43
16,619	9,637	2,658	3,581	744	3,391	4,129	1,613	3,882	2,080	7,539	8,477	8,825	44
8,948	5,008	2,013	1,619	309	1,432	1,869	1,001	1,776	1,390	575	3,311	(¹)	45

[4] Includes other vehicle expenses and public transportation.   [5] Includes entertainment, personal care, reading, education, tobacco and smoking supplies, cash contributions, and miscellaneous expenditures. For additional data on entertainment and reading, see table 384.

Source: U.S. Bureau of Labor Statistics, *Consumer Expenditures in 1990* (BLS News Release, USDL: 91-607.)

No. 693. Average Annual Expenditures of All Consumer Units: 1984 to 1990

[In dollars, except as indicated. For explanation of average annual percent change, see Guide to Tabular Presentation. Minus sign (-) indicates decrease. See headnote, table 692]

ITEM	1984	1985	1988	1989	1990	AVERAGE ANNUAL PERCENT CHANGE	
						1984-90	1989-90
All consumer units (1,000)	90,233	91,564	94,862	95,818	96,968	1	1
Total expenditures	21,975	23,490	25,892	27,810	28,369	4	2
Food, total	3,290	3,477	3,748	4,152	4,296	5	3
Food at home, total	1,970	2,037	2,136	2,390	2,485	4	4
Cereal and bakery products.	262	283	312	359	368	6	3
Meats, poultry, fish, and eggs	586	579	551	611	668	2	9
Dairy products	253	266	274	304	295	3	-3
Fruits and vegetables.	313	322	373	408	408	5	(Z)
Other food at home	556	585	625	708	746	5	3
Food away from home	1,320	1,441	1,612	1,762	1,811	5	3
Alcoholic beverages.	275	306	269	284	293	1	3
Tobacco products and smoking supplies . .	228	219	242	261	274	3	5
Housing, total	6,674	7,087	8,079	8,609	8,886	5	3
Shelter	3,489	3,833	4,493	4,835	5,032	6	4
Fuels, utilities, and public services.	1,638	1,648	1,747	1,835	1,890	2	3
Household operations and furnishings . .	1,241	1,282	1,477	1,546	1,557	4	1
Housekeeping supplies	307	325	361	394	406	5	3
Apparel and services	1,319	1,420	1,489	1,582	1,617	3	2
Transportation, total.	4,304	4,587	5,093	5,187	5,122	3	-1
Vehicles	1,813	2,043	2,361	2,291	2,129	3	-7
Gasoline and motor oil	1,058	1,035	932	985	1,047	(-Z)	6
Other transportation	1,433	1,509	1,800	1,911	1,946	5	2
Health care	1,049	1,108	1,298	1,407	1,480	6	5
Life insurance	300	278	314	346	345	2	(Z)
Pensions and Social Security.	1,598	1,738	1,935	2,125	2,248	6	6
Other expenditures [1]	2,936	3,269	3,426	3,857	3,806	4	-1

Z Less than 0.5 percent.   [1] Includes entertainment, personal care, reading, education, cash contributions, and miscellaneous expenditures. For data on entertainment and reading, see table 384.

No. 694. Average Annual Expenditures of All Consumer Units for Selected Metropolitan Statistical Areas: 1990

[In dollars. Metropolitan areas defined June 30, 1983, CMSA=Consolidated Metropolitan Statistical Area; MSA=Metropolitan Statistical Area; PMSA=Primary Metropolitan Statistical Area. See text, section 1 and Appendix II. Based on Consumer Expenditure Survey, integrated data from the Interview and Diary surveys, see headnote, table 692]

METROPOLITAN STATISTICAL AREA	Total expenditures [1]	Food	HOUSING		Apparel and services	TRANSPORTATION			Health care
			Total [1]	Shelter		Total [1]	Vehicle purchases	Gasoline and motor oil	
Anchorage, AK MSA.	43,434	5,554	13,396	8,529	2,016	8,610	4,221	1,195	1,671
Atlanta, GA MSA	32,760	4,158	10,775	6,401	2,108	5,543	2,109	1,058	1,798
Baltimore, MD MSA	30,768	4,529	9,895	6,074	1,978	5,100	2,059	1,005	1,453
Boston-Lawrence-Salem, MA-NH CMSA.	30,518	4,036	11,461	7,624	1,659	4,896	1,762	884	1,165
Buffalo-Niagara Falls, NY CMSA. . . .	24,530	4,530	7,759	4,511	1,315	4,513	1,994	714	1,162
Chicago-Gary-Lake County, IL-IN-WI CMSA	32,890	5,151	10,728	6,487	2,184	5,301	2,180	986	1,256
Cincinnati-Hamilton, OH-KY-IN CMSA .	27,862	4,687	8,035	4,448	1,740	5,439	2,352	1,085	1,450
Cleveland-Akron-Lorain, OH CMSA . .	26,357	4,166	7,468	3,853	2,043	4,502	1,623	874	1,340
Dallas-Fort Worth, TX CMSA	34,534	4,530	10,296	5,453	1,982	6,948	3,085	1,328	1,552
Detroit-Ann Arbor, MI CMSA	28,658	3,760	9,521	5,644	1,262	5,883	2,483	1,160	1,157
Honolulu, HI MSA.	33,320	5,455	10,359	6,770	1,477	5,200	2,002	858	1,691
Houston-Galveston-Brazoria, TX CMSA.	30,217	4,195	9,063	5,077	1,589	6,278	2,483	1,231	1,469
Kansas City, MO-Kansas City, KS CMSA.	27,345	4,389	8,457	4,620	1,343	4,789	1,771	1,011	1,927
Los Angeles-Long Beach, CA PMSA . .	36,061	5,236	12,656	7,995	2,404	6,004	2,520	1,087	1,633
Miami-Fort Lauderdale, FL CMSA	33,205	4,926	10,470	6,204	1,587	6,839	3,125	954	1,742
Milwaukee, WI PMSA	26,021	3,966	8,724	5,548	1,544	4,396	1,866	820	1,088
Minneapolis-St. Paul, MN-WI MSA. . . .	32,827	4,621	10,340	6,543	1,816	5,295	1,727	1,196	1,374
New York-Northern New Jersey-Long Island, NY-NJ-CT CMSA.	32,680	5,120	11,169	6,968	2,290	4,866	1,771	766	1,490
Philadelphia-Wilmington-Trenton, PA-NJ-DE-MD CMSA.	31,429	4,619	10,173	5,562	2,037	5,223	1,940	847	1,646
Pittsburgh-Beaver Valley, PA CMSA . .	26,168	4,292	8,324	3,936	1,646	4,138	1,584	792	1,208
Portland-Vancouver, OR-WA CMSA. . .	27,467	3,866	8,773	5,467	1,440	4,758	1,782	972	1,291
San Diego, CA MSA	32,024	4,351	11,642	7,179	1,849	5,019	1,491	1,182	1,285
San Francisco-Oakland-San Jose, CA CMSA.	38,927	5,292	13,727	9,449	2,556	6,470	2,570	1,024	1,348
Seattle-Tacoma, WA CMSA	33,426	4,750	10,759	6,721	1,667	5,761	2,179	1,009	1,578
St. Louis-East St. Louis-Alton, MO-IL CMSA	27,491	3,813	8,793	4,386	1,340	4,888	1,932	1,013	1,428
Washington, DC-MD-VA MSA.	37,505	4,825	12,905	8,172	2,469	5,922	2,377	1,014	1,918

[1] Includes other items not shown separately.

Sources of tables 693 and 694: U.S. Bureau of Labor Statistics, *Consumer Expenditures in 1990,* (BLS News Release, USDL: 91-607); and unpublished data.

No. 695. Money Income of Households—Percent Distribution, by Income Level in Constant (1990) Dollars, by Race and Hispanic Origin of Householder: 1970 to 1990

[Households as of **March** of **following year.** Based on Current Population Survey; see text, sections 1 and 14, and Appendix III. Hispanic persons may be of any race. For definitions of household and race, see text, section 1. For definition of median, see Guide to Tabular Presentation]

RACE AND HISPANIC ORIGIN OF HOUSEHOLDER AND YEAR	Number of house-holds (1,000)	Under $10,000	$10,000-$14,999	$15,000-$24,999	$25,000-$34,999	$35,000-$49,999	$50,000-$74,999	$75,000 and over	Median income (dol.)
ALL HOUSEHOLDS [1]									
1970	64,778	15.6	8.7	17.6	18.6	20.0	13.8	5.6	29,421
1975	72,867	15.7	10.1	18.4	16.7	19.6	13.8	5.8	28,667
1980	82,368	16.3	9.7	18.9	16.6	18.6	13.6	6.4	28,091
1985 [2]	88,458	16.2	9.6	18.3	15.7	17.7	14.5	8.0	28,688
1987 [3]	91,124	15.5	9.4	17.4	15.3	17.7	15.3	9.4	29,984
1988	92,830	15.4	9.2	17.4	15.3	17.7	15.3	9.7	30,079
1989	93,347	14.7	9.4	17.2	15.6	17.4	15.5	10.2	30,468
1990	94,312	14.9	9.5	17.7	15.8	17.5	14.9	9.7	29,943
WHITE									
1970	57,575	14.3	8.2	17.1	18.9	20.8	14.6	6.1	30,644
1975	64,392	14.1	9.6	18.1	17.0	20.3	14.6	6.2	29,978
1980	71,872	14.4	9.3	18.8	16.8	19.4	14.5	6.9	29,636
1985 [2]	76,576	14.4	9.2	18.1	16.0	18.5	15.2	8.7	30,255
1987 [3]	78,519	13.4	9.0	17.2	15.7	18.5	16.2	10.1	31,591
1988	79,734	13.2	8.8	17.3	15.7	18.5	16.1	10.4	31,798
1989	80,163	12.7	9.1	17.0	15.9	18.0	16.2	11.0	32,049
1990	80,968	12.8	9.2	17.7	16.1	18.0	15.8	10.4	31,231
BLACK									
1970	6,180	28.0	13.5	22.3	15.6	12.1	7.0	1.5	18,652
1975	7,489	30.0	14.0	20.5	14.4	13.3	6.3	1.5	17,997
1980	8,847	31.8	13.5	20.2	14.5	11.7	6.6	1.7	17,073
1985 [2]	9,797	31.0	13.0	20.3	13.3	12.2	7.8	2.5	18,000
1987 [3]	10,192	31.7	12.3	19.5	13.2	12.0	7.7	3.5	18,031
1988	10,561	31.6	12.5	18.6	12.8	12.1	9.0	3.5	18,127
1989	10,486	29.9	11.9	19.5	13.3	12.5	9.2	3.7	19,060
1990	10,671	30.8	11.6	19.1	13.5	13.1	8.1	3.8	18,676
HISPANIC									
1975	2,948	20.3	13.8	24.2	17.4	15.5	6.9	2.0	21,536
1980	3,906	21.0	13.2	22.9	16.6	14.9	8.6	2.8	21,653
1985 [2]	5,213	23.2	13.8	20.5	15.9	14.2	9.2	3.1	21,214
1987 [3]	5,642	22.4	12.9	20.8	15.2	14.4	9.6	4.6	22,247
1988	5,910	22.0	12.2	20.7	15.9	15.2	9.4	4.5	22,493
1989	5,933	20.3	12.3	20.8	15.8	15.3	10.6	4.9	23,105
1990	6,220	21.1	12.9	21.1	16.5	14.8	9.1	4.3	22,330

[1] Includes other races not shown separately. [2] Beginning 1985, based on revised Hispanic population controls; data not directly comparable with prior years. [3] Beginning 1987, based on revised processing procedures; data not directly comparable with prior years. See text, section 14, and source.

No. 696. Money Income of Households—Median Household Income in Current and Constant (1990) Dollars, by Race and Hispanic Origin of Householder: 1970 to 1990

[See headnote, table 695. Minus sign (-) indicates decrease. For definition of median, see Guide to Tabular Presentation]

YEAR	MEDIAN INCOME IN CURRENT DOLLARS				MEDIAN INCOME IN CONSTANT (1990) DOLLARS				ANNUAL PERCENT CHANGE OF MEDIAN INCOME OF ALL HOUSEHOLDS	
	All house-holds [1]	White	Black	His-panic [2]	All house-holds [1]	White	Black	His-panic [2]	Current dollars	Constant (1990) dollars
1970	8,734	9,097	5,537	(NA)	29,421	30,644	18,652	(NA)	[3]7	[3]2
1975	11,800	12,340	7,408	8,865	28,667	29,978	17,997	21,536	6	-1
1977	13,572	14,272	8,422	10,647	29,272	30,781	18,164	22,963	7	1
1978	15,064	15,660	9,411	11,803	30,197	31,392	18,865	23,660	11	3
1979 [4]	16,461	17,259	10,133	13,042	29,634	31,071	18,242	23,479	9	-2
1980	17,710	18,684	10,764	13,651	28,091	29,636	17,073	21,653	8	-5
1981	19,074	20,153	11,309	15,300	27,425	28,977	16,261	21,999	8	-2
1982	20,171	21,117	11,900	15,178	27,320	28,601	16,210	20,557	6	(-Z)
1983 [5]	21,018	22,035	12,473	15,794	27,581	28,915	16,368	20,726	4	1
1984	22,415	23,647	13,471	16,992	28,197	29,747	16,946	21,375	7	2
1985	23,618	24,908	14,819	17,465	28,688	30,255	18,000	21,214	5	2
1986	24,897	26,175	15,080	18,352	29,690	31,214	17,983	21,885	5	4
1987 [6]	26,061	27,458	15,672	19,336	29,984	31,591	18,031	22,247	5	1
1988	27,225	28,781	16,407	20,359	30,079	31,798	18,127	22,493	5	(Z)
1989	28,906	30,406	18,083	21,921	30,468	32,049	19,060	23,105	6	1
1990	29,943	31,231	18,676	22,330	29,943	31,231	18,676	22,330	4	-2

NA Not available. Z Less than 0.5 percent. [1] Includes other races not shown separately. [2] Hispanic persons may be of any race. [3] Change from 1967. [4] Population controls based on 1980 census; see text, sections 1 and 14. [5] Beginning 1983, data based on revised Hispanic population controls; data not directly comparable with prior years. [6] Beginning 1987, based on revised processing procedures; data not directly comparable with prior years. See text, section 14, and source.
Source of tables 695 and 696: U.S. Bureau of the Census, *Current Population Reports*, series P-60, No. 174; and unpublished data.

No. 697. Money Income of Households—Percent Distribution, by Income Level and Selected Characteristics: 1990

[Households as of **March 1991**. For definition of median, see Guide to Tabular Presentation. For composition of regions, see table 25]

CHARACTERISTIC	Number of house-holds (1,000)	PERCENT DISTRIBUTION OF HOUSEHOLDS BY INCOME LEVEL								Median income (dollars)
		Under $5,000	$5,000-$9,999	$10,000-$14,999	$15,000-$24,999	$25,000-$34,999	$35,000-$49,999	$50,000-$74,999	$75,000 and over	
Total [1]	94,312	5.2	9.7	9.5	17.7	15.8	17.5	14.9	9.7	29,943
Age of householder:										
15 to 24 years	4,882	13.3	14.2	14.7	24.3	16.6	11.2	4.6	1.1	18,002
25 to 34 years	20,323	5.0	6.9	8.2	19.8	19.3	20.9	14.2	5.8	30,359
35 to 44 years	21,304	3.3	4.5	5.8	14.0	16.5	21.7	21.4	12.8	38,561
45 to 54 years	14,751	3.3	5.0	5.3	12.4	14.1	19.5	21.6	18.7	41,922
55 to 64 years	12,524	5.5	7.9	8.4	16.7	15.1	17.8	16.1	12.5	32,365
65 years and over . .	20,527	6.6	21.4	17.0	22.5	12.9	9.5	5.7	4.4	16,855
White	80,968	4.0	8.8	9.2	17.7	16.1	18.0	15.8	10.4	31,231
Black	10,671	14.1	16.7	11.6	19.1	13.5	13.1	8.1	3.8	18,676
Hispanic [2]	6,220	7.5	13.7	12.9	21.1	16.5	14.8	9.1	4.3	22,330
Northeast	19,271	4.4	10.1	8.4	15.3	14.6	17.7	17.0	12.5	32,676
Midwest	23,223	5.1	10.0	9.6	17.7	15.8	18.0	15.2	8.6	29,897
South	32,312	6.6	10.2	10.4	19.2	16.0	16.7	13.0	7.9	26,942
West	19,506	3.8	8.4	8.8	17.6	16.5	17.8	15.7	11.5	31,761
Size of household:										
One person	23,590	10.9	22.5	15.7	21.9	13.9	9.0	4.2	1.9	15,344
Two persons	30,181	3.5	6.0	9.3	19.8	17.3	18.8	15.3	10.0	31,358
Three persons	16,082	4.0	5.6	6.4	14.8	16.4	20.6	19.6	12.7	36,765
Four persons	14,556	2.7	4.6	4.8	12.4	14.9	22.9	22.5	15.3	41,473
Five persons	6,206	2.3	5.0	6.3	12.8	16.2	21.2	21.4	14.8	39,275
Six persons	2,237	2.4	5.5	7.3	15.7	14.6	20.8	19.2	14.4	38,159
Seven persons or more	1,459	2.7	5.8	7.4	18.1	14.6	18.2	19.0	14.1	36,108
Family households. . . .	66,322	3.4	5.6	7.3	16.3	16.3	20.2	18.5	12.5	35,707
Married-couple families	52,147	1.3	3.3	5.9	15.0	16.4	21.9	21.3	14.9	39,996
Male householder, wife absent	2,907	3.5	6.5	8.0	20.3	18.3	21.2	15.3	6.9	31,552
Female householder, husband absent . . .	11,268	13.0	16.2	13.4	21.2	15.2	11.9	6.7	2.5	18,069
Nonfamily households .	27,990	9.5	19.5	14.6	21.2	14.5	11.0	6.4	3.3	17,690
Male householder. . .	12,150	7.0	12.1	13.1	22.4	16.9	14.2	9.2	5.2	22,489
Female householder .	15,840	11.4	25.3	15.7	20.3	12.7	8.6	4.2	1.8	14,099
Education attainment of householder: [3]										
Elementary school, 8 years or less	10,146	12.2	25.1	16.8	22.0	11.4	7.4	3.8	1.3	13,523
High school.	42,120	5.5	11.0	11.2	20.4	17.7	18.0	12.1	4.7	25,953
1 to 3 years	10,077	9.4	18.0	14.3	22.7	14.7	12.0	6.6	2.3	18,191
4 years	32,043	4.2	8.8	10.3	19.7	17.9	19.9	13.8	5.5	28,744
College.	37,163	1.9	3.5	4.8	12.6	15.3	20.5	22.5	18.9	43,112
1 to 3 years	16,451	2.8	5.3	6.7	16.5	17.3	21.7	20.2	9.4	35,724
4 years or more . .	20,712	1.3	2.0	3.3	9.5	13.7	19.5	24.3	26.4	50,549
Tenure:										
Owner occupied. . . .	60,395	2.7	6.5	7.7	15.5	15.5	19.6	19.0	13.5	36,298
Renter occupied. . . .	32,218	9.4	15.4	12.5	21.7	16.3	14.0	7.7	3.1	20,722
Occupier paid no cash rent.	1,698	14.0	18.5	15.1	20.9	14.3	8.8	6.3	2.2	15,868

[1] Includes other races not shown separately.   [2] Hispanic persons may be of any race.   [3] 25 years old and over.

Source: U.S. Bureau of the Census, *Current Population Reports*, series P-60, No. 174; and unpublished data.

No. 698. Money Income of Households—Aggregate and Mean Income, by Race and Hispanic Origin of Householder: 1990

[As of **March 1991**. See headnote, table 695. For number of households by characteristic, see table 62. For definition of mean, see Guide to Tabular Presentation. For composition of regions, see table 25]

CHARACTERISTIC	ALL RACES [1]		WHITE		BLACK		HISPANIC [2]	
	Aggregate money income (bil.dol.)	Mean income (dol.)	Aggregate money income (bil.dol.)	Mean income (dol.)	Aggregate money income (bil.dol.)	Mean income (dol.)	Aggregate money income (bil.dol.)	Mean income (dol.)
Total	3,528	37,403	3,151	38,912	265	24,814	174	27,972
Age of householder:								
15 to 24 years old	105	21,484	92	22,727	10	14,068	12	20,098
25 to 34 years old	701	34,484	620	36,322	57	22,014	48	26,385
35 to 44 years old	960	45,076	846	46,987	80	30,906	48	31,307
45 to 54 years old	738	50,003	652	52,014	56	33,198	33	34,076
55 to 64 years old	519	41,459	473	43,483	33	24,775	22	32,667
65 years old and over	505	24,586	468	25,363	29	16,286	12	17,900
Region:								
Northeast	789	40,953	717	42,479	53	26,979	30	26,571
Midwest	845	36,387	782	37,628	52	24,310	12	29,245
South	1,104	34,180	954	36,549	134	23,306	53	26,539
West	789	40,443	698	40,547	27	31,184	80	29,411
Size of household:								
One person.	487	20,644	433	21,314	42	15,193	15	15,826
Two persons	1,184	39,233	1,094	40,726	67	25,061	36	26,310
Three persons	699	43,436	623	45,837	56	27,820	35	28,884
Four persons	702	48,223	620	50,342	51	30,573	37	31,552
Five persons	291	46,834	251	48,802	25	31,598	27	32,690
Six persons	101	45,251	82	47,331	12	33,395	12	31,372
Seven persons or more	64	43,914	47	47,351	10	29,790	13	36,618

[1] Includes other races not shown separately.   [2] Hispanic persons may be of any race.

Source: U.S. Bureau of the Census, *Current Population Reports,* series P-60, No. 174.

No. 699. Household Type, by Median Income and Income Level: 1990

[Households as of **March 1991.** See headnote, table 695]

ITEM	All households	FAMILY HOUSEHOLDS				NONFAMILY HOUSEHOLDS		
		Total	Married couple	Male householder, wife absent	Female householder, husband absent	Total [1]	Single-person household	
							Male householder	Female householder
MEDIAN INCOME (dollars)								
All households.	29,943	35,707	39,996	31,552	18,069	17,690	19,964	12,548
White	31,231	37,219	40,433	32,869	20,867	18,449	20,900	13,094
Black	18,676	21,899	33,893	24,048	12,537	11,789	13,126	7,674
Hispanic [2]	22,330	24,552	28,584	25,456	12,603	14,274	13,716	8,933
NUMBER (1,000)								
All households.	94,312	66,322	52,147	2,907	11,268	27,990	9,450	14,141
Under $5,000	4,901	2,241	674	101	1,466	2,660	806	1,771
$5,000 to $9,999.	9,184	3,712	1,700	189	1,823	5,471	1,378	3,918
$10,000 to $14,999	8,925	4,841	3,102	233	1,506	4,084	1,349	2,365
$15,000 to $19,999	8,296	5,176	3,626	293	1,257	3,120	1,200	1,578
$20,000 to $24,999	8,427	5,601	4,175	298	1,128	2,826	1,066	1,318
$25,000 to $34,999	14,864	10,808	8,564	531	1,713	4,057	1,599	1,691
$35,000 to $49,999	16,469	13,394	11,442	616	1,337	3,075	1,143	973
$50,000 and over	23,246	20,546	18,864	647	1,037	2,699	909	529

[1] Includes other nonfamily households not shown separately.   [2] Hispanic persons may be of any race.

Source: U.S. Bureau of the Census, *Current Population Reports,* series P-60, No. 174; and unpublished data.

No. 700. Money Income of Households—Percent Distribution, by Income Quintile and Top 5 Percent for Selected Characteristics: 1990

[As of **March, 1991**. See headnote, table 695. For composition of regions, see table 25]

CHARACTERISTIC	Number (1,000)	PERCENT DISTRIBUTION						
		Total	Lowest fifth	Second fifth	Third fifth	Fourth fifth	Highest fifth	Top 5 percent
All households	94,312	100.0	20.0	20.0	20.0	20.0	20.0	5.0
White	80,968	100.0	17.7	19.9	20.4	20.7	21.3	5.4
Black	10,671	100.0	37.4	21.9	17.5	14.2	9.0	1.4
Hispanic [1]	6,220	100.0	28.5	24.3	21.2	15.8	10.3	2.0
Northeast.	19,271	100.0	19.0	17.5	18.3	20.6	24.6	6.5
Midwest.	23,223	100.0	20.0	20.5	20.0	20.7	18.8	4.2
South	32,312	100.0	22.5	21.6	20.4	18.9	16.6	3.9
West.	19,506	100.0	16.9	19.2	21.0	20.4	22.6	6.3
Family households.	66,322	100.0	12.7	17.8	20.6	23.5	25.4	6.4
Married-couple families	52,147	100.0	7.5	16.0	20.8	25.9	29.8	7.7
Male householder.	2,907	100.0	13.5	22.6	22.5	23.7	17.7	3.5
Female householder.	11,268	100.0	36.5	24.8	19.3	12.4	6.9	1.1
Nonfamily households	27,990	100.0	37.2	25.3	18.5	11.7	7.3	1.7
Male householder.	12,150	100.0	26.2	26.0	21.4	15.4	11.1	2.8
Living alone	9,450	100.0	30.9	27.9	21.5	12.6	7.1	1.8
Female householder.	15,840	100.0	45.7	24.8	16.4	8.8	4.4	0.9
Living alone	14,141	100.0	49.9	25.4	15.3	7.0	2.4	0.5
15 to 24 years old	4,882	100.0	35.7	28.1	20.8	11.4	4.0	0.5
25 to 34 years old	20,323	100.0	16.1	21.5	24.5	23.1	14.8	2.4
35 to 44 years old	21,304	100.0	10.9	15.0	20.7	26.1	27.3	6.3
45 to 54 years old	14,751	100.0	11.2	13.0	18.0	23.1	34.7	9.7
55 to 64 years old	12,524	100.0	17.7	18.5	19.3	20.6	23.8	7.4
65 years old and over	20,527	100.0	37.3	27.8	16.5	10.0	8.4	2.5
65 to 74 years old	12,001	100.0	29.7	27.9	19.3	12.5	10.7	3.1
75 years old and over	8,526	100.0	47.9	27.6	12.7	6.5	5.3	1.5
Worked	68,658	100.0	10.2	18.2	21.9	24.3	25.4	6.4
Worked at full-time jobs	60,886	100.0	7.3	17.3	22.5	25.8	27.1	6.8
Worked at part-time jobs	7,771	100.0	32.4	25.5	17.2	13.2	11.7	3.1
Did not work.	25,654	100.0	46.3	24.8	14.9	8.4	5.6	1.3

[1] Hispanic persons may be of any race.

Source: U.S. Bureau of the Census, *Current Population Reports*, series P-60, No. 174.

No. 701. Median Income of Households, by State, in Constant (1990) Dollars: 1984 to 1990

[Based on the Current Population Survey. The CPS is designed to collect reliable data on income primarily at the national level and secondarily at the regional level. When the income data are tabulated by State, the estimates are considered less reliable and, therefore, particular caution should be used when trying to interpret the results; see source for additional detail]

STATE	1984	1985	1988 [1]	1989	1990	STATE	1984	1985	1988 [1]	1989	1990
U.S.	28,197	28,688	30,079	30,468	29,943	MO . . .	26,134	26,649	25,900	27,929	27,332
AL . . .	21,775	22,269	22,039	22,434	23,357	MT . . .	24,575	24,580	24,561	24,972	23,375
AK . .	40,702	42,249	36,573	37,951	39,298	NE . . .	26,916	26,479	27,796	27,741	27,482
AZ . .	26,951	29,003	29,206	30,095	29,224	NV . . .	32,425	28,271	30,916	30,925	32,023
AR . .	19,717	21,197	22,286	22,591	22,786	NH . . .	32,598	32,071	38,254	39,560	40,805
CA . .	31,810	32,773	33,462	34,793	33,290	NJ . . .	34,941	37,631	40,091	41,234	38,734
CO . .	32,456	34,232	28,962	28,254	30,733	NM . . .	25,951	24,807	21,319	23,823	25,039
CT . .	37,677	37,765	40,009	44,608	38,870	NY . . .	27,709	28,714	31,946	33,198	31,591
DE . .	32,479	27,913	33,702	33,801	30,804	NC . . .	25,875	26,056	26,974	27,833	26,329
DC . .	25,672	25,601	29,544	28,197	27,392	ND . . .	26,129	25,757	26,617	26,592	25,264
FL . .	24,888	25,925	28,069	27,494	26,685	OH . . .	29,087	30,578	30,648	30,589	30,013
GA . .	25,139	25,568	29,351	29,030	27,561	OK . . .	26,603	25,757	26,148	24,946	24,384
HI . .	36,326	35,178	36,486	36,928	38,921	OR . . .	26,619	26,594	30,656	30,070	29,281
ID . . .	26,532	25,218	25,908	25,986	25,305	PA . . .	25,594	27,788	29,545	30,240	29,005
IL	29,879	30,209	32,619	32,991	32,542	RI . . .	27,187	29,912	32,970	31,752	31,968
IN . . .	28,643	27,543	29,049	27,297	26,928	SC . . .	25,548	24,337	28,209	25,084	28,735
IA . . .	24,986	25,420	26,853	27,684	27,288	SD . . .	24,415	22,037	24,631	25,411	24,571
KS . .	30,982	27,680	28,246	28,313	29,917	TN . . .	21,111	21,595	23,042	23,833	22,592
KY . .	22,240	21,088	21,994	24,541	24,780	TX . . .	28,963	28,840	27,580	27,285	28,228
LA . .	23,837	25,726	22,645	24,096	22,405	UT . . .	29,004	30,656	29,071	32,377	30,142
MN . .	25,974	24,924	29,169	29,746	27,464	VT . . .	28,402	31,582	32,026	32,986	31,098
MD . .	37,371	36,606	40,383	37,962	38,857	VA . . .	33,367	34,532	36,070	35,961	35,073
MA . .	33,913	34,263	36,694	38,036	36,247	WA . . .	31,470	29,152	35,175	33,688	32,112
MI . .	28,889	29,446	32,561	32,438	29,937	WV . . .	21,187	19,414	21,382	22,848	22,137
MN .	30,739	28,978	32,136	31,816	31,465	WI . . .	26,093	28,237	32,675	30,697	30,711
MS . .	19,410	19,937	20,070	20,993	20,178	WY . .	29,959	26,821	29,188	31,116	29,460

[1] Beginning 1988, based on revised processing procedures; data not directly comparable with prior years. See text, section 14, and source.

Source: U.S. Bureau of the Census, *Current Population Reports*, series P-60, No. 174.

No. 702. Money Income of Families—Percent Distribution by Income Level in Constant (1990) Dollars, by Race and Hispanic Origin of Householder: 1970 to 1990

[Families as of **March** of following year. Beginning with 1980, based on householder concept and restricted to primary families. For definition of race, family, and householder, see text, section 1. Based on Current Population Survey; see text, sections 1 and 14 and Appendix III. For definition of median, see Guide to Tabular Presentation. See also *Historical Statistics, Colonial Times to 1970*, series G 1-8, G 16-23, G 190-192, and G 197-199]

RACE AND HISPANIC ORIGIN OF HOUSEHOLDER AND YEAR	Number of families (1,000)	PERCENT DISTRIBUTION OF FAMILIES, BY INCOME LEVEL							Median income (dol.)
		Under $10,000	$10,000-$14,999	$15,000-$24,999	$25,000-$34,999	$35,000-$49,999	$50,000-$74,999	$75,000 and over	
ALL FAMILIES									
1970	52,227	8.7	7.5	17.6	20.3	23.1	16.2	6.5	33,238
1975	56,245	8.6	8.5	17.9	18.3	23.0	16.6	7.0	33,328
1980	60,309	9.5	8.0	17.9	17.9	21.9	16.8	7.9	33,346
1985 [1]	63,558	10.4	7.9	17.4	16.4	20.3	17.5	10.0	33,689
1987 [2]	65,204	9.7	7.4	16.4	15.9	20.2	18.7	11.7	35,632
1988	65,837	9.5	7.6	16.2	15.9	20.1	18.7	12.0	35,565
1989	66,090	9.3	7.7	15.8	15.9	19.7	18.8	12.8	36,062
1990	66,322	9.4	7.5	16.4	16.2	20.1	18.2	12.3	35,353
WHITE									
1970	46,535	7.4	6.9	16.9	20.6	24.1	17.0	7.1	34,481
1975	49,873	7.1	7.9	17.4	18.6	23.8	17.6	7.6	34,662
1980	52,710	7.6	7.3	17.6	18.2	22.9	17.8	8.6	34,743
1985	54,991	8.5	7.3	17.0	16.7	21.1	18.5	10.8	35,410
1987 [2]	56,086	7.5	6.8	16.0	16.3	21.1	19.8	12.5	37,260
1988	56,492	7.4	6.9	15.9	16.3	21.0	19.8	12.8	37,470
1989	56,590	7.1	7.0	15.5	16.3	20.5	19.7	13.8	37,919
1990	56,803	7.2	7.0	16.0	16.5	20.8	19.3	13.2	36,915
BLACK									
1970	4,928	20.9	13.6	23.9	17.6	13.9	8.3	1.6	21,151
1975	5,586	21.8	14.5	21.9	16.3	15.8	8.0	1.8	21,327
1980	6,317	24.3	14.1	20.9	15.7	14.1	8.7	2.2	20,103
1985	6,921	25.8	12.4	21.2	14.2	14.2	9.3	3.0	20,390
1987 [2]	7,202	25.7	11.7	20.1	13.8	14.3	9.9	4.5	21,177
1988	7,409	25.2	12.8	19.0	13.3	13.9	11.3	4.4	21,355
1989	7,470	24.6	12.6	19.4	13.8	14.1	11.0	4.5	21,301
1990	7,471	25.6	11.3	19.5	14.0	15.0	9.8	4.7	21,423
HISPANIC [3]									
1975	2,499	16.7	13.6	24.5	18.7	16.9	7.5	2.2	23,203
1980	3,235	17.1	13.2	23.5	17.7	16.4	9.1	3.0	23,342
1985	4,206	19.5	13.7	20.9	17.0	15.1	10.3	3.6	23,112
1987 [2]	4,576	19.5	12.9	21.2	15.8	15.0	10.8	4.7	23,356
1988	4,823	18.8	11.9	21.0	16.7	16.0	10.8	4.7	24,051
1989	4,840	17.4	12.1	21.0	16.3	16.7	11.3	5.2	24,713
1990	4,981	18.6	12.6	21.7	16.6	15.7	10.0	4.8	23,431

[1] Beginning 1985, data based on revised Hispanic population controls; data not directly comparable with prior years. [2] Beginning 1987, based on revised processing procedures; data not directly comparable with prior years. See text, section 14, and source. [3] Hispanic persons may be of any race.

No. 703. Money Income of Families—Median Family Income in Current and Constant (1990) Dollars, by Race and Hispanic Origin of Householder: 1970 to 1990

[See headnote, table 702. Minus sign (-) indicates decrease]

YEAR	MEDIAN INCOME IN CURRENT DOLLARS (dol.)				MEDIAN INCOME IN CONSTANT (1990) DOLLARS (dol.)				ANNUAL PERCENT CHANGE OF MEDIAN INCOME OF ALL FAMILIES	
	All families [1]	White	Black	Hispanic [2]	All families [1]	White	Black	Hispanic [2]	Current dollars	Constant (1990) dollars
1970	9,867	10,236	6,279	(NA)	33,238	34,481	21,151	(NA)	[3]7	[3]3
1973	12,051	12,595	7,269	8,715	35,474	37,076	21,398	25,654	8	2
1974	12,902	13,408	8,006	9,540	34,205	35,546	21,225	25,292	7	-4
1975	13,719	14,268	8,779	9,551	33,328	34,662	21,327	23,203	6	-3
1976	14,958	15,537	9,242	10,259	34,359	35,689	21,225	23,565	9	3
1977	16,009	16,740	9,563	11,421	34,528	36,104	20,625	24,632	7	1
1978	17,640	18,368	10,879	12,566	35,361	36,821	21,808	25,190	10	2
1979	19,587	20,439	11,574	14,169	35,262	36,796	20,836	25,508	11	(Z)
1980	21,023	21,904	12,674	14,716	33,346	34,743	20,103	23,342	7	-5
1981	22,388	23,517	13,266	16,401	32,190	33,814	19,074	23,582	7	-4
1982	23,433	24,603	13,598	16,227	31,738	33,322	18,417	21,978	5	-1
1983 [4]	24,580	25,757	14,506	16,956	32,378	33,905	19,108	22,216	5	2
1984	26,433	27,686	15,432	18,833	33,251	34,827	19,411	23,690	8	3
1985	27,735	29,152	16,786	19,027	33,689	35,410	20,390	23,112	5	1
1986	29,458	30,809	17,604	19,995	35,129	36,740	20,993	23,844	6	4
1987 [5]	30,970	32,385	18,406	20,300	35,632	37,260	21,177	23,356	5	1
1988	32,191	33,915	19,329	21,769	35,565	37,470	21,355	24,051	4	(Z)
1989	34,213	35,975	20,209	23,446	36,062	37,919	21,301	24,713	6	1
1990	35,353	36,915	21,423	23,431	35,353	36,915	21,423	23,431	3	-2

NA Not available. Z Less than 0.5 percent. [1] Includes other races not shown separately. [2] Hispanic persons may be of any race. [3] Change from 1965. [4] Beginning 1983, data based on revised Hispanic population controls; data not directly comparable with prior years. [5] Beginning 1987, data based on revised processing procedures; data not directly comparable with prior years.

Source of tables 702 and 703: U.S. Bureau of the Census, *Current Population Reports*, series P-60, No. 174; and unpublished data.

No. 704. Money Income of Families—Percent Distribution of Aggregate Income Received by Quintile and Income at Selected Positions, in Constant (1990) Dollars: 1980 and 1990

[Families as of **March of following year.** For composition of regions, see table 25. Based on Current Population Survey; see headnote, table 702. See also *Historical Statistics, Colonial Times to 1970,* series G 31-138]

ITEM	All families, 1980	1990						
		All families	RACE		REGION			
			White	Black	North-east	Midwest	South	West
Number (1,000)	60,309	66,322	56,803	7,471	13,450	16,119	23,279	13,474
INCOME AT SELECTED POSITIONS (dollars)								
Upper limit of each fifth:								
Lowest	16,315	16,846	18,656	8,064	19,114	17,500	15,000	18,000
Second	27,583	29,044	30,660	16,251	32,500	30,200	25,700	30,301
Third	39,067	42,040	43,986	27,816	47,030	42,300	38,020	44,050
Fourth	54,777	61,490	63,020	43,900	68,073	60,010	56,040	65,200
Top 5 percent.	85,748	102,358	105,000	73,506	110,000	97,300	94,000	110,049
PERCENT DISTRIBUTION OF AGGREGATE INCOME								
Lowest fifth	5.2	4.6	5.1	3.3	4.6	4.8	4.5	4.8
Second fifth	11.5	10.8	11.1	8.6	11.0	11.3	10.5	10.7
Third fifth.	17.5	16.6	16.6	15.6	16.8	17.0	16.4	16.3
Fourth fifth	24.3	23.8	23.6	25.3	24.0	23.8	23.9	23.5
Highest fifth	41.5	44.3	43.6	47.3	43.7	43.0	44.7	44.8
Top 5 percent.	15.3	17.4	17.1	17.3	17.1	16.8	17.5	17.7

Source: U.S. Bureau of the Census, *Current Population Reports,* series P-60, No. 174; and unpublished data.

No. 705. Money Income of Families—Percent Distribution by Income Quintile and Top 5 Percent for Selected Characteristics: 1990

[As of **March, 1991.** See headnote, table 702]

CHARACTERISTIC	Number (1,000)	PERCENT DISTRIBUTION						
		Total	Lowest fifth	Second fifth	Third fifth	Fourth fifth	Highest fifth	Top 5 percent
All families	66,322	100.0	20.0	20.0	20.0	20.0	20.0	5.0
White	56,803	100.0	17.2	20.0	20.5	21.0	21.3	5.5
Black	7,471	100.0	41.3	21.0	16.5	12.7	8.5	1.2
Hispanic	4,981	100.0	35.8	24.4	18.2	12.9	8.7	1.7
Married-couple families.	52,147	100.0	13.2	19.0	21.3	22.7	23.8	6.1
Male householder	2,907	100.0	25.7	24.9	20.1	17.9	11.4	2.2
Female householder	11,268	100.0	49.9	23.3	14.1	8.2	4.6	0.6
15 to 24 years old.	2,726	100.0	51.9	24.0	16.0	5.9	2.2	0.4
25 to 34 years old	14,590	100.0	24.1	21.8	22.1	20.4	11.7	1.8
35 to 44 years old	17,078	100.0	14.3	16.6	21.0	24.3	23.8	5.3
45 to 54 years old	11,701	100.0	11.2	13.9	18.2	23.4	33.4	9.0
55 to 64 years old	9,326	100.0	15.4	19.2	19.9	20.9	24.6	7.6
65 years old and over	10,900	100.0	28.9	29.2	18.6	12.0	11.3	3.4
65 to 74 years old	7,373	100.0	24.2	29.2	20.4	13.4	12.8	3.7
75 years old and over	3,527	100.0	38.6	29.4	14.8	9.1	8.1	2.7
Size of family:								
Two persons	27,615	100.0	24.1	23.6	19.6	17.1	15.6	4.3
Three persons	15,298	100.0	19.3	18.6	20.0	20.9	21.2	4.8
Four persons	14,098	100.0	14.4	16.0	20.7	23.7	25.2	6.0
Five persons	5,965	100.0	16.1	16.7	21.7	21.4	24.1	5.9
Six persons	2,060	100.0	19.0	18.4	17.8	21.8	23.1	5.9
Seven persons or more	1,285	100.0	20.6	19.9	17.4	21.6	20.5	5.4
Presence of related children under 18 years old:								
No related children	31,819	100.0	17.0	21.0	19.9	20.1	22.1	6.1
One or more related children	34,503	100.0	22.8	19.1	20.1	19.9	18.1	4.0
One child	14,196	100.0	22.4	19.6	19.4	19.2	19.3	4.3
Two children or more	20,307	100.0	23.1	18.7	20.6	20.4	17.2	3.8
Education attainment of householder: [1]								
Total	63,595	100.0	18.6	19.8	20.2	20.6	20.8	5.2
8 years or less	6,545	100.0	45.1	28.4	15.1	7.6	3.9	0.5
High school: Total	30,604	100.0	22.6	24.1	22.5	19.1	11.7	1.8
1 to 3 years	7,053	100.0	35.8	27.8	18.5	11.7	6.3	0.9
4 years	23,551	100.0	18.6	23.0	23.7	21.4	13.3	2.0
College: Total	26,446	100.0	7.5	12.8	18.7	25.5	35.5	10.3
1 to 3 years	11,623	100.0	11.5	17.6	22.6	26.2	22.1	4.1
4 years or more	14,823	100.0	4.4	8.9	15.7	25.0	45.9	15.2
Worked	51,436	100.0	13.0	18.5	21.4	23.1	24.0	6.0
Worked at full-time jobs	46,379	100.0	10.7	18.0	21.9	24.1	25.2	6.3
Worked at part-time jobs	5,057	100.0	34.2	23.3	16.3	13.9	12.4	3.4
Did not work.	14,886	100.0	44.1	25.1	15.3	9.2	6.3	1.5

[1] 25 years old and over.

Source: U.S. Bureau of the Census, *Current Population Reports,* series P-60, No. 174.

No. 706. Money Income of Families—Median Family Income, by Race and Hispanic Origin: 1990

[Families as of **March 1991**. Based on Current Population Survey; see text, section 1, and Appendix III. For composition of regions, see table 25. For definition of median, see Guide to Tabular Presentation]

CHARACTERISTIC	NUMBER (1,000)				MEDIAN FAMILY INCOME (dollars)			
	All families [1]	White	Black	His-panic [2]	All families [1]	White	Black	His-panic [2]
All families	**66,322**	**56,803**	**7,471**	**4,981**	**35,353**	**36,915**	**21,423**	**23,431**
Region:								
Northeast.	13,450	11,805	1,314	879	39,492	41,092	24,681	19,796
Midwest.	16,119	14,427	1,439	326	36,188	37,370	20,512	27,569
South	23,279	18,764	4,169	1,618	31,727	34,242	20,605	23,064
West	13,474	11,806	548	2,159	36,687	36,837	27,947	24,726
Type of family:								
Married-couple families.	52,147	47,014	3,569	3,454	39,895	40,331	33,784	27,996
Wife in paid labor force	30,298	27,008	2,349	1,751	46,777	47,247	40,038	34,778
Wife not in paid labor force . .	21,849	20,006	1,220	1,703	30,265	30,781	20,333	21,168
Male householder [3]	2,907	2,276	472	342	29,046	30,570	21,848	22,744
Female householder [3]	11,268	7,512	3,430	1,186	16,932	19,528	12,125	11,914
With related children [4]	34,503	28,117	5,069	3,497	34,230	36,501	19,359	22,003
Married couple	25,410	22,289	2,104	2,405	41,260	41,685	35,721	27,474
Male householder [3]	1,386	1,042	267	172	25,211	26,168	20,565	20,775
Female householder [3]	7,707	4,786	2,698	921	13,092	14,868	10,306	10,142
Number of earners:								
No earners.	9,519	7,882	1,407	694	15,047	17,369	6,305	7,858
One earner	18,215	15,047	2,591	1,571	25,878	27,670	16,308	16,795
Two earners.	29,536	26,003	2,660	1,948	42,146	43,036	34,050	30,550
Three earners.	6,598	5,770	600	533	53,721	54,632	43,813	39,738
Four or more earners.	2,453	2,100	213	235	67,700	67,753	59,983	52,776

[1] Includes other races not shown separately.   [2] Hispanic persons may be of any race.   [3] No spouse present.   [4] Children under 18 years old.

No. 707. Money Income of Families—Percent Distribution by Income Level, by Race and Hispanic Origin of Householder, and Selected Characteristics: 1990

[Families as of **March of following year.** See headnote, table 702. For definition of median, see Guide to Tabular Presentation. See *Historical Statistics, Colonial Times to 1970,* series G 1-8 for U.S. data on total, White, Black, and other races. For composition of regions, see table 25]

RACE OF HOUSEHOLDER, REGION, AND PRESENCE OF CHILDREN	Number of families (1,000)	PERCENT DISTRIBUTION OF FAMILIES, BY INCOME LEVEL								Median income (dol.)
		Under $5,000	$5,000 to $9,999	$10,000 to $14,999	$15,000 to $24,999	$25,000 to $34,999	$35,000 to $49,999	$50,000 to $74,999	$75,000 and over	
All families [1]	**66,322**	**3.6**	**5.8**	**7.5**	**16.4**	**16.2**	**20.1**	**18.2**	**12.3**	**35,353**
White, total	56,803	2.5	4.7	7.0	16.0	16.5	20.8	19.3	13.2	36,915
Northeast.	11,805	2.1	4.4	5.9	13.6	14.9	20.6	21.8	16.7	41,092
Midwest.	14,427	2.4	4.2	6.8	15.3	16.9	22.5	20.2	11.8	37,370
South	18,764	3.0	5.0	7.8	18.2	17.2	20.0	17.5	11.3	34,242
West	11,806	2.3	5.1	7.1	16.0	16.5	20.1	18.6	14.2	36,837
Black, total	7,471	11.5	14.1	11.3	19.5	14.0	15.0	9.8	4.8	21,423
Northeast.	1,314	10.4	14.8	8.6	16.7	14.8	14.8	13.0	6.7	24,681
Midwest.	1,439	14.1	16.2	9.4	17.3	12.8	14.7	9.6	6.0	20,512
South	4,169	11.6	13.5	12.7	21.4	14.3	15.0	8.2	3.3	20,605
West	548	6.0	12.4	12.0	16.9	13.3	15.8	15.3	8.2	27,947
Hispanic, [2] total	4,981	6.3	12.3	12.6	21.7	16.6	15.7	10.0	4.8	23,431
Northeast.	879	8.6	20.4	11.0	18.7	11.7	11.9	11.5	6.1	19,796
Midwest.	326	6.4	11.3	8.2	21.3	18.0	19.8	9.1	5.8	27,569
South	1,618	7.2	10.3	14.7	22.1	16.7	16.8	7.9	4.3	23,064
West	2,159	4.7	10.8	12.4	22.7	18.2	15.8	11.0	4.4	24,726
Presence of related children under 18 years old:										
All families	66,322	3.6	5.8	7.5	16.4	16.2	20.1	18.2	12.3	35,353
No children	31,819	1.9	4.2	7.6	17.4	16.4	19.8	18.5	14.1	36,539
One or more children	34,503	5.1	7.3	7.4	16.3	10.0	20.3	17.9	10.6	34,230
Married-couple families. . . .	52,147	1.3	3.3	6.0	15.0	16.4	22.0	21.2	14.8	39,895
No children	26,737	1.5	3.7	7.2	16.6	16.6	19.8	19.4	15.7	38,254
One or more children . . .	25,410	1.1	2.9	4.7	13.5	16.8	24.2	23.0	13.9	41,260
Female householder, no husband present	11,268	13.9	17.1	14.0	21.4	14.5	11.2	5.8	2.2	16,932
No children	3,561	4.1	8.2	10.2	23.4	18.6	18.0	12.7	4.7	27,020
One or more children . . .	7,707	18.4	21.2	15.7	20.5	12.6	8.0	2.6	1.1	13,092

[1] Includes other races not shown separately.   [2] Hispanic persons may be of any race.

Source of tables 707 and 708: U.S. Bureau of the Census, *Current Population Reports,* series P-60, No. 174; and unpublished data.

No. 708. Money Income of Families, by Type of Family and Income Level: 1990

[In thousands, except dollars. Families as of **March 1991**. Based on Current Population Survey; see headnote, table 702. For definition of median, see Guide to Tabular Presentation]

TYPE OF FAMILY	Number of families	NUMBER OF FAMILIES BY INCOME LEVEL								Median income (dol.)
		Under $9,999	$10,000-$14,999	$15,000-$19,999	$20,000-$24,999	$25,000-$34,999	$35,000-$49,999	$50,000-$74,999	$75,000 and over	
All families	**66,322**	**6,238**	**4,973**	**5,232**	**5,614**	**10,716**	**13,302**	**12,080**	**8,167**	**35,353**
Married-couple families...	52,147	2,395	3,122	3,644	4,203	8,547	11,459	11,042	7,733	39,895
Wife in paid labor force.	30,298	552	840	1,290	1,903	4,586	7,421	8,145	5,560	46,777
Wife not in paid labor force...........	21,849	1,844	2,281	2,354	2,299	3,961	4,039	2,897	2,174	30,265
Male householder [1].....	2,907	353	279	299	288	534	585	384	186	29,046
Female householder [1]...	11,268	3,489	1,572	1,288	1,123	1,635	1,258	653	246	16,932
With own children [2]..	34,503	4,294	2,551	2,537	2,760	5,513	7,003	6,179	3,666	34,230
Married-couple.......	25,410	1,008	1,193	1,533	1,887	4,264	6,154	5,846	3,527	41,260
Female householder [1]..	7,707	3,051	1,207	860	717	972	617	202	81	13,092

[1] No spouse present. [2] Children under 18 years old. Includes male householders not shown separately.

No. 709. Median Money Income of Families and Unrelated Individuals, in Current and Constant (1990) Dollars: 1970 to 1990

[Unrelated individuals are persons not living with any relatives. See text, sections 1 and 14. For definition of median, see Guide to Tabular Presentation. See also *Historical Statistics, Colonial Times to 1970*, series G 179-188]

ITEM	1970	1975	1980	1984 [1]	1985	1986	1987 [2]	1988	1989	1990
CURRENT DOLLARS Families: [3]										
Married-couple families	10,516	14,867	23,141	29,612	31,100	32,805	34,879	36,389	38,547	39,895
Wife in paid labor force	12,276	17,237	26,879	34,668	36,431	38,346	40,751	42,709	45,266	46,777
Wife not in paid labor force...	9,304	12,752	18,972	23,582	24,556	25,803	26,640	27,220	28,747	30,265
Male householder, no wife present	9,012	12,995	17,519	23,325	22,622	24,962	25,208	26,827	27,847	29,046
Female householder, no husband present...............	5,093	6,844	10,408	12,803	13,660	13,647	14,683	15,346	16,442	16,932
Unrelated individuals:										
Male	4,540	6,612	10,939	13,566	14,921	15,281	16,082	16,976	17,860	17,927
Female...............	2,483	3,978	6,668	9,501	9,865	10,142	11,029	11,881	12,390	12,450
CONSTANT (1990) DOLLARS Families: [3]										
Married-couple families	35,424	36,117	36,705	37,250	37,777	39,121	40,129	40,203	40,630	39,895
Wife in paid labor force	41,352	41,875	42,635	43,610	44,252	45,728	46,885	47,186	47,712	46,777
Wife not in paid labor force...	31,341	30,979	30,093	29,665	29,828	30,771	30,650	30,073	30,300	30,265
Male householder, no wife present	30,357	31,570	27,788	29,341	27,479	29,768	29,003	29,639	29,352	29,046
Female householder, no husband present...............	17,156	16,627	16,509	16,105	16,593	16,274	16,893	16,955	17,330	16,932
Unrelated individuals:										
Male	15,293	16,063	17,351	17,065	18,124	18,223	18,503	18,755	18,825	17,927
Female...............	8,364	9,664	10,577	11,952	11,983	12,095	12,689	13,126	13,059	12,450

[1] Beginning 1984, based on revised Hispanic population controls; data not directly comparable with prior years. [2] Beginning 1987, based on revised processing procedures; data not directly comparable with prior years. See text, section 14, and source. [3] Beginning 1980, based on householder concept. Restricted to primary families, see source.

No. 710. Median Money Income of Year-Round Full-Time Workers With Income, by Sex, Age, Race, and Hispanic Origin: 1980 to 1990

[Age as of **March of following year**. Refers to civilian workers. For definition of median, see Guide to Tabular Presentation]

ITEM	FEMALE					MALE				
	1980	1985 [1]	1988 [2]	1989	1990	1980	1985 [1]	1988 [2]	1989	1990
Total with income..	**$11,591**	**$16,252**	**$18,545**	**$19,643**	**$20,586**	**$19,173**	**$24,999**	**$27,342**	**$28,605**	**$29,172**
15 to 19 years old	6,779	8,372	[3]13,183	[3]13,653	[3]13,955	7,753	9,050	[3]14,863	[3]15,501	[3]15,580
20 to 24 years old	9,407	11,757	(NA)	(NA)	(NA)	12,109	13,827	(NA)	(NA)	(NA)
25 to 34 years old	12,190	16,740	18,486	19,706	20,178	17,724	22,321	24,284	24,991	25,502
35 to 44 years old	12,239	18,032	20,635	21,498	22,483	21,777	28,900	31,847	32,370	32,611
45 to 54 years old	12,116	17,009	20,174	20,905	21,937	22,323	29,880	32,701	35,356	35,731
55 to 64 years old	11,931	16,761	18,347	19,895	20,765	21,053	28,387	31,645	34,505	33,180
65 years old and over....	12,342	18,336	19,493	21,505	22,866	17,307	26,146	29,070	34,110	35,520
White..............	11,703	16,482	18,823	19,873	20,840	19,720	25,693	28,262	29,846	30,186
Black..............	10,915	14,590	16,867	17,908	18,518	13,875	17,971	20,716	20,706	21,540
Hispanic [4]	9,887	13,522	15,201	16,006	16,186	13,790	17,344	18,190	18,570	19,314

NA Not available. [1] Beginning 1985, based on revised Hispanic population controls; data not directly comparable with prior years. [2] Beginning 1988, based on revised processing procedures; data not directly comparable with prior years. See text, section 14, and source. [3] 15 to 24 years old. [4] Persons of Hispanic origin may be of any race.

Source of tables 708-710: U.S. Bureau of the Census, *Current Population Reports*, series P-60, No. 174, earlier issues; and unpublished data.

No. 711. Money Income of Persons—Percent Distribution, by Income Level and Median Income in Constant (1990) Dollars: 1970 to 1990

[As of **March of following year.** For 1970 and 1975, persons 14 years old and over; thereafter, 15 years old and over. Based on Current Population Survey; see headnote, table 702. For definition of median, see Guide to Tabular Presentation. See *Historical Statistics, Colonial Times to 1970*, series G 257-268. For composition of regions, see table 25]

SEX, YEAR, AGE, RACE, HISPANIC ORIGIN, AND REGION	All persons (mil.)	PERSONS WITH INCOME									
		Total (mil.)	Percent distribution by income level—								Median income (dol.)
			$1 to $2,499 or loss [1]	$2,500 to $4,999	$5,000 to $9,999	$10,000 to $14,999	$15,000 to $24,999	$25,000 to $49,999	$50,000 to $74,999	$75,000 and over	
MALE											
1970	70.6	65.0	8.5	6.1	11.0	10.0	20.5	34.7	6.4	2.8	22,468
1975	77.6	71.2	7.9	5.7	12.4	11.3	20.7	32.8	6.4	2.7	21,507
1980	82.9	78.7	7.8	6.1	13.0	11.6	21.8	31.3	5.7	2.8	19,875
1981	84.0	79.7	8.2	6.5	13.1	12.8	20.8	29.9	6.2	2.4	19,372
1982	85.0	79.7	8.7	6.5	13.5	12.9	21.0	28.7	6.0	2.8	18,894
1983 [2]	86.0	80.8	8.7	6.6	13.3	12.3	21.4	28.6	6.3	2.9	19,239
1984	87.3	82.2	8.1	6.4	13.3	12.1	20.4	29.5	6.9	3.2	19,624
1985	88.5	83.6	8.1	6.2	13.0	12.6	21.0	29.1	6.9	3.2	19,813
1986	89.4	84.5	7.8	5.7	12.9	12.2	20.4	29.9	7.2	3.7	20,409
1987 [3]	90.3	85.7	7.5	5.8	12.4	12.9	20.4	29.7	7.5	3.7	20,463
1988	91.0	86.6	7.1	5.7	12.6	12.1	21.0	30.3	7.2	4.0	20,890
1989	92.0	87.5	6.7	5.5	12.6	12.6	20.8	29.9	7.5	4.3	20,968
1990	**92.8**	**88.2**	**6.8**	**5.5**	**12.8**	**12.8**	**21.7**	**29.2**	**7.3**	**3.9**	**20,293**
15 to 24 years old . .	17.4	14.0	28.1	15.1	22.0	14.9	14.8	4.9	0.3	-	6,319
25 to 34 years old . .	21.3	20.9	3.1	3.7	10.0	13.8	28.6	34.4	4.7	1.7	21,393
35 to 44 years old . .	19.0	18.8	2.6	2.8	6.5	8.3	20.1	41.8	11.8	6.0	29,773
45 to 54 years old . .	12.4	12.2	3.0	2.4	6.3	8.5	18.4	39.3	13.9	8.1	31,007
55 to 64 years old . .	10.2	10.0	3.1	4.1	10.8	11.2	21.1	33.1	10.1	6.4	24,804
65 yr. old and over . .	12.5	12.5	1.9	5.8	24.7	20.9	24.2	16.0	3.9	2.6	14,183
White	80.0	76.5	6.2	4.9	12.1	12.5	21.8	30.4	7.8	4.3	21,170
Black	10.1	8.8	10.7	10.5	18.6	15.0	21.1	20.7	2.7	0.7	12,868
Hispanic [4]	7.5	6.8	7.4	8.1	20.0	19.2	23.2	18.3	2.7	1.1	13,470
Northeast	19.1	18.1	6.5	4.9	11.4	11.6	21.0	31.4	8.6	4.7	21,907
Midwest	22.3	21.4	7.1	5.5	12.4	11.5	22.3	30.8	7.0	3.2	20,673
South	31.6	29.9	7.0	6.4	14.0	14.2	22.3	26.5	6.3	3.3	18,429
West	19.8	18.9	6.2	4.7	12.7	13.0	20.9	29.7	8.0	4.9	20,989
FEMALE											
1970	77.6	51.6	21.4	16.6	20.4	15.3	17.7	8.0	0.4	0.2	7,535
1975	85.0	60.8	17.9	15.8	24.2	15.4	17.9	8.3	0.4	0.1	8,223
1980	91.1	80.8	21.6	14.9	22.5	14.3	17.6	8.3	0.6	0.2	7,804
1981	92.2	82.1	21.1	14.7	22.5	15.6	17.0	8.4	0.5	0.2	7,848
1982	93.1	82.5	21.0	14.6	22.5	15.0	16.9	9.1	0.6	0.3	7,973
1983 [2]	94.3	83.8	20.1	13.9	22.2	14.5	18.0	10.1	0.8	0.3	8,405
1984	95.3	85.6	19.2	13.5	22.5	14.3	18.0	11.2	1.0	0.4	8,640
1985	96.4	86.5	19.2	13.7	22.0	14.3	17.7	11.6	1.1	0.3	8,766
1986	97.3	87.8	18.5	13.1	22.0	14.3	18.0	12.5	1.1	0.5	9,075
1987 [3]	98.2	89.7	17.5	13.1	21.6	14.6	18.4	13.1	1.3	0.5	9,544
1988	99.0	90.6	16.8	13.0	21.5	14.3	18.8	13.6	1.4	0.5	9,815
1989	99.8	91.4	16.0	12.7	21.3	14.7	18.9	14.1	1.6	0.6	10,144
1990	**100.7**	**92.2**	**15.8**	**12.7**	**21.2**	**14.7**	**19.0**	**14.3**	**1.7**	**0.6**	**10,070**
15 to 24 years old . .	17.5	13.7	31.0	19.7	22.8	13.1	10.5	2.7	0.1	-	4,902
25 to 34 years old . .	21.6	20.0	15.7	8.8	16.5	15.3	25.0	17.2	1.2	0.4	12,589
35 to 44 years old . .	19.6	18.5	14.9	7.6	14.8	13.8	23.0	22.2	2.7	1.0	14,504
45 to 54 years old . .	13.3	12.3	14.7	7.9	15.3	14.2	21.7	22.2	3.0	1.0	14,230
55 to 64 years old . .	11.2	10.4	17.0	14.8	20.4	14.5	17.0	13.0	2.5	0.8	9,400
65 yr. old and over . .	17.5	17.3	5.0	19.4	37.0	16.7	13.8	6.8	0.9	0.5	8,044
White	85.0	73.6	16.0	12.0	20.8	14.8	19.3	14.6	1.8	0.6	10,317
Black	12.1	10.7	13.8	18.5	24.0	13.9	16.8	11.9	0.8	0.3	8,328
Hispanic [4]	7.6	5.9	19.1	15.8	25.4	15.3	15.1	8.4	0.7	0.2	7,532
Northeast	21.2	19.5	14.6	11.7	21.4	13.5	19.6	16.2	2.2	0.8	10,732
Midwest	24.2	22.9	15.8	12.8	21.0	15.5	19.7	13.5	1.3	0.4	10,119
South	34.7	31.3	16.8	14.4	20.8	14.9	18.7	12.6	1.3	0.5	9,417
West	20.6	18.6	15.5	10.9	21.9	14.7	18.0	16.0	2.1	0.8	10,467

- Represents or rounds to zero.   [1] Includes persons with income deficit.   [2] Beginning 1983, based on revised Hispanic population controls; data not directly comparable with prior years.   [3] Beginning 1987, based on revised processing procedures; data not directly comparable with prior years.   [4] Hispanic persons may be of any race.

Source: U.S. Bureau of the Census, *Current Population Reports*, series P-60, No. 174; and unpublished data.

No. 712. Median Income of Married-Couple Families, by Work Experience of Husbands and Wives and Race: 1990

[As of **March 1991**. Based on Current Population Survey; see text, sections 1 and 14 and Appendix III]

WORK EXPERIENCE OF HUSBAND	NUMBER (1,000)				MEDIAN INCOME (dollars)			
	Total	Wife worked		Wife did not work	Total	Wife worked		Wife did not work
		Total	Worked year-round, full-time			Total	Worked year-round, full-time	
All families [1]	52,147	33,290	17,437	18,857	39,895	46,006	51,479	28,972
Husband worked	42,241	30,994	16,324	11,247	44,346	47,334	52,642	35,522
Worked year-round, full-time	33,322	25,060	13,656	8,262	47,576	50,290	55,068	39,083
Husband did not work	9,907	2,296	1,113	7,610	22,323	27,770	32,640	20,807
White	47,014	29,816	15,276	17,198	40,331	46,411	52,004	29,523
Husband worked	38,044	27,828	14,303	10,216	44,804	47,687	53,215	36,130
Worked year-round, full-time	30,008	22,504	11,953	7,504	48,079	50,690	55,668	39,903
Husband did not work	8,970	1,989	973	6,982	23,153	28,666	33,285	21,599
Black	3,569	2,474	1,518	1,095	33,784	39,604	46,178	19,134
Husband worked	2,852	2,233	1,407	619	38,129	41,487	47,593	25,867
Worked year-round, full-time	2,225	1,794	1,175	431	40,699	43,982	49,265	30,065
Husband did not work	717	242	111	475	14,731	21,188	26,523	12,022
Hispanic [2]	3,454	1,929	986	1,524	34,266	34,124	40,581	20,083
Husband worked	2,961	1,786	910	1,174	30,326	35,124	41,667	22,281
Worked year-round, full-time	2,153	1,326	917	828	33,946	38,634	45,307	24,434
Husband did not work	493	143	75	350	15,709	22,623	27,969	14,172

[1] Includes other races not shown seperately. [2] Persons of Hispanic origin may be of any race.

No. 713. Mean Money Earnings of Persons, by Educational Attainment, Sex, and Age: 1990

[In dollars. For year-round full-time workers 25 years old and over. As of **March 1991**. See headnote, table 712]

AGE AND SEX	Total	Elementary, 8 years or less	HIGH SCHOOL			COLLEGE			
			Total	1-3 years	4 years	Total	1-3 years	4 years	5 or more years
Male, total	**34,886**	**19,188**	**27,131**	**22,564**	**28,043**	**43,217**	**34,188**	**44,554**	**55,831**
25 to 34 years old	27,743	15,887	23,355	19,453	24,038	33,003	28,298	35,534	39,833
35 to 44 years old	37,958	18,379	28,205	23,621	28,927	45,819	36,180	47,401	58,542
45 to 54 years old	40,231	19,686	31,235	24,133	32,862	50,545	39,953	50,718	62,902
55 to 64 years old	37,469	22,379	29,460	25,280	30,779	50,585	36,954	55,518	61,647
65 years old and over	33,145	17,028	24,003	19,530	25,516	44,424	34,323	43,092	52,149
Female, total	**22,768**	**13,322**	**18,469**	**15,381**	**18,954**	**27,493**	**22,654**	**28,911**	**35,827**
25 to 34 years old	21,337	11,832	16,673	13,385	17,076	25,194	20,872	27,210	32,563
35 to 44 years old	24,453	13,714	19,344	15,695	19,886	29,287	23,307	31,631	37,599
45 to 54 years old	23,429	13,490	19,500	16,651	19,986	29,334	24,608	29,242	38,307
55 to 64 years old	21,388	13,941	18,607	15,202	19,382	26,930	23,364	27,975	33,383
65 years old and over	19,194	(B)	18,281	(B)	18,285	23,277	(B)	(B)	(B)

B Base figure too small to meet statistical standards for reliability of derived figure.

No. 714. Per Capita Money Income in Current and Constant (1990) Dollars, by Race and Hispanic Origin: 1970 to 1990

[In dollars. See headnote, table 711]

YEAR	CURRENT DOLLARS				CONSTANT (1990) DOLLARS			
	All races	White	Black	Hispanic [1]	All races	White	Black	Hispanic [1]
1970	3,177	3,354	1,869	(NA)	10,702	11,298	6,296	(NA)
1975	4,818	5,072	2,972	2,847	11,705	12,322	7,220	6,916
1980	7,787	8,233	4,804	4,865	12,351	13,059	7,620	7,717
1981	8,476	8,979	5,129	5,349	12,187	12,910	7,375	7,691
1982	8,980	9,527	5,360	5,448	12,163	12,903	7,260	7,379
1983 [2]	9,548	10,125	5,755	5,852	12,529	13,287	7,552	7,679
1984	10,328	10,939	6,277	6,401	12,992	13,761	7,896	8,052
1985	11,013	11,671	6,840	6,613	13,377	14,177	8,308	8,033
1986	11,670	12,352	7,207	7,000	13,917	14,730	8,594	8,348
1987 [3]	12,391	13,143	7,645	7,653	14,256	15,121	8,796	8,805
1988	13,123	13,896	8,271	7,956	14,499	15,353	9,138	8,790
1989	14,056	14,896	8,747	8,390	14,815	15,701	9,220	8,843
1990	14,387	15,265	9,017	8,424	14,387	15,265	9,017	8,424

NA Not available. [1] Hispanic persons may be of any race. [2] Beginning 1983, based on revised Hispanic population controls; data not directly comparable with prior years. [3] Beginning 1987, based on revised processing procedures; data not directly comparable with prior years.
Source of tables 712-714: U.S. Bureau of the Census, *Current Population Reports*, series P-60, No. 174.

No. 715. Per Capita Money Income, 1969 to 1987, and Median Family Income, 1969 and 1979, by State

[**In dollars**. For definition of median, see Guide to Tabular Presentation. See also *Historical Statistics, Colonial Times to 1970*, series G 205-256 and Appendix III]

STATE	PER CAPITA INCOME			MEDIAN FAM-ILY INCOME		STATE	PER CAPITA INCOME			MEDIAN FAM-ILY INCOME	
	1969	1979	1987	1969	1979		1969	1979	1987	1969	1979
U.S.	**3,119**	**7,298**	**11,923**	**9,586**	**19,917**	Missouri	2,952	6,917	11,203	8,908	18,784
Alabama	2,317	5,894	9,615	7,263	16,347	Montana	2,696	6,589	9,322	8,509	18,413
Alaska	3,725	10,193	13,263	12,441	28,395	Nebraska	2,797	6,934	11,139	8,562	19,122
Arizona	2,937	7,042	11,521	9,185	19,017	Nevada	3,554	8,453	12,603	10,687	21,311
Arkansas	2,142	5,614	9,061	6,271	14,641	New Hampshire	2,985	6,966	13,529	9,682	19,723
California	3,614	8,294	13,197	10,729	21,537	New Jersey . . .	3,674	8,127	15,028	11,403	22,906
Colorado	3,106	7,998	12,271	9,552	21,279						
						New Mexico . . .	2,437	6,119	9,434	7,845	16,928
Connecticut . . .	3,885	8,511	16,094	11,808	23,149	New York	3,608	7,496	13,167	10,609	20,180
Delaware	3,265	7,449	12,785	10,209	20,817	North Carolina .	2,474	6,132	10,856	7,770	16,792
Dist. of Col. . . .	3,842	8,960	14,778	9,576	19,099	North Dakota . .	2,469	6,417	9,641	7,836	18,023
Florida	3,058	7,260	12,456	8,261	17,280	Ohio	3,199	7,284	11,323	10,309	20,909
Georgia	2,640	6,380	11,406	8,165	17,414	Oklahoma	2,694	6,854	9,927	7,720	17,688
Hawaii	3,373	7,740	12,290	11,552	22,750						
						Oregon	3,148	7,556	11,045	9,487	20,027
Idaho	2,644	6,248	9,159	8,380	17,492	Pennsylvania . .	3,066	7,075	11,544	9,554	19,995
Illinois	3,495	8,064	12,437	10,957	22,746	Rhode Island . .	3,121	6,897	12,351	9,733	19,448
Indiana	3,070	7,142	11,078	9,966	20,535	South Carolina .	2,303	5,884	9,967	7,620	16,978
Iowa	2,884	7,136	11,198	9,016	20,052	South Dakota . .	2,387	5,696	8,910	7,490	15,993
Kansas	2,929	7,350	11,520	8,690	19,707	Tennessee . . .	2,464	6,212	10,448	7,446	16,564
Kentucky	2,425	5,973	9,380	7,439	16,444	Texas	2,792	7,203	10,645	8,486	19,618
Louisiana	2,330	6,425	8,961	7,527	18,088						
						Utah	2,697	6,305	9,288	9,320	20,024
Maine	2,548	5,768	10,478	8,205	16,167	Vermont	2,772	6,177	11,234	8,928	17,205
Maryland	3,512	8,293	14,697	11,057	23,112	Virginia	2,996	7,475	13,658	9,044	20,018
Massachusetts .	3,408	7,458	14,389	10,833	21,166	Washington . . .	3,357	8,073	12,184	10,404	21,696
Michigan	3,357	7,688	11,973	11,029	22,107	West Virginia . .	2,333	6,142	9,807	7,414	17,308
Minnesota	3,038	7,451	12,281	9,928	21,185	Wisconsin	3,032	7,241	11,417	10,065	20,915
Mississippi	1,925	5,183	8,088	6,068	14,591	Wyoming	2,895	7,927	9,826	8,944	22,430

Source: U.S. Bureau of the Census, *1970 Census of Population*, vol. 1; *1980 Census of Population*, vol. 1, chapter C (PC 80-1C), and *Current Population Reports*, series P-26, No. 88.

No. 716. Per Capita Money Income for 50 Largest Cities: 1979 and 1987

CITIES RANKED BY POPULATION-SIZE, 1988	1979	1987	Percent change, 1979-1987	CITIES RANKED BY POPULATION-SIZE, 1988	1979	1987	Percent change, 1979-1987
New York, NY	7,271	12,926	77.8	Denver, CO	8,553	12,980	51.8
Los Angeles, CA	8,415	13,592	61.5	Nashville-Davidson, TN. . .	7,276	12,583	72.9
Chicago, IL.	6,933	10,806	55.9	Austin, TX	7,368	11,860	61.0
Houston, TX	8,826	12,007	36.0	Kansas City, MO	7,480	12,077	61.5
Philadelphia, PA	6,053	10,002	65.2	Oklahoma City, OK	7,999	11,547	44.4
San Diego, CA	8,016	12,978	61.9	Fort Worth, TX	7,336	11,082	51.1
Detroit, MI	6,215	9,662	55.5	Atlanta, GA.	6,539	11,689	78.8
Dallas, TX	8,607	13,489	56.7	Portland, OR.	8,104	11,830	46.0
San Antonio, TX	5,763	8,779	52.3	Long Beach, CA	8,342	12,947	55.2
Phoenix, AZ	7,552	12,375	63.9	St. Louis, MO	5,877	9,718	65.4
Honolulu, HI [1]	7,912	12,734	60.9	Tucson, AZ.	6,537	10,204	56.1
Baltimore, MD	5,877	9,989	70.0	Albuquerque, NM.	7,440	11,988	61.1
San Jose, CA	8,377	13,711	63.7	Pittsburgh, PA	6,845	10,988	60.5
San Francisco, CA.	9,265	15,137	63.4	Miami, FL.	6,084	9,830	61.6
Indianapolis, IN	7,585	12,111	59.7	Cincinnati, OH.	6,874	11,223	63.3
Memphis, TN	6,466	10,347	60.0	Tulsa, OK.	8,842	12,829	45.1
Jacksonville, FL.	6,767	11,514	70.1	Charlotte, NC	7,965	13,970	75.4
Washington, DC	8,959	14,778	65.0	Virgina Beach, VA	7,704	13,141	70.6
Milwaukee, WI.	7,029	10,593	50.7	Oakland, CA.	7,701	12,215	58.6
Boston, MA	6,555	12,984	98.1	Omaha, NE.	7,718	12,480	61.7
Columbus, OH.	6,783	10,811	59.4	Minneapolis, MN	7,940	13,092	64.9
New Orleans, LA	6,463	9,340	44.5	Toledo, OH.	7,050	10,872	54.2
Cleveland, OH.	5,770	8,690	50.6	Sacramento, CA	7,558	11,580	53.2
El Paso, TX	5,431	8,027	47.8	Newark, NJ.	4,525	7,622	68.4
Seattle, WA	9,282	14,438	55.5	Buffalo, NY.	5,929	9,364	57.8

[1] Data are for Honolulu County.

Source: U.S. Bureau of the Census, *1980 Census of Population*, vol. 1, chapter C (PC 80-1-C) and *Current Population Reports*, series P-26, No. 88.

No. 717. Persons Below Poverty Level and Below 125 Percent of Poverty Level: 1959 to 1990

[Persons as of **March of the following year**. For explanation of poverty level, see text, section 14]

YEAR	NUMBER BELOW POVERTY LEVEL (mil.)				PERCENT BELOW POVERTY LEVEL				BELOW 125 PERCENT OF POVERTY LEVEL		AVERAGE INCOME CUTOFFS FOR NON-FARM FAMILY OF 4 [3]	
	All races [1]	White	Black	His-panic [2]	All races [1]	White	Black	His-panic [2]	Number (mil.)	Per-cent of total popula-tion	At poverty level	At 125 percent of poverty level
1959	39.5	28.5	9.9	(NA)	22.4	18.1	55.1	(NA)	54.9	31.1	$2,973	$3,716
1960	39.9	28.3	(NA)	(NA)	22.2	17.8	(NA)	(NA)	54.6	30.4	3,022	3,778
1966	28.5	20.8	8.9	(NA)	14.7	12.2	41.8	(NA)	41.3	21.3	3,317	4,146
1969	24.1	16.7	7.1	(NA)	12.1	9.5	32.2	(NA)	34.7	17.4	3,743	4,679
1970	25.4	17.5	7.5	(NA)	12.6	9.9	33.5	(NA)	35.6	17.6	3,968	4,960
1975	25.9	17.8	7.5	3.0	12.3	9.7	31.3	26.9	37.2	17.6	5,500	6,875
1976	25.0	16.7	7.6	2.8	11.8	9.1	31.1	24.7	35.5	16.7	5,815	7,269
1977	24.7	16.4	7.7	2.7	11.6	8.9	31.3	22.4	35.7	16.7	6,191	7,739
1978 [4]	24.5	16.3	7.6	2.6	11.4	8.7	30.6	21.6	34.2	15.8	6,662	8,328
1979 [4]	26.1	17.2	8.1	2.9	11.7	9.0	31.0	21.8	36.6	16.4	7,412	9,265
1980	29.3	19.7	8.6	3.5	13.0	10.2	32.5	25.7	40.7	18.1	8,414	10,518
1981	31.8	21.6	9.2	3.7	14.0	11.1	34.2	26.5	43.7	19.3	9,287	11,609
1982 [5]	34.4	23.5	9.7	4.3	15.0	12.0	35.6	29.9	46.5	20.3	9,862	12,328
1983 [5]	35.3	24.0	9.9	4.6	15.2	12.1	35.7	28.0	47.2	20.3	10,178	12,723
1984	33.7	23.0	9.5	4.8	14.4	11.5	33.8	28.4	45.3	19.4	10,609	13,261
1985	33.1	22.9	8.9	5.2	14.0	11.4	31.3	29.0	44.2	18.7	10,989	13,736
1986 [6]	32.4	22.2	9.0	5.1	13.6	11.0	31.1	27.3	43.5	18.2	11,203	14,004
1987 [6]	32.2	21.2	9.5	5.4	13.4	10.4	32.4	28.0	43.0	17.9	11,611	14,514
1988	31.7	20.7	9.4	5.4	13.0	10.1	31.3	26.7	42.6	17.5	12,092	15,115
1989	31.5	20.8	9.3	5.4	12.8	10.0	30.7	26.2	42.7	17.3	12,674	15,843
1990	33.6	22.3	9.8	6.0	13.5	10.7	31.9	28.1	44.8	18.0	13,359	16,699

NA Not available. [1] Includes other races not shown separately. [2] Hispanic persons may be of any race. [3] Beginning 1981, income cutoffs for nonfarm families are applied to all families, both farm and nonfarm. [4] Population controls based on 1980 census; see text, sections 1 and 14. [5] Beginning 1983, based on revised Hispanic population controls; data not directly comparable with prior years. [6] Beginning 1987, based on revised processing procedures; data not directly comparable with prior years.

Source: U.S. Bureau of the Census, *Current Population Reports*, series P-60, No. 175, and earlier reports.

No. 718. Children Below The Poverty Level, by Race And Hispanic Origin: 1970 to 1990

[Persons as of **March of the following year**. Covers only related children in families under 18 years old. Based on Current Population Survey; see headnote, table 702. For explanation of poverty, see text, section 14]

YEAR AND REGION	NUMBER BELOW POVERTY LEVEL (1,000)				PERCENT BELOW POVERTY LEVEL			
	All races [1]	White	Black	Hispanic [2]	All races [1]	White	Black	Hispanic [2]
1970	10,235	6,138	3,922	(NA)	14.9	10.5	41.5	(NA)
1971	10,344	6,341	3,836	(NA)	15.1	10.9	40.7	(NA)
1972	10,082	5,784	4,025	(NA)	14.9	10.1	42.7	(NA)
1973	9,453	5,462	3,822	1,364	14.2	9.7	40.6	27.8
1974	9,967	6,079	3,713	1,414	15.1	11.0	39.6	28.6
1975	10,882	6,748	3,884	1,619	16.8	12.5	41.4	33.1
1976	10,081	6,034	3,758	1,424	15.8	11.3	40.4	30.1
1977	10,028	5,943	3,850	1,402	16.0	11.4	41.6	28.0
1978	9,722	5,674	3,781	1,354	15.7	11.0	41.2	27.2
1979	9,993	5,909	3,745	1,505	16.0	11.4	40.8	27.7
1980	11,114	6,817	3,906	1,718	17.9	13.4	42.1	33.0
1981	12,068	7,429	4,170	1,874	19.5	14.7	44.9	35.4
1982 [3]	13,139	8,282	4,388	2,117	21.3	16.5	47.3	38.9
1983 [3]	13,427	8,534	4,273	2,251	21.8	17.0	46.2	37.7
1984	12,929	8,086	4,320	2,317	21.0	16.1	46.2	38.7
1985	12,483	7,838	4,057	2,512	20.1	15.6	43.1	39.6
1986 [4]	12,257	7,714	4,039	2,413	19.8	15.3	42.7	37.1
1987 [4]	12,275	7,398	4,234	2,606	19.7	14.7	44.4	38.9
1988	11,935	7,095	4,148	2,576	19.0	14.0	42.8	37.3
1989	12,001	7,165	4,257	2,496	19.0	14.1	43.2	35.5
1990	12,715	7,696	4,412	2,750	19.9	15.1	44.2	39.7

NA Not available. [1] Includes persons of other races, not shown separately. [2] Hispanic persons may be of any race. [3] Beginning 1983, based on revised Hispanic population controls; data not directly comparable with prior years. [4] Beginning 1987, based on revised processing procedures; data not directly comparable with prior years.

Source: U.S. Bureau of the Census, *Current Population Reports*, series P-60, No. 175, and earlier reports.

No. 719. Distribution of All Children and of Poor Children, by Family Type and Race: 1990

[Based on published and unpublished tabulations from the 1991 March Supplement to the Current Population Survey. Numbers and percentages may not add due to rounding]

AGE, RACE, AND FAMILY TYPE	ALL CHILDREN		CHILDREN BELOW POVERTY LINE		Pov-erty rate	AGE, RACE, AND FAMILY TYPE	ALL CHILDREN		CHILDREN BELOW POVERTY LINE		Pov-erty rate
	Num-ber (mil.)	Per-cent	Num-ber (mil.)	Per-cent			Num-ber (mil.)	Per-cent	Num-ber (mil.)	Per-cent	
ALL FAMILIES						Married-couple	13.1	84.7	1.0	51.8	8.6
Children under 18 years:						Single-parent [1]	2.4	15.3	1.1	48.2	44.5
All family types	63.9	100.0	12.7	100.0	19.9	Mother-only	2.0	12.8	1.0	45.2	49.9
Married-couple	48.0	75.1	4.9	38.5	10.2	Black:					
Single-parent [1]	15.9	24.9	7.8	61.5	49.1	All family types	3.5	100.0	1.7	100.0	50.0
Mother-only	11.9	18.6	6.5	51.1	54.6	Married-couple	1.3	36.1	0.3	14.6	20.2
Children under 6 years:						Single-parent [1]	2.2	63.9	1.5	85.4	66.7
All family types	22.6	100.0	5.2	100.0	23.0	Mother-only	2.1	60.2	1.4	83.2	69.1
Married-couple	17.1	75.6	2.1	39.8	12.1	Hispanic: [2]					
Single-parent [1]	5.5	24.4	3.1	60.2	56.7	All family types	2.7	100.0	1.1	100.0	40.2
Mother-only	4.9	21.6	3.0	57.3	61.0	Married-couple	2.0	72.5	0.6	53.5	29.6
CHILDREN UNDER 6 YEARS OLD						Single-parent [1]	0.7	27.5	0.5	46.6	68.0
						Mother-only	0.7	24.2	0.5	43.4	72.0
White:											
All family types	15.5	100.0	2.7	100.0	14.1						

[1] Includes father-only, relative-only, and nonrelative-only families, not shown separately.   [2] Hispanic persons may be of any race.

Source: National Center for Children in Poverty, Columbia University, New York, New York, *Five Million Children: Data Sourcebook*.

No. 720. Persons Below Poverty Level, by Race, Hispanic Origin, Age, and Region: 1990

[Persons as of **March 1991**. Based on Current Population Survey; see headnote, table 702. For explanation of poverty level, see text, section 14. For composition of regions, see table 25]

AGE AND REGION	NUMBER BELOW POVERTY LEVEL (1,000)				PERCENT BELOW POVERTY LEVEL			
	All races [1]	White	Black	Hispanic [2]	All races [1]	White	Black	Hispanic [2]
Total	33,585	22,326	9,837	6,006	13.5	10.7	31.9	28.1
Under 16 years old.	12,342	7,605	4,166	2,632	21.1	16.3	45.6	39.2
16 to 21 years old	3,351	2,162	1,020	669	16.2	13.0	32.9	29.7
22 to 44 years old	10,170	7,045	2,688	1,922	11.0	9.1	24.0	23.0
45 to 54 years old	2,002	1,358	569	311	7.8	6.2	21.1	17.9
55 to 59 years old	963	681	246	122	9.0	7.4	22.0	18.5
60 to 64 years old	1,098	768	288	105	10.3	8.2	27.9	18.1
65 years old and over . . .	3,658	2,707	860	245	12.2	10.1	33.8	22.5
Northeast	5,794	4,006	1,604	1,287	11.4	9.2	28.9	36.4
Midwest	7,458	5,027	2,156	318	12.4	9.5	36.0	22.7
South.	13,456	7,708	5,538	1,777	15.8	11.6	32.6	26.9
West	6,877	5,584	538	2,624	13.0	12.2	23.7	26.6

[1] Includes other races not shown separately.   [2] Hispanic persons may be of any race.
Source: U.S. Bureau of the Census, *Current Population Reports*, series P-60, No. 175.

No. 721. Persons 65 Years Old and Over Below Poverty Level, by Selected Characteristics: 1970 to 1990

[Persons as of **March of following year**. See headnote, table 720]

CHARACTERISTIC	NUMBER BELOW POVERTY LEVEL (1,000)					PERCENT BELOW POVERTY LEVEL				
	1970	1979 [1]	1985 [2]	1989 [3]	1990	1970	1979 [1]	1985 [2]	1989 [3]	1990
Persons, 65 yr. and over [4]	4,793	3,682	3,456	3,363	3,658	24.6	15.2	12.6	11.4	12.2
White.	4,011	2,911	2,698	2,539	2,707	22.0	13.3	11.0	9.6	10.1
Black.	735	740	717	763	860	47.7	36.3	31.5	30.7	33.8
Hispanic [5].	(NA)	154	219	211	245	(NA)	26.8	23.9	20.6	22.5
In families.	2,013	1,380	1,173	1,204	1,172	14.8	8.4	6.4	6.1	5.8
Unrelated individuals.	2,779	2,299	2,281	2,160	2,479	47.2	29.4	25.6	22.0	24.7
Persons, 60 yr. and over	5,977	4,753	4,677	4,380	4,756	21.3	13.9	12.3	10.9	11.7

NA Not available.   [1] Population controls based on 1980 census; see text, section 14.   [2] Beginning 1985, based on revised Hispanic population controls; data not directly comparable with prior years.   [3] Beginning 1989, based on revised processing procedures; data not directly comparable with prior years.   [4] Beginning 1979, includes members of unrelated subfamilies not shown separately. For earlier years, unrelated subfamily members are included in the "In families" category.   [5] Hispanic persons may be of any race.
Source: U.S. Bureau of the Census, *Current Population Reports*, series P-60, No. 175, and earlier issues.

No. 722. Persons Below Poverty Level, by Race of Householder and Family Status: 1979 to 1990

[Persons as of March of following year. For explanation of poverty level, see text, section 14]

RACE OF HOUSEHOLDER AND FAMILY STATUS	NUMBER BELOW POVERTY LEVEL (mil.)					PERCENT BELOW POVERTY LEVEL				
	1979 [1]	1985	1988 [2]	1989	1990	1979 [1]	1985	1988 [2]	1989	1990
All persons [3]	**26.1**	**33.1**	**31.7**	**31.5**	**33.6**	**11.7**	**14.0**	**13.0**	**12.8**	**13.5**
In families	20.0	25.7	24.0	24.1	25.2	10.2	12.6	11.6	11.5	12.0
Householder	5.5	7.2	6.9	6.8	7.1	9.2	11.4	10.4	10.3	10.7
Related children under 18 years	10.0	12.5	11.9	12.0	12.7	16.0	20.1	19.0	19.0	19.9
Other family members	4.5	6.0	5.2	5.3	5.4	6.1	7.7	6.6	6.6	6.7
Unrelated individuals	5.7	6.7	7.1	6.8	7.4	21.9	21.5	20.6	19.2	20.7
White	**17.2**	**22.9**	**20.7**	**20.8**	**22.3**	**9.0**	**11.4**	**10.1**	**10.0**	**10.7**
In families	12.5	17.1	15.0	15.2	15.9	7.4	9.9	8.6	8.6	9.0
Householder	3.6	5.0	4.5	4.4	4.6	6.9	9.1	7.9	7.8	8.1
Related children under 18 years	5.9	7.8	7.1	7.2	7.7	11.4	15.6	14.0	14.1	15.1
Other family members	3.0	4.3	3.4	3.6	3.6	4.7	6.4	5.0	5.3	5.2
Unrelated individuals	4.5	5.3	5.3	5.1	5.7	19.7	19.6	18.1	16.9	18.6
Black	**8.1**	**8.9**	**9.4**	**9.3**	**9.8**	**31.0**	**31.3**	**31.3**	**30.7**	**31.9**
In families	6.8	7.5	7.7	7.7	8.2	30.0	30.5	30.0	29.7	31.0
Householder	1.7	2.0	2.1	2.1	2.2	27.8	28.7	28.2	27.8	29.3
Related children under 18 years	3.7	4.1	4.1	4.3	4.4	40.8	43.1	42.8	43.2	44.2
Other family members	1.3	1.5	1.4	1.4	1.6	18.2	17.7	16.8	15.9	17.6
Unrelated individuals	1.2	1.3	1.5	1.5	1.5	37.3	34.7	36.8	35.2	35.1
In families with female householder, no husband present [3]	**13.5**	**16.4**	**16.2**	**15.9**	**17.2**	**32.0**	**33.5**	**32.1**	**30.9**	**32.4**
In families	9.4	11.6	12.0	11.7	12.6	34.9	37.6	37.2	35.9	37.2
Householder	2.6	3.5	3.6	3.5	3.8	30.4	34.0	33.4	32.2	33.4
Related children under 18 years	5.6	6.7	7.0	6.8	7.4	48.6	53.6	52.9	51.1	53.4
Other family members	1.1	1.4	1.4	1.4	1.4	16.9	17.3	16.9	16.3	17.6
Unrelated individuals	3.8	4.2	4.2	4.2	4.6	26.0	24.8	23.1	22.2	24.0
In all other families [3]	**12.6**	**16.7**	**14.9**	**14.9**	**15.0**	**7.0**	**8.9**	**7.8**	**7.7**	**7.8**
In families	10.6	14.1	12.1	12.4	12.7	6.3	8.2	6.9	7.0	7.1
Householder	2.8	3.7	3.2	3.3	3.3	5.5	7.0	5.9	5.9	6.0
Related children under 18 years	4.4	5.8	5.0	5.2	5.4	8.5	11.7	10.0	10.4	10.7
Other family members	3.4	4.6	3.9	3.9	4.0	5.1	6.6	5.4	5.5	5.5
Unrelated individuals	2.0	2.5	2.8	2.8	2.9	16.9	17.4	17.7	17.7	16.9

[1] Population controls based on 1980 census; see text section 14.   [2] Beginning 1986, based on revised processing procedures; data not directly comparable with prior years.   [3] Includes races and members of unrelated subfamilies not shown separately.

Source: U.S. Bureau of the Census, *Current Population Reports*, series P-60, No. 175; and unpublished data.

No. 723. Percent of Persons Below Poverty Level, by State: 1984 to 1990

[Based on the Current Population Survey. The CPS is designed to collect reliable data on income primarily at the national level and secondarily at the regional level. When the income data are tabulated by State, the estimates are considered less reliable and, therefore, particular caution should be used when trying to interpret the results; for additional detail, see source]

STATE	1984	1985	1986	1987 [1]	1988	1989	1990	STATE	1984	1985	1986	1987 [1]	1988	1989	1990
U.S.	14.4	14.0	13.6	13.4	13.0	12.8	13.5	MO	14.5	13.7	14.4	14.0	12.7	12.6	13.4
AL	19.1	20.6	23.8	21.3	19.3	18.9	19.2	MT	13.8	16.0	16.5	18.0	14.6	15.6	16.3
AK	9.6	8.7	11.4	12.0	11.0	10.5	11.4	NE	13.3	14.8	13.6	11.9	10.3	12.8	10.3
AZ	18.2	10.7	14.3	12.8	14.1	14.1	13.7	NV	10.5	14.4	8.1	10.4	8.6	10.8	9.8
AR	23.9	22.9	21.3	21.8	21.6	18.3	19.6	NH	7.1	6.0	3.7	4.8	6.7	7.7	6.3
CA	13.2	13.6	12.7	12.3	13.2	12.9	13.9	NJ	10.1	8.3	8.9	8.3	6.2	8.2	9.2
CO	8.9	10.2	13.5	12.5	12.5	12.1	13.7	NM	19.5	18.5	21.3	19.4	23.0	19.5	20.9
CT	6.9	7.6	6.0	6.6	4.0	2.9	6.0	NY	16.0	15.8	13.2	14.3	13.4	12.6	14.3
DE	10.3	11.4	12.4	6.6	8.6	10.0	6.9	NC	14.6	14.2	14.3	13.8	12.6	12.2	13.0
DC	21.1	20.4	12.8	14.9	15.2	18.0	21.1	ND	15.4	15.9	13.5	11.4	11.6	12.2	13.7
FL	15.1	13.4	11.4	12.4	13.6	12.5	14.4	OH	13.5	12.8	12.8	12.7	12.4	10.6	11.5
GA	16.9	17.7	14.6	14.6	14.0	15.0	15.8	OK	13.3	16.0	14.7	17.0	17.3	14.7	15.6
HI	9.3	10.7	10.7	8.8	11.1	11.3	11.0	OR	12.8	11.9	12.3	14.2	10.4	11.2	9.2
ID	17.3	16.0	18.5	15.1	12.5	12.4	14.9	PA	15.6	10.5	10.1	10.6	10.3	10.4	11.0
IL	15.0	15.6	13.3	14.4	12.7	12.7	13.7	RI	12.8	9.0	9.1	8.1	9.8	6.7	7.5
IN	12.9	12.0	12.7	11.1	10.1	13.7	13.0	SC	17.2	15.2	17.3	15.6	15.5	17.0	16.2
IA	14.6	17.9	12.9	14.5	9.4	10.3	10.4	SD	14.5	17.3	17.0	15.2	14.2	13.2	13.3
KS	10.7	13.8	11.1	9.2	8.1	10.8	10.3	TN	17.4	18.1	18.3	16.9	18.0	18.4	16.9
KY	19.1	19.4	17.7	17.3	17.6	16.1	17.3	TX	15.7	15.9	17.3	17.6	18.0	17.1	15.9
LA	20.6	18.1	22.0	25.1	22.8	23.3	23.6	UT	11.1	10.9	12.6	10.2	9.8	8.2	8.2
ME	13.0	11.9	10.2	11.7	13.2	10.4	13.1	VT	12.6	9.2	11.0	9.3	8.1	8.0	10.9
MD	8.7	8.7	9.2	9.2	9.8	9.0	9.9	VA	10.0	10.0	9.7	9.9	10.8	10.9	11.1
MA	8.9	9.2	9.2	8.2	8.5	8.8	10.7	WA	11.3	12.0	12.9	10.0	8.7	9.6	8.9
MI	16.7	14.5	13.9	12.2	12.1	13.2	14.3	WV	20.4	22.3	22.4	21.6	17.9	15.7	18.1
MN	9.1	12.6	12.5	11.3	11.6	11.2	12.0	WI	15.5	11.6	10.7	9.0	7.8	8.4	9.3
MS	25.1	25.1	26.6	25.0	27.2	22.0	25.7	WY	10.9	12.0	14.6	10.8	9.6	10.9	11.0

[1] Beginning 1987, based on revised processing procedures; data not directly comparable with prior years. See text, section 14, and source.

Source: U.S. Bureau of the Census, *Current Population Reports*, series P-60, No. 175.

No. 724. Families Below Poverty Level and Below 125 Percent of Poverty Level: 1959 to 1990

[Families as of **March of the following year.** For explanation of poverty level, see text, section 14]

YEAR	NUMBER BELOW POVERTY LEVEL (1,000)				PERCENT BELOW POVERTY LEVEL				BELOW 125 PERCENT OF POVERTY LEVEL	
	All races [1]	White	Black	His-panic [2]	All races [1]	White	Black	His-panic [2]	Number (1,000)	Percent
1959	8,320	6,185	1,860	(NA)	18.5	15.2	48.1	(NA)	11,790	26.2
1960	8,243	6,115	(NA)	(NA)	18.1	14.9	(NA)	(NA)	11,525	25.4
1970	5,260	3,708	1,481	(NA)	10.1	8.0	29.5	(NA)	7,516	14.4
1972	5,075	3,441	1,529	(NA)	9.3	7.1	29.0	(NA)	7,347	13.5
1973	4,828	3,219	1,527	468	8.8	6.6	28.1	19.8	7,044	12.8
1974	4,922	3,352	1,479	526	8.8	6.8	26.9	21.2	7,195	12.9
1975	5,450	3,838	1,513	627	9.7	7.7	27.1	25.1	7,974	14.2
1976	5,311	3,560	1,617	598	9.4	7.1	27.9	23.1	7,647	13.5
1977	5,311	3,540	1,637	591	9.3	7.0	28.2	21.4	7,713	13.5
1978 [4]	5,280	3,523	1,622	559	9.1	6.9	27.5	20.4	7,417	12.8
1979 [3]	5,461	3,581	1,722	614	9.2	6.9	27.8	20.3	7,784	13.1
1980	6,217	4,195	1,826	751	10.3	8.0	28.9	23.2	8,764	14.5
1981	6,851	4,670	1,972	792	11.2	8.8	30.8	24.0	9,568	15.7
1982	7,512	5,118	2,158	916	12.2	9.6	33.0	27.2	10,279	16.7
1983 [4]	7,647	5,220	2,161	981	12.3	9.7	32.3	25.9	(NA)	(NA)
1984	7,277	4,925	2,094	991	11.6	9.1	30.9	25.2	9,901	15.8
1985	7,223	4,983	1,983	1,074	11.4	9.1	28.7	25.5	9,753	15.3
1986	7,023	4,811	1,987	1,085	10.9	8.6	28.0	24.7	9,476	14.7
1987 [5]	7,005	4,567	2,117	1,168	10.7	8.1	29.4	25.5	9,338	14.3
1988	6,874	4,471	2,089	1,141	10.4	7.9	28.2	23.7	9,284	14.1
1989	6,784	4,409	2,077	1,133	10.3	7.8	27.8	23.4	9,267	14.0
1990	7,098	4,622	2,193	1,244	10.7	8.1	29.3	25.0	9,564	14.4

NA Not available.   [1] Includes other races not shown separately.   [2] Hispanic persons may be of any race.   [3] Population controls based on 1980 census; see text, section 14.   [4] Beginning 1983, data based on revised Hispanic population controls; data not directly comparable with prior years.   [5] Beginning 1987, based on revised processing procedures; data not comparable with prior years. See text, section 14, and source.

Source: U.S. Bureau of the Census, *Current Population Reports*, series P-60, No. 175.

No. 725. Families Below Poverty Level—Selected Characteristics, by Race and Hispanic Origin: 1990

[Families as of **March 1991.** For explanation of poverty, see text, section 14. For composition of regions, see table 25]

CHARACTERISTIC	NUMBER BELOW POVERTY LEVEL (1,000)				PERCENT BELOW POVERTY LEVEL			
	All races [1]	White	Black	His-panic [2]	All races [1]	White	Black	His-panic [2]
Total	7,098	4,622	2,193	1,244	10.7	8.1	29.3	25.0
Age of householder:								
15 to 24 years old................	955	617	311	182	35.0	28.5	65.3	43.0
25 to 34 years old................	2,377	1,568	734	441	16.3	12.9	37.8	29.5
35 to 44 years old................	1,648	1,063	482	322	9.6	7.4	23.8	24.4
45 to 54 years old................	806	508	263	161	6.9	5.1	21.0	20.0
55 to 64 years old................	627	422	180	67	6.7	5.1	21.0	12.7
65 years old and over	686	443	224	69	6.3	4.5	24.2	17.0
Northeast......................	1,234	839	360	297	9.2	7.1	27.4	33.8
Midwest.......................	1,583	1,050	479	73	9.8	7.3	33.3	22.5
South.........................	2,942	1,661	1,231	385	12.6	8.9	29.5	23.8
West	1,339	1,072	123	488	9.9	9.1	22.4	22.6
Size of family:								
Two persons	2,234	1,587	566	235	8.1	6.5	22.7	19.1
Three persons	1,698	1,053	587	285	11.1	8.1	30.3	24.0
Four persons	1,507	954	488	295	10.7	8.0	30.5	25.8
Five persons	876	570	284	214	14.7	11.6	36.0	27.5
Six persons	415	275	108	117	20.2	17.1	33.0	34.2
Seven persons or more	368	183	160	98	28.6	21.3	50.0	32.9
Mean size	3.55	3.45	3.71	4.09	(X)	(X)	(X)	(X)
Mean number of children per family with children .	2.24	2.17	2.34	2.53	(X)	(X)	(X)	(X)
Education of householder: [3]								
Elementary: Less than 8 years.............	910	595	268	344	26.3	22.6	38.7	31.6
8 years	479	365	107	104	17.0	14.6	39.5	34.5
High school: 1 to 3 years	1,460	889	540	270	20.7	15.9	41.5	35.9
4 years	2,188	1,411	703	190	9.3	6.9	26.2	15.0
College: 1 year or more	996	675	238	93	3.8	2.9	11.9	9.3
Work experience of householder in 1989: [4]								
Total [5]	7,098	4,622	2,193	1,244	10.7	8.1	29.3	25.0
Worked	3,533	2,481	931	626	7.0	5.6	18.1	16.7
50 to 52 weeks	1,442	1,029	360	291	3.6	2.9	9.6	10.7
49 weeks or less	2,091	1,452	571	335	19.5	16.1	40.8	32.5
Did not work..................	3,527	2,114	1,252	614	23.7	17.2	56.7	51.8

X Not applicable.   [1] Includes other races not shown separately.   [2] Hispanic persons may be of any race.   [3] Householder 25 years old and over.   [4] Restricted to families with civilian workers.   [5] Includes Armed Forces not shown separately.
Source: U.S. Bureau of the Census, *Current Population Reports*, series P-60, No. 175.

No. 726. Persons Below Poverty Level and Poverty Rate, by Definition of Income: 1990

[Persons as of **March 1991**. Based on Current Population Survey; see text, sections 1 and 14. For explanation of definitions of income, see text, section 14 and source]

Defi-nition num-ber	DEFINITION OF INCOME	NUMBER BELOW POVERTY LEVEL (1,000)				PERCENT BELOW POVERTY LEVEL			
		All races [1]	White	Black	His-panic [2]	All races [1]	White	Black	His-panic [2]
	All persons.	248,644	208,611	30,806	21,405	(X)	(X)	(X)	(X)
	INCOME BEFORE TAXES								
1	Money income excluding capital gains (current) measure [3]	33,585	22,326	9,837	6,006	13.5	10.7	31.9	28.1
2	Definition 1 less government money transfers .	50,944	36,827	12,235	7,221	20.5	17.7	39.7	33.7
3	Definition 2 plus capital gains	50,754	36,659	12,223	7,148	20.4	17.6	39.7	33.4
4	Definition 3 plus health insurance supplements to wage or salary income [4]	49,423	35,717	11,889	6,956	19.9	17.1	38.6	32.5
	INCOME AFTER TAXES								
5	Definition 4 less Social Security payroll taxes . .	51,875	37,589	12,372	7,429	20.9	18.0	40.2	34.7
6	Definition 5 less Federal income taxes (excluding EITC) [5]	52,367	37,962	12,470	7,550	21.1	18.2	40.5	35.3
7	Definition 6 plus EITC [5]	51,285	37,170	12,235	7,323	20.6	17.8	39.7	34.2
8	Definition 7 less State income taxes	51,758	37,576	12,293	7,378	20.8	18.0	39.9	34.5
9	Definition 8 plus nonmeans-tested government cash transfers [6]	36,526	24,330	10,588	6,516	14.7	11.7	34.4	30.4
11	Definition 9 plus nonmeans-tested government noncash transfers [8]	35,450	23,542	10,349	6,344	14.3	11.3	33.6	29.6
12	Definition 11 plus means-tested government cash transfers [7]	32,884	22,050	9,504	5,963	13.2	10.6	30.8	27.9
14	Definition 12 plus means-tested government noncash transfers [9]	27,279	18,722	7,478	4,856	11.0	9.0	24.3	22.7
15	Definition 13 plus net imputed return on equity in own home [10]	24,406	16,532	6,865	4,580	9.8	7.9	22.3	21.4

X Not applicable. [1] Includes other races not shown separately. [2] Hispanic persons may be of any race. [3] Official definition of income based on money income before taxes and includes government cash transfers. [4] Employer contributions to the health insurance plans of employees. [5] Earned Income Tax Credit. [6] Includes Social Security and Railroad Retirement, veterans payments, and unemployment and workers' compensation. [7] Includes Medicare and subsidies from regular price school lunches. [8] Includes AFDC or other assistance or welfare payments and Supplemental Security Income. Households must meet certain eligibility requirements in order to qualify for these benefits. (See section 12.) [9] Includes Medicaid, food stamps, subsidies from free or reduced-price school lunches, and rent subsidies. [10] Estimated amount of income a household would receive if it chose to shift amount held as home equity into an interest bearing account.

Source: U.S. Bureau of the Census, *Current Population Reports*, series P-60, No. 176-RD.

No. 727. Families Below Poverty Level—Alternative Inflation Adjustment: 1970 to 1990

[**In thousands, except percent.** Families as of **March of following year.** Based on Current Population Survey. Families include unrelated individuals and are therefore not directly comparable to Census Bureau definitions; see text, section 1. Adjustments for family size and inflation were made to family income and poverty thresholds; see text, section 14]

ITEM	1970	1975	1980	1984	1985	1986	1987	1988	1989	1990
NUMBER OF FAMILIES BELOW POVERTY LEVEL										
All families [1]	9,775	9,630	10,869	12,091	12,203	12,269	12,468	12,515	12,141	13,158
Families with children [1]	3,330	3,903	4,432	5,230	5,177	5,199	5,231	5,179	5,054	5,441
Married couples	1,558	1,629	1,555	1,877	1,803	1,644	1,638	1,515	1,498	1,610
Single mothers	1,509	2,050	2,498	2,918	2,957	3,121	3,142	3,195	3,072	3,302
Nonelderly units:										
Childless families	662	611	587	907	898	826	795	796	767	755
Unrelated individuals	2,146	2,677	3,307	3,890	3,990	4,016	4,100	4,214	4,077	4,532
Elderly units:										
Childless families	965	504	574	408	420	413	466	492	455	474
Unrelated individuals	2,672	1,936	1,969	1,656	1,718	1,815	1,876	1,834	1,787	1,956
PERCENT BELOW POVERTY LEVEL										
All families [1]	15	13	12	13	13	13	13	12	12	13
Families with children [1]	11	12	13	16	15	15	15	15	15	16
Married couples	6	7	6	8	7	7	7	6	6	7
Single mothers	45	44	42	44	44	46	45	45	43	44
Nonelderly units:										
Childless families	4	4	3	4	4	4	4	4	4	4
Unrelated individuals	23	20	17	18	18	18	17	17	16	18
Elderly units:										
Childless families	14	6	6	4	4	4	4	5	4	4
Unrelated individuals	46	28	25	19	19	20	20	19	18	19

[1] Includes other types of families not shown separately.

Source: Congressional Budget Office, *Trends in Family Income: 1970-1986*, February 1988, and unpublished data.

No. 728. Adjusted Poverty Thresholds, Weighted Average by Family Size: 1980 to 1990

[Adjustments for changes in family size and for inflation using the CPI-U-X1 have been made; see text, section 14]

SIZE OF UNIT	1980	1982	1983	1984	1985	1986	1987	1988	1989	1990
One person (unrelated individual). .	3,843	4,458	4,604	4,801	4,974	5,068	5,308	5,534	5,807	6,121
Under 65 years	3,935	4,566	4,713	4,912	5,088	5,186	5,428	5,654	5,937	6,257
65 years and over	3,623	4,208	4,345	4,529	4,690	4,780	5,004	5,212	5,472	5,767
Two persons	4,920	5,714	5,899	6,151	6,366	6,493	6,795	7,077	7,431	7,829
Householder under 65 years . . .	5,079	5,901	6,093	6,352	6,578	6,706	7,019	7,310	7,676	8,091
Householder 65 years and over .	4,571	5,309	5,480	5,715	5,915	6,031	6,313	6,575	6,902	7,273
Three persons	6,022	6,998	7,222	7,529	7,799	7,948	8,319	8,667	9,095	9,587
Four persons	7,719	8,972	9,260	9,651	9,997	10,191	10,666	11,108	11,662	12,293
Five persons	9,142	10,629	10,963	11,431	11,832	12,061	12,619	13,141	13,792	14,530
Six persons	10,338	12,015	12,401	12,924	13,369	13,633	14,247	14,834	15,569	16,414
Seven persons	11,706	13,679	14,103	14,642	15,152	15,509	16,212	16,763	17,631	18,624
Eight persons.	13,025	15,210	15,622	16,339	16,840	17,094	17,926	18,628	19,624	20,778
Nine or more persons	15,499	17,920	18,479	19,328	20,089	20,465	21,224	22,169	23,444	24,703

Source: Congressional Budget Office, *Trends in Family Income: 1970 to 1986*, February 1988 and Congressional Budget Office tabulations.

No. 729. Persons Below Poverty Level—Alternative Inflation Adjustment: 1974 to 1990

[Based on Current Population Survey. Annual adjustment for cost-of-living changes are based on the CPI-U-X1; see text, section 14]

YEAR	NUMBER BELOW POVERTY LEVEL (1,000)				PERCENT BELOW POVERTY LEVEL			
	All races [1]	White	Black	Hispanic [2]	All races [1]	White	Black	Hispanic [2]
1974	22,076	14,870	6,773	2,448	10.5	8.2	28.6	21.9
1975	24,232	16,547	7,170	2,787	11.5	9.0	29.8	25.1
1976	23,347	15,513	7,202	2,570	11.0	8.4	29.5	22.8
1977	22,933	15,190	7,230	2,480	10.7	8.2	29.3	20.6
1978	22,472	14,829	7,085	2,416	10.4	8.0	28.4	20.0
1979	23,504	15,382	7,388	2,614	10.5	8.0	28.5	19.5
1980	25,869	17,283	7,671	3,134	11.5	9.0	29.0	23.0
1981	27,731	18,456	8,311	3,302	12.2	9.5	31.0	23.6
1982	30,288	20,385	8,824	3,842	13.2	10.4	32.4	26.7
1983	31,649	21,180	9,130	4,215	13.7	10.7	33.0	25.5
1984	29,971	20,043	8,765	4,367	12.8	10.1	31.2	25.8
1985	29,558	20,157	8,284	4,712	12.5	10.0	29.1	26.1
1986	29,101	19,629	8,391	4,570	12.2	9.7	29.1	24.4
1987	28,890	18,777	8,744	4,899	12.0	9.2	29.8	25.3
1988	28,544	18,326	8,707	4,914	11.7	8.9	29.2	24.5
1989	27,967	18,152	8,504	4,827	11.4	8.8	28.0	23.3
1990	30,097	19,677	9,145	5,401	12.1	9.4	29.7	25.2

[1] Includes races not shown separately.   [2] Hispanic persons may be of any race.

Source: U.S. Bureau of the Census, *Current Population Reports*, series P-60, No. 176-RD.

No. 730. Weighted Average Poverty Thresholds Based on the CPI-U-X1, by Size: 1980 to 1990

SIZE OF UNIT	1980	1983	1984	1985	1986	1987	1988	1989	1990
One person (unrelated individual). . . .	3,851	4,657	4,856	5,032	5,127	5,316	5,543	5,807	6,121
Under 65 years	3,942	4,766	4,969	5,146	5,246	5,437	5,663	5,936	6,257
65 years and over	3,629	4,394	4,581	4,744	4,835	5,012	5,221	5,472	5,767
Two persons	3,729	5,965	6,222	6,439	6,568	6,806	7,089	7,431	7,829
Householder under 65 years	5,088	6,162	6,425	6,653	6,783	7,031	7,322	7,676	8,091
Householder 65 years and over . . .	4,579	5,542	5,780	5,983	6,100	6,323	6,586	6,902	7,273
Three persons	6,033	7,304	7,616	7,888	8,039	8,333	8,681	9,095	9,587
Four persons	7,732	9,365	9,761	10,111	10,308	10,683	11,126	11,662	12,292
Five persons	9,159	11,086	11,562	11,968	12,200	12,640	13,162	13,792	14,530
Six persons	10,356	12,541	13,072	13,522	13,789	14,270	14,859	15,569	16,414
Seven persons	(NA)	14,262	14,810	15,325	13,687	16,239	16,790	17,631	18,624
Eight persons.	(NA)	15,798	16,526	17,033	17,290	17,956	18,659	19,624	20,778
Nine or more persons	(NA)	18,687	19,550	20,319	20,700	21,259	22,205	23,444	24,703

NA Not available.

Source: U.S. Bureau of the Census, *Current Population Reports*, series P-60, No. 176-RD; and unpublished data.

No. 731. Money Income of Households—Percent Distribution by Quintile and Index of Income Concentration, by Definition of Income: 1990

[Based on 94,312,000 households as of **March 1991**. Based on Current Population Survey; see text, sections 1 and 14. For explanation of money income definitions, see text, section 14. For definition of median, see Guide to Tabular Presentation]

Defi-nition num-ber	DEFINITION OF INCOME	Total income (bil. dol.)	SHARE OF AGGREGATE INCOME BY QUINTILE					Index of income con-centra-tion [1]	Median income (dol.)
			Lowest quintile	Second quintile	Third quintile	Fourth quintile	Highest quintile		
	INCOME BEFORE TAXES								
1	Money income excluding capital gains (current) measure [2]	3,528	3.9	9.6	16.0	24.1	46.4	0.426	29,943
2	Definition 1 less government money transfers	3,248	1.2	8.3	15.7	25.0	49.7	0.480	27,263
3	Definition 2 plus capital gains	3,358	1.2	8.1	15.4	24.5	50.9	0.491	27,437
4	Definition 3 plus health insurance supplements to wage or salary income [3]	3,493	1.1	7.9	15.5	24.7	50.7	0.490	28,779
	INCOME AFTER TAXES								
5	Definition 4 less Social Security payroll taxes	3,302	1.1	7.9	15.4	24.5	51.1	0.492	26,963
6	Definition 5 less Federal income taxes (excluding the EITC) [4]	2,880	1.3	8.5	16.1	25.2	48.8	0.471	24,673
7	Definition 6 plus EITC [4]	2,886	1.3	8.6	16.1	25.2	48.7	0.469	24,713
8	Definition 7 less State income taxes	2,762	1.4	8.9	16.4	25.2	48.1	0.463	23,947
9	Definition 8 plus nonmeans-tested government cash transfers [5]	3,011	3.7	10.4	16.6	24.2	45.1	0.412	26,379
11	Definition 9 plus nonmeans-tested government noncash transfers [6]	3,085	3.9	10.8	16.7	24.2	44.3	0.402	27,328
12	Definition 11 plus means-tested government cash transfers [7]	3,116	4.6	10.9	16.6	24.0	43.9	0.394	27,442
14	Definition 12 plus means-tested government noncash transfers [8]	3,153	5.1	11.1	16.5	23.8	43.5	0.384	27,720
15	Definition 14 plus net inputed return on equity in own home [9]	3,374	5.2	11.1	16.6	23.6	43.5	0.383	29,615

[1] A statistical measure of income equality ranging from 0 to 1. A measure of 1 indicates perfect inequality (i.e. one person having all the wealth and the rest having none.) A measure of 0 indicates perfect equality (i.e. all persons having equal shares of wealth.)   [2] Official definition of income based on money income before taxes and includes government cash transfers.   [3] Employer contributions to the health insurance plans of employees.   [4] Earned Income Tax Credit   [5] Includes Social Security and Railroad Retirement, Veterans payments, and unemployment and workers' compensation.   [6] Includes Medicare and subsidies from regular price school lunches.   [7] Includes AFDC or other assistance or welfare payments and Supplemental Security Income. Households must meet certain eligibility requirements in order to qualify for these benefits (see Section 12.)   [8] Includes Medicaid, food stamps, subsidies from free or reduced price school lunches, and rent subsidies.   [9] Estimated amount of income a household would receive if it chose to shift amount held as home equity into an interest bearing account.

Source: U.S. Bureau of the Census, *Current Population Reports*, series P-60, No. 176-RD.

No. 732. Family Net Worth—Mean and Median of Net Worth, by Selected Characteristics: 1983 and 1989

[**Mean and median value in thousands of constant 1989 dollars.** Constant dollar figures are based on consumer price index data published by U.S. Bureau of Labor Statistics; see table 738, section 15. See headnote, table 733]

CHARACTERISTIC	1983			1989		
	Percent of families	Net worth		Percent of families	Net worth	
		Mean	Median		Mean	Median
All families	100	**149.1**	**42.7**	100	**183.7**	**47.2**
White	82	173.0	54.3	87	203.8	58.5
Nonwhite and Hispanic	18	37.6	6.9	13	45.9	4.0
Under 35 years old	31	40.9	8.5	26	46.9	6.8
35 to 44 years old	19	110.5	49.8	23	148.3	52.8
45 to 54 years old	15	215.9	69.4	14	286.4	86.7
55 to 64 years old	15	242.2	84.4	15	292.5	91.3
65 to 74 years old	12	272.6	76.3	13	278.3	77.6
75 years old and over	7	166.8	49.8	9	194.5	66.1
Under 55 years old:						
Unmarried, no children	11	48.9	6.0	11	47.5	8.4
Married, no children	6	80.1	20.1	5	147.9	27.3
Unmarried, children	13	57.8	10.8	13	54.2	5.7
Married, children	35	140.6	51.3	34	196.9	62.0
55 years and over:						
In labor force	14	363.1	108.0	12	438.3	104.5
Retired	18	153.6	63.9	18	211.6	94.1
Managerial and professional specialities	24	328.5	95.8	25	382.0	104.5
Technical, sales, and administrative support	12	105.1	39.1	12	139.7	32.6
Service occupations	7	33.6	12.1	7	46.1	8.4
Precision production, craft, and repair	12	70.4	40.0	12	91.5	46.0
Operators, fabricators, and laborers	12	49.3	28.6	9	67.3	18.8
Farming, forestry, and fishing	2	343.9	185.0	2	322.3	107.3
Not working	31	110.7	30.0	33	138.9	44.0
Income (**1989** dollars):						
Less than $10,000	19	30.0	3.8	20	30.1	2.3
$10,000 to $19,999	23	53.0	19.3	20	63.1	27.1
$20,000 to $29,999	19	69.5	36.9	17	89.6	37.0
$30,000 to $49,999	23	117.6	67.7	23	150.2	69.2
$50,000 and over	17	550.5	176.1	20	586.7	185.6

Source: Board of Governors of the Federal Reserve System, *Federal Reserve Bulletin*, January 1992.

No. 733. Family Net Worth—Percent of Families Owning Selected Nonfinancial Assets, by Selected Characteristics: 1983 and 1989

[Families include one-person units; for definition of family, see text, section 1. Based on Survey of Consumer Finance; see Appendix III. For data on financial assets, see table 768, section 16]

CHARACTERISTIC	Total	Vehicles	Principal residence	Investment real estate	Business	Other assets
1983						
All families	90.3	84.4	64.4	20.9	14.2	7.4
White	94.3	88.7	68.0	23.1	16.1	8.5
NonWhite and Hispanic	71.3	64.4	42.2	10.9	5.4	2.5
Under 35 years old	87.2	83.3	38.7	10.4	10.3	9.1
35 to 44 years old	94.0	91.2	68.4	22.9	18.3	10.3
45 to 54 years old	92.7	90.3	78.0	24.9	18.2	6.4
55 to 64 years old	93.1	87.7	76.8	32.6	18.1	5.9
65 to 74 years old	91.8	80.2	78.9	27.2	12.3	5.6
75 years old and over	79.6	57.8	69.5	16.9	6.4	1.4
Under 55 years old:						
Unmarried, no children	79.1	71.9	23.4	10.0	9.1	13.9
Married, no children	97.0	96.4	51.8	14.6	14.3	13.0
Unmarried, children	78.3	73.1	42.7	12.0	6.4	6.2
Married, children	97.8	96.2	73.5	22.5	19.3	7.6
55 years and over:						
In labor force	95.1	89.5	78.1	36.3	24.1	7.3
Out of labor force, retired	86.2	74.4	74.8	22.1	6.1	3.4
Income (**1989** dollars):						
Less than $10,000	67.4	50.5	40.1	6.9	4.5	3.3
$10,000 to $19,999	89.1	83.2	52.6	14.1	6.9	5.5
$20,000 to $29,999	96.1	93.3	60.3	17.9	12.0	7.2
$30,000 to $49,999	98.6	97.0	77.2	25.8	18.7	8.0
$50,000 and over	99.4	96.4	88.9	42.7	31.5	14.3
1989						
All families	90.2	84.0	64.7	20.4	11.5	22.1
White	93.2	87.9	67.9	21.9	12.6	23.3
NonWhite and Hispanic	70.0	56.8	42.8	10.5	4.4	13.2
Under 35 years old	84.4	80.7	36.8	8.1	8.4	20.5
35 to 44 years old	92.8	89.5	65.9	20.9	17.0	24.9
45 to 54 years old	93.3	90.9	76.6	28.5	16.2	25.6
55 to 64 years old	92.1	86.9	82.2	31.3	11.3	23.9
65 to 74 years old	93.8	81.9	80.2	25.6	7.9	20.4
75 years old and over	87.3	66.9	72.8	16.9	4.7	13.3
Under 55 years old:						
Unmarried, no children	82.1	75.5	23.7	10.9	10.5	28.6
Married, no children	97.2	95.4	56.9	19.8	13.0	26.9
Unmarried, children	71.6	64.7	35.2	9.2	5.0	22.2
Married, children	97.7	96.6	74.9	22.3	17.5	21.6
55 years and over:						
In labor force	94.8	91.1	82.0	34.3	17.6	28.7
Out of labor force, retired	93.5	82.6	82.2	25.0	4.7	17.4
Income (**1989** dollars):						
Less than $10,000	66.9	51.6	36.2	5.9	2.3	12.1
$10,000 to $19,999	90.5	82.1	57.0	14.4	8.0	18.5
$20,000 to $29,999	96.7	94.4	63.5	15.0	10.1	23.8
$30,000 to $49,999	98.0	95.5	76.2	27.1	12.0	25.4
$50,000 and over	99.4	96.8	90.0	38.7	25.4	30.7

Source: Board of Governors of the Federal Reserve System, *Federal Reserve Bulletin*, January 1992.

No. 734. Family Net Worth—Composition of Assets and Debts of All Families: 1983 and 1989

In percent. See headnote, table 733]

ASSETS	1983	1989	DEBTS	1983	1989
Total	100.0	100.0	Total	100.0	100.0
Financial	25.6	27.7	Home mortgages	58.1	53.1
Nonfinancial	74.4	72.3	Investment real estate	20.5	25.0
Vehicles	3.6	3.0	Home equity lines of credit	0.5	2.6
Principal residence	33.4	32.2	Other lines of credit	2.8	1.0
Real estate and land investment	16.0	15.1	Credit cards	1.8	2.2
Business investment	20.4	17.8	Car loans	6.1	8.0
Other	1.0	3.3	Other	10.2	8.1

Source: Board of Governors of the Federal Reserve System, *Federal Reserve Bulletin*, January 1992.

No. 735. Gross and Net Stock of Fixed Reproducible Tangible Wealth in Current and Constant (1987) Dollars: 1970 to 1990

[In billions of dollars. As of December 31]

ITEM	1970	1980	1981	1982	1983	1984	1985	1986	1987	1988	1989	1990
CURRENT DOLLARS												
Gross stock, total. . .	4,428	14,306	15,670	16,527	17,277	18,259	19,330	20,503	21,774	22,966	24,285	25,588
Private	2,689	9,364	10,387	11,005	11,477	12,083	12,747	13,536	14,388	15,078	15,944	16,821
Nonresidential equipment	680	2,389	2,723	2,939	3,067	3,214	3,374	3,599	3,775	4,010	4,202	4,447
Nonresidential structures	790	2,683	3,032	3,247	3,376	3,573	3,783	3,951	4,156	4,478	4,732	4,986
Residential.	1,219	4,292	4,632	4,819	5,034	5,296	5,590	5,986	6,457	6,590	7,010	7,388
Government	1,060	2,979	3,141	3,237	3,368	3,568	3,772	3,916	4,084	4,306	4,518	4,720
Equipment	274	488	543	583	621	657	695	732	764	814	874	946
Structures	786	2,491	2,599	2,654	2,748	2,912	3,077	3,184	3,319	3,492	3,644	3,774
Federal	424	885	968	1,018	1,067	1,119	1,176	1,227	1,269	1,325	1,397	1,471
Military	276	493	536	566	601	638	678	715	738	776	818	871
State and local	636	2,094	2,173	2,219	2,302	2,449	2,596	2,690	2,814	2,981	3,121	3,249
Consumer durable goods. .	680	1,963	2,142	2,285	2,433	2,608	2,811	3,051	3,303	3,582	3,824	4,048
Net stock, total.	2,708	8,619	9,374	9,792	10,172	10,734	11,367	12,063	12,803	13,458	14,196	14,891
Private	1,674	5,814	6,413	6,737	6,987	7,348	7,752	8,224	8,729	9,108	9,600	10,077
Government	662	1,791	1,875	1,921	1,991	2,105	2,225	2,311	2,414	2,542	2,665	2,780
Consumer durable goods. .	372	1,014	1,086	1,134	1,194	1,282	1,391	1,528	1,660	1,808	1,931	2,034
CONSTANT (1987) DOLLARS												
Gross stock, total. . .	12,476	17,469	17,963	18,370	18,845	19,441	20,091	20,753	21,400	22,062	22,701	23,314
Private	8,131	11,585	11,936	12,217	12,523	12,909	13,322	13,728	14,112	14,504	14,871	15,215
Nonresidential equipment	1,839	3,009	3,126	3,206	3,285	3,397	3,518	3,633	3,737	3,855	3,966	4,069
Nonresidential structures	2,411	3,255	3,384	3,506	3,606	3,730	3,870	3,983	4,088	4,191	4,290	4,390
Residential.	3,881	5,321	5,427	5,505	5,632	5,783	5,934	6,112	6,287	6,458	6,614	6,755
Government	3,001	3,544	3,603	3,648	3,705	3,770	3,849	3,934	4,026	4,115	4,203	4,309
Equipment	662	625	630	634	647	670	698	730	768	802	836	876
Structures	2,340	2,918	2,973	3,014	3,058	3,100	3,152	3,204	3,259	3,313	3,367	3,433
Federal	1,142	1,122	1,138	1,142	1,156	1,177	1,204	1,233	1,266	1,293	1,319	1,351
Military	723	641	643	644	652	668	691	716	743	767	785	810
State and local	1,860	2,422	2,465	2,506	2,549	2,593	2,645	2,701	2,760	2,822	2,884	2,958
Consumer durable goods. .	1,344	2,340	2,424	2,505	2,617	2,762	2,920	3,092	3,262	3,444	3,628	3,791
Net stock, total.	7,691	10,524	10,755	10,902	11,112	11,441	11,824	12,214	12,577	12,942	13,278	13,574
Private	5,074	7,198	7,384	7,499	7,643	7,866	8,112	8,346	8,558	8,774	8,965	9,128
Government	1,884	2,123	2,148	2,167	2,191	2,223	2,269	2,321	2,380	2,430	2,481	2,539
Consumer durable goods. .	733	1,203	1,223	1,236	1,278	1,352	1,442	1,547	1,639	1,738	1,833	1,906

Source: U.S. Bureau of Economic Analysis, *Survey of Current Business*, January 1992.

No. 736. Top Wealthholders With Gross Assets of $500,000 or More, by Size of Net Worth and Sex: 1986

[All figures are estimates based on estate tax return samples. Net worth equals assets minus debts and mortgages]

ITEM	Unit	Total	SIZE OF NET WORTH ($1,000)						
			Under $250 [1]	$250 to $499	$500 to $999	$1,000 to $2,499	$2,500 to $4,999	$5,000 to $9,999	$10,000 or more
Top wealthholders, number . .	1,000 . .	3,329.4	291.2	548.9	1,548.3	710.0	150.3	55.5	25.0
Total assets	Mil. dol .	4,321,202	118,635	306,901	1,182,818	1,148,848	574,279	412,160	577,561
Net worth	Mil. dol .	3,766,706	6,460	219,171	1,066,541	1,050,716	513,217	373,847	536,756
MALE									
Top wealthholders, number . .	1,000 . .	1,957.4	248.6	389.1	789.0	389.2	93.0	32.2	16.4
Total assets	Mil. dol .	2,557,364	103,475	211,403	618,115	642,995	356,532	242,260	382,584
Net worth	Mil. dol .	2,162,692	777	152,548	543,976	579,562	318,340	216,925	350,564
FEMALE									
Top wealthholders, number . .	1,000 . .	1,372.0	42.7	159.8	759.3	320.7	57.3	23.3	8.7
Total assets	Mil. dol .	1,763,838	15,159	95,499	564,703	505,853	217,748	169,900	194,976
Net worth	Mil. dol .	1,604,014	5,683	66,623	522,565	471,153	194,876	156,921	186,192

[1] Includes those wealthholders with negative net worth.

Source: U.S. Internal Revenue Service, *Statistics of Income Bulletin*, spring 1990.

Prices

This section presents indexes of producer and consumer prices, actual prices for selected commodities and energy prices. The primary sources of these data are monthly publications of the Department of Labor, Bureau of Labor Statistics (BLS), which include *Monthly Labor Review, Consumer Price Index, Detailed Report;* and *Producer Price Indexes.* The Bureau of Economic Analysis of the Department of Commerce is the source for gross national product implicit price deflators; see table 750.

Producer price index (PPI).—This index, dating from 1890, is the oldest continuous statistical series published by BLS. It is designed to measure average changes in prices received by producers of all commodities, at all stages of processing, produced in the United States.

PPI—Stage of Processing: 1960–91

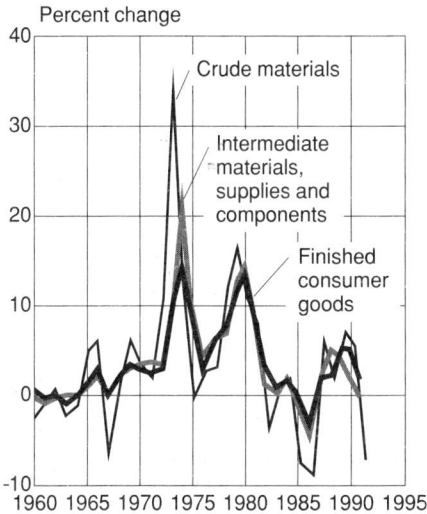

Source: Chart prepared by U.S. Bureau of the Census. For data, see table 747.

The index has undergone several revisions (see *Monthly Labor Review,* February 1962, April 1978, and August 1988). It is now based on approximately 3,100 commodity price series. Indexes for the net output of manufacturing and mining industries have been added in recent years. Prices used in constructing

In Brief

Consumer price changes: 1990-91:

*All items index up 4.2 percent
Medical care index up 8.7 percent
Fuel oil index down -6.3 percent*

the index are collected from sellers, and generally, apply to the first significant large-volume commercial transaction for each commodity—i.e., the manufacturer's or other producer's selling price or the selling price on an organized exchange or at a central market.

The weights used in the index represent the total net selling value of commodities produced or processed in this country. Values are f.o.b. (free-on-board) production point and are exclusive of excise taxes. Effective with the release of data for January 1988, many important producer price indexes were changed to a new reference base year, 1982=100, from 1967=100. The reference year of the PPI shipment weights have been taken primarily from the 1987 Census of Manufactures.

Consumer price indexes (CPI).—The CPI is a measure of the average change in prices over time in a fixed "market basket" of goods and services purchased either by urban wage earners and clerical workers or by all urban consumers.

In 1919, BLS began to publish complete indexes at semiannual intervals, using a weighting structure based on data collected in the expenditure survey of wage-earner and clerical-worker families in 1917-19 (BLS Bulletin 357, 1924). The first major revision of the CPI occurred in 1940, with subsequent revisions in 1953, 1964, 1978, and 1987.

Beginning with the release of data for January 1988 in February 1988, most Consumer Price Indexes shifted to a new reference base year. All indexes previously expressed on a base of 1967=100, or any other base through December 1981, have been rebased to 1982-84=100. Selection of the 1982-84 period was made to coincide with the updated expenditure weights, which are based upon data tabulated from the Consumer Expenditure Surveys for 1982, 1983, and 1984.

BLS publishes CPI's for two population groups: (1) a CPI for All Urban Consumers (CPI-U) which covers approximately 80 percent of the total population; and (2) a CPI for Urban Wage Earners and Clerical Workers (CPI-W) which covers 32 percent of the total population. The CPI-U includes, in addition to wage earners and clerical workers, groups which historically have been excluded from CPI coverage, such as professional, managerial, and technical workers; the self-employed; short-term workers; the unemployed; and retirees and others not in the labor force.

CPI—Selected Items: 1960–91

Percent change

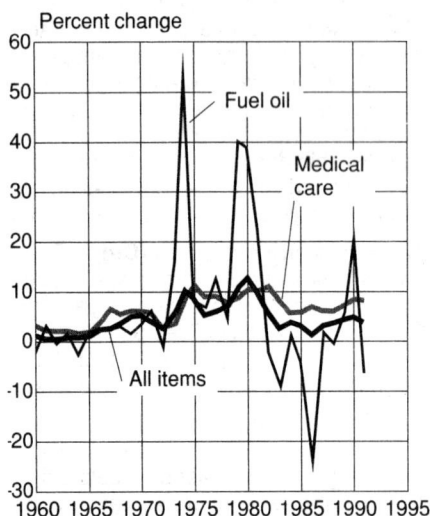

Source: Chart prepared by U.S. Bureau of the Census. For data, see table 739.

The current CPI is based on prices of food, clothing, shelter, fuels, transportation fares, charges for doctors' and dentists' services, drugs, etc., purchased for day-to-day living. Prices are collected in 85 areas across the country from over 57,000 housing units and 19,000 establishments. Area selection was based on the 1980 census. All taxes directly associated with the purchase and use of items are included in the index. Prices of food, fuels, and a few other items are

obtained every month in all 85 locations. Prices of most other commodities and services are collected monthly in the five largest geographic areas and every other month in other areas.

In calculating the index, each item is assigned a weight to account for its relative importance in consumers' budgets. Price changes for the various items in each location are then averaged. Local data are then combined to obtain a U.S. city average. Separate indexes are also published for regions, area size-classes, cross-classifications of regions and size-classes, and for 29 local areas, usually consisting of the Metropolitan Statistical Area (MSA); see Appendix II. Area definitions are those established by the Office of Management and Budget in 1983. Definitions do not include revisions made since 1983. Area indexes do not measure differences in the level of prices among cities; they only measure the average change in prices for each area since the base period. For further detail regarding the CPI, see the BLS *Handbook of Methods,* Bulletin 2285, Chapter 19; the Consumer Price Index, and Report 736, the CPI: 1987 Revision.   In January 1983, the method of measuring homeownership costs in the CPI-U was changed to a rental equivalence approach. This treatment calculates homeowner costs of shelter based on the implicit rent owners would pay to rent the homes they own. The rental equivalence approach was introduced into the CPI-W in 1985.

Other price indexes.—The *fixed-weighted price index* is a weighted average of the detailed price indexes used in the deflation of goods and services that make up the Gross domestic product (GDP). These price indexes are combined using weights that reflect the composition of GDP in 1987. Because the same weights are used for each period, changes in this index measure changes in prices over any period.

The *implicit price deflator* is a by-product of the deflation of GDP. It is derived as the ratio of current- to constant-dollar GDP (multiplied by 100). It is a weighted average of the detailed price indexes used in the deflation of GNP, but they are combined using weights that reflect the composition of GNP in each period.

Thus, changes in the implicit price deflator reflect not only changes in prices but also changes in the composition of GNP. All of the above GNP measures are published by the Bureau of Economic Analysis of the Department of Commerce.

Selected Fixed-Weighted Price Indexes: 1960–91

Percent change

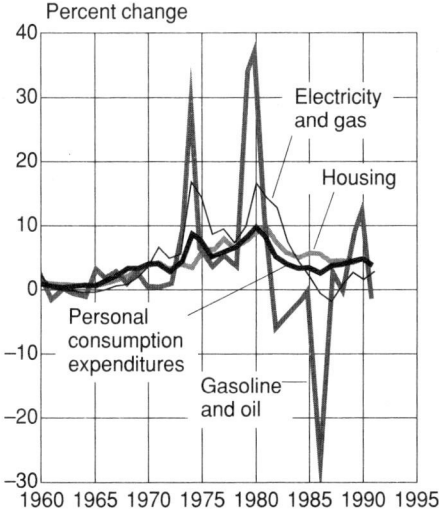

Source: Chart prepared by U.S. Bureau of the Census. For data, see table 751.

Measures of inflation.—Inflation is defined as a time of generally rising prices for goods and factors of production. The U.S. Bureau of Labor Statistics samples prices of items in a representative market basket and publishes the results as the CPI. The media invariably announce the inflation rate as the percent change in the CPI from month to month. A much more meaningful indicator of inflation is the percent change from the same month of the prior year.

The Producer Price Index (PPI) measures prices at the wholesale level only. The PPI shows the same general pattern of inflation as does the CPI, but is more volatile. The PPI can be roughly viewed as a leading indicator. It often tends to foreshadow trends that later occur in the CPI and the GNP implicit price deflator.

Other measures of inflation include the index of industrial materials prices; the Dow Jones Commodity Spot Price Index; Futures Price Index; the Employment Cost Index, the Hourly Compensation Index, or the Unit Labor Cost Index as a measure of the change in cost of the labor factor of production; and changes in long-term interest rates that are often used to measure changes in the cost of the capital factor of production.

Statistical reliability.—For a discussion of statistical collection and estimation, sampling procedures, and measures of statistical reliability pertaining to the producer price index and the CPI, see Appendix III.

Historical statistics.—Tabular headnotes provide cross-references, where applicable, to *Historical Statistics of the United States, Colonial Times to 1970.* See Appendix IV.

No. 737. Purchasing Power of the Dollar: 1950 to 1991

[Indexes: PPI, 1982=$1.00; CPI, 1982–84=$1.00. Producer prices prior to 1961, and consumer prices prior to 1964, exclude Alaska and Hawaii. Producer prices based on finished goods index. Obtained by dividing the average price index for the 1982=100, PPI; 1982–84=100, CPI base periods (100.0) by the price index for a given period and expressing the result in dollars and cents. Annual figures are based on average of monthly data]

YEAR	ANNUAL AVERAGE AS MEASURED BY—		YEAR	ANNUAL AVERAGE AS MEASURED BY—		YEAR	ANNUAL AVERAGE AS MEASURED BY—	
	Producer prices	Consumer prices		Producer prices	Consumer prices		Producer prices	Consumer prices
1950	$3.546	$4.151	1964	2.985	3.220	1978	1.433	1.532
1951	3.247	3.846	1965	2.933	3.166	1979	1.289	1.380
1952	3.268	3.765	1966	2.841	3.080	1980	1.136	1.215
1953	3.300	3.735	1967	2.809	2.993	1981	1.041	1.098
1954	3.289	3.717	1968	2.732	2.873	1982	1.000	1.035
1955	3.279	3.732	1969	2.632	2.726	1983	0.984	1.003
1956	3.195	3.678	1970	2.545	2.574	1984	0.964	0.961
1957	3.077	3.549	1971	2.469	2.466	1985	0.955	0.928
1958	3.012	3.457	1972	2.392	2.391	1986	0.969	0.913
1959	3.021	3.427	1973	2.193	2.251	1987	0.949	0.880
1960	2.994	3.373	1974	1.901	2.029	1988	0.926	0.846
1961	2.994	3.340	1975	1.718	1.859	1989	0.880	0.807
1962	2.985	3.304	1976	1.645	1.757	1990	0.839	0.766
1963	2.994	3.265	1977	1.546	1.649	1991	0.822	0.734

Source: U.S. Bureau of Labor Statistics. Monthly data in U.S. Bureau of Economic Analysis, Survey of Current Business.

Figure 15.1
Annual Percent Change in Consumer and Producer Price Indexes: 1970 to 1991

Consumer Price Index

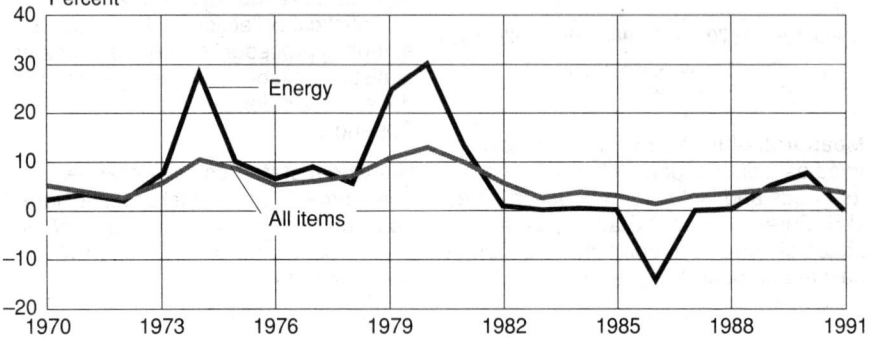

Producer Price Index by Stage of Processing

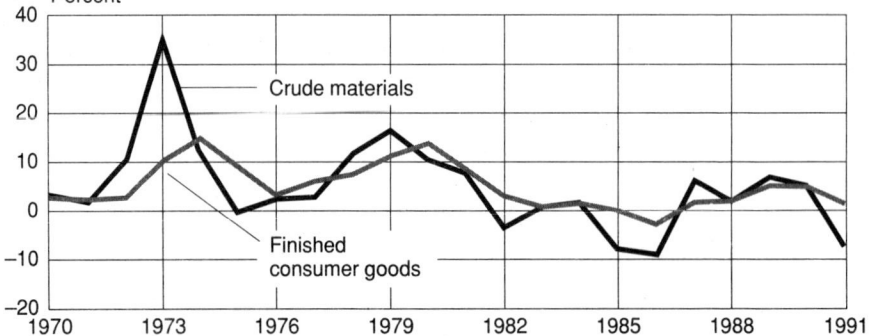

Source: Chart prepared by U.S. Bureau of the Census. For data, see tables 739 and 747.

No. 738. Consumer Price Indexes, by Major Groups: 1960 to 1991

[1982-84 = 100. Represents annual averages of monthly figures. Reflects buying patterns of all urban consumers. See text. See *Historical Statistics, Colonial Times to 1970*, series E 135-173 for similar data]

YEAR	All items	Energy	Food	Shelter	Apparel and upkeep	Transportation	Medical care	Fuel oil	Electricity	Utility (piped gas)	Telephone services	All commodities
1960	29.6	22.4	30.0	25.2	45.7	29.8	22.3	13.5	29.9	17.6	58.3	33.6
1961	29.9	22.5	30.4	25.4	46.1	30.1	22.9	14.0	29.9	17.9	58.5	33.8
1962	30.2	22.6	30.6	25.8	46.3	30.8	23.5	14.0	29.9	17.9	58.5	34.1
1963	30.6	22.6	31.1	26.1	46.9	30.9	24.1	14.3	29.9	17.9	58.6	34.4
1964	31.0	22.5	31.5	26.5	47.3	31.4	24.6	14.0	29.8	17.9	58.6	34.8
1965	31.5	22.9	32.2	27.0	47.8	31.9	25.2	14.3	29.7	18.0	57.7	35.2
1966	32.4	23.3	33.8	27.8	49.0	32.3	26.3	14.7	29.7	18.1	56.5	36.1
1967	33.4	23.8	34.1	28.8	51.0	33.3	28.2	15.1	29.9	18.1	57.3	36.8
1968	34.8	24.2	35.3	30.1	53.7	34.3	29.9	15.6	30.2	18.2	57.3	38.1
1969	36.7	24.8	37.1	32.6	56.8	35.7	31.9	15.9	30.8	18.6	58.0	39.9
1970	38.8	25.5	39.2	35.5	59.2	37.5	34.0	16.5	31.8	19.6	58.7	41.7
1971	40.5	26.5	40.4	37.0	61.1	39.5	36.1	17.6	33.9	21.0	61.6	43.2
1972	41.8	27.2	42.1	38.7	62.3	39.9	37.3	17.6	35.6	22.1	65.0	44.5
1973	44.4	29.4	48.2	40.5	64.6	41.2	38.8	20.4	37.4	23.1	66.7	47.8
1974	49.3	38.1	55.1	44.4	69.4	45.8	42.4	32.2	44.1	26.0	69.5	53.5
1975	53.8	42.1	59.8	48.8	72.5	50.1	47.5	34.9	50.0	31.1	71.7	58.2
1976	56.9	45.1	61.6	51.5	75.2	55.1	52.0	37.4	53.1	36.3	74.3	60.7
1977	60.6	49.4	65.5	54.9	78.6	59.0	57.0	42.4	56.6	43.2	75.2	64.2
1978	65.2	52.5	72.0	60.5	81.4	61.7	61.8	44.9	60.9	47.5	76.0	68.8
1979	72.6	65.7	79.9	68.9	84.9	70.5	67.5	63.1	65.6	55.1	75.8	76.6
1980	82.4	86.0	86.8	81.0	90.9	83.1	74.9	87.7	75.8	65.7	77.7	86.0
1981	90.9	97.7	93.6	90.5	95.3	93.2	82.9	107.3	87.2	74.9	84.6	93.2
1982	96.5	99.2	97.4	96.9	97.8	97.0	92.5	105.0	95.8	89.8	93.2	97.0
1983	99.6	99.9	99.4	99.1	100.2	99.3	100.6	96.5	98.9	104.7	99.2	99.8
1984	103.9	100.9	103.2	104.0	102.1	103.7	106.8	98.5	105.3	105.5	107.5	103.2
1985	107.6	101.6	105.6	109.8	105.0	106.4	113.5	94.6	108.9	104.8	111.7	105.4
1986	109.6	88.2	109.0	115.8	105.9	102.3	122.0	74.1	110.4	99.7	117.2	104.4
1987	113.6	88.6	113.5	121.3	110.6	105.4	130.1	75.8	110.0	95.1	116.5	107.7
1988	118.3	89.3	118.2	127.1	115.4	108.7	138.6	75.8	111.5	94.5	116.0	111.5
1989	124.0	94.3	125.1	132.8	118.6	114.1	149.3	80.3	114.7	97.1	117.2	116.7
1990	130.7	102.1	132.4	140.0	124.1	120.5	162.8	98.6	117.4	97.3	117.7	122.8
1991	136.2	102.5	136.3	146.3	128.7	123.8	177.0	92.4	121.8	98.5	119.7	126.6

Source: U.S. Bureau of Labor Statistics, *Monthly Labor Review* and *Handbook of Labor Statistics*, periodic.

No. 739. Consumer Price Indexes—Percent Change in Major Groups: 1960 to 1991

[In percent. See table 738]

YEAR	All items	Energy	Food	Shelter	Apparel and upkeep	Transportation	Medical care	Fuel oil	Electricity	Utility (piped gas)	Telephone services	All commodities
1960	1.7	2.3	1.0	2.0	1.6	-	3.7	-1.5	1.4	6.7	1.6	0.9
1961	1.0	0.4	1.3	0.8	0.9	1.0	2.7	3.7	-	1.7	0.3	0.6
1962	1.0	0.4	0.7	1.6	0.4	2.3	2.6	-	-	-	-	0.9
1963	1.3	-	1.6	1.2	1.3	0.3	2.6	2.1	-	-	0.2	0.9
1964	1.3	-0.4	1.3	1.5	0.9	1.6	2.1	-2.1	-0.3	-	-	1.2
1965	1.6	1.8	2.2	1.9	1.1	1.6	2.4	2.1	-0.3	0.6	-1.5	1.1
1966	2.9	1.7	5.0	3.0	2.5	1.3	4.4	2.8	-	0.6	-2.1	2.6
1967	3.1	2.1	0.9	3.6	4.1	3.1	7.2	2.7	0.7	-	1.4	1.9
1968	4.2	1.7	3.5	4.5	5.3	3.0	6.0	3.3	1.0	0.6	-	3.5
1969	5.5	2.5	5.1	8.3	5.8	4.1	6.7	1.9	2.0	2.2	1.2	4.7
1970	5.7	2.8	5.7	8.9	4.2	5.0	6.6	3.8	3.2	5.4	1.2	4.5
1971	4.4	3.9	3.1	4.2	3.2	5.3	6.2	6.7	6.6	7.1	4.9	3.6
1972	3.2	2.6	4.2	4.6	2.0	1.0	3.3	-	5.0	5.2	5.5	3.0
1973	6.2	8.1	14.5	4.7	3.7	3.3	4.0	15.9	5.1	4.5	2.6	7.4
1974	11.0	29.6	14.3	9.6	7.4	11.2	9.3	57.8	17.9	12.6	4.2	11.9
1975	9.1	10.5	8.5	9.9	4.5	9.4	12.0	8.4	13.4	19.6	3.2	8.8
1976	5.8	7.1	3.0	5.5	3.7	10.0	9.5	7.2	6.2	16.7	3.6	4.3
1977	6.5	9.5	6.3	6.6	4.5	7.1	9.6	13.4	6.6	19.0	1.2	5.8
1978	7.6	6.3	9.9	10.2	3.6	4.6	8.4	5.9	7.6	10.0	1.1	7.2
1979	11.3	25.1	11.0	13.9	4.3	14.3	9.2	40.5	7.7	16.0	-0.3	11.3
1980	13.5	30.9	8.6	17.6	7.1	17.9	11.0	39.0	15.5	19.2	2.5	12.3
1981	10.0	10.6	7.8	11.7	4.8	12.2	10.7	22.3	15.0	14.0	8.9	8.4
1982	6.2	1.5	4.1	7.1	2.6	4.1	11.6	-2.1	9.9	19.9	10.2	4.1
1983	3.2	0.7	2.1	2.3	2.5	2.4	8.8	-8.1	3.2	16.6	6.4	2.9
1984	4.3	1.0	3.8	4.9	1.9	4.4	6.2	2.1	6.5	0.8	8.4	3.4
1985	3.6	0.7	2.3	5.6	2.8	2.6	6.3	-4.0	3.4	-0.7	3.9	2.1
1986	1.9	-13.2	3.2	5.5	0.9	-3.9	7.5	-21.7	1.4	-4.9	4.9	-0.9
1987	3.6	0.5	4.1	4.7	4.4	3.0	6.6	2.3	-0.4	-4.6	-0.6	3.2
1988	4.1	0.8	4.1	4.8	4.3	3.1	6.5	-	1.4	-0.6	-0.4	3.5
1989	4.8	5.6	5.8	4.5	2.8	5.0	7.7	5.9	2.9	2.8	1.0	4.7
1990	5.4	8.3	5.8	5.4	4.6	5.6	9.0	22.8	2.4	0.2	0.4	5.2
1991	4.2	0.4	2.9	4.5	3.7	2.7	8.7	-6.3	3.7	1.2	1.7	3.1

- Represents zero.

Source: Bureau of Labor Statistics, *Monthly Labor Review*.

No. 740. Consumer Price Indexes for Selected Items and Groups: 1970 to 1991

[1982-84 = 100. Annual averages of monthly figures. See headnote, table 738]

ITEM	1970	1980	1985	1986	1987	1988	1989	1990	1991
All items	**38.8**	**82.4**	**107.6**	**109.6**	**113.6**	**118.3**	**124.0**	**130.7**	**136.2**
Food and beverages	40.1	86.7	105.6	109.1	113.5	118.2	124.9	132.1	136.8
Food	39.2	86.8	105.6	109.0	113.5	118.2	125.1	132.4	136.3
Food at home	39.9	88.4	104.3	107.3	111.9	116.6	124.2	132.3	135.8
Cereals and bakery products	37.1	83.9	107.9	110.9	114.8	122.1	132.4	140.0	145.8
Cereals and cereal products	(NA)	84.2	107.2	110.4	113.9	122.5	133.8	141.1	147.5
Cereals	(NA)	76.3	111.3	117.3	124.1	132.9	147.9	158.6	168.1
Rice, pasta, and cornmeal	(NA)	90.9	102.1	102.2	101.7	114.4	120.0	122.0	126.5
Bakery products	(NA)	83.8	108.2	111.1	115.0	121.8	131.5	139.2	144.7
White bread	43.1	85.9	105.8	107.7	110.7	118.6	129.4	136.4	139.3
Cookies, cakes, and cupcakes	(NA)	81.5	110.2	113.4	118.3	125.0	134.5	142.7	151.1
Meats, poultry, fish and eggs	44.6	92.0	100.1	104.5	110.5	114.3	121.3	130.0	132.6
Meats	43.8	92.7	98.9	102.0	109.6	112.2	116.7	128.5	132.5
Beef and veal	43.5	98.4	98.2	98.8	106.3	112.1	119.3	128.8	132.4
Ground beef excl. canned	47.0	104.6	95.9	94.9	100.2	103.4	108.6	118.1	119.9
Chuck roast	42.8	99.8	95.6	95.0	103.8	108.1	116.8	130.3	135.8
Round steak	45.8	98.9	97.0	98.4	105.3	110.6	116.6	125.1	129.5
Sirloin steak	42.4	96.2	99.7	102.3	111.2	120.0	126.0	130.6	133.5
Pork	45.4	81.9	99.1	107.2	116.0	112.5	113.2	129.8	134.1
Bacon	41.9	73.5	101.3	108.5	114.6	100.9	95.8	113.4	119.8
Chops	49.1	82.9	98.7	109.5	120.5	118.8	122.7	140.2	141.7
Ham	(NA)	85.5	99.8	107.4	115.8	116.5	117.3	132.4	139.9
Poultry	53.2	93.7	106.2	114.2	112.6	120.7	132.7	132.5	131.5
Fresh whole chicken	52.4	94.4	104.5	115.4	113.3	125.1	137.1	134.9	131.7
Fresh, frozen chicken parts	(NA)	91.7	104.6	114.6	114.4	123.3	135.7	135.9	134.7
Fish and seafood	31.3	87.5	107.5	117.4	129.9	137.4	143.6	146.7	148.3
Canned fish and seafood	(NA)	93.7	97.8	98.6	103.9	117.0	124.3	119.5	119.0
Fresh and frozen fish and seafood	(NA)	84.1	112.9	127.7	143.6	144.2	155.2	161.4	163.8
Eggs	65.6	88.6	91.0	97.2	91.5	93.6	118.5	124.1	121.2
Dairy products	44.7	90.9	103.2	103.3	105.9	108.4	115.6	126.5	125.1
Fruits and vegetables	37.8	82.1	108.4	109.4	119.1	128.1	138.0	149.0	155.8
Fresh fruits	35.6	84.8	116.3	118.7	132.0	143.0	152.4	170.9	193.9
Apples	37.1	92.1	113.1	130.6	131.0	134.2	140.5	147.5	172.8
Bananas	39.0	91.5	99.9	105.0	104.2	119.2	131.3	138.2	145.0
Oranges, tangerines	30.6	72.6	119.7	108.6	135.9	144.6	147.0	160.6	249.4
Fresh vegetables	39.4	79.0	103.5	107.7	121.6	129.3	143.1	151.1	154.4
Potatoes	38.0	81.0	101.6	96.1	116.0	119.1	153.5	162.6	144.6
Lettuce	35.4	77.8	106.1	112.7	136.4	148.6	151.5	150.3	159.8
Tomatoes	46.3	81.9	103.6	111.3	116.8	123.1	136.2	160.8	153.1
Processed fruits	38.4	82.1	109.5	106.3	110.6	122.0	125.9	136.9	131.8
Processed vegetables	36.6	83.1	104.4	104.2	107.1	112.2	124.2	127.5	128.5
Coffee	31.7	111.6	105.5	132.7	116.2	115.0	120.4	117.5	115.3
Lunch away from home	(NA)	83.8	107.8	112.0	116.6	121.5	127.6	133.9	138.4
Dinner away from home	(NA)	84.2	108.8	112.7	117.0	121.6	126.9	132.3	136.3
Alcoholic beverages	52.1	86.4	106.4	111.1	114.1	118.6	123.5	129.3	142.8
Alcoholic beverages at home	(NA)	87.3	105.2	109.3	111.5	114.2	117.9	123.0	137.8
Beer and ale	49.2	84.8	106.7	108.7	110.9	114.4	118.2	123.6	138.4
Distilled spirits	(NA)	89.8	105.3	113.3	114.4	116.1	119.9	125.7	139.2
Wine	49.7	89.5	100.2	102.4	105.7	107.8	110.9	114.4	129.9
Alcoholic beverages away from home	(NA)	82.9	111.1	118.5	123.4	130.6	137.4	144.4	156.9
Housing	36.4	81.1	107.7	110.9	114.2	118.5	123.0	128.5	133.6
Shelter	35.5	81.0	109.8	115.8	121.3	127.1	132.8	140.0	146.3
Renters' cost	(NA)	(NA)	115.4	121.9	128.1	133.6	138.9	146.7	155.6
Rent, residential	46.5	80.9	111.8	118.3	123.1	127.8	132.8	138.4	143.3
Tenants' insurance	(NA)	78.9	109.4	115.8	120.4	124.9	128.3	130.6	133.2
Homeowners' costs	(NA)	(NA)	113.1	119.4	124.8	131.1	137.3	144.6	150.2
Owners' equivalent rent	(NA)	(NA)	113.2	119.4	124.8	131.1	137.4	144.8	150.4
Household insurance	(NA)	(NA)	112.4	119.2	124.0	129.0	132.6	135.3	138.4
Maintenance and repair	35.8	82.4	106.5	107.9	111.8	114.7	118.0	122.2	126.3
Fuels and other utilities	29.1	75.4	106.5	104.1	103.0	104.4	107.8	111.6	115.3
Fuels	23.1	74.8	104.5	99.2	97.3	98.0	100.9	104.5	106.7
Fuel oil and other	17.0	86.1	95.9	77.6	77.9	78.1	81.7	99.3	94.6
Fuel oil	16.5	87.7	94.6	74.1	75.8	75.8	80.3	98.6	92.4
Gas (piped) and electricity	25.4	71.4	107.1	105.7	103.8	104.6	107.5	109.3	112.6
Electricity	31.8	75.8	108.9	110.4	110.0	111.5	114.7	117.4	121.8
Utility (piped) gas	19.6	65.7	104.8	99.7	95.1	94.5	97.1	97.3	98.5
Telephone services	58.7	77.7	111.7	117.2	116.5	116.0	117.2	117.7	119.7
Local charges	(NA)	72.8	120.4	132.7	139.3	141.3	146.5	149.3	153.9
Interstate toll charges	(NA)	83.3	94.9	88.4	75.3	72.3	70.0	68.2	67.6
Intrastate toll charges	(NA)	85.2	106.8	106.8	104.7	101.5	97.0	95.1	93.1
Water and sewerage maintenance	34.3	74.0	113.4	119.4	125.8	132.7	140.8	150.2	161.1
Cable television	(NA)	(NA)	110.6	115.5	123.1	132.9	144.0	158.4	175.7
Refuse collection	(NA)	(NA)	109.9	118.7	130.3	142.5	155.6	171.2	189.2

See footnotes at end of table.

No.740 Consumer Price Indexes for Selected Items and Groups: 1970 to 1991—Continued

[1982-84 = 100. Annual averages of monthly figures. See headnote, table 738]

ITEM	1970	1980	1985	1986	1987	1988	1989	1990	1991
Household furnishings and operations.........	46.8	86.3	103.8	105.2	107.1	109.4	111.2	113.3	116.0
Housefurnishings....................	55.5	88.5	101.7	102.2	103.6	105.1	105.5	106.7	107.5
Furniture and bedding.............	52.9	88.0	104.9	107.2	109.7	113.2	113.9	115.7	116.6
Bedroom furniture...............	(NA)	83.5	107.4	113.9	114.1	117.7	117.6	118.5	120.1
Sofas.......................	(NA)	(NA)	103.0	105.9	110.9	114.3	117.0	118.4	118.3
Living room chairs and tables......	(NA)	(NA)	103.2	105.3	107.2	111.0	112.5	116.7	118.4
Appliances and electronic equip..........	69.3	93.5	95.2	92.8	91.4	90.2	89.1	87.8	86.0
Video and audio equipment...........	(NA)	100.7	91.9	88.0	86.0	83.6	82.2	80.8	79.4
Television...................	100.0	104.6	88.7	83.2	79.7	77.6	76.1	74.6	72.9
Video products other than TV........	(NA)	(NA)	(NA)	(NA)	(NA)	(NA)	96.8	91.5	84.6
Audio products..................	(NA)	97.7	94.4	91.8	93.0	92.7	92.8	93.2	94.6
Housekeeping supplies..................	36.6	83.2	106.2	108.2	111.5	114.7	120.9	125.2	128.9
Housekeeping services.................	37.9	84.3	106.1	108.5	110.6	114.3	117.3	120.1	127.5
Postage.........................	34.9	76.2	108.8	110.2	110.2	121.4	125.1	125.1	143.6
Apparel and upkeep.....................	59.2	90.9	105.0	105.9	110.6	115.4	118.6	124.1	128.7
Apparel commodities...................	63.3	92.9	104.0	104.2	108.9	113.7	116.7	122.0	126.4
Apparel commodities less footwear........	64.5	93.0	104.3	104.7	109.6	114.4	117.1	122.8	127.4
Men's and boy's apparel.............	62.2	89.4	105.0	106.2	109.1	113.4	117.0	120.4	124.2
Women's and girl's apparel..........	71.8	96.0	104.9	104.0	110.4	114.9	116.4	122.6	127.6
Infants' and toddlers'..............	39.2	85.5	107.2	111.8	112.1	116.4	119.1	125.8	128.9
Footwear.........................	56.8	91.8	102.3	101.9	105.1	109.9	114.4	117.4	120.9
Transportation........................	37.5	83.1	106.4	102.3	105.4	108.7	114.1	120.5	123.8
Private transportation.................	37.5	84.2	106.2	101.2	104.2	107.6	112.9	118.8	121.9
New vehicles....................	53.1	88.5	106.1	110.6	114.4	116.5	119.2	121.4	126.0
New cars.......................	53.0	88.4	106.1	110.6	114.6	116.9	119.2	121.0	125.3
New trucks.....................	(NA)	(NA)	105.5	110.2	112.2	113.5	117.0	121.6	127.0
Used cars......................	31.2	62.3	113.7	108.8	113.1	118.0	120.4	117.6	118.1
Motor fuel.....................	27.9	97.4	98.7	77.1	80.2	80.9	88.5	101.2	99.4
Automobile maintenance and repair........	36.6	81.5	106.8	110.3	114.8	119.7	124.9	130.1	136.0
Automobile insurance.................	42.0	82.0	119.2	135.0	142.6	156.6	166.6	177.9	191.5
Automobile finance charges.............	(NA)	86.4	94.5	86.0	84.9	91.3	100.5	99.6	98.0
Vehicle rental, registration, other..........	(NA)	78.3	111.7	117.2	123.0	128.1	135.0	148.1	154.8
Public transportation..................	35.2	69.0	110.5	117.0	121.1	123.3	129.5	142.6	148.9
Airline fares......................	28.3	68.0	112.5	117.1	122.8	124.2	131.6	148.4	155.2
Other intercity transportation...........	(NA)	73.1	114.7	125.5	126.7	132.6	138.5	143.3	149.0
Intracity transportation................	(NA)	69.7	107.7	115.8	118.8	121.7	125.2	133.5	138.9
Medical care........................	34.0	74.9	113.5	122.0	130.1	138.6	149.3	162.8	177.0
Medical care commodities..............	46.5	75.4	115.2	122.8	131.0	139.9	150.8	163.4	176.8
Prescription drugs.................	47.4	72.5	120.1	130.4	140.8	152.0	165.2	181.7	199.7
Nonprescription drugs, medical sup.......	(NA)	(NA)	(NA)	(NA)	103.1	108.1	114.6	120.6	126.3
Medical care services	32.3	74.8	113.2	121.9	130.0	138.3	148.9	162.7	177.1
Professional medical services..........	37.0	77.9	113.5	120.8	128.8	137.5	146.4	156.1	165.7
Physicians' services.............	34.5	76.5	113.3	121.5	130.4	139.8	150.1	160.8	170.5
Dental services.................	39.2	78.9	114.2	120.6	128.8	137.5	146.1	155.8	167.4
Eye care......................	(NA)	(NA)	(NA)	(NA)	103.5	108.7	112.4	117.3	121.9
Hospital and related services..........	(NA)	69.2	116.1	123.1	131.6	143.9	160.5	178.0	196.1
Hospital rooms.................	23.6	68.0	115.4	122.3	131.1	143.3	158.1	175.4	191.9
Entertainment	47.5	83.6	107.9	111.6	115.3	120.3	126.5	132.4	138.4
Entertainment commodities..............	46.1	84.5	105.8	107.9	110.5	115.0	119.8	124.0	128.6
Reading materials	(NA)	77.7	110.7	115.6	119.5	124.3	129.5	136.2	144.7
Newspapers....................	39.8	79.4	109.3	113.7	118.4	123.7	129.2	134.6	146.5
Magazines, periodacls, and books	(NA)	75.9	112.1	117.7	120.7	125.0	130.0	137.9	143.3
Sporting goods, equipment	(NA)	88.5	104.6	104.0	104.3	108.1	111.1	114.9	118.5
Sport vehicles, including bicycles	(NA)	87.9	106.3	105.6	105.5	108.9	112.3	115.3	117.5
Toys, hobbies; other entertainment	(NA)	86.5	103.3	105.3	108.4	113.2	118.5	121.5	123.9
Pet supplies and expenses	(NA)	83.3	106.4	108.7	111.0	114.5	120.7	124.6	129.1
Entertainment services................	49.4	82.3	110.9	116.8	122.0	127.7	135.4	143.2	150.6
Club membership.................	(NA)	(NA)	(NA)	(NA)	101.0	107.2	112.6	117.0	122.5
Admissions....................	(NA)	83.8	112.8	117.9	124.4	131.1	141.4	151.2	159.3
Tobacco and smoking products	43.1	72.0	102.6	112.4	124.7	133.6	145.8	164.4	181.5
Personal care.......................	43.5	81.9	108.3	111.9	115.1	119.4	125.0	130.4	134.9
Personal care services...............	44.2	83.7	108.9	112.5	116.2	120.7	126.8	132.8	137.0
Beauty parlor services for women........	42.9	83.4	108.8	112.2	116.0	120.3	126.5	133.0	137.2
Haircuts, etc. for men...............	(NA)	84.4	109.0	113.1	116.5	121.7	127.3	131.5	135.9
Personal and educational expenses	35.5	70.9	119.1	128.6	138.5	147.9	158.1	170.2	183.7
School books and supplies..............	38.8	71.4	118.2	128.1	138.1	148.1	158.0	171.3	180.3
Personal and educational services........	34.8	70.8	119.2	128.7	138.7	148.0	158.3	170.4	184.2
Tuition and other school fees...........	(NA)	71.2	119.7	129.6	140.0	151.0	162.7	175.7	191.4
College tuition..................	(NA)	70.8	119.9	129.6	139.4	150.0	161.9	175.0	192.8
Elementary and high school tuition	(NA)	72.3	119.0	129.2	141.3	154.6	168.0	182.8	198.0
Day care and nursery school............	(NA)	(NA)	(NA)	(NA)	(NA)	(NA)	(NA)	(NA)	103.2
All commodities......................	41.7	86.0	105.4	104.4	107.7	111.5	116.7	122.8	126.6
All commodities less food	43.4	85.7	105.2	101.7	104.3	107.7	112.0	117.4	121.3
Energy...........................	25.5	86.0	101.6	88.2	88.6	89.3	94.3	102.1	102.5

NA Not available.

Source: U.S. Bureau of Labor Statistics, *Monthly Labor Review* and *CPI Detailed Report*, January issues.

No. 741. Consumer Price Indexes—Selected Areas: 1970 to 1991

[1982-84 = 100, except as indicated. Represents annual averages of monthly figures, except as noted. Local area CPI indexes are byproducts of the national CPI program. Each local index has a smaller sample size than the national index and is therefore, subject to substantially more sampling and other measurement error. As a result, local area indexes show greater volatility than the national index, although their long- term trends are similar. Area definitions are those established by the Office of Management and Budget in 1983. For further detail see the U.S. Bureau of Labor Statistics Handbook of Methods, Bulletin 2285, Chapter 19, the Consumer Price Index, and Report 736, the CPI: 1987 Revision. See also text, section 15]

AREA	1970	1975	1980	1985	1987	1988	1989	1990	1991
U.S. city average.	38.8	53.8	82.4	107.6	113.6	118.3	124.0	130.7	136.2
Anchorage, AK MSA.	41.1	57.1	85.5	105.8	108.2	108.6	111.7	118.6	124.0
Atlanta, GA MSA	38.6	53.6	80.3	108.9	116.5	120.4	126.1	131.7	135.9
Baltimore, MD MSA	39.1	55.2	83.7	108.2	114.2	119.3	124.5	130.8	136.4
Boston-Lawrence-Salem, MA-NH CMSA.	40.2	55.8	82.6	109.4	117.1	124.2	131.3	138.9	145.0
Buffalo-Niagara Falls, NY CMSA.	41.2	57.4	83.5	108.6	113.0	117.4	121.6	127.7	133.4
Chicago-Gary-Lake County, IL-IN-WI CMSA ...	38.9	52.8	82.2	107.7	114.5	119.0	125.0	131.7	137.0
Cincinnati-Hamilton, OH-KY-IN CMSA	37.4	51.8	82.1	106.6	111.9	116.1	120.9	126.5	131.4
Cleveland-Akron-Lorain, OH CMSA	37.2	50.2	78.9	107.8	112.7	116.7	122.7	129.0	134.2
Dallas-Fort Worth, TX CMSA	37.6	50.4	81.5	108.2	112.9	116.1	119.5	125.1	130.8
Denver-Boulder, CO CMSA	34.5	48.4	78.4	107.1	110.8	113.7	115.8	120.9	125.6
Detroit-Ann Arbor, MI CMSA	39.5	53.9	86.5	106.8	111.7	116.1	122.3	128.6	133.1
Honolulu, HI MSA.	41.5	56.3	83.0	106.8	114.9	121.7	128.7	138.1	148.0
Houston-Galveston-Brazoria, TX CMSA	36.4	51.4	82.7	104.9	106.5	109.5	114.1	120.6	125.1
Kansas City, MO-KS CMSA	39.0	53.2	83.6	107.7	113.1	117.4	121.6	126.0	131.2
Los Angeles-Anaheim-Riverside, CA CMSA ...	38.7	53.3	83.7	108.4	116.7	122.1	128.3	135.9	141.4
Miami-Fort Lauderdale, FL CMSA	(NA)	(NA)	81.1	106.5	111.8	116.8	121.5	128.0	132.3
Milwaukee, WI PMSA	37.5	50.8	81.4	107.0	111.5	115.9	120.8	126.2	132.2
Minneapolis-St. Paul, MN-WI MSA.	37.4	51.2	78.9	107.0	111.6	117.2	122.0	127.0	130.4
New Orleans, LA MSA [1]	(NA)	(NA)	(NA)	(NA)	100.0	102.7	107.2	111.5	116.0
New York-Northern New Jersey-Long Island, NY-NJ-CT CMSA	41.2	57.6	82.1	108.7	118.0	123.7	130.6	138.5	144.8
Philadelphia-Wilmington-Trenton, PA-NJ-DE- MD CMSA.	40.8	56.8	83.6	108.8	116.8	122.4	128.3	135.8	142.2
Pittsburgh-Beaver Valley, PA CMSA	38.1	52.4	81.0	106.9	111.4	114.9	120.1	126.2	131.3
Portland-Vancouver, OR-WA CMSA.	38.7	53.5	87.2	106.7	110.9	114.7	120.4	127.4	133.9
San Diego, CA MSA	34.1	47.6	79.4	110.4	117.5	123.4	130.6	138.4	143.4
San Francisco-Oakland-San Jose, CA CMSA ..	37.7	51.8	80.4	108.4	115.4	120.5	126.4	132.1	137.9
Seattle-Tacoma, WA CMSA.	37.4	51.1	82.7	105.6	109.2	112.8	118.1	126.8	134.1
St. Louis-East St. Louis, MO-IL CMSA	38.8	52.6	82.5	107.1	112.2	115.7	121.8	128.1	132.1
Tampa-St. Petersburg-Clearwater, FL MSA [1].	(NA)	(NA)	(NA)	(NA)	100.0	103.7	107.2	111.7	116.4
Washington, DC-MD-VA MSA.	39.8	54.7	82.9	109.0	116.2	121.0	128.0	135.6	141.2

NA Not available. [1] 1987 = 100.

Source: U.S. Bureau of Labor Statistics, *Monthly Labor Review* and *CPI Detailed Report*, January issues.

No. 742. CPI—Major Commodity Groups, by Selected Areas: 1991

[1982-84 = 100, except as noted. See table 741]

AREA	All items	Food and bever- ages	Food	Hous- ing	Ap- parel and upkeep	Trans- porta- tion	Med- ical care	Enter- tain- ment	Fuel and other utilities
U.S. City Average.	136.2	136.8	136.3	133.6	128.7	123.8	177.0	138.4	115.3
Anchorage, AK MSA.	124.0	127.7	126.3	111.2	126.6	121.7	173.5	148.8	136.5
Atlanta, GA MSA.	135.9	135.3	137.0	130.6	148.4	118.7	191.6	156.7	121.6
Baltimore, MD MSA	136.4	140.6	141.1	131.0	132.9	125.5	171.9	143.8	107.7
Boston-Lawrence-Salem, MA-NH CMSA.	145.0	142.5	142.0	140.9	144.6	125.5	202.7	152.2	109.1
Buffalo-Niagara Falls, NY CMSA.	133.4	136.0	135.3	139.4	112.0	112.2	159.0	148.2	107.4
Chicago-Gary-Lake County, IL-IN-WI CMSA ...	137.0	135.5	134.7	136.4	125.3	121.2	177.9	145.9	111.9
Cincinnati-Hamilton, OH-KY-IN CMSA	131.4	131.7	131.4	126.5	121.6	120.1	175.5	134.6	104.2
Cleveland-Akron-Lorain, OH CMSA	134.2	135.4	135.3	132.5	121.9	123.1	171.7	138.6	113.9
Dallas-Fort Worth, TX CMSA	130.8	136.3	135.6	118.6	151.7	120.7	174.8	142.4	116.2
Denver-Boulder, CO CMSA	125.6	128.3	127.8	114.1	94.8	127.8	191.8	130.8	111.9
Detroit-Ann Arbor, MI CMSA	133.1	131.1	130.5	128.6	131.8	123.9	171.0	132.7	111.2
Honolulu, HI MSA.	148.0	145.9	145.9	152.8	110.5	139.3	171.3	134.3	101.3
Houston-Galveston-Brazoria, TX CMSA	125.1	131.6	130.9	109.5	134.8	119.6	177.7	139.6	104.2
Kansas City, MO-KS CMSA	131.2	130.9	131.3	125.4	124.7	119.2	173.5	149.3	115.9
Los Angeles-Anaheim-Riverside, CA CMSA ...	141.4	136.6	135.0	144.9	130.9	126.6	178.2	135.4	133.0
Miami-Fort Lauderdale, FL CMSA	132.3	137.7	138.9	123.7	140.4	126.0	162.8	126.4	111.5
Milwaukee, WI PMSA	132.2	135.2	135.8	132.2	125.4	119.1	159.5	124.0	97.8
Minneapolis-St. Paul, MN-WI MSA.	130.4	141.5	140.6	120.6	130.9	119.4	171.8	141.6	103.1
New Orleans, LA [1]	116.0	118.7	119.2	106.0	130.9	116.6	136.9	126.2	119.6
New York- Northern New Jersey-Long Island, NY-NJ-CT CMSA	144.8	144.3	143.8	145.7	124.5	127.9	186.6	140.8	105.6
Philadelphia-Wilmington-Trenton, PA-NJ-DE- MD CMSA.	142.2	135.4	133.8	145.6	103.7	132.3	183.5	138.0	116.8
Pittsburgh-Beaver Valley, PA CMSA	131.3	129.2	127.8	131.4	129.5	112.9	175.7	143.0	131.2
Portland-Vancouver, OR-WA CMSA.	133.9	130.7	130.2	130.4	122.3	130.1	166.0	132.6	107.8
St. Louis-East St. Louis, MO-IL CMSA	132.1	139.6	139.2	127.7	122.5	118.5	171.7	134.5	115.2
San Diego, CA MSA	143.4	140.3	137.9	144.1	124.1	129.6	133.8	188.3	104.8
San Francisco-Oakland-San Jose, CA CMSA ..	137.9	140.3	139.9	142.7	113.1	117.1	172.9	152.4	134.7
Seattle-Tacoma, WA CMSA.	134.1	140.6	140.6	134.0	113.4	119.9	169.4	135.9	97.4
Washington, DC-MD-VA MSA.	141.2	137.7	136.3	140.8	142.4	126.2	176.4	142.7	112.3
Tampa-St. Petersburg-Clearwater, FL [1]	116.4	116.4	116.3	111.2	127.9	112.2	147.2	105.8	107.6

[1] 1987 = 100.

Source: U.S. Bureau of Labor Statistics, *Monthly Labor Review,* and *CPI Detailed Report*, January issues.

Prices

473

No. 743. Consumer Price Index, by Region: 1975 to 1991

[1982-84 = 100. For composition of regions, see table 25]

ITEM	1975	1980	1981	1982	1983	1984	1985	1986	1987	1988	1989	1990	1991
U.S. city average, all items . .	53.8	82.4	90.9	96.5	99.6	103.9	107.6	109.6	113.6	118.3	124.0	130.7	136.2
Food.	59.8	86.8	93.6	97.4	99.4	103.2	105.6	109.0	113.5	118.2	125.1	132.4	136.3
Housing.	50.7	81.1	90.4	96.9	99.5	103.6	107.7	110.9	114.2	118.5	123.0	128.5	133.6
Gas (piped) and electricity.	40.1	71.4	81.9	93.2	101.5	105.4	107.1	105.7	103.8	104.6	107.5	109.3	112.6
Northeast:													
All items	55.8	82.2	91.0	95.8	99.8	104.5	108.4	111.1	116.0	121.8	128.6	136.3	142.5
Food.	60.4	86.5	93.4	97.3	99.4	103.3	106.2	110.1	115.8	121.1	128.7	135.9	139.8
Housing.	(NA)	80.7	90.7	95.7	99.7	104.6	109.0	112.7	117.3	124.0	130.8	138.0	144.4
Gas (piped) and electricity.	(NA)	73.8	85.4	94.4	100.9	104.7	105.9	104.6	101.2	100.2	105.4	109.6	113.4
North Central:													
All items	53.0	82.4	90.1	96.5	99.9	103.6	106.8	108.0	111.9	116.1	121.5	127.4	132.4
Food.	60.3	88.5	94.9	98.1	99.3	102.7	104.4	107.5	111.8	116.0	122.2	129.6	133.5
Housing.	(NA)	80.0	87.7	96.3	100.3	103.5	107.0	109.4	112.4	115.9	119.9	124.1	128.5
Gas (piped) and electricity.	(NA)	70.1	79.1	90.7	103.3	106.1	108.6	107.1	104.6	104.3	105.5	104.0	105.6
South:													
All items	53.3	81.9	90.7	96.5	99.7	103.8	107.1	108.9	112.4	116.4	121.5	127.9	132.9
Food.	59.7	86.6	93.5	97.1	99.3	103.6	105.7	108.8	113.1	117.6	124.2	131.6	135.0
Housing.	(NA)	80.8	90.4	97.5	99.6	103.0	106.3	109.0	111.0	113.9	117.2	121.8	125.6
Gas (piped) and electricity.	(NA)	70.2	82.6	94.1	100.9	105.0	106.0	105.1	104.3	106.1	108.2	110.4	112.9
West:													
All items	52.6	83.3	91.9	97.4	99.0	103.6	108.0	110.5	114.3	119.0	124.6	131.5	137.3
Food.	57.8	85.2	92.3	96.7	99.7	103.6	106.1	109.0	112.9	117.6	124.9	132.0	136.4
Housing.	(NA)	83.3	92.6	98.4	98.2	103.3	108.8	113.0	116.5	120.7	124.8	130.9	136.9
Gas (piped) and electricity.	(NA)	72.1	80.3	94.6	99.9	105.6	108.1	105.8	105.5	108.8	112.9	115.8	122.9

NA Not available.

Source: U.S. Bureau of Labor Statistics, *Monthly Labor Review and CPI Detailed Report,* January issues.

No. 744. Annual Percent Changes in Consumer Prices, United States and OECD Countries: 1970 to 1990

[Covers member countries of Organization for Economic Cooperation and Development (OECD). For consumer price indexes for OECD countries, see section 31]

COUNTRY	1970	1975	1979	1980	1981	1982	1983	1984	1985	1986	1987	1988	1989	1990
United States	5.8	9.1	11.3	13.5	10.3	6.1	3.2	4.3	3.5	1.9	3.7	4.1	4.8	5.4
OECD, total.	6.0	11.8	10.7	14.2	10.9	8.1	5.7	5.8	5.1	3.2	3.9	4.8	5.8	6.3
OECD, Europe.	6.1	14.4	12.7	17.7	13.4	11.5	9.5	9.0	7.9	5.3	5.1	7.1	8.3	8.6
Australia	3.9	15.1	9.1	10.2	9.7	11.1	10.1	3.9	6.8	9.1	8.5	7.2	7.6	7.3
Canada	3.3	10.7	9.1	10.2	12.4	10.8	5.8	4.3	4.0	4.2	4.4	4.0	5.0	4.8
Japan.	7.7	11.8	3.7	7.8	4.9	2.7	1.9	2.2	2.0	0.6	-0.1	0.7	2.3	3.1
New Zealand.	6.5	14.7	13.7	17.2	15.4	16.2	7.3	6.2	15.4	13.2	15.8	6.4	5.7	6.1
Austria	4.4	8.4	3.7	6.4	6.8	5.4	3.3	5.6	3.2	1.7	1.4	2.0	2.5	3.3
Belgium	3.9	12.8	4.5	6.6	7.1	8.7	7.7	6.3	4.9	1.3	1.6	1.2	3.1	3.4
Denmark.	5.8	9.6	9.6	12.3	11.7	10.1	6.9	6.3	4.7	3.6	4.0	4.6	4.8	2.7
Finland.	2.8	17.9	7.5	11.6	12.0	9.6	8.3	7.1	5.9	2.9	4.1	5.1	6.6	6.1
France	5.2	11.8	10.8	13.6	13.4	11.8	9.6	7.4	5.8	2.7	3.1	2.7	3.6	3.4
Greece.	3.2	13.4	19.0	24.9	24.5	21.0	20.2	18.4	19.3	23.0	16.4	13.5	13.7	20.4
Ireland	8.2	20.9	13.3	18.2	20.4	17.1	10.5	8.6	5.4	3.8	3.1	2.1	4.1	3.3
Italy [1]	5.1	17.2	15.7	21.1	18.7	16.3	15.0	10.6	8.6	6.1	4.6	5.0	6.6	6.1
Luxembourg	4.6	10.7	4.5	6.3	8.1	9.4	8.7	5.6	4.1	0.3	-0.1	1.4	3.4	3.7
Netherlands	3.6	10.2	4.2	6.5	6.7	5.9	2.7	3.3	2.3	0.1	-0.7	0.7	1.1	2.5
Norway.	10.6	11.7	4.8	10.9	13.7	11.3	8.4	6.3	5.7	7.2	8.7	6.7	4.6	4.1
Portugal [2]	6.3	20.4	23.9	16.6	20.0	22.4	25.5	28.8	19.6	11.8	9.4	9.7	12.6	13.4
Spain	5.9	16.9	15.6	15.6	14.5	14.4	12.2	11.3	8.8	8.8	5.2	4.8	6.8	6.7
Sweden	7.0	9.8	7.2	13.7	12.1	8.6	8.9	8.0	7.4	4.3	4.2	5.8	6.4	10.5
Switzerland	3.6	6.7	3.6	4.0	6.5	5.6	3.0	2.9	3.4	0.8	1.4	1.9	3.2	5.4
Turkey [2]	28.7	19.5	58.7	110.2	36.6	29.7	31.4	48.4	45.0	34.6	38.9	75.4	63.3	60.3
United Kingdom	6.4	24.2	13.4	18.0	11.9	8.6	4.6	5.0	6.1	3.4	4.1	4.9	7.8	9.5
Germany	3.4	6.0	4.1	5.5	6.3	5.3	3.3	2.4	2.2	-0.1	0.2	1.3	2.8	2.7

[1] Households of wage and salary earners.   [2] Excludes rent.

Source: Organization for Economic Cooperation and Development, Paris, France, *Main Economic Indicators,* monthly.

Prices

No. 745. Cost of Living Index—Selected Metropolitan Areas: Third Quarter 1991

[This cost of living index measures relative price levels for consumer goods and services in participating areas for a midmanagement standard of living. The national average equals 100, and each participant's index is read as a percentage of the national average. For example, the Albany-Schenectady-Troy, NY MSA's composite cost of living is 5.7 percent above the national average. The index does not measure inflation, but compares prices at a single point in time. Excludes taxes. Metropolitan areas defined as defined by the Office of Management and Budget. For definitions and components of MSA's, see Appendix II. See source for details]

METROPOLITAN AREA	Composite index	Grocery items	Housing	Utilities	Transportation	Health care
Akron, OH PMSA	95.4	96.8	84.2	118.4	104.6	96.1
Albany-Schenectady-Troy, NY MSA	105.7	107.7	101.3	130.7	101.9	102.4
Albuquerque, NM MSA	99.1	91.3	100.6	95.6	98.2	105.4
Amarillo, TX MSA	96.0	106.7	86.7	83.1	96.8	91.4
Anchorage, AK MSA	129.1	127.0	151.8	101.2	105.8	183.1
Appleton-Oshkosh-Neenah, WI MSA	92.7	91.0	100.0	78.6	94.1	92.7
Atlanta, GA MSA	100.1	98.1	99.2	114.1	98.9	108.8
Augusta, GA-SC MSA	100.4	97.0	88.4	115.9	104.5	90.9
Austin, TX MSA:						
Georgetown, TX	92.6	97.8	80.1	89.7	95.9	92.4
Baton Rouge, LA MSA	99.1	104.2	85.2	115.7	99.5	87.8
Beaumont-Port Arthur, TX MSA	97.6	100.4	76.6	103.6	111.8	99.4
Binghamton, NY MSA	101.0	101.2	94.6	114.4	110.2	95.1
Birmingham, AL MSA	101.4	96.8	95.2	110.1	100.3	100.4
Boise City, ID MSA	98.0	94.6	109.1	76.1	90.2	108.6
Boston, MA PMSA:						
Framingham-Natick, MA	134.8	109.3	186.9	131.9	131.7	142.6
Boulder-Longmont, CO PMSA	106.7	96.2	118.5	95.5	104.2	120.7
Brownsville-Harlingen, TX MSA:						
Harlingen, TX	99.0	104.5	73.2	119.9	104.6	96.8
Canton, OH MSA	92.0	99.0	83.1	103.7	88.8	95.2
Charleston, SC MSA	101.4	98.4	100.9	87.8	97.6	98.6
Charlotte-Gastonia-Rock Hill, NC-SC MSA	100.1	97.6	101.7	95.7	95.5	101.3
Chicago, IL PMSA:						
Schaumburg, IL	124.0	110.7	173.0	111.3	110.5	111.4
Cincinnati, OH-KY-IN PMSA	105.8	97.9	114.8	96.2	108.1	96.5
Cleveland, OH PMSA	114.3	106.2	117.1	128.1	115.8	104.7
Colorado Springs, CO MSA	93.8	100.3	94.7	70.4	93.7	99.3
Columbia, SC MSA	97.1	96.4	99.1	86.0	98.0	95.6
Columbus, GA-AL MSA	93.1	98.7	82.1	97.6	95.7	86.4
Columbus, OH MSA	107.3	99.5	113.7	108.6	126.3	96.5
Corpus Christi, TX MSA	92.9	95.4	79.8	110.7	88.4	87.6
Dallas, TX PMSA	104.7	102.0	100.0	117.1	108.8	112.4
Davenport-Rock Island-Moline, IL-IA MSA:						
Quad-Cities, IL-IA	98.5	101.2	98	95.2	98.1	93.3
Denver, CO PMSA	100.0	93.7	101.8	95.9	105.3	117.6
Des Moines, IA MSA	99.6	94.0	90.6	108.8	104.1	96.4
Dothan, AL MSA	90.1	96.3	79.2	98.1	99.4	82.6
El Paso, TX MSA	96.4	96.3	85.8	86.0	110.1	96.6
Eugene-Springfield, OR MSA	100.6	95.1	113.3	68.9	96.1	127.0
Evansville, IN-KY MSA	91.5	101.3	82.7	85.4	91.6	87.9
Fayetteville-Springdale, AR MSA	89.4	98.8	79.3	82.2	99.0	73.4
Fort Collins-Loveland, CO MSA	95.1	97.1	98.5	66.7	96.9	110.0
Fort Wayne, IN MSA	91.7	96.6	88.8	95.4	98.4	88.4
Fort Worth-Arlington, TX PMSA	93.4	98.2	81.1	108.0	96.9	100.2
Fresno, CA MSA	118.4	111.0	139.2	111.0	105.4	126.4
Green Bay, WI MSA	97.0	97.1	98.9	90.8	100.0	94.2
Greensboro-Winston-Salem-High Point NC MSA	98.9	95.5	95.5	96.7	98.1	87.5
Greenville-Spartanburg, SC MSA	94.0	96.7	91.5	103.3	94.1	75.8
Harrisburg-Lebanon-Carlisle, PA MSA	103.4	96.4	98.8	120.2	107.1	105.6
Hickory-Morganton, NC MSA	95.8	93.5	100.7	95.6	83.6	83.8
Houston, TX PMSA	102.6	105.8	91.4	100.8	115.1	103.5
Huntsville, AL MSA	99.1	93.3	94.8	82.0	111.8	101.4
Indianapolis, IN MSA	97.2	97.9	95.7	86.3	97.4	97.1
Jacksonville, FL MSA	98.2	98.3	86.5	108.7	111.3	105.5
Janesville-Beloit, WI MSA	93.9	96.1	93.6	91.9	87.4	97.6
Johnson City-Kingsport-Bristol, TN-VA MSA	96.1	94.2	100.1	78.6	98.9	85.8
Kansas City, MO-KS MSA	97.0	96.3	96.8	91.8	98.3	100.4
Killeen-Temple, TX MSA:						
Killeen-Harker Heights, TX	87.8	96.9	71.7	115.3	83.9	82.8
Knoxville, TN MSA	94.4	91.6	89.0	98.2	101.7	81.3

See footnote at end of table.

No. 745. Cost of Living Index—Selected Metropolitan Areas: Third Quarter 1991—Continued

[See headnote, page 474]

METROPOLITAN AREAS	Com- posite index	Grocery items	Housing	Utilities	Transpor- tation	Health care
Lancaster, PA MSA	110.6	101.9	116.6	128.4	118.2	92.4
Lansing-East Lansing, MI MSA	103.4	103.2	118.4	88.3	99.6	112.9
Lexington-Fayette, KY MSA	98.1	100.0	100.2	82.6	93.0	97.7
Lincoln, NE MSA	89.4	91.9	84.0	80.6	101.0	87.3
Little Rock-North Little Rock, AR MSA	95.1	94.6	83.1	116.0	99.8	87.9
Los Angeles-Long Beach CA PMSA	124.6	102.8	196.3	76.0	107.8	134.1
Louisville, KY-IN MSA	93.6	90.7	91.1	78.8	97.5	85.3
Lubbock, TX MSA	92.8	103.1	82.6	73.6	95.5	89.3
Memphis, TN-AR-MS MSA	94.5	99.4	84.0	92.0	101.9	88.5
Miami-Hialeah, FL PMSA	112.2	97.9	117.7	127.5	108.4	129.4
Milwaukee, WI PMSA	103.4	101.5	123.4	92.4	102.1	100.7
Minneapolis-St. Paul, MN-WI MSA:						
St. Paul, MN	99.6	90.4	98.5	100.3	109.0	111.3
Mobile, AL MSA	96.2	101.8	79.3	102.9	109.7	92.3
Montgomery, AL MSA	101.0	97.6	94.7	111.9	107.0	97.9
Nashville, TN MSA	91.7	93.2	90.9	91.0	93.9	75.5
Nassau-Suffolk, NY PMSA	147.9	121.6	195.1	198.9	129.5	131.2
New Orleans, LA MSA	93.5	100.5	83.1	98.8	98.2	85.0
New York, NY PMSA	213.3	144.6	417.3	202.1	120.8	199.1
Norfolk-Virginia Beach-Newport News, VA MSA:						
Hampton Roads/SE Virginia	104.6	103.6	97.3	112.6	111.6	95.2
Ocala, FL MSA	93.1	99.3	82.0	102.3	96.3	83.3
Oklahoma City, OK MSA	96.0	101.1	76.9	104.9	99.9	93.5
Olympia, WA MSA:						
Olympia-Lacey-Tumwater, WA	102.7	100.1	115.7	71.6	95.7	135.3
Omaha, NE-IA MSA	89.9	92.7	82.4	91.9	104.2	79.5
Orlando, FL MSA	100.6	96.0	104.3	101.7	105.7	104.6
Pensacola, FL MSA	94.5	97.0	77.6	92.7	100.1	95.9
Peoria, IL MSA	102.6	101.6	111.3	98.9	101.8	94.8
Philadelphia, PA-NJ PMSA	127.2	112.7	139.3	185.0	110.6	130.4
Phoenix, AZ MSA	101.7	94.6	94.3	99.8	106.8	122.3
Portland, OR PMSA	108.0	100.9	134.0	71.6	103.4	129.0
Prova-Orem, UT MSA	93.1	91.8	75.3	86.2	96.6	102.3
Raleigh-Durham, NC MSA	96.4	95.9	98.7	104.8	91.9	96.9
Reno, NV MSA:						
Reno-Sparks, NV	104.0	96.9	125.1	81.8	98.0	116.2
Richmond-Petersburg, VA MSA	105.5	100.4	104.6	112.4	104.8	107.0
Riverside-San Bernardino, CA PMSA	111.3	102.1	138.0	87.1	107.7	131.1
Roanoke, VA MSA	96.8	95.0	99.9	86.2	104.3	91.4
Rockford, IL MSA	105.2	98.1	106.2	125.5	102.5	104.1
Sacramento, CA MSA	106.1	100.2	112.7	82.2	109.3	118.6
Saginaw-Bay City-Midland, MI MSA:						
Midland, MI	103.5	106.4	118.4	90.8	98.1	105.0
Salem, OR MSA	98.9	97.3	106.9	79.5	99.3	115.6
Salt Lake City-Ogden, UT MSA	93.8	98.4	81.3	92.2	101.4	94.9
San Antonio, TX MSA	93.1	98.2	85.3	73.0	114.4	94.0
San Diego, CA MSA	128.5	103.4	204.0	70.8	121.1	141.5
Savannah, GA MSA	97.3	99.1	89.3	99.0	102.6	104.5
Scranton-Wilkes Barre, PA MSA:						
Wilkes-Barre, PA	102.3	107.0	103.2	145.3	86.3	87.7
Seattle, WA PMSA	111.9	105.2	147.8	62.3	109.6	133.9
Shreveport, LA MSA	98.0	93.5	90.9	100.8	104.8	99.9
South Bend-Mishawaka, IN MSA	92.4	90.1	91.2	86.4	93.1	91.0
Springfield, IL MSA	98.2	100.6	97.6	89.4	101.2	101.6
Springfield, MA MSA	119.6	113.2	146.0	124.4	113.8	114.2
Springfield, MO MSA	90.6	97.2	76.1	97.4	96.1	95.2
St. Cloud, MN MSA	97.4	97.9	80.4	100.1	106.1	98.5
St. Louis, MO-IL MSA	97.7	98.0	96.8	105.2	98.9	100.4
Syracuse, NY MSA	103.2	106.9	92.6	115.8	109.7	108.8
Tacoma, WA MSA	100.3	107.6	100.0	59.6	104.1	137.0
Tampa-St. Petersburg-Clearwater, FL MSA	98.3	96.0	90.1	101.2	110.7	101.9
Toledo. OH MSA	106.1	101.8	113.9	118.7	106.4	92.0
Tucson, AZ MSA	104.2	95.5	99.0	89.8	102.1	121.3
Tulsa, OK MSA	94.7	95.5	71.8	91.5	100.1	105.8
Visalia-Tulare-Porterville, CA MSA	113.4	100.0	131.2	120.2	102.3	109.7
Waco, TX MSA	98.2	98.6	77.7	129.2	99.7	92.4
Washington, DC-MD-VA MSA	131.7	118.2	167.1	115.0	130.5	141.2
West Palm Beach-Boca Raton-Delray Beach, FL MSA	114.7	97.4	131.3	122.3	98.1	136.2
Wichita, KS MSA	95.5	79.7	91.4	116.2	93.0	102.6
Yakima, WA MSA	101.4	106.3	93.1	89.0	109.3	126.0
Youngstown-Warren, OH MSA	93.8	98.4	86.8	112.5	89.9	88.7

Source: American Chamber of Commerce Researchers Association (ACCRA), Alexandria, VA, *Cost of Living Index,* Third Quarter 1991, (copyright).

No. 746. Producer Price Indexes, by Stage of Processing: 1950 to 1991

[1982 = 100. See text, section 15. See *Historical Statistics, Colonial Times to 1970,* series E 73-86 for similar data]

YEAR	Crude materials	Crude foodstuffs and feedstuffs	Intermediate materials	Finished goods	Finished consumer goods	Capital equipment	YEAR	Crude materials	Crude foodstuffs and feedstuffs	Intermediate materials	Finished goods	Finished consumer goods	Capital equipment
1950...	32.7	43.4	25.3	28.2	32.7	23.2	1972...	39.9	51.5	38.2	41.8	46.9	42.8
1951...	37.6	50.2	28.4	30.8	36.7	25.5	1973...	54.5	72.6	42.4	45.6	56.5	44.2
1952...	34.5	47.3	27.5	30.6	36.4	25.9	1974...	61.4	76.4	52.5	52.6	64.4	50.5
1953...	31.9	42.3	27.7	30.3	34.5	26.3	1975...	61.6	77.4	58.0	58.2	69.8	58.2
1954...	31.6	42.3	27.9	30.4	34.2	26.7	1976...	63.4	76.8	60.9	60.8	69.6	62.1
1955...	30.4	38.4	28.4	30.5	33.4	27.4	1977...	65.5	77.5	64.9	64.7	73.3	66.1
1956...	30.6	37.6	29.6	31.3	33.3	29.5	1978...	73.4	87.3	69.5	69.8	79.9	71.3
1957...	31.2	39.2	30.3	32.5	34.4	31.3	1979...	85.9	100.0	78.4	77.6	87.3	77.5
1958...	31.9	41.6	30.4	33.2	36.5	32.1	1980...	95.3	104.6	90.3	88.0	92.4	85.8
1959...	31.1	38.8	30.8	33.1	34.8	32.7	1981...	103.0	103.9	98.6	96.1	97.8	94.6
1960...	30.4	38.4	30.8	33.4	35.5	32.8	1982...	100.0	100.0	100.0	100.0	100.0	100.0
1961...	30.2	37.9	30.6	33.4	35.4	32.9	1983...	101.3	101.8	100.6	101.6	101.0	102.8
1962...	30.5	38.6	30.6	33.5	35.7	33.0	1984...	103.5	104.7	103.1	103.7	105.4	105.2
1963...	29.9	37.5	30.7	33.4	35.3	33.1	1985...	95.8	94.8	102.7	104.7	104.6	107.5
1964...	29.6	36.6	30.8	33.5	35.4	33.4	1986...	87.7	93.2	99.1	103.2	107.3	109.7
1965...	31.1	39.2	31.2	34.1	36.8	33.8	1987...	93.7	96.2	101.5	105.4	109.5	111.7
1966...	33.1	42.7	32.0	35.2	39.2	34.6	1988...	96.0	106.1	107.1	108.0	112.6	114.3
1967...	31.3	40.3	32.2	35.6	38.5	35.8	1989...	103.1	111.2	112.0	113.6	118.7	118.0
1968...	31.8	40.9	33.0	36.6	40.0	37.0	1990...	108.9	113.1	114.5	119.2	124.4	122.9
1969...	33.9	44.1	34.1	38.0	42.4	38.3	1991...	101.2	105.5	114.4	121.7	124.1	126.9
1970...	35.2	45.2	35.4	39.3	43.8	40.1							
1971...	36.0	46.1	36.8	40.5	44.5	41.7							

Source: U.S. Bureau of Labor Statistics, *Producer Price Indexes,* monthly and annual.

No. 747. Stage of Processing Producer Prices—Annual Percent Change: 1960 to 1991

[1982 = 100. Yearly averages. See table 746]

YEAR	FINISHED GOODS			Finished consumer goods except foods	Intermediate materials, supplies and components	Intermediate materials, less food and feedstuffs	CRUDE MATERIALS			
	Total	Consumer goods	Capital equipment				Total	Crude foodstuffs and feedstuffs	Crude nonfood materials excluding fuel	Crude fuel
1960	0.9	0.9	0.3	0.6	-	0.7	-2.3	-1.0	-4.3	1.0
1961	-	-	0.3	-0.3	-0.6	-1.3	-0.7	-1.3	1.1	-
1962	0.3	0.3	0.3	-	-	-0.3	1.0	1.8	-0.4	-1.0
1963	-0.3	-0.6	0.3	-	0.3	-0.3	-2.0	-2.8	-1.5	1.0
1964	0.3	0.3	0.9	-0.3	0.3	0.7	-1.0	-2.4	1.9	-
1965	1.8	1.8	1.2	0.9	1.3	1.3	5.1	7.1	1.8	1.0
1966	3.2	3.5	2.4	1.5	2.6	2.0	6.4	8.9	2.2	2.8
1967	1.1	0.6	3.5	1.8	0.6	1.3	-5.4	-5.6	-6.4	3.7
1968	2.8	2.5	3.4	2.3	2.5	2.5	1.6	1.5	2.3	1.8
1969	3.8	3.8	3.5	2.3	3.3	3.4	6.6	7.8	4.8	4.3
1970	3.4	3.2	4.7	3.0	3.8	3.6	3.8	2.5	2.5	15.0
1971	3.1	2.8	4.0	3.5	4.0	4.0	2.3	2.0	1.0	13.8
1972	3.2	3.2	2.6	1.8	3.8	4.1	10.8	11.7	9.9	7.0
1973	9.1	10.8	3.3	4.6	11.0	7.7	36.6	41.0	32.8	10.7
1974	15.4	15.4	14.3	17.0	23.8	24.4	12.7	5.2	27.0	33.3
1975	10.6	9.6	15.2	10.4	10.5	12.1	0.3	1.3	-8.3	23.4
1976	4.5	3.8	6.7	6.2	5.0	6.0	2.9	-0.8	9.8	12.7
1977	6.4	6.5	6.4	7.3	6.6	6.8	3.3	0.9	2.6	21.7
1978	7.9	7.9	7.9	7.1	7.1	7.0	12.1	12.6	9.9	14.8
1979	11.2	11.7	8.7	13.3	12.8	12.8	17.0	14.5	22.0	18.9
1980	13.4	14.3	10.7	18.5	15.2	15.5	10.9	4.6	21.6	21.1
1981	9.2	9.0	10.3	10.3	9.2	9.8	8.1	-0.7	19.6	22.2
1982	4.1	3.5	5.7	4.1	1.4	1.8	-2.9	-3.8	-8.9	17.9
1983	1.6	1.3	2.8	1.2	0.6	0.5	1.3	1.8	-1.2	5.1
1984	2.1	2.0	2.3	1.0	2.5	2.5	2.2	2.8	2.2	-
1985	1.0	0.5	2.2	1.1	-0.4	-	-7.4	-9.5	-6.6	-2.3
1986	-1.4	-2.3	2.0	-4.6	-3.5	-3.6	-8.5	-1.7	-19.4	-10.2
1987	2.1	2.2	1.8	2.2	2.4	2.4	6.8	3.2	16.4	-8.8
1988	2.5	2.5	2.3	2.4	5.5	5.1	2.5	10.3	15.0	-2.4
1989	5.2	5.6	3.9	5.6	4.6	4.7	7.4	4.8	3.7	3.9
1990	4.9	5.4	3.5	5.9	2.2	2.3	5.6	1.7	12.0	-0.6
1991	2.1	1.9	3.1	2.9	-0.1	0.1	-7.1	-6.7	-9.2	-2.4

- Represents zero.

Source: U.S. Bureau of Labor Statistics, *Monthly Labor Review.*

No. 748. Producer Price Indexes for Selected Commodity Groupings, by Stage of Processing: 1960 to 1991

[1982=100 except as indicated]

COMMODITY	1960	1970	1980	1985	1988	1989	1990	1991
Finished goods	**33.4**	**39.3**	**88.0**	**104.7**	**108.0**	**113.6**	**119.2**	**121.7**
Finished consumer goods	33.6	39.1	88.6	103.8	106.2	112.1	118.2	121.5
Finished consumer foods	35.5	43.8	92.4	104.6	112.6	118.7	124.4	124.1
Fresh fruits............................	42.8	42.3	100.3	108.1	113.5	113.2	118.1	129.4
Fresh and dried vegetables	39.0	47.5	88.9	99.5	105.5	116.7	118.1	103.8
Eggs	68.5	71.0	95.7	95.7	88.6	119.6	117.6	110.7
Bakery products	32.3	40.0	90.0	113.9	126.4	135.4	141.0	146.6
Milled rice	51.5	52.4	131.5	105.0	118.1	104.9	102.5	110.0
Beef and veal	38.8	46.7	106.2	90.3	101.4	108.9	116.0	112.1
Pork	34.5	44.6	78.4	89.1	95.0	97.7	119.8	113.0
Processed young chickens	66.0	61.2	106.8	106.5	113.1	120.3	111.0	105.1
Processed turkeys	67.2	69.1	109.2	121.3	100.4	110.6	107.6	107.2
Fish...................................	19.3	29.7	87.8	114.6	148.7	142.9	147.2	151.3
Dairy products.........................	34.6	44.7	92.7	100.2	102.2	110.6	117.2	114.6
Processed fruits and vegetables.........	33.8	40.3	83.3	108.0	113.8	119.9	124.7	119.5
Soft drinks	25.6	37.8	81.8	107.7	114.3	117.7	122.3	125.6
Roasted coffee	28.7	37.7	110.4	107.2	113.5	115.9	113.0	107.9
Shortening and cooking oils............	37.8	47.7	99.5	124.0	118.8	116.6	123.2	116.4
Finished consumer goods excl. foods	33.5	37.4	87.1	103.3	103.1	108.9	115.3	118.7
Alcoholic beverages....................	49.6	53.3	88.9	107.7	111.8	115.2	117.2	123.7
Women's apparel.......................	56.9	62.8	86.9	105.4	111.3	113.5	116.1	117.8
Men's and boys' apparel.................	41.1	51.2	91.3	105.0	113.0	116.8	120.2	122.7
Girls', children's, and infants' apparel	47.6	58.8	87.1	103.1	107.5	110.5	115.3	117.6
Textile housefurnishings	40.3	43.4	86.8	100.6	104.4	106.6	109.5	111.8
Footwear	35.8	46.2	95.2	104.8	115.1	120.8	125.6	128.6
Natural gas...........................	NA	7.9	63.3	102.9	77.4	82.0	80.4	79.0
Gasoline	14.5	14.4	93.3	83.3	57.3	65.1	78.7	69.9
Fuel oil No. 2	(NA)	(NA)	82.8	81.6	49.5	58.0	73.3	65.2
Pharmaceutical preps, ethical (Prescription)	(NA)	52.0	80.6	132.0	169.0	184.4	200.8	217.0
Pharmaceut'l preps, propri.; Over-counter.	(NA)	42.3	81.3	121.6	144.4	152.1	156.8	165.7
Soaps and synthetic detergents	37.5	41.5	85.8	107.9	114.7	119.4	117.7	117.1
Cosmetics and other toilet preparations.......	40.9	47.8	83.8	109.0	116.3	119.3	121.6	124.5
Tires, tubes, tread, etc	38.0	42.7	92.8	93.0	94.0	97.2	96.8	98.3
Sanitary papers and health products	26.5	32.5	91.9	106.6	115.0	126.0	135.3	136.4
Household furniture	39.2	48.6	89.1	108.5	117.6	121.8	125.1	128.1
Floor coverings	59.3	54.9	90.0	105.6	114.7	117.6	119.0	120.2
Household appliances	54.0	52.9	87.5	106.7	106.0	108.7	110.8	111.3
Home electronic equipment..............	133.8	106.0	103.8	90.8	87.2	86.9	82.7	83.2
Household glassware	20.6	33.1	84.7	121.8	128.1	134.7	132.5	136.0
Household flatware	20.7	32.7	148.0	98.6	113.0	125.7	122.1	119.4
Lawn and garden equip., ex. tractors.........	39.2	46.8	87.5	110.3	114.6	119.8	123.0	124.9
Passenger cars........................	48.5	50.0	88.9	106.9	113.0	115.5	118.3	124.1
Toys, games, and children's vehicles	43.3	48.5	89.2	103.8	110.8	115.6	118.1	120.3
Sporting and athletic goods..............	45.5	52.7	90.6	99.7	105.9	108.8	112.6	115.2
Tobacco products	27.9	35.2	76.0	132.5	171.9	194.8	221.4	249.3
Mobile homes.........................	(NA)	(NA)	(NA)	101.7	109.3	114.0	117.5	120.4
Capital equipment.................	**32.8**	**40.1**	**85.8**	**107.5**	**114.3**	**118.8**	**122.9**	**126.7**
Agricultural machinery and equipment	27.7	36.4	83.3	108.7	112.7	117.7	121.7	125.2
Construction machinery and equipment	25.0	33.7	84.2	105.4	111.8	117.2	121.6	125.2
Metal cutting machine tools..............	(NA)	30.8	85.1	107.3	117.4	123.4	129.8	134.6
Metal forming machine tools	(NA)	28.6	85.7	107.0	113.2	118.1	128.7	133.5
Tools, dies, jigs, fixtures, and ind. molds	(NA)	(NA)	(NA)	106.3	110.9	113.8	117.2	122.6
Pumps, compressors, and equipment	23.9	33.0	82.8	102.6	108.9	115.0	119.2	124.6
Industrial material handling equipment........	30.9	39.8	88.4	102.7	107.5	111.7	115.0	117.4
Textile machinery......................	35.8	45.4	87.2	107.6	119.4	123.9	128.8	135.0
Paper industries machinery (June 1982=100). ..	(NA)	(NA)	(NA)	109.8	119.4	128.5	134.8	140.1
Printing trades machinery	26.9	42.5	89.7	109.0	120.1	123.0	124.9	126.7
Transformers and power regulators........	49.5	44.7	82.4	105.0	108.8	117.3	120.9	123.8
Oil field and gas field machinery...........	20.7	27.0	76.3	96.8	97.0	99.1	102.4	108.6
Mining machinery and equipment	24.5	30.9	85.2	105.4	110.2	116.3	121.0	125.2
Office and store machines and equipment	63.0	68.3	93.1	101.6	107.0	109.5	109.5	109.7
Commercial furniture	33.4	41.6	85.7	111.9	124.2	129.0	133.4	136.2
Light motor trucks	(NA)	42.0	83.3	112.2	125.0	129.5	130.0	135.5
Heavy motor trucks	(NA)	36.3	82.3	108.8	112.4	117.2	120.3	123.5
Truck trailers..........................	(NA)	(NA)	(NA)	106.2	106.6	110.4	110.8	112.2
Railroad equipment	(NA)	33.2	90.4	104.9	107.5	114.0	118.6	122.2
Photographic and photocopy equipment	71.4	72.0	94.9	89.5	91.8	94.1	97.2	99.4
Intermed. materials, supplies, comp'nts	**30.8**	**35.4**	**90.3**	**102.7**	**107.1**	**112.0**	**114.5**	**114.4**
Intermediate foods and feeds	(NA)	45.6	105.5	97.3	109.5	113.8	113.3	111.1
Flour..................................	47.9	55.3	102.3	98.9	105.7	114.6	103.6	97.6
Crude vegetable oils...................	57.6	75.8	127.1	137.6	116.6	103.1	115.8	103.2
Prepared animal feeds	37.2	49.1	107.3	90.1	116.0	116.6	107.4	106.8

See footnotes at end of table.

No. 748. Producer Price Indexes for Selected Commodity Groupings by Stage of Processing: 1960 to 1991—Continued

[1982=100 except as indicated]

COMMODITY	1960	1970	1980	1985	1988	1989	1990	1991
Intermediate materials less foods and feeds....	**30.7**	**34.8**	**89.4**	**103.0**	**106.9**	**111.9**	**114.5**	**114.6**
Leather	30.1	34.6	99.8	113.4	167.5	170.4	177.5	168.4
Liquefied petroleum gas	(NA)	(NA)	102.3	86.3	51.6	52.7	77.4	75.3
Electric power.	24.9	26.1	79.1	111.6	111.2	114.8	117.6	124.3
Jet fuels.	(NA)	(NA)	87.5	81.0	52.1	58.1	76.0	66.4
No. 2 Diesel fuel	(NA)	(NA)	85.8	81.2	49.7	58.9	74.1	65.5
Residual fuel.	9.3	10.6	81.3	83.2	41.1	47.6	57.7	46.9
Industrial chemicals	29.3	28.6	91.9	96.0	106.8	114.8	113.2	111.8
Prepared paint	35.0	42.8	89.5	105.3	112.2	119.5	124.8	129.9
Paint materials	36.7	33.3	89.9	109.5	115.7	129.1	136.3	135.8
Medicinal and botanical chemicals	53.9	44.4	91.0	91.8	93.5	100.3	102.2	109.1
Fats and oils, inedible.	37.5	49.7	111.6	110.6	110.9	95.5	88.1	86.8
Mixed fertilizers.	35.2	35.2	90.0	96.1	104.8	105.9	103.3	105.1
Nitrogenates.	48.4	32.7	90.0	96.3	93.3	94.9	92.3	98.5
Phosphates	28.4	27.5	93.0	91.6	103.3	105.6	96.5	98.2
Other agricultural chemicals.	(NA)	23.2	80.1	98.7	107.4	115.1	119.9	125.4
Plastic resins and materials	38.2	32.0	98.5	107.5	132.4	133.4	124.1	120.1
Synthetic rubber	34.8	34.0	85.3	96.8	108.9	108.5	111.9	106.0
Plastic construction products	(NA)	65.5	103.9	108.6	121.1	120.1	117.2	115.4
Softwood lumber	28.8	35.2	107.3	107.4	120.0	127.1	123.8	125.7
Hardwood lumber	34.6	43.7	96.0	117.1	131.0	128.2	131.0	128.5
Millwork	33.3	41.5	93.2	111.7	121.9	127.3	130.4	135.4
Plywood.	47.2	46.7	106.2	99.6	103.4	115.9	114.2	114.3
Woodpulp.	27.0	28.9	100.3	91.4	136.7	157.4	151.3	119.8
Paper	32.4	38.8	89.7	106.0	123.2	129.6	128.8	127.0
Paperboard.	41.0	39.7	92.0	107.7	133.2	140.1	135.7	130.2
Paper boxes and containers	40.3	43.3	89.4	108.8	123.5	129.8	129.9	128.6
Building paper and board	46.1	42.2	86.1	107.4	113.3	115.6	112.2	111.8
Commercial printing (June 1982=100)	(NA)	(NA)	(NA)	111.6	119.5	124.9	128.0	130.0
Foundry and forge shop products	26.6	32.4	89.7	105.2	109.6	114.6	117.2	119.0
Steel mill products	27.6	32.7	86.6	104.7	110.7	114.5	112.1	109.6
Primary nonferrous metals.	29.5	44.9	132.7	93.6	144.3	149.2	133.4	114.1
Aluminum mill shapes.	37.1	36.7	89.3	107.8	130.9	135.4	127.9	123.2
Copper and brass mill shapes	39.7	63.4	112.6	106.9	162.7	182.0	174.6	161.0
Nonferrous wire and cable.	39.8	62.6	107.5	100.9	129.6	146.1	142.6	139.3
Metal containers	27.3	34.3	90.9	109.0	110.2	111.5	114.0	115.6
Hardware	32.2	39.8	85.8	109.1	113.7	120.4	125.9	130.2
Plumbing fixtures and brass fittings	33.5	39.9	88.5	111.9	128.7	137.7	144.3	149.7
Heating equipment.	44.6	46.6	87.0	109.5	119.2	125.1	131.6	134.1
Fabricated structural metal products	31.4	36.7	88.8	103.2	114.3	120.3	121.8	122.4
Mechanical power transmission equipment.	27.3	36.9	84.5	108.2	116.0	121.1	125.3	129.1
Ball and roller bearings	34.2	33.1	80.0	105.9	114.0	124.1	130.6	136.7
Wiring devices.	(NA)	35.9	81.9	111.7	123.8	129.7	132.2	133.9
Motors, generators, motor generator sets.	34.3	37.7	86.0	113.3	121.8	129.0	132.9	135.0
Switchgear, switchboard, etc., equipment.	34.7	40.5	88.4	106.7	113.2	119.0	124.4	128.5
Electronic components and accessories	(NA)	57.4	88.8	112.4	117.5	119.4	118.4	118.8
Internal combustion engines	28.4	34.5	81.7	104.9	111.4	114.7	120.2	126.0
Machine shop products.	(NA)	31.1	81.0	112.8	116.8	121.3	124.3	126.0
Flat glass	(NA)	52.2	88.7	101.7	109.7	109.7	107.5	106.0
Concrete products	32.6	37.7	92.0	107.5	110.0	111.2	113.5	116.6
Asphalt felts and coatings.	24.4	25.8	99.6	102.6	94.7	95.8	97.1	98.3
Gypsum products.	38.7	38.9	100.1	132.3	112.9	110.0	105.2	99.5
Glass containers	27.6	33.9	82.3	106.8	112.3	115.2	120.4	125.4
Motor vehicle parts	(NA)	32.9	72.9	102.5	107.2	109.7	111.2	112.3
Photographic supplies.	34.7	41.0	97.2	107.4	113.1	123.0	127.6	126.1
Crude materials for further processing.	**30.4**	**35.2**	**95.3**	**95.8**	**96.0**	**103.1**	**108.9**	**101.2**
Crude foodstuffs and feedstuffs.	38.4	45.2	104.6	94.8	106.1	111.2	113.1	105.5
Wheat	51.2	39.7	108.3	87.6	93.7	109.5	87.6	79.5
Corn	46.0	54.5	119.2	105.9	97.1	102.4	100.9	97.0
Cattle	40.0	46.9	104.9	91.2	109.5	113.8	122.5	115.8
Hogs.	32.8	45.5	74.5	80.7	81.8	80.5	94.1	82.7
Live chickens (broilers and fryers).	63.1	48.5	103.4	110.5	125.4	131.7	119.5	111.9
Live turkeys	67.5	59.9	112.2	144.6	108.4	119.1	116.9	109.5
Fluid milk	30.0	40.8	96.0	93.7	89.4	98.8	100.8	89.3
Soybeans.	35.0	45.3	117.0	94.2	124.8	114.3	100.8	95.1
Cane sugar, raw	31.0	39.9	148.3	104.6	111.9	115.5	119.2	113.7
Crude nonfood materials.	**(NA)**	**23.8**	**84.6**	**96.9**	**85.5**	**93.4**	**101.5**	**94.6**
Raw cotton.	65.8	43.6	135.7	97.7	95.5	105.6	118.2	116.2
Leaf tobacco.	33.1	40.3	82.1	101.2	87.2	93.8	95.8	100.4
Cattle hides	33.5	30.4	104.6	126.1	205.8	213.1	217.8	173.5
Coal	17.9	28.1	87.4	102.2	95.4	95.5	97.5	97.2
Natural gas.	(NA)	7.9	63.3	102.9	77.4	82.0	80.4	79.0
Crude petroleum	13.4	14.5	75.9	84.5	46.2	56.3	71.0	61.9
Logs, timber, etc..	(NA)	(NA)	(NA)	96.0	117.7	131.9	142.8	144.0
Wastepaper	95.4	103.2	172.2	122.9	183.6	157.1	138.9	121.3
Iron ore	38.7	35.9	87.8	97.5	82.8	82.8	83.3	83.6
Iron and steel scrap	47.3	59.6	140.9	112.6	177.1	173.7	166.0	147.3
Nonferrous metal ores (Dec. 1983=100)	(NA)	(NA)	(NA)	73.2	108.1	109.6	98.3	82.9
Copper base scrap.	48.8	100.9	138.9	95.4	157.9	179.8	181.3	170.0
Aluminum base scrap.	35.0	34.4	183.9	123.4	219.5	204.4	172.6	142.7
Construction sand, gravel, and crushed stone. . .	33.5	40.9	85.3	110.7	120.6	122.8	125.4	128.6

NA Not available.

Source: U.S. Bureau of Labor Statistics, *Producer Price Indexes,* monthly and annual.

No. 749. Producer Price Indexes for the Net Output of Selected Industries: 1980 to 1991

[Indexes are based on selling prices reported by establishments of all sizes by probability sampling. Industries ranked by value added. N.e.c.= not elsewhere classified. See text section 27]

SIC code [1]	ITEM	Date	1980	1985	1988	1989	1990	1991
3711	Motor vehicles and passenger car bodies	06/82	86.0	107.2	114.1	117.4	119.9	125.3
2834	Pharmaceutical preparations	06/81	(NA)	141.3	175.6	190.2	203.5	217.1
3714	Motor vehicle parts and accessories	12/82	(NA)	100.6	105.3	107.4	108.9	110.3
2711	Newspaper publishing	12/79	106.8	164.0	193.9	206.9	220.4	235.6
2869	Industrial organic chemicals, n.e.c	12/82	(NA)	101.3	120.0	128.7	125.6	128.9
2911	Petroleum refining	06/85	104.6	98.3	65.4	73.6	90.1	80.8
2752	Commercial printing, lithographic	06/82	(NA)	111.0	118.5	124.1	127.9	129.8
2111	Cigarettes	12/82	62.5	110.7	150.8	173.1	197.6	224.6
3721	Aircraft	12/85	(NA)	(NA)	101.5	110.2	116.0	120.4
3312	Blast furnaces and steel mills	06/82	87.8	104.9	109.4	113.0	110.8	108.5
3674	Semiconductors and related devices	06/81	100.5	106.6	108.3	107.5	105.0	103.1
2621	Paper mill products except building paper	06/81	93.5	109.5	127.4	134.6	134.0	131.2
3861	Photographic equipment and supplies	12/83	(NA)	101.5	105.3	109.3	112.2	111.9
2721	Periodical publishing	12/79	105.5	157.9	183.8	194.0	205.7	217.7
3728	Aircraft parts and auxiliary equipment, n.e.c	06/85	(NA)	(NA)	109.6	113.1	116.3	120.1
2821	Plastic materials and resins	12/80	101.5	113.6	144.0	147.3	139.5	138.0
2844	Toilet preparations	03/80	(NA)	135.4	145.6	149.8	153.2	157.8
3724	Aircraft engines and engine parts	12/85	(NA)	(NA)	103.8	106.6	112.6	117.9
3599	Machinery, except electrical, n.e.c	06/84	(NA)	102.0	106.0	110.8	113.9	114.5
2731	Book publishing	12/80	(NA)	134.1	155.1	165.4	175.2	183.9
2819	Industrial inorganic chemicals, n.e.c	12/82	(NA)	100.4	104.7	116.2	117.9	119.4
2051	Bread, cake, and related products	06/80	(NA)	127.1	142.8	153.6	159.4	165.0
3661	Telephone & telegraph apparatus	12/85	(NA)	(NA)	108.3	110.2	112.0	112.8
2086	Bottled and canned soft drinks	06/81	(NA)	112.5	119.5	122.5	127.2	130.4
3679	Electronic components, n.e.c.	06/82	(NA)	108.6	112.5	113.9	115.1	115.2
3585	Refrigeration and heating equipment	12/82	88.3	104.7	110.8	115.5	119.0	119.6
2082	Malt beverages	06/82	(NA)	110.0	113.2	115.4	115.2	121.3
2631	Paperboard mills	12/82	97.3	112.0	141.6	149.9	146.0	140.7
2841	Soap and other detergents	06/83	(NA)	104.2	110.5	115.5	115.2	115.7
3531	Construction machinery	12/80	95.7	119.5	125.8	132.4	137.6	142.0
2851	Paints and allied products	06/83	(NA)	104.9	111.7	119.5	125.0	130.3
2011	Meat packing plants	12/80	98.2	90.9	101.7	108.2	119.8	115.0
3544	Special tools, dies, jigs, fixtures and indus. molds	06/81	(NA)	113.5	118.2	121.1	124.5	129.3
3011	Tires and inner tubes	06/81	93.9	96.8	99.5	102.9	103.0	105.1
2033	Canned fruits and vegetables	06/81	89.0	112.7	121.0	128.8	129.9	129.4
3731	Ship building and repairing	12/85	(NA)	(NA)	105.5	110.2	114.0	116.2
3465	Automotive stampings	12/82	94.5	110.4	108.1	109.9	112.6	111.7
2421	Sawmills and planing mills	12/80	(NA)	97.3	107.1	111.6	109.9	111.4
2759	Commercial printing, n.e.c.	06/82	(NA)	112.9	128.2	133.7	136.1	140.8
3523	Farm machinery and equipment	12/82	80.8	105.3	108.1	113.0	116.8	120.5
2824	Noncellulosic manmade fibers	06/81	84.5	97.6	96.8	101.5	102.7	101.9
2653	Corrugated and solid fiber boxes	03/80	(NA)	119.7	140.2	143.6	139.6	134.4
2026	Fluid milk	12/82	(NA)	102.6	106.0	112.8	121.4	119.0
3273	Ready-mixed concrete	06/81	92.7	108.6	109.7	111.5	114.3	117.0
3559	Special industry machinery, n.e.c	12/81	(NA)	116.4	127.2	132.9	137.5	142.4
2099	Food preparations, n.e.c.	12/85	(NA)	(NA)	104.8	110.4	114.3	117.3
2013	Sausages and other prepared meats	12/82	81.8	95.7	99.2	102.4	112.7	113.0
2899	Chemicals and chemical preparations, n.e.c.	06/85	(NA)	104.3	111.3	112.5	115.8	
3519	Internal combustion engines, n.e.c	12/82	78.9	103.4	106.7	110.6	115.7	120.7
3444	Sheet metal work	12/82	(NA)	107.2	121.4	128.4	129.4	128.2
2052	Cookies and crackers	06/83	(NA)	112.0	126.3	134.6	141.9	148.6
3469	Metal stampings, n.e.c.	06/84	(NA)	101.4	111.5	118.8	121.1	122.6
3357	Nonferrous wire drawing and insulating	12/82	(NA)	100.5	132.7	153.5	148.7	145.0
3429	Hardware, n.e.c.	06/85	(NA)	(NA)	100.7	106.5	110.6	113.3
2511	Wood household furniture, except upholstered	12/79	105.3	133.3	147.2	153.7	158.9	163.4
2411	Logging camps and logging contractors	12/81	(NA)	94.8	112.8	128.0	135.6	134.9
3443	Fabricated plate work	03/80	(NA)	120.8	129.6	137.1	142.3	145.8
3321	Gray iron foundries	12/80	97.2	115.6	118.3	120.9	123.4	125.6
2761	Manifold business forms	12/83	(NA)	106.2	120.3	124.9	124.6	123.9
3441	Fabricated structural metal	06/82	(NA)	103.0	113.0	118.0	118.6	117.3
3621	Electric motors and generators	06/83	82.3	108.2	116.4	123.3	127.5	129.8
2865	Cyclic (coal tar) crudes & intermediates	12/82	(NA)	96.9	105.8	112.7	114.1	113.3
2431	Millwork	06/83	(NA)	103.2	113.5	118.9	120.4	125.8
3499	Fabricated metal products, n.e.c.	06/85	(NA)	(NA)	109.6	114.6	117.6	119.0
2038	Frozen specialties	12/82	87.6	110.8	118.4	123.5	127.3	130.5
2842	Specialty cleaning, polish. and sanitation preps.	06/83	(NA)	103.9	110.2	115.6	118.6	121.5
3411	Metal cans	06/81	95.7	110.4	111.2	113.7	116.6	118.2
2221	Synthetic fiber and silk broadwoven fabric	06/81	91.0	101.2	101.1	110.1	112.3	115.2
2095	Coffee	06/81	112.9	111.5	117.8	120.4	120.0	116.6
2335	Women's, misses', and juniors' dresses	12/80	98.6	108.0	116.7	122.0	125.6	129.0

NA Not available. [1] Standard Industrial Classification code.

Source: U.S. Bureau of Labor Statistics, *Producer Price Indexes*, monthly.

No. 750. Fixed-Weighted Price Indexes for Personal Consumption Expenditures: 1960 to 1991

[1987 = 100.]

YEAR	Personal consumption expenditures [1]	Motor vehicles and parts	Furniture [2]	Food	Clothing and shoes	Gasoline and oil	Housing	Household operation	Electricity and gas	Transportation	Medical care
1960	30.9	40.6	78.5	27.4	46.1	30.5	28.8	32.0	24.6	25.5	17.8
1961	31.2	40.6	77.7	27.7	46.4	30.2	29.2	32.2	24.7	26.5	18.3
1962	31.4	40.8	76.1	28.0	46.5	30.4	29.5	32.3	24.8	26.8	18.8
1963	31.6	40.8	75.3	28.4	46.9	30.3	29.9	32.5	24.9	26.4	19.2
1964	32.0	41.0	74.8	29.0	47.3	30.1	30.2	32.6	24.7	26.4	19.9
1965	32.3	40.5	73.2	29.5	47.7	31.2	30.5	32.6	24.6	27.1	20.5
1966	32.9	40.1	71.7	30.7	49.0	32.0	30.9	32.5	24.6	27.9	21.5
1967	33.8	40.6	72.2	31.2	51.1	33.0	31.5	33.0	24.8	28.4	22.9
1968	35.1	41.9	73.3	32.3	54.0	33.5	32.3	33.6	25.0	29.2	24.6
1969	36.4	42.6	74.5	33.7	57.1	34.6	33.4	34.5	25.5	30.8	26.1
1970	38.0	43.8	75.2	35.9	59.4	34.9	34.8	35.6	26.4	33.8	27.9
1971	39.6	45.9	76.0	36.9	51.3	35.2	36.4	38.0	28.2	37.3	29.3
1972	40.9	45.9	76.6	38.6	62.7	35.7	37.7	39.9	29.7	38.6	30.7
1973	42.8	46.2	77.4	42.6	64.9	39.1	39.4	41.6	31.3	39.4	32.1
1974	46.8	49.1	81.1	48.7	69.5	52.7	40.9	45.8	36.6	42.1	34.7
1975	50.6	53.9	86.5	52.7	72.2	56.2	43.6	49.8	41.9	44.5	38.3
1976	53.4	57.8	88.9	54.4	74.5	58.6	46.5	53.6	45.6	49.3	41.7
1977	56.7	61.2	90.6	57.9	77.6	62.0	50.4	57.0	50.0	54.7	45.7
1978	60.7	65.3	93.6	63.1	79.5	64.7	54.0	60.2	53.8	57.9	50.0
1979	65.9	70.3	97.6	69.4	81.7	86.8	58.3	63.6	59.1	62.2	54.4
1980	72.6	75.6	98.5	75.9	85.2	120.7	63.8	69.7	69.0	71.9	60.4
1981	78.9	81.3	101.7	82.1	88.2	134.4	70.4	78.1	79.0	79.2	67.6
1982	83.2	85.1	103.6	85.4	90.0	127.5	75.9	86.7	89.1	83.0	74.7
1983	86.7	87.9	102.6	87.6	91.8	123.4	80.5	92.1	95.8	86.9	80.1
1984	89.9	90.5	101.7	91.1	93.0	121.5	84.9	96.3	100.0	89.6	85.0
1985	93.3	92.9	100.8	93.4	95.8	122.5	90.0	98.9	102.2	91.0	90.4
1986	96.1	95.7	99.5	96.5	95.8	96.2	95.4	100.4	101.7	94.0	94.6
1987	100.0	100.0	100.0	100.0	100.0	100.0	100.0	100.0	100.0	100.0	100.0
1988	104.3	101.5	101.0	104.0	104.2	100.9	104.9	101.4	100.8	104.9	107.1
1989	109.3	104.8	101.6	109.8	106.7	110.2	109.6	103.7	103.7	109.6	115.8
1990	115.0	106.4	102.4	115.7	111.4	125.6	115.3	105.7	105.4	114.5	123.6
1991	119.7	109.8	102.9	120.1	115.4	123.8	120.1	109.6	108.5	122.0	131.8

[1] Includes items not shown seperately.   [2] Includes household equipment.

No. 751. Fixed Weighted Price Indexes for Personal Consumption Expenditures—Annual Percent Change: 1960 to 1991

YEAR	Personal consumption expenditures [1]	Motor vehicles and parts	Furniture [2]	Food	Clothing and shoes	Gasoline and oil	Housing	Household operation	Electricity and gas	Transportation	Medical care
1960	1.3	-1.7	0.1	1.3	1.2	2.9	1.5	2.2	2.4	3.5	3.6
1961	0.9	0.0	-1.0	0.9	0.5	-0.9	1.3	0.7	0.5	3.7	2.7
1962	0.7	0.5	-2.0	1.2	0.2	0.6	1.2	0.4	-	1.3	2.8
1963	0.9	-	-1.0	1.4	1.0	-0.2	1.1	0.7	-0.1	-1.5	2.6
1964	1.1	0.4	-0.7	2.1	0.7	-0.6	1.0	0.3	-0.3	-0.1	3.2
1965	1.0	-1.2	-2.1	1.8	1.0	3.8	1.0	-0.2	-0.3	2.8	3.3
1966	1.8	-1.0	-2.0	3.9	2.6	2.3	1.4	-0.2	0.1	2.8	4.7
1967	2.6	1.3	0.6	1.7	4.2	3.3	1.9	1.5	0.7	2.0	6.6
1968	3.7	3.1	1.6	3.5	5.7	1.5	2.5	1.8	0.9	2.8	7.5
1969	3.7	1.9	1.5	4.6	5.7	3.3	3.4	2.6	2.0	5.3	5.9
1970	4.4	2.8	1.0	6.3	4.1	0.9	4.2	3.3	3.7	9.7	6.9
1971	4.4	4.8	1.0	2.9	3.2	0.8	4.6	6.6	6.8	10.3	5.1
1972	3.3	-	0.8	4.6	2.2	1.3	3.6	5.1	5.0	3.5	5.0
1973	4.6	0.6	1.0	10.4	3.6	9.5	4.4	4.2	5.6	2.1	4.4
1974	9.3	6.2	4.8	14.3	7.1	34.9	3.9	10.1	17.0	6.8	8.4
1975	8.1	9.9	6.6	8.2	3.8	6.7	6.6	8.6	14.5	5.7	10.1
1976	5.6	7.3	2.8	3.3	3.3	4.2	6.7	7.7	8.8	10.9	9.0
1977	6.3	5.7	1.9	6.5	4.1	5.8	8.5	6.3	9.6	10.9	9.6
1978	7.0	6.8	3.2	9.0	2.4	4.4	7.0	5.6	7.5	5.9	9.2
1979	8.5	7.6	4.3	10.0	2.9	34.2	8.0	5.7	9.9	7.3	9.0
1980	10.3	7.6	0.9	9.3	4.3	39.0	9.4	9.5	16.8	15.7	10.9
1981	8.6	7.5	3.3	8.2	3.5	11.3	10.3	12.1	14.4	10.2	11.8
1982	5.4	4.7	1.9	4.0	2.1	5.1	7.8	11.1	12.8	4.7	10.6
1983	4.3	3.2	-1.0	2.6	2.0	-3.3	6.1	6.2	7.5	4.8	7.2
1984	3.7	3.0	-0.8	3.9	1.3	-1.5	5.4	4.6	4.5	3.1	6.1
1985	3.8	2.7	-1.0	2.6	3.0	0.8	6.1	2.7	2.2	1.5	6.4
1986	3.0	3.0	-1.2	3.3	-	-21.5	6.0	1.5	-0.5	3.3	4.6
1987	4.1	4.5	0.5	3.6	4.3	4.0	4.8	-0.4	-1.7	6.4	5.7
1988	4.3	1.5	1.0	4.0	4.2	0.9	4.9	1.4	0.8	4.9	7.1
1989	4.8	3.2	0.5	5.6	2.4	9.2	4.6	2.2	2.8	4.5	8.1
1990	5.2	1.6	0.8	5.3	4.3	14.0	5.2	2.0	1.7	4.5	6.8
1991	4.1	3.2	0.5	3.8	3.7	-1.4	4.1	3.7	2.9	6.6	6.7

- Represents or rounds to zero.   [1] Includes items not shown seperately.   [2] Includes household equipment.

Source: U.S. Bureau of Economic Analysis, *The National Income and Product Accounts of the United States: Volume 2, 1959-88;* and *Survey of Current Business,* July issues.

No. 752. Fixed-Weighted Price Indexes: 1980 to 1991

[1987 = 100]

ITEM	1980	1982	1983	1984	1985	1986	1988	1989	1990	1991
Gross domestic product	(NA)	84.80	88.10	91.10	94.30	97.00	103.90	108.40	113.10	117.6
Personal consumption expenditures.	72.6	83.2	86.7	89.9	93.3	96.1	104.3	109.3	115.0	119.7
Durable goods	84.8	92.4	93.7	94.9	96.0	97.1	102.0	104.6	106.8	109.4
Nondurable goods.	79.6	88.8	91.1	93.7	96.2	96.2	103.8	109.5	116.2	120.5
Services	65.3	77.4	82.4	86.4	90.9	95.8	105.1	110.4	116.3	121.8
Gross private domestic investment:										
Fixed investment.	(NA)	95.8	95.0	94.8	95.8	97.9	103.2	106.2	108.7	110.5
Nonresidential	(NA)	100.6	98.5	97.0	97.5	98.9	102.7	105.5	107.9	110.2
Structures	78.5	93.0	92.5	94.1	96.9	98.5	104.6	109.0	111.9	113.6
Producers' durable equipment	(NA)	104.6	101.7	98.6	97.8	99.2	101.6	103.6	105.9	108.1
Residential	75.3	85.3	87.3	89.8	92.1	95.8	104.3	107.8	110.4	111.4
Exports of goods and services	(NA)	100.1	99.5	99.8	98.2	97.3	105.7	108.1	109.8	111.6
Imports of goods and services	(NA)	101.5	98.0	97.0	94.6	93.8	105.4	108.6	113.3	113.6
Government purchases	73.3	85.0	88.5	92.2	95.4	97.6	103.7	107.9	112.4	116.3
Federal	75.2	88.5	92.2	95.6	97.9	99.0	102.8	107.2	112.1	116.4
National defense	76.3	89.7	93.5	96.9	98.8	99.5	103.1	107.3	112.2	116.3
Nondefense	72.0	84.8	88.4	91.4	94.9	97.5	102.0	106.9	111.5	116.8
State and local	71.9	82.3	85.5	89.6	93.5	96.5	104.3	108.5	112.7	116.2

NA Not available.

Source: U.S. Bureau of Economic Analysis, *The National Income and Product Accounts of the United States, 1929-1982*, and *Survey of Current Business*, July issues.

No. 753. Fixed-Weighted Price Indexes—Annual Percent Change: 1980 to 1991

[1987 = 100]

ITEM	1980 –81	1982 –83	1983 –84	1984 –85	1985 –86	1986 –87	1987 –88	1988 –89	1989 –90	1990 –91
Gross domestic product.	(NA)	3.89	3.41	3.51	2.86	3.09	3.90	4.33	4.34	3.98
Personal consumption expenditures	8.7	4.2	3.7	3.8	3.0	4.1	4.3	4.8	5.2	4.1
Durable goods.	5.5	1.4	1.3	1.2	1.1	3.0	2.0	2.5	2.1	2.4
Nondurable goods	8.0	2.6	2.9	2.7	-	4.0	3.8	5.5	6.1	3.7
Services.	10.1	6.5	4.9	5.2	5.4	4.4	5.1	5.0	5.3	4.7
Gross private domestic investment:										
Fixed investment	(NA)	–0.8	–0.2	1.1	2.2	2.1	3.2	2.9	2.4	1.7
Nonresidential	(NA)	–2.1	–1.5	0.5	1.4	1.1	2.7	2.7	2.3	2.1
Structures.	11.2	–0.5	1.7	3.0	1.7	1.5	4.6	4.2	2.7	1.5
Producers' durable equipment	(NA)	–2.8	–3.0	–1.2	1.4	0.8	1.6	2.0	2.2	2.1
Residential	8.0	2.3	2.9	2.6	4.0	4.4	4.3	3.4	2.4	0.9
Exports of goods and services	(NA)	–0.6	0.3	–1.6	–0.9	2.8	5.7	2.3	1.6	1.6
Imports of goods and services	(NA)	–3.4	–1.0	–2.5	–0.8	6.6	5.4	3.0	4.3	0.3
Government purchases	8.6	4.1	4.2	3.5	2.3	2.5	3.7	4.1	4.2	3.5
Federal	9.4	4.2	3.7	2.4	1.1	1.0	2.8	4.3	4.6	3.8
National defense	9.2	4.2	3.6	2.0	0.7	0.5	3.1	4.1	4.6	3.7
Nondefense.	9.9	4.2	3.4	3.8	2.7	2.6	2.0	4.8	4.3	4.8
State and local	7.9	3.9	4.8	4.4	3.2	3.6	4.3	4.0	3.9	3.1

- Represents or rounds to zero.   NA Not available.

Source: U.S. Bureau of Economic Analysis, *The National Income and Product Accounts of the United States, 1929-1982*, and *Survey of Current Business*, July issues.

No. 754. Selected Mineral Products—Average Prices: 1975 to 1990

[**Represents average price, except as noted.** Excludes Alaska and Hawaii, except as noted. See also *Historical Statistics, Colonial Times to 1970*, series M96, 139, 148, 209, 248, and 262]

MINERAL	Unit	1975	1980	1981	1982	1983	1984	1985	1986	1987	1988	1989	1990, prel.
Aluminum [1]	Cents/lb.	39.8	71.6	76.0	76.0	77.8	81.0	81.0	81.0	72.3	110.1	87.8	74.0
Bituminous coal [2][3] . . .	Dol./sh. ton . .	19.2	24.5	26.3	27.1	25.9	25.5	25.1	23.7	23.0	22.0	21.8	22.0
Cobalt [4].	Dol./lb.	4.0	25.0	12.9	8.6	5.8	10.4	11.4	7.5	6.6	7.1	7.6	10.1
Copper, electrolytic . . .	Cents/lb.	64.2	101.3	84.2	72.8	76.5	66.8	67.0	66.1	82.5	120.5	130.9	(NA)
Gold	Dol./fine oz . .	161.0	613.0	460.0	376.0	424.0	361.0	318.0	368.0	448.0	438.0	382.6	386.9
Lead (NY)	Cents/lb.	21.5	42.5	36.5	25.5	21.7	25.6	19.1	22.1	35.9	37.1	39.4	46.02
Natural gas [2][5]	Dol./1,000 cu. ft	0.5	1.6	2.0	2.5	2.6	2.7	2.5	1.9	1.7	1.7	1.7	1.72
Nickel [6].	Dol./lb.	2.2	3.0	2.7	2.2	2.2	2.2	2.2	2.3	1.8	2.2	6.3	(NA)
Petroleum, crude [2]. . . .	Dol./bbl	7.7	21.6	31.8	28.5	26.2	25.9	24.1	12.5	15.4	12.6	15.9	20.03
Platinum [7]	Dol./troy oz . .	164.0	439.0	475.0	475.0	475.0	475.0	475.0	519.0	600.0	600.0	600.0	600.0
Silver	Dol./fine oz . .	4.4	20.6	10.5	8.0	11.4	8.1	6.1	5.5	7.0	6.5	5.5	4.8
Tungsten concentrate [8]	Dol./lb.	5.3	8.4	8.0	6.4	4.7	5.2	4.2	3.2	2.9	(NA)	(NA)	(NA)
Zinc [9]	Cents/lb.	39.0	37.4	44.6	38.5	41.4	48.6	40.4	38.0	41.9	60.2	82.1	(NA)

NA Not available.　[1] 99.5 percent primary aluminum ingot.　[2] Average value at point of production; includes Alaska. Source: U.S. Energy Information Administration, *Annual Energy Review* and *Monthly Energy Review.*　[3] Includes subbituminous coal and lignite.　[4] Weighted average based on the market price quoted by a major U.S. cobalt dealer, otherwise based on range of prices.　[5] Average value of marketed production.　[6] 1975, peak price quoted U.S. buyers by International Nickel Co., Inc., for electrolytic nickel, includes U.S. duty f.o.b. Port Colborne, Ontario; thereafter, from New York dealer.　[7] Producer prices.　[8] Average value of shipments.　[9] Delivered price.

Source: Except as noted, U.S. Bureau of Mines, *Minerals Yearbook.*

No. 755. Indexes of Spot Primary Market Prices: 1970 to 1990

[**1967 = 100.** Index computed weekly through 1981; daily, beginning May 27, 1981. Represents unweighted geometric average of price quotations of 23 commodities. This index is much more sensitive to changes in market conditions than is a monthly producer price index]

ITEMS AND NUMBER OF COMMODITIES	1970 (6-16)	1975 (6-24)	1980 (6-24)	1982 (5-25)	1983 (5-23)	1984 (5-22)	1985 (5-21)	1986 (5-20)	1987 (5-26)	1988 (5-27)	1989 (5-26)	1990 (5-25)
All commodities (22).	113.6	189.9	265.1	247.6	249.8	293.9	251.4	218.0	250.0	270.3	281.3	279.2
Foodstuffs (9)	112.2	215.3	260.9	252.8	246.1	299.9	248.1	205.5	215.2	230.1	222.5	231.5
Raw industrials (13).	114.4	174.1	268.0	243.9	252.3	289.7	253.6	226.9	277.3	302.0	329.0	317.0
Livestock and products (5)	123.6	240.8	250.5	312.1	278.1	364.5	284.5	231.2	303.3	316.1	285.2	306.9
Metals (5)	125.2	166.8	257.9	218.2	225.9	253.4	220.2	191.2	239.5	276.7	347.1	313.9
Textiles and fibers (4)	99.9	158.8	234.7	206.6	208.0	248.1	220.8	216.9	247.1	247.3	253.5	259.4
Fats and oils (4)	128.6	213.6	229.5	255.7	225.9	363.5	172.1	168.5	201.2	230.4	208.1	193.3

Source: 1970-80, U.S. Bureau of Labor Statistics, *Tuesday Spot Market Price Indexes and Prices,* weekly and monthly; thereafter, Commodity Research Bureau, a Knight-Ridder Business Information Service, New York, NY, *CRB Commodity Index Report,* weekly (copyright).

No. 756. Commodity Research Bureau Futures Price Index: 1975 to 1989

[**1967 = 100.** Index computed daily. Represents unweighted geometric average of commodity futures prices (through 9 months forward) of 21 major commodity futures markets. Represents end of year index]

ITEM	1975	1978	1979	1980	1981	1982	1983	1984	1985	1986	1987	1988	1989
All commodities	191.0	227.6	281.5	308.5	254.9	234.0	277.6	244.2	229.2	209.1	232.5	251.8	229.9
Imported	259.4	345.0	425.3	426.0	357.0	269.0	326.0	291.7	398.2	321.2	356.1	365.2	271.7
Industrial	154.8	222.1	354.8	324.6	249.2	249.9	249.0	217.0	211.7	210.4	252.5	248.2	249.6
Grains	195.6	187.8	251.9	312.1	251.3	215.1	249.6	224.9	198.5	164.6	186.1	261.9	205.7
Oilseeds	181.6	240.6	258.1	314.6	271.0	236.9	316.6	273.5	245.4	189.8	223.6	309.6	254.2
Livestock and meats	180.8	196.4	195.0	217.4	195.3	219.9	229.7	240.8	206.9	200.2	189.9	199.1	206.5
Metals (precious) [1]	141.0	230.4	658.0	531.4	319.7	366.0	328.5	243.3	256.6	296.6	346.4	318.7	296.9

[1] Prior to 1979, index for metals only.

Source: Commodity Research Bureau (CRB), New York City, NY, *CRB Commodity Index Report,* weekly, (copyright).

No. 757. Weekly Food Cost for Families, by Type of Family: 1975 to 1991

[In dollars. As of **December**, except as indicated. Based on moderate-cost food plan; assumes all meals are eaten at home or taken from home]

FAMILY TYPE	1975	1980	1984	1985	1986	1987	1988	1989	1990	1991 Jan.	1991 May
Couple, 20 to 50 years old [1]	37.10	52.00	56.50	58.30	60.40	63.50	66.70	70.40	74.70	76.30	77.00
Couple, 51 years and over [1]	32.40	45.90	53.90	55.70	57.80	60.70	64.00	67.50	71.80	73.50	74.10
Couple [2] with children:											
One child, 1 to 5 years old	44.90	62.90	69.20	71.30	73.90	77.50	81.60	86.40	91.70	93.70	94.50
One child, 15 to 19 years old	53.50	74.80	80.50	83.00	85.80	90.10	94.80	100.60	106.50	108.70	109.70
Two children, 1 to 5 years old	51.80	72.60	80.50	82.90	85.80	90.00	94.90	100.60	106.60	109.00	109.90
Two children, 6 to 11 years old	63.00	88.10	97.10	99.80	103.30	108.30	114.10	121.00	128.30	130.90	132.00
Two children, 12 to 19 years old	67.20	93.80	101.80	104.60	108.20	113.50	119.40	126.60	134.90	137.50	138.60

[1] 1975 and 1980, costs based on 1974 food plans with age groups 20 to 54 years old and 55 years old and over. [2] Couple 20 to 50 years old.

Source: U.S. Dept. of Agriculture, *Human Nutrition Information Service, Adm. 329,* monthly.

No. 758. Food—Retail Prices of Selected Items: December 1985 to 1991
[In dollars per pound, except as indicated. As of December]

FOOD	1985	1986	1987	1988	1989	1990	1991
Ground beef	1.28	1.26	1.32	1.40	1.50	1.63	1.58
Chuck, ground	1.68	1.65	1.75	1.79	1.88	2.02	1.93
Rib roast	3.37	3.39	3.57	4.03	4.21	4.54	4.59
Round steak	2.83	2.80	2.93	3.01	3.17	3.42	3.38
Sirloin steak, bone-in	2.98	2.93	3.17	3.23	3.46	3.65	3.78
T-bone steak	4.05	3.97	4.27	4.97	5.04	5.45	5.21
Bacon, sliced	1.92	2.16	2.02	1.79	1.96	2.28	1.99
Chops, center cut	2.39	2.75	2.67	2.65	2.85	3.32	3.12
Sausage	1.78	2.05	1.99	1.92	2.12	2.42	2.24
Chicken, fresh, whole	0.78	0.87	0.74	0.89	0.88	0.86	0.86
Chicken breast	1.74	1.99	1.72	2.06	2.01	2.00	2.02
Turkey, frozen	1.03	1.02	0.89	0.97	0.95	0.96	0.91
Tuna, canned	2.04	1.94	2.11	2.18	2.04	2.11	2.05
Eggs, Grade A, large, (dozen)	0.91	0.91	0.73	0.83	1.14	1.00	1.01
Milk, fresh, whole (1/2 gal.)	1.11	1.13	1.16	1.21	1.37	1.39	1.40
Ice cream (1/2 gal.)	2.29	2.41	2.44	2.54	2.67	2.54	2.63
Apples, red Delicious	0.68	0.66	0.55	0.71	0.57	0.77	0.86
Bananas	0.32	0.33	0.38	0.41	0.42	0.43	0.42
Pears, Anjou	0.69	0.72	0.57	0.64	0.76	0.79	0.88
Potatoes, white	0.17	0.26	0.25	0.30	0.31	0.32	0.28
Lettuce, iceberg	0.71	0.56	1.25	0.77	0.52	0.58	0.69
Tomatoes, field grown	0.95	0.94	1.00	0.81	0.90	0.86	0.79
Margarine, stick	0.80	0.76	0.68	0.80	0.83	0.87	0.83
Peanut butter	1.57	1.68	1.82	1.82	1.82	2.07	2.04
Sugar, white	0.35	0.35	0.36	0.38	0.41	0.43	0.42
Coffee, roasted	2.51	3.25	2.55	2.93	2.94	2.94	2.63

Source: U.S. Bureau of Labor Statistics, *CPI Detailed Report,* January issues.

No. 759. Average Prices of Selected Fuels and Electricity: 1975 to 1990

[In dollars per unit, except electricity, in cents per kWh. Represents price to end-users, except as noted]

ITEM	Unit [1]	1975	1980	1981	1982	1983	1984	1985	1986	1987	1988	1989	1990
Crude oil, composite [2]	Barrel	10.38	28.07	35.24	31.87	28.99	28.63	26.75	14.55	17.90	14.67	17.97	22.23
Motor gasoline: [3]													
Leaded regular	Gallon	0.57	1.19	1.31	1.22	1.16	1.13	1.12	0.86	0.90	0.90	1.00	1.15
Unleaded regular	Gallon	(NA)	1.25	1.38	1.30	1.24	1.21	1.20	0.93	0.95	0.95	1.02	1.16
Unleaded premium	Gallon	(NA)	1.47	1.42	1.38	1.37	1.34	1.09	1.09	1.11	1.20	1.35
No. 2 heating oil	Gallon	(NA)	0.79	0.91	0.91	0.92	0.92	0.85	0.56	0.58	0.54	0.59	0.73
No. 2 diesel fuel	Gallon	(NA)	0.82	1.00	0.94	0.83	0.82	0.79	0.48	0.55	0.50	0.59	0.73
Residual fuel oil	Gallon	(NA)	0.61	0.76	0.68	0.65	0.69	0.61	0.34	0.42	0.33	0.39	0.44
Natural gas, residential	1,000 cu/ft	1.71	3.68	4.29	5.17	6.06	6.12	6.12	5.83	5.54	5.47	5.64	5.77
Electricity, residential	kWh	3.5	5.4	6.2	6.9	7.2	7.5	7.8	7.4	7.4	7.5	7.6	7.8

NA Not available. [1] See headnote. [2] Refiner acquisition cost. [3] Average, all service.

Source: U.S. Energy Information Administration, *Monthly Energy Review,* July 1991.

No. 760. Import Price Indexes—Selected Commodities: 1980 to 1991

[1985 = 100, except as noted. **As of June quarter.** Indexes are weighted by the 1985 Tariff Schedule of the United States Annotated, a scheme for describing and reporting product composition and value of U.S. imports. Import prices are based on U.S. dollar prices paid by importer. F.o.b. = Free on board; c.i.f. = Cost, insurance, and freight; n.e.s. = Not elsewhere specified]

COMMODITY	1980	1984	1985 [1]	1986	1987	1988	1989	1990	1991
All commodities	(NA)	103.9	99.2	98.7	110.0	116.8	119.8	118.9	122.4
Food	105.1	104.2	98.9	107.3	108.3	114.0	111.3	111.9	116.1
Meat	112.5	107.9	94.0	96.0	108.0	107.0	109.7	136.5	144.1
Meat, edible meat offals, fresh, chilled or frozen	114.5	109.4	93.2	91.1	102.0	104.6	108.0	133.4	136.8
Meat and edible meat offals, prepared or preserved, n.e.s.; fish extracts	108.7	105.8	95.6	106.5	120.6	111.5	113.3	143.5	159.9
Dairy products and eggs	(NA)	100.7	98.7	108.7	122.3	125.0	120.2	132.6	131.6
Fish	94.5	101.9	98.6	110.5	126.0	129.3	122.7	126.2	140.4
Shellfish, fresh, chilled, frozen, salted, or dried, c.i.f.	84.0	106.7	99.4	113.3	123.2	123.1	115.1	114.0	125.5
Fish in airtight containers, c.i.f.	111.8	102.3	98.1	103.6	113.7	130.2	124.9	125.8	133.1
Bakery goods [2]	95.7	98.4	97.1	112.5	126.2	139.8	140.2	151.7	148.2
Fruits and vegetables	79.2	107.4	103.0	100.0	110.1	120.3	123.2	125.9	132.4
Sugar [3]	(NA)	101.8	102.3	104.6	109.6	110.0	111.8	116.7	113.2
Coffee, tea, cocoa	114.9	105.6	96.8	117.2	87.0	93.3	85.3	66.3	62.1
Beverages and tobacco	85.7	98.2	99.2	105.2	112.8	116.2	117.2	127.6	142.5
Beverages	87.2	98.3	98.9	106.1	114.2	120.0	120.7	129.5	143.8
Alcoholic	87.2	98.2	98.9	105.8	113.7	119.3	120.5	129.2	143.8
Wine of fresh grapes, c.i.f.	92.7	96.2	98.7	109.7	121.0	127.3	125.3	135.5	151.3
Beer, c.i.f.	(NA)	98.5	100.1	103.2	111.4	114.2	114.8	117.0	123.6
Spirits, c.i.f.	80.5	99.4	98.5	104.1	109.1	115.6	119.2	130.0	147.6
Crude materials	(NA)	108.4	100.5	106.4	116.2	137.8	144.3	131.7	123.9
Crude rubber [4]	(NA)	120.9	101.0	99.5	103.7	151.1	103.4	104.0	101.1
Wood	(NA)	99.8	105.0	104.3	110.2	111.4	112.4	115.1	121.0
Lumber	94.8	99.6	105.4	104.6	110.0	111.1	110.8	112.8	118.6
Pulp and waste paper	(NA)	121.3	101.4	100.3	132.0	160.5	190.0	183.3	141.1
Crude minerals	(NA)	96.0	100.6	99.0	99.6	101.0	104.7	97.5	98.8
Metalliferous ores and metal scrap	(NA)	114.5	95.6	121.6	124.5	167.6	213.2	160.7	149.2
Ores and concentrates of base metals, n.e.s.	(NA)	120.4	94.5	134.0	136.4	192.9	258.1	179.7	166.4
Crude vegetable and animal materials, n.e.s.	(NA)	91.6	94.8	111.3	109.0	148.2	110.3	117.4	117.1
Fuels and related products	(NA)	108.7	99.7	51.5	74.1	63.4	73.3	63.7	72.5
Crude petroleum and petroleum products	(NA)	107.2	99.5	49.0	74.4	63.6	74.4	64.0	73.5
Crude petroleum	120.3	107.7	100.5	45.8	68.7	57.5	67.1	54.2	66.0
Natural gas and LNG	(NA)	131.0	102.3	79.7	67.8	58.7	61.0	60.0	56.5
Fats and oils	(NA)	174.3	110.0	66.7	87.9	112.4	117.4	95.7	97.3
Chemicals and related products	(NA)	104.5	100.4	99.7	104.8	116.4	120.4	118.2	120.9
Intermediate manufactured products	105.9	104.2	99.1	103.6	112.5	132.2	136.1	135.0	134.7
Leather and furskins	103.1	105.8	97.9	106.3	116.6	137.0	133.8	143.8	142.5
Rubber manufactures	100.4	102.2	99.5	101.2	104.6	107.0	112.2	115.6	116.5
Cork and wood manufactures	103.7	104.4	99.2	111.0	124.3	138.2	139.8	144.4	141.8
Paper and paperboard products	84.3	95.7	99.9	100.8	104.9	118.3	120.8	121.2	122.0
Paper and paperboard	83.8	95.1	100.0	98.9	102.5	115.5	117.9	118.3	119.5
Newsprint, c.i.f.	83.0	94.0	100.1	99.2	105.0	119.1	119.6	120.5	121.3
Textiles	101.5	99.4	98.9	105.4	111.8	120.6	122.1	125.8	131.3
Non-metallic mineral manufactures	100.9	106.0	96.2	110.5	126.7	142.5	149.5	159.9	165.5
Iron and steel	99.2	102.9	100.2	98.9	106.6	127.2	133.6	125.9	125.4
Non-ferrous metals	(NA)	118.1	100.2	98.9	112.4	159.7	158.6	143.3	129.3
Silver platinum, other metals of platinum group, c.i.f.	(NA)	132.9	94.6	106.8	141.7	136.4	119.0	124.3	119.8
Copper	129.7	104.6	100.6	103.9	107.8	149.0	172.1	172.2	154.8
Nickel, c.i.f.	(NA)	98.1	105.7	88.1	83.5	262.4	258.0	161.8	165.5
Zinc	91.2	126.9	109.4	83.2	101.3	147.1	210.3	219.0	149.2
Tin, c.i.f.	148.5	108.6	103.9	49.0	60.4	62.0	83.6	59.9	50.7
Metal manufactures, n.e.s.	103.3	100.5	99.2	107.9	112.7	126.9	132.6	134.6	137.7
Machinery and transport equipment	(NA)	100.5	98.9	110.4	119.9	127.3	129.2	130.1	133.9
Machinery specialized for particular industries	(NA)	100.1	96.4	116.9	136.1	149.8	145.7	158.8	166.0
Metalworking machinery	109.6	102.1	98.3	113.0	128.1	142.4	139.5	149.6	152.5
General industrial machinery, parts, n.e.s.	(NA)	101.8	98.0	116.2	130.8	143.7	143.0	153.0	159.0
Office machines [5]	109.9	105.8	98.5	109.1	114.0	119.5	119.3	115.7	112.7
Telecommunications [6]	115.0	107.4	100.2	106.4	110.3	113.8	115.7	111.4	108.7
Electric machinery and equipment	(NA)	107.2	100.3	106.4	115.8	124.2	129.6	127.8	130.2
Road vehicles and parts	(NA)	97.2	98.8	110.8	120.5	127.6	129.6	129.5	136.3
Misc. manufactured articles	100.3	102.7	99.2	106.8	117.8	125.7	126.6	132.0	134.2
Plumbing, heating and lighting fixtures	87.8	98.3	98.6	108.6	117.0	126.9	131.5	140.8	140.2
Furniture and parts	106.8	102.5	98.6	109.0	116.5	124.0	125.3	132.1	134.9
Clothing	88.1	98.5	99.8	100.7	109.2	114.9	119.9	122.8	120.7
Footwear, c.i.f.	101.1	102.0	98.1	108.0	119.8	129.6	127.9	137.6	140.3
Professional, scientific and controlling instruments, and apparatus	109.4	102.3	96.1	117.9	135.9	142.5	136.5	145.5	152.5
Photographic apparatus [7]	111.1	101.5	98.9	113.8	126.0	129.3	127.9	131.8	134.7
Misc. manufactured articles, n.e.s.	(NA)	103.0	99.6	108.1	121.1	132.1	131.4	137.3	142.8

NA Not available. [1] June 1985 may not equal 100 because indexes were reweighted to an "average" trade value in 1985. [2] Includes pasta products, grain and grain preparations. [3] Includes sugar preparations and honey. [4] Includes synthetic and reclaimed rubber. [5] Includes automatic data processing equipment. [6] Includes sound recording and reproducing equipment. [7] Includes photographic supplies, optical goods, watches and clocks.

Source: U.S. Bureau of Labor Statistics, *News,* quarterly.

No. 761. Export Price Indexes—Selected Commodities: 1980 to 1991

[1985= 100, except as noted. **June quarter.** Indexes are weighted by 1980 export values according to the Schedule B classification system of the U.S. Bureau of the Census. Prices used in these indexes were collected from a sample of U.S. manufacturers of exports and are factory transaction prices, except as noted. F.a.s. = free alongside ship. N.e.s. = not elsewhere specified. F.o.b. = free on board]

COMMODITY	1980	1984	1985 [1]	1986	1987	1988	1989	1990	1991
All commodities	(NA)	104.1	100.4	99.1	102.2	109.5	113.2	113.3	114.7
Food	(NA)	116.3	100.5	97.1	89.9	103.4	115.5	108.8	105.1
Meat	(NA)	102.1	98.8	105.2	121.2	131.0	128.2	123.7	128.0
Fish	(NA)	96.3	101.2	108.6	125.8	145.0	158.9	126.9	122.1
Grain and grain preparations	106.5	121.8	102.5	89.0	71.0	87.2	106.4	101.8	90.8
Wheat	113.7	110.2	99.8	80.7	66.8	87.8	116.1	96.9	78.8
Rice	128.3	107.2	101.6	67.9	59.1	105.7	95.7	93.1	102.7
Corn, yellow, f.o.b.	99.7	131.3	104.0	95.2	72.7	83.7	101.5	104.8	94.3
Other grain	(NA)	(NA)	106.3	96.5	77.7	87.6	104.9	106.0	98.8
Fruits and vegetables	(NA)	102.8	100.1	108.6	112.4	104.3	113.6	115.2	137.2
Feedstuff for animals	(NA)	129.9	90.9	114.8	123.8	158.1	144.0	118.4	121.2
Miscellaneous food products	(NA)	100.5	99.9	97.0	100.6	102.8	108.0	110.2	110.8
Beverages and tobacco	(NA)	102.4	100.1	97.4	105.0	110.6	117.6	124.5	132.6
Tobacco and tobacco products	(NA)	102.5	100.1	97.1	105.0	110.7	117.9	124.9	132.8
Crude materials	(NA)	123.6	101.6	102.2	114.5	139.9	143.0	137.3	130.3
Raw hides and skins	76.4	118.1	97.4	117.1	149.6	166.8	149.9	162.0	125.6
Oilseeds and oleaginous fruit	109.3	154.1	105.5	98.1	101.6	143.0	129.8	110.4	112.9
Crude rubber, f.a.s.	(NA)	100.3	99.8	99.9	101.0	106.1	114.6	115.5	120.3
Wood	122.9	101.3	98.7	101.2	116.2	149.6	170.7	179.2	171.9
Pulp and waste paper	(NA)	127.5	100.3	116.4	149.9	179.5	193.5	174.3	150.8
Textile fibers	108.3	120.5	103.5	98.0	112.4	109.9	115.5	124.5	129.7
Cotton	120.5	133.0	103.4	95.5	114.4	108.8	110.9	122.7	127.6
Crude minerals and fertilizers	79.2	88.9	100.4	98.4	94.0	94.2	99.2	99.7	100.7
Metal ores and scrap	(NA)	117.2	100.9	98.0	107.0	146.0	157.2	142.6	127.2
Scrap metal (iron or steel) f.a.s.	123.4	112.1	100.2	96.1	95.8	147.7	154.3	137.1	128.2
Nonferrous base metal waste and scrap, n.e.s., f.a.s.	(NA)	118.9	98.9	101.3	126.9	185.6	197.0	174.0	147.4
Fuels and related products	(NA)	101.5	101.8	76.8	82.8	82.1	86.0	88.7	87.5
Coal and coke	(NA)	(NA)	100.5	94.0	88.2	92.0	94.3	97.5	96.1
Crude petroleum and petroleum products [2]	(NA)	(NA)	(NA)	(NA)	(NA)	97.2	105.4	108.7	103.7
Fats and oils	(NA)	130.9	113.4	67.7	78.8	97.3	87.3	94.6	86.2
Vegetable oils	(NA)	125.8	116.8	70.6	71.9	93.7	84.4	101.7	89.5
Chemicals and related products	(NA)	102.4	100.2	98.0	106.7	121.6	121.9	115.5	118.1
Organic chemicals	(NA)	106.8	100.6	93.1	118.4	144.6	145.0	118.8	118.2
Hydrocarbons, n.e.s. and derivatives, f.a.s.	136.3	113.9	101.4	86.4	142.8	169.0	157.6	128.0	104.6
Alcohols, phenols, phenol-alcohols, and deriv., f.a.s.	117.6	107.2	99.9	96.9	102.7	143.8	186.8	122.3	129.3
Carboxylic acids, f.a.s.	101.1	104.2	100.7	99.0	103.2	127.5	120.9	112.6	126.6
Fertilizers, manufactured	(NA)	107.1	97.2	93.0	91.6	109.8	108.0	102.8	111.0
Pesticides, starches, glue, gas and oil additives, chemical materials and products, n.e.s.	(NA)	97.1	99.9	101.8	97.7	101.7	109.4	113.7	119.1
Intermediate manufactured products	(NA)	101.6	100.2	102.5	107.9	117.7	123.1	123.0	123.3
Leather and fur skins	103.4	104.5	99.1	103.8	126.9	125.1	120.7	126.0	118.1
Rubber manufactures	82.6	98.7	100.2	100.1	102.5	108.8	112.9	114.4	121.5
Paper and paperboard products	86.0	102.0	100.5	104.7	117.0	129.0	133.7	130.3	130.2
Textiles [3]	(NA)	(NA)	100.2	102.9	103.7	107.9	115.4	118.3	123.7
Non-metallic mineral manufactures [3]	(NA)	(NA)	(NA)	102.4	108.7	114.1	122.4	126.9	128.9
Iron and steel	(NA)	100.4	99.5	100.2	102.9	110.8	117.2	117.4	119.1
Non-ferrous metals	(NA)	111.6	102.0	103.1	113.0	143.5	145.8	132.6	116.5
Metal manufactures, n.e.s.	(NA)	98.3	99.7	100.8	101.3	107.6	113.9	117.1	120.5
Machinery and transport equipment [4]	79.1	97.8	100.0	100.8	101.8	104.0	107.2	110.1	113.5
Power generating machinery [5]	70.5	93.2	100.1	102.4	103.7	108.4	112.8	117.2	123.0
Internal combustion piston engines, parts	73.5	99.8	99.8	101.4	102.9	107.1	108.9	112.5	118.2
Electric motors, generators, other rotating plant, f.o.b., factory	84.5	95.7	101.0	103.2	107.7	117.9	124.9	131.1	133.9
Machinery specialized for particular industries	76.9	98.1	100.0	100.3	100.1	103.6	108.8	113.2	117.8
Agricultural machinery and parts [6]	72.6	97.6	99.7	100.4	101.2	102.1	104.9	111.5	113.8
Civil engineering and contractors, plant and equip. [7]	77.4	99.6	100.3	98.4	96.0	98.5	105.3	109.3	114.9
Metalworking machinery	77.5	97.0	99.7	102.0	106.7	110.8	117.3	121.1	129.4
General industrial machines, parts, n.e.s.	76.6	97.2	100.0	101.6	104.5	108.1	113.3	118.2	122.9
Office machines [8]	101.6	102.4	99.8	99.0	96.1	95.7	94.8	94.6	92.7
Telecommunications [9]	88.8	99.0	99.6	98.9	101.4	104.6	107.5	111.2	118.2
Electrical machinery, equipment	87.6	98.4	100.9	99.2	102.1	103.4	106.5	105.5	108.2
Road vehicles and parts	76.8	97.5	100.1	101.7	103.5	104.9	107.8	111.0	114.1
Other transport equipment [4]	64.4	94.5	99.2	103.1	105.5	109.6	114.7	121.3	136.5
Miscellaneous manufactured articles	(NA)	99.7	100.3	103.5	105.2	108.1	112.8	116.4	122.4

NA Not available. [1] June 1985 may not equal 100 because indexes were reweighted to an "average" trade value in 1985. [2] December 1987 = 100. [3] September 1985 = 100. [4] Excludes military and commercial aircraft. [5] Includes equipment. [6] Excludes tractors. [7] Includes parts. [8] Includes data processing equipment. [9] Includes sound recording and reproducing equipment.

Source: U.S. Bureau of Labor Statistics, *News,* quarterly.

No. 762. Refiner/Reseller Sales Price of Motor Gasoline, by Grade and State: 1989 to 1991

[In cents per gallon. As of **March**. Represents all refinery and gas plant operators' sales through company-operated retail outlets. Gasoline prices exclude excise taxes]

STATE	Gasoline excise taxes 1991 [1]	AVERAGE, ALL GRADES			LEADED REGULAR			UNLEADED REGULAR			PREMIUM		
		1989	1990	1991	1989	1990	1991	1989	1990	1991	1989	1990	1991
United States . .	(NA)	70.5	76.8	(NA)	66.7	74.5	(NA)	66.9	72.5	(NA)	81.7	88.8	(NA)
Northeast:													
New England:													
Maine	19	80.0	85.8	90.0	76.9	(D)	(NA)	76.1	81.6	86.9	91.4	99.0	102.2
New Hampshire . . .	18	78.4	84.9	85.2	76.1	(D)	(D)	73.9	79.1	82.0	88.0	97.0	95.7
Vermont	15	80.6	88.8	91.6	75.1	96.3	(D)	76.5	84.2	88.2	91.1	100.4	102.8
Massachusetts	21	79.8	82.9	83.1	73.1	(D)	86.4	74.0	76.1	78.8	90.1	96.6	94.4
Rhode Island	26	77.3	81.7	82.9	74.2	(NA)	(NA)	71.7	75.2	78.9	86.4	93.9	91.7
Connecticut	25	82.8	82.9	83.0	74.8	(D)	(D)	78.3	75.1	78.5	92.3	96.4	93.7
Middle Atlantic:													
New York	8	75.5	78.7	87.0	70.5	77.7	87.1	70.4	72.9	83.2	87.7	92.2	99.5
New Jersey	11	79.1	80.3	83.4	69.9	(D)	(NA)	71.3	72.3	77.9	90.6	90.4	94.2
Pennsylvania	12	70.7	77.1	82.4	67.7	79.8	(D)	64.3	70.5	78.5	83.6	89.9	94.2
North Central:													
East North Central:													
Ohio	21	71.7	75.0	73.4	71.0	79.2	78.4	67.2	70.5	70.7	86.3	90.1	84.6
Indiana	15	66.8	75.1	77.3	69.0	83.8	84.8	63.8	71.3	75.0	77.7	85.5	87.6
Illinois	19	69.2	73.2	76.1	68.6	77.7	88.2	65.5	69.5	73.4	79.8	83.9	86.2
Michigan	15	66.9	72.7	74.0	70.8	75.5	79.2	63.7	69.6	71.7	77.9	83.5	84.9
Wisconsin	22	67.5	72.8	76.8	68.2	79.2	82.2	65.2	69.7	75.1	75.2	84.2	86.6
West North Central:													
Minnesota	20	69.5	77.9	77.6	69.5	79.2	79.3	67.7	76.1	76.1	78.2	87.2	85.0
Iowa	20	67.9	75.9	80.0	68.4	77.0	83.7	66.9	74.6	79.1	77.5	84.6	86.4
Missouri	11	66.0	71.8	75.6	65.5	73.1	78.7	63.2	67.8	73.1	76.6	83.6	85.5
North Dakota	17	72.5	85.3	82.8	72.1	86.9	85.5	72.2	84.4	82.2	79.0	93.2	85.6
South Dakota	18	70.5	83.1	80.8	70.2	82.4	80.2	70.4	82.3	79.9	79.8	90.7	90.4
Nebraska	23	70.3	73.0	80.9	70.1	72.9	78.6	70.2	72.3	79.0	73.0	78.9	87.9
Kansas	17	66.2	73.0	76.2	66.8	73.4	77.8	64.5	71.4	74.9	74.1	82.6	85.3
South:													
South Atlantic:													
Delaware	19	73.0	81.0	83.8	68.9	(NA)	(NA)	67.1	74.4	78.8	85.1	94.9	98.4
Maryland	19	74.7	84.4	78.8	69.2	(D)	(NA)	70.2	78.7	73.0	85.3	95.0	93.3
District of Columbia .	18	(D)	0.0	(D)	(D)	(D)	(D)	(D)	(D)	(D)	(D)	(D)	(D)
Virginia	18	74.5	80.5	77.2	65.6	75.0	72.4	69.3	74.4	72.7	84.7	91.5	89.1
West Virginia	16	75.1	81.0	81.1	71.4	0.0	(D)	69.9	74.5	76.9	88.1	97.2	95.8
North Carolina	23	69.4	76.3	76.2	63.2	70.8	(D)	65.1	70.5	72.3	80.8	88.9	88.3
South Carolina	16	69.1	78.9	75.6	64.4	77.6	(D)	65.5	73.1	71.3	82.4	94.1	91.0
Georgia	8	68.5	74.6	75.9	61.7	80.1	75.9	63.4	68.9	71.3	79.4	86.2	89.2
Florida	4	73.4	80.9	78.5	67.1	79.2	0.0	68.2	75.4	73.9	81.8	90.9	89.1
East South Central:													
Kentucky	15	70.6	76.6	78.6	67.6	76.8	83.8	67.0	72.2	75.5	82.7	89.6	90.2
Tennessee	21	68.3	73.8	74.4	63.0	70.7	(D)	63.8	67.6	70.0	80.8	87.8	87.5
Alabama	11	69.6	83.1	78.4	66.4	79.3	(D)	66.8	77.7	75.1	78.8	95.8	90.1
Mississippi	18	74.7	78.1	78.9	69.6	77.8	(D)	69.5	73.1	75.2	86.1	92.0	90.4
West South Central:													
Arkansas	19	65.4	75.8	77.5	63.0	75.9	79.5	63.3	72.2	74.8	74.1	88.4	90.6
Louisiana	20	70.0	76.2	77.2	66.0	76.4	(D)	66.7	71.4	73.2	78.8	86.0	88.4
Oklahoma	16	66.2	72.7	75.8	66.0	74.2	77.6	64.7	70.8	74.3	72.7	79.9	81.6
Texas	20	67.9	76.4	76.1	64.3	76.7	79.0	64.2	72.2	73.1	77.6	86.6	85.5
West:													
Mountain:													
Montana	21	69.2	79.5	81.3	68.7	78.6	80.4	68.4	78.2	90.6	73.4	85.4	86.6
Idaho	22	68.5	71.5	67.0	67.9	71.0	66.0	66.0	67.7	66.4	77.7	81.1	77.8
Wyoming	9	70.6	78.9	79.4	69.7	77.8	78.9	69.7	77.7	78.2	77.7	86.6	87.0
Colorado	22	69.5	69.7	73.4	65.7	68.3	73.3	68.9	67.4	71.3	78.1	79.6	83.0
New Mexico	16	73.4	78.6	77.8	71.4	78.1	75.6	73.2	77.3	76.9	82.0	88.6	88.1
Arizona	18	70.4	80.4	78.6	65.6	76.8	75.9	68.8	79.2	77.5	85.5	91.2	89.3
Utah	19	66.7	71.1	66.2	64.2	69.5	65.3	66.0	69.4	64.4	73.2	79.1	73.8
Nevada	18	67.5	74.6	79.2	63.8	69.4	74.5	65.7	73.3	77.6	80.1	87.8	90.4
Pacific:													
Washington	23	66.7	73.6	72.4	62.6	69.5	68.1	64.9	71.6	71.1	79.1	86.3	84.3
Oregon	20	71.5	78.7	75.8	68.5	75.7	71.5	70.9	77.6	75.1	84.6	91.8	89.8
California	15	73.2	77.9	65.3	67.8	72.6	61.4	71.0	75.3	63.2	84.6	89.9	75.2
Alaska	8	94.3	101.0	108.7	98.1	107.3	0.0	92.5	98.1	108.6	(D)	106.5	109.2
Hawaii	22	87.8	96.9	99.1	82.5	(NA)	0.0	83.4	90.3	93.0	100.9	109.9	110.3

D Withheld to avoid disclosure of individual company data. NA Not available. [1] Source: U.S. Advisory Commission on Intergovernmental Relations, *Significant Features of Fiscal Federalism*, 1992 Edition, Vol. I, based on CCH, *State Tax Reporter*.

Source: Except as noted, U.S. Energy Information Administration, *Petroleum Marketing Monthly June 1991.*

Banking, Finance, and Insurance

This section presents data on the Nation's finances, various types of financial institutions, money and credit, securities, and insurance. The primary sources of these data are publications of several departments of the Federal Government, especially the Treasury Department, and independent agencies such as the Federal Deposit Insurance Corporation, the Federal Reserve System, and the Securities and Exchange Commission. National data on insurance are available primarily from private organizations, such as the American Council of Life Insurance.

In Brief

1989, percent of families owning:

Checking accounts	75%
Savings accounts	44%
Retirement accounts	33%
Stocks	19%

Dow-Jones industrial average:

1980	891.4
1990	2,678.9
1991	2,929.3

Flow of funds.—The flow of funds accounts of the Federal Reserve System (see tables 764 to 767) bring together statistics on all of the major forms of financial transactions and financial claims to present an economy-wide view of asset and liability relationships. In flow form, the accounts relate borrowing and lending to one another and to the nonfinancial activities that generate income and production. Each claim outstanding is included simultaneously as an asset of the lender and as a liability of the debtor. The accounts also indicate the balance between asset totals and liability totals over the economy as a whole. Several publications of the Board of Governors of the Federal Reserve System contain information on the flow of funds accounts: Summary data on flows and outstandings, in the *Federal Reserve Bulletin, Flow of Funds Accounts* (quarterly), and *Annual Statistical Digest;* and concepts and organization of the accounts, in *Introduction to Flow of Funds* (June 1980).

Banking system.—Banks in this country are organized under the laws of both the States and the Federal Government and are regulated by several bank supervisory agencies. State-chartered banks are supervised by officials of the respective States. National banks are supervised by the Comptroller of the Currency. *Reports of Condition* have been collected from national banks since 1863. Summaries of these reports are published in the Comptroller's *Annual Report,* which also

presents data on the structure of the national banking system.

The Federal Reserve System was established in 1913 to exercise central banking functions, some of which are shared with the U.S. Treasury. It includes national banks and such State banks that voluntarily join the System. Statements of State bank members are consolidated by the Board of Governors of the Federal Reserve System with data for national banks collected by the Comptroller of the Currency into totals for all member banks of the System. Balance sheet data for member banks and other commercial banks are published quarterly in the *Federal Reserve Bulletin*. The Federal Deposit Insurance Corporation (FDIC), established in 1933, insures each depositor up to $100,000 currently in banks that are members of the Federal Reserve System and in such nonmember banks that join the Bank Insurance Fund. Major item balance sheets for all commercial banks are published monthly in the *Federal Reserve Bulletin.*

Savings institutions.—Savings institutions are primarily involved in credit extension in the form of mortgage loans. Statistics on savings institutions are collected by the U.S. Office of Thrift Supervision. The Financial Institutions Reform, Recovery, and Enforcement Act of 1989 (FIRREA) authorized the establishment of the Resolution Trust Corporation (RTC). The RTC is responsible for the disposal of assets from failed savings institutions. Under FIRREA, the FDIC Board of Directors acts as the RTC Board. FIRREA also gave the FDIC the job of managing the federal deposit insurance fund for savings institutions (SAIF=Savings Association Insurance Fund).

Other credit agencies.—Insurance companies, finance companies dealing primarily in installment sales financing, credit unions, and personal loan companies represent important sources of funds for the credit market. Statistics on loans, investments, cash, etc., of life insurance companies are published principally by the American Council of Life Insurance in its *Life Insurance Fact Book.* Consumer credit data are published currently in the *Federal Reserve Bulletin.*

Federally chartered credit unions are under the supervision of the National Credit Union Administration, established in 1970. State-chartered credit unions are supervised by the respective State supervisory authorities. The Administration publishes comprehensive program and statistical information on all Federal and federally insured State credit unions in the *Annual Report of the National Credit Union Administration.* Deposit insurance (up to $100,000 per account) is provided to members of all Federal and those State credit unions that are federally-insured by the National Credit Union Share Insurance Fund which was established in 1970. Deposit insurance for State chartered credit unions is also available in some States under private or State-administered insurance programs.

Government corporations and credit agencies make available credit of specified types or to specified groups of private borrowers, either by lending directly or by insuring or guaranteeing loans made by private lending institutions. Data on operations of Government credit agencies, along with other Government corporations, are available in reports of individual agencies; data on their debt outstanding are published in the *Federal Reserve Bulletin.*

Currency.—Currency, including coin and paper money, represents more than 30 percent of all media of exchange in the United States, with most payments made

by check. All currency is now issued by the Federal Reserve Banks.

Securities.—The Securities and Exchange Commission (SEC) was established in 1934 to protect the interests of the public and investors against malpractices in the securities and financial markets and to provide the fullest possible disclosure of information regarding securities to the investing public. Statistical data are published in the *SEC Annual Report.*

Insurance.—Insuring companies, which are regulated by the various States or the District of Columbia, are classified as either life or property. Companies that underwrite accident and health insurance only and those that underwrite accident and health insurance in addition to one or more property lines are included with property insurance. Insuring companies, other than those classified as life, are permitted to underwrite one or more property lines provided they are so licensed and have the necessary capital or surplus.

There are a number of published sources for statistics on the various classes of insurance—life, health, fire, marine, and casualty. Individual States collect data on all insurers operating within their respective jurisdictions, and many of the States publish an annual insurance report giving individual company data and aggregates of certain items for the companies operating within the State. Organizations representing certain classes of insurers publish reports for these classes. Among them are the annual commercial publishers, such as The National Underwriter Company whose *Argus Health Chart* (annual) contains financial and operating data for individual health and accident insurance companies, including Blue Cross and Blue Shield Plans. The American Council of Life Insurance publishes statistics on life insurance purchases, ownership, benefit payments, and assets in its biennial *Life Insurance Fact Book.*

Historical statistics.—Tabular headnotes provide cross-references, where applicable, to *Historical Statistics of the United States, Colonial Times to 1970.* See Appendix IV.

Figure 16.1
SAIF[1]—Insured Savings Institutions: 1980 to 1990

Institutions

Number (in thousands)

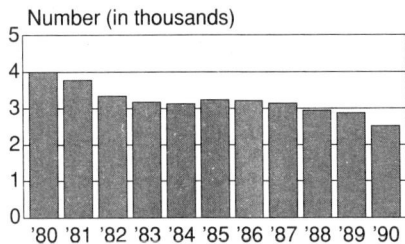

Mortgage Loans Foreclosed[2]

Percent

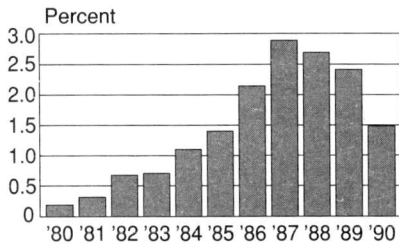

Net Income After Taxes

Billions of dollars

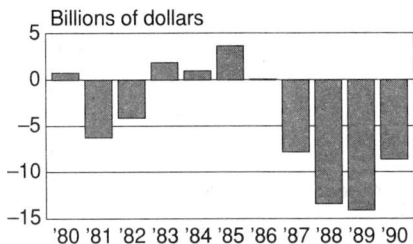

Return on Assets[3]

Percent

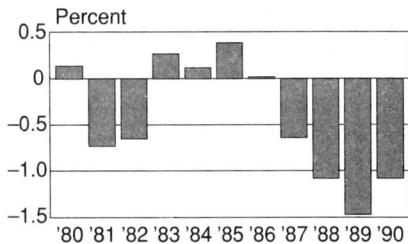

[1]Savings Association Insurance Fund. [2]Based on amount of mortgages foreclosed.
[3]Net income after taxes as a percent of assets.
Source: Chart prepared by U.S. Bureau of the Census. For data, see tables 784, 786, and 787.

Figure 16.2
Interest Rates: 1970 to 1991

Percent per annum

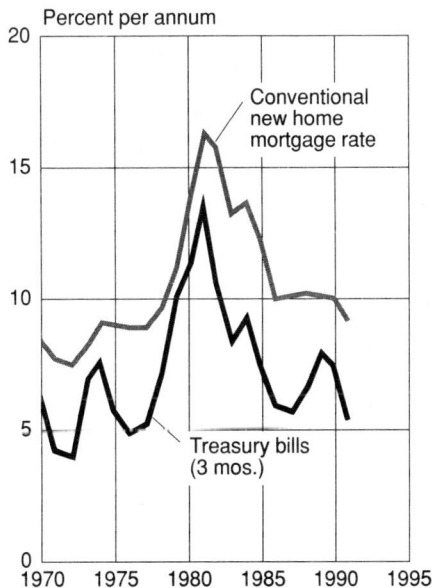

Conventional
new home
mortgage rate

Treasury bills
(3 mos.)

Percent per annum

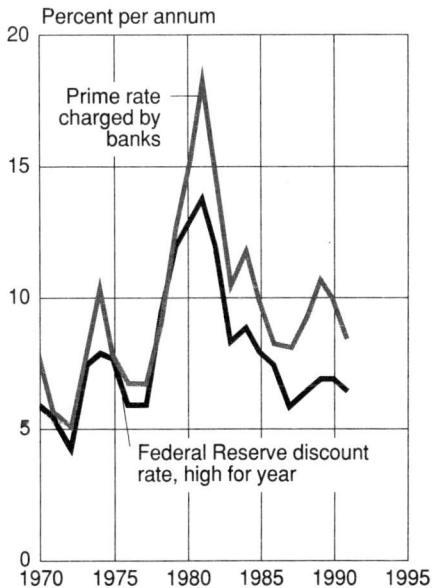

Prime rate
charged by
banks

Federal Reserve discount
rate, high for year

Source: Chart prepared by U.S. Bureau of the Census. For data, see tables 805 and 806.

No. 763. Gross National Product in Finance, Insurance, and Real Estate in Current and Constant (1982) Dollars: 1980 to 1989

[In billions of dollars, except percent. For definition of gross national product, see text, section 14. These data are not fully consistent with other gross domestic product tables because they do not yet reflect the results of the comprehensive National Income and Product Accounts revision; see text, section 14. Based on 1972 Standard Industrial Classification]

INDUSTRY	1980	1982	1983	1984	1985	1986	1987	1988	1989
CURRENT DOLLARS									
Finance, insurance, real estate, total ...	400.6	475.1	536.4	572.8	639.5	696.3	761.6	826.8	896.7
Percent of gross national product......	14.7	15.0	15.7	15.2	15.9	16.5	16.9	17.0	17.2
Banking	51.1	59.8	68.1	70.6	79.4	80.3	88.7	100.2	119.4
Credit agencies other than banks	5.5	5.4	10.6	9.8	11.6	15.7	18.0	15.7	20.5
Security and commodity brokers, and services .	9.7	13.1	20.7	19.7	24.1	30.1	35.8	42.3	43.8
Insurance carriers.....................	37.0	29.8	36.5	34.9	40.7	49.5	55.4	62.0	60.4
Insurance agents and brokers, and services ...	14.4	12.7	17.6	20.1	22.4	25.6	30.6	34.6	37.4
Real estate........................	281.5	342.7	374.2	409.1	449.0	478.6	517.3	561.6	607.1
Holding and other investment companies.....	1.3	7.2	8.7	8.5	12.3	16.4	15.9	10.2	8.1
CONSTANT (1982) DOLLARS									
Finance, insurance, real estate, total ...	468.9	475.1	492.9	509.8	528.3	535.6	560.6	590.0	604.0
Percent of gross national product......	14.7	15.0	14.6	14.6	14.6	14.4	14.6	14.7	14.7
Banking	56.7	59.8	60.1	60.6	61.5	62.5	62.8	62.4	63.1
Credit agencies other than banks	5.2	5.4	6.0	6.6	7.0	7.8	8.3	8.4	8.3
Security and commodity brokers, and services .	11.2	13.1	18.6	17.0	18.8	23.1	29.8	36.4	37.9
Insurance carriers.....................	38.7	29.8	33.2	35.9	39.5	36.0	34.4	37.0	36.7
Insurance agents and brokers, and services ...	15.9	17.0	16.3	17.5	18.0	17.8	20.0	21.4	22.1
Real estate........................	335.0	342.7	351.4	364.1	374.5	378.6	394.5	413.0	424.4
Holding and other investment companies.....	6.3	7.2	7.4	8.2	9.0	9.8	10.9	11.4	11.5

Source: U.S. Bureau of Economic Analysis, *Survey of Current Business*, January and April 1991.

No. 764. Flow of Funds Accounts—Financial Assets of Financial and Nonfinancial Institutions, by Holder Sector: 1980 to 1991

[In billions of dollars. As of **Dec. 31**. See also *Historical Statistics, Colonial Times to 1970*, series X 192, X 229, X 821, and X 835]

SECTOR	1980	1983	1984	1985	1986	1987	1988	1989	1990	1991
All sectors...............	13,205	17,152	18,825	21,485	24,243	25,953	28,343	31,290	32,585	35,203
Households [1].............	6,350	8,066	8,588	9,707	10,666	11,235	12,222	13,606	13,969	15,190
Nonfinancial business	1,372	1,697	1,833	1,975	2,187	2,357	2,585	2,721	2,860	2,968
Farm...................	24	29	29	33	36	38	41	44	47	49
Nonfarm noncorporate	148	231	279	318	357	372	412	440	460	473
Nonfinancial corporations	1,200	1,437	1,525	1,624	1,794	1,948	2,132	2,238	2,353	2,446
State and local government	257	331	375	524	593	661	706	732	734	732
U.S. Government	230	293	330	366	376	367	352	359	425	493
U.S. Government-sponsored credit agencies and mortgage pools. ...	307	500	585	692	877	1,043	1,165	1,323	1,495	1,662
Monetary authorities [2]..........	173	203	218	243	274	285	304	315	343	365
Commercial banking [2]...........	1,486	1,892	2,133	2,381	2,622	2,777	2,955	3,235	3,340	3,458
Domestic commercial banks	1,267	1,603	1,800	1,992	2,168	2,258	2,386	2,545	2,644	2,681
Foreign banking offices in U.S.....	101	112	126	147	187	237	269	362	372	452
Nonbank finance	2,574	3,597	4,101	4,801	5,627	6,050	6,686	7,398	7,730	8,575
Savings and loan associations [3]....	623	819	977	1,058	1,141	1,247	1,360	1,233	1,097	924
Mutual savings banks [4]	170	193	203	217	237	261	285	284	264	249
Credit unions	68	96	111	135	163	178	192	202	217	237
Life insurance...............	464	633	697	796	906	1,005	1,133	1,251	1,367	1,518
Other insurance	174	225	241	289	342	391	435	492	513	563
Private pension funds...........	470	640	680	841	947	928	1,009	1,171	1,163	1,427
State and local govt. retirement funds.	198	311	357	405	469	517	606	735	752	877
Finance companies	221	290	328	388	460	496	565	613	781	801
Real estate investment trusts	3	4	6	8	9	11	14	13	13	13
Investment companies..........	62	112	137	240	414	460	478	555	579	852
Money market funds	76	179	234	244	292	316	338	428	498	540
Security brokers, dealers	45	91	118	156	185	138	136	237	262	315
SCO [5] issuers................	-	4	14	25	64	103	136	185	225	259
Rest of the world	457	573	664	797	1,022	1,179	1,368	1,602	1,690	1,760

- Represents zero. [1] Includes personal trusts and nonprofit organizations. [2] Includes other sectors not shown separately. [3] Includes most Federal savings banks insured by Savings Association Insurance Fund. A few of them are included with mutual savings banks, not shown separately. [4] Includes Federal savings banks insured by Bank Insurance Fund and a few insured by Savings Association Insurance Fund. [5] Securitized credit obligations.

Source: Board of Governors of the Federal Reserve System, *Annual Statistical Digest*.

No. 765. Flow of Funds Accounts—Financial Assets and Liabilities of Financial and Nonfinancial Institutions, by Sector and Type of Instrument: 1991

[In billions of dollars. As of Dec. 31. Preliminary. A=Assets; L=Liabilities, SDR=Special drawing rights, IMF=International Monetary Fund. RPs=Repurchase Agreements. "N.e.c."=Not elsewhere classified]

TYPE OF INSTRUMENT	ALL SECTORS, TOTAL		PRIVATE DOMESTIC NONFINANCIAL INSTITUTIONS — Total		Households[1]		Business		State and local govts.		U.S. GOVERNMENT		FINANCIAL INSTITUTIONS — Total[2]		Commercial banking		Nonbank finance		Federally sponsored credit agencies and mortgage pools		FOREIGN SECTOR	
	A	L	A	L	A	L	A	L	A	L	A	L	A	L	A	L	A	L	A	L	A	L
Total	35,203	27,895	18,889	10,116	15,190	4,190	2,968	5,007	732	918	493	3,157	14,060	13,572	3,458	3,331	8,575	8,223	1,662	1,653	1,760	1,051
Gold stock and SDR's	22	10	-	-	-	-	-	-	-	-	11	-	11	-	-	-	-	-	-	-	-	-
IMF position	10	46	-	-	-	-	-	-	-	-	10	-	-	-	-	-	-	-	-	-	-	10
Official foreign exchange	46	-	-	-	-	-	-	-	-	-	19	-	27	-	-	-	-	-	-	-	-	46
Treasury currency, SDR certificates	31	26	-	-	-	-	-	-	-	-	-	26	31	-	-	-	-	-	-	-	-	-
Checkable deposits, currency	975	1,011	828	-	583	-	221	-	25	-	50	-	76	1,011	4	619	71	99	-	-	21	-
Time and savings accounts	2,836	2,836	2,600	-	2,322	-	233	-	45	-	2	2	193	2,836	-	1,779	193	1,056	-	1	42	-
Fed. funds and security RP's	383	359	164	-	-	-	78	-	86	-	-	-	203	359	-	230	117	129	-	-	17	-
Money market fund shares	540	540	496	-	472	-	24	-	-	-	-	-	44	540	-	-	44	540	69	-	-	-
Foreign deposits	54	54	32	-	-	-	32	-	-	-	-	-	22	-	-	-	22	-	-	-	-	54
Life insurance reserves	409	409	409	-	409	-	-	-	-	-	-	12	-	397	-	-	-	397	-	-	-	-
Pension fund reserves	3,473	3,473	3,473	-	3,473	-	-	-	-	-	-	276	-	3,197	-	-	-	3,197	-	-	-	-
Interbank claims	69	61	-	-	-	-	-	-	-	-	-	-	64	61	58	-2	5	-	-	-	4	-
Mutual fund shares[3]	852	852	750	-	734	-	16	-	-	-	-	-	103	852	4	-	99	852	-	-	-	-
Other corporate equities[4]	4,367	-	2,334	-	2,334	-	-	-	-	-	-	-	1,742	-	5	-	1,737	-	-	-	291	-
Credit market instruments[5]	14,182	14,182	2,781	8,453	1,995	4,061	258	3,510	529	883	250	2,776	10,317	2,648	2,861	173	5,620	900	1,564	1,575	834	304
U.S. Treasury securities[6]	2,758	2,758	930	-	505	-	86	-	339	-	-	2,758	1,372	-	234	-	818	-	53	-	456	-
Federal agency securities[7]	1,589	1,589	396	-	334	-	1	-	61	-	-	-	1,128	1,571	336	-	770	16	16	1,571	65	-
Tax-exempt securities	1,082	1,082	584	1,082	554	95	16	114	15	873	-	-	498	-	104	-	395	-	-	-	-	-
Corporate and foreign bonds	1,758	1,758	178	1,060	178	-	37	1,060	-	-	-	-	1,340	561	96	110	1,244	451	-	-	240	137
Mortgages	4,049	4,049	399	4,045	248	2,998	66	1,047	-	-	100	-	3,549	4	882	-	1,317	4	1,351	-	-	-
Consumer credit	793	793	66	793	-	793	-	-	-	-	-	-	726	-	367	-	360	-	-	-	-	-
Bank loans, n.e.c.	796	796	-	731	-	54	-	677	-	-	-	-	796	42	796	-	-	42	-	-	-	23
Open-market paper	566	566	228	99	177	-	51	99	-	-	-	-	332	386	11	62	310	324	11	-	6	82
Security credit	171	171	74	50	74	50	-	-	-	-	-	-	97	121	47	-	50	121	-	-	-	-
Proprietors' equity[8]	2,568	-	2,568	-	2,568	-	-	-	-	-	-	-	-	-	-	-	-	-	-	-	-	-
Trade credit[8]	1,117	982	979	878	-	61	979	782	-	-	43	59	52	18	-	-	52	18	-	-	44	26
Taxes payable	52	61	48	58	-	-	-	58	48	36	4	3	-	-	-	-	-	-	-	-	-	-
Miscellaneous claims	3,048	2,823	1,354	676	227	19	1,127	657	-	-	105	7	1,081	1,528	480	531	567	911	28	78	508	611

- Represents or rounds to zero. [1] Includes personal trusts and nonprofit organizations. [2] Includes monetary authority, not shown separately. [3] Nonbank finance liability is redemption value of shares of open-end investment companies. [4] Assets shown at market value. No specific liability attributed to issuers of stocks other than open-end investment companies for amounts outstanding. [5] Includes "Other loans," not shown separately. [6] Includes savings bonds and other nonmarketable debt held by public. [7] Issues by agencies in the budget and by sponsored credit agencies in financial sectors, issues backed by mortgage pools, and loan participation certificates. [8] Asset is corporate only; noncorporate credit deducted in liability total to conform to quarterly flow tables.

Source: Board of Governors of the Federal Reserve System, *Annual Statistical Digest*.

No. 766. Flow of Funds Accounts—Assets and Liabilities of Households: 1980 to 1991

[As of **December 31.** Includes personal trusts and nonprofit organizations. See also *Historical Statistics, Colonial Times to 1970*, series X 114-147]

TYPE OF INSTRUMENT	TOTAL (bil. dol.)							PERCENT DISTRIBUTION		
	1980	1985	1987	1988	1989	1990	1991	1980	1990	1991
Total financial assets	**6,350**	**9,707**	**11,235**	**12,222**	**13,606**	**13,969**	**15,190**	**100.0**	**100.0**	**100.0**
Deposit and market instrument [1]	2,101	3,546	4,179	4,584	5,002	5,339	5,371	33.1	38.2	35.4
Checkable deposits and currency. . .	260	381	480	479	497	516	583	4.1	3.7	3.8
Small time and savings deposits . . .	1,141	1,830	2,005	2,137	2,226	2,277	2,297	18.0	16.3	15.1
Money market fund shares	65	211	279	306	392	439	472	1.0	3.1	3.1
Large time deposits.	112	98	117	145	150	104	25	1.8	0.7	0.2
Credit market instruments.	523	1,027	1,297	1,517	1,738	2,004	1,995	8.2	14.3	13.1
U.S. Government securities	241	448	492	622	739	822	838	3.8	5.9	5.5
Treasury issues.	194	357	355	410	432	492	505	3.1	3.5	3.3
Savings bonds.	73	80	101	110	118	126	138	1.1	0.9	0.9
Other Treasury	122	277	254	300	314	366	367	1.9	2.6	2.4
Agency issues	47	91	136	212	308	330	334	0.7	2.4	2.2
Tax-exempt obligations	102	305	398	465	527	549	554	1.6	3.9	3.6
Corporate and foreign bonds	31	19	91	52	65	195	178	0.5	1.4	1.2
Mortgages	107	127	165	182	213	226	248	1.7	1.6	1.6
Open-market paper	43	129	151	196	195	212	177	0.7	1.5	1.2
Mutual fund shares.	52	207	406	418	481	496	734	0.8	3.6	4.8
Other corporate equities	1,111	1,700	1,751	1,877	2,205	2,008	2,334	17.5	14.4	15.4
Life insurance reserves	216	257	300	326	352	377	409	3.4	2.7	2.7
Pension fund reserves [2]	916	1,795	2,182	2,451	2,848	2,963	3,473	14.4	21.2	22.9
Equity in noncorporate business	1,863	2,035	2,207	2,339	2,463	2,507	2,568	29.3	17.9	16.9
Security credit	16	35	39	41	53	62	74	0.3	0.4	0.5
Miscellaneous assets	74	133	171	188	202	217	227	1.2	1.6	1.5
Total liabilities	**1,485**	**2,395**	**2,972**	**3,292**	**3,609**	**4,008**	**4,190**	**100.0**	**100.0**	**100.0**
Credit market instruments	1,430	2,296	2,875	3,189	3,502	3,898	4,061	96.3	97.3	96.9
Mortgages	974	1,484	1,970	2,228	2,473	2,848	2,998	65.6	71.1	71.5
Installment consumer credit	302	527	620	675	731	748	744	20.3	18.7	17.7
Other consumer credit	53	75	74	69	64	61	49	3.6	1.5	1.2
Tax-exempt debt.	17	81	78	80	82	82	86	1.1	2.1	2.3
Bank loans, not elsewhere classified	30	44	42	40	52	43	54	2.0	1.1	1.3
Other loans	55	84	92	98	100	112	121	3.7	2.8	2.9
Security credit	25	51	42	44	43	39	50	1.7	1.0	1.2
Trade credit	17	34	40	44	49	55	61	1.2	1.4	1.4
Unpaid life insurance premiums [3] . . .	13	15	15	16	16	17	19	0.9	0.4	0.5

[1] Excludes corporate equities.   [2] See also table 577.   [3] Includes deferred premiums.

Source: Board of Governors of the Federal Reserve System, *Annual Statistical Digest.*

No. 767. Flow of Funds Accounts—Credit Market Debt Outstanding: 1980 to 1991

[**In billions of dollars; except percent.** As of Dec. 31. N.e.c.=Not elsewhere classified]

ITEM	1980	1983	1984	1985	1986	1987	1988	1989	1990	1991
Credit market debt	**4,671**	**6,317**	**7,235**	**8,325**	**9,508**	**10,524**	**11,498**	**12,472**	**13,561**	**14,182**
Government.	1,045	1,559	1,792	2,151	2,427	2,653	2,857	3,067	3,356	3,659
Federal	735	1,167	1,364	1,590	1,806	1,950	2,105	2,251	2,498	2,776
State and local	310	392	427	561	621	704	753	816	858	883
Non-government.	3,625	4,758	5,444	6,174	7,082	7,871	8,640	9,405	10,205	10,523
Financial [1]	565	862	1,015	1,204	1,513	1,786	2,000	2,219	2,512	2,648
Sponsored credit agencies [2] . .	163	212	242	264	279	308	353	378	399	407
Mortgage pools.	114	245	289	369	532	670	745	871	1,020	1,168
Commercial banks [3]	91	150	174	185	192	213	215	220	191	173
Savings and loan associations.	53	64	82	99	120	139	159	145	114	74
Finance companies	138	181	208	252	312	328	361	393	536	542
SCO trusts [4].	-	4	14	25	64	103	136	185	225	259
Foreign	192	221	229	238	245	254	256	265	289	304
Private domestic nonfinancial . . .	2,868	3,676	4,199	4,732	5,323	5,830	6,385	6,920	7,404	7,570
Corporations [1]	829	1,049	1,224	1,364	1,574	1,747	1,928	2,099	2,172	2,194
Bonds	412	507	574	670	787	866	969	1,042	1,090	1,174
Mortgages	85	50	53	34	62	115	113	127	122	118
Bank loans, n.e.c.	230	341	391	424	474	482	519	554	555	536
Open-market paper	28	37	59	72	63	74	86	107	117	99
Nonbank finance loans	44	58	75	88	101	120	142	154	167	170
Individuals [1]	2,039	2,626	2,975	3,368	3,750	4,004	4,457	4,821	5,233	5,377
By sector:										
Households [5]	1,430	1,792	2,018	2,296	2,592	2,875	3,189	3,502	3,898	4,061
Farm.	162	188	188	173	157	145	138	139	141	143
Nonfarm noncorporate. . .	448	646	769	899	1,001	1,063	1,131	1,181	1,194	1,173
By type of instrument:										
Mortgages.	1,360	1,745	1,964	2,214	2,513	2,795	3,091	3,370	3,746	3,887
Consumer credit	355	438	519	602	660	693	744	795	809	793
Policy loan	43	55	56	56	55	55	56	60	65	71
Bank loans, n.e.c	136	156	169	178	189	187	191	206	199	196
Other loans	124	163	184	198	214	234	256	269	288	296
Tax-exempt debt.	17	41	51	81	79	78	80	82	86	95

- Represents zero.   [1] Includes other types, not shown separately.   [2] U.S. Government.   [3] Includes bank affiliates.   [4] Securitized credit obligations.   [5] See footnote 1, table 765.

Source: Board of Governors of the Federal Reserve System, *Annual Statistical Digest.*

No. 768. Financial Assets Held by Families—Ownership and Median Value: 1983 and 1989

[Median value in thousands of constant 1989 dollars. Constant dollar figures are based on consumer price index data published by U.S. Bureau of Labor Statistics; see table 738. Families include one-person units; for definition of family, see text, section 1. Based on Survey of Consumer Finance; see Appendix III. For definition of median, see Guide to Tabular Presentation]

AGE OF FAMILY HEAD AND FAMILY INCOME	Total [1]	Checking accounts	Savings accounts	Money market accounts	Certifi-cates of deposit	Retire-ment accounts	Stocks	Bonds	Non-taxable bonds
PERCENT OF FAMILIES OWNING ASSET									
1983, total	87.8	78.6	61.7	15.0	20.1	24.2	20.4	3.0	2.1
1989, total	87.5	75.4	43.5	22.2	19.6	33.3	19.0	4.4	4.4
Under 35 years old	82.2	68.4	45.0	14.9	8.5	23.0	11.4	0.8	0.9
35 to 44 years old	88.4	76.1	50.0	20.4	15.5	44.0	21.2	3.4	3.5
45 to 54 years old	90.4	78.9	44.6	27.0	21.1	45.5	23.1	3.5	4.3
55 to 64 years old	87.5	76.7	38.9	23.0	20.9	42.6	22.0	5.9	7.5
65 to 74 years old	91.5	79.9	37.7	28.3	31.6	30.0	20.8	9.1	9.4
75 years old and over	90.6	79.3	36.2	30.5	39.4	6.6	21.3	9.6	4.9
Less than $10,000	59.1	46.2	21.9	7.8	8.6	3.1	2.0	0.8	(B)
$10,000 to $19,999	85.6	69.7	40.7	14.6	21.2	14.9	10.9	2.4	(B)
$20,000 to $29,999	95.2	80.3	47.6	21.0	20.6	34.4	16.9	3.0	4.2
$30,000 to $49,999	98.2	88.8	52.9	23.2	21.0	44.9	20.8	5.0	4.2
$50,000 and more	99.7	91.5	53.9	44.7	26.5	69.2	44.6	12.7	12.6
MEDIAN VALUE [2]									
1983, total	4.5	0.6	1.4	11.0	12.5	5.0	6.2	12.5	52.9
1989, total	10.4	0.9	1.5	5.0	11.0	10.0	7.5	17.3	25.0
Under 35 years old	2.5	0.6	0.7	2.6	5.0	4.0	2.7	0.1	15.0
35 to 44 years old	11.2	0.9	1.5	5.0	10.0	8.0	3.0	6.2	11.7
45 to 54 years old	14.5	1.0	1.5	2.7	9.0	14.0	6.0	12.0	10.0
55 to 64 years old	20.0	1.0	4.5	11.0	12.0	22.0	18.3	20.0	25.0
65 to 74 years old	18.2	1.0	2.0	10.0	17.0	15.0	25.0	20.0	32.0
75 years old and over	21.0	5.0	8.0	25.0	25.0	25.0	18.0	26.0	50.0
Less than $10,000	1.3	0.4	1.0	4.0	10.0	3.3	30.0	13.0	(B)
$10,000 to $19,999	4.5	0.7	1.0	5.0	10.0	4.0	7.0	15.0	(B)
$20,000 to $29,999	6.8	0.8	1.2	3.5	10.0	6.0	4.0	6.2	5.0
$30,000 to $49,999	12.2	1.0	2.0	4.0	12.0	8.5	5.5	26.0	25.0
$50,000 and more	41.5	1.5	3.0	10.0	15.0	21.2	12.0	20.0	35.0

B Base figure too small.   [1] Includes other types of financial assets, not shown separately.   [2] Median value of financial asset for families holding such assets.

No. 769. Financial Debts Held by Families, by Type of Debt: 1983 and 1989

[Median debt in thousands of constant 1989 dollars. See headnote, table 768]

AGE OF FAMILY HEAD AND FAMILY INCOME	Total [1]	Home mortgage	Investment real estate	Home equity lines	Other lines of credit	Credit cards	Car loans
PERCENT OF FAMILIES CARRYING DEBT							
1983, total	69.6	36.9	7.6	0.5	11.2	37.0	28.7
1989, total	72.7	38.7	7.0	3.3	3.3	39.9	35.1
Under 35 years old	79.5	32.8	2.6	1.0	4.5	44.0	37.4
35 to 44 years old	89.6	57.7	10.2	4.3	4.7	52.4	51.5
45 to 54 years old	85.9	56.3	12.3	6.3	4.0	50.0	48.7
55 to 64 years old	74.0	37.5	10.7	6.1	1.9	34.1	29.3
65 to 74 years old	47.9	19.9	3.9	1.0	0.6	25.4	14.0
75 years old and over	23.8	8.6	1.4	(B)	(B)	10.6	5.3
Less than $10,000	47.2	8.8	1.0	(B)	1.5	15.0	11.1
$10,000 to $19,999	58.7	21.3	1.5	1.3	2.2	27.3	21.8
$20,000 to $29,999	79.5	36.8	4.7	2.4	1.6	48.9	39.4
$30,000 to $49,999	86.5	53.1	8.8	4.5	4.1	55.0	50.9
$50,000 and more	91.8	72.4	18.7	7.7	6.7	53.1	51.7
MEDIAN DEBT [2]							
1983, total	13.4	27.0	23.3	7.5	1.2	0.6	3.8
1989, total	15.2	32.0	30.0	17.5	2.0	0.9	5.8
Under 35 years old	11.0	44.0	20.0	18.9	1.7	1.0	5.1
35 to 44 years old	31.1	40.0	39.0	15.0	3.3	1.2	6.6
45 to 54 years old	23.7	26.0	21.0	16.0	1.3	1.0	6.4
55 to 64 years old	10.8	21.0	16.3	30.0	2.0	0.9	5.8
65 to 74 years old	5.0	11.0	15.0	30.0	2.0	0.5	4.0
75 years old and over	3.0	4.5	18.0	(B)	(B)	0.2	3.3
Less than $10,000	1.9	7.5	3.6	(B)	2.0	0.3	1.8
$10,000 to $19,999	5.0	13.0	24.0	25.0	0.9	0.6	3.0
$20,000 to $29,999	12.5	21.0	13.5	8.3	0.5	0.8	5.5
$30,000 to $49,999	26.2	33.0	17.5	16.0	2.5	1.0	6.5
$50,000 and more	55.5	48.0	47.0	20.0	3.3	1.7	7.2

B Base figure too small.   [1] Includes other types of debt, not shown separately.   [2] Median amount of financial debt for families carrying such debt.

Source of tables 768 and 769: Board of Governors of the Federal Reserve System, *Federal Reserve Bulletin*, January 1992.

No. 770. Persons Working in Finance, Insurance, and Real Estate Industries: 1987 to 1990

[In thousands. Data represent worker-years of full-time equivalent employment by persons working for wages or salaries and number of active partners and proprietors of unincorporated businesses who devote a majority of their working hours to their unincorporated businesses. Based on 1987 Standard Industrial Classification]

INDUSTRY	1987	1988	1989	1990
Finance, insurance, real estate, total	6,969	7,096	7,134	7,230
Average annual percent change [1]	(X)	1.8	0.5	1.3
Depository institutions.	2,155	2,154	2,166	2,161
Nondepository institutions	363	364	362	378
Security and commodity brokers.	522	514	497	491
Insurance carriers	1,373	1,401	1,423	1,462
Insurance agents, brokers, and services	844	882	891	927
Real estate.	1,521	1,584	1,597	1,603
Holding and other investment offices.	191	197	198	208

X Not applicable.　　[1] For explanation of average annual percent change, see Guide to Tabular Presentation.

Source: U.S. Bureau of Economic Analysis, *Survey of Current Business,* January 1992.

No. 771. Finance, Insurance, and Real Estate—Establishments, Employees, and Payroll: 1987 to 1989

[Covers establishments with payroll. Excludes government employees, railroad employees, self-employed persons, etc. For statement on methodology, see Appendix III]

1987 SIC code [1]	KIND OF BUSINESS	ESTABLISHMENTS (1,000)			EMPLOYEES (1,000)		PAYROLL (bil. dol.)	
		1987	1988	1989	1988	1989	1988	1989
(H)	**Finance, insurance, real estate** . .	535.7	518.2	529.3	6,659.6	6,801.6	177.2	184.5
60	Depository institutions [2]	77.8	76.3	80.1	1,959.8	2,029.9	42.9	46.2
601	Central reserve depository.	(NA)	0.1	0.1	25.6	26.0	0.7	0.7
602	Commercial banks	(NA)	49.6	51.3	1,454.6	1,463.4	32.1	33.6
603	Savings institutions.	(NA)	20.2	22.0	383.7	434.7	7.7	9.0
606	Credit unions.	(NA)	3.6	3.7	44.9	47.7	0.8	0.9
609	Functions closely related to banking . . .	(NA)	2.6	2.3	37.9	40.0	1.0	1.2
61	Nondepository institutions [2].	42.6	43.6	41.8	542.2	484.9	13.8	13.1
611	Federal and Federally-sponsored credit .	(NA)	2.8	0.6	88.7	17.8	2.1	0.5
614	Personal credit institutions	(NA)	25.6	25.3	212.8	217.8	4.6	5.0
615	Business credit institutions	(NA)	3.6	3.7	86.2	85.1	2.7	2.8
616	Mortgage bankers and brokers	(NA)	11.3	10.7	153.3	149.6	4.4	4.5
62	Security and commodity brokers [2]	22.4	21.6	21.5	426.6	406.1	27.5	25.3
621	Security brokers and dealers	(NA)	13.3	13.3	332.7	312.6	22.6	20.3
622	Commodity contracts brokers, dealers . .	(NA)	1.2	1.1	15.3	15.6	0.7	0.7
623	Security and commodity exchanges. . . .	(NA)	0.1	0.1	7.5	7.5	0.3	0.3
628	Security and commodity services	(NA)	6.3	6.2	69.6	67.8	3.8	3.8
63	Insurance carriers [2]	41.1	39.9	44.2	1,326.5	1,390.0	35.4	37.8
631	Life insurance	(NA)	14.4	14.3	538.3	568.8	13.7	14.8
632	Medical service and health insurance [2] .	(NA)	2.1	2.0	173.8	181.9	4.3	4.6
6321	Accident and health insurance. . . .	(NA)	1.2	1.1	44.0	45.9	1.0	1.1
6324	Hospital and medical service plans. . .	(NA)	0.9	0.9	128.6	135.3	3.2	3.4
633	Fire, marine, and casualty insurance . .	(NA)	16.2	17.3	518.1	524.7	14.9	15.3
635	Surety insurance	(NA)	0.5	0.6	10.4	14.0	0.3	0.4
636	Title insurance.	(NA)	3.0	3.2	54.2	56.4	1.4	1.5
637	Pension, health and welfare funds.	(NA)	2.6	5.7	17.3	26.9	0.4	0.7
64	Insurance agents, brokers, and service . . .	109.3	105.1	107.5	686.0	694.4	18.0	18.8
65	Real estate [2]	216.6	208.0	210.6	1,286.6	1,326.6	25.4	27.4
651	Real estate operators and lessors.	(NA)	93.7	93.0	483.8	492.5	7.8	8.2
653	Real estate agents and managers.	(NA)	82.9	70.2	616.4	567.1	13.5	13.2
654	Title abstract offices	(NA)	3.1	3.0	25.0	23.6	0.5	0.5
655	Subdividers and developers [2]	(NA)	18.6	19.2	124.4	132.2	2.9	3.1
6552	Subdividers and developers, n.e.c. [3] . .	(NA)	10.6	10.6	78.1	82.3	1.9	2.1
6553	Cemetery subdividers and developers.	(NA)	4.6	4.6	35.3	35.6	0.6	0.6
67	Holding and other investment offices [2] . . .	23.7	21.5	21.2	239.6	254.0	8.6	9.2
671	Holding offices.	(NA)	5.6	5.8	116.6	124.5	4.9	5.2
673	Trusts	(NA)	7.8	7.6	58.4	63.7	1.2	1.4
6732	Educational, religious, etc. trusts	(NA)	3.3	3.3	30.7	37.7	0.6	0.8
679	Miscellaneous investing.	(NA)	6.7	4.8	52.5	41.4	1.7	1.5
6794	Patent owners and lessors	(NA)	0.8	0.8	15.3	14.9	0.4	0.4
	Administrative and auxiliary.	2.2	2.2	2.4	192.4	215.8	5.6	6.5

NA Not available.　　[1] Standard Industrial Classification; see text, section 13.　　[2] Includes industries not shown separately.
[3] N.e.c.=Not elsewhere classified.

Source: U.S. Bureau of the Census, *County Business Patterns,* annual.

No. 772. Selected Financial Institutions—Number and Assets, by Asset Size: 1990

[As of **December.** BIF=Bank Insurance Fund; SAIF=Savings Association Insurance Fund]

ASSET SIZE	NUMBER OF INSTITUTIONS				ASSETS (bil. dol.)			
	B.I.F.-insured commercial banks	S.A.I.F.-insured savings institutions	B.I.F.-insured savings institutions	Credit unions [1]	B.I.F.-insured commercial banks [2]	S.A.I.F.-insured savings institutions	B.I.F.-insured savings institutions	Credit unions [1]
Total	**12,345**	**2,526**	**469**	**12,860**	**3,388.9**	**1,085.3**	**259.0**	**198.2**
Less than $5.0 million	(3)	(3)	(3)	7,995	(3)	(3)	(3)	12.2
$5.0 million to $9.9 million	(3)	(3)	(3)	1,692	(3)	(3)	(3)	12.0
$10.0 million to $24.9 million.	[3]3,330	[3]261	[3]22	1,581	[3]51.9	[3]4.0	[3]0.3	25.3
$25.0 million to $49.9 million.	3,145	424	41	795	113.9	15.5	1.5	27.9
$50.0 million to $99.9 million.	2,782	587	72	415	193.8	41.8	5.2	29.1
$100.0 million to $499.9 million	2,461	905	216	354	481.2	196.3	48.7	65.9
$500.0 million to $999.9 million	253	151	57	[4]28	173.9	105.9	39.0	[4]25.8
$1.0 billion to $2.9 billion	202	135	43	(4)	354.6	233.3	65.2	(4)
$3.0 billion or more	172	63	18	(4)	2,019.6	488.5	99.1	(4)
	PERCENT DISTRIBUTION							
Total	**100.0**	**100.0**	**100.0**	**100.0**	**100.0**	**100.0**	**100.0**	**100.0**
Less than $5.0 million	(3)	(3)	(3)	62.2	(3)	(3)	(3)	6.2
$5.0 million to $9.9 million	(3)	(3)	(3)	13.1	(3)	(3)	(3)	6.0
$10.0 million to $24.9 million.	[3]27.0	[3]10.3	[3]4.7	12.3	[3]1.5	[3]0.4	[3]0.1	12.8
$25.0 million to $49.9 million.	25.5	16.8	8.7	6.2	3.4	1.4	0.6	14.1
$50.0 million to $99.9 million.	22.5	23.2	15.4	3.2	5.7	3.8	2.0	14.7
$100.0 million to $499.9 million	19.9	35.8	46.1	2.8	14.2	18.1	18.8	33.2
$500.0 million to $999.9 million	2.0	6.0	12.2	[4]0.2	5.1	9.8	15.1	[4]13.0
$1.0 billion to $2.9 billion	1.6	5.3	9.2	(4)	10.5	21.5	25.2	(4)
$3.0 billion or more	1.4	2.5	3.8	(4)	59.6	45.0	38.2	(4)

[1] Source: National Credit Union Administration, *National Credit Union Administration Yearend Statistics 1990.* Excludes nonfederally insured State chartered credit unions and federally insured corporate credit unions. [2] Includes foreign branches of U.S. banks. [3] Data for institutions with assets less than $10 million included with those with assets of $10.0 million to $24.9 million. [4] Data for institutions with assets of $1 billion or more included with those with assets of $500.0 million to $999.9 million.

Source: Except as noted, U.S. Federal Deposit Insurance Corporation, *Statistics on Banking, 1990.*

No. 773. Banking Offices, by Type of Bank: 1970 to 1990

[As of **December 31.** Includes Puerto Rico and outlying areas. Covers all FDIC-insured commercial banks and all Bank Insurance Fund-insured savings banks as well as those State-chartered Savings Association Insurance Fund-insured savings banks that are regulated by the FDIC. Beginning 1982, excludes automatic teller machines that were previously being reported by many banks as branches. See also *Historical Statistics, Colonial Times to 1970,* series X 716-724]

ITEM	1970	1980	1984	1985	1986	1987	1988	1989	1990
All banking offices	**37,166**	**57,232**	**60,067**	**60,890**	**61,897**	**62,914**	**63,960**	**64,570**	**66,945**
Commercial banks, total.	35,585	53,649	57,010	57,764	58,565	59,423	60,200	60,796	63,160
Member, Federal Reserve System .	21,989	29,985	32,809	33,854	34,542	35,196	35,763	36,755	38,201
National banks	17,191	24,217	27,037	27,844	28,218	28,744	29,270	30,019	31,279
State banks	4,798	5,768	5,772	6,010	6,324	6,452	6,493	6,736	6,922
Nonmember banks.	13,596	23,664	24,201	23,910	24,023	24,227	24,437	24,041	24,959
Insured	13,332	23,186	23,535	23,910	24,023	24,227	24,437	24,041	24,959
Noninsured	264	478	666	(NA)	(NA)	(NA)	(NA)	(NA)	(NA)
Savings banks, total	1,581	3,583	3,057	3,126	3,332	3,491	3,760	3,774	3,785
Insured	1,223	3,066	2,728	3,126	3,332	3,491	3,760	3,774	3,785
Noninsured	358	517	329	(NA)	(NA)	(NA)	(NA)	(NA)	(NA)

NA Not available.

Source: U.S. Federal Deposit Insurance Corporation, 1970 and 1980, *Annual Report* and, beginning 1984, *Statistics on Banking,* annual.

No. 774. Changes in Number of Operating Banking Offices: 1970 to 1990

[As of **December 31.** Includes Puerto Rico and outlying areas. See headnote, table 773. Beginning 1985, excludes noninsured institutions]

TYPE OF CHANGE	1970	1980	1984	1985	1986	1987	1988	1989	1990
Banking offices [1]	**37,166**	**57,232**	**60,067**	**60,890**	**61,897**	**62,914**	**63,960**	**64,570**	**66,945**
Number of banks	14,199	15,330	15,489	14,809	14,681	14,207	13,629	13,201	12,819
Number of branches [1]	22,967	41,902	44,578	46,081	47,216	48,707	50,331	51,369	54,126
Net change during year	**1,584**	**2,306**	**1,017**	**1,759**	**1,007**	**1,017**	**1,046**	**610**	**2,375**
Offices opened	1,864	2,800	2,338	2,874	2,756	3,144	3,537	3,342	4,154
Banks.	186	271	486	482	396	271	248	202	193
Branches.	1,678	2,529	1,852	2,392	2,360	2,873	3,289	3,140	3,961
Offices closed.	280	494	1,321	1,115	1,749	2,127	2,491	2,732	1,779
Banks.	165	142	427	460	524	745	826	630	575
Branches.	115	352	894	655	1,225	1,382	1,665	[2]2,102	1,204

[1] See headnote, table 773. [2] Includes 366 Federal nonmember contractual branches in Michigan that were previously reported as branches. "Contractual branches" are established among affiliated banks and allow the banks' branches to act as branches for each other.

Source: U.S. Federal Deposit Insurance Corporation, *Statistics on Banking,* annual.

No. 775. 500 Largest Banks in the World—Number and Deposits, by Location of Bank: 1970 to 1990

[Deposits in billions of dollars, except percent. Data cover U.S. commercial banks and foreign banks that conduct a commercial banking business; beginning 1983, includes U.S. and foreign savings banks. Beginning 1982, covers top 500 banks in assets available. Number of banks includes banks more than 50 percent owned by other banks. To avoid double-counting of deposits, banks more than 50 percent owned by other banks are excluded from deposit totals if their parent bank consolidates their deposits]

LOCATION OF BANK	1970	1980	1983	1984	1985	1986	1987	1988	1989	1990	PERCENT		
											1970	1980	1990
NUMBER													
U.S. banks	185	93	102	115	110	102	90	107	108	96	37	19	19
Foreign banks	315	407	398	385	390	398	410	393	392	404	63	81	81
Japan	71	78	95	95	96	108	111	111	108	106	14	16	21
United Kingdom . .	27	34	26	22	22	20	18	18	20	22	5	7	4
Germany	37	38	40	39	39	38	42	38	37	39	7	8	8
France	19	28	21	19	20	23	23	20	20	20	4	6	4
Italy	25	27	29	26	29	31	32	29	28	31	5	5	6
DEPOSITS													
Total	890	4,994	5,683	5,854	7,022	9,220	12,090	12,837	13,565	15,854	100	100	100
U.S. banks	296	754	882	961	1,014	1,084	1,108	1,347	1,352	1,329	33	15	8
Foreign banks	594	4,240	4,801	4,893	6,008	8,136	10,982	11,489	12,214	14,525	67	85	92
Japan	151	1,131	1,587	1,750	2,179	3,350	4,936	5,333	5,236	5,888	17	24	37
United Kingdom . .	60	349	375	343	403	458	588	646	673	822	7	7	5
Germany	80	603	550	500	684	912	1,208	1,151	1,309	1,692	9	12	11
France	40	483	436	440	502	650	836	822	970	1,175	5	10	7
Italy	62	290	309	296	395	527	647	606	708	870	7	6	5

Source: American Banker-Bond Buyer, New York, NY, *American Banker Ranking The Banks*, annual, (copyright).

No. 776. Insured Commercial Banks—Assets and Liabilities: 1980 to 1991

[In billions of dollars, except as indicated. As of Dec. 31. Includes outlying areas. Except as noted, includes foreign branches of U.S. banks. See *Historical Statistics, Colonial Times to 1970*, series X 588-609, for related data]

ITEM	1980	1984	1985	1986	1987	1988	1989	1990	1991 [1]
Number of banks	14,434	14,481	14,404	14,200	13,696	13,139	12,713	12,345	11,920
Assets, total	**1,856**	**2,509**	**2,731**	**2,941**	**2,999**	**3,131**	**3,299**	**3,389**	**3,430**
Net loans and leases.	1,006	1,490	1,608	1,728	1,779	1,886	2,004	2,054	1,996
Real estate loans.	269	386	438	515	600	677	762	830	851
Commercial and industrial loans . . .	391	565	578	601	589	599	619	615	559
Loans to individuals	187	267	309	336	351	378	401	403	391
Farm loans.	32	40	36	32	29	30	31	33	35
Other loans and leases.	137	250	270	273	259	249	246	229	215
Less: Reserve for losses.	10	19	23	29	50	47	54	56	55
Temporary investments	(²)	410	452	464	451	466	482	451	501
Securities over 1 year in length	(²)	252	298	358	397	383	402	450	514
Other	²849	357	374	392	373	397	411	434	419
Domestic office assets.	1,533	2,109	2,326	2,533	2,575	2,726	2,897	2,999	3,033
Foreign office assets.	323	400	406	408	425	405	402	390	397
Liabilities and capital, total	1,856	2,509	2,731	2,941	2,999	3,131	3,299	3,389	3,430
Noninterest-bearing deposits [3]	432	432	471	532	478	479	483	489	480
Interest-bearing deposits [4]	1,049	1,531	1,646	1,751	1,858	1,952	2,065	2,162	2,207
Subordinated debt.	7	10	15	17	18	17	20	24	25
Other liabilities	260	381	429	458	466	485	526	496	486
Equity capital	108	154	169	182	181	197	205	219	232
Domestic office deposits	1,187	1,645	1,796	1,970	1,994	2,117	2,237	2,357	2,383
Foreign office deposits.	294	318	322	314	342	315	312	293	305

[1] Preliminary.   [2] Temporary investments and securities over one year in length included in other.   [3] Prior to 1984, demand deposits.   [4] Prior to 1984, time and savings deposits.
Source: U.S. Federal Deposit Insurance Corporation, *The FDIC Quarterly Banking Profile, Annual Report*, and *Statistics on Banking*, annual.

No. 777. FDIC-Insured Commercial and Savings Banks Closed or Assisted Due to Financial Difficulties and Problem Banks: 1980 to 1991

[rectors of banks. F.D.I.C. = Federal Deposit Insurance Corporation. See also *Historical Statistics, Colonial Times to 1970*, series X 741, 748, 756, and 761]

ITEM	Unit	1980	1982	1983	1984	1985	1986	1987	1988	1989	1990	1991
Total banks closed or assisted	Number .	11	42	48	80	120	145	203	221	207	169	127
Agricultural banks [1]	Number .	(NA)	7	7	31	62	59	57	29	13	7	(NA)
Deposits, closed and assisted banks.	Mil. dol .	5,216	9,908	5,442	29,883	8,059	6,597	8,568	37,215	24,097	14,489	(NA)
Agricultural banks [1]	Mil. dol .	(NA)	112	114	421	866	1,408	906	492	173	166	(NA)
Problem banks [2].	Number .	217	369	642	848	1,140	1,484	1,575	1,406	1,109	1,046	1,069

NA Not available.   [1] Banks with at least 25 percent of their portfolios devoted to farm loans.   [2] FDIC-insured commercial and savings banks considered to be problem banks by the supervisory authorities, end-of-period.
Source: U.S. Federal Deposit Insurance Corporation, *Annual Report, The FDIC Quarterly Banking Profile*; and *Failed Bank Cost Analysis Report*, 1991.

No. 778. Insured Commercial Banks—Income and Selected Measures of Financial Condition: 1980 to 1991

[In billions of dollars, except as indicated. Includes outlying areas. Includes foreign branches of U.S. banks. See *Historical Statistics, Colonial Times to 1970*, series X 588-609, for related data]

ITEM	1980	1984	1985	1986	1987	1988	1989	1990	1991 [1]
Interest income	177.4	264.2	248.2	237.8	244.8	272.3	317.3	320.4	289.2
Interest expense	120.1	181.2	157.3	142.8	144.9	165.0	205.1	204.9	167.3
Net interest income	57.3	83.0	90.9	95.0	99.9	107.3	112.2	115.5	121.9
Provisions for loan losses	4.5	13.7	17.7	22.1	37.5	17.0	31.0	32.1	33.9
Noninterest income	13.3	27.7	31.0	35.9	41.5	44.9	51.1	55.1	59.7
Noninterest expense	46.7	76.4	82.3	90.2	97.3	101.3	108.1	115.7	124.5
Income taxes	5.0	4.9	5.6	5.3	5.4	10.0	9.7	7.8	8.4
Net operating income	14.5	15.7	16.3	13.3	1.1	23.9	14.5	15.0	14.8
Securities gain/loss, net	-0.5	-0.1	1.6	4.0	1.4	0.3	0.8	0.5	3.0
Extraordinary gains, net	-	0.2	0.2	0.3	0.2	0.8	0.3	0.6	0.8
Net income	14.0	15.8	18.1	17.5	2.8	25.1	15.6	16.1	18.6
RATIOS OF CONDITION									
Return on assets [2] (percent)	0.80	0.65	0.70	0.63	0.12	0.82	0.49	0.49	0.56
Return on equity [3] (percent)	13.66	10.73	11.31	9.94	2.00	13.30	7.78	7.61	8.32
Equity capital to assets (percent)	5.80	6.15	6.20	6.19	6.04	6.28	6.21	6.46	6.77
Nonperforming assets	(NA)	49.5	51.0	57.7	73.8	67.1	75.4	98.1	102.5
Nonperforming assets to assets (percent)	(NA)	1.97	1.87	1.95	2.46	2.14	2.26	2.90	2.99
Net charge-offs [4]	3.6	10.8	13.6	16.5	16.4	18.5	22.9	29.7	32.6
Net charge-offs to loans and leases (percent)	0.36	0.76	0.84	0.99	0.92	1.00	1.16	1.44	1.60
Net interest margin [5] (percent)	3.66	3.95	4.09	3.98	3.89	4.06	3.31	3.41	4.18
Percentage of banks losing money	3.7	13.1	17.1	19.8	17.7	14.7	12.5	13.4	10.8

- Represents or rounds to zero. NA Not available. [1] Preliminary. [2] Net income (including securities transactions and nonrecurring items) as a percentage of average total assets. [3] Net income as a percentage of average total equity capital. [4] Total loans and leases charged off (removed from balance sheet because of uncollectibility), less amounts recovered on loans and leases previously charged off. [5] Interest income less interest expense as a percentage of average earning assets (i.e. the profit margin a bank earns on its loans and investments).

Source: U.S. Federal Deposit Insurance Corporation, *Annual Report; Statistics on Banking*, annual; and *FDIC Quarterly Banking Profile*.

No. 779. Insured Commercial Banks—Assets, Deposits, and Problem Banks, States and Other Areas: 1990

[Includes foreign branches of U.S. banks]

STATE	ALL BANKS [1]			BANKS CLOSED OR ASSISTED		STATE	ALL BANKS [1]			BANKS CLOSED OR ASSISTED	
	Number	Assets (bil. dol.)	Deposits (bil. dol.)	Number	Deposits (bil. dol.)		Number	Assets (bil. dol.)	Deposits (bil. dol.)	Number	Deposits (bil. dol.)
Total	12,345	3,388.9	2,650.0	169	14.5	WV	180	17.4	14.8	-	-
U.S.	12,327	3,369.1	2,632.9	169	14.5	NC	78	80.2	58.4	-	-
Northeast	881	1,121.7	830.5	16	6.1	SC	85	25.2	18.5	-	-
N.E.	257	172.9	139.9	9	2.7	GA	409	70.3	53.2	-	-
ME	21	8.2	6.9	-	-	FL	430	137.2	117.0	7	0.4
NH	45	10.0	8.3	1	(Z)	E.S.C.	929	149.1	123.7	2	0.1
VT	27	6.1	5.3	-	-	KY	332	41.4	33.5	1	(Z)
MA	85	97.9	76.6	7	2.6	TN	253	47.4	39.9	1	0.1
RI	11	14.7	11.0	-	-	AL	221	38.9	31.9	-	-
CT	68	36.1	31.7	1	0.1	MS	123	21.4	18.5	-	-
M.A.	624	948.8	690.6	7	3.5	W.S.C.	2,090	256.5	221.0	118	5.9
NY	193	682.2	476.0	5	3.3	AR	256	21.5	19.1	1	(Z)
NJ	131	94.2	78.3	2	0.1	LA	231	37.4	32.6	4	0.4
PA	300	172.4	136.3	-	-	OK	419	26.9	23.7	10	0.2
Midwest	5,338	740.9	598.7	7	0.1	TX	1,184	170.8	145.6	103	5.2
E.N.C.	2,384	509.6	408.7	1	(Z)	West	1,553	551.3	447.8	18	0.6
OH	288	113.1	89.7	1	(Z)	Mt.	898	119.4	97.5	14	0.3
IN	301	58.3	47.6	-	-	MT	156	7.3	6.3	-	-
IL	1,087	196.9	154.7	-	-	ID	22	8.6	6.9	-	-
MI	235	93.8	76.9	-	-	WY	71	4.6	4.1	-	-
WI	473	47.5	39.8	-	-	CO	446	26.9	22.7	7	0.2
W.N.C.	2,954	231.3	190.1	6	0.1	NM	91	11.1	9.6	2	(Z)
MN	626	55.5	45.4	1	(Z)	AZ	38	32.6	28.4	5	0.1
IA	562	34.6	29.2	-	-	UT	66	13.0	10.6	-	-
MO	544	64.7	54.3	1	(Z)	NV	19	14.4	8.9	-	-
ND	150	7.6	6.7	3	(Z)	Pac.	655	431.9	350.2	4	0.3
SD	125	19.2	10.9	-	-	WA	94	39.7	32.8	-	-
NE	392	20.2	17.6	-	-	OR	50	22.9	18.0	-	-
KS	555	29.5	26.0	1	(Z)	CA	482	345.3	279.7	4	0.3
						AK	8	4.5	3.5	-	-
South	4,555	955.2	756.0	128	7.6	HI	21	19.4	16.3	-	-
S.A.	1,536	549.5	411.2	8	1.6						
DE	47	74.3	34.3	-	-	AM	1	(Z)	(Z)	-	-
MD	103	57.0	45.0	-	-	PR	15	19.4	16.6	-	-
DC	26	18.1	15.4	1	1.3	GU	1	0.5	0.5	-	-
VA	178	69.6	54.7	-	-	Pac. Is	1	(Z)	(Z)	-	-

- Represents zero. Z Less than $50 million. [1] As of December 31.

Source: U.S. Federal Deposit Insurance Corporation, *Statistics on Banking*, annual, and *Annual Report*.

No. 780. Insured Commercial Banks—Selected Measures of Financial Condition, by Asset Size and Region: 1991

[In percent. Preliminary. See headnote, table 778]

ASSET SIZE AND REGION	Return on assets	Return on equity	Equity capital to assets	Nonperforming assets to total assets	Net charge-offs to loans and leases	Percentage of banks losing money
Total	0.56	8.32	6.77	2.99	1.60	10.8
Less than $100 million	0.79	8.62	9.12	1.62	0.66	11.3
$100 million to $1 billion	0.78	10.05	7.81	2.06	0.93	8.3
$1 billion to $10 billion.	0.58	8.52	6.97	2.81	1.70	17.2
$10 billion or more	0.37	6.79	5.48	3.95	2.03	24.5
Northeast [1]	0.30	5.04	6.07	4.13	2.36	26.1
Southeast [2]	0.64	8.83	7.25	2.21	1.22	14.1
Central [3]	0.90	12.39	7.34	1.63	0.88	6.1
Midwest [4]	1.10	13.66	8.15	1.51	1.05	4.2
Southwest [5]	0.66	9.75	6.88	2.39	1.25	10.5
West [6]	0.45	6.69	6.74	3.36	1.31	18.3

[1] CT, DE, DC, ME, MD, MA, NH, NJ, NY, PA, PR, RI, and VT. [2] AL, FL, GA, MS, NC, SC, TN, VA, and WV. [3] IL, IN, KY, MI, OH, and WI. [4] IA, KS, MN, MO, NE, ND, and SD. [5] AR, LA, NM, OK, and TX. [6] AK, AZ, CA, CO, HI, ID, MT, NV, OR, Pacific Islands, UT, WA, and WY.

Source: U.S. Federal Deposit Insurance Corporation, *The FDIC Quarterly Banking Profile.*

No. 781. U.S. Banking Offices of Foreign Banks—Summary: 1975 to 1990

[In billions of dollars, except as indicated. As of December, except as indicated. Covers agencies, branches, subsidiary commercial banks, New York State investment companies, and, for data by country only, finance companies]

YEAR	Assets	LOANS		Deposits	COUNTRY	NUMBER OF—			Loans, com- mercial and indus- trial	Deposits
		Total	Busi- ness			Banks with U.S. offices	U.S. offices	Assets		
1975	52.4	29.9	19.9	22.6	**1990, total** [2] .	288	718	757.4	189.9	377.6
1980	200.6	121.4	59.6	80.4	Japan	45	137	408.9	113.9	189.0
1985	440.8	247.4	108.8	236.7	United Kingdom.	11	42	38.6	12.3	28.8
1987	592.6	310.9	147.9	316.1	Italy	13	27	46.6	10.3	14.3
1988	650.6	338.8	167.3	335.1	Canada	6	49	42.8	9.8	19.4
1989	735.7	369.8	184.3	376.1	Hong Kong . . .	10	30	25.9	5.6	19.7
1990	784.8	395.2	192.8	378.7	France	15	37	33.2	5.3	15.9
Share: [1] 1975 . .	5.3	5.7	10.4	2.9	Netherlands . . .	4	27	15.7	4.7	9.0
1980 . .	11.9	13.4	18.2	6.6	Israel	4	23	12.5	3.3	10.9
1985 . .	16.1	15.4	22.5	12.1	Switzerland . . .	6	17	22.4	3.0	12.1
1990 . .	21.2	17.9	30.6	14.3	Spain	8	27	13.2	2.9	9.2

[1] Percent of "domestically owned" commercial banks plus U.S. offices of foreign banks. [2] As of June 30. Includes other countries not shown separately. Source: American Banker-Bond Buyer, New York, NY, *American Banker Ranking The Banks,* annual, (copyright).

Source: Except as noted, Board of Governors of the Federal Reserve System, unpublished data.

No. 782. Foreign Lending by U.S. Banks, by Type of Borrower and Country: 1991

[In millions of dollars. As of December. Covers 159 U.S. banking organizations which do nearly all of the foreign lending in the country. Data represent claims on foreign residents and institutions held at all domestic and foreign offices of covered banks. Data cover only cross-border and non-local currency lending. These result from a U.S. bank's office in one country lending to residents of another country or lending in a currency other than that of the borrower's country. Excludes local currency loans and other claims and local currency liabilities held by banks' foreign offices on residents of the country in which the office was located (e.g. Deutsche mark loans to German residents booked at the German branch of the reporting U.S. bank). Criteria for country selection is $1.8 billion or more]

COUNTRY	Total	Bank	Public	Private non- bank	COUNTRY	Total	Bank	Public	Private non- bank
Total [1]	196,429	87,912	48,937	56,580	Italy.	5,342	2,871	1,794	676
					Japan	21,731	16,082	461	5,188
Argentina	3,813	263	1,470	2,079	Mexico.	16,516	1,654	12,533	2,332
Australia.	3,991	1,363	640	1,988	Netherlands	3,183	968	411	1,802
Bahamas, The.	4,273	3,949	7	317	Philippines	3,005	397	2,193	415
Belgium-Luxembourg .	6,527	3,973	1,148	1,406	Singapore.	4,017	2,593	218	1,206
Brazil.	6,897	1,041	4,378	1,479	South Africa	1,878	1,091	495	293
British West Indies. . .	10,047	8,278	6	1,764	South Korea	3,799	1,840	322	1,636
Canada	9,420	3,174	681	5,564	Spain.	2,864	761	1,621	483
Chile	2,730	431	1,515	785	Sweden	2,091	1,238	117	737
France.	8,647	6,581	1,140	927	Switzerland.	2,621	858	17	1,746
Germany	4,125	2,003	884	1,239	United Kingdom.	26,626	15,688	211	10,727
Hong Kong	5,182	2,830	61	2,292	Venezuela	6,806	122	5,669	1,015

[1] Includes other countries, not shown separately.

Source: Board of Governors of the Federal Reserve System, Federal Financial Institutions Examination Council, statistical release.

No. 783. Federal and State-Chartered Credit Unions—Summary: 1970 to 1990

[As of **December 31**. Federal data include District of Columbia, Puerto Rico, Canal Zone, Guam, and Virgin Islands. Excludes State-insured, privately-insured and non-insured State-chartered credit unions and corporate central credit unions which have mainly other credit unions as members. See also *Historical Statistics, Colonial Times to 1970*, series X 864-878]

YEAR	OPERATING CREDIT UNIONS		MEMBERS (1,000)		ASSETS (mil. dol.)		LOANS OUTSTANDING (mil. dol.)		SAVINGS (mil. dol.)	
	Federal	State	Federal	State	Federal	State	Federal	State	Federal	State
1970	12,977	(¹)	11,966	(¹)	8,861	(¹)	6,969	(¹)	7,629	(¹)
1980	12,440	4,910	24,519	12,338	40,092	20,870	26,350	14,582	36,263	18,469
1985	10,125	4,920	29,579	15,689	78,188	41,525	48,241	26,168	71,616	37,917
1986	9,758	4,935	31,041	17,363	95,484	52,244	55,305	30,834	87,954	48,097
1987	9,401	4,934	32,067	17,999	105,190	56,972	64,104	35,436	96,346	52,083
1988	9,118	4,760	34,438	18,519	114,565	60,740	73,766	39,977	104,431	55,217
1989	8,821	4,550	35,612	18,858	120,666	63,175	80,272	42,373	109,653	57,658
1990	8,511	4,349	36,241	19,454	130,073	68,133	83,029	44,102	117,892	62,082

¹ Federal insurance for State-chartered credit unions was not effective until 1971.

Source: National Credit Union Adminstration, *Annual Report of the National Credit Union Adminstration*, and unpublished data.

No. 784. Savings Institutions—Financial Summary, by Type: 1970 to 1990

[**In billions of dollars, except number of institutions**. As of **December 31**. Includes Puerto Rico, Guam, and Virgin Islands. SAIF = Savings Association Insurance Fund. BIF = Bank Insurance Fund. See also *Historical Statistics, Colonial Times to 1970*, series X 834-844]

TYPE OF INSTITUTION	1970	1980	1984	1985	1986	1987	1988	1989	1990
NUMBER OF INSTITUTIONS									
Savings institutions, total. . . .	**6,162**	**5,076**	**3,978**	**3,939**	**3,959**	**3,869**	**3,667**	**3,500**	**(NA)**
Savings and loan associations	5,669	4,613	3,362	3,233	3,084	2,886	2,554	2,271	(NA)
SAIF-insured.	4,365	4,002	2,907	2,944	2,817	2,648	2,328	2,138	1,650
State insured and non-insured . . .	1,304	611	455	289	267	238	226	133	(NA)
Savings banks	493	463	616	706	875	983	1,113	1,229	1,345
SAIF-insured.	(X)	3	229	302	403	499	621	740	871
BIF-insured [1]	328	323	291	392	472	484	492	489	474
Federally chartered	(X)	(X)	24	28	26	22	21	20	18
State chartered	328	323	267	364	446	462	471	469	456
State insured and non-insured . . .	165	137	96	12	-	-	-	-	-
SAIF-insured institutions.	4,365	4,005	3,136	3,246	3,220	3,147	2,949	2,878	2,521
BIF-insured institutions [1]	328	323	291	392	472	484	492	489	474
State insured and non-insured.	1,469	748	551	301	267	238	226	133	(NA)
ASSETS									
Savings institutions, total. . . .	**255**	**797**	**1,207**	**1,315**	**1,422**	**1,521**	**1,644**	**1,518**	**(NA)**
Savings and loan associations	176	630	902	948	962	974	933	756	(NA)
SAIF-insured.	171	619	879	938	954	967	925	751	507
State insured and non-insured . . .	6	11	23	10	8	8	9	5	(NA)
Savings banks	79	167	305	367	460	546	710	762	838
SAIF-insured.	(X)	2	98	132	210	284	426	483	578
BIF-insured [1]	69	153	179	205	250	262	284	280	261
Federally chartered	(X)	(X)	44	48	52	45	46	(NA)	(NA)
State chartered	69	153	136	157	198	217	238	(NA)	(NA)
State insured and non-insured . . .	11	12	27	30	-	-	-	-	-
SAIF-insured institutions.	171	621	978	1,070	1,164	1,251	1,351	1,234	1,085
BIF-insured institutions [1]	69	153	179	205	250	262	284	280	261
State insured and non-insured.	16	23	50	40	8	8	9	5	(NA)
DEPOSITS									
Savings institutions, total. . . .	**219**	**674**	**988**	**1,057**	**1,097**	**1,144**	**1,193**	**(NA)**	**(NA)**
Savings and loan associations	147	511	725	749	740	736	674	(NA)	(NA)
SAIF-insured.	142	501	705	741	733	729	674	597	401
State insured and non-insured . . .	5	10	20	9	7	7	(NA)	(NA)	(NA)
Savings banks	72	163	264	308	357	408	519	572	648
SAIF-insured.	(X)	2	80	104	158	203	298	349	434
BIF-insured [1]	63	150	160	179	199	205	221	224	214
Federally chartered	(X)	(X)	38	40	39	31	32	(NA)	(NA)
State chartered	63	150	122	139	160	174	189	(NA)	(NA)
State insured and non-insured . . .	9	11	24	26	-	-	-	-	-
SAIF-insured institutions.	142	503	785	844	891	933	972	946	836
BIF-insured institutions [1]	63	150	160	179	199	205	221	224	214
State insured and non-insured.	14	21	44	35	7	7	-	(NA)	(NA)

- Represents zero. NA Not available. X Not applicable. [1] Source: U.S. Federal Deposit Insurance Corporation, *Annual Report* (for 1970 and 1980), *Statistics on Banking*, annual, and *The FDIC Quarterly Banking Profile*, (for 1990). Includes those State-chartered, SAIF-insured savings banks that are regulated by the FDIC.

Source: Except as noted, U.S. Office of Thrift Supervision, 1970-1989, *Savings and Home Financing Source Book*, annual; 1990, *Quarterly Thrift Financial Aggregates*.

No. 785. Savings Institutions (SAIF-Insured) Approved for Merger: 1980 to 1990

[Covers all institutions approved for merger by the U.S. Office of Thrift Supervision except for holding company acquisitions. See headnote, table 787]

YEAR	NUMBER					ASSETS (bil. dol.)				
	Total	Voluntary	Supervisory	SAIF-assisted	Transfers to RTC [1]	Total	Voluntary	Supervisory	SAIF-assisted	Transfers to RTC [1]
1980	120	88	21	11	(X)	10.1	7.2	1.4	1.5	(X)
1985	77	49	6	22	(X)	23.7	17.4	2.8	3.5	(X)
1986	75	45	5	25	(X)	23.7	16.8	7.0	6.2	(X)
1987	107	74	4	29	(X)	34.1	27.2	0.4	6.5	(X)
1988	222	34	9	179	(X)	109.2	10.5	1.0	97.7	(X)
1989	354	36	(X)	(X)	318	143.4	8.2	(X)	(X)	135.1
1990	251	38	(X)	(X)	213	145.5	17.4	(X)	(X)	128.1

X Not applicable.   [1] RTC=Resolution Trust Corporation. This government agency is charged with disposal of failed thrifts. More often than not, the RTC sold the deposit base of the failed institution to a commercial bank.

No. 786. Savings Institutions (SAIF-Insured)—Deposit Accounts and Mortgage Activity: 1970 to 1990

[See headnote, table 787]

ITEM	Unit	1970	1980	1984	1985	1986	1987	1988	1989	1990
DEPOSIT ACCOUNTS										
Number of accounts	Millions . .	46.5	92.2	111.9	111.5	110.1	110.6	110.1	108.3	93.8
Average balance	Dollars . .	3,045	5,410	7,008	7,572	8,087	8,433	8,825	8,733	8,904
Net deposit gain [1]	Bil. dol. . .	10.8	41.0	113.9	53.0	55.1	46.4	44.0	-15.7	-26.6
Net new deposits received [2]	Bil. dol. . .	5.3	10.7	57.2	-4.6	-3.3	-1.8	-8.4	-72.8	-79.2
MORTGAGE LOANS										
Number of borrowers	Millions . .	10.6	15.7	15.8	15.0	14.1	13.6	13.7	12.5	12.9
Average balance	Dollars . .	13,728	31,311	37,510	43,168	46,359	49,967	52,999	56,556	47,668
Mortgage loans closed [3]	Bil. dol. . .	20.8	85.5	181.3	196.8	265.5	253.4	240.3	188.7	153.5
Purchase of 1- to 4-family homes. . .	Bil. dol. . .	12.3	60.2	95.7	107.8	175.7	173.1	159.1	154.1	133.7
Refinancing loans	Bil. dol. . .	1.7	10.6	31.7	(NA)	(NA)	71.6	42.4	30.9	21.0
Delinquent mortgage loans: [4]										
Amount	Bil. dol. . .	(NA)	7.3	12.6	21.7	32.6	37.7	33.3	36.1	36.3
Percent of mortgage holdings. . . .	Percent. .	(NA)	1.48	2.12	3.36	4.97	5.56	4.58	4.96	5.72
Mortgage loans foreclosed: [5]										
Number.	1,000 . . .	(NA)	20.3	57.0	75.2	90.9	100.0	100.8	74.9	52.8
Percent of mortgages held.	Percent . .	(NA)	0.13	0.37	0.33	0.63	0.73	0.76	0.59	0.34
Amount	Bil. dol. . .	0.3	0.9	6.2	8.7	13.9	19.1	18.9	18.2	17.1
Percent of mortgages held.	Percent . .	0.22	0.15	1.11	1.41	2.15	2.90	2.70	2.42	1.49

NA Not available.   [1] Net new deposits received plus interest credited.   [2] New deposits received less deposits withdrawn.   [3] Reported on a gross basis including refinancing and combination construction-purchase loan.   [4] Prior to 1987, covers all mortgage loans 60 or more days delinquent. Beginning 1987, covers construction and land loans past due, permanent loans secured by 1-4 dwelling unit properties 60 or more days delinquent, and all other permanent loans past due.   [5] Foreclosures are reported as of judgment date, even if subject to a redemption period.

No. 787. Savings Institutions (SAIF-Insured)—Selected Financial Items and Ratios of Condition: 1970 to 1990

[As of **Dec. 31** for assets, liabilities and net worth; calendar year for other items. Includes Puerto Rico, Guam, and Virgin Islands. SAIF=Savings Association Insurance Fund. Beginning 1983, includes SAIF-insured savings and loan associations which changed to SAIF-insured savings banks. Minus sign (-) indicates either loss or outflow]

ITEM	Unit	1970	1980	1984	1985	1986	1987	1988	1989	1990
Assets [1]	Bil. dol .	170.6	620.6	977.5	1,070.0	1,163.9	1,250.9	1,350.5	1,233.6	1,084.8
Mortgage assets [2]	Bil. dol .	146.0	494.9	593.0	645.5	655.7	679.2	726.6	708.9	615.6
Mortgage-backed securities.	Bil. dol .	(X)	27.3	112.7	115.5	158.2	201.8	214.6	170.5	156.3
Cash and securities	Bil. dol .	15.8	57.0	136.7	143.5	164.8	169.7	187.0	166.0	146.6
Liabilities [1].	Bil. dol .	158.8	588.0	940.3	1,023.4	1,111.6	1,204.5	1,295.3	1,225.2	1,052.2
Deposit accounts.	Bil. dol .	141.7	503.2	784.5	843.9	890.7	932.6	971.7	945.7	835.5
FHLB advances.	Bil. dol .	10.5	47.0	71.7	84.4	100.0	116.4	134.2	124.6	100.4
Other borrowed money	Bil. dol .	0.3	17.2	66.2	73.3	96.9	133.5	165.2	131.4	95.2
Net worth	Bil. dol .	11.8	32.6	37.2	46.7	52.3	46.4	55.2	23.6	31.1
Net worth to total assets ratio .	**Ratio** . .	**6.9**	**5.2**	**3.8**	**4.4**	**4.5**	**3.7**	**4.1**	**1.9**	**2.9**
Operating income	Bil. dol .	10.7	56.1	101.2	110.6	110.8	107.5	113.6	125.9	(NA)
Operating expenses	Bil. dol .	1.9	7.9	15.3	19.2	22.6	24.1	23.8	26.6	(NA)
Interest expense.	Bil. dol .	7.7	47.5	85.0	87.7	83.5	80.5	89.3	97.5	79.4
Net income before taxes	Bil. dol .	1.2	1.2	1.8	5.8	3.3	-5.1	-11.6	-13.4	-7.5
Net income after taxes	Bil. dol .	0.9	0.8	1.0	3.7	0.1	-7.8	-13.4	-14.1	-7.0
Average cost of funds	Percent.	5.30	8.94	10.03	9.19	8.06	7.20	7.49	8.26	7.83
Average effective dividend rate paid.	Percent.	5.14	8.78	9.92	9.02	7.84	6.92	7.20	7.91	7.60
Average interest return on mortgages	Percent.	6.56	9.34	11.65	11.52	10.65	9.70	9.62	10.32	10.38
Return on assets [3] **. . . . .**	**Percent**	**0.57**	**0.14**	**0.12**	**0.39**	**0.02**	**-0.64**	**-1.08**	**-1.47**	**-1.08**

NA Not available.   X Not applicable.   [1] Includes other items, not shown separately.   [2] Beginning 1983, reflects deductions from asset accounts.   [3] Net income after taxes as a percent of average assets.

Source of tables 785-787: U.S. Office of Thrift Supervision, 1970-89, *Savings and Home Financing Source Book*, annual; 1990, *Quarterly Thrift Financial Aggregate*.

No. 788. Savings Institutions (SAIF-Insured)—Selected Financial Items, by State and Other Areas: 1990

[See headnote, table 787]

DIVISION AND STATE	Mortgage loans foreclosed [1] (percent)	Net income after taxes (mil. dol.)	Return on assets [2] (percent)	DIVISION AND STATE	Mortgage loans foreclosed [1] (percent)	Net income after taxes (mil. dol.)	Return on assets [2] (percent)	DIVISION AND STATE	Mortgage loans foreclosed [1] (percent)	Net income after taxes (mil. dol.)	Return on assets [2] (percent)
Total	1.49	-8,583	-1.08	IA	1.08	-14	-	AR	0.81	-156	-4.62
				MO	2.26	-29	-0.35	LA	1.43	-383	-4.66
U.S. . . .	(NA)	-8,570	(NA)	ND	0.31	34	0.45	OK	3.00	-97	-1.93
N.E	(NA)	-396	(NA)	SD	0.36	-12	-0.78	TX	6.67	-1,723	-4.01
ME. . . .	0.52	(-Z)	-	NE	0.57	11	-0.04	Mt.	(NA)	-920	(NA)
NH. . . .	1.14	-24	-1.13	KS	1.07	-162	1.13	MT	0.25	9	0.72
VT	2.10	2	0.32	S.A.	(NA)	-1,203	(NA)	ID	0.24	-1	0.04
MA. . . .	3.88	-212	-9.74	DE	0.10	2	0.52	WY	0.74	2	-0.11
RI	2.45	-13	-0.44	MD	2.09	-11	-0.12	CO	6.39	-140	-2.67
CT	1.42	-149	-1.55	DC	0.44	10	0.44	NM	0.74	-285	-9.50
M.A.	(NA)	-1,697	(NA)	VA	3.15	-409	-1.37	AZ	1.67	-518	-14.04
NY	0.64	-355	-0.65	WV	0.49	1	0.02	UT	1.78	3	-0.05
NJ	1.60	-649	-1.66	NC	1.05	24	0.08	NV	0.51	10	0.20
PA	0.66	-694	0.01	SC	1.04	10	0.10	Pac.	(NA)	-1,954	(NA)
E.N.C	(NA)	290	(NA)	GA. . . .	1.64	-37	-0.28	WA	0.15	105	0.67
OH. . . .	0.60	27	0.01	FL	2.16	-792	-1.29	OR	0.26	-232	0.23
IN	0.22	65	0.45	E.S.C.	(NA)	-141	(NA)	CA	1.38	-1,909	-0.63
IL.	0.27	145	0.10	KY	0.51	33	0.42	AK	2.36	1	0.58
MI	0.70	-4	0.05	TN	1.48	-71	-0.43	HI	0.01	81	1.12
WI	0.21	56	-0.11	AL	2.23	-38	-0.55	PR	0.30	-17	(NA)
W.N.C	(NA)	-191	(NA)	MS. . . .	0.96	-64	-2.44	GU	(NA)	3	(NA)
MN. . . .	1.33	-19	-0.73	W.S.C	(NA)	-2,358	(NA)				

- Represents or rounds to zero.   NA Not available.   Z Less than $500 thousand.   [1] Percent of average mortgage balances. See footnote 5, table 786.   [2] Net income after taxes as a percent of average assets.

Source: U.S. Office of Thrift Supervision, *Quarterly Thrift Financial Aggregates.*

No. 789. Mortgage Debt Outstanding, by Type of Property and Holder: 1970 to 1990

[In billions of dollars. As of Dec. 31. Includes Puerto Rico and Guam. See also *Historical Statistics, Colonial Times to 1970,* series N 273 and N 276]

TYPE OF PROPERTY AND HOLDER	1970	1980	1982	1983	1984	1985	1986	1987	1988	1989	1990
Mortgage debt, total	474	1,460	1,638	1,825	2,051	2,303	2,634	2,986	3,270	3,556	3,858
Residential nonfarm	358	1,107	1,226	1,359	1,520	1,716	1,981	2,242	2,493	2,733	3,017
One- to four-family homes.	297	965	1,080	1,198	1,334	1,501	1,724	1,963	2,201	2,430	2,710
Savings institutions	167	487	458	482	529	554	559	602	672	669	600
Mortgage pools or trusts [1]	3	125	201	271	322	407	553	702	790	921	1,078
Commercial banks	42	160	174	183	196	213	236	276	334	390	456
Individuals and others [2]	36	99	134	140	151	176	202	206	216	246	339
Federal and related agencies	22	61	78	87	98	110	127	124	134	143	165
Finance companies.	1	14	19	21	24	29	34	40	44	49	60
Life insurance companies.	27	18	17	15	14	12	13	13	11	12	12
Five or more units	60	142	146	161	185	214	257	279	291	303	307
Commercial	86	255	301	352	419	482	556	657	692	739	756
Farm	30	97	111	114	112	106	96	88	85	84	84
TYPE OF HOLDER											
Savings institutions	208	603	578	627	710	760	778	860	925	910	802
Commercial banks	73	263	301	331	379	429	503	592	674	767	844
Life insurance companies.	74	131	142	151	157	172	194	212	233	254	267
Finance companies.	1	14	19	21	24	29	34	40	44	49	60
Individuals and others [2]	79	189	235	251	272	307	357	370	383	420	527
Mortgage pools or trusts [1]	5	146	224	297	351	439	565	718	812	947	1,107
Government National Mortgage Assoc . . .	(Z)	94	119	160	180	212	263	318	341	368	404
Federal Home Loan Mortgage Corp	-	17	43	58	71	100	171	213	226	273	316
Federal National Mortgage Association . . .	-	-	14	25	36	55	97	140	178	228	300
Farmers Home Administration [3]	4	32	40	42	45	48	(Z)	(Z)	(Z)	(Z)	(Z)
Federal and related agencies	34	115	139	148	159	167	204	193	201	209	251
Federal National Mortgage Association . . .	16	57	72	78	88	00	98	97	103	111	117
Farmers Home Administration [3]	2	3	2	2	1	1	48	43	42	42	41
Federal Land Banks	7	38	51	52	52	47	40	34	32	30	29
Federal Home Loan Mortgage Corp	(Z)	5	5	8	10	14	12	13	17	22	22
Federal Housing and Veterans Admin . . .	4	6	5	5	5	5	5	6	6	6	9
Government National Mortgage Assoc . . .	5	5	4	3	2	1	1	(Z)	(Z)	(Z)	(Z)
Resolution Trust Corporation	(X)	(X)	(X)	(X)	(X)	(X)	(X)	(X)	(X)	(X)	33

- Represents zero.   X Not applicable.   Z Less than $500 million.   [1] Outstanding principal balances of mortgage pools backing securities insured or guaranteed by the agency indicated. Includes private pools not shown separately.   [2] Includes mortgage companies, real estate investment trusts, State and local retirement funds, noninsured pension funds, credit unions, and other U.S. agencies.   [3] FmHA-guaranteed securities sold to the Federal Financing Bank were reallocated from FmHA mortgage pools to FmHA mortgage holdings in 1986 because of accounting changes by the Farmers Home Administration.

Source: Board of Governors of the Federal Reserve System, *Federal Reserve Bulletin,* monthly.

No. 790. Volume of Long-Term Mortgage Loans Originated, by Type of Property, 1970 to 1990, and by Lender, 1990

[In billions of dollars. Covers credit extended in primary mortgage markets for financing real estate acquisitions]

TYPE OF PROPERTY	1970	1980	1984	1985	1986	1987	1988	1989	1990, BY LENDER				
									Total [1]	Commercial banks	Mortgage companies	Savings and loan	Life insurance companies
Loans, total	59.8	197.2	319.2	430.0	706.4	729.4	673.6	642.3	711.9	329.8	169.2	135.1	41.1
1-4 unit family home . .	35.6	133.8	203.7	289.8	499.4	507.2	446.3	452.9	458.4	153.3	161.2	121.0	0.6
New units	12.6	49.1	53.7	59.0	72.5	79.0	85.2	90.4	110.7	57.4	30.3	18.5	0.1
Existing units	23.0	84.6	150.0	230.8	426.9	428.2	361.1	362.5	347.8	95.8	130.9	102.6	0.5
Multifamily residential .	8.8	12.5	27.6	31.9	49.9	45.1	38.2	31.1	32.5	11.0	5.5	9.2	2.2
New units	7.0	8.6	11.1	10.6	15.3	14.1	9.0	8.3	6.4	2.2	0.8	0.5	0.5
Existing units	1.8	3.9	16.4	21.3	34.6	31.0	29.2	22.8	26.0	8.8	4.8	8.7	1.7
Non-residential	12.5	35.9	77.3	99.4	147.4	168.7	181.6	150.0	209.5	157.3	2.5	4.8	37.6
Farm properties	3.0	15.0	10.5	9.0	9.8	8.4	7.6	8.3	11.5	8.3	-	-	0.7

- Represents zero.   [1] Includes other lenders not shown separately.

Source: U.S. Dept. of Housing and Urban Development, *Survey of Mortgage Lending Activity, 1970-1979*, and monthly and quarterly press releases based on the Survey of Mortgage Lending Activity.

No. 791. Characteristics of Conventional First Mortgage Loans for Purchase of Single-Family Homes: 1970 to 1991

[In percent, except as indicated. Annual averages, except as indicated. Refers to loans originated directly by Savings Association Insurance Fund-insured savings institutions, mortgage bankers, commercial banks, and Federal Deposit Insurance Corporation-insured savings banks. Excludes interim construction loans, refinancing loans, junior liens, and federally underwritten loans]

LOAN CHARACTERISTICS	1970	1980	1982	1983	1984	1985	1986	1987	1988	1989	1990	1991, June
NEW HOMES												
Contract interest rate, [1] all loans	8.3	12.3	14.5	12.1	11.9	11.1	9.7	8.9	8.8	9.8	9.7	9.2
Fixed-rate loans.	(NA)	(NA)	14.4	12.3	12.5	11.9	10.0	9.5	10.0	10.2	10.1	9.5
Adjustable-rate loans [2]	(NA)	(NA)	14.7	11.8	11.5	10.4	9.0	8.2	8.1	9.0	8.9	8.3
Initial fees, charges [3]	1.03	2.09	2.96	2.39	2.66	2.52	2.48	2.26	2.19	2.08	1.98	1.69
Effective interest rate, [4] all loans	8.5	12.7	15.1	12.6	12.4	11.6	10.2	9.3	9.2	10.1	10.1	9.5
Fixed-rate loans.	(NA)	(NA)	14.9	12.7	13.0	12.4	10.5	9.9	10.4	10.6	10.4	9.8
Adjustable-rate loans [2]	(NA)	(NA)	15.4	12.3	12.0	10.8	9.4	8.5	8.5	9.3	9.2	8.6
Term to maturity (years)	25.1	28.1	27.5	26.7	27.8	27.0	26.8	27.8	28.0	28.1	27.3	26.8
Purchase price ($1,000)	35.5	83.2	94.1	93.9	96.8	105.0	119.8	137.2	150.5	160.1	154.1	166.7
Loan to price ratio.	71.7	73.2	76.6	77.3	78.6	77.1	75.3	75.2	75.6	74.6	74.9	74.2
Percent of number of loans with												
adjustable rates	(NA)	(NA)	41	37	59	51	27	41	19	35	31	26
EXISTING HOMES												
Contract interest rate, [1] all loans	8.2	12.5	14.8	12.3	12.0	11.2	9.8	8.9	9.0	9.8	9.8	9.2
Fixed-rate loans.	(NA)	(NA)	14.8	12.6	12.7	11.9	10.1	9.5	10.1	10.2	10.1	9.5
Adjustable-rate loans [2]	(NA)	(NA)	14.7	11.9	11.6	10.5	9.1	8.2	8.2	9.2	8.9	7.9
Initial fees, charges [3]	0.92	1.91	2.55	2.40	2.54	2.50	2.13	2.02	1.88	1.79	1.74	1.52
Effective interest rate, [4] all loans	8.4	12.9	15.3	12.8	12.5	11.6	10.2	9.3	9.3	10.1	10.1	9.4
Fixed-rate loans.	(NA)	(NA)	15.4	13.0	13.2	12.4	10.5	9.9	10.4	10.5	10.4	9.8
Adjustable-rate loans [2]	(NA)	(NA)	15.3	12.3	12.1	10.9	9.4	8.5	8.5	9.4	9.2	8.1
Term to maturity (years)	22.8	26.9	24.9	25.9	26.5	25.5	25.4	26.6	27.7	27.7	27.0	27.3
Purchase price ($1,000)	30.0	68.3	70.7	79.3	82.2	92.7	108.5	117.7	126.6	138.4	140.3	148.7
Loan to price ratio.	71.1	73.5	71.9	74.3	76.8	75.7	73.9	75.4	76.4	75.2	74.9	74.8
Percent of number of loans with												
adjustable rates	(NA)	(NA)	39	41	64	50	31	44	24	37	27	23

NA Not available.   [1] Initial interest rate paid by the borrower as specified in the loan contract.   [2] Loans with a contractual provision for periodic adjustments in the contract interest rate.   [3] Includes all fees, commisions, discounts and "points" paid by the borrower, or seller, in order to obtain the loan. Excludes those charges for mortgage, credit, life or property insurance; for property transfer; and for title search and insurance.   [4] Contract interest rate plus fees and charges amortized over a 10-year period.

Source: U.S. Federal Housing Finance Board, annual and monthly press releases.

No. 792. Mortgage Delinquency Rates, by Division: 1980 to 1991

[In percent. Annual average of quarterly figures. Covers one- to four-family residential nonfarm mortgage loans. Represents number of loans delinquent 30 days or more as percentage of loans serviced in survey. Excludes loans in foreclosure. For composition of divisions, see table 25]

YEAR	U.S., total	New England	Middle Atlantic	East North Central	West North Central	South Atlantic	East South Central	West South Central	Mountain	Pacific
1980	4.97	3.52	6.23	6.29	4.60	4.55	5.32	4.12	4.40	4.29
1985	5.83	4.22	6.31	7.18	4.96	5.11	5.98	6.54	6.10	4.96
1987	4.97	2.85	5.08	5.94	3.93	4.54	5.36	7.37	5.48	3.82
1988	4.79	2.74	4.67	5.42	4.04	4.55	5.55	6.83	5.58	3.67
1989	4.80	3.13	4.65	5.32	4.18	4.61	6.24	7.14	5.35	3.31
1990	4.66	3.53	4.54	5.06	3.82	4.80	6.33	6.45	5.10	3.21
1991	5.02	4.14	5.05	5.20	3.99	5.53	6.70	6.41	5.01	3.45

Source: Mortgage Bankers Association of America, Washington, DC, *National Delinquency Survey*, quarterly.

No. 793. Mortgage Delinquency and Foreclosure Rates and Private Mortgage Insurance: 1980 to 1991

[In percent, except as indicated. Covers one- to four-family residential nonfarm mortgage loans]

ITEM	1980	1984	1985	1986	1987	1988	1989	1990	1991
Number of mortgage loans outstanding (1,000)	30,033	32,366	34,316	36,439	37,232	41,603	43,836	47,002	48,260
Delinquency rates: [1]									
Total.	5.0	5.7	5.8	5.6	5.0	4.8	4.8	4.7	5.0
Conventional loans.	3.1	3.9	4.0	3.8	3.2	2.9	3.1	3.0	3.3
VA loans.	5.3	6.4	6.6	6.6	6.2	6.2	6.4	6.4	6.8
FHA loans	6.6	7.3	7.5	7.2	6.6	6.6	6.7	6.7	7.3
Foreclosure rates: [2]									
Total.	0.5	0.9	1.0	1.2	1.3	1.2	1.0	0.9	1.0
Conventional loans.	0.2	0.6	0.7	0.8	0.8	0.7	0.6	0.7	0.8
VA loans.	0.6	1.0	1.1	1.4	1.6	1.6	1.3	1.2	1.3
FHA loans	0.7	1.2	1.3	1.5	1.8	1.8	1.4	1.3	1.4
Claims paid by private mortgage insurers [3] (mil. dol.)	59	472	971	1,262	1,574	992	834	(NA)	(NA)

NA Not available. [1] Number of loans delinquent 30 days or more as percentage of mortgage loans serviced in survey. Annual average of quarterly figures. [2] Percentage of loans in the foreclosure process at yearend, not seasonally adjusted. [3] Source: Mortgage Insurance Companies of America, Washington, DC, unpublished data.

Source: Except as noted, Mortgage Bankers Association of America, Washington, DC, *National Delinquency Survey*, quarterly.

No. 794. Home Equity Loans—Insured Domestic Commercial Banks Offering Loans and Home Equity Balances, 1987 to 1990, and by Asset-Size of Bank, 1990

[As of December 31]

ITEM	1987	1988	1989	1990 Total	1990 Less than $100 million	1990 $100 to $249 million	1990 $250 to $999 million	1990 $1 billion or more
Banks offering home equity loans	4,346	4,707	4,861	5,054	2,767	1,285	674	328
Percent of all commercial banks	32	36	38	41	30	67	84	89
Home equity debt outstanding (bil. dol.)	29.0	39.9	50.8	61.3	2.9	4.7	8.8	44.9
All commercial banks:								
Home equity debt as percent of consumer loans plus home equity debt.	8	10	12	14	8	12	15	15
Home equity debt as percent of consumer loans plus all loans secured by homes.	5	6	7	8	3	6	8	9
Banks offering home equity loans:								
Home equity debt as percent of consumer loans plus home equity debt.	10	12	15	17	17	17	17	17
Home equity debt as percent of consumer loans plus all loans secured by homes.	6	8	9	9	8	8	9	10

Source: Board of Governors of the Federal Reserve System, *Domestic Offices, Commercial Bank Assets and Liabilities, Consolidated Report of Condition*, quarterly.

No. 795. Consumer Credit—Installment Credit Finance Rates: 1980 to 1991

[In percent. Annual averages]

TYPE OF CREDIT	1980	1981	1982	1983	1984	1985	1986	1987	1988	1989	1990	1991
Commercial banks:												
New automobiles (48 months) [1]	14.30	16.54	16.83	13.92	13.71	12.91	11.33	10.46	10.85	12.07	11.78	11.14
Mobile homes (120 months) [1]	14.99	17.45	18.05	16.08	15.58	14.96	14.00	13.38	13.54	14.11	14.02	13.70
Other consumer goods (24 months) . .	15.47	18.09	18.65	16.68	16.47	15.94	14.83	14.23	14.68	15.44	15.46	15.18
Credit-card plans	17.31	17.78	18.51	18.78	18.77	18.69	18.26	17.93	17.79	18.02	18.17	18.23
Finance companies:												
New automobiles.	14.82	16.17	16.15	12.58	14.62	11.98	9.44	10.73	12.60	12.62	12.54	12.41
Used automobiles	19.10	20.00	20.75	18.74	17.85	17.59	15.95	14.61	15.11	16.18	15.99	15.60

[1] For 1980-82, maturities were 36 months for new car loans and 84 months for mobile home loans.

Source: Board of Governors of the Federal Reserve System, *Federal Reserve Bulletin*, monthly; *Annual Statistical Digest*; and unpublished data.

No. 796. Consumer Credit Outstanding: 1970 to 1991

[In billions of dollars, except percent. Estimated amounts of seasonally adjusted credit outstanding as of end of year. See also *Historical Statistics, Colonial Times to 1970*, series X 551-560]

TYPE OF CREDIT	1970	1980	1981	1982	1983	1984	1985	1986	1987	1988	1989	1990	1991
Credit outstanding	131.6	350.3	366.9	383.1	431.2	511.3	592.1	649.1	681.9	731.2	781.2	794.4	777.3
Ratio to disposable personal income [1] (percent)	18.2	18.0	16.9	16.5	17.3	18.5	20.1	20.7	20.7	20.6	20.6	19.6	18.4
Installment.	103.9	298.2	311.3	325.8	369.0	442.6	518.3	573.0	610.5	664.0	718.9	735.1	729.4
Automobile paper	36.3	112.0	119.0	125.9	143.6	173.6	210.2	247.4	265.9	284.2	290.7	284.6	267.9
Revolving.	4.9	55.1	61.1	66.5	79.1	100.3	121.8	135.9	153.1	174.1	199.1	220.1	234.5
Mobile home paper	2.4	18.7	20.1	22.6	23.6	25.9	26.8	27.1	25.9	25.3	22.5	21.0	19.1
All other loans.	60.2	112.4	111.1	110.8	122.8	142.9	159.4	162.6	165.6	180.4	206.6	209.5	207.9
Noninstallment.	27.7	52.1	55.6	57.3	62.2	68.7	73.8	76.1	71.4	67.1	62.3	59.3	47.9

[1] Based on fourth quarter seasonally adjusted disposable personal income at annual rates as published by the U.S. Bureau of Economic Analysis in sources listed in table 682.

Source: Board of Governors of the Federal Reserve System, *Federal Reserve Bulletin*, monthly; *Annual Statistical Digest*; and unpublished data.

No. 797. Delinquency Rates on Bank Installment Loans, by Type of Loan: 1980 to 1991

[In percent, except as indicated. As of end of year; seasonally adjusted, except as noted. Number of loans having an installment past due for 30 days or more as a percentage of total installment loans outstanding]

TYPE OF CREDIT	1980	1982	1983	1984	1985	1986	1987	1988	1989	1990	1991
DELINQUENCY RATES											
Closed-end installment loans, total	2.82	2.39	1.94	2.09	2.32	2.26	2.47	2.49	2.64	2.57	2.58
Personal loans [1]	3.53	3.04	2.84	3.16	3.63	3.11	3.66	3.34	3.52	3.37	2.95
Automobile, direct loans [2]	1.81	1.68	1.53	1.47	1.64	1.80	1.59	1.92	2.03	2.22	2.14
Automobile, indirect loans [3]	2.29	1.73	1.50	1.77	2.02	2.09	2.20	2.46	2.61	2.59	2.66
Property improvement [4]	1.93	1.98	2.14	2.00	1.91	1.77	1.88	2.06	2.25	2.30	2.38
Home equity and second mortgage loans [5] . .	(NA)	(NA)	1.94	1.77	2.06	1.85	2.01	1.86	1.85	1.45	2.06
Mobile home loans	3.14	2.69	2.44	2.56	2.39	3.04	2.57	3.12	2.51	3.03	2.86
Recreational vehicle loans	1.94	1.88	1.58	1.87	1.84	1.92	1.99	2.07	2.24	2.63	2.25
Bank card loans.	2.72	2.38	2.08	2.81	2.95	3.15	2.33	2.19	2.24	2.86	3.29
Revolving credit loans.	2.70	2.16	1.44	1.50	1.96	1.53	2.33	2.87	2.92	3.00	2.75
Home equity lines of credit loans (open-end) [5] .	(NA)	(NA)	(NA)	(NA)	(NA)	(NA)	0.74	0.68	0.78	0.85	0.88
REPOSSESSIONS PER 1,000 LOANS OUTSTANDING											
Mobile home	1.57	1.14	1.23	1.29	1.21	2.50	1.58	1.77	1.63	1.19	1.62
Automobile, direct loans [2]	1.10	0.90	0.70	0.72	1.11	1.15	0.86	1.03	1.03	1.75	1.17
Automobile, indirect loans [3]	2.75	2.13	1.56	1.58	2.08	1.95	2.04	1.86	1.70	1.61	2.07

NA Not available. [1] Beginning 1983, includes home appliance loans. [2] Made directly by bank's lending function. [3] Made by automobile dealerships; loans in bank's portfolio. [4] Beginning 1983, own plan and FHA Title I loans. [5] Seasonally not adjusted.

Source: American Bankers Association, Washington, DC, *Consumer Credit Delinquency Bulletin*, quarterly.

No. 798. Credit Cards—Holders, Numbers, Spending, and Debt, 1980 and 1991, and Projections, 2000

TYPE OF CREDIT CARD	CARDHOLDERS (mil.)			NUMBER OF CARDS (mil.)			CREDIT CARD SPENDING (bil. dol.)			CREDIT CARD DEBT (bil. dol.)		
	1980	1991	2000, proj.	1980	1991	2000, proj.	1980	1991	2000, proj.	1980	1991	2000, proj.
Total [1]	86.1	111.3	124.8	526	1,027	1,319	201.2	481.0	882.0	80.2	257.9	432.9
Bank.	63.3	79.7	90.0	111	221	296	52.9	260.0	493.6	25.0	166.6	278.7
Oil company.	68.5	79.9	91.1	110	122	131	28.9	26.5	53.5	2.2	3.4	6.9
Phone.	(NA)	98.0	111.6	(NA)	145	195	(NA)	12.4	23.1	(NA)	1.0	2.0
Retail store	83.0	95.0	108.9	277	463	610	74.4	76.4	135.2	47.3	51.9	78.7
Travel and entertainment	10.5	23.1	26.4	10	28	36	21.2	89.4	146.6	2.7	20.2	33.5
Other [2]	13.4	7.1	7.3	19	48	52	23.8	21.3	37.9	3.0	14.9	33.2

NA Not available. [1] Cardholders may hold more than one type of card. [2] Includes airline, automobile rental, Discover (except for cardholders), hotel, motel, and other miscellaneous credit cards.

Source: HSN Consultants Inc., Santa Monica, CA, *The Nilson Report*, bimonthly. (Copyright used by permission.)

No. 799. Use of Financial Services by Households, by Type of Financial Institution: 1989

[In percent, except as indicated. Use of a financial institution consists of use of one or more of the types of accounts shown in table 800. Savings institutions consist of savings and loan associations and savings banks. Other nondepository financial institutions include mortgage banks and insurance companies. An institution is local if the office or branch used by the household is located 30 miles or less from the household or workplace of the primary user. Based on the Survey of Consumer Finance, see headnote, table 768. For definition of mean, see Guide to Tabular Presentation]

ITEM	All finan-cial institu-tions	DEPOSITORY				NONDEPOSITORY			
		Total	Com-mercial bank	Savings	Credit union	Total	Finance com-pany	Bro-kerage firm	Other financial
Percentage of households using financial institutions, total [1]	90.3	88.6	77.6	39.4	26.5	42.8	21.3	14.0	18.1
Local	89.5	87.8	75.4	37.4	23.0	28.5	13.3	10.1	7.2
Nonlocal	17.8	11.7	6.8	3.5	4.4	17.5	9.0	4.6	10.9
Mean number of accounts used per household, total	4.73	3.92	2.40	0.91	0.61	0.81	0.29	0.30	0.22
Institutions identified by household as—									
Primary financial institution [2]	100.0	96.4	64.7	22.0	9.7	3.6	2.0	1.3	0.4
Main checking institution [3]	100.0	99.5	69.2	21.2	9.1	0.5	0.2	0.4	(Z)

Z Less than .05 percent. [1] Sum of local and nonlocal exceeds total because some households use both local and nonlocal institutions. [2] 84.7 percent of households designated a primary financial institution. [3] 81.3 percent of households designated a main checking institution.

No. 800. Use of Financial Services by Households, by Type of Account and Locality of Institution: 1989

[See headnote, table 799]

TYPE OF ACCOUNT	PERCENT OF HOUSEHOLDS USING FINANCIAL INSTITUTIONS			Mean number of accounts per house-hold	TYPE OF ACCOUNT	PERCENT OF HOUSEHOLDS USING FINANCIAL INSTITUTIONS			Mean number of accounts per house-hold
	Total	Local	Non-local			Total	Local	Non-local	
All types	**90.3**	**89.5**	**17.8**	**4.73**	Brokerage	8.4	6.9	1.9	0.10
					Trust	3.2	2.0	1.4	0.04
Asset	86.2	85.4	9.9	2.84	Credit	74.9	68.6	15.0	1.89
Checking [1]	75.6	74.3	2.9	1.05	Bank credit card	55.8	51.1	6.1	0.71
Other liquid asset	61.2	58.4	6.6	1.27	Mortgage	37.2	30.1	9.0	0.46
Savings [2]	43.4	41.1	3.8	0.71	Motor vehicle	33.8	28.8	5.8	0.42
Money market [3]	21.6	20.0	2.3	0.30	Home equity or other				
Certificate of deposit	19.5	18.7	3.2	0.27	credit line	10.6	9.3	1.4	0.12
IRA or Keogh	23.0	20.6	3.2	0.38	Other [4]	13.8	12.3	1.7	0.18

[1] Consists of regular checking, NOW, and share draft accounts. Excludes money market accounts. [2] Consists of passbook, share, and statement savings accounts. [3] Consists of money market deposit accounts and mutual fund accounts. [4] Includes personal loans and home improvement loans.

No. 801. Percent of Households Using Financial Accounts, by Type of Account and Source: 1989

[See headnote, table 799]

TYPE OF ACCOUNT	Any source	FINANCIAL INSTITUTIONS									Non-finan-cial [1]
		Total	Depository				Nondepository				
			Total	Com-mer-cial bank	Sav-ings	Credit union	Total	Fi-nance com-pany	Bro-kerage	Other	
All types of accounts	**92.4**	**90.3**	**88.6**	**77.6**	**39.4**	**26.5**	**42.8**	**21.3**	**14.0**	**18.1**	**27.9**
Asset	86.3	86.2	86.1	65.9	30.6	22.8	17.3	0.3	13.9	4.6	3.8
Checking [2]	75.6	75.6	75.4	55.5	18.3	9.6	0.8	0.1	0.7	-	(Z)
Other liquid asset	61.3	61.2	59.4	34.9	21.4	18.2	6.3	0.1	5.6	0.7	0.9
Savings [3]	43.5	43.4	42.9	21.5	12.0	16.3	0.9	0.1	0.7	0.2	0.4
Money market [4]	21.8	21.6	17.8	10.7	0.0	2.4	5.2	(Z)	4.8	0.5	0.4
Certificate of deposit	19.5	19.5	19.0	11.6	8.5	2.0	0.9	(Z)	0.8	0.1	0.1
IRA or Keogh	24.2	23.0	15.6	9.4	5.2	2.2	9.8	0.1	7.0	3.0	1.9
Brokerage	8.4	8.4	0.9	0.8	0.1	(Z)	7.6	(Z)	7.6	-	(Z)
Trust	4.3	3.2	1.1	0.7	0.2	0.1	2.2	0.1	0.9	1.4	1.2
Credit	80.0	74.9	68.0	56.6	20.9	13.7	32.8	21.1	1.1	14.8	25.0
Bank credit card	56.5	55.8	54.0	45.5	5.9	6.3	7.9	0.2	0.8	7.1	1.5
Mortgage	40.8	37.2	26.3	14.1	12.8	1.1	13.3	5.3	0.1	8.2	5.8
Motor vehicle	34.9	33.8	21.8	13.7	3.1	6.0	13.7	13.5	(Z)	0.1	1.3
Home equity, other credit line	10.8	10.6	8.8	5.6	1.5	1.9	2.1	1.8	0.3	-	0.3
Other [5]	28.2	13.8	10.4	6.2	2.2	2.6	4.1	4.0	(Z)	0.1	18.6

- Represents zero. Z Less than .05 percent. [1] Includes individuals, retailers, other nonfinancial businesses, government agencies, and nonprofit organizations. [2] See footnote 1, table 800. [3] See footnote 2, table 800. [4] See footnote 3, table 800. [5] See footnote 4, table 800.

Source of tables 799-801: Board of Governors of the Federal Reserve System, *Federal Reserve Bulletin*, March 1992.

No. 802. Money Stock and Liquid Assets: 1980 to 1991

[In billions of dollars. As of December. Seasonally adjusted averages of daily figures. See *Historical Statistics, Colonial Times to 1970*, series X 410-417 for similar data]

ITEM	1980	1981	1982	1983	1984	1985	1986	1987	1988	1989	1990	1991
M1, total	409	437	475	521	552	620	725	750	787	794	826	898
Currency [1]	115	123	133	146	156	168	181	197	212	223	247	267
Travelers checks [2]	4	4	4	5	5	6	6	7	7	7	8	8
Demand deposits [3]	261	231	234	238	244	267	302	287	287	279	277	289
Other checkable deposits [4]	28	78	104	132	147	180	235	259	281	285	294	333
M2, total	1,629	1,794	1,952	2,186	2,374	2,569	2,811	2,911	3,071	3,227	3,339	3,439
M1	409	437	475	521	552	620	725	750	787	794	826	898
Nontransaction components in M2 [5]	1,221	1,356	1,477	1,665	1,822	1,949	2,087	2,160	2,284	2,433	2,513	2,541
Overnight repurchase (RP) agreements and Eurodollars [6]	29	37	40	56	61	73	82	84	83	78	75	76
Money market funds, general purpose and broker/dealer	62	151	185	138	167	176	208	222	242	316	349	[7] 361
Money market deposit accounts	(Z)	(Z)	43	379	418	515	572	525	502	487	507	[7] 1,043
Commercial banks	(Z)	(Z)	26	230	267	332	357	357	350	353	379	[7] 665
Thrift institutions	(Z)	(Z)	17	150	152	183	195	169	151	133	128	[7] 378
Savings deposits	398	342	355	305	286	300	368	412	424	404	411	(7)
Commercial banks	185	158	163	133	122	125	156	178	192	188	199	(7)
Thrift institutions	214	184	193	172	164	175	212	233	232	216	211	(7)
Small time deposits [8]	727	820	847	781	885	882	855	917	1,033	1,148	1,169	1,063
Commercial banks	286	346	378	349	385	384	366	388	447	531	606	599
Thrift institutions	441	474	469	432	499	498	489	530	586	618	562	464
M3, total	1,987	2,234	2,441	2,693	2,987	3,203	3,494	3,681	3,923	4,060	4,115	4,172
M2	1,629	1,794	1,952	2,186	2,374	2,569	2,811	2,911	3,071	3,227	3,339	3,439
Nontransaction components in M3 [5]	358	441	489	507	613	634	683	770	852	832	776	733
Large time deposits [9]	258	299	323	325	416	436	440	489	541	559	495	437
Commercial banks [10]	213	245	260	228	269	284	289	326	367	398	374	354
Thrift institutions	45	54	64	97	147	152	150	163	174	161	121	83
Term RP's and term Eurodollars [8][11]	84	103	115	141	141	139	164	197	227	179	158	129
Money market funds, institution only	15	38	51	43	64	67	87	93	91	108	134	180
L, total	2,324	2,596	2,850	3,154	3,529	3,830	4,134	4,339	4,678	4,892	4,967	4,989
M3	1,987	2,234	2,441	2,693	2,987	3,203	3,494	3,681	3,923	4,060	4,115	4,172
Savings bonds	72	68	68	71	74	79	92	101	109	118	126	138
Short-term Treasury securities [12]	133	149	184	212	261	298	280	253	270	326	333	316
Bankers acceptances	32	40	44	45	45	42	37	44	40	40	34	23
Commercial paper [13]	99	105	114	133	161	208	231	261	336	349	359	340

Z Less than $500 million. [1] Currency outside U.S. Treasury, Federal Reserve Banks and the vaults of depository institutions. [2] Outstanding amount of nonbank issuers. [3] At commercial banks and foreign-related institutions. [4] Consists of negotiable order of withdrawal (NOW) and automatic transfer service (ATS) accounts at all depository institutions, credit union share draft balances and demand deposits at thrift institutions. [5] This sum is seasonally adjusted as a whole. [6] Not seasonally adjusted. [7] Data for savings deposits included with money market deposit accounts. [8] Issued in amounts of less than $100,000. Includes retail repurchase agreements. Excludes individual retirement accounts (IRAs) and Keogh accounts. [9] Issued in amounts of $100,000 or more. Excludes those booked at international banking facilities. [10] Excludes those held by money market mutual funds, depository institutions and foreign banks and official institutions. [11] Excludes those held by depository institutions and money market mutual funds. [12] U.S. Treasury bills and coupons with remaining maturities of less than 12 months held by other than depository institutions, Federal Reserve banks, money market mutual funds and foreign entities. [13] Excludes commercial paper held by money market mutual funds.

Source: Board of Governors of the Federal Reserve System, *Federal Reserve Bulletin*, monthly, and *Money Stock, Liquid Assets, and Debt Measures, Federal Reserve Statistical Release H.6*, weekly.

No. 803. Commercial Paper Outstanding, by Type of Company: 1980 to 1991

[In billions of dollars. As of December 31. Seasonally adjusted. Commercial paper is an unsecured promissory note having a fixed maturity of no more than 270 days]

TYPE OF COMPANY	1980	1982	1983	1984	1985	1986	1987	1988	1989	1990	1991
All issuers	124.4	166.4	187.7	237.6	298.8	330.0	359.0	458.5	525.8	561.1	530.3
Financial companies [1]	87.7	118.7	141.0	167.0	213.8	252.9	277.1	354.7	394.6	415.0	397.6
Dealer-placed paper [2]	19.9	34.7	44.8	56.5	78.4	101.1	102.7	159.8	183.6	215.1	214.4
Directly-placed paper [3]	67.8	84.0	96.2	110.5	135.3	151.8	174.3	194.9	210.9	199.8	183.2
Nonfinancial companies [4]	36.7	47.7	46.7	70.6	85.0	77.1	81.9	103.8	131.3	146.2	132.7

[1] Institutions engaged primarily in activities such as, but not limited to, commercial, savings, and mortgage banking; sales, personal, and mortgage financing; factoring, finance leasing, and other business lending; insurance underwriting; and other investment activities. [2] Includes all financial company paper sold by dealers in the open market. [3] As reported by financial companies that place their paper directly with investors. [4] Includes public utilities and firms engaged primarily in such activities as communications, construction, manufacturing, mining, wholesale and retail trade, transportation, and services.

Source: Board of Governors of the Federal Reserve System, *Federal Reserve Bulletin*, monthly.

No. 804. Bank Debits and Deposit Turnover: 1970 to 1990

[Debits in trillions of dollars; turnover as ratio of debits to deposits. Annual averages of monthly data]

ITEM	1970	1980	1981	1982	1983	1984	1985	1986	1987	1988	1989	1990
Debits to—												
Demand deposits, all banks [1]	11.3	63.1	81.3	96.5	112.3	131.6	156.3	188.8	214.9	219.9	256.4	277.7
Major New York City banks	4.1	25.3	34.1	39.8	47.6	57.3	70.7	91.6	110.4	115.5	129.5	131.9
Other banks..........	7.3	37.9	47.2	56.7	64.7	74.2	85.6	97.1	104.5	104.4	126.9	145.8
ATS/NOW accounts [2]	(NA)	0.2	0.7	1.0	1.4	1.6	1.8	2.2	2.2	2.5	2.9	3.3
Money market deposit accounts	(NA)	(NA)	(NA)	(NA)	0.6	0.9	1.2	1.6	1.9	2.3	2.7	2.9
Savings deposits [3]	(NA)	0.7	0.7	0.7	0.5	0.4	0.4	0.4	0.5	0.5	0.5	0.6
Deposit turnover:												
All banks [1]	64	203	286	343	386	441	501	557	608	623	736	800
Major New York City banks	171	816	1,116	1,354	1,522	1,840	2,200	2,500	2,669	2,897	3,428	3,815
Other banks..........	47	135	186	225	249	278	306	322	335	333	408	467

NA Not available. [1] Represents accounts of individuals, partnerships, and corporations, and of States and political subdivisions at insured commercial banks. [2] Accounts authorized for negotiable orders of withdrawal (NOW) and accounts authorized for automatic transfer to demand deposits (ATS). [3] Excludes ATS and NOW accounts, money market deposit accounts, and special club accounts, such as Christmas and vacation clubs.

No. 805. Federal Reserve Bank of New York—Discount Rates: 1979 to 1992

[**Percent per year**. Rates for short-term adjustment credit. For rates applicable to other types of discount window credit, see source. See also *Historical Statistics, Colonial Times to 1970*, series X 454-455]

EFFECTIVE DATE	Rate	EFFECTIVE DATE	Rate	EFFECTIVE DATE	Rate	EFFECTIVE DATE	Rate
1979: July 20.....	10	Dec. 5	13	Dec. 15	$8\frac{1}{2}$	**1988:** Aug. 9	$6\frac{1}{2}$
Aug. 17	$10\frac{1}{2}$	**1981:** [1] May 5	14	**1984:** April 9	9	**1989:** Feb. 24	7
Sept. 19	11	Nov. 2	13	Nov. 21	$8\frac{1}{2}$	**1990:** Dec. 19	$6\frac{1}{2}$
Oct. 8	12	Dec. 4.....	12	Dec. 24	8	**1991:** Feb. 1	6
1980: [1] Feb. 15 ...	13	**1982:** July 20.....	$11\frac{1}{2}$	**1985:** May 20.....	$7\frac{1}{2}$	April 30	$5\frac{1}{2}$
May 30.....	12	Aug. 2	11	**1986:** March 7	7	Sept. 13	5
June 13	11	Aug. 16	$10\frac{1}{2}$	April 21	$6\frac{1}{2}$	Nov. 6	$4\frac{1}{2}$
July 28.....	10	Aug. 27	10	July 11.....	6	Dec. 20	$3\frac{1}{2}$
Sept. 26	11	Oct. 12.....	$9\frac{1}{2}$	Aug. 21	$5\frac{1}{2}$	In effect, **March 31,**	
Nov. 17	12	Nov. 22 ...	9	**1987:** Sept. 4.....	6	**1992.........**	$3\frac{1}{2}$

[1] See table 806, footnote 5.

No. 806. Money Market Interest Rates and Mortgage Rates: 1980 to 1991

[**Percent per year**. Annual averages of monthly data, except as indicated. See also *Historical Statistics, Colonial Times to 1970*, series X 444-453]

TYPE	1980	1981	1982	1983	1984	1985	1986	1987	1988	1989	1990	1991
Federal funds, effective rate [1] [2]	13.35	16.39	12.24	9.09	10.23	8.10	6.80	6.66	7.57	9.21	8.10	5.69
Commercial paper, 3-month [1] [2]	12.61	15.34	11.90	8.88	10.12	7.95	6.49	6.82	7.66	8.99	8.06	5.87
Prime rate charged by banks	15.26	18.87	14.85	10.79	12.04	9.93	8.33	8.21	9.32	10.87	10.01	8.46
Eurodollar deposits, 3-month	14.00	16.79	13.12	9.57	10.75	8.27	6.70	7.07	7.85	9.16	8.16	5.86
Finance paper, 3-month [2] [3]	11.49	14.08	11.23	8.70	9.73	7.77	6.38	6.54	7.38	8.72	7.87	5.71
Bankers acceptances, 90-day [2] [4] .	12.67	15.34	11.89	8.91	10.17	7.91	6.38	6.75	7.56	8.87	7.93	5.70
Large negotiable CDs, 3-month,												
secondary market	13.07	15.91	12.27	9.07	10.37	8.05	6.52	6.86	7.73	9.09	8.15	5.83
Federal Reserve discount rate [5] .	10-13	12-14	$8\frac{1}{2}$ -12	$8\frac{1}{2}$	8-9	$7\frac{1}{2}$ -8	$5\frac{1}{2}$ -$7\frac{1}{2}$	$5\frac{1}{2}$ -6	6-$6\frac{1}{2}$	$6\frac{1}{2}$ -7	$6\frac{1}{2}$ -7	$3\frac{1}{2}$ -$6\frac{1}{2}$
Taxable money market funds [6] ...	12.68	16.82	12.23	8.58	10.04	7.71	6.26	6.12	7.11	8.87	7.82	5.71
Certificates of deposit (CDs): [7]												
6-month.................	(NA)	(NA)	(NA)	(NA)	9.99	7.83	6.51	6.47	7.18	8.34	7.35	5.67
1-year.................	(NA)	(NA)	(NA)	(NA)	10.37	8.29	6.75	6.77	7.47	8.41	7.42	5.88
2 1/2-year...............	(NA)	(NA)	(NA)	10.06	10.82	9.00	7.13	7.16	7.77	8.33	7.52	6.29
5-year.................	(NA)	(NA)	(NA)	(NA)	11.25	9.66	7.60	7.66	8.11	8.30	7.71	6.83
U.S. Government securities: [8]												
3-month Treasury bill	11.39	14.04	10.60	8.62	9.54	7.47	5.97	5.78	6.67	8.11	7.50	5.38
6-month Treasury bill	11.32	13.81	11.06	8.74	9.78	7.65	6.02	6.03	6.91	8.03	7.46	5.44
1-year Treasury bill	10.85	13.16	11.07	8.80	9.94	7.81	6.07	6.33	7.13	7.92	7.35	5.52
Home mortgages: [9]												
HUD series: [10]												
FHA insured, secondary												
market [10]	13.44	16.31	15.30	13.11	13.81	12.24	9.91	10.16	10.49	10.49	10.17	9.25
Conventional, new-home [11] [12]	13.95	16.52	15.79	13.43	13.80	12.28	10.07	10.17	10.30	10.21	10.08	9.20
Conventional, existing-home [11]	13.95	16.55	15.82	13.44	13.81	12.29	10.09	10.17	10.31	10.22	10.08	9.20
Conventional, 15 yr. fixed [7]	(NA)	(NA)	(NA)	(NA)	(NA)	(NA)	10.05	10.04	10.14	10.05	9.67	8.76
Conventional, 30 yr. fixed [7]	(NA)	(NA)	(NA)	(NA)	(NA)	(NA)	10.39	10.40	10.38	10.26	10.01	9.09

NA Not available. [1] Based on daily offering rates of dealers. [2] Yields are quoted on a bank-discount basis, rather than an investment yield basis (which would give a higher figure). [3] Placed directly; averages of daily offering rates quoted by finance companies. [4] Based on representative closing yields. From Jan. 1, 1981, rates of top-rated banks only. [5] Federal Reserve Bank of New York, low and high. The discount rates for 1980 and 1981 do not include the surcharge applied to frequent borrowings by large institutions. The surcharge reached 3 percent in 1980 and 4 percent in 1981. Surcharge was eliminated in Nov. 1981. [6] 12 month yield for period ending December 31. Source: IBC/Donoghue, Inc., Ashland, MA, *IBC/Donoghue's Money Market Insight*, monthly (copyright). [7] Annual averages. Source: Financial Rates, Inc., North Palm Beach, FL, *Bank Rate Monitor*, weekly (copyright). [8] Averages based on daily closing bid yields in secondary market, bank discount basis. [9] HUD=Housing and Urban Development. [10] Averages based on quotations for 1 day each month as compiled by FHA. [11] Primary market. [12] Average contract rates on new commitments.

Source of tables 804-806: Except as noted, Board of Governors of the Federal Reserve System, *Federal Reserve Bulletin*, monthly, and *Annual Statistical Digest*.

No. 807. Selected Time Deposits and Other Accounts at Insured Commercial Banks— Deposits and Interest Rates: 1985 to 1991

[As of **December**, except as noted. Estimates based on data collected from a sample of about 500 banks]

TYPE OF DEPOSIT	AMOUNT OUTSTANDING (bil. dol.)						AVERAGE RATE PAID (percent)					
	1985	1987	1988	1989	1990	1991 [1]	1985	1987	1988	1989	1990	1991 [1]
NOW accounts [2]	44.5	174.8	190.5	196.8	209.2	229.5	5.99	4.95	4.96	5.02	4.93	4.39
Interest-bearing time deposits: [3]												
7-91 day	26.3	30.5	31.2	45.4	50.2	49.8	7.10	6.20	7.11	7.64	6.94	5.09
92-182 day	147.8	132.4	136.3	152.8	167.6	160.8	7.50	6.75	7.84	7.83	7.19	5.26
183 day-1 year	66.1	96.8	128.0	177.4	220.8	215.2	7.77	7.14	8.19	7.86	7.33	5.49
1-2½ year	81.2	89.6	107.2	125.0	150.0	168.9	8.24	7.46	8.30	7.88	7.43	5.86
2½ year or more	115.4	121.3	133.0	129.2	138.1	158.5	8.73	7.86	8.39	7.86	7.52	6.50
All IRA and Keogh Plan deposits	59.4	83.2	94.0	109.2	131.2	146.4	(NA)	(NA)	(NA)	(NA)	(NA)	(NA)

NA Not available. [1] As of October. [2] Negotiable order of withdrawal accounts containing an agreement between depositor and depository such that some or all funds deposited are eligible to earn more than 5.25 percent. As of January 1, 1986 interest rate ceilings were removed from all NOW accounts. Beginning with the December 1987 data the NOW accounts category includes all NOW accounts, including those accounts which were subject to a 5.25 percent regulatory interest rate restriction prior to January 1, 1986. Estimates for NOW accounts beginning in December 1987 are based on reports of deposits. [3] All interest-bearing time deposits and open account time deposits with balances of less than $100,000, including those held in IRA's and Keogh Plan deposits.

Source: Board of Governors of the Federal Reserve System, *Money Stock, Liquid Assets, and Debt Measures, Federal Reserve Statistical Release H.6*, weekly.

No. 808. Security Prices: 1980 to 1991

[Annual averages of monthly figures, except as noted. See also *Historical Statistics, Colonial Times to 1970*, series X 492- 498]

CLASS OR ITEM	1980	1983	1984	1985	1986	1987	1988	1989	1990	1991
Bond prices (dollars per $100 bond):										
Standard & Poor's: Municipal [1] [2]	57.4	51.4	47.9	53.0	65.1	62.7	62.0	66.1	66.0	68.8
Dow Jones and Co., Inc.: [3]										
Yearly high	76.6	77.8	72.9	83.7	93.7	95.5	91.3	94.2	93.0	98.9
Yearly low	61.0	69.4	64.8	72.3	83.7	81.3	86.9	87.4	88.4	91.3
Stock prices:										
Standard & Poor's common index										
(500 stocks)(1941-43=10) [4]	118.7	160.4	160.5	186.8	236.3	268.8	265.9	323.1	334.6	376.2
Industrial	134.5	180.5	181.3	207.8	262.2	330.5	306.5	392.9	391.4	445.8
N.Y. Stock Exchange common										
stock index										
(Dec. 31, 1965=50):										
Composite	68.1	92.6	92.5	108.1	136.0	161.7	150.0	180.1	183.5	206.4
Yearly high [5]	81.0	99.6	98.1	121.9	145.8	188.0	159.4	199.3	201.1	229.4
Yearly low [5]	55.3	79.8	85.1	94.6	117.8	125.9	136.7	155.0	162.2	171.0
Industrial	78.6	107.5	108.0	123.8	155.9	195.3	180.8	228.0	225.8	258.2
Transportation	60.5	89.4	85.6	104.1	119.9	140.4	134.0	174.9	158.6	174.0
Utility	37.3	47.0	46.4	56.8	71.4	74.3	72.2	94.3	90.6	92.6
Finance	64.3	95.3	89.3	114.2	147.2	146.5	127.4	162.0	133.2	150.8
American Stock Exchange										
Market Value Index										
(Aug. 31, 1973=50)	150.6	216.5	208.0	229.1	264.4	316.4	295.1	356.7	338.3	360.3
NASDAQ OTC composite [6]	202.3	278.6	247.4	324.9	348.8	330.5	381.4	454.8	373.9	586.3
Industrial	261.4	323.7	260.7	330.2	349.3	338.9	379.0	448.0	406.1	669.0
Insurance	166.8	257.6	283.1	382.1	404.1	351.1	429.1	546.0	451.8	601.1
Banks	118.4	203.8	229.8	349.4	412.5	390.7	435.3	391.0	254.9	350.6
Dow Jones and Co., Inc.:										
Composite (65 stocks) [1] [7]	328.2	472.2	463.1	541.6	702.5	849.5	772.2	966.9	965.2	1,048.3
Industrial (30 stocks)	891.4	1,190.3	1,178.5	1,328.2	1,792.8	2,276.0	2,060.8	2,508.9	2,678.9	2,929.3
Transportation (20 stocks)	307.2	544.6	513.8	645.1	785.4	929.2	863.8	1,194.3	1,040.2	1,170.2
Utility (15 stocks)	110.4	130.0	131.8	157.6	195.2	202.2	179.7	205.7	211.5	210.3
Wilshire 5000 equity index										
(Dec. 31, 1980=1404.596) [8]	1,220.7	1,691.5	1,644.6	1,923.8	2,418.8	2,843.7	2,636.9	3,172.6	3,187.3	3,590.1
Standard & Poor's:										
Dividend-price ratio (percent)	5.26	4.40	4.64	4.25	3.48	3.08	3.64	3.45	3.61	3.25
Earnings-price ratio (percent)	12.66	8.02	10.02	8.12	6.09	5.48	8.00	7.41	8.96	8.17

[1] Source: U.S. Bureau of Economic Analysis. [2] Derived from average yields on basis of assumed 4 percent, 20-year bond; Wednesday closing prices. [3] Source: Dow Jones and Co., Inc., New York, NY. A 20-bond average consisting of 10 utility bonds and 10 industrial bonds. [4] The index includes 400 industrial stocks, 20 transportation, 40 public utility, and 40 financial stocks. [5] Source: New York Stock Exchange, Inc., New York, NY, *Fact Book*, annual. [6] Source: National Association of Securities Dealers, Washington, DC, *Fact Book*, annual. OTC=over-the-counter. December monthly closing values. [7] Based on stocks listed on the New York Stock Exchange. [8] Represents return on the market value of all common equity securities for which daily pricing is available. Annual average of daily figures. Source: Wilshire Associates, Santa Monica, CA, releases.

Source: Except as noted, Board of Governors of the Federal Reserve System, *Federal Reserve Bulletin*, monthly and unpublished data.

No. 809. Bond and Stock Yields: 1980 to 1991

[Percent per year. Annual averages of monthly data, except as indicated. See also *Historical Statistics, Colonial Times to 1970*, series X 474-491]

TYPE	1980	1982	1983	1984	1985	1986	1987	1988	1989	1990	1991
U.S. Treasury, constant maturities: [1][2]											
3-year	11.51	12.93	10.45	11.92	9.64	7.06	7.68	8.26	8.55	8.26	6.82
5-year	11.45	13.01	10.79	12.26	10.12	7.30	7.94	8.47	8.50	8.37	7.37
10-year	11.43	13.01	11.10	12.46	10.62	7.67	8.39	8.85	8.49	8.55	7.86
U.S. Govt., long-term bonds [2][3] . . .	10.81	12.23	10.84	11.99	10.75	8.14	8.64	8.98	8.58	8.74	8.16
State and local govt. bonds, Aaa [4] . . .	7.86	10.86	8.80	9.61	8.60	6.95	7.12	7.36	7.00	6.96	6.56
State and local govt. bonds, Baa [4] . . .	9.02	12.46	10.17	10.38	9.58	7.75	8.17	7.84	7.40	7.29	6.99
High-graded municipal bonds (Standard & Poor's) [5]	8.51	11.57	9.47	10.15	9.18	7.38	7.73	7.74	7.24	7.25	6.89
Municipal (Bond Buyer, 20 bonds) . . .	8.59	11.66	9.51	10.10	9.11	7.32	7.63	7.68	7.23	7.27	6.92
Corporate Aaa seasoned [4]	11.94	13.79	12.04	12.71	11.37	9.02	9.38	9.71	9.26	9.32	8.77
Corporate Baa seasoned [4]	13.67	16.11	13.55	14.19	12.72	10.39	10.58	10.83	10.18	10.36	9.80
Corporate (Moody's) [4][6]	12.75	14.94	12.78	[7]13.49	12.05	9.71	9.91	10.18	9.66	9.77	9.23
Industrials (49 bonds) [8]	12.35	14.54	12.25	13.21	11.80	9.96	9.83	9.91	9.66	9.77	9.25
Public utilities (51 bonds) [9]	13.15	15.33	13.31	[7]14.03	12.29	9.46	9.98	10.45	9.66	9.76	9.21
Stocks (Standard & Poor's): [5]											
Preferred (10 stocks) [10]	10.60	12.53	11.02	11.59	10.49	8.76	8.37	9.23	9.04	8.96	8.17
Common: Composite (500 stocks) . .	5.26	5.81	4.40	4.64	4.25	3.48	3.08	3.64	3.45	3.61	3.24
Industrials (400 stocks)	4.95	5.48	4.04	4.05	3.76	3.09	2.62	3.14	3.01	3.16	2.82

[1] Yields on the more actively traded issues adjusted to constant maturities by the U.S. Treasury.   [2] Yields are based on closing bid prices quoted by at least five dealers.   [3] Averages (to maturity or call) for all outstanding bonds neither due nor callable in less than 10 years, including several very low yielding "flower" bonds.   [4] Source: Moody's Investors Service, New York, NY.   [5] Source: Standard & Poor's Corp., New York, NY, *Standard & Poor's Outlook*, weekly.   [6] For 1980-88, includes railroad bonds which were discontinued as part of composite in 1989.   [7] The Aaa public utility average was suspended on Jan. 17, 1984 because of a lack of appropriate issues. The average corporate does not include Aaa utilities from Jan. 17 to Oct. 12. The Aaa utility average was reinstated on Oct. 12. Thirty public utility bonds were used during the period Jan. 17-Oct. 12, 1984.   [8] Covers 40 bonds for period 1980-83, 38 bonds for 1984-86, and 37 bonds for 1987 and 1988.   [9] Covers 40 bonds for period 1980-88.   [10] Yields based on 10 stocks, 4 yields. Issues converted to a price equivalent to $100 par and a 7 percent annual dividend before averaging.

Source: Except as noted, Board of Governors of the Federal Reserve System, *Federal Reserve Bulletin*, monthly.

No. 810. Sales of Stocks and Options on Registered Exchanges: 1970 to 1990

[Excludes over-the-counter trading. See also *Historical Statistics, Colonial Times to 1970*, series X 517-530]

EXCHANGE	Unit	1970	1980	1983	1984	1985	1986	1987	1988	1989	1990
Market value of all sales, all exchanges [1][2]	Bil. dol	136	522	1,023	1,004	1,260	1,868	2,492	1,702	2,010	1,751
New York	Bil. dol	108	398	816	815	1,024	1,453	1,987	1,380	1,581	1,394
American.	Bil. dol	15	47	48	32	38	63	102	59	80	65
Midwest	Bil. dol	5	21	60	62	79	102	122	87	101	74
Chicago	Bil. dol	-	28	39	35	38	56	124	64	88	81
Pacific.	Bil. dol	5	13	31	31	40	55	71	49	64	53
Philadelphia.	Bil. dol	3	11	20	19	23	35	48	34	50	41
STOCKS [3]											
Shares sold, all exchanges [2] . . .	Million.	4,539	15,488	30,146	30,456	37,046	48,338	63,771	52,533	54,239	53,338
New York	Million.	3,213	12,390	24,253	25,150	30,222	39,258	53,038	44,018	44,140	43,829
American.	Million.	879	1,659	2,209	1,584	2,115	2,999	3,496	2,576	3,248	3,125
Midwest	Million.	149	598	1,662	1,843	2,274	2,784	3,329	2,771	2,960	2,511
Pacific.	Million.	165	435	1,070	1,006	1,352	1,750	2,034	1,576	1,791	1,682
Market value, all exchanges [2] . . .	Bil. dol	131	476	957	951	1,200	1,705	2,284	1,587	1,845	1,612
New York	Bil. dol	103	398	815	814	1,023	1,450	1,983	1,378	1,577	1,390
American.	Bil. dol	14	35	31	21	26	43	53	31	43	36
Midwest	Bil. dol	5	21	60	62	79	102	122	87	101	74
Pacific.	Bil. dol	5	11	27	28	37	51	57	41	52	45
OPTIONS [4]											
Contracts traded, all exchanges [2].	Million.	(NA)	97	149	197	233	289	305	196	227	210
Chicago	Million.	(NA)	53	82	123	149	180	182	112	127	130
American.	Million.	(NA)	29	39	40	49	65	71	45	50	41
Market value of contracts traded, all exchanges [2]	Bil. dol	(NA)	45.8	64.2	53.0	59.1	87.9	118.9	62.6	76.8	79.0
Chicago	Bil. dol	(NA)	27.9	39.4	34.9	38.4	55.9	76.9	39.7	47.3	55.4
American.	Bil. dol	(NA)	12.5	15.8	10.5	11.6	19.0	25.7	13.4	16.1	12.0
Options exercised:											
Number of contracts	Million.	(NA)	4.9	13.6	11.9	10.5	14.5	17.0	11.4	15.6	12.1
Value	Bil. dol	(NA)	20.4	65.1	55.6	49.2	72.8	85.9	51.5	85.2	55.8

- Represents zero.   NA Not available.   [1] Includes market value of rights and warrants and, for 1970, bond sales. Excludes the value of options exercised.   [2] Includes other registered exchanges, not shown separately.   [3] Includes voting trust certificates, American Depository Receipts, and certificate of deposit for stocks.   [4] Includes non-equity options as of October 1982.

Source: U.S. Securities and Exchange Commission, *SEC Monthly Statistical Review* (discontinued Feb. 1989) and unpublished data.

No. 811. Foreign Purchases and Sales of U.S. Securities, by Type of Security, 1980 to 1991, and by Selected Country, 1990 and 1991

[In billions of dollars. Covers transactions in all types of long-term domestic securities by foreigners as reported by banks, brokers, and other entities in the United States (except non-marketable U.S. Treasury notes, foreign series; and nonmarketable U.S. Treasury bonds and notes, foreign currency series). Data cover new issues of securities, transactions in outstanding issues, and redemptions of securities. Includes transactions executed in the United States for the account of foreigners, and transactions executed abroad for the account of reporting institutions and their domestic customers. Data by country show the country of domicile of the foreign buyers and sellers of the securities; in the case of outstanding issues, this may differ from the country of the original issuer. The term "foreigner" covers all institutions and individuals domiciled outside the United States, including U.S. citizens domiciled abroad, and the foreign branches, subsidiaries and other affiliates abroad of U.S. banks and businesses; the central governments, central banks, and other official institutions of foreign countries; and international and regional organizations. "Foreigner" also includes persons in the United States to the extent that they are known by reporting institutions to be acting on behalf of foreigners. Minus sign (-) indicates net sales by foreigners or a net outflow of capital from the United States]

YEAR AND COUNTRY	NET PURCHASES					TOTAL TRANSACTIONS [4]				
	Total	Treasury bonds and notes [1]	U.S. Govt. corporations [2] bonds	Corporate rate bonds [3]	Corporate rate stocks	Total	Treasury bonds and notes [1]	U.S. Govt. corporations [2] bonds	Corporate rate bonds [3]	Corporate rate stocks
1980	15.8	4.9	2.6	2.9	5.4	198.0	97.4	16.9	8.5	75.2
1985	78.3	29.2	4.3	39.8	4.9	1,256.1	968.0	45.6	83.5	159.0
1987	69.4	25.6	5.0	22.5	16.3	3,315.4	2,649.3	80.6	103.6	482.0
1988	74.8	48.8	6.7	21.2	-2.0	3,581.1	3,071.9	56.1	88.7	364.4
1989	96.6	54.2	15.1	17.4	9.9	4,766.8	4,140.3	87.8	120.4	418.2
1990, total [5]	19.4	17.9	6.3	10.4	-15.1	4,213.3	3,634.6	103.9	113.5	361.4
Japan.	-16.9	-14.8	0.4	0.3	-2.9	1,533.9	1,418.6	40.3	17.2	57.9
United Kingdom	5.4	-2.0	2.0	8.4	-3.0	1,213.3	1,051.0	20.2	49.2	93.0
Canada	-1.8	-4.6	0.7	1.2	0.9	174.4	127.0	3.1	6.2	38.1
Germany	5.1	5.9	(-Z)	-0.4	-0.4	97.3	82.0	0.2	2.9	12.2
Netherlands Antilles	11.6	10.8	1.5	0.5	-1.1	80.1	44.5	15.5	3.2	16.9
Sweden	1.5	1.2	(Z)	(-Z)	0.3	65.9	63.6	0.1	0.4	1.8
1991, total [5]	61.1	22.5	9.8	17.7	11.1	4,651.4	3,963.6	123.4	154.1	410.3
United Kingdom	14.6	5.7	1.3	8.0	-0.3	1,414.1	1,211.5	22.3	69.1	111.2
Japan.	2.9	-4.1	4.7	1.1	1.2	1,376.4	1,251.4	56.4	21.1	47.4
Canada	2.4	-2.7	0.3	1.0	3.8	220.9	163.8	2.3	9.0	45.7
Bermuda.	-1.9	-2.2	(-Z)	0.5	-0.2	126.2	107.5	2.7	5.5	10.5
Netherlands Antilles	7.0	6.2	(-Z)	0.3	0.6	115.5	86.1	4.0	5.7	19.7
France	-0.2	-1.0	0.4	0.4	(Z)	115.4	96.1	1.0	3.4	14.9

Z Less than $50 million.   [1] Marketable bonds and notes.   [2] Includes federally-sponsored agencies.   [3] Includes transactions in directly placed issues abroad by U.S. corporations and issues of States and municipalities.   [4] Total purchases plus total sales.   [5] Includes other countries, not shown separately.

Source: U.S. Dept. of Treasury, *Treasury Bulletin*, quarterly.

No. 812. Ownership of Public Debt Securities by Private Investors: 1980 to 1991

[As of **December**. Par values. Estimated]

INVESTOR	AMOUNT (bil. dol.)								PERCENT DISTRIBUTION		
	1980	1985	1986	1987	1988	1989	1990	1991	1980	1990	1991
Total privately held.	616	1,417	1,602	1,731	1,859	2,016	2,288	2,563	100	100	100
Commercial banks [1]	112	189	198	194	185	165	172	222	18	7	9
Nonbank investors	504	1,228	1,405	1,537	1,674	1,851	2,117	2,341	82	93	91
Individuals [2]	117	155	163	172	190	216	234	264	19	10	10
Insurance companies	24	81	102	108	119	125	142	168	4	6	7
Money market funds	4	25	29	15	12	15	46	80	1	2	3
Corporations [3]	19	59	69	85	86	93	109	151	3	5	6
State and local governments [4] . .	88	304	347	418	472	488	490	490	14	21	19
Foreign and international [5]	130	225	263	300	362	393	422	458	21	18	18
Other investors [6]	123	380	433	439	433	521	674	731	20	29	29

[1] Consists of domestically chartered banks, U.S. branches and agencies of foreign banks, NY investment companies majority owned by foreign banks, and Edge Act corporations owned by domestically chartered and foreign banks.   [2] Includes partnerships and personal trust accounts.   [3] Exclusive of banks and insurance companies.   [4] Includes State and local pension funds.   [5] Consists of the investment of foreign balances and international accounts in the United States.   [6] Consists of savings and loan associations, credit unions, mutual savings banks, nonprofit institutions, corporate pension trust funds, and dealers and brokers. Also included are certain government deposit accounts and government-sponsored agencies.

Source: U.S. Dept. of the Treasury, *Treasury Bulletin*, quarterly.

No. 813. New Security Issues of Corporations, by Type of Offering and Industry Group: 1985 to 1990

[In billions of dollars. Represents gross proceeds of issues maturing in more than one year. Figures are the principal amount or the number of units multiplied by the offering price. Excludes secondary offerings, employee stock plans, investment companies other than closed-end, intracorporate transactions, equities sold abroad, and Yankee bonds. Stock data include ownership securities issued by limited partnerships]

TYPE OF OFFERING AND INDUSTRY GROUP	1985	1987	1988	1989	1990	TYPE OF OFFERING AND INDUSTRY GROUP	1985	1987	1988	1989	1990
Total	239.2	392.6	410.9	377.8	339.1	Stocks, total	35.5	66.5	57.8	57.9	40.2
Bonds, total	203.7	326.1	353.1	320.0	298.6	Preferred.	6.5	10.1	6.5	6.2	4.0
Public, domestic . .	119.7	209.7	202.0	179.7	188.8	Common.	29.0	43.2	35.9	26.0	19.4
Private placement, domestic	46.2	92.1	127.7	117.4	87.0	Private placement	(NA)	13.2	15.3	25.6	16.7
Sold abroad.	37.8	24.3	23.1	22.9	23.1						
Manufacturing . .	63.6	60.9	70.3	76.2	52.6	Manufacturing . . .	5.7	13.9	7.6	9.3	5.6
Commercial and miscellaneous . .	17.2	49.8	62.8	49.5	40.0	Commercial and miscellaneous. .	9.1	12.9	8.4	7.4	10.2
Transportation . . .	6.0	12.0	10.3	10.0	12.7	Transportation . . .	1.5	2.4	1.5	1.9	0.4
Public utility	13.6	23.0	20.8	18.7	17.6	Public utility	2.0	4.3	1.9	3.1	0.4
Communication . .	10.9	7.3	5.6	8.5	6.6	Communication . .	1.0	1.5	0.5	1.9	3.8
Real estate and financial	92.3	173.1	183.3	157.2	169.2	Real estate and financial	16.2	31.5	37.8	34.0	19.7

NA Not available.

Source: Board of Governors of the Federal Reserve System, *Federal Reserve Bulletin,* monthly, and *Annual Statistical Digest.*

No. 814. Volume of Trading on New York Stock Exchange: 1980 to 1991

[Round lot: A unit of trading or a multiple thereof. On the NYSE the unit of trading is generally 100 shares in stocks. For some inactive stocks, the unit of trading is 10 shares. Odd lot: An amount of stock less than the established 100-share unit or 10-share unit of trading]

ITEM	Unit	1980	1983	1984	1985	1986	1987	1988	1989	1990	1991
Shares traded	Million .	11,562	21,846	23,309	27,774	36,009	48,143	41,118	42,022	39,947	45,599
Round lots.	Million . .	11,352	21,590	23,071	27,511	35,680	47,801	40,850	41,699	39,665	45,266
Average daily shares	Million . .	44.9	85.3	91.2	109.2	141.0	189.0	161.5	165.5	156.8	178.9
High day.	Million . .	84.3	129.4	236.6	181.0	244.3	608.1	343.9	416.4	292.4	317.4
Low day	Million . .	16.1	53.0	46.4	62.1	48.9	86.7	72.1	68.9	56.9	69.6
By size: [1]											
100 to 900 shares [2]	Percent .	24.7	14.6	11.3	10.6	10.8	13.6	12.6	13.4	22.3	21.9
1,000 to 4,900 shares [3] . . .	Percent .	32.2	26.7	25.1	24.1	25.7	21.1	19.8	20.7	12.9	12.9
5,000 or more shares [4] . . .	Percent .	43.1	58.7	63.6	65.3	63.5	65.3	67.6	65.9	64.8	65.2
Odd lots	Million . .	209	256	238	263	329	342	268	324	282	[5]333
Value of shares traded . .	Bil. dol. .	382	775	773	981	1,389	1,889	1,366	1,556	1,336	1,533
Round lots.	Bil. dol. .	375	765	765	971	1,374	1,874	1,356	1,543	1,325	1,520
Odd lots	Bil. dol. .	8	10	9	10	15	15	10	13	11	[5]13
Bond volume [6]	Mil. dol .	5,190	7,572	6,982	9,046	10,464	9,727	7,702	8,836	10,894	12,698
Daily average.	Mil. dol. .	20.5	29.9	27.6	35.9	41.4	38.4	30.4	35.1	43.1	50.2

[1] Share volume of reported trades by size (percent of total) on New York Stock Exchange. [2] 1988 and 1989, at 100 to 1,000 shares. Beginning 1990, at 100 to 2,000 shares. [3] 1988 and 1989, at 1,100 to 4,900 shares. Beginning 1990, at 2,100 to 4,900 shares. [4] Includes bunched orders at the opening and re-opening of trading. [5] Excludes odd lot statistics for February which were not available. [6] Par value.

Source: New York Stock Exchange, Inc., New York, NY, *Fact Book,* annual.

No. 815. NASDAQ—Securities Listed and Volume of Trading: 1980 to 1991

ITEM	Unit	1980	1983	1984	1985	1986	1987	1988	1989	1990	1991
Companies listed.	Number. . .	2,894	3,901	4,097	4,136	4,417	4,706	4,451	4,293	4,132	4,094
Issues.	Number. . .	3,050	4,467	4,728	4,784	5,189	5,537	5,144	4,963	4,706	4,684
Shares traded.	Million. . .	6,692	15,909	15,159	20,699	28,737	37,890	31,070	33,530	33,380	41,311
Average daily volume . . .	Million. . . .	26.5	62.9	59.9	82.1	113.6	149.8	122.8	133.1	131.9	163.3
Value of shares traded. . . .	Bil. dol. . . .	68.7	188.3	153.5	233.5	378.2	499.9	347.1	431.4	452.4	693.9

Source: National Association of Securities Dealers, Washington, DC, *Fact Book,* annual.

No. 816. Securities Listed on N.Y. Stock Exchange: 1980 to 1991

[As of **December 31**, except **cash dividends** are for **calendar year**]

ITEM	Unit	1980	1982	1983	1984	1985	1986	1987	1988	1989	1990	1991
Bonds:												
Number of issuers....	Number .	1,045	1,031	1,034	1,024	1,010	951	885	846	794	743	706
Number of issues	Number .	3,057	3,233	3,600	3,751	3,856	3,611	3,346	3,106	2,961	2,912	2,727
Face value.........	Bil. dol ..	602	793	965	1,084	1,327	1,380	1,651	1,610	1,435	1,689	2,219
Market value	Bil. dol..	508	766	898	1,022	1,339	1,458	1,621	1,561	1,412	1,610	2,227
Average price.......	Percent .	84.41	96.67	93.04	94.29	100.90	105.66	98.20	96.94	98.42	95.31	100.34
Stocks:												
Companies.........	Number .	1,570	1,526	1,550	1,543	1,541	1,575	1,647	1,681	1,720	1,774	1,885
Number of issues	Number .	2,228	2,225	2,307	2,319	2,298	2,257	2,244	2,234	2,246	2,284	2,426
Shares listed	Billion...	33.7	39.5	45.1	49.1	52.4	59.6	72.0	76.1	83.0	90.7	99.6
Market value	Bil. dol .	1,243	1,305	1,584	1,586	1,950	2,199	2,216	2,457	3,030	2,820	3,713
Average price.......	Dollars ..	36.87	33.03	35.11	32.31	37.20	36.89	30.87	32.30	36.51	31.08	37.27
Cash dividends on common stock.....	Bil. dol ..	53.1	62.2	67.1	68.2	74.2	76.2	84.4	102.2	101.8	103.2	125.3

Source: New York Stock Exchange, Inc., New York, NY, *Fact Book*, annual.

No. 817. Commodity Futures Trading on U.S. Exchanges—Volume of Trading: 1980 to 1991

[In millions. For year ending Sept. 30]

COMMODITY	1980	1982	1983	1984	1985	1986	1987	1988	1989	1990	1991
Number of contracts traded.	82.7	107.6	136.1	148.8	152.6	183.1	213.5	241.8	267.7	272.2	261.4
Grain...................	18.3	14.9	17.8	15.9	10.7	10.3	10.9	15.9	15.9	17.0	16.6
Oilseeds/products	15.7	15.8	19.8	23.5	14.9	13.8	14.2	22.5	21.1	20.4	19.8
Livestock/products	11.8	11.0	11.1	8.4	7.9	8.6	8.8	9.6	8.2	8.0	6.9
Other agriculturals	7.8	4.9	6.3	6.0	5.1	6.7	5.7	9.8	10.7	11.0	9.5
Energy products	1.1	2.3	3.2	4.9	7.0	11.5	20.3	26.3	31.3	35.2	31.8
Metals..................	14.1	19.3	26.3	22.4	18.4	16.2	19.4	18.9	17.9	17.8	13.9
Financial instruments	10.2	31.3	40.2	51.0	72.1	96.9	114.3	117.6	136.7	135.7	134.1
Currencies	3.7	8.3	11.4	16.7	16.4	19.1	19.9	21.2	25.7	27.2	28.8

Source: U.S. Commodity Futures Trading Commission, *Annual Report*.

No. 818. Mutual Funds—Summary: 1980 to 1990

[See also *Historical Statistics, Colonial Times to 1970*, series X 536-539]

TYPE OF FUND	Unit	1980	1983	1984	1985	1986	1987	1988	1989	1990
Number of funds, total ...	**Number..**	564	1,026	1,246	1,531	1,843	2,323	2,718	2,918	3,122
Money market funds..........	Number ..	96	307	329	348	360	389	432	463	508
Equity funds	Number ..	288	396	466	574	700	847	1,015	1,081	1,133
Income and bond funds.......	Number ..	128	179	240	323	409	565	681	735	777
Municipal bond funds	Number ..	42	78	114	174	247	368	415	438	467
Short-term municipal bond funds [1]	Number ..	10	66	97	112	127	154	175	201	237
Shareholder accounts, total	**Millions..**	12.1	24.6	28.2	35.0	46.1	54.7	54.8	58.3	61.8
Equity, bond, and income funds ..	Millions ..	7.3	12.1	14.4	20.0	29.8	37.0	36.2	37.0	39.6
Money market funds and short-term municipal bond funds [1] ...	Millions ..	4.8	12.5	13.8	15.0	16.3	17.7	18.6	21.3	22.2
Assets, total...........	**Bil. dol ..**	135	293	371	496	716	770	810	982	1,069
Money market funds..........	Bil. dol...	74	163	210	208	228	255	272	359	415
Equity funds	Bil. dol...	44	77	83	117	162	181	195	249	246
Income and bond funds.......	Bil. dol...	11	22	33	95	187	196	191	199	205
Municipal bond funds	Bil. dol...	3	15	21	39	76	77	87	106	120
Short-term municipal bond funds [1].	Bil. dol...	2	17	24	36	64	61	66	69	84
Sales, total............	**Bil. dol ..**	248	548	680	954	1,206	1,252	1,177	1,445	1,566
Money market funds..........	Bil. dol...	232	463	572	730	792	869	903	1,135	1,219
Equity funds	Bil. dol...	6	22	20	30	58	72	31	55	72
Income and bond funds.......	Bil. dol...	3	9	16	65	118	90	44	45	50
Municipal bond funds	Bil. dol...	2	9	10	19	40	29	21	27	29
Short-term municipal bond funds [1].	Bil. dol...	5	45	62	109	198	192	178	185	197
Redemptions, total	**Bil. dol ..**	217	566	607	865	1,016	1,179	1,167	1,327	1,471
Money market funds..........	Bil. dol...	204	509	531	732	776	866	899	1,055	1,183
Equity funds	Bil. dol...	6	9	11	18	27	40	35	38	46
Income and bond funds.......	Bil. dol...	2	3	5	11	31	59	45	41	39
Municipal bond funds	Bil. dol...	1	2	4	4	9	17	13	12	14
Short-term municipal bond funds [1].	Bil. dol...	4	42	56	99	172	197	175	181	190

[1] The average maturity of the portfolio is generally less than 2 years.

Source: Investment Company Institute, Washington, DC, *Mutual Fund Fact Book*, annual, (copyright).

No. 819. Securities Industry—Revenues and Expenses: 1980 to 1991

[In millions of dollars. Data provided by U.S. Securities and Exchange Commission cover all securities firms. Minus sign (-) indicates net loss]

TYPE	ALL SECURITIES FIRMS								MEMBERS OF NY STOCK EXCHANGE [1]	
	1980	1984	1985	1986	1987	1988	1989	1990	1990	1991
Revenues, total..........	19,829	39,607	49,844	64,424	66,104	66,100	76,864	71,424	54,034	58,970
Commissions	6,777	9,270	10,955	13,977	16,574	11,932	13,452	12,040	8,878	10,092
Trading/investment gains	5,091	10,761	14,549	18,145	14,423	16,667	16,247	15,806	12,892	16,592
Underwriting profits	1,571	3,249	4,987	6,743	5,719	5,607	4,537	3,728	3,243	5,404
Margin interest	2,151	2,971	2,746	3,022	3,493	3,155	3,860	3,179	3,075	2,583
Mutual fund sales	278	1,452	2,754	4,540	4,069	2,644	3,038	3,242	1,669	1,962
Other	3,960	11,905	13,854	17,998	21,825	26,096	35,731	33,429	24,276	22,340
Expenses, total	16,668	36,751	43,342	56,123	62,894	62,623	74,041	70,631	54,196	53,738
Interest expense..............	3,876	10,693	11,470	14,233	16,473	19,502	29,822	28,100	22,717	19,621
Compensation	7,619	14,431	18,112	23,936	25,583	23,418	23,740	22,962	17,715	19,935
Commissions/clearance paid	1,055	1,907	2,314	2,995	3,563	2,804	3,057	2,968	1,731	1,671
Other	4,119	9,720	11,446	14,959	17,276	16,899	17,422	16,600	12,032	12,511
Net income, pre-tax.......	3,160	2,857	6,502	8,301	3,210	3,477	2,823	794	-162	5,233

[1] Covers all members of New York Stock Exchange doing public business. Source: Securities Industry Association, New York, NY, *Securities Industry Trends*, periodic.

Source: Except as noted, U.S. Securities and Exchange Commission, *Annual Report*.

No. 820. Health Insurance—Premium Income and Benefit Payments of Insurance Companies: 1970 to 1989

[In billions of dollars. Beginning 1975, includes Puerto Rico and other U.S. outlying areas. Represents premium income of and benefits paid by insurance companies only. Excludes Blue Cross-Blue Shield plans, medical-society sponsored plans, and all other independent plans]

ITEM	1970	1975	1980	1981	1982	1983	1984	1985	1986	1987	1988	1989
Premiums [1]	11.5	20.8	43.7	49.0	58.3	63.2	70.4	75.2	75.5	84.1	98.2	108.0
Group policies [2]	8.1	15.9	36.8	42.5	50.0	54.9	60.8	64.4	65.9	74.0	87.6	96.1
Individual and family policies..	3.4	4.9	6.9	6.5	8.3	8.3	9.6	10.8	9.6	10.1	10.6	11.8
Benefit payments [3]. . .	9.1	16.5	37.0	41.6	49.2	51.7	56.0	60.0	64.3	72.5	83.0	89.4
Group policies [2]	7.5	14.2	33.0	37.7	44.2	46.9	50.3	53.7	58.9	66.5	76.4	82.2
Individual and family policies..	1.6	2.3	4.0	3.9	4.9	4.8	5.7	6.3	5.4	5.9	6.6	7.2
Type of coverage:												
Loss of income	1.8	2.7	5.3	5.2	5.5	4.9	5.2	5.6	5.6	6.4	6.4	7.2
Medical expense	7.1	13.2	28.9	33.0	39.6	42.4	45.9	49.0	53.4	58.7	68.6	74.0
Dental	0.1	0.6	2.8	3.5	4.0	4.4	4.9	5.3	5.3	5.9	6.3	6.5

[1] 1970 refers to written premiums; thereafter, refers to earned premiums.   [2] Beginning 1975, insurance company group premiums and benefit payments include administrative service agreements and minimum premium plans. Amounts for 1970 contain only a portion of these data.   [3] Beginning 1987, includes Medicare supplement policies which are not available by type of coverage.

Source: Health Insurance Association of America, Washington, DC, *Source Book of Health Insurance Data*, annual.

No. 821. Property and Casualty Insurance—Summary: 1987 to 1991

[In billions of dollars. Minus sign (-) indicates loss]

ITEM	1987	1988	1989	1990	1991, est.
Premiums, net written.....................	193.2	202.0	208.4	217.8	224.9
Automobile...........................	81.2	86.4	90.9	95.4	(NA)
Auto liability.....................	49.2	52.5	56.0	60.1	(NA)
Auto physical damage................	32.0	33.9	34.8	35.3	(NA)
Liability other than auto	24.9	23.1	22.7	22.1	(NA)
Fire and allied lines	7.7	6.9	7.0	7.1	(NA)
Homeowners' multiple peril	16.7	17.1	17.7	18.6	(NA)
Commercial multiple peril	17.2	17.7	17.5	17.7	(NA)
Workers' compensation	23.4	26.1	28.5	31.0	(NA)
Marine, inland and ocean	5.5	5.5	5.6	5.7	(NA)
Accident and health......................	3.8	4.7	4.6	5.0	(NA)
Other lines...........................	12.8	14.5	14.2	15.2	(NA)
Underwriting gain/loss	-7.1	-8.4	-16.5	-18.2	-20.5
Net investment income	24.0	27.7	31.2	32.9	34.7
Operating earnings after taxes	11.0	12.9	9.1	8.8	8.5
Assets...............................	426.7	476.9	527.0	556.3	601.4
Policyholders' surplus	104.0	118.2	134.0	138.4	151.8

NA Not available.

Source: U.S. Department of Commerce, International Trade Administration, *U.S. Industrial Outlook, 1992*.

No. 822. U.S. Life Insurance Companies—Summary: 1980 to 1990

[As of **December 31** or **calendar year**, as applicable. Covers domestic and foreign business of U.S. companies. See also *Historical Statistics, Colonial Times to 1970*, series X 879 and X 890-917]

ITEM	Unit	1980	1982	1983	1984	1985	1986	1987	1988	1989	1990
U.S. companies	Number .	1,958	2,060	2,117	2,193	2,261	2,254	2,337	2,343	2,270	2,200
Sales	**Bil. dol. .**	**655**	**920**	**1,279**	**1,390**	**1,530**	[1]**1,578**	**1,656**	**1,716**	**1,788**	**2,024**
Ordinary.	Bil. dol . .	462	661	972	1,074	1,187	1,178	1,267	1,287	1,343	1,368
Group	Bil. dol . .	190	257	306	315	342	[1]400	388	428	444	655
Industrial	Bil. dol . .	4	2	2	1	1	(Z)	(Z)	(Z)	(Z)	(Z)
Income.	**Bil. dol. .**	**130.9**	**170.0**	**176.0**	**206.1**	**234.0**	**282.3**	**314.3**	**338.1**	**367.3**	**402.2**
Life insurance premiums	Bil. dol . .	40.8	50.8	50.3	51.3	60.1	66.2	76.7	73.5	73.3	76.7
Percent of total	Percent .	31.2	29.9	28.6	24.9	25.7	23.5	24.4	21.7	20.0	19.1
Annuity considerations	Bil. dol . .	22.4	34.6	30.5	42.8	53.9	83.7	88.7	103.3	115.0	129.1
Health insurance premiums . . .	Bil. dol . .	29.4	35.0	38.2	40.7	41.8	44.2	47.6	52.3	56.1	58.2
Investment and other	Bil. dol . .	38.3	49.6	57.0	71.3	78.2	88.2	101.3	109.0	122.9	138.2
Disbursements . . . .[2][3]	**Bil. dol. .**	**88.2**	**113.3**	**123.5**	**138.5**	**151.8**	**186.5**	**202.3**	**221.4**	**246.8**	**277.1**
Payments to policyholders[2][3]	Bil. dol . .	59.0	71.2	80.9	89.8	95.7	131.4	144.4	156.8	178.3	200.9
Percent of total	Percent .	66.9	62.8	65.5	64.8	63.0	70.5	71.4	70.8	72.2	72.5
Death payments	Bil. dol . .	12.9	14.5	16.8	17.6	18.5	19.6	20.7	22.4	23.5	25.5
Matured endowments	Bil. dol . .	0.8	0.6	0.6	0.7	0.8	0.8	0.8	0.8	0.8	0.8
Annuity payments	Bil. dol . .	7.4	10.3	12.7	18.0	19.7	17.8	20.3	21.9	26.0	28.6
Policy dividends	Bil. dol . .	8.1	9.6	10.8	11.4	12.4	12.4	13.0	13.8	14.9	15.7
Surrender values[3]	Bil. dol . .	6.4	9.8	12.5	14.5	15.9	49.6	53.7	58.1	73.4	90.2
Disability benefits	Bil. dol . .	0.5	0.5	0.5	0.4	0.5	0.5	0.5	0.4	0.5	0.5
Commissions, expenses, etc.[3]	Bil. dol . .	27.8	40.3	40.7	46.0	53.1	51.4	54.7	61.3	63.5	70.2
Dividends to stockholders	Bil. dol . .	1.4	1.8	1.9	2.7	3.0	3.7	3.3	3.4	5.0	6.0
BALANCE SHEET											
Assets	**Bil. dol. .**	**479**	**588**	**655**	**723**	**826**	**938**	**1,045**	**1,167**	**1,300**	**1,408**
Government securities	Bil. dol . .	33	56	77	100	125	145	151	160	178	211
Corporate securities	Bil. dol . .	227	269	297	323	374	433	502	585	664	711
Percent of total assets . . .	Percent .	47.4	45.7	45.3	44.6	45.3	46.2	48.1	50.1	51.1	50.5
Bonds.	Bil. dol . .	180	213	232	259	297	342	406	480	538	583
Stocks	Bil. dol . .	47	56	65	63	78	91	97	104	126	128
Mortgages	Bil. dol . .	131	142	151	157	172	194	214	233	254	270
Real estate.	Bil. dol . .	15	21	22	26	29	32	34	37	40	43
Policy loans	Bil. dol . .	41	53	54	55	54	54	54	54	57	63
Other.	Bil. dol . .	32	49	54	64	72	81	90	98	106	110
Interest earned on assets[4]	Percent .	8.02	8.91	8.96	9.45	9.63	9.35	9.10	9.03	9.10	8.89
Liabilities[2][5]	Bil. dol . .	445	547	609	673	769	873	977	1,092	1,216	1,317
Policy reserves[2] **. . . . .**	**Bil. dol. .**	**390**	**479**	**532**	**584**	**665**	**762**	**862**	**969**	**1,084**	**1,197**
Annuities.	Bil. dol . .	182	252	297	342	411	489	562	642	730	815
Group	Bil. dol . .	140	192	222	255	303	356	393	434	474	516
Individual[6]	Bil. dol . .	41	61	75	87	108	133	169	208	256	299
Life insurance	Bil. dol . .	198	214	221	226	236	252	276	300	324	349
Health insurance	Bil. dol . .	11	13	15	17	19	21	24	27	30	33
Capital and surplus[2]	Bil. dol . .	34	42	46	50	57	64	67	75	84	91

Z Less than $500 million.   [1] Includes Servicemen's Group Life Insurance, $51 billion, and Federal Employees' Group Life Insurance, $11 billion.   [2] Includes operations of accident and health departments of life insurance companies.   [3] Beginning in 1986, data not comparable to prior years due to change in accounting method.   [4] Net rate.   [5] Includes other obligations not shown separately.   [6] Includes reserves for supplementary contracts with and without life contingencies.

No. 823. Life Insurance Purchases in the United States— Number and Amount: 1980 to 1990

[Excludes revivals, increases, dividend additions, and reinsurance acquired. Includes long-term credit insurance (life insurance on loans of more than 10 years' duration). See also headnote, table 824]

YEAR	NUMBER OF POLICIES PURCHASED (1,000)						AMOUNT PURCHASED (bil. dol.)					
	Total	Ordinary			Group	Indus-trial	Total	Ordinary			Group	Indus-trial
		Total	Percent—					Total	Percent—			
			Whole life[1]	Term[2]					Whole life[1]	Term[2]		
1980	29,007	14,750	78	22	11,379	2,878	573	386	43	57	183	4
1983	32,021	17,737	77	23	13,450	834	1,026	753	47	53	272	1
1984	33,012	17,695	77	23	14,605	712	1,115	820	55	45	294	1
1985	33,880	17,104	78	22	16,243	533	1,231	911	62	38	320	1
1986	34,623	16,811	77	23	17,507	305	[3]1,309	934	61	39	[3]375	(Z)
1987	33,153	16,225	75	25	16,698	230	1,353	987	57	43	366	(Z)
1988	31,589	15,579	81	19	15,793	217	1,407	996	61	39	411	(Z)
1989	29,960	14,694	80	20	15,110	156	1,442	1,021	59	41	421	(Z)
1990	28,791	14,066	79	21	14,592	133	1,529	1,070	58	42	459	(Z)

Z Less than $500 million.   [1] Life insurance payable to a beneficiary at the death of the insured whenever that occurs. Premiums may be payable for a specified number of years or for life. Includes a small number of endowment and retirement income policies.   [2] Life insurance payable to a beneficiary only when an insured dies within a specified period.   [3] Includes Servicemen's Group Life Insurance, $51 billion, and Federal Employees' Group Life Insurance, $11 billion.

Source of tables 822 and 823: American Council of Life Insurance, Washington, DC, *Life Insurance Fact Book*, biennial.

No. 824. Life Insurance in Force in the United States—Summary: 1980 to 1990

[As of **December 31** or **calendar year**, as applicable. Covers life insurance with life insurance companies only. Represents all life insurance in force on lives of U.S. residents whether issued by U.S. or foreign companies. For definition of household, see text, section 1. See also *Historical Statistics, Colonial Times to 1970*, series X 879-889]

YEAR	Number of policies, total (mil.)	LIFE INSURANCE IN FORCE					AVERAGE SIZE POLICY IN FORCE (dollars)				AVERAGE AMOUNT ($1,000)		Disposable personal income per household ($1,000)
		Value (bil. dol.)					Ordinary	Group	Industrial	Credit [1]	Per household	Per insured household	
		Total	Ordinary	Group	Industrial	Credit [1]							
1980	402	3,541	1,761	1,579	36	165	11,920	13,410	620	2,110	41.9	51.1	23.7
1981	400	4,064	1,978	1,889	35	162	13,310	15,400	630	2,220	46.2	56.3	25.8
1982	389	4,477	2,217	2,066	33	161	15,140	16,630	630	2,410	51.1	63.1	27.1
1983	387	4,966	2,544	2,220	31	171	17,380	17,530	630	2,650	56.3	69.5	28.9
1984	385	5,500	2,888	2,392	30	190	19,970	18,780	630	2,880	61.4	75.7	31.3
1985	386	6,053	3,247	2,562	28	216	22,780	19,720	640	3,100	66.6	82.2	32.7
1986	391	6,720	3,658	2,801	27	234	25,540	20,720	650	3,310	72.2	89.1	34.1
1987	395	7,452	4,139	3,043	27	243	28,510	22,380	650	3,330	78.7	97.2	35.5
1988	391	8,020	4,512	3,232	26	251	31,390	23,410	660	3,570	84.5	104.3	38.0
1989	394	8,694	4,940	3,469	24	260	34,410	24,510	670	3,600	89.9	111.0	40.1
1990	389	9,393	5,367	3,754	24	248	37,910	26,630	670	3,500	98.4	121.4	42.9

[1] Insures borrower to cover consumer loan in case of death.

Source: American Council of Life Insurance, Washington, DC, *Life Insurance Fact Book*, biennial.

No. 825. Life Insurance—Insurance in Force and Benefit Payments, by State: 1990

[Applies to policyholders and payments in the United States]

REGION, DIVISION, AND STATE	INSURANCE IN FORCE		Avg. per household (dol.)	Benefit payments [1] (mil. dol.)	REGION, DIVISION, AND STATE	INSURANCE IN FORCE		Avg. per household (dol.)	Benefit payments [1] (mil. dol.)
	Policies (1,000)	Value (bil. dol.)				Policies (1,000)	Value (bil. dol.)		
U.S.	389,186	9,393	98,400	88,385	DC.	2,166	68	244,400	467
					VA.	14,175	263	109,600	1,804
Northeast	78,939	2,175	111,000	24,954	WV	2,851	45	66,400	493
N.E.	20,788	589	113,900	6,258	NC	12,737	242	92,300	1,893
ME	1,785	38	77,900	338	SC	7,982	120	92,500	812
NH	1,669	42	99,500	367	GA	12,609	273	109,600	2,023
VT	1,037	20	91,800	227	FL	17,571	412	77,000	4,282
MA	8,398	248	107,200	2,971	E.S.C	32,016	507	87,400	3,834
RI	1,821	39	98,500	404	KY	6,163	108	76,000	880
CT	6,078	202	153,200	1,951	TN	9,767	175	92,000	1,451
M.A	58,151	1,586	109,900	18,696	AL	11,702	150	97,100	1,010
NY	24,464	735	107,500	9,341	MS	4,384	74	79,300	493
NJ	11,661	382	130,400	4,018	W.S.C	40,488	930	94,100	7,298
PA	22,026	469	100,800	5,337	AR	2,905	61	65,000	466
Midwest	97,170	2,294	99,000	23,233	LA	8,074	145	93,700	1,109
E.N.C	69,115	1,606	99,100	16,901	OK	3,908	96	78,500	1,006
OH	18,048	409	95,900	4,174	TX	25,601	628	101,600	4,717
IN	9,318	207	95,300	1,891	West	60,322	1,822	92,000	15,276
IL	19,479	481	110,600	5,261	Mt	18,578	462	88,100	4,163
MI	14,547	344	97,100	3,855	MT	1,189	24	77,500	221
WI	7,723	165	88,000	1,720	ID	1,373	33	86,800	291
W.N.C	28,055	688	98,500	6,332	WY	666	17	97,000	132
MN	6,476	173	99,600	1,588	CO	5,161	138	103,600	1,217
IA	4,676	105	96,100	1,190	NM	1,852	45	79,300	427
MO	8,779	201	98,600	1,765	AZ	4,589	113	79,100	1,169
ND	896	25	98,500	210	UT	2,436	57	100,600	406
SD	952	25	91,200	202	NV	1,312	35	72,200	300
NE	2,431	63	101,900	574	Pac	41,744	1,360	93,500	11,113
KS	3,845	96	99,200	803	WA	5,546	164	83,500	1,367
South	152,755	3,102	94,200	24,922	OR	3,295	87	74,700	905
S.A	80,251	1,665	96,600	13,790	CA	30,380	1,041	95,900	8,296
DE	1,885	41	157,000	288	AK	534	19	96,000	155
MD	8,275	201	110,600	1,728	HI	1,989	49	133,100	390

[1] Comprises death payments, matured endowments, disability and annuity payments, surrender values, and policy dividends.

Source: American Council of Life Insurance, Washington, DC, *Life Insurance Fact Book*, biennial.

Figure 17.1
Bankruptcy Petitions Filed, by State: 1991
(Thousands)

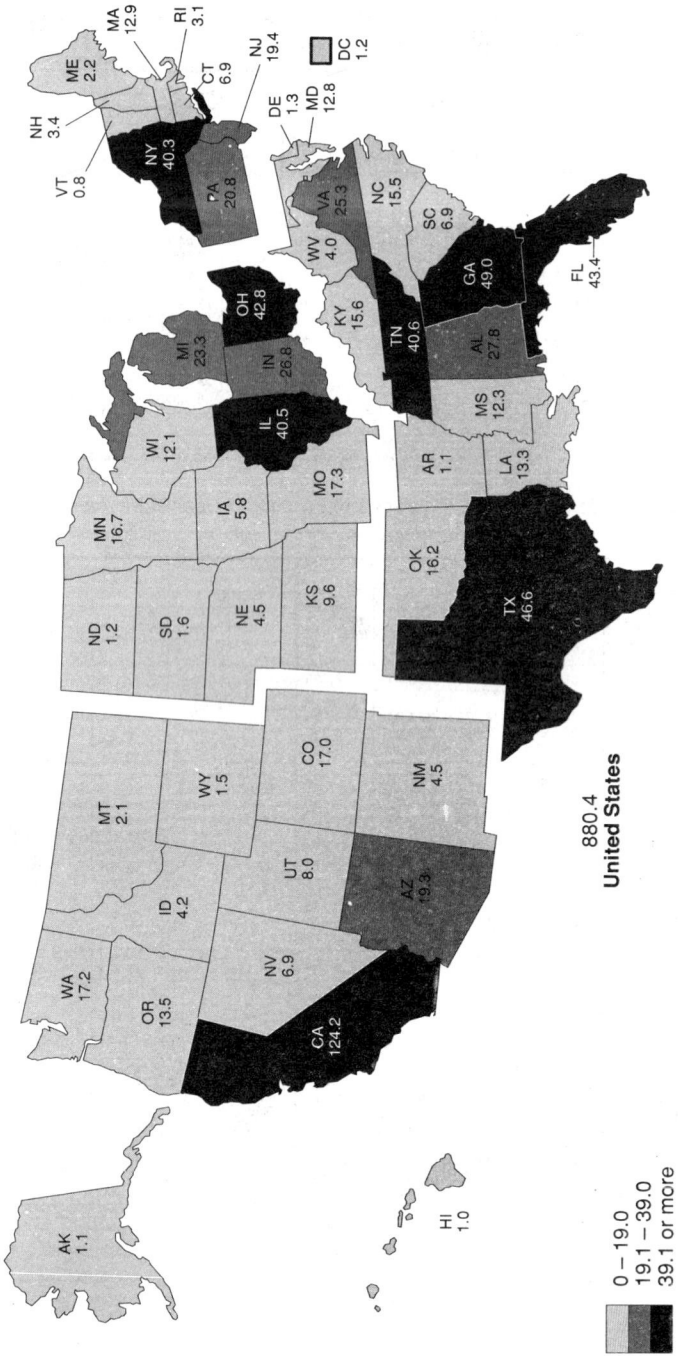

☐	0 – 19.0
▨	19.1 – 39.0
■	39.1 or more

Source: Chart prepared by U.S. Bureau of the Census. For data, see table 848.

Business Enterprise

This section relates to the place and behavior of the business firm and to business initiative in the American economy. It includes data on the number, type, and size of businesses; financial data of domestic and multinational U.S. corporations and their foreign affiliates; business investment, expenditures, and profits; sales and inventories; and business failures. Additional business data may be found in other sections, particularly 27 and 28.

The principal sources of these data are the *Survey of Current Business,* published by the Bureau of Economic Analysis (BEA); the *Federal Reserve Bulletin,* issued by the Board of Governors of the Federal Reserve System; the annual *Statistics of Income* reports of the Internal Revenue Service (IRS); *The Business Failure Record* issued by The Dun & Bradstreet Corporation, New York; and *Fortune* and *The Fortune Directory,* issued by Time, Inc., New York.

Business firms.—A firm is generally defined as a business organization under a single management and may include one or more establishments (i.e., a single physical location at which business is conducted). The terms firm, business, company, and enterprise are used interchangeably throughout this section. Examples of series where the industrial distribution is based on data collected from establishments are those on capital stock (table 863), those on gross national product by industry (table 674), and those on employment and earnings (section 13). Examples of company-based series are those on business expenditures for new plant and equipment (table 862), those from IRS *Statistics of Income* (tables 835 and 836), and those on corporation profits by industry (tables 872 and 873). A firm doing business in more than one industry is classified by industry according to the major activity of the firm as a whole. The industrial classification is based on the *Standard Industrial Classification (SIC) Manual* (see text, section 13). The IRS concept of a business firm relates primarily to the legal entity used for tax reporting purposes. The IRS *Statistics of Income* reports present data, based on a sample of tax returns before audit, separately for

In Brief

Patents issued in 1990: 46,200
*Percent issued to foreign country
residents:* 47%

Bankruptcies filed in 1991: 880,399
Business: 8%
Nonbusiness: 92%

sole proprietorships, partnerships, and corporations. Data presented are for active enterprises only. A *sole proprietorship* is an unincorporated business owned by one person including large enterprises with many employees and hired managers to the part-time operations in which the owner is the only person involved. A *partnership* is an unincorporated business owned by two or more persons, each of whom has a financial interest in the business. The "persons" could be individuals, estates, trusts, other partnerships or corporations. A *corporation* is a business that is legally incorporated under State laws. The IRS recognizes many types of businesses as corporations, including joint-stock companies, insurance companies, and unincorporated associations such as business trusts, etc. While many corporations file consolidated tax returns, most corporate tax returns represent individual corporations, some of which are affiliated through common ownership or control with other corporations filing separate returns.

Assets and liabilities.—In its annual report, *Statistics of Income, Corporation Income Tax Returns,* the IRS presents balance sheet and income estimates for all active U.S. corporations. The Bureau of the Census issues the *Quarterly Financial Report for Manufacturing, Mining, and Trade Corporations* (QFR), which presents quarterly income account and balance sheet data for manufacturing, mining, and trade industries. This report was prepared by the Federal Trade Commission until responsibilities for QFR were transferred to Census beginning with the fourth quarter 1982 report.

One of the most comprehensive measures of the investment position of the business sector (and the only measure adjusted to current replacement cost) is the BEA capital stock series. See *Survey of Current Business,* January 1992.

Income, profits, dividends, and taxes.— Several agencies, among them IRS and BEA, compile corporate income account data. These data, however, are not comparable because of differing definitions and methods of compilation. A reconciliation of the two can be found in table 8.22 of *Survey of Current Business,* published by BEA. The IRS publishes financial data for all business enterprises. These data appear in *Statistics of Income, Corporation Income Tax Returns* and the *Statistics of Income Bulletin* (partnerships and sole proprietorships). Data on international income and taxes reported by U.S. corporations are also included in the *Statistics of Income Bulletin* and in the periodic *Compendium of Studies of International Income and Taxes.*

Corporate data issued by BEA are a part of its national income and product accounts (see text, section 14). The primary sources for BEA estimates of profits, taxes, dividends, and undistributed profits are the original corporate tax returns submitted to IRS. Various adjustments of IRS data are required by the national income treatment—particularly with respect to profits which would be disclosed if all tax returns were audited: depletion, capital gain or loss, treatment of bad debts, measurement of income received from abroad, and intercorporate dividends—to make the figures comparable with other entries in the national income accounts. For a discussion of two types of adjustments (inventory valuation and capital consumption), see text, section 14. The BEA's corporate profits data also include net earnings of Federal Reserve banks, credit unions, private noninsured pension funds, and several quasi-government credit agencies not included in IRS data.

Sources and uses of corporate funds.— These data (table 832, Federal Reserve Board) show capital requirements of corporations and the manner in which they are financed. Sources of funds should be equal to their uses. Certain discrepancies, however, interfere with this equality due to omission of (1) money accruing to corporations from an excess of sales over purchases of used plant and equipment, (2) transactions in securities held as perma-

nent investments except public offerings, and (3) net purchases of land. Also, the balance sheet data upon which many of the financial flow estimates are based are not fully comparable with the tax-return based estimates of internal sources or the establishment series underlying the figures on inventory change.

Sales, assets, net income, stockholder's equity, and total returns to investors.—Sales include service and rental revenues but exclude dividends, interest, and other non-operating revenues. All companies must have derived more than 50 percent of their sales from manufacturing and/or mining. Sales of subsidiaries are included when they are consolidated. **Assets** are those shown at the company's year-end. **Net income** is shown after taxes and after extraordinary credits or charges when any are shown on the income statement. **Stockholder's equity** is the sum of capital stock, surplus, and retained earnings at the company's year-end. Redeemable preferred stock is excluded when its redemption is either mandatory or outside the control of the company, except in the case of cooperatives. **Total returns to investors** include both price appreciation and dividend yield. Returns are adjusted for stock splits, stock dividends, recapitalizations, and corporate reorganizations as they occur. For further discussion, see Time, Inc., New York, NY, *The Fortune Directories.*

Economic censuses.—The economic censuses constitute comprehensive and periodic canvasses of the Nation's industrial and business activities. The first economic census of the United States was conducted as part of the 1810 decennial census, when inquiries on manufacturing were included with the census of population. Minerals data were collected in 1840. The first censuses of construction and business were taken for 1929. An integrated economic census program was begun for 1954. In that year, the censuses covered the retail and wholesale trades, selected service industries, manufactures, and mineral industries. The economic censuses are taken at 5-year intervals covering years ending in "2" and "7." Special surveys are conducted every 5 years as part of the economic censuses to determine the extent of business ownership by specific minority groups and women.

No. 826. Number of Returns and Business Receipts, by Size of Receipts and Type of Business: 1970 to 1988

[Covers active enterprises only. Figures are estimates based on sample of unaudited tax returns; see Appendix III. The industrial distribution is based on data collected from companies; see text, section 17. See also *Historical Statistics, Colonial Times to 1970,* series V 1-12]

SIZE-CLASS OF RECEIPTS	RETURNS (1,000)					BUSINESS RECEIPTS [1] (bil. dol.)				
	1970	1980	1985	1987	1988	1970	1980	1985	1987	1988
Corporate returns	**1,665**	**2,711**	**3,277**	**3,612**	**3,563**	**1,706**	**6,172**	**8,050**	**9,185**	**9,804**
Under $25,000 [2]	452	557	711	788	818	3	4	5	5	5
$25,000-$49,999	171	208	237	267	228	6	8	9	10	8
$50,000-$99,999	220	323	330	369	350	16	22	24	27	26
$100,000-$499,999.	517	926	1,110	1,191	1,134	123	224	278	300	288
$500,000-$999,999.	141	280	352	391	409	99	197	249	276	288
$1,000,000 or more	165	418	538	605	623	1,459	5,717	7,484	8,568	9,189
Partnership returns	**936**	**1,380**	**1,714**	**1,648**	**1,654**	**92**	**286**	**349**	**411**	**464**
Under $25,000 [2]	502	638	1,036	1,052	1,045	4	5	4	2	2
$25,000-$49,999	125	182	154	123	120	5	7	6	3	3
$50,000-$99,999	120	184	152	142	151	9	13	11	7	7
$100,000-$499,999.	162	290	281	240	234	33	64	61	46	44
$500,000-$999,999.	17	48	48	45	50	12	33	34	28	30
$1,000,000 or more	10	37	42	44	54	30	164	234	326	378
Non-farm proprietorship returns [3].	**6,494**	**9,730**	**11,929**	**13,091**	**13,679**	**199**	**411**	**540**	**611**	**672**
Under $25,000 [2]	4,738	6,916	8,250	8,984	9,347	30	44	54	60	64
$25,000-$49,999	746	1,079	1,394	1,559	1,601	27	39	50	55	57
$50,000-$99,999	562	836	1,094	1,172	1,226	40	59	77	83	88
$100,000-$499,999.	420	796	1,060	1,232	1,337	76	159	213	251	277
$500,000-$999,999.	21	74	89	102	118	14	50	61	69	82
$1,000,000 or more	7	29	41	43	50	12	60	85	93	105

[1] Excludes investment income except for partnerships (through 1985) and corporations in finance, insurance, and real estate. In 1987, partnerships and S corporations exclude gross income from rental real estate and other rental activities and portfolio income distributed directly to partners or shareholders. S corporations have no more than 35 shareholders (10 prior to 1983) most of which are individuals, electing to be taxed at the shareholder level.   [2] Includes firms with no receipts.   [3] Number of businesses for 1970 and 1980. Number of non-farm sole proprietorship returns is not available prior to 1981. However, the number of returns and the number of businesses are very closely related. Since 1970, the ratio of number of returns to the number of businesses has remained approximately 1 to 1.1.

Source: U.S. Internal Revenue Service, *Statistics of Income, Statistics of Income Bulletin;* and unpublished data.

No. 827. Number of Returns, Receipts, and Net Income, by Type of Business, 1970 to 1988, and by Industry, 1988

[Covers active enterprises only. Figures are based on sample of unaudited tax returns; see Appendix III. See also *Historical Statistics, Colonial Times to 1970,* series V 1-12 and V 42-53. Minus sign (-) indicates net loss]

YEAR AND INDUSTRY	NUMBER OF RETURNS (1,000)			BUSINESS RECEIPTS [2] (bil. dol.)			NET INCOME (less loss) [3] (bil. dol.)		
	Non-farm proprietor-ships [1]	Partner-ships	Corpo-rations	Non-farm proprietor-ships [1]	Partner-ships	Corpo-rations	Non-farm proprietor-ships [1]	Partner-ships	Corpora-tions
1970.	5,770	936	1,665	198.6	91.8	1,706.1	30.5	9.8	65.9
1980.	8,932	1,380	2,711	411.2	286.0	6,172.2	54.9	8.2	239.0
1985.	11,929	1,714	3,277	540.0	349.2	8,049.6	78.8	-8.9	240.1
1986.	12,394	1,703	3,429	559.4	378.7	8,281.9	90.4	-17.4	269.6
1987.	13,091	1,648	3,612	610.8	411.4	9,185.5	105.5	-5.4	328.2
1988 [4].	**13,679**	**1,654**	**3,563**	**672.0**	**464.0**	**9,803.8**	**126.3**	**14.5**	**413.0**
Agriculture, forestry, and fishing [5] . . .	351	122	120	15.4	9.0	80.5	2.1	1.0	1.6
Mining.	140	48	41	7.0	16.0	87.3	(-Z)	0.9	4.1
Construction	1,696	75	381	96.8	31.0	485.7	16.5	3.2	11.3
Manufacturing	355	25	300	20.0	43.7	3,118.1	2.3	1.5	205.1
Transportation, public utilities	599	20	149	30.3	21.6	779.6	4.1	-2.3	46.9
Wholesale and retail trade [6]	2,414	179	985	230.0	83.6	2,891.3	13.2	3.4	42.8
Wholesale	335	11	315	39.0	25.7	1,396.3	4.3	0.8	22.9
Retail.	2,022	167	666	189.1	57.7	1,491.4	8.4	2.5	19.9
Finance, insurance, real estate	1,233	868	572	46.1	115.4	1,714.4	16.4	-19.3	91.9
Services.	6,457	296	995	212.0	141.9	643.7	68.3	25.6	9.3

Z Less than $50 million.   [1] Through 1980, includes both individually owned business and farm returns; thereafter, includes only nonfarm business returns.   [2] Excludes investment income except for partnerships (through 1986) and corporations in finance, insurance, and real estate. In 1987, partnerships and S corporations exclude gross income from rental real estate and other rental activities and portfolio income distributed directly to partners or shareholders. For definition of S corporation, see table 826, footnote 1.   [3] Net income (less loss) is defined differently by form of organization, basically as follows: (a) Proprietorships: Total taxable receipts less total deductions, including cost of sales and operations (except charitable contributions and owners' salary), investment and other income are excluded; (b) Partnerships: Total taxable receipts less total deductions, including cost of sales and operations (except investment and other income (except capital gains); (c) Corporations: Total taxable receipts less total deductions, including cost of sales and operations; investment and other income, such as capital gains and income from foreign corporations considered received for tax purposes only; net income is before income tax.   [4] Includes business not specifically allocated to industries below.   [5] Represents agricultural services only.   [6] Includes trade business not identified as wholesale or retail.

Source: U.S. Internal Revenue Service, *Statistics of Income,* various publications.

No. 828. Number of Returns, Business Receipts, and Net Income, by Industry, Type of Business, and Size of Business Receipts: 1988

[Number in thousands; receipts and net income in billions of dollars. Covers active enterprises only. Figures are estimates based on a sample of unaudited tax returns; see appendix III. The industrial distribution is based on data collected from establishments; see text, section 17. See also *Historical Statistics, Colonial Times to 1970*, series V 42-53, for number of active corporations. Minus sign (-) indicates net loss]

INDUSTRY	Non-farm proprietor-ships, total	Partner-ships, total	CORPORATIONS				
			Under $1 mil. [1]	$1 mil.-$4.9 mil.	$5 mil.-$9.9 mil.	$10 mil.-$49.9 mil.	$50 mil. or more
All industrial divisions: [2]							
Number	13,679	1,654	2,940	469	75	65	14
Business receipts [3]	672.0	464.0	614.7	997.7	520.2	1,290.4	6,380.7
Net income (less loss)	126.3	14.5	-4.7	14.4	11.1	39.3	352.9
Agriculture, forestry, fishing: [4]							
Number	351	122	108	10	1	1	(Z)
Business receipts [5]	15.4	9.0	17.2	19.9	8.9	15.7	18.8
Mining:							
Number	140	48	36	4	(Z)	(Z)	(Z)
Business receipts [3]	7.0	16.0	4.4	8.4	3.0	9.0	62.6
Construction:							
Number	1,696	75	303	63	9	6	1
Business receipts [3]	96.8	31.0	82.2	134.5	63.9	106.0	99.1
Manufacturing:							
Number	355	26	197	69	15	14	4
Business receipts [3]	20.0	43.7	53.0	157.2	102.7	288.3	2,516.8
Transportation, public utilities:							
Number	599	20	119	24	3	2	1
Business receipts [3]	30.3	21.6	25.0	51.2	22.2	43.5	637.7
Wholesale and retail trade:							
Number	2,414	180	726	191	33	30	5
Business receipts [3]	230.0	83.6	201.0	407.8	228.9	598.2	1,455.5
Finance, insurance, real estate:							
Number	1,233	869	524	33	6	7	3
Business receipts [3]	46.1	115.4	61.2	72.1	41.6	140.1	1,399.4
Services:							
Number	6,457	296	909	73	7	5	1
Business receipts [3]	212.0	141.9	169.6	145.4	49.0	89.1	190.6

Z Less than 500 returns.   [1] Includes businesses without receipts.   [2] Includes businesses not allocable to individual industries.   [3] Excludes investment income except for corporations (other than S corporations; see table 826, footnote 1) in finance, insurance and real estate. For partnerships, excludes gross income from rental real estate and other rental activities and portfolio income distributed directly to partners.   [4] Represents agricultural services only.

Source: U.S. Internal Revenue Service, *Statistics of Income*, various publications; and unpublished data.

No. 829. Nonfarm Sole Proprietorship Returns—Selected Income and Deduction Items: 1970 to 1989

[In millions of dollars, except as indicated. All figures are estimates based on sample. Tax law changes have affected the comparability of the data over time. See *Statistics of Income* reports for a description of appropriate years tax law changes; see Appendix III. See also *Historical Statistics, Colonial Times to 1970*, series V 4-6]

ITEM	1970	1980	1983	1984	1985	1986	1987	1988	1989
Number of returns, total (1,000) [1] . .	5,770	8,932	10,704	11,262	11,929	12,394	13,091	13,679	14,298
Businesses with net income (1,000).	(NA)	(NA)	7,390	8,003	8,641	9,248	9,884	10,492	11,017
Inventory, end of year	11,061	21,996	(NA)	23,233	24,970	24,477	26,333	27,313	30,060
Business receipts, total [2]	198,582	411,206	465,169	516,037	540,045	559,384	610,823	671,970	692,811
Income from sales and operations .	(NA)	407,169	455,382	507,234	528,675	548,273	598,315	658,687	678,616
Business deductions, total [2]	168,045	356,258	404,809	445,270	461,273	468,960	505,362	545,735	560,175
Cost of goods sold/operations	109,149	209,890	212,631	229,906	232,294	232,135	255,045	277,880	283,709
Purchases	88,586	168,302	(NA)	(NA)	(NA)	(NA)	173,400	197,220	204,681
Labor costs	7,704	10,922	9,871	13,009	14,504	17,318	19,631	21,143	22,540
Materials and supplies	6,216	12,909	(NA)	(NA)	(NA)	(NA)	23,842	27,800	29,870
Commissions	1,274	3,333	(NA)	(NA)	(NA)	(NA)	6,262	6,540	6,843
Salaries and wages (net).	15,107	26,561	31,666	34,686	38,266	38,691	42,330	43,007	45,469
Car and truck expenses	(NA)	13,378	14,758	17,524	17,044	16,381	17,470	19,640	20,789
Rent paid	4,637	9,636	11,831	14,278	15,259	15,654	16,358	19,470	17,976
Repairs	2,445	5,032	(NA)	(NA)	(NA)	(NA)	7,438	8,104	8,149
Taxes paid	3,776	7,672	(NA)	(NA)	(NA)	(NA)	8,449	9,495	9,948
Utilities.	(NA)	4,790	(NA)	(NA)	(NA)	(NA)	13,362	14,618	13,601
Insurance	2,310	6,003	(NA)	(NA)	(NA)	(NA)	10,783	11,719	12,879
Interest paid	1,784	7,190	9,926	11,025	11,914	11,504	11,616	12,071	13,280
Depreciation	5,452	13,953	22,070	23,900	26,291	26,418	25,557	26,078	24,479
Pension and profit sharing plans. . .	73	141	123	258	311	638	548	450	568
Net income (less loss)	30,537	54,947	60,359	70,767	78,773	90,423	105,461	126,323	132,738
Businesses with net income.	33,736	68,010	78,618	89,849	98,776	110,497	123,783	145,518	152,416

NA Not available.   [1] Through 1980, includes both individually owned business and farm returns; thereafter, includes only nonfarm business returns.   [2] Includes other amounts not shown separately.

Source: U.S. Internal Revenue Service, *Statistics of Income Bulletin*.

No. 830. Partnerships—Selected Items, by Industry: 1980 to 1989

[In millions of dollars, except partners and partnerships in thousands. Covers active partnerships only. Includes partnerships not allocable by nature of business. Figures are estimates based on samples. See Appendix III]

INDUSTRY AND YEAR	NUMBER OF PARTNERSHIPS			Number of part-ners	Total assets	Business re-ceipts [1][2]	Total deduc-tions [2]	Net income less loss [2]	Net income	Net loss
	Total	With net income	With net loss							
All industries:										
1980	1,380	774	605	8,420	597,504	285,967	283,749	8,249	45,062	36,813
1985	1,714	876	838	13,245	1,269,434	349,169	376,001	-8,884	77,045	85,928
1986	1,703	851	851	15,229	1,403,750	378,703	414,673	-17,371	80,215	97,586
1987	1,648	865	783	16,963	1,381,297	411,457	423,499	-5,419	87,654	93,073
1988	1,654	901	753	17,291	1,580,194	463,956	464,991	14,493	111,384	96,892
1989	1,635	898	737	18,432	1,791,027	464,952	475,434	14,099	113,886	99,787
Agriculture, forestry, and fishing:										
1980	126	72	54	381	24,595	21,611	22,859	472	2,539	2,067
1985	136	76	60	585	27,027	6,529	10,495	-1,049	2,797	3,846
1986	148	78	69	642	24,749	6,085	9,825	-938	2,746	3,684
1987	149	97	52	592	26,402	6,756	9,146	2,015	4,488	2,472
1988	122	80	42	555	24,106	8,988	11,602	1,079	3,827	2,748
1989	131	83	48	591	25,219	7,708	10,133	1,380	3,679	2,299
Mining:										
1980	35	15	20	722	24,742	13,201	18,248	-4,208	3,920	8,128
1985	62	33	30	2,207	66,930	19,922	21,920	1,482	7,884	6,402
1986	53	23	30	2,351	66,969	14,749	21,290	-3,458	5,214	8,672
1987	60	24	36	2,742	71,492	15,332	19,424	-1,360	5,698	7,058
1988	48	31	17	2,467	65,652	15,977	18,759	934	6,641	5,707
1989	46	26	20	3,771	62,073	19,701	20,751	1,965	7,027	5,062
Construction:										
1980	67	51	16	160	9,811	18,407	17,202	1,560	2,119	559
1985	57	41	16	134	15,008	21,476	20,080	2,207	2,743	536
1986	61	41	20	137	16,556	26,823	25,123	2,498	3,206	708
1987	62	48	14	153	17,077	26,295	24,293	2,766	3,350	584
1988	74	60	14	179	20,070	30,978	28,712	3,284	3,929	645
1989	62	46	16	165	21,150	30,052	28,397	2,647	3,313	666
Transportation and public utilities:										
1980	20	11	10	73	9,291	5,868	5,821	248	1,092	844
1985	25	15	10	186	26,468	11,253	14,814	-3,066	1,360	4,426
1986	21	7	14	223	33,567	12,599	16,276	-3,029	1,682	4,712
1987	30	13	17	429	42,015	19,795	24,228	-3,781	2,028	5,809
1988	20	12	8	433	45,003	21,639	25,389	-2,292	2,951	5,244
1989	22	10	12	435	54,171	26,727	30,319	-1,977	3,695	5,671
Manufacturing:										
1980	30	20	10	92	11,252	15,327	16,142	-472	1,199	1,671
1985	30	12	18	105	24,838	22,588	24,225	-1,085	1,228	2,314
1986	28	17	11	108	25,299	22,227	23,187	-458	1,512	1,970
1987	35	18	17	178	30,965	32,356	32,576	806	2,504	1,698
1988	26	12	14	173	41,714	43,724	43,345	1,540	3,598	2,058
1989	26	14	12	185	56,601	55,336	55,816	1,398	4,154	2,756
Wholesale and retail trade:										
1980	200	123	77	487	17,727	65,793	63,988	2,475	3,374	900
1985	201	113	88	493	20,568	69,079	68,119	1,977	3,467	1,490
1986	174	105	69	409	23,007	68,495	67,216	2,272	3,717	1,445
1987	185	100	85	476	26,105	70,560	69,277	2,697	4,215	1,518
1988	180	104	76	490	26,512	83,640	56,375	3,351	4,742	1,391
1989	173	98	75	496	27,294	90,306	89,418	2,529	4,550	2,021
Finance, insurance, and real estate:										
1980	637	313	325	5,566	454,531	87,133	91,382	-4,249	15,169	19,418
1985	844	369	475	7,755	979,787	92,309	118,237	-25,929	30,383	56,311
1986	853	350	503	9,459	1,068,220	112,594	145,574	-32,980	32,477	65,457
1987	828	365	463	10,327	1,040,671	123,239	139,480	-26,777	36,061	62,837
1988	869	398	471	10,880	1,200,673	115,415	127,356	-19,258	47,842	67,100
1989	853	419	434	11,327	1,394,319	71,243	91,965	-20,824	47,753	68,576
Services:										
1980	263	169	94	938	45,510	58,627	48,106	12,424	15,649	3,224
1985	341	207	134	1,713	106,597	104,197	96,202	16,541	26,942	10,400
1986	325	208	117	1,744	123,461	111,701	102,362	18,563	29,021	10,458
1987	291	194	97	2,042	125,134	116,379	104,296	18,092	29,118	11,025
1988	296	197	00	2,000	154,548	141,909	126,505	25,639	37,527	11,888
1989	299	189	110	2,370	148,688	162,325	147,280	26,652	39,296	12,643

[1] Business plus investment receipts for partnerships in finance, insurance, and real estate, and business receipts for all other industries through 1986. Beginning 1987, excludes gross income from rental real estate and other rental activities and portfolio income distributed directly to partners.   [2] Beginning 1985, the agriculture, forestry, and fishing industries are based on revised collection procedures. See source for detail.

Source: U.S. Internal Revenue Service, *Statistics of Income, Partnership Returns—1978-1982*, and *Statistics of Income Bulletin*.

No. 831. Partnership Returns—Selected Income Statement and Balance Sheet Items: 1980 to 1989

[In billions of dollars, except as indicated. Covers active partnerships only. All figures are estimates based on samples. See headnote, table 829. See also Appendix III and *Historical Statistics, Colonial Times to 1970*, series V 7-9]

ITEM	1980	1982	1983	1984	1985	1986	1987	1988	1989
Partnerships, number (1,000)	**1,380**	**1,514**	**1,542**	**1,644**	**1,714**	**1,703**	**1,648**	**1,654**	**1,635**
Number with net income (1,000). . . .	774	791	784	845	876	851	865	901	898
Number with balance sheets (1,000)	1,194	1,223	1,191	1,191	1,215	1,227	1,203	1,129	1,155	1,149
Number of partners (1,000)	**8,420**	**9,765**	**10,589**	**12,427**	**13,245**	**15,229**	**16,963**	**17,291**	**18,432**
Assets, total [1] [2]	**597.5**	**845.3**	**887.0**	**1,030.8**	**1,269.4**	**1,403.8**	**1,381.3**	**1,580.2**	**1,791.0**
Depreciable assets (net)	239.1	310.8	345.9	581.6	695.9	779.9	567.5	621.2	669.8
Inventories, end of year	33.2	100.7	77.1	61.8	27.3	47.4	45.1	51.2	59.4
Land	70.2	87.8	98.4	122.0	152.2	179.1	177.9	200.3	213.9
Liabilities, total [1]	**488.7**	**701.6**	**745.2**	**855.4**	**1,269.4**	**1,175.7**	**1,385.7**	**1,580.2**	**1,791.0**
Accounts, payable	33.9	37.3	34.7	32.8	46.9	43.6	41.3	48.9	51.7
Short-term debt [3]	48.0	73.3	67.3	68.6	102.8	92.5	81.7	86.6	86.9
Long-term debt [4]	178.0	236.2	268.3	322.3	382.0	429.2	429.9	473.6	512.1
Nonrecourse loans.	118.9	154.5	194.8	260.2	327.6	365.0	388.4	436.9	461.0
Partner's capital accounts	108.8	143.7	141.8	175.5	200.2	228.0	247.4	267.1	355.8
Total receipts [1] [5] [6]	**292.0**	**296.7**	**291.3**	**375.2**	**367.1**	**397.3**	**473.8**	**540.2**	**550.3**
Business receipts [5] [6]	271.1	251.6	243.2	318.3	302.7	327.4	411.5	464.0	465.0
Interest received [7]	10.9	15.3	15.0	16.7	20.6	21.7	17.9	19.0	20.9
Deductions, total [1] [6]	**283.7**	**304.0**	**293.9**	**378.7**	**376.0**	**414.7**	**423.5**	**465.0**	**475.4**
Cost of goods sold/operations. . . .	113.9	144.6	125.3	180.9	146.3	164.2	237.2	252.6	232.8
Salaries and wages	22.3	23.2	24.7	28.5	33.9	36.3	40.7	47.1	54.1
Taxes paid	9.6	5.3	5.9	6.7	7.7	7.9	6.9	8.0	8.9
Interest paid	28.4	21.5	22.4	25.4	28.7	29.5	20.0	23.2	32.7
Depreciation	21.6	32.4	37.3	19.8	22.6	23.4	19.3	19.8	19.6
Net income (less loss) [6]	**8.2**	**−7.3**	**−2.6**	**−3.5**	**−8.9**	**−17.4**	**−5.4**	**14.5**	**14.1**
Businesses with net income.	45.1	53.6	60.3	69.7	77.0	80.2	87.7	111.4	113.9

[1] Includes other amounts not shown separately.   [2] Total assets, total liabilities, and partner's capital accounts are somewhat understated because not all partnership returns filed contained a complete balance sheet.   [3] Represents mortgages, notes, and bonds payable in less than 1 year.   [4] Represents mortgages, notes, and bonds payable in 1 year or more.   [5] Beginning 1987, excludes gross income from rental real estate and other rental activities and portfolio income distributed directly to partners.   [6] Beginning 1987, receipts, deductions, and net income from trade or business only. Except for total receipts, excludes income and expenses related to certain investment activities. See source for detail.   [7] Beginning 1982, includes both interest and dividends.

Source: U.S. Internal Revenue Service, *Statistics of Income Bulletin*, various publications.

No. 832. Corporate Funds—Sources and Uses: 1970 to 1990

[In billions of dollars, except percent. Covers nonfarm nonfinancial corporate business. See text, section 17]

SOURCE AND USE	1970	1980	1984	1985	1986	1987	1988	1989	1990	1991
Sources, total.	**102.9**	**320.6**	**491.4**	**464.3**	**521.5**	**545.0**	**586.7**	**549.3**	**470.6**	**472.5**
Internal	63.9	199.7	336.4	351.9	336.8	376.1	404.4	404.9	381.5	391.5
Domestic undistributed profits . . .	8.6	52.9	35.0	10.7	−18.9	26.7	44.4	30.2	7.6	−11.3
IVA and CCA [1]	−1.1	−61.4	24.1	54.4	53.4	30.6	15.7	7.0	10.8	−0.7
Capital consumption allowances. .	49.4	173.3	246.2	256.1	269.3	279.3	295.2	313.9	324.5	337.8
Foreign earnings [2]	7.2	35.0	31.1	30.8	32.9	39.5	49.1	53.8	60.2	65.7
External [3]	38.9	120.8	155.0	112.3	184.7	168.9	182.3	144.4	89.1	81.0
Percent of total	37.8	37.7	31.5	24.2	35.4	31.0	31.1	26.3	18.9	17.2
Credit market funds	34.1	68.4	92.5	52.4	126.7	63.0	63.0	42.1	16.5	39.7
Securities and mortgages.	26.2	27.8	−13.0	−4.5	60.9	27.5	−13.0	−41.8	−13.5	97.7
Equity issues	5.7	10.4	−79.0	−84.5	−85.0	−75.5	−129.5	−124.2	−63.0	17.5
Bonds and mortgages [4]	20.5	17.4	65.9	80.0	145.9	103.0	116.5	82.3	49.5	80.2
Loans and short-term paper . . .	7.8	40.6	105.5	56.9	65.8	35.4	76.0	83.9	30.0	−58.0
Other.	4.9	52.5	62.5	59.9	58.0	106.0	119.3	102.3	72.6	41.4
Profit taxes payable.	−3.7	−0.8	4.4	−0.4	5.3	4.9	2.2	2.9	2.7	-
Trade debt	7.1	38.0	33.7	34.0	13.7	39.9	59.1	27.8	31.1	19.6
Foreign direct investments in U.S	1.5	15.3	24.4	26.3	39.0	61.2	57.9	71.6	38.8	21.8
Uses, total	**100.6**	**353.7**	**506.2**	**458.1**	**505.1**	**477.5**	**558.3**	**525.2**	**489.7**	**452.9**
Capital expenditures	81.9	254.2	399.1	375.3	353.9	365.8	394.5	421.4	403.2	365.6
Increase in financial assets.	18.7	99.4	107.2	82.8	151.2	111.7	163.8	103.9	86.5	87.3
Discrepancy (sources less uses) . . .	*2.2*	*−33.1*	*−14.8*	*6.2*	*16.4*	*67.5*	*28.4*	*24.1*	*−19.1*	*19.6*

- Represents or rounds to zero.   [1] Inventory valuation and capital consumption adjustment.   [2] Foreign branch profits, dividends, and subsidiaries' earnings retained abroad.   [3] Net increases in liability.   [4] Includes industrial pollution control revenue bonds, issued by State and local governments.

Source: Board of Governors of the Federal Reserve System. Data derived from *Flow of Funds Accounts*, annual.

No. 833. Nonfinancial Corporate Business-Sector Balance Sheet: 1970 to 1990

[In billions of dollars. Represents year-end outstandings]

ITEM	1970	1980	1981	1982	1983	1984	1985	1986	1987	1988	1989	1990
Total assets	1,304	3,999	4,473	4,644	4,862	5,198	5,437	5,759	6,126	6,500	6,858	7,111
Tangible assets (current cost)	934	2,983	3,357	3,502	3,606	3,844	3,993	4,151	4,380	4,635	4,874	5,030
Reproducible	823	2,666	2,988	3,102	3,181	3,380	3,499	3,625	3,828	4,058	4,271	4,413
Land	112	317	369	400	424	463	494	526	553	577	603	617
Financial assets	370	1,015	1,116	1,142	1,257	1,355	1,444	1,609	1,746	1,866	1,985	2,081
Liquid assets [1]	69	197	220	267	302	326	355	416	441	436	451	474
Checkable deposits and currency	44	57	47	53	62	75	94	113	120	135	128	128
Time deposits	5	38	48	59	71	74	80	88	92	92	99	105
Consumer credit	15	25	25	25	29	31	32	32	35	36	35	37
Mutual fund shares	1	2	2	3	5	7	11	16	13	11	14	14
Trade credit	191	482	507	492	544	592	634	664	725	787	814	839
Miscellaneous assets	94	310	361	354	377	398	412	481	532	596	671	717
Total liabilities	537	1,290	1,436	1,490	1,624	1,863	2,052	2,313	2,542	2,817	3,080	3,194
Credit market instruments	352	829	927	970	1,049	1,224	1,362	1,571	1,725	1,900	2,065	2,142
Profit taxes payable	11	30	24	14	19	22	18	22	26	26	24	26
Trade debt	160	348	376	381	418	452	486	500	520	563	591	622
Foreign direct investment in U.S	13	83	109	125	137	165	185	220	272	329	401	404
Net worth	767	2,709	3,037	3,154	3,239	3,336	3,386	3,447	3,584	3,684	3,778	3,917

[1] Includes other assets not shown separately.
Source: Board of Governors of the Federal Reserve System, *Balance Sheets for the U.S. Economy*.

No. 834. Corporation Income Tax Returns—Selected Financial Items: 1980 to 1988

[In billions of dollars, except number of returns. Covers active corporations only. All corporations are required to file returns except those specifically exempt. See source for changes in law affecting comparability of historical data. Based on samples; see Appendix III. See also *Historical Statistics, Colonial Times to 1970*, series Y 381-392]

ITEM	1980	1981	1982	1983	1984	1985	1986	1987	1988
Number of returns, total (1,000)	2,711	2,812	2,926	2,999	3,171	3,277	3,429	3,612	3,563
Number with net income (1,000)	1,597	1,597	1,608	1,676	1,778	1,820	1,908	1,995	1,909
S Corporation returns [1] (1,000)	545	541	564	648	701	725	826	1,128	1,257
BALANCE SHEET									
Assets, total [2]	7,617	8,547	9,358	10,201	11,107	12,773	14,163	15,311	16,568
Cash	529	533	541	590	596	683	763	754	785
Notes and accounts receivable	1,985	2,240	2,420	2,677	2,897	3,318	3,594	3,763	4,099
Inventories	535	588	581	599	664	715	733	829	846
Investments in Government obligations	472	515	606	685	726	917	1,059	1,092	1,095
Mortgage and real estate	894	934	942	982	1,127	1,259	1,377	1,455	1,605
Other investments	1,214	1,388	1,605	1,798	1,973	2,414	2,848	3,227	3,614
Depreciable assets	2,107	2,353	2,583	2,730	2,913	3,174	3,383	3,603	3,821
Depletable assets	72	84	95	108	115	112	116	123	124
Land	93	102	110	119	128	141	150	159	177
Liabilities [2]	7,617	8,547	9,358	10,201	11,107	12,773	14,163	15,311	16,568
Accounts payable	542	620	679	671	741	892	909	998	1,023
Mortgages, notes, and bonds, short-term [3]	505	586	667	760	867	1,001	1,084	1,247	1,431
Mortgages, notes, and bonds, long-term [4]	987	1,058	1,224	1,323	1,494	1,699	1,958	2,141	2,352
Capital stock	417	533	658	787	839	920	1,191	1,292	1,429
Paid-in or capital surplus	532	671	782	874	1,066	1,421	1,726	1,988	2,154
Retained earnings [5]	1,070	1,170	1,228	1,274	1,308	1,366	1,394	1,417	1,493
Net worth	1,944	2,244	2,470	2,645	2,884	3,304	3,698	3,947	4,207
INCOME STATEMENT									
Receipts, total [2][6]	6,361	7,026	7,024	7,135	7,861	8,398	8,669	9,582	10,265
Business receipts [6][7]	5,732	6,245	6,157	6,335	6,948	7,370	7,535	8,415	8,950
Interest [8]	367	494	530	511	580	635	662	706	805
Rents and royalties	54	68	83	83	90	105	110	113	116
Deductions, total [2][6]	6,125	6,814	6,869	6,945	7,629	8,158	8,395	9,244	9,853
Cost of sales and operations [7]	4,205	4,509	4,271	4,308	4,693	4,894	4,923	5,596	5,945
Compensation of officers	109	120	129	141	157	171	185	200	203
Rent paid on business property	72	82	95	105	119	135	145	154	161
Taxes paid	163	170	166	173	192	201	203	211	222
Interest paid	345	477	515	475	536	569	573	590	672
Depreciation	157	186	213	241	265	304	313	317	328
Advertising	52	60	65	72	82	92	99	107	114
Net income (less loss), total [6]	239	214	154	188	233	240	270	328	413
Net income	297	301	274	297	349	364	409	465	556
Deficit	58	87	120	109	116	124	139	137	143
TAX ITEMS									
Income subject to tax	247	240	205	219	257	266	276	312	383
Income tax before credits [9]	104	101	85	90	106	109	109	115	127
Tax credits, total [2]	42	44	40	40	44	48	37	31	35
Foreign tax credit	25	22	19	20	21	24	21	21	27
Income tax after credits [9]	62	57	45	51	62	61	72	84	92

[1] Represents corporations with no more than 35 shareholders (10 prior to 1983), most of which are individuals, electing to be taxed at the shareholder level. [2] Includes items not shown separately. [3] Payable in less than one year. [4] Payable in one year or more. [5] Appropriated and unappropriated. [6] Beginning 1987, receipts, deductions and net income of S corporations (footnote 1) limited to those from trade or business. Except for total receipts, excludes income and expenses related to certain investment activities. [7] Beginning 1987, includes sales and cost of sales of securities, commodities and real estate by exchanges, brokers or dealers selling on their own account. [8] Includes tax-exempt interest on Government obligations issued by U.S., State, and local governments. [9] Consists of regular (and alternative tax); excludes minimum tax and adjustments for certain prior year credits.
Source: U.S. Internal Revenue Service, *Statistics of Income, Corporation Income Tax Returns*, annual.

No. 835. Corporation Income Tax Returns—Financial Summary, by Industry: 1980 to 1988

[In **billions of dollars, except as indicated.** Covers active corporations only. Industrial distribution based on data collected from companies; see text, section 17. Excludes corporations not allocable by nature of business]

ITEM	1980	1982	1983	1984	1985	1986	1987	1988
Agriculture, forestry, and fishing:								
Returns (1,000)	81	91	92	98	103	107	117	120
Assets	40.7	50.4	50.3	50.7	52.7	53.5	55.4	60.5
Liabilities [1]	29.3	36.3	36.7	36.4	37.2	36.4	37.2	40.2
Receipts [2]	52.1	65.4	59.2	66.6	70.5	77.5	77.1	86.3
Deductions [2]	51.4	65.4	59.4	66.4	70.6	76.3	75.4	84.6
Net income (less loss) [2]	0.7	(-Z)	-0.2	0.2	-0.1	1.1	1.6	1.6
Mining:								
Returns (1,000)	26	37	37	41	41	40	42	41
Assets	126.9	192.4	194.4	209.0	240.8	206.1	220.1	225.6
Liabilities [1]	72.9	112.5	108.8	114.7	136.0	107.5	110.6	113.8
Receipts [2]	176.7	203.1	132.4	123.5	142.0	98.6	96.8	100.4
Deductions [2]	169.1	203.0	134.3	124.6	145.4	102.1	96.7	96.8
Net income (less loss) [2]	7.8	0.5	-1.6	-0.4	-2.5	-3.1	0.3	4.1
Construction:								
Returns (1,000)	272	282	284	307	318	342	371	381
Assets	132.9	153.1	161.4	195.3	215.3	218.9	222.1	241.4
Liabilities [1]	100.1	114.2	119.8	144.9	160.6	166.1	168.1	178.9
Receipts [2]	267.2	281.7	290.8	338.6	387.2	412.5	454.8	499.7
Deductions [2]	262.1	279.6	288.6	335.7	382.8	406.7	446.1	488.4
Net income (less loss) [2]	5.3	2.3	2.3	2.9	4.4	5.8	8.7	11.3
Manufacturing:								
Returns (1,000)	243	259	262	272	277	285	294	300
Assets	1,709.5	2,060.7	2,233.0	2,417.6	2,644.4	2,931.6	3,111.7	3,390.4
Liabilities [1]	960.3	1,163.8	1,279.9	1,392.6	1,544.7	1,807.2	1,920.0	2,137.2
Receipts [2]	2,404.3	2,488.3	2,552.8	2,768.2	2,831.1	2,810.7	3,141.4	3,349.0
Deductions [2]	2,290.6	2,423.3	2,469.3	2,661.2	2,733.1	2,723.7	3,012.1	3,170.0
Net income (less loss) [2]	125.7	75.8	95.3	121.2	113.8	101.8	145.5	205.1
Transportation and public utilities:								
Returns (1,000)	111	115	123	128	138	138	148	149
Assets	758.4	919.9	998.9	1,084.9	1,246.4	1,310.2	1,352.5	1,411.2
Liabilities [1]	467.7	567.0	604.6	660.9	755.9	807.7	842.4	891.8
Receipts [2]	523.8	632.3	657.4	725.6	772.4	762.2	786.2	838.8
Deductions [2]	504.0	614.4	638.2	697.2	747.8	740.7	749.0	792.5
Net income (less loss) [2]	20.0	18.3	19.5	28.9	25.1	21.0	37.5	46.9
Wholesale and retail trade:								
Returns (1,000)	800	840	852	897	917	939	972	985
Assets	646.9	753.4	804.2	899.0	1,010.0	1,073.5	1,177.7	1,295.8
Liabilities [1]	424.6	501.9	539.0	609.7	723.7	773.4	861.2	963.9
Receipts [2]	1,955.5	2,017.7	2,119.4	2,307.6	2,473.9	2,547.4	2,766.7	2,978.0
Deductions [2]	1,919.5	1,989.7	2,084.5	2,265.8	2,440.4	2,512.1	2,728.5	2,935.5
Net income (less loss) [2]	35.8	28.4	35.3	42.0	33.1	34.0	38.0	42.8
Finance, insurance, and real estate:								
Returns (1,000)	493	462	480	497	518	537	521	572
Assets	4,022.2	4,987.5	5,487.2	5,939.0	7,029.5	7,985.6	8,732.3	9,411.5
Liabilities [1]	3,491.7	4,220.5	4,670.4	5,037.3	5,867.5	6,483.4	7,097.4	7,632.1
Receipts [2]	697.5	949.9	902.8	1,033.1	1,182.0	1,365.1	1,589.2	1,714.4
Deductions [2]	652.6	915.2	856.7	985.7	1,104.6	1,245.5	1,476.7	1,596.0
Net income (less loss) [2]	33.1	21.8	31.7	32.7	60.7	99.8	87.4	91.9
Services:								
Returns (1,000)	671	820	848	899	939	1,012	1,120	995
Assets	178.2	237.9	269.8	307.9	331.0	381.6	435.6	530.3
Liabilities [1]	125.3	170.1	198.1	223.1	241.1	281.4	323.1	402.2
Receipts [2]	279.9	380.8	416.5	490.3	534.6	591.9	663.1	695.3
Deductions [2]	271.8	373.7	410.5	485.0	528.7	584.3	654.0	686.3
Net income (less loss) [2]	8.2	7.2	6.0	5.5	5.9	7.0	9.3	9.3
ANNUAL PERCENT CHANGE RECEIPTS [3]								
Agriculture, forestry, and fishing	-2.4	0.5	-9.4	12.6	5.9	9.9	-0.5	11.9
Mining.	33.3	1.5	-34.8	-6.7	15	-30.6	-1.8	3.7
Construction.	5.7	0.6	3.2	16.4	14.4	6.5	10.2	9.8
Manufacturing.	11.7	-4.8	2.6	8.4	2.3	-0.7	11.7	6.6
Transportation and public utilities	17.5	5.6	4.0	10.3	6.4	-1.3	3.1	6.6
Wholesale and retail trade	11.6	-1.1	5.0	8.9	7.2	3.0	8.6	7.6
Finance, insurance, and real estate	24.3	8.2	-5.0	14.4	14.4	15.5	16.4	7.8
Services	14.2	9.8	9.4	17.7	9.0	10.7	12.0	4.8

Z Less than half the measure. [1] Liabilities does not include net worth. [2] Beginning 1987, receipts, deductions, and net income of S corporations limited to those from trade or business; those from investments are generally excluded. For definition of S corporation, see table 834, footnote 1. [3] Change from preceding year.

Source: U.S. Internal Revenue Service, *Statistics of Income, Corporation Income Tax Returns,* annual.

No. 836. Corporation Income Tax Returns, by Asset Size-Class and Industry: 1988

[In millions of dollars, except returns. Covers active corporations only. Excludes corporations not allocable by nature of business. The industrial distribution is based on data collected from companies; see text, section 17. Detail may not add to total because of rounding. See table 834. See also *Historical Statistics, Colonial Times to 1970*, series V 167-183 and V 193-196]

INDUSTRY AND ITEM	Total	ASSET SIZE-CLASS					
		Under 10 mil. dol.[1]	10-24.9 mil. dol.	25-49.9 mil. dol.	50-99.9 mil. dol.	100-249.9 mil. dol.	250 mil. dol. and over
Agriculture, forestry, and fishing:							
Returns	119,902	119,457	275	94	44	25	7
Assets	60,492	43,143	4,251	3,207	2,984	3,916	2,990
Receipts	86,258	61,770	5,071	4,568	4,602	6,516	3,732
Deductions	84,637	60,667	5,027	4,490	4,526	6,363	3,565
Net income (less loss)	1,616	1,086	44	72	76	154	183
Mining:							
Returns	41,080	40,199	432	168	115	87	79
Assets	225,639	14,551	6,465	5,966	9,871	22,612	166,175
Receipts	100,427	19,232	4,580	4,073	6,154	14,494	51,894
Deductions	96,765	19,462	4,628	3,988	5,976	13,551	49,161
Net income (less loss)	4,112	-238	-53	81	180	944	3,198
Construction:							
Returns	381,499	379,275	1,579	375	166	64	40
Assets	241,395	134,333	23,015	12,832	12,271	9,442	49,502
Receipts	499,690	364,098	43,008	21,850	17,950	14,794	37,990
Deductions	488,357	356,888	41,689	21,232	17,473	14,613	36,463
Net income (less loss)	11,344	7,192	1,310	605	471	170	1,596
Manufacturing:							
Returns	299,538	288,882	5,648	2,057	1,083	868	1,001
Assets	3,390,434	194,615	87,983	72,596	76,611	139,738	2,818,890
Receipts	3,348,966	483,382	159,781	114,768	108,311	174,596	2,308,128
Deductions	3,169,975	473,621	154,637	110,426	103,054	166,170	2,162,067
Net income (less loss)	205,084	9,949	5,180	4,391	5,312	8,811	171,441
Transportation and public utilities:							
Returns	149,248	147,278	920	343	195	171	341
Assets	1,411,201	52,415	13,677	18,724	13,436	28,647	1,284,302
Receipts	838,753	129,322	17,487	18,029	12,464	22,262	639,190
Deductions	792,540	128,408	17,208	17,717	12,116	21,910	595,182
Net income (less loss)	46,944	907	275	295	358	425	44,683
Wholesale and retail trade:							
Returns	984,553	976,118	5,398	1,540	687	447	364
Assets	1,295,819	402,038	81,015	52,854	47,318	70,917	641,677
Receipts	2,977,983	1,406,785	233,016	141,783	117,288	161,378	917,733
Deductions	2,935,533	1,394,309	228,841	139,490	115,510	158,450	898,933
Net income (less loss)	42,845	12,425	4,178	2,300	1,780	2,983	19,180
Finance, insurance, and real estate:							
Returns	572,418	548,300	7,977	5,286	4,360	3,405	3,091
Assets	9,411,547	222,585	130,048	189,849	307,738	532,439	8,028,889
Receipts	1,714,352	200,608	35,925	37,340	54,376	98,156	1,287,947
Deductions	1,596,045	196,071	34,650	35,802	50,541	89,338	1,189,642
Net income (less loss)	91,893	4,195	984	953	2,646	6,882	76,233
Services:							
Returns	995,425	992,063	1,914	647	372	259	171
Assets	530,326	167,526	29,260	28,151	26,387	41,070	237,932
Receipts	695,265	441,757	34,509	26,292	27,605	36,632	128,469
Deductions	686,268	437,842	34,880	25,613	27,227	36,145	124,562
Net income (less loss)	9,277	3,884	-387	666	434	494	4,186
PERCENT DISTRIBUTION RECEIPTS							
Agriculture, forestry, and fishing	100.0	71.6	5.9	5.3	5.3	7.6	4.3
Mining	100.0	19.2	4.6	4.1	6.1	14.4	51.7
Construction	100.0	72.9	8.6	4.4	3.6	3.0	7.6
Manufacturing	100.0	14.4	4.8	3.4	3.2	5.2	68.9
Transportation and public utilities	100.0	15.4	2.1	2.1	1.5	2.7	76.2
Wholesale and retail trade	100.0	47.2	7.8	4.8	3.9	5.4	30.8
Finance, insurance, and real estate	100.0	11.7	2.1	2.2	3.2	5.7	75.1
Services	100.0	63.5	5.0	3.8	4.0	5.3	18.5

[1] Includes returns with zero assets.

Source: U.S. Internal Revenue Service, *Statistics of Income, Corporation Income Tax Returns*, annual.

No. 837. Employees and Payroll, by Employment-Size Class: 1975 to 1989

[Excludes government employees, railroad employees, self-employed persons, etc. See "General Explanation" in source for definitions and statement on reliability of data. An **establishment** is a single physical location where business is conducted or where services or industrial operations are performed]

EMPLOYMENT-SIZE CLASS	Unit	1975	1980	1983	1984	1985	1986	1987	1988	1989
Employees, total [1]	1,000	60,519	74,844	72,974	78,021	81,111	83,379	85,484	87,882	91,631
Under 20 employees	1,000	16,393	19,423	20,136	21,171	21,810	22,296	23,069	23,583	23,992
20 to 99 employees	1,000	16,272	21,168	20,806	22,449	23,539	24,311	25,221	25,930	26,829
100 to 499 employees	1,000	13,713	17,840	16,794	18,348	19,410	20,260	20,615	21,307	22,387
500 to 999 employees	1,000	4,872	5,689	5,186	5,614	5,716	5,780	5,922	6,078	6,442
1,000 or more employees	1,000	9,315	10,716	10,050	10,413	10,645	10,734	10,657	10,984	11,981
Annual payroll [1]	Bil. dol	596	1,035	1,269	1,339	1,514	1,608	1,724	1,860	1,990
Under 20 employees	Bil. dol.	138	231	298	326	352	375	414	440	461
20 to 99 employees	Bil. dol.	147	261	319	358	388	414	449	485	514
100 to 499 employees	Bil. dol.	135	249	297	334	362	391	417	452	488
500 to 999 employees	Bil. dol.	53	91	107	120	126	132	140	152	163
1,000 or more employees	Bil. dol.	123	208	248	269	286	298	305	331	364

[1] Prior to 1987, totals for employees and annual payroll have been revised. Detail may not add to totals because revisions for size class are not available.

Source: U.S. Bureau of the Census, *County Business Patterns,* annual.

No. 838. Establishments, Employees, and Payroll, by Industry: 1975 to 1989

[See headnote, table 837. For 1975-85, data are based on the *1972 Standard Industrial Classification (SIC) Manual.* 1989 data are based on the *1987 SIC Manual*]

INDUSTRY	ESTABLISHMENTS (1,000)				EMPLOYEES (1,000)				PAYROLL (bil. dol.)			
	1975	1980	1985	1989	1975	1980	1985	1989	1975	1980	1985	1989
All industries [1]	4,114	4,543	5,701	6,107	60,519	74,844	81,111	91,631	596	1,035	1,513	1,990
Agricultural services [2]	40	46	64	79	195	290	380	489	2	3	5	8
Mining	24	30	37	30	720	994	943	711	10	22	28	25
Contract construction	364	418	476	547	3,322	4,473	4,480	5,036	44	75	98	127
Manufacturing [3]	306	319	358	363	18,372	21,165	19,429	19,492	213	355	458	533
Transportation [3]	147	168	203	228	3,908	4,623	4,809	5,418	51	88	123	154
Wholesale trade	350	385	438	460	4,332	5,211	5,624	6,153	52	89	130	170
Retail trade	1,190	1,223	1,407	1,495	12,271	15,047	16,851	19,335	76	124	178	229
Finance and insurance [4]	372	421	488	529	4,247	5,295	6,005	6,802	42	77	132	184
Services	1,118	1,278	1,712	1,977	12,655	17,186	21,549	27,339	102	197	346	544

[1] Includes nonclassifiable establishments, not shown separately.   [2] Includes forestry and fisheries.   [3] Includes other public utilities.   [4] Includes real estate.

Source: U.S. Bureau of the Census, *County Business Patterns,* annual.

No. 839. Establishments, Employees, and Payroll, by Employment-Size Class and Industry: 1989

[See headnote, table 837. Data are based on the *1987 Standard Industrial Classification Manual*]

EMPLOYMENT SIZE-CLASS	Unit	All industries [1]	Agricultural services [2]	Mining	Contract construction	Manufacturing	Transportation [3]	Wholesale trade	Retail trade	Finance and insurance [4]	Services
Establishments, total	1,000	6,107	79	30	547	363	228	460	1,495	529	1,977
Under 20 employees	1,000	5,305	75	24	496	234	183	390	1,265	472	1,774
20 to 99 employees	1,000	668	4	5	46	91	36	62	206	48	164
100 to 499 employees	1,000	119	(Z)	1	5	33	8	7	23	8	34
500 to 999 employees	1,000	9	(Z)	(Z)	(Z)	4	1	(Z)	1	1	3
1,000 or more employees	1,000	5	(Z)	(Z)	(Z)	2	(Z)	(Z)	(Z)	(Z)	2
Employees, total	1,000	91,631	489	711	5,036	19,492	5,418	6,153	19,335	6,802	27,339
Under 20 employees	1,000	23,992	277	117	2,089	1,453	900	2,148	6,789	1,946	7,591
20 to 99 employees	1,000	26,829	136	203	1,745	4,039	1,482	2,373	8,174	1,888	6,614
100 to 499 employees	1,000	22,387	58	225	869	6,787	1,472	1,230	3,768	1,542	6,436
500 to 999 employees	1,000	6,442	(D)	(D)	154	2,510	460	232	371	522	2,101
1,000 or more employees	1,000	11,981	(D)	(D)	178	4,704	1,104	170	233	903	4,596
Annual payroll	Bil. dol	1,990	7.8	24.9	127.3	533.1	153.5	170.4	228.6	184.5	543.8
Under 20 employees	Bil. dol	461	4.5	3.2	45.4	31.8	19.7	55.6	77.2	46.4	162.6
20 to 99 employees	Bil. dol	514	2.1	6.2	46.3	93.8	37.7	63.9	90.0	49.5	122.9
100 to 499 employees	Bil. dol	488	0.9	8.6	25.7	166.7	42.6	37.0	49.5	43.5	113.0
500 to 999 employees	Bil. dol	163	(D)	(D)	4.3	69.4	15.2	7.9	6.6	14.8	41.6
1,000 or more employees	Bil. dol	364	(D)	(D)	5.6	171.4	38.3	6.1	5.3	30.3	103.6

D Withheld to avoid disclosing data for individual companies; data are included in higher-level totals.   Z Less than 500 establishments or $500 million.   [1] Includes nonclassifiable establishments not shown separately.   [2] Includes forestry and fisheries.   [3] Includes other public utilities.   [4] Includes real estate.

Source: U.S. Bureau of the Census, *County Business Patterns,* annual.

No. 840. Women-Owned Firms—Major Industry Statistics: 1982 and 1987

1972 SIC [1] code	INDUSTRY	1982 Number of firms (1,000)	1982 Sales and receipts (mil. dol.)	1987 Number of firms Total (1,000)	1987 Number of firms Percent change, 1982-87	1987 Number of firms Percent of U.S.	1987 Sales and receipts Total (mil. dol.)	1987 Sales and receipts Percent change, 1982-87	1987 Sales and receipts Percent of U.S.
(X)	All industries [2]	2,612.6	98,292	4,114.8	57	30	278,138	183	17
(A)	Agriculture [3]	19.5	686	48.0	146	13	1,933	182	9
(B)	Mining	19.8	2,221	26.4	33	22	1,934	-13	13
(C)	Construction [2]	59.0	4,565	94.3	60	6	20,302	345	9
15	General building contractors.	11.1	1,483	21.3	92	6	7,625	414	9
17	Special trade contractors.	44.9	2,497	67.1	50	5	9,152	267	9
(D)	Manufacturing [2]	44.9	5,303	94.0	109	22	30,914	483	14
23	Apparel and other textile products. .	4.7	526	17.9	280	55	2,641	402	16
27	Printing and publishing	13.0	847	19.7	52	26	3,999	372	16
(E)	Transportation, public utilities [2]	38.9	3,229	79.8	105	13	10,936	239	14
42	Trucking and warehousing	16.2	1,342	27.4	69	8	4,654	247	11
47	Transportation services	13.7	1,282	30.4	121	35	3,968	210	28
(F)	Wholesale trade	32.1	9,190	82.5	157	19	42,805	366	14
(G)	Retail trade [2]	631.3	35,861	798.7	27	36	85,418	138	16
52	Building materials and garden supplies	9.5	1,186	11.3	18	18	4,096	245	12
53	General merchandise stores.	6.3	1,182	10.2	62	32	1,198	1	15
54	Food stores.	36.8	6,047	48.5	32	24	14,428	139	18
55	Auto dealers, service stations.	14.0	4,754	20.9	50	10	20,224	325	10
56	Apparel accessory stores	27.7	2,446	40.6	47	43	5,216	113	28
58	Eating and drinking places	66.2	6,684	90.8	37	28	14,167	112	19
(H)	Finance, insurance, real estate [2]	246.4	6,370	437.4	77	36	17,833	180	14
64	Insurance agents, brokers	29.2	882	53.2	82	17	2,306	162	10
65	Real estate [4]	212.0	4,733	335.4	58	46	12,641	167	18
(I)	Services [2]	1,284.8	26,278	2,269.0	77	38	61,123	133	15
70	Hotels and other lodging places . . .	17.5	1,671	22.2	27	30	3,201	92	12
72	Personal services	394.6	5,500	561.7	42	52	10,289	87	34
73	Business services.	(NA)	(NA)	690.5	(X)	38	18,936	(X)	19
75	Auto repair, services, and garages .	11.0	929	23.5	114	7	2,644	184	9
76	Miscellaneous repair services.	13.3	430	24.0	81	10	1,167	171	10
79	Amusement and recreation services	45.0	1,132	99.5	121	26	3,100	174	16
80	Health services	123.1	3,989	235.3	91	37	9,618	141	12
81	Legal services	23.3	853	41.9	80	17	2,220	160	4
83	Social services	(NA)	(NA)	269.2	(X)	83	3,047	(X)	56

NA Not available. X Not applicable. [1] Standard Industrial Classification; see text, section 13. [2] Includes industries not shown separately. [3] Includes agricultural services, forestry, and fishing. [4] Excludes industry 6552 which is included in construction industries.

Source: U.S. Bureau of the Census, *1987 Survey of Women-Owned Businesses*, series WB87-1.

No. 841. Women-Owned Firms—Number and Receipts, by State: 1982 and 1987

STATE	1982 Firms (1,000)	1982 Sales and receipts (mil. dol.)	1987 Number of firms Total (1,000)	1987 Number of firms Per-cent of U.S. total	1987 Sales and receipts Total (mil. dol.)	1987 Sales and receipts Per-cent of U.S. total	STATE	1982 Firms (1,000)	1982 Sales and receipts (mil. dol.)	1987 Number of firms Total (1,000)	1987 Number of firms Per-cent of U.S. total	1987 Sales and receipts Total (mil. dol.)	1987 Sales and receipts Per-cent of U.S. total
U.S..	2,612.6	98,292	4,114.8	30	278,138	14	MO ..	54.1	1,989	87.7	30	5,349	14
AL...	30.9	1,268	48.0	27	3,624	14	MT...	12.8	499	17.7	28	930	17
AK...	9.5	379	14.0	29	829	17	NE...	22.7	717	32.3	31	1,649	14
AZ...	35.1	1,027	60.6	32	2,911	13	NV...	11.7	450	18.8	31	1,414	14
AR...	24.5	1,069	35.5	26	2,008	13	NH...	11.9	392	22.7	28	1,858	14
CA...	354.7	12,023	559.8	31	31,027	13	NJ...	63.2	3,573	117.4	29	13,554	14
CO...	57.4	1,829	89.4	34	4,261	16	NM...	16.3	576	25.4	31	1,166	16
CT...	35.5	1,401	60.9	31	5,320	15	NY...	176.5	8,352	284.9	31	29,970	14
DE...	5.7	196	9.7	31	753	16	NC...	57.4	1,860	93.5	28	6,813	15
DC...	8.9	334	11.0	38	774	12	ND...	8.8	340	12.7	30	572	14
FL...	125.4	4,789	221.4	30	16,828	17	OH...	102.5	3,615	154.1	30	8,872	12
GA...	53.3	1,848	88.1	29	5,874	14	OK...	49.2	2,123	63.7	28	2,948	15
HI ...	14.4	356	21.7	36	857	13	OR...	40.5	1,357	58.9	32	4,279	19
ID ...	13.4	427	19.0	28	813	12	PA...	106.2	4,186	167.4	28	13,339	11
IL....	110.3	4,567	177.1	31	13,884	14	RI ...	0.0	270	14.5	28	1,340	13
IN ...	62.0	3,192	89.9	31	8,913	18	SC ...	27.1	983	42.6	29	2,950	16
IA ...	36.1	1,137	53.6	31	2,905	16	SD ...	9.4	368	13.4	28	726	14
KS ...	36.8	1,235	53.5	32	2,661	16	TN ...	44.6	1,707	67.4	27	4,226	12
KY ...	36.6	1,583	53.5	28	3,265	14	TX ...	199.8	8,074	298.1	29	13,385	12
LA ...	38.3	2,201	55.9	27	2,962	14	UT ...	19.1	665	29.8	30	1,392	14
ME...	14.5	420	23.9	27	1,635	16	VT ...	8.0	267	13.8	31	766	15
MD...	48.4	1,530	81.9	34	5,509	13	VA ...	56.9	1,753	94.4	32	5,952	14
MA...	63.2	1,778	111.4	31	11,140	17	WA ...	59.3	1,599	90.3	32	4,689	13
MI ...	87.1	2,790	134.0	31	7,889	12	WV ..	15.7	616	22.5	29	1,114	16
MN...	56.2	1,751	88.1	31	4,991	14	WI ...	44.4	1,562	69.2	29	4,667	15
MS...	20.4	955	29.0	26	2,062	16	WY ..	8.4	312	10.8	31	524	15

Source: U.S. Bureau of the Census, *1987 Survey of Women-Owned Business Enterprises*, series WB87-1.

No. 842. Women- and Minority-Owned Firms, by Selected Metropolitan Area: 1987

[Metropolitan areas as defined June 30, 1987. MSA = Metropolitan Statistical Area. PMSA = Primary Metropolitan Statistical Area; see text, section 1]

METROPOLITAN AREAS RANKED BY 1990 POPULATION	WOMEN-OWNED		BLACK-OWNED		HISPANIC-OWNED		AMERICAN INDIANS, ALASKA NATIVES, ASIAN AND PACIFIC ISLANDERS-OWNED	
	Firms	Sales and receipts (mil. dol.)	Firms	Sales and receipts (mil. dol.)	Firms	Sales and receipts (mil. dol.)	Firms	Sales and receipts (mil. dol.)
Los Angeles-Long Beach, CA PMSA	162,417	10,775	23,932	1,300	56,679	3,346	63,139	6,873
New York, NY PMSA	136,209	17,314	28,063	1,235	23,014	1,240	29,248	2,435
Chicago, IL PMSA	89,424	9,195	15,374	909	7,848	506	12,593	1,211
Philadelphia, PA-NJ PMSA.	68,032	6,749	10,249	613	1,930	202	5,521	758
Detroit, MI PMSA	58,791	4,183	9,852	514	1,288	75	3,058	296
Houston, TX PMSA.	59,866	2,653	12,989	372	15,967	584	8,777	805
Boston, MA PMSA	58,975	7,545	3,191	198	1,420	72	2,637	188
Atlanta, GA MSA	49,340	3,075	11,804	747	1,424	110	3,042	329
Nassau-Suffolk, NY PMSA.	50,471	6,001	3,990	392	3,313	215	3,985	431
Riverside-San Bernardino, CA PMSA.	34,214	1,773	2,788	139	10,195	577	4,366	480
Dallas, TX PMSA	55,452	2,722	7,857	235	6,747	294	5,650	396
San Diego, CA MSA	47,450	2,201	2,481	105	10,373	559	6,731	442
Minneapolis-St. Paul, MN-WI MSA.	52,427	3,442	1,333	113	568	23	1,595	151
Anaheim-Santa Ana, CA PMSA.	54,367	3,266	1,318	81	9,683	651	15,407	1,425
Baltimore, MD MSA	36,891	2,628	8,593	331	680	71	2,619	273
Phoenix, AZ MSA.	37,407	1,900	1,218	67	4,507	223	1,826	170
Oakland, CA PMSA	45,590	1,899	6,541	247	6,046	354	12,011	1,057
Tampa-St. Petersburg-Clearwater, FL MSA .	35,218	2,688	2,630	165	4,513	342	1,299	110
Seattle, WA PMSA	43,335	2,030	1,639	87	1,034	55	5,696	588
Miami-Hialeah, FL PMSA.	32,937	2,954	6,747	276	47,725	3,771	1,845	195
Cleveland, OH PMSA	25,794	1,726	4,755	218	433	19	1,126	88
Newark, NJ PMSA	28,420	3,567	5,641	446	2,877	235	2,941	254
Denver, CO PMSA	45,449	2,390	2,198	84	4,760	222	2,523	149
San Francisco, CA PMSA	46,000	3,255	3,131	140	6,472	431	17,260	1,740

Source: U.S. Bureau of the Census, *1987 Survey of Minority-Owned Enterprises*, series MB87-1, MB87-2, MB87-3, and *1987 Survey of Women-Owned Businesses*, series WB87-1.

No. 843. Minority-Owned Firms—Major Industry Statistics: 1987

1972 SIC [1] code	INDUSTRY	BLACK-OWNED		HISPANIC-OWNED		AMERICAN INDIAN AND ALASKA NATIVE-OWNED		ASIAN AND PACIFIC ISLANDER-OWNED	
		Number of firms	Sales and receipts (mil. dol.)	Number of firms	Sales and receipts (mil. dol.)	Number of firms	Sales and receipts (mil. dol.)	Number of firms	Sales and receipts (mil. dol.)
(X)	All industries [2]	424,165	19,763	422,373	24,732	21,380	911	355,331	33,124
(A)	Agriculture [3]	7,316	217	16,365	695	3,661	104	9,726	365
(C)	Construction [2]	36,763	2,174	55,516	3,439	2,832	156	13,391	1,224
15	General building contractors	6,285	636	7,990	861	461	34	2,632	486
17	Special trade contractors	29,631	1,314	46,383	2,266	2,268	97	10,331	579
(D)	Manufacturing [2]	8,004	1,023	11,090	1,450	911	64	10,121	1,461
23	Apparel and other textile products . . .	552	65	1,713	279	76	(D)	4,265	(D)
(E)	Transportation, public utilities [2]	36,958	1,573	26,955	1,381	917	44	11,940	691
41	Local and interurban passenger trans .	11,566	218	4,522	106	95	3	6,049	133
42	Trucking and warehousing	19,663	1,010	17,304	907	590	32	2,214	122
47	Transportation services	4,053	223	3,617	285	134	6	2,959	388
(F)	Wholesale trade.	5,519	1,327	10,154	2,445	360	36	10,654	4,189
(G)	Retail trade [2]	66,229	5,890	69,911	7,644	3,090	268	88,761	13,316
54	Food stores	8,952	1,001	9,599	1,836	301	54	17,263	3,786
55	Auto dealers, service stations	3,690	2,156	5,627	2,100	222	65	2,831	1,881
56	Apparel accessory stores	3,061	140	3,472	231	85	6	6,208	677
58	Eating and drinking places	11,834	1,084	14,003	1,645	464	35	24,863	3,600
(H)	Finance, insurance, real estate [2]	26,989	804	22,106	864	614	20	27,297	1,087
64	Insurance agents, brokers.	7,956	189	6,013	209	152	5	6,829	176
65	Real estate [4]	15,552	506	12,872	472	370	13	16,794	692
(I)	Services [2]	209,547	6,120	184,372	6,031	7,604	178	165,342	9,881
70	Hotels and other lodging places.	1,734	128	973	113	102	6	7,809	1,366
72	Personal services	56,772	960	44,872	893	1,719	27	36,392	1,318
73	Business services	59,177	1,570	59,948	1,420	2,532	49	46,066	1,523
75	Auto repair, services, and garages . . .	11,801	427	15,824	837	538	21	5,072	499
76	Miscellaneous repair services	5,197	154	8,337	302	300	11	3,601	163
79	Amusement and recreation services . .	13,250	503	9,528	204	556	16	5,307	142
80	Health services.	30,026	1,351	16,322	1,326	488	21	34,590	3,755
81	Legal services	4,920	336	3,690	287	169	11	2,186	180
83	Social services	13,210	224	8,840	100	451	4	4,038	85

D Withheld to avoid disclosing data for individual companies; data are included in higher-level totals.   [1] Standard Industrial Classification code; see text, section 13.   [2] Includes industries not shown separately.   [3] Includes agricultural services, forestry, and fishing.   [4] Excludes industry 6552 which is included in contruction industries.
Source: U.S. Bureau of the Census, *1987 Survey of Minority-Owned Business Enterprises*, series MB87-4.

No. 844. Minority-Owned Firms, by State: 1987

[A firm is classified as minority owned if sole owner or at least half of the partners or shareholders are of minority ancestry]

STATE	BLACK OWNED		HISPANIC OWNED		AMERICAN INDIAN AND ALASKA NATIVE OWNED		ASIAN AND PACIFIC ISLANDER OWNED	
	Firms	Sales and receipts (mil. dol.)	Firms	Sales and receipts (mil. dol.)	Firms	Sales and receipts (mil. dol.)	Firms	Sales and receipts (mil. dol.)
United States	424,165	19,763	422,373	24,732	21,380	911	355,331	33,124
Alabama.	10,085	440	397	30	90	5	917	126
Alaska	507	14	502	27	4,006	118	1,028	78
Arizona.	1,811	91	9,845	513	872	50	2,526	253
Arkansas	4,392	215	324	14	91	3	567	53
California	47,728	2,364	132,212	8,120	3,280	162	144,353	14,620
Colorado.	2,871	106	9,516	394	351	14	3,192	216
Connecticut.	4,061	226	2,235	176	88	(D)	1,963	(D)
Delaware	1,399	78	184	6	43	(D)	436	(D)
District of Columbia	8,275	412	762	64	28	1	779	133
Florida	25,527	1,212	64,413	4,949	349	(D)	8,553	(D)
Georgia	21,283	1,180	1,931	145	129	6	4,092	463
Hawaii	399	12	1,226	58	106	6	31,300	1,656
Idaho.	94	5	974	31	80	7	433	31
Illinois	19,011	1,100	9,636	589	193	7	14,679	1,438
Indiana.	5,867	350	1,427	106	90	3	1,718	205
Iowa	703	45	475	20	43	1	574	54
Kansas.	2,323	154	1,541	62	231	(D)	1,135	(D)
Kentucky	3,738	120	359	17	24	2	875	96
Louisiana	15,331	532	2,697	136	225	(D)	2,583	(D)
Maine.	131	5	139	12	68	4	165	23
Maryland	21,678	720	2,931	185	123	9	7,831	702
Massachusetts.	4,761	252	2,636	174	132	5	3,784	292
Michigan.	13,708	701	2,654	126	305	(D)	4,424	(D)
Minnesota.	1,448	125	751	29	340	18	1,684	154
Mississippi	9,667	532	308	12	50	(D)	1,128	(D)
Missouri	7,832	336	1,247	50	137	2	2,056	165
Montana.	77	7	304	10	405	17	207	13
Nebraska	863	31	619	19	66	2	385	30
Nevada	1,002	39	1,767	142	150	9	1,245	84
New Hampshire	229	31	244	13	29	(D)	304	(D)
New Jersey.	14,556	996	12,094	902	135	(D)	12,530	(D)
New Mexico	587	27	14,299	702	1,258	37	897	67
New York	36,289	1,886	28,254	1,556	445	25	35,812	3,193
North Carolina	19,487	746	918	93	1,758	(D)	2,069	(D)
North Dakota.	57	1	88	2	210	(D)	119	(D)
Ohio	15,983	626	1,989	192	152	(D)	3,859	(D)
Oklahoma.	3,461	94	1,516	50	2,051	57	1,700	98
Oregon.	848	34	1,598	110	333	19	3,007	332
Pennsylvania	11,728	747	2,650	247	140	(D)	7,049	(D)
Rhode Island.	489	18	426	40	36	(D)	436	(D)
South Carolina.	12,815	444	393	16	47	4	918	84
South Dakota.	63	5	109	4	267	11	108	6
Tennessee	10,423	386	554	35	90	(D)	1,574	(D)
Texas.	35,725	1,084	94,754	4,108	929	28	21,753	1,787
Utah	202	9	1,300	47	110	(D)	1,129	(D)
Vermont	98	7	118	5	9	(D)	102	(D)
Virginia.	18,781	811	2,716	141	190	(D)	7,973	(D)
Washington.	2,583	176	2,686	141	682	48	7,559	745
West Virginia.	727	39	177	14	28	1	523	75
Wisconsin.	2,381	191	894	74	307	(D)	1,144	(D)
Wyoming	81	4	584	22	79	(D)	154	(D)

D Figure withheld to avoid disclosure pertaining to a specific organization or individual.

Source: U.S. Bureau of the Census, *Survey of Minority-Owned Business Enterprises*, series MB87-4.

No. 845. New Business Incorporations and Business Failures—Number and Liabilities: 1970 to 1991

[1970 excludes Hawaii; 1970 and 1975 exclude Alaska. Total concerns and failure data prior to 1984 exclude agriculture, forestry and fishing, finance, insurance, and real estate, and services; therefore, are not directly comparable with data for 1984 and later. See also *Historical Statistics, Colonial Times to 1970*, series V 20-30]

YEAR	Total concerns in business [1] (1,000)	Index of net business formations [2] (1967 =100)	New incorporations (1,000)	FAILURES [3] Number	FAILURES [3] Rate per 10,000 concerns	FAILURES [3] Current liabilities [4] (mil. dol.)	YEAR	Total concerns in business [1] (1,000)	Index of net business formations [2] (1967 =100)	New incorporations (1,000)	FAILURES [3] Number	FAILURES [3] Rate per 10,000 concerns	FAILURES [3] Current liabilities [4] (mil. dol.)
1970....	2,442	108.8	264	10,748	44	1,888	1985....	4,990	120.9	663	57,078	115	36,937
1975....	2,679	109.9	326	11,432	43	4,380	1986....	5,119	120.4	702	61,616	120	44,724
1980....	2,780	129.9	532	11,742	42	4,635	1987....	6,004	121.2	685	61,111	102	34,724
1981....	2,745	124.8	581	16,794	61	6,955	1988....	5,804	124.1	685	57,098	98	39,126
1982....	2,806	116.4	566	24,908	88	15,611	1989....	7,694	124.7	677	50,361	65	44,261
1983....	2,851	117.5	602	31,334	110	16,073	1990....	8,039	120.7	647	60,432	75	64,044
1984....	4,885	121.3	635	52,078	107	29,269	1991, prel.	8,218	115.4	629	(NA)	(NA)	(NA)

NA Not available. [1] Data through 1983 represent number of names listed in July issue of *Dun & Bradstreet Reference Book*. Data for 1984-91 represent the number of establishments listed in the Dun's Census of American Business. The base has been changed due to expanded business failure coverage. [2] Source: U.S. Bureau of Economic Analysis, *Survey of Current Business*. [3] Includes concerns discontinued following assignment, voluntary or involuntary petition in bankruptcy, attachment, execution, foreclosure, etc.; voluntary withdrawals from business with known loss to creditors; also enterprises involved in court action, such as receivership and reorganization or arrangement which may or may not lead to discontinuance; and businesses making voluntary compromise with creditors out of court. [4] Liabilities exclude long-term publicly held obligations; offsetting assets are not taken into account.

Source: Except as noted, Dun & Bradstreet Corporation, New York, NY, *New Business Incorporations*, monthly; *The Failure Record Through 1991*; and *Monthly Failure Report*.

No. 846. New Business Incorporations and Number of Failures, by State: 1989 to 1991

[1991 preliminary. See headnote, table 845]

DIVISION AND STATE	NEW BUSINESS INCORPORATIONS 1990	NEW BUSINESS INCORPORATIONS 1991	NUMBER OF FAILURES 1989	NUMBER OF FAILURES 1990	DIVISION AND STATE	NEW BUSINESS INCORPORATIONS 1990	NEW BUSINESS INCORPORATIONS 1991	NUMBER OF FAILURES 1989	NUMBER OF FAILURES 1990
United States ...	647,366	628,580	50,361	60,432	Virginia	17,376	16,883	1,177	1,585
					West Virginia.......	2,542	2,219	162	231
New England	31,363	28,864	1,282	3,057	North Carolina......	12,376	11,944	762	1,030
Maine	2,428	2,326	132	197	South Carolina	7,158	5,700	182	415
New Hampshire.....	2,679	2,387	125	275	Georgia	18,891	18,098	1,787	1,937
Vermont..........	1,650	1,486	51	74	Florida...........	82,172	81,083	3,160	3,655
Massachusetts ...	12,468	11,706	771	1,898	**East South Central** ...	24,456	24,806	2,866	3,655
Rhode Island	3,000	2,458	56	183	Kentucky	6,669	6,782	676	1,048
Connecticut	9,138	8,501	147	430	Tennessee........	8,290	8,306	1,164	1,474
Middle Atlantic	113,281	109,142	4,176	6,736	Alabama	6,092	6,116	490	676
New York..........	65,569	63,808	1,964	3,281	Mississippi	3,405	3,602	536	457
New Jersey	28,281	27,994	606	1,246	**West South Central**...	57,760	55,943	8,414	9,738
Pennsylvania......	19,431	17,340	1,606	2,209	Arkansas	6,111	5,326	307	260
East North Central ...	87,519	84,261	8,822	8,308	Louisiana	8,974	8,973	1,402	1,153
Ohio	18,094	17,895	1,713	2,254	Oklahoma.........	7,152	7,073	1,266	1,587
Indiana	10,608	10,205	929	1,164	Texas	35,523	34,571	5,439	6,738
Illinois	29,279	29,068	3,382	2,124	**Mountain**	46,017	47,033	4,213	4,781
Michigan	22,204	20,099	2,080	2,100	Montana	1,519	1,572	191	191
Wisconsin.........	7,334	6,994	718	666	Idaho............	1,909	1,944	233	309
West North Central ...	32,941	32,499	3,164	3,823	Wyoming.........	1,171	1,386	118	177
Minnesota	9,678	9,564	323	522	Colorado	12,257	13,581	1,516	2,077
Iowa	4,381	4,531	560	554	New Mexico	2,854	2,713	393	318
Missouri..........	9,761	9,521	1,150	1,216	Arizona	10,129	9,832	1,250	1,084
North Dakota	860	820	105	145	Utah	4,147	4,973	281	372
South Dakota	1,078	1,040	142	270	Nevada	12,031	11,030	231	253
Nebraska	2,934	3,093	216	358	**Pacific**	64,723	61,499	9,887	10,614
Kansas	4,249	3,930	668	758	Washington	11,948	11,521	1,316	854
South Atlantic	189,306	184,533	7,537	9,720	Oregon	8,525	8,375	444	588
Delaware	29,861	29,887	31	80	California	39,111	36,561	7,814	8,902
Maryland	16,674	16,463	232	686	Alaska	1,345	1,250	143	123
District of Columbia ..	2,256	2,256	44	101	Hawaii	3,794	3,792	170	147

Source: Dun & Bradstreet Corporation, New York, NY, *New Business Incorporations*, monthly; and *Business Failure Record*, annual, (copyright).

No. 847. Business Failures—Number and Rate, by Industry: 1985 to 1990

INDUSTRY	NUMBER					RATE PER 10,000 FIRMS				
	1985	1986	1987	1989	1990	1985	1986	1987	1989	1990
Total [1]	57,253	61,616	61,111	50,361	60,432	115	120	102	65	75
Agriculture, forestry, fishing.	2,699	2,649	3,766	1,540	1,727	197	175	194	49	50
Mining.	796	921	627	351	381	193	223	148	79	86
Construction.	7,005	7,109	6,735	7,120	8,072	109	108	92	86	90
Manufacturing.	4,869	4,772	4,273	3,933	4,709	119	114	95	79	91
Food and kindred products	261	239	191	216	226	127	113	87	87	89
Textile mill products	110	72	73	75	101	129	82	77	72	96
Apparel, other textile products . .	338	287	265	204	318	128	108	96	73	114
Lumber and wood products	415	392	374	368	417	136	125	107	91	96
Furniture and fixtures	236	244	200	253	257	161	164	128	154	150
Paper and allied products	55	46	60	46	66	100	81	101	72	101
Printing and publishing	659	606	633	679	728	94	85	79	71	73
Chemicals and allied products . .	172	129	116	102	134	126	92	79	63	83
Petroleum refining	26	35	21	21	21	145	189	106	83	83
Rubber and misc. products	157	145	145	109	160	117	103	101	71	102
Leather and leather products . . .	47	48	34	30	40	130	137	96	84	113
Stone, clay, and glass products .	159	164	164	114	165	98	101	94	59	82
Primary metal products	122	133	107	71	114	169	177	135	79	122
Fabricated metal products	484	528	461	374	396	125	132	111	87	90
Machinery, exc. electric.	721	739	639	511	650	110	111	91	67	84
Electric and electronic										
equipment	329	332	262	256	288	154	151	113	104	114
Transportation equipment	197	226	175	190	240	165	185	131	117	146
Instruments and related										
equipment	110	140	112	108	119	85	103	78	66	68
Miscellaneous	271	267	241	206	269	101	97	76	58	73
Transportation, public utilities	2,536	2,565	2,236	2,115	2,610	151	140	109	82	93
Wholesale trade	4,836	4,869	4,336	3,687	4,376	102	100	82	66	76
Retail trade	13,494	13,620	12,240	11,120	12,826	109	110	81	56	65
Finance, insurance, real estate . . .	2,676	2,797	2,550	2,932	3,881	62	65	54	47	61
Services	16,649	20,967	23,802	13,679	17,673	115	139	128	53	64

[1] Includes industries not shown separately.

Source: The Dun and Bradstreet Corporation, New York, NY, *Business Failure Record,* annual, (copyright).

No. 848. Bankruptcy Petitions Filed, by State: 1981 to 1991

[In thousands. For years ending June 30. Includes outlying areas, not shown separately. Covers only b filed under the Bankruptcy Reform Act of 1978. **Bankruptcy:** legal recogition that a company or indivi and must restructure or liquidate. Petitions "filed" means the commencement of a proceeding through the present a petition to the clerk of the court]

STATE	1981	1985	1988	1989	1990	1991	STATE	1981	1985	1988	1989	1990	1991
U.S.. . . .	360.3	364.5	594.6	643.0	725.5	880.4	MO	7.9	7.4	10.7	12.0	13.4	17.3
AL	10.8	10.9	18.4	20.9	24.7	27.8	MT	1.1	1.1	1.8	1.9	1.8	2.1
AK	0.4	0.5	1.4	1.4	1.2	1.1	NE	2.8	2.8	3.4	3.3	3.8	4.5
AZ	4.3	5.2	12.7	14.9	17.7	19.3	NV	2.6	2.9	5.5	5.7	6.2	6.9
AR	2.6	3.9	5.9	6.0	6.8	7.7	NH	0.7	0.5	0.7	1.0	1.8	3.4
CA	50.2	61.8	96.4	99.3	103.2	124.2	NJ	7.0	6.7	8.3	9.3	12.6	19.4
CO	6.7	7.0	17.0	18.3	17.1	17.0	NM	1.5	1.6	2.8	3.4	4.0	4.5
CT	2.5	1.8	2.4	3.0	4.4	6.9	NY	24.2	14.2	18.8	21.9	29.0	40.3
DE	0.6	0.5	0.7	0.7	0.9	1.3	NC	8.3	5.4	8.1	8.9	10.7	15.5
DC	0.7	0.7	1.1	1.1	1.0	1.2	ND	0.6	0.7	1.1	1.1	1.1	1.2
FL	6.8	9.1	20.0	25.3	31.9	43.4	OH	27.3	19.5	29.1	31.7	36.8	42.8
GA	11.7	14.4	25.0	29.5	38.7	49.0	OK	4.7	7.1	14.3	14.1	14.3	16.2
HI	0.8	0.6	0.9	0.9	0.9	1.0	OR	5.5	6.5	10.1	10.1	11.3	13.5
ID	2.2	2.4	3.9	3.9	4.1	4.2	PA	10.0	9.8	13.3	13.5	15.8	20.8
IL	26.6	25.6	31.1	32.5	35.8	40.5	RI	1.0	0.8	0.9	1.0	1.7	3.1
IN	13.5	12.2	18.8	20.0	22.2	26.8	SC	1.6	2.3	4.1	4.6	4.8	6.9
IA	4.5	4.7	5.1	4.9	5.5	5.8	SD	0.6	0.9	1.3	1.2	1.4	1.6
KS	4.5	4.8	7.0	7.3	8.1	9.6	TN	13.8	14.7	26.0	29.3	34.2	40.6
KY	7.8	7.0	10.4	12.0	13.6	15.6	TX	9.6	16.8	40.4	41.4	41.7	46.6
LA	5.2	7.7	13.7	12.5	12.9	13.3	UT	3.8	4.0	7.3	7.9	8.0	8.0
ME	1.0	0.6	0.9	1.1	1.5	2.2	VT	0.3	0.2	0.3	0.3	0.5	0.8
MD	5.3	3.9	7.6	8.1	9.2	12.8	VA	9.9	9.2	14.7	16.3	19.3	25.3
MA	3.4	2.0	3.0	4.2	7.6	12.9	WA	8.4	11.3	17.5	18.3	17.0	17.2
MI	15.1	8.6	15.3	16.5	18.8	23.3	WV	2.2	1.9	3.1	3.4	3.5	4.0
MN	5.4	5.4	9.9	11.6	14.0	16.7	WI	5.8	7.4	8.9	9.3	10.2	12.1
MS	5.1	4.8	8.7	9.8	10.6	12.3	WY	0.6	1.0	1.5	1 4	1 5	1.6

Source: Compiled by U.S. Bureau of the Census; based on unpublished data from Adminstrative Office of the U.S. Courts.

No. 849. Bankruptcy Petitions Filed and Pending, by Type and Chapter: 1981 to 1991

[For years ending June 30. Covers only bankruptcy cases filed under the Bankruptcy Reform Act of 1978. **Bankruptcy:** legal recognition that a company or individual is insolvent and must restructure or liquidate. Petitions "filed" means the commencement of a proceeding through the presentation of a petition to the clerk of the court; "pending" is a proceeding in which the administration has not been completed]

ITEM	1981	1984	1985	1986	1987	1988	1989	1990	1991
Total, filed	**360,329**	**344,275**	**364,536**	**477,856**	**561,278**	**594,567**	**642,993**	**725,484**	**880,399**
Business [1]	47,415	62,170	66,651	76,281	88,278	68,501	62,534	64,688	69,193
Nonbusiness [2]	312,914	282,105	297,885	401,575	473,000	526,066	580,459	660,796	811,206
Voluntary	358,997	342,828	362,939	476,214	559,658	593,158	641,528	723,886	878,626
Involuntary	1,332	1,447	1,597	1,642	1,620	1,409	1,465	1,598	1,773
Chapter 7 [3]	265,721	232,994	244,650	332,679	397,551	423,796	457,240	505,337	612,330
Chapter 9 [4]	1	4	3	7	10	3	7	7	20
Chapter 11 [5]	7,828	19,913	21,425	24,443	22,566	18,891	17,465	19,591	22,495
Chapter 12 [6]	(X)	(X)	(X)	(X)	4,824	3,099	1,717	1,351	1,358
Chapter 13 [7]	86,778	91,358	98,452	120,726	136,300	148,771	166,539	199,186	244,192
Section 304 [8]	1	6	6	1	27	7	25	12	4
Total, pending . .	**361,664**	**577,567**	**608,945**	**728,577**	**808,504**	**814,195**	**869,340**	**961,919**	**1,123,433**

X Not applicable.   [1] Business bankruptcies include those filed under chapters 7, 9, 11, or 12.   [2] Bankruptcies include those filed under chapters 7, 11, or 13.   [3] Chapter 7, liquidation of non-exempt assets of businesses or individuals.   [4] Chapter 9, adjustment of debts of a municipality.   [5] Chapter 11, individual or business reorganization.   [6] Chapter 12, adjustment of debts of a family farmer with regular annual income, effective November 26, 1986.   [7] Chapter 13, adjustment of debts of an individual with regular income.   [8] 11 U.S.C., Section 304, cases ancillary to foreign proceedings.

Source: Administrative Office of the U.S. Courts, *Annual Report of the Director.*

No. 850. Small Business Administration Loans to All Small Businesses: 1980 to 1991

[For fiscal year ending in year shown; see text, section 9. A small business must be independently owned and operated, must not be dominant in its particular industry, and must meet standards set by the Small Business Administration as to its annual receipts or number of employees. Loans include both direct and guaranteed loans to small business establishments. Does not include Disaster Assistance Loans]

LOANS APPROVED	Unit	1980	1982	1983	1984	1985	1986	1987	1988	1989	1990	1991
Loans, all businesses	1,000. . .	31.7	15.4	19.2	21.3	19.3	16.8	17.1	17.1	17.0	18.8	19.4
Loans, minority-owned businesses. .	1,000. . .	6.0	2.5	2.7	3.1	2.8	2.0	2.1	2.2	2.4	2.4	2.9
Percent of all business loans	Percent . .	19	16	14	15	15	12	12	13	14	13	15
Value of total loans [1]	Mil. dol. .	3,858	2,038	3,007	3,450	3,217	3,013	3,232	3,434	3,490	4,354	4,625
Value of loans to minority-operated businesses [2]	Mil. dol. .	470	238	295	383	324	265	299	343	385	473	601

[1] Includes both SBA and bank portions of loans.   [2] SBA direct loans and guaranteed portion of bank loans only.

Source: U.S. Small Business Administration, unpublished data.

No. 851. Job Creation, by Firm Size and Industry: 1976 to 1990

YEAR	Total (1,000)	SHARE OF JOBS BY EMPLOYMENT-SIZE OF FIRM			More than 500 employees
		Less than 500 employees			
		Total	Less than 20	20 to 499	
1976 to 1978.	6,062	4,407	2,316	2,091	1,655
1978 to 1980.	5,777	2,605	1,519	1,086	3,172
1980 to 1982.	1,542	1,473	1,510	−37	69
1982 to 1984.	4,318	3,312	2,107	1,205	1,006
1984 to 1986.	4,611	2,412	1,637	775	2,199
1986 to 1988.	6,169	2,770	1,487	1,283	3,399
1988 to 1990.	**2,664**	**3,165**	**4,015**	**−849.8**	**−501**
Agriculture, forestry, fishing	201	180	185	−4.1	21
Mining	−76	−5	3	−8.1	−70
Construction	3	21	261	−239.8	−18
Manufacturing	−974	8	220	−212.3	−982
Transportation, communications, and public utilities . . .	139	99	134	−35.7	40
Wholesale trade.	−93	38	139	−100.5	−132
Retail trade.	760	605	686	−81.3	155
Finance, insurance, real estate	338	254	278	−24.5	84
Services.	2,366	1,967	2,111	−143.9	400

Source: U.S. Small Business Administration, Office of Advocacy, Small Business Data Base, linked 1988-1990 USEEM files, unpublished data.

No. 852. Federal Contract Actions—Small and Minority-Owned Small Businesses Share, by State of Principal Place of Performance: 1989 and 1990

[In millions of dollars, except percent. For fiscal year. Excludes Guam, Puerto Rico, and Virgin Islands. Represents contract awards of $25,000 or more awarded to establishments. A contract may consist of more than one action. Minus sign (-) indicates decrease]

REGION, DIVISION, AND STATE	TOTAL CONTRACT ACTIONS			SMALL BUSINESS SHARE				SMALL MINORITY-OWNED SHARE			
	1989	1990	Percent change 1989-90	1989	1990 Amount	1990 Percent of total	Percent change 1989-90	1989	1990 Amount	1990 Percent of total	Percent change 1989-90
U.S.	159,112	163,775	3	23,105	25,399	19	33	5,103	5,757	4	15
Northeast	33,268	31,730	-5	3,721	3,859	12	4	599	655	2	9
New England. . . .	17,273	15,399	-11	1,427	1,263	8	-12	183	212	1	16
Maine.	389	921	137	61	59	6	-3	4	4	(Z)	-
New Hampshire .	509	419	-18	63	61	15	-3	8	5	1	-38
Vermont	184	96	-48	19	19	20	-	2	1	1	-50
Massachusetts. .	9,347	9,008	-4	815	715	8	-12	117	141	2	21
Rhode Island. . .	433	580	34	140	137	24	-2	19	31	5	63
Connecticut. . . .	6,411	4,375	-32	329	272	6	-17	33	30	1	-9
Middle Atlantic . .	15,995	16,331	2	2,294	2,596	16	13	416	443	3	7
New York	8,412	8,238	-2	821	1,098	13	34	111	203	3	83
New Jersey	3,938	4,127	5	701	784	19	12	103	121	3	18
Pennsylvania. . .	3,645	3,966	9	772	714	18	-8	202	119	3	-41
Midwest.	25,073	24,250	-3	3,516	3,526	15	(Z)	560	653	3	33
East North Central	13,670	12,929	-5	2,443	2,559	20	5	399	438	3	10
Ohio	6,660	5,879	-12	847	925	16	9	231	263	5	14
Indiana.	1,854	1,888	2	197	222	12	13	29	31	2	7
Illinois	2,249	2,357	5	553	574	24	4	120	112	5	-7
Michigan.	1,542	1,597	4	412	421	26	2	12	26	2	117
Wisconsin.	1,365	1,208	-12	434	417	35	-4	7	6	1	-14
West North Central	11,403	11,321	-1	1,073	967	9	-10	161	215	3	91
Minnesota.	1,891	2,015	7	162	140	7	-14	1	13	1	1,200
Iowa	584	652	12	69	58	9	-16	5	4	1	-20
Missouri	7,111	6,884	-3	386	349	5	-10	66	51	1	-23
North Dakota. . .	162	159	-2	117	94	59	-20	43	44	28	2
South Dakota. . .	141	120	-15	61	53	44	-13	17	56	47	229
Nebraska	373	402	8	141	134	33	-5	7	10	25	43
Kansas.	1,141	1,089	-5	137	139	13	2	22	37	3	68
South	52,221	58,205	12	9,975	12,069	30	74	2,623	3,060	5	17
South Atlantic . . .	28,741	33,528	17	6,096	6,972	37	101	1,705	2,184	7	28
Delaware	191	116	-39	36	36	31	-	5	10	9	100
Maryland	6,104	6,798	11	1,170	1,269	19	9	430	559	8	30
District of Columbia.	2,861	3,096	8	664	874	28	32	321	424	14	32
Virginia.	7,305	10,434	43	2,003	2,403	23	20	607	768	7	27
West Virginia. . .	341	305	-11	151	151	50	(Z)	64	88	29	38
North Carolina. .	1,406	1,533	9	376	361	24	-4	27	41	3	52
South Carolina. .	2,450	2,664	9	296	377	14	27	39	39	2	-
Georgia	2,063	2,147	4	512	456	21	-11	97	80	4	-18
Florida	6,020	6,435	7	889	1,045	16	18	114	175	3	54
East South Central	8,727	10,156	16	1,350	2,576	25	91	333	355	4	7
Kentucky	1,145	1,972	72	153	1,075	55	603	59	49	3	-17
Tennessee	3,966	3,241	-18	406	603	19	49	76	134	4	76
Alabama.	2,242	3,352	50	616	713	21	16	171	133	4	-22
Mississippi	1,374	1,591	16	175	185	12	6	26	39	3	50
West South Central	14,753	14,521	-2	2,529	2,521	17	(-Z)	586	521	4	-11
Arkansas	496	361	-27	253	152	42	-40	22	15	4	-32
Louisiana	2,414	2,332	-3	400	586	25	47	56	51	2	-9
Oklahoma.	767	845	10	329	292	35	-11	140	159	19	14
Texas.	11,076	10,983	-1	1,547	1,491	14	-4	367	296	3	-19
West	48,550	49,590	2	5,893	5,945	12	1	1,321	1,389	3	5
Mountain	13,980	15,004	7	1,642	1,687	11	3	451	459	3	2
Montana.	155	156	1	99	122	78	23	20	29	19	45
Idaho.	1,079	854	-21	90	83	10	-8	17	15	2	-12
Wyoming	139	131	-6	95	89	68	-6	9	6	5	-33
Colorado.	3,921	4,651	10	425	437	9	3	108	125	3	16
New Mexico . . .	3,110	3,245	4	277	303	9	9	117	128	4	9
Arizona.	3,144	3,625	15	316	290	8	-8	99	68	2	-31
Utah	1,507	1,529	2	215	264	17	23	31	56	4	81
Nevada	925	813	-12	124	99	12	-20	49	32	4	-35
Pacific	34,570	34,586	(Z)	4,251	4,258	12	(Z)	870	930	3	7
Washington. . . .	4,099	3,878	-5	414	419	11	1	89	80	2	-10
Oregon.	327	530	62	163	201	38	23	22	20	4	-9
California	28,920	29,110	1	3,119	3,211	11	3	607	687	2	13
Alaska	615	529	-14	290	190	36	-35	35	48	9	37
Hawaii	609	539	-12	265	237	44	-11	118	95	18	-20

- Represents or rounds to zero. Z Less than $500,000 or .5 percent.

Source: U.S. Small Business Administration, *The State of Small Business: A Report of the President*, annual. Data from Federal Procurement Data Center, March 13, 1991.

No. 853. Mergers and Acquisitions—Summary: 1980 to 1990

[Covers transactions valued at $1 million or more. Values based on transactions for which price data revealed. **All activity** includes mergers, acquisitions, acquisitions of interest, acquisitions of controlling interest, divestitures, and leveraged transactions that result in a change in ownership. **Divestiture:** sale of a business, division, or subsidiary by corporate owner to another party. **Leveraged buyout:** acquisition of a business in which buyers use mostly borrowed money to finance purchase price and incorporate debt into capital structure of business after change in ownership]

ITEM	Unit	1980	1983	1984	1985	1986	1987	1988	1989	1990
All activity: Number	Number . .	1,558	2,395	3,176	3,489	4,463	4,024	4,233	4,167	4,168
Value.	Mil. dol. . .	32,830	52,708	126,140	145,978	205,958	177,900	240,177	254,020	172,319
Divestitures: Number	Number . .	104	661	794	1,041	1,419	1,221	1,336	1,333	1,406
Value.	Mil. dol. . .	5,090	12,949	30,572	43,534	72,427	57,797	83,979	66,685	59,605
Leveraged buyouts: Number .	Number . .	11	231	254	255	337	279	383	382	254
Value.	Mil. dol. . .	236	4,519	18,718	19,670	45,160	36,228	47,068	66,915	16,022
Form of payment: All cash. . . .	Percent . .	8	24	36	40	43	54	60	43	46
All stock	Percent . .	19	13	12	10	12	11	5	10	6
Combination cash, stock debt, other.	Percent . .	17	28	26	24	20	18	25	37	33
Undisclosed [1]	Percent . .	56	35	26	26	25	17	10	10	15
Ownership status of acquisition targets:										
Public acquired company:										
Number	Number . .	398	554	835	823	865	1,011	984	1,124	915
Value.	Mil. dol. . .	11,948	31,899	85,692	91,653	109,217	103,029	130,385	168,852	89,974
Private acquired company:										
Number	Number . .	1,059	1,195	1,555	1,621	2,168	1,739	1,848	1,600	1,695
Value.	Mil. dol. . .	15,911	8,344	10,069	10,608	24,454	15,067	24,089	18,236	17,939

[1] Price was given but form of payment was not.

No. 854. Mergers and Acquisitions—Number and Value of Transactions by, Industry: 1990

[See headnote table 853]

INDUSTRY	TOTAL		U.S. COMPANY ACQUIRING U.S. COMPANY		FOREIGN COMPANY ACQUIRING U.S. COMPANY		U.S. COMPANY ACQUIRING FOREIGN COMPANY	
	Number	Value (mil. dol.)	Number	Value (mil. dol.)	Number	Value (mil. dol.)	Number	Value (mil. dol.)
Total activity [1]	4,168	172,319	3,244	107,210	599	47,595	325	17,514
Agriculture, forestry, fishing.	13	57	10	54	2	3	1	(NA)
Mining.	208	11,646	165	6,401	29	5,091	14	154
Construction.	35	281	30	229	5	52	-	(X)
Manufacturing:								
Food and kindred products	92	9,246	65	3,716	16	781	11	4,749
Textile mill products	29	212	21	83	1	43	7	86
Apparel, other textile products	25	544	21	134	1	410	3	(NA)
Lumber and wood products	14	258	10	202	3	56	1	(NA)
Paper and allied products	41	5,682	24	5,314	4	235	13	133
Printing and publishing	130	3,953	95	2,162	29	1,334	6	457
Chemicals and allied products	193	15,612	119	3,787	54	11,545	20	280
Rubber and plastic products.	53	2,298	40	1,399	6	877	7	22
Stone, clay, glass, and concrete	43	4,839	21	1,579	17	3,030	5	230
Primary metals industries.	51	1,572	32	620	17	309	2	643
Fabricated metal products	89	2,715	64	1,536	21	947	4	232
Industrial machinery, computer equipment .	233	5,978	170	4,263	43	1,638	20	77
Electrical and electronic equipment	186	6,381	131	3,885	37	1,811	18	685
Transportation equipment	63	4,837	40	1,552	12	570	11	2,715
Instruments and related products	144	2,778	108	1,094	26	1,661	10	23
Transportation and public utilities	343	19,838	292	14,224	32	1,321	19	4,293
Wholesale trade	266	3,132	190	1,888	38	1,008	38	236
Retail trade	158	7,373	126	4,660	23	2,650	9	63
Finance, insurance, real estate	905	28,142	808	21,337	78	6,015	19	790
Services	744	32,746	585	26,161	86	5,504	73	1,081

- Represents or rounds to zero.   NA Not available.   X Not applicable.   [1] Includes other industries, not shown separately.
Source of tables 853 and 854: MLR Publishing Company, Philadelphia, PA, *Mergers and Acquisitions,* 1991, (copyright). Publication contains extract from database, M&A Database.

No. 855. Employee Stock Ownership Plans—Number of Plans and Participants: 1975 to 1990

[As of **end of year**]

YEAR	Number of plans	Number of employees (1,000)	YEAR	Number of plans	Number of employees (1,000)	YEAR	Number of plans	Number of employees (1,000)
1975.	1,601	248	1981.	5,680	4,537	1986.	8,046	7,860
1977.	3,137	1,658	1982.	6,082	4,745	1987.	8,514	8,860
1978.	4,028	2,800	1983.	6,456	5,397	1988.	8,862	9,076
1979.	4,551	3,039	1984.	6,904	6,576	1989.	9,385	10,631
1980.	5,009	4,048	1985.	7,402	7,353	1990.	9,870	11,271

Source: National Center for Employee Ownership, Inc., Oakland, CA, unpublished data.

No. 856. Patents and Trademarks: 1980 to 1990

[**In thousands.** Calendar year data. Covers patents issued to citizens of the United States and residents of foreign countries. For data on copyrights, see table 902. For data on foreign countries, see table 1390. See also *Historical Statistics, Colonial Times to 1970*, series W 96-108]

ITEM	1980	1982	1983	1984	1985	1986	1987	1988	1989	1990
Patent applications filed	113.0	118.4	112.4	120.6	127.1	133.0	139.8	151.9	166.3	176.7
Inventions	104.3	109.6	103.7	111.3	117.0	122.4	127.9	139.8	152.8	164.5
Designs.	7.8	8.2	8.1	8.7	9.6	9.9	11.2	11.3	12.6	11.3
Botanical plants	0.2	0.2	0.3	0.3	0.2	0.3	0.4	0.4	0.4	0.4
Reissues	0.6	0.4	0.3	0.3	0.3	0.3	0.4	0.4	0.5	0.5
Patents issued	66.2	63.3	62.0	72.7	77.2	76.9	89.4	84.3	102.5	99.1
Inventions	61.8	57.9	56.9	67.2	71.7	70.9	83.0	77.9	95.5	90.4
Individuals.	13.3	11.9	10.5	12.3	12.9	13.3	15.3	14.3	17.9	17.3
Corporations: United States	29.4	25.8	25.7	30.1	31.3	29.6	33.8	31.4	38.7	36.1
Foreign [1]	18.2	19.2	19.6	23.6	26.4	27.0	32.9	31.4	38.0	36.0
U.S. Government	1.0	1.0	1.0	1.2	1.1	1.0	1.0	0.7	0.9	1.0
Designs.	3.9	4.9	4.6	4.9	5.1	5.5	6.0	5.7	6.1	8.0
Botanical plants	0.1	0.2	0.2	0.2	0.2	0.2	0.2	0.4	0.6	0.3
Reissues	0.3	0.3	0.4	0.3	0.3	0.3	0.2	0.2	0.3	0.4
U.S. residents [2]	40.8	37.7	36.6	42.2	43.3	42.0	47.7	44.6	54.6	52.9
Foreign country residents [2]	25.4	25.6	25.4	30.5	33.9	34.9	41.7	39.7	47.9	46.2
Percent of total	38	41	41	42	44	45	47	47	47	47
Other published documents [3]	(Z)	(Z)	(Z)	(Z)	(Z)	0.2	0.2	0.2	0.2	0.1
Trademarks:										
Applications filed.	46,837	63,745	55,545	62,600	65,134	69,091	71,292	78,345	94,401	127,346
Issued:	24.7	48.4	46.8	54.0	71.7	51.8	51.4	54.3	63.1	60.8
Trademarks.	18.9	42.4	40.5	48.6	65.8	46.7	47.3	47.4	55.3	53.6
Trademark renewals	5.9	6.0	6.2	5.4	5.9	5.1	4.1	6.9	7.8	7.2

Z Less than 50. [1] Includes patents to foreign governments. [2] Includes patents for inventions, designs, botanical plants, and reissues. [3] Includes Defensive Publications, a practice which began in November 1968 and ended in July 1986; and Statutory Invention Registrations, the current practice, which began May 1985. These documents are patent applications, which are published to provide the defensive properties of a patent, but do not have the enforceable rights of a patent.

Source: U.S. Patent and Trademark Office. Fiscal-year figures are published in the *Commissioner of Patents and Trademarks Annual Report.*

No. 857. Patents, by State: 1990

[Includes only U.S. patents granted to residents of the United States and territories]

STATE	Total	Inventions	Designs	Botanical plants	Reissue	STATE	Total	Inventions	Designs	Botanical plants	Reissue
U.S. [1] . .	52,855	47,393	5,068	153	241	MT.	72	66	5	-	1
						NE.	147	133	13	-	1
AL.	355	308	46	-	1	NV.	127	105	19	-	3
AK.	34	31	2	-	1	NH.	328	303	23	-	2
AZ.	737	664	72	-	1	NJ	3,090	2,830	240	12	8
AR.	148	125	23	-	-	NM.	198	192	4	-	2
CA.	7,922	6,944	866	75	37	NY.	4,524	4,059	445	1	19
CO.	830	746	78	-	6	NC.	848	740	106	1	1
CT.	1,512	1,360	151	-	1	ND.	50	41	9	-	-
DE.	434	417	16	-	1	OH.	2,727	2,374	326	15	12
DC.	48	39	9	-	-	OK.	632	564	64	1	3
FL.	1,904	1,663	212	14	15	OR.	640	542	90	3	5
GA.	723	628	79	9	7	PA.	2,820	2,625	173	6	16
HI	84	71	12	-	1	RI	181	142	39	-	-
ID	190	164	25	1	-	SC.	407	373	30	-	4
IL.	2,935	2,608	309	1	17	SD.	41	33	8	-	-
IN	1,049	935	111	-	3	TN	559	513	44	-	2
IA	388	346	40	-	2	TX	3,176	2,926	232	2	16
KS	328	242	83	1	2	UT.	368	324	43	-	1
KY	310	284	25	-	1	VT.	145	128	17	-	-
LA	505	469	32	-	4	VA.	824	746	78	-	-
ME.	113	99	14	-	-	WA	951	869	72	7	3
MD.	889	825	53	1	10	WV	166	154	12	-	-
MA.	2,113	1,957	151	-	5	WI	1,216	1,068	140	-	8
MI	2,707	2,529	170	-	8	WY	36	27	9	-	-
MN.	1,474	1,316	148	3	7						
MS.	129	116	11	-	2	PR	16	12	4	-	-
MO	702	616	84	-	2	VI	2	2	-	-	-

- Represents zero. [1] Includes patents not distributed by State.

Source: U.S. Patent and Trademark Office, *Technology Assessment and Forecast Data Base.*

No. 858. Patents, by Industry: 1970 to 1990

[Includes all patents for inventions granted to residents of the United States, its territories, and foreign citizens. Number of patents by industry may not add to total since a patent may be recorded in more than one industry category. Except for totals, data for all years have been revised to reflect the U.S. Patent Classification System as of 1990]

SIC [1] code	INDUSTRY	1970	1980	1985	1988	1989	1990
(X)	**Total**	**64,429**	**61,819**	**71,661**	**77,924**	**95,539**	**90,366**
(X)	Durable goods:						
32	Stone, clay, glass and concrete products	1,227	1,289	1,380	1,481	1,859	1,729
33, 3462-3	Primary metals	639	623	689	758	858	737
34	Fabricated metal products [2]	5,142	5,146	5,629	5,882	7,203	6,969
35	Machinery, except electrical	15,758	14,361	16,781	17,331	20,092	18,466
36, 3825	Electrical and electronic equipment, and supplies	13,038	10,449	13,644	16,145	20,100	18,850
37, 348	Transportation and other public utilities	3,053	2,911	3,569	4,061	4,586	4,405
38	Professional and scientific instruments [3]	7,293	7,665	9,166	10,707	13,571	13,010
(X)	Nondurable goods:						
20	Food and kindred products	488	482	545	531	803	726
22	Textile mill products	480	420	498	498	621	501
28	Chemicals and allied products	8,806	9,828	10,238	10,090	12,704	12,377
13, 29	Petroleum, oil and gas extraction	829	729	959	794	962	830
30	Rubber and miscellaneous plastics products	2,478	2,647	3,119	3,308	4,009	3,892
(X)	All other SIC [1] groups	5,100	5,259	5,432	6,213	7,892	7,486

X Not applicable.   [1] Standard Industrial Classification.   [2] Excludes SIC groups 3462, 3463, and 348.   [3] Excludes SIC group 3825.

Source: U.S. Patent and Trademark Office, *Patenting Trends in the United States, State Country Report, 1963-1990.*

No. 859. Consumer Packaged Goods—New Product Introductions: 1980 to 1991

[**Consumer packaged goods:** consumable products packaged by the manufacturer for retail sale primarily through grocery and drug stores. **New product:** a product not previously offered for sale by a particular manufacturer including new varieties, formats, sizes, and packaging for existing products]

ITEM	Food	Bever-ages	Health and beauty	House-hold prod-ucts	Pet prod-ucts	Miscella-neous products
Domestic and imports:						
1980	1,192	256	834	331	86	197
1981	1,356	262	868	315	74	237
1982	1,762	332	919	390	103	113
1983	3,013	587	1,355	473	138	105
1984	2,678	569	1,094	303	108	227
1985	2,327	585	1,222	463	139	294
1986	2,764	657	1,327	365	107	194
1987	2,895	634	1,526	362	152	292
1988	2,781	597	1,496	310	151	222
1989	2,866	524	1,492	313	204	206
1990	3,453	630	1,531	432	164	154
1991, total	**3,130**	**589**	**1,614**	**422**	**175**	**113**
Percent:						
New brands [1]	33.8	37.9	27.0	30.6	40.6	43.4
Brand extensions [2]	0.9	0.5	0.8	1.2	0.6	1.8
Line extensions [3]	65.3	61.6	72.2	68.2	58.8	54.8
Types of new product innovation (percent): [4]						
Formulation [5]	56.5	63.6	44.3	47.7	59.3	42.9
New market [6]	0.5	-	1.5	-	-	-
Packaging [7]	12.1	9.0	15.7	20.5	11.1	14.2
Positioning [8]	29.0	27.4	36.4	31.8	29.6	42.9
Technology [9]	1.9	-	2.1	-	-	-
CUMULATIVE						
Domestic, except imports, 1980-91	26,768	5,148	14,230	4,274	1,541	2,189
Imports, 1980-91 [10]	3,449	1,074	1,048	205	60	165
International, 1985-91 [11]	10,289	2,979	9,054	1,980	427	736

- Represents or rounds to zero.   [1] Product introduced under completely or partly new brand name.   [2] Product introduced in a category with an existing brand name which has not been used in the category before.   [3] Introduction of a new variety, format, size or package of an existing product/brand name.   [4] Product which offers consumers something significantly different from existing products.   [5] Added or new ingredient which offers a benefit not previously provided by existing products in its category.   [6] Special category for new products which do not compete with any existing category of products.   [7] New product packaged in a way that makes it easier to store, handle, prepare, or dispense than others in its category.   [8] New product presented for new users or uses compared to existing products in its category.   [9] New product with added consumer benefits resulting from use of a new technology.   [10] New products introduced in the U.S. by foreign companies.   [11] New products introduced by U.S. and foreign companies outside the United States.

Source: Marketing Intelligence Service Ltd., Naples, New York, *Product Alert Weekly.* Publication contains extract from database, Productscan.

No. 860. Gross Stock of Fixed Private Capital, Nonresidential and Residential, by Industry: 1970 to 1990

[In billions of dollars. Estimates as of Dec. 31. Based on the *1987 Standard Industrial Classification Manual;* see text, section 13]

INDUSTRY	CURRENT DOLLARS				CONSTANT (1987) DOLLARS			
	1970	1980	1985	1990	1970	1980	1985	1990
Fixed private capital.	2,689.0	9,364.1	12,746.6	16,821.0	8,131.2	11,584.7	13,322.3	15,214.5
Nonresidential	1,469.6	5,072.1	7,156.4	9,433.0	4,250.1	6,263.6	7,388.5	8,459.1
Agriculture, forestry and fisheries	96.7	333.2	398.2	418.1	300.6	436.1	418.5	369.5
Farms	90.7	308.6	363.1	370.6	282.6	405.0	382.0	326.9
Agr. serv., forestry and fisheries	6.0	24.6	35.1	47.6	18.0	31.1	36.6	42.5
Mining	83.5	403.3	541.4	516.1	282.4	383.7	495.8	445.7
Metal mining	6.9	30.6	40.0	42.0	21.3	39.6	41.7	37.0
Coal mining	4.7	31.0	46.0	49.9	15.1	39.3	47.8	43.9
Oil and gas extraction.	67.2	323.2	431.4	395.5	231.2	280.8	381.4	339.7
Nonmetallic minerals, exc. fuels	4.7	18.4	23.9	28.8	14.8	24.0	25.0	25.1
Construction.	28.1	91.8	96.4	113.3	87.3	120.0	102.4	100.9
Manufacturing.	338.4	1,144.5	1,598.6	2,088.7	1,001.1	1,480.7	1,694.1	1,873.3
Durable goods.	184.0	622.6	873.1	1,122.2	533.7	797.9	922.5	1,013.7
Lumber and wood products	7.8	31.0	37.1	41.8	24.2	40.5	39.5	37.3
Furniture and fixtures.	2.6	9.6	13.7	19.1	7.7	12.6	14.5	17.3
Stone, clay, glass products.	14.6	47.8	57.9	63.1	44.9	61.4	61.4	57.5
Primary metal industries.	49.0	143.2	178.0	203.3	144.3	185.6	188.7	179.9
Fabricated metal products	19.8	70.0	95.5	124.4	57.6	90.2	101.6	111.6
Machinery, exc. electrical.	28.2	99.8	148.1	194.0	75.7	123.2	155.1	178.9
Elec. and elec. equipment	16.5	65.4	115.6	167.4	46.8	84.8	121.2	152.0
Motor vehicles and equipment	22.4	73.3	95.1	116.5	65.8	93.6	101.3	104.6
Other transp. equipment	12.7	41.2	65.4	95.9	36.6	53.1	68.9	86.4
Instruments, related products	7.1	29.5	51.4	77.8	20.4	37.6	54.1	71.3
Misc. mfg. industries	3.4	11.8	15.2	18.9	9.8	15.3	16.2	16.9
Nondurable goods	154.4	521.9	725.5	966.5	467.4	682.8	771.7	859.6
Food and kindred products.	33.9	103.8	141.8	189.2	103.5	137.2	151.8	168.6
Tobacco manufacturers	1.4	5.3	10.7	14.5	4.0	7.0	11.3	13.0
Textile mill products	11.5	34.7	43.4	51.1	36.9	47.1	47.0	45.6
Apparel; other textile products.	3.2	11.8	15.3	18.0	9.4	15.4	16.4	16.1
Paper and allied products.	20.8	69.8	98.7	143.4	63.9	91.9	105.0	126.5
Printing and publishing.	10.7	36.1	52.7	81.0	33.3	47.8	56.2	74.2
Chemicals, allied products	41.0	149.6	202.6	271.5	119.5	192.1	213.9	239.3
Petroleum and coal products	21.7	71.4	107.5	127.0	65.6	92.6	113.4	112.8
Rubber; misc. plastic products	9.3	36.7	49.4	66.9	28.3	48.0	52.9	59.9
Leather and leather products	1.0	2.8	3.5	4.4	3.0	3.2	3.7	3.6
Transportation and public utilities	483.2	1,498.3	1,940.5	2,423.9	1,348.7	1,810.2	1,978.5	2,143.3
Transportation.	192.6	492.4	572.1	617.1	555.1	603.1	580.5	553.0
Railroad transportation.	114.1	232.0	253.1	251.4	332.6	281.1	252.0	226.0
Local, interurban pass. transit	5.1	8.9	10.3	12.6	14.4	11.2	10.7	11.5
Trucking and warehousing	20.7	77.5	100.9	106.4	60.5	101.6	105.2	96.1
Water transportation	14.5	46.6	51.0	54.8	39.3	56.5	53.3	48.5
Transportation by air	19.0	64.0	83.1	106.2	51.5	78.9	85.5	95.7
Pipelines, exc. natural gas	9.8	33.3	37.4	41.3	28.5	40.1	37.9	35.8
Transportation services	9.3	30.0	36.4	44.4	28.2	33.8	35.9	39.4
Communication	101.8	360.2	492.9	622.2	249.7	426.7	505.8	561.4
Telephone and telegraph	95.8	336.4	444.6	539.5	233.3	395.3	455.5	485.9
Radio and TV broadcasting	6.0	23.8	48.4	82.7	16.5	31.4	50.3	75.5
Elec., gas, and sanitary services.	188.7	645.7	875.5	1,184.6	544.0	780.4	892.2	1,028.9
Electric services	136.5	492.6	677.1	916.4	391.7	596.3	690.2	791.8
Gas services	46.6	135.3	170.7	210.1	136.2	163.6	174.0	183.2
Sanitary services	5.6	17.8	27.7	58.2	16.0	20.4	28.0	53.8
Wholesale trade	40.7	160.5	276.3	394.8	107.6	199.6	286.6	366.7
Retail trade	75.8	259.6	412.8	606.2	216.5	334.8	432.3	547.8
Finance, insurance, real estate.	216.8	794.3	1,302.7	2,031.9	619.8	1,006.3	1,362.9	1,842.3
Banking	22.4	126.1	235.4	407.9	60.9	151.2	244.5	377.7
Credit agencies other than banks	6.2	39.1	58.2	105.5	16.7	44.8	59.9	95.9
Security and commodity brokers and services	1.1	3.8	8.6	12.9	2.6	4.4	8.8	12.4
Insurance carriers	5.6	21.8	56.2	122.4	13.4	25.3	57.2	120.2
Insurance agents, brokers, and services . . .	1.9	4.8	5.4	5.9	3.9	5.0	5.5	5.7
Real estate.	177.5	589.6	919.5	1,349.6	517.8	765.5	967.4	1,203.4
Holding, other investment companies	2.1	9.0	19.3	27.7	4.6	10.2	19.6	27.0
Services.	106.3	386.7	589.6	840.1	286.1	492.1	617.3	769.7
Hotels, other lodging places	20.1	63.2	96.0	129.5	60.0	82.4	101.0	115.4
Personal services	7.9	20.7	24.2	32.1	19.9	26.0	25.2	29.7
Business services	18.7	88.4	149.7	216.9	48.0	111.2	157.2	198.3
Auto repair; serv., garages.	16.3	68.2	103.4	145.6	43.9	86.5	107.0	136.8
Misc. repair services.	2.4	9.4	12.3	14.9	7.0	12.0	12.9	13.5
Motion pictures	2.8	9.0	11.4	19.8	6.8	10.8	12.1	18.4
Amusement, recreation services.	10.0	28.5	34.8	41.7	27.3	36.4	36.3	37.5
Other services.	28.1	99.5	157.8	239.6	73.3	126.8	164.8	220.0
Health services	14.0	50.6	83.0	130.0	38.8	64.9	86.9	117.7
Legal services	2.8	7.9	14.5	25.5	7.0	9.9	15.1	24.2
Educational services	1.4	2.6	3.6	5.5	2.9	3.1	3.8	5.0
Other [1]	9.8	38.4	56.7	78.6	24.6	48.9	59.0	73.0
Residential	1,219.4	4,292.0	5,590.2	7,387.9	3,881.1	5,321.2	5,933.8	6,755.4
Farms.	50.9	129.1	144.7	159.8	161.6	160.8	153.1	146.4
Real estate	1,168.5	4,162.9	5,445.5	7,228.1	3,719.5	5,160.4	5,780.7	6,609.0

[1] Consists of social services, membership organizations, and miscellaneous professional services.

Source: U.S. Bureau of Economic Analysis, *Survey of Current Business,* January 1992.

No. 861. Fixed Nonresidential Private Capital Valued in Current and Constant (1987) Dollars: 1980 to 1991

[In billions of dollars. Stocks as of **Dec. 31;** depreciation over entire calendar year. Data refer to privately owned assets and are based on the fixed capital formation components of the gross domestic product. Excludes residential capital and government enterprises; includes nonprofit institutions. Gross stocks allow for retirement; net stocks allow for retirement and depreciation. Net stock and depreciation estimates are based on the straight-line depreciation formula. For manufacturing industry, see table 1307]

ITEM	CURRENT DOLLARS						CONSTANT (1987) DOLLARS					
	1980	1985	1988	1989	1990	1991	1980	1985	1988	1989	1990	1991
Gross stocks	5,072.1	7,156.4	8,488.0	8,933.7	9,433.0	9,748.7	6,263.6	7,388.5	8,045.3	8,256.3	8,459.1	8,641.2
Equipment	2,388.7	3,373.6	4,009.9	4,201.7	4,447.2	4,659.8	3,008.8	3,518.4	3,854.6	3,965.9	4,069.2	4,178.4
Structures	2,683.4	3,782.8	4,478.2	4,732.0	4,985.8	5,088.9	3,254.8	3,870.1	4,190.8	4,290.4	4,389.8	4,462.8
Net stocks	2,974.2	4,112.7	4,810.3	5,033.7	5,280.3	5,413.0	3,677.4	4,247.8	4,561.9	4,657.5	4,742.4	4,809.5
Equipment	1,359.8	1,851.8	2,173.9	2,262.6	2,373.4	2,471.6	1,709.2	1,929.0	2,092.0	2,142.3	2,181.5	2,227.6
Structures	1,614.5	2,260.8	2,636.4	2,771.0	2,906.9	2,941.4	1,968.3	2,318.9	2,469.8	2,515.2	2,560.9	2,581.9
Depreciation	239.6	357.9	419.6	448.6	466.6	486.4	307.8	367.8	408.1	425.0	434.2	446.2
Equipment	161.3	239.7	285.5	304.0	318.2	333.9	211.0	249.8	280.9	293.3	302.3	312.6
Structures	78.4	118.2	134.1	144.6	148.4	152.5	96.9	118.0	127.3	131.6	131.9	133.6

Source: U.S. Bureau of Economic Analysis, *Survey of Current Business,* January 1992; and unpublished data.

No. 862. Business Expenditures for New Plant and Equipment: 1980 to 1992

[In billions of dollars. Based on sample and subject to sampling variability; see text, section 17. Represents expenditures facilities and for expansion or replacement of existing facilities that are chargeable to fixed asset accounts and for which depreciation or amortization accounts are ordinarily maintained. Excludes expenditures for land and mineral rights; maintenance and repair; used plant and equipment, including that purchased or acquired through mergers or acquisitions; assets located in foreign countries; residential structures; etc. They also differ from the nonresidential fixed investment data in type of detail, data sources, coverage, and timing. For further information, see the February 1985 *Survey of Current Business]*

INDUSTRY	1980	1983	1984	1985	1986	1987	1988	1989	1990	1991	1992, plans
All industries [1]	286.4	321.2	373.8	410.1	399.4	410.5	455.5	507.4	532.6	530.0	558.6
(1987 dollars) [2]	354.6	337.7	390.9	424.5	405.9	410.6	443.2	482.3	498.1	492.8	521.0
Manufacturing	112.6	117.4	139.6	152.9	138.0	141.1	163.5	183.8	192.6	184.3	184.1
Durable goods [3]	54.8	51.6	64.6	70.9	65.7	68.0	77.0	82.6	82.6	77.0	79.4
Primary metals	6.7	5.9	6.8	7.5	6.7	8.6	11.0	12.0	12.2	11.0	10.0
Electrical machinery	10.2	12.7	16.2	17.1	15.6	16.8	20.8	20.5	22.0	21.2	22.7
Machinery, except electrical	10.7	12.0	13.6	13.8	11.4	11.9	13.7	14.6	13.7	12.3	12.5
Transportation equipment	16.1	11.9	16.6	19.6	18.9	16.7	15.8	18.7	17.9	16.7	17.8
Nondurable goods [3]	57.8	65.7	75.0	82.0	72.3	73.0	86.4	101.2	110.0	107.3	104.7
Food and beverage	8.5	8.5	9.7	11.4	11.6	12.1	14.2	15.9	16.4	17.7	18.8
Paper	6.4	5.7	6.9	8.1	8.3	8.5	10.9	15.6	16.5	11.9	10.6
Chemicals	10.6	11.6	13.5	14.4	14.5	13.9	16.6	18.5	20.6	21.2	22.5
Petroleum	22.8	29.5	32.6	34.1	23.1	22.1	26.0	30.1	34.8	37.2	31.9
Mining	12.7	10.6	11.9	12.0	8.2	8.3	9.3	9.2	9.9	10.1	9.5
Public utilities	41.3	53.0	57.5	59.6	56.6	56.3	60.4	66.3	67.2	66.0	71.4
Transportation	13.6	10.8	13.4	14.6	15.1	15.1	16.6	18.8	21.5	22.2	26.2
Wholesale and retail trade	32.0	44.5	53.4	60.1	65.4	68.5	76.4	84.5	95.6	(NA)	(NA)
Finance and insurance	22.6	32.0	37.9	45.2	49.6	54.1	59.2	70.3	69.0	(NA)	(NA)
Personal and business services [4]	24.9	25.1	28.5	28.8	28.4	30.1	32.9	34.6	33.7	(NA)	(NA)
Communication	26.8	27.9	31.6	37.1	38.2	37.2	37.2	39.8	43.1	(NA)	(NA)

NA Not available. [1] Surveyed quarterly. [2] For preparation of constant-dollar estimates, see source for detail. [3] Includes industries not shown separately. [4] Includes construction.
Source: U.S. Bureau of the Census, *Plant and Equipment Expenditures and Plans,* quarterly.

No. 863. Gross Private Domestic Investment: 1970 to 1990

[In billions of dollars]

YEAR	CURRENT DOLLARS						CONSTANT (1987) DOLLARS					
	Gross private domestic investment				Less: Capital consumption allowances [2]	Equals: Net private domestic investment	Gross private domestic investment				Less: Capital consumption allowances [2]	Equals: Net private domestic investment
	Total [1]	Fixed investment	Non-residential	Residential			Total [1]	Fixed investment	Non-residential	Residential		
1970	150	148	107	41	89	62	430	424	292	132	258	172
1980	468	477	354	123	312	156	594	603	438	165	401	194
1985	715	690	504	186	455	260	746	724	522	202	472	274
1986	718	709	492	217	479	239	735	727	500	226	487	248
1987	749	723	498	225	502	247	749	723	498	225	502	247
1988	794	777	545	232	534	260	773	753	531	223	519	255
1989	838	802	571	231	575	263	789	757	542	214	542	247
1990	803	803	587	216	595	208	745	744	549	196	551	194

[1] Includes change in inventories, not shown separately. [2] With capital consumption adjustment.
Source: U.S. Bureau of Economic Analysis, *Survey of Current Business,* January 1992; and unpublished data.

No. 864. Composite Indexes of Economic Cyclical Indicators: 1980 to 1990

[1990 figures are preliminary. See source for discussion of composite indexes. Minus sign (-) indicates decrease. **Leading indicators** are economic time series that tend to reach their cyclical high and low points earlier than the corresponding peaks and troughs in the overall economy. **Coincident indicators** are economic time series that tend to reach their cyclical high and low points about the same time as the corresponding peaks and troughs in the overall economy. **Lagging indicators** are economic time series that tend to reach their cyclical high and low points later than the corresponding peaks and troughs in the overall economy]

ITEM	Unit	1980	1982	1983	1984	1985	1986	1987	1988	1989	1990
LEADING INDICATORS											
Composite index	1982=100. . .	99.2	100.0	116.2	121.7	124.0	132.4	140.1	142.4	145.0	144.0
Building permits [1]	1967=100. . .	96.7	80.7	131.1	134.8	138.1	141.2	122.9	115.8	107.7	89.5
Common stock prices, index [2]	1941-43=100.	118.8	119.7	160.4	160.5	186.8	236.4	286.6	265.8	322.8	334.6
Initial claims, unemployment insurance . .	1,000	480	578	426	366	383	370	314	305	327	383
Change in sensitive materials prices [3][4] . .	Percent	0.4	-0.9	1.1	0.2	-0.8	0.4	1.1	0.4	0.1	-0.3
Vendor performance, slower deliveries . .	Percent	41	44	57	57	48	57	58	58	48	48
Average workweek, manufacturing [5] . . .	Hours	39.7	38.9	40.1	40.7	40.5	40.7	41.0	41.1	41.0	40.8
Plant and equipment contracts and orders (1982 dol.)	Bil. dol.	332	280	288	350	381	383	433	496	550	546
New orders, manufacturing, consumer goods and materials (1982 dol.)	Bil. dol.	909	837	934	1,016	1,022	1,043	1,098	1,120	1,129	1,109
Money supply (M2) [6] (1982 dol.)	Bil. dol.	1,836	1,875	2,044	2,119	2,228	2,365	2,433	2,458	2,437	2,433
Consumer expectations index [7]	1966=100. . .	56.8	62.7	84.7	92.7	86.5	85 8	81.3	85.2	85.3	70.2
Change in manufacturers' unfilled orders, durable goods (1982 dol.) [4]	Bil. dol.	-12	-31	16	30	3	2	18	17	27	9
COINCIDENT INDICATORS											
Composite index	1982=100. . .	107.2	100.0	101.9	112.3	116.3	119.0	123.6	130.0	133.5	132.8
Industrial production index	1987=100. . .	84.1	81.9	84.9	92.8	94.4	95.3	100.0	105.4	108.1	109.2
Employees, nonagricultural payrolls	Million	90.4	89.6	90.2	94.5	97.5	99.5	102.2	105.5	108.3	110.0
Personal income less transfer payments (1987 dol.)	Bil. dol.	2,722	2,776	2,812	3,015	3,110	3,200	3,260	3,357	3,441	3,483
Sales, mfg. and trade (1982 dol.)	Bil. dol.	4,341	4,184	4,362	4,726	4,870	5,046	5,338	5,587	5,722	5,747
LAGGING INDICATORS											
Composite index	1982=100. . .	105.5	100.0	91.4	100.7	107.5	111.4	110.6	114.3	119.3	119.2
Change in labor cost per unit of output, manufacturing [4]	Percent	10.1	4.1	-3.3	1.6	1.8	-0.2	-2.6	3.1	1.2	2.2
Ratio, consumer installment credit to personal income	Percent	13.2	11.8	12.0	13.0	14.3	15.3	15.5	15.7	16.0	15.6
Average prime rate charged by banks. . .	Percent	15.3	14.9	10.8	12.0	9.9	8.3	8.2	9.3	10.9	10.0
Average duration of unemployment	Weeks	11.9	15.6	20.0	18.2	15.6	15.0	14.5	13.5	11.9	12.1
Ratio, inventories to sales, mfg. and trade (1982 dol.) [8]	Ratio.	1.6	1.7	1.6	1.6	1.6	1.5	1.5	1.5	1.5	1.5
Commercial and industrial loans outstanding (1982 dol.) [8]	Bil. dol.	225	268	261	296	329	349	354	364	390	402
Change in CPI for services [4][9]	Percent	15.2	6.8	3.1	5.6	5.0	4.8	4.2	4.7	5.0	5.9

[1] New private housing units authorized. [2] Standard and Poor's 500 stocks. [3] Producer prices of selected crude and intermediate materials and spot market prices of selected raw industrial materials. [4] Smoothed by an autoregressive-moving-average filter developed by Statistics Canada. [5] Production workers. [6] See table 803. [7] Copyrighted by the University of Michigan's Survey Research Center. [8] Includes commercial paper issued by nonfinancial companies. [9] Consumer Price Index.

Source: U.S. Bureau of Economic Analysis, *Survey of Current Business,* monthly.

No. 865. Business Cycle Expansions and Contractions—Months of Duration: 1919 to 1990

[A trough is the low point of a business cycle; a peak is the high point. Contraction or recession, is the period from peak to subsequent trough; expansion is the period from trough to subsequent peak. Business cycle reference dates are determined by the National Bureau of Economic Research, Inc.]

BUSINESS CYCLE REFERENCE DATE		Contraction (trough from previous peak)	Expansion (trough to peak)	LENGTH OF CYCLE	
Trough	Peak			Trough from previous trough	Peak from previous peak
March 1919.	January 1920	[1]7	10	[2]51	[1]17
July 1921	May 1923	18	22	28	40
July 1924	October 1926	14	27	36	41
November 1927.	August 1929.	13	21	40	34
March 1933.	May 1937	43	50	64	93
June 1938.	February 1945	13	80	63	93
October 1945	November 1948	8	37	88	45
October 1949	July 1953.	11	45	48	56
May 1954	August 1957.	10	39	55	49
April 1958.	April 1960	8	24	47	32
February 1961.	December 1969	10	106	34	116
November 1970.	November 1973	11	36	117	47
March 1975.	January 1980	16	58	52	74
July 1980	July 1981.	6	12	64	18
November 1982.	July 1990.	16	92	28	108
Average, all cycles:					
1919 to 1945 (six cycles)	. . . .	18	35	53	53
1945 to 1990 (eight cycles). . . .	. . . .	11	[3]50	56	[3]61

[1] Previous peak: August 1918. [2] Previous trough: December 1914. [3] For nine cycles.

Source: U.S. Bureau of Economic Analysis, *Survey of Current Business,* April 1992.

No. 866. Manufacturing and Trade—Sales and Inventories in Current and Constant (1982) Dollars: 1980 to 1991

[In billions of dollars, except ratios]

ITEM	1980	1981	1982	1983	1984	1985	1986	1987	1988	1989	1990	1991
CURRENT DOLLARS												
Sales, average monthly	**328**	**357**	**349**	**370**	**412**	**424**	**432**	**459**	**496**	**526**	**543**	**535**
Manufacturing	154	168	163	173	191	195	195	206	224	237	243	239
Retail trade	80	87	89	98	107	115	121	129	138	145	151	152
Merchant wholesalers	93	102	96	100	113	115	116	124	135	144	149	145
Inventories [1]	**494**	**538**	**581**	**575**	**627**	**657**	**667**	**687**	**740**	**797**	**819**	**815**
Manufacturing	264	283	319	307	329	337	327	328	352	380	388	381
Retail trade	116	128	133	140	159	174	188	200	212	232	240	240
Merchant wholesalers	113	127	130	128	139	146	153	159	175	185	192	195
Inventory-sales ratio [2]	**1.51**	**1.51**	**1.66**	**1.55**	**1.52**	**1.55**	**1.54**	**1.50**	**1.49**	**1.52**	**1.51**	**1.52**
Manufacturing	1.71	1.68	1.96	1.77	1.72	1.73	1.68	1.59	1.57	1.60	1.60	1.59
Retail trade	1.45	1.47	1.49	1.43	1.49	1.51	1.55	1.55	1.54	1.60	1.59	1.58
Merchant wholesalers	1.22	1.25	1.35	1.28	1.23	1.27	1.32	1.28	1.30	1.28	1.29	1.34
CONSTANT (1982) DOLLARS												
Sales, average monthly [3]	**372**	**357**	**346**	**383**	**403**	**414**	**432**	**457**	**478**	**482**	**(NA)**	**(NA)**
Manufacturing	175	167	159	178	186	189	192	214	224	224	(NA)	(NA)
Retail trade	93	91	94	102	108	112	120	121	127	126	(NA)	(NA)
Merchant wholesalers	104	99	93	102	109	113	120	122	127	132	(NA)	(NA)
Inventories	**591**	**602**	**582**	**584**	**631**	**638**	**642**	**669**	**689**	**702**	**(NA)**	**(NA)**
Manufacturing	327	330	315	309	330	321	316	323	330	334	(NA)	(NA)
Retail trade	130	136	133	142	158	169	171	186	192	199	(NA)	(NA)
Merchant wholesalers	134	136	134	133	143	149	155	160	166	169	(NA)	(NA)
Inventory-sales ratios [4]	**1.59**	**1.68**	**1.68**	**1.53**	**1.56**	**1.54**	**1.49**	**1.46**	**1.44**	**1.46**	**(NA)**	**(NA)**
Manufacturing	1.87	1.98	1.99	1.74	1.77	1.70	1.64	1.51	1.47	1.49	(NA)	(NA)
Retail trade	1.40	1.48	1.41	1.39	1.46	1.51	1.43	1.54	1.52	1.58	(NA)	(NA)
Merchant wholesalers	1.29	1.37	1.44	1.30	1.31	1.32	1.29	1.31	1.31	1.28	(NA)	(NA)

NA Not available.   [1] Book value; seasonally adjusted end-of-year data. See text, section 17.   [2] Average inventories to average sales. Average inventories based on weighted averages of end-of-month figures.   [3] Average monthly sales for fourth quarter.   [4] End of fourth quarter inventories to average monthly sales for fourth quarter.

Source: Current dollars from U.S. Bureau of the Census, *Current Business Reports*, "Manufacturing and Trade Inventories and Sales" February 1990 and unpublished data; constant dollars from U.S. Bureau of Economic Analysis, *Survey of Current Business*, September issues.

No. 867. Manufacturing Corporations, Assets, and Profits, by Asset Size: 1970 to 1990

[Corporations and assets as of **end of 4th quarter**; profit for **entire year.** Through 1979, corporations under $10 million based on sample; $10 million and over based on complete canvass. The asset value for complete canvass was raised in 1980 to $25 million and again in 1988 to $50 million. Asset sizes less than these values continue to be sampled, except as noted. For details regarding methodology, see source for first quarter, 1988]

YEAR AND ITEM	Unit	Total	ASSET-SIZE CLASS						
			Under [1] $10 mil.	$10-$25 mil.	$25-$50 mil.	$50-$100 mil.	$100-$250 mil.	$250 mil. -$1 bil.	$1 bil. and over
Corporations:									
1970 [2]	Number	197,807	[3]195,000	1,202	533	366	289	218	102
1980	Number	(NA)	(NA)	1,777	941	590	491	369	244
1983	Number	(NA)	(NA)	(NA)	863	683	559	403	275
1984	Number	(NA)	(NA)	(NA)	872	703	601	420	287
1985	Number	(NA)	(NA)	(NA)	896	744	608	428	281
1986	Number	(NA)	(NA)	(NA)	962	741	628	445	291
1987	Number	(NA)	(NA)	(NA)	1,007	811	676	481	318
1988	Number	(NA)	(NA)	(NA)	(NA)	783	729	550	334
1989	Number	(NA)	(NA)	(NA)	(NA)	781	750	579	347
1990	Number	(NA)	(NA)	(NA)	(NA)	834	774	597	367
Assets:									
1970	Mil. dol	578,234	69,101	20,471	20,138	25,946	47,783	112,475	282,320
1980	Mil. dol	1,384,474	126,639	43,569	34,930	41,963	75,284	179,959	882,129
1983	Mil. dol	1,704,951	149,791	54,506	41,766	52,673	87,391	194,212	1,124,612
1984	Mil. dol	1,853,457	156,671	59,549	49,419	53,517	94,315	206,698	1,233,288
1985	Mil. dol	1,932,766	153,883	64,324	52,669	58,019	96,748	208,403	1,298,720
1986	Mil. dol	1,994,120	140,864	67,663	55,974	58,233	97,908	217,341	1,356,137
1987	Mil. dol	2,135,266	147,919	65,623	50,171	60,874	109,458	235,368	1,465,853
1988	Mil. dol	2,339,690	149,276	77,068	53,461	62,190	110,411	261,880	1,625,404
1989	Mil. dol	2,501,097	144,814	73,487	56,548	68,149	117,014	282,056	1,759,029
1990	Mil. dol	2,629,542	142,619	74,488	55,947	72,593	123,847	287,512	1,872,536
Net profit: [4]									
1970	Mil. dol	28,572	2,812	811	836	1,101	2,315	5,862	14,832
1980	Mil. dol	92,443	7,770	2,235	1,904	2,479	4,502	11,485	62,041
1983	Mil. dol	85,834	7,438	2,893	2,149	2,466	3,861	6,134	60,893
1984	Mil. dol	107,648	10,037	3,417	2,527	2,877	4,864	9,278	74,648
1985	Mil. dol	87,647	8,601	2,551	2,305	2,819	3,628	7,312	60,431
1986	Mil. dol	83,122	6,659	2,988	2,129	2,514	3,884	7,572	57,376
1987	Mil. dol	115,600	7,273	3,849	2,753	3,338	5,237	9,636	83,514
1988	Mil. dol	154,583	11,364	4,488	3,199	3,978	5,473	13,994	112,086
1989	Mil. dol	136,490	10,381	5,173	2,921	3,105	4,434	11,824	98,651
1990	Mil. dol	111,549	8,529	5,152	2,769	2,681	3,520	7,245	81,652

NA Not available.   [1] Beginning 1986, excludes estimates for corporations with less than $250,000 in assets at time of sample selection. Prior periods include estimates for corporations in this size category.   [2] Source: U.S. Securities and Exchange Commission.   [3] Data derived from U.S. Internal Revenue Service, *Statistics of Income,* annual.   [4] After taxes.

Source: Except as noted, through 1980, U.S. Federal Trade Commission; thereafter, U.S. Bureau of the Census, *Quarterly Financial Report for Manufacturing, Mining and Trade Corporations.*

No. 868. Largest Industrial Corporations—Sales, Assets, and Profits by Sales Group Rank: 1987 and 1991

[In billions of dollars, except percent. Excludes large privately owned companies that do not publish sales. Includes service and rental revenues, but companies must derive more than 50 percent of revenues from manufacturing or mining for years ending not later than **Dec. 31 of year stated,** sales exclude excise taxes collected by manufacturer and include discontinued operations. Minus sign (-) indicates decrease]

RANK BY SALES GROUP	SALES			ASSETS [1]			PROFITS [2]		
	1987	1991	Percent change, 1987-91	1987	1991	Percent change, 1987-91	1987	1991	Percent change 1987-1991
500 largest	1,880	2,263	20	1,706	2,458	44	91	55	-39
Top 100	1,307	1,619	24	1,217	1,844	51	66	38	-41
101-200	287	323	13	240	328	37	14	9	-36
201-300	142	160	13	123	151	23	5	4	-21
301-400	88	96	8	73	77	6	2	3	12
401-500	56	65	16	52	57	9	3	1	-72
Percent of total:									
Top 100	70	72	(X)	71	75	(X)	73	70	(X)
101-200	15	14	(X)	14	13	(X)	16	17	(X)
201-300	8	7	(X)	7	6	(X)	6	8	(X)
301-400	5	4	(X)	4	3	(X)	3	5	(X)
401-500	3	3	(X)	3	2	(X)	3	1	(X)

X Not applicable. [1] Total assets employed in business at end of fiscal year, less depreciation and depletion. [2] After taxes, special charges, and credits.

Source: Time Warner, New York, NY, *The Fortune Directories,* (copyright).

No. 869. 500 Largest Industrial Corporations—Selected Financial Items: 1970 to 1991

ITEM	Unit	1970	1980	1984	1985	1986	1987	1988	1989	1990	1991
Sales per employee	$1,000. . . .	29.5	71.1	100.6	106.0	110.7	124.4	137.9	146.0	154.1	159.7
Changes in profits.	Percent . . .	(NA)	(NA)	24.9	-19.1	-7.9	41.3	26.9	-8.1	-11.7	-41.0
Sales per dollar of stockholder's equity. .	Dollar	2.4	3.12	2.78	2.80	2.79	2.77	2.93	2.96	2.95	2.81
Return on stockholder's equity	Percent . . .	9.5	14.1	13.6	11.6	11.6	14.4	16.2	15.0	13.0	10.2
Return on sales	Percent . . .	3.9	4.5	4.5	3.9	4.1	5.1	5.5	4.6	4.1	3.2
Total return to investors [1]	Percent . . .	6.5	21.6	-0.8	26.3	16.1	6.6	14.1	17.5	-10.2	29.5

NA Not available. [1] Includes both price appreciation and dividend yield, i.e., to an investor in the company's stock.
Source: Time Warner, New York, NY, *The Fortune Directories,* (copyright).

No. 870. 500 Largest Industrial Corporations—Selected Financial Items, by Industry: 1987 and 1991

[Data are medians and are ranked based on sales per employee for latest year shown. See headnote, table 868. Minus sign (-) indicates decrease. For definition of median, see Guide to Tabular Presentation]

INDUSTRY	SALES PER EMPLOYEE ($1,000)		CHANGES IN PROFITS FROM PREVIOUS YEAR (percent)		SALES PER DOLLAR OF STOCKHOLDER'S EQUITY (dol.)		RETURN ON STOCKHOLDER'S EQUITY (percent)		RETURN ON SALES (percent)		TOTAL RETURN TO INVESTORS [1] (percent)	
	1987	1991	1987	1991	1987	1991	1987	1991	1987	1991	1987	1991
Total	124.4	159.7	41.3	11.6	2.77	2.81	14.4	10.2	5.1	3.2	6.6	29.5
Petroleum refining	416.5	555.2	0.1	-52.1	3.05	3.44	10.2	8.5	3.4	1.5	6.8	0.7
Mining, crude-oil production	248.7	414.5	14.2	-61.9	1.86	1.64	7.0	7.7	3.3	4.8	24.5	-5.5
Soaps, cosmetics	181.1	241.1	13.6	-12.9	3.64	3.11	16.2	14.7	4.9	5.1	6.0	19.4
Food	178.3	239.0	19.5	13.2	5.32	4.82	16.1	19.7	3.5	3.5	3.4	26.7
Chemicals	173.1	227.3	29.4	-17.8	2.41	2.36	14.2	12.6	6.0	3.7	8.5	31.9
Beverages	160.6	201.1	11.2	5.9	2.06	2.48	14.0	21.1	7.0	5.5	0.2	32.3
Metals	157.1	176.7	53.6	-51.8	2.73	2.50	11.1	5.2	4.3	1.5	50.5	18.2
Tobacco	150.3	257.1	24.6	27.2	2.63	5.20	20.0	12.1	8.3	2.3	19.2	137.3
Forest products	145.6	174.1	59.7	39.6	2.22	1.77	14.7	4.6	6.5	2.9	9.1	37.5
Building materials . . . . . , ...	140.8	157.9	17.2	-53.8	2.14	1.95	13.4	-0.7	6.8	-3.6	25.2	39.8
Transportation equipment [2]	125.9	118.4	(NA)	-11.7	5.51	3.72	23.1	8.9	3.1	2.4	-1.1	54.3
Pharmaceuticals	123.5	168.9	15.1	16.0	1.97	1.85	22.7	26.1	13.2	12.8	11.7	61.5
Rubber and plastic products	107.2	152.7	51.9	13.3	3.48	3.23	13.1	11.6	5.6	3.4	15.7	90.3
Metal products	105.1	123.0	35.3	-1.0	2.93	3.43	14.3	11.8	5.4	3.4	12.0	40.9
Computers (incl. office equip.)	105.0	163.7	26.9	1.1	2.17	2.38	14.6	10.2	8.2	4.9	6.3	12.3
Publishing, printing	103.3	133.0	15.6	-10.3	2.13	2.14	18.9	10.7	8.4	5.1	8.7	19.4
Motor vehicles and parts	101.9	129.9	20.6	-58.7	3.48	3.37	11.6	1.0	3.5	0.4	-7.7	16.7
Aerospace	98.9	135.7	3.9	0.7	4.21	3.91	14.3	12.4	3.7	3.3	-24.5	35.5
Industrial and farm equipment	97.7	137.7	42.4	28.9	2.98	3.34	11.2	6.0	3.3	1.5	10.0	15.0
Scientific, photographic equipment .	94.5	130.0	21.9	16.3	1.92	2.50	16.3	14.3	8.3	5.3	0.5	50.2
Electronics	85.1	111.2	17.1	-9.3	2.46	2.78	14.1	10.7	5.0	2.7	1.4	37.6
Furniture	75.4	105.5	8.0	20.6	2.61	3.17	15.2	9.2	5.2	2.3	-7.0	41.5
Textiles	71.3	93.4	24.3	-49.5	3.26	2.97	12.8	4.6	4.1	1.4	-6.3	45.2
Apparel	52.2	73.9	29.0	1.1	3.14	3.96	14.1	13.6	3.9	3.4	-18.9	52.6

NA Not available. [1] Includes both price appreciation and dividend yield, i.e., to an investor in the company's stock. [2] Excludes motor vehicles and aircraft.
Source: Time Warner, New York, NY, *The Fortune Directories,* (copyright).

No. 871. Corporate Profits, Taxes, and Dividends: 1980 to 1991

[**In billions of dollars.** Covers corporations organized for profit and other entities treated as corporations. Represents profits to U.S. residents, without deduction of depletion charges and exclusive of capital gains and losses; intercorporate dividends from profits of domestic corporations are eliminated; net receipts of dividends, reinvested earnings of incorporated foreign affiliates, and earnings of unincorporated foreign affiliates are added]

ITEM	1980	1981	1982	1983	1984	1985	1986	1987	1988	1989	1990	1991
Profits before taxes	240.9	228.9	176.3	210.7	240.5	225.0	217.8	287.9	347.5	344.5	332.3	312.7
Less: Income tax liability [1]	84.8	81.1	63.1	77.2	94.0	96.5	106.5	127.1	137.0	138.0	135.3	124.6
Equals: Profits after taxes	156.1	147.8	113.2	133.5	146.4	128.5	111.3	160.8	210.5	206.6	197.0	188.1
Less: Net dividends [2]	59.0	69.2	70.0	81.2	82.7	92.4	109.8	106.2	115.3	127.9	133.7	137.8
Equals: Undistributed profits	97.1	78.6	43.2	52.3	63.8	36.1	1.6	54.6	95.2	78.7	63.3	50.3
Capital consumption allowances [3]	164.9	198.2	228.8	268.1	293.7	333.3	338.3	354.1	372.3	375.2	366.3	374.9
Profits after tax plus capital consumption allowances [3]	321.0	346.0	342.0	401.6	440.1	461.8	449.6	514.9	582.8	581.8	563.3	563.0

[1] Federal, State, and local.   [2] Disbursements to U.S. residents, measured after eliminations of intercorporate dividends.
[3] Without capital consumption adjustment. Includes depreciation and accidental damages.
Source: U.S. Bureau of Economic Analysis, *Survey of Current Business*, March 1992, and unpublished data.

No. 872. Corporate Profits, by Industry: 1987 to 1990

[**In billions of dollars.** Profits are without inventory valuation and capital consumption adjustments. Minus sign (-) indicates loss. See headnote, table 871]

INDUSTRY	BEFORE TAXES				AFTER TAXES			
	1987	1988	1989	1990	1987	1988	1989	1990
Total	**287.9**	**347.5**	**344.5**	**332.3**	**160.8**	**210.5**	**206.6**	**197.0**
Domestic industries	**248.4**	**298.5**	**290.7**	**272.1**	**121.3**	**161.4**	**152.7**	**136.8**
Agriculture [1]	1.9	1.8	1.9	2.0	1.3	1.2	1.3	1.4
Mining.	-1.4	0.5	1.9	2.8	-2.2	-0.7	0.4	1.0
Construction.	11.3	12.5	13.5	14.3	8.4	9.8	10.5	11.1
Manufacturing.	93.9	130.1	118.4	99.4	50.3	76.8	68.9	53.1
Transportation	4.2	7.0	4.3	1.9	1.2	2.6	1.8	-0.2
Communications.	19.5	19.1	22.3	24.9	11.8	11.6	13.6	15.4
Public utilties	18.9	20.9	19.7	18.6	10.3	12.9	10.9	9.1
Wholesale and retail trade	47.1	49.4	51.2	48.9	29.5	33.5	35.0	32.9
Finance, insurance [2]	38.0	42.3	39.1	39.5	0.9	3.7	-3.6	-2.6
Services	15.1	14.9	18.4	19.8	9.8	10.0	14.0	15.6
Rest of world [3]	**39.5**	**49.1**	**53.9**	**60.2**	**39.5**	**49.1**	**53.9**	**60.2**

[1] Includes forestry and fisheries.   [2] Includes real estate.   [3] Consists of receipts by all U.S. residents, including both corporations and persons, of earnings of unincorporated foreign affiliates, dividends from their incorporated foreign affiliates, and their share of their incorporated foreign affiliates, net of corresponding outflows.
Source: U.S. Bureau of Economic Analysis, *Survey of Current Business*, January 1992.

No. 873. Corporate Profits With Inventory Valuation and Capital Consumption Adjustments—Financial and Nonfinancial Industries: 1970 to 1991

[**In billions of dollars.** Minus sign (-) indicates loss. See headnote, table 871]

ITEM	1970	1980	1983	1984	1985	1986	1987	1988	1989	1990	1991
Corporate profits with IVA [1] and CCA [2]	**77.5**	**177.7**	**212.7**	**264.2**	**280.8**	**271.6**	**319.8**	**365.0**	**351.7**	**319.0**	**307.1**
Domestic industries	70.4	142.7	182.3	233.0	250.0	238.7	280.3	315.9	297.8	258.8	241.0
Financial.	13.3	22.0	22.4	18.7	28.6	34.9	36.1	41.5	36.9	34.5	35.6
Nonfinancial	57.1	120.7	159.9	214.3	221.4	203.8	244.2	274.4	261.0	224.3	205.4
Rest of the world	7.1	35.0	30.4	31.2	30.8	32.9	39.5	49.1	53.9	60.2	66.1
Corporate profits with IVA [1] . .	**71.8**	**197.8**	**202.2**	**236.4**	**225.3**	**227.6**	**273.4**	**320.3**	**327.0**	**318.2**	**315.8**
Domestic industries	64.7	162.9	171.9	205.2	194.5	194.6	233.9	271.2	273.1	258.0	249.7
Financial.	13.1	24.3	24.5	20.3	28.7	35.8	36.4	41.8	39.2	39.6	41.8
Federal Reserve banks	3.5	11.8	14.6	16.4	16.3	15.5	15.7	17.6	20.2	21.3	20.7
Other	9.6	12.6	9.9	3.9	12.4	20.3	20.7	24.2	19.0	18.3	21.1
Nonfinancial	51.6	138.5	147.4	185.0	165.8	158.9	197.5	229.4	233.9	218.3	207.9
Manufacturing.	27.1	75.8	71.4	86.7	80.1	59.0	87.0	117.5	113.6	95.7	81.9
Durable goods [3]	10.4	17.9	18.4	37.2	29.0	30.0	42.2	52.2	50.2	37.2	23.5
Primary metal industries	0.8	2.6	-4.9	-0.4	-0.9	0.9	2.6	5.9	6.4	4.6	2.2
Fabricated metal products . . .	1.1	4.3	3.1	4.5	4.7	5.3	5.2	6.4	6.9	5.6	4.6
Machinery, except electrical . .	3.0	7.5	4.4	6.3	5.3	3.2	7.3	10.5	10.3	10.2	8.5
Electric and electronic equipment.	1.3	5.0	3.4	4.8	2.4	2.6	6.2	7.6	8.7	7.9	6.4
Motor vehicles and equipment.	8.2	-4.3	28.9	39.9	8.9	7.3	4.4	3.7	5.7	1.7	-7.1	-11.1
Nondurable goods [3]	16.8	57.8	53.0	49.5	51.1	29.0	44.8	65.3	63.4	58.5	58.4
Food and kindred products . . .	3.2	6.0	5.8	7.3	8.4	7.5	11.4	11.8	11.8	12.6	15.6
Chemicals and allied products .	3.9	5.5	6.8	7.3	6.0	8.0	15.1	19.3	19.9	20.3	20.2
Petroleum and coal products. .	3.6	33.6	22.1	15.9	17.1	-8.5	-3.6	10.4	7.2	6.5	4.0
Transportation and public utilities. .	8.2	18.3	28.9	39.9	34.1	36.5	43.4	47.5	45.0	44.5	45.3
Wholesale and retail trade	10.3	22.8	38.7	49.7	43.1	46.3	39.9	37.1	42.8	39.8	46.1
Other	5.9	21.6	8.4	8.7	8.5	17.1	27.2	27.3	32.6	38.4	34.6

[1] Inventory valuation adjustment.   [2] Capital consumption adjustment.   [3] Includes other industries not shown separately.
Source: U.S. Bureau of Economic Analysis, *Survey of Current Business*, March 1992, and unpublished data.

No. 874. Selected Corporate Profits and Stockholders' Equity Ratios, by Industry: 1980 to 1990

[Averages of quarterly figures at annual rates. Beginning 1989, manufacturing data exclude estimates for corporations with less than $250,000 in assets at time of sample selection. Data are not necessarily comparable from year to year due to changes in accounting procedures, industry classifications, sampling procedures, etc.; for detail, see source. Based on sample; see source for discussion of methodology. Minus sign (-) indicates loss]

INDUSTRY GROUP	RATIO OF PROFITS TO STOCKHOLDERS' EQUITY (percent)				PROFITS PER DOLLAR OF SALES (cents)				RATIO OF STOCKHOLDERS' EQUITY TO DEBT			
	1980	1985	1989	1990	1980	1985	1989	1990	1980	1985	1989	1990
All manufacturing corporations [1]	13.9	10.1	13.7	10.7	4.9	3.8	5.0	4.0	2.3	1.9	1.4	1.3
Durable goods industries............	11.2	9.2	11.0	8.0	4.0	3.4	4.1	3.0	2.2	2.2	1.6	1.6
Stone, clay, and glass products	10.8	7.9	10.4	5.4	4.2	3.1	3.3	1.8	1.9	1.7	0.8	0.8
Primary metal industries	11.7	-7.9	18.4	9.5	4.1	-2.6	4.6	2.6	1.7	1.2	1.1	1.1
Iron and steel...................	9.0	-11.0	20.2	6.6	2.9	-2.6	2.7	1.0	1.7	0.8	0.6	0.6
Nonferrous metals	15.6	-5.7	17.7	10.4	5.8	-2.5	6.3	4.0	1.8	1.6	1.5	1.6
Fabricated metal products...........	13.9	9.2	13.6	11.7	4.2	2.8	3.8	3.4	2.1	1.6	1.3	1.3
Machinery, exc. electrical	15.0	9.3	7.4	8.1	6.5	4.7	3.8	4.4	2.2	2.6	2.1	2.2
Electrical and electronic equipment.....	15.1	8.3	10.9	7.5	5.0	3.4	4.4	3.0	2.6	2.7	1.8	1.6
Transportation equipment	-0.6	15.4	11.1	3.8	-0.3	4.1	3.6	1.3	2.7	2.9	2.1	1.9
Motor vehicles and equipment	-9.3	18.2	10.9	-1.0	-3.4	4.9	3.6	-0.5	3.4	4.2	2.4	2.2
Aircraft, guided missiles and parts	16.0	11.1	10.7	11.5	4.3	3.1	3.3	3.4	2.8	2.6	1.9	1.6
Instruments and related products	17.5	10.1	12.4	12.9	9.3	5.7	6.2	6.6	4.3	3.5	1.6	1.6
Nondurable goods industries..........	16.4	11.0	16.3	13.3	5.6	4.1	5.9	4.9	2.3	1.7	1.2	1.2
Food and kindred products [2]	14.7	15.3	17.1	16.1	3.4	4.1	4.2	4.1	1.9	1.4	0.8	0.8
Tobacco manufactures..............	19.8	(2)	(2)	(2)	11.7	(2)	(2)	(2)	1.8	(2)	(2)	(2)
Textile mill products................	8.5	8.6	10.0	3.4	2.2	2.4	2.5	0.8	2.0	1.5	0.8	0.7
Paper and allied products	12.1	9.7	15.6	10.6	5.1	4.0	6.2	4.2	2.0	1.7	1.3	1.1
Printing and publishing	16.4	19.2	15.0	8.3	5.5	6.5	5.7	3.6	2.1	1.7	1.1	1.2
Chemicals and allied products	15.4	9.4	19.7	17.3	7.1	4.7	8.8	8.2	2.2	2.1	1.5	1.4
Industrial...................	11.9	4.2	17.9	13.8	5.4	2.2	8.3	7.0	1.9	1.8	1.5	1.4
Drugs......................	19.9	15.2	28.0	27.1	13.2	9.8	15.1	15.7	3.0	3.2	2.1	2.2
Petroleum and coal products	20.0	8.5	14.6	12.8	7.7	4.0	7.4	5.7	3.4	1.6	1.6	1.7
Rubber and misc. plastics products.....	6.7	9.5	12.1	6.9	2.0	2.6	3.0	1.8	1.6	1.6	1.0	1.0
Mining corporations, total [3]	19.2	-4.0	6.0	8.1	11.3	-3.2	4.5	5.7	1.3	1.0	1.2	1.3
Retail trade corporations, total [3] ...	13.2	12.5	13.2	8.4	1.7	2.2	1.9	1.1	1.2	1.4	0.7	0.6
Wholesale trade corporations, total [3]	17.3	8.7	9.0	5.0	1.8	1.0	1.1	0.6	1.2	1.0	1.0	1.0

[1] Includes other industries not shown separately.   [2] Beginning 1985, tobacco included in food and kindred products.   [3] For 1985, represents results of companies with assets over $25 million; thereafter, asset cut-off raised to $50 million.

Source: 1980, U.S. Federal Trade Commission; thereafter, U.S. Bureau of the Census, *Quarterly Financial Report for Manufacturing, Mining and Trade Corporations*. In U.S. Council of Economic Advisers, *Economic Report of the President,* annual.

No. 875. Manufacturing Corporations—Sales, Profits, Stockholders' Equity, and Debt: 1970 to 1990

[**In billions of dollars.** Data are not necessarily comparable from year to year due to changes in accounting procedures, industry classifications, sampling procedures, etc.; for detail, see source. See also *Historical Statistics, Colonial Times to 1970,* series P 93-106]

YEAR	ALL MANUFACTURING CORPS.					DURABLE GOODS INDUSTRIES					NONDURABLE GOODS INDUSTRIES				
	Sales	Profits		Stock-hold-ers' equi-ty [1]	Debt [1]	Sales	Profits		Stock-hold-ers' equi-ty [1]	Debt [1]	Sales	Profits		Stock-hold-ers' equi-ty [1]	Debt [1]
		Before taxes	After taxes				Before taxes	After taxes				Before taxes	After taxes		
1970 ..	709	48	29	307	134	363	23	13	155	71	346	25	16	152	63
1975 ..	1,065	80	49	423	183	521	35	21	208	94	544	45	28	215	89
1976 ..	1,203	105	65	463	188	590	51	31	224	91	614	54	34	238	97
1977 ..	1,328	115	70	497	200	657	58	35	240	95	671	57	36	257	106
1978 ..	1,496	133	81	541	222	761	70	42	263	106	736	63	39	278	117
1979 ..	1,742	154	99	600	252	866	72	45	292	123	876	82	54	308	129
1980 ..	1,897	145	92	665	292	883	57	36	316	143	1,014	88	57	349	149
1981 ..	2,145	159	101	743	335	979	67	42	350	159	1,165	91	60	393	176
1982 ..	2,039	108	71	770	371	913	35	22	356	177	1,126	74	49	415	193
1983 ..	2,114	133	86	813	368	973	49	30	372	168	1,141	84	56	440	200
1984 ..	2,335	166	108	864	405	1,100	70	49	396	166	1,228	90	59	469	239
1985 .	2,331	137	88	866	454	1,143	61	39	421	187	1,189	76	49	445	267
1986 [2] .	2,221	129	83	875	501	1,126	52	33	436	203	1,096	78	51	438	298
1987 ..	2,378	173	116	901	553	1,178	78	53	444	229	1,200	95	63	457	324
1988 ..	2,596	216	155	958	622	1,285	92	67	469	265	1,312	124	88	489	357
1989 ..	2,745	189	136	999	733	1,357	75	56	501	308	1,388	114	81	498	425
1990 ..	2,811	160	112	1,044	781	1,357	58	41	515	328	1,454	102	71	529	453

[1] Annual data are average equity or debt for the year (using four end-of-quarter figures).   [2] Beginning 1986, data exclude estimates for corporations with less than $250,000 in assets at time of sample selection. Prior periods include estimates for corporations in this size category.

Source: Through 1981, U.S. Federal Trade Commission; thereafter, U.S. Bureau of Census, *Quarterly Financial Report for Manufacturing, Mining and Trade Corporations*. In U.S. Council of Economic Advisers, *Economic Report of the President,* annual.

No. 876. Corporate Philanthropy as a Percent of Worldwide Pretax Net Income: 1985 to 1989

[Data are based on a sample greater than 1,200 corporations. Medians by industry]

INDUSTRY CLASS	1985	1987	1988	1989	INDUSTRY CLASS	1985	1987	1988	1989
All firms, median	**1.0**	**0.9**	**0.8**	**0.9**	Paper and like products. . . .	1.2	0.7	0.6	0.7
Manufacturing firms,					Petroleum and gas [2]	0.7	0.9	0.5	0.8
median	**1.1**	**1.0**	**0.8**	**0.9**	Pharmaceuticals.	1.0	1.0	1.1	1.0
Chemicals.	1.1	0.8	0.7	0.8	Primary metal industries . . .	1.1	([1])	([1])	([1])
Electrical machinery and					Printing and publishing	1.3	0.8	2.3	1.7
equipment.	1.6	1.2	0.6	0.7	Stone, clay and glass				
Fabricated metal products . .	0.8	[1]1.2	[1]0.8	[1]1.0	products	1.5	([1])	([1])	([1])
Food, beverage and					Textiles	([3])	([3])	([3])	0.8
tobacco	1.2	1.3	1.0	1.4	Transportation equipment [4] .	1.0	0.9	1.1	1.2
Machinery, nonelectrical . . .	1.1	1.0	0.9	0.7	**Nonmanufacturing firms,**				
					median	**0.9**	**0.7**	**0.9**	**1.0**

[1] Primary metals and stone, clay, and glass firms included with fabricated metal firms.   [2] Mining firms included with petroleum firms.   [3] Fewer than 4 companies reporting.   [4] Rubber and miscellaneous plastic firms included with transportation firms.

Source: The Conference Board, New York, NY, *Annual Survey of Corporate Contributions*, (copyright).

No. 877. U.S. Largest Public Companies, Profitability and Growth: 1991

[In percent, except ranks. For fiscal years ending in the 12 month period ending September 30. Included in the Forbes Universe of 1,177 companies is every firm with revenue of over $400 million in **1991**, electric and banking firms $800 million. Represents industry medians; calculated by listing companies in rank order and selecting the midpoint. Where there is an even number of companies, an arithmetic average of the two middle companies is substituted]

INDUSTRY	PROFITABILITY					GROWTH					
	Return on equity [1]			1991		Sales [3]			Earnings per share		
	5-year rank	5-year average	Latest 12 months, 1991	Return on capital, [2] latest 12 months	Debt/ capital	5-year rank	5-year average	Latest 12 months, 1991	5-year rank	5-year average	Latest 12 months, 1991
All-industry medians .	(X)	13.2	9.9	7.6	32.4	(X)	11.3	3.7	(X)	4.5	−5.9
Food, drink and tobacco . .	1	20.0	17.0	12.4	30.6	14	10.6	7.0	1	14.8	7.4
Consumer nondurables . . .	2	18.0	13.6	9.4	32.4	5	12.3	7.6	5	10.8	10.3
Health	3	17.9	16.9	14.2	18.9	4	12.5	10.8	2	14.7	18.5
Chemicals.	4	16.7	13.0	9.4	30.8	6	12.2	4.0	3	13.9	−11.1
Entertainment and informa-											
tion	5	15.4	8.4	7.6	31.6	12	11.0	0.7	12	−0.7	−22.6
Business services and sup-											
plies	6	14.8	10.3	9.0	31.4	7	11.7	2.6	7	8.5	−10.1
Forest products and pack-											
aging.	7	14.4	5.5	4.3	33.3	9	11.6	−1.8	4	12.6	−48.1
Food distribution.	8	14.2	12.0	10.0	39.7	8	11.6	3.5	6	9.0	7.0
Retailing	9	14.0	10.5	9.3	32.4	2	13.5	7.7	11	4.5	−5.9
Metals	10	13.2	3.7	3.7	31.2	13	10.7	−5.7	8	7.5	−66.9
Computers and communi-											
cations.	11	13.2	9.4	7.4	25.0	1	14.3	4.5	16	−13.6	−19.1
Capital goods.	12	13.2	7.5	7.2	28.9	11	11.3	−0.8	9	7.1	−29.8
Electric utilities.	13	12.4	12.2	7.0	40.4	20	3.2	3.7	14	−11.7	1.7
Aerospace and defense. . .	14	12.2	9.4	7.6	32.8	19	6.8	2.2	17	−18.7	1.5
Insurance	15	12.1	10.7	9.9	19.5	15	9.6	5.4	10	4.9	1.3
Financial services	16	11.1	12.0	8.7	27.2	10	11.3	0.1	19	(NS)	(NS)
Consumer durables	17	11.0	4.3	5.3	34.5	16	9.4	−2.3	18	(NS)	−51.1
Transport	18	10.8	9.9	6.7	36.8	17	8.8	4.3	13	−6.7	2.9
Energy	19	10.7	9.6	7.2	37.7	21	−4.2	6.0	19	(NS)	−4.7
Construction	20	9.6	0.8	3.5	39.5	18	8.6	−8.2	15	−11.7	−87.8
Travel.	21	9.4	0.2	2.3	50.4	3	12.6	9.0	19	(NS)	([4])

NS Not significant.   X Not applicable.   [1] Represents primary earnings per share before extraordinary item divided by common shareholders' equity per share. Common shareholders' equity is total shareholders' equity including the stated value of all preferred stock at the beginning of each year minus the involuntary liquidating value of non-convertible preferred shares. [2] After-tax profits, the amount remaining if the interest paid on long-term debt was taxed, and minority interest divided by a firm's total capitalization. Total capitalization is long-term debt, common and preferred equity, deferred taxes, investment tax credits and minority interest in consolidated subsidiaries.   [3] Net sales plus other operating revenue.   [4] Profit to deficit.

Source: Forbes, Inc., New York, NY, *Forbes Annual Report on American Industry.* (copyright).

No. 878. Foreign Corporate Activity in the United States: 1988

[Includes corporations controlled or owned by any foreign person (i.e., an individual, partnership, corporation, estate, or trust), directly or indirectly, based on 50 percent or more of a U.S. corporations's voting stock at the end of the tax year]

AREA AND COUNTRY [1]	Number of returns	Total assets (bil. dol.)	Total receipts [2] (bil. dol.)	Net income (less deficit) (mil. dol.)	TOTAL U.S. INCOME TAX	
					Before credits (mil. dol.)	After credits (mil. dol.)
All corporations in the United States	**3,562,789**	**16,568**	**10,265**	**412,983**	**131,367**	**95,896**
Corporations controlled by a foreign person [3].	**46,298**	**1,199**	**826**	**11,201**	**7,071**	**5,824**
Canada	7,545	116	83	935	562	485
Latin America	7,170	39	37	7	272	209
Other Western Hemisphere	459	11	9	−6	58	50
Europe, total. . . . .·.	16,454	682	442	9,639	4,757	3,806
European Economic Community countries [3] .	13,693	612	382	8,595	4,256	3,430
Belgium	179	9	10	735	236	115
France.	1,876	62	43	711	429	363
Netherlands	1,877	148	93	1,854	792	668
United Kingdom.	5,043	301	150	4,673	2,193	1,783
West Germany	3,291	74	74	675	540	439
Sweden	265	15	14	410	160	107
Switzerland	1,803	43	39	719	307	238
Africa	659	2	1	−14	1	1
Asia [3]	8,527	315	232	389	1,254	1,190
Hong Kong	1,172	35	6	−216	18	17
Japan.	5,345	248	209	956	1,160	1,112
South Korea	148	4	8	−5	8	8
Oceania.	653	29	14	87	64	32
Puerto Rico and U.S. possessions	179	2	1	180	67	15
Country not stated.	4,651	4	6	−15	37	36

[1] Geographic location of the foreign owners country of residence, incorporation, organization, creation, or administration.
[2] Total receipts includes business plus investment receipts.   [3] Some countries not shown separately.

Source: U.S. Internal Revenue Service, *Statistics of Income Bulletin, Fall 1991.*

No. 879. U.S. Multinational Companies—Assets, Sales, Employment, Employee Compensation, and U.S. Exports and Imports: 1989

[In billions of dollars, except as indicated. Consists of non-bank U.S. parent companies and their foreign affiliates. U.S. parent is a U.S. person that owns or controls directly or indirectly, 10 percent or more of the voting securities of an incorporated foreign business enterprise, or an equivalent interest in an unincorporated foreign business enterprise. A U.S. person can be an incorporated business enterprise. A foreign affiliate is a foreign business enterprise owned or controlled by a U.S. parent company]

INDUSTRY [1]	U.S. PARENTS				FOREIGN AFFILIATES				U.S. exports shipped to foreign affiliates	U.S. imports shipped from foreign affiliates
	Total assets	Sales	Employ-ment (1,000)	Em-ployee com-pensa-tion	Total assets	Sales	Employ-ment (1,000)	Em-ployee com-pensa-tion		
All industries	**4,905**	**3,134**	**18,721**	**662**	**1,314**	**1,266**	**6,621**	**162**	**102**	**94**
Petroleum	502	353	628	29	193	224	291	11	2	11
Manufacturing	1,878	1,545	10,138	391	491	641	4,189	101	70	72
Food and kindred products	187	193	1,136	29	48	69	479	9	2	1
Chemical and allied products. . . .	295	232	1,253	54	102	115	580	16	8	4
Primary and fabricated metals . . .	107	104	691	26	23	26	222	5	2	2
Machinery (except electrical)	220	174	1,267	57	74	104	553	18	12	12
Electric and electronic equipment .	207	137	1,016	38	52	61	650	13	8	9
Transportation equipment	447	359	2,083	94	99	160	833	22	29	34
Other.	416	346	2,693	93	94	106	872	20	8	9
Wholesale trade	99	225	424	14	112	221	535	19	27	8
Finance (except banking), insur-ance, real estate.	1,620	376	1,081	46	403	59	160	6	(Z)	(Z)
Services	136	111	1,726	43	48	41	483	12	(Z)	(D)
Other industries	671	524	4,724	140	67	79	964	12	2	(D)

D Withheld to avoid disclosure.   Z Less than $500 million.   [1] Represents industry of U.S. parent or industry of foreign affiliate.

Source: U.S. Bureau of Economic Analysis, *Survey of Current Business,* October 1991.

Figure 18.1
Households With Selected Media: 1980 and 1990

Percent

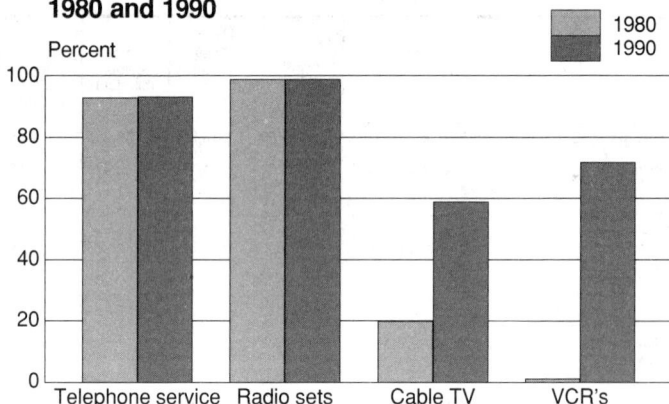

Source: Chart prepared by U.S. Bureau of the Census. For data, see table 884.

Figure 18.2
Telephone Communications: 1990

Operating revenue

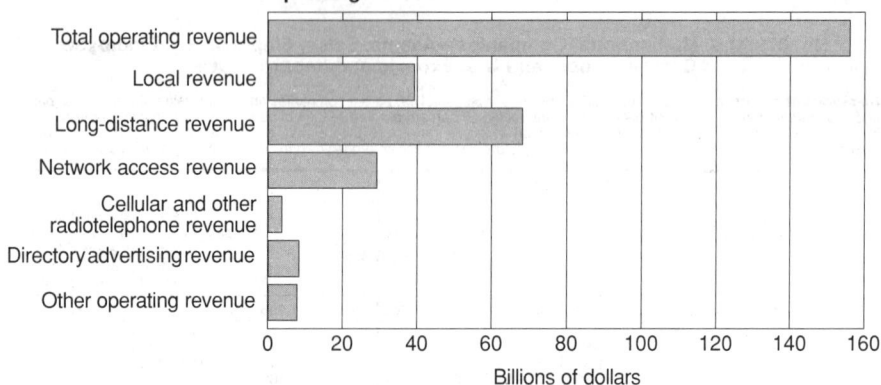

Billions of dollars

1989 to 1990 change in revenue

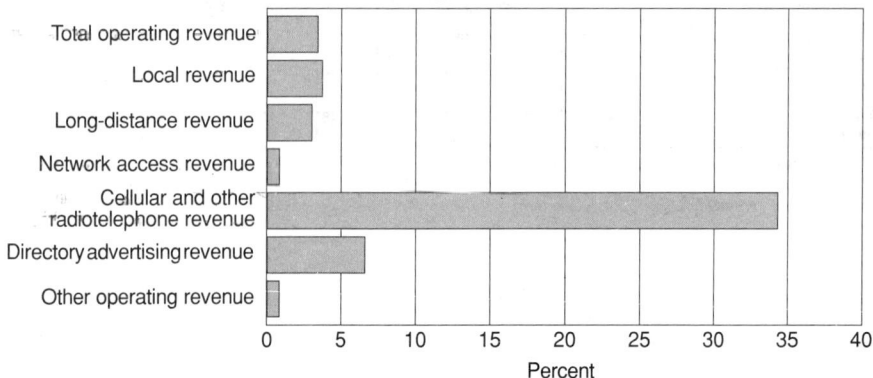

Percent

Source: Chart prepared by U.S. Bureau of the Census. For data, see table 887.

Communications

This section presents statistics on the usage, finances, and operations of the Postal Service and of the various communications media: telephone, telegraph, radio, television, newspapers, and periodicals. Expenditure data for advertising in the media are also included.

Postal Service.—The Postal Service provides mail processing and delivery services within the United States. The Postal Reorganization Act of 1970 created the Postal Service, effective July 1971, as an independent establishment of the Federal Executive Branch.

Revenue and cost analysis describes the Postal Service's system of attributing revenues and costs to classes of mail and service. This system draws primarily upon probability sampling techniques to develop estimates of revenues, volumes, and weights, as well as costs by class of mail and special service. The costs attributed to classes of mail and special services are primarily incremental costs which vary in response to changes in volume; they account for roughly 60 percent of the total costs of the Postal Service. The balance represents "institutional costs." Statistics on revenues, volume of mail, and distribution of expenditures are presented in the Postal Service's annual report, *Cost and Revenue Analysis,* and its *Annual Report of the Postmaster General.*

Communication media.—The Bureau of the Census *Annual Survey of Communication Services* (ASCS) covers all employer firms with one or more establishments that are primarily engaged in providing point-to-point communication services, whether by wire or radio, and whether intended to be received aurally or visually. This includes telephone communications, including cellular and other radiotelephone services; telegraph and other message communications, such as electronic mail services, facsimile transmission services, telex services, and so on; radio and television broadcasting stations and networks; cable and other pay television services; and other communication services, such as radar station operations, satellite earth stations, satellite or missile tracking stations, and so

In Brief

Households in 1989 with:

Telephone service	93%
Radio sets	94%
Television	98%
Cable television	59%
VCR's	72%

on. The report presents statistics that are summarized by kind-of-business classification based on the 1972 edition of the *Standard Industrial Classification Manual.*

The Federal Communications Commission (FCC), established in 1934, regulates wire and radio communications. Only the largest carriers and holding companies file annual or monthly financial reports. The FCC has jurisdiction over interstate and foreign communication services, but not over intrastate or local services. The gross operating revenues of the telephone carriers reporting annually to the FCC, however, are estimated to cover about 90 percent of the revenues of all U.S. telephone companies. Data are not comparable with Bureau of the Census *Annual Survey of Communication Services* because of coverage (*ASCS* includes all domestic long-distance telephone companies, all local exchange carriers, and all cellular telephone companies) and different accounting practices for those telephone companies which report to the FCC.

Reports filed by the broadcasting industry cover substantially all radio and television stations operating in the United States. The private radio services represent the largest and most diverse group of licensees regulated by the FCC. These services provide voice, data communications, point-to-point and point-to-multipoint radio communications for fixed and mobile communicators. Major users of these services are small business, the aviation industry, the maritime trades, the land transportation industry, manufacturing industries, State and local public safety and governmental authorities, emergency medical service providers, amateur radio operators, and personal radio operations (CB and the General Mobile Radio Service). The FCC also licenses entities as private and common carriers. Private and common carriers provide fixed and land mobile communications service on a for-profit basis. Principal sources of wire, radio, and television data are the FCC's *Annual Report* and its annual *Statistics of Communications Common Carriers.*

Statistics on the printed media are available from the U.S. Bureau of the Census, as well as from various private agencies. The censuses of manufactures (conducted by the Census Bureau every 5 years, for the years ending in "2" and "7") provide statistics on the number and circulation of newspapers and periodicals and on sales of books and pamphlets. Editor & Publisher Co. New York, NY presents annual data on the number and circulation of daily and Sunday newspapers in its *International Year Book.* Monthly data on new books and new editions appear in *Publishers Weekly,* issued by R. R. Bowker Company, New York. (See table 386 for annual data.)

Advertising.—Data on advertising expenditures are compiled primarily by McCann-Erickson, Inc., which compiles certain of the data shown (see tables 903-904). Monthly index figures of advertising in certain media are also published periodically by McCann-Erickson in *Advertising Age.*

The Broadcast Advertisers Reports distinguishes between spot and local advertising primarily on the basis of the type of advertiser to whom the time is sold, rather than how and by whom it is sold. In general, time purchased on behalf of retail or service establishments in the market is considered local, even though the establishments may be part of a national or regional chain. That is, spot advertising promotes a product, while local advertising promotes a given establishment. Network advertising, mutually exclusive of spot and local, is broadcast through the network system.

Statistical reliability.—For a discussion of statistical collection and estimation, sampling procedures, and measures of statistical reliability applicable to Census Bureau data, see Appendix III.

Historical statistics.—Tabular headnotes provide cross-references, where applicable, to *Historical Statistics of the United States, Colonial Times to 1970.* See Appendix IV.

No. 880. U.S. Postal Service—Summary: 1975 to 1990

[Employees in thousands; revenue and expenditures in millions of dollars, except as indicated. For fiscal years; see text, section 9. Includes Puerto Rico and all outlying areas except Canal Zone. See text, section 18. See also *Historical Statistics, Colonial Times to 1970*, series R 163-171]

ITEM	1975	1980	1984	1985	1986	1987	1988	1989	1990
Number of post offices	30,754	30,326	29,750	29,557	29,344	29,319	29,203	29,083	28,959
Pieces of mail handled (est.) (bil.)	89.3	106.3	131.5	140.1	147.4	153.9	161.0	161.6	166.3
First-class, number (bil.) [1]	51.4	60.3	68.4	72.4	76.2	78.9	84.7	85.9	89.3
Percent	57.6	56.7	52.0	51.7	51.7	51.3	52.6	53.2	53.7
Second class (bil.).	9.1	8.4	9.5	10.4	10.6	10.3	10.4	10.5	10.7
Employees, total.	**702**	**667**	**702**	**744**	**785**	**791**	**824**	**817**	**809**
Regular	559	536	561	586	606	751	764	764	747
Postmasters.	30	29	28	28	27	28	28	27	27
Office supervisors and tech. personnel . .	37	36	45	46	49	55	55	55	53
Office clerks and mail handlers [2]	239	229	235	249	260	345	347	345	333
City carriers and vehicle drivers	167	160	171	179	187	237	243	243	240
Rural carriers	31	33	35	35	36	37	39	40	42
Other	55	49	47	48	47	49	52	54	52
Substitute (part-time).	143	130	141	159	179	40	60	53	62
Compensation and employee benefits (mil. dol.)	10,805	16,541	22,157	24,349	25,576	27,229	30,749	32,368	34,214
Avg. salary per employee (dol.) [3]	15,392	24,799	31,562	32,727	32,581	34,424	36,989	39,619	42,292
Pieces of mail per employee, avg	127	159	187	188	188	195	195	198	206
Total revenue [4]	**11,590**	**19,106**	**26,474**	**28,956**	**31,021**	**32,297**	**35,939**	**38,920**	**40,074**
Operating postal revenue.	10,015	17,143	25,314	27,736	30,102	31,528	35,036	37,979	39,201
Stamps, postal cards, etc	2,819	4,287	6,023	6,520	6,969	7,246	7,784	8,381	8,638
Second-class postage paid in money (pound rates) [5]	284	881	1,056	1,339	1,271	1,326	1,455	1,594	1,580
Other postage paid under permit and meter	6,241	10,828	16,067	17,747	19,294	20,280	22,676	24,534	25,311
Box rents.	67	160	188	230	259	273	296	362	394
Miscellaneous.	556	892	1,847	1,774	2,174	2,255	2,683	2,959	3,124
Money-order revenues	53	95	132	126	135	148	142	148	154
Government appropriations	1,533	1,610	879	970	716	650	517	436	453
Percent of total revenue	13.2	8.4	3.3	3.3	2.3	2.0	1.4	1.1	1.1
Investment income, net	37	353	282	250	203	119	386	504	420
Mail and service:									
First-class mail [1]	5,798	10,146	15,216	16,740	18,035	18,786	21,402	23,234	24,023
Priority mail [6]	411	612	928	960	1,011	1,086	1,329	1,416	1,555
Second-class publishers' mail [7]	277	864	1,025	1,093	1,222	1,280	1,400	1,519	1,509
Third-class mail [8]	1,348	2,412	4,241	4,887	5,606	6,148	7,311	7,924	8,082
Bulk rate.	1,167	2,168	4,039	4,697	5,414	5,947	7,096	7,668	7,844
Single piece rate and fees	181	244	202	190	193	200	215	256	238
Fourth-class mail [9]	718	805	774	763	814	823	929	908	920
Zone rate mail (parcels, catalogs, etc.).	577	500	519	524	550	563	647	612	655
Special fourth-class rate	130	272	210	199	213	203	223	235	215
Library rate and fees.	11	33	45	40	51	57	59	61	50
Government mail [10]	484	745	901	934	992	907	(NA)	(NA)	(NA)
International mail [11]	390	596	859	882	934	957	992	1,081	1,163
Special services	251	518	868	918	979	1,030	1,136	1,314	1,310
Express mail	(X)	184	490	544	491	499	524	572	631
Mailgrams	(X)	15	13	15	17	13	12	10	8
Other [12].	1,913	2,205	1,159	1,220	919	769	903	938	873
Expenditures [13]	**12,578**	**19,412**	**26,357**	**29,207**	**30,716**	**32,520**	**36,119**	**38,370**	**40,490**

NA Not available.   X Not applicable.   [1] Items mailed at 1st-class rates and weighing 12 ounces or less.   [2] Includes mobile unit employees.   [3] Includes fringe benefits.   [4] Net revenues after refunds of postage. Includes operating reimbursements, embossed envelope purchases, indemnity claims, and miscellaneous revenue and expenditure offsets. Shown in year which gave rise to the earnings.   [5] Includes controlled circulation publications.   [6] Items otherwise qualified as 1st-class or airmail that exceeds 12 ounces and 8 ounces, respectively.   [7] Includes mail paid at other than bulk rates. Publishers' mail includes printed publications periodically issued and mailed at a known post office to paid subscribers, such as regular rate newspapers and magazines, and classroom and nonprofit rate publications. See source for further detail.   [8] Items less than 16 ounces in weight not mailed at either 1st- or 2d-class rates.   [9] Items not mailed at 1st-, 2d-, or 3d-class rates, except government and international mail. May include parcel post, catalogs weighing 16 ounces or more, books, films, and records.   [10] Penalty and franked. Beginning in 1989 penalty and franked mail are included in their appropriate classes of mail.   [11] Mail from U.S. to foreign countries paid at international mail rates.   [12] Consists of unassignable revenues; 1975 includes domestic airmail.   [13] Shown in year in which obligation was incurred.

Source: U.S. Postal Service, *Annual Report of the Postmaster General.*

No. 881. U.S. Postal Service—Volume of Mail, by Class: 1970 to 1990

[In millions, except per capita. **For fiscal years;** see text section 9. Includes Puerto Rico and all outlying areas except Canal Zone. For definition of classes of mail, see footnotes, table 880. See also *Historical Statistics, Colonial Times to 1970*, series R 172-186]

CLASS OF MAIL	PIECES OF MAIL					WEIGHT OF MAIL (lb.)				
	1970	1980	1985	1989	1990	1970	1980	1985	1989	1990
Total	84,882	106,311	140,098	161,603	166,875	13,281	12,958	16,783	18,412	18,826
Domestic	83,986	105,348	139,269	160,880	166,077	13,055	12,742	16,564	18,184	18,577
1st class and airmail [1]	50,174	60,332	72,517	85,926	89,917	1,636	2,213	2,807	3,315	3,452
Priority mail.	185	248	308	471	518	371	591	672	939	1,007
2d class	9,914	10,221	10,380	10,523	10,680	3,641	3,478	3,966	4,170	4,233
3d class	19,974	30,381	52,170	62,779	63,725	2,032	3,240	6,453	7,479	7,648
4th class.	977	633	576	626	663	4,786	2,661	2,156	2,196	2,109
Penalty.	2,544	2,992	2,608	(NA)	(NA)	540	503	470	(NA)	(NA)
Franked and free for blind . . .	218	540	710	555	574	49	56	40	84	127
International	896	963	829	724	798	226	216	219	228	249
Per capita: [2]										
Total, all domestic mail [3] . .	411	464	585	651	666	64	56	70	74	74
1st class and airmail	245	266	304	348	360	8	10	12	13	14
2d class	49	45	44	43	43	18	15	17	17	17
3d class	98	134	219	254	255	10	14	27	30	31
4th class.	5	3	2	3	3	23	12	9	9	4

NA Not available.   [1] Beginning 1980, includes express mail established as a class of mail on October 9, 1977, and mailgrams. [2] 1970, 1980, and 1990 based on April 1 population, including Armed Forces abroad; otherwise, based on estimated total population as of Jan. 1, including Armed Forces abroad.   [3] Includes types of mail not shown separately.

Source: U.S. Postal Service, *Annual Report of the Postmaster General.*

No. 882. U.S. Postal Service Rates for Letters and Post Cards: 1958 to 1991

[Domestic airmail letters discontinued in 1973 at 13 cents per ounce; superceded by express mail. See also *Historical Statistics, Colonial Times to 1970*, series R 188-191]

DATE OF RATE CHANGE	SURFACE MAIL			Postal and post cards	Ex-press mail [1]	DATE OF RATE CHANGE	SURFACE MAIL			Postal and post cards	Ex-press mail [1]
	Letters		Each added oz.				Letters		Each added oz.		
	Each oz.	First oz.					Each oz.	First oz.			
1958 (Aug. 1) . .	$0.04	(X)	(X)	$0.03	(X)	1978 (May 29). .	(X)	$0.15	$0.13	$0.10	(X)
1963 (Jan. 7). . .	$0.05	(X)	(X)	$0.04	(X)	1981 (Mar. 22). .	(X)	$0.18	$0.17	$0.12	(X)
1968 (Jan. 7). . .	$0.06	(X)	(X)	$0.05	(X)	1981 (Nov. 1) . .	(X)	$0.20	$0.17	$0.13	$9.35
1971 (May 16). .	$0.08	(X)	(X)	$0.06	(X)	1985 (Feb.17) . .	(X)	$0.22	$0.17	$0.14	$10.75
1974 (Mar. 2) . .	$0.10	(X)	(X)	$0.08	(X)	1988 (Apr. 3). . .	(X)	$0.25	$0.20	$0.15	[3]$12.00
1975 (Sept. 14) .	(X)	$0.10	$0.09	$0.07	(X)	1991 (Feb. 3) . .	(X)	$0.29	$0.23	$0.19	[3]$13.95
1975 (Dec. 31). .	[2](X)	[2]$0.13	[2]$0.11	[2]$0.09	(X)						

X Not applicable.   [1] Post Office to addressee rates. Rates shown are for weights up to 2 pounds, all zones. Beginning Feb. 17, 1985, for weights between 2 and 5 lbs, $12.85 is charged. Prior to Nov. 1, 1981, rate varied by weight and distances. Over 5 pounds still varies by distance.   [2] As of October 11, 1975, surface mail service upgraded to level of airmail.   [3] Over 8 ounces and up to 2 pounds.

No. 883. International Air Mail Rates From the United States: 1961 to 1991

[Excludes Canada and Mexico. Zones discontinued as of February 1991]

DATE OF RATE CHANGE	ZONE 1 [1]		ZONE 1 [2]		ZONE 1 [3]		Postal and post cards	Aero-grammes
	Each 1/2 oz. up to 2 ozs.	Each added 1/2 oz.	Each 1/2 oz. up to 2 ozs.	Each added 1/2 oz.	Each 1/2 oz. up to 2 ozs.	Each added 1/2 oz.		
1961 (July 1).	$0.13	$0.13	$0.15	$0.15	$0.25	$0.25	$0.11	$0.11
1967 (May 1).	$0.15	$0.15	$0.20	$0.20	$0.25	$0.25	$0.13	$0.13
1971 (July 1).	$0.17	$0.17	$0.21	$0.21	$0.21	$0.21	$0.13	$0.13
1974 (March 2)	$0.21	$0.17	$0.26	$0.21	$0.26	$0.21	$0.18	$0.18
1976 (January 3)	$0.25	$0.21	$0.31	$0.26	$0.31	$0.26	$0.21	$0.22
1981 (January 1)	$0.35	[4]$0.30	$0.40	[5]$0.35	$0.40	[5]$0.35	$0.28	$0.30
1985 (February 17).	$0.39	[6]$0.33	$0.44	[7]$0.39	$0.44	[7]$0.39	$0.33	$0.36
1988 (April 17) [8]	$0.45	$0.42	$0.45	$0.42	$0.45	$0.42	$0.36	$0.39
1991 (February 3) [8]	[9]$0.50	(X)	(X)	(X)	(X)	(X)	$0.40	$0.45

X Not applicable.   [1] Caribbean, Central and South America. The airmail letter rate to South America, 1961 to 1967, was the same as that to Europe. Beginning January 3, 1976, the airmail letter rate to all South American countries except Colombia and Venezuela is the same as Europe; Colombia and Venezuela are included in the first zone.   [2] Europe and Mediterranean Africa. [3] Rest of world.   [4] Up to 32 oz.; 30 cents per additional ounce over 32.   [5] Up to 32 oz.; 35 cents per additional ounce over 32.   [6] Up to 32 oz.; 33 cents per additional ounce over 32.   [7] Up to 32 oz.; 39 cents per additional ounce over 32.   [8] Air letters collapsed to a single schedule except for Canada and Mexico.   [9] First 1/2 ounce = 50 cents; second 1/2 ounce = 40 cents, 39 cents for each additional 1/2 ounce up to the limit of 64 oz.

Source of tables 882 and 883: U.S. Postal Service, "United States Domestic Postage Rate: Recent History," and unpublished data.

No. 884. Utilization of Selected Media: 1970 to 1991

ITEM	Unit	1970	1975	1980	1984	1985	1986	1987	1988	1989	1990	1991
Households with—												
Telephone service [1]	Percent	87.0	(NA)	93.0	91.8	91.8	92.2	92.5	92.9	93.0	93.3	93.6
Radio sets	Millions	62.0	71.4	78.6	86.7	87.1	88.1	89.9	91.1	92.8	94.4	(NA)
Percentage of households [2]	Percent	98.6	98.6	99.0	99.0	99.0	99.0	99.0	99.0	99.0	99.0	(NA)
Average number of sets	Number	5.1	5.6	5.5	5.5	5.5	5.4	5.4	5.6	5.6	5.6	(NA)
Television households [3]	Millions	59	69	76	84	85	86	87	89	90	92	93
Percent of total households	Percent	95.3	97.1	97.9	98.1	98.1	98.1	98.1	98.1	98.2	98.2	(NA)
Television sets in homes	Millions	81	105	128	149	155	158	163	168	176	193	(NA)
Average number of sets per home	Number	1.4	1.5	1.7	1.8	1.8	1.8	1.9	1.9	1.9	2.1	(NA)
Color set households	Millions	21	47	63	76	78	80	83	85	87	91	91
Cable television [4]	Millions	4	9	15	33	36	39	42	44	48	55	55
Percent of TV households	Percent	6.7	12.6	19.9	39.3	42.8	45.6	47.7	49.4	52.8	58.9	58.9
VCR's [4]	Millions	(NA)	(NA)	1	9	18	31	43	51	58	67	67
Percent of TV households	Percent	(NA)	(NA)	1.1	10.6	20.8	36.0	48.7	58.0	64.6	71.9	71.9
Commercial radio stations: [2]												
AM	Number	4,323	4,463	4,589	4,754	4,718	4,863	4,902	4,932	4,975	4,987	(NA)
FM	Number	2,196	2,767	3,282	3,716	3,875	3,944	4,041	4,155	4,269	4,392	(NA)
Television stations: [6] Total	Number	862	953	1,011	1,138	1,182	1,235	1,290	1,362	1,403	1,442	1,460
Commercial	Number	677	706	734	841	883	919	968	1,028	1,061	1,092	1,099
VHF [3]	Number	501	514	516	523	520	522	524	539	545	547	547
UHF [3]	Number	176	192	218	318	363	397	444	489	516	545	552
Cable television: [7]												
Systems	Number	2,490	3,506	4,225	6,200	6,844	7,600	7,900	8,500	(NA)	(NA)	(NA)
Subscribers served	Millions	4.5	9.8	15.5	30.0	31.3	37.5	41.0	43.8	47.8	(NA)	(NA)
Daily newspaper circulation: [8]												
Number	Millions	62	61	62	63	63	63	63	63	(NA)	62.3	(NA)
Per capita [9]	Number	0.305	0.282	0.275	0.267	0.263	0.260	0.258	0.256	(NA)	0.251	0.251

NA Not available. [1] For occupied housing units. 1970, 1980, and 1990 as of April 1; all other years as of March. Source: U.S. Bureau of the Census, *Census of Housing: 1970, 1980, and 1990* vol. 1, and unpublished data. [2] As of Dec. 31, except as noted. Source: Radio Advertising Bureau, New York, NY, *Radio Facts*, annual (copyright). Number of stations on the air compiled from Federal Communications Commission reports. [3] 1970-1975, as of Sept. of prior year; all other years as of Jan. of year shown. Excludes Alaska and Hawaii. Source: Television Bureau of Advertising, Inc., *Trends in Television*, annual (copyright). [4] As of February. Excludes Alaska and Hawaii. Source: See footnote 3. [5] As of February 1986. [6] As of Jan. 1 of year shown. Number of television stations on the air. Source: See footnote 3. [7] As of Jan. 1 of year shown. Source: Cable Advertising Bureau. [8] As of Sept. 30. Source: Editor & Publisher, Co., New York, NY, *Editor & Publisher International Year Book*, annual (copyright). [9] Per capita based on enumerated total resident population as of April 1 1970, 1980, and 1990. For all other years, based on estimates as of July 1. Estimates do not reflect revisions based on the 1990 Census of Population. Source: See footnote 3.

Source: Compiled from sources mentioned in footnotes.

No. 885. Multimedia Audiences—Summary: 1991

[In percent, except as indicated. As of spring. For persons 18 years old and over. Based on sample and subject to sampling error; see source for details]

ITEM	Total population (1,000)	Television viewing/ coverage	Television prime time viewing/ coverage	Cable viewing/ coverage	Radio listening/ coverage	Newspaper reading/ coverage
Total	183,814	92.8	79.4	56.1	84.7	83.9
18 to 24 years old	25,866	91.7	74.9	56.3	93.8	78.5
25 to 34 years old	44,367	92.0	79.0	57.1	91.9	84.2
35 to 44 years old	36,739	92.3	79.0	59.2	89.6	86.7
45 to 54 years old	25,123	91.5	77.9	59.0	85.6	86.9
55 to 64 years old	21,937	95.2	82.0	57.9	76.6	84.7
65 years old and over	29,782	94.9	83.6	46.9	65.0	81.4
Male	87,656	93.3	78.0	58.6	86.8	84.6
Female	96,158	92.4	80.6	53.8	82.7	83.2
White	158,153	92.4	78.6	58.1	84.8	85.5
Black	20,734	95.8	85.2	44.9	84.5	76.3
Other	4,926	92.5	79.6	41.0	80.1	64.4
Spanish speaking	13,949	94.8	82.9	39.4	87.9	72.4
Not high school graduate	41,614	93.5	81.0	40.3	75.5	65.4
High school graduate	71,872	93.1	80.9	58.5	85.2	86.2
Attended college	34,878	93.2	77.7	62.9	89.5	89.9
College graduate	35,449	91.1	76.1	63.1	89.6	95.1
Employed:						
Full-time	101,332	92.2	77.7	59.8	90.8	87.8
Part-time	14,797	91.4	77.9	58.4	88.3	86.2
Not employed	67,685	94.0	82.3	50.1	74.6	77.5
Household income:						
Less than $10,000	21,383	93.3	80.3	35.0	73.2	60.9
$10,000 to $19,999	30,690	94.0	82.2	44.2	78.7	76.5
$20,000 to $29,999	30,246	93.4	80.2	52.3	83.3	84.3
$30,000 to $34,999	15,122	92.8	78.9	60.6	85.2	85.8
$35,000 to $39,999	13,333	94.5	80.4	61.1	87.9	87.9
$40,000 to $49,999	21,970	92.6	78.3	64.6	90.3	90.1
$50,000 or more	51,070	91.2	77.2	68.1	90.4	93.3

Source: Mediamark Research Inc., New York, NY, *Multimedia Audiences*, fall 1991, (copyright).

No. 886. Telephone and Telegraph Systems: 1970 to 1990

[Covers principal carriers filing annual reports with Federal Communications Commission. Minus sign (-) indicates loss. See *Historical Statistics, Colonial Times to 1970,* series R 46-70 and R 75-88, for data on telegraph systems]

ITEM	Unit	1970	1980	1984	1985	1986	1987	1988	1989	1990
Domestic telephone: [1]										
Carriers [2]	Number	56	59	61	39	39	37	54	53	53
Access lines	Million	(NA)	(NA)	100	103	106	111	122	126	126
Miles of wire	Million	628	1,131	1,290	1,313	1,338	1,371	1,483	1,502	1,525
Gross book cost of plant	Bil. dol.	59.9	147.4	183.0	195.1	207.4	222.0	250.2	260.1	264.7
Depreciation reserves [3]	Bil. dol.	13.2	26.5	42.9	50.0	58.7	69.8	84.7	94.2	97.6
Ratio to book cost	Percent	22.1	18.0	23.5	25.6	28.3	31.4	33.9	36.2	36.9
Capital stock and premium	Bil. dol.	16.4	31.3	46.9	48.1	41.5	42.8	45.4	45.7	46.3
Operating revenues	Bil. dol.	18.2	55.6	98.9	104.8	106.4	106.3	116.7	117.3	117.7
Operating expenses [4]	Bil. dol.	11.7	37.3	74.7	78.6	79.0	79.8	90.8	91.7	91.6
Net operating income [5]	Bil. dol.	3.1	10.0	12.4	13.4	13.9	14.5	16.5	16.2	16.3
Net income	Bil. dol.	2.3	6.6	8.5	9.5	10.4	11.1	12.6	12.4	12.8
Employees	1,000.	839	938	742	(NA)	(NA)	(NA)	688	663	648
Compensation of employees	Bil. dol.	7.0	20.2	22.7	(NA)	(NA)	(NA)	24.9	24.4	25.9
Overseas telephone:										
Number of overseas calls	Million	23.4	199.6	427.6	411.7	477.6	579.6	705.7	1,007.8	1,200.7
Revenue from overseas calls	Mil. dol.	252	1,535	1,772	1,799	1,841	2,127	2,573	3,513.4	4,362.2
Ocean cable systems	Number	17	24	26	26	26	26	26	23	24
Communications satellites [6]	Number	4	5	6	6	11	11	14	15	16
Domestic and overseas telegraph: [7]										
Carriers	Number	7	8	7	7	7	7	6	6	3
Revenue messages transmitted	Million	102	75	48	42	29	25	(NA)	(NA)	(NA)
Message revenues [8]	Mil. dol.	358	676	732	708	678	594	483	521	259
Total operating revenues	Mil. dol.	596	1,232	1,382	1,367	1,206	1,076	882	1,019	408
Operating revenue deductions	Mil. dol.	524	1,008	1,323	1,292	1,243	1,125	942	995	447
Operating income [9]	Mil. dol.	72	147	48	102	-37	-48	-56	24	-39
Return on investment: [10]										
Telephone	Percent	7.1	8.7	9.2	9.4	9.4	9.6	10.0	9.8	9.8
Overseas telegraph	Percent	10.6	15.9	3.3	6.7	-1.5	2.5	-5.5	3.9	-9.4

NA Not available. [1] Includes Puerto Rico and Virgin Islands. Excludes intercompany duplications. Gross operating revenues of carriers reporting estimated at 90 percent of all carriers. Beginning 1988, based on new accounting rules; prior years not directly comparable. [2] Beginning 1985, number of carriers changed due to change in dollar requirement of reporting carriers from $1,000,000 to $100,000,000. [3] Includes amortization reserves. [4] Excludes taxes. [5] After tax deductions. [6] Excludes contingency and retired satellites. [7] Excludes South American and most Caribbean operations of All America Cables and Radio, Inc. [8] Includes telex service; for domestic telegraph, excludes TWX. [9] After Federal income taxes. [10] Ratio of net operating income (after taxes) to average net book cost of communications plant.
Source: U.S. Federal Communications Commission, *Statistics of Communications Common Carriers,* annual; and unpublished data.

No. 887. Telephone Communications—Operating Revenue and Expenses: 1989 and 1990

[Covers employer firms with one or more establishments that are primarily engaged in furnishing telephone communication services. Based on the *1972 Standard Industrial Classification Manual;* see text, section 13]

ITEM	1989 Total (mil. dol.)	1989 Percent of total	1990 Total (mil. dol.)	1990 Percent of total	Percent change, 1989-90
OPERATING REVENUE					
Total	150,935	100.0	156,003	100.0	3.4
Local service	37,816	25.1	39,231	25.2	3.7
Long-distance service	66,165	43.8	68,128	43.7	3.0
Network access	28,971	19.2	29,189	18.7	0.8
Cellular and other radiotelephone	2,652	1.8	3,563	2.3	34.3
Directory advertising	7,683	5.1	8,187	5.3	6.6
Other operating revenue	7,647	5.1	7,705	4.9	0.8
OPERATING EXPENSES					
Total	123,131	100.0	126,775	100.0	3.0
Annual payroll	29,205	23.7	30,799	24.3	5.5
Employer contributions to Social Security and other supplemental benefits	7,166	5.8	7,303	5.8	1.9
Access charges	24,783	20.1	25,003	19.7	0.9
Depreciation	22,561	18.3	22,817	18.0	1.1
Buildings, offices, and structures	756	0.6	769	0.6	1.6
Communication systems	18,336	14.9	18,320	14.5	-0.1
Vehicles, machinery and equipment, and other tangible assets	3,469	2.8	3,728	2.9	7.5
Lease and rental	3,592	2.9	3,442	2.7	-4.2
Buildings, offices, and structures	1,426	1.2	1,520	1.2	6.6
Communication systems	1,215	1.0	1,178	0.9	-3.0
Vehicles, machinery and equipment, and other tangible assets	951	0.8	744	0.6	-21.8
Purchased repairs	2,624	2.1	2,819	2.2	7.4
Insurance	170	0.1	171	0.1	0.4
Telephone and other purchased communication services	406	0.3	485	0.4	19.4
Purchased utilities	882	0.7	889	0.7	0.7
Purchased advertising	1,625	1.3	2,004	1.6	23.3
Taxes	4,930	4.0	5,106	4.0	3.6
Other operating expenses	25,186	20.5	25,939	20.5	3.0

Source: U.S. Bureau of the Census, *Annual Survey of Communication Services: 1990.*

No. 888. Telephone Companies—Summary: 1980 to 1990

[As of Dec. 31 or **calendar year,** as applicable. January 1, 1988 marked the beginning of significant rules changes in the way that local exchange carriers account for assets, liabilities, revenue, expenses, and income. Any comparisons with earlier data would not be meaningful. See also *Historical Statistics, Colonial Times to 1970,* series R 31-45]

ITEM	Unit	INDEPENDENT COMPANIES [1]				ALL TELEPHONE COMPANIES				
		1980	1985	1989	1990	1984	1985	1988	1989	1990
All companies	Number .	1,483	1,402	1,332	1,310	1,440	1,426	1,371	1,354	1,332
Access lines	Millions .	20.8	24.3	32.2	32.2	114.5	118.2	130.0	135.0	138.1
Total telephone plant	Bil. dol. .	35.3	49.1	61.8	64.7	193.8	207.3	238.3	249.0	256.0
Operating revenues.	Bil. dol. .	10.5	17.2	21.7	22.1	73.9	78.4	89.9	89.1	90.1
Avg. daily conversations [2] . .	Millions .	192	226	(NA)	(NA)	1,199	1,264	1,700	9,569	9,515
Local calls	Millions .	177	203	(NA)	(NA)	1,111	1,162	(NA)	(NA)	(NA)
Toll calls	Millions .	15	20	(NA)	(NA)	88	102	(NA)	(NA)	(NA)
Reporting companies [3]	Number .	765	653	579	594	655	677	607	601	616
Access lines	Millions .	19.4	23.4	29.8	30.3	113.6	117.4	129.7	132.7	136.3
Telephone plant in service [4] .	Bil. dol. .	32.5	45.5	60.0	62.8	186.2	200.0	233.3	243.9	250.9
Depreciation reserves [5]	Bil. dol. .	7.8	14.3	22.0	23.7	45.7	52.9	80.0	89.6	95.0
Operating revenues	Bil. dol. .	10.2	16.7	21.7	22.1	73.3	77.9	85.9	87.9	89.1
Operating expenses [6]	Bil. dol. .	7.3	11.9	15.3	15.6	59.8	63.7	61.2	63.9	65.2
Net income	Bil. dol. .	1.3	2.4	3.3	3.4	9.3	10.1	11.8	11.5	11.6
Stockholders' equity	Bil. dol. .	9.6	13.9	20.9	22.1	63.1	66.5	75.8	76.8	80.4
Net income to stockholders equity	Percent .	13.2	17.5	15.8	15.4	14.7	15.1	15.6	15.0	14.4
Employees	1,000 . .	189	170	163	161	724	695	639	626	606
Wages and salaries.	Bil. dol. .	3.4	4.6	(NA)	(NA)	22.1	21.4	(NA)	(NA)	(NA)

NA Not available.   [1] Companies independent of the Bell System, prior to divestiture of January 1984.   [2] Average business day minutes of use beginning 1989.   [3] Comprises only companies submitting operating information to source cited below.   [4] Total property plant and equipment beginning 1989.   [5] Total accumulated depreciation and amortization beginning 1989.   [6] Excludes Federal income tax.

Source: United States Telephone Association, Washington, DC, *Statistics of the Local Exchange Carriers,* annual, (copyright).

No. 889. Cellular Telephone Industry: 1984 to 1991

[**Calendar year data.** Based on a survey mailed to 1,252 cellular systems]

ITEM	Unit	1984	1985	1986	1987	1988	1989	1990	1991
Systems	Number .	32	102	166	312	517	584	751	1,252
Subscribers	1,000. . .	92	340	682	1,231	2,069	3,509	5,283	7,557
Cell sites [1]	Number .	346	913	1,531	2,305	3,209	4,169	5,616	7,847
Employees	Number .	1,404	2,727	4,334	7,147	11,400	15,927	21,382	26,327
Service revenue . . . [2]	Mil. dol. .	178	482	823	1,152	1,960	3,341	4,549	5,709
Roamer revenue [2]	Mil. dol. .	(NA)	(NA)	(NA)	(NA)	89	295	456	704
Capital investment . . [3]	Mil. dol. .	355	556	526	798	1,039	1,206	1,801	2,390
Average monthly bill [3]	Dollars. .	(NA)	(NA)	(NA)	96.83	98.02	89.30	80.90	72.74
Average call length [3]	Minutes .	(NA)	(NA)	(NA)	2.33	2.26	2.48	2.20	2.38

NA Not available.   [1] The basic geographic unit of a cellular system. A city or county is divided into smaller "cells," each of which is equipped with a low-powered radio transmitter/receiver. The cells can vary in size depending upon terrain, capacity demands, etc. By controlling the transmission power, the radio frequencies assigned to one cell can be limited to the boundaries of that cell. When a cellular phone moves from one cell toward another, a computer at the Switching Office monitors the movement and at the proper time, transfers or hands off the phone call to the new cell and another radio frequency.   [2] Service revenue generated by subscribers' calls outside of their home system areas. Excludes taxes and tolls.   [3] As of December 31.

Source: Cellular Telecommunications Industry Association, Washington, DC, *State of the Cellular Industry,* annual, (copyright).

No. 890. Private Radio Stations Authorized, by Class: 1985 to 1990

[In thousands. As of Sept. 30. Includes Puerto Rico and Virgin Islands. See also *Historical Statistics, Colonial Times to 1970*, series R 140-148]

CLASS	1985	1988	1989	1990	CLASS	1985	1988	1989	1990
Private radio services [1]	2,420	2,748	2,828	2,880	Railroad	13.8	15.4	16.0	16.2
Personal [1]	(X)	475.3	501.7	528.0	Taxicab	6.1	5.9	5.9	5.7
General mobile	33.6	36.2	34.4	32.3	Interurban property	4.4	5.4	5.6	5.8
Amateur and disaster	415.4	439.1	467.3	495.7	Other	13.4	13.4	12.9	12.4
Aviation	245.7	248.5	251.2	250.9	Marine	525.3	605.4	620.4	622.9
Aircraft	207.3	207.9	210.2	209.6	Ship	510.4	589.4	604.6	607.2
Aeronautical and fixed	10.9	11.7	11.7	12.1	Alaskan	2.7	2.7	2.5	2.4
Civil air patrol	23.0	23.9	24.2	24.4	Coastal and other	12.2	13.3	13.3	13.3
Other	4.5	5.0	5.1	4.8	Public safety	194.5	221.4	228.5	234.5
Industrial	811.3	875.6	873.9	864.8	Police	42.3	47.8	49.1	50.5
Power	34.4	42.8	44.3	45.7	Fire	36.6	41.3	42.8	44.0
Business	593.5	641.7	638.0	628.1	Forestry conservation	9.6	10.7	11.1	11.3
Petroleum	25.2	26.8	27.0	26.8	Highway maintenance	12.7	14.3	14.6	15.0
Forest products	9.8	11.3	11.6	11.7	Special emergency	37.4	40.5	40.9	41.1
Special industrial	115.0	117.0	115.4	113.5	Other	55.9	66.8	70.0	72.6
Other	33.4	36.0	37.6	39.0	Operational fixed				
Land transportation	37.7	40.1	40.4	40.1	services [2]	23.1	29.2	29.9	32.9

X Not applicable.   [1] Includes items not shown separately. Each license, construction permit, or combination construction permit and license is counted one station; therefore, a station might include a transmitter and many mobile units.   [2] Includes microwave operations.

Source: U.S. Federal Communications Commission, *Annual Report*, and unpublished data.

No. 891. Radio and Television Broadcasting Services—Operating Revenue and Expenses: 1989 and 1990

[In millions of dollars. Based on the *1972 Standard Industrial Classification Manual*; see text, section 13. Based on a sample; see Appendix III]

ITEM	TOTAL BROAD-CASTING		RADIO		TELEVISION	
	1989	1990	1989	1990	1989	1990
OPERATING REVENUE						
Total	27,882	28,684	7,341	7,391	20,540	21,293
Station time sales	18,511	18,847	6,658	6,670	11,854	12,176
Network compensation	587	592	124	131	464	461
National/regional advertising	6,868	7,090	1,687	1,712	5,181	5,378
Local advertising	11,056	11,164	4,847	4,827	6,209	6,337
Network time sales	7,893	8,178	324	328	7,569	7,850
Other operating revenue	1,477	1,660	360	392	1,118	1,267
OPERATING EXPENSES						
Total	23,810	24,948	6,688	6,788	17,122	18,160
Annual payroll	6,478	6,681	2,577	2,636	3,901	4,045
Employer contributions to Social Security and other supplemental benefits	1,008	1,056	351	361	657	696
Broadcast rights	7,458	8,085	438	445	7,020	7,641
Music license fees	364	357	151	152	212	205
Network compensation fees	513	525	90	103	423	422
Depreciation	1,377	1,372	525	516	852	856
Lease and rental	511	514	167	173	344	340
Purchased repairs	244	249	84	86	160	163
Insurance	149	147	70	69	78	78
Telephone and other purchased communication services	238	241	114	113	124	128
Purchased utilities	250	255	95	98	155	157
Purchased advertising	963	951	419	392	544	559
Taxes	179	174	62	61	117	113
Other operating expenses	4,079	4,341	1,544	1,582	2,535	2,758

Source: U.S. Bureau of the Census, *Annual Survey of Communication Services: 1990*.

No. 892. Public Television Stations: 1976 to 1988

[Calendar year data for 1976; fiscal year data thereafter. General programing is directed at the general community. Instructional programing is directed at students in the classroom or otherwise in the general context of formal education]

ITEM	1976	1978	1980	1982	1984	1986	1988
Stations broadcasting . . .	253	272	281	291	303	305	(NA)
Number of broadcasters [1]	152	156	160	164	169	178	169
Average annual hours per broadcaster.	4,542	4,894	5,128	5,421	5,542	5,650	6,135
BROADCAST HOURS, PERCENT DISTRIBUTION							
Program content [2]	100.0	100.0	100.0	100.0	100.0	100.0	100.0
General [2]	66.5	70.7	71.3	72.0	73.2	74.5	72.9
News and public affairs [3]	11.9	11.0	12.2	12.4	14.1	16.4	16.3
Information and skills	19.9	23.6	22.8	24.5	25.5	29.5	21.7
Cultural	20.9	22.1	21.9	22.8	20.1	20.5	17.9
General children's and youth's	10.0	8.7	8.9	7.5	7.9	6.5	5.8
Instructional	16.6	14.9	14.7	14.3	13.0	14.5	15.5
The Electric Co., Villa Alegre [4]	1.8	1.6	1.5	1.1	1.0	0.4	(NA)
Other [5]	14.8	13.3	13.2	13.2	12.0	14.1	(NA)
Sesame Street and The Electric Company [4]	17.8	16.1	15.5	14.8	11.4	11.4	11.7
Producer [2]	100.0	100.0	100.0	100.0	100.0	100.0	100.0
Local	10.1	7.7	7.0	6.7	5.7	5.2	5.2
Major public television production center, and other	48.2	52.2	46.2	45.6	44.4	37.6	27.1
Consortium	1.7	1.8	2.7	2.6	3.3	3.1	9.8
Children's television workshop.	18.8	16.8	17.1	15.8	16.4	29.1	16.1
Independent and commercial producers	8.9	8.0	11.1	15.2	12.0	(NA)	23.8
Foreign producer, international coproduction	7.6	9.1	12.5	10.1	13.2	15.1	14.0
Distributor [2]	100.0	100.0	100.0	100.0	100.0	100.0	100.0
Local distribution only	10.0	7.4	6.8	6.2	5.6	4.9	6.4
Public broadcasting service	69.3	71.6	69.6	67.1	65.3	63.9	62.0
Regional public television network	6.2	5.4	7.6	10.8	13.0	14.0	17.8

NA Not available.   [1] In 1988, only broadcasters in the 50 U.S. States were surveyed.   [2] Includes other items not shown separately.   [3] In 1986 and 1988, this category includes "Business or Consumer".   [4] After 1976 "Electric Company" was double counted if aired during school hours when school is in session.   [5] Excluding "Sesame Street" and "The Electric Company" but including "Mister Rogers." Includes adult educational.

Source: Corporation for Public Broadcasting, Washington, DC, PTV Programming Survey, biennial.

No. 893. Public Broadcasting Systems—Income, by Source: 1980 to 1990

[In millions of dollars, except percent. Stations as of Dec. 31; fiscal year data for income. Includes nonbroadcast income]

NUMBER OF STATIONS AND INCOME SOURCE	1980	1985	1986	1987	1988	1989	1990	PERCENT DISTRIBUTION		
								1980	1985	1990
CPB-qualified public radio stations. . . .	217	288	295	299	308	313	315	(X)	(X)	(X)
Public television stations	290	317	322	323	324	340	341	(X)	(X)	(X)
Total income.	705	1,096	1,134	1,295	1,368	1,549	1,581	100.0	100.0	100.0
Federal government	193	179	186	243	248	264	267	27.3	16.3	16.9
State and local government [1]	272	358	379	389	416	454	474	38.5	32.7	30.0
Subscribers and auction/marathon . . .	102	248	269	298	321	347	364	14.5	22.6	23.0
Business and industry	72	171	171	196	213	242	262	10.3	15.6	16.6
Foundation	24	43	38	48	51	69	71	3.3	3.9	4.5
Other	43	97	92	121	120	173	143	6.0	8.9	9.0

X Not applicable.   [1] Includes income received from State colleges and universities.
Source: Corporation for Public Broadcasting (CPB), Washington, DC, Public Broadcasting Income, Fiscal Year, 1990; and unpublished data.

No. 894. Cable Television—Systems and Subscribers: 1970 to 1991

[Subscribers in thousands, except percent. Estimated]

YEAR (As of Jan. 1)	Sys-tems	Sub-scribers	YEAR (As of Jan. 1)	Sys-tems	Sub-scribers	SUBSCRIBER SIZE-GROUP	NUMBER OF [1]—		PERCENT OF [1]—	
							Sys-tems	Sub-scribers	Sys-tems	Sub-scribers
1970	2,490	4,500	1982	4,825	21,000	1991, total [2]	10,704	50,770	100	100
1973	2,991	7,300	1983	5,600	25,000	50,000 and over	203	19,647	2	39
1974	3,158	8,700	1984	6,200	30,000	20,000 to 49,999.	410	12,783	4	25
1975	3,506	9,800	1985	6,600	32,000	10,000 to 19,999.	496	7,018	5	14
1976	3,681	10,800	1986	7,600	37,500	5,000 to 9,999	635	4,453	6	9
1977	3,832	11,900	1987	7,900	41,100	3,500 to 4,999	401	1,665	4	3
1978	3,875	13,000	1988	8,500	44,000	1,000 to 3,499	1,774	3,377	17	7
1979	4,150	14,100	1989	9,050	47,500	500 to 999	1,339	954	13	2
1980	4,225	16,000	1990	9,575	50,000	250 to 499	1,411	508	13	1
1981	4,375	18,300	1991	10,704	51,000	Less than 250	2,787	364	26	1

[1] As of April 1, 1991.   [2] Excludes 1,248 systems not available by subscriber size-group.
Source: Warren Publishing, Inc., Washington, DC, Television & Cable Factbook, annual, (copyright).

No. 895. Cable and Pay TV—Summary: 1955 to 1990

[Cable TV for calendar year. Pay TV, as of **Dec. 31** of year shown]

YEAR	CABLE TV				PAY TV					
	Avg. basic sub-scribers (1,000)	Avg. monthly basic rate (dol.)	Revenue [1] (mil. dol.)		Units [2] (1,000)		Monthly rate (dollars)		Pay cable units	
			Total	Basic	Total pay [3]	Pay cable	Total pay [3]	Pay cable	Percent of homes passed	Percent basic
1955	250	5.00	20	20	(X)	(X)	(X)	(X)	(X)	(X)
1960	750	5.00	50	50	(X)	(X)	(X)	(X)	(X)	(X)
1965	1,500	5.00	95	95	(X)	(X)	(X)	(X)	(X)	(X)
1970	5,100	5.50	345	345	(X)	(X)	(X)	(X)	(X)	(X)
1975	9,800	6.50	804	774	469	469	(X)	7.85	11.1	23.6
1976	11,000	6.72	976	897	1,021	978	(NA)	7.87	10.6	22.3
1977	12,200	7.00	1,221	1,035	1,733	1,642	8.12	7.92	12.2	25.3
1978	13,400	7.26	1,496	1,177	3,580	3,289	8.62	8.09	17.9	35.0
1979	15,000	7.53	1,906	1,367	6,409	5,732	9.37	8.44	22.3	41.3
1980	17,500	7.85	2,603	1,668	10,389	9,144	9.78	8.80	27.9	50.6
1981	21,500	8.14	3,717	2,140	17,521	15,450	10.13	9.02	37.6	68.8
1982	25,400	8.46	5,097	2,628	23,179	20,791	10.36	9.57	46.2	84.0
1983	29,450	8.76	6,512	3,151	28,115	26,418	10.25	9.84	47.3	84.3
1984	32,850	9.20	7,892	3,696	31,027	29,966	10.32	10.08	49.5	87.5
1985	35,430	10.24	9,305	4,522	31,055	30,596	10.53	10.42	47.1	83.3
1986	38,740	11.09	10,520	5,341	32,428	32,064	10.40	10.31	46.2	80.8
1987	41,200	13.27	12,374	6,778	35,110	34,793	10.21	10.15	47.5	81.6
1988	44,200	14.45	13,979	7,883	39,144	38,819	10.22	10.18	50.3	85.0
1989	47,390	15.97	15,933	9,322	41,234	41,095	10.26	10.21	49.6	83.3
1990	[4]50,455	17.58	[4]17,784	[4]10,074	(NA)	41,505	(NA)	10.38	(NA)	80.2

NA Not available.   X Not applicable.   [1] Includes installation revenue.   [2] Individual program services sold to subscribers.
[3] Includes multipoint distribution service (MDS) and satellite TV (STV).   [4] Projection.

Source: Paul Kagan Associates, Inc., Carmel, CA, *The Cable TV Financial Databook,* annual, (copyright); *The Kagan Census of Cable; and Pay TV,* 1991, and *The Pay TV Newsletter,* June 29, 1991.

No. 896. Cable and Other Pay Television Services—Operating Revenue: 1989 and 1990

[Cable and other pay television services include establishments primarily engaged in the dissemination of visual and textual television programs on a subscription or fee basis. Based on the *1972 Standard Industrial Classification Manual;* see text, section 13]

OPERATING REVENUE	1989		1990		Percent change, 1989-90
	Total (mil. dol.)	Percent of total	Total (mil. dol.)	Percent of total	
Total	18,739	100.0	21,309	100.0	13.7
Advertising	1,254	6.7	1,602	7.5	27.7
Program revenue	861	4.6	1,103	5.2	28.2
Basic service.	10,042	53.6	11,475	53.9	14.3
Pay and other premium service.	5,284	28.2	5,643	26.5	6.8
Installation fees	298	1.6	330	1.6	10.9
Other cable and pay television revenue	1,000	5.3	1,156	5.4	15.6

Source: U.S. Bureau of the Census, *Annual Survey of Communication Services: 1990.*

No. 897. Publishing Industry—Summary: 1982 to 1990

[**In millions of dollars, except as noted.** Number in parentheses represents Standard Industrial Classification code; see text, section 13. Based on the censuses of manufactures and the Annual Survey of Manufactures (ASM). For the 1990 ASM, a major change in the survey was introduced. This change resulted from a backlog of previously unclassified single-establishment companies, now classified as manufacturing; for details, see text, section 27 and Appendix III]

ITEM	NEWSPAPERS (271)				PERIODICALS (272)				BOOKS (273)			
	1982	1987	1989	1990	1982	1987	1989	1990	1982	1987	1989	1990
Establishments	8,846	9,091	(NA)	(NA)	3,328	4,020	(NA)	(NA)	2,130	2,298	(NA)	(NA)
With 20 or more employees	2,554	2,617	(NA)	(NA)	690	876	(NA)	(NA)	419	424	(NA)	(NA)
Employees [1] (1,000)	402	435	431	443	94	110	116	115	67	70	74	74
Payroll	6,555	9,025	9,842	10,407	1,986	2,983	3,423	3,659	1,327	1,860	2,132	2,300
Value of receipts	21,276	31,849	34,146	34,642	11,478	17,329	19,787	20,397	7,740	12,620	14,074	15,318
Cost of materials	6,006	7,533	8,218	8,087	4,568	5,873	6,581	6,580	2,420	3,663	4,366	4,466
Value added [2]	15,275	24,311	25,930	26,560	6,911	11,452	13,248	13,848	5,292	9,111	9,916	10,920
New capital expends. . . .	1,029	1,523	1,985	1,886	195	246	272	275	174	240	319	329
Fixed assets, gross assets.	8,701	14,028	(NA)	(NA)	1,370	2,528	(NA)	(NA)	1,109	1,680	(NA)	(NA)
Inventories, Dec. 31	755	857	881	975	724	902	1,107	1,118	1,380	2,091	2,643	2,769

NA Not available.   [1] Represents the average number of production workers plus the number of other employees in mid-March.   [2] By manufacture, derived by subtracting the cost of materials, supplies, containers, fuel, purchased electricity, and contract work from the value of shipments. This result is then adjusted by the addition of value added by merchandising operations, plus the net change in finished goods and work-in-process inventories between the beginning and the end of the year.

Source: U.S. Bureau of the Census, *Census of Manufactures, 1987,* Industry Reports, series MC87-I-27A, and *1990 Annual Survey of Manufactures,* M90(AS)-1.

No. 898. Newspapers and Periodicals—Number, by Type: 1970 to 1992

[Data refer to year of compilation of the Directory cited as the source, i.e., generally to year preceding year shown. See also *Historical Statistics, Colonial Times to 1970*, series R 232-243]

TYPE	1970	1975	1980	1985	1986	1987	1988	1989	1990	1991	1992
Newspapers [1]	11,383	11,400	9,620	9,134	9,144	9,031	10,088	10,457	11,471	11,689	11,339
Semiweekly.	423	506	537	517	495	510	555	567	579	574	562
Weekly.	8,903	8,824	7,159	6,811	6,857	6,750	7,438	7,622	8,420	8,546	8,293
Daily	1,838	1,819	1,744	1,701	1,651	1,646	1,745	1,773	1,788	1,781	1,755
Periodicals [1] . . .	9,573	9,657	10,236	11,090	11,328	11,593	11,229	11,556	11,092	11,239	11,143
Weekly. . . . .᠎. . . .	1,856	1,918	1,716	1,367	1,383	1,400	880	828	553	511	466
Semimonthly [2].	589	537	645	801	789	858	619	622	435	412	371
Monthly	4,314	4,087	3,985	4,088	4,066	4,031	4,192	4,445	4,239	4,340	4,326
Bimonthly	957	1,009	1,114	1,361	1,387	1,402	1,558	1,880	2,087	2,116	2,143
Quarterly	1,108	1,093	1,444	1,759	1,895	1,984	2,245	2,513	2,758	2,861	3,024

[1] Includes other items not shown separately.   [2] Includes fortnightly (every 2 weeks).

Source: Gale Research, Inc., *1992 Gale Directory of Publications and Broadcast Media*, 124th edition, and earlier editions, (copyright).

No. 899. Number and Circulation of Daily and Sunday Newspapers: 1970 to 1990

[Number of newspapers as of Feb. 1 of the following year. Circulation figures as of Sept. 30. For English language newspapers only. See also *Historical Statistics, Colonial Times to 1970*, series R 224-231]

TYPE	1970	1975	1980	1981	1982	1983	1984	1985	1986	1987	1988	1989	1990
NUMBER OF NEWSPAPERS													
Daily: Total [1]	1,748	1,756	1,745	1,730	1,711	1,701	1,688	1,676	1,657	1,645	1,642	1,626	1,611
Morning.	334	339	387	408	434	446	458	482	499	511	529	530	559
Evening.	1,429	1,436	1,388	1,352	1,310	1,284	1,257	1,220	1,188	1,166	1,141	1,125	1,084
Sunday.	586	639	736	755	768	772	783	798	802	820	840	847	863
CIRCULATION (mil.)													
Daily: Total [1]	62.1	60.7	62.2	61.4	62.5	62.6	63.1	62.8	62.5	62.8	62.7	62.6	62.3
Morning.	25.9	25.5	29.4	30.6	33.2	33.8	35.4	36.4	37.4	39.1	40.4	40.7	41.3
Evening.	36.2	35.2	32.8	30.9	29.3	28.8	27.7	26.4	25.1	23.7	22.2	21.8	21.0
Sunday.	49.2	51.1	54.7	55.2	56.3	56.7	57.5	58.8	58.9	60.1	61.5	62.0	62.6

[1] All-day newspapers are counted in both morning and evening columns but only once in total. Circulation is divided equally between morning and evening.

Source: Editor & Publisher Co., New York, NY, *Editor & Publisher International Year Book*, annual, (copyright).

No. 900. Number and Circulation of Daily Newspapers, by Population—Size Class of City: 1975 to 1990

[Number of newspapers as of Feb. 1 of the following year. Circulation as of Sept. 30. For English language newspapers only. See table 37 for number of cities by population size]

TYPE OF DAILY AND POPULATION-SIZE CLASS	NUMBER [1]					NET PAID CIRCULATION [1] (1,000)				
	1975	1980	1985	1989	1990	1975	1980	1985	1989	1990
Morning dailies, total.	339	387	482	530	559	25,491	29,413	36,361	40,759	41,311
In cities of—										
1,000,001 or more	14	20	22	28	18	7,159	8,795	9,367	11,727	6,508
500,001 to 1,000,000 . . .	25	27	24	23	22	5,581	5,705	6,897	5,053	4,804
100,001 to 500,000	89	99	121	130	138	7,836	8,996	12,197	14,890	20,051
50,001 to 100,000	69	75	87	94	100	2,619	2,973	3,653	4,071	4,373
25,001 to 50,000	67	64	83	97	102	1,422	1,701	2,145	2,927	3,209
Less than 25,000	75	102	145	158	179	874	1,243	2,099	2,087	2,365
Evening dailies, total.	1,436	1,388	1,220	1,125	1,084	35,166	32,788	26,407	21,890	21,017
In cities of—										
1,000,001 or more	12	11	8	8	7	4,156	2,984	2,169	1,349	1,423
500,001 to 1,000,000 . . .	24	23	14	14	12	4,573	4,101	1,626	1,569	1,350
100,001 to 500,000	127	123	102	77	71	8,918	8,178	6,987	5,035	4,687
50,001 to 100,000	175	156	127	105	94	5,379	4,896	3,942	3,336	2,941
25,001 to 50,000	248	246	229	209	204	4,898	5,106	4,606	4,065	1,278
Less than 25,000 , , , , , .	850	820	740	712	696	7,242	7,523	7,075	6,533	6,338

[1] All-day newspapers are counted in both morning and evening columns; circulation is divided equally between morning and evening.

Source: Editor & Publisher Co., New York, NY, *Editor & Publisher International Year Book*, annual, (copyright).

No. 901. Daily and Sunday Newspapers—Number and Circulation, by State: 1990

[Number of newspapers as of Feb. 1 of the following year. Circulation figures as of Sept. 30. For English language newspapers only. New York, Massachusetts, and Virginia Sunday newspapers include national circulation]

STATE	DAILY			SUNDAY		STATE	DAILY			SUNDAY	
	Num-ber	Circulation [1]		Num-ber	Net paid circula-tion (1,000)		Num-ber	Circulation [1]		Num-ber	Net paid circula-tion (1,000)
		Net paid (1,000)	Per cap-ita [2]					Net paid (1,000)	Per cap-ita [2]		
Total.	1,611	62,328.0	0.25	863	62,634.5	MO	44	1,092.6	0.21	20	1,336.2
AL	27	766.5	0.19	21	766.9	MT	11	188.7	0.24	7	194.0
AK	7	136.3	0.25	4	151.0	NE	20	471.3	0.30	7	436.8
AZ	20	737.4	0.20	12	820.9	NV	8	261.9	0.22	4	301.8
AR	32	566.0	0.24	17	675.2	NH	9	215.5	0.19	4	158.3
CA	116	6,591.3	0.22	71	6,753.9	NJ	23	1,685.9	0.22	17	1,925.1
CO	29	1,007.9	0.31	11	1,159.8	NM	18	314.1	0.21	13	289.0
CT	21	847.8	0.26	11	830.6	NY	71	7,418.1	0.41	40	5,902.4
DE	2	144.7	0.22	2	171.9	NC	53	1,453.4	0.22	35	1,452.7
DC	2	877.8	1.45	1	1,137.0	ND	10	187.3	0.29	7	185.6
FL	43	3,175.0	0.25	36	3,920.0	OH	87	2,745.6	0.25	34	2,893.2
GA	36	1,211.4	0.19	18	1,311.6	OK	49	744.2	0.24	43	907.3
HI	6	244.3	0.22	5	262.0	OR	20	673.1	0.24	10	701.1
ID	12	208.8	0.21	8	226.8	PA	91	3,277.8	0.28	29	3,165.3
IL	69	2,596.6	0.23	27	2,748.0	RI	6	294.6	0.29	3	306.8
IN	74	1,512.0	0.27	22	1,370.5	SC	17	675.5	0.19	13	727.5
IA	37	724.9	0.26	10	738.1	SD	12	168.0	0.24	4	136.6
KS	46	531.1	0.21	17	492.6	TN	28	969.5	0.20	16	1,082.6
KY	23	662.4	0.18	12	673.7	TX	98	3,586.3	0.21	89	4,599.5
LA	28	780.4	0.18	21	892.1	UT	6	285.3	0.17	6	327.5
ME	8	282.3	0.23	2	189.7	VT	9	149.8	0.27	3	103.4
MD	15	738.5	0.15	7	679.0	VA	34	2,525.4	0.41	15	990.3
MA	40	2,015.9	0.34	14	1,770.1	WA	26	1,181.9	0.24	15	1,207.7
MI	52	2,373.3	0.26	23	2,431.4	WV	23	436.0	0.24	11	412.0
MN	25	949.9	0.22	13	1,147.1	WI	36	1,145.2	0.23	15	1,118.4
MS	22	403.2	0.16	14	379.5	WY	10	95.6	0.21	4	74.2

[1] Circulation figures based on the principal community served by a newspaper which is not necessarily the same location as the publisher's office.   [2] Per capita based on enumerated resident population as of April 1.

Source: Editor & Publisher Co., New York, NY, *Editor & Publisher International Year Book,* annual, (copyright).

No. 902. Copyright Registration, by Subject Matter: 1985 to 1991

[In thousands. For years ending Sept. 30. Comprises claims to copyright registered for both U.S. and foreign works. See also *Historical Statistics, Colonial Times to 1970,* series W 82-95]

SUBJECT MATTER OF COPYRIGHT	1985	1990	1991	SUBJECT MATTER OF COPYRIGHT	1985	1990	1991
Total	539.8	643.5	663.7	Sound recordings	22.7	37.5	36.8
Monographs [1]	154.5	179.7	193.8	Renewals	43.8	51.8	52.3
Semiconductor chip products	0.9	1.0	1.2	Musical works [2]	147.9	185.3	191.2
Serials	120.0	111.5	109.2	Works of the visual arts [3]	50.0	76.7	79.2

[1] Includes computer software and machine readable works.   [2] Includes dramatic works, accompanying music, choreography, pantomimes, motion pictures, and filmstrips.   [3] Two-dimensional works of fine and graphic art, including prints and art reproductions; sculptural works; technical drawings and models; photographs; commercial prints and labels; works of applied arts, cartographic works, and multimedia works.

Source: The Library of Congress, *Annual Report.*

No. 903. Advertising—Estimated Expenditures: 1950 to 1991

[In millions of dollars. National advertising is defined as advertising done for companies whose products are distributed nationally and for which national media rates are paid. Local advertising is defined as advertising done for companies which market products locally and which may pay special "local" media rates. See also *Historical Statistics, Colonial Times to 1970,* series T 444-446]

YEAR	Total	National	Local	YEAR	Total	National	Local	YEAR	Total	National	Local
1950.	5,700	3,260	2,440	1975.	27,900	15,200	12,700	1984.	87,820	49,690	38,130
1955.	9,150	5,380	3,770	1976.	33,300	18,355	14,945	1985.	94,750	53,355	41,395
1960.	11,960	7,305	4,655	1977.	37,440	20,595	16,845	1986.	102,140	56,850	45,290
1965.	15,250	9,340	5,910	1978.	43,330	23,720	19,610	1987.	109,650	60,625	49,025
1970.	19,550	11,350	8,200	1979.	48,780	26,695	22,085	1988.	118,050	65,610	52,440
1971.	20,700	11,755	8,945	1980.	53,550	29,815	23,735	1989.	123,930	68,990	54,940
1972.	23,210	12,980	10,230	1981.	60,430	33,890	26,540	1990.	128,640	72,780	55,860
1973.	24,980	13,700	11,280	1982.	66,580	37,785	28,795	1991 [1] . . .	126,680	72,690	53,990
1974.	26,620	14,700	11,920	1983.	75,850	42,525	33,325				

[1] Projection.

Source: McCann-Erickson, Inc., New York, NY. Compiled for Crain Communications, Inc. In *Advertising Age,* (copyright).

No. 904. Advertising—Indexes of National Advertising Expenditures, by Medium: 1970 to 1990

[1982-84 = 100. Based on the average monthly expenditure for those major media which give national coverage. See also *Historical Statistics, Colonial Times to 1970*, series T 472-484]

MEDIUM	1970	1980	1981	1982	1983	1984	1985	1986	1987	1988	1989	1990
General index	26	71	79	87	98	114	118	124	128	136	141	(NA)
Network television	23	72	78	86	97	116	113	117	119	128	128	131
Spot television	25	67	77	89	99	112	123	134	140	146	150	159
Magazines	30	73	82	86	99	115	120	124	131	142	156	159
Newspapers	32	71	82	89	99	112	122	123	127	130	135	140

NA Not available.
Source: McCann-Erickson, Inc., New York, NY. Compiled for Crain Communications, Inc. In *Advertising Age*, (copyright).

No. 905. Advertising—Estimated Expenditures, by Medium: 1970 to 1990

[In millions of dollars, except percent. See text, section 18 for a discussion of types of advertising. See also *Historical Statistics, Colonial Times to 1970*, series R 106-109, R 123-126, and T 444-471]

MEDIUM	EXPENDITURES							PERCENT			
	1970	1980	1985	1987	1988	1989	1990	1970	1980	1985	1990
Total	19,550	53,550	94,750	109,650	118,050	123,930	128,640	100	100	100	100
National	11,350	29,815	53,355	60,625	65,610	68,990	72,780	58	56	56	57
Local	8,200	23,735	41,395	49,025	52,440	54,940	55,860	42	44	44	43
Newspapers	5,704	14,794	25,170	29,412	31,197	32,368	32,281	29	28	27	25
National	891	1,963	3,352	3,494	3,586	3,720	3,867	5	4	4	3
Local	4,813	12,831	21,818	25,918	27,611	28,648	28,414	25	24	23	22
Magazines	1,292	3,149	5,155	5,607	6,072	6,716	6,803	7	6	5	5
Weeklies	617	1,418	2,297	2,445	2,646	2,813	2,864	3	3	2	2
Women's	301	782	1,294	1,417	1,504	1,710	1,713	2	1	1	1
Monthlies	374	949	1,564	1,745	1,922	2,193	2,226	2	2	2	2
Farm publications	62	130	186	196	196	212	215	(Z)	(Z)	(Z)	(Z)
Television	3,596	11,469	21,022	23,904	25,686	26,891	28,405	18	21	22	22
Three networks	1,658	5,130	8,060	8,500	9,172	9,110	9,383	9	10	9	7
Cable networks	-	45	594	760	942	1,197	1,393	-	(Z)	1	1
Syndication (nat'l)	-	50	520	762	901	1,288	1,589	-	(Z)	1	1
Spot (national)	1,234	3,269	6,004	6,846	7,147	7,354	7,788	6	6	6	6
Spot (local)	704	2,967	5,714	6,833	7,270	7,612	7,856	4	6	6	6
Cable (non-network)	-	8	130	203	254	330	396	-	(Z)	(Z)	(Z)
Radio	1,308	3,702	6,490	7,206	7,798	8,323	8,726	7	7	7	7
Network	56	183	365	413	425	476	482	(Z)	(Z)	(Z)	(Z)
Spot	371	779	1,335	1,330	1,418	1,547	1,635	2	2	1	1
Local	881	2,740	4,790	5,463	5,955	6,300	6,609	5	5	5	5
Yellow Pages	(NA)	2,900	5,800	7,300	7,781	8,330	8,926	(NA)	5	6	7
National	(NA)	330	695	830	944	1,011	1,132	(NA)	1	1	1
Local	(NA)	2,570	5,105	6,470	6,837	7,319	7,794	(NA)	5	5	6
Direct mail	2,766	7,596	15,500	19,111	21,115	21,945	23,370	14	14	16	18
Business papers	740	1,674	2,375	2,458	2,610	2,763	2,875	4	3	3	2
Outdoor	234	578	945	1,025	1,064	1,111	1,084	1	1	1	1
Miscellaneous	3,848	7,558	12,107	13,431	14,531	15,271	15,955	20	14	13	12

- Represents or rounds to zero.   NA Not available.   Z Less than .5 percent.
Source: McCann-Erickson, Inc., New York, NY. Compiled for Crain Communications, Inc. In *Advertising Age*, (copyright). Percentages derived by U.S. Bureau of the Census.

No. 906. Magazine Advertising—Expenditures, by Product Type: 1970 to 1990

[In millions of dollars, except percent. Space cost based on one-time rate; special rates used where applicable. Year-to-year data not strictly comparable, as a few minor publications are added or deleted]

TYPE OF PRODUCT	1970	1980	1985	1986	1987	1988	1989	1990	PERCENT DISTRIBUTION		
									1970	1980	1990
Total	1,193	2,846	4,961	5,120	5,390	5,943	6,611	6,745	100	100	100
Apparel, footwear, and accessories	51	112	251	291	323	363	396	428	4	4	6
Automotive [1]	97	230	549	597	678	801	881	899	8	8	13
Beer, wine, and liquor	98	239	240	225	208	213	255	277	8	8	4
Computers, office equipment, stationery	32	79	250	219	247	252	284	283	3	3	4
Consumer services [2]	74	100	400	404	491	466	522	516	6	7	8
Drugs and remedies	38	79	135	148	142	145	135	163	3	3	2
Food and food products	86	199	342	389	377	377	435	444	7	7	7
Household equipment and supplies	34	65	100	93	97	102	104	118	3	2	2
Household furnishings	38	73	87	103	111	116	126	116	3	2	2
Jewelry, optical goods, camera	30	79	101	113	121	142	156	157	3	3	2
Mail orders/direct response	(NA)	(NA)	328	363	407	467	513	531	(NA)	(NA)	8
Publishing and media	38	146	188	176	186	192	191	212	3	5	3
Retail	53	(NA)	121	143	138	176	211	255	4	(NA)	4
Smoking materials	65	290	383	322	334	352	393	305	5	10	5
Toiletries and toilet goods	119	206	385	390	455	554	651	679	10	7	10
Travel, hotels, and resorts	54	123	245	249	273	311	374	380	5	4	6
All other	289	736	793	815	802	914	984	982	24	26	15

NA Not available.   [1] Includes accessories and equipment.   [2] Includes business services.
Source: Publishers Information Bureau, Inc., New York, NY, as compiled by Leading National Advertisers.

No. 907. Television—Expenditures for Network Advertising: 1980 to 1990

[In millions of dollars. See text, section 18 for a definition of network advertising]

TYPE OF PRODUCT	1980	1985	1989	1990	TYPE OF PRODUCT	1980	1985	1989	1990
Total	5,147	8,313	9,559	10,132	Household equipment,				
Apparel, footwear, and					supplies, and furnishings. . . .	225	275	323	297
accessories	131	161	269	276	Insurance	74	99	158	172
Automotive	529	848	1,491	1,781	Financial planning services. . . .	20	60	63	51
Beer and wine	242	428	364	293	Jewelry and cameras [1]	119	129	111	127
Building material, equipment,					Laundry soaps, cleansers, and				
fixtures.	59	97	84	72	polishes.	306	397	319	317
Computers, office equipment,					Movies	103	138	214	242
and stationery.	57	249	159	149	Pet products	144	175	134	104
Confectionery, soft drinks.	281	388	379	407	Proprietary medicines	430	700	767	817
Consumer services	178	303	437	524	Publishing and media	34	50	61	28
Dept. and discount stores	94	161	196	248	Restaurants and drive-ins.	132	416	604	624
Food and food products.	844	1,502	1,685	1,704	Tobacco products and supplies.	8	6	-	-
Freight and industrial					Toiletries and toilet goods	765	955	850	944
development.	7	40	56	55	Toys and sporting goods	93	152	126	138
Gas, lubricants, etc.	71	49	38	39	Travel, hotels, and resorts	72	102	169	146
Home electronics equipment. . .	50	36	56	85	All other	64	367	408	456
Horticulture	15	30	38	36					

- Represents or rounds to zero. [1] Includes optical goods.

Source: Television Bureau of Advertising, Inc., New York, NY. Data compiled by The Arbitron Co., New York, NY.

No. 908. Television—Estimated Time Charges for Spot Advertising: 1980 to 1990

[In millions of dollars. Data represent activity in the top 75 markets monitored by The Arbitron Co., currently covering approximately 356 stations. Beginning 1989, data exclude National Syndicated activity therefore are not directly comparable to prior years. See text, section 18 for a definition of types of advertising]

TYPE OF PRODUCT	1980	1985	1989	1990	TYPE OF PRODUCT	1980	1985	1989	1990
Total	2,496	4,504	5,423	5,697	Home electronics equipment.	73	67	116	131
Agriculture and farming	15	17	17	12	Horticulture	35	37	47	41
Apparel, footwear, and					Household equipment,				
accessories	105	95	94	105	supplies, and furnishings. .	133	217	175	175
Automotive	228	683	1,415	1,449	Insurance	34	88	104	120
Beer and wine	156	218	208	201	Jewelry, optical goods, and				
Building material, equipment,					cameras	55	68	59	48
and fixtures.	47	58	79	58	Laundry soaps, polishes. . . .	111	175	118	156
Computers, office equip-					Pet products	33	60	41	36
ment and stationery . . .	15	25	32	21	Proprietary medicines	93	148	167	201
Confectionery, soft drinks. . .	212	355	303	338	Publishing and media	78	147	130	124
Consumer services	83	262	380	414	Tobacco products, suppliers.	8	14	5	4
Food and food products. . . .	507	927	958	1,069	Toiletries and toilet goods . .	223	267	281	258
Freight and industrial					Toys and sporting goods . . .	104	211	193	192
development.	5	36	36	33	Travel, hotels, and resorts . .	76	187	215	276
Gasoline, lubricants, etc. . . .	50	102	164	169	All other	17	40	86	66

Source: Television Bureau of Advertising, Inc., New York, NY. Data compiled by The Arbitron Co., New York, NY in the top 75 markets.

No. 909. Television—Expenditures for Retail/Local Advertising: 1980 to 1990

[In millions of dollars. See headnote, table 908]

TYPE OF PRODUCT	1980	1985	1989	1990	TYPE OF PRODUCT	1980	1985	1989	1990
Total	1,983	3,899	5,076	5,200	Financial planning services.	7	29	24	27
Amusements, entertainment . . .	68	121	144	146	Jewelry stores	19	25	26	23
Appliance stores, repair.	38	122	153	178	Legal services	5	38	82	95
Auto repair, service stations	28	73	89	94	Leisure time stores and services .	42	107	134	151
Auto supply, accessory stores. . .	12	41	40	34	Loan, mortgage companies	12	25	30	39
Auto, truck dealers	99	311	321	271	Mail order, catalog showrooms . .	13	23	11	10
Banks, S&L associations	141	195	197	179	Medical, dental services.	13	87	145	150
Builders, home improvement. . . .	20	32	27	26	Movies.	102	103	211	238
Carpet, floor covering stores. . . .	24	40	51	47	Newspapers.	15	32	37	29
Clothing stores.	46	82	144	129	Optical services, supplies.	14	28	77	84
Department stores	131	186	213	169	Political.	70	22	49	203
Discount department stores	74	115	117	121	Radio, cable TV	69	134	183	168
Drug stores	26	67	94	101	Realtors, real estate devel'prs. . .	18	31	34	28
Education services	17	70	132	112	Rental services (non-auto)	15	38	31	30
Food stores, supermarkets.	149	259	341	344	Restaurants, drive-ins	288	672	838	828
Furniture stores	111	187	278	273	Shoe stores.	27	37	44	36
Gas, electric, water companies . .	16	38	50	46	Shopping centers	13	20	26	28
Health clubs, reducing salons . . .	21	39	94	116	Sport, hobby, toy stores.	23	41	47	50
Home centers and hardware. . . .	42	89	106	108	All other	137	278	374	413
Hotels, resorts, U.S.	18	62	82	76					

Source: Television Bureau of Advertising, Inc., New York, NY. Data compiled by The Arbitron Co., New York, NY in the top 75 markets.

Energy

This section presents statistics on fuel resources, energy production and consumption, electric energy, hydroelectric power, nuclear power, solar energy, wood energy and the electric and gas utility industries. The principal sources are the U.S. Department of Energy's Energy Information Administration (EIA), the Edison Electric Institute, Washington, DC, and the American Gas Association, Arlington, VA. For additional data on transportation, see section 21; on fuels, see section 25; and on energy-related housing characteristics, see section 26.

The EIA, in its *Annual Energy Review,* provides statistics and trend data on energy supply, demand, and prices. Information is included on petroleum and natural gas, coal, electricity, hydroelectric power, nuclear power, solar, wood, and geothermal energy. Among its annual reports are *Annual Energy Review, Electric Power Annual, Natural Gas Annual, Petroleum Supply Annual, State Energy Data Report, State Energy Price and Expenditure Report, Financial Statistics of Selected Electric Utilities, Performance Profiles of Major Energy Producers, Annual Energy Outlook,* and *International Energy Annual.* These various publications contain State, national, and international data on production of electricity, net summer capability of generating plants, fuels used in energy production, energy sales and consumption, hydroelectric power. The EIA also issues the *Monthly Energy Review,* which presents current supply, disposition, and price data, and monthly publications on petroleum, coal, natural gas, and electric power. Data on residential energy consumption, expenditures, and conservation activities are available from EIA's Residential Energy Consumption Survey and are published triennially in *Residential Energy Consumption Survey: Consumption and Expenditures,* and *Residential Energy Consumption Survey: Housing Characteristics,* and several other reports.

The Edison Electric Institute's monthly bulletin and annual *Statistical Year Book of the Electric Utility Industry for the Year*

In Brief

Energy consumption, 1990
record 81.4 quadrillion Btu
Nuclear power, 1990
20.6 % of all electric generation
"Renewable" energy sources, 1990
7.9 % of consumption

contain data on the distribution of electric energy by public utilities; information on the electric power supply, expansion of electric generating facilities, and the manufacture of heavy electric power equipment is presented in the annual *Year End Summary of the Electric Power Situation in the United States.* The American Gas Association, in its monthly and quarterly bulletins and its yearbook, *Gas Facts,* presents data on gas utilities, including sales, revenues, customers, prices, and other financial and operating statistics.

Btu conversion factors.—Various energy sources are converted from original units (e.g., short tons, cubic feet, barrels, kilowatt-hours) to the thermal equivalent using British thermal units (Btu). A Btu is the amount of energy required to raise the temperature of 1 pound of water 1 degree Fahrenheit (F) at or near 39.2 degrees F. Factors are calculated annually from the latest final annual data available; some are revised as a result. The following list provides conversion factors used in 1990 for production and consumption, in that order, for various fuels: Petroleum, 5.800 and 5.449 mil. Btu per barrel; total coal, 21.827 and 21.344 mil. Btu per short ton; and natural gas (dry), 1,031 Btu per cubic foot for both. The factors for the production of nuclear power and geothermal power were 10,724 and 21,096 Btu per kilowatt-hour, respectively. The fossil fuel steam-electric power plant generation factor of 10,331 Btu per kilowatt-hour was used for hydroelectric power generation and for wood and waste, wind, photovoltaic, and solar thermal energy consumed at electric utilities.

Energy

No. 910. Total Horsepower of All Prime Movers: 1960 to 1990

[In millions, except percent. As of **January**, except as noted. Prime movers are mechanical engines and turbines, and work animals, which originally convert fuels or force (as wind or falling water) into work and power. Electric motors, which obtain their power from prime movers, are excluded to avoid duplication. See also *Historical Statistics, Colonial Times to 1970*, series S 1-14]

YEAR	Total horse-power	AUTOMOTIVE [1][2]		NONAUTOMOTIVE							
		Total	Percent of total	Total	Facto-ries[3][4]	Mines[3][4]	Rail-roads[5]	Merchant ships and sailing vessels[4]	Farms	Electric central sta-tions[2]	Air-craft[5][6]
1960	11,008	10,367	94.2	641	42	35	47	24	240	217	37
1965	15,096	14,306	94.8	790	48	40	44	24	272	307	55
1970	20,408	19,325	94.7	1,083	54	45	54	22	290	435	183
1975	25,100	23,752	94.6	1,348	60	47	62	22	318	654	185
1976	25,732	24,339	94.6	1,393	61	47	64	22	324	692	184
1977	26,469	25,025	94.5	1,444	62	47	62	23	[7]328	728	194
1978	27,379	25,892	94.6	1,487	63	48	64	25	[7]335	754	198
1979	28,162	26,617	94.5	1,545	63	48	62	26	342	803	201
1980	28,922	27,362	94.6	1,564	64	48	63	28	345	806	210
1981	29,507	27,909	94.6	1,598	64	48	65	29	345	835	212
1982	30,495	28,852	94.6	1,643	64	48	64	29	352	854	232
1983	31,337	29,662	94.7	1,675	64	47	62	29	356	877	240
1984	31,819	30,117	94.7	1,702	65	47	61	30	359	886	254
1985	32,529	30,792	94.7	1,737	65	47	58	29	358	912	268
1986	32,660	30,893	94.6	1,767	65	47	56	29	358	942	270
1987	33,266	31,488	94.7	1,778	65	47	53	29	357	958	269
1988	34,200	32,415	94.8	1,785	65	47	53	28	356	969	267
1989	34,579	32,790	94.8	1,789	65	47	50	28	356	976	267
1990	34,919	33,062	94.7	1,857	66	47	50	28	356	[8]1,043	267

[1] Includes passenger cars, trucks, buses, and motorcycles. [2] As of July 1. [3] Beginning 1965, data are estimates. [4] This is an extensions of trends, since government agencies, suspended compilation of these power capacity statistics. [5] Beginning 1965, not strictly comparable with earlier years. [6] Includes private planes and commercial airlines. [7] Includes estimates of about 3.0 million hp in work animals and 30,000 in windmills. [8] Includes 59,000,000 horsepower in cogenerating and industrial electric power capacity.
Source: John A. Waring, Arlington, VA, unpublished estimates.

No. 911. Energy Production and Consumption, by Major Source: 1960 to 1990

[Btu=British thermal unit. For Btu conversion factors, see text, section 19. See also *Historical Statistics, Colonial Times to 1970*, series M 76-92]

YEAR	Total production (quad. Btu)	PERCENT OF PRODUCTION				Total con-sump-tion (quad. Btu)	PERCENT OF CONSUMPTION				Con-sump-tion/pro-duc-tion ratio
		Coal	Petro-leum[1]	Natural gas[2]	Other[3]		Coal	Petro-leum[1]	Natural gas[2]	Other[3]	
1960	41.5	26.1	36.0	34.0	3.9	43.8	22.5	45.5	28.3	3.8	1.06
1965	49.3	26.5	33.5	35.8	4.3	52.7	22.0	44.1	29.9	4.0	1.07
1970	62.1	23.5	32.9	38.9	4.7	66.4	18.5	44.4	32.8	4.3	1.07
1971	61.3	21.5	32.7	40.5	5.3	67.9	17.1	45.0	33.1	4.8	1.11
1972	62.4	22.6	32.1	39.7	5.6	71.3	16.9	46.2	31.9	5.0	1.14
1973	62.1	22.5	31.4	39.9	6.2	74.3	17.5	46.9	30.3	5.3	1.20
1974	60.8	23.1	30.5	38.9	7.4	72.5	17.5	46.1	30.0	6.5	1.19
1975	59.9	25.0	29.6	36.8	8.6	70.5	17.9	46.4	28.3	7.4	1.18
1976	59.9	26.1	28.8	36.4	8.6	74.4	18.3	47.3	27.4	7.1	1.24
1977	60.2	26.2	29.0	36.4	8.5	76.3	18.2	48.7	26.1	7.0	1.27
1978	61.1	24.4	30.2	35.6	9.9	78.1	17.6	48.6	25.6	8.1	1.28
1979	63.8	27.5	28.4	35.0	9.1	78.9	19.1	47.1	26.2	7.7	1.24
1980	64.8	28.7	28.2	34.2	8.9	76.0	20.3	45.0	26.9	7.8	1.17
1981	64.4	28.5	28.2	34.2	9.1	74.0	21.5	43.2	26.9	8.4	1.15
1982	63.9	29.2	28.7	32.0	10.2	70.8	21.7	42.7	26.1	9.5	1.11
1983	61.2	28.2	30.0	30.6	11.2	70.5	22.5	42.6	24.6	10.3	1.15
1984	65.8	29.9	28.6	30.7	10.7	74.1	23.0	41.9	25.0	10.1	1.13
1985	64.8	29.8	29.3	29.6	11.3	74.0	23.6	41.8	24.1	10.5	1.14
1986	64.2	30.4	28.6	29.0	12.0	74.2	23.3	43.4	22.5	10.8	1.16
1987	64.8	31.1	27.3	29.7	11.9	76.8	23.4	42.8	23.1	10.7	1.19
1988	66.0	31.4	26.2	30.0	12.4	80.2	23.5	42.7	23.1	10.7	1.21
1989	66.1	32.3	24.4	30.2	13.1	81.3	23.3	42.1	23.8	10.8	1.23
1990	[4]67.6	33.5	22.9	29.9	13.7	[5]81.5	23.4	41.3	23.8	11.5	1.20

[1] Production includes crude oil and lease condensate. Consumption includes domestically produced crude oil, natural gas liquids, and lease condensate, plus imported crude oil and products. [2] Production includes natural gas liquids; consumption excludes natural gas liquids. [3] Comprised of hydropower, nuclear power, geothermal energy, and other. [4] Represents peak year for U.S. energy production. [5] Represents peak year for U.S. energy consumption.
Source: U.S. Energy Information Administration, *Annual Energy Review*.

No. 912. Energy Supply and Disposition, by Type of Fuel: 1970 to 1990

[In quadrillion British thermal units (Btu). For Btu conversion factors, see text, section 19]

TYPE OF FUEL	1970	1973	1975	1980	1982	1983	1984	1985	1986	1987	1988	1989	1990
Production[2]	62.1	62.1	59.9	64.8	63.9	61.2	65.8	64.8	64.2	64.8	66.0	66.1	[1]67.6
Crude oil [2]	20.4	19.5	17.7	18.2	18.3	18.4	18.9	19.0	18.4	17.7	17.3	16.1	15.5
Natural gas liquids. . . .	2.5	2.6	2.4	2.3	2.2	2.2	2.3	2.2	2.2	2.2	2.3	2.2	2.2
Natural gas [3]	21.7	22.2	19.6	19.9	18.3	16.5	17.9	16.9	16.5	17.1	17.5	17.8	18.1
Coal	14.6	14.0	15.0	18.6	18.6	17.3	19.7	19.3	19.5	20.1	20.7	21.3	22.6
Nuclear electric power .	0.2	0.9	1.9	2.7	3.1	3.2	3.6	4.2	4.5	4.9	5.7	5.7	6.2
Hydro electric power . .	2.6	2.9	3.2	2.9	3.3	3.5	3.3	2.9	3.0	2.6	2.3	2.8	2.9
Geothermal and other .	(Z)	(Z)	0.1	0.1	0.1	0.1	0.2	0.2	0.2	0.2	0.2	0.2	0.2
Net trade [4]	-5.7	-12.7	-11.8	-12.2	-7.5	-8.3	-9.0	-7.9	-10.4	-11.9	-13.1	-14.2	-13.8
Exports	2.7	2.1	2.4	3.7	4.6	3.7	3.8	4.2	4.1	3.9	4.4	4.8	4.9
Coal.	1.9	1.4	1.8	2.4	2.8	2.0	2.2	2.4	2.2	2.1	2.5	2.6	2.8
Imports	8.4	14.7	14.1	16.0	12.1	12.0	12.8	12.1	14.4	15.8	17.6	18.9	18.7
Crude oil.	2.8	6.9	8.7	11.2	7.4	7.1	7.3	6.8	9.0	10.1	11.0	12.6	12.7
Consumption	66.4	74.3	70.5	76.0	70.8	70.5	74.1	73.9	74.2	76.8	80.2	81.3	[5]81.4
Petroleum products . . .	29.5	34.8	32.7	34.2	30.2	30.1	31.1	30.9	32.2	32.9	34.2	34.2	33.6
Natural gas [3]	21.8	22.5	19.9	20.4	18.5	17.4	18.5	17.8	16.7	17.7	18.6	19.4	19.4
Coal	12.3	13.0	12.7	15.4	15.3	15.9	17.1	17.5	17.3	18.0	18.8	18.9	19.0
Nuclear power	0.2	0.9	1.9	2.7	3.1	3.2	3.6	4.2	4.5	4.9	5.7	5.7	6.2
Hydro electric power [6] .	2.7	3.0	3.2	3.1	3.6	3.9	3.8	3.4	3.4	3.1	2.6	2.9	2.9
Geothermal and other .	(Z)	(Z)	0.1	0.1	0.1	0.1	0.2	0.2	0.2	0.3	0.3	0.2	0.2

Z Less than 50 trillion.   [1] Represents peak year for U.S. energy production.   [2] Includes lease condensate.   [3] Dry marketed gas.   [4] Exports minus imports.   [5] Represents peak year for U.S. energy consumption.   [6] Includes industrial generation of hydropower and net electricity imports.

No. 913. Selected Energy Indicators—Summary: 1970 to 1990

[Btu=British thermal unit. For Btu conversion factors, see text, section 19. Minus sign (-) indicates decrease]

ITEM	1970	1973	1975	1980	1982	1983	1984	1985	1986	1987	1988	1989	1990
AVERAGE ANNUAL PERCENT CHANGE [1]													
Gross national product [2]	-0.3	5.2	-1.3	-0.2	-2.5	3.6	6.8	3.4	2.7	3.4	4.5	2.5	1.0
Energy production, total [3] . . .	5.0	-0.6	-1.6	1.5	-0.8	-4.2	7.6	-1.6	-0.8	0.9	1.8	0.1	2.3
Crude oil [4]	4.1	-2.8	-4.8	0.8	0.9	0.5	2.4	0.8	-3.4	-4.0	-2.3	-7.2	-4.3
Natural gas	5.6	-0.1	-8.0	-0.8	-7.9	-10.4	7.8	-6.1	-2.6	3.4	2.7	1.5	1.5
Coal	5.1	-0.7	6.1	5.7	1.4	-8.1	12.5	-2.0	0.9	3.1	2.9	2.8	5.6
Energy consumption, total [3] . .	3.5	4.2	-2.8	-3.7	-4.3	-0.5	5.1	-0.2	0.4	3.5	4.4	1.4	0.1
Petroleum products	4.0	5.4	-2.2	-8.5	-5.6	-0.6	3.2	-0.4	4.0	2.0	4.0	(Z)	-1.7
Natural gas (dry)	5.1	-0.8	-8.2	-1.3	-7.7	-6.6	6.2	-3.8	-6.3	6.2	4.4	4.3	0.2
Coal	-0.9	7.4	(Z)	2.5	-3.7	3.7	7.4	2.4	-1.2	4.3	4.7	0.5	0.6
PER CAPITA [5] (mil. Btu)													
Energy production	305	294	278	286	275	261	278	271	266	266	269	266	272
Energy consumption	327	351	327	335	305	301	313	310	308	316	326	328	327
Energy consumption per dollar of GNP [2] (1,000 Btu) .	27.5	27.1	26.2	23.8	22.8	21.5	21.2	20.4	20.0	20.0	20.0	19.8	19.6

Z Less than .05 percent.   [1] Represents annual average for period of intervals shown; for 1960, change from 1955. Percent change derived from Btu values. For explanation of average annual percent change, see Guide to Tabular Presentation.   [2] Gross national product in constant (1982) dollars.   [3] Includes types of fuel or power, not shown separately.   [4] Includes lease condensate.   [5] Based on resident population estimated as of July 1.

No. 914. Energy Imports and Exports, by Type of Fuel: 1970 to 1990

[In quadrillion of Btu. For definition of Btu, see text, Section 19]

TYPE OF FUEL	1970	1973	1975	1980	1982	1983	1984	1985	1986	1987	1988	1989	1990
Net imports: [1]													
Coal	-1.93	-1.42	-1.74	-2.39	-2.77	-2.01	-2.12	-2.39	-2.19	-2.05	-2.45	-2.57	-2.70
Natural Gas (dry).	0.77	0.98	0.90	0.96	0.90	0.89	0.79	0.90	0.69	0.94	1.22	1.28	1.41
Petroleum	6.92	12.98	12.51	13.50	9.05	9.08	9.89	8.95	11.53	12.53	14.01	15.33	15.10
Other [2]	-0.04	0.14	0.08	0.18	0.28	0.36	0.40	0.41	0.35	0.48	0.36	0.14	0.02
Imports:													
Coal	(Z)	(Z)	0.02	0.03	0.02	0.03	0.03	0.05	0.06	0.04	0.05	0.07	0.07
Natural Gas (dry).	0.85	1.06	0.98	1.01	0.95	0.94	0.85	0.95	0.75	0.99	1.30	1.39	1.51
Petroleum	7.47	13.47	12.95	14.66	10.78	10.65	11.43	10.61	13.20	14.16	15.75	17.16	16.94
Other [2]	0.07	0.20	0.16	0.28	0.35	0.41	0.45	0.49	0.43	0.56	0.46	0.33	0.23
Exports:													
Coal	1.94	1.43	1.76	2.42	2.79	2.04	2.15	2.44	2.25	2.09	2.50	2.64	2.77
Natural Gas (dry).	0.07	0.08	0.07	0.05	0.05	0.06	0.06	0.06	0.06	0.05	0.07	0.11	0.10
Petroleum	0.55	0.49	0.44	1.16	1.73	1.57	1.54	1.66	1.67	1.63	1.74	1.84	1.84
Other [2]	0.11	0.06	0.08	0.09	0.06	0.05	0.05	0.08	0.07	0.07	0.10	0.18	0.20

Z Less than .005 quadrillion Btu.   [1] Net imports equals imports minus exports.   Minus sign (-) denotes an excess of exports over imports.   [2] Coal coke and small amounts of electricity transmitted across U.S. borders with Canada and Mexico.
Source of tables 912-914: U.S. Energy Information Administration, *Annual Energy Review*, and *Monthly Energy Review*.

No. 915. Energy Consumption—End-Use Sector and Selected Source, by State: 1989

[In trillions of Btu, except as indicated. For Btu conversion factors, see text, section 19.

REGION, DIVISION, AND STATE	Total[1]	Per capita[2] (mil. Btu)	Percent change, 1988-1989	END-USE SECTOR				SOURCE				
				Residential	Commercial	Industrial	Transportation	Petroleum	Natural gas (dry)	Coal	Hydroelectric power	Nuclear electric power
United States . .	81,342	327.6	1.3	16,630	12,867	[3]29,463	22,382	34,209	19,384	18,940	2,884	5,677
Northeast	12,552	247.2	0.1	3,347	2,645	3,130	3,430	6,277	2,462	2,106	432	1,267
New England	3,068	235.2	0.2	927	660	551	929	1,911	416	185	126	355
Maine	341	279.0	8.1	84	50	97	110	226	4	7	49	74
New Hampshire . .	250	226.0	3.0	78	39	56	77	166	14	32	15	-
Vermont	131	231.0	1.7	38	25	25	42	74	6	-	31	39
Massachusetts . . .	1,372	232.0	1.9	417	326	209	420	849	259	121	24	32
Rhode Island	206	206.0	4.0	65	44	36	61	106	35	1	1	-
Connecticut	768	237.0	1.8	245	176	128	219	490	98	24	6	210
Middle Atlantic	9,484	251.4	0.1	2,420	1,985	2,579	2,501	4,366	2,046	1,921	306	912
New York	3,556	198.0	0.8	1,024	977	684	872	1,777	870	363	296	245
New Jersey	2,338	302.0	2.0	529	475	521	813	1,280	469	94	3	247
Pennsylvania	3,590	298.0	0.1	867	533	1,374	816	1,309	707	1,464	13	420
Midwest	19,923	331.2	0.3	4,666	3,151	7,244	4,862	6,941	4,769	6,665	78	1,714
East North Central . .	14,061	332.4	0.5	3,304	2,187	5,343	3,227	4,612	3,460	4,680	24	1,283
Ohio	3,863	354.0	2.3	864	585	1,585	828	1,185	848	1,464	1	136
Indiana	2,494	446.0	0.6	448	274	1,196	576	825	469	1,308	5	-
Illinois	3,527	303.0	2.0	898	643	1,194	793	1,160	1,014	714	1	802
Michigan	2,764	298.0	0.5	731	449	900	684	944	797	801	47	229
Wisconsin	1,413	290.0	1.5	363	236	468	346	498	332	393	16	116
West North Central.	5,862	328.4	0.2	1,362	964	1,901	1,635	2,329	1,309	1,985	102	431
Minnesota	1,335	307.0	1.2	327	195	469	344	509	302	323	4	117
Iowa	925	326.0	1.3	219	138	333	235	324	228	319	7	34
Missouri.	1,513	294.0	0.3	395	286	352	484	637	263	550	11	89
North Dakota	319	483.0	2.8	55	37	160	68	118	32	362	20	-
South Dakota	212	297.0	4.3	57	32	58	65	111	26	33	48	-
Nebraska	526	327.0	2.1	127	112	135	152	211	119	132	12	87
Kansas	1,027	409.0	3.1	182	164	394	287	419	339	266	-	104
South	33,634	393.3	1.6	5,863	4,433	14,510	8,830	14,123	8,672	7,917	545	2,134
South Atlantic	12,435	288.4	0.9	2,899	2,196	3,519	3,822	5,258	1,536	3,813	170	1,424
Delaware	233	346.0	1.7	47	33	88	65	137	36	61	-	-
Maryland	1,262	269.0	1.2	325	164	417	357	550	196	295	18	29
Dist. of Columbia. .	175	290.0	1.3	35	77	33	29	42	34	1	-	-
Virginia	1,839	302.0	0.5	440	376	450	573	772	181	362	4	153
West Virginia	799	430.0	2.7	132	88	429	150	276	140	929	12	-
North Carolina . . .	1,939	295.0	0.9	458	327	604	551	734	167	557	72	313
South Carolina . . .	1,163	331.0	1.8	233	159	479	292	389	120	301	21	437
Georgia.	2,030	315.0	0.3	438	313	603	676	803	325	677	41	268
Florida.	2,995	236.0	2.4	791	659	416	1,129	1,555	337	630	2	224
East South Central .	5,870	381.0	3.5	1,115	685	2,495	1,575	2,216	911	2,099	304	375
Kentucky.	1,475	396.0	5.3	277	176	620	402	538	196	765	46	-
Tennessee.	1,763	357.0	2.6	382	198	710	473	600	229	564	122	167
Alabama	1,643	399.0	2.0	289	205	744	405	602	252	674	136	124
Mississippi	989	377.0	5.2	167	106	421	295	476	234	96	-	84
West South Central.	15,329	567.7	1.5	1,849	1,552	8,496	3,433	6,649	6,225	2,005	71	335
Arkansas.	825	343.0	5.0	164	105	320	236	311	251	203	32	95
Louisiana.	3,523	804.0	0.8	293	241	2,300	689	1,489	1,599	207	-	133
Oklahoma	1,291	401.0	0.3	237	179	517	358	442	612	269	25	-
Texas	9,690	570.0	1.8	1,155	1,027	5,359	2,150	4,407	3,763	1,326	14	107
West	15,201	293.5	3.2	2,749	2,642	4,550	5,261	6,872	3,482	2,253	1,829	562
Mountain	4,413	326.6	3.0	832	846	1,406	1,331	1,697	972	2,085	327	90
Montana	350	434.0	5.1	62	51	153	84	155	47	178	99	-
Idaho	372	367.0	5.2	78	71	136	87	118	47	10	93	-
Wyoming	381	803.0	0.9	35	37	224	86	135	87	421	7	-
Colorado	909	274.0	0.7	205	231	205	267	323	246	324	18	6
New Mexico	559	366.0	6.8	73	99	182	206	233	205	280	2	-
Arizona	916	258.0	2.3	200	208	185	324	354	151	357	82	84
Utah	543	318.0	1.8	100	83	217	144	203	123	345	6	-
Nevada	383	345.0	8.2	79	66	104	133	176	66	170	20	-
Pacific.	10,788	281.8	3.2	1,917	1,796	3,144	3,930	5,175	2,510	168	1,502	472
Washington	1,883	396.0	3.9	376	288	670	550	758	168	97	730	66
Oregon	912	323.0	3.6	203	159	268	281	351	112	7	413	57
California.	7,127	245.0	2.0	1,270	1,244	1,839	2,774	3,540	1,906	58	349	349
Alaska.	567	1075.00	9.0	43	52	298	173	232	321	5	9	-
Hawaii.	299	269.0	13.2	25	53	69	152	294	3	1	1	-

- Represents zero. [1] Sources of energy includes geothermal, wood and waste, and net interstate sales of electricity, including losses, not shown separately. [2] Based on estimated resident population as of July 1. [3] Includes 8.6 trillion Btu of net imports of coal coke not allocated by State.

Source: U.S. Energy Information Administration, *State Energy Data Report, 1960-1989.*

No. 916. Primary Energy Consumption, by End-Use Sector: 1960 to 1990

[Btu = British thermal unit. For residential and commercial, industrial, and transportation, represents consumption of fossil fuels only. For Btu conversion factors, see text, section 19]

YEAR	Total consumption (quad. Btu)	Residential and commercial (quad. Btu)	Industrial and miscellaneous (quad. Btu)	Transportation (quad. Btu)	Electricity generation (quad. Btu)	PERCENT OF TOTAL			
						Residential and commercial	Industrial and miscellaneous	Transportation	Electricity generation
1960	43.8	8.8	16.3	10.6	8.2	20.0	37.1	24.1	18.7
1970	66.4	12.1	21.9	16.1	16.3	18.3	33.0	24.2	24.5
1973	74.3	12.3	23.5	18.6	19.9	16.5	31.7	25.0	26.7
1975	70.6	11.6	20.4	18.2	20.4	16.4	28.9	25.8	28.8
1979	78.9	11.5	22.8	20.4	24.1	14.6	28.9	25.9	30.6
1980	76.0	10.7	21.0	19.7	24.5	14.1	27.7	25.9	32.3
1981	74.0	10.0	19.7	19.5	24.8	13.6	26.6	26.3	33.5
1982	70.9	10.1	17.5	19.0	24.3	14.2	24.6	26.9	34.3
1983	70.5	9.7	16.7	19.1	25.0	13.8	23.7	27.1	35.4
1984	74.1	10.1	18.2	19.8	26.0	13.6	24.5	26.8	35.1
1985	74.0	9.8	17.6	20.1	26.5	13.3	23.7	27.1	35.8
1986	74.2	9.6	17.3	20.7	26.6	12.9	23.3	27.9	35.9
1987	76.8	9.7	18.2	21.3	27.6	12.7	23.7	27.7	35.9
1988	80.2	10.4	19.0	22.1	28.6	12.9	23.7	27.6	35.7
1989	81.4	10.5	19.2	22.3	29.3	12.9	23.6	27.5	36.0
1990	81.4	9.9	19.9	22.0	29.6	12.2	24.4	27.0	36.3

Source: U.S. Energy Information Administration, *Annual Energy Review.*

No. 917. Energy Expenditures and Average Fuel Prices, by Source and Sector: 1970 to 1989

[For definition of Btu, see text, section 19. End-use sector and electric utilities exclude expenditures and prices on energy sources such as hydropower, solar, wind, and geothermal. Also excludes expenditures for reported amounts of energy consumed by the energy industry for production, transportation, and processing operations]

SOURCE AND SECTOR	1970	1973	1975	1980	1983	1984	1985	1986	1987	1988	1989
EXPENDITURES (mil. dol.)											
Total[1][2]	82,579	111,616	171,784	373,901	415,749	433,584	435,901	381,490	393,838	407,749	436,643
Natural gas	10,891	13,933	20,061	51,061	72,000	77,169	72,938	59,702	58,019	61,089	65,419
Petroleum products[2]	48,088	65,305	103,859	238,410	221,469	225,933	223,653	174,772	186,711	189,417	208,536
Motor gasoline	31,596	39,667	59,446	124,408	115,816	114,438	118,044	91,526	99,809	103,211	112,585
Distillate fuel oil	6,253	9,524	15,680	40,797	41,841	44,864	43,611	34,954	37,240	38,362	43,349
Jet fuel	1,441	2,001	4,193	13,923	13,940	15,064	14,747	10,505	11,448	11,318	13,434
Residual fuel	2,046	4,667	10,374	21,573	27,051	29,049	29,719	27,914	27,589	28,372	28,101
Coal	4,593	6,229	13,047	22,648	27,051	29,049	29,719	7,987	7,143	8,218	
Electricity sales	23,351	33,780	50,680	98,098	134,746	142,438	149,242	151,806	154,692	162,065	169,340
Residential sector	20,083	27,078	36,844	68,825	92,350	96,156	98,729	96,628	97,814	103,209	109,171
Commercial sector	10,668	15,104	22,835	46,881	64,943	69,404	70,325	68,320	68,717	71,725	75,605
Industrial sector	16,458	23,531	41,170	94,521	101,412	108,985	105,529	90,436	90,186	91,143	94,891
Transportation sector[2]	35,370	45,904	70,935	163,674	157,044	159,039	161,318	126,107	137,121	141,673	156,977
Motor gasoline	30,525	38,598	57,992	121,809	113,843	112,044	115,201	89,404	97,527	100,988	110,168
Electric utilities	4,316	7,817	16,396	37,435	41,336	43,378	42,558	35,792	36,681	37,435	38,898
AVERAGE FUEL PRICES (dol. per mil. Btu)											
All sectors	1.65	2.02	3.33	6.91	8.47	8.36	8.43	7.36	7.38	7.31	7.72
Residential sector	2.12	2.73	3.83	7.55	10.85	10.86	11.12	10.97	10.93	10.87	11.26
Commercial sector	1.97	2.56	4.09	7.88	11.05	11.29	11.72	11.40	11.05	10.88	11.36
Industrial sector	0.83	1.08	2.20	4.71	6.30	6.21	6.11	5.39	5.18	5.01	5.14
Transportation sector	2.31	2.57	4.02	8.61	8.44	8.24	8.25	6.23	6.59	6.58	7.23
Electric utilities	0.32	0.46	0.96	1.75	1.98	1.97	1.85	1.55	1.51	1.45	1.48

[1] Includes electricity sales; excludes electricity generation. [2] Includes sources or fuel types not shown separately.

Source: U.S. Energy Information Administration, *State Energy Price and Expenditure Report,* annual.

No. 918. Energy Expenditures—End-Use Sector and Selected Source, by State: 1989

[In millions of dollars, except as indicated. End-use sector and electric utilities exclude expenditures on energy sources such as hydropower, solar, wind, and geothermal. Also excludes expenditures for reported amounts of energy consumed by the energy industry for production, transportation, and processing operations]

REGION, DIVISION, AND STATE	Total[1]	Per capita[2] (dol.)	Percent change, 1988-1989	END-USE SECTOR				SOURCE				
				Resi-dential	Com-mercial	Indus-trial	Trans-porta-tion	Petroleum products		Natural gas	Coal	Elec-tricity sales
								Total	Gaso-line			
U.S. . . .	[3]436,643	1,759	7.1	109,171	75,605	[3]94,891	156,977	208,536	112,585	65,419	28,101	169,340
Northeast .	83,281	1,640	8.0	25,847	18,415	13,381	25,638	39,359	19,667	12,620	3,267	33,948
N.E.	22,363	1,714	8.4	7,194	4,523	3,000	7,646	12,525	6,108	2,338	325	8,651
ME . . .	2,227	1,822	1.0	626	308	393	900	1,475	647	21	18	801
NH . . .	1,861	1,681	10.1	619	280	323	640	1,088	555	86	55	759
VT. . . .	983	1,734	9.0	310	173	135	365	590	304	28	1	366
MA . . .	9,838	1,664	10.3	3,164	2,184	1,222	3,268	5,312	2,601	1,367	198	3,801
RI	1,505	1,508	4.9	487	302	192	524	779	424	216	2	526
CT. . . .	5,948	1,836	8.5	1,989	1,276	734	1,949	3,281	1,576	620	51	2,398
M.A	60,918	1,615	7.8	18,653	13,892	10,381	17,992	26,834	13,559	10,282	2,942	25,297
NY. . . .	25,210	1,404	7.4	8,480	7,235	2,849	6,647	10,784	5,480	4,627	590	11,353
NJ. . . .	15,343	1,983	9.0	4,069	3,317	2,446	5,511	7,739	3,626	2,360	153	5,583
PA. . . .	20,365	1,691	7.5	6,105	3,341	5,086	5,834	8,310	4,453	3,295	2,200	8,361
Midwest. . .	108,699	1,807	5.4	28,833	17,456	36,294	26,112	47,861	27,542	19,762	9,847	39,193
E.N.C . . .	76,819	1,816	5.4	20,798	12,613	19,177	24,231	31,761	18,574	15,238	7,389	28,290
OH . . .	20,599	1,889	7.6	5,420	3,408	5,362	6,409	8,333	4,994	3,826	2,208	8,033
IN	11,685	2,089	5.2	2,737	1,434	3,593	3,920	5,028	2,461	2,045	1,953	3,913
IL	20,456	1,755	3.2	5,895	3,877	4,580	6,104	7,744	4,853	4,359	1,261	8,158
MI	16,096	1,736	5.3	4,459	2,700	3,912	5,025	6,855	4,127	3,517	1,377	5,572
WI	7,983	1,640	5.8	2,287	1,194	1,729	2,773	3,801	2,139	1,491	590	2,614
W.N.C . . .	31,880	1,786	5.6	8,035	4,843	6,935	12,067	16,100	8,968	4,524	2,458	10,903
MN . . .	7,217	1,658	5.9	1,880	918	1,640	2,779	3,666	2,225	1,109	406	2,410
IA	4,971	1,750	3.0	1,344	686	1,088	1,853	2,428	1,436	778	398	1,695
MO . . .	8,854	1,716	5.8	2,408	1,559	1,481	3,406	4,257	2,493	1,161	740	3,396
ND . . .	1,525	2,311	6.8	298	174	512	541	772	392	105	437	401
SD. . . .	1,308	1,830	16.9	363	164	258	523	821	408	106	35	383
NE. . . .	2,942	1,826	7.1	674	535	550	1,183	1,533	814	437	113	972
KS. . . .	5,062	2,014	3.7	1,068	806	1,405	1,782	2,623	1,201	829	330	1,647
South	161,732	1,891	6.5	37,101	24,067	40,889	59,673	79,685	41,757	21,528	12,304	64,293
S.A. . . .	72,265	1,676	6.8	19,380	12,473	12,909	27,503	34,367	20,838	6,350	6,285	32,473
DE. . . .	1,308	1,943	6.9	346	193	264	505	745	380	143	106	504
MD . . .	7,587	1,616	8.6	2,090	952	1,661	2,884	3,809	2,279	990	473	2,946
DC. . . .	1,067	1,766	1.7	226	426	155	259	310	209	213	3	567
VA. . . .	10,513	1,744	7.8	2,810	1,924	1,482	4,297	5,293	3,183	851	569	4,308
WV . . .	3,488	1,878	9.3	707	433	1,201	1,146	1,758	872	475	1,326	1,085
NC . . .	11,530	1,755	5.7	3,180	1,820	2,359	4,171	5,234	3,306	719	982	5,479
SC. . . .	6,348	1,808	8.4	1,542	885	1,758	2,163	2,722	1,755	495	514	3,038
GA . . .	11,560	1,796	5.8	2,871	1,972	2,349	4,368	5,111	3,122	1,486	1,182	4,885
FL. . . .	18,864	1,489	6.1	5,606	3,868	1,680	7,709	9,383	5,732	977	1,128	9,661
E.S.C . . .	29,162	1,893	7.8	6,247	3,513	8,225	11,176	14,108	7,738	2,850	3,094	11,749
KY. . . .	7,195	1,931	7.2	1,444	798	2,109	2,844	3,547	1,841	690	934	2,792
TN. . . .	9,196	1,862	6.8	1,993	1,032	2,627	3,545	4,227	2,601	797	765	4,031
AL. . . .	7,992	1,941	9.4	1,775	1,045	2,247	2,924	3,770	2,067	838	1,234	3,140
MS . . .	4,778	1,823	8.1	1,035	637	1,242	1,864	2,563	1,229	525	161	1,787
W.S.C . . .	60,305	2,233	5.5	11,474	8,081	19,755	20,994	31,210	13,181	12,328	2,925	20,071
AR. . . .	4,376	1,819	8.6	1,057	587	1,063	1,670	2,051	1,188	725	333	1,645
LA. . . .	11,983	2,735	3.9	1,911	1,363	4,900	3,810	6,375	1,945	2,431	336	3,604
OK . . .	5,570	1,728	5.3	1,340	877	1,063	2,290	2,722	1,590	1,353	346	2,040
TX. . . .	38,375	2,259	5.7	7,167	5,255	12,730	13,224	20,062	8,458	7,821	1,910	12,782
West	82,794	1,598	9.6	17,389	15,665	14,371	35,366	41,630	23,619	11,508	2,682	31,905
Mt	23,162	1,714	7.7	5,091	4,468	4,138	9,464	11,375	6,714	2,804	2,394	9,052
MT . . .	1,598	1,982	9.5	302	212	403	681	907	465	165	108	519
ID . . .	1,696	1,673	8.0	357	283	397	659	854	487	149	18	675
WY . . .	1,453	3,060	9.5	184	167	487	616	805	309	135	375	467
CO . . .	4,869	1,468	5.6	1,135	1,129	632	1,974	2,257	1,513	837	349	1,775
NM . . .	2,763	1,808	11.3	513	574	513	1,164	1,511	817	355	345	958
AZ. . . .	6,014	1,691	7.1	1,580	1,342	759	2,333	2,572	1,747	511	494	3,030
UT. . . .	2,595	1,520	1.6	572	424	526	1,073	1,251	749	406	452	854
NV. . . .	2,173	1,956	14.7	449	338	421	965	1,217	626	246	253	773
Pac	59,632	1,558	10.4	12,298	11,197	10,233	25,902	30,255	16,905	8,704	288	22,853
WA . . .	7,756	1,629	11.3	1,597	1,092	1,499	3,568	4,174	2,268	628	157	2,984
OR . . .	4,628	1,641	8.6	946	706	896	2,081	2,465	1,423	430	9	1,774
CA. . . .	43,619	1,501	9.4	9,247	8,806	7,410	18,157	20,868	12,504	7,426	112	17,085
AK. . . .	1,772	3,362	19.0	283	276	147	1,065	1,273	231	187	9	380
HI	1,856	1,669	17.8	226	317	282	1,031	1,475	479	33	1	630

[1] Includes sources not shown separately. Total expenditures are the sum of purchases for each source (including electricity sales) less electric utility purchases of fuel. [2] Based on estimated resident population as of July 1. [3] Includes net imports of coal coke not shown separately by State.

Source: U.S. Energy Information Administration, *State Energy Price and Expenditure Report*, annual.

No. 919. Residential Energy Consumption, Expenditures, and Average Prices, 1980 to 1987, and by Region, 1987

[For period April to March for 1980-1985; January to December for 1987. Excludes Alaska and Hawaii in 1980. Covers occupied units only. Excludes household usage of gasoline for transportation and the use of wood or coal. Based on Residential Energy Consumption Survey; see Appendix III. For composition of regions, see table 25. Btu=British thermal unit; see text, section 19]

TYPE OF FUEL	Unit	1980	1981	1982	1983	1985	1987 Total	North-east	Mid-west	South	West
CONSUMPTION											
Total	Quad. Btu...	9.74	9.32	9.51	8.62	9.04	9.13	2.37	2.73	2.61	1.42
Avg. per household	Mil. Btu	126	114	114	103	105	101	124	123	84	78
Natural gas	Quad. Btu	5.31	4.94	5.39	4.77	4.98	4.83	1.03	1.83	1.09	0.88
Electricity	Quad. Btu	2.42	2.46	2.48	2.42	2.48	2.76	0.44	0.61	1.22	0.48
Fuel oil, kerosene	Quad. Btu	1.71	1.55	1.33	1.14	1.26	1.22	0.87	0.16	0.17	0.02
Liquid petroleum gas	Quad. Btu	0.31	0.36	0.31	0.29	0.31	0.32	0.02	0.13	0.12	0.05
EXPENDITURES											
Total	Bil. dol	63.2	74.8	85.0	87.8	97.0	97.7	24.3	25.0	33.4	15.0
Avg. per household	Dollars	815	917	1,022	1,048	1,123	1,080	1,276	1,124	1,081	819
Natural gas	Bil. dol	17.8	19.3	24.5	27.1	29.8	26.1	6.7	9.0	6.1	4.4
Electricity	Bil. dol	32.6	40.1	45.9	48.4	54.5	61.6	12.3	14.1	25.1	10.0
Fuel oil, kerosene	Bil. dol	10.7	12.5	11.8	9.6	9.6	7.2	5.1	1.0	1.1	0.1
Liquid petroleum gas	Bil. dol	2.1	2.9	2.7	2.7	3.1	2.8	0.2	1.0	1.1	0.4
AVERAGE PRICE											
Total	Dol./mil.Btu	6.49	8.03	8.93	10.18	10.73	10.71	10.26	9.18	12.82	10.53
Natural gas	Dol./mil.Btu	3.36	3.90	4.55	5.67	5.97	5.41	6.45	4.93	5.53	5.05
Electricity	Dol./mil.Btu	13.46	16.32	18.51	19.98	21.94	22.34	27.78	23.09	20.61	20.70
Fuel oil, kerosene	Dol./mil.Btu	6.29	8.04	8.89	8.42	7.64	5.89	5.79	5.97	6.29	6.10
Liquid petroleum gas	Dol./mil.Btu	6.71	7.92	8.74	9.42	9.91	8.91	13.24	7.58	9.56	9.30

Source: U.S. Energy Information Administration, *Residential Energy Consumption Survey.* Not conducted in 1984 and 1986.

No. 920. Residential Energy Consumption and Expenditures, by Type of Fuel and Selected Household Characteristic: 1987

[For period January through December 1987. Quad.=quadrillion. See headnote, table 919]

CHARACTERISTIC	CONSUMPTION (Btu's)					EXPENDITURES				
	Total [1] (quad.)	Avg. per house-hold [1] (mil.)	Nat-ural gas (quad.)	Elec-tricity (quad.)	Fuel oil [2] (quad.)	Total [1] (bil. dol.)	Avg. per house-hold [1] (dol.)	Nat-ural gas (bil. dol.)	Elec-tricity (bil. dol.)	Fuel oil [2] (bil. dol.)
Total households	9.13	101	4.83	2.76	1.22	97.7	1,080	26.1	61.6	7.2
Single-family detached	6.32	115	3.30	1.97	0.80	67.6	1,226	17.5	43.1	4.8
Single-family attached	0.53	99	0.29	0.16	0.07	6.0	1,135	1.7	3.8	0.5
Two- to four-unit building	0.94	93	0.61	0.20	0.13	9.1	905	3.4	4.9	0.8
Five or more unit building	0.96	64	0.51	0.28	0.17	10.1	681	2.8	6.5	0.8
Mobile home	0.39	76	0.12	0.16	0.05	4.8	948	0.6	3.3	0.3
Year house built:										
1939 or earlier	2.59	120	1.53	0.48	0.51	23.7	1,105	8.4	11.7	3.0
1940 to 1949	0.85	104	0.48	0.22	0.13	8.6	1,042	2.7	4.9	0.7
1950 to 1959	1.43	110	0.79	0.38	0.22	14.6	1,121	4.2	8.7	1.3
1960 to 1969	1.63	100	0.92	0.50	0.18	17.4	1,060	5.1	11.0	1.0
1970 to 1974	0.92	95	0.49	0.31	0.07	10.2	1,062	2.5	6.8	0.4
1975 to 1979	0.90	86	0.34	0.44	0.08	11.9	1,131	1.7	9.3	0.5
1980 to 1984	0.53	71	0.20	0.28	0.02	7.3	984	1.1	5.8	0.1
1985 or later	0.27	71	0.10	0.15	0.01	4.0	1,049	0.5	3.3	(B)
Heating and cooling degree day zones:[3]										
Less than 2,000 CDD and —										
More than 7,000 HDD	0.94	110	0.42	0.23	0.21	8.8	1,030	2.1	4.8	1.2
5,500 to 7,000 HDD	3.26	126	2.09	0.69	0.44	30.0	1,156	10.6	16.3	2.6
4,000 to 5,499 HDD	2.34	107	1.09	0.67	0.51	24.9	1,138	6.6	14.9	2.9
Less than 4,000 HDD	1.38	77	0.73	0.53	0.05	16.6	931	4.1	11.5	0.4
More than 2,000 CDD and less than 4,000 HDD	1.20	74	0.51	0.64	0.01	17.4	1,068	2.8	14.2	0.1
1987 family income:										
Less than $5,000	0.51	83	0.30	0.13	0.05	5.1	818	1.6	2.8	0.3
$5,000 to $9,999	1.03	90	0.57	0.26	0.16	10.1	881	3.0	5.8	0.9
$10,000 to $14,999	1.15	91	0.62	0.31	0.16	11.7	927	3.3	6.9	0.9
$15,000 to $19,999	0.83	92	0.45	0.24	0.11	8.7	967	2.4	5.3	0.7
$20,000 to $24,999	0.84	96	0.42	0.27	0.12	9.1	1,038	2.2	5.9	0.7
$25,000 to $34,999	1.60	99	0.81	0.52	0.22	17.7	1,091	4.4	11.5	1.3
$35,000 to $49,999	1.50	112	0.77	0.51	0.19	16.8	1,257	4.2	11.2	1.1
$50,000 or more	1.67	129	0.90	0.52	0.22	18.6	1,440	4.9	12.1	1.3

B Base figure too small to meet statistical standards for reliability of derived figure. [1] Includes liquid petroleum gas, not shown separately. [2] Includes kerosene. [3] CDD=Cooling degree day; HDD=Heating degree day.

Source: U.S. Energy Information Administration, *Residential Energy Consumption Survey, 1987.*

No. 921. Residential Energy Expenditures, by Type of End Use and Household Characteristic: 1987

[For period January through December 1987. See headnote, table 919]

CHARACTERISTIC	EXPENDITURES (bil. dol.)					EXPENDITURES PER HOUSEHOLD (dollars)				
	All end uses	End use				All end uses	End use			
		Space heat-ing [1]	Air-condi-tioning [2]	Water heat-ing [1]	Other [3]		Space heat-ing [1]	Air-condi-tioning [2]	Water heat-ing [1]	Other [3]
Total households. . . .	97.7	31.7	9.8	13.9	42.3	1,080	350	109	154	467
Type:										
Single-family detached . .	67.6	21.5	7.0	9.2	29.9	1,226	391	127	167	542
Single-family attached . . .	6.0	2.1	0.6	0.8	2.5	1,135	404	111	148	472
Two- to four-unit building .	9.1	3.4	0.6	1.3	3.8	905	338	60	131	376
Five or more unit building	10.1	3.1	1.3	1.7	4.1	681	206	85	114	276
Mobile home	4.8	1.5	0.4	0.9	2.0	948	297	74	180	397
Year house built:										
1939 or earlier.	23.7	9.7	1.2	3.3	9.6	1,105	452	55	152	446
1940 to 1949.	8.6	2.9	0.7	1.3	3.7	1,042	357	82	152	450
1950 to 1959.	14.6	4.7	1.4	2.0	6.5	1,121	360	111	152	498
1960 to 1969.	17.4	5.3	2.2	2.4	7.5	1,060	324	133	145	459
1970 to 1974.	10.2	3.1	1.2	1.5	4.5	1,062	320	120	154	468
1975 to 1979.	11.9	3.3	1.7	1.7	5.2	1,131	310	163	158	500
1980 to 1984.	7.3	1.7	1.0	1.2	3.4	984	230	130	162	463
1985 or later.	4.0	1.0	0.5	0.7	1.8	1,049	258	137	183	472
1987 family income:										
Less than $5,000	5.1	1.9	0.3	0.8	2.0	818	312	55	135	316
$5,000-$9,999	10.1	3.7	0.7	1.6	4.1	881	324	63	139	354
$10,000-$14,999	11.7	4.0	0.9	1.8	4.9	927	319	75	145	388
$15,000-$19,999	8.7	2.9	0.7	1.3	3.7	967	323	83	148	414
$20,000-$24,999	9.1	2.9	0.9	1.3	4.0	1,038	330	105	152	452
$25,000-$34,999	17.7	5.5	2.0	2.5	7.7	1,091	341	121	153	475
$35,000-$49,999	16.8	5.0	1.9	2.3	7.6	1,257	374	142	171	570
$50,000 or more	18.6	5.7	2.3	2.2	8.4	1,440	440	179	171	650

[1] Heating from the primary and secondary heating equipment. [2] Cooling by refrigeration; does not include dehumidifiers, evaporative coolers, or fans not connected to air-conditioning equipment. [3] Appliance usage; includes fans in central, forced-air furnaces.

Source: U.S. Energy Information Administration, *Residential Energy Consumption Survey, 1987.*

No. 922. Manufacturing Energy Consumption Required to Produce Heat, Power, and Electricity by Type of Fuel and Industry Group: 1988

[Based on the Manufacturing Energy Consumption Survey; therefore, subject to sampling variability]

SIC [1] code	INDUSTRY	TOTAL FUEL CONSUMPTION (tril. Btu)						CONSUMPTION PER—	
		Total	Net elec-tricity [2]	Fuel oil [3]	Natu-ral gas	Coal and coke	Other	Employ-ee (mil. Btu)	Dollar of value added (1,000 Btu)
(X)	**Total. . . . .**	20,534	2,398	810	5,860	2,783	8,684	868	12.1
20	Food and kindred.	994	171	83	489	157	95	694	7.6
21	Tobacco products	25	3	1	2	17	1	580	1.4
22	Textile mill products	275	101	26	93	39	15	451	10.8
23	Apparel and other textile products . .	54	23	4	22	3	2	42	1.3
24	Lumber and wood products	407	56	26	35	2	288	551	13.0
25	Furniture and fixtures	63	19	4	23	3	13	131	3.1
26	Paper and allied products	2,366	189	191	431	315	1,241	3,498	36.7
27	Printing and publishing	116	58	3	49	-	6	73	1.3
28	Chemicals and allied products	4,360	416	137	2,049	317	1,441	3,601	22.4
29	Petroleum and coal products	6,412	106	126	723	8	5,449	28,414	127.0
30	Rubber and misc. plastic products . .	253	107	20	111	9	7	329	5.6
31	Leather and leather products	16	5	4	5	1	(Z)	108	3.3
32	Stone, clay, and glass products	966	115	50	468	301	31	2,037	29.5
33	Primary metal industries	2,875	509	59	751	1,505	51	3,782	45.9
34	Fabricated metal products	346	106	12	204	10	14	251	4.4
35	Machinery, except electrical.	280	114	12	129	18	6	145	2.0
36	Electric and electronic equipment . . .	224	109	10	85	11	9	144	2.2
37	Transportation equipment	350	127	31	139	42	11	193	2.4
38	Instruments and related products . . .	113	49	8	32	22	2	104	1.3
39	Miscellaneous manufacturing	41	14	3	20	2	1	110	2.2

- Represents zero. X Not applicable. Z Less than 0.5 trillion Btu. [1] Standard Industrial Classification; see text, section 13. [2] Net electricity is obtained by aggregating purchases, transfers in, and generation from noncombustible renewable resources minus quantities sold and transferred out. [3] Includes distillate and residual.

Source: U.S. Energy Information Administration, *Manufacturing Energy Consumption Survey: Consumption of Energy,* 1988.

No. 923. Commercial Buildings—Energy Consumption and Expenditures, by Major Fuel Type Used: 1986

[Covers buildings using one or more major fuel. Excludes industrial buildings predominantly residential buildings, and buildings of less than 1,000 sq. ft. Based on a sample survey of building representatives and energy suppliers; therefore, subject to sampling variability. For characteristics of commercial buildings, see tables in the Construction and Housing section. Tril.=trillion]

ITEM	Unit	All major fuels	Elec-tricity	Natural gas	Fuel oil	Pro-pane	District Heat
Number of buildings using the fuel	1,000.	3,992	3,965	2,214	534	344	77
Square footage of floorspace	Million	56,825	56,508	37,263	11,005	3,213	4,625
Square footage per building	1,000.	14.2	14.3	16.8	20.6	9.3	59.7
Energy consumed, total.	Tril. Btu	5,040	2,390	1,723	442	63	422
Energy consumed per building	Mil. Btu	1,262	603	778	827	184	5,446
Energy consumed per square foot of floorspace . . .	1,000 Btu . . .	89	42	46	40	20	91
Energy consumed per employee.	Mil. Btu	69	33	35	28	18	52
Expenditures, total	Mil. dol.	60,762	47,186	8,355	2,059	543	2,620
Expenditures per building.	$1,000.	15.2	11.9	3.8	3.9	1.6	33.8
Expenditures per square foot of floorspace.	Dollars.	1.07	0.84	0.22	0.19	0.17	0.57
Expenditures per million Btu of energy consumed . .	Dollars.	12.06	19.74	4.85	4.66	8.59	6.21

Source: U.S. Energy Information Administration, *Nonresidential Buildings Energy Consumption Survey: Commercial Buildings, Consumption and Expenditure, 1986.*

No. 924. Commercial Buildings—Energy Consumption and Expenditures: 1986

[Covers buildings using one or more major fuel. Excludes industrial buildings, predominantly residential buildings, and buildings of less than 1,000 sq. ft. Based on a sample survey of building representatives and energy suppliers; therefore, subject to sampling variability. For characteristics of commercial buildings, see tables in Section 26. For composition of regions, see table 25]

BUILDING CHARACTERISTIC	ALL BUILDINGS USING ANY MAJOR FUEL		CONSUMPTION (tril. Btu)			EXPENDITURES (mil. dol.)		
	Number (1,000)	Square feet (mil.)	Major fuel, total [1]	Elec-tricity	Natural gas	Major fuel, total [1]	Elec-tricity	Natural gas
All buildings	3,992	56,825	5,040	2,390	1,723	60,762	47,186	8,355
Region:								
Northeast.	639	11,506	1,046	430	244	14,362	10,886	1,472
Midwest.	1,036	15,728	1,603	584	742	15,848	10,869	3,400
South	1,517	18,882	1,485	867	426	17,945	14,856	1,958
West.	800	10,708	906	510	311	12,607	10,575	1,524
Year constructed:								
1900 or before	179	2,294	129	42	54	1,376	891	278
1901 to 1920	237	3,520	274	96	109	3,559	2,597	521
1921 to 1945	596	8,077	666	201	254	6,698	4,233	1,324
1946 to 1960	843	9,410	754	302	308	8,717	6,428	1,495
1961 to 1970	715	11,352	1,252	615	435	14,741	11,574	2,038
1971 to 1973	238	4,290	474	226	158	5,418	4,175	755
1974 to 1979	557	8,186	739	438	196	9,837	8,326	912
1980 to 1983	342	5,179	398	254	102	5,632	4,862	520
1984 to 1986	286	4,517	354	216	106	4,783	4,100	510
Principal activity within building:								
Assembly.	572	7,305	401	164	157	5,009	3,707	811
Education	241	7,292	635	179	254	5,782	3,606	1,189
Food sales/services	303	1,993	411	220	159	5,417	4,374	805
Health care	52	2,107	457	132	205	3,824	2,287	884
Lodging.	137	2,785	311	120	105	3,330	2,251	523
Mercantile/services.	1,280	12,781	1,002	536	332	13,231	10,781	1,706
Office	610	9,532	1,010	641	258	14,777	12,884	1,178
Public order and safety.	53	678	86	30	25	720	475	133
Warehouse	491	8,558	466	252	143	5,620	4,537	722
Other	94	1,704	169	83	46	2,013	1,568	204
Vacant	160	2,090	92	35	38	1,040	715	200
Square footage:								
1,001 to 5,000	2,113	5,943	719	376	248	10,133	8,175	1,316
5,001 to 10,000	901	6,638	598	278	236	7,647	5,962	1,206
10,001 to 25,000	541	8,873	724	312	305	8,374	6,265	1,519
25,001 to 50,000.	239	8,551	662	312	191	7,856	6,060	967
50,001 to 100,000	118	8,217	640	303	220	7,445	5,720	1,057
100,001 to 200,000	51	7,128	577	249	180	6,153	4,514	848
Over 200,000	29	11,475	1,120	560	343	13,154	10,489	1,441

[1] Includes fuel oil, propane, and purchased steam, not shown separately.

Source: U.S. Energy Information Administration, *Nonresidential Buildings Energy Consumption Survey: Commercial Buildings, Consumption and Expenditure, 1986.*

No. 925. Fossil Fuel Prices in Current and Constant (1982) Dollars: 1970 to 1990

[In cents per million British thermal units (Btu), except as indicated. All fuel prices taken as close to the point of production as possible. See text, section 19, for explanation of Btu conversions from mineral fuels]

FUEL	1970	1973	1975	1980	1982	1983	1984	1985	1986	1987	1988	1989	1990
CURRENT DOLLARS													
Composite [1]	31.7	39.8	82.1	204.2	275.8	270.1	264.6	251.2	165.3	170.0	153.3	167.1	184.6
Crude oil	54.8	67.1	132.2	372.2	491.7	451.6	446.2	415.3	215.7	265.5	216.9	273.4	345.3
Natural gas	15.4	20.1	40.2	144.8	222.2	232.3	239.9	225.7	174.8	150.2	152.4	152.7	155.4
Bituminous coal [2]	26.2	36.5	83.9	109.4	122.1	117.2	115.9	114.8	108.2	104.9	100.8	100.0	100.8
Anthracite coal	48.8	61.7	149.5	185.9	214.0	230.0	208.7	204.2	191.1	188.9	189.8	183.6	183.9
CONSTANT (1982) DOLLARS													
Composite [1]	75.5	80.4	138.4	238.3	275.8	260.0	245.7	226.5	145.3	144.8	126.4	132.3	140.4
Crude oil	130.5	135.6	222.9	434.3	491.7	434.6	414.3	374.5	189.5	226.1	178.8	216.5	262.6
Natural gas	36.7	40.6	67.8	169.0	222.2	223.6	222.7	203.5	153.6	127.9	125.6	120.9	118.2
Bituminous coal [2]	62.4	73.7	141.5	127.7	122.1	112.8	107.6	103.5	95.1	89.4	83.1	79.2	76.7
Anthracite coal	116.2	124.6	252.1	216.9	214.0	221.4	193.8	184.1	167.9	160.9	156.5	145.4	139.8
GNP price deflator[3] (1982=100)	42.0	49.5	59.3	85.7	100.0	103.9	107.7	110.9	113.9	117.4	121.3	126.3	131.5

[1] Weighted by relative importance of individual fuels in total fuels production. [2] Includes lignite. [3] GNP=Gross national product; see text, section 15.

Source: U.S. Energy Information Administration, *Annual Energy Review*.

No. 926. World Energy Consumption, by Region and Energy Source: 1960 to 1988

[In tons of coal equivalent. Metric ton=1.1023 short tons. Kilogram=2.205 pounds. See text, section 31 for general comments about the data]

REGION AND ENERGY SOURCE	CONSUMPTION (mil. metric tons)					PER CAPITA (kilograms)				PERCENT DISTRIBUTION			
	1960	1970	1980	1987	1988	1960	1970	1980	1988	1960	1970	1980	1988
World, total	3,924	6,440	8,544	9,655	10,013	1,302	1,748	1,919	1,959	100.0	100.0	100.0	100.0
North America [1]	1,599	2,502	2,796	2,812	2,922	5,951	7,825	7,480	7,011	40.7	38.9	32.7	29.2
United States	1,454	2,217	2,364	2,366	2,458	8,047	10,811	10,386	10,015	37.1	34.4	27.7	24.5
South America	79	143	251	232	297	535	749	1,046	1,042	2.0	2.2	2.9	3.0
Europe	1,039	1,720	2,145	2,192	2,190	2,443	3,745	4,433	4,418	26.5	26.7	25.1	21.9
Asia	514	903	1,579	2,140	2,265	276	386	607	752	13.1	14.0	18.5	22.6
Japan	96	333	435	445	480	1,025	3,246	3,726	3,921	2.4	5.2	5.1	4.8
Soviet Union	595	999	1,473	1,862	1,954	2,777	4,132	5,549	6,888	15.2	15.5	17.2	19.5
Oceania	41	71	105	130	134	2,597	3,675	4,572	5,189	1.0	1.1	1.2	1.3
Energy source:													
Solid fuels	1,940	2,159	2,632	3,168	3,299	644	586	591	645	49.4	33.5	30.8	32.9
Liquid fuels	1,306	2,835	3,778	3,771	3,922	433	770	848	794	33.3	44.0	44.2	39.1
Natural gas	593	1,292	1,834	2,249	2,302	197	351	412	449	15.1	20.1	21.5	23.0
Electricity	84	154	301	·466	490	28	42	68	95	2.1	2.4	3.5	5.0

[1] Includes Central America.

Source: Statistical Office of the United Nations, New York, NY, *Energy Statistics Yearbook*, annual, (copyright).

No. 927. World Primary Energy Production, by Region and Type: 1973 to 1989

[In quadrillion Btu. Btu=British thermal units. For Btu conversion factors, see source]

REGION AND TYPE	1973	1975	1980	1981	1982	1983	1984	1985	1986	1987	1988	1989
World total	244.8	245.0	286.6	281.7	280.2	282.2	297.0	304.3	314.1	322.0	334.2	338.3
North America	73.3	71.1	80.5	80.9	81.3	78.9	84.6	84.1	82.8	84.1	86.2	86.2
United States	62.0	59.8	64.7	64.3	63.8	61.1	65.7	64.6	64.0	64.6	65.8	65.8
Central and South America	12.9	10.6	12.1	12.1	12.0	12.2	13.1	13.5	14.2	14.2	15.2	15.3
Western Europe	19.6	21.4	28.7	29.8	30.7	31.9	32.4	35.0	35.9	36.5	37.0	36.7
Eastern Europe and Soviet Union	51.4	55.9	69.3	69.7	72.5	74.2	76.6	78.7	81.5	83.4	86.2	85.2
Middle East	46.6	43.5	42.2	36.7	29.5	27.3	27.7	25.7	30.6	32.1	36.0	39.6
Africa	14.8	13.3	17.3	15.1	15.4	16.1	17.5	18.4	18.1	18.5	19.4	20.2
Far East and Oceania	26.2	29.3	36.5	37.5	38.8	41.5	45.1	49.0	51.1	53.1	54.2	55.3
Crude oil	117.8	111.6	127.6	119.5	113.9	113.4	116.2	114.7	119.5	120.4	125.4	127.5
Natural gas	43.2	43.9	52.8	54.3	53.7	54.1	59.1	61.4	62.6	65.6	69.0	71.1
Natural gas liquids	4.2	4.4	5.5	5.8	5.8	5.8	6.1	6.2	6.5	6.7	6.8	7.0
Coal	63.8	66.3	75.0	75.2	78.4	78.5	82.2	86.1	88.3	90.4	92.0	91.9
Hydroelectric power	13.5	15.0	18.2	18.4	18.9	19.8	20.4	20.6	21.0	21.1	21.6	21.2
Nuclear electric power	2.2	3.9	7.6	8.5	9.5	10.7	13.0	15.4	16.3	17.8	19.3	19.7

Source: U.S. Energy Information Administration, *International Energy Annual*.

No. 928. U.S. Foreign Trade in Selected Mineral Fuels: 1970 to 1990

[Btu=British thermal units. For Btu conversion factors, see text, section 19. Minus sign (-) indicates an excess of imports over exports. See also *Historical Statistics, Colonial Times to 1970*, series M 100, 101, 127, 128, 140, 141, 178, and 181]

MINERAL FUEL	1970	1973	1975	1980	1983	1984	1985	1986	1987	1988	1989	1990
NATURAL GAS												
Imports:												
Billion cubic feet . . .	821	1,033	953	985	920	843	950	750	993	1,294	1,382	1,505
Trillion Btu	846	1,060	978	1,006	942	847	952	748	992	1,296	1,387	1,511
Exports:												
Billion cubic feet . . .	70	77	73	49	55	55	55	61	54	74	107	99
Trillion Btu	72	79	74	49	55	55	56	62	55	75	109	101
Net trade:												
Billion cubic feet . . .	-751	-956	-880	-936	-865	-788	-894	-689	-939	-1,220	-1,275	-1,406
Trillion Btu	-774	-981	-904	-957	-887	-792	-896	-686	-937	-1,221	-1,278	-1,410
CRUDE OIL												
Imports: [1]												
Million barrels	483	1,184	1,498	1,926	1,215	1,254	1,168	1,525	1,706	1,869	2,133	2,145
Trillion Btu	2,814	6,887	8,721	11,195	7,079	7,302	6,814	9,002	10,067	11,027	12,596	12,674
Exports:												
Million barrels	5	1	2	105	60	66	75	56	55	57	52	42
Trillion Btu	29	4	12	609	348	384	432	326	319	329	300	245
Net trade:												
Million barrels	-478	-1,183	-1,496	-1,821	-1,155	-1,188	-1,094	-1,469	-1,651	-1,812	-2,081	-2,102
Trillion Btu	-2,785	-6,883	-8,708	-10,586	-6,731	-6,918	-6,381	-8,676	-9,748	-10,698	-12,296	-12,429
PETROLEUM PRODUCTS												
Imports:												
Million barrels	765	1,099	712	603	629	736	681	747	731	840	809	759
Trillion Btu	4,656	6,578	4,227	3,463	3,568	4,131	3,796	4,199	4,095	4,720	4,565	4,265
Exports:												
Million barrels	89	84	74	94	210	198	211	230	224	242	262	273
Trillion Btu	520	482	427	551	1,217	1,161	1,225	1,344	1,311	1,412	1,536	1,594
Net trade:												
Million barrels	-675	-1,015	-638	-509	-419	-538	-471	-516	-508	-598	-548	-486
Trillion Btu	-4,136	-6,097	-3,800	-2,912	-2,351	-2,970	-2,570	-2,855	-2,784	-3,308	-3,029	-2,671
COAL												
Imports:												
Thousand short tons	36	127	940	1,194	1,271	1,286	1,952	2,212	1,747	2,134	2,851	2,699
Trillion Btu	1	3	24	30	32	32	49	55	44	53	71	67
Exports:												
Thousand short tons	71,733	53,587	66,309	91,742	77,772	81,482	92,680	85,518	79,607	95,023	100,815	105,804
Trillion Btu	1,936	1,425	1,761	2,421	2,045	2,151	2,438	2,248	2,093	2,499	2,637	2,772
Net trade:												
Thousand short tons	71,697	53,460	65,369	90,548	76,501	80,196	90,728	83,306	77,860	92,889	97,964	103,105
Trillion Btu	1,935	1,422	1,738	2,391	2,013	2,119	2,389	2,193	2,049	2,446	2,566	2,704

Z Less than 500,000 barrels.   [1] Beginning 1979, includes strategic petroleum reserve imports.

Source: U.S. Energy Information Administration, *Annual Energy Review*.

No. 929. Daily International Flow of Crude Oil, by Area: 1988

[In thousands of barrels per day]

EXPORTING AREA	Total [1]	IMPORTING AREA							
		North America		Central and South America	Western Europe	Eastern Europe	Middle East and Africa	Japan	Other Far East and Oceania
		U.S.	Canada						
World total.	25,724	5,107	449	[2]1,617	9,000	2,135	1,132	3,268	3,016
United States	155	(X)	10	142	-	-	-	-	3
North America, except U.S.	1,999	1,355	11	52	344	-	35	180	22
Central and South America	1,463	660	34	484	189	-	16	8	72
Western Europe.	2,515	321	294	-	1,861	16	23	-	£
Eastern Europe and Soviet Union .	2,830	-	-	85	1,194	1,412	46	2	91
Middle East.	10,621	1,401	33	619	3,074	505	748	2,195	2,046
Africa.	4,142	1,011	67	211	2,319	188	249	29	68
Far East and Oceania	1,997	359	-	24	19	14	15	854	712

- Represents zero.   X Not applicable.   [1] Includes stocks at sea, exchanges, transshipments, and other statistical discrepancies, not shown separately.   [2] Includes shipments to Puerto Rico and Virgin Islands.

Source: U.S. Energy Information Administration, *International Energy Annual*.

No. 930. Crude Oil Imports Into the United States, by Country of Origin: 1970 to 1990

[In millions of barrels. Barrels contain 42 gallons]

COUNTRY OF ORIGIN	1970	1973	1975	1980	1982	1983	1984	1985	1986	1987	1988	1989	1990
Total	483	1,184	1,498	1,926	1,273	1,215	1,254	1,168	1,525	1,706	1,869	2,133	2,151
Canada	245	365	219	73	78	100	125	171	208	222	249	230	235
Mexico	-	(Z)	26	186	235	280	241	261	227	220	247	261	251
Norway	-	-	5	53	37	24	41	11	19	25	23	46	35
Trinidad-Tobago	(Z)	22	42	42	34	30	32	36	34	27	26	27	28
United Kingdom	-	-	(Z)	63	161	133	138	102	116	111	93	58	56
OPEC [1]	222	765	1,172	1,414	633	539	553	479	771	876	987	1,232	1,282
Algeria	2	44	96	167	33	64	71	31	28	42	21	22	23
Ecuador	-	17	21	6	12	21	17	20	23	8	12	29	14
Gabon	-	-	10	9	14	21	21	19	9	13	6	18	23
Indonesia	26	73	138	115	82	115	111	107	108	96	68	58	36
Iran	12	79	102	3	13	18	4	10	7	36	(Z)	-	-
Iraq	-	2	1	10	1	4	5	17	29	30	126	161	187
Kuwait	12	15	1	10	1	3	9	1	10	26	29	57	29
Libya	17	49	81	200	8	-	-	-	-	-	-	-	-
Nigeria	17	164	272	308	186	110	76	102	160	193	222	282	286
Qatar	-	3	7	8	3	-	1	-	4	-	-	1	1
Saudi Arabia	15	169	256	458	194	117	113	48	226	234	333	407	436
United Arab Emirates	23	26	43	63	30	7	33	13	14	21	8	7	3
Venezuela	98	126	144	57	56	60	93	112	152	178	161	181	243
Other	16	32	34	95	95	109	124	108	150	225	244	288	264

- Represents zero.   Z Less than 500,000 barrels.   [1] Organization of Petroleum Exporting Countries.

Source: 1970, U.S. Bureau of Mines, *Minerals Yearbooks*, vol. I; thereafter, U.S. Energy Information Administration, *Petroleum Supply Annual*, vol. I.

No. 931. Crude Oil and Refined Products—Summary: 1973 to 1991

[Barrels of 42 gallons. Data are averages]

YEAR AND QUARTER	CRUDE OIL (1,000 bbl. per day)					REFINED OIL PRODUCTS (1,000 bbl. per day)			Total oil imports[2] (1,000 bbl. per day)	CRUDE OIL STOCKS [3] (mil. bbl.)	
	Input to refineries	Domestic production	Imports		Exports	Domestic demand	Imports	Exports		Total	Strategic reserve
			Total [1]	Strategic reserve							
1973	12,431	9,208	3,244	(X)	2	17,308	3,012	229	6,256	242	(X)
1974	12,133	8,774	3,477	(X)	3	16,653	2,635	218	6,112	265	(X)
1975	12,442	8,375	4,105	(X)	6	16,322	1,951	204	6,056	271	(X)
1976	13,416	8,132	5,287	(X)	8	17,461	2,026	215	7,313	285	(X)
1977	14,602	8,245	6,615	21	50	18,431	2,193	193	8,807	348	7
1978	14,739	8,707	6,356	162	158	18,847	2,008	204	8,363	376	67
1979	14,648	8,552	6,519	67	235	18,513	1,937	236	8,456	430	91
1980	13,481	8,597	5,263	44	287	17,056	1,646	258	6,909	466	108
1981	12,470	8,572	4,396	256	228	16,058	1,599	367	5,996	594	230
1982	11,774	8,649	3,488	165	236	15,296	1,625	579	5,113	644	294
1983	11,685	8,688	3,329	234	164	15,231	1,722	575	5,051	723	379
1984	12,044	8,879	3,426	197	181	15,726	2,011	541	5,437	796	451
1985	12,002	8,971	3,201	118	204	15,726	1,866	577	5,067	814	493
1986	12,716	8,680	4,178	48	154	16,281	2,045	631	6,224	843	512
1987	12,854	8,349	4,674	73	151	16,665	2,004	613	6,678	890	541
1988	13,246	8,140	5,107	51	155	17,283	2,295	661	7,402	890	560
1989	13,401	7,613	5,843	56	142	17,325	2,217	717	8,061	921	580
1990	13,409	7,355	5,894	27	109	16,988	2,123	748	8,018	908	586
1st qtr	13,128	7,492	6,081	27	123	16,884	2,444	681	8,422	953	582
2d qtr	13,375	7,281	6,287	48	104	16,952	2,251	647	8,484	971	587
3d qtr	14,153	7,228	6,321	32	74	17,223	2,031	723	8,362	932	590
4th qtr	12,827	7,423	4,940	-	134	16,708	1,775	923	6,717	908	586
1991:[4]											
1st qtr	12,864	7,480	5,304	-	112	16,427	1,515	1,074	6,819	905	568
2d qtr	13,495	7,372	6,079	-	135	16,319	1,942	803	8,021	916	568

- Represents zerol.   X Not applicable.   [1] Includes Strategic Petroleum Reserve.   [2] Crude oil (including Strategic Petroleum Reserve imports) plus refined products.   [3] End of year or quarter.   [4] Preliminary.

Source: U.S. Energy Information Administration, *Monthly Energy Review*, August 1991.

No. 932. Strategic Petroleum Reserve: 1977 to 1990

[**Million barrels, except as noted.** The Strategic Petroleum Reserve is a stock of petroleum maintained by the Federal Government for use during periods of major supply interruption]

YEAR	Crude oil imports	Domestic crude oil deliveries	STOCKS AT YEAREND			Days of net petroleum imports [3]
			Quantity [1]	Percent of crude oil stocks [2]	Percent of total petroleum stocks	
1977	7.54	[4]0.37	7.46	2.1	0.6	1
1980	16.07	1.30	107.80	23.1	7.7	17
1981	93.30	28.79	230.34	38.8	15.5	43
1982	60.19	3.79	293.83	45.7	20.5	68
1983	85.29	0.42	379.09	52.4	26.1	88
1984	72.04	0.05	450.51	56.6	28.9	96
1985	43.12	0.17	493.32	60.6	32.5	115
1986	17.56	1.21	511.57	60.7	32.1	94
1987	26.52	2.69	540.65	60.8	33.6	91
1988	18.76	(Z)	559.52	62.9	35.0	85
1989	20.35	-	579.86	62.9	36.7	81
1990	9.77	-	585.69	64.5	36.1	83

- Represents zero.   Z Less than .005 million barrels.   [1] Stocks do not include imported quantities in transit to Strategic Petroleum Reserve terminals, pipeline fill, and above ground storage.   [2] Including lease condensate stocks.   [3] Derived by dividing end-of-year strategic petroleum reserve stocks by annual average daily net imports of all petroleum. Calculated prior to rounding.   [4] The quantity of domestic fuel oil which was in storage prior to injection of foreign crude oil.
Source: U.S. Energy Information Administration, *Annual Energy Review.*

No. 933. World Petroleum Consumption, by Major Consuming Country: 1970 to 1990

[**Million barrels per day.** OECD=Organization for Economic Cooperation Development. For a complete list of OECD countries, see Section 31]

COUNTRY	1970	1973	1975	1980	1983	1984	1985	1986	1987	1988	1989	1990
World, total . . .	46.81	57.24	56.20	63.07	58.70	59.79	59.87	61.52	62.78	64.50	65.80	(NA)
OECD countries, total	33.27	39.90	36.98	38.60	33.79	34.50	34.27	35.28	35.91	37.09	37.56	37.53
United States	14.70	17.31	16.32	17.06	15.23	15.73	15.73	16.28	16.67	17.28	17.33	16.99
Australia	0.52	0.57	0.64	0.59	0.59	0.61	0.63	0.63	0.64	0.65	0.68	([1])
Canada	1.52	1.73	1.78	1.87	1.45	1.47	1.50	1.51	1.55	1.69	1.73	1.70
France	1.94	2.60	2.25	2.26	1.84	1.75	1.78	1.77	1.79	1.80	1.86	1.81
West Germany . . .	2.61	3.06	2.65	2.71	2.32	2.32	2.34	2.50	2.42	2.42	2.28	2.38
Italy	1.71	2.07	1.86	1.93	1.75	1.65	1.72	1.74	1.86	1.84	1.93	1.84
Japan	3.82	4.95	4.62	4.96	4.40	4.58	4.38	4.44	4.48	4.75	4.98	5.22
Spain	0.58	0.78	0.87	0.99	1.01	0.91	0.85	0.88	0.90	0.98	1.03	([1])
United Kingdom . .	2.10	2.34	1.91	1.73	1.53	1.85	1.63	1.65	1.60	1.70	1.74	1.74
Other OECD.	3.79	4.50	4.08	4.50	3.67	3.63	3.72	3.90	4.00	3.98	4.00	5.85
Brazil	0.53	0.78	0.92	1.15	0.98	1.03	1.08	1.24	1.26	1.30	1.32	(NA)
China	0.62	1.12	1.36	1.77	1.73	1.74	1.78	1.92	2.08	2.15	2.28	(NA)
Mexico	0.50	0.67	0.75	1.27	1.35	1.45	1.47	1.49	1.52	1.55	1.66	(NA)
U.S.S.R.	5.31	6.60	7.52	9.00	8.95	8.91	8.95	8.98	9.00	8.89	8.80	(NA)

NA Not available.   [1] Included in OECD total.
Source: U.S. Energy Information Administration, *Annual Energy Review,* and *Monthly Energy Review,* August 1991 issue.

No. 934. Energy Producing Companies—Selected Financial and Investment Indicators: 1979 to 1989

[Based on data from major publicly-owned domestic crude oil producing companies which either had at least one percent of domestic production or reserves of oil, natural gas, coal, or uranium, or at least one percent of refining capacity or petroleum product sales. There were 26 companies during 1979 through 1982; 25 in 1983; 22 during 1984 through 1987; and 23 in 1988]

ITEM	1979	1980	1981	1982	1983	1984	1985	1986	1987	1988	1989
INCOME STATEMENT (bil. dol.)											
Operating revenues	392.6	518.6	575.7	549.7	511.0	517.4	492.5	378.5	417.4	419.8	433.6
Operating expenses	345.8	455.9	520.8	504.2	462.8	467.3	444.2	354.4	383.7	381.6	397.7
Operating income.	46.8	62.7	54.8	45.5	48.2	50.1	48.3	24.0	33.7	38.2	35.9
Pretax income	48.6	66.9	60.0	45.2	47.4	47.6	43.6	20.6	25.0	34.3	35.3
Net income	23.5	31.0	30.0	21.8	21.9	21.3	17.4	9.2	11.3	22.3	19.8
Funds from operations[1]	45.4	59.0	61.6	60.4	60.7	63.6	63.5	53.1	51.6	57.8	48.3
BALANCE SHEET (bil. dol.)											
Net property, plant, and equipment	159.3	188.9	224.9	265.5	278.4	292.4	297.7	291.1	297.6	293.6	293.4
Net investment in place [2]	169.9	202.6	240.8	282.5	296.3	309.1	315.4	310.0	310.4	000.0	000.0
Total assets	282.8	333.0	372.5	411.9	421.8	442.9	438.4	427.0	443.6	437.8	434.5
RATIOS (percent)											
Net income to operating revenues.	6.0	6.0	5.2	4.0	4.3	4.1	3.5	2.4	2.7	5.3	4.6
Net income to total assets.	8.3	9.3	8.0	5.3	5.2	5.0	4.0	2.2	2.5	5.1	4.6
Net income to stockholders' equity	18.8	21.1	18.1	11.9	11.4	12.1	10.5	5.6	6.8	13.5	12.3
Long-term debt to stockholders' equity [3] . .	33.7	31.5	32.2	37.1	34.8	49.5	54.3	56.0	57.6	56.6	56.5
Long-term debt to total assets[3]. . . .	14.9	13.9	14.3	16.6	15.9	20.6	20.5	21.6	21.5	21.3	20.9

[1] The sum of net income, depreciation, depletion and amortization, deferred taxes, dry hole expenses, etc. [2] Composed of net property, plant and equipment plus investment and advances to unconsolidated subsidiaries. [3] Long-term debt includes amounts applicable to capitalized leases.
Source: U.S. Energy Information Administration, *Performance Profiles of Major Energy Producers,* annual.

No. 935. Petroleum and Coal Products Corporations—Sales, Net Profit, and Profit Per Dollar of Sales: 1975 to 1990

[Represents SIC group 29. Profit rates are averages of quarterly figures at annual rates. Beginning 1986, excludes estimates for corporations with less than $250,000 in assets]

ITEM	Unit	1975	1980	1981	1982	1983	1984	1985	1986	1987	1988	1989	1990
Sales................	Bil. dol..	121.8	333.2	376.1	357.1	312.7	338.4	320.9	226.5	248.3	252.2	265.3	318.5
Net profit:													
Before income taxes.....	Bil. dol..	13.3	39.1	35.3	27.8	27.1	24.5	17.7	9.8	14.2	27.3	23.7	23.3
After income taxes......	Bil. dol..	9.3	25.5	23.7	19.7	19.3	17.2	12.7	8.8	10.9	21.2	19.5	18.0
Depreciation[1]...........	Bil. dol..	5.6	11.6	13.7	16.3	17.5	20.7	22.1	21.9	20.3	20.0	18.5	18.6
Profits per dollar of sales:													
Before income taxes.....	Cents..	10.9	11.7	9.4	7.8	8.7	7.2	5.5	4.1	5.8	10.8	9.0	7.4
After income taxes......	Cents..	7.6	7.7	6.3	5.5	6.2	5.1	4.0	3.8	4.5	8.5	7.4	5.7
Profits on stockholders' equity:													
Before income taxes.....	Percent.	17.9	30.7	25.6	18.7	17.8	14.3	11.7	6.8	10.1	19.2	17.8	16.6
After income taxes......	Percent.	12.5	20.0	17.2	13.2	12.7	10.0	8.5	6.1	7.7	14.9	14.6	12.8

[1] Includes depletion and accelerated amortization of emergency facilities.
Source: Through 1981, U.S. Federal Trade Commission and, beginning 1982, U.S. Bureau of the Census, *Quarterly Financial Report for Manufacturing, Mining and Trade Corporations.*

No. 936. Major Petroleum Companies—Financial Data Summary: 1973 to 1990

[Data represent a composite of approximately 42 major worldwide petroleum companies aggregated on a consolidated, total company basis]

ITEM	1973	1975	1980	1982	1983	1984	1985	1986	1987	1988	1989	1990
FINANCIAL DATA (bil. dol.)												
Net income...................	11.8	11.6	32.9	21.1	20.6	22.7	19.4	10.8	15.0	24.6	24.7	26.8
Depreciation, depletion, etc.........	10.5	11.3	32.5	37.2	45.3	45.3	53.0	43.7	45.0	34.3	33.7	40.5
Cash flow[1]...................	22.3	22.8	65.4	58.3	58.1	68.0	72.4	54.5	60.0	58.9	58.4	67.3
Dividends paid.................	4.0	4.7	9.3	10.6	10.5	11.6	12.0	12.1	12.4	14.0	16.0	16.8
Net internal funds available for investment or debt repayment[2]...............	18.3	18.1	56.1	47.7	47.6	56.4	60.4	42.4	47.6	44.9	42.4	50.5
Capital and exploratory expenditures...	16.3	26.9	62.1	67.8	50.7	57.5	58.3	38.3	50.1	62.4	55.1	60.2
Long-term capitalization...........	102.9	121.1	211.4	243.8	240.0	285.7	272.1	279.9	282.2	287.8	290.0	304.6
Long-term debt...............	22.5	28.9	49.8	62.6	61.0	95.8	93.5	95.5	88.4	88.5	91.4	91.2
Preferred stock...............	0.4	0.4	2.0	3.5	3.5	5.2	3.3	3.7	4.1	4.5	6.4	5.4
Common stock and retained earnings[3].	80.0	91.9	159.6	177.7	175.5	184.7	175.3	180.7	189.7	194.8	192.2	208.0
Excess of expenditures over cash income[4]...................	-2.0	8.9	6.0	20.1	3.1	1.1	-2.1	3.0	-2.5	17.5	12.7	9.7
RATIOS [5] (percent)												
Long-term debt to long-term capitalization................	22.0	23.8	23.6	25.7	25.4	33.5	34.4	34.1	31.3	30.8	31.5	29.9
Net income to total average capital....	12.0	10.0	17.0	8.6	8.8	8.6	7.0	4.0	4.6	8.6	8.3	9.0
Net income to average common equity..	15.6	13.1	22.5	11.5	12.0	12.5	10.8	6.2	7.3	12.8	12.4	13.4

[1] Generally represents internally-generated funds from operations. Sum of net income and noncash charges such as depreciation, depletion, and amortization. [2] Cash flow minus dividends paid. [3] Includes common stock, capital surplus, and earned surplus accounts after adjustments. [4] Capital and exploratory expenditures plus dividends paid minus cash flow. [5] Represents approximate year-to-year comparisons because of changes in the makeup of the group due to mergers and other corporate changes.
Source: Carl H. Pforzheimer & Co., New York, NY, *Comparative Oil Company Statements, 1990-1989,* and earlier reports.

No. 937. Electric Utility Sales and Average Prices, by End-Use Sector: 1970 to 1990

[Prior to 1980, covers Class A and B privately-owned electric utilities; thereafter, Class A utilities whose electric operating revenues were $100 million or more during the previous year]

YEAR	SALES (bil. kWh)				AVERAGE PRICE OF ELECTRICITY SOLD (cents per kWh)							
					Current dollars				Constant (1982) dollars [2]			
	Total [1]	Resi-dential	Com-mer-cial	Indus-trial	Total [1]	Resi-dential	Com-mer-cial	Indus-trial	Total [1]	Resi-dential	Com-mer-cial	Indus-trial
1970.....	1,392	466	307	571	1.7	2.2	2.1	1.0	4.0	5.2	5.0	2.4
1973.....	1,713	579	388	686	2.0	2.5	2.4	1.3	4.0	5.1	4.8	2.6
1975.....	1,747	588	403	688	2.9	3.5	3.5	2.1	4.9	5.9	5.9	3.5
1979.....	2,071	683	473	842	4.0	4.6	4.7	3.1	5.1	5.9	6.0	3.9
1980.....	2,094	717	488	815	4.7	5.4	5.5	3.7	5.5	6.3	6.4	4.3
1981.....	2,147	722	514	826	5.5	6.2	6.3	4.3	5.9	6.6	6.7	4.6
1982.....	2,086	730	526	745	6.1	6.9	6.9	5.0	6.1	6.9	6.9	5.0
1983.....	2,151	751	544	776	6.3	7.2	7.0	5.0	6.1	6.9	6.7	4.8
1984.....	2,286	780	583	838	6.3	7.2	7.1	4.8	5.8	6.7	6.6	4.5
1985.....	2,324	794	606	837	6.4	7.4	7.3	5.0	5.8	6.7	6.6	4.5
1986.....	2,369	819	631	831	6.4	7.4	7.2	4.9	5.6	6.5	6.3	4.3
1987.....	2,457	850	660	858	6.4	7.5	7.1	4.8	5.5	6.3	6.0	4.1
1988.....	2,578	893	699	896	6.4	7.5	7.0	4.7	5.3	6.2	5.8	3.9
1989.....	2,647	906	726	926	6.5	7.6	7.2	4.7	5.1	6.0	5.7	3.7
1990.....	2,705	922	753	938	6.6	7.8	7.3	4.7	5.0	5.9	5.6	3.6

[1] Includes other sectors not shown separately. [2] Based on the GNP implicit price deflator.
Source: U.S. Energy Information Administration, *Annual Energy Review.*

No. 938. Electric Utility Industry—Net Generation, Net Summer Capability, Generating Units, and Consumption of Fuels: 1970 to 1990

[Net Generation for **calendar years;** other data as of **December 31.** See also *Historical Statistics, Colonial Times to 1970,* series S 32-52, S 78-82, and S 86-10

ITEM	Unit	1970	1980	1984	1985	1986	1987	1988	1989	1990
NET GENERATION										
Total	Bil. kWh . .	1,532	2,286	2,416	2,470	2,487	2,572	2,704	2,784	2,805
Average annual change [1]	Percent . . .	7.3	1.8	4.4	2.2	0.7	3.4	4.9	2.9	0.7
Net generation, kWh per kW of net summer capability [2]	Rate	4,554	3,952	3,805	3,771	3,741	3,816	3,990	4,067	4,073
Investor owned.	Bil. kWh. . .	1,183	1,783	1,849	1,918	1,928	2,022	2,146	2,192	2,201
Percent of total utilities	Percent . . .	77.2	78.0	76.5	77.7	77.5	78.6	79.4	78.7	78.5
Publicly owned.	Bil. kWh. . .	349	503	567	552	559	550	559	592	606
Municipal	Bil. kWh. . .	71	87	75	74	79	86	97	100	98
Federal	Bil. kWh. . .	186	235	254	233	225	205	201	224	235
Cooperatives and other.	Bil. kWh. . .	91	182	239	245	255	258	261	269	273
Source of energy:										
Coal [3]	Percent . . .	46.0	51.0	55.9	57.2	56.2	57.4	57.4	56.2	55.9
Nuclear	Percent . . .	1.4	11.0	13.6	15.5	16.6	17.7	19.5	19.0	20.6
Oil.	Percent . . .	12.0	10.8	5.0	4.1	5.5	4.6	5.5	5.7	4.2
Gas.	Percent . . .	24.3	15.1	12.3	11.8	10.0	10.6	9.3	9.6	9.4
Hydro	Percent . . .	16.2	12.1	13.3	11.4	11.7	9.7	8.2	9.5	10.0
Type of prime mover: [4]										
Hydro	Bil. kWh. . .	248	276	321	281	291	250	223	265	280
Steam conventional [5]	Bil. kWh. . .	1,240	1,726	1,742	1,778	1,756	1,837	1,921	1,950	1,916
Gas turbine and internal combustion	Bil. kWh. . .	22	28	17	16	15	18	22	29	22
Steam nuclear.	Bil. kWh. . .	22	251	328	384	414	455	527	529	577
Other.	Bil. kWh. . .	1	6	9	11	12	12	12	11	11
NET SUMMER CAPABILITY										
Total [6]	Mil. kW . . .	336	579	635	655	665	674	678	685	689
Average annual change [1] . . .	Percent . . .	7.2	1.6	2.2	3.1	1.4	1.4	0.5	1.0	0.6
Hydro	Mil. kW . . .	64	82	85	89	89	90	90	91	91
Steam conventional [7]	Mil. kW . . .	248	397	431	437	441	440	442	444	446
Gas turbine	Mil. kW . . .	13	43	44	44	43	44	44	45	46
Steam nuclear	Mil. kW . . .	7	52	70	79	85	94	95	98	100
Internal combustion.	Mil. kW . . .	4	5	5	5	5	5	5	5	5
Geothermal and other	Mil. kW . . .	(Z)	1	1	2	2	2	2	2	2
NUMBER OF GENERATING UNITS										
Total [8]	Number . .	9,717	11,084	(NA)	(NA)	10,611	10,406	10,305	10,325	10,296
Hydro	Number . . .	3,108	3,275	(NA)	(NA)	3,489	3,488	3,496	3,479	3,479
Steam conventional	Number . . .	2,813	2,862	(NA)	(NA)	2,536	2,437	2,383	2,363	2,354
Gas turbine	Number . . .	658	1,447	(NA)	(NA)	1,439	1,408	1,397	1,438	1,460
Steam nuclear	Number . . .	16	74	(NA)	(NA)	99	109	108	110	111
Internal combustion.	Number . . .	3,118	3,410	(NA)	(NA)	2,998	2,917	2,872	2,889	2,847
CONSUMPTION OF FUELS										
Net generation by fuel [9]	Bil. kWh . .	1,284	2,010	2,095	2,189	2,197	2,322	2,481	2,519	2,525
Average annual change [1] . .	Percent . . .	52.5	2.1	5.6	4.3	0.4	5.4	6.4	1.4	0.2
Coal	Bil. kWh. . .	704	1,162	1,342	1,402	1,386	1,464	1,541	1,554	1,557
Percent of total	Percent . . .	54.8	57.8	64.1	64.0	63.1	63.0	62.1	61.7	61.7
Petroleum	Bil. kWh. . .	184	246	120	100	137	118	149	158	117
Gas	Bil. kWh. . .	373	346	297	292	249	273	253	267	263
Nuclear.	Bil. kWh. . .	22	251	328	384	414	455	527	529	577
Fuel consumed:										
Total energy equivalent.	Quad. Btu . .	13.40	18.57	18.53	18.79	18.59	19.37	20.12	20.56	20.28
Coal	Mil. sh. tons	320	569	664	694	685	718	758	767	772
Oil.	Mil. bbl. . . .	339	421	206	175	232	201	250	267	196
Gas.	Bil cu. ft. . .	3,932	3,682	3,111	3,044	2,602	2,844	2,636	2,787	2,776

NA Not available. Z Less than .5 million kWh. [1] Change from immediate prior year, except for 1970, change from 1960. For explanation of average annual percent change, see Guide to Tabular Presentation. [2] Net summer capability is the steady hourly output that generating equipment is expected to supply to system load, exclusive of auxiliary power as demonstrated by test at the time of summer peak demand. [3] Includes small percentage (.5%) from wood and waste, geothermal, and petroleum coke. [4] A prime mover is the engine, turbine, water wheel, or similar machine which drives an electric generator. [5] Fossil fuels only. [6] Includes wind, solar thermal, and photovoltaic, not shown separately. [7] Includes fossil steam, wood, and waste. [8] Each prime mover type in combination plants counted separately. Includes geothermal, wind, and solar, not shown separately. [9] Includes small amounts of wood, waste, wind, geothermal, solar thermal, and photovoltaic.

Source: 1970, U.S. Federal Power Commission, *Electric Power Statistics,* and press releases; thereafter, U.S. Energy Information Administration, 1975 and 1980, *Power Production, Fuel Consumption, and Installed Capacity Data-Annual,* and unpublished data; thereafter, *Electric Power Annual, Annual Energy Review,* and unpublished data.

No. 939. Electric Utility Industry—Capability, Peak Load, and Capacity Margin: 1970 to 1990

[Excludes Alaska and Hawaii. Capability represents the maximum kilowatt output with all power sources available and with hydraulic equipment under actual water conditions, allowing for maintenance, emergency outages, and system operating requirements. Capacity margin is the difference between capability and peak load]

YEAR	CAPABILITY AT THE TIME OF—				NON-COINCIDENT PEAK LOAD		CAPACITY MARGIN			
	Summer peak load (1,000 kW)		Winter peak load[1] (1,000 kW)		Summer	Winter[1]	Summer		Winter[1]	
	Amount	Change from prior year[2]	Amount	Change from prior year[2]			Amount (1,000 kW)	Percent of capability	Amount (1,000 kW)	Percent of capability
1970	326,900	26,600	339,050	27,600	274,650	248,550	52,250	16.0	90,500	26.7
1975	479,300	34,900	492,450	25,050	356,800	331,100	122,500	25.6	161,350	32.8
1976	498,750	19,450	511,000	18,550	370,900	349,850	127,850	25.6	161,150	31.5
1977	516,000	17,250	537,600	26,600	396,350	360,200	119,650	23.2	177,400	33.0
1978	545,700	29,700	561,550	23,950	408,050	383,100	137,650	25.2	178,450	31.8
1979 [3]	544,506	(X)	554,525	(X)	398,424	368,876	146,082	26.8	185,649	33.5
1980	558,237	13,731	572,195	17,670	427,058	384,567	131,179	23.5	187,628	32.8
1981	572,219	13,982	586,569	14,374	429,349	397,800	142,870	25.0	188,769	32.2
1982	586,142	13,923	598,066	11,497	415,618	373,985	170,524	29.1	224,081	37.5
1983	596,449	10,307	612,453	14,387	447,526	410,779	148,923	25.0	201,674	32.9
1984	604,240	7,791	622,125	9,673	451,150	436,374	153,090	25.3	185,751	29.9
1985	621,597	17,357	636,475	14,350	460,503	423,660	161,094	25.9	212,815	33.4
1986	633,291	11,694	646,721	10,246	476,320	422,857	156,971	24.8	223,864	34.6
1987	648,118	14,827	662,977	16,256	496,185	448,277	151,933	23.4	214,700	32.4
1988	661,580	13,462	676,940	13,963	529,460	466,533	132,120	20.0	210,407	31.1
1989	673,316	11,736	685,249	8,309	523,432	496,378	149,884	22.3	188,871	27.6
1990	685,091	11,775	696,757	11,508	545,537	484,014	139,554	20.4	212,743	30.5

X Not applicable.   [1] 1970 is for the month of December.   [2] For 1970 and 1975, change from 1969 and 1974, respectively.   [3] Beginning 1979, data are not entirely comparable with prior years due to change in data source.

Source: Edison Electric Institute, Washington, DC, *Statistical Yearbook of the Electric Utility Industry*, annual.

No. 940. Electric Energy Sales, by Class of Service, 1970 to 1990, and by State, 1990

[In billions of kilowatthours]

REGION, DIVISION, AND STATE	Total[1]	Resi-dential	Com-mercial	Indus-trial	REGION, DIVISION, AND STATE	Total[1]	Resi-dential	Com-mercial	Indus-trial
1970	1,392.3	466.3	306.7	570.9	**South**	1,128.4	417.8	283.1	391.5
1973	1,712.9	579.2	388.3	686.1	**South Atlantic**	532.2	210.4	152.2	152.5
1975	1,747.1	588.1	403.0	687.7	Delaware	8.3	2.7	2.3	3.3
1980	2,094.4	717.5	488.2	815.1	Maryland	49.7	19.0	10.4	19.6
1985	2,309.5	791.0	609.0	824.5	Dist. of Columbia	9.8	1.5	5.1	3.0
1986	2,350.8	817.7	641.5	808.3	Virginia	72.6	28.0	20.0	16.6
1987	2,457.3	850.4	660.4	858.2	West Virginia	23.4	7.7	5.0	10.5
1988	2,578.1	892.9	699.1	896.5	North Carolina	89.5	33.1	23.7	31.1
1989	2,646.7	904.0	725.2	926.4	South Carolina	55.5	17.6	11.9	25.2
					Georgia	80.3	29.5	22.9	27.0
1990, total	2,705.5	921.6	752.6	937.8	Florida	143.1	71.4	50.9	16.2
					East South Central	230.6	77.9	39.0	109.1
Northeast	412.6	135.5	140.6	120.1	Kentucky	62.3	16.6	9.3	34.0
New England	104.3	37.7	37.5	27.1	Tennessee	76.6	28.4	12.0	35.4
Maine	11.5	3.9	2.7	4.7	Alabama	59.7	20.8	11.1	27.3
New Hampshire	9.1	3.5	2.0	3.5	Mississippi	31.9	12.1	6.7	12.5
Vermont	4.8	1.9	1.5	1.4	**West South Central**	365.6	129.5	92.0	129.8
Massachusetts	45.3	15.6	18.5	10.0	Arkansas	26.7	10.5	6.0	9.6
Rhode Island	6.4	2.4	2.5	1.4	Louisiana	62.9	21.1	13.5	25.7
Connecticut	27.2	10.4	10.4	6.1	Oklahoma	38.3	14.8	10.3	11.1
Middle Atlantic	308.3	97.9	103.2	92.9	Texas	237.7	83.1	62.2	83.5
New York	130.1	38.6	46.9	32.2	**West**	515.4	163.8	167.6	162.9
New Jersey	62.6	20.5	27.0	15.0	**Mountain**	160.3	49.2	51.3	53.4
Pennsylvania	115.6	38.8	29.6	45.7	Montana	13.2	3.3	2.7	6.6
					Idaho	18.0	5.7	5.0	7.1
Midwest	649.0	204.4	161.2	263.3	Wyoming	11.7	1.7	2.2	7.6
East North Central	459.5	134.1	111.2	199.5	Colorado	31.2	9.8	14.5	6.0
Ohio	141.9	37.7	30.6	69.2	New Mexico	13.7	3.6	4.6	4.3
Indiana	73.6	21.9	15.4	35.6	Arizona	40.4	15.3	13.7	9.6
Illinois	112.2	32.7	31.7	40.0	Utah	15.2	4.2	4.7	5.6
Michigan	82.7	25.2	20.8	35.5	Nevada	16.9	5.6	3.9	6.9
Wisconsin	49.2	16.6	12.8	19.1	**Pacific**	355.1	114.6	116.3	109.5
West North Central	189.5	70.3	50.0	63.9	Washington	88.5	29.0	16.9	38.8
Minnesota	47.4	15.0	8.2	23.3	Oregon	42.6	15.2	11.6	15.4
Iowa	29.1	10.5	6.6	11.1	California	211.4	66.4	83.7	51.2
Missouri	54.7	22.1	17.7	13.8	Alaska	4.3	1.7	2.0	0.4
North Dakota	7.1	3.0	1.8	1.8	Hawaii	8.3	2.3	2.2	3.7
South Dakota	6.3	2.8	1.5	1.6					
Nebraska	17.8	7.2	5.1	4.2					
Kansas	27.1	9.5	9.2	8.0					

[1] Includes other service, not shown separately.

Source: U.S. Energy Information Association, *Electric Power Annual* and *Electric Power Monthly*, December 1990 issue.

No. 941. Electric Energy—Net Generation and Installed Generating Capacity, by State: 1980 to 1990

[Capacity as of **Dec. 31.** Covers utilities for public use]

DIVISION AND STATE	NET GENERATION (bil. kWh)		1990		INSTALLED CAPACITY (mil. kW)		DIVISION AND STATE	NET GENERATION (bil. kWh)		1990		INSTALLED CAPACITY (mil. kW)	
	1980	1989	Total	Per-cent from coal	1980	1990		1980	1989	Total	Per-cent from coal	1980	1990
U.S....	2,286.4	2,784.3	2,805.3	55.5	613.5	735.1	VA	34.3	43.4	47.2	44.5	11.7	14.6
							WV	70.8	82.9	77.4	99.1	15.2	15.1
N.E	78.2	97.4	94.1	17.6	21.1	23.9	NC	72.1	87.1	79.8	58.4	15.6	20.9
ME	7.9	11.6	9.1	0.0	2.4	2.4	SC	41.9	67.0	69.3	33.0	11.7	16.3
NH	6.0	7.1	10.8	27.4	1.6	2.6	GA	63.3	92.4	97.6	69.3	16.3	21.3
VT	3.8	4.8	5.0	0.0	0.9	1.1	FL	95.9	124.3	123.5	47.8	29.0	36.2
MA	34.8	39.2	36.5	30.9	9.6	10.1	E.S.C....	214.1	243.4	246.8	74.3	53.3	64.0
RI	1.0	0.5	0.6	0.0	0.3	0.3	KY	57.1	70.8	73.8	95.6	13.6	17.3
CT	24.7	34.3	32.2	7.3	6.3	7.4	TN	60.2	74.0	73.9	68.0	15.9	18.2
M.A	260.5	326.4	330.8	40.4	78.4	85.2	AL	78.3	77.6	76.2	69.9	18.2	21.3
NY	108.6	130.5	128.7	19.1	31.4	33.3	MS	18.5	21.1	23.0	41.1	5.5	7.2
NJ	29.4	41.1	36.5	19.3	12.6	14.9	W.S.C....	313.1	364.5	374.0	48.3	84.7	107.5
PA	122.5	154.8	165.7	61.6	34.4	37.0	AR	19.7	33.4	37.1	51.7	7.2	9.9
E.N.C....	397.0	482.7	485.8	74.6	107.9	123.9	LA	45.7	54.3	57.4	30.5	12.9	18.1
OH	110.2	131.4	126.5	90.9	27.4	28.9	OK	44.6	44.4	45.1	55.9	11.3	13.6
IN	70.6	88.6	97.7	98.2	17.1	22.9	TX	203.0	232.4	234.5	50.7	53.3	66.0
IL	103.4	126.8	127.0	42.4	29.9	36.9	Mt	158.8	235.5	247.3	75.7	35.8	52.3
MI	74.8	91.5	89.0	73.3	22.7	24.1	MT	15.5	25.8	25.7	57.9	3.2	4.9
WI	37.8	44.4	45.6	70.6	10.7	11.1	ID	9.5	8.9	8.6	0.0	2.0	2.1
W.N.C ...	168.2	215.9	216.2	75.3	49.0	58.6	WY	22.4	36.8	39.4	98.2	4.1	6.2
MN	31.5	40.4	39.5	64.6	8.8	9.2	CO	23.6	32.3	31.3	94.5	6.1	6.7
IA	21.8	28.1	29.0	85.7	7.3	8.6	NM	24.7	28.3	28.5	90.6	5.0	5.5
MO	48.9	59.4	59.0	82.2	13.8	16.7	AZ	36.9	53.1	62.3	50.8	9.4	16.5
ND	15.8	25.7	26.8	93.5	3.4	4.7	UT	12.1	30.5	32.3	97.7	2.1	5.2
SD	8.6	7.0	6.4	38.5	2.2	2.7	NV	14.1	19.7	19.3	78.1	3.9	5.1
NE	16.3	21.1	21.6	58.5	5.1	5.9	Pac	278.8	276.7	276.5	3.2	71.9	81.9
KS	25.1	34.2	33.9	70.0	8.3	10.8	WA	92.3	87.1	100.5	7.3	23.0	23.4
S.A	417.8	541.9	533.7	60.3	111.5	137.9	OR	36.6	45.0	49.0	2.2	8.5	10.6
DE	6.7	8.5	7.1	69.1	1.6	2.1	CA	140.3	132.3	114.6	0.0	37.8	44.5
MD	32.2	35.8	31.5	74.0	9.2	10.5	AK	3.1	4.4	4.5	6.9	1.1	1.8
DC	0.7	0.7	0.4	0.0	1.2	0.9	HI	6.5	7.9	8.0	0.0	1.1	1.5

Source: U.S. Energy Information Administration, 1980, *Power Production, Fuel Consumption, and Installed Capacity Data*, annual; thereafter, *Electric Power Annual, Electric Power Monthly*, December 1989 issue, and *Inventory of Power Plants in the United States*, annual.

No. 942. Nuclear Power Plants—Number of Units, Net Generation, and Net Summer Capability, by State: 1990

DIVISION AND STATE	Number of units	NET GENERATION Total (mil. kW)	Percent of total[1]	NET SUMMER CAPABILITY Total (mil. kW)	Percent of total[1]	DIVISION AND STATE	Number of units	NET GENERATION Total (mil. kW)	Percent of total[1]	NET SUMMER CAPABILITY Total (mil. kW)	Percent of total[1]
U.S.....	111	576,784	20.6	99.6	14.4	KS	1	7,874	23.3	1.1	11.9
						South	42	215,169	18.6	39.3	13.5
Northeast ..	28	142,585	33.6	24.0	23.6	S.A	27	140,354	26.3	23.6	18.3
N.E	9	37,404	39.8	6.6	28.0	MD	2	1,251	4.0	1.7	16.9
ME	1	4,861	53.6	0.9	35.7	VA	4	23,820	50.5	3.4	24.8
NH	1	4,081	37.7	1.2	43.6	NC	5	25,905	32.5	4.7	23.3
VT	1	3,616	72.4	0.5	46.6	SC	7	42,881	61.9	6.3	42.6
MA	2	5,070	13.9	0.8	8.4	GA	4	24,797	25.4	3.7	18.0
CT	4	19,776	61.5	3.2	45.0	FL	5	21,699	17.6	3.8	11.7
M.A	19	105,181	31.8	17.4	22.3	E.S.C....	8	33,477	13.6	8.3	13.9
NY	6	23,623	18.4	4.8	15.5	TN	2	14,003	19.0	2.3	13.5
NJ	4	23,770	65.1	3.9	28.1	AL	5	12,052	15.8	4.8	24.2
PA	9	57,787	34.9	8.7	26.2	MS	1	7,422	32.3	1.1	16.3
Midwest ...	31	153,923	21.9	25.8	15.4	W.S.C....	7	41,000	11.1	7.4	7.3
E.N.C....	23	115,388	23.8	20.2	17.8	AR	2	11,282	30.4	1.7	17.6
OH	2	10,664	8.4	2.0	7.6	LA	2	14,197	24.7	2.0	12.0
IL	13	71,887	56.6	12.6	38.7	TX	3	15,859	6.8	3.7	5.9
MI	5	21,610	24.3	4.0	18.0	West......	10	65,110	12.4	10.6	8.1
WI	3	11,226	24.6	1.5	14.3	Mt	3	20,598	8.3	3.7	7.4
W.N.C ...	8	38,535	17.8	5.6	10.3	AZ	3	20,598	33.1	3.7	24.6
MN	3	12,139	30.8	1.5	17.4	Pac	7	44,512	16.9	7.0	8.5
IA	1	3,012	10.4	0.5	6.7	WA	1	5,742	5.7	1.1	4.6
MO	1	7,998	13.6	1.1	7.4	OR	1	6,074	12.4	1.1	9.8
NE	2	7,511	34.7	1.3	23.0	CA	5	32,696	28.5	4.7	10.9

[1] For total capability and generation, see table 941.

Source: U.S. Energy Information Administration, *Electric Power Monthly*, December 1990 issue.

No. 943. Nuclear Power Plants—Number, Capacity, and Generation: 1965 to 1990

ITEM	1965	1970	1975	1980	1983	1984	1985	1986	1987	1988	1989	1990
Operable generating units[1]......	6	18	54	70	80	86	95	100	107	108	110	111
Net summer capability[1][2] (mil. kW)..	0.8	7.0	37.3	51.8	63.0	69.7	79.4	85.2	93.6	94.7	98.2	99.6
Electricity generated (bil. kWh)	0.4	21.8	172.5	251.1	293.7	327.6	383.7	414.0	455.3	527.0	529.4	576.8
Percent of total electric utility generation	0.3	1.4	9.0	11.0	12.7	13.6	15.5	16.6	17.7	19.5	19.0	20.6
Capacity factor[3]	(NA)	(NA)	55.9	56.3	54.4	56.3	58.0	56.9	57.4	63.5	62.2	66.1

NA Not available. [1] As of yearend. [2] Net summer capability is the peak steady hourly output that generating equipment is expected to supply to system load, exclusive of auxiliary and other powerplant, as demonstrated by test at the time of summer peak demand. [3] Weighted average of monthly capacity factors. Monthly factors are derived by dividing actual monthly generation by the maximum possible generation for the month (hours in month times net maximum dependable capacity).

Source: U.S. Energy Information Administration, *Annual Energy Review.*

No. 944. Commercial Nuclear Power Generation, by Country: 1970 to 1991

[Generation for **calendar years;** other data as of **December**]

COUNTRY	REACTORS				GROSS ELECTRICITY GENERATED (bil. kWh)				GROSS CAPACITY (1,000 kW)			
	1970	1980	1990	1991	1970	1980	1990	1991	1970	1980	1990	1991
Total......	64	208	368	362	73.9	617.8	1,743.9	1,844.0	15,186	128,847	301,745	302,020
United States ..	15	74	112	112	23.2	265.2	606.4	643.5	5,211	56,529	105,998	105,998
Argentina	-	1	2	2	0.0	2.3	7.0	7.5	-	357	1,005	1,005
Belgium	1	3	7	7	0.3	12.5	42.7	42.9	11	1,744	5,740	5,740
Brazil........	-	-	1	1	0.0	0.0	2.0	1.4	-	-	657	657
Canada	1	9	19	19	0.9	40.4	74.0	86.1	220	5,588	13,855	13,904
China: Taiwan ..	-	2	6	6	0.0	8.2	32.9	35.3	-	1,272	5,146	5,146
Finland.......	-	4	4	4	0.0	7.0	18.9	19.2	-	2,296	2,400	2,400
France.......	4	22	58	57	5.7	61.2	314.1	331.4	1,606	15,412	58,862	59,224
Germany	4	11	22	22	5.3	43.7	147.2	147.2	907	8,996	23,973	23,983
Great Britain ...	27	33	42	37	26.5	37.2	68.8	70.4	4,783	9,012	15,274	14,813
Hungary......	-	-	4	4	0.0	0.0	13.6	13.7	-	-	1,760	1,820
India	2	4	6	7	2.2	2.9	6.0	5.4	400	860	1,330	1,565
Italy	3	4	2	-	3.3	2.2	0.0	0.0	631	1,490	1,132	-
Japan	3	22	40	42	3.3	81.0	191.9	205.8	828	15,117	31,645	33,399
Mexico.......	-	-	1	1	0.0	0.0	2.1	4.2	-	-	675	675
Netherlands ...	1	2	2	2	0.4	4.2	3.4	3.3	55	529	540	540
Pakistan	-	1	1	1	0.0	0.1	0.4	0.4	-	137	137	137
South Africa ...	-	-	2	2	0.0	0.0	8.9	9.7	-	-	1,930	1,930
South Korea ...	-	1	9	9	0.0	3.5	52.8	56.3	-	587	7,616	7,616
Spain	1	3	10	9	0.9	5.2	54.3	55.6	160	1,117	7,984	7,368
Sweden	1	8	12	12	(Z)	26.7	68.2	76.8	12	5,770	10,344	10,359
Switzerland ...	1	4	5	5	1.9	14.3	23.6	22.9	364	2,034	3,079	3,079
Yugoslavia	-	-	1	1	0.0	0.0	4.6	5.0	-	-	664	664

- Represents zero. Z Less than 50 million kWh.

Source: McGraw-Hill, Inc., New York, NY, *Nucleonics Week,* January issues, (copyright).

No. 945. Uranium Supply, Enrichment, and Discharged Commercial Reactor Fuel: 1970 to 1990

[Years ending **Dec. 31,** except as noted. For additional data on uranium, see section 25 on mining. For explanation of kilogram, see weights and measures]

ITEM	Unit	1970	1975	1980	1984	1985	1986	1987	1988	1989	1990
URANIUM CONCENTRATE											
Production	Mil. lb	25.81	23.20	43.70	14.88	11.31	13.51	12.99	13.13	13.84	8.90
Exports.................	Mil. lb	4.20	1.00	5.80	2.20	5.30	1.60	1.00	3.30	2.10	2.00
Imports.................	Mil. lb	-	1.40	3.60	12.50	11.70	13.50	15.10	15.80	13.10	23.70
Delivered price...........	Dol./lb....	(NA)	10.50	26.00	32.65	31.43	30.01	27.37	25.65	19.56	15.70
ENRICHMENT [3]											
Enriched product [1]	Mil. Swu[2]..	5.10	9.92	10.69	11.2	10.2	8.6	8.1	9.9	11.9	10.2
For domestic customers...	Mil. Swu[2]..	3.74	4.36	6.89	5.8	6.0	4.9	3.4	6.3	7.6	6.8
For foreign customers	Mil. Swu[2]..	1.36	5.56	3.80	5.4	4.2	3.7	4.7	3.6	4.3	3.4
Sales.................	Mil. dol ...	(NA)	376	1,379	1,457	1,403	1,085	921	1,094	1,320	1,148
DISCHARGED COMMERCIAL REACTOR FUEL [4]											
Annual discharge	Metric tons.	82	499	1,193	1,257	1,330	1,431	1,615	(NA)	(NA)	(NA)
Inventory, yearend [5]	Metric tons.	118	1,538	6,434	11,006	12,481	13,881	(NA)	(NA)	(NA)	(NA)

- Represents zero. NA Not available. [1] Based on sales. [2] Separative work units. The standard measure of enrichment services is based on operating tails assay in effect at the time the enriched product was placed in inventory. [3] Beginning 1984, represents fiscal years. [4] Uranium content. Source: Nuclear Assurance Corporation, Atlanta, GA. [5] Reprocessed fuel not included as inventory.

Source: Except as noted, U.S. Energy Information Administration, *Annual Energy Review, Uranium Industry Annual;* and unpublished data.

No. 946. Electric Utilities—Generation, Sales, Revenue, and Customers: 1970 to 1990

[Sales and revenue are to and from ultimate customers]

CLASS	Unit	1970	1975	1980	1984	1985	1986	1987	1988	1989	1990, prel.
Generation [1]	Bil. kWh	1,532	1,918	2,286	2,416	2,470	2,487	2,572	2,704	2,784	2,807
Sales [2]	Bil. kWh	1,391	1,733	2,126	2,281	2,306	2,355	2,435	2,554	2,621	2,667
Residential or domestic	Bil. kWh	448	586	734	783	793	820	846	886	899	910
Percent of total	Percent	32.2	33.8	34.5	34.3	34.4	34.8	34.8	34.7	34.3	34.1
Commercial [3]	Bil. kWh	313	418	524	578	606	629	658	698	716	735
Industrial [4]	Bil. kWh	573	662	794	835	820	819	844	882	913	926
Revenue [2]	Bil. dol	22.1	46.9	95.5	143.1	149.2	152.5	155.7	162.4	169.6	175.5
Residential or domestic	Bil. dol	9.4	18.8	37.6	56.1	58.6	60.9	63.0	66.4	68.8	71.2
Percent of total	Percent	42.7	40.1	39.4	39.2	39.3	39.9	40.5	40.9	40.5	40.6
Commercial [3]	Bil. dol	6.3	13.5	27.4	41.3	44.1	45.4	46.7	49.1	51.6	53.9
Industrial [4]	Bil. dol	5.4	12.7	27.3	40.8	41.4	40.9	40.6	41.6	43.7	44.8
Ultimate customers, Dec. 31 [2]	Million	72.5	81.8	92.7	99.4	101.6	103.0	104.6	106.4	108.5	109.8
Residential or domestic	Million	64.0	72.6	82.2	87.9	89.8	91.0	92.4	93.9	95.6	96.8
Commercial [3]	Million	7.9	8.6	9.7	10.6	10.9	11.1	11.4	11.6	12.0	12.1
Industrial [4]	Million	0.4	0.4	0.5	0.5	0.5	0.5	0.5	0.5	0.5	0.5
Avg. kWh used per customer	1,000	19.4	21.4	23.2	23.2	22.9	23.1	23.5	24.2	24.4	24.5
Residential	1,000	7.1	8.2	9.0	9.0	8.9	9.1	9.2	9.5	9.5	9.5
Commercial [3]	1,000	40.0	49.0	54.5	55.2	56.1	57.2	58.4	60.4	60.6	61.1
Avg. annual bill per customer	Dollar	307	579	1,040	1,453	1,482	1,494	1,501	1,536	1,576	1,610
Residential	Dollar	149	262	462	644	658	675	688	712	725	741
Commercial [3]	Dollar	804	1,580	2,848	3,940	4,080	4,127	4,147	4,256	4,363	4,478
Avg. revenue per kWh sold	Cents	1.59	2.70	4.49	6.27	6.47	6.47	6.39	6.36	6.47	6.58
Residential	Cents	2.10	3.21	5.12	7.17	7.39	7.43	7.45	7.49	7.65	7.82
Commercial [3]	Cents	2.01	3.23	5.22	7.14	7.27	7.22	7.10	7.04	7.20	7.33
Industrial [4]	Cents	0.95	1.92	3.44	4.88	5.04	4.99	4.82	4.71	4.79	4.83

[1] Source: 1970 and 1975, U.S. Federal Power Commission; thereafter, U.S. Energy Information Administration, *Monthly Energy Review,* August 1991. [2] Includes other types not shown separately. [3] Small light and power. [4] Large light and power.
Source: Except as noted, Edison Electric Institute, Washington, DC, *Statistical Yearbook.*

No. 947. Electric Utilities—Balance Sheet and Income Account of Privately Owned Companies: 1970 to 1989

[In billions of dollars. As of Dec. 31. See also *Historical Statistics, Colonial Times to 1970,* series S 133-146 and V 197-212]

ITEM	CLASS A AND B INVESTOR-OWNED ELECTRIC UTILITIES [1]				MAJOR-INVESTOR-OWNED ELECTRIC UTILITIES [2]								
	1970	1980	1981	1981	1982	1983	1984	1985	1986	1987	1988	1989
COMPOSITE BALANCE SHEET												
Assets and other debits	87.4	260.0	286.0	285.1	315.0	342.4	375.6	404.7	426.1	446.3	454.3	465.7
Electric utility plant [3]	93.3	266.9	292.7	291.6	321.2	347.9	364.7	396.9	419.5	434.6	449.4	462.4
Depreciation and amortization	20.3	55.5	61.5	61.1	67.6	74.3	77.1	85.1	93.9	103.2	113.5	125.0
Net electric utility plant	73.1	211.5	231.2	230.5	253.6	273.6	287.5	311.8	325.6	331.4	335.9	337.5
Other utility plant	9.0	14.8	15.7	15.7	16.7	17.5	17.6	19.9	21.2	23.1	24.6	26.3
Depreciation and amortization	2.1	4.5	4.9	4.9	5.3	5.8	6.1	6.5	7.2	7.8	8.5	9.2
Net other utility plant	6.9	10.3	10.8	10.8	11.4	11.8	12.1	13.4	14.0	15.2	16.1	17.1
Total utility plant	102.3	281.7	308.4	307.3	337.9	365.5	395.3	431.1	455.9	475.7	493.0	507.9
Depreciation and amortization	22.3	60.0	66.4	66.0	72.9	80.1	88.0	97.4	107.7	118.7	131.3	144.6
Net total utility plant	79.9	221.7	242.0	241.3	265.0	285.4	307.3	333.8	348.2	357.0	361.6	363.2
Other property and investments	1.7	6.5	7.9	7.9	9.1	10.3	10.8	12.1	13.5	15.6	15.2	16.2
Current and accrued assets	5.3	26.2	28.7	28.6	31.7	33.3	37.9	39.4	38.4	40.9	39.1	41.5
Deferred debits	0.4	5.5	7.3	7.3	9.3	13.4	19.3	19.4	26.1	32.9	38.3	44.8
Liabilities and other credits [4]	87.4	260.0	286.0	285.1	315.0	342.4	375.3	404.7	426.1	446.3	454.3	465.7
Capital stock	20.8	59.3	63.9	63.7	70.3	75.9	79.0	82.8	81.6	79.9	80.7	82.9
Other paid-in capital	4.4	21.5	24.0	23.9	27.7	31.0	34.0	36.3	38.4	40.3	40.4	39.1
Retained earnings	9.4	22.7	25.0	24.8	27.9	31.9	37.1	41.1	46.0	48.0	47.1	47.7
Subsidiary earnings [5]	(X)	1.1	1.3	1.3	1.6	1.7	1.9	2.2	2.3	2.6	2.5	2.8
Long-term debt	41.9	105.3	115.5	115.2	124.0	131.6	140.6	152.7	157.2	158.4	160.7	162.9
Current and accrued liabilities	7.3	26.3	28.4	26.1	28.6	29.5	32.0	32.0	34.0	39.3	38.4	42.0
Deferred credits and operating reserves	0.9	9.8	11.5	11.0	15.1	16.6	19.0	20.9	22.4	25.6	28.1	28.5
Deferred income taxes [6]	2.2	14.1	16.7	16.6	19.4	23.6	28.1	32.7	39.6	45.9	50.2	53.3
COMPOSITE INCOME ACCOUNTS												
Electric operating revenues	19.8	87.1	102.3	101.7	109.0	116.7	128.3	136.2	136.3	138.5	143.9	150.9
Electric operating expenses	15.3	73.4	86.0	85.5	91.1	96.2	105.5	111.1	110.2	111.6	115.3	121.6
Net electric operating revenues	4.5	13.6	16.3	16.2	18.1	20.5	22.8	24.1	26.1	27.0	28.6	29.4
Other utility operating income	0.4	0.7	0.9	0.9	0.9	0.9	1.1	1.2	1.1	1.1	1.2	1.2
Total utility operating income	4.9	14.4	17.0	17.0	19.1	21.4	24.0	25.3	27.2	28.1	29.8	30.6
Other income	0.8	3.6	4.4	4.4	5.3	6.5	6.8	7.4	7.2	6.6	5.0	5.2
Total income	5.7	18.0	21.4	21.3	24.4	28.0	30.8	32.7	34.4	34.6	34.8	35.8
Income deductions	2.3	7.3	8.7	8.7	9.4	10.1	11.1	14.0	14.0	15.6	18.8	18.5
Net income [7]	3.4	10.7	12.7	12.7	15.0	17.9	19.7	18.7	20.4	19.0	16.0	17.3

X Not applicable. [1] There were 197 utilities of this type in 1981. [2] There were 181 utilities of this type in 1987. [3] Includes construction work in progress. [4] Includes contributions in aid of construction through 1970. [5] Unappropriated undistributed. [6] Cumulative. [7] Beginning 1980, includes net extraordinary income.
Source: 1970, U.S. Federal Power Commission and 1980, U.S. Energy Information Administration, *Statistics of Privately Owned Electric Utilities in the United States,* annual; 1981-84 U.S. Energy Information Administration, *Financial Statistics of Selected Electric Utilities,* annual; thereafter, U.S. Energy Information Administration, *Financial Statistics of Selected Investor-Owned Electric Utilities,* annual.

No. 948. Water Power—Developed and Undeveloped Capacity, by Division: 1950 to 1990

[In millions of kilowatts. As of **Dec. 31.** Excludes Alaska and Hawaii for 1950 and all capacity of reversible equipment at pumped storage projects. Also excludes capacity precluded from development due to wild and scenic river legislation. For composition of division, see table 25. See also *Historical Statistics, Colonial Times to 1970,* series S 160-175]

DIVISION	DEVELOPED INSTALLED CAPACITY							ESTIMATED UNDEVELOPED CAPACITY						
	1950	1960	1970	1980	1985	1989	1990	1950	1960	1970	1980	1985	1989	1990
United States	18.7	33.2	52.0	64.4	68.8	71.8	73.0	87.6	114.2	128.0	129.9	76.4	75.2	73.9
New England	1.2	1.5	1.5	1.5	1.7	1.9	1.9	3.3	2.9	3.3	4.7	4.4	4.5	4.4
Middle Atlantic	1.7	2.5	4.3	4.3	4.5	4.8	4.9	6.6	7.6	4.5	5.1	5.4	5.2	5.1
East North Central	0.9	0.9	0.9	0.9	1.1	1.1	1.1	2.3	3.0	1.6	2.0	1.8	1.7	1.7
West North Central	0.6	1.6	2.7	2.8	2.9	3.1	3.1	5.8	6.4	4.4	3.4	3.1	3.1	3.1
South Atlantic	2.8	3.8	5.3	5.9	6.5	6.7	6.7	8.2	8.4	9.6	9.6	7.4	7.1	7.0
East South Central	2.7	3.8	5.2	5.6	5.9	5.9	5.9	4.7	4.6	3.8	3.3	2.7	2.4	2.4
West South Central	0.5	0.9	1.9	2.3	2.3	2.4	2.7	3.6	3.9	3.3	4.7	5.4	4.8	4.6
Mountain	2.3	4.6	6.2	7.4	8.1	8.9	9.2	23.4	23.6	26.7	34.2	19.4	19.3	19.4
Pacific	6.0	13.6	23.9	33.7	35.8	37.0	37.5	29.8	53.8	70.9	62.9	26.8	27.1	26.2

Source: U.S. Federal Energy Regulatory Commission (formerly U.S. Federal Power Commission), *Hydroelectric Power Resources of the United States, Developed and Undeveloped,* January 1, 1988; and unpublished data.

No. 949. Solar Collector Shipments, by Type, End-Use, and Market Sector: 1975 to 1989

[In thousands of square feet, except number of manufacturers. Solar collector is a device for intercepting sunlight, converting the light to heat, and carrying the heat to where it will be either used or stored. 1985 data are not available]

YEAR	Number of manufacturers	Total shipments [1]	COLLECTOR TYPE		END USE			MARKET SECTOR		
			Low temperature	Medium temperature, special, other	Pool heating	Hot water	Space heating	Residential	Commercial	Industrial
1975	131	3,743	3,026	717	(NA)	(NA)	(NA)	(NA)	(NA)	(NA)
1976	186	5,801	3,876	1,925	(NA)	(NA)	(NA)	(NA)	(NA)	(NA)
1977	321	10,312	4,743	5,569	6,334	1,713	1,699	7,978	1,680	105
1978	340	10,860	5,872	4,988	5,970	2,513	1,736	8,095	1,848	263
1979	349	14,251	8,395	5,857	8,551	2,958	1,722	11,387	2,015	314
1980	233	19,398	12,233	7,165	12,029	4,790	1,688	16,077	2,417	488
1981	203	20,133	8,677	11,456	9,781	7,204	2,017	15,773	2,561	1,518
1982	265	18,621	7,476	11,145	7,035	7,444	2,367	13,729	3,789	560
1983	203	16,828	4,853	11,975	4,839	9,323	2,082	11,780	3,039	1,665
1984	225	17,191	4,479	11,939	4,427	8,930	2,370	13,980	2,091	289
1986 [2]	98	9,360	3,751	1,111	3,494	1,181	127	4,131	703	13
1987 [2]	59	7,269	3,157	957	3,111	964	23	3,775	305	11
1988 [2]	51	8,174	3,326	732	3,304	726	7	3,796	255	7
1989	44	11,482	4,283	1,989	4,688	1,374	205	5,804	424	42

NA Not available.   [1] Includes other end uses and market sectors not shown separately.   [2] Declines between 1984 and 1988 are primarily due to the expiration of the Federal energy tax credit and industry consolidation.
Source: U.S. Energy Information Administration, *Solar Collector Manufacturing Activity,* annual.

No. 950. Wood Energy Consumption, by Region and Sector: 1980 to 1989

[In trillions of Btu, except percent. For composition of regions, see table 25. X Not applicable]

YEAR	Total	Percent of total energy consumption	REGION				SECTOR			
			Northeast	Midwest	South	West	Residential	Industrial	Commercial	Electric utilities
1980	2,483	3.3	386	329	1,380	388	859	1,600	21	4
1981	2,412	3.3	389	331	1,291	402	869	1,519	21	3
1982	2,395	3.4	351	339	1,334	372	937	1,434	22	2
1983	2,556	3.6	369	318	1,471	396	925	1,606	22	3
1984	2,633	3.6	349	341	1,482	461	923	1,679	22	9
1987	2,437	3.2	350	474	1,147	467	852	1,576	(X)	9
1989	2,487	3.1	413	527	1,109	438	918	1,556	(X)	13

No. 951. Households That Burn Wood: 1980 to 1987

[Based on Residential Energy Consumption Survey; see Appendix III]

ITEM	Unit	HOUSEHOLDS THAT BURN WOOD					HOUSEHOLDS THAT BURN WOOD AS MAIN HEATING FUEL				
		1980	1981	1982	1984	1987	1980	1981	1982	1984	1987
Number of households	Millions	21.6	22.8	21.4	22.9	22.5	4.7	5.3	5.6	6.4	5.0
Percent of all households	Percent	26.4	27.4	25.6	26.6	24.8	5.8	6.4	6.7	7.5	5.6
Number of cords burned	Millions	42.7	44.0	48.6	49.0	42.6	22.4	24.7	28.7	29.4	23.5
Average number per household	Number	2.0	1.9	2.3	2.1	1.9	4.7	4.6	5.1	4.6	4.7
Median number per household	Number	0.7	1.0	1.0	1.0	0.7	3.3	3.0	4.0	4.0	4.0
Wood energy consumption	Tril. Btu	854	881	971	981	853	448	493	574	589	470

Source of tables 950 and 951: U.S. Energy Information Administration, *Annual Energy Review.*

No. 952. Renewable Energy Consumption Estimates by Type: 1988 to 1990

SOURCES	QUANTITY (Quadrillion Btu)			PERCENT CHANGE	
	1988	1989	1990	1988 -1989	1989 -1990
Adjusted Total energy consumption estimates [1] . . .	83.63	84.54	84.99	1.1	0.5
Total renewable energy consumption estimates . . .	6.31	6.29	6.70	−0.3	6.5
Percent of adjusted total.	7.50	7.40	7.90	−1.3	6.8
Reported renewable energy consumption	2.88	3.10	3.15	7.6	1.6
Hydroelectric power	2.64	2.88	2.94	9.1	2.1
Electric utilities	2.28	2.74	2.89	20.2	5.5
Industrial	0.03	0.03	0.03	-	-
Imported electricity	0.40	0.27	0.21	−32.5	−22.2
Exported electricity	0.07	0.17	0.19	142.9	11.8
Geothermal energy at electric utilities	0.22	0.20	0.18	−9.1	−10.0
Wood and waste energy at electric utilities	0.02	0.02	0.02	-	-
Wind energy at electric utilities	(Z)	(Z)	(Z)	(X)	(X)
Additional renewable energy consumption estimates	3.43	3.19	3.55	−7.0	11.3
Biofuels	3.15	2.90	3.23	−7.9	11.4
Residential, commercial, and industrial use	3.09	2.83	3.15	−8.4	11.3
Transportation use	0.06	0.07	0.08	16.7	14.3
Geothermal energy (nonelectric utilities)	0.13	0.14	0.16	7.7	14.3
Solar energy (nonelectric utilities)	0.09	0.09	0.08	-	−11.1
Wind energy (nonelectric utilities)	0.03	0.03	0.04	-	33.3
Hydroelectric power (additional industrial use)	0.03	0.03	0.04	-	33.3

- Represents zero or rounds to zero. X Not applicable. Z Less than 50 billion. [1] Adjusted total energy consumption estimates will differ from other energy consumption estimates shown in tables 911-916.

Source: U.S. Energy Information Administration, *Annual Energy Review*.

No. 953. Privately Owned Gas Utility Industry—Balance Sheet and Income Account: 1970 to 1990

[In millions of dollars. The gas utility industry consists of pipeline and distribution companies. Excludes operations of companies distributing gas in bottles or tanks. See also *Historical Statistics, Colonial Times to 1970*, series S 205-218]

ITEM	1970	1980	1984	1985	1986	1987	1988	1989	1990
COMPOSITE BALANCE SHEET									
Assets, total [1]	34,929	75,851	98,933	104,478	104,008	109,390	121,667	123,820	121,763
Total utility plant.	38,541	67,071	83,118	88,121	91,606	93,540	99,933	106,017	112,894
Depreciation and amortization . . .	10,696	26,162	35,542	36,377	36,776	41,162	44,423	47,054	49,500
Utility plant (net).	27,845	40,909	47,576	51,744	54,830	52,378	55,510	58,963	63,394
Investment and fund accounts [1] . .	3,024	15,530	21,872	23,871	21,850	25,660	31,552	28,111	23,895
Current and accrued assets	3,674	17,243	25,367	24,771	21,477	21,025	23,402	24,836	23,279
Deferred debits [2]	386	2,169	4,118	4,092	5,851	8,633	9,658	10,364	9,603
Liabilities, total [1]	34,929	75,851	98,933	104,478	104,008	109,390	121,667	123,820	121,763
Capitalization, total [1].	28,646	51,382	64,458	65,799	66,660	66,312	69,875	74,753	75,003
Capital stock [1]	12,965	29,315	38,959	39,517	39,902	38,212	39,898	43,889	43,839
Long-term debts	15,681	22,067	25,499	26,282	26,758	28,100	29,977	30,864	31,164
Current and accrued liabilities. . . .	4,832	18,119	23,043	26,125	23,855	26,664	33,735	31,005	29,562
Deferred income taxes [3]	788	4,149	7,000	7,769	8,363	9,901	10,685	11,292	11,371
Other liabilities and credits	663	2,201	4,432	4,785	5,130	6,513	7,372	6,770	5,827
COMPOSITE INCOME ACCOUNT									
Operating revenues, total . .	16,380	85,918	115,491	103,945	80,978	69,566	69,754	70,363	66,049
Operating expenses [4]	14,306	81,789	109,165	98,320	75,470	64,409	64,696	64,262	60,157
Operation and maintenance . . .	11,636	74,508	98,953	88,572	66,032	56,054	57,032	55,990	51,644
Federal, State, and local taxes .	1,569	4,847	7,146	6,590	6,133	5,179	4,241	4,843	4,958
Operating income.	2,074	4,129	6,326	5,625	5,508	5,157	5,058	6,101	5,892
Utility operating income.	2,159	4,471	6,047	6,030	5,943	5,452	5,202	6,274	6,079
Income before interest charges [1] .	2,457	6,929	9,068	7,636	7,085	6,845	7,472	8,764	8,083
Net income [1]	1,427	4,194	5,619	3,785	3,390	2,971	3,352	4,641	4,411
Dividends	1,006	2,564	4,471	4,060	3,882	3,453	3,113	3,151	3,192

[1] Beginning 1980, not comparable with 1970 due to Federal Power Commission ruling requiring adoption of the equity method in reporting earnings of subsidiaries. [2] Includes capital stock discount and expense and reacquired securities. [3] Includes reserves for deferred income taxes. [4] Includes expenses not shown separately.

Source: American Gas Association, Arlington, VA, *Gas Facts*, annual, (copyright).

No. 954. Gas Utility Industry—Summary: 1970 to 1990

[Covers natural, manufactured, mixed, and liquid petroleum gas. Based on questionnaire mailed to all privately and municipally owned gas utilities in U.S., except those with annual revenues less than $25,000. See also *Historical Statistics, Colonial Times to 1970*, series S 190-204]

ITEM	Unit	1970	1975	1980	1984	1985	1986	1987	1988	1989	1990
Customers [1]	**1,000**	41,482	44,555	47,223	49,325	49,971	50,704	51,576	52,422	53,356	54,293
Residential.	1,000	38,097	40,950	43,489	45,367	45,929	46,583	47,362	48,133	48,980	49,830
Commercial	1,000	3,131	3,367	3,498	3,730	3,816	3,892	3,980	4,069	4,161	4,249
Industrial and other	1,000	254	237	236	228	226	229	234	220	215	214
Sales [2]	**Tril. Btu** . .	16,044	14,863	15,413	13,162	12,616	11,125	10,543	10,705	10,551	9,846
Residential.	Tril. Btu . . .	4,923	4,991	4,826	4,628	4,513	4,381	4,385	4,695	4,798	4,471
Percent of total	Percent . .	30.7	33.6	31.3	35.2	35.8	39.4	41.6	43.9	45.5	45.4
Commercial	Tril. Btu . . .	2,007	2,387	2,453	2,396	2,338	2,239	2,156	2,306	2,322	2,194
Industrial	Tril. Btu . . .	8,439	6,837	7,957	5,991	5,635	4,338	3,848	3,544	3,243	3,011
Other	Tril. Btu . . .	674	648	177	147	130	167	155	160	188	171
Revenues [2]	**Mil. dol** . . .	10,283	19,101	48,303	67,496	63,293	51,201	45,492	46,162	47,493	45,174
Residential.	Mil. dol . . .	5,207	8,445	17,432	27,485	26,864	24,759	23,622	24,828	26,172	25,014
Percent of total	Percent . .	50.6	44.2	36.1	40.7	42.4	48.4	51.9	53.8	55.1	55.4
Commercial	Mil. dol . . .	1,620	3,302	8,183	13,205	12,722	11,274	10,271	10,681	11,074	10,610
Industrial	Mil. dol . . .	3,181	6,745	22,215	26,094	23,086	14,495	11,069	10,113	9,666	8,997
Other	Mil. dol . . .	274	608	473	712	621	673	530	538	581	553
Prices per mil. Btu [3]	**Dollars** . . .	0.64	1.29	3.13	5.13	5.02	4.60	4.32	4.31	4.50	4.59
Residential.	Dollars . . .	1.06	1.69	3.61	5.94	5.95	5.65	5.39	5.29	5.45	5.59
Commercial	Dollars . . .	0.81	1.38	3.34	5.51	5.44	5.04	4.77	4.63	4.77	4.84
Industrial	Dollars . . .	0.38	0.99	2.79	4.36	4.10	3.34	2.88	2.85	2.98	2.99
Gas mains mileage	**1,000**	913	980	1,052	1,102	1,119	1,134	1,151	1,169	1,185	1,206
Field and gathering	1,000	66	68	84	94	94	94	94	92	91	89
Transmission	1,000	252	263	266	272	271	271	274	276	276	280
Distribution.	1,000	595	649	702	736	754	769	784	801	818	837
Construction expenditures [4]	**Mil. dol** . . .	2,506	2,466	5,350	4,645	5,671	5,342	5,328	6,166	7,341	7,899
Transmission	Mil. dol . . .	1,019	590	1,583	1,301	1,562	1,448	1,295	1,568	2,081	2,886
Distribution.	Mil. dol . . .	913	910	1,869	2,266	2,577	2,920	3,055	3,389	3,980	3,714
Production and storage . . .	Mil. dol . . .	370	831	1,546	543	965	383	251	268	276	309

[1] Annual average.   [2] Excludes sales for resale.   [3] For definition, see text, section 19.   [4] Includes general.

Source: American Gas Association, Arlington, VA, *Gas Facts*, annual, (copyright).

No. 955. Gas Utility Industry—Customers, Sales, and Revenues, by State: 1989

[See headnote, table 954. For definition of Btu, see text, section 19]

DIVISION AND STATE	CUSTOMERS[1] Total[2]	CUSTOMERS[1] Residential	SALES[3] (tril. Btu) Total[2]	SALES[3] (tril. Btu) Residential	REVENUES[3] (mil. dol.) Total[2]	REVENUES[3] (mil. dol.) Residential	DIVISION AND STATE	CUSTOMERS[1] Total[2]	CUSTOMERS[1] Residential	SALES[3] (tril. Btu) Total[2]	SALES[3] (tril. Btu) Residential	REVENUES[3] (mil. dol.) Total[2]	REVENUES[3] (mil. dol.) Residential
U.S. . . .	54,293	49,830	9,846	4,471	45,174	25,014	DC . . .	147	133	31	12	204	94
							VA . .	680	611	119	50	633	333
Northeast.	10,944	10,032	1,724	946	10,383	6,505	WV . .	404	370	64	41	341	236
N.E.	2,045	1,850	389	170	2,372	1,309	NC . . .	583	513	130	37	565	220
ME. . . .	16	12	4	1	26	5	SC . . .	374	333	96	19	422	128
NH. . .	85	73	16	7	103	50	GA . . .	1,412	1,303	204	99	1,091	636
VT . . .	25	21	7	2	34	14	FL . . .	480	436	222	13	734	101
MA. . .	1,230	1,121	239	101	1,391	772	**E.S.C.** . . .	2,513	2,258	449	180	1,948	943
RI . . .	213	195	31	19	206	135	KY . . .	684	618	103	58	463	276
CT . . .	476	428	92	40	611	333	TN . . .	683	596	159	48	645	230
M.A. . . .	8,899	8,182	1,335	776	8,011	5,196	AL . . .	733	673	111	48	542	302
NY . . .	4,202	3,893	571	352	3,647	2,491	MS. . .	413	371	76	26	299	135
NJ . . .	2,199	1,977	354	176	1,947	1,128	**W.S.C.** . . .	5,877	5,382	1,685	357	5,447	1,948
PA . . .	2,498	2,312	410	248	2,416	1,578	AR . . .	552	489	84	38	358	190
Midwest . .	16,707	15,256	2,917	1,777	13,357	8,744	LA . . .	973	910	211	54	754	324
E.N.C . . .	12,001	11,020	2,085	1,343	9,818	6,678	OK. . .	897	809	217	67	633	312
OH. . .	2,991	2,755	491	322	2,362	1,622	TX . . .	3,455	3,174	1,173	198	3,702	1,122
IN . . .	1,449	1,320	262	146	1,275	787	**West**	13,238	12,344	2,056	867	9,249	4,666
IL. . . .	3,548	3,250	621	426	2,871	2,046	**Mt.**	3,336	3,025	486	259	2,160	1,284
MI . . .	2,779	2,573	481	335	2,198	1,572	MT. . .	199	176	39	19	151	78
WI . . .	1,234	1,122	230	115	1,112	651	ID . . .	136	117	17	9	75	42
W.N.C . . .	4,706	4,236	832	434	3,539	2,066	WY . . .	123	109	23	12	100	55
MN. . .	1,062	961	224	108	917	502	CO. . .	1,099	986	165	94	699	424
IA . . .	700	705	149	71	613	347	NM. . .	405	365	53	31	256	163
MO . . .	1,317	1,210	195	120	934	610	AZ . . .	618	571	80	29	380	193
ND. . .	98	86	18	10	79	43	UT. . .	479	444	73	47	328	231
SD. . .	119	105	21	10	92	51	NV . . .	277	257	36	18	171	98
NE. . .	485	422	90	43	365	193	**Pac.**	9,902	9,319	1,570	608	7,089	3,382
KS. . .	835	747	134	72	539	319	WA . .	513	452	134	41	478	202
South.	13,404	12,199	3,150	881	12,186	5,099	OR. . .	364	317	56	24	282	147
S.A.	5,014	4,559	1,016	344	4,791	2,208	CA . . .	8,909	8,449	1,337	528	6,158	2,970
DE. . .	97	89	22	7	101	44	AK. . .	82	70	40	14	128	53
MD. . .	837	771	129	66	700	416	HI . . .	34	31	3	1	43	10

[1] Averages for the year.   [2] Includes other service, not shown separately.   [3] Excludes sales for resale.

Source: American Gas Association, Arlington, VA, *Gas Facts*, annual, (copyright).

Science and Technology

This section presents statistics on scientific, engineering, and technological resources, with emphasis on patterns of research and development (R&D) funding and on scientific, engineering, and technical personnel, education, and employment. Also included are statistics on space program outlays and accomplishments. Principal sources of these data are the National Science Foundation (NSF) and the National Aeronautics and Space Administration (NASA).

NSF gathers data chiefly through recurring surveys. Current NSF publications containing data on funds for research and development and on scientific and engineering personnel include the *Science Resources Studies Highlights* summaries series; Detailed Statistical Tables; and annual, biennial, triennial, and special reports. Titles or the areas of coverage of these reports include the following: *Science and Engineering Indicators; National Patterns of R&D Resources; Science and Engineering Personnel-A National Overview; Women and Minorities in Science and Engineering;* science and technology data presented in chart and tabular form in a pocket-size publication; *International Science and Technology Data Update;* profiles on human resources and funding in individual fields of science and engineering; *Federal Funds for Research and Development; Federal R&D Funding by Budget Function; Federal Support to Universities, Colleges, and Selected Nonprofit Institutions; Scientific and Engineering Facilities at Universities and Colleges; Geographic Distribution of Industrial R&D Expenditures; Research and Development in Industry;* R&D funds and graduate enrollment and support in academic science and engineering; characteristics of doctoral scientists and engineers and of recent graduates in the United States; *U.S. Scientists and Engineers;* and scientists, engineers, and technicians in manufacturing, nonmanufacturing, and trade and regulated industries. Statistical surveys in these areas pose problems of concept and definition and the data should, therefore, be regarded as broad estimates

In Brief

R&D expenditures in constant (1982) dollars:

1970	62.4 bil.
1980	73.3 bil.
1990	110.5 bil.

Nondefense R&D spending as percent of GNP: 1989

Japan	3.0
West Germany	2.8
United States	1.9
France	1.8
United Kingdom	1.6

rather than precise quantitative statements. See sources for details.

The National Science Board's biennial *Science and Engineering Indicators* contains data and analyses of international and domestic science and technology, including measures of inputs and outputs. *The Budget of the United States Government,* published by the U.S. Office of Management and Budget, contains summary financial data on Federal R&D programs.

Research and development outlays.—NSF defines research as a "systematic and intensive study directed toward a fuller knowledge of the subject studied" and development as "the systematic use of scientific knowledge directed toward the production of useful materials, devices, systems, methods, or processes." National coverage of R&D expenditures is developed primarily from periodic surveys in four principal economic sectors: (1) *Government,* made up primarily of Federal executive agencies; (2) *industry,* consisting of manufacturing and nonmanufacturing firms and the federally funded research and development centers (FFRDC's) they administer; (3) *universities and colleges,* composed of universities, colleges, and their affiliated institutions, agricultural experiment stations, and associated schools of agriculture, and FFRDC's administered by educational institutions; and (4) *other nonprofit institutions,* consisting of such organizations as private philanthropic foundations, nonprofit research institutes, voluntary health agencies, and FFRDC's administered by nonprofit organizations. The R&D funds reported consist of current operating costs, including planning and administration costs, except as otherwise noted. They exclude funds for routine testing, mapping and surveying, collection of general-purpose data, dissemination of scientific information, and training of scientific personnel.

Scientists, engineers, and technicians.—Scientists and engineers are defined as persons engaged in scientific and engineering work at a level requiring a knowledge of sciences equivalent at least to that acquired through completion of a 4-year college course. Technicians are defined as persons engaged in technical work at a level requiring knowledge acquired through a technical institute, junior college, or other type of training less extensive than 4-year college training. Craftsmen and skilled workers are excluded.

Historical statistics.—Tabular headnotes provide cross-references, where applicable, to *Historical Statistics of the United States, Colonial Times to 1970.* See Appendix IV.

Figure 20.1
Top 15 Universities—Federal Research and Development Obligations: 1989

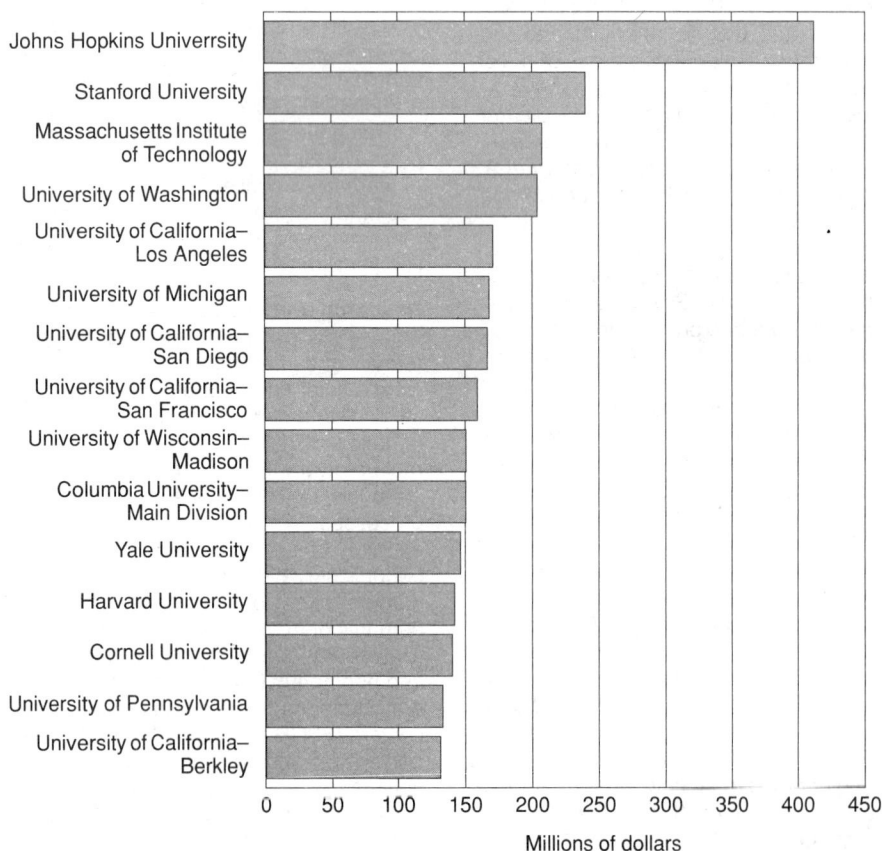

Source: Chart prepared by U.S. Bureau of the Census. For data, see table 965.

No. 956. Research and Development (R&D)—Expenditures: 1960 to 1990

[Includes basic research, applied research, and development. Defense-related outlays comprise all research and development spending by Dept. of Defense, including space activities, and a portion of Department of Energy funds. Space-related outlays are those of the National Aeronautics and Space Administration; they exclude space activities of other Federal agencies, estimated at less than 5 percent of all space research and development spending. Minus sign (-) indicates decrease]

YEAR OR PERIOD	CURRENT DOLLARS (bil. dol.)			CONSTANT (1982) DOLLARS [1]		ANNUAL PERCENT CHANGE [3]		PERCENT OF TOTAL R&D OUTLAYS					
								Federally funded defense/space-related			Other outlays		
	Total	Defense space related	Other	Total (bil. dol.)	Per-cent of GNP [2]	Cur-rent dollars	Con-stant dollars	Total	Defense	Space	Total	Non-Federal	Federal
1960	13.5	7.4	6.1	43.6	2.6	9.4	7.5	55	52	3	45	35	10
1961	14.3	8.0	6.3	45.8	2.7	5.9	4.9	56	50	6	44	35	9
1962	15.4	8.6	6.8	48.2	2.7	7.5	5.2	56	49	7	44	36	8
1963	17.1	9.2	7.8	52.6	2.8	10.8	9.2	54	41	13	46	34	12
1964	18.9	10.6	8.3	57.2	2.9	10.5	8.8	56	37	19	44	34	10
1965	20.0	10.8	9.2	59.4	2.8	6.3	3.8	54	33	21	46	35	11
1966	21.8	11.1	10.7	62.6	2.8	9.0	5.5	51	32	19	49	36	13
1967	23.1	11.3	11.8	64.4	2.8	6.0	2.9	49	35	14	51	38	13
1968	24.6	12.1	12.5	65.5	2.8	6.3	1.6	49	35	14	51	39	12
1969	25.6	11.5	14.1	64.7	2.7	4.2	-1.2	45	34	11	55	42	13
1970	26.1	11.2	14.9	62.4	2.6	2.0	-3.5	43	33	10	57	43	14
1971	26.7	11.5	15.2	60.4	2.4	2.1	-3.2	43	33	10	57	44	13
1972	28.5	11.7	16.8	61.4	2.4	6.7	1.7	41	33	8	59	44	15
1973	30.7	12.0	18.7	62.4	2.3	7.9	1.7	39	32	7	61	47	14
1974	32.9	11.8	21.0	61.5	2.2	7.0	-1.5	36	29	7	64	49	15
1975	35.2	12.0	23.2	59.9	2.2	7.2	-2.6	34	27	7	66	49	17
1976	39.0	13.7	25.4	62.1	2.2	10.8	3.8	35	27	8	65	49	16
1977	42.8	14.5	28.2	63.7	2.2	9.6	2.4	34	27	7	66	50	16
1978	48.1	15.4	32.7	66.8	2.1	12.5	4.9	32	26	6	68	50	18
1979	55.0	17.0	37.9	70.1	2.2	14.2	5.0	31	25	6	69	51	18
1980	62.6	18.2	44.5	73.3	2.3	13.9	4.5	29	24	5	71	53	18
1981	71.9	20.8	51.0	76.6	2.4	14.8	4.6	29	24	5	71	54	17
1982	80.0	24.0	56.0	80.0	2.5	11.3	4.4	30	26	4	70	54	16
1983	89.1	26.7	62.4	85.8	2.6	11.4	7.2	30	27	3	70	54	16
1984	101.1	31.4	69.8	93.8	2.7	13.5	9.4	31	28	3	69	55	14
1985	113.8	37.6	76.3	102.5	2.8	12.5	9.2	33	30	3	67	54	13
1986	119.5	40.6	78.9	104.9	2.8	5.0	2.3	34	31	3	66	55	11
1987	125.4	43.9	81.5	106.6	2.8	4.9	1.7	35	32	3	65	54	11
1988	133.7	45.5	88.3	110.2	2.7	6.7	3.3	34	31	3	66	54	12
1989	140.5	46.4	94.1	111.1	2.7	5.0	0.9	33	29	4	67	55	12
1990	145.5	46.5	98.9	110.5	2.7	3.5	-0.6	32	28	4	68	56	12

[1] Based on GNP implicit price deflator. [2] GNP = Gross National Product. [3] Change from prior year shown; 1960 change from 1955.
Source: U.S. National Science Foundation, *National Patterns of R&D Resources: 1990;* and unpublished data.

No. 957. Research and Development (R&D)—Source of Funds and Performance Sector: 1970 to 1990

[In millions of dollars. See headnote, table 958]

YEAR	Total	SOURCE OF FUNDS				PERFORMANCE SECTOR				
		Federal Govt.	Industry	Univ., col-leges	Other [1]	Federal Govt.	Industry	Univ., col-leges	Associated FFRDC's [2]	Other [1]
Current dollars:										
1970	26,134	14,891	10,444	462	337	4,079	18,067	2,335	737	916
1975	35,213	18,109	15,820	749	535	5,354	24,187	3,409	987	1,276
1980	62,610	29,461	30,912	1,334	903	7,632	44,505	6,077	2,246	2,150
1982	80,018	36,578	40,692	1,731	1,017	9,141	58,650	7,323	2,479	2,425
1983	89,139	40,832	45,251	1,929	1,127	10,582	65,268	7,877	2,737	2,675
1984	101,194	45,641	52,204	2,104	1,190	11,572	74,800	8,617	3,150	3,000
1985	113,818	52,120	57,977	2,376	1,345	12,945	84,239	9,686	3,523	3,425
1986	119,529	54,273	61,076	2,790	1,410	13,535	87,823	10,926	3,895	3,350
1987	125,352	57,904	62,642	3,200	1,606	13,413	92,155	12,153	4,206	3,425
1988	133,741	61,499	66,953	3,473	1,816	14,281	97,889	13,465	4,531	3,575
1989	140,486	62,688	71,767	3,948	2,083	15,121	101,599	14,987	4,729	4,050
1990	145,450	64,000	74,700	4,450	2,300	16,100	104,200	16,000	4,800	4,350
Constant (1982) dollars: [3]										
1970	62,403	35,632	24,851	1,114	807	9,833	42,986	5,629	1,777	2,179
1975	59,882	30,985	26,679	1,302	916	9,308	40,781	5,926	1,716	2,151
1980	73,255	34,557	36,065	1,574	1,059	9,006	51,919	7,171	2,650	2,508
1981	76,641	35,690	38,257	1,667	1,027	9,040	55,140	7,345	2,667	2,448
1982	80,018	36,578	40,692	1,731	1,017	9,141	58,650	7,323	2,479	2,425
1983	85,753	39,251	43,568	1,851	1,083	10,152	62,842	7,557	2,626	2,576
1984	93,790	42,286	48,456	1,945	1,102	10,696	69,433	7,965	2,912	2,785
1985	102,462	46,870	52,252	2,130	1,209	11,606	75,925	8,684	3,159	3,087
1986	104,866	47,555	53,639	2,436	1,235	11,820	77,160	9,542	3,401	2,943
1987	106,616	49,201	53,341	2,711	1,364	11,364	78,477	10,296	3,563	2,917
1988	110,166	50,635	55,361	2,856	1,315	11,742	80,680	11,072	3,726	2,947
1989	111,129	49,553	56,815	3,115	1,646	11,931	80,436	11,825	3,731	3,206
1990	110,470	48,591	56,757	3,376	1,746	12,213	79,173	12,137	3,641	3,305

[1] Nonprofit institutions. [2] University associated federally-funded R&D centers. [3] Based on gross national product implicit price deflator.
Source: U.S. National Science Foundation, *National Patterns of R&D Resources: 1990.*

No. 958. Research and Development (R&D) Funds, by Performance Sector and Source: 1970 to 1990

[In millions of dollars, except percent. Data primarily on calendar year basis-calendar year data for industry and other nonprofit institutions combined with Federal and university fiscal year data. Data refer, in general, to natural sciences including engineering, and to social sciences in all but industry sector. Excludes capital expenditures data. Expenditures at associated federally funded research and development centers administered by industry and other nonprofit institutions included in totals of respective sectors. See also *Historical Statistics, Colonial Times to 1970*, series W 109-125]

PERFORMANCE SECTOR AND SOURCE OF FUNDS	1970	1980	1983	1984	1985	1986	1987	1988	1989	1990
Total R&D [1]	26,134	62,610	89,139	101,139	113,818	119,529	125,352	133,741	140,486	145,450
In 1982 dollars [2]	62,403	73,255	85,753	93,790	102,462	104,866	106,616	110,166	111,129	110,470
Percent Federal as source	57.0	47.1	45.8	45.1	45.8	45.4	46.2	46.0	44.6	44.0
Percent of gross national product	2.6	2.3	2.6	2.7	2.8	2.8	2.8	2.7	2.7	2.7
Federal Government	4,079	7,632	10,582	11,572	12,945	13,535	13,413	14,281	15,121	16,100
Industry	18,067	44,505	65,268	74,800	84,239	87,823	92,155	97,889	101,599	104,200
Federal funds	7,779	14,029	20,680	23,396	27,196	27,891	30,752	32,306	31,366	31,200
Industry funds	10,288	30,476	44,588	51,404	57,043	59,932	61,403	65,583	70,233	73,000
Universities and colleges	2,335	6,077	7,877	8,617	9,686	10,926	12,153	13,465	14,987	16,000
Federal funds	1,647	4,104	4,983	5,423	6,056	6,702	7,333	8,181	8,972	9,250
Industry funds	61	236	388	475	559	699	789	870	984	1,100
University and college funds [3]	462	1,334	1,929	2,104	2,376	2,790	3,200	3,473	3,948	4,450
Other nonprofit institutions funds [3]	165	403	577	615	695	735	831	941	1,083	1,200
Universities and colleges, associated federally funded R&D centers	737	2,246	2,737	3,150	3,523	3,895	4,206	4,531	4,729	4,800
Other nonprofit institutions	916	2,150	2,675	3,000	3,425	3,350	3,425	3,575	4,050	4,350
Federal funds	649	1,450	1,850	2,100	2,400	2,250	2,200	2,200	2,500	2,650
Industry funds	95	200	275	325	375	425	450	500	550	600
Other [4]	172	500	550	575	650	675	775	875	1,000	1,100
Total research, basic and applied [2]	9,269	22,292	32,328	35,760	40,029	44,156	46,095	48,548	53,185	55,815
In 1982 dollars [2]	22,198	26,154	31,077	33,133	35,999	38,698	39,167	39,972	42,044	42,379
Percent Federal as source	60.1	55.3	52.4	51.5	51.4	47.1	47.6	47.4	47.4	47.2
Federal Government	1,904	3,666	4,710	4,764	5,056	5,160	5,438	5,338	5,982	6,400
Industry	4,029	9,775	16,150	18,373	21,117	23,807	24,136	25,001	27,086	27,800
Federal funds	1,207	2,190	4,104	4,700	5,836	5,229	5,400	5,449	5,920	5,900
Industry funds	2,822	7,585	12,046	13,673	15,281	18,578	18,736	19,552	21,166	21,900
Universities and colleges	2,223	5,739	7,450	8,194	9,232	10,406	11,566	12,820	14,266	15,195
Federal funds	1,563	3,904	4,758	5,223	5,856	6,477	7,083	7,906	8,672	8,925
Industry funds	56	219	361	442	520	650	734	809	915	1,020
University and college funds [3]	449	1,241	1,794	1,957	2,210	2,595	2,976	3,230	3,672	4,130
Other nonprofit institutions funds [3]	155	375	537	572	646	684	773	875	1,007	1,120
Universities and colleges, associated federally funded R&D centers	485	1,627	2,198	2,479	2,584	2,633	2,705	2,919	3,051	3,250
Other nonprofit institutions	628	1,485	1,820	1,950	2,040	2,150	2,250	2,470	2,800	3,170
Federal funds	409	930	1,180	1,250	1,250	1,300	1,300	1,400	1,600	1,850
Industry funds	77	160	220	260	300	340	360	400	440	480
Other [4]	142	395	420	440	490	510	590	670	760	840
Total basic research	3,531	8,432	11,634	12,909	14,198	16,590	17,999	18,673	19,885	21,920
In 1982 dollars [2]	8,483	9,922	11,172	11,946	12,749	14,515	15,273	15,365	15,704	16,636
Percent of total R&D	13.5	13.5	13.1	12.8	12.5	13.9	14.4	14.0	14.2	15.1
Percent Federal as source	70.0	70.1	66.8	65.8	64.6	60.2	60.4	61.8	64.2	62.3
Federal Government	559	1,182	1,690	1,861	1,923	2,019	2,046	2,050	2,371	2,600
Industry	602	1,325	2,223	2,608	2,862	4,047	4,323	4,244	4,000	4,750
Federal funds	158	290	463	476	489	551	740	891	1,095	1,150
Industry funds	444	1,035	1,760	2,132	2,373	3,496	3,583	3,353	2,905	3,600
Universities and colleges	1,796	4,041	5,304	5,735	6,559	7,495	8,398	8,827	9,685	10,350
Federal funds	1,296	2,863	3,544	3,827	4,338	4,862	5,369	5,629	6,127	6,400
Industry funds	40	141	236	284	342	436	496	527	582	650
University and college funds [3]	350	796	1,173	1,257	1,454	1,739	2,011	2,101	2,335	2,600
Other nonprofit institutions funds [3]	110	241	351	367	425	458	522	570	641	700
Universities and colleges, associated federally funded R&D centers	269	1,124	1,472	1,675	1,749	1,859	2,012	2,222	2,329	2,500
Other nonprofit institutions	305	760	945	1,030	1,105	1,170	1,220	1,330	1,500	1,720
Federal funds	189	450	600	650	675	700	700	750	850	1,000
Industry funds	44	95	125	150	170	200	210	230	250	280
Other [4]	72	215	220	230	260	270	310	350	400	440
Total development	16,865	40,318	56,811	65,379	73,789	75,373	79,257	85,193	87,301	89,635
In 1982 dollars [2]	40,206	47,101	54,676	60,657	66,463	66,167	67,449	70,194	69,085	68,092
Percent of total R&D	64.5	64.4	63.7	64.6	64.8	63.1	63.2	63.7	62.1	61.6
Percent Federal as source	55.3	42.5	42.0	41.6	42.7	44.4	45.4	45.2	42.9	42.0

[1] Basic research, applied research, and development.   [2] Based on gross national product implicit price deflator.   [3] Includes State and local government funds received by these institutions and used for research and development.   [4] Includes estimates for independent nonprofit hospitals and voluntary health agencies.

Source: U.S. National Science Foundation, *National Patterns of R&D Resources: 1990*; and unpublished data.

No. 959. Funds for Research and Development—Performance Sector, by State: 1989

[In millions of dollars. See headnote, table 958. Data may differ slightly due to revisions not available on the State level]

REGION, DIVISION, AND STATE	Total	Federal government	Industry	Universities and colleges [1]	Other nonprofit [2]	REGION, DIVISION, AND STATE	Total	Federal government	Industry	Universities and colleges [1]	Other nonprofit [2]
U.S. . . .	140,486	15,121	101,599	19,716	4,050	VA	2,536	1,018	1,126	272	120
Northeast . .	34,628	1,458	27,873	4,486	811	WV	(NA)	63	([7])	58	2
N.E	11,710	665	8,789	1,721	535	NC	1,826	60	1,305	425	36
ME	72	4	33	20	15	SC	576	60	386	120	10
NH	(NA)	22	([3])	62	(Z)	GA	1,302	158	719	417	8
VT	(NA)	4	([4])	43	3	FL	3,375	642	2,341	386	6
MA	7,949	401	5,825	1,232	491	E.S.C	3,132	864	1,640	589	39
RI	428	196	139	80	13	KY	343	31	226	84	2
CT	2,745	38	2,410	284	13	TN	1,302	135	930	223	14
M.A.	22,918	793	19,084	2,765	276	AL	1,223	568	428	207	20
NY	7,229	430	6,381	396	22	MS	264	130	56	75	3
NJ	9,898	89	8,071	1,587	151	W.S.C . . .	7,589	571	5,580	1,345	93
PA	5,791	274	4,632	782	103	AR	121	25	51	44	1
Midwest . . .	29,877	1,454	24,615	3,587	221	LA	384	36	168	179	1
E.N.C. . . .	23,347	1,288	19,308	2,600	151	OK	507	46	332	113	16
OH	5,465	1,056	3,946	417	46	TX	6,576	464	5,028	1,009	75
IN	2,120	75	1,815	227	3	West	42,035	3,739	30,859	6,664	773
IL	5,307	59	4,050	1,133	65	Mt	7,109	1,021	4,095	1,867	126
MI	9,057	71	8,468	486	32	MT	(NA)	21	([8])	32	1
WI	1,399	27	1,030	337	5	ID	(NA)	19	([9])	33	1
W.N.C . . .	6,530	166	5,307	987	70	WY	(NA)	9	([10])	23	21
MN	2,399	31	2,066	259	43	CO	1,649	117	1,162	290	80
IA	616	20	363	231	2	NM	2,680	594	1,034	1,039	13
MO	2,710	58	2,380	255	17	AZ	1,293	118	917	251	7
ND	79	20	27	28	4	UT	620	66	387	165	2
SD	23	6	4	12	(Z)	NV	141	77	29	34	1
NE	182	22	64	94	2	Pac	34,925	2,718	26,764	4,796	647
KS	523	9	404	108	2	WA	3,225	111	2,716	277	121
South	28,500	7,973	15,320	4,686	521	OR	579	42	355	161	21
S.A	17,779	6,538	8,100	2,752	389	CA	30,881	2,478	23,675	4,231	497
DE	(NA)	3	([5])	37	2	AK	118	51	9	57	1
MD	5,091	3,012	1,088	922	69	HI	123	36	9	71	7
DC	(NA)	1,522	([6])	114	136	Other [11]	5,446	497	2,932	294	1,724

NA Not available.   Z Less than $0.5 million.   [1] Distribution by States includes R&D performed in only Doctoral degree granting institutions; U.S. total includes R&D performed in all institutions.   [2] For other sector, funds distributed by State include only Federal obligations to organizations in the nonprofit sector. Nonprofit R&D performance using non-Federal funds are undistributed.   [3] Between $95 and $140 million.   [4] Between $242 and $287 million.   [5] Between $845 and $1,032 million.   [6] Between $23 and $210 million.   [7] Between $80 and $267 million.   [8] Between $5 and $405 million.   [9] Between $161 and $561 million.   [10] Below $400 million.   [11] Includes unknown.

Source: U.S. National Science Foundation, as reported in the National Science Board, *Science and Engineering Indicators—1991.*

No. 960. Federal Obligations for Research and Development, by Agency in Current and Constant (1982) Dollars: 1975 to 1991

[In millions of dollars. For fiscal years ending in year shown; see text, section 9. Includes those agencies with obligations of $1 billion dollars or more in 1991. See *Historical Statistics, Colonial Times to 1970,* series W 142, for total R&D expenditures]

AGENCY	1975	1980	1984	1985	1986	1987	1988	1989	1990, est.	1991, est.
CURRENT DOLLARS										
Obligations, total [1]	**19,039**	**29,830**	**42,225**	**48,360**	**51,412**	**55,253**	**56,935**	**61,406**	**62,320**	**66,107**
Dept. of Defense.	9,013	13,981	25,373	29,792	32,938	35,232	35,415	37,577	35,899	36,918
Dept. of Health and Human Services.	2,281	3,780	4,831	5,451	5,658	6,606	7,158	7,903	8,457	8,888
National Aeronautics and Space Administration	3,064	3,234	2,822	3,327	3,420	3,787	4,330	5,394	6,635	8,322
Dept. of Energy	2,047	4,754	4,674	4,966	4,688	4,757	5,036	5,193	5,698	6,006
National Science Foundation.	595	882	1,203	1,346	1,353	1,471	1,533	1,670	1,766	1,983
Dept. of Agriculture	420	688	866	943	929	948	1,017	1,038	1,104	1,158
CONSTANT (1982) DOLLARS [2]										
Obligations, total [1]	**33,098**	**35,202**	**39,028**	**43,359**	**44,898**	**46,823**	**46,822**	**48,450**	**47,277**	**48,022**
Dept. of Defense.	15,668	16,499	23,452	26,711	28,764	29,856	29,125	29,649	27,233	26,818
Dept. of Health and Human Services.	3,965	4,461	4,465	4,887	4,941	5,598	5,887	6,236	6,416	6,456
National Aeronautics and Space Administration	5,327	3,816	2,608	2,983	2,986	3,209	3,561	4,256	5,033	6,045
Dept. of Energy	3,559	5,610	4,320	4,452	4,094	4,031	4,142	4,097	4,323	4,363
National Science Foundation.	1,034	1,041	1,112	1,206	1,182	1,246	1,261	1,318	1,340	1,441
Dept. of Agriculture	730	811	801	845	811	803	836	819	838	841

[1] Includes other agencies, not shown separately.   [2] See footnote 1, table 956.
Source: U.S. National Science Foundation, *Federal Funds for Research and Development,* annual.

No. 961. Federal Funding for Research and Development, by Selected Budget Function, in Current and Constant (1982) Dollars: 1980 to 1992

[In millions of dollars. For fiscal years ending in year shown; see text, section 9. Excludes R&D plant. Represents budget authority. Functions shown are those for which $1 billion or more was authorized for 1992. See *Historical Statistics, Colonial Times to 1970*, series W 126, for total obligations]

FUNCTION	1970	1980	1984	1985	1986	1987	1988	1989	1990	1991, est.	1992, est.
CURRENT DOLLARS											
Total [1]	15,339	29,739	44,214	49,887	53,249	57,069	59,106	62,115	63,794	64,135	72,070
8 functions, percent of total	96.6	96.5	98.1	98.3	98.3	98.2	98.3	98.2	98.0	97.7	97.8
National defense	7,981	14,946	29,287	33,698	36,926	39,152	40,099	40,665	39,925	37,788	43,247
Health	1,084	3,694	4,779	5,418	5,565	6,556	7,076	7,773	8,314	9,090	9,655
Space research and technology	3,606	2,738	2,300	2,725	2,894	3,398	3,683	4,555	5,765	6,428	7,656
General science	452	1,233	1,676	1,862	1,873	2,042	2,160	2,373	2,410	2,632	2,962
Energy	574	3,603	2,581	2,389	2,286	2,053	2,126	2,419	2,715	2,885	2,920
Natural resources and environment	340	999	963	1,059	1,062	1,133	1,160	1,255	1,386	1,553	1,602
Transportation	535	887	1,040	1,030	917	908	896	1,064	1,045	1,251	1,380
Agriculture	238	585	762	836	815	822	882	907	957	1,057	1,098
CONSTANT (1982) DOLLARS [2]											
Total [1]	36,975	35,094	40,866	44,728	46,502	48,350	48,600	49,009	48,393	46,590	50,298
National defense	19,259	17,637	27,070	30,213	32,247	33,170	32,971	32,085	30,286	27,451	30,182
Health	2,613	4,359	4,417	4,858	4,860	5,554	5,818	6,133	6,307	6,603	6,738
Space research and technology	8,692	3,231	2,126	2,443	2,527	2,879	3,028	3,594	4,373	4,670	5,343
General science	1,090	1,455	1,549	1,669	1,636	1,730	1,776	1,872	1,828	1,912	2,067
Energy	1,384	4,252	2,386	2,142	1,996	1,739	1,748	1,909	2,060	2,096	2,038
Natural resources and environment	820	1,179	890	949	927	960	954	990	1,051	1,128	1,118
Transportation	1,290	1,047	961	923	801	769	737	840	793	909	963
Agriculture	574	690	704	750	712	696	725	716	726	768	766

[1] Includes other functions, not shown separately.   [2] See footnote 1, table 956.
Source: U.S. National Science Foundation, *Federal R&D Funding by Budget Function*, annual.

No. 962. National Research and Development (R&D) Expenditures as a Percent of Gross National Product, by Country: 1975 to 1990

YEAR	TOTAL R&D					NON DEFENSE R&D [1]				
	United States	France	West Germany	Japan	United Kingdom	United States	France	West Germany	Japan	United Kingdom
1975	2.2	1.8	2.2	2.0	2.1	1.6	1.5	2.1	2.0	1.5
1980	2.3	1.8	2.4	2.2	(NA)	1.7	1.4	2.3	2.2	(NA)
1985	2.8	2.3	2.8	2.8	2.3	2.0	1.8	2.7	2.8	1.6
1987	2.8	2.3	2.9	2.8	2.3	1.9	1.8	2.8	2.8	1.8
1988	2.7	2.3	2.9	2.9	2.2	1.9	1.8	2.7	2.9	1.7
1989	2.7	2.3	2.9	3.0	2.0	1.9	1.8	2.8	3.0	1.6
1990	2.7	(NA)	(NA)	(NA)	(NA)	1.9	(NA)	(NA)	(NA)	(NA)

NA Not available.   [1] Estimated.
Source: U.S. National Science Foundation, *Science Indicators*, biennial; *National Patterns of R&D Resources: 1990*; and *International Science and Technology Data Update*, annual.

No. 963. Research and Development (R&D) Expenditures in Science and Engineering at Universities and Colleges in Current and Constant (1982) Dollars: 1981 to 1990

[In millions of dollars]

CHARACTERISTIC	1981	1988	1989	1990	CHARACTERISTIC	1981	1988	1989	1990
CURRENT DOLLARS					CONSTANT (1982) DOLLARS [1]				
Total	6,846	13,464	15,009	16,325	Total	7,345	11,070	11,842	12,384
Basic research	4,597	8,827	9,710	10,431	Basic research	4,932	7,258	7,661	7,913
Applied R&D	2,249	4,637	5,299	5,894	Applied R&D	2,413	3,813	4,181	4,471
Source of funds:					Source of funds:				
All governments	5,111	9,288	10,218	10,949	All governments	5,483	7,637	8,062	8,306
Institutions' own funds	1,008	2,364	2,712	3,017	Institutions' own funds	1,081	1,944	2,140	2,289
Industry	291	871	998	1,135	Industry	312	716	787	861
Other	436	941	1,081	1,223	Other	468	774	853	928
Fields:					Fields:				
Physical sciences	765	1,545	1,641	1,781	Physical sciences	821	1,270	1,295	1,351
Environmental sciences	549	885	989	1,047	Environmental sciences	589	728	780	794
Mathematical sciences	87	199	215	221	Mathematical sciences	93	164	169	168
Computer sciences	132	410	468	503	Computer sciences	142	337	369	381
Life sciences	3,698	7,256	8,088	8,763	Life sciences	3,967	5,966	6,381	6,648
Psychology	127	214	238	260	Psychology	136	176	188	197
Social sciences	366	553	637	702	Social sciences	393	455	502	533
Other sciences	145	305	330	365	Other sciences	156	251	261	277
Engineering	977	2,097	2,404	2,682	Engineering	1,048	1,724	1,897	2,034

[1] See footnote 1, table 956.
Source: U.S. National Science Foundation, *Survey of Scientific and Engineering Expenditures at Universities and Colleges*, annual.

No. 964. Federal Obligations to Universities and Colleges: 1970 to 1989

[In millions of dollars, except percent. For fiscal years ending in year shown; see text, section 9. Total and nonscience/engineering activities for 1983 are estimates based on revised student aid data from the Dept. of Education. Minus sign (-) indicates decrease]

ITEM	1970	1975	1980	1983	1984	1985	1986	1987	1988	1989
CURRENT DOLLARS										
Federal obligations, total	3,237	4,547	8,299	9,345	10,039	10,972	11,619	13,433	14,066	15,658
Annual percent change [1]	6.5	1.5	9.1	6.5	7.4	9.3	5.9	15.6	4.7	11.3
Academic science/engineering obligations	2,188	2,806	4,791	5,681	6,308	7,258	7,431	8,565	9,133	10,073
Percent of total	67.6	61.7	57.7	60.8	62.8	66.2	64.0	63.8	64.9	64.3
Research and development.	1,447	2,246	4,161	5,024	5,449	6,246	6,457	7,241	7,719	8,517
Research and development plant	45	45	38	38	50	114	106	230	203	237
Other science/engineering activities . .	696	515	593	619	809	898	868	1,095	1,211	1,319
Nonscience/engineering activities	1,049	1,741	3,508	3,664	3,731	3,714	4,188	4,868	4,933	5,584
CONSTANT (1982) DOLLARS [2]										
Federal obligations, total	7,802	7,905	9,793	8,965	9,279	9,838	10,147	11,381	11,566	12,354
Annual percent change [1]	0.6	-8.0	0.3	2.1	3.5	6.0	3.1	12.2	1.6	6.8
Academic science/engineering obligations	5,273	4,878	5,654	5,450	5,830	6,508	6,489	7,257	7,509	7,948
Percent of total	67.6	61.7	57.7	60.8	62.8	66.2	64.0	63.8	64.9	64.3
Research and development.	3,487	3,905	4,910	4,820	5,036	5,600	5,639	6,135	6,347	6,720
Research and development plant	108	78	45	36	46	102	93	195	167	187
Other science/engineering activities . .	1,678	895	699	594	748	805	758	928	996	1,041
Nonscience/engineering activities	2,529	3,027	4,139	3,515	3,449	3,330	3,657	4,124	4,056	4,406

[1] Percent change from immediate prior year. [2] See footnote 1, table 956.
Source: U.S. National Science Foundation, *Survey of Federal Support to Universities, Colleges, and Selected Nonprofit Institutions*, annual.

No. 965. Federal R&D Obligations to Selected Universities and Colleges: 1981 to 1989

[For fiscal years ending in year shown; see text, section 9. For the top 45 institutions receiving Federal R&D funds in 1989. Awards to the administrative offices of university systems are excluded from totals for individual institutions because that allocation of funds is unknown, but these awards are included in "total all institutions"]

MAJOR INSTITUTION RANKED BY TOTAL 1989 FEDERAL R&D OBLIGATIONS	OBLIGATIONS ($1,000)				RANK			
	1981	1985	1988	1989	1981	1985	1988	1989
Total, all institutions [1]	**4,410,931**	**6,246,181**	**7,719,162**	**8,516,849**	**(X)**	**(X)**	**(X)**	**(X)**
45 institutions, percent of total	62.2	61.4	61.1	60.8	(X)	(X)	(X)	(X)
Johns Hopkins University.	363,429	297,374	431,593	411,879	1	1	1	1
Stanford University.	106,073	174,961	210,572	239,847	3	3	2	2
Massachusetts Institute of Technology. . . .	146,035	189,558	187,558	207,157	2	2	3	3
University of Washington	99,965	146,179	181,301	203,691	4	4	4	4
University of California—Los Angeles.	94,945	128,211	154,964	170,839	5	5	5	5
University of Michigan.	73,999	108,035	148,446	167,865	11	11	6	6
University of California—San Diego	91,403	103,633	139,149	166,601	6	13	8	7
University of California—San Francisco . . .	64,814	98,536	147,553	159,027	15	16	7	8
University of Wisconsin—Madison.	86,918	124,604	131,186	150,474	8	7	12	9
Columbia University—Main Division	83,659	127,331	139,108	150,263	9	6	9	10
Yale University.	73,526	109,227	135,421	146,245	12	10	10	11
Harvard University	87,830	109,414	125,242	141,760	7	9	13	12
Cornell University	72,671	119,966	134,493	139,954	13	8	11	13
University of Pennsylvania.	76,136	103,119	120,029	132,805	10	15	14	14
University of California—Berkeley	64,065	106,710	106,844	131,070	16	12	16	15
University of Minnesota.	72,001	103,272	119,831	128,727	14	14	15	16
Pennsylvania State University.	47,099	76,726	105,443	119,435	21	19	18	17
University of Southern California	49,221	89,706	99,399	114,766	20	17	19	18
Duke University	44,287	69,169	92,763	108,611	23	26	23	19
Washington University.	54,170	71,978	95,368	102,974	17	22	21	20
University of Colorado.	46,146	71,424	105,772	101,345	22	23	17	21
University of Illinois—Urbana	53,583	83,122	95,748	100,062	19	18	20	22
University of Rochester.	42,983	70,379	94,885	98,550	25	25	22	23
University of NC at Chapel Hill	38,447	63,105	84,918	93,244	30	27	24	24
University of Pittsburgh	38,512	58,620	79,380	91,094	29	28	28	25
University of Chicago.	53,992	71,194	84,668	90,611	18	24	25	26
University of Texas at Austin	43,756	72,379	84,400	84,619	24	21	26	27
University of Arizona.	36,308	49,740	65,258	82,913	33	37	33	28
New York University	40,636	74,577	79,516	77,761	28	20	27	29
University of Iowa.	35,300	55,117	72,309	76,059	34	31	30	30
Ohio State University	42,899	56,065	62,946	72,702	26	30	36	31
University of Alabama—Birmingham	29,970	44,093	59,933	70,702	44	46	38	32
Case Western Reserve University	33,744	47,994	62,989	69,589	38	40	35	33
Baylor College of Medicine	35,062	45,897	63,117	69,499	35	45	34	34
California Institute of Technology	32,959	55,083	65,982	69,335	40	32	32	35
Yeshiva University	42,590	56,988	67,096	68,553	27	29	31	36
Woods Hole Oceanographic Institution. . . .	27,633	31,392	35,285	67,289	48	63	66	37
University of Massachusetts.	22,418	46,046	62,300	67,183	55	44	37	38
Vanderbilt University.	27,426	39,909	58,389	63,978	49	48	39	39
Purdue University.	36,549	51,544	45,907	62,751	32	34	53	40
University of Utah.	38,163	50,938	56,686	61,361	31	36	41	41
Georgia Institute of Technology	33,616	51,585	55,486	60,949	39	33	43	42
University of Maryland—College Park.	27,313	51,073	54,580	60,252	50	35	45	43
University of Miami.	28,956	33,709	58,241	60,135	46	59	40	44
University of California—Davis	31,757	43,156	55,239	60,100	42	47	44	45

X Not applicable. [1] Includes other institutions, not shown separately.
Source: U.S. National Science Foundation, *Federal Support to Universities and Colleges and Selected Nonprofit Institutions*, annual.

No. 966. Funds for Performance of Industrial Research and Development (R&D), by Source of Funds and Selected Industries, in Current and Constant (1982) Dollars: 1970 to 1989

[In millions of dollars. Covers basic research, applied research, and development. See also *Historical Statistics, Colonial Times to 1970*, series W 144-160]

1972 SIC [1] code	INDUSTRY	1970	1975	1980	1985	1986	1987	1988	1989
(X)	CURRENT DOLLARS								
(X)	**Total funds**	18,067	24,187	44,505	84,239	87,823	92,155	97,889	101,599
28	Chemicals and allied products	1,773	2,727	4,636	8,540	8,843	9,635	10,772	11,537
13,29	Petroleum refining and extraction	515	693	1,552	(D)	(D)	1,897	1,944	2,066
35	Machinery	1,729	3,196	5,901	12,216	(D)	(D)	(D)	(D)
36	Electrical equipment	4,220	5,105	9,175	14,432	14,980	15,848	16,242	16,768
371	Motor vehicles and motor vehicles equipment	1,591	2,340	4,955	6,984	(D)	(D)	(D)	(D)
372,376	Aircraft and missiles	5,219	5,713	9,198	22,231	21,050	24,458	25,900	25,654
38	Professional and scientific instruments	744	1,173	3,029	5,013	5,103	5,222	5,426	5,763
(X)	All other [2]	2,276	3,240	6,059	(D)	(D)	(D)	(D)	(D)
(X)	**Company funds**	10,288	15,582	30,476	57,043	59,932	61,403	65,583	70,233
28	Chemicals and allied products	1,593	2,490	4,264	8,310	8,664	9,445	10,573	11,449
13,29	Petroleum refining and extraction	493	(D)	1,401	2,194	1,971	1,883	1,923	2,050
35	Machinery	1,469	2687	5,254	10,701	10,701	10,577	11,992	13,216
36	Electrical equipment	2,008	2,798	5,431	9,271	9,767	10,449	10,872	11,546
371	Motor vehicles and motor vehicles equipment	1,278	2,022	4,300	6,164	7,171	7,167	7,769	8,726
372,376	Aircraft and missiles	1,213	1,285	2,570	5,649	6,066	5,939	6,023	6,020
38	Professional and scientific instruments	550	1,001	2,456	4,622	4,752	4,950	5,306	5,638
(X)	All other [2]	1,684	(D)	4,800	10,132	10,840	10,993	11,125	11,588
(X)	CONSTANT (1982) DOLLARS [3]								
(X)	**Total funds**	42,986	40,781	51,919	75,925	77,160	78,477	80,680	80,436
28	Chemicals and allied products	4,218	4,598	5,408	7,697	7,769	8,205	8,878	9,134
13,29	Petroleum refining and extraction	1,225	1,168	1,811	(D)	(D)	1,615	1,602	1,636
35	Machinery	4,114	5,389	6,884	11,010	(D)	(D)	(D)	(D)
36	Electrical equipment	10,040	8,607	10,703	13,008	13,161	13,406	13,387	13,275
371	Motor vehicles and motor vehicles equipment	3,785	3,945	5,780	6,295	(D)	(D)	(D)	(D)
372,376	Aircraft and missiles	12,417	9,632	10,730	20,037	18,494	20,828	21,347	20,310
38	Professional and scientific instruments	1,770	1,978	3,534	4,518	4,483	4,447	4,472	4,563
(X)	All other [2]	5,415	5,463	7,068	(D)	(D)	(D)	(D)	(D)
(X)	**Company funds**	24,478	26,272	35,553	51,413	52,655	52,289	54,053	55,604
28	Chemicals and allied products	3,790	4,198	4,974	7,490	7,612	8,043	8,714	9,064
13,29	Petroleum refining and extraction	1,173	(D)	1,634	1,977	1,732	1,604	1,585	1,623
35	Machinery	3,495	4,530	6,129	9,645	9,402	9,007	9,884	10,463
36	Electrical equipment	4,778	4,718	6,336	8,356	8,581	8,898	8,961	9,141
371	Motor vehicles and motor vehicles equipment	3,041	3,409	5,016	5,556	6,300	6,103	6,403	6,908
372,376	Aircraft and missiles	2,886	2,167	2,998	5,091	5,329	5,057	4,964	4,766
38	Professional and scientific instruments	1,309	1,688	2,865	4,166	4,175	4,215	4,373	4,464
(X)	All other [2]	4,007	(D)	5,600	9,132	9,524	9,361	9,169	9,174

D Figure withheld to avoid disclosure of information pertaining to a specific organization or individual.   X Not applicable.
[1] 1972 Standard Industrial Classification. See text, section 13.   [2] All other manufacturing and nonmanfacturing.   [3] See footnote 1, table 956.

Source: U.S. National Science Foundation, *Research and Development in Industry*, annual.

No. 967. R&D Funds as a Percent of Net Sales in R&D—Performing Manufacturing Companies, by Industry: 1970 to 1989

1972 SIC [1] code	INDUSTRY GROUP	TOTAL R&D FUNDS AS A PERCENT OF NET SALES					COMPANY R&D FUNDS AS A PERCENT OF NET SALES				
		1970	1980	1985	1988	1989	1970	1980	1985	1988	1989
(X)	Total [2]	3.7	3.0	4.4	4.7	4.7	2.2	2.1	3.0	3.1	3.1
20	Food and kindred products [3]	0.5	0.4	(D)	(D)	(D)	0.5	(D)	0.6	0.5	0.5
26	Paper and allied products	0.9	1.0	(D)	(D)	0.7	(D)	1.0	0.8	0.7	0.7
28	Chemicals and allied products	3.9	3.6	5.0	5.4	5.4	3.5	3.3	4.9	5.3	5.3
13,29	Petroleum refining and extraction	1.0	0.6	(D)	1.0	1.0	0.9	0.5	0.9	1.0	1.0
30	Rubber products	2.3	2.2	(D)	(D)	(D)	1.7	(D)	1.8	1.6	1.7
32	Stone, clay, and glass products	1.8	1.4	(D)	(D)	(D)	1.7	1.3	2.3	2.2	2.3
33	Primary metals	0.8	0.7	(D)	0.8	0.9	0.8	0.5	0.9	0.8	0.9
34	Fabricated metal products	1.2	1.4	1.5	1.3	1.3	1.1	1.2	1.4	1.0	1.1
35	Machinery	4.0	5.0	7.6	(D)	(D)	3.4	4.5	6.7	7.2	7.8
36	Electrical equipment	7.3	6.6	7.6	7.8	7.7	3.4	3.9	4.8	5.2	5.3
371	Motor vehicles and motor vehicle equipment	3.5	4.9	3.8	(D)	(D)	2.8	4.2	3.1	3.4	3.8
372,376	Aircraft and missiles	16.2	13.7	14.9	15.6	15.5	3.8	3.8	3.9	3.6	3.6
38	Professional and scientific instruments	5.7	7.5	8.9	7.5	7.4	4.2	6.1	8.3	7.3	7.2

D Figure withheld to avoid disclosure of information pertaining to a specific organization or individual.   X Not applicable.
[1] 1972 Standard Industrial Classification. See text, section 13.   [2] Includes all manufacturing industries.   [3] Includes tobacco products (SIC 21) for 1985-89.

Source: U.S. National Science Foundation, *Research and Development in Industry*, annual.

No. 968. Federal Obligations for Research, by Field of Science in Current and Constant (1982) Dollars: 1980 to 1991

[In millions of dollars. For fiscal years ending in year shown; see text, section 9. See headnote, table 961]

FIELD	1980	1983	1984	1985	1986	1987	1988	1989	1990	1991, est.
CURRENT DOLLARS										
Research, total	11,597	14,254	14,979	16,133	16,502	17,940	18,650	20,765	21,683	23,220
Basic	4,674	6,260	7,067	7,819	8,153	8,942	9,474	10,602	11,348	12,255
Applied	6,923	7,993	7,911	8,315	8,349	8,998	9,176	10,163	10,335	10,965
Life sciences	4,192	5,178	5,636	6,363	6,464	7,341	7,725	8,495	8,914	9,407
Psychology	199	241	267	327	334	370	390	422	448	510
Physical sciences	2,001	2,891	2,969	3,046	3,069	3,253	3,317	3,705	3,895	4,191
Environmental sciences	1,261	1,251	1,276	1,404	1,482	1,512	1,607	1,773	2,104	2,345
Mathematics and computer sciences . .	241	419	440	575	615	641	643	735	721	792
Engineering	2,830	3,517	3,624	3,618	3,739	3,906	3,956	4,442	4,361	4,684
Social sciences . . . . [1]	524	435	436	460	416	480	486	551	621	646
Other sciences, n.e.c. [1]	350	320	331	342	383	438	527	642	619	645
CONSTANT (1982) DOLLARS [2]										
Research, total	13,686	13,675	13,845	14,465	14,411	15,203	15,335	16,384	16,449	16,867
Basic	5,516	6,006	6,532	7,010	7,120	7,578	7,790	8,365	8,609	8,902
Applied	8,170	7,669	7,312	7,455	7,291	7,625	7,545	8,019	7,840	7,965
Life sciences	4,947	4,968	5,209	5,705	5,645	6,221	6,351	6,703	6,762	6,834
Psychology	235	231	247	293	292	313	321	333	340	370
Physical sciences	2,361	2,774	2,744	2,731	2,680	2,756	2,728	2,923	2,955	3,045
Environmental sciences	1,488	1,200	1,179	1,259	1,294	1,281	1,321	1,399	1,596	1,703
Mathematics and computer sciences . .	284	402	407	515	537	543	529	580	547	575
Engineering	3,340	3,374	3,350	3,244	3,265	3,310	3,253	3,505	3,308	3,403
Social sciences . . . . [1]	618	418	403	412	363	407	399	435	471	469
Other sciences, n.e.c. [1]	413	307	305	306	335	371	433	506	470	468

[1] N.e.c. = Not elsewhere classified.   [2] See footnote 1, table 956.
Source: U.S. National Science Foundation, *Federal Funds for Research and Development*, annual.

No. 969. Research and Development Scientists and Engineers—Average Full-Time-Equivalent Employment and Cost, by Industry: 1975 to 1988

[Data are estimates; on average full-time-equivalent (FTE) basis. See *Historical Statistics, Colonial Times to 1970*, series W 167, for total cost per scientist or engineer]

1972 SIC [1] code	INDUSTRY	1975	1980	1981	1982	1983	1984	1985	1986	1987	1988
(X)	EMPLOYED SCIENTISTS										
(X)	**Average FTE of scientists**										
(X)	**and engineers (1,000)** [2] [3]	363.9	469.2	498.8	525.4	562.5	603.3	646.8	684.2	703.0	716.8
28	Chemicals [4]	44.8	53.1	58.2	64.5	68.6	70.5	73.5	74.4	74.4	76.6
35	Machinery	54.3	65.7	72.6	77.8	83.3	84.4	85.7	93.1	97.4	99.1
36	Electrical equipment [5]	81.5	100.7	108.4	109.2	110.9	113.2	115.6	123.1	130.4	136.2
371	Motor vehicles	25.7	36.7	32.6	29.5	28.8	28.7	31.3	42.1	48.8	46.6
372,376	Aircraft and missiles	67.2	90.6	93.2	97.1	107.3	120.9	137.5	137.5	133.3	139.3
(X)	CONSTANT (1982) DOLLARS [6]										
(X)	**Cost per scientist or**										
(X)	**engineer ($1,000)** [3] [7]	112.1	110.7	110.6	111.6	111.7	115.1	117.4	113.2	114.1	114.4
28	Chemicals [4]	102.7	102.0	102.8	102.5	100.9	104.4	104.8	104.5	113.1	115.9
35	Machinery	99.3	104.9	99.9	103.8	104.4	115.6	128.4	(D)	(D)	(D)
36	Electrical equipment [5]	105.7	106.3	101.4	100.0	110.1	113.0	112.6	106.9	104.9	101.3
371	Motor vehicles	153.6	157.7	156.9	162.6	177.8	196.2	201.1	(D)	(D)	(D)
372,376	Aircraft and missiles	143.5	118.5	136.7	148.8	138.3	144.8	145.7	134.5	156.6	152.0

D Withheld to avoid disclosure.   X Not applicable.   [1] 1972 Standard Industrial Classification; see text, section 13.   [2] The mean number of FTE R&D scientists and engineers employed in January of the year shown and the following January.   [3] Includes industries not shown separately.   [4] Includes allied products.   [5] Includes communication.   [6] See footnote 1, table 956.   [7] Represents the arithmetic mean of the numbers of R&D scientists and engineers reported in each industry for January in two consecutive years divided into total R&D expenditures in each industry.
Source: U.S. National Science Foundation, *Research and Development in Industry*, annual.

No. 970. Scientists and Engineers Employed in Research and Development: 1970 to 1988

[In thousands of full-time equivalent employees. Data are estimates. Yearly averages for industry sector only. Excludes those employed by State and local government agencies. DOD=Dept. of Defense. FFRDC's = federally funded R&D centers]

SECTOR	1970	1980	1981	1982	1983	1984	1985	1986	1987	1988
Total	543.8	651.2	683.3	711.9	751.7	797.8	849.2	896.5	923.3	949.2
Industry (excl. social scientists) [1] . .	375.6	469.2	498.8	525.4	562.5	603.3	646.8	684.2	703.0	716.8
Universities and colleges, total [1] . .	79.5	95.9	98.3	99.5	100.4	103.4	108.5	118.0	126.5	135.1
Scientists and engineers	61.3	72.7	73.9	74.5	75.5	77.3	81.1	89.1	95.2	101.8
Graduate students	18.2	23.2	24.4	25.0	24.9	26.1	27.4	28.9	31.3	33.3
Federal Government (incl. DOD) . .	67.5	58.6	59.2	60.0	61.3	62.1	62.9	63.3	62.3	65.8
Other nonprofit institutions [1]	21.2	27.5	27.0	27.0	27.5	29.0	31.0	31.0	31.5	31.5

[1] Includes professional R&D personnel employed at FFRDC's administered by organizations in their respective sectors.
Source: U.S. National Science Foundation, *National Patterns of R&D Resources: 1990.*

No. 971. Science and Engineering Degree Recipients in 1988 and 1989—Selected Characteristics: 1990

[Based on survey and subject to sampling error; see source for details]

DEGREE AND FIELD	Graduates 1988 and 1989	PERCENT DISTRIBUTION—1990				Median salary ($1,000)
		In school [1]	Employed		Not employed	
			In S&E [2]	In other		
Bachelor's recipients.	643.2	20	44	32	5	26.0
All science fields	494.5	22	35	38	5	23.8
Physical sciences	29.4	39	38	18	5	25.1
Math/statistics	35.2	18	50	26	6	23.6
Computer science.	69.3	6	77	13	4	30.1
Environmental science.	7.3	30	49	15	5	23.7
Life sciences	111.2	32	34	28	6	21.0
Psychology	86.7	21	20	54	6	18.6
Social Sciences	156.4	20	19	55	5	21.9
All engineering fields [3]	148.7	11	73	12	3	33.0
Civil	15.2	10	78	9	3	30.1
Electrical/electronics.	55.5	11	76	10	3	34.0
Industrial.	12.3	5	72	18	5	31.1
Mechanical	30.0	11	76	10	4	34.0
Master's recipients.	136.6	23	61	13	4	37.0
All science fields	93.7	25	55	16	4	33.8
Physical sciences	9.2	41	49	8	2	34.9
Math/statistics	10.6	18	67	13	2	32.8
Computer science.	22.2	9	78	10	3	42.1
Environmental science.	5.2	21	71	6	2	33.8
Life sciences	19.3	35	47	15	4	26.9
Psychology	7.3	34	36	26	4	32.0
Social Sciences	19.9	26	37	30	7	31.0
All engineering fields [3]	42.9	17	73	6	3	41.4
Civil	4.7	11	85	4	-	35.2
Electrical/electronics.	13.8	19	72	4	5	46.5
Industrial.	2.6	8	62	23	8	40.3
Mechanical	8.0	15	79	5	1	42.1

[1] Full-time graduate students.   [2] In science and engineering.   [3] Includes other fields, not shown separately.
Source: National Science Foundation/SRS, *Characteristics of Recent Science and Engineering Graduates: 1990.*

No. 972. Professional Scientific, Engineering, and Technical Personnel in the Federal Government, by Occupational Group: 1970 to 1989

[In thousands, except percent. As of October. Excludes health professional personnel]

OCCUPATIONAL GROUP	1970	1980	1985 [1]	1987 [1]	1988 [1][2]	1989 [1][2]	PERCENT FEMALE					
							1970	1980	1985 [1]	1987 [1]	1988 [1][2]	1989 [1][2]
Total	180.3	206.9	238.0	240.0	217.6	223.3	6.7	9.5	13.8	15.4	13.8	14.7
Scientific personnel .	77.2	88.0	91.4	89.1	86.7	87.7	8.0	12.7	15.6	22.7	17.6	18.6
Physical sciences.	29.8	27.6	27.6	27.1	26.5	26.6	6.4	9.5	12.5	13.9	14.4	14.8
Mathematics [3] . . .	8.6	11.1	11.0	10.4	9.8	9.7	17.4	19.8	22.8	23.7	23.4	24.0
Life sciences . . .	26.9	30.5	33.5	33.1	33.2	33.8	4.1	8.7	12.1	14.2	15.0	16.3
Social sciences [4] .	6.6	10.5	10.1	10.1	10.4	10.2	16.2	23.3	25.1	26.3	26.4	28.8
Economics. . . .	4.3	5.9	5.9	5.6	5.5	5.5	11.1	17.4	20.6	21.3	21.5	22.1
Other	2.3	4.6	4.2	4.5	4.9	4.7	25.1	30.8	31.5	32.6	31.9	36.6
Geography [5]	3.3	4.9	5.7	4.9	3.6	4.1	8.5	14.8	17.0	18.0	19.2	19.2
Psychology	2.2	3.3	3.4	3.5	3.3	3.4	13.7	16.8	21.4	23.6	23.0	24.7
Engineering personnel	83.0	89.6	105.1	109.7	108.2	111.4	0.5	1.9	5.3	6.7	7.2	7.8
Computer specialists.	20.1	29.3	41.5	41.2	22.7	24.3	21.1	23.3	31.4	34.8	31.2	32.0

[1] Excludes U.S. Post Office.   [2] Not comparable with previous years. Excludes employees with less than a bachelor's degree.   [3] Includes statistics.   [4] Includes community planning.   [5] Includes cartography and land surveying.
Source: U.S. National Science Foundation. Compiled from data supplied by the U.S. Office of Personnel Management.

No. 973. Civilian Employment of Scientists, Engineers, and Technicians, by Occupation and Major Industrial Sector: 1990

[In thousands. Based on sample and subject to sampling error. For details, see source]

OCCUPATION	Total [1]	WAGE AND SALARY WORKERS								Self employed
		Min-ing [2]	Con-struc-tion	Manu-facturing	Trans-por-tation [3]	Trade	FIRE [4]	Serv-ices	Govern-ment	
Scientists and engineers..	2,600.7	48.0	24.9	927.2	117.7	61.8	87.1	711.1	451.4	161.0
Scientists..............	1,081.7	22.6	1.3	182.9	33.6	27.5	72.5	356.9	250.2	125.0
Physical scientists.........	199.5	19.0	0.1	59.3	2.6	2.0	0.2	61.8	43.1	11.0
Life scientists...........	173.5	0.2	-	23.6	1.0	1.6	0.6	64.4	66.6	7.0
Mathematical scientists.....	21.6	-	-	2.5	1.7	-	2.0	9.1	6.3	-
Social scientists..........	223.9	0.4	-	0.0	1.8	-	10.0	87.6	58.8	65.0
Systems analysts, EDP.....	463.2	3.1	1.2	97.4	26.6	23.8	59.7	133.9	75.4	42.0
Engineers [5]............	1,519.0	25.4	23.6	744.3	84.1	34.4	14.6	354.2	201.2	36.0
Civil engineers...........	198.0	1.0	8.9	9.4	7.4	0.4	1.1	79.0	83.6	7.0
Electrical/electronics.......	426.2	1.1	4.5	196.7	40.5	18.8	0.9	117.3	40.4	6.0
Mechanical engineers......	233.3	1.7	4.7	141.6	5.8	5.4	0.9	54.0	14.3	5.0
Engineering and science technicians..........	1,326.4	18.0	24.6	481.9	77.0	99.6	7.1	412.3	173.8	24.0
Electrical/electronics technicians...............	363.0	0.8	5.0	145.6	32.0	78.8	1.6	64.7	29.6	5.0
Engineering technicians......	391.8	5.5	5.4	137.5	24.0	9.1	1.6	105.2	97.6	5.0
Drafters................	325.2	4.1	14.1	106.4	17.4	7.6	1.7	148.0	13.8	10.0
Science technicians.........	246.4	7.6	0.0	92.3	3.8	4.1	2.3	94.3	32.8	4.0
Surveyors	108.0	2.7	2.8	-	2.9	-	0.5	68.2	24.3	6.0
Computer programmers..	564.7	3.2	2.1	99.7	26.6	56.3	77.4	233.6	50.4	15.0

- Represents or rounds to zero. [1] Includes agriculture, forestry, and fishing not shown separately. [2] Includes oil and gas extraction. [3] Includes communications and public utilities. [4] Finance, insurance, and real estate. [5] Includes kinds of engineers and technicians not shown separately.

Source: U.S. Bureau of Labor Statistics, *Monthly Labor Review*, November 1991. (Data collected biennially.)

No. 974. Doctoral Scientists and Engineers—Selected Characteristics: 1975 to 1989

[In thousands]

CHARACTERISTIC	1975	1985	1989		CHARACTERISTIC	1975	1985	1989	
			Num-ber	Em-ployed				Num-ber	Em-ployed
Total.............	270.4	424.6	485.2	448.7	Women..............	25.6	64.0	84.5	77.2
Field:					Race:				
Life scientists.........	68.3	109.9	127.0	115.8	White...............	245.4	377.9	432.0	397.2
Physical scientists......	58.5	73.1	78.3	70.2	Black..............	2.6	5.9	7.6	7.2
Psychologists.........	31.3	54.9	64.8	60.6	Asian/Pacific Islander....	13.9	35.5	42.6	41.1
Social scientists........	38.6	68.5	76.8	70.0	Other and not reported ...	8.4	5.2	2.9	3.2
Economists	12.6	19.1	20.5	18.6	Employment status:				
Other social scientists ..	26.0	49.4	56.3	51.4	Full-time employed......	240.6	371.9	411.0	411.0
Engineers............	43.5	67.9	78.4	74.8	Part-time employed......	7.3	16.7	22.9	22.9
Mathematical scientists ...	14.2	17.5	18.8	17.6	Postdoctorates.........	8.2	11.8	14.8	14.8
Computer specialists.....	3.5	15.0	19.9	19.8	Unemployed/seeking	2.5	3.4	3.8	(X)
Environmental scientists ..	12.5	18.0	21.1	19.8	Unemployed/not seeking..	2.4	3.9	4.2	(X)
Sex:					Retired/not employed	8.7	16.2	27.4	(X)
Men................	244.9	360.6	400.6	371.5	Other and not reported ...	0.9	0.8	1.1	(X)

X Not applicable.

Source: U.S. National Science Foundation, *Characteristics of Doctoral Scientists and Engineers in the United States*, biennial series.

No. 975. Graduate Science/Engineering Students in Doctorate-Granting Institutions of Higher Education, by Sex, Citizenship, and Enrollment Status: 1975 to 1990

[As of **fall.** Includes outlying areas]

FIELD OF SCIENCE OR ENGINEERING	TOTAL (1,000)				PERCENT—								
					Female			Foreign		Part-time			
	1975	1980	1989	1990	1980	1989	1990	1989	1990	1975	1980	1989	1990
Total, all surveyed fields .	291.8	322.7	384.0	398.4	32.6	36.7	37.5	25.2	25.2	29.2	30.9	30.5	30.9
Science/engineering	268.9	286.3	338.6	350.0	27.7	31.5	32.2	27.5	27.6	29.3	29.9	28.2	28.6
Engineering, total..........	65.2	69.9	96.9	100.3	8.7	13.2	13.6	36.1	36.0	43.0	40.0	35.5	36.0
Sciences, total............	203.7	216.4	241.7	249.8	33.9	38.8	39.6	24.0	24.1	24.9	26.7	25.3	25.6
Physical sciences	24.9	25.4	31.8	32.5	16.6	22.9	23.3	35.8	36.9	13.9	12.3	10.6	11.3
Environmental..........	11.1	12.8	12.7	12.9	22.7	27.9	29.1	20.1	20.4	19.2	19.3	23.4	23.5
Mathematical sciences....	14.7	13.6	16.9	17.3	25.4	30.1	30.4	37.6	35.2	30.8	31.3	23.0	23.7
Computer sciences	7.4	11.4	26.5	27.7	21.8	23.4	22.8	31.8	33.1	43.5	48.0	46.9	46.9
Agricultural sciences	10.1	11.6	10.4	10.4	23.5	28.0	29.5	26.3	27.3	15.5	17.2	17.5	18.1
Biological sciences	41.7	42.8	45.8	47.1	38.1	44.9	45.4	23.2	24.2	15.7	16.2	13.9	14.7
Psychology	27.8	30.0	33.6	34.7	52.2	63.7	65.5	4.4	4.6	27.2	26.0	26.5	28.1
Social sciences........	66.1	69.0	64.0	67.2	37.1	41.9	43.0	22.7	21.7	33.1	37.3	33.4	32.1
Health fields, total..........	22.9	36.4	45.4	48.4	71.0	75.8	76.2	8.2	8.5	28.0	38.8	47.5	47.8

Source: U.S. National Science Foundation, *Survey of Graduate Science and Engineering Students and Postdoctorates*, annual.

No. 976. Doctorates Conferred, by Recipients' Characteristics, 1980 to 1990, and by Selected Science and Engineering Fields, 1990

[In percent, except as indicated]

CHARACTERISTIC	ALL FIELDS		1990									
	1980	1985	All fields [1]	Engineer-ing	Physical sciences [2]	Earth sciences	Mathematics	Computer sciences	Biological sciences [3]	Agricultural	Social sciences [4]	Psychology
Total conferred (number)	31,020	31,297	36,027	4,892	3,494	769	892	704	4,333	1,176	3,146	3,267
Male	69.7	65.7	22,966	4,478	2,843	620	734	594	2,727	930	2,112	1,361
Female	30.3	34.3	13,061	414	651	149	158	110	1,606	246	1,034	1,906
Median age [5]	32.2	33.3	33.9	31.2	29.8	32.4	30.9	31.7	31.4	33.6	34.4	33.9
CITIZENSHIP [6]												
Total conferred (number)	30,156	29,921	33,588	4,494	3,265	715	829	659	4,109	1,103	2,913	2,975
U.S. citizen	83.6	78.1	24,190	1,927	2,077	521	369	343	3,104	622	1,865	2,790
Foreign citizen	16.4	21.9	9,398	2,567	1,188	194	460	316	1,005	481	1,048	185
RACE/ETHNICITY [7]												
Total conferred (number)	26,512	24,693	25,844	2,303	2,244	544	416	396	3,288	679	2,047	2,859
White [8]	84.7	86.2	22,345	1,818	1,929	502	367	334	2,908	597	1,721	2,551
Black [8]	4.2	4.2	972	40	27	2	4	1	41	15	100	110
Asian/Pacific [8]	4.2	4.3	1,260	345	161	17	25	46	193	30	100	51
Indian/Alaskan [8]	0.3	0.4	93	4	3	1	1	-	3	4	6	18
Hispanic	1.8	2.6	813	53	70	13	10	5	88	23	86	103
Other/unknown	4.9	2.2	361	43	54	9	9	10	55	10	34	26

- Represents or rounds to zero.   [1] Includes other fields, not shown separately.   [2] Astronomy, physics, and chemistry. [3] Biochemistry, botany, microbiology, physiology, zoology, and related fields.   [4] Anthropology, sociology, political science, economics, and international relations.   [5] For definition of median, see Guide to Tabular Presentation.   [6] For those with known citizenship. Includes those with temporary visas.   [7] Excludes those with temporary visas.   [8] Non-Hispanic.

Source: U.S. National Science Foundation, Division of Science Resources Studies, *Survey of Earned Doctorates.*

No. 977. Nobel Prize Laureates in Chemistry, Physics, and Physiology/Medicine—Selected Countries: 1901 to 1990

[Presented by location of award-winning research and by date of award]

COUNTRY	1901-1990				1901-1915	1916-1930	1931-1945	1946-1960	1961-1975	1976-1990
	Total	Physics	Chemistry	Physiology/Medicine						
Total	406	140	115	151	52	41	49	74	92	98
United States	162	57	36	69	3	3	14	38	41	63
United Kingdom	69	21	24	24	7	8	11	14	20	9
West Germany [1]	57	17	28	12	15	12	11	4	8	7
France	22	8	7	7	10	3	2	-	5	2
Soviet Union	10	7	1	2	2	-	-	4	3	1
Japan	4	3	1	-	-	-	-	1	2	1
Other countries	82	27	18	37	15	15	11	13	13	15

- Represents zero.   [1] Includes East Germany before 1946.

Source: U.S. National Science Foundation, unpublished data.

No. 978. Federal Space Program—Budget Authority, by Agency: 1960 to 1991

[In millions of dollars, except percent. For fiscal years ending in year shown; see text, section 9. NASA = National Aeronautics and Space Administration]

YEAR	Total	NASA [1]		DEFENSE		Other	YEAR	Total	NASA [1]		DEFENSE		Other
		Total	Percent of total	Total	Percent of total				Total	Percent of total	Total	Percent of total	
1960	1,066	462	43.3	561	52.6	43	1979	7,244	4,030	55.6	3,036	41.9	178
1965	6,956	5,138	73.9	1,574	22.6	244	1980	8,689	4,680	53.9	3,848	44.3	160
1966	6,970	5,065	72.7	1,689	24.2	217	1981	9,978	4,992	50.0	4,828	48.4	158
1969	5,976	3,822	64.0	2,013	33.7	141	1982	12,441	5,528	44.4	6,679	53.7	234
1970	5,341	3,547	66.4	1,678	31.4	115	1983	15,589	6,328	40.6	9,019	57.9	242
1971	4,741	3,101	65.4	1,512	31.9	127	1984	17,136	6,648	38.8	10,195	59.5	293
1972	4,575	3,071	67.1	1,407	30.8	97	1985	20,167	6,925	34.3	12,768	63.3	474
1973	4,825	3,093	64.1	1,623	33.6	109	1986	21,659	7,165	33.1	14,126	65.2	368
1974	4,640	2,759	59.4	1,766	38.1	116	1987	26,448	[3]9,809	37.1	16,287	61.6	352
1975	4,914	2,915	59.3	1,892	38.5	107	1988	26,607	8,302	31.2	17,679	66.4	626
1976 [2]	6,660	4,075	61.2	2,444	36.7	142	1989	28,443	10,098	35.5	17,906	63.0	440
1977	5,983	3,440	57.5	2,412	40.3	131	1990	31,854	12,142	38.1	19,382	60.8	330
1978	6,518	3,623	55.6	2,738	42.0	157	1991 [4]	34,419	13,603	39.5	20,443	59.4	373

[1] Includes budget authority for the space transportation system of $3.1 billion in 1982; $4.1 billion in 1983; and $4.0 billion in 1984.   [2] Includes transition quarter, July 1 to Sept. 30, 1976.   [3] Includes $2.1 billion for replacement of shuttle orbiter Challenger.   [4] Estimated.

Source: U.S. National Aeronautics and Space Administration, *Aeronautics and Space Report of the President,* annual. Data from U.S. Office of Management and Budget.

No. 979. Space Vehicle Systems—Net Sales and Backlog Orders: 1965 to 1990

[In millions of dollars. Backlog orders as of Dec. 31. Based on data from major companies engaged in manufacture of aerospace products. Includes parts but excludes engines and propulsion units]

YEAR	NET SALES			BACKLOG ORDERS			YEAR	NET SALES			BACKLOG ORDERS		
	Total	Military	Non-military	Total	Military	Non-military		Total	Military	Non-military	Total	Military	Non-military
1965..	2,449	602	1,847	2,203	503	1,700	1984..	5,225	3,019	2,206	4,624	3,099	1,525
1970..	1,956	1,025	931	1,184	786	398	1985..	6,300	4,241	2,059	6,707	4,941	1,766
1975..	2,119	1,096	1,023	1,304	1,019	285	1986..	6,304	4,579	[1]1,725	8,063	6,028	[1]2,035
1980..	3,483	1,461	2,022	1,814	951	863	1987..	8,051	5,248	[1]2,803	12,393	9,460	[1]2,933
1981..	3,856	1,736	2,120	3,174	2,164	1,010	1988..	8,622	6,190	[1]2,432	10,838	7,880	[1]2,958
1982..	4,749	2,606	2,143	4,337	2,403	1,934	1989..	9,758	6,457	[1]3,301	13,356	9,192	[1]4,164
1983..	4,940	2,420	2,520	4,865	2,733	2,132	1990..	9,663	6,288	[1]3,375	13,258	8,719	[1]4,539

[1] Includes data for non-military missile systems and parts.
Source: U.S. Bureau of the Census, Current Industrial Reports, MA-37D, Aerospace Industry (Orders, Sales, and Backlog).

No. 980. National Aeronautics and Space Administration—Budget Summary: 1989 to 1991

[In millions of dollars]

ITEM	1989	1990	1991	ITEM	1989	1990	1991
Appropriations, total	10,898	12,296	15,078	Physics and astronomy	712	847	954
				Planetary exploration.	406	381	470
Research and development .	4,267	5,221	6,024	Life sciences	78	105	136
Space station	885	1,724	1,875	Space applications	578	632	835
Space transportation capability [1] . .	660	546	589	Operating account	104	94	102
Space lab	88	119	129	Adjustment	32	-7	-
Upper stages	132	80	76	**Space flight, control and**			
Engineering and technical base. .	161	182	209	**data communication pro-**			
Commercial programs.	44	56	87	**grams**	4,464	4,555	6,334
Aeronautics and space technology .	727	765	869	Space flight	3,721	3,818	4,287
Space research and technology .	274	274	280	Shuttle production/operation. . . .	1,117	1,190	1,310
Aeronautical research and				Space transportation operations .	2,604	2,628	2,977
technology	385	434	495	Space tracking and data systems . .	813	898	974
Transatmospheric research and				Operating account	14	9	10
technology	69	58	94	Adjustment	-84	-171	1,063
Tracking and data advanced				**Research and program**			
systems	19	19	20	**management. . . . .**	1,862	1,923	2,212
Safety, reliability, and quality				**Construction of facilities** . . .	305	588	498
assurance	22	22	33	Trust funds.	1	1	1
University space science and				**Inspector General**	(X)	8	9
technology program	(X)	37	54				
Space science and applications . . .	1,774	1,965	2,395				

- Represents or rounds to zero.   X Not applicable.   [1] Includes other items not shown separately.
Source: U.S. National Aeronautics and Space Administration, NASA News.

No. 981. NASA Financial Summary: 1970 to 1991

[In millions of dollars, except personnel. For fiscal year ending in year shown; see text, section 9]

YEAR	Appropriations	Direct obligations	OUTLAYS					Personnel (number)
			Total	R&D	Communications [1]	Facility construction	Research and program management	
1970	3,749	3,859	3,753	2,992	-	54	707	32,548
1975	3,231	3,266	3,267	2,420	-	85	761	25,638
1980	5,243	5,098	4,852	3,701	-	140	1,010	23,470
1984	7,243	7,135	7,048	2,792	2,915	109	1,232	21,870
1985	7,552	7,638	7,318	2,118	3,707	170	1,323	22,316
1986	7,764	7,463	7,404	2,615	3,267	189	1,332	21,960
1987	10,621	8,604	7,591	2,436	3,597	149	1,409	22,646
1988	9,002	9,915	9,092	2,916	4,362	166	1,648	22,823
1989 [2]	10,898	11,316	11,052	3,922	5,030	190	1,908	23,893
1990 [2]	12,290	13,069	12,429	5,094	5,117	218	1,991	23,625
1991 [2]	15,078	13,974	13,878	5,765	5,590	326	2,185	(NA)

- Represents zero.   NA Not available.   [1] Space flight, control, and data communications.   [2] Outlays include trust funds outlays and outlays for the Inspector General, not shown separately.

Source: National Aeronautics and Space Administration, NASA News.

No. 982. Space Shuttle System Expenditures by NASA in Constant (1982) Dollars: 1973 to 1991

[In millions of dollars. For year ending Sept. 30. These data cannot be used alone to estimate the total shuttle cost. Only operating expenditures correspond to an annual cost in the economic sense, and even those estimates require adjustment for the three-year period over which the cost of a shuttle flight is incurred and reimbursements are received. For details, see source]

YEAR	Total	D.D.T. and E.[1]	Con-struction	Produc-tion	Opera-tions	YEAR	Total	D.D.T. and E.[1]	Con-struction	Produc-tion	Opera-tions
1973. . . .	58	-	58	-	-	1983. . . .	3,014	-	26	1,635	1,354
1974. . . .	325	216	109	-	-	1984. . . .	3,127	-	73	690	2,364
1975. . . .	1,543	1,407	136	-	-	1985. . . .	2,636	-	42	1,376	1,218
1976. . . .	2,619	2,541	79	-	-	1986. . . .	2,606	-	-	1,184	1,422
1977. . . .	2,258	2,089	60	109	-	1987. . . .	4,165	-	-	2,611	1,553
1978. . . .	2,062	1,898	103	61	-	1988. . . .	2,538	-	-	948	1,590
1979. . . .	2,251	1,713	42	496	-	1989. . . .	3,084	-	-	943	2,141
1980. . . .	2,751	1,339	42	907	463	1990. . . .	2,996	-	-	968	2,028
1981. . . .	2,724	1,041	13	1,093	578	1991. . . .	2,989	-	-	938	2,051
1982. . . .	2,932	894	20	1,283	735						

- Represents or rounds to zero.   [1] Design, development, testing, and evaluation.

Source: U.S. Congress, Congressional Budget Office, unpublished data.

No. 983. Space Shuttle Flights—Summary: 1981 to 1992

FLIGHT NUMBER	Date	Mission/ Orbiter name	Crew size	Days duration	FLIGHT NUMBER	Date	Mission/ Orbiter name	Crew size	Days duration
1	4/12/81	Columbia	2	2	27	12/2/88	Atlantis	4	4
4	6/27/81	Columbia	2	7	29	3/13/89	Discovery	5	5
2	11/12/81	Columbia	2	2	30	5/4/89	Atlantis	5	4
3	3/22/82	Columbia	2	8	28	8/8/89	Columbia	5	5
5	11/11/82	Columbia	4	5	34	10/18/89	Atlantis	5	5
6	4/4/83	Challenger	4	5	33	11/22/89	Discovery	5	5
7	6/18/83	Challenger	5	6	32	1/9/90	Columbia	5	10
8	8/30/83	Challenger	5	6	36	2/28/90	Atlantis	5	5
9	11/28/83	Columbia	6	10	31	4/24/90	Discovery	5	6
10	2/3/84	Challenger	5	8	41	10/6/90	Discovery	5	4
11	4/6/84	Challenger	5	7	38	11/15/90	Atlantis	5	4
12	8/30/84	Discovery	6	6	35	12/2/90	Columbia	7	9
13	10/5/84	Challenger	7	8	39	4/28/91	Discovery	7	8
14	11/8/84	Discovery	5	8	37	4/5/91	Atlantis	5	6
15	1/24/85	Discovery	5	3	40	6/5/91	Columbia	7	9
16	4/12/85	Discovery	7	7	43	8/2/91	Atlantis	5	9
17	4/29/85	Challenger	7	7	44	11/24/91	Atlantis	6	7
18	6/17/85	Discovery	7	7	42	1/92	Discovery	7	7
19	7/29/85	Challenger	7	8	45	5/92	Atlantis	7	8
20	8/27/85	Discovery	5	7	49	5/92	Endeavour	7	7
21	10/3/85	Atlantis	5	4	50	6/92	Columbia	7	13
22	10/30/85	Challenger	8	7	46	9/92	Atlantis	7	7
23	11/26/85	Atlantis	7	7	47	9/92	Endeavour	7	7
24	1/12/86	Columbia	7	6	52	11/92	Columbia	6	9
25	1/28/86	Challenger	7	-	53	12/92	Discovery	5	4
26	9/29/88	Discovery	5	4					

- Represents zero.

Source: U.S. National Aeronautics and Space Administration, *Payload Flight Assignments NASA Mixed Fleets,* monthly, and "Upcoming Shuttle Flights," November 1991.

No. 984. World-Wide Successful Space Launches: 1957 to 1990

[Criterion of success is attainment of Earth orbit or Earth escape]

COUNTRY	Total	1957-1964	1965-1969	1970-1974	1975-1979	1980-1984	1985-1989	1985	1986	1987	1988	1989	1990
Total.	3,308	289	586	555	607	605	550	120	103	110	116	101	116
Soviet Union	2,255	82	302	405	461	483	447	97	91	95	90	74	75
United States.	932	207	279	139	126	93	61	17	6	8	12	18	27
Japan.	41	-	-	5	10	12	11	2	2	3	2	2	3
ESA [1]	35	-	-	-	1	8	21	3	2	2	7	7	5
China: Mainland	28	-	-	2	6	6	9	1	2	2	4	-	5
France	10	-	4	3	3	-	-	-	-	-	-	-	-
India.	3	-	-	-	-	3	-	-	-	-	-	-	-
Israel	2	-	-	-	-	-	1	-	-	-	1	-	1
Australia	1	-	1	-	-	-	-	-	-	-	-	-	-
United Kingdom	1	-	-	1	-	-	-	-	-	-	-	-	-

- Represents zero.   [1] European Space Agency.

Source: Library of Congress, Congressional Research Service, Science Policy Research Division, *Space Activities of the United States, Soviet Union and Other Launching Countries/Organization: 1957-1990,* July 1991.

Transportation—Land

This section presents statistics on revenues, passenger and freight traffic volume, and employment in various revenue-producing modes of the transportation industry, including motor vehicles, trains, and pipelines. Data are also presented on commuting travel; highway mileage and finances; motor vehicle travel, accidents, sales, and registrations; automobile operating costs; and characteristics of public transit, railroads, and pipelines.

In Brief

Transportation outlays reached $954 billion in 1990

State gasoline tax rates for 1991—
*Lowest rate, 7.5 percent
in Georgia
Highest rate, 26 percent
in Rhode Island*

The principal compiler of data on public roads and on operation of motor vehicles is the U.S. Department of Transportation's (DOT) Federal Highway Administration (FHWA). These data appear in FHWA's annual *Highway Statistics* and other publications. The U.S. Interstate Commerce Commission (ICC) presents data on interstate land transport in its publications, the *Annual Report to Congress* and the *Transport Statistics in the United States,* which contain data on railroads and motor carriers subject to ICC regulations.

The U.S. National Highway Traffic Safety Administration issues data on traffic accident deaths and death rates in two annual reports: the *Fact Book* and the *Fatal Accident Reporting System Annual Report.* DOT's Federal Railroad Administration presents data on accidents involving railroads in its annual *Accident/Incident Bulletin,* and the *Rail-Highway Crossing Accident/Incident and Inventory Bulletin.*

Various censuses and surveys conducted by the U.S. Bureau of the Census also provide data. Results of the censuses of transportation are presented in the *Truck Inventory and Use Survey.* The *Annual Survey of Manufactures* and reports of the censuses of manufactures, wholesale and retail trade, and service industries contain statistics on the motor vehicle and equipment industry and on retail, wholesale, and services aspects of this industry. Data on persons commuting to work were collected as part of the 1980 census and are in various census reports.

Data are also presented in many nongovernment publications. Among them are the weekly and annual *Cars of Revenue Freight Loaded* and the annual *Yearbook of Railroad Facts,* both published by the Association of American Railroads, Washington, DC; *Bus Facts,* issued annually by the American Bus Association, Washington, DC; and the *Transit Fact Book,* containing electric railway and motorbus statistics, published annually by the American Public Transit Association, Washington, DC. Useful annual handbooks in the field of transportation are *Motor Vehicle Facts and Figures* and *World Motor Vehicle Data,* issued by the Motor Vehicle Manufacturers Association of the United States, Inc., Detroit, MI; *Accident Facts,* issued by the National Safety Council, Chicago, IL; and *Transportation in America,* issued by the ENO Foundation for Transportation, Westport, Connecticut.

Urban and rural highway mileage.— Beginning 1980, mileage is classified in urban and rural categories, rather than municipal and rural. Urban denotes the Federal-aid legislation definition of an area. Such areas include, as a minimum, a census place with a population of 5,000 to 49,999 or a designated urbanized area with a population of 50,000 or more. These Federal-aid urban areas may extend beyond corporate and census boundaries, and thus are not necessarily coextensive with municipal boundaries. Rural in 1980 refers to non-Federal-aid urban area mileage. Prior to 1980, municipal referred to roads within incorporated places, densely populated New England towns, and certain of the more populous unincorporated areas and rural to non-municipal roads.

Federal-aid highway systems.— Federal law provides that Federal funds be matched in varying proportions with State funds for the costs of planning, engineering, right-of-way acquisition, and construction of highways. Other costs, such as maintenance and policing, are borne entirely by the States and local agencies.

Effective July 1, 1976, a uniform road classification system was implemented which shortened the mileage of the highway system and redefined the three main systems of Federal-aid routes. The Federal-aid primary system is comprised of a network of main roads important to interstate, statewide, and regional travel. The system consists of main rural roads and their extensions into or through urban areas. The Federal-aid secondary system consists of rural roads of a more local nature, such as those which connect county seats and the larger population centers not served by the primary system. The Federal-aid urban system is located in urban places of 5,000 or more persons and consists of major urban roads and streets, except those on the primary system.

Regulatory bodies.—The ICC, created by the U.S. Congress to regulate transportation in interstate commerce, has jurisdiction over railroads, trucking companies, bus lines, freight forwarders, water carriers, coal slurry pipelines, and transportation brokers. The Federal Energy Regulatory Commission is responsible for setting rates and charges for transportation and sale of natural gas and for establishing rates or charges for transportation.

Motor carriers.—For 1960-73, class I for-hire motor carriers of freight were classified by the ICC as those with $1 million or more of gross annual operating revenue; 1974-79, the class I minimum was $3 million. Effective January 1, 1980, class I carriers are those with $5 million or more in revenue. For 1960-68, class I motor carriers of passengers were classified by the ICC as those with $200,000 or more of gross annual operating revenue; for 1969-76, as those with revenues of $1

million or more; and since 1977, as those with $3 million or more. Effective January 1, 1988, class I motor carriers of passengers are those with $5 million or more in operating revenues; class II less than $5 million in operating revenues.

Railroads.—Railroad companies reporting to the ICC are divided into specific groups as follows: (1) Regular line-haul (interstate) railroads (and their non-operating subsidiaries); (2) switching and terminal railroads; (3) private railroads prior to 1964 (identified by ICC as "circular" because they reported on brief circulars); and (4) unofficial railroads, so designated when their reports are received too late for tabulation. For the most part, the last three groups are not included in the statistics shown here.

For years prior to 1978, class I railroads were those with annual revenues of $1 million or more for 1950-55; $3 million or more for 1956-64; $5 million or more for 1965-75; and $10 million or more for 1976-77. In 1978, the classification became class I, those having more than $50 million gross annual operating revenue; class II, from $10 million to $50 million; and class III, less than $10 million. Effective January 1, 1982, the ICC adopted a procedure to adjust the threshold for inflation by restating current revenues in constant 1978 dollars. In 1990, the criteria for class I and class II railroads were $94.4 million and $18.9 million, respectively. Also effective January 1, 1982, the ICC adopted a *Carrier Classification Index Survey Form* for carriers not filing annual report form R-1 with the commission. Class II and class III railroads are currently exempted from filing any financial report with the Commission. The form is used for reclassifying carriers.

Statistical reliability.—For a discussion of statistical collection and estimation, sampling procedures, and measures of statistical reliability, see Appendix III.

Historical statistics.—Tabular headnotes provide cross-references, where applicable, to *Historical Statistics of the United States, Colonial Times to 1970.* See Appendix IV.

No. 985. Passenger and Freight Transportation Outlays, by Type of Transport: 1970 to 1990

[In billions of dollars. Freight data include outlays for mail and express. ICC=Interstate Commerce Commission]

TYPE OF TRANSPORT	1970	1975	1978	1979	1980	1981	1982	1983	1984	1985	1986	1987	1988	1989	1990
Total outlays [1]	**195.6**	**297.8**	**453.2**	**492.4**	**540.9**	**595.8**	**588.7**	**638.7**	**706.0**	**755.6**	**769.6**	**802.5**	**865.1**	**906.3**	**954.3**
Passenger, total	114.9	187.4	287.5	307.6	336.9	373.5	377.6	409.0	455.7	493.3	502.6	520.8	566.8	592.6	621.6
Private transportation [2]	99.6	161.3	249.9	263.9	284.8	317.4	320.6	347.2	387.0	419.3	426.6	440.8	473.9	496.7	520.7
Automobiles [2]	97.0	156.6	244.1	256.8	276.7	308.0	312.4	339.8	378.8	411.0	418.4	432.1	464.4	487.3	510.8
New and used cars	32.1	46.0	80.4	77.1	73.3	82.6	85.7	105.6	125.7	139.3	156.7	149.2	165.6	161.6	164.6
Tires, tubes, accessories	7.1	12.4	17.2	19.8	22.2	24.6	24.9	26.9	27.5	29.4	31.3	33.2	36.8	38.2	40.1
Gasoline and oil	29.9	53.9	68.3	78.3	99.7	111.3	106.3	105.9	106.7	108.9	86.9	90.6	90.4	98.6	110.4
Insurance less claims	4.4	4.5	10.2	10.3	11.5	10.8	11.2	12.5	12.0	11.6	14.8	18.2	19.8	20.0	21.4
Interest on debt	4.7	7.3	13.0	15.4	17.5	21.0	21.8	19.6	25.1	26.7	26.5	29.1	33.7	36.7	35.7
Registration and operator's permit fees	1.9	2.3	3.0	3.1	3.3	3.5	3.8	4.1	4.5	5.3	5.6	5.9	6.2	6.6	6.9
Repair, greasing, was-ing. parking, tolls [3]	13.2	22.1	33.0	36.7	38.0	41.5	43.5	45.7	50.4	56.8	60.9	66.4	73.5	81.9	90.4
Air	2.6	4.7	5.8	7.1	8.1	9.4	8.2	7.4	8.2	8.3	8.1	8.7	9.4	9.5	9.9
For-hire transportation	15.3	26.2	37.6	43.3	52.2	56.1	57.1	61.8	68.7	74.2	76.0	82.3	92.9	95.8	100.9
Local [4]	5.4	10.5	15.4	15.4	18.5	20.4	21.3	22.3	23.6	27.7	29.0	30.5	33.1	32.9	33.1
Bus and transit [5]	1.8	4.7	6.7	7.5	9.2	10.1	10.0	11.4	11.7	15.1	15.1	15.8	17.4	15.7	15.6
School bus	1.2	2.2	2.7	3.2	3.8	4.7	5.0	5.3	5.8	5.6	6.4	6.8	7.1	7.3	7.5
Taxi	2.1	3.4	4.4	4.5	5.2	5.2	5.6	5.3	5.5	5.6	6.0	6.4	6.9	7.1	7.5
Intercity	7.7	12.9	19.6	23.3	28.4	30.6	30.5	33.5	38.5	39.5	39.8	42.6	48.6	50.8	53.3
Air	6.6	11.2	17.1	20.4	25.1	26.8	26.8	29.7	33.6	35.9	36.4	39.3	44.9	46.9	49.5
Rail [6]	0.3	0.6	1.3	1.4	1.6	1.6	1.8	1.8	1.8	1.5	1.5	1.8	1.6	1.7	1.7
Bus	0.8	1.0	1.2	1.4	1.7	1.8	1.9	2.0	2.0	2.0	1.9	1.8	2.0	2.2	2.0
International	2.2	2.7	3.8	4.6	5.3	5.3	5.4	6.0	6.6	7.0	7.1	9.2	11.2	12.1	14.5
Freight, total [4]	83.8	115.5	172.9	192.9	212.1	234.6	220.9	240.5	262.1	272.3	279.6	292.6	311.5	330.1	349.7
Highway	62.5	84.8	127.2	142.7	155.4	173.3	162.7	180.5	195.6	208.6	214.1	224.7	239.2	257.0	272.6
Truck, intercity	33.6	47.4	77.9	90.2	94.6	100.2	99.9	111.1	120.7	126.2	129.1	136.3	143.2	151.3	160.6
Truck, local	28.8	37.3	49.1	52.3	60.5	72.8	72.8	69.2	74.7	82.2	84.8	89.6	95.8	105.5	111.8
Rail	11.9	16.5	21.9	24.8	27.7	30.5	27.1	27.3	30.5	29.2	27.8	28.4	29.6	29.9	30.4
Water	5.1	7.9	12.9	13.4	14.8	15.7	15.6	16.2	17.8	18.7	19.0	19.1	20.2	19.8	20.7
Oil pipeline	1.4	2.2	5.5	6.2	7.1	7.4	7.9	8.3	8.7	8.9	8.6	8.5	8.6	7.8	8.4
Air carrier	1.2	1.8	2.7	2.8	4.0	4.3	4.4	5.0	6.0	6.8	8.7	8.7	10.2	11.9	13.7

[1] Total outlays less than sum of passenger and freight totals, as estimated freight costs included in costs of new cars, gasoline, oil, tires, and tubes have been excluded to prevent duplication. [5] Includes Federal. State, and local government operating subsidies and capital grants.
[2] Includes business-owned vehicles. [3] Includes storage and rental. [4] Includes items not shown separately.
[6] Includes Federal operating subsidies and capital grants for Amtrak.

Source: ENO Foundation for Transportation, Westport, CT, *Transportation in America*, May 1990, with periodic supplements, (copyright).

Transportation—Land

No. 986. Employment and Earnings in Transportation, by Industry: 1980 to 1991

[Annual averages of monthly figures. Based on Current Employment Statistics program; see Appendix III. See also *Historical Statistics, Colonial Times to 1970*, series Q36-42]

SIC [1] code	INDUSTRY	1980	1984	1985	1986	1987	1988	1989	1990	1991
(X)	NUMBER (1,000)									
(X)	**Total transportation**	**2,960**	**2,916**	**3,001**	**3,056**	**3,163**	**3,312**	**3,428**	**3,554**	**3,562**
40	Railroads	532	376	359	332	309	298	293	280	269
4011	Class I railroads	482	345	323	294	271	259	252	241	231
41	Local and interurban passengers	265	271	278	287	296	312	329	343	361
42	Trucking and warehousing.	1,280	1,318	1,363	1,396	1,468	1,552	1,600	1,638	1,638
44	Water transportation.	211	190	185	175	173	172	173	174	174
45	Air transportation.	453	489	522	567	603	646	684	751	750
46	Pipelines, exc. natural gas.	21	19	19	18	19	19	19	19	19
47	Transportation services.	198	253	276	282	296	313	331	350	352
(X)	AVERAGE WEEKLY EARNINGS (dol.)									
4011	Class I railroads.	427	573	595	608	627	674	693	727	707
41	Local and interurban passengers	217	258	261	274	281	293	305	307	314
42	Trucking and warehousing.	358	407	405	408	414	419	437	451	456
46	Pipelines, exc. natural gas.	441	597	629	637	644	662	671	711	733

X Not applicable.   [1] 1987 Standard Industrial Classification, see text, section 13.

Source: U.S. Bureau of Labor Statistics, Bulletin 2370 and, Supplement to Employment and Earnings, July 1991, *Employment and Earnings*, monthly.

No. 987. Volume of Domestic Intercity Freight and Passenger Traffic, by Type of Transport: 1970 to 1990

[Freight traffic in bil. ton-miles; passenger traffic in bil. passenger-miles. A ton-mile is the movement of 1 ton (2,000 pounds) of freight for the distance of 1 mile. A passenger-mile is the movement of 1 passenger for the distance of 1 mile. Comprises public and private traffic, both revenue and nonrevenue. See also *Historical Statistics, Colonial Times to 1970*, series Q1-22]

TYPE OF TRANSPORT	TRAFFIC VOLUME						PERCENT DISTRIBUTION					
	1970	1975	1980	1985	1989	1990	1970	1975	1980	1985	1989	1990
Freight traffic, total	**1,936**	**2,066**	**2,487**	**2,458**	**2,807**	**2,855**	**100.0**	**100.0**	**100.0**	**100.0**	**100.0**	**100.0**
Railroads.	771	759	932	895	1,048	1,071	39.8	36.7	37.5	36.4	37.3	37.5
Truck:												
ICC truck	167	200	242	250	302	311	8.6	9.7	9.7	10.2	10.8	10.9
Non-ICC truck.	245	254	313	360	414	424	12.7	12.3	12.6	14.7	14.8	14.9
Water:												
Rivers/canals	205	243	311	306	363	377	10.6	11.8	12.5	12.5	12.9	13.2
Great Lakes	114	99	96	76	86	85	5.9	4.8	3.9	3.1	3.1	3.0
Oil pipelines.	431	507	588	564	584	577	22.3	24.5	23.6	23.0	20.8	20.2
Domestic airways [1] . .	3	4	5	7	10	11	0.2	0.2	0.2	0.3	0.4	0.4
Passenger traffic, total . . .	**1,181**	**1,354**	**1,557**	**1,744**	**2,012**	**2,054**	**100.0**	**100.0**	**100.0**	**100.0**	**100.0**	**100.0**
Private automobiles. . .	1,026	1,171	1,300	1,418	1,627	1,660	86.9	86.5	83.5	81.3	80.9	80.8
Domestic airways [2] . .	119	148	219	291	347	358	10.1	10.9	14.1	16.7	17.3	17.4
Bus [3]	25	25	27	24	24	23	2.1	1.9	1.7	1.4	1.2	1.1
Railroads [4]	11	10	11	11	13	13	0.9	0.7	0.7	0.6	0.7	0.6

[1] Revenue service only for scheduled and non-scheduled carriers, with small section 418 all-cargo carriers included from 1980. Includes express, mail, and excess baggage.   [2] Includes general aviation (mostly private business) flying.   [3] Excludes school and urban transit buses.   [4] Includes intercity (Amtrak) and rail commuter service.

Source: Eno Foundation for Transportation, Westport, CT, *Transportation in America*, May 1990, with periodic supplements (copyright).

No. 988. Passenger Transportation Arrangement: 1988 to 1990

[In millions of dollars, except percent. Represents SIC 4722]

SOURCE OF RECEIPTS	1988	1989	1990	OPERATING EXPENSES	1988	1989	1990
Receipts, total [1] . . .	**8,082**	**8,945**	**9,453**	**Expenses, total** [1]	**7,297**	**8,017**	**8594**
Air carriers	4,622	5,135	5,369	Payroll, annual	2,963	3,239	3,507
Water carriers	342	374	422	Employer contributions [2].	372	440	478
Hotels and motels	458	531	556	Lease and rental payments	748	792	828
Motor coaches.	318	321	342	Advertising and promotion	473	528	604
Railroads	47	56	56	Taxes and licenses	126	141	145
Rental cars	148	160	173	Utilities	297	336	373
Package tours	1,664	1,817	1,971	Depreciation.	293	287	298
Other	483	551	563	Office Supplies	251	284	283
				Repair Services	95	93	106

[1] Receipts for firms primarily engaged in arranging passenger transportation. These estimates exclude receipts of transportation companies (airlines, railroads, etc.).   [2] Includes contributions to Social Security and other supplemental benefits.

Source: U.S. Bureau of the Census, *Service Annual Survey*.

No. 989. Transportation Accidents, Deaths, and Injuries: 1970 to 1990
[For related data, see also table 1008, and 1032]

YEAR AND CASUALTY	Total (1,000)	Motor vehi-cle [1] (1,000)	Rail-road [2]	TYPE OF TRANSPORT					Gen-eral avia-tion [6]	Recre-ational boat-ing [7]	Gas pipe-lines [8]	Liquid pipe-lines [9]	Water-borne [10]	Haz-ardous mate-rials [11]
				Air carriers										
				Total	Air-lines [3]	Com-muter air car-riers [4]	On demand air carr-iers [5]							
Accidents:														
1970....	16,013	16,000	8,095	(NA)	55	(NA)	(NA)		4,712	3,803	1,019	351	2,582	(NA)
1975....	16,524	16,500	8,041	237	37	48	152		3,995	6,308	1,373	254	3,310	10,951
1980....	17,925	17,900	8,451	228	19	38	171		3,590	5,513	1,996	219	4,624	15,737
1985....	19,348	19,300	3,275	195	22	21	152		2,737	6,237	331	183	3,439	6,014
1989....	12,832	12,800	2,898	160	30	17	113		2,201	6,063	257	161	3,270	[12]7,545
1990....	11,531	11,500	2,879	144	26	14	104		2,138	6,411	199	177	1,227	[12]8,687
Deaths:														
1970....	54.8	52.6	785	(NA)	146	(NA)	(NA)		1,310	1,418	22	4	178	(NA)
1975....	48.2	44.5	575	221	124	28	69		1,252	1,466	14	7	243	27
1980....	54.5	51.1	584	143	1	37	105		1,239	1,360	11	3	206	19
1985....	47.3	43.8	454	639	526	37	76		951	1,116	26	5	131	8
1989....	49.1	45.6	523	397	278	31	88		757	896	36	3	79	8
1990....	47.9	44.5	599	83	39	4	40		736	865	5	3	14	4
Injuries:														
1970....	2,024	2,000	21,327	(NA)	(NA)	(NA)	(NA)		(NA)	780	347	21	105	(NA)
1975....	1,858	1,800	54,306	109	71	6	32		728	2,136	819	17	97	648
1980....	2,066	2,000	62,246	74	17	14	43		675	2,650	310	12	176	626
1985....	1,705	1,700	31,592	89	30	16	43		517	2,757	106	18	187	253
1989....	1,734	1,700	23,847	61	23	4	34		423	3,635	78	38	187	329
1990....	1,734	1,700	22,736	83	40	11	32		424	3,822	67	7	25	390

NA Not available.   [1] Data on deaths are from U.S. National Highway Traffic Safety Administration and are based on 30 day definition; see table 1008. Other data are from National Safety Council.   [2] Accidents which result in damages to railroad property. Grade crossing accidents are also included when classified as a train accident. Deaths exclude fatalities in railroad-highway grade crossing accidents.   [3] Includes scheduled and non-scheduled (charter) air carriers. Represents serious injuries.   [4] All scheduled service. Represents serious injuries.   [5] All non-scheduled service. Represents serious injuries.   [6] 1975 excludes commuter and on-demand air taxis.   [7] Accidents resulting in death; injury or requiring medical treatment beyond first aid; damages exceeding $200; or a person's disappearance.   [8] Pipeline accidents/incidents are credited to year of occurrence. Beginning 1985; prior data are credited to the year filed. Fatalities and injuries as reported in annual report.   [9] Pipelines carrying hazardous materials, petroleum, and liquid petroleum products.   [10] Covers accidents involving commercial vessels which must be reported to U.S. Coast Guard if there is property damage exceeding $1,500; material damage affecting the seaworthiness or efficiency of a vessel; stranding or grounding; loss of life; or injury causing a person's incapacity for more than 3 days.   [11] Accidents, deaths, and injuries involving hazardous materials cover all types of transport.   [12] Preliminary.

Source: U.S. Dept. of Transportation, Transportation Systems Center, Cambridge, MA, *Transportation Safety Information Report*, annual.

No. 990. Federal Outlays for Transportation, by Function: 1970 to 1991
[In millions of dollars. For fiscal years ending in year shown; see text, section 9]

FUNCTION	1970	1975	1980	1983	1984	1985	1986	1987	1988	1989	1990	1991, est.
Total outlays	7,008	10,918	21,329	21,334	23,669	25,838	28,117	26,222	27,272	27,608	29,485	31,099
Ground transportation .	4,678	7,027	15,274	14,265	16,158	17,606	18,725	17,150	18,148	17,946	18,954	19,545
Air transportation.....	1,408	2,387	3,723	4,000	4,415	4,895	5,287	5,520	5,897	6,622	7,234	8,184
Water transportation ...	895	1,430	2,229	2,969	3,010	3,201	3,964	3,461	3,111	2,916	3,151	3,148
Other transportation. . .	26	74	104	99	85	137	140	91	116	124	146	223

Source: U.S. Office of Management and Budget, *Budget of the United States Government*, annual.

No. 991. Expedited Domestic Package Express Volume and Growth: 1977 and 1988
[Year ended December 31. Represents the activity of domestic package express companies. Companies such as Federal Express Inc. and United Parcel Service Inc. Also includes package express services offered by trucking companies, the postal service, passenger airlines, freight forwarders, couriers, Amtrak, and bus companies. The Department of Transportation defines package express as the transpotation of parcels of 150 pounds or less, with overnight or second-day delivery]

EXPEDITED PACKAGE EXPRESS	Unit	1977	1988	Percent change 1977-88	Average annual percent change, 1977-88
Expedited package express, total:					
Shipments	Millions	628	3,176	406.6	40.6
Weight	Mil. lbs	9,409	37,258	296.0	29.6
Revenue	Mil. dol	2,487	20,771	741.9	74.2
Air: Shipments.................	Millions	81	544	571.8	57.2
Weight	Mil. lbs	4,485	8,914	98.7	9.9
Revenue	Mil. dol	1,384	11,403	724.1	72.4
Surface express: Shipments..........	Millions	547	2,632	381.0	38.1
Weight	Mil. lbs	4,924	28,344	475.6	47.6
Revenue	Mil. dol	1,083	9,368	764.8	76.5

Source: U.S. Department of Commerce, *Journal of Commerce.*

Transportation—Land

No. 992. Highway Mileage—Urban and Rural, by Type and Control, and Federal-Aid Highway System: 1970 to 1990

[In thousands, except percent. As of Dec. 31. Beginning 1980, data for urban and rural mileage are not comparable to prior years because of classification changes; see text, section 21. See also *Historical Statistics, Colonial Times to 1970*, series Q 50, 51, and 55]

TYPE AND CONTROL	1970	1975	1980	1983	1984	1985	1986	1987	1988	1989	1990
Total mileage [1]	3,730	3,838	[2]3,955	3,880	3,892	3,862	3,880	3,874	3,871	3,877	3,380
Urban mileage [3]	561	639	624	662	674	691	701	710	739	754	757
Under State control	74	84	79	100	103	111	94	95	97	97	96
Under local control	487	555	543	562	571	578	606	614	642	656	661
Rural mileage	3,169	3,199	[2]3,331	3,217	3,218	3,171	3,178	3,164	3,132	3,123	3,123
Percent surfaced [4]	76.1	77.6	77.5	86.0	87.5	88.1	88.4	88.4	88.1	88.4	88.6
Under State control	707	711	702	817	818	773	704	704	704	706	703
Under local control	2,275	2,261	2,270	2,138	2,134	2,173	2,243	2,249	2,244	2,238	2,242
Under Federal control	188	227	262	262	266	225	231	212	183	178	178
Fed.-aid highway system: [5]											
Primary (urban and rural) . .	272	266	300	300	300	301	303	302	304	304	305
Interstate	32	37	41	43	43	44	44	44	45	45	45
Urban	(X)	65	124	137	140	144	146	148	147	148	148
Secondary	647	643	398	397	398	398	398	398	400	400	400

X Not applicable. [1] Prior to 1980, includes public and nonpublic road mileage; beginning 1983, includes only public road mileage as defined 23 USC 402. [2] Includes 98,000 miles of nonpublic road mileage previously contained in other rural categories. [3] Prior to 1980, represents municipal mileage; see text, section 21. [4] Covers soil-surfaced roads and roads with slag, gravel, stone, bituminous, or concrete surfaces. [5] For definition, see text, section 21. Beginning 1980, data represent actual mileage open to traffic rather than total highway miles carrying interstate traffic.

Source: U.S. Federal Highway Administration, *Highway Statistics*, annual.

No. 993. Highway Mileage—Urban, Rural, and Federal-Aid Highway System: 1990

[As of Dec. 31. For definition of urban, rural, and Federal-aid highway system roads, see text, section 21]

STATE	Urban	Rural	FEDERAL-AID HIGHWAY SYSTEM [1]				STATE	Urban	Rural	FEDERAL-AID HIGHWAY SYSTEM [1]			
			Total		Urban	Sec-ondary				Total		Urban	Sec-ondary
			Pri-mary	Inter-state [2]						Pri-mary	Inter-state [2]		
U.S. .	757,363	3,122,788	305,347	45,074	147,680	399,974	MO . .	15,039	105,488	8,197	1,177	2,483	18,093
AL. . .	16,854	73,818	7,651	889	2,792	11,581	MT . .	2,271	69,116	6,645	1,191	342	4,744
AK . .	1,549	11,936	2,108	1,089	238	1,816	NE . .	4,952	87,451	7,675	481	1,064	11,458
AZ . .	14,667	36,945	5,276	1,169	1,833	3,256	NV . .	3,084	42,440	2,401	545	557	2,315
AR . .	7,677	69,408	5,757	542	1,160	7,374	NH . .	2,433	12,403	1,357	224	726	1,232
CA . .	73,922	89,652	13,477	2,399	17,791	11,176	NJ . .	22,502	11,750	1,875	396	5,388	1,687
CO . .	11,272	66,408	5,247	942	2,394	3,410	NM . .	5,498	49,238	4,888	1,000	573	3,640
CT . .	10,905	9,086	1,611	341	2,955	902	NY . .	37,913	73,329	9,946	1,500	8,733	6,293
DE . .	1,615	3,829	484	41	321	605	NC . .	19,245	75,445	5,381	937	2,995	10,325
DC . .	1,102	-	190	12	233	-	ND . .	1,811	84,706	6,110	570	501	10,628
FL. . .	48,034	60,051	9,436	1,426	4,603	4,396	OH . .	31,428	82,172	8,161	1,572	7,866	11,793
GA . .	21,728	87,873	11,367	1,245	3,982	14,011	OK . .	12,083	99,682	6,237	930	2,995	11,809
HI . . .	1,512	2,587	554	43	322	435	OR . .	8,410	86,559	5,773	727	2,056	7,817
ID . . .	2,429	60,006	3,362	605	725	4,057	PA . .	28,344	88,164	11,482	1,569	7,053	7,980
IL . . .	32,003	103,941	11,838	1,961	6,645	12,922	RI . . .	4,588	1,523	504	70	930	201
IN . . .	17,868	74,040	6,153	1,148	4,714	9,740	SC . .	9,343	54,703	6,473	791	1,168	8,534
IA . . .	8,786	103,755	9,535	782	2,443	13,566	SD . .	1,734	72,962	6,477	678	390	11,094
KS . .	9,105	124,473	8,922	872	1,651	22,655	TN . .	15,340	69,299	7,227	1,062	3,168	5,456
KY . .	7,692	61,976	4,609	763	2,008	7,172	TX . .	88,776	217,175	20,003	3,229	8,198	32,638
LA. . .	12,290	46,330	3,976	844	2,167	7,349	UT . .	5,575	37,669	3,553	938	927	2,706
ME . .	2,494	19,895	2,376	366	706	2,742	VT . .	1,180	12,941	1,444	320	349	1,913
MD . .	12,290	16,462	2,605	400	2,155	1,911	VA . .	15,251	52,449	6,489	1,076	3,450	10,200
MA . .	20,846	13,230	2,777	567	5,905	2,007	WA . .	16,260	65,039	5,782	759	4,236	7,320
MI . . .	26,676	90,773	8,454	1,227	5,466	17,059	WV . .	3,076	31,516	2,964	517	808	6,351
MN . .	14,208	115,189	10,208	905	2,256	16,604	WI . . .	14,395	95,481	9,966	640	2,982	13,040
MS . .	7,356	65,164	6,461	684	1,719	11,695	WY . .	1,952	37,261	3903	913	558	2,266

- Represents zero. [1] Highway mileage open to traffic. [2] Although the interstate system is part of the Federal-aid primary system, its mileage is shown separately.

Source: U.S. Federal Highway Administration, *Highway Statistics*, annual.

No. 994. Highway Pavement Condition, by Type of Road System: 1980 to 1990

[Highway pavement condition is classified by the Present Serviceability Rating (PSR) system (5.0 - 0.1). The reported ranges are defined as: PSR 5.0-3.5, pavements give a first class ride and exhibit few, if any, visible signs of surface wear. Of the quality of new or nearly new pavements. PSR 3.4-2.0, pavements have a riding quality somewhat inferior to that of new pavements or may even be barely tolerable at high speeds. Surfaces may show signs of cracking, substantial patching, and rutting. PSR 1.9-0.1, pavements show extensive wear to the point of needing resurfacing or may even need complete reconstruction]

PAVEMENT CONDITION	INTERSTATE ROAD				ARTERIAL ROAD				COLLECTOR ROAD			
	1980	1985	1989	1990	1980	1985	1989	1990	1980	1985	1989	1990
URBAN AREAS												
Percent of road mileage rated—												
PSR 0.1-1.9 (0.1-2.4) [1]	6	7	7	6	7	5	4	4	9	7	14	13
PSR 2.0-3.4 (2.5-3.4) [1]	26	38	36	35	42	53	54	52	50	58	54	55
PSR 3.5-5.0	68	55	57	59	51	42	42	44	41	35	32	32
RURAL AREAS												
Percent of road mileage rated—												
PSR 0.1-1.9 (0.1-2.4) [1]	5	7	7	6	6	4	3	2	16	10	9	8
PSR 2.0-3.4 (2.5-3.4) [1]	26	33	35	35	46	51	49	48	55	59	55	54
PSR 3.5-5.0	69	60	58	59	48	45	48	50	29	31	36	38

[1] PSR range shown in parentheses applies to Interstate roads only.

No. 995. Receipts and Disbursements for Highways, by Type: 1970 to 1991

[In millions of dollars. Data compiled from reports of State and local authorities. For Federal highway trust fund receipts, disbursements, and balances, see table 493. State data include District of Columbia]

TYPE	1970	1980	1985	1988	1989	1990, prel.	1991, proj.		
							Total [1]	Federal	State
Total receipts.	21,747	39,715	61,506	69,002	72,775	73,919	79,995	17,215	40,635
Current income.	19,861	37,604	54,957	64,593	67,623	68,547	74,577	17,215	37,437
Imposts on highway users [2]	15,311	22,559	35,599	41,588	44,079	44,172	48,994	15,286	32,163
Other taxes and fees	3,732	11,808	15,127	18,158	17,987	18,438	19,714	873	3,151
Investment income, other receipts. . . .	818	3,237	4,231	4,847	5,557	5,937	5,869	1,056	2,123
Bond issue proceeds [3]	1,886	2,111	6,549	4,409	5,152	5,372	5,418	(X)	3,198
Intergovernmental payments . . . ,.	(X)	(X)	(X)	(X)	(X)	(X)	(X)	-14035	5,650
Funds from (+) or to (-) reserves [4].	-912	2,080	-4058	-393	-1852	966	-2874	-2333	-47
Total funds available.	20,835	41,795	57,448	68,609	70,923	74,885	77,121	847	46,238
Total disbursements.	20,835	41,795	57,448	68,609	70,923	74,885	77,121	847	46,238
Current disbursements.	19,583	40,084	54,725	66,044	67,311	71,573	73,787	847	44,364
Capital outlay	11,575	20,337	27,138	32,982	33,204	35,481	36,236	410	26,316
Maintenance and traffic services.	4,720	11,445	16,032	18,969	18,952	19,742	21,643	112	8,861
Administration and research.	1,275	3,022	4,033	5,124	5,683	6,355	5,707	325	3,477
Law enforcement and safety	1,303	3,824	5,334	6,142	6,647	6,922	7,105	-	3,830
Interest on debt	710	1,456	2,188	2,827	2,825	3,073	3,096	-	1,880
Debt retirement [3]	1,252	1,711	2,723	2,565	3,612	3,312	3,334	-	1,874

- Represents zero.   X Not applicable.   [1] Includes other levels of government not shown separately.   [2] Excludes amounts later allocated for nonhighway purposes.   [3] Par value. Excludes issue and redemption of short-term notes or refunding bonds. Premiums and discounts on sale of bonds and accrued interest are investment income and other receipts. Redemption premiums and discounts are included with interest on debt.   [4] Plus sign (+) indicates net receipt of funds from other levels of government; minus sign (-) indicates net disbursement of funds to other levels.

Source of tables 994 and 995: U.S. Federal Highway Administration, *Highway Statistics,* annual; and releases.

No. 996. Disbursements of State Highway Funds, by State: 1980 to 1990

[In millions of dollars. Comprises disbursements from current revenues or loans for construction, maintenance, interest and principal payments on highway bonds, transfers to local units, and miscellaneous. Includes transactions by State toll authorities. Excludes amounts allocated for collection and nonhighway purposes, and bonds redeemed by refunding. See also *Historical Statistics, Colonial Times to 1970,* series Q 90-94]

STATE	1980	1985	1990	STATE	1980	1985	1990	STATE	1980	1985	1990
U.S.	30,049	40,891	53,536	KY	913	901	1,008	OH.	1,032	1,622	2,271
AL	517	875	866	LA	682	879	923	OK.	461	668	827
AK	274	383	336	ME.	164	238	332	OR.	482	492	765
AZ	365	778	1,525	MD.	663	988	1,464	PA	1,557	2,340	2,885
AR	405	408	166	MA.	704	786	1,055	RI	72	139	214
CA	1,930	3,006	4,294	MI	997	1,275	1,526	SC	309	420	585
CO	411	563	714	MN.	611	980	1,228	SD.	151	211	232
CT	393	565	1,204	MS.	468	845	529	TN	609	800	1,174
DE	152	234	315	MO	555	854	937	TX	1,882	1,825	3,001
DC	57	142	273	MT.	224	286	302	UT.	241	394	355
FL	1,261	1,647	1,677	NE	274	358	449	VT	87	135	165
GA	762	1,115	1,278	NV	169	241	309	VA	894	1,165	1,874
HI	134	137	297	NH.	152	219	299	WA	787	1,040	1,251
ID	153	229	300	NJ	662	1,229	1,831	WV	672	582	605
IL	1,652	2,087	2,645	NM.	197	384	409	WI	468	669	979
IN	688	919	1,218	NY	1,650	2,022	2,874	WY	192	298	297
IA	504	746	869	NC	807	986	1,428				
KS	440	506	697	ND.	143	199	189				

Source: U.S. Federal Highway Administration, *Highway Statistics,* annual.

No. 997. Federal Grants to State and Local Governments for Highway Trust Fund and Urban Mass Transportation Administration (UMTA), by State: 1990

[Year ending Sept. 30]

STATE	HIGHWAY TRUST FUND Total (mil. dol.)	Per cap-ita [1]	UMTA Total (mil. dol.)	Per cap-ita [1]	STATE	HIGHWAY TRUST FUND Total (mil. dol.)	Per cap-ita [1]	UMTA Total (mil. dol.)	Per cap-ita [1]	STATE	HIGHWAY TRUST FUND Total (mil. dol.)	Per cap-ita [1]	UMTA Total (mil. dol.)	Per cap-ita [1]
U.S.	13,557	54.5	3,731	15.0	KS...	162	65.3	7	2.7	ND...	70	110.2	2	2.9
AL...	292	72.3	15	3.6	KY...	161	43.6	11	3.1	OH...	404	37.2	109	10.1
AK...	160	291.1	2	2.8	LA...	302	40		9.5	OK...	175	55.6	14	4.4
AZ...	186	50.8	26	7.1	ME...	66	53.9	11	8.9	OR...	159	55.9	29	10.1
AR...	128	54.6	7	2.8	MD...	365	76.3	96	20.1	PA...	759	63.9	179	15.1
CA...	1,344	45.2	488	16.4	MA...	181	30.1	134	22.3	RI...	126	125.8	8	8.3
CO...	250	75.9	28	8.6	MI...	356	38.3	57	6.2	SC...	161	46.1	11	3.3
CT...	391	119.0	46	14.0	MN...	281	64.1	34	7.7	SD...	95	136.8	2	2.6
DE...	40	60.1	4	6.4	MS...	124	48.3	7	2.8	TN...	271	55.5	18	3.6
DC...	67	110.5	324	534.2	MO...	272	53.1	67	13.1	TX...	1,026	60.4	108	6.4
FL...	478	37.0	93	7.2	MT...	96	120.0	2	3.0	UT...	121	70.3	22	12.7
GA...	387	59.7	87	13.5	NE...	103	65.6	8	5.4	VT...	55	97.4	2	3.1
HI...	125	112.5	14	13.1	NV...	90	74.9	5	4.6	VA...	316	51.1	32	5.2
ID...	126	125.2	3	2.8	NH...	56	50.2	3	2.8	WA...	401	82.3	71	14.6
IL...	502	44.0	324	28.4	NJ...	354	45.8	222	28.7	WV..	108	60.5	6	3.6
IN...	259	46.8	28	2.0	NM...	96	63.3	11	7.2	WI...	222	45.3	33	6.8
IA...	186	67.1	17	6.0	NY...	604	33.6	843	46.8	WY...	111	245.7	2	4.9
					NC...	386	58.2	17	2.6					

[1] Based on Bureau of the Census resident population as of April 1, 1990.

Source: U.S. Bureau of the Census, *Federal Expenditures by State for Fiscal Year*, annual.

No. 998. State Gasoline Tax Rates, 1990 and 1991, and Motor Fuel Tax Receipts, 1990

[See also *Historical Statistics, Colonial Times to 1970*, series Q 233-234]

STATE	RATE [1] (cents/gal.) 1990	1991	Re-ceipts, [2] 1990 (mil. dol.)	STATE	RATE [1] (cents/gal.) 1990	1991	Re-ceipts, [2] 1990 (mil. dol.)	STATE	RATE [1] (cents/gal.) 1990	1991	Re-ceipts, [2] 1990 (mil. dol.)
Federal .	14.1	14.1	(NA)	KS ...	16.0	17.0	225	ND...	17.0	17.0	69
State...	(NA)	(NA)	(NA)	KY [3]	15.4	15.4	357	OH...	20.0	21.0	1,043
AL...	13.0	13.0	352	LA...	20.0	20.0	452	OK [4].	17.0	17.0	316
AK...	8.0	8.0	25	ME...	17.0	19.0	121	OR...	18.0	20.0	244
AZ...	18.0	18.0	344	MD...	18.5	18.5	444	PA...	17.8	22.4	1,018
AR...	13.7	18.7	215	MA...	17.0	21.0	347	RI...	20.0	26.0	84
CA...	9.0	15.0	1,324	MI...	15.0	15.0	668	SC...	16.0	16.0	348
CO...	20.0	22.0	320	MN...	20.0	20.0	437	SD ...	18.0	18.0	80
CT...	22.0	25.0	306	MS...	18.2	18.2	282	TN [5]	20.0	20.0	610
DE...	16.0	19.0	64	MO...	11.0	11.0	358	TX...	15.0	20.0	1,511
DC...	18.0	18.0	30	MT...	20.0	20.0	105	UT...	19.0	19.0	166
FL...	10.9	11.2	701	NE...	21.7	23.8	204	VT ...	16.0	16.0	56
GA...	7.5	7.5	329	NV...	18.0	21.5	149	VA [3]	17.7	17.7	612
HI...	11.0	16.0	45	NH...	16.6	18.6	84	WA...	22.0	23.0	538
ID...	18.0	21.0	106	NJ...	10.5	10.5	408	WV..	20.4	20.4	152
IL...	19.0	19.0	1,059	NM...	17.0	17.0	159	WI...	21.5	22.2	539
IN...	15.0	15.0	579	NY...	14.4	20.8	529	WY...	9.0	9.0	43
IA...	20.0	20.0	318	NC...	21.5	22.6	833				

NA Not available. [1] In effect Dec. 31. [2] Represents net gallonage receipts. [3] Trucks or combinations with more than 2 axles pay tax of 2 cents per gallon more in Kentucky, and 3.5 cents per gallon more in Virginia. [4] .08 cents per gallon is for inspection fee. [5] Includes 1 cent per gallon inspection fee.

No. 999. Public Highway Debt—State and Local Governments: 1970 to 1991

[In millions of dollars. Long-term obligations. State data are for calendar years; local data for varying fiscal years. Excludes duplicated and interunit obligations. Municipal debt includes other political subdivisions urban in character. See also *Historical Statistics, Colonial Times to 1970*, series Q 136-147]

ITEM	1970	1980	1983	1984	1985	1986	1987	1988	1989	1990 [1]	1991 [2]
Total debt issued [3] ...	1,886	2,094	2,566	3,151	6,074	6,296	3,802	4,261	5,268	5,413	5,418
State............	1,305	1,128	1,072	1,715	3,404	3,946	1,927	2,384	3,096	3,233	3,198
County and township ...	174	276	475	524	1,387	1,200	451	567	650	580	800
Municipal	407	690	1,019	912	1,283	1,150	1,424	1,310	1,522	1,600	1,420
Total debt redeemed [4].	1,252	1,706	2,172	2,411	2,737	3,132	2,685	2,735	3,606	3,302	3,478
State.............	782	1,022	1,191	1,507	1,580	1,875	1,625	1,396	2,063	1,602	2,070
County and township ...	152	209	303	216	378	432	349	353	618	750	375
Municipal	318	475	678	688	779	825	711	986	925	950	1,033
Total debt outstanding .	19,107	25,851	27,224	27,964	31,301	34,465	36,565	38,091	39,716	41,827	43,767

[1] Preliminary. [2] Projection. [3] Excludes refunding issues. [4] Excludes redemptions by refunding.

Source of tables 998 and 999: U.S. Federal Highway Administration, *Highway Statistics*, annual.

No. 1000. Motor Vehicles—Summary: 1980 to 1990

ITEM	Unit	1980	1984	1985	1986	1987	1988	1989	1990
Passenger car production	1,000. . .	6,376	7,773	8,185	7,829	7,099	7,113	6,823	6,077
Passenger car factory sales . . . . , . . .	1,000. . .	6,400	7,621	8,002	7,516	7,085	7,105	6,807	6,050
Passenger car (new), retail sales [1] . . .	1,000. . .	8,979	10,390	11,042	11,460	10,277	10,530	9,772	9,300
Domestic [2]	1,000. . .	6,581	7,952	8,205	8,215	7,081	7,526	7,073	6,897
Subcompact [3]	1,000. . .	1,604	2,322	1,297	1,325	1,101	1,019	926	(NA)
Compact [3]	1,000. . .	1,659	1,336	2,563	2,461	2,389	2,781	2,606	(NA)
Standard [3]	1,000. . .	1,358	1,817	1,882	1,888	1,565	1,722	1,629	(NA)
Intermediate [3]	1,000. . .	1,957	2,484	2,464	2,540	2,026	2,017	1,916	(NA)
Imports [4]	1,000. . .	2,398	2,439	2,838	3,245	3,196	3,004	2,699	2,403
Truck and bus production	1,000. . .	1,634	3,151	3,468	3,506	3,826	4,101	4,051	3,703
Truck and bus factory sales	1,000. . .	1,667	3,075	3,357	3,393	3,821	4,121	4,062	3,719
Truck and bus retail sales [5]	1,000. . .	2,232	3,538	3,984	4,031	4,174	4,608	4,483	4,261
Light duty (up to 14,000 GVW) [6]	1,000. . .	1,964	3,261	3,700	3,766	3,885	4,273	4,171	3,984
Med. duty (14,001-26,000 GVW) [6]	1,000. . .	92	61	53	51	55	83	73	71
Heavy duty (over 26,000 GVW) [6]	1,000. . .	176	216	231	214	234	251	239	207
Motorcycle registrations, new [7]	1,000. . .	876	772	722	631	550	410	294	269
Motorcycle (new) retail sales [8]	1,000. . .	1,070	1,305	1,260	1,075	970	710	515	462
All-terrain vehicles.	1,000. . .	(NA)	550	550	480	405	290	200	145
All-terrain vehicle imports	1,000. . .	(NA)	635	683	498	320	210	121	100
Motorcycle imports, total [9]	1,000. . .	1,120	441	733	550	318	287	253	169
Value [10]	Mil. dol. .	1,142	523	783	763	463	512	542	361
Passenger cars(new), exported [1][11] . . .	1,000. . .	617	616	704	673	633	781	778	794
Passenger cars (new), imported [1][12] . .	1,000. . .	3,116	3,559	4,398	4,691	4,589	4,450	4,043	3,945
Canada	1,000. . .	595	1,073	1,145	1,162	927	1,191	1,151	1,220
Germany, Federal Republic of	1,000. . .	339	335	473	452	378	264	217	245
Japan	1,000. . .	1,992	1,949	2,527	2,619	2,418	2,123	2,052	1,868
Trucks (new) exports	1,000. . .	186	159	183	205	222	230	189	151
Trucks (new) imports [12]	1,000. . .	747	1,025	1,253	1,351	1,177	938	953	766
Japan	1,000. . .	483	567	800	976	772	542	420	302
Import value, new passenger cars [1] . . .	Mil. dol. .	16,675	29,264	36,474	45,302	47,858	47,005	44,417	45,716
Trucks and buses, new [1]	Mil. dol. .	1,985	6,541	7,734	8,504	8,729	8,089	8,591	8,155
Export value [1][13]	Mil. dol. .	16,015	20,776	22,820	21,955	24,812	29,519	31,574	38,086
Passenger cars (new) [13]	Mil. dol. .	3,932	4,876	6,027	6,258	6,695	8,318	8,895	9,708
Trucks and buses (new) [13]	Mil. dol. .	2,977	2,479	2,789	2,953	3,375	3,683	3,471	2,845
Parts and accessories [14]	Mil. dol. .	9,106	13,421	14,004	12,744	14,742	17,518	19,208	24,996
Cars in use, total	Million .	104.6	112.0	114.7	117.3	119.8	121.5	122.8	123.3
Under 3 years.	Million .	26.8	22.0	24.8	27.9	28.1	27.8	27.1	26.0
3-5 years.	Million .	25.5	26.8	23.9	22.7	24.7	27.7	30.5	30.5
6-8 years.	Million .	25.2	26.8	27.8	26.5	24.4	21.6	20.7	22.6
9-11 years.	Million .	14.6	17.4	17.2	18.7	21.4	22.4	21.1	19.1
12 years and over	Million .	12.5	19.0	21.0	21.5	21.2	22.0	23.4	25.1
Average age.	Years .	6.6	7.5	7.6	7.6	7.6	7.6	7.6	7.8
Cars retired from use [15]	1,000. . .	8,405	6,675	7,729	8,442	8,103	8,754	8,981	8,897
Trucks in use, total	Million .	35.2	40.1	42.4	44.8	47.3	50.2	53.2	56.0
Under 3 years.	Million .	8.8	7.2	9.0	11.1	11.9	12.5	12.5	12.8
3-5 years.	Million .	8.1	8.0	6.3	6.6	8.3	10.3	12.6	13.2
6-8 years.	Million .	7.4	9.2	10.2	8.9	7.4	5.9	6.3	8.0
9-11 years.	Million .	4.4	6.2	6.2	6.7	8.0	8.9	7.9	6.6
12 years and over	Million .	6.5	9.6	10.7	11.5	11.8	12.6	14.0	15.5
Average age.	Years .	7.1	8.2	8.1	8.0	8.0	7.9	7.9	8.0
Trucks retired from use [15]	1,000. . .	1,732	1,602	2,100	2,309	2,364	2,251	2,189	2,177
Tires, passenger car, total [16]	Million .	145.9	201.6	200.9	202.7	210.8	218.8	214.8	213.6
Radials.	Million .	83.5	156.6	164.7	174.0	187.3	200.2	200.4	202.1
Replacement	Million .	106.9	144.6	141.5	144.3	151.9	155.3	151.2	152.3
Tires, truck and bus, total [16]	Million .	31.1	40.8	41.1	40.6	44.4	46.0	46.9	46.9
Radials.	Million .	3.8	16.0	19.7	21.1	26.0	29.4	30.6	32.5
Replacement	Million .	24.4	31.7	32.1	32.4	34.5	33.9	35.2	36.6
Batteries, total [17]	Million .	61.7	74.7	74.4	75.7	75.7	80.1	80.3	79.7
Replacement automobile batteries . .	Million .	50.1	59.3	58.7	60.3	59.9	63.5	64.4	65.2

NA Not available. [1] Based on data from U.S. Dept. of Commerce. [2] Includes domestic models produced in Canada and Mexico. [3] Source: Board of Governors of the Federal Reserve System, unpublished data. Represents total auto sales data from Ward's Automotive Reports. Criteria by which each year's car models are grouped into the major size categories vary among those collecting data. Data shown here follow Automotive News classifications. Beginning 1987, data from Wards Automotive Yearbooks. Beginning 1980, cars produced in U.S. by foreign manufacturers are included. [4] Excludes domestic models produced in Canada. [5] Excludes motorcoaches and light-duty imports from foreign manufacturers. Beginning 1980, includes imports sold by franchised dealers of U.S. manufacturers. Starting in 1986, includes sales of trucks over 10,000 lbs. GVW by foreign manufacturers. [6] Gross vehicle weight (fully loaded vehicle). [7] Source: R. L. Polk & Company, Detroit, MI, New Motorcycle Registrations by States. 1980-1986 excludes Oklahoma; 1984, excludes New York. Reproduction prohibited without Polk permission. [8] Estimates by Motorcycle Industry Council Inc., Irvine, CA. Includes all-terrain vehicles and scooters. Excludes mopeds/motorized bicycles. [9] Source: Motorcycle Industry Council, Inc., Irvine, CA. Data from U.S. Dept. of Commerce. Excludes mopeds/motorized bicycles and all-terrain vehicles. Excludes moped imports (motorcycle imports less than 51 cc's) from all countries (except Japan). [10] Dutiable value for customs purposes prior to 1980, thereafter, c.i.f. value. [11] Beginning 1980, includes chassis. [12] Includes other countries, not shown separately. [13] Covers assembled and unassembled vehicles. [14] Includes rubber tires and tubes and used vehicles. [15] For years ending June 30. Represents vehicles failing to re-register. [16] Includes original equipment. Also includes exports, not shown separately. Source: The Rubber Manufacturers Association, Inc., Washington, D.C., RMA Monthly Tire Report. [17] Source: Battery Council International, Chicago, IL, and U.S. Bureau of the Census.

Source: Except as noted, Motor Vehicle Manufacturers Association of the United States, Inc., Detroit, MI, Motor Vehicle Facts and Figures, annual; and World Motor Vehicle Data, annual.

No. 1001. Motor Vehicle Registrations, 1980 to 1990, Vehicle Miles of Travel, 1990, and Drivers Licenses, 1990, by State

[In thousands, except as indicated. Motor vehicle registrations cover publicly, privately, and commercially owned vehicles. For uniformity, figures have been adjusted to a calendar-year basis as registration years in States differ; figures represent net numbers where possible, excluding re-registrations and nonresident registrations]

STATE	AUTOMOBILES, TRUCKS, AND BUSES [1]					1990				
				1990		Public road and street mileage (1,000 mi.)	Vehicle miles of travel		Drivers licenses	Motor-cycles [1] (incl. official)
	1980	1985	1989	Total	Automobiles (incl. taxis)		Total (bil. mi.)	Per mile of road (1,000)		
U.S.	155,796	171,654	188,261	188,655	143,026	3,880	2,147.0	553	167,015	4,259
AL.	2,938	3,338	3,623	3,744	2,733	91	42.3	466	2,753	44
AK.	262	353	364	477	302	14	4.0	296	314	12
AZ.	1,917	2,235	2,775	2,825	2,002	52	35.5	688	2,393	80
AR.	1,574	1,384	1,433	1,448	934	77	21.0	272	1,722	15
CA.	16,873	18,899	21,671	21,926	16,972	164	258.9	1,583	19,846	641
CO	2,342	2,759	3,154	3,155	2,300	78	27.2	350	2,043	108
CT.	2,147	2,465	2,651	2,623	2,472	20	26.3	1,315	2,214	51
DE.	397	465	522	526	406	5	6.5	1,204	485	9
DC.	268	326	259	262	245	1	3.4	3,091	412	3
FL.	7,614	9,865	11,207	10,950	8,695	108	110.0	1,018	9,231	206
GA	3,818	4,580	5,270	5,489	3,834	110	72.7	663	4,478	74
HI	570	651	736	771	672	4	8.1	1,976	678	20
ID	834	854	1,039	1,054	636	62	9.8	157	704	42
IL	7,477	7,727	8,022	7,873	6,300	136	83.3	613	7,295	180
IN	3,826	4,024	4,322	4,366	3,197	92	53.7	584	3,601	97
IA	2,329	2,696	2,583	2,632	1,880	113	23.0	204	1,872	173
KS.	2,007	2,148	1,987	2,012	1,405	134	22.8	171	1,715	76
KY.	2,593	2,615	2,843	2,909	1,915	70	33.6	482	2,402	35
LA.	2,779	3,012	2,976	2,995	1,998	59	37.7	643	2,575	30
ME	724	840	939	977	742	22	11.9	531	887	38
MD	2,803	3,276	3,527	3,607	2,970	29	40.5	1,406	3,362	56
MA	3,749	3,738	3,804	3,726	3,224	34	46.1	1,352	4,229	56
MI	6,488	6,727	7,139	7,209	5,613	117	81.1	691	6,440	177
MN	3,091	3,385	3,283	3,508	2,742	129	38.9	301	2,529	122
MS	1,577	1,746	1,867	1,875	1,434	73	24.4	337	1,885	26
MO	3,271	3,558	3,844	3,905	2,760	121	50.9	422	3,688	68
MT	680	652	741	783	457	71	8.3	116	604	22
NE.	1,254	1,257	1,362	1,384	913	92	14.0	152	1,089	22
NV.	655	709	826	853	592	46	10.2	224	846	19
NH	704	974	936	946	751	15	9.8	662	843	40
NJ.	4,761	4,909	5,636	5,652	5,180	34	58.9	1,717	5,585	86
NM	1,068	1,176	1,295	1,301	806	55	16.1	294	1,074	33
NY.	8,002	9,042	10,021	10,196	8,831	111	106.9	961	10,254	198
NC	4,532	4,450	5,113	5,162	3,677	95	62.7	662	4,551	57
ND	627	655	636	630	372	87	5.9	68	425	20
OH	7,771	8,102	9514	8,410	6,818	114	87.0	766	7,427	228
OK	2,583	2,864	2,568	2,649	1,711	112	33.1	296	2,278	61
OR	2,081	2,204	2,379	2,445	1,839	95	26.7	281	2,212	64
PA.	6,926	7,209	7,909	7,971	6,384	117	85.7	736	7,899	173
RI	623	610	671	672	563	6	7.0	1,148	671	24
SC.	1,996	2,222	2,469	2,521	1,878	64	34.4	538	2,373	31
SD.	601	650	705	704	425	75	7.0	94	492	30
TN.	3,271	3,754	4,316	4,444	3,553	85	46.7	552	3,334	80
TX.	10,475	12,444	12,565	12,800	8,714	306	162.2	530	11,137	174
UT.	992	1,099	1,175	1,206	789	43	14.6	338	1,046	28
VT.	347	398	462	462	342	14	5.8	411	412	18
VA.	3,626	4,253	4,860	4,938	3,776	68	60.2	889	4,389	62
WA	3,225	3,526	4,090	4,257	2,979	81	44.7	550	3,377	119
WV	1,320	1,143	1,214	1,225	753	35	15.4	445	1,284	22
WI	2,941	3,187	3,471	3,672	2,757	110	44.3	403	3,328	189
WY	467	500	487	528	309	39	5.8	148	334	20

[1] Excludes vehicles owned by military services.

Source: U.S. Federal Highway Administration, *Highway Statistics*, annual; and *Selected Highway Statistics and Charts*, annual.

No. 1002. Motor Vehicles—Registrations, Factory Sales, and Retail Sales: 1960 to 1990

[For definition of average annual percent change, see Guide to Tabular Presentation. See also *Historical Statistics, Colonial Times to 1970*, series Q 148-155]

YEAR	REGISTRATION [1] (mil.)			Motor-cycle regis-trat-ions [1] (1,000)	FACTORY SALES (1,000)			RETAIL SALES (1,000)					
	Total cars, trucks, buses	Pas-senger cars [2]	Trucks and buses		Total cars, trucks, buses	Pas-senger cars	Trucks and buses [3]	Passenger cars			Trucks		
								Total	Do-mestic	Imports	Total	Do-mestic	Imports
1960	74	62	12	574	7,869	6,675	1,194	6,641	6,142	499	963	926	37
1965	90	75	15	1,382	11,057	9,306	1,752	9,332	8,763	569	1,553	1,539	14
1970	108	89	19	2,824	8,239	6,547	1,692	8,400	7,119	1,280	1,811	1,746	65
1975	133	107	26	4,964	8,985	6,713	2,272	8,624	7,053	1,571	2,478	2,249	229
1976	139	110	28	4,933	11,480	8,500	2,979	10,110	8,611	1,498	3,181	2,944	237
1977	142	112	30	4,881	12,642	9,201	3,441	11,183	9,109	2,074	3,675	3,352	323
1978	148	117	32	4,868	12,871	9,165	3,706	11,314	9,312	2,002	4,109	3,773	336
1979	152	118	33	5,422	11,456	8,419	3,037	10,673	8,341	2,332	3,480	3,010	470
1980	156	122	34	5,694	8,067	6,400	1,667	8,979	6,581	2,398	2,487	2,001	486
1981	158	123	35	5,831	7,956	6,255	1,701	8,536	6,209	2,327	2,260	1,809	451
1982	160	124	36	5,754	6,955	5,049	1,906	7,982	5,759	2,224	2,560	2,146	414
1983	164	126	37	5,585	9,153	6,739	2,414	9,182	6,795	2,387	3,129	2,658	471
1984	166	128	38	5,480	10,696	7,621	3,075	10,390	7,952	2,439	4,093	3,475	618
1985	172	132	40	5,444	11,359	8,002	3,357	11,042	8,205	2,838	4,682	3,902	780
1986	176	135	41	5,262	10,909	7,516	3,393	11,460	8,215	3,245	4,863	3,921	942
1987	179	137	42	4,886	10,907	7,085	3,821	10,277	7,081	3,196	4,912	4,055	857
1988	184	141	43	4,584	11,225	7,105	4,121	10,530	7,526	3,004	5,149	4,508	641
1989	187	143	44	4,434	10,869	6,807	4,062	9,772	7,073	2,699	4,941	4,403	538
1990	189	144	45	4,259	9,769	6,050	3,719	9,301	6,897	2,404	4,846	4,215	631

[1] Includes publicly owned vehicles. Excludes military vehicles.   [2] Includes taxis.   [3] Includes standard equipment.

Source: Registrations—U.S. Federal Highway Administration, *Selected Highway Statistics and Charts*, annual; sales—Motor Vehicle Manufacturers Association of the United States, Inc., Detroit, MI, *MVMA Motor Vehicle Facts and Figures*, annual.

No. 1003. Automobile Output and Trade in National Income Accounts: 1970 to 1990

[In billions of current and constant (1982) dollars, except percent. Vehicle output equals final dollar sales value of new vehicles, plus net dollar value of used vehicle sales adjusted for changes in inventories and net balance of vehicle exports and imports]

ITEM	1970	1975	1980	1984	1985	1986	1987	1988	1989	1990
Current dollar auto output	**28.5**	**40.3**	**59.2**	**104.2**	**115.8**	**120.4**	**118.9**	**129.1**	**133.9**	**130.3**
Final sales	29.7	41.9	60.1	101.0	111.3	118.9	112.1	128.1	132.2	135.0
Personal consumption expenditures	26.8	36.8	57.2	98.7	111.7	125.7	121.6	131.6	132.5	132.4
New autos	21.9	29.3	46.4	77.6	87.4	100.3	93.5	101.0	100.0	96.6
Net purchases of used autos	4.8	7.4	10.8	21.2	24.3	25.4	28.2	30.5	32.5	35.8
Producers' durable equipment	5.3	8.6	14.3	26.2	27.7	30.2	28.9	32.3	31.2	35.5
New autos	7.6	12.6	20.8	40.2	44.0	46.1	45.1	51.2	49.7	55.0
Net purchases of used autos	-2.3	-3.9	-6.5	-14.0	-16.3	-15.9	-16.2	-18.9	-18.6	-19.6
Net exports	-2.9	-4.2	-12.8	-25.8	-30.0	-39.0	-40.6	-38.0	-33.7	-35.4
Exports	0.8	2.9	4.0	4.9	6.1	6.3	7.4	9.0	10.8	10.5
Imports	3.7	7.1	16.8	30.7	36.1	45.3	47.9	47.1	44.5	45.9
Government purchases	0.5	0.7	1.4	2.0	2.0	2.0	2.1	2.2	2.3	2.5
Change in business inventories (new and used) .	-1.2	-1.5	-0.9	3.2	4.5	1.5	6.8	1.0	1.6	-4.7
New	-1.0	-1.9	-0.1	2.6	4.0	1.4	6.3	0.2	0.9	-4.2
Used	-0.1	0.4	-0.8	0.6	0.5	0.1	0.5	0.9	0.8	-0.6
Addenda:										
Domestic output of new autos [1]	23.8	33.7	49.3	87.1	95.9	98.1	95.5	101.9	104.9	99.7
Sales of imported new autos [2]	5.8	10.4	21.8	38.5	45.7	55.4	55.1	60.5	57.5	59.3
Constant dollar auto output	**65.4**	**74.8**	**79.1**	**115.8**	**125.0**	**124.4**	**118.9**	**127.3**	**127.1**	**121.1**
Final sales	68.3	78.5	80.5	113.1	120.7	124.8	112.1	126.7	125.4	126.5
Personal consumption expenditures	68.3	73.5	80.9	111.4	122.4	133.3	121.6	129.6	126.2	124.9
New autos	47.4	53.3	60.2	86.4	94.5	103.9	93.5	99.1	96.1	91.5
Net purchases of used autos	20.9	20.3	20.8	25.0	27.9	29.4	28.2	30.5	30.1	33.4
Producers' durable equipment	10.0	14.8	16.8	31.8	32.2	31.7	28.9	31.9	30.1	33.1
New autos	16.4	22.8	26.9	44.7	47.6	47.8	45.1	50.2	47.8	52.1
Net purchases of used autos	-6.3	-8.0	-10.1	-13.0	-15.4	-16.1	-16.2	-18.3	-17.6	-19.0
Net exports	-11.5	-11.4	-19.2	-32.4	-36.1	-42.3	-40.6	-37.0	-33.1	-33.8
Exports	1.8	5.2	5.3	5.5	6.5	6.5	7.4	8.9	9.5	9.7
Imports	13.3	16.6	24.5	37.9	42.6	48.8	47.9	45.8	42.6	43.6
Government purchases	1.5	1.5	2.0	2.3	2.2	2.1	2.1	2.2	2.2	2.3
Change in business inventories of new and used.	-3.0	-3.7	-1.5	2.7	4.3	-0.4	6.8	0.6	1.7	-5.3
New	-2.6	-4.5	-0.1	2.3	3.9	-0.5	6.3	-0.3	0.9	-4.8
Used	-0.3	0.8	-1.3	0.5	0.4	0.1	0.5	0.9	0.8	-0.5
Addenda:										
Domestic output of new autos [1]	51.7	61.6	64.6	97.9	104.7	102.1	95.5	99.9	100.0	93.5
Sales of imported new autos [2]	11.7	17.9	27.5	41.5	47.9	55.7	55.1	59.3	55.3	56.2

[1] Consists of final sales and change in business inventories of new autos assembled in the United States.   [2] Consists of personal consumption expenditures, producers' durable equipment, and government purchases.

Source: U.S. Bureau of Economic Analysis, *The National Income and Product Accounts of the United States, 1929-82*, and *Survey of Current Business*, July issues.

No. 1004. New Trucks—Retail Sales, by Weight Class and Type: 1980 to 1989

WEIGHT CLASS AND TYPE	NUMBER (1,000)							PERCENT CHANGE			
	1980	1985	1986	1987	1988	1989	1990	1986-1987	1987-1988	1988-1989	1989-1990
Total	2,232	3,984	4,031	4,174	4,608	4,483	4,261	3.5	10.4	-2.7	-5.0
Under 6,000 pounds	985	2,408	2,541	2,696	2,926	2,854	2,866	6.1	8.5	-2.4	0.4
Utility.	51	429	387	403	445	447	490	4.0	10.5	0.6	9.6
Pickup, conventional.	545	644	582	566	593	600	614	-2.8	4.8	1.2	2.3
Pickup, compact	254	696	757	861	901	840	786	13.7	4.7	-6.8	-6.4
Domestic.	26	625	679	795	848	811	774	17.2	6.7	-4.4	-4.6
Import (U.S. manufactures). . .	229	70	79	66	53	29	12	-16.7	-18.8	-45.6	-58.6
Van	79	115	112	89	47	43	31	-20.5	-47.0	-8.5	-27.9
Mini van (cargo).	(X)	103	110	101	105	97	83	-8.2	4.0	-7.8	-14.4
Station wagon (truck chassis). . .	(X)	86	98	108	138	138	112	11.1	27.6	-	-18.8
Mini passenger carrier	(X)	301	460	546	692	688	750	18.8	26.6	-0.5	9.0
6,000 to 10,000 pounds [1] . .	975	1,280	1,214	1,175	1,333	1,297	1,097	-3.2	13.4	-2.7	-15.4
Utility.	108	108	101	91	90	93	68	-9.6	-1.2	3.0	-26.9
Van	172	261	261	254	302	289	254	-2.8	19.0	-4.2	-12.1
Pickup, conventional.	546	628	582	569	666	663	568	-2.2	17.0	-0.4	-14.3
Station wagon (truck chassis). . .	39	95	98	91	104	100	85	-7.5	14.3	-4.2	-15.0
10,001 pounds and over . .	271	295	276	302	349	331	298	9.6	15.3	-5.0	-10.0

- Represents zero.   X Not applicable.   [1] Includes vehicles not shown separately.

Source: Motor Vehicle Manufacturers Association, Detroit, MI, *Motor Vehicle Facts and Figures*, annual.

No. 1005. New Car Buyers—Characteristics, by Type of Vehicle Purchased: 1990

[In percent, except as indicated. Based on Newsweek's survey of 33,780 buyers of 1990 new cars. Forty-three percent of new car buyers responded]

CHARACTERISTIC	All cars	Domestic	Asian	European	CHARACTERISTIC	All cars	Domestic	Asian	European
Household income:					Education:				
Less than $35,000	31	34	27	7	High school or less. . . .	31	37	18	15
$35,000-$49,999	22	22	22	10	Some college	27	27	28	19
$50,000-$74,999	22	22	23	20	College graduate or				
$75,000 and over.	24	22	28	63	more.	39	34	51	65
Mean ($1,000)	62.6	59.5	65.5	116.4					
Median ($1,000).	48.1	46.2	50.9	96.0	Employed	74	70	84	82
Sex: Male	56	57	52	62					
Female.	44	43	48	38	Occupation				
Age: Under 25 years	8	7	10	3	(Base=Employed):				
25-54 years	59	54	70	70	Prof./manager	64	61	68	84
55 years and over	33	38	20	27	Blue collar	15	18	11	5
Median (years).	44.6	47.6	40.3	42.9					

Source: Newsweek, Inc., New York, NY, *1990 Buyers of New Cars*. (Copyright. All rights reserved. Reprinted by permission.)

No. 1006. Recreational Vehicles—Number and Retail Value of Shipments: 1970 to 1990

ITEM	1970	1975	1980	1982	1983	1984	1985	1986	1987	1988	1989	1990
NUMBER (1,000)												
Total	380.3	339.6	181.4	258.0	358.0	398.2	359.2	379.5	400.2	427.3	395.7	354.5
Motorized homes	30.3	96.6	99.9	152.5	223.7	257.3	233.5	249.6	255.7	277.1	261.6	226.5
Travel trailers	138.0	150.6	52.0	65.5	90.0	92.4	82.9	86.0	92.8	96.9	90.3	87.6
Folding camping trailers	116.1	48.1	24.5	34.3	37.5	40.9	35.9	36.5	41.6	42.3	33.9	30.7
Truck campers	95.9	44.3	5.0	5.7	6.8	7.6	6.9	7.4	10.1	11.0	9.9	9.7
RETAIL VALUE (mil. dol.)												
Total	1,122	2,320	1,952	3,505	6,324	7,610	7,029	7,564	8,400	9,188	9,027	8,223
Motorized homes	318	1,251	1,381	2,701	5,099	6,262	5,724	6,155	6,826	7,543	7,420	6,660
Travel trailers	445	856	485	666	1,067	1,157	1,122	1,213	1,331	1,381	1,378	1,342
Folding camping trailers	175	101	69	110	122	145	137	144	167	175	147	134
Truck campers	183	112	17	28	36	46	46	53	76	88	81	86

Source: Recreation Vehicle Industry Association, Reston, VA, *RVs ... A Year-End Report/1989*. Data also in Motor Vehicle Manufacturers Association of the United States, Inc., Detroit, MI, *Motor Vehicle Facts and Figures*, annual.

No. 1007. Motorcycles—Travel, Registration, and Fuel Consumption: 1970 to 1989

ITEM	Unit	1970	1975	1980	1982	1983	1984	1985	1986	1987	1988	1989
Vehicle-miles of travel.	Million .	2,979	5,629	10,214	9,910	8,760	8,784	9,086	9,397	9,506	10,024	10,371
Number of registered vehicles . . .	1,000 .	2,824	4,964	5,694	5,754	5,585	5,480	5,444	5,199	4,917	4,584	4,434
Average travel per vehicle	Miles. .	1,055	1,134	1,794	1,722	1,568	1,603	1,669	1,807	1,933	2,187	2,339
Fuel consumption, total	Mil. gal	59.6	112.6	204.3	198.2	175.2	175.7	181.7	187.9	190.1	200.5	207.4
Average per vehicle.	Gallon .	21	23	36	34	31	32	33	36	39	44	47

Source: U.S. Federal Highway Administration, *Highway Statistics Summary to 1985* and *Highway Statistics*, annual.

No. 1008. Motor Vehicle Accidents—Number and Deaths: 1970 to 1990

[See also *Historical Statistics, Colonial Times to 1970,* series Q 208 and Q 224-232]

ITEM	Unit	1970	1972 [1]	1980	1985	1986	1987	1988	1989	1990
Motor vehicle accidents [2]	Million .	16.0	17.0	17.9	19.3	17.7	20.8	20.6	12.8	11.5
Cars	Million .	23.5	24.5	22.8	25.6	27.7	25.9	28.2	15.3	14.3
Trucks	Million .	3.2	3.5	5.5	6.1	6.1	6.0	6.8	6.5	4.4
Motorcycles	1,000 .	305	343	560	480	440	380	370	211	180
Motor vehicle deaths within 1 yr. [3]	1,000 .	54.6	56.3	53.2	45.9	47.9	48.3	49.1	47.1	46.3
Noncollision accidents	1,000 .	15.4	15.8	14.7	12.6	13.1	5.2	5.3	5.0	4.9
Collision accidents:										
With other motor vehicles	1,000 .	23.2	23.9	23.0	19.9	20.8	20.7	20.9	20.0	19.4
With pedestrians	1,000 .	9.9	10.3	9.7	8.5	8.9	7.5	7.7	7.6	7.4
With fixed objects	1,000 .	3.8	3.9	3.7	3.2	3.3	13.2	13.4	12.6	12.9
Deaths within 30 days [4]	1,000 .	52.6	54.6	51.1	43.8	46.1	46.4	47.1	45.6	(NA)
Vehicle occupants	1,000 .	40.6	41.4	36.8	31.5	33.7	34.5	35.5	34.9	(NA)
Pedestrians	1,000 .	9.0	9.2	8.1	6.8	6.8	6.7	6.9	6.6	(NA)
Motorcyclists [5]	1,000 .	2.3	3.0	5.1	4.6	4.6	4.0	3.7	3.1	(NA)
Bicyclists	1,000 .	0.8	1.0	1.0	0.9	0.9	0.9	0.9	0.8	(NA)
Traffic death rates: [4][6]										
Per 100,000 resident population	Rate . .	25.8	26.2	22.6	18.4	19.1	19.1	19.2	18.4	(NA)
Per 100,000 registered vehicles	Rate . .	47.3	44.5	31.6	24.8	25.4	25.2	24.9	23.6	(NA)
Per 100 million vehicle miles	Rate . .	4.7	4.3	3.3	2.5	2.5	2.4	2.3	2.2	(NA)
Per 100,000 licensed drivers	Rate . .	47.2	46.1	35.2	27.9	28.9	28.7	28.9	27.6	(NA)
Motor vehicle accidents [7]	Million .	22.1	24.9	24.1	32.5	33.3	33.9	34.2	34.4	33.4
Injuries [7]	1,000 .	4,983	5,190	5,230	5,044	5,300	5,400	5,500	5,560	5,560
Economic loss [7][8]	Bil. dol.	23.5	28.7	57.1	76.0	80.0	85.0	89.0	93.9	95.9

NA Not available. [1] Represents peak year for deaths from motor vehicle accidents. [2] Covers only accidents occurring on the road. [3] Deaths that occur within one year of accident. Includes collision categories not shown separately. [4] Within 30 days of accident. Source: U.S. National Highway Traffic Safety Administration, unpublished data from Fatal Accident Reporting System. [5] Includes motor scooters and motorized bicycles (mopeds). [6] Based on 30-day definition of traffic deaths. [7] Source: Insurance Information Institute, New York, NY, *Insurance Facts.* Estimates based on official reports from a representative cross-section of States. Includes all motor vehicle accidents on and off the road and all injuries regardless of length of disability. 1986 data for economic loss based on information from the National Center for Health Statistics, National Health Survey. [8] Wage loss; legal, medical, hospital, and funeral expenses; insurance administrative costs; and property damage.

Source: Except as noted, National Safety Council, Itasca, IL, *Accident Facts,* annual (copyright).

No. 1009. Motor Vehicle Deaths, by State: 1985 to 1990

[Includes both traffic and nontraffic motor vehicle deaths. See source for definitions]

STATE	1985	1988	1989	1990	MILEAGE RATE [1]		STATE	1985	1988	1989	1990	MILEAGE RATE [1]	
					1985	1990						1985	1990
U.S. . . .	**45,901**	**49,391**	**47,100**	**46,300**	**2.6**	**2.2**	DC. . .	96	123	75	55	3.0	1.6
							VA. . .	1,021	1,093	999	1,073	2.1	1.8
Northeast.	**6,797**	**7,412**	**6,708**	**6,243**	**(NA)**	**(NA)**	WV . .	461	491	468	481	3.6	3.2
N.E.	**1,873**	**1,960**	**1,702**	**1,528**	**(NA)**	**(NA)**	NC. . .	1,553	1,669	1,464	1,383	3.1	2.3
ME. . .	224	268	190	212	2.4	1.8	SC. . .	943	1,012	996	983	3.5	2.9
NH. . .	198	175	190	158	2.6	1.6	GA. . .	1,462	1,756	1,632	1,563	2.7	2.0
VT. . .	117	129	116	89	2.5	1.5	FL . . .	2,968	3,247	3,016	2,951	3.4	2.7
MA. . .	761	750	700	607	1.9	1.3	**E.S.C. . .**	**3,664**	**4,196**	**3,616**	**3,868**	**(NA)**	**(NA)**
RI . . .	124	145	100	84	2.1	1.3	KY . . .	749	843	782	850	2.6	2.6
CT. . .	449	493	406	378	2.0	1.5	TN . . .	1,219	1,404	1,081	1,172	3.4	2.6
M.A. . . .	**4,924**	**5,452**	**5,006**	**4,715**	**(NA)**	**(NA)**	AL . . .	1,005	1,158	1,025	1,095	2.9	2.6
NY . .	2,121	2,345	2,239	2,183	2.3	2.0	MS. . .	691	791	728	751	3.6	3.2
NJ . . .	986	1,079	890	886	1.9	1.5	**W.S.C. . .**	**6,197**	**5,753**	**5,521**	**5,405**	**(NA)**	**(NA)**
PA . . .	1,817	2,028	1,877	1,646	2.4	1.9	AR . . .	580	667	648	604	3.4	2.9
Midwest. .	**9,760**	**10,874**	**9,993**	**9,601**	**(NA)**	**(NA)**	LA . . .	1,011	946	857	912	3.0	2.5
E.N.C . .	**6,602**	**7,417**	**6,871**	**6,509**	**(NA)**	**(NA)**	OK. . .	781	649	655	646	2.5	2.0
OH. . .	1,581	1,755	1,700	1,550	2.1	1.8	TX . . .	3,825	3,491	3,361	3,243	2.7	2.0
IN . . .	1,045	1,142	973	1,044	2.6	1.8	**West . . .**	**10,352**	**10,803**	**9,847**	**9,944**	**(NA)**	**(NA)**
IL. . . .	1,594	1,925	1,748	1,589	2.3	1.9	**Mt. . . . .**	**3,409**	**3,371**	**3,100**	**3,098**	**(NA)**	**(NA)**
MI . . .	1,605	1,749	1,633	1,563	2.4	1.9	MT. . .	233	215	181	212	3.1	2.5
WI . . .	777	846	817	763	2.1	1.8	ID . . .	268	278	238	243	3.5	2.9
W.N.C . .	**3,158**	**3,457**	**3,122**	**3,092**	**(NA)**	**(NA)**	WY . .	145	159	127	125	2.7	2.2
MN. . .	657	675	605	568	2.0	1.5	CO. . .	628	544	522	543	2.4	1.9
IA . . .	478	556	511	459	2.4	2.1	NM. . .	561	538	538	499	4.2	3.1
MO . . .	1,005	1,163	1,052	1,006	2.6	2.3	AZ . . .	942	1,003	884	863	4.4	2.5
ND. . .	117	121	81	112	2.2	1.9	UT. . .	335	313	303	270	2.8	2.0
SD. . .	142	160	151	153	2.3	2.3	NV. . .	297	321	307	343	3.9	3.6
NE . . .	259	288	296	262	2.1	1.9	**Pac. . . .**	**6,943**	**7,432**	**6,747**	**6,846**	**(NA)**	**(NA)**
KS . . .	500	494	426	442	2.6	2.1	WA . .	786	817	781	825	2.3	1.9
South. . . .	**19,250**	**20,302**	**18,655**	**18,631**	**(NA)**	**(NA)**	OR. . .	605	726	630	578	2.8	2.2
S.A.	**9,389**	**10,353**	**9,518**	**9,358**	**(NA)**	**(NA)**	CA . . .	5,294	5,632	5,105	5,173	2.6	2.0
DE. . .	119	169	118	143	2.2	2.2	AK . . .	124	104	84	95	3.2	2.1
MD. . .	766	793	750	726	2.3	1.9	HI . . .	134	153	147	175	2.0	2.3

NA Not available. [1] Deaths per 100 million vehicle miles.

Source: 1985: National Center for Health Statistics; thereafter, National Safety Council, Itasca, IL, *Accident Facts, 1991,* (copyright).

No. 1010. Fatal Motor-Vehicle Accidents, by Type of Vehicle: 1980 to 1990

[Based on data from the Fatal Accident Reporting System]

TYPE OF VEHICLE	ACCIDENTS [1]					OCCUPANT FATALITIES				
	1980	1985	1988	1989	1990	1980	1985	1988	1989	1990
Total [2]	**45,284**	**39,195**	**42,130**	**60,834**	**59,193**	**41,927**	**36,043**	**39,170**	**38,087**	**37,081**
Passenger cars [3]	31,550	27,142	29,534	35,384	33,972	27,455	23,214	25,808	25,063	24,025
Mini-compact	3,263	3,973	4,445	4,145	4,207	2,966	3,429	3,794	3,481	3,523
Subcompact	4,875	5,445	6,137	6,144	5,949	4,158	4,422	4,945	4,785	4,698
Compact	1,118	3,445	6,122	6,751	7,198	927	2,635	4,764	4,987	5,272
Intermediate	5,224	6,064	6,941	7,037	6,959	3,878	4,391	5,016	4,943	4,833
Full size	7,026	4,906	4,490	4,024	3,824	4,831	2,974	2,840	2,569	2,363
Largest size	10,817	6,452	5,095	4,476	3,988	6,746	3,612	2,904	2,534	2,247
Unknown	5,134	2,699	2,378	2,807	1,847	3,943	1,751	1,515	1,747	1,089
Motorcycles	4,879	4,342	3,480	3,194	3,270	5,144	4,564	3,662	3,036	3,238
Moped, mini bike	180	151	164	76	86	183	147	170	71	83
Light trucks [2]	10,841	10,470	12,626	13,801	15,601	7,486	6,689	8,306	8,551	8,593
Pickup	8,796	8,375	9,629	10,262	10,272	5,463	4,886	5,880	5,864	5,951
Van	2,009	1,807	2,378	2,563	2,419	1,000	791	1,001	1214	1,079
Medium and heavy trucks	5112	4871	4936	4,982	4,761	1261	971	911	857	704
Single-unit heavy trucks [4]	377	370	406	442	443	89	48	68	66	58
Two-unit [5]	3,396	3,411	3,256	(NA)	(NA)	812	692	607	(NA)	(NA)
Multi-unit	148	182	253	(NA)	(NA)	41	31	43	(NA)	(NA)
Buses	329	304	284	311	288	46	55	54	50	32

NA Not available.   [1] Each accident involving multiple types of vehicles is recorded in each category; therefore, the aggregate of all types will exceed the total number of accidents.   [2] Includes other types and unknown, not shown separately.   [3] Mini-compact wheel base less than 95 in.; subcompact, 95 in. to 99 in.; compact, 100 in. to 104 in.; intermediate, 105 in. to 109 in.; full size, 110-114 in.; and largest size greater than 115 in.   [4] Gross vehicle weight greater than 26,000 lbs.   [5] Tractor-trailer combination.

Source: U.S. National Highway Traffic Safety Administration, *Fatal Accident Reporting System,* annual.

No. 1011. Highway Mileage, Vehicle Miles of Travel, Accidents, and Fatalities, 1975 to 1989, and by Type of Highway System, 1990

YEAR AND TYPE OF SYSTEM	Highway mileage (1,000)	Vehicle miles of travel (bil.)	Daily vehicle miles per mile	FATAL ACCIDENTS		NONFATAL INJURY ACCIDENTS		FATALITIES [2]	
				Number	Rate [1]	Number (1,000)	Rate [1]	Number	Rate [1]
1975	3,838	1,328	948	39,993	3.01	1,861	140	45,500	3.43
1980	3,857	1,527	1,082	45,284	2.96	2,008	131	51,091	3.35
1985	3,862	1,774	1,259	39,168	2.21	2,219	125	43,795	2.47
1986	3,880	1,835	1,298	41,062	2.23	2,254	123	46,056	2.51
1987	3,874	1,921	1,361	41,434	2.15	2,294	119	46,385	2.41
1988	3,871	2,026	1,430	42,119	2.08	2,302	114	47,093	2.32
1989	3,877	2,096	1,489	40,718	1.93	2,384	113	45,555	2.16
1990, total	**3,880**	**2,148**	**1,516**	**39,779**	**1.85**	**2,501**	**116**	**44,529**	**2.07**
Urban	757	1,277	4,620	17,382	1.36	1,833	143	18,750	1.47
Rural	3,123	870	764	22,397	2.57	669	77	25,779	2.96
interstate	45	479	29,114	4,223	0.88	185	34	4,941	1.03
Urban	12	278	66,171	1,965	0.71	121	43	2,228	0.80
Rural	34	201	16,380	2,258	1.13	44	22	2,713	1.35
Noninterstate	3,921	1,669	1,166	35,556	2.13	2,337	140	39,588	2.37
Urban	746	999	3,669	15,417	1.54	1,712	171	16,522	1.65
Rural	3,089	670	594	20,139	3.01	625	93	23,066	3.44
Federal-aid highway system	853	1,733	5,568	30,063	1.73	1,593	92	33,962	1.96
Urban	193	1,022	14,474	13,704	1.34	1,181	116	14,850	1.45
Rural	660	712	2,956	16,359	2.30	411	58	19,112	2.69
Interstate	45	479	29,114	4,223	0.88	185	34	4,941	1.03
Other primary arterial	260	614	6,468	11,919	1.94	515	84	13,743	2.24
Urban	34	287	22,988	3,716	1.30	314	109	4,081	1.42
Rural	226	328	3,969	8,203	2.50	201	81	9,662	2.95
Urban (arterial and collector)	148	456	8,457	8,023	1.76	747	164	8,541	1.87
Secondary (collector)	340	184	1,258	5,898	3.21	166	90	6,737	3.67
Non-Federal-aid highway system	3,027	414	375	9,716	2.35	909	219	10,567	2.55
Arterial	10	35	9,235	410	1.16	24	69	476	1.35
Urban	8	32	10,798	216	0.68	22	70	232	0.73
Rural	2	4	4,147	194	5.21	2	56	244	6.56
Collector	353	85	661	2,110	2.48	93	110	2,318	2.72
Urban	23	27	3,263	222	0.82	28	104	234	0.87
Rural	330	58	482	1,888	3.25	65	112	2,084	3.58
Local	2,664	294	302	7,196	2.45	791	269	7,773	2.65
Urban	533	197	1,011	3,240	1.65	601	305	3,434	1.75
Rural	2,130	97	125	3,958	4.08	190	196	4,339	4.48

[1] Rate per 100 million vehicle miles of travel.   [2] Represents fatalities occurring within 30 days of accident. Excludes nontraffic accidents which, for example, occur outside the rights-of-way or other boundaries of roads that are open for public use.

Source: U.S. Federal Highway Administration, *Fatal and Injury Accident Rates on Public Roads in the United States,* annual.

No. 1012. State Legislation—Alcohol and Road Safety Laws: Various Years

STATE	ALCOHOL LEGISLATION			MANDATORY BELT USE LAW			Child safety seat law date [5]	Motorcycle helmet law [6]	65 SPEED LIMIT	
	21 year drinking age since [1]	Open container law [2]	BAC limit [3]	Effective date	Enforcement [4]	Seating positions			Effective date [7]	Applicable vehicles
Northeast:										
N.E:										
ME	1985	no	0.08	none	(X)	(X)	9/83	[8][9]15	6/87	all
NH	1985	no	0.10	none	(X)	(X)	(1)	18	4/87	all
VT	1986	no	0.10	none	(X)	(X)	7/84	yes	4/87	all
MA	1985	no	0.10	repealed	(X)	(X)	1/82	yes	none	(X)
RI	1984	no	[10]0.10	none	(X)	(X)	7/87	([11])	none	(X)
CT	1985	no	0.10	1/86	1	front	1982	18	none	(X)
M.A:										
NY	1990	no	(NA)	12/84	1	front	4/82	yes	none	(X)
NJ	1982	no	0.10	3/85	2	front	4/83	yes	none	(X)
PA	1935	no	0.10	11/87	2	front	11/83	yes	none	(X)
Midwest:										
E.N.C:										
OH	1987	yes	[10]0.10	5/86	2	front	6/83	[9]18	7/87	some
IN	1935	no	0.10	7/87	2	front	1/84	18	6/87	some
IL	1980	yes	0.10	7/85	2	front	7/83	no	4/87	some
MI	1978	yes	(NA)	7/85	2	front	3/82	yes	12/87	some
WI	1986	yes	[10]0.10	12/87	2	front	4/84	[8]18	6/87	all
W.N.C:										
MN	1986	yes	0.10	8/86	2	front	8/83	[8]18	6/87	all
IA	1986	yes	0.10	7/86	1	front	1/85	no	5/87	all
MO	1945	no	0.10	9/85	2	front	1/84	yes	4/87	some
ND	1936	yes	0.10	none	(X)	(X)	1/84	18	4/87	all
SD	1987	yes	0.10	none	(X)	(X)	7/84	18	4/87	all
NE	1985	no	0.10	repealed	(X)	(X)	8/83	yes	4/87	all
KS	1985	yes	0.10	7/86	2	front	7/81	18	5/87	some
South:										
S.A:										
DE	1983	yes	0.10	none	(X)	(X)	6/82	[8][12]19	none	(X)
MD	1982	no	0.10	7/86	2	[13]front	1/84	18	none	(X)
DC	1986	no	0.10	12/85	2	[13]front	7/83	yes	none	(X)
VA	1986	yes	0.10	1/88	2	front	1/83	yes	7/88	some
WV	1986	yes	0.10	none	(X)	(X)	7/81	yes	5/87	all
NC	1986	yes	0.10	10/85	1	front	7/85	yes	4/87	all
SC	1986	yes	0.10	7/89	2	front	1/89	21	7/87	all
GA	1986	no	0.12	9/88	2	front	7/84	yes	2/88	all
FL	1985	yes	0.10	7/86	2	front	7/83	yes	4/87	all
E.S.C:										
KY	1938	no	0.10	none	(X)	(X)	7/82	yes	6/87	all
TN	1984	no	0.10	4/86	2	front	1/78	yes	5/87	all
AL	1985	no	0.10	none	(X)	(X)	1982	yes	1987	all
MS	1986	no	0.10	3/90	1	front	7/83	yes	4/87	all
W.S.C:										
AR	1957	no	0.10	none	(X)	(X)	8/83	yes	4/87	all
LA	1987	no	0.10	7/86	2	front	1/85	yes	4/87	all
OK	1983	yes	0.10	2/87	2	front	11/83	18	4/87	all
TX	1985	no	0.10	9/85	1	front	1/85	yes	5/87	some
West:										
Mt:										
MT	1987	no	(NA)	10/87	2	all	10/83	18	4/87	all
ID	1987	[14]Yes	0.10	7/86	2	front	1/85	18	5/87	all
WY	1988	no	0.10	6/89	2	front	4/85	18	5/87	all
CO	1987	no	0.10	7/87	2	front	1/84	no	4/87	all
NM	1934	yes	0.10	1/86	1	front	5/83	18	4/87	all
AZ	1984	no	0.10	1/91	2	front	1984	18	4/87	all
UT	1935	yes	0.08	4/86	2	front	4/83	18	5/87	all
NV	1933	no	0.10	7/87	2	all	7/83	yes	4/87	all
Pac										
WA	1934	yes	0.10	6/86	2	all	1/84	yes	4/87	some
OR	1935	yes	[10]0.08	12/90	1	all	1/84	yes	10/87	some
CA	1933	yes	0.08	1/86	2	all	1/83	15.5	5/87	some
AK	1983	yes	0.10	9/90	2	front	7/85	19	none	(X)
HI	1986	Yes	0.10	12/85	1	front	1983	18	none	(X)

X Not applicable. [1] Year in which original law became effective, not when grandfather causes expired. [2] Law prohibiting open liquor containers in motor vehicles. [3] Percent blood alcohol concentration (BAC) which constitutes the threshold of legal intoxication. [4] "1" indicates primary enforcement (law can be enforced on its own), "2" indicates secondary enforcement. (Law enforced only if vehicle stopped for a separate offense). [5] Effective data of original law, not of subsequent revisions. [6] Presence of law or age below which riders are required to wear helmet. [7] Includes administrative action as well as legislation. [8] Plus instruction permit holders. [9] Plus novice license holders. [10] Different legal limit for minors. [11] Passengers only. [12] Possession of helmet required by all. [13] Excluding front center seat. [14] Does not include beer.

Source: National Safety Council, Itasca, IL, *Accident Facts*, annual.

No. 1013. Motor Vehicle Safety Defect Recalls, by Domestic and Foreign Manufacturers: 1980 to 1989

[Covers manufacturers reporting to U.S. National Highway Traffic Administration under section 151 of National Traffic and Motor Vehicle Safety Act of 1966, as amended]

MANUFACTURER	Unit	1980	1981	1982	1983	1984	1985	1986	1987	1988	1989
Motor vehicles:											
Total recall											
campaigns [1]	Number	167	156	135	140	164	173	174	199	197	237
Domestic	Number.	129	128	107	110	127	137	139	150	152	182
Foreign.	Number.	38	28	28	30	37	36	35	49	45	55
Total vehicles											
recalled	1,000 ..	4,863	9,405	1,914	6,114	7,220	5,629	2,880	9,091	4,486	7,033
Domestic	1,000 ..	3,939	7,379	1,401	3,090	6,283	4,995	1,731	7,297	3,171	6,070
Vehicles recalled by											
Four leading auto											
manufacturers	1,000 ..	3,730	7,247	1,324	3,021	6,148	4,811	1,382	6,945	[2]2,900	5,842
Foreign.	1,000 ..	924	2,026	513	3,024	937	634	1,149	1,793	1,315	963
Motor vehicle tires:											
Recall campaigns [1]	Number.	24	25	17	21	16	19	14	16	12	11
Tires recalled	1,000 ..	7,070	125	131	95	81	28	164	43	214	115

[1] A recall campaign is the notification to the Secretary of the U.S. Dept. of Transportation and to owners, purchasers, and dealers, of a motor vehicle safety defect.   [2] Three leading automobile manufacturers.

Source: U.S. National Highway Traffic Safety Administration, *Motor Vehicles Defect Recall Campaigns*, annual.

No. 1014. Licensed Drivers and Estimated Arrests for Driving Under the Influence, by Age: 1975 and 1986

[**Total drivers and arrests in thousands.** Represents licensed drivers and arrests for those 16 years old and over]

AGE	1975			1986			Percent change in rate, 1975-86
	Drivers	Arrests	Arrests per 100,000 drivers	Drivers	Arrests	Arrests per 100,000 drivers	
Total	129,671	946	729	158,494	1,792	1,130	55
Percent distribution	100.0	100.0	(X)	100.0	100.0	(X)	(X)
16 to 17 years old	3.7	1.8	352	2.6	1.5	647	84
18 to 24 years old	18.9	25.3	979	15.7	28.8	2,075	112
25 to 29 years old	12.9	15.0	847	13.0	22.0	1,909	125
30 to 34 years old	10.3	12.2	867	12.2	15.8	1,471	70
35 to 39 years old	8.5	10.6	909	10.9	11.1	1,158	27
40 to 44 years old	7.9	9.8	904	8.5	7.2	968	7
45 to 49 years old	8.0	8.9	812	6.9	4.9	805	-1
50 to 54 years old	7.9	7.3	675	6.3	3.4	609	-10
55 to 59 years old	6.8	4.6	490	6.3	2.4	434	-11
60 to 64 years old	5.7	2.7	347	5.9	1.6	299	-14
65 years old and over	9.5	1.8	141	11.9	1.2	118	-16

X Not applicable.

Source: U.S. Bureau of Justice Statistics, *Drunk Driving, Special Report.*

No. 1015. Licensed Drivers, Fatal Motor-Vehicle Accidents, and Alcohol Involvement, by Age of Driver: 1989

ITEM	Unit	Total	AGE OF DRIVER							
			16-17 years	18-21 years	22-24 years	25-34 years	35-44 years	45-54 years	55-64 years	65 years and over
Licensed drivers (estimated) [1]	1,000..	164,912	4,146	12,248	10,859	41,089	34,126	22,477	18,897	21,070
Percent distribution	Percent .	100.0	2.5	7.4	6.6	24.9	20.7	13.6	11.5	12.8
Licensed drivers involved in fatal accidents	Number .	60,398	2,900	8,537	5,709	15,919	10,100	6,031	4,200	5,426
Percent distribution	Percent .	100.0	4.8	14.1	9.5	26.4	16.7	10.0	7.0	9.0
Drinking drivers involved in fatal accidents	Number .	19,256	568	3,210	2,567	6,400	3,161	1,442	762	548
Percent distribution	Percent .	100.0	2.9	16.7	13.3	33.2	16.4	7.5	4.0	2.8

[1] Source: U.S. Federal Highway Administration, *Selected Highway Statistics and Charts*, annual.

Source: Except as noted, U.S. National Highway Traffic Safety Administration, unpublished data from the Fatal Accident Reporting System.

No. 1016. Police-Reported Traffic Crashes, by Age Group: 1990

[Based on probability sample of police-reported crashes. See source for details]

Item	Total	15 yrs. and under	16 to 20 yrs.	21 to 24 yrs.	25 to 34 yrs.	35 to 44 yrs.	45 to 54 yrs.	55 to 64 yrs.	65 yrs. and older
Crash-involved.	11,253,000	40,000	1,962,000	1,398,000	3,041,000	2,095,000	1,153,000	750,000	815,000
Percent male	62.0	67.0	62.0	63.0	62	60	62	63	63
Percent female	38.0	33.0	38.0	37.0	38	40	38	37	37
Percent alcohol-involved	4.0	4.0	4.0	6.0	6	4	3	2	1
Passengers injured or killed	1,033,000	236,000	246,000	108,000	180,000	96,000	60,000	46,000	61,000
Percent male	41.0	[1]42.0	[2]45.0	50.0	43	36	31	19	[3]19
Percent female	59.0	[1]58.0	[2]55.0	50.0	57	64	69	81	[3]81
Pedestrians injured or killed	109,000	[1]34,000	[2]13,000	[4]9,000	(NA)	[5]34,000	[6]10,000	(NA)	10,000
Percent during day. . . .	63.0	[1]75.0	[7]49.0	[4]35.0	(NA)	[5]56.0	[6]71.0	(NA)	76.0
Percent at night.	37.0	[1]25.0	[7]51.0	[4]65.0	(NA)	[5]44.0	[6]29.0	(NA)	24.0
Pedalcyclists injured or killed	77,000	[1]31,000	[7]14,000	[4]10,000	(NA)	[5]17,000	(NA)	(NA)	[8]5,000

NA Not available.   [1] 14 years and under.   [2] 15 to 20 years.   [3] 65 to 74 years.   [4] 20 to 24 years.   [5] 25 to 44 years.   [6] 45 to 64 years.   [7] 15 to 19 years.

Source: U.S. National Highway Traffic Safety Administration, *General Estimates System,* annual.

No. 1017. Cost of Owning and Operating an Automobile: 1975 to 1990

ITEM	Unit	1975	1980	1985	1986	1987	1988	1989	1990
Cost per mile [1]	Cents	18.31	27.95	27.20	29.59	32.64	33.40	38.20	41.0
Cost per 10,000 miles [1] . . .	Dollars. . . .	1,831	2,795	2,720	2,959	3,264	3,341	3,820	41.0
Variable cost	Cents/mile .	6.45	7.62	8.04	6.52	7.20	7.60	7.90	8.4
Gas and oil.	Cents/mile .	4.82	5.86	6.16	4.48	4.80	5.20	5.20	5.4
Maintenance.	Cents/mile .	0.97	1.12	1.23	1.37	1.60	1.60	1.90	2.1
Tires	Cents/mile .	0.66	0.64	0.65	0.67	0.80	0.80	0.80	0.9
Fixed cost	Dollars. . . .	1,186	2,033	2,441	2,596	2,782	3,061	3,534	[2]3,256
Insurance.	Dollars. . . .	383	490	503	509	535	573	663	675
License and registration	Dollars. . . .	30	82	115	130	140	139	151	165
Depreciation	Dollars. . . .	773	1,038	1,253	1,320	1,506	1,784	2,094	2,357
Finance charge	Dollars. . . .	(NA)	423	570	637	601	565	626	680

NA Not available.   [1] Beginning 1985, not comparable to previous data.   [2] Not comparable to previous years. Ownership costs based on a 6 year or 60,000 mile retention cycle.

Source: Motor Vehicle Manufacturers Association of the United States, Inc., Detroit, MI, *Motor Vehicle Facts and Figures,* annual.

No. 1018. New Car Prices and Consumer Expenditures per New Car: 1970 to 1990

[In dollars, except as indicated]

YEAR	CONSUMER EXPENDITURE PER NEW CAR [1]			ESTIMATED AVG. NEW CAR PRICE FOR A 1967 "COMPARABLE CAR"			WEEKS OF MEDIAN FAMILY INCOME TO EQUAL	
							Cost of comparable car	
	Domestic	Import	Average	With added safety and emissions equipment [2]	Without added safety and emissions equipment [3]	Average new car expend. [4]	With added safety and emissions equipment [5]	Without added safety and emissions equipment [6]
1970	3,708	2,648	3,542	3,601	3,459	18.7	19.0	18.2
1980	7,609	7,482	7,574	6,863	5,764	18.7	17.0	14.3
1985	11,733	12,875	12,022	8,984	6,958	23.0	17.2	13.3
1989	14,959	16,127	15,292	10,248	7,825	24.5	16.4	12.5
1990	15,641	17,010	16,012	10,581	7,938	24.5	16.2	12.2

[1] Average transaction price per new car.   [2] 1967 "average consumer expenditures per new car" plus the value of added safety and emissions equipment, all inflated to current dollars.   [3] 1967 average consumer expenditure per new car inflated to current dollars.   [4] Average consumer expenditures divided by annual median family income multiplied by 52 weeks.   [5] Estimated average new car price of comparable cars with new safety equipment added, divided by annual median family income, multiplied by 52 weeks. This index is a good reflection of price as seen by the car purchasers who would not otherwise buy safety/emissions equipment.   [6] Estimated average new car price of comparable cars without new safety and emissions equipment divided by annual median family income, multiplied by 52 weeks. This index is a good reflection of price as seen by purchasers who place full value on new safety/emissions equipment.

Source: Motor Vehicle Manufacturers Association of the United States, Inc., Detroit, MI *Motor Vehicle Facts and Figures,* annual.

No. 1019. Domestic Motor Fuel Consumption, by Type of Vehicle: 1970 to 1990

[Comprises all fuel types used for propulsion of vehicles under State motor fuels laws. Excludes Federal purchases for military use. Minus sign (-) indicates decrease. See also *Historical Statistics, Colonial Times to 1970*, series Q 156-162]

YEAR	FUEL CONSUMPTION					AVG. FUEL CONSUMPTION PER VEHICLE (gal.)			AVG. MILES PER GALLON		
	All vehicles (bil. gal.)	Avg. annual percent change [1]	Cars [2] (bil. gal.)	Buses [3] (bil. gal.)	Trucks [4] (bil. gal.)	Cars [2]	Buses [3]	Trucks [4]	Cars [2]	Buses [3]	Trucks [4]
1970 ..	92.3	5.4	67.8	0.8	23.6	760	2,172	1,257	13.52	5.54	7.85
1975 ..	109.0	2.5	76.4	1.1	31.4	716	2,279	1,217	13.52	5.75	8.99
1980 ..	115.0	-5.9	71.9	1.0	41.9	591	1,926	1,243	15.46	5.95	9.54
1981 ..	114.5	-0.4	71.0	1.1	42.2	576	1,938	1,219	15.94	5.92	9.59
1982 ..	113.4	-0.9	70.1	1.0	42.1	566	1,756	1,191	16.65	5.93	9.80
1983 ..	116.1	2.4	69.9	0.9	45.1	553	1,507	1,229	17.14	5.92	9.77
1984 ..	118.7	2.3	68.7	0.8	49.0	536	1,359	1,308	17.83	5.85	9.83
1985 ..	121.3	2.2	69.3	0.8	51.0	525	1,407	1,302	18.20	5.84	9.79
1986 ..	125.2	3.2	71.4	0.9	52.9	526	1,463	1,320	18.27	5.84	9.81
1987 ..	127.5	1.8	70.6	0.9	55.8	514	1,500	1,357	19.20	5.89	9.87
1988 ..	130.1	2.0	71.9	0.9	57.2	509	1,496	1,345	19.95	5.93	10.16
1989 ..	131.8	1.3	72.7	0.9	57.9	509	1,518	1,328	20.40	5.96	10.41
1990 ..	131.6	-0.2	72.4	0.9	58.1	505	1,436	1,305	21.00	5.36	10.62

[1] From prior year, except 1970, change from 1965.   [2] Includes taxicabs.   [3] Includes school buses.   [4] Includes combinations.

Source: U.S. Federal Highway Administration, *Highway Statistics Summary to 1985*, and *Highway Statistics*, annual.

No. 1020. Household Motor Vehicle Transportation, by Vehicle Model Year: 1988

[Preliminary. Household vehicles include all motorized vehicles used for personal transportation, excluding motorcycles, mopeds, large trucks, and buses. The reporting unit for 1988 is all households which owned a vehicle at any time during 1988. Based on the Residential Transportation Energy Consumption Survey; subject to sampling variability. For composition of regions, see fig. I, inside front cover]

HOUSEHOLD CHARACTERISTICS	Households with motor vehicles (mil.)	VEHICLES (millions)					MILES PER GALLON				
		Total	Model year				Average	Model year			
			1974 and earlier	1975 to 1980	1981 to 1985	1986 to 1989		1976 and earlier	1981 or 1982	1986	1988 or 1989
Total	81.3	147.5	13	29	35	23	18.3	12.3	20.7	21.9	22.1
Northeast	15.2	26.6	8	24	40	28	19.6	12.2	21.8	22.3	21.5
Midwest	20.4	37.8	11	32	35	22	18.2	12.2	20.7	21.5	23.0
South.	28.3	50.6	12	29	34	24	18.0	12.0	19.7	21.8	21.9
West	17.3	32.5	21	29	30	20	18.0	12.7	21.5	22.3	22.3

Source: U.S. Energy Information Administration, *Household Vehicles Energy Consumption, 1988*.

No. 1021. Household Vehicles—Annual Mileage, Fuel Consumption, and Fuel Expenditures: 1988

[See headnote, table 1020]

HOUSEHOLD AND VEHICLE CHARACTERISTICS	NUMBER OF—			MILES DRIVEN		GALLONS CONSUMED		FUEL EXPENDITURES	
	Households [1] (millions)	Vehicles (millions)	Vehicles per household	Total (billion)	Percent	Total (billion)	Percent	Total (bil. dol.)	Percent
Total	**81.3**	**147.5**	**1.8**	**1,511**	**100.0**	**82.4**	**100.0**	**81.1**	**100.0**
Metropolitan status:									
Metropolitan...........	63.0	113.9	1.8	1,171	77.5	62.6	76.0	61.9	76.3
Nonmetropolitan	18.3	33.6	1.8	341	22.5	19.8	24.0	19.2	23.7
Origin of householder: White .	71.5	132.2	1.8	1,346	89.0	73.5	89.2	72.3	89.1
Black	7.2	10.6	1.5	115	7.6	6.2	7.5	6.2	7.6
Other	2.6	4.7	1.8	51	3.4	2.8	3.3	2.7	3.3
Family income 1988:									
Less than $10,000.	10.2	13.3	1.3	111	7.4	6.6	8.0	6.4	7.9
$10,000-$14,999........	11.8	17.0	1.4	153	10.2	9.0	10.9	8.8	10.8
$15,000-$19,999........	8.3	13.3	1.6	132	8.7	7.3	8.9	7.2	8.9
$20,000-$24,999........	8.6	15.1	1.7	154	10.2	8.5	10.3	8.3	10.3
$25,000-$34,999........	16.0	29.2	1.8	297	19.7	16.4	19.9	16.1	19.9
$35,000-$49,999........	12.9	28.3	2.2	313	20.7	16.5	20.0	16.3	20.1
$50,000-$74,999........	8.8	20.5	2.3	226	15.0	11.8	14.3	11.6	14.3
$75,000 or more	4.5	10.8	2.4	124	8.2	6.3	7.7	6.3	7.8

[1] Includes only households with vehicles.

Source: U.S. Energy Information Administration, *Household Vehicles Energy Consumption 1988*.

No. 1022. Motor Vehicle Travel, by Type of Vehicle, and by Speed: 1970 to 1990

[Travel in billions of vehicle-miles, except as indicated. Travel estimates based on automatic traffic recorder data. Speed trend data for 1970-1975 were collected by several State highway agencies, normally during summer months; beginning Oct. 1975 all States have monitored speeds at locations on several highway systems as part of 55 mile per hour Speed Limit Monitoring Program. See also *Historical Statistics, Colonial Times to 1970*, series Q 199-207]

YEAR	VEHICLE-MILES OF TRAVEL (bil.)				AVG. MILES PER VEHICLE (1,000)			MOTOR VEHICLE SPEED [2]				
	Total	Cars [1]	Buses	Trucks	Passenger vehicles		Trucks	Vehicles recorded (1,000) [3]	Avg. speed (miles per hour)	Percent of vehicles exceeding—		
					Cars [1]	Buses				55 mph	60 mph	65 mph
1970	1,110	920	4.5	186	10.0	12.0	9.9	200	63.8	87	69	44
1980	1,527	1,122	6.1	399	8.8	11.5	11.9	667	57.5	66	25	7
1983	1,653	1,207	5.2	441	9.1	8.9	12.0	7,856	59.1	74	41	15
1984	1,720	1,234	4.6	482	9.2	8.0	12.8	8,067	59.3	75	43	16
1985	1,774	1,270	4.9	500	9.2	8.2	12.7	8,449	59.5	75	44	17
1986	1,834	1,311	5.1	519	9.3	8.5	13.0	8,549	59.7	76	46	18
1987	1,921	1,365	5.3	551	9.6	8.8	13.4	7,992	59.7	74	46	19
1988	2,025	1,439	5.5	581	9.9	8.9	13.6	7,566	59.5	74	46	19
1989	2,096	1,488	5.7	603	10.1	9.0	13.8	7,488	60.1	77	49	22
1990	2,148	1,525	5.7	617	10.3	9.1	13.9	7,511	60.4	78	50	23

[1] Includes motorcycles.   [2] Represents speed on rural interstate highways. Beginning 1980, for year ending Sept. 30.
[3] Citations issued for 55 mph violations.

Source: U.S. Federal Highway Administration, *Highway Statistics Summary to 1985*, and *Highway Statistics*, annual.

No. 1023. Passenger Transit Industry—Summary: 1980 to 1990

[Includes Puerto Rico. Includes aggregate information for all transit systems in the United States. Except as noted, prior-to-1984 data exclude commuter railroad, automated guideway, urban ferry boat, and demand response, as well as most transit systems outside of urbanized areas. Data are noncontinuous between 1983 and 1984. Non-transit services such as taxicab, school bus, unregulated jitney, sightseeing bus, intercity bus, and special application mass transportation systems (e.g., amusement parks, airports, island, and urban park ferries) are excluded. Beginning in 1984, only active vehicles are counted]

ITEM	Unit	1980	1984	1985	1986	1987	1988	1989	1990, prel.
Operating systems	Number. . .	1,044	4,938	4,972	5,018	5,047	5,036	5,046	5,073
Motorbus systems [1]	Number. . .	1,040	2,604	2,631	2,655	2,671	2,671	2,665	2,686
Publicly owned systems [1] .	Number. . .	576	(NA)	1,435	(NA)	(NA)	(NA)	(NA)	1,580
Passenger vehicles owned [2 3]	Number. . .	75,388	96,901	94,368	96,127	96,127	97,209	92,293	93,752
Motorbus [2]	Number. . .	59,411	67,294	64,258	66,218	63,017	62,572	58,919	59,753
Trolley bus.	Number. . .	823	664	676	680	671	710	725	832
Heavy rail [2]	Number. . .	9,641	9,083	9,326	10,386	10,168	10,539	10,506	10,419
Light rail [2]	Number. . .	1,013	733	717	697	766	831	755	913
Commuter rail.	Number. . .	4,500	4,075	4,035	4,440	4,686	4,649	4,472	4,415
Demand response.	Number. . .	(NA)	14,164	14,490	15,346	15,944	16,812	15,856	16,222
Total revenue	Mil. dol .	6,510	11,623	12,195	13,342	14,091	14,537	14,985	15,982
Passenger revenue	Mil. dol . .	2,557	4,448	4,575	5,113	5,114	5,225	5,420	5,858
Other operating revenue [4]. .	Mil. dol . .	248	781	702	737	777	841	837	904
Operating assistance	Mil. dol . .	3,705	6,395	6,918	7,491	8,200	8,471	8,728	9,220
Federal.	Mil. dol . .	1,094	996	940	941	955	901	937	863
State and local	Mil. dol . .	2,611	5,399	5,979	4,245	4,681	4,893	4,995	5,338
Local	Mil. dol . .	(NA)	(NA)	(NA)	2,306	2,565	2,677	2,796	3,019
Total expense	Mil. dol . .	6,711	12,957	14,077	14,726	15,405	16,442	17,169	18,340
Operating expense	Mil. dol . .	6,247	11,574	12,381	12,952	13,472	14,287	14,972	16,058
Transportation	Mil. dol . .	3,248	5,142	5,655	5,690	5,790	6,052	6,275	6,768
Maintenance	Mil. dol . .	1,774	3,062	3,672	4,029	4,094	4,313	4,493	4,682
Administration	Mil. dol . .	1,224	3,370	3,054	3,298	3,714	4,041	4,223	3,588
Reconciling expense	Mil. dol . .	464	1,383	1,696	1,774	1,933	2,155	2,196	2,282
Capital expenditure, Federal. .	Mil. dol . .	2,787	2,876	2,510	3,138	2,475	2,521	2,590	2,380
Vehicle-miles operated [3] . . .	Million. . .	2,287	2,750	2,791	2,986	3,055	3,157	3,203	3,274
Motorbus.	Million. . .	1,677	1,845	1,863	2,002	2,079	2,097	2,109	2,153
Trolley bus.	Million. . .	13	15	16	15	15	15	15	14
Heavy rail	Million. . .	385	436	451	476	490	517	532	537
Light rail	Million. . .	18	17	17	17	18	21	21	24
Commuter rail.	Million. . .	179	168	183	189	189	202	210	213
Demand response.	Million. . .	(NA)	256	247	275	250	289	300	317
Passengers carried [3]	Million. . .	8,567	8,829	8,636	8,777	8,735	8,666	8,931	8,873
Motorbus.	Million. . .	5,837	5,908	5,675	5,753	5,614	5,500	5,620	5,751
Trolley bus.	Million. . .	142	165	142	139	141	136	130	126
Heavy rail	Million. . .	2,108	2,231	2,290	2,333	2,402	2,308	2,542	2,346
Light rail	Million. . .	133	135	132	130	133	154	162	176
Commuter rail.	Million. . .	280	267	275	306	311	325	330	329
Demand response.	Million. . .	(NA)	62	59	63	64	73	70	62
Avg.revenue per passenger . .	Cents	31.0	50.3	52.8	58.1	58.4	60.1	60.5	65.8
Employees, number (avg.) . . .	1,000	187	263	270	277	278	277	276	276
Payroll, employee.	Mil. dol . . .	3,281	5,488	5,843	6,119	6,324	6,675	6,898	7,325
Fringe benefits, employee . . .	Mil. dol . . .	1,353	2,717	2,868	3,126	3,267	3,529	3,737	4,049

NA Not available.   [1] Includes systems with combined services including motorbuses, heavy rail cars, light rail cars, trolley coaches, cable cars, and inclined plane cars. Beginning 1984, combined services also include suburban rail cars, urban ferry boats, vanpools, aerial tramways, automated guideways, and demand response vehicles.   [2] Beginning 1984, includes active vehicles only. Includes other vehicles not shown separately.   [3] Includes other not shown separately.   [4] Includes other operating revenue, non-operating revenue, and auxiliary income.

Source: American Public Transit Association, Washington, DC, *Transit Fact Book*, annual.

No. 1024. Class I Intercity Motor Carriers of Passengers: 1975 to 1990

[Carriers subject to ICC regulations. See text, section 21. Minus sign (-) indicates deficit. See also *Historical Statistics, Colonial Times to 1970,*

ITEM	Unit	1975	1980	1982	1983	1984	1985	1986	1987	1988	1989	1990
Carriers reporting [1]	Number.	77	48	50	45	43	43	29	32	21	20	21
Number of employees, average. . . .	1,000 . .	31	31	30	25	25	24	20	(NA)	(NA)	(NA)	(NA)
Compensation of employees.	Mil. dol .	383	599	646	570	551	518	443	(NA)	(NA)	(NA)	(NA)
Operating revenue . .	Mil. dol .	942	1,397	1,447	1,276	1,255	1,233	1,117	1,079	1,122	1,205	943
Passenger revenue [2]	Mil. dol .	651	947	969	876	861	836	765	751	825	890	738
Special bus revenue and other. . .	Mil. dol .	291	215	229	180	180	184	155	165	155	165	90
Operating expenses	Mil. dol .	880	1,318	1,416	1,283	1,254	1,168	1,082	1,081	1,059	1,133	1,015
Net operating revenue	Mil. dol .	61	79	30	-7	1	65	35	-2	63	72	-72
Ordinary income:												
Before income taxes	Mil. dol .	83	107	35	16	53	65	50	-11	(NA)	(NA)	(NA)
After income taxes.	Mil. dol .	56	90	37	26	43	53	36	-21	(NA)	12	-180
Passenger vehicles in service [2]	1,000 . .	9.7	8.6	8.1	7.3	7.0	8.4	8.3	(NA)	(NA)	(NA)	(NA)
Vehicle-miles, passenger	Million. .	835	781	717	591	585	567	495	(NA)	(NA)	(NA)	(NA)
Revenue passengers carried.	Million. .	147	134	112	94	89	88	74	82	55	54	43
Expense per vehicle-mile	Dollar . .	1.05	1.69	1.98	2.17	2.14	2.06	2.18	(NA)	(NA)	(NA)	(NA)

NA Not available. [1] Excludes carriers preponderantly in local or suburban service and carriers engaged in transportation of both property and passengers. [2] Regular route, intercity, and local.

Source: U.S. Interstate Commerce Commission, *Transport Statistics in the United States,* part 2, annual.

No. 1025. Intercity Bus Lines—Summary of Operations: 1970 to 1987

ITEM	Unit	1970	1975	1979	1980	1981	1982	1983	1984	1985	1986	1987
Operating companies	Number.	1,000	950	1,200	1,330	1,470	1,520	(NA)	(NA)	(NA)	(NA)	3,550
Buses	1,000 . .	22.0	20.5	21.3	21.4	21.7	20.9	20.4	20.1	20.1	19.1	18.4
Miles of highway served (Dec. 31) [1] .	1,000 . .	267	274	280	279	276	273	270	266	263	257	249
Employees (Dec. 31) [2]	1,000 . .	50	47	48	49	50	48	45	44	43	41	39
Bus miles, total	Million. .	1,209	1,126	1,153	1,162	1,151	1,115	1,027	1,016	997	945	914
Revenue passengers.	Million. .	401	351	368	370	370	359	352	352	353	346	333
Charter and tour passengers.	Million. .	92	145	185	195	204	206	209	(NA)	(NA)	(NA)	(NA)
Revenue passenger-miles	Billion . .	25.3	25.4	27.7	27.4	268	27.3	25.4	35.2	23.8	22.5	21.9
Operating revenue, all services	Mil. dol .	901	1,172	1,664	1,943	2,097	2,070	1,953	1,914	1,898	1,838	1,717
Operating expenses	Mil. dol .	812	1,103	1,572	1,811	1,982	2,013	1,938	1,896	1,839	1,781	1,669
Net operating revenue [3]	Mil. dol .	89	69	92	132	115	57	15	18	59	57	48

NA Not available. [1] Includes duplication between carriers. [2] Operating companies only. [3] Before income taxes.

Source: American Bus Association, Washington, DC, *Bus Facts,* annual; and *Annual Report.*

No. 1026. Warehousing Services—Revenues, Expenses, and Payroll: 1985 to 1990

[In millions of dollars]

SIC [1] code	KIND OF BUSINESS	OPERATING REVENUES		OPERATING EXPENSES		ANNUAL PAYROLL	
		1985	1990	1985	1990	1985	1990
42	Motor frgt transport.and warehousing srvs. [2]	91,663	121,171	87,448	120,321	28,091	37,495
421	Trucking, local and long distance.	82,212	120,190	78,819	114,120	25,576	35,675
422	Public warehousing	4,415	6,923	3,847	6,148	1,322	1,798
4221	Farm product warehousing and storage.	518	670	457	564	(D)	(D)
4222	Refrigerated warehousing.	1,007	1,343	872	1,144	313	391
4224	Household goods warehousing, storage	233	264	200	212	53	83

D Data do not meet publication standards because of high sampling error or high imputation rate. [1] Standard Industrial Classification. [2] Includes SIC 4231 and 4225,6 not shown separately.

Source: U.S. Bureau of the Census, *Current Business Reports, 1988 Motor Freight Transportation and Warehousing Survey.*

No. 1027. Trucking Costs and Rates for Fresh Fruit and Vegetables: 1980 to 1989

[Dollars per box, except as indicated]

SELECTED ITEMS	1980	1982	1983	1984	1985	1986	1987	1988	1989
Truck costs for fleet operators [1] (dollars per mile) . .	0.97	1.11	1.13	1.15	1.17	1.14	1.17	1.18	1.23
Truck rates by commodity and origin/destination: [2]									
Lettuce [3], California to New York City	3.36	3.62	3.62	3.65	3.62	3.75	3.83	3.69	3.76
Citrus and vegetables, Southern California to New York City	2.77	2.91	2.98	3.18	3.06	3.16	3.23	3.14	3.2
Apples, Washington to New York City.	3.09	3.20	3.41	3.19	3.20	3.21	3.28	3.30	3.31

[1] Truck costs developed by Office of Transportation, USDA. [2] Average rates reported by Agricultural Marketing Service, Market News Service, USDA, for the first week of the month. [3] January to April: Imperial Valley, California to New York City; May to December: Salinas, California to New York City.

Source: U.S. Dept. of Agriculture, Economic Research Service, *Food Cost Review,* 1989.

No. 1028. Trucking Services—Operating Revenues, Operating Expenses, and Equipment, by Type of Carrier: 1985 to 1990

[In millions of dollars, except as indicated. Data cover SIC group 421. Estimates include both regulated and nonregulated carriers; excluded are non-employers (i.e., firms with no paid employees) and private fleets operated as auxiliary establishments to nontransportation companies. Some unpublished estimates may be derived from this table by subtraction, but such figures are subject to high sampling variability and should be used with caution]

ITEM	ALL CARRIERS			SPECIALTY FREIGHT CARRIERS			GENERAL FREIGHT CARRIERS		
	1985	1989	1990	1985	1989	1990	1985	1989	1990
Operating revenues:									
Total [1]	86,858	112,263	120,190	30,435	39,524	40,904	56,423	72,739	79,286
Motor carrier	81,347	105,158	112,572	26,974	34,705	35,805	54,373	70,453	76,767
Local trucking	17,548	22,287	23,859	9,084	12,610	13,380	8,464	9,677	10,479
Intercity trucking	63,799	82,871	88,713	17,890	22,095	22,425	45,909	60,776	66,288
Operating expenses:									
Total	83,266	107,432	114,120	28,933	37,790	39,186	54,333	69,642	74,934
Annual payroll	26,722	34,161	35,675	7,600	9,788	10,201	19,122	24,373	25,474
Employer contributions to Social Security and other benefits	6,113	8,282	8,708	1428	2,015	2,088	4,685	6,267	6,620
Purchased fuels	6,825	7,737	9,186	2,191	2,443	2,772	4,634	5,294	6,414
Cost of purchased transportation	(NA)	23,050	24,162	(NA)	9,438	9,355	(NA)	13,612	14,807
Lease and rental payments	1,314	2,063	2,258	504	876	925	810	1,187	1,333
Cost of insurance	(NA)	4,426	4,580	(NA)	1,624	1,583	(NA)	2,802	2,997
Maintenance and repair costs	(NA)	6,054	6,509	(NA)	2,319	2,408	(NA)	3,735	4,101
Depreciation	4,193	5,820	6,141	1,596	2,183	2,122	2,597	3,637	4,019
Taxes and licenses	1,950	2,370	2,493	619	778	804	1,331	1,592	1,689
Other	(NA)	13,469	14,408	(NA)	6,326	6,928	(NA)	7,143	7,480
Equipment (1,000 units): [2]									
Trucks	201	247	259	94	104	107	(S)	143	152
Truck-tractors	461	541	549	167	170	167	302	371	382
Trailers, full and semi	1,055	1,178	1,214	246	295	299	765	883	915

NA Not available. S Data do not meet publication standards. [1] Includes other revenues not shown separately.
[2] Represents revenue generating freight equipment as of December 31. Includes owned and leased equipment.

Source: U.S. Bureau of the Census, *Current Business Reports, Motor Freight Transportation and Warehousing Survey,* annual.

No. 1029. Class I Intercity Motor Carriers of Property, by Carrier: 1980 to 1990

[See headnote, table 1024. Common carriers are carriers offering regular scheduled service. Contract carriers provide service at request of user. Minus sign (-) indicates loss]

ITEM	Unit	1980	1985	1989	1990	1980	1985	1989	1990
		COMMON CARRIER, GENERAL FREIGHT				COMMON CARRIER OTHER THAN GENERAL FREIGHT			
Carriers reporting	Number	298	237	192	191	441	397	337	322
Number of employees, average	1,000	413	376	461	465	101	76	84	87
Compensation of employees	Mil. dol.	9,803	10,217	12,854	13,556	1,931	1,783	2,105	2,236
Operating revenues	Mil. dol.	19,725	22,314	27,405	29,682	8,792	7,962	8,321	9,042
Intercity freight	Mil. dol.	19,480	22,080	27,289	29,517	8,339	7,664	8,024	8,762
Operating expenses	Mil. dol.	18,870	21,037	26,242	28,340	8,426	7,752	8,081	8,702
Ordinary income before taxes	Mil. dol.	701	1,198	988	1,146	230	123	117	198
Net income	Mil. dol.	-72	658	659	746	14	94	88	153
Total power units, intercity service	1,000	102	108	(NA)	(NA)	95	77	(NA)	(NA)
Trucks, tractors owned in operation, avg.	1,000	73	82	(NA)	(NA)	33	29	(NA)	(NA)
Intercity vehicle-miles	Million	6,547	5,760	6,557	6,804	6,889	5,714	6,320	6,566
Tons of intercity revenue freight carried	Million	178	136	145	157	324	303	278	302
		CONTRACT CARRIER OTHER THAN GENERAL FREIGHT				CARRIERS OF HOUSEHOLD GOODS			
Carriers reporting	Number	69	64	77	87	28	40	36	36
Number of employees, average	1,000	14	22	29	34	10	11	12	13
Compensation of employees	Mil. dol.	336	630	893	1,082	157	240	276	296
Operating revenues	Mil. dol.	1,272	1,942	2,946	3,486	1,824	2,684	3,114	3,152
Intercity freight	Mil. dol.	1,172	1,792	2,693	3,209	1,676	2,388	2,703	2,702
Operating expenses	Mil. dol.	1,207	1,807	2,888	3,422	1,781	2,635	3,059	3,129
Ordinary income before taxes	Mil. dol.	48	103	15	3	74	79	41	12
Net income	Mil. dol.	28	69	3	-13	42	54	28	8
Total power units, intercity service	1,000	13	16	(NA)	(NA)	25	35	(NA)	(NA)
Trucks, tractors owned in operation, avg.	1,000	7	11	(NA)	(NA)	1	1	(NA)	(NA)
Intercity vehicle-miles	Million	934	1,227	1,826	2,044	969	1,171	1,229	1,366
Tons of intercity revenue freight carried	Million	37	41	80	80	5	7	7	8

NA Not available.

Source: U.S. Interstate Commerce Commission, *Transport Statistics in the United States,* part 2, annual.

No. 1030. Trucks—Percent Distribution, Operational Characteristics: 1977 to 1987

[See headnote, table 1031]

CHARACTERISTIC	1977	1982	1987	CHARACTERISTIC	1977	1982	1987
Total	100.0	100.0	100.0	Purchased used	50.0	51.5	50.1
				Leased [5]	2.4	2.8	2.6
Major use:				Fleet size: [6] 1	71.6	77.8	65.1
Agriculture [1]	17.0	12.2	8.5	2 to 5	16.3	10.9	24.9
Construction	6.7	11.2	10.0	6 to 19.	6.6	5.3	5.4
Manufacturing	1.4	1.6	1.3	20 or more	5.5	6.0	4.6
Wholesale and retail trade.	7.6	6.8	5.6	Truck-type:			
Personal transportation.	54.4	56.7	65.7	Single-unit	96.8	95.7	96.3
All other.	13.0	11.4	8.8	Combination	3.2	4.3	3.7
Body type:				Annual miles:			
Pickup and panel [2].	83.3	85.8	89.0	Less than 5,000	23.9	26.0	25.3
Platform and cattlerack	6.8	5.1	3.7	5,000 to 9,999.	24.0	25.5	23.4
Van [3].	4.5	3.8	3.2	10,000 to 19,999	37.0	35.0	34.5
All other.	5.5	5.2	4.0	20,000 to 29,999	9.2	8.4	10.7
Vehicle size: [4] Light.	85.4	89.3	91.9	30,000 miles or more	5.9	5.0	6.1
Medium	6.0	3.5	2.3	Range of operation: [7]			
Light-heavy.	3.1	2.4	1.7	Local.	84.8	76.6	75.6
Heavy-heavy.	5.5	4.8	4.1	Short-range	8.4	10.3	14.8
Year model:				Long-range.	2.1	3.1	4.5
1 to 2 years old.	17.1	8.9	17.2	Off-the-road [5]	4.7	10.0	5.1
3 to 4 years old.	17.5	16.5	16.5	Fuel type:			
4 years or more.	65.4	74.6	66.3	Gasoline	96.0	94.3	93.7
Vehicle acquisition:				Diesel and LPG.	3.9	5.5	6.2
Purchased new	47.6	45.7	47.3	Not reported	-	0.2	0.1

- Represents zero. [1] Includes forestry and lumbering. [2] Also includes walk-in, mini-van, station wagon, and utility trucks. [3] Includes multi-stop or walk-in. [4] See footnote 6, table 1031. [5] Includes not reported. [6] See footnote 8, table 1031. [7] See footnote 9, table 1031.

No. 1031. Trucks and Truck-Miles, by Vehicle and Operational Characteristics: 1987

[Data are based on a stratified probability sample of trucks drawn from current registrations on file with motor vehicle departments in the 50 States and DC]

ITEM	TRUCKS (1,000)		TRUCK-MILES (bil.)	ITEM	TRUCKS (1,000)		TRUCK-MILES (bil.)
	Total	Excl. pickups, panels [1]			Total	Excl. pickups, panels [1]	
Total	44,572	4,886	529.3	Range of operation: [9]			
Major use:				Local.	33,685	3,027	350.9
Agriculture [2]	3,819	1,114	39.0	Short-range	6,612	920	108.3
Construction	4,479	997	63.7	Long-range.	1,997	490	56.0
Manufacturing	581	241	12.5	Off-the-road [7]	2,278	449	14.1
Wholesale and retail trade.	2,507	830	43.3	Products carried:			
Personal transportation.	29,292	250	287.0	Farm products.	1,558	769	16.2
All other.	3,894	1,455	83.8	Building materials	1,141	640	18.6
Body type:				Mixed cargoes.	686	325	21.1
Pickup and panel [3].	39,686	(X)	427	Craftsman's equipment.	2,476	319	34.5
Platform [4].	1,668	1,668	25.0	Personal transportation.	29,290	251	286.9
Van [3].	1,424	1,424	48.8	All other.	9,422	2,583	152.0
All other.	1,794	1,794	28.5	Hazardous materials			
Vehicle size: [6] Light.	40,947	1,356	439.3	carried:			
Medium	1,030	939	10.8	Less than 10 percent of time. .	114	107	7.2
Light-heavy.	766	764	7.6	10-25 percent of time.	28	19	1.2
Heavy-heavy.	1,829	1,828	71.6	26-49 percent of time.	18	15	0.7
Year model:				50-74 percent of time.	25	24	1.0
1 to 2 years old.	7,678	473	123.6	75-100 percent of time	94	89	2.8
3 to 4 years old.	7,338	549	120.5	Not reported	61	25	1.7
4 years or more.	29,543	3,864	285.1				
Vehicle acquisition:				Types of hazardous			
Purchased new	21,087	2,138	292.3	material: [10]			
Purchased used	22,325	2,511	215.2	Flammables liquids	198	175	9.3
Leased [7]	1,160	237	21.8	Combustible liquids	95	95	5.8
Fleet size: [8] 1	29,026	1,170	308.7	Corrosive liquids	70	66	4.6
2 to 5	11,094	1,547	122.9	Flammable solids.	29	28	2.3
6 to 19.	2,397	1,007	40.1	Oxidizers	28	28	2.3
20 or more	2,054	1,163	57.6	Flammable gas	26	26	2.2
Truck type:				Nonflammable gas.	26	26	2.2
Single-unit	42,917	3,587	462.0	Corrosive solids.	21	21	1.9
Combination	1,656	1,300	67.3	Not reported	139	101	5.1

X Not applicable. [1] Also excludes mini-vans, utilities, and station wagons. [2] Includes forestry and lumbering. [3] Also includes multi-stop, mini-vans, station wagons, and utility trucks. [4] Includes livestock truck. [5] Includes multi-stop or walk-in. [6] Average vehicle weight (empty-weight of the vehicle plus the average weight of load carried). Light=10,000 lbs. or less; medium=10,001-19,500 lbs.; light-heavy=19,501-26,000 lbs.; and heavy-heavy=26,001 lbs. or more. [7] Includes not reported. [8] A fleet size of one truck was assumed when no response was obtained. [9] Area in which usually operated. Local=less than 50 miles; short-range=50 to 200 miles; long-range=more than 200 miles. [10] Detail does not add to totals because items were not applicable or multiple responses were possible.

Source of tables 1030 and 1031: U.S. Bureau of the Census, *1987 Census of Transportation, TC87-T-52.*

No. 1032. Railroads, Class I—Summary: 1970 to 1990

[As of **Dec. 31**, or **calendar year** data, except as noted. Compiled from annual reports of class I railroads only, except where noted. Beginning 1983, financial data are not comparable with earlier years due to change in method of accounting for track and related structures. Minus sign (-) indicates deficit. See also *Historical Statistics, Colonial Times to 1970*, series Q 284-312, Q 319, Q 330, Q 356-378, and Q 400-401]

ITEM	Unit	1970	1980	1984	1985	1986	1987	1988	1989	1990
Class I line-hauling companies [1] . . .	Number.	71	40	29	23	22	18	17	15	14
Employees [2]	1,000 . .	566	459	323	302	276	249	236	228	216
Compensation	Mil. dol .	5,711	11,318	11,004	10,563	9,900	9,373	9,301	9,043	8,654
Average per hour.	Dollars .	4.14	10.2	13.8	14.3	14.8	15.1	15.6	15.8	15.8
Average per year.	Dollars .	10,086	24,659	34,064	34,991	35,894	37,716	39,431	39,742	39,987
Mileage:										
Railroad line owned [3]	1,000 . .	206	179	157	155	154	152	150	149	144
Railroad track owned [4]	1,000 . .	336	290	264	257	256	254	251	249	239
Equipment:										
Locomotives in service	Number.	27,077	28,094	22,548	22,932	20,790	19,358	19,364	19,015	18,835
Average horsepower	1,000 lb	1,926	2,302	2,415	2,469	2,531	2,554	2,579	2,624	2,665
Cars in service:										
Passenger train	Number.	11,177	4,347	[5]2,580	2,502	2,307	2,350	2,332	(NA)	(NA)
Freight train [6]	1,000 . .	1,784	1,711	1,486	1,422	1,339	1,288	1,239	1,224	1,212
Freight cars [7]	1,000 . .	1,424	1,168	948	867	799	749	725	682	659
Average capacity [7] . . .	Tons. . .	67.1	78.5	83.4	83.2	84.1	85.0	86.4	87.8	87.5
Aggregate capacity [7] . . .	Mil. tons	95.6	92.7	80.0	72.2	67.2	63.6	55.9	55.0	53.0
Box [7]	1,000 . .	590	347	245	216	180	163	144	133	123
Gondola and hopper [7] .	1,000 . .	724	636	552	505	473	445	437	423	411
Other [7]	1,000 . .	140	185	151	145	146	141	144	132	125
Income and expenses:										
Operating revenues.	Mil. dol .	11,992	28,258	29,453	27,586	26,204	26,622	27,934	27,956	28,370
Operating expenses	Mil. dol .	11,478	26,355	25,800	25,225	24,896	23,878	24,811	25,038	24,652
Net revenue from operations . . .	*Mil. dol .*	*514*	*1,902*	*3,653*	*2,361*	*1,308*	*2,744*	*3,123*	*2,918*	*3,718*
Income before fixed charges. . . .	Mil. dol .	994	2,897	4,893	3,393	2,480	3,932	4,460	4,162	4,627
Provision for taxes [8]	Mil. dol .	88	592	1,185	660	163	1,051	1,162	1,040	1,088
Ordinary income	Mil. dol .	227	1,129	2,654	1,788	747	1,965	2,286	2,009	1,961
Net income	Mil. dol .	227	1,129	2,701	1,882	544	2,055	2,382	2,203	1,977
Net railway operating income . . .	Mil. dol .	486	1,339	2,537	1,746	507	1,756	1,980	1,894	2,648
Total taxes [9]	Mil. dol .	1,069	2,585	3,605	3,169	2,728	3,553	3,871	3,742	3,780
Indus. return on net investment. .	Percent.	1.7	4.2	5.7	4.6	1.3	4.8	6.7	6.3	8.1
Gross capital expenditures	Mil. dol .	1,351	3,238	4,121	4,485	3,645	3,076	3,546	3,865	3,591
Equipment	Mil. dol .	993	2,280	806	965	693	657	1,027	1,171	996
Roadway and structures	Mil. dol .	358	953	2,938	3,458	2,908	2,314	2,654	2,538	2,644
Other.	Mil. dol .	-	5	377	62	44	105	-135	156	-49
Balance sheet:										
Total property investment.	Mil. dol .	38,213	43,923	63,471	64,241	64,781	66,760	68,550	67,661	70,348
Accrued depreciation and										
amortization	Mil. dol .	10,027	10,706	20,098	19,756	20,490	21,070	21,497	21,481	22,222
Net investment.	Mil. dol .	28,186	33,419	45,435	46,237	45,344	45,690	47,053	47,370	48,126
Shareholder's equity	Mil. dol .	17,323	19,860	27,986	27,605	25,442	25,616	26,467	25,753	23,663
Net working capital	Mil. dol .	-59	897	1,844	1,084	743	1,241	-190	-2119	-3505
Cash dividends.	Mil. dol .	421	610	1,066	1,444	1,376	1,252	1,814	1,910	2,074
AMTRAK passenger traffic:										
Passenger revenue	Mil. dol .	(NA)	(NA)	556.7	604.9	633.6	681.1	784.2	893.0	941.9
Revenue passengers carried. . . .	1,000 . .	(NA)	21,303	20,065	20,945	20,165	20,727	21,490	21,394	22,383
Revenue passenger miles	Million. .	(NA)	4,645	4,566	4,977	5,015	5,368	5,686	5,912	6,125
Averages:										
Revenue per passenger	Dollars .	(NA)	(NA)	28.2	28.9	31.4	32.9	36.5	41.8	42.1
Revenue per passenger mile . .	Cents . .	(NA)	(NA)	12.4	12.2	12.6	12.7	13.8	15.1	15.4
Trip per passenger.	Miles . .	(NA)	218.1	227.6	237.6	248.7	259.0	264.6	276.3	273.7
Freight service:										
Freight revenue	Mil. dol .	10,922	26,200	28,472	26,688	25,344	25,797	27,092	27,059	24,471
Per ton-mile	Cents . .	1.4	2.8	3.1	3.0	2.9	2.7	2.7	2.7	2.7
Per ton originated	Dollar . .	7.7	17.7	19.9	20.2	19.4	18.8	19.0	19.3	19.3
Revenue-tons originated	Million. .	1,485	1,492	1,429	1,320	1,087	1,372	1,430	1,402	1,425
Revenue-tons carried	Million. .	2,616	2,434	2,119	1,985	1,938	1,984	2,045	1,988	2,024
Tons carried one mile	Billion . .	765	919	922	877	868	944	996	1,014	1,034
Average miles of road operated . .	1,000 . .	209	179	165	161	155	147	141	138	133
Revenue ton-miles per mile of										
road	1,000 . .	3,652	5,133	5,578	5,446	5,587	6,395	7,052	7,373	7,763
Revenue per ton-mile	Cents . .	1.428	3	3	3	3	3	3	3	2,657
Train miles	Million. .	427	428	369	347	347	361	379	382	380
Net ton-miles per train-mile [10] . . .	Number.	1,820	2,175	2,543	2,574	2,552	2,644	2,662	2,683	2,755
Net ton-miles per loaded										
car-mile [10]	Number.	44.9	63.5	62.4	62.7	63.2	64.0	65.5	67.0	69.0
Train-miles per train-hour	Miles . .	20.1	18.2	21.9	21.9	22.5	22.2	21.5	23.0	24.0
Haul per ton, U.S. as a system . .	Miles . .	490	616	645	664	664	688	697	723	726
Accident: [11]										
Persons killed	Number.	2,255	1,417	1,247	1,036	1,091	1,165	1,199	1,324	1,297
Persons injured	Number.	21,327	62,246	38,570	34,304	26,923	26,033	27,054	26,715	25,143

- Represents zero.   NA Not available.   [1] See text, section 21 for definition of Class I.   [2] Average mid-month count. [3] Represents the aggregate length of roadway of all line-haul railroads. Excludes yard tracks, sidings, and parallel lines. (Includes estimate for class II and III railroads.)   [4] Includes multiple main tracks, yard tracks, and sidings owned by both line-haul and switching and terminal. (Includes estimate for class II and III railroads.)   [5] Excludes Long Island Railroad, which was reclassified.   [6] Includes cars owned by all railroads, private car companies, and shippers.   [7] Class I railroads only.   [8] Includes State income taxes beginning 1980.   [9] Includes payroll, income, and other taxes.   [10] Revenue and non-revenue freight. [11] Includes highway grade crossing casualties. 1970 not comparable with later years due to change in requirements for reporting injuries.

Source: Association of American Railroads, Washington, DC, *Railroad Facts, Statistics of Railroads of Class I*, annual, and *Analysis of Class I Railroads*, annual. Accident data: U.S. Federal Railroad Administration, *Accident Bulletin*, annual.

No. 1033. Railroads, Class I-Cars of Revenue Freight Loaded, 1970 to 1990, and by Commodity Group, 1989 and 1990

[In thousands. Figures are 52-week totals. N.e.c.= Not elsewhere classified]

YEAR	CARLOADS		COMMODITY GROUP	CARLOADS		COMMODITY GROUP	CARLOADS	
	Total	Piggy-back		1989	1990		1989	1990
1970 . .	27,160	1,450	Coal	5,969	6,296	Metals and products	421	454
1975 . .	23,217	1,308	Metallic ores	514	506	Stone, clay, and glass products . .	509	489
1980 . .	22,598	1,661	Chemicals, allied products. . . .	1,382	1,421	Crushed stone, gravel, sand	717	710
1985 . .	19,574	2,863	Grain.	1,472	1,428	Nonmetalic minerals, n.e.c	492	459
1986 . .	19,783	3,279	Motor vehicles and equipment .	958	882	Waste and scrap materials	416	414
1987 . .	21,133	3,294	Pulp, paper, allied products	494	485	Lumber, wood products, n.e.c. [1]. .	339	301
1988 . .	16,422	(NA)	Primary forest products.	431	410	Coke.	274	281
1989 . .	16,030	(NA)	Food and kindred prod., n.e.c. .	448	448	Petroleum product.	253	255
1990 . .	16,177	(NA)	Grain mill products.	513	520	All other carloads	527	418

NA Not available.   [1] Excludes furniture.

Source: Association of American Railroads, Washington, DC, *Weekly Railroad Traffic,* annual.

No. 1034. Railroads, Class I Line-Haul-Revenue Freight Originated, by Commodity Group: 1970 to 1990

[See *Historical Statistics, Colonial Times to 1970,* series Q 332, for total carloads originated]

COMMODITY GROUP	1970	1975	1980	1983	1984	1985	1986	1987	1988	1989	1990
Carloads (1,000) [1].	27,015	22,930	22,223	19,013	20,946	19,501	19,587	20,602	21,600	21,226	21,401
Coal.	5,296	4,844	5,789	5,276	6,061	5,684	5,433	5,430	5,621	5,672	5,912
Farm products	2,374	1,873	1,866	1,642	1,757	1,494	1,602	1,907	1,977	1,781	1,689
Chemicals, allied products	1,576	1,313	1,322	1,216	1,312	1,296	1,287	1,410	1,497	1,486	1,531
Food and kindred products	2,706	2,154	1,767	1,316	1,234	1,224	1,276	1,326	1,318	1,284	1,307
Nonmetallic minerals [2]	2,204	1,895	1,474	1,079	1,204	1,196	1,113	1,188	1,290	1,254	1,202
Transportation equipment	1,059	1,135	1,004	954	1,141	1,202	1,148	1,085	1,160	1,141	1,091
Lumber and wood products [3] . . .	2,048	1,615	1,384	1,075	1,051	948	965	986	910	843	780
Pulp, paper, allied products	1,197	1,015	954	746	741	703	672	561	646	615	611
Petroleum and coal products . . .	699	787	596	495	529	491	477	520	568	561	573
Stone, clay, and glass products . .	1,231	906	776	543	576	551	530	559	577	565	539
Metallic ores	1,602	1,338	1,258	812	1,001	511	508	494	582	523	508
Primary metal products	1,486	796	756	440	487	449	389	428	479	452	477
Waste and scrap materials.	805	744	632	417	480	429	402	440	471	444	439
Machinery, exc. electrical.	200	156	77	38	40	35	31	33	40	38	39
Fabricated metal products [4]	398	244	72	33	37	31	26	24	26	27	31
Tons (mil.) [1]	1,485	1,395	1,492	1,293	1,429	1,320	1,306	1,372	1,429	1,403	1,425
Coal.	405	408	522	494	567	538	518	523	543	551	579
Farm products	134	134	156	142	151	127	136	163	170	154	147
Chemicals, allied products	92	91	108	99	107	106	106	116	123	123	126
Nonmetallic minerals [2]	163	151	125	97	108	108	101	109	115	111	109
Food and kindred products	110	100	92	75	72	74	78	81	81	79	81
Lumber and wood products [3] . . .	102	89	86	72	70	63	65	67	62	57	53
Metallic ores	127	106	105	68	86	47	46	45	52	47	47
Stone, clay, and glass products . .	71	57	54	42	45	44	42	44	46	47	44
Petroleum and coal products	36	46	38	34	35	33	33	35	39	39	40
Primary metal products	82	51	53	32	36	34	30	33	38	36	38
Pulp, paper, allied products	43	41	42	37	38	36	36	36	35	34	33
Waste and scrap materials.	40	38	34	25	29	26	25	28	30	28	28
Transportation equipment	24	27	24	22	26	27	26	24	25	24	23
Machinery, exc. electrical.	5	4	2	1	1	1	1	1	1	1	1
Fabricated metal products [4]	11	8	2	1	1	1	1	1	1	1	1
Gross revenue (mil. dol.) [1].	11,388	15,899	26,938	26,710	29,866	28,225	27,186	27,657	29,529	29,328	29,775
Coal.	1,381	2,146	4,956	5,969	6,965	6,556	6,089	6,097	6,430	6,581	6,954
Chemicals, allied products	1,137	1,681	2,946	3,078	3,360	3,342	3,342	3,477	3,795	3,788	3,933
Transportation equipment	734	1,283	1,977	2,292	2,859	3,110	2,997	2,866	3,218	3,269	3,100
Farm products	1,068	1,472	2,801	2,374	2,483	1,977	2,007	2,246	2,534	2,444	2,422
Food and kindred products	1,363	1,822	2,387	2,349	2,309	2,226	2,192	2,171	2,198	2,128	2,188
Pulp, paper, allied products [3] . . .	730	977	1,652	1,671	1,762	1,641	1,572	1,542	1,540	1,514	1,486
Lumber and wood products [3] . . .	832	1,066	1,543	1,527	1,611	1,525	1,563	1,660	1,626	1,500	1,390
Primary metal products	813	848	1,332	816	955	872	787	863	1,013	972	979
Stone, clay, and glass products . .	512	651	1,025	908	1,024	960	907	914	065	960	931
Petroleum and coal products	305	573	865	844	913	861	800	809	903	917	918
Nonmetallic minerals [2]	409	596	948	834	997	949	839	854	890	868	885
Waste and scrap materials.	232	359	513	423	496	446	425	474	526	492	504
Metallic ores	333	468	597	450	567	403	375	348	415	397	408
Machinery, exc. electrical.	148	200	176	75	81	72	58	57	63	66	67
Fabricated metal products [4]	210	221	110	52	57	48	40	37	38	38	42

[1] Includes commodity groups and small packaged freight shipments, not shown separately.   [2] Except fuels.   [3] Except furniture.   [4] Except ordnance, machinery, and transport.

Source: 1970-1975, U.S. Interstate Commerce Commission, *Freight Commodity Statistics—Class I Railroads in the United States,* annual; thereafter, Association of American Railroads, Washington, DC, *Freight Commodity Statistics,* annual.

No. 1035. Railroad Freight—Producer Price Indexes: 1970 to 1991

[Dec. 1984 = 100. Reflects prices for shipping a fixed set of commodities under specified and unchanging conditions]

COMMODITY	1970	1975	1980	1983	1984	1985	1986	1987	1988	1989	1990	1991
Total railroad freight	29.1	45.3	75.9	95.0	99.3	99.9	100.7	100.1	104.8	106.4	107.5	109.3
Coal	26.9	44.0	75.8	96.5	99.9	100.0	100.7	100.1	104.3	105.3	104.2	105.2
Farm products	29.7	45.2	75.6	94.0	98.7	99.0	99.6	99.3	105.5	108.5	110.4	111.5
Food products	28.9	44.8	75.2	94.8	99.1	100.0	99.9	98.6	103.1	103.9	105.4	108.2
Metallic ores	26.4	43.2	74.5	95.9	99.4	100.2	100.5	99.0	103.9	105.8	106.5	106.7
Chemicals or allied products	30.0	46.5	75.6	94.3	98.7	100.1	101.2	100.8	106.9	110.0	111.7	113.5
Nonmetallic minerals	25.4	40.5	72.2	94.6	98.9	100.1	101.6	101.1	106.1	108.3	111.7	116.0
Wood or lumber products	28.3	42.8	72.7	93.3	99.7	100.0	100.9	100.4	105.3	105.9	107.5	108.7
Transportation equipment	31.7	50.3	81.7	95.6	99.8	100.0	100.8	99.3	103.4	106.4	107.5	109.7
Pulp, paper, or allied products	31.5	47.1	76.7	95.6	99.9	100.0	101.0	100.6	104.0	105.1	108.0	111.5
Primary metal products	29.9	47.8	77.8	95.4	99.7	99.7	100.2	99.7	108.8	112.3	113.1	116.1
Clay, concrete, glass, or stone products .	26.9	43.0	74.2	94.4	98.8	100.0	102.2	102.2	107.5	110.5	114.1	117.3

Source: U.S. Bureau of Labor Statistics, *Producer Price Indexes,* monthly and annual.

No. 1036. Petroleum Pipeline Companies—Characteristics: 1975 to 1990

[1975, covers pipeline companies operating in interstate commerce and subject to jurisdiction of Interstate Commerce Commission; thereafter, Federal Energy Regulatory Commission]

ITEM	Unit	1975	1980	1982	1983	1984	1985	1986	1987	1988	1989	1990
Miles of pipeline,												
total	1,000	171	173	173	168	174	171	170	168	171	169	168
Gathering lines . . .	1,000	40	36	36	31	36	35	34	35	34	33	32
Trunk lines	1,000	130	136	137	137	138	136	136	133	136	135	136
Total deliveries	Mil. bbl.	9,391	10,600	10,181	10,310	10,224	10,745	11,002	11,194	11,484	11,281	11,378
Crude oil	Mil. bbl.	5,729	6,405	5,968	6,020	5,671	6,239	6,286	6,278	6,509	6,435	6,563
Products	Mil. bbl.	3,662	4,195	4,213	4,289	4,552	4,506	4,716	4,917	4,974	4,847	4,816
Total trunk line												
traffic	Bil. bbl-miles .	2,892	3,405	3,442	3,328	3,406	3,342	3,467	3,524	3,619	3,505	3,500
Crude oil	Bil. bbl-miles .	1,551	1,948	1,938	1,875	1,855	1,842	1,893	1,932	1,970	1,918	1,891
Products	Bil. bbl-miles .	1,341	1,458	1,484	1,452	1,551	1,500	1,573	1,592	1,649	1,587	1,609
Carrier property												
value	Mil. dol.	10,740	19,752	21,942	22,255	19,397	21,605	22,384	21,353	24,332	24,638	25,828
Operating revenues .	Mil. dol.	1,869	6,356	7,140	7,472	7,824	7,461	7,287	7,057	6,861	6,512	7,149
Net income	Mil. dol.	456	1,912	2,162	2,353	2,545	2,431	2,051	2,475	2,505	2,227	2,340

Source: PennWell Publishing Co., Tulsa, OK, *Oil & Gas Journal,* November 25, 1991, and earlier issues. (copyright)

No. 1037. Major Interstate Natural Gas Pipeline Companies—Summary: 1982 to 1989

[In 1984, the reporting criteria were changed from that of prior years. The classification of A and B interstate natural gas pipeline companies was changed to major companies and nonmajor companies. Major natural gas pipeline companies are those whose combined sales for resale and natural gas transported or stored for a fee exceed 50 billion cubic feet. They account for more than 85 percent of all interstate natural gas]

ITEM	Unit	1982	1983	1984	1985	1986	1987	1988	1989
Sales	Tril. cu. ft. .	14.4	12.9	13.2	11.3	7.8	6.5	6.4	5.6
Residential	Tril. cu. ft. .	0.3	0.3	0.3	0.3	0.2	0.2	0.3	0.1
Commercial, industrial	Tril. cu. ft. .	1.2	1.0	1.2	1.1	0.5	0.4	0.5	0.5
For resale	Tril. cu. ft. .	13.0	11.6	11.6	9.9	7.1	5.8	5.6	4.9
Operating revenues	Mil. dol . . .	56,203	56,792	56,326	49,106	33,859	27,565	27,501	25,695
From sales [1]	Mil. dol . . .	53,601	53,710	52,529	44,996	29,508	22,942	22,512	19,786
Residential	Mil. dol . . .	1,273	1,725	1,927	1,879	1,122	1,094	1,553	819
Commercial, industrial	Mil. dol . . .	4,453	4,233	5,180	4,466	1,909	1,464	1,544	1,452
For resale	Mil. dol . . .	47,776	47,661	45,268	38,545	26,413	20,351	19,420	17,505
From transportation of gas of others. . . .	Mil. dol . . .	1,259	1,787	1,923	2,272	3,027	3,622	4,059	4,959
Other	Mil. dol . . .	1,344	1,296	1,874	1,838	1,325	1,002	929	950
Operation, maintenance expenses.	Mil. dol . . .	49,989	49,391	48,411	42,528	27,460	21,794	22,742	20,829
Production	Mil. dol . . .	44,449	43,516	42,407	36,739	22,208	16,955	17,625	15,257
Storage	Mil. dol . . .	405	441	415	418	420	409	436	458
Transmission	Mil. dol . . .	3,629	3,729	3,760	3,409	2,984	2,598	2,589	2,589
Distribution	Mil. dol . . .	103	131	131	132	80	80	127	94
Administrative, general, and other	Mil. dol . . .	1,402	1,576	1,697	1,830	1,768	1,752	1,966	2,430
Pipeline mileage:									
Transmission lines.	1,000	178.0	176.7	183.4	189.7	184.6	181.2	191.6	194.1
Field lines	1,000	64.6	63.7	65.2	69.6	64.5	62.9	55.5	55.1
Storage	1,000	6.9	6.5	4.6	4.8	4.6	4.3	4.8	4.8

[1] Includes other ultimate customers not shown separately.

Source: U.S. Energy Information Administration, *Statistics of Interstate Natural Gas Pipeline Companies,* annual.

Figure 22.1
Domestic Scheduled Operations of Air Carriers: 1970 to 1990

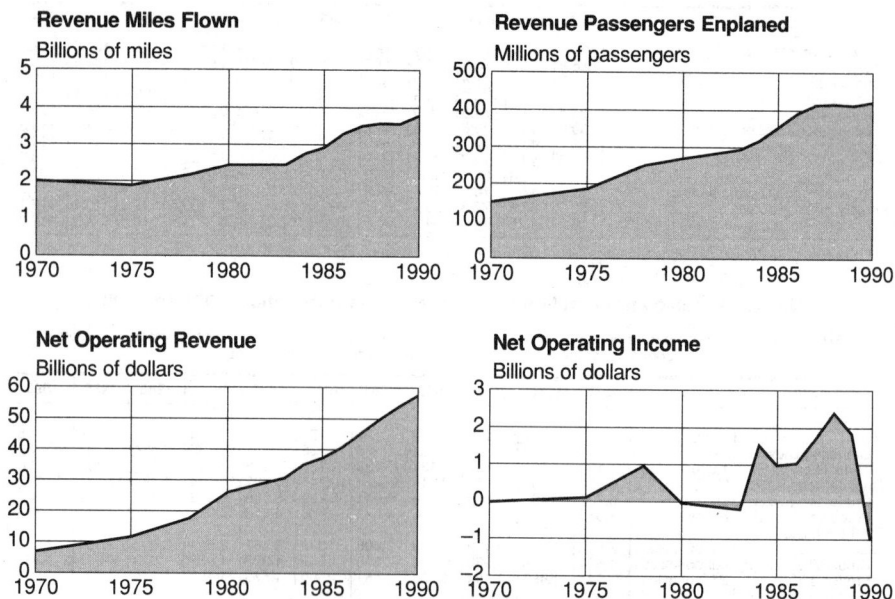

Revenue Miles Flown
Billions of miles

Revenue Passengers Enplaned
Millions of passengers

Net Operating Revenue
Billions of dollars

Net Operating Income
Billions of dollars

Source: Chart prepared by U.S. Bureau of the Census. For data, see table 1038.

Figure 22.2
Revenue Passengers Enplaned—
Top 10 Airports: 1990

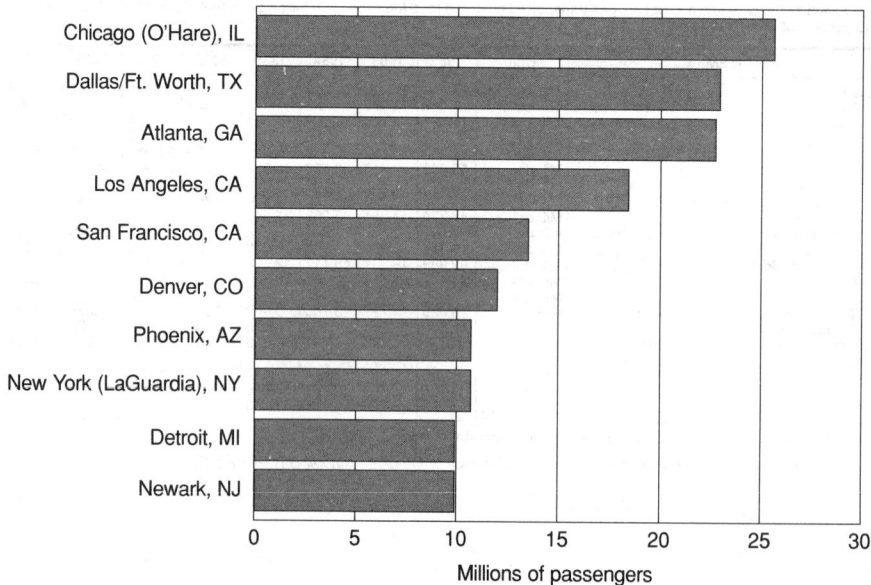

Millions of passengers

Source: Chart prepared by U.S. Bureau of the Census. For data, see table 1044.

Transportation— Air and Water

This section presents data on civil air transportation, both passenger and cargo, and on water transportation, including inland waterways, oceanborne commerce, the merchant marine, cargo and vessel tonnages, and shipbuilding. Comparative data on various types of transportation carriers are presented in section 21.

Principal sources of these data are the annual *FAA Statistical Handbook of Aviation* issued by the Federal Aviation Administration (FAA); the annual *Waterborne Commerce of the United States* issued by the Corps of Engineers of the Department of the Army; the monthly and annual issues of *U.S. Waterborne Exports and General Imports,* and the annual *Vessel Entrances and Clearances,* and the monthly *Highlights of U.S. Export and Import Trade,* issued by the Bureau of the Census. In addition, the Bureau of the Census in its commodity transportation survey (part of the census of transportation, taken every 5 years, for years ending in "2" and "7") provides data on the type, weight, and value of commodities shipped by manufacturing establishments in the United States, by means of transportation, origin, and destination.

Air transportation data are also presented annually by the Air Transport Association of America, Washington, DC in *Air Transport Facts and Figures.* Additional sources of data on water transportation include *Merchant Fleets of the World* issued by the U.S. Maritime Administration; *The Bulletin,* issued monthly by the American Bureau of Shipping, New York, NY; and the *Annual Summary of Merchant Ships Completed in the World* and the *Register Book,* published by Lloyd's Register of Shipping, London, England.

Civil aviation.—Federal promotion and regulation of civil aviation have been carried out by the FAA and the Civil Aeronautics Board (CAB). The CAB promoted and regulated the civil air transportation

In Brief

DOMESTIC AIR CARRIERS
Revenue passengers enplaned:

1970	153 million
1980	273 million
1990	424 million

Net operating income:

1970	+$3 million
1980	-$6 million
1990	-$1,012 million

industry within the United States and between the United States and foreign countries. The Board granted licenses to provide air transportation service, approved or disapproved proposed rates and fares, and approved or disapproved proposed agreements and corporate relationships involving air carriers. In December 1984, the CAB ceased to exist as an agency. Some of its functions were transferred to the Department of Transportation (DOT), as outlined below. The responsibility for investigation of aviation accidents resides with the National Transportation Safety Board.

The Office of the Secretary, DOT aviation activities include the following: negotiation of international air transportation rights, selection of U.S. air carriers to serve capacity controlled international markets, oversight of international rates and fares, maintenance of essential air service to small communities, and consumer affairs. DOT's Research and Special Programs Administration (RSPA) handles aviation information functions formerly assigned to CAB.

The principal activities of the FAA include the promotion of air safety; controlling the use of navigable airspace; prescribing regulations dealing with the competency of airmen, airworthiness of aircraft, and air traffic control; operation of air route traffic control centers, airport traffic control towers, and flight service stations; the design, construction, maintenance, and inspection of navigation, traffic control, and communications equipment; and the development of general aviation.

The CAB published monthly and quarterly financial and traffic statistical data for the certificated route air carriers. RSPA continues these publications, including both certificated and noncertificated (commuter) air carriers. The FAA publishes annually data on the use of airway facilities; data related to the location of airmen, aircraft, and airports; the volume of activity in the field of nonair carrier (general aviation) flying; and aircraft production and registration.

General aviation comprises all civil flying (including such commercial operations as small demand air taxis, agriculture application, powerline patrol, etc.) but excludes certificated route air carriers, supplemental operators, large-aircraft commercial operators and commuter airlines.

Air carriers and service.—The CAB previously issued "certificates of public convenience and necessity" under Section 401 of the Federal Aviation Act of 1958 for scheduled and nonscheduled (charter) passenger services and cargo services. It also issued certificates under Section 418 of the Act to cargo air carriers for domestic all-cargo service only. The DOT Office of the Secretary now issues the certificates under a "fit, willing, and able" test of air carrier operations. Carriers operating only 60 seat or less aircraft are given exemption authority to carry passengers, cargo, and mail in scheduled and nonscheduled service under Part 298 of the DOT (formerly CAB) regulations. Exemption authority carriers who offer scheduled passenger service to an essential air service point must meet the "fit, willing, and able" test.

Vessel shipments, entrances, and clearances.—Shipments by dry cargo vessels comprise shipments on all types of watercraft, except tanker vessels; shipments by tanker vessels comprise all types of cargo, liquid and dry, carried by tanker vessels.

A vessel is reported as entered only at the first port which it enters in the United States, whether or not cargo is unloaded at that port. A vessel is reported as cleared only at the last port at which clearance is made to a foreign port, whether or not it takes on cargo. Army and Navy vessels entering or clearing without commercial cargo are not included in the figures.

Units of measurement.—Cargo (or freight) tonnage and shipping weight both represent the gross weight of the cargo including the weight of containers, wrappings, crates, etc. However, shipping weight excludes lift and cargo vans and similar substantial outer containers. Other tonnage figures generally refer to stowing capacity of vessels, 100 cubic feet being called 1 ton. Gross tonnage comprises the space within the frames and the ceiling of the hull, together with those closed-in spaces above deck available for cargo, stores, passengers, or crew, with certain minor exceptions. Net or registered tonnage is the gross tonnage less the spaces occupied by the propelling machinery, fuel, crew quarters, master's cabin, and navigation spaces. Substantially, it represents space available for cargo and passengers. The net tonnage capacity of a ship may bear little relation to weight of cargo. Deadweight tonnage is the weight in long tons required to depress a vessel from light water line (that is, with only the machinery and equipment on board) to load line. It is, therefore, the weight of the cargo, fuel, etc., which a vessel is designed to carry with safety.

Historical statistics.—Tabular headnotes provide cross-references, where applicable, to *Historical Statistics of the United States, Colonial Times to 1970.* See Appendix IV.

No. 1038. Certificated Route Air Carriers—Summary: 1970 to 1990

[As of **Dec. 31 or for calendar years.** See text, section 22. Operations between conterminous United States, Puerto Rico, and outlying areas included with international. Minus sign (-) indicates loss. See also *Historical Statistics, Colonial Times to 1970,* series Q 577-590 and Q 624-633]

ITEM	Unit	1970	1975	1978	1980	1985	1988	1989	1990
Domestic operators [1]	Number...	35	33	34	72	86	66	62	60
Operating revenue	Mil. dol....	7,131	11,911	17,943	26,404	37,629	50,187	54,314	57,991
Operating expenses	Mil. dol....	7,128	11,781	16,948	26,409	36,611	47,739	52,460	59,004
Net operating income	Mil. dol....	3	129	995	-6	1,018	2,448	1,855	-1,012
International operators	Number...	6	2	2	(1)	(1)	(1)	(1)	(1)
Operating revenue	Mil. dol....	1,913	3,063	4,332	6,543	8,302	13,402	14,911	17,976
Operating expenses	Mil. dol....	1,894	3,059	4,008	6,766	7,984	12,403	14,954	18,878
Net operating income	Mil. dol....	19	4	324	-223	319	998	-43	-902
Employment, total [2]	1,000....	297	290	329	371	355	481	507	545
Pilots, copilots, and other flight personnel	1,000....	33	32	36	39	40	52	52	56
Flight attendants	1,000....	34	39	48	57	63	76	78	83
Mechanics	1,000....	48	45	44	45	43	55	57	61
Aircraft and traffic servicing personnel	1,000....	84	83	96	122	101	212	225	252
Other	1,000....	98	91	104	108	108	86	95	94
Fixed-wing aircraft in operation [3]	Number...	2,421	2,260	2,345	2,505	2,860	4,439	4,477	4,665
Turbojet	Number...	2,041	2,022	2,184	2,336	2,740	3,913	3,939	4,145
Two-engine	Number...	519	500	579	652	1,235	1,944	2,052	2,275
Three-engine	Number...	631	961	1,140	1,311	1,277	1,542	1,459	1,438
Four-engine	Number...	891	561	465	373	228	427	428	432
Turboprop	Number...	316	193	155	163	110	438	447	438
Piston	Number...	64	45	6	6	10	88	91	82
Average available seats: [4][5]									
Domestic operations	Number...	110.4	130.4	140	143.1	152.5	153.1	152.1	151.9
International operations	Number...	154.9	224.8	244.1	274.5	296.6	281.3	277.1	275.7
Average speed: [5]									
Domestic operations	Mi. per h...	403	403	409	405	409	409	406	408
International operations	Mi. per h...	482	482	489	494	497	488	486	489
Jet fuel consumed [6]	Mil. gal...	10,083	9,507	10,534	11,311	12,603	15,094	15,624	16,252
Domestic operations	Mil. gal...	7,842	7,558	8,621	9,218	10,115	11,902	12,087	12,461
International operations	Mil. gal...	2,241	1,949	1,913	2,093	2,488	3,192	3,537	3,791
Revenue-miles flown [5]	Millions...	2,426	2,241	2,520	2,816	3,320	4,141	4,193	4,491
Domestic operations	Millions...	2,027	1,909	2,201	2,471	2,950	3,603	3,591	3,818
International operations	Millions...	399	332	319	345	370	538	602	674
Revenue passengers enplaned [5]	Millions...	169	205	275	297	382	455	454	466
Domestic operations	Millions...	153	189	254	273	357	419	416	424
International operations	Millions...	16	16	21	24	25	35	37	42
Revenue passenger-miles flown [5]	Billions...	131.7	162.8	226.8	255.2	336.4	423.3	432.7	457.9
Domestic operations	Billions...	104.1	131.7	182.7	200.8	270.6	329.3	330.0	340.2
International operations	Billions...	27.6	31.1	44.1	54.4	65.8	94.0	102.7	117.7
Available seat-miles [5]	Billions...	265.2	303.0	368.7	432.5	547.8	676.8	684.4	733.4
Domestic operations	Billions...	213.2	241.3	299.5	346.0	445.8	536.7	530.1	563.0
International operations	Billions...	52.0	61.7	69.2	86.5	102.0	140.1	154.3	170.3
Passenger load factor [5]	Percent...	49.7	53.7	61.5	59.0	61.4	62.5	63.2	62.4
Domestic operations	Percent...	48.9	54.6	61.0	58.0	60.7	61.4	62.3	60.4
International operations	Percent...	53.0	50.4	63.7	62.8	64.6	67.1	66.6	69.1
Revenue passenger-miles per gallon of fuel	Number...	13.1	17.1	21.5	22.6	26.7	28.0	27.7	28.2
Domestic operations	Number...	13.3	17.4	21.2	21.8	26.8	26.7	27.3	27.3
International operations	Number...	12.3	16.0	23.1	26.0	26.4	29.4	29.0	31
Average passenger-mile rate: [5][7]									
Domestic operations	Dollars...	0.060	0.077	0.085	0.113	0.123	0.123	0.131	0.134
International operations	Dollars...	0.050	0.072	0.075	0.075	0.098	0.104	0.104	0.108
Express and freight revenue, ton-miles flown [5]	Millions...	3,515	4,796	5,818	5,742	6,020	9,632	10,275	10,600
Domestic operations	Millions...	2,216	2,747	3,505	3,277	3,133	4,843	4,916	5,076
International operations	Millions...	1,299	2,049	2,313	2,465	2,887	4,789	5,359	5,524
Mail, ton-miles flown [5]	Millions...	1,264	1,109	1,181	1,342	1,659	1,837	1,911	2,004
Domestic operations	Millions...	715	683	807	949	1,214	1,367	1,415	1,490
International operations	Millions...	549	426	374	393	445	470	496	513

[1] The Airline Deregulation Act of 1978 lifted some restrictions on entering new markets. As a result there is no longer a clear distinction between domestic and international operators. Includes all cargo. Carrier count as of end of year. Revenue and expense data exclude carriers which report system totals only. [2] Scheduled airlines only. Source: Air Transport Association of America, Washington, DC, *Air Transport Facts and Figures,* annual. [3] Excludes those used for crew training and general utility purposes, or held for disposal. Beginning 1980, includes aircraft operated by the scheduled all-cargo certificated route air carriers. Beginning in 1988 also includes large aircraft (passenger seating capacity of more than 30 or a payload of more than 7,500 pounds) operated by commuters and air taxis. [4] Seats per aircraft mile. Passenger seat-miles divided by revenue-miles flown in passenger service. [5] Scheduled services of all certificated route air carriers; includes all cargo. [6] Includes all cargo. Beginning 1980 includes very small amount of gasoline. Beginning 1988, excludes fuel consumption for airlines with a waiver for reporting. [7] Passenger revenues divided by revenue passenger-miles flown.

Source: Except as noted, U.S. Dept. of Transportation, Federal Aviation Administration and Research and Special Programs Administration, *Air Carrier Traffic Statistics,* monthly and *Air Carrier Financial Statistics,* quarterly. Includes data from U.S. National Transportation Safety Board.

No. 1039. Airline Cost Indexes: 1970 to 1990

[Covers U.S. major and national service carriers. Major carriers have operating revenues of $1 billion or more; nationals have operating revenues from $75 million to $1 billion]

ITEM	INDEX (1972=100)									PERCENT DISTRIBUTION OF CASH OPERATING EXPENSES [1]			
	1970	1975	1980	1985	1986	1987	1988	1989	1990	1970	1985	1980	1990
Composite.........	87.8	142.5	262.5	313.4	293.1	299.5	310.0	329.6	353.2	100.0	100.0	100.0	100.0
Labor..............	82.9	129.8	211.4	277.8	272.1	276.3	286.6	295.4	301.1	45.8	35.1	34.9	32.5
Interest [2]...........	99.0	125.0	167.2	198.8	191.2	184.5	187.9	210.2	202.3	3.6	2.9	3.5	2.5
Fuel...............	94.3	250.8	770.3	689.6	473.6	479.2	457.7	515.0	658.7	12.8	29.7	22.3	17.6
Passenger food......	97.4	120.8	153.6	167.0	167.7	173.3	182.3	199.9	215.0	3.9	2.9	3.2	3.6
Advertising and promotion....	99.5	102.7	141.5	203.3	210.4	184.7	197.2	218.0	221.7	2.7	1.7	2.3	2.1
Landing fees..........	82.2	136.1	192.9	217.6	242.6	262.5	276.8	294.0	316.7	2.2	1.7	1.7	1.9
Passenger traffic commissions.	80.2	154.0	322.8	491.4	499.9	540.8	619.0	679.0	733.4	2.6	4.8	7.4	9.7
All other.............	95.5	127.6	184.4	239.2	245.4	253.2	260.9	271.8	282.8	26.4	21.3	24.6	30.1

[1] Total operating expenses plus interest on long term debt, less depreciation and amortization.   [2] Interest on debt.
Source: Air Transport Association of America, Washington, DC, *Air Transport, 1990*, annual; and unpublished data.

No. 1040. Aircraft in Operation and Aircraft Age, by Type of Aircraft: 1983 to 1989

[As of January 1. For U.S. domestic and major services. Major carriers have operating revenue of $1 billion or more; national carriers have operating revenues of $75 million to $1 billion]

TYPE OF AIRCRAFT	AIRCRAFT IN OPERATION				MEAN AGE (years) [1]			
	1983	1985	1987	1989	1983	1985	1987	1989
Industry total................	2,360	2,790	2,816	3,190	10.5	10.8	11.8	12.0
Majors....................	1,953	2,185	2,386	2,850	10.9	11.6	12.0	12.2
Nationals..................	407	605	430	340	8.4	8.0	10.6	10.6
Type of aircraft:								
Boeing 727 [2]	1,001	996	993	956	10.5	12.0	13.9	15.5
Boeing 737	270	365	547	698	8.9	9.1	8.8	8.2
Boeing 747	130	136	124	136	10.9	11.8	15.0	15.8
Boeing 757	2	23	73	107	1.0	2.0	2.4	3.6
Boeing 767	14	54	61	111	1.0	2.6	3.9	4.3
Airbus A300/A310............	30	134	59	76	3.4	1.9	5.7	5.3
Lockheed L-1011 [2]	119	184	107	111	7.3	7.5	11.0	13.0
McDonnell Douglas DC-8 [2]	98	72	52	40	15.8	17.2	18.8	20.9
McDonnell Douglas DC-9 [2]	541	658	433	455	11.9	9.9	16.7	18.5
McDonnell Douglas DC-10 [2]	155	168	161	159	9.1	9.8	12.5	14.6
McDonnell Douglas MD-80	(X)	(X)	206	341	(X)	(X)	3.1	3.9

X Not applicable.   [1] For definition of mean, see Guide to Tabular Presentation.   [2] No longer in production.
Source: AVMARK, Arlington, VA. Compiled from data by the U.S. Dept. of Transportation and Aviation Information Services Limited, London, England, *The World's Jet and Turboprop Airliner Fleet*.

No. 1041. Net New Firm Orders Booked for U.S. Civil Jet Transport Aircraft: 1983 to 1990

[Value in millions of dollars. Minus sign (-) indicates net cancellations]

TYPE OF AIRCRAFT AND CUSTOMER	1983	1984	1985	1986	1987	1988	1989	1990
Total number [1]	158	319	468	332	519	956	1,015	670
U.S. customers	89	212	242	134	217	404	507	259
Foreign customers	69	107	226	198	302	552	508	411
Boeing 737, total	82	144	253	106	234	311	397	189
U.S. customers	50	116	146	45	105	173	216	38
Foreign customers	32	28	107	61	129	138	181	151
Boeing 747, total	19	32	37	68	61	57	57	153
U.S. customers	5	-	13	6	15	22	4	24
Foreign customers	14	32	24	62	46	35	53	129
Boeing 757, total	3	22	51	21	44	186	190	66
U.S. customers	-1	21	39	11	18	101	137	33
Foreign customers	4	1	12	10	26	85	53	33
Boeing 767, total	9	12	10	22	42	87	138	60
U.S. customers	-2	-6	4	3	11	32	40	23
Foreign customers	11	18	6	19	31	55	98	37
Boeing 777, total	-	-	-	-	-	-	-	34
U.S. customers	-	-	-	-	-	-	-	34
Foreign customers.	-	-	-	-	-	-	-	-
McDonnell Douglas MD-11, total ...	-	-	-	-	29	59	38	52
U.S. customers	-	-	-	-	2	11	17	16
Foreign customers	-	-	-	-	27	48	21	36
McDonnell Douglas MD-80/90, total.	44	97	114	112	105	254	195	116
U.S. customers	37	75	37	68	65	65	93	91
Foreign customers	7	22	77	44	40	189	102	25
Total value	4,258	9,624	14,811	13,948	18,737	39,806	47,470	45,485
U.S. customers	1,530	4,981	7,869	3,394	6,999	16,308	20,304	14,828
Foreign customers	2,728	4,643	6,942	10,554	11,738	23,498	27,166	30,657

- Represents zero.   [1] Includes types of aircraft not shown separately.
Source: Aerospace Industries Association of America, Washington, DC, Research Center, Statistical Series 23.

No. 1042. Worldwide Airline Fatalities: 1970 to 1990

[Passenger deaths for scheduled air transport operations]

YEAR	Aircraft fatal accidents	Passenger deaths	Death rate [1]	YEAR	Aircraft fatal accidents	Passenger deaths	Death rate [1]
1970.	29	700	0.29	1981.	21	362	0.06
1971.	32	884	0.35	1982.	26	764	0.13
1972.	41	1,209	0.42	1983.	20	809	0.13
1973.	29	862	0.27	1984.	16	223	0.03
1974.	21	1,299	0.38	1985. [2]	22	1,066	0.15
1975.	20	467	0.13	1986. [2]	22	546	0.06
1976.	24	734	0.19	1987. [2]	26	901	0.09
1977.	25	516	0.12	1988. [2]	28	729	0.07
1978.	31	754	0.15	1989. [2]	27	817	0.05
1979.	31	877	0.16	1990. [2][3]	25	495	0.03
1980.	22	814	0.14				

[1] Rate per 100 million passenger miles flown.   [2] Includes USSR which began reporting in 1986.   [3] Preliminary.
Source: International Civil Aviation Organization, Montreal, Canada, *Civil Aviation Statistics of the World*, annual.

No. 1043. Aircraft Accidents and Hijackings: 1975 to 1990

[For years ending December 31]

ITEM	Unit	1975	1980	1985	1986	1987	1988	1989	1990
Aircraft accidents: [1]									
General aviation [2]	Number. . .	3,995	3,590	2,737	2,576	2,464	2,354	2,201	2,138
Fatal	Number. . .	633	618	497	473	431	447	423	424
Rate per 100,000 aircraft hours flown	Rate.	2.20	1.69	1.62	1.61	1.47	1.51	1.38	1.39
Fatalities	Number. . .	1,252	1,239	951	965	807	777	757	736
Air carrier, all services [3]	Number. . .	(NA)	19	22	24	36	29	30	26
Fatal	Number. . .	(NA)	1	7	3	5	3	11	6
Rate per 1,000,000 aircraft miles flown	Rate.	(X)	-	0.002	0.001	0.001	-	0.002	0.001
Fatalities	Number. . .	(NA)	1	526	8	232	285	278	39
Air carrier, scheduled services	Number. . .	29	15	17	21	32	28	25	24
Fatal	Number. . .	2	-	4	2	4	3	8	6
Rate per 1,000,000 aircraft miles flown	Rate.	0.001	0.000	0.001	-	0.001	0.001	0.002	0.001
Fatalities	Number. . .	122	-	197	5	231	285	131	39
Commuter air carriers [4]	Number. . .	48	38	21	15	32	19	17	14
Fatal	Number. . .	12	8	7	2	10	2	5	2
Rate per 1,000,000 aircraft miles flown	Rate.	0.07	0.04	0.02	0.01	0.03	0.01	0.01	0.01
Fatalities	Number. . .	28	37	37	4	59	21	31	4
Air taxis [5]	Number. . .	152	171	152	116	97	96	113	104
Fatal	Number. . .	24	46	35	31	30	27	26	26
Rate per 100,000 aircraft hours flown	Rate.	0.95	1.27	1.26	1.06	1.04	0.95	0.83	0.82
Fatalities	Number. . .	69	105	76	65	65	58	88	40
Hijacking incidents, worldwide	Number. . .	25	39	35	12	15	17	24	46
U.S. registered aircraft	Number. . .	12	21	4	4	4	3	6	4
Successful [6]	Number. . .	4	13	2	-	-	-	-	(NA)
Foreign-registered aircraft.	Number. . .	13	18	31	8	11	14	18	42
Successful [6]	Number. . .	3	9	18	2	5	-	-	(NA)
Bomb threats:									
U.S. airports	Number. . .	449	268	256	238	376	178	487	448
Explosions	Number. . .	4	1	-	-	-	-	-	-
U.S. worldwide and foreign aircraft in U.S . . .	Number. . .	1,853	1,179	372	401	898	372	479	338
Explosions	Number. . .	2	1	1	1	1	1	2	-

- Represents or rounds to zero.   NA Not available.   X Not applicable.   [1] Data from National Transportation Safety Board.   [2] See text, section 22.   [3] U.S. Air Carriers operating under 14 CFR 121.   [4] All scheduled service of U.S. Air Carriers operating under 14 CFR 135.   [5] All nonscheduled service of U.S. Air Carriers operating under 14 CFR 135.   [6] Hijacker controls flight and reaches destination or objective.
Source: U.S. Federal Aviation Administration, *FAA Statistical Handbook of Aviation*, annual; and unpublished data. Includes data from U.S. Department of Transportation, Research and Special Programs Administration.

No. 1044. Top 10 Airports—Traffic Summary: 1990

[In thousands, except percent change. For calendar year. Airports ranked by revenue passengers enplaned, 1990]

AIRPORT	Rank	AIRCRAFT DEPARTURES			REVENUE PASSENGERS ENPLANED		ENPLANED REVENUE TONS		
		Total [1]	Scheduled		Total	Percent change, 1980-1990	Total [2]	Freight and express	U.S. mail
			Number	Completed					
All airports [2]	(X)	6,642	6,759	6,601	438,544	57.1	6,299	4,733	1,566
Atlanta, Hartsfield International . . .	3	286	289	285	22,666	13.4	259	166	93
Chicago, O'Hare	1	322	332	322	25,636	33.3	441	300	140
Dallas/Ft. Worth International	2	267	270	266	22,899	119.5	229	143	87
Denver, Stapleton International . . .	6	154	156	154	11,962	24.4	105	67	38
Detroit, Metro Wayne	9	135	138	134	9,903	97.1	75	43	32
Los Angeles International	4	213	216	212	18,438	30.2	424	353	72
New York, LaGuardia	8	130	131	129	10,725	27.7	59	23	36
Newark International	10	130	133	129	9,854	134.3	197	163	34
Phoenix, Sky Harbor International .	7	148	149	148	10,727	217.4	66	43	24
San Francisco International	5	172	188	172	13,475	43.3	77	22	55

X Not applicable.   [1] Includes completed scheduled and unscheduled.   [2] Includes other airports, not shown separately.
Source: U.S. Federal Aviation Administration and Research and Special Programs Administration, *Airport Activity Statistics*, annual.

No. 1045. On-Time Flight Arrivals and Departures at Major U.S. Airports: 1990 and 1991

[In percent. Quarterly, based on gate arrival and departure times for domestic scheduled operations in the 48 contiguous states of major U.S. airlines, per DOT reporting rule effective September 1987. All U.S. airlines with one percent or more of total U.S. domestic scheduled airline passenger revenues are required to report on-time data. A flight is considered on time if it operated less than 15 minutes after the scheduled time shown in the carrier's computerized reservation system. Cancelled and diverted flights are considered late. Excludes flight operations delayed/cancelled due to aircraft mechanical problems reported on FAA maintenance records (4-5% of the reporting airlines' scheduled operations). See source for data on individual airlines]

	ON-TIME ARRIVALS						ON-TIME DEPARTURES					
	1990		1991				1990		1991			
AIRPORT	3d qtr.	4th qtr.	1st qtr.	2d qtr.	3d qtr.	4th qtr.	3d qtr.	4th qtr.	1st qtr.	2d qtr.	3d qtr.	4th qtr.
Total, all airports	81.3	79.1	78.5	84.1	85.2	82.0	87.6	85.0	84.1	89.1	90.2	87.5
Total 29 major airports	80.1	78.4	77.5	83.0	83.8	80.9	86.2	84.1	82.9	87.9	88.7	86.1
Atlanta, Hartsfield International	78.8	77.5	78.0	80.0	80.7	81.1	85.3	82.8	82.4	84.9	88.4	88.1
Baltimore/Washington International .	81.1	83.4	84.6	86.6	85.8	84.1	87.4	88.5	88.6	91.2	90.6	89.4
Boston, Logan International	74.9	77.7	76.8	81.2	79.6	75.4	83.6	85.3	84.7	88.3	85.6	83.3
Charlotte, Douglas	84.3	82.9	85.0	85.7	83.7	86.4	87.1	86.3	88.2	89.9	87.9	87.6
Chicago, O'Hare	80.0	78.1	76.0	82.9	85.6	77.0	85.0	82.5	80.3	86.6	89.0	80.8
Dallas/Ft. Worth International	83.5	75.4	78.7	84.1	83.7	77.1	89.0	81.2	84.4	87.7	90.7	84.3
Denver, Stapleton International	82.1	76.4	75.9	78.1	82.4	77.0	87.0	82.2	82.8	84.3	87.5	83.1
Detroit, Metro Wayne	81.7	83.4	85.1	88.6	90.8	87.9	86.9	86.1	87.2	90.6	91.9	89.8
Dulles International	83.5	85.3	83.8	84.6	85.4	85.8	88.4	88.9	87.2	88.4	90.1	88.8
Houston Intercontinental	81.9	79.5	78.3	78.0	85.3	81.3	89.1	86.2	85.2	83.7	89.4	87.1
Las Vegas, McCarran International .	86.4	77.7	74.2	84.9	87.0	86.0	90.0	83.5	79.2	88.7	88.9	89.0
Los Angeles International	80.7	75.7	70.0	79.1	78.5	76.0	87.4	84.1	78.0	86.3	85.9	83.9
Miami International	81.7	83.4	82.5	84.1	78.2	77.8	86.8	89.7	87.3	90.7	89.2	88.6
Minneapolis/St. Paul International . .	81.0	84.1	82.3	88.1	88.6	81.1	85.5	85.8	84.9	90.7	91.0	83.8
Newark International	70.2	72.8	74.4	80.1	79.4	80.1	80.1	82.1	82.3	87.2	85.3	87.0
New York, Kennedy International. . .	69.9	76.5	76.9	81.2	78.5	78.1	74.5	81.4	82.1	85.5	80.2	81.2
New York, LaGuardia	73.2	78.5	81.1	81.6	82.5	83.1	84.4	87.2	86.4	89.1	88.8	88.9
Orlando International	78.8	81.6	79.8	84.0	83.8	84.1	88.7	90.3	87.6	90.0	90.6	91.3
Philadelphia International	70.7	78.6	80.2	82.9	82.3	81.5	80.4	84.8	84.2	88.9	88.4	86.1
Phoenix, Sky Harbor International . .	83.0	75.5	72.7	86.7	88.8	85.0	86.5	77.6	74.1	87.0	88.6	85.7
Pittsburgh, Greater International . . .	78.2	82.7	81.7	85.6	85.1	80.9	81.9	83.0	83.6	88.1	86.9	81.0
Raleigh/Durham	87.4	85.8	88.9	91.5	88.9	90.3	89.9	88.5	90.1	93.4	92.5	92.6
St. Louis, Lambert.	84.0	75.8	69.6	83.4	86.7	81.2	86.7	80.2	75.7	89.5	91.2	85.7
Salt Lake City International.	85.3	79.7	77.8	87.5	87.2	80.7	90.8	85.2	83.7	91.8	90.9	87.1
San Diego International, Lindbergh .	83.7	76.4	72.2	83.2	85.2	82.5	87.5	83.6	78.7	88.2	88.3	86.5
San Francisco International	78.2	75.4	62.3	73.4	75.1	79.6	87.2	84.7	74.5	82.9	83.3	85.7
Seattle-Tacoma International	78.0	65.7	74.7	81.1	84.9	75.6	84.7	79.9	83.7	88.6	88.1	86.6
Tampa International	80.2	82.1	80.6	84.9	83.2	83.6	89.2	90.3	86.7	92.1	92.9	92.8
Washington National	81.1	84.3	84.9	86.0	86.3	84.9	88.2	88.7	89.8	90.9	91.3	89.9

Source: U.S. Department of Transportation, Office of Consumer Affairs, *Air Travel Consumer Report,* monthly.

No. 1046. Consumer Complaints Against U.S. Airlines: 1986 to 1991

[Calendar year data. See source for data on individual airlines]

COMPLAINT CATEGORY	COMPLAINTS						PERCENT			RANK		
	1986	1987	1988	1989	1990	1991	1986	1989	1991	1986	1989	1991
Total	10,802	40,985	21,493	10,553	7,703	6,126	100.0	100.0	100.0	(X)	(X)	(X)
Flight problems [1]	3,390	18,019	8,831	4,111	3,034	1,883	31.4	39.0	30.7	1	1	1
Baggage.	2,149	7,438	3,938	1,702	1,329	888	19.9	16.1	14.5	2	2	2
Refunds	1,627	3,313	1,667	1,023	701	787	15.1	9.7	12.8	3	3	3
Customer service [2]	702	3,888	2,120	1,002	758	714	6.5	9.5	11.7	5	4	4
Ticketing/boarding [3]	687	2,458	1,445	821	624	661	6.4	7.8	10.8	6	5	5
Fares [4]	468	937	455	341	312	388	4.3	3.2	6.3	7	7	6
Oversales [5]	849	2,122	1,353	607	399	304	7.9	5.8	5.0	4	6	7
Advertising	122	344	141	89	96	96	1.1	0.8	1.6	9	9	8
Smoking.	311	888	546	232	74	30	2.9	2.2	0.5	8	8	9
Tours	33	90	37	22	29	23	0.3	0.2	0.4	11	10	10
Credit.	40	101	35	19	5	10	0.4	0.2	0.2	10	11	11
Other	424	1,387	925	584	342	342	3.9	5.5	5.6	(X)	(X)	(X)

X Not applicable. [1] Cancellations, delays etc. from schedule. [2] Unhelpful employees, inadequate meals or cabin service, treatment of delayed passengers. [3] Errors in reservations and ticketing; problems in making reservations and obtaining tickets. [4] Incorrect or incomplete information about fares, discount fare conditions and availability, etc. [5] All bumping problems, whether or not airline complied with DOT regulations.

Source: U.S. Dept. of Transportation, Office of Consumer Affairs, *Air Travel Consumer Report,* monthly.

No. 1047. Commuter/Regional Airline Operations—Summary: 1980 to 1990

[Calendar year data. Commuter/regional airlines operate primarily aircraft of predominately 60 passengers or less and 18,000 pounds of payload capacity serving short haul and small community markets. Represents operations within all North America by U.S. Regional Carriers. Averages are mean. For definition of mean, see Guide to Tabular Presentation]

ITEM	Unit	1980	1983	1984	1985	1986	1987	1988	1989	1990
Passenger carriers operating	Number .	214	196	203	179	179	169	163	151	150
Passengers enplaned	Millions .	14.8	21.8	26.1	[1]26.0	28.4	31.8	35.2	37.4	42.1
Average passengers enplaned per carrier	1,000 . .	69.2	111.2	128.1	152.4	158.4	187.7	213.9	247.4	277.5
Revenue passenger miles (RPM).	Billions .	1.92	3.24	4.17	[1]4.41	4.47	5.0	6.04	6.77	7.61
Average RPMs per carrier	Millions .	8.97	16.53	20.46	[1]24.64	24.98	29.60	37.05	44.84	50.75
Airports served.	Number .	732	854	853	854	824	834	861	817	811
Average trip length	Miles. . .	129	149	160	173	158	158	173	181	183
Passenger aircraft operated	Number .	1,339	1,545	1,747	1,745	1,806	1,841	1,801	1,907	1,917
Average seating capacity (seats)	Number .	13.9	18.1	18.4	19.2	18.4	19.7	20.5	21.8	22.1
Fleet flying hours	1,000 . .	1,740	2,415	2,764	2,854	2,929	2,942	3,078	3,266	3,447
Average annual utilization aircraft	Hours . .	1,299	1,563	1,582	1,635	1,622	1,598	1,709	1,712	1,798

[1] Adjusted to exclude a merger in 1986.
Source: Regional Airline Association, Washington, DC, *1991 Annual Report of the Regional Airline Industry* (copyright).

No. 1048. Civil Flying—Summary: 1970 to 1990

[As of **Dec. 31** or for years ending **Dec. 31,** except as noted. See also *Historical Statistics, Colonial Times to 1970,* series Q 604-623]

ITEM	Unit	1970	1980	1985	1986	1987	1988	1989	1990
Airports in operation [1]	Number .	11,261	15,161	16,318	16,582	17,015	17,327	17,446	17,490
Heliports	Number .	790	2,336	3,120	3,336	3,653	3,913	4,016	4,085
Public	Number .	4,260	4,814	5,861	4,924	4,984	5,043	5,084	5,078
Private	Number .	7,001	10,347	10,457	11,658	12,031	12,284	12,362	12,412
Airports with runway lights	Number .	3,554	4,738	4,941	4,954	4,922	4,890	4,443	4,822
Airports with paved runways	Number .	3,805	5,833	6,721	6,948	7,232	7,429	7,612	7,694
Miles (nautical) of Federal airways. . . .	1,000. . .	324.7	411.1	368.5	332.0	332.9	334.8	366.6	(NA)
Airport Improvement Program [2]	Mil. dol. .	50.5	639.0	842.1	1,615.3	919.4	1,278.3	1,271.2	1,244.7
Total civil aircraft.	1,000. . .	154.5	259.4	274.9	275.7	275.1	272.7	274.8	275.9
Active aircraft [3]	1,000. . .	134.5	214.8	215.4	224.9	222.4	215.9	225.4	218.9
Air carriers, total [4]	1,000. . .	2.8	3.8	4.7	4.9	5.2	5.6	5.7	6.7
General aviation aircraft [5]	1,000. . .	131.7	211.0	210.7	220.0	217.2	210.3	219.7	212.2
Fixed-wing aircraft:									
Multi-engine:									
Multi-engine.	1,000. . .	18.4	31.7	33.6	34.3	33.0	32.2	34.1	32.7
Single-engine:									
4-place and over	1,000. . .	64.6	107.9	105.6	109.4	107.5	105.2	107.8	104.6
3-place and less.	1,000. . .	44.9	60.5	58.8	62.4	63.5	59.6	62.6	60.5
Rotorcraft [6]	1,000. . .	2.2	6.0	6.4	6.9	6.3	6.4	7.5	7.4
Balloons, blimps, gliders, etc	1,000. . .	1.6	5.0	6.3	7.0	6.8	6.9	7.7	7.0
Airman certificates held	1,000. . .	1,002	1,195	1,105	1,119	1,128	1,143	1,168	1,195
Pilot [7]	1,000. . .	733	827	710	709	700	694	700	703
Held by women	Percent .	4.0	6.4	6.1	6.1	6.1	6.1	6.1	5.8
Airline transport	1,000. . .	34	70	83	87	91	97	102	108
Commercial	1,000. . .	187	183	152	148	144	143	145	149
Private	1,000. . .	304	357	311	306	301	300	293	299
Student.	1,000. . .	196	200	147	150	146	137	143	128
Nonpilot [8]	1,000. . .	269	368	395	410	428	449	468	492
Ground technicians [9]	1,000. . .	241	321	341	353	367	385	401	421
FAA employees: Total	Number .	53,125	55,340	47,245	46,809	47,907	49,210	50,977	51,269
Air traffic control specialists [10]	Number .	(NA)	27,190	23,580	23,515	24,132	24,803	24,368	24,339
Full performance [11]	Number .	(NA)	16,317	11,672	12,533	11,617	12,180	12,640	12,985
Developmental [11]	Number .	(NA)	4,387	4,304	3,976	5,462	5,495	5,574	5,042
Assistants [11]	Number .	(X)	(X)	1,465	1,479	1,481	1,283	1,316	1,153
Traffic management coordinators [12] .	Number .	(X)	(X)	(X)	(X)	278	347	350	370
Electronic technicians	Number .	(NA)	8,871	6,856	6,600	6,788	6,627	6,508	6,458
Aviation safety inspectors	Number .	(NA)	2,038	1,897	2,204	2,305	2,499	2,766	2,984
Engineers.	Number .	(NA)	2,436	2,457	2,417	2,579	2,640	2,657	2,745
Other.	Number .	(NA)	14,805	12,455	12,073	12,058	12,641	14,678	14,743
General aviation: [5]									
Hours flown	Million . .	26.0	41.0	34.1	34.4	33.4	33.6	35.0	34.8
Fuel consumed: [13]									
Gasoline	Mil. gal. .	362	520	420	410	402	398	343	353
Jet fuel [14]	Mil. gal. .	415	766	691	732	672	746	688	663

NA Not available.   X Not applicable.   [1] Existing airports, heliports, seaplane bases, etc. recorded with FAA. Includes military airports with joint civil and military use. Includes U.S. outlying areas. Airport-type definitions: Public—publicly owned and under control of a public agency; private owned by a private individual or corporation. May or may not be open for public use.
[2] Fiscal year data. Does not include System Planning Grants. Includes U.S. outlying areas. 1970-1980 data are obligated Federal funds for the Airport Development Aid Program. 1985-1990 data are appropriated Federal funds under the Airport and Airway Improvement Act of 1982.   [3] Registered aircraft that flew 1 or more hours during the year.   [4] Includes helicopters.   [5] See text, section 22.   [6] Includes autogyros; excludes air carrier helicopters.   [7] Includes all active pilots. An active pilot is one with a pilot certificate and a valid medical certificate. Also includes pilots who hold only a helicopter, glider, or lighter than air certificate, not shown separately.   [8] Includes dispatchers, flight navigators and engineers, and ground technicians—mechanics, parachute riggers, and ground instructors.   [9] No medical examinations are required, therefore, data represent all certificates on record and include retired or otherwise inactive technicians.   [10] Includes all air traffic control specialists (staff positions, managers, supervisors, and for 1970-1986 traffic management coordinators, not shown separately) and air traffic assistants.   [11] Serving in-flight service stations, towers, and centers.   [12] Prior to 1987, included in total air traffic control specialists.   [13] Source: 1970, U.S. Bureau of Mines; thereafter, FAA General Aviation Activity and Avionics Survey.   [14] Includes kerosene-type and naphtha-type jet fuels.
Source: Except as noted, U.S. Federal Aviation Administration, *FAA Statistical Handbook of Aviation,* annual; and unpublished data. Includes data from U.S. Department of Transportation, Research and Special Programs Administration.

No. 1049. U.S. Aircraft Shipments, 1970 to 1991, and Projections, 1992

[Value in millions of dollars]

YEAR	TOTAL		CIVIL						MILITARY	
	Units	Value	Large transports [1]		General Aviation [2]		Helicopters		Units	Value
			Units	Value	Units	Value	Units	Value		
1970	11,632	7,511	311	3,158	7,292	337	495	49	3,534	3,967
1975	17,030	9,136	315	3,779	14,072	1,033	864	274	1,779	4,050
1980	14,681	18,950	387	9,895	11,881	2,507	1,366	656	1,047	5,892
1981	11,978	20,093	387	9,706	9,457	2,920	1,072	597	1,062	6,870
1982	6,244	19,257	232	6,246	4,266	1,999	587	365	1,159	10,647
1983	4,409	22,519	262	8,000	2,691	1,470	403	303	1,053	12,746
1984	3,935	21,933	185	5,689	2,438	1,698	376	330	936	14,216
1985	3,610	28,386	278	8,448	2,029	1,431	384	506	919	18,001
1986	3,258	34,809	330	10,308	1,495	1,262	326	287	1,107	22,952
1987	3,010	35,925	357	10,507	1,085	1,364	358	277	1,210	23,777
1988	3,254	34,875	423	13,603	1,143	1,918	383	334	1,305	19,020
1989	3,675	34,229	398	15,074	1,535	1,804	515	251	1,227	17,100
1990	3,418	41,920	521	22,215	1,144	2,007	603	254	1,150	17,444
1991 [3]	3,244	44,273	583	26,200	1,024	1,838	632	188	1,005	16,047
1992 [4]	3,132	43,989	534	26,829	1,068	1,897	660	200	870	15,063

[1] Capacity over 70 seats. [2] Includes aircraft kits for exports. [3] Estimated. [4] Forecast.

Source: U.S. Department of Commerce, International Trade Administration, U.S. Industrial Outlook, 1992.

No. 1050. Employment and Earnings in Aircraft Industries: 1975 to 1991

[Annual averages of monthly figures]

1987 SIC [1] code	ITEM	Unit	1975	1980	1985	1987	1988	1989	1990	1991
(X)	Employment: Total	1,000..	596	746	794	883	893	906	892	821
3721	Aircraft........................	1,000..	293	349	326	356	369	382	377	343
3724	Aircraft engines and engine parts	1,000..	126	163	148	158	156	154	151	142
3728	Aircraft equipment, n.e.c. [2]	1,000..	84	123	143	163	160	176	178	166
376	Guided missiles, space vehicles, and parts ..	1,000..	93	111	177	206	208	194	186	170
(X)	Average weekly earnings: [3]									
3721	Aircraft........................	Dollars .	256	404	(NA)	(NA)	(NA)	(NA)	(NA)	(NA)
3724	Aircraft engines and parts	Dollars .	247	394	542	567	582	616	637	654
376	Guided missiles, space vehicles, and parts ..	Dollars .	245	378	518	541	567	589	612	632
(X)	Average hourly earnings: [3]									
3721	Aircraft [4].......................	Dollars .	6.21	9.66	13.18	13.74	14.18	14.89	15.66	16.72
3724	Aircraft engines and parts	Dollars .	6.04	9.42	12.85	13.33	13.33	13.80	14.42	15.38
376	Guided missiles, space vehicles, and parts ..	Dollars .	6.02	9.22	12.14	12.73	13.13	13.70	14.39	14.90

NA Not available. X Not applicable. [1] 1987 Standard Industrial Classification; see text, section 13. [2] N.e.c.=Not elsewhere classified. [3] For production workers. [4] Excludes lump-sum payments. Earnings which include proration of lump-sum payments were; $13.40 in 1985; $14.32 in 1987; $14.65 in 1988; $15.41 in 1989; $16.32 in 1990 and $17.16 in 1991.

Source: U.S. Bureau of Labor Statistics, Bulletin 2370; and Employment and Earnings, monthly.

No. 1051. Aerospace Industry—Summary, 1980 to 1991, and Projections, 1992

[For calendar year, except employment and earnings annual averages of monthly figures. Includes Standard Industrial Classification Codes 372 and 376. Industry shipments refer to the total value of all products shipped by establishments classified in that industry. Product shipments refer to the total value of specific products shipped, irrespective of how the establishments which made them are classified]

ITEM	Unit	1980	1984	1985	1986	1987	1988	1989	1990	1991 [1]	1992 [2]
INDUSTRY DATA											
Value of shipments	Mil. dol.	58,483	77,826	90,795	100,999	103,589	107,746	113,477	123,705	123,933	124,558
In 1987 dollars	Mil. dol.	(NA)	(NA)	(NA)	(NA)	103,589	107,671	109,073	114,340	109,529	105,800
Employment, total.......	1,000..	721	693	746	798	810	820	823	814	749	741
Production workers	1,000..	387	344	372	400	407	399	400	395	364	360
Average hourly earnings ..	Dol ...	9.90	13.24	13.88	14.37	14.92	15.35	15.84	(NA)	(NA)	(NA)
Capital expenditures	Mil. dol.	1,923	3,050	3,784	4,144	3,612	3,388	3,921	(NA)	(NA)	(NA)
PRODUCT DATA											
Value of shipments	Mil. dol.	53,296	70,200	80,625	90,907	97,185	102,242	106,320	117,226	117,249	117,396
In 1987 dollars	Mil. dol.	(NA)	(NA)	(NA)	(NA)	97,185	101,850	101,671	108,189	103,410	100,712

NA Not available. [1] Estimated. [2] Forecast.

Source: U.S. Department of Commerce, International Trade Administration, U.S. Industrial Outlook, 1992.

No. 1052. Aerospace—Sales, New Orders, and Backlog: 1970 to 1990

[In billions of dollars, except as indicated. Reported by establishments in which the principal business is the development and/or production of aerospace products]

ITEM	1970	1975	1980	1983	1984	1985	1986	1987	1988	1989 [1]	1990 [1]
Net sales	24.8	29.5	58.4	83.5	88.9	100.5	105.6	110.3	113.5	122.1	141.6
Percent of U.S. Government	66.3	58.7	45.6	58.8	62.7	63.2	61.9	62.2	60.0	58.0	55.0
Complete aircraft and parts [2]	10.4	11.3	22.6	27.3	28.3	34.2	38.0	37.0	35.7	38.4	50.0
Aircraft engines and parts.	3.1	3.4	6.9	8.6	9.1	9.7	9.8	12.0	15.0	15.4	16.4
Missiles and space vehicles, parts . .	5.4	6.3	8.4	12.7	13.6	16.7	17.5	20.7	21.5	22.6	21.9
Other products, services.	5.9	8.5	20.5	34.8	38.0	39.8	40.3	40.5	41.3	45.7	53.4
Net, new orders	21.2	29.0	70.4	91.6	104.9	111.0	110.8	121.2	147.1	173.6	147.3
Backlog, Dec. 31	24.7	35.0	90.5	116.6	132.5	143.0	148.2	158.7	191.5	252.4	264.2

[1] Data beginning 1989 are not comparable with earlier years. Data are being reported which were previously not available. The extent of this noncomparabilty is not known. [2] Except engines sold separately.

Source: U.S. Bureau of the Census, *Current Industrial Reports*, series MA-37D.

No. 1053. Aerospace Industry Sales, by Product Group and Customer: 1980 to 1992

[In billions of dollars. Due to reporting practices and tabulating methods, figures may differ from those in table 1052]

ITEM	CURRENT DOLLARS						CONSTANT (1982) DOLLARS [3]					
	1980	1985	1989 [1]	1990	1991 [1]	1992 [2]	1980	1985	1989	1990	1991 [1]	1992 [2]
Total sales.	54.7	96.6	117.6	134.2	140.3	142.9	68.1	86.6	98.4	107.8	108.9	107.0
PRODUCT GROUP												
Aircraft, total	31.5	50.5	61.0	70.8	75.6	77.3	39.2	45.3	51.0	56.9	58.6	58.0
Civil [4]	16.3	13.7	22.1	30.9	36.4	40.3	20.3	12.3	18.5	24.9	28.2	30.2
Military	15.2	36.8	38.9	39.9	39.2	37.0	18.9	33.0	32.5	32.0	30.4	27.8
Missiles	6.5	11.4	11.2	12.1	10.5	10.0	8.1	10.3	9.4	9.8	8.2	7.5
Space . . . . [5] . .	7.9	18.6	25.8	28.9	30.8	31.8	9.9	16.6	21.6	23.2	23.9	23.8
Related products and services [5] . .	8.8	16.1	19.6	22.4	23.4	23.8	11.0	14.4	16.4	18.0	18.1	17.9
CUSTOMER GROUP												
Aerospace, total.	45.9	80.5	98	111.8	116.9	119.1	57.1	72.2	82.0	89.9	90.7	89.3
DOD [6]	22.8	53.2	58.5	60.6	57.9	54.7	28.4	47.7	48.9	48.7	44.9	41.1
NASA [7] and other agencies . . .	4.1	6.3	9.6	11.1	12.8	13.9	5.1	5.6	8.1	9.6	9.9	10.4
Other customers [8] . . . . . . [5] . .	19.0	21.0	29.9	40.1	46.2	50.4	23.6	18.9	25.0	32.3	35.8	37.8
Related products and services [5] . .	8.8	16.1	19.6	22.4	23.4	23.8	11.0	14.4	16.4	18.0	18.1	17.9

[1] Preliminary. [2] Estimate. [3] Based on aerospace composite price deflator supplied by the U.S. International Trade Administration. [4] All civil sales of aircraft (domestic and export sales of jet transports, commuters, business and personal aircraft and helicopters). [5] Electronics, software, and ground support equipment, plus sales of non-aerospace products which are produced by aerospace-manufacturing establishments and which use technology, processes, and materials derived from aerospace products. [6] Department of Defense. [7] National Aeronautics and Space Administration. [8] Includes civil aircraft sales (see footnote 4), commercial space sales, all exports of military aircraft and missiles and related propulsion and parts.

Source: Aerospace Industries Association of America, Inc., Washington, DC, *Aerospace Facts and Figures, 1991/92*.

No. 1054. Aerospace Industry—Net Profits After Taxes: 1976 to 1991

YEAR	AEROSPACE INDUSTRY PROFITS				ALL MANUFACTURING CORPORATIONS PROFITS AS PERCENT OF—		
	Total (mil. dol.)	As percent of—			Sales	Assets	Equity
		Sales	Assets	Equity			
1976	1,091	3.4	4.7	12.8	5.4	7.5	14.0
1977	1,427	4.2	5.7	14.9	5.3	7.6	14.2
1978	1,816	4.4	5.5	15.7	5.4	7.8	15.0
1979	2,614	5.0	6.3	18.4	5.7	8.4	16.5
1980	2,588	4.3	5.2	16.0	4.8	6.9	13.9
1981	2,966	4.4	5.2	16.0	4.7	6.7	13.6
1982	2,193	3.3	3.7	12.0	3.5	4.5	9.2
1983	2,829	3.5	4.1	12.1	4.1	5.1	10.5
1984	3,639	4.1	4.7	14.1	4.6	6.0	12.5
1985	3,274	3.1	3.6	11.1	3.8	4.6	10.1
1986	3,093	2.8	3.1	9.4	3.7	4.2	9.5
1987	4,582	4.1	4.4	14.6	4.9	5.6	12.8
1988	4,883	4.3	4.4	14.9	6.0	6.9	16.2
1989	3,866	3.3	3.3	10.7	5.0	5.6	13.7
1990	4,487	3.4	3.4	11.5	4.0	4.3	10.7
1991	2,486	1.8	1.9	6.1	2.5	2.6	6.5

Source: Aerospace Industries Association of America, Washington, DC, *Aerospace Facts and Figures*, annual.

No. 1055. U.S. Exports of Aerospace Vehicles and Equipment, 1988 to 1991, and Projections, 1992

ITEM	NUMBER OF UNITS					VALUE (mil. dol.)				
	1988	1989	1990	1991 [1]	1992 [2]	1988	1989	1990	1991 [1]	1992 [2]
Aerospace vehicles and equipment .	(NA)	(NA)	(NA)	(NA)	(NA)	26,915	32,884	39,030	42,413	44,758
Civilian aircraft	2,784	3,940	3,446	3,288	3,247	10,294	14,257	18,110	20,881	22,438
Under 4,536 kg. unladen weight, new .	619	1,638	799	600	624	298	265	318	250	260
4,536-15,000 kg. unladen weight, new.	24	48	79	70	74	49	164	245	292	304
Over 15,000 kg. unladen weight, new .	217	260	306	356	365	8,766	13,122	16,691	19,499	21,059
Rotocraft, new	280	294	349	388	372	219	155	161	173	180
Other new aircraft, n.e.c. [3]	(NA)	(NA)	(NA)	(NA)	(NA)	323	18	15	24	20
Used, rebuilt, and converted	1,644	1,700	1,913	1,874	1,837	639	533	680	643	615
Military aircraft, new and used.	(NA)	846	445	498	480	2,157	892	1,481	1,826	2,020
Aircraft engines and parts	(NA)	(NA)	(NA)	(NA)	(NA)	5,420	6,629	6,870	7,058	7,273
Piston engines and parts.	(NA)	(NA)	(NA)	(NA)	(NA)	389	438	421	443	460
Complete engines, new and used . .	6,260	8,653	6,411	7,300	7,000	57	131	110	108	110
Engine parts	(NA)	(NA)	(NA)	(NA)	(NA)	332	307	311	335	350
Turbine engines and parts.	(NA)	(NA)	(NA)	(NA)	(NA)	5,031	6,191	6,449	6,615	6,813
Complete engines, new and used . .	2,486	3,917	3,008	2,860	2,900	1,705	2,053	1,846	2,067	2,130
Engine parts	(NA)	(NA)	(NA)	(NA)	(NA)	3,326	4,138	4,603	4,548	4,683
Propellers and parts	(NA)	(NA)	(NA)	(NA)	(NA)	75	271	343	316	320
Landing gear and parts	(NA)	(NA)	(NA)	(NA)	(NA)	125	273	276	315	322
Aircraft parts, n.e.c. [3]	(NA)	(NA)	(NA)	(NA)	(NA)	7,228	8,198	8,982	9,038	9,220
Guided missiles and parts	(NA)	(NA)	(NA)	(NA)	(NA)	434	1,042	1,306	1,403	1,500
Flight simulators	(NA)	(NA)	(NA)	(NA)	(NA)	159	206	255	220	215
Space launch equipment	(NA)	(NA)	(NA)	(NA)	(NA)	622	384	660	537	550
Avionics	(NA)	(NA)	(NA)	(NA)	(NA)	401	732	747	819	900

NA Not available.   [1] Estimated.   [2] Forecast.   [3] N.e.c.=Not elsewhere classified.
Source: U.S. Dept. of Commerce, International Trade Administration, *U.S. Industrial Outlook*, 1992.

No. 1056. U.S. Receipts and Payments for International Transportation: 1970 to 1989

[In millions of dollars. Data are international transportation transactions recorded for balance of payment purposes (see table 1314). Receipts include freight on exports carried by U.S.-operated carriers and foreign carrier expenditures in U.S. ports. Payments include freight on imports carried by foreign carriers and U.S. carrier port expenditures abroad. Freight on exports carried by foreign carriers is excluded since such payments are directly or indirectly for foreign account. Similarly, freight on U.S. imports carried by U.S. carriers is a domestic rather than an international transaction. Minus sign (-) indicates excess of payments over receipts. See *Historical Statistics, Colonial Times to 1970*, series U 3 and U 10, for totals]

ITEM	1970	1980	1982	1983	1984	1985	1986	1987	1988	1989
Total receipts	3,672	14,208	15,491	16,200	17,823	18,997	20,915	23,854	27,710	30,517
Ocean transportation.	2,256	7,757	7,685	8,133	8,449	8,846	9,169	10,060	11,135	11,628
Export freight earnings	604	2,641	2,549	2,881	2,702	2,866	2,610	2,806	2,959	3,065
Freight earnings on shipments between foreign countries	209	588	555	575	563	574	576	595	708	755
Port expenditures.	1,406	4,435	4,468	4,562	5,457	5,274	5,843	6,514	7,315	7,609
Charter hire	37	93	113	115	127	132	140	145	153	199
Air transportation	1,243	5,946	7,326	7,596	8,459	9,670	10,877	12,809	15,563	17,913
Export freight earnings	187	742	762	576	645	706	783	982	1,385	1,719
Passenger fares	544	2,591	3,174	3,610	4,014	4,323	5,457	6,866	8,771	10,101
Port expenditures.	512	2,613	3,390	3,410	3,800	4,641	4,637	4,961	5,407	6,093
Other transportation	173	505	480	471	515	481	869	985	1,012	976
Total payments	4,058	15,397	16,482	18,225	20,721	22,293	23,381	25,496	27,607	29,313
Ocean transportation.	2,380	8,447	8,307	8,624	10,560	11,018	11,619	11,649	12,641	12,641
Import freight payments	1,444	5,809	5,562	5,827	7,755	8,114	8,636	8,657	9,505	9,483
Passenger fares	245	268	290	305	305	320	320	328	328	322
Port expenditures.	316	1,905	1,957	1,980	1,972	2,048	2,125	2,114	2,244	2,228
Charter hire	375	465	498	512	528	536	538	550	564	608
Air transportation	1,581	6,705	7,938	9,361	9,918	11,049	11,473	13,515	14,585	16,280
Import freight payments	115	562	725	1,066	1,633	1,666	2,051	2,242	2,226	2,197
Passenger fares	970	3,339	4,482	5,698	5,573	6,330	6,346	7,083	7,604	8,200
Port expenditures.	496	2,804	2,731	2,597	2,712	3,053	3,076	4,190	4,755	5,883
Other transportation	97	245	237	240	243	226	289	332	381	392
Balance.	-386	-1,189	-991	-2,025	-2,898	-3,296	-2,466	-1,642	103	1,204

Source: U.S. Bureau of Economic Analysis, *Survey of Current Business,* June issues; and unpublished data.

No. 1057. Exports and Imports, by Method of Transport: 1970 to 1990

[Exports are free alongside ship (f.a.s.) value (see text, section 29) for all years; imports are f.a.s. value for 1980 and customs value for other years. Export data include both domestic and foreign; import data for general imports only. For details, see source]

ITEM	Unit	EXPORTS						IMPORTS					
		1970	1980	1985	1988	1989	1990	1970	1980	1985	1988	1989	1990
All methods [1]	Bil. dol.	43.2	220.7	213.1	320.4	363.8	393.0	40.0	240.8	345.3	441.3	473.4	495.3
Vessel	Bil. dol.	24.6	120.9	91.7	126.0	146.3	150.8	24.8	165.1	208.4	255.8	269.9	283.4
Air.	Bil. dol.	6.1	46.1	52.3	91.6	101.9	110.5	3.4	28.0	51.3	77.5	84.4	90.9
Shipping weight: Vessel . . .	Bil. kg.	218.0	363.7	317.7	361.8	390.6	372.4	271.4	443.1	361.5	466.8	494.7	496.3
Air.	Bil. kg.	0.4	1.0	0.8	1.4	1.6	1.5	0.3	0.6	1.3	1.5	4.3	1.7

[1] Includes types other than vessel and air and revisions that are not distributed by method of transport.
Source: U.S. Bureau of the Census, Highlights of U.S. Export and Import Trade, through 1988, FT 990, monthly; thereafter, U.S. Merchandise Trade: Selected Highlights, FT-920, monthly.

No. 1058. Federal Expenditures for Civil Functions of the Corps of Engineers, United States Army: 1960 to 1990

[In millions of dollars. For fiscal years ending in year shown, see text, section 9. These expenditures represent the work of the Corps of Engineers to plan, design, construct, operate, and maintain civil works projects and activities, particularly in the management and improvement of rivers, harbors, and waterways for navigation, flood control, and multiple purposes. The amounts listed below do not include the expenditure of funds contributed, advanced, or reimbursed by other government agencies or local interests. Includes Puerto Rico and outlying areas]

FISCAL YEAR	Total program [1]	Navigation	Flood control	Multiple purpose	FISCAL YEAR	Total program [1]	Navigation	Flood control	Multiple purpose
1960.....	873	310	293	270	1982.....	2,940	1,331	1,083	453
1965.....	1,169	426	447	283	1983.....	2,959	1,290	1,088	482
1970.....	1,128	398	379	331	1984.....	3,085	1,383	1,154	445
1975.....	2,070	694	904	439	1985.....	2,956	1,234	1,187	419
1977.....	2,340	792	918	594	1986.....	3,163	1,345	1,300	402
1978.....	2,645	951	1,069	583	1987.....	2,937	1,135	1,272	411
1979.....	2,934	1,083	1,218	577	1988.....	3,086	1,271	1,271	423
1980.....	3,061	1,225	1,228	551	1989.....	3,252	1,395	1,253	462
1981.....	3,198	1,339	1,273	527	1990.....	3,297	1,391	1,397	375

[1] Includes expenditures which are not associated with a specific purpose (e.g., headquarters staff supervision, management, and administration activities, and some research and development activities).
Source: U.S. Army Corps of Engineers, *Report of Civil Works Expenditures by State and Fiscal Year*, annual.

No. 1059. Freight Carried on Inland Waterways, by System: 1960 to 1989

[In billions of ton-miles. Excludes Alaska and Hawaii, except as noted. Includes waterways, canals, and connecting channels]

ITEM	1960	1970	1980	1981	1982	1983	1984	1985	1986	1987	1988	1989
Total	220.3	318.6	406.9	410.2	351.2	359.0	399.0	381.7	392.6	410.7	438.2	448.7
Atlantic coast waterways....	28.6	28.6	30.4	28.3	25.4	22.5	24.7	24.8	25.7	25.9	28.1	28.2
Gulf coast waterways	16.9	28.6	36.6	35.1	31.8	32.4	36.7	36.5	39.0	37.9	44.6	42.5
Pacific coast waterways [1]	6.0	8.4	14.9	14.4	12.8	13.2	20.5	19.9	20.8	22.8	24.5	24.0
Mississippi River system [2] ...	69.3	138.5	228.9	234.4	218.0	223.0	234.6	224.7	239.3	251.6	257.8	268.1
Great Lakes System [3]	99.5	114.5	96.0	98.0	63.2	67.9	82.5	75.8	67.9	72.5	83.1	85.8

[1] Includes Alaskan waterways.   [2] Comprises main channels and all tributaries of the Mississippi, Illinois, Missouri, and Ohio Rivers.   [3] Does not include traffic between foreign ports.
Source: U.S. Army Corps of Engineers, *Waterborne Commerce of the United States*, annual.

No. 1060. Domestic and Foreign Waterborne Commerce, by Type of Commodity: 1970 to 1989

[In millions of short tons. Domestic trade includes all commercial movements between United States ports and on inland rivers, Great Lakes, canals, and connecting channels of the United States, Puerto Rico, and Virgin Islands. Figures may differ from those shown in table 1061 due to minor differences in basic concepts]

COMMODITY	1970 Total	1970 Domestic	1980 Total	1980 Domestic	1985 Total	1985 Domestic	1989 Total	1989 Domestic	1989 Foreign Imports	1989 Foreign Exports
Net total	1,531.7	950.7	1,998.9	1,077.5	1,788.4	1,014.1	2,140.4	1,102.5	589.5	448.4
Petroleum products [1] ...	394.7	287.3	423.2	339.2	368.8	259.0	441.9	289.2	108.8	43.9
Gasoline	89.3	88.7	87.3	81.0	94.0	78.0	107.9	86.2	19.8	1.9
Distillate fuel oil	78.8	76.9	74.6	72.1	70.0	55.0	75.2	58.1	12.9	4.2
Residual fuel oil	170.5	78.8	188.0	141.3	130.0	83.7	147.5	91.4	42.8	13.3
Crude petroleum	210.5	116.3	480.2	174.2	357.7	194.7	480.8	181.9	298.8	0.1
Coal and lignite	225.4	154.1	256.4	164.1	273.9	179.9	304.8	203.8	2.4	98.6
Nonmetallic minerals [1][2] ..	166.6	132.6	157.1	111.6	150.7	108.5	158.7	111.6	25.7	21.4
Sand and gravel [3]	78.4	73.9	65.1	60.8	66.4	62.0	58.8	54.9	2.1	1.8
Limestone	42.0	34.1	34.2	23.9	24.5	21.9	41.3	35.5	2.3	3.5
Phosphate rock......	16.6	5.8	23.7	9.5	19.4	8.4	15.8	6.1	0.8	8.9
Iron and concentrates...	129.3	75.2	98.4	64.9	72.7	50.0	86.5	59.6	21.4	5.5
Farm products [1]	90.4	28.5	216.8	63.4	172.8	60.0	216.3	70.5	8.7	137.1
Corn	27.2	11.7	98.6	30.8	70.3	20.0	96.4	35.8	0.1	60.5
Wheat............	25.0	5.8	53.4	14.3	38.0	10.6	55.8	16.5	0.2	39.1
Soybeans	21.2	8.3	39.6	16.1	32.9	14.9	28.8	12.8	(Z)	16.0
Chemicals and allied products	62.0	39.7	91.9	49.4	108.5	53.3	123.3	61.9	15.9	45.5
Food and kindred products	35.0	11.0	54.8	20.4	52.5	17.6	54.3	20.6	11.5	22.2
Lumber and wood products [4]	49.9	27.3	52.0	22.7	47.2	18.8	56.9	21.0	4.7	31.2
Primary metal products ..	42.4	10.8	28.9	9.0	33.4	8.5	31.5	8.7	17.9	4.9
Waste and scrap	25.9	16.0	31.1	18.8	37.4	23.9	54.6	37.3	0.9	16.4
Other.............	99.7	51.9	108.1	39.8	112.8	40.0	130.8	36.4	72.8	21.6

Z Less than 50,000.   [1] Includes categories not shown separately.   [2] Excludes fuels.   [3] Includes crushed rock.   [4] Excludes furniture.
Source: U.S. Army Corps of Engineers, *Waterborne Commerce of the United States*, annual.

No. 1061. Waterborne Imports and Exports—Cargo Tonnage and Value, by Coastal District: 1970 to 1990

[Exports are free alongside ship (f.a.s.) value for all years; imports are f.a.s. value for 1980 and customs value for other years see text, section 29. Includes commodities classified for security reasons as "Special Category" (exports only) and exports by Dept. of Defense (grant-aid shipments), and merchandise shipped in transit through the United States. See Appendix III]

DISTRICT	CARGO TONNAGE (mil. sh. tons)							VALUE (bil. dol.)						
	1970	1980	1985	1987	1988	1989	1990	1970	1980	1985	1987	1988	1989	1990
Imports:														
Atlantic	219	183	190	224	234	211	207	15.0	71.5	94.4	105.8	107.4	109.3	110.8
Gulf.	47	243	141	184	212	217	225	2.9	56.4	32.8	30.5	31.2	36.1	41.0
Pacific	31	56	51	56	55	55	55	5.5	45.0	90.4	118.4	126.5	140.9	143.3
Great Lakes	26	16	17	14	16	16	16	1.3	1.9	2.8	2.0	2.5	3.7	7.6
Exports:														
Atlantic	79	117	93	78	92	94	101	11.9	51.0	35.2	38.7	48.2	56.3	62.4
Gulf.	78	163	144	155	162	152	148	6.9	41.5	31.8	31.6	37.9	40.9	41.2
Pacific	48	78	81	95	110	103	100	4.1	25.2	25.8	31.9	43.3	50.1	53.7
Great Lakes	36	45	34	32	37	34	26	1.4	4.6	2.4	2.1	3.2	3.6	1.7

Source: U.S. Bureau of the Census, *U.S. Waterborne Exports and General Imports*, through 1988, FT 985, annual; thereafter TM 985, monthly.

No. 1062. Vessels Entered and Cleared in Foreign Trade—Net Registered Tonnage, by Flag of Carrier Vessel: 1966 to 1990

[**In millions of net tons, except as indicated.** Includes Puerto Rico and Virgin Islands. Seaports comprise all ports except Great Lakes ports. See also *Historical Statistics, Colonial Times to 1970*, series Q 507-517]

YEARLY AVERAGE OR YEAR	Number of vessels	ALL PORTS				SEAPORTS					
		Tonnage, all vessels				Tonnage, all vessels			Tonnage, with cargo		
		Total	U.S.	Percent U.S.	Foreign	Total	U.S.	Foreign	Total	U.S.	Foreign
Entered:											
1966-70.	53,459	232	29	12.5	203	206	27	180	157	18	139
1971-75.	53,760	319	30	9.5	290	292	28	264	220	24	196
1976-80.	53,700	458	40	8.7	418	425	38	387	316	30	286
1981-85.	50,124	452	57	12.4	395	424	55	369	277	36	241
1986-90.	61,978	548	46	8.4	502	521	45	476	346	30	315
1970.	53,293	254	26	10.3	226	227	24	202	171	19	152
1975.	51,443	355	32	9.9	323	326	30	297	240	26	215
1980.	53,645	492	52	10.6	440	460	50	410	310	34	276
1985.	53,531	451	53	11.7	398	426	52	374	283	34	249
1986.	56,859	489	49	10.0	439	463	48	415	310	32	278
1987.	59,563	518	48	9.3	470	492	47	445	333	29	304
1988.	62,097	556	47	8.5	509	527	46	481	352	30	322
1989.	64,946	587	44	7.4	543	558	42	516	367	31	335
1990.	66,424	589	41	7.0	548	564	40	524	367	30	337
Cleared:											
1966-70.	52,415	232	30	12.8	202	206	27	179	122	23	99
1971-75.	53,039	324	31	9.9	293	296	29	267	149	21	127
1976-80.	52,931	453	41	9.1	412	420	38	382	203	26	177
1981-85.	50,291	460	57	12.4	403	432	55	377	251	34	217
1986-90.	60,249	551	47	8.6	504	524	46	478	284	31	253
1970.	52,195	253	27	10.6	226	226	25	201	132	20	112
1975.	51,017	363	34	10.3	329	334	31	303	168	23	144
1980.	52,928	487	54	11.1	433	456	51	405	246	33	213
1985.	53,095	461	55	11.9	406	435	53	382	253	36	217
1986.	55,710	491	51	10.4	441	466	49	417	246	33	212
1987.	58,307	521	49	9.4	472	495	48	447	269	31	238
1988.	60,540	561	49	8.7	512	531	47	484	295	31	264
1989.	63,042	590	45	7.6	545	561	44	517	304	30	274
1990.	63,648	592	43	7.3	550	566	41	525	304	29	275

Source: U.S. Bureau of the Census, *Vessel Entrances and Clearances*, through 1986, FT 975, annual; thereafter TA 987, annual.

No. 1063. Domestic Merchant Vessels Completed by U.S. Shipyards: 1970 to 1988

[**Vessels of 1,000 gross tons and over.** See also *Historical Statistics, Colonial Times to 1970*, series Q 438-48]

TYPE	Unit	1970	1975	1979	1980	1981	1982	1983	1984	1985	1986	1987	1988
Merchant vessels	Number	13	15	15	10	12	11	13	5	8	5	4	4
Gross tons	1,000	342	452	1,149	375	275	337	376	118	172	215	153	153
Cargo	Number	6	3	4	6	2	6	6	-	4	2	3	3
Gross tons	1,000	120	65	53	105	53	221	228	-	113	66	58	58
Deadweight tons	1,000	134	71	47	114	73	219	219	-	97	53	63	63
Tankers	Number	7	12	11	4	10	5	7	5	4	3	1	1
Gross tons	1,000	222	387	1,096	270	222	116	148	118	59	149	95	95
Deadweight tons	1,000	427	742	1,901	354	358	226	277	210	92	271	209	209

- Represents zero.

Source: U.S. Maritime Administration, *New Ship Construction*, annual.

No. 1064. United States Flag Merchant Vessels—Number and Vessel Deadweight Tonnage: 1990

[As of **end of fiscal year;** see text, section 9. Covers ocean-going vessels of 1,000 gross tons and over engaged in foreign and domestic trade, and inactive vessels. Excludes special types such as tugs, barges, cable ships, fishing trawlers, and vessels employed on Great Lakes. See also *Historical Statistics, Colonial Times to 1970,* series Q 487-502]

VESSEL TYPE	NUMBER						DEADWEIGHT TONNAGE (1,000)					
	Total	Pas-sen-ger [1]	Car-go [2]	Inter-modal	Bulk car-rier	Tanker	Total	Pas-sen-ger [1]	Car-go [2]	Inter-modal	Bulk car-rier	Tanker
Total.............	635	9	199	168	26	233	24,262	86	2,546	4,711	1,270	15,649
Active vessels............	423	7	55	153	22	186	18,374	59	857	4,339	972	12,147
Privately owned	368	2	38	122	22	184	17,329	14	617	3,629	972	12,097
U.S. foreign trade........	131	-	27	66	15	23	5,119	-	426	2,271	785	1,637
Foreign-to-foreign........	25	-	-	9	-	16	2,103	-	-	227	-	1,876
Domestic trade	158	2	2	26	7	121	8,624	14	24	549	187	7,850
Coastal	83	-	2	-	5	76	3,134	-	24	-	132	2,978
Noncontiguous.........	75	2	-	26	2	45	5,490	14	-	549	55	4,872
Military Sea Lift Command..	54	-	9	21	-	24	1,483	-	167	582	-	734
Government owned........	55	5	17	31	-	2	1,045	45	240	710	-	50
Ready reserve force......	45	2	13	29	-	1	935	23	188	691	-	33
Inactive vessels............	212	2	144	15	4	47	5,888	27	1,689	372	298	3,502
Privately owned	38	1	6	8	3	20	3,200	16	70	263	273	2,578
Temporarily inactive	2	-	-	1	-	1	214	-	-	41	-	173
Laid-up.............	28	1	2	6	3	16	2,754	16	15	192	273	2,258
Laid-up (CHARAD Custody) [3].............	8	-	4	1	-	3	232	-	55	30	-	147
Government owned (CHARAD Custody) [3]	174	1	138	7	1	27	2,688	11	1,619	109	25	924
National defense reserve fleet...............	165	1	133	7	-	24	2,382	11	1,560	109	-	702
Ready reserve fleet.....	51	-	37	4	-	10	829	-	495	72	-	262
Other reserve.........	114	1	96	3	-	14	1,553	11	1,065	37	-	440
Nonretention [4]..........	5	-	5	-	-	-	59	-	59	-	-	-
Other Government owned ..	4	-	-	-	1	3	247	-	-	-	25	222

- Represents zero.   [1] Includes combination passenger and cargo vessels.   [2] General cargo.   [3] In the custody of the Maritime Administration.   [4] Vessels not actively maintained.

Source: U.S. Maritime Administration, *Employment Report of the United States Flag Merchant Fleet Ocean-going Vessels 1,000 Gross Tons and Over,* annual.

No. 1065. Private Shipyards—Summary: 1970 to 1991

[For calendar year, unless noted. See also *Historical Statistics, Colonial Times to 1970,* series Q 449-458 and series Q 467-472]

ITEM	Unit	1970	1980	1984	1985	1986	1987	1988	1989	1990	1991
Employment	1,000...	133.4	177.3	142.0	130.3	120.6	120.4	121.0	123.4	[1]121.8	[1]125.0
Production workers	1,000...	108.5	141.8	111.0	99.0	90.3	90.8	90.9	88.6	[1]86.4	[1]94.3
Value of work done	Mil. dol.	2,682	9,269	8,944	9,358	8,840	8,531	(NA)	(NA)	(NA)	(NA)
On ships only..........	Mil. dol.	2,594	8,889	8,308	9,483	8,913	8,377	(NA)	(NA)	(NA)	(NA)
Value added	Mil. dol.	1,616	5,338	5,206	5,740	5,426	5,227	(NA)	(NA)	(NA)	(NA)
Building activity:											
Merchant vessels: [2]											
Under construction [3]....	Number .	49	69	10	10	7	6	-	-	-	3
Ordered	Number .	13	7	5	-	-	-	-	-	-	3
Delivered	Number .	13	23	5	3	1	4	-	-	-	-
Cancelled	Number .	-	4	-	-	-	2	-	-	-	-
Under contract [4]	Number .	49	49	10	7	6	-	-	-	3	3
Naval vessels: [2]											
Under construction [3]....	Number .	108	99	111	100	85	79	83	105	98	89
Ordered	Number .	6	11	11	11	16	20	32	16	7	(NA)
Delivered	Number .	32	19	22	26	20	16	10	23	15	(NA)
Under contract [4]	Number .	82	91	100	85	[5]79	83	105	98	[6]89	(NA)
Repairs/conversions:											
Commercial ships	Mil. dol. .	431	1,335	1,631	852	847	806	(NA)	(NA)	(NA)	(NA)
Naval ships ...,.......	Mil. dol. .	359	1,134	1,641	2,311	2,008	1,930	(NA)	(NA)	(NA)	(NA)
Unfinished work: [3]											
Commercial ships	Mil. dol.	765	2,070	100	450	315	53	-	-	-	(NA)
Naval ships	Mil. dol. .	1,719	7,107	14,003	12,091	9,595	8,265	10,500	16,010	(NA)	(NA)

- Represents zero.   NA Not available.   [1] Estimate as of July.   [2] Vessels of 1,000 tons or larger.   [3] As of Jan. 1.   [4] As of Dec. 31.   [5] Two ships were cancelled during 1986.   [6] One contract was terminated in December 1990.

Source: Shipbuilders Council of America, Washington, DC, *Annual Report,* through 1980; thereafter, unpublished data.

No. 1066. Employees in Government and Private Shipyards: 1960 to 1991

[In thousands. Annual average employment in establishments primarily engaged in building and repairing all types of ships, barges, canal boats, and lighters of 5 gross tons and over, whether propelled by sail or motor power, or towed by other craft. Includes all full- and part-time employees]

YEAR	Total	Private yards	Navy yards	YEAR	Total	Private yards	Navy yards	YEAR	Total	Private yards	Navy yards
1960.	208	112	96	1980.	251	178	73	1986.	206	131	75
1970.	216	134	83	1981.	264	187	77	1987.	199	124	75
1975.	217	154	65	1982.	252	172	80	1988.	197	124	73
1977.	242	174	68	1983.	227	143	84	1989.	197	126	71
1978.	243	172	71	1984.	229	146	83	1990.	197	129	68
1979.	244	173	71	1985.	219	138	80	1991.	190	127	63

Source: U.S. Bureau of Labor Statistics, Bulletin 2370; *Employment and Earnings,* monthly; and unpublished data.

No. 1067. Employment on U.S. Flag Merchant Vessels, 1970 to 1991, and Basic Monthly (January) Wage Scale for Able-Bodied Seamen, 1970 to 1992

[Employment in thousands. See also *Historical Statistics, Colonial Times to 1970,* series Q 414-416]

YEAR	Employ- ment[1]	YEAR	Employ- ment[1]	YEAR	East coast wage rate[2]	West coast wage rate[2]	YEAR	East coast wage rate[2]	West coast wage rate[2]
1970.	37.6	1985	13.1	1970	$470	$652	1986	$1,419	$2,132
1975.	20.5	1986	11.5	1975	612	900	1987	1,419	2,132
1980.	19.6	1987	10.4	1979	865	1,287	1988	1,419	2,175
1981.	18.3	1988	10.7	1980	967	1,414	1989	1,448	2,218
1982.	16.7	1989	9.9	1983	1,320	1,862	1990	1,505	2,218
1983.	15.3	1990	11.1	1984	1,419	2,029	1991	1,581	2,329
1984.	13.7	1991	11.7	1985	1,419	2,069	1992	1,655	2,438

[1] As of June 30, except beginning 1980, as of Sept. 30. Estimates of personnel employed on merchant ships, 1,000 gross tons and over. Excludes vessels on inland waterways, Great Lakes, and those owned by, or operated for, U.S. Army and Navy, and special types such as cable ships, tugs, etc. [2] Basic monthly wage, over and above subsistence (board and room); excludes overtime and fringe pay benefits. West coast incorporates extra pay for Saturdays and Sundays at sea into base wages but east coast does not.

Source: U.S. Maritime Administration, *U.S. Merchant Marine Data Sheet,* monthly; and unpublished data.

No. 1068. Worldwide Tanker Casualties: 1975 to 1991

[Data for 1975 and 1980 covers tankers, ore/oil carriers and bulk/oil vessels of 6,000 deadweight tons and over; beginning 1983, 10,000 deadweight tons and over; excludes liquid gas carriers. Incident is counted in the year it is reported. Based on data from "Lloyd's List" published by Lloyd's of London. "Casualties" include weather damage, strandings, collisions and other contact, fires and explosions, machinery damage, and other mishaps]

ITEM	Unit	1975	1980	1983	1984	1985	1986	1987	1988	1989	1990	1991
Casualties.	Number	906	(NA)	(NA)	(NA)	340	451	408	456	528	541	507
Total losses[1]	Number	22	15	11	14	12	8	5	3	8	10	10
Deaths	Number	90	132	14	68	53	23	12	63	74	119	205
Oil spills	Number	45	32	17	15	9	8	12	13	31	31	26
Amount	1,000 tons . .	188	136	388	22	80	5	9	178	188	61	439

NA Not available. [1] Excludes losses due to hostilities.

Source: Tanker Advisory Center, Inc., New York, NY, "Worldwide Tanker Casualty Returns," quarterly.

No. 1069. Merchant Vessels—World and United States: 1960 to 1990

[Vessels of 100 gross tonnage and above. Excludes sailing ships, nonpropelled craft, and all ships built of wood. See also *Historical Statistics, Colonial Times to 1970,* series Q 473-480]

YEAR	WORLD: COMPLETED		WORLD: OWNED		U.S.: COMPLETED		U.S.: REGISTERED	
	Number	Gross tonnage (1,000)	Number	Gross tonnage (1,000)	Number	Gross tonnage (1,000)	Number	Gross tonnage (1,000)
1960	2,005	8,382	36,311	129,770	49	379	4,059	24,837
1970	2,814	20,980	52,444	227,490	156	375	2,983	18,463
1980	2,412	13,101	73,832	419,911	205	555	5,579	18,464
1984	2,210	18,334	76,068	418,682	73	84	6,441	19,292
1985	1,964	18,157	76,395	416,269	66	180	6,447	19,518
1986	1,634	16,845	75,266	404,910	36	223	6,496	19,901
1987	1,528	12,259	75,240	403,498	29	164	6,427	20,178
1988	1,575	10,909	75,680	403,406	60	11	6,442	20,832
1989	1,593	13,236	76,100	410,481	10	4	6,375	20,588
1990	1,672	15,885	78,336	423,627	16	15	6,348	21,328

Source: Lloyd's Register of Shipping, London, England, *Statistical Tables,* annual; and *Annual Summary of Merchant Ships Completed in the World.*

No. 1070. Merchant Vessels—Ships and Tonnage Lost Worldwide, by Type of Ship: 1980 to 1990

[For merchant vessels of 100 gross tonnage and above. Excludes ships which have been declared constructive losses but have undergone repair during the year. Loss counted in the year the casualty occurred, providing that information was available at time of relevant publication]

TYPE OF SHIP	SHIPS LOST					GROSS TONNAGE LOST (1,000)				
	1980	1985	1988	1989	1990	1980	1985	1988	1989	1990
Total [1]	387	307	231	211	188	1,804	1,651	865	667	1126
Tankers	24	19	9	13	8	707	776	327	135	138
Ore/bulk carriers [2]	21	22	8	12	15	458	405	133	182	687
General cargo	211	155	110	92	87	478	363	227	250	202
Container ships	2	5	4	2	-	6	41	26	3	-
Passenger [3]	9	-	2	1	-	112	-	11	12	-
Fishing	96	66	60	67	50	30	26	22	29	20

- Represents zero.   [1] Includes types not shown separately.   [2] Includes ore/bulk/oil carriers.   [3] Includes passenger cargo ships.

Source: Lloyd's Register of Shipping, London, England, *Casualty Return,* annual.

No. 1071. Merchant Fleets of the World: 1980 to 1989

[Vessels of 1,000 gross tons and over. As of Jan. 1 of the following year. Specified countries have 100 or more ships]

YEAR AND COUNTRY OF REGISTRY, 1989	TOTAL		PASSENGER/ CARGO COMB.		FREIGHTERS		BULK CARRIERS [1]		TANKERS	
	Number	Average age (yr.)	Number	Average age (yr.)	Number	Average age (yr.)	Number	Average age (yr.)	Number	Average age (yr.)
1980, world total. . .	24,867	13	468	24	14,242	14	4,798	10	5,359	12
United States	864	23	65	34	471	23	20	22	308	20
Foreign.	24,003	13	403	22	13,771	13	4,778	10	5,051	11
1985, world total. . .	25,555	14	375	25	13,937	15	5,787	11	5,456	13
United States	737	23	37	38	417	25	25	9	258	19
Foreign.	24,818	14	338	23	13,520	15	5,762	11	5,198	13
1988, world total. . .	23,468	14	368	23	12,518	15	5,332	12	5,250	14
United States	675	22	21	41	381	24	26	12	247	19
Foreign.	22,793	14	347	22	12,137	15	5,306	12	5,003	13
1989, world total [2] .	22,983	14	320	23	12,195	15	5,335	12	5,133	14
United States	655	22	19	41	371	24	26	12	239	19
Privately-owned	407	16	4	36	171	14	26	12	206	18
Government-owned . . .	248	33	15	43	200	32	-	(X)	33	31
Foreign.	22,328	14	301	22	11,824	15	5,309	12	4,894	13
Argentina.	135	18	-	-	69	18	17	16	49	17
Brazil	293	14	2	28	114	19	94	9	83	13
British Colonies.	545	15	6	16	252	17	176	12	111	15
Bulgaria.	114	15	2	16	52	16	46	14	14	17
China: Mainland	1,281	18	13	25	860	19	240	15	168	17
Taiwan.	226	12	1	18	147	13	63	10	15	13
Cyprus	1,054	15	3	32	537	15	410	15	104	15
Denmark (DIS) [3]	199	7	-	-	136	8	9	8	54	7
East Germany	147	14	1	8	125	15	17	13	4	10
Egypt	131	17	4	27	100	18	16	7	11	20
France	134	12	4	10	64	11	15	8	51	14
Greece	914	15	31	28	238	18	442	13	203	16
Honduras.	139	25	1	34	107	26	11	24	20	23
India	296	13	3	24	112	15	118	11	63	10
Indonesia.	323	19	7	13	217	21	13	8	86	16
Iran.	123	13	-	-	38	17	50	10	35	15
Italy	479	16	9	19	181	16	67	14	222	17
Japan.	1,007	8	14	10	411	7	287	9	295	8
Liberia.	1,409	12	13	16	311	12	511	12	574	11
Malaysia	158	15	-	-	103	17	21	10	34	12
Malta	293	18	2	56	144	18	79	18	68	18
Netherlands	326	9	4	9	256	9	13	8	53	8
Norway (NIS) [3]	587	12	11	8	138	12	177	12	261	12
Panama.	3,189	12	38	29	1,707	13	854	10	590	11
Philippines	558	13	10	28	225	15	285	8	38	25
Poland	245	13	3	9	143	13	92	12	7	14
Romania	304	12	-	-	220	12	70	12	14	10
Singapore	407	12	-	-	216	14	70	9	121	11
South Korea.	429	14	-	-	211	15	154	12	64	14
Soviet Union.	2,428	17	32	25	1,722	17	244	12	420	15
Spain	301	13	-	1	178	13	43	12	80	15
Sweden.	162	13	4	17	80	12	17	16	61	14
Thailand	124	21	1	-	88	22	2	19	33	21
Turkey.	317	14	4	35	202	12	58	16	53	16
United Kingdom	198	14	12	16	89	13	29	10	68	15
West Germany	310	6	6	11	244	6	10	5	50	8
Yugoslavia	272	14	3	26	167	14	90	13	12	13
All others.	2,771	(NA)	57	(NA)	1,610	(NA)	399	(NA)	705	(NA)

- Represents zero.   NA Not available.   X Not applicable.   [1] Includes bulk/oil, ore/oil, and ore/bulk/oil carriers.
[2] Average age for the previous year.   [3] International Shipping Registry which is an open registry under which the ship flies the flag of the specified nation but is exempt from certain taxation and other regulations.

Source: U.S. Maritime Administration, *Merchant Fleets of the World,* summary report, annual.

Figure 23.1
Cash Receipts From Farm Marketings: 1980 and 1990

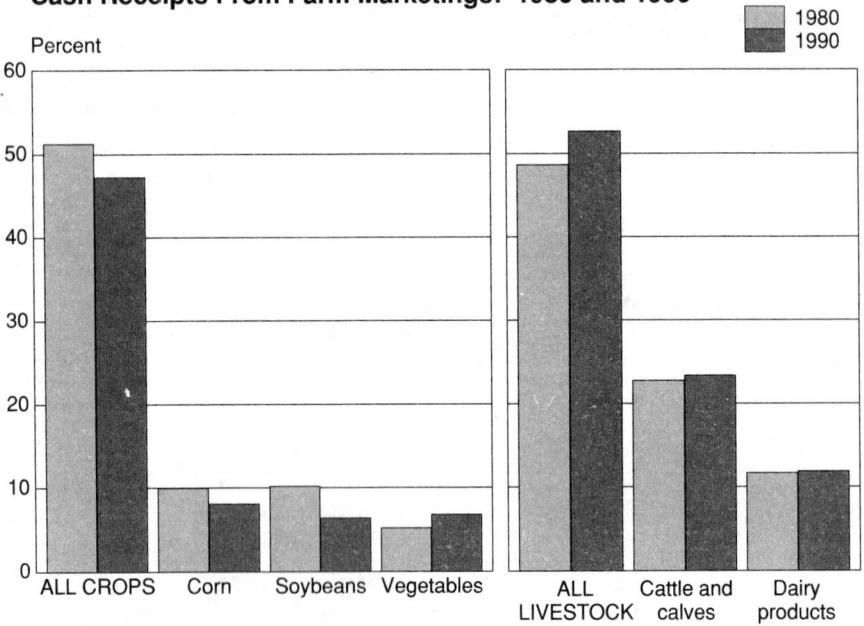

Source: Chart prepared by U.S. Bureau of the Census. For data, see table 1094.

Figure 23.2
**Corn, Soybeans, and Wheat—
U.S. Production and Exports: 1991**

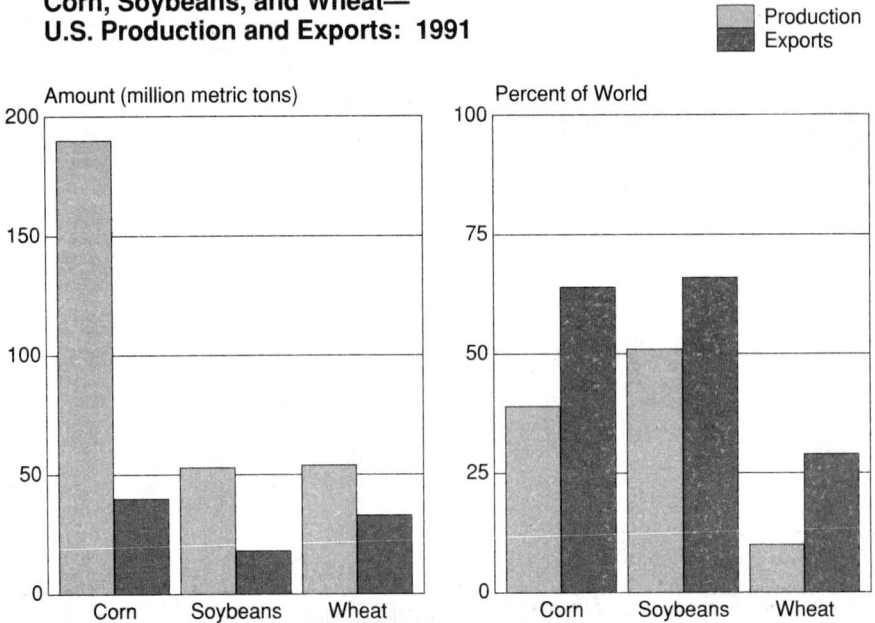

Source: Chart prepared by U.S. Bureau of the Census. For data, see table 1107.

Agriculture

This section presents statistics on farms and farm population; land use and irrigation; farm cooperatives; farm income, expenditures, and debt; farm output, productivity, and marketings; foreign trade in agricultural products; specific crops; and livestock, poultry, and their products.

The principal sources are the reports issued by the U.S. Bureau of the Census and by the National Agricultural Statistics Service (NASS) and the Economic Research Service (ERS) of the U.S. Department of Agriculture. The Bureau of the Census has taken a census of agriculture every 10 years from 1840 to 1920 and every 5 years from 1925 through 1974. Two 4-year censuses, taken for 1978 and 1982, adjusted the data reference year to coincide with the economic censuses. The 1987 Census of Agriculture is the most recent census for which reports are presently available. The Department of Agriculture publishes annually *Agricultural Statistics,* a general reference book on agricultural production, supplies, consumption, facilities, costs, and returns. The Economic Research Service publishes a series of annual reports, *Economic Indicators of the Farm Sector.* This series comprises five reports: *National Financial Summary, State Financial Summary, Production and Efficiency Statistics, Costs of Production— Livestock and Dairy,* and *Costs of Production—Major Field Crops.* Sources of current data on agricultural exports and imports include *Foreign Agricultural Trade of the United States,* published by the ERS, and the reports of the Bureau of the Census, particularly *U.S. Imports for Consumption and General Imports— HTSUSA Commodity by Country of Origin* (FT 247), *U.S. Exports, Harmonized Schedule B, Commodity by Country* (FT447), and *U.S. Merchandise Trade: Exports, General Imports, and Imports for Consumption* (FT925).

The 45 field offices of the NASS collect data on crops, livestock and products, agricultural prices, farm employment, and other related subjects mainly through sample surveys. Information is obtained on some 75 crops and 50

In Brief

Number of farms, 1991: 2.1 million
  Leading States—
  Texas *185,000*
  Missouri *107,000*
  Iowa *102,000*
Farm marketings cash receipts, 1990: $170 billion
  Leading commodities—
  Cattle, calves *$40 billion*
  Dairy products *$20 billion*
  Corn *$14 billion*

livestock items as well as scores of items pertaining to agricultural production and marketing. State estimates and supporting information are sent to the Agricultural Statistics Board of NASS which reviews the estimates and issues reports containing State and national data. Among these reports are annual summaries such as *Crop Production, Crop Values, Agricultural Prices,* and *Livestock Production, Disposition and Income.* For more information about concepts and methods underlying USDA's statistical series, see *Major Statistical Series of the U.S. Department of Agriculture* (Agricultural Handbook No. 671), a 12-volume set of publications.

Farms and farmland.—The Bureau of the Census has used varying definitions of a farm. Data from the census of agriculture reflect the definition of farm used for the census year. For the 1974, 1978, 1982, and 1987 Censuses of Agriculture, a farm was defined as any place from which $1,000 or more of agricultural products were produced and sold or normally would have been sold during the census year. Control may have been exercised through ownership or management, or through a lease, rental, or cropping arrangement. In the case of landowners who had one or more tenants or renters, the land operated by each was counted as a separate farm. The effect of the change in definition must be considered when comparing farms in the 1974, 1978, 1982, and 1987 censuses with those in previous censuses. In the 1969 census, as well as the 1959 and 1964 censuses, places of less than 10 acres were counted as farms if estimated sales of agricultural products for the year amounted to at least $250 and places of 10 or more acres if such sales amounted to at least $50.

Unless otherwise stated in the specific tables of this section, the definition of a farm applicable to data originated by the Department of Agriculture is the one used by the Bureau of the Census for the agriculture census immediately preceding the year or years for which the data are shown. Farmland refers to all land under the control of a farm operator, including land not actually under cultivation or not used for pasture or grazing. Land used for pasture or grazing on a per head basis that was neither owned nor leased by a farm operator is not included except for grazing lands controlled by grazing associations leased on a per acre basis. Coverage estimates for 1978, 1982, and 1987 indicate about 3.4, 9.1, and 7.2 percent of all farms, respectively, were not included in census totals. Farms undercounted in these censuses were usually small and accounted for approximately 1 percent of the total value of agricultural products sold and approximately 2 percent of the land in farms. For more explanation about mail list compilation and census coverage, see appendixes A and C, *1987 Census of Agriculture,* volume 1 reports, and *Coverage Evaluation, Volume 2, Part 2.*

Farm population.—Farm population consists of all persons living on farms in rural areas. Farm population data shown for 1960 to 1975 are based on the definition of a farm used for the 1959, 1964, and 1969 Censuses of Agriculture. Farm population data for 1980 to 1983 are shown on the basis of both the 1969 and 1974 census farm definitions and are so indicated. Beginning in 1984, farm population data are based only on the farm definition adopted for the 1974 Census of Agriculture.

Farm income.—Gross farm income comprises cash receipts from farm marketings of crops and livestock, Federal government payments made directly to farmers for farm-related activities, rental value of farm homes, value of farm products consumed in farm homes, and other farm-related income such as machine hire and custom work. Farm marketings represent quantities of agricultural products sold by farmers multiplied by prices received per unit of production at the local market. Information on prices received for farm products is generally obtained by the NASS Agricultural Statistics Board from surveys of firms (such as grain elevators, packers, and processors) purchasing agricultural commodities directly from producers. In some cases, the price information is obtained directly from the producers.

Crops.—Estimates of crop acreage and production by the NASS are based on current sample survey data obtained from individual producers and objective yield counts, reports of carlot shipments, market records, personal field observations by field statisticians, and reports from other sources. Prices received by farmers are marketing year averages. These averages are based on U.S. monthly prices weighted by monthly marketings during specific periods. U.S. monthly prices are State average prices weighted by marketings during the month. Marketing year average prices do not include allowances for outstanding loans, government purchases, deficiency payments or disaster payments.

All State prices are based on individual State marketing years, while U.S. marketing year averages are based on standard marketing years for each crop. For a listing of the crop marketing years and the participating States in the monthly program, see *Crop Values,* January 1992. Value of production is computed by multiplying State prices by each State's production. The U.S. value of production is the sum of State values for all States. Value of production figures shown in tables 1115-1117, 1119, and 1120 should not be confused with cash receipts from farm marketings which relate to sales during a calendar year, irrespective of the year of production.

Price supports.—Agricultural income is supplemented through two basic Government-support mechanisms available to producers of eligible commodities: (1) *a market price support* (loan rate) through which producers may place any portion of their production in approved storage and receive a loan at a specified rate. The farmer may repay the loan with interest and retain the commodity or, at the end of the loan period, forfeit the commodity as full payment of the loan; (2) *a farm income support* (target price) whose payments vary inversely with the market price of the specified commodity. "Deficiency payments" are made when market prices for a specified period are below the target prices. The payment rate is the difference between the target price and market price, or between the target price and loan rate, whichever is smaller.

Livestock.—Annual inventory numbers of livestock and estimates of livestock,

dairy, and poultry production prepared by the Department of Agriculture are based on information from farmers and ranchers obtained by probability survey sampling methods.

Statistical reliability.—For a discussion of statistical collection and estimation, sampling procedures, and measures of statistical reliability pertaining to Census Bureau and Department of Agriculture data, see Appendix III.

Historical statistics.—Tabular headnotes provide cross-references, where applicable, to *Historical Statistics of the United States, Colonial Times to 1970.* See Appendix IV.

Figure 23.3
Consumer Expenditures for Farm Foods: 1970, 1980 and 1990
(In billions of dollars)

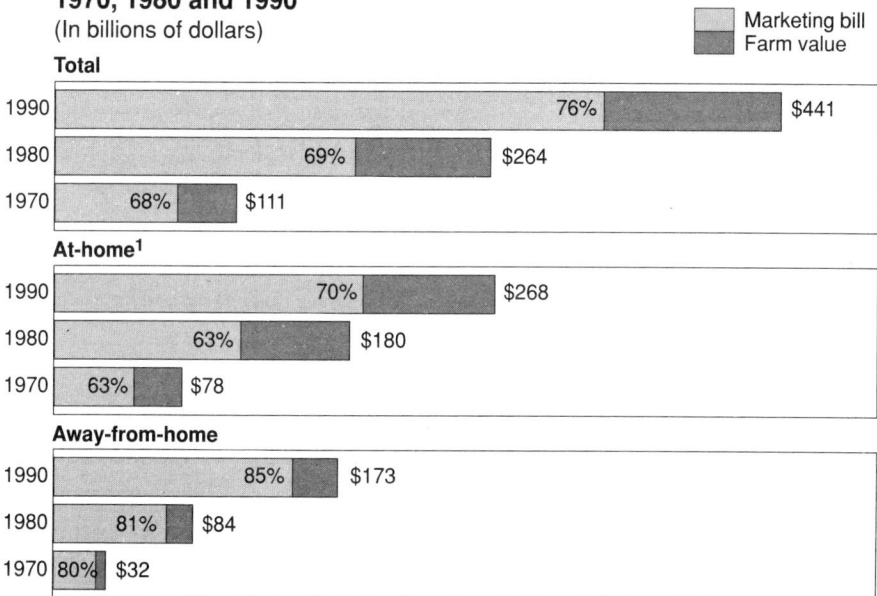

☐ Marketing bill
■ Farm value

Total

1990	76%	$441
1980	69%	$264
1970	68%	$111

At-home[1]

1990	70%	$268
1980	63%	$180
1970	63%	$78

Away-from-home

1990	85%	$173
1980	81%	$84
1970	80%	$32

[1]Food purchased from retail food stores for use at home.
Source: Chart prepared by U.S. Bureau of the Census. For data, see table 1101.

No. 1072. Food and Fiber Sector of Domestic Economy—Employment and Value Added: 1975 to 1990

[Employment in millions; value added in billions of dollars, except as indicated]

SECTOR	1975	1980	1983	1984	1985	1986	1987	1988	1989	1990
EMPLOYMENT										
Food and fiber sector, total . . . [1]	20.3	21.4	21.5	21.4	21.1	20.7	20.1	19.8	21.0	20.7
Percent of domestic economy [1]	21.6	20.1	19.3	18.9	18.2	17.6	16.7	16.3	17.0	16.6
Farm sector.	3.0	2.6	2.8	2.7	2.3	2.2	1.9	1.9	2.2	2.1
Nonfarm sector	17.2	18.9	18.7	18.7	18.7	18.6	18.2	17.9	18.8	18.6
Food processing	1.5	1.5	1.5	1.4	1.5	1.4	1.3	1.2	1.3	1.3
Manufacturing	3.3	3.3	3.1	3.0	2.9	2.8	2.6	2.6	2.7	2.6
Transportation, trade, and retailing .	5.7	6.4	6.5	6.6	6.7	6.7	6.6	6.5	6.8	6.8
Eating establishments.	3.1	3.6	3.6	3.6	3.6	3.6	3.8	3.8	3.8	3.8
Other.	3.7	4.0	4.0	4.1	4.1	4.0	3.9	3.8	4.1	4.1
VALUE ADDED [2]										
Food and fiber sector, total . . .	325.7	499.9	602.7	660.6	698.7	713.8	715.3	731.1	820.1	843.5
Percent of domestic economy .	20.4	18.3	17.7	17.5	17.4	16.9	15.8	15.0	15.8	15.4
Farm sector.	43.3	55.1	49.8	64.6	71.4	66.0	59.9	53.0	71.4	76.2
Nonfarm sector	282.4	444.8	552.9	596.0	627.4	647.8	655.4	678.1	748.7	767.2
Food processing	38.7	56.0	70.4	75.6	83.7	87.3	83.1	83.0	93.9	96.8
Manufacturing	57.0	83.0	98.0	101.5	102.1	104.7	101.3	105.0	115.9	117.9
Transportation, trade, and retailing .	96.8	157.5	196.8	209.8	220.9	226.3	232.2	241.9	262.8	270.1
Eating establishments.	25.7	42.0	52.0	55.7	57.5	60.2	65.8	70.3	73.5	76.4
Other.	64.2	106.3	135.7	153.5	163.2	169.3	173.0	177.9	202.6	206.1

[1] Based on civilian labor force.   [2] Value added equals profits, rent, interest, wages, indirect business taxes, and depreciation.

Source: U.S. Dept. of Agriculture, Economic Research Service, unpublished data.

No. 1073. Farm Population and Employment: 1970 to 1991

[In thousands, except percent. For definition of farm population, see text, section 23. See also *Historical Statistics, Colonial Times to 1970*, series C 76 and K 1-2 and K 174-176]

ITEM	1970	1980	1982	1983	1984	1985	1986	1987	1988	1989	1990	1991
Farm population (**1974** definition) [1] . . .	(NA)	6,051	5,628	5,787	5,754	5,355	5,226	4,986	4,951	4,801	4,591	(NA)
Percent of resident population.	(NA)	2.8	2.5	2.5	2.5	2.3	2.2	2.1	2.1	2.0	1.9	(NA)
Farm population (**1969** definition) [1] . . .	9,712	7,241	6,880	7,029	(NA)	(NA)	(NA)	(NA)	(NA)	(NA)	(NA)	(NA)
Percent of resident population.	4.8	3.3	3.0	3.0	(NA)	(NA)	(NA)	(NA)	(NA)	(NA)	(NA)	(NA)
Farm employment, total [2] . . . . [3]	4,523	3,705	4,043	3,749	3,405	3,115	2,912	2,897	2,954	2,863	2,891	2,877
Self-employed and unpaid workers [3].	3,348	2,402	2,494	2,271	2,175	2,017	1,873	1,846	1,917	1,935	1,999	1,967
Hired workers [4].	1,175	1,303	1,549	1,478	1,230	1,098	1,039	1,051	1,037	928	892	910

NA Not available.   [1] April-centered five-quarter averages for 1970 to 1983; annual average for 1984 to 1990.   [2] 1970, averages of monthly estimates of employed during last full calendar week ending at least one day before end of month; 1980 and 1989-91, average from Jan., April, July and Oct. surveys; 1982-83 based on July survey; 1984, average from July and Oct. surveys; 1985-88 average from April, July and Oct. surveys.   [3] Includes farm operators doing 1 or more hours of farm work and unpaid workers doing 15 or more hours of farm work during survey week.   [4] Includes all persons doing 1 or more hours of farm work for pay during survey week. Members of operators' families doing any farm work for cash wages are counted as hired workers.
Source: Population—U.S. Dept. of Agriculture, Economic Research Service and U.S. Bureau of the Census. Published in U.S. Bureau of the Census, *Current Population Reports*, series P-20, No. 457 and earlier series P-20 and series P-27 reports. Farm employment—U.S. Dept. of Agriculture, National Agricultural Statistics Service, *Farm Labor*, periodic.

No. 1074. Characteristics of Farm and Nonfarm Families: 1970 to 1990

[As of **March**. 1970 based on 1969 census farm definition and 1980 and 1990 based on 1974 definition; see text, section 23. 1970, 1980 and 1990 data are based on population controls from 1960, 1970, and 1980 censuses respectively; see text, section 1. Based on Current Population Survey, see text, section 1 and Appendix III. For definition of median, see Guide to Tabular Presentation]

CHARACTERISTIC	1970			1980			1990		
	Total	Farm	Nonfarm	Total	Farm	Nonfarm	Total	Farm	Nonfarm
Total families (1,000)	51,237	2,457	48,781	58,426	1,666	56,760	66,090	1,390	64,701
Persons per family	3.62	3.77	3.61	3.28	3.35	3.27	3.17	3.09	3.17
With own children under 18 (1,000) . . .	28,665	1,169	27,496	30,517	745	29,772	32,289	553	31,736
Mean number of own children	2.33	2.61	2.32	1.89	2.00	1.89	1.83	1.95	1.83
Percent distribution:									
Married couple	86.7	90.5	86.5	82.5	92.3	82.2	79.2	92.5	78.9
Male householder, no wife present . . .	2.4	4.2	2.3	2.9	3.4	2.9	4.4	3.6	4.4
Female householder, no husband present .	10.9	5.3	11.2	14.6	4.4	14.9	16.5	3.9	16.7
Two-person families	34.5	37.0	34.3	39.2	42.7	39.1	41.8	45.6	41.7
Three- to five-person families	52.7	46.4	53.1	53.7	47.1	53.9	53.4	49.6	53.5
Six-or-more person families	12.9	16.6	12.6	7.1	10.3	7.0	4.8	4.7	4.8

Source: U.S. Bureau of the Census, *Current Population Reports*, series P-20, No 457; and earlier series P-27 reports; and unpublished data.

No. 1075. Farm Population, by Characteristics: 1970 to 1990

[1970 and 1980, **April-centered five-quarter averages; 1985 and 1990 annual averages.** For definition of farm population, see text, section 23]

CHARACTERISTIC	FARM POPULATION (1,000)							PERCENT DISTRIBUTION			
	1969 definition		1974 definition					1969 defini-tion, 1970	1974 definition		
	1970	1980	1980	1985	1990				1980	1985	1990
					Total	Male	Female				
Total, all ages	**9,712**	**7,241**	**6,051**	**5,355**	**4,591**	**2,383**	**2,208**	**100.0**	**100.0**	**100.0**	**100.0**
White.	8,775	6,828	5,714	5,195	4,478	2,328	2,150	90.4	94.4	97.0	97.5
Black and other races.	938	413	337	160	113	55	58	9.7	5.6	3.0	2.5
Under 15 years old	[1]2,490	[1]1,391	[1]1,146	1,100	940	480	459	[1]25.6	[1]18.9	20.5	20.5
15-19 years old	[2]1,316	[2]926	[2]790	456	356	190	166	[2]13.6	[2]13.1	8.5	7.8
20-24 years old	502	502	444	381	232	134	99	5.2	7.3	7.1	5.1
25-34 years old	770	735	606	640	532	285	247	7.9	10.0	12.0	11.6
35-44 years old	1,061	862	712	687	633	314	319	10.9	11.8	12.8	13.8
45-64 years old	2,452	1,892	1,607	1,342	1,197	616	582	25.2	26.6	25.1	26.1
65 years old and over.	1,122	934	746	747	702	365	338	11.6	12.3	13.9	15.3
Total, 15 years old and over.	[3]7,222	[3]5,851	[3]4,905	4,255	3,651	1,902	1,749	[3]100.0	[3]100.0	100.0	100.0
In labor force	4,293	3,682	3,139	2,853	2,528	1,539	990	59.4	64.0	67.1	69.2
Employed, agriculture	2,333	1,722	1,642	1,363	1,157	913	245	32.3	33.5	32.0	31.7
Percent of labor force . . .	54.3	46.8	52.3	47.8	45.8	59.3	24.7	(X)	(X)	(X)	(X)
Self-employed.	1,411	1,083	1,034	896	804	664	140	19.5	21.1	21.1	22.0
Wage and salary workers . .	395	344	326	318	269	217	52	5.5	6.6	7.5	7.4
Unpaid family workers. . . .	526	295	282	149	84	31	53	7.3	5.7	3.5	2.3
Employed, nonagriculture	1,878	1,853	1,415	1,402	1,318	599	719	26.0	28.8	32.9	36.1
Self-employed.	159	210	161	159	141	77	64	2.2	3.3	3.7	3.9
Wage and salary workers . .	1,698	1,624	1,239	1,237	1,170	522	648	23.5	25.3	29.1	32.0
Unpaid family workers. . . .	21	19	16	7	7	-	6	0.3	0.3	0.2	0.2
Unemployed	82	106	82	88	53	27	27	1.1	1.7	2.1	1.5
Not in labor force.	2,929	2,169	1,766	1,402	1,123	364	759	40.6	36.0	32.9	30.8

- Represents or rounds to zero.   X Not applicable.   [1] Persons under 14 years old.   [2] Persons 14 to 19 years old.
[3] Persons 14 years old and over.

Source: U.S. Bureau of the Census, *Current Population Reports,* series P-20, No. 457; series P-27, No. 59 and earlier reports; and unpublished data.

No. 1076. Farm Operator Off-Farm Employment, by Age of Operator: 1988

[Based on a sample survey of 44,125 farm operators conducted as part of the Agricultural Economics and Land Ownership Survey. Subject to sampling variability; see source]

TYPE OF OFF-FARM EMPLOYMENT	NUMBER (1,000)				PERCENT DISTRIBUTION			
	All farms	Under 35 years	35 to 64 years	65 years old and over	All farms	Under 35 years	35 to 64 years	65 years old and over
Total	**1,879.6**	**245.2**	**1,224.2**	**410.1**	**100.0**	**100.0**	**100.0**	**100.0**
Farms reporting off-farm work	924.7	149.7	700.2	74.8	49.2	61.0	57.2	18.2
Only operator	336.3	55.7	246.1	34.4	17.9	22.7	20.1	8.4
Only spouse	69.7	8.5	49.5	11.6	3.7	3.5	4.0	2.8
Both operator and spouse	518.7	85.4	404.6	28.7	27.6	34.8	33.0	7.0
Farms reporting no off-farm work	586.8	60.3	322.2	204.3	31.2	24.6	26.3	49.8
Farms not responding	368.1	35.2	201.8	131.1	19.6	14.3	16.5	32.0
Operators reporting off-farm work.	855.0	141.2	650.7	63.1	100.0	100.0	100.0	100.0
Employee of another farm	54.9	10.2	35.2	9.5	6.4	7.2	5.4	15.1
Employee of private business.	349.7	70.3	263.8	15.6	40.9	49.8	40.5	24.7
Government employee	135.3	14.5	112.9	7.9	15.8	10.3	17.3	12.5
Self-employed:								
Farm related business	75.0	15.1	52.4	7.5	8.8	10.7	8.1	11.8
Nonfarm related business or profession.	94.5	11.7	73.2	9.6	11.1	8.3	11.2	15.2
Type of employment not reported	145.6	19.4	113.2	13.0	17.0	13.7	17.4	20.7
Spouses reporting off-farm work	588.4	90.0	454.1	40.4	100.0	100.0	100.0	100.0
Employee of another farm	17.1	1.1	13.4	2.6	2.9	1.2	2.9	6.4
Employee of private business.	267.4	49.5	200.9	17.1	45.4	52.7	44.2	42.2
Government employee	140.0	19.4	112.8	7.8	23.8	20.7	24.8	19.4
Self-employed:								
Farm related business	18.3	3.1	13.3	2.0	3.1	3.3	2.9	4.9
Nonfarm related business or profession.	48.3	5.8	36.6	5.8	8.2	6.2	8.1	14.4
Type of employment not reported	97.2	15.0	77.1	5.1	16.5	16.0	17.0	12.5

Source: U.S. Bureau of the Census, *1987 Census of Agriculture, Vol. 3, Related Surveys, Part 2, Agricultural Economics and Land Ownership Survey (1988).*

No. 1077. Farms—Number and Acreage: 1959 to 1991

[Based on census year definition indicated; for definition of farms and farmland, see text, section 23. Data for census years (indicated by italics) have been adjusted for underenumeration and are used as reference points along with data from acreage and livestock surveys in estimating data for other years. Minus sign (-) indicates decrease. See also *Historical Statistics, Colonial Times to 1970*, series K 4-7]

YEAR	FARMS Number (1,000)	FARMS Annual change [1] (1,000)	LAND IN FARMS Total (mil. acres)	LAND IN FARMS Average per farm (acres)	YEAR	FARMS Number (1,000)	FARMS Annual change [1] (1,000)	LAND IN FARMS Total (mil. acres)	LAND IN FARMS Average per farm (acres)
1969 DEFINITION					**1974 DEFINITION**				
1959	*4,105*	*-139*	*1,183*	*288*	1975	2,521	(X)	1,059	420
1960	*3,963*	*-142*	*1,176*	*297*	1976	2,497	-24	1,054	422
1964	*3,457*	*-127*	*1,146*	*332*	1977	2,456	-41	1,048	427
1965	*3,356*	*-101*	*1,140*	*340*	*1978*	*2,436*	*-20*	*1,045*	*429*
1969	*3,000*	*-89*	*1,108*	*369*	1979	2,437	1	1,042	428
					1980	2,440	3	1,039	426
1970	2,949	-51	1,102	374	1981	2,440	-	1,034	424
1971	2,902	-47	1,097	378	*1982*	*2,407*	*-33*	*1,028*	*427*
1972	2,860	-42	1,092	382	1983	2,379	-28	1,023	430
1973	2,823	-37	1,088	385	1984	2,334	-45	1,018	436
1974	*2,795*	*-28*	*1,084*	*388*	1985	2,293	-41	1,012	441
					1986	2,250	-43	1,005	447
1975	2,767	-28	1,081	391	*1987*	*2,213*	*-37*	*999*	*451*
1976	2,738	-29	1,078	394	1988	2,197	-16	995	453
1977	2,706	-32	1,075	397	1989	2,171	-26	991	457
1978	*2,672*	*-34*	*1,072*	*401*	1990	2,140	-31	987	461
					1991, prel.	2,105	-35	983	467

- Represents zero.   X Not applicable.   [1] Average annual change from preceding year shown. For 1959, change from 1954.

Source: U.S. Dept. of Agriculture, National Agricultural Statistics Service, *Number of Farms and Land in Farms, 1959-70* (Statistical Bulletin No. 507); *Farms and Land in Farms, 1969-75* (Statistical Bulletin No. 594); *Farm Numbers, 1975-80; Farms and Land in Farms, Final Estimates by States, 1979-1987;* and *Crop Production* (August releases).

No. 1078. Farms—Number and Acreage, by State: 1990 and 1991

[Based on 1974 census definition of farms and farmland; see text, section 23. See also *Historical Statistics, Colonial Times to 1970*, series K 4-7]

STATE	FARMS (1,000) 1990	FARMS (1,000) 1991, prel.	ACREAGE (mil.) 1990	ACREAGE (mil.) 1991, prel.	ACREAGE PER FARM 1990	ACREAGE PER FARM 1991, prel.	STATE	FARMS (1,000) 1990	FARMS (1,000) 1991, prel.	ACREAGE (mil.) 1990	ACREAGE (mil.) 1991, prel.	ACREAGE PER FARM 1990	ACREAGE PER FARM 1991, prel.
U.S.	**2,140**	**2,105**	**987**	**983**	**461**	**467**	Missouri	108	107	30	30	281	284
							Montana	25	25	61	60	2,449	2,431
Alabama	47	45	10	10	215	218	Nebraska	57	56	47	47	826	841
Alaska	1	1	1	1	1,724	1,768	Nevada	3	3	9	9	3,560	3,560
Arizona	8	8	36	36	4,615	4,500	New Hampshire	3	3	(Z)	(Z)	169	166
Arkansas	47	46	16	16	330	337	New Jersey	8	8	1	1	107	106
California	85	84	31	30	362	361	New Mexico	14	14	45	44	3,296	3,281
Colorado	27	26	33	33	1,249	1,262	New York	39	38	8	8	218	218
Connecticut	4	4	(Z)	(Z)	108	108	North Carolina	62	60	10	10	156	160
Delaware	3	3	1	1	197	197	North Dakota	34	33	41	40	1,191	1,224
Florida	41	40	11	11	266	263	Ohio	84	80	16	16	187	196
Georgia	48	46	13	12	260	263	Oklahoma	70	70	33	33	471	471
Hawaii	5	5	2	2	372	372	Oregon	37	37	18	18	488	481
Idaho	22	21	14	14	628	631	Pennsylvania	53	53	8	8	153	153
Illinois	83	82	29	29	343	348	Rhode Island	1	1	(Z)	(Z)	95	94
Indiana	68	65	16	16	240	246	South Carolina	25	24	5	5	208	213
Iowa	104	102	34	34	322	328	South Dakota	35	35	44	44	1,266	1,263
Kansas	69	69	48	48	694	694	Tennessee	89	87	12	12	139	143
Kentucky	93	91	14	14	152	155	Texas	186	185	132	131	710	708
Louisiana	32	30	9	9	278	293	Utah	13	13	11	11	856	850
Maine	7	7	1	1	201	203	Vermont	7	7	2	2	216	219
Maryland	15	15	2	2	148	146	Virginia	46	45	9	9	193	196
Massachusetts	7	7	1	1	99	99	Washington	37	37	16	16	432	432
Michigan	54	54	11	11	200	200	West Virginia	21	20	4	4	180	185
Minnesota	89	88	30	30	337	341	Wisconsin	80	79	18	18	220	222
Mississippi	40	38	13	13	325	337	Wyoming	9	9	35	35	3,910	3,867

Z Less than 500,000 acres.

Source: U.S. Dept. of Agriculture, National Agricultural Statistics Service, *Crop Production* (August 1991 release).

No. 1079. Farms—Number, 1974 to 1987, and Acreage, 1978 to 1987, by Size of Farm

[See also *Historical Statistics, Colonial Times to 1970*, series K 162-173]

SIZE OF FARM	NUMBER OF FARMS (1,000)				LAND IN FARMS (mil. acres)			CROPLAND HARVESTED (mil. acres)			PERCENT DISTRIBUTION, 1987		
	1974	1978	1982	1987	1978	1982	1987	1978	1982	1987	Number of farms	All land in farms	Cropland harvested
Total	2,314	2,258	2,241	2,088	1,014.8	986.8	964.5	317.1	326.3	282.2	100.0	100.0	100.0
Under 10 acres.......	128	151	188	183	0.6	0.7	0.7	0.2	0.3	0.2	8.8	0.1	0.1
10 to 49 acres	380	392	449	412	10.9	12.1	11.1	4.5	4.5	3.9	19.8	1.2	1.4
50 to 99 acres	385	356	344	311	25.9	24.8	22.5	10.2	9.5	7.9	14.9	2.3	2.8
100 to 179 acres.....	443	403	368	334	55.0	49.9	45.3	23.3	21.2	17.1	16.0	4.7	6.1
180 to 259 acres.....	253	234	211	192	50.6	45.7	41.5	23.7	21.7	17.2	9.2	4.3	6.1
260 to 499 acres.....	363	348	315	286	124.6	113.0	103.0	64.5	60.5	47.3	13.7	10.7	16.8
500 to 999 acres.....	207	213	204	200	146.7	140.5	138.5	75.2	77.6	67.4	9.6	14.4	23.9
1,000 to 1,999 acres ..	93	98	97	102	133.0	132.4	138.8	58.2	64.5	61.1	4.9	14.4	21.7
2,000 acres and over..	62	63	65	67	467.4	467.5	463.2	57.3	66.6	60.2	3.2	48.0	21.3

No. 1080. Farms—Number and Acreage, by Tenure of Operator: 1974 to 1987

[*Full owners* own all the land they operate. *Part owners* own a part, and rent from others the rest of the land they operate. See also *Historical Statistics, Colonial Times to 1970*, series K 109-113 and 142-146]

ITEM AND YEAR	Unit	Total	Full owner	Part owner	Tenant	PERCENT DISTRIBUTION			
						Total	Full owner	Part owner	Tenant
Number of farms:									
1974..........................	1,000....	2,314	1,424	628	262	100.0	61.5	27.2	11.3
1978..........................	1,000....	2,258	1,298	681	279	100.0	57.5	30.1	12.4
1982..........................	1,000....	2,241	1,326	656	259	100.0	59.2	29.3	11.5
1987..........................	1,000....	2,088	1,239	609	240	100.0	59.3	29.2	11.5
Under 50 acres.............	1,000....	596	483	59	53	100.0	81.1	9.9	9.0
50 to 179 acres.............	1,000....	645	449	130	66	100.0	69.6	20.1	10.3
180 to 499 acres	1,000....	478	217	195	67	100.0	45.3	40.8	13.9
500 to 999 acres	1,000....	200	53	117	31	100.0	26.3	58.3	15.4
1,000 acres or more..........	1,000....	169	37	108	23	100.0	22.1	64.2	13.7
Land in farms:									
1974..........................	Mil. acres .	1,017	359	535	122	100.0	35.4	52.6	12.0
1978..........................	Mil. acres .	1,015	332	561	122	100.0	32.7	55.3	12.0
1982..........................	Mil. acres .	987	342	531	114	100.0	34.7	53.8	11.6
1987..........................	Mil. acres .	964	318	520	127	100.0	32.9	53.9	13.2

No. 1081. Farm Operators—Tenure and Characteristics: 1982 and 1987

[**In thousands, except as indicated**. See also *Historical Statistics, Colonial Times to 1970*, series K 82-113]

CHARACTERISTIC	ALL FARMS		FARMS WITH SALES OF $10,000 AND OVER		CHARACTERISTIC	ALL FARMS		FARMS WITH SALES OF $10,000 AND OVER	
	1982	1987	1982	1987		1982	1987	1982	1987
Total operators	2,241	2,088	1,143	1,060	Principal occupation:				
White	2,187	2,043	1,127	1,046	Farming	1,235	1,138	901	811
Black.................	33	23	7	4	Other	1,006	950	242	248
American Indian, Eskimos, and									
Aleuts..............	7	7	2	2	Place of residence: [2]				
Asian or Pacific Islander	8	8	5	5	On farm operated.......	1,581	1,488	833	776
Other	6	7	2	2	Not on farm operated	429	443	202	215
Operators of Hispanic origin [1].	16	17	6	6					
					Years on present farm: [2]				
Female	122	132	37	42	2 years or less.........	127	114	53	49
Under 25 years old	62	36	39	21	3 to 4 years...........	193	135	83	56
25 to 34 years old	204	243	173	147	5 to 9 years...........	360	304	167	138
35 to 44 years old	443	411	223	212	10 years or more	1,098	1,163	638	653
45 to 54 years old	505	455	264	228					
55 to 64 years old.......	536	496	288	263	Days worked off farm: [2]				
65 years old and over	400	447	156	188	None	862	844	591	561
Average age (years)......	50.5	52.0	49.1	50.6	Less than 100 days	224	200	141	124
Full owner	1,326	1,239	482	445	100 to 199 days........	189	178	77	80
Part owner	656	609	491	454	200 days or more	775	737	213	219
Tenant................	259	240	170	161					

[1] Operators of Hispanic origin may be of any race. [2] Excludes not reported.

Source of tables 1079-1081: U.S. Bureau of the Census, *Census of Agriculture: 1974*, vol. II; *1982*, vol. 1; and *1987*, vol. 1.

No. 1082. Farms—Number, Acreage, and Value, by Type of Organization: 1982 and 1987

[Data for 1982 exclude abnormal farms (institutional farms, experimental and research farms, Indian reservations, etc.)]

ITEM	Unit	Total [1]	Individual or family	Partnership	Corporation	PERCENT DISTRIBUTION Total [1]	Individual or family	Partnership	Corporation
ALL FARMS									
Number of farms: 1982	1,000 ...	2,239	1,946	223	60	100.0	86.9	10.0	2.7
1987	1,000 ...	2,088	1,809	200	67	100.0	86.7	9.6	3.2
Land in farms: 1982	Mil. acres.	932	642	152	127	100.0	68.9	16.3	13.6
1987	Mil. acres.	964	628	153	119	100.0	65.1	15.9	12.4
Value of land and buildings: [2] 1982	Bil. dol. ..	763	547	119	90	100.0	71.7	15.6	11.8
1987	Bil. dol. ..	604	424	95	69	100.0	70.1	15.7	11.4
Value of farm products sold: 1982	Bil. dol. ..	132	78	22	31	100.0	59.2	16.4	23.9
1987	Bil. dol. ..	136	77	23	35	100.0	56.3	17.1	25.6
FARMS WITH SALES OF $10,000 AND OVER									
Number of farms: 1982	1,000 ...	1,143	934	152	52	100.0	81.7	13.3	4.6
1987	1,000 ...	1,060	861	136	56	100.0	81.3	12.8	5.3
Land in farms: 1982	Mil. acres.	811	536	141	124	100.0	66.1	17.4	15.3
1987	Mil. acres.	829	525	143	116	100.0	63.3	17.3	14.0

[1] Includes other types, not shown separately.   [2] Based on a sample of farms.

No. 1083. Farms—Number, Acreage, and Value, by State: 1987

[See also *Historical Statistics, Colonial Times to 1970*, series K 17-18]

REGION, DIVISION, AND STATE	ALL FARMS Number of farms (1,000)	Land in farms (mil. acres)	Average size of farm (acres)	FARMS WITH SALES OF $10,000 OR MORE Number of farms (1,000)	Land in farms (mil. acres)	Average size of farm (acres)	REGION, DIVISION, AND STATE	ALL FARMS Number of farms (1,000)	Land in farms (mil. acres)	Average size of farm (acres)	FARMS WITH SALES OF $10,000 OR MORE Number of farms (1,000)	Land in farms (mil. acres)	Average size of farm (acres)
U.S. ...	2,088	964.5	462	1,060	829.0	782	MD	15	2.4	162	7	1.9	278
Northeast ..	123	21.4	174	61	16.0	261	VA	45	8.7	194	16	5.9	377
N.E	25	4.2	169	11	2.8	260	WV	17	3.4	196	3	1.4	431
ME	6	1.3	214	3	0.9	332	NC	59	9.4	159	26	7.1	276
NH	2	0.4	169	1	0.2	283	SC	20	4.8	232	7	3.3	491
VT	6	1.4	240	3	1.1	325	GA	44	10.7	247	18	7.9	439
MA	6	0.6	99	2	0.4	153	FL	37	11.2	306	15	9.4	638
RI	1	0.1	84	(Z)	(Z)	116	**E.S.C...**	250	45.6	183	82	30.4	372
CT	4	0.4	111	1	0.3	179	KY	92	14.0	152	34	9.4	276
M.A	98	17.2	175	50	13.1	262	TN	80	11.7	147	22	7.2	329
NY	38	8.4	223	21	6.7	327	AL	43	9.1	211	14	5.9	424
NJ	9	0.9	99	3	0.7	191	MS	34	10.7	315	12	7.9	662
PA	51	7.9	153	26	5.7	221	**W.S.C ...**	335	184.4	551	129	153.3	1,184
							AR	48	14.4	298	21	11.2	522
Midwest ...	862	350.5	407	556	314.5	565	LA	27	8.0	293	11	6.4	607
E.N.C ...	365	86.6	237	219	76.3	348	OK	70	31.5	449	29	25.1	878
OH	79	15.0	189	40	12.1	305	TX	189	130.5	691	69	110.5	1,606
IN	70	16.2	229	40	14.4	355							
IL	89	28.5	321	63	27.0	431	**West .....**	278	311.3	1,118	139	277.5	1,999
MI	51	10.3	202	24	8.2	340	**Mt .....**	124	244.1	1,965	67	218.3	3,271
WI	75	16.6	221	52	14.5	280	ID	24	13.9	577	14	12.0	881
W.N.C ...	497	263.8	531	337	238.3	707	WY	9	33.6	3,650	5	28.4	5,183
MN	85	26.6	312	58	23.8	407	CO	27	34.0	1,248	15	30.6	2,030
IA	105	31.6	301	83	30.2	365	NM	14	46.0	3,230	6	41.3	7,319
MO	106	29.2	275	50	22.7	457	AZ	8	36.3	4,732	4	33.7	9,411
ND	35	40.3	1,143	28	37.9	1,339	UT	14	10.0	710	6	8.6	1,452
SD	36	44.2	1,214	28	37.9	1,339	NV	3	10.0	3,300	1	9.3	6,288
NE	60	45.3	749	47	43.0	918	**Pac .....**	154	67.3	466	72	59.2	821
KS	69	46.6	680	43	42.8	1,002	WA	34	16.1	480	15	13.8	901
							OR	32	17.8	556	12	15.4	1,319
South	824	281.2	341	304	221.0	727	CA	83	30.6	368	43	27.7	647
S.A	240	51.2	214	93	37.4	403	AK	1	1.0	1,789	(Z)	0.6	3,411
DE	3	0.6	205	2	0.5	291	HI	5	1.7	353	2	1.6	798

Z Less than 500 farms or 50,000 acres.

Source of tables 1082 and 1083: U.S. Bureau of the Census, *Census of Agriculture: 1987*, vol. 1.

No. 1084. Irrigated Farms and Acreage, by State: 1982 and 1987

[See also *Historical Statistics, Colonial Times to 1970*, series J 85-91]

STATE	IRRIGATED FARMS Number (1,000) 1982	1987	Percent of all farms 1982	1987	LAND IN IRRIGATED FARMS Acreage (1,000) 1982	1987	Percent of all land in farms 1982	1987	IRRIGATED LAND Acreage (1,000) 1982	1987	Percent of all land in farms 1982	1987
U.S. [1]	278.3	291.6	12.4	13.9	246,603	241,069	24.9	24.9	49,002	46,386	5.0	4.8
Arizona.	4.4	4.2	60.4	55.3	18,871	17,167	49.9	47.3	1,098	914	2.9	2.5
California	58.4	58.9	70.8	70.7	18,402	17,567	57.2	57.4	8,461	7,596	26.3	24.8
Colorado.	15.2	14.9	56.1	54.6	17,351	16,729	51.7	49.1	3,201	3,014	9.5	8.9
Florida	10.6	12.0	29.0	32.7	5,529	4,670	43.1	41.7	1,585	1,623	12.4	14.5
Idaho	17.4	16.6	70.2	68.8	9,168	9,053	65.8	64.9	3,450	3,219	24.8	23.1
Kansas.	7.3	7.4	9.8	10.7	10,345	10,654	21.9	22.8	2,675	2,463	5.7	5.3
Louisiana	3.7	3.9	11.6	14.3	2,273	2,337	25.4	29.1	694	647	7.8	8.1
Montana.	9.2	9.5	39.1	38.7	24,171	23,259	39.9	38.6	2,023	1,997	3.3	3.3
Nebraska	22.2	22.6	36.8	37.3	22,679	22,499	50.4	49.6	6,039	5,682	13.4	12.5
Nevada	2.2	2.2	79.2	73.3	7,881	7,806	78.9	78.1	830	779	8.3	7.8
New Mexico . . .	6.2	7.0	45.9	49.2	14,755	12,385	31.3	26.9	807	718	1.7	1.6
Oregon.	15.3	14.4	44.9	45.0	11,382	11,340	64.1	63.6	1,808	1,648	10.2	9.3
Texas.	19.8	19.8	10.6	10.4	22,161	20,270	16.8	15.5	5,576	4,271	4.2	3.3
Utah	11.2	11.1	79.9	79.2	7,598	7,594	77.7	76.0	1,082	1,161	11.1	11.6
Washington. . . .	16.3	15.4	45.0	45.9	6,003	5,468	36.4	33.9	1,638	1,519	9.9	9.4
Wyoming	5.3	5.2	59.6	56.7	18,132	18,207	54.1	54.1	1,565	1,518	4.7	4.5

[1] Includes other States not shown separately.
Source: U.S. Bureau of the Census, *1987 Census of Agriculture*, vol. 1.

No. 1085. Foreign Ownership of U.S. Agricultural Land: 1991

[In thousands of acres, except percent. Covers "foreign persons" reporting under the Agricultural Foreign Investment Disclosure Act of 1978. As defined in the Act, a "foreign person" is any person who is not a U.S. citizen and who is not a permanent resident alien of the U.S. Foreign governments and entities are also "foreign persons." Also, each successive link in a chain of U.S. entities containing foreign interests is considered a "foreign person." An entity is deemed a "foreign person" if it is 10 percent or more owned by a single foreign person or foreign persons acting in concert, or 50 percent foreign owned by a group of foreign persons not acting in concert, none of whom individually holds a 10 percent or greater interest in the entity. Therefore, acreage figures reported do not necessarily mean that they are wholly owned by foreign investors. Covers reports received and accepted as of December 31, 1991]

CHARACTERISTIC	ACREAGE OWNED [1] Total	Per-cent	ACREAGE ACQUIRED [2] Total	Per-cent	CHARACTERISTIC	ACREAGE OWNED [1] Total	Per-cent	ACREAGE ACQUIRED [2] Total	Per-cent
Total [3]	14,809	100.0	227	100.0	Country of foreign owner: Canada	1,971	13.3	6	2.5
Type of owner:					Germany	757	5.1	19	8.2
Corporation	10,762	72.7	166	73.0	Netherlands Antilles . . .	367	2.5	(Z)	(Z)
Partnership	2,859	19.3	41	17.8	Switzerland	300	2.0	1	0.5
Individual	942	6.4	10	4.6	United Kingdom	1,803	12.2	14	6.0
Other	245	1.7	11	4.6	Through U.S. interest: [4]				
Size:					Canada	1,691	11.4	6	2.5
Less than 100 acres. . . .	106	0.7	3	1.1	France	1,020	6.9	29	12.6
100-299 acres	296	2.0	8	3.5	Germany	445	3.0	1	0.3
300-999 acres	892	6.0	20	8.7	Japan	268	1.8	65	28.4
1,000 acres or more . . .	13,515	91.3	197	86.7	Luxembourg	234	1.6	(Z)	(Z)
Land use:					Mexico	323	2.2	1	0.5
Cropland.	2,495	16.9	35	15.3	Netherlands	316	2.1	2	0.8
Pasture	3,904	26.4	31	13.8	Switzerland	333	2.3	46	20.0
Forest	7,316	49.4	146	64.3	United Kingdom	1,327	9.0	6	2.8
Other agriculture	673	4.5	6	2.7					
Other nonagriculture . . .	420	2.8	9	4.0					

Z Less than 500 acres or .05 percent.   [1] Landholdings by foreign interests as of Dec. 31.   [2] Acquisitions by foreign interests from Jan. 1-Dec. 31, 1991.   [3] Includes other countries not shown separately.   [4] Reports filed by U.S. corporations with foreign shareholders.
Source: U.S. Dept. of Agriculture, Economic Research Service, *Foreign Ownership of U.S. Agricultural Land Through December 31, 1991* (Economic Research Service Staff Report AGES 9211), 1992.

No. 1086. Farm Real Estate—Summary: 1980 to 1991

[1980 and 1986-89, value data as of Feb. 1; 1982-85, as of April 1; 1990-91, as of January 1. Excludes Alaska and Hawaii. Total value of land and buildings is estimated by multiplying the number of acres of farmland by the average value per acre of land and buildings. Per acre values are based on data from the census of agriculture. For intercensal years, estimates are based on surveys conducted by the U.S. Dept. of Agriculture]

ITEM	Unit	1980	1982	1983	1984	1985	1986	1987	1988	1989	1990	1991
Total value	Bil. dol	763.3	843.3	803.9	812.9	719.4	641.1	597.1	626.9	653.5	658.5	672.2
Average value per acre.	Dollars.	737	823	788	801	713	640	599	632	661	668	682
Average value, operating unit. . .	$1,000	313.5	351.2	338.7	349.1	314.5	285.6	270.5	286.0	301.8	308.0	314.4

Source: U.S. Dept. of Agriculture, Economic Research Service, 1980-1984, *Farm Real Estate Market Developments*, annual; thereafter, *Agricultural Resources, Agricultural Land Values and Markets, Situation and Outlook Report*, annual.

No. 1087. Farm Real Estate—Value of Land and Buildings, by State: 1985 to 1991

[See headnote, table 1086. See also *Historical Statistics, Colonial Times to 1970,* series K 16]

STATE	VALUE OF LAND AND BUILDINGS (mil. dol.)			AVERAGE VALUE OF LAND AND BUILDINGS, PER ACRE			STATE	VALUE OF LAND AND BUILDINGS (mil. dol.)			AVERAGE VALUE OF LAND AND BUILDINGS, PER ACRE		
	1985	1990	1991	1985	1990	1991		1985	1990	1991	1985	1990	1991
U.S ..	719,398	658,451	672,235	$713	$668	$682	MT	14,800	14,399	14,702	243	238	243
							NE	22,911	25,905	26,188	485	550	556
AL	8,929	8,642	8,147	797	839	791	NV	2,171	1,727	1,949	244	194	219
AZ	11,062	9,468	10,260	295	263	285	NH	777	1,096	1,053	1,439	2,237	2,148
AR	14,425	11,625	11,935	907	750	770	NJ	2,833	4,032	4,273	2,951	4,634	4,912
CA	59,829	52,483	55,040	1,841	1,704	1,787	NM	8,324	8,722	10,235	185	196	230
CO	15,042	11,850	13,571	437	358	410	NY	7,464	8,182	8,660	820	974	1,031
CT	1,442	1,855	1,781	3,005	4,417	4,240	NC	14,373	12,251	12,057	1,331	1,263	1,243
DE	1,037	1,288	1,281	1,596	2,259	2,248	ND	15,253	13,770	14,904	373	340	368
FL	19,346	22,727	23,250	1,599	2,085	2,133	OH	19,203	18,903	19,107	1,215	1,204	1,217
GA	11,968	12,650	12,438	886	1,012	995	OK	19,691	16,401	16,038	597	497	486
ID	10,711	9,056	9,028	739	661	659	OR	11,077	10,164	10,377	615	571	583
IL	39,647	39,587	40,841	1,381	1,389	1,433	PA	12,416	14,637	14,232	1,427	1,807	1,757
IN	22,049	20,277	20,783	1,344	1,244	1,275	RI	218	357	343	2,990	5,028	4,827
IA	36,653	36,917	38,760	1,091	1,102	1,157	SC	4,939	4,727	4,930	898	909	948
KS	23,443	22,130	22,369	448	462	467	SD	12,856	14,543	15,561	289	328	351
KY	13,849	13,832	13,564	955	981	962	TN	12,650	12,350	12,251	944	996	988
LA	13,791	8,235	8,145	1,407	915	905	TX	94,025	65,340	63,492	694	495	481
ME	1,153	1,478	1,418	774	1,019	978	UT	5,947	4,396	4,554	513	389	403
MD	5,711	5,445	4,941	2,197	2,420	2,196	VT	1,515	1,797	1,724	947	1,190	1,142
MA	1,616	2,559	2,456	2,377	3,763	3,612	VA	10,566	13,492	11,526	1,112	1,516	1,295
MI	12,517	10,854	11,718	1,108	1,005	1,085	WA	15,187	12,464	12,768	943	779	798
MN	27,311	24,150	26,190	898	805	873	WV	2,186	2,268	2,313	607	613	625
MS	12,054	9,464	9,802	855	728	754	WI	16,905	14,133	15,013	944	803	853
MO	21,234	20,642	20,946	689	679	689	WY	6,287	5,185	5,324	181	149	153

Source: U.S. Dept. of Agriculture, Economic Research Service, *Agricultural Resources, Agricultural Land Values and Markets, Situation and Outlook Report,* annual.

No. 1088. Balance Sheet of the Farming Sector in Current and Constant (1982) Dollars: 1970 to 1990

[In billions of dollars, except as indicated. As of **December 31.** Includes farm operator households. See *Historical Statistics, Colonial Times to 1970,* series K 204-219, for data before revisions]

ITEM	1970	1980	1982	1983	1984	1985	1986	1987	1988	1989	1990
CURRENT DOLLARS											
Assets	324.3	1,089.2	1,056.8	1,064.3	975.9	892.8	848.0	911.4	956.8	976.0	996.2
Physical assets:											
Real estate	224.5	850.1	819.1	829.3	735.0	657.0	613.0	658.6	687.0	692.7	702.6
Non-real estate	76.6	199.8	194.9	190.4	193.2	186.5	181.2	196.1	211.8	224.6	232.4
Livestock and poultry [1]	23.7	60.6	53.0	49.5	49.5	46.3	47.8	58.0	62.2	66.2	69.1
Machinery, motor vehicles . .	34.4	86.9	92.6	92.1	91.1	88.3	86.1	84.5	86.7	90.2	91.7
Crops stored	8.5	32.8	26.4	24.4	26.3	22.9	16.6	17.8	22.7	23.3	22.4
Household furnishings, equipment	10.0	19.4	23.0	24.4	24.3	27.8	28.7	32.9	37.0	42.2	46.3
Purchased inputs	(NA)	(NA)	(NA)	(NA)	2.0	1.2	2.1	3.0	3.3	2.7	2.8
Financial assets.	23.2	39.3	42.8	44.6	47.7	49.3	53.8	56.7	58.0	58.7	61.2
Investment in cooperatives. . .	7.2	19.3	21.9	22.8	24.3	24.3	24.4	25.3	25.1	26.1	27.6
Other financial assets	16.0	20.0	20.9	21.8	23.4	25.0	29.4	31.4	32.9	32.5	33.5
Claims	324.3	1,089.2	1,056.8	1,064.3	975.9	892.8	848.0	911.4	956.8	976.0	996.2
Debt	52.8	178.7	203.1	206.5	204.3	187.9	166.6	153.7	148.5	146.0	145.1
Real estate debt.	30.5	97.5	111.3	113.7	112.3	105.7	95.9	87.7	83.0	80.5	78.4
Non-real estate debt	22.3	81.2	91.8	92.7	92.0	82.2	70.8	66.0	65.6	65.5	66.7
Equity	271.5	910.5	853.7	857.9	771.5	704.9	681.3	757.7	808.3	830.0	851.1
Farm debt/asset ratio (percent)	16.3	16.4	19.2	19.4	20.9	21.0	19.7	16.9	15.5	15.0	14.6
CONSTANT **(1982)** DOLLARS [2]											
Assets	772.1	1,270.9	1,056.8	1,024.4	906.1	805.0	745.1	776.3	788.8	772.8	757.5
Debt	125.6	208.5	203.1	198.7	189.7	169.4	146.4	130.9	122.5	115.6	110.3
Equity	646.5	1,062.4	853.7	825.7	716.4	635.6	598.7	645.4	666.4	657.2	647.2

NA Not available. [1] Excludes horses and mules. [2] Constant dollar figures are based on gross national product implicit price deflators for year.

Source: U.S. Dept. of Agriculture, Economic Research Service, *Economic Indicators of the Farm Sector: National Financial Summary, 1990.*

No. 1089. Percent Distribution of Farms and Farm Debt, by Debt/Asset Ratio: 1987 to 1990

[Value of sales for calendar year shown; balance sheet data as of January 1 of the following year. A farm is a crop or livestock farm if 50 percent or more of its commodity receipts derive from the sale of crop or animal products, respectively. A crop or livestock farm is further categorized as a particular type if 50 percent of its crop or, if applicable, livestock receipts come from a specific commodity area. Based on Farm Costs and Returns Survey conducted in February-March of following year]

VALUE OF SALES AND TYPE OF FARM	FARMS					FARM DEBT				
	Total	Less than 11 percent	11 to 40 percent	41 to 70 percent	Over 70 percent	Total	Less than 11 percent	11 to 40 percent	41 to 70 percent	Over 70 percent
1987	100	58	24	11	7	100	6	34	30	29
1988	100	62	24	9	5	100	7	40	31	21
1989	100	62	24	9	4	100	8	44	31	17
1990, total.	100	61	26	10	4	100	8	46	32	13
Less than $40,000	100	70	20	7	3	100	12	43	31	14
$40,000 to $99,999	100	47	34	14	5	100	8	46	31	15
$100,000 to $249,999. . .	100	35	43	17	5	100	7	48	33	12
$250,000 to $499,999 . . .	100	31	45	20	4	100	7	48	35	10
$500,000 and over	100	33	45	16	6	100	7	45	31	16
Cash grain	100	51	32	12	5	100	7	46	33	14
Tobacco.	100	63	26	9	2	100	9	44	24	23
Cotton	100	42	29	16	13	100	7	33	32	28
Other field crops	100	56	27	13	4	100	6	41	39	14
Vegetable, fruit, and nut .	100	72	17	7	4	100	17	44	28	11
Nursery, greenhouse. . . .	100	66	24	7	3	100	8	55	16	22
Beef, hog, and sheep . . .	100	68	21	8	3	100	10	47	32	11
Poultry	100	38	34	17	11	100	5	33	32	31
Dairy	100	41	40	15	4	100	6	51	34	10
Other livestock	100	65	24	9	3	100	9	43	33	16

Source: U.S. Dept. of Agriculture, Economic Research Service, *Financial Characteristics of U.S. Farms,* annual.

No. 1090. Farms, Farm Income, Assets, and Debt, by Value of Sales: 1990

FARMS WITH VALUE OF SALES OF—	Number of farms [1] (1,000)	Gross cash income [2] (bil. dol.)	Cash receipts (bil. dol.)	Govt. payments (bil. dol.)	Net cash income [2] (bil. dol.)	Assets [3] (bil. dol.)	Debt (bil. dol.)	Debt/asset ratio [3] (percent)	PERCENT DISTRIBUTION		
									Number of farms [1]	Gross cash income [2]	Assets [3]
Total	2,140	186.0	170.0	9.3	61.8	996.2	145.1	14.6	100	100	100
Less than $20,000. . .	1,254	9.1	7.2	0.2	-0.5	287.7	25.6	8.9	59	5	31
$20,000 to $39,999 . .	259	9.0	7.8	0.5	2.4	103.3	11.6	11.2	12	5	11
$40,000 to $99,999 . .	306	24.0	21.0	1.8	7.9	175.1	25.4	14.5	14	13	18
$100,000 to $249,999.	214	39.4	34.8	3.2	15.1	195.5	33.4	17.1	10	21	19
$250,000 to $499,999.	64	25.8	23.1	2.1	10.2	89.9	18.8	20.9	3	14	8
$500,000 to $999,999.	27	21.2	19.9	1.0	7.5	62.5	13.0	20.7	1	11	6
$1 million and over . .	16	57.4	56.2	0.4	19.3	82.1	17.3	21.0	1	31	8

[1] Based on 1974 census definition. See text, section 23.　[2] For components of income, see table 1093. Minus sign (-) indicates loss.　[3] Data as of December 31. Includes farm households.

No. 1091. Net Cash Income and Net Cash Flow From Farming: 1970 to 1990

[In billions of dollars. Net cash income measures the cash income from a farm operator's farm business and net cash flow measures the cash flow within the agricultural sector. Minus sign (-) indicates net loan redemption or decrease]

ITEM	1970	1980	1981	1982	1983	1984	1985	1986	1987	1988	1989	1990
Net cash income.	18.4	34.2	32.8	38.1	38.4	37.4	47.1	47.8	55.3	57.4	59.4	61.8
Gross cash income	54.8	143.3	146.0	151.3	151.1	156.1	157.9	152.8	165.1	171.9	179.9	186.0
Cash expenses	36.4	109.1	113.2	113.2	112.8	118.7	110.7	105.0	109.8	114.5	120.5	124.2
Change in loans outstanding. .	2.3	15.3	15.6	6.4	2.3	2.7	-16.2	-20.6	-12.6	-5.0	-2.2	-0.7
Real estate loans.	1.1	10.0	9.1	3.0	1.4	3.5	-6.6	-9.7	-8.0	-4.8	-2.3	-1.9
Nonreal estate loans [1]	1.2	5.3	6.5	3.4	0.9	-0.8	-9.6	-11.0	-4.6	-0.3	0.1	1.3
Net change in other financial assets	0.1	0.1	0.2	0.2	0.3	0.2	0.7	1.1	-0.2	0.5	0.1	0.4
Net rent received by nonoperator landlords.	2.1	6.1	6.2	5.5	5.2	8.2	7.7	6.1	7.3	7.4	7.9	8.2
Capital expenditures	6.8	18.0	16.8	13.3	12.7	12.5	9.2	8.5	11.2	11.3	12.8	13.4
Net cash flow [2].	16.1	37.6	37.9	37.0	33.4	36.0	30.1	25.9	38.7	49.0	52.6	56.4

[1] Excludes Commodity Credit Corporation loans.　[2] Net cash income plus change in loans outstanding plus net change in other financial assets plus net rent received by nonoperator landlords minus capital expenditures.

Source of tables 1090 and 1091: U.S. Dept. of Agriculture, Economic Research Service, *Economic Indicators of the Farm Sector: National Financial Summary,* annual.

No. 1092. Gross Farm Product—Summary: 1970 to 1990

[In billions of dollars. For definition of gross product, see text, section 14. Minus sign (-) indicates decrease]

ITEM	1970	1980	1982	1983	1984	1985	1986	1987	1988	1989	1990
CURRENT DOLLARS											
Farm output, total [1]	55.1	142.9	152.0	135.1	160.0	152.7	144.0	152.1	158.2	178.4	184.8
Cash receipts from farm marketings	51.3	140.3	135.3	140.2	144.6	136.3	135.2	147.7	159.3	166.6	172.8
Farm housing	3.3	5.1	5.0	5.1	5.1	5.0	4.9	4.9	4.9	5.0	4.9
Other farm income	0.5	2.4	4.8	4.1	3.5	4.6	4.4	5.1	4.6	5.7	4.4
Change in farm inventories	-0.8	-6.1	5.8	-15.4	5.7	5.8	-1.5	-6.4	-11.3	0.5	2.0
Less: Intermediate goods and services purchased [2]	28.9	86.8	86.9	85.9	91.4	85.6	81.1	86.1	90.6	96.3	99.1
Equals: **Gross farm product**	26.2	56.1	65.1	49.2	68.5	67.1	62.9	66.0	67.6	82.1	85.7
Less: Consumption of fixed capital	6.1	19.4	22.8	23.2	23.2	22.9	22.5	22.0	21.6	21.9	21.7
Indirect business tax [3]	2.0	3.0	3.0	3.2	3.1	3.3	3.3	3.6	3.6	3.8	4.2
Plus: Subsidies to operators	3.3	1.0	2.2	7.5	7.0	6.3	9.5	13.9	11.8	9.3	7.7
Equals: **Farm national income**	21.4	34.7	41.6	30.3	49.2	47.2	46.6	54.3	54.2	65.6	67.6
CONSTANT (1987) DOLLARS											
Farm output, total [1]	119.7	137.1	142.2	133.2	139.0	146.0	146.4	152.1	146.5	151.2	156.4
Cash receipts from farm marketings	108.8	130.7	127.9	131.2	127.8	133.1	137.9	147.7	143.9	142.0	145.9
Farm housing	8.0	6.3	5.5	5.4	5.4	5.3	5.1	4.9	4.7	4.6	4.5
Other farm income	1.6	2.3	4.5	3.8	3.1	4.3	4.6	5.1	4.1	4.7	3.8
Change in farm inventories	-0.5	-3.4	3.1	-8.3	1.7	2.4	-2.1	-6.4	-7.0	-0.7	1.7
Less: Intermediate goods and services purchased [2]	70.3	86.1	82.0	79.5	83.9	81.8	82.2	86.1	83.3	84.0	85.0
Equals: **Gross farm product**	49.5	51.0	60.2	53.7	55.1	64.2	64.3	66.0	63.2	67.2	71.4
Less: Consumption of fixed capital	19.1	26.7	26.5	25.8	25.1	24.3	23.1	22.0	21.1	20.4	19.5
Indirect business tax [3]	2.7	2.8	3.3	2.9	3.0	3.5	3.5	3.6	3.5	3.7	3.9
Plus: Subsidies to operators	8.7	11.9	11.1	11.6	10.7	11.4	12.3	13.9	12.9	12.8	13.4
Equals: **Farm national income**	36.3	33.4	41.5	36.5	37.7	47.8	49.9	54.3	51.6	55.8	61.4

- Represents zero.   [1] Includes farm products consumed in farm households where raised, not shown separately.   [2] Includes rent paid to nonoperator landlords.   [3] Includes nontax liability.

Source: U.S. Bureau of Economic Analysis, *Survey of Current Business*, January 1992; and unpublished data.

No. 1093. Farm Income and Expenses: 1970 to 1990

[In billions of dollars. See also *Historical Statistics, Colonial Times to 1970*, series K 192, K 259-260, K 264-285, and K 326]

ITEM	1970	1980	1981	1982	1983	1984	1985	1986	1987	1988	1989	1990
Gross farm income	58.8	149.3	166.3	164.1	153.9	168.0	161.2	156.1	168.4	174.5	190.3	195.1
Cash income	54.8	143.3	146.0	151.3	151.1	156.1	157.9	152.8	165.1	171.9	179.9	186.0
Farm marketings	50.5	139.7	141.6	142.6	136.8	142.8	144.1	135.3	141.8	151.1	160.9	170.0
Crops [1]	21.0	71.7	72.5	72.3	67.2	69.9	74.3	63.7	65.8	71.6	76.8	80.4
Livestock and products	29.5	68.0	69.2	70.3	69.6	72.9	69.8	71.6	76.0	79.4	84.1	89.6
Government payments	3.7	1.3	1.9	3.5	9.3	8.4	7.7	11.8	16.7	14.5	10.9	9.3
Other farm income [1]	0.6	2.3	2.5	5.2	5.1	4.9	6.0	5.7	6.6	6.3	8.1	6.7
Value of home consumption	0.8	1.2	1.2	1.1	1.0	1.0	0.9	0.9	0.7	0.7	0.7	0.7
Rental value of dwellings [2]	3.3	11.0	12.6	13.1	12.6	4.9	4.7	4.6	4.9	5.4	5.5	5.6
Value of inventory adjustment [3]	(Z)	-6.3	6.5	-1.4	-10.9	6.0	-2.3	-2.2	-2.3	-3.5	4.3	2.9
Expenses of farm production	44.5	133.1	139.4	140.3	139.6	141.9	142.4	124.2	125.1	128.7	133.9	144.3
Intermediate products	25.2	76.1	76.6	75.4	75.8	78.0	72.3	70.6	74.9	79.4	83.8	85.9
Farm origin	13.3	34.9	33.3	31.4	32.1	32.3	29.3	30.4	32.6	36.5	37.7	39.0
Feed purchased	8.0	21.0	20.9	18.6	20.6	19.4	16.9	17.5	17.5	20.4	21.0	20.7
Livestock, poultry purchased	4.3	10.7	9.0	9.7	8.8	9.5	9.2	9.8	11.8	12.8	13.1	14.7
Seed purchased [4]	0.9	3.2	3.4	3.2	2.7	3.4	3.1	3.2	3.3	3.4	3.6	3.6
Manufactured inputs	5.4	22.4	23.9	22.1	20.1	22.4	20.2	18.2	18.1	18.9	19.7	20.8
Fertilizer and lime	2.4	9.5	9.4	8.0	7.1	8.4	7.5	6.8	6.5	6.9	7.2	7.1
Pesticides	1.0	3.5	4.2	4.3	3.9	4.7	4.3	4.3	4.5	4.6	5.4	5.7
Fuel and oil	1.7	7.9	8.6	7.7	7.2	7.3	6.4	5.3	5.0	5.1	5.0	6.0
Electricity	0.3	1.5	1.7	2.0	2.0	2.1	1.9	1.8	2.2	2.3	2.0	1.9
Repairs and maintenance [5]	2.8	7.1	7.0	6.4	6.5	6.4	6.4	6.4	6.8	6.8	7.3	7.3
Other [6]	3.7	11.8	12.4	15.5	17.1	16.9	16.5	15.5	17.5	17.2	19.2	18.8
Interest	3.4	16.3	19.9	21.8	21.4	21.1	18.6	16.5	15.0	14.7	14.7	14.5
Real estate	1.8	7.5	9.1	10.5	10.8	10.7	9.9	9.1	8.2	7.9	7.8	7.7
Non-real estate	1.6	8.7	10.7	11.3	10.6	10.4	8.7	7.4	6.8	6.8	6.9	6.8
Contract, hired labor expenses [7] [8]	4.3	9.3	8.9	9.4	8.9	9.4	10.0	9.5	10.0	10.4	11.1	12.5
Net rent to nonoperator landlords [8]	2.1	6.1	6.2	5.5	5.2	8.1	7.7	6.1	7.3	7.4	7.9	8.2
Capital consumption [9]	6.9	21.5	23.6	24.2	23.8	20.8	19.3	17.8	16.7	17.1	17.6	17.5
Property taxes	2.6	3.9	4.2	4.0	4.5	4.3	4.5	4.6	4.9	4.8	5.1	5.6
Net farm income	14.4	16.1	26.9	23.8	14.2	26.1	28.8	31.0	39.7	40.6	50.1	50.8

Z Less than $50 million.   [1] Forest product sales are included in cash receipts for crops for 1970 and in other farm income beginning 1980.   [2] Data for 1970 to 1983 are not comparable with later data.   [3] Minus sign (-) indicates decrease in inventories.   [4] Includes bulbs, plants, and trees.   [5] Expenditures for repairs and maintenance of farm buildings, motor vehicles, and machinery.   [6] Includes machine hire and custo expenses; marketing, storage, and transportation expenses and miscellaneous expenses. Beginning 1980 data not strictly comparable with prior years.   [7] payments and perquisites.   [8] Data for periods 1970, 1980-83, and 1984 and later are based on different sources, creating potential inconsistencies in estimates among these periods.   [9] Depreciation and accidental damage.

Source: U.S. Dept. of Agriculture, Economic Research Service, *Economic Indicators of the Farm Sector: National Financial Summary*, annual.

No. 1094. Farm Income—Cash Receipts From Farm Marketings: 1980 to 1990

[Represents gross receipts from commercial market sales as well as net Commodity Credit Corporation loans. See also *Historical Statistics, Colonial Times to 1970*, series K 286-302]

COMMODITY	FARM MARKETINGS (mil. dol.)								PERCENT		
	1980	1984	1985	1986	1987	1988	1989	1990	1980	1985	1990
Total	139,737	142,784	144,114	135,303	141,759	151,082	160,893	169,987	100.0	100.0	100.0
All crops [1]	71,746	69,889	74,293	63,749	65,764	71,645	76,761	80,364	51.3	51.6	47.3
Barley	736	1,087	1,039	835	754	862	765	768	0.5	0.7	0.5
Corn	13,959	10,909	16,880	12,315	9,924	8,928	11,388	13,716	10.0	11.7	8.1
Cotton lint, seed.	4,447	3,674	3,687	3,371	4,189	4,546	5,040	5,234	3.2	2.6	3.1
Hay	1,917	2,363	2,390	2,246	2,533	3,132	3,395	3,357	1.4	1.7	2.0
Oats	(NA)	(NA)	298	178	260	305	268	232	(NA)	0.2	0.1
Peanuts	607	1,233	1,005	1,074	1,027	1,116	1,117	1,260	0.4	0.7	0.7
Rice.	1,519	1,096	1,042	738	707	1,088	942	1,089	1.1	0.7	0.6
Sorghum.	1,392	1,469	1,981	1,332	1,100	1,068	1,240	1,038	1.0	1.4	0.6
Soybean.	14,241	11,957	11,161	9,235	10,017	12,138	10,524	10,887	10.2	7.7	6.4
Sunflower/safflower	(NA)	(NA)	242	254	211	224	212	229	(NA)	0.2	0.1
Tobacco.	2,672	2,813	2,699	1,894	1,816	2,083	2,415	2,736	1.9	1.9	1.6
Wheat . . . . . , . .	8,854	8,576	7,909	4,975	5,044	6,356	7,286	6,772	6.3	5.5	4.0
Vegetables [2]	7,307	9,152	8,572	8,865	9,902	9,787	11,461	11,533	5.2	5.9	6.8
Dry beans	(NA)	(NA)	439	437	444	421	688	675	(NA)	0.3	0.4
Snap beans	(NA)	(NA)	167	150	171	166	228	205	(NA)	0.1	0.1
Broccoli.	(NA)	(NA)	239	240	240	292	276	268	(NA)	0.2	0.2
Carrots	(NA)	(NA)	206	335	248	268	297	273	(NA)	0.1	0.2
Celery	(NA)	(NA)	190	211	199	231	268	215	(NA)	0.1	0.1
Sweet corn	(NA)	(NA)	368	360	372	360	468	467	(NA)	0.3	0.3
Cucumbers.	(NA)	(NA)	181	170	188	196	203	216	(NA)	0.1	0.1
Lettuce	(NA)	(NA)	675	758	1,003	1,040	950	847	(NA)	0.5	0.5
Onions	(NA)	(NA)	372	415	536	498	538	551	(NA)	0.3	0.3
Potatoes	(NA)	1,921	1,601	1,377	1,707	1,625	2,334	2,679	(NA)	1.1	1.6
Tomatoes . . , ...	(NA)	1,240	1,198	1,265	1,466	1,415	1,824	1,622	(NA)	0.8	1.0
Fruits, tree nuts [2]	6,557	6,734	6,946	7,252	8,062	9,204	9,257	9,306	4.7	4.8	5.5
Apples	(NA)	951	892	927	1,060	1,109	1,114	1,159	(NA)	0.6	0.7
Avocados	(NA)	(NA)	139	163	120	213	221	216	(NA)	0.1	0.1
Grapefruit	(NA)	(NA)	319	358	408	471	440	317	(NA)	0.2	0.2
Grapes	(NA)	983	961	1,177	1,362	1,600	1,866	1,668	(NA)	0.7	1.0
Lemons	(NA)	(NA)	237	157	226	188	223	278	(NA)	0.2	0.2
Oranges	(NA)	1,359	1,404	1,184	1,363	1,825	1,777	1,707	(NA)	1.0	1.0
Peaches	(NA)	(NA)	295	315	311	382	364	365	(NA)	0.2	0.2
Pears	(NA)	(NA)	193	198	196	218	252	266	(NA)	0.1	0.2
Plums and prunes	(NA)	(NA)	196	200	207	255	252	293	(NA)	0.1	0.2
Strawberries.	(NA)	(NA)	451	504	554	536	520	560	(NA)	0.3	0.3
Almonds	(NA)	(NA)	361	462	648	600	481	592	(NA)	0.3	0.3
Pecans	(NA)	(NA)	163	197	140	167	179	248	(NA)	0.1	0.1
Walnuts.	(NA)	(NA)	175	194	243	194	245	235	(NA)	0.1	0.1
Sugar beets	(NA)	750	774	902	1,025	1,022	1,038	1,157	(NA)	0.5	0.7
Sugarcane	(NA)	(NA)	717	742	803	854	879	857	(NA)	0.5	0.5
Mushrooms.	(NA)	(NA)	491	491	519	573	630	667	(NA)	0.3	0.4
Greenhouse, nursery. . . .	(NA)	5,176	5,407	5,983	6,755	7,069	7,601	8,145	(NA)	3.8	4.8
All livestock and products [1] .	67,991	72,895	69,822	71,553	75,994	79,437	84,131	89,623	48.7	48.4	52.7
Cattle and calves	31,819	30,589	29,002	28,865	33,583	36,810	36,894	39,748	22.8	20.1	23.4
Dairy products	16,365	17,931	18,055	17,724	17,727	17,641	19,396	20,199	11.7	12.5	11.9
Hogs	8,942	9,701	9,033	9,734	10,337	9,207	9,475	11,516	6.4	6.3	6.8
Broilers.	4,303	6,020	5,668	6,784	6,177	7,435	8,778	8,366	3.1	3.9	4.9
Eggs	3,247	4,110	3,262	3,543	3,209	3,067	3,862	4,044	2.3	2.3	2.4
Turkeys	1,273	1,655	1,820	1,949	1,703	1,951	2,234	2,383	0.9	1.3	1.4
Sheep and lambs	(NA)	(NA)	514	481	558	476	487	412	(NA)	0.4	0.2
Horses and mules	(NA)	(NA)	560	500	540	540	524	490	(NA)	0.4	0.3
Aquaculture.	(NA)	(NA)	205	230	290	324	407	460	(NA)	0.1	0.3

NA Not available.   [1] Includes other commodities not shown separately.   [2] Melons included with vegetables.

Source: U.S. Dept. of Agriculture, Economic Research Service, *Economic Indicators of the Farm Sector: National Financial Summary*, annual.

No. 1095. Government Payments to Farms, by Program: 1980 to 1990

[**In millions of dollars.** See also *Historical Statistics, Colonial Times to 1970*, series K 326-329]

PROGRAM	1980	1984	1985	1986	1987	1988	1989	1990
Total	1,285	8,431	7,705	11,814	16,747	14,480	10,887	9,298
Feed grain.	382	367	2,861	5,158	8,490	7,219	3,141	2,701
Wheat.	211	1,795	1,950	3,500	2,931	1,842	603	2,311
Cotton	172	275	1,106	1,042	1,204	924	1,184	441
Rice	2	192	577	423	475	465	671	465
Wool	28	118	98	112	144	117	81	96
Conservation . . , . .	214	191	189	254	1,531	1,607	1,771	1,898
Miscellaneous [1] . .	276	5,493	924	1,325	1,972	2,306	3,436	1,386

[1] Includes value of commodities transferred to farmers under the payment-in-kind program (PIK).

Source: U.S. Dept. of Agriculture, Economic Research Service, *Economic Indicators of the Farm Sector: National Financial Summary, 1990*.

No. 1096. Farm Assets, Debt, and Income, by State: 1989 and 1990

[Assets and debt, as of December 31. Includes farm operator households. Farm income data are after inventory adjustment]

DIVISION AND STATE	ASSETS (mil. dol.)		DEBT (mil. dol.)		DEBT/ASSET RATIO (percent)		GROSS FARM INCOME (mil. dol.)		NET FARM INCOME (mil. dol.)	
	1989	1990 [1]	1989	1990	1989	1990	1989	1990	1989	1990
United States	975,985	997,935	145,966	145,067	15.0	14.6	190,293	195,123	50,074	50,832
New England:										
Maine	2,367	2,296	340	332	14.4	14.4	513	520	148	151
New Hampshire.	1,665	1,671	73	76	4.4	4.6	164	167	41	40
Vermont.	2,797	2,751	350	371	12.5	13.5	481	485	134	127
Massachusetts	4,826	4,697	265	317	5.5	6.8	490	480	173	149
Rhode Island.	605	565	30	37	5.0	6.5	86	79	45	37
Connecticut.	4,320	4,022	216	231	5.0	5.7	462	496	164	188
Middle Atlantic:										
New York	13,868	14,597	2,363	2,313	17.0	15.8	3,141	3,267	880	935
New Jersey.	8,935	9,370	401	435	4.5	4.6	768	757	277	247
Pennsylvania.	21,945	21,551	2,392	2,406	10.9	11.2	4,000	4,050	1,108	1,139
East North Central:										
Ohio	28,746	29,229	3,453	3,367	12.0	11.5	4,546	4,783	1,096	1,173
Indiana.	29,604	30,093	4,926	4,754	16.6	15.8	5,444	5,468	1,270	1,054
Illinois	53,354	54,616	7,473	7,364	14.0	13.5	8,957	8,898	2,017	1,705
Michigan.	17,449	18,802	2,912	2,774	16.7	14.8	3,755	3,724	1,101	941
Wisconsin.	26,783	28,236	5,297	5,102	19.8	18.1	6,675	6,387	2,283	1,863
West North Central:										
Minnesota.	38,168	40,935	7,000	6,592	18.3	16.1	8,270	8,398	2,607	2,504
Iowa	54,269	56,987	9,972	9,911	18.4	17.4	11,497	12,045	2,722	2,964
Missouri	32,138	32,952	4,756	4,687	14.8	14.2	4,866	4,705	1,073	874
North Dakota.	20,980	22,360	3,570	3,622	17.0	16.2	3,107	3,463	616	802
South Dakota	21,477	23,026	3,281	3,399	15.3	14.8	3,658	4,078	982	1,285
Nebraska	37,297	38,502	6,474	6,594	17.4	17.1	10,142	10,408	1,748	2,128
Kansas.	32,813	33,448	5,603	5,808	17.1	17.4	7,797	8,561	707	1,378
South Atlantic:										
Delaware	1,752	1,715	278	333	15.9	19.4	698	668	190	171
Maryland	7,677	6,877	996	988	13.0	14.4	1,476	1,492	412	427
Virginia.	19,131	17,105	2,013	2,049	10.5	12.0	2,418	2,435	569	542
West Virginia.	3,671	3,787	440	434	12.0	11.5	415	459	52	76
North Carolina.	18,435	18,060	2,759	2,659	15.0	14.7	5,366	5,643	1,810	1,968
South Carolina.	7,215	7,398	1,011	974	14.0	13.2	1,400	1,277	398	274
Georgia	18,630	18,564	3,065	2,901	16.5	15.6	4,407	4,203	1,297	1,076
Florida	28,395	28,626	3,711	3,764	13.1	13.1	6,435	5,888	2,930	2,273
East South Central:										
Kentucky	21,510	21,453	2,796	2,717	13.0	12.7	3,429	3,492	1,135	1,038
Tennessee	19,765	19,677	2,160	2,155	10.9	11.0	2,497	2,456	553	461
Alabama.	13,142	12,420	1,565	1,521	11.9	12.2	3,032	3,102	844	823
Mississippi	14,195	14,351	2,877	2,656	20.3	18.5	2,807	2,815	652	616
West South Central:										
Arkansas	16,720	17,129	3,019	3,116	18.0	18.2	4,809	4,810	1,242	1,204
Louisiana	11,060	10,512	2,072	1,953	18.7	18.6	2,160	2,239	599	602
Oklahoma.	24,511	24,690	4,113	3,991	16.8	16.2	4,327	4,429	998	1,110
Texas	89,777	88,900	10,238	10,139	11.4	11.4	13,227	14,489	2,419	3,371
Mountain:										
Montana.	19,680	20,314	2,724	2,647	13.8	13.0	2,162	2,098	532	387
Idaho.	13,409	13,466	2,408	2,456	18.0	18.2	3,176	3,332	994	1,090
Wyoming	7,239	7,512	770	882	10.6	11.7	803	857	83	120
Colorado	17,598	19,467	3,107	3,011	17.7	17.0	4,571	4,785	767	873
New Mexico	10,934	12,541	1,065	1,031	9.7	8.2	1,584	1,641	352	337
Arizona	10,715	11,529	1,637	1,443	15.3	12.5	2,106	2,039	704	582
Utah	6,023	6,343	737	698	12.2	11.0	832	883	210	240
Nevada	3,344	3,742	287	267	8.6	7.1	325	341	96	87
Pacific:										
Washington.	17,620	18,126	2,981	3,057	16.9	16.9	4,360	4,525	1,380	1,401
Oregon.	14,930	15,495	2,565	2,563	17.2	16.5	2,804	2,898	840	852
California	80,428	83,217	13,068	13,779	16.2	16.6	19,209	19,962	6,714	7,030
Alaska	552	593	33	27	6.0	4.8	34	32	9	8
Hawaii	3,523	3,618	322	367	9.2	10.1	605	614	106	84

[1] Reflects revisions subsequent to publication of report.

Source: U.S. Dept. of Agriculture, Economic Research Service, *Economic Indicators of the Farm Sector: State Financial Summary, 1990*; and unpublished data.

No. 1097. Farm Income—Farm Marketings, 1989 and 1990, Government Payments, 1990, and Principal Commodities, 1990, by State

[In millions of dollars. Cattle include calves; sheep include lambs; and greenhouse includes nursery]

DIVISION AND STATE	1989 Farm marketings Total	1989 Farm marketings Crops	1989 Farm marketings Livestock and products	1990 Farm marketings Total	1990 Farm marketings Crops	1990 Farm marketings Livestock and products	1990 Government payments	State rank for total farm marketings and four principal commodities in order of marketing receipts
U.S....	160,893	76,761	84,131	169,987	80,364	89,623	9,298	Cattle, dairy products, corn, hogs
N.E....	1,951	978	973	1,976	971	1,005	20	(X)
ME ...	444	228	216	460	240	220	7	42-Potatoes, dairy products, eggs, blueberries
NH ...	139	73	65	134	71	63	2	48-Dairy products, greenhouse, apples, cattle
VT...	429	50	379	447	49	398	6	43-Dairy products, cattle, hay, greenhouse
MA ...	434	321	113	418	303	116	3	45-Greenhouse, dairy products, cranberries, eggs
RI ...	78	65	13	71	58	13	(Z)	49-Greenhouse, dairy products, eggs, potatoes
CT....	426	240	186	446	250	196	2	44-Greenhouse, eggs, dairy products, tobacco
M.A	7,118	2,373	4,745	7,421	2,528	4,893	116	(X)
NY...	2,854	917	1,937	3,006	1,023	1,983	59	23-Dairy products, greenhouse, cattle, apples
NJ...	662	464	197	647	452	196	16	39-Greenhouse, dairy products, eggs, soybeans
PA...	3,602	992	2,611	3,767	1,053	2,714	41	18-Dairy products, cattle, greenhouse, mushrooms
E.N.C ...	23,369	11,933	11,437	25,930	13,577	12,353	1,298	(X)
OH ...	3,787	2,088	1,698	4,172	2,335	1,836	197	14-Corn, soybeans, dairy products, hogs
IN ...	4,281	2,456	1,826	4,931	2,871	2,060	244	10-Corn, soybeans, hogs, cattle
IL ...	6,979	4,727	2,251	7,938	5,461	2,477	507	5-Corn, soybeans, hogs, cattle
MI ...	2,923	1,611	1,311	3,183	1,785	1,398	169	21-Dairy products, corn, cattle, greenhouse
WI ...	5,400	1,050	4,350	5,706	1,125	4,581	181	9-Dairy products, cattle, corn, hogs
W.N.C..	39,890	15,972	23,918	42,995	17,025	25,970	3,902	(X)
MN ...	6,513	2,820	3,693	7,011	3,253	3,758	512	6-Dairy products, corn, soybeans, hogs
IA ...	9,049	3,755	5,293	10,319	4,437	5,882	754	3-Hogs, corn, cattle, soybeans
MO ...	3,920	1,751	2,169	3,939	1,668	2,271	299	15-Cattle, soybeans, hogs, dairy products
ND ...	2,152	1,483	669	2,537	1,724	813	545	26-Wheat, cattle, barley, sunflower
SD...	2,982	951	2,031	3,349	1,036	2,313	333	20-Cattle, hogs, wheat, soybeans
NE....	8,726	3,080	5,646	8,845	2,808	6,037	625	4-Cattle, corn, hogs, soybeans
KS....	6,548	2,132	4,416	6,995	2,099	4,896	835	7-Cattle, wheat, corn, hogs
S.A.....	20,329	10,811	9,518	20,039	10,346	9,693	363	(X)
DE...	662	159	503	644	184	460	3	40-Broilers, soybeans, corn, greenhouse
MD ...	1,336	477	859	1,345	517	828	17	35-Broilers, dairy products, greenhouse, soybeans
VA...	2,039	694	1,345	2,120	741	1,379	32	29-Cattle, dairy products, broilers, tobacco
WV ...	310	60	250	338	70	269	6	46-Cattle, broilers, dairy productss, turkeys
NC ...	4,593	2,082	2,510	4,867	2,214	2,653	73	11-Tobacco, broilers, hogs, turkeys
SC...	1,235	680	554	1,176	599	577	63	36-Tobacco, cattle, broilers, soybeans
GA ...	3,908	1,626	2,281	3,842	1,574	2,268	131	16-Broilers, peanuts, eggs, cattle
FL...	6,246	5,031	1,215	5,708	4,448	1,260	37	8-Oranges, greenhouse, sugar, dairy products
E.S.C ..	9,817	3,807	6,010	10,307	4,094	6,213	441	(X)
KY....	2,924	1,266	1,658	3,098	1,400	1,698	82	22-Tobacco, cattle, horses, dairy products
TN...	1,946	863	1,082	2,039	928	1,111	91	30-Cattle, dairy products, soybeans, tobacco
AL...	2,671	696	1,975	2,737	655	2,083	82	25-Broilers, cattle, greenhouse, eggs
MS ...	2,276	981	1,295	2,433	1,111	1,322	186	27-Cotton, broilers, cattle, soybeans
W.S.C ...	20,303	7,790	12,513	21,715	8,297	13,419	1,761	(X)
AR...	4,157	1,496	2,661	4,259	1,553	2,706	313	12-Broilers, cattle, soybeans, rice
LA...	1,708	1,094	614	1,921	1,284	637	155	31-Cotton, soybeans, cattle, rice
OK ...	3,515	1,137	2,377	3,554	1,191	2,363	319	19-Cattle, wheat, greenhouse, broilers
TX...	10,923	4,063	6,861	11,981	4,268	7,712	975	2-Cattle, cotton, dairy products, greenhouse
Mt	13,479	5,726	7,754	14,003	5,687	8,316	848	(X)
MT ...	1,554	625	929	1,606	742	864	300	33-Cattle, wheat, barley, hay
ID ...	2,745	1,662	1,084	2,935	1,781	1,154	133	24-Cattle, potatoes, dairy products, wheat
WY ...	827	163	664	767	157	610	31	37-Cattle, sugar beets, hay, sheep
CO ...	3,969	1,321	2,649	4,213	1,184	3,029	237	13-Cattle, corn, wheat, dairy products
NM ...	1,459	485	974	1,529	483	1,046	64	34-Cattle, dairy products, hay, chili peppers
AZ....	1,926	1,182	744	1,865	1,046	819	43	32-Cattle, cotton, dairy products, hay
UT....	755	188	567	755	179	576	35	38-Cattle, dairy products, hay, turkeys
NV....	244	102	142	333	115	218	5	47-Cattle, hay, dairy products, potatoes
Pac	24,638	17,373	7,264	25,601	17,839	7,762	549	(X)
WA ...	3,688	2,457	1,230	3,616	2,420	1,096	205	17-Dairy products, cattle, apples, wheat
OR ...	2,285	1,546	738	2,312	1,557	755	89	28-Cattle, greenhouse, dairy products, wheat
CA ...	18,050	12,857	5,193	18,859	13,344	5,515	252	1-Dairy products, greenhouse, cattle, grapes
AK ...	29	20	9	27	19	8	1	50-Greenhouse, dairy products, potatoes, hay
HI ...	585	493	92	588	499	88	1	41-Sugar, pineapples, greenhouse, nuts

X Not applicable.   Z Less than $500 thousand.

Source: U.S. Dept. of Agriculture, Economic Research Service, *Economic Indicators of the Farm Sector: State Financial Summary, 1990.*

No. 1098. Commodity Credit Corporation—Summary: 1980 to 1991

[In millions of dollars. As of end of fiscal year or for fiscal year ending in year shown; see text, section 9. The Commodity Credit Corporation is a wholly government-owned corporation. Its purpose is stabilizing, supporting, and protecting farm income and prices; assisting in maintenance of balanced adequate supplies of agricultural commodities; and facilitating orderly distribution of agricultural commodities. See also *Historical Statistics, Colonial Times to 1970*, series K 330-343]

ITEM	1980	1982	1983	1984	1985	1986	1987	1988	1989	1990	1991
LOAN ACTIVITY [1]											
Loans made...............	4,228	11,454	13,710	5,131	10,187	17,391	16,566	13,302	7,068	5,943	6,630
Loans repaid.............	4,148	4,629	9,373	10,581	4,458	5,675	13,894	17,979	9,394	6,894	6,827
Loans cancelled by acquisition of collateral......	115	363	860	1,032	1,638	5,583	6,144	2,110	1,055	871	993
Loans outstanding [2].........	5,119	11,633	15,084	8,571	12,631	18,668	15,174	8,354	4,922	3,071	1,858
Wheat...................	837	3,321	4,162	3,414	4,591	3,753	2,836	1,608	865	796	500
Corn...................	1,617	4,210	5,274	1,236	2,766	7,878	7,424	3,803	1,921	1,031	149
Cotton..................	35	714	960	67	376	1,076	450	569	594	40	19
Tobacco.................	815	867	1,738	2,084	2,539	2,336	2,071	1,616	1,236	924	787
COMMODITY INVENTORY OPERATIONS											
Acquisitions, value [2].........	2,759	2,968	8,634	8,741	4,294	9,912	17,617	12,167	3,193	2,130	2,726
Purchases...............	2,643	2,593	7,644	7,676	2,616	4,195	11,212	9,901	2,201	1,225	1,690
Collateral acquired from loans ...	116	375	990	1,065	1,678	5,717	6,405	2,266	992	904	1,036
Wheat..................	601	27	1,600	1,983	919	2,196	1,802	1,051	294	307	436
Corn...................	416	179	3,132	2,591	192	2,287	10,218	8,484	1,418	852	996
Cotton..................	1	(Z)	175	1,056	53	559	1,273	138	73	32	1
Dairy products............	1,262	2,282	2,716	1,983	1,820	2,036	956	1,125	611	399	757
Commodities owned, value [2]....	2,737	5,103	10,227	7,358	6,921	11,050	11,735	5,588	3,771	2,149	2,796
Wheat..................	705	679	1,533	1,510	1,951	3,491	3,272	1,208	697	505	639
Corn...................	596	709	3,392	1,045	757	1,757	4,172	2,197	1,253	625	962
Cotton..................	1	2	174	74	46	226	24	2	34	7	(Z)
Sorghum................	93	91	520	290	359	725	1,244	1,268	936	447	162
Dairy products............	1,266	3,442	4,219	4,102	3,014	2,830	1,439	734	681	522	1,010

Z Less than $500,000.   [1] Covers commodity loans and storage facility and equipment loans. The latter were not available after July 1982.   [2] Includes amounts for commodities and storage facilities, not shown separately.

No. 1099. Commodity Credit Corporation—Net Outlays, by Commodity and Function: 1980 to 1991

[In millions of dollars. For fiscal year ending in year shown; see text, section 9. Excludes value of commodity certificates which may also be issued to farmers in lieu of cash under certain programs. Minus sign (-) indicates a net receipt (excess of repayments or other receipts over gross outlays of funds)]

COMMODITY AND FUNCTION	1980	1982	1983	1984	1985	1986	1987	1988	1989	1990	1991
Total	2,752	11,652	18,851	7,315	17,683	25,841	22,408	12,461	10,523	6,471	10,110
Feed grains...............	1,286	5,397	6,815	-758	5,211	12,211	13,967	9,053	3,384	2,721	2,722
Wheat...................	879	2,238	3,419	2,536	4,691	3,440	2,836	678	53	806	2,958
Cotton, upland............	64	1,190	1,363	244	1,553	2,142	1,786	666	1,461	-79	382
Dairy....................	1,011	2,182	2,528	1,502	2,085	2,337	1,166	1,295	679	505	839
Rice....................	-76	164	664	333	990	947	906	128	631	667	867
Wool....................	35	54	94	132	109	123	152	[1]5	93	104	172
Honey...................	9	27	48	90	81	89	73	100	42	47	19
Peanuts.................	28	12	-6	1	12	32	8	7	13	1	48
Sugar...................	-405	-5	49	10	184	214	-65	-246	-25	15	-20
Tobacco.................	-88	103	880	346	455	253	-346	-453	-367	-307	-143
Soybeans	116	169	288	-585	711	1,597	-476	-1,676	-86	5	40
Operating expense [2]........	157	294	328	362	346	457	535	614	620	618	625
Interest expenditure	518	-13	3,525	1,064	1,435	1,411	1,219	395	98	632	745
Export programs [3].........	-669	65	398	743	134	102	276	200	-102	-34	733
1988/89 disaster/livestock assistance	(X)	(X)	(X)	(X)	(X)	(X)	(X)	(X)	3,919	[4]161	121
Other	-113	-225	-1,542	1,295	-314	486	371	1,695	110	609	2
Price support loans [5]..........	-66	7,015	8,438	-27	6,272	13,628	12,199	4,579	-926	-399	418
Direct payments [6]...........	418	1,491	3,600	2,117	7,827	6,746	5,862	4,245	6,011	4,370	6,341
Deficiency payments	79	1,184	2,780	612	6,302	6,166	4,833	3,971	5,798	4,178	6,224
Diversion payments	56	(Z)	705	1,504	1,525	64	382	8	-1		
1988/89 crop disaster..........	(X)	(X)	(X)	(X)	(X)	(X)	(X)	(X)	3,386	[4]5	6
Emergency livestock/forage assistance	23	16						31	533	156	115
Purchases................	1,681	2,031	2,540	1,470	1,331	1,670	-479	-1,131	116	-48	646
Producer storage payments	254	679	964	268	329	485	832	658	174	185	1
Processing, storage and transportation	259	355	665	639	657	1,013	1,659	1,113	659	317	394
Operating expense [2]	157	294	328	362	346	457	535	614	620	618	625
Interest expenditure	518	-13	3,525	1,064	1,435	1,411	1,219	425	98	632	745
Export programs [3]............	-669	65	398	743	134	102	276	200	-102	-34	733
Other	177	-281	-1,607	679	-648	329	305	1,727	-46	669	86

- Represents zero.   X Not applicable.   Z Less than $500,000.   [1] Fiscal year 1988 wool and mohair program outlays were $130,635,000 but include a one-time advance appropriation of $126,108,000, which was recorded as a wool program receipt by U.S. Department of Treasury.   [2] Excludes CCC transfers to the general sales manager.   [3] Covers the direct export credit sales program, the export guarantee program, and transfers to the general sales manager.   [4] Approximately $1.5 billion in benefits to farmers under the Disaster Assistance Act of 1989 were paid in generic certificates and were not recorded directly as disaster assistance outlays.   [5] Price support loans made less loans repaid.   [6] Includes disaster payments; beginning 1986 includes dairy termination program.   [7] Purchases less sales proceeds.

Source of tables 1098 and 1099: U.S. Agricultural Stabilization and Conservation Service, *Commodity Credit Corporation Report of Financial Condition and Operations*, annual, and *Agricultural Outlook*, monthly.

No. 1100. Indexes of Prices Received and Paid by Farmers: 1980 to 1991

[1977 = 100, except as noted. See also *Historical Statistics, Colonial Times to 1970*, series K 344-353]

ITEM	1980	1985	1990	1991	ITEM	1980	1985	1990	1991
Prices received, all products.	134	128	149	146	**Prices paid, total** [3]	138	162	184	189
Crops [1]	125	120	127	130	Production [1]	138	151	171	173
Food grains	165	133	123	115	Feed	123	116	128	123
Feed grains and hay	132	122	123	118	Feeder livestock	177	154	213	214
Cotton	114	93	107	108	Seed	118	152	165	163
Tobacco.	125	153	152	159	Fertilizer.	134	135	131	134
Oil-bearing crops	102	84	93	90	Agricultural chemicals. . . .	102	128	139	151
Fruits.	124	180	188	270	Fuels and energy.	188	201	204	203
Commercial vegetables [2] .	113	129	142	135	Farm and motor supplies . .	134	146	154	157
Livestock and products	144	136	170	162	Interest payable per acre . .	174	228	173	172
Meat animals	156	142	193	186	Taxes payable per acre . . .	115	133	156	160
Dairy products.	135	131	141	126	Wage rates [4]	127	154	191	201
Poultry and eggs	112	119	131	125	**Parity ratio (1910-14 = 100)** [5] .	65	52	54	51

[1] Includes other items not shown separately. [2] Excludes potatoes and dry beans. [3] Includes production items, interest, taxes, wage rates, and a family living component. The family living component is the Consumer Price Index for all urban consumers from the Bureau of Labor Statistics. See text, section 15, and table 738. [4] Straight average of seasonally adjusted indexes. [5] Ratio of prices received by farmers to prices paid.
Source: U.S. Dept. of Agriculture, National Agricultural Statistics Service, *Agricultural Prices: Annual Summary*.

No. 1101. Civilian Consumer Expenditures for Farm Foods—Farm Value and Marketing Bill: 1970 to 1990

[In billions of dollars, except percent. Excludes imported and nonfarm foods, such as coffee and seafood, as well as food consumed by the military, or exported. See *Historical Statistics, Colonial Times to 1970*, series K 358-360 for data before revisions]

ITEM	1970	1980	1982	1983	1984	1985	1986	1987	1988	1989	1990
Consumer expenditures, total	110.6	264.4	298.9	315.0	332.0	345.4	359.6	375.5	398.8	419.4	440.8
Farm value, total	35.5	81.7	81.4	85.3	89.8	86.4	88.8	90.4	96.8	103.8	106.6
Marketing bill, total [1]	75.1	182.7	217.5	229.7	242.2	259.0	270.8	285.1	301.9	315.6	334.2
Percent of total consumer expenditures	67.9	69.1	72.8	72.9	73.0	75.0	75.3	75.9	75.7	75.3	75.8
At-home expenditures [2]	78.2	180.1	196.7	204.6	213.1	220.8	226.0	230.2	242.1	255.5	267.9
Farm value	29.1	65.9	64.1	66.5	69.5	66.6	67.6	67.5	72.5	77.9	79.8
Marketing bill [1]	49.1	114.2	132.6	138.1	143.6	154.2	158.4	162.7	169.6	177.6	188.1
Percent of at-home expenditures	62.8	63.4	67.4	67.5	67.4	69.8	70.1	70.7	70.1	69.5	70.2
Away-from-home expenditures	32.4	84.3	102.2	110.4	118.9	124.6	133.6	145.3	156.7	163.9	172.9
Farm value	6.4	15.8	17.3	18.8	20.3	19.8	21.2	22.9	24.3	25.9	26.8
Marketing bill [1]	26.0	68.5	84.9	91.6	98.6	104.8	112.4	122.4	132.4	138.0	146.1
Percent of away-from-home expenditures. .	80.2	81.3	83.1	83.0	82.9	84.1	84.1	84.2	84.5	84.2	84.5
Marketing bill cost components:											
Labor cost [3]	32.2	81.5	96.6	102.4	109.3	115.6	122.9	130.0	137.9	145.1	153.8
Packaging materials	8.2	21.0	23.7	24.7	26.2	26.9	27.7	29.9	32.6	35.2	36.2
Rail and truck transport [4]	5.2	13.0	14.7	15.4	15.9	16.5	16.8	17.2	17.8	18.6	19.6
Corporate profits before taxes	3.6	9.9	9.3	9.6	9.6	10.4	10.3	11.1	11.6	11.8	14.1
Fuels and electricity	2.2	9.0	11.0	11.7	12.5	13.1	13.2	13.6	14.1	15.3	16.3
Other [5]	23.7	48.3	62.2	65.9	68.7	76.5	79.9	83.3	87.9	89.6	94.2
Processing	29.7	66.3	75.6	77.8	80.8	88.4	91.0	93.9	99.7	103.8	110.3
Wholesaling	8.7	20.4	25.9	27.1	28.6	29.8	30.5	31.8	33.8	35.2	37.3
Transportation.	5.2	13.0	14.9	15.4	16.0	16.6	16.8	17.6	17.7	18.6	19.6
Retailing and food service	31.5	83.0	101.1	109.4	116.8	124.2	132.5	141.8	150.8	158.0	167.0
SELECTED FOOD COMMODITY GROUPS											
Meat products:											
Total expenditures	33.7	83.3	91.9	97.9	101.7	103.2	106.3	110.0	117.6	121.5	124.7
Farm value	14.4	30.8	31.5	31.4	32.4	30.5	30.5	32.7	33.5	34.0	37.0
Percent of total	42.7	37.0	34.3	32.1	31.9	29.6	29.1	29.7	28.5	28.0	29.7
Marketing bill [1]	19.3	52.5	60.4	66.5	69.3	72.7	75.4	77.3	84.1	87.5	87.7
Poultry and eggs:											
Total expenditures	9.1	18.3	20.3	21.7	24.2	26.0	27.6	29.4	31.3	33.9	36.4
Farm value	4.0	8.4	8.5	9.3	11.0	10.2	11.5	10.3	12.1	14.2	13.9
Percent of total	44.0	45.9	41.9	42.9	45.5	39.2	41.7	35.0	38.7	41.9	38.2
Marketing bill [1]	5.1	9.9	11.8	12.4	13.2	15.8	16.1	19.1	19.2	19.7	22.5
Dairy products:											
Total expenditures	16.7	37.8	42.0	45.0	47.4	49.4	51.4	54.0	55.8	58.1	59.9
Farm value	6.9	16.0	16.7	18.0	18.1	17.7	17.8	18.2	17.9	19.6	20.6
Percent of total	41.3	42.3	39.8	40.0	38.2	35.8	34.6	33.7	32.1	33.7	34.4
Marketing bill [1]	9.8	21.8	25.3	27.0	29.3	31.7	33.6	35.8	37.9	38.5	39.3
Fruits and vegetables:											
Total expenditures	22.6	55.5	66.7	70.0	74.7	78.5	81.6	84.7	89.3	96.0	101.7
Farm value	5.1	11.7	11.5	12.9	13.5	13.3	14.6	14.3	16.2	17.8	16.6
Percent of total	22.6	21.1	17.2	18.4	18.1	16.9	17.9	16.9	18.1	18.5	16.3
Marketing bill [1]	17.5	43.8	55.2	57.1	61.2	65.2	67.0	70.4	73.1	78.2	85.1
Bakery, grain mill products:											
Total expenditures	13.6	35.2	39.6	40.6	43.3	45.5	48.3	49.9	54.7	57.7	63.6
Farm value	2.0	5.1	4.8	4.9	5.1	4.7	4.0	3.8	4.9	5.9	5.1
Percent of total	14.7	14.5	12.1	12.1	11.8	10.3	8.3	7.6	9.0	10.2	8.0
Marketing bill [1]	11.6	30.1	34.8	35.7	38.2	40.8	44.3	46.1	49.8	51.8	58.5

[1] The difference between expenditures for domestic farm-originated food products and the farm value or payment farmers received for the equivalent farm products. [2] Food primarily purchased from retail food stores for use at home. [3] Covers employee wages and salaries, and their health and welfare benefits. Also includes imputed earnings of proprietors, partners, and family workers not receiving stated remuneration. [4] Excludes local hauling. [5] Represents advertising, rent, depreciation, interest on borrowed capital, taxes other than income, and other costs.
Source: U.S. Dept. of Agriculture, Economic Research Service, *Food Cost Review, 1990*, AER No. 651, June 1991; *National Food Review*, periodic; and *Agricultural Statistics*, annual.

No. 1102. Farmer Marketing and Farm Supply Cooperatives—Summary: 1970 to 1990

[1970 for **fiscal years** of cooperatives ending between **July 1, 1969** and **June 30, 1970.** Beginning **1980,** reports of cooperatives are for the **calendar year.** Comprises independent local associations, federations, large-scale centralized associations, and sales agencies. Memberships and businesses are estimated. See also *Historical Statistics, Colonial Times to 1970*, series K 195-203]

ITEM	1970	1980	1982	1983	1984	1985	1986	1987	1988	1989	1990
Cooperatives listed	7,790	6,293	6,125	5,989	5,782	5,625	5,369	5,109	4,937	4,799	4,663
Marketing [1]	5,015	3,924	3,826	3,781	3,646	3,589	3,398	3,168	3,101	2,996	2,946
Farm supply	2,775	2,369	2,299	2,208	2,136	2,036	1,971	1,941	1,836	1,803	1,717
Memberships [2] (1,000).	6,355	5,379	5,136	4,955	4,842	4,781	4,600	4,440	4,195	4,134	4,119
Marketing [1] (1,000)	3,133	2,574	2,469	2,402	2,445	2,383	2,290	2,158	2,053	2,099	2,114
Farm supply (1,000)	3,222	2,804	2,666	2,553	2,397	2,398	2,310	2,282	2,142	2,035	2,006
Business [3] (mil. dol.)	19,080	66,254	69,150	66,755	73,047	65,601	58,395	60,318	66,430	72,129	77,266
Marketing [1] (mil. dol.)	15,207	50,120	52,788	50,812	56,078	48,961	43,300	46,047	51,006	55,222	60,178
Farm supply (mil. dol.)	3,873	16,134	16,362	15,943	16,969	16,641	15,095	14,271	15,424	16,907	17,088

[1] Includes cooperatives whose major activity is providing services related to marketing and purchasing activities. [2] Excludes nonvoting patrons. [3] Value of commodities sold or purchased for patrons. Business dollar volume for marketing includes service receipts for charges related to marketing and purchasing. Represents net volume after eliminating intercooperative business.

Source: U.S. Dept. of Agriculture, Agricultural Cooperative Service, *Farmer Cooperative Statistics*, annual.

No. 1103. Selected Indexes of Farm Inputs: 1970 to 1990

[**1977 = 100.** Inputs based on physical quantities of resources used in production. See *Historical Statistics, Colonial Times to 1970*, series K 486-495 for data before revisions]

INPUT	1970	1980	1982	1983	1984	1985	1986	1987	1988	1989	1990
Total	**96**	**103**	**98**	**96**	**95**	**91**	**89**	**89**	**87**	**87**	**88**
Farm labor . . . . . , ...	112	96	93	97	92	85	80	78	75	76	(NA)
Farm real estate [1]	105	103	102	101	99	97	96	95	94	93	93
Mechanical power and machinery	85	101	89	86	85	80	77	74	74	73	71
Agricultural chemicals [2].	75	123	118	102	120	115	109	111	112	119	122
Feed, seed, and livestock purchases [3].	96	114	107	103	103	102	109	116	111	111	113
Taxes and interest	102	100	95	99	93	96	97	100	97	94	(NA)
Miscellaneous	89	96	116	101	110	116	110	122	119	123	(NA)

NA Not available. [1] Includes service buildings, improvements. [2] Includes fertilizer, lime, and pesticides. [3] Includes nonfarm portion.

Source: U.S. Dept. of Agriculture, Economic Research Service, *Economic Indicators of the Farm Sector: Production and Efficiency Statistics*, annual. Also in U.S. Council of Economic Advisers, *Economic Report of the President*, annual.

No. 1104. Farm Machinery and Equipment: 1970 to 1990

[See also *Historical Statistics, Colonial Times to 1970*, series K 184-191]

ITEM	Unit	1970	1980	1981	1982	1983	1984	1985	1986	1987	1988	1989	1990
Value of farm implements and machinery [1]	Bil. dol. .	34.4	86.9	92.5	92.6	92.1	91.1	92.4	86.1	84.5	86.7	90.2	91.7
Farmers' expenditures:													
Motor vehicles [2]	Mil. dol. .	2,030	5,813	5,652	4,436	4,724	4,583	3,699	3,227	4,275	4,812	5,266	5,383
Tractors	Mil. dol. .	1,123	3,683	3,740	2,597	2,606	2,539	1,937	1,513	2,104	2,477	2,763	2,865
Machinery, equipment	Mil. dol. .	2,888	6,956	6,481	5,068	4,735	4,682	3,232	3,094	4,297	4,150	4,916	5,322
Repair and maintenance. . .	Mil. dol. .	1,910	5,205	5,278	4,635	4,793	4,908	4,834	4,825	4,972	5,163	5,706	5,363
Tractors, machinery and equipment	Mil. dol. .	1,126	3,746	3,771	3,557	3,616	3,592	3,442	3,428	3,508	3,559	3,925	3,735
Autos and trucks	Mil. dol. .	[3]784	1,459	1,507	1,079	1,178	1,316	1,392	1,397	1,464	1,604	1,781	1,628
Retail sales: [4]													
Tractors, total [5].	1,000. . .	135.5	119.3	103.8	77.2	71.3	66.7	58.5	47.1	48.3	52.0	59.7	66.3
Two-wheel drive.	1,000. . .	135.5	108.4	94.1	70.4	66.2	62.7	55.5	45.1	46.6	49.3	55.5	61.2
Four-wheel drive	1,000. . .	(NA)	10.9	9.7	6.8	5.1	4.0	3.0	2.0	1.7	2.7	4.2	5.1
Combines	1,000. . .	26.7	25.7	26.8	16.2	12.8	11.4	8.4	7.7	7.2	6.0	9.1	10.4
Field forage harvesters. . . .	1,000. . .	15.0	9.5	7.6	5.1	4.1	3.5	2.5	2.2	2.3	2.4	2.8	3.3

NA Not available. [1] Farm inventory valuations as of December 31. Includes family automobiles. [2] For farm business use. [3] Includes insurance, registration fees, and licensing fees. [4] Source: Equipment Manufacturers Institute, Chicago, IL, unpublished data. [5] Beginning 1980, covers tractors over 40 hp. only.

Source: Except as noted, U.S. Dept. of Agriculture, Economic Research Service, *Economic Indicators of the Farm Sector: National Financial Summary*, annual. Also in *Agricultural Statistics*, annual.

No. 1105. Hired Farmworkers—Workers and Weekly Earnings: 1990

[Represents average number of persons 15 years old and over in the civilian noninstitutional population who were employed at hired farmwork at any time during the year. Preliminary. Based on Current Population Survey; see text, section 1 and Appendix III. For definition of median, see Guide to Tabular Presentation]

CHARACTERISTIC	Workers (1,000)	Median weekly earnings [1]	CHARACTERISTIC	Workers (1,000)	Median weekly earnings [1]
All workers	**886**	**$200**	White [2]	540	201
			Black and other races [2]	85	175
15 to 19 years old	144	100	Hispanic.	260	213
20 to 24 years old	135	206			
25 to 34 years old	251	240	Years of school completed:		
35 to 44 years old	170	250	Less than 5 years.	98	204
45 to 54 years old	90	200	5 to 8 years.	191	200
55 years old and over.	95	200	9 to 11 years	202	168
			12 years	278	240
Male	735	216	13 or more years	116	260
Female	151	175			

[1] The weekly earnings the farmworker usually earns at his farmwork job before deductions and includes any overtime pay or commissions.   [2] Excludes persons of Hispanic origin.
Source: U.S. Dept. of Agriculture, Economic Research Service, unpublished data.

No. 1106. Farm Output Indexes: 1970 to 1991

[1977 = 100. See also *Historical Statistics, Colonial Times to 1970*, series K 414-429]

ITEM	1970	1980	1982	1983	1984	1985	1986	1987	1988	1989	1990, prel.	1991, prel.
Farm output [1]	**84**	**104**	**116**	**96**	**112**	**118**	**111**	**110**	**102**	**114**	**119**	**120**
Per unit of total input	87	101	119	100	118	129	124	124	116	130	135	(NA)
Gross production:												
Livestock and products [2]	99	108	107	109	107	110	110	113	116	116	117	119
Meat animals	102	107	101	104	101	102	100	102	105	104	104	104
Dairy products	95	105	110	114	110	117	116	116	118	117	120	121
Poultry and eggs	93	115	119	120	123	128	133	144	148	153	162	168
Crops [3]	77	101	117	88	111	118	109	108	92	107	114	111
Feed grains	71	97	122	67	116	134	123	106	73	108	112	106
Hay and forage	92	98	109	100	107	106	106	102	89	101	101	103
Food grains	69	121	138	117	129	121	107	107	98	107	136	104
Vegetables	96	104	116	107	117	122	117	126	115	132	(NA)	(NA)
Fruits and nuts.	81	119	113	110	114	119	111	137	137	129	(NA)	(NA)
Sugar crops	95	97	96	93	95	97	106	111	105	105	107	112
Cotton	72	79	85	55	91	94	69	103	107	86	109	122
Tobacco	100	93	104	75	90	81	63	62	72	71	84	87
Oil crops	66	99	121	91	106	117	110	108	89	106	107	114

NA Not available.   [1] Annual production available for eventual human use.   [2] Includes livestock products not shown separately and excludes horses and mules.   [3] Includes crops not shown separately.

Source: U.S. Dept. of Agriculture, Economic Research Service, *Economic Indicators of the Farm Sector: Production and Efficiency Statistics*, annual. Also in *Agricultural Outlook*, monthly.

No. 1107. Selected Farm Products—United States and World Production and Exports: 1989 to 1991

[**In metric tons, except as indicated.** Metric ton=1.102 short tons or .984 long tons]

ITEM	Unit	AMOUNT						UNITED STATES AS PERCENT OF WORLD		
		United States			World			1989	1990	1991
		1989	1990	1991	1989	1990	1991			
PRODUCTION [1]										
Wheat	Million.	55	74	54	538	593	545	10.3	12.6	9.9
Corn for grain	Million.	191	202	190	462	479	483	41.3	42.1	39.4
Soybeans	Million.	52	52	53	107	103	105	48.8	50.9	50.8
Rice, rough	Million.	7.0	7.0	7.2	509	520	509	1.4	1.4	1.4
Tobacco, unmanufactured [2]	1,000	620	737	746	7,110	7,061	6,983	8.7	10.4	10.7
Cotton [3]	Million bales [4].	15.4	12.2	15.5	84.6	80.0	87.1	18.2	15.2	17.8
EXPORTS [5]										
Wheat [6]	Million.	33.6	29.1	33.3	107.5	110.1	117.0	31.2	26.4	28.5
Corn	Million.	60.2	43.9	40.0	78.7	63.1	62.3	76.5	69.5	64.3
Soybeans	Million.	17.0	15.2	17.7	28.2	24.8	26.7	60.1	61.2	66.3
Rice, milled basis	Million.	2.5	2.3	2.2	12.0	12.7	12.9	21.2	18.3	16.7
Tobacco, unmanufactured [7]	1,000	220	223	225	1,409	1,493	1,640	15.6	15.0	13.7
Cotton [3]	Million.	1.3	1.7	1.7	5.6	5.2	5.1	23.8	32.1	33.5

[1] Production years vary by commodity. In most cases, includes harvests from July 1 of the year shown through June 30 of the following year.   [2] Farm sales weight basis.   [3] For production and trade years ending in year shown.   [4] Bales of 480 lb. net weight.   [5] Trade years may vary by commodity.   [6] Includes wheat flour on a grain equivalent.   [7] Dried weight basis.
Source: U.S. Department of Agriculture, Foreign Agricultural Service, *Foreign Agricultural Commodity Circular Series*, periodic.

No. 1108. Agricultural Exports and Imports—Volume, by Principal Commodities: 1980 to 1990

[In thousands of metric tons]

EXPORTS	1980	1985	1989	1990	IMPORTS	1980	1985	1989	1990
Animal products [1]	2,575	2,517	2,919	2,730	Fruits, nuts, vegetables . . .	2,325	3,326	4,335	4,315
Wheat and products [2]	37,130	26,123	37,525	28,240	Bananas	2,352	2,969	2,920	3,094
Feed grains and products	72,970	51,735	66,975	61,449	Green coffee	1,089	1,122	1,163	1,174
Rice.	3,075	1,961	3,047	2,525	Cocoa and products	252	565	569	716
Feeds and fodders	6,888	6,710	11,014	12,287	Meat and products [5]	931	1,139	1,110	1,165
Oilseeds and products [3]	31,042	23,673	21,733	21,858	Vegetable oils	704	961	1,054	1,183
Fruits, nuts, vegetables [4]	4,147	3,255	4,283	5,554	Sugar	3,744	2,178	1,569	1,856
Cotton	1,880	1,135	1,581	1,733					
Tobacco	272	249	220	223					

[1] Includes meat and products, poultry meats, dairy products, and fats, oils and greases. Excludes live animals, hides, skins, and eggs.   [2] Includes flour and bulgur.   [3] Includes soybeans, sunflowerseeds, peanuts, cottonseed, safflowerseed, flaxseed, and nondefatted soybean flour.   [4] Excludes fruit juices.   [5] Excludes poultry.

Source: U.S. Dept. of Agriculture, Economic Research Service, *Foreign Agricultural Trade of the United States*, annual, and *Foreign Agricultural Trade of the United States*, Jan./Feb. 1991.

No. 1109. Agricultural Exports and Imports—Value: 1970 to 1990

[In billions of dollars, except percent. Includes Puerto Rico. Excludes forest products and distilled liquors; includes crude rubber and similar gums (now mainly plantation products). Includes shipments under foreign aid programs. See also *Historical Statistics, Colonial Times to 1970*, series K 251-255]

YEAR	Trade balance	Exports, domestic products	Percent of all exports	Imports for consumption	Percent of all imports	YEAR	Trade balance	Exports, domestic products	Percent of all exports	Imports for consumption	Percent of all imports
1970 to 1974, average	5.5	12.8	21	7.3	12	1977	10.2	23.6	20	13.4	9
1975 to 1979, average	13.5	26.5	20	13.0	11	1978	14.6	29.4	21	14.8	9
1980 to 1984, average	21.9	39.0	18	17.1	6	1979	18.0	34.7	19	16.7	8
1985 to 1989, average	11.3	32.2	12	20.9	5	1980	23.9	41.2	18	17.4	7
1970	1.5	7.3	17	5.8	15	1981	26.6	43.3	18	16.8	6
1972	2.9	9.4	19	6.5	12	1982	21.2	36.6	17	15.4	6
1973	9.3	17.7	25	8.4	12	1983	19.5	36.1	18	16.6	7
1974	11.7	21.9	23	10.2	10	1984	18.5	37.8	17	19.3	6
1975	12.6	21.9	21	9.3	10	1985	9.1	29.0	13	20.0	6
1976	12.0	23.0	20	11.0	9	1986	4.8	26.2	13	21.5	6
						1987	8.3	28.7	12	20.4	5
						1988	16.1	37.1	12	21.0	. 5
						1989	18.2	39.9	11	21.7	5
						1990	16.6	39.3	10	22.8	5

Source: U.S. Dept. of Agriculture, Economic Research Service, *U.S. Foreign Agricultural Trade Statistical Report*, annual, and *Foreign Agricultural Trade of the United States*, Jan.-Feb. issues. Also in *Agricultural Statistics*, annual.

No. 1110. Agricultural Imports—Value, by Selected Commodity, 1970 to 1990, and by Leading Countries of Origin, 1990

[In millions of dollars]

COMMODITY	1970	1980	1985	1987	1988	1989	1990	Leading countries of origin, 1990
Total	5,770	17,366	19,968	20,402	20,951	21,749	22,771	Canada, Mexico, Brazil
Competitive products.	3,609	10,374	13,067	13,781	14,688	15,624	17,225	Canada, Mexico, Australia
Beef and veal	680	1,780	1,276	1,562	1,679	1,662	1,871	Australia, New Zealand, Canada
Pork	272	486	861	1,096	933	754	940	Canada, Denmark, Poland
Dairy products.	126	488	765	831	875	857	911	New Zealand, Ireland, Italy
Fruits and preparations. .	146	564	1,738	1,718	1,866	1,820	2,218	Brazil, Chile, Mexico
Vegetables and preparations	296	864	1,385	1,535	1,615	2,049	2,268	Mexico, Canada, Spain
Wine	145	692	998	966	939	930	917	France, Italy, Spain
Malt beverages	32	367	633	882	918	855	923	Netherlands, Canada, Mexico
Grains and feeds.	99	371	623	748	909	1,217	1,183	Canada, Thailand, Italy
Sugar and related products.	798	2,205	1,190	630	690	956	1,172	Brazil, Dominican Republic, Canada
Noncompetitive products . .	2,161	6,992	6,902	6,621	6,263	6,125	5,546	Indonesia, Brazil, Ecuador
Coffee and products. . . .	1,213	4,186	3,322	2,908	2,470	2,432	1,915	Brazil, Mexico, Colombia
Rubber, crude natural. . .	236	817	654	760	1,023	958	707	Indonesia, Malaysia, Thailand
Cocoa and products. . . .	279	920	1,351	1,194	1,003	977	1,072	Brazil, Ivory Coast, Canada
Bananas and plantains . .	194	430	763	819	832	871	938	Ecuador, Costa Rica, Honduras

Source: U.S. Dept. of Agriculture, Economic Research Service, *Foreign Agricultural Trade of the United States*, annual.

No. 1111. Spices—Imports, by Type of Spice: 1970 to 1990

[In millions of pounds. Data shown are annual averages. The United States produces only three major spices - capsicum (red pepper), paprika, and mustard - in any profitable degree. Unground or unprocessed spices enter duty-free. Most spices imported into the United States are unground or unprocessed]

SPICE	1970-74	1975-79	1980-84	1985-89	1990	SPICE	1970-74	1975-79	1980-84	1985-89	1990
Total [1]	254.4	298.1	351.0	405.6	590.0	Mace	0.6	0.5	0.6	0.6	0.7
						Mustard seed	89.7	76.1	79.5	106.9	160.3
Anise seed	0.6	1.0	1.4	2.2	2.2	Nutmeg	4.2	4.4	4.8	4.2	4.0
Capsicum	13.7	10.2	13.9	23.4	46.0	Paprika	15.3	12.3	10.5	12.6	10.0
Caraway seed	5.9	6.5	7.5	7.6	8.0	Pepper, black and white	54.2	59.0	72.5	77.5	92.6
Cassia and cinnamon	13.9	18.6	23.4	28.7	26.6	Pimento	1.4	1.5	1.7	1.9	2.4
Celery seed	4.0	4.2	4.7	5.4	5.2	Poppy seed	5.7	6.1	7.2	8.8	7.9
Cloves	2.7	2.5	2.1	2.3	4.2	Sage	3.0	2.9	3.7	4.3	3.8
Coriander seed	3.4	6.8	10.4	7.6	5.2	Sesame seed	49.1	62.5	80.4	81.1	100.1
Cumin seed	6.2	8.1	8.8	9.0	11.1	Turmeric	3.3	3.2	3.7	4.3	3.8
Fennel seed	1.3	1.9	3.4	4.7	6.8	Vanilla beans	2.2	2.3	1.6	2.4	2.4
Ginger root	5.9	7.8	9.5	11.2	18.0						

[1] The United States also imports limited amounts of other spices which are not included in the total.

Source: U.S. Dept. of Agriculture, Economic Research Service, *Foreign Agricultural Trade of the United States*, annual, and U.S. Bureau of the Census, *U.S. Imports for Consumption, Annual 1990*, series FT247.

No. 1112. Agricultural Exports—Value, by Principal Commodities and Selected Countries of Destination: 1970 to 1990

[See headnote, table 1109. Data by country of destination for 1970 and 1980 are not adjusted for transshipments]

COMMODITY AND COUNTRY	VALUE (mil. dol.)								PERCENT		
	1970	1980	1985	1986	1987	1988	1989	1990	1970	1980	1990
Total agricultural exports [1]	7,255	41,233	29,041	26,222	28,709	37,126	39,909	39,327	100.0	100.0	100.0
Grains and feeds [2]	2,720	19,117	11,882	8,656	9,423	13,979	17,187	14,410	37.5	46.4	36.6
Feed grains and products	1,093	9,831	6,112	3,176	3,917	5,970	7,870	7,157	15.1	23.8	18.2
Corn	818	8,492	5,206	2,605	3,209	5,040	6,580	6,033	11.3	20.6	15.3
Wheat and products	1,136	6,660	3,898	3,290	3,280	5,117	6,136	4,034	15.7	16.2	10.3
Rice	313	1,289	665	625	576	806	971	802	4.3	3.1	2.0
Oilseeds and products [2]	1,931	9,393	5,794	6,467	6,446	7,753	6,313	5,684	26.6	22.8	14.5
Soybeans	1,228	5,880	3,732	4,326	4,378	4,920	3,942	3,551	16.9	14.3	9.0
Soybean oil cake and meal	344	1,665	870	1,229	1,211	1,580	1,181	987	4.7	4.0	2.5
Vegetable oils and waxes	295	1,216	870	672	626	983	872	809	4.1	2.9	2.1
Animals and animal products [2]	865	3,768	4,150	4,547	5,156	6,422	6,378	6,668	11.9	9.1	17.0
Hides and skins, incl. furskins	187	1,046	1,295	1,522	1,731	1,829	1,717	1,751	2.6	2.5	4.5
Cattle hides	130	623	1,007	1,219	1,328	1,466	1,383	1,369	1.8	1.5	3.5
Meats and meat products	132	890	905	1,130	1,366	1,974	2,348	2,558	1.8	2.2	6.5
Beef and veal	25	249	467	634	771	1,109	1,420	1,579	0.3	0.6	4.0
Fats, oils, and greases	246	769	619	413	431	577	512	424	3.4	1.9	1.1
Poultry and poultry products	82	603	384	504	602	689	713	907	1.1	1.5	2.3
Cotton, excluding linters	372	2,864	1,633	812	1,631	1,975	2,250	2,783	5.1	6.9	7.1
Tobacco, unmanufactured	517	1,334	1,521	1,223	1,090	1,253	1,301	1,441	7.1	3.2	3.7
Fruits and preparations	334	1,335	1,186	1,306	1,484	1,762	1,836	2,360	4.6	3.2	6.0
Fresh fruits	164	739	743	851	939	1,093	1,133	1,486	2.3	1.8	3.8
Vegetables and preparations	219	1,188	930	1,085	1,158	1,361	1,601	2,302	3.0	2.9	5.9
Nuts and preparations	69	757	683	753	804	884	846	976	1.0	1.8	2.5
Other	232	1,477	1,262	1,373	1,517	1,737	2,197	2,703	3.2	3.6	6.9
Asia [1]	2,717	14,886	11,191	10,617	12,535	16,871	18,828	17,600	37.5	36.1	44.8
Japan	1,214	6,111	5,409	5,141	5,723	7,640	8,162	8,058	16.7	14.8	20.5
South Korea	224	1,797	1,413	1,306	1,833	2,283	2,593	2,644	3.1	4.4	6.7
China: Taiwan	134	1,095	1,231	1,171	1,285	1,661	1,754	1,660	1.9	2.7	4.2
Mainland	-	2,210	157	58	362	759	1,435	814	-	5.4	2.1
Hong Kong	57	437	389	400	466	489	611	701	0.8	1.1	1.8
Western Europe [1,3]	2,534	11,744	6,937	7,056	7,309	7,877	6,995	7,320	34.9	28.5	18.6
European Economic Community [4]	2,316	11,033	6,477	6,627	6,880	7,338	6,503	6,817	29.4	22.4	17.3
Netherlands	526	3,412	1,869	2,073	1,985	2,066	1,722	1,582	7.3	8.3	4.0
West Germany	529	1,831	944	1,048	1,285	1,215	1,000	1,119	7.3	4.4	2.8
Spain [5]	143	1,129	837	703	666	883	703	830	2.0	2.7	2.1
United Kingdom	411	928	604	681	661	835	637	713	5.7	2.3	1.8
Italy	210	1,094	669	727	697	693	458	528	2.9	2.7	1.3
France	164	748	403	439	524	534	820	937	2.3	1.8	2.4
Latin America [1]	688	6,150	4,224	3,681	3,678	4,927	5,337	5,092	9.5	14.9	12.9
Mexico	155	2,468	1,439	1,080	1,202	2,227	2,724	2,554	2.1	6.0	6.5
Canada	820	1,852	1,022	1,542	1,008	2,010	2,221	4,197	11.4	4.5	10.7
Soviet Union	16	1,047	1,923	658	938	2,252	3,597	2,268	0.2	2.5	5.8
Eastern Europe	169	2,071	479	434	436	540	401	577	2.3	5.0	1.5
Africa [1]	254	2,179	2,488	2,008	1,766	2,385	2,260	1,935	3.5	5.3	4.9
Algeria	19	176	227	287	310	596	504	513	0.3	0.4	1.3
Egypt	26	770	891	811	679	841	989	693	0.4	1.9	1.8

- Represents or rounds to zero.   [1] Includes areas not shown separately.   [2] Includes commodities not shown separately.
[3] Includes Canary Islands and Madeira Islands for all years.   [4] Includes Belgium, Luxembourg, Denmark, France, Greece, Ireland, and Portugal, not shown separately. As of Jan. 1, 1973, United Kingdom, Denmark, and Ireland became members of EEC. As of Jan. 1, 1981, Greece became a member of EEC. As of Jan. 1, 1986, Spain and Portugal became members of EEC. For consistency, data for all years are shown on same basis.   [5] As of Jan. 1, 1984, includes Canary Islands and Spanish Africa, not elsewhere classified.

Source: U.S. Dept. of Agriculture, Economic Research Service, *U.S. Foreign Agricultural Trade Statistical Report*, annual. Also in *Agricultural Statistics*, annual, and *Foreign Agricultural Trade of the United States*, Jan/Feb 1991.

No. 1113. Cropland Used for Crops and Acreages of Crops Harvested: 1970 to 1990

[See also *Historical Statistics, Colonial Times to 1970*, series K 496-501]

YEAR	CROPLAND USED FOR CROPS						ACREAGES OF CROPS HARVESTED [2]				
	Number (mil. acres)				Index (1977=100)	Index of crop production per acre (1977=100)	Total (mil. acres)	Used to produce goods for—			
								Domestic use		Exports	
	Total	Crop-land harvest-ed [1]	Crop failure	Culti-vated sum-mer fallow				Amount (mil. acres)	Per capita (acres) [3]	Amount (mil. acres)	Per-cent of total
1970 . . .	332	289	5	38	88	88	293	221	1.08	72	24.6
1980 . . .	382	342	10	30	101	100	352	215	0.94	137	38.9
1985 . . .	372	334	7	31	98	120	342	263	1.10	81	23.7
1986 . . .	357	316	9	32	94	116	325	229	0.95	96	29.5
1987 . . .	331	293	6	32	88	123	302	196	0.80	106	35.1
1988 . . .	327	287	10	30	86	107	297	179	0.73	118	39.7
1989 . .	341	306	8	27	90	119	318	215	0.86	103	32.4
1990 [4] . .	341	310	6	25	90	126	322	239	0.95	83	25.8

[1] Land supporting one or more harvested crops. [2] Area in principal crops harvested as reported by Crop Reporting Board plus acreages in fruits, tree nuts, and farm gardens. [3] Based on Bureau of the Census estimated total population, including Armed Forces overseas, as of July 1. [4] Preliminary.

Source: U.S. Dept. of Agriculture, Economic Research Service, *Economic Indicators of the Farm Sector: Production and Efficiency Statistics*, annual. Also in *Agricultural Statistics*, annual.

No. 1114. Crops—Acreage and Value, by State: 1988 to 1991

STATE	ACREAGE HARVESTED (1,000)				FARM VALUE (mil. dol.)				
	1988	1989	1990	1991, prel.	1988	1989	1990	1991, prel.	
								Value	Rank
U.S. [1]	289,846	305,596	308,935	304,308	72,746	80,347	80,864	79,858	(X)
AL.	2,389	2,338	2,342	2,240	570	575	464	593	34
AZ.	784	830	802	770	1,060	1,003	894	925	30
AR.	7,538	7,603	8,080	7,863	1,780	1,611	1,648	1,760	18
CA.	5,107	4,900	4,797	4,340	9,763	10,401	10,649	9,833	1
CO	5,609	5,677	5,862	5,580	1,366	1,341	1,194	1,138	24
CT.	124	128	129	125	93	95	112	99	46
DE.	504	537	496	556	128	127	139	142	43
FL.	1,115	1,128	1,076	1,040	3,247	3,603	2,766	3,445	7
GA	3,754	4,205	3,793	3,774	1,305	1,400	1,273	1,603	20
HI	86	81	79	74	402	407	413	383	36
ID	4,018	4,333	4,281	4,215	1,684	1,966	1,735	1,624	19
IL	21,581	22,977	22,759	22,906	4,242	6,045	5,809	5,360	3
IN	11,082	11,631	11,485	11,555	2,397	3,151	3,023	2,529	9
IA	23,092	24,097	23,276	23,376	4,632	5,767	5,818	5,663	2
KS.	19,191	18,794	20,978	20,712	2,774	2,237	2,610	2,529	10
KY.	4,968	5,487	5,505	5,495	1,395	1,685	1,721	1,782	17
LA.	4,308	4,093	4,367	3,571	1,251	1,093	1,184	1,162	23
ME	346	364	361	351	212	219	180	157	42
MD	1,493	1,602	1,552	1,561	356	362	386	370	37
MA	143	136	135	136	169	167	149	175	41
MI	6,401	6,360	6,510	6,713	1,576	1,842	1,839	1,926	15
MN	18,767	18,661	18,779	18,719	3,134	4,174	4,177	4,052	4
MS	5,149	4,614	4,723	4,481	1,204	1,042	1,149	1,220	22
MO	12,684	13,249	12,685	12,900	2,138	2,254	2,083	2,120	14
MT	7,118	9,475	8,926	8,687	640	1,061	881	1,079	26
NE.	16,765	17,450	18,044	18,316	3,661	3,420	3,621	3,724	6
NV.	549	554	520	495	149	171	154	106	45
NH	99	93	91	92	30	27	29	27	48
NJ.	368	380	364	382	167	164	170	185	40
NM	936	968	881	1,047	338	404	401	407	35
NY.	3,439	3,560	3,538	3,443	878	887	916	914	31
NC	4,104	4,526	4,370	4,428	1,852	1,850	1,981	2,129	13
ND	16,216	20,660	21,229	20,925	1,301	1,843	2,082	2,196	12
OH	9,731	10,259	10,132	9,972	2,165	2,477	2,597	2,237	11
OK	8,482	9,396	9,688	8,614	1,203	1,172	1,142	945	29
OR	2,168	2,339	2,290	2,260	1,011	1,063	1,035	1,023	27
PA	4,199	4,198	4,094	4,067	1,119	1,264	1,358	1,137	25
RI	11	10	10	10	6	5	5	5	49
SC.	2,022	2,283	2,049	1,827	603	635	517	634	33
SD	13,508	15,210	15,552	15,640	1,158	1,434	1,638	1,596	21
TN.	4,548	4,570	4,477	4,379	950	905	954	976	28
TX.	16,527	16,697	18,550	17,608	3,656	3,318	4,023	3,945	5
UT.	1,026	983	992	973	260	254	257	221	39
VT.	453	442	441	434	72	75	77	71	47
VA.	2,708	2,768	2,726	2,660	741	816	846	801	32
WA	3,890	4,045	4,168	4,046	2,199	2,222	2,527	2,603	8
WV	644	664	668	615	97	107	114	106	44
WI	8,430	8,615	8,550	8,449	1,325	1,921	1,830	1,896	16
WY	1,674	1,628	1,735	1,889	284	285	292	304	38

X Not applicable. [1] Excludes Alaska.

Source: U.S. Dept. of Agriculture, National Agricultural Statistics Service, *Crop Production*, annual; and *Crop Values*, annual.

No. 1115. Principal Crops—Production, Supply, and Disappearance: 1986 to 1991

[Marketing year beginning May 1 for hay, June 1 for wheat, August 1 for cotton and rice, and September 1 for soybeans, corn, and sorghum. Acreage, production, and yield of all crops periodically revised on basis of census data. See also *Historical Statistics, Colonial Times to 1970*, series K 506-563]

CROP AND YEAR	ACREAGE (mil.)— Set aside[1]	Planted	Harvested	Yield per acre	Production	Farm price[2]	Farm value (mil. dol.)	Total supply[3]	DISAPPEARANCE Total[4]	Exports	Ending stocks
Corn for grain:				Bu.	Mil. bu.	$/bu.			Mil. bu.		
1987......	23.1	66.2	59.5	119.8	7,131	1.94	14,108	12,016	7,757	1,716	4,259
1988......	20.5	67.7	58.3	84.6	4,929	2.54	12,661	9,191	7,260	2,026	1,930
1989......	10.8	72.2	64.7	116.3	7,525	2.36	17,897	9,458	8,113	2,368	1,344
1990......	10.7	74.2	67.0	118.5	7,934	2.28	18,009	9,282	7,761	1,725	1,521
1991, prel ...	7.4	76.0	68.8	108.6	7,474	(NA)	(NA)	9,016	7,925	1,525	1,091
Hay:				Sh. tons	Mil. sh. tons	$/ton			Mil. sh. tons		
1986......	-	(NA)	62.4	2.49	156	[5][6]59.80	8,611	182	150	(NA)	32
1987......	-	(NA)	60.1	2.45	148	[5][6]65.00	8,845	180	153	(NA)	27
1988......	-	(NA)	65.1	1.94	126	[5][6]85.20	10,457	153	136	(NA)	18
1989......	-	(NA)	63.3	2.30	146	[5][6]87.40	11,514	163	136	(NA)	27
1990......	-	(NA)	61.6	2.39	147	[5][6]83.20	11,138	174	147	(NA)	27
Soybeans:				Bu.	Mil. bu.	$/bu.			Mil. bu.		
1987......	-	58.2	57.2	33.9	1,938	5.88	11,391	2,375	2,073	802	302
1988......	-	58.8	57.4	27.0	1,549	7.42	11,488	1,855	1,673	527	182
1989......	-	60.8	59.5	32.3	1,924	5.69	10,732	2,109	1,870	623	239
1990......	-	57.8	56.5	34.0	1,926	5.75	11,215	2,167	1,838	557	329
1991, prel ...	-	59.1	58.0	34.3	1,986	(NA)	(NA)	2,320	1,995	665	325
Wheat:				Bu.	Mil. bu.	$/bu.			Mil. bu.		
1987......	23.9	65.8	55.9	37.7	2,108	2.57	5,498	3,945	2,684	1,598	1,261
1988......	22.5	65.5	53.2	34.1	1,812	3.72	6,684	3,096	2,394	1,419	702
1989......	9.6	76.6	62.2	32.7	2,037	3.72	7,542	2,762	2,225	1,233	536
1990......	7.5	77.2	69.3	39.5	2,736	2.61	7,299	3,309	2,443	1,068	866
1991, prel ...	15.4	69.9	57.7	34.3	1,981	(NA)	(NA)	2,882	2,492	1,275	390
Cotton:				Lb.	bales[7]	cents/lb.			bales[7]		
1987......	4.0	10.4	10.0	706	[8]14.8	64.3	4,555	19.8	14.2	6.6	[9]5.8
1988......	2.2	12.5	11.9	619	[8]15.4	56.6	4,190	21.2	13.9	6.1	[9]7.1
1989......	3.5	10.6	9.5	614	[8]12.2	66.2	3,877	19.3	16.5	7.7	[9]3.0
1990......	2.0	12.3	11.7	634	[8]15.5	68.2	5,040	18.5	16.5	7.8	[9]2.3
1991, prel ...	0.9	14.1	12.8	656	[8]17.5	(NA)	(NA)	19.9	16.1	6.8	[9]3.9
Tobacco: [10]				Lb.	Mil. lb.	$/lb.			Mil. lb.		
1987......	(NA)	(NA)	0.6	2,028	1,189	[6]1.57	1,870	4,597	1,688	573	2,909
1988......	(NA)	(NA)	0.6	2,160	1,370	[6]1.65	2,261	4,279	1,565	555	2,714
1989......	(NA)	(NA)	0.7	2,016	1,367	[6]1.71	3,338	4,081	1,677	558	2,404
1990......	(NA)	(NA)	0.7	2,218	1,625	[6]1.74	2,828	3,999	1,808	635	2,191
1991, prel ...	(NA)	(NA)	0.8	2,143	1,638	[6]1.79	2,932	3,653	(NA)	(NA)	(NA)
Potatoes:				Cwt.	Mil. cwt.	$/cwt.			Mil. cwt.		
1987......	(NA)	1.3	1.3	301	389	4.38	1,682	574	[11]307	[12]11	(NA)
1988......	(NA)	1.3	1.3	283	356	6.02	2,144	558	[11]300	[12]16	(NA)
1989......	(NA)	1.3	1.3	289	370	7.36	2,717	555	[11]315	[12]15	(NA)
1990......	(NA)	1.4	1.4	293	402	6.08	2,431	582	[11]327	[12]16	(NA)
1991, prel ...	(NA)	1.4	1.4	304	418	5.05	2,095	(NA)	(NA)	(NA)	(NA)
Sorghum for grain:				Bu.	Mil. bu.	$/bu.			Mil. bu.		
1987......	4.1	11.8	10.5	69.4	731	1.70	1,179	1,474	812	232	663
1988......	3.9	11.1	9.0	63.8	577	2.27	1,337	1,239	800	312	440
1989......	3.3	12.6	11.1	55.4	615	2.10	1,288	1,055	835	303	220
1990......	3.3	10.5	9.1	63.1	573	2.12	1,202	793	651	232	143
1991, prel ...	2.3	11.0	9.8	59.0	579	(NA)	(NA)	722	605	200	117
Rice, rough:				Lb.	Mil. cwt.	$/cwt.			Mil. cwt.		
1987......	1.6	2.4	2.3	5,555	130	7.27	945	184	153	72	31
1988......	1.1	2.9	2.9	5,514	160	6.83	1,092	195	168	86	27
1989......	1.2	2.7	2.7	5,749	155	7.35	1,134	186	159	77	26
1990......	1.0	2.9	2.8	5,529	156	6.70	991	187	163	71	25
1991, prel ...	0.7	2.9	2.8	5,617	155	(NA)	(NA)	185	155	60	30

- Represents zero. NA Not available. [1] Acreage set aside under diversion, PIK (payment-in-kind) and acreage reduction programs. [2] Except as noted, marketing year average price. U.S. prices are computed by weighting U.S. monthly prices by estimated monthly marketings and do not include an allowance for outstanding loans and government purchases and payments. [3] Comprises production, imports, and beginning stocks. [4] Includes feed, residual, and other domestic uses not shown separately. [5] Prices are for hay sold baled. [6] Season average prices received by farmers. U.S. prices are computed by weighting State prices by estimated sales and include an allowance for outstanding loans and government purchases, if any, for crops under government programs. [7] Bales of 480 pounds, net weight. [8] State production figures, which conform with U.S. Bureau of the Census annual ginning enumeration with allowance for cross-State ginnings, rounded to thousands and added for U.S. totals. [9] Stock estimates based on Census Bureau data which results in an unaccounted difference between supply and use estimates and changes in ending stocks. [10] Flue-cured and cigar wrapper, crop year July-June; all other types October-September. Farm-sales-weight basis. [11] Covers potatoes used for table use, frozen and canned products, chips, and dehydration. [12] Covers fresh potatoes and frozen and dehydrated products.

Source: Production—U.S. Dept. of Agriculture, National Agricultural Statistics Service. In *Crop Production*, annual; *Field Crops* (Statistical Bulletin No. 708); *Crop Values* (Statistical Bulletin No. 729). Supply and disappearance—U.S. Dept. of Agriculture, Economic Research Service, *Feed Situation*, quarterly; *Fats and Oils Situation*, quarterly; *Wheat Situation*, quarterly; *Tobacco Situation*, quarterly; *Cotton and Wool Outlook Statistics*, periodic; and *Agricultural Supply and Demand Estimates*, periodic. All data are also in *Agricultural Statistics*, annual; and *Agricultural Outlook*, monthly.

No. 1116. Selected Crops—Acreage, Production, and Value, by Leading States: 1988 to 1990

[One bushel of corn=56 pounds; one bushel of soybeans or wheat= 60 pounds. See also *Historical Statistics, Colonial Times to 1970,* series K 502-508, 521, 553-558, and 561-563]

STATE	ACREAGE HARVESTED (1,000 acres)			YIELD PER ACRE			PRODUCTION			PRICE			FARM VALUE (mil. dol.)		
	1988	1989	1990	1988	1989	1990	1988	1989	1990	1988	1989	1990	1988	1989	1990
CORN				(bu.)			(mil. bu.)			($/bu.)					
U.S.[1]	58,250	64,703	66,952	85	116	119	4,929	7,525	7,933	2.54	2.36	2.30	12,661	17,897	18,009
IA	10,700	12,250	12,400	84	118	126	899	1,446	1,562	2.45	2.29	2.20	2,202	3,310	3,437
IL	9,600	10,750	10,400	73	123	127	701	1,322	1,321	2.59	2.40	2.30	1,815	3,173	3,038
NE	6,600	7,000	7,300	124	121	128	818	847	934	2.48	2.30	2.30	2,030	1,948	2,149
MN	4,700	5,600	6,150	74	125	124	348	700	763	2.40	2.27	2.15	835	1,589	1,640
IN	5,000	5,200	5,450	83	133	129	415	692	703	2.65	2.47	2.25	1,100	1,708	1,582
OH	3,000	2,900	3,450	85	118	121	255	342	417	2.61	2.49	2.25	666	852	939
WI	1,950	2,800	3,000	67	111	118	131	311	354	2.55	2.31	2.20	333	718	779
MI	1,600	1,970	2,070	70	113	115	112	223	238	2.53	2.28	2.20	283	508	524
SD	2,400	2,650	3,000	55	72	78	132	191	234	2.38	2.14	2.00	314	408	468
MO	2,020	2,290	1,960	76	96	105	154	220	206	2.63	2.38	2.30	404	523	473
SOYBEANS				(bu.)			(mil. bu.)			($/bu.)					
U.S.[1]	57,373	59,538	56,502	27	32	34	1,549	1,924	1,922	7.42	5.69	5.85	11,488	10,916	11,215
IL	8,700	8,850	9,100	27	40	39	235	354	355	7.45	5.76	6.00	1,750	2,039	2,129
IA	8,100	8,280	7,900	31	39	41	251	323	324	7.33	5.62	5.75	1,841	1,815	1,862
MN	4,800	5,000	4,600	26	37	39	125	185	179	7.30	5.58	5.70	911	1,032	1,023
IN	4,200	4,550	4,180	28	37	41	116	166	171	7.55	5.79	5.85	872	962	1,003
OH	3,700	3,980	3,480	27	32	39	100	125	136	7.54	5.73	5.85	753	718	794
MO	4,230	4,350	4,150	27	28	30	112	122	125	7.45	5.60	5.80	835	682	722
AR	3,200	3,200	3,350	26	24	27	83	75	90	7.55	5.88	6.05	628	442	547
NE	2,360	2,560	2,360	30	32	35	71	82	81	7.31	5.45	5.70	518	446	464
SD	1,730	1,880	1,920	24	26	28	42	49	54	7.21	5.35	5.65	299	262	304
KS	2,000	1,850	1,950	23	27	24	46	50	47	7.26	5.45	5.70	334	272	267
WHEAT				(bu.)			(mil. bu.)			($/bu.)					
U.S.[1]	53,189	62,189	69,353	34	33	40	1,812	2,037	2,739	3.72	3.72	2.61	6,684	7,542	7,299
KS	9,500	8,900	11,800	34	24	40	323	214	472	3.58	3.74	2.60	1,156	799	1,227
ND	7,230	10,330	10,910	14	24	35	103	242	385	4.02	3.45	2.47	416	836	953
OK	4,800	5,700	6,300	36	27	32	173	154	202	3.57	3.79	2.65	617	583	534
WA	2,060	2,270	2,480	61	49	61	125	111	150	4.19	4.04	2.75	522	447	413
MT	3,830	5,235	5,185	16	28	28	60	145	146	3.98	3.66	2.73	239	531	398
MN	2,250	2,699	2,865	23	38	48	52	103	139	3.79	3.63	2.50	196	372	347
TX	3,200	3,000	4,200	28	20	31	90	60	130	3.39	3.79	2.75	304	227	358
SD	2,638	3,520	3,789	14	24	34	38	83	128	3.73	3.60	2.56	142	299	327
ID	1,150	1,370	1,370	66	67	73	76	91	100	4.01	3.67	2.60	303	335	259
IL	1,250	1,780	1,900	54	59	48	68	105	91	3.50	3.80	2.75	236	399	251
COTTON				(lb.)			(1,000 bales)[2]			(cents/lb.)					
U.S.[1]	11,948	9,538	11,732	619	614	634	15,412	12,196	15,499	56.6	66.2	67.8	4,190	3,878	5,041
TX	5,342	3,828	5,057	475	376	479	5,282	2,999	5,046	52.4	60.4	63.7	1,329	875	1,543
CA	1,337	1,058	1,116	1,015	1,226	1,201	2,827	2,701	2,791	64.8	72.2	76.3	879	936	1,022
MS	1,190	1,021	1,221	736	731	728	1,825	1,556	1,852	53.7	62.9	64.4	470	470	573
LA	645	620	790	705	672	715	948	868	1,177	54.5	63.9	65.7	248	266	371
AR	675	595	750	742	687	692	1,044	851	1,081	54.4	63.2	65.3	273	258	339
AZ	477	484	472	1,113	1,118	1,016	1,106	1,126	999	70.4	79.6	76.1	374	424	365
TOBACCO				(lb.)			(mil. lb.)			($/lb.)					
U.S.[1]	634	678	730	2,160	2,016	2,201	1,370	1,367	1,607	1.65	1.71	1.73	2,254	2,335	2,786
NC	250	267	286	2,211	2,029	2,240	553	541	640	1.61	1.68	1.68	890	906	1,075
KY	158	178	194	2,247	2,059	2,248	355	367	437	1.64	1.68	1.76	581	617	769
SC	45	48	51	2,225	2,160	2,155	100	104	110	1.61	1.66	1.59	162	172	174
VA	47	50	53	1,973	1,892	2,055	92	94	109	1.59	1.68	1.71	147	157	187
GA	38	40	43	2,260	2,180	2,400	86	87	103	1.63	1.67	1.68	140	146	174
TN	49	46	49	1,920	1,754	2,031	93	80	99	1.71	1.73	1.76	159	138	175

[1] Includes other States, not shown separately.   [2] Bales of 480 lb. net weight.

Source: U.S. Dept. of Agriculture, National Agricultural Statistics Service, *Crop Production,* annual; and *Crop Values,* annual.

No. 1117. Sugar Beets, Sugarcane, and Sugar—Summary: 1985 to 1990

[Data are for crop year. See also *Historical Statistics, Colonial Times to 1970*, series K 542-546]

ITEM	Unit	SUGAR BEETS			SUGARCANE FOR SUGAR AND SEED			YEAR	SUGAR PRODUCTION (1,000 tons)	
		1985	1989	1990	1985	1989	1990		Raw value [1]	Refined basis [2]
Acreage harvested . .	1,000 acres .	1,103	1,295	1,378	770	852	791	Beet: 1985.	3,000	2,804
Yield per acre	Sh. tons. . . .	20.4	19.4	20.0	36.6	34.5	34.2	1989 .	3,442	3,217
Production . ₃.	Mil. tons . .	22.5	25.1	27.6	28.2	29.4	27.1	1990 .	3,809	3,560
Price per ton [3].	Dollars	33.80	42.10	(NA)	[4]26.70	[4]29.20	(NA)	Cane: 1985	3,033	2,835
Farm value	Mil. dol	761	1,058	(NA)	[5]752	[5]858	(NA)	1989 .	3,176	2,967
								1990 .	3,004	2,807

NA Not available.   [1] Raw value equals 96 degree sugar as defined in Sugar Act of 1948.   [2] Calculated on the basis of 100 lbs. of raw sugar required to produce 93.46 lbs. of refined sugar.   [3] Season average prices received by farmers. Prices exclude Government payments under Sugar Act.   [4] Price per ton for sugar.   [5] Price per ton of cane for sugar used in evaluating value of production for seed.
Source: U.S. Dept. of Agriculture, National Agricultural Statistics Service, *Field Crops* (Statistical Bulletin 793); *Crop Production*, June issue and annual; and *Crop Values*, annual.

No. 1118. Fruits and Planted Nuts—Bearing Areas, by Type: 1980 to 1990

[In thousands of acres]

TYPE	1980	1982	1983	1984	1985	1986	1987	1988	1989	1990
Total	3,556	3,544	3,572	3,545	3,494	3,432	3,458	3,485	3,495	3,540
Citrus fruit [1] . . . . ₂. . . .	1,143	1,124	1,092	1,008	899	819	826	833	848	890
Major deciduous fruits [2] ₃. . . .	1,608	1,640	1,674	1,704	1,725	1,728	1,739	1,748	1,748	1,756
Miscellaneous noncitrus [3]	242	201	207	210	212	216	217	217	213	206
Planted nuts [4]	563	579	599	624	657	670	675	686	687	688

[1] Grapefruit, lemons, limes, oranges, tangelos, tangerines, and temples. Acreage is for the year of harvest.   [2] Commercial apples, apricots, cherries, grapes, nectarines, peaches, pears, plums, and prunes.   [3] Avocados, bananas, cranberries (beginning 1983), dates, figs, kiwifruit, olives, papayas, pineapples, and pomegranates.   [4] Almonds, filberts, macadamia nuts, walnuts, and pistachios.
Source: U.S. Dept. of Agriculture, National Agricultural Statistics Service, *Noncitrus Fruits and Nuts*, annual.

No. 1119. Fruits and Nuts—Utilized Production and Value, 1988 to 1990, and Leading Producing States, 1990

FRUIT OR NUT	UTILIZED PRODUCTION [1]				FARM VALUE (mil. dol.)			Leading States in order of production, 1990
	Unit	1988	1989	1990	1988	1989	1990	
Apples (35 States) [2]	Mil. lb	9,078	9,917	9,658	1,150	1,034	1,449	WA, NY, CA, MI
Apricots	1,000 tons . .	94	119	120	34	40	41	CA, WA, UT
Avocados	1,000 tons . .	193	139	145	220	251	189	CA, FL, HI
Bananas	Mil. lb	13	12	11	4	4	4	HI
Cherries, sweet	1,000 tons . .	185	191	132	145	136	119	WA, OR, CA, MI
Cherries, tart	Mil. lb . . . ₃.	234	243	203	44	35	37	MI, NY, UT, OR
Cranberries	1,000 bbl. [3] .	4,080	3,748	3,370	186	165	147	MA, WI, NJ, OR
Dates	1,000 tons . .	22	22	24	20	23	21	CA
Figs (fresh)	1,000 tons . .	56	48	46	20	18	15	CA
Grapefruit (4 States)	Mil. boxes [4] .	69	70	49	479	416	372	FL, CA, AZ
Grapes (13 States)	1,000 tons . .	6,032	5,930	5,660	1,607	1,863	1,662	CA, WA, NY
Kiwifruit.	1,000 tons ₅.	30	37	34	22	15	14	CA
Lemons (2 States)	Mil. boxes [5] .	21	20	19	202	235	280	CA, AZ
Limes (FL).	Mil. boxes [6] .	1	2	1	23	21	23	FL
Nectarines.	1,000 tons . .	200	200	211	79	80	100	CA
Olives.	1,000 tons ₇.	88	123	131	45	57	64	CA
Oranges and tangerines (4 States). .	Mil. boxes [7] .	205	215	184	1,854	1,932	1,476	FL, CA, AZ
Papayas	Mil. lb	69	74	69	12	14	15	HI
Peaches (32 States)	Mil. lb	2,449	2,209	2,111	382	361	365	CA, GA, SC, PA
Pears	1,000 tons . .	860	917	964	235	254	264	WA, CA, OR, NY
Pineapples	1,000 tons . .	659	580	575	107	98	99	HI
Plums and prunes (fresh)	1,000 tons . .	734	1,015	728	230	281	267	CA, OR, WA, ID
Pomegranates	1,000 tons ₇.	18	18	(NA)	6	5	(NA)	(NA)
Tangelos (FL)	Mil. boxes [8] .	4	3	3	33	31	21	FL
Temples (FL)	Mil. boxes [8] ,	4	4	1	28	28	11	FL
Almonds (shelled basis)	Mil. lb	452	395	532	600	481	592	CA
Filberts (in the shell)	1,000 tons . .	17	13	22	14	11	17	OR, WA
Macadamia nuts	Mil. lb	46	51	50	41	45	41	HI
Pecans (in the shell) (11 States) . . .	Mil. lb	308	251	216	167	179	248	GA, TX, NM, LA
Pistachios	Mil. lb	94	39	118	115	64	127	CA
Walnuts, English (in the shell)	1,000 tons . .	209	229	227	193	245	245	CA

NA Not available.   [1] Excludes quantities not harvested or not marketed.   [2] Production in commercial orchards with 100 or more bearing age trees.   [3] Barrels of 100 pounds.   [4] Approximate average, net weight, is 65 lb. in AZ and CA, 85 in FL, and 80 in TX.   [5] About 76 lb. net.   [6] Approximate net weight is 80 lb.   [7] Net contents of box varies. In CA and AZ approximate average for oranges and tangerines is 75 lb.; FL oranges, 90 lb.; TX oranges, 85 lb.; and FL tangerines, 95 lb.   [8] Approximate net weight is 90 lb.
Source: U.S. Dept. of Agriculture, National Agricultural Statistics Service, *Noncitrus Fruits and Nuts*, annual; and *Citrus Fruits*, annual.

No. 1120. Commercial Vegetable and Other Specified Crops—Area, Production, and Value, 1988 to 1990, and Leading Producing States, 1989

[Relates to commercial production for fresh market and processing combined. Includes market garden areas but excludes minor producing acreage in minor producing States. Excludes production for home use in farm and nonfarm gardens. Value is for season or crop year and should not be confused with calendar-year income]

CROP	AREA [1] (1,000 acres)			PRODUCTION [2] (1,000 short tons)			VALUE [3] (mil. dol.)			Leading States in order of production, 1989
	1988	1989	1990	1988	1989	1990	1988	1989	1990	
Asparagus	101	99	96	121	125	122	152	150	148	CA, WA, MI.
Beans, snap [4]	218	249	246	588	870	796	99	151	145	WI, OR, IL.
Beans, dry edible. .	1,353	1,651	2,086	963	1,186	1,621	575	677	609	MI, NE, ID.
Broccoli	114	117	111	640	676	617	292	276	268	CA, AZ, TX.
Carrots	98	102	94	1,293	1,449	1,462	268	297	273	CA, WA, TX.
Cauliflower	63	68	66	394	392	393	202	205	190	CA, AZ, OR.
Celery	34	35	38	971	1,014	990	231	268	215	CA, FL, MI.
Corn, sweet	625	643	675	3,140	3,756	3,954	360	470	467	WI, MN, WA.
Cucumbers [4]	119	124	116	652	643	657	130	131	137	MI, NC, TX.
Honeydew melons .	31	30	27	262	257	226	75	62	82	CA, TX, AZ.
Lettuce	240	243	231	3,525	3,762	3,672	1,040	950	847	CA, AZ, FL.
Peppermint.	81	101	102	2.7	3.3	3.5	85	87	97	OR, WA, ID.
Spearmint. [5]	23	26	34	0.9	0.9	1.3	22	26	38	WA, WI, IN.
Mushrooms	131	133	138	316	334	357	544	596	645	PA, CA, MI.
Onions.	129	133	138	2,337	2,395	2,639	414	497	489	CA, CO, TX.
Peas, green [4]	284	317	341	313	505	528	73	120	131	WI, MN, WA.
Potatoes	1,259	1,282	1,371	17,822	18,522	20,106	2,144	2,718	2,431	ID, WA, WI.
Strawberries	47	46	45	590	571	629	544	538	594	CA, FL, OR.
Sweet potatoes . . .	86	86	90	547	568	651	141	186	139	NC, LA, CA.
Tomatoes.	415	462	489	9,203	11,280	12,033	1,422	1,848	1,622	CA, FL, OH.

[1] Area of crops for harvest for fresh market, including any partially harvested or not harvested because of low prices or other factors, plus area harvested for processing.   [2] Excludes some quantities not marketed.   [3] Fresh market vegetables valued at f.o.b. shipping point. Processing vegetables are equivalent returns at packinghouse door.   [4] Processing only.   [5] Area is shown in million square feet. All data are for marketing year ending June 30.

Source: U.S. Dept. of Agriculture, National Agricultural Statistics Service, *Vegetables*, annual summary. Also in *Agricultural Statistics*, annual.

No. 1121. Red Meats—Slaughtering, Supply, and Use: 1980 to 1991

[**Quantities in millions of pounds** (carcass weight equivalent), except as noted. Carcass weight equivalent is the weight of the animal minus entrails, head, and hide; includes internal organs, fat, and bone. Covers inspected, noninspected, retail, and farm slaughter. See also *Historical Statistics, Colonial Times to 1970*, series K 583-594]

YEAR AND TYPE OF MEAT	Animals slaughtered (mil. head)	Produc- tion	Imports	Supply, [1] total	Con- sump- tion [2]	Exports	Ending stocks
All red meats:							
1980	139.7	38,978	2,668	42,481	41,170	429	882
1985	131.3	39,409	3,255	43,505	42,311	461	733
1988	131.0	40,004	3,594	44,356	42,599	887	870
1989	130.5	39,602	3,138	43,610	41,663	1,287	660
1990	126.4	38,787	3,313	42,760	40,805	1,248	707
1991	128.6	39,585	3,242	43,534	41,235	1,474	825
Beef:							
1980	34.1	21,643	2,064	24,166	23,561	173	432
1985	36.6	23,728	2,071	26,271	25,523	328	420
1988	35.3	23,589	2,380	26,355	25,252	681	422
1989	34.1	23,087	2,179	25,688	24,330	1,023	335
1990	33.4	22,743	2,356	25,434	24,031	1,006	397
1991	32.9	22,916	2,406	25,719	24,112	1,188	419
Pork:							
1980	97.2	16,617	550	17,521	16,838	252	431
1985	84.9	14,807	1,128	16,282	15,866	128	288
1988	88.1	15,684	1,136	17,180	16,548	195	437
1989	89.0	15,813	896	17,146	16,571	262	313
1990	85.4	15,354	898	16,565	16,030	239	296
1991	88.4	15,999	776	17,071	16,395	283	393
Veal:							
1980	2.7	400	21	431	420	2	9
1985	3.5	515	20	549	534	5	11
1988	2.6	396	27	427	412	10	5
1989	2.2	355	(NA)	360	356	(NA)	4
1990	1.8	327	(NA)	331	325	(NA)	6
1991	1.5	306	(NA)	312	305	(NA)	7
Lamb and mutton:							
1980	5.7	318	33	362	351	2	9
1985	6.3	358	36	401	387	1	13
1988	5.4	335	51	394	387	1	6
1989	5.6	347	63	416	406	2	8
1990	5.7	363	59	430	419	3	8
1991	5.8	364	60	432	423	3	6

NA Not available.   [1] Total supply equals production plus imports plus ending stocks of previous year.   [2] Includes shipments to territories.

Source: U.S. Dept. of Agriculture, Economic Research Service, *Livestock and Meat Statistics*, quarterly. Also published in *Agricultural Outlook*, monthly.

No. 1122. Livestock Inventory and Production: 1980 to 1991

[Production in live weight; includes animals for slaughter market, younger animals shipped to other States for feeding or breeding purposes, farm slaughter and custom slaughter consumed on farms where produced, minus livestock shipped into States for feeding or breeding with an adjustment for changes in inventory. See also *Historical Statistics, Colonial Times to 1970*, series K 564-569 and 575-582]

TYPE OF LIVESTOCK	Unit	1980	1982	1983	1984	1985	1986	1987	1988	1989	1990	1991
ALL CATTLE [1]												
Inventory: [2] Number on farms	Mil	111.2	115.4	115.0	113.4	109.6	105.4	102.1	99.6	98.1	98.2	99.4
Total value	Bil. dol. .	55.8	47.9	46.7	44.8	44.0	41.2	41.6	52.1	56.9	60.3	64.9
Value per head.	Dol	502	415	406	396	402	391	407	523	580	614	653
Production: Quantity	Bil. lb . .	40.3	40.7	40.4	40.1	40.1	40.6	40.5	40.6	40.2	40.7	(NA)
Beef, price per 100 lb . .	Dol	62.40	56.70	55.50	57.30	53.70	52.60	61.10	66.60	69.50	74.60	(NA)
Calves, price per 100 lb .	Dol	76.80	59.80	61.70	59.90	62.10	61.10	78.50	89.20	90.80	95.60	(NA)
Value of production. . . .	Bil. dol. .	25.5	22.6	22.0	22.1	21.2	21.0	24.8	27.2	28.0	30.5	(NA)
HOGS AND PIGS												
Inventory: [3] Number on farms	Mil	67.3	58.7	54.5	56.7	54.1	52.3	51.0	54.4	55.5	53.8	54.5
Total value	Bil. dol. .	3.8	4.1	4.9	3.3	4.1	3.6	4.7	4.1	3.7	4.3	4.7
Value per head.	Dol	56.00	70.10	89.90	58.80	75.00	69.60	91.90	76.00	66.30	79.10	85.40
Production: Quantity	Bil. lb . .	23.4	19.7	21.2	20.2	20.2	19.5	20.4	21.7	21.9	23.5	(NA)
Price per 100 lb	Dol	38.00	52.30	46.80	47.10	44.00	49.30	51.20	42.30	42.50	53.70	(NA)
Value of production. . . .	Bil. dol. .	8.9	10.3	9.9	9.5	8.9	9.6	10.4	9.1	9.3	11.3	(NA)
SHEEP AND LAMBS												
Inventory: [2] Number on farms	Mil	12.7	13.0	12.1	11.6	10.7	10.1	10.6	10.9	10.9	11.4	11.2
Total value	Mil. dol .	993	742	629	603	654	684	799	985	895	902	735
Value per head.	Dol	78.20	57.10	51.80	52.10	61.10	67.40	75.70	90.00	82.40	79.30	65.60
Production: Quantity	Mil. lb . .	746	785	769	700	704	726	733	707	776	757	(NA)
Sheep, price per 100 lb .	Dol	21.30	19.50	15.70	16.40	23.90	25.60	29.50	25.60	24.40	23.20	(NA)
Lambs, price per 100 lb .	Dol	63.60	53.10	53.90	60.10	67.70	69.00	77.60	69.10	66.10	55.50	(NA)
Value of production. . . .	Mil. dol .	403	356	356	378	434	445	503	420	420	446	361	(NA)

NA Not available.   [1] Includes milk cows.   [2] As of Jan. 1.   [3] As of Dec. 1 of preceding year.
Source: U.S. Dept. of Agriculture, National Agricultural Statistics Service, *Meat Animals—Production, Disposition, and Income*, annual; and annual livestock summaries. Also in *Agricultural Statistics*, annual.

No. 1123. Cattle and Calves; and Hogs and Pigs—Number, Production, and Value, by State: 1988 to 1991

[See headnote, table 1122]

STATE	NUMBER ON FARMS [1] (1,000)			QUANTITY PRODUCED (mil. lb.)			VALUE OF PRODUCTION (mil. dol.)			COMMERCIAL SLAUGHTER [2] (mil. lb.)		
	1989	1990	1991	1988	1989	1990	1988	1989	1990	1988	1989	1990
CATTLE AND CALVES [3]												
U.S. [4]	98,065	98,162	99,436	40,557	40,241	40,743	27,220	28,031	30,519	39,294	38,467	37,758
AL	1,800	1,750	1,800	672	647	684	431	440	500	283	297	288
CA	4,700	4,800	4,750	2,111	2,025	2,003	1,314	1,274	1,315	1,408	1,362	1,408
CO	2,850	2,900	2,800	1,818	1,791	1,946	1,296	1,320	1,546	2,541	2,542	2,363
ID	1,650	1,660	1,740	824	810	859	525	527	593	899	825	763
IL	1,950	1,950	2,000	778	760	806	547	578	633	1,463	1,389	(5)
IA	4,500	4,500	4,750	2,062	2,078	1,955	1,390	1,467	1,488	2,213	2,162	2,134
KS	5,600	5,700	5,700	3,050	3,083	3,109	2,176	2,262	2,417	7,012	7,001	7,091
KY	2,480	2,420	2,500	701	697	744	473	499	568	107	105	100
MN	2,700	2,600	2,760	1,279	1,233	1,149	807	812	820	1,309	1,209	1,264
MO	4,400	4,400	4,500	1,221	1,242	1,173	904	959	984	433	390	351
MT	2,450	2,300	2,400	923	955	999	631	671	736	19	16	30
NE	5,500	5,800	6,000	3,618	3,714	3,735	2,541	2,728	2,858	6,659	6,698	6,804
OH	1,730	1,650	1,580	561	498	750	361	339	539	472	331	262
OK	5,050	5,250	5,550	2,025	2,033	1,961	1,290	1,371	1,461	126	82	62
SD	3,380	3,380	3,400	1,781	1,792	1,781	1,239	1,272	1,404	704	751	702
TN	2,300	2,300	2,250	726	652	665	439	426	455	173	105	(5)
TX	13,400	13,200	13,400	5,699	5,639	5,926	3,839	3,982	4,564	6,267	6,282	6,100
WA	1,300	1,330	1,340	610	589	653	401	402	481	1,074	986	(5)
WI	4,130	4,170	4,170	1,280	1,244	1,220	798	800	887	1,464	1,436	1,368
HOGS AND PIGS												
U.S. [4]	55,469	53,821	54,362	21,670	21,942	21,275	9,145	9,204	11,333	21,838	22,027	21,230
IL	5,600	5,700	5,700	2,471	2,324	2,225	1,026	986	1,192	2,063	2,178	2,250
IN	4,300	4,350	4,300	1,671	1,666	1,667	696	696	870	1,037	919	876
IA	14,000	13,500	13,800	5,507	5,544	5,394	2,359	2,379	2,912	6,257	6,421	6,571
MN	4,690	4,450	4,500	1,739	1,787	1,715	752	780	948	1,093	1,228	1,382
MO	2,850	2,700	2,800	1,192	1,078	1,040	510	460	566	990	899	685
NE	4,150	4,200	4,300	1,557	1,657	1,624	655	707	881	1,165	1,243	1,299
NC	2,700	2,570	2,800	1,065	1,178	1,190	446	493	607	672	698	654
OH	2,210	2,080	2,000	882	889	837	367	373	437	754	757	642
SD	1,810	1,720	1,770	772	771	753	329	328	410	1,053	998	1,154

[1] Cattle and calves, as of January 1; hogs and pigs as of December 1 of preceding year.   [2] Data for cattle and calves cover cattle only. Includes slaughter in federally inspected and other slaughter plants; excludes animals slaughtered on farms.   [3] Includes milk cows.   [4] Includes other States not shown separately.   [5] Included in U.S. total. Not printed to avoid disclosing individual operation.
U.S. Dept. of Agriculture, National Agricultural Statistics Service, *Meat Animals-Production, Disposition and Income*, annual and *Livestock and Meat Statistics*, annual.

No. 1124. Milk Production and Commercial Use: 1980 to 1991

[In billions of pounds milkfat basis]

YEAR	Pro-duc-tion	Farm use	COMMERCIAL		Imports	Commer-cial supply, total	CCC net remov-als [1]	COMMERCIAL		Milk price per 100 lb. [2] (dol.)
			Farm market-ings	Begin-ning stock				End-ing stock	Disap-pear-ance	
1980	128.4	2.3	126.1	5.4	2.1	133.6	8.8	5.7	119.0	13.1
1985	143.0	2.5	140.6	4.8	2.8	148.2	13.3	4.5	130.4	12.8
1987	142.7	2.3	140.5	4.1	2.5	147.1	6.8	4.6	135.7	12.5
1988	145.2	2.2	142.9	4.6	2.4	149.9	9.1	4.3	136.5	12.3
1989	144.2	2.1	142.2	4.3	2.5	149.0	9.4	4.1	135.5	13.6
1990	148.3	2.0	146.3	4.1	2.7	153.1	9.0	5.1	139.0	13.7
1991	148.5	2.0	146.5	5.1	2.6	154.3	10.5	4.5	139.3	12.2

[1] Removals from commercial supply to Commodity Credit Corporation stocks.   [2] Wholesale price received by farmers for all milk delivered to plants and dealers.

Source: U.S. Dept. of Agriculture, *Agricultural Outlook*, monthly.

No. 1125. Milk Production and Manufactured Dairy Products: 1970 to 1990

[See also *Historical Statistics, Colonial Times to 1970*, series K 595-601]

ITEM	Unit	1970	1980	1984	1985	1986	1987	1988	1989	1990
Cows and heifers that have calved, kept for milk, Jan. 1 [1]	Mil. head	13.3	10.8	10.8	11.0	10.8	10.3	10.3	10.1	10.1
Milk produced on farms	Bil. lb	117	128	135	143	143	143	145	144	148
Production per cow	1,000 lb.	9.8	11.9	12.5	13.0	13.3	13.8	14.1	14.2	14.6
Whole milk sold from farms [2]	Bil. lb	113	126	132	141	141	140	143	142	146
Sales to plants and dealers	Bil. lb	110	125	131	139	140	139	142	141	145
Value of milk produced	Bil. dol.	6.8	16.9	18.3	18.4	18.0	18.0	17.9	19.7	20.5
Gross farm income, dairy products	Bil. dol.	6.7	16.7	18.0	18.1	17.8	17.8	17.7	19.5	20.3
Cash receipts from marketing of milk and cream [2]	Bil. dol.	6.5	16.6	17.9	18.1	17.7	17.7	17.6	19.4	20.2
Sales to plants and dealers	Bil. dol.	6.3	16.3	17.7	17.8	17.5	17.5	17.4	19.1	20.0
Number of dairy manufacturing plants	Number	3,749	2,257	2,059	2,061	1,998	1,933	1,846	1,750	1,714
Manufactured dairy products:										
Butter (incl. whey butter)	Mil. lb	1,137	1,145	1,103	1,248	1,202	1,104	1,208	1,295	1,302
Cheese, total [3]	Mil. lb	2,201	3,984	4,674	5,081	5,209	5,344	5,572	5,615	6,061
American (excl. full-skim American)	Mil. lb	1,428	2,376	2,648	2,855	2,798	2,717	2,757	2,674	2,891
Cream and Neufchatel	Mil. lb	126	229	276	294	322	342	376	401	431
All Italian varieties	Mil. lb	394	983	1,319	1,491	1,633	1,800	1,937	2,043	2,209
Cottage cheese: Creamed [4]	Mil. lb	978	825	736	716	705	675	647	570	531
Curd, pot, and bakers	Mil. lb	726	667	606	599	600	574	557	527	493
Condensed bulk milk	Mil. lb	1,237	952	1,159	1,232	1,362	1,383	1,364	1,417	1,426
Evaporated and condensed canned milk	Mil. lb	1,293	740	666	656	602	597	612	545	615
Nonfat dry milk solids [5]	Mil. lb	1,456	1,168	1,168	1,398	1,294	1,077	998	893	900
Dry whey [6]	Mil. lb	621	690	898	987	1,031	1,097	1,137	1,069	1,143
Ice cream of all kinds	Mil. gal	762	830	894	901	924	928	882	831	816
Ice milk	Mil. gal	287	293	300	301	315	328	355	377	349

[1] For 1970, cows and heifers 2 years old and over.   [2] Comprises sales to plants and dealers, and retail sales by farmers direct to consumers.   [3] Includes varieties not shown separately. Beginning 1980, includes fullskim.   [4] Includes partially creamed (low fat).   [5] Includes dry skim milk for animal feed.   [6] Includes animal but excludes modified whey production.

Source: U.S. Dept. of Agriculture, National Agricultural Statistics Service, *Production of Manufactured Dairy Products*, annual; and *Milk Production, Disposition, and Income*, annual.

No. 1126. Milk Cows—Number, Production, and Value, by State: 1988 to 1990

STATE	NUMBER ON FARMS [1] (1,000)			MILK PRODUCED ON FARMS (mil. lb.)			VALUE OF PRODUCTION [2] (mil. dol.)		
	1988	1989	1990	1988	1989	1990	1988	1989	1990
U.S. [3]	10,262	10,126	10,127	145,152	144,239	148,284	17,921	19,688	20,483
California	1,083	1,104	1,135	18,607	19,420	20,953	2,078	2,446	2,562
Idaho	168	171	179	2,628	2,669	2,949	294	328	360
Illinois	206	197	195	2,805	2,743	2,820	342	373	361
Iowa	307	309	305	4,040	4,202	4,330	477	555	576
Michigan	350	345	344	5,228	5,152	5,233	650	702	739
Minnesota	783	734	710	10,413	10,108	10,006	1,215	1,322	1,323
Missouri	230	228	230	3,000	2,975	3,040	366	396	413
New York	794	776	768	11,444	11,071	11,102	1,446	1,576	1,626
Ohio	351	349	342	4,785	4,535	4,495	577	610	625
Pennsylvania	717	698	683	10,204	9,998	9,933	1,359	1,469	1,513
Texas	375	386	386	4,874	5,170	5,539	646	741	814
Washington	221	225	237	3,966	4,097	4,398	496	559	604
Wisconsin	1,760	1,739	1,753	25,000	24,000	24,400	2,993	3,228	3,282

[1] Average number during year. Represents cows and heifers that have calved, kept for milk; excluding heifers not yet fresh.
[2] Valued at average returns per 100 pounds of milk in combined marketings of milk and cream. Includes value of milk fed to calves.   [3] Includes other States not shown separately.

Source: U.S. Dept. of Agriculture, National Agricultural Statistics Service, *Production of Manufactured Dairy Products*, annual; and *Milk Production, Disposition, and Income*, annual.

No. 1127. Poultry—Number on Farms, Value, Production, and Prices: 1970 to 1990

[For year ending November 30, except as noted. See also *Historical Statistics, Colonial Times to 1970*, series K 609-623]

ITEM	Unit	1970	1980	1982	1983	1984	1985	1986	1987	1988	1989	1990
Chickens:[1] Number [2]	Million . .	433	392	379	365	374	370	373	380	356	356	351
Value per head [2]	Dollars. .	1.21	1.88	1.85	1.96	2.02	1.90	1.87	1.87	2.04	2.16	2.29
Value, total [2]	Mil. dol. .	525	737	701	717	757	704	698	711	726	771	806
Number sold [3]	Million . .	233	238	242	237	225	220	218	218	224	199	208
Price per lb. [3]	Cents . .	9.1	11.0	10.3	12.7	15.9	14.8	12.5	11.0	9.2	14.9	9.6
Value of sales [3]	Mil. dol. .	107	129	121	145	170	152	128	112	95	138	95
PRODUCTION												
Broilers:[4] Number	Million . .	2,987	3,963	4,149	4,184	4,283	4,470	4,649	5,004	5,238	5,517	5,865
Weight	Bil. lb. . .	10.8	15.5	16.8	17.0	17.9	18.9	19.7	21.5	22.5	24.0	25.6
Price per lb	Cents . .	13.6	27.7	26.9	28.6	33.7	30.1	34.5	28.7	33.1	36.6	32.6
Production value	Mil. dol. .	1,475	4,303	4,502	4,873	6,020	5,668	6,784	6,177	7,435	8,779	8,366
Turkeys: Number.	Million . .	116	165	165	171	171	185	207	240	242	261	283
Weight	Bil. lb. . .	2.2	3.1	3.2	3.3	3.3	3.4	3.7	4.1	4.9	5.1	5.5	6.0
Price per lb	Cents . .	22.6	41.3	39.5	38.0	48.9	49.1	47.1	34.8	38.6	40.9	39.4
Gross income.	Mil. dol. .	498	1,272	1,255	1,269	1,655	1,819	1,948	1,703	1,951	2,234	2,383

[1] Excludes commercial broilers. [2] As of Dec. 1. [3] 1970-84, represents number produced and production value. [4] Young chickens of the heavy breeds and other meat-type birds, to be marketed at 2-5 lbs. live weight and from which no pullets are kept for egg production. Not included in sales of chickens.

Source: U.S. Dept. of Agriculture, National Agricultural Statistics Service, *Hatchery Production—Annual; Poultry—Production and Value; Turkeys;* and *Chickens and Eggs.*

No. 1128. Poultry—Production, by State: 1988 to 1990

[In millions of pounds, liveweight production. See *Historical Statistics, Colonial Times to 1970,* series K 614 and 621 for U.S. totals]

STATE	BROILERS			TURKEYS			STATE	BROILERS			TURKEYS		
	1988	1989	1990	1988	1989	1990		1988	1989	1990	1988	1989	1990
U.S. [1] . .	22,464	23,979	25,634	5,059	5,465	6,042	NE.	6	14	20	31	36	38
AL.	2,881	3,150	3,642	(NA)	(NA)	(NA)	NC.	2,300	2,444	2,593	939	992	1,160
AR.	3,677	3,866	3,995	371	412	453	OH.	62	72	96	94	110	135
CA.	997	1,049	1,109	572	664	723	OK.	472	527	540	(NA)	(NA)	(NA)
DE.	1,087	1,132	1,159	(NA)	(NA)	(NA)	OR.	83	92	111	32	38	44
FL.	505	519	490	(NA)	(NA)	(NA)	PA.	533	549	520	158	168	169
GA.	3,400	3,573	3,760	71	54	61	SC.	283	308	343	164	153	168
IL.	(NA)	(NA)	(NA)	35	86	99	SD.	(NA)	(NA)	(NA)	67	63	80
IN	(NA)	(NA)	(NA)	261	280	288	TN.	365	427	436	(NA)	(NA)	(NA)
IA	26	33	63	187	186	228	TX.	1,118	1,254	1,454	(NA)	(NA)	(NA)
MD.	1,085	1,108	1,141	3	2	2	UT.	(NA)	(NA)	(NA)	90	85	90
MI	3	3	3	84	102	125	VA.	791	802	882	306	319	316
MN.	156	181	198	705	784	852	WA	130	140	157	(NA)	(NA)	(NA)
MS.	1,480	1,627	1,693	(NA)	(NA)	(NA)	WV	130	131	156	42	55	72
MO	240	308	362	335	353	360	WI	56	54	62	(NA)	(NA)	(NA)

NA Not available.   [1] Includes other States not shown separately.

Source: U.S. Dept. of Agriculture, National Agricultural Statistics Service, *Poultry—Production and Value;* and *Turkeys,* annual.

No. 1129. Egg Production, Supply, and Use: 1980 to 1991

YEAR	PRODUCTION [1]			SUPPLY (mil. dozen)			USE (mil. dozen)			
	Number produced (bil.)	Price per dozen (cents)	Production value (mil. dol.)	Total [2]	Production	Imports	Total	Consumption [3]	Hatching use	Exports
1980	69.7	56.3	3,268	5,830	5,806	5	5,811	5,169	499	143
1985	68.4	57.2	3,262	5,734	5,710	13	5,723	5,104	548	71
1007	70.4	54.7	3,209	5,884	5,868	6	5,870	5,160	599	111
1988	69.7	52.8	3,067	5,804	5,784	5	5,709	5,041	606	142
1989	67.2	68.9	3,854	5,639	5,598	25	5,628	4,892	644	92
1990	67.8	71.6	4,857	5,685	5,665	9	5,673	4,896	677	101
1991	(NA)	(NA)	(NA)	5,771	5,758	2	5,758	4,899	705	154

NA Not available.   [1] For year ending November 30.   [2] Includes beginning stocks, not shown separately.   [3] Includes shipments to territories.

Source: U.S. Dept. of Agriculture, National Agricultural Statistics Service, *Layers and Egg Production—Annual;* and Economic Research Service, *Agricultural Outlook,* monthly.

Figure 24.1
**Domestic Consumption of Selected
Timber Products: 1970 to 1988**

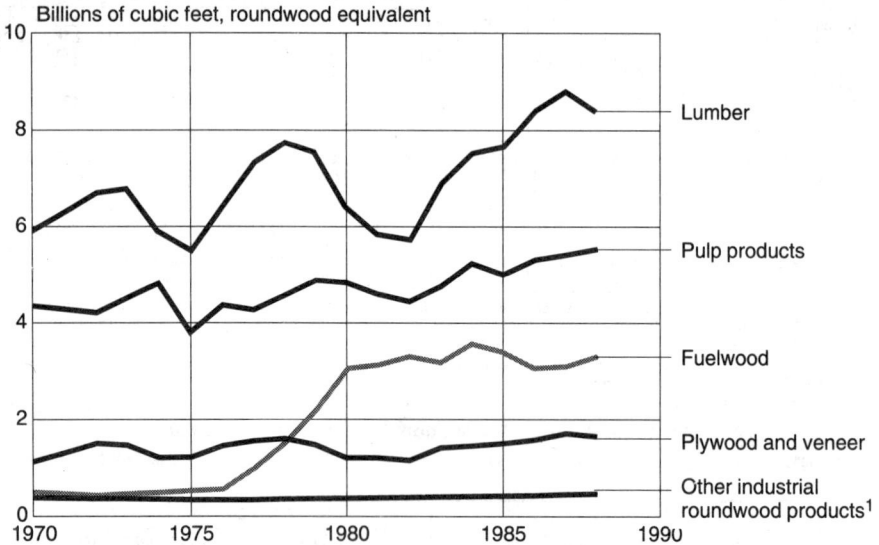

Billions of cubic feet, roundwood equivalent

— Lumber

— Pulp products

— Fuelwood

— Plywood and veneer

— Other industrial
roundwood products[1]

[1] Includes cooperage logs, poles and piling, fence posts, hewn ties, round mine timbers, box bolts, etc.
Source: Chart prepared by U.S. Bureau of the Census. For data, see table 1136.

Figure 24.2
**Fishery Products—
Domestic Catch and Imports: 1960 to 1990**

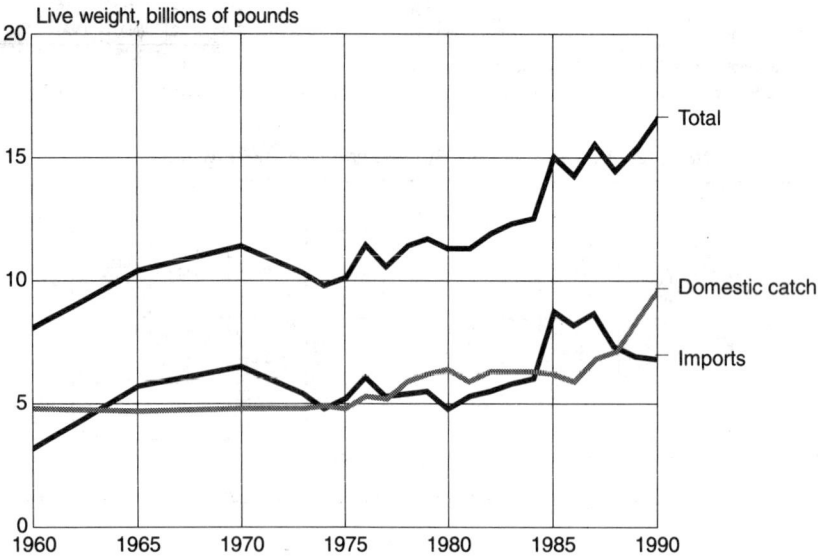

Live weight, billions of pounds

— Total

— Domestic catch

— Imports

Source: Chart prepared by U.S. Bureau of the Census. For data, see table 1149.

Forests and Fisheries

This section presents data on the area, ownership, and timber resource of commercial timberland; forestry statistics covering the National Forests and Forest Service cooperative programs; product data for lumber, pulpwood, woodpulp, paper, and paperboard; and similar data. In addition, data are presented on commercial fishing and the fish processing industry.

The principal sources of data relating to forests and forest products are *An Analysis of the Timber Situation in the United States, 1989-2040, Part I: The Current Resource and Use Situation,* and *Part II: The Future Resource Situation,* forthcoming; *Forest Statistics of the United States, 1987; U.S. Timber Production, Trade, Consumption, and Price Statistics, 1960-88; Land Areas of the National Forest System,* issued annually by the Forest Service of the Department of Agriculture; *Agricultural Statistics* issued by the Department of Agriculture; and reports of the census of manufactures (taken every 5 years) and the annual *Current Industrial Reports,* issued by the Bureau of the Census. Additional information is published in the monthly *Survey of Current Business* of the Bureau of Economic Analysis; and the annual *Wood Pulp and Fiber Statistics* and *The Statistics of Paper, Paperboard, and Wood Pulp* of the American Paper Institute, New York, NY.

The Bureau of the Census also collects data on foreign trade of forest products. The Bureau of Labor Statistics publishes monthly and annual statistics of producer prices for lumber.

The completeness and reliability of statistics on forests and forest products vary considerably. The data for forest land area and stand volumes are much more roliable for areas recently surveyed than for those for which only estimates are available. In general, more data are available for lumber and other manufactured products such as veneer and plywood, etc., than for the primary forest products such as poles and piling and fuelwood.

The principal sources of data relating to fisheries are *Fishery Statistics of the United States,* and *Fisheries of the*

> **In Brief**
> 1991
> Production:
> Paper and board   81.0 mil. sh. tns
> Consumption:
> Recovered paper   23.5 mil. sh. tns

United States, both issued annually by the National Marine Fisheries Service (NMFS), National Oceanic and Atmospheric Administration (NOAA).

The NMFS collects and disseminates data on commercial landings of fish and shellfish. Quarterly data are published on U.S. output of fish sticks, fish portions, and breaded shrimp. Annual reports include quantity and value of commercial landings of fish and shellfish, etc. Reports for the fish-processing industry include annual output of canned, packaged, and industrial products and, for the wholesaling and fish processing establishments, annual and seasonal employment, and number of firms, by product and State.

The Magnuson Fishery Conservation and Management Act of 1976 (Magnuson Act), Public Law 94-265 as amended, provides for the conservation and management of all fishery resources within the U.S. Exclusive Economic Zone (EEZ), except highly migratory species of tuna, and gives the Federal Government exclusive authority over domestic and foreign fisheries within 200 nautical miles of U.S. shores and over certain living marine resources beyond the EEZ. Within the EEZ, the total allowable level of foreign fishing, if any, is that portion of the "optimum yield" not harvested by U.S. vessels. Adjustments in the "optimum yield" level may occur periodically. For details, see *Fisheries of the United States, 1988.* The NMFS collects and disseminates data on catches by foreign fishing vessels in the EEZ.

Historical statistics.—Tabular headnotes provide cross-references, where applicable, to *Historical Statistics of the United States, Colonial Times to 1970.* See Appendix IV.

No. 1130. National Forest System Land and Purchases: 1970 to 1990

[Area as of **June 30** except, beginning **1980**, as of **Sept. 30**; purchases for years ending **June 30**, except as noted. Includes Puerto Rico. Prior to Oct. 1976, lands to be purchased under the Weeks Law and related acts were approved by the National Forest Reservation Commission which also set prices on such lands. With the passage of the National Forest Management Act, all functions of the Commission were transferred to the Secretary of Agriculture. Actual purchases are made by U.S. Department of Agriculture. See also *Historical Statistics, Colonial Times to 1970*, series L 10-14]

ITEM	Unit	1970	1975	1980	1984	1985	1986	1987	1988	1989	1990
Gross area [1]	Mil. acres. .	226	226	226	230	230	230	230	230	231	231
National forest system [2]	Mil. acres. .	187	188	187	191	191	191	191	191	191	191
Approved for purchase	1,000 acres	92	12	42	8	16	23	87	42	99	51
Average price per acre.	Dollars . . .	125	275	664	544	431	308	437	561	346	464
Total price.	Mil. dol . . .	11.5	3.3	27.9	4.2	6.9	7.0	38.0	23.5	34.0	24.0
Purchases completed	1,000 acres	113	34	27	35	7	33	53	18	46	38
Average price per acre.	Dollars . . .	96	267	617	407	653	295	360	153	428	556
Total price.	Mil. dol . . .	10.9	9.1	17.1	14.0	4.2	9.8	19.0	7.2	20.0	21.0
Gross area of purchase units . .	Mil. acres. .	56	56	56	58	58	58	58	58	58	58
Purchase completed, net area [3]	Mil. acres. .	20	20	20	20	20	20	20	20	20	20
Average price per acre.	Dollars . . .	6	9	12	15	15	16	17	17	17	19
Total price.	Mil. dol . . .	125	179	250	298	305	314	333	340	360	381

[1] Comprises all publicly and privately owned land within authorized boundaries of National forests, Purchase units, National grasslands, land utilization projects, research and experimental areas, and other areas.   [2] Federally owned land within the "Gross area."   [3] Cumulative total. Under the March 1, 1911 Act of Congress (Weeks Law), as amended, and related acts.

Source: U.S. National Forest Reservation Commission, *Final Report to October 1976;* and U.S. Forest Service, *Land Areas of the National Forest System,* annual; and unpublished data.

No. 1131. National Forest System—Summary: 1970 to 1990

[**For fiscal years ending in year shown;** see text, section 9. Includes Alaska and Puerto Rico, except as noted. See *Historical Statistics, Colonial Times to 1970*, series J 33-34, for similar but not comparable grazing data, and L 15-31]

ITEM	Unit	1970	1980	1984	1985	1986	1987	1988	1989	1990
Timber cut, total value	Mil. dol.	309	737	764	725	790	1,019	1,243	1,313	1,191
Commercial and cost sales: [1]										
Volume	Mil. bd..	11,527	9,178	10,549	10,941	11,786	12,712	12,649	11,951	10,500
Value	Mil. dol.	308	730	760	721	787	1,016	1,240	1,310	1,188
Free use:										
Volume	Mil. bd..	179	2,070	570	399	308	209	223	214	151
Value [2]	Mil. dol.	0.3	5.7	2.6	2.2	1.4	1.1	1.2	1.2	1.0
Misc. forest products:										
Value	Mil. dol.	0.7	1.1	1.7	1.7	1.6	1.9	2.0	2.2	2.6
Livestock grazing: [3]										
Cattle and horses [4]	1,000 .	1,607	1,521	1,521	1,545	1,491	1,410	1,313	1,526	1,206
Sheep and goats	1,000 .	2,105	1,328	1,129	1,183	1,168	1,134	1,067	972	974
Roads and trails:										
Road construction [5]	Miles..	942	925	1,667	1,903	1,252	2,394	1,352	866	857
Trail construction [5][6]	Miles..	278	2,419	874	987	1,092	1,046	1,834	1,944	1,637
Receipts, total	Mil. dol.	300	703	637	636	832	898	980	1,051	971
Timber use	Mil. dol.	284	625	544	515	745	808	888	910	850
Grazing use	Mil. dol.	4	16	10	9	9	8	9	11	10
Special land use, etc	Mil. dol.	11	62	84	112	78	82	83	130	112
Payments to local govt. [7]	Mil. dol.	73	240	235	229	271	295	326	368	368
25-percent fund [8]	Mil. dol.	72	234	225	212	262	285	317	354	358
Other [9]	Mil. dol.	1	7	10	17	9	10	8	15	10
Allotments to Forest										
Service, total [10]	Mil. dol.	30	73	62	60	82	88	105	111	106
Roads and trails.	Mil. dol.	29	66	58	56	78	84	92	96	91
Other.	Mil. dol.	1	8	4	5	4	4	12	15	15

[1] Includes land exchanges.   [2] Includes some free use timber not reducible to board feet.   [3] For 1970, data for livestock permitted to graze; 1980-89 for number actually grazed. Calendar-year data, prior to 1980. Excludes Puerto Rico.   [4] Excludes animals under 6 months of age. 1970 includes swine. Includes burros beginning in 1980.   [5] Includes reconstruction. [6] Beginning 1980, includes work accomplished by Human Resource Programs and volunteers.   [7] Payments made in following year.   [8] Includes Tongass Alaska suspense account.   [9] Includes Arizona and New Mexico School Fund (through 1982), State of Minnesota, and receipts paid to counties under Bankhead-Jones Farm Tenant Act.   [10] For use in following year.

Source: U.S. Forest Service. In *Agricultural Statistics,* annual, and unpublished data.

No. 1132. National Forest System Land—States and Other Areas: 1990

[In thousands of acres. As of Sept. 30. See also *Historical Statistics, Colonial Times to 1970*, series L 10-11]

STATE	Gross area within unit boundaries [1]	National forest system land [2]	Other lands within unit boundaries	STATE	Gross area within unit boundaries [1]	National forest system land [2]	Other lands within unit boundaries
Total	**230,839**	**191,268**	**39,570**	NV	6,009	5,743	266
AL.	1,275	651	623	NH	825	720	105
AK	24,233	22,437	1,796	NM	10,367	9,320	1,046
AZ	11,889	11,242	647	NY	13	13	-
AR	3,490	2,495	995	NC	3,165	1,221	1,944
CA	24,434	20,588	3,845	ND	1,106	1,106	(Z)
CO	16,027	14,444	1,582	OH	833	191	642
CT	(Z)	(Z)	-	OK	461	296	165
FL.	1,246	1,122	124	OR	17,496	15,634	1,862
GA	1,846	858	988	PA	743	512	231
HI	(Z)	(Z)	-	SC	1,376	605	770
ID	21,694	20,457	1,238	SD	2,342	1,997	345
IL	840	264	576	TN	1,212	626	586
IN	644	188	456	TX	1,994	753	1,241
KS	116	108	8	UT	9,128	8,041	1,086
KY	2,102	667	1,435	VT	630	327	302
LA.	1,023	601	422	VA	3,226	1,642	1,584
ME	93	53	40	WA	10,045	9,147	898
MI	4,872	2,801	2,071	WV	1,861	1,021	840
MN	5,467	2,808	2,659	WI	2,023	1,513	510
MS	2,310	1,149	1,161	WY	9,704	9,255	449
MO	3,082	1,474	1,608	PR	56	28	28
MT	19,101	16,796	2,305	VI	(Z)	(Z)	-
NE	442	352	90				

- Represents zero. Z Less than 500 acres. [1] Comprises all publicly and privately owned land within authorized boundaries of National forests, Purchase units, National grasslands, Land utilization projects, Research and experimental areas, and Other areas. [2] Federally owned land within the "Gross area within unit boundaries."

Source: U.S. Forest Service, *Land Areas of the National Forest System*, annual.

No. 1133. Forest Land—Total and Timberland Area, Volume of Sawtimber, and Growing Stock: 1952 to 1987

[As of **Jan. 1.** See table 25 for composition of regions]

YEAR AND REGION	Total forest land (mil. acres)	TIMBERLAND, OWNERSHIP [1]					SAWTIMBER, NET VOLUME [3]		GROWING STOCK, NET VOLUME [4]	
		All owner- ships (mil. acres)	Feder- ally owned or man- aged [2] (mil. acres)	State, county, and munic- ipal (mil. acres)	Private		Total (bil. bd. ft.)	Soft- wood (bil. bd. ft.)	Total (bil. cu. ft.)	Soft- wood (bil. cu. ft.)
					Total (mil. acres)	Per- cent of total				
United States, 1952........	664	509	125	27	356	70.0	2,520	2,089	610	430
North	209	158	13	18	127	80.0	231	62	106	28
South	197	205	15	3	187	91.4	411	198	143	59
West....................	258	146	97	6	42	29.1	1,878	1,829	361	343
United States, 1962........	759	515	125	27	363	70.4	2,558	2,062	659	448
North	178	160	13	18	130	80.9	268	74	131	35
South	220	209	15	3	191	91.4	494	250	168	73
West....................	360	146	97	6	42	28.9	1,795	1,738	361	340
United States, 1970........	754	504	122	29	354	70.2	2,587	2,035	694	458
North	186	158	13	18	127	80.5	305	87	148	40
South	212	203	15	3	185	90.9	569	302	191	87
West....................	355	143	94	7	42	29.2	1,713	1,646	355	331
United States, 1977........	737	491	113	31	347	70.6	2,635	2,021	725	465
North	178	157	12	19	126	80.4	350	102	166	46
South	207	198	15	3	180	90.6	648	345	215	99
West....................	352	136	85	9	41	30.1	1,637	1,574	344	320
United States, 1987........	731	483	103	34	347	71.8	2,829	2,032	756	451
North	170	158	13	19	126	79.6	471	133	190	49
South	203	195	16	4	176	89.9	757	380	238	104
West....................	358	130	74	11	45	34.9	1,601	519	327	200

[1] Timberland is forest land that is producing or is capable of producing crops of industrial wood and not withdrawn from timber utilization by statute or administrative regulation. Areas qualifying as timberland have the capability of producing in excess of 20 cubic feet per acre per year of industrial wood in natural stands. Currently inaccessible and inoperable areas are included. [2] Includes Indian lands. [3] Sawtimber is timber suitable for sawing into lumber. Live trees of commercial species containing at least one 12-foot sawlog or two noncontiguous 8-foot logs, and meeting regional specifications for freedom from defect. Softwood trees must be at least 9.0-inches diameter, and hardwood trees must be at least 11.0-inches diameter at 4 1/2 feet above ground. International 1/4-inch rule. [4] Live trees of commercial species meeting specified standards of quality or vigor. Cull trees are excluded. Includes only trees 5.0-inches diameter or larger at 4 1/2 feet above ground.

Source: U.S. Forest Service, *Forest Statistics of the United States, 1987.*

No. 1134. Timber-Based Industries—Summary of Manufactures: 1987 to 1990

[Data based on *1987 Standard Industrial Classification Manual,* published by the Office of Management and Budget, see text, section 27. Based on Census of Manufactures, except where noted. N.e.c. = Not elsewhere classified]

SIC [1] code	INDUSTRY	1987 All employees Number (1,000)	1987 All employees Payroll (mil. dol.)	1987 Value of shipments (bil. dol.)	1989 All employees Number (1,000)	1989 All employees Payroll (mil. dol.)	1989 Value of shipments (bil. dol.)	1990 [2] All employees Number (1,000)	1990 [2] All employees Payroll (mil. dol.)	1990 [2] Value of shipments (bil. dol.)
242	Logging and sawmills	266.0	4,805	30.1	256.8	5,040	32.5	254.2	5,076	32.2
2411	Logging	85.7	1,516	10.9	81.7	1,596	12.0	83.4	1,647	12.2
2421	Sawmills/planing mills, gen.	148.2	2,817	17.4	143.7	2,937	18.5	138.9	2,913	17.9
2426	Hardwood dimension and flooring mills	29.9	441	1.7	29.2	472	1.8	29.3	475	1.8
2429	Special product sawmills, n.e.c. . .	2.2	33	0.1	2.3	36	0.2	2.5	41	0.2
243	**Millwork and veneer [3] . . . .**	**240.0**	**4,657**	**22.6**	**233.0**	**4,866**	**23.7**	**229.4**	**4,823**	**23.2**
2431	Millwork	89.0	1,810	9.3	90.9	1,977	9.7	90.5	1,961	9.5
2434	Wood kitchen cabinets	67.0	1,185	4.4	61.6	1,197	4.4	62.8	1,217	4.6
2435	Hardwood veneer and plywood. . .	20.5	340	2.1	20.1	356	2.2	18.7	335	2.1
2436	Softwood veneer and plywood . . .	38.9	888	4.9	36.5	888	5.3	35.6	881	5.0
2439	Structural wood members, n.e.c. . .	24.6	435	1.9	23.9	449	2.1	21.8	429	2.0
244	**Wood containers . . . .**	**37.0**	**483**	**2.1**	**42.2**	**600**	**2.6**	**41.5**	**636**	**2.9**
2441	Nailed and lock corner wood boxes and shook	5.9	85	0.3	6.2	95	0.4	6.0	98	0.4
2448	Wood pallets and skids	25.7	328	1.5	29.1	395	1.8	28.3	417	1.9
2449	Wood containers, n.e.c	5.4	70	0.2	6.9	111	0.4	7.2	122	0.5
245	**Wood buildings and mobile homes . . . .**	**65.3**	**1,208**	**6.6**	**62.8**	**1,211**	**6.4**	**61.4**	**1,217**	**6.5**
2451	Mobile homes	39.9	734	4.1	39.9	769	4.1	38.8	769	4.2
2452	Prefab. wood bldgs/components .	25.4	473	2.5	22.9	442	2.3	22.6	448	2.3
249	**Miscellaneous wood products . .**	**89.9**	**1,536**	**8.3**	**91.0**	**1,643**	**9.2**	**96.4**	**1,745**	**9.6**
2491	Wood preserving	11.8	208	2.2	12.1	223	2.4	13.0	246	2.6
2493	Reconstituted wood products	22.0	505	2.9	22.2	547	3.2	22.3	554	3.0
2499	Wood products, n.e.c	56.1	824	3.3	56.6	873	3.6	61.1	945	3.9
261	Pulp mills	14.2	535	4.3	15.2	603	6.4	16.1	668	6.2
262	Paper mills	129.1	4,597	28.9	130.1	4,927	35.4	130.1	5,062	35.3
263	Paperboard mills	52.3	1,859	13.7	52.1	1,958	16.3	53.1	2,049	15.9
265	Paperboard containers and boxes .	193.6	4,618	25.9	202.3	5,144	30.5	200.3	5,245	30.5
2652	Setup paperboard boxes	8.7	131	0.4	8.7	141	0.5	8.8	146	0.6
2653	Corrugated and solid fiber boxes .	105.8	2,610	16.1	111.1	2,928	18.9	110.1	2,984	18.6
2655	Fiber cans, tubes, drums, and similar prod.	12.6	281	1.5	13.3	329	1.8	13.3	341	1.9
2656	Sanitary food containers, except folding.	15.8	340	2.1	17.2	383	2.5	17.5	392	2.5
2657	Folding paperboard boxes, including sanitary	50.7	1,256	5.7	51.8	1,364	6.7	50.7	1,382	7.0
267	**Converted paper and paperboard products [4] . . . . .**	**222.1**	**5,251**	**36.2**	**229.9**	**5,765**	**42.8**	**228.5**	**5,923**	**43.5**
2671	Packaging paper and plastic film. .	15.0	406	2.4	16.3	458	2.9	16.4	489	3.0
2672	Coated and laminated paper, n.e.c.	30.9	839	5.9	35.9	973	7.1	35.0	985	7.1
2673	Plastics, foil, and coated paper bags.	36.6	784	4.6	39.0	882	5.6	37.4	870	5.5
2674	Uncoated paper and multiwall bags.	17.1	348	2.4	17.0	358	2.8	16.9	374	2.8
2675	Die-cut paper and paperboard and cardboard	15.7	308	1.7	16.1	384	2.0	16.8	395	2.1
2676	Sanitary paper products	38.4	1,155	11.7	37.8	1,235	14.3	39.0	1,299	14.7
2677	Envelopes.	27.6	613	2.6	27.3	645	2.8	26.1	648	2.8
2678	Stationery, tablets, and related products	11.2	206	1.2	10.5	203	1.3	10.1	203	1.3
2679	Converted paper and paperboard products, n.e.c	29.6	593	3.6	30.1	627	3.8	30.7	659	4.1

[1] Standard Industrial Classification code; see text, section 13.   [2] Source: U.S. Bureau of the Census, *Annual Survey of Manufactures* .   [3] Includes plywood and structural members.   [4] Except containers and boxes.

Source: Except as noted, U.S. Bureau of the Census, *Census of Manufactures, 1987 Final Industry Series,* MC87-I-24A-D and MC87-I-26A-C.

No. 1135. Timber-Based Industries—Employment and Average Hourly Earnings: 1970 to 1991

[Data for production workers.]

SIC [1] code	ITEM	EMPLOYEES (1,000)						EARNINGS (dollars)					
		1970	1980	1985	1989	1990	1991	1970	1980	1985	1989	1990	1991
24	Lumber and wood products [2] . .	564	587	593	628	610	571	2.97	6.57	8.25	8.84	9.09	9.28
241	Logging.	(NA)	71	67	72	70	66	(NA)	8.64	10.92	11.13	11.23	11.15
242	Sawmills and planing mills . .	196	190	172	177	174	164	2.84	6.70	8.52	9.03	9.23	9.42
243	Millwork, plywood, and structural members	(NA)	170	195	220	213	195	(NA)	6.44	8.09	8.73	9.05	9.30
26	Paper and allied products	540	519	509	522	524	520	3.44	7.84	10.83	11.96	12.30	12.70
25	Furniture and fixtures	362	376	394	419	403	378	2.77	5.49	7.17	8.25	8.52	8.77

NA Not available. [1] 1987 Standard Industrial Classification; see text, section 27. [2] Includes other industries, not shown separately.

Source: U.S. Bureau of Labor Statistics, Bulletin 2370 Supplement to Employment and Earnings, July 1991, and *Employment and Earnings*, monthly.

No. 1136. Timber Products—Production, Foreign Trade, and Consumption, by Type of Product: 1970 to 1988

[In millions of cubic feet, roundwood equivalent. See also *Historical Statistics, Colonial Times to 1970*, series L 72-86]

ITEM	1970	1975	1980	1982	1983	1984	1985	1986	1987	1988, prel.
Industrial roundwood:										
Domestic production [1]	11,105	10,575	12,120	10,910	12,065	12,725	12,515	13,845	14,670	14,985
Softwoods	8,635	8,380	9,290	8,450	9,285	9,790	9,690	10,595	11,390	11,430
Hardwoods	2,470	2,195	2,825	2,465	2,780	2,935	2,825	3,250	3,280	3,555
Imports	2,430	2,215	3,250	3,015	3,710	4,165	4,340	4,375	4,575	4,445
Exports . . . . [2] . . .	1,540	1,685	2,350	1,995	2,110	2,060	2,070	2,300	2,650	3,200
Consumption [2]	11,995	11,105	13,020	11,930	13,665	14,830	14,785	15,920	16,595	16,230
Softwoods	9,425	8,875	10,345	9,575	10,975	11,965	11,960	12,735	13,430	12,970
Hardwoods	2,565	2,230	2,675	2,355	2,690	2,865	2,825	3,180	3,165	3,260
Lumber:										
Domestic production	5,215	4,890	5,300	4,635	5,370	5,770	5,665	6,545	6,990	6,920
Imports	955	930	1,540	1,460	1,915	2,130	2,345	2,285	2,380	2,225
Exports	195	255	395	320	360	340	305	385	510	720
Consumption	5,970	5,565	6,450	5,780	6,925	7,560	7,700	8,445	8,860	8,425
Plywood and veneer:										
Domestic production	1,020	1,165	1,175	1,135	1,365	1,400	1,420	1,505	1,650	1,630
Imports	170	170	120	115	160	145	165	185	190	165
Exports	15	70	45	50	65	45	40	65	80	100
Consumption	1,170	1,265	1,250	1,200	1,460	1,500	1,550	1,625	1,760	1,695
Pulp products:										
Domestic production	3,835	3,485	4,390	3,980	4,165	4,355	4,165	4,545	4,670	4,885
Imports	1,280	1,105	1,565	1,415	1,605	1,860	1,810	1,895	1,985	2,045
Exports	720	715	1,070	900	965	930	920	1,080	1,195	1,345
Consumption	4,400	3,875	4,885	4,495	4,805	5,290	5,055	5,360	5,465	5,585
Logs:										
Imports	25	15	25	20	30	30	20	15	15	15
Exports	465	455	560	550	565	600	655	620	705	825
Pulpwood chips, exports.	145	195	275	175	155	145	145	150	160	215
Other industrial prod. [3] consumption	425	385	415	435	445	455	465	475	495	510
Fuelwood consumption	**540**	**570**	**3,105**	**3,355**	**3,235**	**3,620**	**3,450**	**3,115**	**3,150**	**3,360**

[1] Includes log exports. [2] Includes log imports. [3] Includes cooperage logs, poles and piling, fence posts, hewn ties, round mine timbers, box bolts, etc.

No. 1137. Timber Products—Per Capita Consumption: 1970 to 1988

[Based on total population estimated as of **July 1**. See also *Historical Statistics, Colonial Times to 1970*, series L 87-97]

PRODUCT	Unit	1970	1975	1980	1982	1983	1984	1985	1986	1987	1988, prel.
All products	Cu. ft	61.1	54.0	70.8	65.7	72.0	77.9	76.2	78.8	81.0	79.5
Industrial roundwood	Cu. ft	58.5	51.4	57.2	51.3	58.2	62.6	61.8	65.9	68.0	65.9
Lumber	Cu. ft	29.1	25.8	28.3	24.9	29.5	31.9	32.2	35.0	36.3	34.2
Plywood and veneer. . . .	Cu. ft	5.7	5.9	5.5	5.2	6.2	6.3	6.5	6.7	7.2	6.9
Pulp products	Cu. ft	21.4	17.9	21.4	19.3	20.5	22.3	21.1	22.2	22.4	22.7
Other products	Cu. ft	2.1	1.8	1.8	1.9	1.9	1.9	1.9	2.0	2.0	2.1
Fuelwood	Cu. ft	2.6	2.6	13.6	14.4	13.8	15.3	14.4	12.9	12.9	13.6
Lumber.	Bd. ft	193	171	188	161	190	205	207	224	233	221
Plywood and veneer	Bd. ft	34	32	30	28	34	34	35	37	39	37
Pulp products.	Cords (128 cu. ft.) . . .	0.3	0.2	0.3	0.2	0.3	0.3	0.3	0.3	0.3	0.3

Source of tables 1136 and 1137: U.S. Forest Service, *U.S. Timber Production, Trade, Consumption, and Price Statistics, 1960-88*, annual.

No. 1138. Lumber Consumption, by Species Group and End Use: 1962 to 1986

[In million board feet, except per capita in board feet.] Per capita consumption based on estimated resident population as of July 1]

ITEM	1962	1970	1976	1986	END-USE	1962	1970	1976	1986
Total	39,078	39,869	44,653	57,203	New housing	14,160	13,350	17,000	19,320
					Residential upkeep and				
Per capita	210	194	205	237	improvements	4,330	4,980	6,260	9.930
					New non-residential				
Species group:					construction [1]	4,200	4,700	4,470	5,310
Softwoods	30,773	31,959	36,627	47,094	Manufacturing	4,540	4,670	4,865	4,805
Hardwoods	8,305	7,910	8,026	10,109	Shipping	4,550	5,725	5,915	6,785
					Other [2]	7,298	6,444	6,143	11,053

[1] In addition to new construction, includes railroad ties laid as replacements in existing track and lumber used by railroads for railcar repair. [2] Includes upkeep and improvement of non-residential buildings and structures; made-at-home projects, such as furniture, boats, and picnic tables; made-on-the-job items such as advertising and display structures; and miscellaneous products and uses.

Source: U.S. Forest Service. *Analysis of the Timber Situation in the United States: 1989-2040*, forthcoming.

No. 1139. Selected Timber Products—Producer Price Indexes: 1980 to 1990

[See also *Historical Statistics, Colonial Times to 1970*, series L 206-210]

PRODUCT	Unit	1980	1985	1987	1988	1989	1990
Lumber and wood products, except furniture. . .	Dec. 1984 = 100 . . .	(NA)	100.3	105.3	109.2	115.3	117.0
Logging camps and logging contractors	Dec. 1981 = 100 . . .	(NA)	94.8	100.4	112.8	128.0	135.6
Sawmills and planing mills	Dec. 1984 = 100 . . .	(NA)	99.7	106.7	110.2	114.6	113.7
Millwork, veneer, and plywood [1]	Dec. 1984 = 100 . . .	(NA)	99.9	105.3	107.5	114.1	115.4
Softwood plywood	Dec. 1980 = 100 . . .	91.4	90.0	93.8	93.0	104.8	102.5
Wood containers	June 1985 = 100 . . .	(NA)	(NA)	101.3	103.8	109.7	113.9
Wood buildings and mobile homes	Dec. 1984 = 100 . . .	(NA)	100.6	103.6	107.9	112.1	115.5
Particleboard	Dec. 1982 = 100 . . .	92.1	110.0	120.3	124.6	127.8	117.1
Paper and allied products	Dec. 1984 = 100 . . .	(NA)	98.8	104.9	113.7	120.8	121.9
Pulp mills	Dec. 1982 = 100 . . .	105.5	100.9	117.0	141.7	161.3	153.8
Paper mill products; except building paper . . .	June 1981 = 100 . . .	93.5	109.5	115.5	127.4	134.6	134.0
Paperboard mills	Dec. 1982 = 100 . . .	97.3	112.0	126.2	141.6	149.9	146.0
Converted paper and paperboard products [2] . .	June 1985 = 100 . . .	(NA)	(NA)	101.4	105.7	110.5	111.3
Paperboard containers and boxes	Dec. 1984 = 100 . . .	(NA)	98.4	104.3	111.7	117.2	117.7
Building paper and building board mills	Dec. 1985 = 100 . . .	(NA)	(NA)	104.2	108.8	114.4	(NA)

NA Not available. [1] Includes structural wood members. [2] Excludes containers and boxes.

Source: U.S. Bureau of Labor Statistics, *Producer Price Indexes*, monthly.

No. 1140. Selected Species—Stumpage Prices In Current and Constant (1982) Dollars: 1975 to 1990

[In dollars per 1,000 board feet. Stumpage prices are based on sales of sawtimber from National Forests. See also *Historical Statistics, Colonial Times to 1970*, series L 199-205]

SPECIES	1975	1980	1981	1982	1983	1984	1985	1986	1987	1988	1989	1990
CURRENT DOLLARS												
Softwoods:												
Douglas-fir [1]	170	432	350	118	162	133	126	161	190	256	390	466
Southern pine [2]	57	155	172	127	141	139	91	104	136	142	131	127
Sugar pine [3]	99	667	225	72	138	84	110	170	288	260	289	285
Ponderosa pine [3][4]	71	206	195	67	104	123	101	157	209	182	292	252
Western hemlock [5]	69	213	163	45	62	62	51	75	105	163	223	203
Hardwoods:												
All eastern hardwoods [6].	34	52	51	56	60	90	65	70	88	151	136	146
Oak, white, red, and												
black [6]	30	66	63	71	88	145	95	108	147	146	179	188
Maple, sugar [7]	42	70	68	71	55	81	70	66	81	108	129	135
CONSTANT (1982) DOLLARS [8]												
Softwoods:												
Douglas-fir [1]	290	481	357	118	160	128	122	160	185	240	347	401
Southern pine [2]	98	173	176	127	139	134	88	103	132	133	117	109
Sugar pine [3]	170	742	230	72	136	81	106	169	280	244	258	245
Ponderosa pine [3][4]	122	230	199	67	103	118	98	156	204	170	260	217
Western hemlock [5]	118	237	167	45	61	60	49	75	103	152	199	175
Hardwoods:												
All eastern hardwoods [6].	58	58	52	56	59	87	63	70	86	142	121	126
Oak, white, red, and												
black [6]	51	73	65	71	87	140	92	108	143	137	159	162
Maple, sugar [7]	72	78	69	71	54	78	68	66	78	101	115	116

[1] Western Washington and western Oregon. [2] Southern region. [3] Pacific Southwest region (formerly California region). [4] Includes Jeffrey pine. [5] Pacific Northwest region. [6] Eastern and Southern regions. [7] Eastern region. [8] Deflated by the producer price index, all commodities.

Source: U.S. Forest Service, *U.S. Timber Production, Trade, Consumption, and Price Statistics, 1960-89*, annual, forthcoming.

No. 1141. Lumber Production and Consumption, by Kind of Wood: 1980 to 1990

[In millions of board feet, except as indicated. Based on sample survey; see source for sampling variability. See also *Historical Statistics, Colonial Times to 1970*, series L 98-112 and L 122-137]

ITEM	1980	1983	1984	1985	1986	1987	1988	1989	1990 [1]	1990 [2]
Total production	35,354	34,572	37,065	36,445	41,999	44,886	44,576	43,576	43,942	41,204
Softwoods [3][4]	28,239	28,927	30,801	30,479	34,815	37,410	36,845	36,040	36,602	33,692
Cedar	722	744	752	759	860	924	863	828	965	944
Douglas fir	6,853	6,434	7,809	7,751	9,600	10,422	9,986	10,045	8,888	7,614
Hemlock	1,855	1,316	(NA)	(NA)	(NA)	(NA)	(NA)	(NA)	(NA)	(NA)
Ponderosa pine	3,269	2,869	3,679	3,773	3,967	4,125	3,940	3,914	3,744	3,412
Redwood	770	852	999	1,155	984	1,157	1,157	1,048	1,096	1,085
Southern yellow pine [4]	8,217	10,181	10,648	10,230	11,443	12,043	12,474	12,031	13,131	12,921
White fir [5]	1,643	1,316	2,017	2,272	2,659	2,899	2,919	3,296	3,221	2,808
Hardwoods [3][4]	7,115	5,644	6,264	5,966	7,184	7,476	7,731	7,536	7,340	7,512
Ash	(S)	224	219	218	257	265	293	278	217	189
Beech	183	112	111	89	125	116	120	105	83	83
Cottonwood and aspen	303	197	133	216	247	235	234	217	187	201
Elm	149	(NA)	(NA)	(NA)	(NA)	(NA)	(NA)	(NA)	(NA)	(NA)
Maple	[6]225	524	538	532	587	636	619	589	544	596
Oak	3,356	2,163	2,786	2,793	3,410	3,804	3,790	3,546	2,640	2,556
Sweet gum [7]	371	278	300	293	375	330	356	306	246	262
Yellow poplar	661	475	569	544	724	805	828	802	674	721
Domestic consumption	44,536	48,674	52,661	53,468	57,448	61,754	58,834	58,847	54,482	(X)
Percent net imports [8]	16.8	18.6	18.7	24.4	23.1	24.4	16.5	16.7	15.7	(X)
Softwoods	33,812	39,611	42,832	44,240	47,492	50,558	48,513	47,975	45,003	(X)
Mill stocks, yearend	4,228	4,606	4,594	4,765	4,905	4,840	4,999	4,888	4,854	(X)
Exports	1,956	1,745	1,599	1,515	1,877	2,423	3,264	3,319	2,970	(X)
Imports	9,540	11,977	13,270	14,608	14,238	14,680	13,806	13,638	12,148	(X)
Hardwoods	10,724	9,063	9,829	9,228	9,956	11,196	10,321	10,872	9,480	(X)
Mill stocks, yearend	1,572	1,334	1,561	1,719	1,636	(NA)	(NA)	(NA)	(NA)	(X)
Exports	379	478	467	397	498	775	1,232	856	878	(X)
Imports	293	261	328	364	347	511	390	375	255	(X)

NA Not available. S Figure does not meet publication standards. X Not applicable. [1] Based on old sample and represent the bridge between the old and new sample. [2] New sample, based on the new MA-24T sample. [3] Includes types not shown separately. [4] Beginning 1986, data not directly comparable to previous years due to inclusion of 200 sawmills in the survey for the first time; see source. [5] Beginning 1988, also includes hemfir, and other western truefirs. [6] Excludes hard maple. [7] Red and sap. [8] Imports minus exports.

Source: U.S. Bureau of the Census, *Current Industrial Reports*, series MA-24T, annual.

No. 1142. Lumber Production, by Geographic Area: 1970 to 1988

[In billion board feet. Data based in part on a sample of sawmills and are subject to sampling variability; see source. See *Historical Statistics, Colonial Times to 1970*, series L 113-121, for data by regions]

SECTION AND DIVISION	1970	1975	1978	1979	1980	1982	1983	1984	1985	1986	1987	1988
United States	34.7	32.6	[1]40.5	[1]40.6	[1]35.4	30.0	34.6	37.1	36.4	42.0	44.9	44.7
North [2][3]	4.4	4.1	(NA)	(NA)	(NA)	3.8	4.3	4.5	4.2	4.9	5.3	5.2
Hardwood	3.4	3.0	(NA)	(NA)	(NA)	2.7	3.0	3.3	3.0	3.6	3.8	3.9
Softwood	1.0	1.1	(NA)	(NA)	(NA)	1.1	1.3	1.2	1.2	1.4	1.5	1.4
South [2]	10.8	9.7	(NA)	(NA)	(NA)	10.8	12.7	13.4	13.0	15.1	15.7	16.3
Hardwood	3.6	2.7	(NA)	(NA)	(NA)	2.0	2.4	2.8	2.7	3.4	3.4	3.6
Softwood	7.2	7.0	(NA)	(NA)	(NA)	8.8	10.3	10.7	10.2	11.7	12.3	12.7
West [2]	19.4	18.8	21.7	21.1	17.2	15.4	17.6	19.1	19.3	22.0	23.9	23.2
Hardwood	0.1	0.1	0.2	0.2	0.3	0.2	0.2	0.2	0.2	0.2	0.3	0.3
Softwood	19.3	18.6	21.4	20.9	16.9	15.1	17.4	19.0	19.1	21.7	23.6	22.9
New England	0.7	0.8	1.0	1.0	1.1	1.0	1.1	1.1	1.1	1.2	1.2	1.2
Middle Atlantic	0.8	0.7	0.9	0.9	0.9	0.8	0.8	0.8	0.7	0.9	0.9	0.9
East North Central	1.2	1.1	1.4	1.4	1.3	1.1	1.2	1.3	1.3	1.5	1.6	1.5
West North Central	0.6	0.5	0.7	0.6	0.6	0.3	0.4	0.4	0.6	0.7	0.6	0.6
South Atlantic	5.2	4.7	5.4	5.8	5.2	5.4	6.5	6.7	6.4	7.4	7.7	8.1
East South Central	3.4	3.0	3.7	3.6	3.2	3.2	3.8	4.2	4.1	5.0	5.3	5.3
West South Central	3.2	3.0	3.6	3.2	2.9	2.8	3.1	3.3	3.1	3.4	3.7	3.9
Mountain	4.2	3.9	4.7	4.5	3.3	3.8	3.8	4.4	4.3	4.8	(4)	(4)
Pacific	15.3	14.8	17.0	16.6	13.4	12.2	13.6	14.8	14.8	17.0	[5]23.9	[5]23.2

NA Not available. [1] Includes amounts not specified by division. [2] Source: U.S. Forest Service, *U.S. Timber Production, Trade, Consumption, and Price Statistics, 1960-88*, annual. Sections are as defined by the Forest Service. [3] Includes Kentucky. [4] Included with Pacific. [5] Includes Mountain.

Source: Except as noted, U.S. Bureau of the Census, *Current Industrial Reports*, series MA-24T, annual.

No. 1143. Wood Products—Production: 1970 to 1990

ITEM	Unit	1970	1975	1980	1983	1984	1985	1986	1987	1988	1989	1990, prel.
Hardwood flooring.	Mil. bd. ft........	307	99	78	98	110	122	145	174	193	206	205
Softwood plywood	Bil. sq. ft., 3/8"....	14.1	15.1	15.5	18.3	18.9	19.3	20.4	21.1	22.9	21.4	20.7
Insulation boards [1]	1,000 short tons ...	1,219	1,249	1,051	713	785	735	732	605	529	460	474
Hardboard [1].....	Mil. sq. ft., 1/8" ...	4,340	5,681	6,140	7,303	6,837	6,300	5,822	5,458	5,118	5,196	5,025
Particleboard	Mil. sq. ft., 3/4" ...	1,731	2,503	2,950	3,009	3,196	3,331	3,603	3,706	3,829	3,858	3,806

[1] Beginning 1983, data are for shipments.

Source: U.S. Dept. of Commerce, International Trade Administration, *Forest Products Review*, monthly (discontinued April 1983); and unpublished data. Based on reports of U.S. Bureau of the Census, National Oak Flooring Manufacturers Association and National Particleboard Association.

No. 1144. Paper and Paperboard—Production and Consumption: 1970 to 1991

[In millions of short tons. See also *Historical Statistics, Colonial Times to 1970*, series L 172, L 174, and L 178-191]

ITEM	PRODUCTION						CONSUMPTION [1]					
	1970	1980	1985	1989	1990	1991	1970	1980	1985	1989	1990	1991
Total paper and paperboard ..	51.7	63.6	68.7	78.4	80.4	81.0	56.0	67.2	76.1	85.2	86.7	84.8
Paper: Newsprint............	3.5	4.7	5.4	6.1	6.6	6.8	9.8	11.4	12.8	13.1	13.3	12.5
Coated printing, converting....	3.2	4.6	5.9	7.2	7.5	7.3	3.2	4.6	6.3	7.8	8.3	7.8
Uncoated free sheet	5.1	8.0	9.7	11.1	11.5	11.6	5.1	8.0	10.0	11.5	12.0	11.9
Other printing, writing, etc.....	2.6	2.9	2.9	3.3	3.3	3.2	2.8	3.5	4.4	5.1	5.2	5.0
Packaging and industrial converting	5.3	5.5	5.2	4.9	4.6	4.5	5.1	5.2	5.2	5.0	4.7	4.6
Tissue and other machine creped..............	3.7	4.4	4.9	5.6	5.8	5.7	3.7	4.4	5.0	5.7	5.9	5.7
Paperboard: Unbleached kraft...	11.5	15.3	16.4	19.5	20.4	20.9	9.9	13.0	14.6	17.2	17.8	17.8
Bleached kraft	3.3	3.8	3.9	4.5	4.4	4.6	3.2	3.3	3.4	3.8	3.7	3.8
Semichemical.............	3.5	4.7	5.1	5.7	5.7	5.7	3.4	4.4	5.0	5.7	5.7	5.6
Recycled finish	7.0	7.1	7.6	8.8	9.0	9.1	7.0	7.0	7.6	[3]9.1	9.3	9.5
Construction paper and board [2].	3.0	2.6	[3]1.7	[3]1.6	[3]1.6	[3]1.6	3.0	3.0	2.0	[3]1.7	[3]1.7	[3]1.6

[1] Total consumption of paper and paperboard includes net imports of paper and paperboard conot available by grade.
[2] Source: 1970-80, U.S. Bureau of the Census, *Current Industrial Reports*. Includes wetately 100,000-160,000 tons per year.
[3] Estimated.

Source: Except as noted, American Paper Institute, Inc., New York, NY, *Statistics of Paper, Paperboard, and Woodpulp*, annual.

No. 1145. Newsprint—Production, Stocks, Consumption, Imports, and Price Index: 1970 to 1990

[In thousands of metric tons, except price index and imports (imports in short tons). See also *Historical Statistics, Colonial Times to 1970*, series L 198-198]

COUNTRY AND ITEM	1970	1975	1980	1983	1984	1985	1986	1987	1988	1989	1990
Canada: Production	7,808	6,966	8,625	8,486	9,013	8,988	9,289	9,669	9,840	9,640	9,068
Shipments from mills	7,795	7,010	8,622	8,439	9,018	8,996	9,302	9,757	9,740	9,607	9,074
Stocks at mills, end of year....	214	86	165	303	298	290	277	189	288	321	315
United States:											
Estimated consumption [1]	8,805	8,395	10,088	10,529	11,349	11,507	11,873	12,303	12,244	12,241	12,127
Production	3,142	3,348	4,239	4,688	5,025	4,924	5,107	5,300	5,427	5,523	5,997
Shipments from mills	3,136	3,347	4,234	4,674	5,065	4,927	5,115	5,310	5,415	5,515	6,007
Stocks, end of year: At mills ...	30	19	21	99	60	57	49	36	48	56	46
At and in transit to publishers..	680	666	732	790	874	910	849	900	933	749	802
Imports [2]................	6,635	5,847	7,280	6,919	7,899	8,472	8,589	8,976	8,592	8,765	(NA)
Producer price index (1982=100)	34.1	58.3	[3]88.5	95.9	102.3	105.3	103.3	112.3	127.6	122.5	119.5

NA Not available. [1] By all users. Based on American Paper Institute data. [2] Source: Reports of U.S. Bureau of the Census. Includes Puerto Rico and beginning 1983, Virgin Islands. [3] Average for 11 months.

Source: Except as noted, U.S. Bureau of Economic Analysis, *Survey of Current Business*, monthly. Data from American Paper Institute, Inc., New York, NY, and Canadian Pulp & Paper Association.

No. 1146. Recovered Paper Utilization and Recovery Rates: 1970 to 1991

[In millions of short tons, except percent. Recovery rate is ratio of total recovered paper to new supply. Recovered paper utilization is the ratio of recovered paper consumption at paper and board mills to paper and board production. See *Historical Statistics, Colonial Times to 1970*, series L 175, for U.S. wastepaper consumption]

ITEM	1970	1980	1984	1985	1986	1987	1988	1989	1990	1991
Paper and board, production [1]	51.7	63.5	70.2	68.7	72.5	75.9	78.1	78.4	80.4	81.0
Recovered paper consumption	11.8	14.9	16.7	16.4	17.9	18.7	19.7	20.2	21.7	23.5
Recovered paper utilization rate (percent)..	22.8	23.5	23.8	23.8	24.7	24.6	25.2	25.8	27.1	29.0
Other recovered paper uses [2]	0.42	0.47	0.46	0.53	0.59	0.66	0.70	0.72	1.00	1.10
Recovered paper exports	0.41	2.64	3.46	3.56	4.09	4.81	5.95	6.31	6.51	6.60
Total paper recovered..............	12.6	17.9	20.5	20.4	22.5	24.0	26.2	27.1	29.1	31.1
Paper and board, new supply [3]	56.0	67.2	76.9	76.1	79.8	83.5	85.5	85.2	86.7	84.8
Recovery rate (percent).............	22.4	26.7	26.7	26.8	28.2	28.8	30.6	31.8	33.6	36.7

[1] Excludes hard pressed board; includes construction paper and board, and wet machine board. [2] Estimated. [3] Excludes production of hard pressed board.

Source: American Paper Institute, Inc., New York, NY, *Statistics of Paper, Paperboard, and Woodpulp*, annual; and unpublished data.

No. 1147. Selected Wood Products—Production and Consumption: 1970 to 1989

[See also *Historical Statistics, Colonial Times to 1970*, series L 151-170]

ITEM	Unit	1970	1975	1980	1984	1985	1986	1987	1988	1989
PULPWOOD										
Receipts, total	Mil. cords [1]	68.9	65.4	81.0	88.0	85.4	90.6	93.9	95.1	97.0
Softwood	Mil. cords [1]	52.4	49.3	60.2	62.9	60.2	63.3	65.3	65.8	67.1
Hardwood	Mil. cords [1]	16.5	16.2	20.8	25.2	25.1	27.3	28.6	29.3	29.9
Consumption, total	Mil. cords [1]	67.6	65.4	79.7	87.0	84.8	91.1	92.4	95.3	96.1
Softwood	Mil. cords [1]	51.3	48.9	58.8	62.0	59.7	63.1	64.2	65.9	66.3
Hardwood	Mil. cords [1]	16.3	16.5	20.9	24.9	25.1	28.1	28.2	29.4	29.7
Inventories [2]	Mil. cords [1]	6.6	6.6	6.7	5.2	5.1	4.7	5.6	5.3	5.8
WOODPULP										
Production	Mil. short tons	43.9	43.1	53.0	57.8	57.7	60.6	62.4	64.1	64.6
Consumption, [3] total	Mil. short tons	43.2	42.4	52.4	57.5	56.6	60.0	61.2	62.8	62.7
Own pulp	Mil. short tons	38.9	38.5	46.6	50.3	49.7	52.6	53.8	54.9	54.9
Purchased pulp	Mil. short tons	4.3	3.9	5.9	7.2	7.0	7.5	7.4	7.9	7.8
PLYWOOD										
Softwood:										
Production	Mil. sq. ft. [4]	14,149	15,706	15,483	18,865	19,341	20,363	22,312	22,233	20,919
Consumption, total	Mil. sq. ft. [4]	(NA)	(NA)	15,145	18,526	19,122	19,880	21,503	22,277	20,904
Value	Mil. dol.	949	(NA)	2,582	2,995	3,080	3,237	3,483	3,513	3,734
Hardwood:										
Production	Mil. sq. ft. [5]	1,904	1,280	1,311	1,185	1,016	1,088	1,256	1,217	1,213
Consumption, total	Mil. sq. ft. [5]	5,772	4,970	3,416	3,831	4,311	4,884	4,918	4,193	(NA)
Value	Mil. dol.	516	586	977	1,199	1,192	1,320	1,471	1,405	1,392

NA Not available.   [1] Standard cords. 128 cubic feet roughwood bases.   [2] As of Dec. 31.   [3] In the manufacture of paper and board.   [4] 3/8'' basis.   [5] Surface measure.
Source: U.S. Bureau of the Census, *Current Industrial Reports*, series MA26-A, MA24-H, and MA24-F.

No. 1148. Selected Timber Products—Imports and Exports: 1970 to 1989

ITEM	Unit	1970	1980	1982	1983	1984	1985	1986	1987	1988	1989, prel.
IMPORTS [1]											
Lumber, total [2]	Mil. bd. ft.	6,114	9,866	9,360	12,254	13,632	14,996	14,619	15,234	14,226	15,277
From Canada	Percent	96.0	97.5	98.2	98.3	97.9	97.6	97.5	96.9	97.5	91.3
Softwoods	Mil. bd. ft.	5,778	9,573	9,150	11,993	13,304	14,632	14,272	14,723	13,841	14,928
Value	Mil. dol	434	1,826	1,624	2,569	2,681	2,898	2,969	3,060	2,939	2,875
Hardwoods	Mil. bd. ft.	337	293	211	260	328	364	347	511	386	349
Value	Mil. dol	62	152	104	134	173	180	168	273	238	152
Logs, total	Mil. bd. ft. [3]	144	128	117	165	147	99	78	83	68	42
From Canada	Percent	79.6	97.4	98.6	97.9	97.4	81.8	77.9	91.6	91.9	61.5
Softwoods	Mil. bd. ft. [3]	107	114	99	142	117	71	52	69	56	24
Value	Mil. dol	9	17	23	24	15	17	7	19	15	12
Hardwoods	Mil. bd. ft. [3]	38	13	18	23	30	28	26	14	12	18
Value	Mil. dol	5	3	3	3	5	4	4	3	3	17
Paper and board [4]	1,000 tons	7,115	8,780	8,024	8,986	11,075	11,522	11,936	12,837	13,110	13,100
Value	Mil. dol	1,039	3,418	3,682	4,019	5,324	5,698	6,036	6,928	8,002	8,330
Woodpulp	1,000 tons	3,518	4,051	3,656	4,093	4,490	4,466	4,564	4,848	4,938	5,105
Value	Mil. dol	483	1,684	1,493	1,472	1,845	1,521	1,606	2,069	2,608	3,037
Plywood	Mil. sq. ft	4,171	2,477	2,270	3,393	3,056	3,609	3,941	4,094	3,358	(NA)
Value	Mil. dol	208	409	331	451	438	463	519	638	577	(NA)
EXPORTS											
Lumber, total [2]	Mil. bd. ft.	1,243	2,494	2,021	2,270	2,150	1,945	2,427	3,217	4,527	4,236
To: Canada	Percent	21.7	25.3	20.7	29.3	25.8	23.7	22.0	20.9	17.6	15.5
Japan	Percent	30.8	26.0	31.1	27.8	28.0	32.1	36.4	36.8	34.5	38.2
Europe	Percent	24.1	23.8	20.3	20.2	16.0	15.1	16.6	16.9	20.5	16.7
Softwoods	Mil. bd. ft.	1,115	2,007	1,635	1,756	1,624	1,518	1,878	2,424	3,266	3,379
Value	Mil. dol	163	789	582	609	541	497	644	856	1,143	1,404
Hardwoods	Mil. bd. ft.	128	487	386	514	527	427	548	793	1,261	856
Value	Mil. dol	31	272	229	305	300	263	350	493	683	653
Logs, total	Mil. bd. ft. [3]	2,741	3,261	3,208	3,307	3,495	3,843	3,627	4,110	4,798	4,773
To: Canada	Percent	10.6	9.7	9.4	10.5	12.1	11.6	12.2	10.3	7.9	5.8
Japan	Percent	86.3	78.0	61.7	55.4	50.4	49.4	57.3	58.3	50.3	63.2
China: Mainland	Percent	(NA)	2.7	17.1	17.1	21.9	24.8	27.8	17.0	14.1	10.1
Softwoods	Mil. bd. ft. [3]	2,672	3,109	3,115	3,196	3,369	3,732	3,488	3,960	4,594	4,557
Value	Mil. dol	320	1,452	1,174	1,068	1,079	1,169	1,129	1,526	2,090	2,177
Hardwoods	Mil. bd. ft. [3]	69	152	93	112	126	111	139	149	204	216
Value	Mil. dol	36	129	84	98	101	91	97	118	160	230
Paper and board [4]	1,000 tons	2,817	5,214	4,246	4,569	4,387	4,071	4,687	5,304	5,691	6,300
Value	Mil. dol	602	2,773	2,589	2,481	2,552	2,266	2,540	3,104	3,753	4,261
Woodpulp	1,000 tons	3,095	3,806	3,395	3,644	3,594	3,796	4,459	4,869	5,528	6,231
Value	Mil. dol	464	1,652	1,415	1,362	1,502	1,354	1,663	2,251	2,915	3,513
Plywood	Mil. sq. ft	183	420	493	615	407	365	656	855	1,108	(NA)
Value	Mil. dol	16	108	117	143	94	86	145	194	247	(NA)

NA Not available.   [1] Customs value of imports; see text, section 29.   [2] Includes railroad ties.   [3] Log scale.   [4] Includes paper and board products. Excludes hardboard.
Source: U.S. Forest Service, *U.S. Timber Production, Trade, Consumption, and Price Statistics: 1960-89*.

No. 1149. Fishery Products—Domestic Catch and Imports, Summary: 1970 to 1990

[Live weight, in millions of pounds, except percent. 1979-1989 preliminary. For data on com.nercial catch for selected countries, see table 1478, section 31. See *Historical Statistics, Colonial Times to 1970*, series L 224-226, for domestic catch]

ITEM	1970	1980	1981	1982	1983	1984	1985	1986	1987	1988	1989	1990
Total	11,474	11,357	11,353	12,011	12,352	12,552	15,150	14,368	15,744	14,628	15,485	16,653
For human food.......	6,213	8,006	8,267	7,968	8,413	8,498	9,337	9,620	10,561	10,505	12,268	12,967
Finfish..	(NA)	6,139	6,316	6,090	6,358	6,303	6,991	7,087	7,919	7,786	9,735	10,426
Shellfish [1]	(NA)	1,867	1,951	1,878	2,055	2,195	2,346	2,533	2,642	2,719	2,533	2,541
For industrial use	5,261	3,351	3,086	4,043	3,939	4,054	5,813	4,748	5,183	4,123	3,217	3,686
Domestic catch	4,917	6,482	5,977	6,367	6,439	6,438	6,258	6,031	6,896	7,192	8,463	9,708
Percent of total ..	42.8	57.1	52.7	53.0	52.1	51.3	41.3	42.0	43.8	49.2	54.7	58.3
For human food	2,537	3,654	3,547	3,285	3,238	3,320	3,294	3,393	3,946	4,588	6,204	7,346
Finfish ..	(NA)	2,516	2,414	2,324	2,351	2,348	2,273	2,240	2,769	3,306	4,897	6,053
Shellfish [1]	(NA)	1,138	1,133	961	887	972	1,021	1,153	1,177	1,282	1,307	1,293
For industrial use	2,380	2,828	2,430	3,082	3,201	3,118	2,964	2,638	2,950	2,604	2,259	2,362
Imports [2]	6,557	4,875	5,376	5,644	5,913	6,114	8,892	8,337	8,848	7,436	7,022	6,945
Percent of total ..	57.2	42.9	47.3	47.0	47.9	48.7	58.7	58.0	56.2	50.8	45.3	41.7
For human food	3,676	4,352	4,720	4,683	5,175	5,178	6,043	6,227	6,615	5,917	6,064	5,621
Finfish	(NA)	3,623	3,902	3,766	4,007	3,955	4,718	4,847	5,150	4,480	4,838	4,373
Shellfish [1]	(NA)	729	818	917	1,168	1,223	1,325	1,380	1,465	1,437	1,226	1,248
For industrial use [3] ...	2,881	523	656	961	738	936	2,849	2,110	2,233	1,519	958	1,324

NA Not available.   [1] For univalve and bivalve mollusks (conchs, clams, oysters, scallops, etc.), the weight of meats, excluding the shell, is reported.   [2] Excludes imports of edible fishery products consumed in Puerto Rico; includes landings of tuna caught by foreign vessels in American Samoa.   [3] Fish meal and sea herring.

Source: U.S. National Oceanic and Atmospheric Administration, National Marine Fisheries Service, *Fishery Statistics of the United States*, annual; and *Fisheries of the United States*, annual.

No. 1150. Fisheries—Employment, Fishing Craft, and Establishments: 1970 to 1989

[In thousands. As of Dec. 31. 1979-89 preliminary. Data for employment and establishments exclude Alaska. See also *Historical Statistics, Colonial Times to 1970*, series L 254-261]

ITEM	1970	1975	1979	1980	1981	1982	1983	1984	1985	1986	1987	1988	1989
Persons employed in U.S.	227	260	267	296	303	314	333	340	351	347	359	364	(NA)
Fishermen	140	168	184	193	198	216	223	230	239	247	256	274	(NA)
Shore workers [1]	87	92	83	103	105	98	110	110	112	100	103	90	73
Craft used	88	103	103	113	115	123	127	127	130	128	[2]93	[2]110	111
Vessels, 5 net tons and over .	14	16	18	19	20	20	21	24	24	38	[2]23	[2]32	36
Motorboats..............	72	85	84	93	93	102	105	102	104	88	[2]68	[2]78	75
Other boats	2	2	1	1	2	1	1	1	2	2	[2]2	(NA)	1
Fishery shore establishments.	3.7	3.6	3.4	3.6	3.6	3.6	3.9	4.0	4.0	4.0	4.2	4.6	4.5

NA Not available.   [1] Seasonal average for processors and wholesaling plants.   [2] Excludes Maryland and Virginia.

Source: U.S. National Oceanic and Atmospheric Administration, National Marine Fisheries Service, *Fishery Statistics of the United States*, annual; and *Fisheries of the United States*, annual.

No. 1151. Fisheries—Quantity and Value of Domestic Catch: 1960 to 1990

[1979-1990 preliminary. See also *Historical Statistics, Colonial Times to 1970*, series L 224-226, L 229, and L 310]

YEAR	QUANTITY (mil. lb. [1])			Value (mil. dol.)	Average price per lb. (cents)	YEAR	QUANTITY (mil. lb. [1])			Value (mil. dol.)	Average price per lb. (cents)
	Total	For human food	For industrial products [2]				Total	For human food	For industrial products [2]		
1960.....	4,942	2,498	2,444	354	7.2	1980.....	6,482	3,654	2,828	2,237	34.5
1965.....	4,777	2,587	2,190	446	9.3	1981.....	5,977	3,547	2,430	2,388	40.0
1970.....	4,917	2,537	2,380	613	12.5	1982.....	6,367	3,285	3,082	2,390	37.5
1972.....	4,806	2,435	2,371	748	15.6	1983.....	6,439	3,238	3,201	2,355	36.6
1973.....	4,858	2,398	2,460	937	19.3	1984.....	6,438	3,320	3,118	2,350	36.5
1974.....	4,967	2,496	2,471	932	18.7	1985.....	6,258	3,294	2,964	2,326	37.2
1975.....	4,877	2,465	2,412	977	20.0	1986.....	6,031	3,393	2,638	2,763	45.8
1976.....	5,388	2,775	2,613	1,349	25.0	1987.....	6,896	3,946	2,950	3,115	45.2
1977.....	5,271	2,952	2,319	1,554	29.5	1988.....	7,192	4,588	2,604	3,520	48.9
1978.....	6,028	3,177	2,851	1,854	30.7	1989.....	8,463	6,204	2,259	3,238	38.3
1979.....	6,267	3,318	2,949	2,234	35.6	1990.....	9,708	7,346	2,362	3,572	36.8

[1] Live weight.   [2] Meal, oil, fish solubles, homogenized condensed fish, shell products, bait, and animal food.

Source: U.S. National Oceanic and Atmospheric Administration, National Marine Fisheries Service, *Fishery Statistics of the United States*, annual; and *Fisheries of the United States*, annual.

No. 1152. Fisheries—Quantity and Value of Catch, by State, and Catch of Principal Species, by Area: 1980 to 1990

[Catch in millions of pounds, live weight, except as indicated; value in millions of dollars. Preliminary. See also *Historical Statistics, Colonial Times to 1970*, series L 262-293]

AREA, STATE, CATCH, AND VALUE	1980	1985	1989	1990
Total:				
Catch	6,482	6,258	8,463	9,708
Value	2,237	2,326	3,238	3,572
New England:				
Catch	788	590	565	649
Value	327	419	509	543
Maine:				
Catch	245	175	151	169
Value	93	101	133	130
New Hampshire:				
Catch	19	8	11	11
Value	5	5	10	10
Massachusetts:				
Catch	438	296	269	328
Value	178	232	273	303
Rhode Island:				
Catch	81	104	125	132
Value	46	70	75	73
Connecticut:				
Catch	5	7	9	9
Value	5	12	18	27
Catch for certain species:				
Clams	15	22	16	15
Cod	118	83	78	95
Crabs	7	8	11	9
Flounder	118	98	50	60
Haddock	55	14	4	5
Herring, sea	184	52	90	113
Lobster, American	36	44	49	55
Ocean perch, Atlantic	24	10	1	1
Pollock	40	43	23	21
Scallops, sea	17	10	21	25
Squid	6	15	47	36
Whiting	18	31	23	28
Middle Atlantic:				
Catch	244	151	172	207
Value	97	101	133	150
New York:				
Catch	39	39	37	49
Value	45	38	51	56
New Jersey:				
Catch	201	108	128	149
Value	50	61	79	89
Delaware:				
Catch	4	5	7	9
Value	2	2	3	4
Catch for certain species:				
Clams (meats)	40	73	80	93
Scup or porgy	8	2	4	4
Squid	3	8	17	6
Chesapeake Bay:				
Catch	717	815	778	867
Value	130	124	152	160
Maryland:				
Catch	80	92	85	81
Value	45	47	52	54
Virginia:				
Catch	637	723	693	787
Value	85	76	100	107
Catch for certain species:				
Crabs	65	91	89	91
Clams	36	47	38	27
Scallops, sea	6	3	8	9
Flounder	10	6	4	2
Oysters	21	8	4	4
South Atlantic:				
Catch	473	311	256	262
Value	148	156	169	170
North Carolina:				
Catch	356	215	164	176
Value	69	65	71	72
South Carolina:				
Catch	21	13	20	14
Value	20	14	25	24
Georgia:				
Catch	19	17	16	13

AREA, STATE, CATCH, AND VALUE	1980	1985	1989	1990
Value	20	21	20	20
Florida (east coast):				
Catch	77	66	56	58
Value	39	57	53	54
Catch for certain species:				
Menhaden	218	105	68	74
Shrimp	33	28	34	28
Crabs	55	48	52	54
Scallops	1	13	5	2
Gulf States:				
Catch	1,979	2,412	1,790	1,625
Value	463	597	649	640
Florida (west coast):				
Catch	115	117	141	122
Value	86	114	132	116
Alabama:				
Catch	25	30	25	23
Value	25	41	38	36
Mississippi:				
Catch	334	471	298	320
Value	25	40	44	42
Louisiana:				
Catch	1,412	1,693	1,228	1,061
Value	174	225	265	263
Texas:				
Catch	94	103	96	99
Value	153	177	170	182
Catch for certain species:				
Crabs	45	53	61	51
Mullet	31	17	27	24
Oysters (meats)	17	25	15	11
Shrimp	208	263	228	247
Great Lakes: [1]				
Catch	44	54	38	45
Value	14	15	20	20
Mississippi River and tributaries:				
Catch	85	92	(NA)	(NA)
Value	21	29	(NA)	(NA)
Pacific Coast:				
Catch	2,140	1,816	4,840	6,027
Value	1,025	863	1,560	1,825
Washington:				
Catch	156	167	163	137
Value	86	93	135	118
Oregon:				
Catch	126	101	170	139
Value	56	46	79	70
California:				
Catch	804	363	418	347
Value	323	133	123	127
Alaska:				
Catch	1,054	1,185	4,089	5,404
Value	560	591	1,223	509
Catch for certain species:				
Anchovies	107	15	13	13
Bonito	14	5	2	8
Cod	20	120	372	544
Crabs	347	129	199	281
Flounder	60	68	133	430
Hake	12	16	17	21
Halibut	19	61	75	70
Herring, sea	107	142	119	108
Jack mackerel	44	21	28	9
Mackerel	65	75	89	84
Oysters	7	8	8	11
Pollock	3	93	2,362	3,157
Rockfish	106	82	134	170
Sablefish	22	00	08	00
Salmon	614	727	785	733
Shrimp	98	35	81	59
Tuna	387	64	56	34
Hawaii:				
Catch	11	17	24	26
Tuna catch	7	11	14	14
Value	12	22	47	65

NA Not available.   [1] Collected largely by State fishery agencies and compiled by State fishery agencies and National Marine Fisheries Service. Includes, in addition to the Great Lakes, small amounts for Lake St. Clair, Lake of the Woods, Namakan Lake, and Rainy Lake.

Source: U.S. National Oceanic and Atmospheric Administration, National Marine Fisheries Service, *Fishery Statistics of the United States*, annual; and *Fisheries of the United States*, annual.

No. 1153. Domestic Fisheries—Catch by Selected Ports: 1985 to 1990

[See *Historical Statistics, Colonial Times to 1970,* series L 236-253, for data on quantity and value of catch]

PORT	CATCH (mil. lb.)					VALUE (mil. dol.)				
	1985	1987	1988	1989	1990	1985	1987	1988	1989	1990
New Bedford, MA.	90.6	78.7	90.3	90.4	114.8	103.2	143.7	140.9	141.0	160.4
Dutch Harbor-Unalaska, AK	106.3	128.2	377.3	504.3	509.9	21.3	62.7	100.9	107.0	126.2
Kodiak, AK	96.1	204.1	304.6	213.2	272.5	65.8	132.1	[1]166.3	100.2	101.7
Dulac-Chauvin, LA	398.6	331.7	244.1	210.9	164.4	59.9	65.6	56.5	50.0	52.7
Empire-Venice, LA	224.5	357.4	297.2	272.7	244.2	34.3	60.1	67.7	49.2	46.3
Gloucester, MA	116.5	93.0	107.4	98.5	126.2	37.1	34.0	30.8	30.0	40.5
Petersburg, AK	(NA)	42.4	50.4	113.5	67.5	(NA)	36.9	58.5	61.4	39.4
Cordova, AK	(NA)	69.6	42.5	55.3	70.8	(NA)	41.9	46.4	35.3	36.8
Cape May-Wildwood, NJ	30.3	56.8	47.9	54.0	69.2	18.1	30.5	28.4	30.8	34.4
Point Judith, RI	56.8	46.6	49.6	48.3	58.7	28.0	27.4	25.4	23.6	32.2
Portland, ME	36.1	43.8	43.9	49.0	48.9	17.2	35.8	30.4	34.4	31.7
Ketchikan, AK	(NA)	27.6	28.3	91.6	52.6	(NA)	22.8	43.5	45.6	28.3
Beaufort-Morehead City, NC.	133.2	85.7	110.0	95.0	102.0	22.7	22.7	27.0	25.0	23.0
Cameron, LA.	673.6	672.4	438.9	352.7	232.6	29.9	31.9	33.2	20.5	20.6
Morgan City-Berwick, LA	7.7	27.0	43.3	68.1	146.5	(NA)	11.0	16.7	17.8	19.7
Pascagoula-Moss Point, MS.	423.2	391.6	292.0	282.1	303.9	18.4	20.3	28.2	16.9	18.8
Los Angeles, CA	150.3	203.1	232.0	177.6	133.8	32.5	55.6	34.0	20.3	17.6
Astoria, OR.	25.5	46.6	44.2	51.0	41.2	9.5	24.6	24.3	20.0	16.2
Port Hueneme-Oxnard-Ventura, CA	19.9	42.3	55.0	50.9	24.2	5.4	8.1	10.0	7.9	9.2
Intercoastal City, LA	(NA)	314.3	209.7	207.2	173.0	(NA)	13.4	14.7	9.5	(NA)

NA Not available. [1] Record.

Source: U.S. National Oceanic and Atmospheric Administration, National Marine Fisheries Service, *Fisheries of the United States,* annual.

No. 1154. Domestic Fish and Shellfish Catch and Value, by Species: 1985 to 1990

SPECIES	QUANTITY (1,000 lb.)				VALUE ($1,000)		
	1985-89 5 year average	1985	1989	1990	1985	1989	1990
Total	(X)	6,257,642	8,463,080	9,708,421	2,326,237	3,238,440	3,572,437
Fish, total [1]	(X)	5,214,363	7,145,154	8,395,918	1,193,427	1,726,247	1,950,539
Anchovies.	13,335	14,566	13,389	13,189	2,704	2,696	2,723
Bluefish	14,044	13,743	10,429	13,802	2,363	2,245	3,239
Butterfish	8,605	10,338	7,051	6,532	3,537	4,108	3,334
Cod: Atlantic	71,511	82,823	78,423	95,881	35,140	47,772	61,329
Pacific.	206,934	120,275	372,137	544,203	18,556	55,375	94,590
Croaker	10,681	11,088	8,287	6,786	3,658	4,114	3,437
Flounder.	199,118	195,718	202,489	502,218	129,121	119,831	159,315
Haddock.	8,459	14,416	3,808	5,440	13,545	4,538	5,967
Halibut.	74,321	61,032	75,168	70,454	38,376	85,145	96,700
Herring, sea; Atlantic. . . .	80,221	57,133	89,657	113,095	2,968	5,041	5,746
Herring, sea; Pacific	129,243	142,074	119,346	108,120	47,025	24,391	32,178
Jack mackerel.	24,433	20,852	28,422	8,959	1,770	1,927	535
Mackerel, Pacific	88,732	75,453	88,667	83,721	6,324	6,023	5,081
Menhaden	2,383,569	2,739,401	1,988,726	1,962,160	100,680	84,462	93,896
Mullet.	27,442	21,205	31,594	28,554	5,720	15,023	12,738
Ocean perch, Atlantic	4,837	9,666	1,392	1,322	3,179	919	703
Ocean perch, Pacific.	15,770	9,034	22,332	60,972	1,757	4,646	8,494
Pollock, Atlantic	39,978	43,477	23,249	21,042	6,978	9,922	10,516
Pollock, Alaska	878,909	92,833	2,361,988	3,157,406	5,409	186,921	272,640
Rockfish	109,934	82,109	133,623	170,647	23,107	42,338	40,532
Sablefish	91,209	63,380	97,590	89,802	28,692	73,272	58,864
Salmon.	667,900	726,946	785,868	733,146	439,795	591,234	612,367
Scup or porgy	14,082	15,996	9,582	11,452	9,338	7,720	8,677
Sea trout, gray.	17,930	16,400	14,187	9,880	7,330	7,160	5,777
Shark, Dogfish.	11,944	11,563	12,804	35,793	842	1,602	3,801
Snapper, red.	4,303	5,181	3,959	3,101	10,661	10,329	8,411
Swordfish	11,255	12,258	11,768	13,797	33,191	38,321	40,851
Tuna	94,337	83,054	89,413	62,393	52,515	103,543	105,040
Whiting.	38,813	44,545	39,353	44,500	8,274	9,403	11,281
Shellfish, total [1]	(X)	1,043,279	1,317,926	1,312,503	1,132,810	1,512,193	1,621,898
Clams	140,041	150,551	138,166	139,198	128,349	134,943	130,194
Crabs.	398,733	337,632	458,378	499,416	203,044	414,401	483,837
Lobsters: American.	47,866	46,152	52,926	61,017	114,895	149,115	154,677
Oysters	37,268	44,173	29,926	29,193	70,053	83,585	93,718
Scallops: Calico	8,146	12,513	6,580	1,135	12,524	5,928	1,281
Sea	26,435	15,829	33,757	39,917	74,562	132,594	153,696
Shrimp	355,881	333,691	351,514	346,494	472,850	467,571	491,433
Squid: Atlantic	38,551	7,157	66,829	59,809	7,256	25,592	21,178
Pacific	49,728	22,276	60,509	36,082	4,047	5,509	2,636

X Not applicable. [1] Includes other types of fish and shellfish, not shown separately.
Source: U.S. National Oceanic and Atmospheric Administration, National Marine Fisheries Service, *Fisheries of the United States,* annual.

No. 1155. Disposition of U.S. Domestic Catch: 1970 to 1990

[Live weight catch in millions of pounds. 1980-90 preliminary. In addition to whole fish, a large portion of waste (400-500 million lb.) derived from canning, filleting, and dressing fish and shellfish is utilized in production of fish meal and oil in each year shown. See *Historical Statistics, Colonial Times to 1970*, series L 305-310, for similar but not entirely comparable data]

DISPOSITION	1970	1975	1980	1982	1983	1984	1985	1986	1987	1988	1989	1990
Total	4,917	4,877	6,482	6,367	6,439	6,438	6,258	6,031	6,896	7,192	8,463	9,708
Fresh and frozen	1,595	1,744	2,621	2,550	2,304	2,336	2,242	2,487	3,157	3,813	5,585	6,805
Canned	1,150	907	1,161	891	1,087	1,128	1,232	1,134	1,009	1,017	798	751
Cured.................	71	55	96	85	80	82	70	60	89	86	128	126
Reduced to meal, oil, etc.	2,101	2,171	2,604	2,841	2,968	2,892	2,714	2,350	2,641	2,276	1,952	2,026

Source: U.S. National Oceanic and Atmospheric Administration, National Marine Fisheries Service, *Fishery Statistics of the United States*, annual; and *Fisheries of the United States*, annual.

No. 1156. Joint Venture Catches in the U.S. Exclusive Economic Zone (EEZ), by Species: 1985 to 1990

[Joint venture—An operation authorized under the Magnuson Fishery Conservation and Management Act (MFCMA) in which a permitted foreign vessel receives fish in the U.S. Exclusive Economic Zone (EEZ) from a U.S. vessel. The fish received from the U.S. vessel are part of the U.S. harvest]

SPECIES	QUANTITY (1,000 lb.)				VALUE ($1,000)			
	1985	1988	1989	1990	1985	1988	1989	1990
Total	2,008,889	3,201,487	1,700,293	800,565	104,320	221,090	112,165	51,341
Atka mackerel	88,047	43,253	-	-	6,109	3,571	-	-
Cod	80,189	245,871	97,937	17,809	7,799	30,429	12,495	1,763
Flounder............	396,084	727,778	426,436	219,547	24,833	53,763	34,179	23,527
Hake, Pacific	(D)	299,343	448,808	376,927	(D)	14,660	21,628	18,429
Ocean perch	619	-	-	-	56	-	-	-
Mackerel, Atlantic......	8,350	12,533	(Z)	(D)	584	760	(Z)	(D)
Pollock, Alaska	1,354,368	1,822,242	634,385	49,376	59,730	116,102	40,378	2,139
Rockfish............	154	4,636	-	-	14	705	-	-
Sablefish	207	112	-	-	30	14	-	-
Squid	7,987	(D)	-	-	1,194	(D)	-	-
Other	72,884	45,719	92,727	136,906	3,971	1,086	3,485	5,483

- Represents zero.   D Figure withheld to avoid disclosure.   Z Less than $500.

Source: U.S. National Oceanic and Atmospheric Administration, National Marine Fisheries Service, *Fisheries of the United States*, annual.

No. 1157. U.S. Catch and Value of Fish and Shellfish, by Distance Caught Off U.S. Shores—Selected Species: 1990

[Preliminary. Catch is shown in **live weight,** except as indicated. Includes landings by U.S. flag vessels at Puerto Rico and other ports outside the 50 States and joint venture catches, therefore will not agree with other tables; see table 1156]

SPECIES	Total U.S. catch (mil. lb.)	BY DISTANCE FROM U.S. SHORES						Value of U.S. catch [1] (mil. dol.)
		Catch (mil. lb.)			Percent of U.S. catch			
		3 miles or less [1]	3 to 200 miles	International waters [2]	3 miles or less [1]	3 to 200 miles	International waters [2]	
Total	11,021	4,570	5,964	487	41	54	5	3,860
Fish [3]	9,703	3,888	5,328	487	40	55	5	2,227
Cod	658	83	575	-	13	87	-	158
Flounder.....................	722	361	361	-	50	50	-	183
Halibut	70	47	23	-	67	33	-	97
Herring, sea.................	221	140	81	-	63	37	-	38
Mackerel....................	117	4	113	-	3	97	-	16
Menhaden...................	1,962	1,658	304	-	85	15	-	94
Pollock	3,228	473	2,754	-	15	85	-	285
Salmon, Pacific	733	726	7	-	99	1	-	612
Tuna	514	4	26	484	1	5	94	310
Shellfish [3]	1,318	682	636	-	52	48	-	1,633
Clams (meals)	139	38	101	-	27	73	-	130
Crabs	499	264	235	-	53	47	-	404
Lobsters	68	53	15	-	78	22	-	178
Scallops (meats).	42	3	39	-	7	93	-	158
Shrimp	346	180	166	-	52	48	-	491
Squid	96	28	68	-	29	71	-	24

- Represents or rounds to zero.   [1] Includes all landings in Great Lakes and other inland waters.   [2] Greater than 200 nautical miles seaward from the U.S. shores except for two States. The boundaries for the Gulf Coast of Florida and Texas are 9 nautical miles.   [3] Includes other species, not shown separately.

Source: U.S. National Oceanic and Atmospheric Administration, National Marine Fisheries Service, *Fishery Statistics of the United States*, annual; and *Fisheries of the United States*, annual.

No. 1158. U.S. Private Aquaculture—Production and Value: 1980 to 1987

[Production is shown in live weight, except as indicated. Aquaculture is the commercial growing of fish or other aquatic life in a controlled environment]

SPECIES	PRODUCTION (1,000 lbs.)					VALUE ($1,000)				
	1980	1984	1985	1986	1987	1980	1984	1985	1986	1987
Total	203,178	455,733	535,764	619,959	721,089	191,977	398,168	422,736	496,329	613,653
Baitfish [1]	22,046	23,598	24,807	25,247	26,000	44,000	47,045	51,280	51,522	71,500
Catfish	76,842	239,800	271,357	326,979	372,000	53,572	191,840	189,194	228,886	277,000
Clams [2]	561	1,698	1,588	2,506	2,215	2,295	4,178	4,717	8,307	9,243
Crawfish	23,917	59,400	64,999	97,500	95,000	12,951	29,700	32,500	48,750	35,525
Freshwater prawns	300	317	267	178	200	1,200	1,698	1,540	893	1,250
Mussels [2]	(NA)	917	928	1,206	1,077	(NA)	1,584	1,248	1,725	1,746
Oysters [2]	23,755	24,549	22,473	24,090	24,315	37,085	38,970	39,977	42,797	43,756
Pacific salmon	7,616	45,086	84,305	74,398	124,308	3,400	17,252	25,439	32,751	55,906
Shrimp	-	528	440	1,354	2,655	-	1,566	1,687	3,408	7,206
Trout	48,141	49,940	50,600	51,000	56,247	37,474	54,435	55,154	55,590	57,336
Other species	(NA)	9,900	14,000	15,500	[3]17,072	(NA)	9,900	20,000	21,700	[3]53,285

- Represents or rounds to zero. NA Not available. [1] Not used for food consumption. [2] Production is shown in meat weight. [3] Includes tropical fish or ornamentals; production of 22,000 pounds and value of $21 million.
Source: U.S. Dept. of Agriculture, Office of Aquaculture, *Agricultural Outlook*, June 1989.

No. 1159. Supply of Selected Fishery Items: 1980 to 1990

[**In millions of pounds.** Totals available for U.S. consumption are supply minus exports plus imports. Round weight is the complete or full weight as caught. Data are preliminary]

ITEM	Unit	1980	1982	1983	1984	1985	1986	1987	1988	1989	1990
Tuna, canned	Canned weight. . .	666	626	713	777	759	873	866	843	1,034	865
Shrimp	Heads-off weight .	425	458	541	584	633	706	773	767	743	734
Clams	Meat weight	102	119	126	144	164	162	151	145	150	152
Salmon, canned	Canned weight. . .	126	71	127	150	113	87	76	59	159	148
American lobster	Round weight. . . .	69	81	93	100	108	113	115	121	94	111
Spiny lobster.	Round weight. . . .	127	127	137	153	154	152	151	139	106	95
Scallops	Meat weight	51	55	67	87	72	70	81	75	81	81
Sardines, canned.	Canned weight. . .	69	67	46	58	76	68	77	63	61	61
Oysters	Meat weight	71	82	81	84	90	91	92	78	67	57
Crab meat, canned	Canned weight. . .	9	7	8	7	8	9	8	8	8	9
Snow crab	Round weight. . . .	54	25	30	23	45	49	29	31	(NA)	(NA)
King crab	Round weight. . . .	133	28	23	13	11	19	14	10	(NA)	(NA)

NA Not available.
Source: U.S. National Oceanic and Atmospheric Administration, National Marine Fisheries Service, *Fisheries of the United States*, annual.

No. 1160. Canned, Fresh, and Frozen Fishery Products: 1980 to 1990

[Fresh fishery products exclude Alaska and Hawaii. Canned fishery products data are for natural pack only. See also *Historical Statistics, Colonial Times to 1970*, series L 338-357 (production data in cases) and L 358]

PRODUCT	PRODUCTION (mil. lb.)						VALUE (mil. dol.)					
	1980	1985	1987	1988	1989	1990 [1]	1980	1985	1987	1988	1989	1990 [1]
Canned, [2]	1,516	1,161	1,186	1,131	1,455	1,178	1,928	1,360	1,562	1,481	1,992	1,562
Tuna	602	545	654	598	686	581	1,144	821	1,016	960	1,058	902
Salmon	200	159	105	88	197	196	376	228	262	219	514	366
Clam products	77	117	117	127	135	110	66	109	88	98	91	76
Mackerel [3]	38	15	15	18	18	23	12	7	6	9	7	11
Sardines, Maine	20	20	13	19	13	13	32	38	22	24	17	17
Shrimp	16	4	4	4	3	1	80	19	22	25	9	3
Crabs	5	1	(Z)	(Z)	1	1	19	2	1	2	3	4
Oysters [4]	(Z)	2	4	3	4	1	(Z)	2	2	2	1	1
Fish fillets and steaks [5] .	202	246	356	378	371	434	261	440	753	767	724	820
Cod	31	57	78	62	73	66	43	89	165	137	136	134
Flounder	49	69	58	53	44	53	87	157	168	163	142	149
Haddock	17	8	9	8	7	7	29	19	32	30	26	24
Ocean perch, Atlantic	7	2	3	2	2	1	9	3	6	5	3	1
Rockfish	14	18	18	36	25	36	13	25	27	57	40	58
Pollock, Atlantic	9	15	18	14	11	12	9	17	30	21	18	21
Pollock, Alaska	(NA)	11	75	110	106	164	(NA)	24	82	110	98	174
Other	74	66	97	93	103	95	71	106	243	244	279	259

NA Not available. Z Less than 500,000 pounds or $500,000. [1] Preliminary. [2] Includes other products, not shown separately. [3] Includes Jack and a small amount of Pacific mackerel. [4] Includes oyster specialties. [5] Fresh and frozen.
Source: U.S. National Oceanic and Atmospheric Administration, National Marine Fisheries Service, *Fisheries of the United States*, annual.

No. 1161. Processed Fishery Products—Production and Value: 1980 to 1990

[Includes Puerto Rico and American Samoa. See *Historical Statistics, Colonial Times to 1970*, series L 362-365, for meal, scrap, and oil]

PRODUCT	PRODUCTION (mil. lb.)						VALUE (mil. dol.)					
	1980	1985	1987	1988	1989	1990 [1]	1980	1985	1987	1988	1989	1990 [1]
Total [2]	(X)	(X)	(X)	(X)	(X)	(X)	4,456	4,936	5,951	5,369	6,889	7,401
Fresh and frozen [3] . .	(X)	(X)	(X)	(X)	(X)	(X)	2,110	3,242	4,041	3,562	4,517	5,430
Fillets	197	232	338	362	345	410	247	408	696	707	656	747
Steaks.	5	13	18	22	26	24	14	32	58	70	86	73
Fish sticks	88	96	99	80	89	65	89	111	143	114	116	75
Fish portions	344	330	324	301	280	294	388	368	446	439	400	414
Breaded shrimp . .	83	95	109	99	121	114	254	355	372	293	404	371
Canned products [4] . .	1,516	1,161	1,186	1,130	1455	1178	1,928	1,360	1,562	1,481	1,992	1,562
Fish and shellfish .	1,009	913	965	907	1110	957	1,782	1,269	1,476	1,388	1,754	1,415
Animal food	507	248	221	223	345	221	146	91	85	93	238	147
Industrial products . .	(X)	(X)	(X)	(X)	(X)	(X)	270	182	212	236	206	207
Meal and scrap. . .	724	722	787	644	618	577	134	84	121	131	115	121
Oil (body and liver)	312	285	298	225	225	282	58	42	36	44	24	29
Solubles	267	323	249	223	233	186	14	19	17	15	18	14
Other	(X)	(X)	(X)	(X)	(X)	(X)	64	37	38	47	50	43

X Not applicable. [1] Preliminary. [2] Includes cured fish. [3] Includes items not shown (dressed fish, shellfish not breaded, specialties). [4] Includes salmon eggs for bait.

Source: U.S. National Oceanic and Atmospheric Administration, National Marine Fisheries Service, *Fisheries of the United States*, annual.

No. 1162. Imports and Exports: 1970 to 1990

[Imports include landings of tuna by foreign vessels at American Samoa. See also *Historical Statistics, Colonial Times to 1970*, series L 227-235]

YEAR	IMPORTS					EXPORTS				
	Total U.S. value (mil. dol.)	Fishery products				Total U.S. value (mil. dol.)	Fishery products			
		Total value (mil. dol.)	Edible products		Noned- ible, value (mil. dol.)		Total value (mil. dol.)	Edible products		Noned- ible, value (mil. dol.)
			Quantity (mil. lb.)	Value (mil. dol.)				Quantity (mil. lb.)	Value (mil. dol.)	
1970.	39,756	1,037	1,873	813	225	43,224	118	140	94	24
1980.	244,007	3,648	2,145	2,687	962	220,783	1,006	574	904	102
1985.	343,553	6,679	2,754	4,064	2,614	213,146	1,084	648	1,010	73
1986.	368,657	7,626	2,979	4,813	2,813	217,304	1,356	735	1,290	66
1987.	402,066	8,818	3,201	[1]5,711	3,106	252,866	1,660	783	1,577	83
1988.	437,140	8,872	2,968	5,442	3,430	320,385	2,275	1,060	2,156	119
1989.	472,977	9,604	3,243	5,498	4,107	(NA)	4,707	1,374	2,283	2,424
1990, prel . . .	490,554	9,048	2,885	5,233	3,815	(NA)	[1]5,639	[1]1,920	[1]2,779	2,860

NA Not available. [1] Record. [2] Increase from 1988 due to change in classification of products in new harmonized system; see text, section 29.

No. 1163. Selected Fishery Products—Imports and Exports: 1985 to 1990

[See *Historical Statistics, Colonial Times to 1970*, series L 312-318, for selected imports]

PRODUCT	QUANTITY (mil. lb.)					VALUE (mil. dol.)				
	1985	1987	1988	1989	1990, prel.	1985	1987	1988	1989	1990, prel.
Imports, edible [1]	2,754	3,201	2,968	3,243	2,885	4,064	5,711	5,442	5,498	5,233
Fresh or frozen [1]	2,229	2,662	2,473	2,612	2,336	3,462	5,022	4,780	4,695	4,521
Salmon [2]	27	42	50	99	104	76	113	155	229	253
Tuna [3]	479	573	550	650	454	266	331	372	402	339
Groundfish fillets, blocks [4] .	640	630	501	484	418	655	1,004	759	702	677
Other fillets and steaks . . .	231	394	320	253	257	334	651	533	490	458
Scallops (meats)	42	40	32	41	40	147	162	116	139	131
Lobster, American, spiny . .	77	81	78	72	74	465	576	547	453	440
Shrimp and prawn	343	461	490	492	492	1,121	1,677	1,726	1,685	1,639
Canned	414	420	424	533	458	466	516	551	642	543
Sardines and herring [5]	40	43	37	41	42	30	34	33	34	31
Tuna	214	212	245	348	285	209	207	299	376	294
Oysters	29	33	27	20	14	30	36	40	37	27
Pickled or salted	57	57	56	51	45	53	75	67	55	49
Cod, haddock, hake, pollock, cusk	35	32	31	17	4	41	61	53	25	5
Nonedible scrap and meal . . .	511	394	265	171	239	62	53	49	32	39
Exports: Canned salmon	48	36	33	40	49	83	86	92	90	104
Fish oil, nonedible	279	249	149	195	222	37	23	22	20	24

[1] Includes products not shown separately. [2] Excludes fillets. [3] Includes landings of tuna by foreign vessels at American Samoa. [4] Includes cod, cusk, haddock, hake, pollock, Atlantic ocean perch, and whiting. [5] Not in oil.

Source of tables 1162 and 1163: U.S. National Oceanic and Atmospheric Administration, National Marine Fisheries Service, *Fisheries of the United States*, annual. Compiled from U.S. Bureau of the Census data.

Figure 25.1
**Wells Drilled and Drilling Costs for Crude Petroleum
and Natural Gas: 1980 to 1990**

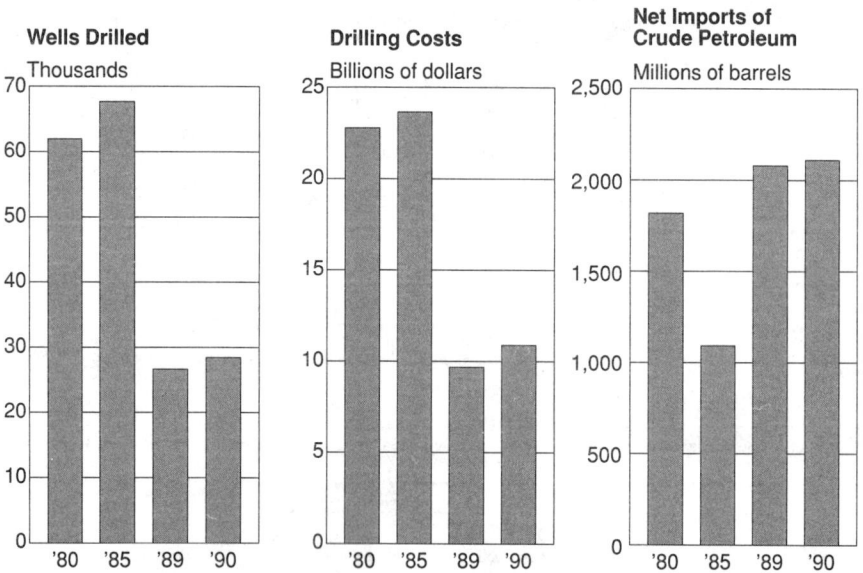

Source: Chart prepared by U.S. Bureau of the Census. For data, see tables 1181 and 1184.

Figure 25.2
U.S. Mineral Production as a Percentage of World: 1989

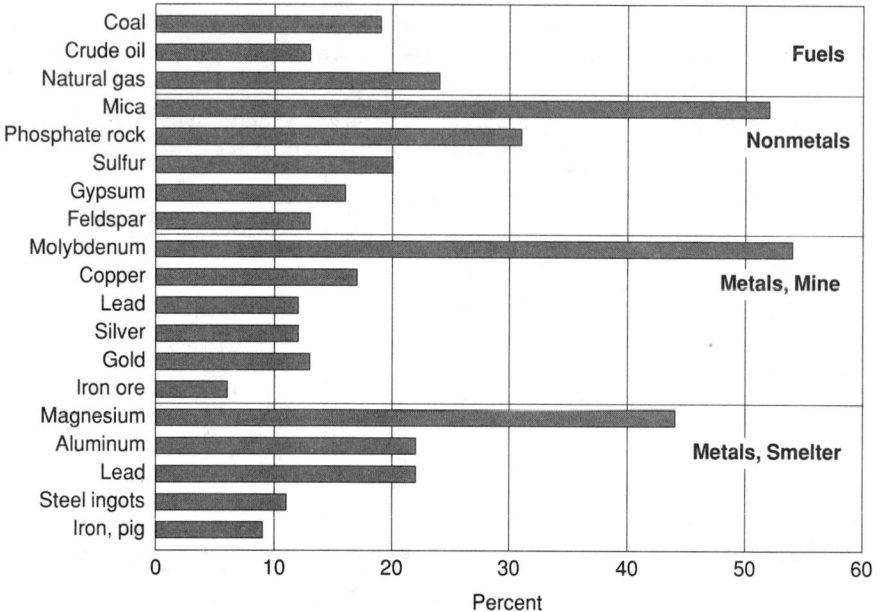

Source: Chart prepared by U.S. Bureau of the Census. For data, see table 1174.

Mining and Mineral Products

This section presents data relating to mineral industries and their products, general summary measures of production and employment, and more detailed data on production, prices, imports and exports, consumption, and distribution for specific industries and products. Data on mining and mineral products may also be found in sections 27 and 31 of this *Abstract;* data on mining employment may be found in section 13.

Mining comprises the extraction of minerals occurring naturally (coal, ores, crude petroleum, natural gas) and quarrying, well operation, milling, refining and processing, and other preparation customarily done at the mine or well site or as a part of extraction activity. (Mineral preparation plants are usually operated together with mines or quarries.) Exploration for minerals is included as is the development of mineral properties.

The principal governmental sources of these data are the *Minerals Yearbook,* published by the Bureau of Mines, Department of the Interior, and various monthly and annual publications of the Energy Information Administration, Department of Energy. See text, section 19 for list of Department of Energy publications. In addition, the Bureau of the Census conducts a census of mineral industries every 5 years. Nongovernment sources include the *Annual Statistical Report* of the American Iron and Steel Institute, Washington, DC; *Metals Week* and the monthly *Engineering and Mining Journal,* issued by the McGraw-Hill Publishing Co., New York, NY; *The Iron Age,* issued weekly by the Chilton Co., Philadelphia, PA; and the *Joint Association Survey of the U.S. Oil and Gas Industry,* conducted jointly by the American Petroleum Institute, Independent Petroleum Association of America, and Mid-Continent Oil and Gas Association.

Mineral statistics, with principal emphasis on commodity detail, have been collected by the Geological Survey or by the Bureau of Mines since 1880. Current data in Bureau of Mines publications include quantity and value of nonfuel minerals produced, sold or used by producers, or shipped; quantity of minerals stocked; crude

In Brief

Petroleum balance, 1990:
Production	6.2 billion barrels
Net imports	2.1 billion barrels
Stocks	1.6 billion barrels

materials treated and prepared minerals recovered; and consumption of mineral raw materials. The U.S. Mine Safety and Health Administration also collects and publishes data on workhours, employment, accidents, and injuries in the mineral industries, except petroleum and natural gas. In October 1977, mineral fuel data collection activities of the Bureau of Mines were transferred to the Energy Information Administration.

Censuses of mineral industries have been conducted by the Bureau of the Census at various intervals since 1840. Beginning with the 1967 census, legislation provides for a census to be conducted every 5th year for years ending in "2" and "7." The censuses provide, for the various types of mineral establishments, information on operating costs, capital expenditures, labor, equipment, and energy requirements in relation to their value of shipments and other receipts. Commodity statistics on many manufactured mineral products are also collected by the Bureau at monthly, quarterly, or annual intervals and issued in its *Current Industrial Reports* series.

In general, figures shown in the individual commodity tables include data for outlying areas and may therefore not agree with detailed table 1168. Except for crude petroleum and refined products, the export and import figures include foreign trade passing through the customs districts of United States and Puerto Rico, but exclude shipments between U.S. territories and the customs districts.

Historical statistics. Tabular headnotes provide cross-references, where applicable, to *Historical Statistics of the United States, Colonial Times to 1970.* See Appendix IV.

Mining and Mineral Production

No. 1164. Summary of Mineral Operations: 1958 to 1987

[Represents mineral operations only. Beginning 1967, excludes single unit establishments without paid employees. See also *Historical Statistics, Colonial Times to 1970*, series M 1-11]

ITEM	Unit	1958	1963	1967	1972	1977	1982	1987
Establishments	Number	36,392	38,651	28,579	25,269	31,359	42,241	33,617
With 20 or more employees	Number	6,045	5,499	5,682	5,312	6,632	(NA)	6,299
Including all operations in manufactures	Number	37,966	40,532	29,688	26,178	31,967	42,585	34,041
Excluding oil and gas extraction	Number	19,444	19,290	13,330	11,680	13,520	12,267	10,707
Employees, total	1,000	734	616	567	595	799	1,114	698
Production workers [1]	1,000	565	482	433	443	593	762	451
All other	1,000	169	134	134	152	206	352	247
Worker-hours, production workers [1]	Million	1,081	973	892	909	1,183	1,578	942
Worker-hours per production workers	1,000	1.9	2.0	2.1	2.1	2.0	2.1	2.1
Payroll, total	Mil. dol	3,749	3,743	4,187	6,226	13,167	28,637	21,739
Wages, production workers [1]	Mil. dol	2,623	2,680	2,888	4,250	9,082	18,030	12,443
Salaries, all other employees	Mil. dol	1,126	1,063	1,299	1,976	4,085	10,607	9,296
Cost of supplies, etc. [2]	Mil. dol	7,521	8,974	10,576	14,884	46,079	109,697	62,423
Value added in mining	Mil. dol	13,385	15,910	19,330	26,471	68,013	188,056	110,959
Metal mining	Mil. dol	1,180	1,418	1,557	2,382	3,504	3,215	4,610
Coal mining	Mil. dol	1,780	1,727	2,091	3,754	11,266	18,631	17,068
Oil and gas extraction	Mil. dol	9,033	11,020	13,394	17,612	48,587	159,937	80,049
Nonmetallic minerals mining	Mil. dol	1,392	1,745	2,288	2,723	4,656	6,273	9,233
Value of shipments and receipts [3]	Mil. dol	16,373	18,804	22,784	36,319	96,375	250,000	157,964
Capital expenditures	Mil. dol	2,804	3,264	4,058	5,036	17,718	47,753	15,418

NA Not available.   [1] See footnote 4, table 1167.   [2] Includes purchased machinery installed.   [3] See footnote 6, table 1167.

Source: U.S. Bureau of the Census, *Census of Mineral Industries, 1972, 1977, 1982,* and *1987.*

No. 1165. Gross National Product (GNP) in Mining: 1980 to 1989

[**In millions of dollars, except percent.** For definition of gross national product, see text, section 14. Based on 1972 Standard Industrial Classification]

MINING INDUSTRY	1980	1982	1983	1984	1985	1986	1987	1988	1989
Current dollars, total	107,257	132,122	118,351	119,362	114,174	74,289	76,836	80,017	80,254
Percent of total GNP	3.9	4.2	3.5	3.2	2.8	1.8	1.7	1.6	1.5
Metal mining	3,836	2,321	2,527	2,216	1,750	1,768	2,449	2,928	3,570
Coal mining	12,909	15,108	14,301	14,597	13,881	13,168	13,189	13,171	13,647
Oil and gas extraction	84,947	110,228	96,412	96,385	92,444	52,449	54,010	55,799	55,660
Nonmetallic minerals, exc. fuels	5,565	4,465	5,111	6,164	6,099	6,904	7,188	8,119	7,377
Constant (1982) dollars, total	143,544	132,122	129,926	137,874	138,950	128,250	127,514	129,536	127,187
Percent of total GNP	4.5	4.2	4.0	3.9	3.8	3.4	3.3	3.2	3.1
Metal mining	2,054	2,321	2,246	2,463	2,423	2,597	2,687	2,625	3,294
Coal mining	13,944	15,108	15,484	16,514	16,391	16,972	18,050	19,567	21,599
Oil and gas extraction	121,505	110,228	107,048	112,647	114,053	102,075	100,172	99,919	95,662
Nonmetallic minerals, exc. fuels	6,041	4,465	5,148	6,250	6,083	6,606	6,605	7,425	6,632

Source: U.S. Bureau of Economic Analysis, *The National Income and Product Accounts of the United States, 1929-82,* and *Survey of Current Business,* July issues.

No. 1166. Mining and Primary Metal Production Indexes: 1970 to 1991

[**1987 = 100.** See also *Historical Statistics, Colonial Times to 1970*, series M 68-71]

INDUSTRY GROUP	1970	1975	1980	1983	1984	1985	1986	1988	1989	1990	1991
Mining	100.4	98.0	110.0	104.8	111.9	109.0	101.0	101.8	100.5	102.6	101.1
Coal	67.2	71.5	90.2	85.4	97.5	96.3	97.1	105.0	105.7	113.2	109.2
Anthracite	274.1	175.0	169.6	115.1	116.9	132.8	120.8	115.6	96.3	103.2	72.7
Bituminous	66.0	71.0	89.7	85.2	97.4	96.1	96.9	105.0	105.8	113.3	109.4
Oil and gas extraction	104.8	101.8	112.1	109.3	115.5	111.9	102.0	99.4	99.5	95.5	95.8
Crude oil and natural gas	122.3	107.5	108.4	102.1	106.4	105.0	101.7	99.2	95.6	93.7	95.5
Oil and gas drilling	65.2	109.7	181.2	197.1	226.6	198.9	109.8	100.0	93.7	109.0	93.3
Metal mining	129.5	106.4	108.8	83.5	91.7	91.3	95.2	122.7	141.4	153.1	150.2
Iron ore	194.4	172.1	149.4	82.0	111.0	104.9	84.4	119.8	123.3	118.1	118.2
Nonferrous ores	111.5	88.7	95.0	84.0	84.8	86.4	99.1	123.3	145.1	160.5	156.9
Copper ore	123.2	101.5	93.1	83.0	85.9	86.9	91.2	113.8	118.4	125.3	129.1
Lead and zinc ores	192.2	189.9	166.7	138.1	109.7	120.1	103.3	119.8	130.4	174.3	185.1
Primary metals, manufacturing	115.2	107.2	110.8	91.0	102.4	101.8	93.8	110.3	109.2	108.4	99.5
Nonferrous metals	77.1	75.3	92.5	84.9	98.2	98.5	97.3	106.2	109.0	106.2	101.5
Copper	135.2	103.0	94.7	85.6	97.0	99.8	99.1	113.5	115.5	120.2	116.7
Aluminum	107.8	105.2	138.7	100.1	122.2	104.7	90.9	117.6	120.8	121.1	123.2
Iron and steel	148.2	133.5	126.0	96.1	105.9	104.5	90.8	113.8	109.3	109.9	98.0

Source: Board of Governors of the Federal Reserve System, *Federal Reserve Bulletin,* monthly.

No. 1167. Mineral Industries—Summary: 1977 to 1987

[N.e.c. means not elsewhere classified. See also *Historical Statistics, Colonial Times to 1970*, series M1-12]

MINERAL INDUSTRY	1977 Establishments	1977 All employees, payroll[1] (mil. dol.)	1977 Value added in mining[2] (mil. dol.)	1982 Estab. Total[7]	1982 Estab. With 20 or more employees	1982 All emp. Number[3] (1,000)	1982 All emp. Payroll[1] (mil. dol.)	1982 Value added in mining[2] (mil. dol.)	1987 Estab. Total	1987 Estab. With 20 or more employees	1987 All emp. Number[3] (1,000)	1987 All emp. Payroll[1] (mil. dol.)	1987 Prod. workers[4] Number[3] (1,000)	1987 Prod. workers Hours[5] (millions)	1987 Prod. workers Wages (mil. dol.)	1987 Value added in mining[2] (mil. dol.)	1987 Value of shipments and receipts[6] (mil. dol.)	1987 Capital expenditures (mil. dol.)
All industries	31,359	13,167	68,013	42,241	(NA)	1,114	28,637	188,056	33,617	6,299	698	21,739	451	942	12,443	110,959	157,964	15,418
Metal mining	1,206	1,485	3,504	1,434	(NA)	68	1,860	3,215	1,027	260	44	1,354	34	68	952	4,610	6,852	899
Iron ores	97	544	1,046	78	40	12	340	770	51	16	7	224	6	11	166	768	1,362	24
Copper ores	133	546	1,067	81	51	22	604	672	61	33	14	405	11	21	283	1,301	2,150	205
Lead and zinc ores	88	105	329	71	28	4	112	201	39	19	2	58	1	3	40	176	268	12
Gold and silver ores	175	71	161	371	80	10	263	650	372	101	13	423	10	21	305	1,814	2,261	555
Ferroalloy ores, except vanadium	56	107	256	69	16	5	150	146	58	10	1	46	1	2	24	24	110	8
Metal mining services	270	52	112	313	(NA)	3	61	90	268	42	3	81	2	5	60	176	251	26
Miscellaneous metal ores	387	234	533	451	91	12	332	686	178	42	4	116	3	5	75	313	449	70
Coal mining	5,451	4,171	11,266	5,087	(NA)	251	6,805	18,631	3,905	1,418	163	5,567	129	259	4,251	17,068	25,955	1,665
Bituminous coal and lignite mining	4,944	4,005	10,837	4,513	1,787	241	6,570	18,041	3,507	1,335	158	5,410	124	249	4,125	16,679	25,347	1,614
Anthracite mining	156	48	116	152	40	3	67	172	107	26	2	41	2	3	32	109	206	12
Coal mining services	351	119	313	422	(NA)	7	168	418	291	57	4	116	3	7	94	280	402	39
Oil and gas extraction	18,447	5,902	48,587	29,974	(NA)	625	17,693	159,937	22,910	3,167	378	11,961	206	437	5,283	80,049	112,363	11,717
Crude petroleum and natural gas	8,573	2,738	38,327	12,087	236	204	8,084	126,035	10,203	1,171	199	7,510	69	142	2,154	67,955	76,518	10,549
Natural gas liquids	692	227	3,286	793	14	14	402	8,865	714	210	13	433	10	20	320	4,025	24,750	383
Oil and gas field services	9,182	2,936	6,974	17,094	(NA)	406	9,207	25,037	11,993	1,786	167	4,018	127	275	2,809	8,069	11,035	786
Drilling oil and gas wells	2,625	1,317	3,307	4,385	(NA)	166	4,007	11,316	2,591	620	55	1,318	46	93	1,012	2,549	3,626	321
Oil, gas exploration services	1,252	220	545	2,934	(NA)	42	391	2,307	1,917	143	17	452	13	27	311	771	1,096	69
Oil, gas field services, n.e.c.	5,305	1,399	3,122	9,775	(NA)	199	4,391	11,415	7,485	1,023	95	2,248	69	154	1,486	4,748	6,373	395
Nonmetallic mining[8]	6,255	1,609	4,656	5,746	(NA)	110	2,278	6,273	5,775	1,454	113	2,858	83	178	1,956	9,233	12,795	1,136
Dimension stone[8]	154	17	39	154	22	2	21	50	149	25	1	25	1	2	18	65	86	4
Crushed and broken stone[9]	2,055	543	1,501	1,932	567	37	701	1,787	2,002	711	44	1,082	33	72	754	3,465	4,768	521
Sand and gravel[9]	2,807	418	1,017	2,758	343	28	520	1,336	2,750	436	33	772	24	51	551	2,320	3,139	238
Clay and related minerals[9]	255	136	358	224	97	11	212	510	197	100	10	272	7	15	165	827	1,249	111
Chemical and fertilizer minerals[9]	205	372	1,433	196	114	26	681	2,237	148	79	16	501	12	24	336	1,999	2,772	192
Nonmetallic minerals, services[9]	176	36	70	167	(NA)	2	35	35	177	23	2	45	2	3	32	119	165	25
Miscellaneous[9]	548	87	238	315	72	6	109	283	352	86	7	162	5	10	101	438	616	46

NA Not available. [1] Gross earnings paid to all employees on payroll. [2] Computed by subtracting cost of supplies, minerals received for preparation, purchased fuel and electric energy, contract work, and purchased machinery from the value of shipments and capital expenditures. [3] Excludes proprietors and firm members of unincorporated concerns. [4] Represents employees up through the working foreman level engaged in manual work. Includes development and exploration workers. [5] Excludes paid vacations, holidays, and sick leave; includes actual overtime hours (not straight-time equivalent). [6] Represents value of shipments of primary and secondary products of the industry and amount received for services performed for other establishments on a contract, fee, or other basis. [7] Redefined to conform to 1987 and pre-1982 definition of establishment; for detail, see source. [8] Excludes data for dimension stone quarries operated in conjunction with dressing plants. [9] Excludes data for mining included in establishments classified in manufacturing industries.

Source: U.S. Bureau of the Census, *Census of Mineral Industries: 1977, 1982,* and *1987,* final industry series reports.

No. 1168. Mineral Production and Value: 1980 to 1990

[Data represent production as measured by mine shipments, mine sales, or marketable production

	MINERAL	Unit	PRODUCTION QUANTITY						
			1980	1985	1986	1987	1988	1989	1990
1	Total mineral production	(X)	(X)	(X)	(X)	(X)	(X)	(X)	(X)
2	**Mineral fuels**	(X)	**(X)**	**(X)**	**(X)**	**(X)**	**(X)**	**(X)**	**(X)**
3	Coal: Bituminous and lignite	Mil. sh. ton.	824	879	886	915	947	977	1,033
4	Pennsylvania anthracite	Mil. sh. ton.	6	5	4	4	4	3	3
5	Natural gas (wet)	Tril. cu. ft.	20.18	17.27	16.86	17.43	1792	1,810	1,856
6	Petroleum (crude).	Mil. bbl. [1]	3,146	3,274	3,168	3,047	2,979	2,779	2,685
7	Uranium [2]	Mil. lb.	43.7	11.3	13.5	13.0	13.1	13.8	8.9
8	**Industrial minerals**	(X)	**(X)**	**(X)**	**(X)**	**(X)**	**(X)**	**(X)**	**(X)**
9	Abrasive stone [3]	Metric tons.	(NA)	(NA)	(D)	11,587	13,313	1,257	3,734
10	Asbestos	1,000 metric ton	(NA)	57	51	51	51	17	(D)
11	Asphalt and related bitumens (native) [4]	1,000 sh. ton	1,252	(D)	(D)	(NA)	(NA)	(NA)	(NA)
12	Barite	1,000 metric ton	(NA)	(NA)	(NA)	(NA)	404	290	439
13	Boron minerals	1,000 metric ton	(NA)	(NA)	(NA)	1,256	1,149	1,114	1,094
14	Bromine	Mil. kilograms	(NA)	(NA)	(NA)	(NA)	163	175	177
15	Calcium chloride	1,000 sh. ton	581	(D)	(D)	(D)	(D)	(D)	(D)
16	Carbon dioxide, natural (estimate)	Mil. cu. ft.	1,628	-	-	-	-	-	-
17	Cement: Portland	Mil. sh. ton.	71.6	74.3	75.2	74.9	74.1	74.2	75.6
18	Masonry	Mil. sh. ton.	3.0	3.2	3.5	3.7	3.6	3.3	3.3
19	Clays	1,000 metric ton	(NA)	(NA)	(NA)	43,234	44,515	42,254	42,904
20	Diatomite	1,000 metric ton	(NA)	(NA)	(NA)	597	629	617	631
21	Feldspar	1,000 metric ton	(NA)	(NA)	(NA)	(NA)	649	654	630
22	Fluorspar	Metric ton	(NA)	(NA)	(NA)	64	64	66	64
23	Garnet (abrasive)	1,000 sh. ton	26.9	36.7	32.3	38	43	43	47
24	Gem stones (estimate)	(X)	(NA)	(NA)	(NA)	(NA)	(NA)	(NA)	(NA)
25	Gypsum	Mil. sh. ton.	12.4	14.4	15.4	15.6	16.4	17.6	16.4
26	Helium [6]	Mil. cu. ft.	1,458	1,865	1,941	2,230	2,574	2,879	3,059
27	Lime	Mil. sh. ton.	19.0	15.7	14.5	15.7	17.1	17.2	17.5
28	Magnesium compounds [7]	1,000 sh. ton	(D)	(D)	(D)	(D)	(D)	(D)	(D)
29	Mica: Scrap.	1,000 metric ton	(NA)	(NA)	(NA)	146	130	119	109
30	Peat.	1,000 sh. ton	788	882	1,038	958	908	775	795
31	Perlite	1,000 sh. ton	638	507	507	533	645	601	639
32	Phosphate rock	Mil. metric ton.	(NA)	50.8	40.3	41.0	45.4	49.8	46.3
33	Potassium salts (K_2O equivalent)	1,000 metric ton	(NA)	1,266	1,147	1,262	1,521	1,595	1,716
34	Pumice.	1,000 metric ton	(NA)	(NA)	(NA)	356	353	424	443
35	Pyrites	1,000 lg. ton.	834	(D)	(D)	(D)	(D)	(D)	(D)
36	Salt (common).	Mil. sh. ton.	40.4	40.1	36.7	36.5	38.0	38.4	40.7
37	Sand and gravel.	Mil. sh. ton.	793	830	910	923	952	927	939
38	Sodium carbonate (natural)	1,000 sh. ton	(D)	(D)	(D)	(D)	9,632	(D)	(D)
39	Sodium sulfate (natural).	1,000 metric ton	(NA)	(NA)	(NA)	(NA)	361	340	349
40	Stone [8]	Mil. sh. ton.	982	1,002	1,024	1,200	1,248	1,213	1,222
41	Sulfur: Frasch mines (shipments)	1,000 metric ton	(NA)	4,678	4,180	3,610	4,341	3,780	3,676
42	Talc, soapstone, pyrophyllite	1,000 metric ton	(NA)	(NA)	(NA)	(NA)	1,234	1,253	(D)
43	Tripoli.	1,000 metric ton	(NA)	(NA)	(NA)	(NA)	100	105	94
44	Vermiculite	1,000 sh. ton	337	314	317	303	304	293	230
45	Nonmetallic minerals, undistributed [9]	(X)	(X)	(X)	(X)	(X)	(X)	(X)	(X)
46	**Metals.**	(X)	**(X)**	**(X)**	**(X)**	**(X)**	**(X)**	**(X)**	**(X)**
47	Antimony ore and concentrate	Metric ton [10].	311	(D)	(D)	(D)	(D)	(D)	(D)
48	Bauxite (dried)	1,000 metric ton [12]	1,559	674	510	576	588	(D)	(D)
49	Copper [2]	1,000 metric ton	1,181	1,106	1,147	1,244	1,417	1,498	1,587
50	Gold [2]	1,000 kilograms	(NA)	(NA)	(NA)	154	201	266	290
51	Iron ore [13]	Mil. metric ton [14].	70.7	50.2	42.0	48.0	57.1	58.3	57.0
52	Lead [2]	1,000 metric ton	550	414	340	311	385	411	474
53	Manganiferous ore [15]	1,000 sh. ton [14]	174	20	14	(D)	(D)	(D)	(D)
54	Mercury	76 lb. flasks	30,657	16,530	(D)	(D)	(D)	(D)	(D)
55	Molybdenum [16]	Mil. lb.	149	112	95	70	46	61	62
56	Nickel [17]	1,000 sh. ton	11.0	6.0	2.0	-	-	0.4	4.1
57	Silver [2]	Metric ton	(NA)	(NA)	(NA)	1,241	1,661	2,007	2,170
58	Titanium concentrate: Ilmenite [2]	1,000 metric ton [14]	539	(D)	(D)	(D)	(D)	(D)	(D)
59	Tungsten ore and concentrate	Metric ton [18]	(NA)	983	817	(D)	(D)	(D)	(D)
60	Vanadium [2]	Sh. ton	4,806	(D)	(D)	(D)	(D)	(D)	(D)
61	Zinc mine production [2]	1,000 metric ton	317	227	203	216	244	276	515
62	Metals, undistributed [9]	(X)	(X)	(X)	(X)	(X)	(X)	(X)	(X)

- Represents zero.   D Withheld to avoid disclosing individual company data.   NA Not available.   X Not applicable. [1] 42 gal. bbl.   [2] Recoverable content of ores, etc.   [3] Crude production. Grindstones, pulpstones, millstones, grinding pebbles, sharpening stones, and tubemill liners.   [4] Contains bituminous limestone and sandstone, and gilsonite.   [5] Value included in "Industrial minerals, undistributed."   [6] 1980, crude and refined; thereafter, refined only.   [7] From sea water and brines, except for metals (M_gO equiv.).   [8] Excludes abrasive stone, bituminous limestone and sandstone, and ground soapstone, all included elsewhere in table. Includes calcareous marl and slate.

and Principal Producing States, 1990

(including consumption by producers). See *Historical Statistics, Colonial Times to 1970,* series M 13-37 for selected values]

PRODUCTION VALUE (mil.dol.)							Principal producing States ranked by quantity, **1990**	
1980	**1985**	**1986**	**1987**	**1988**	**1989**	**1990**		
146,750	168,154	117,408	123,840	119,102	128,603	141,741	(X)	1
121,612	**144,847**	**93,944**	**97,499**	**89,088**	**96,378**	**108,422**	(X)	2
20,197	22,063	21,001	21,050	20,827	21,268	22,719	WY, KY, WV, PA.	3
259	215	190	157	159	142	133	PA.	4
32,090	43,343	32,717	29,008	30,287	30,627	31,658	TX, LA, OK, NM.	5
67,930	78,871	39,632	46,930	37,479	44,071	53,772	AK, TX, CA, LA, OK.	6
1,136	356	405	356	336	270	140	TX, WY, NM.	7
16,213	**17,678**	**17,647**	**18,894**	**19,805**	**20,357**	**20,891**	(X)	8
2	1	(D)	1	1	-	-	AR, WI, OH.	9
31	21	17	17	(D)	(D)	(D)	CA and VT.	10
25	(5)	(NA)	(NA)	(NA)	(NA)	(NA)	(NA)	11
66	22	12	16	16	13	16	GA, NV, MO, CA.	12
367	405	426	475	430	430	436	CA.	13
95	80	93	107	144	189	97	AR.	14
48	(5)	(5)	(5)	(5)	(5)	(5)	MI and CA.	15
3	-	(NA)	(NA)	(NA)	(NA)	(NA)	(X)	16
3,613	3,817	3,760	3,647	3,576	3,592	3,683	CA, TX, PA, MI.	17
189	213	232	260	244	229	225	IN, FL, MI, PA.	18
899	1,011	1,095	1,202	1,401	1,515	1,620	GA, CA, WY, SC.	19
101	127	128	134	144	137	138	CA, NV, WA, OR.	20
23	23	26	26	28	28	27	NC, CA, CT, GA.	21
13	(D)	(D)	12	(D)	(D)	(D)	IL, UT, NV.	22
2	3	3	4	5	4	7	ID and NY.	23
7	7	9	21	44	43	53	(X)	24
103	112	100	107	109	128	100	IA, MI, OK, NV.	25
30	70	73	83	95	107	113	KS, WY, TX, NM.	26
843	809	758	786	818	852	902	MO, OH, PA, KY.	27
(5)	(5)	(5)	(5)	(5)	(5)	(5)	MI, CA, FL, DE.	28
6	6	7	8	7	6	6	NC, GA, NM, SC.	29
16	22	24	21	20	18	19	MI, FL, MN, IL	30
17	17	16	17	18	16	15	NM, AZ, CA, ID.	31
1,257	1,236	897	793	888	1,083	1,075	FL, NC, ID, TN.	32
(NA)	178	152	196	240	272	303	NM, UT, CA, MI.	33
4	5	6	5	4	8	11	CA, OR, AZ, NM.	34
14	(5)	(5)	(5)	(5)	(5)	(5)	AZ.	35
656	740	665	684	680	777	827	NY, OH, LA, MI.	36
2,289	2,812	3,107	3,367	3,514	3,659	3,686	CA, TX, MI, AZ.	37
(5)	(5)	(5)	594	(5)	(5)	(5)	WY and CA.	38
36	36	34	33	31	31	34	CA, TX, UT.	39
3,394	4,225	4,228	5,439	5,558	5,326	5,591	PA, VA, FL, GA.	40
721	574	509	387	431	379	335	TX and LA.	41
26	29	31	29	31	(D)	(D)	MT, TX, NC, VT.	42
1	(D)	1	1	1	3	3	IL, AR, OK, PA.	43
24	32	34	33	34	33	19	SC, MT, VA.	44
941	1,046	994	375	(NA)	(NA)	(NA)	(X)	45
8,921	**5,629**	**5,817**	**7,447**	**10,209**	**11,868**	**12,428**	(X)	46
(11)	(11)	(11)	(NA)	(NA)	(NA)	(NA)	ID.	47
22	13	10	11	11	(D)	(D)	AR and AL.	48
2,667	1,633	1,671	2,262	3,764	4,324	4,310	AZ, NM, UT, MT.	49
594	771	1,377	2,216	2,831	3,269	3,610	NV, CA, UT, SD.	50
2,544	2,077	1,473	1,503	1,717	1,840	1,741	MN, MI, MO, UT.	51
515	174	165	247	315	356	481	MO, AK, ID, CO.	52
2	(D)	(D)	(D)	(D)	(D)	(D)	SC.	53
12	(D)	(D)	(D)	(D)	(D)	(D)	NV, UT, CA.	54
1,344	348	241	179	271	427	346	CO, AZ, ID, MT.	55
(11)	(D)	(D)	-	-	5	33	OR.	56
667	242	189	280	349	355	336	NV, ID, AK, MT.	57
32	(11)	(11)	(11)	(11)	(11)	(11)	FL and CA.	58
50	9	6	(D)	(D)	(D)	(D)	CA.	59
64	(11)	(11)	(11)	(11)	(11)	(11)	CO, ID, AR, UT.	60
262	202	170	200	324	499	847	AK, TN, NY, MO.	61
145	2,235	1,563	1,637	(NA)	(NA)	(NA)	(X)	62

[9] Comprises value of items that cannot be disclosed. [10] Antimony content. [11] Included with "Metals, undistributed." [12] Dried equivalent. [13] Represents shipments; includes byproduct ores. [14] Gross weight. [15] 5 to 35 percent manganiferous ore. [16] Content of concentrate. [17] Content of ore and concentrate. [18] Tungsten content.

Source: U.S. Bureau of Mines, *Minerals Yearbook.* Mineral fuels: U.S. Energy Information Administration, *Annual Energy Review, Uranium Industry Annual; Petroleum Supply Annual,* vol. 1; *Natural Gas Annual;* and *Quarterly Coal Report.*

No. 1169. Nonfuel Mineral Commodities—Summary: 1991

[Preliminary estimates]

MINERAL	Unit	MINERAL DISPOSITION Production	Exports	Net import reliance [1] (percent)	Consumption, apparent	Average price per unit (dollars)	Employment (number)
Aluminum	1,000 metric tons	5,400	1,700	[2]	5,000	[3]60.00	23,600
Antimony (contained)	Metric tons	[4]36,500	7,000	57	39,700	[3]82.00	115
Arsenic	Metric tons	-	-	100	20,000	[5]68.00	(NA)
Asbestos	1,000 metric tons	(D)	22	95	37	(D)	70
Barite	1,000 metric tons	430	10	70	1,420	36.80	400
Bauxite and alumina	1,000 metric tons	(D)	1,415	100	4,595	15-20	35
Beryllium (contained)	Metric tons	176	25	[2]	170	[6]225.00	425
Bismuth (contained)	Metric tons	(D)	90	(D)	[7]1,300	3.10	30
Boron (B_2O_3 content)	1,000 Metric tons	608	620	[2]	340	272.00	1,100
Bromine (contained)	1,000 metric tons	170	19	1	172	[3]1.24	300
Cadmium (contained)	Metric tons	1,600	300	54	3,500	[8]2.05	190
Cement	1,000 sh. tons	71,127	600	11	79,014	[9]50.00	18,000
Cesium (contained)	Kilograms	(D)	(NA)	100	(NA)	[10]4,420.00	25
Chromium	1,000 metric tons	[11]84	10	80	420	[12]130.00	(NA)
Clays	1,000 sh. tons	43,000	4,000	[2]	39,000	[5]	11,000
Columbium (contained)	1,000 lb	-	250	100	7,300	[13]2.83	(NA)
Copper (Mine, contained)	1,000 metric tons	1,630	260	[2]	2,120	[14]110.00	13,000
Diamond (industrial)	Mil. carats	93.2	83.2	[2]	83.3	[15]0.81	(NA)
Diatomite	1,000 metric tons	621	150	[2]	471	[16]219.00	1,000
Feldspar	1,000 metric tons	573	6	2	583	[16]41.88	450
Fluorspar	1,000 metric tons	145	20	87	460	(NA)	180
Gallium (contained)	Kilograms		(NA)	(NA)	(NA)	525.00	20
Garnet (industrial)	Metric tons	50,930	10,000	[2]	43,636	60-2,000	150
Gem stones	Mil. dol.	128.2	1,901	98	2,867	[17]	800
Germanium (contained)	Kilograms	15,000	(NA)	(NA)	[7]33,000	[18]1,060.00	100
Gold (gold contained)	Metric tons	300	270	(NA)	260	[19]370.00	15,000
Graphite (crude)	1,000 metric tons	-	14	100	15	[20]617.00	(NA)
Gypsum	1,000 sh. tons	15,300	40	30	23,000	[21]6.20	6,800
Indium	Metric tons	(NA)	(NA)	(NA)	[7]30	[22]218.00	(NA)
Iodine	metric tons	1,926	2,900	14	2,200	[23]10.70	50
Iron ore (usable)	Mil. metric tons	53.7	2.0	14	62.3	[24]72.5-74	7,300
Iron and steel scrap (metal)	Mil. sh. tons	72.6	18	[2]	63.2	[25]94.54	105,000
Iron and steel slag (metal)	1,000 sh. tons	25,000	6	(NA)	(NA)	[21]5.62	3,000
Lead (contained)	1,000 metric tons	1,180	80	4	1,220	[3]34.00	2,400
Lime	1,000 sh. tons	16,800	49	1	16,920	[9]51.75	5,500
Magnesium metal	1,000 metric tons	[26]130	50	[2]	133	[27]1.43	450
Magnesium compounds	1,000 metric tons	510	60	15	600	(NA)	650
Manganese	1,000 sh. tons	-	40	100	660	[28]3.70	(NA)
Mercury	Metric tons	50	300	(D)	(D)	[29]110.00	3
Mica, scrap and flake	1,000 metric tons	178	5	9	92	[9]55.00	80
Molybdenum	1,000 metric tons	60	42	[2]	22	[10]7.39	1,000
Nickel	1,000 sh. tons	8.1	36	74	160	[30]3.80	295
Nitrogen (fixed)-ammonia	1,000 sh. tons	14,000	650	14	16,279	[31]115.00	2,500
Peat	1,000 sh. tons	770	-	44	1,393	[9]24.40	650
Perlite	1,000 sh. tons	603	30	5	663	[9]28.42	120
Phosphate rock	1,000 metric tons	47,000	6,000	[2]	41,450	[9]24.00	5,800
Platinum-group, refined	Kilograms	55,000	30,000	88	105,924	[32]380.00	469
Potash (K_2O equivalent)	1,000 metric tons	1,770	650	67	5,343	131.00	2,001
Pumice and pumicite	1,000 metric tons	439	15	22	559	[16]25.92	55
Rare-earth metals (REO content)	Metric tons	22,700	(NA)	16	26,920	[33]2.87	393
Salt	1,000 sh. tons	40,000	2,000	11	44,300	[34]100.00	4,150
Sand and gravel:							
Construction	Million sh. tons	814.1	0.5	[2]	814.6	[9]3.58	41,000
Industrial	1,000 sh. tons	27,420	1,600	[2]	25,765	[9]15.12	1,500
Silicon	1,000 metric tons	369	34	22	475	[35]38.80	2,400
Silver	Metric tons	1,800	1,500	(NA)	3,600	[19]4.00	2,000
Sodium carbonate (soda ash)	1,000 metric tons	9,300	2,650	[2]	6,807	[36]98.00	2,800
Sodium sulfate	1,000 metric tons	650	110	6	690	[37]114.00	250
Stone (crushed)	Mil. sh. tons	1,081	5	-	1,080	[9]4.53	74,000
Sulfur (all forms)	1,000 metric tons	10,600	1,300	16	12,400	[38]70.00	3,100

- Represents or rounds to zero.   D Withheld to avoid disclosure.   NA Not available.   [1] Net import reliance as a percent of consumption.   [2] Net exporter.   [3] Average cents per pound, except bromine (dollars per kilogram).   [4] Refinery production.   [5] Metal, 99% As_2O_3.   [6] Metal, vacuum-cast ingot.   [7] Reported consumption.   [8] Average dollars per pound, 1 to 5 short ton lots.   [9] Dollars per short ton.   [10] Metal, dollars per pound.   [11] Secondary production.   [12] Turkish, dollars per metric ton.   [13] Columbite, dollars per pound.   [14] Domestic producer cathode, cents per pound.   [15] Dollars, per carat.   [16] Dollars per metric ton.   [17] Variable, depending on size, type and quality.   [18] Zone refined, first reduction quality.   [19] Dollars, per ounce.   [20] Price of flake imports, average dollars per metric ton of foreign imports.   [21] F.O.B. mine, average dollar per short ton.   [22] Average annual dollars per kilogram (99.97% indium).   [23] Average c.i.f. value, dollars per kilogram crude.   [24] Lake Superior pellets. Cents per long ton unit of iron, delivered rail of vessel at lower lake ports.   [25] Average dollars per long ton delivered, No. 1 heavy melting composite price, Iron Age average, Pittsburg, Philadelphia, Chicago.   [26] Primary.   [27] Yearend price, dollars per pound.   [28] Average value, 46%-48% Mn metalurgical ore, dollars per metric ton unit contained Mn, c.i.f. U.S. ports.   [29] Price per flask.   [30] Average price, London Metal Exchange cash, dollars per pound.   [31] Dollars per short ton, yearend quoted, f.o.b. gulf coast.   [32] Dealer price of platinum metal, average dollars per ounce; Palladium price was $89 per ounce; rhodium price was $4,412 per ounce.   [33] Yearend dollars per kilogram, bastnasite concentrate, REO basis.   [34] Vacuum and open pan.   [35] Average cents per pound silicon content, ferrosilicon, 50% Si.   [36] Quoted yearend price, dense, bulk, f.o.b. Green River, WY, dollars per short ton.   [37] Quoted price, bulk, f.o.b. works, East, dollars per short ton.   [38] Reported average dollars per metric ton of elemental sulfur, f.o.b., mine and/or plant.

Source: U.S. Bureau of Mines, *Mineral Commodity Summaries*, annual.

No. 1170. Value of Domestic Nonfuel Mineral Production: 1980 to 1990

[In millions of dollars.]

STATE	1980	1985	1988	1989	1990	Principal minerals in order of value
U.S. [1].....	25,141	23,303	30,015	30,015	33,319	(X)
	1,581	1,964	2,505	2,450	2,475	(X)
Northeast						
N.E........	268	325	525	455	443	(X)
ME	37	41	68	65	63	Sand and gravel, cement, and stone.
NH	25	33	[2]53	33	35	Sand and gravel, stone, and gem stones.
VT........	43	50	77	89	82	Stone, sand and gravel, and talc.
MA	91	117	192	144	127	Stone, sand and gravel, and lime.
RI	6	12	[2]17	11	18	Sand and gravel, stone, and gem stones.
CT.......	66	72	118	113	118	Stone, sand and gravel, and feldspar.
M.A	1,313	1,639	1,980	1,995	2,032	(X)
NY.	496	657	696	745	773	Stone, salt, and cement.
NJ.	149	178	242	249	229	Stone, sand and gravel, and zircon.
PA.	668	804	1,042	1,001	1,030	Stone, cement, and sand and gravel.
	6,611	6,034	6,737	6,980	7,117	(X)
Midwest......						
E.N.C	2,930	2,869	3,524	3,551	3,476	(X)
OH	562	594	737	699	729	Stone, sand and gravel, and salt.
IN	288	303	406	434	432	Stone, cement, and sand and gravel.
IL	443	460	588	633	665	Stone, cement, and sand and gravel.
MI	1,485	1,387	1,588	1,599	1,438	Iron ore, cement, and sand and gravel.
WI	152	125	205	185	212	Stone, sand and gravel, and lime.
W.N.C.....	3,681	3,165	3,213	3,429	3,641	(X)
MN	1,782	1,548	1,267	1,376	1,470	Iron ore, sand and gravel, and stone.
IA	252	228	290	283	316	Cement, stone, and sand and gravel.
MO	1,055	735	968	1,050	1,094	Lead, stone, and cement.
ND	22	24	19	14	27	Sand and gravel, lime, and stone.
SD.......	228	208	286	284	298	Gold, cement, and sand and gravel.
NE.......	80	100	91	104	90	Cement, sand and gravel, and stone.
KS.......	262	322	292	318	346	Salt, stone, and cement.
	5,585	6,292	7,099	7,503	7,718	(X)
South						
S.A.......	3,454	3,998	4,644	4,985	5,093	(X)
DE.......	[2]2	[2]4	[2]6	6	7	Sand and gravel and gem stones.
MD	186	258	363	342	369	Stone, sand and gravel, and cement.
VA.......	305	381	495	509	507	Stone, sand and gravel, and cement.
WV	106	105	127	125	136	Stone, cement, and sand and gravel.
NC	380	466	529	582	565	Stone, phosphate rock, and lithium minerals.
SC	195	276	358	425	450	Stone, cement, and gold.
GA	771	946	1,374	1,387	1,495	Clays, stone, and cement.
FL........	1,509	1,562	1,392	1,608	1,564	Phosphate rock, stone, and cement.
E.S.C	1,030	1,251	1,493	1,537	1,694	(X)
KY.......	204	268	345	331	359	Stone, lime, and cement.
TN.......	394	473	586	638	663	Stone, zinc, and cement.
AL.......	328	407	459	461	561	Stone, cement, and lime.
MS	104	103	103	108	112	Sand and gravel, clays, and cement.
W.S.C	1,101	1,043	962	981	931	(X)
AR.......	293	270	307	382	303	Bromine, stone, and sand and gravel.
LA.......	584	521	435	380	368	Sulfur, salt, and sand and gravel.
OK	224	252	220	219	260	Stone, cement, and iodine.
TX.......	1,735	1,737	1,469	1,462	1,457	Cement, stone, and magnesium metal.
	9,629	7,276	12,205	13,814	14,546	(X)
West						
Mt	7,223	4,669	8,665	9,985	10,372	(X)
MT	280	200	548	566	568	Gold, copper, and molybdenum.
ID	522	359	291	365	400	Phosphate rock, silver, and molybdenum.
WY	761	551	710	827	911	Soda ash, clays, and helium.
CO	1,265	408	364	458	386	Molybdenum, sand and gravel, and cement.
NM	766	657	1,019	1,122	1,098	Copper, potash, and sand and gravel.
AZ.	2,471	1,550	2,773	3,046	3,065	Bromine, stone, and sand and gravel.
UT.......	764	313	1,015	1,290	1,334	Copper, gold, and magnesium metal.
NV.......	394	631	1,945	2,310	2,611	Gold, silver, and sand and gravel.
Pac	2,406	2,607	3,540	3,828	4,173	(X)
WA	207	222	459	481	473	Sand and gravel, gold, and magnesium metal.
OR	152	130	178	188	237	Stone, sand and gravel, and cement.
CA.......	1,872	2,112	2,709	2,854	2,780	Sand and gravel, cement, and boron.
AK.......	115	90	119	213	577	Zinc, lead, and silver.
HI	60	53	75	92	106	Stone, cement, and sand and gravel.

X Not applicable.   [1] Includes undistributed not shown separately.   [2] Partial data only.

Source: U.S. Bureau of Mines, *Minerals Yearbook*, annual

No. 1171. Mineral Industries—Gross Assets and Capital Expenditures: 1972 to 1987

[In millions of dollars]

INDUSTRY AND YEAR	END OF YEAR GROSS VALUE OF DEPRECIABLE ASSETS					CAPITAL EXPENDITURES					
	Total [1]	Buildings and other structures	Machinery and equipment	Mineral exploration and development [1]	Mineral land and rights [1]	Total [1]	New buildings and other structures	New machinery and equipment	Used buildings and other structures	Used machinery and equipment	Mineral exploration and development [1]
Mineral industries: [2]											
1972	21,690	4,244	15,038	([3])	[3]2,409	2,802	317	1,407	([3])	[3]128	230
1977	44,664	6,099	33,068	2,625	2,871	6,802	785	5,068	30	399	520
1982	94,613	10,228	73,419	5,036	5,930	13,472	1,229	10,551	78	937	677
1987	84,286	9,314	64,143	5,034	5,795	4,869	349	3,234	88	797	401
Crude oil, nat. gas:											
1972	47,500	(NA)	(NA)	(NA)	(NA)	2,954	403	842	([3])	[3]44	1,666
1977	94,414	(NA)	(NA)	(NA)	(NA)	10,916	571	2,269	14	93	7,969
1982	233,052	(NA)	(NA)	(NA)	(NA)	34,281	1,967	5,550	20	215	26,529
1987	(NA)	(NA)	(NA)	(NA)	(NA)	10,549	590	3,176	18	218	6,548

NA Not available. [1] Excludes data for mineral exploration and development, and mineral land and rights portions for mining service industries and natural gas liquids industry. [2] Excludes crude petroleum and natural gas. [3] Not collected separately. Data for mineral exploration and development are combined with mineral land and rights. Data for used buildings and other structures are combined with used machinery and equipment.

Source: U.S. Bureau of the Census, *Census of Mineral Industries, 1987.*

No. 1172. Mineral Industries—Employment, Hours, and Earnings: 1985 to 1991

ITEM	Unit	1985	1990	1991	ITEM	Unit	1985	1990	1991
All mining:					Avg. weekly hours.	No . . .	44.2	43.9	44.5
All employees	1,000 .	927	711	697	Avg. weekly earnings. . .	Dol . . .	489	568	602
Production workers	1,000 .	658	510	496	Metal mining:				
Avg. weekly hours.	No . . .	43.4	44.1	44.4	All employees	1,000 .	46	59	59
Avg. weekly earnings. . .	Dol . . .	520	604	631	Production workers	1,000 .	34	46	47
Coal mining:					Avg. weekly hours.	No . . .	40.9	42.7	42.9
All employees	1,000 .	187	148	139	Avg. weekly earnings. . .	Dol . . .	547	601	640
Production workers	1,000 .	153	120	113	Nonmetallic minerals,				
Avg. weekly hours.	No . . .	41.3	44.0	44.6	except fuels:				
Avg. weekly earnings. . .	Dol . . .	626	736	763	All employees	1,000 .	110	111	107
Oil and gas extraction:					Production workers	1,000 .	84	84	80
All employees	1,000 .	583	394	392	Avg. weekly hours.	No . . .	44.5	645.3	44.6
Production workers	1,000 .	387	260	257	Avg. weekly earnings. . .	Dol . . .	453	524	530

Source: U.S. Bureau of Labor Statistics, *Bulletin 2370* and *Employment and Earnings*, monthly.

No. 1173. Selected Mineral Products—Average Prices: 1970 to 1990

[Excludes Alaska and Hawaii, except as noted. See *Historical Statistics, Colonial Times to 1970*, series M 96, M 139, M 209, M 248, and M 262, for bituminous coal, crude petroleum, iron ore, lead, and aluminum, respectively]

YEAR	Tantalum (dol. per lb.) [1]	Copper, electrolytic [2] (cents per lb.)	Platinum [3] (dol./ troy oz.)	Gold (dol./ fine oz.)	Silver (dol./ fine oz.)	Lead [4] (cents per lb.)	Tin (New York) [5] (cents per lb.)	Zinc [6] (cents per lb.)	Sulfur [7] (dol./ metric ton)	Bituminous coal [8] (dol./ short ton)	Crude petroleum [8] (dol./ bbl.)	Natural gas [8] (dol./ 1,000 cu. ft.)
1970	9.15	58	133	36	1.77	15.7	174.2	15.3	[9]22.77	6.26	3.18	0.17
1975	18.32	64	164	161	4.42	21.5	339.8	39.0	[9]44.91	19.23	7.67	0.45
1976	20.31	69	162	125	4.35	23.1	379.8	37.1	[9]45.72	19.43	8.19	0.58
1977	25.64	66	162	148	4.62	30.7	534.6	34.4	[9]44.38	19.82	8.57	0.79
1978	34.19	66	237	194	5.40	33.7	629.6	31.0	45.17	21.78	9.00	0.91
1979	80.00	92	352	308	11.09	52.6	753.9	37.3	55.75	23.65	12.64	1.18
1980	126.37	101	439	613	20.64	42.5	846.0	37.4	89.06	24.52	21.59	1.59
1981	99.51	84	475	460	10.52	36.5	733.0	44.6	111.48	26.29	31.77	1.98
1982	49.95	73	475	376	7.95	25.5	653.9	38.5	108.27	27.14	28.52	2.46
1983	30.60	77	475	424	11.44	21.7	654.8	41.4	87.24	25.85	26.19	2.59
1984	37.44	67	475	361	8.14	25.6	623.8	48.6	94.31	25.51	25.88	2.66
1985	33.68	67	475	318	6.14	19.1	596.0	40.4	106.46	25.10	24.09	2.51
1986	23.74	66	519	368	5.47	22.1	383.2	38.0	105.22	23.70	12.51	1.94
1987	27.08	83	600	448	7.01	35.9	418.8	41.9	89.78	23.00	15.40	1.67
1988	47.37	120	600	438	6.53	37.1	441.4	60.2	85.95	22.00	12.58	1.69
1989	44.93	131	600	383	5.50	39.4	520.2	83.0	88.00	21.76	15.86	1.69
1990, prel . .	38.06	123	600	387	4.82	46.02	366.3	(NA)	(NA)	22.00	20.03	1.72

NA Not available. [1] Dollars per pound of tantalum content. [2] Average producer prices, delivered. [3] Average annual producer prices. [4] 1970, New York prices; beginning 1975, nationwide delivered basis. [5] Straits tin through 1975; thereafter, composite price. [6] Prime western. Beginning 1975, delivered price. [7] F.O.B. works. [8] Average value at the point of production. Source: U.S. Energy Information Administration, *Annual Energy Review.* [9] Per long ton.

Source: Except as noted, U.S. Bureau of Mines, *Mineral Facts and Problems*, 1980 edition; and *Mineral Commodity Summaries*, annual.

No. 1174. Principal Fuels, Nonmetals, and Metals-U.S. Production as Percent of World Production: 1980 to 1990

MINERAL	Unit	WORLD PRODUCTION				PERCENT U.S. OF WORLD			
		1980	1985	1989, prel.	1990, est.	1980	1985	1989, prel.	1990, est.
Fuels: [1]									
Coal	Bil. sh. ton	4.2	4.8	5.2	(NA)	20	18	19	(NA)
Petroleum (crude)	Bil. bbl	21.7	19.6	21.8	(NA)	14	17	13	(NA)
Natural gas (dry, marketable).	Tril. cu. ft	53.1	62.0	71.9	(NA)	37	26	24	(NA)
Natural gas plant liquids	Bil. bbl	1.4	1.5	1.7	(NA)	43	38	35	(NA)
Nonmetals:									
Asbestos	Mil. metric ton . .	5	4	4	4	2	1	(Z)	(D)
Barite	Mil. short ton . . .	8.3	6.7	6.1	6.1	27	11	5	8
Feldspar.	Mil. short ton . . .	3.5	4.5	5.7	5.5	20	16	13	13
Fluorspar	Mil. short ton . . .	5.5	5.5	6.2	5.6	2	1	1	1
Gypsum	Mil. short ton . . .	86.4	97.3	109.0	107.7	13	15	16	15
Mica (incl. scrap) . . . . [2] . . .	1,000 short ton .	251.6	281.1	253.0	236.5	46	49	52	51
Nitrogen, agricultural [2]	Mil. short ton . . .	81.2	100.3	109.7	107.9	20	14	13	13
Phosphate rock.	Mil. metric ton . .	144	149	159	154	38	34	31	30
Potash.	Mil. metric ton . .	28	29	29	29	8	4	5	6
Sulfur, elemental	Mil. metric ton . .	55	54	59	58	22	22	20	20
Metals, mine basis:									
Bauxite	Mil. metric ton . .	89	84	106	109	2	1	(D)	(D)
Columbian concentrates (columbian content)	Mil. lb.	33.4	32.7	30.3	27.1	-	-	-	-
Copper [3]	Mil. metric ton . .	7	8	9	9	16	14	17	18
Gold	Mil. troy oz	39.2	49.2	64.3	65.9	2	5	13	14
Iron ore	Mil. metric ton . .	891	861	926	919	8	6	6	6
Lead [3]	1,000 metric ton.	3,470	3,431	3,368	3,367	17	12	12	15
Mercury . . . . [2]	1,000 flasks [4] . .	197	178	182	168	16	8	7	(NA)
Molybdenum [3]	Mil. lb.	244	217	257	246	62	50	54	55
Nickel [3]	1,000 short ton .	859	896	1,067	1,029	2	1	-	(Z)
Silver.	Mil. troy oz	343	420	475	486	9	9	14	14
Tantalum concentrates (tantalum content).	Mil. lb.	1.2	0.7	0.8	0.8	-	-	-	-
Titanium concentrates:									
Ilmenite.	Mil. short ton . . .	4.1	3.8	4.7	4.5	14	(D)	(D)	(D)
Tungsten	1,000 metric ton.	52	47	42	40	5	2	(D)	(D)
Vanadium [3].	1,000 short ton .	40.7	33.3	37	37.3	12	(D)	(D)	(D)
Zinc	Mil. metric ton . .	6	7	7	7	5	4	4	7
Metals, smelter basis:									
Aluminum	1,000 metric ton.	15,383	15,398	18,020	17,817	30	23	22	23
Cadmium	1,000 metric ton.	18.2	18.9	21.1	20.2	9	8	7	8
Copper	Mil. metric ton . .	8	9	10	9	14	14	16	16
Iron, pig (incl. ferroalloys) . . .	Mil. short ton . . .	567	550	603	594	12	9	9	9
Lead	1,000 metric ton.	5,397	5,641	5,987	5,942	23	20	22	22
Magnesium	1,000 metric ton.	348	358	379	387	49	42	44	40
Steel ingots and castings . . .	Mil. short ton . . .	790	792	862	851	14	11	11	12
Tin	1,000 metric ton.	245	181	250	250	1	2	1	(NA)
Zinc	1,000 metric ton.	6,049	6,798	7,203	7,041	6	5	5	5

- Represents or rounds to zero.   D Withheld to avoid disclosing company data.   NA Not available.   Z Less than half the unit of measure.   [1] Source: Energy Information Administration, *International Energy Annual*.   [2] For fiscal years ending in year shown; see text, section 9. U.S. production includes Puerto Rico.   [3] Content of ore and concentrate.   [4] 76-lb. flasks.

Source: Except as noted, U.S. Bureau of Mines, *Minerals Yearbook*, annual.

No. 1175. Federal Strategic and Critical Materials Inventory: 1980 to 1990

[As of **Dec. 31**. Covers strategic and critical materials essential to military and industrial requirements in time of national emergency. Market values are estimated current trade values of similar materials and not necessarily amounts that would be realized at time of sale]

MINERAL	Unit	QUANTITY [1]				VALUE (mil. dol.)			
		1980	1985	1989	1990	1980	1985	1989	1990
Tin.	1,000 metric ton.	200	185	171	169	3,158	2,324	1,182	962
Silver.	1,000 troy oz. .	139,500	136,006	98,174	92,151	2,288	801	543	374
Cobalt . [2]	Mil. lb.	41	53	53	53	1,020	590	406	443
Bauxite [2]. . [2]	1,000 lg. ton . . .	14,333	17,957	18,032	18,033	583	871	888	888
Manganese [?].	1,000 sh. ton . .	5,130	4,470	4,109	4,017	599	520	881	962
Tungsten [4]	Mil. lb.	97	87	80	82	817	369	291	253
Zinc.	1,000 sh. ton. . .	380	378	379	379	317	268	556	483
Titanium	1,000 sh. ton. . .	43	48	37	37	432	405	402	402
Platinum . [5]	1,000 troy oz. . .	466	466	453	453	215	154	231	186
Chromium [5].	1,000 sh. ton. . .	804	854	1,022	1,074	773	836	952	917
Diamonds: Stones . .	Carat	19,224	12,549	7,777	7,777	349	336	267	267
Industrial, bort. . . .	Carat	23,693	22,001	22,001	17,353	73	39	21	16

[1] Consists of stockpile and nonstockpile grades and reflects uncommitted balances.   [2] Consists of abrasive grade, metallic grade Jamaica, metallic grade Suriname, and refractory.   [3] Consists of chemical grade, dioxide battery natural, dioxide battery synthetic, electrolytic, ferro-high carbon, ferro-med. carbon, ferro-silicon, and metal.   [4] Consists of carbide powder, ferro, metal powder, and ores and concentrates.   [5] Consists of ferro-high carbon, ferro-low carbon, ferro-silicon, and metal.

Source: U.S. Defense Logistics Agency, *Statistical Supplement, Stockpile Report to the Congress* (AP-3).

Mineral and Mining Products

No. 1176. Selected Mineral and Metal Products—Quantity and Value of Imports and Exports: 1980 to 1990

[Imports represent imports for consumption. Exports include shipments under foreign aid programs. Includes trade of Puerto Rico with foreign countries]

PRODUCT		QUANTITY				VALUE (mil. dol.)			
	Unit	1980	1985	1989	1990	1980	1985	1989	1990
IMPORTS									
Petroleum (crude) [1]	Mil. bbl	1,975	1,625	(NA)	(NA)	61,899	22,608	(NA)	(NA)
Gem stones: Diamonds	Mil. carat	4.2	8.2	10.0	7.5	2,251	3,007	4,358	3955
Ores and concentrates:									
Chromium (Cr_2O_3 content)	1,000 metric ton	372	160	525	306	57	20	44	22
Copper	1,000 metric ton	14	3	47	91	73	2	51	131
Iron	Mil. lg. ton	25.1	15.8	19.3	17.8	773	452	522	560
Tungsten	Mil. lb	11.4	10.5	17.4	14.2	87	37	45	31
Metals:									
Aluminum	1,000 sh. ton	581	958	1,017	1058	778	1,017	1,898	1,597
Cobalt [2]	Mil. lb	15.0	16.6	12.8	13.8	359	181	97	109
Copper refined ingots, etc.	1,000 metric ton	427	378	304	262	935	492	866	675
Gold (bullion)	1,000 troy oz	4,090	6,361	3118	2,082	2,507	2,109	1,199	795
Iron and steel products									
(major)	Mil. sh. ton	15.5	24.3	17.3	17.2	7,713	10,874	7,591	[3]8,300
Platinum group [4]	1,000 troy oz	3,502	3,990	3642	4,030	1,177	1,026	1,382	1,906
Silver (bullion)	Mil. troy oz	64.9	137.4	98.4	86.7	1,332	856	579	437
Zinc: Blocks, pigs, slabs	1,000 sh. ton	452	673	784	696	319	508	1,184	992
EXPORTS									
Fuels: [1]									
Bituminous coal	Mil. sh. ton	89.9	84.0	(NA)	(NA)	4,523	3,862	(NA)	(NA)
Petroleum (crude)	Mil. bbl	30.6	6.0	(NA)	(NA)	751	117	(NA)	(NA)
Nonmetallic minerals:									
Gem stones: Diamonds	Mil. carat	1.3	2.4	1.1	1.0	1,041	571	1,244	1,899
Nitrogen compounds (maj.)	Mil. sh. ton	11.1	10.8	13.8	13.1	1,842	1,553	(NA)	(NA)
Phosphatic fertilizers [5]	Mil. sh. ton	7.2	6.1	10.6	10.2	1,383	1,225	1,760	1,515
Metals:									
Aluminum: Ingots, slabs,									
crude	1,000 sh. ton	715	383	654	749	1,107	442	1,261	1,161
Plates, sheets, bars, etc	1,000 sh. ton	306	185	492	482	716	411	1,380	1,406
Gold (refined bullion)	1,000 troy oz	4,702	2,888	3,974	4,531	2,787	919	1,490	1,719
Iron and steel products									
(major) [6]	Mil. sh. ton	4.1	0.9	4.6	4.3	3,504	1,321	2,063	[3]2,800
Magnesium [6]	1,000 sh. ton	56.8	40.3	62.4	57.1	128	114	170	164
Molybdenum [7]	1,000 lb	614	574	253	180	5	2	3	2
Silver (refined bullion)	Mil. troy oz	57.2	12.6	13.8	23.7	1,327	82	78	120
Scrap exports:									
Aluminum	1,000 sh. ton	445	413	633	592	483	351	769	719
Iron and steel	Mil. sh. ton	11.4	10.2	12.5	12.8	1,257	940	1,777	1,653

NA Not available. [1] Source: U.S. Bureau of the Census, *U.S. Imports for Consumption and General Imports, TSUSA Commodity and Country*, FT 246, annual; and *U.S. Exports, Schedule B Commodity and Country*, FT 446, annual; 1989 and 1990, *U.S. Exports of Merchandise* and *U.S. Imports of Merchandise* compact discs, December issues. [2] Includes unwrought metal, waste and scrap. [3] Estimate. [4] Unwrought and semimanufactured. [5] Superphosphates and ammonium phosphates. [6] Metal and alloys, scrap, semimanufactured forms. [7] Metals and alloys, crude and scrap.

Source: Except as noted, U.S. Bureau of Mines, *Minerals Yearbook*.

No. 1177. Mineral Industries—Lost Workday Injuries and Fatalities: 1980 to 1990

[Excludes office workers. Lost workday injuries are nonfatal occurrences that result in days away from work, days of restricted work activity or a permanent disability. Data for all years includes injuries to independent contractors at mine sites. Beginning with 1985, rates for the non-coal industries are based only on employment and hours worked by mine employees. See also *Historical Statistics, Colonial Times to 1970*, series M 271-286]

ITEM	COAL MINING			QUARRYING; RELATED INDUSTRY [1]			METAL; NONMETAL MINING [2]		
	1980	1985	1990	1980	1985	1990	1980	1985	1990
Injuries, total	18,822	9,141	12,292	3,551	2,571	3,812	6,923	2,234	3,804
Fatal	133	68	66	42	26	18	46	22	26
Rate per million work-hrs:									
Fatal	0.3	0.2	0.2	0.3	0.2	0.13	0.2	0.2	0.2
Nonfatal	43	27	41	21	19	28	28	17	25
Fatalities per 1,000 employed [3]	0.55	0.36	0.4	0.5	0.4	0.2	0.3	0.3	0.3

[1] Includes cement. [2] Nonmetal mines exclude extraction of Frasch process sulfur. [3] Average number of persons at work each day mines were active.

Source: U.S. Mine Safety and Health Administration, Denver, CO, unpublished data.

No. 1178. Net U.S. Imports of Selected Minerals and Metals as Percent of Apparent Consumption, 1980 to 1991, and by Major Foreign Sources, 1982 to 1991

[In percent. Figures based on net imports which equal the difference between imports and exports plus or minus government stockpile and industry stock changes]

MINERAL	1980	1985	1987	1988	1989	1990	1991,	Rank of major foreign sources, 1982-91
Columbium	100	100	100	100	100	100	100	Brazil, Canada, Thailand.
Manganese	98	100	100	100	100	100	100	South Africa, France, Gabon.
Mica (sheet)	100	100	100	100	100	100	100	India, Belgium, France.
Strontium	100	100	100	100	100	100	100	Mexico, Spain.
Bauxite [1]	94	96	96	97	96	98	100	Australia, Guinea, Jamaica.
Asbestos	78	65	40	75	90	90	95	Canada, South Africa.
Platinum group	88	92	91	91	90	88	88	So. Africa, United Kingdom, U.S.S.R.
Tantalum	90	89	85	80	86	86	85	Thailand, Germany, Brazil.
Cobalt	93	94	87	87	83	84	82	Zaire, Zambia, Canada.
Chromium	91	75	75	78	78	79	80	South Africa, Turkey, Zimbabwe.
Tungsten	53	68	79	76	77	73	75	China, Bolivia, Canada.
Nickel	71	71	79	73	69	72	74	Canada, Norway, Australia.
Tin	79	72	74	78	77	71	73	Brazil, Thailand, Malaysia.
Barium	44	74	65	74	77	69	70	China, Morocco, India.
Potassium	65	76	75	71	65	68	67	Canada, Israel, U.S.S.R.
Antimony	48	63	63	65	56	51	57	China, South Africa.
Cadmium	55	57	64	48	62	46	54	Canada, Australia, Mexico.
Selenium	59	(D)	(D)	52	55	46	52	Canada, United Kingdom, Japan.
Petroleum [2] [3]	37	27	36	38	42	42	(NA)	Mexico, Canada, Venezuela.
Zinc	60	70	71	69	61	41	30	Canada, Mexico, Peru.
Gypsum	35	38	38	36	35	36	30	Canada, Mexico, Spain.
Iron ore	25	21	22	18	22	21	14	Canada, Brazil, Venezuela.
Iron and steel	15	22	20	19	13	13	12	E.E.C. [4], Japan, Canada.
Sulfur	14	5	7	16	9	11	15	Canada, Mexico.
Natural gas [3]	5	5	5	7	7	8	(NA)	Canada, Algeria.
Copper	14	28	26	13	7	3	(5)	Chile Canada, Peru.
Aluminum	(5)	16	23	7	(5)	(5)	(5)	Canada, Japan, Venezuela.
Silver	7	(NA)	(NA)	(NA)	(NA)	(NA)	(NA)	Canada, Mexico, Peru.
Mercury [6]	26	50	(NA)	NA	(D)	(D)	(D)	Spain, China, Japan.
Titanium [6]	32	(D)	(D)	(D)	(D)	(D)	(D)	Australia, Canada, South Africa.
Vanadium	35	(D)	(D)	(D)	(D)	(D)	(D)	South Africa, E.E.C. [4]

D Withheld to avoid disclosure.   NA Not available.   [1] Includes alumina.   [2] Includes crude and products.   [3] Source: Energy Information Administration, *Annual Energy Review*, and *Monthly Energy Review.*   [4] European Economic Community.   [5] Net exports.   [6] Ilmenite.

Source: Except as noted, U.S. Bureau of Mines, *Mineral Commodity Summaries;* import and export data from U.S. Bureau of the Census.

No. 1179. Federal Offshore Leasing, Exploration, Production, and Revenue: 1975 to 1990

[See source for explanation of terms and for reliability statement]

ITEM	Unit	1975	1980	1984	1985	1986	1987	1988	1989	1990
Tracts offered	Number . .	1,374	483	27,984	15,754	10,724	10,926	33,376	11,013	10,459
Tracts leased	Number . .	321	218	1,400	667	142	640	1,856	1,049	825
Acres offered	1,000	7,247	2,563	154,384	87,029	58,670	59,762	85,366	60,096	56,788
Acres leased	1,000 . . .	1,680	1,134	7,495	3,512	734	45,075	10,040	5,580	4,263
Bonus paid for leased tracts	Bil. dol. . .	1.1	4.2	4.0	1.5	0.2	0.5	1.2	0.6	0.6
New wells being drilled:										
Active	Number . .	97	191	253	195	95	142	116	123	120
Suspended	Number . .	292	739	313	348	279	265	289	361	266
Wells completed	Number . .	6,104	9,638	13,012	12,285	12,536	12,736	12,827	12,938	13,167
Wells plugged and abandoned.	Number . .	5,617	8,057	9,903	10,487	11,909	12,373	13,164	13,846	14,677
Revenue, total [1]	Bil. dol. . .	1.7	6.4	8.0	5.2	2.8	2.9	3.4	2.8	3.3
Bonuses	Bil. dol. . .	1.1	4.2	4.0	1.5	0.2	0.5	1.2	0.6	0.6
Oil and gas royalties [1]	Bil. dol. . .	0.6	2.1	4.0	3.6	2.6	2.3	2.1	2.1	2.6
Rentals	Bil. dol. . .	(Z)	(Z)	(Z)	0.1	0.1	0.1	0.1	0.1	0.1
Production, value [2]	Bil. dol. . .	3.9	13.1	24.0	22.2	15.7	14.6	12.9	13.0	16.5
Crude oil	Bil. dol. . .	2.2	4.8	9.6	9.6	5.8	5.6	4.2	4.4	5.9
Condensate	Bil. dol. . .	0.2	0.4	1.2	1.0	0.7	0.7	0.7	0.8	1.1
Natural gas	Bil. dol. . .	1.5	7.9	13.2	11.5	9.3	8.1	7.9	7.8	9.5
Production: [2]										
Crude oil	Mil. bbls. . .	303	259	330	352	350	325	279	260	274
Condensate	Mil. bbls. . .	27	19	40	37	39	41	41	45	51
Natural gas	Tril. cu. ft. . .	3,459	4,641	4,537	4,000	3,949	4,425	4,425	4,310	4,200	(NA)

NA Not available.   Z Less than $50 million.   [1] Includes condensate royalties.   [2] Production value is value at time of production, not current value.

Source: U.S. Dept. of the Interior, Minerals Management Service, *Federal Offshore Statistics,* annual.

No. 1180. Petroleum Industry—Summary: 1975 to 1990

ITEM	Unit	1975	1980	1984	1985	1986	1987	1988	1989	1990, est.
Crude oil producing wells (Dec. 31).	1,000...	500	548	621	647	623	620	612	603	588
Daily output per well	Bbl.....	16.8	15.9	14.3	13.9	13.9	13.5	13.5	12.6	12.4
Completed wells drilled, total	1,000...	39	70	85	70	40	36	32	28	29
Crude oil...................	1,000...	17	32	43	35	19	16	13	10	12
Gas	1,000...	8	17	17	14	8	8	8	9	10
Dry.......................	1,000...	14	20	26	21	13	12	10	8	8
Crude oil production, total	Mil. bbl. .	3,057	3,146	3,250	3,275	3,168	3,047	2,979	2,785	2,685
Value at wells	Bil. dol..	23.5	67.9	84.1	78.9	39.6	46.9	37.5	44.1	53.4
Average price per barrel	Dollars..	7.67	21.59	25.88	24.09	12.51	15.40	12.58	15.86	20.03
Refinery input of crude oil	Mil. bbl. .	4,541	4,934	4,408	4,381	4,641	4,692	4,848	4,891	4,895
Imports: Crude oil	Mil. bbl. .	1,498	1,926	1,254	1,168	1,525	1,706	1,869	2,133	2,145
Refined petroleum products	Mil. bbl. .	712	603	736	681	747	731	840	809	759
Import value.................	Mil. dol. .	25,059	74,440	54,310	50,368	34,790	41,495	39,981	49,028	60,747
Export value	Mil. dol. .	1,007	2,871	4,801	5,121	3,883	3,922	2,802	2,859	4,419
Operable refineries.	Number .	279	319	247	223	216	219	213	204	205
Capacity (Jan. 1)	Mil. bbl. .	5,461	6,584	5,906	5,716	5,643	5,681	5,825	5,714	5,683
Output	Mil. bbl. .	4,995	5,352	5,007	5,019	5,301	5,339	5,498	5,539	5,570
Utilization rate	Percent .	85.5	75.4	76.2	77.6	82.9	83.1	84.7	86.6	87.3
Proved reserves	Bil. bbl .	32.7	29.8	28.4	28.4	26.9	27.3	26.8	26.5	26.3

Source: U.S. Energy Information Administration, *Annual Energy Review,* and *Petroleum Supply Annual.*

No. 1181. Crude Petroleum and Natural Gas Wells Drilled—Summary: 1970 to 1990

[Includes all costs incurred for drilling and equipping wells to point of completion as productive wells or abandonment after drilling becomes unproductive. Based on sample of operators of different size drilling establishments]

ITEM	Unit	1970	1975	1980	1984	1985	1986	1987	1988	1989	1990
Wells drilled	Number...	27,177	36,960	62,011	77,210	67,821	37,173	33,041	29,741	26,693	28,513
Offshore	Number...	1,058	1,028	1,272	1,421	1,247	898	709	866	746	704
Footage drilled........	Mil. ft....	136.9	177.6	296.0	350.6	314.5	176.3	157.4	150.2	131.5	143.8
Drilling cost.........	Mil. dol...	2,579	6,571	22,800	25,206	23,697	13,552	9,239	10,550	9,669	10,937
Average depth per well..	Feet.....	5,037	4,806	4,773	4,541	4,637	4,742	4,762	5,051	4,925	5,043
Average cost per well...	$1,000...	95	178	368	326	349	365	280	355	362	384
Offshore	$1,000...	566	1,142	3,024	3,536	4,073	4,004	2,896	3,112	3,197	3,112
Average cost per foot...	Dollars ...	18.84	36.99	77.02	71.90	75.35	76.88	58.71	70.23	73.55	76.07

Source: American Petroleum Institute, *Joint Association Survey of Drilling Costs,* annual.

No. 1182. Domestic Motor Gasoline Supply: 1975 to 1990

[In 1,000 barrels per day, except as noted]

ITEM	1975	1980	1982	1983	1984	1985	1986	1987	1988	1989	1990
Supply [1]	6,675	6,579	6,539	6,622	6,693	6,831	7,034	7,206	7,336	7,328	7,235
Unleaded.......	(NA)	3,067	3,409	3,647	3,987	4,406	4,854	5,470	5,995	6,507	6,850
Production	6,520	6,506	6,338	6,340	6,453	6,419	6,752	6,841	6,956	6,963	6,959
Net imports......	182	139	177	237	293	371	293	349	383	330	287
Stocks (mil. bbl.) [2] .	235	261	235	222	243	223	233	226	228	213	220

NA Not available.   [1] Production plus net imports less net increase in primary stocks.   [2] End of year, includes motor gasoline blending components.

Source: U.S. Energy Information Administration, *Monthly Energy Review.*

No. 1183. Natural Gas Plant Liquids—Production and Value: 1970 to 1990

[Barrels of 42 gallons. See also *Historical Statistics, Colonial Times to 1970,* series M 143-146]

ITEM	Unit	1970	1975	1980	1984	1985	1986	1987	1988	1989	1990
Field production [1]........	Mil. bbl ...	606	596	576	596	587	566	582	595	564	566
Pentanes plus..........	Mil. bbl ...	197	149	126	107	103	98	106	111	113	112
Liquefied petroleum gases .	Mil. bbl ...	400	444	441	488	479	474	474	483	451	454
Natural gas processed	Tril. cu. ft..	19	18	15	14	13	[2]13	13	13	13	15

[1] Includes other finished petroleum products, not shown separately.   [2] Estimated.

Source: Through 1975, U.S. Bureau of Mines, *Minerals Yearbook;* thereafter, U.S. Energy Information Administration, *Energy Data Reports, Petroleum Statement Annual, Petroleum Supply Annual,* and *Natural Gas Annual.*

No. 1184. U.S. Petroleum Balance: 1980 to 1990
[In millions of barrels]

ITEM	1980	1984	1985	1986	1987	1988	1989	1990
Petroleum products supplied	6,242	5,756	5,740	5,942	6,083	6,308	6,324	6,201
New supply of products	6,249	5,800	5,676	5,995	6,053	6,290	6,270	6,259
Production of products	5,765	5,392	5,363	5,604	5,680	5,849	5,874	5,934
Crude input to refineries	4,934	4,408	4,381	4,641	4,692	4,835	4,891	4,894
Oil, field production.	3,146	3,250	3,275	3,168	3,047	2,979	2,779	2,685
Alaska.	592	631	666	681	716	738	684	647
Lower 48 States	2,555	2,619	2,608	2,487	2,331	2,241	2,095	2,037
Net imports	1,821	1,188	1,094	1,468	1,651	1,807	2,081	2,112
Imports (gross excluding SPR) [1] . . .	1,910	1,182	1,125	1,507	1,679	1,845	2,112	2,142
SPR [1] imports.	16	72	43	18	27	19	20	10
Exports	-105	66	75	56	55	57	52	40
Other sources	33	29	12	4	7	57	32	98
Natural gas plant liquids (NGPL), supply .	577	596	604	575	585	593	563	574
Other liquids.	253	371	378	388	403	418	420	465
Net imports of refined products.	484	407	313	391	373	441	396	326
Imports	578	604	523	621	596	681	656	598
Exports	94	197	210	229	223	240	260	272
Stock withdrawal, refined products	-7	-44	64	-53	30	17	53	-59
Ending stocks, all oils	1,392	1,556	1,519	1,593	1,607	1,597	1,581	1,621
Crude oil and lease condensate.	358	345	321	331	349	330	341	323
Srategic Petroleum Reserve (SPR) [1]	108	451	493	512	541	560	580	586
Unfinished oils	124	94	107	94	93	100	(NA)	(NA)
Gasoline blending components	17	39	33	39	38	39	(NA)	(NA)
Pentanes plus.	(NA)	8	8	7	7	7	(NA)	(NA)
Finished refined products	785	621	557	609	580	562	580	712
PRODUCT TYPE SUPPLIED								
Total products	6,242	5,756	5,740	5,942	6,083	6,326	6,324	6,201
Finished motor gasoline	2,407	2,449	2,493	2,567	2,630	2,678	2,675	2,641
Distillate fuel oil	1,049	1,041	1,047	1,064	1,086	1,140	1,152	1,103
Residual fuel oil	918	501	439	518	462	5,030	500	449
Liquified petroleum gases [2]	414	576	584	552	588	604	609	568
Pentanes plus, other liquids, etc	1,454	1,165	1,155	1,223	1,304	1,369	1,378	1,431
Crude oil	(NA)	23	22	18	12	15	10	9

NA Not available.   [1] SPR=Strategic petroleum reserve. For more information, see table 932.   [2] Includes ethane.

Source: U.S. Energy Information Administration, *Petroleum Supply Annual.*

No. 1185. Crude Petroleum and Natural Gas—Production, by State: 1985 to 1990
[See also *Historical Statistics, Colonial Times to 1970,* series M 138, M 142, and M 147-161]

STATE	CRUDE PETROLEUM						NATURAL GAS MARKETED PRODUCTION [1]					
	Quantity (mil. bbl.)			Value (mil. dol.)			Quantity (bil. cu. ft.)			Value (mil. dol.)		
	1985	1989	1990	1985	1989	1990	1985	1989	1990	1985	1989	1990
Total [2] . . .	3,274	2,779	2,685	78,884	44,071	53,772	17,270	18,095	18,562	43,343	30,627	31,658
AL.	22	18	18	579	316	387	107	128	135	398	349	373
AK.	666	693	658	10,655	8,135	10,086	321	394	403	236	536	554
AR.	19	11	10	443	191	222	155	174	175	393	420	360
CA.	424	325	322	8,386	4,564	5,732	491	363	363	1,653	841	857
CO	30	29	31	758	542	722	178	217	243	517	329	377
FL	11	7	6	(NA)	(NA)	(NA)	11	8	6	26	15	15
IL	30	20	20	795	371	467	1	1	1	4	3	1
IN	5	3	3	134	60	73	(Z)	(Z)	(Z)	1	1	1
KS.	75	58	59	1,939	1,058	1,359	528	601	574	671	867	893
KY.	8	5	5	201	92	124	73	72	75	174	154	169
LA.	508	154	148	5,387	2,838	3,409	5,014	5,078	5,242	13,355	9,256	9,587
MI	27	22	20	726	396	458	132	156	140	475	492	420
MS	31	31	30	796	528	630	144	103	95	456	202	167
MT	30	21	20	734	356	429	52	51	50	125	79	90
NE.	7	6	5	163	102	119	2	1	1	6	2	2
NM	79	66	66	2,028	1,182	1,472	905	855	965	2,370	1,337	1,629
NY.	1	1	(Z)	25	8	9	32	20	25	106	45	55
ND	51	39	39	1,307	662	849	73	51	52	138	91	93
OH	15	9	8	361	164	196	182	160	155	560	408	393
OK	162	124	117	4,256	2,253	2,690	1,936	2,550	2,258	4,930	2,237	3,548
PA.	5	2	2	114	44	51	150	192	178	474	460	417
TX.	889	686	674	23	12,219	15,060	6,053	6,241	6,343	14,097	9,671	9,939
UT.	41	25	23	773	464	524	83	120	146	293	190	249
WV	4	2	2	86	36	43	145	177	178	558	551	568
WY	129	107	103	3,061	1,784	2,169	417	666	736	1,252	823	856

NA Not available.   Z Less than 500 million cubic feet or less than $500,000.   [1] Excludes nonhydrocarbon gases.
[2] Includes other States not shown separately. State production does not include State offshore production.

Source: U.S. Energy Information Administration, *Energy Data Reports, Petroleum Supply Annual, Natural Gas Annual,* and *Natural Gas Monthly.*

No. 1186. Natural Gas—Supply, Consumption, Reserves, and Marketed Production: 1970 to 1990

[See also *Historical Statistics, Colonial Times to 1970*, series M 147-161]

ITEM	Unit	1970	1973	1975	1980	1984	1985	1986	1987	1988	1989	1990
Producing wells (yearend)	1,000	117	124	130	182	234	243	242	249	257	262	270
Production value at wells.	Bil. dol	3.7	5.0	8.9	32.1	48.5	43.2	32.6	29.0	30.3	30.6	31.7
Avg. per 1,000 cu. ft . .	Dollars	0.17	0.22	0.44	1.59	2.66	2.51	1.94	1.67	1.69	1.69	1.72
Proved reserves [1]	Tril. cu. ft . .	291	250	228	199	198	193	192	187	168	167	169
Marketed production [2]. . .	Tril. cu. ft . .	21.9	22.7	20.1	20.2	18.3	17.3	16.9	17.4	17.9	18.1	18.6
Drawn from storage	Tril. cu. ft . .	1.5	1.5	1.8	2.0	2.1	2.4	1.8	1.9	2.3	2.9	2.0
Imports [3]	Tril. cu. ft . .	0.8	1.0	1.0	1.0	0.8	1.0	0.8	1.0	1.3	1.4	1.5
Consumption, total	Tril. cu. ft . .	21.1	22.1	19.5	19.9	18.0	17.3	16.2	17.2	18.0	18.8	18.7
Residential	Tril. cu. ft . .	4.8	4.9	4.9	4.8	4.6	4.4	4.3	4.3	4.6	4.8	4.4
Commercial [4]	Tril. cu. ft . .	2.4	2.6	2.5	2.6	2.5	2.4	2.3	2.4	2.7	2.7	2.7
Industrial	Tril. cu. ft . .	9.3	10.2	8.4	8.2	7.2	6.9	6.5	7.1	7.5	7.9	8.5
Lease and plant fuel .	Tril. cu. ft . .	1.4	1.5	1.4	1.0	1.1	1.0	0.9	1.2	1.1	1.1	1.2
Other industrial	Tril. cu. ft . .	7.9	8.7	7.0	7.2	6.2	5.9	5.6	6.0	6.4	6.8	7.0
Electric utilities	Tril. cu. ft . .	3.9	3.7	3.2	3.7	3.1	3.0	2.6	2.8	2.6	2.8	2.8
Transportation [5]	Tril. cu. ft . .	0.7	0.7	0.6	0.6	0.5	0.5	0.5	0.5	0.6	0.6	0.7
Extraction losses [6]	Tril. cu. ft . .	0.9	0.9	0.9	0.8	0.8	0.8	0.8	0.8	0.8	0.8	0.8
Exports.	Tril. cu. ft . .	0.1	0.1	0.1	0.1	0.1	0.1	0.1	0.1	0.1	0.1	0.1
Additions to storage [7] . . .	Tril. cu. ft . .	1.9	2.0	2.1	2.0	2.3	2.2	2.0	1.9	2.2	2.5	2.5
Unaccounted for gas [8] . .	Tril. cu. ft . .	0.2	0.2	0.2	0.6	0.1	0.4	0.4	0.4	0.3	0.2	0.2
World production (dry). . .	Tril. cu. ft . .	(NA)	43.2	44.1	53.1	59.7	62.0	63.3	66.2	69.8	71.9	(NA)
U.S. production (dry) . .	Tril. cu. ft . .	21.0	21.7	19.2	19.4	17.4	16.4	16.0	16.5	17.0	17.3	17.6
Percent U.S. of world	Percent . . .	56.0	50.4	43.6	36.5	29.2	26.4	25.3	25.0	24.4	24.0	(NA)

NA Not available.   [1] Estimated; end of year. Source: 1970-1975; American Gas Association, Arlington, VA (copyright.); thereafter, U.S. Energy Information Administration, *U.S. Crude Oil, Natural Gas, and Natural Gas Liquids Reserves*, annual.
[2] Marketed production includes gross withdrawals from reservoirs less quantities used for reservoir repressuring and quantities vented or flared. For 1980 and thereafter, it excludes the nonhydrocarbon gases subsequently removed.   [3] Includes imports of liquefied natural gas.   [4] Includes deliveries to municipalities and public authorities for institutional heating and other purposes.
[5] Pipeline fuel.   [6] Volumetric reduction in natural gas resulting from the extraction of natural gas constituents at natural gas processing plants.   [7] Beginning with 1980, includes liquefied natural gas (LNG) storage in above ground tanks.   [8] Derived by subtracting the sum of additions to storage, exports and consumption from total supply.

Source: Except as noted, U.S. Energy Information Administration, *Annual Energy Review, International Energy Annual, Natural Gas Annual*, Volume I and II and *Monthly Energy Review*, August 1991.

No. 1187. Liquefied Petroleum Gases—Summary: 1980 to 1990

[In millions of 42-gallon barrels. Includes ethane]

ITEM	1980	1985	1989	1990	ITEM	1980	1985	1989	1990
Production	561	622	654	638	Consumption.	538	584	609	568
At natural gas plants.	441	479	452	456	Ethane [1] [2]	164	210	170	186
At refineries.	121	143	202	182	Propane [1] [2]	298	322	361	335
Imports	79	68	66	68	Butane (incl. isobutane) [2]. .	76	52	69	47
Refinery input	85	111	115	107	Stocks, Dec. 31.	116	74	80	98
Exports	9	23	13	14				Tc	

[1] Reported consumption of ethane-propane mixtures have been allocated 70 percent ethane and 30 percent propane.
[2] Reported consumption of butane-propane mixtures have been allocated 60 percent butane and 40 percent propane.

Source: U.S. Energy Information Administration, *Petroleum Supply Annual*.

No. 1188. World Coal Trade: 1975 to 1989

[In millions of short tons]

COUNTRIES	1975	1980	1981	1982	1983	1984	1985	1986	1987	1988	1989
Exporting countries, total [1]	212.5	277.2	288.4	292.0	284.5	332.9	370.2	376.3	383.0	415.0	423.5
United States	66.3	88.7	106.5	106.5	78.2	82.0	93.2	85.5	79.6	94.9	100.8
Australia	33.5	46.6	54.3	48.8	62.3	82.2	96.6	101.3	111.9	109.8	108.5
South Africa	3.0	30.7	33.3	30.5	32.7	40.9	49.8	50.1	46.9	47.4	51.6
Soviet Union	28.8	26.2	22.5	23.0	22.8	22.8	26.5	36.9	39.1	46.0	43.9
West Germany.	16.2	13.8	13.1	11.2	11.5	12.4	10.5	7.9	6.9	5.5	5.9
Canada	12.9	16.1	17.9	16.6	18.6	26.8	30.3	28.6	29.5	35.0	36.1
Poland	42.4	34.6	16.6	30.6	38.7	47.2	39.7	37.9	34.2	05.5	31.8
China: Mainland	0.5	4.2	4.1	5.1	6.8	7.7	8.6	10.9	14.4	16.2	16.9
Importing countries, total [1]	212.5	277.2	288.4	292.0	284.5	332.9	370.2	376.3	383.0	415.0	423.5
Western Europe/Mediterranean	80.8	126.9	129.4	126.5	112.9	132.4	152.3	149.0	145.6	146.2	154.7
Japan.	68.5	75.6	86.0	86.5	82.8	96.2	103.0	99.6	100.2	111.6	111.7
Eastern Europe	35.1	34.8	30.1	37.0	39.7	39.9	39.1	45.4	44.9	45.1	39.6
Canada	16.8	17.4	16.3	17.3	16.7	20.3	16.1	14.7	15.8	19.3	15.1

[1] Includes areas not shown separately.   [2] Includes trade with Japan only.

Source: U.S. Energy Information Administration, 1975-84, *Outlook for U.S. Coal Imports;* thereafter, *Annual Prospects for World Coal Trade.*

No. 1189. Coal and Coke—Summary: 1970 to 1990

[Includes coal consumed at mines. Demonstrated coal reserve base for United States on Jan. 1, 1989, was an estimated 473 billion tons. Recoverability varies between 40 and 90 percent for individual deposits; 50 percent or more of overall U.S. coal reserve base is believed to be recoverable. See also *Historical Statistics, Colonial Times to 1970*, series M 93-126]

ITEM	Unit	1970	1975	1980	1985	1987	1988	1989	1990 [1]
Coal production, total [2]	**Mil. sh. tons.**	**613**	**655**	**830**	**884**	**919**	**950**	**981**	**1,036**
Value	Mil. dol.	3,882	12,670	20,453	22,277	21,101	20,890	21,330	(NA)
Anthracite production	Mil. sh. tons .	9.7	6.2	6.1	4.7	3.6	3.6	3.3	3.1
Bituminous coal and lignite: [3]									
Number of mines	Number . . .	5,601	6,168	5,598	4,547	3,894	3,462	3,511	(NA)
Production	Mil. sh. tons .	603	648	824	879	915	947	977	1,033
Value, total	Mil. dol.	3,774	12,469	20,196	22,061	21,050	20,828	21,268	22,720
Average per ton	Dollars.	6.26	19.23	24.52	25.10	23.00	22.00	21.76	22.00
Exports	Mil. sh. tons .	71	66	90	91	78	94	100	105
Value.	Mil. dol.	961	3,259	4,627	4,403	3,354	3,975	4,255	4,481
Imports	1,000 sh. tns.	36	940	1,194	1,952	1,747	2,134	2,851	2,699
Method of mining:									
Underground.	Mil. sh. tons .	339	293	337	350	372	382	393	416
Surface	Mil. sh. tons .	264	356	487	529	543	565	584	617
Percent of total prod . .	Percent	43.8	54.8	59.1	60.2	59.4	59.7	59.8	59.7
Value	Mil. dol.	(Z)	22	30	70	(NA)	(NA)	(NA)	(NA)
Consumption [4]	Mil. sh. tons .	515	558	699	815	834	881	888	890
Electric power utilities . . .	Mil. sh. tons .	318	404	568	693	717	757	766	770
Industrial.	Mil. sh. tons .	184	146	126	116	112	118	117	114
Productivity average: [5]									
Daily employment	1,000.	140	190	225	169	143	135	131	(NA)
Days worked	Number	228	232	210	204	207	211	214	(NA)
Tons per worker:									
Per day	Sh./tons. . . .	18.84	14.74	16.32	23.13	28.19	30.30	31.75	(NA)
Per year	Sh./tons. . . .	4,296	3,420	3,427	4,719	5,835	6,393	6,795	(NA)
Production, by State:									
Alabama	Mil. sh. tons .	20.6	22.6	26.4	27.8	25.5	26.5	28.0	28.7
Illinois	Mil. sh. tons .	65.1	59.5	62.5	59.2	59.2	58.6	59.3	60.2
Indiana	Mil. sh. tons .	22.3	25.1	30.9	33.3	34.2	31.3	33.6	36.3
Kentucky	Mil. sh. tons .	125.3	143.6	150.1	152.3	163.7	157.9	167.4	173.6
Montana	Mil. sh. tons .	3.4	22.1	29.9	33.3	34.4	38.9	37.7	37.8
Ohio	Mil. sh. tons .	55.4	46.8	39.4	35.6	35.6	34.0	33.7	34.9
Pennsylvania	Mil. sh. tons .	90.2	90.3	93.1	71.4	66.4	67.1	70.6	70.5
Virginia	Mil. sh. tons .	35.0	35.5	41.0	40.9	44.2	45.9	43.0	48.5
West Virginia	Mil. sh. tons .	144.1	109.3	121.6	127.8	135.9	145.0	153.6	168.2
Wyoming	Mil. sh. tons .	7.2	23.8	94.9	140.7	146.8	164.0	171.6	184.7
Other States.	Mil. sh. tons .	44.1	75.9	139.7	161.3	165.8	177.6	182.3	185.5
World production	Mil. sh. tons .	3,295	3,665	4,173	4,844	5,070	5,166	5,154	(NA)
Coke production [6]	**Mil. sh. tons.**	**66.5**	**57.2**	**46.1**	**28.7**	**28.0**	**32.4**	**33.0**	**28.9**
Oven coke [7]	Mil. sh. tons .	65.7	56.5	46.1	28.7	28.0	32.4	33.0	28.9
Value of product at plant . .	Mil. dol.	2,193	5,261	6,029	(NA)	(NA)	(NA)	(NA)	(NA)
Coke and breeze.	Mil. dol.	1,899	4,607	4,784	(NA)	(NA)	(NA)	(NA)	(NA)
Avg. market value per ton . .	Dollars.	28	84	103	103	(NA)	(NA)	(NA)	(NA)
Coal carbonized	Mil. sh. tons .	96.5	83.6	66.7	41.1	37.0	41.9	41.4	39.8
Average value per ton	Dollars.	12.47	44.21	56.26	54.30	46.55	47.70	47.50	47.79
Yield of coke from coal . . .	Percent	69.1	68.4	69.2	69.8	75.9	77.3	79.8	72.7

NA Not available. Z Less than $500,000. [1] Preliminary. [2] Includes bituminous coal, lignite, and anthracite. [3] All domestic product data for 1970 and 1975 are for mines producing 1,000 short tons or more per year; thereafter, data are for all mines. [4] Includes some categories not shown separately. [5] Data for 1970 and 1975 are for mines producing 1,000 short tons or more per year; thereafter, for mines producing 10,000 short tons or more. Beginning 1984, includes anthracite. [6] Includes beehive coke. [7] Prior to 1980, excludes screenings or breeze; thereafter, includes beehive and other nonrecoverables.

Source: 1970 and 1975, U.S. Bureau of Mines, *Minerals Yearbook;* thereafter, U.S. Energy Information Administration, *Coal Production,* annual; *Annual Energy Review,* and *Quarterly Coal Report.*

No. 1190. Uranium Concentrate (U$_3$O$_8$) Industry—Summary: 1980 to 1990

[Middle demand case. See table 981. See also *Historical Statistics, Colonial Times to 1970*, series M 266-267]

ITEM	Unit	1980	1982	1983	1984	1985	1986	1987	1988	1989	1990
Production	1,000 sh. tons .	21.9	13.4	10.6	7.4	5.6	6.8	6.5	6.5	6.9	4.4
Net imports (U$_3$O$_8$)	1,000 sh. tons .	−1.1	6.3	2.4	5.2	3.2	6.0	6.9	6.2	5.5	(NA)
Utility and Suppliers inventories											
(U$_3$O$_8$ equivalent).	1,000 sh. tons .	54.4	68.6	80.0	[1]74.7	[1]68.3	[1]66.2	[1]64.5	[1]59.1	[1]54.9	66.0
Price (1988 dol./lb. U$_3$O$_8$):											
Long-term contract price . . .	Dollars	41.4	30.2	31.7	26.4	24.7	19.3	18.5	(NA)	(NA)	(NA)
Spot market price.	Dollars	45.0	24.3	26.8	19.4	17.0	18.1	17.3	14.5	14.2	(NA)
Delivered price.	Dollars	39.9	48.5	44.6	[2]36.5	[2]33.6	[2]31.9	[2]19.6	[2]25.7	[2]27.8	(NA)
Capital expenditures											
(1988 dollars)	Mil. dol.	1,107	202	78	43	37	29	63	36	35	(NA)
Employment.	1,000	19.9	9.0	5.6	3.6	2.4	2.1	2.0	2.1	1.6	1.3

NA Not available. [1] Includes natural U$_3$O$_8$ (uranium oxide), natural UF$_6$ (uranium hexafluoride), natural UF$_6$ under usage agreement, UF$_6$ at enrichment suppliers, enriched UF$_6$ and fabricated fuel. [2] Average U.S. contract prices and market price settlements.

Source: U.S. Department of Energy, *Domestic Uranium Mining and Milling Industry,* annual, and *Uranium Industry,* annual.

Mining and Mineral Products

No. 1191. Cobalt—Summary: 1980 to 1990

[In millions of pounds of contained cobalt, except price]

ITEM	1980	1982	1983	1984	1985	1986	1987	1988	1989	1990
Production: Secondary (scrap) [1]	1.2	0.9	0.7	0.9	0.9	2.6	2.3	2.2	2.6	2.7
Imports [2]	16.3	12.9	17.2	25.3	17.7	12.3	19.5	15.5	12.8	14.4
Zaire.	6.2	5.0	7.7	11.8	4.8	0.7	9.4	5.4	2.4	4.0
Zambia	2.2	1.2	2.3	3.8	4.3	3.5	2.9	2.7	3.1	3.6
Canada	1.1	1.5	2.0	3.1	3.1	3.4	3.4	3.6	2.7	2.9
Exports [3]	0.6	0.6	0.8	0.7	0.6	1.0	0.8	1.2	2.0	3.0
Consumption (reported)	15.3	9.5	11.3	12.9	12.4	14.3	14.7	16.0	15.6	16.5
Inventories	45.0	48.2	48.8	49.3	56.0	56.1	57.6	57.0	56.3	56.9
Government [4]	40.8	45.7	46.0	46.2	53.2	53.1	53.1	53.1	53.1	[5]52.8
Private [6]	4.2	2.5	2.8	3.1	2.8	3.0	4.5	3.9	3.2	4.1
Price per pound [7] (dollars)	25.00	8.56	5.76	10.40	11.43	7.49	6.56	7.09	7.64	10.09

[1] Reported consumption.   [2] Includes countries not shown separately.   [3] 1980 to 1988-estimated content of unwrought cobalt and waste and scrap. 1989 also includes oxides, acetates and chlorides.   [4] Includes cobalt sold but not delivered.   [5] Inventory following upgrading program. Class 1 cobalt only.   [6] Stocks held by consumers and chemical processors.   [7] 1980 price is producer price, thereafter; prices are weighted average based on the market price quoted by *Metals Week*.

No. 1192. Tin—Summary: 1980 to 1990

[In metric tons, except price.]

ITEM	1980	1983	1984	1985	1986	1987	1988	1989	1990
Production: Domestic smelters	3,000	2,500	4,000	3,000	3,213	3,905	1,467	1,000	-
Secondary sources	18,638	14,205	15,417	14,109	14,850	16,159	15,249	15,213	13,200
Imports for consumption:									
Metal	45,982	34,048	41,224	33,830	35,768	41,150	43,493	33,988	33,810
Ore (tin content)	840	969	3,272	1,616	3,936	2,953	2,837	216	-
Exports	595	1,340	1,429	1,478	1,547	1,318	1,209	904	658
Price of Straits tin at NY, dol. per lb.[1] . .	8.46	6.55	6.24	[2]5.96	[2]3.83	4.19	4.41	5.20	3.86
Consumption, primary and secondary. .	56,362	45,547	48,315	48,669	43,524	44,219	45,601	46,456	44,363
World mine production, est	247,300	196,942	188,183	180,725	172,471	178,131	200,150	216,457	222,000

- Represents zero.   [1] See footnote 5, table 1173.   [2] Average of monthly prices quoted for 10 months only.

No. 1193. Tungsten Concentrate—Summary: 1970 to 1990

[Excludes Alaska and Hawaii. See *Historical Statistics, Colonial Times to 1970*, series M 225-226, for related data]

ITEM	Unit	1970	1980	1983	1984	1985	1986	1987	1988	1989	1990
Production:	1,000 sh.										
Concentrates (60% WO_2 basis) . . .	ton. . . .	10.1	6.4	2.3	2.8	2.3	1.8	0.1	(D)	(D)	(D)
Tungsten content	Mil. lb.	9.6	6.0	2.2	2.7	2.2	1.7	0.1	(D)	(D)	(D)
Shipments from mines:											
Reported value f.o.b. mines	Mil. dol.	23.8	50.6	10.5	13.4	9.1	5.8	0.2	(D)	(D)	(D)
Avg. value per lb. of tungsten	Dollars .	2.55	8.38	4.70	5.18	4.22	3.21	2.88	(D)	(D)	(D)
Imports for consumption [2]	Mil. lb.	[3]1.3	11.4	6.3	12.8	10.5	5.6	9.7	17.7	17.4	14.2
Consumption [2]	Mil. lb.	16.7	20.4	11.4	18.9	15.1	10.6	12.1	17.3	17.0	13.0
Stocks, [2] end of year	Mil. lb.	2.3	1.4	2.5	2.2	2.5	1.1	0.7	1.1	2.8	2.4
World production [2]	Mil. lb.	71.4	114.6	90.2	101.8	102.7	95.9	93.6	93.0	92.8	89.0

D Withheld to avoid disclosure.   [1] A short ton of 60% tungsten trioxide (WO_8) contains 951.72 pounds of tungsten.   [2] Estimated.   [2] Tungsten content.   [3] General imports.

Source of tables 1191-1193: U.S. Bureau of Mines, *Minerals Yearbook*.

No. 1194. Zinc—Summary: 1980 to 1990

[**Production in thousands of metric tons,** except value. Excludes Alaska and Hawaii. See *Historical Statistics, Colonial Times to 1970*, series M 249-250, for production in short tons]

ITEM AND STATE	1980	1982	1983	1984	1985	1986	1987	1988	1989	1990
Smelter production, primary slab zinc	**340**	**228**	**236**	**253**	**261**	**253**	**261**	**241**	**260**	**263**
Value (mil. dol.)	280	194	215	271	232	212	241	320	476	(NA)
From domestic ores	232	193	210	198	198	191	205	196	165	158
From foreign ores	108	35	26	55	63	62	56	45	95	105
Production, redistilled secondary slab zinc	29	74	69	78	73	63	83	88	98	96
Avg. price of common zinc (cents per lb.)	37.4	38.5	41.4	48.6	40.4	38.0	41.9	60.2	82.1	(NA)
World smelter production, est.	6,049	5,894	6,249	6,527	6,798	6,693	7,038	7,113	7,203	7,041
World smelter and refining capacity	7,650	(NA)	7,200	7,800	7,900	7,900	7,900	7,950	[1]7,992	[1]8,236
Mine production, recoverable zinc	**317**	**303**	**275**	**253**	**227**	**203**	**216**	**244**	**276**	**515**
Colorado	14	(D)	(D)	(D)	(D)	(D)	(D)	(D)	(D)	(D)
Idaho	28	(D)	(D)	(D)	(D)	(D)	(D)	(D)	(D)	(D)
Missouri	63	64	57	45	49	38	35	41	51	49
New York	34	52	57	(D)	(D)	(D)	(D)	(D)	(D)	(D)
Tennessee	112	121	110	117	104	102	116	120	(D)	(D)
Other States.	66	66	51	91	74	63	65	83	225	466

D Withheld to avoid disclosure of individual company data.   NA Not available.   [1] Smelter capacity only.

Source: U.S. Bureau of Mines, *Minerals Yearbook*, and *Mineral Facts and Problems*.

No. 1195. Bauxite—Summary: 1980 to 1990

[See *Historical Statistics, Colonial Times to 1970*, series M 256-257, for bauxite in short ton

ITEM	Unit	1980	1985	1986	1987	1988	1989	1990 [1]
Production:								
Crude ore	Mil. metric ton.	1.9	0.8	0.6	0.7	0.7	(D)	(D)
Dried bauxite	Mil. metric ton.	1.6	0.7	0.5	0.6	0.7	(D)	(D)
Value	Mil. dol.	22.4	12.9	10.4	10.9	10.6	(D)	(D)
Imports [2] (crude, dried)	Mil. metric ton.	14.1	7.2	6.5	9.2	10.0	10.7	(NA)
Jamaica.	Mil. metric ton.	6.1	1.5	2.1	2.8	2.7	3.3	(NA)
Guinea.	Mil. metric ton.	4.1	3.8	3.4	4.3	4.5	3.4	(NA)
Suriname.	Mil. metric ton.	1.4	12.0	0.1	0.1	-	-	(NA)
Value	Mil. dol.	380.5	210.1	188.8	229.2	250.9	304.5	343.9
Exports (as shipped).	1,000 metric ton . . .	21.0	56.0	69.0	201.0	63	44	(NA)
Consumption (dry equivalent)	Mil. metric ton.	16.0	8.2	6.9	9.5	10.1	11.8	(NA)
World production, est	Mil. metric ton.	89.2	84.5	86.1	90.3	97.9	105.0	(NA)

- Represents or rounds to zero.   D Withheld to avoid disclosure.   NA Not available.   [1] Preliminary.   [2] Includes countries not shown separately.

Source: U.S. Bureau of Mines, *Minerals Yearbook*.

No. 1196. Platinum-Group Metals—Summary: 1980 to 1990

[1980-87: **In thousands of troy ounces; thereafter, in kilograms; except as indicated.** The platinum group is comprised of six closely related metals. The metals commonly occur together in nature and are among the scarcest of the metallic elements. The metals are refracto are chemically inert toward a wide variety of materials even at high temperatures; are used as catalysts in the chemical, petroleum refining, and automotive industries, and as corrosion-resistant materials in the chemical, electrical, glass, and dental-medical industries]

ITEM	1980	1984	1985	1986	1987	1988 [1]	1989 [1]	1990 [1]
World mine production, total [2]	**6,848**	**7,653**	**7,941**	**8,365**	**8,796**	**281,853**	**283,158**	**286,704**
United States	3	15	(D)	(D)	100	4,970	6,280	7,740
Soviet Union	3,250	3,700	3,800	3,900	4,000	127,500	127,500	125,000
South Africa	3,100	3,500	3,700	3,961	4,221	133,300	135,800	137,500
Refinery production, total domestic .	**1,413**	**1,521**	**1,304**	**1,513**	**1,615**	**51,488**	**50,525**	**52,311**
Primary refined	3	24	7	4	6	297	339	64
Secondary refined	1,410	1,497	1,297	1,509	1,609	51,191	50,186	52,247
Imports	3,502	4,474	3,990	4,477	3,807	124,324	113,278	125,354
Value (mil. dol.).	1,177	1,118	1,026	1,347	1,240	1,348	1,382	1,906
Exports.	765	1,162	889	751	708	28,787	38,301	55,044
Value (mil. dol.).	341	275	187	202	225	310	399	416
Consumption [3]	2,206	2,200	2,271	2,080	1,938	70,998	78,483	77,487
Industry stocks, Jan. 1	761	943	1,319	1,129	1,292	35,515	32,543	30,324
Producer price per troy ounce (dol.):								
Platinum	439	475	475	519	600	600	600	600
Palladium.	214	147	127	131	150	150	150	150
Rhodium.	766	625	915	1,196	1,239	1,275	1,275	1,275
Iridium.	505	600	600	600	532	420	(NA)	(NA)

D Withheld to avoid disclosing company proprietary data.   NA Not available.   [1] Data reported in kilograms.   [2] Includes countries not shown separately.   [3] Reported sales to industry.

Source: U.S. Bureau of Mines, *Minerals Yearbook*.

No. 1197. Titanium—Summary: 1980 to 1990

[**In 1,000 metric tons, except as indicated.** In 1985, approximately 63 percent of the titanium metal was used in jet engines, airframes, and space and mis approximately 20 percent was used in the chemical processing industry, power generation, and in marine and ordinance applications; and 17 percent in steel and other alloys]

ITEM	1980	1983	1984	1985	1986	1987	1988	1989	1990
Ilmenite concentrate:									
Mine shipments	539	(D)	(D)	(D)	(D)	(D)	(D)	(D)	(D)
Value (mil. dol.)	32.0	(D)	(D)	(D)	(D)	(D)	(D)	(D)	(D)
Imports	324	235	372	460	423	308	394	412	(NA)
Value (mil. dol.)	6.7	9.3	11.1	14.6	16.8	12.0	19.5	25.5	(NA)
Consumption	770	663	711	686	731	744	679	660	689
Titanium dioxide pigments:									
Production	660	689	758	784	844	879	927	1,007	979
Imports for consumption.	80	159	176	178	184	174	185	166	148
Apparent consumption	684	774	831	893	908	966	992	947	925
Price, Dec. 31:									
Anatase (cents per lb.)	57	69	69	72	77	77	95	102	99
Rutile (cents per lb.)	64	75	75	78	82	82	97	105	101
World production:									
Ilmenite concentrate	3,725	[1]2,674	[1]3,476	[1]3,457	[1]3,420	[1]3,937	[1]4,035	[1]4,236	[1]4,051
Titanium slag	1,192	1,052	1,143	1,280	1,285	1,575	1,725	1,765	1485
Rutile concentrate, natural [1] . . .	436	315	341	373	394	439	434	476	452

D Withheld to avoid disclosing company proprietary data.   NA Not available.   [1] Preliminary.   [2] Excludes U.S. production data to avoid disclosing company proprietary data.

Source of tables 1195-1197: U.S. Bureau of Mines, *Minerals Yearbook*.

Mining and Mineral Products

No. 1198. Chromite—Summary: 1980 to 1990

[In thousands of metric tons, except as indicated]

ITEM	1980	1983	1984	1985	1986	1987	1988	1989	1990
Imports for consumption [1]	891	172	277	376	443	490	615	525	306
Value (mil. dol.)	57	10	15	20	22	24	42	44	22
South Africa	367	131	214	273	309	251	387	368	260
Exports	5	10	50	91	84	1	4	40	6
Re-exports	40	5	4	3	1	5	1	2	4
Consumption, total	886	290	465	508	388	506	551	561	402
Metallurgical industry	741	225	376	449	342	459	495	517	359
Refractory industry	145	65	88	56	45	48	56	44	44
Stocks, Dec. 31 (consumer)	613	413	297	272	285	332	390	392	355
World production [1]	9,902	8,210	9,776	10,935	11,797	11,637	12,593	13,542	12,846
South Africa	3,414	2,466	3,407	3,699	3,907	3,789	4,245	4,951	4,498

[1] Includes countries not shown separately.
Source: U.S. Bureau of Mines, *Minerals Yearbook.*

No. 1199. Diamond Industrial—Summary: 1985 to 1991

[In million carats, unless noted]

ITEM	1985	1986	1987	1988	1989	1990	1991
Bort, grit, and powder and dust, natural and synthetic:							
Production: Manufactured diamond	76.0	80.0	(D)	(D)	90.0	90.0	90.0
Secondary (est.)	1.0	3.1	3.0	6.6	3.0	5.9	3.2
Imports for consumption	36.4	37.1	45.0	64.3	61.6	85.4	70.6
Exports and re-exports [1]	51.6	51.2	56.8	74.5	78.2	71.0	83.2
Sales of Govt. stockpile excesses	-	-	-	-	-	3.0	3.3
Consumption, apparent	61.2	68.4	(D)	(D)	75.8	112.7	83.3
Price, value of imports, dollars per carat	1.27	1.25	1.28	1.03	0.72	0.76	0.81

- Represents or rounds to zero. D Witheld to avoid disclosing company proprietary data.   [1] Includes diamonds in manufactured abrasive products.

No. 1200. Manganese Compounds—Summary: 1985 to 1991

[In thousand short tons of manganese content, unless noted]

ITEM	1985	1986	1987	1988	1989	1990	1991
Salient Statistics—United States: [1]							
Imports for consumption:							
Manganese ore	387	463	341	512	639	338	290
Ferromanganese	367	396	368	531	476	419	335
Exports:							
Manganese ore	56	42	63	68	57	77	30
Ferromanganese	7	4	3	3	9	8	10
Shipments from Govt. stockpile excesses: [2]							
Manganese ore	191	150	228	78	78	146	160
Ferromanganese	-	−81	-	−52	−55	−56	−74
Consumption, reported: [3]							
Manganese ore	545	500	533	554	616	548	510
Ferromanganese	466	376	409	468	440	455	380
Consumption, apparent, manganese [4]	698	730	699	752	797	695	660
Price, [5] average value, 46%-48% Mn metallurgical ore, dollars per ltu cont. Mn, c.i.f. U.S. ports	1.43	1.34	1.27	1.75	2.76	3.78	3.70
Stocks, producer and consumer, yearend:							
Manganese ore	589	455	456	458	518	418	355
Ferromanganese	100	93	48	91	75	62	50
Net import reliance [6] as a percent of apparent consumption	100	100	100	100	100	100	100

- Represents or rounds to zero.   [1] Manganese content typically ranges from 35% to 54% for manganese ore and from 74% to 95% for ferromanganese.   [2] Net quantity including effect of stockpile upgrading program.   [3] Total manganese consumption cannot be approximated from consumption of manganese ore and ferromanganese because of the use of ore in making manganese ferroalloys and metal.   [4] Thousand short tons, manganese content. Based on estimates of average content for all significant components except imports for which content is reported.   [5] Thousand short tons, manganese content.   [6] Defined as imports - exports + adjustments for Government and industry stock changes.

Source of tables 1199 and 1200: U.S. Bureau of Mines, *Mineral Commodity Summaries,* annual.

Construction and Housing

This section presents data on the construction industry and on various indicators of its activity and costs; on housing units and their characteristics and occupants; and on the characteristics and vacancy rates for commercial buildings. Considerable data from the 1990 census are featured in tables 1223 to 1229.

The principal source of these data is the U.S. Bureau of the Census, which issues a variety of current publications. Construction statistics compiled by the Bureau appear in its monthly *Current Construction Reports* series with various quarterly or annual supplements; *Housing Starts* and *Housing Completions* present data by type of structure and by 4 major census regions; *New One-Family Houses Sold and For Sale* also provides statistics annually on physical and financial characteristics for all new housing by the 4 major census regions; *Price Index of New One-Family Houses Sold* presents quarterly figures and annual regional data; and *Housing Units Authorized by Building Permits* covers approximately 17,000 permit-issuing jurisdictions in the United States. Statistics on expenditures by owners of residential properties are issued quarterly and annually in *Expenditures for Residential Upkeep and Improvements. Value of New Construction Put in Place* presents data on all types of construction and includes monthly composite cost indexes. Reports of the censuses of construction industries (see below) are also issued on various topics.

Other Census Bureau publications include the *Current Housing Reports* series, which comprises the quarterly *Housing Vacancies*, the quarterly *Market Absorption of Apartments*, the American Housing Survey (formerly Annual Housing Survey) and reports of the censuses of housing and of construction industries. *Construction Review,* published quarterly by the International Trade Administration, U.S. Department of Commerce, contains many of the census series and other construction statistics series from the Federal Government and private agencies.

Other sources include the monthly *Dodge Construction Potentials* of F. W. Dodge Division, McGraw-Hill Information

In Brief

Housing units, 1990	102 mil.
Median home value, 1990	$79,100
Value of new construction, 1991	$405 bil.
New homes sold, 1991	504,000
Private housing starts, 1991	1,014,000

Systems Company, New York, NY, which presents State data on construction contracts; the National Association of Home Builders with State-level data on housing starts; the NATIONAL ASSOCIATION OF REALTORS, which presents data on existing home sales; and the Society of Industrial and Office Realtors and Oncor International on commercial office space; and the Bureau of Economic Analysis, which presents data on residential capital and gross housing product; and the U.S. Energy Administration, which provides data on commercial buildings through its periodic sample surveys.

Censuses and surveys.—Censuses of the construction industry were first conducted by the Bureau of the Census for 1929, 1935, and 1939; beginning in 1967, a census has been taken every five years (for years ending in "2" and "7"). The latest reports are for 1987.

The 1987 Census of Construction Industries, in accordance with the 1987 *Standard Industrial Classification Manual* (see text, section 13), covers all employer establishments primarily engaged in (1) building construction by general contractors or operative builders; (2) heavy (non-building) construction by general contractors; and (3) construction by special trade contractors.

From 1850 through 1930, the Bureau of the Census collected some housing data as part of its censuses of population and agriculture. Beginning in 1940, separate censuses of housing have been taken at 10-year intervals. For the 1970 and 1980 censuses, data on year-round housing units were collected and issued on occupancy and structural characteristics, plumbing facilities, value, and rent.

Evaluation studies of the 1950, 1960, 1970, and 1980 censuses estimated the underenumeration of occupied housing units at 2.9 percent, 2.4 percent, 1.7 percent, and 1.5 percent respectively. The missed rate in 1980 for all housing units was 2.6 percent or approximately 2.3 million units, 1 million of which were vacant housing units. The rate for 1990 is not available at this tiime.

The American Housing Survey (*Current Housing Reports* series H-150 and H-170), which began in 1973, provided an annual and ongoing series of data on selected housing and demographic characteristics until 1983. In 1984 the name of the survey was changed from the Annual Housing Survey. It is currently based on a biennial national sample and on 11 annual MSA samples. All samples represent a cross section of the housing stock in their respective areas. Estimates are subject to both sampling and non-sampling errors; caution should therefore, be used in making comparisons with 1970 and 1980 census data.

Data on residential mortgages were collected continuously from 1890 to 1970, except 1930, as part of the decennial census by the Bureau of the Census. Since 1973, mortgage status data, which are limited to single family homes on less than ten acres with no business on the property, have been presented in the American Housing Survey.

Housing units.—In general, a housing unit is a group of rooms or a single room occupied or intended for occupancy as separate living quarters; that is, the occupants do not live and eat with any other persons in the structure and there is direct access from the outside or through a common hall. Transient accommodations, barracks for workers, and institutional-type quarters are not counted as housing units.

Statistical reliability.—For a discussion of statistical collection and estimation, sampling procedures, and measures of statistical reliability applicable to Census Bureau data, see Appendix III.

Historical statistics.—Tabular headnotes provide cross-references, where applicable, to *Historical Statistics of the United States, Colonial Times to 1970.* See Appendix IV.

No. 1201. Construction Industries—Summary, by Industry: 1987

[Based on a probability sample of about 160,000 construction establishments with payroll in 1987; see Appendix III. N.e.c.= Not elsewhere classified]

SIC [1] code	INDUSTRY	Estab-lish-ments with payroll (1,000)	EMPLOYEES (1,000) Total	EMPLOYEES (1,000) Con-struction workers	PAYROLL (mil. dol.) Total	PAYROLL (mil. dol.) Con-struction workers	VALUE OF CONSTRUC-TION WORK (mil. dol.) Total	VALUE OF CONSTRUC-TION WORK (mil. dol.) Net[2]	Value added [3] (mil. dol.)
(X)	**All industries, total**	544.2	5,054	3,989	111,067	79,742	499,982	367,746	230,174
	Contract construction.	536.3	5,015	3,979	110,200	79,589	495,346	365,241	227,934
15	General building contractors.	157.6	1,278	926	27,870	17,204	212,629	111,019	65,514
1521	Single-family houses	90.4	396	307	6,272	4,343	39,098	27,319	14,970
1522	Other residential buildings.	8.1	82	61	1,752	1,130	13,316	6,257	3,659
1531	Operative builders	20.8	169	80	4,385	1,478	48,960	26,837	15,173
1541	Industrial buildings and warehouses . .	7.0	143	111	3,619	2,497	21,462	11,095	6,882
1542	Nonresidential buildings, n.e.c	31.3	488	367	11,843	7,756	89,793	39,510	24,831
16	Heavy construction contractors.	36.6	827	683	20,408	15,461	82,285	68,435	44,940
1611	Highway and street construction	11.0	284	239	7,041	5,397	34,161	27,984	17,120
1622	Bridge, tunnel, and elevated highway .	1.2	47	40	1,192	910	5,481	4,187	2,430
1623	Water, sewer, and utility lines	10.0	198	166	4,513	3,428	17,010	15,055	10,090
1629	Heavy construction, n.e.c	14.5	298	238	7,662	5,726	25,633	21,209	15,301
17	Special trade contractors.	342.0	2,909	2,370	61,921	46,923	200,434	185,786	117,480
1711	Plumbing, heating, air-conditioning . . .	69.6	617	471	14,330	10,311	49,503	44,518	25,912
1721	Painting and paperhanging	29.9	170	145	2,979	2,386	7,953	7,446	5,716
1731	Electrical work	49.4	509	406	12,664	9,622	35,838	34,658	21,817
1741	Masonry and other stonework	23.3	169	150	2,947	2,462	8,714	8,269	5,476
1742	Plastering, drywall, insulation.	17.8	254	217	5,485	4,348	16,427	15,137	9,748
1743	Terrazzo, tile, marble, and mosaic work	5.1	34	28	734	554	2,272	2,182	1,318
1751	Carpentry.	36.0	190	164	3,272	2,610	11,244	10,039	6,078
1752	Floorlaying and other floor work.	8.2	45	35	906	645	3,651	3,371	1,880
1761	Roofing, siding, and sheet metal work.	25.7	231	187	4,314	3,111	15,028	14,183	8,524
1771	Concrete work	23.4	218	187	4,175	3,278	15,056	13,854	8,443
1781	Water well drilling	3.4	18	14	335	249	1,330	1,299	780
1791	Structural steel erection	4.0	65	55	1,594	1,232	4,863	4,510	3,253
1793	Glass and glazing work	4.6	41	29	919	607	3,222	3,142	1,701
1794	Excavation work	13.4	95	79	2,060	1,598	8,244	7,491	5,708
1795	Wrecking and demolition work.	1.2	14	12	261	195	912	845	782
1796	Installing building equipment, n.e.c . . .	3.8	62	50	1,858	1,447	5,360	5,010	3,723
1799	Special trade contractors, n.e.c.	23.2	176	142	3,089	2,269	10,814	9,833	6,622
6552	Land subdividers and developers, n.e.c.	8.0	40	9	867	153	4,636	2,505	2,240

X Not applicable.   [1] Standard Industrial Classification; see, text, section 13.   [2] Value of construction work less payments for construction work subcontracted to others, not shown separately.   [3] Dollar value of business done less (a) payments for materials, components, and supplies, and (b) payments for construction work subcontracted to others, not shown separately.
Source: U.S. Bureau of the Census, *Census of Construction Industries, 1987,* series CC87-I-28.

No. 1202. Construction Materials—Producer Price Indexes: 1970 to 1991

[1982 = 100, except as noted. For discussion of producer price index, see text, section 15. This index, more formally known as the special commodity grouping index for construction materials, covers materials incorporated as integral part of a building or normally installed during construction and not readily removable. Excludes consumer durables such as kitchen ranges, refrigerators, etc. This index is not the same as the stage-of-processing index of intermediate materials and components for construction. See *Historical Statistics, Colonial Times to 1970,* series N 140-155 for similar data]

COMMODITY	1970	1975	1980	1984	1985	1986	1987	1988	1989	1990	1991
Construction materials	39.1	60.4	92.5	106.4	107.6	107.3	109.5	115.7	119.5	119.6	120.4
Interior solvent based paint	40.1	60.2	91.3	103.9	107.3	109.9	111.6	120.3	128.8	133.0	140.2
Plastic construction products	65.5	83.5	103.9	115.5	108.6	106.4	108.4	121.1	120.1	117.2	115.4
Douglas fir, dressed	40.8	79.6	132.6	123.2	126.5	124.5	125.1	135.7	151.6	138.4	139.4
Southern pine, dressed	40.1	61.3	104.0	111.9	105.2	104.9	114.1	112.4	108.0	111.2	111.0
Millwork	41.5	57.4	93.2	104.2	111.7	113.7	117.7	121.9	127.3	130.4	135.4
Softwood plywood	40.3	71.1	109.5	107.6	107.4	109.4	109.8	109.1	124.2	119.6	120.7
Hardwood plywood and related products . . .	56.6	66.0	97.5	99.6	89.9	91.0	92.9	94.2	99.8	102.7	102.9
Softwood plywood veneer, ex. reinforced/backed	(NA)	75.2	126.0	103.3	100.1	105.9	108.4	117.3	142.1	142.3	138.5
Building paper and building board mill products .	42.2	53.1	86.1	108.2	107.4	108.8	111.2	113.3	115.6	112.2	111.8
Tube, drawn, 6000 alloy series	35.6	56.5	85.6	109.7	109.7	109.8	111.2	128.9	131.0	127.1	124.1
Builders hardware	41.7	58.7	84.9	109.3	113.5	115.8	117.4	122.5	127.8	133.0	138.1
Plumbing fixtures and brass fittings	39.9	58.2	88.5	108.6	111.9	115.5	119.7	128.7	137.7	144.3	149.7
Heating equipment	46.6	63.5	87.0	106.6	109.5	113.0	115.5	119.2	125.1	131.6	134.1
Metal doors, sash, and trim	30.9	55.0	87.8	106.6	106.7	108.9	120.0	122.4	130.0	131.4	134.7
Incandescent outdoor lighting fixtures	34.4	53.0	82.7	109.2	109.2	112.0	117.2	122.4	128.0	137.3	136.2
Bright nails	31.4	66.1	90.9	99.4	100.2	99.8	101.2	104.7	110.4	(NA)	(NA)
Welded steel wire fabric for concrete reinforcing.	40.6	(NA)	98.9	101.9	101.3	98.8	98.3	109.2	108.6	109.7	99.7
Elevators, escalators, and other lifts	42.3	62.0	87.3	97.1	97.7	99.2	100.4	103.6	107.1	110.1	108.8
Stamped metal outlet box	31.4	(NA)	82.7	114.9	119.7	152.0	160.1	168.7	171.7	179.4	179.7
Concrete ingredients and related products	36.3	55.6	88.4	105.1	108.5	109.4	110.4	112.0	113.2	115.3	118.5
Concrete products	37.7	57.3	92.0	103.9	107.5	109.2	109.4	110.0	112.3	113.5	115.6
Clay construction products exc. refractories . . .	42.1	58.0	88.8	110.0	113.5	118.0	121.4	124.9	127.0	129.9	130.2
Prep. asphalt and tar roofing and siding products.	28.8	61.7	105.5	97.7	100.5	96.8	91.9	94.4	95.6	97.1	98.3
Gypsum products	38.9	56.2	100.1	135.4	132.3	137.0	125.2	112.9	110.0	105.2	99.5
Insulation materials.	34.6	55.0	80.7	104.0	105.2	105.7	105.0	105.8	106.7	108.4	110.9
Paving mixtures and blocks	18.1	44.0	83.7	106.1	111.6	104.9	100.8	102.7	101.0	101.2	103.2

NA Not available.

Source: U.S. Bureau of Labor Statistics, *Producer Price Indexes,* monthly and annual.

No. 1203. Price and Cost Indexes for Construction: 1970 to 1991

[**1987**=**100.** Excludes Alaska and Hawaii. Indexes from certain of these sources are published on bases different from those shown here. See *Historical Statistics, Colonial Times to 1970,* series N 118-137, for construction cost indexes on a 1947-49 base]

NAME OF INDEX	1970	1975	1980	1984	1985	1986	1988	1989	1990	1991
Bureau of the Census:										
Composite fixed-weighted [1]	31.7	48.4	77.6	90.2	93.1	96.5	103.8	107.4	110.1	110.9
Implicit price deflator [2]	32.6	50.2	79.1	91.2	93.9	96.8	104.1	108.3	110.8	111.4
Bureau of the Census houses under construction: [3]										
Fixed-weighted	30.2	45.0	75.6	88.8	91.0	95.6	103.6	107.0	109.8	110.2
Price deflator	31.4	46.8	77.9	90.1	92.0	95.8	104.1	108.4	110.9	110.8
Federal Highway Administration, composite [4]	36.8	58.1	97.2	92.6	102.0	101.1	106.6	107.7	108.5	107.5
Bureau of Reclamation composite [5]	34	55	81	96	98	99	103	107	111	114
Turner Construction Co.: Building construction [6] . . .	32	50	69	91	94	97	104	107	111	113
E. H. Boeckh, building cost index: [7]										
Residences	(NA)	(NA)	(NA)	93.5	96.2	98.0	102.5	106.3	109.9	113.0
Apartments, hotels, and office buildings	(NA)	(NA)	(NA)	94.8	96.3	98.0	102.7	106.2	109.0	112.0
Commercial and factory buildings.	(NA)	(NA)	(NA)	95.0	96.7	98.3	103.0	107.2	110.8	114.2
Engineering News-Record: [8]										
Buildings	32.9	51.4	76.5	95.1	95.5	97.7	102.2	103.6	106.3	108.3
Construction.	31.4	50.2	73.5	94.1	95.2	97.5	102.6	104.7	107.4	109.7
Handy-Whitman public utility: [9]										
Buildings	32	57	83	94	96	98	104	107	108	105
Electric [10]	32	55	80	97	98	99	107	111	115	116
Gas	34	54	79	100	100	97	106	111	114	116
Water [11]	32	54	81	94	97	98	103	106	108	108
C. A. Turner Telephone Plant [12]	51	69	102	99	101	100	101	110	113	114

NA Not available.   [1] Weighted average of the various indexes used to deflate the Construction Put in Place series. In calculating the index, the weights (i.e., the composition of current dollar estimates in 1987 by category) are held constant. [2] Derived ratio of total current to constant dollar Construction Put in Place (multiplied by 100).   [3] Excludes value of site.   [4] Based on average contract unit bid prices for composite mile (involving specific average amounts of excavation, paving, reinforcing steel, structural steel, and structural concrete).   [5] Derived from the four quarterly indexes which are weighted averages of costs of labor, materials, and equipment for the construction of dams and reclamation projects.   [6] Based on firm's cost experience with respect to labor rates, materials prices, competitive conditions, efficiency of plant and management, and productivity.   [7] Average of 20 cities for types shown. Weights based on surveys of building costs.   [8] Building index computed on the basis of a hypothetical unit of construction requiring 6 bbl. of portland cement, 1,088 M bd. ft. of 2'' x 4'' lumber, 2,500 lb. of structural steel, and 68.38 hours of skilled labor. Construction index based on same materials components combined with 200 hours of common labor.   [9] Based on data covering public utility construction costs in six geographic regions. Covers skilled and common labor. [10] As derived by U.S. Bureau of the Census. Covers steam generation plants only.   [11] As derived by U.S. Bureau of the Census. Reflects costs for structures and improvements at water pumping and treatment plants.   [12] Computed by the Census Bureau by averaging the weighted component indexes published for six geographic regions.

Source: U.S. Bureau of the Census. In U.S. Department of Commerce, International Trade Administration, *Construction Review,* bimonthly.

No. 1204. Value of New Construction Put in Place: 1964 to 1991

[**In millions of dollars.** Represents value of construction put in place during year; differs from building permit and construction contract data in timing and coverage. Includes installed cost of normal building service equipment and selected types of industrial production equipment (largely site fabricated). Excludes cost of shipbuilding, land, and most types of machinery and equipment. For methodology, see Appendix III. See also *Historical Statistics, Colonial Times to 1970,* series N 1-29 and N 66-69]

YEAR	CURRENT DOLLARS					CONSTANT (**1987**) DOLLARS				
	Total	Private			Public	Total	Private			Public
		Total	Residential buildings	Nonresidential buildings			Total	Residential buildings	Nonresidential buildings	
1964	72,124	51,921	30,526	14,412	20,203	294,569	211,627	124,768	60,892	82,942
1970	100,727	72,819	35,863	23,008	27,908	309,244	225,168	114,138	71,796	84,077
1971	117,311	87,612	48,514	24,204	29,699	337,451	254,502	145,554	69,621	82,949
1972	133,318	103,288	60,693	26,568	30,030	360,780	281,593	170,190	71,490	79,187
1973	146,826	114,477	65,085	30,683	32,348	364,938	285,937	166,249	76,259	79,001
1974	147,476	109,344	55,967	32,195	38,132	319,362	242,274	130,126	70,029	77,089
1975	145,623	102,330	51,581	28,397	43,293	290,137	208,991	109,920	58,990	81,147
1976	165,441	121,462	68,273	27,936	43,979	315,865	235,338	136,685	55,617	80,527
1977	193,126	150,044	92,004	30,871	43,083	340,833	266,393	165,926	57,134	74,440
1978	230,178	180,032	109,838	39,135	50,146	362,862	285,880	174,695	65,343	76,982
1979	259,839	203,194	116,444	51,732	56,646	364,554	288,789	165,116	77,359	75,766
1980	259,746	196,100	100,381	58,290	63,646	328,435	252,645	128,926	78,972	75,790
1981	271,950	207,259	99,241	68,450	64,691	320,950	247,427	118,343	85,091	73,523
1982	260,594	197,531	84,676	73,953	63,064	297,759	226,510	97,595	87,505	71,249
1983	294,945	231,494	125,521	70,438	63,450	332,625	261,398	143,108	80,888	71,227
1984	348,817	278,600	153,849	87,493	70,217	382,435	306,152	170,732	96,664	76,284
1985	377,366	299,543	158,474	103,455	77,823	401,967	321,706	172,338	111,262	80,260
1986	407,693	323,100	187,148	98,674	84,593	421,367	335,709	195,377	102,596	85,658
1987	419,264	328,636	194,656	100,933	90,628	419,250	328,535	194,622	100,877	90,715
1988	432,223	337,441	198,101	106,994	94,782	415,004	324,332	190,292	103,037	90,673
1989	443,721	345,417	196,551	113,988	98,305	409,775	318,653	181,321	105,711	91,122
1990	446,434	337,777	182,856	117,971	108,657	402,770	304,057	164,887	106,369	98,714
1991	404,892	295,736	160,961	96,763	109,156	363,204	265,345	145,162	86,934	97,859

Source: U.S. Bureau of the Census, *Current Construction Reports,* series C30, and press release, CB-91-14.

No. 1205. Value of New Construction Put in Place in Current and Constant (1987) Dollars: 1985 to 1991

[In millions of dollars. Represents value of construction put in place during year; differs from building permit and construction contract data in timing and coverage. Includes installed cost of normal building service equipment and selected types of industrial production equipment (largely site fabricated). Excludes cost of shipbuilding, land, and most types of machinery and equipment. For details on derivation of constant values and description of revised series, see source. For description of nature of revisions and deflators used, see *Construction Reports*, series C30-9005. For methodology, see Appendix III. See also *Historical Statistics, Colonial Times to 1970*, series N 1-29 and N 66-69]

TYPE OF CONSTRUCTION	CURRENT DOLLARS					CONSTANT (1987) DOLLARS				
	1985	1988	1989	1990	1991, prel.	1985	1988	1989	1990	1991, prel.
Total new construction .	377,366	432,223	443,721	446,434	404,892	401,967	415,004	409,775	402,770	363,204
Private construction	299,543	337,441	345,417	337,777	[1]295,736	321,706	324,332	318,653	304,057	[1]265,345
Residential buildings	158,474	198,101	196,551	182,856	160,961	172,338	190,292	181,321	164,887	145,162
New housing units	114,662	138,947	139,202	127,987	110,816	124,699	133,469	128,435	115,414	99,927
One unit	86,123	116,649	116,898	108,737	95,841	93,659	112,045	107,849	98,053	86,408
Two or more units	28,539	22,298	22,304	19,250	14,975	31,040	21,424	20,586	17,362	13,519
Improvements	43,812	59,154	57,349	54,869	(NA)	47,639	56,823	52,886	49,472	(NA)
Nonresidential buildings . . .	103,455	106,994	113,988	117,971	96,763	111,262	103,037	105,711	106,369	86,934
Industrial.	17,116	16,452	20,410	23,848	21,709	18,408	15,838	18,919	21,502	19,505
Office.	34,276	30,902	31,538	28,722	22,676	36,867	29,761	29,263	25,902	20,373
Hotels, motels	7,925	7,486	8,401	9,673	6,279	8,524	7,213	7,791	8,723	5,643
Other commercial.	30,443	33,122	33,958	34,140	25,357	32,734	31,893	31,482	30,780	22,781
Religious	2,615	3,110	3,278	3,390	3,394	2,811	2,995	3,040	3,055	3,049
Educational	2,058	3,209	3,648	4,219	3,901	2,213	3,091	3,382	3,803	3,505
Hospital and institutional .	6,060	7,954	8,312	9,450	9,255	6,521	7,662	7,711	8,519	8,316
Miscellaneous [2]	2,962	4,760	4,443	4,528	4,190	3,186	4,583	4,122	4,083	3,764
Farm nonresidential.	2,197	2,270	2,295	2,670	(NA)	2,366	2,187	2,129	2,407	(NA)
Public utilities	32,692	27,949	29,881	30,953	(NA)	32,989	26,784	26,993	27,371	(NA)
Telecommunications	8,397	9,556	9,465	9,565	(NA)	8,264	9,475	8,525	8,499	(NA)
Other public utilities	24,295	18,393	20,416	21,388	(NA)	24,725	17,309	18,468	18,872	(NA)
Railroads	4,046	2,382	2,650	2,726	(NA)	4,079	2,275	2,452	2,477	(NA)
Electric light and power .	16,460	11,978	13,038	12,882	(NA)	16,871	11,240	11,769	11,302	(NA)
Gas	3,517	3,656	4,386	5,369	(NA)	3,504	3,439	3,939	4,731	(NA)
Petroleum pipelines.	272	377	342	411	(NA)	271	354	307	362	(NA)
All other private [3]	2,726	2,126	2,702	3,326	3,608	2,751	2,033	2,501	3,024	3,206
Public construction.	77,823	94,782	98,305	108,657	109,156	80,260	90,673	91,122	98,714	97,859
Buildings	27,861	36,362	39,567	45,825	49,574	30,000	35,009	36,668	41,309	44,548
Housing and development	2,893	3,276	3,621	3,733	3,544	3,146	3,147	3,341	3,368	3,198
Industrial.	1,968	1,413	1,300	1,433	1,828	2,118	1,361	1,205	1,292	1,642
Educational	9,329	14,397	17,012	20,566	23,247	10,033	13,860	15,769	18,533	20,881
Hospital	2,497	2,708	2,514	2,610	2,658	2,686	2,608	2,332	2,354	2,388
Other [4]	11,174	14,569	15,120	17,482	18,297	12,016	14,033	14,021	15,761	16,439
Highways and streets.	23,741	29,228	28,174	30,593	29,041	23,455	27,586	26,138	28,211	26,165
Military facilities.	3,235	3,579	3,520	2,732	1,849	3,341	3,417	3,261	2,492	1,664
Conservation and development	5,144	4,739	4,989	4,718	5,347	5,279	4,577	4,609	4,233	4,688
Sewer systems	6,960	8,818	9,405	10,403	10,255	7,139	8,519	8,687	9,327	8,990
Water supply facilities	2,580	4,000	3,999	4,973	4,941	2,671	3,872	3,755	4,588	4,566
Miscellaneous public [5]	8,302	8,055	8,651	9,413	8,148	8,374	7,693	8,004	8,554	7,239

NA Not available. [1] Includes estimates for types of construction indicated as (NA). [2] Includes amusement and recreational buildings, bus and airline terminals, animal hospitals and shelters, etc. [3] Includes privately owned streets and bridges, parking areas, sewer and water facilities, parks and playgrounds, golf courses, airfields, etc. [4] Includes federal administrative buildings, prisons, police and fire stations, courthouses, civic centers, passenger terminals, space facilities, postal facilities, etc. [5] Includes open amusement and recreational facilities, power generating facilities, transit systems, airfields, open parking facilities, etc.

Source: U.S. Bureau of the Census, *Current Construction Reports*, series C30, and press release, CB-91-14.

No. 1206. Value of Privately Owned Nonresidential Building Projects, by Construction Status, 1980 to 1990, and by Type of Project, 1990

[In billions of dollars]

CONSTRUCTION STATUS	1980	1983	1984	1985	1986	1987	1988	1989	1000			
									Total	Industrial	Office building	Other commercial	Other[1]
Value of projects—													
Started	53.8	67.8	91.3	98.5	97.1	95.7	107.7	109.9	89.5	15.2	23.2	27.5	23.6
Completed	53.0	64.7	73.5	89.9	107.5	91.4	101.6	107.7	114.0	19.4	29.5	35.9	29.1

[1] Privately owned hotels and motels, religious, educational, hospital and institutional, and miscellaneous nonresidential building projects.

Source: U.S. Bureau of the Census, *Current Construction Reports*, series C30.

No. 1207. Construction Contracts—Value of Construction and Floor Space of Buildings, by Class of Construction: 1980 to 1991

[Includes new structures and additions, and major alterations to existing structures which affect only valuation, since no additional floor area is created by "alteration." See also *Historical Statistics, Colonial Times to 1970*, series N 7888-100]

YEAR	Total	Resi-dential build-ings	NONRESIDENTIAL BUILDINGS									Non-build-ing con-struc-tion
			Total	Com-mer-cial [1]	Manu-fac-turing	Educa-tional [2]	Hos-pital	Public build-ings	Reli-gious	Social and recrea-tional	Mis-cella-neous	
VALUE (bil. dol.)												
1980	151.8	60.4	56.9	27.7	9.2	7.4	5.4	1.6	1.2	2.7	1.7	34.5
1981	157.3	56.3	65.5	35.2	9.3	6.6	6.4	1.4	1.2	3.4	2.0	35.4
1982	157.1	55.0	64.6	32.3	9.6	6.8	8.0	1.9	1.2	2.8	2.0	37.5
1983	194.1	88.4	67.9	38.3	5.4	7.1	8.5	2.1	1.5	2.9	2.1	37.8
1984	214.3	95.3	82.1	48.2	7.9	8.5	7.4	2.7	1.7	3.3	2.4	36.9
1985	235.8	102.1	92.3	54.6	8.1	10.0	7.8	3.1	2.0	4.0	2.5	41.4
1986	249.3	115.6	91.6	52.4	7.3	11.7	7.9	3.2	2.1	4.2	2.8	42.1
1987	259.0	114.1	98.8	53.7	8.6	13.2	9.0	4.7	2.1	4.3	3.2	46.1
1988	262.2	116.2	97.9	51.6	9.5	14.1	8.2	4.4	2.2	4.7	3.2	48.1
1989	271.3	116.2	106.1	53.6	12.7	15.9	8.8	5.2	2.0	5.0	2.8	49.0
1990	246.4	101.0	95.6	45.1	8.4	16.6	9.2	5.7	2.2	5.3	3.1	49.8
1991	228.6	94.3	85.0	32.7	7.8	18.9	9.4	6.0	2.4	4.9	2.9	49.2
FLOOR SPACE (mil. sq. ft.)												
1980	3,102	1,839	1,263	738	220	103	55	18	28	49	52	(X)
1981	2,805	1,562	1,243	787	188	83	60	14	25	46	41	(X)
1982	2,455	1,440	1,015	631	119	82	71	19	25	38	30	(X)
1983	3,387	2,276	1,111	716	112	84	84	20	29	36	31	(X)
1984	3,661	2,311	1,350	901	157	100	70	23	29	37	34	(X)
1985	3,853	2,324	1,529	1,039	165	111	73	28	32	44	38	(X)
1986	3,935	2,481	1,454	960	148	129	73	30	32	44	39	(X)
1987	3,756	2,288	1,469	933	160	139	78	42	32	46	38	(X)
1988	3,594	2,181	1,413	883	162	142	71	38	32	49	37	(X)
1989	3,516	2,115	1,401	867	158	152	72	41	27	48	35	(X)
1990	3,025	1,818	1,207	698	128	152	69	47	29	51	32	(X)
1991	2,591	1,621	971	475	97	176	71	48	29	43	32	(X)

X Not applicable.   [1] Includes nonindustrial warehouses.   [2] Includes science.

No. 1208. Construction Contracts—Value, by State: 1985 to 1991

[In millions of dollars. See headnote, table 1207. Represents value of construction in States in which work was actually done]

STATE	1985	1989	1990	1991 Total (incl. non-bldg.)	1991 Resi-den-tial	1991 Non-resi-den-tial	STATE	1985	1989	1990	1991 Total (incl. non-bldg.)	1991 Resi-den-tial	1991 Non-resi-den-tial
U.S.	232,277	270,654	246,236	226,760	97,416	80,491	MO	3,851	4,180	3,833	3,904	1,581	1,323
							MT	698	440	332	451	124	163
AL	2,886	3,022	2,940	2,664	1,187	951	NE	1,040	1,128	1,318	1,225	501	345
AK	1,500	648	1,919	735	207	165	NV	1,629	3,702	3,335	2,434	1,249	817
AZ	6,629	5,070	4,554	4,617	2,499	1,179	NH	1,355	1,292	1,021	815	355	257
AR	1,649	1,836	1,437	1,627	715	461	NJ	8,077	7,820	6,192	6,221	1,750	2,405
CA	32,456	43,496	37,442	29,366	12,623	11,121	NM	1,771	1,271	1,123	1,504	544	415
CO	4,667	2,797	3,240	4,483	1,713	1,539	NY	11,366	17,349	14,226	12,294	4,271	4,766
CT	3,385	3,679	3,012	2,783	880	1,224	NC	6,671	7,419	6,629	6,852	3,290	2,505
DE	715	884	787	793	343	303	ND	557	460	506	490	178	163
DC	985	1,282	795	626	52	434	OH	6,943	10,302	9,897	9,460	4,064	3,595
FL	17,820	21,141	17,023	15,474	8,070	4,771	OK	2,650	1,912	2,164	2,049	796	693
GA	7,566	7,970	7,124	6,831	3,472	2,172	OR	1,634	2,545	3,102	2,484	1,409	689
HI	873	2,263	2,829	2,713	1,349	878	PA	7,008	10,831	10,095	9,661	3,643	4,008
ID	758	775	986	1,054	627	223	RI	828	1,396	594	675	263	217
IL	7,513	11,992	10,777	9,149	3,865	3,477	SC	3,446	3,444	3,666	3,451	1,629	1,226
IN	4,045	5,496	6,311	5,196	2,575	1,750	SD	485	501	468	373	169	118
IA	1,532	1,812	2,036	2,329	829	753	TN	4,394	5,027	4,388	4,277	2,055	1,293
KS	2,227	2,089	2,171	2,237	923	697	TX	21,305	14,645	13,197	14,297	5,444	5,684
KY	2,843	3,294	3,175	3,719	1,382	1,320	UT	1,633	1,698	1,884	1,719	860	489
LA	3,869	3,201	3,193	2,942	848	1,069	VT	487	634	515	544	254	133
ME	785	952	895	769	381	215	VA	7,586	9,057	7,192	6,307	3,040	2,060
MD	5,703	7,368	6,052	5,083	2,475	1,800	WA	4,409	5,402	6,179	6,082	2,852	2,374
MA	5,806	6,560	5,136	4,870	1,687	1,471	WV	858	836	1,253	885	226	269
MI	5,827	8,262	7,669	7,196	3,250	2,693	WI	3,038	4,461	4,647	4,215	1,948	1,438
MN	4,285	5,046	4,947	4,431	2,277	1,485	WY	693	407	461	513	131	105
MS	1,543	1,561	1,569	1,887	562	787							

Source of tables 1207 and 1208: F. W. Dodge, National Information Services Division, McGraw-Hill Information Systems Company, New York, NY. Figures reported currently in *Dodge Construction Potentials*.

No. 1209. New Privately-Owned Housing Units Authorized, by State: 1990 and 1991

[Based on about 17,000 places in United States having building permit systems]

STATE	HOUSING UNITS (1,000) 1990	1991 Total	1991 1 unit	VALUATION (mil. dol.) 1990	1991 Total	1991 1 unit	STATE	HOUSING UNITS (1,000) 1990	1991 Total	1991 1 unit	VALUATION (mil. dol.) 1990	1991 Total	1991 1 unit
U.S.	1,110.8	948.8	753.5	86,522	78,772	69,723	MO . . .	15.3	16.1	13.1	1,089	1,122	1,020
AL. . . .	12.5	11.3	8.8	683	692	624	MT . . .	1.2	1.5	1.0	86	111	87
AK . . .	0.7	1.0	0.9	92	137	128	NE . . .	6.8	6.2	4.6	355	387	340
AZ . . .	23.0	23.5	21.4	1,963	2,262	2,172	NV . . .	25.1	21.0	15.3	1,427	1,280	1,094
AR . . .	5.9	6.9	5.0	333	386	340	NH . . .	4.1	3.5	3.3	361	304	298
CA . . .	163.2	106.0	73.9	17,233	11,990	9,677	NJ. . . .	17.5	14.9	12.9	1,398	1,245	1,144
CO . . .	11.9	14.1	12.9	1,157	1,512	1,453	NM . . .	6.0	6.1	5.4	464	471	448
CT . . .	7.6	7.5	5.9	649	667	614	NY . . .	35.0	28.6	21.7	2,782	2,421	2,002
DE . . .	5.1	4.3	3.8	274	238	225	NC . . .	40.8	39.0	33.2	2,753	2,803	2,622
DC . . .	0.4	0.3	0.1	21	17	7	ND . . .	1.5	2.1	1.0	89	112	85
FL. . . .	126.3	95.3	71.0	8,424	7,087	6,080	OH . . .	38.5	35.8	27.1	3,039	3,147	2,855
GA . . .	41.3	37.6	33.6	2,720	2,701	2,568	OK . . .	5.3	5.9	5.7	401	488	482
HI . . .	8.7	9.2	4.7	1,008	1,138	571	OR . . .	22.9	16.4	11.8	1,657	1,382	1,201
ID. . . .	5.7	6.6	5.5	445	519	476	PA . . .	37.2	34.6	29.4	2,896	2,798	2,568
IL. . . .	38.3	32.8	26.0	3,515	3,189	2,865	RI . . .	3.0	2.4	2.0	233	181	171
IN. . . .	25.0	23.9	19.4	2,033	1,995	1,844	SC . . .	21.3	18.7	16.2	1,445	1,353	1,268
IA. . . .	7.6	8.0	5.9	531	603	524	SD . . .	2.8	2.5	1.6	140	147	114
KS . . .	8.5	7.8	6.6	659	644	600	TN . . .	20.2	19.3	16.9	1,317	1,359	1,282
KY . . .	11.8	12.0	9.2	771	784	705	TX . . .	47.1	51.9	41.7	3,869	4,301	4,010
LA. . . .	6.5	7.2	6.7	440	509	494	UT . . .	7.3	8.9	8.1	594	778	737
ME. . . .	4.8	3.7	3.5	325	280	270	VT . . .	2.4	2.0	1.8	189	167	158
MD. . . .	32.0	25.2	21.0	2,180	1,915	1,744	VA . . .	42.1	33.7	29.5	2,798	2,490	2,337
MA . . .	14.3	12.7	11.3	1,321	1,265	1,197	WA . .	48.4	33.0	23.7	3,487	2,644	2,200
MI. . . .	38.9	33.8	28.2	2,748	2,597	2,358	WV . . .	1.8	2.0	1.7	110	126	120
MN . . .	23.5	21.1	18.1	1,867	1,882	1,746	WI. . . .	27.3	25.1	16.5	1,792	1,798	1,470
MS . . .	5.9	5.2	4.4	298	285	267	WY . . .	0.7	0.6	0.6	62	62	58

Source: U.S. Bureau of the Census, *Construction Reports*, series C40, annual.

No. 1210. Valuation of Construction Authorized by Permit, by Type of Construction and State: 1991

[In millions of dollars]

STATE	Total [1]	Resi-dential	NONRESIDENTIAL Total [2]	Indus-trial	Office	Stores	STATE	Total [1]	Resi-dential	NONRESIDENTIAL Total [2]	Indus-trial	Office	Stores
U.S..	153,409	78,772	32,674	4,975	6,998	9,282	MO . . .	2,522	1,122	657	81	93	164
AL . . .	1,648	692	471	49	115	123	MT . . .	282	111	63	3	19	28
AK . . .	295	137	74	5	12	34	NE . . .	739	387	142	18	31	37
AZ . . .	3,207	2,262	488	56	71	182	NV . . .	2,256	1,280	403	67	48	153
AR . . .	804	386	248	44	39	80	NH. . . .	609	304	140	9	32	57
CA . . .	24,480	11,990	5,098	855	1,233	1,570	NJ. . . .	3,734	1,245	733	99	226	115
CO . . .	2,536	1,512	301	50	32	59	NM. . . .	786	471	131	46	21	30
CT . . .	1,602	667	247	11	33	55	NY . . .	5,947	2,421	1,449	141	202	442
DE . . .	572	238	147	39	28	34	NC . . .	5,227	2,803	1,282	297	270	296
DC . . .	170	17	71	-	58	7	ND . . .	262	112	48	7	9	18
FL . . .	12,007	7,087	2,195	119	313	736	OH . . .	6,245	3,147	1,357	247	249	407
GA . . .	4,730	2,701	993	144	203	342	OK . . .	957	488	227	46	43	84
HI . . .	2,116	1,138	471	53	214	44	OR . . .	2,421	1,382	473	108	93	98
ID . . .	824	519	168	36	30	43	PA . . .	5,662	2,798	1,259	182	265	323
IL . . .	6,711	3,189	1,538	268	416	431	RI . . .	328	181	26	5	2	6
IN . . .	3,453	1,995	826	177	149	272	SC . . .	2,503	1,353	670	120	130	168
IA . . .	1,249	603	329	51	60	103	SD . . .	363	147	102	7	28	25
KS . . .	1,185	644	206	48	36	52	TN . . .	2,667	1,359	620	90	111	186
KY . . .	1,424	784	368	62	107	99	TX . . .	8,161	4,301	1,860	276	369	584
LA . . .	1,101	509	287	15	93	83	UT . . .	1,271	778	289	34	30	97
ME. . .	569	280	105	12	12	41	VT . . .	352	167	89	13	10	18
MD . . .	3,623	1,915	563	125	106	163	VA . . .	4,979	2,490	1,206	127	408	256
MA . . .	2,889	1,265	396	50	58	83	WA . .	4,794	2,644	1,093	202	303	282
MI . . .	5,075	2,597	1,079	231	256	289	WV . .	302	126	82	6	12	20
MN	3,628	1,882	671	70	104	215	WI . . .	3,412	1,798	759	157	193	169
MS. . .	592	285	143	16	17	62	WY . .	105	62	31	2	4	18

- Represents zero.   [1] Includes residential and nonresidential additions and alterations, residential nonhousekeeping buildings, and residential garages and carports, not shown separately.   [2] Includes other types of construction not shown separately.

Source: U.S. Bureau of the Census, unpublished data.

No. 1211. New Privately-Owned Housing Units Started—Selected Characteristics: 1970 to 1991

[In thousands. For composition of regions, see table 25. See also *Historical Statistics, Colonial Times to 1970*, series N 156-163 and 170]

YEAR	Total units	STRUCTURES WITH— One unit	STRUCTURES WITH— 2 to 4 units	STRUCTURES WITH— 5 or more units	REGION North-east	REGION Mid-west	REGION South	REGION West	CONDOMINIUM UNITS [1] Total	CONDOMINIUM UNITS [1] Single-family	CONDOMINIUM UNITS [1] Multi-family	TYPE OF ASSISTANCE FHA	TYPE OF ASSISTANCE VA
1970	1,434	813	85	536	218	294	612	311	(NA)	(NA)	(NA)	421	61
1971	2,052	1,151	120	781	264	434	869	486	(NA)	(NA)	(NA)	528	94
1972	2,357	1,309	141	906	330	443	1,057	527	(NA)	(NA)	(NA)	371	104
1973	2,045	1,132	118	795	277	440	899	429	241	69	172	163	86
1974	1,338	888	68	382	183	317	553	285	175	46	130	95	73
1975	1,160	892	64	204	149	294	442	275	65	20	45	98	77
1976	1,538	1,162	86	289	169	400	569	400	95	30	64	144	100
1977	1,987	1,451	122	414	202	465	783	538	118	41	77	178	131
1978	2,020	1,433	125	462	200	451	824	545	156	42	114	178	127
1979	1,745	1,194	122	429	178	349	748	470	198	43	156	178	122
1980	1,292	852	110	331	125	218	643	306	186	35	150	177	95
1981	1,084	705	91	288	117	165	562	240	181	36	145	145	75
1982	1,062	663	80	320	117	149	591	205	170	40	130	152	73
1983	1,703	1,068	113	522	168	218	935	382	276	77	199	121	107
1984	1,750	1,084	121	544	204	243	866	436	291	96	194	63	97
1985	1,742	1,072	93	576	252	240	782	468	225	79	146	159	90
1986	1,805	1,179	84	542	294	296	733	483	214	80	134	266	80
1987	1,620	1,146	65	409	269	298	634	420	196	73	123	176	58
1988	1,488	1,081	59	348	235	274	575	404	148	53	95	117	52
1989	1,376	1,003	55	318	179	266	536	396	118	37	82	(NA)	(NA)
1990	1,193	895	37	260	131	253	479	329	75	22	53	(NA)	(NA)
1991	1,014	840	36	138	113	233	414	254	60	21	39	(NA)	(NA)

NA Not available.   [1] Type of ownership under which the owners of the individual housing units are also joint owners of the common areas of the building or community. Includes a small number of cooperatively-owned units.

Source: U.S. Bureau of the Census, *Construction Reports*, series C20, and press release, CB92-11.

No. 1212. New Privately-Owned Housing Units Started, by State: 1985 to 1991

[In thousands of units]

REGION, DIVISION, AND STATE	1985	1989	1990	1991 Total units	1991 Single-family units	REGION, DIVISION, AND STATE	1985	1989	1990	1991 Total units	1991 Single-family units
U.S. . . .	1,741.0	1,374.0	1,193.0	1,015.0	842.0	DC. . .	0.7	3.5	0.3	0.2	0.2
						VA. . .	74.6	66.8	43.8	34.3	28.3
Northeast.	251.0	177.0	131.0	113.0	99.0	WV . .	2.0	1.7	2.5	2.2	2.0
N.E.	90.8	58.3	39.2	33.3	30.6	NC. . .	82.6	51.2	51.4	42.0	37.7
ME. . .	7.8	6.7	5.4	3.9	3.6	SC. . .	30.8	24.0	22.3	19.8	18.0
NH. . .	15.5	6.5	4.8	3.6	3.3	GA. . .	67.9	53.7	43.4	40.8	35.5
VT . .	3.7	3.7	2.8	2.2	2.0	FL . . .	193.8	165.4	126.1	98.1	80.7
MA. . .	34.6	21.9	14.7	12.8	12.0	E.S.C. . .	93.6	61.6	67.5	60.7	52.2
RI . .	4.8	5.0	3.2	2.8	2.5	KY . . .	19.9	14.3	15.2	13.8	11.8
CT . . .	24.3	14.5	8.3	8.1	7.2	TN. . .	45.5	28.3	26.7	24.0	21.3
M.A. . . .	160.2	119.2	91.8	79.7	68.4	AL. . .	19.3	12.0	18.5	16.5	13.7
NY. . .	60.4	42.9	36.6	27.6	22.3	MS. . .	8.9	7.0	7.1	6.5	5.4
NJ . . .	56.3	34.4	17.5	16.2	14.4	W.S.C. . .	191.9	62.3	83.9	87.8	77.6
PA . . .	43.5	41.9	37.7	35.8	31.6	AR. . .	9.9	6.7	10.6	9.1	8.2
Midwest . .	241.0	266.0	253.0	234.0	192.0	LA . . .	17.2	7.0	6.7	8.4	6.9
E.N.C . .	149.2	192.9	183.6	162.3	131.9	OK. . .	14.0	7.1	7.3	8.2	7.6
OH. . .	30.2	47.3	45.2	41.1	33.5	TX . . .	150.8	41.6	59.3	62.0	54.9
IN . . .	21.3	31.0	29.4	27.5	24.3	West . . .	467.0	394.0	329.0	254.0	197.0
IL. . . .	42.4	46.9	39.5	35.5	29.7	Mt.	157.5	81.6	85.9	85.4	70.9
MI . . .	38.3	40.8	41.2	32.7	25.6	MT. . .	2.8	0.6	2.8	3.3	2.6
WI . . .	17.1	26.9	28.2	25.5	18.9	ID . . .	4.2	4.8	6.7	8.5	7.8
W.N.C . .	91.8	73.1	69.6	71.7	60.1	WY . . .	3.8	0.5	1.4	2.0	1.9
MN. . .	25.7	22.9	21.7	21.9	20.1	CO. . .	33.6	10.7	12.6	15.4	12.5
IA . . .	4.6	9.0	9.3	9.5	7.6	NM. . .	9.8	5.3	4.7	4.6	4.2
MO . . .	33.4	19.5	17.4	18.1	15.2	AZ. . .	72.1	24.1	23.6	25.4	23.0
ND. . .	1.9	2.3	1.8	2.9	1.5	UT. . .	17.3	5.5	7.4	8.9	8.4
SD . . .	2.7	2.6	3.2	2.7	2.2	NV . . .	14.0	30.2	26.7	17.5	10.5
NE . . .	5.4	7.1	7.3	7.1	5.6	Pac. . . .	309.5	313.4	243.5	168.6	126.1
KS . . .	18.1	9.7	9.0	9.4	7.9	WA . . .	34.4	45.9	48.3	34.2	26.1
South. . . .	782.0	535.0	479.0	414.0	354.0	OR. . .	11.5	13.5	15.4	15.3	10.5
S.A . . .	496.5	411.8	328.0	265.6	224.4	CA . . .	253.4	245.5	171.6	109.1	82.7
DE. . .	4.9	7.0	6.1	5.5	4.8	AK. . .	4.3	0.6	1.2	1.6	1.3
MD. . .	39.3	38.6	32.1	22.7	17.2	HI . . .	5.9	7.8	7.0	8.3	5.5

Source: National Association of Home Builders, Economics Division, Washington, DC. Data provided by the Econometric Forecasting Service.

No. 1213. Characteristics of New Privately Owned One-Family Houses Completed: 1970 to 1991

[Percent distribution, except as indicated. Data beginning 1980 show percent distribution of characteristics for all houses completed (includes new houses completed, houses built for sale completed, contractor-built and owner-built houses completed, and houses completed for rent). Data for 1970 cover contractor-built, owner-built, and houses for rent for year construction started and houses sold for year of sale. Percents exclude houses for which characteristics specified were not reported]

CHARACTERISTIC	1970	1980	1985	1990	1991	CHARACTERISTIC	1970	1980	1985	1990	1991
Total houses (1,000) ...	793	957	1,072	966	838	Bedrooms..........	100	100	100	100	100
						2 or less..........	13	17	25	15	14
Financing	100	100	100	100	100	3................	63	63	57	57	59
Mortgage	84	81	81	82	81	4 or more	24	20	18	29	27
FHA-insured.......	30	16	15	14	13	Bathrooms	100	100	100	100	100
VA-guaranteed.....	7	8	7	4	5	1 1/2 or less.......	20	10	11	5	13
Conventional	47	55	57	62	61	2................	32	48	48	42	43
Farmers Home						2 1/2 or more	16	25	29	45	44
Administration	(¹)	3	3	2	2	Heating fuel	100	100	100	100	100
Cash or equivalent	16	18	19	18	19	Electricity	28	50	44	33	32
						Gas..............	62	41	49	59	60
Floor area...........	100	100	100	100	100	Oil...............	8	3	3	5	4
Under 1,200 sq. ft	36	21	20	11	12	Other.............	1	5	4	3	4
1,200 to 1,599 sq. ft...	28	29	30	22	22	Heating system	100	100	100	100	100
1,600 to 1,999 sq. ft...	16	22	21	22	21	Warm air furnace	71	57	54	65	65
2,000 to 2,399 sq. ft ...	21	13	12	17	17	Electric heat pump	(NA)	24	30	23	23
2,400 sq. ft. and over ...	(²)	15	17	29	28	Other.............	29	19	15	12	12
Average (sq. ft.)......	1,500	1,740	1,785	2,080	2,075	Central air-conditioning .	100	100	100	100	100
Median (sq. ft.)	1,385	1,595	1,605	1,905	1,890	With..............	34	63	70	76	75
						Without	66	37	30	24	25
Number of stories	100	100	100	100	100	Fireplaces..........	100	100	100	100	100
1................	74	60	52	46	48	No fireplace	65	43	41	34	37
2 or more	17	31	42	49	47	1 or more	35	56	59	66	63
Split level	10	8	6	4	5	Parking facilities	100	100	100	100	100
Foundation	100	100	100	100	100	Garage............	58	69	70	82	81
Full or partial basement.	37	36	35	38	40	Carport............	17	7	5	2	3
Slab..............	36	45	48	40	38	No garage or carport ..	25	24	25	16	16
Crawl space	27	19	18	21	22						

NA Not available. ¹ Included with "Conventional" financing.

No. 1214. New Privately Owned One-Family Houses Sold, by Region and Type of Financing, 1970 to 1991, and by Sales-Price Group, 1991

[In thousands. Based on a national probability sample of monthly interviews with builders or owners of one-family houses for which building permits have on which construction has started. For details, see source. For composition of regions, see table 25]

YEAR AND SALES-PRICE GROUP	Total sales	REGION				FINANCING TYPE			
		North-east	Midwest	South	West	Conventional	FHA and VA	Farmers Home Admin.	Cash
1970	485	61	100	203	121	¹213	244	(¹)	27
1971	656	82	127	270	176	¹314	314	(¹)	28
1972	718	96	130	305	187	¹447	242	(¹)	30
1973	634	95	120	257	161	¹465	134	(¹)	34
1974	519	69	103	207	139	¹378	112	(¹)	28
1975	549	71	106	222	150	363	122	43	22
1976	646	72	128	247	199	458	134	23	31
1977	819	86	162	317	255	592	166	24	38
1978	817	78	145	331	262	575	174	26	43
1979	709	67	112	304	225	469	186	18	36
1980	545	50	81	267	145	302	196	14	32
1981	436	46	60	219	112	244	142	14	36
1982	412	47	48	219	99	193	173	11	34
1983	623	76	71	323	152	350	217	8	49
1984	639	94	76	309	160	423	149	9	58
1985	688	112	82	323	170	403	208	11	64
1986	750	136	96	322	196	411	268	12	59
1987	671	117	97	271	186	408	190	6	64
1988	676	101	97	276	202	437	171	6	62
1989	650	86	102	260	202	416	162	14	58
1990	534	71	89	225	149	337	138	10	50
1991, prel..	509	57	93	215	144	329	128	9	43
Under $80,000.	98	(B)	22	62	12	32	50	(B)	8
$80,000 to $119,999.	153	11	29	73	40	81	59	(B)	13
$120,000 to $149,999.	86	13	15	32	27	64	13	(B)	9
$150,000 to $199,999.	82	14	14	24	29	71	(B)	(B)	6
$200,000 and over	89	17	13	24	35	81	(B)	(B)	7

B Withheld because estimate did not meet publication standards on the basis of sample size.   ¹ Houses financed by Farmers Home Administration included under conventional financing.

Source: U.S. Bureau of the Census and U.S. Dept. of Housing and Urban Development, *Construction Reports*, series C25, *Characteristics of New Housing*, annual; and *New One-Family Houses Sold*, monthly.

Construction and Housing

No. 1215. Median Sales Price of New Privately Owned One-Family Houses Sold, by Region: 1970 to 1991

[In dollars. For definition of median, see Guide to Tabular Presentation. For composition of regions, see table 25]

YEAR	U.S.	North-east	Midwest	South	West	YEAR	U.S.	North-east	Midwest	South	West
1970.....	23,400	30,300	24,400	20,300	24,000	1981.....	68,900	76,000	65,900	64,400	77,800
1971.....	25,200	30,600	27,200	22,500	25,500	1982.....	69,300	78,200	68,900	66,100	75,000
1972.....	27,600	31,400	29,300	25,800	27,500	1983.....	75,300	82,200	79,500	70,900	80,100
1973.....	32,500	37,100	32,900	30,900	32,400	1984.....	79,900	88,600	85,400	72,000	87,300
1974.....	35,900	40,100	36,100	34,500	35,800	1985.....	84,300	103,300	80,300	75,000	92,600
1975.....	39,300	44,000	39,600	37,300	40,600	1986.....	92,000	125,000	88,300	80,200	95,700
1976.....	44,200	47,300	44,800	40,500	47,200	1987.....	104,500	140,000	95,000	88,000	111,000
1977.....	48,800	51,600	51,500	44,100	53,500	1988.....	112,500	149,000	101,600	92,000	126,500
1978.....	55,700	58,100	59,200	50,300	61,300	1989.....	120,000	159,600	108,800	96,400	139,000
1979.....	62,900	65,500	63,900	57,300	69,600	1990.....	122,900	159,000	107,900	99,000	147,500
1980.....	64,600	69,500	63,400	59,600	72,300	1991.....	120,000	155,400	110,000	100,000	142,300

Source: U.S. Bureau of the Census and U.S. Dept. of Housing and Urban Development, *Current Construction Reports*, series C25, *Characteristics of New Housing*, annual; and *New One-Family Houses Sold*, monthly.

No. 1216. New Mobile Homes Placed for Residential Use and Average Sales Price, by Region: 1975 to 1991

[A mobile home is a moveable dwelling, 10 feet or more wide and 35 feet or more long, designed to be towed on its own chassis and without need of a permanent foundation. Excluded are travel trailers, motor homes, and modular housing. Data are based on a probability sample and subject to sampling variability; see source. For composition of regions, see table 25]

YEAR	UNITS PLACED (1,000)					AVERAGE SALES PRICE (dol.)				
	Total	North-east	Mid-west	South	West	U.S.	North-east	Mid-west	South	West
1975	229.3	14.7	48.5	110.8	55.2	10,600	10,500	10,700	9,000	13,600
1980	233.7	12.3	32.3	140.3	48.7	19,800	18,500	18,600	18,200	25,400
1981	229.2	12.0	30.1	143.5	43.6	19,900	19,000	18,900	18,400	25,600
1982	234.1	12.4	25.6	161.1	35.0	19,700	19,800	20,000	18,500	24,700
1983	278.1	16.3	34.3	186.0	41.4	21,000	21,400	20,400	19,700	27,000
1984	287.9	19.8	35.2	193.4	39.4	21,500	22,200	21,100	20,200	27,400
1985	283.4	20.2	38.6	187.6	36.9	21,800	22,700	21,500	20,400	28,700
1986	256.1	21.2	37.2	162.3	35.4	22,400	24,400	21,800	20,700	29,900
1987	239.2	23.6	40.0	145.5	30.1	23,700	25,600	23,700	21,900	31,000
1988	224.3	22.7	39.1	130.7	31.8	25,100	27,000	24,600	22,700	33,900
1989	202.8	20.2	39.1	112.8	30.6	27,200	30,200	26,700	24,100	37,800
1990	195.4	18.8	37.7	108.4	30.6	27,800	30,000	27,000	24,500	39,300
1991, prel.	174.0	14.4	35.5	97.2	26.9	27,800	30,500	27,600	24,500	38,600

Source: U.S. Bureau of the Census, *Current Construction Reports*, series C20.

No. 1217. Existing One-Family Houses Sold and Price, by Region: 1970 to 1991

[Based on data (adjusted and aggregated to regional and national totals) reported by participating real estate multiple listing services. see Guide to Tabular Presentation. For composition of regions, see fig. I, inside front cover]

YEAR	HOUSES SOLD (1,000)					MEDIAN SALES PRICE (dol.)				
	Total	North-east	Mid-west	South	West	Total	North-east	Mid-west	South	West
1970	1,612	251	501	568	292	23,000	25,200	20,100	22,200	24,300
1971	2,018	311	583	735	389	24,800	27,100	22,100	24,300	26,500
1972	2,252	361	630	788	473	26,700	29,800	23,900	26,400	28,400
1973	2,334	367	674	847	446	28,900	32,800	25,300	29,000	31,000
1974	2,272	354	645	839	434	32,000	35,800	27,700	32,300	34,800
1975	2,476	370	701	862	543	35,300	39,300	30,100	34,800	39,600
1976	3,064	439	881	1,033	712	38,100	41,800	32,900	36,500	46,100
1977	3,650	515	1,101	1,231	803	42,900	44,400	36,700	39,800	57,300
1978	3,986	516	1,144	1,416	911	48,700	47,900	42,200	45,100	66,700
1979	3,827	526	1,061	1,353	887	55,700	53,600	47,800	51,300	77,400
1980	2,973	403	806	1,092	672	62,200	60,800	51,900	58,300	89,300
1981	2,419	353	632	917	516	66,400	63,700	54,300	64,400	96,200
1982	1,990	354	490	780	366	67,800	63,500	55,100	67,100	98,900
1983	2,719	493	709	1,035	481	70,300	72,200	56,600	69,200	94,900
1984	2,868	511	755	1,073	529	72,400	78,700	57,100	71,300	95,800
1985	3,214	622	866	1,172	554	75,500	88,900	58,900	75,200	95,400
1986	3,565	703	991	1,261	610	80,300	104,800	63,500	78,200	100,900
1987	3,526	685	959	1,282	600	85,600	133,300	66,000	80,400	113,200
1988	3,594	673	929	1,350	642	89,300	143,000	68,400	82,200	124,900
1989	3,346	531	855	1,185	775	93,100	145,200	71,300	84,500	139,900
1990	3,211	469	831	1,202	709	95,500	141,200	74,000	85,900	139,900
1991	3,220	479	840	1,199	702	100,300	141,900	77,800	88,900	147,200

Source: NATIONAL ASSOCIATION OF REALTORS, Washington, DC, *Home Sales*, monthly, and *Home Sales Yearbook: 1990*, (copyright).

No. 1218. Median Sales Price of Existing One-Family Homes, by Selected Metropolitan Area: 1985 to 1991

[In thousands of dollars. Areas are metropolitan statistical areas (MSA's) except as indicated; for definitions and components, see Appendix II]

METROPOLITAN AREA	1985	1989	1990	1991	METROPOLITAN AREA	1985	1989	1990	1991
U.S., all areas	75.5	93.1	95.5	100.3	Louisville, KY-IN	50.6	58.4	60.8	65.4
					Memphis, TN-AR-MS	64.6	78.1	78.1	82.5
Akron, OH PMSA	52.7	64.5	67.7	71.8	Miami-Hialeah, FL PMSA	80.5	86.9	89.3	93.7
Albany-Schenectady-Troy, NY	60.3	104.9	106.9	110.3	Milwaukee, WI PMSA	67.5	79.6	84.4	90.0
Albuquerque, NM	76.8	83.0	84.5	86.8	Minneapolis-St. Paul, MN-WI	75.2	87.2	88.7	91.1
Anaheim-Santa Ana, CA PMSA	134.7	241.9	242.4	239.7	Nashville, TN	66.1	79.9	81.8	86.9
Baltimore, MD	72.6	96.3	105.9	110.1	New York-Northern New Jersey-				
Baton Rouge, LA	74.6	63.8	64.9	69.4	Long Island, NY-NJ-CT CMSA	134.0	183.2	174.9	173.5
Birmingham, AL	64.5	78.5	80.8	86.0	Oklahoma City, OK	64.7	53.5	53.2	57.0
Boston, MA PMSA	134.2	181.9	174.1	170.1	Omaha, NE-IA	58.3	60.6	63.0	66.5
Buffalo-Niagara Falls, NY CMSA	46.7	72.5	77.2	79.7	Orlando, FL	70.3	79.8	82.8	86.3
Chicago, IL PMSA	81.1	107.0	116.8	131.1	Philadelphia, PA-NJ PMSA	74.0	103.9	108.7	118.4
Cincinnati, OH-KY-IN PMSA	60.2	75.8	79.8	84.9	Phoenix, AZ	74.8	78.8	84.0	85.5
Cleveland, OH PMSA	64.4	75.2	80.6	86.2	Portland, OR PMSA	61.5	70.1	79.5	88.5
Columbus, OH	62.2	77.9	81.6	85.2	Providence, RI PMSA	67.5	130.2	127.9	124.3
Dallas, TX PMSA	94.0	93.4	89.5	88.3	Riverside/San Bernardino, CA				
Denver, CO PMSA	84.3	85.5	86.4	89.1	PMSA	85.0	124.1	132.1	135.4
Des Moines, IA	52.5	57.5	60.5	68.2	Rochester, NY	64.2	78.5	79.8	81.5
Detroit, MI PMSA	51.7	73.7	76.7	80.6	St. Louis, MO-IL	65.7	76.9	76.7	79.4
Ft. Lauderdale-Hollywood-					Salt Lake City-Ogden, UT	66.7	69.4	69.4	72.8
Pompano Beach, FL PMSA	74.6	83.9	92.6	96.2	San Antonio, TX	67.7	64.2	63.6	64.9
Ft. Worth, TX PMSA	74.9	79.9	76.7	77.6	San Diego, CA	107.4	181.9	183.2	187.5
Hartford, CT PMSA	99.6	165.9	157.3	148.2	San Francisco-Oakland-				
Honolulu, HI	162.1	270.0	352.0	353.8	San Jose, CA CMSA	145.1	260.7	259.3	256.6
Houston, TX PMSA	78.6	66.7	70.7	74.0	Seattle/Tacoma, WA CMSA	(NA)	115.0	142.0	143.1
Indianapolis, IN	55.0	71.2	74.8	79.1	Syracuse, NY	58.8	79.3	80.7	77.7
Jacksonville, FL	58.4	69.3	72.4	73.7	Tampa-St. Petersburg-				
Kansas City, MO-KS	61.4	71.6	74.1	76.6	Clearwater, FL	58.4	71.9	71.4	71.3
Las Vegas, NV	75.1	85.7	93.0	101.4	Tulsa, OK	66.7	62.6	63.9	66.4
Los Angeles-Long Beach, CA					Washington, DC-MD-VA	97.1	144.4	150.5	156.7
PMSA	125.2	214.8	212.1	214.9	West Palm Beach-Boca Raton-				
					Delray Beach, FL	88.3	102.6	108.0	116.3

NA Not available.
Source: NATIONAL ASSOCIATION OF REALTORS, Washington, DC, *Home Sales*, monthly, and *Home Sales Yearbook: 1990*, (copyright).

No. 1219. Existing Home Sales, by State: 1985 to 1991

[In thousands]

REGION, DIVISION, AND STATE	1985	1988	1989	1990	1991	REGION, DIVISION, AND STATE	1985	1988	1989	1990	1991
U.S. [1]	3,214.0	3,594.0	3,346.0	3,211.0	3,220.0	DC	9.2	8.0	15.5	13.1	12.5
						VA	116.0	130.7	116.0	96.9	90.3
Northeast	624.6	697.7	603.4	523.1	537.6	WV	31.1	36.4	36.8	42.0	43.3
N.E.	156.9	178.4	142.8	100.1	112.4	NC	107.9	134.7	127.5	135.9	139.9
ME	21.8	18.4	9.0	(NA)	(NA)	SC	48.4	55.0	52.2	57.8	53.9
NH	14.5	13.8	9.7	7.9	9.3	GA	58.7	78.2	73.6	73.2	70.7
VT	7.5	9.5	6.2	6.1	8.1	FL	142.7	179.2	177.6	183.3	176.0
MA	60.2	76.5	67.4	44.0	49.6	E.S.C.	230.6	252.9	253.3	254.9	259.0
RI	10.3	11.0	9.5	7.8	7.8	KY	51.8	60.9	62.2	66.4	67.8
CT	42.6	49.2	41.0	34.3	37.6	TN	89.3	93.9	95.2	92.7	92.0
M.A.	467.7	519.3	460.6	423.0	425.2	AL	54.8	61.5	59.4	61.1	64.0
NY	150.0	160.5	140.2	125.5	127.2	MS	34.7	36.6	36.5	34.7	35.2
NJ	160.2	133.6	126.6	114.8	118.8	W.S.C.	312.1	359.3	350.5	379.8	385.0
PA	157.5	225.2	193.8	182.7	179.2	AR	49.9	47.5	47.5	44.8	43.4
Midwest	851.7	924.0	918.8	890.2	900.6	LA	36.4	39.8	40.8	41.6	47.1
E.N.C.	581.5	633.1	633.4	609.3	618.9	OK	42.3	46.8	49.1	53.4	52.5
OH	147.6	160.6	163.4	151.6	149.8	TX	183.5	225.2	213.1	240.0	242.0
IN	88.4	81.6	81.6	80.1	76.0	West	767.6	950.9	941.6	866.2	828.0
IL	130.2	168.1	162.7	160.9	168.1	Mt.	243.0	236.3	230.5	250.6	256.7
MI	153.4	147.6	151.6	145.0	145.0	MT	11.7	12.5	13.0	12.7	13.9
WI	61.9	75.2	74.1	71.7	80.0	ID	14.2	13.1	15.0	18.1	19.0
W.N.C.	270.2	290.9	285.4	280.9	281.7	WY	8.0	7.4	7.3	7.4	8.2
MN	67.4	70.8	62.7	64.8	66.3	CO	64.4	60.9	53.9	54.2	59.6
IA	36.4	57.9	54.6	51.9	54.1	NM	22.2	20.5	21.9	23.6	24.4
MO	78.9	73.0	81.0	84.1	82.7	AZ	83.6	80.3	77.7	86.3	79.7
ND	8.8	10.2	10.3	10.4	10.1	UT	22.1	20.7	20.3	22.1	26.3
SD	10.5	11.4	10.8	11.6	11.3	NV	16.8	20.9	21.4	26.2	25.6
NE	22.6	20.0	20.9	19.3	19.9	Pac.	524.6	714.6	711.1	615.6	571.3
KS	45.6	47.6	45.1	38.8	37.1	WA	61.8	73.4	90.8	87.7	86.9
South	1,139.3	1,328.4	1,291.6	1,313.7	1,307.8	OR	36.1	48.9	53.2	56.6	48.1
S.A.	596.6	716.2	687.8	679.0	663.8	CA [2]	404.9	562.8	539.3	452.1	424.1
DE	11.3	12.4	11.8	9.7	10.4	AK	9.5	9.1	6.6	(NA)	(NA)
MD	71.3	81.6	76.8	67.1	66.8	HI	12.3	20.4	21.2	19.2	12.2

NA Not available. [1] U.S. totals are derived independently and therefore are not equal to the sum of the States. [2] Provided by the California Association of Realtors.
Source: NATIONAL ASSOCIATION OF REALTORS, Washington, DC, *Existing Home Sales*, monthly, (copyright).

No. 1220. New Apartments Completed and Rented in 3 Months, by Region: 1980 to 1990

[Structures with 5 or more units, privately financed, nonsubsidized, unfurnished apartments. Based on sample and subject to sampling variability. For composition of regions, see table 25]

YEAR AND RENT	NUMBER (1,000)					PERCENT RENTED IN 3 MONTHS				
	U.S.	North-east	Mid-west	South	West	U.S.	North-east	Mid-west	South	West
1980	196.1	14.2	43.8	91.5	46.6	75	77	77	74	75
1981	135.3	4.9	36.9	68.4	25.1	80	85	86	78	75
1982	117.0	4.6	21.9	66.8	23.7	72	74	79	70	72
1983	191.5	3.5	41.1	115.1	31.8	69	73	86	63	69
1984	313.2	3.8	41.2	194.4	73.9	67	64	79	63	70
1985	365.2	8.1	54.0	166.1	137.0	65	69	72	59	68
1986	407.6	16.9	64.5	171.7	154.5	66	70	70	62	67
1987	345.6	11.3	66.0	124.5	143.9	63	73	65	59	64
1988	284.5	8.7	60.4	91.7	123.8	66	52	73	58	69
1989	247.8	13.4	45.8	86.3	102.3	70	74	74	68	69
1990	**214.8**	**12.8**	**44.3**	**77.3**	**80.4**	**67**	**67**	**75**	**64**	**65**
Less than $350	13.8	1.0	4.9	5.1	3.0	66	100	93	69	9
$350-$449	26.0	3.4	10.4	8.4	3.9	82	90	87	78	71
$450-$549	45.9	3.9	10.8	18.6	12.7	70	51	78	66	75
$550-$649	43.9	1.0	7.1	19.0	16.9	67	62	77	63	67
$650-$749	33.3	1.3	5.9	11.6	14.6	61	51	54	59	66
$750 or more	51.8	2.6	5.2	14.6	29.4	60	63	49	55	64
Median asking rent	$599	$510	$513	$584	$676	(X)	(X)	(X)	(X)	(X)

X Not applicable.

Source: U.S. Bureau of the Census, *Current Housing Reports*, series H-130 and H-131, and unpublished data.

No. 1221. Gross Housing Product—Summary: 1970 to 1990

[**In billions of dollars.** For definition of current and constant dollars, see Guide to Tabular Presentation]

ITEM	CURRENT DOLLARS						CONSTANT (1982) DOLLARS					
	1970	1980	1985	1988	1989	1990	1970	1980	1985	1988	1989	1990
Housing output [1]	90.5	245.3	377.0	464.2	493.3	525.4	257.6	383.1	418.7	442.9	450.2	456.5
Nonfarm housing	87.3	240.2	372.0	459.4	488.4	520.5	249.6	376.9	413.5	438.2	445.6	452.0
Owner-occupied	61.3	178.4	271.0	334.1	355.8	379.7	174.4	278.7	301.3	317.6	322.7	326.8
Tenant-occupied	26.0	61.8	101.0	125.3	132.6	140.8	75.1	98.2	112.2	120.6	122.8	125.2
Farm housing	3.3	5.1	5.0	4.9	5.0	4.9	8.0	6.3	5.3	4.7	4.6	4.5
Less: Intermediate goods and												
services consumed	13.0	35.8	49.9	63.1	64.3	71.1	37.0	55.9	55.4	60.2	60.5	61.9
Equals: **Gross housing product**	77.5	209.5	327.1	401.2	429.0	454.3	220.6	327.2	363.3	382.7	389.7	394.7

[1] Equals personal consumption expenditures (see text, section 14) for housing, less expenditures for transient hotels, motels, clubs, schools, and other group housing.

Source: U.S. Bureau of Economic Analysis, *Survey of Current Business*, March 1992 issue, and unpublished data.

No. 1222. Residential Capital—Yearend Stocks and Average Age: 1970 to 1991

[As of **Dec. 31.** Data based on fixed residential capital formation components of the gross national product. For definition of current and constant dollars, see Guide to Tabular Presentation]

ITEM	CURRENT DOLLARS (bil. dol.)					CONSTANT (1987) DOLLARS (bil. dol.)					AVERAGE AGE [1] (years)				
	1970	1980	1985	1990	1991	1970	1980	1985	1990	1991	1970	1980	1985	1990	1991
Gross stocks [2]	1,244	4,380	5,706	7,543	7,869	3,961	5,430	6,057	6,897	7,014	24.8	23.2	23.7	23.6	23.8
Private nonfarm:															
1 to 4 units	1,001	3,502	4,566	6,075	6,345	3,208	4,356	4,852	5,557	5,659	25.3	23.9	24.3	24.2	24.3
5 or more units	131	522	701	933	974	421	647	746	853	864	17.7	17.8	18.7	19.8	20.3
Farm (1 to 4 units)	55	136	150	163	167	176	170	159	150	148	43.9	42.8	43.4	43.2	42.9
Private nonhouse-															
keeping	10	24	27	32	32	32	29	29	29	29	14.6	19.3	22.0	23.6	23.9
Mobile homes	15	79	104	124	129	31	88	106	112	110	5.1	7.7	9.2	10.7	11.0
Public: Federal, State															
and local	25	88	116	155	163	80	100	123	141	145	14.9	19.3	21.1	22.4	22.7
Net stocks [2][3]	813	2,900	3,715	4,896	5,080	2,590	3,594	3,945	4,475	4,529	16.2	15.8	16.6	16.9	17.1
Private nonfarm:															
1 to 4 units	656	2,334	2,998	3,991	4,149	2,102	2,902	3,186	3,650	3,702	16.8	16.3	17.1	17.2	17.4
5 or more units	93	371	487	629	649	301	459	518	574	575	13.8	14.8	15.2	15.7
Farm (1 to 4 units)	24	58	62	68	70	76	73	66	62	62	28.7	26.4	27.2	26.6	26.3
Private nonhouse-															
keeping	6	12	12	14	14	21	15	13	12	12	9.0	16.0	18.5	18.4	18.3
Mobile homes	11	48	57	62	62	23	54	58	55	53	3.8	6.0	6.7	7.5	7.7
Public: Federal, State															
and local	18	60	76	99	103	60	74	81	90	92	12.7	15.9	16.9	17.3	17.4

[1] Constant-dollar stocks.   [2] Includes equipment, not shown separately.   [3] Based on straight-line depreciation.

Source: U.S. Bureau of Economic Analysis, *Fixed Reproducible Tangible Wealth in the United States, 1925-89*, forthcoming, and *Survey of Current Business*, January 1992 issue, and unpublished data.

No. 1223. Housing Units—Selected Characteristics, by State: 1990
[As of **April 1**]

REGION, DIVISION, AND STATE	Total (1,000)	Percent change, 1980-90	1 unit detached	1 unit attached	2-4 units	5-9 units	10 or more units	Mobile homes, trailers	OCCUPIED UNITS Total (1,000)	With 1.01 or more persons per room	VACANT UNITS Total (1,000)	Vacancy rate (percent)
U.S. . . .	102,264	15.7	60,383	5,378	9,876	4,936	13,169	7,400	91,947	4,549	10,316	10.1
Northeast .	20,811	9.0	10,253	1,657	3,488	1,019	3,464	637	18,873	735	1,938	9.3
N.E.	5,570	14.8	3,050	211	1,133	327	620	153	4,943	112	628	11.3
ME . . .	587	17.2	378	12	74	29	26	55	465	8	122	20.7
NH . . .	504	30.4	298	23	68	27	46	35	411	7	93	18.6
VT. . . .	271	21.5	168	9	41	14	10	23	211	4	61	22.3
MA . . .	2,473	12.0	1,238	89	597	159	339	24	2,247	57	226	9.1
RI	415	11.2	219	11	109	23	43	5	378	9	37	8.8
CT. . . .	1,321	14.0	749	67	244	75	155	12	1,230	28	90	6.8
M.A	15,240	7.1	7,203	1,446	2,355	692	2,844	483	13,930	623	1,310	8.6
NY. . . .	7,227	5.2	2,929	302	1,320	375	1,998	195	6,639	432	588	8.1
NJ. . . .	3,075	10.9	1,637	235	527	146	453	34	2,795	109	281	9.1
PA. . . .	4,938	7.4	2,637	910	507	171	393	255	4,496	83	442	9.0
Midwest. . .	24,493	7.3	16,218	754	2,394	1,080	2,470	1,339	22,317	558	2,176	8.9
E.N.C .	17,028	6.6	11,044	544	1,825	827	1,759	861	15,597	413	1,431	8.4
OH . . .	4,372	6.4	2,897	148	461	204	416	206	4,088	72	284	6.5
IN	2,246	7.4	1,574	57	171	100	168	157	2,065	45	181	8.0
IL	4,506	4.3	2,557	158	648	291	663	151	4,202	167	304	6.7
MI	3,848	7.2	2,673	131	268	151	337	246	3,419	91	429	11.1
WI. . . .	2,056	10.3	1,342	50	277	81	175	101	1,822	38	234	11.4
W.N.C. .	7,465	9.0	5,175	211	569	253	711	478	6,720	145	744	10.0
MN . . .	1,848	14.6	1,231	69	115	45	276	91	1,648	34	201	10.9
IA	1,144	1.1	853	18	87	41	77	57	1,064	16	79	6.9
MO . . .	2,199	10.6	1,490	57	212	85	172	164	1,961	48	238	10.8
ND . . .	276	6.8	173	10	21	12	30	27	241	5	35	12.8
SD. . . .	292	5.6	202	5	19	10	22	31	259	8	33	11.4
NE. . . .	661	5.7	479	16	40	25	59	37	602	11	58	8.8
KS. . . .	1,044	9.3	747	35	74	35	75	71	945	24	99	9.5
South	36,065	22.6	22,007	1,725	2,349	1,724	4,068	3,835	31,822	1,524	4,243	11.8
S.A. . . .	18,719	27.4	10,607	1,250	1,269	978	2,352	2,095	16,503	675	2,216	11.8
DE. . . .	290	21.5	156	40	14	10	33	35	247	6	42	14.6
MD . . .	1,892	20.4	939	393	104	106	294	43	1,749	53	143	7.6
DC. . . .	278	0.5	35	71	31	21	118	-	250	21	29	10.4
VA. . . .	2,496	23.5	1,532	216	144	136	287	159	2,292	65	205	8.2
WV . . .	781	4.5	546	11	46	20	29	119	689	13	93	11.9
NC . . .	2,818	23.9	1,830	74	178	131	151	430	2,517	73	301	10.7
SC. . . .	1,424	23.4	898	34	92	67	80	241	1,258	51	166	11.7
GA . . .	2,638	30.1	1,639	73	198	168	233	305	2,367	96	272	10.3
FL. . . .	6,100	39.3	3,033	336	462	321	1,128	763	5,135	298	965	15.8
E.S.C .	6,214	13.1	4,213	130	408	260	406	735	5,652	192	562	9.0
KY. . . .	1,507	10.1	1,011	25	109	65	96	185	1,380	36	127	8.4
TN. . . .	2,026	15.9	1,358	55	146	93	166	189	1,854	51	172	8.5
AL. . . .	1,670	13.8	1,134	32	96	66	102	224	1,507	53	164	9.8
MS . . .	1,010	10.8	710	17	57	36	41	137	911	53	99	9.8
W.S.C . .	11,132	20.6	7,187	345	673	485	1,310	1,006	9,668	657	1,465	13.2
AR. . . .	1,001	11.4	709	18	61	27	44	132	891	33	109	10.9
LA . . .	1,716	10.8	1,084	79	152	59	125	196	1,499	89	217	12.6
OK . . .	1,406	13.7	1,005	33	69	56	100	130	1,206	40	200	14.2
TX . . .	7,009	26.3	4,389	215	391	343	1,041	548	6,071	495	938	13.6
West	20,895	22.3	11,905	1,242	1,645	1,113	3,166	1,589	18,935	1,732	1,960	9.4
Mt	5,864	29.3	3,422	300	399	231	751	691	5,033	271	831	14.2
MT . . .	361	10.0	238	8	29	10	17	54	306	9	55	15.2
ID . . .	413	10.2	286	9	29	12	17	57	361	15	53	12.7
WY . . .	203	8.1	129	6	16	6	10	33	169	5	35	17.0
CO . . .	1,477	23.7	884	87	90	64	249	89	1,282	38	195	13.2
NM . . .	632	24.5	388	28	39	16	48	103	543	43	89	14.1
AZ. . . .	1,659	49.4	868	110	88	61	257	251	1,369	102	291	17.5
UT. . . .	598	22.1	393	24	58	21	62	35	537	30	61	10.2
NV. . . .	519	52.6	236	27	50	41	90	70	466	30	53	10.1
Pac	15,031	19.8	8,483	942	1,246	882	2,415	898	13,902	1,461	1,129	7.5
WA . . .	2,032	20.3	1,273	48	139	91	275	188	1,872	73	160	7.9
OR . . .	1,194	10.2	764	32	86	47	119	134	1,103	40	90	7.6
CA. . . .	11,183	20.5	6,119	812	966	706	1,900	555	10,381	1,275	802	7.2
AK. . . .	233	42.9	124	16	30	16	21	20	189	16	44	18.8
HI	390	16.6	203	34	24	22	100	(Z)	356	57	34	8.6

- Represents zero.   Z Less than 500 units.

Source: U.S. Bureau of the Census, *1990 Census of Housing, General Housing Characteristics*, series CH-1, forthcoming, and *Census of Population and Housing, 1990: Summary Tape File 1C on CD-ROM.*

No. 1224. Occupied Housing Units—Tenure, by Race of Householder: 1920 to 1990

[In thousands, except as indicated. As of **April 1**. Prior to **1960**, excludes Alaska and Hawaii. Statistics on the number of occupied units are essentially comparable although identified by various terms—the term "family" applies to figures for 1920 and 1930; "occupied dwelling unit," 1940 and 1950; and "occupied housing unit," 1960 to 1990. For 1920, includes the small number of quasifamilies; for 1930, represents private families only. See also *Historical Statistics, Colonial Times to 1970*, series N 238-245]

RACE OF HOUSEHOLDER AND TENURE	1920	1930	1940	1950	1960	1970	1980	1990
ALL RACES								
Occupied units, total	24,352	29,905	34,855	42,826	53,024	63,445	80,390	91,947
Owner occupied	11,114	14,280	15,196	23,560	32,797	39,886	51,795	59,025
Percent of occupied	45.6	47.8	43.6	55.0	61.9	62.9	64.4	64.2
Renter occupied	13,238	15,624	19,659	19,266	20,227	23,560	28,595	32,923
WHITE								
Occupied units, total	21,826	26,983	31,561	39,044	47,880	56,606	68,810	76,880
Owner occupied	10,511	13,544	14,418	22,241	30,823	37,005	46,671	52,433
Percent of occupied	48.2	50.2	45.7	57.0	64.4	65.4	67.8	68.2
Renter occupied	11,315	13,439	17,143	16,803	17,057	19,601	22,139	24,447
BLACK AND OTHER								
Occupied units, total	2,526	2,922	3,293	3,783	5,144	6,839	11,580	15,067
Owner occupied	603	737	778	1,319	1,974	2,881	5,124	6,592
Percent of occupied	23.9	25.2	23.6	34.9	38.4	42.1	44.2	43.8
Renter occupied	1,923	2,185	2,516	2,464	3,170	3,959	6,456	8,475

Source: U.S. Bureau of the Census, *Census of Housing: 1960*, vol. 1; *1970*, vol. 1; *1980 Census of Housing*, vol. 1, chapter A (HC80-1-A); and *1990 Census of Housing, General Housing Characteristics*, series CH-90-1, forthcoming reports.

No. 1225. Occupied Housing Units—Tenure, by Race and Hispanic Origin of Householder: 1980 and 1990

[As of **April 1**. Based on the Census of Population and Housing; see Appendix III]

RACE AND HISPANIC ORIGIN OF HOUSEHOLDER	ALL HOUSEHOLDS			OWNER OCCUPIED		PERCENT OWNER OCCUPIED		RENTER OCCUPIED	
	1980 (1,000)	1990 (1,000)	Percent change, 1980-1990	1980	1990	1980	1990	1980	1990
Total units	80,389,673	91,947,410	14.4	51,794,545	59,024,811	64.4	64.2	28,595,128	32,922,599
White	68,810,123	76,880,105	11.7	46,670,775	52,432,648	67.8	68.2	22,139,348	24,447,457
Black	8,381,668	9,976,161	19.0	3,724,251	4,327,265	44.4	43.4	4,657,417	5,648,896
American Indian, Eskimo, or Aleut	397,252	591,372	48.9	212,209	318,001	53.4	53.8	185,043	273,371
Asian or Pacific Islander .	993,458	2,013,735	102.7	521,230	1,050,182	52.5	52.2	472,228	963,553
Other race	1,807,172	2,486,037	37.6	666,080	896,715	36.9	36.1	1,141,092	1,589,322
Hispanic origin [1]	4,007,896	6,001,718	49.7	1,738,920	2,545,584	43.4	42.4	2,268,976	3,456,134

[1] Persons of Hispanic origin may be of any race.

U.S. Bureau of the Census, *1980 Census of Housing*, vol. 1, chapter A (HC80-1-A); and *1990 Census of Housing, General Housing Characteristics*, series CH-1, forthcoming reports.

No. 1226. Occupied Housing Units—Tenure, by Age of Householder: 1980 and 1990

[As of April 1]

AGE OF HOUSEHOLDER	OWNER OCCUPIED				RENTER OCCUPIED			
	Number (1,000)		Percent		Number (1,000)		Percent	
	1980	1990	1980	1990	1980	1990	1980	1990
Total units	51,797	59,024	64.4	64.2	28,594	32,922	35.6	35.8
15 to 24 years old	1,459	862	22.1	17.1	5,137	4,187	77.9	82.9
25 to 34 years old	9,439	9,000	51.6	45.3	8,844	10,849	48.4	54.7
35 to 44 years old	9,895	13,503	71.2	66.2	3,997	6,890	28.8	33.8
45 to 54 years old	[1]19,563	10,774	[1]77.3	75.3	[1]5,744	3,529	[1]22.7	24.7
55 to 64 years old	([1])	9,864	([1])	79.7	([1])	2,515	([1])	20.3
65 to 74 years old	[2]11,441	9,072	[2]70.1	78.8	[2]4,872	2,445	[2]29.9	21.2
75 years old and over	([2])	5,949	([2])	70.4	([2])	2,507	([2])	29.6

[1] Householders age 55 to 64 years old are included with householders 45 to 54 years. [2] Householders age 75 years old and over are included with householders 65 to 74 years old.

U.S. Bureau of the Census, *1980 Census of Housing*, vol. 1, chapter A (HC80-1-A); and *1990 Census of Housing, General Housing Characteristics*, series CH-1, forthcoming reports.

No. 1227. Occupied Housing Units—Housing Value and Contract Rent, by Region: 1990

[Specified owner–occupied units are limited to one–unit structures on less than 10 acres and no business on property. Specified renter–occupied units exclude one–unit on 10 acres or more. Based on the American Housing Survey; see Appendix III]

CATEGORY	NUMBER (1,000)					PERCENT DISTRIBUTION				
	Total units	North-east	Mid-west	South	West	Total units	North-east	Mid-west	South	West
VALUE										
Specified owner occupied units	44,918.0	8,762.9	11,794.7	15,595.6	8,764.8	100.0	100.0	100.0	100.0	100.0
Less than $15,000	1,177.0	114.8	412.0	583.6	66.6	2.6	1.3	3.5	3.7	0.8
$15,000 to $19,999	761.0	85.8	293.1	343.5	38.6	1.7	1.0	2.5	2.2	0.4
$20,000 to $24,999	1,018.8	118.2	392.2	451.2	57.2	2.3	1.3	3.3	2.9	0.7
$25,000 to $29,999	1,232.9	137.5	475.9	544.8	74.7	2.7	1.6	4.0	3.5	0.9
$30,000 to $34,999	1,572.0	168.5	597.5	698.1	107.9	3.5	1.9	5.1	4.5	1.2
$35,000 to $39,999	1,737.5	172.9	642.2	787.2	135.1	3.9	2.0	5.4	5.0	1.5
$40,000 to $44,999	1,985.6	202.0	717.8	887.9	178.0	4.4	2.3	6.1	5.7	2.0
$45,000 to $49,999	1,917.7	187.4	683.0	844.2	203.2	4.3	2.1	5.8	5.4	2.3
$50,000 to $59,999	3,940.0	410.5	1,361.4	1,673.5	494.6	8.8	4.7	11.5	10.7	5.6
$60,000 to $74,999	5,959.6	703.8	1,923.1	2,440.9	891.9	13.3	8.0	16.3	15.7	10.2
$75,000 to $99,999	7,057.8	1,162.6	1,961.0	2,639.2	1,295.0	15.7	13.3	16.6	16.9	14.8
$100,000 to $124,999	3,808.2	941.1	873.3	1,188.4	805.3	8.5	10.7	7.4	7.6	9.2
$125,000 to $149,999	2,965.1	944.5	534.9	789.4	696.3	6.6	10.8	4.5	5.1	7.9
$150,000 to $174,999	2,316.2	886.8	312.4	507.5	609.5	5.2	10.1	2.6	3.3	7.0
$175,000 to $199,999	1,701.0	688.3	181.4	315.2	516.1	3.8	7.9	1.5	2.0	5.9
$200,000 to $249,999	2,084.3	776.4	187.8	354.6	765.4	4.6	8.9	1.6	2.3	8.7
$250,000 to $299,999	1,292.6	416.7	96.1	203.5	576.3	2.9	4.8	0.8	1.3	6.6
$300,000 to $399,999	1,206.8	344.1	78.7	176.8	607.2	2.7	3.9	0.7	1.1	6.9
$400,000 to $499,999	501.3	131.1	31.1	70.1	269.2	1.1	1.5	0.3	0.4	3.1
$500,000 and over	682.5	169.8	39.8	96.2	376.7	1.5	1.9	0.3	0.6	4.3
Median value (dol.)	$79,100	$124,400	$62,500	$66,000	$126,200	(X)	(X)	(X)	(X)	(X)
CONTRACT RENT										
Specified renter occupied units	31,966.8	7,193.3	6,807.2	10,378.1	7,588.1	100.0	100.0	100.0	100.0	100.0
Less than $100	1,406.0	191.3	351.0	732.4	131.2	4.4	2.7	5.2	7.1	1.7
$100 to $149	1,557.8	366.3	398.8	605.1	187.5	4.9	5.1	5.9	5.8	2.5
$150 to $199	1,961.7	346.4	566.8	779.3	269.2	6.1	4.8	8.3	7.5	3.5
$200 to $249	2,552.7	437.2	750.5	1,014.2	350.9	8.0	6.1	11.0	9.8	4.6
$250 to $299	3,046.8	485.0	878.3	1,180.7	502.9	9.5	6.7	12.9	11.4	6.6
$300 to $349	3,214.0	599.5	842.3	1,158.5	613.7	10.1	8.3	12.4	11.2	8.1
$350 to $399	3,189.3	630.1	776.4	1,104.3	678.5	10.0	8.8	11.4	10.6	8.9
$400 to $449	2,709.6	659.1	582.1	823.9	644.5	8.5	9.2	8.6	7.9	8.5
$450 to $499	2,212.2	561.6	424.5	628.4	597.8	6.9	7.8	6.2	6.1	7.9
$500 to $549	1,903.1	568.2	297.8	459.8	577.3	6.0	7.9	4.4	4.4	7.6
$550 to $599	1,404.0	400.0	193.9	318.9	491.2	4.4	5.6	2.8	3.1	6.5
$600 to $649	1,231.7	402.9	138.3	246.5	444.0	3.9	5.6	2.0	2.4	5.9
$650 to $699	942.1	290.1	90.4	178.3	383.4	2.9	4.0	1.3	1.7	5.1
$700 to $749	707.3	235.5	60.1	119.5	292.2	2.2	3.3	0.9	1.2	3.9
$750 to $999	1,626.6	498.2	117.9	246.3	764.2	5.1	6.9	1.7	2.4	10.1
$1,000 or more	825.5	276.4	54.9	122.0	372.2	2.6	3.8	0.8	1.2	4.9
No cash rent	1,476.2	245.5	283.2	660.0	287.5	4.6	3.4	4.2	6.4	3.8
Median contract rent (dol.) ...	$374	$432	$319	$324	$473	(X)	(X)	(X)	(X)	(X)

X Not applicable.
Source: U.S. Bureau of the Census, 1990 Census of Housing, *General Housing Characteristics*, series CH–1, forthcoming.

Figure 26.1
Occupied Housing Units-Contract Rent, by Region: 1990

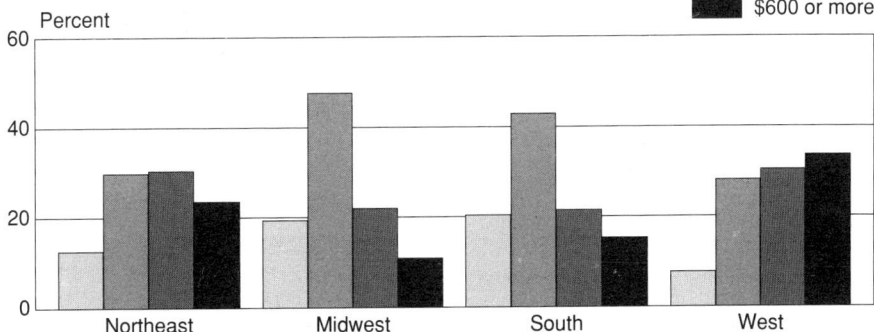

Percent

Legend: $199 or less / $200–$399 / $400–$599 / $600 or more

Source: Chart prepared by U.S. Bureau of the Census. For data, see table 1227.

Construction and Housing

No. 1228. Occupied Housing Units—

[**In thousands of units,** except as indicated. As of **April.**

STATE	Total housing units	SPECIFIED OWNER OCCUPIED UNITS								
		Value categories						Lower quartile value[1] (dol.)	Median (dol.)	Upper quartile value[1] (dol.)
		Less than $50,000	$50,000 to $99,999	$100,000 to $149,000	$150,000 to $199,000	$200,000 to $299,000	$300,000 or more			
United States ..	**44,918.0**	**11,402.5**	**16,957.5**	**6,773.3**	**4,017.2**	**3,376.9**	**2,390.7**	**49,500**	**79,100**	**137,800**
Alabama	753.8	343.9	310.7	62.5	20.1	11.3	5.4	35,500	53,700	78,800
Alaska.	77.5	11.0	31.9	23.0	7.5	3.2	0.9	66,400	94,400	128,500
Arizona	668.7	98.7	372.7	118.8	40.6	23.9	14.0	59,800	80,100	109,900
Arkansas	427.7	235.6	156.9	23.3	6.8	3.5	1.6	31,100	46,300	68,700
California	4,690.3	119.0	636.6	812.1	851.5	1,151.0	1,120.0	127,100	195,500	294,800
Colorado	637.6	84.1	363.1	122.8	37.4	19.9	10.3	62,500	82,700	109,700
Connecticut	643.5	4.6	36.7	165.3	188.0	150.3	98.5	139,000	177,800	246,000
Delaware	137.5	11.8	56.8	38.5	15.6	10.5	4.3	74,800	100,100	143,900
District of Columbia . .	71.5	1.7	25.2	15.0	6.9	8.4	14.4	86,700	123,900	258,700
Florida.	2,378.2	433.1	1,239.1	381.9	151.5	100.6	72.0	56,100	77,100	112,200
Georgia	1,138.8	314.5	531.2	163.2	66.9	39.9	23.1	47,300	71,300	102,100
Hawaii	144.4	3.3	13.1	16.7	21.1	39.7	50.5	156,800	245,300	358,800
Idaho	177.3	66.8	89.4	14.2	3.7	2.0	1.2	42,100	58,200	79,700
Illinois	2,084.7	525.1	786.6	403.2	183.7	114.5	71.6	49,800	80,900	128,300
Indiana	1,137.8	514.3	484.0	92.8	27.0	13.7	6.0	36,500	53,900	78,200
Iowa	566.6	317.8	209.7	27.7	7.0	3.3	1.1	30,200	45,900	65,900
Kansas	500.6	238.0	199.6	41.1	12.3	6.4	3.1	32,400	52,200	78,000
Kentucky	662.2	326.9	260.5	47.5	15.9	8.0	3.4	33,400	50,500	73,400
Louisiana	733.9	289.1	344.5	63.0	19.8	11.5	6.1	38,200	58,500	83,000
Maine	214.7	37.5	95.2	49.3	18.0	10.0	4.7	60,100	87,400	123,300
Maryland	970.9	87.3	300.9	274.2	139.6	103.3	65.6	79,000	116,500	169,300
Massachusetts	1,004.6	9.5	93.5	310.8	298.3	196.4	96.1	126,800	162,800	216,000
Michigan	1,916.1	737.2	814.5	219.2	79.3	46.0	20.0	38,500	60,600	90,600
Minnesota	894.3	204.9	482.3	138.2	38.6	21.1	9.2	52,200	74,000	98,200
Mississippi	441.8	249.3	156.1	24.2	7.0	3.6	1.6	31,400	45,600	67,800
Missouri.	1,005.4	385.1	452.6	102.0	33.6	20.3	11.9	38,800	59,800	87,100
Montana	132.4	52.3	68.3	8.4	2.1	1.0	0.3	40,000	56,600	74,200
Nebraska	314.4	155.3	132.4	18.5	4.7	2.4	1.0	32,800	50,400	70,400
Nevada	183.8	8.4	93.3	51.3	16.0	9.1	5.6	75,400	95,700	129,400
New Hampshire . . .	199.4	6.3	45.6	79.9	39.9	21.1	6.6	98,400	129,400	167,600
New Jersey	1,466.3	45.5	241.4	348.8	367.3	301.5	161.9	112,300	162,300	225,000
New Mexico	262.3	73.5	128.2	37.3	12.8	7.2	3.3	46,700	70,100	97,800
New York.	2,387.6	243.8	674.4	431.6	439.0	381.0	217.8	76,200	131,600	200,400
North Carolina	1,218.0	382.8	575.7	155.2	56.3	33.1	15.0	44,700	65,800	94,900
North Dakota	103.7	50.6	46.3	5.1	1.1	0.5	0.1	30,800	50,800	70,000
Ohio	2,241.3	734.0	1,102.8	260.5	80.8	42.9	20.3	43,900	63,500	90,200
Oklahoma	616.3	323.7	235.6	36.8	10.9	6.1	3.3	30,800	48,100	71,000
Oregon	511.8	133.3	281.2	62.7	19.5	10.5	4.7	49,200	67,100	92,600
Pennsylvania	2,581.3	829.2	1,017.8	395.9	180.6	109.1	48.7	42,500	69,700	109,500
Rhode Island	176.5	3.0	31.0	78.4	35.6	19.4	9.0	106,000	133,500	171,800
South Carolina	615.4	225.7	280.1	63.5	23.7	14.8	7.6	41,100	61,100	89,100
South Dakota	113.1	64.2	42.4	4.6	1.0	0.5	0.2	27,300	45,200	64,500
Tennessee.	938.4	371.8	416.4	91.5	32.2	17.8	8.7	39,600	58,400	85,300
Texas	2,949.1	1,151.2	1,261.1	314.8	111.3	66.5	44.2	38,300	59,600	89,200
Utah	303.7	61.1	188.6	35.2	10.6	5.7	2.5	53,100	68,900	92,000
Vermont.	89.2	7.9	41.3	25.5	8.4	4.4	1.7	73,100	95,500	130,000
Virginia	1,192.1	206.7	466.2	203.9	132.8	116.5	66.0	60,100	91,000	155,800
Washington	896.4	124.0	371.3	192.7	101.0	67.8	39.6	63,700	93,400	145,400
West Virginia	350.1	185.3	136.8	18.9	5.4	2.8	0.9	31,200	47,900	69,400
Wisconsin	916.7	287.2	492.2	95.3	24.7	12.3	5.1	45,600	62,500	86,100
Wyoming	78.4	25.9	43.8	6.2	1.5	0.7	0.4	43,900	61,600	82,100

[1] This measure divides the distribution of value and rent categories into four equal parts. The lower quartile value is the value that defines the upper limit of the lowest one-quarter of the cases. The upper quartile value defines the lower limit of the upper one-quarter of the cases in the distribution.

Housing Value and Contract Rent, by State: 1990

Based on the Census of Population and Housing; see appendix III]

| | SPECIFIED RENTER OCCUPIED UNITS | | | | | | | | |
| Total housing units | Rent categories | | | | | Lower quartile value[1] (dol.) | Median (dol.) | Upper quartile value[1] (dol.) | STATE |
	Less than $250	$250 to $499	$500 to $749	$750 to $999	$1,000 or more				
30,490.5	7,478.2	14,371.9	6,188.4	1,626.6	825.5	252	374	527	**United States**
386.2	214.4	155.0	14.4	1.6	0.8	136	229	326	Alabama
70.6	5.8	29.2	23.8	8.5	3.4	377	503	666	Alaska
456.9	73.9	290.5	76.5	10.5	5.6	288	370	473	Arizona
227.6	129.5	90.5	6.2	0.9	0.6	154	230	310	Arkansas
4,400.1	330.3	1,385.0	1,692.5	668.5	323.8	414	561	728	California
452.9	88.7	271.3	76.5	10.9	5.3	271	362	472	Colorado
401.3	56.7	135.1	152.1	38.2	19.1	366	510	648	Connecticut
68.2	12.7	36.0	16.7	1.8	1.0	304	425	518	Delaware
148.6	23.9	65.5	37.6	12.7	8.8	317	441	618	District of Columbia
1,591.5	261.3	892.4	355.6	49.4	32.7	302	402	515	Florida
759.5	251.8	362.0	127.4	13.1	5.1	202	344	466	Georgia
139.3	15.1	36.8	43.8	25.2	18.4	401	599	837	Hawaii
92.9	43.0	44.1	4.6	0.9	0.3	184	261	348	Idaho
1,416.3	352.3	703.8	283.2	53.5	23.4	251	369	503	Illinois
554.7	204.4	310.1	33.4	4.4	2.3	210	291	380	Indiana
268.4	125.1	129.1	12.3	1.3	0.6	182	261	350	Iowa
270.8	108.0	136.0	22.4	2.7	1.6	196	285	385	Kansas
351.2	175.3	160.4	12.9	1.5	1.1	163	250	335	Kentucky
452.1	211.8	213.9	21.8	3.2	1.5	167	260	346	Louisiana
123.0	30.2	68.6	21.4	1.9	0.8	252	358	468	Maine
574.1	88.1	223.0	196.8	51.0	15.2	321	473	635	Maryland
879.2	164.9	265.6	308.2	98.6	41.9	323	506	668	Massachusetts
925.3	233.0	536.9	128.9	17.8	8.7	249	343	450	Michigan
431.8	104.0	217.4	93.6	12.8	3.5	255	384	503	Minnesota
214.3	126.9	80.1	6.2	0.6	0.4	123	215	313	Mississippi
548.6	223.9	275.8	40.8	5.3	2.8	189	282	384	Missouri
85.5	42.4	40.3	2.4	0.2	0.2	175	251	332	Montana
174.1	69.6	91.6	11.0	1.2	0.7	194	282	375	Nebraska
202.8	19.1	111.1	62.9	7.6	2.1	351	445	552	Nevada
121.8	14.7	52.0	45.1	7.8	2.2	363	479	600	New Hampshire
942.1	106.6	321.8	381.9	92.5	39.3	381	521	657	New Jersey
157.1	49.8	88.3	16.1	2.0	1.0	220	312	406	New Mexico
3,059.9	529.1	1,387.2	764.7	223.1	155.8	302	428	596	New York
709.7	288.2	360.7	52.0	4.9	3.9	190	284	386	North Carolina
69.8	31.4	35.6	2.5	0.2	0.1	178	266	349	North Dakota
1,231.5	431.2	692.2	87.8	11.5	8.8	212	296	388	Ohio
341.1	159.7	162.6	15.6	2.0	1.2	184	259	345	Oklahoma
378.5	82.4	241.8	44.5	6.4	3.4	262	344	433	Oregon
1,216.4	397.0	601.6	174.4	28.8	14.6	217	322	447	Pennsylvania
146.3	30.7	69.4	38.5	5.7	2.1	286	416	535	Rhode Island
332.5	145.1	161.6	21.7	2.7	1.3	174	276	379	South Carolina
72.8	38.1	31.4	3.0	0.3	0.1	155	242	339	South Dakota
524.2	229.0	260.1	29.4	3.7	2.0	176	273	370	Tennessee
2,192.6	573.8	1,321.2	240.0	36.4	21.2	245	328	423	Texas
161.6	46.3	101.2	11.3	2.1	0.7	237	300	383	Utah
57.8	11.2	34.1	10.4	1.5	0.6	280	378	481	Vermont
698.8	150.6	297.1	165.4	60.4	25.0	271	411	596	Virginia
655.7	122.1	373.6	130.9	21.3	7.8	280	383	497	Washington
146.1	88.9	53.4	3.3	0.3	0.2	151	221	295	West Virginia
560.5	146.2	343.6	61.5	6.8	2.3	245	331	425	Wisconsin
46.7	20.0	24.1	2.4	0.2	0.1	198	270	353	Wyoming

Source: U.S. Bureau of the Census, *1990 Census of Housing, General Housing Characteristics*, series CH-1, forthcoming, and *Census of Population and Housing, 1990: Summary Tape File 1C on CD-ROM.*

Construction and Housing

No. 1229. Occupied Housing Units—Housing Value and Contract Rent in Constant (1990) Dollars, by State: 1970 to 1990

[As of **April 1**. Constant dollar figures were calculated using the Consumer Price Index for "All items"; see tables 738 and 740]

STATE	MEDIAN VALUE					MEDIAN CONTRACT RENT				
	1970 (dol.)	1980 (dol.)	1990 (dol.)	Percent change		1970 (dol.)	1980 (dol.)	1990 (dol.)	Percent change	
				1970-1980	1980-1990				1970-1980	1980-1990
U.S.	53,800	75,000	79,100	39.4	5.5	282	314	374	11.3	19.1
AL.	38,600	53,800	53,700	39.4	−0.2	152	189	229	24.3	21.2
AK.	71,800	121,200	94,400	68.8	−22.1	541	540	503	−0.2	−6.9
AZ.	51,600	87,000	80,100	68.6	−7.9	285	360	370	26.3	2.8
AR.	33,200	49,400	46,300	48.8	−6.3	168	202	230	20.2	13.9
CA.	73,100	134,200	195,500	83.6	45.7	358	402	561	12.3	39.6
CO	54,800	101,800	82,700	85.8	−18.8	307	354	362	15.3	2.3
CT.	80,700	104,200	177,800	29.1	70.6	332	322	510	−3.0	58.4
DE.	54,100	70,500	100,100	30.3	42.0	282	321	425	13.8	32.4
DC.	67,400	109,300	123,900	62.2	13.4	348	329	441	−5.5	34.0
FL.	47,500	71,600	77,100	50.7	7.7	291	330	402	13.4	21.8
GA	46,200	58,600	71,300	26.8	21.7	206	243	344	18.0	41.6
HI	111,100	187,500	245,300	68.8	30.8	380	430	599	13.2	39.3
ID	44,600	72,400	58,200	62.3	−19.6	222	272	261	22.5	−4.0
IL	62,700	83,800	80,900	33.7	−3.5	339	319	369	−5.9	15.7
IN	43,700	59,100	53,900	35.2	−8.8	260	264	291	1.5	10.2
IA	44,000	64,500	45,900	46.6	−28.8	244	278	261	13.9	−6.1
KS.	38,300	60,000	52,200	56.7	−13.0	237	267	285	12.7	6.7
KY.	39,900	54,300	50,500	36.1	−7.0	199	240	250	20.6	4.2
LA.	46,200	68,300	58,500	47.8	−14.3	196	248	260	26.5	4.8
ME	40,500	60,200	87,400	48.6	45.2	218	273	358	25.2	31.1
MD	59,200	92,600	116,500	56.4	25.8	348	353	473	1.4	34.0
MA	65,200	76,900	162,800	17.9	111.7	282	313	506	11.0	61.7
MI	55,400	61,900	60,600	11.7	−2.1	294	311	343	5.8	10.3
MN	57,000	84,300	74,000	47.9	−12.2	320	337	384	5.3	13.9
MS	35,400	49,900	45,600	41.0	−8.6	146	173	215	18.5	24.3
MO	45,600	58,300	59,800	27.9	2.6	234	243	282	3.8	16.0
MT	44,300	73,800	56,600	66.6	−23.3	225	262	251	16.4	−4.2
NE.	39,200	60,300	50,400	53.8	−16.4	244	270	282	10.7	4.4
NV.	70,900	109,100	95,700	53.9	−12.3	389	426	445	9.5	4.5
NH	51,900	76,200	129,400	46.8	69.8	250	326	479	30.4	46.9
NJ.	74,100	95,600	162,300	29.0	69.8	351	359	521	2.3	45.1
NM	41,100	71,900	70,100	74.9	−2.5	228	281	312	23.2	11.0
NY.	71,200	72,400	131,600	1.7	81.8	301	333	428	10.6	28.5
NC	40,500	57,200	65,800	41.2	15.0	187	213	284	13.9	33.3
ND	41,100	69,700	50,800	69.6	−27.1	244	278	266	13.9	−4.3
OH	55,700	71,300	63,500	28.0	−10.9	263	265	296	0.8	11.7
OK	35,100	56,500	48,100	61.0	−14.9	203	260	259	28.1	−0.4
OR.	48,700	90,400	67,100	85.6	−25.8	272	337	344	23.9	2.1
PA.	43,000	62,100	69,700	44.4	12.2	231	275	322	19.0	17.1
RI	57,600	74,300	133,500	29.0	79.7	206	251	416	21.8	65.7
SC.	41,100	55,700	61,100	35.5	9.7	158	206	276	30.4	34.0
SD.	36,100	58,100	45,200	60.9	−22.2	218	235	242	7.8	3.0
TN.	39,600	56,500	58,400	42.7	3.4	196	235	273	19.9	16.2
TX.	38,000	62,100	59,600	63.4	−4.0	241	338	328	40.2	−3.0
UT.	53,200	91,000	68,900	71.1	−24.3	253	297	300	17.4	1.0
VT.	51,900	67,000	95,500	29.1	42.5	241	276	378	14.5	37.0
VA.	54,100	76,200	91,000	40.9	19.4	291	329	411	13.1	24.9
WA	58,600	95,100	93,400	62.3	−1.8	298	348	383	16.8	10.1
WV	35,800	61,100	47,900	70.7	−21.6	165	216	221	30.9	2.3
WI	54,800	77,200	62,500	40.9	−19.0	288	294	331	2.1	12.6
WY	48,400	95,000	61,600	96.3	−35.2	228	345	270	51.3	−21.7

Source: U.S. Bureau of the Census, *1990 Housing Highlights,* series CH-S-1-1 - 52.

No. 1230. Housing Units—Summary of Characteristics and Equipment, by Tenure and Region: 1987

[In thousands of units, except as indicated. Based on the American Housing Survey; see Appendix III. For composition of regions, see table 25]

ITEM	Total housing units	Sea-sonal	YEAR-ROUND UNITS Occupied — Total	Owner	Renter	North-east	Mid-west	South	West	Vacant
Total units	**102,652**	**2,837**	**90,888**	**58,164**	**32,724**	**18,953**	**22,267**	**31,270**	**18,397**	**8,927**
Percent distribution	100.0	2.8	88.5	56.7	31.9	20.9	24.5	34.4	20.2	8.7
Units in structure:										
Single family detached	61,775	1,741	56,559	48,162	8,397	9,644	15,097	20,694	11,125	3,475
Single family attached	5,496	74	4,820	2,456	2,364	1,378	878	1,619	944	602
2 to 4 units	10,987	156	9,472	1,872	7,601	3,265	2,297	2,172	1,739	1,359
5 to 9 units	5,358	63	4,533	325	4,209	988	973	1,469	1,103	761
10 to 19 units	4,766	57	3,948	279	3,669	767	780	1,487	914	761
20 to 49 units	3,625	63	2,936	256	2,680	895	553	629	859	626
50 or more units	3,957	79	3,352	544	2,808	1,520	642	617	573	526
Mobile home or trailer	6,688	604	5,267	4,270	997	496	1,048	2,583	1,140	817
Stories in structure: [1]										
1 story	2,643	42	2,241	243	1,999	114	309	1,109	709	360
2 stories	8,407	108	6,877	664	6,213	729	909	2,963	2,277	1,422
3 stories	7,034	97	6,018	1,185	4,834	2,397	2,046	882	693	919
4 to 6 stories	8,073	132	6,930	818	6,112	2,837	1,679	1,095	1,319	1,012
7 or more stories	2,537	40	2,175	367	1,808	1,358	301	325	190	321
Foundation:										
Full or partial basement	30,711	369	29,049	25,392	3,657	9,526	12,150	4,679	2,695	1,292
Crawlspace	18,356	666	16,196	12,684	3,512	540	2,268	8,736	4,653	1,494
Concrete slab	16,402	403	14,868	11,651	3,217	843	1,347	8,178	4,500	1,130
Other	1,802	375	1,265	891	375	114	210	720	221	161
Year structure built: [2]										
1939 and earlier	24,104	575	21,215	12,110	9,105	7,735	6,793	4,233	2,455	2,314
1940 to 1949	9,038	340	7,945	4,997	2,948	1,692	1,816	2,789	1,647	753
1950 to 1959	14,249	367	13,056	9,559	3,497	2,730	3,367	4,162	2,797	825
1960 to 1969	16,768	473	15,136	10,110	5,025	2,594	3,475	5,641	3,425	1,160
1970 to 1979	24,825	749	21,829	13,777	8,054	2,868	4,894	8,764	5,304	2,246
1980 or later	13,668	334	11,706	7,611	4,095	1,335	1,922	5,681	2,768	1,627
Median year	1962	1963	1962	1962	1962	1950	1958	1968	1967	1965
Main heating equipment:										
Warm-air furnace	54,929	818	49,854	35,049	14,805	6,770	16,059	17,341	9,684	4,258
Electric heat pump	4,361	118	3,688	2,809	878	222	339	2,621	506	556
Steam or hot water system	15,102	100	13,855	7,190	6,665	9,456	2,785	915	699	1,147
Floor, wall, or pipeless furnace	6,059	103	5,450	2,583	2,867	207	424	1,701	3,118	506
Built-in electric units.	7,255	329	6,092	2,873	3,220	1,352	1,280	1,724	1,736	833
Room heaters with flue	3,331	276	2,629	1,403	1,226	217	475	1,505	432	426
Room heaters without flue	2,741	36	2,346	1,313	1,033	30	51	2,167	98	359
Stoves	4,501	427	3,762	2,895	867	546	626	1,690	900	312
Fireplaces	1,377	145	1,150	971	178	47	102	512	489	83
None	1,297	389	659	282	377	14	21	202	422	249
Portable elec. heaters	820	71	671	320	351	8	26	442	194	79
Other	879	27	732	476	256	85	78	449	120	120
Air conditioning:										
Central	36,752	529	33,006	23,378	9,628	2,526	7,929	17,484	5,067	3,217
Percent of total units.	35.8	18.6	36.3	40.2	29.4	13.3	35.6	55.9	27.5	36.0
1 or more room units	28,220	369	26,547	16,885	9,660	7,551	6,988	9,058	2,948	1,305
Source of water:										
Public system or private company . .	86,952	1,376	77,944	47,446	30,498	16,097	18,361	26,347	17,139	7,631
Percent of total units.	84.7	48.5	85.8	81.6	93.2	84.9	82.5	84.3	93.2	85.5
Well serving 1 to 5 units.	14,232	941	12,183	10,145	2,038	2,696	3,759	4,558	1,170	1,109
Other	1,468	520	761	573	188	160	148	365	88	187
Means of sewage disposal:										
Public sewer.	77,130	975	69,345	40,150	29,195	14,672	17,431	21,770	15,472	6,811
Percent of total units.	75.1	34.4	76.3	69.0	89.2	77.4	78.3	69.6	84.1	76.3
Septic tank, cesspool, chemical toilet.	24,769	1,537	21,281	17,886	3,395	4,255	4,817	9,002	2,008	1,951
Other	752	325	262	128	134	26	20	198	18	165

[1] Limited to multiunit structures in 1987.   [2] For mobile home, oldest category is 1939 or earlier.

Source: U.S. Bureau of the Census, *Current Housing Reports*, series H-150-87, American Housing Survey.

No. 1231. Heating Equipment and Fuels for Occupied Units: 1950 to 1990

[Based on the Census of Population and Housing; see Appendix III]

ITEM	NUMBER (1,000)					PERCENT DISTRIBUTION				
	1950	1960	1970	1980	1990	1950	1960	1970	1980	1990
Occupied units, total	42,826	53,024	63,445	80,390	91,947	100.0	100.0	100.0	100.0	100.0
Heating equipment:										
Warm air furnace	[1]11,508	17,378	27,515	39,279	(NA)	[1]26.9	32.8	43.4	48.9	(NA)
Heat pumps	(NA)	(NA)	(NA)	2,835	(NA)	(NA)	(NA)	(NA)	3.5	(NA)
Steam or hot water.	10,071	11,990	13,211	13,859	(NA)	23.5	22.6	20.8	17.2	(NA)
Floor, wall, or pipeless furnace . .	([1])	6,088	5,552	4,693	(NA)	([1])	11.5	8.8	5.8	(NA)
Built-in electric units	-	664	3,236	6,370	(NA)	-	1.3	5.1	7.9	(NA)
Room heaters with flue	[2]15,399	[2]11,183	7,209	6,098	(NA)	[2]36.0	[2]21.1	11.4	7.6	(NA)
Room heaters without flue.	5,268	5,218	3,558	2,736	(NA)	12.3	9.8	5.6	3.4	(NA)
Fireplaces, stoves, portable heaters or other	([2])	([2])	2,766	3,977	(NA)	([2])	([2])	4.4	4.9	(NA)
None	581	503	398	541	(NA)	1.4	0.9	0.6	0.7	(NA)
House heating fuel:										
Utility gas	11,387	22,851	35,014	42,658	46,851	26.6	43.1	55.2	53.1	51.0
Fuel oil, kerosene, etc.	9,686	17,158	16,473	14,655	11,244	22.6	32.4	26.0	18.2	12.2
Electricity	283	933	4,876	14,768	23,697	0.7	1.8	7.7	18.3	25.8
Bottled, tank, or LP gas.	787	2,686	3,807	4,535	5,243	1.8	5.1	6.0	5.6	5.7
Wood and other fuel.	4,855	2,460	1,060	2,729	4,009	11.3	4.6	1.7	3.4	4.4
Coal or coke	14,828	6,456	1,821	504	359	34.6	12.2	2.9	0.6	0.4
None	999	478	395	541	544	2.3	0.9	0.6	0.7	0.6
Cooking fuel:										
Electricity	6,403	16,351	25,768	41,906	(NA)	15.0	30.8	40.6	52.1	(NA)
Gas [3]	25,501	33,787	36,558	37,944	(NA)	59.6	63.7	57.6	47.2	(NA)
Other fuel	10,796	2,603	908	398	(NA)	25.2	4.9	1.4	0.5	(NA)
None	124	280	213	142	(NA)	0.3	0.5	0.3	0.2	(NA)

- Represents zero. NA Not available. [1] "Floor, wall, or pipeless furnace" included in "Warm air furnace." [2] "Fireplaces, stoves, or portable heaters" included in "Room heaters with flue." [3] Includes utility, bottled, tank, and LP gas.

Source: U.S. Bureau of the Census, *Census of Housing, 1960,* vol. 1, and *1980,* vol. 1; 1990, *1990 Census of Population and Housing,* CPH-L-80.

No. 1232. Appliances Used by Households, by Region and Family Income: 1987

[In millions, except percent. As of **November**. Represents appliances possessed and generally used by the household. Based on Residential Energy Consumption Survey; see Appendix III. For composition of regions, see table 25]

TYPE OF APPLIANCE	HOUSEHOLDS USING APPLIANCE		REGION				FAMILY INCOME IN **1987**			
	Number	Percent of total	North-east	Midwest	South	West	Under $15,000	$15,000 -$24,999	$25,000 -$34,999	$35,000 and over
Total households . .	90.5	100.0	19.0	22.3	30.9	18.3	30.3	17.8	16.2	26.3
Air conditioners: Room . .	26.9	29.8	7.4	7.9	9.2	2.4	10.1	6.0	4.6	6.2
Central system [1]	30.7	33.9	3.0	7.2	16.2	4.3	5.9	5.2	6.4	13.2
Clothes washer	67.8	74.9	13.8	17.1	23.8	13.1	18.4	13.0	12.7	23.7
Clothes dryer	59.6	65.8	11.3	16.2	20.1	12.0	13.5	11.5	11.7	23.0
Dehumidifier	9.0	10.0	2.9	4.7	1.3	0.1	1.4	1.5	2.2	4.0
Dishwasher	39.0	43.1	7.4	7.6	14.0	10.0	5.1	6.5	8.4	19.1
Evaporative cooler [2]	3.0	3.4	-	0.1	0.6	2.3	1.3	0.6	0.5	0.7
Freezer	30.8	34.0	4.8	9.2	11.3	5.4	8.8	5.2	5.8	10.9
Humidifier	13.2	14.6	2.8	7.2	2.3	1.0	2.7	2.6	2.6	5.3
Microwave oven [3]	55.0	60.8	9.8	14.9	18.7	11.7	12.1	10.8	10.9	21.2
Motor vehicles: [4] One . . .	30.8	34.0	6.3	7.5	11.2	5.7	15.0	7.4	4.7	3.7
Two or more	48.6	53.7	8.9	12.3	16.4	11.0	6.6	9.0	10.8	22.2
Outdoor gas grill	18.3	20.2	4.6	5.4	5.2	3.2	2.1	3.0	3.6	9.6
Outdoor gas light	1.3	1.4	0.1	0.4	0.6	0.1	0.2	0.3	0.2	0.5
Oven: Electric	51.2	56.6	9.3	11.5	20.1	10.4	13.9	10.2	10.2	17.0
Gas	37.1	40.9	9.4	10.3	9.9	7.4	15.3	6.9	5.9	9.0
Portable electric heater . .	9.0	10.0	1.2	2.1	3.5	2.3	3.8	1.9	1.4	2.0
Portable kerosene heater.	5.3	5.8	1.0	1.3	2.8	0.2	1.8	1.0	1.1	1.4
Range: Electric	51.4	56.8	9.0	11.6	20.4	10.3	14.1	10.3	10.1	16.9
Gas	38.7	42.7	9.8	10.7	10.2	8.0	15.9	7.4	6.0	9.4
Refrigerator: Frost-free . .	60.9	67.3	11.0	14.5	22.9	12.5	15.8	11.9	11.6	21.6
Nonfrost-free [5]	29.4	32.5	8.0	7.6	7.9	5.9	14.3	5.9	4.6	4.7
Television set: Color	83.9	92.7	17.9	20.7	28.4	17.0	25.7	16.6	15.7	25.9
Black and white	32.4	35.8	7.1	8.8	10.8	5.6	11.0	5.7	5.7	10.0
Water heater: [6] Gas	42.1	46.5	7.0	13.1	11.7	10.3	13.1	7.5	7.4	14.1
Electric	30.5	33.7	4.0	5.6	16.1	4.8	10.0	6.6	5.8	8.2
Other fuel	3.6	4.0	2.9	0.1	0.2	0.4	0.5	0.6	0.6	1.8
Whole house cooling fan . .	8.6	9.5	1.5	2.4	3.6	1.1	1.7	1.3	1.6	3.9
Window or ceiling fan . . .	41.8	46.2	7.8	10.3	17.9	5.8	12.0	8.3	8.0	13.5

- Represents zero. [1] Includes the .9 million households with both Central air conditioning and window or wall air conditioning units. [2] An air-cooling unit used in dry climates that turns air into moist, cool air by saturating the air with water vapor. [3] Microwave is first or second most used oven. [4] All motorized vehicles used by U.S. households for personal transportation excluding motorcycles, mopeds, large trucks, and buses. [5] Includes refrigerators without freezer compartments. [6] Excludes water heaters that serve more than one household.

Source: U.S. Energy Information Administration, *Residential Energy Consumption Survey, 1987.*

No. 1233. Expenditures by Residential Property Owners for Improvements and Maintenance and Repairs, by Type of Property and Activity: 1970 to 1990

[In millions of dollars]

YEAR AND TYPE OF EXPENDITURE	Total	1-unit proper-ties with owner occu-pant	Other proper-ties	ADDITIONS AND ALTERATIONS				To property outside of struc-tures	Major replace-ments	Mainte-nance and repairs
				Total	To structures					
					Addi-tions	Alter-ations				
1970.	14,770	9,469	5,301	6,246	1,411	3,539	1,296	2,629	5,895
1975.	25,239	15,684	9,556	10,997	1,971	6,844	2,182	4,484	9,758
1976.	29,034	18,854	10,180	12,314	3,493	6,367	2,454	5,341	11,379
1977.	31,280	21,761	9,519	14,237	2,655	8,505	3,077	5,699	11,344
1978.	37,461	24,189	13,272	16,458	3,713	8,443	4,302	8,094	12,909
1979.	42,231	28,280	13,951	18,285	3,280	9,642	5,363	8,996	14,950
1980.	46,338	31,481	14,857	21,336	4,183	11,193	5,960	9,816	15,187
1981.	46,351	30,201	16,150	20,414	3,164	11,947	5,303	9,915	16,022
1982.	45,291	29,779	15,512	18,774	2,641	10,711	5,423	9,707	16,810
1983.	49,295	32,524	16,771	20,271	4,739	11,673	3,859	10,895	18,128
1984.	69,784	43,781	26,003	27,822	6,007	14,486	7,329	13,067	28,894
1985.	80,267	47,742	32,525	28,775	3,966	17,599	7,211	16,134	35,358
1986.	91,274	54,298	36,976	38,608	7,377	21,192	10,040	16,695	35,971
1987.	94,082	54,791	39,291	39,978	9,557	21,641	8,779	15,875	38,229
1988, total [1]	101,117	60,822	40,295	43,339	11,333	22,703	9,303	16,893	40,885
Heating and air-conditioning [2]	7,460	4,838	2,622	1,357	(NA)	1,357	(NA)	3,352	2,751
Plumbing.	8,610	4,414	4,196	1,619	(NA)	1,619	(NA)	2,968	4,024
Roofing.	6,665	3,317	3,348	(NA)	(NA)	(NA)	(NA)	4,799	1,866
Painting.	12,467	6,159	6,308	(NA)	(NA)	(NA)	(NA)	(NA)	12,467
1989, total [1]	100,891	59,858	41,033	39,786	6,828	23,129	9,828	18,415	42,689
Heating and air-conditioning [2]	5,841	3,589	2,252	1,484	(NA)	1,484	(NA)	2,167	2,191
Plumbing.	9,875	5,258	4,617	1,607	(NA)	1,607	(NA)	3,314	4,954
Roofing.	10,075	6,266	3,809	(NA)	(NA)	(NA)	(NA)	6,299	3,777
Painting.	11,319	5,192	6,127	(NA)	(NA)	(NA)	(NA)	(NA)	11,319
1990, total [1]	106,773	59,683	47,090	37,253	8,561	21,920	6,771	18,215	51,305
Heating and air-conditioning [2]	7,646	4,920	2,726	1,634	(NA)	1,634	(NA)	3,394	2,618
Plumbing.	10,838	5,842	4,996	1,867	(NA)	1,867	(NA)	3,382	5,589
Roofing.	7,914	4,159	3,755	(NA)	(NA)	(NA)	(NA)	4,508	3,406
Painting.	13,768	5,260	8,508	(NA)	(NA)	(NA)	(NA)	(NA)	13,768

NA Not available.   [1] Includes types of expenditures not separately specified.   [2] Central air-conditioning.

Source: U.S. Bureau of the Census, *Current Construction Reports*, series C50.

No. 1234. Vacancy Rates for Housing Units—Characteristics: 1985 to 1991

[In percent. Annual averages. Based on Current Population Survey and Quarterly Household Survey. Rate is relationship between vacant housing for rent or for sale and the total rental and homeowner supply, which comprises occupied units, units rented or sold and awaiting occupancy, and vacant units availa For composition of regions, see fig. I, inside front cover. See also *Historical Statistics, Colonial Times to 1970*, series N 249-258]

CHARACTERISTIC	RENTAL UNITS					HOMEOWNER UNITS				
	1985	1988	1989	1990	1991	1985	1988	1989	1990	1991
Total units	6.5	7.7	7.4	7.2	7.4	1.7	1.6	1.8	1.7	1.7
Inside MSA's.	6.3	7.8	7.4	7.1	7.5	1.7	1.6	1.7	1.7	1.7
Outside MSA's.	7.1	7.3	7.7	7.6	7.3	1.9	1.6	1.9	1.8	1.8
Northeast	3.5	4.8	4.7	6.1	6.9	1.0	1.6	1.5	1.6	1.5
Midwest	5.9	6.9	6.8	6.4	6.7	1.6	1.2	1.4	1.3	1.3
South.	9.1	10.1	9.7	8.8	8.9	2.1	1.9	2.2	2.1	2.2
West	6.2	7.7	7.1	6.6	6.5	2.1	1.6	1.6	1.8	1.7
Units in structure:										
One unit	3.8	3.6	4.2	4.0	3.9	1.4	1.3	1.4	1.4	1.4
Two units or more	7.9	9.8	9.2	9.0	9.4	6.6	6.1	7.1	7.1	6.8
Five units or more	8.8	11.4	10.1	9.6	10.4	10.1	9.7	9.6	8.4	7.9
Units with—										
Three rooms or less . .	8.8	10.6	10.3	10.3	10.8	5.8	5.6	10.8	10.2	10.5
Four rooms	6.9	8.7	8.2	8.0	8.1	2.3	2.6	3.1	3.2	3.0
Five rooms	5.0	5.3	5.6	5.7	5.9	2.0	1.6	2	2.0	1.9
Six rooms or more. . . .	3.2	3.3	3.4	3.0	3.1	1.4	1.2	1.2	1.1	1.2

Source: U.S. Bureau of the Census, *Current Housing Reports*, series H-111.

No. 1235. Recent Home Buyers—General Characteristics: 1976 to 1990

[As of **October.** Based on a sample survey; subject to sampling variability]

ITEM	Unit	1976	1980	1984	1985	1986	1987	1988	1989	1990
Median purchase price ..	Dollars ...	43,340	68,714	89,400	90,400	93,680	99,260	121,910	129,800	131,200
First-time buyers	Dollars ...	37,670	61,450	81,500	75,100	74,700	84,730	97,100	105,200	106,000
Repeat buyers [1]	Dollars ...	50,090	75,750	100,400	106,200	114,860	115,430	141,400	144,700	149,400
Average monthly mortgage										
payment	Dollars ...	329	599	868	896	852	939	1,008	1,054	1,127
Percent of income....	Percent ...	24.0	32.4	30.3	30.0	28.6	29.3	32.8	31.8	33.8
Percent buying—										
New houses........	Percent ...	15.1	22.4	22.3	23.8	25.7	23.8	26.2	21.8	21.2
Existing houses......	Percent ...	84.9	77.6	77.7	76.2	74.3	76.2	73.8	78.2	78.8
Single-family houses ...	Percent ...	88.8	82.4	89.9	87.0	85.1	87.3	83.3	84.8	83.8
Condominiums [2]	Percent ...	11.2	17.6	10.1	10.6	14.2	12.5	12.4	13.5	13.1
For the first time	Percent ...	44.8	32.9	37.7	36.6	35.5	36.8	37.8	40.2	41.9
Average age:										
First-time buyers	Years	28.1	28.3	29.1	28.4	30.9	29.6	30.3	29.6	30.5
Repeat buyers [1]	Years	35.9	36.4	37.8	38.4	39.5	39.1	38.9	39.4	39.1
Downpayment/sales price	Percent ...	25.2	28.0	20.9	24.8	23.4	27.2	24.0	24.4	23.3
First-time buyers	Percent ...	18.0	20.5	13.2	11.4	13.4	20.4	14.6	15.8	15.7
Repeat buyers [1]	Percent ...	30.8	32.7	25.6	32.7	28.9	31.3	29.7	30.3	28.9

[1] Buyers who previously owned a home. [2] Includes multiple-family houses.
Source: Chicago Title Insurance Company, Chicago, IL, *The Guarantor*, bimonthly, (copyright).

No. 1236. Low-Income Public Housing Units, by Progress Stage: 1960 to 1988

[In thousands. As of **Dec.** 31. Housing for the elderly intended for persons 62 years old or over, disabled, or handicapped. Includes Puerto Rico and Virgin Islands. Covers units subsidized by HUD under annual contributions contracts. See also *Historical Statistics, Colonial Times to 1970,* series N 186-191]

YEAR	Total[1]	Occupied units [2]	Under con-struction	YEAR	Total[1]	Occupied units [2]	Under con-struction
1960........	593.3	478.2	36.4	1985........	1,378.0	1,344.6	9.6
Elderly.....	18.9	1.1	4.1	Elderly.....	373.5	361.1	2.1
1970........	1,155.3	893.5	126.8	1987........	1,443.0	1,406.4	9.7
Elderly.....	249.4	143.4	65.7	Elderly.....	378.6	374.2	1.3
1980........	1,321.1	1,195.6	20.9	1988........	1,448.8	1,413.3	9.7
Elderly.....	358.3	317.7	11.5	Elderly.....	382.5	374.7	1.4

[1] Inclues units to be constructed or to go directly "under management" because no rehabilitation needed, not shown separately. [2] Under management or available for occupancy.
Source: U.S. Dept. of Housing and Urban Development, unpublished data.

No. 1237. Office Buildings—Vacancy Rates for Major Cities, 1980 to 1991, and Status of Supply, 1991

[As of **December;** except **1991, as of June.** Excludes government owned and occupied, owner-occupied, and medical office buildings]

CITY	VACANCY RATE FOR EXISTING SPACE (percent)									SUPPLY STATUS, June 1991 (mil. sq. ft.)			
										Existing space		Space under construction	
	1980	1984	1985	1986	1987	1988	1989	1990	1991, June	Total	Avail-able for lease	Total	Avail-able for lease
Total [1].......	4.6	15.5	16.9	18.6	19.0	18.6	19.5	20.0	20.0	2,236.6	447.1	47.6	33.3
Atlanta, GA....	10.0	14.5	21.0	20.1	19.6	18.3	19.9	19.1	18.3	83.1	15.2	3.5	2.1
Baltimore, MD	7.2	11.9	11.5	15.9	15.8	13.4	16.4	20.0	17.6	32.2	5.7	1.2	0.9
Boston, MA.....	3.8	8.9	13.1	13.0	12.6	14.1	15.3	19.6	19.3	131.4	25.3	2.1	2.0
Charlotte, NC	(NA)	16.7	16.7	15.5	15.1	16.5	14.3	16.5	16.6	17.1	2.8	1.7	1.0
Chicago, IL......	7.0	14.8	16.5	19.6	17.0	15.9	17.0	18.6	19.6	191.8	37.5	5.4	3.8
Dallas, TX.......	8.6	18.7	23.0	30.9	29.1	29.7	26.9	25.8	24.8	113.0	28.0	-	-
Denver, CO.......	6.6	20.6	24.7	25.1	27.9	27.6	26.1	24.8	23.7	68.6	16.3	-	-
Houston, TX	4.0	25.0	27.6	30.6	31.8	29.2	27.5	24.9	24.0	137.2	33.0	0.6	0.2
Indianapolis, IN	(NA)	(NA)	(NA)	(NA)	(NA)	21.3	20.0	21.2	21.7	20.5	4.4	0.1	0.1
Kansas City, MO	4.2	18.6	16.2	18.2	18.2	19.9	15.8	14.1	16.6	32.4	5.4	0.2	0.1
Los Angeles, CA ...	0.9	20.4	15.3	13.2	19.0	15.8	19.7	16.8	19.5	198.3	38.7	9.9	7.8
Milwaukee, WI	(NA)	(NA)	(NA)	(NA)	16.8	19.3	20.4	22.9	17.5	21.2	3.7	0.3	0.3
New Orleans, LA	(NA)	22.4	21.8	25.5	24.3	25.6	25.7	29.0	26.9	23.3	6.3	-	-
New York, NY [2] ...	3.1	6.8	7.9	8.9	9.7	11.5	15.1	16.0	17.0	224.3	38.1	2.2	1.7
Philadelphia, PA....	6.3	9.0	14.5	15.5	16.5	15.8	16.3	18.2	17.5	70.5	12.3	2.2	1.1
Pittsburgh, PA.....	1.2	14.2	(NA)	12.0	12.3	17.6	16.3	16.3	14.7	36.2	5.3	0.8	0.8
San Diego, CA.....	(NA)	21.8	24.7	25.4	22.8	20.1	17.6	19.5	22.7	38.5	8.7	0.8	0.6
San Francisco, CA ..	0.4	9.0	13.7	16.6	15.0	15.5	15.7	14.7	15.2	56.1	8.5	-	-
Seattle, WA......	(NA)	(NA)	(NA)	(NA)	(NA)	13.2	12.4	12.3	12.3	29.7	3.6	0.5	0.2
St. Louis, MO	(NA)	(NA)	(NA)	(NA)	15.6	18.4	22.6	21.0	21.6	33.1	7.2	-	-
Washington, DC....	2.5	9.6	9.0	13.6	13.4	13.2	14.4	19.0	18.5	176.2	32.6	4.6	3.2

- Represents zero. NA Not available. [1] Includes other cities not shown separately. In 1990, 49 cities were covered.
[2] Refers to Manhattan.
Source: ONCOR International, Houston, TX, 1980-1985, *National Office Market Report*, semi-annual; thereafter, *International Office Market Report*, semi-annual, (copyright).

No. 1238. Commercial Office Space—Inventory and Vacancy Rates for the 50 Largest Metropolitan Areas: 1991

[As of December 31. Central business district is the area located near the historical urban core, commonly associated with the traditional government and financial districts in most cities; outside the central business districts is comprised of the suburban area and "urban clusters" with areas of high office space concentrations. Class A space is in "excellent" locations, with high quality finish, well maintained, an professionally managed; Class B space is in "good" locations, professionally managed, with fairly high quality construction and tenancy. Data based on responses from individuals knowledgeable in the local markets]

METROPOLITAN AREAS RANKED BY POPULATION-SIZE, **1990** [1]	INVENTORY (1,000 square feet)				VACANCY RATE [2] (percent)			
	Inside central business district		Outside central business district		Inside central business district		Outside central business district	
	Class A	Class B	Class A	Class B	Class A	Class B	Class A	Class B
Los Angeles-Long Beach, CA PMSA .	17,578.7	6,726.3	36,573.8	24,473.2	17.6	22.9	17.8	20.2
New York, NY PMSA.	251,537.0	109,737.2	7,200.0	12,400.0	16.5	20.0	14.3	22.1
Chicago, IL PMSA.	47,147.1	44,939.0	24,680.0	31,786.3	18.0	18.7	20.2	21.5
Philadelphia, PA-NJ PMSA	31,184.9	6,764.5	49,212.1	23,815.8	13.5	14.3	17.2	23.1
Detroit, MI PMSA	6,489.7	7,036.8	21,432.1	25,021.4	11.5	12.2	20.1	21.3
Washington, DC-MD-VA MSA	92,500.0		167,200.0		15.4	-	20.9	
Boston, MA NECMA	35,000.0	11,000.0	45,000.0	(NA)	18.3	20.9	21.1	(NA)
Houston, TX PMSA.	25,205.7	9,155.6	33,744.6	67,112.8	13.6	30.6	13.8	30.6
Atlanta, GA MSA	³21,126.5	(³)	³59,212.3	(³)	³17.3	(³)	³16.4	(³)
Nassau-Suffolk, NY PMSA	-	-	22,365.0	13,419.0	-	-	20.1	20.8
Riverside-San Bernardino, CA PMSA .	2,872.0	3,300.1	182.3	1,125.2	37.7	28.8	29.6	24.7
Dallas, TX PMSA	13,059.0	16,816.0	46,491.0	40,953.0	16.4	34.9	22.1	28.3
San Diego, CA MSA	5,824.4	3,614.8	21,813.2	10,703.8	19.0	19.0	20.8	17.0
Minneapolis-St. Paul, MN-WI MSA . . .	10,756.3	4,607.5	8,308.8	20,053.3	16.2	18.2	20.2	20.7
St. Louis, MO-IL MSA	7,023.3	6,113.3	21,096.8	(NA)	21.1	36.0	14.7	(NA)
Anaheim-Santa Ana, CA PMSA.	52,359.6	(NA)	(NA)	(NA)	19.3	(NA)	(NA)	(NA)
Baltimore, MD MSA.	6,967.5	5,101.1	11,610.1	4,918.7	14.5	28.4	19.1	15.6
Phoenix, AZ MSA.	17,225.7	(NA)	20,949.5	(NA)	22.7	(NA)	28.3	(NA)
Oakland, CA PMSA.	10,771.3	1,753.1	21,052.6	2,919.7	13.8	20.1	17.8	19.0
Tampa-St.Petersburg-Clearwater, FL MSA.	4,321.6	1,274.0	7,346.1	6,340.3	18.7	41.8	16.0	15.5
Seattle, WA PMSA	22,844.3	4,503.7	8,961.9	5,322.6	13.1	15.1	11.0	16.4
Miami-Hialeah, FL PMSA	7,200.0	4,700.0	5,400.0	12,200.0	31.9	35.1	22.2	16.4
Cleveland, OH PMSA	10,949.4	10,327.7	10,176.5	2,608.5	18.7	16.8	19.6	18.4
Newark, NJ PMSA [4]	-	-	24,040.0	23,795.0	-	-	16.1	23.1
Denver, CO PMSA	12,286.2	9,391.3	7,292.2	26,554.4	16.3	24.1	14.3	20.5
San Francisco, CA PMSA.	30,771.0	17,726.0	3,086.0	6,864.0	15.0	17.4	16.6	16.8
Kansas City, MO-KS MSA	5,240.0	6,000.0	13,210.0	7,600.0	8.6	18.5	11.0	14.5
Sacramento, CA MSA	4,500.0	3,300.0	10,000.0	12,000.0	6.7	6.1	8.0	24.2
Cincinnati, OH-KY-IN PMSA	6,774.9	7,148.2	5,411.0	3,840.1	19.1	17.7	18.0	21.8
Milwaukee, WI PMSA	5,324.7	7,603.9	3,725.6	8,121.4	14.6	15.4	14.7	19.8
Norfolk-Virginia Beach-Newport News, VA MSA	2,317.6	1,491.1	3,844.5	7,206.0	13.5	21.1	19.5	14.7
Columbus, OH MSA	4,500.0	3,400.0	5,183.7	5,000.0	9.3	11.6	14.0	14.4
San Antonio, TX MSA	2,043.0	3,223.0	4,982.0	9,828.5	22.9	38.6	20.3	28.4
Fort Lauderdale-Hollywood-Pompano Beach, FL PMSA	2,373.2	552.0	5,018.5	7,707.2	22.4	22.0	₂25.0	24.4
Indianapolis, IN MSA.	6,514.8	2,191.5	³12,291.2	(³)	19.2	26.4	³23.4	(³)
Portland, OR PMSA	7,617.1	1,873.4	3,267.3	3,033.5	14.1	19.5	11.1	15.0
New Orleans, LA PMSA.	9,452.8	6,095.0	2,220.7	2,699.4	24.6	34.7	18.9	15.6
Charlotte-Gastonia-Rock Hill, NC-SC MSA	(NA)	(NA)	(NA)	(NA)	(NA)	(NA)	(NA)	(NA)
Orlando, FL MSA	3,705.0	2,055.1	4,037.3	12,806.3	13.9	21.2	12.9	15.2
Salt Lake City-Ogden, UT MSA	3,400.0	2,500.0	1,700.0	2,000.0	14.7	14.0	11.8	17.5
Nashville, TN MSA	(NA)	(NA)	(NA)	(NA)	(NA)	(NA)	(NA)	(NA)
Memphis, TN-AR-MS MSA.	1,947.9	3,438.0	8,548.0	2,631.0	7.4	32.8	12.9	16.0
Buffalo, NY PMSA	2,948.4	1,769.5	848.6	1,160.2	20.4	18.6	8.5	12.2
Oklahoma City, OK MSA	3,351.0	2,460.0	4,901.0	3,679.0	29.9	48.6	10.2	26.4
Dayton-Springfield, OH MSA.	1,961.9	1,252.8	1,921.0	1,543.9	21.9	28.7	16.9	12.5
Greensboro-Winston-Salem-High Point, NC MSA.	1,473.0	830.0	2,000.0	285.0	16.0	24.1	15.8	28.1
Birmingham, AL MSA	2,832.9	1,980.0	4,031.3	3,570.5	17.4	33.4	12.5	20.1
Jacksonville, FL MSA	4,914.0	2,168.0	2,411.5	3,107.5	21.5	28.5	14.2	18.1
Albany-Schenectady-Troy, NY MSA . .	1,447.0	2,845.8	3,443.7	2,956.2	8.6	10.4	6.6	14.9

- Represents zero.   NA Not available.   [1] List excludes San Jose, CA MSA; Fort Worth-Arlington, TX PMSA; Bergen-Passaic, NJ PMSA; Rochester, NY MSA; Middlesex-Somerset-Hunterdon, NJ PMSA; Monmouth-Ocean, NJ PMSA; and Louisville, KY-IN MSA.   [2] Represents the total vacant space divided by the total inventory of space in that area.   [3] Class A includes Class B; data not available separately.   [4] Data are for area identified by source as New Jersey-Central with a market area of Hunterdon, Mercer, Middlesex, Monmouth, Somerset, and Union counties.

Source: Society of Industrial and Office REALTORS, Washington, DC, 1992 Guide to Industrial and Office Real Estate Markets, (copyright).

No. 1239. Commercial Buildings—Selected Characteristics, by Square Footage of Floorspace: 1989

[Excludes buildings 1,000 square feet or smaller. Building type based on predominant activity in which the occupants were engaged. Based on a sample survey of building representatives conducted between January and April 1986; therefore, subject to sampling variability. For composition of regions, see table 25]

CHARACTERISTIC	Number of build-ings (1,000)	FLOORSPACE (mil. sq. ft.)							Mean sq. ft. per building (1,000)	Median sq. ft. per building (1,000)
		Total	Within all buildings having square footage of—							
			5,000 or less	5,001 to 10,000	10,001 to 25,000	25,001 to 50,000	50,001 to 100,000	100,001 and over		
All buildings	4,528	63,184	6,790	6,532	10,393	8,801	9,130	21,538	14.0	4.5
Region:										
Northeast	783	13,569	1,047	1,271	1,980	1,722	1,507	6,041	17.3	5.2
Midwest	1,046	16,955	1,612	1,468	2,250	2,049	2,362	6,215	15.3	4.5
South	1,847	22,040	2,853	2,530	4,109	3,322	3,632	5,595	11.9	4.0
West	851	11,620	1,279	1,263	2,054	1,708	1,630	3,686	13.7	4.8
Year constructed:										
1900 or before	172	1,654	270	299	353	451	(S)	(S)	9.6	4.5
1901 to 1920	242	4,245	338	399	375	680	729	(S)	17.5	4.8
1921 to 1945	680	8,098	1,178	928	1,089	994	1,395	2,514	11.9	4.0
1946 to 1960	868	10,511	1,363	1,233	2,046	1,369	1,191	(S)	12.1	4.1
1961 to 1970	821	12,167	1,197	1,027	2,064	1,648	1,889	4,343	14.8	4.3
1970 to 1979	884	13,329	1,266	1,340	2,180	1,884	1,628	5,031	15.1	5.0
1980 to 1983	317	4,274	465	440	943	480	563	1,385	13.5	4.8
1984 to 1986	329	5,670	419	541	858	853	924	(S)	17.2	5.4
1987 to 1989	215	3,235	294	325	485	443	600	1,088	15.1	4.5
Principal activity within building:										
Assembly	615	6,838	1,006	1,183	1,390	1,230	635	(S)	11.1	5.0
Education	284	8,148	279	400	892	1,425	1,818	(S)	28.7	9.0
Food sales	102	792	223	33	177	(S)	(S)	(S)	7.7	4.8
Food service	241	1,167	417	263	260	(S)	(S)	(S)	4.8	3.0
Health care	80	2,054	136	(S)	166	(S)	123	1,510	25.7	3.5
Lodging	140	3,476	123	278	617	469	709	(S)	24.8	8.5
Mercantile/services	1,278	12,365	2,120	1,753	2,639	1,395	1,378	3,081	9.7	3.9
Office	679	11,802	961	90	1,721	1,459	1,575	5,267	17.4	4.2
Parking garage	45	983	55	821	79	(S)	(S)	656	22.0	4.8
Public order and safety	50	616	73	91	(S)	(S)	(S)	(S)	12.3	4.0
Warehouse	618	9,253	800	1,031	1,667	1,921	1,369	2,465	15.0	5.8
Other	62	1,529	63	87	160	128	701	(S)	24.7	6.7
Vacant	333	4,161	533	440	566	334	530	(S)	12.5	3.7
Government owned	577	14,342	645	908	1,752	1,892	2,475	6,670	24.8	7.1
Nongovernment owned	3,951	48,842	6,145	5,624	8,641	6,609	6,655	14,868	12.4	4.2
Fuels used alone or in combination:										
Electricity	4,297	61,587	6,411	6,302	9,989	8,682	8,918	21,286	14.3	4.6
Natural gas	2,439	41,593	3,441	3,985	5,793	5,487	6,397	16,489	17.1	5.0
Fuel oil	586	12,684	832	698	1,499	1,352	1,685	6,618	21.6	5.0
Propane	348	4,695	587	454	738	461	748	(S)	13.5	4.5
District heat	105	6,856	43	115	566	512	848	4,772	65.4	19.5
District chilled water	25	2,101	(S)	32	86	148	282	1,548	84.6	34.5
Any other [1]	130	1542	206	184	342	138	(S)	(S)	11.9	4.0
Workers:										
Fewer than 5	2,280	13,292	4,271	2,717	2,841	1,432	727	(S)	5.8	3.0
5 to 9	906	7,939	1,471	1,606	2,132	1,105	749	(S)	8.8	4.6
10 to 19	507	6,445	544	1,228	1,921	1,317	828	(S)	12.7	7.5
20 to 49	381	9,665	167	693	2,330	2,415	2,201	(S)	25.4	16.0
50 to 99	132	7,389	(S)	(S)	684	1,584	1,919	(S)	56.1	36.5
100 to 249	79	6,771	(S)	(S)	124	629	2,062	3,924	85.9	69.9
250 or more	32	9,829	(S)	(S)	(S)	95	394	9,340	308.0	200.1
Weekly operating hours:										
39 or less	876	6,073	1,574	1,159	1,157	885	634	(S)	6.9	3.5
40 to 48	1,117	13,905	1,628	1,830	2,628	2,163	2,386	3,269	12.4	5.0
49 to 60	987	13,473	1,450	1,409	2,614	2,081	1,925	3,995	13.6	5.0
61 to 84	625	10,777	891	824	1,601	1,235	1,530	4,697	17.2	4.8
85 to 167	515	9,387	776	680	1,159	1,296	1,272	(S)	18.2	4.5
168 (open continuously)	408	9,569	682	631	1,235	1,141	1,384	4,707	23.5	5.8

S Figure does not meet publication standards. [1] Active solar, coal, wood, and biomass.

Source: U.S. Energy Information Administration, *Commercial Buildings Characteristics, 1989.*

No. 1240. Commercial Buildings—Number and Square Footage of Floorspace, by Type of Building and Characteristic: 1989

[For composition of regions, see table 25]

BUILDING CHARACTERISTICS	All build-ings [1]	As-sembly	Educa-tion	Food sales	Food service	Health care	Lodg-ing	Mer-cantile/serv-ices	Offices	Public order and safety	Ware-house
NUMBER (1,000)											
All buildings	**4,528**	**615**	**284**	**102**	**241**	**80**	**140**	**1,278**	**679**	**50**	**618**
Region:											
Northeast	783	96	38	(S)	54	12	21	259	108	(S)	95
Midwest	1,046	134	54	(S)	59	21	24	303	139	(S)	177
South	1,847	275	108	45	87	30	50	523	275	(S)	243
West	851	109	84	(S)	41	17	44	193	157	(S)	104
Year constructed:											
1900 or before	172	53	(S)	(S)	(S)	(S)	(S)	43	27	(S)	(S)
1901 to 1920	242	41	14	(S)	(S)	(S)	(S)	61	36	(S)	27
1921 to 1945	680	125	32	(S)	34	(S)	17	194	85	(S)	67
1946 to 1960	868	138	87	(S)	38	15	18	254	109	(S)	113
1961 to 1970	821	82	65	(S)	35	24	36	227	129	(S)	107
1970 to 1979	884	97	52	(S)	57	10	32	227	128	(S)	137
1980 to 1983	317	32	10	(S)	(S)	(S)	9	78	62	(S)	50
1984 to 1986	329	31	14	(S)	(S)	(S)	10	78	71	(S)	74
1987 to 1989	215	17	9	(S)	(S)	(S)	(S)	67	39	(S)	35
Government owned	577	87	192	(S)	13	9	14	33	70	39	65
Nongovernment owned	3,951	528	92	99	228	71	126	1,246	609	(S)	553
FLOORSPACE (mil. sq. ft.)											
All buildings	**63,184**	**6,838**	**8,148**	**7,921**	**1,167**	**2,054**	**3,476**	**12,365**	**11,802**	**616**	**9,253**
Region:											
Northeast	13,569	1,507	1,888	(S)	284	378	549	2,647	2,703	(S)	1,811
Midwest	15,955	1,408	2,221	(S)	339	912	982	3,059	2,281	(S)	2,639
South	22,040	2,750	2,404	278	370	472	1,215	4,778	3,817	(S)	3,422
West	11,620	1,174	1,634	(S)	173	292	730	1,882	3,001	(S)	1,381
Year constructed:											
1900 or before	1,654	386	(S)	(S)	(S)	(S)	(S)	428	289	(S)	(S)
1901 to 1920	4,245	492	435	(S)	(S)	(S)	(S)	514	552	(S)	348
1921 to 1945	8,098	926	1,244	(S)	147	(S)	442	1,322	1,166	(S)	1,448
1946 to 1960	10,511	1,470	2,267	(S)	152	371	358	1,694	1,849	(S)	1,279
1961 to 1970	12,167	1,249	2,201	(S)	282	355	1,042	2,458	1,736	(S)	1,702
1971 to 1973	13,329	1,410	1,391	(S)	268	586	578	3,464	2,425	(S)	2,178
1980 to 1983	4,274	373	155	(S)	(S)	(S)	216	873	1,174	(S)	650
1984 to 1986	5,670	293	158	(S)	(S)	(S)	510	896	1,860	(S)	1,003
Government owned	14,342	1,394	6,312	(S)	109	495	622	399	2,353	575	597
Nongovernment owned	48,842	5,443	1,835	787	1,058	1,559	2,854	11,966	9,449	(S)	8,656

S Figure does not meet publication standards.   [1] Includes parking garages, vacant, and other commercial buildings, not shown separately.

Source: U.S. Energy Information Administration, *Commercial Building Characteristics, 1989.*

No. 1241. Commercial Buildings and Workers—Selected Building Characteristics, by Floorspace: 1986

[See headnote, table 1239]

BUILDING CHARACTERISTICS	NUMBER OF BUILDINGS (1,000)							WORKERS		
	Total	Square footage of—						Number (1,000)	Average sq. ft. per worker	Median sq. ft. per worker
		5,000 or less	5,001 to 10,000	10,001 to 25,000	25,001 to 50,000	50,001 to 100,000	100,001 and over			
All buildings	**4,154**	**2,220**	**931**	**557**	**242**	**123**	**81**	**73,436**	**792.9**	**1,000.9**
Region:										
Northeast	663	298	183	90	53	21	18	16,183	731.0	1,000.5
Midwest	1,096	559	277	147	56	33	24	17,636	909.2	1,251.9
South	1,570	905	312	200	83	47	22	25,099	774.0	975.8
West	825	458	158	120	51	22	16	14,518	753.4	833.9
Principal activity within building:										
Assembly	575	274	138	106	33	16	(S)	4,303	1,705.7	2,901.9
Education	241	72	50	44	37	21	(S)	6,833	1,071.5	932.5
Food sales/service	303	204	(S)	(S)	(S)	(S)	(S)	5,073	830.8	855.4
Health care	52	27	(S)	(S)	6	(S)	4	5,050	417.3	422.7
Lodging	137	48	29	31	16	9	(S)	2,277	1,223.2	2,001.3
Mercantile/services	1,287	757	309	142	46	23	10	15,870	806.9	900.7
Office	614	343	133	74	35	15	15	25,010	381.7	437.9
Public order and safety	55	26	(S)	13	(S)	(S)	(S)	1,367	497.8	875.3
Warehouse	549	274	123	72	44	21	(S)	5,343	1,683.6	3,001.8
Other	103	58	(S)	18	(S)	5	(S)	1,566	1,102.2	1,601.3
Vacant	238	136	47	30	15	8	(S)	745	3,933.8	(X)
Nongovernment owned	3,661	2,024	828	471	188	94	56	57,505	800.6	1,000.9
Owner occupied	2,396	1,338	546	301	120	59	32	35,691	811.5	1,000.9
Nonowner occupied	1,265	686	282	170	69	35	23	21,814	783.0	1,033.3
Government owned	493	196	104	86	54	29	25	15,931	765.0	1,000.1

S Figure does not meet publication standards.   X Not applicable.

Source: U.S. Energy Information Administration, *Nonresidential Buildings Energy Consumption Survey: Characteristics of Commercial Buildings, 1986.* Data for 1989 will be forthcoming in late 1992.

Figure 27.1
Summary of Manufactures: 1977 to 1990

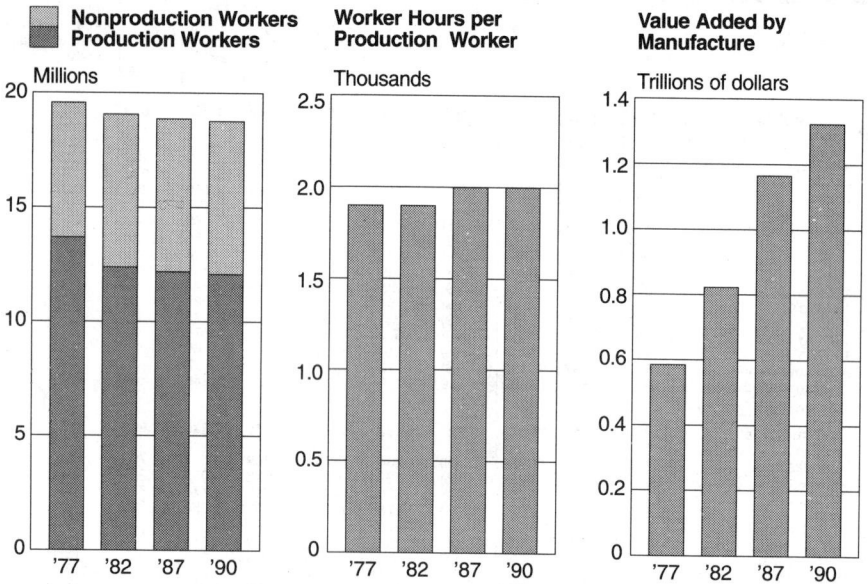

Nonproduction Workers
Production Workers

Worker Hours per Production Worker

Value Added by Manufacture

Millions

Thousands

Trillions of dollars

'77 '82 '87 '90

'77 '82 '87 '90

'77 '82 '87 '90

Source: Chart prepared by U.S. Bureau of the Census. For data, see table 1243.

Figure 27.2
Capital in Manufacturing Establishments: 1980 to 1989

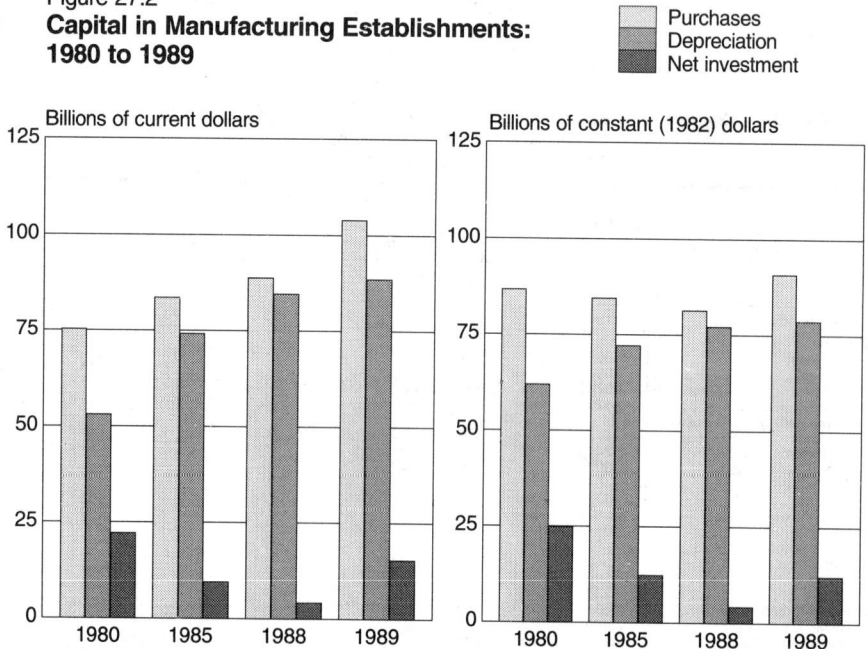

Purchases
Depreciation
Net investment

Billions of current dollars

Billions of constant (1982) dollars

1980 1985 1988 1989

1980 1985 1988 1989

Source: Chart prepared by U.S. Bureau of the Census. For data, see table 1249.

Manufactures

This section presents summary data for manufacturing as a whole and more detailed information for major industry groups and selected specific products. The types of measures shown at the different levels include data for establishments; employment and wages; raw materials, fuels, and electricity consumed; plant and equipment expenditures; value and quantity of production and shipments; value added by manufacture; inventories; and various indicators of financial status.

The principal sources of these data are Bureau of the Census reports of the censuses of manufactures conducted every 5 years; the *Annual Survey of Manufactures;* and the *Current Industrial Reports* series, which presents monthly, quarterly, or annual data on production, shipments, and stocks for particular commodities. Indexes of industrial production are presented monthly in the Federal Reserve Board's *Federal Reserve Bulletin.* Reports on current activities of industries, or current movements of individual commodities, are compiled by such government agencies as the Bureau of Labor Statistics; the Economic Research Service of the Department of Agriculture; the International Trade Administration; and by private research or trade associations such as The Conference Board, Inc., New York, NY and the American Iron and Steel Institute, Washington, DC.

Data on financial aspects of manufacturing industries are collected by the Bureau of Economic Analysis (BEA) and the Bureau of the Census. Industry aggregates in the form of balance sheets, profit and loss statements, analyses of sales and expenses, lists of subsidiaries, and types and amounts of security issues are published for leading manufacturing corporations registered with the Securities and Exchange Commission. The BEA issues data on capital in manufacturing industries and capacity utilization rates in manufacturing. See also section 17, Business Enterprise, in this edition.

Censuses and annual surveys.—The first census of manufactures covered the year 1809. Between 1809 and 1963, a

In Brief
Revenue from total computer shipments topped $50 billion in 1991.

Personal computer shipments topped 7 million units in 1991.

1-megabit DRAM chips:

	1965	1990
Revenue (mil. dol.)	5	4,623
Price (dollars)	162.50	6.33

census was conducted at periodic intervals. Since 1967 it has been taken every 5 years (for years ending in "2" and "7"). Census data, either direct reports or estimates from administrative records, are obtained for every manufacturing plant with one paid employee or more.

The *Annual Survey of Manufactures (ASM),* conducted for the first time in 1949, collects data for the years between censuses for the more general measures of manufacturing activity covered in detail by the censuses. The annual survey data are estimates derived from a scientifically selected sample of establishments. The 1990 annual survey is based on a sample of about 55,000 establishments of an approximate total of 200,000. These establishments represent all manufacturing establishments of multiunit companies and all single-establishment manufacturing companies mailed schedules in the 1987 Census of Manufactures. The 1989 through 1993 ASM sample is similar to the previous sample. For the current panel, all establishments of companies with 1987 shipments in manufacturing in excess of $500 million were included in the survey with certainty. For the remaining portion of the mail survey, the establishment was defined as the sampling unit. For this portion, all establishments with 250 employees or more and establishments with a very large value of shipments also were included. Therefore, of the 55,000 establishments included in the ASM panel, approximately 28,000 are selected with certainty. These establishments account for approximately 80 percent of total value of shipments in the 1987 census. Smaller establishments in the remaining portion of the mail survey were selected by sample.

The basic statistical measures of manufacturing activity, such as employment, payrolls, value added, etc., are defined in essentially the same way for both the annual surveys and the census of manufactures. However, the bases for computing average employment vary for different years. For example, beginning with 1949, average employment was calculated from the figures reported for the pay periods ending nearest the 15th of March, May, August, and November; whereas, for 1947 such averages were based on 12 monthly employment figures. In 1967, the average employment calculation was revised to the pay periods which include the 12th of March, May, August, and November to provide data more comparable with other statistical series.

Establishments and classification.—The censuses of manufactures for 1947 through 1987 cover operating manufacturing establishments as defined in the *Standard Industrial Classification Manual (SIC),* issued by the U.S. Office of Management and Budget (see text, section 13). The *Manual* is also used for classifying establishments in the annual surveys. The comparability of manufactures data over time is affected by changes in the official definitions of industries as presented in the *Manual.* It is important to note, therefore, that the 1987 edition of the *Manual* was used for the 1987 census; and the 1972 edition of the *Manual* and the *1977 Supplement* was used for the 1972 through 1982 censuses. For the censuses from 1947 to 1963, reports were required from all establishments employing one or more persons at any time during the census year. Beginning with the 1967 census, an effort was made to relieve the very small establishments from the necessity of filing a census report. Approximately 150,000 small single-unit manufacturing firms identified as having less than 20 employees (cutoff varied by industry) benefited from this procedure. Data for these single-unit companies were estimated on the basis of government administrative records and industry averages. Each of the establishments tabulated was classified in one of the approximately 459 manufacturing industries as defined by the *SIC Manual* in 1987. The *Manual* defines an industry as a number of establishments producing a single product or a closely related group of products. In the main, an establishment is classified in a particular industry if its production of a product or product group exceeds in value added its production of any other product group. While some establishments produce only the products of the industry in which they are classified, few within an industry specialize to that extent. The statistics on employment, payrolls, value added, inventories, and expenditures, therefore, reflect both the primary and secondary activities of the establishments in that industry. For this reason, care should be exercised in relating such statistics to the total shipments figures of products primary to the industry.

The censuses for 1947 through 1987 were conducted on an establishment basis. The term "establishment" signifies a single physical plant site or factory. It is not necessarily identical to the business unit or company, which may consist of one or more establishments. A company operating establishments at more than one location is required to submit a separate report for each location. An establishment engaged in distinctly different lines of activity and maintaining separate payroll and inventory records is also required to submit separate reports.

Durable goods.—Items with a normal life expectancy of three years or more. Automobiles, furniture, household appliances, and mobile homes are common examples.

Nondurable goods.—Items which generally last for only a short time (three years or less). Food, beverages, clothing, shoes, and gasoline are common examples.

Statistical reliability.—For a discussion of statistical collection and estimation, sampling procedures and measures of statistical reliability applicable to Census Bureau data, see Appendix III.

Historical statistics.—Tabular headnotes provide cross-references, where applicable, to *Historical Statistics of the United States, Colonial Times to 1970.* See Appendix IV.

No. 1242. Gross National Product in Manufacturing: 1977 to 1989

[In millions of dollars. For definition of gross national product, see text, section 14. Based on 1972 Standard Industrial Classification]

ITEM	1977	1978	1979	1980	1981	1982	1983	1984	1985	1986	1987	1988	1989
CURRENT DOLLARS													
Manufacturing †	465,346	518,752	561,765	581,018	643,098	634,648	683,205	771,884	789,537	832,420	875,539	940,656	965,997
Durable goods †	277,673	317,351	345,242	351,820	385,824	362,512	385,633	451,120	458,774	478,079	499,874	527,137	540,995
Lumber and wood products	15,890	19,010	20,823	18,658	17,125	16,041	20,543	22,843	24,777	24,690	29,441	31,118	32,163
Stone, clay, and glass	15,251	17,975	19,573	19,012	19,039	18,160	20,179	22,934	24,777	26,915	25,737	25,695	26,299
Primary metal industries	33,471	40,623	45,225	44,286	49,804	35,281	30,344	36,286	34,803	39,248	36,053	43,241	44,376
Fabricated metal products	35,438	39,965	44,765	46,017	49,632	46,281	47,626	55,053	57,845	57,917	60,412	65,325	68,029
Machinery, exc. electrical	55,421	62,384	70,631	76,861	86,166	80,005	75,346	85,445	82,687	82,699	88,916	96,157	97,300
Electric and electronic equip	39,490	45,640	49,326	54,961	60,695	61,814	67,694	79,888	82,193	82,656	89,626	90,461	96,894
Motor vehicles and equip.	35,846	38,428	35,811	26,698	31,539	29,453	39,037	49,647	53,718	53,219	52,505	53,311	50,072
Instruments and related products	13,174	15,120	16,485	18,962	22,260	22,631	23,845	26,949	25,809	27,138	26,840	30,256	30,541
Nondurable goods †	187,673	201,401	216,523	229,198	257,274	272,136	297,572	320,764	330,763	354,341	375,665	413,519	425,002
Food and kindred products	42,665	44,839	47,859	52,198	57,879	61,427	64,662	66,648	69,830	70,926	75,096	80,863	81,458
Tobacco	14,047	(NA)	14,785	14,962	15,891	8,916	11,942	12,762	12,156	14,386	14,105	14,445	16,096
Textile mill	14,468	15,442	16,040	17,093	18,671	14,827	20,270	20,716	20,640	21,907	22,478	20,217	20,803
Apparel and other textile	18,030	19,839	22,219	23,126	25,052	18,931	21,907	22,769	23,609	24,738	22,840	23,553	24,603
Paper and allied products	23,326	26,202	28,810	31,553	35,228	26,718	27,769	31,907	33,123	35,501	40,152	45,682	46,827
Printing and publishing	35,190	37,097	41,124	37,048	38,588	38,364	42,374	47,578	52,512	56,865	61,112	65,505	68,236
Chemicals and allied	52,959	55,055	56,700	50,021	53,986	55,257	59,581	61,972	63,823	70,789	80,938	95,819	98,763
Petroleum and coal	14,542	15,200	15,078	16,757	19,784	24,352	28,260	33,747	32,219	35,174	29,599	34,515	33,682
CONSTANT (1982) DOLLARS													
Manufacturing †	664,755	694,744	712,184	673,936	678,555	634,648	674,223	752,407	779,230	803,179	852,178	917,448	929,042
Durable goods †	403,295	423,307	433,149	408,468	408,606	362,512	383,817	448,614	471,548	482,717	515,552	570,796	583,684
Lumber and wood products	19,504	19,348	21,665	21,328	16,515	16,041	18,831	20,921	19,824	21,307	24,993	26,439	25,646
Stone, clay, and glass	22,674	23,327	23,546	21,254	20,583	18,160	19,671	21,300	22,158	22,874	22,018	22,847	23,552
Primary metal industries	47,867	52,825	52,669	48,231	50,583	35,281	28,856	33,360	32,682	32,156	34,752	37,750	36,863
Fabricated metal products	51,534	53,382	56,040	53,692	52,975	46,281	48,761	54,781	56,234	54,774	58,908	66,218	65,816
Machinery, exc. electrical	78,381	80,915	85,588	86,051	89,564	80,005	84,816	105,663	124,180	129,447	138,112	163,910	174,853
Electric and electronic equip	50,087	56,175	60,159	63,346	64,897	61,814	64,559	73,540	74,315	74,141	82,891	88,060	90,839
Motor vehicles and equip.	56,988	58,103	51,587	35,160	34,783	29,453	37,613	47,322	50,332	46,516	44,788	49,503	47,283
Instruments and related products	19,735	20,315	22,397	21,922	23,763	22,631	23,070	25,157	24,244	25,687	25,748	27,946	26,639
Nondurable goods †	261,460	271,437	279,035	265,468	269,949	272,136	290,406	303,793	307,682	320,462	336,627	346,651	345,358
Food and kindred products	51,702	56,566	59,526	59,762	58,900	61,427	62,655	62,063	64,818	65,592	66,665	67,836	70,284
Tobacco	9,525	9,924	9,852	9,561	9,931	8,916	7,784	6,248	6,248	7,039	5,164	3,725	3,080
Textile mill	17,628	16,595	17,029	16,368	15,792	14,827	16,230	16,025	15,598	17,043	17,374	16,727	16,720
Apparel and other textile	20,760	21,538	21,334	21,068	20,284	18,931	20,096	20,421	20,096	20,993	21,952	22,406	22,396
Paper and allied products	27,531	28,901	28,667	25,800	25,502	26,718	28,978	29,498	30,214	31,579	33,658	34,560	32,992
Printing and publishing	35,190	36,228	37,097	37,048	38,588	38,364	39,642	40,772	42,532	43,130	44,723	46,5?5	45,116
Chemicals and allied	52,959	55,055	56,700	50,021	53,986	55,257	59,642	59,398	59,057	64,563	71,944	77,501	76,128
Petroleum and coal	23,453	22,673	24,124	22,937	21,811	24,352	29,780	39,520	39,363	41,139	42,599	44,463	44,906

NA Not available.   † Includes industries not shown separately.

Source: U.S. Bureau of Economic Analysis, *The National Income and Product Accounts of the United States, 1929-82*, and *Survey of Current Business*, July issues.

No. 1243. Manufactures—Summary: 1963 to 1990

[For establishment coverage, see text, section 27. Data based on Census of Manufactures, except as noted. For composition of regions, see fig. I, inside front cover. See also, *Historical Statistics, Colonial Times to 1970*, series P 1-12]

ITEM	Unit	1963	1967	1972	1977	1982	1987	1989 [1]	1990 [1]
ALL ESTABLISHMENTS									
Number of establishments [2] ...	1,000	312	311	321	360	358	369	(NA)	(NA)
With 20 or more employees ...	1,000	102	110	114	119	123	126	(NA)	(NA)
Employee size-class:									
Establishments [3]	1,000	305	306	313	351	348	359	(NA)	(NA)
Under 20	1,000	207	199	203	237	230	238	(NA)	(NA)
20 to 99.................	1,000	70	74	76	78	84	86	(NA)	(NA)
100 to 249	1,000	18	20	21	22	21	22	(NA)	(NA)
250 to 999	1,000	10	11	11	12	11	11	(NA)	(NA)
1,000 and over	1,000	3	3	3	2	2	2	(NA)	(NA)
Form of organization:									
Corporate	1,000	176.2	153.9	233.2	284.2	283.2	287.4	(NA)	(NA)
Noncorporate, total [4]	1,000	130.4	33.2	87.5	75.7	74.0	81.5	(NA)	(NA)
Individual proprietorship.	1,000	99.2	24.9	42.5	52.3	45.6	35.4	(NA)	(NA)
Partnership	1,000	27.7	6.7	17.7	18.3	15.0	13.2	(NA)	(NA)
Value added by region:									
Northeast.................	Percent . . .	29.8	29.1	26.3	23.7	23.7	23.7	(NA)	(NA)
North Central	Percent . . .	35.4	35.0	34.9	34.4	29.8	29.8	(NA)	(NA)
South	Percent . . .	21.5	22.7	25.5	27.4	29.5	29.5	(NA)	(NA)
West....................	Percent . . .	13.3	13.0	13.4	14.5	17.0	17.0	(NA)	(NA)
All employees, [5] **annual average** [6] ..	Million . . .	17.0	19.3	19.0	19.6	19.1	18.9	19.0	18.8
Payroll, all employees	Bil. dol. . .	100	132	174	264	380	476	519	532
Payroll per employee	$1,000. . . .	5.9	6.8	9.2	13.5	19.9	25.2	27.3	28.3
Production workers, annual average ..	Million....	12.2	14.0	13.5	13.7	12.4	12.2	12.3	12.1
Percent of all employees	Percent . . .	71.8	72.5	71.1	69.9	64.9	64.6	64.7	64.4
Hours, production workers	Billion	24.5	27.8	26.7	26.7	23.5	24.3	24.7	24.3
Hours per worker	1,000	2.0	2.0	2.0	1.9	1.9	2.0	2.0	2.0
Wages, production workers	Bil. dol. . . .	62	81	106	157	205	251	269	272
Percent of payroll for all									
employees	Percent . . .	62.0	61.4	60.9	59.5	53.9	52.8	51.8	51.1
Wages per worker..............	$1,000. . . .	5.1	5.8	7.9	11.5	16.5	20.6	21.9	22.5
Wages per worker hour	Dollar . . .	2.53	2.91	3.97	5.89	8.72	10.35	10.89	11.19
Value added by manufacture [7].....	**Bil. dol.. . .**	192	262	354	585	824	1,166	1,308	1,326
Per production worker	$1,000. . . .	15.7	18.7	26.2	42.7	66.5	95.5	106.3	109.6
Per production worker hour.	Dollar . . .	7.84	9.42	13.26	21.91	35.06	47.97	52.96	54.57
Per dollar of workers' wages......	Dollar . . .	3.10	3.23	3.34	3.73	4.02	4.64	4.86	4.88
Cost of materials . . [8]	**Bil. dol.. . .**	230	299	407	782	1,130	1,320	1,503	1,554
Value of shipments [8].	**Bil. dol.. . .**	421	557	757	1,359	1,960	2,476	2,793	2,874
Per production worker	$1,000. . . .	34.5	39.8	56.1	99.2	158.1	203.0	227.1	237.5
End-of-year inventories	Bil. dol. . . .	60	84	108	188	307	333	381	393
Capital expenditures, new [9]	Bil. dol. . . .	11.4	21.5	24.1	47.5	75.0	78.6	97.2	102.0
Ratios:									
Value added to shipments	Ratio.....	45.6	47.0	46.7	42.9	42.0	47.1	(NA)	(NA)
Inventories to shipments.	Ratio.....	14.2	15.0	14.2	13.8	15.7	13.4	(NA)	(NA)
Payroll to value added	Ratio.....	52.0	50.3	49.1	45.2	46.1	40.8	(NA)	(NA)
Gross book value of depreciable									
assets	Bil. dol. . . .	158	218	301	439	692	868	(NA)	(NA)
Machinery and equipment.	Bil. dol. . . .	(NA)	157	218	328	527	671	(NA)	(NA)
Assets per employee	$1,000. . . .	9.3	11.3	16.4	22.4	36.2	48.6	(NA)	(NA)
MULTIUNIT COMPANIES									
Establishments	1,000	45.9	51.7	70.2	81.2	81.7	80.9	(NA)	(NA)
Employees	Million	11.0	13.3	14.3	15.0	14.3	13.8	(NA)	(NA)
Production workers	Million	8.1	9.8	9.8	10.1	8.8	8.5	(NA)	(NA)
Payroll, all employees	Bil. dol. . . .	68.2	93.8	138.8	214.2	307.5	377.3	(NA)	(NA)
Wages, production workers.......	Bil. dol. . . .	44.7	60.9	81.9	124.9	159.1	191.8	(NA)	(NA)
Value added by manufacture	Bil. dol. . . .	146.6	206.4	286.1	485.0	678.4	953.6	(NA)	(NA)
Capital expenditures, new	Bil. dol. . . .	8.9	18.6	20.0	41.0	65.2	66.5	(NA)	(NA)
SINGLE UNIT COMPANIES [10]									
Establishments	1,000	260.8	254.0	250.5	278.7	276.3	288.0	(NA)	(NA)
Employees	Million....	5.2	5.2	4.8	4.6	4.8	5.1	(NA)	(NA)
Payroll, all employees	Bil. dol. . . .	25.1	28.5	35.4	49.8	72.1	98.3	(NA)	(NA)
Value added by manufacture	Bil. dol. . . .	45.5	55.5	67.9	100.1	145.7	212.1	(NA)	(NA)

NA Not available.   [1] Estimated data based on *Annual Survey of Manufactures;* see text, section 27.   [2] Includes administrative and auxiliary units, except as noted.   [3] Excludes administrative offices and auxiliary units.   [4] Includes forms of organization not shown separately.   [5] Includes data for employees of manufacturing establishments engaged in distribution and construction work.   [6] Data are based on pay periods ending nearest 15th of March, May, August, and November.   [7] Adjusted value added; takes into account (a) value added by merchandising operations (that is, difference between the sales value and cost of merchandise sold without further manufacture, processing, or assembly), plus (b) net change in finished goods and work-in-process inventories between beginning and end of year.   [8] Includes extensive and unmeasurable duplication from shipments between establishments in the same industry classification.   [9] Includes plants under construction and not yet in operation.   [10] Beginning 1967, includes data obtained from Federal administrative records.

Source: U.S. Bureau of the Census, *Census of Manufactures, 1963, 1967, 1972, 1977, 1982,* and *1987;* and *Annual Survey of Manufactures.*

No. 1244. Manufactures—Summary, by Industry Group: 1982, 1987, and 1990

[Data based on various editions of the *Standard Industrial Classification Manual*, published by the Office of Management and Budget; see text, section 27. N.e.c.=Not elsewhere classified. See also *Historical Statistics, Colonial Times to 1970*, series P-58-67]

SIC[1] code	INDUSTRY GROUP	1982 Establishments (number)	1982 All employees — Number[2] (1,000)	1982 All employees — Payroll (mil. dol.)	1982 Value of shipments (mil. dol.)	1987 Establishments, total	1987 All employees — Number (1,000)	1987 All employees — Payroll (mil. dol.)	1987 Value of shipments (mil. dol.)	1990 All employees — Number (1,000)	1990 All employees — Payroll (mil. dol.)	1990 Production workers	1990 Value added by manufacture (mil. dol.)	1990 Value of shipments (mil. dol.)
(X)	All manufacturing establishments	358,061	19,094	379,627	1,960,206	368,897	18,950	475,651	2,475,901	18,840	532,317	12,129	1,326,362	2,873,502
20	Food and kindred products	22,130	1,488	26,088	280,529	20,624	1,449	30,268	329,725	1,470	33,470	1,061	140,973	384,009
201	Meat products	3,623	318	4,993	67,602	3,267	341	5,701	77,002	377	6,693	319	18,435	90,777
202	Dairy products	2,724	140	2,553	38,771	2,366	142	3,217	44,755	139	3,482	85	13,234	50,962
203	Preserved fruits and vegetables	(NA)	(NA)	(NA)	(NA)	1,912	209	3,784	36,343	218	4,441	181	20,419	44,495
204	Grain mill products	2,745	108	2,197	31,386	2,610	102	2,704	36,737	103	3,001	70	19,295	46,538
205	Bakery products	(NA)	(NA)	(NA)	(NA)	2,850	217	4,761	23,677	208	5,144	126	15,971	26,121
206	Sugar and confectionery products	1,033	96	1,661	15,576	1,094	90	1,991	18,887	92	2,252	74	9,475	21,045
207	Fats and oils	724	39	774	16,752	595	30	702	15,881	29	751	19	4,118	19,499
208	Beverages	2,584	194	4,244	38,801	2,214	161	4,521	47,327	146	4,499	73	25,034	52,198
209	Miscellaneous foods and kindred products	3,941	158	2,300	23,959	3,716	158	2,887	29,116	157	3,208	114	14,993	32,375
21	Tobacco products	163	58	1,324	16,061	138	45	1,486	20,757	41	1,516	30	22,561	29,922
211	Cigarettes	14	42	1,094	12,127	11	32	1,234	17,372	28	1,230	20	20,628	25,522
212	Cigars	60	5	59	254	20	3	36	192	2	39	2	137	230
213	Chewing and smoking tobacco	29	3	52	665	29	3	77	1,114	3	84	2	1,106	1,474
214	Tobacco stemming and redrying	60	8	120	3,015	78	7	139	2,079	8	164	5	690	2,697
22	Textile mill products	6,630	717	9,046	47,515	6,412	672	11,410	62,786	633	11,586	548	26,542	65,951
221	Broadwoven fabric mills, cotton	269	77	965	3,972	301	72	1,260	5,508	63	1,137	56	2,457	5,325
222	Broadwoven fabric mills, manmade	523	141	1,815	8,191	441	88	1,596	8,049	85	1,688	75	3,619	8,578
223	Broadwoven fabric mills, wool	131	13	176	763	119	14	236	1,051	16	291	14	675	1,798
224	Narrow fabric mills	281	18	216	852	277	19	296	1,136	17	307	15	671	1,260
225	Knitting mills	(NA)	(NA)	(NA)	(NA)	2,130	203	2,988	13,531	198	3,159	175	6,791	14,597
226	Textile finishing, except wool	753	58	834	4,972	971	56	1,036	7,042	49	998	41	2,365	6,304
227	Carpets and rugs	505	42	603	5,808	477	53	1,039	9,795	52	1,059	41	2,917	10,038
228	Yarn and thread mills	714	109	1,098	7,036	610	114	1,850	10,277	101	1,754	92	3,753	10,575
229	Miscellaneous textile goods	(NA)	(NA)	(NA)	(NA)	1,086	53	1,109	6,398	52	1,192	40	3,292	7,478
23	Apparel and other textile products	24,391	1,189	12,129	53,388	22,872	1,081	13,904	64,243	993	14,111	845	33,034	64,414
231	Men's and boys' suits and coats	529	75	878	3,062	347	55	779	2,863	48	768	41	1,501	2,622
232	Men's and boys' furnishings	2,544	299	2,837	12,727	2,195	280	3,246	15,441	259	3,275	228	8,051	14,873
233	Women's and misses' outerwear	10,838	419	4,110	18,225	10,290	349	4,297	19,389	318	4,316	272	10,192	19,339
234	Women's and children's undergarments	755	82	783	3,323	557	68	839	3,738	60	798	51	1,859	3,424

See footnotes at end of table.

No. 1244. Manufactures—Summary, by Industry Group: 1982, 1987, and 1990—Continued

[See headnote, p. 733]

SIC [1] code	INDUSTRY GROUP	1982 Establishments (number)	1982 All employees Number [2] (1,000)	1982 All employees Payroll (mil. dol.)	1982 Value of shipments (mil. dol.)	1987 Establishments, total	1987 All employees Number (1,000)	1987 All employees Payroll (mil. dol.)	1987 Value of shipments (mil. dol.)	1990 All employees Number (1,000)	1990 All employees Payroll (mil. dol.)	1990 Production workers	1990 Value added by manufacture (mil. dol.)	1990 Value of shipments (mil. dol.)
	Apparel, other textile products—Con													
235	Hats, caps, and millinery	419	16	157	522	461	17	204	663	17	227	14	424	737
236	Girls' and children's outerwear	968	71	671	2,711	834	72	826	3,753	61	812	51	2,046	3,698
237	Fur goods	504	3	60	419	380	2	48	423	2	46	2	104	379
238	Miscellaneous apparel and accessories	1,223	50	513	2,118	986	41	518	2,229	38	546	32	1,238	2,256
239	Miscellaneous fabricated textile products	6,611	174	2,120	10,281	6,822	198	3,143	15,744	189	3,323	155	7,619	17,086
24	**Lumber and wood products** [3]	**32,984**	**576**	**8,445**	**42,935**	**33,982**	**698**	**12,707**	**69,747**	**683**	**13,496**	**571**	**28,597**	**74,287**
241	Logging	11,658	81	1,208	8,274	11,952	86	1,518	10,938	83	1,647	69	4,313	12,229
242	Sawmills and planing mills	7,403	158	2,306	11,132	6,696	180	3,297	19,220	171	3,429	153	7,175	19,935
243	Millwork, plywood, and structural members	6,545	165	2,596	11,683	7,930	240	4,658	22,614	229	4,823	188	9,578	23,245
244	Wood containers	2,250	36	391	1,635	2,216	37	483	2,069	42	636	35	1,189	2,850
245	Wood buildings and mobile homes	1,163	60	880	4,955	1,077	65	1,215	6,575	61	1,217	48	1,365	6,471
25	**Furniture and fixtures** [3]	**10,003**	**436**	**6,084**	**24,129**	**11,613**	**511**	**9,082**	**37,462**	**499**	**9,851**	**398**	**21,645**	**41,682**
251	Household furniture	5,475	263	3,162	12,776	5,606	284	4,452	18,559	275	4,718	231	9,878	19,913
253	Public building and related furniture	413	19	295	1,103	484	22	397	2,088	26	544	20	1,147	3,112
254	Partitions and fixtures	2,148	60	1,025	3,710	2,455	74	1,552	5,537	73	1,701	53	3,409	6,193
259	Miscellaneous furniture and fixtures	1,267	36	551	2,390	2,084	50	892	3,740	51	991	38	2,491	4,434
26	**Paper and allied products**	**(NA)**	**(NA)**	**(NA)**	**(NA)**	**6,342**	**611**	**16,860**	**108,989**	**628**	**18,946**	**480**	**59,823**	**131,445**
261	Pulp mills	43	17	468	3,110	39	14	535	4,314	16	668	12	3,416	6,239
262	Paper mills	299	129	3,431	20,995	281	129	4,597	28,918	130	5,062	99	16,600	35,322
263	Paperboard mills	222	56	1,502	9,531	199	52	1,859	13,730	53	2,049	41	8,123	15,919
265	Paperboard containers and boxes	2,781	188	3,517	19,192	2,796	194	4,618	25,863	200	5,245	153	11,082	30,510
267	Miscellaneous converted paper products	3,006	213	3,961	26,701	3,027	222	5,251	36,165	229	5,923	175	20,602	43,454
27	**Printing and publishing**	**53,406**	**1,292**	**22,707**	**85,797**	**61,774**	**1,494**	**33,440**	**136,196**	**1,538**	**38,807**	**818**	**103,179**	**157,060**
271	Newspapers	8,846	402	6,555	21,276	9,079	434	9,022	31,850	443	10,407	149	26,560	34,642
272	Periodicals	3,328	94	1,986	11,478	4,017	110	2,983	17,329	115	3,659	22	13,848	20,397
273	Books	2,811	112	2,090	10,132	2,856	114	2,821	15,876	122	3,463	55	13,320	19,450
274	Miscellaneous publishing	2,057	45	706	2,871	2,376	70	1,513	7,810	65	1,708	22	6,656	8,875
275	Commercial printing	(NA)	(NA)	(NA)	(NA)	36,103	553	12,301	44,786	580	14,271	421	29,001	52,904
276	Manifold business forms	810	50	934	5,059	853	53	1,281	7,397	50	1,326	35	4,038	7,808
277	Greeting cards	154	21	344	1,894	162	22	471	2,911	25	625	12	2,828	3,721
278	Blankbooks and bookbinding	1,487	61	903	2,803	1,545	69	1,265	4,080	70	1,396	54	3,219	4,549
279	Printing trade services	(NA)	(NA)	(NA)	(NA)	4,783	69	1,784	4,157	67	1,952	48	3,709	4,715

See footnotes at end of table.

No. 1244. Manufactures—Summary, by Industry Group: 1982, 1987, and 1990—Continued

[See headnote, p. 733]

SIC[1] code	INDUSTRY GROUP	1982 Establishments (number)	1982 All employees Number (1,000)	1982 All employees Payroll (mil. dol.)	1982 Value of shipments (mil. dol.)	1987 Establishments (number)	1987 All employees Number (1,000)	1987 All employees Payroll (mil. dol.)	1987 Value of shipments (mil. dol.)	1990 All employees Number (1,000)	1990 All employees Payroll (mil. dol.)	1990 Production workers	1990 Value added by manufacture (mil. dol.)	1990 Value of shipments (mil. dol.)
28	Chemicals and allied products	11,901	873	20,836	170,737	12,109	814	25,016	229,546	853	30,082	484	153,032	288,184
281	Industrial inorganic chemicals	1,365	108	2,795	17,280	1,405	94	3,099	19,774	101	3,843	55	16,100	26,691
282	Plastics materials and synthetics	606	141	3,451	28,428	680	123	4,013	40,851	132	4,802	88	20,511	48,420
283	Drugs	1,281	166	3,966	24,695	1,356	172	5,304	39,263	183	6,851	81	38,245	53,720
284	Soap, cleaners, and toilet goods	2,379	127	2,581	26,031	2,399	119	3,099	34,748	126	3,683	78	25,008	41,438
285	Paints and allied products	1,441	54	1,158	9,162	1,431	55	1,492	12,702	54	1,628	27	6,766	14,239
286	Industrial organic chemicals	969	144	4,005	38,157	961	126	4,541	51,158	126	5,187	75	28,813	65,696
287	Agricultural chemicals	1,127	51	1,156	14,653	973	40	1,171	14,267	43	1,445	27	8,060	18,307
289	Miscellaneous chemical products	2,733	82	1,725	12,330	2,904	85	2,298	16,782	89	2,643	53	9,531	19,674
29	Petroleum and coal products	2,322	152	4,339	208,919	2,254	116	3,996	130,414	112	4,474	74	27,214	172,589
291	Petroleum refining	(NA)	(NA)	(NA)	(NA)	331	75	2,845	118,186	72	3,196	47	22,822	159,411
295	Asphalt paving and roofing materials	1,307	30	629	5,948	1,367	28	786	7,749	27	848	19	2,735	7,799
299	Miscellaneous petroleum and coal products	582	14	312	3,614	556	13	365	4,479	13	431	7	1,657	5,379
30	Rubber and misc. plastics products	13,449	682	11,597	55,416	14,515	831	17,581	86,634	870	20,236	674	49,889	101,398
301	Tires and inner tubes	164	70	1,734	9,340	164	65	2,070	10,427	68	2,315	55	6,489	11,861
302	Rubber and plastics footwear	65	18	197	706	66	11	153	557	11	159	9	339	650
305	Hose and belting and plastics and packing	635	55	999	3,612	693	52	1,159	4,648	56	1,375	42	3,143	5,570
306	Fabricated rubber products, n.e.c.	(NA)	(NA)	(NA)	(NA)	1,573	104	2,245	9,227	103	2,336	80	5,225	10,559
308	Miscellaneous plastics products, n.e.c.	(NA)	(NA)	(NA)	(NA)	12,019	599	11,955	61,775	633	14,052	489	34,693	72,758
31	Leather and leather products	2,735	200	2,219	9,719	2,193	129	1,831	9,082	117	1,888	99	4,587	9,887
311	Leather tanning and finishing	384	20	311	1,753	344	15	292	2,219	12	282	10	780	2,411
313	Footwear cut stock	161	7	81	368	128	5	70	324	5	94	4	196	413
314	Footwear, except rubber	751	121	1,250	5,269	479	71	913	4,073	62	896	54	2,120	4,232
315	Leather gloves and mittens	96	4	37	178	77	3	34	185	3	34	2	59	155
316	Luggage	292	16	194	789	241	11	196	929	14	244	11	618	1,169
317	Handbags and personal leather goods	636	25	271	1,035	529	17	232	942	13	207	10	510	912
319	Leather goods, n.e.c.	415	7	76	327	395	7	95	411	9	132	7	303	595

See footnotes at end of table.

No. 1244. Manufactures—Summary, by Industry Group: 1982, 1987, and 1990—Continued

[See headnote, page 733]

SIC[1] code	INDUSTRY GROUP	1982 Establishments (number)	1982 All employees Number[2] (1,000)	1982 All employees Payroll (mil. dol.)	1982 Value of shipments (mil. dol.)	1987 Establishments (number)	1987 All employees Number (1,000)	1987 All employees Payroll (mil. dol.)	1987 Value of shipments (mil. dol.)	1990 All employees Number (1,000)	1990 All employees Payroll (mil. dol.)	1990 Production workers (1,000)	1990 Value added by manufacture (mil. dol.)	1990 Value of shipments (mil. dol.)
32	**Stone, clay, and glass products**	**16,545**	**532**	**10,097**	**45,181**	**16,166**	**524**	**12,349**	**61,477**	**509**	**13,169**	**395**	**34,140**	**63,468**
321	Flat glass	69	15	414	1,666	81	15	507	2,549	15	509	12	1,395	2,279
322	Glass and glassware, pressed or blown	459	97	2,032	7,941	522	77	1,959	8,339	72	2,059	62	5,343	8,918
323	Products of purchased glass	1,337	41	696	2,977	1,432	51	1,060	5,429	54	1,250	42	3,342	6,141
324	Cement, hydraulic	237	25	636	3,542	215	19	599	4,335	18	599	13	2,197	4,251
325	Structural clay products	628	30	491	1,868	598	35	689	2,915	34	756	27	1,853	3,087
326	Pottery and related products	910	37	598	1,762	1,006	38	762	2,416	38	832	30	1,839	2,613
327	Concrete, gypsum, and plaster products	9,933	167	2,995	14,947	9,814	203	4,632	24,427	195	4,806	145	11,662	24,595
328	Cut stone and stone products	711	11	156	555	745	13	243	841	14	297	11	575	989
329	Miscellaneous nonmetallic mineral products	(NA)	(NA)	(NA)	(NA)	1,753	73	1,898	10,226	71	2,062	53	5,936	10,595
33	**Primary metal industries[3]**	**7,061**	**854**	**20,603**	**104,667**	**6,771**	**701**	**19,771**	**120,248**	**712**	**22,477**	**548**	**53,367**	**146,052**
331	Blast furnace and basic steel products	1,068	366	8,267	46,720	1,241	253	8,166	51,815	259	9,386	200	23,766	62,121
332	Iron and steel foundries	1,438	157	3,113	9,642	1,231	130	3,426	10,628	133	3,781	107	6,692	12,065
333	Primary nonferrous metals	161	44	1,307	11,321	169	32	996	10,869	35	1,281	27	4,266	15,507
334	Secondary nonferrous metals	458	19	402	4,852	397	13	312	4,431	15	418	11	1,108	6,130
335	Nonferrous rolling and drawing	1,022	167	3,636	25,463	1,066	163	4,298	33,282	157	4,713	116	11,833	39,331
336	Nonferrous foundries (castings)	(NA)	(NA)	(NA)	(NA)	1,687	80	1,805	6,315	80	1,954	64	3,548	7,159
34	**Fabricated metal products**	**35,560**	**1,460**	**28,283**	**119,444**	**36,105**	**1,458**	**35,000**	**147,366**	**1,439**	**37,790**	**1,061**	**79,952**	**163,053**
341	Metal cans and shipping containers	566	59	1,533	12,172	538	48	1,527	12,114	43	1,504	36	4,091	14,666
342	Cutlery, handtools, and hardware	2,238	141	2,585	10,082	2,327	145	3,389	13,481	139	3,525	105	8,504	14,666
343	Plumbing and heating, except electric	1,177	48	821	4,003	828	46	1,005	5,283	43	1,095	31	3,080	5,897
344	Fabricated structural metal products	12,681	422	7,897	34,904	12,579	407	9,042	40,416	406	9,991	289	19,935	44,936
345	Screw machine products, bolts, etc.	2,690	94	1,727	5,834	2,569	95	2,270	7,890	95	2,525	73	4,536	8,723
346	Metal forgings and stampings	4,019	236	5,110	20,057	4,062	255	7,235	28,410	249	7,504	196	13,666	29,663
347	Metal services, n.e.c.	5,070	97	1,518	5,125	5,251	113	2,167	7,790	117	2,534	93	5,410	9,442
348	Ordnance and accessories, n.e.c.	349	79	1,780	4,993	374	88	2,458	7,644	71	2,256	41	4,741	6,725
349	Miscellaneous fabricated metal products	6,770	284	5,312	22,274	7,577	262	5,906	24,340	275	6,857	197	15,376	29,445
35	**Industrial machinery and equipment**	**52,912**	**2,189**	**46,911**	**187,896**	**52,135**	**1,844**	**50,553**	**217,670**	**1,877**	**56,424**	**1,184**	**132,166**	**256,345**
351	Engines and turbines	341	112	2,850	13,040	356	87	2,906	14,570	83	2,976	56	7,159	16,581
352	Farm and garden machinery	2,078	114	2,386	13,018	1,804	82	1,917	11,474	94	2,409	68	7,985	16,456
353	Construction and related machinery	3,952	326	7,332	32,038	3,467	188	5,272	24,622	203	6,098	129	13,928	30,697
354	Metalworking machinery	(NA)	(NA)	(NA)	(NA)	11,470	268	7,301	22,004	281	8,555	200	16,516	27,035
355	Special industry machinery	(NA)	(NA)	(NA)	(NA)	4,550	169	4,588	17,096	172	5,424	100	11,003	21,258
356	General industrial machinery	(NA)	(NA)	(NA)	(NA)	3,929	240	6,203	24,121	260	7,510	164	16,811	30,339
357	Computer and office equipment	(NA)	(NA)	(NA)	(NA)	2,134	328	10,668	60,627	288	10,269	106	31,283	64,073
358	Refrigeration and service machinery	1,937	172	3,344	16,450	2,129	190	4,752	23,235	186	5,048	129	12,159	26,218
359	Industrial machinery, n.e.c.	(NA)	(NA)	(NA)	(NA)	22,296	292	6,946	19,921	310	8,133	232	15,323	23,687

See footnotes at end of table.

No. 1244. Manufactures—Summary, by Industry Group: 1982, 1987, and 1990—Continued

[See headnote, page 733]

SIC [1] code	INDUSTRY GROUP	1982 Establishments (number)	1982 All employees Number [2] (1,000)	1982 All employees Payroll (mil. dol.)	1982 Value of shipments (mil. dol.)	1987 Establishments (number)	1987 All employees Number (1,000)	1987 All employees Payroll (mil. dol.)	1987 Value of shipments (mil. dol.)	1990 All employees Number (1,000)	1990 All employees Payroll (mil. dol.)	1990 Production workers	1990 Value added by manufacture (mil. dol.)	1990 Value of shipments (mil. dol.)
36	**Electronics; other electric equip.**	(NA)	(NA)	(NA)	(NA)	15,962	1,565	38,738	171,286	1,497	42,067	950	106,984	194,848
361	Electric distribution equipment	(NA)	(NA)	(NA)	(NA)	766	77	1,791	8,197	75	1,946	53	5,207	9,729
362	Electrical industrial apparatus	(NA)	(NA)	(NA)	(NA)	2,213	166	3,882	15,266	162	4,207	109	10,127	18,159
363	Household appliances	(NA)	(NA)	(NA)	(NA)	480	117	2,642	16,498	111	2,604	88	7,836	18,069
364	Electric lighting and wiring equipment	1,993	159	2,718	12,048	1,986	167	3,732	18,004	157	3,893	114	10,769	19,322
365	Household audio and video equipment	(NA)	(NA)	(NA)	(NA)	854	44	850	7,833	45	999	33	3,150	9,377
366	Communications equipment	(NA)	(NA)	(NA)	(NA)	1,437	260	7,537	34,001	250	8,661	119	22,350	38,452
367	Electronic components and accessories	(NA)	(NA)	(NA)	(NA)	5,911	546	13,623	50,258	536	15,293	326	37,270	60,844
369	Misc. electrical equipment and supplies	(NA)	(NA)	(NA)	(NA)	2,315	188	4,682	21,230	162	4,465	107	10,276	20,887
37	**Transportation equipment**	9,443	1,596	40,812	201,346	10,500	1,817	58,790	332,936	1,774	62,855	1,154	146,916	367,927
371	Motor vehicles and equipment	3,867	616	15,393	112,270	4,422	751	23,910	205,923	704	24,793	567	69,649	214,964
372	Aircraft and parts	1,471	539	14,718	52,027	1,618	596	20,590	77,304	616	22,906	324	44,903	94,640
373	Ship and boat building and repairing	2,566	205	4,326	13,326	2,766	177	4,266	13,857	175	4,667	134	8,555	15,854
374	Railroad equipment	200	35	790	3,457	173	22	631	2,471	30	870	21	1,839	4,694
375	Motorcycles, bicycles, and parts	273	13	225	1,341	246	7	158	1,063	9	214	8	571	1,476
376	Guided missiles, space vehicles, parts	105	146	4,481	14,398	156	214	8,114	26,285	200	8,438	73	19,284	30,554
379	Miscellaneous transportation equipment	961	43	879	4,528	1,119	49	1,122	6,033	39	968	28	2,116	5,746
38	**Instruments and related products**	(NA)	(NA)	(NA)	(NA)	10,326	982	28,778	107,325	949	31,572	481	81,666	123,777
381	Search and navigation equipment	(NA)	(NA)	(NA)	(NA)	1,137	369	12,368	36,267	314	12,258	130	24,932	36,734
382	Measuring and controlling devices	(NA)	(NA)	(NA)	(NA)	4,240	285	7,807	26,042	284	8,950	145	19,629	31,456
384	Medical instruments and supplies	2,973	189	3,559	15,133	3,443	204	5,027	22,865	235	6,603	139	20,286	30,934
385	Ophthalmic goods	410	26	409	1,273	494	24	475	1,689	28	605	20	1,626	2,275
386	Photographic equipment and supplies	795	119	3,193	17,038	791	88	2,878	19,241	79	2,937	41	14,527	21,018
387	Watches, clocks, watchcases and parts	237	17	248	1,188	221	12	223	1,221	9	218	7	665	1,360
39	**Miscel. manufacturing industries**	15,871	383	5,647	26,891	16,544	374	6,884	32,012	386	7,805	278	20,096	37,205
391	Jewelry, silverware, and plated ware	2,882	50	770	4,379	2,978	50	941	5,554	49	1,040	35	2,591	5,754
393	Musical instruments	452	18	258	916	425	12	218	814	12	234	9	548	873
394	Toys and sporting goods	2,570	99	1,389	8,256	2,711	89	1,512	8,798	99	1,886	73	5,920	11,044
395	Pens, pencils, office, and art supplies	1,026	32	485	2,372	1,020	29	540	2,536	30	611	21	1,780	3,310
396	Costume jewelry and notions	(NA)	(NA)	(NA)	(NA)	1,013	32	498	2,062	28	491	20	1,364	2,223
399	Miscellaneous manufactures	(NA)	(NA)	(NA)	(NA)	8,397	163	3,174	12,248	169	3,543	119	7,894	14,002
(X)	Administrative and auxiliary [4]	9,676	1,276	38,220	-	9,480	1,234	47,202	-	1,261	59,695	-	-	-

- Represents zero.   NA Not applicable.   X Not applicable.   [1] Standard Industrial Classification Code; see text, section 27.   [2] All employees represents the average of *production workers* plus all other employees for the payroll period ending nearest the 15th of March.   [3] Includes other industries, not shown separately.   [4] Manufacturing concerns often report separately for central offices or auxiliaries which serve the manufacturing establishment of a company, rather than the general public. Separate reports were obtained from such units if at a different location or if they serviced more than one establishment.

Source: U.S. Bureau of the Census, *Census of Manufactures, 1987*, and *Annual Survey of Manufactures.*

No. 1245. Manufactures—Summary, by Industry Group; Ranked by Value Added: 1982, 1987, and 1990

[Data based on various editions of the Standard Industrial Classification Manual, published by the Office of Management and Budget; see text, section 27. N.e.c.=Not elsewhere classified. See also Historical Statistics, Colonial Times to 1970, series P-58-67]

SIC code	INDUSTRY GROUP	1982 Establishments (number)	1982 All employees Number² (1,000)	1982 Payroll (mil. dol.)	1982 Value of shipments (mil. dol.)	1987 Establishments (number)	1987 All employees Number (1,000)	1987 All employees Payroll (mil. dol.)	1987 Value of shipments (mil. dol.)	1990 All employees Number (1,000)	1990 All employees Payroll (mil. dol.)	1990 Production workers (1,000)	1990 Value added by manufacture (mil. dol.)	1990 Value of shipments (mil. dol.)
3711	Motor vehicles and car bodies	355	240.1	6,822	70,740	413	284.4	10,376	133,346	239.5	10,060	200.0	39,504	140,417
2834	Pharmaceutical preparations	683	124.4	3,053	18,998	732	131.6	4,168	32,094	143.8	5,531	61.5	32,745	44,182
3714	Motor vehicle parts and accessories	2,420	321.4	7,614	36,293	2,807	389.1	11,947	62,007	388.7	13,037	308.4	26,871	64,875
2711	Newspapers	8,846	401.5	6,555	21,276	9,091	434.6	9,025	31,849	443.4	10,407	149.2	26,560	34,642
3812	Search and navigation equipment	(NA)	(NA)	(NA)	(NA)	1,084	369.4	12,373	36,267	313.6	12,258	130.3	24,932	36,734
2869	Industrial organic chemicals, n.e.c.	(NA)	(NA)	(NA)	(NA)	699	100.3	3,696	42,189	100.3	4,216	58.8	24,492	54,160
2911	Petroleum refining	(NA)	(NA)	(NA)	(NA)	309	74.6	2,846	118,216	71.9	3,196	47.3	22,822	159,411
2752	Commercial printing, lithographic	17,842	311.9	5,746	19,442	24,980	403.0	9,132	32,698	423.3	10,607	307.3	21,230	38,877
2111	Cigarettes	14	41.5	1,094	12,127	12	32.0	1,234	17,372	27.8	1,230	20.2	20,628	25,522
3721	Aircraft	165	275.1	7,744	28,024	155	268.2	9,680	39,093	289.3	11,225	139.7	20,235	51,370
3089	Plastics products, n.e.c.	(NA)	(NA)	(NA)	(NA)	8,571		4,953	33,774	404.2	8,536	313.8	19,856	38,946
3571	Electronic computers	(NA)	(NA)	(NA)	(NA)	342	151.9	6,451	38,663	134.1	5,265	44.0	19,666	39,294
3312	Blast furnaces and steel mills	301	295.8	8,678	36,824		188.9	5,495	33,627	188.5	7,328	146.0	18,283	45,950
3674	Semiconductors and related devices	766	166.5	3,785	12,430	853	184.6	4,597	28,916	181.8	6,432	87.7	17,856	25,977
2621	Paper mills	299	129.0	3,431	20,995	282	129.1	6,415	21,566	130.1	5,062	98.6	16,600	35,322
3761	Guided missiles and space vehicles	29	99.6	3,159	10,219	40	166.7	6,088	19,241	156.2	6,743	54.2	15,783	25,083
3861	Photographic equipment and supplies	795	119.3	3,193	17,038	787	88.0	2,878	17,329	79.3	2,937	41.2	14,527	21,018
2721	Periodicals	3,328	94.0	1,986	11,478	4,020	110.0	2,983	17,923	115.2	3,659	21.6	13,848	20,397
3728	Aircraft parts and equipment, n.e.c.	966	132.8	3,429	10,193	1,013	187.7	6,088	26,246	197.5	6,852	111.3	12,609	20,458
2821	Plastics materials and resins	440	54.7	1,434	15,769	480	56.3	2,006	14,593	62.4	2,486	37.9	12,195	31,326
2844	Toilet preparations	639	60.4	1,102	10,183	694	58.5	1,353	20,262	61.1	1,621	38.1	12,104	17,048
3724	Aircraft engines and engine parts	340	130.7	3,544	13,809	453	139.6	4,814	14,229	129.0	4,830	72.6	12,059	22,813
3599	Industrial machinery, n.e.c.	(NA)	(NA)	(NA)	(NA)	21,545	228.4	5,119	13,692	247.2	6,312	190.3		
3663	Radio and television communications equip.	(NA)	(NA)	(NA)	(NA)	655	126.0	3,776	13,212	135.4	4,652	62.4	11,741	18,759
2731	Book publishing	2,130	67.1	1,327	7,740	2,298	70.1	1,860	16,202	73.5	2,300	17.3	10,920	15,318
2819	Industrial inorganic chemicals, n.e.c.	645	81.7	2,134	12,060	662	72.2	2,425	17,583	76.6	2,998	40.0	10,800	17,719
2051	Bread, cake, and related products	2,305	170.7	3,254	13,143	2,357	161.6	3,556	22,006	149.0	3,763	82.4	10,476	17,019
3661	Telephone and telegraph apparatus	(NA)	(NA)	(NA)	(NA)	469	112.3	3,178	17,027	82.4	3,421	46.5	9,619	17,297
2086	Bottled and canned soft drinks	1,626	113.8	2,146	16,808	1,190	95.6	2,277	23,219	92.7	2,132	32.0	9,075	23,848
3585	Refrigeration and heating equipment	(NA)	(NA)	(NA)	(NA)	2,900	162.6	3,891	18,663	159.9	4,108	101.1	8,727	17,222
3679	Electronic components, n.e.c.	865		2,393	12,390	892	133.3	3,355	19,730	126.9	3,507	92.4	8,340	19,043
2082	Malt beverages	109	42.0	1,308	11,183	134	31.9	1,355	13,730	32.6	1,425	23.5	8,193	15,186
2631	Paperboard mills	222	55.6	1,502	9,531	205	52.3	1,859	13,619	53.1	2,049	40.7	8,123	15,919
2841	Soap and other detergents	723	35.4	827	9,167	764	31.7	956	11,559	36.3	1,198	22.8	7,971	15,373
2676	Sanitary paper products	138	36.7	863	9,086	133	38.4	1,155	11,698	39.0	1,299	31.0	7,896	14,709
3842	Surgical appliances and supplies	1,367	68.8	1,211	5,667	1,500	78.5	1,786	8,533	86.6	2,195	55.8	7,163	11,128
3841	Surgical and medical instruments	859	56.9	1,000	4,085	1,136	73.1	1,786	7,780	88.9	2,434	53.8	7,078	10,262
3531	Construction machinery	939	115.5	2,653	11,658	955	81.2	2,429	12,773	89.9	2,878	60.7	6,797	16,070
2851	Paints and allied products	1,441	54.1	1,158	9,162	1,426	55.2	1,491	12,701	53.9	1,628	27.2	6,766	14,239
2011	Meat packing plants	1,780	134.4	2,549	44,854	1,434	113.2	2,141	44,991	118.4	2,256	100.1	6,667	51,069
2741	Miscellaneous publishing	2,057	45.3	706	2,871	2,369	69.4	1,513	7,810	65.2	1,708	22.3	6,656	8,875

See footnotes at end of table.

No. 1245. Manufactures—Summary, by Industry Group; Ranked by Value Added: 1982, 1987, and 1990—Continued

[Data based on various editions of the *Standard Industrial Classification Manual*, published by the Office of Management and Budget; see text, section 27. N.e.c.=Not elsewhere classified. See also *Historical Statistics, Colonial Times to 1970*, series P-58-67]

SIC code[1]	INDUSTRY GROUP	1982 Estab. (number)	1982 All emp. Number[2] (1,000)	1982 All emp. Payroll (mil. dol.)	1982 Value of shipments (mil. dol.)	1987 Estab. (number)	1987 All emp. Number (1,000)	1987 All emp. Payroll (mil. dol.)	1987 Value of shipments (mil. dol.)	1990 All emp. Number (1,000)	1990 All emp. Payroll (mil. dol.)	1990 Production workers	1990 Value added by manufacture (mil. dol.)	1990 Value of shipments (mil. dol.)
3544	Special dies, tools, jigs, and fixtures	7,255	102.9	2,293	5,375	7,317	114.4	3,107	10,427	119.8	3,805	92.2	6,525	9,487
3011	Tires and inner tubes	164	70.3	1,734	9,340	163	65.4	2,070	10,479	67.7	2,315	54.7	6,489	11,861
2015	Poultry slaughtering and processing	532	117.7	1,237	10,471	463	147.7	1,919	14,912	176.8	2,597	157.6	6,452	20,928
2033	Canned fruits and vegetables	715	70.5	1,040	9,283	647	65.6	1,163	11,890	68.0	1,408	58.2	6,405	14,698
3731	Ship building and repairing	689	166.7	3,738	10,967	590	120.2	3,218	8,504	121.2	3,606	91.0	6,363	10,856
2043	Cereal breakfast foods	52	15.6	435	4,132	53	16.0	599	6,566	16.1	684	13.1	6,325	8,705
3465	Automotive stampings	668	90.5	2,293	8,777	713	119.8	3,977	15,252	110.6	3,888	91.3	6,300	14,545
2421	Sawmills and planing mills, general	6,316	131.9	2,020	10,065	5,742	148.2	2,817	14,472	138.9	2,913	124.5	6,184	17,923
2759	Commercial printing, n.e.c.	(NA)	(NA)	(NA)	(NA)	10,796	126.2	2,490	8,973	133.2	2,964	93.8	6,029	10,390
3523	Farm machinery and equipment	1,903	96.1	2,067	10,743	1,634	57.7	1,416	10,112	69.6	1,883	49.9	5,979	11,546
2824	Organic fibers, noncellulosic	70	60.2	1,382	8,263	72	45.7	1,347	6,880	48.1	1,539	36.1	5,930	11,427
2653	Corrugated and solid fiber boxes	1,492	94.4	1,862	10,558	946	105.8	2,610	16,107	110.1	2,984	80.0	5,902	18,572
2026	Fluid milk	1,190	78.2	1,469	18,736	1,601	72.4	1,681	20,591	69.6	1,832	34.0	5,780	22,704
3273	Ready-mixed concrete	5,379	81.4	1,475	8,163	5,321	96.9	2,289	8,275	91.8	2,353	70.4	5,634	12,830
3559	Special industry machinery, n.e.c.	(NA)	(NA)	(NA)	(NA)	2,531	83.3	2,286	9,787	84.2	2,710	47.3	5,517	10,247
2099	Food preparations, n.e.c.	(NA)	(NA)	(NA)	(NA)	1,658	57.9	1,110	7,703	55.7	1,190	38.1	5,458	11,048
3825	Instruments to measure electricity	749	89.7	1,888	6,094	930	85.2	2,477	7,854	78.4	2,604	38.7	5,352	8,390
2013	Sausages and other prepared meats	1,311	65.5	1,206	12,278	1,344	79.1	1,619	16,623	81.7	1,840	61.2	5,316	18,780
2879	Agricultural chemicals, n.e.c.	330	16.5	404	5,436	277	16.1	518	6,300	17.7	664	10.2	5,143	8,539
3672	Printed circuit boards	(NA)	(NA)	(NA)	(NA)	1,009	66.6	1,379	4,673	76.7	2,104	51.0	4,997	7,844
2899	Chemical preparations, n.e.c.	1,443	39.7	837	6,344	1,529	37.9	1,021	8,024	40.9	1,205	23.9	4,907	9,418
3519	Internal combustion engines, n.e.c.	253	79.6	1,979	9,363	278	64.0	2,043	11,123	61.3	2,118	42.9	4,900	12,224
3444	Sheet metal work	3,795	81.1	1,495	6,854	4,297	100.3	2,237	9,700	99.1	2,445	73.5	4,867	10,249
2052	Cookies and crackers	358	45.6	950	4,665	380	45.4	1,010	6,309	48.7	1,181	34.7	4,823	7,804
3469	Metal stampings, n.e.c.	2,843	100.4	1,783	6,438	2,815	95.5	2,132	8,331	98.4	2,383	74.7	4,747	9,380
3625	Relays and industrial controls	(NA)	(NA)	(NA)	(NA)	1,168	66.6	1,631	6,101	66.0	1,819	38.9	4,688	7,854
3357	Nonferrous wiredrawing and insulating	440	67.6	1,270	8,217	487	64.9	1,504	10,827	60.2	1,601	44.6	4,621	12,609
3429	Hardware, n.e.c.	1,185	80.1	1,521	5,741	1,240	85.6	2,056	8,175	78.8	2,016	60.6	4,593	8,462
2511	Wood household furniture	2,607	125.6	1,403	5,057	2,948	135.8	2,017	7,980	130.9	2,097	112.6	4,399	8,303
3572	Computer storage devices	(NA)	(NA)	(NA)	(NA)	106	43.3	1,443	6,395	42.6	1,490	15.4	4,359	8,751
2064	Candy and other confectionery products	(NA)	(NA)	(NA)	(NA)	685	45.8	900	6,980	49.2	1,073	39.5	4,355	7,992
2411	Logging	11,658	80.8	1,208	8,274	11,936	85.7	1,516	10,880	83.4	1,647	68.9	4,313	12,229
3081	Unsupported plastics film and sheet	(NA)	(NA)	(NA)	(NA)	594	48.4	1,256	8,140	51.4	1,431	36.8	4,294	9,285
3443	Fabricated plate work (boiler shops)	1,929	102.9	2,180	8,225	1,740	74.6	1,842	6,795	76.1	2,113	53.1	4,199	8,654
3321	Gray and ductile iron foundries	925	97.3	1,965	6,202	774	82.4	2,290	7,213	81.0	2,428	66.4	4,111	7,825
2761	Manifold business forms	810	49.5	934	5,059	853	53.2	1,276	7,359	50.3	1,326	35.1	4,038	7,808
3441	Fabricated structural metal	2,740	103.6	1,990	8,853	2,454	80.9	1,881	8,667	82.7	2,152	59.1	4,035	9,788
3621	Motors and generators	472	84.2	1,546	6,060	462	74.6	1,664	6,753	72.6	1,751	55.1	4,005	7,672

NA Not available. [1] Standard Industrial Classification Code, see text, section 27. [2] All employees represents the average of production workers plus all other employees for the payroll period ended nearest the 15th of the month.

Source: U.S. Bureau of the Census, *Census of Manufactures, 1987* and *Annual Survey of Manufactures*.

No. 1246. Manufactures Summary,

[Sum of State totals may not add to U.S. total

	1982				1987				
DIVISION AND STATE	Establishments, total[1]	All employees[2]		Value of shipments (mil. dol.)	Establishments, total[1]	All employees[2]		Value added by manufacture (mil. dol.)	Value of shipments (mil. dol.)
		Number[3] (1,000)	Payroll (mil. dol.)			Number[3] (1,000)	Payroll (mil. dol.)		
1 U.S.	358,061	19,094	379,627	1,960,206	368,897	18,950	475,651	1,165,917	2,476,071
2 Northeast ..	91,102	4,798	95,919	400,767	88,287	4,357	112,222	259,074	483,748
3 N.E.	25,659	1,445	27,603	105,938	26,393	1,350	34,455	78,908	136,989
4 ME......	2,009	110	1,775	8,649	2,172	102	2,192	5,271	10,662
5 NH......	1,981	107	1,792	7,636	2,328	108	2,509	8,189	12,214
6 VT	1,104	47	863	3,730	1,262	49	1,140	2,543	4,753
7 MA......	11,017	643	12,353	48,204	11,006	591	15,211	35,770	62,794
8 RI.	2,855	114	1,760	7,652	2,878	112	2,292	4,788	9,166
9 CT	6,693	424	9,060	30,067	6,747	389	11,111	22,349	37,400
10 M.A.	65,443	3,353	68,316	294,829	61,894	3,007	77,767	180,165	346,759
11 NY......	32,651	1,419	29,156	121,469	29,608	1,279	33,916	80,033	145,657
12 NJ......	15,126	754	15,845	70,420	14,442	691	18,550	42,527	82,451
13 PA......	17,666	1,180	23,315	102,940	17,844	1,038	25,302	57,605	118,651
14 Midwest...	91,318	5,609	117,830	596,245	94,269	5,508	148,994	351,139	787,123
15 E.N.C.	67,378	4,337	92,400	440,702	69,756	4,186	116,148	266,248	590,487
16 OH......	16,960	1,102	24,740	112,278	17,544	1,100	30,765	71,707	158,560
17 IN......	7,960	585	12,559	63,332	8,641	602	15,757	39,279	83,788
18 IL......	18,618	1,069	22,681	112,929	18,404	990	26,235	63,350	132,204
19 MI	15,158	884	22,223	99,715	16,010	980	30,628	60,259	146,339
20 WI	8,682	697	10,197	52,448	9,157	514	12,763	31,653	69,596
21 W.N.C.	23,940	1,272	25,430	155,543	24,513	1,322	32,846	84,891	196,637
22 MN......	6,775	350	7,423	35,321	7,112	374	10,142	23,322	47,774
23 IA......	3,598	213	4,403	31,397	3,569	206	4,971	14,469	35,409
24 MO......	7,069	406	8,013	41,459	7,290	419	10,390	25,917	59,889
25 ND......	587	15	246	2,465	627	15	310	979	2,574
26 SD	748	25	398	3,005	764	28	498	1,476	3,859
27 NE	1,928	92	1,624	15,143	1,876	91	1,938	5,819	16,076
28 KS	3,235	171	3,323	26,753	3,275	189	4,597	12,909	31,056
29 South	99,304	5,819	101,293	647,918	104,500	5,839	128,278	354,380	800,875
30 S.A.	48,855	2,930	48,588	256,625	53,478	3,104	66,893	179,075	373,181
31 DE......	632	68	1,743	8,383	673	67	2,091	3,866	10,730
32 MD......	3,883	234	4,859	21,282	4,244	230	5,956	14,020	28,009
33 DC......	514	17	394	1,537	486	17	494	1,525	2,128
34 VA......	5,568	391	6,649	36,803	6,137	429	9,740	26,857	51,902
35 WV.....	1,662	96	2,007	9,869	1,619	84	2,108	5,404	11,561
36 NC.....	10,133	799	11,717	64,176	10,995	842	16,293	47,007	95,317
37 SC	4,206	368	5,540	27,836	4,534	366	7,324	19,112	41,212
38 GA.....	8,534	503	7,906	48,056	9,187	570	11,933	33,708	75,709
39 FL	13,723	454	7,773	38,683	15,603	499	10,954	27,574	56,613
40 E.S.C.	18,573	1,241	20,132	119,698	19,718	1,303	26,524	74,296	164,862
41 KY......	3,502	247	4,639	29,639	3,693	252	5,865	18,092	41,827
42 TN	6,417	462	7,378	40,777	6,864	485	9,869	27,050	57,753
43 AL	5,528	330	5,234	29,794	5,843	347	6,963	18,652	40,901
44 MS	3,126	202	2,881	19,488	3,318	219	3,827	10,503	24,381
45 W.S.C.	31,876	1,648	32,573	271,595	31,304	1,432	34,861	101,009	262,832
46 AR.....	3,313	190	2,824	19,747	3,390	206	3,815	10,827	25,308
47 LA	4,107	202	4,304	57,058	3,816	161	4,176	16,426	50,700
48 OK	4,168	197	4,010	23,116	3,728	151	3,629	9,857	24,074
49 TX	20,288	1,059	21,435	171,674	20,370	914	23,241	63,899	162,751
50 West	76,337	3,074	64,587	315,277	81,841	3,246	86,158	201,325	404,325
51 Mt	14,854	556	10,863	56,997	16,479	596	14,689	35,822	73,554
52 MT	1,090	20	379	3,668	1,239	20	426	1,112	3,498
53 ID......	1,404	48	865	5,370	1,491	53	1,149	3,057	7,005
54 WY.....	511	10	183	2,558	500	8	180	493	2,074
55 CO......	4,406	192	3,983	17,963	4,718	184	4,958	12,046	23,236
56 NM.....	1,223	33	521	3,815	1,322	35	713	1,653	4,226
57 AZ	3,407	150	3,037	12,907	4,151	184	4,669	11,299	20,758
58 UT	1,962	83	1,539	8,960	2,083	89	2,073	4,883	10,287
59 NV	851	20	356	1,756	975	24	521	1,279	2,470
60 Pac	61,483	2,518	53,724	258,280	65,362	2,650	71,469	165,503	330,771
61 WA.....	6,788	291	6,681	34,665	7,630	310	8,842	19,016	46,532
62 OR.....	5,659	185	3,783	17,897	6,353	203	4,767	11,610	25,352
63 CA.....	47,625	2,005	42,630	199,695	49,930	2,104	57,148	132,638	252,729
64 AK.....	445	13	270	2,580	427	11	272	834	2,711
65 HI.......	966	24	360	3,443	1,022	22	440	1,405	3,448

[1] Includes central administrative offices and auxiliary units.　[2] Includes employment and payroll at administrative offices and auxiliary units.　[3] **All employees** represents the average of production workers plus all other employees for the payroll period ended nearest the 12th of March. **Production workers** represents the average of the employment for the payroll periods ended nearest the 12th of March, May, August, and November.

by State: 1982 to 1990

because U.S. and State figures were independently derived]

	1990						
	All employees [2]			Production workers [2]		Value added by manu- facture [4] (mil. dol.)	Value of ship- ments [5] (mil. dol.)
Number [3] (1,000)	Payroll						
	Amount (mil. dol.)	Per employee (dol.)	Number [3] (1,000)	Wages (mil. dol.)			
18,840	532,317	28,254	12,129	272,068	1,326,362	2,873,502	1
4,002	119,838	29,944	2,370	54,093	273,541	519,990	2
1,215	36,515	30,061	715	16,643	78,765	141,252	3
103	2,499	24,265	76	1,628	5,886	12,477	4
92	2,554	27,675	58	1,344	5,569	9,727	5
44	1,236	28,082	29	615	3,233	5,592	6
529	16,321	30,835	301	7,122	35,102	63,796	7
101	2,364	23,404	67	1,237	5,149	9,761	8
345	11,541	33,441	184	4,696	23,826	39,898	9
2,787	83,323	29,893	1,655	37,451	194,776	378,738	10
1,150	35,145	30,555	655	14,697	85,532	154,714	11
627	20,353	32,451	340	7,986	45,179	87,498	12
1,010	27,826	27,550	660	14,768	64,065	136,526	13
5,553	166,888	30,053	3,612	90,544	396,725	902,270	14
4,169	129,372	31,029	2,730	71,161	297,974	669,480	15
1,085	33,318	30,705	711	18,798	80,377	177,787	16
616	18,920	30,739	438	10,982	44,924	98,619	17
1,008	30,515	30,282	619	15,002	70,784	156,675	18
913	31,699	34,716	590	17,803	64,799	153,386	19
548	14,920	27,226	371	8,577	37,090	83,013	20
1,384	37,516	27,111	882	19,382	98,751	232,790	21
395	11,790	29,885	225	5,026	25,804	55,244	22
230	6,012	26,092	158	3,636	19,503	45,927	23
423	11,557	27,340	266	5,807	30,255	67,355	24
16	351	21,540	11	193	1,110	3,013	25
30	564	18,997	22	369	1,630	4,533	26
99	2,296	23,126	71	1,418	7,450	20,370	27
191	4,946	25,909	129	2,933	12,998	36,349	28
5,942	146,361	24,630	4,154	82,525	423,958	962,574	29
3,058	74,584	24,388	2,119	41,024	205,326	427,439	30
66	2,486	37,781	30	816	4,512	12,901	31
212	6,357	29,973	123	3,055	15,724	30,679	32
14	541	38,369	4	115	1,573	2,152	33
423	10,683	25,262	303	6,158	32,511	61,042	34
82	2,262	27,512	59	1,468	6,342	12,938	35
832	18,315	22,019	619	10,930	57,674	116,245	36
368	8,348	22,686	276	5,224	21,075	46,734	37
564	13,210	23,443	401	7,661	36,123	83,997	38
498	12,382	24,867	304	5,596	29,793	60,750	39
1,384	31,141	22,505	1,050	19,943	88,029	200,241	40
279	7,013	25,155	211	4,457	23,629	53,777	41
504	11,407	22,647	369	6,966	30,245	67,404	42
368	8,194	22,277	283	5,401	21,362	48,748	43
233	4,527	19,394	187	3,120	12,793	30,313	44
1,500	40,636	27,084	986	21,558	130,604	334,894	45
219	4,359	19,905	172	2,973	12,468	30,493	46
171	4,812	28,106	123	3,060	22,617	65,807	47
168	4,482	26,759	109	2,399	11,889	28,010	48
943	26,983	28,623	582	13,126	83,630	210,584	49
3,343	99,230	29,687	1,993	44,906	232,138	488,669	50
619	17,039	27,531	375	8,149	41,529	88,989	51
20	450	22,515	13	298	1,190	4,040	52
61	1,508	24,762	45	936	3,928	9,184	53
10	248	24,265	7	149	844	2,756	54
180	5,528	30,727	104	2,519	13,819	27,701	55
40	862	21,599	28	509	2,252	5,548	56
181	5,321	29,414	98	2,187	11,916	22,886	57
102	2,494	24,572	64	1,210	6,111	13,950	58
26	628	24,543	17	340	1,470	2,925	59
2,724	82,192	30,178	1,618	36,757	190,609	399,680	60
367	11,344	30,886	211	5,082	24,871	67,538	61
216	5,657	26,178	153	3,373	13,213	31,073	62
2,106	64,352	30,558	1,230	27,772	149,578	293,190	63
14	362	26,603	11	260	1,390	3,676	64
21	477	23,029	13	263	1,558	4,203	65

[4] For defintion, see footnote 6, table 1243.   [5] See footnote 7, table 1243.

Source: U.S. Bureau of the Census, *Census of Manufactures, 1982* and *1987* and *Annual Survey of Manufactures*.

No. 1247. Average Hourly Earnings of Production Workers in Manufacturing Industries, by State: 1980 to 1990

[In dollars]

REGION, DIVISION, AND STATE	1980	1984	1985	1986	1987	1988	1989	1990
U.S.	7.27	9.18	9.54	9.73	9.91	10.19	10.48	10.83
Northeast								
New England:								
ME	6.00	8.05	8.40	8.65	8.77	9.31	9.92	10.59
NH	5.87	7.85	8.39	8.77	9.29	9.97	10.37	10.83
VT	6.14	8.03	8.41	8.83	9.12	9.47	9.99	10.52
MA	6.51	8.50	9.00	9.24	9.77	10.40	10.87	11.39
RI	5.59	7.23	7.59	7.90	8.20	7.64	9.06	9.45
CT	7.08	9.22	9.57	10.07	10.46	10.78	11.21	11.53
Middle Atlantic:								
NY	7.18	9.22	9.67	9.92	10.09	10.43	10.67	11.11
NJ	7.31	9.50	9.86	10.12	10.40	10.86	11.17	11.76
PA	7.59	9.28	9.57	9.74	9.98	10.33	10.66	11.04
Midwest.								
East North Central:								
OH	8.57	10.96	11.38	11.56	11.73	12.00	12.26	12.64
IN	8.49	10.45	0.00	10.81	0.00	0.00	11.70	12.03
IL	8.02	10.08	10.37	10.67	10.85	10.98	11.21	11.44
MI	9.52	12.18	12.64	12.80	12.97	13.31	13.51	13.86
WI	8.03	10.03	10.26	10.35	10.55	10.61	10.77	11.11
West North Central:								
MN	7.61	9.75	10.05	10.20	10.37	10.59	10.95	11.23
IA	8.67	10.25	10.32	10.35	10.62	10.56	10.82	11.27
MO	7.26	9.32	9.57	9.83	10.00	10.24	10.49	10.74
ND	6.56	7.86	8.05	8.19	8.43	8.36	8.80	9.27
SD	6.50	7.15	7.43	7.75	7.92	8.09	8.30	8.48
NE	7.38	8.93	9.02	9.26	9.33	9.38	9.53	9.66
KS	7.37	9.40	9.45	9.76	9.97	10.24	10.68	10.94
South								
South Atlantic:								
DE	7.58	9.30	9.86	10.05	10.67	11.49	12.36	12.39
MD	7.61	9.45	9.73	9.91	10.11	10.71	11.19	11.57
DC	8.46	10.10	10.48	10.40	10.73	11.10	11.79	12.51
VA	6.22	8.12	8.51	8.83	9.14	9.37	9.69	10.07
WV	8.08	9.93	10.24	10.38	10.55	10.81	11.17	11.53
NC	5.37	7.01	7.29	7.54	7.84	8.12	8.42	8.79
SC	5.59	7.28	7.61	7.92	8.10	8.30	8.54	8.84
GA	5.77	7.58	8.10	8.35	8.49	8.65	8.87	9.17
FL	5.98	7.62	7.86	8.02	8.16	8.39	8.67	8.98
East South Central:								
KY	7.34	9.28	9.53	9.86	10.02	10.16	10.37	10.70
TN	6.08	7.93	8.29	8.58	8.78	8.96	9.22	9.55
AL	6.49	7.97	8.48	8.64	8.76	8.95	9.10	9.39
MS	5.44	6.95	7.22	7.46	7.59	7.83	8.03	8.37
West South Central:								
AR	5.71	7.31	7.57	7.76	7.88	8.07	8.26	8.51
LA	7.74	10.06	10.43	10.60	10.90	10.94	11.13	11.61
OK	7.36	9.64	9.86	9.80	10.14	10.35	10.48	10.73
TX	7.15	9.04	9.41	9.65	9.85	9.97	10.25	10.47
West								
Mountain:								
MT	8.78	10.74	10.95	10.94	10.61	10.68	11.15	11.51
ID	7.55	9.34	9.41	9.66	9.75	10.00	10.21	10.60
WY	7.01	8.86	9.64	9.68	9.75	10.27	10.58	10.83
CO	7.63	9.24	9.52	9.82	10.05	10.38	10.44	10.94
NM	5.79	7.97	8.41	8.75	8.74	8.87	8.74	9.04
AZ	7.29	9.09	9.48	9.88	9.97	9.85	9.92	10.21
UT	7.02	8.95	9.64	9.98	9.96	10.11	10.14	10.32
NV	7.72	9.12	9.15	9.36	9.76	10.08	10.33	11.05
Pacific:								
WA	(NA)	(NA)	11.63	11.65	11.73	11.90	12.12	12.61
OR	8.65	10.44	10.50	10.57	10.56	10.60	10.81	11.15
CA	7.70	9.77	10.12	10.36	10.75	10.80	11.16	11.48
AK	10.22	12.25	12.19	11.62	11.79	11.98	12.01	12.46
HI	6.83	8.35	8.65	8.86	9.30	9.84	10.37	10.99

NA Not available.

Source: U.S. Bureau of Labor Statistics, *Employment and Earnings*, monthly.

No. 1248. Finances of Manufacturing Corporations: 1970 to 1990

[In billions of dollars. Beginning 1986, data exclude estimates for corporations with less than $250,000 in assets at time of sample selection. Prior period includes estimates for corporations in this size category. See table 874 for individual industry data]

ITEM	1970	1975	1980	1981	1982	1983	1984	1985	1986	1987	1988	1989	1990
Net sales	709	1,065	1,897	2,145	2,039	2,114	2,335	2,331	2,221	2,378	2,596	2,745	2,811
Net operating profit.........	50	77	129	144	105	125	159	138	125	159	190	182	173
Net profit:													
Before taxes............	48	80	145	158	108	133	166	137	129	173	216	189	160
After taxes.............	29	49	92	101	71	86	108	88	83	116	155	136	112
Cash dividends...........	15	20	36	40	41	42	45	46	46	50	57	65	62
Net income retained in business	14	29	58	61	30	44	63	42	37	66	98	71	49

Source: Through 1981, U.S. Federal Trade Commission; thereafter, U.S. Bureau of the Census. *Quarterly Financial Report for Manufacturing, Mining, and Trade Corporations.*

No. 1249. Capital in Manufacturing Establishments: 1980 to 1989

[In billions of dollars, except percent. Minus sign (-) indicates decline. Data refer to privately owned manufacturing establishments and are based on the capital expenditures data from the Census of Manufactures, the Annual Survey of Manufactures, and the inventory investment component of GNP. For details, see source]

ITEM	CURRENT DOLLARS						CONSTANT (1982) DOLLARS					
	1980	1985	1986	1987	1988	1989	1980	1985	1986	1987	1988	1989
Purchases of equipment												
and structures	75.3	83.7	76.9	78.8	88.9	104.0	86.8	84.6	75.5	74.6	81.4	90.9
Percent equipment	80.4	80.0	80.6	81.1	81.7	80.6	80.4	82.4	82.9	83.4	83.8	82.9
Depreciation (straight line) [1] .	53.1	74.2	78.4	81.7	84.7	88.6	62.0	72.2	74.3	75.8	77.2	78.7
Percent equipment	78.7	78.6	79.0	78.9	79.0	78.8	78.9	80.4	80.8	81.1	81.3	81.6
Net investment [2]	22.2	9.5	-1.5	-2.9	4.2	15.4	24.9	12.4	1.1	-1.2	4.2	12.2
Net stock, end of year [1] ...	944.6	1,145.1	1,174.1	1,215.6	1,276.7	1,339.9	1,034.0	1,078.6	1,076.0	1,083.4	1,096.2	1,113.6
Equipment and structures.	633.9	811.7	845.8	872.1	906.9	957.2	707.2	758.0	760.5	760.6	766.4	780.0
Percent equipment....	67.0	66.8	67.4	67.3	67.9	67.8	67.4	68.7	69.0	69.3	69.7	70.1
Inventories	310.7	333.4	328.3	343.5	369.9	382.7	326.8	320.6	315.5	322.7	329.8	333.6

[1] Depreciation and net stock estimates for equipment and structures are derived using the perpetual inventory method and the straight-line depreciation formula. [2] Represents the difference between purchases and depreciation.

Source: U.S. Bureau of Economic Analysis, *The National Income and Product Accounts of the United States, 1929-82, Fixed Reproducible Tangible Wealth in the United States, 1925-85,* and *Survey of Current Business,* July 1987, August 1987, July 1989, August 1989, July 1990, and August 1990.

No. 1250. Manufacturers' Shipments, Inventories, and Orders: 1950 to 1991

[In billions of dollars, except ratio. See also *Historical Statistics, Colonial Times to 1970,* series P 74-92]

YEAR	Ship-ments, total	Invento-ries, total (Dec. 31) [1]	Ratio of invento-ries to ship-ments [2]	New orders, total	Unfilled orders, total (Dec. 31)	YEAR	Ship-ments, total	Invento-ries, total (Dec. 31) [1]	Ratio of invento-ries to ship-ments [2]	New orders, total	Unfilled orders, total (Dec. 31)
1950.....	224	32	1.41	242	41	1971.....	671	102	1.76	672	107
1951.....	261	39	1.78	287	67	1972.....	756	108	1.58	770	120
1952.....	270	42	1.71	279	76	1973.....	875	124	1.63	913	158
1953.....	298	44	1.90	283	60	1974.....	1,018	158	1.86	1,047	187
1954.....	280	42	1.71	268	48						
						1975.....	1,039	160	1.77	1,023	171
1955.....	318	45	1.63	330	60	1976.....	1,186	175	1.66	1,194	180
1956.....	333	51	1.74	340	68	1977.....	1,358	188	1.58	1,381	202
1957.....	345	52	1.90	331	53	1978.....	1,523	209	1.55	1,580	259
1958.....	327	50	1.75	324	47	1979.....	1,727	239	1.61	1,771	303
1959.....	363	53	1.68	369	52						
						1980.....	1,853	262	1.61	1,876	326
1960.....	371	54	1.79	363	45	1981.....	2,018	280	1.74	2,015	323
1961.....	371	55	1.67	373	47	1982.....	1,960	307	1.91	1,947	309
1962.....	400	58	1.76	401	48	1983.....	2,071	308	1.80	2,105	343
1963.....	421	60	1.66	426	53	1984.....	2,288	334	1.78	2,315	370
1964.....	448	63	1.62	460	65						
						1985.....	2,334	330	1.72	2,348	384
1965.....	492	68	1.50	505	70	1986.....	2,336	318	1.66	2,342	390
1966.....	538	78	1.70	557	97	1987.....	2,475	333	1.64	2,513	427
1967.....	558	84	1.71	565	104	1988.....	2,682	361	1.64	2,724	469
1968.....	603	90	1.76	608	110	1989.....	2,840	377	1.62	2,889	518
1969.....	642	98	1.81	647	115	1990.....	2,917	382	1.60	2,924	524
1970.....	634	101	1.91	625	106	1991.....	2,864	369	1.57	2,847	508

[1] Beginning in 1982 inventories are stated at current cost and are not comparable to the book value estimates for prior years. [2] Ratio based on December seasonally adjusted data.

Source: U.S. Bureau of the Census, *Current Industrial Reports, Manufacturers' Shipments, Inventories, and Orders: 1982-1990,* series M3; and monthly press releases.

Manufactures

No. 1251. Value of Manufactures Shipments and Inventories—Selected Industries: 1980 to 1989

[In billions of dollars. See also *Historical Statistics, Colonial Times to 1970,* series P 74-79]

SIC[1] code	INDUSTRY	1980	1984	1985	1986	1987	1988	1989
(X)	Shipments, total	1,852.7	2,254.4	2,280.2	2,260.3	2,390.0	2,611.6	2,781.4
(X)	Durable goods industries[2]	930.6	1,159.5	1,188.2	1,199.9	1,263.5	1,388.2	1,472.0
32	Stone, clay, and glass products	46.1	53.4	55.1	57.3	62.1	64.0	64.8
33	Primary metals	133.9	119.1	110.5	105.6	117.1	142.2	145.4
34	Fabricated metal products₂	116.2	135.9	139.6	138.0	135.0	144.1	162.6
35	Machinery, exc. electrical[2]	180.7	210.4	215.2	208.5	216.6	247.2	266.0
351	Engines and turbines₄	13.7	15.5	14.9	14.1	14.4	16.1	13.7
353	Construction, mining[3]	33.6	27.1	27.7	25.9	25.8	29.9	33.6
357	Office and computing machines	32.4	59.7	62.2	58.8	61.2	67.9	70.1
36	Electrical machinery[2]	128.6	187.6	193.4	196.2	210.7	227.1	239.6
361-2	Elec. transmission and distrib.	21.3	24.7	24.7	24.6	25.9	27.6	29.8
363	Household appliances	12.9	16.3	16.2	16.6	18.0	18.1	19.4
365	Radio amd TV	8.5	9.9	11.4	11.9	11.5	11.7	12.5
366	Communication equipment	36.0	56.7	65.4	67.4	70.8	74.5	78.1
367	Electronic components ₅	27.6	48.0	42.9	42.0	47.1	54.7	58.1
37	Transportation equipment[2]	186.5	281.2	301.4	313.8	323.0	351.9	372.9
371	Motor vehicles and parts	104.6	179.3	188.5	191.6	197.0	219.3	232.9
372, 6	Aircraft, missiles, and parts.	58.5	78.8	90.8	101.0	103.7	107.6	113.7
38	Instruments and related products[2]	44.1	59.4	61.0	61.9	66.8	72.5	77.0
381-4	Scientific and engineering equip.	25.6	38.3	40.6	40.8	44.7	48.9	51.2
(X)	Nondurable goods industries[2]	922.1	1,095.0	1,092.0	1,060.5	126.0	1,223.4	1,309.3
20	Food and kindred products[2]	256.2	300.0	301.6	308.5	325.0	356.8	388.1
208	Beverages.	33.0	41.2	43.2	45.6	44.9	47.8	50.5
21	Tobacco products	12.2	17.4	18.5	19.1	19.9	22.2	24.1
22	Textile mill products . . . . . . ₅	47.3	55.5	53.3	55.3	57.5	59.8	63.5
26	Paper and allied products[2]	72.8	94.8	93.4	97.9	110.3	124.4	130.4
261-3, 6	Paper, pulp, paperboard mill products.	31.8	41.4	39.2	41.0	47.0	55.2	57.7
265	Paperboard containers.	17.2	22.6	22.7	23.1	26.8	30.6	32.3
28	Chemicals and allied products[2]	162.5	198.2	197.3	197.1	212.7	240.5	255.5
281	Industrial inorganic chemicals	57.3	61.5	59.5	54.1	59.5	67.8	68.9
283-4	Drugs, soaps, toiletries	41.9	57.5	60.9	65.8	67.1	73.1	82.0
29	Petroleum and coal products	198.7	189.0	179.1	124.9	124.5	124.2	138.5
30	Rubber and plastics products.	47.3	69.5	71.3	73.4	80.5	91.1	95.8
(X)	Inventories, total (Dec. 31)	261.7	329.6	322.4	311.1	325.7	348.5	364.8
(X)	Durable goods industries[2]	172.2	214.5	209.9	204.2	212.3	229.0	241.3
32	Stone, clay, and glass products	5.8	7.1	7.0	7.0	7.1	7.4	7.7
33	Primary metals	23.1	21.9	19.5	17.6	18.0	20.2	20.5
34	Fabricated metal products₂	19.2	22.6	21.9	21.4	22.4	23.1	23.0
35	Machinery, exc. electrical[2]	40.3	47.4	44.6	41.2	41.1	45.8	47.1
351	Engines and turbines₄	2.6	3.0	2.6	2.5	2.5	2.8	2.7
353	Construction, mining[3]	9.2	9.1	7.7	6.8	6.5	7.6	7.4
357	Office and computing machines	8.4	13.2	11.6	10.4	10.5	11.8	12.5
36	Electrical machinery[2]	25.4	37.6	37.6	37.5	38.4	39.7	39.8
361-2	Elec. transmission and distrib.	4.1	5.3	5.0	4.8	4.8	5.1	5.1
363	Household appliances	1.8	2.7	2.5	2.6	2.7	2.7	2.8
365	Radio and TV.	1.3	1.4	1.3	1.4	1.3	1.4	1.8
366	Communication equipment	8.8	14.7	15.6	15.8	16.1	15.6	15.5
367	Electronic components ₅	5.4	8.0	7.6	7.2	7.7	8.7	8.5
37	Transportation equipment[2]	35.3	49.5	50.9	50.9	50.9	55.9	61.7	71.0
371	Motor vehicles and parts	9.6	11.6	11.7	11.1	11.4	11.8	11.8
372, 6	Aircraft, missiles, and parts.	21.7	34.4	35.9	36.4	40.8	45.9	54.7
38	Instruments and related products[2]	8.8	12.2	12.4	12.2	12.3	13.7	13.7
381-4	Scientific and engineering equip.	6.0	8.9	9.1	9.2	9.2	10.1	10.2
(X)	Nondurable goods industries[2]	89.5	115.1	112.5	106.9	113.4	119.4	123.5
20	Food and kindred products[2]	22.4	24.4	24.0	24.0	25.2	26.9	26.9
208	Beverages.	3.8	4.4	4.6	4.8	4.5	4.5	4.2
21	Tobacco products	3.9	6.9	6.2	5.9	5.9	5.9	5.7
22	Textile mill products . . . . . . ₅	6.5	7.5	7.0	6.9	7.2	7.3	7.8
26	Paper and allied products[2]	7.7	10.1	9.9	10.2	11.1	11.9	12.5
261-3, 6	Paper, pulp, paperboard mill products.	2.9	3.8	3.8	3.7	3.9	4.3	5.0
265	Paperboard containers.	1.9	2.7	2.5	2.6	2.9	3.2	3.2
28	Chemicals and allied products[2]	19.6	25.5	25.1	24.2	24.8	27.3	28.7
281	Industrial inorganic chemicals	6.5	8.0	7.5	6.6	6.6	7.2	8.0
283-4	Drugs, soaps, toiletries	5.9	7.5	7.7	8.1	8.7	9.3	9.6
29	Petroleum and coal products	9.9	14.3	13.9	9.2	9.9	8.8	10.2
30	Rubber and plastics products.	6.0	8.2	8.4	8.3	9.0	10.1	10.4

X Not applicable.   [1] Standard Industrial Classification.   [2] Includes industries not shown separately.   [3] Also includes material handling industries.

Source: U.S. Bureau of the Census, *Current Industrial Reports, Manufactures' Shipments, Inventories, and Orders: 1982-1988,* series M3-1.86 M3-1(88), and monthly press releases.

No. 1252. Industrial Production Indexes, by Industry: 1970 to 1991

[1987 = 100. Based on 1977 *Standard Industrial Classification Manual;* see text, section 6. See also *Historical Statistics, Colonial Times to 1970*, series P 13 and P 18-39]

SIC [1] code	MAJOR INDUSTRY GROUP	1970	1975	1980	1983	1984	1985	1986	1988	1989	1990	1991
(X)	Industrial production	61.4	66.3	84.1	84.9	92.8	94.4	95.3	105.4	108.1	109.2	107.1
(X)	Manufacturing	56.4	61.1	78.8	80.9	89.3	91.6	94.3	105.8	108.9	109.9	107.4
(X)	Durable goods	53.3	56.7	75.7	76.8	88.4	91.8	93.9	107.6	110.9	111.6	107.1
24	Lumber and products	66.7	66.5	76.9	79.9	86.0	88.0	95.1	104.6	103.0	101.6	94.2
25	Furniture and fixtures	55.6	59.4	78.5	79.6	87.9	88.1	92.5	103.6	105.3	105.9	99.1
32	Clay, glass, and stone products . .	71.1	77.8	92.0	87.2	94.2	93.6	97.1	106.4	108.0	105.7	94.6
33	Primary metals	115.2	107.2	110.8	91.0	102.4	101.8	93.8	110.3	109.2	108.4	99.5
34	Fabricated metal products	75.9	76.7	92.5	85.5	93.3	94.5	93.8	106.2	107.2	105.9	100.4
35	Nonelectrical machinery	32.8	38.1	60.6	64.3	80.8	86.8	90.4	113.8	121.8	126.5	123.5
36	Electrical machinery	40.5	45.1	73.3	80.3	94.1	93.1	94.3	106.5	109.5	111.4	110.1
37	Transportation equipment	55.5	59.7	72.3	72.7	83.1	91.8	96.9	105.0	107.2	105.5	98.6
38	Instruments	38.8	52.4	78.8	83.2	92.1	95.7	95.1	110.1	116.4	116.8	118.2
(X)	Nondurable goods	61.1	67.7	83.1	87.0	90.8	91.5	94.9	103.6	106.4	107.8	107.9
20	Food	64.0	71.4	84.6	90.1	92.1	94.9	97.4	102.8	105.5	107.6	108.6
21	Tobacco products	90.6	92.7	103.6	97.1	97.2	97.3	95.8	101.4	99.7	98.6	99.7
22	Textile mill products	74.4	77.7	92.1	93.2	93.7	89.7	93.9	99.8	101.9	100.8	100.5
26	Paper and products	62.9	65.9	83.1	89.0	93.5	92.2	97.1	102.9	103.2	105.3	105.1
27	Printing and publishing	52.7	53.7	70.3	79.0	84.5	87.6	90.7	103.6	108.5	111.9	112.3
28	Chemicals and products	55.9	69.1	87.8	87.5	91.4	91.4	94.6	105.4	108.5	110.3	110.9
29	Petroleum products	83.9	91.5	99.0	89.6	92.8	92.6	98.9	103.4	106.1	108.2	107.5
30	Rubber and plastics products . . .	37.6	47.4	61.7	74.3	83.8	85.8	90.8	105.9	108.9	110.2	110.0
31	Leather and products	208.0	182.5	161.7	140.9	126.5	112.5	102.6	99.6	103.7	100.0	88.1
(X)	Mining	100.4	98.0	110.0	104.8	111.9	109.0	101.0	101.8	100.5	102.6	101.1
(X)	Utilities	72.9	84.3	95.9	93.6	97.0	99.5	96.3	104.4	107.1	108.0	109.2

X Not applicable. [1] Standard Industrial Classifications.
Source: Board of Governors of the Federal Reserve System, *Federal Reserve Bulletin*, monthly.

No. 1253. Index of Manufacturing Capacity: 1950 to 1991

[1987 output = 100. Annual figures are averages of quarterly data. Capacity represents estimated quantity of output, relative to output in 1967, which the *current* stock of plant and equipment in manufacturing industries was capable of producing. Primary processing industries comprise textiles, lumber, paper and pulp, petroleum, rubber, stone, clay, glass, primary metals, fabricated metals, and a portion of chemicals. Advanced processing industries comprise chemical products, food, beverages, tobacco, apparel, furniture, printing and publishing, leather, machinery, transportation equipment, instruments, ordnance, and miscellaneous industry groups]

YEAR	Index of capacity	RELATION OF OUTPUT TO CAPACITY (percent)			YEAR	Index of capacity	RELATION OF OUTPUT TO CAPACITY (percent)		
		All manu-facturing	Primary pro-cessing	Advanced pro-cessing			All manu-facturing	Primary pro-cessing	Advanced pro-cessing
1950	29	83	88	80	1984	111	80	80	80
1955	36	87	92	84	1985	115	80	80	79
1960	44	80	80	80	1986	119	79	81	78
1965	54	90	91	89	1987	123	81	85	80
1970	71	80	80	79	1988	126	84	88	82
1975	84	73	73	74	1989	130	84	87	83
1980	98	80	78	81	1990	134	82	85	81
1981	102	79	78	79					
1982	105	73	69	75	1991: 1st qtr . .	136	78	79	77
1983	108	75	75	75	2d qtr . .	137	78	79	77

Source: Board of Governors of the Federal Reserve System, *Industrial Production and Capacity Utilization*, G.17(419) . (Based on data from Federal Reserve Board, U.S. Dept. of Commerce, U.S. Bureau of Labor Statistics, and McGraw-Hill Information Systems Company, New York, NY; and other sources.)

No. 1254. Large Manufacturing Companies—Adequacy of Capital Facilities: 1970 to 1989

[Percent distribution. As of July. Number of companies weighted by company assets. Based on replies to the question, "In view of the current rate of order bookings and customer inquiries, are your plant-and-equipment facilities now: Inadequate, Sufficient, or More than adequate?," as part of a quarterly survey conducted among the 1,000 largest manufacturing companies as listed by total assets]

YEAR	Inadequate	Sufficient	More than adequate	YEAR	Inadequate	Sufficient	More than adequate
1970	28	60	12	1984	8	55	37
1975	19	43	38	1985	10	52	38
1980	12	57	31	1986	8	55	37
1981	9	51	40	1987	8	71	21
1982	8	45	47	1988	12	74	14
1983	6	48	46	1989	12	69	19

Source: The Conference Board, New York, NY, *Quarterly Survey of Capital Investment and Supply Conditions in Manufacturing*, (copyright).

No. 1255. Large Manufacturing Companies—Capital Appropriations and Expenditures, by Industry: 1980 to 1989

[In millions of dollars. Based on reports submitted by the 1,000 largest manufacturing companies listed by total assets responding to The Conference Board's *Quarterly Survey of Capital Appropriations*. **Appropriations:** Authorizations by management to spend funds for new plant and equipment; **expenditures:** Cost of new plant and equipment]

INDUSTRY	APPROPRIATIONS					EXPENDITURES				
	1980	1985	1987	1988	1989	1980	1985	1987	1988	1989
Total	103,579	108,855	119,168	157,195	165,366	87,007	99,358	103,935	132,448	146,331
Food and beverages.	6,650	8,139	10,180	20,977	24,151	6,017	6,535	9,357	16,069	15,327
Paper and allied products	3,515	3,200	7,308	14,608	13,197	3,839	3,951	5,407	7,535	10,754
Chemicals and allied products . .	12,160	11,528	14,272	17,009	22,907	10,906	10,610	11,624	15,717	20,242
Petroleum and coal products . . .	33,597	25,823	15,841	15,647	18,498	22,044	21,866	14,298	14,461	13,687
Primary iron and steel.	2,890	1,943	2,693	3,920	4,529	3,525	2,551	1,629	2,490	3,150
Elec. mach. and equip.	6,519	8,284	22,297	30,902	28,686	6,183	9,185	18,698	27,616	30,424
Machinery, except electrical. . . .	8,891	11,446	8,689	7,100	7,615	9,301	10,222	6,608	6,977	7,242
Motor vehicles and equipment . .	7,012	11,849	6,584	8,732	9,264	5,558	10,275	9,104	9,559	10,479
Other transportation equipment. .	3,633	5,835	6,220	6,078	7,860	3,744	5,163	5,822	5,702	7,217
Instruments and photo. equip. . .	3,153	4,008	3,913	4,257	2,900	2,873	3,786	3,536	4,815	2,816
Rubber products	873	4,744	1,608	2,325	4,980	803	3,439	1,361	2,385	3,085
Other manufacturing	14,686	12,056	19,563	25,640	20,779	12,214	11,775	16,491	19,122	21,908

Source: The Conference Board, New York, NY, *Quarterly Survey of Capital Appropriations*, (copyright).

No. 1256. U.S. Share of World Exports of Manufactures: 1980 to 1990

[World exports = exports from 15 major trading countries: United States, Austria, Belgium-Luxembourg, Canada, Denmark, France, West Germany, Italy, Japan, Netherlands, Norway, Sweden, Switzerland, and United Kingdom. Percents are calculated from the values of exports of the 5 commodity groups from each of the 15 countries. Percentage shares are based on dollar values calculated at current exchange rates. Details are reported according to the United Nations Standard International Trade Classification (SITC), Revision 2 (1980-87), Revision 3 (1988 —).]

PRODUCT CATEGORY	TOTAL (bil. dol.)						PERCENT OF WORLD EXPORTS					
	1980	1985	1987	1988	1989	1990	1980	1985	1987	1988	1989	1990
Total [1]	147.2	150.7	179.4	225.5	275.0	300.3	16.8	16.7	13.9	15.1	17.1	16.3
Machinery	57.1	62.7	73.0	94.6	112.2	119.7	21.4	21.4	17.2	18.9	20.6	20.2
Transport equipment . .	28.9	35.2	40.6	47.8	55.2	62.9	18.3	18.7	15.5	16.6	17.9	17.6
Chemicals	20.8	21.5	26.7	32.7	38.0	39.5	17.9	17.9	15.3	16.0	18.0	16.6
Basic manufactures [2] .	23.3	15.0	18.0	23.8	31.6	33.9	10.1	7.9	6.9	7.8	9.6	9.3
Misc. articles [3]	17.0	16.3	21.1	26.7	38.1	43.1	16.0	14.6	12.4	13.6	17.8	16.8

[1] Represents manufactures exports. Excludes mineral fuel products, processed food, fats, oils, firearms of war, and ammunition. [2] Includes semimanufactures of various materials, such as metals, fibers, wood, glass, leather, rubber, and certain finished products of metal. [3] Includes mainly nondurable consumer goods and professional and scientific instruments.

Source: U.S. Dept. of Commerce, International Trade Administration, Office of Finance, Industry, and Trade Information; *Business America,* biweekly; and unpublished data.

No. 1257. Foreign Direct Investment Position in the United States for Manufacturing: 1989 and 1990

[In millions of dollars. Minus sign (-) indicates a negative position. See table 1321]

AREA OR COUNTRY	TOTAL [1]		FOOD PRODUCTS		CHEMICALS AND ALLIED PRODUCTS		PRIMARY AND FABRICATED METALS		MACHINERY	
	1989	1990	1989	1990	1989	1990	1989	1990	1989	1990
All countries [2]	151,820	159,998	24,054	22,875	36,997	41,678	13,583	17,596	30,673	29,677
Canada	9,934	9,327	894	392	452	508	2,034	1,816	1,953	1,875
Europe [2]	120,132	125,568	22,070	21,256	32,082	34,604	8,461	12,504	23,856	22,586
France	11,355	14,692	1,369	1,631	2,995	4,016	(D)	(D)	(D)	(D)
Netherlands	23,709	24,446	6,744	7,267	7,557	8,126	1,186	1,495	4,723	4,454
United Kingdom	51,789	52,955	10,481	8,793	8,507	8,882	2,482	4,914	8,800	7,943
Sweden.	3,783	4,938	-	-	512	589	200	170	2,223	3,209
Switzerland	10,412	9,113	(D)	(D)	3,167	2,656	(D)	(D)	3,362	2,057
Germany [3]	15,722	15,216	589	91	8,318	8,552	1,033	1,121	2,779	2,962
Africa	(D)	(D)	4	2	161	(D)	(D)	(D)	2	4
Latin America	4,815	5,619	54	32	1,932	1,821	-348	-156	28	-41
Middle East.	(D)	(D)	-	-	7	(D)	(D)	(D)	8	9
Asia and Pacific [2].	16,365	18,801	1,031	1,193	2,363	4,483	3,041	3,023	4,828	5,244
Japan	13,978	15,169	641	662	2,272	3,918	2,248	2,090	4,150	4,210

- Represents or rounds to zero. D Withheld to avoid disclosure of data of individual companies. [1] Includes other manufacturing, not shown separately. [2] Includes other countries, not shown separately. [3] For 1989, includes only the Federal Republic of Germany. For 1990, also includes the former German Democratic Republic (GDR). This change has no effect on the data because, prior to 1990, there were no U.S. affiliates of the former GDR.

Source: U.S. Bureau of Economic Analysis, *Survey of Current Business,* October 1984 and August 1991 issues.

No. 1258. Employment Related to Manufactured Exports, by Industry: 1977 to 1987

[Total employment related to manufactured exports is the sum of employment directly calculated for the plants shipping the exported product, the supplying industries and service organizations and the central administrative offices and auxiliaries. For manufacturing industries, employment is limited to paid employees in manufacturing plants, while for nonmanufacturing it includes an estimate for working proprietors and partners]

INDUSTRY	EMPLOYMENT RELATED TO MANUFACTURED EXPORTS								CIVILIAN EMPLOYMENT (1,000)			
	Employees(1,000)				Percent of civilian employment							
	1977	1980	1985	1987	1977	1980	1985	1987	1977	1980	1985	1987
U.S	3,258	4,808	4,413	5,573	3.6	4.8	4.0	4.9	89,369	100,260	110,136	114,840
Manufacturing . .	1,990	2,639	2,295	2,771	10.2	12.8	12.2	14.7	19,590	20,647	18,788	18,900
Nonmfg	1,268	2,170	2,118	2,802	1.8	2.7	2.3	2.9	69,779	79,613	91,348	95,940
Trade	489	845	949	1,207	2.9	4.3	4.3	5.3	16,653	19,737	21,999	22,922
Business serv.	215	575	227	317	1.3	3.3	1.1	1.4	16,750	17,245	21,139	23,048
Transp. [1]	185	305	282	379	3.9	4.8	4.6	6.1	4,797	6,369	6,155	6,223
Agriculture . . .	129	144	127	146	4.2	4.5	3.7	4.3	3,044	3,225	3,423	3,425
Mining	34	69	50	64	4.6	7.3	4.9	7.3	747	947	1,016	871
Other	216	233	483	689	0.8	0.7	1.3	1.7	27,788	32,090	37,616	39,451

[1] Includes communications and utilities.

No. 1259. Manufacturing Establishments—Export-Related Shipments and Employment, 1977 to 1987, and by Industry, 1987

[The export-related employment data shown do not include the jobs involved in the export of nonmanufactured goods and various services sold to foreign buyers. Thus, jobs in the manufacturing sector that relate to the export of nonmanufactured goods are excluded from the estimates. In addition, all of the indirect exports being reported are domestically produced, that is, they exclude imports. See source for further details on methodology]

SIC [1] code	INDUSTRY GROUP	MANUFACTURER'S SHIPMENT VALUE				MANUFACTURING EMPLOYMENT			
		Total [2] (bil. dol.)	Export related		Export related as percent of shipments	Total (1,000)	Export related		Export related as percent of total employment
			Total (bil. dol.)	Direct exports [3] (bil. dol.)			Total (1,000)	Direct exports [4] (1,000)	
(X)	1977	1,358.4	142.4	85.8	10.4	19,590	1,990	1,106	10.2
(X)	1980	1,852.7	249.8	151.2	13.5	20,647	2,639	1,486	12.8
(X)	1981	2,017.5	271.7	164.3	13.4	20,264	2,604	1,486	12.9
(X)	1983	2,055.3	246.4	141.6	12.0	18,737	2,173	1,118	11.6
(X)	1984	2,253.8	268.3	151.0	11.9	19,141	2,179	1,083	11.4
(X)	1985	2,278.9	286.7	156.9	12.6	18,788	2,295	1,083	12.2
(X)	1986	2,260.3	294.3	159.4	13.0	18,371	2,318	1,061	12.6
(X)	**1987, total**	**2,475.9**	**378.8**	**193.6**	**15.3**	**18,900**	**2,771**	**1,185**	**14.7**
20	Food and kindred products	329.7	17.7	12.8	5.4	1,449	68	50	4.7
21	Tobacco products	20.8	2.9	2.5	13.8	45	8	7	17.4
22	Textile mill products	62.8	5.5	2.1	8.7	672	54	18	8.1
23	Apparel, other textile products . . .	64.2	2.6	1.8	4.1	1,081	30	18	2.8
24	Lumber and wood products	69.7	6.9	3.6	9.9	698	54	23	7.7
25	Furniture and fixtures	37.5	1.2	0.6	3.2	511	15	6	2.9
26	Paper and allied products	109.0	16.0	5.0	14.7	611	82	19	13.4
27	Printing and publishing	136.2	6.7	1.1	4.9	1,494	68	11	4.6
28	Chemical and allied products	229.5	43.7	25.6	19.1	814	139	83	17.1
29	Petroleum and coal products	130.4	13.3	3.3	10.2	116	10	4	9.0
30	Rubber, misc. plastics products . .	86.6	12.9	4.0	14.8	831	119	33	14.3
31	Leather, leather products	9.1	1.0	0.8	10.6	129	7	5	5.7
32	Stone, clay, glass products	61.5	4.9	1.8	8.0	524	42	14	7.9
33	Primary metal industries	120.2	33.4	4.7	27.8	701	192	14	27.3
34	Fabricated metal products	147.4	22.2	6.1	15.1	1,458	223	56	15.3
35	Machinery, except electric	217.7	61.5	30.1	28.3	1,844	464	276	25.1
36	Electric, electronic equipment . . .	171.3	54.8	21.4	32.0	1,565	534	187	34.1
37	Transportation equipment	332.9	50.7	40.9	15.2	1,817	260	204	14.3
38	Instruments and related products .	107.3	17.2	13.0	16.0	982	160	119	16.3
39	Misc. manufacturing	32.0	3.7	3.0	11.6	374	36	27	9.7
—	Administrative and auxiliary	-	-	-	-	1,183	205	-	17.3

- Represents zero.   X Not applicable.   [1] Standard Industrial Classification; see text, section 13.   [2] Includes total domestic and export shipments for all manufacturing establishments.   [3] Includes only the value of manufactured products exported by the producing plants.   [4] Employment is limited to paid employees in manufacturing plants producing the export product. The number of employees related to export shipments was calculated for each establishment, aggregated by industry and by States, and inflated to a level comparable to the plant value of exports reported in the official foreign trade statistics

Source of tables 1258 and 1259: U.S. Bureau of the Census, *Census of Manufactures, 1977* and *1987; and Annual Survey of Manufactures.*

No. 1260. Export-Related Shipments and Employment of Manufacturing Establishments, by State: 1987

[Advance data. See headnote, table 1259. Includes employees of central administrative and auxiliary offices]

	MANUFACTURES SHIPMENT VALUE					MANUFACTURING EMPLOYMENT				
		Export related			Export related as percent of total ship-ments		Export related			Export related as percent of total employ-ment
REGION, DIVISION, AND STATE	Total (bil. dol.)	Total (bil. dol.)	Direct exports (bil. dol.)	Sup-porting exports (bil. dol.)		Total (1,000)	Total (1,000)	Direct exports (1,000)	Sup-porting exports (1,000)	
U.S..........	2,475.9	378.8	193.6	185.2	15.3	18,900.1	2,770.6	1,184.5	1,586.1	14.7
Northeast	484.0	75.1	36.8	38.3	15.5	4,337.1	666.2	271.6	394.6	15.4
N.E...........	137.1	26.5	14.3	12.4	19.3	1,347.3	245.9	110.5	135.4	18.3
ME	10.7	1.6	0.8	0.8	14.9	101.4	13.0	5.9	7.1	12.8
NH	12.2	2.6	1.2	1.5	21.7	108.0	20.8	8.4	12.4	19.3
VT..........	4.8	1.2	0.6	0.6	25.7	48.5	11.4	5.5	5.9	23.5
MA	62.8	11.9	6.3	5.6	19.0	591.4	109.8	47.2	62.6	18.6
RI	9.2	1.5	0.7	0.9	16.1	111.9	17.1	7.4	9.7	15.3
CT..........	37.4	7.7	4.7	3.0	20.7	386.1	73.8	36.1	37.7	19.1
M.A	346.9	48.6	22.5	25.9	14.0	2,989.8	420.3	161.1	259.2	14.1
NY..........	145.7	22.0	11.8	10.1	15.1	1,269.8	187.7	83.8	103.9	14.8
NJ..........	82.5	9.6	4.0	5.6	11.6	684.3	86.8	27.3	59.5	12.7
PA..........	118.7	17.0	6.7	10.2	14.3	1,035.7	145.8	50.0	95.8	14.1
Midwest......	787.1	113.8	58.8	55.1	14.5	5,495.1	816.3	330.5	486.1	14.9
E.N.C	590.5	87.6	43.2	44.4	14.8	4,175.6	636.3	245.3	391.0	15.2
OH	158.6	25.8	13.0	12.8	16.3	1,096.6	176.8	69.8	107.0	16.1
IN	83.8	12.5	5.0	7.5	14.9	600.7	87.3	31.2	56.1	14.5
IL	132.2	19.0	8.7	10.3	14.4	985.0	144.6	50.1	94.5	14.7
MI	146.3	21.7	12.4	9.3	14.8	979.0	155.1	65.2	89.9	15.8
WI..........	69.6	8.6	4.1	4.5	12.4	514.3	72.5	29.0	43.5	14.1
W.N.C.......	196.6	26.2	15.6	10.7	13.3	1,319.5	180.3	85.2	95.1	13.7
MN	47.6	8.0	4.7	3.3	16.8	373.5	62.3	28.2	34.1	16.7
IA	35.4	4.3	2.6	1.7	12.1	206.0	25.9	13.4	12.5	12.6
MO	59.9	8.3	5.1	3.2	13.9	417.7	56.1	26.4	29.7	13.4
ND	2.6	0.3	0.2	0.1	12.8	15.4	1.4	0.8	0.6	9.1
SD..........	3.9	0.5	0.3	0.2	12.3	27.3	3.5	1.6	1.9	12.8
NE..........	16.1	1.5	0.8	0.7	9.3	90.6	9.3	3.9	5.4	10.3
KS..........	31.1	3.3	1.9	1.5	10.7	189.0	21.8	10.9	10.9	11.5
South	800.9	115.3	55.1	60.2	14.4	5,825.2	720.4	298.6	421.8	12.4
S.A..........	373.1	49.8	24.6	25.1	13.3	3,097.6	365.3	142.3	223.0	11.8
DE..........	10.7	1.1	0.5	0.6	10.1	66.6	8.2	2.0	6.2	12.3
MD	28.0	3.7	1.9	1.7	13.1	230.5	29.3	12.6	16.7	12.7
DC..........	2.1	0.2	0.1	0.1	8.3	17.0	1.0	0.3	0.7	5.9
VA..........	51.9	6.8	3.7	3.1	13.1	426.3	46.4	19.1	27.3	10.9
WV	11.6	2.6	1.1	1.4	22.1	83.8	13.8	4.8	9.0	16.5
NC	95.3	12.3	5.7	6.6	12.9	841.5	86.9	31.9	55.0	10.3
SC..........	41.2	6.6	3.2	3.4	16.0	366.2	48.1	20.8	27.3	13.1
GA	75.7	7.7	3.6	4.2	10.2	567.5	53.9	21.2	32.7	9.5
FL..........	56.6	8.8	4.8	4.0	15.5	498.2	77.7	29.6	48.1	15.6
E.S.C	164.9	22.4	10.3	12.1	13.6	1,304.4	145.0	59.3	85.7	11.1
KY..........	41.8	6.0	2.9	3.1	14.3	251.5	30.5	10.7	19.8	12.1
TN..........	57.8	7.3	3.6	3.7	12.7	484.7	52.2	22.1	30.1	10.8
AL..........	40.9	5.8	2.1	3.7	14.3	348.5	42.0	18.0	24.0	12.1
MS	24.4	3.3	1.7	1.6	13.4	219.7	20.3	8.5	11.8	9.2
W.S.C........	262.9	43.1	20.2	23.0	16.4	1,423.2	210.1	97.0	113.1	14.8
AR..........	25.3	3.1	1.4	1.8	12.4	205.4	22.2	8.7	13.5	10.8
LA..........	50.7	7.7	3.4	4.3	15.2	160.4	19.2	8.9	10.3	12.0
OK	24.1	2.9	1.4	1.5	11.9	151.3	19.9	9.6	10.3	13.2
TX..........	162.8	29.4	14.0	15.4	18.1	906.1	148.8	69.8	79.0	16.4
West..........	404.3	74.6	42.8	31.7	18.5	3,242.9	565.5	281.8	283.7	17.4
Mt	73.6	12.3	5.8	6.4	16.7	596.6	99.6	43.9	55.7	16.7
MT	3.5	0.5	0.1	0.4	14.2	20.1	1.9	0.4	1.5	9.5
ID	7.0	1.2	0.8	0.4	17.0	52.9	8.8	4.8	4.0	16.6
WY	2.1	0.2	0.0	0.1	9.0	7.9	0.7	0.2	0.5	8.9
CO	23.2	3.3	1.8	1.4	14.0	183.7	28.6	14.5	14.1	15.6
NM	4.2	0.7	0.2	0.5	16.3	34.7	3.9	1.2	2.7	11.2
AZ..........	20.8	4.8	2.1	2.7	23.2	184.7	40.3	16.2	24.1	21.8
UT..........	10.3	1.3	0.6	0.7	12.9	88.9	11.9	4.7	7.2	13.4
NV..........	2.5	0.3	0.2	0.2	13.8	23.7	3.5	1.9	1.6	14.8
Pac	330.7	62.3	37.0	25.3	18.8	2,646.3	465.9	237.9	228.0	17.6
WA	46.5	13.6	10.8	2.8	29.3	309.7	71.3	51.5	19.8	23.0
OR	25.4	4.0	2.1	1.8	15.6	203.0	31.5	16.4	15.1	15.5
CA..........	252.7	43.4	23.0	20.5	17.2	2,100.6	357.7	165.6	192.1	17.0
AK..........	2.7	1.0	0.9	0.1	37.8	11.0	4.4	4.0	0.4	40.0
HI	3.4	0.3	0.2	0.1	9.2	22.0	1.0	0.4	0.6	4.5

Source: U.S. Bureau of the Census, *Exports from Manufacturing Establishments* AR87-1.

No. 1261. Alcoholic Beverages—Summary: 1970 to 1989

[For fiscal years ending in year shown; see text, section 9. Includes Puerto Rico. Excludes imports. See *Historical Statistics, Colonial Times to 1970*, series P 235 for beer production, and P 236a for distilled spirits]

ITEM	Unit	1970	1980	1984	1985	1986	1987	1988	1989
Beer: Breweries operated . . .	Number	154	86	96	103	103	120	183	231
Production	Mil. bbl. [1]	135	193	193	194	194	196	197	198
Value of shipments (SIC 2082) [2]	Mil. dol.	3,822	9,362	11,868	12,216	12,678	13,619	13,871	14,321
Tax-paid withdrawals	Mil. bbl. [1]	123	172	176	175	177	178	178	179
Stocks on hand, June 30 . .	Mil. bbl. [1]	15	15	14	14	14	14	14	14
Per capita consumption [3] . .	Gallons	(NA)	24.5	23.9	23.7	24.0	23.7	(NA)	(NA)
Distilled spirits:									
Production facilities operated.	Number	140	143	112	117	117	102	105	119
Warehouses operated	Number	274	200	202	214	216	211	186	191
Production, total [4]	Mil. tax gal. [5] . .	355	236	134	117	102	90	99	135
Whisky	Mil. tax gal. [5] . .	160	87	77	65	54	42	38	75
Tax-paid withdrawals, total [6]	Mil. tax gal. [5] . .	256	330	301	306	265	271	255	256
Whisky	Mil. tax gal. [5] . .	112	42	(NA)	(NA)	(NA)	(NA)	(NA)	(NA)
Stocks on hand, June 30, total [4]	Mil. tax gal. [5] . .	1,091	696	636	588	546	508	456	456
Whisky	Mil. tax gal. [5] . .	960	566	490	467	445	409	370	361
Bottled for consumption, total	Mil. wine gal. [7] .	312	392	368	371	328	337	317	312
Whisky	Mil. wine gal. [7] .	192	165	142	138	121	119	111	109
Per capita [3]	Wine gal. [7] . .	(NA)	2.0	1.8	1.7	1.6	1.6	(NA)	(NA)
Still wines: Production [8] . .	Mil. wine gal. [7] .	713	982	684	622	667	677	538	611
Distilling materials . . [9] . . .	Mil. wine gal. [7] .	(NA)	184	169	148	149	155	119	122
Tax-paid withdrawals [9] . . .	Mil. wine gal. [7] .	204	340	376	414	441	451	451	409
Stocks on hand, June 30 [10]	Mil. wine gal. [7] .	207	486	577	602	601	618	570	538
Per capita [3]	Wine gal. [7] . .	(NA)	2.1	2.3	2.4	2.3	2.2	(NA)	(NA)
Effervescent wines: [11]									
Production	Mil. wine gal. [7] .	20.0	26.8	34.6	32.0	32.1	~ 29.2	29.8	30.9
Tax-paid withdrawals	Mil. wine gal. [7] .	17.1	24.1	31.9	30.9	31.4	31.2	29.2	27.0
Stocks on hand, June 30 . .	Mil. wine gal. [7] .	8.1	11.9	20.5	21.3	19.3	18.7	18.2	19.4
Per capita [3]	Wine gal. [7] . .	0.15	0.17	0.21	(NA)	(NA)	(NA)	(NA)	(NA)
Of domestic output	Wine gal. [7] . .	0.13	0.12	0.17	(NA)	(NA)	(NA)	(NA)	(NA)

NA Not available. [1] Barrels of 31 wine gallons (see footnote 8). [2] Source: U.S. Bureau of the Census, *Census of Manufactures, 1977, 1982* and *1987*, and *Annual Survey of Manufactures*. [3] Source: U.S. Dept. of Commerce, International Trade Administration. Based on resident population as of July 1, including Armed Forces abroad. [4] Excludes alcohol produced for industrial use. [5] A tax gallon for spirits of 100 proof or over is equivalent to the proof gallon; for spirits of less than 100 proof to the wine gallon. (See footnote 8.) A proof gallon is the alcoholic equivalent of a U.S. gallon at 60° F, containing 50 percent of ethyl alcohol by volume. [6] Includes ethyl alcohol. [7] A wine gallon is the U.S. gallon equivalent to the volume of 231 cubic inches. [8] Production represents total amount removed from fermenters, including distilling material, and includes increase after fermentation (by amelioration, sweetening, and addition of wine spirits). [9] Includes special natural wines. [10] Excludes distilling materials. [11] Includes champagne, other effervescent wines, and artificially carbonated wines.

Source: Except as noted, U.S. Bureau of Alcohol, Tobacco, and Firearms, *Alcohol and Tobacco Summary Statistics*, annual.

No. 1262. Tobacco Products—Production, Consumption, and Expenditures: 1970 to 1990

[Production data are for calendar years. Excludes cigars produced in customs bonded manufacturing warehouses. See also *Historical Statistics, Colonial Times to 1970*, series P 239-241]

ITEM	Unit	1970	1975	1980	1982	1983	1984	1985	1986	1987	1988	1989	1990
Production:													
Cigarettes	Billions .	583	651	714	694	667	669	665	658	689	695	677	710
Nonfilter tip	Billions .	116	80	54	47	43	39	36	33	30	28	24	23
Regular	Billions .	54	36	23	21	19	18	16	15	14	12	11	11
King	Billions .	62	44	30	26	24	21	20	18	16	16	13	12
Filter tip	Billions .	467	571	661	647	625	630	629	625	660	667	654	687
Long and king.	Billions .	362	404	439	404	384	380	378	373	397	400	392	417
Extra long	Billions .	105	167	222	243	241	251	252	252	263	267	261	270
Cigars	Billions .	8.4	5.7	4.0	3.7	3.6	3.5	3.1	2.9	2.1	2.0	2.0	1.9
Tobacco [1]	Mil. lb.	165	152	163	163	162	163	158	147	143	142	141	142
Per capita consumption: [2]													
All products	Lb. [3] . . .	9.7	9.1	7.9	7.5	7.2	6.9	6.8	6.6	6.3	6.1	5.7	5.5
Cigarettes	1,000 .	4.0	4.1	3.8	3.7	3.5	3.4	3.4	3.3	3.2	3.1	2.9	2.8
Cigars [4]	Number.	60	39	24	22	21	20	18	17	15	14	14	13
Expenditures (consumer)	Mil. dol .	11.5	15.5	21.0	25.3	28.7	30.7	32.2	33.7	35.4	37.8	40.9	43.8
Cigarettes	Mil. dol .	10.4	14.3	19.4	23.5	26.8	28.8	30.3	31.8	33.6	35.9	38.3	41.6
Cigars	Mil. dol .	0.7	0.7	0.7	0.7	0.7	0.7	0.7	0.7	0.6	0.6	0.7	0.7
Other	Mil. dol .	0.4	0.6	0.9	1.1	1.2	1.2	1.2	1.2	1.3	1.4	1.4	1.5

[1] Smoking and chewing tobaccos and snuff output. [2] Based on U.S. Bureau of the Census estimated population 18 years old and over, as of July 1, including Armed Forces abroad. [3] Unstemmed processing weight equivalent. [4] Weighing over 3 pounds per 1,000.

Source: U.S. Dept. of Agriculture, Economic Research Service, *Tobacco Situation and Outlook,* quarterly.

No. 1263. Cotton, Wool, and Manmade Fibers—Consumption and Distribution in Selected Consumer Products: 1980 to 1990

[Represents products manufactured by U.S. mills. Excludes glass fiber]

END-USE AND YEAR	Total (mil. lb.)	COTTON Total (mil. lb.)	COTTON Percent end-use	WOOL Total (mil. lb.)	WOOL Percent end-use	MAN-MADE FIBERS Total (mil. lb.)	Percent end-use	Cellulosic [1] Total (mil. lb.)	Cellulosic Percent end-use	Non-cellulosic [2] Total (lb.)	Non-cellulosic Percent end-use
Total:											
1980	11,205	3,125	27.9	167	1.5	7,913	70.6	748	6.7	7,165	63.9
1985	11,538	3,176	26.8	194	1.7	8,168	71.5	542	4.7	7,626	66.8
1986	12,922	3,940	30.5	215	1.6	8,767	67.9	606	4.7	8,161	63.2
1987	13,913	4,520	32.5	226	1.6	9,167	65.9	587	4.2	8,580	61.7
1988	13,528	4,033	29.8	210	1.6	9,285	68.6	613	4.5	8,672	64.1
1989	14,006	4,584	32.7	210	1.5	9,212	65.8	600	4.3	8,612	61.5
1990	14,001	4,699	33.6	185	1.3	9,117	65.1	598	4.3	8,519	60.8
Apparel:											
1980	4,696	1,652	35.2	125	2.7	2,919	62.1	297	6.3	2,622	55.8
1985	4,282	1,766	41.2	141	3.3	2,375	55.5	208	4.9	2,167	50.6
1986	5,138	2,343	59.5	158	73.5	2,637	30.1	257	42.4	2,380	29.2
1987	5,564	2,769	61.3	157	69.5	2,638	28.8	236	40.2	2,402	28.0
1988	5,164	2,513	62.3	139	66.2	2,512	27.1	276	45.0	2,236	25.8
1989	5,457	2,834	61.8	138	65.7	2,485	27.0	274	45.7	2,211	25.7
1990	5,333	3,028	64.4	118	63.8	2,187	24.0	294	49.2	1,893	22.2
Home furnishings:											
1980	1,717	787	45.8	15	0.9	915	53.3	169	9.9	746	43.4
1985	1,895	912	48.1	18	0.9	965	51.0	125	6.6	840	44.4
1986	2,000	1,082	27.5	18	8.4	900	10.3	131	21.6	769	9.4
1987	2,162	1,232	27.3	18	8.0	912	9.9	139	23.7	773	9.0
1988	2,052	1,079	26.8	19	9.0	954	10.3	130	21.2	824	9.5
1989	2,236	1,290	28.1	19	9.0	927	10.1	123	20.5	804	9.3
1990	2,097	1,188	25.3	14	7.6	895	9.8	104	17.4	791	9.3
Floor coverings:											
1980	1,926	15	0.8	10	0.5	1,901	98.7	-	-	1,901	98.7
1985	2,565	15	0.6	12	0.5	2,538	98.9	1	-	2,537	98.9
1986	2,799	15	0.4	17	7.9	2,767	31.6	2	0.3	2,765	33.9
1987	2,975	18	0.4	23	10.2	2,934	32.0	1	0.2	2,933	34.2
1988	3,050	12	0.3	21	10.0	3,017	32.5	1	0.2	3,016	34.8
1989	2,996	13	0.3	24	11.4	2,959	32.1	1	0.2	2,958	34.3
1990	3,068	18	0.4	21	11.4	3,029	33.2	-	0.0	3,029	35.6
Exports of domestic products:											
1980	617	259	42.0	6	1.0	352	57.0	31	5.0	321	52.0
1985	328	108	33.0	10	3.0	210	64.0	16	4.9	194	59.1
1986	384	143	3.5	9	4.2	232	2.6	19	3.2	213	2.6
1987	406	127	2.7	15	6.5	264	2.9	22	3.7	242	2.8
1988	456	124	3.0	19	9.1	313	3.3	25	4.1	288	3.3
1989	492	135	3.0	20	9.5	337	3.6	27	4.4	310	3.7
1990	532	146	3.1	22	11.8	364	4.0	29	4.8	335	3.9
Industrial: [3]											
1980	2,249	412	18.3	11	0.5	1,826	81.2	251	11.2	1,575	70.0
1985	2,468	375	15.1	13	0.5	2,080	84.4	192	7.9	1,888	76.5
1986	2,601	357	9.1	13	6.0	2,231	25.4	197	32.5	2,034	24.9
1987	2,806	374	8.3	13	5.8	2,419	26.4	189	32.2	2,230	26.0
1988	2,806	305	7.6	12	5.7	2,489	26.8	181	29.5	2,308	26.6
1989	2,825	312	6.8	9	4.3	2,504	27.2	175	29.2	2,329	27.0
1990	2,971	319	6.8	10	5.4	2,642	29.0	171	28.6	2,471	29.0

- Represents zero.   [1] Rayon and acetate.   [2] Nylon, polyester, acrylic, olefin, except as noted.   [3] Includes consumer-type products.

Source: Fiber Economics Bureau, Inc., Roseland, NJ, *Textile Organon,* monthly, (copyright).

No. 1264. U.S. Exports and Imports of Textiles and Apparel Products: 1989 to 1991

[In millions of dollars. Excludes glass fibers, linoleum, rubber and leather apparel and clothing donated for charity. Minus sign (-) indicates deficit]

PRODUCT	EXPORTS 1989	1990	1991	GENERAL IMPORTS 1989	1990	1991	BALANCE 1989	1990	1991
Total	5,984	7,401	8,669	30,653	31,931	33,197	24,669	24,530	24,528
Textile yarn fabrics	3,897	4,922	5,457	6,094	6,398	6,991	2,197	1,476	1,534
Textile yarn	1,032	1,242	1,254	742	697	831	-290	-545	-423
Cotton fabric, woven	369	503	542	1,063	1,120	1,281	694	617	739
Woven fabric of manmade textiles	577	673	703	969	974	1,106	392	301	403
Woven fabric of textile material	132	129	141	641	647	677	509	518	536
Special yarns	830	1,053	1,166	633	695	724	-197	-358	-442
Other	957	1,322	1,651	2,046	2,265	2,372	1,089	943	721
Apparel	2,087	2,479	3,212	24,559	25,533	26,206	22,472	23,054	22,994

Source: U.S. Bureau of the Census, *U.S. Merchandise Trade: Exports, General Imports, and Imports for Consumption,* Report FT925, monthly.

No. 1265. Iron and Steel Industry—Summary: 1980 to 1990

[The universe for financial data for 1988 represents companies who produced 75 percent of the reported raw steel production. The financial data represents the operations of the steel segment of companies. Minus sign (-) indicates net loss]

ITEM	Unit	1980	1982	1983	1984	1985	1986	1987	1988	1989	1990
Steel mill products, apparent supply . . .	Mil. tons [1] . .	95.2	76.4	83.5	98.9	96.4	90.0	95.9	102.7	96.8	97.8
Net shipments	Mil. tons [1] . .	83.9	61.6	67.6	73.7	73.0	70.3	76.7	83.8	84.1	85.0
Exports	Mil. tons [1] . .	4.1	1.8	1.2	1.0	1.0	1.0	1.1	2.1	4.6	4.3
Imports	Mil. tons [1] . .	15.5	16.7	17.1	26.2	24.3	20.7	20.4	20.9	17.3	17.2
Scrap consumed	Mil. tons [1] . .	66.6	43.7	49.0	51.8	53.2	49.7	51.7	56.3	51.7	50.1
Scrap inventory	Mil. tons [1] . .	6.9	5.5	5.0	4.4	4.0	3.4	3.8	3.5	3.5	3.6
Iron and steel products: Exports	Mil. tons [1] . .	5.1	2.6	1.8	1.7	1.6	1.5	1.7	2.8	5.4	5.3
Imports	Mil. tons [1] . .	17.9	18.8	19.3	29.5	27.6	24.2	23.8	25.7	22.1	21.9
Capacity by steelmaking process	Mil. net tons	153.7	154.0	150.6	135.3	133.6	127.9	112.2	112.0	115.9	116.7
Revenue	Bil. dol.	37.7	28.7	25.0	30.3	28.4	25.0	27.1	32.7	31.8	29.6
Net income	Bil. dol.	0.7	-3.4	-2.2	(-Z)	-1.8	-4.1	1.0	-0.6	1.6	0.2
Stockholders' equity	Bil. dol.	14.5	11.3	8.2	9.4	6.9	2.4	3.0	2.2	2.1	2.0
Total assets	Bil. dol.	30.8	27.9	25.5	26.2	24.0	21.0	21.9	24.2	24.6	25.6
Capital expenditures	Bil. dol.	2.7	2.3	1.9	1.2	1.6	0.9	1.2	1.8	2.3	2.5
Working capital ratio [2]	Ratio	1.6	1.5	1.3	1.4	1.3	1.6	1.5	1.7	1.6	1.5
Inventories	Bil. dol.	4.7	4.0	3.3	4.2	3.5	3.0	3.4	3.8	4.0	4.5
Average employment	1,000 . .	399	289	243	236	208	175	163	169	169	164
Hours worked	Million	758	526	475	474	419	356	354	363	360	350
Producer price indexes: [3]											
Iron and steel, total	1982=100 .	90.0	100.0	101.3	105.3	104.8	101.1	104.6	115.7	119.1	117.2
Steel mill products	1982=100 .	86.6	100.0	100.9	104.7	104.7	99.8	102.3	110.7	114.5	112.1
Blast and electric furnace products . .	1982=100 .	97.1	100.0	97.7	97.3	95.6	94.2	97.1	119.6	129.4	120.1
Iron ore	1982=100 .	87.8	100.0	101.2	101.2	97.5	91.5	84.2	82.8	82.8	83.3
Scrap, iron and steel	1982=100 .	140.9	100.0	107.4	123.7	112.6	109.6	128.4	177.1	173.7	166.0
Foundry and forge shop products . . .	1982=100 .	89.7	100.0	101.6	104.4	105.2	105.2	105.7	109.6	114.6	117.2

Z Less than $50 million. [1] In millions of short tons. [2] Current assets to current liabilities. [3] Source: U.S. Bureau of Labor Statistics, *Producer Price Indexes*, monthly and annual.

Source: Except as noted, American Iron and Steel Institute, Washington, DC, *Annual Statistical Report*, (copyright).

No. 1266. Raw Steel, Pig Iron, and Ferroalloys Production: 1970 to 1990

[In millions, except percent. See also *Historical Statistics, Colonial Times to 1970*, series P 265-269]

ITEM	1970	1975	1980	1983	1984	1985	1986	1987	1988	1989	1990
Raw steel (net tons):											
World production	654.2	712.0	790.4	730.9	782.6	792.9	788.9	811.1	859.2	865.3	849.6
U.S. production	131.5	116.6	111.8	84.6	92.5	88.3	81.6	89.2	99.9	97.9	98.9
Percent of world	20.1	16.4	14.2	11.6	11.8	11.1	10.3	11.0	11.6	11.3	11.6
Basic oxygen process . . .	63.3	71.8	67.6	52.1	52.8	51.9	47.9	52.5	58.0	58.3	58.5
Electric	20.2	22.7	31.2	26.6	31.4	29.9	30.4	34.0	36.8	35.2	36.9
Open hearth	48.0	22.2	13.0	5.9	8.3	6.4	3.3	2.7	5.1	4.4	3.5
Carbon	117.4	100.4	94.7	73.8	79.9	76.7	71.4	78.0	86.8	86.2	86.6
Alloy and stainless	14.1	16.3	17.1	10.8	12.6	11.6	10.2	11.2	13.1	11.7	12.3
Pig iron and ferroalloys,											
production (sh. tons) [1]	93.5	79.9	68.7	48.7	51.9	50.4	44.0	48.4	55.7	55.9	54.8

[1] Beginning 1975, includes blast furnace ferroalloys.

No. 1267. Steel Products—Net Shipments, by Market Classes: 1970 to 1990

[In thousands of short tons. Comprises carbon, alloy, and stainless steel]

MARKET CLASS	1970	1975	1980	1985	1986	1987	1988	1989	1990
Total [1]	90,798	79,957	83,853	73,043	70,263	76,654	83,840	84,100	84,981
Automotive	14,475	15,214	12,124	12,950	11,889	11,343	12,555	11,763	11,100
Steel service centers, distributors	16,025	12,700	16,172	18,439	17,478	19,840	21,037	20,769	21,111
Construction, incl. maintenance	8,913	8,119	8,742	7,900	7,336	7,681	8,607	8,318	9,245
Containers, packaging, shipping	7,775	6,053	5,551	4,089	4,113	4,372	4,421	4,459	4,474
Machinery, industrial equipment, tools . . .	5,169	5,173	4,543	2,271	2,076	2,277	2,798	2,409	2,388
Steel for converting and processing . . .	3,443	3,255	4,117	5,484	5,635	7,195	8,492	8,235	9,441
Rail transportation	3,098	3,152	3,155	1,061	798	758	1,146	1,229	1,080
Contractors' products	4,440	3,927	3,148	3,330	3,278	3,337	3,495	3,182	2,870
Oil and gas industries	3,550	4,171	5,371	2,044	1,023	1,489	1,477	1,203	1,892
Electrical equipment	2,094	2,170	2,441	1,860	2,113	2,373	2,459	2,449	2,453
Appliances, utensils, and cutlery	2,160	1,653	1,725	1,466	1,648	1,633	1,638	1,721	1,540

[1] Includes other classes not shown and nonclassified shipments.

Source of tables 1266 and 1267: American Iron and Steel Institute, Washington, DC, *Annual Statistical Report*, (copyright).

No. 1268. Manufacturing Technology—Percent of Establishments Using and Planning to Use: 1988

ESTABLISHMENT CHARACTERISTIC	ESTABLISHMENTS USING SELECTED TECHNOLOGIES									PLANNING TO USE WITHIN 2 YEARS				
	Computer aided design (CAD) or computer aided engineering	Numerically controlled machines	Automated material handling	Automated sensor based inspection or testing	Communication and control					Design and engineering	Fabrication/machining, assembly	Automated material handling	Automated sensor based inspection or testing	Communication and control
					Programmable controllers	Computer control on factory floor	LAN[1] For technical data	LAN[1] For factory use	Inter-company computer network					
Major SIC[2] group:														
34, Fabricated metal products	26.8	32.2	1.8	15.0	26.8	21.1	13.4	11.6	14.9	20.4	14.7	1.3	6.5	38.8
35, Industrial mach. and equip.	43.2	56.7	5.3	18.4	33.9	28.1	18.5	16.3	12.4	30.8	14.9	2.6	8.2	40.3
36, Electronic and other	48.5	34.9	6.7	38.4	38.0	34.5	24.9	21.1	16.2	26.6	21.9	3.3	12.0	49.5
37, Transportation equip.	39.9	37.3	8.0	27.1	32.0	27.4	22.0	18.7	21.7	25.8	20.2	3.5	7.1	36.3
38, Instruments, related prod.	48.9	33.6	5.5	27.6	32.7	32.3	25.8	21.3	13.8	29.7	19.4	2.5	12.0	45.4
Employment size:														
20 to 99	29.8	35.9	1.7	13.8	22.5	18.9	13.1	11.0	9.7	23.3	11.4	1.2	6.2	36.2
100 to 499	54.4	50.0	5.4	31.6	48.1	41.0	25.9	22.9	22.7	32.6	26.9	3.8	13.4	53.0
500 and over	82.6	69.8	37.5	85.8	77.8	68.0	58.6	50.7	41.8	32.6	40.7	10.3	16.0	55.9
Age of plant (years):														
Less than 5	44.4	37.3	3.7	24.7	29.5	27.3	21.3	18.0	11.9	32.0	19.5	1.7	13.4	50.3
5 to 15	42.6	42.3	4.4	24.8	34.5	29.8	21.3	17.4	16.2	28.8	19.9	3.3	9.9	48.1
16 to 30	41.3	48.0	4.7	23.7	34.9	29.0	19.4	17.1	16.6	27.5	17.6	2.2	7.9	45.1
Over 30	43.1	50.0	7.3	24.9	39.0	32.1	20.7	18.7	18.0	27.0	17.0	2.6	7.9	38.5
Manufacturing process:														
Fabrication/machining	31.1	53.5	2.4	20.6	31.2	24.7	13.7	12.2	14.6	24.1	15.6	1.6	9.9	45.1
Assembly	49.9	15.1	7.4	30.5	30.5	32.6	26.2	22.5	18.3	22.9	19.5	3.9	11.0	45.7
Both	47.2	55.0	5.7	25.2	38.7	32.1	21.8	18.8	16.6	33.3	20.1	2.7	9.0	46.0
Neither	18.5	9.6	2.7	14.8	24.6	17.4	15.9	12.1	11.9	13.7	10.9	1.3	6.0	36.3
Market for most products:														
Consumer	27.6	23.9	4.6	21.2	34.5	27.1	16.1	17.2	17.5	21.7	21.3	3.0	10.6	42.3
Commercial	49.1	41.7	6.5	25.9	34.3	33.0	24.4	22.0	16.4	32.1	18.7	2.8	9.8	43.5
Industrial	42.8	49.5	3.9	21.3	34.5	27.6	19.1	15.9	13.6	29.9	16.4	2.2	8.5	45.8
Transportation	45.7	47.9	8.3	35.4	44.3	34.5	24.8	20.4	32.6	34.1	29.9	3.6	11.9	57.0
Government	57.0	62.0	7.9	42.2	39.4	41.0	28.8	22.8	13.9	29.0	20.1	3.7	13.5	51.9
Other	36.6	36.9	4.5	14.6	24.5	24.0	16.7	13.3	12.2	16.6	12.4	1.5	5.4	31.6
Market price for most products:														
Less than $5	28.6	29.0	2.2	27.0	39.3	26.4	16.7	15.1	21.5	25.4	22.1	1.7	13.4	47.6
$5 to $100	33.3	45.1	3.5	25.6	35.7	29.9	16.4	17.7	19.0	28.2	22.1	3.7	11.9	47.1
$101 to $1,000	41.0	51.5	4.5	24.9	31.6	29.6	20.0	16.1	13.7	27.6	18.5	1.9	8.0	47.0
$1,001 to $2,000	50.2	49.2	6.0	25.8	32.1	30.5	22.1	18.5	14.1	29.9	16.9	3.6	10.5	43.3
$2,001 to $10,000	50.9	45.0	4.9	21.2	28.0	30.7	22.0	17.4	11.8	30.7	13.5	2.0	6.7	41.1
Over $10,000	61.8	48.8	9.8	22.2	39.8	31.9	29.9	21.8	14.4	33.5	16.0	3.0	6.0	46.5

[1] Local area network.   [2] Standard Industrial Classification; see text, section 13.

Source: U.S. Bureau of the Census, *Current Industrial Reports, Manufacturing Technology, 1988.*

No. 1269. Machine Tool Orders and Shipments: 1970 to 1990

[In millions of dollars. These data represent total industry volume based on reports from over 200 manufacturers]

YEAR	METAL CUTTING TYPE TOOLS					METAL FORMING TYPE TOOLS				
	New orders (net)		Shipments		Order backlog, end of period	New orders (net)		Shipments		Order backlog, end of period
	Total	Domestic	Total	Domestic		Total	Domestic	Total	Domestic	
1970.	651	507	993	827	471	261	227	450	412	235
1975.	916	781	1,879	1,548	1,062	361	284	573	485	388
1980.	3,885	3,496	3,681	3,206	4,750	870	744	1,011	879	701
1981.	2,228	1,946	4,105	3,552	2,873	717	617	991	824	427
1982.	1,064	890	2,895	2,599	1,043	433	372	710	600	151
1983.	1,152	1,069	1,372	1,200	823	545	489	474	430	222
1984.	1,916	1,700	1,607	1,484	1,132	1,000	932	679	609	542
1985.	1,853	1,652	1,742	1,549	1,243	675	610	803	743	414
1986.	1,544	1,377	1,890	1,685	897	581	507	688	621	307
1987.	1,451	1,294	1,677	1,499	672	667	536	647	538	327
1988.	2,708	2,316	1,575	1,400	1,806	883	749	825	702	386
1989.	1,977	1,723	2,359	2,059	1,423	832	719	837	704	380
1990.	2,070	1,772	2,330	2,004	1,164	894	761	970	851	304

Source: NMTBA-The Association For Manufacturing Technology, McLean, VA; data published in U.S. Bureau of Economic Analysis, *Business Statistics, 1979*, for 1970-78; thereafter, *Survey of Current Business*, monthly.

No. 1270. U.S. Factory Sales of Electronics Shipments: 1975 to 1990

[In millions of dollars]

TYPE OF ELECTRONICS	1975	1980	1984	1985	1986	1987	1988	1989	1990
Total value [1]	42,269	100,550	169,391	172,974	174,865	189,818	200,667	205,372	211,471
Computers and industrial electronics.	13,457	39,272	69,747	70,310	69,942	76,048	78,748	80,616	83,350
Communications equip. and systems.	14,302	30,772	49,529	57,095	59,823	62,368	63,705	63,606	66,575
Electronic components	9,286	25,571	43,306	39,459	38,829	45,335	50,988	54,937	55,164
Consumer electronics (excl. imports).	5,224	4,935	6,809	6,110	6,271	6,067	7,226	6,213	6,382

[1] Beginning 1984, includes other products and related services not shown separately.

Source: Electronic Industries Association, Washington, DC, *Electronic Market Data Book,* annual.

No. 1271. Communications Equipment—Factory Shipments: 1985 to 1990

[In millions of dollars, except percent change. Minus sign (-) indicates decrease. N.e.c. Not elsewhere classified]

ITEM	1985	1987	1988	1989	1990	PERCENT CHANGE	
						1980-90	1989-90
Shipments, total	40,968	46,373	47,650	48,848	51,375	161.8	7.8
Search, detection, navigation and guidance systems and equip. [1]	27,057	31,426	31,689	30,983	31,900	162.8	3.0
Radar systems and equipment.	4,321	3,751	3,659	3,646	3,800	134.7	4.2
Missile and space-vehicle-borne equip	2,732	4,169	4,453	4,312	4,440	264.5	3.0
Navigation systems and equip. [2]	2,971	3,820	4,001	4,634	4,800	123.2	3.6
Counter measures equipment	2,682	3,527	3,315	2,814	2,800	271.4	-0.5
Tracking radar	2,208	2,900	2,916	3,247	3,400	199.6	4.7
Search, detect., ident., and tracking n.e.c	1,961	1,964	1,784	1,810	1,880	131.0	3.9
Sonar search, detect., tracking systems	1,885	1,835	1,736	1,701	1,760	120.0	3.5
Specialized elect. and comm. intelligence equip . .	1,810	2,049	2,272	2,209	2,275	169.2	3.0
Commercial, industrial,and military communications equipment [1]	10,607	11,395	12,213	13,880	15,400	162.2	11.0
Space satellite communications systems	2,281	2,224	2,387	2,491	2,580	187.3	3.6
Receivers, radio communications	1,953	1,764	1,762	1,914	2,050	162.3	7.1
Intercommunications systems [3]	1,743	1,944	1,944	2,137	2,175	82.3	1.8
Broadcast studio and related elect. equip [4]	1,562	1,608	1,804	1,849	1,900	60.1	2.8

[1] Includes shipments not shown separately.   [2] For aircraft, ship, and ground navigation. Represents autopilots, beacons, collision warning devices, direction finders equipment, etc.   [3] Includes alarm systems and traffic control shipment.   [4] Includes video, cable TV, and audio equipment.

Source: Electronic Industries Association, Washington, DC, *Electronic Market Data Book,* annual.

No. 1272. Robots—Units Shipped and Value: 1985 to 1989

[Based on a survey of all known manufacturers of robots, robot accessories, and components. Shipment value represents the net sales price, f.o.b. plant, to the customer or branch to which the products are shipped, net of discounts, allowances, freight charges, and returns. A robot is a reprogrammable multi-functional manipulator designed to move materials, parts, tools, or specialized devices through variable programmed motions for the performance of a variety of tasks]

ROBOTS, ACCESSORIES, AND COMPONENTS	UNITS SHIPPED (number)			VALUE OF SHIPMENTS (mil. dol.)		
	1985	1988	1989	1985	1988	1989
Robots, robot accessories, and components	**(X)**	**(X)**	**(X)**	**345.2**	**238.0**	**256.0**
Robots, complete	5,466	4,603	2,217	275.7	164.1	150.6
Servo-controlled robots	2,978	2,072	1,840	254.9	137.7	135.7
Point-to-point type:						
Welding, soldering, brazing, and/or cutting (welding type). .	839	304	273	74.6	32.3	29.3
Foundry, forging, and/or heat treating [1]	65	31	34	4.5	3.2	9.3
Assembly for non-electronic and electronic products	547	296	238	17.8	8.0	8.1
Material handling and/or parts transfer	463	247	162	44.9	27.0	26.0
Continuous-path type:						
Welding, soldering, brazing, and/or cutting.	287	79	31	22.4	3.7	2.2
Spraying, painting, gluing, and/or sealing.	339	292	254	41.4	30.1	35.1
Fettling, grinding, polishing, and/or deburring [2]	438	823	848	49.4	33.4	25.6
Nonservo-controlled robots	460	336	377	18.0	17.1	14.9
Other robots	2,028	2,195	([3])	2.8	9.3	([3])
Robot accessories, subassemblies, etc	(X)	(X)	(X)	69.5	73.9	105.4
Miscellaneous receipts	(X)	(X)	(X)	9.2	5.8	2.5

X Not applicable.   [1] Includes all point-to-point robots, except assembly, material handling and/or parts transfer.   [2] Includes other continuous-path type, not elsewhere classified.   [3] Beginning in 1989, other robots which included educational, hobby, experimental and non-industrial robots are no longer collected in this survey.

Source: U.S. Bureau of the Census, *Current Industrial Reports*, series MA 35X(88-1).

No. 1273. Computer Shipments and Revenues: 1987 to 1991

[Revenue is in if-sold, end-user dollars]

ITEM	Unit	1987	1988	1989	1990	1991
Factory revenue	**Mil. dol.** . . .	**44,383**	**44,130**	**47,387**	**49,362**	**50,886**
Supercomputer	Mil. dol. . . .	593	701	683	697	724
Mainframe	Mil. dol. . . .	14,055	13,378	12,340	12,457	11,739
Midrange	Mil. dol. . . .	13,485	11,820	10,705	10,992	10,925
Workstation	Mil. dol. . . .	1,391	2,216	2,885	3,192	3,755
Personal computer	Mil. dol. . . .	14,859	16,015	20,773	22,024	23,742
Unit shipments	**1,000**	**4,642.5**	**5,946.7**	**6,591.4**	**7,148.8**	**7,618.8**
Supercomputer	1,000	0.4	0.4	0.4	0.4	0.4
Mainframe	1,000	6.1	5.6	3.8	3.9	3.8
Midrange	1,000	396.4	349.6	304.7	342.1	340.8
Workstation	1,000	61.2	97.4	135.5	163.8	221.2
Personal computer	1,000	4,178.4	5,493.7	6,147.0	6,638.7	7,052.6

Source: Dataquest Inc., San Jose, CA, Consolidated Data Base, November 12, 1991.

No. 1274. Domestic Personal Computer Sales and Use: 1981 to 1988

[In millions of units, except as indicated]

ITEM	1981	1982	1983	1984	1985	1986	1987	1988
Personal computers (PC's) sold	1.11	3.53	6.90	7.61	6.75	7.04	8.34	9.50
Value (mil. dol.)	3,143	5,925	9,779	14,269	17,077	18,888	23,458	27,700
Personal computers in use, total [1]	2.12	5.53	12.17	19.18	25.27	31.15	37.84	45.08
Workplace	1.24	2.26	4.00	6.44	9.26	12.22	15.91	20.33
Business: 1-49 employees	0.30	0.55	0.99	1.71	2.57	3.47	4.55	5.84
50-999 employees	0.24	0.44	0.77	1.26	1.82	2.46	3.25	4.23
Over 999 employees	0.47	0.88	1.61	2.65	3.73	4.82	6.14	7.73
Government	0.24	0.40	0.62	0.82	1.14	1.47	1.97	2.53
Education	0.13	0.27	0.54	0.78	1.15	1.55	1.96	2.36
Kindergarten through grade 12	0.10	0.21	0.40	0.59	0.87	1.17	1.48	1.76
College/university	0.03	0.06	0.14	0.20	0.28	0.38	0.49	0.60
Homes	0.75	3.00	7.64	11.95	14.86	17.38	19.97	22.38
Personal computer-related equipment in use:								
Impact printers	0.72	1.90	4.25	8.70	12.80	17.21	22.49	27.30
Nonimpact printers	0.02	0.10	0.31	0.68	1.19	1.83	2.76	3.42
Plotters	0.02	0.05	0.12	0.22	0.39	0.61	0.88	1.07
Monochrome monitors	0.97	2.24	4.68	7.00	9.74	12.56	15.59	18.65
Color monitors	0.13	0.48	1.29	2.98	5.01	7.73	11.68	13.97
Modems	0.18	0.53	1.41	3.00	4.66	6.55	8.91	10.91
Add-in-boards [2]	2.41	5.68	11.43	19.36	29.62	41.22	55.17	65.26
PC hardware maintenance (mil. dol.) [3]	76	166	279	568	951	1,061	1,750	2,298

[1] Excluding multiuser personal computers.   [2] Excluding add-in modem boards.   [3] Excluding education and home.

Source: Future Computing/Datapro, Inc. Delran, NJ, unpublished data.

No. 1275. Semiconductors and Related Devices: 1980 to 1990

[In millions of dollars, except percent. Semiconductors and related devices represent SIC 3674]

ITEM	1980	1984	1985	1986	1987	1988	1989	1990
Semiconductors: [1]								
North American market consumption [2]	6,053	13,006	9,420	10,844	12,858	15,844	17,937	17,386
Capital expenditures (North America) [3]	1,438	3,039	2,072	1,438	1,911	2,649	3,004	3,208
Percent of sales	22.6	23.4	22.0	13.3	14.9	16.7	16.7	18.5
Japanese capital expenditures as a percent of revenues	17.2	43.0	40.0	16.0	16.0	21.4	23.3	23.4
R&D (North America)	423	1,007	1,159	1,250	1,448	1,661	(NA)	(NA)
Semiconductor imports, total [4]	2,223	6,699	4,870	5,044	6,656	9,502	10,758	(NA)
Integrated circuits, total	1,909	6,055	4,365	4,459	6,000	8,683	9,957	(NA)
Transistors	193	332	242	279	318	402	401	(NA)
Diodes and rectifiers	121	312	263	306	338	417	400	(NA)
Semiconductors and related devices:								
Shipments	9,455	17,819	15,253	14,930	17,929	20,332	23,488	23,978
Integrated microcircuits	6,768	13,484	10,872	10,925	13,300	14,857	16,682	16,372
Semiconductor devices, n.e.c. [5]	1,398	2,543	2,569	2,303	2,586	3,337	4,875	5,584
Assets, beginning of year	4,014	9,789	12,200	(NA)	16,515	(NA)	(NA)	(NA)
New capital expenditures	1,596	2,818	2,832	2,220	1,921	2,681	3,132	3,439
Used capital expenditures	40	96	390	66	94	56	46	37
Retirements	230	543	896	(NA)	1,442	(NA)	(NA)	(NA)
Assets, end of year	5,420	12,159	14,526	(NA)	17,088	(NA)	(NA)	(NA)
Depreciation charges	601	1,309	1,512	(NA)	1,719	(NA)	(NA)	(NA)
Rental payments	74	173	184	(NA)	203	(NA)	(NA)	(NA)

NA Not available. [1] Source: Dataquest Inc., San Jose, CA, unpublished data. [2] Revenue from shipments by all companies into Canada and the United States. [3] Capital expenditures by all companies in Canada and the United States. [4] Imports for consumption. Includes imports not shown separately. [5] N.e.c.=Not elsewhere classified.

Source: Except as noted, U.S. Bureau of the Census, *Current Industrial Reports*, series MA-36Q; *U.S. Imports, FT 210, 1980-1988: Import CD-Rom disc 1989;* and *Annual Survey of Manufactures.*

No. 1276. Microcontrollers and Chip Shipments: 1984 to 1990

ITEM	Unit	1984	1985	1986	1987	1988	1989	1990
Microcontrollers, worldwide: Units	Mil. units	357.0	340.8	493.9	729.2	948.3	1,152.8	1,357.5
8-bit	Mil. units	163.5	163.6	218.0	333.5	477.8	461.3	562.9
4-bit	Mil. units	193.4	177.0	271.9	392.3	465.0	682.1	777.2
16-bit	Mil. units	0.1	0.2	0.4	3.4	5.5	9.4	17.4
Revenue	Mil. dol.	1,407	1,114	1,392	2,072	2,706	3,262	3,530
8-bit	Mil. dol.	930	728	831	1,251	1,725	2,002	1,987
4-bit	Mil. dol.	476	382	555	792	935	1,173	1,391
16-bit	Mil. dol.	1	4	7	29	47	86	152
32-bit processor—Units:								
RISC [1]	Mil. units	(NA)	-	-	0.1	0.2	0.7	0.9
CISC [2]	Mil. units	-	0.1	0.5	1.7	4.9	8.1	10.2
Revenue RISC [1]	Mil. dol.	3	19	88	301	889	1,552	1,965
RISC [1]	Mil. dol.	(NA)	3	4	12	39	(NA)	(NA)
CISC [2]	Mil. dol.	3	16	84	288	850	(NA)	(NA)
256K DRAM [3] chips	Mil. units	200.0	237.9	620.0	775.0	947.1	853.7	646.1
Revenue	Mil. dol.	695	868	1,432	1,829	2,898	2,772	1,366
Price	Dollars	25.00	3.65	2.31	2.36	3.06	3.25	2.11
1-Megabit DRAM chips	Mil. units	(NA)	-	4.3	42.6	211.6	503.0	730.8
Revenue	Mil. dol.	(NA)	5	134	636	3,576	7,048	4,623
Price	Dollars	(NA)	162.50	31.16	14.93	16.90	14.01	6.33

- Represents or rounds to zero. NA Not available. [1] RISC=Reduced Instruction Set Computer. [2] CISC=Complex Instruction Set Computer. [3] DRAM=Dynamic Random Access Memory.

Source: Dataquest, Inc., San Jose, CA, unpublished data.

No. 1277. Computers and Industrial Electronic Equipment—Shipments, by Type: 1975 to 1990

[In millions of dollars]

TYPE OF EQUIPMENT	1975	1980	1982	1983	1984	1985	1986	1987	1988	1989	1990
Total [1]	13,457	39,272	53,320	57,265	69,474	70,310	69,942	76,048	78,748	80,616	83,350
Computer and peripheral equipment	7,478	24,320	33,286	37,131	46,486	47,629	47,031	51,889	53,721	53,997	56,155
Computers	2,123	9,580	14,557	16,288	22,532	23,801	24,836	27,778	28,126	29,072	30,575
Peripheral equipment [1]	3,732	14,740	18,728	20,844	23,954	23,828	22,195	24,111	25,595	24,925	25,580
Controlling, processing equipment	2,492	5,627	6,523	6,186	7,294	7,410	7,677	7,892	8,535	9,361	9,550
Testing, measuring equipment	1,552	3,584	4,695	5,200	6,279	6,008	5,736	6,009	5,807	5,701	5,415
Medical electronic equipment	829	2,703	4,402	4,845	5,148	5,028	5,111	5,576	6,015	6,911	7,480
Nuclear electronic equipment	292	304	540	400	480	510	560	601	614	636	675

[1] Includes other types of equipment not shown separately.

Source: Electronic Industries Association, Washington, DC, *Electronic Market Data Book*, annual.

No. 1278. Factory Sales of Electronic Components and Consumer Electronic Products: 1981 to 1990

[In millions of dollars]

PRODUCT	1981	1982	1983	1984	1985	1986	1987	1988	1989	1990
Electronic components	**28,784**	**29,561**	**33,856**	**43,306**	**39,459**	**38,829**	**45,335**	**50,988**	**54,937**	**55,164**
Solid state products	10,309	10,729	12,570	17,032	14,650	14,408	16,819	19,790	22,376	21,950
Parts	7,647	7,403	8,318	10,155	9,329	9,169	10,664	10,871	10,560	10,225
Electron tubes	1,959	1,885	2,049	2,137	2,055	2,125	2,176	2,289	2,596	2,574
Other components [1]	8,869	9,544	10,919	13,982	13,423	13,121	15,676	18,038	19,405	20,415
Consumer electronic products	**12,438**	**12,499**	**14,560**	**17,594**	**23,652**	**21,480**	**21,835**	**22,139**	**22,340**	**22,191**
Color TV receivers	4,349	4,253	5,002	5,538	5,565	6,040	6,303	6,277	6,530	6,247
Car audio	2,000	2,100	1,900	2,500	2,761	3,135	3,523	3,937	4,125	4,292
Video cassette recorders	1,127	1,303	2,162	3,585	4,739	5,258	3,442	2,848	2,625	2,439
Camcorders	(NA)	(NA)	(NA)	(NA)	565	1,280	1,651	1,972	2,007	2,260
Separate audio components	1,363	1,181	1,268	913	1,132	1,358	1,715	1,854	1,871	1,935
Portable audio tape equipment	1,157	971	1,102	1,191	1,140	1,389	1,469	1,547	1,595	1,645
Audio systems	720	573	630	976	1,372	1,370	1,048	1,225	1,217	1,270
Blank video cassettes	(NA)	357	580	770	1,055	1,235	1,006	936	923	948
Projection TV	287	236	268	385	488	529	527	529	478	626
Home radios	501	530	565	661	379	408	409	377	379	360
Blank audio cassettes	227	202	234	256	270	300	375	354	367	376
Monochrome TV receivers	505	507	465	419	328	373	341	236	156	132
Video disc players	55	54	81	45	23	26	26	34	50	72
Color cameras	147	232	303	355	228	59	(NA)	(NA)	(NA)	(NA)

NA Not available.   [1] Includes sockets, delay lines, loudspeakers, magnetic components, transducers, printed circuit boards, microwave components, assemblies, and parts.

Source: Electronic Industries Association, Washington, DC, *Electronic Market Data Book,* annual, (copyright).

No. 1279. Selected Electric Home Appliances and Consumer Electronic Products— Shipments and Retail Value: 1985 to 1989

[Compiled from report of associations and manufacturers. Retail value represents median price of product times the number of units shipped. Except as indicated, covers electric appliances only]

PRODUCT	MANUFACTURES SHIPMENTS (1,000 units)					RETAIL VALUE (mil. dol.)				
	1985	1986	1987	1988	1989	1985	1986	1987	1988	1989
Major appliances:										
Air conditioners	2,900	2,765	3,659	4,379	4,909	1,286	1,130	1,502	1,774	2,012
Refrigerators [1]	5,874	6,284	6,724	6,973	6,799	4,121	4,299	4,557	4,860	4,881
Microwave ovens	10,633	12,658	12,741	11,189	10,848	3,468	3,600	3,541	2,726	2,541
Ranges, electric	3,218	3,532	3,362	3,186	3,068	1,517	1,589	1,643	1,545	1,524
Freezers [2]	1,140	1,154	1,180	1,250	1,189	546	517	526	555	544
Ranges, gas	1,807	1,895	2,132	2,132	2,068	821	880	992	989	960
Dryers	3,701	4,114	4,421	4,363	4,404	1,326	1,451	1,544	1,536	1,422
Washers	4,925	5,430	5,610	5,708	5,765	2,231	2,379	2,470	2,514	2,341
Video:										
TV, color	16,894	18,855	18,473	19,173	20,955	7,250	7,632	8,221	8,434	8,749
Videocassette recorders	11,912	12,685	11,700	10,998	9,843	(NA)	5,067	4,553	4,348	3,767
Camcorders	(NA)	1,090	1,600	2,108	2,348	(NA)	1,213	1,674	2,082	2,170
Video cameras	402	181	110	90	81	266	118	77	62	51
Video cassette players	(NA)	150	182	213	234	(NA)	28	28	32	35
Audio/HiFi:										
Components [3]	8,800	10,914	12,085	12,858	14,050	1,653	2,041	2,232	2,571	3,060
Compact disc players	850	1,384	2,490	2,237	2,338	264	356	514	512	511
Tape decks	908	1,508	1,458	1,457	1,542	176	284	282	283	289
Portable tape equipment	27,626	30,635	30,753	29,556	31,085	1,333	1,449	1,442	1,372	1,452
Radios	27,528	29,896	30,678	27,252	28,371	808	845	818	761	815
Headphones	3,167	3,425	3,534	3,477	3,755	134	140	149	146	160
Cartridges	3,047	2,795	2,539	1,803	1,533	94	86	78	58	42
Mobile electronics:										
ID [4] cassette/radio combo . . .	4,030	3,989	4,053	4,256	4,098	789	814	848	905	865
Radios only	867	757	687	664	551	81	65	59	58	49
Car speakers (in pairs)	15,162	15,010	16,241	17,540	18,294	979	942	993	1,070	1,104
Radar detectors	1,227	1,688	1,834	1,953	2,051	187	263	277	295	341
Cellular telephones	(NA)	265	331	700	1,081	(NA)	423	509	578	667
Auto security systems	(NA)	1,028	1,371	1,759	2,023	(NA)	257	308	358	360
Home office:										
Electronic typewriters	850	2,038	2,186	2,481	2,580	185	458	533	672	740
Personal computers	4,025	3,075	3,598	4,192	4,737	(NA)	2,983	3,313	3,810	4,694
Facsimile machines	(NA)	181	525	900	1,400	(NA)	584	1,335	1,335	1,540
Blank floppy disks	205,063	425,000	545,403	651,757	706,505	(NA)	680	764	878	883
Satellite earth stations	630	255	252	277	294	1,386	513	508	624	657
Telephone equipment:										
Corded telephones	22,403	23,768	21,900	20,805	20,493	983	1,006	840	808	798
Cordless telephones	4,076	4,279	5,450	8,000	9,200	380	410	455	680	796
Telephone answering equip . .	3,306	4,856	7,332	10,100	12,160	371	535	654	873	986

NA Not available.   [1] 6.5 cu. ft. and over.   [2] 10 cu. ft. and over.   [3] Includes others not shown separately.   [4] ID = in dash.

Source: Dealerscope Merchandising, Philadelphia, PA, 68th Annual *Statistical and Marketing Report.*

Domestic Trade and Services

This section presents statistics relating to the distributive trades and service industries. Data shown for the trades, classified by kind of business, and for the various categories of services (e.g., personal, business, repair, hotel) cover sales or receipts, establishments, employees, payrolls, and other items. Also included are data for franchised businesses. The principal sources of these data are census reports and survey reports of the Bureau of the Census. Data on gross product in trade and service industries usually appear in the July issues of the *Survey of Current Business*, issued by the U.S. Bureau of Economic Analysis. Financial data for firms engaged in retail, wholesale, or service activities appear in the annual *Statistics of Income*, published by the Internal Revenue Service.

Censuses.—Censuses of retail trade and wholesale trade have been taken at various intervals since 1929. Limited coverage of the service industries started in 1933. Beginning with the 1967 census, legislation provides for a census of each area to be conducted every 5 years (for years ending in "2" and "7"). The industries covered in the censuses and surveys of business are those classified in three divisions defined in the *Standard Industrial Classification Manual* (see text, section 13). *Retail trade* refers to places of business primarily engaged in selling merchandise for personal or household consumption; *wholesale trade,* to establishments primarily engaged in selling goods to dealers and distributors for resale or to purchasers who buy for business and farm uses; and *services,* to establishments primarily engaged in providing a wide range of services for individuals and for businesses.

Beginning with the 1954 Censuses of Retail Trade and Service Industries, data for nonemployer establishments are included and published separately. The census of wholesale trade excludes establishments with no paid employees. Beginning in 1977, sales taxes and finance charges are excluded from sales (or receipt) figures of the three censuses.

In Brief

Retail sales, 1991:
Total	$1.8 trillion
Automotive dealers	$.4 trillion
Food stores	$.4 trillion

Annual receipts of taxable service firms ($ billions):
	1985	1990
Business services	207	345
Health services	147	246

In 1982 and prior censuses, the count of establishments represented the number in business at the end of the year. For 1987, the count of establishments represents those in business at any time during 1987.

The 1987 Census of Service Industries includes hospitals whereas the 1982 census did not. For 1987, hospitals operated by governmental organizations are included. Government-operated facilities in other service kind-of-business classifications are excluded from the census. In 1982 and 1987, data were not collected for elementary and secondary schools, colleges and universities, labor unions and similar organizations, and political organizations.

The census of retail trade beginning in 1977, excludes nonemployer direct sellers. Beginning 1982, the census treated each leased department in a store as a separate establishment and classified it according to the kind of business it conducted. In prior years, data for leased departments were consolidated with the data for stores in which they were located.

Current surveys. Current sample surveys conducted by the Bureau of the Census cover various aspects of the retail and wholesale trade and selected service industries. Its *Monthly Retail Trade Report* contains monthly estimates of sales, inventories, inventory/sales ratios, and sales of organizations operating 11 or more retail stores, for the United States, by kind of business. In addition, monthly retail sales data for census regions and divisions, large States, metropolitan areas, and cities are included. Annual figures on sales, year-end inventories, and sales/inventory ratios, by kind of business, appear in the *Annual Retail Trade Report.*

Statistics from the Bureau's monthly wholesale trade survey include national estimates of merchant wholesalers' sales, inventories, and stock-sales ratios by major summary groups—durable and nondurable—and selected kinds of business. Merchant wholesalers are those wholesalers who take title to the goods they sell (e.g., jobbers, exporters, importers, major distributors). These data, based on reports submitted by a sample of firms, appear in the *Monthly Wholesale Trade Report.* Annual figures on sales, sales-inventory ratios, and yearend inventories appear in the *Annual Wholesale Trade Report.* The *Service Annual Survey* provides annual estimates of receipts for selected service

kinds of business for the United States as a whole.

For the current sample survey programs, retail trade coverage is the same as for the census; wholesale trade coverage is limited to merchant wholesalers; and selected services coverage is less inclusive than the census.

Estimates obtained from annual and monthly surveys are based on sample data and are not expected to agree exactly with results that would be obtained from a complete census of all establishments. Data include estimates for sampling units not reporting.

Statistical reliability.—For a discussion of statistical collection and estimation, sampling procedures, and measures of statistical reliability applicable to Census Bureau data, see Appendix III.

Historical statistics.—Tabular headnotes provide cross-references, where applicable, to *Historical Statistics of the United States, Colonial Times to 1970.* See Appendix IV.

Figure 28.1
Distribution of Retail Sales, by Kind of Business: 1980 and 1991

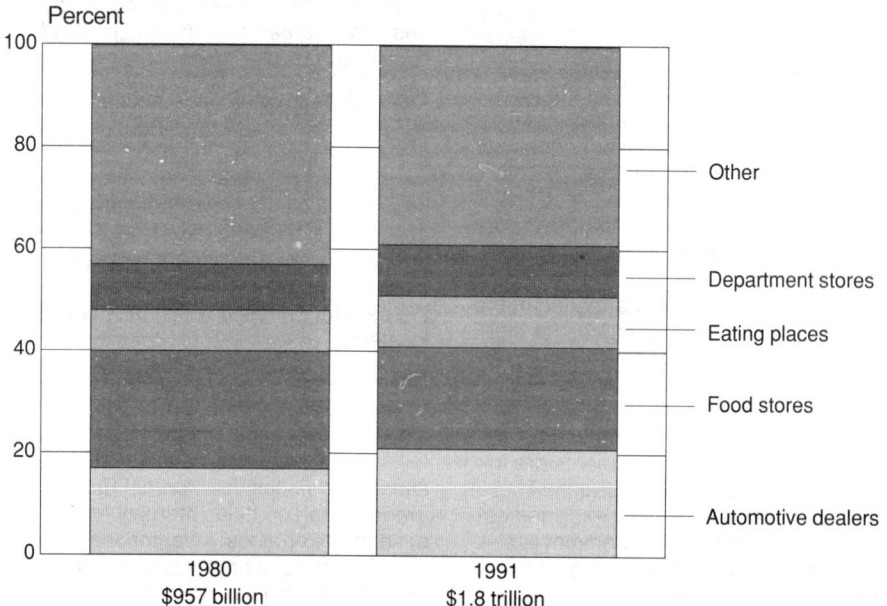

Source: Chart prepared by U.S. Bureau of the Census. For data, see table 1287.

No. 1280. Gross National Product in Domestic Trade and Service Industries in Current and Constant (1982) Dollars: 1980 to 1989

[Based on 1972 Standard Industrial Classification]

INDUSTRY	1980	1982	1983	1984	1985	1986	1987	1988	1989
CURRENT DOLLARS									
Wholesale and retail trade	**438.8**	**506.5**	**542.9**	**614.0**	**658.2**	**682.6**	**721.1**	**777.3**	**825.4**
Percent of gross national product	16.1	16.0	15.9	16.3	16.4	16.1	16.0	15.9	15.9
Wholesale trade.	193.9	219.0	226.5	263.1	280.8	282.0	294.8	317.4	339.5
Retail trade.	245.0	287.5	316.4	350.8	377.4	400.5	426.4	459.9	486.0
Services	**374.0**	**463.6**	**515.5**	**580.2**	**648.1**	**717.6**	**793.6**	**885.2**	**970.5**
Percent of gross national product	13.7	14.6	15.1	15.4	16.1	17.0	17.6	18.2	18.7
Hotels and other lodging places	18.9	21.7	24.3	27.0	30.4	32.4	36.0	41.2	44.5
Personal services.	18.8	21.3	23.1	25.0	29.7	31.9	34.0	38.5	43.0
Business services.	68.8	90.7	104.8	125.3	145.8	163.6	180.1	202.1	222.9
Auto repair, services, and garages	21.1	23.5	26.1	29.2	33.2	36.3	38.1	40.5	43.6
Miscellaneous repair services.	9.2	9.6	10.8	12.8	12.4	13.7	13.8	15.6	16.9
Motion pictures	5.0	6.3	6.6	7.3	9.0	10.5	12.5	13.5	14.7
Amusement and recreation services	12.4	15.1	16.8	17.8	19.9	22.1	24.8	27.4	29.8
Health services	108.1	142.0	156.1	169.0	184.6	200.3	226.1	250.3	273.3
Legal services	23.3	30.6	35.0	41.6	46.3	54.1	60.0	68.7	75.2
Educational services.	16.0	19.1	21.0	23.5	25.8	27.6	29.5	32.5	35.5
Social services, membership organizations	26.3	30.5	32.8	35.7	38.3	41.7	45.8	51.2	56.0
Miscellaneous professional services	39.6	45.7	49.9	56.9	63.6	74.4	83.6	93.9	104.9
Private households.	6.6	7.6	8.2	8.9	9.0	9.1	9.1	9.7	10.3
CONSTANT (1982) DOLLARS									
Wholesale and retail trade	**481.8**	**506.5**	**530.0**	**589.0**	**621.5**	**662.2**	**655.9**	**689.8**	**716.6**
Percent of gross national product	15.1	16.0	16.2	16.8	17.2	17.8	17.1	17.2	17.4
Wholesale trade.	200.1	219.0	222.2	254.9	267.1	284.7	284.3	290.6	304.7
Retail trade.	281.7	287.5	307.8	334.0	354.4	377.5	371.6	399.2	412.0
Services	**450.9**	**463.6**	**480.4**	**509.7**	**538.6**	**565.8**	**592.6**	**623.3**	**652.3**
Percent of gross national product	14.1	14.6	14.6	14.6	14.9	15.2	15.4	15.5	15.8
Hotels and other lodging places	22.3	21.7	23.6	24.3	26.0	26.6	28.2	31.2	32.5
Personal services.	22.3	21.3	21.7	22.2	25.2	25.9	26.3	28.6	30.3
Business services.	83.9	90.7	97.3	111.0	120.8	129.8	139.7	147.7	158.7
Auto repair, services, and garages	24.8	23.5	24.5	26.2	28.7	29.0	28.4	28.3	28.8
Miscellaneous repair services.	10.6	9.6	10.5	11.8	10.7	11.2	10.8	11.7	12.2
Motion pictures	5.7	6.3	6.2	6.3	7.5	8.6	8.9	9.5	9.8
Amusement and recreation services	13.4	15.1	16.1	16.3	17.5	18.4	20.1	21.8	22.8
Health services	133.8	142.0	143.7	145.0	148.6	150.5	158.0	161.1	164.4
Legal services	30.6	30.6	30.1	32.5	33.5	36.7	36.9	40.6	41.8
Educational services.	18.9	19.1	19.9	21.1	22.1	22.4	22.7	23.3	24.1
Social services, membership organizations	30.2	30.5	31.1	32.3	33.3	34.7	36.5	39.0	40.9
Miscellaneous professional services	47.0	45.7	47.7	52.1	56.0	63.3	67.4	71.3	76.4
Private households.	7.4	7.6	8.1	8.8	8.8	8.8	8.7	9.2	9.5

Source: U.S. Bureau of Economic Analysis, *Survey of Current Business*, January and April 1991.

No. 1281. Persons Working in Domestic Trade and Service Industries: 1987 to 1990

[In thousands. Data represent worker-years of full-time equivalent employment by persons working for wages or salaries and number of active partners and proprietors of unincorporated businesses who devote a majority of their working hours to their unincorporated businesses. Based on 1987 Standard Industrial Classification]

INDUSTRY	1987	1988	1989	1990
Wholesale and retail	**23,121**	**23,741**	**24,527**	**24,573**
Wholesale trade.	6,029	6,188	6,436	6,362
Retail trade.	17,092	17,553	18,091	18,211
Services	**26,412**	**27,664**	**29,125**	**30,267**
Hotels and other lodging places	1,684	1,788	1,851	1,865
Personal services.	1,535	1,632	1,618	1,592
Business services.	4,659	5,075	5,399	5,733
Auto repair, services, and parking	1,177	1,231	1,258	1,289
Miscellaneous repair services.	550	569	582	602
Motion pictures	327	395	437	456
Amusement and recreation services	895	895	977	1,029
Health services	6,708	6,848	7,194	7,529
Legal services	1,080	1,132	1,169	1,141
Educational services.	1,515	1,549	1,600	1,623
Social services and membership organizations	2,928	3,129	3,289	3,538
Social services	1,530	1,625	1,698	1,860
Membership organizations	1,398	1,504	1,591	1,678
Other services [1]	2,680	2,704	2,921	3,048
Private households.	734	717	830	822

[1] Consists of museums, botanical, zoological gardens; engineering and management services; and services, not elsewhere classified.

Source: U.S. Bureau of Economic Analysis, *Survey of Current Business*, January 1992.

Domestic Trade and Services

No. 1282. Retail Trade—Establishments, Employees, and Payroll: 1987 to 1989

[Excludes government employees, railroad employees, self-employed persons, etc. For statement on methodology, see Appendix III]

1987 SIC code [1]	KIND OF BUSINESS	ESTABLISHMENTS (1,000)			EMPLOYEES (1,000)		PAYROLL (bil. dol.)	
		1987	1988	1989	1988	1989	1988	1989
(G)	**Retail trade, total**	**1,514.0**	**1,472.9**	**1,495.0**	**18,802**	**19,335**	**215.9**	**228.6**
52	Building materials and garden supplies [2] ...	73.0	71.4	71.2	679	698	10.8	11.4
521	Lumber and other building materials.....	(NA)	27.1	27.0	386	402	6.8	7.3
523	Paint, glass, and wallpaper stores	(NA)	10.2	10.0	53	54	0.9	0.9
525	Hardware stores.................	(NA)	19.1	19.3	140	142	1.7	1.8
526	Retail nurseries and garden stores......	(NA)	10.4	9.9	76	72	0.9	1.0
53	General merchandise stores [2]	36.7	35.1	35.8	2,066	2,082	20.1	21.9
531	Department stores	(NA)	10.0	10.1	1,687	1,675	16.4	17.7
533	Variety stores..................	(NA)	10.2	10.1	118	116	0.9	1.0
539	Misc. general merchandise stores	(NA)	14.6	14.8	261	288	2.8	3.2
54	Food stores [2]	197.1	183.2	183.9	2,886	3,012	31.7	33.6
541	Grocery stores..................	(NA)	132.3	132.8	2,544	2,661	28.7	30.5
542	Meat and fish markets.............	(NA)	10.3	9.7	57	55	0.6	0.6
546	Retail bakeries.................	(NA)	20.4	20.1	178	175	1.4	1.5
55	Automotive dealers and service stations [2] ..	209.8	208.3	208.2	2,076	2,129	38.7	39.4
551	New and used car dealers	(NA)	27.4	26.7	953	960	24.5	24.1
552	Used car dealers	(NA)	13.8	14.8	54	57	0.9	1.0
553	Auto and home supply stores	(NA)	44.2	44.2	287	298	4.5	4.9
554	Gasoline service stations	(NA)	108.1	105.8	683	699	7.0	7.3
56	Apparel and accessory stores [2]	149.6	148.3	147.5	1,157	1,168	11.0	11.5
561	Men's and boys' clothing stores	(NA)	15.4	15.0	115	113	1.5	1.5
562	Women's clothing stores	(NA)	52.8	50.1	451	434	3.7	3.8
563	Women's accessory and specialty stores .	(NA)	7.1	7.2	39	40	0.4	0.4
565	Family clothing stores	(NA)	17.8	17.3	265	269	2.5	2.7
566	Shoe stores...................	(NA)	38.5	38.4	203	213	2.0	2.1
569	Misc. apparel and accessory stores.....	(NA)	8.1	8.2	42	44	0.4	0.5
57	Furniture and home furnishings stores [2] ...	108.0	105.0	104.6	712	734	11.2	11.8
571	Furniture and home furnishings stores [2] ..	(NA)	61.4	60.4	427	432	6.8	7.1
5712	Furniture stores..............	(NA)	31.3	31.0	247	248	4.2	4.3
5713	Floor covering stores	(NA)	13.0	12.7	76	77	1.4	1.5
5719	Misc. homefurnishings stores........	(NA)	13.4	13.0	87	90	1.0	1.1
572	Household appliance stores	(NA)	10.4	9.8	63	63	1.0	1.1
573	Radio, television, and computer stores ...	(NA)	32.3	32.5	220	233	3.3	3.5
5731	Radio, TV, and electronic stores......	(NA)	17.8	16.4	122	120	2.0	2.0
5734	Computer and software stores	(NA)	3.8	4.2	23	28	0.5	0.6
5735	Record and prerecorded tape stores...	(NA)	6.3	6.4	50	55	0.4	0.5
58	Eating and drinking places [2]	388.4	378.5	391.5	6,097	6,288	43.2	46.1
5812	Eating places..................	(NA)	317.8	303.4	5,762	5,803	40.7	42.3
5813	Drinking places.................	(NA)	52.5	47.2	295	276	2.0	2.0
59	Miscellaneous retail [2]	337.7	326.6	334.7	2,317	2,386	28.5	30.7
591	Drug stores and proprietary stores......	(NA)	50.8	50.6	577	588	7.0	7.6
592	Liquor stores	(NA)	31.9	31.7	148	144	1.5	1.5
593	Used merchandise stores...........	(NA)	13.9	13.8	70	73	0.8	0.8
5941	Sporting goods and bicycle shops	(NA)	20.6	20.8	128	133	1.4	1.5
5942	Book stores...................	(NA)	10.6	11.5	75	78	0.7	0.7
5944	Jewelry stores	(NA)	27.0	27.4	160	159	2.2	2.3
5945	Hobby, toy, and game shops	(NA)	9.2	9.0	80	83	0.7	0.8
5947	Gift, novelty, and souvenir shops.......	(NA)	30.2	28.8	157	159	1.2	1.3
5949	Sewing, needlework, and piece goods ...	(NA)	8.8	8.4	62	63	0.4	0.5
5961	Catalog and mail-order houses	(NA)	6.9	6.9	132	137	2.2	2.4
5962	Merchandising machine operators	(NA)	5.0	4.9	82	78	1.2	1.3
5963	Direct selling establishments.	(NA)	9.3	8.9	121	107	1.6	1.6
598	Fuel dealers...................	(NA)	12.4	12.0	99	99	2.1	2.1
5992	Florists.....................	(NA)	25.3	25.9	125	129	1.1	1.2
5995	Optical goods stores..............	(NA)	13.7	13.4	61	69	1.0	1.0
	Administrative and auxiliary	13.7	16.4	17.6	811	838	20.8	22.2

NA Not available. [1] Based on 1987 Standard Industrial Classification; see text, section 13. [2] Includes kinds of business not shown separately.

Source: U.S. Bureau of the Census, *County Business Patterns*, annual.

No. 1283. Retail Trade—Summary: 1958 to 1987

[1972 through 1982 based on 1972 Standard Industrial Classification (SIC) code; 1987 based on 1987 SIC code. Prior years based on earlier editions of SIC. Comparability of data over time is affected by changes in the SIC code. See also *Historical Statistics, Colonial Times to 1970*, series T 43-47 and T 79-91]

ITEM	Unit	1958	1963	1967	1972	1977	1982	1987
Firms, total [1]	1,000	(NA)	1,532	1,577	1,665	1,567	1,573	1,992
Multiunit establishments [1][2]	1,000	[3]183	220	220	301	343	415	498
Establishments, total [1]	1,000	1,795	1,708	1,763	1,780	1,855	1,923	2,420
With payroll	1,000	1,185	1,206	1,192	1,265	1,304	1,324	1,504
With sales of $1,000,000 or more	1,000	(NA)	(NA)	(NA)	74	119	193	259
Consumer Price Index: [4]								
All items	1982-84 = 100	28.9	30.6	33.4	41.8	60.6	96.5	113.6
All commodities	1982-84 = 100	33.3	34.4	36.8	44.5	64.2	97.0	107.7
Sales	Bil. dol.	200	244	310	457	723	1,066	1,540
By establishments with payroll	Bil. dol.	188	233	295	440	700	1,039	1,493
By multiunit establishments [2]	Bil. dol.	[3]67	90	124	202	341	567	844
Percent of total sales	Percent	33.5	36.6	39.8	44.0	47.1	53.2	56.5
Percent of multiunit sales by 100-or-more establishment multiunits [2][5]	Percent	42.4	43.1	46.7	55.8	55.8	54.5	54.6
In 1982 dollars [6]	Bil. dol.	(NA)	645	764	943	1,054	1,066	1,393
Percent of sales by corporations	Percent	53.0	61.9	67.4	76.4	79.8	84.6	88.9
Per capita sales: [7]								
Current dollars	Dollars	1,156	1,296	1,571	2,186	3,291	4,599	6,328
Constant (1982) dollars [6]	Dollars	(NA)	3,423	3,869	4,508	4,798	4,599	5,722
Sales as percent of personal income	Percent	[3]55.5	52.4	49.3	48.1	46.9	41.5	40.9
Sales, inside metropolitan areas [8]	Bil. dol.	[3]133	170	221	(NA)	552	845	[9]1,230
Percent of total sales	Percent	66.4	69.5	71.4	(NA)	76.3	79.3	[9]82.4
Payroll, entire year	Bil. dol.	21.7	27.6	36.2	55.4	85.9	123.6	177.5
Percent of sales	Percent	[3]11.5	11.3	11.7	12.1	11.9	11.6	11.5
Paid employees, March 12 pay period [10]	1,000	7,942	8,410	9,381	11,211	13,040	14,468	17,780

NA Not available. [1] Through 1982, represents the number of establishments and firms in business at the end of the year. For 1987, represents the number of establishments and firms in business at any time during year. [2] Establishments operated by firms which operate at two or more locations. Beginning 1982, includes single units operated by multiunit establishments. 1972 and 1977 data revised since originally published. [3] Excludes Alaska and Hawaii. [4] Source: U.S. Bureau of Labor Statistics, *Monthly Labor Review*. Beginning 1982, CPI-U annual averages, see text, section 14. [5] Prior to 1982, data provided for percent of multiunit sales by 101-or-more establishment units. [6] Based on implicit price deflators for retail sales supplied by U.S. Bureau of Economic Analysis. [7] Based on estimated resident population as of July 1. [8] Through 1982 based on Standard Metropolitan Statistical Area definitions. Data for 1987 based on Metropolitan Statistical Area definitions. See Appendix II. [9] Covers only establishments with payroll. [10] 1958 and 1963 data for week including November 15.

Source: Except as noted, U.S. Bureau of the Census, *U.S. Census of Business: 1958*, vol. I; *1963*, vol. I; *1967*, vol. I; and *Census of Retail Trade, 1972*, RC72-S-1; *1977*, RC77-52; *1982*, RC82-A-52 and RC82-I-1; and *1987*, RC87-A-52, RC87-N-1, and RC87-S-1.

No. 1284. Retail Trade—Sales, by Broad Merchandise Lines: 1982 and 1987

[For establishments with payroll]

MERCHANDISE LINES	1982			1987			
	Estab-lish-ments [1] (1,000)	Sales of specified merchandise lines		Estab-lish-ments [1] (1,000)	Sales of specified merchandise lines		Percent of total sales of estab-lishments handling line
		Total (mil. dol.)	Percent distri-bution		Total (mil. dol.)	Percent distri-bution	
Retail trade, total [2]	[3]1,330	1,039,029	100.0	[3]1,504	1,493,309	100.0	(X)
Groceries and other food	267	198,705	19.1	369	247,410	16.6	42.9
Meals and snacks	391	92,677	8.9	478	137,954	9.2	40.7
Packaged alcoholic beverages	157	25,633	2.5	179	29,651	2.0	11.3
Cigars, cigarettes, and tobacco	241	14,664	1.4	275	23,231	1.6	5.0
Drugs, health and beauty aids	187	42,337	4.1	219	69,040	4.6	13.2
Men's, boys' wear, except footwear	104	29,461	2.8	117	41,647	2.8	16.9
Women's, girls' wear, except footwear	146	57,553	5.5	175	85,617	5.7	29.2
Footwear, except infant'o and toddler's	112	17,017	1.6	111	22,732	1.5	11.4
Furniture and sleep equipment	68	19,086	1.8	70	30,949	2.0	14.4
Kitchenware and home furnishings	150	15,642	1.5	167	21,512	1.4	6.4
Jewelry	95	12,133	1.2	118	20,691	1.4	8.3
Sporting goods	70	13,038	1.3	73	21,190	1.4	12.0
Hardware, tools, plumbing, and electrical supplies	103	13,978	1.3	107	20,784	1.4	8.3
Lumber and building materials	(NA)	(NA)	(NA)	65	45,491	3.0	33.3
Cars, trucks, powered vehicles	49	139,687	13.4	51	251,243	16.8	84.0
Automotive fuels	156	89,288	8.6	151	87,432	5.9	55.6
Automobile tires, batteries, accessories	166	31,050	3.0	158	37,734	2.5	8.1
Nonmerchandise receipts	249	30,355	2.9	342	52,381	3.5	8.2

NA Not available. X Not applicable. [1] Excludes establishments not in business at end of year. [2] Includes other merchandise lines not shown separately. [3] Detail will not add to total because establishments may carry more than one merchandise line.

Source: U.S. Bureau of the Census, *Census of Retail Trade, 1982*, and *1987, Merchandise Line Sales*, RC82-L and RC87-S-3.

No. 1285. Retail Trade Establishments—Number, Sales, Payroll, and Employees, by Kind of Business: 1987

[Each kind-of-business classification includes leased departments classified in that kind of business as if they were separate establishments. See *Historical Statistics, Colonial Times to 1970*, series T 79-196 for similar but not comparable data]

1987 SIC code [1]	KIND OF BUSINESS	ALL ESTABLISHMENTS Number [2] (1,000)	ALL ESTABLISHMENTS Sales (mil. dol.)	ESTABLISHMENTS WITH PAYROLL Number [2] (1,000)	Sales Total (mil. dol.)	Sales Per establishment ($1,000)	Annual payroll (mil. dol.)	Paid employees [3] (1,000)
	Retail trade, total	[4]2,420	[4]1,540,263	1,504	1,493,309	993	177,548	17,780
52	Building materials, garden supplies stores	107	83,454	74	81,487	1,104	9,760	668
521, 3	Building materials, supply stores	51	61,302	38	60,525	1,593	6,929	432
525	Hardware stores	27	11,036	20	10,535	525	1,564	138
526	Retail nurseries, lawn and garden supply stores	21	5,809	11	5,411	506	822	71
527	Mobile home dealers	8	5,307	5	5,015	993	445	27
53	General merchandise stores	57	181,971	35	181,147	5,112	19,586	2,003
531	Department stores (incl. leased depts.) [5][6]	10	153,679	10	153,679	15,305	(NA)	(NA)
531	Department stores (excl. leased depts.) [5][6]	10	144,017	10	144,017	14,343	16,365	1,651
533	Variety stores	21	7,134	10	6,762	649	926	121
539	Misc. general merchandise stores	26	30,819	15	30,368	2,029	2,294	231
54	Food stores [7]	290	309,460	191	301,847	1,583	29,819	2,855
541	Grocery stores	197	290,979	138	285,481	2,075	27,084	2,502
542	Meat and fish (seafood) markets	(NA)	(NA)	11	5,616	494	606	59
546	Retail bakeries	31	5,194	22	4,871	224	1,353	185
543	Fruit and vegetable markets	(NA)	(NA)	3	1,802	551	186	20
544	Candy, nut, confectionery stores	(NA)	(NA)	6	1,182	193	199	31
55 ex. 554	Automotive dealers [7]	194	342,896	103	333,420	3,246	28,688	1,373
551	New and used car dealers	28	280,529	28	280,529	9,906	22,205	940
552	Used car dealers	75	18,295	15	10,849	726	809	55
553	Auto and home supply stores	67	26,622	46	25,460	551	4,152	286
555	Boat dealers	(NA)	(NA)	5	6,824	1,319	620	35
556	Recreational vehicle dealers	(NA)	(NA)	3	5,538	1,842	437	25
557	Motorcycle dealers	(NA)	(NA)	4	3,475	828	382	27
554	Gasoline service stations [7]	137	104,769	115	101,997	889	6,414	702
56	Apparel and accessory stores [7]	197	79,322	149	77,391	519	9,725	1,121
561	Men's and boys' clothing stores	19	9,017	17	8,869	537	1,361	115
562, 3	Women's clothing, specialty stores	77	29,208	60	28,531	477	3,519	455
562	Women's clothing stores	64	26,366	52	25,868	495	3,150	419
565	Family clothing stores	27	21,472	18	21,117	1,145	2,362	268
566	Shoe stores	43	14,594	39	14,411	365	1,880	205
564	Children's and infants' wear stores	(NA)	(NA)	6	2,101	342	245	37
57	Furniture and homefurnishings stores	180	78,072	110	74,783	682	9,904	703
5712	Furniture stores	46	26,740	33	25,997	793	3,828	247
5713, 4, 9	Homefurnishings stores	63	17,737	32	16,374	512	2,389	176
572	Household appliance stores	17	8,642	11	8,332	744	953	65
573	Radio, television, computer, and music stores	54	24,953	34	24,080	714	2,734	215
5734	Computer and software stores	8	2,799	4	2,651	687	325	22
58	Eating and drinking places	490	153,462	391	148,776	380	38,582	6,100
5812	Eating places [7]	402	142,627	333	139,282	419	36,633	5,787
5812 pt.	Restaurants and lunchrooms	(NA)	(NA)	155	66,364	429	18,796	2,822
5812 pt.	Refreshment places	(NA)	(NA)	138	56,870	412	13,269	2,352
5813	Drinking places	88	10,834	59	9,495	162	1,950	313
591	Drug and proprietary stores	56	54,142	52	53,824	1,031	6,476	574
59 ex. 591	Miscellaneous retail stores [7]	[4]710	[4]152,716	284	138,636	489	18,594	1,682
592	Liquor stores	45	19,826	35	18,597	528	1,454	157
593	Used merchandise stores	89	5,217	15	3,502	236	663	69
594	Misc. shopping goods stores [7]	263	53,777	123	49,460	403	6,481	706
5941	Sporting goods, bicycle shops	50	11,256	22	10,077	467	1,218	121
5942	Book stores	19	5,338	11	5,116	462	581	72
5943	Stationery stores	7	1,942	5	1,814	376	287	27
5944	Jewelry stores	50	12,925	28	11,994	428	1,921	163
5945	Hobby, toy, and game shops	28	7,451	10	7,031	730	614	76
5946	Camera, photo supply stores	6	2,383	4	2,294	605	276	21
5947	Gift, novelty, souvenir shops	79	8,446	32	7,459	231	1,055	151
5949	Sewing, needlework, and piece goods stores	22	3,138	10	2,836	294	406	65
596	Nonstore retailers	[4]66	[4]34,878	23	33,894	1,470	4,523	318
5961	Catalog and mail-order houses	31	20,765	7	20,347	2,815	1,932	123
5962	Merchandising machine operators	24	6,258	5	5,692	1,074	1,090	74
5963	Direct selling establishments	[4]11	[4]7,855	11	7,855	746	1,501	121
598	Fuel dealers	17	14,503	13	14,198	1,114	1,824	99
5992	Florists	50	5,441	27	4,810	180	1,019	125
5995	Optical goods stores	15	3,480	14	3,415	251	811	54

NA Not available. [1] Based on 1987 Standard Industrial Classification; see text, section 13. [2] Represents the number of establishments in business at any time during year. [3] For pay period including March 12. [4] Excludes nonemployer direct sellers, SIC 5963. [5] Includes sales from catalog order desks. [6] Establishments defined as department stores with 50 employees or more. [7] Includes other kinds of businesses, not shown separately.

Source: U.S. Bureau of the Census, *1987 Census of Retail Trade*, RC87-A-52 and RC87-N-1.

No. 1286. Retail Trade Sales—Summary: 1970 to 1991

[Sales and inventories for leased departments and concessions are tabulated in the kind-of-business category of the leased department or concession. Based on Current Business Survey, see Appendix III. Minus sign (-) indicates decrease. See also *Historical Statistics, Colonial Times to 1970*, series T 245, 246, and 255]

| YEAR | CURRENT DOLLARS | | | | | | | CONSTANT (1982) dollars [4] | | |
| | Total sales (bil. dol.) | Annual percent change [1] | Per capita [2] (dol.) | Index of sales (1982= 100) | Durable goods (bil. dol.) | Nondurable goods (bil. dol.) | | Total sales (bil. dol.) | Annual percent change [1] | Per capita [2] (dol.) |
						Total	Dept. stores [3]			
1970	375.2	6.4	1,839	35.1	114.8	260.3	37.4	822.7	2.5	4,033
1971	414.2	10.4	2,002	38.7	135.4	278.8	41.8	874.7	6.3	4,229
1972	458.5	10.7	2,191	42.9	156.3	302.2	45.9	945.6	8.1	4,518
1973	511.9	11.6	2,422	47.9	177.2	334.7	51.0	990.7	4.8	4,687
1974	542.0	5.9	2,541	50.7	172.9	369.1	53.8	937.4	-5.4	4,394
1975	588.1	8.5	2,730	55.0	185.9	402.2	57.5	944.0	0.7	4,381
1976	656.4	11.6	3,017	61.4	220.4	436.0	63.5	1,007.2	6.7	4,629
1977	722.5	10.1	3,288	67.6	249.4	473.1	71.1	1,053.3	4.6	4,793
1978	804.2	11.3	3,621	75.2	281.4	522.7	78.0	1,096.0	4.1	4,935
1979	896.8	11.5	3,993	83.9	307.5	589.2	82.5	1,112.8	1.5	4,955
1980	957.4	6.7	4,213	89.5	299.2	658.1	88.3	1,074.8	-3.4	4,730
1981	1,038.7	8.5	4,527	97.1	324.8	713.9	98.9	1,078.5	0.3	4,700
1982	1,069.4	3.0	4,616	100.0	336.2	733.2	103.3	1,069.4	-0.8	4,616
1983	1,170.8	9.5	5,008	109.5	391.6	779.3	112.1	1,145.6	7.1	4,900
1984	1,287.8	10.0	5,460	120.4	455.3	832.5	124.1	1,228.8	7.3	5,210
1985	1,375.7	6.8	5,781	128.6	498.8	876.9	129.8	1,285.7	4.6	5,403
1986	1,450.3	5.4	6,039	135.6	541.5	908.9	137.8	1,359.2	5.7	5,660
1987	1,542.1	6.3	6,364	144.2	576.6	965.5	147.2	1,394.3	2.6	5,754
1988	1,651.4	7.1	6,753	154.4	627.4	1,024.0	155.1	1,448.6	3.9	5,924
1989	1,741.7	5.5	7,057	162.9	652.2	1,089.6	164.4	1,473.6	1.7	5,970
1990	1,807.2	3.8	7,246	169.0	654.8	1,152.5	170.7	1,466.9	-0.5	5,881
1991	1,821.5	0.8	7,223	170.3	644.8	1,176.7	177.3	1,439.9	-1.8	5,710

[1] Change from immediate prior year.   [2] Based on Bureau of the Census estimates of resident population as of July 1.   [3] Excludes leased departments.   [4] Based on implicit price deflators for retail sales supplied by U.S. Bureau of Economic Analysis.

No. 1287. Retail Trade—Sales, by Kind of Business: 1980 to 1991

[In billions of dollars. See headnote, table 1286. Based on Current Business Survey, see Appendix III. See also *Historical Statistics, Colonial Times to 1970*, series T 245-271]

1972 SIC code [1]	KIND OF BUSINESS	1980	1985	1986	1987	1988	1989	1990	1991
	Retail trade, total	957.4	1,375.7	1,450.3	1,542.1	1,651.4	1,741.7	1,807.2	1,821.5
	Durable goods stores, total [2]	299.2	498.8	541.5	576.6	627.4	652.2	654.8	644.8
55 exc. 554	Automotive dealers	164.1	303.3	326.3	342.9	371.6	383.6	382.0	374.5
551,2,5,6,7,9	Motor vehicle, misc. automotive dealers . . .	146.2	278.1	301.2	316.3	341.8	353.8	351.0	343.5
551,2	Motor vehicle dealers.	137.7	263.1	284.5	298.8	323.8	335.3	334.0	326.8
551	Motor vehicle dealers, franchised	130.5	251.6	270.4	280.5	302.4	309.7	308.4	299.6
553	Auto and home supply stores	18.0	25.2	25.1	26.6	29.7	29.8	31.0	31.0
52	Building materials, hardware, garden supply, mobile home dealers [2]	50.8	71.2	77.1	83.5	91.2	92.7	92.5	92.7
521,3	Building materials, supply stores	35.0	50.8	56.5	61.3	66.6	67.0	66.8	68.0
525	Hardware stores	8.3	10.5	10.7	11.0	11.9	12.6	13.3	13.1
57	Furniture, home furnishings, equipment [2]	44.2	68.3	75.7	78.1	85.4	91.5	93.0	90.1
571	Furniture, home furnishings stores	26.3	38.3	43.0	44.5	47.5	51.1	51.6	48.9
5722,32	Household appliance, radio, TV	14.0	25.1	27.0	27.1	30.5	32.4	33.0	32.3
	Nondurable goods stores, total [2]	658.1	876.9	908.9	965.5	1,024.0	1,089.6	1,152.5	1,176.7
56	Apparel and accessory stores [2]	49.3	70.2	75.6	79.3	84.9	91.4	94.7	95.6
561	Men's, boys' clothing, furnishings	7.7	8.5	8.6	9.0	9.4	9.5	9.5	9.2
562,3,8	Women's clothing, specialty stores, furriers. .	17.6	26.1	28.6	29.2	30.8	32.6	33.1	32.8
562	Women's ready-to-wear stores	15.9	23.6	25.7	26.4	27.5	29.3	29.9	30.2
565	Family clothing stores	10.8	17.8	19.3	21.5	23.6	25.8	28.0	29.8
566	Shoe stores	10.5	13.1	13.9	14.6	15.4	17.2	17.9	17.6
591	Drug and proprietary stores.	31.0	47.0	50.5	54.1	57.4	62.5	68.6	74.9
58	Eating and drinking places	90.1	127.9	139.4	153.5	166.9	173.9	182.0	189.5
5812	Eating places.	80.4	117.6	128.6	142.6	155.4	162.2	170.3	177.4
54	Food stores	220.2	285.1	297.0	309.5	326.5	345.1	362.4	370.6
541	Grocery stores.	205.6	269.5	280.8	291.0	307.2	324.0	338.7	346.3
554	Gasoline service stations	94.1	113.3	102.1	104.8	107.9	117.8	131.7	128.5
53	General merchandise group stores	108.7	158.6	169.2	182.0	191.8	204.4	211.9	217.6
531	Department stores [3]	88.3	129.8	137.8	147.2	155.1	164.4	170.7	177.3
533	Variety stores	7.8	8.5	7.4	7.1	7.2	7.4	7.3	7.1
539	Misc. gen. merchandise group stores [4]	12.6	20.3	24.0	27.7	29.5	32.7	33.9	33.2
592	Liquor stores	16.9	19.5	19.9	19.8	19.6	20.0	20.8	21.4
596	Non-store retailers.	22.8	28.3	30.3	35.9	41.2	45.2	50.3	50.2
5961 pt.	Mail-order houses (department store merchandise)	4.3	4.7	4.3	4.1	4.4	4.7	4.7	4.5

[1] Based on 1972 Standard Industrial Classification code; see text, section 13.   [2] Includes kinds of business, not shown separately.   [3] Excludes leased departments.   [4] Includes catalog showroom stores.

Source of tables 1286 and 1287: U.S. Bureau of the Census, *Current Business Reports, Revised Monthly Retail Sales and Inventories, January 1981 Through December 1990*, (BR/90-R), prior issues, and unpublished data.

No. 1288. Retail Trade—Sales of Multiunit Organizations, by Kind of Business: 1980 to 1991

[Data based on sales of companies which had 11 or more retail establishments according to the most recent update of multiestablishment files selected with certainty (i.e., their sales size exceeded specified dollar volume cutoffs which varied by kind of business). For details, see source. See also *Historical Statistics, Colonial Times to 1970*, series T 197-219]

1972 SIC code [1]	KIND OF BUSINESS	SALES (bil. dol.)						PERCENT OF TOTAL RETAIL SALES		
		1980	1985	1988	1989	1990	1991	1980	1990	1991
	Total sales	357.2	514.3	608.4	648.4	685.9	705.5	37.3	38.0	38.7
	Durable goods stores	34.2	54.6	72.9	77.1	81.1	83.5	11.4	12.4	12.9
553	Auto and home supply stores. . . .	4.7	5.9	7.5	7.9	8.6	8.9	26.2	27.7	28.7
	Nondurable goods stores [2]	322.9	459.7	535.4	571.2	604.8	622.0	49.1	52.5	52.9
56	Apparel and accessory stores [2]	21.1	35.9	45.5	50.1	53.3	55.4	42.7	56.3	58.9
562,3,8	Women's clothing specialty stores, furriers . . .	8.3	13.6	16.4	18.0	18.8	19.4	47.1	56.7	59.1
566	Shoe stores.	5.3	7.7	9.6	10.8	11.3	11.1	50.8	63.2	63.1
591	Drug and proprietary stores	16.8	27.9	33.8	37.5	41.9	46.1	54.3	61.2	61.5
54	Food stores	119.8	162.5	185.1	193.0	202.9	208.7	54.4	56.0	56.3
541	Grocery stores	118.1	160.2	182.7	190.4	200.0	205.8	57.4	59.1	59.4
53	General merchandise group.	98.5	145.9	176.3	187.5	194.5	199.8	90.6	91.8	91.8
531	Department stores	84.9	125.7	151.0	158.9	165.5	172.3	96.1	96.9	97.2
533	Variety stores.	6.3	7.0	5.7	5.8	5.6	5.3	80.9	77.4	74.6
539	Misc. general merchandise group stores	7.3	13.2	20.5	22.8	23.3	22.2	58.1	68.8	66.9
5812	Eating places	22.6	33.8	42.0	44.4	46.0	46.5	28.1	27.0	26.2

[1] Based on 1972 Standard Industrial Classification code; see text, section 13.   [2] Includes kinds of business not shown separately.

Source: U.S. Bureau of the Census, *Current Business Reports, Revised Monthly Retail Sales and Inventories, January 1981 Through December 1990* (BR/90-R) and prior issues; and unpublished data.

No. 1289. Retail Trade—Merchandise Inventories and Sales-Inventory Ratios, by Kind of Business: 1985 to 1991

[As of **Dec. 31**. Includes warehouses. See headnote, table 1286]

1972 SIC code [1]	KIND OF BUSINESS	INVENTORIES AT COST [2] (bil. dol.)				SALES-INVENTORY RATIOS [3]			
		1985	1989	1990	1991, prel.	1985	1989	1990	1991, prel.
	Total.	176.9	233.3	236.3	240.1	7.8	7.5	7.7	7.6
	Total (excluding automotive dealers) . .	130.4	166.7	170.4	177.9	8.2	8.2	8.5	8.1
	Durable goods stores [4]	87.8	121.3	120.7	118.7	5.7	5.4	5.5	5.4
55 exc. 554	Automotive dealers	46.4	66.6	65.9	62.2	6.5	5.8	5.8	6.0
551,2,5,6,7,9	Motor vehicle and misc. automotive dealers . .	41.7	61.3	60.2	56.9	6.7	5.8	5.9	6.0
551,2	Motor vehicle dealers	38.2	56.4	55.4	(NA)	6.9	5.9	6.0	(NA)
551	Motor vehicle dealers (franchised)	36.5	52.7	52.1	(NA)	6.9	5.9	6.0	(NA)
553	Automotive and home supply stores.	4.7	5.3	5.7	5.2	5.4	5.7	5.7	6.0
52	Building materials, hardware, garden supplies, mobile home dealers	13.1	15.9	15.5	16.1	5.5	5.8	6.1	5.8
521,3,5	Building materials, supply, hardware stores . . .	11.2	13.4	13.3	(NA)	5.5	6.0	6.2	(NA)
521,3	Building materials and supply stores	8.4	10.4	10.3	(NA)	6.0	6.5	6.8	(NA)
525	Hardware stores	2.8	3.0	3.0	(NA)	3.8	4.2	4.1	(NA)
57	Furniture, home furnishings, equipment stores [4] .	13.7	16.9	16.9	16.9	5.0	5.4	5.4	5.3
571	Furniture, home furnishings	7.1	9.1	8.8	(NA)	5.4	5.6	5.8	(NA)
5712	Furniture stores.	4.9	6.0	5.4	(NA)	4.9	5.0	5.1	(NA)
5722,32	Household appliance, radio, TV.	5.2	5.7	5.6	(NA)	4.8	5.7	5.8	(NA)
5722	Household appliance stores.	1.5	1.7	1.6	(NA)	5.9	5.6	5.5	(NA)
5944	Jewelry stores.	4.6	5.8	6.0	(NA)	2.4	2.4	2.4	(NA)
	Nondurable goods stores [4]	89.1	112.0	115.6	121.4	9.8	9.8	10.1	9.7
56	Apparel and accessory stores [4]	14.6	17.7	17.9	18.0	4.8	5.2	5.3	5.3
561	Men's, boys' clothing, furnishings	2.1	2.3	2.1	(NA)	4.1	4.2	4.2	(NA)
562	Women's ready-to-wear stores	3.8	4.4	4.5	(NA)	6.2	6.7	6.8	(NA)
565	Family clothing stores	3.7	5.0	5.0	(NA)	4.8	5.2	5.4	(NA)
566	Shoe stores	3.2	4.2	4.4	(NA)	4.1	4.1	4.0	(NA)
591	Drug and proprietary stores	8.8	11.8	12.8	14.9	5.4	5.3	5.4	5.0
58	Eating and drinking places.	3.2	3.5	3.7	(NA)	39.5	50.1	50.1	(NA)
54	Food stores	19.5	23.9	25.5	26.4	14.6	14.6	14.6	14.0
541	Grocery stores	18.7	22.9	24.4	25.4	14.4	14.3	14.3	13.6
554	Gasoline service stations	3.3	3.3	3.5	3.7	34.2	35.4	37.2	34.7
53	General merchandise group stores	31.3	40.1	39.8	43.0	5.1	5.1	5.3	5.1
531,9	Dept. stores, misc. general merchandise stores	29.1	38.1	37.9	(NA)	5.2	5.2	5.4	(NA)
531	Department stores.	24.0	31.2	30.8	(NA)	5.4	5.3	5.5	5.1
533	Variety stores.	2.1	2.0	1.9	(NA)	4.0	3.7	3.9	(NA)
592	Liquor stores.	2.3	2.5	2.6	(NA)	8.4	8.0	8.3	(NA)

NA Not available.   [1] Based on 1972 Standard Industrial Classification code; see text, section 13.   [2] Excludes supplies and equipment used in store and warehouse operations that are not for resale. Not adjusted for seasonal variation.   [3] Relates annual sales to yearend inventories.   [4] Includes kinds of business not shown separately.

Source: U.S. Bureau of the Census, *Current Business Reports*, series BR, *Annual* and *Monthly Retail Trade Reports*.

No. 1290. Retail Trade—Summary of Establishments, by State: 1987

[Kind-of-business classification based on 1987 Standard Industrial Classification code; see text, section 13]

DIVISION AND STATE	Estab-lish-ments	Sales (mil. dol.)	Annual payroll (mil. dol.)	Paid employees [1] (1,000)	DIVISION AND STATE	Estab-lish-ments	Sales (mil. dol.)	Annual payroll (mil. dol.)	Paid employees [1] (1,000)
U.S ..	2,419,641	1,540,263	177,548	17,780	VA	52,634	39,785	4,557	453
					WV	17,621	9,349	994	109
N.E	137,866	101,632	11,900	1,115	NC	69,125	40,651	4,423	465
ME	15,242	8,940	959	92	SC	36,493	19,750	2,177	237
NH	12,928	10,212	1,122	102	GA	61,686	41,186	4,792	487
VT	7,981	4,177	473	47	FL....	130,508	90,295	10,297	1,023
MA	58,623	45,997	5,493	530	E.S.C	155,670	83,825	8,952	972
RI.....	10,276	6,521	772	76	KY	38,507	19,872	2,132	244
CT	32,816	25,785	3,081	268	TN	50,423	29,694	3,198	338
M.A	364,778	236,566	27,338	2,564	AL....	40,218	22,268	2,357	250
NY	171,579	106,453	12,774	1,150	MS	26,522	11,991	1,265	140
NJ....	74,524	56,326	6,467	566	W.S.C	277,131	152,359	17,171	1,798
PA	118,675	73,787	8,097	848	AR	27,040	12,319	1,246	139
E.N.C....	381,109	255,197	29,029	3,081	LA.....	40,465	22,446	2,570	278
OH	96,973	64,705	7,434	804	OK	35,949	16,913	1,859	207
IN	53,633	33,992	3,727	412	TX	173,677	100,682	11,496	1,174
IL	99,468	69,937	8,078	820	Mt	134,395	80,171	9,487	977
MI....	80,743	58,026	6,584	673	MT	10,720	4,511	503	57
WI....	50,292	28,537	3,206	372	ID	10,953	5,082	556	63
W.N.C ...	189,743	105,042	11,685	1,317	WY	6,023	2,614	308	33
MN	42,874	28,008	3,086	347	CO	36,131	21,287	2,668	268
IA	32,338	15,581	1,705	204	NM	15,168	8,202	941	105
MO	52,540	31,142	3,538	376	AZ	31,519	22,360	2,624	261
ND	7,803	3,849	408	48	UT	13,827	8,620	963	109
SD	8,736	3,822	408	49	NV	10,054	7,495	924	81
NE	17,896	8,776	970	118	Pac	360,529	243,233	29,661	2,693
KS	27,556	13,863	1,570	175	WA	44,759	27,939	3,402	329
S.A	418,420	282,239	32,326	3,263	OR	29,488	17,340	2,027	204
DE	6,380	5,077	566	56	CA	268,873	185,959	22,732	2,022
MD	39,495	32,680	3,945	378	AK	6,266	3,728	484	36
DC	4,478	3,465	575	55	HI	11,143	8,267	1,016	102

[1] For pay period including March 12.

Source: U.S. Bureau of the Census, *1987 Census of Retail Trade,* Geographic Area Series, RC87-A-1 to 52; and Nonemployer Statistics Series, RC87-N-1 to 4.

No. 1291. Retail Trade—Sales, by Metropolitan Area: 1990

[Covers only establishments with payroll. Areas as defined by U.S. Office of Management and Budget, June 30, 1987. CMSA=consolidated metropolitan statistical area. MSA=metropolitan statistical area. NECMA=New England county metropolitan area. For definition, see Appendix II]

METROPOLITAN AREAS RANKED BY VOLUME OF SALES	Total sales (mil. dol.)	Sales per house-hold [1] (dol.)	METROPOLITAN AREAS RANKED BY VOLUME OF SALES PER HOUSEHOLD	Total sales (mil. dol.)	Sales per house-hold [1] (dol.)
New York-Northern New Jersey-Long Island, NY-NJ-CT CMSA [2]	132,199	20,028	St. Cloud, MN MSA	2,385	36,640
Los Angeles-Anaheim-Riverside, CA CMSA	111,467	22,285	Portland, ME NECMA..........	3,115	32,650
Chicago-Gary-Lake County, IL-IN-WI CMSA......................	61,391	21,045	Honolulu, HI MSA	8,377	31,340
San Francisco-Oakland-San Jose, CA CMSA	51,794	21,946	Anchorage, AK MSA	2,484	29,963
Philadelphia-Wilmington-Trenton, PA-NJ-DE-MD CMSA............	44,689	20,609	Terre Haute, IN MSA	1,453	29,663
Detroit-Ann Arbor, MI CMSA	35,737	20,701	Portsmouth-Dover-Rochester, NH NECMA	3,754	29,032
Washington, DC-MD-VA MSA....	32,926	22,207	Manchester-Nashua, NH NECMA.....	3,608	28,502
Boston-Lawrence-Salem-Lowell-Brockton, MA NECMA	32,454	22,936	Rapid City, SD MSA.............	830	26,777
Dallas-Fort Worth, TX CMSA	32,245	21,793	Bridgeport-Stamford-Norwalk-Danbury, CT NECMA	7,971	26,151
Miami-Fort Lauderdale, FL CMSA ...	27,178	21,918	Grand Forks, ND MSA...........	641	25,139
Houston-Galveston-Brazoria, TX CMSA .	26,777	19,940	Atlantic City, NJ MSA...........	3,110	24,982
Atlanta, GA MSA	24,168	22,233	Rochester, MN MSA	1,010	24,934
Seattle-Tacoma, WA CMSA	21,747	21,340	Bangor, ME NECMA	1,350	24,808
Minneapolis-St. Paul, MN-WI MSA.....	20,447	21,534	Orlando, FL MSA	9,896	23,897
Cleveland-Akron-Lorain, OH CMSA	19,013	18,006	Burlington, VT NECMA..........	1,204	23,558

[1] Based on number of households estimated as of July 1, 1990. [2] Includes Bridgeport-Stamford-Norwalk-Danbury, CT NECMA.

Source: Market Statistics, New York, NY, *The Survey of Buying Power Data Service,* annual, (copyright).

No. 1292. Retail Sales—

[**In millions of dollars, except as indicated**. Kind-of-business classification based on

REGION, DIVISION, AND STATE	ALL STORES [1]				FOOD STORES				GENERAL MERCHANDISE STORES			
	1987, total	1990			Total		Supermarkets		Total		Department stores	
		Total	Sales per household [2] Amount (dol.)	Percent change 1987-90	1987	1990	1987	1990	1987	1990	1987	1990
U.S. . . .	1,540,268	1,807,183	19,488	14.9	309,482	362,667	290,475	340,455	182,311	211,806	144,367	167,761
Northeast .	338,193	383,482	20,228	12.9	66,968	80,089	60,964	72,943	36,809	38,527	30,011	31,392
N.E	101,628	112,582	22,638	6.8	18,703	23,176	17,114	21,216	10,699	10,656	8,445	8,387
ME . . .	8,940	10,399	22,149	9.8	1,857	2,414	1,757	2,284	828	865	570	594
NH . . .	10,212	11,860	28,373	9.7	1,937	2,532	1,846	2,413	1,190	1,250	847	887
VT . . .	4,173	4,512	21,223	4.8	865	1,040	813	978	305	296	211	206
MA . . .	45,997	50,757	22,488	7.6	8,241	10,144	7,401	9,112	4,966	4,914	3,917	3,874
RI . . .	6,521	7,325	19,276	7.4	1,206	1,512	1,052	1,319	778	785	611	616
CT . . .	25,785	27,729	22,435	3.3	4,597	5,535	4,244	5,110	2,632	2,547	2,288	2,211
M.A	236,566	270,900	19,371	15.3	48,266	56,913	43,850	51,727	26,110	27,871	21,565	23,005
NY . . .	106,453	124,479	18,667	18.1	22,005	26,457	19,612	23,612	11,546	12,572	9,246	10,073
NJ . . .	56,326	63,431	22,579	13.4	11,409	13,222	10,508	12,182	5,754	6,039	4,884	5,120
PA . . .	73,787	82,990	18,413	12.8	14,851	17,234	13,730	15,933	8,810	9,260	7,435	7,813
Midwest . .	360,253	422,324	18,873	16.5	67,790	77,593	63,697	72,926	45,712	55,423	37,656	45,614
E.N.C . . .	255,190	298,075	19,069	16.3	47,580	53,229	44,434	49,703	32,018	38,647	26,810	32,367
OH . . .	64,705	73,206	17,880	12.3	13,183	14,304	12,400	13,453	8,372	9,808	6,862	8,038
IN. . . .	33,992	37,574	18,153	8.1	6,135	6,492	5,859	6,202	4,086	4,668	3,254	3,722
IL. . . .	69,930	83,479	19,840	21.8	12,669	14,490	11,801	13,491	8,084	9,986	6,857	8,467
MI. . . .	58,026	67,785	19,765	14.9	10,182	11,420	9,304	10,443	8,063	9,739	7,119	8,607
WI . . .	28,537	36,031	19,691	24.6	5,410	6,523	5,070	6,114	3,413	4,446	2,718	3,533
W.N.C . . .	105,063	124,249	18,419	17.1	20,211	24,364	19,262	23,223	13,694	16,776	10,846	13,247
MN . . .	28,006	33,315	20,050	14.0	4,966	6,038	4,706	5,723	3,767	4,667	2,796	3,394
IA . . .	15,581	18,818	17,724	25.5	3,328	4,084	3,199	3,926	1,947	2,430	1,526	1,916
MO . . .	31,128	36,032	18,281	12.2	5,899	6,946	5,664	6,670	4,191	5,017	3,535	4,233
ND . . .	3,848	4,467	18,630	20.5	694	819	668	788	501	601	386	466
SD . . .	3,822	4,649	17,921	25.6	750	930	720	894	393	493	294	372
NE . . .	8,814	10,313	17,113	18.4	1,734	2,072	1,559	1,861	1,092	1,326	870	1,064
KS . . .	13,863	16,656	17,540	19.7	2,839	3,475	2,747	3,361	1,803	2,242	1,440	1,803
South	518,372	607,087	18,885	13.5	107,769	125,704	102,889	120,043	61,493	74,534	48,012	53,272
S.A	282,219	325,787	19,454	8.7	55,821	64,629	53,100	61,489	31,388	37,645	24,707	29,679
DE . . .	5,077	6,041	24,145	9.9	916	1,088	850	1,009	698	860	606	745
MD . . .	32,680	36,837	20,790	5.2	6,243	7,045	5,859	6,616	3,750	4,388	2,993	3,493
DC . . .	3,465	3,815	15,360	12.8	598	637	537	573	315	348	272	301
VA . . .	39,785	47,472	20,459	8.6	8,236	9,856	7,951	9,517	4,334	5,373	3,358	4,168
WV . . .	9,349	10,060	14,718	14.6	2,226	2,404	2,095	2,262	1,322	1,481	884	1,003
NC . . .	40,650	45,756	17,995	5.9	8,146	9,223	7,878	8,919	4,063	4,769	2,999	3,526
SC . . .	19,750	23,754	18,685	17.2	4,244	5,126	4,101	4,953	2,029	2,541	1,533	1,925
GA . . .	41,168	46,748	19,417	6.5	7,924	9,019	7,644	8,700	4,920	5,809	3,987	4,708
FL . . .	90,295	105,304	20,056	8.9	17,289	20,231	16,185	18,940	9,955	12,077	8,076	9,809
E.S.C . . .	83,815	96,459	17,010	14.5	18,110	18,482	17,271	17,621	10,734	13,030	8,282	10,077
KY . . .	19,868	23,861	17,283	18.4	4,516	4,810	4,312	4,593	2,579	3,269	1,985	2,520
TN . . .	29,691	32,422	17,384	7.0	5,909	5,698	5,625	5,421	3,824	4,397	3,012	3,470
AL . . .	22,268	26,373	17,435	19.2	4,740	4,963	4,516	4,727	2,682	3,349	2,152	2,696
MS . . .	11,988	13,803	15,131	17.5	2,944	3,010	2,818	2,880	1,650	2,016	1,133	1,390
W.S.C . .	152,338	184,842	18,998	21.5	33,839	42,593	32,518	40,933	19,370	23,859	15,023	18,516
AR . . .	12,319	15,386	17,205	24.3	2,625	3,406	2,537	3,293	1,730	2,196	1,437	1,825
LA . . .	22,446	28,778	19,260	36.2	5,655	7,508	5,402	7,173	3,045	3,950	2,272	2,949
OK . . .	16,913	20,218	16,780	25.6	3,778	4,684	3,611	4,478	2,095	2,543	1,678	2,041
TX . . .	100,661	120,459	19,631	17.0	21,781	26,995	20,968	25,989	12,500	15,171	9,636	11,702
West.	323,449	394,289	20,478	17.6	66,954	79,282	62,925	74,543	38,297	43,323	28,688	32,482
Mt	80,197	94,172	18,465	14.7	17,304	20,409	16,695	19,689	9,016	10,827	6,771	8,166
MT . . .	4,511	5,333	17,478	24.6	1,042	1,240	1,007	1,198	428	518	325	398
ID . . .	5,082	6,004	16,591	17.6	1,157	1,375	1,123	1,335	486	589	366	448
WY . . .	2,614	2,726	16,314	15.9	548	575	535	562	265	284	194	209
CO . . .	21,311	24,383	18,864	15.2	4,345	4,987	4,198	4,817	2,538	2,967	1,982	2,314
NM . . .	8,204	9,378	17,044	13.6	1,692	1,944	1,614	1,854	943	1,103	662	784
AZ . . .	22,360	26,137	18,703	0.8	5,041	5,916	4,880	5,728	2,488	2,975	1,730	2,071
UT . . .	8,620	10,581	19,501	20.1	1,921	2,367	1,842	2,270	1,026	1,288	799	1,006
NV . . .	7,495	9,630	19,938	11.9	1,558	2,007	1,495	1,926	842	1,103	712	935
Pac	243,252	300,117	21,204	18.5	49,650	58,872	46,229	54,854	29,281	32,496	21,917	24,316
WA . . .	27,939	36,762	19,370	23.3	6,297	8,010	6,029	7,669	3,362	3,945	2,500	2,938
OR . . .	17,340	22,417	20,159	23.3	3,402	4,268	3,202	4,015	2,533	2,953	1,795	2,088
CA . . .	185,978	225,066	21,245	16.8	37,425	43,261	34,630	40,044	21,601	23,505	16,256	17,688
AK . . .	3,728	4,669	24,533	22.7	927	1,197	899	1,161	527	592	370	412
HI . . .	8,267	11,204	31,121	29.4	1,599	2,137	1,470	1,964	1,258	1,502	997	1,191

[1] Includes other types of stores, not shown separately.　[2] Based on number of households as of July 1 as estimated by source.　[3] Includes hardware dealers.　[4] Includes home furnishings stores.

by Type of Store and State: 1987 and 1990

1987 Standard Industrial Classification code; see text, section 13. Data are estimates]

AUTOMOTIVE DEALERS		EATING AND DRINKING PLACES		GASOLINE SERVICE STATIONS		BUILDING MATERIALS DEALERS [3]		APPAREL AND ACCESSORIES STORES		FURNITURE AND APPLIANCE STORES [4]		REGION, DIVISION, AND STATE
1987	1990	1987	1990	1987	1990	1987	1990	1987	1990	1987	1990	
342,927	381,799	153,488	182,107	104,762	131,381	83,366	92,730	79,454	94,645	78,098	92,595	**U.S.**
70,902	76,991	31,600	38,489	18,896	22,359	18,209	17,209	20,983	23,396	17,581	21,577	**Northeast**
22,498	22,903	9,472	12,059	6,060	6,855	6,513	6,032	5,707	5,861	4,841	5,801	**N.E**
1,977	2,111	711	951	569	677	693	672	343	371	310	391	ME
2,476	2,658	772	1,038	501	599	827	806	443	482	542	686	NH
937	931	370	459	276	305	382	348	179	179	170	199	VT
10,059	10,175	4,808	6,093	2,576	2,900	2,541	2,333	2,832	2,900	2,184	2,605	MA
1,313	1,353	665	858	441	505	395	369	369	385	264	321	RI
5,737	5,676	2,147	2,660	1,697	1,869	1,676	1,505	1,542	1,544	1,370	1,599	CT
48,404	54,088	22,128	26,430	12,836	15,504	11,696	11,176	15,275	17,535	12,739	15,776	**M.A**
19,036	21,749	10,768	13,098	5,052	6,237	5,199	5,055	7,698	8,994	6,081	7,672	NY
12,905	14,185	4,824	5,656	3,227	3,839	2,637	2,499	3,807	4,288	3,320	4,037	NJ
16,463	18,154	6,536	7,675	4,557	5,428	3,861	3,623	3,771	4,253	3,339	4,066	PA
80,739	92,223	36,100	40,526	28,463	37,823	20,094	23,966	16,729	19,807	17,484	19,620	**Midwest**
57,712	64,296	25,961	28,767	19,095	25,908	13,766	16,720	12,266	14,490	12,627	15,131	**E.N.C**
14,743	15,950	6,690	7,184	5,026	6,596	3,302	3,889	2,639	3,018	3,017	3,499	OH
8,050	8,491	3,321	3,478	2,693	3,459	2,045	2,349	1,396	1,556	1,495	1,691	IN
15,028	17,140	7,233	8,189	4,727	6,563	3,467	4,307	4,140	4,991	3,652	4,466	IL
13,797	15,388	5,653	6,259	4,316	5,822	3,249	3,946	2,986	3,520	3,011	3,602	MI
6,094	7,328	3,063	3,656	2,334	3,468	1,703	2,229	1,105	1,404	1,452	1,873	WI
23,027	27,928	10,139	11,759	9,369	11,916	6,329	7,246	4,463	5,318	4,857	4,489	**W.N.C**
5,672	6,945	2,656	3,111	2,293	2,941	1,871	2,162	1,241	1,492	1,429	1,332	MN
3,483	4,305	1,431	1,691	1,478	1,918	906	1,056	651	790	653	615	IA
7,136	8,461	3,115	3,532	2,816	3,501	1,789	2,001	1,295	1,507	1,340	1,210	MO
895	1,063	355	403	383	478	251	282	170	199	142	128	ND
869	1,083	354	421	400	523	236	278	158	193	154	147	SD
1,853	2,229	899	1,034	816	1,027	473	536	378	447	478	437	NE
3,119	3,842	1,330	1,566	1,183	1,528	802	932	571	690	661	621	KS
122,728	136,393	50,087	58,025	36,730	43,879	28,530	30,498	25,453	29,546	25,417	28,801	**South**
67,736	70,886	27,921	32,715	19,203	23,197	16,728	18,114	13,557	15,350	15,141	16,856	**S.A**
1,158	1,242	449	540	291	360	324	360	222	258	275	314	DE
7,903	8,056	3,084	3,527	2,159	2,539	1,598	1,687	1,789	1,976	1,817	1,971	MD
176	170	843	910	132	147	72	71	329	343	200	205	DC
9,617	10,383	3,625	4,392	2,845	3,570	2,208	2,471	1,874	2,193	2,204	2,532	VA
2,071	2,020	756	827	724	814	623	630	338	358	362	376	WV
9,707	9,926	3,934	4,514	2,823	3,332	3,063	3,245	1,931	2,141	2,313	2,518	NC
4,435	4,839	1,889	2,313	1,543	1,943	1,419	1,603	1,042	1,232	1,012	1,175	SC
9,689	9,962	4,059	4,683	3,062	3,637	2,585	2,753	1,909	2,127	2,103	2,302	GA
22,980	24,288	9,283	11,008	5,623	6,855	4,836	5,294	4,122	4,722	4,855	5,462	FL
20,080	23,433	7,337	8,390	6,295	7,431	4,831	5,087	3,812	4,677	3,638	4,230	**E.S.C**
4,214	5,145	1,866	2,230	1,623	2,000	1,183	1,301	773	990	838	1,020	KY
7,455	8,256	2,687	2,912	2,292	2,563	1,689	1,683	1,365	1,586	1,417	1,565	TN
5,680	6,830	1,864	2,193	1,566	1,904	1,291	1,398	1,177	1,487	938	1,125	AL
2,732	3,202	921	1,056	814	964	668	705	498	614	444	520	MS
34,912	42,074	14,829	16,920	11,231	13,252	6,970	7,297	8,084	9,519	6,639	7,715	**W.S.C**
2,940	3,659	945	1,113	1,011	1,229	829	893	524	638	461	553	AR
4,377	5,566	2,119	2,552	1,619	2,015	1,062	1,169	1,104	1,373	945	1,159	LA
4,074	4,850	1,672	1,884	1,254	1,459	779	802	913	1,062	707	811	OK
23,522	27,999	10,093	11,370	7,347	8,549	4,301	4,432	5,543	6,447	4,526	5,192	TX
68,557	76,191	35,701	45,068	20,673	27,320	16,533	21,058	16,289	21,896	17,617	22,598	**West**
17,585	19,547	8,408	9,681	6,285	7,016	4,346	5,199	3,362	4,349	3,950	4,797	**Mt**
950	1,065	496	576	416	470	276	332	177	230	190	233	MT
1,188	1,331	472	549	454	511	317	382	200	261	230	282	ID
547	541	280	288	316	314	138	147	110	126	88	95	WY
4,542	4,016	2,133	2,722	1,569	1,707	1,062	1,237	921	1,159	1,112	1,313	CO
1,846	1,999	885	995	676	740	501	581	351	441	348	412	NM
5,021	5,556	2,274	2,611	1,602	1,782	1,143	1,360	857	1,103	1,161	1,403	AZ
1,880	2,185	780	940	725	847	456	570	416	562	487	617	UT
1,611	1,955	787	992	527	646	452	590	331	467	334	442	NV
50,972	56,644	27,293	35,387	14,388	20,304	12,187	15,859	12,927	17,547	13,666	17,801	**Pac**
5,484	6,503	3,030	4,155	1,763	2,650	1,575	2,190	1,395	1,977	1,411	1,957	WA
3,925	4,607	1,764	2,403	1,075	1,603	860	1,179	781	1,117	819	1,125	OR
39,821	43,475	20,658	26,290	10,931	15,110	9,301	11,908	9,958	13,289	11,026	14,153	CA
511	584	474	625	185	250	216	242	198	272	117	153	AK
1,232	1,476	1,366	1,913	434	692	235	339	595	892	293	413	HI

Source: Market Statistics, New York, NY, *The Survey of Buying Power Data Service,* annual (copyright).

No. 1293. Retail Foodstores—Number and Sales, by Type: 1980 to 1990

TYPE OF FOODSTORE	NUMBER [1] (1,000)					SALES [2] (bil. dol.)					PERCENT DISTRIBUTION			
											Number		Sales	
	1980	1985	1988	1989	1990	1980	1985	1988	1989	1990	1980	1990	1980	1990
Total	253.4	255.9	255.9	254.4	253.0	220.2	285.1	326.5	349.3	362.4	100.0	100.0	100.0	100.0
Grocery stores . . .	178.3	177.2	174.5	172.3	170.1	205.6	269.5	307.2	329.4	338.7	70.4	67.2	93.4	93.5
Supermarkets [3] .	26.3	26.2	24.6	24.1	23.8	157.0	201.8	230.6	247.3	260.1	10.4	9.4	71.3	71.8
Convenience stores [4]	35.8	45.4	52.5	52.0	51.7	18.9	33.7	38.3	43.9	46.5	14.1	20.4	8.6	12.8
Superette [5] . . .	116.2	105.6	97.4	96.2	94.6	29.7	34.0	38.2	38.1	32.0	45.9	37.4	13.5	8.8
Specialized food stores [6]	75.0	78.7	81.3	82.1	83.0	14.6	15.5	19.3	19.9	23.7	29.6	32.8	6.6	6.5

[1] Estimated.   [2] Includes nonfood items.   [3] A grocery store, primarily self-service in operation, providing a full range of departments, and having at least $2.5 million in annual sales in 1985 dollars.   [4] A small grocery store selling a limited variety of food and nonfood products, typically open extended hours.   [5] A grocery store, primarily self-service in operation, selling a wide variety of food and nonfood products with annual sales below $2.5 million (1985 dollars).   [6] Primarily engaged in the retail sale of a single food category such as meat and seafood stores and retail bakeries.

No. 1294. Supermarkets—Number and Sales, by Type of Format: 1980 to 1990

[For definition of supermarket, see footnote 3, table 1293]

SUPERMARKET FORMAT	NUMBER				SALES (bil. dol.)			PERCENT DISTRIBUTION			
								Number		Sales	
	1980	1985	1989	1990	1980	1989	1990	1980	1990	1980	1990
Supermarkets, total	26,321	26,229	24,083	23,813	157.0	247.3	260.1	100.0	100.0	100.0	100.0
Conventional.	21,009	16,568	13,273	12,550	114.7	103.9	90.7	79.8	52.7	73.1	34.9
Superstore [1]	3,150	4,854	5,642	5,810	27.8	75.7	87.6	12.0	24.4	17.7	33.7
Warehouse [2]	1,670	3,483	3,395	3,381	6.6	30.4	33.1	6.3	14.2	4.2	12.7
Combination food and drug [3] . . .	475	1,047	1,273	1,619	6.3	21.8	34.8	1.8	6.8	4.0	13.4
Superwarehouse [4]	7	207	385	333	1.6	9.9	12.6	(Z)	1.4	1.0	4.8
Hypermarket [5]	10	70	115	120	(NA)	5.7	1.3	(Z)	0.5	(NA)	0.5

NA Not available.   Z Less than .05 percent.   [1] Contains greater variety of products than conventional supermarkets, including specialty and service departments, and considerable nonfood (general merchandise) products.   [2] Contains limited product variety and fewer services provided, incorporating case lot stocking and shelving practices.   [3] Contains a pharmacy, a nonprescription drug department, and a greater variety of health and beauty aids than that carried by conventional supermarkets.   [4] A larger warehouse store that offers expanded product variety and often service meat, deli, or seafood departments.   [5] A very large store offering a greater variety of general merchandise—like clothes, hardware, and seasonal goods—and personal care products than other grocery stores.

Source of tables 1293 and 1294: U.S. Dept. of Agriculture, Economic Research Service, *Food Marketing Review*, annual.

No. 1295. Commercial and Institutional Groups—Food and Drink Sales: 1980 to 1991

[Excludes military. Data refer to sales to consumers of food and alcoholic beverages. Sales are estimated. For details, see source]

TYPE OF GROUP	Number, 1990	SALES (mil. dol.)							
		1980	1985	1986	1987	1988	1989	1990	1991 [1]
Total	720,043	119,004	172,787	184,189	198,741	212,859	225,644	237,700	246,958
Commercial foodservice [2] [3]	546,996	101,529	151,762	162,528	176,312	189,289	200,583	211,083	219,474
Eating places [2]	338,724	72,276	111,657	120,138	128,867	138,542	146,716	154,227	161,771
Restaurants, lunchrooms	163,514	39,307	57,939	61,474	65,184	69,356	72,727	76,072	79,192
Limited menu restaurants [4]	149,786	28,699	47,477	51,940	56,431	61,397	65,775	69,458	73,570
Bars and taverns [5]	37,227	7,785	8,338	8,563	8,742	8,899	8,952	9,212	8,554
Food contractors [2]	15,739	6,818	9,460	10,095	11,075	12,071	13,198	14,149	14,990
Manufacturing and industrial plants. .	(NA)	2,121	2,721	2,824	3,042	3,356	3,669	3,856	3,845
Colleges and universities	(NA)	1,140	1,738	1,882	2,057	2,284	2,569	2,788	3,174
Lodging places [2]	27,158	6,768	10,557	11,187	12,031	12,933	13,606	14,272	14,285
Hotel restaurants	16,532	4,964	8,986	9,714	10,608	11,533	12,215	12,907	12,922
Motel restaurants	8,828	1,151	975	911	872	850	836	820	812
Retail hosts [2] [6]	107,807	3,264	5,254	5,651	7,956	8,605	9,276	9,888	10,643
Department store restaurants	4,980	857	865	827	831	875	925	950	(NA)
Grocery store restaurants [6]	44,766	830	2,074	2,381	4,552	4,979	5,379	5,733	(NA)
Gasoline service stations	33,788	492	1,052	1,164	1,254	1,381	1,523	1,681	(NA)
Recreation and sports	14,447	1,452	1,972	2,074	2,382	2,546	2,787	2,916	2,968
Institutional foodservice [2]	173,047	17,475	21,025	21,661	22,429	23,570	25,061	26,617	27,483
Employee foodservice	7,717	1,635	1,971	1,975	1,979	1,985	1,994	1,985	1,871
Industrial, commercial organizations .	3,091	1,377	1,682	1,694	1,680	1,658	1,641	1,603	(NA)
Educational foodservice	95,883	4,610	5,978	6,253	6,542	6,883	7,237	7,671	7,960
Elementary and secondary schools .	93,104	2,312	2,919	3,060	3,189	3,347	3,478	3,700	3,747
Hospitals	6,613	6,668	7,104	7,170	7,436	7,826	8,396	8,968	9,434
Miscellaneous [2]	29,403	1,521	2,077	2,197	2,365	2,489	2,677	2,845	2,969
Clubs	10,310	1,056	1,537	1,620	1,743	1,809	1,914	1,993	(NA)

NA Not available.   [1] Projection.   [2] Includes other types of groups, not shown separately.   [3] Data for establishments with payroll.   [4] Fast-food restaurants.   [5] For establishments serving food.   [6] Beginning 1987, a portion of deli sales in grocery stores are considered foodservice.

Source: National Restaurant Association, Washington, DC, *Foodservice Numbers: A Statistical Digest for the Foodservice Industry*, 1992; *Foodservice Industry in Review*, annual; and *National Restaurant Association Foodservice Industry Forecast*, December 1991, (copyright).

No. 1296. Shopping Centers—Number, Gross Leasable Area, and Retail Sales, by Gross Leasable Area: 1986 to 1991

[As of **December 31**. A shopping center is a group of architecturally unified commercial establishments built on a site which is planned, developed, owned and managed as an operating unit related in its location, size, and type of shops to the trade area that the unit serves. The unit provides on-site parking in definite relationship to the types and total size of the stores. The data base attempts to include all centers with three or more stores. Estimates are based on a sample of data available on shopping center properties; for details, contact source]

YEAR	Total	GROSS LEASABLE AREA (sq. ft.)					
		Less than 100,001	100,001-200,000	200,001-400,000	400,001-800,000	800,001-1,000,000	More than 1 million
NUMBER							
1986.	28,496	18,230	6,692	2,083	918	261	312
1989.	34,683	22,016	8,337	2,637	1,065	280	348
1990.	36,515	23,231	8,756	2,781	1,102	288	357
1991.	37,975	23,997	9,226	2,953	1,141	294	364
Percent distribution	100.0	63.2	24.3	7.8	3.0	0.8	1.0
Percent change, 1990-91	4.0	3.3	5.4	6.2	3.5	2.1	2.0
GROSS LEASABLE AREA							
1986 (mil. sq. ft.)	3,523	901	917	555	522	234	393
1989 (mil. sq. ft.)	4,214	1,074	1,146	699	598	252	444
1990 (mil. sq. ft.)	4,390	1,125	1,197	734	618	259	457
1991 (mil. sq. ft.)	4,586	1,168	1,267	781	640	265	466
Percent distribution	100.0	25.5	27.6	17.0	14.0	5.8	10.2
Percent change, 1990-91	4.5	3.8	5.8	6.4	3.6	2.3	2.0
RETAIL SALES							
1986 (bil. dol.)	556.5	160.3	140.4	84.8	73.9	36.2	60.8
1989 (bil. dol.)	682.8	198.3	173.4	104.4	88.7	43.6	74.4
1990 (bil. dol.)	706.4	205.1	179.5	108.0	91.7	45.1	77.0
1991 (bil. dol.)	716.9	208.3	182.2	109.5	93.0	45.8	78.2
Percent distribution	100.0	29.0	25.4	15.3	13.0	6.4	10.9
Percent change, 1990-91	1.5	1.6	1.5	1.4	1.4	1.6	1.6

Source: National Research Bureau, 225 West Wacker Drive, Chicago, IL 60606-1229. Data for 1986 published by Communication Channels Inc., Atlanta, GA, in *Shopping Center World*, February issues, (copyright). Data for 1989-91 published by Monitor Publishing, Clearwater, FL, in *Monitor Magazine*, November/December issues, (copyright).

No. 1297. Shopping Centers—Number, Gross Leasable Area, and Retail Sales, by State: 1991

[Minus sign (-) indicates decrease. See headnote, table 1296]

DIVI-SION AND STATE	Num-ber	Gross leasa-ble area (mil. sq. ft.)	Retail sales (bil. dol.)	PERCENT CHANGE, 1990-91			DIVI-SION AND STATE	Num-ber	Gross leasa-ble area (mil. sq. ft.)	Retail sales (bil. dol.)	PERCENT CHANGE, 1990-91		
				Num-ber	Gross leasa-ble area	Retail sales per sq. ft.					Num-ber	Gross leasa-ble area	Retail sales per sq. ft.
U.S.	37,975	4,586	716.9	4.0	4.5	-2.8	VA. . .	1,089	141	21.5	3.5	4.3	-2.1
							WV . .	153	21	2.8	2.7	5.7	-5.7
N.E. . . .	2,206	238	37.0	5.0	4.9	-3.4	NC . .	1,303	140	20.3	5.7	5.2	-3.0
ME . .	176	15	2.7	5.4	5.5	-3.7	SC . .	715	71	11.1	5.1	2.8	-1.1
NH . .	188	20	2.7	6.2	17.3	-12.6	GA . .	1,354	142	22.1	3.3	4.7	-2.3
VT . .	98	7	1.1	5.4	6.0	-4.1	FL . . .	2,937	371	62.3	2.6	2.7	0.1
MA . .	882	98	15.8	3.5	2.7	-1.6	**E.S.C** . .	2,618	284	43.7	2.1	3.2	-2.1
RI . . .	182	16	2.6	2.2	2.5	-1.3	KY . .	565	61	10.0	2.4	1.6	-0.9
CT . . .	680	82	12.2	7.3	5.1	-3.7	TN . .	1,075	118	16.2	1.7	4.0	-2.6
M.A . .	3,816	540	78.5	5.9	5.2	-4.3	AL . . .	583	67	11.3	2.3	2.9	-1.8
NY . .	1,458	204	31.4	4.8	4.7	-3.9	MS . .	395	37	6.2	2.3	4.0	-3.0
NJ . .	946	133	18.9	7.1	5.5	-4.3	**W.S.C.** .	4,283	483	90.0	1.5	1.9	-0.4
PA . .	1,412	202	28.1	6.2	5.6	-4.7	AR . . .	331	31	5.5	1.2	1.8	-0.6
E.N.C . .	5,601	728	102.0	4.7	5.6	-4.8	LA . . .	654	77	13.4	1.1	1.1	-0.7
OH . .	1,465	208	29.7	5.5	5.5	-4.7	OK . .	546	56	9.8	4.6	3.5	-2.6
IN . . .	803	107	15.4	1.8	2.7	-2.1	TX . . .	2,752	319	61.3	1.0	1.8	0.1
IL . . .	1,847	222	28.9	6.4	8.6	-7.6	**Mt**	2,529	303	50.5	2.8	4.1	-1.8
MI . . .	926	122	17.8	4.2	4.0	-3.3	MT . .	89	8	1.4	3.5	3.2	-2.6
WI . . .	560	69	10.1	2.6	3.7	-2.7	ID . . .	125	15	2.4	5.0	4.5	-3.1
W.N.C. .	2,262	285	46.0	2.1	3.2	-2.3	WY . .	51	6	1.0	4.1	3.7	-3.6
MN . .	113	59	9.7	2.7	4.2	-3.0	CO . .	660	85	15.4	0.2	0.1	1.6
IA . . .	266	34	5.4	1.9	2.5	-2.4	NM . .	261	26	4.5	4.8	3.9	-1.6
MO . .	794	99	16.1	1.5	2.3	-1.3	AZ . .	885	104	16.6	2.5	4.6	-1.6
ND . .	77	9	1.5	4.1	2.6	-2.2	UT . .	195	28	4.7	3.2	4.2	-2.6
SD . .	47	6	0.9	4.4	3.4	-2.5	NV . .	260	30	4.4	7.4	15.1	-10.3
NE . .	224	29	4.1	1.4	5.2	-4.4	**Pac** . . .	6,139	705	107.8	6.2	6.8	-4.4
KS . .	442	49	8.3	2.6	3.1	-2.3	WA . .	619	82	12.1	4.0	3.5	-1.6
S.A. . . .	8,521	1,021	161.4	3.6	3.7	-1.4	OR . .	414	48	6.4	7.0	6.3	-5.1
DE. . .	116	18	2.9	10.5	2.4	-0.8	CA . .	4,897	553	85.4	6.6	7.6	-4.9
MD . .	791	110	17.2	2.9	3.5	-1.8	AK . . .	57	7	1.3	1.8	1.8	0.7
DC. . .	63	8	1.2	5.0	3.4	-2.9	HI . . .	152	14	2.6	2.7	1.1	0.6

Source: National Research Bureau, 225 West Wacker Drive, Chicago, IL 60606-1229. Data published by Monitor Publishing, Clearwater, FL, in *Monitor Magazine*, November/December 1991, (copyright).

No. 1298. Domestic and International Franchising—Summary: 1980 to 1991

[Franchising is a form of marketing or distribution in which a parent company customarily grants an individual or a company the right, or privilege, to do business in a prescribed manner over a certain period of time in a specified place. The parent company is termed the franchisor; the receiver of the privilege the franchisee; and the right, or privilege, the franchise]

ITEM	Unit	1980	1983	1984	1985	1986	1987	1988	1989	1990	1991 [1]
DOMESTIC [2]											
Number of franchised establishments.	1,000	442	442	444	455	462	479	481	493	521	543
Company-owned [3]	1,000	85	86	87	86	88	89	94	95	97	101
Franchisee-owned	1,000	357	355	357	369	374	390	387	398	424	442
Sales of products and services	Bil. dol.	336	423	492	543	569	599	648	678	714	758
Company-owned [3]	Bil. dol.	47	59	64	68	85	90	98	107	117	127
Franchisee-owned	Bil. dol.	289	364	428	475	484	509	550	570	597	631
Average sales per establishment	$1,000	760	958	1,108	1,193	1,231	1,251	1,348	1,376	1,369	1,396
Employment	1,000	4,668	5,165	5,671	6,283	6,501	(NA)	(NA)	(NA)	(NA)	(NA)
INTERNATIONAL											
U.S. companies operating foreign outlets	Number.	279	305	328	342	354	(NA)	374	(NA)	(NA)	(NA)
Foreign outlets	1,000	20.4	25.7	27.0	30.2	31.6	(NA)	35.0	(NA)	(NA)	(NA)

NA Not available.　[1] Estimated by respondents to annual survey of franchisors.　[2] Excludes foreign outlets of U.S. companies.　[3] Represents establishments owned by the parent company.

Source: U.S. Dept. of Commerce, International Trade Administration, *Franchising in the Economy, 1986-88*, 1988. Beginning 1988, International Franchise Association Educational Foundation, Inc., Washington, DC and Horwath International, New York, NY, *Franchising in the Economy*, annual.

No. 1299. Domestic Franchising—Number of Establishments and Sales, by Kind of Franchised Business: 1980 to 1990

[See headnote, table 1298, for definition of franchising. Excludes foreign outlets of U.S. companies]

KIND OF FRANCHISED BUSINESS	NUMBER OF ESTABLISHMENTS (1,000)						SALES (bil. dol.)					
	1980	1985	1987	1988	1989 [1]	1990 [1]	1980	1985	1987	1988	1989 [1]	1990 [1]
All franchising, total	442.4	455.2	479.1	480.8	498.8	533.0	336.2	543.0	599.4	648.1	678.8	716.4
Auto and truck dealers [2]	29.4	27.5	27.6	27.8	27.6	27.6	143.9	282.6	319.7	345.1	353.6	362.3
Percent	6.6	6.0	5.8	5.8	5.5	5.2	42.8	52.0	53.3	53.2	52.1	50.6
Restaurants (all types)	60.0	73.9	83.3	90.3	94.3	102.1	27.9	47.7	56.8	64.3	69.1	76.5
Percent	13.6	16.2	17.4	18.8	18.9	19.2	8.3	8.8	9.5	9.9	10.2	10.7
Gasoline service stations [2]	158.5	124.6	115.9	113.2	112.0	111.7	94.5	100.8	89.2	101.9	108.5	115.1
Percent	35.8	27.4	24.2	23.5	22.1	20.9	28.1	18.6	14.9	15.7	16.0	16.1
Retailing (nonfood)	35.2	45.1	47.9	46.2	49.2	54.1	10.5	20.6	25.4	23.3	26.0	28.6
Percent	8.0	9.9	10.0	9.6	9.7	10.2	3.1	3.8	4.2	3.6	3.8	4.0
Auto, truck rental services	7.3	11.2	10.0	9.5	9.9	10.6	3.1	5.7	6.5	6.6	7.0	7.6
Automotive products and services [3]	40.2	36.5	39.3	34.7	35.8	38.6	7.1	10.7	12.3	11.4	12.2	13.6
Business aids and services	40.7	49.8	56.7	55.6	59.8	67.3	6.7	12.0	14.7	15.7	17.1	19.5
Employment services	4.4	4.8	6.1	6.5	6.6	7.4	1.6	2.7	3.7	4.7	5.0	5.8
Tax preparation services	9.2	8.1	8.5	8.3	8.2	8.5	0.3	0.4	0.5	0.6	0.7	0.7
Accounting, credit, collection, and general	2.4	2.1	2.0	1.7	1.7	1.9	0.1	0.2	0.2	0.2	0.2	0.2
Real estate [4]	17.3	13.9	15.2	15.3	16.0	17.0	3.6	4.6	5.6	5.9	6.2	6.8
Printing and copying	2.8	4.5	5.6	5.9	6.5	7.4	0.4	0.9	1.2	1.5	1.6	1.9
Other	4.8	16.4	19.4	17.9	20.8	25.1	0.8	3.1	3.5	3.0	3.4	4.1
Construction, home improvement, maintenance, and cleaning	14.3	17.5	21.7	22.0	24.7	28.3	1.5	4.1	5.2	5.3	6.0	6.8
Convenience stores	15.6	15.1	16.3	17.2	17.3	17.5	7.8	10.8	12.3	13.9	14.1	14.4
Educational products and services	3.2	8.2	9.6	11.6	11.9	13.3	0.3	0.8	1.0	1.7	1.9	2.3
Equipment rental services	2.2	2.5	2.8	3.0	3.0	3.4	0.4	0.7	0.7	0.7	0.7	0.8
Food retailing [5]	15.5	18.7	20.5	21.6	23.0	25.4	7.4	10.1	11.1	10.2	10.9	11.9
Hotels and motels [6]	6.4	7.5	9.3	9.3	10.1	11.1	9.5	14.8	17.7	19.7	21.3	23.9
Laundry, dry cleaning services . . .	3.4	2.3	2.2	2.3	2.5	2.6	0.3	0.3	0.3	0.3	0.3	0.3
Recreation, entertainment, travel. .	4.6	7.8	8.2	8.8	9.5	10.3	0.5	2.3	4.0	3.5	4.1	4.7
Soft drink bottlers [2] [7]	1.9	1.4	1.1	0.9	0.8	0.8	14.4	18.3	20.9	22.7	24.2	25.8
Miscellaneous	3.6	5.5	6.8	6.9	7.3	8.4	0.4	0.9	1.5	1.7	1.9	2.2

[1] Estimated by respondents.　[2] Estimated by source on basis of Bureau of the Census and trade association data. [3] Includes some establishments with significant sales of nonautomotive products such as household appliances, garden supplies, etc.　[4] Gross commissions.　[5] Excludes convenience stores.　[6] Includes campgrounds.　[7] Includes soft drinks, fruit drinks and ades, syrups, flavoring agents and bases. Excludes independent private label and contract-filler bottling companies, which accounted for 22 percent of the value of shipments of the total industry in recent years.

Source: U.S. Dept. of Commerce, International Trade Administration, *Franchising in the Economy, 1986-88*, 1988. Beginning 1988, International Franchise Association Educational Foundation, Inc., Washington, DC and Horwath International, New York, NY, *Franchising in the Economy, 1988-1990*, 1990. Equipment rental services included with auto, truck rental services.

No. 1300. Franchised New Car Dealerships—Summary: 1970 to 1990

[Calendar year, except as indicated]

ITEM	Unit	1970	1980	1983	1984	1985	1986	1987	1988	1989	1990
Dealerships [1]	Number.	30,800	27,900	24,725	24,725	24,725	24,825	25,150	24,950	24,925	24,825
Sales	Bil. dol . .	51.8	130.5	187.7	225.9	251.6	270.4	280.5	302.4	309.7	308.4
New cars.	1,000. . .	8,393	8,979	9,182	10,390	11,038	11,455	10,277	10,639	9,771	9,296
Used vehicles.	1,000. . .	11,283	9,717	10,930	12,420	13,330	13,460	13,400	14,940	14,510	14,290
Employment	1,000. . .	702.9	745.2	722.4	794.8	856.9	896.7	926.0	960.1	959.2	947.6
Annual payroll	Bil. dol . .	5.5	11.0	14.5	17.8	20.1	21.7	22.6	24.7	25.2	25.4
Advertising expenses	Bil. dol . .	0.4	1.2	1.7	2.1	2.8	3.2	3.7	4.1	3.9	3.6
Dealer pretax profits as a percentage of sales	Percent .	2.00	0.61	2.14	2.18	2.20	2.16	1.88	1.71	1.00	1.00
Inventory: [2] Domestic: [3]											
Total	1,000. . .	1,409	1,506	1,209	1,413	1,510	1,687	1,724	1,543	1,677	1,450
Days' supply	Days . . .	60	71	55	55	58	63	75	63	72	66
Imported: [3]											
Total	1,000. . .	(NA)	458	260	216	271	392	551	626	648	597
Days' supply	Days . . .	(NA)	55	34	26	30	37	53	62	70	74

NA Not available.   [1] At beginning of year.   [2] Annual average.   [3] Classification based on where automobiles are produced (i.e., automobiles manufactured by foreign companies but produced in the United States are classified as domestic).

Source: National Automobile Dealers Association, McLean, VA, *NADA Data*, annual.

No. 1301. Wholesale Trade—Summary: 1958 to 1987

[Data prior to 1972 based on earlier editions of Standard Industrial Classification (SIC) code. Comparability of data over time is affected by changes in the SIC code; for details, see source. See also *Historical Statistics, Colonial Times to 1970*, series T 43-47, and T 274-279]

ITEM	Unit	1958	1963	1967	1972 [1]	1977 [1]	1982 [1]	1987 [1]	1987 [2]
Firms, total [3]	1,000. . .	(NA)	232	233	276	289	335	(NA)	364
Establishments, total [3]	1,000. . .	287	308	311	370	383	435	467	470
With sales of $1,000,000 or more.	1,000. . .	(NA)	62	75	103	152	(NA)	(NA)	222
Sales, all establishments	Bil. dol . .	286	358	460	695	1,258	1,998	2,524	2,525
Merchant wholesalers	Bil. dol . .	122	157	206	354	678	1,159	1,477	1,478
Inventories, end of year.	Bil. dol . .	15.0	20.1	28.1	45.7	82.3	130.7	(NA)	165.1
Payroll, entire year	Bil. dol . .	13.2	18.1	23.9	36.9	58.3	95.2	133.2	133.4
Paid employees, Mar. 12 workweek [4]	1,000. . .	2,808	3,089	3,519	4,026	4,397	4,985	5,581	5,596

NA Not available.   [1] Based on 1972 SIC code.   [2] Based on 1987 SIC code.   [3] Through 1977 number of firms and establishments in business at end of year; beginning 1982 number of firms and establishments in business at any time during year.   [4] 1958 and 1963 data for workweek including Nov. 15.

No. 1302. Wholesale Trade, by Type of Operation and Kind of Business: 1982 and 1987

[Based on 1972 Standard Industrial Classification code; see text, section 13. See *Historical Statistics, Colonial Times to 1970*, series T 274-287 and T 352-369 for similar but not comparable data]

TYPE OF OPERATION AND KIND OF BUSINESS	ESTABLISH-MENTS [1] (1,000)		SALES (mil. dol.)		ANNUAL PAYROLL (mil. dol.)		PAID EMPLOYEES [2] (1,000)	
	1982	1987	1982	1987	1982	1987	1982	1987
Wholesale trade	435.1	466.7	1,997,895	2,523,688	95,209	133,153	4,985	5,581
Merchant wholesalers	353.1	388.1	1,159,334	1,477,132	69,936	100,210	3,918	4,461
Other operating types	82.1	78.6	838,561	1,046,557	25,273	32,944	1,067	1,120
Durable goods	267.4	292.8	881,212	1,258,483	57,368	82,248	2,913	3,303
Motor vehicles, automotive equipment	41.1	43.0	187,607	(D)	7,524	(D)	433	(D)
Furniture, home furnishings	13.1	14.5	32,452	48,123	2,367	3,652	126	153
Lumber, construction materials	17.9	19.1	50,694	79,946	3,429	5,476	184	231
Sporting, recreational, photographic goods [3] .	7.6	8.9	26,980	40,965	1,646	2,312	85	97
Metals and minerals, except petroleum	10.6	11.1	102,690	114,528	3,359	4,038	148	143
Electrical goods	30.4	35.3	120,062	(D)	7,462	(D)	357	(D)
Hardware, plumbing, heating equipment	21.6	23.1	43,529	57,126	4,051	5,610	217	235
Machinery, equipment, supplies	103.4	114.4	263,309	336,976	24,804	35,612	1,192	1,353
Miscellaneous.	21.7	23.4	53,889	75,506	2,726	3,777	171	184
Nondurable goods	167.8	173.9	1,116,683	1,265,205	37,841	50,905	2,072	2,278
Paper, paper products	14.5	16.8	53,493	83,173	3,586	5,202	187	228
Drugs, drug proprietaries [4]	4.0	4.9	33,987	64,280	1,975	2,968	106	120
Apparel, piece goods, notions	15.0	16.9	55,897	81,476	2,897	4,661	144	181
Groceries and related products	40.4	42.1	288,659	380,945	12,269	16,729	674	763
Farm-product raw materials.	14.4	12.6	153,419	117,606	1,839	1,847	136	117
Chemicals, allied products	11.2	12.7	76,103	94,620	2,902	3,847	124	131
Petroleum, petroleum products	20.3	16.7	296,995	234,874	3,433	3,658	188	175
Beer, wines, distilled alcoholic beverages . . .	6.7	5.8	42,122	49,433	3,091	3,849	141	146
Miscellaneous.	41.2	45.3	116,008	158,800	5,849	8,143	372	417

D Data withheld to avoid disclosure.   [1] Number of establishments in business at any time during the year.   [2] For pay period including March 12.   [3] Includes toys, hobby goods, and supplies.   [4] Includes druggists sundries.

Source of tables 1301 and 1302: U.S. Bureau of the Census, *U.S. Census of Business: 1958*, vol. III; *1963*, vol. IV; *1967*, vol. III; and *Census of Wholesale Trade: 1972*, vol. I; *1977*, WC77-A-52; *1982*, WC82-A-52; and *1987*, WC87-A-52.

No. 1303. Merchant Wholesalers—Summary: 1986 to 1991

[**Inventories and stock/sales ratios,** as of **December, seasonally adjusted.** Data reflect latest revision. Based on Current Business Survey; see Appendix III. See *Historical Statistics, Colonial Times to 1970*, series T 280-371, for related sales data]

1987 SIC code [1]	KIND OF BUSINESS	1986	1987	1988	1989	1990	1991
	SALES (bil. dol.)						
	Merchant wholesalers	**1,395.9**	**1,492.1**	**1,623.1**	**1,728.5**	**1,790.4**	**1,741.6**
50	**Durable goods**	**698.1**	**747.1**	**815.6**	**863.2**	**890.3**	**846.5**
501	Motor vehicles and automotive equipment....	152.0	156.2	165.6	164.7	169.7	154.4
502	Furniture and home furnishings	24.5	26.9	29.2	29.7	30.5	28.1
503	Lumber and other construction material	51.8	58.4	58.9	57.6	55.8	52.6
504	Professional and commercial equipment and supplies.......................	74.2	84.7	94.6	110.8	116.1	116.4
505	Metals and minerals, except petroleum......	58.9	67.6	81.6	86.9	88.9	76.3
506	Electrical goods	86.9	91.7	99.4	110.5	113.1	113.7
507	Hardware, plumbing and heating equipment. ..	39.0	41.4	42.9	44.0	45.1	41.3
508	Machinery, equipment and supplies	115.7	120.0	139.4	149.6	157.3	156.2
509	Miscellaneous durable goods	95.1	100.2	104.0	109.4	113.7	107.3
51	**Nondurable goods**	**697.8**	**745.0**	**807.4**	**865.2**	**900.2**	**895.1**
511	Paper and paper products.............	35.8	40.8	46.6	50.0	50.7	48.6
512	Drugs, drug proprietaries and druggists' sundries.......................	29.2	34.0	39.3	43.0	47.9	54.2
513	Apparel, piece goods and notions	42.4	46.6	51.9	59.0	60.8	60.7
514	Groceries and related products	222.4	223.0	228.1	242.7	246.6	254.4
515	Farm-product raw materials..............	94.1	102.2	127.9	129.5	123.2	118.0
516	Chemicals and allied products............	23.6	26.5	35.9	37.6	43.0	44.8
517	Petroleum and petroleum products........	116.4	124.9	124.4	140.7	156.3	138.7
518	Beer, wine, and distilled beverages.........	39.3	41.6	42.1	42.9	45.4	47.1
519	Miscellaneous nondurable goods	94.6	105.5	111.4	119.8	126.2	128.6
	INVENTORIES (bil. dol.)						
	Merchant wholesalers	**155.4**	**165.8**	**180.7**	**188.6**	**196.9**	**199.0**
50	**Durable goods**	**104.2**	**110.0**	**119.7**	**125.8**	**130.8**	**130.6**
501	Motor vehicles and automotive equipment....	19.3	21.2	22.5	22.1	23.8	24.3
502	Furniture and home furnishings	3.6	4.2	4.4	4.4	4.3	4.0
503	Lumber and other construction material	5.1	5.5	5.7	5.8	5.5	5.7
504	Professional and commercial equipment and supplies.......................	11.8	11.7	12.8	14.3	14.9	15.2
505	Metals and minerals, except petroleum......	8.3	8.7	10.6	10.6	10.2	8.9
506	Electrical goods	12.6	13.0	14.0	15.3	15.7	15.8
507	Hardware, plumbing and heating equipment. ..	6.4	6.6	6.7	7.2	6.9	6.6
508	Machinery, equipment and supplies	26.3	27.7	31.6	34.3	38.3	37.2
509	Miscellaneous durable goods	10.8	11.4	11.3	11.8	11.2	12.8
51	**Nondurable goods**	**51.2**	**55.8**	**61.0**	**62.8**	**66.1**	**68.4**
511	Paper and paper products.............	3.4	3.5	4.0	4.1	4.3	4.0
512	Drugs, drug proprietaries and druggists' sundries.......................	4.1	4.8	5.3	5.7	6.1	7.1
513	Apparel, piece goods and notions	7.4	7.7	8.2	9.8	10.2	10.0
514	Groceries and related products	12.1	12.5	12.5	13.1	13.2	14.8
515	Farm-product raw materials..............	6.2	7.2	9.2	7.8	8.3	8.2
516	Chemicals and allied products............	2.3	2.5	2.9	2.6	3.0	2.9
517	Petroleum and petroleum products........	3.7	3.4	3.6	3.9	4.4	4.6
518	Beer, wine, and distilled beverages.........	3.9	4.0	3.9	3.9	4.0	4.3
519	Miscellaneous nondurable goods	8.2	10.2	11.5	11.8	12.5	12.6
	STOCK/SALES RATIO						
	Merchant wholesalers	**1.31**	**1.31**	**1.28**	**1.28**	**1.32**	**1.37**
50	**Durable goods**	**1.73**	**1.74**	**1.67**	**1.73**	**1.80**	**1.85**
501	Motor vehicles and automotive equipment....	1.44	1.59	1.58	1.70	1.76	1.94
502	Furniture and home furnishings	1.75	1.82	1.71	1.80	1.75	1.81
503	Lumber and other construction material	1.13	1.12	1.12	1.29	1.33	1.25
504	Professional and commercial equipment and supplies.......................	1.76	1.65	1.47	1.43	1.49	1.55
505	Metals and minerals, except petroleum......	1.62	1.43	1.46	1.51	1.40	1.42
506	Electrical goods	1.68	1.76	1.58	1.58	1.73	1.67
507	Hardware, plumbing and heating equipment. ..	1.93	1.90	1.86	1.94	1.83	1.92
508	Machinery, equipment and supplies	2.58	2.75	2.56	2.75	2.92	2.79
509	Miscellaneous durable goods	1.48	1.33	1.27	1.21	1.20	1.45
51	**Nondurable goods**	**0.88**	**0.88**	**0.88**	**0.84**	**0.87**	**0.92**
511	Paper and paper products.............	1.09	0.93	1.01	0.97	1.04	0.98
512	Drugs, drug proprietaries and druggists' sundries.......................	1.54	1.63	1.51	1.48	1.53	1.46
513	Apparel, piece goods, and notions	2.16	1.89	1.83	1.82	1.88	1.96
514	Groceries and related products	0.66	0.66	0.61	0.64	0.65	0.69
515	Farm-product raw materials..............	0.79	0.84	0.86	0.75	0.84	0.84
516	Chemicals and allied products............	1.13	0.96	0.99	0.79	0.79	0.78
517	Petroleum and petroleum products........	0.39	0.34	0.35	0.29	0.32	0.41
518	Beer, wine, and distilled beverages.........	1.15	1.16	1.11	1.07	0.96	1.07
519	Miscellaneous nondurable goods	1.00	1.12	1.19	1.11	1.19	1.20

[1] Based on 1987 Standard Industrial Classification code; see text, section 13.

Source: U.S. Bureau of the Census, *Current Business Reports, Revised Monthly Wholesale Trade Sales and Inventories, January 1986 Through March 1992*, (BW/91-RV).

No. 1304. Wholesale Trade—Summary, by State: 1987

[Kind-of-business classification based on 1972 Standard Industrial Classification code; see text, section 13]

DIVISION AND STATE	Estab-lish-ments [1]	Sales (bil. dol.)	Paid employ-ees [2] (1,000)	Annual payroll (mil. dol.)	DIVISION AND STATE	Estab-lish-ments [1]	Sales (bil. dol.)	Paid employ-ees [2] (1,000)	Annual payroll (mil. dol.)
U.S ..	466,680	2,523.7	5,580.8	133,153	VA	8,369	44.7	114.6	2,618
					WV....	2,421	5.9	24.2	476
N.E	23,628	146.1	322.6	8,482	NC	12,037	57.0	139.8	3,059
ME	1,845	6.5	22.6	460	SC	5,229	17.1	54.3	1,063
NH	1,952	6.8	22.5	560	GA	13,580	86.8	177.8	4,111
VT	976	2.8	10.2	205	FL.....	25,482	97.3	261.0	5,545
MA	11,029	74.7	160.5	4,386	E.S.C	24,778	109.3	296.3	6,031
RI	1,708	6.0	22.2	489	KY	5,582	24.4	63.3	1,237
CT	6,116	49.2	84.6	2,382	TN	8,745	48.3	115.8	2,517
M.A	78,914	532.7	983.3	25,987	AL....	6,626	24.3	77.3	1,545
NY	41,647	283.7	465.4	12,636	MS	3,825	12.2	39.9	732
NJ....	17,575	144.6	270.7	7,524	W.S.C. ...	52,344	256.6	569.0	12,555
PA	19,692	104.4	247.2	5,827	AR	3,976	12.8	38.8	704
E.N.C....	75,156	431.6	941.4	22,925	LA.....	7,598	31.5	80.3	1,650
OH	18,577	104.0	247.5	5,757	OK	5,913	20.2	54.7	1,115
IN	9,611	40.5	107.8	2,338	TX	34,857	192.1	395.2	9,085
IL	23,521	167.4	305.9	8,072	Mt	24,666	84.1	256.1	5,444
MI.....	14,682	86.0	178.7	4,562	MT	1,792	4.4	14.8	264
WI.....	8,765	33.7	101.4	2,195	ID	2,112	5.1	20.7	353
W.N.C ...	40,506	196.0	441.1	9,608	WY	1,016	2.2	6.3	125
MN	9,436	55.3	114.1	2,820	CO	7,038	30.0	76.1	1,768
IA	6,983	24.5	65.8	1,279	NM	2,373	5.1	22.0	421
MO....	10,605	53.5	124.8	2,815	AZ	5,826	20.8	64.5	1,418
ND	2,044	6.0	17.5	324	UT	2,934	11.1	34.1	717
SD	1,783	5.2	15.3	255	NV	1,575	5.5	17.6	378
NE	3,949	21.3	43.0	834	Pac	71,398	406.6	875.7	22,075
KS	5,706	30.2	60.6	1,281	WA	9,250	41.5	102.3	2,374
S.A	75,290	360.7	895.3	20,048	OR	5,878	29.9	63.7	1,461
DE	985	7.9	15.5	452	CA	53,508	327.2	682.4	17,622
MD	6,636	41.1	99.3	2,493	AK	773	2.7	7.1	204
DC	551	2.8	8.8	231	HI.....	1,989	5.4	20.1	415

[1] Number of establishments in business at any time during the year.   [2] For the pay period including March 12.

Source: U.S. Bureau of the Census, *1987 Census of Wholesale Trade,* Geographic Area Series, WC87-A-1 to 52.

No. 1305. Wholesale Trade—Establishments and Sales by Selected Metropolitan Areas: 1987

[Kind-of-business classification based on 1987 Standard Industrial Classification code; see text, section 13. Metropolitan statistical areas (MSA's) and consolidated metropolitan statistical areas (CMSA's) are as defined by the U.S. Office of Management and Budget as of June 30, 1987; see Appendix II for definitions and components]

METROPOLITAN AREA	ALL ESTABLISHMENTS [1]			MERCHANT WHOLESALERS	
	Estab-lish-ments	Sales		Estab-lish-ments	Sales (bil. dol.)
		Amount (bil. dol.)	Percent of U.S. total		
New York-Northern New Jersey-Long Island, NY-NJ-CT CMSA.	47,892	398.6	15.8	40,796	271.7
Los Angeles-Anaheim-Riverside, CA CMSA.	28,918	203.5	8.1	24,155	137.7
Chicago-Gary-Lake County, IL-IN-WI CMSA.	17,043	139.8	5.5	12,978	63.9
San Francisco-Oakland-San Jose, CA CMSA.	12,714	83.4	3.3	10,089	40.4
Philadelphia-Wilmington-Trenton, PA-NJ-DE-MD CMSA	11,192	73.6	2.9	8,859	33.6
Houston-Galveston-Brazoria, TX CMSA	8,258	72.4	2.9	6,651	42.5
Dallas-Fort Worth, TX CMSA	10,158	71.1	2.8	7,523	27.3
Atlanta, GA MSA	7,963	70.0	2.8	5,655	23.1
Boston-Lawrence-Salem, MA-NH CMSA.	8,694	66.5	2.6	6,807	36.0
Detroit-Ann Arbor, MI CMSA.	8,122	60.5	2.4	6,141	23.0
Minneapolis-St. Paul, MN-WI MSA	5,645	44.7	1.8	4,189	24.3
Cleveland-Akron-Lorain, OH CMSA	5,675	34.2	1.4	4,270	14.4
Miami-Fort Lauderdale, FL CMSA	9,924	33.5	1.3	8,637	24.1
St. Louis, MO-IL MSA	5,057	31.7	1.3	3,875	15.1
Seattle-Tacoma, WA CMSA	5,745	31.3	1.2	4,490	18.2
Washington, DC-MD-VA MSA	4,353	31.2	1.2	3,509	13.5
Kansas City, MO-KS MSA	3,710	30.1	1.2	2,726	14.6
Cincinnati-Hamilton, OH-KY-IN CMSA.	3,283	26.9	1.1	2,358	9.5
Pittsburgh-Beaver Valley, PA CMSA.	4,051	26.5	1.1	3,140	10.7
Charlotte-Gastonia-Rock Hill, NC-SC MSA	3,394	25.7	1.0	2,477	7.7

[1] Includes other types of operations, not shown separately.

Source: U.S. Bureau of the Census, *1987 Census of Wholesale Trade,* Geographic Area Series, WC87-A-52.

No. 1306. Selected Service Industries—Summary: 1982 and 1987

[For establishments with payroll]

1972 SIC code [1]	KIND OF BUSINESS	ESTABLISH-MENTS [2] (1,000)		RECEIPTS OR EXPENSES [3] (mil. dol.)		PAID EMPLOYEES [4] (1,000)	
		1982	1987	1982	1987	1982	1987
(X)	**Firms subject to Federal income tax [5]**	**1,339.2**	**1,624.6**	**426,982**	**752,474**	**11,106**	**15,688**
70	Hotels, rooming houses, camps, and other lodging places	44.3	46.8	33,215	51,865	1,102	1,411
72	Personal services	179.6	196.1	22,980	35,133	970	1,209
73	Business services	230.1	339.3	106,866	216,807	3,152	5,250
75	Automotive repair, services, and parking	123.6	151.2	30,695	51,423	553	785
76	Miscellaneous repair services	58.2	65.5	14,133	20,838	300	346
78, 79	Amusement and recreation services [6]	73.0	74.3	33,115	52,808	804	929
80 ex. 806	Health services, except hospitals	360.4	405.4	95,610	162,569	2,433	3,226
81	Legal services	122.7	138.2	34,325	66,998	569	808
823, 4, 9	Selected educational services	7.8	10.6	2,400	4,882	68	109
83	Social services	29.7	43.1	3,636	7,330	222	357
891	Engineering, architectural, surveying services	47.6	62.3	34,315	53,563	581	747
893	Accounting, auditing, and bookkeeping services . . .	55.3	69.8	14,596	24,483	330	448
(X)	**Firms exempt from Federal income tax [5]** . . .	**151.6**	**169.9**	**54,522**	**87,448**	**2,280**	**2,773**
805, 8, 9	Selected health services.	10.2	13.2	10,438	19,084	476	684
83	Social services	54.2	63.0	16,455	26,884	904	1,110
861,2,4,9	Selected membership organizations	63.2	68.0	15,093	22,028	493	539

X Not applicable. [1] Based on 1972 Standard Industrial Classification; see text, section 13. [2] Number of establishments in business at any time during the year. [3] Receipts refer to establishments subject to Federal income tax. Expenses refer to establishments exempt from Federal income tax. [4] For pay period including March 12. [5] Excludes hospitals. Includes other kinds of business, not shown separately. [6] Includes motion pictures.

Source: U.S. Bureau of the Census, *1987 Census of Service Industries*, Geographic Area Series, SC87-A-52.

No. 1307. Service Industries—Summary of Establishments, by State: 1987

[Based on 1987 Standard Industrial Classification code; see text, section 13]

DIVISION AND STATE	FIRMS SUBJECT TO FEDERAL INCOME TAX			TAX-EXEMPT FIRMS [3]		DIVISION AND STATE	FIRMS SUBJECT TO FEDERAL INCOME TAX			TAX-EXEMPT FIRMS [3]	
	Establishments [1] (1,000)	Receipts (mil. dol.)	Paid employees [2] (1,000)	Establishments [1]	Revenues (mil. dol.)		Establishments [1] (1,000)	Receipts (mil. dol.)	Paid employees [2] (1,000)	Establishments [1]	Revenues (mil. dol.)
U.S	**6,254.5**	**868,343**	**16,055**	**175,829**	**267,490**	VA. .	137.3	22,172	439	3,885	6,304
						WV . .	32.2	3,249	67	1,407	1,625
N.E . . .	**385.9**	**55,493**	**997**	**13,154**	**19,577**	NC . .	130.9	14,354	331	3,884	5,083
ME. .	32.8	2,728	58	1,406	1,258	SC . .	62.6	7,146	170	1,756	2,217
NH. .	32.1	3,541	68	1,127	984	GA. .	134.3	20,644	415	3,140	5,131
VT . .	18.2	1,591	37	897	587	FL . .	340.8	50,997	975	7,028	9,875
MA. .	184.0	30,252	523	6,005	11,115	**E.S.C .**	**286.0**	**33,760**	**723**	**8,638**	**11,777**
RI . .	24.5	2,955	61	895	1,417	KY . .	74.9	7,267	166	2,213	2,655
CT . .	94.3	14,426	250	2,824	4,216	TN . .	101.5	13,449	283	3,010	4,320
M.A. . .	**940.7**	**156,935**	**2,582**	**28,944**	**54,676**	AL . .	69.1	9,198	190	1,947	3,024
NY . .	476.5	83,524	1,293	13,891	30,583	MS . .	40.5	3,846	84	1,468	1,778
NJ . .	198.3	35,953	596	4,196	7,618	**W.S.C .**	**682.4**	**81,375**	**1,545**	**14,803**	**19,660**
PA . .	265.9	37,458	694	10,857	16,475	AR . .	49.1	4,295	94	1,579	1,751
E.N.C .	**925.7**	**120,455**	**2,459**	**30,592**	**49,332**	LA . .	92.3	11,583	241	2,087	3,334
OH. .	232.1	29,471	648	8,222	12,973	OK . .	91.1	7,575	149	2,133	2,616
IN . .	117.5	12,605	282	4,396	5,389	TX . .	449.9	57,922	1,061	9,004	11,959
IL . .	277.0	40,742	730	7,907	15,201	**Mt. . . .**	**393.6**	**50,083**	**994**	**9,868**	**11,371**
MI . .	203.5	26,574	533	6,205	10,827	MT. .	24.6	1,680	36	1,170	779
WI . .	95.6	11,063	265	3,862	4,942	ID . .	25.7	2,355	48	727	594
W.N.C .	**459.9**	**46,696**	**1,021**	**17,372**	**20,282**	WY . .	14.4	1,041	22	640	403
MN . .	121.9	13,196	295	4,412	5,781	CO . .	125.8	13,236	256	2,780	3,580
IA . .	69.0	5,830	131	3,122	2,928	NM . .	36.4	4,655	88	1,232	1,124
MO .	122.9	15,173	324	3,679	6,078	AZ . .	91.8	11,981	244	2,020	3,241
ND. .	16.6	1,244	28	920	843	UT . .	44.6	4,407	94	768	1,114
SD. .	17.9	1,177	27	957	757	NV . .	30.3	10,728	206	531	536
NE . .	42.3	4,004	89	1,679	1,583	**Pac. . .**	**1,180.2**	**175,020**	**2,802**	**25,457**	**38,437**
KS . .	69.3	6,072	128	2,603	2,312	WA . .	131.3	14,495	277	4,238	4,578
S.A. . . .	**1,000.3**	**148,531**	**2,932**	**27,001**	**42,376**	OR. .	82.1	7,509	157	2,467	2,611
DE. .	15.1	2,313	46	562	730	CA . .	918.5	146,288	2,248	17,048	29,382
MD. .	125.0	19,369	369	3,156	5,570	AK . .	18.2	1,826	28	706	644
DC. .	22.1	8,287	121	2,183	5,841	HI . .	30.1	4,902	92	998	1,222

[1] Number of establishments in business at any time during year. [2] For the pay period including March 12. [3] Covers only establishments with payroll.

Source: U.S. Bureau of the Census, *1987 Census of Service Industries*, Geographic Area Series, SC87-A-1 to 52 and Nonemployer Statistics Series, SC87-N-1 to 4.

No. 1308. Service Industries—Summary of Establishments, by Tax Status: 1987

[Data for firms subject to Federal income tax cover all establishments, except as noted. Data for firms exempt from Federal income tax cover only establishments with payroll. See *Historical Statistics, Colonial Times to 1970*, series T 391-443, for similar but not comparable data]

1987 SIC code [1]	KIND OF BUSINESS	Establishments [2] (1,000)	Receipts or revenues [3] (mil. dol.)	Annual payroll (mil. dol.)	Paid employees [4] (1,000)	Receipts or revenues per establishment [3] ($1,000)	Annual payroll per employee (dol.)
(X)	**Firms subject to Federal income tax [5]** ...	6,254.5	868,343	289,807	16,054.7	138.8	18,051
70 ex. 704	Hotels, rooming houses, camps, and other lodging places [5] [6]	85.7	53,630	14,452	1,410.8	625.8	10,244
701	Hotels and motels	63.4	51,633	14,135	1,380.2	814.4	10,241
72	Personal services [5]	1,037.4	43,247	10,853	1,105.0	41.7	9,822
721	Laundry, cleaning, and garment services	108.6	14,184	4,388	408.3	130.6	10,746
722	Photographic studios, portrait	56.2	2,929	514	50.1	52.1	10,253
723, 4	Beauty and barber shops	407.3	11,990	3,538	390.7	29.4	9,055
726	Funeral service and crematories	22.3	5,668	1,362	82.6	254.2	16,479
73	Business services [5]	1,433.2	188,856	66,456	4,414.4	131.8	15,054
731	Advertising	79.2	16,802	5,537	181.6	212.1	30,493
732	Consumer credit, mercantile reporting agencies [7]	[8] 7.1	[8] 4,124	1,415	82.8	[8] 582.8	17,078
733	Mailing, reproduction, commercial art [9]	[8] 27.2	[8] 12,407	3,945	210.6	[8] 455.6	18,729
734	Services to dwellings and other buildings	290.4	15,649	6,555	746.0	53.9	8,788
735	Miscellaneous equipment rental and leasing	49.1	15,472	3,579	185.3	315.1	19,319
736	Personnel supply services	43.2	20,336	13,590	1,397.1	470.7	9,727
737	Computer programming, data processing [10]	140.5	56,004	19,142	637.4	398.6	30,031
7381, 2	Detective agencies and protective services	45.2	9,303	5,040	475.8	205.8	10,594
75	Automotive repair, services, and parking	388.2	58,278	11,690	785.3	150.1	14,886
751	Automotive rental and leasing, without drivers	19.9	16,679	2,366	134.6	838.1	17,578
752	Automobile parking	10.5	2,691	491	45.7	256.3	10,751
753	Automotive repair shops	301.3	34,182	7,727	485.6	113.4	15,913
754	Automotive services, except repair	56.4	4,726	1,106	119.4	83.8	9,258
76	Miscellaneous repair services [5]	247.6	24,597	6,416	345.8	99.3	18,551
762	Electrical repair shops	65.7	7,584	2,107	107.4	115.4	19,618
78, 79, 84	Amusement and recreation services [5] [11]	467.0	64,524	15,474	1,094.4	138.2	14,139
781, 2	Motion picture prod., distribution, services	37.1	20,778	4,973	171.3	560.1	29,029
783	Motion picture theaters	8.6	4,056	584	94.1	471.6	6,211
784	Video tape rental	24.7	2,920	581	79.6	118.2	7,300
792	Theatrical producers, bands, entertainers [12]	186.9	7,725	1,607	55.2	41.3	29,092
793	Bowling centers	8.3	2,597	702	99.8	313.1	7,039
794	Commercial sports	50.6	5,966	2,047	75.5	117.9	27,106
7991	Physical fitness facilities	22.3	2,721	745	104.9	122.0	7,097
7996	Amusement parks	[8] 0.7	[8] 3,470	820	60.4	[8] 4,663.8	13,566
7997	Membership sports and recreation clubs	[8] 7.7	[8] 3,700	1,173	112.7	[8] 483.1	10,403
80	Health services [5]	800.6	196,211	78,820	3,592.5	245.1	21,940
801	Offices and clinics of doctors of medicine	297.7	96,698	43,856	1,131.6	324.8	38,756
802	Offices and clinics of dentists	131.3	25,258	8,760	491.5	192.4	17,822
8041	Offices and clinics of chiropractors	31.4	3,707	900	58.0	118.0	15,504
8042	Offices and clinics of optometrists	23.1	3,755	893	57.9	162.8	15,429
805	Nursing and personal care facilities	38.3	20,570	9,465	961.6	537.1	9,843
806	Hospitals	[8] 1.4	[8] 19,720	6,582	366.5	[8] 14,136.2	17,958
807	Medical and dental laboratories	[9] 14.8	[8] 7,114	2,567	131.8	[8] 479.4	19,474
808	Home health care services	[8] 5.1	[8] 3,024	1,578	184.8	[8] 595.3	8,542
81	Legal services	273.2	72,115	26,078	807.6	264.0	32,291
823, 4, 9	Selected educational services [5]	155.9	6,102	1,657	109.4	39.1	15,144
824	Vocational schools	[8] 3.7	[8] 3,058	1,086	65.3	[8] 826.1	16,637
83	Social services [5]	319.5	9,561	2,971	357.3	29.9	8,315
835	Child day care services	248.7	4,284	1,307	199.7	17.2	6,547
871	Engineering, architectural, and surveying services	195.3	57,051	23,109	747.0	292.1	31,024
872	Accounting, auditing, and bookkeeping services	250.1	26,612	10,204	448.1	106.4	22,768
873 ex. 8733	Research, development, and testing services [13]	[8] 12.4	[8] 14,184	5,615	222.2	[8] 1,144.8	25,266
874	Management and public relations services	418.8	43,381	14,515	551.8	103.6	26,303
(X)	**Firms exempt from Federal income tax [5]**	175.8	267,490	117,976	6,736.7	1,521.3	17,513
7997	Membership sports and recreation clubs	6.5	3,694	1,467	116.4	564.0	12,607
84	Museums, art galleries, botanical gardens, and zoos	2.7	2,597	778	52.1	961.9	14,933
805	Nursing and personal care facilities	4.1	8,201	4,264	371.5	1,995.5	11,479
806	Hospitals	5.9	172,001	82,342	3,964.1	29,137.9	20,772
83	Social services [5]	63.0	31,552	11,617	1,109.5	500.8	10,470
832	Individual and family social services	21.9	8,585	3,629	312.7	392.7	11,606
833	Job training, vocational rehabilitation services	5.0	3,664	1,741	238.2	732.0	7,307
836	Residential care	10.5	6,125	2,768	240.5	584.8	11,507
861	Business associations	12.3	6,756	1,996	87.5	549.3	22,819
862	Professional membership organizations	5.6	4,110	1,133	49.3	732.6	22,981
864	Civic, social, and fraternal associations	40.4	8,569	2,779	322.9	212.0	8,604
873	Research, development, and testing services	3.2	8,303	3,088	107.8	2,623.5	28,643

X Not applicable. [1] Based on 1987 Standard Industrial Classification; see text, section 13. [2] Represents the number of establishments in business at any time during year. [3] Receipts refer to establishments subject to Federal income tax. Revenues refer to establishments exempt from Federal income tax. [4] For pay period including March 12. [5] Includes other kinds of businesses, not shown separately. [6] Excludes membership lodging. [7] Includes adjustment and collection agencies. [8] Covers only establishments with payroll. [9] Includes photography and stenographic services. [10] Includes other computer related services. [11] Includes motion pictures and museums. [12] Excludes motion picture producers and includes orchestras. [13] Excludes noncommercial research organizations.

Source: U.S. Bureau of the Census, *1987 Census of Service Industries*, SC87-A-52 and SC87-N-1. # #end# #

No. 1309. Services—Establishments, Employees, and Payroll: 1987 to 1989

[Covers establishments with payroll. Excludes government employees, railroad employees, self-employed persons, etc. For statement on methodology, see Appendix III]

1987 SIC code [1]	KIND OF BUSINESS	ESTABLISHMENTS (1,000)			EMPLOYEES (1,000)		PAYROLL (bil. dol.)	
		1987	1988	1989	1988	1989	1988	1989
(l)	**Services, total [2]**	1,980.1	1,937.5	1,977.3	25,143	27,339	477.8	543.8
70	Hotels and other lodging places [2]	51.4	49.0	50.0	1,385	1,468	15.8	17.4
701	Hotels and motels	(NA)	38.8	39.5	1,333	1,409	15.2	16.7
72	Personal services [2]	184.4	177.3	181.2	1,101	1,142	11.7	12.5
721	Laundry, cleaning, and garment services [2] .	(NA)	48.1	49.4	406	409	4.7	4.9
7215	Coin-operated laundries and cleaning . . .	(NA)	11.7	11.6	45	45	0.4	0.4
7216	Drycleaning plants, except rug.	(NA)	19.4	19.6	158	156	1.6	1.6
723	Beauty shops	(NA)	75.3	74.9	363	357	3.5	3.6
726	Funeral service and crematories	(NA)	15.1	15.1	81	85	1.5	1.6
73	Business services [2]	248.0	250.5	263.6	4,385	4,749	78.0	87.1
731	Advertising	(NA)	17.9	17.7	194	199	6.5	6.8
7311	Advertising agencies	(NA)	12.0	11.0	136	139	4.9	5.1
733	Mailing, reproduction, and stenographic services	(NA)	25.2	24.5	219	221	4.6	4.7
734	Services to buildings.	(NA)	44.0	45.3	743	765	7.3	7.7
735	Miscellaneous equipment rental and leasing	(NA)	24.0	22.3	193	207	4.3	4.7
736	Personnel supply services [2]	(NA)	24.4	25.2	1,247	1,390	16.2	18.1
7361	Employment agencies	(NA)	11.8	12.0	169	202	2.9	3.4
7363	Help supply services	(NA)	12.6	12.5	1,076	1,154	13.2	14.3
737	Computer and data processing services [2] . .	(NA)	37.9	37.8	679	722	22.7	25.0
7371	Computer programming services	(NA)	13.2	12.1	203	208	7.8	8.1
7374	Data processing and preparation	(NA)	6.8	6.8	218	223	5.4	5.8
738	Miscellaneous business services.	(NA)	60.5	55.4	1,001	1,019	14.3	15.6
7381	Detective and armored car services . . .	(NA)	9.4	8.9	436	438	4.4	4.7
75	Automotive repair, services, and parking [2] . . .	149.8	145.5	151.1	813	843	13.2	14.0
751	Automotive rentals, no drivers	(NA)	11.4	10.7	150	144	2.8	2.8
753	Automotive repair shops [2]	(NA)	108.2	111.2	483	495	8.5	9.0
7532	Top and body repair and paint shops . . .	(NA)	30.7	30.3	162	161	3.0	3.1
7538	General automotive repair shops	(NA)	52.2	54.4	202	211	3.4	3.6
754	Automotive services, except repair	(NA)	15.5	16.3	128	140	1.3	1.4
76	Miscellaneous repair services	64.1	61.8	62.9	356	373	7.3	7.8
762	Electrical repair shops.	(NA)	17.1	16.5	107	111	2.4	2.5
78	Motion pictures [2].	34.9	33.5	35.2	370	348	6.7	6.9
781	Motion picture production and services . . .	(NA)	9.0	8.8	159	129	4.5	4.6
784	Video tape rental	(NA)	15.5	17.2	87	96	0.6	0.7
79	Amusement and recreation services [2]	72.4	70.5	70.3	909	956	13.2	14.1
7997	Membership sports and recreation clubs . .	(NA)	13.5	13.1	223	232	3.0	3.2
80	Health services [2].	424.2	417.2	425.1	7,222	8,430	159.1	195.6
801	Offices and clinics of medical doctors	(NA)	192.0	192.2	1,242	1,304	51.1	55.7
802	Offices and clinics of dentists.	(NA)	102.2	103.3	499	513	10.0	10.6
8041	Offices and clinics of chiropractors	(NA)	20.1	21.7	61	67	1.0	1.2
8042	Offices and clinics of optometrists.	(NA)	15.3	15.0	58	59	1.0	1.0
805	Nursing and personal care facilities	(NA)	18.0	18.2	1,358	1,420	15.1	16.6
806	Hospitals	(NA)	5.2	6.2	3,213	4,197	67.2	94.5
807	Medical and dental laboratories	(NA)	14.3	14.6	139	149	3.0	3.4
808	Home health care services	(NA)	7.5	7.5	303	318	3.2	3.9
81	Legal services	139.8	135.7	137.3	849	892	30.3	32.9
82	Educational services [2]	34.2	33.2	34.1	1,631	1,704	25.0	27.2
821	Elementary and secondary schools	(NA)	14.5	14.3	434	440	5.7	6.1
822	Colleges and universities.	(NA)	3.0	3.1	1,013	1,055	16.3	17.8
83	Social services [2]	104.2	104.8	108.5	1,532	1,630	16.6	18.4
832	Individual and family services	(NA)	25.9	26.0	355	377	4.4	4.9
833	Job training and related services.	(NA)	6.7	6.6	271	280	2.3	2.5
835	Child day care services	(NA)	39.2	38.8	368	383	2.8	3.1
836	Residential care.	(NA)	19.3	19.7	358	388	4.2	4.8
86	Membership organizations [2]	221.6	214.3	219.7	1,778	1,837	19.4	20.9
861	Business associations.	(NA)	12.0	12.2	92	95	2.3	2.5
863	Labor organizations	(NA)	20.0	19.5	179	179	2.5	2.6
864	Civic and social associations	(NA)	39.0	39.6	330	346	3.1	3.4
866	Religious organizations	(NA)	126.8	131.8	1,036	1,072	8.7	9.4
87	Engineering and management services [2]	204.1	199.0	189.6	2,302	2,384	67.7	72.7
8711	Engineering services.	(NA)	35.6	32.7	592	624	21.0	22.5
8712	Architectural services	(NA)	17.1	16.0	141	143	4.5	4.7
872	Accounting, auditing, and bookkeeping. . . .	(NA)	66.2	64.9	498	509	11.9	12.7
873	Research and testing services	(NA)	15.1	13.9	360	371	10.3	11.1
8731	Commercial physical research.	(NA)	3.9	3.4	159	159	5.6	6.0
8741	Management services.	(NA)	17.1	15.1	283	285	6.9	7.3
8742	Management consulting services	(NA)	26.0	22.7	218	217	7.4	7.7

NA Not available.   [1] Based on 1987 Standard Industrial Classification; see text, section 13.   [2] Includes kinds of business not shown separately.

Source: U.S. Bureau of the Census, *County Business Patterns*, annual.

No. 1310. Service Industries—Annual Receipts of Taxable Firms: 1980 to 1990

[**In billions of dollars.** Estimated]

1972 SIC code [1]	KIND OF BUSINESS	1980	1985	1986	1987	1988	1989	1990
70	Hotels, camps, and other lodging places	(NA)	45.9	48.1	54.1	58.9	61.1	63.7
701	Hotels, motels, and tourist courts	27.0	43.5	45.8	51.6	56.1	58.1	60.5
72	Personal services [2]	25.1	39.4	42.8	47.0	54.1	59.6	65.2
721	Laundry, cleaning, and garment services	9.2	12.8	13.3	14.2	15.8	16.7	17.5
722	Photographic studios, portrait	(NA)	2.4	2.7	2.9	3.3	3.5	3.8
723	Beauty shops	5.8	9.0	9.7	10.6	11.7	13.0	13.6
726	Funeral service and crematories	3.5	5.2	5.4	5.7	6.1	6.2	6.5
73	Business services [2]	(NA)	207.3	226.9	247.8	289.1	318.2	345.1
731	Advertising	(NA)	14.9	15.8	16.8	18.3	19.0	19.9
7311	Advertising agencies	(NA)	11.1	11.7	12.0	13.2	13.6	14.1
732	Credit reporting and collection agencies	(NA)	4.2	4.5	5.3	5.5	6.1	6.7
733	Mailing, reproduction, and stenographic services	(NA)	12.9	14.1	15.8	17.8	19.4	21.4
7331	Direct mail advertising services	(NA)	4.2	4.8	5.2	6.0	6.0	6.7
7333	Commercial photography, art, and graphics	(NA)	5.7	5.9	6.7	7.3	8.1	9.1
734	Services to dwellings and other buildings	(NA)	13.3	14.6	15.6	17.5	20.1	22.1
7342	Disinfecting and exterminating services	(NA)	2.7	2.8	3.2	3.5	3.7	4.0
7349	Cleaning and maintenance services to dwellings, and other buildings, n.e.c. [3]	(NA)	10.5	11.7	12.3	13.8	16.2	17.8
736	Personnel supply services [2]	(NA)	17.7	20.0	24.0	28.6	31.6	34.8
7361	Employment agencies	(NA)	3.4	3.7	3.9	4.8	5.6	6.7
7362	Temporary help supply services	(NA)	11.2	12.7	16.3	19.9	21.6	23.4
737	Computer and data processing services	(NA)	45.2	50.6	56.0	66.4	74.1	80.3
7372	Computer programming and other software services . .	(NA)	21.0	24.0	28.1	34.8	40.5	43.7
7374	Data processing services	(NA)	15.2	16.4	17.0	18.9	20.0	21.3
7379	Computer related services, n.e.c. [3]	(NA)	9.0	10.1	10.9	12.8	13.6	15.3
7391	Research and development laboratories [4]	(NA)	7.7	8.8	9.2	11.2	12.9	14.6
7392	Management, consulting, and public relations services [4] .	(NA)	38.5	42.3	44.3	52.5	57.3	61.2
7393	Detective agencies and protective services	(NA)	7.3	8.2	9.3	10.9	11.4	11.3
7394	Equipment rental and leasing services	(NA)	15.7	16.3	16.9	20.0	21.3	22.4
7395	Photofinishing laboratories	(NA)	4.7	4.9	5.1	5.6	6.1	6.0
7397	Commercial testing laboratories . . . . . [2]	(NA)	2.7	2.8	3.1	4.1	5.0	6.0
75	Automotive repair, services, and garages [2]	30.5	51.8	53.9	58.3	66.2	71.4	74.5
751	Automotive rental and leasing [2]	8.8	14.6	15.5	16.7	18.7	19.4	20.4
7512	Passenger car rental and leasing	4.7	8.8	9.4	10.0	11.2	11.7	12.5
7513	Truck rental and leasing	4.0	5.5	5.8	6.5	7.3	7.4	7.6
752	Automobile parking	(NA)	2.1	2.4	2.7	3.2	3.6	3.7
753	Automotive repair shops	18.1	30.6	31.6	34.2	38.5	41.9	43.5
76	Miscellaneous repair services	15.4	20.7	22.4	24.6	27.4	29.4	31.8
78	Motion pictures	12.5	18.9	20.9	24.8	27.4	30.6	33.0
781,2	Motion picture production, distribution, allied services . . .	8.9	15.1	17.0	20.8	23.3	26.1	28.4
783	Motion picture theaters	(NA)	3.8	3.9	4.1	4.2	4.5	4.6
79	Amusement and recreation services [2]	(NA)	29.8	32.2	34.5	37.8	40.0	44.1
792	Theatrical producers, bands, orchestras, and entertainers [4]	(NA)	6.4	7.6	7.7	8.2	7.6	9.4
793	Bowling alleys and billiard and pool establishments	(NA)	2.7	2.7	2.7	2.9	3.1	3.3
794	Commercial sports	3.3	5.0	5.1	6.0	6.7	7.3	8.2
7996	Amusement parks	(NA)	2.6	3.0	3.5	3.9	4.3	4.6
7997	Membership sports and recreation clubs	(NA)	4.0	4.4	4.6	4.9	5.0	5.4
80	Health services [2 5]	(NA)	146.5	161.6	182.3	204.3	221.7	245.7
801	Offices of physicians	38.8	66.8	72.6	83.8	94.4	101.7	111.9
802	Offices of dentists	12.6	20.4	21.7	23.8	25.7	27.6	29.7
804	Offices of other health practitioners	3.9	7.9	8.8	10.3	12.0	12.4	14.2
8041	Offices of chiropractors	(NA)	2.7	3.0	3.3	4.0	4.5	4.9
8042	Offices of optometrists	(NA)	2.8	3.0	3.5	3.8	3.9	4.4
805	Nursing and personal care facilities [4]	(NA)	17.5	19.0	20.1	21.2	23.1	26.0
806	Hospitals [4]	(NA)	15.7	18.1	19.7	21.7	22.7	25.2
8071	Medical laboratories	(NA)	3.9	4.5	5.5	7.0	8.4	10.0
808	Outpatient care facilities [4]	(NA)	7.1	8.8	10.7	12.6	15.5	16.4
81	Legal services [4 5]	25.7	52.8	58.9	67.0	76.0	83.1	91.1
835	Child day care services	(NA)	2.6	2.9	2.9	3.6	3.9	4.4
891	Engineering and architectural services	(NA)	49.3	51.3	57.1	62.9	71.3	79.6
893	Accounting, auditing, and bookkeeping	(NA)	21.2	22.9	26.6	29.7	33.3	34.2
4722	Arrangement of passenger transportation	(NA)	6.3	6.6	7.3	8.1	8.9	9.5
653	Real estate agents and managers [5]	(NA)	31.3	34.9	38.1	42.1	44.1	44.0
824	Correspondence schools and vocational schools	(NA)	2.9	3.3	3.4	4.2	4.4	4.3

NA Not available. [1] Standard Industrial Classification; see text, section 13. [2] Includes other kinds of businesses, not shown separately. [3] N.e.c. means not elsewhere classified. [4] For data on tax-exempt organizations, see table 1311. [5] Excludes nonemployers.

Source: U.S. Bureau of the Census, *Current Business Reports*, series BS, *1990 Service Annual Survey*.

No. 1311. Selected Service Industries—Annual Revenues of Tax-Exempt Firms: 1985 to 1990

[In billions of dollars. Estimated]

1972 SIC code [1]	KIND OF BUSINESS	1985	1986	1987	1988	1989	1990
7391,2,7 792,7997, 7999	Selected business services [2]	3.6	4.0	5.1	5.5	6.1	6.5
	Selected amusement services [3]	5.2	5.5	6.4	6.9	7.4	8.1
805,6,8,9	Selected health services [4]	115.5	126.1	143.3	160.9	181.3	208.9
805	Nursing and personal care facilities	6.8	7.4	8.2	9.3	10.4	11.8
806	Hospitals	99.1	108.0	123.5	138.3	155.3	178.8
808	Outpatient care facilities	7.0	7.8	8.3	9.4	11.4	13.2
81	Legal services	0.5	0.6	0.7	0.7	0.8	0.9
833	Job training and vocational rehabilitation services	3.1	3.4	3.7	4.1	4.4	4.7
835	Child day care services	1.8	1.9	2.2	2.4	2.7	2.8
836	Residential care	4.9	5.4	6.1	7.1	8.0	8.7
892	Noncommercial educational, scientific, and research organizations	3.5	3.9	4.1	4.5	4.8	5.5

[1] Standard Industrial Classification; see text, section 13.   [2] Covers research and development laboratories (SIC 7391); management, consulting, and public relations services (SIC 7392); and commercial testing laboratories (SIC 7397).   [3] Covers theatrical producers, bands, orchestras, and entertainers (SIC 7999); membership sports and recreation clubs (SIC 7997); and amusement and recreation services, not elsewhere classified (SIC 7999).   [4] Includes health and allied services, not elsewhere classified (SIC 809).

Source: U.S. Bureau of the Census, *Current Business Reports*, series BS, *1990 Service Annual Survey.*

No. 1312. Computer Programming and Data Processing—Establishments, Employees, and Payroll: 1989

[Covers establishments with payroll. Excludes government employees, railroad employees, self-employed persons, etc. For statement on methodology, see Appendix III]

1987 SIC code [1]	KIND OF BUSINESS	Establishments	Employees (1,000)	Annual payroll (mil. dol.)	STATE	COMPUTER PROGRAMMING, DATA PROCESSING (SIC 737)		
						Establishments	Employees (1,000)	Annual payroll (mil. dol.)
737	Computer programming, data processing, total	37,752	721.8	25,033	CA	6,190	115.2	4,361
7371	Computer programming services	12,057	208.4	8,086	FL	1,680	30.6	917
7372	Prepackaged software	3,643	68.0	2,883	IL	1,906	33.9	1,159
7373	Computer integrated systems design	3,191	72.2	2,946	MD	1,172	35.0	1,300
7374	Computer processing and data preparation and processing services	6,776	222.7	5,818	MA	1,442	39.2	1,632
7375	Information retrieval services	446	14.5	436	NJ	2,226	37.8	1,414
7376	Computer facilities managements services	640	22.7	645	NY	3,104	43.7	1,550
7377	Computer rental and leasing	865	11.5	476	TX	2,653	49.9	1,800
7378	Computer maintenance and repair	3,261	51.2	1,818	VA	1,436	47.3	1,713
7379	Computer related services, n.e.c. [2]	5,348	46.4	1,769				

[1] Based on 1987 Standard Industrial Classification; see text, section 13.   [2] N.e.c. means not elsewhere classified.

Source: U.S. Bureau of the Census, *County Business Patterns 1989.*

No. 1313. National Nonprofit Associations—Number, by Type: 1980 to 1991

[Data compiled during last few months of year previous to year shown and the beginning months of year shown]

TYPE	1980	1985	1990	1991	TYPE	1980	1985	1990	1991
Total	14,726	19,121	22,289	22,389	Fraternal, foreign interest, nationality, ethnic	435	492	573	565
Trade, business, commercial	3,118	3,719	3,918	3,911	Religious	797	953	1,172	1,177
Agriculture	677	882	940	1,055	Veteran, hereditary, patriotic	208	281	462	542
Legal, governmental, public admin., military	529	658	792	794	Hobby, avocational	910	1,311	1,475	1,499
Scientific, engineering, tech	1,039	1,270	1,417	1,378	Athletic sports	504	737	840	849
Educational	[1]2,376	[1]2,822	1,291	1,301	Labor unions	235	252	253	253
Cultural	([1])	([1])	1,886	1,884	Chambers of Commerce [2]	105	142	168	168
Social welfare	994	1,450	1,705	1,742	Greek and non-Greek letter societies	318	331	340	341
Health, medical	1,413	1,886	2,227	2,229	Fan clubs	(NA)	(NA)	581	519
Public affairs	1,068	1,935	2,249	2,182					

NA Not available.   [1] Data for cultural associations included with educational associations.   [2] National and binational.

Source: Gale Research Inc., Detroit, MI. Compiled from *Encyclopedia of Associations*, annual, (copyright).

Foreign Commerce and Aid

This section presents data on the flow of goods, services, and capital between the United States and other countries; changes in official reserve assets of the United States; international investments; foreign assistance programs; and import duties.

The Bureau of Economic Analysis publishes current figures on U.S. international transactions and the U.S. international investment position in its monthly *Survey of Current Business.* Statistics for the foreign aid programs are presented by the Agency for International Development (AID) in its annual *U.S. Overseas Loans and Grants and Assistance from International Organizations;* and by the Department of Agriculture in its *Foreign Agricultural Trade of the United States.*

The principal source of merchandise import and export data is the Bureau of the Census. Current data are presented monthly in *U.S. Merchandise Trade*, report series FT 900, and *U.S. Merchandise Trade: Exports, General Imports, and Imports for Consumption,* report series FT 925. The *Bureau of the Census Catalog* and the *Guide to Foreign Trade Statistics* lists the Bureau's monthly and annual reports in this field. In addition, the International Trade Administration and the Bureau of Economic Analysis present summary as well as selected commodity and country data for U.S. foreign trade in the *Overseas Business Reports* and the *Survey of Current Business,* respectively. The merchandise trade data in the latter source include balance of payments adjustments to the Census data. The Treasury Department's *Monthly Treasury Statement of Receipts and Outlays of the United States Government* contains information on import duties.

International accounts.—The international transactions tables (Nos. 1314 to 1316) show, for given time periods, the transfer of goods, services, grants, and financial assets and liabilities between the United States and the rest of the world. The international investment position table (No. 1317) presents, for specific dates, the value of U.S. investments

In Brief	
U.S. merchandise trade,	
net balance	-66.2 bil. dol.
Exports, 1991	422 bil. dol.
General imports, 1991	488 bil. dol.
U.S. foreign assistance,	
1990	15.7 bil. dol.

abroad and of foreign investments in the United States. The movement of foreign and U.S. capital as presented in the balance of payments is not the only factor affecting the total value of foreign investments. Among the other factors are changes in the valuation of assets or liabilities, including changes in prices of securities, defaults, expropriations, and write-offs.

Direct investment abroad means the ownership or control, directly or indirectly, by one person of 10 percent or more of the voting securities of an incorporated business enterprise or an equivalent interest in an unincorporated business enterprise. Direct investment position is the value of U.S. parents' claims on the equity of, and receivables due from, foreign affiliates, less foreign affiliates' receivables due from their U.S. parents. Income consists of parents' shares in the earnings of their affiliates plus net interest received by parents on intercompany accounts, less withholding taxes on dividends and interest.

Foreign aid.—Foreign assistance is divided into three major categories—grants (military supplies and services and other grants), credits, and other assistance (through net accumulation of foreign currency claims from the sale of agricultural commodities). *Grants* are transfers for which no payment is expected (other than a limited percentage of the foreign currency "counterpart" funds generated by the grant), or which at most involve an obligation on the part of the receiver to extend aid to the United States or other countries to achieve a common objective. *Credits* are loan disbursements or transfers under other agreements which give rise to specific obligations to repay, over a period of years, usually with interest. All known returns to the U.S. Government stemming from grants and credits (reverse grants, returns of grants, and payments of principal) are taken into account in net grants and net credits, but no allowance is made for interest or commissions. *Other assistance* represents the transfer of U.S. farm products in exchange for foreign currencies (plus, since enactment of Public Law 87-128, currency claims from principal and interest collected on credits extended under the farm products program), *less* the Government's disbursements of the currencies as grants, credits, or for purchases. The net acquisition of currencies represents net transfers of resources to foreign countries under the agricultural programs, in addition to those classified as grants or credits.

The basic instrument for extending military aid to friendly nations has been the Mutual Defense Assistance Program authorized by the Congress in 1949. Prior to 1952, economic and technical aid was authorized in the Foreign Assistance Act of 1948, the 1950 Act for International Development, and other legislation which set up programs for specific countries. In 1952, these economic, technical, and military aid programs were combined under the Mutual Security Act, which in turn was followed by the Foreign Assistance Act passed in 1961. Appropriations to provide military assistance were also made in the Department of Defense Appropriation Act (rather than the Foreign Assistance Appropriation Act) beginning in 1966 for certain countries in Southeast Asia and in other legislation concerning program for specific countries (such as Israel). Figures on activity under the Foreign Assistance Act as reported in the *Foreign Grants and Credits* series differ from data published by AID or its immediate predecessors, due largely to differences in reporting, timing, and treatment of particular items.

Exports.—The Bureau of the Census compiles export data primarily from Shipper's Export Declarations required to be filed with customs officials for shipments leaving the United States. They include U.S. exports under mutual security programs and exclude shipments to U.S. Armed Forces for their own use.

The value reported in the export statistics is generally equivalent to a free alongside ship (f.a.s.) value at the U.S. port of export, based on the transaction price, including inland freight, insurance, and other charges incurred in placing the merchandise alongside the carrier at the U.S. port of exportation. This value, as defined, excludes the cost of loading merchandise aboard the exporting carrier and also excludes freight, insurance, and any other charges or transportation and other costs beyond the U.S. port of exportation. The country of destination is defined as the country of ultimate destination or country where the merchandise is to be consumed, further processed, or manufactured, as known to the shipper at the time of exportation. When ultimate destination is not known, the shipment is statistically credited to the last country to which the shipper knows the merchandise will be shipped in the same form as exported.

For certain "low-valued" shipments, the export statistics include estimates based upon selected samples of such shipments. The dollar value of the "low-valued" shipments have varied. For instance, effective January 1987 through September 1989, data are estimated for shipments valued under $1,501; from October 1989 through December 1989, data are estimated for shipments valued under $2,501 to all countries.

Effective January 1990, the United States is substituting Canadian import statistics for U.S. exports to Canada. As a result of the data exchange between the U.S. and Canada, the U.S. has adopted the Canadian import exemption level for its export statistics based on shipments to Canada.

Data are estimated for shipments valued under $2,501 to all countries, except Canada, using factors based on the ratios of low-valued shipments to individual country totals. These shipments represent slightly less than 2.5 percent of the monthly value of U.S. exports to those countries. Data are estimated for shipments reported on Canadian import documents which total less than $900 (Canadian). Such shipments represent 2 percent of the monthly value of U.S. exports to Canada.

From 1978-1988 exports were based on Schedule B, Statistical Classification of Domestic and Foreign Commodities Exported from the United States. These statistics were retabulated and published using Schedule E, Standard International Trade Classification, Revision 2. Beginning in 1989, Schedule B classifications were based on the Harmonized System and made to coincide with the Standard International Trade Classification, Revision 3. This revision will affect the comparability of most export series beginning with the 1989 data.

Imports.—The Bureau of the Census compiles import data from various customs forms required to be filed with customs officials. From 1974-1981, data on import values were presented on three bases: The transaction values f.a.s. (free alongside ship) at the foreign port of export, the c.i.f. (cost, insurance, and freight), and the previously reported customs import value (as appraised by the U.S. Customs Service in accordance with legal requirements of the Tariff Act of 1930, as amended). This latter valuation, primarily used for collection of import duties, frequently did not reflect the actual transaction value. Beginning 1982, import data are based on customs values, i.e., the price paid by the buyer to the seller in accordance with the 1979 Trade Agreement Act amendments to the 1930 Tariff Act. For the c.i.f. imports, the new customs value was substituted for the arms-length transaction value used for 1981 and earlier years. The f.a.s. transaction values were discontinued as of January 1982. Country of origin is defined as country where the merchandise was grown, mined, or manufactured. If country of origin is unknown, country of shipment is reported.

Imports are classified either as "General imports" or "Imports for consumption." General imports are a combination of entries for immediate consumption, entries into customs bonded warehouses, and entries into U.S. Foreign Trade Zones, thus generally reflecting total arrivals of merchandise. Imports for consumption are a combination of entries for immediate consumption, withdrawals from warehouses for consumption, and entries of merchandise into U.S. customs territory from U.S. Foreign Trade Zones, thus generally reflecting the total of the commodities entered into U.S. consumption channels.

Since July 1953, the import statistics include estimates, not classified by commodity, for certain low-valued shipments. For instance, from January 1985 through September 1989, import statistics include estimates for shipments valued under $1,001. Effective October 1989, import statistics are fully compiled on shipments valued over $1,250 or, under certain textile programs, for any article which must be reported on a formal entry. Value data for shipments valued under $1,251 and not required to be reported on formal entries are estimated for individual countries using factors based on the ratios of low-valued shipments to individual country totals for past periods. The estimated low-valued shipments generally amount to slightly less than 4 percent of the import total.

From 1978-1988, imports were based on the Tariff Schedule of the United States Annotated. The statistics were retabulated and published using Schedule A, Standard International Trade Classification, Revision 2. Beginning in 1989, the statistics are based on the Harmonized Tariff Schedule of the United States, which coincides with the Standard International Trade Classification, Revision 3. This revision will affect the comparability of most import series beginning with the 1989 data.

Area coverage.—Except as noted, the geographic area covered by the export and import trade statistics is the United States Customs area (includes the 50 States, the District of Columbia and Puerto Rico), the U.S. Virgin Islands (effective January 1981), and U.S. Foreign Trade Zones (effective July 1982). Data for selected tables and total values for 1980, have been revised to reflect the U.S. Virgin Islands' trade with foreign countries, where possible.

No. 1314. U.S. International Transactions, by Type of Transaction: 1980 to 1991

[In millions of dollars. Minus sign (-) indicates debits. See also Historical Statistics, Colonial Times to 1970, series U 1-25]

TYPE OF TRANSACTION	1980	1982	1983	1984	1985	1986	1987	1988	1989	1990	1991
Exports of goods and services [1]	**343,241**	**356,060**	**343,877**	**379,318**	**366,049**	**384,135**	**431,890**	**533,441**	**606,593**	**652,936**	**676,498**
Merchandise, excl. military [2][3]	224,269	211,198	201,820	219,900	215,935	223,367	250,266	320,337	361,451	389,550	416,517
Foods, feeds, and beverages	36,417	32,228	32,116	32,197	24,513	23,790	25,252	23,734	37,403	35,423	36,053
Industrial supplies and materials	72,297	64,269	59,146	64,148	61,140	64,923	69,976	89,990	99,908	105,201	109,817
Capital goods, except automotive	76,259	76,026	71,308	77,041	79,618	82,908	92,352	119,005	139,341	153,839	166,992
Automotive vehicles and parts [4]	17,350	17,422	18,620	22,581	25,144	25,331	28,131	33,869	34,941	37,394	39,841
Consumer goods (nonfood) [5]	17,698	16,162	15,040	14,982	14,381	16,275	20,275	26,869	36,565	43,271	45,842
Services	47,584	59,516	60,085	66,483	67,832	79,786	91,088	102,435	116,491	133,295	144,675
Transfers under U.S. military agency sales contracts	9,029	12,572	12,524	9,969	8,699	8,596	11,141	9,384	8,391	9,899	10,429
Travel	10,588	12,393	10,947	[6] 17,050	17,663	20,273	23,366	28,935	35,173	40,579	45,551
Passenger fares	2,591	3,174	3,610	[6] 4,014	4,323	5,457	6,866	8,771	10,374	12,251	13,836
Other transportation	11,618	12,317	12,590	13,809	14,674	15,458	16,989	19,022	20,708	22,407	23,114
Royalties and license fees	7,085	5,177	5,276	5,629	5,995	7,254	9,060	10,846	11,934	15,291	16,330
Other private services	6,276	13,308	14,472	15,296	15,601	[6] 22,153	23,140	24,804	29,299	32,173	34,736
U.S. Government misc. services	398	576	666	714	878	595	526	672	612	695	679
Income on U.S. assets abroad	71,388	85,346	81,972	92,935	82,282	80,982	90,536	110,669	128,651	130,091	115,306
Direct investment	37,146	24,717	26,822	29,984	28,295	30,900	40,588	50,437	53,997	54,444	51,754
Other private receipts	31,680	56,512	50,318	57,725	48,487	43,669	44,638	53,530	69,014	65,702	56,011
U.S. Government receipts	2,562	4,118	4,832	5,227	5,499	6,413	5,311	6,703	5,640	9,945	7,541
Imports of goods, services and income	**-333,774**	**-352,154**	**-374,065**	**-465,703**	**-472,908**	**-513,519**	**-577,418**	**-644,735**	**-697,407**	**-722,730**	**-704,842**
Merchandise, excl. military [2][3]	-249,750	-247,642	-268,900	-332,422	-338,083	-368,425	-409,766	-447,323	-477,368	-497,665	-490,103
Foods, feeds, and beverages	-18,548	-17,462	-18,871	-21,873	-21,873	-24,346	-24,809	-24,929	-25,077	-26,650	-26,487
Industrial supplies and materials	-132,256	-110,922	-109,193	-124,026	-113,678	-104,263	-113,746	-122,683	-135,113	-144,619	-132,226
Capital goods, except automotive	-31,420	-38,407	-43,193	-60,460	-61,434	-72,139	-85,129	-102,203	-112,453	-116,389	-121,316
Automotive vehicles and parts [4]	-28,058	-34,040	-43,218	-56,561	-65,071	-78,110	-85,174	-87,948	-87,380	-87,314	-84,848
Consumer goods (nonfood) [5]	-34,222	-39,661	-47,200	-61,155	-66,345	-79,179	-88,824	-96,424	-103,453	-105,666	-108,059
Services	-41,491	-47,415	-50,616	-63,739	-68,710	-75,081	-84,744	-92,096	-94,076	-106,919	-106,796
Direct defense expenditures	-10,851	-12,460	-12,687	-12,116	-12,795	-13,503	-14,803	-15,127	-14,595	-17,119	-15,709
Travel	-10,397	-12,394	-13,149	[6] -22,305	-25,155	-26,746	-30,022	-33,098	-34,548	-38,671	-39,418
Passenger Fares	-3,607	-4,772	-6,003	[6] -5,878	-6,650	-6,666	-7,411	-7,932	-8,387	-8,963	-9,269
Other transportation	-11,710	-11,710	-12,222	-14,843	-15,643	-16,715	-17,794	-19,542	-20,699	-23,463	-23,467
Royalties and license fees	-724	-617	-723	-955	-891	-1,062	-1,416	-2,125	-2,158	-2,644	-3,409
Other private services	-2,909	-4,003	-4,264	-5,108	-5,840	[6] -8,703	-11,405	-12,312	-11,644	-13,819	-15,030
U.S. Government miscellaneous services	-1,214	-1,460	-1,568	-1,534	-1,735	-1,686	-1,893	-1,960	-2,045	-2,240	-2,474
Income on foreign assets in U.S.	-42,532	-57,097	-54,549	-69,542	-66,115	-70,013	-82,908	-105,317	-125,963	-118,146	-105,943
Direct investment	-8,635	-3,155	-5,598	-9,229	-6,079	-5,379	-7,198	-13,627	-11,513	-1,782	-361
Other private payments	-21,214	-34,659	-29,958	-39,158	-37,064	-40,563	-50,419	-61,526	-78,594	-78,494	-66,743
U.S. Government payments	-12,684	-19,282	-18,993	-21,155	-22,972	-24,071	-25,291	-30,164	-35,856	-37,870	-38,839
Unilateral transfers (excl. military grants, net	**-8,349**	**-9,775**	**-9,956**	**-12,621**	**-15,473**	**-16,009**	**-14,674**	**-14,943**	**-15,491**	**-22,329**	**19,728**
U.S. Government grants	-5,486	-6,087	-6,469	-8,696	-11,268	-11,867	-10,287	-10,506	-11,071	-17,486	25,111
U.S. Government pensions	-1,818	-2,251	-2,207	-2,159	-2,138	-2,197	-2,221	-2,501	-2,517	-2,947	-3,187
Private remittances and other transfers	-1,044	-1,438	-1,280	-1,766	-2,068	-1,946	-2,166	-1,937	-1,903	-1,896	-2,196

TYPE OF TRANSACTION	1980	1982	1983	1984	1985	1986	1987	1988	1989	1990	1991
U.S. assets abroad, net (increase/capital outflow (-))	-86,118	-124,490	-56,100	-31,070	-27,721	-92,030	-62,937	-86,057	-128,610	-57,706	-67,747
U.S. official reserve assets, net	-8,155	-4,965	-1,196	-3,131	-3,358	312	9,149	-3,912	-25,293	-2,158	5,763
Special drawing rights	-16	-1,371	-66	-979	-897	-246	-509	127	-535	-192	-177
Reserve position in the International Monetary Fund	-1,667	-2,552	-4,434	-995	908	1,501	2,070	1,025	471	731	-367
Foreign currencies	-6,472	-1,041	3,304	-1,156	-3,869	-942	7,588	-5,064	-25,229	-2,697	6,307
U.S. Govt. assets, other than official reserve assets, net	-5,162	-6,131	-5,006	-5,489	-2,821	-2,022	1,006	2,966	1,320	2,976	3,572
U.S. credits and other long-term assets	-9,860	-10,063	-9,967	-9,599	-7,657	-9,084	-6,506	-7,683	-5,563	-7,319	-11,916
Repayments on U.S. credits and other long-term assets	4,456	4,292	5,012	4,490	4,719	6,089	7,625	10,373	6,726	10,327	16,466
U.S. foreign currency holdings and U.S. short-term assets, net	242	-360	-51	-379	117	973	-113	276	157	-32	-979
U.S. private assets, net	-72,802	-113,394	-49,898	-22,451	-21,043	-90,321	-73,091	-85,111	-104,637	-58,524	-77,082
Direct investments abroad	-19,222	6,967	-6,695	-11,587	-13,162	-18,679	-31,045	-17,879	-33,388	-33,437	-29,497
Foreign securities	-3,568	-7,983	-6,762	-4,756	-7,481	-4,271	-5,251	-7,846	-22,575	-28,476	-46,215
U.S. claims on unaffiliated foreigners reported by U.S. nonbanking concerns	-3,174	6,626	-6,513	5,019	923	-7,396	5,324	-3,064	2,581	-1,944	(NA)
U.S. claims reported by U.S. banks, n.i.e. [8]	-46,838	-111,070	-29,928	-11,127	-1,323	-59,975	-42,119	-56,322	-51,255	5,333	3,428
Foreign assets in the U.S., net (increase/capital inflow (+))	58,112	93,746	84,869	102,621	130,012	221,539	229,828	221,534	216,549	86,303	79,503
Foreign official assets in the U.S., net	15,497	3,593	5,845	3,140	-1,083	35,588	45,343	39,657	8,624	32,425	20,585
U.S. Government securities	11,895	5,085	6,496	4,703	-1,138	33,150	44,802	43,050	1,532	29,310	19,459
U.S. Treasury securities	9,708	5,779	6,972	4,690	-838	34,364	43,238	41,741	149	28,643	18,623
Other	2,187	-694	-476	13	-301	-1,214	1,564	1,309	1,383	667	926
Other U.S. Government liabilities	615	605	602	739	880	2,135	-2,370	-568	281	1,703	1,603
U.S. liabilities reported by U.S. banks, n.i.e. [8]	-159	545	545	555	645	1,187	3,918	-319	4,976	2,998	-1,856
Other foreign official assets	3,145	-350	-1,798	-2,857	-1,469	-884	-1,007	-2,506	1,835	-1,586	1,289
Other foreign assets in the U.S., net	42,615	90,154	79,023	99,481	131,096	186,011	184,485	181,877	207,925	53,879	58,918
Direct investments in U.S.	16,918	13,792	11,946	25,359	19,022	34,091	58,119	59,424	70,551	37,213	22,197
U.S. Treasury securities	2,645	7,027	8,689	23,001	20,433	3,809	-7,643	20,239	29,618	1,131	16,861
U.S. securities other than U.S. Treasury securities	5,457	6,085	8,164	12,568	50,962	70,969	42,120	26,353	38,920	1,781	35,417
U.S. liabilities to unaffiliated foreigners reported by U.S. nonbanking concerns	6,852	-2,383	-118	4,704	-366	-2,641	2,863	5,626	5,454	3,779	(NA)
U.S. liabilities reported by U.S. banks, n.i.e. [8]	10,743	65,633	50,342	33,849	41,045	79,783	89,026	70,235	63,382	9,975	-15,046
Allocations of special drawing rights	1,152										
Statistical discrepancy	25,736	36,612	11,374	27,456	20,041	15,824	-6,690	-9,240	18,366	63,526	-3,138
Balance on merchandise trade	-25,481	-36,444	-67,080	-112,522	-122,148	-145,058	-159,500	-126,986	-115,917	-108,115	-73,586
Balance on services	6,093	12,101	9,469	2,744	-877	4,706	6,344	10,340	22,415	26,376	35,879
Balance on investment income	28,856	28,250	27,423	23,394	16,166	10,969	7,629	5,353	2,688	11,945	9,363
Balance on goods, services, and income	9,467	3,907	-30,188	-86,385	-106,859	-129,384	-145,527	-111,294	-90,814	-69,794	-28,344
Unilateral transfers, net	-8,349	-9,775	-9,956	-12,621	-15,473	-16,009	-14,674	-14,943	-15,491	-22,329	-19,728
Balance on current account	1,119	-5,868	-40,143	-99,006	-122,332	-145,393	-160,201	-126,236	-106,305	-92,123	-8,616

- Represents zero. NA Not available. [1] Excludes transfers of goods and services under U.S. military grant programs. [2] Excludes exports of goods under U.S. military agency sales contracts identified in Bureau of the Census export documents, excludes imports of goods under direct defense expenditures identified in Census import documents, and reflects various other adjustments (for valuation, coverage, and timing) of Census statistics to a balance of payments basis. [3] Includes other, end-use items, not shown separately. [4] Includes engines. [5] Excludes automotive. [6] Break in series due to inclusion of new data. See Technical Note in Survey of Current Business, June 1979. [7] Includes sales of foreign obligations to foreigners. [8] Not included elsewhere. [9] Includes foreign currency notes sold to private residents abroad.

Source: U.S. Bureau of Economic Analysis, Survey of Current Business, March 1992.

No. 1315. U.S. International Transactions—Summary: 1960 to 1991

[In billions of dollars. Reserve assets are for end of period. Minus sign (-) indicates debits, see headnote, table 1314]

YEAR	Merchandise trade balance [1]	Net investment income	Net military transactions	Net travel and transportation receipts	Other services, net	Balance on goods, services, and income.	Unilateral transfers [1]	Balance on current account	Net foreign assets in U.S.	Net U.S. assets abroad	Net U.S. official reserve assets
1960.	4.9	3.4	-1.1	-1.0	0.6	6.9	-4.1	2.8	2.3	-4.1	19.4
1965.	5.0	5.3	-0.5	-1.3	1.5	10.0	-4.6	5.4	0.7	-5.7	15.5
1966.	3.8	5.0	-1.0	-1.3	1.5	8.0	-5.0	3.0	3.7	-7.3	14.9
1967.	3.8	5.3	-1.2	-1.8	1.7	7.9	-5.3	2.6	7.4	-9.8	14.8
1968.	0.6	6.0	-0.6	-1.5	1.8	6.2	-5.6	0.6	9.9	-11.0	15.7
1969.	0.6	6.0	-0.7	-1.8	2.0	6.1	-5.7	0.4	12.7	-11.6	17.0
1970.	2.6	6.2	-0.6	-2.0	2.3	8.5	-6.2	2.3	6.4	-9.3	14.5
1971.	-2.3	7.3	0.7	-2.3	2.6	6.0	-7.4	-1.4	23.0	-12.5	12.2
1972.	-6.4	8.2	1.1	-3.1	3.0	2.7	-8.5	-5.8	21.5	-14.5	13.2
1973.	0.9	12.2	0.7	-3.2	3.4	14.1	-6.9	7.1	18.4	-22.9	14.4
1974.	-5.5	15.5	0.2	-3.2	4.2	11.2	-9.2	2.0	34.2	-34.7	15.9
1975.	8.9	12.8	1.5	-2.8	4.9	25.2	-7.1	18.1	15.7	-39.7	16.2
1976.	-9.5	16.0	0.9	-2.6	5.0	9.9	-5.7	4.2	36.5	-51.3	18.7
1977.	-31.1	18.0	1.7	-3.6	5.7	-9.3	-5.2	-14.5	51.3	-34.8	19.3
1978.	-33.9	20.1	0.9	-3.6	6.9	-9.6	-5.8	-15.4	64.0	-61.1	18.7
1979.	-27.5	30.1	-1.3	-2.9	7.3	5.6	-6.6	-1.0	38.8	-64.3	19.0
1980.	-25.5	28.9	-1.8	-1.0	8.9	9.5	-8.3	1.1	58.1	-86.1	26.8
1981.	-28.0	31.3	-0.8	0.1	12.6	15.2	-8.3	6.9	83.0	-111.0	30.1
1982.	-36.4	28.3	0.1	-1.0	13.0	3.9	-9.8	-5.9	93.7	-124.5	34.0
1983.	-67.1	27.4	-0.2	-4.2	13.9	-30.2	-10.0	-40.1	84.9	-56.1	33.7
1984.	-112.5	23.4	-2.1	-9.2	14.0	-86.4	-12.6	-99.0	102.6	-31.1	34.9
1985.	-122.1	16.2	-4.1	-10.8	14.0	-106.9	-15.5	-122.3	130.0	-27.7	43.2
1986.	-145.1	11.0	-4.9	-8.9	18.6	-129.4	-16.0	-145.4	221.6	-92.0	48.5
1987.	-159.5	7.6	-3.7	-8.0	18.0	-145.5	-14.7	-160.2	229.8	-62.9	45.8
1988.	-127.0	5.4	-5.7	-3.8	21.0	-111.3	-14.9	-126.2	221.5	-86.1	47.8
1989.	-115.9	2.7	-6.2	2.6	26.0	-90.8	-15.5	-106.3	216.5	-128.6	74.6
1990.	-108.1	11.9	-7.2	4.1	29.5	-69.8	-22.3	-92.1	86.3	-57.7	83.3
1991, prel. . . .	-73.6	9.4	-5.3	10.3	30.8	-28.3	19.7	-8.6	79.5	-67.7	77.7

[1] Excludes military.

Source: U.S. Council of Economic Advisers, *Economic Indicators*, monthly; and *Economic Report of the President*, annual.

No. 1316. U.S. Balances on International Transactions, by Area and Selected Country: 1989 to 1991

[In millions of dollars. Minus sign (-) indicates debits]

AREA OR COUNTRY	1989, BALANCE ON—			1990, BALANCE ON—			1991, BALANCE ON—		
	Merchandise trade [1]	Goods, services, and income	Current account	Merchandise trade [1]	Goods, services, and income	Current account	Merchandise trade [1]	Goods, services, and income	Current account
All areas.	-115,917	-90,814	-106,305	-108,115	-69,794	-92,123	-73,586	-28,344	-8,616
Western Europe.	-3,990	-14,258	-14,071	2,121	-2,214	-1,797	14,724	10,024	14,865
European Economic Community [2]	-994	-10,760	-10,055	4,950	-1,024	206	15,394	9,988	16,227
United Kingdom	2,381	-9,821	-9,213	2,999	-10,557	-9,834	3,186	-10,504	-9,780
Belgium-Luxembourg . . .	3,910	5,456	5,423	5,796	7,774	7,735	6,553	(NA)	(NA)
France	-1,327	1,476	1,325	620	4,010	3,901	2,137	(NA)	(NA)
West Germany.	-8,280	-14,353	-13,410	-9,664	-14,644	-13,276	(NA)	(NA)	(NA)
Italy	-4,806	-4,182	-4,455	-4,849	4,899	4,873	-3,231	(NA)	(NA)
Netherlands	6,313	7,321	7,296	7,841	12,180	12,148	8,420	(NA)	(NA)
Other Western Europe	-2,996	-3,498	-4,016	-2,829	-1,190	-2,003	(NA)	(NA)	(NA)
Eastern Europe	3,480	4,299	3,876	2,074	2,370	1,618	3,071	3,258	1,114
Canada	-9,277	5,266	4,912	-9,454	4,094	3,804	-7,976	7,638	7,283
Latin America, other Western Hemisphere.	-8,660	-6,681	-9,874	-10,048	-9,547	-12,943	296	3,442	-2,127
Mexico	-2,450	-2,081	-2,635	-2,392	-2,887	-3,473	1,611	(NA)	(NA)
Venezuela	-3,795	-2,992	-3,019	-6,424	-5,952	-5,988	-3,597	(NA)	(NA)
Australia.	4,246	7,732	7,674	3,893	7,337	7,272	4,269	7,087	7,011
Japan [3]	-49,669	-42,711	-42,844	-41,690	-31,748	-31,467	-44,107	-32,761	-23,924
Other Asia and Africa	-52,220	-47,635	-57,928	-55,569	-44,277	-61,352	-44,253	-31,092	-15,218
South Africa.	122	751	708	34	496	448	(NA)	(NA)	(NA)
Int'l. and unallocated.	173	3,174	1,949	558	4,191	2,741	390	4,059	2,380

NA Not available.   [1] Adjusted to balance of payments basis; excludes exports under U.S. military sales contracts and imports under direct defense expenditures.   [2] Includes Denmark, Greece, Ireland, Spain, Portugal, European Atomic Energy Community, European Coal and Steel Community, and European Investment Bank, not shown separately.   [3] Includes Ryukyu Islands.

Source: U.S. Bureau of Economic Analysis, *Survey of Current Business*, March 1992.

No. 1317. International Investment Position: 1980 to 1990

[In billions of dollars. Estimates for end of year; subject to considerable error due to nature of basic data. See *Historical Statistics, Colonial Times to 1970*, series U 26-39, for similar data]

TYPE OF INVESTMENT	1980	1984	1985	1986	1987	1988	1989	1990
U.S. net international investment position:								
Current cost	379,623	163,972	64,306	-74,122	-134,960	-305,976	-439,656	-412,163
Market value	(NA)	111,034	64,502	14,588	-42,237	-150,562	-267,711	-360,598
U.S. assets abroad:								
Current cost	921,527	1,104,622	1,173,850	1,319,094	1,463,400	1,533,692	1,672,532	1,764,055
Market value	(NA)	1,022,251	1,174,772	1,424,416	1,555,825	1,707,549	1,944,218	1,880,096
U.S. official reserve assets	171,412	105,040	117,930	139,875	162,370	144,179	168,714	174,664
Gold	155,816	81,202	85,834	102,428	127,648	107,434	105,164	102,406
Special drawing rights	2,610	5,641	7,293	8,395	10,283	9,637	9,951	10,989
Reserve position in IMF	2,852	11,541	11,947	11,730	11,349	9,745	9,048	9,076
Foreign currencies	10,134	6,656	12,856	17,322	13,090	17,363	44,551	52,193
U.S. Government assets, other	63,865	84,971	87,752	89,637	88,596	85,565	84,207	81,209
U.S. loans and other long-term assets	62,023	82,883	85,814	88,710	87,580	84,858	83,675	80,661
U.S. foreign currency holdings and short-term assets	1,842	2,088	1,938	927	1,016	707	532	548
U.S. private assets:								
Current cost	686,250	914,611	968,168	1,089,582	1,212,434	1,303,948	1,419,611	1,508,182
Market value	(NA)	832,240	969,090	1,194,904	1,304,859	1,477,805	1,691,297	1,624,223
Direct investments abroad								
Current cost.	385,059	350,007	379,556	414,091	485,178	504,980	536,057	598,062
Market value	(NA)	267,636	380,478	519,413	577,603	678,837	807,743	714,103
Foreign securities.	62,653	88,917	112,226	131,736	146,714	156,775	190,259	222,317
U.S. claims on unaffiliated foreigners [1]	34,672	30,056	29,023	36,417	31,085	34,157	31,574	33,518
U.S. claims reported by U.S. banks [2]	203,866	445,631	447,363	507,338	549,457	608,036	661,721	654,285
Foreign assets in the U.S.								
Current cost	541,904	940,650	1,109,544	1,393,216	1,598,360	1,839,668	2,112,188	2,176,218
Market value	(NA)	911,217	1,110,270	1,409,828	1,598,062	1,858,111	2,211,929	2,240,694
Foreign official assets in the U.S.	176,062	199,690	202,544	241,199	283,024	321,891	337,278	369,607
U.S. Government securities . .	118,189	144,665	145,063	178,915	220,548	260,934	265,708	296,036
Other U.S. Government liabilities	13,367	14,971	15,865	18,005	15,635	15,067	15,348	17,052
U.S. liabilities reported by U.S. banks [2]	30,381	26,090	26,734	27,920	31,838	31,520	36,496	39,494
Other foreign official assets . .	14,125	13,964	14,882	16,359	15,003	14,370	19,726	17,025
Other foreign assets in the U.S:								
Current cost.	365,842	740,960	907,000	1,152,017	1,315,336	1,517,777	1,774,910	1,806,611
Market value	(NA)	711,527	907,726	1,168,629	1,315,038	1,536,220	1,874,651	1,871,087
Direct investments:								
Current cost.	124,120	207,159	227,223	266,541	316,012	372,569	433,741	465,916
Market value	(NA)	177,726	227,949	283,153	315,714	391,012	533,482	530,392
U.S. securities other than U.S. Treasury securities	74,114	128,477	207,868	310,883	346,187	395,584	489,127	475,120
U.S. liabilities to unaffiliated foreigners [1]	30,426	31,024	29,458	26,902	29,818	35,003	40,437	44,134
U.S. liabilities reported by U.S. banks [2]	121,069	312,179	354,497	451,613	540,731	613,744	677,117	687,041
U.S. Treasury securities	16,113	62,121	87,954	96,078	82,588	100,877	134,488	134,391

NA Not available. [1] Reported by U.S. nonbanking concerns. [2] Not included elsewhere.

Source: U.S. Bureau of Economic Analysis, *Survey of Current Business*, June 1991.

No. 1318. U.S. Reserve Assets: 1980 to 1991

[In billions of dollars. As of end of year, except as indicated]

TYPE	1980	1981	1982	1983	1984	1985	1986	1987	1988	1989	1990	1991
Total	26.8	30.1	34.0	33.7	34.9	43.2	48.5	45.8	47.8	74.6	83.3	77.7
Gold stock [1]	11.2	11.2	11.1	11.1	11.1	11.1	11.1	11.1	11.1	11.1	11.1	11.1
Special drawing rights	2.6	4.1	5.3	5.0	5.6	7.3	8.4	10.3	9.6	10.0	11.0	11.2
Foreign currencies	10.1	9.8	10.2	6.3	6.7	12.9	17.3	13.1	17.4	44.6	52.2	45.9
Reserve position in IMF [2]	2.9	5.1	7.3	11.3	11.5	11.9	11.7	11.3	9.7	9.0	9.1	9.5

[1] Includes gold in Exchange Stabilization Fund; excludes gold held under earmark at Federal Reserve banks for foreign and interternational accounts. Beginning 1975, gold assets were valued at $42.22 pursuant to the amending of Section 2 of the Par Value Modification Act, PL-93-110, approved September 21, 1973. [2] International Monetary Fund.

Source: Board of Governors of the Federal Reserve System, *Federal Reserve Bulletin*, monthly; and Department of the Treasury, *Treasury Bulletin*, monthly.

No. 1319. Foreign Direct Investment Position in the U.S.—Value, by Area and Industry: 1980 to 1990

[In millions of dollars. Book value at year end. 1970 covers U.S. firms, including real estate investments in which foreign interest or ownership was 25 percent or more; thereafter, ownership of 10 percent or more. Minus sign (-) indicates a negative position. See also Historical Statistics, Colonial Times to 1970, series U 47-74]

AREA AND INDUSTRY	1980	1982	1983	1984	1985	1986	1987	1988	1989	1990, prel.
All areas [1]	**83,046**	**124,677**	**137,061**	**164,583**	**184,615**	**220,414**	**263,394**	**314,754**	**373,763**	**403,735**
Petroleum	12,200	17,660	18,209	25,400	28,270	29,094	37,815	36,006	37,201	38,004
Manufacturing	32,993	44,065	47,665	51,802	59,584	71,963	93,865	122,582	151,820	159,998
Finance and insurance	12,027	17,933	10,934	24,881	27,429	34,978	39,455	44,010	58,215	58,437
Trade, wholesale and retail . .	15,210	23,604	26,513	31,219	35,873	42,920	45,399	53,590	55,310	61,996
Canada	**12,162**	**11,708**	**11,434**	**15,286**	**17,131**	**20,318**	**24,684**	**26,566**	**28,686**	**27,733**
Petroleum	1,817	1,550	1,391	1,544	1,589	1,432	1,088	1,181	1,233	1,417
Manufacturing	5,227	3,500	3,313	4,115	4,607	6,108	8,085	9,730	9,934	9,327
Finance and insurance	1,612	1,801	1,061	3,245	4,008	4,283	5,797	5,769	7,227	7,325
Europe	**54,688**	**83,193**	**92,936**	**108,211**	**121,413**	**144,181**	**181,006**	**208,942**	**242,961**	**256,496**
Petroleum	10,137	15,071	16,326	23,142	25,636	26,139	35,700	33,499	32,476	31,197
Manufacturing	21,953	33,032	36,866	39,083	45,841	56,016	74,300	95,641	120,132	125,568
Finance and insurance	8,673	12,601	8,450	15,945	17,022	21,787	26,336	27,121	31,609	30,329
United Kingdom	14,105	28,447	32,152	38,387	43,555	55,935	75,519	95,698	105,511	108,055
Petroleum	-257	5,444	5,955	7,061	12,155	11,758	17,950	19,522	16,545	15,310
Manufacturing	6,159	8,504	9,221	9,179	11,687	16,500	30,372	41,708	51,798	52,955
Finance and insurance . .	3,350	5,661	3,777	5,485	6,483	10,163	9,801	11,256	11,859	13,139
Netherlands	19,140	26,191	29,182	33,728	37,056	40,717	46,636	48,128	56,316	64,333
Petroleum	9,265	8,098	8,646	9,981	11,481	(D)	(D)	9,045	9,889	10,527
Manufacturing	4,777	9,901	11,222	12,497	13,351	13,293	15,615	17,843	23,709	24,446
Switzerland	5,070	6,378	7,464	8,146	10,568	12,058	13,772	14,372	18,772	17,512
Manufacturing	3,116	3,584	4,165	4,774	6,881	7,520	6,921	7,613	10,412	9,113
Finance and insurance . .	1,033	1,473	1,830	(D)	5,425	2,517	3,211	3,506	4,671	4,947
West Germany	7,596	9,850	10,845	12,330	14,816	17,250	21,905	25,250	29,015	27,770
Manufacturing	3,875	4,239	4,487	4,389	6,015	7,426	10,298	13,980	15,722	15,216
Finance and insurance . .	1,248	1,426	1,416	1,902	(D)	1,962	3,442	2,683	3,396	2,767
Other Europe [2]	8,777	12,327	13,293	15,620	15,417	18,221	23,174	25,494	33,347	38,826
Petroleum	991	1,380	1,679	2,080	(D)	(D)	(D)	4,580	4,920	4,760
Manufacturing	4,026	6,804	7,771	7,704	7,907	11,277	11,094	14,497	18,491	23,838
Finance insurance	1,193	429	-908	(D)	(D)	(D)	2,189	406	2,574	1,119
Japan	**4,723**	**9,677**	**11,336**	**16,044**	**19,313**	**26,824**	**34,421**	**51,126**	**67,319**	**83,498**
Other areas	**11,472**	**20,099**	**21,356**	**25,043**	**26,758**	**29,091**	**23,283**	**28,120**	**34,797**	**36,008**

D Withheld to avoid disclosure of data of individual companies. [1] Area totals include industries not shown separately. [2] Direct investments in 1990 (in millions of dollars): Belgium and Luxembourg, 6,061; France, 19,550; Italy, 1,552; and Sweden, 5,450.

Source: U.S. Bureau of Economic Analysis, Survey of Current Business, August 1991, and earlier issues.

No. 1320. U.S. Affiliates of Foreign Companies—Assets, Sales, Employment, Land, Exports, and Imports: 1989

[A U.S. affiliate is a U.S. business enterprise in which one foreign owner (individual, branch, partnership, association, trust, corporation, or government) has a direct or indirect voting interest of 10 percent or more. Universe estimates based on a sample survey of nonbank affiliates with assets, sales, or net income of $10 million or more]

INDUSTRY	Total assets (mil. dol.)	Sales [1] (mil. dol.)	Employ-ment [2] (1,000)	Employee compen-sation (mil. dol.)	GROSS BOOK VALUE (mil. dol.) Plant and equip-ment [3]	GROSS BOOK VALUE (mil. dol.) Land	Land owned (1,000 acres)	Merchan-dise exports [4] (mil. dol.)	Mer-chandise imports [4] (mil. dol.)
Total	**1,402,174**	**1,040,887**	**4,440.1**	**140,592**	**437,285**	**44,749**	**18,702**	**84,263**	**169,745**
Petroleum	91,381	91,651	135.3	6,287	87,464	3,556	1,322	1,962	14,131
Manufacturing	367,452	347,023	2,123.4	74,674	177,130	7,430	6,187	31,281	39,227
Chemicals and allied products	105,964	93,969	442.5	19,279	68,321	1,536	834	9,377	7,688
Wholesale trade [5]	131,226	342,922	390.8	14,132	26,920	2,078	725	47,645	113,059
Motor vehicles and auto parts and supplies	37,842	86,746	81.7	3,130	9,968	555	25	4,558	45,178
Farm-product raw materials . .	8,400	43,040	17.3	590	1,636	214	34	17,292	3,398
Retail trade	48,474	71,816	818.0	12,009	20,609	2,100	18	1,533	2,686
Finance, except banking	380,743	42,026	93.9	7,918	4,705	387	19	6	(Z)
Insurance	171,055	55,393	111.6	4,157	4,088	683	13	-	-
Real estate	89,968	14,745	37.8	1,025	52,346	18,655	2,908	3	2
Services	57,970	28,666	404.9	9,505	25,315	2,707	329	279	176
Other	63,905	46,643	324.2	10,885	38,709	7,153	7,181	1,555	465

- Represents zero.   Z Less than $500,000.   [1] Excludes returns, discounts, allowances, and sales and excise taxes. [2] Average number of full-time and part-time employees.   [3] Includes other property, value of mineral rights owned and capitalized value of mineral rights leased.   [4] F.a.s. value at port of exportation.   [5] Includes industries not shown separately.

Source: U.S. Bureau of Economic Analysis, Survey of Current Business, July 1991, and Foreign Direct Investment in the United States, Operations of U.S. Affiliates of Foreign Companies, preliminary 1989 estimates.

No. 1321. Foreign Direct Investment in the United States—Gross Book Value of Property, Plant, and Equipment and Employment of U.S. Affiliates of Foreign Companies, by State: 1981 and 1989

[A U.S. affiliate is a U.S. business enterprise in which one foreign owner (individual, branch, partnership, association, trust corporation, or government) has a direct or indirect voting interest of 10 percent or more. Universe estimates based on a sample survey of nonbank affiliates with assets, sales, or net income of $10 million or more]

DIVISION, STATE, AND OTHER AREA	GROSS BOOK VALUE OF PROPERTY, PLANT, AND EQUIPMENT (mil. dol.)		TOTAL EMPLOYMENT			MANUFACTURING EMPLOYMENT, 1989	
				1989			
	1981	1989	1981	Total (1,000)	Percent of all businesses	Total (1,000)	Percent of all manufacturing
Total	187,956	482,035	2,416.6	4,440.1	(X)	1,834.4	(X)
United States.	178,003	461,313	2,402.3	4,406.0	4.8	1,816.2	9.3
New England	5,686	16,982	143.9	291.1	5.1	115.4	8.9
Maine	1,637	2,110	17.7	27.1	6.0	8.4	7.9
New Hampshire	409	1,141	13.9	25.6	5.5	11.6	10.1
Vermont	315	502	6.0	8.4	3.8	3.0	6.1
Massachusetts	1,712	7,580	55.6	129.0	4.7	49.0	8.7
Rhode Island	359	931	9.9	13.3	3.2	7.2	6.6
Connecticut	1,254	4,718	40.8	87.7	6.0	36.2	10.0
Middle Atlantic	20,216	62,988	480.2	794.7	5.5	292.8	10.1
New York	7,892	31,993	210.3	370.9	5.5	96.5	8.1
New Jersey	6,552	16,011	134.9	222.4	7.0	89.2	13.8
Pennsylvania	5,772	14,984	135.0	201.4	4.5	107.1	10.2
East North Central	19,215	59,600	388.6	759.8	4.7	391.9	9.1
Ohio	5,178	17,315	99.9	207.6	5.0	114.9	10.2
Indiana	1,883	8,106	47.0	96.5	4.5	63.9	9.9
Illinois	5,646	19,610	113.6	238.6	5.3	103.5	10.5
Michigan	4,188	10,220	65.9	140.1	4.2	67.4	7.0
Wisconsin	2,320	4,349	62.2	77.0	4.0	42.2	7.5
West North Central	8,400	25,784	112.2	233.0	3.5	98.5	7.0
Minnesota	2,902	11,410	33.0	81.2	4.5	30.2	7.5
Iowa	1,032	2,356	21.6	30.6	3.0	18.8	8.0
Missouri.	1,894	5,024	32.6	71.6	3.6	30.9	7.0
North Dakota	1,155	1,121	3.5	3.1	1.5	1.1	6.7
South Dakota	299	456	1.3	3.0	1.4	1.6	5.1
Nebraska.	241	700	5.6	13.5	2.3	6.2	6.3
Kansas	877	4,717	14.6	30.0	3.4	9.7	5.2
South Atlantic	33,271	77,901	476.0	875.6	5.4	361.8	11.3
Delaware.	1,869	5,378	36.0	41.5	14.4	11.8	16.0
Maryland	2,103	4,812	45.1	68.6	3.8	25.1	12.0
District of Columbia	547	2,433	3.2	8.8	2.2	0.3	2.2
Virginia	3,046	9,137	49.8	106.1	4.6	44.9	10.4
West Virginia	3,992	5,511	35.4	29.8	6.2	17.7	20.1
North Carolina	5,543	13,869	89.0	174.5	6.7	101.6	11.7
South Carolina	5,318	8,572	65.1	100.1	8.1	51.9	13.3
Georgia	4,558	13,873	78.5	159.7	6.5	67.8	11.9
Florida.	6,295	14,316	73.9	186.5	4.1	40.7	7.6
East South Central	9,802	23,982	121.7	246.4	4.9	142.4	9.9
Kentucky	1,848	6,750	26.0	55.5	4.7	36.2	12.7
Tennessee.	3,747	8,771	57.4	112.3	6.1	66.6	12.7
Alabama.	2,776	5,855	27.0	55.8	4.3	26.2	6.7
Mississippi	1,431	2,606	11.3	22.8	3.1	13.4	5.5
West South Central	34,651	71,826	268.5	401.6	4.7	140.9	9.1
Arkansas	636	2,263	17.5	32.0	4.2	17.6	7.6
Louisiana	7,872	15,661	47.0	64.6	5.2	19.9	11.3
Oklahoma	2,760	5,726	25.0	41.2	4.5	13.3	8.1
Texas	23,383	48,176	179.0	263.8	4.7	90.1	9.2
Mountain	12,353	27,087	97.9	161.0	3.4	41.2	6.4
Montana	1,235	1,917	3.0	4.1	1.8	1.4	6.4
Idaho	312	618	3.8	8.2	2.7	4.0	6.6
Wyoming	2,144	1,958	4.2	4.1	2.8	0.8	8.9
Colorado	2,369	5,716	24.7	40.0	3.2	10.6	5.5
New Mexico	997	3,881	7.9	15.6	3.7	2.7	6.3
Arizona	2,949	5,859	30.6	54.2	4.4	13.1	7.0
Utah	1,791	3,391	16.8	16.1	2.9	7.2	7.0
Nevada	556	3,747	6.9	10.7	3.6	1.4	5.6
Pacific	34,409	95,162	313.3	642.8	4.4	231.3	8.2
Washington	2,430	5,914	26.0	67.2	3.9	19.7	5.4
Oregon	845	2,299	13.1	28.5	2.8	10.8	4.9
California	20,404	61,142	248.4	496.4	4.5	196.3	9.0
Alaska.	(D)	18,919	8.8	8.0	5.0	2.8	17.5
Hawaii.	(D)	6,888	17.0	42.7	10.1	1.7	8.0
Puerto Rico.	413	997	9.5	19.6	(X)	12.3	(X)
Other territories and offshore	7,496	17,579	3.1	8.8	(X)	2.1	(X)
Foreign.	2,044	2,146	1.6	5.7	(X)	3.8	(X)

X Not applicable.   D Withheld to avoid disclosure of data of individual companies.   X Not applicable.

Source: U.S. Bureau of Economic Analysis, *Survey of Current Business*, July 1991, and *Foreign Direct Investment in the United States, Operations of U.S. Affiliates of Foreign Companies*, preliminary 1989 estimates.

No. 1322. U.S. Businesses Acquired or Established by Foreign Direct Investors, by Industry of U.S. Business Enterprise: 1989 and 1990

[Foreign direct investment is the ownership or control, directly or indirectly, by one foreign individual branch, partnership, association, trust, corporation, or government of 10 percent or more of the voting securities of a U.S. business enterprise or an equivalent interest in an unincorporated one. Data represent number and full cost of acquisitions of existing U.S. business enterprises, including business segments or operating units of existing U.S. business enterprises and establishments of new enterprises. Investments may be made by the foreign direct investor itself, or indirectly by an existing U.S. affiliate of the foreign direct investor. Covers investments in U.S. business enterprises with assets of over $1 million, or ownership of 200 acres of U.S. land]

INDUSTRY	1989						1990					
	Investments			Investors			Investments			Investors		
	Total	Acquisition	Establishments	Total	Foreign direct investors	U.S. affiliates	Total	Acquisition	Establishments	Total	Foreign direct investors	U.S. affiliates
NUMBER OF INVESTMENTS [1]												
Total	1,580	837	743	1,742	727	1,015	1,617	839	778	1,768	670	1,098
Petroleum	42	32	10	43	9	34	23	17	6	24	3	21
Manufacturing	522	417	105	579	219	360	507	414	93	556	192	364
Wholesale trade	112	81	31	116	37	79	105	69	36	114	40	74
Retail trade	45	34	11	47	15	32	39	28	11	40	7	33
Banking	13	2	11	13	12	1	32	16	16	33	22	11
Finance, except banking	77	23	54	94	65	29	61	28	33	64	23	41
Insurance	20	14	6	21	2	19	26	21	5	26	7	19
Real estate	457	55	402	507	229	278	503	40	463	568	268	300
Services	195	132	63	219	98	121	203	139	64	217	68	149
Other [2]	97	47	50	103	41	62	118	67	51	126	40	86
INVESTMENT OUTLAYS (mil. dol.)												
Total	71,163	59,708	11,455	71,163	22,538	48,625	65,932	55,315	10,617	65,932	14,026	51,906
Petroleum	1,189	1,125	64	1,189	122	1,068	1,141	1,013	128	1,141	6	1,135
Manufacturing	35,958	33,236	2,723	35,958	12,073	23,885	23,898	22,789	1,109	23,898	5,708	18,190
Wholesale trade	2,634	2,504	130	2,634	1,747	887	1,676	1,484	192	1,676	509	1,167
Retail trade	1,861	1,838	23	1,861	299	1,562	1,250	1,197	53	1,250	28	1,222
Banking	349	280	69	349	78	271	897	816	81	897	115	781
Finance, except banking	4,186	2,853	1,334	4,186	2,564	1,623	2,121	875	1,246	2,121	252	1,869
Insurance	1,901	1,768	133	1,901	28	1,873	2,093	2,007	87	2,093	1,134	959
Real estate	6,438	1,409	5,029	6,438	2,329	4,109	7,771	1,873	5,898	7,771	4,330	3,441
Services	10,058	8,333	1,725	10,058	3,057	7,001	19,369	17,912	1,457	19,369	906	18,463
Other [2]	6,587	6,362	225	6,587	242	6,346	5,716	5,349	367	5,716	1,037	4,678

[1] Excludes investments that do not meet asset or acreage criteria in headnote.   [2] Includes agriculture, forestry, and fishing; mining; construction; transportation; and communication and public utilities.

Source: U.S. Bureau of Economic Analysis, *Survey of Current Business*, May 1992.

No. 1323. U.S. Businesses Acquired by Foreign Direct Investors Assets, Sales, and Employment, by Industry of U.S. Business Enterprise: 1989 and 1990

[See headnote, table 1322. Minus sign (-) indicates loss]

INDUSTRY	1989					1990				
	Total assets (mil. dol.)	Sales (mil. dol.)	Net income (mil. dol.)	Employment (1,000)	Acres of land owned (1,000)	Total assets (mil. dol.)	Sales (mil. dol.)	Net income (mil. dol.)	Employment (1,000)	Acres of land owned (1,000)
Total	99,306	72,710	345	705.1	364.8	95,184	60,165	332	454.8	289.4
Petroleum	2,859	1,854	-69	4.1	(D)	(D)	864	22	2.9	1.5
Manufacturing	36,790	39,306	302	380.5	289.0	28,987	31,451	859	235.2	167.9
Wholesale trade	(D)	4,018	-52	17.5	0.7	2,156	4,320	26	9.2	4.8
Retail trade	5,488	8,139	69	175.3	2.1	957	1,427	11	36.2	0.5
Banking	(D)	(D)	(D)	(D)	(D)	10,057	438	51	2.7	(D)
Finance, except banking	22,054	2,447	186	7.0	4.2	6,079	832	-56	3.6	(D)
Insurance	(D)	3,346	32	8.1	0.1	2,093	1,580	106	9.2	(D)
Real estate	1,529	(D)	(D)	(D)	3.4	4,322	1,123	110	3.0	4.1
Services	8,066	4,799	-34	56.5	5.5	26,469	7,970	140	79.8	19.3
Other [1]	9,417	8,213	-129	52.7	35.2	11,266	10,160	-937	73.1	87.0

D Withheld to avoid disclosure of data of individual companies.   [1] Includes agriculture, forestry, and fishing; mining; construction; transportation; and communication and public utilities.

Source: U.S. Bureau of Economic Analysis, *Survey of Current Business*, May 1992.

No. 1324. U.S. Investment Position Abroad, by Country: 1980 to 1990

[In millions of dollars. Direct investments represent private enterprises in one country owned or controlled by investors in another country or in the management of which foreign investors have an important role. Negative position occurs when U.S. parent company's liabilities to the foreign affiliate are greater than its equity in, and loans to the foreign affiliate. See also *Historical Statistics, Colonial Times to 1970*, series U 41-46]

COUNTRY	1980	1985	1987	1988	1989	1990 Total [1]	1990 Manufacturing	1990 Petroleum	1990 Finance [2]
All countries	215,375	230,250	314,307	335,893	370,091	421,494	168,220	59,736	98,889
Developed countries	158,214	172,058	237,508	252,649	274,564	312,186	134,658	41,551	67,917
Canada	45,119	46,909	57,783	62,656	65,548	68,431	33,231	10,691	12,025
Europe [3]	96,287	105,171	150,439	157,077	175,213	204,204	83,992	24,356	52,227
Austria	524	493	691	669	588	767	63	(D)	(D)
Belgium	6,259	5,038	7,267	7,501	7,941	9,462	4,331	327	2,059
Denmark	1,266	1,281	1,070	1,161	1,234	1,633	286	(D)	295
France	9,347	7,643	11,868	13,041	14,069	17,134	11,051	(D)	960
Greece	347	210	132	195	264	300	84	37	(D)
Ireland	2,319	3,693	5,425	5,886	5,522	6,776	4,885	-41	1,549
Italy	5,397	5,906	9,264	9,496	10,294	12,971	8,535	605	1,005
Luxembourg	652	690	660	841	1,127	1,119	539	22	238
Netherlands	8,039	7,129	14,842	16,145	18,133	22,778	8,144	1,636	8,642
Norway	1,679	3,215	3,843	4,371	3,547	3,633	121	2,954	(D)
Portugal	257	237	495	546	488	590	285	(D)	(D)
Spain	2,678	2,281	4,076	4,966	6,096	7,480	4,998	116	3
Sweden	1,474	933	1,139	1,119	1,129	1,526	1,060	16	36
Switzerland	11,280	15,766	19,665	18,734	19,209	23,733	1,177	(D)	11,049
Turkey	207	234	247	246	310	507	117	173	(Z)
United Kingdom	28,460	33,024	44,512	49,459	59,827	64,983	20,636	11,331	23,071
West Germany	15,415	16,764	24,388	21,832	24,550	27,715	17,489	3,136	2,863
Japan	6,225	9,235	15,684	18,009	18,488	20,994	10,623	3,419	2,240
Australia	7,654	8,772	11,363	12,823	13,331	14,529	6,060	2,615	1,116
New Zealand	579	576	743	833	1,140	3,139	341	(D)	257
South Africa	2,350	1,394	1,497	1,252	843	889	411	(D)	54
Developing countries	53,206	52,764	73,017	80,060	92,098	105,721	33,562	15,658	30,972
Latin America	38,761	28,261	47,551	53,506	62,727	72,467	23,802	5,275	27,250
South America [3]	16,342	17,623	21,227	21,815	23,612	24,920	15,242	2,038	2,065
Argentina	2,540	2,705	2,744	2,597	2,684	2,889	1,566	437	164
Brazil	7,704	8,893	10,951	12,609	14,522	15,416	11,286	650	1,351
Chile	536	88	348	672	1,069	1,341	275	(D)	418
Colombia	1,012	2,148	3,104	2,248	1,977	2,043	799	(D)	30
Ecuador	322	361	466	431	393	389	174	121	(D)
Peru	1,665	1,243	1,022	976	939	600	78	-2	(D)
Venezuela	1,908	1,588	2,095	1,903	1,503	1,581	963	278	74
Central America	10,193	9,658	12,218	13,380	16,050	18,911	8,171	2,269	5,647
Mexico	5,986	5,088	4,913	5,712	7,280	9,360	7,314	80	314
Panama	3,170	3,959	6,622	6,874	7,889	8,521	363	1,927	5,312
Other [3]	1,037	611	683	794	881	1,029	494	263	21
Costa Rica	303	113	141	169	163	193	(NA)	(NA)	(NA)
El Salvador	105	73	51	56	57	66	(NA)	(NA)	(NA)
Guatemala	229	213	174	201	215	245	(NA)	(NA)	(NA)
Honduras	288	171	185	240	317	315	(NA)	(NA)	(NA)
Other W. Hemisphere [3]	12,226	980	14,106	18,311	23,065	28,636	389	967	19,539
Bahamas, The	2,712	3,795	3,814	4,112	4,257	4,301	60	235	841
Bermuda	11,045	13,116	19,215	19,022	17,717	18,972	-	-60	18,185
Dominican Republic	316	212	156	138	361	478	(NA)	(NA)	(NA)
Jamaica	407	122	103	134	223	276	152	(D)	3
Netherlands Antilles	-4,336	-20,499	-14,235	-9,983	-5,956	-1,401	38	(D)	-1,689
Trinidad and Tobago	951	484	400	447	503	413	9	(D)	6
Other Africa [3]	3,778	4,497	4,372	4,219	3,993	3,780	416	2,716	265
Egypt	1,038	1,926	1,669	1,637	1,744	1,451	45	1,117	-4
Libya	575	325	310	315	252	246	-	228	-
Nigeria	18	44	894	660	406	210	67	163	-
Middle East [3]	2,163	4,606	4,084	3,806	4,166	4,755	911	2,033	884
Israel	379	717	635	701	756	818	311	(D)	(D)
Saudi Arabia	1,037	2,442	2,092	1,782	1,955	2,523	576	558	(D)
United Arab Emirates	384	792	694	672	652	584	13	(D)	(D)
Bahrain	-16	-440	-340	-311	-28	-100	(NA)	(NA)	(NA)
Other Asia and Pacific	8,505	15,400	17,010	18,528	21,212	24,719	8,433	5,635	2,573
China: Taiwan	498	750	1,372	1,621	1,921	2,273	1,449	-9	127
Hong Kong	2,078	3,295	4,389	5,240	5,948	6,537	775	188	2,007
India	398	383	439	436	527	639	511	11	-1
Indonesia	1,014	1,475	3,070	2,921	3,770	3,827	135	3,209	(D)
Malaysia	632	1,140	952	1,135	1,174	1,425	561	679	17
Philippines	1,259	1,032	1,396	1,513	1,657	1,655	818	149	95
Singapore	1,204	1,874	2,384	2,311	2,318	3,971	2,361	775	126
South Korea	575	743	1,178	1,501	1,855	2,096	920	7	98
Thailand	361	1,074	1,274	1,132	1,271	1,515	461	719	23
Other	186	635	556	719	772	782	141	207	(D)
China: Mainland	-6	311	207	307	371	289	(NA)	(NA)	(NA)
International	3,955	5,428	3,782	3,184	3,430	3,586	-	2,527	-
Addendum-OPEC [4]	6,090	10,383	9,899	8,827	9,046	9,828	1,930	5,516	941

- Represents zero. NA Not available. D Suppressed to avoid disclosure of data of individual companies. [1] Includes industries not shown separately. [2] Includes insurance. [3] Includes countries not shown separately. [4] OPEC=Organization of Petroleum Exporting Countries. Includes Algeria, Ecuador, Gabon, Indonesia, Iran, Iraq, Kuwait, Libya, Nigeria, Qatar, Saudi Arabia, United Arab Emirates, and Venezuela.

Source: U.S. Bureau of Economic Analysis, *Survey of Current Business*, August 1991.

No. 1325. U.S. Government Foreign Grants and Credits: 1946 to 1990

[In millions of dollars. "P.L." means Public Law. For explanation of minus sign (-), see headnote, table 1326. See also text, section 29, and *Historical Statistics, Colonial Times to 1970*, series U 75-101]

PROGRAM	1946-1955, total	1956-1965, total	1966-1975, total	1976-1985, total	1986	1987	1988	1989	1990, prel.
Total, net.	**51,509**	**49,723**	**70,368**	**104,189**	**15,017**	**9,403**	**8,082**	**10,206**	**14,143**
Investment in international financial institutions [1] .	635	655	2,719	10,432	1,481	1,212	1,314	1,173	1,301
Under assistance programs, net.	**50,875**	**49,067**	**67,649**	**93,757**	**13,536**	**8,191**	**6,768**	**9,033**	**12,843**
Developed countries [2]	35,150	5,834	616	757	815	-801	-131	66	36
Developing countries [2]	15,725	43,233	67,033	93,000	12,721	8,990	6,899	8,967	12,807
Net new military grants	14,200	21,564	30,236	14,957	4,125	3,131	3,576	3,728	6,638
Developed countries [2]	8,910	7,931	691	1,369	162	261	305	321	551
Developing countries [2]	5,291	13,633	29,545	13,587	3,963	2,870	3,272	3,408	6,087
Gross new grants	14,434	21,805	30,281	14,993	4,128	3,136	3,578	3,732	6,643
Foreign Assistance Act [3].	13,427	21,769	30,281	14,993	4,128	3,136	3,578	3,732	6,643
Military supplies and services	12,282	20,662	9,802	2,438	99	57	92	44	73
Military assistance, service funded [4]. . . .	-	8	18,161						
Financing of military purchases [5].	-	-	1,584	10,122	3,873	2,816	3,185	3,369	6,017
Relocation of facilities in Israel	-	-	-	800	-	-	-	-	-
Other special programs	1,145	1,100	734	1,633	157	263	301	319	553
Other.	1,007	36	-	-	-	-	-	-	-
Less: Reverse grants and returns	234	241	45	36	3	5	2	3	5
Other grants, credits, and other assistance (through net accumulation of foreign currency claims).	36,675	27,503	37,413	78,800	9,411	5,060	3,192	5,305	6,205
Developed countries [2]	26,240	-2,097	-75	-612	653	-1,062	436	-255	-515
Developing countries [2]	10,434	29,600	37,488	79,412	8,758	6,122	3,627	5,560	6,720
Net new economic and technical aid grants [6]	27,529	17,675	21,748	43,302	7,898	7,419	7,231	7,662	10,153
Developed countries [2]	19,424	780	-182	464	98	67	72	56	-599
Developing countries [2]	8,104	16,896	21,929	42,839	7,801	7,352	7,160	7606	10,751
Gross new grants	28,769	17,993	22,003	43,311	7,950	7,419	7,231	7,662	15,670
Foreign Assistance Act [3]	17,711	12,189	12,191	31,525	6,439	5,886	5,559	5,784	6,704
Farm products disposals:									
Foreign currencies, P.L. 83-480 [7]	-	2,048	4,234	186	3	6	1	1	1
Famine and other urgent relief	530	2,704	2,862	5,026	568	687	740	912	817
Payment of transportation	-	494	946	1,890	265	222	177	85	156
Food for development loan forgiveness.	-	-	-	353	53	37	133	7	166
Supplies to military or trusteeship administration areas.	5,528	132	536	1,246	217	173	202	155	50
Peace Corps	-	232	912	979	130	126	151	151	151
Forgiveness of Foreign Debt.	-	-	-	-	-	-	-	207	7,206
Other	5,000	194	321	2,106	275	284	269	360	391
Less: Reverse grants and returns	1,240	318	255	9	52	-	-	-	-
Less: Receipts from Persian Gulf partners .	-	-	-	-	-	-	-	-	5,517
Net new credits [8]	8,605	7,025	16,955	35,785	1,507	2332	-4,003	-2,335	-3,915
Developed countries [2]	6,627	-3,207	310	-1,019	557	-1,091	481	-294	90
Developing countries [2]	1,978	10,232	16,645	36,805	950	-1,241	-3,521	-2,060	-4,005
New credits	11,958	15,429	37,424	72,195	7,165	4,845	5,913	3,923	6,172
Export-Import Bank Act	4,241	5,257	15,506	22,096	1,251	990	1,060	761	2,423
Foreign Assistance Act [3]	1,919	6,196	12,053	35,324	2,932	2,529	3,476	1,578	2,238
Country program loans	1,765	5,722	8,362	10,733	595	347	455	384	215
Financing or military purchases	9	247	3,089	24,288	2,307	2,169	2,992	1,159	1,993
Social Progress Trust Fund	-	226	487	142	-5	-9	-4	-1	-14
Other.	145	2	116	162	35	22	34	36	45
P.L. 83-480 [7]	48	3,839	7,161	8,142	991	826	959	793	863
Loans of foreign currency:									
To foreign governments.	48	3,285	1,843	10	-	2	(Z)	(Z)	3
To private enterprises.	-	202	217	310	2	3	11	9	37
Long-term credit sales	-	352	5,101	8,116	988	821	948	784	823
P.L. 80-806 [9]	-	-	2,433	5,559	1,982	500	418	790	649
Other	5,750	137	271	1,074					
Less: Principal collections	3,353	8,404	20,469	36,410	5,648	7,176	9,915	6,277	10,087
Export-Import Bank Act	1,787	4,458	9,282	15,222	2,915	4,293	1,501	1,395	1,786
Foreign Assistance Act [3]	38	1,263	3,557	11,234	1,674	2,336	7,718	3,861	7,261
Country program loans	1	944	2,481	4,212	537	470	489	745	599
Financing of military purchases	2	222	852	6,492	1,095	1,835	7,197	3,083	6,636
Social Progress Trust Fund	-	9	198	354	17	16	15	11	11
Other.	35	88	25	177	25	14	18	21	14
P.L. 83-480 [7]	-	180	3,753	2,923	368	275	468	355	577
Loans of foreign currency:									
To foreign governments.	-	111	2,354	551	37	29	24	27	31
To private enterprise	-	43	175	96	3	1	1	2	4
Long-term credit sales	-	27	1,223	2,276	327	245	444	237	542
Lend-lease, surplus property, and grant settlements.	675	2,001	1,438	386	20	16	16	16	16
P.L. 80-806 [9]	-	-	1,763	4,748	569	152	106	548	340
Other	853	501	677	1,897	101	105	106	103	107

See footnotes at end of table.

No. 1325. U.S. Government Foreign Grants and Credits: 1946 to 1990—Continued

[In millions of dollars. See headnote, p. 790]

PROGRAM	1946-1955, total	1956-1965, total	1966-1975, total	1976-1985, total	1986	1987	1988	1989	1990, prel.
Other assistance (through net accumulation of foreign currency claims) [10]	541	2,802	-1,290	-287	5	-27	-36	-2	-34
Developed countries [3]	190	330	-203	-56	-3	-38	-26	-17	-7
Developing countries [2]	351	2,472	-1,086	-231	8	11	-10	14	-26
Currency claims acquired	813	11,498	6,888	1,227	134	84	82	66	76
Sales of farm products	813	11,170	3,013	114	49	41	35	25	13
Second-stage operations [11]	-	329	3,875	1,113	85	43	46	42	63
Less: Currencies disbursed.	*272*	*8,696*	*8,177*	*1,514*	*129*	*111*	*118*	*68*	*109*
Economic grants and credits to purchasing country	182	6,863	6,238	180	10	15	16	10	37
Other uses	90	1,833	1,940	1,334	119	96	101	58	72

- Represents zero. Z Less than $500,000. [1] For details, see table 1326. [2] Developed countries include Australia, Canada, Japan, New Zealand, South Africa, all countries listed under "Western Europe" in table 1326, except Portugal, Spain (through 1981), Yugoslavia, and Malta, and all countries listed under "Eastern Europe" in table 1326. Developing countries include all other countries listed in table 1326 (including Spain through 1981). [3] Foreign Assistance Act of 1961 (P.L. 87-195), as amended. Also includes predecessor and related programs. [4] Includes military assistance under Dept. of Defense Appropriation Act, 1966 (P.L. 89-394) and later acts. [5] Includes funds made available under Public Law 93-199 and subsequent legislation to release Israel from its contractual liability to pay for defense articles and services purchased under other legislation. [6] Net new grants are not adjusted for settlements for postwar relief and other grants under agreements, and net new credits exclude prior grants converted into credits, which were as follows: 1946-55, $1,463 million; 1956-65, $491 million; 1972, $994 million. Repayments on these settlements are included in net new credits. [7] Agricultural Trade Development and Assistance Act. [8] Outstanding credits on Dec. 31, 1990, totaled $60,650 million representing net credits extended since organization of Export-Import Bank, Feb. 12, 1934, less chargeoffs and net adjustments due to exchange rates ($2,055 million), and excluding World War I debts. The amount repayable in dollars at U.S. Government option was $59,325 million; the remainder was repayable in foreign currencies, commodities, or services, at the option of the borrowers. [9] Commodity Credit Corporation Charter Act. [10] Equivalent value of currencies still available to be used, including some funds advanced from foreign governments and after loss by exchange rate fluctuation ($1,592 million), was $44 million on Dec. 31, 1990. [11] Includes foreign currencies acquired from triangular trade operations and principal and interest collections on credits, originally extended under P.L. 83-480, which—since enactment of P.L. 87-128—are available for the same purposes as P.L. 83-480 currencies.

Source: U.S. Bureau of Economic Analysis, press releases, and unpublished data.

No. 1326. U.S. Government Foreign Grants and Credits, by Type and Country: 1946 to 1990

[In millions of dollars. See text, section 29. Negative figures (-) occur when the total of grant returns, principal repayments, and/or foreign currencies disbursed by the U.S. Government exceeds new grants and new credits utilized and/or acquisitions of foreign currencies through new sales of farm products. See also *Historical Statistics, Colonial Times to 1970*, series U 75-186]

TYPE AND COUNTRY	1946-1955, total	1956-1965, total	1966-1975, total	1976-1985, total	1986	1987	1988	1989	1990, prel.
Total, net	51,509	49,723	70,368	104,189	15,017	9,403	8,082	10,206	14,143
Investment in financial institutions	635	655	2,719	10,432	1,481	1,212	1,314	1,173	1,301
African Development Bank	-	-	-	54	15	20	9	7	19
African Development Fund	-	-	-	125	53	45	40	34	75
Asian Development Bank	-	-	110	602	110	95	111	160	127
Inter-American Development Bank	-	300	1,321	2,770	351	189	124	97	90
Special Facility For Sub-Saharan Africa	-	-	-	-	24	65	48	-	-
International Bank for Reconstruction and Development	635	-	13	353	241	232	95	23	61
International Development Association	-	320	1,275	6,417	658	546	826	852	842
International Finance Corporation	-	35	-	111	28	7	25	-	75
Inter-American Investment Corporation	-	-	-	-	-	-	13	-	13
Under assistance programs	50,875	49,067	67,649	93,757	13,536	8,191	6,768	9,033	12,843
Developed Countries	35,150	5,834	616	757	815	-801	-131	66	36
Developing Countries	15,725	43,233	67,033	92,999	12,721	8,992	6,899	8,967	12,807
Western Europe	33,067	6,752	-1,004	1,626	-9	-167	118	-247	-58
Austria	1,001	193	-19	34	-9	-9	-9	-11	-10
Belgium and Luxembourg	1,570	305	17	-46	-9	-9	-9	-9	-9
Denmark	596	276	64	-58	-7	-6	-	-	-
Finland	86	-26	-19	21	-47	8	6	7	-8
France	8,661	-171	-93	-222	-26	-13	-14	-14	-15
Germany	-	-	-	-	-	-	-	-	-338
Germany, Federal Republic of	3881	10	-117	-117	-	-3	-	-1	-
Iceland	34	33	-8	-12	-2	-2	-4	(Z)	(Z)
Ireland	146	-16	-51	7	2	-2	-6	-7	2
Italy	3,851	1,435	85	133	-107	-21	-28	-28	-30
Netherlands	1,716	322	116	-180	-1	-1	-	-	-
Norway	697	362	379	-257	-16	-4	-	-	-
Portugal	248	241	34	1,003	178	8	66	71	56
Spain	258	1,203	607	965	66	-11	-113	-474	-122
Sweden	107	-20	17	-1	-6	-5	-3	-2	-
United Kingdom	7,458	105	-546	-964	-202	-347	-105	-109	-111
Yugoslavia	1,356	1,151	84	174	-21	-41	-2	11	-39
Other [1] and unspecified	1,399	1,351	454	1,146	199	290	338	320	566

See footnotes at end of table.

No. 1326. U.S. Government Foreign Grants and Credits, by Type and Country: 1946 to 1990—Continued

[In millions of dollars. See headnote, p. 791]

COUNTRY	1946-1955, total	1956-1965, total	1966-1975, total	1976-1985, total	1986	1987	1988	1989	1990, prel.
Eastern Europe	**823**	**501**	**226**	**1,029**	**1,249**	**−161**	**−121**	**419**	**784**
Czechoslovakia	136	-	-	−5	-	-	-	-	(Z)
Poland	350	555	−75	1,017	1,348	−44	−53	524	749
Romania	-	-	92	55	−26	−50	−1	−59	64
Soviet Union	292	−59	214	−44	−66	−66	−66	−46	−30
Other and unspecified	45	5	−5	6	−6	-	-	-	1
Near East and South Asia	**4,944**	**16,828**	**17,195**	**50,793**	**7,926**	**6,276**	**2,128**	**4,440**	**6,563**
Afghanistan	31	227	185	56	−3	29	30	76	57
Bangladesh	-	-	701	1,670	178	150	170	138	172
Cyprus	-	19	20	138	21	17	14	19	16
Egypt	41	1,009	271	13,600	2,729	1,614	3,490	2,085	4,977
Greece	2,026	1,281	905	362	72	304	488	306	282
India	370	4,890	3,810	1,021	36	66	139	69	−32
Iran	314	1,061	914	−847	-	-	−19	-	-
Iraq	13	81	−5	5	−5	21	29	−16	−7
Israel	390	483	3,760	25,417	4,030	3,115	−1,826	1,902	4,377
Jordan	26	495	618	1,320	7	109	−231	162	135
Kuwait	-	-	-	-	-	-	-	-	−2,506
Lebanon	15	78	90	233	−12	−4	−7	(Z)	5
Nepal	3	86	105	177	20	22	19	15	19
Oman	-	-	(Z)	79	12	−33	9	8	4
Pakistan	189	3,092	2,048	1,971	347	235	389	−388	522
Saudi Arabia	12	35	23	−20	−1	-	-	-	−1,614
Sri Lanka	(Z)	89	153	512	65	40	43	43	72
Syria	1	57	15	262	(Z)	(Z)	(Z)	-	(Z)
Turkey	1,295	3,020	2,703	3,760	298	449	−720	−91	367
United Arab Emirates	-	-	-	-	-	-	(Z)	-	−361
Yemen (Sanaa)	-	40	24	216	39	47	33	42	14
Yemen	-	-	-	-	-	-	-	-	28
UNRWA [2]	-	274	296	596	67	61	54	39	7
Other and unspecified	98	510	559	263	27	34	26	29	27
Africa	**147**	**2,272**	**3,610**	**11,074**	**1,300**	**1,110**	**1,258**	**980**	**1,792**
Algeria	1	135	263	345	−128	−98	−58	−77	59
Angola	-	-	6	115	27	24	2	−13	−16
Benin	-	7	12	44	3	3	5	12	5
Botswana	-	(Z)	35	169	20	28	20	15	17
Burkina	-	5	40	287	30	24	18	14	14
Burundi	-	4	5	62	5	5	5	3	18
Cameroon	-	16	50	150	11	13	24	18	42
Cape Verde	-	-	1	68	9	7	6	4	6
Chad	(Z)	5	20	145	25	35	38	15	24
Ethiopia	13	200	297	310	88	13	71	37	51
Ghana	(Z)	64	203	152	13	10	17	46	13
Guinea	-	58	68	74	16	24	19	5	15
Ivory Coast	-	14	57	57	5	−3	27	2	27
Kenya	(Z)	34	76	549	39	46	47	54	109
Lesotho	-	(Z)	27	197	23	24	23	19	15
Liberia	24	139	86	459	52	23	27	13	20
Madagascar	(Z)	7	13	86	21	17	19	7	30
Malawi	-	5	30	56	11	19	34	44	31
Mali	-	12	58	199	45	34	50	27	31
Mauritania	-	1	20	161	19	12	11	14	11
Morocco	7	464	413	948	177	85	185	−5	94
Mozambique	-	-	1	175	34	69	56	48	75
Niger	-	5	64	223	39	43	25	34	33
Nigeria	(Z)	87	284	267	1	1	169	44	156
Rwanda	-	2	13	91	24	16	16	9	13
Senegal	-	18	48	361	45	49	45	46	60
Sierra Leone	(Z)	22	36	85	12	12	8	12	2

See footnotes at end of table.

No. 1326. U.S. Government Foreign Grants and Credits, by Type and Country: 1946 to 1990—Continued

[In millions of dollars. See headnote, p. 791]

COUNTRY	1946-1955, total	1956-1965, total	1966-1975, total	1976-1985, total	1986	1987	1988	1989	1990, prel.
Africa—Continued									
Somalia	(Z)	42	47	582	111	69	62	38	77
Sudan	-	86	52	1,358	164	101	110	118	145
Swaziland	-	(Z)	8	58	9	16	12	11	14
Tanzania	2	34	123	259	10	40	16	16	40
Togo	-	9	18	60	10	13	9	15	10
Tunisia	2	407	376	563	7	-7	-175	56	38
Uganda	-	12	33	40	4	17	21	20	31
Zaire	(Z)	258	342	938	104	112	141	72	241
Zambia	-	1	35	331	77	36	18	21	58
Zimbabwe	-	(Z)	(Z)	271	22	33	6	12	10
Other and unspecified	96	118	350	781	117	154	133	157	173
Far East and Pacific	9,678	16,199	34,780	9,635	-64	-2,614	308	381	-132
Australia	-9	(Z)	276	-12	-118	-30	-26	-18	-34
Burma	25	134	43	31	7	10	9	1	1
Cambodia	28	327	1,771	-	-	-	-	-	-
China: Mainland	-	-	-	49	-8	9	48	35	71
Taiwan	1,267	2,681	1,523	648	-262	-970	-8	-7	-7
Hong Kong	3	35	41	11	-11	-8	-8	-8	-8
Indonesia	246	501	1,390	1,661	13	-12	-3	36	48
Japan and Ryukyu Islands	3,267	1,318	-345	-210	-88	-319	-4	-1	-635
Laos	37	647	1,868	-	-	-	-	-	-
Malaysia	1	30	86	39	-15	-12	-9	-36	-1
New Zealand	3	2	95	-68	-10	-4	-4	-4	-2
Pacific Islands, Trust Territory of the [3]	28	89	488	1,260	219	166	138	156	52
Philippines	1,028	554	729	1,466	449	331	421	310	557
Singapore	-	(Z)	78	110	-184	1	1	1	2
South Korea	1,420	4,744	5,426	3,518	-146	-1,717	-383	-132	-192
Thailand	192	727	996	733	62	-77	72	12	-21
Vietnam	244	3,566	19,721	-	-	-	-	-	-
Other and unspecified	1,898	844	595	400	27	18	65	36	39
Western Hemisphere	1,248	5,181	6,816	9,861	1,815	2,100	1,448	1,117	1,887
Argentina	86	342	34	21	85	27	16	-6	64
Bolivia	77	288	270	414	111	124	82	131	109
Brazil	509	1,400	1,518	399	7	34	(Z)	-202	235
Canada	-1	4	272	317	-61	-158	-50	-30	-41
Chile	100	740	724	-565	56	26	11	-46	-32
Colombia	43	446	846	298	63	22	-23	-36	-29
Costa Rica	15	83	103	687	139	159	107	143	103
Dominican Republic	2	184	360	550	230	78	52	52	26
Ecuador	32	131	144	153	59	60	47	23	46
El Salvador	3	56	93	1,681	376	418	405	406	300
Guatemala	23	146	160	270	91	159	142	161	92
Guyana	(Z)	7	71	36	2	8	5	8	42
Haiti	27	75	42	370	87	94	41	76	49
Honduras	6	53	113	801	224	212	194	133	218
Jamaica	16	3	120	643	121	92	95	138	107
Mexico	225	178	305	1,162	-29	543	62	-100	131
Nicaragua	8	67	150	197	(Z)	(Z)	(Z)	(Z)	97
Panama	10	103	210	205	24	10	13	8	99
Paraguay	4	67	86	22	(Z)	(Z)	(Z)	1	(Z)
Peru	55	304	274	757	98	74	67	36	79
Trinidad and Tobago	-	35	21	151	-32	-33	-11	16	5
Uruguay	8	90	116	-9	11	-3	9	-6	-4
Venezuela	6	156	115	-35	-31	-38	-28	-21	-18
Central American Bank for Economic Integration	*	6	121	36	-5	-4	-3	-1	-5
Caribbean Development Bank	-	-	8	108	-1	-1	2	-2	-2
Other [4] and unspecified	-6	218	543	1,193	189	197	219	233	215
Other international organizations and unspecified areas	969	1,335	4,018	9,739	1,319	1,648	1,623	1,943	2,007

- Represents zero.   Z Less than $500,000.   [1] Includes European Atomic Energy Community, European Coal and Steel Community, European Payments Union, European Productivity Agency, North Atlantic Treaty Organization, and Organization for European Economic Cooperation.   [2] United Nations Relief and Works Agency for Palestine refugees.   [3] Excludes transactions after October 1986, with Commonwealth of the Northern Mariana Islands; includes transactions with Federated States of Micronesia, Republic of the Marshall Islands, and Republic of Palau.   [4] Includes Andean Development Corporation, Eastern Caribbean Central Bank, Inter-American Institute of Agricultural Sciences, Organization of American States, and Pan American Health Organization.

Source: U.S. Bureau of Economic Analysis, press releases; and unpublished data.

No. 1327. U.S. Foreign Economic and Military Aid Programs: 1946 to 1990

[In millions of dollars. For years ending June 30 except, beginning 1977, ending Sept. 30. Economic aid shown here represents I U.S. economic aid-not just aid under Foreign Assistance Act. Major components in recent years include AID, Food for Peace, Peace Corps, and paid-in subscriptions to international financial institutions, such as IBRD, and IDB. Cumulative totals for 1946-1990 are true totals net of deobligation; annual figures however, are gross unadjusted program figures. Military aid includes Military Assistance Program (MAP) grants, foreign military credit sales, service-funded programs, and excess defense articles]

PERIOD OR YEAR AND REGION	Total economic and military aid	ECONOMIC AID			MILITARY AID		
		Total	Loans	Grants	Total	Loans	Grants
1946-1990, total	374,046	232,971	56,364	176,607	141,075	40,983	100,092
1946-1952	41,661	31,116	8,518	22,598	10,545	-	10,545
1953-1961	43,358	24,053	5,850	18,203	19,305	161	19,144
1962-1969	50,254	33,392	15,421	17,972	16,862	1,620	15,242
1970-1979	65,714	26,902	9,995	16,907	38,812	14,179	24,633
1980-1986	96,368	63,081	10,941	52,140	33,287	19,758	13,529
1980-1987	111,650	73,261	12,194	61,067	38,389	20,711	17,678
1980-1988	125,442	82,222	13,046	69,176	43,220	21,474	21,746
1980-1989	140,130	92,082	13,740	78,342	48,048	21,884	26,164
1980-1990	155,857	102,916	14,496	88,420	52,941	22,288	30,653
1970	6,568	3,676	1,389	2,288	2,892	70	2,822
1975	6,916	4,908	1,679	3,229	2,009	750	1,259
1976	6,412	3,878	1,759	2,119	2,535	1,442	1,093
1976, TQ [1]	2,603	1,931	840	1,091	672	494	178
1977	7,784	5,594	2,083	3,511	2,190	1,411	779
1978	9,014	6,661	2,530	4,131	2,353	1,601	752
1979	13,845	7,120	1,900	5,220	6,725	5,173	1,552
1980	9,695	7,573	1,993	5,580	2,122	1,450	672
1981	10,550	7,305	1,460	5,845	3,245	2,546	699
1982	12,324	8,129	1,454	6,675	4,195	3,084	1,111
1983	14,202	8,603	1,619	6,984	5,599	3,932	1,667
1984	15,524	9,038	1,621	7,417	6,486	4,401	2,085
1985	18,128	12,327	1,579	10,748	5,801	2,365	3,436
1986	16,739	10,900	1,330	9,570	5,839	1,980	3,859
1987	14,488	9,386	1,138	8,248	5,102	953	4,149
1988	13,792	8,961	852	8,109	4,831	763	4,068
1989	14,688	9,860	694	9,166	4,828	410	4,418
1990	15,727	10,834	756	10,078	4,893	404	4,489
Near East and South Asia	7,377	3,136	373	2,763	4,241	404	3,837
East Asia	687	535	21	514	152	-	152
Europe	373	284	64	220	89	-	89
Latin America	2,144	1,910	184	1,726	234	-	234
Africa.	1,176	1,062	111	951	114	-	114
Oceania and other	25	25	-	25	(Z)	-	(Z)
Non-regional	3,945	3,883	3	3,880	63	-	63

- Represents zero.   Z Less than $500,000.   [1] Transition quarter, July-Sept.

No. 1328. U.S. Foreign Military Aid, by Region and Selected Countries: 1985 to 1990

[In millions of dollars. For years ending Sept. 30. Military aid data include Military Assistance Program (MAP foreign military credit sales, International Military Education and Training, and excess defense articles]

REGION AND COUNTRY	1985	1987	1988	1989	1990	REGION AND COUNTRY	1985	1987	1988	1989	1990
Total	5,801	5,102	4,831	4,828	4,893	Cameroon	5	1	(Z)	(Z)	(Z)
Europe	531	191	88	105	89	Djibouti	3	1	1	1	2
Portugal	128	83	85	103	87	Gabon	(Z)	(Z)	(Z)	(Z)	(Z)
Spain	403	108	2	2	2	Kenya	22	12	6	16	11
Near East and						Liberia	13	1	1	1	(Z)
South Asia	4,248	4,299	4,231	4,202	4,241	Morocco	50	46	53	53	44
Egypt.	1,177	1,302	1,302	1,302	1,296	Niger	5	2	1	1	2
Greece	501	344	344	351	349	Somalia	34	8	7	1	1
Israel	1,400	1,800	1,800	1,800	1,792	Sudan	46	6	1	1	2
Jordan.	92	42	28	12	70	Tunisia.	67	34	28	31	31
Lebanon	1	1	(Z)	(Z)	(Z)	Zaire	8	5	4	4	4
Oman	40	(Z)	(Z)	(Z)	(Z)	**Latin America** [1] . . .	269	215	144	164	234
Pakistan.	326	314	261	231	230	Colombia	1	5	4	8	73
Turkey.	704	494	493	504	501	Costa Rica	11	2	(Z)	(Z)	(Z)
Yemen.	6	2	2	2	2	Dominican Rep . .	9	3	1	1	21
East Asia	416	171	182	157	152	Ecuador	7	5	1	5	1
Indonesia	34	12	6	3	2	El Salvador.	136	112	82	81	81
Malaysia	5	1	1	1	2	Haiti	1	1	(Z)	(Z)	1
Philippines	42	103	128	128	143	Honduras	67	61	41	41	21
South Korea	232	2	2	2	2	Jamaica.	8	3	(Z)	4	1
Thailand.	102	52	46	24	5	Panama.	11	4	-	-	-
Africa [1]	279	139	116	118	114	Peru	9	(Z)	(Z)	3	2
Botswana.	9	2	(Z)	1	2	**Nonregional**	58	88	70	82	63

- Represents zero.   Z Less than $500,000.   [1] Includes countries not shown separately.
Source of tables 1327 and 1328: U.S. Agency for International Development, *U.S. Overseas Loans and Grants and Assistance from International Organizations,* annual.

No. 1329. U.S. Foreign Aid—Commitments for Economic Assistance, by Region and Selected Countries: 1985 to 1990

[In millions of dollars. For years ending Sept. 30. Falls under economic portion of the Foreign Assistance Act. Data cover commitments for economic and technical assistance by AID. See text, section 29]

REGION AND COUNTRY	1985	1987	1988	1989	1990
Total	8,132	6,355	5,705	6,136	6,964
Europe	94	106	77	54	141
Italy	2	(Z)	-	-	-
Portugal	80	65	32	50	39
Spain	12	5	3	-	-
Near East and South Asia [1]	3,867	2,763	2,523	2,562	2,565
Bangladesh	76	80	49	53	56
Cyprus	15	15	10	20	5
Egypt	1,065	820	718	817	901
Israel	1,950	1,200	1,200	1,200	1,195
Jordan	100	111	24	16	4
Lebanon	20	13	5	3	8
Nepal	18	16	12	15	17
Oman	20	15	13	15	13
Pakistan	250	276	385	265	276
Sri Lanka	35	26	28	29	21
Turkey	175	102	32	60	14
Yemen (Sanaa)	28	25	22	24	23
Regional	23	-5	-	-	12
East Asia	313	440	225	541	482
Burma	15	7	6	-	-
Indonesia	72	88	42	50	48
Philippines	183	253	78	347	314
Thailand	36	27	25	23	14
East Asia Regional	7	65	74	122	106
Africa [1]	900	620	644	748	666
Botswana	10	6	13	9	9
Burkina	8	9	4	6	4
Burundi	4	2	6	2	20
Cameroon	24	31	19	33	22
Cape Verde	3	2	3	3	3
Chad	16	11	17	16	11
Congo	1	1	1	1	1
Djibouti	4	2	4	3	1
Equatorial Guinea	1	1	1	1	1
Gambia, The	6	9	4	4	5
Ghana	2	3	7	10	15
Guinea	4	2	18	16	15
Guinea-Bissau	4	1	1	2	3
Kenya	40	37	43	56	36
Lesotho	11	13	26	10	7

REGION AND COUNTRY	1985	1987	1988	1989	1990
Liberia	60	27	10	21	(Z)
Malawi	25	13	44	21	23
Mali	32	12	21	27	21
Mauritania	11	4	4	2	1
Mauritius	7	3	15	2	(Z)
Morocco	38	28	31	32	31
Niger	28	27	35	24	20
Rwanda	19	9	5	9	12
Senegal	44	35	24	49	37
Seychelles	2	3	3	3	3
Sierra Leone	(Z)	1	1	1	1
Somalia	51	36	10	13	1
Sudan	149	21	17	5	8
Swaziland	9	9	16	7	7
Tanzania	(Z)	58	9	10	9
Togo	4	5	4	4	4
Tunisia	23	18	12	13	14
Uganda	9	7	25	14	43
Zaire	36	33	31	36	31
Zambia	42	17	13	7	17
Zimbabwe	41	6	13	29	28
Regional	96	52	65	110	73
Latin America [1]	1,506	1,310	967	937	1,486
Belize	23	13	8	8	6
Bolivia	18	29	38	37	58
Costa Rica	196	161	101	115	78
Dominican Rep.	126	20	33	20	18
Ecuador	33	37	15	27	17
El Salvador	376	415	266	253	200
Grenada	11	-	-	-	-
Guatemala	76	154	110	114	86
Guyana	-	-	-	-	21
Haiti	31	75	31	40	42
Honduras	205	175	130	53	167
Jamaica	115	44	40	65	28
Nicaragua	-	-	-	4	220
Panama	74	12	1	-	396
Paraguay	1	1	1	1	1
Peru	38	21	28	22	22
ROCAP [2]	107	58	59	48	30
Regional	30	29	74	100	88
Nonregional	1,453	1,116	1,269	1,296	1,625

- Represents zero.   Z Less than $500,000.   [1] Includes countries not shown separately.   [2] Regional programs covering Costa Rica, El Salvador, Guatemala, Honduras, Nicaragua, and Panama.

Source: U.S. Agency for International Development, *U.S. Overseas Loans and Grants and Assistance from International Organizations,* annual; and unpublished data.

No. 1330. U.S. Exports and Imports of Merchandise: 1970 to 1991

[**In billions of dollars, except percent.** Includes silver ore and bullion; beginning 1974, includes shipments of nonmonetary gold. Data may differ from those shown in other tables due to revisions and inclusion of the Virgin Islands since 1974. For basis of dollar values, see text, section 29. See also *Historical Statistics, Colonial Times to 1970*, series U 190-195 and U 207-212]

YEAR	Merchandise trade balance	EXPORTS [1]					GENERAL IMPORTS [4]				AVERAGE ANNUAL PERCENT CHANGE [5]	
		Total [2]	Domestic				Total [3]	Petro-leum	Machin-ery	Trans-port equip-ment	Domestic exports	General imports
			Total [3]	Agri-cultural	Machin-ery	Trans-port equip-ment						
1970	2.7	42.7	42.0	7.2	11.4	6.5	40.0	2.8	5.3	5.9	14.1	10.8
1971	-2.0	43.5	42.9	7.7	11.6	7.9	45.6	3.3	6.0	7.9	1.9	14.0
1972	-6.4	49.2	48.4	9.4	13.2	8.3	55.6	4.3	7.8	9.6	13.1	21.9
1973	1.3	70.8	69.7	17.7	17.7	17.1	69.5	7.6	10.0	11.1	43.9	25.0
1974	-4.5	98.1	96.5	22.0	23.7	14.5	102.6	24.3	11.6	12.5	38.6	47.6
1975	9.1	107.7	106.1	21.9	28.5	17.2	98.5	24.8	12.0	12.2	9.8	-4.0
1976	-8.3	115.2	113.5	23.0	31.3	18.2	123.5	31.8	15.2	14.6	7.0	25.4
1977	-29.2	121.2	118.9	23.7	32.5	18.5	150.4	41.5	17.7	17.8	5.2	21.8
1978	-31.1	143.7	141.0	29.4	37.0	22.3	174.8	39.1	24.4	23.2	18.6	16.2
1979	-27.6	181.9	178.6	34.8	44.7	25.8	209.5	56.0	28.0	25.6	26.6	19.9
1980	-24.2	220.6	216.5	41.3	55.8	28.8	244.9	77.6	31.9	28.6	21.3	16.9
1981	-27.3	233.7	228.9	43.3	62.9	32.8	261.0	75.6	38.2	31.4	5.9	6.6
1982	-31.8	212.3	207.1	36.6	60.3	23.6	244.0	59.4	39.7	33.6	-9.2	-6.5
1983	-57.5	200.5	196.0	36.1	54.3	28.3	258.0	52.3	47.0	39.2	-5.6	5.7
1984	-107.9	217.9	212.1	37.8	60.3	29.7	325.7	55.9	68.4	50.8	8.7	26.2
1985	-132.1	213.1	206.9	29.2	59.5	34.8	345.3	49.6	75.3	62.0	-2.2	6.0
1986	-152.7	217.3	206.4	26.1	60.4	34.9	370.0	34.1	87.5	74.0	2.0	7.2
1987	-152.1	254.1	243.9	28.6	69.6	39.0	406.2	41.5	99.4	78.4	16.9	9.8
1988	-118.6	322.4	310.0	37.0	88.4	46.7	441.0	38.8	117.3	79.8	26.9	8.6
1989	-109.6	363.8	349.4	40.0	98.3	50.5	473.4	49.1	126.8	79.0	12.8	7.3
1990	-101.7	393.6	375.1	38.7	122.4	32.1	495.3	60.5	134.8	72.4	8.2	4.6
1991	-66.2	421.9	400.9	38.5	139.7	34.9	488.1	50.1	131.8	70.6	7.2	-1.5

[1] Includes "Special Category" items and beginning 1974, includes trade of Virgin Islands with foreign countries. F.a.s. value basis. [2] Domestic and foreign exports excluding M.A.P. Grant-Aid shipments, through 1985; 1986 through 1988 include Grant-Aid shipments. [3] Includes commodity groups not shown separately. [4] 1970-73, 1982-91, customs value basis; 1974-81, f.a.s. value basis. Beginning 1974, includes trade of Virgin Islands with foreign countries. [5] 1970, change from 1965; thereafter, from previous year. For explanation of average annual percent change, see Guide to Tabular Presentation.

Source: U.S. Bureau of the Census, 1970-88, *Highlights of U.S. Export and Import Trade*, FT 990, monthly; beginning 1989, *U.S. Merchandise Trade: Export, General Imports, and Imports for Consumption*, FT 925, monthly.

No. 1331. U.S. Exports, by State of Origin: 1989 to 1991

[**In millions of dollars.** Exports are on a f.a.s. value basis]

STATE	1989	1990	1991 Total	1991 Rank	STATE	1989	1990	1991 Total	1991 Rank
Total	364,350	394,045	421,851	(X)	MT	283	229	279	48
					NE	669	693	960	40
U.S.	271,830	315,065	351,343	(X)	NV	283	394	427	44
AL	2,950	2,834	3,325	26	NH	935	973	988	39
AK	2,024	2,850	3,134	28	NJ	6,492	7,633	8,740	13
AZ	3,300	3,729	4,465	20	NM	192	249	309	47
AR	728	920	1,147	37	NY	19,580	22,072	23,261	4
CA	40,231	44,520	50,415	1	NC	6,571	8,010	8,540	14
CO	2,153	2,274	2,574	29	ND	299	360	335	45
CT	3,667	4,356	4,995	19	OH	10,172	13,378	14,855	7
DE	841	1,344	1,441	36	OK	1,428	1,646	1,770	33
DC	229	320	269	(X)	OR	3,878	4,065	4,264	22
FL	10,196	11,634	13,257	9	PA	6,809	8,491	9,411	12
GA	4,859	5,763	6,815	15	RI	526	595	679	43
HI	160	179	148	50	SC	2,875	3,116	3,741	23
ID	750	898	958	41	SD	129	205	218	49
IL	10,434	12,965	14,025	8	TN	2,918	3,746	4,344	21
IN	4,246	5,273	5,724	16	TX	30,020	32,931	40,079	2
IA	2,172	2,189	2,263	30	UT	1,114	1,596	1,906	32
KS	1,674	2,113	2,148	31	VT	1,016	1,154	1,091	38
KY	2,509	3,175	3,217	27	VA	7,657	9,333	10,004	11
LA	15,033	14,199	15,456	6	WA	19,305	24,432	27,053	3
ME	691	870	915	42	WV	1,234	1,550	1,656	35
MD	2,441	2,592	3,363	25	WI	4,129	5,158	5,319	18
MA	8,619	9,501	10,018	10	WY	237	264	328	46
MI	14,881	18,474	20,236	5					
MN	4,413	5,091	5,376	17	PR	2,901	3,600	3,657	(X)
MS	1,466	1,605	1,738	34	VI	63	51	171	(X)
MO	2415	3,130	3,367	24	Other [1]	89,556	75,328	66,680	(X)

X Not applicable.   [1] Includes unreported, not specified, special category, estimated shipments, foreign trade zone, and re-exports

Source: U.S. Bureau of the Census, *U.S. Merchandise Trade*, series FT 900, December issues.

No. 1332. U.S. Exports and Imports for Consumption of Merchandise, by Coastal Area and Customs District: 1980 to 1991

[In billions of dollars. Exports are f.a.s. (free alongside ship) value all years; imports are on customs value basis for years 1983 to present; f.a.s. value basis for 1980. See also *Historical Statistics, Colonial Times to 1970*, series U 264-273]

U.S. COASTAL AREA AND CUSTOMS DISTRICT	EXPORTS							IMPORTS FOR CONSUMPTION						
	1980	1985	1987	1988	1989	1990	1991	1980	1985	1987	1988	1989	1990	1991
Total [1]	220.8	213.1	252.9	320.4	363.8	393.0	421.9	244.0	343.6	402.1	437.1	468.0	490.6	483.0
North Atlantic area	68.8	46.5	53.4	69.2	79.2	85.7	90.6	79.8	107.1	123.0	126.3	126.8	128.7	123.6
Portland, ME.	4.3	0.6	0.8	1.0	1.2	1.7	2.1	1.6	2.3	3.3	3.4	3.5	4.3	3.8
St. Albans, VT.	0.7	1.1	1.6	1.9	2.7	4.0	4.1	1.6	2.7	3.2	3.6	4.2	5.2	5.2
Boston, MA	0.8	3.0	4.4	5.7	6.2	5.6	4.3	5.0	8.2	12.0	12.6	12.0	12.2	11.8
Providence, RI	2.7	0.1	(Z)	(Z)	(Z)	(Z)	(Z)	1.5	2.3	1.6	1.5	1.4	1.3	1.1
New York, NY.	38.9	28.5	32.8	42.4	47.0	50.9	54.6	43.4	60.5	68.4	69.7	70.4	68.0	67.4
Philadelphia, PA	3.2	2.0	2.4	3.4	3.9	4.0	4.4	15.6	15.8	15.6	15.6	16.0	18.3	16.1
Baltimore, MD.	9.0	5.5	5.4	6.8	7.7	6.7	8.0	6.0	8.8	11.8	12.1	11.8	11.2	10.1
Norfolk, VA [2]	8.0	5.4	5.5	7.3	9.4	11.7	11.5	4.7	6.0	6.3	7.0	6.8	7.4	7.4
Washington, DC	0.3	0.5	0.5	0.7	1.1	1.1	1.6	0.4	0.5	0.7	0.8	0.7	0.8	0.7
South Atlantic area	14.7	15.0	18.7	24.2	27.7	31.0	34.5	15.5	20.4	26.6	28.4	31.5	34.5	33.6
Wilmington, NC	1.3	1.3	1.1	1.4	2.1	3.0	2.8	1.1	1.9	2.5	2.9	3.0	3.3	3.4
Charleston, SC [2]	3.1	2.9	3.6	5.0	6.2	6.7	7.2	1.8	3.3	5.9	6.1	6.5	6.8	6.3
Savannah, GA.	2.4	3.4	4.4	6.0	6.8	7.4	8.4	2.2	5.1	7.4	8.3	4.5	9.8	10.1
San Juan, PR	0.9	1.2	1.4	1.7	2.1	2.5	2.4	3.7	4.0	3.9	4.1	4.7	5.4	4.8
Virgin Islands of the U.S..	0.1	0.1	0.1	0.1	0.1	0.2	0.3	4.1	1.7	1.7	1.0	1.6	2.1	1.7
Miami, FL.	6.9	6.1	8.1	9.9	10.4	11.2	13.4	2.6	4.4	5.7	6.0	6.2	7.1	7.3
Gulf area	51.1	38.4	39.0	49.7	56.9	58.2	66.0	62.3	50.5	53.1	56.3	64.1	72.3	67.6
Tampa, FL	2.8	2.8	2.7	3.6	4.0	4.3	5.2	3.7	6.6	7.4	7.3	6.7	7.0	6.8
Mobile, AL [2]	2.6	1.1	1.4	1.4	1.9	1.9	2.2	3.0	2.8	2.9	2.8	3.4	3.4	3.3
New Orleans, LA	19.5	13.9	14.0	16.9	18.5	18.0	18.8	22.5	14.7	15.9	17.1	20.6	24.1	22.3
Port Arthur, TX	2.0	0.8	0.9	1.1	1.2	0.9	0.7	9.4	2.7	1.9	1.8	2.8	3.2	2.8
Laredo, TX	8.3	7.2	7.5	10.6	13.4	15.2	18.2	2.7	4.8	6.8	7.9	9.4	10.0	10.4
St. Louis, MO	0.2	0.1	0.2	0.2	0.5	0.3	0.4	0.9	1.6	2.3	2.7	3.0	3.0	2.8
Houston/Galveston, TX .	15.7	12.5	12.5	15.9	17.4	17.6	20.5	20.1	17.3	16.0	16.7	18.2	21.6	19.2
Pacific area	43.8	49.6	61.1	82.8	98.9	111.2	120.0	43.1	80.4	101.6	111.8	121.4	125.7	127.3
San Diego, CA	1.4	1.6	1.7	2.5	3.0	3.4	3.9	1.0	1.8	2.7	3.4	4.0	4.3	4.7
Los Angeles, CA	14.8	19.5	23.7	32.0	38.6	42.1	46.0	20.0	44.1	53.6	58.0	62.3	64.1	66.4
San Francisco, CA	10.6	11.3	14.3	19.1	21.4	23.1	23.9	8.3	15.5	21.8	25.1	27.1	28.0	29.2
Portland, OR.	3.8	3.5	3.7	5.6	6.2	5.8	6.0	2.6	3.8	4.6	5.8	5.7	5.6	5.3
Seattle, WA	12.0	12.1	15.7	20.9	26.6	32.6	35.0	9.2	13.4	17.2	17.8	20.2	20.9	18.9
Anchorage, AK	1.0	1.3	1.7	2.2	2.6	3.7	4.6	0.2	0.2	0.1	0.2	0.4	0.7	0.9
Honolulu, HI	0.2	0.4	0.4	0.6	0.5	0.5	0.6	1.8	1.6	1.6	1.6	1.7	2.1	1.9
Great Lakes area	35.0	46.5	54.8	62.6	63.9	78.7	80.6	37.0	72.3	81.9	95.9	103.7	107.5	108.1
Ogdensburg, NY	3.8	4.1	4.7	5.3	5.6	7.9	7.5	4.6	6.8	7.9	8.5	9.2	9.8	9.9
Buffalo, NY.	6.3	8.4	9.5	10.5	9.5	15.8	15.7	7.4	14.7	15.4	18.1	19.0	19.2	18.7
Pembina, ND	2.3	2.2	2.5	2.8	3.4	3.4	4.3	3.0	3.2	2.7	3.3	3.9	4.1	4.1
Minneapolis, MN	0.1	0.2	0.3	0.5	0.8	0.9	0.9	0.3	1.0	1.4	1.6	1.9	2.0	2.2
Duluth, MN.	1.5	0.9	0.7	1.2	1.2	0.8	0.8	3.0	3.0	2.9	3.2	3.5	3.9	3.3
Milwaukee, WI.	0.4	0.2	0.1	0.1	0.1	0.1	0.1	0.4	1.0	0.9	1.1	0.9	1.1	1.1
Detroit, MI	14.6	22.8	26.6	30.1	28.9	35.6	36.0	12.7	27.4	29.7	35.7	38.7	37.8	37.6
Chicago, IL.	4.2	5.4	6.9	8.7	10.0	10.2	11.3	4.1	11.4	13.8	16.1	17.4	18.3	19.4
Cleveland, OH.	1.8	2.1	3.4	3.4	3.9	4.0	4.0	1.5	3.8	7.3	8.3	9.2	11.3	11.8
Other statistical areas [3] . .	7.4	17.1	25.9	31.8	37.7	28.2	30.2	6.3	12.7	15.8	18.5	19.8	21.9	22.8
El Paso, TX	1.8	2.1	2.6	3.8	4.0	3.9	4.7	1.4	2.5	3.4	4.5	5.1	5.0	5.5
Nogales, AZ	0.8	0.8	1.0	1.3	1.5	2.1	2.2	1.2	2.0	3.1	3.2	3.7	4.2	4.4
Great Falls, MT.	1.8	1.5	1.2	1.6	1.8	2.4	3.3	3.2	4.0	3.7	4.0	4.1	4.7	4.6
Dallas/Fort Worth, TX . . .	0.5	1.0	1.5	2.1	2.7	3.4	2.6	1.2	2.4	3.3	4.1	4.1	4.8	4.9

Z Less than $50 million. [1] Totals shown for exports reflect the value of estimated parcel post and Special Category shipments, and beginning 1987, adjustments for undocumented exports to Canada which are not distributed by coastal area/customs district. Beginning 1985, the value of bituminous coal exported through Norfolk, VA; Charleston, SC; and Mobile, AL is reflected in the total but not distributed by district. Total bituminous coal exports for the 3 customs districts were valued at $2.3 billion in 1984, $2.6 billion in 1985, $2.3 billion in 1986, $1.9 billion in 1987, and $2.4 billion in 1988. [2] Beginning 1985, excludes exports of bituminous coal. [3] Includes estimated shipments and vessel-own power.

Source: U.S. Bureau of the Census, 1980-1988, *Highlights of U.S. Export and Import Trade*, FT 990; beginning 1989, *U.S. Merchandise Trade: Selected Highlights*, series FT 920, monthly.

No. 1333. Export and Import Unit Value Indexes—Selected Countries: 1986 to 1991

[Indexes in U.S. dollars, 1985 = 100. A unit value is an implicit price derived from value and quantity data. NA Not available]

COUNTRY	EXPORT UNIT VALUE						IMPORT UNIT VALUE					
	1986	1987	1988	1989	1990	1991	1986	1987	1988	1989	1990	1991
United States	101	103	110	113	114	(NA)	97	104	109	112	116	(NA)
Australia.	97	106	132	141	(NA)	(NA)	105	116	127	127	(NA)	(NA)
Austria	133	156	161	155	182	(NA)	125	144	147	143	167	(NA)
Belgium-Luxembourg	119	139	145	146	167	162	111	129	135	135	156	152
Canada	95	103	112	119	119	118	97	101	107	112	116	116
Denmark.	127	148	149	146	170	165	119	134	138	137	156	152
France	123	140	146	144	166	159	110	125	130	129	149	143
Germany	131	154	159	156	179	173	114	129	133	134	152	150
Italy	122	142	149	150	175	174	105	120	124	127	144	138
Japan.	120	131	144	142	142	152	85	92	98	101	107	105
Norway.	87	93	96	101	117	(NA)	116	131	140	140	155	(NA)
Sweden	120	138	148	151	168	(NA)	111	128	138	137	152	(NA)
United Kingdom	103	119	130	130	148	148	110	124	135	133	149	149

Source: International Monetary Fund, Washington, DC, *International Financial Statistics*, monthly.

No. 1334. U.S. Domestic Exports and General Imports of Selected Commodities—Value, by Area: 1990

[In millions of dollars. Includes nonmonetary gold. Exports are f.a.s. (free alongside ship) transaction value basis; imports are customs value basis]

SELECTED MAJOR COMMODITIES	Total [1]	WESTERN HEMISPHERE		WESTERN EUROPE				ASIA		
		Canada	Mexico	United King-dom	Ger-many[1]	France	Italy	Japan	China: Taiwan	South Korea
Domestic exports, total	393,592	83,674	28,279	23,490	18,760	13,664	7,992	48,580	11,491	14,404
Meat and meat preparations	3,219	496	270	8	10	65	16	1,567	15	129
Fish (except marine mammal) crustaceans, etc., preparations	2,907	391	26	100	66	86	26	1,799	43	107
Cereals and cereal preparations	12,629	347	931	42	72	48	107	2,419	659	827
Vegetables and fruit	5,544	2,123	208	240	297	127	70	938	171	56
Feeding stuff for animals not including unmilled cereal	2,938	328	131	76	31	94	92	370	55	15
Miscellaneous edible products and preparations	1,005	246	55	14	8	7	2	66	40	24
Tobacco and tobacco manufactures	6,516	12	3	59	253	24	61	1,622	159	115
Hides, skins, and furskins, raw	1,768	120	99	4	12	20	42	457	114	780
Oil seeds and oleaginous fruits	3,914	135	232	132	227	39	77	848	413	197
Cork and wood	5,254	686	166	111	116	38	177	2,690	112	316
Pulp and waste paper	4,073	298	323	160	289	198	281	777	203	405
Textile fibers & their wastes (excluding wool tops, etc)	3,904	151	118	55	208	13	199	629	140	508
Crude fertilizers & crude minerals [2]	1,320	278	71	37	61	15	49	292	41	61
Metalliferous ores and metal scrap	5,094	934	231	175	153	58	133	1,036	202	646
Crude animal and vegetable materials, n.e.s.	1,065	216	110	49	64	23	37	147	14	29
Coal, coke and briquettes	4,639	615	25	245	45	296	538	597	178	186
Petroleum, petroleum products, and related materials	6,721	988	610	81	48	175	214	722	309	550
Organic chemicals	10,556	1,150	604	359	451	197	230	1,137	873	698
Inorganic chemicals	3,894	473	224	127	243	57	51	987	129	217
Dyeing, tanning and coloring materials	1,603	429	99	104	54	20	16	116	37	88
Medicinal and pharmaceutical products	4,177	462	106	221	328	271	293	765	50	53
Essential oils, etc; toilet, polishing, preparations	2,024	412	131	128	73	64	27	249	53	51
Fertilizers [3]	2,590	189	46	5	37	58	15	160	2	82
Plastics in primary forms	6,457	1,184	537	257	206	84	56	448	255	264
Plastics in nonprimary forms	2,657	745	325	136	144	70	58	196	46	62
Chemical materials and products, n.e.s.	5,576	1,127	253	209	273	308	111	569	94	204
Rubber manufactures, n.e.s.	2,134	991	204	78	73	26	17	235	17	32
Cork and wood manufactures other than furniture	1,277	279	109	137	117	10	24	109	40	54
Paper, paperboard and articles	5,055	1,336	633	244	154	64	91	513	94	127
Textile yarn, fabrics, made-up articles, n.e.s.	5,065	1,248	516	300	189	94	138	272	65	106
Nonmetallic mineral manufactures, n.e.s.	4,589	1,164	231	184	114	69	54	548	71	89
Iron and steel	3,515	1,462	563	108	62	59	57	215	28	150
Nonferrous metals	5,293	1,435	370	226	135	123	72	1,574	358	168
Manufactures of metals, n.e.s.	6,075	2,288	907	360	286	141	72	366	90	138
Power generating machinery and equipment	16,111	4,262	863	1,263	699	2,067	198	912	471	354
Machinery specialized for particular industries	15,767	3,389	965	904	685	554	276	1,001	288	549
Metalworking machinery	2,868	563	214	207	205	75	66	217	96	194
General industrial machinery, equipment, parts	16,178	4,928	1,415	898	688	540	259	855	498	704
Office machines and automatic data processing machines	27,788	4,180	941	3,171	2,710	1,471	716	3,678	469	656
Telecommunications, sound recording, reproduction apparatus and equipment	9,927	1,582	1,529	746	548	218	208	973	577	306
Electrical machinery, apparatus, and appliances, n.e.s.	31,764	7,669	3,749	1,763	1,402	1,009	586	2,390	1,440	1,395
Road vehicles (incl. air-cushion vehicles)	30,981	18,062	3,274	445	1,191	361	106	1,584	846	242
Transport equipment, n.e.s.	32,340	1,883	522	4,091	2,132	1,435	686	3,689	430	962
Furniture, bedding, mattresses, etc.	1,639	747	325	80	44	24	8	80	13	10
Articles of apparel and clothing accessories	2,559	236	403	94	46	69	54	306	7	8
Professional scientific and control instruments and apparatus	12,614	2,036	770	1,001	1,018	705	473	1,613	276	471
Photo apparatus, equipment and optical goods n.e.s.; watch and clocks	3,942	592	197	437	238	333	85	601	46	51
Miscellaneous manufactured articles	20,971	4,033	1,148	1,821	1,315	811	344	3,448	442	501
Special transactions and commodities not classified by kind	2,962	1,040	201	132	135	48	22	145	80	33
Gold, nonmonetary (excluding ores & concentrates)	2,991	530	94	689	97	336	8	16	3	4
Shipments under $10,000 and under $1,500 documented exports	9,011	1,183	1,264	722	485	374	196	618	168	135

See footnotes at end of table.

No. 1334. U.S. Domestic Exports and General Imports of Selected Commodities—Value, by Area: 1990—Continued

[In millions of dollars. See headnote, page 798]

SELECTED MAJOR COMMODITIES	Total [1]	WESTERN HEMISPHERE		WESTERN EUROPE				ASIA		
		Canada	Mexico	United King-dom	Ger-many[1]	France	Italy	Japan	China: Taiwan	South Korea
Imports, total	495,310	91,380	30,157	20,188	28,162	13,153	12,751	89,684	22,666	18,485
Meat and meat preparations	2,958	649	3	(Z)	1	4	6	4	(Z)	(Z)
Fish (except marine mammal) crustaceans, etc., preps	5,192	1,174	278	24	3	9	2	147	168	124
Vegetables and fruit.	5,795	278	1,441	15	76	17	42	38	71	26
Coffee, tea, cocoa, spices manufactures thereof	3,355	149	374	30	80	10	16	4	13	1
Beverages	3,806	543	248	633	192	893	355	30	3	4
Cork and wood	3,123	2,785	111	1	3	1	9	(Z)	11	(Z)
Pulp and waste paper	2,867	2,546	2	(Z)	2	(Z)	-	(Z)	1	(Z)
Metalliferous ores and metal scrap.	3,990	1,209	282	37	39	33	2	16	3	2
Petroleum, petroleum products, and related materials	60,468	6,583	5,101	2,068	64	354	522	26	(Z)	9
Gas, natural and manufactured	3,443	2,836	161	14	8	11	8	2	-	(Z)
Organic chemicals.	7,427	847	156	764	1,072	420	354	844	42	73
Inorganic chemicals.	3,204	1,057	236	242	400	187	47	158	10	3
Medicinal and pharmaceutical products. .	2,491	100	15	456	337	114	179	213	4	3
Chemical materials and products, n.e.s.	2,022	236	51	158	348	126	43	250	11	4
Rubber manufactures, n.e.s	3,544	831	72	112	228	153	111	1,061	185	255
Cork and wood manufactures other than furniture.	2,103	700	100	11	27	43	53	11	288	12
Paper, paperboard and articles	8,491	6,286	191	156	292	121	71	237	60	73
Textile yarn, fabrics, made-up articles, n.e.s.	6,424	403	292	294	318	203	479	580	445	490
Nonmetallic mineral manufactures, n.e.s..	9,882	701	437	602	412	327	700	739	384	123
Iron and steel.	9,866	1,505	358	391	877	665	252	2,155	161	574
Nonferrous metals.	9,792	3,923	521	390	432	172	38	467	28	8
Manufactures of metals, n.e.s	8,911	1,361	499	289	625	239	235	1,584	1,559	568
Power generating machinery and equipment.	14,552	2,742	1,074	1,830	1,605	1,897	183	3,284	95	82
Machinery specialized for particular industries	12,990	1,420	140	1,072	3,073	593	790	3,349	314	69
Metalworking machinery	3,677	246	8	222	672	62	158	1,519	162	36
General industrial machinery, equipment, parts	14,461	1,717	737	925	2,142	379	732	3,856	846	416
Office machines and automatic data processing machines	26,862	1,877	709	794	521	247	234	10,978	3,092	1,351
Telecommunications, sound recording, reproduction apparatus and equipment.	22,230	969	2,773	209	140	107	53	9,348	1,450	1,706
Electrical machinery, apparatus and appliances, n.e.s.	33,564	3,316	4,563	936	2,018	603	297	8,897	2,192	2,507
Road vehicles (incl air-cushion vehicles) .	72,305	26,121	3,646	1,374	6,722	699	788	27,356	870	1,292
Transport equipment, n.e.s	7,254	2,422	31	1,159	181	1,055	332	526	65	80
Furniture, bedding, mattresses, etc.	5,006	1,208	580	93	201	69	534	166	1,008	67
Travel goods, handbags and similar containers.	2,223	17	46	7	16	72	195	9	407	446
Articles of apparel and clothing accessories.	25,622	251	712	213	138	227	929	160	2,491	3,259
Footwear.	9,564	53	164	43	28	48	986	5	1,525	2,565
Professional scientific and control instruments and apparatus.	6,206	526	523	651	958	242	86	1,643	180	91
Photo apparatus, equipment and optical goods, n.e.s.; watch and clocks	7,128	181	135	224	368	270	305	2,781	348	135
Miscellaneous manufactured articles, n.e.s.	25,000	1,277	779	1,482	1,007	833	1,554	4,622	2,987	1,562
Special transactions and commodities not classified by kind	11,890	3,579	1,007	1,265	887	574	193	827	98	104
Estimate of low valued import transactions	3,442	878	292	212	343	115	115	528	152	40

- Represents zero.   Z Less than $500,000.   X Not applicable.   [1] Effective October 3, 1990 East Germany ceased to exist as a sovereign state and became a part of West Germany. However, trade statistics for Germany comprise of statistics for West Germany and East Germany combined for the period shown.   [2] Other than fertilizers covered in SITC division 56 (Fertilizers). [3] Other than crude fertilizers covered in SITC division 272.

Source: U.S. Bureau of the Census, *U.S. Merchandise Trade: Exports, General Imports, and Imports for Consumption,* series FT 927.

No. 1335. U.S. Exports, Imports, and Merchandise Trade Balance, by Continent, Area, and Country: 1985 to 1991

[In millions of dollars, except percent. Includes silver ore and bullion. Country totals include exports of special category commodities, if any. Data include nonmonetary gold beginning 1985, data include trade of Virgin Islands with foreign countries, if any, except for exception, see footnote 2 for exception. Minus sign (-) denotes an excess of imports over exports. See Historical Statistics, Colonial Times to 1970, series U 317-352, for selected countries]

COUNTRY	EXPORTS, DOMESTIC AND FOREIGN				GENERAL IMPORTS [1]				MERCHANDISE TRADE BALANCE			
	1985	1989	1990	1991	1985	1989	1990	1991	1985	1989	1990	1991
Total [2]	213,146	363,812	393,592	421,851	345,276	473,211	495,311	488,055	-132,130	-109,399	-101,718	-66,205
Afghanistan	3	5	4	3	7	5	5	5	-4			-2
Algeria	430	756	951	727	2,333	1,829	2,626	2,100	-1,903	-1,074	-1,674	-1,372
Angola	137	97	152	188	1,054	1,929	1,904	1,786	-917	-1,832	-1,752	-1,598
Anguilla	199	17	15	11	95			1	104	17	15	10
Argentina	721	1,039	1,179	2,049	1,069	1,391	1,511	1,291	-348	-352	-333	758
Australia	5,441	8,331	8,538	8,416	2,837	3,873	4,447	4,010	2,604	4,458	4,091	4,406
Austria	441	873	875	1,055	834	1,136	1,318	1,274	-393	-263	-444	-219
Bahamas, The	786	772	800	721	626	462	509	470	160	310	291	251
Bahrain	107	489	721	501	84	80	81	87	23	409	640	414
Bangladesh	219	282	181	179	196	428	539	524	23	-147	-357	-345
Barbados	173	180	161	167	202	46	31	32	-29	134	130	135
Belgium and Luxembourg	4,918	8,522	10,458	10,791	3,387	4,555	4,585	4,139	1,531	3,968	5,872	6,652
Belize	56	101	105	114	47	43	47	46	9	58	58	69
Bermuda	258	354	255	233	7	11	12	9	251	343	242	224
Bolivia	120	145	138	190	99	118	203	209	21	27	-65	-18
Botswana	16	30	19	31	29	17	14	13	-13	13	-6	6
Brazil	3,140	4,804	5,048	6,154	7,526	8,410	7,898	6,727	-4,386	-3,606	-2,850	-573
Bulgaria	104	181	84	142	36	59	47	56	68	122	37	86
Burma	10	5	20	24	14	17	23	27	-4	-12	-3	-3
Cameroon	69	35	47	46	324	426	147	127	-255	-391	-100	-81
Canada	47,251	78,809	83,674	85,103	69,006	87,953	91,380	91,141	-21,755	-9,144	-7,707	-6,039
Cayman Islands	75	204	183	116	11	48	21	18	64	155	162	99
Central African Republic	1	6	8	14	8	3	2	1	-7	3	6	14
Chad	25	35							25	35		
Chile	682	1,414	1,664	1,840	745	1,292	1,313	1,304	-63	122	351	536
China: Mainland	3,886	5,755	4,806	6,287	3,862	11,990	15,237	18,976	24	-6,235	-10,431	-12,689
Colombia	1,468	1,924	2,029	1,947	1,331	2,555	3,168	2,734	137	-631	-1,139	-787
Costa Rica	422	882	986	1,034	501	962	1,005	1,154	-79	-81	-19	-120
Cuba		3		(Z)		(Z)	(Z)	(Z)				
Cyprus	45	109	129	119	14	15	19	13	31	94	111	106
Czechoslovakia	63	53	91	124	76	85	87	144	-13	-32	4	-20

COUNTRY	EXPORTS, DOMESTIC AND FOREIGN				GENERAL IMPORTS [1]				MERCHANDISE TRADE BALANCE			
	1985	1989	1990	1991	1985	1989	1990	1991	1985	1989	1990	1991
Denmark	706	1,051	1,311	1,572	1,665	1,535	1,678	1,666	-959	-484	-367	-94
Dominican Republic	742	1,645	1,656	1,743	982	1,646	1,752	2,017	-240	-1	-96	-274
East Germany [3]	73	94	62	(X)	92	139	85	(X)	-19	-45	-23	(X)
Ecuador	591	643	678	948	1,837	1,474	1,376	1,328	-1,246	-832	-697	-380
Egypt	2,323	2,612	2,249	2,721	79	227	398	206	2,244	2,385	1,851	2,514
El Salvador	445	520	554	534	396	245	238	303	49	275	316	231
Ethiopia	203	67	157	210	43	70	40	15	160	-3	117	196
Finland	438	969	1,126	951	895	1,370	1,262	1,089	-457	-402	-136	-138
France	6,096	11,579	13,665	15,365	9,482	13,014	13,153	13,372	-3,386	-1,435	511	1,993
French Guiana	114	270	271	150	13	5	2	1	101	265	269	149
Gabon	91	46	49	85	502	437	701	712	-411	-390	-652	-627
Gambia	11	10	9	11	2	1	2	2	9	9	7	9
Germany [3]	9,050	16,956	18,760	21,317	20,239	24,971	28,162	26,229	-11,189	-8,015	-9,402	-4,913
Ghana	54	121	140	142	90	127	169	152	-36	-7	-29	-10
Gibraltar	13	2	32	10	1	1	1	1	12	1	31	9
Greece	498	697	763	1,036	395	473	509	433	103	224	255	603
Greenland	6	4	6	4	4	2	1	4	2	2	5	-0
Guadeloupe	28	34	53	83	409	609	1	2	-381	-575	52	82
Guatemala	405	662	764	951	390	374	794	900	15	288	-31	51
Guyana	43	78	76	86	47	56	53	84	-4	22	23	3
Haiti	396	472	477	392	390	461	343	285	6	11	134	107
Honduras	308	515	564	627	375	328	491	557	-67	187	73	70
Hong Kong	2,786	6,291	6,817	8,140	8,396	9,722	9,622	9,286	-5,610	-3,431	-2,805	-1,146
Hungary	94	122	156	256	218	328	347	367	-124	-207	-191	-111
Iceland	38	179	232	156	248	208	163	208	-210	-29	69	-52
India	1,642	2,458	2,486	2,003	2,295	3,315	3,197	3,197	-653	-857	-711	-1,195
Indonesia	795	1,247	1,897	1,892	4,569	3,529	3,341	3,239	-3,774	-2,282	-1,444	-1,347
Iran	74	55	163	527	725	9	7	231	-651	47	156	296
Iraq	427	1,169	732	-	474	2,415	3,008	6	-47	-1,246	-2,276	-6
Ireland	1,342	2,483	2,540	2,683	901	1,566	1,755	1,956	441	917	784	727
Israel	2,239	2,827	3,203	3,856	2,123	1,576	3,313	3,497	116	1,251	-110	359
Italy	4,625	7,215	7,992	8,579	9,674	11,933	12,751	11,788	-5,049	-4,718	-4,760	-3,209
Ivory Coast	70	79	79	82	525	234	200	221	-455	-155	-121	-139
Jamaica	404	1,006	943	963	273	509	569	576	131	497	374	387
Japan	22,631	44,494	48,580	48,147	68,783	93,553	89,684	91,583	-46,152	-49,059	-41,105	-43,436
Jordan	377	380	309	220	14	8	11	7	363	372	298	213

See footnotes at end of table.

No. 1335. U.S. Exports, Imports, and Merchandise Trade Balance, by Country: 1985 to 1991—Continued

[See headnote, page 800]

COUNTRY	EXPORTS, DOMESTIC AND FOREIGN				GENERAL IMPORTS [1]				MERCHANDISE TRADE BALANCE			
	1985	1989	1990	1991	1985	1989	1990	1991	1985	1989	1990	1991
Kampuchea	-	(Z)	-	(Z)	-	-	-	-	-	-	-	-
Kenya	97	133	116	92	92	68	58	69	5	65	58	23
Kuwait	551	853	403	1,228	184	973	569	36	367	-120	-166	1,192
Laos	(Z)	(Z)	1	1	4	1	2	2	-4	-1	-1	-1
Lebanon	141	94	98	165	19	30	24	28	122	63	74	138
Liberia	73	98	44	47	83	106	49	9	-10	-8	-5	38
Libya	311	(Z)	(Z)	-	44	-	-	-	267	-	-	-
Macao	(Z)	11	8	10	342	654	736	583	-341	-643	-728	-573
Madagascar	33	11	14	14	53	41	44	47	-20	-30	-30	-33
Malaysia	1,539	2,870	3,425	3,902	2,300	4,744	5,272	6,103	-761	-1,874	-1,847	-2,201
Malta	26	48	45	57	34	60	40	65	-8	-12	5	-9
Mauritania	26	13	15	22	4	11	24	12	22	2	-9	10
Mexico	13,635	24,982	28,279	33,276	19,132	27,162	30,157	31,194	-5,497	-2,180	-1,878	2,082
Morocco	279	394	495	403	39	98	109	151	240	296	386	251
Mozambique	56	41	50	101	16	20	29	23	40	21	21	78
Namibia	19	13	44	33	12	2	33	36	7	11	11	-3
Nepal	7	9	10	6	44	47	51	55	-37	-38	-41	-49
Netherlands	7,269	11,364	13,022	13,528	4,081	4,810	4,952	4,827	3,188	6,554	8,071	8,701
Netherlands Antilles	427	412	543	629	808	383	429	656	-381	29	114	-28
New Zealand	727	1,117	1,135	1,009	860	1,209	1,197	1,212	-133	-91	-62	-202
Niger	42	9	58	147	41	2	6	60	1	7	52	88
Nigeria	676	490	553	833	3,002	5,284	5,982	5,360	-2,326	-4,794	-5,429	-4,527
Norway	666	1,037	1,281	1,489	1,164	1,991	1,830	1,626	-498	-955	-549	-138
Pakistan	1,042	1,134	1,143	951	274	523	610	663	768	612	533	288
Panama	675	723	869	981	410	268	234	270	265	455	635	711
Paraguay	99	168	307	375	24	45	51	43	75	123	256	332
Peru	496	695	772	840	1,087	814	802	778	-591	-119	-30	63
Philippines	1,379	2,202	2,471	2,269	2,145	3,068	3,384	3,472	-766	-866	-913	-1,203
Poland	238	414	406	458	220	387	408	357	18	26	-2	101
Portugal	695	925	922	792	546	800	832	697	149	125	91	95
Qatar	64	100	115	147	16	50	53	30	48	50	62	118
Romania	208	155	369	209	882	354	231	69	-674	-199	138	140

COUNTRY	EXPORTS, DOMESTIC AND FOREIGN				GENERAL IMPORTS [1]				MERCHANDISE TRADE BALANCE			
	1985	1989	1990	1991	1985	1989	1990	1991	1985	1989	1990	1991
Saudi Arabia	4,474	3,574	4,049	6,572	1,907	7,157	10,021	10,978	2,567	-3,583	-5,971	-4,406
Senegal	61	69	52	76	5	41	6	12	56	27	46	65
Sierra Leone	13	25	27	25	16	53	46	48	-3	-28	-19	-23
Singapore	3,476	7,345	8,023	8,808	4,260	9,003	9,800	9,976	-784	-1,658	-1,778	-1,169
Somalia	57	21	12	7	2	3	-	3	55	18	11	5
South Africa	1,205	1,659	1,732	2,113	2,071	1,531	1,698	1,733	-866	128	34	380
South Korea	5,956	13,459	14,404	15,518	10,013	19,737	18,485	17,025	-4,057	-6,278	-4,081	-1,506
Soviet Union	2,423	4,284	3,087	3,578	409	709	1,059	813	2,014	3,574	2,028	2,765
Spain	2,524	4,796	5,213	5,482	2,515	3,317	3,311	2,854	9	1,479	1,901	2,627
Sri Lanka	73	143	137	121	282	449	538	605	-209	-306	-401	-484
Sudan	243	81	42	92	9	20	16	16	234	61	26	77
Suriname	86	140	156	135	60	74	50	52	26	66	106	83
Sweden	1,925	3,139	3,405	3,288	4,124	4,892	4,937	4,502	-2,199	-1,753	-1,533	-1,214
Switzerland	2,288	4,911	4,943	5,558	3,476	4,714	5,587	5,585	-1,188	197	-645	-27
Syria	106	91	150	207	3	98	52	25	103	-7	98	182
China: Taiwan	4,700	11,335	11,491	13,191	16,396	24,313	22,666	23,036	-11,696	-12,978	-11,175	-9,845
Tanzania	46	29	48	35	10	53	16	15	36	-24	33	20
Thailand	849	2,288	2,995	3,758	1,428	4,380	5,289	6,125	-579	-2,091	-2,293	-2,368
Togo	17	28	31	24	12	3	4	3	5	25	27	21
Trinidad and Tobago	504	563	428	469	1,258	768	1,020	856	-754	-205	-592	-387
Tunisia	256	160	177	171	13	55	40	33	243	105	137	138
Turkey	1,295	2,003	2,243	2,423	602	1,372	1,183	1,009	693	632	1,061	1,414
Turks and Caicos Islands	12	46	39	40	4	3	4	4	8	43	36	36
Uganda	5	23	26	13	113	41	15	18	-108	-17	11	-4
United Kingdom	11,273	20,837	23,490	22,064	14,937	18,319	20,188	18,520	-3,664	2,518	3,302	3,544
Uruguay	64	134	144	216	557	219	206	238	-493	-85	-62	-21
Venezuela	3,399	3,025	3,108	4,668	6,537	6,771	9,480	8,229	-3,138	-3,746	-6,371	-3,560
Yugoslavia	595	499	565	370	542	799	776	677	53	-300	-211	-306
Zaire	105	122	138	62	401	330	325	302	-296	-208	-187	-240
Zambia	60	50	80	24	58	24	29	42	2	26	52	-19
Zimbabwe	46	121	135	53	52	127	119	89	-6	-6	16	-35

- Represents zero. Z Less than $500,000. [1] Imports are on a customs value basis. Exports are f.a.s. value. [2] Includes revisions not carried to area values; therefore, area values will not add to total. [3] Effective October 3, 1990, East Germany ceased to exist as a sovereign state and became a part of West Germany. Accordingly, trade statistics for East Germany reflect trade for January through September 1990. Trade statistics for 1990 for former West Germany reflect this unification beginning with October 1990. Data for Germany reflect the consolidation of the two countries for 1991.

Source: U.S. Bureau of the Census, 1985, *Highlights of U.S. Export and Import Trade*, FT 990, monthly; and 1989-1991, *U.S. Merchandise Trade*, series FT 900, monthly.

No. 1336. Domestic Exports and General Imports, by Selected Commodity Groups: 1989 to 1991

[In millions of dollars]

COMMODITY GROUP	DOMESTIC EXPORTS [1]			GENERAL IMPORTS [2]		
	1989	1990	1991	1989	1990	1991
Total	363,811.5	393,592.3	421,850.7	473,210.8	495,310.5	488,055.4
Agricultural commodities	41,319.4	38,722.9	38,462.6	22,035.5	22,343.1	22,171.2
Animal feeds	3,081.1	2,868.2	3,178.7	279.0	283.8	313.7
Bulbs	427.2	109.2	112.5	343.2	161.9	177.9
Cereal flour	694.5	685.7	811.2	558.1	568.5	641.2
Cocoa	22.0	38.1	22.5	732.0	783.1	823.2
Coffee	12.7	11.8	9.8	2,273.5	1,766.4	1,735.6
Corn	6,734.2	6,195.5	5,147.3	551.0	23.3	39.3
Cotton, raw and linters	2,267.5	2,799.5	2,492.0	9.5	19.9	16.3
Dairy products; eggs	446.5	371.7	453.7	4,409.0	501.0	452.4
Furskins, raw	173.3	144.3	106.5	115.8	78.3	56.7
Grains, unmilled	1,045.2	811.0	701.0	162.6	110.3	117.9
Hides and skins	1,576.6	1,612.5	1,278.2	97.9	94.4	109.8
Live animals	531.7	514.1	686.6	869.6	1,184.7	1,174.2
Meat and preparations	2,963.8	3,189.1	3,627.8	2,560.0	2,958.2	2,913.2
Oils/fats, animal	37.9	425.3	446.5	0.4	21.2	28.7
Oils/fats, vegetable	739.6	664.6	598.6	655.5	715.7	742.1
Plants	92.6	102.7	99.6	71.5	99.1	107.8
Rice	981.4	798.2	752.2	61.9	71.7	80.3
Seeds	224.1	245.9	273.0	125.5	119.4	132.1
Soybeans	4,011.5	3,597.3	3,997.7	23.9	15.3	27.4
Sugar	3.3	7.8	12.1	605.3	848.0	708.3
Tobacco, unmanufactured.	1,339.9	1,444.7	1,427.6	667.6	679.6	991.3
Vegetables and fruit.	4,530.4	5,015.0	5,329.3	4,908.6	5,794.6	5,396.2
Wheat	5,907.1	3,886.7	3,348.1	57.5	80.1	66.1
Other agricultural.	3,475.3	3,184.1	3,550.1	5,877.1	5,364.6	5,319.5
Manufactured goods.	272,166.4	298,236.4	325,850.9	379,425.4	388,819.7	393,069.6
ADP equipment, office machinery. . .	23,992.2	24,735.5	25,953.6	25,714.5	26,862.2	30,064.3
Airplanes.	14,432.6	19,641.3	24,158.2	2,947.8	2,733.1	3,436.1
Airplane parts.	8,791.6	9,814.9	10,263.6	2,929.1	3,556.0	4,085.4
Aluminum	2,988.2	2,856.6	3,124.6	3,143.5	2,843.0	2,409.1
Artwork/antiques.	1,653.0	2,281.9	1,240.2	2,172.2	2,340.1	1,980.8
Basketware, etc	966.0	1,097.3	1,288.6	1,800.6	1,836.8	1,913.0
Chemicals, cosmetics	1,553.5	1,964.4	2,360.8	1,157.6	1,322.8	1,417.3
Chemicals, dyeing	1,248.9	1,591.4	1,647.5	1,131.0	1,286.8	1,415.8
Chemicals, fertilizers	2,707.8	2,577.9	2,980.0	1,003.2	921.2	919.2
Chemicals, inorganic	4,319.0	3,822.6	4,102.0	3,244.2	3,204.4	3,298.7
Chemicals, medicinal	3,692.5	4,102.9	4,606.2	2,087.6	2,490.8	3,052.8
Chemicals, organic	10,872.9	10,427.0	10,927.9	7,004.2	7,427.2	8,156.8
Chemicals, plastics	8,559.1	9,073.7	10,322.4	3,308.9	3,744.4	3,785.1
Chemicals, n.e.s.	5,106.7	5,489.9	6,019.8	1,777.1	2,022.1	2,123.0
Clothing.	2,290.7	2,471.7	3,211.6	24,537.4	25,621.5	26,205.8
Copper	945.8	1,213.0	1,325.6	2,140.4	1,774.1	1,600.9
Electrical machinery.	25,409.3	28,405.7	29,935.2	32,373.0	33,564.1	35,103.1
Footwear.	532.2	476.9	542.5	8,393.8	9,563.6	9,561.6
Furniture and parts	1,294.8	1,605.4	2,113.2	4,907.9	5,006.0	4,938.3
Gem diamonds.	1,097.6	320.5	209.2	4,347.3	3,973.6	4,006.1
General industrial machinery	15,034.5	15,828.1	17,107.1	14,486.9	14,461.3	14,422.5
Glass	979.0	1,086.6	1,127.8	788.8	759.9	770.7
Glassware	342.9	400.7	447.9	889.4	939.4	938.0
Gold, nonmonetary	2,544.9	2,970.0	3,295.1	1,498.5	1,081.4	1,934.8
Iron and steel mill products.	3,559.2	3,270.3	4,214.1	9,392.7	8,805.2	8,312.3
Lighting, plumbing	623.7	680.4	874.0	1,159.5	1,233.5	1,247.2
Metal manufactures, n.e.s.	4,494.4	4,782.7	5,169.2	6,371.6	6,440.9	6,376.2
Metalworking machinery	2,738.5	2,759.3	2,706.3	3,867.9	3,677.3	3,622.6
Motorcycles, bicycles.	729.2	935.0	1,302.6	1,552.5	1,438.0	1,635.9
Nickel	243.6	227.9	217.9	1,521.9	1,101.8	1,062.7
Optical goods	544.5	638.7	711.5	1,371.4	1,470.2	1,485.5
Paper and paperboard	4,585.5	5,004.3	5,961.8	8,491.8	8,490.6	8,024.4
Photographic equipment.	2,535.0	2,773.1	2,926.2	3,435.6	3,340.9	3,652.7
Plastic articles, n.e.s.	1,700.0	1,945.1	2,236.7	2,998.6	3,138.4	3,115.4
Platinum	226.6	224.0	313.8	1,365.3	1,856.2	1,663.9
Pottery	69.6	71.1	87.1	1,243.9	1,222.3	1,244.8
Power generating machinery	15,348.7	15,795.8	16,967.5	14,257.1	14,552.2	14,230.3
Printed materials.	3,002.2	3,164.3	3,578.8	1,617.8	1,668.8	1,705.3
Records/magnetic media	2,957.2	3,877.4	4,263.0	2,446.5	2,531.4	2,786.5
Rubber articles, n.e.s.	670.5	504.7	574.5	912.5	649.7	704.8
Rubber tires and tubes.	819.1	1,147.6	1,272.7	2,383.8	2,591.1	2,310.2

See footnotes at end of table.

No. 1336. Domestic Exports and General Imports, by Selected SITC Commodity Groups: 1989 to 1991—Continued

[In millions of dollars]

COMMODITY GROUP	DOMESTIC EXPORTS [1]			GENERAL IMPORTS [2]		
	1989	1990	1991	1989	1990	1991
Manufactured goods—Continued						
Scientific instruments	11,488.6	12,121.2	13,487.6	5,848.9	6,206.4	6,757.4
Ships, boats	1,050.2	1,276.9	1,154.3	578.7	329.2	248.1
Silver and bullion	68.4	163.3	238.8	576.6	450.8	366.2
Spacecraft	554.0	598.5	257.3	80.0	0.1	-
Specialized industrial machinery	14,351.9	15,276.8	16,565.2	12,839.4	12,990.3	10,914.2
Telecommunications equipment	8,131.7	9,138.7	9,965.8	23,233.8	22,230.4	23,469.0
Textile yarn, fabric	4,301.7	4,947.0	5,457.1	6,087.1	6,423.9	6,990.8
Toys/games/sporting goods	1,630.9	1,818.6	2,085.5	8,396.1	9,080.2	8,823.6
Travel goods	114.0	133.0	159.0	2,127.6	2,222.8	2,345.3
Vehicles/new cars, Canada	6,823.7	6,231.6	6,189.5	12,870.6	13,348.3	13,543.5
Vehicles/new cars, Japan	327.0	530.6	497.3	19,912.2	19,219.5	20,387.7
Vehicles/new cars, Other	2,274.3	2,464.6	3,077.2	11,370.7	12,542.0	10,853.2
Vehicles/trucks	2,842.8	3,083.9	3,869.2	8,807.2	8,579.8	8,261.4
Vehicles/chassis/bodies	207.3	206.9	239.9	1,095.0	518.3	406.8
Vehicles/parts	13,224.8	14,463.1	14,301.5	15,248.3	15,230.0	14,073.0
Watches/clocks/parts	177.3	209.2	225.3	907.7	2,247.3	2,286.6
Wood manufactures	1,064.9	1,222.2	1,244.0	2,028.7	2,034.4	1,907.8
Zinc	48.9	47.1	39.4	1,198.6	1,017.3	651.5
Other manufactured goods	17,281.1	22,245.5	25,108.7	28,042.9	30,604.6	30,064.2
Mineral fuel	**10,124.0**	**12,233.4**	**12,033.3**	**52,778.9**	**64,661.4**	**54,342.7**
Coal	4,087.1	4,636.2	4,720.3	84.1	288.1	309.3
Crude oil	205.4	137.1	35.4	35,529.2	43,784.8	37,153.2
Petroleum preparations	2,783.3	4,072.4	4,409.7	11,650.1	16,094.3	12,374.7
Liquified propane/butane	110.3	160.9	256.0	480.3	808.4	862.7
Natural gas	215.5	203.1	293.4	1,849.7	2,328.1	2,426.9
Electricity	189.3	493.2	53.7	521.2	462.5	486.7
Other mineral fuels	2,533.1	2,530.6	2,264.8	2,664.3	895.4	729.1
Selected commodities:						
Fish and preparations	2,396.2	2,800.7	3,056.3	5,388.8	5,192.1	5,638.3
Cork, wood, lumber	5,203.5	5,236.3	5,102.7	3,499.4	3,122.6	3,056.9
Pulp and waste paper	4,394.5	4,043.2	3,604.0	3,050.4	2,866.9	2,163.5
Metal ores; scrap	5,520.9	4,948.6	3,989.4	3,866.4	3,989.9	3,590.5
Crude fertilizers	1,359.1	1,266.1	1,367.1	1,145.8	1,129.1	987.0
Cigarettes	3,362.4	4,757.4	4,231.8	49.3	53.0	129.9
Alcoholic bev, distilled	222.4	254.3	279.0	1,587.7	1,724.9	1,594.3
All other	1,457.9	2,576.2	2,821.4	383.2	1,407.8	1,379.0
Re-exports	16,284.8	18,516.7	21,011.2	(X)	(X)	(X)
Agricultural commodities	885.0	847.9	856.9	(X)	(X)	(X)
Manufactured goods	14,851.1	17,119.0	19,525.8	(X)	(X)	(X)
Mineral fuels	127.3	150.9	223.0	(X)	(X)	(X)
Other, reexports	548.7	398.9	405.4	(X)	(X)	(X)
Timing adjustment	(X)	(X)	41.0	(X)	(X)	(X)

- Represents zero.   X Not applicable.   [1] F.A.S. basis.   [2] Customs value basis.
Source: U.S. Bureau of the Census, *U.S. Merchandise Trade*, series FT 900, December issues.

No. 1337. Imports for Consumption—Values and Duties: 1970 to 1991

[Imports are on customs value basis. Beginning 1970, includes silver ores and bullion, and beginning 1980, includes trade of Virgin Islands with foreign countries. For basis of dollar values and for area coverage, see text, section 29. See also *Historical Statistics, Colonial Times to 1970*, series U 207-212]

YEAR	VALUES				Duties calculated [1] (mil. dol.)	RATIO OF DUTIES TO VALUES		Duties per capita [2] (dollar)
	Total (mil. dol.)	Free (mil. dol.)	Dutiable (mil. dol.)	Percent free		Total imports (percent)	Dutiable imports (percent)	
1970	39,756	13,870	25,886	35	2,584	6.5	10.0	12.60
1975	96,516	31,030	65,486	32	3,780	3.9	5.8	17.50
1976	121,121	37,190	83,931	31	4,675	3.9	5.6	21.44
1977	147,075	43,633	103,442	30	5,485	3.7	5.3	24.91
1978	[3]172,912	51,827	121,125	30	7,162	4.1	5.9	32.17
1979	[3]205,850	103,278	102,645	50	7,202	3.5	7.0	31.99
1980	[3]244,007	106,992	132,951	45	7,535	3.1	5.7	33.09
1981	259,012	76,338	182,674	29	8,893	3.4	4.9	38.67
1982	242,340	75,856	166,484	31	8,688	3.6	5.2	37.40
1983	256,679	83,397	173,283	32	9,430	3.7	5.4	40.21
1984	322,989	102,977	220,012	32	12,042	3.7	5.5	50.90
1985	343,553	106,035	237,518	31	13,067	3.8	5.5	54.73
1986	368,657	121,742	246,915	33	13,312	3.6	5.4	55.10
1987	402,066	132,152	269,914	33	13,923	3.5	5.2	57.08
1988	437,140	151,693	285,447	35	15,054	3.4	5.3	61.12
1989	468,012	156,365	311,647	33	16,096	3.4	5.2	64.70
1990	490,554	161,108	329,446	33	16,339	3.3	5.0	65.38
1991	483,028	167,641	315,386	35	16,197	3.4	5.1	64.10

NA Not available.   [1] Customs duties (including import excise taxes) calculated on the basis of reports of quantity and value of imports of merchandise entered directly for consumption or withdrawn from bonded customs warehouses.   [2] Based on estimated population including Armed Forces abroad as of July 1.   [3] Total includes revisions not carried to free and dutiable values.

Source: U.S. Bureau of the Census, 1970-1988, *Highlights of U.S. Export and Import Trade*, series FT 990, monthly; beginning 1989, *U.S. Merchandise Trade: Selected Highlights*, series FT 920, and unpublished data.

No. 1338. Domestic Exports and Imports for Consumption of Merchandise, by Selected SIC-Based Product Category: 1985 to 1991

[**In millions of dollars.** Includes nonmetary gold]

SIC [1] code	SIC-BASED PRODUCT CATEGORY	1985	1986	1987	1988	1989	1990	1991
(X)	**Domestic exports, total [2]**	**212,961**	**216,555**	**243,859**	**310,346**	**349,433**	**374,537**	**400,842**
	Agricultural, forestry and fishery							
(X)	products.....................	20,074	15,968	17,718	24,464	27,198	26,225	25,052
01	Agricultural products..............	19,199	15,088	16,678	21,508	24,142	22,597	21,075
02	Livestock and livestock products......	735	740	855	1,014	821	829	970
08	Forestry products................	122	120	155	266	270	281	306
09	Fish, fresh or chilled; and other							
	marine products [3]	18	20	30	1,676	1,965	2,518	2,701
(X)	Mineral commodities	6,394	5,600	5,058	6,559	7,030	7,335	7,442
10	Metallic ores and concentrates.......	686	590	597	883	1,247	1,137	1,014
11,12	Bituminous, lignite and anthracite coal . .	4,465	3,930	3,368	4,014	4,287	4,513	4,623
13	Crude petroleum and natural gas	476	306	271	485	490	638	675
14	Nonmetallic minerals, fuels	767	774	822	1,177	1,006	1,047	1,130
(X)	Manufactured commodities	175,752	179,401	208,438	261,755	290,536	330,403	359,635
20	Food and kindred products	10,055	11,250	12,320	14,788	15,205	16,160	17,492
21	Tobacco manufactures	1,268	1,522	2,310	2,901	3,632	5,040	4,574
22	Textile mill products	1,462	1,653	1,891	2,415	2,794	3,635	4,108
23	Apparel and related products	1,019	1,213	1,518	1,824	2,349	2,848	3,679
24	Lumber and related products	2,668	3,018	3,961	5,326	6,050	6,523	6,477
25	Furniture and fixtures	483	466	550	841	1,011	1,589	2,086
26	Paper and allied products	3,886	4,479	5,676	7,197	8,126	8,631	9,214
27	Printing and publishing	1,250	1,298	1,525	1,996	2,598	3,150	3,590
28	Chemicals and allied products	21,797	22,562	26,090	31,722	35,825	37,806	41,483
29	Petroleum and coal products	5,433	4,228	4,479	3,926	5,019	6,794	7,026
30	Rubber and misc. plastics products....	2,765	2,941	3,710	4,412	5,010	6,398	7,049
31	Leather and leather products	478	521	688	953	1,131	1,388	1,413
32	Stone, clay, and glass products	1,792	1,723	2,045	2,272	2,638	3,295	3,533
33	Primary metal products	4,747	4,803	5,806	12,362	12,110	13,116	15,243
34	Fabricated metal products	5,765	5,542	6,185	8,318	9,117	11,138	11,962
35	Machinery, except electrical.........	37,478	36,358	41,054	51,803	55,524	61,229	65,300
36	Electric and electronic machinery	18,908	20,415	24,359	27,033	32,718	39,807	42,330
37	Transportation equipment	38,024	37,977	42,371	49,768	56,875	68,113	76,172
38	Instruments and related products	8,623	9,237	10,191	17,160	17,327	19,524	21,699
39	Misc. manufactured commodities	1,773	2,080	2,719	4,443	4,553	4,296	4,621
(X)	**Imports for consumption,**							
	total [2]	**343,553**	**368,657**	**402,066**	**437,140**	**468,012**	**490,554**	**483,028**
(X)	Agricultural, forestry and fishery products .	12,805	14,754	14,402	12,759	13,251	12,750	13,148
01	Agricultural products..............	7,483	8,792	7,444	5,786	6,109	5,925	6,107
02	Livestock and livestock products......	933	993	999	1,235	1,290	1,453	1,501
08	Forestry products................	830	786	933	1,326	1,235	1,015	978
09	Fish, fresh or chilled; and other							
	marine products [3]	3,559	4,183	5,026	4,412	4,617	4,357	4,562
(X)	Mineral commodities	39,011	27,780	33,615	31,540	41,264	51,391	44,581
10	Metallic ores and concentrates.......	1,265	1,318	1,130	1,126	1,425	1,500	1,244
11,12	Bituminous, lignite and anthracite coal . .	70	80	56	65	97	93	112
13	Crude petroleum and natural gas	35,872	24,463	30,843	29,573	38,842	48,917	42,415
14	Nonmetallic minerals, exc. fuels	1,804	1,919	1,586	776	900	881	810
(X)	Manufactured commodities	280,089	314,140	341,141	379,172	396,903	407,043	406,550
20	Food and kindred products	12,521	12,521	13,180	15,043	15,122	16,564	16,298
21	Tobacco manufactures	78	82	90	86	88	94	199
22	Textile mill products	3,616	4,136	4,697	5,506	7,294	6,807	7,132
23	Apparel and related products	15,710	18,171	21,503	20,890	22,841	24,644	25,497
24	Lumber and related products	5,105	5,374	5,959	5,720	5,848	5,446	5,229
25	Furniture and fixtures	3,220	3,997	4,575	4,796	5,158	5,235	5,130
26	Paper and allied products	7,493	7,983	9,461	11,001	11,880	11,669	10,431
27	Printing and publishing	1,200	1,488	1,583	1,776	1,807	1,849	1,878
28	Chemicals and allied products	12,790	13,281	14,400	18,602	20,118	21,611	22,999
29	Petroleum and coal products	18,282	12,836	13,123	11,027	11,979	14,472	11,097
30	Rubber and misc. plastics products....	4,721	5,381	6,331	9,590	9,488	9,731	9,855
31	Leather and leather products	7,724	8,648	9,930	9,578	9,837	10,994	10,714
32	Stone, clay, and glass products	4,296	4,910	5,560	5,921	5,775	5,845	5,558
33	Primary metal products	20,439	22,580	19,254	25,075	25,563	23,232	22,262
34	Fabricated metal products	7,754	8,475	9,562	11,215	11,568	11,608	11,396
35	Machinery, except electrical.........	31,310	38,234	44,807	50,301	54,051	55,021	55,578
36	Electric and electronic machinery	37,951	42,734	46,566	52,539	55,316	55,736	58,610
37	Transportation equipment	65,944	79,887	84,347	86,717	87,972	89,599	88,004
38	Instruments and related products	8,805	10,646	11,547	15,430	15,364	16,846	18,668
39	Misc. manufactured commodities	11,130	12,776	14,666	18,359	19,844	20,090	20,015

X Not applicable.   NA Not available.   [1] Standard Industrial Classification.   [2] Includes scrap and waste, used or secondhand merchandise, and manufactured commodities not identified by kind.   [3] Includes frozen and packaged fish.

Source: U.S. Bureau of the Census, 1980-1988, *Highlights of U.S. Export and Import Trade*, series FT 990; beginning 1989, *U.S. Merchandise Trade*, series FT 900.

Outlying Areas

This section presents summary economic and social statistics for Puerto Rico, Virgin Islands, Guam, American Samoa, and the Northern Mariana Islands.

Primary sources are the decennial censuses of population and housing, and the censuses of agriculture, business, manufactures, and construction (taken every 5 years) conducted by the Bureau of the Census; the annual *Vital Statistics of the United States,* issued by the National Center for Health Statistics; and the annual *Income and Product* of the Puerto Rico Planning Board, San Juan.

Jurisdiction.—The United States gained jurisdiction over these areas as follows:

The islands of *Puerto Rico* and *Guam,* surrendered by Spain to the United States in October 1898, were ceded to the United States by the Treaty of Paris, ratified in 1899. Puerto Rico became a Commonwealth on July 25, 1952, thereby achieving a high degree of local autonomy under its own constitution. The *Virgin Islands,* comprising 50 islands and cays, was purchased by the United States from Denmark in 1917. *American Samoa,* a group of seven islands, was acquired by the United States in accordance with a convention among the United States, Great Britain, and Germany, ratified in 1900 (Swains Island was annexed in 1925).

By an agreement approved by the Security Council and the United States, the Northern Mariana Islands, previously under Japanese mandate, was administered by the United States between 1947 and 1986 under the United Nations trusteeship system. The Northern Mariana Islands became a Commonwealth in 1986.

For a brief summary of U.S. territorial development, see table 341.

Censuses.—Because characteristics of the outlying areas differ, the presentation of census data for them is not uniform. The 1960 Census of Population covered

In Brief

Persons per household, 1990:

Puerto Rico	*3.3*
Virgin Islands	*3.1*
Guam	*4.0*
American Samoa	*7.0*
Northern Mariana Islands	*4.6*

all of the places listed above except the Northern Mariana Islands (their census was conducted in April 1958 by the Office of the High Commissioner), while the 1960 Census of Housing also excluded American Samoa. The 1970, 1980 and 1990 Censuses of Population and Housing covered all five areas. The 1959, 1969, and 1978 Censuses of Agriculture covered Puerto Rico, American Samoa, Guam, and the Virgin Islands; the 1964, 1974, and 1982 censuses covered the same areas except American Samoa; and the 1969, 1978, and 1987 censuses included the Northern Mariana Islands. Beginning in 1967, Congress authorized the economic censuses, to be taken at 5-year intervals, for years ending in "2" and "7." Prior economic censuses were conducted in Puerto Rico for 1949, 1954, 1958, and 1963 and in Guam and the Virgin Islands for 1958 and 1963. In 1967, the census of construction industries was added for the first time in Puerto Rico; in 1972, Virgin Islands and Guam were covered. For 1982 and 1987, the economic censuses covered the Northern Mariana Islands.

Information in other sections.—In addition to the statistics presented in this section, other data are included as integral parts of many tables showing distribution by States in various sections of the *Abstract.* See "Outlying areas of the United States" in the index. For definition and explanation of terms used, see section 1, Population; section 4, Education; section 23, Agriculture; section 26, Construction and Housing; section 27, Manufactures; and section 28, Domestic Trade and Services.

Figure 30.1
Selected Outlying Areas of the United States

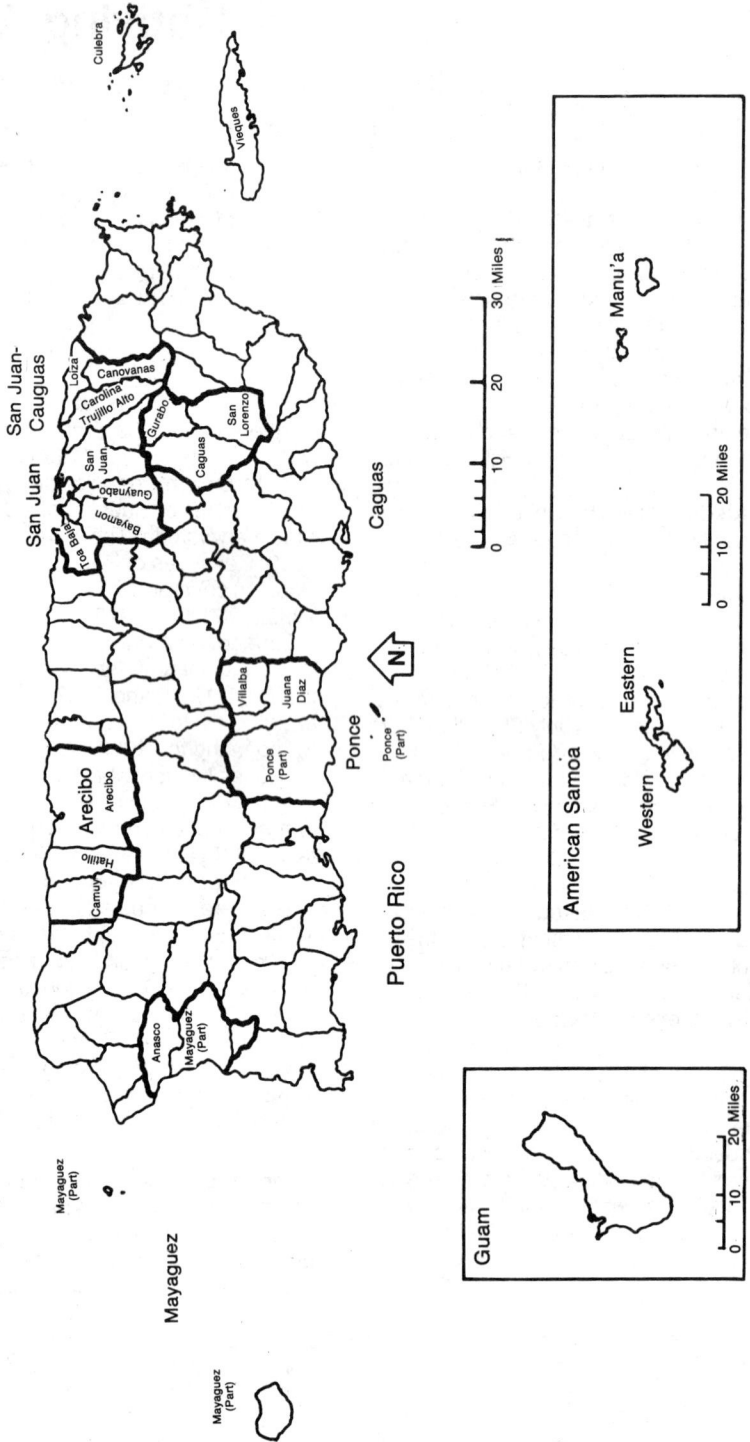

No. 1339. Estimated Resident Population, by Area: 1950 to 1990

[In thousands. As of July 1, except 1990, as of April 1. Includes estimates of Armed Forces stationed in area]

AREA	1950	1960	1970	1975	1980	1985	1987	1988	1990
Puerto Rico.	2,218	2,362	2,716	2,933	3,206	3,282	3,292	3,291	3,522
American Samoa	19	20	27	30	32	36	38	40	47
Guam.	60	66	86	102	107	124	130	133	133
Virgin Islands.	27	32	63	94	98	111	106	103	102
Northern Mariana Islands [1]	(NA)	(NA)	12	15	17	19	20	21	43

NA Not available. [1] Data consistent with apportionment census of September 1973 which showed a total population of 14,333 for the Marianas.
Source: U.S. Bureau of the Census, 1950-1988: *Current Population Reports,* series P-25, Nos. 80, 336, 943, and 1049; 1990: press releases, CB91-142, 242, 276, 263, and 243.

No. 1340. Estimates of Components of Population Change, by Area: 1970 to 1980 and 1980 to 1988

[In thousands, except percent. Resident population, including Armed Forces stationed in area. See table 1341 for population totals. Minus sign (-) indicates decrease. For explanation of methodology, see source]

AREA	APRIL 1, 1970 to APRIL 1, 1980					APRIL 1, 1980 to JULY 1, 1988				
	Net change		Births	Deaths	Net migra-tion [1]	Net change		Births	Deaths	Net migra-tion [1]
	Number	Percent				Number	Percent			
Puerto Rico.	484.5	17.9	744.0	193.7	-65.9	95.0	3.0	546.0	185.0	-267.0
American Samoa	5.1	18.9	10.6	1.4	-4.1	7.2	22.4	11.2	1.3	-2.7
Guam.	21.0	24.7	30.7	4.1	-5.7	27.0	25.5	25.9	3.7	4.9
Virgin Islands.	34.1	54.6	26.6	5.0	12.5	6.6	6.9	20.1	4.4	-9.0
Northern Mariana Islands [2] . .	4.6	37.5	5.3	0.9	([3])	4.4	26.1	5.9	0.9	([3])

[1] Includes error of closure (the amount necessary to make the components of change add to the net change between censuses). [2] See footnote 1, table 1339. [3] Migration is derived as a residual. Because part of the residual migration in these areas reflects under-registration of vital statistics, migration figures are not shown.
Source: U.S. Bureau of the Census, *Current Population Reports,* series P-25, Nos. 943 and 1049.

No. 1341. Population and Median Age, by Area and Sex: 1970 to 1990

[As of April 1. For definition of median, see Guide to Tabular Presentation]

AREA AND SEX	POPULATION (1,000)			MEDIAN AGE (years)			AREA AND SEX	POPULATION (1,000)			MEDIAN AGE (years)		
	1970	1980	1990	1970	1980	1990		1970	1980	1990	1970	1980	1990
Puerto Rico . .	2,712.0	3,196.5	3,522.0	21.6	24.6	28.5	Guam	85.0	106.0	133.2	20.4	22.3	25.0
Male.	1,329.9	1,556.7	1,706.0	20.9	23.7	(NA)	Male.	47.3	55.3	70.9	21.6	22.4	25.2
Female. . . .	1,382.2	1,639.8	1,816.0	22.2	25.5	(NA)	Female	37.7	50.7	62.2	18.2	22.1	24.9
							Virgin Islands .	62.5	96.6	101.8	23.0	22.5	28.2
American							Male.	31.3	46.2	49.2	23.1	21.1	(NA)
Samoa. . .	27.2	32.3	46.8	16.1	18.8	20.9	Female	31.3	50.4	52.6	23.0	23.6	(NA)
Male.	13.7	16.4	24.0	16.1	18.4	20.6	No. Mariana Is.	9.6	16.8	43.3	15.2	19.7	27.4
Female. . . .	13.6	15.9	22.8	16.1	19.2	21.2	Male.	4.9	8.8	22.8	15.4	20.9	29.9
							Female	4.7	8.0	20.5	15.0	18.5	24.9

NA Not available.
Source: U.S. Bureau of the Census, *Census of Population: 1970,* vol. I, *Characteristics of the Population,* parts 53-58; *1980,* vol. 1, chapter B, *Characteristics of the Population,* parts 53-57a; and *1990,* CPH-1, parts 53A and 55; CPH-6, parts G (Guam), AS (American Samoa), and CNMI (Commonwealth of the Northern Mariana Islands); and Summary Tape File 1A, (Puerto Rico) and Summary Tape File 2 (Virgin Islands).

No. 1342. Population, by Place of Birth and Year of Immigration—Area and Year

[As of April 1]

ITEM	1980		1990		
	Puerto Rico	Virgin Islands	Guam	American Samoa	Northern Mariana Islands
All persons	3,196,520	96,569	133,152	46,773	43,345
Born in this area	2,881,641	43,234	63,504	25,573	16,752
Percent of total	90.1	44.8	47.7	54.7	38.6
Born in the United States	199,524	11,964	28,010	3,519	1,271
Born in elsewhere [1]	70,768	36,006	41,638	17,681	25,322
Place of birth not reported	44,587	5,365	(X)	(X)	(X)
Born outside area.	(NA)	(NA)	69,648	21,200	26,593
Year of entry:					
1985 to 1990.	(NA)	(NA)	43,575	9,302	21,984
1980 to 1984.	(NA)	(NA)	8,768	5,025	2,491
1970 to 1979.	(NA)	(NA)	10,994	4,423	1,600
1960 to 1969.	(NA)	(NA)	4,143	1,758	274
Before 1960	(NA)	(NA)	2,168	692	244

NA Not available. X Not applicable. [1] Includes persons born in other outlying areas under United States jurisdiction and persons born abroad with at least one parent who is a United States citizen, or both, are foreign born persons.
Source: U.S. Bureau of the Census, *1980 Census of Population,* vol. 1, chapter C, parts 53A and 55 and *1990 Census of Population and Housing,* CPH-6, parts G (Guam), AS (American Samoa), and CNMI (Commonwealth of the Northern Mariana Islands).

No. 1343. Land Area and Population and Housing Characteristics, by Area: 1990

[As of **April 1**. See also table 341, for gross area (land and water). For definition of median, see Guide to Tabular Presentation]

ITEM	Puerto Rico	Virgin Islands	Guam	American Samoa	Northern Mariana Islands
Land area (sq. miles)	3,427	134	209	77	184
Total resident population	**3,522,037**	**101,809**	**133,152**	**46,773**	**43,345**
Per square mile	1,027.9	760.9	637.1	607.4	235.6
Percent increase, 1980-90	10.2	5.4	25.6	44.8	158.3
Urban	(NA)	(NA)	50,801	15,599	12,151
Rural	(NA)	(NA)	82,351	31,174	31,194
Male	1,705,642	49,210	70,945	24,023	22,802
Female	1,816,395	52,599	62,207	22,750	20,543
Males per 100 females	93.9	93.6	114.0	105.6	111.0
Median age (years)	28.5	28.2	25.0	20.9	27.4
Male (years)	(NA)	(NA)	25.2	20.6	29.9
Female (years)	(NA)	(NA)	24.9	21.2	24.9
Marital status, persons					
15 years old and over	**2,563,818**	**72,365**	**93,200**	**28,952**	**33,030**
Never married	711,470	27,539	30,759	11,412	13,810
Married [1]	1,499,449	35,199	54,717	15,958	17,869
Widowed or divorced	352,899	9,627	7,724	1,582	1,351
Households and families:					
Households	1,054,924	32,020	31,373	6,607	6,873
Persons in households	3,487,667	100,488	124,596	46,267	31,856
Persons per household	3.31	3.14	3.97	7.00	4.63
Families	886,339	23,012	27,313	6,301	5,312
Husband-wife families	634,872	13,197	21,342	5,153	3,947
Children ever born per					
1,000 females 15 to 44 years	**(NA)**	**(NA)**	**1,523**	**1,757**	**1,226**

NA Not available. [1] For Puerto Rico, includes consensually married couples and for all areas, includes separated couples.
Source: U.S. Bureau of the Census, *1990 Census of Population and Housing,* CPH-1, parts 53A and 55; CPH-6, parts G (Guam), AS (American Samoa), and CNMI (Commonwealth of the Northern Mariana Islands); *1990 Census of Population and Housing,* Summary Tape File 1A, (Puerto Rico) and Summary Tape File 2 (Virgin Islands).

No. 1344. Selected Social and Economic Characteristics, by Area and Year

CHARACTERISTIC	1980		1990		
	Puerto Rico	Virgin Islands	Guam	American Samoa	Northern Mariana Islands
EDUCATIONAL ATTAINMENT [1]					
Persons 25 years and over	1,577,682	44,986	66,700	19,570	24,633
Elementary: 0-8 years	753,742	15,997	9,238	3,664	4,285
High school: 1-3 years	200,269	6,475	8,602	5,239	4,016
4 years or more	332,770	11,543	22,220	6,253	8,659
College, one or more years	290,901	10,971	26,640	4,414	7,673
EMPLOYMENT STATUS					
Total persons, 16 years old					
and over	2,114,673	59,310	90,990	27,991	32,522
In labor force	869,856	38,082	66,138	14,198	26,589
Percent of total	41.1	64.2	72.7	50.7	81.8
Armed forces	4,137	84	11,952	11	8
Civilian labor force	865,719	37,998	54,186	14,187	26,581
Employed	733,922	35,652	52,144	13,461	25,965
Unemployed	131,797	2,346	2,042	726	616
Percent of civilian labor force	15.2	6.2	3.8	5.1	2.3
Not in labor force	1,244,817	21,228	24,852	13,793	5,933
FAMILY INCOME, PRIOR YEAR					
Families, census year	757,645	20,855	27,313	6,301	5,312
Percent distribution by income class	100.0	100.0	100.0	100.0	100.0
Less than $5,000	43.4	14.4	4.0	11.0	8.2
$5,000 to $9,999	28.4	26.7	4.7	19.2	13.9
$10,000 to $14,999	13.3	19.8	8.3	17.0	13.1
$15,000 to $24,999	10.3	22.3	21.1	23.6	21.6
$25,000 or more	4.6	16.7	61.9	29.1	43.2
Median income (dollars)	5,923	11,914	31,178	15,979	21,275
RESIDENCE 5 YEARS PRIOR					
Persons 5 years and over	[2]2,857,152	[2]85,856	118,055	39,821	39,206
Same house	1,960,988	47,380	54,665	30,759	11,479
Different house in this area	682,746	22,618	24,763	2,763	6,870
Outside area 5 years before census	148,064	11,537	38,627	6,299	20,857
LANGUAGE SPOKEN AT HOME					
Persons 5 years and over	2,857,152	85,856	118,055	39,821	39,206
Speak only English at home	1,208,145	69,754	44,048	1,203	1,878

[1] For educational attainment, in 1990, high school 4 years, no diploma included in 1-3 years; "college" includes high school graduates. [2] "Residence in 1975 not reported" included in total.
Source: U.S. Bureau of the Census, *1980 Census of Population,* vol. 1, chapter C, parts 53A and 55 and *1990 Census of Population and Housing,* CPH-6, parts G (Guam), AS (American Samoa), and CNMI (Commonwealth of the Northern Mariana Islands).

No. 1345. Vital Statistics—Specified Areas: 1960 to 1988

[Births, deaths, and infant deaths by place of residence; marriages and divorces by place of occurrence. Rates for 1960, 1970, and 1980 based on population enumerated as of **April 1;** for all other years, on population estimated as of **July 1**]

AREA AND YEAR	BIRTHS		DEATHS		INFANT DEATHS		MARRIAGES		DIVORCES [3]	
	Number	Rate [1]	Number	Rate [1]	Number	Rate [2]	Number	Rate [1]	Number	Rate [1]
Puerto Rico:										
1960.	76,314	32.5	15,791	6.7	3,307	43.3	[4]20,212	[4]8.6	5,218	2.2
1970.	67,628	24.8	18,080	6.7	1,930	28.6	29,905	11.0	9,688	3.6
1980.	72,986	22.8	20,413	6.4	1,351	18.5	33,167	10.4	15,276	4.8
1985.	63,547	19.4	23,071	7.0	944	14.9	30,355	9.2	14,686	4.5
1986.	63,479	19.4	23,182	7.1	869	13.7	32,339	9.9	13,563	4.1
1987.	64,331	19.5	23,829	7.2	916	14.2	33,285	10.1	14,165	4.3
1988.	63,991	19.4	24,940	7.6	801	12.5	32,214	9.8	13,930	4.2
Guam:										
1965.	2,523	32.8	336	4.4	82	32.5	471	6.2	53	0.7
1970.	2,842	28.8	355	5.8	62	21.6	874	9.9	84	1.0
1980.	2,945	27.8	393	3.7	43	14.6	(NA)	(NA)	(NA)	(NA)
1985.	3,049	24.6	415	3.4	35	11.5	(NA)	(NA)	(NA)	(NA)
1986.	3,276	25.8	429	3.4	29	8.9	(NA)	(NA)	(NA)	(NA)
1987.	3,330	25.5	472	3.6	25	7.5	(NA)	(NA)	(NA)	(NA)
1988.	3,509	26.4	464	3.5	27	7.7	(NA)	(NA)	(NA)	(NA)
Virgin Islands:										
1960.	1,180	36.8	332	10.3	42	35.6	359	11.1	135	4.2
1970.	2,898	46.8	469	7.9	72	24.6	1,149	18.4	270	4.3
1980.	2,504	25.9	504	5.2	61	24.4	1,112	11.5	478	4.9
1985.	2,375	21.4	506	4.6	42	17.7	1,448	13.1	363	3.3
1986.	2,257	20.6	476	4.3	28	12.4	1,804	16.5	314	2.9
1987.	2,322	21.9	527	5.0	46	19.8	1,902	17.9	258	2.4
1988.	2,216	21.5	501	4.9	29	13.1	2,161	20.9	373	3.6

NA Not available.   [1] Per 1,000 population.   [2] Per 1,000 live births.   [3] Includes reported annulments.   [4] Data are incomplete.

Source: U.S. National Center for Health Statistics, *Vital Statistics of the United States,* annual.

No. 1346. Public Elementary and Secondary Schools, by Areas: 1988

[For school year ending in year shown, unless otherwise indicated]

ITEM	Puerto Rico	Guam	Virgin Islands	American Samoa	ITEM	Puerto Rico	Guam	Virgin Islands	American Samoa
Enrollment, fall	672,837	25,936	24,020	11,248	Percent of enrollment .	92.4	89.3	92.0	94.1
Elementary					Staff, fall 1986	62,322	2,778	3,322	1,255
(kindergarten-grade					School district staff . .	1,961	8	405	92
8)	498,853	18,713	17,131	8,313	School staff	39,550	1,725	2,267	834
Secondary (grades					Teachers.	33,357	1,403	1,597	674
9-12 and post					Other support				
graduates)	173,984	7,223	6,889	2,935	services staff.	20,811	1,045	650	329
					Current expenditures [1]				
Average daily					($1,000).	935,392	76,359	89,217	20,186
attendance	621,731	23,172	22,103	10,579	Per pupil [2] (dol.)	1,504	3,295	4,036	1,908

[1] Public elementary and secondary day schools.   [2] Annual expenditures per pupil in average daily attendance.

Source: U.S. National Center for Education Statistics, unpublished data.

No. 1347. Federal Direct Payments for Individuals, by Selected Program and Outlying Area: 1989 and 1990

[**In thousands of dollars.** For fiscal years ending **September 30**]

PROGRAM PAYMENTS	1989				1990			
	Puerto Rico	Guam	Virgin Islands	American Samoa	Puerto Rico	Guam	Virgin Islands	American Samoa
Total	3,196,033	79,742	84,759	13,264	3,487,697	83,199	95,396	14,615
Pell Grants	251,106	1,371	506	220	240,545	1,260	432	113
Medicare: Hospital Insurance . .	156,718	1,906	4,172	-	186,950	1,907	4,977	-
Supplemental medical								
insurance.	175,104	1,861	3,110	-	209,525	2,273	3,722	-
Social Security: Disability								
insurance.	537,588	1,920	5,467	2,032	560,910	1,907	5,692	2,410
Retirement insurance	1,001,509	9,697	30,654	3,919	1,077,133	11,372	31,601	4,330
Survivors insurance	426,667	5,873	10,339	3,437	461,999	6,430	11,056	3,873
Veterans: Pension and								
disability	269,523	3,303	1,960	1,223	280,799	3,578	1,794	1,354
Education assistance	3,247	306	38	88	3,086	178	28	37
Federal retirement and								
disability	156,824	30,501	9,632	1,535	161,315	34,150	8,326	1,605
Food Stamps	[1]900,688	16,640	12,744	-	[1]931,131	14,362	18,403	-
Other	217,747	6,364	6,137	810	305,435	5,782	9,365	893

- Represents or rounds to zero.   [1] Food stamp program in Puerto Rico was replaced by the Nutritional Assistance Grant Program. Figures shown represent grants to State and local governments, not included in totals.

Source: U.S. Bureau of the Census, *Federal Expenditures by State for Fiscal Year,* annual.

No. 1348. Puerto Rico—Summary: 1970 to 1990

ITEM	Unit	1970	1980	1984	1985	1986	1987	1988	1989	1990
POPULATION										
Total [1]	1,000	2,722	3,184	3,349	3,378	3,406	3,433	3,461	3,497	3,528
Persons per family	Number...	4.6	4.3	3.9	3.9	3.8	3.8	3.8	3.7	3.7
EDUCATION [2]										
Enrollment, total.	1,000	925.8	1,092.1	1,102.9	1,126.1	1,113.4	1,109.0	(NA)	(NA)	(NA)
Public day school	1,000	672.3	716.1	701.9	692.9	686.9	679.5	672.8	661.6	651.2
Other public	1,000	103.9	149.5	152.0	152.0	153.7	152.1	156.3	(NA)	(NA)
Private schools	1,000	89.1	95.2	95.4	102.3	122.5	122.6	128.6	137.2	145.8
College and university	1,000	57.3	130.1	160.2	155.7	156.8	158.6	155.7	156.9	156.1
Expenses	Mil. dol ...	288.8	825.0	1,117.0	1,171.8	1,212.9	1,282.3	1,434.0	1,564.2	1,696.5
As percent of GNP	Percent ...	6.2	7.5	7.9	7.8	7.6	7.5	7.7	7.8	7.9
Public	Mil. dol ...	254.6	612.2	782.2	810.2	814.4	847.9	932.7	990.8	1064.3
Private	Mil. dol ...	34.2	212.8	334.8	361.6	398.5	434.4	501.3	573.4	632.2
LABOR FORCE [3]										
Total [4]	1,000	765	907	952	964	977	1,013	1,039	1,060	1,067
Employed [5]	1,000	686	753	743	758	777	834	873	907	915
Agriculture [6]	1,000	68	38	40	38	40	35	31	34	33
Manufacturing	1,000	132	143	142	138	140	152	157	158	160
Trade	1,000	128	138	145	147	149	159	173	178	176
Government	1,000	106	184	177	180	180	197	201	209	211
Unemployed	1,000	79	154	209	206	200	179	165	153	153
Unemployment rate [7]	Rate	10	17	22	21	20	18	16	14	14
Compensation of employees .	Mil. dol ...	2,800	7,200	8,891	9,442	9,929	10,681	11,786	12,817	13,591
Avg. compensation	Dollar	4,082	9,563	11,967	12,456	12,779	12,806	13,447	14,131	14,854
Salary and wages	Mil. dol ...	2,555	6,290	7,666	8,137	8,496	9,182	10,118	10,965	11,632
INCOME [8]										
Personal income:										
Current dollars	Mil. dol ...	3,753	11,002	13,674	14,588	15,448	16,465	17,756	19,170	20,727
Constant (1954) dollars ...	Mil. dol ...	2,654	3,985	4,105	4,274	4,509	4,766	4,982	5,192	5,463
Disposable personal income:										
Current dollars	Mil. dol ...	3,565	10,403	12,913	13,760	14,391	15,420	16,529	18,142	19,536
Constant (1954) dollars ...	Mil. dol ...	2,521	3,768	3,877	4,032	4,200	4,463	4,638	4,914	5,149
Average family income:										
Current dollars	Dollar	6,366	14,858	15,990	16,914	17,305	18,297	19,562	20,387	21,834
Constant (1954) dollars ...	Dollar	4,503	5,381	4,801	4,957	5,050	5,297	5,491	5,520	5,754
BANKING [9]										
Assets	Mil. dol ...	3,322	10,223	19,968	21,209	22,534	26,101	24,660	27,179	27,902
TOURISM [8]										
Number of visitors	1,000	1,225.0	2,140.0	2,018.7	2,061.6	2,144.6	2,619.3	3,004.2	3221.2	3420.1
Visitor expenditures	Mil. dol ...	235.4	618.7	712.4	757.7	792.6	955.4	1,121.4	1,254.0	1,367.0
Average per visitor	Dollar	192	289	353	368	370	365	373	389	400
Net income from tourism	Mil. dol ...	89.8	202.2	205.1	223.1	239.3	285.8	333.1	372.8	387.2

NA Not available.   [1] 1970, and 1980 enumerated as of April 1; all other years estimated as of July 1.   [2] Enrollment for the first school month. Expenses for school year ending in year shown.   [3] Annual average of monthly figures. For fiscal years. [4] Beginning 1980, for population 16 years old and over; 1970, for population 14 years and over.   [5] Includes other employment, not shown separately.   [6] Includes forestry and fisheries.   [7] Percent unemployed of the labor force.   [8] For fiscal years.   [9] As of June 30.

Source: Puerto Rico Planning Board, San Juan, PR, *Income and Product,* annual; and *Socioeconomics Statistics,* annual.

No. 1349. Puerto Rico—Employment Status, 1970 to 1990, and by Sex, 1990

[In thousands. For 1970, for persons 14 years old and over; beginning 1980, 16 years old and over. Annual averages for calendar years of the civilian noninstitutional population]

EMPLOYMENT STATUS	1970	1980	1983	1984	1985	1986	1987	1988	1989	1990		
										Total	Male	Female
Total	1,743	2,116	2,251	2,273	2,293	2,303	2,310	2,321	2,339	2,362	1,096	1,268
In the labor force	777	916	942	958	969	998	1,019	1,058	1,063	1,072	675	398
Employed	693	758	722	759	758	809	848	900	907	920	565	355
Working	657	712	683	719	710	768	804	848	858	(NA)	(NA)	(NA)
35 hours or more	569	535	498	521	508	579	570	614	651	(NA)	(NA)	(NA)
Less than 35 hours ...	88	177	185	198	203	189	235	234	207	(NA)	(NA)	(NA)
Not working	35	48	39	40	47	41	44	52	49	(NA)	(NA)	(NA)
Unemployed	84	156	220	198	211	188	171	158	155	152	109	43
Percent	10.7	17.0	23.4	20.7	21.8	18.9	16.8	15.0	14.6	14.2	16.2	10.7
Not in labor force	966	1,200	1,309	1,315	1,324	1,305	1,291	1,263	1,277	1,290	421	870

NA Not available.

Source: Puerto Rico Dept. of Labor and Human Resources, Bureau of Labor Statistics, San Juan, PR.

No. 1350. Puerto Rico—Gross Product, by Major Industrial Sector: 1980 to 1991

[In millions of dollars. For fiscal years ending June 30]

ITEM	1980	1983	1984	1985	1986	1987	1988	1989	1990	1991
Gross product	11,065	13,048	14,183	15,002	16,014	17,153	18,550	19,954	21,491	22,831
Agriculture	380	391	345	357	373	411	399	443	430	470
Manufacturing	5,306	6,406	7,371	7,909	8,549	9,483	10,513	11,133	12,181	12,672
Contract construction and mining [1]	369	301	326	334	331	418	551	662	721	764
Transportation [2]	1,279	1,600	1,714	1,709	1,905	2,045	2,262	2,315	2,459	2,672
Trade	2,273	2,570	2,912	3,159	3,361	3,745	4,125	4,375	4,732	4,851
Finance, insurance, real estate	1,486	2,230	2,421	2,547	2,867	3,183	3,545	3,750	3,832	4,152
Services	1,279	1,576	1,714	1,837	1,993	2,184	2,505	2,699	2,920	3,125
Government	1,897	2,040	2,173	2,346	2,445	2,680	2,918	3,187	3,337	3,538
Commonwealth	1,574	1,734	1,849	1,996	2,078	2,293	2,506	2,745	2,884	3,063
Municipalities	323	306	324	350	367	387	413	442	453	475
Rest of the world	-3,372	-4,228	-4,980	-5,287	-5,955	-6,725	-7,629	-8,313	-9,045	-9,638
Statistical discrepancy. . .	166	162	187	91	147	-270	-639	-298	-75	225

[1] Mining includes only quarries.   [2] Includes other public utilities.
Source: Puerto Rico Planning Board, San Juan, PR, *Economic Report of the Governor, 1990-91.*

No. 1351. Puerto Rico—Net Income, by Industrial Origin: 1980 to 1991

[In millions of dollars. For fiscal years ending June 30]

INDUSTRY	1980	1984	1985	1986	1987	1988	1989	1990	1991
All industries.	9,007	11,408	12,182	13,166	14,414	15,699	16,662	17,790	18,741
Agriculture	435	425	410	420	465	447	494	487	525
Manufacturing	4,756	6,568	7,117	7,862	8,760	9,704	10,299	11,311	11,778
Chemicals and allied products . .	1,535	2,233	2,720	3,247	3,872	4,349	4,613	5,243	5,742
Metal products and machinery. .	1,445	2,253	2,367	2,420	2,551	2,709	2,822	3,106	3,120
Food and related products	524	772	833	967	1,044	1,154	1,304	1,427	1,467
Apparel and related products . .	410	481	450	409	437	496	499	489	513
Other manufacturing	842	829	747	819	856	996	1,061	1,046	936
Mining	9	9	10	13	15	22	24	26	27
Contract construction	337	303	309	299	380	516	624	680	722
Transp. and other public utilities [1].	1,022	1,275	1,248	1,442	1,574	1,646	1,681	1,765	1,956
Trade.	1,609	2,106	2,285	2,451	2,648	2,942	3,154	3,432	3,534
Finance, insurance, and real estate.	1,200	2,039	2,141	2,442	2,707	2,978	3,136	3,228	3,532
Services	1,114	1,490	1,606	1,748	1,911	2,154	2,377	2,570	2,767
Commonwealth Government [2] . . .	1,897	2,174	2,346	2,445	2,680	2,918	3,187	3,337	3,538
Rest of the world	-3,372	-4,980	-5,287	-5,955	-6,725	-7,629	-8,313	-9,045	-9,638

[1] Includes radio and television.   [2] Includes public enterprises, not elsewhere classified.
Source: Puerto Rico Planning Board, San Juan, PR, *Economic Report of the Governor, 1990-91.*

No. 1352. Puerto Rico—Transfers Between Federal and State Governments and Other Nonresidents: 1980 to 1991

[In million of dollars. For fiscal years ending June 30]

ITEM	1980	1984	1985	1986	1987	1988	1989	1990	1991
Total receipts.	2,665	3,485	3,531	3,837	3,992	4,073	4,289	4,877	4,958
Federal government [1]	2,538	3,256	3,348	3,672	3,785	3,840	4,082	4,655	4,694
Transfers to individuals [1]	2,477	3,194	3,283	3,589	3,715	3,761	4,014	4,584	4,616
Veterans benefits.	229	301	317	329	339	323	337	349	363
Medicare	118	187	220	266	273	292	320	368	415
Old age, disability, survivors . .	1,041	1,528	1,581	1,658	1,743	1,826	1,940	2,055	2,243
Nutritional assistance	812	765	780	791	804	822	853	880	916
Industry subsidies	61	61	65	84	70	80	68	71	79
Private institutions	21	28	33	35	34	35	35	37	36
U.S. State governments.	13	16	17	15	15	15	17	18	18
Other nonresidents.	114	213	166	150	192	217	191	205	246
Total payments	834	1,104	1,180	1,275	1,345	1,524	1,664	1,804	1,847
Federal government [1]	827	1,078	1,145	1,257	1,332	1,512	1,651	1,759	1,830
Old age, disability, survivors . . .	636	793	849	900	992	1,135	1,232	1,322	1,380
Medicare	21	38	44	47	53	70	89	97	100
Unemployment insurance	129	183	189	240	213	223	237	247	243
U.S. State governments.	2	3	3	2	2	2	2	2	3
Other nonresidents.	5	23	33	16	11	10	11	43	14
Net balance.	1,831	2,381	2,351	2,562	2,647	2,550	2,625	3,073	3,111
Federal government	1711	2178	2203	2415	2452	2328	2,431	2,896	2,865
U.S. State governments.	11	13	14	13	13	14	14	16	15
Other nonresidents.	109	190	134	134	134	181	208	180	162	232

[1] Includes other receipts and payments, not shown separately.
Source: Puerto Rico Planning Board, San Juan, PR, *Economic Report of the Governor, 1990-91.*

No. 1353. Puerto Rico—Economic Summary, by Industry: 1989

[Excludes employees of establishments totally exempt from the Federal Insurance Contributions Act: government workers, railroad employment jointly covered by Social Security and railroad retirement programs, self-employed persons, domestic service, agriculture production employees, and employees on oceanborne vessels or in foreign countries]

1987 SIC code [1]	INDUSTRY	Total establishments	Employment-size class					Employees [2]	Annual payroll (Mil. dol.)
			1 to 4	5 to 9	10 to 19	20 to 49	50 or more		
(X)	**Total** [3]	34,712	20,876	5,506	3,801	2,779	1,750	542,474	6,737.2
A	Agricultural services, forestry, and fishing	69	42	17	6	4	-	366	2.9
B	Mining..........................	35	12	5	5	11	2	728	9.2
14	Nonmetallic minerals, except fuels	27	7	5	5	9	1	447	6.1
C	Construction [3]	921	373	128	119	143	158	33,978	325.4
15	General contractors and operative builders........................	380	130	48	40	66	96	21,779	198.9
17	Special trade contractors..........	462	227	68	64	57	46	8,386	77.9
D	Manufacturing [3]	1,769	412	204	276	312	565	148,203	2,177.1
20	Food and kindred products	246	71	43	43	34	55	19,177	287.2
22	Textile mill products	17	4	2	2	4	5	2,342	27.4
23	Apparel and other textile products.....	259	41	15	24	48	131	31,450	245.9
25	Furniture and fixtures	110	37	17	28	22	6	2,055	18.4
26	Paper and allied products	43	6	3	11	7	16	1,870	28.6
27	Printing and publishing	152	69	25	31	18	9	3,670	51.3
28	Chemicals and allied products	166	21	10	19	31	85	23,137	555.2
29	Petroleum and coal products	16	3	2	3	1	7	1,139	30.1
30	Rubber and misc. plastic products.....	85	13	6	18	19	29	7,606	101.0
31	Leather and leather products	29	3	1	3	4	18	5,814	55.4
32	Stone, clay, and glass products	118	32	21	24	31	10	3,383	56.0
34	Fabricated metal products	113	22	18	25	23	25	4,184	53.6
35	Industrial machinery and equip	82	26	14	8	16	18	6,483	121.5
36	ELectronic and other electronic equip ...	111	9	1	8	12	81	19,755	284.8
38	Instruments and related products	64	12	1	5	6	40	8,313	141.8
E	Transportation and public utilities [3]	736	380	138	86	77	55	24,322	447.7
42	Trucking and warehousing	253	144	46	27	30	6	2,262	23.2
44	Water transportation.............	53	21	8	5	7	12	5,581	88.6
45	Air transportation	44	14	9	6	5	10	2,916	65.6
47	Transportation services...........	223	154	36	14	12	7	1,864	27.7
48	Communication	92	12	20	27	19	14	10,635	228.7
49	Electric, gas, and sanitary services	15	2	4	1	3	5	698	11.7
F	Wholesale trade [3]	1,904	749	378	349	278	150	33,090	550.5
50	Durable goods.................	961	366	193	199	142	61	14,890	243.2
51	Nondurable goods	927	380	183	146	132	86	17,708	294.6
G	Retail trade [3]	9,378	5,302	1,866	1,097	768	345	101,388	903.8
52	Building materials, garden supplies	580	333	122	65	47	13	4,863	49.8
53	General merchandise stores........	421	176	59	58	56	72	16,261	150.2
54	Food stores....................	1,292	763	190	131	94	114	18,966	148.8
55	Automotive dealers and service stations.	1,520	984	331	116	69	20	9,395	97.5
56	Apparel and accessory stores	1,212	541	313	222	118	18	11,835	93.7
57	Furniture and home furnishings......	662	377	176	73	31	5	4,421	43.6
58	Eating and drinking places.......	1,686	899	265	247	218	57	18,871	136.3
H	Finance, insurance, and real estate [3]	1,660	746	309	328	179	98	34,966	610.6
60	Depository institutions............	288	45	33	133	53	24	14,027	257.0
61	Nondepository institutions	409	110	110	107	61	21	7,170	116.0
63	Insurance carriers...............	84	15	16	17	19	17	4,088	78.4
64	Insurance agents, brokers, and service .	200	101	41	24	17	17	3,665	66.0
65	Real estate	631	448	102	45	23	13	4,897	56.0
I	Services [3]	7,280	4,837	972	656	438	377	113,162	1,174.3
72	Personal services...............	532	375	69	62	19	7	3,091	25.1
73	Business services................	690	320	115	79	76	100	26,040	227.6
75	Auto repair, services, and parking	528	376	90	36	18	8	3,042	29.8
78	Motion pictures	95	42	22	20	8	3	969	11.9
79	Amusement and recreation services ...	149	87	23	20	14	5	1,705	14.7
80	Health services	2,493	1,995	281	105	47	65	24,847	254.8
81	Legal services..................	728	608	45	55	12	8	2,961	47.9
82	Education services...............	429	115	48	73	105	88	21,057	209.4
83	Social services	207	88	41	41	17	20	5,339	37.9
86	Membership organizations	483	308	65	47	42	21	5,718	46.9
87	Engineering and management services .	525	299	93	66	43	24	6,067	102.1

- Represents or rounds to zero.   X Not applicable.   [1] 1987 Standard Industrial Classification (SIC) code; see text, section 13.   [2] For the pay period including March 12.   [3] Includes other establishments, not shown separately.
Source: U.S. Bureau of the Census, *County Business Patterns*, 1989.

No. 1354. Puerto Rico—Merchandise Imports and Exports: 1970 to 1990

[In millions of dollars]

ITEM	1970	1975	1979	1980	1981	1982	1983	1984	1985	1986	1987	1988	1989	1990
Imports.	2,681	4,885	7,834	9,018	9,329	8,167	8,708	10,116	10,162	10,321	11,308	13,096	15,010	16,200
From U.S.... .	2,070	3,029	4,788	5,345	5,801	5,300	5,162	5,738	6,130	6,467	7,307	8,788	10,193	10,792
From other... .	611	1,856	3,046	3,673	3,528	2,867	3,546	4,378	4,032	3,854	4,001	4,308	4,817	5,408
Exports.	1,680	3,000	6,539	6,576	7,047	8,888	8,242	9,426	11,087	11,854	12,508	14,436	17,455	20,402
To U.S.	1,563	2,633	5,720	5,643	6,024	7,624	6,936	8,074	9,873	10,524	11,153	12,756	15,334	17,915
To other	117	367	819	933	1,023	1,264	1,306	1,352	1,214	1,330	1,355	1,680	2,121	2,487

Source: U.S. Bureau of the Census, *Foreign Commerce and Navigation of the United States*, annual; *U.S. Trade with Puerto Rico and U.S. Possessions, FT 895;* and, through 1988, *Highlights of U.S. Export and Import Trade, FT990;* thereafter, FT990 supplement.

No. 1355. Puerto Rico, Guam, and Virgin Islands—Agriculture: 1982 and 1987

[1 cuerda=.97 acre. Tons specified are short tons]

ITEM	1982	1987	ITEM	1982	1987	ITEM	AMOUNT HARVESTED [1] Unit	1982	1987	SALES ($1,000) 1982	1987
PUERTO RICO											
Farms.........	21,820	20,245	Tenure of operator: Percent—			Dairy products.	(X)	(X)	(X)	152,126	157,864
Percent— Less than 10 cuerdas.....	45.1	48.7	Full-owners .	79.3	77.5	Poultry [2].....	(X)	(X)	(X)	45,945	70,560
10 to 19 cuerdas.	20.9	19.5				Coffee......	1,000 cwt.[3]	243.9	246.2	39,302	41,786
20 to 49 cuerdas.	18.0	16.7	Part-owners .	11.5	13.1	Cattle and calves.....	(X)	(X)	(X)	28,579	30,206
50 to 99 cuerdas.	7.1	6.7	Managers ..	1.8	2.3	Sugarcane ..	1,000 tons	1,462	1,170	26,663	26,643
100 to 174 cuerdas......	3.9	3.7	Tenants....	7.4	7.1	Fruits/nuts ...	(X)	(X)	(X)	14,060	20,645
175 or more cuerdas.....	5.0	4.7	Avg. farm size- cuerdas— Full-owners .	31.1	30.6	Pineapples ...	1,000 tons	44	69	9,534	15,495
			Part-owners ..	99.3	85.7	Hogs........	(X)	(X)	(X)	6,903	9,525
Cuerdas in farms........	982,457	886,846	Managers .. Tenants....	122.8 90.9	128.0 84.0	Vegetables...	Cuerdas..	6,669	6,179	9,547	8,236
GUAM											
Farms.........	297	351	Tenure of operator: Percent—			Chicken eggs .	(X)	(X)	(X)	791.9	651.1
Percent—						Fish.........	(X)	(X)	(X)	121.3	235.0
Less than 1 acre.	9.4	6.3	Full-owners .	62.0	64.1	Cucumbers...	1,000 lbs.	623.3	587.1	217.8	233.5
1 to 2 acres....	36.0	35.9	Permittees ..	21.9	20.5	Green beans..	1,000 lbs.	116.5	303.8	81.7	230.2
3 to 7 acres ..	28.6	29.1	Tenants....	9.1	4.3	Watermelons .	1,000 lbs.	400.3	632.6	115.6	178.6
8 or more acres .	26.0	28.8	Part-owners .	5.1	4.6	Tomatoes....	1,000 lbs.	88.0	142.7	64.3	108.6
			Nonpermittees. Others......	1.3 0.7	6.0 0.6	Hogs and pigs.	(X)	(X)	(X)	117.0	106.4
Acres in farms....	17,787	13,134									
VIRGIN ISLANDS											
Farms.........	259	267	Tenure of operator:			Milk........	(X)	(X)	(X)	922.8	1,042.7
Percent— Less than 3 acres........	29.0	30.0	Percent—			Cattle and calves.....	(X)	(X)	(X)	488.6	613.4
3 to 9 acres	34.7	30.3	Full-owners .	79.9	75.3	Hogs and pigs.	(X)	(X)	(X)	130.0	125.2
10 to 19 acres ..	9.3	12.0	Part-owners .	10.4	13.5						
20 or more acres.	27.0	27.7	Tenants....	9.3	8.6	Tomatoes....	Acres ...	8	16	33.7	113.7
						Lettuce	Acres ...	2	8	7.8	49.5
			Managers	0.4	2.6	Mangoes	1,000....	205.0	171.1	(D)	44.0
Acres in farms....	17,778	17,785				Poultry [2]....	(X)	(X)	(X)	315.6	16.8

D Withheld to avoid disclosure of information pertaining to a specific organization or individual.   X Not applicable.
[1] Includes amounts not sold.   [2] Includes poultry products.   [3] Cwt=hundredweight (100 lbs.).
Source: U.S. Bureau of the Census, *1987 Census of Agriculture*, vol. 1, parts 52, 53, and 54.

No. 1356. Guam, Virgin Islands, and Northern Mariana Islands—Economic Summary: 1987

[Sales and payroll in millions of dollars]

ITEM	Guam	Virgin Islands	No. Mariana Islands	ITEM	Guam	Virgin Islands	No. Mariana Islands
Total: Establishments	1,490	2,604	768	**Wholesale trade:**			
Sales.................	1,510	(D)	374	Establishments	94	84	28
Annual payroll	221	255	57	Sales................	245	211	50
Paid employees [1].......	10,502	20,700	0,000	Annual payroll	19	20	2
Unpaid family workers [2]....	371	209	167	Paid employees [1].......	1,392	1,322	187
Construction: Establishments.	79	92	72	Unpaid family workers [2]....	6	2	-
Sales.................	127	124	43	**Retail trade:**			
Annual payroll	35	29	12	Establishments	804	1,311	383
Paid employees [1].......	2,705	2,170	2,061	Sales................	786	703	155
Unpaid family workers [2]....	1	3	6	Annual payroll	79	85	14
Manufacturing:				Paid employees [1].......	7,344	8,529	2,304
Establishments	38	66	39	Unpaid family workers [2]....	273	168	126
Sales.................	81	(D)	58	**Services:** Establishments....	475	1,051	246
Annual payroll	17	44	14	Sales................	271	296	67
Paid employees [1].......	1,320	2,102	2,257	Annual payroll	71	76	16
Unpaid family workers [2]....	1	-	3	Paid employees [1].......	5,821	6,586	2,281
				Unpaid family workers [2]....	90	36	32

- Represents zero.   D Withheld to avoid disclosure of information pertaining to a specific organization or individual.   [1] For pay period including March 12.   [2] Includes those who worked 15 hours or more during the week including March 12.
Source: U.S. Bureau of the Census, *1987 Economic Census of Outlying Areas*, OAC 87-5 to OAC 87-7.

Comparative International Statistics

This section presents statistics for the world as a whole and for many countries on a comparative basis with the United States. Selected data are shown for area and population, births and deaths, social and industrial indicators, finances, agriculture, communication, and military affairs.

Statistics of the individual nations may be found primarily in official national publications, generally in the form of yearbooks, issued by most of the nations at various intervals in their own national languages and expressed in their own or customary units of measure. (For a listing of selected publications, see Guide to Sources.) For handier reference, especially for international comparisons, the Statistical Office of the United Nations compiles data as submitted by member countries and issues a number of international summary publications, generally in English and French. Among these are the *Statistical Yearbook;* the *Demographic Yearbook;* the *Yearbook of International Trade Statistics;* the *Yearbook of National Accounts Statistics: Vol. II, International Tables; Population and Vital Statistics Reports* (quarterly); the *Monthly Bulletin of Statistics;* and the *Energy Statistics Yearbook.* Specialized agencies of the United Nations also issue international summary publications on agricultural, labor, health, and education statistics. Among these are the *Production Yearbook* and *Trade Yearbook* issued by the Food and Agriculture Organization, the *Yearbook of Labour Statistics* issued by the International Labour Office, the *World Health Statistics* issued by the World Health Organization, and the *Statistical Yearbook* issued by the Educational, Scientific, and Cultural Organization.

The Bureau of the Census, in *Country Demographic Profiles,* series ISP-DP, presents data on individual countries for both a recent census year and the current period; and in the *World Population Profile* series, estimates of basic demographic measures for countries and regions of the world. The *International Population Statistics Reports,* series P-90

In Brief

Ten largest countries in 1991:

China, Mainland	1,151,487
India	869,515
Soviet Union (former)	293,048
United States	252,502
Indonesia	193,560
Brazil	155,356
Japan	124,017
Nigeria	122,471
Pakistan	117,490
Bangladesh	116,601

and P-91, issued by the Bureau of the Census, also present population figures for many foreign countries. Detailed population statistics are also available from the Bureau of the Census' computerized International Data Base.

The U.S. Arms Control and Disarmament Agency and the International Monetary Fund (IMF) also compile data on international statistics. In its *World Military Expenditures and Arms Transfers,* published annually, the ACDA presents data on various economic indicators, as well as basic military data. Among the topics presented have been military expenditures, gross national product, imports and exports, and armed forces, by region and/or country. The IMF publishes a series of reports relating to financial data. These include *International Financial Statistics, Direction of Trade,* and *Balance of Payments Yearbook,* published in English, French, and Spanish.

Statistical coverage, country names, and classifications.—Problems of space and availability of data limit the number of countries and the extent of statistical coverage shown. The list of countries included is based almost entirely on a list of sovereign nations, dependencies, and areas of special sovereignty published by the U.S. Department of State in *Status of the World's Nations.* Country names are shown here as specified in that publication. In the few cases where a lack of comparability exists between State Department and

United Nations' terminology, the State Department's preferences are used.

In 1990 and 1991, several important changes took place in the status of the world's nations. Two nations, Yemen and Germany, were formed in 1990, each by unification of two formerly separate nations. In the case of Germany, the former German Democratic Republic (East) was subsumed by the Federal Republic of Germany (West). In most cases, data presented in the *Statistical Abstract* are for former West Germany. The Republic of Yemen was formed by union of the former Yemen Arab Republic and the People's Democratic Republic of Yemen. Also in 1990, Namibia finally realized its independence; the United Nations terminated its status as a South African mandate in 1966.

The year 1990 also began a period of turmoil in the former Soviet Union. The independence of three Baltic States—Estonia, Latvia, and Lithuania—was recognized by the central Soviet government in August 1991. The United States established diplomatic relations with the democratically elected governments of the Baltic States in September 1991. In December 1991, the 12 former Soviet republics became separate sovereign nations—Armenia, Azerbaijan, Byelarus, Georgia, Kazakhstan, Kyrgyzstan, Moldova, Russia, Tajikistan, Turkmenistan, Ukraine, and Uzbekistan. Eleven of the 12 have formed a Commonwealth of Independent States (Georgia has not joined). Data presented in the *Statistical Abstract* are for former Soviet Union.

The population estimates and projections used in tables 1459-1461 were prepared by the Census Bureau. For each country, the data on population, by age and sex, fertility, mortality, and international migration were evaluated and, where necessary, adjusted for inconsistencies and errors in the data. In most instances, comprehensive projections were made by the component method, resulting in distributions of the population by age and sex, and requiring an assessment of probable future trends of fertility, mortality, and international migration.

Economic associations.—The Organization for European Economic Co-operation (OEEC), a regional grouping of Western European countries established in 1948 for the purpose of harmonizing national economic policies and conditions, was succeeded on September 30, 1961, by the Organization for Economic Cooperation and Development (OECD). The member nations of the OECD are Australia, Austria, Belgium, Canada, Denmark, Finland, France, Germany, Greece, Iceland, Ireland, Italy, Japan, Luxembourg, the Netherlands, New Zealand, Norway, Portugal, Spain, Sweden, Switzerland, Turkey, the United Kingdom, and the United States, plus Yugoslavia in special status category.

Quality and comparability of the data.—The quality and comparability of the data presented here are affected by a number of factors:

(1) The year for which data are presented may not be the same for all subjects for a particular country, or for a given subject for different countries, though the data shown are the most recent available. All such variations have been noted. The data shown are for calendar years except as otherwise specified.

(2) The bases, methods of estimating, methods of data collection, extent of coverage, precision of definition, scope of territory, and margins of error may vary for different items within a particular country, and for like items for different countries. Footnotes and headnotes to the tables give a few of the major time-period and coverage qualifications attached to the figures; considerably more detail is presented in the source publications. Many of the measures shown are, at best, merely rough indicators of magnitude.

(3) Figures shown in this section for the United States may not always agree with figures shown in the preceding sections. Disagreements may be attributable to the use of differing original sources, a difference in the definition of geographic limits (the 50 States, conterminous United States only, or the United States including certain outlying areas and possessions), or to possible adjustments made in the U.S. figures by the United Nations or other sources in order to make them more

comparable with figures from other countries.

International comparisons of national accounts data.—In order to compare national accounts data for different countries, it is necessary to convert each country's data into a common unit of currency, usually the U.S. dollar. The market exchange rates which are often used in converting national currencies do not necessarily reflect the relative purchasing power in the various countries. For example, using table 1370, it should not be concluded that the United Kingdom's individual standard of living in 1990 was only 78 percent of that of the United States, as the statistics may imply. It is obviously necessary that the goods and services produced in different countries should be valued consistently if the differences observed are meant to reflect real differences in the volumes of goods and services produced. The use of purchasing power parities (see table 1375) instead of exchange rates is intended to achieve this objective.

The method used to present the data shown in table 1375 is to construct volume measures directly by revaluing the goods and services sold in different countries at a common set of international prices. By dividing the ratio of the gross domestic products of two countries expressed in their own national currencies by the corresponding ratio calculated at constant international prices, it is possible to derive the implied purchasing power parity (PPP) between the two currencies concerned. PPP's show how many units of currency are needed in one country to buy the same amount of goods and services which one unit of currency will buy in the other country. For further information, see *National Accounts, Main Aggregates,* volume I, issued annually by the Organization for Economic Cooperation and Development, Paris, France.

International Standard Industrial Classification.—The original version of the International Standard Industrial Classification of All Economic Activities (ISIC) was adopted in 1948. Wide use has been made both nationally and internationally in classifying data according to kind of economic activity in the fields of production, employment, national income, and other economic statistics. A number of countries have utilized the ISIC as the basis for devising their industrial classification scheme. Substantial comparability has been attained between the industrial classifications of many other countries, including the United States, and the ISIC by ensuring, as far as practicable, that the categories at detailed levels of classification in national schemes fitted into only one category of the ISIC. For more detail, see Bureau of the Census, *The International Standard Industrial Classification and the U.S. Standard Industrial Classification,* Technical Paper No. 14 and text, section 27. The United Nations, the International Labour Organization, the Food and Agriculture Organization, and other international bodies have utilized the ISIC in publishing and analyzing statistical data. Revisions of the ISIC were issued in 1958, 1968, and 1989.

No. 1357. World Summary: 1970 to 1989

[See text, section 31, for general comments concerning quality of the data]

ITEM	Unit	1970	1980	1982	1983	1984	1985	1986	1987	1988	1989
Population.	Millions	3,698	4,448	4,604	4,685	4,768	4,851	4,936	5,023	5,111	5,201
Agriculture, forestry, and fishing: [1]											
Barley	Mil. metric tons.	121.7	159.8	164.0	161.7	172.2	176.2	181.5	179.8	167.1	167.6
Coffee	Mil. metric tons.	3.8	4.8	5.0	5.6	5.2	5.9	5.3	6.5	5.7	6.0
Corn	Mil. metric tons.	267.0	398.0	452.4	350.0	455.1	485.7	481.7	454.0	402.1	470.5
Cotton (lint)	Mil. metric tons.	12.0	13.9	14.9	14.2	18.2	17.4	15.2	16.6	18.3	16.7
Meats	Mil. metric tons.	98.9	134.4	138.2	142.4	146.0	151.2	155.5	160.3	167.3	169.9
Peanuts (groundnuts)	Mil. metric tons.	18.0	16.9	17.9	19.0	20.0	20.9	21.1	21.5	24.9	23.0
Rice	Mil. metric tons.	316.7	399.2	423.9	451.5	469.4	472.1	471.3	464.4	492.1	512.7
Tobacco.	Mil. metric tons.	4.6	5.3	6.9	5.9	6.5	7.0	6.1	6.2	6.8	7.1
Wheat	Mil. metric tons.	316.4	446.0	481.6	493.0	516.0	504.6	534.7	511.5	506.3	542.0
Wool, greasy.	Mil. metric tons.	2.9	2.8	2.9	2.9	2.9	3.0	3.0	3.1	3.1	3.2
Roundwood	Mil. cubic meters	2,614	2,942	2,941	3,038	3,126	3,158	3,254	3,352	(NA)	(NA)
Fish catches	Mil. metric tons.	68.0	72.0	76.6	77.4	83.5	86.0	92.4	92.7	(NA)	(NA)
Industrial production:											
Wine	Mil. metric tons.	(NA)	35.2	37.0	34.8	32.9	31.0	32.6	31.8	27.6	28.5
Sugar	Mil. metric tons.	72.9	84.0	102.2	97.4	99.9	98.5	101.1	101.8	105.3	109.4
Wheat flour.	Mil. metric tons.	121.2	187.2	198.2	197.0	196.9	198.2	201.4	200.9	202.9	203.2
Coal	Mil. metric tons.	2,143	2,728	2,828	2,831	2,999	3,161	3,249	3,335	3,454	3,474
Lignite and brown coal	Mil. metric tons.	793	1,042	1,106	1,130	1,153	1,202	1,219	1,246	1,257	1,257
Crude petroleum [2]	Bil. bbl.	16.74	21.72	19.41	19.33	19.84	19.58	20.39	20.55	21.41	21.76
Natural gas (dry) [2]	Trl. cu. ft	37.54	53.11	54.12	54.57	59.66	62.00	63.25	66.17	69.80	71.88
Electricity	Bil. kWh.	4,962	8,247	8,476	8,826	9,326	9,747	10,055	10,587	11,035	11,427
Iron ore	Mil. metric tons.	421	841	781	740	829	862	868	890	916	920
Pig iron and ferroalloys	Mil. metric tons.	440	542	509	461	466	500	507	496	504	506
Tin [3]	1,000 metric tons	184	231	212	195	196	196	191	194	210	210
Crude steel.	Mil. metric tons.	594	699	623	638	679	685	671	682	685	676
Cement	Mil. metric tons.	(NA)	872	880	906	933	949	996	1,045	1,109	1,137
Non-cellulosic fibers [3]	Mil. metric tons.	4.9	10.0	9.6	10.4	11.0	11.7	11.9	12.4	11.6	11.6
Sawnwood	Mil. cubic meters	413	447	419	438	458	464	480	502	503	498
Woodpulp.	Mil. metric tons.	97.2	124.4	118.2	135.1	134.2	133.8	139.1	144.5	150.6	151.7
Newsprint.	Mil. metric tons.	21.6	25.4	25.2	25.6	27.6	28.0	29.0	30.0	31.3	31.6
Merchant vessels, launched . .	Mil. gross tons.	21.7	13.9	17.3	14.9	17.7	17.3	14.9	9.6	11.8	12.7
Motor vehicles	Millions	29.3	38.9	36.4	39.9	42.0	43.9	43.9	45.9	48.2	49.0
External trade:											
Imports, c.i.f	Bil. U.S. dollars .	331	2,047	1,900	1,874	1,983	2,006	2,199	2,547	2,899	3,108
Exports, f.o.b	Bil. U.S. dollars .	314	1,998	1,829	1,805	1,901	1,931	2,124	2,481	2,811	2,992
Transport:											
Railway freight	Bil. metric ton-km	5,027	6,754	6,635	6,855	7,138	7,285	(NA)	(NA)	(NA)	(NA)
Merchant shipping, freight [4] . .	Mil. metric tons.	(NA)	3,676	3,290	3,290	3,410	3,362	3,363	3,506	3,692	3,891
Civil aviation, kilometers flown [5]	Millions	4,353	9,362	9,010	9,320	9,950	10,565	11,455	12,208	13,026	13,564

NA Not available.   [1] Source: U.S. Department of Agriculture, Economic Research Service, *World Agriculture-Trends and Indicators.*   [2] Source: U.S. Energy Information Administration, *International Energy Annual* and *Annual Energy Review.* [3] Excludes China: Mainland. Tin and merchant vessels exclude Soviet Union. For other exclusions, see source.   [4] Freight loaded. [5] Scheduled services of members of International Civil Aviation Organization. Excludes Soviet Union.

Source: Except as noted, Statistical Office of the United Nations, New York, NY, *Monthly Bulletin of Statistics*, (copyright).

No. 1358. World Population, 1990 and 1991, and Area, 1991, by Size of Country

[Covers only countries listed in table 1359, except for newly independent Soviet and Yugoslavia republics. See headnote, table 1359]

POPULATION CLASS IN **1991**	POPULATION, 1990		1991					
			Population		Countries		Area	
	Total (mil.)	Percent of total	Total number	Percent of total	Total (mil.)	Percent of total	Total sq. miles	Percent of total
Total	5,329	100.0	5,423	100.0	206	100.0	50,524	100.0
Under 1 million	15	0.3	15	0.3	74	35.9	544	1.1
1 to 5 million	114	2.1	117	2.2	40	19.4	4,048	8.0
5 to 10 million.	193	3.6	197	3.6	26	12.6	3,690	7.3
10 to 25 million.	464	8.7	475	8.8	30	14.6	7,518	14.9
25 to 50 million.	457	8.6	466	8.6	14	6.8	9,538	18.9
Over 50 million	4,085	76.7	4,153	76.6	22	10.7	25,186	49.9

Source: Compiled from U.S. Bureau of the Census, unpublished data.

Comparative International Statistics

No. 1359. Population and Area, by Country, 1990 and 1991, and Projections, 2000 and 2010

[Population data generally are de facto figures for the present territory. Population estimates were derived from information available as of mid-1990. See table 1361 for country components of regions. See text, section 31, for general comments concerning the data. Data compiled from the International Data Base; see text, section 31. For details of methodology, coverage, and reliability, see sources. Minus sign (-) indicates decrease]

COUNTRY	MIDYEAR POPULATION (1,000)				Population rank, 1991	ANNUAL RATE OF GROWTH [1] (percent)		Population per sq. mile, 1991	Area [2] (sq. mile)
	1990	1991	2000, proj.	2010, proj.		1990-2000	2000-2010		
World total.	5,329,407	5,422,908	6,284,643	7,239,935	(X)	1.6	1.4	107	50,523,913
Afghanistan	15,564	16,450	24,935	32,358	53	4.7	2.6	66	250,000
Albania	3,273	3,335	3,824	4,265	124	1.6	1.1	315	10,579
Algeria.	25,377	26,022	32,024	39,106	36	2.3	2.0	28	919,591
Andorra	52	53	63	72	204	2.0	1.2	305	174
Angola.	8,449	8,668	11,424	14,887	77	3.0	2.6	18	481,351
Antigua and Barbuda	64	64	69	76	200	0.7	1.0	376	170
Argentina	32,291	32,664	36,036	39,884	31	1.1	1.0	31	1,056,637
Armenia	3,357	(NA)	3,552	3,685	119	0.6	0.4	[3]287	11,700
Aruba	64	64	67	70	199	0.6	0.4	860	75
Australia.	17,037	17,288	19,511	21,689	50	1.4	1.1	6	2,941,285
Austria.	7,644	7,666	7,762	7,660	83	0.2	-0.1	240	31,942
Azerbaijan	7,212	(NA)	8,177	8,911	87	1.3	0.9	[3]213	33,930
Bahamas, The.	249	252	283	313	175	1.3	1.0	65	3,888
Bahrain	520	537	694	863	159	2.9	2.2	2,247	239
Bangladesh	113,930	116,601	143,226	176,562	10	2.3	2.1	2,255	51,703
Barbados	254	255	260	272	174	0.2	0.4	1,534	166
Belgium	9,909	9,922	9,989	9,889	69	0.1	-0.1	850	11,672
Belize	220	228	301	377	176	3.2	2.2	26	8,803
Benin.	4,674	4,832	6,509	8,939	103	3.3	3.2	113	42,710
Bhutan.	1,566	1,598	1,909	2,277	142	2.0	1.8	88	18,147
Bolivia	6,989	7,157	8,721	10,574	89	2.2	1.9	17	418,683
Bosnia and Herzegovina . .	4,517	(NA)	4,828	5,039	105	0.7	0.4	(NA)	(NA)
Botswana.	1,224	1,258	1,554	1,869	146	2.4	1.8	6	226,012
Brazil.	152,505	155,356	180,536	207,462	5	1.7	1.4	48	3,265,061
Brunei	372	398	562	660	166	4.1	1.6	195	2,035
Bulgaria	8,934	8,911	9,004	9,072	75	0.1	0.1	209	42,683
Burkina	9,078	9,360	12,464	17,158	73	3.2	3.2	89	105,714
Burma	41,277	42,112	49,787	58,601	25	1.9	1.6	166	253,954
Burundi	5,646	5,831	7,731	10,423	94	3.1	3.0	589	9,903
Byelarus.	10,257	(NA)	10,629	10,901	67	0.4	0.3	[3]126	81,120
Cambodia.	6,991	7,146	8,498	10,023	88	2.0	1.6	105	68,154
Cameroon	11,092	11,390	14,453	18,625	61	2.6	2.5	63	181,251
Canada	26,538	26,835	29,301	31,464	32	1.0	0.7	8	3,560,219
Cape Verde	375	387	504	649	165	3.0	2.5	248	1,556
Central African Republic . .	2,877	2,952	3,702	4,712	127	2.5	2.4	12	240,533
Chad	5,017	5,122	6,204	7,652	99	2.1	2.1	11	486,178
Chile	13,083	13,287	15,025	16,817	57	1.4	1.1	46	289,112
China: Mainland.	1,133,683	1,151,487	1,303,342	1,420,312	1	1.4	0.9	320	3,600,930
Taiwan.	20,435	20,659	22,441	24,065	42	0.9	0.7	1,659	12,456
Colombia [4]	33,076	33,778	39,745	45,603	30	1.8	1.4	84	401,042
Comoros [4]	460	477	656	920	161	3.5	3.4	569	838
Congo	2,242	2,309	2,995	3,908	134	2.9	2.7	18	131,853
Costa Rica	3,033	3,111	3,803	4,546	126	2.3	1.8	159	19,560
Cote d'Ivoire	12,478	12,978	18,144	25,263	59	3.7	3.3	106	122,780
Croatia.	4,686	(NA)	4,717	4,729	102	0.1	(Z)	(NA)	(NA)
Cuba	10,620	10,732	11,613	12,277	62	0.9	0.6	251	42,803
Cyprus.	702	709	768	830	155	0.9	0.8	199	3,568
Czechoslovakia	15,683	15,725	16,303	16,824	52	0.4	0.3	325	48,440
Denmark	5,131	5,133	5,147	5,095	98	(Z)	-0.1	314	16,359
Djibouti	337	346	440	571	171	2.7	2.6	41	8,486
Dominica	85	86	101	118	192	1.7	1.5	298	290
Dominican Republic	7,241	7,385	8,676	10,080	86	1.8	1.5	395	18,680
Ecuador	10,507	10,752	12,997	15,543	64	2.1	1.8	101	106,888
Egypt.	53,212	54,452	66,498	81,750	21	2.2	2.1	142	384,344
El Salvador.	5,310	5,419	6,471	7,628	97	2.0	1.6	677	8,000
Equatorial Guinea	369	379	477	615	167	2.6	2.5	35	10,830
Estonia	1,584	(NA)	1,675	1,770	141	0.6	0.6	[3]96	16,464
Ethiopia	51,407	53,191	69,374	93,593	23	3.0	3.0	125	425,097
Fiji	738	744	823	932	154	1.1	1.2	105	7,054
Finland	4,977	4,991	5,075	5,088	100	0.2	(Z)	42	117,942
France.	56,358	56,596	58,548	59,708	19	0.4	0.2	269	210,668
Gabon.	1,068	1,080	1,231	1,423	149	1.4	1.5	11	99,486
Gambia, The.	848	875	1,151	1,553	151	3.1	3.0	227	3,861
Georgia	5,479	(NA)	5,865	6,184	95	0.7	0.5	[3]201	27,300
Germany	79,123	79,548	81,532	82,189	12	0.3	0.1	588	135,236
West Germany (former) .	63,232	64,039	(NA)	(NA)	(X)	(NA)	(NA)	667	95,976
Ghana	15,130	15,617	20,527	27,141	54	3.1	2.8	176	88,811
Greece	10,028	10,043	10,166	10,160	68	0.1	(Z)	199	50,502
Grenada.	84	84	83	96	193	-0.1	1.4	640	131
Guatemala	9,038	9,266	11,315	13,537	74	2.2	1.8	221	41,865
Guinea.	7,269	7,456	9,232	11,562	85	2.4	2.2	79	94,927
Guinea-Bissau.	999	1,024	1,265	1,579	150	2.4	2.2	95	10,811
Guyana	753	750	728	807	153	-0.3	1.0	10	76,004
Haiti	6,142	6,287	7,649	9,421	92	2.2	2.1	591	10,641
Honduras	4,804	4,949	6,243	7,660	101	2.6	2.0	115	43,201
Hungary.	10,569	10,558	10,604	10,602	63	(Z)	(Z)	296	35,653
Iceland	257	260	280	296	173	0.9	0.6	7	38,707

See footnotes at end of table.

No. 1359. Population and Area, by Country, 1990 and 1991, and Projections, 2000 and 2010—Continued

[See headnote, page 820]

COUNTRY	MIDYEAR POPULATION (1,000)				Popu-lation rank, 1991	ANNUAL RATE OF GROWTH [1] (percent)		Popu-lation per sq. mile, 1991	Area [2] (sq. mile)
	1990	1991	2000, proj.	2010, proj.		1990-2000	2000-2010		
India [5]	852,667	869,515	1,018,092	1,172,101	2	1.8	1.4	757	1,147,950
Indonesia	190,136	193,560	223,820	256,818	4	1.6	1.4	274	705,189
Iran	57,003	59,051	78,246	107,406	18	3.2	3.2	93	631,660
Iraq	18,782	19,525	27,205	38,047	45	3.7	3.4	117	167,556
Ireland	3,500	3,489	3,509	3,685	118	(Z)	0.5	131	26,598
Israel	4,436	4,558	5,321	6,103	106	1.8	1.4	581	7,849
Italy	57,664	57,772	58,592	58,011	15	0.2	-0.1	509	113,521
Jamaica	2,469	2,489	2,762	3,155	131	1.1	1.3	595	4,181
Japan	123,567	124,017	128,144	130,480	7	0.4	0.2	814	152,411
Jordan	3,273	3,413	4,880	6,810	123	4.0	3.3	97	35,344
Kazakhstan	16,757	(NA)	18,272	19,718	51	0.9	0.8	[3]16	1,059,630
Kenya	24,342	25,242	34,259	45,498	37	3.4	2.8	115	219,788
Kiribati	70	71	81	90	196	1.5	1.0	257	277
Kuwait	2,124	2,204	2,879	3,635	137	3.0	2.3	320	6,880
Kyrgyzstan	4,394	(NA)	5,207	6,029	107	1.7	1.5	[3]57	77,610
Laos	4,024	4,113	4,964	5,951	112	2.1	1.8	46	89,112
Latvia	2,695	(NA)	2,840	3,008	129	0.5	0.6	[3]107	25,194
Lebanon	3,339	3,385	4,058	4,934	120	1.9	2.0	857	3,950
Lesotho	1,755	1,801	2,242	2,776	140	2.4	2.1	154	11,718
Liberia	2,640	2,730	3,674	4,977	130	3.3	3.0	73	37,189
Libya	4,223	4,353	5,599	7,067	110	2.8	2.3	6	679,359
Liechtenstein	28	28	30	31	211	0.5	0.3	458	62
Lithuania	3,726	(NA)	4,589	4,726	114	0.4	0.3	[3]147	25,428
Luxembourg	384	388	410	409	164	0.7	(Z)	389	998
Macedonia	2,132	(NA)	2,324	2,478	136	0.9	0.6	(NA)	(NA)
Madagascar	11,801	12,185	16,185	21,954	60	3.2	3.0	54	224,533
Malawi	9,197	9,438	11,892	16,450	72	2.6	3.2	260	36,324
Malaysia	17,556	17,982	21,950	26,562	47	2.2	1.9	142	126,853
Maldives	218	226	312	427	177	3.6	3.1	1,953	116
Mali	8,142	8,339	10,667	14,398	79	2.7	3.0	18	471,042
Malta	353	356	377	393	168	0.6	0.4	2,876	124
Mauritania	1,935	1,996	2,652	3,624	139	3.2	3.1	5	397,838
Mauritius	1,072	1,081	1,168	1,270	148	0.9	0.8	1,514	714
Mexico	88,010	90,007	108,754	129,017	11	2.1	1.7	121	742,486
Moldova	4,393	(NA)	4,589	4,726	108	0.4	0.3	[3]331	13,260
Monaco	29	30	32	34	210	0.7	0.6	38,477	1
Mongolia	2,187	2,247	2,836	3,579	135	2.6	2.3	4	604,247
Montenegro	645	(NA)	696	733	156	0.8	0.5	(NA)	(NA)
Morocco	25,630	26,182	31,392	37,349	35	2.0	1.7	152	172,317
Mozambique	14,539	15,113	20,936	27,494	56	3.6	2.7	50	302,737
Namibia	1,453	1,521	2,081	2,895	144	3.6	3.3	5	317,873
Nauru	9	9	10	11	221	1.3	0.7	1,151	8
Nepal	19,146	19,612	24,340	30,622	44	2.4	2.3	371	52,819
Netherlands	14,936	15,022	15,642	15,814	55	0.5	0.1	1,146	13,104
New Zealand	3,296	3,309	3,400	3,441	121	0.3	0.1	32	103,734
Nicaragua	3,602	3,752	4,729	5,858	117	2.7	2.1	81	46,430
Niger	7,879	8,154	11,056	15,323	81	3.4	3.3	17	489,073
Nigeria	118,819	122,471	160,751	213,042	8	3.0	2.8	348	351,649
North Korea	21,412	21,815	25,491	28,491	40	1.7	1.1	469	46,490
Norway	4,253	4,273	4,411	4,463	109	0.4	0.1	36	118,865
Oman [6]	1,481	1,534	2,099	2,990	143	3.5	3.5	19	82,031
Pakistan [6]	114,649	117,490	149,147	195,215	9	2.6	2.7	391	300,664
Panama	2,425	2,476	2,937	3,433	132	1.9	1.6	84	29,340
Papua New Guinea	3,823	3,913	4,806	5,924	113	2.3	2.1	22	174,405
Paraguay	4,660	4,799	6,023	7,381	104	2.6	2.0	31	153,398
Peru	21,906	22,362	26,435	30,880	39	1.9	1.6	45	494,208
Philippines	64,404	65,759	77,734	90,261	14	1.9	1.5	571	115,124
Poland	37,777	37,800	38,889	40,599	28	0.3	0.4	322	117,571
Portugal	10,354	10,388	10,652	10,764	66	0.3	0.1	294	35,382
Qatar	491	518	743	954	160	4.1	2.5	122	4,247
Romania	23,273	23,397	24,534	25,417	38	0.5	0.4	263	88,934
Russia	148,254	(NA)	152,910	157,946	6	0.3	0.3	[3]22	6,659,250
Rwanda	7,609	7,903	11,047	15,787	84	3.7	3.6	820	9,633
Saint Kitts and Nevis	40	40	44	51	208	0.9	1.5	290	139
Saint Lucia	150	153	186	226	184	2.2	2.0	649	236
Saint Vincent and the Grenadines	113	114	132	156	187	1.6	1.6	873	131
San Marino	23	23	24	26	214	0.6	0.6	1,004	23
Sao Tome and Principe	125	128	166	211	186	2.9	2.9	347	371
Saudi Arabia	17,116	17,870	25,003	34,134	49	3.8	3.8	22	829,996
Senegal	7,714	7,953	10,482	14,090	82	3.1	3.1	107	74,131
Serbia	9,883	(NA)	10,425	10,892	70	0.5	0.4	(NA)	(NA)
Seychelles	68	69	74	80	197	0.8	0.8	392	176
Sierra Leone	4,166	4,275	5,399	6,980	111	2.6	2.6	155	27,653
Singapore	2,721	2,756	3,021	3,233	128	1.0	1.0	11,441	241
Slovenia	1,954	(NA)	1,998	2,025	138	0.2	0.1	(NA)	(NA)
Solomon Islands	335	347	469	620	172	3.4	3.4	33	10,633
Somalia	6,654	6,709	9,409	12,849	91	3.5	2.1	28	242,216
South Africa	39,539	40,601	51,375	66,005	26	2.6	2.6	86	471,444
South Korea	42,792	43,134	45,962	48,063	24	0.7	0.7	1,138	37,911
Spain	39,269	39,385	40,456	40,998	27	0.3	0.1	204	192,819

See footnotes at end of table.

No. 1359. Population and Area, by Country, 1990 and 1991, and Projections, 2000 and 2010—Continued

[See headnote, page 820]

COUNTRY	MIDYEAR POPULATION (1,000)				Popula-tion rank, 1991	ANNUAL RATE OF GROWTH [1] (percent)		Popula-tion per sq. mile, 1991	Area [2] (sq. mile)
	1990	1991	2000, proj.	2010, proj.		1990-2000	2000-2010		
Sri Lanka	17,198	17,424	19,296	21,435	48	1.2	1.1	697	24,996
Sudan	26,425	27,220	35,870	46,980	33	3.1	2.7	30	917,375
Suriname	397	402	463	535	163	1.5	1.4	6	62,344
Swaziland	837	859	1,124	1,545	152	3.0	3.2	129	6,641
Sweden	8,526	8,564	8,761	8,728	76	0.3	(Z)	54	158,927
Switzerland	6,742	6,784	7,018	6,989	90	0.4	(Z)	442	15,355
Syria	12,483	12,966	18,212	25,947	58	3.8	3.5	182	71,062
Tajikistan	5,342	(NA)	6,967	8,577	96	2.7	2.1	[3]96	55,770
Tanzania	25,971	26,869	36,489	50,795	34	3.4	3.3	79	342,100
Thailand	56,002	56,814	63,832	70,740	20	1.3	1.0	288	197,595
Togo	3,674	3,811	5,248	7,336	115	3.6	3.3	181	21,000
Tonga	101	102	110	119	189	0.8	0.8	369	277
Trinidad and Tobago	1,271	1,285	1,425	1,601	145	1.1	1.2	649	1,981
Tunisia	8,104	8,276	9,713	11,203	80	1.8	1.4	138	59,985
Turkey	57,285	58,581	70,368	83,494	17	2.1	1.7	197	297,591
Turkmenistan	3,658	(NA)	4,428	5,118	116	1.9	1.4	[3]19	190,320
Tuvalu	9	9	11	12	222	1.6	1.4	928	10
Uganda	18,016	18,690	25,802	36,002	46	3.6	3.3	242	77,108
Ukraine	51,791	(NA)	32,361	52,949	22	0.1	0.1	[3]220	235,560
United Arab Emirates	2,254	2,390	3,598	4,920	133	4.7	3.1	74	32,278
United Kingdom	57,366	57,515	58,719	59,178	16	0.2	0.1	617	93,278
United States	**250,410**	**252,502**	**268,266**	**282,575**	**3**	**0.7**	**0.5**	**71**	**3,539,227**
Uruguay	3,102	3,121	3,289	3,469	125	0.6	0.5	47	67,035
Uzbekistan	20,569	(NA)	24,988	29,034	41	1.9	1.5	[3]118	174,330
Vanuatu	165	170	221	279	183	2.9	2.4	30	5,699
Venezuela	19,698	20,189	24,596	29,518	43	2.2	1.8	59	340,560
Vietnam	66,171	67,568	79,801	92,027	13	1.9	1.4	538	125,622
Western Samoa	186	190	235	289	180	2.3	2.1	173	1,100
Yemen	9,746	10,063	13,603	18,985	71	3.3	3.3	49	203,849
Zaire	36,613	37,832	50,043	67,540	29	3.1	3.0	43	875,521
Zambia	8,154	8,446	11,572	16,181	78	3.5	3.4	30	285,992
Zimbabwe	10,394	10,720	13,806	17,559	65	2.8	2.4	72	149,293
AREAS OF SPECIAL SOVEREIGNTY AND DEPENDENCIES									
American Samoa	42	43	52	57	207	2.1	1.0	560	77
Anguilla	7	7	7	8	224	0.7	0.6	197	35
Bermuda	58	58	59	60	201	0.1	0.1	3,089	19
British Virgin Islands	12	12	14	16	218	1.2	1.3	214	58
Cayman Islands	26	27	36	46	212	3.1	2.5	274	100
Cook Islands	18	18	19	20	215	0.5	0.5	192	93
Faroe Islands	48	48	52	55	205	0.8	0.6	89	541
Federated States of Micronesia	105	108	125	130	188	1.8	0.4	397	271
French Guiana	98	102	132	163	191	2.9	2.1	3	34,421
French Polynesia	190	195	242	296	179	2.4	2.0	138	1,413
Gaza Strip	622	642	838	1,060	157	3.0	2.4	4,366	147
Gibraltar	30	30	30	30	209	0.1	(Z)	12,783	2
Greenland	56	57	62	66	203	1.0	0.7	(Z)	131,931
Guadeloupe	342	345	376	406	169	1.0	0.8	507	680
Guam	141	145	179	209	185	2.4	1.5	694	209
Guernsey	57	58	60	62	202	0.5	0.3	769	75
Hong Kong	5,818	5,856	6,146	6,370	93	0.5	0.4	15,335	382
Isle of Man	65	64	66	66	198	0.1	(Z)	282	227
Jersey	84	84	90	93	194	0.7	0.4	1,867	45
Macau	442	446	474	487	162	0.7	0.3	72,239	6
Marshall Islands	46	48	68	100	206	3.9	3.8	688	70
Martinique	342	345	374	396	170	0.9	0.6	844	409
Mayotte	72	75	106	153	195	3.9	3.7	517	145
Montserrat	12	13	13	13	219	0.2	0.1	324	39
Netherlands Antilles	184	184	192	204	181	0.5	0.6	496	371
New Caledonia	168	172	200	229	182	1.7	1.3	24	7,243
Northern Mariana Islands	23	23	29	32	213	2.4	1.1	128	184
Pacific Islands, Trust Territory of the [7]	14	14	15	16	217	0.7	0.6	81	177
Puerto Rico	3,291	3,295	3,406	3,688	122	0.3	0.8	953	3,459
Reunion	596	607	708	808	158	1.7	1.3	629	965
Saint Helena	7	7	7	7	223	0.6	0.6	42	158
Saint Pierre and Miquelon	6	6	7	7	225	0.3	0.2	68	93
Turkes and Caicos Islands	10	10	12	13	220	1.7	1.0	60	166
Virgin Islands	99	99	110	127	190	1.0	1.5	736	135
Wallis and Futuna	16	17	22	28	216	2.9	2.5	157	106
West Bank	1,075	1,105	1,380	1,697	147	2.5	2.1	507	2,178
Western Sahara	192	197	246	304	178	2.5	2.1	2	102,703

NA Not available. X Not applicable. Z Less than .05 percent or .5. [1] Computed by the exponential method. For explanation of average annual percent change, see Guide to Tabular Presentation. [2] Data from U.S. Central Intelligence Agency, *The World Factbook Nineteen and Eighty-Six;* U.S. Department of State, *Status of the World's Nations,* periodic; and Statistical Office of the United Nations, New York, NY, *Demographic Yearbook.* [3] 1990 population per square mile. [4] Excludes Mayotte, an area subject to dispute over sovereignty. [5] Includes the Indian-held part of Jammu and Kashmir. [6] Excludes the Pakistani-held part of Jammu and Kashmir. [7] Includes only the Republic of Palau.

Source: Except as noted, U.S. Bureau of the Census, *World Population Profile: 1991;* and unpublished data.

No. 1360. World Population, by Age Group, 1991, and Projections, 2000

[In percent. Covers countries with 10 million or more population in 1991. See table 1361 for country components of regions. Data compiled from the International Data Base; see text, section 31]

COUNTRY	1991				2000			
	Under 5 years old	5 to 14 years old	15 to 64 years old	65 years old and over	Under 5 years old	5 to 14 years old	15 to 64 years old	65 years old and over
World total	**11.8**	**20.4**	**61.6**	**6.1**	**10.9**	**20.2**	**62.1**	**6.8**
United States	**7.3**	**14.4**	**65.7**	**12.7**	**6.3**	**13.9**	**66.8**	**13.0**
Afghanistan	16.8	26.2	54.3	2.7	16.2	26.1	54.7	3.0
Algeria	14.5	28.5	53.4	3.7	12.6	23.9	59.6	3.9
Argentina	9.6	19.7	61.5	9.2	9.1	17.4	63.6	9.8
Australia	7.4	14.6	66.7	11.3	6.8	14.2	66.9	12.1
Bangladesh	14.9	27.4	54.7	3.0	14.1	23.7	59.2	3.1
Brazil	11.9	23.2	60.6	4.3	10.3	20.2	64.4	5.1
Burma	14.1	24.0	57.9	4.0	12.6	23.2	59.9	4.3
Cameroon	16.9	26.7	53.3	3.1	16.3	26.2	54.5	3.1
Canada	7.0	13.7	67.6	11.7	6.0	13.0	67.9	13.1
Chile	10.3	19.4	64.0	6.2	9.0	18.1	65.5	7.4
China: Mainland	10.3	16.7	67.1	5.9	9.0	18.3	65.7	7.0
Taiwan	8.0	18.7	66.9	6.5	7.2	14.6	69.7	8.4
Colombia	12.3	21.7	62.0	4.0	9.9	20.7	64.4	4.9
Cote D'Ivoire	19.4	27.6	51.1	2.0	18.7	28.6	50.4	2.2
Cuba	8.5	14.0	68.6	8.9	7.3	15.6	67.3	9.8
Czechoslovakia	6.8	15.5	65.8	11.9	6.8	13.1	67.1	13.0
Ecuador	13.7	25.0	57.5	3.8	11.8	22.5	61.5	4.2
Egypt	14.4	25.5	56.2	3.8	13.2	23.4	59.2	4.2
Ethiopia	18.2	27.6	51.4	2.7	17.9	27.5	51.8	2.8
France	6.7	13.3	65.7	14.3	6.2	12.9	65.0	15.9
Germany	5.6	10.5	68.8	15.1	5.2	11.1	67.1	16.7
Ghana	19.0	25.5	52.5	3.0	17.7	28.4	50.9	3.0
Greece	5.3	13.4	66.9	14.3	5.4	10.7	65.9	18.0
Hungary	5.8	13.6	67.0	13.6	6.0	11.6	67.0	15.4
India	13.3	22.7	60.2	3.8	11.5	21.8	62.3	4.4
Indonesia	12.1	23.7	61.2	3.1	10.2	20.3	65.2	4.4
Iran	19.0	27.7	49.8	3.5	17.5	28.3	50.3	3.9
Iraq	19.0	28.7	49.1	3.2	18.0	28.6	50.4	3.0
Italy	5.0	11.2	68.8	15.0	5.3	10.2	66.8	17.6
Japan	5.3	12.7	69.8	12.3	5.5	10.2	67.6	16.7
Kenya	19.2	29.8	48.8	2.2	17.2	28.7	51.8	2.4
Madagascar	19.1	27.4	50.2	3.3	18.2	28.2	50.5	3.1
Malaysia	13.8	22.9	59.6	3.7	12.4	23.0	60.6	4.0
Mexico	13.5	24.5	58.1	3.9	11.9	22.5	61.1	4.6
Morocco	13.6	24.6	57.6	4.2	11.6	22.3	61.3	4.7
Mozambique	18.2	26.7	52.6	2.5	17.4	27.4	52.5	2.6
Nepal	16.3	26.8	54.1	2.8	15.3	25.4	56.3	3.0
Netherlands	6.3	11.9	68.8	13.0	5.9	12.1	67.6	14.3
Nigeria	18.0	26.8	53.0	2.2	17.7	26.9	52.7	2.7
North Korea	10.9	18.5	66.9	3.8	10.2	19.2	65.9	4.7
Pakistan	17.6	26.2	52.1	4.0	16.7	26.9	52.6	3.9
Peru	12.9	24.6	58.7	3.8	10.9	21.4	63.2	4.5
Philippines	13.6	25.2	57.6	3.6	11.6	22.5	61.8	4.0
Poland	7.4	17.3	65.1	10.2	6.4	13.8	67.5	12.2
Portugal	5.9	14.3	66.5	13.4	5.8	11.6	67.3	15.3
Romania	7.7	15.5	66.2	10.6	6.9	14.5	65.2	13.3
Saudi Arabia	15.6	21.7	60.8	1.9	14.8	23.3	59.5	2.5
South Africa	15.2	24.5	56.3	4.0	14.7	24.7	56.5	4.1
South Korea	7.4	18.2	69.4	4.9	6.6	13.8	72.9	6.8
Soviet Union (former) [1]	8.9	17.1	64.3	9.7	7.9	16.3	64.4	11.5
Spain	5.4	13.9	67.0	13.7	5.7	10.8	67.0	16.5
Sri Lanka	9.8	21.4	63.5	5.3	8.7	17.4	67.5	6.4
Sudan	18.2	27.9	51.5	2.3	17.0	27.5	53.2	2.2
Syria	19.0	28.4	49.6	3.0	18.5	28.5	50.0	3.0
Tanzania	19.9	28.4	48.8	2.8	19.3	28.9	49.2	2.7
Thailand	9.9	21.2	64.8	4.1	8.5	17.4	68.6	5.5
Turkey	13.1	23.4	58.7	4.8	11.3	21.8	61.1	5.8
Uganda	20.9	28.3	48.6	2.1	19.7	30.0	48.3	2.0
United Kingdom	6.8	12.3	65.3	15.7	6.1	13.1	64.7	16.0
Venezuela	13.2	24.0	58.8	4.0	11.4	21.8	61.9	4.9
Vietnam	13.8	24.4	57.0	4.7	11.4	22.8	60.8	5.0
Yemen	20.1	28.9	48.3	2.7	20.0	29.5	47.9	2.6
Yugoslavia (former) [1]	7.2	15.3	67.9	9.7	6.4	13.5	66.8	13.3
Zaire	18.8	27.4	51.0	2.8	17.7	28.2	51.1	2.9
Zimbabwe	18.1	20.4	40.8	2.7	15.5	27.0	54.2	2.0

[1] Data for newly independent republics not available.

Source: U.S. Bureau of the Census, *World Population Profile: 1991*.

No. 1361. Birth and Death Rates and Other Vital Statistics, 1991, and Projections, 2000—Selected Countries

[Covers countries with 2 million or more population in 1991. AFR - Africa, EAS - East Asia, SAS - South Asia, CAR - Carribbean, MAM - Middle America, SAM - South America, NAM - North America, EUR - Europe, SOV - Soviet Union, OCE - Oceania. Data compiled from the International Data Base; see text, section 31]

COUNTRY	Region	CRUDE BIRTH RATE [1]		CRUDE DEATH RATE [2]		EXPECTATION OF LIFE AT BIRTH (years)		INFANT MORTALITY RATE [3]		TOTAL FERTILITY RATE [4]	
		1991	2000	1991	2000	1991	2000	1991	2000	1991	2000
United States.	NAM	14.6	12.6	8.7	8.8	75.7	77.0	10.3	9.3	1.85	1.84
Afghanistan	SAS	43.7	40.3	20.0	16.6	43.5	47.9	163.5	134.3	6.32	5.58
Albania	EUR	23.8	16.8	5.4	5.0	75.1	77.5	49.9	31.0	2.87	2.10
Algeria	AFR	31.8	26.8	6.8	5.4	66.7	69.6	57.0	40.7	4.24	3.20
Angola.	AFR	46.5	42.5	19.8	15.9	44.3	48.9	150.9	121.0	6.66	6.05
Argentina	SAM	19.8	19.2	8.7	8.6	70.9	72.3	31.2	26.0	2.74	2.50
Australia.	OCE	14.7	13.2	7.4	7.4	77.0	78.7	7.9	6.6	1.84	1.80
Austria.	EUR	11.5	9.8	10.7	10.1	77.3	78.9	5.4	3.3	1.46	1.50
Bangladesh	SAS	36.2	32.5	13.0	10.2	53.0	57.5	117.8	89.8	4.72	4.00
Belgium	EUR	11.9	10.3	10.6	10.2	77.1	78.8	5.5	3.4	1.59	1.60
Benin.	AFR	49.0	44.9	15.8	12.1	50.5	54.7	118.8	96.9	7.00	6.32
Bolivia	SAM	33.9	29.0	9.3	7.5	61.5	65.5	83.0	59.5	4.62	3.75
Brazil.	SAM	25.8	22.2	7.4	7.0	65.2	67.5	68.3	60.2	3.07	2.60
Bulgaria	EUR	13.0	12.4	11.6	10.8	72.7	76.0	12.5	6.5	1.91	1.80
Burkina	AFR	49.7	45.8	16.3	12.4	52.2	56.4	119.0	97.6	7.12	6.48
Burma	SAS	32.4	28.1	12.5	10.7	54.9	58.0	95.2	79.5	4.08	3.51
Burundi	AFR	46.7	41.6	14.5	11.1	52.4	56.4	109.1	88.5	6.89	6.25
Cambodia.	SAS	37.7	28.8	15.9	12.1	49.3	54.6	124.9	96.4	4.47	3.96
Cameroon	AFR	41.3	38.2	14.8	12.0	51.0	55.2	117.6	95.7	5.63	5.00
Canada	NAM	13.8	11.8	7.5	7.7	77.5	79.2	7.2	6.1	1.68	1.68
Central African Republic	AFR	43.7	39.2	18.0	14.7	47.1	51.5	137.8	113.7	5.58	5.07
Chad	AFR	42.3	39.7	21.6	18.4	39.8	43.5	133.5	112.9	5.33	5.08
Chile	SAM	21.1	18.1	5.8	5.9	73.4	75.1	17.8	13.4	2.49	2.29
China: Mainland.	EAS	22.3	16.9	6.7	6.5	70.0	72.4	32.9	24.3	2.30	2.10
Taiwan	EAS	16.5	14.5	5.4	6.2	74.6	76.3	5.9	5.6	1.81	1.80
Colombia	SAM	26.1	19.5	5.0	4.4	71.0	74.1	36.9	28.5	2.83	2.25
Congo	AFR	42.7	38.3	13.2	10.4	54.2	58.3	108.0	92.6	5.73	5.01
Costa Rica	MAM	27.5	22.5	3.7	3.4	76.8	78.9	15.3	11.7	3.23	2.82
Cote d'Ivoire	AFR	47.7	43.8	12.4	9.9	54.3	58.3	97.4	77.8	6.84	6.21
Cuba	CAR	17.9	14.1	6.7	7.1	75.6	76.4	11.9	11.0	1.86	1.86
Czechoslovakia	EUR	13.6	13.6	10.8	8.9	72.9	76.3	10.9	7.8	1.95	1.80
Denmark	EUR	11.6	10.9	11.4	10.9	75.9	78.0	6.1	3.8	1.57	1.60
Dominican Republic	CAR	27.2	22.2	6.8	5.6	67.2	70.2	59.9	44.2	3.12	2.57
Ecuador	SAM	29.8	24.8	6.9	5.9	66.2	69.0	52.6	46.7	3.70	2.93
Egypt.	AFR	32.7	29.2	9.5	7.6	60.8	65.0	82.0	56.3	4.52	3.78
El Salvador.	MAM	33.7	29.6	6.9	5.4	65.5	69.6	47.3	31.0	4.05	3.30
Ethiopia	AFR	45.1	42.6	14.6	12.0	51.3	55.4	113.5	92.4	6.97	6.33
Finland	EUR	12.4	10.8	9.9	9.6	75.8	78.1	6.0	5.3	1.71	1.70
France.	EUR	13.5	12.3	9.4	9.1	77.8	79.3	6.1	4.3	1.82	1.80
Germany	EUR	11.3	9.8	11.2	10.5	75.8	77.9	7.1	5.8	1.45	1.55
Ghana	AFR	45.6	40.6	13.0	10.8	54.6	57.5	85.5	72.3	6.34	5.76
Greece	EUR	10.9	10.9	9.5	9.7	77.7	79.3	10.0	7.6	1.54	1.60
Guatemala	MAM	35.3	28.3	8.2	6.5	63.2	66.9	57.8	42.8	4.78	3.50
Guinea.	AFR	46.6	39.6	21.4	17.2	42.8	47.0	144.2	122.0	6.02	5.46
Haiti	CAR	43.5	35.3	15.2	12.1	53.6	56.1	105.7	94.0	6.28	5.16
Honduras	MAM	38.2	29.0	7.3	5.3	66.0	70.0	56.3	37.5	4.98	3.50
Hungary	EUR	11.7	12.1	12.6	10.6	71.6	75.5	14.0	9.3	1.77	1.70
India	SAS	30.4	24.7	11.0	9.1	57.2	61.4	83.5	63.0	3.74	3.04
Indonesia	SAS	25.9	21.5	8.3	6.7	61.0	66.6	72.5	53.9	3.03	2.43
Iran	SAS	44.2	39.3	8.6	6.2	64.5	69.1	65.8	45.7	6.55	5.88
Iraq.	SAS	45.7	40.1	7.2	5.1	67.0	71.0	65.7	50.5	7.16	5.81
Ireland	EUR	14.6	12.7	8.8	8.2	75.5	77.9	6.2	5.4	2.06	1.80
Israel.	SAS	21.7	20.6	6.4	6.0	77.0	78.5	9.4	7.6	2.98	2.68
Italy.	EUR	10.6	10.6	9.6	9.6	78.1	79.6	6.0	4.5	1.38	1.50
Jamaica	CAR	23.5	19.6	5.9	5.2	73.6	75.9	18.3	13.1	2.63	2.24
Japan	EAS	10.2	11.4	6.7	7.9	79.2	80.8	4.4	4.0	1.56	1.60
Jordan	SAS	45.6	40.6	4.7	3.9	71.2	73.2	38.1	32.6	7.09	5.99
Kenya	AFR	44.5	38.1	8.4	6.7	61.5	64.6	69.4	53.8	6.37	5.04
Kuwait	SAS	29.1	26.4	2.4	2.4	73.6	76.7	14.5	9.1	3.71	3.69
Laos	SAS	36.8	31.8	14.9	12.0	50.2	54.7	123.8	105.6	5.01	3.98
Lebanon.	SAS	27.8	27.6	6.9	6.0	68.4	71.4	47.8	38.9	3.61	3.00
Liberia	AFR	44.8	41.0	13.3	10.9	56.4	60.4	124.2	104.1	6.55	5.95
Libya	AFR	36.3	30.5	6.2	4.7	68.1	72.5	62.1	45.3	5.05	3.84
Madagascar	AFR	46.6	42.7	14.6	11.5	52.6	56.7	95.3	78.1	6.88	6.25
Malawi.	AFR	52.2	47.6	17.8	14.3	49.2	52.9	135.7	120.5	7.64	6.94
Malaysia	SAS	29.8	25.6	6.0	5.3	68.1	70.9	28.6	21.0	3.61	3.31
Mali.	AFR	50.7	46.8	20.6	16.6	46.1	50.3	114.1	101.2	7.01	6.31
Mexico.	MAM	28.7	24.3	4.9	4.2	72.2	75.4	29.3	19.0	3.36	2.77
Mongolia	EAS	34.4	30.7	7.5	6.0	65.1	68.4	48.2	34.7	4.58	3.94
Morocco.	AFR	30.1	24.7	7.9	5.8	64.6	69.8	76.1	56.4	3.84	2.95
Mozambique	AFR	46.1	42.1	17.3	14.0	47.4	51.5	133.8	108.8	6.43	5.84
Nepal	SAS	38.7	35.6	14.7	11.7	50.6	55.2	97.7	82.5	5.52	4.68
Netherlands	EUR	12.8	11.4	8.4	8.5	77.8	79.3	6.9	5.9	1.57	1.60
New Zealand	OCE	15.4	12.8	8.2	8.0	75.5	78.0	9.5	7.2	1.95	1.80
Nicaragua.	MAM	37.1	29.9	7.4	5.5	62.5	66.8	59.6	41.4	4.72	3.50
Niger.	AFR	50.2	46.0	16.0	12.5	51.0	55.5	128.6	110.8	7.03	6.38
Nigeria.	AFR	46.1	43.1	16.3	13.8	48.9	52.7	117.6	103.4	6.52	5.99
North Korea	EAS	24.3	19.9	5.6	5.4	69.0	71.5	30.4	22.2	2.47	2.21
Norway	EUR	13.6	12.3	10.7	10.3	77.1	78.8	6.7	4.5	1.83	1.80
Pakistan	SAS	43.3	39.8	13.0	11.0	56.6	59.6	109.1	98.4	6.64	5.94

See footnotes at end of table.

No. 1361. Birth and Death Rates and Other Vital Statistics, 1991, and Projections, 2000—Selected Countries—Continued

[See headnote, page 824]

COUNTRY	Region	CRUDE BIRTH RATE [1]		CRUDE DEATH RATE [2]		EXPECTATION OF LIFE AT BIRTH (years)		INFANT MORTALITY RATE [3]		TOTAL FERTILITY RATE [4]	
		1991	2000	1991	2000	1991	2000	1991	2000	1991	2000
Panama	MAM	25.8	22.0	4.8	4.4	74.0	76.5	21.0	16.8	3.02	2.60
Papua New Guinea	OCE	34.1	31.4	10.8	9.1	55.4	59.1	66.2	51.5	4.91	4.02
Paraguay	SAM	34.9	26.9	6.0	5.3	69.7	71.4	47.0	40.1	4.69	3.50
Peru	SAM	27.9	23.2	7.5	6.2	64.3	68.1	65.8	53.2	3.51	2.70
Philippines	SAS	29.0	24.4	7.2	6.6	64.6	66.9	53.6	43.3	3.64	2.88
Poland	EUR	14.1	13.0	9.3	8.5	72.9	76.1	12.4	6.4	2.06	1.80
Portugal	EUR	12.1	11.5	9.7	9.3	74.7	77.4	13.3	9.1	1.53	1.50
Romania	EUR	15.9	13.4	9.9	8.6	71.9	75.6	18.2	10.9	2.12	1.80
Rwanda	AFR	52.4	47.8	14.6	11.1	52.5	56.8	110.2	88.3	8.42	7.65
Saudi Arabia	SAS	36.6	33.6	6.3	4.7	65.9	70.6	69.2	50.6	6.71	6.31
Senegal	AFR	43.7	40.6	13.2	10.1	55.1	60.0	85.5	72.1	6.24	5.57
Sierra Leone	AFR	46.2	42.3	20.4	16.3	44.8	49.7	151.1	124.6	6.13	5.57
Singapore	SAS	17.8	13.6	5.2	5.4	74.8	76.9	8.0	6.0	1.97	1.97
Somalia	AFR	45.8	42.0	13.2	9.8	55.9	60.9	116.4	84.4	7.19	6.53
South Africa	AFR	34.2	32.4	7.8	6.8	64.2	67.0	51.1	40.0	4.45	4.24
South Korea	EAS	14.8	13.1	6.2	6.5	69.7	72.3	23.4	17.3	1.58	1.50
Soviet Union (former) [5]	SOV	17.3	16.2	10.3	9.4	69.8	73.2	22.7	14.7	2.35	2.27
Spain	EUR	11.2	11.5	8.3	8.8	78.3	79.7	6.2	5.5	1.45	1.50
Sri Lanka	SAS	19.9	17.8	5.9	6.0	71.1	73.0	21.4	16.8	2.26	2.05
Sudan	AFR	44.0	38.9	13.1	10.3	53.0	56.8	84.6	68.7	6.37	5.46
Sweden	EUR	13.0	11.4	11.4	10.9	77.8	79.3	5.9	5.3	1.92	1.80
Switzerland	EUR	12.1	10.4	9.1	9.3	79.1	80.1	4.7	3.6	1.57	1.60
Syria	SAS	43.5	40.9	5.5	3.9	69.4	73.2	36.7	27.1	6.66	6.00
Tanzania	AFR	49.6	46.1	15.2	12.0	52.0	56.1	104.9	86.4	7.03	6.39
Thailand	SAS	20.3	17.3	6.0	5.6	68.5	72.1	37.1	23.7	2.21	1.89
Togo	AFR	49.4	44.7	13.1	9.9	55.6	59.7	110.2	94.7	7.10	6.45
Tunisia	AFR	25.9	20.2	5.2	4.7	71.9	74.8	38.3	24.0	3.31	2.33
Turkey	SAS	28.4	23.5	6.2	4.9	69.8	74.5	54.3	27.7	3.56	2.90
Uganda	AFR	51.4	46.2	14.7	11.3	51.0	55.0	93.5	74.8	7.29	6.62
United Arab Emirates	SAS	30.1	25.1	3.0	2.9	70.9	73.0	23.3	16.7	4.85	4.25
United Kingdom	EUR	13.7	11.8	11.1	10.1	76.5	78.5	7.2	6.0	1.82	1.80
Uruguay	SAM	17.2	16.6	10.0	10.3	72.6	72.9	22.4	21.5	2.39	2.21
Venezuela	SAM	27.8	23.6	4.2	3.8	74.2	77.1	26.2	20.1	3.39	2.88
Vietnam	SAS	29.5	23.2	8.1	6.4	64.7	68.8	48.2	34.4	3.70	2.80
Yemen	SAS	51.2	48.3	16.2	12.4	49.9	54.6	121.2	96.5	7.40	6.73
Yugoslavia (former) [5]	EUR	14.3	12.8	8.7	8.1	73.0	76.3	21.2	12.3	1.93	1.80
Zaire	AFR	45.8	41.2	13.1	10.3	53.9	57.9	99.0	77.4	6.17	5.60
Zambia	AFR	49.0	43.9	11.7	9.1	56.4	60.4	79.2	63.4	6.94	6.30
Zimbabwe	AFR	40.6	32.9	8.3	6.1	61.7	65.7	60.6	42.9	5.60	4.15

[1] Number of births during 1 year per 1,000 persons (based on midyear population). [2] Number of deaths during 1 year per 1,000 persons (based on midyear population). [3] Number of deaths of children under 1 year of age per 1,000 live births in a calendar year. [4] Average number of children that would be born if all women lived to the end of their childbearing years and, at each year of age, they experienced the birth rates occurring in the specified year. [5] Data for newly independent republics not available.

Source: U.S. Bureau of the Census, *World Population Profile: 1991.*

No. 1362. Population and Average Annual Rates of Growth for World's 94 Largest Cities: 1991 to 2000

[Cities are defined as population clusters of continuous built-up area with a population density of at least 5,000 persons per square mile]

CITY AND COUNTRY	Rank	MIDYEAR POPULATION (1,000)			AVERAGE ANNUAL GROWTH RATE (percent)		Area (square miles)	Population per square mile, 1991
		1991	1995	2000	1991-1995	1995-2000		
Tokyo-Yokohama, Japan	1	27,245	28,447	29,971	0.9	1.0	1,089	25,018
Mexico City, Mexico	2	20,899	23,913	27,872	2.7	3.1	522	40,037
Sao Paulo, Brazil	3	18,701	21,539	25,354	2.8	3.3	451	41,466
Seoul, South Korea	4	16,792	19,065	21,976	2.5	2.8	342	49,101
New York, United States	**5**	**14,625**	**14,638**	**14,648**	**(Z)**	**(Z)**	**1,274**	**11,480**
Osaka-Kobe-Kyoto, Japan	6	13,872	14,060	14,287	0.3	0.3	495	20,025
Bombay, India	7	12,109	13,532	15,357	2.2	2.5	95	127,461
Calcutta, India	8	11,898	12,885	14,088	1.6	1.8	209	56,927
Rio de Janeiro, Brazil	9	11,688	12,786	14,169	1.8	2.1	260	44,952
Buenos Aires, Argentina	10	11,657	12,232	12,911	1.0	1.1	535	21,790
Moscow, Soviet Union (former)	11	10,446	10,769	11,121	0.6	0.6	379	27,562
Manila, Philippines	12	10,156	11,342	12,846	2.2	2.5	188	54,024
Los Angeles, United States	**13**	**10,130**	**10,414**	**10,714**	**0.6**	**0.6**	**1,110**	**9,126**
Cairo, Egypt	14	10,099	11,155	12,512	2.0	2.3	104	97,106
Jakarta, Indonesia	15	9,882	11,151	12,804	2.4	2.8	76	130,026
Tehran, Iran	16	9,779	11,681	14,251	3.6	4.0	112	87,312
London, United Kingdom	17	9,115	8,897	8,574	-0.5	-0.7	874	10,429
Delhi, India	18	8,778	10,105	11,849	2.8	3.2	138	63,612
Paris, France	19	8,720	8,764	8,803	0.1	0.1	432	20,185
Karachi, Pakistan	20	8,014	9,350	11,299	3.1	3.8	190	42,179

See footnotes at end of table.

Comparative International Statistics

No. 1362. Population and Average Annual Rates of Growth for World's 94 Largest Cities: 1991 to 2000—Continued

[See headnote, page 825]

CITY AND COUNTRY	Rank	MIDYEAR POPULATION (1,000)			AVERAGE ANNUAL GROWTH RATE (percent)		Area (square miles)	Population per square mile, 1991
		1991	1995	2000	1991-1995	1995-2000		
Lagos, Nigeria	21	7,998	9,799	12,528	4.1	4.9	56	142,821
Essen, Germany	22	7,452	7,364	7,239	-0.2	-0.3	704	10,585
Shanghai, China	23	6,936	7,194	7,540	0.7	0.9	78	88,924
Lima, Peru	24	6,815	7,853	9,241	2.8	3.3	120	56,794
Taipei, Taiwan	25	6,695	7,477	8,516	2.2	2.6	138	48,517
Istanbul, Turkey	26	6,678	7,624	8,875	2.6	3.0	165	40,476
Chicago, United States	**27**	**6,529**	**6,541**	**6,568**	**(Z)**	**0.1**	**762**	**8,568**
Bangkok, Thailand	28	5,955	6,657	7,587	2.2	2.6	102	58,379
Bogota, Colombia	29	5,913	6,801	7,935	2.8	3.1	79	74,851
Madras, India	30	5,896	6,550	7,384	2.1	2.4	115	51,270
Beijing, China	31	5,762	5,865	5,993	0.4	0.4	151	38,156
Hong Kong, Hong Kong	32	5,693	5,841	5,956	0.5	0.4	23	247,501
Santiago, Chile	33	5,378	5,812	6,294	1.6	1.6	128	42,018
Pusan, South Korea	34	5,008	5,748	6,700	2.8	3.1	54	92,735
Tianjin, China	35	4,850	5,041	5,298	0.8	1.0	49	98,990
Bangalore, India	36	4,802	5,644	6,764	3.2	3.6	50	96,041
Nagoya, Japan	37	4,791	5,017	5,303	0.9	1.1	307	15,606
Milan, Italy	38	4,749	4,795	4,839	0.2	0.2	344	13,806
Leningrad, Soviet Union (former)	39	4,672	4,694	4,738	0.1	0.2	139	33,614
Madrid, Spain	40	4,513	4,772	5,104	1.1	1.4	66	68,385
Dhaka, Bangladesh	41	4,419	5,296	6,492	3.6	4.1	32	138,108
Lahore, Pakistan	42	4,376	4,986	5,864	2.6	3.2	57	76,779
Shenyang, China	43	4,289	4,457	4,684	0.8	1.0	39	109,974
Barcelona, Spain	44	4,227	4,492	4,834	1.2	1.5	87	48,584
Baghdad, Iraq	45	4,059	4,566	5,239	2.4	2.8	97	41,843
Manchester, United Kingdom	46	4,030	3,949	3,827	-0.4	-0.6	357	11,287
Philadelphia, United States	**47**	**4,003**	**3,988**	**3,979**	**-0.1**	**-0.1**	**471**	**8,499**
San Francisco, United States	**48**	**3,987**	**4,104**	**4,214**	**0.6**	**0.5**	**428**	**9,315**
Belo Horizonte, Brazil	49	3,812	4,373	5,125	2.7	3.2	79	48,249
Kinshasa, Zaire	50	3,747	4,520	5,646	3.8	4.5	57	65,732
Ho Chi Minh City, Vietnam	51	3,725	4,064	4,481	1.7	2.0	31	120,168
Ahmadabad, India	52	3,709	4,200	4,837	2.5	2.8	32	115,893
Hyderabad, India	53	3,673	4,149	4,765	2.4	2.8	88	41,741
Sydney, Australia	54	3,536	3,619	3,708	0.5	0.5	338	10,460
Athens, Greece	55	3,507	3,670	3,866	0.9	1.0	116	30,237
Miami, United States	**56**	**3,471**	**3,679**	**3,894**	**1.2**	**1.1**	**448**	**7,748**
Guadalajara, Mexico	57	3,370	3,839	4,451	2.6	3.0	78	43,205
Guangzhou, China	58	3,360	3,485	3,652	0.7	0.9	79	42,537
Surabaya, Indonesia	59	3,248	3,428	3,632	1.1	1.2	43	75,544
Caracas, Venezuela	60	3,217	3,338	3,435	0.7	0.6	54	59,582
Wuhan, China	61	3,200	3,325	3,495	0.8	1.0	65	49,225
Toronto, Canada	62	3,145	3,296	3,296	0.9	-	154	20,420
Porto Alegre, Brazil	63	3,114	3,541	4,109	2.6	3.0	231	13,479
Rome, Italy	64	3,033	3,079	3,129	0.3	0.3	69	43,949
Greater Berlin, Germany	65	3,021	3,018	3,006	(Z)	-0.1	274	11,026
Naples, Italy	66	2,978	3,051	3,134	0.5	0.5	62	48,032
Casablanca, Morocco	67	2,973	3,327	3,795	2.2	2.6	35	84,953
Detroit, United States [1]	**68**	**2,969**	**2,865**	**2,735**	**-0.7**	**-0.9**	**468**	**6,343**
Alexandria, Egypt	69	2,941	3,114	3,304	1.1	1.2	35	84,022
Monterrey, Mexico	70	2,939	3,385	3,974	2.8	3.2	77	38,169
Montreal, Canada	71	2,916	2,996	3,071	0.5	0.5	164	17,779
Melbourne, Australia	72	2,915	2,946	2,968	0.2	0.2	327	8,914
Ankara, Turkey	73	2,872	3,263	3,777	2.6	2.9	55	52,221
Rangoon, Burma	74	2,864	3,075	3,332	1.4	1.6	47	60,927
Kiev, Soviet Union (former)	75	2,796	2,943	3,237	1.3	1.6	62	45,095
Dallas, United States	**76**	**2,787**	**2,972**	**3,257**	**1.3**	**1.8**	**419**	**6,652**
Singapore, Singapore	77	2,719	2,816	2,913	0.7	0.7	78	34,856
Taegu, South Korea	78	2,651	3,201	4,051	3.8	4.7	(NA)	(NA)
Harbin, China	79	2,643	2,747	2,887	0.8	1.0	30	88,110
Washington, United States	**80**	**2,565**	**2,637**	**2,707**	**0.6**	**0.5**	**357**	**7,184**
Poona, India	81	2,547	2,987	3,647	3.2	4.0	(NA)	(NA)
Boston, United States	**82**	**2,476**	**2,480**	**2,485**	**(Z)**	**(Z)**	**303**	**8,172**
Lisbon, Portugal	83	2,426	2,551	2,717	1.0	1.3	(NA)	(NA)
Tashkent, Soviet Union (former)	84	2,418	2,640	2,947	1.8	2.2	(NA)	(NA)
Chongqing, China	85	2,395	2,632	2,961	1.9	2.4	(NA)	(NA)
Chengdu, China	86	2,372	2,465	2,591	0.8	1.0	25	94,870
Vienna, Austria	87	2,344	2,474	2,647	1.1	1.4	(NA)	(NA)
Houston, United States	**88**	**2,329**	**2,456**	**2,651**	**1.1**	**1.5**	**310**	**7,512**
Budapest, Hungary	89	2,303	2,313	2,335	0.1	0.2	138	16,691
Salvador, Brazil	90	2,298	2,694	3,286	3.2	4.0	(NA)	(NA)
Bucharest, Romania	91	2,163	2,271	2,271	0.5	0.5	52	41,589
Birmingham, United Kingdom	92	2,162	2,130	2,078	-0.3	-0.5	223	9,695
Havana, Cuba	93	2,130	2,218	2,333	0.8	1.0	(NA)	(NA)
Kanpur, India	94	2,129	2,356	2,673	2.0	2.5	(NA)	(NA)

- Represents zero.   NA Not available.   Z Less than .05 percent.   [1] Includes Windsor, Canada.

Source: U.S. Bureau of the Census, *World Population Profile: 1991.*

No. 1363. Percent Distribution of Households, by Type—Selected Countries

COUNTRY AND YEAR	Total	MARRIED-COUPLE [1]			Single parent [2]	One-person	Other [3]
		Total	With children [2]	Without children [2]			
United States:							
1960	100	74	44	30	4	13	8
1970	100	71	40	30	5	17	7
1980	100	61	31	30	8	23	9
1987	100	58	28	30	8	24	11
1988	100	57	27	30	8	24	11
1989	100	56	27	30	8	25	11
1990	100	56	26	30	8	25	11
Canada:							
1961	100	[4]78	[4]51	[4]27	[4]4	9	[4]9
1971	100	74	47	28	5	13	8
1981	100	67	36	31	5	20	8
1986	100	65	32	32	6	22	8
Japan:							
1960	100	65	49	16	3	17	14
1970	100	64	45	20	2	20	13
1980	100	68	43	26	2	20	10
1985	100	67	39	28	3	21	9
1990	100	65	33	32	2	23	10
Denmark: [5]							
1976	100	45	24	21	5	(NA)	(NA)
1983	100	44	23	21	5	(NA)	(NA)
1988	100	41	20	21	5	(NA)	(NA)
1989	100	41	20	21	5	(NA)	(NA)
France:							
1968	100	70	44	27	4	20	5
1975	100	69	42	27	4	22	5
1982	100	67	40	27	4	25	4
1988	100	63	36	27	5	27	4
1989	100	64	36	28	5	27	4
Netherlands:							
1961	100	78	55	22	6	12	5
1971	100	74	52	22	5	17	4
1981	100	67	44	23	6	21	6
1985	100	60	39	22	7	28	6
1989	100	57	35	22	7	29	7
Sweden:							
1960	100	66	36	31	4	20	10
1970	100	64	30	34	3	25	7
1980	100	58	25	33	3	33	6
1985	100	55	22	33	3	36	6
1990	100	52	20	32	3	40	5
United Kingdom: [6]							
1961	100	74	38	36	2	12	12
1971	100	70	34	35	3	18	9
1981	100	64	31	34	5	22	9
1987	100	64	28	36	4	25	7
1988	100	62	26	36	5	26	7
1989	100	62	26	36	5	25	8
Germany: [7]							
1961	100	67	44	22	11	21	2
1970	100	65	42	23	6	27	3
1980	100	61	37	24	7	30	3
1988	100	54	31	23	7	35	4
1989	100	54	31	23	7	35	4
1990	100	54	31	23	6	35	4

NA Not available.   [1] May include unmarried cohabitating couples. Such couples are explicitly included under married couples in Canada (beginning in 1981) and France. For Sweden, beginning in 1980, all cohabitants are included as married couples, and the figures for 1970 have been adjusted to include all cohabitants. For Denmark, from 1983 onward, persons reported separately as living in consensual unions with joint children have been classified here as married couples. In other countries, some unmarried cohabitants are included as married couples, while some are classified under "other households", depending on responses to surveys and censuses.   [2] Children are defined as unmarried children living at home according to the following age limits: Under 18 years old in the United States, Canada, Japan, Denmark, and the United Kingdom, except that the United Kingdom includes 16- and 17-year-olds only if they are in full-time education; under 25 years old in France; under 16 years old in Sweden; and children of all ages in the Netherlands and Germany.   [3] Includes both family and nonfamily households not elsewhere classified. These households comprise, for example, siblings residing together, other households composed of relatives, and households made up of roommates. Some unmarried cohabitating couples may also be included in the "other" group. See footnote 1.   [4] Estimated by the U.S. Bureau of Labor Statistics.   [5] From family-based statistics. However, one person living alone constitutes a family in Denmark. In this respect, the Danish data are closer to household statistics.   [6] Great Britain only (excludes Northern Ireland).   [7] Formerly West Germany (prior to unification).

Source: U.S. Bureau of Labor Statistics, *Monthly Labor Review*, March 1990; and unpublished data.

Comparative International Statistics

No. 1364. Marriage and Divorce Rates, Selected Countries: 1960 to 1989

COUNTRY	MARRIAGE RATE PER 1,000 POPULATION, AGES 15 TO 64						DIVORCE RATE PER 1,000 MARRIED WOMEN					
	1960	1970	1980	1987	1988	1989	1960	1970	1980	1987	1988	1989
United States [1]	14	17	16	15	15	15	9	15	23	21	21	(NA)
Canada	12	14	12	11	11	11	2	6	11	14	13	13
Denmark	12	12	8	9	9	9	6	8	11	13	13	14
France	11	12	10	7	7	8	3	3	6	8	8	8
Italy	12	11	9	8	8	8	(NA)	1	1	2	2	2
Japan	15	14	10	8	8	8	4	4	5	5	5	5
Netherlands	13	15	10	9	9	9	2	3	8	8	8	8
Sweden	10	8	7	8	8	[2]20	5	7	11	11	11	12
United Kingdom	12	14	12	11	11	11	[3]2	[3]5	[3]12	12	12	(NA)
West Germany	14	12	9	9	9	9	4	5	6	9	9	(NA)

NA Not available. [1] Beginning 1980, includes unlicensed marriages registered in California. [2] Increase in Swedish marriage rate in 1989 is due to change in inheritance laws which caused many cohabiting couples to marry. [3] England and Wales only.

Source: U.S. Bureau of Labor Statistics, *Monthly Labor Review*, March 1990; and unpublished data.

No. 1365. Births to Unmarried Women, Selected Countries: 1960 to 1989

[For U.S. figures, beginning 1980, marital status is inferred from a comparison of the childs' and parents' surnames on the birth certificate for those States that do not report on marital status. No estimates are included for misstatements on birth records or failures to register births]

COUNTRY	1960		1970		1980		1989	
	Total live births (1,000)	Percent born to unmarried women	Total live births (1,000)	Percent born to unmarried women	Total live births (1,000)	Percent born to unmarried women	Total live births (1,000)	Percent born to unmarried women
United States	4,258	5	3,731	11	3,612	18	4,041	27
Canada	479	4	372	10	360	13	384	23
Denmark	76	8	71	11	57	33	62	46
France	820	6	850	7	800	11	766	28
Italy	910	2	902	2	640	4	567	6
Japan	1,624	1	1,932	1	1,616	1	1,269	1
Netherlands	239	1	239	2	181	4	189	11
Sweden	102	11	110	18	97	40	116	52
United Kingdom	918	5	904	8	754	12	777	27
West Germany	969	6	811	6	621	8	662	11

Source: U.S. Bureau of Labor Statistics, *Monthly Labor Review*, March 1990; and unpublished data.

No. 1366. Death Rates, by Selected Causes—Selected Countries

[**Age-standardized death rate per 100,000 population.** For explanation of age-adjustment, see text, section 2. The standard population for this table is the European standard; see source for details. Deaths classified according to ninth revision of *International Classification of Diseases;* see text, section 2]

COUNTRY	Year	Ischemic heart disease	Cerebrovascular disease	MALIGNANT NEOPLASM OF—			Bronchitis,[1] emphysema, asthma	Chronic liver disease and cirrhosis	Motor vehicle traffic accidents	Suicide and self-inflicted injury
				Lung, trachea, bronchus	Stomach	Female breast				
United States	1988	188.1	53.6	55.4	5.4	32.0	9.1	11.7	18.7	12.2
Australia	1988	200.5	77.9	40.4	9.0	29.6	14.6	8.1	17.8	13.3
Austria	1989	149.6	102.5	34.4	18.3	31.5	17.8	26.2	17.6	23.0
Belgium	1986	110.4	83.0	55.5	13.8	38.1	26.3	12.6	19.6	21.0
Bulgaria	1989	222.8	226.3	31.5	22.3	21.7	17.5	17.3	12.8	15.6
Canada	1988	182.3	53.7	54.3	8.5	34.3	9.0	8.9	14.7	13.3
Czechoslovakia	1989	293.4	180.8	52.3	20.8	28.3	27.5	23.2	11.2	18.2
Denmark	1988	222.2	69.6	53.7	9.4	40.8	36.6	12.4	12.8	24.7
Finland	1988	250.1	100.8	35.4	15.7	25.8	17.6	9.7	12.2	27.5
France	1988	67.4	62.2	34.2	10.0	28.2	10.0	19.6	17.2	19.7
Hungary	1989	234.8	172.0	57.1	24.3	32.3	39.3	50.4	21.1	40.0
Italy	1988	97.4	102.3	44.1	20.5	29.5	23.9	24.9	14.2	7.0
Japan	1989	37.4	93.0	27.0	37.0	8.5	10.7	13.0	11.2	16.4
Netherlands	1988	141.4	67.9	56.2	14.2	39.0	16.7	5.3	8.4	10.1
New Zealand	1987	248.6	88.8	45.5	10.9	40.2	19.8	4.2	22.8	14.2
Norway	1988	196.1	84.8	28.5	12.3	28.4	15.0	6.5	8.0	16.7
Poland	1989	118.9	73.5	49.9	21.8	21.7	27.0	11.6	20.4	12.0
Portugal	1989	76.5	194.1	18.6	26.1	24.1	12.8	24.0	26.3	7.0
Spain	1986	75.7	106.8	29.1	17.1	22.0	11.8	21.4	15.7	7.1
Sweden	1987	213.7	68.8	23.5	10.6	25.1	12.5	6.4	8.4	17.3
Switzerland	1989	109.4	57.8	34.2	10.5	34.5	18.1	9.1	12.9	20.9
United Kingdom:										
England and Wales	1989	216.6	89.0	53.8	13.3	42.0	15.2	5.5	8.7	7.0
Scotland	1989	276.3	120.2	69.1	13.5	41.6	12.5	8.4	10.1	10.2
West Germany	1989	150.0	87.3	35.8	16.3	32.8	22.3	20.1	11.1	14.5

[1] Chronic and unspecified.

Source: World Health Organization, Geneva, Switzerland, *1990 World Health Statistics Annual.*

No. 1367. Suicide Rates for Selected Countries, by Sex and Age Group

[Rate per 100,000 population. Includes deaths resulting indirectly from self-inflicted injuries. Deaths classified according to the ninth revision of the *International Classification of Diseases*; see text, section 2]

SEX AND AGE	United States, 1988	Aus- tralia, 1988	Aus- tria, 1989	Can- ada, 1988	Den- mark, 1988	France, 1988	Italy, 1987	Japan, 1989	Nether- lands, 1988	Poland, 1989	Swe- den, 1987	United King- dom, [1] 1989	West Ger- many, 1988
MALE													
Total [2]	20.1	21.0	36.1	21.4	33.3	30.2	11.7	21.5	13.2	19.3	26.0	11.2	25.0
15 to 24 years old. .	21.9	27.8	27.1	26.9	15.9	13.9	5.1	9.7	8.2	14.5	16.9	10.3	15.8
25 to 34 years old. .	25.0	28.2	35.6	29.2	33.6	32.5	10.3	19.9	16.1	26.4	30.0	14.7	22.7
35 to 44 years old. .	22.9	26.0	38.2	26.1	44.7	38.2	10.0	23.8	14.3	29.5	30.2	16.0	24.4
45 to 54 years old. .	21.7	24.4	45.1	24.2	50.5	40.0	14.1	33.2	17.2	33.2	41.9	14.1	33.0
55 to 64 years old. .	25.0	23.8	52.4	28.0	52.6	41.2	18.5	33.7	20.0	30.3	29.7	13.0	35.5
65 to 74 years old. .	33.0	27.7	71.6	26.2	47.2	47.5	29.1	38.7	21.2	25.8	39.4	13.3	41.3
75 yrs. old and over	57.8	39.8	96.0	30.6	69.2	109.0	47.1	68.0	41.3	29.6	50.2	20.4	77.8
FEMALE													
Total [2]	5.0	5.6	14.7	5.9	19.0	11.7	4.2	13.1	7.5	3.7	10.9	3.7	10.8
15 to 24 years old. .	4.2	4.5	8.3	4.9	5.5	4.2	1.4	5.3	2.4	2.8	5.6	1.9	4.7
25 to 34 years old. .	5.7	7.2	10.6	7.1	12.0	9.0	2.4	9.4	8.3	3.6	10.3	3.5	7.7
35 to 44 years old. .	6.9	7.5	13.2	9.8	20.6	12.7	3.6	10.5	9.3	5.0	14.8	3.6	9.5
45 to 54 years old. .	7.9	8.2	19.0	9.9	33.2	19.8	5.6	14.8	11.2	5.9	20.1	5.8	13.6
55 to 64 years old. .	7.2	8.7	20.0	6.9	33.2	17.6	7.5	18.2	14.0	6.5	13.2	6.0	14.6
65 to 74 years old. .	6.8	7.4	25.2	6.1	36.0	22.9	9.0	29.4	13.1	6.0	12.6	5.5	19.5
75 yrs. old and over	6.4	10.0	36.2	6.2	33.1	25.3	11.7	51.6	10.7	7.2	18.3	7.1	24.1

[1] England and Wales only.   [2] Includes under 15 years old not shown separately.

Source: World Health Organization, Geneva, Switzerland, *1990 World Health Statistics Annual.*

No. 1368. Health Expenditures—Selected Countries: 1980 to 1990

[G.D.P. = gross domestic product; for explanation, see text, section 14. For explanation of purchasing power parities, see text, section 31]

COUNTRY	TOTAL HEALTH EXPENDITURES						PUBLIC HEALTH EXPENDITURES			
	Percent of gross domestic product					Per capita, 1990, on basis of G.D.P. pur- chasing power parities [1]	1980		1990 [1]	
	1980	1985	1988	1989 [1]	1990 [1]		Percent of gross domestic product	Percent of total health expendi- tures	Percent of gross domestic product	Percent of total health expendi- tures
United States	9.3	10.7	11.4	11.7	12.4	2,566	3.9	42.0	5.2	42.4
Australia	7.4	7.8	7.7	7.6	7.5	1,151	4.6	62.9	5.2	69.6
Austria	7.9	8.1	8.4	8.4	8.4	1,192	5.4	68.8	5.6	66.5
Belgium	6.7	7.4	7.5	7.4	7.4	1,087	5.5	82.8	6.1	82.5
Canada	7.4	8.5	8.7	8.7	9.0	1,795	5.5	74.7	6.7	74.1
Denmark	6.8	6.3	6.5	6.4	6.2	963	5.8	85.2	5.2	84.2
Finland	6.5	7.2	7.2	7.2	7.4	1,156	5.1	79.0	6.2	83.3
France	7.6	8.5	8.6	8.8	8.9	1,379	6.0	78.8	6.6	74.2
Germany	8.4	8.7	8.9	8.2	8.1	1,287	6.3	75.0	5.9	72.7
Greece	4.3	4.9	5.0	5.3	5.3	406	3.6	82.2	4.0	76.0
Iceland	6.5	7.4	8.5	8.6	8.5	1,372	5.7	88.2	7.4	87.5
Ireland	9.0	8.3	7.9	7.3	7.1	693	8.0	88.8	5.8	82.0
Italy	6.9	7.0	7.6	7.6	7.7	1,138	5.6	81.2	5.9	75.9
Japan	6.4	6.5	6.6	6.6	6.5	1,145	4.5	70.8	4.6	71.4
Luxembourg	6.8	6.8	7.3	7.4	7.2	1,300	6.3	92.8	6.5	91.4
Netherlands	8.0	8.0	8.2	8.1	8.0	1,182	6.0	74.7	5.8	72.6
New Zealand	7.2	6.6	7.4	7.3	7.2	853	6.0	83.6	5.9	81.7
Norway	6.6	6.4	7.5	7.6	7.2	1,281	6.5	98.4	6.9	95.7
Portugal	5.9	7.0	7.1	7.2	6.7	529	4.3	72.4	4.1	61.7
Spain	5.6	5.7	6.0	6.3	6.6	730	4.5	79.9	5.2	78.4
Sweden	9.2	8.8	8.5	8.7	8.7	1,421	8.7	94.4	7.8	89.3
Switzerland	7.3	7.6	7.8	7.7	7.7	1,436	4.9	67.5	5.2	68.1
Turkey	4.0	2.8	3.7	3.9	4.0	197	1.1	27.3	1.4	35.6
United Kingdom	5.8	6.0	6.0	6.0	6.2	932	5.2	89.6	5.2	84.5

[1] Preliminary estimates.

Source: Organization for Economic Cooperation and Development, Paris, France, *OECD Health Data,* 1991, and *OECD Health Systems: Facts and Trends,* 1992.

No. 1369. Proficiency Test Scores in Mathematics and Science for 13-Year-Old Students, by Selected Countries: 1991

[Based on the average scores of students participating in the second International Assessment of Educational Progress (IAEP), conducted in 1991 by the Educational Testing Service. The IAEP is an international comparative study of the mathematics and science skills of samples of 9- and 13-year-old students from 20 countries. The IAEP was designed to collect and report data on what students know and can do, on the educational and cultural factors associated with achievement, and on students' attitudes, backgrounds, and classroom experiences; for detail, see source]

AREA	Average days of instruction in year	Rank	Per-cent correct	MATHEMATICS [1] Average minutes of mathematics instruction each week	Percent of students who spend 2 hours or more on homework per day	Percent of students who watch television 5 hours or more per day	Rank	Per-cent correct	SCIENCE [2] Average minutes of science instruction each week	Percent of students who spend 2 hours or more on homework per day	Percent of students who watch television 5 hours or more per day
Canada	188	9	62	225	27	14	9	69	156	26	15
France	174	6	64	230	55	5	10	69	174	55	4
Hungary	177	5	68	186	58	13	4	73	207	61	16
Ireland	173	11	61	189	63	9	14	63	159	66	9
Israel [3]	215	8	63	205	50	20	8	70	181	49	20
Italy [4]	204	7	64	219	79	5	7	70	138	78	7
Jordan	191	15	40	180	56	7	15	57	180	54	10
Scotland	191	10	61	210	14	24	11	68	179	15	23
Slovenia	190	12	57	188	28	4	6	70	283	27	5
South Korea . .	222	1	73	179	41	11	1	78	144	38	10
Soviet republics [5] . . .	198	4	70	258	52	17	5	71	387	52	19
Spain [6] . . . ., . .	188	13	55	235	64	10	12	68	189	62	11
Switzerland [7] . .	207	3	71	251	20	7	3	74	152	21	7
Taiwan	222	2	73	204	41	10	2	76	245	44	7
United States . .	178	14	55	228	29	20	13	67	233	31	22

[1] Includes 75 questions on numbers and operations, measurement, geometry, data analysis, statistics, and probability, and algebra and functions. [2] Includes 64 questions on life, physical, earth and space sciences, and nature of science. [3] Hebrew-speaking schools only. [4] Emilia-Romagna province only. [5] Russian-speaking schools, 14 out of 15 republics only. [6] Spanish speaking schools, Cataluna excluded. [7] 15 out of 26 Cantons only.

Source: National Center of Education Statistics, U.S. Department of Education, and the National Science Foundation, *Learning Mathematics* and *Learning Science*, February 1992.

No. 1370. Organization for Economic Cooperation and Development (OECD)—Gross National Product: 1980 to 1990

[For interpretation of the absolute levels of GNP and per capita GNP, the market exchange rates used in converting national currencies do not necessarily reflect the relative purchasing power in the various countries. As a consequence, it should not be concluded, for instance, that the United Kingdom's individual standard of living in 1990 was only 78 percent of that of the United States, as the statistics may imply. Minus sign (-) indicates decrease. For explanation of annual percent change, see Guide to Tabular Presentation]

COUNTRY	GROSS NATIONAL PRODUCT (GNP) Total in constant (1990) dollars (bil.)			Annual percent change		GNP PER CAPITA In constant (1990) dollars [1]			Annual percent change		Inflation rate, [2] 1989-1990
	1980	1985	1990	1980-1990	1989-1990	1980	1985	1990	1980-1990	1989-1990	(percent)
United States . . .	4,182.6	4,757.1	5,465.1	2.7	1.0	19,466	19,948	21,863	1.8	-0.1	4.1
OECD Europe [3] . .	5,526.7	5,974.4	6,974.1	2.4	2.8	14,505	14,798	16,639	1.7	1.8	5.9
Belgium	158.3	164.4	192.4	2.0	3.5	16,542	16,673	19,953	2.0	3.6	3.5
Denmark	103.0	117.4	123.5	1.8	1.0	22,016	22,975	24,027	1.8	0.8	2.7
France	954.0	1,028.6	1,187.7	2.2	2.5	18,369	18,644	21,044	1.7	2.0	2.7
Germany [4]	1,216.1	1,291.5	1,507.1	2.2	4.2	20,733	21,183	23,885	1.9	2.3	3.4
Greece	57.6	61.6	67.3	1.6	1.2	6,040	6,203	6,697	1.1	1.0	20.1
Ireland	31.2	32.4	37.4	1.8	4.4	9,065	9,153	10,685	1.5	4.8	3.6
Italy	855.1	925.5	1,078.0	2.4	2.6	15,825	16,197	18,696	2.1	2.3	7.5
Luxembourg . . .	6.4	7.2	9.0	3.5	2.6	19,000	19,568	24,270	3.2	5.4	3.4
Netherlands . . .	232.6	243.2	276.5	1.7	3.0	16,470	16,776	18,481	1.1	2.2	3.1
Portugal	44.7	46.7	58.0	2.6	3.9	4,490	4,596	5,505	1.8	3.3	14.2
Spain	364.6	390.4	486.9	2.9	3.5	9,953	10,148	12,497	2.5	3.3	7.5
United Kingdom .	753.0	829.3	975.0	2.6	1.6	14,722	14,647	17,004	2.4	0.9	6.1
Austria	126.8	135.5	158.0	2.2	4.5	17,510	17,923	20,493	2.0	3.2	3.4
Finland	99.2	114.6	137.3	3.3	1.4	22,725	23,388	27,518	2.9	1.1	6.0
Iceland	4.4	4.8	5.4	2.1	-0.1	19,458	20,125	21,680	1.3	-0.2	12.5
Norway	75.8	89.4	105.0	3.3	3.0	20,507	21,672	24,764	2.9	2.7	4.0
Sweden	185.1	202.5	224.7	2.0	0.9	23,753	24,251	26,250	1.6	0.1	9.2
Switzerland	192.2	206.0	235.4	2.1	2.5	30,838	31,829	35,081	1.4	1.6	6.5
Turkey	66.6	83.4	109.9	5.1	7.6	1,479	1,660	1,873	2.2	4.1	53.1
Australia	213.5	250.0	294.2	3.3	2.2	15,259	15,833	17,215	1.7	0.6	3.8
Canada	415.1	477.8	558.0	3.0	1.1	18,267	18,990	21,094	2.0	-0.1	3.1
Japan	1,893.2	2,307.4	2,910.4	4.4	6.1	18,319	19,045	23,558	3.8	5.7	1.9
New Zealand . . .	34.5	41.3	41.9	2.0	0.7	11,981	12,708	12,507	1.2	-0.5	2.9

[1] National currency values converted into dollars by the average 1989 Market Rate, as published by the International Monetary Fund, Washington, DC. [2] GNP or GDP (gross domestic product) implicit price deflators; totals weighted by 1989 (base year) GNP. [3] See text, section 31. [4] Former West Germany (prior to unification).

Source: U.S. Department of State, Bureau of Intelligence and Research, *Economic Growth of OECD Countries, 1980-1990*, Report No. IRR 22 (Revised), 1991; and unpublished data.

No. 1371. Gross National Product in Current and Constant (1989) Dollars and Per Capita: 1980 to 1989

[In billions of dollars, except per capita. For explanation of conversion to U.S. dollars, see headnote, table 1413. For explanation of gross national product (GNP), see text, section 14]

COUNTRY	CURRENT DOLLARS				CONSTANT (1989) DOLLARS				Per capita (dol.)		
	1980	1985	1988	1989	1980	1985	1988	1989	1980	1985	1989
United States	2,732.0	4,015.0	4,874.0	5,201.0	4,025.0	4,571.0	5,073.0	5,201.0	17,670	[1]19,100	20,910
Afghanistan.	2.7	[1]2.9	(NA)	(NA)	4.0	[1]3.3	(NA)	(NA)	269	239	(NA)
Algeria	23.9	40.0	42.4	45.3	35.3	45.6	44.1	45.3	1,870	2,054	1,831
Argentina	43.9	48.5	56.5	54.1	64.6	55.2	58.8	54.1	2,289	1,818	1,694
Austria	71.5	99.0	115.9	125.2	105.3	112.7	120.6	125.2	13,950	14,920	16,430
Bangladesh.	10.0	15.5	18.8	20.0	14.7	17.6	19.6	20.0	167	174	180
Belgium	89.4	119.4	141.8	154.6	131.8	135.9	147.6	154.6	13,380	13,780	15,620
Brazil	260.6	348.6	430.5	462.3	384.0	396.9	448.2	462.3	3,124	2,874	3,090
Bulgaria	30.6	41.2	48.0	49.6	45.0	46.9	49.9	49.6	5,093	5,246	5,530
Burma	9.8	15.8	14.6	16.3	14.4	17.9	15.2	16.3	429	482	404
Canada	270.2	401.3	496.5	531.0	398.0	456.9	516.8	531.0	16,540	18,140	20,240
Chile	12.6	15.2	20.2	23.3	18.5	17.4	21.1	23.3	1,670	1,438	1,809
China:											
Mainland [1]	186.4	386.3	559.1	603.5	274.6	439.8	582.0	603.5	279	422	547
Taiwan	49.7	90.6	134.6	150.2	73.3	103.2	140.1	150.2	4,104	5,317	7,390
Colombia	19.4	27.3	34.1	36.9	28.6	31.0	35.4	36.9	1,077	1,046	1,139
Czechoslovakia	71.2	97.8	117.1	123.2	104.9	111.3	121.9	123.2	6,874	7,182	7,876
East Germany	89.6	127.4	151.3	159.4	132.0	145.0	157.5	159.4	7,885	8,707	9,669
Egypt.	30.6	53.0	64.9	69.8	45.1	60.4	67.6	69.8	1,082	1,277	1,342
Ethiopia	3.3	4.3	5.6	6.0	4.9	4.8	5.8	6.0	128	111	120
France	536.2	740.9	884.2	954.1	790.0	843.5	920.5	954.1	14,660	15,290	17,000
Ghana	2.9	3.6	4.6	5.1	4.3	4.1	4.8	5.1	396	322	350
Greece.	32.4	43.4	49.6	52.9	47.8	49.4	51.7	52.9	4,954	4,977	5,286
Hungary	39.3	52.6	63.3	64.7	57.9	59.9	65.9	64.7	5,408	5,621	6,119
India	112.4	188.2	246.2	267.4	165.5	214.2	256.3	267.4	240	279	321
Indonesia	35.1	61.1	79.8	89.4	51.7	69.5	83.1	89.4	334	403	479
Iran [1]	37.8	71.1	71.3	77.5	55.6	80.9	74.3	77.5	1,422	1,716	1,440
Iraq [1]	55.6	41.3	39.6	(NA)	81.9	47.0	41.3	(NA)	6,188	2,992	(NA)
Italy	479.0	665.5	800.6	860.0	705.7	757.6	833.4	860.0	12,500	13,260	14,940
Japan.	1,328.0	2,090.0	2,586.0	2,820.0	1,956.0	2,379.0	2,692.0	2,820.0	16,750	19,700	22,900
Kenya	3.8	5.6	7.3	7.9	5.6	6.3	7.6	7.9	336	314	338
Madagascar	1.6	1.9	2.2	2.3	2.4	2.2	2.3	2.3	279	213	205
Malaysia	15.1	24.1	31.2	36.0	22.3	27.4	32.5	36.0	1,619	1,765	2,099
Mexico	114.1	159.2	174.1	186.7	168.1	181.2	181.3	186.7	2,415	2,310	2,170
Morocco.	10.7	15.8	20.3	21.7	15.7	18.0	21.1	21.7	764	780	866
Mozambique	0.9	0.9	1.0	1.1	1.4	1.0	1.0	1.1	84	76	78
Nepal.	1.3	2.1	2.7	2.8	1.9	2.3	2.8	2.8	123	138	150
Netherlands	129.9	176.4	205.0	222.5	191.4	200.8	213.4	222.5	13,530	13,860	14,980
Nigeria	18.9	22.4	25.2	27.5	27.8	25.5	26.2	27.5	309	248	239
North Korea [1]	21.9	26.3	29.2	30.0	32.3	29.9	30.4	30.0	1,793	1,527	1,427
Pakistan	14.3	25.6	33.7	36.8	21.1	29.1	35.1	36.8	247	293	330
Peru	29.3	36.4	43.3	40.8	43.2	41.5	45.1	40.8	2,497	2,113	1,903
Philippines	25.9	31.8	40.0	44.0	38.2	36.2	41.7	44.0	750	629	697
Poland	108.1	144.4	170.9	174.7	159.3	164.3	177.9	174.7	4,477	4,417	4,625
Portugal	23.8	31.5	40.5	44.6	35.0	35.8	42.2	44.6	3,583	3,525	4,323
Romania.	75.0	99.3	112.3	113.4	110.5	113.1	117.0	113.4	4,977	4,977	4,896
South Africa	49.6	70.5	83.6	86.8	73.1	80.3	87.0	86.8	2,414	2,317	2,253
South Korea	62.3	120.6	188.4	210.1	91.9	137.2	196.1	210.1	2,409	3,343	4,920
Soviet Union	1,532.0	2,145.0	2,526.0	2,664.0	2,257.0	2,442.0	2,630.0	2,664.0	8,473	8,757	9,226
Spain.	196.2	271.0	340.2	370.7	289.1	308.5	354.2	370.7	7,711	8,014	9,471
Sri Lanka	3.3	5.5	6.5	6.9	4.9	6.3	6.8	6.9	330	392	409
Sudan	9.0	11.7	13.6	15.6	13.3	13.3	14.2	15.6	702	567	608
Sweden	106.0	147.6	174.8	185.8	156.1	168.0	182.0	185.8	18,790	20,110	21,900
Switzerland	103.7	146.4	172.3	184.3	152.8	166.7	179.4	184.3	23,930	25,510	27,510
Syria	11.2	16.7	19.5	19.3	16.6	19.0	20.3	19.3	1,904	1,832	1,608
Tanzania.	1.6	2.1	2.5	2.6	2.3	2.4	2.6	2.6	124	108	105
Thailand	24.4	41.3	58.7	68.8	36.0	47.0	61.1	68.8	766	908	1,246
Turkey	34.1	55.6	73.1	77.3	50.3	63.2	76.1	77.3	1,115	1,241	1,380
Uganda	2.0	2.8	3.6	4.0	3.0	3.2	3.8	4.0	232	216	233
United Kingdom	442.8	632.7	783.3	834.4	652.5	720.2	815.4	834.4	11,590	12,720	14,580
Venezuela.	29.3	34.7	44.7	41.5	43.1	39.6	46.6	41.5	2,869	2,285	2,158
West Germany.	685.6	942.9	1,112.0	1,207.0	1,010.0	1,073.0	1,158.0	1,207.0	16,410	17,590	19,520
Yugoslavia	39.0	51.2	55.9	58.6	57.4	58.2	58.2	58.6	2,574	2,518	2,474
Zaire	5.5	7.5	8.9	9.2	8.1	8.6	9.3	9.2	304	276	258

NA Not available. [1] Estimated.

Source: U.S. Arms Control and Disarmament Agency, *World Military Expenditures and Arms Transfers*, annual. Data from International Bank for Reconstruction and Development and U.S. Central Intelligence Agency.

No. 1372. Annual Growth Rates of Real Gross Domestic Product—International Comparisons, Selected Periods: 1970 to 1989

[In percent. Minus sign (-) indicates decline. See also *Historical Statistics, Colonial Times to 1970*, series F 10-16]

COUNTRY	1970-80	1980-89	1980-81	1981-82	1982-83	1983-84	1984-85	1985-86	1986-87	1987-88	1988-89
United States.	2.5	3.1	2.3	-2.6	3.9	7.2	3.8	3.2	3.5	4.5	2.8
Per capita	1.6	2.1	1.2	-3.6	2.9	6.2	2.8	2.2	2.5	3.5	1.8
Canada	4.1	3.2	3.7	-3.2	3.2	6.3	4.8	3.3	4.0	4.4	3.0
Per capita	3.0	2.3	2.4	-4.2	2.3	5.5	4.0	2.5	2.9	3.2	1.8
France.	2.9	2.1	1.2	2.3	0.8	1.5	1.8	2.4	2.0	3.6	3.6
Per capita	2.4	1.7	0.6	1.7	0.3	1.1	1.4	2.0	1.5	3.1	3.1
West Germany	2.5	1.9	0.2	-0.6	1.5	2.8	2.0	2.3	1.7	3.7	3.3
Per capita	2.3	1.8	-	-0.6	1.9	3.2	2.2	2.3	1.7	3.1	2.4
Italy.	3.4	2.3	1.0	0.3	1.1	3.0	2.6	2.5	3.0	4.2	3.2
Per capita	3.0	2.1	0.8	0.1	0.8	2.7	2.4	2.4	2.8	4.0	3.0
Japan	4.2	4.1	3.9	2.8	3.2	5.0	4.7	2.5	4.4	5.7	4.9
Per capita	3.1	3.5	3.1	2.1	2.5	4.3	4.1	1.8	3.9	5.3	4.5
United Kingdom.	1.7	2.8	-1.3	1.7	3.7	2.1	3.6	3.9	4.7	4.6	2.2
Per capita	1.6	2.6	-1.4	1.8	3.7	1.9	3.3	3.6	4.4	4.4	1.9

- Represents or rounds to zero.

Source: Organization for Economic Cooperation and Development, Paris, France, *National Accounts, 1960-1989*.

No. 1373. Gross Domestic Product of Selected Countries as Percent of United States: 1970 to 1989

[Comparisons are based on constant (1985) price data converted to U.S. dollars using 1985 exchange rates]

COUNTRY	GROSS DOMESTIC PRODUCT								PER CAPITA GROSS DOMESTIC PRODUCT							
	1970	1975	1980	1985	1986	1987	1988	1989	1970	1975	1980	1985	1986	1987	1988	1989
United States.	100	100	100	100	100	100	100	100	100	100	100	100	100	100	100	100
Canada.	7	8	9	9	9	9	9	9	70	80	83	83	83	84	84	84
France	13	14	14	13	13	13	13	11	54	58	60	57	57	56	56	57
Italy	10	11	11	11	11	11	11	11	39	41	46	45	45	45	45	46
Japan.	26	29	32	33	33	33	34	35	52	57	62	66	66	67	68	70
United Kingdom	13	13	12	11	11	12	12	12	48	49	48	48	49	50	50	51
West Germany.	17	17	17	16	16	15	15	15	58	59	63	61	62	61	61	61

Source: Organization for Economic Cooperation and Development, Paris, France, *National Accounts, 1960-1989*.

No. 1374. Selected International Economic Indicators: 1970 to 1989

[Data cover gross national product (GNP) at market prices, except for France, Italy, and the United Kingdom, which relate to gross domestic product. Gross fixed capital formation covers private and government sectors except military. Savings data are calculated by deducting outlays—such as personal consumption expenditures, interest paid, and transfer payments to foreigners—from disposable personal income. Minus sign (-) indicates decline]

YEAR	United States	France	West Germany	Italy	Nether- lands	United Kingdom	Japan	Canada
GNP growth rates [1] (constant **1982** prices):								
1970	-0.3	5.7	-0.5	5.3	5.4	2.3	10.8	2.5
1980	-0.2	1.6	1.5	4.2	0.8	-2.2	4.3	1.5
1984	6.8	1.3	3.3	3.0	3.2	2.1	5.1	6.1
1985	3.4	1.9	1.9	2.6	2.6	3.6	4.9	4.8
1986	2.7	2.5	2.3	2.5	2.0	3.9	2.5	3.1
1987	3.4	2.2	1.6	3.0	1.1	4.7	4.6	4.4
1988	4.5	3.8	3.7	4.2	2.8	4.6	5.7	4.2
1989	2.5	3.6	3.9	3.2	3.5	2.2	4.9	2.7
Ratio of gross fixed capital formation to GNP (current prices):								
1970	17.7	24.3	25.4	24.5	27.2	18.7	35.6	21.7
1980	19.0	23.0	22.6	24.2	21.1	18.0	31.6	23.9
1984	18.0	19.3	20.0	21.2	18.6	16.7	27.9	19.6
1985	18.1	19.3	19.6	20.8	19.2	16.9	27.7	20.3
1986	17.8	19.2	19.4	19.9	20.1	16.7	27.5	20.7
1987	17.3	19.5	19.4	20.1	20.2	17.4	28.7	21.5
1988	17.1	20.3	19.8	20.0	21.3	18.9	30.4	22.5
1989	16.7	20.8	20.6	20.2	21.9	19.4	31.9	22.8
Ratio of savings to disposable personal income:								
1970	8.1	18.7	14.7	30.3	13.2	9.0	18.2	5.5
1980	7.1	17.6	14.1	30.5	11.0	13.1	17.9	13.3
1984	6.1	14.5	12.8	25.5	13.1	10.5	16.0	14.8
1985	4.4	14.0	12.7	24.7	12.7	9.7	16.0	13.1
1986	4.1	12.9	13.5	23.7	13.1	8.2	16.4	10.5
1987	2.9	11.1	13.6	22.3	12.1	6.6	15.1	9.2
1988	4.2	12.1	13.9	22.8	12.5	5.4	14.8	9.9
1989	4.6	12.3	13.5	(NA)	13.4	6.7	(NA)	10.8

NA Not available.   [1] Growth rates represent percentage change from preceding year.

Source: U.S. Dept. of Commerce, International Trade Administration, Office of Finance, Industry, and Trade Information, based on official statistics of listed countries.

No. 1375. Gross Domestic Product, Total and Per Capita, Using Purchasing Power Parities—Selected Countries: 1970 to 1989

[The goods and services produced in different countries should be valued consistently if the differences observed are meant to reflect real differences in the volumes of goods and services produced. The use of purchasing power parities (PPP) instead of exchange rates is intended to achieve this objective. PPP's show how many units of currency are needed in one country to buy the same amount of goods and services which one unit of currency will buy in the other country. For further explanation of PPP, see text, section 31]

COUNTRY	GROSS DOMESTIC PRODUCT (bil. dol.)						GROSS DOMESTIC PRODUCT PER CAPITA (dollars)					
	1970	1980	1985	1987	1988	1989	1970	1980	1985	1987	1988	1989
United States ...	1,008.6	2,686.2	3,962.2	4,452.9	4,809.1	5,132.0	4,919	11,794	16,559	18,254	19,525	20,630
OECD Europe [1] ..	1,044.1	2,863.0	3,980.2	4,453.4	4,766.0	5,114.2	3,060	7,847	10,586	11,685	12,460	13,262
Belgium	28.5	79.7	106.2	115.9	125.2	135.0	3,310	9,076	12,067	13,147	14,206	15,231
Denmark......	17.0	43.0	62.8	68.1	70.2	73.9	3,724	9,085	13,295	14,503	15,053	15,802
France	167.4	468.1	646.6	710.3	760.2	818.0	3,696	9,740	13,141	14,345	15,319	16,397
Germany	205.0	544.3	738.7	808.8	866.5	929.0	3,884	10,170	13,876	15,122	16,100	17,093
Greece.......	13.5	43.6	59.7	63.4	68.2	72.8	1,507	4,426	5,883	6,216	6,670	7,145
Ireland	5.2	16.9	24.5	26.8	28.7	31.6	1,853	5,190	7,246	7,930	8,568	9,526
Italy	152.9	449.9	624.2	693.9	746.7	799.7	3,123	8,743	11,859	13,197	14,161	15,126
Luxembourg ...	1.2	3.3	4.8	5.4	5.9	6.5	3,919	9,610	13,825	15,483	16,802	18,345
Netherlands ...	45.1	122.1	164.3	177.7	188.5	203.6	3,499	9,233	12,137	12,971	13,664	14,671
Portugal	12.3	39.7	53.2	61.4	65.9	72.1	1,545	4,511	5,811	6,641	7,105	7,732
Spain........	75.5	215.6	295.8	339.5	369.2	401.9	2,366	6,126	8,159	9,308	10,089	10,952
United Kingdom .	180.2	443.3	625.5	715.7	773.5	820.6	3,399	8,259	11,590	13,207	14,188	15,023
Austria	20.4	59.4	81.2	88.4	94.6	102.1	3,158	9,081	12,408	13,397	14,356	25,402
Finland.......	13.2	37.9	56.1	62.7	68.3	74.5	3,007	8,342	12,028	13,353	14,504	15,808
Iceland.......	0.6	2.3	3.2	3.9	4.0	4.0	2,764	9,448	12,532	15,079	15,211	15,400
Norway.......	11.9	38.4	58.0	64.8	67.0	70.5	2,812	8,622	12,818	14,212	14,532	15,079
Sweden	30.7	75.8	106.3	117.7	124.4	131.9	3,986	9,517	13,286	14,611	15,368	16,224
Switzerland....	29.9	68.7	94.3	104.1	110.7	119.0	5,351	12,087	16,218	17,675	18,641	19,949
Turkey.......	33.6	111.1	179.7	220.0	236.1	247.6	628	1,673	2,390	2,810	2,948	3,018
Australia	43.7	123.6	184.2	206.0	221.2	240.4	3,644	9,003	12,548	13,693	14,412	15,324
Canada.......	82.8	263.1	388.8	441.8	478.7	507.0	3,733	10,509	14,852	16,500	17,648	18,544
Japan........	286.9	918.2	1,425.4	1,604.3	1,752.1	1,908.5	2,932	8,225	12,246	13,614	14,875	16,090
New Zealand	9.4	22.7	33.0	35.8	36.5	38.4	3,474	7,836	11,159	11,976	12,164	12,745

[1] See text, section 31.
Source: Organization for Economic Cooperation and Development, Paris, France, *National Accounts of OECD Countries*, vol. I, annual.

No. 1376. Food and Beverage Expenditures as a Percent of Total Private Consumption Expenditures—Selected Countries: 1988

COUNTRY	Total	Food	Nonalcoholic beverages	Alcoholic beverages	COUNTRY	Total	Food	Nonalcoholic beverages	Alcoholic beverages
United States ...	11.9	10.2	0.6	1.2	Mexico [3]	35.3	31.9	1.2	2.2
Australia [1]	19.5	15.2	(NA)	4.4	Netherlands.....	16.6	14.3	(NA)	1.8
Austria	19.8	16.7	0.7	2.4	Norway........	23.1	18.7	1.2	3.2
Belgium	18.1	16.2	0.5	1.4	Philippines......	64.8	62.2	2.7	0.0
Canada [1]......	14.4	11.5	(NA)	2.9	Portugal [2]......	36.4	34.1	0.3	2.0
Denmark.......	19.3	15.1	0.6	3.5	South Africa.....	34.8	27.4	1.6	5.7
Finland........	21.5	16.8	0.6	4.2	South Korea [2] ...	40.3	36.1	0.9	3.3
France	18.5	16.1	0.5	2.0	Soviet Union [3] ...	38.0	28.0	(NA)	10.0
Greece........	36.3	32.5	1.0	2.8	Spain [2]........	26.6	25.1	0.4	1.1
India.........	52.4	51.3	0.1	1.1	Sweden	20.0	16.4	0.5	3.1
Ireland [2]	35.7	22.7	1.4	11.6	Switzerland [4] ...	26.9	19.7	7.2	(NA)
Israel	25.8	23.4	2.3	0.6	United Kingdom [2] .	15.3	12.8	0.6	1.8
Italy	21.3	19.8	0.4	1.2	West Germany ...	20.1	20.0	(NA)	(NA)
Japan........	41.8	36.0	1.6	4.2					

NA Not available.   [1] Food expenditures include nonalcoholic beverages.   [2] Data for 1987.   [3] Data for 1986.   [4] Food expenditures include all beverages.
Source: U.S. Dept. of Agriculture, Economic Research Service. Based on data from the United Nations, New York, NY, *National Accounts Statistics*, annual.

No. 1377. Per Capita Consumption of Pork, Poultry, Beef, and Veal: 1991

[Preliminary. In pounds per capita. Beef, veal, and pork quantities are as of September and in carcass-weight equivalents; poultry quantities are as of July and are on ready-to-cook basis]

COUNTRY	PORK		COUNTRY	POULTRY		COUNTRY	BEEF AND VEAL	
	Quantity	Rank		Quantity	Rank		Quantity	Rank
Hungary..........	147.5	1	United States	94.8	1	Argentina	153.9	1
Denmark	144.2	2	Israel	81.8	2	Uruguay..........	122.8	2
Germany	121.5	3	Hong Kong	76.5	3	United States......	97.0	3
Czechoslovakia.....	116.9	4	Singapore	75.2	4	Australia..........	84.0	4
Austria	116.4	5	Canada	63.5	5	Canada	80.3	5
Poland............	116.4	6	Saudi Arabia	56.7	6	New Zealand	76.7	6
Belgium-Luxembourg .	104.7	7	Taiwan	56.2	7	France...........	66.2	7
Spain............	103.2	8	Spain	51.6	8	Soviet Union [1].....	65.9	8
Bulgaria..........	97.7	9	Spain	50.7	9	Italy.............	58.9	9
Netherlands	92.4	10	Hungary	49.2	10	Switzerland.......	56.2	10
United States......	65.5	22						

[1] Former Soviet Union. Data for newly independent republics are not available.
Source: U.S. Department of Agriculture, Foreign Agricultural Service, *World Poultry Situation*, August 1991, and *World Livestock Situation*, November 1991.

No. 1378. Percent of Households Owning Selected Appliances—Selected Countries: 1990

APPLIANCE	United States [1]	Bel- gium	Den- mark	France	Ger- many [2]	Italy	Nether- lands	Spain	Sweden	Swit- zerland	United King- dom
Cassette recorder. . .	(NA)	75	82	76	74	64	80	67	88	82	82
Clothes washer	76	88	76	88	88	96	91	87	72	78	78
Dishwasher.	43	26	26	33	34	18	12	11	31	32	11
Food processor. . . .	(NA)	91	83	83	92	41	84	50	77	91	80
Microwave oven. . . .	61	21	14	25	36	6	19	9	37	15	48
Radio.	(NA)	90	98	98	84	92	97	95	93	99	90
Television set:											
Color/mono	93	97	98	94	97	98	98	98	97	93	98
Tumbledrier.	[3]51	39	22	12	17	10	23	5	18	27	32
Vacuum cleaner. . . .	(NA)	92	96	89	96	56	98	29	97	93	98
Video recorder.	(NA)	42	39	35	42	25	48	40	48	41	58

NA Not available.   [1] 1987 data. Represents appliances possessed and generally used by the household (as of November). Source: U.S. Energy Information Administration, *Annual Energy Review, 1989.*   [2] Former West Germany (prior to unification).   [3] Electric tumbledriers.

Source: Except as noted, Euromonitor Publications Limited, London, England, *European Marketing Data and Statistics,* annual (copyright).

No. 1379. Motor-Vehicle Deaths, Rates, and Vehicle Registrations, by Nation

[Deaths are included if they occur within 30 days after the accident, except as noted. Death data must be compared cautiously because of differences in the volume and kinds of traffic, numbers of vehicles, population density, definitions of deaths, and other factors]

COUNTRY	MOTOR VEHICLE TRAFFIC DEATHS			1989 VEHICLE REGISTRATIONS			
				All vehicles		Passenger cars	
	Year	Number	Rate [1]	Number (mil.)	Persons per vehicle	Number (mil.)	Persons per car
Argentina	1986	3,075	10.0	5.6	5.8	4.1	7.9
Australia.	1988	3,078	18.6	9.5	1.8	7.4	2.2
Austria	1989	1,460	19.2	3.2	2.4	2.9	2.6
Belgium	1986	[2]2,057	20.9	4.1	2.4	3.7	2.7
Bulgaria	1989	1,173	13.0	1.4	6.4	1.2	7.3
Canada	1988	[3]3,971	15.3	15.7	1.7	11.2	2.4
Chile	1987	879	7.0	1.0	13.0	0.7	19.0
Costa Rica	1988	352	12.3	0.3	10.0	0.2	18.0
Czechoslovakia .	1989	1,746	11.2	3.4	4.6	3.1	5.0
Denmark.	1988	723	14.1	1.9	2.7	1.6	3.2
Dominican Republic.	1985	557	8.9	0.2	39.0	0.1	64.0
East Germany . .	1989	1,909	11.5	4.4	3.8	3.9	4.3
Ecuador	1988	2,037	20.0	0.2	45.0	0.1	150.0
Finland.	1988	627	12.7	2.2	2.3	1.9	2.6
France	1988	[4]10,165	18.2	27.8	2.0	23.0	2.4
Greece.	1988	1,863	18.6	2.4	4.3	1.6	6.3
Hong Kong	1987	283	5.0	0.4	16.0	0.2	27.0
Hungary	1989	2,289	21.6	2.1	5.1	1.7	6.1
Ireland	1988	458	12.9	1.0	3.6	0.8	4.6
Israel	1987	463	10.6	0.9	4.9	0.7	5.9
Italy	1988	[4]8,885	15.5	26.4	2.2	24.3	2.4
Japan.	1989	14,276	11.7	55.1	2.2	32.6	3.8
Kuwait	1987	343	18.3	0.6	3.4	0.5	4.4
Netherlands . . .	1988	1,316	8.9	5.9	2.5	5.4	2.8
New Zealand. . .	1987	815	24.6	1.9	1.8	1.6	2.2
Norway.	1988	363	8.6	1.9	2.2	1.6	2.6
Panama	1987	388	17.1	0.2	11.0	0.2	14.0
Paraguay	1986	241	10.6	0.1	49.0	0.1	72.0
Poland	1989	7,452	19.6	5.9	6.5	4.8	7.9
Portugal	1989	2,795	27.1	1.9	5.5	1.5	7.1
Puerto Rico. . . .	1987	652	18.3	1.5	2.2	1.3	2.5
Singapore	1987	233	8.9	0.4	6.9	0.3	10.0
Sweden	1987	764	9.1	3.9	2.2	3.6	2.3
Switzerland	1989	939	14.1	3.2	2.1	2.9	2.3
Syrian Arab Republic.	1985	176	1.7	0.3	49.0	0.1	106.0
Thailand	1987	4,441	8.3	2.2	25.0	0.8	67.0
United States . .	**1988**	**[3]48,024**	**19.5**	**187.3**	**1.3**	**143.1**	**1.7**
Uruguay	1987	290	9.5	0.3	12.0	0.2	18.0
West Germany. .	1989	7,615	12.3	32.1	1.9	30.2	2.0
Yugoslavia	1988	3,626	15.4	4.1	5.8	3.2	7.4

[1] Deaths per 100,000 population.   [2] Deaths occurring at the accident scene only.   [3] Deaths occurring within one year after the accident.   [4] Deaths occurring within three days after the accident.

Source: World Health Organization, Geneva, Switzerland, unpublished data; and Motor Vehicle Manufacturers Association of the United States, Inc., Detroit, MI, *MVMA Motor Vehicle Facts & Figures,* annual (copyright).

No. 1380. Communications—Telephones, Newspapers, Television, and Radio, by Country

[See text, section 31, for general comments about the data. For additional data qualifications for countries, see source]

COUNTRY	Telephones per 100 population,[1] 1987	Daily newspaper circulation, copies per 1,000 population,[2] 1988	Television receivers per 1,000 population,[3] 1989	Radio receivers per 1,000 population,[4] 1989	COUNTRY	Telephones per 100 population,[1] 1987	Daily newspaper circulation, copies per 1,000 population,[2] 1988	Television receivers per 1,000 population,[3] 1989	Radio receivers per 1,000 population,[4] 1989
United States	[5]76.0	[6]259	813.6	2,122	Jamaica	[6 12]6.0	(NA)	123.5	409
Algeria	3.8	21	72.8	232	Japan	[7 12]55.5	[6]566	610.4	895
Argentina	11.6	(NA)	219.3	673	Kenya	1.4	[6]13	8.6	95
Australia	[7]55.0	252	483.9	1,262	Kuwait	18.1	209	280.6	337
Austria	52.5	362	475.3	622	Lebanon	(NA)	97	326.5	834
Bangladesh	[8]0.1	10	4.4	41	Luxembourg	[15]41.2	395	252.0	623
Belgium	47.8	219	447.1	776	Madagascar	[6]0.4	6	19.8	198
Bolivia	[6]2.9	[5]50	98.4	597	Malaysia	9.1	(NA)	143.6	428
Brazil	9.3	[6]48	203.6	373	Mexico	[6]9.6	127	126.8	242
Bulgaria	[9]20.0	267	249.1	436	Morocco	1.5	(NA)	69.6	209
Burma	[9]0.1	[7]75	1.7	81	Netherlands	63.9	(NA)	484.8	902
Cambodia	(NA)	(NA)	8.1	107	New Zealand	[12]69.7	327	371.6	922
Canada	78.0	231	626.3	1,023	Nicaragua	[5]1.6	[5]47	61.4	247
Chile	6.5	67	200.6	340	Nigeria	[5]0.3	[8]6	28.6	171
China:					Norway	[5]62.2	551	422.7	796
Mainland	0.7	[5]29	26.7	184	Pakistan	0.7	64	15.8	86
Taiwan	[10]35.9	(NA)	(NA)	(NA)	Panama	10.7	69	164.6	222
Colombia	8.0	(NA)	108.1	167	Paraguay	2.5	(NA)	48.2	169
Costa Rica	14.7	86	136.1	259	Peru	[6]3.1	[16]31	94.6	251
Cuba	5.4	129	203.4	343	Philippines	[5]1.5	56	41.1	136
Cyprus	39.8	125	141.4	289	Poland	12.2	184	291.5	428
Czechoslovakia	24.6	345	410	583	Portugal	20.2	[6]41	176.2	216
Denmark	86.4	359	528.2	1,012	Puerto Rico	[6 12]20.3	185	265.7	720
Dominican Republic	[11]2.9	[6]42	81.9	168	Romania	(NA)	159	193.8	195
East Germany	23.3	585	779.1	687	Saudi Arabia	[5]11.3	(NA)	276.5	[17]280
Ecuador	3.6	[8]64	82.3	314	Singapore	44.2	289	372.4	306
Egypt	2.8	38	97.7	322	South Africa	[12]14.3	48	101.4	324
El Salvador	2.7	45	87.1	403	South Korea	25.5	(NA)	207.3	1,003
Ethiopia	0.3	1	2.1	188	Soviet Union	[7]11.3	474	323.3	685
Finland	[7]61.7	[7]547	488.3	998	Spain	39.6	82	388.7	304
France	[7]60.8	[6]193	400.2	895	Sri Lanka	0.8	35	32.3	194
Ghana	0.6	33	14.5	295	Sudan	[5]0.4	[5]5	61.3	235
Greece	41.3	(NA)	194.5	419	Sweden	[9]89.0	526	470.5	885
Guatemala	[7]1.6	(NA)	44.7	64	Switzerland	[6]85.6	504	405.8	851
Honduras	1.2	41	70.3	384	Syria	5.9	[6]15	58.7	248
Hong Kong	47.0	(NA)	260.3	642	Thailand	[6]1.9	87	109.3	182
Hungary	15.2	273	409.3	592	Trinidad and Tobago	[9]9.6	108	301.3	460
Iceland	[9]52.5	500	318.7	785	Tunisia	4.1	[5]39	75.1	188
India	[12]0.6	[6]28	27.0	78	Turkey	[9]9	55	173.6	161
Indonesia	0.5	21	55.3	144	United Kingdom	[5 12]52.4	394	434.3	1,145
Iran	[13]3.9	[5]5	65.8	245	Uruguay	14.9	(NA)	227.2	600
Iraq	[7]5.6	(NA)	68.4	202	Venezuela	9.2	[8]186	156.0	432
Ireland	[7]26.5	205	271.0	583	West Germany	65.0	331	506.4	949
Israel	[12]44.5	(NA)	265.5	468	Yugoslavia	[6]15.4	100	196.8	245
Italy	[14]48.8	105	422.9	794	Zimbabwe	3.2	24	26.6	85

NA Not available. [1] As of December 31, except as noted. Comprises public and private telephones installed which can be connected to a central exchange. [2] Publications containing general news and appearing at least 4 times a week, may range in size from a single sheet to 50 or more pages. Circulation data refer to average circulation per issue or number of printed copies per issue and include copies sold outside the country. [3] Estimated number of sets in use. [4] Data cover estimated number of receivers in use, except as noted, and apply to all types of receivers for radio broadcasts to the public, including receivers connected to a radio "redistribution system" but excluding television sets. [5] For 1984. [6] For 1986. [7] For 1985. [8] For 1982. [9] For 1983. [10] For 1988. [11] For 1980. [12] As of March 31. [13] As of March 21. [14] Includes San Marino. [15] For 1981. [16] Lima only. [17] Number of licenses issued.

Source: Except Taiwan, International Telecommunications Union, Geneva, Switzerland, *Telecommunication Statistics*, and United Nations Educational, Scientific, and Cultural Organization, Paris, France, *Statistical Yearbook* (copyright); Taiwan, U.S. Bureau of the Census. Data from Republic of China publications.

No. 1381. Tax Revenues—Selected Countries: 1980 to 1989

[Covers national and local taxes and Social Security contributions]

COUNTRY	TAX REVENUES, 1989		PERCENT CHANGE IN TOTAL TAX REVENUE AS EXPRESSED IN NATIONAL CURRENCY					TAX REVENUES AS PERCENT OF GROSS DOMESTIC PRODUCT				
	Total (bil. dol.)	Per capita (dol.)	1980-1989	1985-1986	1986-1987	1987-1988	1988-1989	1980	1985	1987	1988	1989
United States	1,522.2	6,119	96.6	5.4	10.2	6.7	8.3	29.5	29.2	30.2	29.8	30.1
Australia	88.6	5,269	180.8	12.7	13.8	11.8	8.5	28.5	30.0	30.8	30.3	30.1
Austria	51.8	6,805	67.5	5.1	2.8	4.9	4.3	41.2	43.1	42.6	42.0	41.0
Belgium	67.7	6,813	74.0	4.1	5.0	3.8	4.3	44.4	47.6	47.2	46.1	44.3
Canada	196.9	7,501	130.8	7.7	13.4	8.2	9.8	31.6	33.1	34.8	34.6	35.3
Denmark	52.9	10,314	127.6	12.2	6.6	4.3	2.9	45.5	49.0	51.5	51.1	49.9
Finland	44.0	8,867	197.1	11.0	2.3	18.6	13.1	33.0	37.0	35.9	37.8	38.1
France	421.4	7,503	129.5	6.7	6.4	5.9	7.0	41.7	44.5	44.5	43.9	43.8
Greece	18.0	1,795	481.8	25.4	14.6	12.0	11.9	28.4	35.1	37.5	34.8	33.2
Ireland	12.8	3,629	182.4	8.4	7.5	12.3	1.7	34.0	38.2	39.3	41.2	37.6
Italy	328.8	5,716	285.6	15.7	9.7	12.9	12.6	30.2	34.4	36.3	37.0	37.8
Japan	893.8	7,260	97.5	7.4	9.3	8.6	8.0	25.4	27.6	29.7	30.3	30.6
Luxembourg	3.4	9,017	119.1	3.9	4.4	8.2	10.6	41.0	44.0	42.5	42.2	42.4
Netherlands	103.0	6,936	41.6	4.6	5.1	4.3	0.4	45.8	44.9	48.5	48.4	46.0
New Zealand . . .	16.5	4,931	202.4	21.8	22.2	6.7	13.8	33.1	34.1	37.9	37.4	39.4
Norway	41.4	9,790	112.9	7.9	4.8	3.6	2.5	47.1	47.6	47.9	47.8	45.5
Portugal	15.9	1,624	595.3	32.4	10.4	27.7	20.5	28.7	31.6	31.5	34.6	35.1
Spain	130.9	3,343	323.3	22.0	18.8	12.3	17.4	23.8	28.8	32.6	32.9	34.4
Sweden	106.5	12,537	164.9	15.0	14.0	7.8	11.4	49.1	50.4	56.1	55.5	56.1
Switzerland	56.3	8,381	75.8	8.6	3.0	7.1	5.5	30.8	32.0	32.0	32.6	31.8
Turkey	22.9	416	5,087.2	65.2	57.0	63.6	111.6	21.7	19.7	24.1	22.8	29.0
United Kingdom	306.0	5,349	128.9	6.6	8.3	11.6	7.8	35.3	37.9	37.0	37.0	36.5
West Germany	452.7	7,304	51.5	4.6	4.0	4.5	7.8	38.0	38.0	37.7	37.4	38.1

Source: Organization for Economic Cooperation and Development, Paris, France, *Revenue Statistics of OECD Member Countries*, annual.

No. 1382. Percent Distribution of Tax Receipts, by Type of Tax—Selected Countries: 1980 to 1989

COUNTRY	Total [1]	INCOME AND PROFITS TAXES [2]			SOCIAL SECURITY CONTRIBUTIONS			TAXES ON GOODS AND SERVICES [5]		
		Total [3]	Individual	Corporate	Total [4]	Employees	Employers	Total [3]	General consumption taxes [6]	Taxes on specific goods, services [7]
United States: 1980	100.0	47.0	36.9	10.2	26.2	10.0	15.5	16.6	6.6	7.8
1988	100.0	43.2	34.8	8.4	29.5	11.5	16.8	16.9	7.5	7.3
1989	100.0	44.2	35.7	8.5	29.2	11.5	16.5	16.2	7.4	6.8
Canada: 1980	100.0	46.6	34.1	11.6	10.5	3.7	6.6	32.5	11.5	13.0
1988	100.0	46.2	37.1	8.4	13.8	4.7	8.9	29.8	15.2	10.9
1989	100.0	47.4	38.4	8.5	13.0	4.4	8.4	29.5	15.3	10.6
France: 1980	100.0	18.1	12.9	5.1	42.7	11.1	28.4	30.4	21.1	8.4
1988	100.0	17.4	12.1	5.2	43.3	12.5	27.2	29.5	19.7	8.9
1989	100.0	17.4	11.8	5.5	43.9	13.0	27.2	28.7	19.3	8.6
Italy: 1980	100.0	31.1	23.1	7.8	38.0	6.9	28.4	26.5	15.6	9.7
1988	100.0	35.7	26.8	9.4	33.3	6.6	23.4	28.0	15.2	10.5
1989	100.0	37.1	26.7	10.1	33.2	6.4	23.8	26.9	14.1	10.3
Japan: 1980	100.0	46.1	24.3	21.8	29.1	10.2	14.8	16.3	-	14.1
1988	100.0	47.9	23.2	24.7	28.0	10.0	14.5	12.8	-	11.0
1989	100.0	49.1	24.7	24.4	27.9	10.1	14.5	12.6	3.3	7.6
Netherlands: 1980	100.0	32.8	26.3	6.6	38.1	15.7	17.8	25.2	15.8	7.3
1988	100.0	27.8	20.5	7.3	42.5	18.9	17.1	25.9	16.5	7.1
1989	100.0	28.8	21.1	7.7	41.0	19.0	16.4	26.1	16.3	7.5
Sweden: 1980	100.0	43.5	41.0	2.5	28.8	-	27.6	24.0	13.4	9.2
1988	100.0	43.9	38.8	5.2	25.1	-	24.3	24.2	13.3	10.0
1989	100.0	42.9	39.2	3.8	26.2	-	24.9	24.1	13.6	9.6
United Kingdom: 1980	100.0	38.2	29.8	8.3	16.6	6.7	9.5	29.2	14.4	13.1
1988	100.0	37.4	26.6	10.8	18.5	8.3	9.7	31.1	16.4	13.1
1989	100.0	38.9	26.6	12.3	17.6	7.5	9.5	30.9	16.8	12.5
West Germany: 1980	100.0	35.1	29.6	5.5	34.4	15.3	18.5	27.1	16.6	9.3
1988	100.0	34.2	28.9	5.3	37.4	16.2	19.1	25.2	15.6	8.6
1989	100.0	35.0	29.5	5.5	36.3	15.6	18.5	25.6	15.4	9.0

- Represents zero. [1] Includes property taxes, employer payroll taxes other than Social Security contributions, and miscellaneous taxes, not shown separately. [2] Includes taxes on capital gains. [3] Includes other taxes, not shown separately. [4] Includes contributions of self-employed, not shown separately. [5] Taxes on the production, sales, transfer, leasing and delivery of goods and services and rendering of services. [6] Primary value-added and sales taxes. [7] For example, excise taxes on alcohol, tobacco, and gasoline.

Source: Organization for Economic Cooperation and Development, Paris, France, *Revenue Statistics of OECD Member Countries*, annual.

No. 1383. Employee-Employer Payroll Tax Rates for Social Security Programs—Selected Countries: 1981 to 1989

[In percent. Covers old-age, disability and survivors insurance, public health or sickness insurance, workers' compensation, unemployment insurance, and family allowance programs]

COUNTRY	ALL SOCIAL SECURITY PROGRAMS					OLD-AGE, DISABILITY AND SURVIVORS INSURANCE				
	1981, total	1985, total	1989			1981, total	1985, total	1989		
			Total	Employ-er	Employ-ee			Total	Employ-er	Employ-ee
United States ...	17.60	18.90	19.72	12.21	7.51	10.70	11.40	12.12	6.06	6.06
Austria	35.80	39.90	42.40	24.20	18.20	21.10	22.78	22.80	12.55	10.25
Belguim........	34.70	39.71	52.94	40.24	12.70	15.11	16.36	16.36	8.86	7.50
Canada	[1]7.92	[1]9.24	[1]8.88	[1]4.83	4.05	3.60	3.60	4.20	2.10	2.10
France	47.55	51.23	53.03	36.96	16.07	[2]13.00	[2]14.00	[2]15.90	[2]8.20	[2]7.70
Ireland........	14.95	23.60	21.76	14.01	7.75	12.00	20.7	18.83	12.33	6.50
Italy	54.30	55.91	53.11	45.16	8.05	24.46	24.36	25.21	18.06	7.15
Japan	[3]21.41	[3]21.61	[3]23.40	[3]12.45	10.95	[4]10.60	[4]10.60	[4]12.40	[4]6.20	[4]6.20
Luxembourg.....	34.25	34.30	30.20	18.00	12.20	16.00	16.00	16.00	8.00	8.00
Netherlands.....	54.85	51.18	43.03	21.93	21.10	32.45	24.63	21.90	6.20	15.70
Sweden........	32.65	30.45	34.11	34.11	-	21.15	19.95	20.95	20.95	-
Switzerland	11.9	12.0	12.2	7.1	5.1	9.40	9.4	9.60	4.80	4.80
United Kingdom ..	21.45	19.45	19.45	10.45	9.00	(NA)	(NA)	(NA)	(NA)	(NA)
West Germany ...	34.80	34.30	36.18	18.73	17.40	18.50	18.70	18.70	9.35	9.35

- Represents zero.   NA Not available.   [1] Excludes work-injury compensation program.   [2] Disability and survivors benefits financed through sickness insurance.   [3] Rate refers to male employees and contributions for employee pension and health insurance only.   [4] Rate refers to male employees and contributions for employee pension insurance only.
Source: U.S. Social Security Administration, Office of International Policy, unpublished data.

No. 1384. Consumer Prices—Annual Percent Changes, by Country: 1986 to 1991

[See text, section 31, for general comments concerning the data. For additional qualifications of the data for individual countries, see source. Minus sign (-) indicates decrease]

COUNTRY	1986-1987	1987-1988	1988-1989	1989-1990	1990-1991	COUNTRY	1986-1987	1987-1988	1988-1989	1989-1990	1990-1991
United States..	3.7	4.0	4.8	5.4	4.2	Kenya	5.2	8.3	9.8	11.7	14.8
Argentina	131.7	343.0	3,080	2,314	(NA)	Malaysia	0.9	2.6	2.8	2.6	4.4
Australia......	8.5	7.2	7.6	7.3	7.2	Mexico.......	131.8	114.2	20.0	26.7	22.7
Austria	1.4	1.9	2.6	3.3	3.3	Netherlands ...	-0.7	0.7	1.1	2.5	3.9
Bangladesh....	9.5	9.3	10.0	8.1	7.2	Nigeria	10.2	54.5	50.5	7.4	13.0
Belgium......	1.6	1.2	3.1	3.4	3.2	Norway.......	8.7	6.7	4.6	4.1	3.4
Bolivia	14.6	16.0	15.0	17.0	21.0	Pakistan......	4.7	8.8	7.8	9.1	6.6
Brazil	229.7	682.3	1,287	2,938	440.8	Peru........	85.8	667.0	3,399	7,482	409.5
Canada	4.4	4.0	5.0	4.8	5.6	Philippines	3.8	8.8	12.2	14.1	18.7
Chile	19.9	14.7	17.0	26.0	21.8	Portugal	9.4	9.6	12.6	13.4	11.4
Colombia	23.3	28.1	25.8	29.1	30.4	Romania	(NA)	2.8	0.7	4.2	(NA)
Ecuador.....	29.5	58.2	75.6	48.5	48.7	South Africa ...	16.1	12.8	14.7	14.4	15.3
Egypt.......	19.7	17.7	21.3	16.8	19.8	South Korea ...	3.0	7.1	5.7	8.6	9.7
France.......	3.3	2.7	3.5	3.4	3.1	Spain	5.3	4.8	6.8	6.7	5.9
Ghana	39.8	31.4	25.2	37.3	(NA)	Sri Lanka	7.7	14.0	11.6	21.5	12.2
Greece.......	16.4	13.5	13.7	20.4	19.5	Sweden	4.2	5.8	6.4	10.5	9.3
Guatemala	12.3	10.8	11.4	41.2	(NA)	Switzerland	1.4	1.9	3.2	5.4	5.8
India	8.8	9.4	6.4	9.0	13.9	Thailand......	2.5	3.9	5.4	5.9	(NA)
Indonesia	9.3	8.0	6.4	7.5	9.2	Turkey	38.8	75.4	63.3	60.3	(NA)
Iran	28.6	28.7	22.3	7.6	17.1	United Kingdom .	4.1	4.9	7.8	9.5	5.9
Israel	19.8	16.3	20.2	17.2	19.0	Venezuela.....	28.1	29.5	84.2	40.8	34.2
Italy........	4.7	5.1	6.3	6.4	6.4	West Germany.	0.2	1.3	2.8	2.7	3.5
Japan........	-	0.7	2.3	3.1	3.3	Zaire	90.4	82.7	104.1	81.3	2,155

- Represents or rounds to zero.   NA Not available.
Source: International Monetary Fund, Washington, DC, *International Financial Statistics*, monthly.

No. 1385. Civilian Employment-Population Ratios, by Sex, and Females as Percent of Total Civilian Employment—Selected Countries: 1970 to 1990

[See headnote, table 1386]

COUNTRY	CIVILIAN EMPLOYMENT-POPULATION RATIOS [1]										FEMALES AS PERCENT OF CIVILIAN EMPLOYMENT				
	Women					Men									
	1970	1980	1985	1989	1990	1970	1980	1985	1989	1990	1970	1980	1985	1989	1990
United States.....	40.8	47.7	50.4	54.3	54.4	76.2	72.0	70.9	72.5	71.9	37.7	42.4	44.1	45.2	45.4
Australia.........	39.3	41.9	42.9	48.6	49.3	83.2	75.1	70.4	72.0	71.3	32.4	36.4	38.4	40.8	41.3
Canada	36.1	46.2	48.8	53.3	53.7	73.4	73.0	68.7	71.1	69.8	33.6	39.7	42.7	44.1	44.7
France	38.1	40.1	39.6	[2]40.1	[2]40.4	76.3	68.5	62.3	[2]61.0	[2]61.3	36.0	39.5	41.4	[2]42.3	[2]42.3
Germany [3]	(NA)	37.7	37.1	[2]39.5	[2]40.2	(NA)	70.9	66.4	[2]65.6	[2]65.3	(NA)	38.0	39.0	[2]40.2	[2]40.8
Italy............	25.0	27.9	27.8	28.6	[2]29.0	71.9	66.0	62.5	59.9	[2]60.5	27.7	31.7	32.8	34.3	[2]34.5
Japan...........	48.2	45.7	46.3	47.4	48.0	80.5	77.9	75.9	75.1	75.4	39.0	38.4	39.4	40.1	40.3
Netherlands	(NA)	31.0	33.4	37.4	(NA)	(NA)	74.1	67.6	66.4	(NA)	(NA)	30.2	34.0	37.0	(NA)
Sweden	49.1	58.0	59.7	62.8	[2]62.8	77.4	73.6	70.5	71.9	[2]71.8	39.5	45.2	47.2	47.8	[2]47.8
United Kingdom....	41.2	44.8	44.3	[2]49.1	[2]49.8	79.2	72.8	67.1	[2]70.5	[2]70.4	36.7	40.4	42.0	[2]43.1	[2]43.5

NA Not available.   [1] Civilian employment as a percent of the civilian working age population.   [2] Break in series.   [3] Former West Germany (prior ot unification).
Source: U.S. Bureau of Labor Statistics, *Comparative Labor Force Statistics for Ten Countries, 1959-1990*, November 1991.

No. 1386. Civilian Labor Force, Employment, and Unemployment—Selected Countries: 1970 to 1990

[Data based on U.S. labor force definitions adopted in 1967 (see text, section 13) except that minimum age for population base varies as follows: United States, France, Sweden, and, beginning 1980, United Kingdom, 16 years; Australia, Canada, Japan, Netherlands, Germany, and, for 1970, United Kingdom, 15 years; Italy, 14 years]

YEAR	United States	Aus-tralia	Canada	France	Ger-many [1]	Italy	Japan	Nether-lands	Sweden	United King-dom
Civilian labor force (mil.):										
1970	82.8	5.5	8.4	20.8	26.2	19.7	50.7	(NA)	3.9	25.1
1980	106.9	6.7	11.6	22.8	27.3	21.1	55.7	5.9	4.3	26.5
1981	108.7	6.8	11.9	23.0	27.5	21.3	56.3	6.1	4.3	26.6
1982	110.2	6.9	11.9	23.2	27.7	21.4	57.0	6.2	4.4	26.6
1983	111.6	7.0	12.1	23.1	[2]27.7	21.6	58.1	[2]6.1	4.4	26.6
1984	113.5	7.1	12.3	23.3	27.8	21.7	58.5	6.2	4.4	27.0
1985	115.5	7.3	12.5	23.4	28.0	21.8	58.8	6.2	4.4	27.2
1986	117.8	7.6	12.7	23.4	28.2	[2]22.3	59.4	6.4	4.4	27.4
1987	119.9	7.8	13.0	23.6	28.4	22.4	60.0	6.5	[2]4.5	27.7
1988	121.7	8.0	13.3	23.6	[3]28.6	22.7	60.9	6.5	4.5	28.2
1989	123.9	8.2	13.5	23.7	[3]28.8	22.5	61.9	[3]6.6	4.6	[3]28.4
1990	124.8	8.5	13.7	23.9	[3]29.4	[3]22.7	63.0	[3]6.8	4.6	[3]28.6
Labor force participation rate: [4]										
1970	60.4	62.1	57.8	57.5	56.9	49.0	64.5	(NA)	64.0	61.1
1980	63.8	62.1	64.1	57.2	54.7	48.2	62.6	55.4	66.9	62.5
1981	63.9	61.9	64.8	57.1	54.7	48.3	62.6	56.7	66.8	62.2
1982	64.0	61.7	64.1	57.1	54.6	47.7	62.7	56.6	66.8	61.9
1983	64.0	61.4	64.4	56.6	[2]54.3	47.5	63.1	[2]55.7	66.7	61.6
1984	64.4	61.5	64.8	56.6	54.4	47.3	62.7	55.7	66.6	62.1
1985	64.8	61.6	65.3	56.3	54.7	47.2	62.3	55.5	66.9	62.2
1986	65.3	62.8	65.7	56.1	54.9	[2]47.8	62.1	55.8	67.0	62.2
1987	65.6	63.0	66.2	55.9	55.0	47.6	61.9	56.3	[2]67.1	62.6
1988	65.9	63.3	66.7	55.5	[3]55.1	47.4	61.9	56.1	67.6	63.4
1989	66.5	64.2	67.0	[3]55.3	[3]54.9	47.3	62.2	[3]56.4	68.0	[3]63.9
1990	66.4	64.7	67.0	[3]55.4	[3]54.9	[3]47.3	62.6	[3]57.3	[3]68.2	[3]64.1
Civilian employment (mil.):										
1970	78.7	5.4	7.9	20.3	26.1	19.1	50.1	(NA)	3.8	24.3
1980	99.3	6.3	10.7	21.3	26.5	20.2	54.6	5.5	4.2	24.7
1981	100.4	6.4	11.0	21.2	26.4	20.3	55.1	5.6	4.2	23.8
1982	99.5	6.4	10.6	21.2	26.2	20.2	55.6	5.5	4.2	23.6
1983	100.8	6.3	10.7	21.2	[2]25.8	20.3	56.6	[2]5.4	4.2	23.4
1984	105.0	6.5	10.9	21.0	25.8	20.4	56.9	5.5	4.2	23.8
1985	107.2	6.7	11.2	20.9	26.0	20.5	57.3	5.6	4.3	24.2
1986	109.6	7.0	11.5	21.0	26.4	[2]20.6	57.7	5.7	4.3	24.3
1987	112.4	7.1	11.9	21.0	26.6	20.6	58.3	5.8	[2]4.4	24.9
1988	115.0	7.4	12.2	21.2	[3]26.8	20.9	59.3	5.9	4.5	25.7
1989	117.3	7.7	12.5	21.5	[3]27.2	20.8	60.5	[3]6.1	4.5	[3]26.4
1990	117.9	7.9	12.6	21.7	[3]27.9	[3]21.1	61.7	[3]6.2	4.6	[3]26.6
Employment-population ratio: [5]										
1970	57.4	61.1	54.5	56.0	56.6	47.4	63.8	(NA)	63.1	59.2
1980	59.2	58.3	59.3	53.5	53.1	46.1	61.3	52.1	65.6	58.1
1981	59.0	58.4	59.9	52.8	52.5	45.9	61.2	51.7	65.1	55.7
1982	57.8	57.3	57.1	52.3	51.6	45.2	61.2	50.8	64.7	54.9
1983	57.9	55.3	56.8	51.8	[2]50.6	44.7	61.4	[2]49.3	64.4	54.3
1984	59.5	56.0	57.5	51.0	50.5	44.5	61.0	49.3	64.5	54.8
1985	60.1	56.5	58.5	50.4	50.7	44.4	60.6	50.1	65.0	55.2
1986	60.7	57.7	59.4	50.2	51.3	[2]44.2	60.4	50.3	65.2	55.2
1987	61.5	57.9	60.4	49.9	51.5	43.8	60.1	50.7	[2]65.8	56.2
1988	62.3	58.7	61.6	49.8	[3]51.6	43.7	60.4	50.8	66.5	58.0
1989	63.0	60.2	62.0	[3]50.0	[3]51.8	43.6	60.8	[3]51.6	67.1	[3]59.3
1990	62.7	60.2	61.5	[3]50.3	[3]52.1	[3]44.0	61.3	[3]52.7	[3]67.2	[3]59.6
Unemployment rate:										
1970	4.9	1.6	5.7	2.5	0.5	3.2	1.2	(NA)	1.5	3.1
1980	7.1	6.1	7.5	6.4	2.8	4.4	2.0	6.0	2.0	7.0
1981	7.6	5.8	7.5	7.6	4.0	4.9	2.2	8.9	2.5	10.5
1982	9.7	7.2	11.0	8.3	5.6	5.4	2.4	10.2	3.1	11.3
1983	9.6	10.0	11.8	8.5	[2]6.9	5.9	2.7	[2]11.4	3.5	11.8
1984	7.5	9.0	11.2	10.0	7.1	5.9	2.8	11.5	3.1	11.8
1985	7.2	8.3	10.5	10.4	7.2	6.0	2.6	9.6	2.8	11.2
1986	7.0	8.1	9.5	10.6	6.6	[2]7.5	2.8	9.7	2.6	11.2
1987	6.2	8.1	8.8	10.7	6.3	7.9	2.9	10.0	[2]1.9	10.3
1988	5.5	7.2	7.8	10.2	[3]6.3	7.9	2.5	9.3	1.6	8.6
1989, total	5.3	6.2	7.5	9.6	[3]5.7	7.8	2.3	[3]8.6	1.3	[3]7.1
1990, total	5.5	6.9	8.1	9.2	[3]5.2	[3]7.0	2.1	[3]8.0	1.5	[3]6.9
Under 25 years old	11.1	13.1	12.8	(NA)	(NA)	21.8	[3]4.2	(NA)	3.5	[6]10.1
Teenagers [7]	15.5	16.9	14.2	(NA)	(NA)	27.3	[3]6.8	(NA)	4.5	[6]11.5
20 to 24 years old	8.8	10.2	11.8	(NA)	(NA)	19.2	[3]3.6	(NA)	3.0	[6]9.3
25 years old and over	4.4	5.1	7.0	(NA)	(NA)	4.3	[3]1.8	(NA)	1.2	[6]5.9

NA Not available. [1] Former West Germany (prior to unification). [2] Preliminary [3] Break in series. [4] Civilian labor force as a percent of the civilian working age population. [5] Civilian employment as a percent of the civilian working age population. [6] French data are for March; Italian data are for April; United Kingdom data are for April-June. [7] 16 to 19 years old in the United States, France, Sweden, and the United Kingdom; 15 to 19 years old in Canada, Australia, and Japan; and 14 to 19 years old in Italy and Germany.

Source: U.S. Bureau of Labor Statistics, *Comparative Labor Force Statistics for Ten Countries, 1959-1990*, November 1991, and *Monthly Labor Review*.

No. 1387. Labor Force Participation Rates, by Sex and Age-Group—Selected Countries: 1980 and 1990

[Participation rates represent percent of population of each specified group in labor force]

COUNTRY AND SEX	15 TO 19 YEARS OLD		20 TO 24 YEARS OLD		25 TO 54 YEARS OLD		55 TO 64 YEARS OLD		65 YEARS AND OVER	
	1980	1990	1980	1990	1980	1990	1980	1990	1980	1990
United States: Total	[1]56.5	53.9	77.5	77.9	78.4	83.2	55.1	55.4	11.9	11.2
Male	[1]60.5	55.9	85.7	84.0	93.4	92.6	71.2	67.1	18.3	15.8
Female	[1]52.4	51.7	69.1	71.6	63.8	73.9	41.0	45.0	7.6	8.1
Canada: Total	55.1	57.5	79.6	79.7	77.4	84.3	53.9	49.9	8.9	7.1
Male	57.9	58.9	86.3	82.8	94.8	93.3	76.2	64.9	14.8	11.4
Female	52.2	55.9	73.0	76.5	60.1	75.6	33.6	35.7	4.4	3.9
France: Total	22.0	11.4	73.7	61.3	79.8	81.3	53.4	38.2	5.0	2.4
Male	25.7	14.5	80.2	65.1	96.4	90.1	68.5	45.8	7.5	3.7
Female	18.3	8.1	67.5	57.4	63.0	72.6	39.7	31.3	3.3	1.5
Germany [2]: Total	43.9	(NA)	73.8	(NA)	74.0	(NA)	42.8	(NA)	4.5	(NA)
Male	47.0	(NA)	79.2	(NA)	93.6	(NA)	65.5	(NA)	7.0	(NA)
Female	40.5	(NA)	68.0	(NA)	53.6	(NA)	27.2	(NA)	3.1	(NA)
Italy: Total	31.1	23.1	65.1	66.5	[3]65.9	69.5	[4]24.5	22.3	7.5	4.6
Male	33.3	24.7	72.5	70.2	[3]93.1	90.7	[4]39.6	35.9	12.6	8.0
Female	28.9	21.4	57.9	62.8	[3]39.9	49.0	[4]11.0	10.1	3.5	2.2
Japan: Total	17.9	18.1	69.8	73.4	76.8	80.9	63.0	64.7	26.3	24.3
Male	17.4	18.3	69.6	71.7	97.0	97.5	85.4	83.3	41.0	36.5
Female	18.5	17.8	70.0	75.1	56.7	64.2	45.3	47.2	15.5	16.2
Sweden: Total	55.6	49.1	83.1	82.7	89.3	91.3	66.8	70.7	8.6	8.5
Male	55.3	47.7	84.5	84.7	95.4	94.9	78.7	75.4	14.2	12.3
Female	55.8	50.6	81.6	80.6	82.9	91.3	55.3	66.3	3.7	5.1
United Kingdom: Total	74.4	72.5	77.1	80.7	79.5	83.4	59.4	53.1	6.2	5.4
Male	73.6	74.2	86.0	86.3	95.4	93.6	81.6	68.1	10.3	8.6
Female	75.3	70.7	67.9	74.8	63.4	73.0	39.1	38.9	3.6	3.3

NA Not available. [1] Persons 16 to 19 years old. [2] Former West Germany (prior to unification). [3] Persons 25 to 59 years old. [4] Persons 60 to 64 years old.

Source: Organization for Economic Cooperation and Development, Paris, France, *Labour Force Statistics*, annual.

No. 1388. Organization for Economic Cooperation and Development (OECD)—Index of Industrial Production: 1980 to 1990

[Industrial production index measures output in the manufacturing, mining, and electric and gas utilities industries. Minus sign (-) indicates decrease. For explanation of average annual percent change, see Guide to Tabular Presentation]

COUNTRY	INDEX (1985=100)							AVERAGE ANNUAL PERCENT CHANGE					
	1980	1984	1986	1987	1988	1989	1990	1980-1990	1985-1986	1986-1987	1987-1988	1988-1989	1989-1990
OECD, total	90.6	97.3	101.1	104.8	110.8	114.8	116.9	2.6	1.1	3.6	5.7	3.7	1.8
United States	89.1	98.3	100.9	105.9	111.7	114.5	115.7	2.6	0.9	5.0	5.4	2.6	1.0
Australia [1]	98.1	96.2	101.0	102.0	105.4	111.2	111.0	1.2	1.0	1.0	3.3	5.5	-0.1
Austria	92.2	95.7	101.1	102.1	106.6	112.9	121.2	2.8	1.1	1.0	4.4	6.0	7.4
Belgium [2]	96.0	97.6	100.8	103.0	109.7	113.4	118.3	2.1	0.8	2.1	6.5	3.4	4.3
Canada [2]	86.2	94.7	99.3	104.1	109.8	109.6	104.9	2.0	-0.7	4.9	5.5	-0.1	-4.3
Finland	86.0	96.1	100.8	105.0	111.1	113.8	113.9	2.8	0.8	4.2	5.8	2.4	0.1
France [3]	101.9	95.8	100.9	102.8	107.6	112.0	113.6	1.1	0.9	1.9	4.6	4.1	1.5
Germany [3]	97.2	95.7	102.1	102.5	106.2	111.5	117.2	1.9	2.1	0.4	3.6	5.0	5.1
Greece	92.5	96.0	99.0	97.5	102.5	104.4	101.9	0.4	-1.0	-1.5	5.2	1.8	-2.4
Ireland	78.0	86.8	96.8	102.3	111.3	123.2	137.5	6.3	2.2	8.9	10.7	11.6	4.7
Italy	103.2	98.7	104.1	106.8	114.2	118.7	117.9	1.3	-0.2	2.6	6.9	3.9	-0.7
Japan	84.4	96.5	99.8	103.3	112.8	119.7	125.4	4.0	-0.2	3.4	9.3	6.0	4.7
Luxembourg	82.3	93.5	101.9	101.2	110.0	118.6	118.0	3.7	1.9	-0.6	8.7	7.8	-0.5
Netherlands	94.6	95.8	100.2	101.3	101.3	106.5	109.0	1.4	0.2	1.1	-0.1	5.1	2.4
Norway	82.4	94.8	103.5	111.3	117.0	136.1	141.1	5.5	3.5	7.5	5.1	16.3	3.7
Portugal	84.9	99.3	107.3	112.0	116.2	124.1	135.2	4.8	7.3	4.4	3.8	6.7	9.0
Spain	96.7	98.1	103.1	107.8	111.1	116.1	116.2	1.9	3.1	4.6	3.1	4.5	(Z)
Sweden [4]	90.2	97.1	100.4	103.0	104.3	108.1	105.2	1.6	-0.4	2.5	1.3	3.7	-2.7
Switzerland [5]	96.8	94.7	103.8	105.0	111.6	114.9	118.0	2.0	3.8	1.2	6.2	3.0	2.7
United Kingdom	92.5	94.9	102.3	105.7	109.7	109.9	109.2	1.7	2.3	3.3	3.8	0.2	-0.6

Z Less than .05 percent. [1] Index of Real Gross Product in industry. [2] Gross domestic product in industry at factor cost and 1986 prices. [3] Former West Germany (prior to unification). [4] Mining and manufacturing. [5] Exludes mining and quarrying.

Source: Organization for Economic Cooperation and Development, Paris, France, *Main Economic Indicators, Historical Statistics, 1969-1988*, 1990; and *Main Economic Indicators*, monthly.

No. 1389. International Economic Composite Indexes—Average Annual Percent Change: 1979 to 1991

[The coincident index changes are for calendar years and the leading index changes are for years ending June 30 because they lead the coincident indexes by about 6 months, on average. The G-7 countries are United States, Canada, France, Germany, Italy, United Kingdom and Japan. Average annual percent changes derived from indexes with base 1980=100. Minus sign (-) indicates decrease]

COUNTRIES	1979-1980	1980-1981	1981-1982	1982-1983	1983-1984	1984-1985	1985-1986	1986-1987	1987-1988	1988-1989	1989-1990	1990-1991
LEADING INDEX												
Total, 11 countries	2.3	-0.8	-0.9	1.4	9.5	2.8	2.1	4.7	7.9	5.1	2.3	-1.6
10 countries, excluding U.S.	6.5	-2.0	0.6	0.7	6.0	4.4	1.8	5.2	8.1	5.7	3.2	-0.9
G-7 countries	2.2	-0.9	-0.9	1.4	9.5	2.6	2.0	4.5	7.8	5.0	2.2	-1.6
North America	-3.0	1.2	-3.4	2.4	14.2	1.0	2.5	4.0	7.4	4.0	0.6	-2.9
United States	-3.3	0.9	-3.0	3.0	14.3	0.9	2.5	4.0	7.3	3.9	0.5	-3.1
Canada	3.2	1.1	-6.4	0.5	11.9	4.4	3.0	2.6	5.4	1.1	-2.4	-5.2
4 European countries.	2.8	-1.4	0.6	1.2	4.2	2.3	2.4	3.6	3.1	4.1	1.3	1.0
France. . , ...	4.5	-0.6	0.9	0.8	3.8	2.6	2.1	6.1	5.2	5.6	-	1.8
Germany [1]	2.7	-2.9	-1.0	2.0	6.1	2.0	2.9	1.6	3.5	5.3	4.5	3.7
Italy.	3.6	4.8	-0.1	-1.2	1.9	2.3	5.3	3.8	0.3	1.2	0.4	-1.8
United Kingdom.	0.5	-4.3	3.6	2.2	3.3	2.1	0.4	3.4	2.2	2.3	-1.2	-2.0
5 Pacific region countries	13.9	-3.4	1.7	-0.2	8.3	7.6	0.9	7.8	15.9	8.8	6.2	-2.5
Australia.	6.0	2.0	-4.1	-4.0	9.9	6.7	2.9	3.4	7.2	4.8	-1.5	-3.7
China: Taiwan	4.8	5.7	5.0	8.1	11.8	6.4	8.2	13.5	14.6	12.2	7.4	1.3
Japan	16.6	-4.9	2.0	-0.5	7.9	8.0	-0.2	7.7	17.6	9.0	7.2	-2.9
South Korea	-2.4	5.0	6.8	8.0	9.3	4.6	9.7	16.7	12.8	8.9	4.0	3.0
New Zealand	1.8	0.5	2.9	-1.7	6.4	5.3	-1.1	2.8	-1.5	0.9	1.6	-3.1
COINCIDENT INDEX												
Total, 11 countries	0.2	0.5	-1.9	1.7	6.0	3.8	3.3	4.2	6.0	4.8	3.6	0.1
10 countries, excluding U.S.	2.4	0.5	0.7	1.2	3.7	4.0	3.6	4.3	6.7	6.0	5.6	2.6
G-7 countries	0.1	0.3	-2.0	1.8	5.8	3.7	3.1	4.1	5.9	4.7	3.6	0.1
North America	-2.5	0.7	-5.6	2.4	9.2	3.7	2.8	4.1	5.1	2.7	0.2	-4.0
United States	-2.7	0.5	-5.6	2.3	9.6	3.5	2.5	4.1	4.9	2.8	0.2	-4.1
Canada	2.0	3.8	-4.8	2.0	6.3	5.2	3.5	4.9	5.8	2.7	0.3	-3.7
4 European countries.	1.5	-1.7	-0.3	0.6	2.0	2.9	3.6	3.8	5.9	5.7	5.7	2.1
France.	1.4	0.3	2.9	1.9	0.5	1.5	3.8	5.1	7.8	8.6	7.1	3.6
Germany [1]	2.6	-0.9	-2.4	-0.6	2.7	3.5	4.3	3.0	3.6	5.1	6.8	4.5
Italy.	5.3	-1.4	-0.3	-1.1	3.5	2.4	1.7	1.5	5.3	2.1	4.6	1.9
United Kingdom.	-2.0	-5.4	-0.8	1.6	2.2	4.2	3.3	5.0	7.3	5.6	3.0	-3.3
5 Pacific region countries	3.8	3.6	2.9	2.2	5.7	5.4	3.8	4.8	7.9	7.0	6.4	4.1
Australia.	4.9	5.9	-2.5	-6.8	9.2	7.5	5.2	3.5	7.7	10.6	0.6	-7.9
China: Taiwan	7.1	5.1	2.9	7.4	12.0	4.9	10.8	11.6	6.0	6.1	1.7	4.8
Japan	4.1	3.1	3.5	2.6	4.9	5.1	3.0	4.2	7.9	6.8	7.2	5.2
South Korea	-5.0	6.6	6.2	11.4	9.0	5.5	11.9	13.9	10.8	6.1	8.5	7.6
New Zealand	2.0	2.4	0.9	0.8	3.6	2.1	1.4	1.4	-1.0	-0.4	1.3	-1.1

- Represents or rounds to zero. [1] Former West Germany (prior to unification).
Source: Center for International Business Cycle Research, Columbia Business School, New York, NY, *International Economic Indicators*, monthly.

No. 1390. Patents, Top Countries: 1990

[Includes only U.S. patents granted to residents of areas outside of the United States and its territories]

TOP COUNTRIES	Total [1]	Inventions	Designs	TOP COUNTRIES	Total [1]	Inventions	Designs
Total, foreign country residents	**46,223**	**42,973**	**2,956**	Sweden	885	768	114
Japan	20,726	19,524	1,137	China: Taiwan	861	732	129
Germany	7,858	7,610	182	Australia	517	432	81
France	3,093	2,866	184	Austria	423	393	29
United Kingdom.	3,015	2,790	202	Belgium	352	313	37
Canada	2,089	1,861	213	Israel	311	299	7
Italy.	1,499	1,260	227	Denmark	204	158	43
Switzerland.	1,347	1,284	57	Finland	315	304	10
Netherlands	1,044	958	46	South Korea	289	224	65
				Other countries	1,395	1,197	193

[1] Includes patents for botanical plants and reissues, not shown separately.
Source: U.S. Patent and Trademark Office, *Technology Assessment and Forecast Data Base*.

No. 1391. World's 500 Largest Industrial Corporations: 1989

[Sales as of December 31, 1989, assets as of company's fiscal year-end. Companies must have derived more than 50% of their sales from manufacturing and/or mining. Sales of consolidated subsidiaries are included and exclude excise taxes collected by manufacturers. Profits are shown after taxes and extraordinary credits or charges]

COUNTRY	Number of companies	Sales ($1,000)	Profits ($1,000)	Assets ($1,000)	Employees (1,000)	COUNTRY	Number of companies	Sales ($1,000)	Profits ($1,000)	Assets ($1,000)	Employees (1,000)
Australia. . . .	10	50.6	2.9	67.7	257.7	Netherlands . .	6	50.8	2.3	52.0	477.9
Canada	13	65.9	5.2	88.5	419.2	South Korea .	11	102.6	1.4	111.2	500.0
Finland	7	26.7	1.2	34.4	138.6	Sweden	15	81.5	3.9	86.2	631.9
France.	29	264.7	12.1	311.5	1,763.9	Switzerland. .	10	96.0	4.8	106.6	707.9
India	6	29.2	1.8	27.5	967.1	U.S.	167	1,714.8	85.1	1,883.2	9,539.6
Italy.	8	154.1	5.8	147.0	1,046.7	U.K.	45	443.9	34.4	419.1	3,131.7
Japan	111	925.3	25.2	936.4	2,952.2	W. Germany .	32	372.1	10.3	314.6	2,861.7

Source: Time Warner, New York, NY, *The Fortune Directories*, (copyright).

No. 1392. Indexes of Hourly Compensation Costs for Production Workers in Manufacturing—Selected Countries: 1980 to 1990

[United States= 100. Compensation costs include pay for time worked, other direct pay, employer expenditures for legally required insurance programs and contractual and private benefit plans, and for some countries, other labor taxes. Data adjusted for exchange rates. Area averages are trade-weighted to account for difference in countries' relative importance to U.S. trade in manufactured goods. The trade weights used are the sum of U.S. imports of manufactured products for consumption (customs value) and U.S. domestic exports of manufactured products (f.a.s. value) in 1986; see source for detail]

AREA OR COUNTRY	1980	1985	1987	1988	1989	1990	AREA OR COUNTRY	1980	1985	1987	1988	1989	1990
United States	100	100	100	100	100	100	China: Taiwan	10	12	17	20	25	27
							Austria [6]	87	56	97	100	95	115
Total [1]	(NA)	54	74	81	81	88	Belgium.	133	69	111	112	106	128
OECD [2]	83	64	90	98	97	105	Denmark	110	62	108	109	101	121
Europe [3]	102	62	101	105	100	118	Finland [7]	83	63	99	112	116	141
Asian newly industrial-							France	91	58	91	93	88	103
izing economies [4] . .	12	12	15	18	23	25	Germany [6][8]	125	74	126	131	124	146
Canada.	85	83	88	97	103	108	Greece	38	28	34	38	38	46
Brazil	14	9	10	10	12	18	Ireland	[9]60	46	69	72	68	80
Mexico [5]	(NA)	12	8	9	11	12	Italy	81	57	91	94	95	111
Australia	86	63	70	81	86	88	Luxembourg.	121	59	96	99	95	(NA)
Hong Kong [5]	15	13	15	17	19	22	Netherlands	122	67	112	114	105	123
Israel	38	31	47	55	54	58	Norway	118	81	128	136	131	148
Japan	57	49	80	92	88	86	Portugal	21	12	19	20	20	25
South Korea.	10	10	12	17	23	26	Spain	60	37	58	63	64	79
New Zealand	54	34	50	59	55	56	Sweden.	127	74	112	121	122	142
Singapore	15	19	17	19	22	26	Switzerland	112	74	126	129	117	141
Sri Lanka.	2	2	2	2	2	(NA)	United Kingdom	75	48	66	75	73	84

NA Not available.   [1] The 27 foreign economies for which 1990 data are available.   [2] Canada, Australia, Japan, New Zealand, and the 16 European countries for which 1990 data are available.   [3] The 16 European countries for which 1990 data are available.   [4] Hong Kong, South Korea, Singapore, and China: Taiwan.   [5] Average of selected manufacturing industries.   [6] Excludes workers in establishments considered handicraft manufactures (including all printing and publishing and miscellaneous manufacturing in Austria).   [7] Includes workers in mining and electrical power plants.   [8] Former West Germany (prior to unification).   [9] Data refer to September.

Source: Bureau of Labor Statistics, Report 817, November 1991.

No. 1393. Structure of Manufacturing Industry for Selected Countries: 1980 to 1988

[In percent. Contribution of each industry group to total manufacturing production. Based on International Standard Industrial Classification; see text, section 31, and source. Numbers in parentheses refer to ISIC codes]

COUNTRY	Food [1] (3100)	Textile [2] (3200)	Wood [3] (3300)	Paper [4] (3400)	Chemical [5] (3500)	Nonmetal [6] (3600)	Basic metal [7] (3700)	Machinery [8] (3800)	Other (3900)
United States: 1980	14.5	5.6	2.8	7.7	22.2	2.5	6.8	36.6	1.3
1985.	14.1	5.3	2.9	9.1	19.9	2.4	4.5	40.8	1.1
1986.	14.6	5.4	3.1	9.7	17.6	2.5	4.3	41.6	1.1
1987.	14.2	5.6	3.3	9.8	18.4	2.6	4.5	40.5	1.2
1988.	14.1	5.3	3.1	9.8	18.4	2.5	5.1	40.5	1.2
Japan: 1980	11.3	5.4	3.6	6.2	19.3	3.9	11.4	37.7	1.2
1985.	11.0	4.9	2.4	6.1	16.7	3.3	8.5	45.7	1.4
1986.	11.7	5.0	2.5	6.6	15.1	3.4	7.3	47.0	1.4
1987.	11.7	5.0	2.7	6.8	14.8	3.5	7.0	47.1	1.4
1988.	11.1	4.7	2.6	6.7	14.3	3.5	7.4	48.4	1.4
France: 1980.	17.0	6.9	3.1	5.6	21.4	3.5	8.4	32.6	1.3
1985.	17.6	6.9	2.5	6.5	21.6	3.0	7.3	33.3	1.3
1986.	17.9	7.1	2.7	6.9	18.9	3.2	7.0	35.0	1.4
1987.	17.3	6.9	2.8	7.1	18.6	3.3	6.6	36.0	1.3
1988.	16.8	6.4	2.8	7.3	18.4	3.4	7.0	36.6	1.3
Italy: 1980.	12.2	11.4	3.2	4.6	19.7	5.6	10.1	32.5	0.8
1985.	12.6	13.5	2.9	5.4	22.5	4.8	9.6	27.8	0.8
1986.	12.7	13.8	2.9	5.2	21.4	4.7	9.0	29.8	0.6
1987.	12.7	14.0	3.4	5.7	20.1	5.1	8.6	29.8	0.6
1988.	12.2	13.4	3.2	5.7	20.1	4.9	8.1	31.8	0.7
Portugal: 1980	18.2	18.9	6.0	6.3	24.5	6.1	2.2	17.6	0.2
1985.	19.5	18.5	3.6	6.8	28.5	4.8	3.3	15.0	0.2
1986.	20.7	20.4	3.9	7.3	24.1	5.2	2.9	15.3	0.2
1987.	20.4	20.8	4.2	8.0	22.0	5.5	2.9	15.9	0.2
1988.	(NA)	(NA)	(NA)	(NA)	(NA)	(NA)	(NA)	(NA)	(NA)
Sweden: 1980	13.3	2.6	8.1	13.5	15.3	2.6	8.5	35.8	0.4
1985.	13.9	2.1	6.4	13.9	15.5	2.1	7.9	37.9	0.3
1986.	14.1	2.1	6.6	14.4	13.3	2.1	7.4	39.6	0.3
1907.	13.6	2.0	6.8	15.3	13.1	2.3	7.1	39.4	0.3
1988.	13.5	1.9	7.0	15.5	12.5	2.3	8.0	39.1	0.3
United Kingdom: 1980. . .	18.6	5.9	2.9	6.8	20.6	3.6	0.0	33.9	0.9
1985.	18.7	5.6	2.7	7.5	21.1	3.5	5.8	34.2	0.9
1986.	19.4	5.8	2.9	8.0	18.4	3.7	5.4	35.4	0.9
1987.	18.2	5.7	3.0	8.1	20.7	3.7	5.3	34.5	0.9
1988.	17.4	5.4	3.2	8.3	19.6	3.9	5.7	35.5	1.0
West Germany: 1980 . . .	12.4	5.4	3.4	4.1	22.9	3.4	7.6	40.3	0.5
1985.	12.2	4.8	2.4	4.2	23.7	2.7	6.6	43.1	0.4
1986.	12.4	4.9	2.6	4.3	21.0	2.8	6.0	45.5	0.5
1987.	12.1	4.8	2.6	4.4	20.7	2.8	5.5	46.6	0.5
1988.	11.7	4.6	2.7	4.4	20.4	2.9	6.1	46.7	0.5

NA Not available.   [1] Manufacture of food, beverages, and tobacco.   [2] Textile, wearing apparel, and leather industries.   [3] Manufacture of wood and wood products including furniture.   [4] Manufacture of paper and paper products; printing and publishing.   [5] Manufacture of chemicals and chemical, petroleum, coal, rubber, and plastic products.   [6] Manufacture of non-metallic products, except petroleum and coal products.   [7] Includes iron and steel basic industries and nonferrous metal basic industries.   [8] Manufacture of fabricated metal products, machinery and equipment.

Source: Organization for Economic Cooperation and Development, Paris, France, OECD Industrial Structure Statistics, 1988.

No. 1394. Selected Indexes of Manufacturing Activity—Selected Countries: 1970 to 1990

[1982=100. Data relate to all employed persons in the United States and Canada; all employees in other countries. Minus sign (-) indicates decrease. For explanation of average annual percent change, see Guide to Tabular Presentation]

INDEX AND YEAR	United States	Bel-gium	Cana-da	Den-mark	France	Ger-many [1]	Italy	Japan	Neth-erlands	Swe-den	United King-dom
Output per hour:											
1970	77.2	44.3	76.9	57.2	58.5	67.0	54.6	52.0	52.9	69.1	70.8
1980	96.6	87.5	99.9	98.0	90.6	98.4	95.5	92.1	93.9	96.4	89.9
1985	114.8	116.4	119.8	105.0	108.8	112.9	122.3	112.0	118.7	112.6	117.8
1988	132.1	129.8	119.6	100.4	120.6	115.4	130.5	126.6	123.4	117.3	137.2
1989	133.3	134.9	120.2	103.1	126.4	120.7	134.5	133.1	126.9	117.6	143.8
1990	136.6	140.5	121.8	105.5	127.7	126.2	138.8	138.0	129.4	118.2	145.0
Average annual percent change:											
1960-1973	3.3	6.9	4.5	6.4	6.4	5.6	6.4	10.2	7.4	6.4	4.2
1973-1990	2.5	5.4	1.7	2.2	3.7	2.8	4.5	4.4	3.9	2.2	3.3
1989-1990	2.5	4.1	1.3	2.3	1.1	4.5	3.2	3.6	1.9	0.5	0.9
Compensation per hour, national currency basis: [2]											
1970	35.8	23.1	28.7	22.3	17.8	34.5	11.6	25.0	27.8	24.4	14.9
1980	83.7	86.3	78.6	83.4	72.8	89.2	70.2	89.0	88.5	84.5	79.7
1985	111.1	121.8	116.8	120.6	130.4	116.3	150.9	110.1	111.5	130.8	122.6
1988	122.9	131.9	130.1	138.1	144.6	131.8	173.1	120.7	119.4	161.4	149.6
1989	127.7	138.9	138.4	144.9	150.6	138.1	189.4	128.0	120.7	176.0	163.8
1990	131.8	148.0	148.1	152.3	156.5	147.7	210 0	134.6	124.6	192.2	182.9
Average annual percent change:											
1960-1973	5.1	11.0	6.2	12.2	10.0	10.3	12.3	15.1	13.0	10.5	9.2
1973-1990	6.8	8.8	8.7	9.1	11.3	6.8	15.7	7.3	6.4	10.7	13.1
1989-1990	3.2	6.6	7.0	5.1	3.9	6.9	10.9	5.2	3.2	9.2	11.7
Real hourly compensation: [2][3]											
1970	89.0	55.1	77.4	70.2	57.3	62.6	60.3	63.6	63.9	72.6	65.8
1980	98.0	101.0	97.9	102.6	92.3	99.9	96.9	96.0	100.0	103.1	97.1
1985	99.7	101.4	101.8	101.4	104.5	107.9	109.3	103.6	102.7	101.9	105.1
1988	100.2	105.6	100.2	102.9	106.5	121.0	107.6	112.0	109.6	110.2	113.5
1989	99.3	107.8	101.5	103.1	107.1	123.3	110.4	116.1	109.4	112.5	115.3
1990	97.3	111.1	103.7	105.6	107.7	128.4	122.4	118.4	110.4	110.4	117.6
Average annual percent change:											
1960-1973	1.9	7.1	2.8	5.6	5.5	6.8	7.3	8.3	7.6	5.4	4.0
1973-1990	0.2	2.6	1.3	1.1	2.8	3.3	2.9	2.1	2.0	1.8	2.5
1989-1990	-2.0	3.0	2.2	2.4	0.5	4.1	10.8	2.0	0.9	-1.9	2.0
Unit labor costs, national currency:											
1970	46.3	52.2	37.3	39.0	30.4	51.4	21.3	48.0	52.7	35.3	21.0
1980	86.7	98.7	78.7	85.1	80.3	90.6	73.5	96.7	94.2	87.7	88.7
1985	96.8	104.7	97.6	114.9	119.9	103.0	123.4	98.4	93.9	116.2	104.0
1988	93.0	101.7	108.7	137.5	119.9	114.2	132.6	95.4	96.8	137.6	109.0
1989	95.8	102.9	115.1	140.6	119.2	114.4	140.8	96.1	95.0	149.6	113.9
1990	96.5	105.4	121.6	144.4	122.6	117.0	151.4	97.5	96.3	162.6	126.1
Average annual percent change:											
1960-1973	1.8	3.8	1.6	5.5	3.4	4.4	5.5	4.4	5.2	3.9	4.8
1973-1990	4.2	3.2	6.9	6.8	7.3	3.9	10.6	2.7	2.4	8.3	9.5
1989-1990	0.7	2.4	5.6	2.7	2.8	2.3	7.5	1.5	1.3	8.7	10.7
Unit labor costs, U.S. dollar basis: [4]											
1970	46.3	48.2	44.1	43.4	36.2	34.2	46.0	33.4	38.9	42.8	28.7
1980	86.7	154.8	83.1	126.2	125.2	121.2	116.3	106.7	126.8	130.2	118.1
1985	96.8	80.8	88.2	90.4	87.8	85.0	87.5	102.7	75.6	84.9	77.2
1988	93.0	126.6	109.1	170.2	132.4	157.8	137.9	185.3	130.8	140.9	111.1
1989	95.8	119.6	120.0	160.2	122.9	147.7	138.9	173.4	119.7	145.7	106.7
1990	96.5	144.4	128.7	194.6	148.0	175.8	171.0	167.5	141.2	172.5	128.7
Average annual percent change:											
1960-1973	1.8	5.8	1.3	6.6	4.2	8.1	6.0	6.7	7.7	5.3	3.7
1973-1990	4.2	4.1	5.9	6.6	6.0	6.9	6.0	6.6	5.0	6.3	7.5
1989-1990	0.7	20.7	7.2	21.5	20.5	19.1	23.1	-3.4	18.0	18.4	20.6
Employment:											
1970	102.4	137.7	96.3	119.6	107.3	115.2	97.6	99.9	135.4	114.7	141.8
1980	107.8	109.9	108.4	103.9	104.9	104.9	107.8	98.5	108.1	107.7	117.5
1985	102.3	95.1	103.6	112.4	92.0	97.4	89.8	106.9	96.5	101.1	91.7
1988	103.0	90.7	114.1	113.1	86.3	99.1	89.4	107.2	100.1	103.0	89.0
1989	103.5	92.6	115.1	112.9	86.6	100.6	89.9	109.7	101.9	100.4	89.0
1990	101.9	91.5	108.9	113.2	87.3	103.5	90.3	112.3	104.0	97.4	88.1
Average annual percent change:											
1960-1973	1.4	0.8	2.0	0.5	1.3	0.5	1.7	3.3	-	0.1	-0.5
1973-1990	-0.3	-2.4	0.3	-0.3	-1.5	-0.6	-0.7	0.4	-1.1	-0.8	-2.5
1989-1990	-1.5	-1.1	-5.4	0.3	0.9	2.9	0.5	2.4	2.0	-3.0	-1.0
Aggregate hours:											
1970	106.5	159.9	102.1	132.3	124.1	129.7	107.0	105.9	152.0	131.7	155.0
1980	109.9	110.1	110.8	103.7	111.0	106.4	108.0	99.3	108.1	106.1	118.1
1985	107.0	92.7	106.0	109.8	91.0	95.6	89.0	108.2	93.6	103.0	93.1
1988	109.4	88.5	117.9	110.5	86.4	95.8	95.8	109.2	96.6	104.6	91.2
1989	109.8	89.9	117.7	109.0	86.2	96.0	96.0	110.5	98.2	105.6	90.7
1990	107.6	90.0	109.9	108.1	86.8	96.6	94.2	111.3	100.1	102.1	89.4
Average annual percent change:											
1960-1973	1.4	-0.3	1.9	-1.1	0.8	-0.5	0.9	2.3	-1.4	-1.3	-1.1
1973-1990	-0.3	-3.0	0.1	-0.7	-2.2	-1.4	-0.8	0.1	-1.8	-1.0	-2.8
1989-1990	-2.0	0.1	-6.6	-0.8	0.7	0.6	-2.0	0.7	2.0	-3.3	-1.3

- Represents or rounds to zero.   [1] Former West Germany (prior to unification).   [2] Compensation includes, but real hourly compensation excludes, adjustments for payroll and employment taxes that are not compensation to employees, but are labor costs to employers.   [3] Index of hourly compensation divided by the index of consumer prices to adjust for changes in purchasing power.   [4] Indexes in national currency adjusted for changes in prevailing exchange rates.

Source: Bureau of Labor Statistics, Office of Productivity and Technology, unpublished data.

No. 1395. Crude Steel Production: 1980 to 1989

[In million metric tons. Data cover both ingots and steel for castings and exclude wrought (puddled) iron]

COUNTRY	1980	1981	1982	1983	1984	1985	1986	1987	1988	1989
World	718.2	708.3	645.1	662.9	708.3	717.1	711.4	731.3	773.3	775.5
United States [1]	101.5	109.6	67.7	76.8	83.9	80.1	74.0	80.9	91.8	88.9
Argentina	2.6	2.4	2.8	2.8	2.5	2.8	3.1	3.5	3.5	[2]3.9
Australia [3]	7.9	8.0	7.3	5.4	4.6	6.3	6.8	6.2	6.1	6.7
Austria	4.6	4.7	4.3	4.4	4.9	4.7	4.3	4.3	4.4	4.9
Belgium	12.3	12.3	10.1	10.3	11.4	10.8	9.8	9.8	11.3	11.0
Brazil	15.5	13.3	13.1	14.7	18.5	20.6	21.3	22.3	24.7	25.1
Bulgaria	2.6	2.5	2.6	2.8	2.9	2.9	3.0	3.0	2.9	2.9
Canada	15.9	14.8	11.9	12.8	14.7	13.5	14.1	14.7	14.8	15.0
China: Mainland	39.0	37.1	38.8	41.9	45.6	49.5	54.8	58.9	62.1	64.2
Czechoslovakia.	15.2	15.3	15.0	15.0	14.8	15.0	15.1	15.4	15.4	15.5
East Germany	7.3	7.5	7.2	7.2	7.6	7.9	8.0	8.2	8.1	7.8
Finland	2.5	2.4	2.4	2.4	2.6	2.5	2.6	2.7	2.8	2.9
France	23.2	21.3	18.4	17.6	19.0	18.8	17.9	17.7	19.1	19.3
Greece	1.1	0.8	0.9	0.9	0.9	1.0	1.0	0.9	1.0	1.0
Hungary	3.8	3.5	3.6	3.5	3.6	3.5	3.6	3.5	3.5	3.3
India . . . . [.]	9.4	10.7	10.9	10.1	10.3	11.2	11.4	12.3	13.0	12.9
Indonesia [4]	0.4	0.5	0.5	0.8	1.0	1.2	1.5	[2]1.5	[2]2.0	[2]2.0
Italy	26.5	24.8	24.0	21.8	24.1	23.9	22.9	22.9	23.9	25.6
Japan	111.4	101.7	99.5	97.2	105.6	105.3	98.3	98.5	105.7	107.9
Luxembourg.	4.6	3.8	3.5	3.3	4.0	3.9	3.7	3.3	3.7	3.7
Mexico	7.0	7.4	6.9	6.7	7.3	7.2	7.0	7.2	7.3	7.4
Netherlands	5.5	5.5	4.3	4.5	5.7	5.5	5.3	5.1	5.5	5.7
North Korea [2][4].	5.8	5.5	5.8	6.1	6.5	6.5	6.5	6.5	8.0	8.0
Poland	18.6	15.1	14.1	16.2	15.2	15.4	16.3	16.3	15.9	12.5
Romania	10.7	10.3	10.1	9.3	10.1	9.7	9.7	9.9	9.8	9.5
South Africa.	9.1	9.0	8.3	7.2	7.8	8.6	8.1	9.0	8.8	9.6
South Korea.	14.4	15.8	16.6	16.4	17.8	18.6	18.8	19.5	21.3	23.7
Soviet Union	147.9	148.4	147.2	152.5	154.2	154.7	160.6	161.9	163.0	160.1
Spain	12.6	13.0	13.4	13.3	13.4	14.7	12.1	11.6	11.7	12.6
Sweden	4.2	3.8	3.9	4.2	4.7	4.8	4.7	4.7	4.8	4.7
Turkey	1.7	1.7	2.0	3.6	4.1	4.7	6.0	7.0	8.0	7.9
United Kingdom	11.3	15.6	13.7	15.0	15.1	15.7	14.7	17.4	19.0	18.7
Venezuela	1.8	1.8	2.2	2.3	2.8	3.1	3.4	3.7	3.7	3.4
West Germany	43.8	41.6	35.9	35.7	39.4	40.5	37.1	36.2	41.0	41.1
Yugoslavia	3.6	4.0	3.9	4.1	4.2	4.5	4.5	4.4	4.5	4.5

[1] Excludes steel for castings made in foundries operated by companies not producing ingots. [2] Estimated. [3] For year ending June 30. [4] Source: U.S. Bureau of Mines.

Source: Except as noted, Statistical Office of the United Nations, New York, NY, *Statistical Yearbook*, and *Industrial Statistics Yearbook*, vol. II, annuals, (copyright).

No. 1396. World Production of Major Mineral Commodities, by Selected Commodity: 1985 to 1989

COUNTRY	Unit	1985	1987	1988, prel.	1989, est.	Leading producers, 1989
MINERAL FUELS						
Coal.	Mil. metric tons .	4,444	4,691	4,814	4,883	China: Mainland, U.S., Soviet Union
Gas, natural, marketed	Tril. cu. ft.	61.5	65.9	68.8	71.3	Soviet Union, U.S., Canada
Natural gas liquids [1]	Mil. barrels [2] . .	1,532	1,650	1,663	1,695	U.S., Soviet Union, Saudi Arabia
Petroleum, crude	Mil. barrels [2] . .	19,664	20,652	21,260	21,915	Soviet Union, U.S., Saudi Arabia
Petroleum, refined	Mil. barrels [2] . .	21,114	22,148	22,626	22,812	U.S., Soviet Union, Japan
NONMETALLIC MINERALS						
Cement, hydraulic.	Mil. metric tons .	960	1,048	1,105	1,123	China: Mainland, Soviet Union, Japan
Diamond, gem and industrial [1].	1,000 carats . . .	66,018	87,603	93,346	94,837	Australia, Zaire, Botswana
Nitrogen in ammonia.	Mil. metric tons .	91.1	94.1	98.5	99.6	Soviet Union, China: Mainland, U.S.
Phosphate rock	Mil. metric tons .	149	144	160	162	U.S., Soviet Union, Morocco
Potash, marketable.	Mil. metric tons .	29.2	30.5	32.1	29.8	U.S., Canada, East Germany
Salt.	Mil. metric tons .	173	179	184	191	U.S., China: Mainland, Soviet Union
Sulfur, elemental basis	Mil. metric tons .	53.8	56.1	58.1	58.3	U.S., Soviet Union, Canada
METALS						
Aluminum [3]	Mil. metric tons .	15.4	16.4	17.6	18.0	U.S., Soviet Union, Canada
Bauxite, gross weight	Mil. metric tons .	85.3	92.8	99.1	106.1	Australia, Guinea, Jamaica
Chromite, gross weight [1]	1,000 metric tons	10,945	11,355	12,167	11,901	South Africa, Soviet Union, India
Copper, metal content [4]	1,000 metric tons	7,989	8,306	8,537	8,887	Chile, U.S., Canada
Gold, metal content	Mil. troy ounces .	47.6	51.6	58.4	61.3	South Africa, U.S., Soviet Union
Iron ore, gross weight [5]	Mil. metric tons .	861	889	906	924	Soviet Union, Brazil, Australia
Lead, metal content [4]	1,000 metric tons	3,439	3,420	3,414	3,395	Australia, Soviet Union, U.S.
Manganese ore,gross weight .	Mil. metric tons .	25.3	23.7	23.9	24.0	Soviet Union, S. Africa, China: Mainland
Nickel, metal content [4]	1,000 metric tons	812	826	872	932	Canada, Soviet Union, New Caledonia
Steel, crude.	Mil. metric tons .	718	733	778	784	Soviet Union, Japan, U.S.
Tin, metal content [4]	1,000 metric tons	181	178	200	216	Brazil, Indonesia, Malaysia
Zinc, metal content [4]	1,000 metric tons	6,758	7,232	7,015	7,062	Canada, Soviet Union, Australia

[1] Excludes China: Mainland. [2] 42-gallon barrels. [3] Unalloyed ingot metal. [4] Mine output. [5] Includes iron ore concentrates and iron ore agglomerates.

Source: U.S. Bureau of Mines, *Minerals Yearbook*.

No. 1397. Energy Consumption and Production, by Country: 1980 and 1989

[See text, section 31, for general comments about the data. For additional data qualifications for countries, see source]

COUNTRY	ENERGY CONSUMED [1] (coal equiv.) Total (mil. metric tons) 1980	1989	Per capita (kilograms) 1980	1989	ELECTRIC ENERGY PRODUCTION [2] (bil. kWh) 1980	1989	CRUDE PETROLEUM PRODUCTION [3] (mil. metric tons) 1980	1989	COAL PRODUCTION [4] (mil. metric tons) 1980	1989
World, total	8,593.1	10,270.8	1,932	1,975	8,236.9	11,449.8	2,982.4	2,956.4	2,728.0	3,562.2
United States	2,364.4	2,504.0	10,381	10,124	[5]2,354.4	[5]2,985.2	424.2	382.7	710.4	810.0
Algeria	24.8	22.7	1,322	936	7.1	15.4	47.4	34.1	(Z)	(Z)
Argentina	49.1	60.6	1,739	1,899	39.7	50.4	25.3	[6]23.5	0.4	[6]0.4
Australia [7]	91.4	120.0	6,222	7,208	96.1	147.8	[6]19.8	22.5	72.5	147.8
Austria	31.2	30.4	4,138	4,014	41.6	50.2	1.5	1.2	-	-
Bahrain	4.4	7.8	12,615	15,601	1.7	3.5	2.4	1.9	(NA)	(NA)
Bangladesh [8]	4.0	7.8	45	69	2.7	7.4	(Z)	(Z)	(X)	(X)
Belgium	62.3	57.0	6,320	5,787	53.1	66.9	(X)	(X)	6.3	[9]3.6
Brazil	92.4	116.6	762	791	139.5	221.7	9.1	29.8	(NA)	(NA)
Bulgaria	47.5	45.5	5,360	5,052	34.8	44.3	[6]0.3	0.1	0.3	0.2
Burma [10]	2.0	2.5	60	62	1.5	2.5	1.6	0.9	(Z)	(Z)
Canada	251.4	287.4	10,457	10,927	377.5	499.5	70.4	76.5	20.2	38.8
Chile	11.4	15.6	1,021	1,206	11.8	17.8	1.6	0.9	1.0	1.9
China: Mainland	545.5	902.5	557	819	300.6	582.0	105.9	137.5	595.8	1,054.0
Taiwan [11]	37.8	62.1	2,126	3,074	(NA)	(NA)	0.2	0.1	2.6	0.8
Colombia	20.2	25.0	753	773	20.6	34.6	6.5	20.4	4.1	18.9
Cuba	13.7	16.1	1,412	1,532	10.0	15.2	0.3	0.7	(X)	(X)
Czechoslovakia	95.2	93.8	6,215	6,003	72.7	87.5	0.1	0.1	[9]28.3	[9]25.1
Denmark	27.7	22.7	5,398	4,413	27.1	22.8	0.3	5.5	(X)	(X)
East Germany	120.6	124.5	7,208	7,631	98.8	119.0	0.1	(Z)	-	-
Ecuador	5.7	6.8	699	662	3.4	5.7	10.4	14.6	(NA)	(NA)
Egypt	20.9	37.9	512	739	18.9	39.3	29.4	43.0	(X)	(X)
Ethiopia	0.8	1.2	21	24	0.7	0.9	(X)	(X)	(NA)	(NA)
Finland [12]	25.7	29.0	5,384	5,839	[5]38.7	[5]53.9	(X)	(X)	(X)	(X)
France [12]	242.9	219.1	4,506	3,915	[5]245.7	[5]406.3	1.2	3.2	[9]20.2	[9]12.3
Greece	20.2	31.2	2,098	3,113	22.7	34.5	-	0.9	(X)	(X)
Hong Kong	7.3	11.5	1,447	1,996	12.6	27.4	(NA)	(NA)	(X)	(X)
Hungary	40.9	34.9	3,815	3,697	23.9	29.6	2.0	2.0	[9]3.1	[9]2.1
India [10]	139.3	256.3	202	307	119.3	266.2	9.4	33.7	109.2	198.7
Indonesia	36.1	56.2	239	311	14.2	41.8	77.6	69.3	0.3	4.6
Iran [13]	45.7	88.1	1,174	1,650	22.4	42.3	72.7	140.4	[6]0.9	1.2
Iraq	10.7	19.4	802	1,059	11.4	28.9	130.1	136.6	(NA)	(NA)
Ireland	11.4	13.4	3,361	3,632	10.6	13.8	(X)	(X)	0.1	(Z)
Israel	8.8	13.8	2,277	3,040	12.5	20.3	(Z)	(Z)	(X)	(X)
Italy [14]	188.9	217.8	3,346	3,813	183.5	207.5	1.8	4.7	-	0.1
Japan [15]	433.4	491.3	3,710	3,995	577.5	798.8	0.4	0.5	18.0	10.2
Kuwait [15]	12.0	17.4	8,735	8,825	9.4	20.5	84.1	74.1	(NA)	(NA)
Libya	7.3	18.8	2,399	4,286	4.8	18.0	88.3	54.3	(X)	(X)
Malaysia	11.3	22.3	821	1,278	10.1	21.7	13.4	28.0	(X)	0.1
Mexico	117.1	150.6	1,663	1,736	[5]67.0	[5]118.1	99.9	130.7	7.0	[6]11.5
Morocco	6.5	8.9	336	366	4.9	9.1	(Z)	(Z)	0.7	0.5
Netherlands	98.5	98.6	6,965	6,639	64.8	73.1	1.3	3.4	-	-
New Zealand [16]	10.0	17.0	3,208	5,053	22.0	29.5	0.3	1.7	2.0	2.5
Nigeria	12.0	21.7	153	207	7.2	9.9	104.2	85.2	0.2	[6]0.1
North Korea	48.5	60.1	2,658	2,814	35.0	53.5	(X)	(X)	[6]36.0	[6]40.7
Norway [17]	26.5	30.2	6,476	7,181	83.6	118.8	24.6	72.6	0.3	0.4
Pakistan [8]	16.6	31.5	195	265	15.0	40.3	0.5	2.3	1.6	2.6
Peru	11.0	10.7	637	505	10.0	13.4	9.7	7.0	(Z)	[6]0.1
Philippines	15.9	18.0	330	295	18.0	25.9	0.5	0.3	0.3	1.4
Poland	176.8	173.1	4,969	4,531	121.9	145.5	0.3	0.2	193.1	177.6
Portugal	12.5	18.6	1,281	1,811	15.3	25.5	(X)	(X)	0.2	0.3
Romania	103.0	103.9	4,637	4,486	67.5	75.9	11.5	9.2	8.1	8.3
Saudi Arabia [15]	25.3	86.5	2,703	6,362	18.9	46.3	495.9	252.4	(NA)	(NA)
South Africa [18]	84.3	105.7	2,604	2,644	89.6	162.3	(X)	(X)	116.6	174.7
South Korea	51.4	93.1	1,349	2,195	40.1	102.9	(X)	(X)	18.6	20.8
Soviet Union	1,507.5	1,877.2	5,677	6,553	1,293.9	1,722.0	603.2	601.5	492.9	577.0
Spain	87.1	97.1	2,321	2,485	109.2	146.6	1.6	1.0	[9]13.1	[9]14.5
Sudan	1.5	1.6	81	64	0.9	1.3	(X)	(X)	(NA)	(NA)
Sweden	44.2	42.7	5,318	5,070	96.3	143.9	(Z)	(Z)	(Z)	-
Switzerland [19]	24.3	24.2	3,834	3,662	[5]47.1	[5]53.8	(X)	(X)	(X)	(X)
Syria	8.6	11.8	981	978	3.8	10.3	9.2	18.3	(X)	(X)
Tanzania	0.9	0.9	46	36	0.8	0.9	(X)	(X)	(Z)	(Z)
Thailand	17.3	35.0	371	637	15.1	39.1	(Z)	1.1	-	-
Trinidad and Tobago	7.5	7.8	6,901	6,160	2.1	3.5	11.0	7.7	(NA)	(NA)
Tunisia	4.1	6.1	643	761	2.8	5.0	5.6	4.9	(X)	(X)
Turkey	31.1	56.2	699	1,027	23.3	52.0	2.3	2.9	3.6	3.0
United Arab Emirates	9.9	31.5	9,749	20,361	6.3	13.3	82.8	89.3	(NA)	(NA)

See footnotes at end of table.

No. 1397. Energy Consumption and Production, by Country: 1980 and 1989—Continued

[See text, section 31, for general comments about the data. For additional data qualifications for countries, see source]

COUNTRY	ENERGY CONSUMED [1] (coal equiv.)				ELECTRIC ENERGY PRODUCTION [2] (bil. kWh)		CRUDE PETROLEUM PRODUCTION [3] (mil. metric tons)		COAL PRODUCTION [4] (mil. metric tons)	
	Total (mil. metric tons)		Per capita (kilograms)							
	1980	1989	1980	1989	1980	1989	1980	1989	1980	1989
United Kingdom	271.8	289.0	4,809	5,043	283.7	313.8	78.9	87.4	[9]130.1	[9]98.3
Venezuela	49.2	58.0	3,278	3,012	35.9	59.3	114.8	100.1	(Z)	2.1
Vietnam.	6.7	8.6	126	132	4.2	7.8	(X)	1.5	5.3	3.9
West Germany	371.6	330.3	6,036	5,391	367.5	437.0	5.2	5.4	94.5	77.5
Yugoslavia	47.9	62.9	2,145	2,656	59.4	86.3	4.2	[6]3.8	0.4	0.3
Zaire	2.0	2.3	75	67	4.4	6.1	1.0	1.4	0.1	[6]0.1
Zambia	2.3	1.6	396	198	[5]9.2	[5]6.7	(X)	(X)	0.6	0.4

- Represents or rounds to zero.   NA Not available.   X Not applicable.   Z Less than 50,000 metric tons.   [1] Based on apparent consumption of coal, lignite, petroleum products, natural gas, and hydro, nuclear, and geothermal electricity.   [2] Comprises production by utilities generating primarily for public use, and production by industrial establishments generating primarily for own use. Relates to production at generating centers, including station use and transmission losses.   [3] Includes shale oil, but excludes natural gasoline.   [4] Excludes lignite and brown coal, except as noted.   [5] Net production, i.e. excluding station use.   [6] Provisional.   [7] For year ending June 30 of year shown.   [8] For year ending June of year shown.   [9] Includes slurries.   [10] For year ending April of year shown.   [11] Source: U.S. Bureau of the Census. Data from Republic of China publications.   [12] Includes Monaco.   [13] For year ending March 20 of year shown.   [14] Includes San Marino.   [15] Includes share of production and consumption in the Neutral Zone.   [16] For year ending March 31 for year shown.   [17] Includes Svalbard and Jan Mayen Islands.   [18] Includes Botswana, Lesotho, Namibia, and Swaziland.   [19] Includes Liechtenstein.
Source: Except as noted, Statistical Office of the United Nations, New York, NY, *Energy Statistics Yearbook*. annual, (copyright).

No. 1398. Selected Petroleum Product Prices—Selected Countries: 1990

[As of January 1, 1990. Includes taxes]

COUNTRY	AUTOMOTIVE FUELS (U.S. dollars per gallon)		RESIDENTIAL (U.S. dollars per gallon)			INDUSTRIAL (U.S. dollars per barrel)	
	Premium gasoline	Diesel fuel	Light fuel oil	Kerosene	Liquified petroleum gases	Light fuel oil	Heavy fuel oil
United States [1]	[2]1.04	[2]0.99	[2]0.81	[2]1.00	[2]0.95	32.47	21.84
Argentina	1.28	0.59	0.41	0.31	0.31	17.14	9.28
Austria [1]	3.15	2.17	0.80	(NA)	1.39	28.56	17.11
Belgium [1]	3.13	1.76	0.96	0.87	1.59	28.14	14.93
Bolivia	1.46	0.95	0.85	0.75	0.51	39.75	(NA)
Brazil	1.41	0.69	0.85	0.79	0.50	12.59	9.55
Canada [1]	1.92	1.55	1.09	1.56	1.28	45.78	23.49
Chile	1.21	1.20	1.17	0.96	0.90	30.39	21.96
Denmark [1]	3.64	1.04	2.32	1.84	2.06	36.96	20.83
Ecuador	0.52	0.37	(NA)	0.06	0.11	15.54	11.78
El Salvador	1.88	1.05	(NA)	1.14	0.70	21.00	21.00
Ethiopia	2.93	1.44	(NA)	1.18	1.28	41.47	47.00
Finland [1]	3.40	2.29	1.21	(NA)	2.90	42.00	25.53
France [1]	3.40	1.78	1.40	(NA)	(NA)	(NA)	18.51
Ghana	0.76	0.69	(NA)	0.52	0.60	22.04	18.36
Greece [1]	2.16	0.89	0.90	0.79	0.76	37.80	24.31
India	1.92	0.78	(NA)	0.50	0.35	33.91	31.46
Ireland [1]	3.63	2.54	1.43	0.48	0.97	42.84	21.79
Israel	2.20	1.67	0.75	1.69	0.49	(NA)	23.03
Italy [1]	4.27	2.34	2.53	2.00	1.84	89.04	24.00
Jamaica	2.02	1.44	(NA)	0.78	(NA)	41.98	25.08
Japan.	3.05	1.75	1.03	(NA)	(NA)	37.80	26.14
Luxembourg [1]	2.32	1.40	0.94	0.98	0.64	36.96	19.81
Mexico	0.88	0.67	0.27	0.63	0.28	28.10	9.74
Morocco [1]	2.86	1.63	0.95	1.47	0.77	35.61	33.48
Netherlands [1]	3.35	1.72	1.25	1.62	1.09	(NA)	26.77
Norway [1]	3.61	1.31	1.38	1.55	1.03	48.30	44.43
Pakistan	1.52	0.68	(NA)	0.53	0.38	12.42	14.28
Panama	1.98	1.19	(NA)	1.10	0.93	46.20	21.21
Paraguay	1.33	0.68	(NA)	0.81	0.46	28.44	17.84
Peru	1.28	0.39	(NA)	0.44	0.33	15.78	11.28
Portugal [1]	3.30	2.06	2.13	2.03	2.07	86.10	25.16
Saudi Arabia	0.54	0.12	(NA)	0.20	0.49	36.00	55.10
South Africa	1.76	1.65	1.59	1.48	1.58	65.09	35.67
Spain [1]	2.73	1.82	1.21	2.04	1.28	45.36	21.22
Sweden [1]	3.23	2.30	1.74	2.18	0.66	63.42	55.61
Switzerland [1]	2.66	2.71	0.88	(NA)	(NA)	33.60	23.42
Thailand	1.24	0.89	(NA)	0.90	0.78	36.30	17.84
Turkey [1]	1.97	1.94	0.96	1.98	0.88	(NA)	36.24
United Kingdom [1]	2.55	2.04	0.81	2.61	(NA)	(NA)	19.59
Uruguay	2.50	1.44	0.98	1.16	1.20	38.32	30.19
Venezuela	0.24	0.06	0.04	0.09	0.21	1.84	1.84
West Germany [1]	2.72	1.91	0.95	(NA)	(NA)	35.11	20.31

NA Not available.   [1] Average for January 1990.   [2] Price excludes tax.
Source: Energy Information Administration, *International Energy Annual 1989.*

No. 1399. Indices of Food Production: 1980 to 1990

[1979-1981 = 100. For explanation of annual percent change, see Guide to Tabular Presentation. Minus sign (-) indicates decrease]

REGION AND COUNTRY	TOTAL FOOD PRODUCTION				Average annual percent change		PER CAPITA FOOD PRODUCTION				Average annual percent change	
	1980	1985	1989	1990	1980-1990	1989-1990	1980	1985	1988	1990	1980-1990	1989-1990
World	99	114	122	124	2.3	1.4	99	105	105	104	0.5	-0.3
Developed countries	99	108	110	110	1.2	0.3	99	105	103	103	0.5	-0.2
United States	96	108	103	105	1.3	1.8	96	102	94	96	0.4	1.3
Canada	99	113	115	126	2.7	9.5	99	108	106	115	1.7	8.4
Europe (including Central)	101	107	109	108	0.7	-0.9	101	106	106	105	0.4	-1.2
Japan	96	109	102	101	0.6	-0.6	96	105	96	95	-	-0.9
Oceania	95	107	108	109	1.6	0.7	95	100	94	93	-	-0.8
South Africa	96	95	112	106	1.5	-5.5	97	85	92	85	-0.8	-7.5
Soviet Union	100	111	123	121	2.1	-1.1	100	106	113	112	1.2	-1.5
Developing countries	100	120	135	139	3.4	2.4	100	108	112	113	1.2	0.3
Latin America	99	114	125	125	2.4	0.3	99	102	103	101	0.2	-1.7
Mexico	100	114	115	122	2.1	6.1	100	101	94	97	-0.2	3.9
Brazil	103	120	140	130	2.5	-7.1	103	107	115	105	0.3	-8.9
Argentina	96	97	108	105	1.0	-2.3	96	90	95	92	-0.4	-3.5
Africa	100	114	130	129	2.6	-0.6	100	98	99	95	-0.5	-3.7
Middle East	100	116	117	125	2.4	7.1	100	101	91	95	-0.4	4.2
Far East	100	124	143	147	4.0	3.1	100	113	121	122	2.1	1.2
India	98	124	147	146	4.2	-0.9	98	111	122	118	2.0	-2.9
China: Mainland	99	128	147	157	4.7	6.5	99	121	131	137	3.3	4.9

- Represents or rounds to zero.

Source: Food and Agriculture Organization of the United Nations, Rome, Italy, FAO AGRISTAT Database.

No. 1400. Wheat, Rice, and Corn—Exports and Imports of 10 Leading Countries: 1980 to 1989

[In millions of dollars. Countries listed are the 10 leading exporters or importers in 1989]

LEADING EXPORTERS	EXPORTS			LEADING IMPORTERS	IMPORTS		
	1980	1985	1989		1980	1985	1989
WHEAT				WHEAT			
United States	6,587	3,781	6,187	China: Mainland	2,437	909	2,573
France	2,542	2,650	3,152	Soviet Union	3,189	3,019	2,297
Canada	3,423	2,838	2,236	Egypt	1,035	1,393	1,758
Australia	2,440	2,233	1,746	Italy	774	793	1,428
West Germany	409	253	852	Japan	1,236	991	1,188
Argentina	825	1,146	661	Algeria	690	752	881
United Kingdom	279	306	568	Iran	252	351	760
Italy	280	345	460	Iraq	531	373	652
Saudi Arabia	2	8	303	West Germany	343	509	502
Soviet Union	455	243	242	South Korea	369	442	436
RICE				RICE			
Thailand	953	830	1,769	Iran	209	171	310
United States	1,285	665	983	China: Mainland	40	36	304
Vietnam	10	15	372	Soviet Union	265	83	221
Pakistan	422	220	310	United Arab Emirates	123	65	216
Italy	289	304	305	France	154	146	209
Belgium-Luxembourg	91	114	156	Iraq	217	175	196
India	173	188	150	United Kingdom	98	126	192
Australia	145	94	122	India	1	14	175
China: Mainland	450	227	94	Saudi Arabia	230	204	174
United Arab Emirates	84	39	90	Hong Kong	158	115	160
CORN				CORN			
United States	8,571	5,312	6,691	Japan	2,011	1,937	2,262
France	869	815	1,592	Soviet Union	1,508	2,315	2,257
China: Mainland	17	742	438	South Korea	376	422	854
Argentina	513	766	236	Taiwan	437	424	617
Thailand	352	280	159	Netherlands	626	422	508
Spain	1	1	112	Mexico	589	255	476
Yugoslavia	86	146	77	West Germany	443	327	327
Netherlands	135	26	68	United Kingdom	547	266	318
Hungary	27	39	56	Belgium-Luxembourg	473	293	276
Kenya	(Z)	3	45	Spain	668	495	238

Z Less than $500,000.

Source: U.S. Dept. of Agriculture, Economic Research Service, World Agriculture-Trends and Indicators.

No. 1401. Wheat, Rice, and Corn Production, by Country: 1980 to 1989

[In thousands of metric tons. Rice data cover paddy. Data for each country pertain to the calendar year in which all or most of the crop was harvested. See text, section 31, for general comments concerning quality of the data]

COUNTRY	WHEAT			RICE			CORN		
	1980	1985	1989	1980	1985	1989	1980	1985	1989
World, total	445,971	504,628	541,952	399,200	472,118	512,728	397,950	485,716	470,526
United States	64,800	65,975	55,407	6,629	6,122	7,007	168,647	225,445	191,197
Argentina	7,780	8,700	10,332	266	400	469	6,400	11,900	4,260
Australia	10,856	16,167	14,120	613	864	805	151	291	201
Austria	1,201	1,563	1,363	(X)	(X)	(X)	1,293	1,727	1,491
Belgium-Luxembourg . . .	907	1,216	1,478	(X)	(X)	(X)	39	51	62
Brazil	2,702	4,320	5,556	9,776	9,025	11,030	20,372	22,018	26,590
Burma	91	206	130	13,317	14,317	13,515	166	299	201
Canada	19,292	24,252	24,334	(X)	(X)	(X)	5,753	6,970	6,379
China: Mainland	55,210	85,805	90,800	139,910	168,569	180,130	62,600	63,826	78,930
Egypt	1,736	1,872	3,183	2,382	2,311	2,680	3,231	3,699	3,748
France	23,781	28,784	31,817	24	62	97	9,365	12,409	12,926
Greece	2,970	1,807	2,005	80	104	110	1,279	1,908	1,700
Hungary	6,077	6,578	6,540	24	38	28	6,673	6,818	6,996
India	31,830	44,069	53,995	80,312	95,818	106,220	6,957	6,644	8,000
Indonesia	(X)	(X)	(X)	29,652	39,033	44,779	3,991	4,330	6,193
Iran	5,922	6,631	5,525	1,449	1,776	1,853	60	50	40
Iraq	976	1,406	491	167	149	232	60	41	104
Italy	9,156	8,461	7,412	968	1,123	1,246	6,377	6,357	6,388
Japan	583	874	1,025	12,189	14,578	12,934	4	2	1
Mexico	2,785	5,214	4,374	445	808	637	12,374	14,104	10,945
Pakistan	10,857	11,703	14,419	4,685	4,378	4,830	970	1,009	1,179
South Korea	92	11	1	5,311	7,855	8,192	154	132	121
Soviet Union	98,182	78,078	92,307	2,791	2,572	2,560	9,454	14,406	15,305
Sweden	1,193	1,338	1,751	(X)	(X)	(X)	(X)	(X)	(X)
Thailand	(X)	(X)	(X)	17,368	20,264	21,000	2,998	4,934	4,393
United Kingdom	8,470	12,046	14,200	(X)	(X)	(X)	1	(NA)	(NA)
West Germany	8,156	9,866	11,032	(X)	(X)	(X)	672	1,204	1,574
Yugoslavia	5,091	4,859	5,599	42	36	28	9,317	9,901	9,415

NA Not available.   X Not applicable.

Source: U.S. Department of Agriculture, Economic Research Service, *World Agriculture-Trends and Indicators.*

No. 1402. Fisheries—Commercial Catch, by Country: 1985 to 1989

[In billions of pounds, live weight. Catch of fish, crustaceans, mollusks (including weight of shells), and other aquatic plants and animals, except whales and seals]

COUNTRY	1985	1986	1987	1988	1989	COUNTRY	1985	1986	1987	1988	1989
World, total [1] .	190.5	204.5	207.8	217.7	219.4	Japan	25.2	26.4	26.1	26.4	24.6
						Mexico	2.7	2.9	3.1	3.0	3.1
United States	11.4	13.2	13.3	13.1	12.7	North Korea (est.) . .	3.7	3.7	3.7	3.7	3.7
Canada	3.2	3.3	3.4	3.5	3.4	Norway	4.7	4.2	4.3	4.1	4.2
Chile	10.6	12.3	10.6	11.5	14.2	Peru	9.1	12.4	10.1	14.6	15.0
China: Mainland . . .	14.9	17.6	20.6	22.8	24.7	Philippines	4.1	4.2	4.4	4.4	4.6
Denmark	3.9	4.1	3.8	4.3	4.2	South Korea	5.8	6.8	6.3	6.0	6.2
Iceland	3.7	3.7	3.6	3.9	3.3	Soviet Union	23.2	24.8	24.6	25.0	24.9
India	6.2	6.4	6.4	6.9	8.0	Spain	3.3	3.2	3.1	3.2	3.0
Indonesia	5.1	5.4	5.7	6.0	6.0	Thailand	4.9	5.6	6.1	6.2	6.2

[1] Includes other countries not shown separately.

Source: U.S. National Oceanic and Atmospheric Administration, National Marine Fisheries Service, *Fisheries of the United States,* annual. Data from Food and Agricultural Organization of the United Nations, Rome, Italy.

No. 1403. Meat—Production, by Country: 1980 to 1989

[In thousands of metric tons, carcass weight. Covers beef and veal (incl. buffalo meat), pork (incl. bacon and ham), mutton and lamb (incl. goat meat), and poultry. Refers to meat from animals slaughtered within the national boundaries irrespective of origin of animals, and relates to commercial and farm slaughter. Excludes lard, tallow, and edible offals. See text, section 31 for general comments concerning the data]

COUNTRY	1980	1985	1989	COUNTRY	1980	1985	1989
World	134,407	151,215	169,887	France	5,300	5,328	5,509
United States	24,599	26,016	28,384	Italy	3,571	3,723	3,897
Argentina	3,622	3,588	3,325	Japan	3,046	3,461	3,634
Australia [1]	2,672	2,461	2,773	Mexico	2,537	2,933	3,644
Brazil	4,551	4,621	5,976	Soviet Union	15,094	17,131	19,936
Canada	2,556	2,758	2,896	United Kingdom	3,070	3,343	3,314
China: Mainland	13,744	19,913	26,400	West Germany	5,199	5,245	5,241

[1] Year ending June 30.

Source: U.S. Department of Agriculture, Economic Research Service, *World Agriculture-Trends and Indicators.*

No. 1404. Foreign Trade of Selected Countries—Source of Imports and Destination of Exports: 1990

[In billions of dollars, except percent. All exports are f.o.b. (free on board) and all imports are c.i.f. (cost insurance freight) except for U.S. and Canadian imports, which are f.o.b.]

COUNTRY	Total [1]	O.E.C.D. [2] Total	O.E.C.D. [2] E.E.C. [3]	Soviet Union and Eastern Europe	China: Mainland, Vietnam, North Korea	O.P.E.C. [4]	Other developing countries [5]	Africa	America [6]	Middle East [7]	Far East [8]
IMPORTS											
United States	495.3	294.8	92.0	2.2	15.2	38.0	145.0	15.9	63.9	18.7	98.8
Australia	39.1	29.9	8.9	0.1	1.1	1.5	6.5	0.1	0.5	1.2	6.7
Austria	48.9	41.5	33.6	2.8	0.4	1.0	3.2	1.2	0.5	0.4	2.0
Belgium-Luxembourg	119.8	104.6	87.9	2.0	0.3	3.2	9.6	4.8	1.9	2.6	3.4
Canada	116.4	101.0	13.4	0.4	1.2	2.0	10.3	0.9	3.9	0.8	7.7
Denmark.	31.8	27.5	16.6	0.8	0.3	0.5	2.7	0.2	1.0	0.4	1.6
France	232.6	187.5	139.2	5.2	2.3	10.3	23.1	12.1	5.2	6.5	10.6
Germany [9]	342.6	276.1	178.5	13.6	4.9	8.8	39.1	10.3	9.4	4.5	23.4
Italy	193.6	147.9	111.4	7.0	2.0	13.6	22.7	16.2	4.9	5.8	7.7
Japan.	234.6	117.9	35.2	4.0	12.9	41.5	58.3	3.8	9.5	31.1	67.5
Netherlands	125.9	104.8	80.4	2.6	0.7	7.1	10.7	3.4	3.3	5.1	6.3
Spain	87.5	68.9	52.1	1.8	0.8	6.3	9.5	5.9	4.1	2.4	3.9
Sweden	54.7	48.4	30.3	1.5	0.4	0.7	3.7	0.3	1.0	0.6	2.8
Switzerland	69.5	62.7	49.8	0.7	0.3	0.9	5.0	1.2	1.4	0.8	2.6
United Kingdom	224.0	189.5	117.3	2.9	1.0	4.7	24.6	5.3	4.0	4.0	15.9
Percent distribution:											
United States	100.0	59.5	18.6	0.4	3.1	7.7	29.3	3.2	12.9	3.8	20.0
Australia	100.0	76.3	22.7	0.3	2.7	3.8	16.7	0.4	1.3	3.2	17.1
Austria	100.0	84.9	68.6	5.7	0.8	2.1	6.6	2.4	1.0	0.7	4.0
Belgium-Luxembourg . . .	100.0	87.4	73.4	1.7	0.3	2.6	8.0	4.0	1.6	2.2	2.8
Canada	100.0	86.8	11.5	0.4	1.0	1.7	8.8	0.8	3.4	0.7	6.6
Denmark	100.0	86.5	52.2	2.4	1.0	1.4	8.6	0.8	3.2	1.2	5.1
France	100.0	80.6	59.8	2.2	1.0	4.4	9.9	5.2	2.2	2.8	4.6
Germany [9]	100.0	80.6	52.1	4.0	1.4	2.6	11.4	3.0	2.7	1.3	6.8
Italy	100.0	76.4	57.5	3.6	1.0	7.1	11.7	8.4	2.5	3.0	4.0
Japan	100.0	50.2	15.0	1.7	5.5	17.7	24.9	1.6	4.1	13.3	28.8
Netherlands	100.0	83.3	63.9	2.1	0.6	5.6	8.5	2.7	2.6	4.1	5.0
Spain	100.0	78.8	59.6	2.0	0.9	7.2	10.8	6.7	4.7	2.8	4.5
Sweden	100.0	88.4	55.3	2.7	0.8	1.2	6.8	0.5	1.8	1.0	5.1
Switzerland	100.0	90.1	71.7	1.0	0.4	1.2	7.3	1.7	2.1	1.2	3.7
United Kingdom . .	100.0	84.6	52.4	1.3	0.5	2.1	11.0	2.4	1.8	1.8	7.1
EXPORTS											
United States	393.0	253.4	98.1	4.2	4.8	13.7	116.3	8.0	54.1	11.2	60.5
Australia	38.9	23.3	5.1	0.5	1.1	2.2	10.9	0.6	0.4	1.4	10.7
Austria	41.0	33.6	26.7	3.2	0.3	1.1	2.8	0.7	0.3	0.8	1.3
Belgium-Luxembourg	118.0	103.8	88.9	1.0	0.4	2.1	9.7	3.0	0.9	3.2	4.7
Canada	126.9	115.5	10.3	1.1	1.4	1.6	7.3	1.0	2.3	0.9	5.9
Denmark.	35.1	30.4	18.3	0.8	0.1	0.7	3.0	1.0	0.6	0.7	1.2
France	209.6	168.1	131.9	2.8	1.5	8.2	28.8	15.4	6.2	5.1	9.3
Germany [9]	398.4	332.0	217.6	14.5	2.5	11.3	37.5	10.0	7.6	9.0	18.9
Italy	181.0	145.4	105.8	5.1	1.1	7.4	21.3	8.1	3.8	5.6	7.8
Japan.	287.0	169.1	54.0	3.2	6.5	13.6	94.6	5.4	9.7	8.7	89.3
Netherlands	131.4	117.9	101.3	1.6	0.2	2.9	7.9	2.8	1.4	2.3	3.7
Spain	55.4	45.5	38.4	0.6	0.3	1.9	5.9	2.6	2.2	1.2	1.4
Sweden	57.5	50.3	31.3	1.1	0.3	1.3	4.6	0.9	1.1	1.1	2.6
Switzerland	63.5	50.9	36.9	1.6	0.3	2.0	8.7	1.3	1.6	2.5	5.2
United Kingdom	184.5	148.6	98.0	2.2	0.8	8.7	22.7	6.5	3.1	8.7	12.6
Percent distribution:											
United States	100.0	64.5	25.0	1.1	1.2	3.5	29.6	2.0	13.8	2.8	15.4
Australia	100.0	59.9	13.2	1.2	2.7	5.6	28.1	1.4	1.0	3.7	27.4
Austria	100.0	82.0	65.2	7.7	0.7	2.7	6.9	1.6	0.7	2.1	3.1
Belgium-Luxembourg . . .	100.0	88.0	75.4	0.9	0.3	1.8	8.3	2.5	0.8	2.7	4.0
Canada	100.0	91.0	8.1	0.8	1.1	1.3	5.7	0.8	1.8	0.7	4.7
Denmark	100.0	86.6	52.2	2.3	0.3	2.1	8.6	2.7	1.8	2.1	3.4
France	100.0	80.2	62.9	1.4	0.7	3.9	13.8	7.3	3.0	2.4	4.4
Germany [9]	100.0	83.3	54.6	3.6	0.6	2.8	9.4	2.5	1.9	2.3	4.7
Italy	100.0	80.3	58.5	2.8	0.6	4.1	11.8	4.5	2.1	3.1	4.3
Japan	100.0	58.9	18.8	1.1	2.3	4.7	32.9	1.9	3.4	3.0	31.1
Netherlands	100.0	89.7	77.1	1.2	0.2	2.2	6.0	2.2	1.0	1.7	2.8
Spain	100.0	82.2	69.4	1.1	0.6	3.5	10.6	4.7	3.9	2.1	2.6
Sweden	100.0	87.5	54.4	1.9	0.5	2.2	7.9	1.6	1.9	2.0	4.5
Switzerland	100.0	80.1	58.1	2.5	0.5	3.1	13.7	2.0	2.4	3.9	8.2
United Kingdom . .	100.0	80.5	53.1	1.2	0.5	4.7	12.3	3.5	1.7	4.7	6.9

[1] Includes other areas not shown separately.   [2] Organization for Economic Cooperation and Development. For member countries, see text, section 31.   [3] European Economic Community comprises Belgium-Luxembourg, Denmark, France, Greece, Ireland, Italy, Netherlands, Portugal, Spain, United Kingdom, and Germany.   [4] Organization of Petroleum Exporting Countries. For member countries, see footnote 4, table 1411.   [5] Comprises trade with all countries other than China: Mainland, North Korea, Vietnam, South Africa, Soviet Union, Eastern Europe, and members of O.P.E.C. and O.E.C.D.   [6] All countries comprising the continent except Canada and the United States.   [7] Comprises Syria, Lebanon, Israel, Gaza Strip, Jordan, Iraq, Saudi Arabia, Yemen (Aden), Yemen (Sanaa), Kuwait, Bahrain, United Arab Emirates, Qatar, Oman, and Iran.   [8] All countries comprising the continent of Asia except Japan, China: Mainland, North Korea, Vietnam, and those countries listed under Middle East.   [9] Former West Germany (prior to unification).

Source: Organization for Economic Cooperation and Development, Paris, France. Data derived from *Monthly Statistics of Foreign Trade.*

No. 1405. Reserve Assets and International Transaction Balances: 1985 to 1991

[**In millions of U.S. dollars.** Assets include holdings of convertible foreign currencies, special drawing rights, and reserve position in International Monetary Fund and exclude gold holdings. Minus sign (-) indicates decrease]

COUNTRY	TOTAL RESERVE ASSETS				CURRENT ACCOUNT BALANCE			MERCHANDISE TRADE BALANCE		
	1985	1990	1991		1985	1989	1990	1985	1989	1990
			Total	Currency holdings [1]						
United States	32,100	72,260	66,660	45,930	122,250	-106,360	92,160	-122,160	-115,920	-108,120
Algeria	2,819	725	1,486	1,484	1,015	-1,081	1,420	4,223	1,162	4,187
Argentina	3,273	4,592	6,615	6,422	-952	-1,305	1,789	4,878	5,709	8,628
Australia	5,768	16,264	16,534	15,894	9,015	-17,853	-15,213	-1,317	-3,990	-31
Austria	4,767	9,376	10,332	9,655	-273	59	958	-4,406	6,605	-7,982
Bangladesh	337	629	1,278	1,207	-458	-1,100	-397	-1,287	-1,995	-1,587
Belgium	4,849	12,151	12,180	11,068	669	3,197	4,548	-472	967	630
Brazil	10,605	7,441	8,033	8,020	-273	1,025	(NA)	12,466	16,112	(NA)
Burma	34	313	258	-	-206	(NA)	(NA)	-202	(NA)	(NA)
Cameroon.	132	26	(NA)	(NA)	-562	(NA)	(NA)	490	(NA)	(NA)
Canada	2,503	17,845	16,252	14,079	-2,279	-17,480	-18,815	12,574	6,732	9,952
Chile	2,450	6,069	7,041	7,041	-1,328	-767	-790	850	1,578	1,273
China: Mainland. . . .	12,728	29,586	43,674	42,664	-11,417	-4,317	11,998	-13,123	-5,620	9,165
Colombia	1,595	4,212	6,029	5,866	-1,809	-195	391	-23	1,474	2,017
Cote d'Ivoire	5	4	13	11	64	-1,210	-1,283	1,351	1,087	1,419
Denmark.	5,429	10,591	7,404	6,807	-2,767	-892	1,541	-764	2,424	4,566
Ecuador	718	839	924	883	114	-472	-136	1,294	661	1,003
Egypt	792	2,684	5,325	5,324	-2,166	-1,309	184	-5,215	-5,933	-6,699
Finland.	3,750	9,644	7,609	7,108	-811	-5,796	-6,682	378	-219	768
France	26,589	36,778	31,284	28,292	-35	-5,623	-13,772	-5,276	-10,655	13,667
Germany [2]	44,380	67,902	63,001	57,517	16,960	57,010	47,370	28,580	77,800	71,590
Ghana	479	219	(NA)	(NA)	-134	-99	-229	-36	-195	-308
Greece.	868	3,412	5,189	5,082	-3,276	-2,561	-3,537	-5,053	-7,383	-10,178
Hungary	2,153	1,070	(NA)	(NA)	-455	-588	379	448	1,043	534
India	6,420	1,521	3,627	3,580	-4,177	(NA)	(NA)	-5,616	(NA)	(NA)
Indonesia	4,974	7,459	9,258	9,151	-1,923	-1,108	-2,369	5,822	6,664	6,098
Ireland	2,940	5,223	5,740	5,320	-690	524	1,433	631	4,007	3,977
Israel	3,680	6,275	6,279	6,279	1,120	1,104	702	-2,364	-1,764	-2,890
Italy	15,595	62,927	48,679	45,495	3,408	-10,886	-12,733	-6,083	-2,167	723
Japan.	26,719	78,501	72,059	61,758	49,170	56,990	35,870	55,990	76,890	63,580
Kenya	391	205	117	98	-113	-588	-477	-327	-1,037	-998
Kuwait	5,471	1,952	3,409	3,067	5,150	9,589	(NA)	5,047	5,872	(NA)
Libya	5,904	5,839	5,695	4,885	1,906	-1,208	2,203	4,599	766	3,780
Malaysia.	4,912	9,754	(NA)	(NA)	-613	-212	-1,672	3,577	3,913	1,924
Mexico.	4,906	9,863	17,726	17,140	1,130	-3,958	-5,255	8,451	-645	-3,026
Morocco.	115	2,066	3,100	2,953	-891	-790	-200	-1,368	-1,679	-2,071
Nepal.	56	295	386	377	-122	-243	-289	-283	-415	-449
Netherlands	10,782	17,484	17,798	16,240	4,190	9,628	10,313	5,393	8,138	10,516
Nigeria	1,667	3,864	4,435	4,435	2,566	1,090	5,126	5,616	4,178	8,653
Norway.	13,917	15,332	13,232	12,209	3,052	214	3,886	4,728	3,770	7,770
Pakistan	807	296	527	519	-1,080	-1,335	-1,578	-3,230	-2,571	-2,699
Peru.	1,842	1,040	2,443	2,443	135	324	-674	1,172	1,242	391
Philippines	615	924	3,246	3,186	-35	-1,456	-2,695	-482	-2,598	-4,020
Poland	870	4,492	3,633	3,625	-982	-1,409	3,067	347	47	3,589
Portugal	1,395	14,485	20,629	20,261	380	153	-139	-1,504	-4,865	-6,580
Romania.	199	373	380	323	1,381	2,514	-3,254	1,772	2,050	-3,344
Saudi Arabia	25,004	11,668	11,673	9,737	-12,932	-9,228	-4,107	7,029	9,068	22,793
Singapore	12,847	27,748	34,128	33,926	-4	2,547	2,350	-2,829	-2,474	-5,119
South Africa	315	1,008	899	897	2,622	1,579	2,253	5,842	5,589	6,338
South Korea	2,869	14,793	13,701	13,306	-887	5,056	-2,172	-19	4,597	-2,004
Spain.	11,175	51,228	65,822	64,295	2,851	-10,933	-16,819	-4,171	-24,495	-29,566
Sri Lanka	451	423	685	685	-419	-414	-296	-523	-550	-473
Sudan	12	11	8	8	155	-150	-369	-139	-507	-322
Sweden	5,793	17,988	18,331	17,476	-1,231	-3,268	-5,463	2,385	4,015	3,402
Switzerland	18,016	29,223	29,004	29,002	6,040	8,042	6,941	-1,561	-4,323	-6,377
Syria	83	(NA)	(NA)	(NA)	-958	1,171	1,827	-2,090	1,192	2,159
Thailand	2,190	13,305	17,517	17,287	-1,537	-2,498	-7,282	-1,332	-2,916	-6,751
Trinidad and Tobago. .	1,129	492	339	337	-90	-66	430	756	489	988
Turkey	1,056	6,050	5,144	5,098	-1,013	961	-2,616	-2,975	-4,219	-9,554
United Kingdom	12,860	35,850	41,890	38,730	4,136	-33,406	-26,086	-3,850	-40,405	-32,500
Venezuela	10,251	8,321	10,665	10,396	3,327	2,161	(NA)	6,782	5,632	10,868
Yugoslavia	1,095	5,474	2,682	2,682	833	2,427	-2,364	-588	58	-2,676
Zaire	190	219	183	183	-289	-611	-643	606	518	600

- Represents or rounds to zero.   NA Not available.   [1] Holdings of convertible foreign currencies.   [2] Former West Germany (prior to unification).

Source: International Monetary Fund, Washington, DC, *International Financial Statistics*, monthly with annual supplements.

No. 1406. Foreign Exchange Rates: 1970 to 1991

[National currency units per dollar, except as noted. Except as indicated, data are annual averages of certified noon buying rates for cable transfers]

YEAR	Australia [1] (dollar)	Austria (schilling)	Belgium (franc)	Canada (dollar)	China: Taiwan (dollar)	Denmark (krone)	France (franc)	Greece (drachma)	Hong Kong (dollar)
1970	111.36	25.880	49.680	1.0103	40.050	7.4890	5.5200	30.00	6.0600
1980	114.00	12.945	29.237	1.1693	36.015	5.6345	4.2250	42.62	4.9760
1981	114.95	15.948	37.194	1.1990	36.849	7.1350	5.4396	55.41	5.5678
1982	101.65	17.060	45.780	1.2344	39.124	8.3443	6.5793	66.87	6.0697
1983	90.14	17.968	51.121	1.2325	40.065	9.1483	7.6203	87.90	7.2569
1984	87.94	20.005	57.749	1.2953	39.633	10.3540	8.7355	112.73	7.8188
1985	70.03	20.676	59.336	1.3658	39.889	10.5980	8.9799	138.40	7.7911
1986	67.09	15.260	44.662	1.3896	37.837	8.0954	6.9256	139.93	7.8037
1987	70.14	12.649	37.357	1.3259	31.756	6.8477	6.0121	135.47	7.7985
1988	78.41	12.357	36.783	1.2306	28.636	6.7411	5.9594	142.00	7.8071
1989	79.19	13.236	39.409	1.1842	26.407	7.3210	6.3802	162.60	7.8008
1990	78.07	11.331	33.424	1.1668	26.918	6.1899	5.4467	158.59	7.7899
1991	77.87	11.687	34.195	1.1460	26.759	6.4038	5.6468	182.63	7.7712

YEAR	India (rupee)	Ireland [1] (pound)	Italy (lira)	Japan (yen)	Malaysia (ringgit)	Netherlands (guilder)	New Zealand [1] (dollar)	Norway (krone)	Portugal (escudo)
1970	7.576	239.59	623.00	357.60	3.0900	3.5970	111.48	7.1400	28.75
1980	7.887	205.77	856.20	226.63	2.1767	1.9875	97.34	4.9381	50.08
1981	8.681	161.32	1,138.60	220.63	2.3048	2.4998	86.85	5.7430	61.74
1982	9.485	142.05	1,354.00	249.06	2.3395	2.6719	75.10	6.4567	80.10
1983	10.104	124.81	1,519.30	237.55	2.3204	2.8543	66.79	7.3012	111.61
1984	11.348	108.64	1,756.10	237.45	2.3448	3.2083	57.84	8.1596	147.70
1985	12.332	106.62	1,908.90	238.47	2.4806	3.3184	49.75	8.5933	172.07
1986	12.597	134.14	1,491.16	168.35	2.5830	2.4484	52.46	7.3984	149.80
1987	12.943	148.79	1,297.03	144.60	2.5185	2.0263	59.33	6.7408	141.20
1988	13.899	152.49	1,302.39	128.17	2.6189	1.9778	65.56	6.5242	144.26
1989	16.213	141.80	1,372.28	138.07	2.7079	2.1219	59.35	6.9131	157.53
1990	17.492	165.76	1,198.27	145.00	2.7057	1.8215	59.62	6.2541	142.70
1991	22.712	158.26	1,241.28	134.59	2.7503	1.8720	57.83	6.4912	144.77

YEAR	Singapore (dollar)	South Africa (rand)	South Korea (won)	Spain (peseta)	Sweden (krona)	Switzerland (franc)	Thailand (baht)	United Kingdom [1] (pound)	Germany (deutsche mark)
1970	3.0800	0.7181	310.57	69.72	5.1700	4.3160	21.000	239.59	(X)
1980	2.1412	0.7796	607.43	71.76	4.2309	1.6772	20.476	232.43	(X)
1981	2.1053	0.8787	681.03	92.40	5.0659	1.9674	21.731	202.43	(X)
1982	2.1406	1.0876	731.93	110.09	6.2838	2.0327	23.014	174.80	(X)
1983	2.1136	1.1146	776.04	143.50	7.6717	2.1006	22.991	151.59	(X)
1984	2.1325	1.4761	807.91	160.78	8.2706	2.3500	23.582	133.66	(X)
1985	2.2008	2.2344	861.89	169.98	8.6031	2.4551	27.193	129.74	(X)
1986	2.1782	2.2919	884.61	140.04	7.1272	1.7979	26.314	146.77	(X)
1987	2.1059	2.0385	825.93	123.54	6.3468	1.4918	25.774	163.98	(X)
1988	2.0132	2.2770	734.51	116.52	6.1369	1.4642	25.312	178.13	(X)
1989	1.9511	2.6214	674.29	118.44	6.4559	1.6369	25.725	163.82	(X)
1990	1.8134	2.5885	710.64	101.96	5.9231	1.3901	25.609	178.41	1.6166
1991	1.7283	2.7633	736.73	104.01	6.0521	1.4356	25.528	176.74	1.6610

X Not applicable.   [1] Value is U.S. cents per unit of foreign currency.
Source: Board of Governors of the Federal Reserve System, *Federal Reserve Bulletin*, monthly.

No. 1407. Exchange Rates—Indexes of Value of Foreign Currency Relative to U.S. Dollar: 1970 to 1990

[1982 = 100]

YEAR	United States	Belgium	Canada	Denmark	France	Germany [1]	Italy	Japan	Netherlands	Norway	Sweden	United Kingdom
1970	100.0	92.2	118.3	111.3	119.0	66.6	215.9	69.5	73.9	90.3	121.2	137.1
1980	100.0	156.8	105.6	148.2	155.9	133.8	158.3	110.4	134.6	130.8	148.6	133.1
1981	100.0	123.7	103.0	116.9	121.0	107.7	118.9	112.9	107.4	112.4	124.0	115.8
1982	100.0	100.0	100.0	100.0	100.0	100.0	100.0	100.0	100.0	100.0	100.0	100.0
1983	100.0	89.6	100.2	91.2	86.3	95.1	89.1	104.8	93.6	88.4	81.9	86.7
1984	100.0	79.3	95.3	80.6	75.3	85.3	77.1	104.9	83.3	79.1	76.0	76.5
1985	100.0	77.2	90.4	78.7	73.3	82.5	70.9	104.4	80.5	75.1	73.0	74.2
1986	100.0	102.5	88.8	103.1	95.0	111.9	90.8	147.9	109.1	87.3	88.2	84.0
1987	100.0	122.6	93.1	121.9	109.4	135.0	104.4	172.2	131.9	95.8	99.0	93.8
1988	100.0	124.5	100.3	123.8	110.4	138.2	104.0	194.3	135.1	99.0	102.4	101.9
1989	100.0	116.2	104.2	114.0	103.1	129.1	98.7	180.4	125.9	93.4	97.3	93.7
1990	100.0	137.0	105.8	134.8	120.8	150.2	113.0	171.8	146.7	103.2	106.1	102.1

[1] Former West Germany (prior to unification).

Source: U.S. Bureau of Labor Statistics, News Release USDL: 90-383, *"International Comparisons of Manufacturing Productivity and Labor Cost Trends"*; July 27, 1990; and unpublished data.

No. 1408. Central Bank Discount Rates, Money Market Rates, and Government Bond Yields—Selected Countries: 1980 to 1992

[In percent per annum. **Central bank discount rates** refer to the rate at which the monetary authority lends or discounts eligible paper for deposit money banks. **Money market rates** refer to the rate at which short-term borrowings are effected between financial institutions. **Government bond yields** refer to one or more series representing average yields to maturity of government bonds or other bonds that would be indicative of longer term rates]

NATIONAL INTEREST RATE AND YEAR	United States	Canada	Japan	France	Germany[1]	Italy	Netherlands	Sweden	Switzerland	United Kingdom
Central bank discount rates: [2]										
1980	13.00	17.26	7.25	9.50	7.50	16.50	8.00	10.00	3.00	14.00
1985	7.50	9.49	5.00	9.50	4.00	15.00	5.00	10.50	4.00	[3]
1988	6.50	11.17	2.50	9.50	3.50	12.50	4.50	8.50	3.50	[3]
1989	7.00	12.47	4.25	9.50	6.00	13.50	7.00	10.50	6.00	[3]
1990	6.50	11.78	6.00	9.50	6.00	12.50	7.25	11.50	6.00	[3]
1991	3.50	8.00	4.50	9.50	8.00	12.00	8.50	8.00	7.00	[3]
1992, February	3.50	8.00	4.50	9.50	8.00	12.00	8.50	8.50	7.00	[3]
Money market rates: [4]										
1980	13.36	13.28	10.93	11.85	9.10	17.17	10.13	12.17	2.29	15.62
1985	8.10	9.57	6.46	9.93	5.20	15.25	6.30	13.85	3.75	10.78
1988	7.61	10.35	3.62	7.52	4.01	11.29	4.48	10.08	2.22	10.31
1989	9.22	12.06	4.87	9.07	6.59	12.69	6.99	11.52	6.50	13.88
1990	8.10	11.62	7.24	9.85	7.92	12.38	8.29	13.45	8.33	14.68
1991	5.70	7.40	7.46	9.49	8.84	12.18	9.01	11.81	7.73	11.75
1992, February	4.06	7.21	5.55	9.92	9.58	(NA)	9.45	12.35	7.71	10.58
Government bond yields:										
1980	11.46	12.48	9.22	13.03	8.50	16.11	10.21	11.74	4.77	13.79
1985	10.62	11.04	6.34	10.94	6.87	13.00	7.34	13.09	4.78	10.62
1988	8.85	10.22	4.27	9.06	6.10	10.16	6.29	11.35	4.15	9.36
1989	8.50	9.92	5.05	8.79	7.09	10.72	7.21	11.18	5.20	9.58
1990	8.55	10.85	7.36	9.96	8.88	11.51	8.93	13.08	6.68	11.08
1991	7.86	9.76	6.53	9.05	8.63	10.10	8.74	10.69	6.35	9.92
1992, February	7.34	8.97	5.41	8.48	8.08	10.54	8.28	9.43	6.16	9.21

NA Not available. [1] Prior to 1990, data for former West Germany. [2] End of period. [3] Minimum lending rate suspended as of August 20, 1981. [4] Period averages.
Source: International Monetary Fund, Washington, DC, *International Financial Statistics*, monthly.

No. 1409. External Debt of Soviet Union and Eastern European Countries: 1980 to 1989

[In billions of dollars. **Gross debt:** total amount owed. **Commercial debt:** money owed to private institutions or indiviuals. **Official debt:** money owed to or guaranteed by a foreign government. Net debt represents gross debt minus assets held with Western commercial banks]

TYPE AND SOURCE	1980	1982	1983	1984	1985	1986	1987	1988	1989
Gross debt, total	**104.2**	**102.7**	**103.9**	**102.0**	**117.3**	**136.6**	**153.8**	**152.4**	**163.8**
Soviet Union: Gross debt	20.5	21.9	22.0	22.3	29.0	36.0	40.8	42.4	47.8
Commercial debt	11.0	12.8	12.6	13.2	19.5	25.9	30.1	33.7	39.0
Official debt	9.5	9.1	9.4	9.1	9.5	10.1	10.7	8.7	8.8
Net debt	10.5	10.0	9.8	10.8	15.7	21.1	25.9	26.9	33.4
Bulgaria: Gross debt	3.5	2.8	2.4	2.2	3.7	4.9	6.1	7.5	10.0
Commercial debt	3.2	2.3	1.9	1.8	3.1	4.2	5.3	6.5	8.8
Official debt	0.3	0.5	0.5	0.5	0.6	0.7	0.9	1.0	1.2
Net debt	2.7	1.8	1.2	0.8	1.5	3.6	5.0	(NA)	(NA)
Czechoslovakia: Gross debt	4.9	4.0	4.0	3.6	3.8	4.5	5.8	6.1	7.8
Commercial debt	4.1	3.1	2.9	2.6	2.8	3.4	4.5	4.8	5.9
Official debt	0.9	0.9	1.1	1.0	1.0	1.1	1.3	1.3	1.9
Net debt	3.7	3.3	3.0	2.6	2.8	3.3	4.2	(NA)	(NA)
East Germany: Gross debt	14.1	13.2	13.1	12.4	14.0	17.0	20.4	19.5	21.2
Commercial debt	11.3	9.6	9.1	8.2	10.1	13.1	16.5	16.2	18.2
Official debt	2.8	3.6	3.9	4.2	3.9	3.9	3.9	3.3	3.0
Net debt	11.6	11.2	9.7	7.8	7.6	9.6	11.4	(NA)	(NA)
Hungary: Gross debt	9.1	7.7	8.2	8.8	11.8	15.1	17.7	18.0	20.7
Commercial debt	8.8	7.0	6.9	7.0	9.8	12.7	15.2	15.6	15.7
Official debt	0.3	0.5	0.7	0.8	0.8	0.9	1.0	1.0	3.2
BIS/IMF [1]	-	0.2	0.6	1.1	1.2	1.5	1.6	1.4	1.8
Net debt	7.0	6.6	6.8	6.7	8.6	12.0	15.5	(NA)	(NA)
Poland: Gross debt	25.0	24.8	26.4	26.8	29.3	33.5	39.2	38.5	39.7
Commercial debt	14.9	13.6	10.9	9.4	10.6	12.1	12.8	11.9	13.4
Official debt	10.1	11.2	15.5	17.4	18.7	21.4	26.4	26.6	26.3
Net debt	24.4	23.8	25.2	25.3	27.7	31.8	36.2	(NA)	(NA)
Romania: Gross debt	9.4	9.8	8.8	7.1	6.6	6.4	5.1	2.2	0.4
Commercial debt	6.5	5.4	4.8	3.4	2.9	2.7	1.7	0.4	0.2
Oficial debt	1.7	1.4	0.9	1.1	1.1	1.1	0.8	0.6	0.2
IMF/World Bank/CEMA bank [1]	1.2	2.9	3.1	2.6	2.6	2.6	2.6	1.2	
Net debt	9.1	9.3	8.2	6.4	6.4	5.8	4.5	(NA)	(NA)
Yugoslavia: Gross debt	17.4	18.5	19.0	18.8	19.2	19.4	18.7	18.2	16.2
Commercial debt	12.8	11.9	10.3	9.0	7.8	7.4	7.6	7.8	6.9
Official debt	2.6	3.1	4.6	5.8	7.1	7.7	6.6	5.4	5.5
IMF/World Bank [1]	2.1	3.5	4.1	4.1	4.3	4.2	4.5	5.0	3.8
Net debt	16.2	17.7	18.1	17.7	18.1	17.9	18.0	(NA)	(NA)

- Represents zero. NA Not available. [1] BIS = Bank of International Settlements. IMF = International Monetary Fund. CEMA = Council for Economic Mutual Assistance.
Source: U.S. Central Intelligence Agency, *Handbook of Economic Statistics, 1990;* and unpublished data.

Comparative International Statistics

No. 1410. Total External Public Debt, 1980 to 1990, and by Type of Creditor, 1990, and Debt Service Payments and Ratio, 1980 to 1990

[**External public debt** is defined as debt repayable to external creditors in foreign currency, goods, or services, with an original or extended maturity of more than one year, which is a direct obligation of, or has repayment guaranteed by, a public body in the borrowing country. Excludes undisbursed debt (amounts not yet drawn by recipient) and unguaranteed private debt, which for some countries is substantial. Debt contracted for the purchase of military equipment is not usually reported. **Debt service** payments represent the sum of interest payments and repayments of principal on external public debt]

COUNTRY	TOTAL EXTERNAL PUBLIC DEBT (mil. dol.)							DEBT SERVICE PAYMENTS (mil. dol.)			DEBT SERVICE RATIO[3] (percent)		
	1980	1985	1989	1990				1980	1985	1990	1980	1985	1990
				Total[1]	Bilateral official	Banks[2]	International organizations						
Argentina[4]	10,181	37,327	51,460	46,146	6,194	33,682	4,883	1,987	4,265	3,792	17.7	41.3	25.2
Bangladesh	3,420	5,975	9,923	11,464	4,852	-	6,414	110	201	433	9.4	12.7	15.8
Bolivia	2,182	3,511	3,429	3,683	1,772	248	1,592	290	248	285	27.7	33.6	28.6
Brazil	40,824	74,557	84,300	82,098	14,301	48,268	11,424	8,065	7,043	4,941	34.6	24.0	14.6
Bulgaria	272	3,944	9,359	9,564	112	4,234	-	29	1,682	1,283	0.3	14.6	16.0
Cameroon	2,005	2,003	3,749	4,785	2,490	324	1,297	186	239	300	10.1	8.5	12.8
Chile	4,705	12,897	10,851	10,339	1,040	4,654	4,143	1,375	1,232	1,571	21.9	26.4	14.9
China: Mainland	4,504	9,963	37,032	45,319	8,390	19,855	6,076	930	1,883	5,904	4.4	5.9	8.7
Colombia	4,089	9,573	13,989	14,681	2,437	4,483	6,103	529	1,416	3,116	8.9	30.0	33.2
Congo	1,242	2,342	3,545	4,380	2,557	882	582	73	383	244	7.1	31.2	14.8
Costa Rica	1,695	3,532	3,560	3,077	1,234	650	1,141	205	452	433	16.8	35.6	21.2
Cote d'Ivoire	4,310	5,778	8,349	10,050	4,145	2,818	2,701	870	600	467	23.9	18.8	12.7
Dominican Republic	1,220	2,691	3,335	3,440	1,634	775	863	154	200	146	10.3	12.6	6.3
Ecuador	3,300	7,199	9,425	9,854	1,937	4,881	2,127	559	946	871	18.8	28.4	26.8
Egypt	16,273	34,677	42,272	34,242	23,294	590	3,724	749	2,298	2,769	8.1	21.0	19.9
Ethiopia	669	1,721	2,886	3,116	1,565	100	1,241	34	101	188	5.8	18.1	30.6
Gabon	1,271	945	2,483	2,945	1,918	247	320	398	225	128	16.4	10.6	4.9
Ghana	1,161	1,299	2,334	2,670	613	13	1,831	108	98	180	8.9	14.5	18.2
Guatemala	549	2,166	2,078	2,179	795	342	990	45	256	163	2.5	21.5	10.3
Honduras	974	2,137	2,822	3,159	1,207	183	1,579	98	159	343	10.1	17.3	31.8
Hungary	6,409	9,965	16,627	18,046	160	14,354	2,555	1,459	3,405	3,804	14.3	34.0	43.2
India[5]	18,372	31,752	56,567	61,097	14,334	9,765	21,797	1,166	2,164	5,437	7.7	13.9	20.4
Indonesia	15,027	26,767	41,205	44,974	18,894	6,162	14,253	1,763	3,972	6,675	7.9	19.7	22.6
Jamaica	1,421	3,122	3,727	3,874	2,140	298	1,176	206	354	525	14.0	26.0	23.6
Jordan	1,491	3,398	6,404	6,486	3,120	1,302	954	182	498	621	7.3	16.0	21.5
Kenya	2,074	2,683	4,117	4,810	1,432	425	2,472	240	363	471	11.6	22.6	21.1
Madagascar	926	2,187	3,361	3,677	2,184	92	1,248	58	100	163	11.2	27.9	33.5
Malaysia	4,008	15,072	15,516	16,107	2,720	9,762	1,812	376	4,348	3,345	2.5	24.5	9.6
Mali	669	1,301	2,044	2,306	1,418	2	870	9	34	40	2.8	11.3	7.1
Mexico	33,915	72,703	76,059	76,204	8,388	47,165	14,303	7,890	10,572	7,980	35.6	35.6	18.3
Morocco	8,325	13,824	20,310	22,097	12,708	3,339	4,469	1,173	997	1,616	27.1	24.2	19.4
Nicaragua	1,661	4,892	7,508	8,067	5,659	1,298	976	87	50	10	16.9	14.5	2.6
Oman	436	1,908	2,627	2,205	201	1,592	136	223	261	744	5.7	4.8	12.6
Pakistan	8,507	10,564	14,467	16,532	8,936	406	6,922	592	1,027	1,360	12.4	15.7	17.1
Panama	2,271	3,320	3,935	3,987	483	2,362	1,019	466	410	140	6.0	6.5	2.6
Papua New Guinea	485	1,069	1,319	1,509	288	342	752	61	125	260	5.6	12.0	16.8
Peru	6,218	10,339	12,670	13,344	4,931	3,968	2,192	1,506	680	237	31.2	17.3	5.4
Philippines	6,363	14,020	22,557	24,108	8,859	7,835	6,274	596	1,252	2,177	7.3	15.6	16.4
Poland	(NA)	29,763	34,452	39,282	27,231	10,238	524	2,758	1,932	848	17.0	14.6	4.3
Portugal	6,728	12,825	14,433	14,432	758	9,375	2,695	1,024	2,914	4,317	10.5	29.0	13.8
Senegal	1,105	2,058	2,671	2,953	1,405	85	1,368	219	98	210	24.2	10.8	14.9
South Korea	15,933	28,279	17,035	17,814	5,476	5,057	3,794	2,783	5,101	4,806	12.3	15.4	6.2
Sri Lanka	1,227	2,836	4,269	4,911	2,729	249	1,620	84	214	281	5.6	11.1	10.1
Sudan	3,822	6,602	8,469	9,156	5,777	1,651	1,724	102	89	22	9.9	7.1	2.6
Syrian	2,918	9,502	15,704	14,959	13,046	-	1,069	302	288	1,374	9.0	10.0	25.2
Tanzania	1,886	2,787	4,611	5,294	3,363	16	1,742	63	61	98	8.2	12.7	17.9
Thailand	3,943	9,860	12,408	12,572	4,295	2,800	3,722	441	1,481	3,301	5.1	14.5	10.5
Tunisia	3,211	4,453	5,989	6,506	3,018	224	2,219	428	673	1,308	11.6	22.2	22.2
Turkey	15,040	19,566	34,832	38,595	8,398	18,416	9,631	1,053	3,526	6,188	18.3	26.9	24.6
Uganda	641	963	1,976	2,301	730	93	1,298	39	62	62	11.8	16.7	34.8
Uruguay	1,127	2,695	2,978	3,044	164	2,173	699	198	407	709	12.4	30.6	29.8
Venezuela	10,614	17,738	25,281	24,643	315	20,029	1,639	2,955	2,386	3,517	13.3	13.9	17.0
Yemen	1,453	2,968	4,546	5,040	3,931	80	1,025	35	95	97	2.2	9.7	5.0
Yugoslavia[6]	4,581	11,201	14,650	13,492	4,152	6,128	3,093	616	1,354	2,042	3.4	7.9	6.6
Zaire	4,261	4,958	7,912	8,851	6,172	529	1,791	396	299	144	16.5	14.9	6.2
Zambia	2,146	3,160	4,196	4,784	2,824	70	1,420	287	90	148	17.7	10.4	10.6
Zimbabwe	696	1,766	2,260	2,449	869	474	638	50	322	365	2.9	22.2	19.1

- Represents or rounds to zero.   NA Not available.   [1] Includes other types of creditors, not shown separately.   [2] Includes other private financial institutions.   [3] Debt service payments as percent of exports.   [4] The increase in debt outstanding from 1980 to 1985 includes the refinancing of short-term private debt by public debt, which matured in 1986-87.   [5] Fiscal year basis.   [6] The bulk of the debt of Yugoslavian enterprises is reported as nonguaranteed.

Source: The World Bank, Washington, DC, *World Debt Tables*, periodic.

No. 1411. Net Flow of Financial Resources to Developing Countries, by Origin and Type of Resource: 1970 to 1990

[In billions of U.S. dollars. Net flow covers loans, grants, and grant-like flows minus amortization on loans. Military flows are excluded. Developing countries cover countries designated by Development Assistance Committee as developing. Official development assistance covers all flows to developing countries and multilateral institutions provided by official agencies, including State and local governments, or by their executive agencies, which are administered with the promotion of economic development and welfare of developing countries as their main objective and whose financial terms are intended to be concessional in character with grant element of at least 25 percent. Other official flows cover export credits and portfolio investment from the official sector]

ORIGIN AND TYPE OF RESOURCE	1970	1980	1983	1984	1985	1986	1987	1988	1989	1990
Development Assistance Committee countries [1]	15.9	75.4	69.8	79.1	45.2	68.8	66.4	85.6	85.3	(NA)
Official development assistance	6.9	27.3	27.6	28.7	29.4	36.7	41.6	48.1	46.7	54.1
Bilateral grants [2]	3.3	14.1	14.2	15.5	17.8	21.1	23.4	26.0	27.3	32.7
Bilateral loans	2.4	4.0	4.4	4.2	4.1	5.2	6.6	7.1	7.0	6.0
Multilateral contributions [3]	1.3	9.2	9.0	9.0	7.5	10.4	11.6	15.0	12.5	15.4
Other official flows	1.1	5.3	4.9	6.2	3.4	2.1	2.0	4.9	5.7	(NA)
Private flows at market terms	7.0	40.4	35.0	41.6	9.4	26.7	18.8	28.3	29.0	(NA)
Direct investment	3.7	10.1	7.8	10.9	6.5	11.0	21.0	25.1	30.1	(NA)
Private export credits	2.2	11.5	5.3	3.5	0.8	-1.7	-2.4	-1.3	5.8	(NA)
Portfolio investment	1.2	18.7	22.2	27.2	2.1	17.4	0.3	4.4	-7.0	(NA)
Private voluntary agencies	0.9	2.4	2.3	2.6	2.9	3.3	4.0	4.2	4.0	(NA)
Organization of Petroleum Exporting Countries [4]	0.6	10.8	5.9	3.7	4.1	(NA)	(NA)	(NA)	(NA)	(NA)
Official development assistance	0.4	9.7	5.0	4.6	3.6	4.7	3.3	2.4	2.4	6.4
Other official flows	0.2	1.1	0.9	-0.9	0.5	(NA)	(NA)	(NA)	(NA)	(NA)
Centrally-planned economies: [5]										
Official development assistance	1.0	2.6	3.5	3.4	3.6	4.6	5.0	5.0	4.7	-2.2
Total net flow to developing countries, by DAC country [1]	15.9	75.4	69.8	79.1	45.2	68.8	66.4	85.6	85.3	(NA)
United States	6.4	13.9	23.0	28.6	1.8	18.2	13.8	17.5	16.4	11.0
Official development assistance	3.2	7.1	8.1	8.7	9.4	9.6	8.9	10.1	7.7	11.4
Bilateral grants [2]	1.4	3.0	4.5	5.6	7.3	7.0	6.7	6.5	6.8	8.4
Bilateral loans	1.3	1.4	1.0	0.8	0.9	0.6	0.3	0.3	-	-0.2
Multilateral contributions [3]	0.5	2.8	2.5	2.3	1.2	2.0	1.9	3.4	0.9	3.0
Other official flows	0.1	1.1	(Z)	1.0	0.2	-0.6	-1.8	1.9	-0.5	-0.5
Private flows at market terms	2.5	4.3	13.6	17.4	-9.3	7.5	4.4	3.2	7.3	-2.4
Direct investment	1.9	3.4	2.3	4.4	0.9	3.1	8.0	4.2	7.8	-3.4
Private export credits and portfolio investment	0.6	0.9	11.2	13.0	-10.2	4.4	-3.6	-1.0	-0.5	-1.0
Private voluntary agencies	0.6	1.3	1.3	1.5	1.5	1.7	1.6	2.3	1.9	2.5
Australia	0.4	0.9	1.0	1.5	1.2	1.1	0.9	3.6	1.5	1.0
Austria	0.1	0.3	0.1	0.1	0.2	0.1	0.2	0.3	0.2	0.6
Belgium	0.3	2.9	0.8	3.5	1.3	-0.8	-0.3	1.8	1.5	(NA)
Canada	0.6	3.2	2.6	2.8	1.7	1.6	2.5	2.7	2.7	3.3
Denmark	0.1	0.8	1.1	0.6	0.4	0.5	0.9	0.7	0.9	1.1
Finland	(Z)	0.2	0.2	0.3	0.3	0.4	0.6	0.8	0.9	(NA)
France	1.8	11.6	9.3	8.9	8.9	9.2	8.7	7.2	7.2	(NA)
Germany [6]	1.5	10.6	7.0	6.5	5.8	7.9	8.8	11.8	12.1	(NA)
Ireland	(NA)	(Z)	(Z)	0.1	0.1	0.1	0.1	0.3	0.1	0.2
Italy	0.7	4.0	3.1	2.3	2.2	2.6	2.0	5.1	5.8	(NA)
Japan	1.8	6.8	7.9	11.7	11.6	14.6	20.3	21.2	24.1	(NA)
Netherlands	0.4	2.4	2.2	2.0	2.6	2.8	3.2	2.7	2.5	3.6
New Zealand	(Z)	0.1	0.1	0.1	0.1	0.1	0.1	0.1	0.1	0.1
Norway	0.1	0.9	0.7	0.6	0.6	0.7	0.9	0.9	0.9	(NA)
Sweden	0.2	1.9	1.3	1.3	1.4	1.7	1.8	2.3	2.3	2.6
Switzerland	0.1	2.7	3.3	3.4	2.5	1.4	-1.6	2.0	2.7	0.8
United Kingdom	1.3	12.2	6.1	4.8	2.5	6.7	3.5	4.7	3.4	-4.4

- Represents or rounds to zero. NA Not available. Z Less than $50 million. [1] Includes flows to OPEC countries (see footnote 4). Comprises as donors Australia, Austria, Belgium, Canada, Denmark, Finland, France, Ireland, Italy, Japan, Netherlands, New Zealand, Norway, Sweden, Switzerland, United Kingdom, United States, and West Germany. [2] Includes "grant-like" flows (i.e., loans repayable in recipients' currencies). [3] Includes capital subscriptions to multilateral organizations in the form of demand instruments as date of issue. [4] Algeria, Ecuador, Gabon, Iran, Iraq, Kuwait, Libya, Nigeria, Qatar, Saudi Arabia, United Arab Emirates, and Venezuela. [5] Bulgaria, Czechoslovakia, East Germany, Hungary, Poland, Romania, and Soviet Union. [6] Former West Germany (prior to unification).
Source: Organization for Economic Cooperation and Development, Paris, France, unpublished data.

No. 1412. Per Capita Public and Private Aid to Developing Countries: 1980 to 1988

[In dollars. See headnote, table 1411. Private aid figures exclude government subsidies to voluntary agencies. Countries are ranked by per capita gross national product in 1988]

COUNTRY	OFFICIAL DEVELOPMENT ASSISTANCE			PRIVATE VOLUNTARY AID			COUNTRY	OFFICIAL DEVELOPMENT ASSISTANCE			PRIVATE VOLUNTARY AID		
	1980	1985	1988	1980	1985	1988		1980	1985	1988	1980	1985	1988
Switzerland	40	46	92	10	8	13	France	77	72	123	1	1	2
Japan	29	31	74	(Z)	(Z)	1	Austria	24	33	40	3	2	3
Denmark	92	86	180	3	3	4	Netherlands	115	78	151	6	7	12
Norway	119	138	234	8	12	13	Belgium	60	45	63	5	2	1
Sweden	116	101	182	7	9	14	Australia	45	47	67	3	3	3
Finland	23	43	123	3	3	3	United Kingdom	33	27	46	2	3	4
West Germany	58	48	77	7	7	11	Italy	12	19	56	(Z)	(Z)	(Z)
United States	31	39	41	6	6	9	New Zealand	23	16	31	2	3	2
Canada	45	64	90	4	7	8	Ireland	9	11	16	-	6	6

- Represents or rounds to zero. Z Less than 50 cents.
Source: Organization for Economic Cooperation and Development, Paris, France, unpublished data.

No. 1413. Military Expenditures in Current and Constant (1989) Dollars: 1980 to 1989

[In millions of dollars, except as indicated. See also table 532. For most countries, data for expenditures and for GNP were based on local currencies which were deflated to constant 1989 local currency values before conversion to U.S. dollar equivalents. In general, the rates used for conversion are the 1989 average par/market exchange rates as supplied by the International Bank for Reconstruction and Development]

COUNTRY	CURRENT DOLLARS				CONSTANT (1989) DOLLARS				Per capita (dollars)		Percent of GNP[1]	
	1980	1985	1988	1989	1980	1985	1988	1989	1980	1989	1980	1989
United States	144,000	265,800	293,100	304,100	212,100	302,600	305,100	304,100	931	1,222	5.3	5.8
Algeria [2]	940	1,040	1,595	2,313	1,385	1,183	1,660	2,313	73	94	3.9	5.1
Argentina	1,559	[2]1,847	1,989	1,858	2,296	[2]2,103	2,070	1,858	81	58	3.6	3.4
Australia	3,226	5,856	6,093	6,153	4,753	6,666	6,342	6,153	325	368	2.3	2.3
Austria	820	[2]1,322	1,310	1,402	1,208	[2]1,505	1,364	1,402	160	184	1.1	1.1
Belgium	2,951	3,592	3,811	3,881	4,348	4,089	3,968	3,881	442	392	3.3	2.5
Brazil [2]	1,899	2,793	5,731	(NA)	2,799	3,180	5,966	(NA)	23	(NA)	0.7	(NA)
Bulgaria [2]	3,993	5,808	5,868	5,885	5,883	6,612	6,109	5,885	665	656	13.1	11.9
Canada	5,176	8,943	10,500	10,840	7,626	10,180	10,930	10,840	317	413	1.9	2.0
Chile [3]	449	619	[2]803	[2]790	662	704	[2]836	[2]790	60	[2]61	3.6	[2]3.4
China:												
Mainland [2]	16,370	19,850	21,830	22,330	24,120	22,600	22,720	22,330	25	20	8.8	3.7
Taiwan	3,222	[2]6,377	[2]6,607	[2]8,060	4,748	[2]7,260	[2]6,877	[2]8,060	266	[2]397	6.5	[2]5.4
Cuba [3]	1,140	1,335	1,350	1,377	1,680	1,520	1,405	1,377	174	131	6.5	3.9
Czechoslovakia [2]	5,249	7,998	9,131	8,361	7,734	9,105	9,505	8,361	507	534	7.4	6.8
Denmark	1,454	1,909	2,135	2,184	2,143	2,173	2,222	2,184	418	426	2.5	2.2
East Germany [2]	7,040	10,810	12,770	13,970	10,370	12,310	13,290	13,970	620	848	7.9	8.8
Egypt [2]	2,923	6,785	5,559	3,499	4,306	7,724	5,786	3,499	103	67	9.5	5.0
El Salvador	120	[2]276	[2]237	[2]252	177	[2]314	[2]247	[2]252	38	[2]48	2.7	[2]4.0
Finland	909	1,435	1,687	1,788	1,339	1,633	1,756	1,788	280	360	1.6	1.6
France	21,230	29,600	33,490	35,260	31,270	33,690	34,860	35,260	581	628	4.0	3.7
Greece	1,779	3,052	3,170	3,097	2,621	3,474	3,300	3,097	272	309	5.5	5.9
Hungary [2]	2,832	3,782	4,396	4,064	4,173	4,305	4,576	4,064	390	384	7.2	6.3
India	3,608	6,662	8,377	8,174	5,316	7,584	8,721	8,174	8	10	3.2	3.1
Indonesia	1,093	1,446	1,402	1,510	1,611	1,646	1,460	1,510	10	8	3.1	1.7
Iran [2]	2,624	(NA)	(NA)	(NA)	3,867	(NA)	(NA)	(NA)	99	(NA)	7.0	(NA)
Israel	6,654	7,027	5,585	5,745	9,805	7,999	5,814	5,745	2,623	1,323	28.8	12.8
Italy	10,110	15,320	19,790	20,720	14,900	17,440	20,600	20,720	264	360	2.1	2.4
Japan	12,330	20,650	26,100	28,410	18,170	23,510	27,170	28,410	156	231	0.9	1.0
Kuwait	892	1,525	1,273	1,964	1,314	1,736	1,325	1,964	959	962	2.9	6.2
Malaysia	664	[2]910	832	1,039	978	[2]1,036	866	1,039	71	61	4.4	2.9
Mexico	456	1,049	962	875	671	1,194	1,002	875	10	10	0.4	0.5
Morocco [2]	763	941	1,102	1,203	1,124	(NA)	1,147	1,203	55	48	7.2	5.5
Netherlands	4,048	5,433	6,070	6,399	5,965	6,185	6,319	6,399	422	431	3.1	2.9
Nicaragua [2]	53	192	(NA)	(NA)	78	218	(NA)	(NA)	28	(NA)	6.2	(NA)
Nigeria	447	294	201	130	658	335	210	130	7	1	2.4	0.5
North Korea [2]	4,380	5,260	5,840	6,000	6,454	5,988	6,079	6,000	359	285	20.0	20.0
Norway	1,320	2,152	2,680	2,925	1,945	2,450	2,790	2,925	476	691	3.0	3.3
Oman	1,059	1,937	1,350	1,552	1,560	2,205	1,405	1,552	1,585	1,085	22.1	20.3
Pakistan	777	1,748	2,309	2,488	1,145	1,990	2,404	2,488	13	22	5.4	6.8
Peru	1,457	[2]2,356	(NA)	(NA)	2,147	[2]2,682	(NA)	(NA)	124	(NA)	5.0	(NA)
Philippines	501	405	675	960	738	461	702	960	15	15	1.9	2.2
Poland [2]	9,644	14,670	15,350	15,480	14,210	16,700	15,980	15,480	399	410	8.9	8.9
Portugal	858	1,051	1,338	1,457	1,265	1,196	1,393	1,457	129	141	3.6	3.3
Romania [2]	4,587	6,840	7,004	6,916	6,759	7,787	7,291	6,916	304	299	6.1	6.1
Saudi Arabia	14,990	21,340	13,600	14,690	22,090	24,290	14,160	14,690	2,176	897	14.3	16.0
Singapore	533	1,125	1,343	1,475	785	1,281	1,398	1,475	325	550	5.2	5.1
South Africa	2,563	2,612	3,555	3,786	3,777	2,974	3,701	3,786	125	98	5.2	4.4
South Korea	3,821	6,109	8,030	9,100	5,629	6,955	8,359	9,100	148	213	6.1	4.3
Soviet Union [2] ...	198,200	277,200	317,900	311,000	292,000	315,600	330,900	311,000	1,096	1,077	12.9	11.7
Spain	4,560	6,639	7,244	7,775	6,719	7,558	7,541	7,775	179	199	2.3	2.1
Sweden	3,257	4,390	4,875	4,872	4,799	4,998	5,075	4,872	577	574	3.1	2.6
Switzerland	2,461	[2]3,487	[2]3,468	[2]3,806	3,626	[2]3,970	[2]3,610	[2]3,806	568	[2]568	2.4	[2]2.1
Syria [3]	1,936	[2]3,627	[2]1,801	2,234	2,852	[2]4,129	[2]1,875	2,234	328	186	17.2	11.6
Thailand	1,011	1,814	1,741	1,843	1,489	2,065	1,813	1,843	32	33	4.1	2.7
Turkey	1,635	2,552	2,826	3,150	2,409	2,906	2,942	3,150	53	56	4.8	4.1
United Arab Emirates	1,724	[2]1,901	1,587	1,471	2,541	[2]2,165	1,652	1,471	2,540	695	5.5	5.3
United Kingdom ..	22,080	32,560	32,710	34,630	32,530	37,070	34,050	34,630	578	605	5.0	4.2
Venezuela	317	358	[2]647	[2]407	467	407	[2]674	[2]407	31	[2]21	1.1	[2]1.0
West Germany	22,400	29,980	32,300	33,600	33,000	34,130	33,630	33,600	536	544	3.3	2.8
Yugoslavia	1,669	1,884	2,528	2,126	2,459	2,144	2,631	2,126	110	90	4.3	3.6

NA Not available.   [1] Military expenditure as percent of gross national product. For additional information on comparisons between communist and noncommunist countries, see footnote 4, table 548.   [2] Estimated.   [3] Data probably omit a major share of total military expenditures, probably including most arms acquisitions.

Source: U.S. Arms Control and Disarmament Agency, *World Military Expenditures and Arms Transfers,* annual.

No. 1414. Armed Forces Personnel—Number and Rate, by Country: 1980 to 1989

[**Personnel data as of July.** Armed Forces refer to active-duty military personnel, including paramilitary forces where those forces resemble regular units in their organization, equipment, training, or mission. Reserve forces are not included]

COUNTRY	ARMED FORCES PERSONNEL (1,000)						ARMED FORCES PER 1,000 POPULATION					
	1980	1985	1986	1987	1988	1989	1980	1985	1986	1987	1988	1989
United States	2,050	2,244	2,269	2,279	2,246	2,241	9.0	9.4	9.4	9.3	9.1	9.0
Algeria	101	170	180	170	126	126	5.4	7.7	7.9	7.2	5.2	5.1
Argentina.	155	129	104	118	95	95	5.5	4.3	3.4	3.8	3.0	3.0
Australia	71	70	71	70	71	70	4.9	4.4	4.4	4.3	4.3	4.2
Austria	40	40	39	70	55	48	5.3	5.3	5.2	9.2	7.2	6.3
Belgium.	108	107	107	109	110	110	11.0	10.9	10.8	11.0	11.1	11.1
Brazil	450	496	527	541	319	319	3.7	3.6	3.7	3.8	2.2	2.1
Bulgaria.	188	189	190	191	160	150	21.2	21.2	21.2	21.3	17.8	16.7
Canada.	82	83	85	86	88	88	3.4	3.3	3.4	3.4	3.4	3.4
Chile.	116	124	127	127	96	95	10.5	10.3	10.3	10.1	7.6	7.4
China: Mainland	4,650	4,100	4,030	3,530	3,783	3,903	26.1	22.7	19.9	18.4	19.4	18.6
Taiwan.	465	440	390	365	390	379	22.8	29.4	29.2	28.9	28.6	28.3
Cuba	220	297	257	297	297	297	22.8	29.4	29.2	28.9	28.6	28.3
Czechoslovakia	190	210	214	215	211	175	12.5	13.5	13.8	13.8	13.5	11.2
Denmark	33	29	28	28	30	31	6.4	5.7	5.5	5.5	5.8	6.0
East Germany	228	242	242	241	242	262	13.6	14.5	14.6	14.5	14.6	15.9
Egypt	447	466	400	450	452	450	10.7	9.9	8.3	9.1	8.9	8.7
El Salvador	16	48	48	49	45	45	3.4	10.0	9.8	9.8	8.8	8.6
Finland	36	40	37	37	40	39	7.5	8.2	7.4	7.4	8.1	7.9
France	575	563	558	559	558	554	10.7	10.2	10.1	10.0	10.0	9.9
Greece	186	201	202	199	199	201	19.3	20.2	20.3	19.9	19.9	20.1
Honduras	14	21	22	22	19	19	3.9	5.0	5.1	4.9	4.2	4.1
Hungary	120	117	116	116	117	109	11.2	11.0	10.9	10.9	11.0	10.3
India	1,104	1,515	1,492	1,502	1,362	1,257	1.6	2.0	1.9	1.9	1.7	1.5
Indonesia	250	281	278	281	284	285	1.6	1.6	1.6	1.6	1.6	1.5
Iran	305	345	345	350	654	604	7.8	7.3	7.1	6.9	12.6	11.2
Iraq	430	788	800	900	1,000	1,000	32.5	50.2	49.2	53.5	57.4	55.3
Israel	196	195	180	180	191	191	52.4	47.8	43.5	42.8	44.7	44.0
Italy	500	531	529	531	533	533	8.9	9.3	9.2	9.3	9.3	9.3
Japan	242	241	245	244	245	247	2.1	2.0	2.0	2.0	2.0	2.0
Kuwait.	12	16	18	20	15	20	8.8	9.3	10.0	10.7	7.7	9.9
Malaysia	83	106	106	106	108	110	6.0	6.8	6.6	6.5	6.5	6.4
Mexico	120	140	141	141	154	154	1.7	1.8	1.8	1.7	1.8	1.8
Morocco	117	165	185	200	195	195	5.7	7.2	7.9	8.3	7.9	7.8
Netherlands	107	103	106	106	107	106	7.6	7.1	7.3	7.2	7.2	7.1
Nicaragua	24	74	75	80	74	74	8.6	22.5	22.2	23.2	21.0	20.4
Nigeria	150	134	138	138	107	107	1.7	1.3	1.3	1.3	1.0	0.9
North Korea.	700	784	838	838	842	1,040	38.9	40.0	42.0	41.3	40.8	49.5
Norway	40	36	38	38	40	43	9.7	8.7	9.1	9.1	9.5	10.2
Oman	15	25	26	27	27	29	15.2	20.2	20.3	22.3	19.3	20.3
Pakistan	467	644	573	572	484	520	5.5	6.5	5.6	5.4	4.5	4.7
Peru	151	128	127	127	111	110	8.7	6.5	6.3	6.2	5.3	5.1
Philippines	155	157	161	161	105	106	3.2	2.7	2.7	2.7	1.7	1.7
Poland	408	439	443	441	430	350	11.5	11.8	11.8	11.7	11.4	9.3
Portugal	88	102	101	105	104	104	9.0	10.0	9.9	10.2	10.1	10.1
Qatar	6	7	9	11	7	7	26.0	20.1	24.0	27.2	16.1	15.1
Romania	211	237	238	248	220	207	9.5	10.4	10.4	10.8	9.5	8.9
Saudi Arabia	79	80	80	80	84	82	7.8	5.9	5.6	5.4	5.3	5.0
Singapore	50	59	56	55	56	56	20.7	23.1	21.5	21.1	21.0	20.7
South Africa.	70	95	90	102	100	100	2.3	2.7	2.5	2.8	2.7	2.6
South Korea.	600	600	604	604	626	647	15.7	14.6	14.5	14.4	14.8	15.1
Soviet Union	3,900	3,900	3,900	3,900	3,900	3,700	14.6	14.0	13.9	13.7	13.6	12.8
Spain	356	314	314	314	304	277	9.5	8.2	8.1	8.1	7.8	7.1
Sweden.	70	69	66	66	65	62	8.4	8.3	7.8	7.8	7.7	7.4
Switzerland	23	23	21	20	23	17	3.6	3.5	3.2	3.0	3.5	2.5
Syria.	250	402	400	400	400	400	28.8	38.8	37.2	35.9	34.5	33.3
Thailand	234	270	275	275	273	273	5.0	5.2	5.2	5.1	5.0	4.9
Turkey	717	814	860	879	847	780	15.9	16.0	16.5	16.4	15.5	13.9
United Arab Emirates.	44	44	44	44	43	43	44.0	28.0	25.7	23.8	21.7	20.3
United Kingdom	330	334	331	328	324	318	5.9	5.9	5.8	5.8	5.7	5.6
Venezuela	55	71	66	69	73	75	3.7	4.1	3.7	3.8	3.9	3.9
Vietnam	900	1,000	1,300	1,300	1,100	1,000	16.9	16.9	21.4	21.0	17.3	15.4
West Germany	490	495	495	495	495	503	8.0	8.1	8.1	8.1	8.1	8.1
Yugoslavia.	260	258	234	234	229	225	11.6	11.2	10.0	10.0	9.7	9.5

Source: U.S. Arms Control and Disarmament Agency, *World Military Expenditures and Arms Transfers*, annual.

Guide to—Sources of Statistics, State Statistical Abstracts, and Foreign Statistical Abstracts

Alphabetically arranged by subject, this guide contains references to the important primary sources of statistical information for the United States. Secondary sources have been included if the information contained in them is presented in a particularly convenient form or if primary sources are not readily available. Nonrecurrent publications presenting compilations or estimates for years later than 1980 or types of data not available in regular series are also included.

Much valuable information may also be found in State reports (see pp. 901–905) and foreign statistical abstracts (see pp. 906 and 907) and in reports for particular commodities, industries, or similar segments of our economic and social structures, many of which are not included here.

Publications listed under each subject are divided into two main groups: "U.S. Government" and "Other." The location of the publisher of each report is given except for Federal agencies located in Washington, DC. Most Federal publications may be purchased from the Superintendent of Documents, U.S. Government Printing Office, Washington, DC 20402, tel. 202-783-3238, or from Government Printing Office bookstores in certain major cities. In some cases, Federal publications may be obtained from the issuing agency.

Major reports, such as the Census of Population, which consist of many volumes, are listed by their general, all-inclusive titles.

Bureau of the Census Publications

In most cases, separate reports of the most recent censuses are available for each State, subject, industry, etc. Complete information on publications of all the censuses and current surveys conducted by the Bureau of the Census appears in the *Bureau of the Census Catalog,* published annually and available from the Superintendent of Documents.

Abortions—*see* Vital Statistics.

Accidents —*see also* Health; Insurance; and Vital Statistics

    U.S. Government

        Bureau of Labor Statistics

            Evaluating Your Firm's Injury and Illness Record, Construction Industries, Report 776 (1990).

            Handbook of Labor Statistics. 1989.

            Heatburn Injuries, Bulletin 2358 (1990).

            Injuries Involving Longshore Operation, Bulletin 2326 (1989).

            Occupational Injuries and Illnesses in the United States by Industry. Annual.

        Department of Transportation

            Transportation Safety Information Report. Quarterly.

        Federal Railroad Administration

Accidents —Con.

    U.S. Government —Con.

        Accident/Incident Bulletin. Summary, statistics, and analysis of accidents on railroads in the United States. Annual.

        Rail-Highway Crossing Accident/Incident and Inventory Bulletin. Annual.

        Mine Safety and Health Administration

            Informational Reports by Mining Industry: Coal; Metallic Minerals; Nonmetallic Minerals (except stone and coal); Stone, Sand, and Gravel. Annual.

            Mine Injuries and Worktime. (Some preliminary data.) Quarterly.

        National Center for Health Statistics

            Vital Statistics of the United States. Annual.

                Volume I, Natality

                Volume II, Mortality

                Volume III, Marriage and Divorce

Agriculture —Con.
  U.S. Government —Con.

      Loans and Discounts of Farm Credit Banks and Associations. Annual.

    National Oceanic and Atmospheric Administration

      Weekly Weather and Crop Bulletin. National summary.

    Soil Conservation Service

      National Resources Inventory, 1982. Periodic.

      Report of Administrator of Soil Conservation Service. Annual.

Air Force —*see* National Defense.

Air Pollution —*see* Environment.

Aliens —*see* Immigration.

American Samoa —*see* Outlying Areas.

Area —*see* Geography.

Army— *see* National Defense.

Aviation— *see* Transportation.

Banks and Banking— *see* Money.

Births— *see* Vital Statistics.

Broadcasting— *see* Communications.

Building Permits— *see* Construction.

Business —*see also* Economic Indexes; Investments; Manufactures; Retail and Wholesale Trade; Science Resources; *and* Service Establishments

  U.S. Government

    Administrative Office of the United States Courts

      Annual Report of the Director.

    Board of Governors of the Federal Reserve System

      Federal Reserve Bulletin. Monthly.

    Bureau of the Census

      Census of Retail Trade. Quinquennial. (1987, most recent.)

      Census of Service Industries. Quinquennial. (1987, most recent.)

      Census of Wholesale Trade. Quinquennial. (1987, most recent.)

      Census of Transportation. Quinquennial. (1987, most recent.)

      County Business Patterns. Annual.

      Characteristics of Business Owners. 1982.

      Current Business Reports. Retail Trade, Sales, and Inventories, BR; and Wholesale Trade, Sales, and Inventories, BW.

      Minority-Owned Businesses. Quinquennial. (1982, most recent.)

      Quarterly Financial Report for Manufacturing, Mining, and Trade Corporations.

    Bureau of Economic Analysis

      Business Statistics, 1961-88. 1989.

      The Detailed Input-Output Structure of the U.S. Economy, 1977. 1984.

      Fixed Reproducible Tangible Wealth in the United States, 1925-85. 1987.

Business —Con.
  U.S. Government —Con.

      The National Income and Product Accounts of the United States, 1929-1982: Statistical Tables. 1986.

      Selected Data on U.S. Direct Investment Abroad, 1950-89. 1990.

      Summary Input-Output Tables of the U.S. Economy: 1980-85. 1990.

      Survey of Current Business. Monthly.

    Council of Economic Advisers

      Economic Indicators. Monthly.

      Economic Report of the President. Annual.

    Federal Trade Commission

      Mergers & Acquisitions, 1972-1974. 1978

    Internal Revenue Service

      Statistics of Income.

        Corporation Income Tax Returns. Annual

      Statistics of Income Bulletin. Quarterly.

    International Trade Administration

      U.S. Industrial Outlook. Annual.

    Patent and Trademark Office

      Commissioner of Patents and Trademarks Annual Report.

      Patenting Trends in the United States, State Country Report, 1963-1988.

      Technology Assessment and Forecast Report - "All Technologies." Annual.

    Securities and Exchange Commission

      Annual Report.

      Statistical Review. Monthly. (Discontinued February 1989.)

    Small Business Administration

      Annual Report.

  Other

    The Conference Board, New York, NY

      Economic Road Maps. Monthly.

    The Dun & Bradstreet Corporation, New York, NY

      The Business Failure Record. Annual.

      Monthly Business Starts Report.

      Monthly Business Failure Report.

      Monthly New Business Incorporations Report.

      Quarterly Survey of Business Expectations.

    Fortune (Time Warner), New York, NY

      The Fortune Directory of the 500 Largest Industrial Corporations. (Annual supplement to Fortune.)

      The Fortune Directory of the 500 Largest Non-industrial Corporations. (Annual supplement to Fortune.)

    National Bureau of Economic Research, Cambridge, MA

      Financial Aspects of the United States Pension System, Zvi Bodie and John B. Shoven, editors. 1983. (University of Chicago Press, Chicago, IL.)

Communications —Con.
Other —Con.

    International Year Book. Annual.
    Market Guide. Annual.

  Electronic Industries Association, Washington, DC

    Electronic Market Data Book. Annual.
    Electronic Market Trends. Monthly.
    Electronics Foreign Trade. Monthly.
    Electronics Foreign Trade 5-Year Summary. Annual.

  Radio Advertising Bureau, New York, NY

    Radio Facts. Annual.

  United States Telephone Association, Washington, DC

    Statistics of the Independent Telephone Industry. Annual.

  Warren Publishing, Inc., Washington, DC

    Cable Action Update. Weekly.
    Cable and Station Coverage Atlas. Annual.
    Television Action Update. Weekly.
    Television and Cable Factbook. Annual.
    TV Station & Cable Ownership Directory. Semiannual.

Construction, Housing, and Real Estate —*see also* Money *and* Roads

  U.S. Government

  Board of Governors of the Federal Reserve System

    Federal Reserve Bulletin. Monthly.

  Bureau of Census

    Census of Construction Industries. Quinquennial. (1987, most recent.)
    Census of Housing. Decennial. (1980, most recent.)
    Current Construction Reports: Housing Starts, C20 (monthly); New Residential Construction in Selected Metropolitan Statistical Areas, C21 (quarterly); Housing Completions, C22 (monthly); New One-Family Houses Sold and for Sale, C25 (monthly with annual report, Characteristics of New Housing); Price Index of New One-Family Houses Sold, C27 (quarterly); Value of New Construction Put in Place, C30 (monthly with occasional historical supplement); Housing Units Authorized by Building Permits, C40 (monthly and annual); Residential Alterations and Repairs, C50 (quarterly and annual).
    Current Housing Reports: Housing Vacancies, H-111 (quarterly and annual); Market Absorption of Apartments, H-130 (quarterly and annual); Characteristics of Apartments Completed, H-131 (annual); Annual Housing Survey, H-150 (series of six biennial reports); Annual Housing Survey—Housing Characteristics for Selected Metropolitan Areas, H-170.
    Social Indicators, 1980.

Construction, Housing, and Real Estate —Con.
  U.S. Government —Con.

  Bureau of Economic Analysis

    Business Statistics, 1961-88. 1989.
    Fixed Reproducible Tangible Wealth in the United States, 1925-85. 1987.
    The National Income and Product Accounts of the United States, 1929-82: Statistical Tables. 1986.
    Survey of Current Business. Monthly.

  Bureau of Labor Statistics

    Compensation and Working conditions. Monthly.
    Employment and Earnings. Monthly.
    Employment, Hours, and Earnings, United States, 1909-90. 1991. Bulletin No. 2370.)
      Supplement to Employment and Earnings
    Evaluating Your Firm's Injury and Illness Record, Construction Industries Report 776, (1990).
    Monthly Labor Review.
    Occupational Employment in Mining, Construction, Finance, and Services. 1992. (Bulletin No. 2397.)
    Occupational Injuries and Illnesses in the United States by Industry. Annual.

  Department of Housing and Urban Development

    Survey of Mortgage Lending Activity. Monthly and quarterly press releases.

  Department of Veterans Affairs

    Loan Guaranty Highlights. Quarterly.
    Trend Data 1964-1988.

  Energy Information Administration

    Residential Energy Consumption Survey: Housing Characteristics. Triennial.

  International Trade Administration

    Construction Review. Bimonthly.

  Office of Thrift Supervision

    Annual Report.
    Savings and Home Financing Source Book. Annual.

  Other

  Dodge, F.W., National Information Services Division, McGraw-Hill Information Systems Co., New York, NY

    Dodge Construction Potentials. Monthly.

  NATIONAL ASSOCIATION OF REALTORS, Washington, DC

    Home Sales. Monthly.

Consumer Income and Expenditures, and Personal Income —*see also* Agriculture; Economic Indexes; Investments; *and* National Income

  U.S. Government

  Board of Governors of the Federal Reserve System

    Federal Reserve Bulletin. Monthly.

  Bureau of the Census

    Census of Population. Decennial. (1980, most recent.)

Economic Indexes —Con.
U.S. Government—Con.

    Federal Reserve Banks. Monthly review published by each Bank with special reference to its own Federal Reserve District.
    Federal Reserve Bulletin. Monthly. (Also monthly releases on industrial production indexes.)

  Bureau of Economic Analysis
    Business Statistics, 1961-88. 1989.
    The National Income and Product Accounts of the United States, 1929-82: Statistical Tables. 1986.
    Survey of Current Business. Monthly.

  Bureau of Labor Statistics
    CPE Detailed Report. Monthly.
    Employment Cost Indexes and Levels. Annual.
    Producer Price Indexes. Monthly, with annual supplement.
    Handbook of Labor Statistics. 1989.
    Monthly Labor Review.

  Council of Economic Advisers
    Economic Indicators. Monthly.
    Economic Report of the President. Annual.

Other

  The Conference Board, New York, NY
    The Conference Board Statistical Bulletin. Monthly.

  National Bureau of Economic Research, Cambridge, MA
    The National Balance Sheet of the United States, 1953-80, by Raymond W. Goldsmith. 1982. (University of Chicago Press, Chicago, IL.)
    The U.S. National Income and Product Accounts: Selected Topics, Murray F. Foss, editor. 1982. (Studies in Income and Wealth, No. 47.) (University of Chicago Press, Chicago, IL.)

Education —*see also* Science Resources; *and* Vocational Rehabilitation

U.S. Government

  Bureau of the Census
    Census of Population. Decennial. (1980, most recent.)
    Current Population Reports. (Series on Population Characteristics, P-20; and Special Studies, P-23.)
    Finances of Public School Systems. Annual. (GF No. 10.)

  Bureau of Labor Statistics
    Educational Attainment of Workers, March 1982-83. 1984. (Bulletin No. 2191.)
    Handbook of Labor Statistics. 1989.
    How Workers Get Their Training. 1985. (Bulletin No. 2226.)
    Labor Force Statistics Derived From the Current Population Survey, 1948-87. 1988. (Bulletin No. 2307.)

Education —Con.
U.S. Government —Con.

    Occupational Projections and Training Data. Biennial.
    Students, Graduates, and Dropouts, October 1980-82. 1983. (Bulletin No. 2192.)

  Department of Education
    Annual Report.
    Inflation Measures for Schools and Colleges. September 1983.

  Employment and Training Administration
    Employment and Training Report of the President. Annual.

  National Center for Education Statistics
    Associate Degrees and Other Formal Awards Below the Baccalaureate. Annual.
    College and University Library Survey. (1985, most recent.)
    The Condition of Education. Annual.
    Digest of Education Statistics. Annual.
    Earned Degrees Conferred. Annual.
    Faculty Salaries, Tenure, and Benefits. Annual.
    Fall Enrollment in Colleges and Universities. Annual.
    High School and Beyond. Reports issued on 1980 high school sophomores and seniors and their transition to further education and labor force participation.
    National Longitudinal Study. Reports issued on high school seniors from class of 1972 and their transition to higher education and the labor force.
    Participation in Adult Education. (1984, most recent.)
    Projections of Education Statistics. Annual.
    Residence and Migration of College Students. (1986, most recent.)
    Revenues and Expenditures for Public Elementary and Secondary Education. Annual.

  National Science Foundation
    Academic Research and Equipment Needs in the Physical Sciences. Report. Biennial.
    Academic Research Equipment and Equipment Needs in Selected Science/Engineering Fields. Report. Biennial.
    Academic Research Equipment in Computer Science, Central Computer Facilities and Engineering. Report. Biennial.
    Academic Science and Engineering: Graduate Enrollment and Support. Detailed Statistical Tables. Annual.
    Academic Science/Engineering: R&D Expenditures. Detailed Statistical Tables. Annual.
    Characteristics of Doctoral Scientists and Engineers in the United States. Detailed Statistical Tables. Biennial.

Education —Con.
  U.S. Government —Con.

Characteristics of Recent Science/Engineering Graduates. Detailed Statistical Tables. Biennial.

Characteristics of Science/Engineering Equipment in Academic Settings: 1989-90. Report.

Federal Support to Universities, Colleges, and Selected Nonprofit Institutions. A report to the President and Congress. Detailed Statistical Tables. Annual.

International Science and Technology Data Update. Report. Annual.

National Patterns of R&D Resources. Report. Annual.

Profiles—Aeronautical/Astronautical Engineering, Agricultural Science, Biological Science, Chemical Engineering, Chemistry, Civil Engineering, Computer Science, Economics, Electrical/Electronic Engineering, Mechanical Engineering, and Psychology: Human Resources and Funding. Special Reports. (NSF 89-314, 89-319, 89-318, 89-312, 87-307, 90-303, 88-324, 88-333, 88-326, 87-309, and 88-325, respectively).

Research and Development Expenditures of State Government Agencies: Fiscal Years 1987 and 1988. Special Report. (NSF 90-309.)

Science and Engineering Degrees. A Source Book. Detailed Statistical Tables. Annual.

Science and Engineering Doctorates. Detailed Statistical Tables. Annual.

Science and Engineering Indicators. Report. Biennial.

Science and Engineering Personnel: A National Overview. Report. Biennial.

Science and Technology Data Book. Report. Annual.

Science Resources Studies Highlights. Frequent.

Favorable Employment Opportunities Continue for Recent S/E Graduates. (NSF 90-315.)

Growth Rate in Non-Federal Academic R&D Support Exceeds That in Federal Support in Last Decade. (NSF 89-309.)

Real Growth in Academic R&D Spending Slowed to 2% in FY 1987, Down from 9% in 1986. (NSF 88-314.)

Scientists and Engineers Now account for over 4 percent of total U.S. Employment. (NSF 88-313.)

Universities Report Improvement in Computer and Physical Science Instrumentation, but Deterioration in Engineering. (NSF 87-316.)

Scientific and Engineering Research Facilities at Universities and Colleges. Report. Biennial.

SRS (Division of Science Resources Studies) Data briefs. Frequent.

Education —Con.
  U.S. Government —Con.

Graduate Enrollments Climb in Science, Engineering, and Health. (NSF 90-326.)

Science and Engineering Doctoral Awards reached Record Highs in 1990. (NSF 91-308.)

S/E Baccalaureates Declined After 1986 As Masters and Doctoral Degrees Increased. (NSF 91-313.)

Women and Minorities in Science and Engineering. Report. Biennial.

Office for Civil Rights

Racial, Ethnic and Sex Enrollment Data, From Institutions of Higher Education. Fall 1982. Biennial.

State and National Summaries of Data from the fall 1982 Civil Rights Survey of Elementary and Secondary Schools. Biennial.

Other

American Council on Education, Washington, DC

A Fact Book on Higher Education. Quarterly.

National Norms for Entering College Freshmen. Annual.

Bowker (R.R.) Company, New York, NY

American Library Directory. Annual.

Book Publishing Annual. (1985, most recent.)

Bowker Annual Library and Book Trade Almanac.

Chronicle of Higher Education, Inc., Washington, DC

Almanac. Annual.

College Entrance Examination Board, New York, NY

National Report on College-Bound Seniors. Annual.

National Catholic Educational Association, Washington, DC

Catholic Schools in America. Annual.

United States Catholic Elementary and Secondary Schools. Staffing and Enrollment. Annual.

U.S. Catholic Elementary Schools and their Finances. Biennial.

U.S. Catholic Secondary Schools and their Finances. Biennial.

National Education Association, Washington, DC

Estimates of School Statistics. Annual.

Rankings of the States. Annual.

Status of the American Public School Teacher, 1985-86. Quinquennial.

Research Associates of Washington, Washington, DC

Inflation Measures for Schools & Colleges. Annual.

State Profiles: Financing Public Higher Education. Annual.

Elections

U.S. Government

Bureau of the Census

Congressional District Data:

1980 Census of Population and Housing, PHC80-4, Congressional Districts of the 98th and 99th Congress.

1980 Census of Population and Housing, PC80-SI-8, Congressional District Profiles, 98th Congress.

Current Population Reports. (Series P-20, Voting and Registration in the Election of November 19—. Biennial survey; and P-25, Projections of the Population of Voting Age for States: November 19—, Biennial projection.)

Commission on Civil Rights

New Evidence on School Desegregation. 1987.

The Economic Status of Americans of Asian Descent. 1988.

The Economic Status of Americans of Southern and Eastern European Ancestry. 1986.

The Voting Rights Act: Unfulfilled Goals. 1981.

Congress. Clerk of the House

Statistics of the Presidential and Congressional Election Years. Biennial.

Congress. Joint Committee on Printing

Congressional Directory. Biennial.

Other

The Council of State Governments, Lexington, KY

The Book of the States and its Supplement I, State Elective Officials and the Legislatures. Biennial.

State Legislative Leadership, Committees, and Staff. Biennial.

Elections Research Center, Chevy Chase MD

America Votes. A handbook of contemporary American election statistics, compiled and edited by Richard M. Scammon and Alice V. McGillivray. Biennial.

Joint Center for Political Studies, Washington, DC

Black Elected Officials: A National Roster. Annual.

Michigan, The University of, Center for Political Studies, Institute for Social Research, Ann Arbor, MI

Who Voted and for Whom. Biennial.

National Association of Latino Elected and Appointed Officials, Washington, DC

National Roster of Hispanic Elected Officials. Annual.

Pharos Books/World Almanac, New York, NY

The World Almanac and Book of Facts. Annual.

Elections —Con.

Other —Con.

World Almanac of U.S. Politics. 1989. 2nd edition, May 1991.

Electric Utilities —*see* Energy.

Emigration —*see* Immigration.

Employment —*see* Federal Government; Labor; *and* State and Local Government.

Energy —*see also* communications; Manufactures; Minerals; *and* Transportation

U.S. Government

Bureau of the Census

Current Industrial Reports. Monthly, quarterly, and annual series on various industries.

Bureau of the Census and Bureau of Mines

Industry Wage Survey: Electric and Gas Utilities, February 1988. (Bulletin 2337.) 1989

Raw Materials in the United States Economy: 1900-1977. (Issued 1980. Working Paper No. 47.)

Technology and Labor in Three Service Industries: Utilities, Retail Trade, and Lodging. (Bulletin 2367.) 1990.

Bureau of Labor Statistics

CPI Detailed Report. Monthly.

Consumer Prices: Energy and Food. Monthly.

Handbook of Labor Statistics. 1989.

Monthly Labor Review.

Energy Information Administration

Annual Energy Outlook.

Annual Energy Review.

Coal Distribution. Quarterly.

Coal Production. Annual.

Cost and Quality of Fuels for Electric Utility Plants. Annual.

Electric Power Annual.

Electric Power Monthly.

Electric Sales, Revenue, and Bills.

Energy Conservation Indicators. Annual.

Financial Statistics of Selected Electric Utilities. Annual.

Historical Plant Cost and Annual Production Expense for Selected

Electric Plants. 1987.

Inventory of Power Plants in the United States. Annual.

International Energy Annual.

Monthly Energy Review.

Natural Gas Annual.

Natural Gas Monthly.

Performance Profiles of Major Energy Producers. Annual.

Petroleum Marketing Monthly.

Petroleum Supply Annual.

Petroleum Supply Monthly.

Quarterly Coal Report.

Energy —Con.
  U.S. Government —Con.

    Residential Energy Consumption Survey: Consumption and Expenditures. Triennial.

    Residential Transportation Energy Consumption Survey. Triennial.

    Short-Term Energy Outlook. Quarterly.

    Solar Collector Manufacturing Activity. Annual.

    State Energy Data Report. Annual.

    State Energy Price and Expenditure Report. Annual.

    Statistics of Interstate Natural Gas Pipeline Companies. Annual.

    Uranium Industry Annual.

    U.S. Crude Oil, Natural Gas, and Natural Gas Liquids Reserves. Annual.

    Weekly Coal Production.

  National Science Foundation

    Federal Funds for Research and Development. Detailed Statistical Tables. Annual.

    Federal R&D Funding by Budget Function. Annual. Research and Development Expenditures of State Government Agencies: Fiscal Years 1987 and 1988. Special Report. (NSF 90-309.) Science and Engineering Indicators. Report. Biennial.

  Rural Electrification Administration

    Annual Statistical Report Rural Electrification Borrowers.

  Other

    American Gas Association, Arlington, VA

    Gas Facts. Annual.

    Gas Stats:

      Monthly Gas Utility Statistical Report.

      Quarterly Report of Gas Industry Operations.

    American Petroleum Institute, Washington, DC

    The Basic Petroleum Data Book. Triennial.

    The Center for Strategic and International Studies, Washington, DC

      Bioenergy and Economic Development: Planning for Biomass Energy Programs in the Third World. 1985.

      Forecasting U.S. Electricity Demand: Trends and Methodologies. 1985.

      Global Security: A Review of Strategic and International Issues. 1987.

      International Security Yearbook, 1984/85. 1985.

      National Security and Strategic Minerals. 1985.

      The Planetary Product in 1982. (World Economic Output, 1970-1982.) 1983.

      The Strategic Consequences of the Oil Price Collapse. 1987.

Energy —Con.
  Other —Con.

      The Strategic Dimension of Military Manpower. 1987.

      The United States and The World Economy. 1985.

    Edison Electric Institute, Washington, DC

      Electric Power Annual Report.

      Statistical Yearbook of the Electric Utility Industry. Annual.

    McGraw-Hill Publications Co., New York, NY

      Electrical World Directory of Electric Utilities. Annual.

    National Coal Association, Washington, DC

      Steam-Electric Plant Factors. Annual.

    Carl H. Pforzheimer & Co., New York, NY

      Comparative Oil Company Statistics, 19881987.

    U.S. Council for Energy Awareness, Washington, DC

      Electricity from Nuclear Energy: The Economic Context. July 1990.

      Electricity from Nuclear Energy. (Map booklet of U.S. Nuclear Power Plants.) 199091.

      Key Data on Nuclear Energy. July 1990.

      U.S. Public Opinion on Nuclear Energy. (Polling reports updated periodically.)

Environment

  U.S. Government

    Bureau of the Census

      Current Industrial Report, Survey of Pollution Abatement Costs and Expenditures, series MA-200.

    Council on Environmental Quality

      Environmental Quality. Annual.

      Environmental Trends. 1981.

      Environmental Protection Agency

      Air Quality Data. Annual.

      Cost of Clean Water. Annual.

      Federal Certification Test Results for Motor Vehicles. Annual.

      Municipal Water Facilities Inventory. Quinquennial.

      National Air Pollutant Emission Estimates, 1940-86.

      National Air Quality and Emissions Trends Report. 1990.

      Needs Survey, Conveyance and Treatment of Municipal Wastewater Summaries of Technical Data. Biennial.

      Pesticides Monitoring Journal. Quarterly.

      Radiation Data and Reports. Monthly.

      Sewage Facility Construction. Annual.

      Summary of Water Enforcement Actions Pursued by EPA since December 3, 1970. (Updated continuously.)

    Geological Survey

Federal Government Finances and Employment
—Con.
U.S. Government —Con.

Occupations of Federal White-Collar and Blue-Collar Workers. Biennial. (Odd Years.)

Pay Structure of the Federal Civil Service. Annual.

Work Years and Personnel Costs. Annual.

Other

Advisory Commission on Intergovernmental Relations, Washington, DC

A Catalog of Federal Grant-in-Aid Programs to State and Local Governments, FY 89. 1989. Every 3 years.

Changing Public Attitudes on Governments and Taxes. Annual.

Significant Features of Fiscal Federalism. Annual.

Moody's Investors Service, New York, NY

Moody's Municipal and Government Manual. Annual with semiweekly supplements.

National Bureau of Economic Research, Cambridge, MA

The National Balance Sheet of the United States, 1953-80, by Raymond W. Goldsmith. 1982. (University of Chicago Press, Chicago, IL)

Tax Foundation, Washington, DC

Facts and Figures on Government Finance. Annual.

Finance —*see* Federal Government; Investments; Money; *and* State and Local Government.

Fisheries

U.S. Government

Department of Agriculture

Aquaculture. Biennially.

National Oceanic and Atmospheric Administration, National Marine Fisheries Service

Fisheries of the United States. Annual.

Fishery Statistics of the United States. (Statistical Digest.) Annual.

Marine Recreational Fishery Statistical Survey, Atlantic and Gulf Coasts. Annual.

Marine Recreational Fishery Statistical Survey, Pacific Coast. Annual.

Food —*see also* Agriculture

U.S. Government

Bureau of the Census

Canned Food Report. (Issued five times a year.) (Last report, July 1981.)

Bureau of Labor Statistics

Consumer Expenditure Survey, integrated Diary and Interview Survey data. Annual press releases.

Consumer Expenditure Survey, 1988-89. 1991. (Bulletin No. 2383.)

Food —Con.
U.S. Government —Con.

Consumer Expenditure Survey, 1987. (Bulletin 2354.) 1990.

Consumer Expenditure Survey: Quarterly Data from the Interview Survey.

Consumer Prices: Energy and Food. Monthly.

CPI Detailed Report. Monthly.

Handbook of Labor Statistics. 1989.

Monthly Labor Review.

Producer Price Indexes. Monthly, with annual supplement.

Department of Agriculture

Agricultural Outlook. 11 issues per year.

Food Consumption Prices, and Expenditures, 1968-89 (SB-804). Revised annually.

Food Cost Review. 1989. (Agricultural Economic Report No. 651.) Revised annually.

Food Review. Quarterly.

Department of Agriculture, Food and Nutrition Service

Annual Historical Review:

Food and Nutrition Service Programs.

Food Program Update. Monthly.

Department of Agriculture, Science and Education Administration.

Family Economics Review. Quarterly.

Other

American Frozen Food Institute, Burlingame, CA

Frozen Food Pack Statistics. Annual.

National Food Processors Association, Washington, DC

Canned Fruit and Vegetable Pack and Stock Situation Reports. Quarterly.

Foreign Commerce —*see also* Economic Indexes; *and* International Accounts and Aid

U.S. Government

Army, Corps of Engineers

Waterborne Commerce of the United States (in five parts). Annual.

Bureau of the Census

Highlights of U.S. Export and Import Trade. Monthly; includes cumulative data. (FT 990.)

Summary of U.S. Export and Import Merchandise Trade. Monthly; includes cumulative data. (FT 900.)

Survey of the Origin of Exports of Manufacturing Establishments. Triennial. (Current Industrial Reports M76(AS)-8.)

U.S. Airborne Exports and General Imports. Monthly and annual. (FT 986.)

U.S. Commodity Exports and Imports as Related to Output. Annual. (Series ES 2.)

Health and Medical Care —Con.
Other —Con.

Survey of Dental Practice. Annual.

American Hospital Association, Chicago, IL
Hospital Statistics. Annual.

American Medical Association, Chicago, IL
Physician Characteristics and Distribution
in the U.S. Annual.
Reference Data on the Profile of Medical
Practice. Annual.
U.S. Medical Licensure Statistics, and
License Requirements. Annual.

American Nurses Association, Kansas City,
MO
Facts About Nursing: A Statistical Sum-
mary. Annual.

American Osteopathic Association. Chicago,
IL
Yearbook and Directory of Osteopathic
Physicians. Annual.

Medical Economics, Montvale, NJ
Physicians' Earnings and Expenses. Published annually in Medical Economics
magazine.

Metropolitan Life Insurance Company, New
York, NY
Health and Safety Education.
Statistical Bulletin. Quarterly.

Hospitals —*see* Health.

Hotels —*see* Service Establishments.

Household Appliances —*see* Construction, Housing,
and Real Estate.

Housing—*see* Construction.

Immigration and Naturalization

U.S. Government

Department of State, Bureau of Consular
Affairs
Report of the Visa Office. Annual. (Dept.
of State Pub. 8810.)

Department of Transportation
Report of Passenger Travel Between the
United States and Foreign Countries.
Annual, semiannual, quarterly, monthly.

Immigration and Naturalization Service
I&N Reporter. Quarterly.
Statistical Yearbook of the Immigration
and Naturalization Service. Annual.

National Science Foundation
Foreign Citizens in U.S. Science and En-
gineering: History, Status, and Outlook.
Special Report. (NSF 86-305, revised.)
Foreign Students Account for Most
Growth in Graduate Science and Engi-
neering Enrollment. Science Resources
Studies Highlights. (NSF 88-316.)
Immigrant Scientists and Engineers. De-
tailed Statistical Tables. Annual.
Science and Engineering Doctoral
Awards Reached Record Highs in
1990. SRS Data Brief. (NSF 91-308.)

Immigration and Naturalization —Con.
U.S. Government —Con.

Survey of Direct U.S. Private Capital Investment in Research and Development Facilities in Japan. (NSF 91-312)
Science and Engineering Doctorates. Detailed Statistical Tables. Annual.

Imports —*see* Foreign Commerce.

Income —*see* Consumer Income; *and* National Income.

Industry —*see* Business; Economic Indexes; *and*
Manufactures.

Institutions —*see* Education; Health; *and* Law Enforcement.

Insurance—*see also* Social Insurance

U.S. Government

Department of Veterans Affairs
Annual Report of The Secretary of Veter-
ans Affairs.
Government Life Insurance Programs for
Veterans and Members of the Service.
Annual.
Trend Data 1964-1988.

Other

American Council of Life Insurance, Washington, DC
Life Insurance Fact Book. Annual.(update
odd years)

Health Insurance Association of America,
Washington, DC
Source Book of Health Insurance Data.
Annual (odd years.) Update (even
years.)

Insurance Information Institute, New York,
NY
Insurance Facts. Annual.

The National Underwriter Co., Cincinnati,
OH
Argus Chart. Health insurance company
financial data. Annual.
Argus F.C. & S. Chart. Property and liabil-
ity insurance company financial data.
Annual.
Life Rates and Data. Premiums, values,
dividends, and contract analysis by
company. Annual.
Life Reports. Life company financial data.
Annual.
Timesaver. Health insurance costs and
contract analysis by company. Annual.

International Accounts and Aid

U.S. Government

Agency for International Development
U.S. Overseas Loans and Grants and
Assistance From International Organi-
zations. Annual.

Board of Governors of the Federal Reserve
System
Federal Reserve Bulletin. Monthly.

Bureau of Economic Analysis
Business Statistics, 1961-1989.

International Accounts and Aid —Con.

U.S. Government —Con.

Survey of Current Business. Monthly. (March, June, September, and December issues contain data on U.S. international transactions. Articles on foreign direct investment in the United States, U.S. direct investment abroad, and other topics appear periodically in other issues.)

U.S. Merchandise Trade: Exports and Imports by End-Use Category. Annually.

Department of Defense

Foreign Military Sales and Military Assistance Facts. Annual.

Department of State

United States Contribution to International Organizations. Issued in the House Documents series. Annual.

Department of the Treasury

Active Foreign Credits of the United States Government. Quarterly.

Treasury Bulletin. Monthly through 1982; beginning 1983, quarterly.

Export-Import Bank of the United States

Annual Report.

Report to the U.S. Congress on Export Credit Competition and the Export-Import Bank of the United States. Annual.

National Advisory Council on International Monetary and Financial Policies

Annual Report to the President and to the Congress.

Office of Management and Budget

The Budget of the United States Government. Annual.

U.S. Arms Control and Disarmament Agency

World Military Expenditures and Arms Transfers. Annual.

Other

International Monetary Fund, Washington, DC

Annual Report.

Balance of Payments Statistics. Monthly with annual yearbook.

Direction of Trade Statistics. Monthly with annual yearbook.

Government Finance Statistics Yearbook.

International Financial Statistics. Monthly with annual yearbook.

The World Bank, Washington, DC

Annual Report.

Social Indicators of Development 1991.

World Bank Atlas. 1991.

World Debt Tables. 1991-92.

World Development Report. 1991.

World Tables: 1991.

International Statistics —*see also* International Accounts

International Statistics —Con.

U.S. Government

Bureau of the Census

Country Demographic Profiles. (Series ISP30.)

International Population Reports. Irregular. (Series P-91.)

Social Indicators, 1980.

World Population Profile: 1989 (most recent).

Bureau of Labor Statistics

Handbook of Labor Statistics. 1989.

International Comparisons of Hourly Compensation Costs for Production Workers in Manufacturing. Quarterly.

International Comparisons of Manufacturing Productivity and Labor Cost Trends. Annual.

Monthly Labor Review.

Energy Information Administration

International Energy Annual.

Internal Revenue Service

Statistics of Income Bulletin. Quarterly. (Includes periodic reports on international income and taxes.)

Compendium of Studies of International Income and Taxes, 1979-1983.

National Science Foundation

International Science and Technology Data Update. Report. Annual.

National Patterns of R&D Resources. Report. Annual.

Science and Engineering Indicators. Report. Biennial.

Science and Technology Data Book. Report. Annual.

Survey of Direct U.S. Private Capital Investment in Research and Development Facilities in Japan. Report. (NSH 91-312.)

The Science and Technology Resources of Japan: A Comparison with the United States. Special Report. (NSF 88-318.)

The Science and Technology Resources of West Germany: A Comparison with the United States. Special Report. (NSF 86-310.)

Other

The Economist Newspaper Ltd., London, England

The Economist Diary. 1987.

World Business Cycles. 1982.

The World in Figures. 1984.

Euromonitor Publications Ltd., London, England

Consumer Europe

Consumer USA

European Marketing Data and Statistics. Annual.

International Marketing Data and Statistics. Annual.

Food and Agriculture Organization of the United Nations, Rome, Italy

Production Yearbook.

International Statistics —Con.
Other —Con.

Trade Yearbook.

Yearbook of Fishery Statistics.

Yearbook of Forest Products.

Inter-American Development Bank, Washington, DC

Annual Report.

Economic and Social Progress in Latin America. Annual Survey.

The International Institute for Strategic Studies, London, England

The Military Balance. Annual.

International Labour Office, Geneva, Switzerland

Economically Active Population, Estimates and Projections: 1950-2025, Vols. 1-6. 3rd Edition. 1986.

Yearbook of Labour Statistics. 49th issue. 1989-1990.

International Monetary Fund, Washington, DC

International Financial Statistics. Monthly with annual yearbook.

Jane's Information Group, Coulsdon, UK and Alexandria, VA

Jane's Air-Launched Weapons. (Binder-4 monthly update.)

Jane's All the World's Aircraft. Annual.

Jane's Armour and Artillery. Annual.

Jane's Avionics. Annual.

Jane's Fighting Ships. Annual.

Jane's Infantry Weapons. Annual.

Jane's Merchant Ships. Annual.

Jane's Military Communications. Annual.

Jane's Military Logistics. Annual.

Jane's Military Training Systems. Annual.

Jane's NATO Handbook. Annual.

Jane's Spaceflight Directory. Annual.

Motor Vehicle Manufacturers Association of the United States, Inc., Detroit, MI

World Motor Vehicle Data. Annual.

Organization for Economic Cooperation and Development, Paris, France

Annual Oil Market Report.

Coal Information. Annual.

Demographic Trends 1950-1990.

Energy Balances of OECD Countries. Annual.

Energy Prices and Taxes. Quarterly.

Energy Statistics. Annual.

Financial Market Trends. Triennial.

Financing and Delivering Health Care, 1987.

Food Consumption Statistics. Irregular.

Geographical Distribution of Financial Flows to Developing Countries.

Historical Statistics of Foreign Trade Series A. Annual.

International Statistics —Con.
Other —Con.

Indicators of Industrial Activity. Quarterly.

Industrial Structure Statistics. Annual.

The Iron and Steel Industry. Annual.

Labour Force Statistics. Annual.

Latest Information on National Accounts of Developing Countries. Annual.

Living Conditions in OECD Countries. 1986.

Main Economic Indicators. Monthly.

Main Science and Technology Indicators. Biennial.

Maritime Transport. Annual.

Measuring Health Care, 1960-1983. 1985.

Meat Balances in OECD Countries. Annual.

Milk and Milk Products Balances in OECD Countries. Annual.

National Accounts of OECD Countries. Annual.

Vol. I: Main Aggregates.

Vol. II: Detailed Tables.

National and International Tourism Statistics. 1974-1985.

OECD Economic Outlook. Bi-annual. Historical Statistics. Annual.

OECD Economic Studies. Annual for member countries.

OECD Employment Outlook. Annual.

OECD Environmental Data-Compendium 1989.

OECD Financial Statistics. Annual (3 vols.) and monthly supplements.

OECD Health Data (Diskette)

OECD Health Systems: Facts and Trends.

OECD Microtables on Foreign Trade by Commodities covering Series B (individual reporting countries) and Series C (total reporting countries). Annual from 1977.

OECD Purchasing Power Parities and Real Expenditures, 1985. (January 1988.)

Oil and Gas Information. Annual.

The Pulp and Paper Industry. Annual.

Quarterly Labor Force Statistics.

Quarterly National Accounts.

Quarterly Oil Statistics and Energy Balances.

Revenue Statistics of OECD Member Countries. Annual.

Review of Fisheries in OECD Member Countries. Annual.

Social Expenditure, 1960-1990. 1985.

Statistical Trends in Transport (ECMT).

Statistics of Area Production and Field of Crop Products in OECD Member Countries.

Statistics of Foreign Trade:

International Statistics —Con.
  Other —Con.
        Monthly Statistics of Foreign Trade. (Series A).
        Foreign Trade by Commodities. (Series C). Annual.
    Tourism Policy and International Tourism in OECD Member Countries. Annual.
    Uranium Resources Production and Demand. Biennial.
    World Energy Statistics and Balances.
    World Steel Trade Developments, 19601983. 1985.

  Pan American Health Organization, Washington DC
    Health Conditions in the Americas. 1990 Edition. Quadrennial.

  United Nations Educational, Scientific and Cultural Organization, Paris, France
    Statistical Yearbook.

  United Nations Population Division, New York, NY
    Global Estimates and Projections of Population by Sex and Age: The 1988 Revision (ST/ESA/SER.R/73). 1989.
    Levels and Trends of Contraceptive Use as Assessed in 1988. 1989 (ST/ESA/SER.A/110).
    Mortality of Children Under Age 5: World Estimates and Projections, 1950-2025 (ST/ESA/SER.A/105). 1988.
    Prospects of World Urbanization, 1988 (ST/ESA/SER.A/112). 1989.
    World Demographic Estimates and Projections, 1950-2025 (ST/ESA/SER.R/79). 1988.
    World Population Prospects, 1988 (ST/ESA/SER.A/106). 1989.

  United Nations Statistical Office, New York, NY
    Compendium of Human Settlements Statistics. (Series N, Quinquennial).
    Demographic Yearbook. (Series R).
    Energy Balances and Electricity Profiles. (Series W).
    Energy Statistics Yearbook. (Series J).
    Industrial Statistics Yearbook: (Series P).
        Volume I, General Industrial Statistics.
        Volume II, Commodity Production Statistics.
    International Trade Statistics Yearbook. (Series G).
    Monthly Bulletin of Statistics. (Series Q).
    National Accounts Statistics: (Series X, Annually).
        Main Aggregates and Detailed Tables.
        Analysis of Main Aggregates.
    Population and Vital Statistics Report. (Series A, Quarterly).
    Social Statistics and Indicators: (Series K, Occasional).

International Statistics —Con.
  Other —Con.
        Compendium of Social Statistics and Indicators
        Compendium of Statistics and Indicators on the Situation of Women
    Statistical Yearbook. (Series S).
    World Statistics in Brief. (Series V, Annually).

  World Health Organization, Geneva, Switzerland
    1990 World Health Statistics. Annual.

International Trade —see Foreign Commerce; and International Statistics.

Investments and Securities —see also Business; Construction; Insurance; International Accounts; and Money

  U.S. Government
    Board of Governors of the Federal Reserve System
        Federal Reserve Bulletin. Monthly.
    Commodity Futures Trading Commission
        Annual Report.
        Commitments of Traders in Commodity Futures. Monthly.
    Securities and Exchange Commission
        Annual Report.
        Statistical Review. Monthly. (Discontinued February 1989.)

  Other
    Commercial and Financial Chronicle. (William B. Dana Co., New York, NY) Semiweekly.
    Investment Company Institute, Washington, DC
        Mutual Fund Fact Book. Annual.
    Moody's Investors Service, New York, NY
        Moody's Manuals. (Volumes on Industriales, OTC, Banks and Finance, International, Municipals and Governments, Transportation, and Public Utilities.) Annual with semi-weekly supplements.
    National Bureau of Economic Research, Cambridge, MA
        Financial Aspects of the United States Pension System, Zvi Bodie and John B. Shoven, editors. 1983. (University of Chicago Press, Chicago,IL.)
    New York Stock Exchange, Inc., New York, NY
        Fact Book. Annual.
        Shareownership, 1980, 1981, 1983, and 1985.
    Securities Industry Association, New York, NY
        Foreign Activity Report. Quarterly.
        International Capital Markets Review. Periodic.
        Investor Activity Report. Monthly.
        Securities Industry Trends. Periodic.

Investments and Securities —Con.

Other —Con.

SIA Fact Book. Annual.

Standard and Poor's Corporation, New York, NY

Analyst's Handbook. Annual with monthly cumulative supplements.

Corporation Records. Six basic volumes; News Supplements, daily; Dividend Record, daily, and cumulative monthly and annual.

Daily Stock Price Records. Quarterly.

Security Owner's Stock Guide. Monthly.

Statistical Service. (Security Price Index Record; business and financial basic statistics with monthly supplement.)

Wall Street Journal. (Dow Jones & Co., New York, NY.) Daily except Saturdays, Sundays, and holidays.

Irrigation, Drainage, and Soil Conservation —*see* Agriculture

Juvenile Court —*see* Law Enforcement.

Labor —*see also* Accidents; Business; Economic Indexes; International Statistics; Science Resources; *and* Social Insurance

U.S. Government

Board of Governors of the Federal Reserve System

Federal Reserve Bulletin. Monthly.

Bureau of the Census

Census of Population. Decennial. (1980, most recent.)

County Business Patterns. Annual.

Current Governments Reports: Public Employment, GE No. 1 (annual); City Employment, GE No. 2 (annual); Local Government Employment in Selected Metropolitan Areas and Large Counties, GE No. 3 (annual); County Government Employment, GE No. 4 (annual).

Labor Force Status and Other Characteristics of Persons With a Work Disability: 1981-1988. (Current Population Reports, Special Studies, Series P-23, No. 160.) 1989.

Population Profile of the United States. (Annual Series P-23.)

Social Indicators, 1980.

Women in the American Economy. (Current Population Reports, Special Studies, Series P-23, No. 146.) 1987.

Bureau of Justice Statistics and Bureau of the Census

Justice Expenditure and Employment in the U.S. Annual.

Bureau of Labor Statistics

Area Wage Surveys: Selected Metropolitan Areas. Annual.

Bargaining Calendar. Annual.

Compensation and Working Conditions. Monthly.

Labor —Con.

U.S. Government —Con.

Employee Benefits in Medium and Large Firms. Biennial.

Employee Benefits in State and Local Governments. Biennial.

Employment and Earnings. Monthly, with annual supplement.

Employment and Earnings Characteristics of Families. Quarterly.

Employment and Wages. Annual.

Employment Cost Index. Quarterly.

Employment, Hours, and Earnings, United States, 1909-90. 1991. (Bulletin 2370.)

Employment in Perspective: Minority Workers. Quarterly.

Employment in Perspective: Women in the Labor Force. Quarterly.

The Employment Situation. Monthly.

Geographic Profile of Employment and Unemployment. Annual.

Handbook of Labor Statistics. 1989.

How Workers Get Their Training. 1985. (Bulletin No. 2226.)

Industry Wage Surveys. (Separate bulletins for selected industries; each industry on a 3- to 5-year cycle.)

Labor Force Statistics Derived from the Current Population Survey, 1948-87. 1988. (Bulletin No. 2307.)

Major Collective Bargaining Settlements. Quarterly.

Major Work Stoppages. Annual.

Mass Layoffs. Annual.

Monthly Labor Review.

Occupational Employment in Manufacturing Industries. 1991. (Bulletin No. 2376.)

Occupational Employment in Mining, Construction, Finance, and Services. 1992. (Bulletin No. 2397.)

Occupational Employment in Selected Nonmanufacturing Industries. 1990. (Bulletin No. 2348.)

Occupational Injuries and Illnesses in the United States, by Industry. Annual.

Occupational Projections and Training Data. Biennial.

Outlook 2000. 1990. (Bulletin No. 2352.)

Permanent Mass Layoffs and Plant Closings, 1987. 1988. (Bulletin 2310.)

Real Earnings. Monthly.

Revised Seasonally Adjusted Labor Force Statistics, 1978-87. 1988. (Bulletin 2506.)

State and Metropolitan Area Employment and Unemployment. Monthly.

Weekly Earnings of Wage and Salary Workers. Quarterly.

White-Collar Pay. Annual.

Work Experience of the Population. Annual.

Labor —Con.

U.S. Government —Con.

Working Woman: A Chartbook. 1991 (Bulletin No. 2385.)

Department of Agriculture

Farm Labor. Monthly.

Department of Labor

Annual Report of the Secretary.

Employment and Training Administration

Employment and Training Report of the President. Annual.

Unemployment Insurance Claims. Weekly.

Interstate Commerce Commission

Monthly Report of Class I Railroad Employees, by Group. (Statement No. 350.)

Wage Statistics of Class I Railroads in the United States. Annual. (Statement No. 300.)

Maritime Administration

Employment Report of United States Flag Merchant Fleet Ocean-going Vessels 1,000 Gross Tons and Over. Annual. (Monthly and quarterly data available from source.)

Seafaring Wage Rates. Biennial.

National Science Foundation

Characteristics of Doctoral Scientists land Engineers in the United States. Detailed Statistical Tables. Biennial.

Characteristics of Recent Science and Engineering Graduates. Detailed Statistical Tables. Biennial.

Immigrant Scientists and Engineers. Detailed Statistical Tables. Biennial.

U.S. Scientists and Engineers. Detailed Statistical Tables. Biennial.

U.S. Scientists and Engineers: 1984 Detailed Statistical Tables.

Woman and Minorities in Science and Engineering. Report. Biennial.

Office of Personnel Management

Affirmative Employment Statistics. Biennial. (Even Years.)

Occupations of Federal White-Collar and Blue-Collar Workers. Biennial. (Odd Years.)

Women's Bureau

Handbook on Women Workers. Periodic.

Other

Aerospace Industries Association of America, Washington, DC

Employment in the Aerospace Industry. Monthly.

Survey of Aerospace Employment. Annual.

The Bureau of National Affairs, Inc., Washington, DC

Basic Patterns in Union Contracts. Annual.

Labor —Con.

Other —Con.

BNA's Employment Outlook. Quarterly.

BNA's Job Absence and Turnover. Quarterly.

Briefing Sessions on Employee Relations Workbook. Annual.

Calendar of Negotiations. Annual.

Directory of U.S. Labor Organizations. Annual.

82 Key Statistics on Work and Family Issues. (The National Report on Work and Family. Special Report No. 9, September 1988.)

National Labor Relations Board Election Statistics. Annual.

NLRB Representation and Decertification Elections Statistics. Quarterly.

101 Key Statistics on Work and Family for the 1990's. (The BNA Special Report Series on Work and Family. Special Report No. 21, September 21, 1989.)

PPF Survey (Personnel Policies Forum.) Three times a year.

Law Enforcement, Courts, and Prisons

U.S. Government

Administrative Office of the United States Courts

Annual Report of the Director ... with, as issued, Reports of the Proceedings of the Judicial Conference of the United States. Includes statistics on Federal Courts.

Calendar Year Reports on Authorized Wiretaps. (State and Federal.)

Calendar Year Reports on the Right to Financial Privacy Act of 1978.

Federal Court Management Statistics. Annual.

Federal Offenders in U.S. District Courts. Annual.

Federal Judicial Workload Statistics. Quarterly.

Grand and Petit Juror Service in U.S. District Courts. Annual.

Bureau of the Census

Census of Population. Decennial. (1980, most recent.)

Social Indicators, 1980.

Bureau of Justice Statistics

American Response to Crime: An Overview of Criminal Justice Systems. December 1983.

Bank Robbery: Federal Offenses and Offenders. August 1984.

Case Filing in State Courts, 1983. October 1984.

Capital Punishment. Annual.

Census of Local Jails, 1988. January 1990.

Law Enforcement, Courts, and Prisons —Con.
U.S. Government —Con.

Children in Custody: Public Juvenile Facilities, 1986. October 1986.

Correctional Populations in the United States, 1988.

Crime Control and Criminal Records. July 1985.

Crime and the Elderly. November 1981.

Crime Prevention Measures. March 1986.

Crime of Rape. March 1985.

Criminal Defense Systems: A National Survey. August 1984.

Criminal Victimization. Annual.

Criminal Victimization in the United States. Annual.

Death-row Prisoners. July 1981.

Economic Cost of Crime to Victims. April 1984.

Electronic Fund Transfer Fraud: Computer Crime. April 1986.

Examining Recidivism. February 1986.

Expenditure and Employment Data for the Criminal Justice System. Annual.

Family Violence. April 1984.

Federal Criminal Cases, 1980-1987.

Federal Drug Law Violators. February 1984.

Federal Justice Statistics. March 1982.

Felony Case Processing in State Courts, 1986. February 1990.

Growth of Appeals: 1973-83 Trends. February 1985.

Habeas Corpus. March 1984.

Hispanic Victims. January 1990.

Household Burglary. January 1986.

Households Touched by Crime. Annual.

Intelligence and Investigative Records: Criminal Justice Information Policy Series: April 1985.

Jail Inmates, Annual.

Justice Agencies in the United States. May 1980.

Justice Expenditure and Employment. 1988 periodic.

Locating City, Suburban, and Rural Crime. December 1986.

Measuring Crime. February 1981.

Parole in the United States. Annual.

Police Departments in Large Cities. 1987.

Police Employment and Expenditure. February 1986.

Pretrial Release and Misconduct: Federal Offenses and Offenders. January 1986.

Prevalence of Crime. April 1981.

Prevalence of Guilty Pleas. December 1984.

Prevalence of Imprisonment. July 1985.

Prison Admissions and Releases, 1983. March 1986.

Law Enforcement, Courts, and Prisons —Con.
U.S. Government —Con.

Prisoners in 1988. Annual.

Prisoners and Alcohol. January 1983.

Prisoners and Drugs. March 1983.

Prisoners in State and Federal Institutions. Annual.

Prisons and Prisoners. January 1982.

Probation and Parole. Annual.

Profile of Felons Convicted in State Courts, 1986. January 1990.

Profile of Jail Inmates. October 1980.

Profile of State and Local Law Enforcement Agencies, 1987.

Profile of State Prison Inmates, 1986. January 1988.

Reporting Crime to the Police. December 1986.

Returning to Prison. November 1984.

Risk of Violent Crime. May 1985.

Severity of Crime. January 1984.

Sourcebook of Criminal Justice Statistics. Annual.

State Court Caseload Statistics, 1977-81. February 1983.

Survey of Youth in Custody, 1987.

Teenage Victims. November 1986.

Time Served in Prison and on Parole. January 1988.

Tracking Offenders, 1984. January 1988.

Tracking Offenders: The Child Victim. December 1984.

Use of Weapons in Committing Crime. January 1986.

Veterans in Prison. October 1981.

Victim and Witness Assistance: New State Laws and the System's Response. May 1983.

Victims of Crime. December 1981.

Violent Crime by Strangers and Nonstrangers. January 1987.

Bureau of Prisons
Statistical Report. Annual through 1985.

Drug Enforcement Administration
Drug Abuse and Law Enforcement Statistics. Irregular.

Federal Bureau of Investigation
Bomb Summary 1988.
Crime in the United States 1988.
Law Enforcement Officers Killed and Assaulted, 1988.

Other

American Bar Foundation, Chicago, IL

The Lawyer Statistical Report: A Statistical Profile of the U.S. Legal Profession in the 1980's. 1985.

Supplement to the Lawyer Statistical Report: The U.S. Legal Profession in 1985. 1986.

Institute for Criminal Justice Ethics, New York, NY

Criminal Justice Ethics. Semiannual.

Law Enforcement, Courts, and Prisons —Con.

Other —Con.

National Center for Juvenile Justice, Pittsburgh, PA

Juvenile Court Statistics: 1985.

National Center for State Courts, Williamsburg, VA

State Court Caseload Statistics. Annual.

State Court Organization, 1987. 1988.

National Governors' Association and National Association of State Budget Officers, Washington, DC

The President's 1990 Budget: Impact on the States.

Libraries — *see* Education.

Livestock —*see* Agriculture.

Lumber —*see* Forests and Lumber.

Manufactures —*see also* Agriculture; Business; Economic Indexes; Forests and Lumber; Investments; Labor; *and* Minerals

U.S. Government

Board of Governors of the Federal Reserve System

Federal Reserve Bulletin. Monthly.

Industrial Production. 1986.

Industrial Production and Capacity Utilization G.17 (419). Monthly.

Bureau of Alcohol, Tobacco, and Firearms

Alcohol and Tobacco Summary Statistics. Annual.

Bureau of the Census

Annual Survey of Manufactures. (1990, most recent.)

Census of Manufactures. Quinquennial. (1987, Industry series, MC 87-I; MC 87-A; MC 87-S.)

Concentration Ratios in Manufacturing Industry. (1987, most recent.)

Cotton Production and Distribution. Annual.

County Business Patterns. Annual.

Current Industrial Reports. Monthly, quarterly, and annual series on various industries.

Exports From Manufacturing Establishments: 1987. (Analytical Report Series AR 87-1.)

Manufacturers' Shipments, Inventories, and Orders. Monthly.

Manufacturers' Shipments, Inventories, and Orders: 1982-91. Annual summary. (Current Industrial Reports M3-1(91).)

Plant and Equipment Expenditures and Plans. Quarterly.

Pollution Abatement Cost and Expenditures. (Current Industrial Reports MA-200.)

Quarterly Financial Report for Manufacturing, Mining, and Trade Corporations.

Manufactures —Con.

U.S. Government —Con.

Shipments to Federal Government Agencies. (Current Industrial Reports MA-175.) (Conducted for economic census years ending in 2 and 7 in the future; 1987 data will be available in 1990.)

Survey of Plant Capacity Utilization. (Current Industrial Reports MQ-C1.) Discontinued March 1992.

U.S. Commodity Exports and Imports as Related to Output. Annual. (Series ES2.)

Bureau of Economic Analysis

Business Statistics, 1961-88. 1989.

Survey of Current Business. Monthly.

Bureau of Labor Statistics

Compensation and Working Conditions. Monthly.

Employment and Earnings. Monthly, with annual supplement.

Employment, Hours, and Earnings, United States, 1909-90. 1991. (Bulletin No. 2370.)

Handbook of Labor Statistics. 1989.

Mass Layoffs. Annual.

Monthly Labor Review.

Occupational Employment in Manufacturing Industries. 1991. (Bulletin No. 2376.)

Occupational Injuries and Illnesses in the United States by Industry. Annual.

Producer Price Indexes. Monthly, with annual supplement.

Trends in Manufacturing: A Chartbook. 1985. (Bulletin No. 2219.)

White-Collar Pay: Private Guards-Producing Industries, March 1990. 1990. (Bulletin 2374.)

International Trade Administration

U.S. Industrial Outlook. Annual.

International Trade Commission

Synthetic Organic Chemicals, U.S. Production and Sales. Annual.

National Science Foundation

A Comparative Analysis of Information on National Industrial R&D Expenditures. Special Report. (NSF 85-311.)

Economic Outlook and Corporate Mergers Dampen Growth in Company R&D. (NSF 88-311.)

Geographic Distribution of Industrial R&D Expenditures. Special Report. (NSF 88-317.)

Geographic Patterns: R&D in the United States. Special Report. (NSF 89-317.)

International Science and Technology Data Update. Report. Annual.

Modest Increase in Company R&D Funding Estimated for 1989. Science Resources Studies Highlights. (NSF 89-310.)

Manufactures —Con.
  Bureau of Economic Analysis —Con.

    Planned R&D Expenditures of Major U.S. Firms. Special Report. (NSF 91-306.)

    Research and Development in Industry. Detailed Statistical Tables. Annual.

    Science and Engineering Indicators. Report. Biennial.

    Science and Engineering Personnel.

    Science and Technology Resources in U.S. Industry. Special Report. (NSF 88-321.)

    Scientists, Engineers, and Technicians in Manufacturing Industries. Detailed Statistical Tables. Triennial.

    Scientists, Engineers, and Technicians in Nonmanufacturing Industries. Detailed Statistical Tables. Triennial.

    Scientists, Engineers, and Technicians in Trade and Regulated Industries. Detailed Statistical Tables. Triennial.

  Other

    Aerospace Industries Association of America, Washington, DC

      Aerospace Facts and Figures. Annual.

      Aerospace Industry Year-End Review and Forecast. Annual.

      AIA Survey of Aerospace Employment. Annual.

      Commercial Helicopter Shipments. Quarterly.

      Manufacturing Production, Capacity, and Utilization in Aerospace and Aircraft and Parts. Monthly.

      Net New Orders, Shipments, and Backlog for Jet Transport Aircraft. Quarterly.

      Orders, Shipments, Backlog and Inventories for Aircraft, Missiles, & Parts. Monthly.

    American Frozen Food Institute, Burlingame, CA

      Frozen Food Pack Statistics. Annual.

    American Iron and Steel Institute, Washington, DC

      Annual Statistical Report.

    Commodity Research Bureau, New York, NY

      Commodity Yearbook. Annual.

    The Conference Board, New York, NY

      Quarterly Survey of Capital Appropriations.

      Quarterly Survey of Capital Investment and Supply Conditions in Manufacturing.

    Dataquest Inc., San Jose, CA

      Consolidated Data Base.

    Dealerscope Merchandising, Philadelphia, PA

      Merchandising. Annual.

    Electronic Industries Association, Washington, DC

Manufactures —Con.
  Other —Con.

      Electronic Market Data Book. Annual.

      Electronic Market Trends. Monthly.

      Electronics Foreign Trade. Monthly.

      Electronics Foreign Trade 5-Year Summary. Annual.

    Motor Vehicle Manufacturers Association of the United States, Inc., Detroit, MI

      Motor Vehicle Facts and Figures. Annual.

    National Association of Hosiery Manufacturers, Charlotte, NC

      Hosiery Statistics. Annual.

    National Food Processors Association, Washington, DC

      Canned Fruit and Vegetable Pack and Stock Situation Reports. Quarterly.

Marine Corps —*see* National Defense.

Marriage —*see* Vital Statistics.

Medical Care; Mental Health —*see* Health.

Merchant Vessels —*see* Transportation

Military Services —see National Defense.

Minerals and Metals —*see also* Economic Indexes; Energy; Foreign Commerce; *and* Manufactures
  U.S. Government

    Census of Mineral Industries. Quinquennial. (1987, Industry series MIC87-I; Geographic Area Series MIC87-A; Subject Series MIC87-S.)

    Bureau of the Census and Bureau of Mines

      Raw Materials in the United States Economy: 1900-1977. (Issued 1980. Working Paper No. 47.)

    Bureau of Mines Apparent Consumption of Industrial Explosives and Blasting Agents in the United States. Annual.

      Mineral Commodity Summaries. Annual.

      Mineral Industry Surveys. (Monthly, quarterly, or annual report.)

      Minerals Today. (Bimonthly survey.)

      Minerals Yearbook. Annual.

    Department of the Treasury

      Treasury Bulletin. Monthly through 1982; beginning 1983, quarterly.

    Energy Information Administration

      Annual Energy Review.

      Coal Production. Annual.

      Domestic Uranium Mining and Milling Industry. Annual.

      International Energy Annual.

      Monthly Energy Review.

      Natural Gas Annual.

      Petroleum Supply Annual.

      Quarterly Coal Report.

      U.S. Crude Oil, Natural Gas, and Natural Gas Liquids Reserves. Annual.

  Other

    American Bureau of Metal Statistics, Inc., Secaucus, NJ

Minerals and Metals —Con.
Other —Con.

Non-Ferrous Metal Data.

American Gas Association, Arlington, VA
Gas Facts. Annual.
Year Book.

American Metal Market, New York, NY
Daily Newspapers.
Metal Statistics. Annual.

American Petroleum Institute, Washington, DC
Quarterly Review of Drilling Statistics for the United States.

American Petroleum Institute, Independent Petroleum Association of America, and MidContinent Oil and Gas Association
Joint Association Survey on Drilling Costs. Annual.

Commodity Research Bureau, New York, NY
Commodity Yearbook. Annual.

Independent Petroleum Association of America, Washington, DC
IPAA Weekly Oil Trends.
IPAA Wholesale Oil Prices. Monthly.
The Oil & Natural Gas Producing Industry in Your State. Annual.
U.S. Petroleum Statistics. Semiannual.

McGraw-Hill Publications Co., New York, NY
Engineering and Mining Journal. Monthly.
Keystone Coal Industry Manual. Annual.

National Coal Association, Washington, DC
Coal Data. Annual.

PennWell Publishing Co., Tulsa, OK
Offshore. Monthly.
Oil and Gas Journal. Weekly.

Carl H. Pforzheimer & Co., New York, NY
Comparative Oil Company Statistics, 1988-1987. Annual.

Money and Banking —*see also* Construction; Insurance; International Accounts; *and* Investments

U.S. Government

Board of Governors of the Federal Reserve System
Annual Statistical Digest.
Domestic Offices, Commercial Bank Assets and Liabilities Consolidated Report of Condition. Quarterly.
Federal Reserve Bulletin. Monthly.
Flow of Funds Accounts: Seasonally Adjusted and Unadjusted. Z.1(780). Quarterly.
Money Stock, Liquid Assets, and Debt Measures. H.6 (508). Weekly.

Bureau of the Mint
Annual Report of the Director.

Comptroller of the Currency
Quarterly Journal.

Money and Banking —Con.
U.S. Government —Con.

Department of the Treasury
Daily Treasury Statement.
Monthly Treasury Statement of Receipts and Outlays of the United States Government.
Statement of United States Currency and Coin. Monthly.
Statistical Appendix to Annual Report of the Secretary of the Treasury on the State of the Finances through 1980.
Treasury Bulletin. Monthly through 1982; beginning 1983, quarterly.

Farm Credit Administration
Annual Report on the Work of the Cooperative Farm Credit System.
Production Credit Association: Summary of Operations. Annual.
Report to the Federal Land Bank Associations. Annual.

Federal Deposit Insurance Corporation
Annual Report.
Data Book-Operating Banks and Branches. Annual.
Quarterly Banking Profile.
Statistics on Banking. Annual.
Trust Assets of Insured Commercial Banks. Annual.

National Credit Union Administration
Annual Report.
Yearend Statistics.
Midyear Statistics.

Office of Thrift Supervision
Annual Report.
Asset and Liability Trends. Annual.
Savings and Home Financing Source Book. Annual.

Other

Credit Union National Association, Inc., Madison, WI
Credit Union Services Profile. Annual.
The Credit Union Report. Annual.
National Member Survey. 1989.
Operating Ratios and Spreads. Semiannual.

William B. Dana Co., New York, NY
The Market Chronicle. Weekly.

Federal National Mortgage Association, Washington, DC
Annual Report.

Investment Company Institute, Washington, DC
Mutual Fund Fact Book. Annual.

National Council of Savings Institutions, Washington, DC

Money and Banking —Con.
Other —Con.

Fact Book of National Council of Savings Institutions. Annual.

National Bureau of Economic Research, Cambridge, MA

Financial Aspects of the United States Pension System, Zvi Bodie and John B. Shoven, editors. 1983. (University of Chicago Press, Chicago, IL)

The National Balance Sheet of the United States, 1953-80, by Raymond W. Goldsmith. 1982. (University of Chicago Press, Chicago, IL)

United States League of Savings Institutions, Chicago, IL

Savings Institutions Sourcebook. Annual.

Mortgages —*see* Construction; *and* Money.

Motor Carriers and Vehicles —*see* Transportation

National Defense —*see also* Federal Government

U.S. Government

Bureau of the Census

Manufacturers' Shipments to Federal Government Agencies. (Current Industrial Reports MA-175.) Conducted for economic census years ending in 2 and 7.)

Department of Defense

Annual Fact Sheet of Department of Defense.

Annual Report of Secretary of Defense.

Atlas/Data Abstract for the United States and Selected Areas. Annual.

The Black in the Armed Forces. Statistical Fact Book. Annual.

Five Year Defense Plan. Annual.

Foreign Military Sales and Military Assistance Facts. Annual.

Military Manpower Statistics. Quarterly.

Military Posture Report. Annual.

Prime Contract Awards. Semiannual.

Prime Contract Awards by State. Semiannual.

Selected Defense Department Economic Indicators. Monthly.

Selected Manpower Statistics. Annual.

Department of Veterans Affairs

Annual Report of the Secretary of Veterans Affairs.

Data on Vietnam Era Veterans, 1984.

National Guard Bureau

Annual Review of the Chief.

Office of Civil Defense

Annual Statistical Report.

Office of Management and Budget

The Budget of the United States Government. Annual.

National Defense —Con.
U.S. Government —Con.

Selective Service System, National Headquarters

Semiannual Report of the Director of Selective Service

U.S. Arms Control and Disarmament Agency

World Military Expenditures and Arms Transfers. Annual.

National Income and Wealth —*see also* Consumer Income; *and* Money and Banking

U.S. Government

Bureau of Economic Analysis

Business Statistics, 1961-88. 1989.

Fixed Reproducible Tangible Wealth in the United States, 1925-85. 1987.

The National Income and Product Accounts of the United States, 1929-82: Statistical Tables. 1986.

Survey of Current Business. Monthly.

Council of Economic Advisers

Economic Indicators. Monthly.

Economic Report of the President. Annual.

Internal Revenue Service

Statistics of Income Bulletin. Quarterly.

Other

National Bureau of Economic Research, Cambridge, MA

The National Balance Sheet of the United States, 1953-80, by Raymond W. Goldsmith. 1982. (University of Chicago Press, Chicago, IL)

The U.S. National Income and Product Accounts: Selected Topics, Murray F. Foss, editor. 1982. (Studies in Income and Wealth, No. 47.) (University of Chicago Press, Chicago, IL)

Naturalization —*see* Immigration.

Navy —*see* National Defense.

Newspapers, Periodicals, and Books —*see also* Communications

U.S. Government

Bureau of the Census

Annual Survey of Manufactures. (1986, most recent.)

Census of Manufactures. Quinquennial. (1987, most recent.)

Library of Congress

Annual Report.

Other

Book Industry Study Group, Inc., New York, NY

Book Industry Trends. Annual.

Bowker (R.R.) Company, New York, NY

Library Journal. Bimonthly.

Publishers Weekly.

School Library Journal. Monthly.

Editor & Publisher Co., New York, NY

International Year Book. Annual.

Market Guide. Annual.

Gale Research Inc., Fort Lauderdale, FL

Public Lands and Park Systems —*see also* Federal Government; *and* Recreation

U.S. Government

Bureau of Land Management

Public Land Statistics. Annual.

General Services Administration

Inventory Report on Real Property Leased to the United States Throughout the World. Annual.

Inventory Report on Real Property Owned by the United States Throughout the World. Annual.

National Park Service

Federal Recreation Fee Report. Annual.

National Park Statistical Abstract. Annual.

Other

National Association of State Park Directors

Annual Information Exchange.

Public Utilities —*see* Communications; Energy; *and* Transportation.

Puerto Rico —*see* Outlying Areas.

Radio —*see* Communications.

Railways —*see* Transportation.

Real Estate —*see* Agriculture; *and* Construction.

Reclamation Projects —*see* Agriculture.

Recreation —*see also* Public Lands

U.S. Government

Bureau of the Census

Census of Transportation. Quinquennial. (1987, most recent.)

Social Indicators, 1980.

Bureau of Economic Analysis

The National Income and Product Accounts of the United States, 1929-82: Statistical Tables. 1986.

Survey of Current Business. Monthly.

Department of Transportation

U.S. International Air Travel Statistics. Annual.

Fish and Wildlife Service

Federal Aid in Fish and Wildlife Restoration. Annual.

National Survey of Fishing, Hunting, and Wildlife-Associated Recreation. Quinquennial. (1985 most recent.)

National Endowment for the Arts

Research Division Notes Nos. 3, 4, 5, 10, 13, and 15. 1983-1986.

National Park Service

Federal Recreation Fee Report. Annual.

National Park Statistical Abstract. Annual.

Other

Association of Racing Commissioners International, Inc., Lexington, KY

Statistical Reports on Greyhound Racing in the United States. Annual.

Recreation —Con.

Other —Con.

Statistical Reports on Horse Racing in the United States. Annual.

Statistical Reports on Jai Alai in the United States. Annual.

National Golf Foundation, Jupiter, FL

Americans' Attitudes Toward Golf in Their Community.

Golf Consumer Spending and Facility Fees.

Golf Facilities in Canada.

Golf Facilities in the United States. 1990.

Golf Participation in Canada.

Golf Participation in the United States. 1990.

Golf Projections 2000. 1989.

Golf Travel in the United States.

Stand-Alone Golf Ranges in the United States.

Trends in the Golf Industry 1986-1990.

Women in Golf.

National Marine Manufacturers Association, Chicago, IL

Boating. (A Statistical Report on America's Top Family Sport.) Annual.

State Boat Registration. Annual.

National Sporting Goods Association, Mt. Prospect, IL

The Sporting Goods Market in 1989. Annual.

Sports Participation in 1988. Annual.

Resources for the Future, Inc., Washington, DC

Statistics on Outdoor Recreation. 1984.

Part I: The Record Through 1956

Part II: The Record Since 1956

Religious Bodies

Other

American Jewish Committee and the Jewish Publication Society, New York, NY

American Jewish Year Book.

Glenmary Research Center, Atlanta, GA

Churches and Church Membership in the United States 1980, by B. Quinn, H. Anderson, M. Bradley, P. Goetting, and P. Shriver. 1982.

National Council of the Churches of Christ in the U.S.A., New York, NY

Yearbook of American and Canadian Churches. Annual.

Research and Development —*see* Science Resources.

Retail and Wholesale Trade —*see also* Commodity Prices; Economic Indexes; *and* Service Establishments

U.S. Government

Board of Governors of the Federal Reserve System

Federal Reserve Bulletin. Monthly.

Retail and Wholesale Trade —Con.

U.S. Government —Con.

Bureau of the Census

Annual Retail Trade Report.

Annual Wholesale Trade Report.

Census of Retail Trade. Quinquennial. (1987, most recent.)

Census of Wholesale Trade. Quinquennial. (1987, most recent.)

County Business Patterns. Annual.

Merchant Wholesalers Measures of Value Produced, Capital Expenditures, Depreciable Assets, and Operating Expenses. (1982, most recent.)

Monthly Retail Trade Report. Sales and Inventories.

Monthly Wholesale Trade Report. Sales and Inventories.

Selected Characteristics of Retail Trade-Measures of Value Produced, Capital Expenditures, Depreciable Assets, and Operating Expenses. (1982, most recent.)

Bureau of Economic Analysis

Business Statistics, 1961-88. 1989.

Survey of Current Business. Monthly.

Bureau of Labor Statistics

Compensation and Working Conditions. Monthly

CPI Detailed Report. Monthly.

Employment and Earnings. Monthly, with annual supplement.

Employment, Hours, and Earnings, United States, 1909-90. 1991. (Bulletin No. 2370.)

Handbook of Labor Statistics. 1989.

Monthly Labor Review.

Occupational Employment in Selected Nonmanufacturing Industries. 1990. (Bulletin No. 2348.)

Occupational Injuries and Illnesses in the United States by Industry. Annual.

Producer Price Indexes. Monthly, with annual supplement.

Productivity Measures for Selected Industries and Government Services. Annual.

Technological Change and Its Labor Impact in Four Industries. 1988. (Bulletin 2316.)

Technology and Labor in Three Service Inductries: Utilities, Retail Trade, and Lodging. 1990. (Bulletin 2367.)

International Trade Administration

Franchising in the Economy. Annual. (Last issued 1988.)

U.S. Industrial Outlook. Annual.

Other

Dealerscope Merchandising, Philadelphia, PA

Merchandising. Annual.

Lebhar-Friedman, Inc., New York, NY

Accounting Today. Biweekly.

Retail and Wholesale Trade —Con.

Other —Con.

Apparel Merchandising. Monthly.

Chain Store Age Executive. Census Issue, August 1989. Monthly.

Discount Store News. July 1989, Statistical Issue. Biweekly.

Drug Store News. May 1989, Statistical Issue. Biweekly.

National Home Center News. May 1989, 2 Statistical Issues. Biweekly.

Nation's Restaurant News. August 1989, Statistical Issue. Weekly.

Market Statistics, New York, NY

The Survey of Buying Power Data Service. Annual.

National Restaurant Association, Washington, DC

Foodservice Industry Forecast. Annual.

Foodservice Industry in Review. Annual.

Foodservice Market Measure. Monthly in Restaurants USA.

Foodservice Numbers: A Statistical Digest for the Foodservice Industry. 1986.

Restaurant Industry Operations Report. Annual.

Restaurants USA. Monthly.

Survey of Wage Rates for Hourly Employees. Biennial.

Compensation for Salaried Personnel in Foodservice. Triennial.

Roads —*see* Transportation.

Sales —*see* Retail and Wholesale Trade.

Savings Institutions —*see* Money.

Science Resources

U.S. Government

Bureau of the Census

Current Industrial Reports, MA37D. Annual.

Energy Research and Development Administration

The Nuclear Industry. Annual.

National Aeronautics and Space Administration

Annual Procurement Report.

The Civil Service Work Force.

Pocket Statistics. Annual.

National Science Foundation

A Comparative Analysis of Information on National Industrial R&D Expenditures. Special Report. (NSF 85-311.)

Academic Research Equipment in Computer Science, Central Computer Facilities and Engineering: 1989.

Academic Research Equipment and Equipment needs in Selected Science/Engineering Fields: 1989-90.

Academic Research and Equipment Needs in the Physical Sciences: 1989.

Science Resources —Con.
U.S. Government —Con.

Academic Science and Engineering:
Graduate Enrollment and Support. Detailed Statistical Tables. Annual.

Academic Science and Engineering: R&D
Expenditures. Detailed Statistical Tables. Annual.

Biotechnology Research and Development Activities in Industry: 1984 and
1985. Special Report. (NSF 87-311.)

Characteristics of Doctoral Scientists and
Engineers in the United States. Detailed Statistical Tables. Biennial.

Characteristics of Recent Scientists and
Engineers. Detailed Statistical Tables.
Biennial.

Characteristics of Science/Engineering
Equipment in Academic Settings: 1989-
90.

Doctoral Scientists and Engineers: A Decade of Change. Special Report. (NSF
88-302.)

Federal R&D Funding by Budget Function. Report. Annual.

Federal Funds for Research and Development. Detailed Statistical Tables. Annual.

Federal Scientists and Engineers. Detailed Statistical Tables. Annual.

Federal Support to Universities, Colleges,
and Selected Nonprofit Institutions. Detailed Statistical Tables. Annual.

Foreign Citizens in U.S. Science and Engineering: History, Status, and Outlook.
Special Report. (NSF 86-305, revised.)

Geographic Distribution of Industrial R&D
Expenditures. Special Report. (NSF 88-
317.)

Geographic Patterns of R&D Expenditures. Special Report. (NSF 89-317.)

Immigrant Scientists and Engineers. Detailed Statistical Tables. Annual.

International Science and Technology
Data Update. Report. Annual.

National Patterns of R&D Resources. Report. Annual.

Planned R&D Expenditures of Major U.S.
firms: 1990-91. Special Report. (NSF
91-306.)

Profiles—Aeronautical/Astronautical Engineering, Agricultural Science, Biological Sciences, Chemical Engineering,
Chemistry, Civil Engineering, Computer
Sciences, Economics,Electrical/Elec-
tronic Engineering, Mechanical Engineering, and Psychology: Human Resources and Funding. Special Reports.
(NSF 89-314, 89-319, 89-318, 89-312,
87-307, 90-303, 88-324, 88-333, 88-
326, 87-309, and 88-325, respectively.)

Research and Development Expenditures
of State Government Agencies: Fiscal
Years 1987 and 1988. Special Report.
(NSF 90-309.)

Science Resources —Con.
U.S. Government —Con.

Research and Development in Industry.
Detailed Statistical Tables. Annual.

Science and Engineering Degrees. A
Source Book. Detailed Statistical Tables. Annual.

Science and Engineering Doctorates. Detailed Statistical Tables. Annual.

Science and Engineering Indicators. Report. Biennial.

Science and Engineering Personnel: A
National Overview. Report. Biennial.

Science and Technology Data Book. Report. Annual.

Science and Technology Resources in
U.S. Industry. Special Report. (NSF 88-
321.)

The Science and Technology Resources
of Japan: A Comparison with the
United States. Special Report. (NSF
88-318.)

The Science and Technology Resources
of West Germany: A Comparison with
the United States. Special Report. (NSF
86-310.)

Science Resources Studies Highlights.
Occasional.

Favorable Employment opportunities Continue for Recent S/E Graduates. (NSF
90-15.)

Federal Academic R&D Support Increased
10% in FY 1989. (NSF 91-301.)

Graduate Enrollments Climb in Science, Engineering, and Health. (NSF
90-326)

Growth Rate in Non-Federal Academic
R&D Support Exceeds That in Federal Support Over Last Decade. (NSF
89-309.)

Industrial Biotechnology R&D Performance Increased an Estimated 12
Percent in 1987 to $1.4 Billion. (NSF
88-306.)

Science and Engineering Doctoral
Awards Reached Record Highs in
1990. (NSF 91-308.)

Scientific and Engineering Research Facilities at Universities and Colleges. Report. Biennial.

Scientists and Engineers Now Account
for Over 4 Percent of Total U.S. Employment. (NSF 88-313.)

Scientists, Engineers, and Technicians in
Manufacturing are Concentrated in High
Technology Industries. (NSF 91-)

S/E Baccalaureates Declined After 1986
as Masters and Doctoral Degrees Increased. (NSF 91-313.)

Scientists, Engineers, and Technicians in
Manufacturing Industries. Detailed Statistical Tables. Triennial.

Scientists, Engineers, and Technicians in
Nonmanufacturing Industries. Detailed
Statistical Tables. Triennial.

Transportation —Con.
U.S. Government —Con.

Merchant Vessels of the United States. Annual.

Polluting Incidents In And Around U.S. Waters. Annual.

Dartment of State, Bureau of Consular Affairs

Summary of Passport Statistics. Annual.

Dartment of Transportation

National Transportation Statistics. Annual.

Transportation Safety Information Report. Quarterly.

U.S. International Air Travel Statistics. Annual.

Federal Aviation Administration

Census of U.S. Civil Aircraft. Annual.

FAA Air Traffic Activity. Annual, for fiscal years.

FAA Aviation Forecasts, for fiscal years.

FAA Statistical Handbook of Aviation. Annual.

General Aviation Activity and Avionics Survey. Annual.

U.S. Civil Airman Statistics. Annual.

Federal Aviation Administration and Research and Special Programs Administration

Airport Activity Statistics of Certificated Route Air Carriers. Annual.

Federal Highway Administration

Drivers Licenses. Annual.

Highway Statistics. Annual.

Highway Statistics, Summary to 1985. (Published every 10 years.)

Selected Highway Statistics and Charts. Annual.

Interstate Commerce Commission

Class I Freight Railroads Selected Earnings Data. Quarterly.

Large Class I Household Goods Carriers Selected Earnings Data. Quarterly.

Large Class I Motor Carriers of Passengers Selected Earnings Data.

Quarterly.

Large Class I Motor Carriers of Property Selected Earnings Data. Quarterly.

Quarterly Report.

Transport Statistics in the United States. Issued annually in two separate parts:

Part 1: Railroads

Part 2: Motor Carriers

Maritime Administration

Annual Report.

Bulk Carriers in the World Fleet. Annual.

Containerized Cargo Statistics. Annual.

Transportation —Con.
U.S. Government —Con.

Employment Report of United States Flag Merchant Fleet Ocean-going Vessels 1,000 Gross Tons and Over. Annual. (Monthly and quarterly data available from source.)

Foreign Flag Merchant Ships Owned by U.S. Parent Companies. Annual.

Maritime Manpower Report. Monthly.

New Ship Construction. Annual.

United States Oceanborne Foreign Trade Routes. Annual.

Research and Special Programs Administration

Air Carrier Financial Statistics. Quarterly.

Air Carrier Industry Scheduled Service Traffic Statistics. Quarterly.

Air Carrier Traffic Statistics. Monthly.

Other

Aerospace Industries Association of America, Washington, DC

Aerospace Facts and Figures. Annual.

Net New Orders, Shipments, and Backlog for Jet Transport Aircraft. Quarterly.

Commercial Helicopter Shipments. Quarterly.

Air Transport Association of America, Washington, DC

Air Transport Facts and Figures. Annual.

American Bureau of Shipping, Paramus, NJ

The Record. Annual with one supplement.

American Public Transit Association, Washington, DC

Transit Fact Book. Annual.

Association of American Railroads, Washington, DC

Analysis of Class I Railroads. Annual.

Cars of Revenue Freight Loaded. Weekly with annual summary.

Freight Commodity Statistics, Class I Railroads in the United States. Annual.

Yearbook of Railroad Facts.

ENO Transportation Foundation, Westport, CT

Transportation in America. May, annually with periodic supplements.

General Aviation Manufacturers Association, Washington, DC

Shipment Report. Quarterly and Annual.

Statistical Databook. Annual.

Lake Carriers' Association, Cleveland, OH

Annual Report.

Monthly Bulk Commodities Report.

Lloyd's Register of Shipping, London, England

Annual Summary of Merchant Ships Completed in the World.

Appendix I

Guide to State Statistical Abstracts

This bibliography includes the most recent statistical abstracts for States and Puerto Rico published since 1980 plus those that will be issued in late 1992 or early 1993. For some States, a near equivalent has been listed in substitution for, or in addition to, a statistical abstract. All sources contain statistical tables on a variety of subjects for the State as a whole, its component parts, or both. The page counts given for publications are approximate.

Alabama

University of Alabama, Center for Business and Economic Research, P.O. Box 870221, Tuscaloosa 35487 205-348-6191

*Economic Abstract of Alabama.*1992. 600 pp.

Alaska

Department of Commerce and Economic Development, Division of Economic Development, P.O. Box 110804, Juneau 99811 907-465-2017 *The Alaska Economy Performance Report. 1988-1989*

Arizona

University of Arizona, Economic and Business Research, College of Business and Public Administration, Tucson 85721 602-621-2155 Fax 602-621-2150

Arizona Statistical Abstract: A 1992 Data Handbook. 600pp.

*Arizona Economic Indicators.*52 pp. (Biannual.)

Arkansas

University of Arkansas at Little Rock, Regional Economic Analysis, Library 512, Little Rock 72204

Arkansas State and County Economic Data. 18 pp. (Revised annually.)

University of Arkansas at Little Rock, State Data Center, Library 508, Little Rock 72204 501-569-8530

Arkansas Statistical Abstract. 500 pp. (Revised biennially.)

California

Department of Finance, 915 L Street, 8th Floor, Sacramento 95814 916-322-2263

California Statistical Abstract, 1992. 210 pp.

Pacific Data Resources, P.O. Box 1911, Santa Barbara, CA 93116-9954 800-422-2546

California Almanac, 5th ed. Biennial. 645 pp.

Colorado

University of Colorado, Business Research Division, Campus Box 420, Boulder 80309 303-4928227

Statistical Abstract of Colorado, 1987. 600 pp.

Connecticut

Connecticut Department of Economic Development, 1990-1991 87 pp. No charge for single copy. 865 Brook St., Rocky Hill 06067-3405

Connecticut Market Data.

Delaware

Delaware Development Office, 99 Kings Highway, P.O. Box 1401, Dover 19903 302-739-4271

Delaware Data Book, 1992. 146 pp.

District of Columbia

Office of Planning, Data Management Division, Presidential Bldg., Suite 500, 415 12th St., N.W. Washington 20004 202-727-6533

Population Estimates and Housing Units, annual.

Office of Policy and Program Evaluation, Executive Office of the Mayor, District Building, Room 208, 1350 Pennsylvania Ave., N.W., Washington 20004 202-727-4016

Indices—A Statistical Index to DC Services, 1990. Annual. 422 pp.

Florida

University of Florida, Bureau of Economic and Business Research, Gainesville 32611-2017 904-392-0171

Florida Statistical Abstract, 1990. 25th ed. 1991. 736 pp.

National Data Consultants, P.O. Box 6381, Athens, Georgia 30604 404-548-8460

45-*Florida County Perspectives: 1991.* Annual. 110 pp.

Georgia

University of Georgia, Selig Center for Economic Growth, Terry College of Business, Athens 30602-6269 (706) 542-4085

Georgia Statistical Abstract, 1990-91. 1990. 483 pp.

University of Georgia, College of Agriculture, Cooperative Extension Service, Athens 30602 404-542-8940

The Georgia County Guide. 1991. 10th ed. Annual. 190 pp.

Office of Planning and Budget, 254 Washington St., S.W., Atlanta 30334-8501 404-656-0911

Georgia Descriptions in Data. 1990-91. 249 pp.

Hawaii

Hawaii State Department of Business, and Economic Development & Tourism, P.O. Box 2359, Honolulu 96804. Inquiries 808-586-2482; Copies 808-586-2404

The State of Hawaii Data Book 1990: A Statistical Abstract. 24th ed. 1990. 667 pp.

Idaho

Department of Commerce, 700 West State St., Boise 83720 208-334-2470

County Profiles of Idaho, 1992

Idaho Community Profiles, 1992.

Idaho Facts, 1992.

Idaho Facts Data Book, 1989.

University of Idaho, Center for Business Development and Research, Moscow 83843 208-885-6611

Idaho Statistical Abstract. 1980. 415 pp. (Out of print.)

Illinois

University of Illinois, Bureau of Economic and Business Research, 428 Commerce West, 1206 South 6th Street, Champaign 61820 217-333-2330

Illinois Statistical Abstract. 1991. 445 pages.

Department of Commerce and Community Affairs, 620 Adams St., Springfield 62701 217-782-1438

Illinois State and Regional Economic Data Book—1989. 419 pp.

Indiana

Indiana University, Indiana Business Research Center, School of Business, Indianapolis 46202-5151 317-274-2204

Indiana Factbook, 1985. 420 pages.

Indiana Factbook, 1989. 165 pages.

Indiana Factbook, 1992. 413 pages.

Iowa

Iowa Department of Economic Development Research Bureau, 200 East Grand Ave., Des Moines 50309

1991 Statistical Profile of Iowa. 111 pp.

Kansas

University of Kansas, Institute for Public Policy and Business Research, 607 Blake Hall, Lawrence 66045-2960 913-864-3701

Kansas Statistical Abstract, 1990-91. 26th ed. 1992.

Kentucky

Department of Existing Business and Industry, Capital Plaza Office Tower, Frankfort 40601 502-564-4886

Kentucky Deskbook of Economic Statistics. 28th ed. 1992.

Louisiana

University of New Orleans, Division of Business and Economic Research, New Orleans 70148 504-286-6248

Statistical Abstract of Louisiana. 8th ed. 1990.

Maine

Maine Department of Economic and Community Development, State House Station 59, Augusta 04333 207-289-2656

Maine: A Statistical Summary. (Updated periodically.)

Maryland

Department of Economic and Employment Development, 217 E. Redwood St., Baltimore 21202 Inquiries 410-333-6953; Copies 410-333-6955

Maryland Statistical Abstract. 1990-91. 274 pp. (Biennial.) 1993-94 available in spring 1993.

Massachusetts

Massachusetts Institute for Social and Economic Research, 128 Thompson Hall, University of Massachusetts at Amherst 01003 (413)5453460 FAX 413-545-3686

*Projected Total Population and Age Distribution for 1995 and 2000: Massachusetts Cities and Towns.*March 1992. 62 pages.

Michigan

Wayne State University, Bureau of Business Research, School of Business Administration, Detroit 48202

Michigan Statistical Abstract. 20th ed. 1986-87. 629 pp.

Minnesota

Department of Trade and Economic Development, Business Development and Analysis Division, 900 American Center Building, St. Paul 55101 612-296-8283

Compare Minnesota: An Economic and Statistical Factbook, 1992-93. 165 pp.

Economic Report to the Governor: State of Minnesota, 1992. 148 pp.

Office of State Demographer, State Planning Agency, 300 Centennial Bldg., St. Paul 55155 612-296-2557

Minnesota Population and Household Estimates, 1988. 74 pp.

Mississippi

Mississippi State University, College of Business and Industry, Division of Research, Mississippi State 39762 601-325-3817

Mississippi Statistical Abstract. 1991. 750 pp.

Missouri

University of Missouri, Business and Public Administration Research Center, Columbia 65211 314-882-4805

Statistical Abstract for Missouri, 1991 Biennial. 350 pp.

Montana

Montana Department of Commerce, Census and Economic Information Center, 1424 9th Ave., Helena 59620 406-444-2896

Montana County Database. (Separate county and state reports; will be available by subject section as well as complete reports by county and state, updated periodically, available in paper microfiche, and diskette.)

Nebraska

Department of Economic Development, Division of Research, Box 94666, Lincoln 68509 402-471-3779

Nebraska Statistical Handbook. 1990-1991. 300 pp.

Nevada

Department of Administration, Planning Division, Capitol Complex, Carson City 89710 702-687-4065

Nevada Statistical Abstract. 1992. Biennial.405 pp.

New Hampshire

Office of State Planning, 2 1/2 Beacon St., Concord 03301 (603)271-2155

*Current Estimates and Trends in New Hampshire's Housing Supply.*Update: 1990. 22 pp.

Selected Economic Characteristics of New Hampshire Municipalities. 1992. 12 pp. (Other series available on population estimates and projections, and taxation.)

New Jersey

New Jersey State Data Center, NJ Department of Labor, CN 388, Trenton 08625-0388 609-984- 2593

New Jersey Statistical Factbook, 1992. 115 pp.

Statistical Source Directory for New Jersey State Government, 1992. 100 pp.

New Mexico

University of New Mexico, Bureau of Business and Economic Research, Albuquerque 87131 505-277-2216

New Mexico Statistical Abstract. 1989. 215 pp.

County Profiles. (Updated continuously.)

New York

Energy Association of New York, 111 Washington Avenue, Suite 601, Albany 12210 518-449-3440

New York at a Glance, 1989-90. 230 pp.

Nelson Rockefeller Institute of Government, 411 State Street, Albany 12203 518-443-5522

*New York State Statistical Yearbook, 1992.*17th ed. 536 pp.

North Carolina

Office of Governor

Office of State Planning, 116 West Jones Street, Raleigh 27603-8003 919-733-4131

Statistical Abstract of North Carolina Counties, 1991. 6th edition.

North Dakota

University of North Dakota, Bureau of Business and Economic Research, Grand Forks 58202 701-777-3365

The Statistical Abstract of North Dakota. 1988. 700 pp.

North Dakota—Con.

North Dakota Department of Economic Development and Finance, 1833 E. Bismark Expressway, Bismark 58504 701-221-5300

North Dakota Economic Data Book. 1988. 100 pp.

Ohio

Department of Development, Ohio Data Users Center (ODUC), P.O. Box 1001, Columbus 43266-0101 614-466-2115

ODUC Products and Services. (Updated continuously.)

Ohio County Profiles, 1992

The Ohio State University, School of Public Policy and Management, 1775 College Road, Columbus 43210-1399 614-292-8696

Benchmark Ohio, 1991. Biennial. 300 pp.

Oklahoma

University of Oklahoma, Center for Economic and Management Research, 307 West Brooks Street, Room 4, Norman 73019 405-325-2931

Statistical Abstract of Oklahoma, 1992. Annual. 626 pp.

Oregon

Secretary of State, Room 136, State Capitol, Salem 97310

Oregon Blue Book. 1991-1992. Biennial. 488 pp.

Pennsylvania

Pennsylvania State Data Center, Institute of State and Regional Affairs, Penn State, Harrisburg, 777 West Harrisburg Pike, Middleton, Pennsylvania 17057-4898.

Pennsylvania Statistical Abstract, 1992. 30th ed. 1992. 249 pp.

Rhode Island

Department of Economic Development, 7 Jackson Walkway, Providence 02903 401-277-2601

Rhode Island Basic Economic Statistics. 1992. 145 pp. $5.00.

South Carolina

Budget and Control Board, Division of Research and Statistical Services, R. C. Dennis Building, Room 425, Columbia 29201 803-734-3781

South Carolina Statistical Abstract: 1992. 392 pp.

South Dakota

University of South Dakota, State Data Center, Vermillion 57069 605-677-5287

Handbook of Manpower Statistics for South Dakota. 294 pp.

1990 South Dakota Community Abstracts. 400 pp.

Tennessee

University of Tennessee, Center for Business and Economic Research, Knoxville 37996-4170 615-974-5441

Tennessee Statistical Abstract, 1992-93. 14th ed. 700 pp. (Annual.)

Texas

Dallas Morning News, Communications Center, P.O. Box 655237, Dallas 75265 214-977-8261

Texas Almanac, 1992-1993. 1991. 656 pp.

University of Texas, Bureau of Business Research, Austin 78712 512-471-5180

Texas Fact Book, 1989. 6th ed. 250 pp.

Utah

University of Utah, Bureau of Economic and Business Research, 401 Kendall D. Garff Building, Salt Lake City 84112 801-581-6333

Statistical Abstract of Utah. 1993. (Triennial.)

Utah Foundation, 10 West 100 South 323, Salt Lake City 84101-1544 801-364-1837

Statistical Review of Government in Utah. 1991. 101 pp.

Vermont

Office of Policy Research and Coordination, Department of Employment and Training, Montpelier 05602 802-229-0311 ext. 323

Demographic and Economic Profiles. (Periodically issued.)

Virginia

University of Virginia, Center for Public Service, Dynamics Building, 4th Floor, 2015 Ivy Road, Charlottesville 22903 804-924-3921

Virginia Statistical Abstract, 1992-93. Biennial. 850 pp.

Washington

Washington State Office of Financial Management, Forecasting Division P.O. Box 43113 Olympia, WA 98504-3113 206-753-5617

Washington State Data Book, 1991. Biennial. 306 pp.
Population Trends for Washington State. Annual. 128 pages.

West Virginia

West Virginia Chamber of Commerce, P.O. Box 2789, Charleston 25330 304-342-1115

West Virginia: Economic-Statistical Profile, 1987-1988. Biennial. 750 pp.

West Virginia Research League, Inc., 405 Capitol Street, Suite 414, Charleston 25301 304-346-9451

Economic Indicators. 1988. 110 pp.
The 1991 Statistical Handbook. 86 pp.

Wisconsin

Wisconsin Legislative Reference Bureau, P.O. Box 2037, Madison 53701-2037 608-266-0341

1991-1992 Wisconsin Blue Book. 1,000 pp. Biennial.

Wyoming

Department of Administration and Information, Division of Economic Analysis, 327 E. Emerson Building, Cheyenne 82002 307-777-7504

Wyoming Data Handbook, 1991. 310 pp.

Puerto Rico

Planning Board, Area of Economic and Social Planning, Bureau of Economic Analysis and Bureau of Statistics, Santurce 00940 809-722-2070

Economic Report to the Governor, 1990. (In Spanish.)
Historic Series of Employment, Unemployment and Labor Force, 1988. 98 pp. (In Spanish.)
Social Statistics Abstract, 1987. 258 pp. (In Spanish.)
Socioeconomic Indicators by Municipios, 1989. (In Spanish.)

Guide to Foreign Statistical Abstracts

This bibliography presents recent statistical abstracts for Mexico, the Soviet Union, and member nations of the Organization for Economic Cooperation and Development. All sources contain statistical tables on a variety of subjects for the individual countries. Many of the following publications provide text in English as well as in the national language(s). For further information on these publications, contact the named statistical agency which is responsible for editing the publication.

Austria

Osterreichisches Statistisches Zentralamt, P.O. Box 9000, A-1033 Vienna

Statistisches Handbuch for die Republik Osterreich. Annual. 1991 592 pp. (In German.)

Australia

Australian Bureau of Statistics, Canberra

Yearbook Australia. Annual. 1991 790 pp. (In English.)

Belgium

Institut National de Statistique, 44 rue de Louvain, 1000 Brussels

Annuaire statistique de la Belgique. Annual. 1988 783 pp. (In French and Dutch.)

Canada

Statistics Canada, Ottawa, Ontario, KIA OT6

Canada Yearbook: A review of economic, social and political developments in Canada. 1990. Irregular. (In English and French.)

Denmark

Danmarks Statistik, Postboks 2550 Sejrogade 11, DK 2100, Copenhagen 0

Statistical Yearbook. 1990. Annual. 541 pp. (In Danish with English translations of table headings.)

Finland

Central Statistical Office of Finland, Box 504 SF-00101 Helsinki

Statistical Yearbook of Finland. Annual. 1991 598 pp. (In English, Finnish, and Swedish.)

France

Institut National de la Statistique et des Etudes Economiques, Paris 18, Bld. Adolphe Pinard, 75675 Paris (Cedex 14)

Annuaire Statistique de la France. Annual. 1989 864 pp. (In French.)

Greece

National Statistical Office, 14-16 Lycourgou St., 101-66 Athens

Statistical Yearbook of Greece. Annual. 1988 240 pp. (plus 7 pages of diagrams). (In English and Greek.)

Iceland

Hagstofa Islands/Statistical Bureau, Hverfisgata 8-10, Reykjavik.

Statistical Abstract of Iceland. 1991. Irregular. 262 pp. (In English and Icelandic.)

Ireland

Central Statistics Office, Earlsfort Terrace, Dublin 2

Statistical Abstract. Annual. 1991 400 pp. (In English.)

Italy

ISTAT (Istituto Centrale di Statistica), Via Cesare Balbo 16, 00100 Rome

Annuario Statistico Italiano. Annual. 1991 701 pp. (In Italian.)

Japan

Statistics Bureau, Management & Coordination Agency, 19-1 Wakamatsucho, Shinjuku Tokyo 162

Japan Statistical Yearbook. Annual. 1991 842 pp. (In English and Japanese.)

Luxembourg

STATEC (Service Central de la Statistique et des Etudes), P.O. Box 304, L-2013, Luxembourg

Annuaire Statistique. Annual. 1991 529 pp. (In French.)

Mexico

Instituto Nacional de Estadistica Geografia e Informatica, Avda. Insurgentes Sur No. 795-PH Col. Napoles, Del. Benito Juarez 03810 Mexico, D.F.

Anuario estadistico de los Estados Unidos Mexicanos. Annual. 1986 706 pp. (In Spanish.)

Netherlands

Centraal Bureau voor de Statistiek. 428 Prinses Beatrixlaan P.O. Box 959, 2270 AZ Voorburg

Statistical Yearbook of the Netherlands. Annual. 1990 491 pp. (In English.)

New Zealand

Department of Statistics, Wellington

New Zealand Official Yearbook. Annual. 1990 707 pp. (In English.)

Norway

Central Bureau of Statistics, Skippergate 15, P.B. 8131 Dep. N-Oslo 1

Statistical Yearbook. Annual. 1988 502 pp. (In English and Norwegian.)

Portugal

INE (Instituto Nacional de Estatistica), Avenida Antonio Jose de Almeida, P-1078 Lisbon Codex

Anuario Estatistico: Continente, Acores e Madeira. Annual. 1990 336 pp. (In Portuguese.)

Soviet Union

Central Statistical Board, Moscow

Narodnoe Khoziaistvo SSSR: Statisticheskii ezhegodnik. Annual. 767 pp. (In Russian.)

Spain

INE (Instituto Nacional de Estadistica), Paseo de la Castellana, 183, Madrid 16

Anuario Estadistico de Espana. Annual. 1989 895 pp. (In Spanish.)

Anuario Estadistico. 1988. (Edicion Manual.) 976 pp.

Sweden

Statistics Sweden, S-11581 Stockholm

Statistical Abstract of Sweden. Annual. 1988 561 pp. (In English and Swedish.)

Switzerland

Bundesamt fur Statistik, Hallwylstrasse 15, CH-3003, Bern

Statistisches Jahrbuch der Schweiz. Annual. 1991 420 pp. (In French and German.)

Turkey

State Institute of Statistics, Prime Ministry, 114 Necatibey Caddesi, Bakanliklar, Yenisehir, Ankara

Statistical Yearbook of Turkey. Published on odd numbered years. 1988 479 pp. (In English and Turkish.)

Turkey —Con.

State Institute of Statistics, Prime Ministry, 114 Necatibey Caddesi, Bakanliklar, Yenisehir, Ankara —Con.

Statistical Pocketbook of Turkey. Published on even numbered years. 1986 294 pp. (In English and Turkish.)

United Kingdom

Central Statistical Office, Great George Street, London SW1P 3AQ

Annual Abstract of Statistics. Annual. 1991 349 pp. (In English.)

West Germany

Statistische Bundesamt, Postfach 5528, 6200 Wiesbaden

Statistisches Jahrbuch fur die Bundesrepublic Deutschland. Annual. 1990 740 pp. (In German.)

Yugoslavia

Savezni Zavod za Statistiku, P.O. Box 203, 11000 Belgrade

Statisticki Godisnjak Jugoslavije. Annual. 1991 779 pp. (In Serbo-Croation with English, French, and Russian translations of table headings.)

Statistical Pocketbook of Yugoslavia. 1991. 161 pp. (In English.)

Metropolitan Area Concepts and Components

Statistics for metropolitan areas shown in the *Statistical Abstract* represent areas designated by the U.S. Office of Management and Budget (OMB) as standard metropolitan statistical areas (SMSA's) or metropolitan statistical areas (MSA's). Effective June 30, 1983, OMB changed the basic term from SMSA to MSA and revised the geographic definitions of many individual metropolitan areas; some new areas were defined, and some areas were redesignated as PMSA's or CMSA's (see further explanation below). The revised definitions appear in OMB press release 83-20 of June 27, 1983. The official standards for defining MSA's appeared in the Federal Register, January 3, 1980 (part 6). Revisions of MSA definitions are made periodically by OMB, mainly to add newly qualified MSA's or central cities.

The list of areas which follows (see p. 898) specifies components and population totals and refers to the definitions in effect on June 30, 1990. On that date, there were 268 MSA's, as well as 21 CMSA's comprising 73 PMSA's (including 4 MSA's, 1 CMSA, and 2 PMSA's in Puerto Rico).

The general concept of a metropolitan area is one of a large population nucleus, together with adjacent communities which have a high degree of economic and social integration with that nucleus. Standard definitions of metropolitan statistical areas were first issued in 1949 by the then Bureau of the Budget (predecessor of OMB), under the designation, "Standard Metropolitan Areas"; the term was changed to SMSA in 1959. From 1977 to 1981, the SMSA's were the responsibility of the Office of Federal Statistical Policy and Standards, Department of Commerce.

The criteria for the establishment and definition of SMSA's were modified in 1958, 1971, and 1975. The current standards were adopted in January 1980; they provide that each MSA must include at least:

(a) One city with 50,000 or more inhabitants, or

(b) A Census Bureau-defined urbanized area of at least 50,000 inhabitants *and* a total MSA population of at least 100,000 (75,000 in New England).

The standards provide that the MSA include as "central county(ies)" the county in which the central city is located, and adjacent counties, if any, with at least 50 percent of their population in the urbanized area. Additional "outlying counties" are included if they meet specified requirements of commuting to the central counties and of metropolitan character (such as population density and percent urban). In New England the MSA's are defined in terms of cities and towns rather than counties. The 1980 standards provide that within metropolitan complexes of 1 million or more population, separate component areas are defined if specified criteria are met. Such areas are designated primary metropolitan statistical areas (PMSA's); and any area containing PMSA's is designated a consolidated metropolitan statistical area (CMSA). Besides the 21 CMSA's, as of 1990 there were 18 MSA's of 1 million or more within which no component PMSA's have been established. Of the 73 PMSA's, most were formerly SMSA's, but some were newly established in 1983. Of the 21 CMSA's, most were previously recognized as standard consolidated statistical areas (SCSA's), but 5 were formerly SMSA's within which PMSA's were newly qualified in 1983. The standards adopted in 1980 were implemented in two stages. First, they were used to defined a group of 36 new areas in June 1981. The 323 SMSA's as of June 30, 1981, were reported in the 1980 census tabulations and publications. Next, the boundaries of all SMSA's were reviewed in 1982-83 under the new standards after 1980 commuting data became available.

Revised 1980 standards for determining central cities and titles were implemented as part of the 1982-83 review. The largest city in each MSA is designated a "central city;" in addition there may be additional central cities if specified requirements are met. The title of each MSA consists of the name(s) of up to three of its central cities and the name of each State into which the MSA extends. However, a central city generally is not included in an MSA title unless it has at least one-third the population of the area's largest city. Prior to 1983, virtually all central cities appeared in the area titles. An MSA may include other cities of 50,000 or more besides its central or title cities.

Standards for defining metropolitan areas after the 1990 census were issued by OMB in March 1990, revising the 1980 standards in a few respects. Effective in April 1990, the areas are collectively termed "metropolitan areas", although each individual area will continue to be designated an MSA, CMSA, or PMSA.

New England MSA's and NECMA's.— Because MSA's in New England are defined in terms of cities and towns rather than counties, some statistical data that are available only for counties cannot be compiled for individual New England MSA's. Therefore, for New England areas, data are shown for both New England County Metropolitan Areas (NECMA's) and MSA's wherever possible. The NECMA's provide a county version of the New

England areas, but do not replace New England MSA's as the standard areas. NECMA's are defined corresponding to the three CMSA's in New England and for the portion of the New York-Northern New Jersey-Long Island CMSA in Connecticut. There are no NECMA definitions corresponding to New England PMSA's.

Effect of changes in MSA definitions.— Changes in the definitions of MSA's since 1949 have consisted chiefly of (1) the recognition of new areas as, for example, cities reached 50,000 population; and (2) the addition of counties (or towns in New England) to existing MSA's as new census data showed them to qualify. Also, several formerly separate MSA's have been merged, and occasionally territory has been transferred from one MSA to another or from an MSA to nonmetropolitan territory. Comparisons of MSA figures over time may be affected in cases where the MSA definitions were changed. To maintain comparability, data for an earlier period have been revised in this volume where possible, to reflect the MSA boundaries of the more recent period. However, this could not always be done; for data based on a sample survey, in particular, it is usually not possible to revise the data to reflect changes in MSA definitions that occurred after the survey was made.

New England County Metropolitan Areas (NECMA's)

[In thousands. As of **April 1**]

NECMA	Population, 1990	NECMA	Population, 1990	NECMA	Population, 1990
Bangor, ME	147	Tolland County	129	Cumberland County	243
Penobscot County	147				
		Lewiston-Auburn, ME	105	Portsmouth-Dover-	
Boston-Lawrence-Salem-		Androscoggin County	105	Rochester, NH	350
Lowell-Brockton, MA	3,784			Rockingham County	246
Essex County	670	Manchester-Nashua, NH	336	Strafford County	104
Middlesex County	1,398	Hillsborough County	336		
Norfolk County	616			Providence-Pawtucket-	
Plymouth County	435	New Bedford-Fall River-		Woonsocket, RI	916
Suffolk County	664	Attleboro, MA	506	Bristol County	49
		Bristol County	506	Kent County	161
Bridgeport-Stamford-				Providence County	596
Norwalk-Danbury, CT	828	New Haven-Waterbury-		Washington County	110
Fairfield County	828	Meriden, CT	804		
		New Haven County	804	Springfield, MA	603
Burlington, VT	137			Hampden County	456
Chittenden County	132	New London-Norwich, CT	255	Hampshire County	147
Grand Isle County	5	New London County	255		
				Worcester-Fitchburg-	
Hartford-New Britain-		Pittsfield, MA	139	Leominster, MA	710
Middletown-Bristol, CT	1,124	Berkshire County	139	Worcester County	710
Hartford County	852				
Middlesex County	143	Portland, ME	243		

Source: U.S. Bureau of the Census, unpublished data.

Appendix II

Metropolitan Areas and Their Components as of June 30, 1990

[Population enumerated as of **April 1, 1990**. All metropolitan areas are arranged alphabetically. For relationship of PMSA's to their CMSA's, see CMSA entry]

	1990 Population (1,000)		1990 Population (1,000)		1990 Population (1,000)
Abilene, TX MSA.	120	Atlanta, GA MSA.	2,834	Bellingham, WA MSA	128
Taylor County.	120	Barrow County	30	Whatcom County.	128
		Butts County	15		
Akron, OH PMSA	658	Cherokee County	90	Benton Harbor, MI MSA. . . .	161
Portage County.	143	Clayton County	182	Berrien County	161
Summit County.	515	Cobb County	448		
		Coweta County	54	Bergen-Passaic, NJ PMSA . .	1,278
Albany, GA MSA.	113	De Kalb County	546	Bergen County	825
Dougherty County	96	Douglas County	71	Passaic County.	453
Lee County	16				
		Fayette County	62	Billings, MT MSA.	113
Albany-Schenectady-Troy,		Forsyth County	44	Yellowstone County.	113
NY MSA.	874	Fulton County.	649		
Albany County	293	Gwinnett County	353	Biloxi-Gulfport, MS MSA . . .	197
Greene County	45	Henry County	59	Hancock County	32
Montgomery County.	52	Newton County	42	Harrison County	165
Rensselaer County	154	Paulding County	42		
Saratoga County	181	Rockdale County.	54	Binghamton, NY MSA	264
Schenectady County	149	Spalding County	54	Broome County.	212
		Walton County	39	Tioga County	52
Albuquerque, NM MSA	481				
Bernalillo County.	481	Atlantic City, NJ MSA	319	Birmingham, AL MSA	908
		Atlantic County	224	Blount County.	39
Alexandria, LA MSA	132	Cape May County	95	Jefferson County.	652
Rapides Parish	132			St. Clair County.	50
		Augusta, GA-SC MSA	397	Shelby County	99
Allentown-Bethlehem-		Columbia County, GA.	66	Walker County	68
Easton, PA-NJ MSA.	687	McDuffie County, GA	20		
Carbon County, PA	57	Richmond County, GA	190	Bismarck, ND MSA	84
Lehigh County, PA.	291	Aiken County, SC	121	Burleigh County	60
Northampton County, PA . .	247			Morton County	24
Warren County, NJ	92	Aurora-Elgin, IL PMSA.	357		
		Kane County	317	Bloomington, IN MSA	109
Altoona, PA MSA	131	Kendall County	39	Monroe County.	109
Blair County	131				
		Austin, TX MSA	782	Bloomington-Normal, IL	
Amarillo, TX MSA	188	Hays County.	66	MSA.	129
Potter County	98	Travis County	576	McLean County.	129
Randall County	90	Williamson County.	140		
				Boise City, ID MSA	206
Anaheim-Santa Ana, CA		Bakersfield, CA MSA.	543	Ada County	206
PMSA.	2,411	Kern County	543		
Orange County	2,411			Boston, MA PMSA	2,871
		Baltimore, MD MSA.	2,382	Bristol County (pt.).	41
Anchorage, AK MSA	226	Anne Arundel County	427	Essex County (pt.).	122
Anchorage Borough.	226	Baltimore County.	692	Middlesex County (pt.)	1,132
		Carroll County.	123	Norfolk County (pt.)	605
Anderson, IN MSA	131	Harford County	182	Plymouth County (pt.).	237
Madison County	131	Howard County	187	Suffolk County	664
		Queen Anne's County	34	Worcester County (pt.)	71
Anderson, SC MSA	145	Baltimore city	736		
Anderson County	145			Boston-Lawrence-Salem,	
		Bangor, ME MSA	89	MA-NH CMSA	4,172
Ann Arbor, MI PMSA.	283	Penobscot County (pt.). . . .	86	Boston, MA PMSA.	2,871
Washtenaw County	283	Waldo County (pt.).	3	Brockton, MA PMSA	189
				Lawrence-Haverhill, MA-NH	
Anniston, AL MSA	116	Baton Rouge, LA MSA	528	PMSA	394
Calhoun County	116	Ascension Parish	58	Lowell, MA-NH PMSA	273
		East Baton Rouge Parish . .	380	Nashua, NH PMSA	181
Appleton-Oshkosh-Neenah,		Livingston Parish.	71	Salem-Gloucester, MA	
WI MSA	315	West Baton Rouge Parish. .	19	PMSA	264
Calumet County	34				
Outagamie County.	141	Battle Creek, MI MSA	136	Boulder-Longmont, CO	
Winnebago County	140	Calhoun County	136	PMSA.	225
				Boulder County	225
Asheville, NC MSA	175	Beaumont-Port Arthur, TX			
Buncombe County.	175	MSA.	361	Bradenton, FL MSA.	212
		Hardin County.	41	Manatee County	212
Athens, GA MSA.	156	Jefferson County.	239		
Clarke County.	88	Orange County	81	Brazoria, TX PMSA	192
Jackson County	30			Brazoria County	192
Madison County	21	Beaver County, PA PMSA . .	186		
Oconee County.	18	Beaver County	186	Bremerton, WA MSA.	190
				Kitsap County	190

Area	1990 Population (1,000)
Bridgeport-Milford, CT PMSA	**444**
Fairfield County (pt.)	335
New Haven County (pt.)	109
Bristol, CT PMSA	**79**
Hartford County (pt.)	68
Litchfield County (pt.)	12
Brockton, MA PMSA	**189**
Bristol County (pt.)	20
Norfolk County (pt.)	5
Plymouth County (pt.)	165
Brownsville-Harlingen, TX MSA	**260**
Cameron County	260
Bryan-College Station, TX MSA	**122**
Brazos County	122
Buffalo, NY PMSA	**969**
Erie County	969
Buffalo-Niagara Falls, NY CMSA	**1,189**
Buffalo, NY PMSA	969
Niagara Falls, NY PMSA	221
Burlington, NC MSA	**108**
Alamance County	108
Burlington, VT MSA	**131**
Chittenden County (pt.)	125
Franklin County (pt.)	4
Grand Isle County (pt.)	3
Canton, OH MSA	**394**
Carroll County	27
Stark County	368
Casper, WY MSA	**61**
Natrona County	61
Cedar Rapids, IA MSA	**169**
Linn County	169
Champaign-Urbana-Rantoul, IL MSA	**173**
Champaign County	173
Charleston, SC MSA	**507**
Berkeley County	129
Charleston County	295
Dorchester County	83
Charleston, WV MSA	**250**
Kanawha County	208
Putnam County	43
Charlotte-Gastonia-Rock Hill, NC-SC MSA	**1,162**
Cabarrus County, NC	99
Gaston County, NC	175
Lincoln County, NC	50
Mecklenburg County, NC	511
Rowan County, NC	111
Union County, NC	84
York County, SC	131
Charlottesville, VA MSA	**131**
Albemarle County	68
Fluvanna County	12
Greene County	10
Charlottesville city	40
Chattanooga, TN-GA MSA	**433**
Hamilton County, TN	286
Marion County, TN	25
Sequatchie County, TN	9
Catoosa County, GA	42
Dade County, GA	13
Walker County, GA	58
Cheyenne, WY MSA	**73**
Laramie County	73
Chicago, IL PMSA	**6,070**
Cook County	5,105
Du Page County	782
McHenry County	183
Chicago-Gary-Lake County (IL), IL-IN-WI CMSA	**8,066**
Aurora-Elgin, IL PMSA	357
Chicago, IL PMSA	6,070
Gary-Hammond, IN PMSA	605
Joliet, IL PMSA	390
Kenosha, WI PMSA	128
Lake County, IL PMSA	516
Chico, CA MSA	**182**
Butte County	182
Cincinnati, OH-KY-IN PMSA	**1,453**
Clermont County, OH	150
Hamilton County, OH	866
Warren County, OH	114
Boone County, KY	58
Campbell County, KY	84
Kenton County, KY	142
Dearborn County, IN	39
Cincinnati-Hamilton, OH-KY-IN CMSA	**1,744**
Cincinnati, OH-KY-IN PMSA	1,453
Hamilton-Middletown, OH PMSA	291
Clarksville-Hopkinsville, TN-KY MSA	**169**
Montgomery County, TN	100
Christian County, KY	69
Cleveland, OH PMSA	**1,831**
Cuyahoga County	1,412
Geauga County	81
Lake County	215
Medina County	122
Cleveland-Akron-Lorain, OH CMSA	**2,760**
Akron, OH PMSA	658
Cleveland, OH PMSA	1,831
Lorain-Elyria, OH PMSA	271
Colorado Springs, CO MSA	**397**
El Paso County	397
Columbia, MO MSA	**112**
Boone County	112
Columbia, SC MSA	**453**
Lexington County	168
Richland County	286
Columbus, GA-AL MSA	**243**
Chattahoochee County, GA	17
Muscogee County, GA	179
Russell County, AL	47
Columbus, OH MSA	**1,377**
Delaware County	67
Fairfield County	103
Franklin County	961
Licking County	128
Madison County	37
Pickaway County	48
Union County	32
Corpus Christi, TX MSA	**350**
Nueces County	291
San Patricio County	59
Cumberland, MD-WV MSA	**102**
Allegany County, MD	75
Mineral County, WV	27
Dallas, TX PMSA	**2,553**
Collin County	264
Dallas County	1,853
Denton County	274
Ellis County	85
Kaufman County	52
Rockwall County	26
Dallas-Fort Worth, TX CMSA	**3,885**
Dallas, TX PMSA	2,553
Fort Worth-Arlington, TX PMSA	1,332
Danbury, CT PMSA	**188**
Fairfield County (pt.)	163
Litchfield County (pt.)	25
Danville, VA MSA	**109**
Pittsylvania County	56
Danville city	53
Davenport-Rock Island-Moline, IA-IL MSA	**351**
Scott County, IA	151
Henry County, IL	51
Rock Island County, IL	149
Dayton-Springfield, OH MSA	**951**
Clark County	148
Greene County	137
Miami County	93
Montgomery County	574
Daytona Beach, FL MSA	**371**
Volusia County	371
Decatur, AL MSA	**132**
Lawrence County	32
Morgan County	100
Decatur, IL MSA	**117**
Macon County	117
Denver, CO PMSA	**1,623**
Adams County	265
Arapahoe County	392
Denver County	468
Douglas County	60
Jefferson County	438
Denver-Boulder, CO CMSA	**1,848**
Boulder-Longmont, CO PMSA	225
Denver, CO PMSA	1,623
Des Moines, IA MSA	**393**
Dallas County	30
Polk County	327
Warren County	36
Detroit, MI PMSA	**4,382**
Lapeer County	75
Livingston County	116
Macomb County	717
Monroe County	134
Oakland County	1,084
St. Clair County	146
Wayne County	2,112
Detroit-Ann Arbor, MI CMSA	**4,665**
Ann Arbor, MI PMSA	283
Detroit, MI PMSA	4,382
Dothan, AL MSA	**131**
Dale County	50
Houston County	81
Dubuque, IA MSA	**86**
Dubuque County	86
Duluth, MN-WI MSA	**240**
St. Louis County, MN	198
Douglas County, WI	42
Eau Claire, WI MSA	**138**
Chippewa County	52
Eau Claire County	85
El Paso, TX MSA	**592**
El Paso County	592
Elkhart-Goshen, IN MSA	**156**
Elkhart County	156

	1990 Population (1,000)
Elmira, NY MSA	95
Chemung County	95
Enid, OK MSA	57
Garfield County	57
Erie, PA MSA	276
Erie County	276
Eugene-Springfield, OR MSA	283
Lane County	283
Evansville, IN-KY MSA	279
Posey County, IN	26
Vanderburgh County, IN . . .	165
Warrick County, IN	45
Henderson County, KY	43
Fall River, MA-RI PMSA	157
Bristol County, MA (pt.) . . .	140
Newport County, RI (pt.) . . .	18
Fargo-Moorhead, ND-MN MSA	153
Cass County, ND	103
Clay County, MN	50
Fayetteville, NC MSA	275
Cumberland County	275
Fayetteville-Springdale, AR MSA	113
Washington County	113
Fitchburg-Leominster, MA MSA	103
Middlesex County (pt.)	3
Worcester County (pt.)	100
Flint, MI MSA	430
Genesee County	430
Florence, AL MSA	131
Colbert County	52
Lauderdale County	80
Florence, SC MSA	114
Florence County	114
Fort Collins-Loveland, CO MSA	186
Larimer County	186
Fort Lauderdale-Hollywood-Pompano Beach, FL PMSA.	1,255
Broward County	1,255
Fort Myers-Cape Coral, FL MSA	335
Lee County	335
Fort Pierce, FL MSA	251
Martin County	101
St. Lucie County	150
Fort Smith, AR-OK MSA . . .	176
Crawford County, AR	42
Sebastian County, AR	100
Sequoyah County, OK	34
Fort Walton Beach, FL MSA.	144
Okaloosa County	144
Fort Wayne, IN MSA	364
Allen County	301
De Kalb County	35
Whitley County	28
Fort Worth-Arlington, TX PMSA	1,332
Johnson County	97
Parker County	65
Tarrant County	1,170
Fresno, CA MSA	667
Fresno County	667

	1990 Population (1,000)
Gadsden, AL MSA	100
Etowah County	100
Gainesville, FL MSA	204
Alachua County	182
Bradford County	23
Galveston-Texas City, TX PMSA	217
Galveston County	217
Gary-Hammond, IN PMSA . .	605
Lake County	476
Porter County	129
Glens Falls, NY MSA	119
Warren County	59
Washington County	59
Grand Forks, ND MSA	71
Grand Forks County	71
Grand Rapids, MI MSA	688
Kent County	501
Ottawa County	188
Great Falls, MT MSA	78
Cascade County	78
Greeley, CO MSA	132
Weld County	132
Green Bay, WI MSA	195
Brown County	195
Greensboro—Winston-Salem—High Point, NC MSA	942
Davidson County	127
Davie County	28
Forsyth County	266
Guilford County	347
Randolph County	107
Stokes County	37
Yadkin County	30
Greenville-Spartanburg, SC MSA	641
Greenville County	320
Pickens County	94
Spartanburg County	227
Hagerstown, MD MSA	121
Washington County	121
Hamilton-Middletown, OH PMSA	291
Butler County	291
Harrisburg-Lebanon-Carlisle, PA MSA	588
Cumberland County	195
Dauphin County	238
Lebanon County	114
Perry County	41
Hartford, CT PMSA	768
Hartford County (pt.)	634
Litchfield County (pt.)	9
Middlesex County (pt.)	7
New London County (pt) . . .	11
Tolland County (pt.)	107
Hartford-New Britain-Middletown, CT CMSA	1,086
Bristol, CT PMSA	79
Hartford, CT PMSA	768
Middletown, CT PMSA	90
New Britain, CT PMSA	148
Hickory-Morganton, NC MSA	222
Alexander County	28
Burke County	76
Catawba County	118
Honolulu, HI MSA	836
Honolulu County	836

	1990 Population (1,000)
Houma-Thibodaux, LA MSA .	183
Lafourche Parish	86
Terrebonne Parish	97
Houston, TX PMSA	3,302
Fort Bend County	225
Harris County	2,818
Liberty County	53
Montgomery County	182
Waller County	23
Houston-Galveston-Brazoria, TX CMSA	3,711
Brazoria, TX PMSA	192
Galveston-Texas City, TX PMSA	217
Houston, TX PMSA	3,302
Huntington-Ashland, WV-KY-OH MSA	313
Cabell County, WV	97
Wayne County, WV	42
Boyd County, KY	51
Carter County, KY	24
Greenup County, KY	37
Lawrence County, OH	62
Huntsville, AL MSA	239
Madison County	239
Indianapolis, IN MSA	1,250
Boone County	38
Hamilton County	109
Hancock County	46
Hendricks County	76
Johnson County	88
Marion County	797
Morgan County	56
Shelby County	40
Iowa City, IA MSA	96
Johnson County	96
Jackson, MI MSA	150
Jackson County	150
Jackson, MS MSA	395
Hinds County	254
Madison County	54
Rankin County	87
Jackson, TN MSA	78
Madison County	78
Jacksonville, FL MSA	907
Clay County	106
Duval County	673
Nassau County	44
St. Johns County	84
Jacksonville, NC MSA	150
Onslow County	150
Jamestown-Dunkirk, NY MSA	142
Chautauqua County	142
Janesville-Beloit, WI MSA . .	140
Rock County	140
Jersey City, NJ PMSA	553
Hudson County	553
Johnson City-Kingsport-Bristol, TN-VA MSA	436
Carter County, TN	52
Hawkins County, TN	45
Sullivan County, TN	144
Unicoi County, TN	17
Washington County, TN . . .	92
Scott County, VA.	23
Washington County, VA . . .	46
Bristol city, VA	18
Johnstown, PA MSA	241
Cambria County	163
Somerset County	78
Joliet, IL PMSA	390
Grundy County	32
Will County	357

	1990 Population (1,000)
Joplin, MO MSA	**135**
Jasper County	90
Newton County	44
Kalamazoo, MI MSA	**223**
Kalamazoo County	223
Kankakee, IL MSA	**96**
Kankakee County	96
Kansas City, MO-KS MSA	**1,566**
Cass County, MO	64
Clay County, MO	153
Jackson County, MO	633
Lafayette County, MO	31
Platte County, MO	58
Ray County, MO	22
Johnson County, KS	355
Leavenworth County, KS	64
Miami County, KS	23
Wyandotte County, KS	162
Kenosha, WI PMSA	**128**
Kenosha County	128
Killeen-Temple, TX MSA	**255**
Bell County	191
Coryell County	64
Knoxville, TN MSA	**605**
Anderson County	68
Blount County	86
Grainger County	17
Jefferson County	33
Knox County	336
Sevier County	51
Union County	14
Kokomo, IN MSA	**97**
Howard County	81
Tipton County	16
La Crosse, WI MSA	**98**
La Crosse County	98
Lafayette, LA MSA	**209**
Lafayette Parish	165
St. Martin Parish	44
Lafayette-West Lafayette, IN MSA	**131**
Tippecanoe County	131
Lake Charles, LA MSA	**168**
Calcasieu Parish	168
Lake County, IL PMSA	**516**
Lake County	516
Lakeland-Winter Haven, FL MSA	**405**
Polk County	405
Lancaster, PA MSA	**423**
Lancaster County	423
Lansing-East Lansing, MI MSA	**433**
Clinton County	58
Eaton County	93
Ingham County	282
Laredo, TX MSA	**133**
Webb County	133
Las Cruces, NM MSA	**136**
Dona Ana County	136
Las Vegas, NV MSA	**741**
Clark County	741
Lawrence, KS MSA	**82**
Douglas County	82
Lawrence-Haverhill, MA-NH PMSA	**394**
Essex County, MA (pt.)	284
Rockingham County, NH (pt.)	110

	1990 Population (1,000)
Lawton, OK MSA	**111**
Comanche County	111
Lewiston-Auburn, ME MSA	**88**
Androscoggin County (pt.)	88
Lexington-Fayette, KY MSA	**348**
Bourbon County	19
Clark County	29
Fayette County	225
Jessamine County	31
Scott County	24
Woodford County	20
Lima, OH MSA	**154**
Allen County	110
Auglaize County	45
Lincoln, NE MSA	**214**
Lancaster County	214
Little Rock-North Little Rock, AR MSA	**513**
Faulkner County	60
Lonoke County	39
Pulaski County	350
Saline County	64
Longview-Marshall, TX MSA	**162**
Gregg County	105
Harrison County	57
Lorain-Elyria, OH PMSA	**271**
Lorain County	271
Los Angeles-Anaheim-Riverside, CA CMSA	**14,532**
Anaheim-Santa Ana, CA PMSA	2,411
Los Angeles-Long Beach, CA PMSA	8,863
Oxnard-Ventura, CA PMSA	669
Riverside-San Bernardino, CA PMSA	2,589
Los Angeles-Long Beach, CA PMSA	**8,863**
Los Angeles County	8,863
Louisville, KY-IN MSA	**953**
Bullitt County, KY	48
Jefferson County, KY	665
Oldham County, KY	33
Shelby County, KY	25
Clark County, IN	88
Floyd County, IN	64
Harrison County, IN	30
Lowell, MA-NH PMSA	**273**
Middlesex County, MA (pt.)	264
Hillsborough County, NH (pt.)	9
Lubbock, TX MSA	**223**
Lubbock County	223
Lynchburg, VA MSA	**142**
Amherst County	29
Campbell County	48
Lynchburg city	66
Macon-Warner Robins, GA MSA	**281**
Bibb County	150
Houston County	89
Jones County	21
Peach County	21
Madison, WI MSA	**367**
Dane County	367
Manchester, NH MSA	**148**
Hillsborough County (pt.)	127
Merrimack County (pt.)	13
Rockingham County (pt.)	8
Mansfield, OH MSA	**126**
Richland County	126

	1990 Population (1,000)
McAllen-Edinburg-Mission, TX MSA	**384**
Hidalgo County	384
Medford, OR MSA	**146**
Jackson County	146
Melbourne-Titusville-Palm Bay, FL MSA	**399**
Brevard County	399
Memphis, TN-AR-MS MSA	**982**
Shelby County, TN	826
Tipton County, TN	38
Crittenden County, AR	50
De Soto County, MS	68
Merced, CA MSA	**178**
Merced County	178
Miami-Fort Lauderdale, FL CMSA	**3,193**
Fort Lauderdale-Hollywood-Pompano Beach, FL PMSA	1,255
Miami-Hialeah, FL PMSA	1,937
Miami-Hialeah, FL PMSA	**1,937**
Dade County	1,937
Middlesex-Somerset-Hunterdon, NJ PMSA	**1,020**
Hunterdon County	108
Middlesex County	672
Somerset County	240
Middletown, CT PMSA	**90**
Middlesex County (pt.)	90
Midland, TX MSA	**107**
Midland County	107
Milwaukee, WI PMSA	**1,432**
Milwaukee County	959
Ozaukee County	73
Washington County	95
Waukesha County	305
Milwaukee-Racine, WI CMSA	**1,607**
Milwaukee, WI PMSA	1,432
Racine, WI PMSA	175
Minneapolis-St. Paul, MN-WI MSA	**2,464**
Anoka County, MN	244
Carver County, MN	48
Chisago County, MN	31
Dakota County, MN	275
Hennepin County, MN	1,032
Isanti County, MN	26
Ramsey County, MN	486
Scott County, MN	58
Washington County, MN	146
Wright County, MN	69
St. Croix County, WI	50
Mobile, AL MSA	**477**
Baldwin County	98
Mobile County	379
Modesto, CA MSA	**371**
Stanislaus County	371
Monmouth-Ocean, NJ PMSA	**986**
Monmouth County	553
Ocean County	433
Monroe, LA MSA	**142**
Ouachita Parish	142
Montgomery, AL MSA	**293**
Autauga County	34
Elmore County	49
Montgomery County	209
Muncie, IN MSA	**120**
Delaware County	120

	1990 Population (1,000)
Muskegon, MI MSA	159
Muskegon County	159
Naples, FL MSA	152
Collier County	152
Nashua, NH PMSA	181
Hillsborough County (pt.)	161
Rockingham County (pt.)	20
Nashville, TN MSA	985
Cheatham County	27
Davidson County	511
Dickson County	35
Robertson County	41
Rutherford County	119
Sumner County	103
Williamson County	81
Wilson County	68
Nassau-Suffolk, NY PMSA	2,609
Nassau County	1,287
Suffolk County	1,322
New Bedford, MA MSA	176
Bristol County (pt.)	161
Plymouth County (pt.)	14
New Britain, CT PMSA	148
Hartford County (pt.)	148
New Haven-Meriden, CT MSA	530
Middlesex County (pt.)	18
New Haven County (pt.)	513
New London-Norwich, CT-RI MSA	267
New London County, CT (pt.)	234
Windham County, CT (pt.)	4
Washington County, RI (pt.)	28
New Orleans, LA MSA	1,239
Jefferson Parish	448
Orleans Parish	497
St. Bernard Parish	67
St. Charles Parish	42
St. John the Baptist Parish	40
St. Tammany Parish	145
New York, NY PMSA	8,547
Bronx County	1,204
Kings County	2,301
New York County	1,488
Putnam County	84
Queens County	1,952
Richmond County	379
Rockland County	265
Westchester County	875
New York-Northern New Jersey-Long Island, NY-NJ-CT CMSA	18,087
Bergen-Passaic, NJ PMSA	1,278
Bridgeport-Milford, CT PMSA	444
Danbury, CT PMSA	188
Jersey City, NJ PMSA	553
Middlesex-Somerset-Hunterdon, NJ PMSA	1,020
Monmouth-Ocean, NJ PMSA	986
Nassau-Suffolk, NY PMSA	2,609
New York, NY PMSA	8,547
Newark, NJ PMSA	1,824
Norwalk, CT PMSA	127
Orange County, NY PMSA	308
Stamford, CT PMSA	203
Newark, NJ PMSA	1,824
Essex County	778
Morris County	421
Sussex County	131
Union County	494
Niagara Falls, NY PMSA	221
Niagara County	221
Norfolk-Virginia Beach-Newport News, VA MSA	1,396
Gloucester County	30
James City County	35
York County	42
Chesapeake city	152
Hampton city	134
Newport News city	170
Norfolk city	261
Poquoson city	11
Portsmouth city	104
Suffolk city	52
Virginia Beach city	393
Williamsburg city	12
Norwalk, CT PMSA	127
Fairfield County (pt.)	127
Oakland, CA PMSA	2,083
Alameda County	1,279
Contra Costa County	804
Ocala, FL MSA	195
Marion County	195
Odessa, TX MSA	119
Ector County	119
Oklahoma City, OK MSA	959
Canadian County	74
Cleveland County	174
Logan County	29
McClain County	23
Oklahoma County	600
Pottawatomie County	59
Olympia, WA MSA	161
Thurston County	161
Omaha, NE-IA MSA	618
Douglas County, NE	416
Sarpy County, NE	103
Washington County, NE	17
Pottawattamie County, IA	83
Orange County, NY PMSA	308
Orange County	308
Orlando, FL MSA	1,073
Orange County	677
Osceola County	108
Seminole County	288
Owensboro, KY MSA	87
Daviess County	87
Oxnard-Ventura, CA PMSA	669
Ventura County	669
Panama City, FL MSA	127
Bay County	127
Parkersburg-Marietta, WV-OH MSA	149
Wood County, WV	87
Washington County, OH	62
Pascagoula, MS MSA	115
Jackson County	115
Pawtucket-Woonsocket-Attleboro, RI-MA PMSA	329
Providence County, RI (pt.)	227
Bristol County, MA (pt.)	85
Norfolk County, MA (pt.)	7
Worcester County, MA (pt.)	10
Pensacola, FL MSA	344
Escambia County	263
Santa Rosa County	82
Peoria, IL MSA	339
Peoria County	183
Tazewell County	124
Woodford County	33
Philadelphia, PA-NJ PMSA	4,857
Bucks County, PA	541
Chester County, PA	376
Delaware County, PA	548
Montgomery County, PA	678
Philadelphia County, PA	1,586
Burlington County, NJ	395
Camden County, NJ	503
Gloucester County, NJ	230
Philadelphia-Wilmington-Trenton, PA-NJ-DE-MD CMSA	5,899
Philadelphia, PA-NJ PMSA	4,857
Trenton, NJ PMSA	326
Vineland-Millville-Bridgeton, NJ PMSA	138
Wilmington, DE-NJ-MD PMSA	579
Phoenix, AZ MSA	2,122
Maricopa County	2,122
Pine Bluff, AR MSA	85
Jefferson County	85
Pittsburgh, PA PMSA	2,057
Allegheny County	1,336
Fayette County	145
Washington County	205
Westmoreland County	370
Pittsburgh-Beaver Valley, PA CMSA	2,243
Beaver County, PA PMSA	186
Pittsburgh, PA PMSA	2,057
Pittsfield, MA MSA	79
Berkshire County (pt.)	79
Portland, ME MSA	215
Cumberland County (pt.)	197
York County (pt.)	18
Portland, OR PMSA	1,240
Clackamas County	279
Multnomah County	584
Washington County	312
Yamhill County	66
Portland-Vancouver, OR-WA CMSA	1,478
Portland, OR PMSA	1,240
Vancouver, WA PMSA	238
Portsmouth-Dover-Rochester, NH-ME MSA	224
Rockingham County, NH (pt.)	77
Strafford County, NH (pt.)	98
York County, ME (pt.)	49
Poughkeepsie, NY MSA	259
Dutchess County	259
Providence, RI PMSA	655
Bristol County	49
Kent County (pt.)	158
Newport County (pt.)	5
Providence County (pt.)	369
Washington County (pt.)	74
Providence-Pawtucket-Fall River, RI-MA CMSA	1,142
Fall River, MA-RI PMSA	157
Pawtucket-Woonsocket-Attleboro, RI-MA PMSA	329
Providence, RI PMSA	655
Provo-Orem, UT MSA	264
Utah County	264
Pueblo, CO MSA	123
Pueblo County	123
Racine, WI PMSA	175
Racine County	175

	1990 Population (1,000)
Raleigh-Durham, NC MSA ..	735
Durham County.........	182
Franklin County.........	36
Orange County.........	94
Wake County..........	423
Rapid City, SD MSA	81
Pennington County	81
Reading, PA MSA	337
Berks County	337
Redding, CA MSA	147
Shasta County	147
Reno, NV MSA	255
Washoe County	255
Richland-Kennewick-Pasco, WA MSA	150
Benton County	113
Franklin County........	37
Richmond-Petersburg, VA MSA	866
Charles City County......	6
Chesterfield County......	209
Dinwiddie County........	21
Goochland County.......	14
Hanover County........	63
Henrico County.........	218
New Kent County	10
Powhatan County	15
Prince George County	27
Colonial Heights city	16
Hopewell city	23
Petersburg city	38
Richmond city..........	203
Riverside-San Bernardino, CA PMSA	2,589
Riverside County........	1,170
San Bernardino County ...	1,418
Roanoke, VA MSA	224
Botetourt County........	25
Roanoke County........	79
Roanoke city	96
Salem city	24
Rochester, MN MSA	106
Olmsted County	106
Rochester, NY MSA	1,002
Livingston County	62
Monroe County.........	714
Ontario County........	95
Orleans County	42
Wayne County.........	89
Rockford, IL MSA	284
Boone County..........	31
Winnebago County	253
Sacramento, CA MSA	1,481
El Dorado County	126
Placer County.........	173
Sacramento County......	1,041
Yolo County	141
Saginaw-Bay City-Midland, MI MSA	399
Bay County	112
Midland County........	76
Saginaw County	212
St. Cloud, MN MSA	191
Benton County	30
Sherburne County	42
Stearns County	119
St. Joseph, MO MSA	83
Buchanan County	83

	1990 Population (1,000)
St. Louis, MO-IL MSA	2,444
Franklin County, MO	81
Jefferson County, MO	171
St. Charles County, MO ...	213
St. Louis County, MO.....	994
St. Louis city, MO	397
Clinton County, IL	34
Jersey County, IL	21
Madison County, IL	249
Monroe County, IL......	22
St. Clair County, IL	263
Salem, OR MSA	278
Marion County	228
Polk County	50
Salem-Gloucester, MA PMSA	264
Essex County (pt.)......	264
Salinas-Seaside-Monterey, CA MSA	356
Monterey County........	356
Salt Lake City-Ogden, UT MSA	1,072
Davis County	188
Salt Lake County.......	726
Weber County	158
San Angelo, TX MSA	98
Tom Green County	98
San Antonio, TX MSA	1,302
Bexar County	1,185
Comal County.........	52
Guadalupe County.......	65
San Diego, CA MSA	2,498
San Diego County.......	2,498
San Francisco, CA PMSA ...	1,604
Marin County	230
San Francisco County	724
San Mateo County......	650
San Francisco-Oakland-San Jose, CA CMSA	6,253
Oakland, CA PMSA	2,083
San Francisco, CA PMSA..	1,604
San Jose, CA PMSA	1,498
Santa Cruz, CA PMSA ...	230
Santa Rosa-Petaluma, CA PMSA	388
Vallejo-Fairfield-Napa, CA PMSA	451
San Jose, CA PMSA	1,498
Santa Clara County......	1,498
Santa Barbara-Santa Maria-Lompoc, CA MSA	370
Santa Barbara County	370
Santa Cruz, CA PMSA	230
Santa Cruz County	230
Santa Fe, NM MSA	117
Los Alamos County	18
Santa Fe County........	99
Santa Rosa-Petaluma, CA PMSA	388
Sonoma County	388
Sarasota, FL MSA	278
Sarasota County........	278
Savannah, GA MSA	243
Chatham County........	217
Effingham County	26

	1990 Population (1,000)
Scranton—Wilkes-Barre, PA MSA	734
Columbia County........	63
Lackawanna County	219
Luzerne County........	328
Monroe County.........	96
Wyoming County........	28
Seattle, WA PMSA	1,973
King County	1,507
Snohomish County	466
Seattle-Tacoma, WA CMSA	2,559
Seattle, WA PMSA	1,973
Tacoma, WA PMSA.....	586
Sharon, PA MSA	121
Mercer County	121
Sheboygan, WI MSA	104
Sheboygan County	104
Sherman-Denison, TX MSA	95
Grayson County	95
Shreveport, LA MSA	334
Bossier Parish	86
Caddo Parish	248
Sioux City, IA-NE MSA	115
Woodbury County, IA ...	98
Dakota County, NE	17
Sioux Falls, SD MSA	124
Minnehaha County	124
South Bend-Mishawaka, IN MSA	247
St. Joseph County.......	247
Spokane, WA MSA	361
Spokane County	361
Springfield, IL MSA	190
Menard County	11
Sangamon County......	178
Springfield, MA MSA	530
Hampden County (pt.)	445
Hampshire County (pt.)...	84
Springfield, MO MSA	241
Christian County........	33
Greene County	208
Stamford, CT PMSA	203
Fairfield County (pt.)	203
State College, PA MSA	124
Centre County	124
Steubenville-Weirton, OH-WV MSA	143
Jefferson County, OH.	80
Brooke County, WV.	27
Hancock County, WV.	35
Stockton, CA MSA	481
San Joaquin County......	481
Syracuse, NY MSA	660
Madison County	69
Onondaga County	469
Oswego County	122
Tacoma, WA PMSA	586
Pierce County..........	586
Tallahassee, FL MSA	234
Gadsden County	41
Leon County..........	192

	1990 Population (1,000)
Tampa-St. Petersburg-	
Clearwater, FL MSA	**2,068**
Hernando County	101
Hillsborough County	834
Pasco County	281
Pinellas County	852
Terre Haute, IN MSA	**131**
Clay County	25
Vigo County	106
Texarkana, TX-Texarkana,	
AR MSA	**120**
Bowie County, TX	82
Miller County, AR	38
Toledo, OH MSA	**614**
Fulton County	38
Lucas County	462
Wood County	113
Topeka, KS MSA	**161**
Shawnee County	161
Trenton, NJ PMSA	**326**
Mercer County	326
Tucson, AZ MSA	**667**
Pima County	667
Tulsa, OK MSA	**709**
Creek County	61
Osage County	42
Rogers County	55
Tulsa County	503
Wagoner County	48
Tuscaloosa, AL MSA	**151**
Tuscaloosa County	151
Tyler, TX MSA	**151**
Smith County	151
Utica-Rome, NY MSA	**317**
Herkimer County	66
Oneida County	251
Vallejo-Fairfield-Napa, CA	
PMSA	**451**
Napa County	111
Solano County	340

	1990 Population (1,000)
Vancouver, WA PMSA	**238**
Clark County	238
Victoria, TX MSA	**74**
Victoria County	74
Vineland-Millville-Bridgeton,	
NJ PMSA	**138**
Cumberland County	138
Visalia-Tulare-Porterville,	
CA MSA	**312**
Tulare County	312
Waco, TX MSA	**189**
McLennan County	189
Washington, DC-MD-VA	
MSA	**3,924**
District of Columbia	607
Calvert County, MD	51
Charles County, MD	101
Frederick County, MD	150
Montgomery County, MD	757
Prince George's County,	
MD	729
Arlington County, VA	171
Fairfax County, VA	819
Loudoun County, VA	86
Prince William County, VA	216
Stafford County, VA	61
Alexandria city, VA	111
Fairfax city, VA	20
Falls Church city, VA	10
Manassas city, VA	28
Manassas Park city, VA	7
Waterbury, CT MSA	**222**
Litchfield County (pt.)	39
New Haven County (pt.)	183
Waterloo-Cedar Falls, IA	
MSA	**147**
Black Hawk County	124
Bremer County	23
Wausau, WI MSA	**115**
Marathon County	115

	1990 Population (1,000)
West Palm Beach-Boca	
Raton-Delray Beach, FL MSA	**864**
Palm Beach County	864
Wheeling, WV-OH MSA	**159**
Marshall County, WV	37
Ohio County, WV	51
Belmont County, OH	71
Wichita, KS MSA	**485**
Butler County	51
Harvey County	31
Sedgwick County	404
Wichita Falls, TX MSA	**122**
Wichita County	122
Williamsport, PA MSA	**119**
Lycoming County	119
Wilmington, DE-NJ-MD	
PMSA	**579**
New Castle County, DE	442
Salem County, NJ	65
Cecil County, MD	71
Wilmington, NC MSA	**120**
New Hanover County	120
Worcester, MA MSA	**437**
Worcester County (pt.)	437
Yakima, WA MSA	**189**
Yakima County	189
York, PA MSA	**418**
Adams County	78
York County	340
Youngstown-Warren, OH	
MSA	**493**
Mahoning County	265
Trumbull County	228
Yuba City, CA MSA	**123**
Sutter County	64
Yuba County	58
Yuma, AZ MSA	**107**
Yuma County	107

Statistical Methodology and Reliability

Introduction.—The data presented in this *Statistical Abstract* came from many sources. The sources include not only Federal statistical bureaus and other organizations that collect and issue statistics as their principal activity, but also governmental administrative and regulatory agencies, private research bodies, trade associations, insurance companies, health associations, and private organizations such as the National Education Association and philanthropic foundations. Consequently, the data vary considerably as to reference periods, definitions of terms and, for ongoing series, the number and frequency of time periods for which data are available.

The statistics presented were obtained and tabulated by various means. Some statistics are based on complete enumerations or censuses while others are based on samples. Some information is extracted from records kept for administrative or regulatory purposes (school enrollment, hospital records, securities registration, financial accounts, social security records, income tax returns, etc.), while other information is obtained explicitly for statistical purposes through interviews or by mail. The estimation procedures used vary from highly sophisticated scientific techniques, to crude "informed guesses."

Each set of data relates to a group of individuals or units of interest referred to as the *target universe* or *target population,* or simply as the *universe* or *population.* Prior to data collection, the target universe should be clearly defined. For example, if data are to be collected for the universe of households in the United States, it is necessary to define a "household." The target universe may not be completely tractable. Cost and other considerations may restrict data collection to a *survey universe* of households on some available list, such list being inaccurate, out of date, defining "household" slightly differently, etc. This list is called a *survey frame* or *sampling frame.*

The data in many tables are based on data obtained for all population units, *a census,* or on data obtained for only a portion, or *sample,* of the population units. When the data presented are based on a sample, the sample is usually a scientifically selected *probability sample.* This is a sample selected from a list or sampling frame in such a way that every possible sample has a known chance of selection and usually each unit selected can be assigned a number, between zero and one, representing its likelihood or probability of selection.

For large-scale sample surveys, the probability sample of units is often selected as a multistage sample. The first stage of a multistage sample is the selection of a probability sample of large groups of population members, referred to as primary sampling units (PSU's). For example, in a national multistage household sample, PSU's are often counties or groups of counties. The second stage of a multistage sample is the selection, within each PSU selected at the first stage, of smaller groups of population units, referred to as secondary sampling units. In subsequent stages of selection, smaller and smaller nested groups are chosen until the ultimate sample of population units is obtained. To qualify a multistage sample as a probability sample, all stages of sampling must be carried out using probability sampling methods.

Prior to selection at each stage of a multistage (or a single stage) sample, a list of the sampling units or sampling frame for that stage must be obtained. For example, for the first stage of selection of a national household sample, a list of the counties and county groups that form the PSU's must be obtained. For the final stage of selection, lists of households, and sometimes persons within the households, have to be compiled in the field. For surveys of economic entities and for the economic census, the Census Bureau generally uses a frame constructed from the Bureau's Standard Statistical Establishment List (SSEL). The SSEL contains all establishments with payroll in the United States including small single establishment firms as well as large multi-establishment firms.

Wherever the quantities in a table refer to an entire universe, but are constructed from data collected in a sample survey, the table quantities are referred to as *sample estimates*. In constructing a sample estimate, an attempt is made to come as close as is feasible to the corresponding universe quantity that would be obtained from a complete census of the universe. Estimates based on a sample will, however, generally differ from the hypothetical census figures. Two classifications of errors are associated with estimates based on sample surveys: (1) *sampling error*—the error arising from the use of a sample, rather than a census, to estimate population quantities and (2) *nonsampling error*—those errors arising from nonsampling sources. As discussed below, the magnitude of the sampling error for an estimate can usually be estimated from the sample data. However, the magnitude of the nonsampling error for an estimate can rarely be estimated. Consequently, actual error in an estimate exceeds the estimated error in the estimate.

The particular sample used in a survey is only one of a large number of possible samples of the same size which could have been selected using the same sampling procedure. Estimates derived from the different samples would, in general, differ from each other. The *standard error* (SE) is a measure of the variation among the estimates derived from all possible samples. The standard error is the most commonly used measure of the sampling error of an estimate. Valid estimates of the standard errors of survey estimates can usually be calculated from the data collected in a probability sample. For convenience, the standard error is sometimes expressed as a percent of the estimate and is called the relative standard error or *coefficient of variation* (CV). For example, an estimate of 200 units with an estimated standard error of 10 units has an estimated CV of 5 percent.

A sample estimate and an estimate of its standard error or CV can be used to construct interval estimates that have a prescribed confidence that the interval includes the average of the estimates derived from all possible samples with a known probability. To illustrate, if all possible samples were selected under essentially the same general conditions, and using the same sample design, and if an estimate and its estimated standard error were calculated from each sample, then: 1) Approximately 68 percent of the intervals from one standard error below the estimate to one standard error above the estimate would include the average estimate derived from all possible samples; 2) approximately 90 percent of the intervals from 1.6 standard errors below the estimate to 1.6 standard errors above the estimate would include the average estimate derived from all possible samples; and 3) approximately 95 percent of the intervals from two standard errors below the estimate to two standard errors above the estimate would include the average estimate derived from all possible samples.

Thus, for a particular sample, one can say with the appropriate level of confidence (e.g., 90 percent or 95 percent) that the average of all possible samples is included in the constructed interval. Example of a confidence interval: An estimate is 200 units with a standard error of 10 units. An approximately 90 percent confidence interval (plus or minus 1.6 standard errors) is from 184 to 216.

All surveys and censuses are subject to nonsampling errors. Nonsampling errors are two kinds—*random* and *nonrandom*. Random nonsampling errors arise because of the varying interpretation of questions (by respondents or interviewers) and varying actions of coders, keyers, and other processors. Some randomness is also introduced when respondents must estimate values. These same errors usually have a nonrandom component. Nonrandom nonsampling errors result from total nonresponse (no usable data obtained for a sampled unit), partial or item nonresponse (only a portion of a response may be usable), inability or unwillingness on the part of respondents to provide correct information, difficulty interpreting questions, mistakes in recording or keying data, errors of collection or processing, and coverage problems (overcoverage and undercoverage of the target universe). Random nonresponse errors usually, but not always, result in an understatement of sampling errors and thus an overstatement of the precision of survey estimates. Estimating the magnitude of nonsampling errors would require special experiments or access to independent data and, consequently, the magnitudes are seldom available.

Nearly all types of nonsampling errors that affect surveys also occur in complete censuses. Since surveys can be conducted on a smaller scale than censuses, nonsampling errors can presumably be controlled more tightly. Relatively more funds and effort can perhaps be expended toward eliciting responses, detecting and correcting response error, and reducing processing errors. As a result, survey results can sometimes be more accurate than census results.

To compensate for suspected nonrandom errors, adjustments of the sample estimates are often made. For example, adjustments are frequently made for nonresponse, both total and partial. Adjustments made for either type of nonresponse are often referred to as *imputations*. Imputation for total nonresponse is usually made by substituting for the questionnaire responses of the nonrespondents the "average" questionnaire responses of the respondents. These imputations usually are made separately within various groups of sample members, formed by attempting to place respondents and nonrespondents together that have "similar" survey characteristics. Imputation for item nonresponse is usually made by substituting for a missing item the response to that item of a respondent having characteristics that are "similar" to those of the nonrespondent.

For an estimate calculated from a sample survey, the *total error* in the estimate is composed of the sampling error, which can usually be estimated from the sample, and the nonsampling error, which usually cannot be estimated from the sample. The total error present in a population quantity obtained from a complete census is composed of only nonsampling errors. Ideally, estimates of the total error associated with data given in the *Statistical Abstract* tables should be given. However, due to the unavailability of estimates of nonsampling errors, only estimates of the levels of sampling errors, in terms of estimated standard errors or coefficients of variation, are available. To obtain estimates of the estimated standard errors from the sample of interest, obtain a copy of the referenced report which appears at the end of each table.

Principal data bases.—Beginning below are brief descriptions of 34 of the sample surveys and censuses that provide a substantial portion of the data contained in this *Abstract*.

SECTION 1. POPULATION

Source and Title: Bureau of the Census, *Census of Population*

Tables: See tables citing *Census of Population* in section 1 and also in sections 2, 4, 6, 8, 13, 14, 26, and 30, as well as the presentation of 1990 Census sample data beginning on page xii.

Universe, Frequency, and Types of Data: Complete count of U.S. population conducted every 10 years since 1790. Data obtained on number and characteristics of inhabitants.

Type of Data Collection Operation: In 1970, 1980, and 1990 complete census for some items—age, sex, race, marital status, and relationship to household head. In 1970, other items collected from a 5 percent and a 15 percent probability (systematic) sample of the population. In 1980, approximately 19 percent of the housing units were included in the sample; in 1990, approximately 17 percent.

Data Collection and Imputation Procedures: In 1970, extensive use of mail questionnaires in urban areas; personal interviews in most rural areas. In 1980 and 1990, mail questionnaires were used in even more areas than in 1970, with personal interviews in the remainder. Extensive telephone and personal followup for nonrespondents was done in the censuses. Imputations were made for missing characteristics.

Estimates of Sampling Error: Sampling errors for data are estimated for all items collected by sample and vary by characteristic and geographic area. The CV's for national and State estimates are generally very small.

Other (nonsampling) Errors: Since 1950, evaluation programs have been conducted to provide information on the magnitude of some sources of nonsampling errors such as response bias and undercoverage in each census. Preliminary results from the evaluation program for the 1990 census indicate that the net under coverage amounted to about 2 percent of the total resident population.

Sources of Additional Material: U.S. Bureau of the Census, *The Coverage of Population in the 1980 Census*, PHC80-E4; *Content Reinterview Study: Accuracy of Data for Selected Population and Housing Characteristics as Measured by Reinterview*, PHC80-E2; *1980 Census of Population*, vol 1., (PC80-1), appendixes B, C, and D.

Source and Title: U.S. Bureau of the Census, *Current Population Survey (CPS)*

Tables: See tables citing *Current Population Reports* primarily in section 1, but also in sections 2, 3, 4, 8, 12, 13, 14, 23, and 30. Many Bureau of Labor Statistics' (BLS) tables in section 13 are CPS based.

Universe, Frequency, and Types of Data: Nationwide monthly sample survey of civilian noninstitutional population, 15 years old or over, to obtain data on employment, unemployment, and a number of other characteristics.

Type of Data Collection Operation: Multistage probability sample of about 60,000 households in 729 PSU's in 1989. Oversampling in some States and the largest MSA's to improve reliability for those areas of employment data on annual average basis. A continual sample rotation system is used. Households are in sample 4 months, out for 8 months, and in for 4 more. Month-to-month overlap is 75 percent; year-to-year overlap is 50 percent.

Data Collection and Imputation Procedures: For first and fifth months that a household is in sample, personal interviews; other months, approximately, 85 percent of the data collected by phone. Imputation is done for both item and total nonresponse. Adjustment for total nonresponse is done by a predefined cluster of units, by MSA size and residence; for item nonresponse imputation varies by subject matter.

Estimates of Sampling Error: Estimated CV's on national annual averages for labor force, total employment, and nonagricultural employment, 0.2 percent; for total unemployment and agricultural employment, 1.0 percent to 2.5 percent. The estimated CV's for family income and poverty rate for all persons in 1986 are 0.5 percent and 1.5 percent, respectively. CV's for subnational areas, such as States, would be larger and would vary by area.

Other (nonsampling) Errors: Estimates of response bias on unemployment are not available, but estimates of unemployment are usually 5 percent to 9 percent lower than estimates from reinterviews. Sample households unavailable for interviews is 4 to 5 percent.

Sources of Additional Material: U.S. Bureau of the Census and Bureau of Labor Statistics, *Concepts and Methods Used in Labor Force Statistics from Current Population Survey* (Census series P-23, No. 62; BLS Report No. 463) and Bureau of the Census, *Current Population Survey* (Tech. Paper 40) and Bureau of Labor Statistics, *Employment and Earnings,* monthly, Explanatory Notes, table A-K and *BLS Handbook of Methods,* chapter 1 (Bulletin 2285).

SECTION 2. VITAL STATISTICS

Source and Title: U.S. National Center for Health Statistics (NCHS), *Vital Registration System*

Tables: See tables citing *Vital Statistics of the United States,* 292 in section 5; and 1345 in section 30.

Universe, Frequency, and Types of Data: Annual data on births and deaths in the United States.

Type of Data Collection Operation: Mortality data based on complete file of death records, except 1972, based on 50 percent sample. Natality statistics 1951-71, based on 50 percent sample of birth certificates, except a 20 percent to 50 percent in 1967, received by NCHS. Beginning 1972, data from some States received through Vital Statistics Cooperative Program (VSCP) and complete file used; data from other States based on 50 percent sample. Beginning 1986, all reporting areas participated in the VSCP.

Data Collection and Imputation Procedures: Reports based on records from registration offices of all States, District of Columbia, New York City, Puerto Rico, Virgin Islands, and Guam.

Estimates of Sampling Error: For recent years, CV's for births are small due to large portion of total file in sample (except for very small estimated totals).

Other (nonsampling) Errors: Data on births and deaths believed to be at least 99 percent complete.

Sources of Additional Material: U.S. National Center for Health Statistics, *Vital Statistics of the United States,* vol. I and vol. II, annual, and *Monthly Vital Statistics Report.*

(See section 1 above for information pertaining to tables 91-93, 96 and 97.)

SECTION 3. HEALTH AND NUTRITION

Source and Title: U.S. National Center for Health Statistics, *National Health Interview Survey (NHIS)*

Tables: 157, 162, 163, 184, 188, 189, 194, 195, 199, 201-203, and 209.

Universe, Frequency, and Types of Data: Continuous data collection covering the civilian noninstitutional population to obtain information on personal and demographic characteristics, illnesses, injuries, impairments, and other health topics.

Type of Data Collection Operation: Multistage probability sample of 42,000 households (in 376 PSU's) selected in groups of about four adjacent households.

Data Collection and Imputation Procedures: Personal household interviews with extensive followup of nonrespondents. Data are adjusted for nonresponse by imputation procedure based on "average" characteristics of persons in interviewed households in the same geographic area.

Estimates of Sampling Error: Estimated CV's: For physician visits by males, 1.5 percent; for workdays lost by males, 3.5 percent; for persons injured at home, 4.7 percent.

Other (nonsampling) Errors: Response rate was 95.7 percent in 1985 for the NHIS.

Sources of Additional Material: U.S. National Center for Health Statistics, "Current Estimates from the National Health Interview Survey, U.S., 1983," Vital and Health Statistics, series 10.

(See section 15 for information pertaining to table 151.)

SECTION 4. EDUCATION

Source and Title: U.S. Department of Education, National Center for Education Statistics, *Higher Education General Information Survey (HEGIS), Fall Enrollment in Institutions of Higher Education;* beginning 1986, *Integrated Postsecondary Education Data Survey (IPEDS), Fall Enrollment*

Tables: 259, 261-264, and 281.

Universe, Frequency, and Types of Data: Annual survey of all institutions and branches listed in the *Directory* to obtain data on total enrollment by sex, level of enrollment, type of program, racial/ethnic characteristics (in alternate years) and attendance status of student, and on first-time students.

Type of Data Collection Operation: Complete census.

Data Collection and Imputation Procedures: Survey package is usually mailed in the spring with surveys due at varying dates in the summer and fall; mail and phone followup procedures for nonrespondents. Missing data are imputed by using data of similar institutions.

Estimates of Sampling Error: Not applicable.

Other (nonsampling) Errors: Approximately 82 percent response rate.

Sources of Additional Material: U.S. Department of Education, National Center for Education Statistics, *Fall Enrollment in Higher Education,* annual.

Source and Title: U.S. Department of Education, National Center for Education Statistics, *Higher Education General Information Survey (HEGIS), Financial Statistics of Institutions of Higher Education;* beginning 1986, *Integrated Postsecondary Education Data Survey (IPEDS), Financial Statistics of Institutions of Higher Education*

Tables: 211, 214, 262, and 266.

Universe, Frequency, and Types of Data: Annual survey of all institutions and branches listed in the *Education Directory,*

Colleges and Universities to obtain data on financial status and operations, including current funds revenues, current funds expenditures, and physical plant assets.

Type of Data Collection Operation: Complete census.

Data Collection and Imputation Procedures: Survey package is usually mailed in the spring with surveys due at varying dates in the summer and fall; mail and phone followup procedures for nonrespondents. Missing data are imputed by using data of similar institutions.

Estimates of Sampling Error: Not applicable.

Other (nonsampling) Errors: For 1990, a 87 percent response rate. Imputed expenditures amounted to about 2.8 percent of total expenditures.

Sources of Additional Material: U.S. Department of Education, National Center for Education Statistics, *Financial Statistics of Institutions of Higher Education,* annual.

Source and Title: U.S. Department of Education, National Center for Education Statistics, *Higher Education General Information Survey (HEGIS), Degrees and Other Formal Awards Conferred.* Beginning 1986, *Integrated Postsecondary Education Data Survey (IPEDS), Degrees and Other Formal Awards Conferred.*

Tables: 278-282.

Universe, Frequency, and Types of Data: Annual survey of all institutions and branches listed in the *Education Directory, Colleges and Universities* to obtain data on earned degrees and other formal awards, conferred by field of study, level of degree, sex, and by racial/ethnic characteristics (in alternate years).

Type of Data Collection Operation: Complete census.

Data Collection and Imputation Procedures: Survey package is usually mailed in the spring with surveys due at varying dates in the summer and fall; mail and phone followup procedures for nonrespondents. Missing data are imputed by using data of similar institutions.

Estimates of Sampling Error: Not applicable.

Other (nonsampling) Errors: For 1989-90, approximately 92.3 percent response rate.

Sources of Additional Material: U.S. Department of Education, National Center for Education Statistics, *Earned Degrees Conferred,* annual.

(See sections 1 and 9 for information pertaining to the Bureau of the Census and section 3 above for the National Center for Health Statistics.)

SECTION 5. LAW ENFORCEMENT, COURTS, AND PRISONS

Source and Title: U.S. Federal Bureau of Investigation, *Uniform Crime Reporting (UCR) Program*

Tables: 287-291, 293, 294, 302, and 304.

Universe, Frequency, and Types of Data: Monthly reports on the number of criminal offenses that become known to law enforcement agencies. Data are collected on crimes cleared by arrest, by age, sex, and race of offender, and on assaults on law enforcement officers.

Type of Data Collection Operation: Crime statistics are based on reports of crime data submitted either directly to the FBI by contributing law enforcement agencies or through cooperating State UCR programs.

Data Collection and Imputation Procedures: States with UCR programs collect data directly from individual law enforcement agencies and forward reports, prepared in accordance with UCR standards, to FBI. Accuracy and consistency edits are performed by FBI.

Estimates of Sampling Error: Not applicable.

Other (nonsampling) Errors: Coverage of 96 percent of the population (98 percent in SMSA's, 93 percent in "other cities," and 89 percent in rural areas) by UCR program, though varying number of agencies report. Some error may be present through incorrect reporting.

Sources of Additional Material: U.S. Federal Bureau of Investigation, *Crime in the United States.*

Source and Title: U.S. Bureau of Justice Statistics (BJS), *National Crime Survey*

Tables: 295-299.

Universe, Frequency, and Types of Data: Monthly survey of individuals and households in the United States to obtain data on criminal victimization of those units for compilation of annual estimates.

Type of Data Collection Operation: National probability sample survey of about 50,000 interviewed households in 376 PSU's selected from a list of addresses from the 1980 census, supplemented by new construction permits and an area sample where permits are not required.

Data Collection and Imputation Procedures: Interviews are conducted every 6 months for 3 years for each household in the sample; 8,000 households are interviewed monthly. Personal interviews are used in the first and fifth interviews; the intervening interviews are conducted by telephone whenever possible.

Estimates of Sampling Error: CV's in 1985: 2.2 percent for crimes of violence; 14.8 percent for estimate of rape counts; 5.5 percent for robbery counts; 2.5 percent for assault counts; 1.4 percent for personal larceny counts; 2.2 percent for burglary counts; 1.8 percent for household larceny; 1.3 percent for all household crimes; and 4.8 percent for motor vehicle theft counts.

Other (nonsampling) Errors: Respondent recall errors which may include reporting incidents for other than the reference period; interviewer coding and processing errors; and possible mistaken reporting or classifying of events. Adjustment is made for a household noninterview rate of about 4 percent and for a smaller within-household noninterview rate.

Sources of Additional Material: U.S. Bureau of Justice Statistics, *Criminal Victimization in the United States,* annual.

(See section 2 for details on table 292 and section 9 for details on table 313.)

SECTION 6. GEOGRAPHY AND ENVIRONMENT

(See section 9 below for information pertaining to table 358.)

SECTION 8. ELECTIONS

(See section 1 above for information pertaining to tables 417 and 435.)

SECTION 9. STATE AND LOCAL GOVERNMENT FINANCES AND EMPLOYMENT

Source and Title: U.S. Bureau of the Census, *Census of Governments*

Tables: See tables in section 9 citing *Census of Governments.*

Universe, Frequency, and Types of Data: Survey of all governmental units in the United States conducted every 5 years to obtain data on government revenue, expenditures, debt, assets, employment and employee retirement systems, property values, public school systems, and number, size, and structure of governments.

Type of Data Collection Operation: Complete census. List of units derived through classification of government units recently authorized in each State and identification, counting, and classification of existing local governments and public school systems.

Data Collection and Imputation Procedures: Data collected through field and office compilation of financial data from official records and reports for States and large local governments; mail canvass of selected data items, like State tax revenue and employee retirement systems; and collection of local government statistics through central collection arrangements with State governments.

Estimates of Sampling Error: Not applicable.

Other (nonsampling) Errors: Some nonsampling errors may arise due to possible inaccuracies in classification, response, and processing.

Sources of Additional Material: U.S. Bureau of the Census, *Census of Governments, 1987,* various reports, and *State Government Finances in 1990,* GF 90, No. 3.

Source and Title: U.S. Bureau of the Census, *Annual Surveys of State and Local Government*

Tables: See tables citing *Public Employment* and *Governmental Finances* in section 9; table 238 in section 4; table 313 in section 5; table 358 in section 6; and table 581 in section 12.

Universe, Frequency, and Types of Data: Sample survey conducted annually to obtain data on revenue, expenditure, debt, and employment of State and local governments. Universe is all governmental units in the United States (about 83,000).

Type of Data Collection Operation: Sample of about 22,000 units includes all State governments, county governments with 50,000+ population, municipalities and townships with 25,000+ population, all school districts with 10,000+ enrollment in October 1986, and other governments meeting certain criteria; probability sample for remaining units.

Data Collection and Imputation Procedures: Field and office compilation of data from official records and reports for States and large local governments; central collection of local governmental financial data through cooperative agreements with a number of State governments; mail canvass of other units with mail and telephone followups of nonrespondents. Data for nonresponses are imputed from previous year data or obtained from secondary sources, if available.

Estimates of Sampling Error: CV's for estimates of major employment and financial items are generally less than 2 percent for most States and less than 1.2 percent for the majority of States.

Other (nonsampling) Errors: Nonresponse rate is less than 15 percent for number of units. Other possible errors may result from undetected inaccuracies in classification, response, and processing.

Sources of Additional Material: U.S. Bureau of the Census, *Public Employment in 1990,* GE 90, No. 1, *Governmental Finances in 1989-90,* GF 90, No. 5, and *Census of Governments, 1987,* various reports.

SECTION 10. FEDERAL GOVERNMENT

Source and Title: U.S. Internal Revenue Service, *Statistics of Income, Individual Income Tax Returns*

Tables: 508-512.

Universe, Frequency, and Types of Data: Annual study of unaudited individual income tax returns, Forms 1040, 1040A, and 1040EZ, filed by U.S. citizens and residents. Data provided on various financial characteristics by size of adjusted gross income, marital status, and by taxable and nontaxable returns. Data by State, based on 100 percent file, also include returns from 1040NR, filed by nonresident aliens plus certain self-employment tax returns.

Type of Data Collection Operation: Annual stratified probability sample of approximately 125,000 returns broken into sample strata based on the larger of total income or total loss amounts as well as the size of business plus farm receipts. Sampling rates for sample strata varied from 0.025 percent to 100 percent.

Data Collection and Imputation Procedures: Computer selection of sample of tax return records. Data adjusted during editing for incorrect, missing, or inconsistent entries to ensure consistency with other entries on return.

Estimates of Sampling Error: Estimated CV's for tax year 1987: Adjusted gross income less deficit 0.13 percent; salaries and wages 0.20 percent; and tax-exempt interest received 4.51 percent. (State data not subject to sampling error.)

Other (nonsampling) Errors: Processing errors and errors arising from the use of tolerance checks for the data.

Sources of Additional Material: U.S. Internal Revenue Service, *Statistics of Income, Individual Income Tax Returns,* annual.

SECTION 12. SOCIAL INSURANCE AND HUMAN SERVICES

Source and Title: U.S. Social Security Administration, *Benefit Data*

Tables: 573 and 574.

Universe, Frequency, and Types of Data: All persons receiving monthly benefits under Title 11 of Social Security Act. Data on number and amount of benefits paid by type and State.

Type of Data Collection Operation: Data based on administrative records. Data based on 100 percent files, as well as 10 percent and 1 percent sample files.

Data Collection and Imputation Procedures: Records used consist of actions pursuant to applications for benefits, updated by subsequent post-entitlement actions.

Estimates of Sampling Error: Varies by size of estimate and sample file size.

Other (nonsampling) Errors: Processing errors, which are believed to be small.

Sources of Additional Material: U.S. Social Security Administration, *Annual Statistical Supplement to the Social Security Bulletin.*

Source and Title: U.S. Social Security Administration, *Supplemental Security Income (SSI) Program*

Tables: 592-595.

Universe, Frequency, and Types of Data: All eligible aged, blind, or disabled persons receiving SSI benefit payments under SSI program. Data include number of persons receiving federally administered SSI, amounts paid, and State administered supplementation.

Type of Data Collection Operation: Data based on administrative records.

Data Collection and Imputation Procedures: Data adjusted to reflect returned checks and overpayment refunds. For federally administered payments, actual adjusted amounts are used.

Estimates of Sampling Error: Not applicable.

Other (nonsampling) Errors: Processing errors, which are believed to be small.

Sources of Additional Material: U.S. Social Security Administration, *Annual Statistical Supplement to the Social Security Bulletin.*

(See section 1 above for information pertaining to the Current Population Survey, section 3 for information pertaining to the National Center for Health Statistics, and section 9 for information pertaining to Annual Surveys of State and Local Government.)

SECTION 13. LABOR FORCE, EMPLOYMENT, AND EARNINGS

Source and Title: U.S. Bureau of Labor Statistics (BLS), *Current Employment Statistics (CES) Program*

Tables: 643-645, 650; in section 21, table 986; in section 22, table 1050; and in section 24, table 1135.

Universe, Frequency, and Types of Data: Monthly survey covering about 5 million nonagricultural establishments to obtain data on employment, hours, and earnings, by industry.

Type of Data Collection Operation: Sample survey of over 350,000 establishments in March 1990.

Data Collection and Imputation Procedures: Cooperating State agencies mail questionnaires to sample establishments to develop State and local estimates; information is forwarded to BLS where national estimates are prepared.

Estimates of Sampling Error: Estimated CV's for average weekly hours paid, 0.1 percent and for average hourly earnings, 0.2 percent.

Other (nonsampling) Errors: Estimates of employment adjusted annually to reflect complete universe. Average adjustment is 0.2 percent.

Sources of Additional Material: U.S. Bureau of Labor Statistics, *Employment and Earnings,* monthly, Explanatory Notes, tables L-Q and *BLS Handbook of Methods,* Chapter 2, Bulletin 2285 (Apr. 1988).

(See section 1 above for information pertaining to the Current Population Survey.)

SECTION 14. INCOME, EXPENDITURES, AND WEALTH

(See section 1 above for information pertaining to the Bureau of the Census.)

SECTION 15. PRICES

Source and Title: U.S. Bureau of Labor Statistics (BLS), *Consumer Price Index (CPI)*

Tables: 737-743, 758, and in section 3, table 151.

Universe, Frequency, and Types of Data: Monthly survey of price changes of all types of consumer goods and services purchased by urban wage earners and clerical workers prior to 1978, and urban consumers thereafter. Both indexes continue to be published.

Type of Data Collection Operation: Prior to 1978, sample of various consumer items in 56 urban areas; thereafter, in 85 PSU's, except from January 1987 through March 1988, when 91 areas were sampled.

Data Collection and Imputation Procedures: Prices of consumer items are obtained from about 57,000 housing units, and 19,000 other reporters in 85 areas. Prices of food, fuel, and a few other items are obtained monthly; prices of most other commodities and services are collected every month in the five largest geographic areas and every other month in others.

Estimates of Sampling Error: Estimates of standard errors are not available at present.

Other (nonsampling) Errors: Errors result from inaccurate reporting, difficulties in defining concepts and their operational implementation, and introduction of product quality changes and new products.

Sources of Additional Material: U.S. Bureau of Labor Statistics, *The Consumer Price Index:* 1987 Revision, Report 736, and *BLS Handbook of Methods,* Bulletin 2285.

Source and Title: U.S. Bureau of Labor Statistics, *Producer Price Index (PPI)*

Tables: 737, 746-749 in section 21, table 1035; in section 24, table 1139; and in section 26, table 1202.

Universe, Frequency, and Types of Data: Monthly survey of producing companies to determine price changes of all commodities produced in the United States for sale in commercial transactions. Data on agriculture, forestry, fishing, manufacturing, mining, gas, electricity, public utilities and a few services.

Type of Data Collection Operation: Probability sample of approximately 3,100 commodities and about 75,000 quotations per month.

Data Collection and Imputation Procedures: Data are collected by mail. If transaction prices are not supplied, list prices are used. Some prices are obtained from trade publications, organized exchanges, and government agencies. To calculate index, price changes are multiplied by their relative weights based on total net selling value of all commodities in 1982.

Estimates of Sampling Error: Not applicable.

Other (nonsampling) Errors: Not available at present.

Sources of Additional Material: U.S. Bureau of Labor Statistics, *BLS Handbook of Methods,* Bulletin 2285.

SECTION 17. BUSINESS ENTERPRISE

Source and Title: U.S. Internal Revenue Service, *Statistics of Income, Sole Proprietorship Returns* and *Statistics of Income Bulletin*

Tables: 826-829.

Universe, Frequency, and Types of Data: Annual study of unaudited income tax returns of nonfarm sole proprietorships, Form 1040 with business schedules. Data provided on various financial characteristics by industry.

Type of Data Collection Operation: Stratified probability sample of approximately 31,000 sole proprietorships for tax year 1990. The sample is classified based on presence or absence of certain business schedules; the larger of total income or loss; and size of business plus farm receipts. Sampling rates vary from 0.043 per cent to 100 percent.

Data Collection and Imputation Procedures: Computer selection of sample of tax return records. Data adjusted during editing for incorrect, missing, or inconsistent entries to ensure consistency with other entries on return.

Estimates of Sampling Error: Estimated CV's for tax year 1990 are not available; for 1987 (the latest available): For sole proprietorships, business receipts, 1.66 percent;

net income, (less loss), 1.33 percent; depreciation 2.17 percent; interest expense 2.80 percent; and employee benefit programs 7.55 percent.

Other (nonsampling) Errors: Processing errors and errors arising from the use of tolerance checks for the data.

Sources of Additional Material: U.S. Internal Revenue Service, *Statistics of Income, Sole Proprietorship Returns* (for years through 1980) and *Statistics of Income Bulletin,* Vol. 10, No. 1 (Summer 1990).

Source and Title: U.S. Internal Revenue Service, *Statistics of Income, Partnership Returns* and *Statistics of Income Bulletin*

Tables: 826-828, 830, and 831.

Universe, Frequency, and Types of Data: Annual study of unaudited income tax returns of partnerships, Form 1065. Data provided on various financial characteristics by industry.

Type of Data Collection Operation: Stratified probability sample of approximately 28,000 partnership returns from a population of 1,660,000 filed during calendar year 1990. The sample is classified based on combinations of gross receipts, net income or loss, and total assets, and on industry. Sampling rates vary from 0.04 percent to 100 percent.

Data Collection and Imputation Procedures: Computer selection of sample of tax return records. Data are adjusted during editing for incorrect, missing, or inconsistent entries to ensure consistency with other entries on return. Data not available due to regulations are not imputed.

Estimates of Sampling Error: Estimated CV's for tax year 1988 (latest available): For number of partnerships, 0.51 percent; business receipts, 0.78 percent; net income, 3.03 percent; net loss, 2.21 percent and total assets, 1.22 percent.

Other (nonsampling) Errors: Processing errors and errors arising from the use of tolerance checks for the data.

Sources of Additional Material: U.S. Internal Revenue Service, *Statistics of Income, Partnership Returns* and *Statistics of Income Bulletin,* Vol. 10, No. 1 (Summer 1990).

Source and Title: U.S. Internal Revenue Service, *Corporation Income Tax Returns*

Tables: 826-828 and 834-836.

Universe, Frequency, and Types of Data: Annual study of unaudited corporation income tax returns, Forms 1120 and 1120 (A, F, L, PC, REIT, RIC, and S), filed by corporations or businesses legally defined as corporations. Data provided on various financial characteristics by industry and size of total assets, and business receipts.

Type of Data Collection Operation: Stratified probability sample of approximately 85,000 returns for 1987, distributed by sample classes generally based on type of return, size of total assets, size of net income or deficit, and selected business activity. Sampling rates for sample strata varied from 0.25 percent to 100 percent.

Data Collection and Imputation Procedures: Computer selection of sample of tax return records. Data adjusted during editing for incorrect, missing, or inconsistent entries to ensure consistency with other entries on return and to achieve statistical definitions.

Estimates of Sampling Error: Estimated CV's for 1988: Number of returns in subgroups ranged from 1.4 percent with assets under $100,000, to 0 percent with assets over $100 mil.; for amount of net income and amount of income tax, 0.18 percent

Other (nonsampling) Errors: Processing errors and errors arising from the use of tolerance checks for the data.

Sources of Additional Material: U.S. Internal Revenue Service, *Statistics of Income, Corporation Income Tax Returns,* annual.

SECTION 18. COMMUNICATIONS

(See section 27 for information pertaining to table 897.)

SECTION 19. ENERGY

Source and Title: U.S. Energy Information Administration, *Residential Energy Consumption Survey*

Tables: 919-921, 951, and table 1232 in section 26.

Universe, Frequency, and Types of Data: Triennial survey of households and fuel suppliers. Data are obtained on energy-related household characteristics, housing unit characteristics, use of fuels, and energy consumption and expenditures by fuel type.

Type of Data Collection Operation: Probability sample of 7,183 eligible units in 129 PSU's. For responding units, fuel consumption and expenditure data obtained from fuel suppliers to those households.

Data Collection and Imputation Procedures: Personal interviews. Extensive followup of nonrespondents including mail questionnaires for some households. Adjustments for nonrespondents were made in weighting for respondents. Most item nonresponses were imputed.

Estimates of Sampling Error: Estimated CV's for household averages: For consumption, 1.3 percent; for expenditures, 1.0 percent; for various fuels, values ranged from 1.4 percent for electricity to 5.9 percent for LPG.

Other (nonsampling) Errors: Household response rate of 86.7 percent. Nonconsumption data were mostly imputed for mail respondents (5.2 percent of eligible units). Usable responses from fuel suppliers for various fuels ranged from 82.8 percent for electricity to 55.7 percent for fuel oil.

Sources of Additional Material: U.S. Energy Information Administration, *Household Energy Consumption and Expenditures, 1987* and *Housing Characteristics,* 1987.

SECTION 21. TRANSPORTATION—LAND

(See section 13 for table 986, and section 15 for table 1035.)

SECTION 22. TRANSPORTATION—AIR AND WATER

Source and Title: U.S. Bureau of the Census, *Foreign Trade—Export Statistics*

Tables: See Bureau of the Census citations for export statistics in source notes in sections 22 and 29 and also tables 1162 and 1163 in section 24; 1176 in section 25; and 1354 in section 30.

Universe, Frequency, and Types of Data: The export declarations collected by Customs are processed each month to obtain data on the movement of U.S. merchandise exports to foreign countries. Data obtained include value, quantity, and shipping weight of exports by commodity, country of destination, Customs district of exportation, and mode of transportation.

Type of Data Collection Operation: Shipper's Export Declarations are required to be filed for the exportation of merchandise valued over $1,500. Customs officials collect and transmit the documents to the Bureau of the Census on a flow basis for data compilation. Value data for shipments valued under $1,501 are estimated, based on established percentages of individual country totals.

Data Collection and Imputation Procedures: Statistical copies of Shipper's Export Declarations are received on a daily basis from Customs ports throughout the country and subjected to a monthly processing cycle. They are fully processed to the extent they reflect items valued over $1,500. Estimates for shipments valued at $1,500 or less are made, based on established percentages of individual country totals.

Estimates of Sampling Error: Not applicable.

Other (nonsampling) Errors: Clerical and complex computer checks intercept most processing errors and minimize otherwise significant reporting errors; other nonsampling errors are caused by undercounting of exports to Canada due to the nonreceipt of some Shipper's Export Declarations.

Sources of Additional Material: U.S. Bureau of the Census, *U.S. Merchandise Trade: Exports, General Imports, and Imports for Consumption, SITC, Commodity by Country,* FT 925.

Source and Title: U.S. Bureau of the Census, *Foreign Trade—Import Statistics*

Tables: See Bureau of the Census citations for import statistics in source notes in sections 22 and 29 and also tables 1162 and 1163 in section 24; 1176 in section 25; and 1354 in section 30.

Universe, Frequency, and Types of Data: The import entry documents collected by Customs are processed each month to obtain data on the movement of merchandise imported into the United States. Data obtained include value, quantity, and shipping weight by commodity, country of origin, Customs district of entry, and mode of transportation.

Type of Data Collection Operation: Import entry documents are required to be filed for the importation of goods into the United States valued over $1,000 or for articles which must be reported on formal entries. Customs officials collect and transmit statistical copies of the documents to the Bureau of the Census on a flow basis for data compilation. Estimates for shipments valued under $1,001 and not reported on formal entries are based on established percentages of individual country totals.

Data Collection and Imputation Procedures: Statistical copies of import entry documents, received on a daily basis from Customs ports of entry throughout the country, are subjected to a monthly processing cycle. They are fully processed to the extent they reflect items valued at $1,001 and over or items which must be reported on formal entries.

Estimates of Sampling Error: Not applicable.

Other (nonsampling) Errors: Verification of statistical data reporting by Customs officials prior to transmittal and a subsequent program of clerical and computer checks are utilized to hold nonsampling errors arising from reporting and/or processing errors to a minimum.

Sources of Additional Material: U.S. Bureau of the Census, *U.S. Merchandise Trade: Exports, General Imports and Imports for Consumption, SITC, Commodity by Country,* FT 925.

(See section 13 for information pertaining to table 1050.)

SECTION 23. AGRICULTURE

Source and Title: U.S. Department of Agriculture, National Agricultural Statistics Service (NASS), *Basic Area Frame Sample*

Tables: See tables citing NASS in source notes in section 23, which pertain to this or the following two surveys.

Universe, Frequency, and Types of Data: Two annual area sample surveys of U.S. farm operators: June agricultural survey collects data on planted acreage and livestock inventories; and a February Farm Costs and Returns survey that collects data on total farm production, expenses and specific commodity costs of production.

Type of Data Collection Operation: Stratified probability sample of about 16,000 land area units of about 1 sq. mile (range from .1 sq. mile in cities to several sq. miles in open grazing areas). Sample includes 60,000 parcels of agricultural land. About 20 percent of the sample replaced annually.

Data Collection and Imputation Procedures: Data collection is by personal enumeration. Imputation is based on enumerator observation or data reported by respondents having similar agricultural characteristics.

Estimates of Sampling Error: Estimated CV's range from 1 percent to 2 percent for regional estimates to 3 percent to 6 percent for State estimates of livestock inventories.

Other (nonsampling) Errors: Minimized through rigid quality controls on the collection process and careful review of all reported data.

Sources of Additional Material: U.S. Department of Agriculture, SRS, *Scope and Methods of the Statistical Reporting Service,* (name changed to National Agricultural Statistics Service), Miscellaneous Publication No. 1308, September 1983 (revised).

Source and Title: U.S. Department of Agriculture, National Agricultural Statistics Service (NASS), *Multiple Frame Survey*

Tables: See tables citing NASS in source notes in section 23, which pertain to this or the following survey.

Universe, Frequency, and Types of Data: Surveys of U.S. farm operators to obtain data on major livestock inventories, selected crop acreages and production, grain stocks, and farm labor characteristics; and to obtain farm economic data for price indexing.

Type of Data Collection Operation: Primary frame is obtained from general or special purpose lists, supplemented by a probability sample of land areas used to estimate for list incompleteness.

Data Collection and Imputation Procedures: Mail, telephone or personal interviews used for initial data collection. Mail nonrespondent followup by phone and personal interviews. Imputation based on average of respondents.

Estimates of Sampling Error: Estimated CV for number of hired farm workers is about 3 percent. Estimated CV's range from 1 percent to 2 percent for regional estimates to 3 percent to 6 percent for State estimates of livestock inventories.

Other (nonsampling) Errors: In addition to above, replicated sampling procedures used to monitor effects of changes in survey procedures.

Sources of Additional Material: U.S. Department of Agriculture, SRS, *Scope and Methods of the Statistical Reporting Service,* (name changed to National Agricultural Statistics Service), Miscellaneous Publication No. 1308, September 1983 (revised).

Source and Title: U.S. Department of Agriculture, National Agricultural Statistics Service (NASS), *Objective Yield Surveys*

Tables: See tables citing NASS in source notes in section 23, which pertain to this or the preceding survey.

Universe, Frequency, and Types of Data: Surveys for data on corn, cotton, potatoes, soybeans, wheat, and rice to forecast and estimate yields.

Type of Data Collection Operation: Random location of plots in probability sample of fields. Fields selected in June from Basic Area Frame Sample (see above).

Data Collection and Imputation Procedures: Enumerators count and measure plant characteristics in sample fields. Production measured from plots at harvest. Harvest loss measured from post harvest gleanings.

Estimates of Sampling Error: CV's for national estimates of production are about 2 percent to 3 percent.

Other (nonsampling) Errors: In addition to above, replicated sampling procedures used to monitor effects of changes in survey procedures.

Sources of Additional Material: U.S. Department of Agriculture, SRS, *Scope and Methods of the Statistical Reporting Service,* (name changed to National Agricultural Statistics Service), Miscellaneous Publication No. 1308, September 1983 (revised).

(See section 1 above for information pertaining to the Census of Population and Current Population Survey.)

SECTION 24. FORESTS AND FISHERIES

(See section 13 for information pertaining to table 1135, section 15 for table 1139, and section 22 for tables 1162 and 1163.)

SECTION 26. CONSTRUCTION AND HOUSING

Source and Title: U.S. Bureau of the Census, *Monthly Survey of Construction*

Tables: 1211, and 1213-1215.

Universe, Frequency, and Types of Data: Survey conducted monthly of newly constructed housing units (excluding mobile homes). Data are collected on the start, completion, and sale of housing. (Annual figures are aggregates of monthly estimates.)

Type of Data Collection Operation: Probability sample of housing units obtained from building permits selected from 17,000 places. For nonpermit places, multistage probability sample of new housing units selected in 169 PSU's. In those areas, all roads are canvassed in selected enumeration districts.

Data Collection and Imputation Procedures: Data are obtained by telephone inquiry and field visit.

Estimates of Sampling Error: Estimated CV of 3 percent to 4 percent for estimates of national totals, but are as high as 20 percent for estimated totals of more detailed characteristics, such as housing units in multiunit structures.

Other (nonsampling) Errors: Response rate is over 90 percent for most items. Nonsampling errors are attributed to definitional problems, differences in interpretation of questions, incorrect reporting, inability to obtain information about all cases in the sample, and processing errors.

Sources of Additional Material: U.S. Bureau of the Census, *Construction Reports,* series C20, *Housing Starts;* C22, *Housing Completions; and* C25, *New One-Family Houses Sold and For Sale..*

Source and Title: U.S. Bureau of the Census, *Value of New Construction Put in Place*

Tables: 1204-1206.

Universe, Frequency, and Types of Data: Survey conducted monthly on total value of all construction put in place in the current month, both public and private projects. Construction values include costs of materials and labor, contractors' profits, overhead costs, cost of architectural and engineering work, and miscellaneous project costs. (Annual figures are aggregates of monthly estimates.)

Type of Data Collection Operation: Varies by type of activity: Total cost of private one-family houses started each month is distributed into value put in place using fixed patterns of monthly construction progress; using a multistage probability sample, data for private multifamily housing are obtained by mail from owners of multiunit projects. Data for residential additions and alterations are obtained in a quarterly survey measuring expenditures; monthly estimates are interpolated from quarterly data. Estimates of value of private nonhousekeeping, nonresidential buildings, and State and local government construction are obtained by mail from owners (or agents) for a probability sample of projects. Estimates of farm nonresidential construction expenditures are based on U.S. Department of Agriculture annual estimates of construction; public utility estimates are obtained from reports submitted to Federal regulatory agencies and from private utility companies; estimates for all other private construction (nonbuilding) are obtained by phasing F. W. Dodge contract award data; estimates of Federal construction are based on monthly data supplied by Federal agencies.

Data Collection and Imputation Procedures: See "Type of Data Collection Operation." Imputation accounts for approximately 20 percent of estimated value of construction each month.

Estimates of Sampling Error: CV estimates for private nonresidential building construction range from 3 percent for estimated value of industrial buildings to 10 percent for miscellaneous buildings. CV is approximately 2 percent for total new private nonresidential buildings.

Other (nonsampling) Errors: For directly measured data series based on samples, some nonsampling errors may arise from processing errors, imputations, and misunderstanding of questions. Indirect data series are dependent on the validity of the underlying assumptions and procedures.

Sources of Additional Material: U.S. Bureau of the Census, *Construction Reports*, series C30, *Value of New Construction Put in Place.*

Source and Title: U.S. Bureau of the Census, *Census of Housing*

Tables: See tables citing *Census of Housing* in source notes in section 26, as well as the presentation of 1990 Census sample data beginning on page xii.

Universe, Frequency, and Types of Data: Census of all occupied and vacant housing, excluding group quarters, conducted every 10 years as part of the decennial census (see section 1 above) to determine characteristics of U.S. housing.

Type of Data Collection Operation: For 1970, 1980, and 1990, a complete count of some housing items (e.g. Owned or rented, and value). In 1970, other items collected from 5 percent and 15 percent probability samples selected from two sets of detailed questions on housing (these two sets having some common items). In 1980, approximately 19 percent of the housing units were included in the sample; in 1990, approximately 17 percent.

Data Collection and Imputation Procedures: In 1970, a self-enumeration census using a mail-out/mail-back procedure was used in most areas. In 1980 and 1990, mail questionnaires were used in even more areas than in 1970, with personal interviews in the remainder. Followup for nonrespondents and identification of vacant units done by phone and personal visit.

Estimates of Sampling Error: Sampling errors for data are estimated for all items collected by sample and vary by characteristic and geographic area.

Other (nonsampling) Errors: Evaluation studies for 1980 estimated the underenumeration of occupied housing units at 1.5 percent. The missed rate in 1980 for all units was 2.6 percent or approximately 2.3 million units, 1 million of which were vacant housing units.

Sources of Additional Material: U.S. Bureau of the Census, *1980 Census of Population and Housing, The Coverage of Housing in the 1980 Census*, PHC80-E1, July 1985.

Source and Title: U.S. Bureau of the Census, *American Housing Survey*

Tables: See tables citing *American Housing Survey* in source notes.

Universe, Frequency, and Types of Data: Conducted nationally in the fall in odd numbered years to obtain data on the approximately 103 million occupied or vacant housing units in the United States (group quarters are excluded). Data include characteristics of occupied housing units, vacant units, new housing and mobile home units, financial characteristics, recent mover households, housing and neighborhood quality indicators, and energy characteristics.

Type of Data Collection Operation: The national sample was a multistage probability sample with about 51,300 units eligible for interview in 1987. Sample units, selected within 394 PSU's, were surveyed over a 5-month period.

Data Collection and Imputation Procedures: For 1987, the survey was conducted by personal interviews. The interviewers obtained the information from the occupants or, if the unit was vacant, from informed persons such as landlords, rental agents, or knowledgeable neighbors.

Estimates of Sampling Error: For the national sample, illustrations of the S.E. of the estimates are provided in the appendix B of the 1987 report. As an example, the estimated CV is about 0.5 percent for the estimated percentage of owner occupied units with two persons.

Other (nonsampling) Errors: Response rate was about 97 percent. Nonsampling errors may result from incorrect or incomplete responses, errors in coding and recording, and processing errors. For the 1985 national sample, approximately 6 percent of the total housing inventory was not adequately represented by the AHS sample.

Sources of Additional Material: U.S. Bureau of the Census, *Current Housing Reports,* series H-150 and H-170, *American Housing Survey.*

(See section 1 above for information pertaining to the Census of Population, section 15 pertaining to table 1202, and section 19 for table 1232.)

SECTION 27. MANUFACTURES

Source and Title: U.S. Bureau of the Census, *Census of Manufactures*

Tables: See tables citing *Census of Manufactures* in source notes in section 27 and also table 897 in section 18 and table 1356 in section 30.

Universe, Frequency, and Types of Data: Conducted every 5 years to obtain information on labor materials, capital input and output characteristics, plant location, and legal form of organization for all plants in the United States with one or more employees. Universe was 350,000 manufacturing establishments in 1987.

Type of Data Collection Operation: Complete enumeration of data items obtained from 200,000 firms. Administrative records from Internal Revenue Service and Social Security Administration are used for 150,000 smaller single-location firms, which were determined by various cutoffs based on size and industry.

Data Collection and Imputation Procedures: Five mail and telephone followups for larger nonrespondents. Data for small single-location firms (generally those with fewer than 10 employees) not mailed census questionnaires were estimated from administrative records of IRS and SSA. Data for nonrespondents were imputed from related responses or administrative records from IRS and SSA. Approximately 8 percent of total value of shipments was represented by fully imputed records in 1987.

Estimates of Sampling Error: Not applicable.

Other (nonsampling) Errors: Based on evaluation studies, estimates of nonsampling errors for 1972 were about 1.3 percent for estimated total payroll; 2 percent for total employment; and 1 percent for value of shipments. Estimates for later years are not available.

Sources of Additional Material: U.S. Bureau of the Census, *1987 Census of Manufactures, Industry Series, Geographic Area Series, and Subject Series.*

Source and Title: U.S. Bureau of the Census, *Annual Survey of Manufactures*

Tables: See tables citing *Annual Survey of Manufactures* in source notes.

Universe, Frequency, and Types of Data: Conducted annually to provide basic measures of manufacturing activity for intercensal years for all manufacturing establishments having one or more paid employees.

Type of Data Collection Operation: Sampling frame is 350,000 establishments in the 1987 Census of Manufactures (see above), supplemented by Social Security Administration lists of new manufacturers and new manufacturing establishments of multi-establishment companies identified annually by the Census Bureau's Company Organization Survey. A probability sample of 66,000 establishments is selected. All establishments of companies with more than $500 million of manufacturing shipments in 1987 are included with certainty. All establishments with 250+ employees are also included with certainty along with a probability sample of smaller establishments.

Data Collection and Imputation Procedures: Survey is conducted by mail with phone and mail followups of nonrespondents. Imputation (for all nonresponse items) is based on previous year reports, or for new establishments in survey, on industry averages.

Estimates of Sampling Error: Estimated CV's for number of employees, new expenditure, and for value added totals are given in annual publications. For U.S. level industry statistics, most estimated CV's are 2 percent or less, but vary considerably for detailed characteristics.

Other (nonsampling) Errors: Response rate is about 85 percent. Nonsampling errors include those due to collection, reporting, and transcription errors, many of which are corrected through computer and clerical checks.

Sources of Additional Material: U.S. Bureau of the Census, *Annual Survey of Manufactures,* and Technical Paper 24.

SECTION 28. DOMESTIC TRADE AND SERVICES

Source and Title: U.S. Bureau of the Census, *Census of Wholesale Trade, Census of Retail Trade, Census of Service Industries*

Tables: See tables citing the above censuses in source notes in section 28 and table 1356 in section 30.

Universe, Frequency, and Types of Data: Conducted every 5 years to obtain data on number of establishments, number of employees, total payroll size, total sales, and other industry-specific statistics. In 1982, universe was all employer establishments primarily engaged in wholesale trade, and employer and nonemployer establishments in retail trade or service industries. Currently for 1987, data are available for establishments with payroll for retail trade, wholesale trade, and services.

Type of Data Collection Operation: All wholesale firms with paid employees surveyed; all retail and service large employer firms surveyed (i.e. all employer firms above the payroll size cutoff established to separate large from small employers) plus a 10-percent sample of smaller employer firms. Firms with no employees were not required to file a census return.

Data Collection and Imputation Procedures: Mail questionnaire is utilized with both mail and telephone followups for nonrespondents. Data for nonrespondents and "nonselected" small employer firms in retail trade and service industries are obtained from administrative records of IRS and the Social Security Administration.

Estimates of Sampling Error: Not applicable.

Other (nonsampling) Errors: Response rate in 1987 of 80 percent for single establishment firms; 83 percent for multi-establishment firms. Item response ranged from 60 percent to 90 percent with higher rates for less detailed questions.

Sources of Additional Material: U.S. Bureau of the Census, appendix A of *Census of Retail Trade; Census of Service Industries; Census of Wholesale Trade;* and *History of the 1982 Economic Censuses,* February 1987.

Source and Title: U.S. Bureau of the Census, *Current Business Surveys*

Tables: 1286-1289, 1303, 1310, 1311, and table 988 in section 21.

Universe, Frequency, and Types of Data: Provides monthly estimates of retail sales by kind of business and geographic area, and end-of-month inventories of retail stores; wholesale sales and end-of-month inventories; and annual receipts of selected service industries.

Type of Data Collection Operation: Probability sample of all firms from a list frame and, additionally, for retail and service an area frame. The list frame is the Bureau's Standard Statistical Establishment List (SSEL) updated quarterly for recent birth Employer Identification (EI) Numbers issued by the Internal Revenue Service and assigned a kind-of-business code by the Social Security Administration. The largest firms are included monthly; a sample of others is included every 3 months on a rotating basis. The area frame covers businesses not subjected to sampling on the list frame.

Data Collection and Imputation Procedures: Data are collected by mail questionnaire with telephone followups for nonrespondents. Imputation made for each nonresponse item and each item failing edit checks.

Estimates of Sampling Error: For the 1989 monthly surveys, CV's are about 0.6 percent for estimated total retail sales, 1.7 percent for wholesale sales, 1.3 percent for wholesale inventories. For dollar volume of receipts, CV's from the *Service Annual Survey* vary by kind of business and range between 1.5 percent to 15.0 percent. Sampling errors are shown in monthly publications.

Other (nonsampling) Errors: Imputation rates are about 18 percent to 23 percent for monthly retail sales, 20 percent to 25 percent for wholesale sales, about 25 percent to 30 percent for monthly wholesale inventories and 14 percent for the *Service Annual Survey.*

Sources of Additional Material: U.S. Bureau of the Census, *Current Business Reports, Monthly Retail Trade, Monthly Wholesale Trade,* and *Service Annual Survey.*

SECTION 30. OUTLYING AREAS

(See section 1 for information pertaining to tables 1343 and 1344, section 2 for table 1345, section 22 for table 1354, section 27 for table 1356.)

Appendix IV

Index to Tables Having Historical Statistics, Colonial Times to 1970 Series

[The most recent historical supplement to the *Statistical Abstract* is the bicentennial edition, *Historical Statistics of the United States, Colonial Times to 1970* (see inside back cover). Listed below are statistical time series (identified by number) appearing in this edition, for which tables in the *Statistical Abstract* present comparable figures. Historical series are listed only where related or comparable data are available for one or more years later than 1970. In a few instances, it may be necessary to combine figures shown in the *Abstract* to obtain totals comparable to the series shown in *Historical Statistics*]

Historical Statistics series	1992 Abstract table number	Historical Statistics series	1992 Abstract table number	Historical Statistics series	1992 Abstract table number	Historical Statistics series	1992 Abstract table number
A		**C—Con.**		**H—Con.**		**K—Con.**	
A 6-8	2	C 149-157	7	H 513-519	211	K 192	1093
A 23-25	12	C 158-160	307	H 535-544	245	K 195-203	1102
A 29-41	12			H 602-617	220	K 204-219	1088
A 119-134	19	**D**		H 690-692	263	K 251-255	1109
A 143-149	15	D 11-19	612	H 699-705	262	K 259-260	1093
A 156-159	83	D 29-41	615	H 705	263	K 264-285	1093
A 158-159	127	D 42-48	609	H 710	262	K 286-302	1094
A 160-171	49	D 49-62	619	H 729-738	266	K 326-329	1095
A 172	25	D 85-86	612	H 747-749	266	K 330-343	1098
A 195-198	25	D 87-101	635	H 751-763	278	K 344-353	1100
A 204-209	27	D 116-126	625	H 793-799	76	K 358-360	1101
A 210-263	340	D 127-141	643	H 806-828	379	K 486-495	1103
A 264-275	31	D 142-151	645	H 829-835	380	K 496-501	1113
A 288-319	56	D 689-704	647	H 862-864	395	K 502-505	1116
A 320-334	57	D 802-810	645	H 865-870	394	K 506-563	1115
A 335-349	58	D 877-892	645	H 871	395	K 561-563	1162
A 353-358	66			H 872	394	K 575-582	1122
A 359-371	74	**E**		H 874	395	K 583-594	1121
		E 73-86	746	H 875-876	391	K 595-608	1125
B		E 135-173	738	H 877	395	K 609-623	1127
B 1-5	80			H 921-940	408	K 614	1128
B 5-10	82	**F**		H 946-951	409	K 621	1128
B 11	84	F 566-594	691	H 952-961	287		
B 12-20	82			H 971-978	292	**L**	
B 20-27	85	**G**		H 979-986	124	L 10-14	1130
B 28-35	89	G 1-8	702	H 987-998	309	L 15-31	1131
B 107-115	103	G 16-23	702	H 1012-1027	310	L 72-86	1136
B 116-125	104	G 31-138	704	H 1028-1062	314	L 87-97	1137
B 136-147	109	G 179-188	709	H 1063-1078	316	L 98-112	1141
B 142	80	G 190-192	702	H 1079-1096	317	L 113-121	1142
B 149-166	114	G 197-199	702	H 1097-1111	318	L 122-137	1141
B 163-165	123	G 205-256	715	H 1112-1118	320	L 151-170	1147
B 167-173	106	G 257-268	711	H 1119-1124	325	L 172	1144
B 181-192	106	G 851-856	208	H 1135-1140	329	L 174	1144
B 214-217	127	G 881-915	205	H 1155-1167	335	L 175	1146
B 218	132					L 192-198	1145
B 221-235	137	**H**		**J**		L 199-205	1140
B 222-232	138	H 1-47	560	J 1-2	341	L 206-210	1139
B 248-261	136	H 51-56	568	J 3-6	342	L 212-223	1135
B 262-272	151	H 57-69	569	J 10-15	524	L 224-226	1151
B 275-290	158	H 115-124	589	J 26-32	524	L 227-235	1162
B 291-303	190	H 172-185	571	J 33-34	1131	L 229	1151
B 305-318	167	H 197-229	573	J 92-103	349	L 254-261	1150
B 331-344	167	H 238-242	572	J 110-136	367	L 262-293	1152
B 359-362	168	H 262-270	580	J 164-267	367	L 305-310	1155
B 384-387	169	H 305-317	583	J 268-278	366	L 312-318	1163
B 413-422	167	H 332-345	584			L 338-357	1160
		H 346-354	593	**K**		L 362-365	1161
C		H 355-367	592	K 1-2	1073		
C 1-10	45	H 392-397	588	K 4-7	1077	**M**	
C 25-75	26	H 398-411	604	K 16	1087	M 1-12	1167
C 76	1073	H 421-429	210	K 82-113	1081	M 13-37	1168
C 89	5	H 442-476	216	K 142-146	1080	M 68-71	1166
C 143-157	6			K 162-173	1079	M 76-92	911
C 144	307			K 174-176	1073	M 93-126	1189
				K 184-191	1104		

Historical Statistics series	1992 Abstract table number	Historical Statistics series	1992 Abstract table number	Historical Statistics series	1992 Abstract table number	Historical Statistics series	1992 Abstract table number
M—Con.		**Q—Con.**		**T**		**X**	
M 127-128	928	Q 224-232	1008	T 43-47	1283	X 114-147	766
M 143-146	1183	Q 233-234	998	T 79-196	1285	X 192, 229	764
M 147-161	1186	Q 238-250	1023	T 197-219	1288	X 410-417	802
M 225-226	1193	Q 284-312	1032	T 245-246, 255	1286	X 444-453	806
M 249-250	1194	Q 319, 330	1032	T 245-271	1287	X 454-455	805
M 256-257	1195	Q 332	1032	T 274-287	1302	X 474-491	809
M 266-267	1190	Q 356-378	1032	T 280-371	1303	X 492-498	808
M 271-286	1177	Q 400-401	1032	T 391-443	1308	X 517-530	810
		Q 414-416	1067	T 444-471	905	X 536-539	818
N		Q 438-448	1063	T 472-484	904	X 551-560	796
		Q 449-458	1065			X 716-724	773
N 1-29	1205	Q 473-480	1069			X 741, 748	777
N 66-69	1205	Q 487-502	1064	**U**		X 756, 761	777
N 78-100	1207	Q 507-517	1062			X 864-878	783
N 118-137	1203	Q 577-590	1038	U 1-25	1314	X 879-889	824
N 140-155	1202	Q 604-623	1048	U 26-39	1317	X 890-917	822
N 156-163	1211	Q 624-633	1038	U 41-46	1324		
N 170	1211			U 47-74	1319		
N 186-191	1236			U 75-186	1326	**Y**	
N 238-245	1224	**R**		U 190-195	1330		
N 249-258	1234			U 207-212	1337	Y 79-83	411
N 273, 276	789	R 31-45	888	U 264-273	1332	Y 84-134	414
		R 46-70	886	U 317-352	1335	Y 135-186	415
		R 75-88	886			Y 189-198	422
P		R 106-109	905			Y 199-203	423
		R 123-126	905	**V**		Y 204-210	421
P 1-12	1243	R 140-148	890			Y 211-214	419
P 13	1252	R 163-171	880	V 20-30	845	Y 272-307	481
P 18-39	1252	R 172-186	881	V 42-53	828	Y 318-331	520
P 58-67	1244	R 188-191	882	V 167-183	836	Y 335-338	495
P 74-92	1250	R 191-216	386	V 197-212	947	Y 339-342	491
P 235, 236a	1261	R 224-231	899			Y 358-373	507
P 239-241	1262	R 232-243	898			Y 393-411	508
P 265-269	1266			**W**		Y 412-439	513
						Y 458-460	527
Q		**S**		W 14, 17, 19	646	Y 497	499
				W 22-25	647	Y 500-504	499
Q 36-42	986	S 1-14	910	W 30-54	646	Y 505-637	450
Q 50-51, 55	992	S 32-52	938	W 62-65	646	Y 638-651	454
Q 69-75	1024	S 78-82	938	W 82-95	902	Y 710-782	461
Q 90-94	996	S 86-107	938	W 96-108	856	Y 856-903	546
Q 136-147	999	S 133-146	947	W 109-125	958	Y 943-956	554
Q 148-155	1002	S 160-175	948	W 126	961	Y 998-999	557
Q 156-162	1019	S 190-204	955	W 142	960		
Q 199-207	1022	S 205-218	953	W 167	969		
Q 208	1008						

Tables Deleted From the 1991 Edition of the Statistical Abstract

1991
table
number

Sec. 1. POPULATION
11	Total Population, by Race: 1960 to 1989
15	Projections of the Hispanic Population, by Age and Sex: 1995 to 2025
16	Projections of Total Population, by Race: 1991 to 2025
17	Projected Components of Population Change, by Race: 1995 to 2025
18	Projections of the Total Population by Age, Sex, and Race: 1995 to 2010
29	State Population Projections: 1995 and 2000
30	Population Projection, by Age—States: 2000
31	White and Black Population Projections, by State: 2000
57	Households, by Type—Projections: 1995 and 2000
79	Religious Congregations—Summary: 1986

Sec. 2. VITAL STATISTICS
87	Projected Fertility Rates, by Race and Age Group: 1990 to 2010
97	Childless Women and Children Ever Born, by Age of Woman: 1980 to 1988
98	Children Ever Born to Single Women, by Age and Race of Woman: 1980 and 1988
127	Deaths—Life Years Lost and Mortality Costs, by Age, Sex, and Cause: 1985
132	Marriages—Age Differences of Bride and Groom, by Age: 1987

Sec. 3. HEALTH AND NUTRITION
156	Persons With Health Insurance Protection, by Type of Insurer: 1960 to 1988
163	Physicians' Median Earnings From Practice: 1975 to 1988
172	Hospitals—Selected Financial Measures: 1980 to 1988
196	Persons With Activity Limitation, by Selected Chronic Conditions: 1985
197	Persons Needing Assistance With Activities, by Type of Activity, Age and Sex: 1986
212	Nutrient Intakes of Persons as Percent of the 1980 Recommended Dietary Allowances (RDA): 1987-88
213	Food Energy for Individuals, by Source and Selected Characteristic: 1987-88

Sec. 4. EDUCATION
225	Years of School Completed, by Age, Race, and Hispanic Origin: 1989
227	Years of School Completed, by Race and Hispanic Origin—States: 1989
228	School Days Lost Associated With Acute Conditions: 1962 to 1988
260	High School Graduates by Sex and Control and General Educational Development (GED) Certificates Issued, by Age: 1960 to 1989
271	General Education Graduation Requirements in Colleges and Universities: 1984 and 1989
274	Undergraduate Students Receiving Financial Aid, by Source of Aid, Control, and Level of Institution: 1986-87
275	Postbaccalaureate Students Receiving Financial Aid by Source of Aid, Level of Study, and Control of Institution: 1986-87
281	Institutions of Higher Education—Tenure Status of Full-Time Faculty, by Type of Institution and Rank of Faculty: 1988
290	College and University Libraries—Summary: 1985

Sec. 5. LAW ENFORCEMENT
301	Crimes Against the Elderly—Number and Rate, by Type: 1973 to 1988
336	State Prison Inmates, by Criminal History and Selected Characteristics of the Inmate: 1986
339	Average Time Served by Prisoners Released From Federal Institutions for First Time, 1970 to 1986, and by Offense, 1986

New Tables

Index

NOTE: Index citations refer to table numbers, not page numbers.

Index

Index 931

Index 931

NOTE: Index citations refer to table numbers, not page numbers.

NOTE: Index citations refer to table numbers, not page numbers.

NOTE: Index citations refer to table numbers, not page numbers.

NOTE: Index citations refer to table numbers, not page numbers.

NOTE: Index citations refer to table numbers, not page numbers.

NOTE: Index citations refer to table numbers, not page numbers.

NOTE: Index citations refer to table numbers, not page numbers.

NOTE: Index citations refer to table numbers, not page numbers.

NOTE: Index citations refer to table numbers, not page numbers.

NOTE: Index citations refer to table numbers, not page numbers.

NOTE: Index citations refer to table numbers, not page numbers.

NOTE: Index citations refer to table numbers, not page numbers.

NOTE: Index citations refer to table numbers, not page numbers.

NOTE: Index citations refer to table numbers, not page numbers.

NOTE: Index citations refer to table numbers, not page numbers.

NOTE: Index citations refer to table numbers, not page numbers.

NOTE: Index citations refer to table numbers, not page numbers.

NOTE: Index citations refer to table numbers, not page numbers.

NOTE: Index citations refer to table numbers, not page numbers.

NOTE: Index citations refer to table numbers, not page numbers.

NOTE: Index citations refer to table numbers, not page numbers.

NOTE: Index citations refer to table numbers, not page numbers.

NOTE: Index citations refer to table numbers, not page numbers.

NOTE: Index citations refer to table numbers, not page numbers.

NOTE: Index citations refer to table numbers, not page numbers.

NOTE: Index citations refer to table numbers, not page numbers.

NOTE: Index citations refer to table numbers, not page numbers.

NOTE: Index citations refer to table numbers, not page numbers.

Table

Table

NOTE: Index citations refer to table numbers, not page numbers.

NOTE: Index citations refer to table numbers, not page numbers.

NOTE: Index citations refer to table numbers, not page numbers.

NOTE: Index citations refer to table numbers, not page numbers.

NOTE: Index citations refer to table numbers, not page numbers.

NOTE: Index citations refer to table numbers, not page numbers.

Table

Table

NOTE: Index citations refer to table numbers, not page numbers.

NOTE: Index citations refer to table numbers, not page numbers.

NOTE: Index citations refer to table numbers, not page numbers.

NOTE: Index citations refer to table numbers, not page numbers.

NOTE: Index citations refer to table numbers, not page numbers.

NOTE: Index citations refer to table numbers, not page numbers.

NOTE: Index citations refer to table numbers, not page numbers.

NOTE: Index citations refer to table numbers, not page numbers.

NOTE: Index citations refer to table numbers, not page numbers.

NOTE: Index citations refer to table numbers, not page numbers.

NOTE: Index citations refer to table numbers, not page numbers.

NOTE: Index citations refer to table numbers, not page numbers.

NOTE: Index citations refer to table numbers, not page numbers.

NOTE: Index citations refer to table numbers, not page numbers.